M.

Literature of the
Western World

LITERATURE OF THE WESTERN WORLD

VOLUME I
The Ancient World Through the Renaissance

BRIAN WILKIE JAMES HURT
University of Illinois

MACMILLAN PUBLISHING CO., INC.
NEW YORK

Macmillan Publishing Company
866 Third Avenue, New York, New York 10022

Collier Macmillan Canada, Inc.

Library of Congress Cataloging in Publication Data
Main entry under title:

Literature of the Western world.

Includes index.
1. Literature—Collections. I. Wilkie, Brian
II. Hurt, James
PN6014.L615 1984   808.8   82-20396
ISBN 0-02-427690-1 (v. 1)
ISBN 0-02-427700-2 (v. 2)

Printing: 1 2 3 4 5 6 7 8   Year: 4 5 6 7 8 9 0

ISBN   0-02-427690-1 (V. 1)

ISBN   0-02-427700-2 (V. 2)

Acknowledgments

ERIC BENTLEY: *Life Is a Dream* by Calderón de la Barca, translated by Roy Campbell, from *The Classic Theatre*, Volume III, edited by Eric Bentley (Anchor Publishing Co., 1959). Reprinted by permission of Eric Bentley.

WALTER J. BLACK, INC.: Selections from Aristotle, *Poetics*, translated by Samuel Henry Butcher and revised by Louise Ropes Loomis, and from *Nicomachean Ethics*, translated by James E. C. Welldon, revised by Louise Ropes Loomis, both from Aristotle, *On Man in the Universe*, the Classics Club Edition published by Walter J. Black, Inc., 1943. Reprinted by verbal permission of Walter J. Black, Inc.

THE BOBBS-MERRILL COMPANY, INC.: Selections from *Song of Roland*, translated by Patricia Terry. Copyright © 1965 by The Bobbs-Merrill Company, Inc., Indianapolis, Indiana. Reprinted by permission of The Bobbs-Merrill Company, Inc.

ALISON M. BOND: Poems numbers 1, 3, 5, 8, 11, 39, 51, 62, 76, 85, 101, 109 from *The Poems of Catullus*, translated by Horace Gregory. Copyright © 1956 by Horace Gregory. Reprinted by permission of the translator from *Poems of Catullus*, W. W. Norton, New York, 1972, through his agent, Alison M. Bond.

CBS COLLEGE PUBLISHING: The complete "Inferno" and selections from "Purgatory" and from "Paradise" from *The Divine Comedy* by Dante Alighieri, translated by H. R. Huse, Holt, Rinehart and Winston, New York, 1954. Copyright © 1954 by Holt, Rinehart and Winston. Reprinted by permission of Holt, Rinehart and Winston, CBS College Publishing.

ROSICA COLIN LIMITED: Selections from *The Decameron* by Boccaccio, translated by Richard Aldington. Copyright © by Catherine Guillaume, 1983. Reprinted by permission of Rosica Colin Limited, authors' representatives, London, England.

DOUBLEDAY & COMPANY, INC.: *The Odyssey* by Homer, translated by Robert Fitzgerald. Translation copyright © 1961 by Robert Fitzgerald. Reprinted by permission of Doubleday & Company, Inc.

HARCOURT BRACE JOVANOVICH, INC.: *Lysistrata* by Aristophanes, An English Version by Dudley Fitts, copyright © 1954 by Harcourt Brace Jovanovich, Inc. Reprinted by permission of the publisher. All rights reserved.

INDIANA UNIVERSITY PRESS: Selections from *Metamorphoses* by Ovid, translated by Rolfe Humphries. Reprinted by permission of Indiana University Press. All rights reserved.

DOROTHY I. LINKER: *Aucassin and Nicolette* (anonymous), translated by Edward Francis Moyer and Carey DeWitt Eldridge, edited and first published by Robert Linker. Reprinted by permission of Dorothy I. Linker as Administrator of the Estate of Robert White Linker.

MACMILLAN PUBLISHING CO., INC., NEW YORK: *King Lear* by William Shakespeare, from *The Living Shakespeare*, edited by Oscar James Campbell. Copyright © 1949 by Macmillan Publishing Co., Inc., renewed 1977 by Robert F. Campbell, Eunice C. Goodale and Emily F. C. Meyer. Reprinted by permission of Macmillan Publishing Co., Inc., New York.

MACMILLAN LTD., LONDON: Selections from *Don Quixote* by Cervantes, translated by Walter Starkie. Reprinted by permission of Macmillan Ltd., London and Basingstoke.

MBI BOOKS DIVISION/THE HERITAGE PRESS: Selections from *The Five Books of Gargantua and Pantagruel* by Rabelais, translated by Jacques Le Clercq. Used by the permission of The Heritage Press, Norwalk, Connecticut.

THE NEW AMERICAN LIBRARY, INC.: *The Symposium* by Plato, from *Great Dialogues of Plato*, translated by W. H. D. Rouse and edited by Eric H. Warmington and Philip G. Rouse. Copyright © 1956 by John Clive Graves Rouse. Reprinted by arrangement with The New American Library, Inc., New York, N.Y.

OXFORD UNIVERSITY PRESS, INC., U.S.A.: *Antigone* by Sophocles, from *Three Theban Plays*, translated by Theodore Howard Banks. Copyright © 1956 by Theodore Howard Banks. Reprinted by permission of Oxford University Press, Inc. *Oedipus the King* by Sophocles, translated by Stephen Berg and Diskin Clay. Copyright © 1978 by Stephen Berg and

Diskin Clay. Reprinted by permission of Oxford University Press, Inc. *Alcestis* by Euripides, translated by William Arrowsmith. Copyright © 1974 by William Arrowsmith. Reprinted by permission of Oxford University Press, Inc. "Authun and the Bear" and "Hrafnkel the Priest of Frey" from *Eirik the Red and Other Icelandic Sagas*, selected and translated by Gwyn Jones. Copyright © 1961 by Oxford University Press. Reprinted by permission of Oxford University Press.

PENGUIN BOOKS LTD.: *Medea* by Euripides, from *MEDEA and Other Plays*, translated by Philip Vellacott (Penguin Classics, 1963). Copyright © 1963 by Philip Vellacott. Reprinted by permission of Penguin Books Ltd., Harmondsworth, Middlesex, England.

SCOTT, FORESMAN AND COMPANY: Selections from *Paradise Lost* by John Milton, from *The Poems of John Milton*, 2nd edition, edited by James Holly Hanford. Copyright © 1953 by Scott, Foresman and Company. Reprinted by permission.

CHARLES SCRIBNER'S SONS: Selections from *The Aeneid* by Virgil, translated by Rolfe Humphries. Copyright © 1951 by Charles Scribner's Sons. Reprinted by permission of Charles Scribner's Sons.

SIMON & SCHUSTER: Books I and II of *Utopia* by Thomas More, translated by Peter K. Marshall. Copyright © 1965 by Washington Square Press, Inc. Reprinted by permission of Simon & Schuster.

UNIVERSITY OF ALABAMA PRESS: Selected poems from *Selected Poems* by Petrarch, translated by Anthony Mortimer. Copyright © 1977 by Anthony Mortimer. Reprinted by permission of the University of Alabama Press.

UNIVERSITY OF CALIFORNIA PRESS: Poems numbered 30, 34, 37, 38, 39, 40, 41, 42, 43, 97 by Sappho, from *Sappho: A New Translation*, translated by Mary Barnard. Copyright © 1958 by The Regents of the University of California. Reprinted by permission of the University of California Press.

VIKING PENGUIN INC.: *The Oresteia* by Aeschylus, translated by Robert Fagles. Copyright © 1966, 1967, 1975 by Robert Fagles. Reprinted by permission of Viking Penguin Inc. All rights reserved. Selections from *The Canterbury Tales* by Geoffrey Chaucer, from *The Portable Chaucer*, translated by Theodore Morrison. Copyright 1949, © 1975, © renewed 1977 by Theodore Morrison. Reprinted by permission of Viking Penguin Inc.

Preface

Our goals in putting together *Literature of the Western World* have been, one, to produce the most comprehensive collection of world literature currently available, and, two, to present that literature as accurately and accessibly as possible. Edgar Lee Masters' unglamorous metaphor for anthologists— "humble gleaners in the fields of literature"—describes one way in which we have seen our role. But our labors in the fields have also given us, not to mention intellectual rewards, a great deal of pleasure; after all, an anthology is literally a "gathering of flowers." We hope the book will provide corresponding rewards and pleasure for its readers.

In selecting works to include, we have started from scratch; we have consciously resisted the notion of a single, unchanging list of canonized great books elevated beyond the shifting winds of human literary tastes and needs. We have recognized, nevertheless, that certain works have an enduring centrality in literary history, and we have honored the claims of this tradition. Here are the *Odyssey*, the great tragedies of ancient Greece, the *Divine Comedy, Don Quixote, King Lear*, and *Paradise Lost*. At the same time, an anthology that included only such monumental works would be as misleading as a map that showed only mountain tops. With the monumental we have included the urgent and immediate, the perhaps unexpected by the side of the inevitable. And so we include Wollstone-craft's *Vindication of the Rights of Woman*, for example, and such acknowl-edged but not easily available masterpieces as Lermontov's *A Hero of Our Time*.

In every selection, the paramount consideration has been to provide a substantial and satisfying reading experience. Whenever possible, we have chosen complete works—representing prose fiction, for example, by five complete short novels, by Voltaire, Goethe, Lermontov, Chopin, and Conrad, and a dozen novellas of the nineteenth and twentieth centuries. For works too long to include in their entirety, such as the *Aeneid* and *Don Quixote*, we have selected sustained units and provided detailed summaries of omitted sections in order to preserve the overall shape of the work. Rather than offer sketchy representations of two authors of equal rank, we have occasionally chosen to represent one of them much more extensively, as with More and Machiavelli, or Tennyson and Browning. The result, we hope, is depth as well as breadth of coverage and a series of substantial works or selections.

In making our choices, we have been acutely aware of T. S. Eliot's conception of literary tradition as fluid and dynamic rather than fixed and unchanging; the new must alter our perception of the "ideal order" of the past. The course of Western literature must look slightly different now from the way it looked even, say, twenty years ago. Certain of the authors and individual works in this book are here because—for sometimes obvious, sometimes more elusive reasons—they seem to have a special appeal for contemporary readers; hence, for example, the complete *Odyssey* rather than the complete *Iliad,* and *King Lear* rather than, say, *Hamlet* or *Macbeth.* We believe the final selection honors equally the claims of old and new and contains, despite its length, nothing of merely historical interest that cannot speak with a special urgency and vitality to a contemporary reader.

In presentation, as in selection, we have tried to keep firmly in mind the needs of teachers and students. Choice of translations was crucial. We live in an age, we have come to realize, of great translations, and choices have often been difficult. We have been guided throughout by considerations of both accessibility and accuracy. We are proud to present a number of distinguished recent translations that combine these virtues: Robert Fagles' translation of the *Oresteia,* for example, which captures, perhaps better than ever before in English, both the lucidity and the wildness of that great dramatic poem of violence, Robert Fitzgerald's wonderfully readable translation of the *Odyssey,* and Mary Barnard's sensitive renderings of Sappho's difficult texts. We are happy, too, to be able to include Stephen Berg's and Diskin Clay's *Oedipus the King,* William Arrowsmith's *Alcestis,* Patricia Terry's *Song of Roland,* Richard Wilbur's *Tartuffe,* Rolf Fjelde's *A Doll House,* Arvid Paulson's *Miss Julie,* and Willa and Edwin Muir's *The Metamorphosis.* But we have never assumed that the most recent translation is necessarily the best and have correspondingly chosen Walter Starkie's earthy, vigorous translation of *Don Quixote* and Tobias Smollett's rollicking English version of *Candide* over more recent but, to our minds, less lively versions. Challenges of translation have also forced upon us the difficult decision to minimize the amount of translated lyric poetry. Poets who travel well in borrowed languages are rare, and so lyric poetry is represented primarily by poets who wrote originally in English, especially those whose forms and themes reflect the currents of Western literature in other languages.

In our introductions to the major periods and to the individual selections, our goal has been to provide the most useful information, while suppressing the professorial temptation to explain everything. Like many other readers in these post-New-Critical days, we have tried to combine a sense of the integrity and autonomy of art with a heightened awareness of the roots of art in particular, time-bound human experience. Our introductions to periods and authors give biography and history their due, especially the history of ideas and culture. For the three period introductions of Volume One we have aimed, within the limits of space, to be at least moderately comprehensive, mentioning the salient facts and tendencies of the three enormously varied periods—the Ancient World, the Middle Ages, and the Renaissance—without attempting to reduce complex historical movements to formulas. The period introductions in Volume Two, on Neoclassicism and Romanticism, Realism and Naturalism, and Modernism, are more thematically organized, but we have tried there too not to be simplistic. In the author introductions, we have done as many of the following things as are relevant to individual authors: give a fairly detailed biographical summary, describe their personal artistic development (including the titles of their most important works), identify their recurrent themes, place them in the context of their times and of the development of literature and ideas, and help readers focus on the selections that follow in this book. Sometimes we venture brief critical commentary, suggesting alternative standard interpretations or advancing our own views, chiefly as whetstones against which we hope students and teachers will hone the edges of their own interpretive tools.

Footnotes are intended to be, above all, functional. From among the dozens of facts worth knowing about Apollo or Stoicism or the French Revolution, we restrict ourselves to the facts relevant to the immediate passage glossed. As in the introductions, our policy is to leave interpretation to our readers. On a very few occasions we depart from this policy for special reasons; in Aeschylus, for example, we stop a few times to point out the richness of meaning and imagery in a passage, by way of alerting readers to the scores of other passages that deserve similar close reading. On matters of general knowledge and of vocabulary, we probably err on the side of over-annotation, hoping that none of our readers will mind being given what they may not need. Among the facts of life that we have tried to keep in mind is that few readers take side trips to the dictionary, especially if they are absorbed in their reading, as we hope our readers will be.

Each period and author introduction is followed by a list of "Further Reading." With a few exceptions, and with some slight modifications, these bibliographies are the work of three people to whom we are deeply indebted: Nancy K. Barry, Frances Stickney Newman, and Willard J. Rusch. Their initials identify the respective reading lists for which they are mainly responsible. They and we have tried to restrict the books listed to reliable and authoritative ones, but a good many works indispensable for advanced scholarly study have been consciously omitted. Each bibliography focuses on a few books we think might be useful to accompany a first reading of the author.

Finally, the obvious: this is a pair of very big books, the most comprehensive collection of world literature, we think, currently available. It is not a course, but a small library from which many courses can be constructed. But despite its size, it contains nothing that has not proved a source of delight to the editors over many years of studying and teaching literature. Our greatest pleasure in making this book has been the hope that it will introduce others to works we love and give them something of the same delight.

By "our" goals, we sometimes mean those of the two editors, but more often we mean those of several dozen teachers, from widely scattered colleges and universities, who before this book was made and while it was in the making have told us what they and their students wanted. In no case did this consensus contradict our own teaching experience, but it has made possible a perspective that no two or even ten anthologists could have achieved confidently on their own. These valued colleagues include:

Professor Jesse T. Airaudi, Baylor University; Professor Beatrice Batson, Wheaton College; Professor J. A. Bryant, University of Kentucky; Professor Leslie Chard, University of Cincinnati; Professor Keith Cohen, University of Wisconsin, Madison; Professor Charles L. Crow, Bowling Green State University; Professor Prescott Evarts, Jr., Monmouth College;

Professor Robert Fagles, Princeton University; Professor Betty S. Flowers, The University of Texas at Austin; Professor Barbara L. Gerber; Professor John F. Hennedy, Providence College; Professor Thomas G. Jones, Jr., Western Kentucky University; Professor Beuford W. Keene, University of Tennessee, Martin; Professor James King, Hillsdale College; Professor Alfred Kloeckner, Norwich University; Professor Stanley J. Kozikowski, Bryant College; Professor Lawrence F. Laban, Virginia Commonwealth University; Professor Frederick Z. Lesher, University of Wisconsin, La Crosse; Professor Irving Lord, South Oregon State College; Professor Christiaan T. Lievestro, University of Santa Clara; Professor John M. Long, Eastern Kentucky University; Professor Littleton Long, University of Vermont; Professor Joan McCarthy, Southern Connecticut State College; Professor H. Thomas McCracken; Professor Ronald E. MacFarland, University of Idaho; Professor Ronald E. McReynolds, Central Missouri State University; Professor Charles Miller, Western State College; Professor Zenobia Mistri, Purdue University, Calumet Campus; Professor Martin Mueller, Northwestern University; Professor Helen H. Naugle, Georgia Institute of Technology; Professor R. W. Parker, Wittenberg University; Professor Erling W. Peterson, Indiana Central University; Professor Willard Potts, Oregon State University; Professor Carroll Y. Rich, North Texas State University; Professor William Patrick Riley, Mississippi Valley State University; Professor J. E. Rivers, University of Colorado, Boulder; Professor Allen Robb, Florida State University; Professor Thomas G. Rosenmeyer, University of California, Berkeley; Professor Silvia Ruffo-Fiore, University of South Florida; Professor Susan Rusinko, Bloomsburg State College; Professor Richard Savage, Bloomsburg State College; Professor Gerald H. Strauss, Bloomsburg State College; Professor Woodruff C. Thomson, Brigham Young University; Professor Willa F. Valencia, Valdosta State College; Professor Robert A. Wiggins, University of California, Davis; Professor Heinz D. Woehlk, Northeast Missouri State University; Professor Edith Williams, Eastern Kentucky University.

For advice on particular authors and periods we warmly thank Lynn Altenbernd, John Bateman, Barbara Bowen, Vincent Bowen, Edward Brandabur, David Bright, Jackson Campbell, Howard Cole, John Dussinger, Chester Fontenot, Eva Frayne, John Frayne, John Friedman, Stanley Gray, Achsah Guibbory, Jan Hinely, Bernard Hirsch, Frank Hodgins, Allan Holaday, Anthony Kaufman, David Kay, Keneth Kinnamon, Joan Klein, Dale Kramer, James Marchand, Donald Masterson, Linda Mazer, Michael Mullin, John K. Newman, Michael Palencia-Roth, Vernon Robbins, Michael Shapiro, Charles Shattuck, Janet Levarie Smarr, Arnold Stein, Jack Stillinger, Zohreh Sullivan, Benjamin Uroff, Leon Waldoff, Emily Watts, and Richard Wheeler.

For their skilled secretarial help we are indebted to Marjorie Beasley, Marlyn Ehlers, Sherri George, Jenny Maden, and Irene Wahlfeldt.

For expert guidance throughout the project we thank D. Anthony English. Our production editor, Patricia Cabeza, helped us immensely with the task of getting the manuscript through the press. Berta Lewis provided excellent design assistance. And finally, we thank Joyce Rappaport, Kevin McLaughlin, and Ann Wilkie for help with the formidable and exacting labor of copyediting and proofreading.

Contents

The Ancient World   1

Introduction   1

THE OLD TESTAMENT 16
KING JAMES VERSION
(Tenth Century B.C. to Second Century B.C.)

FROM Genesis   20
  The Creation of the World   20
  The Fall of Man   21
  Cain and Abel   24
  The Flood   25
  The Tower of Babel   29
  The Story of Abraham   29
  The Story of Isaac and Rebekah   38
  The Story of Jacob   41
The Exodus Saga   53
  The Escape from Egypt   53
  The Song of Moses   66
  The Journey to Sinai   67
  The Giving of the Law   71
  The Golden Calf   72
  The Holiness Code   76
  The Wanderings in the Wilderness   77
  The Death of Moses   87
  The Destruction of Jericho   91
FROM Job   95
FROM Psalms   124
  Psalm   8   124
  Psalm 23   125
  Psalm 91   125
  Psalm 103   126
  Psalm 114   127
  Psalm 130   128
  Psalm 137   129
  Psalm 139   129
Jonah   130

HOMER 133
(*Eighth Century* B.C.)

The Odyssey—*Translated by Robert Fitzgerald*   136
  Book One: A Goddess Intervenes   137
  Book Two: A Hero's Son Awakens   149
  Book Three: The Lord of the Western Approaches   159
  Book Four: The Red-Haired King and his Lady   172
  Book Five: Sweet Nymph and Open Sea   193
  Book Six: The Princess at the River   205
  Book Seven: Gardens and Firelight   213
  Book Eight: The Songs of the Harper   221
  Book Nine: New Coasts and Poseidon's Son   236
  Book Ten: The Grace of the Witch   249
  Book Eleven: A Gathering of Shades   264
  Book Twelve: Sea Perils and Defeat   282
  Book Thirteen: One More Strange Island   295
  Book Fourteen: Hospitality in the Forest   307
  Book Fifteen: How They Came to Ithaka   322
  Book Sixteen: Father and Son   337
  Book Seventeen: The Beggar at the Manor   350
  Book Eighteen: Blows and a Queen's Beauty   369
  Book Nineteen: Recognitions and a Dream   380
  Book Twenty: Signs and a Vision   396
  Book Twenty-One: The Test of the Bow   407
  Book Twenty-Two: Death in the Great Hall   418
  Book Twenty-Three: The Trunk of the Olive Tree   431
  Book Twenty-Four: Warriors, Farewell   441

SAPPHO 455
(*Seventh Century* B.C. *to Sixth Century* B.C.)

Poems—*Translated by Mary Barnard*   457
  30: We drink your health   457
  34: Lament for a maidenhead   458
  37: You know the place   458
  38: Prayer to my lady of Paphos   459
  39: He is more than a hero   460
  40: Yes, Atthis, you may be sure   460
  41: To an army wife, in Sardis   461
  42: I have had not one word from her   462
  43: It was you, Atthis, who said   462
  97: I have often asked you   463

AESCHYLUS 464
(*c. 525–456* B.C.)

The Oresteia—*Translated by Robert Fagles*   467
  Agamemnon   468

The Libation Bearers   520
The Eumenides   555

SOPHOCLES 591
(496–406 B.C.)

Oedipus the King—*Translated by Stephen Berg and
    Diskin Clay*   593
Antigone—*Translated by Theodore Howard Banks*   642

EURIPIDES 673
(c. 480–406 B.C.)

Medea—*Translated by Philip Vellacott*   675
Alcestis—*Translated by William Arrowsmith*   709

ARISTOPHANES 753
(c. 450–c. 386 B.C.)

Lysistrata—*Translated by Dudley Fitts*   755

PLATO 807
(c. 427–c. 348 B.C.)

Symposium (The Banquet)—*Translated by W. H. D. Rouse*   810
FROM The Republic: The Parable of the Cave
    —*Translated by Benjamin Jowett*   850
The Apology—*Translated by Benjamin Jowett*   854

ARISTOTLE 873
(384–322 B.C.)

FROM Poetics—*Translated by Samuel Henry Butcher and
    Louise Ropes Loomis*   876
FROM Nicomachean Ethics—*Translated by James E. C. Welldon and
    Louise Ropes Loomis*   892

CATULLUS 909
(c. 84–c. 54 B.C.)

Poems—*Translated by Horace Gregory*   911
    1: Who shall receive my new-born book   911
    51: He is changed to a god   912
    3: Dress now in sorrow   912
    5: Come, Lesbia, let us live and love   913
    85: I hate and love   913
    109: My life, my love, you say our love
            will last forever   914
    39: Egnatius has white teeth   914
    8: Poor damned Catullus   915
    76: If man can find rich consolation   915
    11: Furius, Aurelius, bound to Catullus   916

62: Twilight and star we hope to see arise   917
101: Dear brother, I have come these many miles   919

VIRGIL   920
(*70–19 B.C.*)

FROM The Aeneid—*Translated by Rolfe Humphries*   924
Book I: The Landing near Carthage   924
Book II: The Fall of Troy   942
Book III: The Wanderings of Aeneas   959
Book IV: Aeneas and Dido   975
FROM Book VI: The Lower World   992

OVID   1004
(*43 B.C.–17 A.D.*)

Metamorphoses—*Translated by Rolfe Humphries*   1006
FROM Book I: 1006
    The Creation   1007
    The Four Ages   1008
    Jove's Intervention   1010
    The Story of Lycaon   1011
    The Flood   1013
    Deucalion and Pyrrha   1014
Book X: 1017
    The Story of Orpheus and Eurydice   1017
    The Story of Cyparissus   1020
    The Story of Ganymede, a Very Brief One   1021
    The Story of Apollo and Hyacinthus   1021
    Two Incidents of Venus' Anger   1023
    The Story of Pygmalion   1023
    The Story of Cinyras and Myrrha   1025
    The Story of Adonis   1030
    Venus Tells Adonis the Story of Atalanta   1031
    The Fate of Adonis   1035
FROM Book XI: 1036
    The Death of Orpheus   1036
    The Story of Midas   1038
    Midas Never Learns   1039

THE NEW TESTAMENT   1041
KING JAMES VERSION
(*First and Second Centuries* A.D.)

The Gospel According to Saint Matthew   1045
FROM The Gospel According to Saint Luke   1091

The Middle Ages 1097

Introduction 1097

FROM THE SONG OF ROLAND 1106
—*Translated by Patricia Terry*
(*c. 1100 A.D.*)

ICELANDIC SAGA 1182
(*Twelfth through Fourteenth Centuries*)
Hrafnkel the Priest of Frey—*Translated by Gwyn Jones* 1184
Authun and the Bear—*Translated by Gwyn Jones* 1203

AUCASSIN AND NICOLETTE 1207
—*Translated by Edward Francis Moyer,
Carey DeWitt Eldridge, and Robert Linker*
(*Twelfth Century*)

DANTE ALIGHIERI 1234
(*1265–1321*)
The Divine Comedy—*Translated by H. R. Huse* 1240
Inferno 1240
FROM Purgatory 1379
FROM Paradise 1428

GEOFFREY CHAUCER 1471
(*1340?–1400*)
The Canterbury Tales —*Translated by Theodore Morrison* 1474
Prologue 1474
Prologue to the Wife of Bath's Tale 1492
The Wife of Bath's Tale 1510
Prologue to the Pardoner's Tale 1517
The Pardoner's Tale 1520
The Knight's Interruption of the Monk's Tale 1531
The Nun's Priest's Tale 1532

EVERYMAN 1545
(*Late Fifteenth Century*)

The Renaissance 1569

Introduction 1569

FRANCIS PETRARCH   1585
(*1304–1374*)

Rhymes—*Translated by Anthony Mortimer*   1588
        I: All you that hear in scattered rhymes   1588
      III: It was that very day on which the sun   1589
       XC: Upon the breeze she spread her golden
             hair   1589
   CXXVI: Waters fresh and sweet and clear   1590
   CXXIX: From thought to thought, from
             mountainside to mountain   1591
 CXXXIV: I find no peace, and have no arms for war   1593
   CCLXV: Fierce heart and bitter, and most cruel will   1593
  CCXCII: The eyes I spoke of once in words that burn   1594
 CCCLXV: I keep lamenting over days gone by   1594

GIOVANNI BOCCACCIO   1595
(*1313–1375*)

The Decameron—*Translated by Richard Aldington*   1597
   The First Day   1597
   Third Day, Tenth Tale   1608
   Fourth Day, Second Tale   1613
   Fifth Day, Eighth Tale   1619
   Fifth Day, Ninth Tale   1623
   Fifth Day, Tenth Tale   1626
   Tenth Day, Tenth Tale   1633
   Conclusion   1641

NICCOLÒ MACHIAVELLI   1644
(*1469–1527*)

FROM The Prince—*Translated by Ninian Hill Thomson*   1647
FROM Discourses on the First Decade of Titus Livius, Book I
   —*Translated by Ninian Hill Thomson*   1672

THOMAS MORE   1674
(*1478–1535*)

Utopia—*Translated by Peter K. Marshall*   1679
   Book I   1679
   Book II   1701

FRANÇOIS RABELAIS   1745
(*1494?–1553*)

Gargantua and Pantagruel—*Translated by Jacques LeClercq*   1748
   FROM the First Book   1749
   FROM the Second Book   1788

MICHEL DE MONTAIGNE 1826
(*1533–1592*)

Essays—*Translated by Charles Cotton* 1830
    Of Cannibals 1830
    Of Repentance 1840
    FROM Of Experience 1851

MIGUEL DE CERVANTES SAAVEDRA 1884
(*1547–1616*)

Don Quixote—*Translated by Walter Starkie* 1887
    FROM Part I 1887
    FROM Part II 1928

WILLIAM SHAKESPEARE 1998
(*1564–1616*)

King Lear 2003

JOHN DONNE 2091
(*1572–1631*)

The Good-Morrow 2093
Song: Go, and catch a falling star 2094
The Canonization 2094
The Funeral 2096
The Sun Rising 2097
Song: Sweetest love, I do not go 2097
The Ecstasy 2098
The Flea 2100
A Valediction: Forbidding Mourning 2101
Love's Diet 2102
Elegy XIX: To His Mistress Going to Bed 2103
Holy Sonnets: 2105
    X: Death be not proud 2105
    XIV: Batter my heart 2105
A Hymn to God the Father 2105

PEDRO CALDERÓN DE LA BARCA 2106
(*1600–1681*)

Life Is a Dream—*Translated by Roy Campbell* 2109

JOHN MILTON 2164
(*1608–1674*)

Paradise Lost 2169
    Book I 2170
    Book II 2191
    Book III 2217

Book IV   2234
Book IX   2260
FROM Book XII   2289

Chronology   2299

Index   2314

The Ancient World

⁂

THE "ancient world," as it is here represented, consists of three civilizations that flourished in the millennium before Christ in a comparatively small area around the Mediterranean Sea: those of the ancient Hebrews, the Greeks, and the Romans. To the far-sighted anthropologist taking a long view of time, such a sampling of the ancient world would be too limited both chronologically and geographically. By the tenth century B.C., man was already old upon the earth and had created many other civilizations, some of them highly developed. Some of them, too, flourished in areas far from the Mediterranean—in the Orient, in Africa, and in the Americas. Nevertheless, it is to the Hebrews, the Greeks, and the Romans that we look for the main literary traditions of Western culture that concern this anthology. These traditions are the riverhead of Western literature, although we can discern other contributions near the source and continuing tributary streams from Africa and the East.

The core of Hebrew culture has always been religion, and it is through religion that it has most strongly influenced the Western world. It would be neither possible nor very useful to review here the course of the development of the Hebrews' culture and conception of God. But much of their view of the world is summed up in the prophet Micah's deceptively simple words: "He has showed you, O man, what is good; and what does the Lord require of you but to do justice, and to love kindness, and to walk humbly with your God?" No Greek or Roman could have written, or even have understood, these words. They imply a cluster of ideas wholly alien to the Greek and Roman world views but at the very heart of Hebraism: the existence of a single God, from whom the idea of "the good" derives, and a moral role for man in which he, along with everything else, is subordinated to God. (Micah's terms for ethical behavior in this world—"justice" and "kindness"—would not have puzzled either a Greek or a Roman, but both would have defined these words differently.) The Hebrew "Yahveh" came to be the God of all mankind and, at the same time, the God of each individual. The result of this personal relationship was a stress upon individual experience, an emphasis upon conscience (including a social conscience), and a concentration upon introspection and the spiritual life. The Hebrews were continually involved in negotiations, individual and collective, with a father-God.

The course of Greek thought was significantly different. When the people we now know as Greeks began to filter into the Greek peninsula in about 2000 B.C., they brought with them a primitive polytheism based on personifications of natural forces, which they humanized and attempted to propitiate by means of prayers, libations, and sacrifices. Greek religion

1

THE ANCIENT
MEDITERRANEAN WORLD

PILLARS OF
HERCULES

IBERIANS

Artemisium
Iberus (Ebro)
Gades
Tingis

Balearic Is.
Palma

LIGURIANS

CORSICA

SARDINIA

CELTS

Rhodanus (Rhône)
Nicaea
Padus (Po)
Hadria
Ancona
Rome
Cumae
Naples
Elea

ITALY

ILLYRIA
ADRIATIC SEA
Epidaurum
Ister (Danube)
Tyras (Dniester)

THRACE

SCYTHIANS
SEA OF AZOV (Kuban)
TAURIS

BLACK SEA

Byzantium

Epidamnus
Corcyra

GREECE
Corinth
Sparta
Athens

AEGEAN
SEA
Troy
Hellespont

LYDIA
Smyrna
Ephesus
Miletus

Halys

Utica
Carthage

SICILY
Syracuse
Malta

Cnossos

CRETE

RHODES

CYPRUS
Paphos

PHOENICIA
Sidon
Tyre
Joppa
Jerusalem

Cyrene

MEDITERRANEAN SEA

0   400
Miles

changed and developed, of course, over its long history, but even in its most fully developed form it carried few if any implications for morality or conscience in the Hebrew sense. The Greek gods were superior to men, in power, beauty, and immortality, but they were not ethically superior, and, unlike Yahveh, they did not demand that men follow an exacting code of morality. The Greeks looked not to their gods for an ethical code, but to their own reason and innate sense of the good. The result was a culture that seems, even to a modern "post-Christian" reader, remarkably serene and guiltfree. The Greeks, it has been said, had a strong sense of crime, but none at all of sin.

The Greeks found the main significance of life not in the relation of man with God, but in man's relations with himself and with his fellows. If, for the sake of focus, we simplify the Greek view of the world as we did the Hebrew, we may find it stated best in the mottoes the Greeks inscribed over the gates of the temple to Apollo at Delphi: "Know thyself" and "Nothing too much." An ancient Hebrew would have misunderstood these phrases as badly as an ancient Greek would have misunderstood Micah's words. "Knowing" himself implied to a Greek none of the spiritual struggles or the wrestling with angels with which the Hebrew was preoccupied. A person came to know himself in Greece through experience, through involvement in the world. The crucial tableau in Hebrew history is one man alone on a mountaintop, learning directly from God "what is good." The Greeks had their mountaintops, too, but the messages they received there from the gods were characteristically riddling and enigmatic; the responsibility for knowledge was thrown squarely back upon the questioner. The Greek tableau corresponding to the man on the mountaintop is a group of men in lively, earnest conversation, exercising the privilege Socrates said was characteristic of free citizens: "They can have their talk out in peace, wandering at will from one subject to another, their only aim to attain the truth."

Or the emblematic tableau might be a group of men at the great Olympic Games, competing in athletics or in horseracing, drama, music, or poetry; or it could be the audience at a production of an Aeschylean tragedy at the City Dionysia in the theater of Dionysus in Athens. For to the Greeks there were no sharp divisions between the intellectual, physical, and spiritual sides of human nature. To "know oneself" was to know one's mind, body, and spirit as a harmonious, balanced system. The Greek view of human nature as a seamless unity was so deep and so thoroughgoing that it provides a stumbling block to our understanding of their institutions and their literature. We attend class, or watch the Rose Bowl on television, or go to a play or to church, and all of these are separate activities, each carried on by specialists and directed at different aspects of our personalities. It is hard for us to understand the very different Greek attitude toward, for example, the Great Games, in which the same contestants might compete in the five athletic events of the *pentathlon* and in music and poetry. The Games were a religious festival as well, dedicated to the worship of Zeus or Apollo or Poseidon. And were the great dramatic festivals artistic events or religious ceremonies? No Greek would have understood such a question, any more than he would have understood our attempts to distinguish between "sin" and "error" in such dramatic characters as King Oedipus. In institu-

3

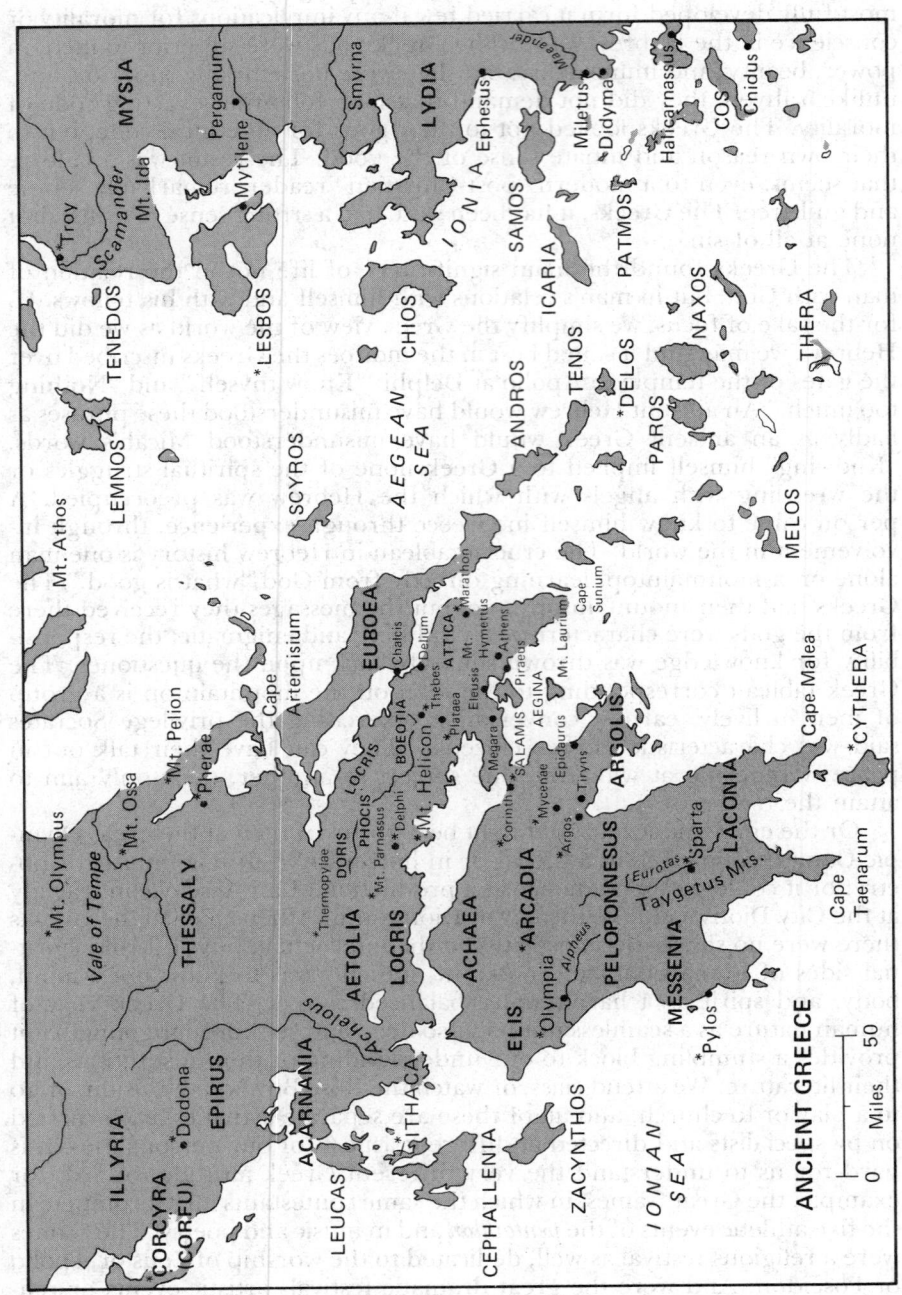

ANCIENT GREECE

0   Miles   50

Ancient Greece. NOTE: Some of the names below are spelled in various ways by translators. Asterisks (*) indicate the places described in the list.

ARCADIA. Setting of much ancient pastoral poetry.

ARGOS. In Aeschylus, the city of Agamemnon, Clytemnestra, Orestes, and Electra.

CORCYRA (Corfu). Conjectural home island of the Phaeacians in Homer's *Odyssey*.

CORINTH. Center of wealth, commerce, and shipbuilding; setting of Euripides' *Medea*.

CYTHERA. Island where Aphrodite came to land after being born of the sea foam.

DELOS. Birthplace of Apollo and Artemis.

DELPHI. Site of the great oracle of Apollo; the center of Greek prophetic utterance. The Omphalos (Navelstone), believed to be the center of the Earth, was located there.

DODONA. Site of the great oracle of Zeus.

HELICON. Mountain sacred to the Muses; location of the Hippocrene, the fountain of poetic inspiration.

ITHACA. Home island of Odysseus.

LESBOS. Home island of Sappho.

MARATHON. Plain (26 miles from Athens) where the Greeks defeated the Persians in 490 B.C.

MYCENAE. Center of a great ancient culture; in Homer, the city of Agamemnon.

OLYMPIA. With Delphi, one of the two greatest religious centers of Greece; site of the ancient Olympic Games.

OLYMPUS. Mountain home of the gods.

OSSA, PELION. Mountains piled atop one another in an attempt by the Titans to take the gods by storm.

PARNASSUS. Mountain associated with Apollo and the Muses and hence with learning and the arts.

PELION. See Ossa.

PHERAE. City of Admetus and Alcestis.

PLATAEA. Site of victory by the Greeks, under Pausanias, over the Persians in 479 B.C.

PYLOS. Home of Nestor; visited by Telemachus in Homer's *Odyssey*.

SALAMIS. Site of defeat of Xerxes and the Persian navy by the Greeks in 480 B.C.

SPARTA. Principal enemy of Athens in the Peloponnesian War (431–404 B.C.); home of Menelaus and Helen of Troy in Homer's *Odyssey*.

THEBES. City of Oedipus and Antigone.

THERMOPYLAE. A mountain pass heroically defended in 480 B.C. by the Spartans, under Leonidas, against the Persian invaders.

TROY. Site of the Trojan War, fought by the Greeks to reclaim Helen.

5

tions, as in human personalities, the Greeks did not differentiate the spirit, the mind, and the flesh.

The other Delphic inscription, "Nothing too much," is also a deceptively simple statement. The concept does not suggest a timid moderation, "playing it safe," but something almost the opposite. It insists that men confront reality unflinchingly, refusing the temptation to retreat into defensive and self-deluding inflations and exaggerations. This principle is consistent with "knowing oneself," since self-knowledge ends in accepting what it is to be human and avoiding the temptation to be either less or more than human. Morally, exaggeration and excess manifest themselves in *hubris*, which is not just pride but also a self-deluding rejection of human limitations. To the fifth-century Greeks, the luxurious and despotic Persian emperor Xerxes represented the sort of overweening man who closed his eyes to human boundaries and whom the gods delighted in cutting down. Greek tragedy is full of parallel examples of men who fall through attempting to be something other than human. Artistically, the principle of "nothing too much" was also expressed in a deep dislike of any elaboration or ornamentation that shielded the viewer from a direct view of "the thing itself." Greek art, whether it be the epics of Homer, the architecture of the Parthenon, or a sculpted Apollo, is characterized by a direct, unblinking view of reality and a combination of passion and restraint that is the essence of classicism. This is not to say that Greek art was "realistic" in the modern sense. Idealization—the attempt to capture the essence of a thing—was also fundamental to Greek art. But the ideal originated in the recognizable.

The leisure which made possible the Greeks' passionate but clear-eyed exploration of themselves and the world around them had a price: slavery and the subjugation of women. The Greek male was freed from demanding physical labor by the existence of a sizable slave class, made up mostly of "barbarians" (non-Greeks) captured in war. The institution of slavery was rarely questioned by the Greeks; one of the ironies of history is that its most freedom-loving culture accepted slavery, for the most part, as a matter of course. Nor did women share in the free exploration of the world men enjoyed. Greek women had few rights and were confined to the home. They managed domestic matters, and they bore and raised the children (at least in Athens; customs differed among the city-states). Greek children were almost exclusively in the company of women until the age of seven and then were rigidly segregated by sex; the result, predictably, was a perpetuation of traditional attitudes on the part of Greek women and a deep-seated distrust and even fear of women on the part of Greek men. This fear expressed itself in widespread homosexuality ("Greek love"), a rigid compartmentalization of sexual qualities, a glorification of "male" at the expense of "female" qualities, and a mythology full of female fright-figures, from the shrewish Hera to the Medusa, whose gaze turned men to stone, to the fearsome Furies, goddesses of blood vengeance, to the fierce Medea, who killed her children to avenge herself upon her faithless husband. (There were, of course, idealized women in myth, too: Athena, the patroness of Athens, was the goddess of wisdom.) The tragedian Euripides, in many ways an ironic commentator upon the ways of his contemporaries, questioned his culture's attitudes toward both slaves and women, but his was a rare voice in an intensely male-oriented society.

6

Greek culture reached its peak in the fifth century B.C. and was centered in Athens, which dominated the city-states of the peninsula and its islands for most of the century. But the power of Athens and Greece alike was severely eroded during a series of bitter internecine wars which ended in 338 B.C. when the kingdom of Macedonia conquered Greece. Greek art and learning had a brief Indian summer, the third-century "Hellenistic" (as opposed to the earlier "Hellenic") period, in the city of Alexandria in northern Egypt. Greek culture maintained some of its integrity through the days of the Roman Empire, and it passed on part of its legacy to Christianity. But the deathblow to even nominal Greek political independence came in 146 B.C., when the armies of the rising Republic of Rome marched into Greece and turned it into a mere province of the growing Roman Empire.

If the Hebrews looked to God for the meaning of life and the Greeks looked for it in the world around them, the Romans looked to earthly, human authority. It was a Roman, Horace, who wrote that it is "sweet and seemly to die for one's country," a phrase which encapsulates a number of Roman attitudes, including the subordination of the individual to the state, an obsession with death, and the cultivation of a stoic denial of personal feeling. Many Greeks suffered or risked death for their country, but it is hard to imagine their idealizing their sacrifice in this way. The Roman tableau to match the Hebrew on his mountaintop and the Greek talking with his friends might be the uniformed centurion marching in a column behind his commander to triumph or death. The Roman empire took shape over centuries of constant war; in our first glimpse of Rome at the end of the sixth century B.C., she is at war, attacking neighbor after neighbor until by 133 B.C. the nation was the undisputed ruler of the whole Mediterranean. The Roman virtues were those of the soldier: discipline, control, and obedience to authority.

Authority hedged the Roman around from his earliest childhood. The Roman family was a miniature of the state, headed by a stern father whose power was almost absolute. He owned all the property and could, by writing a letter, divorce his wife or even condemn her to death. The Greek family, male-oriented as it was, was never paternalistic in the Roman sense; the Greek grew up thinking of himself as an individual, but the Roman was above all else a member of a family and, later, of a clan and a nation. Roman religion reinforced these feelings of subordination to authority. The earliest Roman religion, which continued to be the domestic religion throughout the years of the Empire, rested on a belief in spirits that inhabited particular localities; each household had its own *lares, penates,* and *manes* which, respectively, watched over its lands and buildings, guarded the family's other possessions, and embodied the spirits of its male ancestors. The Roman must have grown up feeling that he was constantly observed by such spirits. When the more generalized gods of the Romans—Jupiter, Juno, Venus, and Mars—were merged, under Greek influence, with the Greek pantheon of Zeus, Hera, Aphrodite, and Ares, the result was a state religion the outward observances of which were enforced with a rigidity totally alien to the Greek mentality. In the late Empire, Stoic philosophy deeply influenced thoughtful Romans; it has been called the true Roman religion. Although Stoicism originated with a Greek—Zeno of Citium—its emphasis upon endurance and the repression of feeling made a strong appeal to the Romans' instinct for authority. The version of Stoicism developed in Rome taught the individual to subordinate his own will to the family, to the state, and to God. He was to do his duty without question, cultivating self-denial and impassive reserve. Altogether, the Stoic view of the world was ideally suited to the Roman temperament.

The great Roman contribution to civilization was the instrument of social organization—law. The Romans were able to extend their sway over so much of the world and maintain it so long because wherever they went they brought with them the concept of authority. In their system, no one was wholly exempt from the rule of an impersonal force. Forbidding as such impersonality may seem, it also left a cherished legacy to posterity. We owe to the Romans the principles that a person must be assumed innocent until proven guilty, that the law must be applied judiciously, with due regard to the particular situation, and that all individuals are equal before the law.

Roman art was largely derivative from the Greeks. After 272 B.C., when the Romans captured the Greek city of Tarentum, Greek artists and scholars poured into Rome, and as Horace expressed it, "Conquered Greece took captive her fierce conqueror." Roman architecture, sculpture, drama, poetry, and painting were all copied from Greek models, often with a considerable distortion through inflation, as in the gigantic Roman temples copied from small Greek originals, or through refinement, as in Seneca's polished imitations of Greek tragedy.

In a survey of ancient literature (limited even to the works of the Hebrews, the Greeks, and the Romans), variety is more apparent than unity. But we can follow a few threads related to the development of the major literary genres: narrative, drama, poetry, and expository literary prose.

The characteristic narrative forms of the ancient world are the folk tale, the epic, and the history. We may pass over the folk tale fairly quickly, since our knowledge of it in the ancient world is indirect and inferential. We know that a large body of folk narrative must have been in oral circulation since earliest times among the Hebrews, the Greeks, and the Romans. But these tales have reached us only as they were incorporated into written narratives. We can detect signs of them in, for example, the Hebrew Bible, Homer, and Virgil.

In narrative, the greatest achievement of the ancient world was the epic. Long heroic poems seem to be a natural form in most early literatures. There are the Exodus epic in the Bible and the *Iliad* and the *Odyssey* at the dawn of Greek literature. But we can also point to, among others, the Babylonian *Gilgamesh* (c. 2000 B.C.), the Indian *Mahabharata* (A.D. 350–500), and the German *Nibelungenlied* (c. A.D. 1200). These are all "folk epics"—that is, although they may have been put into final form by single authors, they were developed by folk poets, over extended periods of time, from traditional materials that dealt with the legendary histories of their peoples. The folk epics have a wide variety of forms, but they are linked by certain recurring characteristics. Though not all are regarded as, like the Bible, "sacred books," all hold special places in their cultures as major statements of national or cultural identity. They purport to tell the stories of the formation or the early history of an entire people; thus they are never regarded as mere fictional entertainment but are held in some degree of reverence. All of them, too, center on heroes, drawn from history or legend, who are regarded not merely as individuals but as embodiments of the special values of their cultures. The settings are vast, ranging across nations or the entire world. Even when the action is confined to a limited place, as in Homer's *Iliad,* that place is the scene of great events determining the fate of nations. The action is similarly grand, involving deeds that exemplify extraordinary qualities treasured by the culture, especially military prowess, physical strength, and spiritual force. Often the action takes the hero on a journey which consists of a series of trials testing his heroism. The gods of the culture often involve themselves in the action, as the Lord does in the Exodus story, or as, in a very different way, the Olympian gods enter the plots of the Homeric epics. The style is at once exalted and simple, grand but not highly embellished. And the point of view is objective; the action is seen from an impersonal angle, without authorial intrusion and with the emphasis upon external action rather than upon inner motivations.

The epic form captured the imaginations of a great many poets who attempted to incorporate its qualities in original works, or art epics. In addition to employing the features of folk epics, these poets developed a number of epic conventions, which refine and develop the features inherent in the folk epic, especially the epics of Homer. The art epic opens with a statement of a grand governing theme and an invocation to an appropriate muse to inspire and instruct the poet. The poet plunges *in medias res,* or "into the middle of things," with earlier action recounted at a later point in the epic. There are, characteristically, catalogues of warriors, ships, armies; extended formal speeches by the main characters; and epic similes, extended set-pieces which develop comparisons at length. The greatest ancient art epic is Virgil's *Aeneid;* Ovid's *Metamorphoses* is another, in some ways, though he introduces the epic conventions in a playful and deliberately trivializing way.

The other major narrative form of the ancient world is the history. The dividing line between epic and history is not always precise; the epic finds its roots in legendary history, and history is often seen through epic lenses. About half of the Old Testament is presented as a history of the Hebrews, though a good part of it—the Exodus saga—blends history with folk epic. But we cannot reconstruct from the Old Testament a factual account of early Israel such as a modern historian would write. Hebrew history is history seen through faith; and the purpose of the Hebrew Bible is not to record precise dates and circumstances, but rather to trace out the underlying design of history as a revelation of religious truth.

History in the modern sense begins in the fifth century B.C. with Herodotus and his Greek history of the Persian Wars. Here too fact and fancy are often mingled; Herodotus begins with a lively travelogue of the Persian Empire, reporting everything he has seen and heard, though he is careful to say he does not necessarily believe all of it. The modern critical and scientific treatment of history begins with Herodotus' younger contemporary Thucydides, whose history of the Peloponnesian War makes a quite modern attempt not only at factual accuracy but also at historical interpretation. The Romans carried on the tradition of historical writing. The romantic and patriotic Livy's *History of Rome* is the historical counterpart to Virgil's epic *Aeneid,* while Tacitus' *Histories* and *Annals* chronicle Rome's later degeneracy, in a savage parallel to the contemporary verse satires of Juvenal. The beginning of modern notions of how to organize and develop a sustained narrative lies as much in the work of these historians as in that of the more frankly "literary" writers.

Of the major literary kinds, drama has had the most sporadic history. Perhaps because a fairly complex set of social and intellectual circumstances are necessary to make theatrical production possible, drama has flourished in only three fairly brief periods in Western history, and the first of these is in the Greece of the fifth century B.C. (The other two ages are the late Renaissance and early neoclassical period, between about 1580 and 1700, and the modern period, since about 1860.)

There is some evidence that a dramatic tradition existed in Egypt as early as 3000 B.C., but practically nothing is known of it. The Hebrews had no theater, although the Book of Job shows some evidence of the influence of Greek tragedy, and the Song of Solomon may have some relation to a quasi-dramatic wedding performance. It is to Greece that we look for the beginnings of Western drama.

Greek drama originated in the sixth century B.C., in the worship of Dionysus. Four annual festivals were consecrated to him: the Rural Dionysia (in December), the Lenaia (in January), the Anthesteria (in February), and the City or Great Dionysia (in March). The god was worshiped at these festivals through the performances of dithyrambs, which were hymns of ecstasy narrating an incident in the life of the god and performed by choruses of singers and dancers. The step from narration to drama presumably was taken when a chorus leader moved from telling about the god to impersonating him and acting out his story. The Greeks believed that this revolutionary innovator was a man named Thespis, who is therefore traditionally regarded as the first actor in history. It was Thespis, too, who won the prize for tragedy in 534 B.C., when the City Dionysia was reorganized and a contest for tragedy was established. Dithyrambic performances took place on the circular stone platforms which were used as threshing floors in the center of Greek villages; these platforms seem to have provided the model for the *orchestra,* or circular dancing place, which served as the central acting area of the fully developed Greek theater.

It is in the fifth century that we emerge from theatrical legend into theatrical history. By the time Aeschylus, the oldest of the Greek dramatists whose works survive, began competing in the tragedy contests in 499 B.C., the contests had been held for about thirty-five years and the methods of production had assumed essentially the form they kept throughout the great age of the Greek theater. The festivals were civic and religious rituals, occasions for exploring the fundamental ideas and values that made Athens a unified community. The annual dramatic festivals were organized, and the plays produced, by a cooperative effort of the civic leaders of the city, eminent private sponsors, and the artists themselves, in accordance with rules that by the fifth century had become standard. The audience consisted, in effect, of the whole citizenry, brought together not in a spirit of playgoing whim but of communal solidarity. (Women attended the tragedies but not the comedies.) During the fifth century, the Great Dionysia, the most important of the annual festivals, included four days devoted to plays. On the first day, five comedies, by different authors, were presented.

Plan of the theater of Dionysus at Athens. A. Orchestra B. Chorus Entrance C. Altar to Dionysus D. Skene.

On each of the next three days, plays by a single author were acted: three tragedies, followed by a broadly comic "satyr play" designed to relieve the intensity of the tragedies. Prizes were awarded to the best actor and to the best combination of playwright and producer.

At Athens, plays were acted in the Theater of Dionysus, a vast outdoor arena located on sloping ground near the Acropolis. Between the sixth and fourth centuries, the most important era of Greek drama, the theater evolved considerably. At first it was little more than a circular acting space, or *orchestra*, at the foot of a concave hillside where the audience sat on the ground. By the fifth century, permanent seats for the audience had been built and a long building called the *skene* had been constructed behind the *orchestra*. The *skene*, which became increasingly elaborate architecturally as time passed, provided dressing rooms, a backdrop for the action (scenery was apparently minimal), and a place through which the principal actors could make their entrances and exits. The *skene* often represented an edifice, integral to the story, where indoor actions could be imagined to happen, offstage—in Agamemnon's palace, for example. (The direct presentation of indoor scenes is unusual in Greek plays, as are killings and other violent episodes.) It is possible, though not certain, that a raised platform directly in front of the *skene* formed a stage slightly elevated above the *orchestra*. At

11

the extreme left and right of the *skene* were corridors, separating it from the seating area, through which the Chorus usually entered near the beginning of the play and exited near the end.

The players—all of them males—consisted of the principal actors and the Chorus. Originally, there was only one principal, but in the course of the fifth century a second actor was added (by Aeschylus) and later a third (by Sophocles), making possible face-to-face confrontations between characters and thus enhancing psychological realism. It must be understood that the number of characters in a play was not limited to the number of actors; one actor often played two or more roles, and conversely the same character could be played by more than one actor. This flexibility was achieved primarily by the use of stylized masks, a device that served several purposes: to maintain elementary verisimilitude (by allowing an adult male to play a young girl or old woman, for example); to help the audience (many of whom sat far from the action) recognize the identity and emotional state of the characters; and to help portray the characters as generalized types rather than simply as individuals.

The Chorus, which probably numbered twelve or fifteen in tragedy and twenty-four in comedy, was a distinctive part of Greek drama. It could represent various groups, from the citizens of Argos in Aeschylus' *Agamemnon,* to the Furies in his *Eumenides,* to the animal grotesques in comedies such as Aristophanes' *The Frogs* or *The Wasps.* Its functions were equally various: it could take part in the play's action, reflect the response the playwright was trying to evoke in the audience, bring out through sympathy or antipathy the salient traits of a principal character, and voice philosophical ideals. Not least, its singing and dancing helped sustain the play's mood and enhance it as spectacle.

Music and dance were important in both tragedy and comedy, helping to create elevated, festive, or ceremonial effects. The choral poems were sung, in a variety of lyric verse forms, to the accompaniment of dance and of musical instruments including the flute. Ordinary dialogue was probably delivered as a quasi-musical chant or in some other way that distinguished it from the tone of ordinary speech. A number of people have pointed out that, in its stylized manner, its spectacle, and its integration of different art media, Greek drama has its closest modern analogue in grand opera. (And indeed, opera originated in a seventeenth-century attempt to reconstruct the staging of Greek drama.)

Only forty-five Greek plays have survived: seven tragedies by Aeschylus, seven tragedies by Sophocles, seventeen tragedies and one satyr play by Euripides, eleven comedies by Aristophanes, and two comedies by Menander (only one of which is intact). Even this small sampling, hardly likely to encompass the full range of Greek drama, is highly varied. Tragedy ranges from the titanic culture-histories of Aeschylus, through the marvelously crafted humanistic dramas of Sophocles, to Euripides' ironic dramas of inner division and self-deception (some of which are more like comedies of manners than like tragedies). Aristophanes' Old Comedy is the Greek dramatic form most remote from modern drama. He strings upon a sketchy, fantastic, often perfunctory plot, scenes of farce, parody, and topical satire, punctuated with choruses of beautiful lyric poetry. It was not Old Comedy but the New Comedy—surviving only in the works of the fourth-

12

century Menander—that was to establish the pattern of later comedy. New Comedy turned from fantasy and satire to deal with contemporary middle-class private life. The choruses were subordinated to intrigue-plots which usually dealt with a young man's attempt to marry against his father's opposition.

The Roman theater, like many aspects of Roman culture, was modeled on that of the Greeks. In Rome, where Greek-inspired plays began to be performed in the third century B.C., plays were performed at festivals honoring the gods, or for special occasions such as a state funeral or a military victory. The theaters were constructed along Greek lines, although by the first century A.D. they had come to be much larger and more elaborate than the Greek theaters, reflecting the Roman love of excess. Thirty-seven Roman plays survive: twenty-one comedies by Plautus (c. 254–184 B.C.); six comedies by Terence (195–159 B.C.); nine tragedies by Seneca (4 B.C.–65 A.D.), the Stoic philosopher and adviser to the Emperor Nero; and one tragedy formerly attributed to Seneca but now agreed to be the work of a later, anonymous author. Roman comedy, like Greek New Comedy, dealt with intrigues arising from middle-class life, while Seneca's stiff, melodramatic dramas, not meant for production, are reworkings of Greek tragedies. (Five of his nine extant plays are adapted from Euripides.)

Greek tragedy expressed the Greek spirit both in its unflinching treatment of basic issues in human life ("Know thyself") and in its strict economy of means ("Nothing too much"). Greek comedy embodied the Greek's freedom of thought and expression, as well as his involvement in public life. Roman drama carried on the Greek achievement and was to be the version of classical drama that initially influenced the theater when it was reborn during the Renaissance.

Of all the genres, lyric poetry travels least well. Narrative and drama lose a great deal with the passage of time and loss of cultural associations. Subtleties disappear with translation into other languages. But the broad outlines of a story and the power of the stage are rugged—thus epic and drama can survive the passing of time and changes in language better than lyric poetry, which depends so much on nuance and the precise word.

"Lyric" originally meant "sung to the lyre," and perhaps the central fact about lyric poetry in the ancient world is its close connection with music. The lyric poet was literally a "lyricist" in Hebrew and Greek culture, as we are reminded by stories of David as a harpist and of Sappho's skill upon the lyre.

The Hebrew Bible is full of song, and the lyric portions of it should be read with imaginary, if not real, music in the background. The role of music and poetry in Hebrew worship is suggested by many passages in the Old Testament, among them the description of David's bringing of the ark to Jerusalem (I Chron. 16:7–36) and the descriptions of worship in the Psalms. In Psalm 42, the speaker tells of leading the throng to the House of God "with glad shouts and songs of thanksgiving," while in Psalm 68 another procession is described, "the singers in front, the minstrels last, between them maidens playing timbrels."

Hebrew poetry, like most ancient Near Eastern poetry, did not depend upon rhyme or a fixed line length, but rather upon a loose rhythm and parallelism. A unit of Hebrew verse characteristically consists of two lines,

13

each with three or four heavily stressed syllables, the second line parallel to the first in that it either paraphrases, develops, or completes it:

What is man, that thou art mindful of him?
and the son of man, that thou visitest him? [PSALMS 8:4]

The simple, exalted power of this form is perceptible even in English translation.

The early Greeks described poetry as either "lyric" or "choric." Lyric poetry was the expression of a single singer accompanied by the lyre, while choric poetry was a group expression, sung by a chorus, usually also with instrumental accompaniment. The greatest school of lyric poets in Greece was centered among the Aeolians, on the eastern coast of the Aegean Sea and on the island of Lesbos, in the sixth century B.C. The great Aeolian lyricists, Sappho and Alcaeus, also inspired an Ionian school of lyricists on the mainland of Greece. The major successor to Sappho and Alcaeus was Anacreon, who was born in Teos in Asia Minor but spent much of his life in Athens. The leader of the "Dorian school" of the fifth century was the "choric" poet Pindar. Late Greek poetry of the Hellenistic period is best represented by Theocritus, whose *Idylls* established the pattern for centuries to come of pastoral poetry, in which the subject matter, whatever it may be, is cast in terms of rural scenes and characters.

In lyric poetry, as in much else, the Greeks set out on paths we still follow. The very conception of a "lyric" voice, intensely individual and personal, uncovering the subtle movements of thought and emotion and linking them to musicality, was Greek. Perhaps the most direct heir to Greek lyricism among the Romans was the first-century B.C. Catullus, whose most famous poems, those about his mistress "Lesbia," seem to explore all the convolutions of a self in the grip of an ambivalent passion. The other great Latin lyricists seem tame by comparison—they are polished and even elegant but they lack the naked self-revelation of the Greeks and of Catullus. Virgil is almost as well known for his *Eclogues* as for the *Aeneid;* in these poems he follows Theocritus in urbanely surveying many subjects under the cloak of the pastoral idiom. The other great Augustan lyricist was Horace, whose polished style, charm, and tone of detached common sense made him the most imitated classical poet of the European Enlightenment. Ovid was primarily a storyteller rather than a lyricist, but in his *Art of Love, Amores,* and *Metamorphoses,* we see again the Greek lyric inspiration, translated into Roman smartness and a cynical, amusing detachment.

Finally, a narrow definition of literary genres should not rule out such masterpieces of discursive prose as we find in much of the Old Testament and in Plato and Aristotle. Such works have had an incalculable impact upon later literature. The voices of the Hebrew prophets, of Plato's genial and humane Socrates, and of Aristotle, the indefatigable analyst of the nature and meaning of almost everything, must be included among the voices of the ancient world.

FURTHER READING *(prepared by J.H.):* An excellent overview of ancient history is provided by Chester G. Starr, *A History of the Ancient World,* 1965. A standard brief introduction to Hebrew history is John Bright, *A History of Israel,* 2nd ed., 1972.

Even briefer and very useful are B. K. Rattey, *A Short History of the Hebrews*, 2nd ed., 1964, and Harry Orlinsky, *Ancient Israel*, 2nd ed., 1960. J. B. Bury's *History of Greece*, revised by R. Meiggs, 1951, and Michael Grant's *History of Rome*, 1978, are recommended for what their titles promise. Also useful are studies of the history of ideas in the ancient world. For the Hebrews, see James Muilenburg, *The Way of Israel*, 1961, and Norman Snaith, *Distinctive Ideas of the Old Testament*, 1947. Important special topics are treated in Frank M. Cross, *Canaanite Myth and Hebrew Epic*, 1973; Dennis J. McCarthy, *Old Testament Covenant: A Survey of Current Opinions*, 1972; and John H. Otwell, *And Sarah Laughed*, 1977, which examines the role of women in the Old Testament. Of special importance in understanding the literary practice of the Hebrews, as well as individual books of the Bible, is Northrop Frye's *The Great Code: The Bible and Literature*, 1982. H. D. F. Kitto's *The Greeks*, 1951, C. M. Bowra's *The Greek Experience*, 1957, A. Andrewes' *The Greeks*, 1967, and K. J. Dover's lavishly illustrated *The Greeks*, 1981, are all clear, accurate introductions to Greek ideas and culture. An important literary history of Greece is Albin Lesky, *A History of Greek Literature*, 1963, trans. James Willis and Cornelis de Heer, 1966. Briefer, but still valuable, overviews are provided by C. M. Bowra, *Ancient Greek Literature*, 1933, and K. J. Dover, ed., *Ancient Greek Literature*, 1980. On Greek drama and the Greek theater, T. B. L. Webster's *Greek Theatre Production*, 1962, Peter Arnott's *Greek Scenic Conventions*, 1962, and Margarete Bieber's *The History of the Greek and Roman Theater*, 2nd ed., 1961, are authoritative. H. D. F. Kitto's *Greek Tragedy*, 3rd ed., 1961, is a standard critical survey; Jan Kott's *The Eating of the Gods*, 1973, surveys the plays from a more recent perspective. M. I. Finley, ed., *The Legacy of Greece*, 1981, collects major essays reappraising the Greek heritage. R. H. Barrow's *The Romans*, 1949, is a useful brief introduction to Roman thought and culture. J. Wight Duff's two-volume history of Roman literature has not been superseded: *A Literary History of Rome from the Origins to the Close of the Golden Age*, 3rd ed., 1953; and *A Literary History of Rome in the Silver Age*, 3rd ed., 1964. Michael Grant's *Roman Literature*, 1954, is also accurate and readable, as is Moses Hadas' *History of Latin Literature*, 1952. Hadas' *Ancilla to Classical Reading*, 1954, is a thoughtful and lively handbook for the student of both Greek and Roman literature. R. M. Ogilvie's *Roman Literature and Society*, 1980, is a good author-by-author introduction and survey.

The Old Testament

(Tenth Century B.C. to Second Century B.C.)

The Old Testament develops a single central theme: the history of the ancient Hebrews' evolving perceptions of God. The setting is the tiny land of Palestine, the characters are the members of a small group of nomadic, Semitic tribes, and the time is a span of about fourteen centuries, from about 1800 B.C. to about 400 B.C. The story is above all a history, for the Hebrews—the ancient people whose culture has been transmitted by the Jews—were unusual, though not unique, among early peoples in conceiving of their religion not as the product of a single magnificent revelation, but as the result of a long series of experiences with their God. To the Hebrews, history was the story of a series of transactions with a stern but loving deity.

Although the Book of Genesis deals with the earliest events in the history of mankind, it was, in its final form, one of the last written books of the Old Testament. A group of Priestly revisers constructed the book, in about the middle of the fourth century B.C. Their sources were a much earlier version (the "J document") and an undetermined number of intermediate accounts.

The book as we have it divides into two parts. The first section is an account of prehistorical racial beginnings, and the second is a history of the origin of the Hebrews, descendants of the three patriarchs Abraham, Isaac, and Jacob. The account of the Creation that opens the book is a poetic treatment that in concrete narrative embodies certain basic Hebrew beliefs. Some of the matters "explained" in this account are fairly trivial: why snakes crawl on the ground, for example, and why women are afraid of them. But most of the questions raised are of the grandest magnitude: Who rules the world? What is man's relationship to God? How can we account for the presence of suffering in the world? Why do people wage war against each other? Genesis provides no final answers to these questions; the rest of the Old Testament, and the New Testament as well, is devoted to exploring the questions more fully, and people today are still engaged in debating some of the issues raised by the Creation story: Should women be subordinate to men, and must there be mistrust between men and women? Is work to be conceived of as a punishment? Are human beings by nature sinful, and is their natural relation to God that of suppliants seeking to atone for their sins?

Such questions do not obscure the major assumptions about the world that the first part of Genesis establishes. The Hebrews maintained that there is a Supreme Being, that He makes certain ethical demands upon human beings, and that man's chief duty is to serve God and to carry out His will.

With the eleventh chapter of Genesis, the focus abruptly narrows from the prehistory of mankind as a whole to the Hebrew people in particular and to their origins in the family of Abraham. The stories of Abraham, Isaac, Jacob, Esau, and Joseph, which follow, bear, like the earlier part of Genesis, the marks of primitive, folktale origins and later, more sophisticated revision. The key episodes, as in the earlier portion, are those in which God reveals Himself to man and establishes a series of "covenants" or agreements. These covenants represent a series of unfolding or developing perceptions of God, from the first (broken) covenant in the Garden, through the covenant of the rainbow, to the great covenant made with Abraham, and subsequently repeatedly renewed, that He would "make of thee a great nation."

16

The books of Exodus, Leviticus, Numbers, Deuteronomy, and Joshua are largely devoted to the Hebrew national epic. These books tell the story of the escape from Egyptian bondage under the leadership of Moses, the forty-years wandering in the Wilderness, and the final triumphant entry into the Promised Land. The books contain much else as well, notably large bodies of legislation, but the selections presented here form the narrative basis of the books. In its grand scope and its nationalistic fervor, the Exodus saga suggests comparisons with the Greek Iliad and Odyssey and the Roman Aeneid. Like these other works, it recounts heroic actions from the early history of a people, centered around strong, dominating heroes. Like the Odyssey and the Aeneid, it is built upon the strong but simple basis of a journey through heroic challenges and perils, a journey that ends in a triumphant "homecoming." And, as in the classical epics, its action moves between the human and divine levels.

The chief difference is in the nature of the divine element in the Hebrew and the Graeco-Roman epics. The Olympian gods, in the classical epics, remain above the action, observing and occasionally intervening either to help or to hinder the hero, but leaving the central action to unfold on the human plane. In the Exodus saga, in contrast, the entire story turns around the complex relationship between the Lord and the Hebrew people, as He both chastises and encourages them in their slow progress not only toward Canaan but toward an understanding of the Lord as God and of themselves as a nation.

Moses emerges almost immediately as the hero of the story, with the romantic tale of his discovery in the bulrushes by the Pharaoh's daughter. We read of his rearing at court, where he is nursed by his own mother in the role of foster mother. He kills an Egyptian oppressor and flees into the land of Midian. And then occurs the mysterious event that sets the epic action in motion: God appears to Moses in a burning bush and tells him to "bring forth the children of Israel out of Egypt." This event thus takes its place in the series of "theophanies," or direct experiences of God, that form the spine of the Pentateuch (the first five books of the Bible). The event is mysterious because no reason is ever given for the Lord's choosing Moses for this great work. Moses must grow into the role God has assigned him. At first he is reluctant and protests that he is not capable of the task God has laid on him. But as the epic progresses, Moses increases in moral stature to true epic proportions: he becomes fearless, commanding, and resourceful—the kind of man the Lord speaks with "face to face, as a man speaketh unto his friend." As the German poet Heinrich Heine wrote, "How tiny the mountain seems when Moses stands upon it!"

The dramatic interest in the Exodus epic is provided not only by the heroic growth of Moses, but also by his struggles with the Hebrew people. It is paradoxical that, in this nationalistic epic, the Hebrews represent themselves as deeply flawed. They are hardly out of Egypt before they are complaining and wishing they were back there, "when we sat by the flesh pots, and when we did eat bread to the full." When Moses obtains the gift of manna for them and conveys the Lord's command that they not store it overnight, they immediately disobey him and "it bred worms and stank." Even when Moses is on Mount Sinai, receiving the law, written upon tablets of stone by the finger of God, the people quickly become discouraged and build a "molten calf" to worship, Egyptian-fashion. No wonder the Lord's recurrent cry is "Behold, it is a stiffnecked people!"

The Exodus saga thus becomes not just a militaristic tale of battles against external enemies, but also the story of an education and a maturation for a whole people. God, through Moses, leads them into the Wilderness for forty years, on the most *circuitous route possible to the Promised Land, not arbitrarily but in order to give them time to transform themselves from a slave people to a nation, with a government, a body of civil and religious law, and a sense of national identity.*

The action of the Exodus saga, though sometimes repetitive and anecdotal, in a folk-like way, is highly unified as a whole. It sweeps toward four great climaxes: the Hebrews' crossing of the Red Sea and their defeat of the forces of the Pharaoh, the receiving of the Law from God atop Mount Sinai, the death of Moses, and the triumphant entry into the Promised Land under Joshua. This last part of the saga, which takes up the entire book of Joshua and which is represented here only by the history of the initial campaign against Jericho, presents the story as a swift and almost wholly triumphant military action under the leadership of a brilliant general. We are later told in Judges and First Samuel that the conquest was a slow and laborious process. The character of Joshua in the earlier books seems to be the result of a deliberate attempt to create an epic hero in a mold more familiar than that of Moses. Joshua is the hero as warrior rather than as spiritual leader. But he never comes fully to life, and Moses remains the memorable figure of the epic.

It is generally agreed that the Book of Job is the literary masterpiece of the Old Testament and one of the great works of all literature. It contains some of the most magnificent poetry in the Bible, and its seemingly simple structure, on rereading, reveals itself as endlessly resonant in its implications. And yet it is somewhat surprising that this book should be in the Bible at all, so sharp is its questioning of traditional Hebrew thought. Its subject is an eternal one—why do the good suffer?—and although of course it arrives at no answer to the unanswerable question, its reasoning is so keen and its emotional power so deep that the careful reader of Job can never again accept easy and shallow answers to the question.

Nothing is known of the author of Job, and its precise date is uncertain, but scholars now generally date it in the fifth century B.C. Such dating would make it roughly contemporary with Aeschylus' Prometheus Bound *and Sophocles'* Oedipus Rex, *both of which also deal profoundly with the question of human suffering. This common theme and the book's dramatic form have tempted critics to speculate that the author was directly influenced by Greek tragedy, though there is no external evidence of such influence.*

Job's debate with his conventional friends Eliphaz, Bildad, and Zophar sharply challenges the traditional Deuteronomic view of human suffering. Job and his "Comforters" agree that his suffering comes from God, but they differ radically on its meaning. The Comforters reconcile God's absolute power and absolute goodness by insisting that Job's suffering is a just punishment for sin. Job insists with equal vehemence that he has not deserved his fate and that no simple equation can be made between sin and suffering. But his lament is directed as much to God Himself as to the Comforters, as he calls into question not only their facile explanations but also the fundamental idea of any sort of justice or "covenant" between limited man and limitless God. "How should man be just with God?" he cries, "If he will contend with Him, he cannot answer Him one of a thousand."

The resolution of the book comes when God speaks "out of the whirlwind" in a theophany which recalls God's other appearances to man throughout the Old Testament. God's reply is simultaneously a rebuke to Job and a vindication of his position that God's power is too great to be reckoned in human terms. Ultimately, God approves the tormented questioner more than the complacent moralizers: "My wrath is kindled against thee, and against thy two friends," He tells Eliphaz, "for ye have not spoken of me the thing that is right, as my servant Job hath." The wager won, God restores to Job all that he has lost, and the book ends. The central question is still unanswered, but the issue has been dramatized more vividly than ever before or since.

The Psalms (a word that literally means "Songs") are thoroughly and obviously an expression of Hebrew ideas, expressed in some of the most beautiful lyric poetry in world literature. Martin Luther called these 150 songs "a Bible in miniature," and indeed they do encapsulate much of Hebrew history, psychology, and theology. Written over almost the entire time-span of the Old Testament, they were used in ancient times for liturgical purposes (the exact nature of which is a subject of controversy) and continue to be so used in modern Jewish and Christian worship. They include hymns, meditations, exhortations, songs of praise, and commentaries on the significance of historical events for the Hebrew people. In tone they range widely, from quietude to rage, from exultation to deep grief. They are deeply Hebraic in their celebration of nature, not for its own sake but as God's handiwork, in their portrayal of God as transcendently great and powerful but in intimate touch with His people, and in their expression of communal ideals through an intensely personal tone.

The Book of Jonah is generally grouped with the Prophetic books, because its protagonist is a prophet (although a surprisingly reluctant and inept one). It is not, however, a prophecy itself, but rather a delightful short story, or perhaps a parable, full of comic irony which makes an essentially serious point, a point about the universality of God's rule and the dangers of narrowness and xenophobia.

The story is full of delicate ironies. Jonah, to whom, as to Moses, God has appeared, tries to escape the task God has demanded of him. The heathen sailors, by contrast, are quite willing to believe in the Lord and to serve Him, once they understand the situation. God saves Jonah from the sea, with a loving charity Jonah himself lacks. (His prayer in the belly of the fish is a later interpolation that suggests a piety he does not have at this point in the story.) The Ninevites, like the sailors, are quite willing to be converted, even by so surly a message as Jonah's: "Yet forty days, and Nineveh shall be overthrown." But Jonah is petty enough to sulk and pout when God does not make good his prophecy that He will kill "sixscore thousand persons" in Nineveh. God teaches Jonah a lesson through the gourd which first flourishes and then dies. We are not told whether or not Jonah profits from the lesson, but the message is clear to us: God does not hate "foreigners," as some of his self-satisfied followers do.

NOTE ON THE TEXT

These selections from the Old Testament are from the King James Version of 1611. There are a number of more accurate, modern translations, but none has had comparable influence upon English speech and literature. The first six books have been condensed for the sake of narrative continuity. Omissions of large sections (such as the Joseph story in Genesis) are marked in footnotes.

FURTHER READING *(prepared by F. S. N.):* George A. Buttrick, ed., *The Interpreter's Bible,* 12 vols., 1952, gives, in addition to background material on the *Old Testament* (vol. 7), introductions, exegesis and exposition on individual books. John E. Steinmueller and Kathryn Sullivan, eds., *Catholic Biblical Encyclopedia: Old Testament,* 1956, have compiled a valuable work of reference. Dealing with the books as literary types is Georg Fohrer's *Introduction to the Old Testament,* 1965, trans. by David E. Green, 1968. Kenneth R. R. Gros Louis, ed., *Literary Interpretations of Biblical Narra-*

tives, 1982, is accurately described by its title. General studies, including information on background, canon, literary merits and individual books, are offered by Otto Eissfeldt, *The Old Testament*, 1934, trans. by Peter R. Ackroyd, 1965, repr. 1974; and by Aage Bentzen, *Introduction to the Old Testament*, 1948, 7th ed. 1967.

THE OLD TESTAMENT

King James Version (1611)

from GENESIS

THE CREATION OF THE WORLD

(Genesis 1:1–2:3)

In the beginning God created the heaven and the earth. And the earth was without form, and void; and darkness was upon the face of the deep. And the Spirit of God moved upon the face of the waters. And God said, "Let there be light": and there was light. And God saw the light, that it was good: and God divided the light from the darkness. And God called the light Day, and the darkness he called Night. And the evening and the morning were the first day.

And God said, "Let there be a firmament in the midst of the waters, and let it divide the waters from the waters." And God made the firmament, and divided the waters which were under the firmament from the waters which were above the firmament: and it was so.[1] And God called the firmament Heaven. And the evening and the morning were the second day.

And God said, "Let the waters under the heaven be gathered together unto one place, and let the dry land appear": and it was so. And God called the dry land Earth; and the gathering together of the waters called he Seas: and God saw that it was good. And God said, "Let the earth bring forth grass, the herb yielding seed, and the fruit tree yielding fruit after his kind, whose seed is in itself, upon the earth": and it was so. And the earth brought forth grass, and herb yielding seed after his kind, and the tree yielding fruit, whose seed was in itself, after his kind: and God saw that it was good. And the evening and the morning were the third day.

And God said, "Let there be lights in the firmament of the heaven to divide the day from the night; and let them be for signs, and for seasons, and for days, and years; and let them be for lights in the firmament of the heaven to give light upon the earth." And it was so. And God made two great lights; the greater light to rule the day, and the lesser light to rule the night: he made the stars also. And God set them in the firmament of the heaven to give light upon the earth. And to rule over the day and over the night, and to divide the light from the darkness: and God saw that it was good. And the evening and the morning were the fourth day.

---

[1] These lines rest upon a belief that the world was created out of a watery chaos. The "firmament" was thought of as a solid dome which divided the "waters above" from the "waters below."

And God said, "Let the waters bring forth abundantly the moving creature that hath life, and fowl that may fly above the earth in the open firmament of heaven." And God created great whales, and every living creature that moveth, which the waters brought forth abundantly, after their kind, and every winged fowl after his kind: and God saw that it was good. And God blessed them, saying, "Be fruitful, and multiply, and fill the waters in the seas, and let fowl multiply in the earth." And the evening and the morning were the fifth day.

And God said, "Let the earth bring forth the living creature after his kind, cattle,[2] and creeping thing, and beast of the earth after his kind": and it was so. And God made the beast of the earth after his kind, and cattle after their kind, and every thing that creepeth upon the earth after his kind: and God saw that it was good.

And God said, "Let us make man in our image, after our likeness: and let them have dominion over the fish of the sea, and over the fowl of the air, and over the cattle, and over all the earth, and over every creeping thing that creepeth upon the earth." So God created man in his own image, in the image of God created he him; male and female created he them. And God blessed them, and God said unto them, "Be fruitful, and multiply, and replenish the earth, and subdue it: and have dominion over the fish of the sea, and over the fowl of the air, and over every living thing that moveth upon the earth." And God said, "Behold, I have given you every herb bearing seed, which is upon the face of all the earth, and every tree, in the which is the fruit of a tree yielding seed; to you it shall be for meat. And to every beast of the earth, and to every fowl of the air, and to every thing that creepeth upon the earth, wherein there is life, I have given every green herb for meat." And it was so. And God saw every thing that he had made, and, behold, it was very good. And the evening and the morning were the sixth day.

Thus the heavens and the earth were finished, and all the host of them. And on the seventh day God ended his work which he had made; and he rested on the seventh day from all his work which he had made. And God blessed the seventh day, and sanctified it: because that in it he had rested from all his work which God created and made. . . .

THE FALL OF MAN

(Genesis 2:4–3:24)
In the day that the Lord God made the earth and the heavens, and every plant of the field before it was in the earth, and every herb of the field before it grew (for the Lord God had not caused it to rain upon the earth, and there was not a man to till the ground) there went up a mist from the earth, and watered the whole face of the ground. And the Lord God formed man of the dust of the ground, and breathed into his nostrils the breath of life; and man became a living soul. And the Lord God planted a garden eastward in Eden; and there he put the man whom he had formed. And out of the ground made the Lord God to grow every tree that is

[2] All domestic animals.

pleasant to the sight, and good for food; the tree of life also in the midst of
the garden, and the tree of knowledge of good and evil. And a river went
out of Eden to water the garden; and from thence it was parted, and became into four heads. The name of the first is Pison: that is it which compasseth the whole land of Havilah, where there is gold; and the gold of that
land is good: there is bdellium[3] and the onyx stone. And the name of the
second river is Gihon: the same is it that compasseth the whole land of
Ethiopia. And the name of the third river is Hiddekel: that is it which goeth
toward the east of Assyria. And the fourth river is Euphrates.

And the Lord God took the man, and put him into the garden of Eden
to dress[4] it and to keep it. And the Lord God commanded the man, saying,
"Of every tree of the garden thou mayest freely eat: but of the tree of the
knowledge of good and evil, thou shalt not eat of it: for in the day that thou
eatest thereof thou shalt surely die."

And the Lord God said, "It is not good that the man should be alone; I
will make him a help meet for him." And out of the ground the Lord God
formed every beast of the field, and every fowl of the air; and brought
them unto Adam[5] to see what he would call them: and whatsoever Adam
called every living creature, that was the name thereof. And Adam gave
names to all cattle, and to the fowl of the air, and to every beast of the field;
but for Adam there was not found a help meet for him. And the Lord God
caused a deep sleep to fall upon Adam, and he slept: and he took one of his
ribs, and closed up the flesh instead thereof; and the rib, which the Lord
God had taken from man, made he a woman, and brought her unto the
man.

And Adam said,

> "This is now bone of my bones,
>   and flesh of my flesh:
> She shall be called Woman,
>   because she was taken out of Man."

Therefore shall a man leave his father and his mother, and shall cleave
unto his wife: and they shall be one flesh. And they were both naked, the
man and his wife, and were not ashamed.

Now the serpent was more subtil than any beast of the field which the
Lord God had made. And he said unto the woman, "Yea, hath God said,
'Ye shall not eat of every tree of the garden'?" And the woman said unto the
serpent, "We may eat of the fruit of the trees of the garden: but of the fruit
of the tree which is in the midst of the garden, God hath said, 'Ye shall not
eat of it, neither shall ye touch it, lest ye die.'" And the serpent said unto
the woman, "Ye shall not surely die: for God doth know that in the day ye
eat thereof, then your eyes shall be opened, and ye shall be as gods, knowing good and evil."[6]

And when the woman saw that the tree was good for food, and that it

---

[3] The meaning of this word is obscure. It may be either a fragrant gum resin or a precious
stone such as carbuncle, crystal, or pearl.
[4] Tend or cultivate.   [5] "Adam" means "man."
[6] Only the tree of "the knowledge of good and evil" is mentioned in the temptation story.
The previously mentioned "tree of life" does not appear.

was pleasant to the eyes, and a tree to be desired to make one wise, she took of the fruit thereof, and did eat, and gave also unto her husband with her; and he did eat. And the eyes of them both were opened, and they knew that they were naked; and they sewed fig leaves together, and made themselves aprons.

And they heard the voice of the Lord God walking in the garden in the cool of the day: and Adam and his wife hid themselves from the presence of the Lord God amongst the trees of the garden. And the Lord God called unto Adam, and said unto him, "Where art thou?" And he said, "I heard thy voice in the garden, and I was afraid, because I was naked; and I hid myself." And he said, "Who told thee that thou wast naked? Hast thou eaten of the tree, whereof I commanded thee that thou shouldest not eat?" And the man said, "The woman whom thou gavest to be with me, she gave me of the tree, and I did eat." And the Lord God said unto the woman, "What is this that thou hast done?" And the woman said, "The serpent beguiled me, and I did eat." And the Lord God said unto the serpent,

> "Because thou hast done this,
> > thou are cursed above all cattle,
> > and above every beast of the field.
> Upon thy belly shalt thou go,
> > and dust shalt thou eat
> > all the days of thy life:
> And I will put enmity between thee and the woman,
> > and between thy seed[7] and her seed;
> It shall bruise thy head,
> > and thou shalt bruise his heel."

Unto the woman he said,

> "I will greatly multiply thy sorrow and thy conception;
> In sorrow thou shalt bring forth children;
> And thy desire shall be to thy husband,
> And he shall rule over thee."

And unto Adam he said, "Because thou hast hearkened unto the voice of thy wife, and hast eaten of the tree, of which I commanded thee, saying, 'Thou shalt not eat of it':

> "Cursed is the ground for thy sake;
> > in sorrow shalt thou eat of it all the days of thy life.
> Thorns also and thistles shall it bring forth to thee;
> > and thou shalt eat the herb of the field;
> In the sweat of thy face
> > shalt thou eat bread,
> Till thou return unto the ground;
> > for out of it wast thou taken:
> For dust thou art,
> > and unto dust shalt thou return."

[7] Descendants.

And Adam called his wife's name Eve; because she was the mother of all living.[8] Unto Adam also and to his wife did the Lord God make coats of skins, and clothed them.

And the Lord God said, "Behold, the man is become as one of us, to know good and evil: and now, lest he put forth his hand, and take also of the tree of life, and eat, and live for ever—" therefore the Lord God sent him forth from the garden of Eden, to till the ground from whence he was taken. So he drove out the man; and he placed at the east of the garden of Eden Cherubims,[9] and a flaming sword which turned every way, to keep the way of the tree of life.

CAIN AND ABEL

(Genesis 4:1–5:5)

And Adam knew[10] Eve his wife; and she conceived, and bore Cain, and said, "I have gotten a man from the Lord." And she again bore his brother Abel. And Abel was a keeper of sheep, but Cain was a tiller of the ground. And in process of time it came to pass that Cain brought of the fruit of the ground an offering unto the Lord. And Abel, he also brought of the firstlings of his flock and of the fat thereof. And the Lord had respect unto Abel and to his offering: but unto Cain and to his offering he had not respect.[11] And Cain was very wroth, and his countenance fell. And the Lord said unto Cain, "Why art thou wroth? and why is thy countenance fallen? If thou doest well, shalt thou not be accepted? and if thou doest not well, sin lieth at the door. And unto thee shall be his desire, and thou shalt rule over him."

And Cain talked with Abel his brother: and it came to pass, when they were in the field, that Cain rose up against Abel his brother, and slew him. And the Lord said unto Cain, "Where is Abel thy brother?" And he said, "I know not: am I my brother's keeper?" And he said, "What hast thou done? the voice of thy brother's blood crieth unto me from the ground. And now art thou cursed from the earth, which hath opened her mouth to receive thy brother's blood from thy hand. When thou tillest the ground, it shall not henceforth yield unto thee her strength; a fugitive and a vagabond shalt thou be in the earth." And Cain said unto the Lord, "My punishment is greater than I can bear. Behold, thou hast driven me out this day from the face of the earth; and from thy face shall I be hid; and I shall be a fugitive and a vagabond in the earth; and it shall come to pass that every one that findeth me shall slay me." And the Lord said unto him, "Therefore whosoever slayeth Cain, vengeance shall be taken on him sevenfold." And the Lord set a mark upon Cain, lest any finding him should kill him. And Cain went out from the presence of the Lord, and dwelt in the land of Nod, on the east of Eden. . . .

[8] "Eve" in Hebrew resembles the word for "living."
[9] Guardians of sacred areas, depicted as winged creatures, half human and half lion.
[10] Had sexual intercourse with.
[11] The Cain and Abel story reflects the tensions between nomadic shepherds and farmers. (Compare the tension between hunter and shepherd in the story of Jacob and Esau.) No reason is given for God's refusal of Cain's offering.

And Adam knew his wife again; and she bore a son, and called his name Seth: "For God," said she, "hath appointed me another seed instead of Abel, whom Cain slew." And to Seth, to him also there was born a son; and he called his name Enos: then began men to call upon the name of the Lord. . . .

And the days of Adam after he had begotten Seth were eight hundred years: and he begot sons and daughters. And all the days that Adam lived were nine hundred and thirty years: and he died. . . .[12]

THE FLOOD

(Genesis 6:1—9:29)

And it came to pass, when men began to multiply on the face of the earth, and daughters were born unto them, that the sons of God saw the daughters of men that they were fair; and they took them wives of all which they chose.[13] And the Lord said, "My spirit shall not always strive with man, for that he also is flesh: yet his days shall be a hundred and twenty years." There were giants in the earth in those days; and also after that, when the sons of God came in unto the daughters of men, and they bore children to them, the same became mighty men which were of old, men of renown. And God saw that the wickedness of man was great in the earth, and that every imagination of the thoughts of his heart was only evil continually. And it repented the Lord that he had made man on the earth, and it grieved him at his heart. And the Lord said, "I will destroy man whom I have created from the face of the earth; both man, and beast, and the creeping thing, and the fowls of the air; for it repenteth me that I have made them." But Noah found grace in the eyes of the Lord. . . .

Noah was a just man and perfect in his generations, and Noah walked with God. And Noah begot three sons, Shem, Ham, and Japheth. . . .

And God said unto Noah, "The end of all flesh is come before me; for the earth is filled with violence through them; and, behold, I will destroy them with the earth.[14] Make thee an ark of gopher wood;[15] rooms shalt thou make in the ark, and shalt pitch it within and without with pitch. And this is the fashion which thou shalt make it of: the length of the ark shall be three hundred cubits,[16] the breadth of it fifty cubits, and the

[12] Various explanations have been offered to account for the extraordinary life spans attributed to figures of the Old Testament. The simplest is that they are exaggerations—such as appear in other national legends—intended to glorify the beginnings of the race.

[13] This account of the mating of "the sons of God" and "the daughters of men" is a good example of the primitive conceptions of divinity which still survive in the Old Testament. The story was perhaps originally intended to account for the existence of the Nephilim, a tribe of men of gigantic size and strength; this narrative may be compared to the stories of the matings of gods and mortal women in Greek mythology.

[14] The Biblical account of the Flood has much in common with other accounts of great floods, especially in the Babylonian Gilgamesh Epic. In this other work, the hero also builds an ark, it comes to rest on a mountain, birds are sent out to see if the flood is subsiding, and the hero makes burnt offerings for his deliverance. The Genesis version differs, however, in that the Flood is not sent capriciously but as a punishment for man's wickedness.

[15] An ark is a large ship. The kind of wood used is unidentified; "gopher" simply means "tree" in Hebrew.

[16] A cubit is an ancient unit of measurement based on the length of the forearm, usually about twenty inches.

height of it thirty cubits. A window shalt thou make to the ark, and in a cubit shalt thou finish it above; and the door of the ark shalt thou set in the side thereof; with lower, second, and third stories shalt thou make it. And, behold, I, even I, do bring a flood of waters upon the earth, to destroy all flesh, wherein is the breath of life, from under heaven; and everything that is in the earth shall die. But with thee will I establish my covenant;[17] and thou shalt come into the ark, thou, and thy sons, and thy wife, and thy sons' wives with thee. And of every living thing of all flesh, two of every sort shalt thou bring into the ark, to keep them alive with thee; they shall be male and female. Of fowls after their kind, and of cattle after their kind, of every creeping thing of the earth after his kind, two of every sort shall come unto thee, to keep them alive. And take thou unto thee of all food that is eaten, and thou shalt gather it to thee; and it shall be for food for thee, and for them." Thus did Noah; according to all that God commanded him, so did he. And the Lord said unto Noah, "Come thou and all thy house into the ark; for thee have I seen righteous before me in this generation. Of every clean beast thou shalt take to thee by sevens, the male and his female; and of beasts that are not clean by two, the male and his female.[18] Of fowls also of the air by sevens, the male and the female; to keep seed alive upon the face of all the earth. For yet seven days, and I will cause it to rain upon the earth forty days and forty nights; and every living substance that I have made will I destroy from off the face of the earth."

And Noah did according unto all that the Lord commanded him. And Noah went in, and his sons, and his wife, and his sons' wives with him, into the ark, because of the waters of the flood. Of clean beasts, and of beasts that are not clean, and of fowls, and of every thing that creepeth upon the earth, there went in two and two unto Noah into the ark, the male and the female, as God had commanded Noah. And it came to pass after seven days that the waters of the flood were upon the earth. In the six hundredth year of Noah's life in the second month, the seventeenth day of the month, the same day were all the fountains of the great deep broken up, and the windows of heaven were opened.[19] And the waters prevailed, and were increased greatly upon the earth; and the ark went upon the face of the waters. And the waters prevailed exceedingly upon the earth; and all the high hills, that were under the whole heaven, were covered. Fifteen cubits

---

[17]This "covenant," or agreement, between God and Noah, which is expanded after the Flood and marked with the sign of the rainbow, is the first of several such covenants in the Old Testament. The agreements culminate in the repeated covenant with Abraham and his descendants, which has become the central idea in Judaism. The conditions under which God allowed Adam and Eve to live in the Garden are an implicit covenant that anticipates these later covenants.

[18]"Clean beasts" include those which have cloven hooves and chew a cud. See Leviticus, Chapter 11. The distinction between clean and unclean here is apparently a later addition, not harmonized with the rest of the text, since Noah takes in two of each animal, regardless of status.

[19]As a result of the blending of different accounts, two explanations are given for the Flood. The first is that it rained for forty days and forty nights, while here it is said that "all the fountains of the great deep [were] broken up, and the windows of heaven were opened." In other words, chaos returned through the opening up of subterranean seas and the opening of the dome-like firmament that restrained "the waters above." See the beginning of Genesis.

upward did the waters prevail; and the mountains were covered. And all flesh died that moved upon the earth, both of fowl, and of cattle, and of beast, and of every creeping thing that creepeth upon the earth, and every man. All in whose nostrils was the breath of life, of all that was in the dry land, died. And every living substance was destroyed which was upon the face of the ground, both man, and cattle, and the creeping things, and the fowl of the heaven; and they were destroyed from the earth: and Noah only remained alive, and they that were with him in the ark. And the waters prevailed upon the earth a hundred and fifty days.

And God remembered Noah, and every living thing, and all the cattle that was with him in the ark: and God made a wind to pass over the earth, and the waters assuaged. The fountains also of the deep and the windows of heaven were stopped, and the rain from heaven was restrained; and the waters returned from off the earth continually: and after the end of the hundred and fifty days the waters were abated. And the ark rested in the seventh month, on the seventeenth day of the month, upon the mountains of Ararat. And the waters decreased continually until the tenth month: in the tenth month, on the first day of the month, were the tops of the mountains seen.

And it came to pass at the end of forty days that Noah opened the window of the ark which he had made: and he sent forth a raven, which went forth to and fro, until the waters were dried up from off the earth. Also he sent forth a dove from him, to see if the waters were abated from off the face of the ground; but the dove found no rest for the sole of her foot, and she returned unto him into the ark, for the waters were on the face of the whole earth: then he put forth his hand, and took her, and pulled her in unto him into the ark. And he stayed yet other seven days; and again he sent forth the dove out of the ark; and the dove came in to him in the evening; and, lo, in her mouth was an olive leaf plucked off: so Noah knew that the waters were abated from off the earth. And he stayed yet other seven days; and sent forth the dove; which returned not again unto him any more.

And it came to pass in the six hundredth and first year, in the first month, the first day of the month, the waters were dried up from off the earth: and Noah removed the covering of the ark, and looked, and, behold the face of the ground was dry. And in the second month, on the seven and twentieth day of the month, was the earth dried. And God spoke unto Noah, saying, "Go forth of the ark, thou, and thy wife, and thy sons, and thy sons' wives with thee. Bring forth with thee every living thing that is with thee, of all flesh, both of fowl, and of cattle, and of every creeping thing that creepeth upon the earth; that they may breed abundantly in the earth, and be fruitful, and multiply upon the earth." And Noah went forth, and his sons, and his wife, and his sons' wives with him. Every beast, every creeping thing, and every fowl, and whatsoever creepeth upon the earth, after their kinds, went forth out of the ark.

And Noah builded an altar unto the Lord; and took of every clean beast, and of every clean fowl, and offered burnt offerings on the altar. And the Lord smelled a sweet savor; and the Lord said in his heart, "I will not again curse the ground any more for man's sake; for the imagination of man's heart is evil from his youth; neither will I again smite any more every thing living, as I have done. While the earth remaineth, seedtime and harvest, and cold and heat, and summer and winter, and day and night shall not cease."

And God blessed Noah and his sons, and said unto them, "Be fruitful, and multiply, and replenish the earth. And the fear of you and the dread of you shall be upon every beast of the earth, and upon every fowl of the air, upon all that moveth upon the earth, and upon all the fishes of the sea; into your hand are they delivered. Every moving thing that liveth shall be meat for you; even as the green herb have I given you all things. But flesh with the life thereof, which is the blood thereof, shall ye not eat. And surely your blood of your lives will I require; at the hand of every beast will I require it, and at the hand of man; at the hand of every man's brother will I require the life of man. Whoso sheddeth man's blood, by man shall his blood be shed: for in the image of God made he man.". . . And God spoke unto Noah, and to his sons with him, saying, "And I, behold, I establish my covenant with you, and with your seed after you; and with every living creature that is with you, of the fowl, of the cattle, and of every beast of the earth with you; from all that go out of the ark, to every beast of the earth. And I will establish my covenant with you; neither shall all flesh be cut off any more by the waters of a flood; neither shall there any more be a flood to destroy the earth."

And God said, "This is the token of the covenant which I make between me and you and every living creature that is with you, for perpetual generations: I do set my bow in the cloud, and it shall be for a token of a covenant between me and the earth. And it shall come to pass, when I bring a cloud over the earth, that the bow shall be seen in the cloud: and I will remember my covenant, which is between me and you and every living creature of all flesh; and the waters shall no more become a flood to destroy all flesh. And the bow shall be in the cloud; and I will look upon it, that I may remember the everlasting covenant between God and every living creature of all flesh that is upon the earth."[20] And God said unto Noah, "This is the token of the covenant, which I have established between me and all flesh that is upon the earth.". . .

And Noah began to be a husbandman, and he planted a vineyard: and he drank of the wine, and was drunken; and he was uncovered within his tent. And Ham, the father of Canaan, saw the nakedness of his father, and told his two brethren without. And Shem and Japheth took a garment, and laid it upon both their shoulders, and went backward, and covered the nakedness of their father; and their faces were backward, and they saw not their father's nakedness.[21] And Noah awoke from his wine, and knew what his younger son had done unto him. And he said, "Cursed be Canaan; a servant of servants shall he be unto his brethren." And he said, "Blessed be the Lord God of Shem; and Canaan shall be his servant. God shall enlarge

[20] The rainbow was often regarded by primitive peoples as God's bow from which he shot arrows of lightning. Here it becomes rather a sign in the heavens that God's anger has abated.

[21] There is some confusion here in names. God places the curse on Canaan rather than on Ham, who is said to have committed the offense. The incident implies that Israel's later subjugation of Canaan was the consequence of the Canaanites' sexual perversions.

Japheth, and he shall dwell in the tents of Shem; and Canaan shall be his servant."

And Noah lived after the flood three hundred and fifty years. And all the days of Noah were nine hundred and fifty years: and he died. . . .

THE TOWER OF BABEL

(Genesis 11:1–11:9)

And the whole earth was of one language, and of one speech. And it came to pass, as they journeyed from the east, that they found a plain in the land of Shinar; and they dwelt there. And they said one to another, "Go to, let us make brick, and burn them thoroughly." And they had brick for stone, and slime had they for mortar. And they said, "Go to, let us build us a city and a tower, whose top may reach unto heaven; and let us make us a name, lest we be scattered abroad upon the face of the whole earth."[22] And the Lord came down to see the city and the tower, which the children of men builded. And the Lord said, "Behold, the people is one, and they have all one language; and this they begin to do: and now nothing will be restrained from them, which they have imagined to do. Go to, let us go down, and there confound their language, that they may not understand one another's speech." So the Lord scattered them abroad from thence upon the face of all the earth: and they left off to build the city. Therefore is the name of it called Babel; because the Lord did there confound the language of all the earth: and from thence did the Lord scatter them abroad upon the face of all the earth. . . .

THE STORY OF ABRAHAM

(Genesis 11:27–23:20)

Now these are the generations of Terah: Terah begot Abram, Nahor and Haran; and Haran begot Lot. And Haran died before his father Terah in the land of his nativity, in Ur of the Chaldees. And Abram and Nahor took them wives: the name of Abram's wife was Sarai; and the name of Nahor's wife, Milcah, the daughter of Haran, the father of Milcah, and the father of Iscah. But Sarai was barren; she had no child.

And Terah took Abram his son, and Lot the son of Haran his son's son, and Sarai his daughter-in-law, his son Abram's wife; and they went forth with them from Ur of the Chaldees, to go into the land of Canaan; and they came unto Haran, and dwelt there. And the days of Terah were two hundred and five years: and Terah died in Haran.

Now the Lord had said unto Abram, "Get thee out of thy country, and from thy kindred, and from thy father's house, unto a land that I will show thee: and I will make of thee a great nation, and I will bless thee, and make

---

[22] Mesopotamian cities were marked by *ziggurats,* pyramid-like towers regarded as the gateways to heaven. The story of the Tower of Babel not only alludes to such structures, but also is an etiological story accounting for the origin of languages and cultural magnificence of Babylon. The episode also emphasizes man's continuing pride and sinfulness even after the Flood.

thy name great; and thou shalt be a blessing. And I will bless them that bless thee, and curse him that curseth thee: and in thee shall all families of the earth be blessed."[23]

So Abram departed, as the Lord had spoken unto him; and Lot went with him: and Abram was seventy and five years old when he departed out of Haran. And Abram took Sarai his wife, and Lot his brother's son, and all their substance that they had gathered, and the souls that they had gotten in Haran; and they went forth to go into the land of Canaan; and into the land of Canaan they came. And Abram passed through the land unto the place of Sichem, unto the plain of Moreh. And the Canaanite was then in the land. And the Lord appeared unto Abram, and said, "Unto thy seed will I give this land." And there built he an altar unto the Lord, who appeared unto him. And he removed from thence unto a mountain on the east of Beth-el, and pitched his tent, having Beth-el on the west, and Hai on the east: and there he builded an altar unto the Lord, and called upon the name of the Lord. And Abram journeyed, going on still toward the south.

And there was a famine in the land: and Abram went down into Egypt to sojourn there; for the famine was grievous in the land. And it came to pass, when he was come near to enter into Egypt, that he said unto Sarai his wife, "Behold now, I know that thou art a fair woman to look upon: therefore it shall come to pass, when the Egyptians shall see thee, that they shall say, 'This is his wife': and they will kill me, but they will save thee alive. Say, I pray thee, thou art my sister: that it may be well with me for thy sake; and my soul shall live because of thee." And it came to pass that, when Abram was come into Egypt, the Egyptians beheld the woman that she was very fair. The princes also of Pharaoh saw her, and commended her before Pharaoh: and the woman was taken into Pharaoh's house. And he entreated Abram well for her sake: and he had sheep, and oxen, and he-asses, and menservants, and maidservants, and she-asses, and camels. And the Lord plagued Pharaoh and his house with great plagues because of Sarai Abram's wife. And Pharaoh called Abram, and said, "What is this that thou hast done unto me? why didst thou not tell me that she was thy wife? Why saidst thou, 'She is my sister'? so I might have taken her to me to wife: now therefore behold thy wife, take her, and go thy way."[24] And Pharaoh commanded his men concerning him: and they sent him away, and his wife, and all that he had.

And Abram went up out of Egypt, he, and his wife, and all that he had, and Lot with him, into the south. And Abram was very rich in cattle, in silver, and in gold. And he went on his journeys from the south even to Beth-el, unto the place where his tent had been at the beginning, between Beth-el and Hai; unto the place of the altar, which he had made there at the first: and there Abram called on the name of the Lord. And Lot also, which went with Abram, had flocks, and herds, and tents. And the land was not able to bear them, that they might dwell together: for their substance was great, so that they could not dwell together. And there was a strife

---

[23] This is the first statement of the often-repeated "covenant" with Israel around which much of Old Testament history revolves.

[24] This story of Abram passing his wife off as his sister does not present the patriarch in a very favorable light. It is probably based on an ancient folk tale, and it appears in other versions in Genesis 20:1–16, where Sarai is actually Abram's half sister, and 26:1–11.

between the herdsmen of Abram's cattle and the herdsmen of Lot's cattle: and the Canaanite and the Perizzite dwelled then in the land.

And Abram said unto Lot, "Let there be no strife, I pray thee, between me and thee, and between my herdsmen and thy herdsmen; for we be brethren. Is not the whole land before thee? separate thyself, I pray thee, from me: if thou wilt take the left hand, then I will go to the right; or if thou depart to the right hand, then I will go to the left." And Lot lifted up his eyes, and beheld all the plain of Jordan, that it was well watered every where, before the Lord destroyed Sodom and Gomorrah, even as the garden of the Lord, like the land of Egypt, as thou comest unto Zoar. Then Lot chose him all the plain of Jordan; and Lot journeyed east: and they separated themselves the one from the other. Abram dwelled in the land of Canaan, and Lot dwelled in the cities of the plain, and pitched his tent toward Sodom. But the men of Sodom were wicked and sinners before the Lord exceedingly. And the Lord said unto Abram, after that Lot was separated from him, "Lift up now thine eyes, and look from the place where thou art northward, and southward, and eastward, and westward: for all the land which thou seest, to thee will I give it, and to thy seed for ever. And I will make thy seed as the dust of the earth: so that if a man can number the dust of the earth, then shall thy seed also be numbered. Arise, walk through the land in the length of it and in the breadth of it; for I will give it unto thee." Then Abram removed his tent, and came and dwelt in the plain of Mamre, which is in Hebron, and built there an altar unto the Lord. . . .

Now Sarai Abram's wife bore him no children: and she had a handmaid, an Egyptian, whose name was Hagar. And Sarai said unto Abram, "Behold now, the Lord hath restrained me from bearing: I pray thee, go in unto my maid; it may be that I may obtain children by her." And Abram hearkened to the voice of Sarai. And Sarai Abram's wife took Hagar her maid the Egyptian, after Abram had dwelt ten years in the land of Canaan, and gave her to her husband Abram to be his wife. And he went in unto Hagar, and she conceived: and when she saw that she had conceived, her mistress was despised in her eyes. And Sarai said unto Abram, "My wrong be upon thee: I have given my maid into thy bosom; and when she saw that she had conceived, I was despised in her eyes: the Lord judge between me and thee." But Abram said unto Sarai, "Behold, thy maid is in thy hand; do to her as it pleaseth thee." And when Sarai dealt hardly with her, she fled from her face. And the angel of the Lord found her by a fountain of water in the wilderness, by the fountain in the way to Shur. And he said, "Hagar, Sarai's maid, whence camest thou? and whither wilt thou go?" And she said, "I flee from the face of my mistress Sarai." And the angel of the Lord said unto her, "Return to thy mistress, and submit thyself under her hands." And the angel of the Lord said unto her, "I will multiply thy seed exceedingly, that it shall not be numbered for multitude." And the angel of the Lord said unto her, "Behold, thou art with child, and shalt bear a son, and shalt call his name Ishmael; because the Lord hath heard thy affliction.[25] And he will be a wild man; his hand will be against every man, and

---

[25]"Ishmael" means "God hears."

every man's hand against him; and he shall dwell in the presence of all his brethren." And she called the name of the Lord that spoke unto her, "Thou God seest me": for she said, "Have I also here looked after him that seeth me?" Wherefore the well was called Beer-lahai-roi; behold, it is between Kadesh and Bered.

And Hagar bore Abram a son: and Abram called his son's name, which Hagar bore, Ishmael. And Abram was fourscore and six years old, when Hagar bore Ishmael to Abram. And when Abram was ninety years old and nine, the Lord appeared to Abram, and said unto him, "I am the Almighty God; walk before me, and be thou perfect. And I will make my covenant between me and thee, and will multiply thee exceedingly." And Abram fell on his face: and God talked with him, saying, "As for me, behold, my covenant is with thee, and thou shalt be a father of many nations. Neither shall thy name any more be called Abram, but thy name shall be Abraham; for a father of many nations have I made thee. . . .[26] This is my covenant, which ye shall keep, between me and you and thy seed after thee; every man child among you shall be circumcised. And ye shall circumcise the flesh of your foreskin; and it shall be a token of the covenant betwixt me and you. And he that is eight days old shall be circumcised among you, every man child in your generations, he that is born in the house, or bought with money of any stranger, which is not of thy seed. He that is born in thy house, and he that is bought with thy money, must needs be circumcised: and my covenant shall be in your flesh for an everlasting covenant. And the uncircumcised man child whose flesh of his foreskin is not circumcised, that soul shall be cut off from his people; he hath broken my covenant."[27]

And God said unto Abraham, "As for Sarai thy wife, thou shalt not call her name Sarai, but Sarah shall her name be.". . .

And Abraham took Ishmael his son, and all that were born in his house, and all that were bought with his money, every male among the men of Abraham's house; and circumcised the flesh of their foreskin in the selfsame day, as God had said unto him. And Abraham was ninety years old and nine, when he was circumcised in the flesh of his foreskin. And Ishmael his son was thirteen years old, when he was circumcised in the flesh of his foreskin. In the selfsame day was Abraham circumcised, and Ishmael his son. And all the men of his house, born in the house, and bought with money of the stranger, were circumcised with him.

And the Lord appeared unto him in the plains of Mamre: and he sat in the tent door in the heat of the day; and he lifted up his eyes and looked, and, lo, three men stood by him: and when he saw them, he ran to meet them from the tent door, and bowed himself toward the ground, and said, "My Lord, if now I have found favor in thy sight, pass not away, I pray thee, from thy servant: let a little water, I pray you, be fetched, and wash your feet, and rest yourselves under the tree: and I will fetch a morsel of bread, and comfort ye your hearts; after that ye shall pass on: for therefore are ye come to your servant." And they said, "So do, as thou hast said." And

[26] "Abraham" means "Father of a multitude."

[27] Ritual circumcision has precedents in other cultures going back as far as 4000 B.C. Despite its mention here, circumcision seems to have been a fairly late addition to Hebrew practice. It is mentioned only in passages in the Pentateuch which were added relatively late, as is true with this example.

Abraham hastened into the tent unto Sarah, and said, "Make ready quickly three measures of fine meal, knead it, and make cakes upon the hearth."

And Abraham ran unto the herd, and fetched a calf tender and good, and gave it unto a young man; and he hastened to dress it. And he took butter, and milk, and the calf which he had dressed, and set it before them; and he stood by them under the tree, and they did eat.

And they said unto him, "Where is Sarah thy wife?" And he said, "Behold, in the tent." And he said, "I will certainly return unto thee according to the time of life; and, lo, Sarah thy wife shall have a son." And Sarah heard it in the tent door, which was behind him. Now Abraham and Sarah were old and well stricken in age; and it ceased to be with Sarah after the manner of women. Therefore Sarah laughed within herself, saying, "After I am waxed old shall I have pleasure, my lord being old also?" And the Lord said unto Abraham, "Wherefore did Sarah laugh, saying, 'Shall I of a surety bear a child, which am old?' Is any thing too hard for the Lord? At the time appointed I will return unto thee, according to the time of life, and Sarah shall have a son." Then Sarah denied, saying, "I laughed not": for she was afraid. And he said, "Nay; but thou didst laugh."

And the men rose up from thence, and looked toward Sodom: and Abraham went with them to bring them on the way. And the Lord said, "Shall I hide from Abraham that thing which I do; seeing that Abraham shall surely become a great and mighty nation, and all the nations of the earth shall be blessed in him? For I know him, that he will command his children and his household after him, and they shall keep the way of the Lord, to do justice and judgment; that the Lord may bring upon Abraham that which he hath spoken of him." And the Lord said, "Because the cry of Sodom and Gomorrah is great, and because their sin is very grievous; I will go down now, and see whether they have done altogether according to the cry of it, which is come unto me; and if not, I will know."

And the men turned their faces from thence, and went toward Sodom: but Abraham stood yet before the Lord. And Abraham drew near, and said, "Wilt thou also destroy the righteous with the wicked? Peradventure there be fifty righteous within the city: wilt thou also destroy and not spare the place for the fifty righteous that are therein? That be far from thee to do after this manner, to slay the righteous with the wicked: and that the righteous should be as the wicked, that be far from thee: shall not the Judge of all the earth do right?" And the Lord said, "If I find in Sodom fifty righteous within the city, then I will spare all the place for their sakes."

And Abraham answered and said, "Behold now, I have taken upon me to speak unto the Lord, which am but dust and ashes. Peradventure there shall lack five of the fifty righteous: wilt thou destroy all the city for lack of five?" And he said, "If I find there forty and five, I will not destroy it." And he spoke unto him yet again, and said, "Peradventure there shall be forty found there." And he said, "I will not do it for forty's sake." And he said unto him, "Oh let not the Lord be angry, and I will speak: peradventure there shall thirty be found there." And he said, "I will not do it, if I find thirty there." And he said, "Behold now, I have taken upon me to speak unto the Lord: peradventure there shall be twenty found there." And he said, "I will not destroy it for twenty's sake." And he said, "Oh let not the Lord be angry, and I will speak yet but this once: peradventure ten shall be found there." And he said, "I will not destroy it for ten's sake." And the Lord went his way, as soon as he had left communing with Abraham; and Abraham returned unto his place.

And there came two angels to Sodom at even; and Lot sat in the gate of Sodom: and Lot seeing them rose up to meet them; and he bowed himself with his face toward the ground. And he said, "Behold now, my lords, turn in, I pray you, into your servant's house, and tarry all night, and wash your feet, and ye shall rise up early, and go on your ways." And they said, "Nay; but we will abide in the street all night." And he pressed upon them greatly; and they turned in unto him, and entered into his house; and he made them a feast, and did bake unleavened bread, and they did eat. But before they lay down, the men of the city, even the men of Sodom, compassed the house round, both old and young, all the people from every quarter: and they called unto Lot, and said unto him, "Where are the men which came in to thee this night? bring them out unto us, that we may know them."[28] And Lot went out at the door unto them, and shut the door after him, and said, "I pray you, brethren, do not so wickedly. Behold now, I have two daughters which have not known man; let me, I pray you, bring them out unto you, and do ye to them as is good in your eyes: only unto these men do nothing; for therefore came they under the shadow of my roof."[29] And they said, "Stand back!" And they said again, "This one fellow came in to sojourn, and he will needs be a judge: now will we deal worse with thee than with them." And they pressed sore upon the man, even Lot, and came near to break the door. But the men put forth their hand, and pulled Lot into the house to them, and shut to the door. And they smote the men that were at the door of the house with blindness, both small and great: so that they wearied themselves to find the door.

And the men said unto Lot, "Hast thou here any besides? sons-in-law, and thy sons, and thy daughters, and whatsoever thou hast in the city, bring them out of this place: for we will destroy this place, because the cry of them is waxen great before the face of the Lord; and the Lord hath sent us to destroy it." And Lot went out, and spoke unto his sons-in-law, which married his daughters, and said, "Up, get you out of this place; for the Lord will destroy this city." But he seemed as one that mocked unto his sons-in-law.

And when the morning arose, then the angels hastened Lot, saying, "Arise, take thy wife, and thy two daughters, which are here; lest thou be consumed in the iniquity of the city." And while he lingered, the men laid hold upon his hand, and upon the hand of his wife, and upon the hand of his two daughters; the Lord being merciful unto him: and they brought him forth, and set him without the city. And it came to pass, when they had brought them forth abroad, that he said, "Escape for thy life; look not behind thee, neither stay thou in all the plain; escape to the mountain, lest thou be consumed." And Lot said unto them, "Oh, not so, my Lord: behold

---

[28] The demand of the men of Sodom that they "know" the strangers suggests that their sin is sodomy; hence the term.

[29] Lot's offer to give up his daughters to be raped rather than deliver his guests seems strange to the modern reader, but his action is in line with Oriental beliefs in the sacred obligation of hospitality to strangers.

now, thy servant hath found grace in thy sight, and thou hast magnified thy mercy, which thou hast showed unto me in saving my life; and I cannot escape to the mountain, lest some evil take me, and I die. Behold now, this city is near to flee unto, and it is a little one. Oh, let me escape thither (is it not a little one?), and my soul shall live." And he said unto him, "See, I have accepted thee concerning this thing also, that I will not overthrow this city, for the which thou hast spoken. Haste thee, escape thither; for I cannot do any thing till thou be come thither." (Therefore the name of the city was called Zoar.)

The sun was risen upon the earth when Lot entered into Zoar. Then the Lord rained upon Sodom and upon Gomorrah brimstone and fire from the Lord out of heaven; and he overthrew those cities, and all the plain, and all the inhabitants of the cities, and that which grew upon the ground. But his wife looked back from behind him, and she became a pillar of salt.[30] And Abraham got up early in the morning to the place where he stood before the Lord. And he looked toward Sodom and Gomorrah, and toward all the land of the plain, and beheld, and, lo, the smoke of the country went up as the smoke of a furnace.

And it came to pass, when God destroyed the cities of the plain, that God remembered Abraham, and sent Lot out of the midst of the overthrow, when he overthrew the cities in the which Lot dwelt. And Lot went up out of Zoar, and dwelt in the mountain, and his two daughters with him; for he feared to dwell in Zoar: and he dwelt in a cave, he and his two daughters. And the firstborn said unto the younger, "Our father is old, and there is not a man in the earth to come in unto us after the manner of all the earth. Come, let us make our father drink wine, and we will lie with him, that we may preserve seed of our father." And they made their father drink wine that night: and the firstborn went in, and lay with her father; and he perceived not when she lay down, nor when she arose. And it came to pass on the morrow that the firstborn said unto the younger, "Behold, I lay yesternight with my father: let us make him drink wine this night also; and go thou in, and lie with him, that we may preserve seed of our father." And they made their father drink wine that night also: and the younger arose, and lay with him; and he perceived not when she lay down, nor when she arose. Thus were both the daughters of Lot with child by their father. And the firstborn bore a son, and called his name Moab: the same is the father of the Moabites unto this day. And the younger, she also bore a son, and called his name Ben-ammi: the same is the father of the children of Ammon unto this day. . . . .[31]

And the Lord visited Sarah as he had said, and the Lord did unto Sarah as he had spoken. For Sarah conceived, and bore Abraham a son in his old age, at the set time of which God had spoken to him. And Abraham called the name of his son that was born unto him, whom Sarah bore to him,

---

[30] This odd story seems to have been originally an explanation of the strange salt formations which can still be seen in the area.

[31] This account of the incest of Lot's daughters with their father is another passage in Genesis which may strike modern readers as peculiar, especially since it is presented with no trace of opprobrium. It may be another etiological story, intended to account for the relation of the tribes of Moab and Ammon to each other and to the Hebrews. "Moab" means "from father," and "Ben-Ammi" means "son of my kinsman."

Isaac. And Abraham circumcised his son Isaac being eight days old, as God had commanded him. And Abraham was a hundred years old, when his son Isaac was born unto him. And Sarah said, "God hath made me to laugh, so that all that hear will laugh with me."[32] And she said, "Who would have said unto Abraham that Sarah should have given children suck? for I have borne him a son in his old age."

And the child grew, and was weaned: and Abraham made a great feast the same day that Isaac was weaned. And Sarah saw the son of Hagar the Egyptian, which she had borne unto Abraham, mocking. Wherefore she said unto Abraham, "Cast out this bondwoman and her son: for the son of this bondwoman shall not be heir with my son, even with Isaac." And the thing was very grievous in Abraham's sight because of his son. And God said unto Abraham, "Let it not be grievous in thy sight because of the lad, and because of thy bondwoman; in all that Sarah hath said unto thee, hearken unto her voice; for in Isaac shall thy seed be called. And also of the son of the bondwoman will I make a nation, because he is thy seed." And Abraham rose up early in the morning, and took bread, and a bottle of water, and gave it unto Hagar, putting it on her shoulder, and the child, and sent her away: and she departed, and wandered in the wilderness of Beer-sheba.

And the water was spent in the bottle, and she cast the child under one of the shrubs. And she went, and sat her down over against him a good way off, as it were a bowshot: for she said, "Let me not see the death of the child." And she sat over against him, and lifted up her voice, and wept. And God heard the voice of the lad; and the angel of God called to Hagar out of heaven, and said unto her, "What aileth thee, Hagar? fear not; for God hath heard the voice of the lad where he is. Arise, lift up the lad, and hold him in thine hand; for I will make him a great nation." And God opened her eyes, and saw a well of water; and she went, and filled the bottle with water, and gave the lad drink. And God was with the lad; and he grew, and dwelt in the wilderness, and became an archer. And he dwelt in the wilderness of Paran: and his mother took him a wife out of the land of Egypt. . . .

And it came to pass after these things that God did tempt Abraham, and said unto him, "Abraham": and he said, "Behold, here I am." And he said, "Take now thy son, thine only son Isaac, whom thou lovest, and get thee into the land of Moriah; and offer him there for a burnt offering upon one of the mountains which I will tell thee of." And Abraham rose up early in the morning, and saddled his ass, and took two of his young men with him, and Isaac his son, and cleft the wood for the burnt offering, and rose up, and went unto the place of which God had told him. Then on the third day Abraham lifted up his eyes, and saw the place afar off. And Abraham said unto his young men, "Abide ye here with the ass; and I and the lad will go yonder and worship, and come again to you." And Abraham took the wood of the burnt offering, and laid it upon Isaac his son; and he took the fire in his hand, and a knife; and they went both of them together.

And Isaac spoke unto Abraham his father, and said, "My father": and he said, "Here am I, my son." And he said, "Behold the fire and the wood:

[32] "Isaac" means "He laughs."

but where is the lamb for a burnt offering?" And Abraham said, "My son, God will provide himself a lamb for a burnt offering": so they went both of them together. And they came to the place which God had told him of; and Abraham built an altar there, and laid the wood in order, and bound Isaac his son, and laid him on the altar upon the wood. And Abraham stretched forth his hand, and took the knife to slay his son. And the angel of the Lord called unto him out of heaven, and said, "Abraham, Abraham": and he said, "Here am I." And he said, "Lay not thine hand upon the lad, neither do thou any thing unto him: for now I know that thou fearest God, seeing thou hast not withheld thy son, thine only son from me." And Abraham lifted up his eyes, and looked, and beheld behind him a ram caught in a thicket by his horns: and Abraham went and took the ram, and offered him up for a burnt offering in the stead of his son. And Abraham called the name of that place Jehovah-jireh: as it is said to this day, "In the mount of the Lord it shall be seen. . . ."[33] So Abraham returned unto his young men, and they rose up and went together to Beer-sheba; and Abraham dwelt at Beer-sheba. . . .

And Sarah was a hundred and seven and twenty years old: these were the years of the life of Sarah. And Sarah died in Kirjath-arba; the same is Hebron in the land of Canaan: and Abraham came to mourn for Sarah, and to weep for her. And Abraham stood up from before his dead, and spoke unto the sons of Heth, saying, "I am a stranger and a sojourner with you: give me a possession of a burying place with you, that I may bury my dead out of my sight." And the children of Heth answered Abraham, saying unto him, "Hear us, my lord: thou art a mighty prince among us: in the choice of our sepulchres bury thy dead; none of us shall withhold from thee his sepulchre, but that thou mayest bury thy dead." And Abraham stood up, and bowed himself to the people of the land, even to the children of Heth. And he communed with them, saying, "If it be your mind that I should bury my dead out of my sight; hear me, and intreat for me to Ephron the son of Zohar, that he may give me the cave of Machpelah, which he hath, which is in the end of his field; for as much money as it is worth he shall give it me for a possession of a burying place amongst you." And Ephron dwelt among the children of Heth: and Ephron the Hittite answered Abraham in the audience of the children of Heth, even of all that went in at the gate of his city, saying, "Nay, my lord, hear me: the field give I thee, and the cave that is therein, I give it thee; in the presence of the sons of my people give I it thee: bury thy dead." And Abraham bowed down himself before the people of the land. And he spake unto Ephron in the audience of the people of the land, saying, "But if thou wilt give it, I pray thee, hear me: I will give thee money for the field; take it of me, and I will bury my dead there." And Ephron answered Abraham, saying unto him, "My lord, hearken unto me: the land is worth four hundred shekels of silver; what is that betwixt me and thee? bury therefore thy dead." And Abraham hearkened unto Ephron; and Abraham weighed to Ephron the

[33] The story of the near-sacrifice of Isaac has many analogues in other religions and literatures, including the story of Agamemnon's sacrifice of his daughter Iphigenia, referred to in the *Iliad* and in Aeschylus' *Agamemnon*. The form the story takes here seems to celebrate perfect faith and to condemn human sacrifice.

silver, which he had named in the audience of the sons of Heth, four hundred shekels of silver, current money with the merchant.

And the field of Ephron, which was in Machpelah, which was before Mamre, the field, and the cave which was therein, and all the trees that were in the field, that were in all the borders round about, were made sure unto Abraham for a possession in the presence of the children of Heth, before all that went in at the gate of his city. And after this, Abraham buried Sarah his wife in the cave of the field of Machpelah before Mamre: the same is Hebron in the land of Canaan. And the field, and the cave that is therein, were made sure unto Abraham for a possession of a burying place by the sons of Heth.

THE STORY OF ISAAC AND REBEKAH

(Genesis 24:1–25:28)
And Abraham was old, and well stricken in age: and the Lord had blessed Abraham in all things. And Abraham said unto his eldest servant of his house, that ruled over all that he had, "Put, I pray thee, thy hand under my thigh: and I will make thee swear by the Lord, the God of heaven, and the God of the earth, that thou shalt not take a wife unto my son of the daughters of the Canaanites, among whom I dwell: but thou shalt go unto my country, and to my kindred, and take a wife unto my son Isaac."[34] And the servant said unto him, "Peradventure the woman will not be willing to follow me unto this land: must I needs bring thy son again unto the land from whence thou camest?" And Abraham said unto him, "Beware thou that thou bring not my son thither again. The Lord God of heaven, which took me from my father's house, and from the land of my kindred, and which spoke unto me, and that swore unto me, saying, 'Unto thy seed will I give this land'; he shall send his angel before thee, and thou shalt take a wife unto my son from thence. And if the woman will not be willing to follow thee, then thou shalt be clear from this my oath: only bring not my son thither again." And the servant put his hand under the thigh of Abraham his master, and swore to him concerning that matter.

And the servant took ten camels of the camels of his master, and departed; for all the goods of his master were in his hand: and he arose, and went to Mesopotamia, unto the city of Nahor. And he made his camels to kneel down without the city by a well of water at the time of the evening, even the time that women go out to draw water. And he said, "O Lord God of my master Abraham, I pray thee, send me good speed this day, and show kindness unto my master Abraham. Behold, I stand here by the well of water; and the daughters of the men of the city come out to draw water. Let it come to pass that the damsel to whom I shall say, 'Let down thy pitcher, I pray thee, that I may drink'; and she shall say, 'Drink, and I will give thy camels drink also': let the same be she that thou hast appointed for

---

[34] The story of the wooing of Rebekah illustrates a number of marriage customs, many of which still survive in the Arab world, including the hostility to intertribal marriage, the use of intermediaries, betrothal gifts, and bride-prices. The odd "oath under the thigh" occurs a number of times in the Old Testament; it appears to reflect the primitive custom of taking oaths while holding the other party's testicles.

thy servant Isaac; and thereby shall I know that thou hast showed kindness unto my master."

And it came to pass, before he had done speaking, that, behold, Rebekah came out, who was born to Bethuel, son of Milcah, the wife of Nahor, Abraham's brother, with her pitcher upon her shoulder. And the damsel was very fair to look upon, a virgin, neither had any man known her: and she went down to the well, and filled her pitcher, and came up. And the servant ran to meet her, and said, "Let me, I pray thee, drink a little water of thy pitcher." And she said, "Drink, my lord"; and she hastened, and let down her pitcher upon her hand, and gave him drink. And when she had done giving him drink, she said, "I will draw water for thy camels also, until they have done drinking." And she hastened, and emptied her pitcher into the trough, and ran again unto the well to draw water, and drew for all his camels. And the man wondering at her held his peace, to wit whether the Lord had made his journey prosperous or not.

And it came to pass, as the camels had done drinking, that the man took a golden earring of half a shekel weight, and two bracelets for her hands of ten shekels' weight of gold; and said, "Whose daughter art thou? tell me, I pray thee: is there room in thy father's house for us to lodge in?" And she said unto him, "I am the daughter of Bethuel the son of Milcah, which she bore unto Nahor." She said moreover unto him, "We have both straw and provender enough, and room to lodge in." And the man bowed down his head, and worshipped the Lord. And he said, "Blessed be the Lord God of my master Abraham, who hath not left destitute my master of his mercy and his truth: I being in the way, the Lord led me to the house of my master's brethren."

And the damsel ran, and told them of her mother's house these things. And Rebekah had a brother, and his name was Laban: and Laban ran out unto the man, unto the well. And it came to pass, when he saw the earring and bracelets upon his sister's hands, and when he heard the words of Rebekah his sister, saying, "Thus spoke the man unto me"; that he came unto the man; and, behold, he stood by the camels at the well. And he said, "Come in, thou blessed of the Lord; wherefore standest thou without? for I have prepared the house, and room for the camels." And the man came into the house; and he ungirded his camels, and gave straw and provender for the camels, and water to wash his feet, and the men's feet that were with him. And there was set meat before him to eat: but he said, "I will not eat until I have told mine errand." And he said, "Speak on."

And he said, "I am Abraham's servant. And the Lord hath blessed my master greatly; and he is become great: and he hath given him flocks, and herds, and silver, and gold, and menservants, and maidservants, and camels, and asses. And Sarah my master's wife bore a son to my master when she was old: and unto him hath he given all that he hath. And my master made me swear, saying, 'Thou shalt not take a wife to my son of the daughters of the Canaanites, in whose land I dwell: but thou shalt go unto my father's house, and to my kindred, and take a wife unto my son.' And I said unto my master, 'Peradventure the woman will not follow me.' And he said unto me, 'The Lord, before whom I walk, will send his angel with thee, and prosper thy way; and thou shalt take a wife for my son of my kindred, and of my father's house: then shalt thou be clear from this my oath, when thou comest to my kindred; and if they give not thee one, thou shalt be clear from my oath.' And I came this day unto the well, and said, 'O Lord God of my master Abraham, if now thou do prosper my way which I go, behold, I stand by the well of water; and it shall come to pass that when the virgin cometh forth to draw water, and I say to her, "Give me, I pray thee, a little water of thy pitcher to drink"; and she say to me, "Both drink thou, and I will also draw for thy camels"; let the same be the woman whom the Lord hath appointed out for my master's son.' And before I had done speaking in mine heart, behold, Rebekah came forth with her pitcher on her shoulder; and she went down unto the well, and drew water: and I said unto her, 'Let me drink, I pray thee.' And she made haste, and let down her pitcher from her shoulder, and said, 'Drink, and I will give thy camels drink also': so I drank, and she made the camels drink also. And I asked her, and said, 'Whose daughter are thou?' And she said, 'The daughter of Bethuel, Nahor's son, whom Milcah bore unto him': and I put the earring upon her face, and the bracelets upon her hands. And I bowed down my head, and worshipped the Lord, and blessed the Lord God of my master Abraham, which had led me in the right way to take my master's brother's daughter unto his son. And now if ye will deal kindly and truly with my master, tell me: and if not, tell me; that I may turn to the right hand, or to the left."

Then Laban and Bethuel answered and said, "The thing proceedeth from the Lord: we cannot speak unto thee bad or good. Behold, Rebekah is before thee, take her, and go, and let her be thy master's son's wife, as the Lord hath spoken."

And it came to pass that, when Abraham's servant heard their words, he worshipped the Lord, bowing himself to the earth. And the servant brought forth jewels of silver, and jewels of gold, and raiment, and gave them to Rebekah: he gave also to her brother and to her mother precious things. And they did eat and drink, he and the men that were with him, and tarried all night; and they rose up in the morning, and he said, "Send me away unto my master." And her brother and her mother said, "Let the damsel abide with us a few days, at the least ten; after that she shall go." And he said unto them, "Hinder me not, seeing the Lord hath prospered my way; send me away that I may go to my master." And they said, "We will call the damsel, and enquire at her mouth." And they called Rebekah, and said unto her, "Wilt thou go with this man?" And she said, "I will go." And they sent away Rebekah their sister, and her nurse, and Abraham's servant, and his men. And they blessed Rebekah, and said unto her, "Thou art our sister, be thou the mother of thousands of millions, and let thy seed possess the gate of those which hate them." And Rebekah arose, and her damsels, and they rode upon the camels, and followed the man: and the servant took Rebekah, and went his way.

And Isaac came from the way of the well Lahai-roi; for he dwelt in the south country. And Isaac went out to meditate in the field at the eventide: and he lifted up his eyes, and saw, and, behold, the camels were coming. And Rebekah lifted up her eyes, and when she saw Isaac, she lighted off the camel. For she had said unto the servant, "What man is this that walketh in the field to meet us?" And the servant had said, "It is my master": therefore she took a veil, and covered herself. And the servant told

Isaac all things that he had done. And Isaac brought her into his mother Sarah's tent, and took Rebekah, and she became his wife; and he loved her: and Isaac was comforted after his mother's death. . . .

And these are the days of the years of Abraham's life which he lived, a hundred threescore and fifteen years. Then Abraham gave up the ghost, and died in a good old age, an old man, and full of years; and was gathered to his people. And his sons Isaac and Ishmael buried him in the cave of Machpelah, in the field of Ephron the son of Zohar the Hittite, which is before Mamre: the field which Abraham purchased of the sons of Heth: there was Abraham buried, and Sarah his wife. . . .

And Isaac was forty years old when he took Rebekah to wife, the daughter of Bethuel the Syrian of Padan-aram, the sister to Laban the Syrian. And Isaac intreated the Lord for his wife, because she was barren: and the Lord was intreated of him, and Rebekah his wife conceived. And the children struggled together within her; and she said, "If it be so, why am I thus?" And she went to enquire of the Lord. And the Lord said unto her,

"Two nations are in thy womb,
    and two manner of people shall be separated from thy bowels;
And the one people shall be stronger than the other people;
    and the elder shall serve the younger."

And when her days to be delivered were fulfilled, behold, there were twins in her womb. And the first came out red, all over like a hairy garment; and they called his name Esau. And after that came his brother out, and his hand took hold on Esau's heel; and his name was called Jacob:[35] and Isaac was threescore years old when she bore them. And the boys grew: and Esau was a cunning hunter, a man of the field; and Jacob was a plain man, dwelling in tents. And Isaac loved Esau, because he did eat of his venison: but Rebekah loved Jacob.

THE STORY OF JACOB

(Genesis 25:29–35:29)
And Jacob sod pottage:[36] and Esau came from the field, and he was faint: and Esau said to Jacob, "Feed me, I pray thee, with that same red pottage; for I am faint" (therefore was his name called Edom). And Jacob said, "Sell me this day thy birthright." And Esau said, "Behold, I am at the point to die: and what profit shall this birthright do to me?" And Jacob said, "Swear to me this day!" And he swore unto him: and he sold his birthright unto Jacob. Then Jacob gave Esau bread and pottage of lentils; and he did eat and drink, and rose up, and went his way: thus Esau despised his birthright. . . .

[35] The name Jacob can mean either "he takes by the heel" or "he supplants." The second meaning is particularly relevant in the light of Jacob's later history. The character of Jacob is a version of the "trickster hero," and his often rather crudely comic exploits in the sections which follow still betray their origins in folk tales.
[36] Cooked food.

And Esau was forty years old when he took to wife Judith the daughter of Beeri the Hittite, and Bashemath the daughter of Elon the Hittite: which were a grief of mind unto Isaac and to Rebekah.

And it came to pass that when Isaac was old, and his eyes were dim, so that he could not see, he called Esau his eldest son, and said unto him, "My son": and he said unto him, "Behold, here am I." And he said, "Behold now, I am old, I know not the day of my death. Now therefore take, I pray thee, thy weapons, thy quiver and thy bow, and go out to the field, and take me some venison; and make me savory meat, such as I love, and bring it to me, that I may eat; that my soul may bless thee before I die."

And Rebekah heard when Isaac spoke to Esau his son. And Esau went to the field to hunt for venison, and to bring it. And Rebekah spoke unto Jacob her son, saying, "Behold, I heard thy father speak unto Esau thy brother, saying, 'Bring me venison, and make me savory meat, that I may eat, and bless thee before the Lord before my death.' Now therefore, my son, obey my voice according to that which I command thee. Go now to the flock, and fetch me from thence two good kids of the goats; and I will make them savory meat for thy father, such as he loveth: and thou shalt bring it to thy father, that he may eat, and that he may bless thee before his death." And Jacob said to Rebekah his mother, "Behold, Esau my brother is a hairy man, and I am a smooth man. My father peradventure will feel me, and I shall seem to him as a deceiver; and I shall bring a curse upon me, and not a blessing." And his mother said unto him, "Upon me be thy curse, my son: only obey my voice, and go fetch me them." And he went, and fetched, and brought them to his mother; and his mother made savory meat, such as his father loved. And Rebekah took goodly raiment of her eldest son Esau, which were with her in the house, and put them upon Jacob her younger son; and she put the skins of the kids of the goats upon his hands, and upon the smooth of his neck; and she gave the savory meat and the bread, which she had prepared, into the hand of her son Jacob.

And he came unto his father, and said, "My father": and he said, "Here am I; who art thou, my son?" And Jacob said unto his father, "I am Esau thy firstborn; I have done according as thou badest me: arise, I pray thee, sit and eat of my venison, that thy soul may bless me." And Isaac said unto his son, "How is it that thou hast found it so quickly, my son?" And he said, "Because the Lord thy God brought it to me." And Isaac said unto Jacob, "Come near, I pray thee, that I may feel thee, my son, whether thou be my very son Esau or not." And Jacob went near unto Isaac his father; and he felt him, and said, "The voice is Jacob's voice, but the hands are the hands of Esau." And he discerned him not, because his hands were hairy, as his brother Esau's hands; so he blessed him. And he said, "Art thou my very son Esau?" And he said, "I am." And he said, "Bring it near to me, and I will eat of my son's venison, that my soul may bless thee." And he brought it near to him, and he did eat: and he brought the wine, and he drank. And his father Isaac said unto him, "Come near now, and kiss me, my son." And he came near, and kissed him: and he smelled the smell of his raiment, and blessed him, and said,

> "See, the smell of my son
>   is as the smell of a field which the Lord hath blessed:

> Therefore God give thee of the dew of heaven,
>> and the fatness of the earth,
>> and plenty of corn and wine:
> Let people serve thee,
>> and nations bow down to thee:
> Be lord over thy brethren,
>> and let thy mother's sons bow down to thee:
> Cursed be every one that curseth thee,
>> and blessed be he that blesseth thee."

And it came to pass, as soon as Isaac had made an end of blessing Jacob, and Jacob was yet scarce gone out from the presence of Isaac his father, that Esau his brother came in from his hunting. And he also had made savory meat, and brought it unto his father, and said unto his father, "Let my father arise, and eat of his son's venison, that thy soul may bless me." And Isaac his father said unto him, "Who art thou?" And he said, "I am thy son, thy firstborn Esau." And Isaac trembled very exceedingly, and said, "Who? where is he that hath taken venison, and brought it me, and I have eaten of all before thou camest, and have blessed him? yea, and he shall be blessed." And when Esau heard the words of his father, he cried with a great and exceeding bitter cry, and said unto his father, "Bless me, even me also, O my father." And he said, "Thy brother came with subtilty, and hath taken away thy blessing." And he said, "Is not he rightly named Jacob? for he hath supplanted me these two times: he took away my birthright; and, behold, now he hath taken away my blessing." And he said, "Hast thou not reserved a blessing for me?" And Isaac answered and said unto Esau, "Behold, I have made him thy lord, and all his brethren have I given to him for servants; and with corn and wine have I sustained him: and what shall I do now unto thee, my son?" And Esau said unto his father, "Hast thou but one blessing, my father? bless me, even me also, O my father." And Esau lifted up his voice, and wept. And Isaac his father answered and said unto him,

> "Behold, thy dwelling shall be the fatness of the earth,
>> and of the dew of heaven from above;
> And by thy sword shalt thou live,
>> and shalt serve thy brother;
> And it shall come to pass when thou shalt have the dominion,
>> that thou shalt break his yoke from off thy neck."

And Esau hated Jacob because of the blessing wherewith his father blessed him: and Esau said in his heart, "The days of mourning for my father are at hand; then will I slay my brother Jacob."[37] And these words of Esau her elder son were told to Rebekah: and she sent and called Jacob her younger son, and said unto him, "Behold, thy brother Esau, as touching thee, doth comfort himself, purposing to kill thee. Now therefore, my son,

---

[37] Jacob's hoodwinking of Isaac reflects the ancient belief in the magical nature of formal blessings and curses; once a blessing had been pronounced, even in error, it could not be withdrawn.

obey my voice; and arise, flee thou to Laban my brother to Haran. And tarry with him a few days, until thy brother's fury turn away; until thy brother's anger turn away from thee, and he forget that which thou hast done to him. Then I will send, and fetch thee from thence: why should I be deprived also of you both in one day?"

And Rebekah said to Isaac, "I am weary of my life because of the daughters of Heth: if Jacob take a wife of the daughters of Heth, such as these which are of the daughters of the land, what good shall my life do me?" And Isaac called Jacob, and blessed him, and charged him, and said unto him, "Thou shalt not take a wife of the daughters of Canaan. Arise, go to Padan-aram, to the house of Bethuel thy mother's father; and take thee a wife from thence of the daughters of Laban thy mother's brother. And God Almighty bless thee, and make thee fruitful, and multiply thee, that thou mayest be a multitude of people; and give thee the blessing of Abraham, to thee, and to thy seed with thee; that thou mayest inherit the land wherein thou art a stranger, which God gave unto Abraham." . . .

And Jacob went out from Beer-sheba, and went toward Haran. And he lighted upon a certain place, and tarried there all night, because the sun was set; and he took of the stones of that place, and put them for his pillows, and lay down in that place to sleep. And he dreamed, and, behold, a ladder set up on the earth, and the top of it reached to heaven: and, behold, the angels of God ascending and descending on it. And, behold, the Lord stood above it, and said, "I am the Lord God of Abraham thy father, and the God of Isaac: the land whereon thou liest, to thee will I give it, and to thy seed; and thy seed shall be as the dust of the earth, and thou shalt spread abroad to the west, and to the east, and to the north, and to the south: and in thee and in thy seed shall all the families of the earth be blessed. And, behold, I am with thee, and will keep thee in all places whither thou goest, and will bring thee again into this land; for I will not leave thee until I have done that which I have spoken to thee of." And Jacob awaked out of his sleep, and he said, "Surely the Lord is in this place; and I knew it not." And he was afraid, and said, "How dreadful is this place! this is none other but the house of God, and this is the gate of heaven."

And Jacob rose up early in the morning, and took the stone that he had put for his pillows, and set it up for a pillar, and poured oil upon the top of it. And he called the name of that place Beth-el:[38] but the name of that city was called Luz at the first. And Jacob vowed a vow, saying, "If God will be with me, and will keep me in this way that I go, and will give me bread to eat, and raiment to put on, so that I come again to my father's house in peace; then shall the Lord be my God: and this stone, which I have set for a pillar, shall be God's house: and of all that thou shalt give me I will surely give the tenth unto thee."

Then Jacob went on his journey, and came into the land of the people of the east. And he looked, and beheld a well in the field, and, lo, there were three flocks of sheep lying by it; for out of that well they watered the flocks: and a great stone was upon the well's mouth. And thither were all the flocks gathered: and they rolled the stone from the well's mouth, and

[38] "The House of God."

watered the sheep, and put the stone again upon the well's mouth in his place. And Jacob said unto them, "My brethren, whence be ye?" And they said, "Of Haran are we." And he said unto them, "Know ye Laban the son of Nahor?" And they said, "We know him." And he said unto them, "Is he well?" And they said, "He is well: and, behold, Rachel his daughter cometh with the sheep." And he said, "Lo, it is yet high day, neither is it time that the cattle should be gathered together: water ye the sheep, and go and feed them." And they said, "We cannot, until all the flocks be gathered together, and till they roll the stone from the well's mouth; then we water the sheep." And while he yet spoke with them, Rachel came with her father's sheep: for she kept them. And it came to pass, when Jacob saw Rachel the daughter of Laban his mother's brother, and the sheep of Laban his mother's brother, that Jacob went near, and rolled the stone from the well's mouth, and watered the flock of Laban his mother's brother. And Jacob kissed Rachel, and lifted up his voice, and wept. And Jacob told Rachel that he was her father's brother, and that he was Rebekah's son: and she ran and told her father.

And it came to pass, when Laban heard the tidings of Jacob his sister's son, that he ran to meet him, and embraced him, and kissed him, and brought him to his house. And he told Laban all these things. And Laban said to him, "Surely thou art my bone and my flesh." And he abode with him the space of a month. And Laban said unto Jacob, "Because thou art my brother, shouldest thou therefore serve me for nought? tell me, what shall thy wages be?" And Laban had two daughters: the name of the elder was Leah, and the name of the younger was Rachel. Leah was tender-eyed;[39] but Rachel was beautiful and well favored. And Jacob loved Rachel; and said, "I will serve thee seven years for Rachel thy younger daughter." And Laban said, "It is better that I give her to thee than that I should give her to another man. Abide with me."

And Jacob served seven years for Rachel; and they seemed unto him but a few days, for the love he had to her. And Jacob said unto Laban, "Give me my wife, for my days are fulfilled, that I may go in unto her." And Laban gathered together all the men of the place, and made a feast. And it came to pass in the evening that he took Leah his daughter, and brought her to him; and he went in unto her. And Laban gave unto his daughter Leah Zilpah his maid for a handmaid. And it came to pass that in the morning, behold, it was Leah: and he said to Laban, "What is this thou hast done unto me? did not I serve with thee for Rachel? wherefore then hast thou beguiled me?" And Laban said, "It must not be so done in our country, to give the younger before the firstborn. Fulfil her week, and we will give thee this also for the service which thou shalt serve with me yet seven other years."[40] And Jacob did so, and fulfilled her week: and he gave him Rachel his daughter to wife also. And Laban gave to Rachel his daughter Bilhah his handmaid to be her maid. And he went in also unto Rachel, and he loved also Rachel more than Leah, and served with him yet seven other years.

---

[39] The word here translated "tender-eyed" apparently means, more precisely, "dull-eyed."
[40] Laban's cheating of Jacob, an example of "the trickster out-tricked," succeeds because of the custom of leading the bride to the bridal tent in darkness.

And when the Lord saw that Leah was hated, he opened her womb: but Rachel was barren. And Leah conceived, and bore a son, and she called his name Reuben: for she said, "Surely the Lord hath looked upon my affliction; now therefore my husband will love me."[41] And she conceived again, and bore a son; and said, "Because the Lord hath heard that I was hated, he hath therefore given me this son also": and she called his name Simeon. And she conceived again, and bore a son; and said, "Now this time will my husband be joined unto me, because I have borne him three sons": therefore was his name called Levi. And she conceived again, and bore a son: and she said, "Now will I praise the Lord": therefore she called his name Judah; and left bearing.

And when Rachel saw that she bore Jacob no children, Rachel envied her sister; and said unto Jacob, "Give me children, or else I die." And Jacob's anger was kindled against Rachel: and he said "Am I in God's stead, who hath withheld from thee the fruit of the womb?" And she said, "Behold my maid Bilhah, go in unto her; and she shall bear upon my knees, that I may also have children by her." And she gave him Bilhah her handmaid to wife: and Jacob went in unto her. And Bilhah conceived, and bore Jacob a son. And Rachel said, "God hath judged me, and hath also heard my voice, and hath given me a son": therefore called she his name Dan.[42] And Bilhah Rachel's maid conceived again, and bore Jacob a second son. And Rachel said, "With great wrestlings have I wrestled with my sister, and I have prevailed": and she called his name Naphtali.

When Leah saw that she had left bearing, she took Zilpah her maid, and gave her Jacob to wife. And Zilpah Leah's maid bore Jacob a son. And Leah said, "A troop cometh": and she called his name Gad.[43] And Zilpah Leah's maid bore Jacob a second son. And Leah said, "Happy am I, for the daughters will call me blessed": and she called his name Asher.[44]

And Reuben went in the days of wheat harvest, and found mandrakes in the field, and brought them unto his mother Leah. Then Rachel said to Leah, "Give me, I pray thee, of thy son's mandrakes."[45] And she said unto her, "Is it a small matter that thou hast taken my husband? and wouldest thou take away my son's mandrakes also?" And Rachel said, "Therefore he shall lie with thee to-night for thy son's mandrakes." And Jacob came out of the field in the evening, and Leah went out to meet him, and said, "Thou must come in unto me; for surely I have hired thee with my son's mandrakes." And he lay with her that night. And God hearkened unto Leah, and she conceived, and bore Jacob the fifth son. And Leah said, "God hath given me my hire, because I have given my maiden to my husband": and she called his name Issachar. And Leah conceived again, and bore Jacob the sixth son. And Leah said, "God hath endued me with a good dowry; now will my husband dwell with me, because I have borne him six sons": and she called his name Zebulun. And afterwards she bore a daughter, and called her name Dinah. And God remembered Rachel, and God hearkened to her, and opened her womb. And she conceived, and bore a son; and

---

[41] "Reuben" means "See, a son!"   [42] "Dan" means "He judged."
[43] "Gad" means "Fortune."   [44] "Asher" means "Happy."
[45] Mandrakes are the roots of a potato-like plant which were thought to have aphrodisiac qualities and to stimulate conception.

said, "God hath taken away my reproach": and she called his name Joseph; and said, "The Lord shall add to me another son."[46]

And it came to pass, when Rachel had borne Joseph, that Jacob said unto Laban, "Send me away, that I may go unto mine own place, and to my country. Give me my wives and my children, for whom I have served thee, and let me go: for thou knowest my service which I have done thee." And Laban said unto him, "I pray thee, if I have found favor in thine eyes, tarry: for I have learned by experience that the Lord hath blessed me for thy sake." And he said, "Appoint me thy wages, and I will give it." And he said unto him, "Thou knowest how I have served thee, and how thy cattle was with me. For it was little which thou hadst before I came, and it is now increased unto a multitude; and the Lord hath blessed thee since my coming: and now when shall I provide for mine own house also?" And he said, "What shall I give thee?" And Jacob said, "Thou shalt not give me any thing: if thou wilt do this thing for me, I will again feed and keep thy flock. I will pass through all thy flock to-day, removing from thence all the speckled and spotted cattle, and all the brown cattle among the sheep, and the spotted and speckled among the goats: and of such shall be my hire. So shall my righteousness answer for me in time to come, when it shall come for my hire before thy face: every one that is not speckled and spotted among the goats, and brown among the sheep, that shall be counted stolen with me." And Laban said, "Behold, I would it might be according to thy word." And he removed that day the he-goats that were ringstreaked and spotted, and all the she-goats that were speckled and spotted, and every one that had some white in it, and all the brown among the sheep, and gave them into the hand of his sons. And he set three days' journey betwixt himself and Jacob: and Jacob fed the rest of Laban's flocks.

And Jacob took him rods of green poplar, and of the hazel and chestnut tree; and peeled white strakes in them, and made the white appear which was in the rods. And he set the rods which he had peeled before the flocks in the gutters in the watering troughs when the flocks came to drink, that they should conceive when they came to drink. And the flocks conceived before the rods, and brought forth cattle ringstreaked, speckled, and spotted.[47] And Jacob did separate the lambs, and set the faces of the flocks toward the ringstreaked, and all the brown in the flock of Laban; and he put his own flocks by themselves, and put them not unto Laban's cattle. And it came to pass, whensoever the stronger cattle did conceive, that Jacob laid the rods before the eyes of the cattle in the gutters, that they might conceive among the rods. But when the cattle were feeble, he put them not in: so the feebler were Laban's, and the stronger Jacob's. And the man increased exceedingly, and had much cattle, and maidservants, and menservants, and camels, and asses.

And he heard the words of Laban's sons, saying, "Jacob hath taken away all that was our father's; and of that which was our father's hath he gotten all this glory." And Jacob beheld the countenance of Laban and, behold, it

---

[46] "Joseph" means "He adds."

[47] Jacob's trick depends upon the notion of prenatal influence, the belief that a pregnant animal's experiences influence her offspring. The cows and ewes see spotted rods and give birth to spotted offspring.

was not toward him as before. And the Lord said unto Jacob, "Return unto
the land of thy fathers, and to thy kindred; and I will be with thee." And
Jacob sent and called Rachel and Leah to the field unto his flock and said
unto them, "I see your father's countenance, that it is not toward me as
before; but the God of my father hath been with me. And ye know that
with all my power I have served your father. And your father hath deceived me, and changed my wages ten times; but God suffered him not to
hurt me. If he said thus, 'The speckled shall be thy wages'; then all the
cattle bore speckled: and if he said thus, 'The ringstreaked shall be thy
hire'; then bore all the cattle ringstreaked. Thus God hath taken away the
cattle of your father, and given them to me. And it came to pass at the time
that the cattle conceived, that I lifted up mine eyes, and saw in a dream,
and, behold, the rams which leaped upon the cattle were ringstreaked,
speckled, and grisled. And the angel of God spoke unto me in a dream,
saying, 'Jacob.' And I said, 'Here am I.' And he said, 'Lift up now thine
eyes, and see, all the rams which leap upon the cattle are ringstreaked,
speckled, and grisled: for I have seen all that Laban doeth unto thee. I am
the God of Beth-el, where thou anointedst the pillar, and where thou
vowedst a vow unto me: now arise, get thee out from this land, and return
unto the land of thy kindred.'" And Rachel and Leah answered and said
unto him, "Is there yet any portion or inheritance for us in our father's
house? Are we not counted of him strangers? for he hath sold us, and hath
quite devoured also our money. For all the riches which God hath taken
from our father, that is ours, and our children's: now then, whatsoever
God hath said unto thee, do."

Then Jacob rose up, and set his sons and his wives upon camels; and he
carried away all his cattle, and all his goods which he had gotten, the cattle
of his getting, which he had gotten in Padan-aram, for to go to Isaac his
father in the land of Canaan. And Laban went to shear his sheep: and
Rachel had stolen the images that were her father's.[48] And Jacob stole away
unawares to Laban the Syrian, in that he told him not that he fled. So he
fled with all that he had; and he rose up, and passed over the river, and set
his face toward the mount Gilead.

And it was told Laban on the third day that Jacob was fled. And he took
his brethren with him, and pursued after him seven days' journey; and
they overtook him in the mount Gilead. And God came to Laban the Syrian
in a dream by night, and said unto him, "Take heed that thou speak not to
Jacob either good or bad."

Then Laban overtook Jacob. Now Jacob had pitched his tent in the
mount: and Laban with his brethren pitched in the Mount of Gilead. And
Laban said to Jacob, "What hast thou done, that thou hast stolen away
unawares to me, and carried away my daughters, as captives taken with the
sword? Wherefore didst thou flee away secretly, and steal away from me;
and didst not tell me, that I might have sent thee away with mirth, and with
songs, with tabret, and with harp? And hast not suffered me to kiss my sons
and my daughters? thou has now done foolishly in so doing. It is in the
power of my hand to do you hurt: but the God of your father spoke unto

[48] These "images," later called "gods," are either small statues of household deities (like the
Roman Lares and Penates) or images of ancestors.

me yesternight, saying, 'Take thou heed that thou speak not to Jacob either good or bad.' And now, though thou wouldest needs be gone, because thou sore longedst after thy father's house, yet wherefore hast thou stolen my gods?" And Jacob answered and said to Laban, "Because I was afraid: for I said, 'Peradventure thou wouldest take by force thy daughters from me.' With whomsoever thou findest thy gods, let him not live: before our brethren discern thou what is thine with me, and take it to thee." For Jacob knew not that Rachel had stolen them.

And Laban went into Jacob's tent, and into Leah's tent, and into the two maidservants' tents; but he found them not. Then went he out of Leah's tent, and entered into Rachel's tent. Now Rachel had taken the images, and put them in the camel's furniture, and sat upon them. And Laban searched all the tent, but found them not. And she said to her father, "Let it not displease my lord that I cannot rise up before thee; for the custom of women is upon me."[49] And he searched, but found not the images.

And Jacob was wroth, and chid with Laban: and Jacob answered and said to Laban, "What is my trespass? what is my sin, that thou hast so hotly pursued after me? Whereas thou hast searched all my stuff, what hast thou found of all thy household stuff? set it here before my brethren and thy brethren, that they may judge betwixt us both. This twenty years have I been with thee; thy ewes and thy she-goats have not cast their young, and the rams of thy flock have I not eaten. That which was torn of beasts I brought not unto thee;[50] I bore the loss of it; of my hand didst thou require it, whether stolen by day, or stolen by night. Thus I was; in the day the drought consumed me, and the frost by night; and my sleep departed from mine eyes. Thus have I been twenty years in thy house; I served thee fourteen years for thy two daughters, and six years for thy cattle: and thou hast changed my wages ten times. Except the God of my father, the God of Abraham, and the fear of Isaac, had been with me, surely thou hadst sent me away now empty. God hath seen mine affliction and the labor of my hands, and rebuked thee yesternight."

And Laban answered and said unto Jacob, "These daughters are my daughters, and these children are my children, and these cattle are my cattle, and all that thou seest is mine: and what can I do this day unto these my daughters, or unto their children which they have borne? Now therefore come thou, let us make a covenant, I and thou; and let it be for a witness between me and thee." And Jacob took a stone, and set it up for a pillar. And Jacob said unto his brethren, "Gather stones"; and they took stones, and made a heap: and they did eat there upon the heap. And Laban called it Jegar-sahadutha: but Jacob called it Galeed.[51] And Laban said, "This heap is a witness between me and thee this day." Therefore was the name of it called Galeed and Mizpah,[52] for he said, "The Lord watch between me and thee, when we are absent one from another. If thou shalt

[49] I.e., she is menstruating.

[50] According to the Code of Hammurabi, then the law in Mesopotamia, a shepherd was not responsible to his employer for animals "torn by beasts." Despite his trickery and sharp dealing, Jacob represents himself as one who goes even beyond the law in his honesty and hard work.

[51] Both these names mean "the heap of witness," in Laban's Aramaic and Jacob's Hebrew.

[52] "Mizpah" means "Watchpost."

afflict my daughters, or if thou shalt take other wives beside my daughters, no man is with us; see, God is witness betwixt me and thee."

And Laban said to Jacob, "Behold this heap, and behold this pillar, which I have cast betwixt me and thee! This heap be witness, and this pillar be witness, that I will not pass over this heap to thee, and that thou shalt not pass over this heap and this pillar unto me, for harm. The God of Abraham, and the God of Nahor, the God of their father, judge betwixt us." Then Jacob offered sacrifice upon the mount, and called his brethren to eat bread: and they did eat bread, and tarried all night in the mount. And early in the morning Laban rose up, and kissed his sons and his daughters, and blessed them: and Laban departed, and returned unto his place.

And Jacob went on his way, and the angels of God met him. And when Jacob saw them, he said, "This is God's host": and he called the name of that place Mahanaim.[53] And Jacob sent messengers before him to Esau his brother unto the land of Seir, the country of Edom. And he commanded them, saying, "Thus shall ye speak unto my lord Esau: 'Thy servant Jacob saith thus, "I have sojourned with Laban, and stayed there until now; and I have oxen, and asses, flocks, and menservants, and womenservants; and I have sent to tell my lord, that I may find grace in thy sight."'"

And the messengers returned to Jacob, saying, "We came to thy brother Esau, and also he cometh to meet thee, and four hundred men with him." Then Jacob was greatly afraid and distressed; and he divided the people that was with him, and the flocks, and herds, and the camels, into two bands; and said, "If Esau come to the one company, and smite it, then the other company which is left shall escape."

And Jacob said, "O God of my father Abraham, and God of my father Isaac, the Lord which saidst unto me, 'Return unto thy country, and to thy kindred, and I will deal well with thee!' I am not worthy of the least of all the mercies, and of all the truth, which thou hast showed unto thy servant; for with my staff I passed over this Jordan; and now I am become two bands. Deliver me, I pray thee, from the hand of my brother, from the hand of Esau: for I fear him, lest he will come and smite me, and the mother with the children. And thou saidst, 'I will surely do thee good, and make thy seed as the sand of the sea, which cannot be numbered for multitude.'"

And he lodged there that same night; and took of that which came to his hand a present for Esau his brother: two hundred she-goats, and twenty he-goats, two hundred ewes, and twenty rams, thirty milch camels with their colts, forty kine, and ten bulls, twenty she-asses, and ten foals. And he delivered them into the hand of his servants, every drove by themselves; and said unto his servants, "Pass over before me, and put a space betwixt drove and drove." And he commanded the foremost, saying, "When Esau my brother meeteth thee, and asketh thee, saying, 'Whose art thou? and whither goest thou? and whose are these before thee?' then thou shalt say, 'They be thy servant Jacob's; it is a present sent unto my lord Esau: and, behold, also he is behind us.'" And so commanded he the second, and the third, and all that followed the droves, saying, "On this manner shall ye speak unto Esau, when ye find him. And say ye moreover, 'Behold, thy

[53] "Two armies."

servant Jacob is behind us.'" For he said, "I will appease him with the present that goeth before me, and afterward I will see his face; peradventure he will accept of me." So went the present over before him: and himself lodged that night in the company.

And he rose up that night, and took his two wives, and his two womenservants, and his eleven sons, and passed over the ford Jabbok. And he took them, and sent them over the brook, and sent over that he had. And Jacob was left alone; and there wrestled a man with him until the breaking of the day. And when he saw that he prevailed not against him, he touched the hollow of his thigh; and the hollow of Jacob's thigh was out of joint, as he wrestled with him. And he said, "Let me go, for the day breaketh." And he said, "I will not let thee go, except thou bless me." And he said unto him, "What is thy name?" And he said "Jacob." And he said, "Thy name shall be called no more Jacob, but Israel: for as a prince hast thou power with God and with men, and hast prevailed." And Jacob asked him, and said, "Tell me, I pray thee, thy name." And he said, "Wherefore is it that thou dost ask after my name?" And he blessed him there. And Jacob called the name of the place Peniel: "For I have seen God face to face, and my life is preserved." And as he passed over Penuel the sun rose upon him, and he halted upon his thigh. Therefore the children of Israel eat not of the sinew which shrank, which is upon the hollow of the thigh, unto this day: because he touched the hollow of Jacob's thigh in the sinew that shrank.[54]

And Jacob lifted up his eyes, and looked, and, behold, Esau came, and with him four hundred men. And he divided the children unto Leah, and unto Rachel, and unto the two handmaids. And he put the handmaids and their children foremost, and Leah and her children after, and Rachel and Joseph hindermost. And he passed over before them, and bowed himself to the ground seven times, until he came near to his brother.

And Esau ran to meet him, and embraced him, and fell on his neck, and kissed him: and they wept. And he lifted up his eyes, and saw the women and the children; and said, "Who are those with thee?" And he said, "The children which God hath graciously given thy servant." Then the handmaidens came near, they and their children and they bowed themselves. And Leah also with her children came near, and bowed themselves: and after came Joseph near and Rachel, and they bowed themselves. And he said, "What meanest thou by all this drove which I met?" And he said, "These are to find grace in the sight of my lord."

And Esau said, "I have enough, my brother; keep that thou hast unto thyself." And Jacob said, "Nay, I pray thee, if now I have found grace in thy sight, then receive my present at my hand: for therefore I have seen thy face, as though I had seen the face of God, and thou wast pleased with me. Take, I pray thee, my blessing that is brought to thee; because God hath dealt graciously with me, and because I have enough."

And he said, "Let us take our journey, and let us go, and I will go before

[54] The meaning of this strange wrestling episode is rather obscure. Jacob's wrestling with God may be intended to represent symbolically his own inner struggle to throw off his rather defective past character and become a worthier man. The reference to the "sinew which shrank" in "the hollow of the thigh" seems to be an attempt to account for the Jewish ritual of removing the sciatic nerves, with the arteries and tendons of the thigh, in meat intended to be eaten.

thee." And he said unto him, "My lord knoweth that the children are tender, and the flocks and herds with young are with me: and if men should overdrive them one day, all the flock will die. Let my lord, I pray thee, pass over before his servant: and I will lead on softly, according as the cattle that goeth before me and the children be able to endure, until I come unto my lord unto Seir."

And Esau said, "Let me now leave with thee some of the folk that are with me." And he said, "What needeth it? let me find grace in the sight of my lord." So Esau returned that day on his way unto Seir. And Jacob journeyed to Succoth, and built him a house, and made booths for his cattle: therefore the name of the place is called Succoth.[55] And Jacob came to Shalem, a city of Shechem, which is in the land of Canaan, when he came from Padan-aram; and pitched his tent before the city. And he bought a parcel of a field, where he had spread his tent, at the hand of the children of Hamor, Shechem's father, for a hundred pieces of money. And he erected there an altar, and called it El-elohe-Israel. . . .[56]

And God said unto Jacob, "Arise, go up to Beth-el, and dwell there: and make there an altar unto God, that appeared unto thee when thou fleddest from the face of Esau thy brother." Then Jacob said unto his household, and to all that were with him, "Put away the strange gods that are among you, and be clean, and change your garments: and let us arise, and go up to Beth-el; and I will make there an altar unto God, who answered me in the day of my distress, and was with me in the way which I went." And they gave unto Jacob all the strange gods which were in their hand, and all their earrings which were in their ears; and Jacob hid them under the oak which was by Shechem.[57] And they journeyed: and the terror of God[58] was upon the cities that were round about them, and they did not pursue after the sons of Jacob.

So Jacob came to Luz, which is in the land of Canaan, that is, Beth-el, he and all the people that were with him. And he built there an altar, and called the place El-beth-el: because there God appeared unto him, when he fled from the face of his brother. But Deborah Rebekah's nurse died, and she was buried beneath Beth-el under an oak: and the name of it was called Allon-bachuth.

And God appeared unto Jacob again, when he came out of Padan-aram, and blessed him. And God said unto him, "Thy name is Jacob: thy name shall not be called any more Jacob, but Israel shall be thy name": and he called his name Israel. And God said unto him, "I am God Almighty: be fruitful and multiply; a nation and a company of nations shall be of thee, and kings shall come out of thy loins; and the land which I gave Abraham and Isaac, to thee I will give it, and to thy seed after thee will I give the land." And God went up from him in the place where he talked with him. And Jacob set up a pillar in the place where he talked with him, even a pillar of stone: and he poured a drink offering thereon, and he poured oil

---

[55] "Booths."   [56] "God, the God of Israel."

[57] The worshipers had to undergo ceremonial purification (washing and changing clothes), and they were required to renounce strange (or foreign) gods. The earrings which they surrendered were magical amulets used in pagan worship.

[58] The "Terror of God" was a mysterious panic said to seize and paralyze the enemy in early accounts of holy wars.

thereon. And Jacob called the name of the place where God spoke with him, Beth-el.

And they journeyed from Beth-el; and there was but a little way to come to Ephrath: and Rachel travailed, and she had hard labor. And it came to pass, when she was in hard labor, that the midwife said unto her, "Fear not; thou shalt have this son also." And it came to pass, as her soul was in departing (for she died), that she called his name Ben-oni: but his father called him Benjamin.[59] And Rachel died, and was buried in the way to Ephrath, which is Beth-lehem. And Jacob set a pillar upon her grave: that is the pillar of Rachel's grave unto this day. And Israel journeyed, and spread his tent beyond the tower of Edar.

And it came to pass, when Israel dwelt in that land, that Reuben went and lay with Bilhah his father's concubine: and Israel heard it. . . .[60]

And Jacob came unto Isaac his father unto Mamre, unto the city of Arbah, which is Hebron, where Abraham and Isaac sojourned. And the days of Isaac were a hundred and fourscore years. And Isaac gave up the ghost, and died, and was gathered unto his people, being old and full of days: and his sons Esau and Jacob buried him. . . .[61]

THE EXODUS SAGA

THE ESCAPE FROM EGYPT

(Exodus 1:8–14:31)

Now there arose up a new king over Egypt, which knew not Joseph.[1] And he said unto his people, "Behold, the people of the children of Israel are more and mightier than we. Come on, let us deal wisely with them; lest they multiply, and it come to pass that, when there falleth out any war, they join also unto our enemies, and fight against us, and so get them up out of the land." Therefore they did set over them taskmasters to afflict them with their burdens. And they built for Pharaoh treasure cities, Pithom and Rameses. But the more they afflicted them, the more they multiplied and grew. And they were grieved because of the children of Israel. And the Egyptians made the children of Israel to serve with rigor: and they made their lives bitter with hard bondage, in mortar, and in brick, and in all manner of service in the field: all their service, wherein they made them serve, was with rigor. And the king of Egypt spoke to the Hebrew mid-

---

[59] "Ben-oni" means "son of my sorrow," but "Benjamin" means "son of my right hand" or "son of the South."

[60] This mysterious episode apparently accounts for Reuben's loss of prestige as the first-born son.

[61] The last fourteen chapters of Genesis, here omitted, tell the story of Jacob's son Joseph and his rise to power in the land of Egypt.

[1] Genesis ends with the long story of Jacob's son Joseph, of how he was sold into slavery in Egypt, and of how he rose to a position of power there, winning favor for his fellow Hebrews. Exodus opens four centuries later, and the Hebrews in Egypt have sunk to the status of slaves, brutally employed in building the Pharaoh's monuments and public works. The "new king" is now thought to belong to a native Egyptian dynasty which drove out the foreign Hyksos kings, who had been friendly to the Hebrews, in the sixteenth century B.C.

wives, of which the name of the one was Shiphrah, and the name of the other Puah: and he said, "When ye do the office of a midwife to the Hebrew women, and see them upon the stools;[2] if it be a son, then ye shall kill him: but if it be a daughter, then she shall live." But the midwives feared God, and did not as the king of Egypt commanded them, but saved the men children alive. And the king of Egypt called for the midwives, and said unto them, "Why have ye done this thing, and have saved the men children alive?" And the midwives said unto Pharaoh, "Because the Hebrew women are not as the Egyptian women; for they are lively, and are delivered ere the midwives come in unto them." Therefore God dealt well with the midwives: and the people multiplied, and waxed very mighty. And it came to pass, because the midwives feared God, that he made them houses. And Pharaoh charged all his people, saying, "Every son that is born ye shall cast into the river, and every daughter ye shall save alive."

And there went a man of the house of Levi, and took to wife a daughter of Levi. And the woman conceived, and bore a son; and when she saw him that he was a goodly child, she hid him three months. And when she could not longer hide him, she took for him an ark of bulrushes,[3] and daubed it with slime and with pitch, and put the child therein; and she laid it in the flags by the river's brink. And his sister stood afar off, to wit[4] what would be done to him.[5] And the daughter of Pharaoh came down to wash herself at the river; and her maidens walked along by the river's side; and when she saw the ark among the flags, she sent her maid to fetch it. And when she had opened it, she saw the child: and, behold, the babe wept. And she had compassion on him, and said, "This is one of the Hebrews' children." Then said his sister to Pharaoh's daughter, "Shall I go and call to thee a nurse of the Hebrew women, that she may nurse the child for thee?" And Pharaoh's daughter said to her, "Go!" And the maid went and called the child's mother.

And Pharaoh's daughter said unto her, "Take this child away, and nurse it for me, and I will give thee thy wages." And the woman took the child, and nursed it. And the child grew, and she brought him unto Pharaoh's daughter, and he became her son. And she called his name Moses; and she said, "Because I drew him out of the water."

And it came to pass in those days, when Moses was grown, that he went out unto his brethren, and looked on their burdens; and he spied an Egyptian smiting an Hebrew, one of his brethren. And he looked this way and that way, and when he saw that there was no man, he slew the Egyptian, and hid him in the sand. And when he went out the second day, behold, two men of the Hebrews strove together: and he said to him that did the wrong, "Wherefore smitest thou thy fellow?" And he said, "Who made thee a prince and a judge over us? intendest thou to kill me, as thou killedst the Egyptian?" And Moses feared, and said, "Surely this thing is known."

Now when Pharaoh heard this thing, he sought to slay Moses. But

---

[2] Birth-stools.   [3] Sedge plants which grow in marshy areas.   [4] To know or find out.
[5] The story of an infant hero being saved by being put in a basket in the water appears in other ancient hero-tales, including that of Sargon of Agade, from about 2600 B.C.

Moses fled from the face of Pharaoh, and dwelt in the land of Midian:[6] and he sat down by a well. Now the priest of Midian had seven daughters: and they came and drew water, and filled the troughs to water their father's flock. And the shepherds came and drove them away: but Moses stood up and helped them, and watered their flock. And when they came to Reuel their father, he said, "How is it that ye are come so soon to-day?" And they said, "An Egyptian delivered us out of the hand of the shepherds, and also drew water enough for us, and watered the flock." And he said unto his daughters, "And where is he? why is it that ye have left the man? call him, that he may eat bread." And Moses was content to dwell with the man: and he gave Moses Zipporah his daughter. And she bore him a son, and he called his name Gershom: for he said, "I have been a stranger in a strange land."[7]

And it came to pass in process of time that the king of Egypt[8] died: and the children of Israel sighed by reason of the bondage, and they cried, and their cry came up unto God by reason of the bondage. And God heard their groaning, and God remembered his covenant with Abraham, with Isaac, and with Jacob. And God looked upon the children of Israel, and God had respect unto them.

Now Moses kept the flock of Jethro his father-in-law, the priest of Midian: and he led the flock to the backside of the desert, and came to the mountain of God, even to Horeb. And the angel of the Lord appeared unto him in a flame of fire out of the midst of a bush: and he looked, and, behold, the bush burned with fire, and the bush was not consumed. And Moses said, "I will now turn aside, and see this great sight, why the bush is not burnt." And when the Lord saw that he turned aside to see, God called unto him out of the midst of the bush, and said, "Moses, Moses." And he said, "Here am I." And he said, "Draw not nigh hither: put off thy shoes from off thy feet, for the place whereon thou standest is holy ground." Moreover he said, "I am the God of thy father, the God of Abraham, the God of Isaac, and the God of Jacob." And Moses hid his face; for he was afraid to look upon God.

And the Lord said, "I have surely seen the affliction of my people which are in Egypt, and have heard their cry by reason of their taskmasters; for I know their sorrows. And I am come down to deliver them out of the hand of the Egyptians, and to bring them up out of that land unto a good land and a large, unto a land flowing with milk and honey; unto the place of the Canaanites, and the Hittites, and the Amorites, and the Perizzites, and the Hivites, and the Jebusites. Now therefore, behold, the cry of the children of Israel is come unto me: and I have also seen the oppression wherewith the Egyptians oppress them. Come now therefore, and I will send thee unto Pharaoh, that thou mayest bring forth my people the children of Israel out of Egypt." And Moses said unto God, "Who am I, that I should go unto

[6] The location of the land of Midian is not known, but it has been suggested that it was from the Midianites and from his father-in-law that Moses acquired his concept of God, especially since his faith before his flight into Midian is not mentioned. Moses' father-in-law, called Reuel here, is later called Jethro (Exodus 3:1) and Raguel (Numbers 10:29). This variation is due to the existence of different compositional strands in the book.

[7] "Gershom," as indicated, means "stranger in a strange land."

[8] The king was probably Seit I; the oppressive new king was Rameses II.

Pharaoh, and that I should bring forth the children of Israel out of Egypt?"
And he said, "Certainly I will be with thee; and this shall be a token unto
thee, that I have sent thee. When thou hast brought forth the people out of
Egypt, ye shall serve God upon this mountain."

And Moses said unto God, "Behold, when I come unto the children of
Israel, and shall say unto them, 'The God of your fathers hath sent me unto
you'; and they shall say to me, 'What is his name?' what shall I say unto
them?" And God said unto Moses, "I AM THAT I AM":[9] and he said, "Thus
shalt thou say unto the children of Israel, I AM hath sent me unto you." And
God said moreover unto Moses, "Thus shalt thou say unto the children of
Israel, 'The Lord God of your fathers, the God of Abraham, the God of
Isaac, and the God of Jacob, hath sent me unto you.' And they shall
hearken to thy voice: and thou shalt come, thou and the elders of Israel,
unto the king of Egypt, and ye shall say unto him, 'The Lord God of the
Hebrews hath met with us: and now let us go, we beseech thee, three days'
journey into the wilderness, that we may sacrifice to the Lord our God.'
And I am sure that the king of Egypt will not let you go, no, not by a mighty
hand. And I will stretch out my hand, and smite Egypt with all my wonders
which I will do in the midst thereof: and after that he will let you go. And I
will give this people favor in the sight of the Egyptians: and it shall come to
pass that, when ye go, ye shall not go empty: but every woman shall borrow
of her neighbor, and of her that sojourneth in her house, jewels of silver,
and jewels of gold, and raiment: and ye shall put them upon your sons, and
upon your daughters; and ye shall spoil the Egyptians."

And Moses answered and said, "But, behold, they will not believe me,
nor hearken unto my voice: for they will say, 'The Lord hath not appeared
unto thee.'" And the Lord said unto him, "What is that in thine hand?"
And he said, "A rod." And he said, "Cast it on the ground." And he cast it
on the ground, and it became a serpent; and Moses fled from before it.
And the Lord said unto Moses, "Put forth thine hand, and take it by the
tail." And he put forth his hand, and caught it, and it became a rod in his
hand. And the Lord said furthermore unto him, "Put now thine hand into
thy bosom." And he put his hand into his bosom: and when he took it out,
behold, his hand was leprous as snow. And he said, "Put thine hand into
thy bosom again." And he put his hand into his bosom again; and plucked
it out of his bosom, and, behold, it was turned again as his other flesh. "And
it shall come to pass, if they will not believe thee, neither hearken to the
voice of the first sign, that they will believe the voice of the latter sign. And
it shall come to pass, if they will not believe also these two signs, neither
hearken unto thy voice, that thou shalt take of the water of the river, and
pour it upon the dry land: and the water which thou takest out of the river
shall become blood upon the dry land."

And Moses said unto the Lord, "O my Lord, I am not eloquent, neither

[9]"I am that I am" is a play on the four Hebrew consonants represented in English as
Y-H-V-H. The English version of the name of the Hebrew God, originally written only in
consonants, has been a source of some confusion. The correct version is apparently "Yahweh,"
but the King James Version regularly uses merely "The Lord." The name "Jehovah," used
only four times in the King James Version, results from a misunderstanding on the part of
early English translators, who inserted the vowels of the Hebrew "Adonai" (Lord) into the
consonants Y (or J)-H-V-H.

heretofore, nor since thou hast spoken unto thy servant: but I am slow of speech, and of a slow tongue." [10] And the Lord said unto him, "Who hath made man's mouth? or who maketh the dumb, or deaf, or the seeing, or the blind? have not I the Lord? Now therefore go, and I will be with thy mouth, and teach thee what thou shalt say." And he said, "O my Lord, send, I pray thee, by the hand of him whom thou wilt send." And the anger of the Lord was kindled against Moses, and he said, "Is not Aaron the Levite thy brother? I know that he can speak well. And also, behold, he cometh forth to meet thee: and when he seeth thee, he will be glad in his heart. And thou shalt speak unto him, and put words in his mouth: and I will be with thy mouth, and with his mouth, and will teach you what ye shall do. And he shall be thy spokesman unto the people: and he shall be, even he shall be to thee instead of a mouth, and thou shalt be to him instead of God. And thou shalt take this rod in thine hand, wherewith thou shalt do signs."

And Moses went and returned to Jethro his father-in-law, and said unto him, "Let me go, I pray thee, and return unto my brethren which are in Egypt, and see whether they be yet alive." And Jethro said to Moses, "Go in peace." And the Lord said unto Moses in Midian, "Go, return into Egypt: for all the men are dead which sought thy life." And Moses took his wife and his sons, and set them upon an ass, and he returned to the land of Egypt: and Moses took the rod of God in his hand. . . .

And Moses and Aaron went and gathered together all the elders of the children of Israel; and Aaron spoke all the words which the Lord had spoken unto Moses, and did the signs in the sight of the people. And the people believed; and when they heard that the Lord had visited the children of Israel, and that he had looked upon their affliction, then they bowed their heads and worshipped.

And afterward Moses and Aaron went in, and told Pharaoh, "Thus saith the Lord God of Israel, 'Let my people go, that they may hold a feast unto me in the wilderness.'" And Pharaoh said, "Who is the Lord, that I should obey his voice to let Israel go? I know not the Lord, neither will I let Israel go." And they said, "The God of the Hebrews hath met with us: let us go, we pray thee, three days' journey into the desert, and sacrifice unto the Lord our God; lest he fall upon us with pestilence, or with the sword." And the king of Egypt said unto them, "Wherefore do ye, Moses and Aaron, let the people from their works? get you unto your burdens." And Pharaoh commanded the same day the taskmasters of the people, and their officers, saying, "Ye shall no more give the people straw to make brick, as heretofore: let them go and gather straw for themselves. [11] And the tale [12] of the bricks, which they did make heretofore, ye shall lay upon them; ye shall not diminish ought thereof: for they be idle; therefore they cry, saying, 'Let us go and sacrifice to our God.' Let there more work be laid upon the men, that they may labor therein; and let them not regard vain words."

---

[10] The tradition that Moses had a speech impediment stems from this passage and from a later passage which says that his brother Aaron spoke for Moses when he reported what the Lord had said to the elders of Israel.

[11] Bricks were made with clay and then dried in the sun (rather than fired). They would be brittle unless the clay was mixed with sand or with chopped straw.

[12] Number or quota.

And the taskmasters of the people went out, and their officers, and they spoke to the people, saying, "Thus saith Pharaoh, 'I will not give you straw. Go ye, get you straw where ye can find it: yet not ought of your work shall be diminished.'" So the people were scattered abroad throughout all the land of Egypt to gather stubble instead of straw. And the taskmasters hastened them, saying "Fulfil your works, your daily tasks, as when there was straw." And the officers of the children of Israel, which Pharaoh's taskmasters had set over them, were beaten, and demanded, "Wherefore have ye not fulfilled your task in making brick both yesterday and to-day, as heretofore?"

Then the officers of the children of Israel came and cried unto Pharaoh, saying, "Wherefore dealest thou thus with thy servants? There is no straw given unto thy servants, and they say to us, 'Make brick': and, behold, thy servants are beaten; but the fault is in thine own people." But he said, "Ye are idle, ye are idle: therefore ye say, 'Let us go and do sacrifice to the Lord.' Go therefore now, and work; for there shall no straw be given you, yet shall ye deliver the tale of bricks." And the officers of the children of Israel did see that they were in evil case, after it was said, "Ye shall not minish[13] ought from your bricks of your daily task." And they met Moses and Aaron, who stood in the way, as they came forth from Pharaoh; and they said unto them, "The Lord look upon you, and judge; because ye have made our savor to be abhorred in the eyes of Pharaoh, and in the eyes of his servants, to put a sword in their hand to slay us."

And Moses returned unto the Lord, and said, "Lord, wherefore hast thou so evil entreated this people? why is it that thou hast sent me? For since I came to Pharaoh to speak in thy name, he hath done evil to this people; neither hast thou delivered thy people at all." . . . And God spoke unto Moses, and said unto him, "I am the Lord; and I appeared unto Abraham, unto Isaac, and unto Jacob, by the name of God Almighty, but by my name JEHOVAH was I not known to them. And I have also established my covenant with them, to give them the land of Canaan, the land of their pilgrimage, wherein they were strangers. And I have also heard the groaning of the children of Israel, whom the Egyptians keep in bondage; and I have remembered my covenant. Wherefore say unto the children of Israel, 'I am the Lord, and I will bring you out from under the burdens of the Egyptians, and I will rid you out of their bondage, and I will redeem you with a stretched out arm, and with great judgments; and I will take you to me for a people, and I will be to you a God; and ye shall know that I am the Lord your God, which bringeth you out from under the burdens of the Egyptians. And I will bring you in unto the land, concerning the which I did swear to give it to Abraham, to Isaac, and to Jacob; and I will give it you for an heritage: I am the Lord.'" And Moses spoke so unto the children of Israel: but they hearkened not unto Moses for anguish of spirit, and for cruel bondage.

And the Lord said unto Moses, "See, I have made thee a god to Pharaoh: and Aaron thy brother shall be thy prophet. Thou shalt speak all that I command thee: and Aaron thy brother shall speak unto Pharaoh, that he send the children of Israel out of his land. And I will harden Pharaoh's

[13] Archaic form of "diminish."

heart, and multiply my signs and my wonders in the land of Egypt. But Pharaoh shall not hearken unto you, that I may lay my hand upon Egypt, and bring forth mine armies, and my people the children of Israel, out of the land of Egypt by great judgments. And the Egyptians shall know that I am the Lord, when I stretch forth mine hand upon Egypt, and bring out the children of Israel from among them." . . .

And the Lord spoke unto Moses and unto Aaron, saying, "When Pharaoh shall speak unto you, saying, 'Show a miracle for you'; then thou shalt say unto Aaron, 'Take thy rod, and cast it before Pharaoh,' and it shall become a serpent." And Moses and Aaron went in unto Pharaoh, and they did so as the Lord had commanded: and Aaron cast down his rod before Pharaoh, and before his servants, and it became a serpent. Then Pharaoh also called the wise men and the sorcerers: now the magicians of Egypt, they also did in like manner with their enchantments. For they cast down every man his rod, and they became serpents: but Aaron's rod swallowed up their rods. And he hardened Pharaoh's heart, that he hearkened not unto them; as the Lord had said. . . .

And the Lord spoke unto Moses, "Say unto Aaron, 'Take thy rod, and stretch out thine hand upon the waters of Egypt, upon their streams, upon their rivers, and upon their ponds, and upon all their pools of water, that they may become blood; and that there may be blood throughout all the land of Egypt, both in vessels of wood, and in vessels of stone.'" And Moses and Aaron did so, as the Lord commanded; and he lifted up the rod, and smote the waters that were in the river, in the sight of Pharaoh, and in the sight of his servants; and all the waters that were in the river were turned to blood.[14] And the fish that was in the river died; and the river stank, and the Egyptians could not drink of the water of the river; and there was blood throughout all the land of Egypt. And the magicians of Egypt did so with their enchantments: and Pharaoh's heart was hardened, neither did he hearken unto them; as the Lord had said. And Pharaoh turned and went into his house, neither did he set his heart to this also. And all the Egyptians digged round about the river for water to drink; for they could not drink of the water of the river. And seven days were fulfilled, after that the Lord had smitten the river.

And the Lord spoke unto Moses, "Say unto Aaron, 'Stretch forth thine hand with thy rod over the streams, over the rivers, and over the ponds, and cause frogs to come up upon the land of Egypt.'" And Aaron stretched out his hand over the waters of Egypt; and the frogs came up, and covered the land of Egypt.[15] And the magicians did so with their enchantments, and brought up frogs upon the land of Egypt.

Then Pharaoh called Moses and Aaron, and said, "Intreat the Lord, that he may take away the frogs from me, and from my people; and I will let the people go, that they may do sacrifice unto the Lord." And Moses said unto Pharaoh, "Glory over me: when shall I intreat for thee, and for

[14] This plague, like the subsequent ones, appears to be a heightening of natural phenomena. The Nile, in the middle of the summer, often turns a reddish color because of small organisms in the water.

[15] Frogs multiply quickly in the muddy lowlands of the Nile, but are usually held in check by the ibis, a frog-eating bird.

thy servants, and for thy people, to destroy the frogs from thee and thy houses, that they may remain in the river only?" And he said, "To-morrow." And he said, "Be it according to thy word: that thou mayest know that there is none like unto the Lord our God. And the frogs shall depart from thee, and from thy houses, and from thy servants, and from thy people; they shall remain in the river only."

And Moses and Aaron went out from Pharaoh: and Moses cried unto the Lord because of the frogs which he had brought against Pharaoh. And the Lord did according to the word of Moses; and the frogs died out of the houses, out of the villages, and out of the fields. And they gathered them together upon heaps: and the land stank. But when Pharaoh saw that there was respite, he hardened his heart, and hearkened not unto them; as the Lord had said.

And the Lord said unto Moses, "Say unto Aaron, 'Stretch out thy rod, and smite the dust of the land, that it may become lice[16] throughout all the land of Egypt.'" And they did so; for Aaron stretched out his hand with his rod, and smote the dust of the earth, and it became lice in man, and in beast; all the dust of the land became lice throughout all the land of Egypt. And the magicians did so with their enchantments to bring forth lice, but they could not: so there were lice upon man, and upon beast. Then the magicians said unto Pharaoh, "This is the finger of God": and Pharaoh's heart was hardened, and he hearkened not unto them; as the Lord had said.

And the Lord said unto Moses, "Rise up early in the morning, and stand before Pharaoh; lo, he cometh forth to the water; and say unto him, 'Thus saith the Lord, "Let my people go, that they may serve me. Else, if thou wilt not let my people go, behold, I will send swarms of flies upon thee, and upon thy servants, and upon thy people, and into thy houses: and the houses of the Egyptians shall be full of swarms of flies, and also the ground whereon they are. And I will sever in that day the land of Goshen, in which my people dwell, that no swarms of flies shall be there; to the end thou mayest know that I am the Lord in the midst of the earth. And I will put a division between my people and thy people: to-morrow shall this sign be."'"

And the Lord did so; and there came a grievous swarm of flies into the house of Pharaoh, and into his servants' houses, and into all the land of Egypt: the land was corrupted by reason of the swarm of flies.

And Pharaoh called for Moses and for Aaron, and said, "Go ye, sacrifice to your God in the land." And Moses said, "It is not meet so to do; for we shall sacrifice the abomination of the Egyptians to the Lord our God: lo, shall we sacrifice the abomination of the Egyptians before their eyes, and will they not stone us? We will go three days' journey into the wilderness, and sacrifice to the Lord our God, as he shall command us." And Pharaoh said, "I will let you go, that ye may sacrifice to the Lord your God in the wilderness; only ye shall not go very far away: intreat for me." And Moses said, "Behold, I go out from thee, and I will intreat the Lord that the swarms of flies may depart from Pharaoh, from his servants, and from his

---

[16] Probably "gnats." The gnats and flies of this and the following miracle are common pests in Egypt.

people, to-morrow: but let not Pharaoh deal deceitfully any more in not letting the people go to sacrifice to the Lord."

And Moses went out from Pharaoh, and intreated the Lord. And the Lord did according to the word of Moses; and he removed the swarms of flies from Pharaoh, from his servants, and from his people; there remained not one. And Pharaoh hardened his heart at this time also, neither would he let the people go.

Then the Lord said unto Moses, "Go in unto Pharaoh, and tell him, 'Thus saith the Lord God of the Hebrews, "Let my people go, that they may serve me." For if thou refuse to let them go, and wilt hold them still, behold, the hand of the Lord is upon thy cattle which is in the field, upon the horses, upon the asses, upon the camels, upon the oxen, and upon the sheep: there shall be a very grievous murrain.[17] And the Lord shall sever between the cattle of Israel and the cattle of Egypt: and there shall nothing die of all that is the children's of Israel.' " And the Lord appointed a set time, saying, "To-morrow the Lord shall do this thing in the land." And the Lord did that thing on the morrow, and all the cattle of Egypt died:[18] but of the cattle of the children of Israel died not one. And Pharaoh sent, and, behold, there was not one of the cattle of the Israelites dead. And the heart of Pharaoh was hardened, and he did not let the people go.

And the Lord said unto Moses and unto Aaron, "Take to you handfuls of ashes of the furnace and let Moses sprinkle it toward the heaven in the sight of Pharaoh. And it shall become small dust in all the land of Egypt, and shall be a boil breaking forth with blains[19] upon man, and upon beast, throughout all the land of Egypt." And they took ashes of the furnace, and stood before Pharaoh; and Moses sprinkled it up toward heaven; and it became a boil breaking forth with blains upon man, and upon beast. And the magicians could not stand before Moses because of the boils; for the boil was upon the magicians, and upon all the Egyptians. And the Lord hardened the heart of Pharaoh, and he hearkened not unto them; as the Lord had spoken unto Moses. . . .

And the Lord said unto Moses, "Stretch forth thine hand toward heaven, that there may be hail in all the land of Egypt, upon man, and upon beast, and upon every herb of the field, throughout the land of Egypt." And Moses stretched forth his rod toward heaven: and the Lord sent thunder and hail, and the fire ran along upon the ground; and the Lord rained hail upon the land of Egypt. So there was hail, and fire mingled with the hail, very grievous, such as there was none like it in all the land of Egypt since it became a nation. And the hail smote throughout all the land of Egypt all that was in the field, both man and beast; and the hail smote every herb of the field, and broke every tree of the field. Only in the land of Goshen, where the children of Israel were, was there no hail.

And Pharaoh sent, and called for Moses and Aaron, and said unto them, "I have sinned this time: the Lord is righteous, and I and my people

---

[17] Any sort of pestilence or plague.

[18] This and the following plague—a disease and boils affecting cattle—are closely related to each other and to the preceding plagues of gnats and flies. The most striking aspect of these miracles is the exemption of the Hebrews from them.

[19] Inflammatory swellings or sores.

are wicked. Intreat the Lord (for it is enough) that there be no more mighty thunderings and hail; and I will let you go, and ye shall stay no longer." . . .

And Moses went out of the city from Pharaoh, and spread abroad his hands unto the Lord: and the thunders and hail ceased, and the rain was not poured upon the earth. And when Pharaoh saw that the rain and the hail and the thunders were ceased, he sinned yet more, and hardened his heart, he and his servants. And the heart of Pharaoh was hardened, neither would he let the children of Israel go; as the Lord had spoken by Moses. . . .

And the Lord said unto Moses, "Stretch out thine hand over the land of Egypt for the locusts, that they may come up upon the land of Egypt, and eat every herb of the land, even all that the hail hath left." And Moses stretched forth his rod over the land of Egypt, and the Lord brought an east wind upon the land all that day, and all that night; and when it was morning, the east wind brought the locusts. And the locusts went up over all the land of Egypt, and rested in all the coasts of Egypt: very grievous were they; before them there were no such locusts as they, neither after them shall be such. For they covered the face of the whole earth, so that the land was darkened; and they did eat every herb of the land, and all the fruit of the trees which the hail had left: and there remained not any green thing in the trees, or in the herbs of the field, through all the land of Egypt.

Then Pharaoh called for Moses and Aaron in haste; and he said, "I have sinned against the Lord your God, and against you. Now therefore forgive, I pray thee, my sin only this once, and intreat the Lord your God, that he may take away from me this death only."

And he went out from Pharaoh, and intreated the Lord. And the Lord turned a mighty strong west wind, which took away the locusts, and cast them into the Red sea; there remained not one locust in all the coasts of Egypt.[20] But the Lord hardened Pharaoh's heart, so that he would not let the children of Israel go.

And the Lord said unto Moses, "Stretch out thine hand toward heaven, that there may be darkness over the land of Egypt, even darkness which may be felt." And Moses stretched forth his hand toward heaven; and there was a thick darkness in all the land of Egypt three days.[21] They saw not one another, neither rose any from his place for three days: but all the children of Israel had light in their dwellings.

And Pharaoh called unto Moses, and said, "Go ye, serve the Lord; only let your flocks and herds be stayed: let your little ones also go with you." And Moses said, "Thou must give us also sacrifices and burnt offerings, that we may sacrifice unto the Lord our God. Our cattle also shall go with us; there shall not a hoof be left behind; for thereof must we take to serve the Lord our God; and we know not with what we must serve the Lord, until we come thither." But the Lord hardened Pharaoh's heart, and he would not let them go. . . .

[20] The plague of the locusts, like the preceding ones, is a heightening of a natural phenomenon, and its beginning and ending can be explained naturalistically; winds brought the locusts and carried them away.

[21] The ninth plague, of thick darkness, has been explained as the thick spring dust storms that still occur in Egypt.

And the Lord said unto Moses, "Yet will I bring one plague more upon Pharaoh, and upon Egypt; afterwards he will let you go hence: when he shall let you go, he shall surely thrust you out hence altogether. Speak now in the ears of the people, and let every man borrow of his neighbor, and every woman of her neighbor, jewels of silver, and jewels of gold." And the Lord gave the people favor in the sight of the Egyptians. Moreover the man Moses was very great in the land of Egypt, in the sight of Pharaoh's servants, and in the sight of the people.

And Moses said, "Thus saith the Lord, 'About midnight will I go out into the midst of Egypt. And all the firstborn in the land of Egypt shall die, from the firstborn of Pharaoh that sitteth upon his throne, even unto the firstborn of the maidservant that is behind the mill; and all the firstborn of beasts. And there shall be a great cry throughout all the land of Egypt, such as there was none like it, nor shall be like it any more.' But against any of the children of Israel shall not a dog move his tongue, against man or beast: that ye may know how the Lord doth put a difference between the Egyptians and Israel. And all these thy servants shall come down unto me, and bow down themselves unto me, saying, 'Get thee out, and all the people that follow thee': and after that I will go out." And he went out from Pharaoh in great anger.

And the Lord said unto Moses, "Pharaoh shall not hearken unto you; that my wonders may be multiplied in the land of Egypt." And Moses and Aaron did all these wonders before Pharaoh: and the Lord hardened Pharaoh's heart, so that he would not let the children of Israel go out of his land. . . .

Then Moses called for all the elders of Israel, and said unto them, "Draw out and take you a lamb according to your families, and kill the passover. And ye shall take a bunch of hyssop,[22] and dip it in the blood that is in the basin, and strike the lintel and the two side posts with the blood that is in the basin; and none of you shall go out at the door of his house until the morning. For the Lord will pass through to smite the Egyptians; and when he seeth the blood upon the lintel, and on the two side posts, the Lord will pass over the door, and will not suffer the destroyer to come in unto your houses to smite you. And ye shall observe this thing for an ordinance to thee and to thy sons for ever. And it shall come to pass, when ye be come to the land which the Lord will give you, according as he hath promised, that ye shall keep this service. And it shall come to pass, when your children shall say unto you, 'What mean ye by this service?' that ye shall say, 'It is the sacrifice of the Lord's passover, who passed over the houses of the children of Israel in Egypt, when he smote the Egyptians, and delivered our houses.'" And the people bowed the head and worshipped. And the children of Israel went away, and did as the Lord had commanded Moses and Aaron, so did they.

And it came to pass that at midnight the Lord smote all the firstborn in the land of Egypt, from the firstborn of Pharaoh that sat on his throne unto the firstborn of the captive that was in the dungeon; and all the firstborn of cattle. And Pharaoh rose up in the night, he, and all his servants, and all the Egyptians; and there was a great cry in Egypt; for there was not a house

---

[22] An aromatic plant, possibly a form of mint.

where there was not one dead.[23] And he called for Moses and Aaron by night, and said, "Rise up, and get you forth from among my people, both ye and the children of Israel; and go, serve the Lord, as ye have said. Also take your flocks and your herds, as ye have said, and be gone; and bless me also."

And the Egyptians were urgent upon the people, that they might send them out of the land in haste; for they said, "We be all dead men."

And the people took their dough before it was leavened, their kneading troughs being bound up in their clothes upon their shoulders. And the children of Israel did according to the word of Moses; and they borrowed of the Egyptians jewels of silver, and jewels of gold, and raiment: and the Lord gave the people favor in the sight of the Egyptians, so that they lent unto them such things as they required. And they spoiled the Egyptians.

And the children of Israel journeyed from Rameses to Succoth, about six hundred thousand on foot that were men, beside children. And a mixed multitude went up also with them; and flocks and herds, even very much cattle. And they baked unleavened cakes of the dough which they brought forth out of Egypt, for it was not leavened; because they were thrust out of Egypt, and could not tarry, neither had they prepared for themselves any victual.

(Now the sojourning of the children of Israel, who dwelt in Egypt, was four hundred and thirty years. And it came to pass at the end of the four hundred and thirty years, even the selfsame day it came to pass, that all the hosts of the Lord went out from the land of Egypt. It is a night to be much observed unto the Lord for bringing them out from the land of Egypt: this is that night of the Lord to be observed of all the children of Israel in their generations.) . . .

And it came to pass, when Pharaoh had let the people go, that God led them not through the way of the land of the Philistines, although that was near; for God said, "Lest peradventure the people repent when they see war, and they return to Egypt": but God led the people about, through the way of the wilderness of the Red Sea.[24] And the children of Israel went up harnessed out of the land of Egypt. And Moses took the bones of Joseph with him: for he had straitly[25] sworn the children of Israel, saying, "God will surely visit you; and ye shall carry up my bones away hence with you." . . . And the Lord went before them by day in a pillar of a cloud, to lead them the way; and by night in a pillar of fire, to give them light; to go by day and night: he took not away the pillar of the cloud by day, nor the pillar of fire by night, from before the people. . . .

---

[23] This story is the basis for the Jewish festival of Passover, one of the oldest religious festivals in the world. It is observed in March or April and lasts for seven or eight days. Work is prohibited on the first and last days; other features of the festival include the eating of unleavened bread ("matzot") and of bitter herbs with the evening meal.

[24] It is possible to reconstruct Moses' route out of Egypt, taking not the direct route to Canaan, about two hundred miles along the coast, but an indirect route southeast to the Sea of Reeds (not the Red Sea). The reason given here is anachronistic, since the Philistines did not settle in Palestine until after the Hebrew invasion. Possibly Moses took the indirect, "wandering" route to allow the Hebrews time to become a disciplined, united people before they invaded Canaan, or perhaps he wanted to lead them toward the mountain where they would receive the Law.

[25] Strictly.

And it was told the king of Egypt that the people fled: and the heart of Pharaoh and of his servants was turned against the people, and they said, "Why have we done this, that we have let Israel go from serving us?" And he made ready his chariot, and took his people with him: and he took six hundred chosen chariots, and all the chariots of Egypt, and captains over every one of them. And the Lord hardened the heart of Pharaoh king of Egypt, and he pursued after the children of Israel: and the children of Israel went out with a high hand. But the Egyptians pursued after them, all the horses and chariots of Pharaoh, and his horsemen, and his army, and overtook them encamping by the sea, beside Pi-hahiroth, before Baal-zephon.

And when Pharaoh drew nigh, the children of Israel lifted up their eyes, and, behold, the Egyptians marched after them; and they were sore afraid: and the children of Israel cried out unto the Lord. And they said unto Moses, "Because there were no graves in Egypt, hast thou taken us away to die in the wilderness? wherefore hast thou dealt thus with us, to carry us forth out of Egypt? Is not this the word that we did tell thee in Egypt, saying, 'Let us alone, that we may serve the Egyptians'? For it had been better for us to serve the Egyptians, than that we should die in the wilderness." And Moses said unto the people, "Fear ye not, stand still, and see the salvation of the Lord, which he will show to you to-day: for the Egyptians whom ye have seen to-day, ye shall see them again no more for ever. The Lord shall fight for you, and ye shall hold your peace." . . .

And the angel of God, which went before the camp of Israel, removed and went behind them; and the pillar of the cloud went from before their face, and stood behind them: and it came between the camp of the Egyptians and the camp of Israel; and it was a cloud and darkness to them, but it gave light by night to these: so that the one came not near the other all night. And Moses stretched out his hand over the sea; and the Lord caused the sea to go back by a strong east wind all that night, and made the sea dry land, and the waters were divided. And the children of Israel went into the midst of the sea upon the dry ground: and the waters were a wall unto them on their right hand, and on their left. And the Egyptians pursued, and went in after them to the midst of the sea, even all Pharaoh's horses, his chariots, and his horsemen. And it came to pass that in the morning watch the Lord looked unto the host of the Egyptians through the pillar of fire and of the cloud, and troubled the host of the Egyptians, and took off their chariot wheels, that they drove them heavily: so that the Egyptians said, "Let us flee from the face of Israel; for the Lord fighteth for them against the Egyptians."

And the Lord said unto Moses, "Stretch out thine hand over the sea, that the waters may come again upon the Egyptians, upon their chariots, and upon their horsemen." And Moses stretched forth his hand over the sea, and the sea returned to his strength when the morning appeared; and the Egyptians fled against it; and the Lord overthrew the Egyptians in the midst of the sea. And the waters returned, and covered the chariots, and the horsemen, and all the host of Pharaoh that came into the sea after them; there remained not so much as one of them. But the children of Israel walked upon dry land in the midst of the sea; and the waters were a wall unto them on their right hand, and on their left.

Thus the Lord saved Israel that day out of the hand of the Egyptians; and Israel saw the Egyptians dead upon the sea shore. And Israel saw that great work which the Lord did upon the Egyptians: and the people feared the Lord, and believed the Lord and his servant Moses.

THE SONG OF MOSES

(Exodus 15:1–15:21)
Then sang Moses and the children of Israel this song unto the Lord, and spoke, saying,

"I will sing unto the Lord, for he hath triumphed gloriously:
    the horse and his rider hath he thrown into the sea.
The Lord is my strength and song,
    and he is become my salvation:
He is my God, and I will prepare him a habitation;
    my father's God, and I will exalt him.
The Lord is a man of war;
    the Lord is his name.

"Pharaoh's chariots and his host hath he cast into the sea:
    his chosen captains also are drowned in the Red Sea.
The depths have covered them:
    they sank into the bottom as a stone.
Thy right hand, O Lord, is become glorious in power:
    thy right hand, O Lord, hath dashed in pieces the enemy.
And in the greatness of thine excellency thou hast overthrown them that
      rose up against thee:
    thy right hand, O Lord, hath dashed in pieces the enemy.
Thou sentest forth thy wrath, which consumed them as stubble,
    and with the blast of thy nostrils the waters were gathered together.
The floods stood upright as a heap,
    and the depths were congealed in the heart of the sea.
The enemy said, 'I will pursue, I will overtake,
    I will divide the spoil; my lust shall be satisfied upon them;
    I will draw my sword, my hand shall destroy them.'
Thou didst blow with thy wind, the sea covered them:
    they sank as lead in the mighty waters.

"Who is like unto thee, O Lord, among the gods?
    who is like thee, glorious in holiness?
    fearful in praises, doing wonders?
Thou stretchedst out thy right hand,
    the earth swallowed them.

"Thou in thy mercy hast led forth the people which thou hast redeemed:
    thou hast guided them in thy strength unto thy holy habitation.
The people shall hear, and be afraid:
    sorrow shall take hold on the inhabitants of Palestina.

Then the dukes of Edom shall be amazed;
> the mighty men of Moab, trembling shall take hold upon them;
> all the inhabitants of Canaan shall melt away.

Fear and dread shall fall upon them;
> by the greatness of thine arm they shall be as still as a stone;

Till thy people pass over, O Lord,
> till the people pass over, which thou hast purchased.

Thou shalt bring them in, and plant them in the mountain of thine inheritance,
> in the place, O Lord, which thou hast made for thee to dwell in,
> in the Sanctuary, O Lord, which thy hands have established.

The Lord shall reign for ever and ever."[26]

. . . And Miriam the prophetess, the sister of Aaron, took a timbrel[27] in her hand; and all the women went out after her with timbrels and with dances. And Miriam answered them,

> "Sing ye to the Lord, for he hath triumphed gloriously;
> the horse and his rider hath he thrown into the sea."

THE JOURNEY TO SINAI

(Exodus 15:22–18:27)
So Moses brought Israel from the Red Sea, and they went out into the wilderness of Shur; and they went three days in the wilderness, and found no water. And when they came to Marah, they could not drink of the waters of Marah, for they were bitter: therefore the name of it was called Marah. And the people murmured against Moses, saying, "What shall we drink?"

And he cried unto the Lord; and the Lord showed him a tree, which when he had cast into the waters, the waters were made sweet: there he made for them a statute and an ordinance, and there he proved them, and said, "If thou wilt diligently hearken to the voice of the Lord thy God, and wilt do that which is right in his sight, and wilt give ear to his command-ments, and keep all his statutes, I will put none of these diseases upon thee, which I have brought upon the Egyptians: for I am the Lord that healeth thee."

And they came to Elim, where were twelve wells of water, and three-score and ten palm trees: and they encamped there by the waters.

And they took their journey from Elim, and all the congregation of the children of Israel came unto the wilderness of Sin, which is between Elim and Sinai, on the fifteenth day of the second month after their departing out of the land of Egypt. And the whole congregation of the children of Israel murmured against Moses and Aaron in the wilderness; and the chil-dren of Israel said unto them, "Would to God we had died by the hand of the Lord in the land of Egypt, when we sat by the flesh pots, and when we

---

[26] This victory song is probably of fairly late date. The oldest portion seems to be the couplet which follows, from which the longer song was elaborated.

[27] A small hand drum or tambourine.

did eat bread to the full; for ye have brought us forth into this wilderness, to kill this whole assembly with hunger."

Then said the Lord unto Moses, "Behold, I will rain bread from heaven for you; and the people shall go out and gather a certain rate every day, that I may prove them, whether they will walk in my law, or no. And it shall come to pass that on the sixth day they shall prepare that which they bring in; and it shall be twice as much as they gather daily." And Moses and Aaron said unto all the children of Israel, "At even, then ye shall know that the Lord hath brought you out from the land of Egypt; and in the morning, then ye shall see the glory of the Lord; for that he heareth your murmurings against the Lord: and what are we, that ye murmur against us?" . . .

And it came to pass, that at even the quails came up, and covered the camp: and in the morning the dew lay round about the host. And when the dew that lay was gone up, behold, upon the face of the wilderness there lay a small round thing, as small as the hoar frost on the ground. And when the children of Israel saw it, they said one to another, "It is manna": for they wist not what it was.[28] And Moses said unto them, "This is the bread which the Lord hath given you to eat. This is the thing which the Lord hath commanded, 'Gather of it every man according to his eating, an omer for every man, according to the number of your persons; take ye every man for them which are in his tents.'" And the children of Israel did so, and gathered, some more, some less. And when they did mete it with an omer,[29] he that gathered much had nothing over, and he that gathered little had no lack; they gathered every man according to his eating. And Moses said, "Let no man leave of it till the morning." Notwithstanding they hearkened not unto Moses; but some of them left of it until the morning, and it bred worms, and stank: and Moses was wroth with them. And they gathered it every morning, every man according to his eating: and when the sun waxed hot, it melted.

And it came to pass that on the sixth day they gathered twice as much bread, two omers for one man: and all the rulers of the congregation came and told Moses. And he said unto them, "This is that which the Lord hath said, 'To-morrow is the rest of the holy sabbath unto the Lord: bake that which ye will bake to-day, and seethe[30] that ye will seethe; and that which remaineth over lay up for you to be kept until the morning.'" And they laid it up till the morning, as Moses bade: and it did not stink, neither was there any worm therein. And Moses said, "Eat that to-day; for to-day is a sabbath unto the Lord: to-day ye shall not find it in the field. Six days ye shall gather it; but on the seventh day, which is the sabbath, in it there shall be none." And it came to pass that there went out some of the people on the seventh day for to gather, and they found none. . . . And the house of Israel called the name thereof Manna: and it was like coriander seed, white; and the taste of it was like wafers made with honey. And Moses said, "This is the thing which the Lord commandeth, 'Fill an omer of it to be

[28]"Manna" means "What is it?"
[29]"Mete" means "measure." An "omer" is an ancient Hebrew unit of dry capacity equal to about a tenth of a bushel.
[30]Boil or stew.

kept for your generations; that they may see the bread wherewith I have fed you in the wilderness, when I brought you forth from the land of Egypt.'" And Moses said unto Aaron, "Take a pot, and put an omer full of manna therein, and lay it up before the Lord, to be kept for your generations."

As the Lord commanded Moses, so Aaron laid it up before the Testimony,[31] to be kept. And the children of Israel did eat manna forty years, until they came to a land inhabited; they did eat manna until they came unto the borders of the land of Canaan. . . .

And all the congregation of the children of Israel journeyed from the wilderness of Sin, after their journeys, according to the commandment of the Lord, and pitched in Rephidim: and there was no water for the people to drink. Wherefore the people did chide with Moses, and said, "Give us water that we may drink." And Moses said unto them, "Why chide ye with me? wherefore do ye tempt the Lord?" And the people thirsted there for water; and the people murmured against Moses, and said, "Wherefore is this that thou hast brought us up out of Egypt, to kill us and our children and our cattle with thirst?" And Moses cried unto the Lord, saying, "What shall I do unto this people? they be almost ready to stone me." And the Lord said unto Moses, "Go on before the people, and take with thee of the elders of Israel; and thy rod, wherewith thou smotest the river, take in thine hand, and go. Behold, I will stand before thee there upon the rock in Horeb; and thou shalt smite the rock, and there shall come water out of it, that the people may drink." And Moses did so in the sight of the elders of Israel. And he called the name of the place Massah, and Meribah, because of the chiding of the children of Israel, and because they tempted the Lord, saying, "Is the Lord among us, or not?"[32]

Then came Amalek, and fought with Israel in Rephidim. And Moses said unto Joshua,[33] "Choose us out men, and go out, fight with Amalek: tomorrow I will stand on the top of the hill with the rod of God in mine hand." So Joshua did as Moses had said to him, and fought with Amalek: and Moses, Aaron, and Hur went up to the top of the hill. And it came to pass, when Moses held up his hand, that Israel prevailed: and when he let down his hand, Amalek prevailed. But Moses' hands were heavy; and they took a stone, and put it under him, and he sat thereon; and Aaron and Hur stayed up his hands, the one on the one side, and the other on the other side; and his hands were steady until the going down of the sun. And Joshua discomfited Amalek and his people with the edge of the sword. . . .

Jethro, the priest of Midian, Moses' father-in-law, heard of all that God had done for Moses, and for Israel his people, and that the Lord had brought Israel out of Egypt. Then Jethro, Moses' father-in-law, took Zipporah, Moses' wife, after he had sent her back, and her two sons; of which the name of the one was Gershom: for he said, "I have been an alien

---

[31] The tablets inscribed with the Mosaic law. The passage anticipates the giving of the Law later in Exodus.

[32] "Massah" means "proof" and "Meribah" means "contention."

[33] This is the first reference to Joshua, the young warrior who was to lead the Israelite armies into Canaan after the death of Moses.

in a strange land," and the name of the other was Eliezer: "For the God of my father," said he, "was mine help, and delivered me from the sword of Pharaoh."[34]

And Jethro, Moses' father-in-law, came with his sons and his wife unto Moses into the wilderness, where he encamped at the mount of God: and he said unto Moses, "I thy father-in-law Jethro am come unto thee, and thy wife, and her two sons with her." And Moses went out to meet his father-in-law, and did obeisance, and kissed him; and they asked each other of their welfare; and they came into the tent. And Moses told his father-in-law all that the Lord had done unto Pharaoh and to the Egyptians for Israel's sake, and all the travail that had come upon them by the way, and how the Lord delivered them. And Jethro rejoiced for all the goodness which the Lord had done to Israel, whom he had delivered out of the hand of the Egyptians. And Jethro said, "Blessed be the Lord, who hath delivered you out of the hand of the Egyptians, and out of the hand of Pharaoh, who hath delivered the people from under the hand of the Egyptians. Now I know that the Lord is greater than all gods: for in the thing wherein they dealt proudly he was above them."

And Jethro, Moses' father-in-law, took a burnt offering and sacrifices for God: and Aaron came, and all the elders of Israel, to eat bread with Moses' father-in-law before God. And it came to pass on the morrow that Moses sat to judge the people: and the people stood by Moses from the morning unto the evening. And when Moses' father-in-law saw all that he did to the people, he said, "What is this thing that thou doest to the people? why sittest thou thyself alone, and all the people stand by thee from morning unto even?" And Moses said unto his father-in-law, "Because the people come unto me to enquire of God. When they have a matter, they come unto me; and I judge between one and another, and I do make them know the statutes of God, and his laws." And Moses' father-in-law said unto him, "The thing that thou doest is not good. Thou wilt surely wear away, both thou, and this people that is with thee: for this thing is too heavy for thee; thou art not able to perform it thyself alone. Hearken now unto my voice, I will give thee counsel, and God shall be with thee: Be thou for the people to God-ward, that thou mayest bring the causes unto God: and thou shalt teach them ordinances and laws, and shalt show them the way wherein they must walk, and the work that they must do. Moreover thou shalt provide out of all the people able men, such as fear God, men of truth, hating covetousness; and place such over them, to be rulers of thousands, and rulers of hundreds, rulers of fifties, and rulers of tens: and let them judge the people at all seasons: and it shall be that every great matter they shall bring unto thee, but every small matter they shall judge: so shall it be easier for thyself, and they shall bear the burden with thee. If thou shalt do this thing, and God command thee so, then thou shalt be able to endure, and all this people shall also go to their place in peace."

So Moses hearkened to the voice of his father-in-law, and did all that he had said. And Moses chose able men out of all Israel, and made them heads over the people, rulers of thousands, rulers of hundreds, rulers of fifties,

---

[34]"Eliezer" means "God is my help."

and rulers of tens. And they judged the people at all seasons: the hard causes they brought unto Moses, but every small matter they judged themselves. And Moses let his father-in-law depart; and he went his way into his own land.

THE GIVING OF THE LAW

(Exodus 19:1–31:18)

In the third month, when the children of Israel were gone forth out of the land of Egypt, the same day came they into the wilderness of Sinai. For they were departed from Rephidim, and were come to the desert of Sinai, and had pitched in the wilderness; and there Israel camped before the mount. And Moses went up unto God, and the Lord called unto him out of the mountain, saying, "Thus shalt thou say to the house of Jacob, and tell the children of Israel: 'Ye have seen what I did unto the Egyptians, and how I bore you on eagles' wings, and brought you unto myself. Now therefore, if ye will obey my voice indeed, and keep my covenant, then ye shall be a peculiar treasure unto me above all people: for all the earth is mine.'"[35]. . . And the Lord said unto Moses, "Go unto the people, and sanctify them to-day and to-morrow, and let them wash their clothes, and be ready against the third day: for the third day the Lord will come down in the sight of all the people upon Mount Sinai. And thou shalt set bounds unto the people round about, saying, 'Take heed to yourselves, that ye go not up into the mount, or touch the border of it: whosoever toucheth the mount shall be surely put to death.' There shall not a hand touch it, but he shall surely be stoned, or shot through; whether it be beast or man, it shall not live: when the trumpet soundeth long, they shall come up to the mount."

And Moses went down from the mount unto the people, and sanctified the people; and they washed their clothes. And he said unto the people, "Be ready against the third day: come not at your wives." And it came to pass on the third day in the morning, that there were thunders and lightnings, and a thick cloud upon the mount, and the voice of the trumpet exceeding loud; so that all the people that was in the camp trembled. And Moses brought forth the people out of the camp to meet with God; and they stood at the nether part of the mount. And Mount Sinai was altogether on a smoke, because the Lord descended upon it in fire; and the smoke thereof ascended as the smoke of a furnace, and the whole mount quaked greatly. And when the voice of the trumpet sounded long, and waxed louder and louder, Moses spoke, and God answered him by a voice. And the Lord came down upon Mount Sinai, on the top of the mount: and the Lord called Moses up to the top of the mount; and Moses went up. . . . .

And God spoke all these words, saying, "I am the Lord thy God, which have brought thee out of the land of Egypt, out of the house of bondage.

---

[35] The first part of this sentence identifies the Hebrews as God's Chosen People or "peculiar treasure," while the last part emphasizes that their God is the God of the entire universe. The sufferings the Hebrews later undergo suggest that they are not "chosen" in the sense of being uniquely favored but rather in the sense of being the medium for God's ethical and spiritual teachings to mankind.

"Thou shalt have no other gods before me.

"Thou shalt not make unto thee any graven image, or any likeness of any thing that is in heaven above, or that is in the earth beneath, or that is in the water under the earth: thou shalt not bow down thyself to them, nor serve them: for I the Lord thy God am a jealous God, visiting the iniquity of the fathers upon the children unto the third and fourth generation of them that hate me; and showing mercy unto thousands of them that love me, and keep my commandments.[36]

"Thou shalt not take the name of the Lord thy God in vain; for the Lord will not hold him guiltless that taketh his name in vain.

"Remember the sabbath day, to keep it holy. Six days shalt thou labor, and do all thy work: but the seventh day is the sabbath of the Lord thy God: in it thou shalt not do any work, thou, nor thy son, nor thy daughter, thy manservant, nor thy maidservant, nor thy cattle, nor thy stranger that is within thy gates: for in six days the Lord made heaven and earth, the sea, and all that in them is, and rested the seventh day: wherefore the Lord blessed the sabbath day, and hallowed it.

"Honor thy father and thy mother: that thy days may be long upon the land which the Lord thy God giveth thee.

"Thou shalt not kill.

"Thou shalt not commit adultery.

"Thou shalt not steal.

"Thou shalt not bear false witness against thy neighbor.

"Thou shalt not covet thy neighbor's house, thou shalt not covet thy neighbor's wife, nor his manservant, nor his maidservant, nor his ox, nor his ass, nor any thing that is thy neighbor's. . . .[37]

And he gave unto Moses, when he had made an end of communing with him upon Mount Sinai, two tables of testimony, tables of stone, written with the finger of God.

THE GOLDEN CALF

(Exodus 32:1–34:32)
And when the people saw that Moses delayed to come down out of the mount, the people gathered themselves together unto Aaron, and said unto him, "Up, make us gods, which shall go before us; for as for this Moses, the man that brought us up out of the land of Egypt, we wot not what is become of him." And Aaron said unto them, "Break off the golden earrings, which are in the ears of your wives, of your sons, and of your daughters, and bring them unto me." And all the people broke off the golden earrings which were in their ears, and brought them unto Aaron.

---

[36] This ban upon "graven images" to be set up for worship is one of the distinctive features of the Hebrew religion. It should be noted that the ban is only against images to be worshiped, not against images of any kind, as in Islam.

[37] A long section is omitted here (Exodus 20:18–31:17), which contains detailed provisions of the Covenant Code, much of it of little contemporary interest. The most important omission is the instructions for the building of the Tabernacle and for public worship.

And he received them at their hand, and fashioned it with a graving tool, after he had made it a molten calf:[38] and they said, "These be thy gods, O Israel, which brought thee up out of the land of Egypt." And when Aaron saw it, he built an altar before it; and Aaron made proclamation, and said, "To-morrow is a feast to the Lord." And they rose up early on the morrow, and offered burnt offerings, and brought peace offerings; and the people sat down to eat and to drink, and rose up to play.

And the Lord said unto Moses, "Go, get thee down; for thy people, which thou broughtest out of the land of Egypt, have corrupted themselves. They have turned aside quickly out of the way which I commanded them: they have made them a molten calf, and have worshipped it, and have sacrificed thereunto, and said, 'These be thy gods, O Israel, which have brought thee up out of the land of Egypt.'" And the Lord said unto Moses, "I have seen this people, and, behold, it is a stiffnecked people. Now therefore let me alone, that my wrath may wax hot against them, and that I may consume them: and I will make of thee a great nation." And Moses besought the Lord his God, and said, "Lord, why doth thy wrath wax hot against thy people, which thou hast brought forth out of the land of Egypt with great power, and with a mighty hand? Wherefore should the Egyptians speak, and say, 'For mischief did he bring them out, to slay them in the mountains, and to consume them from the face of the earth'? Turn from thy fierce wrath, and repent of this evil against thy people. Remember Abraham, Isaac, and Israel, thy servants, to whom thou swforest by thine own self, and saidst unto them, 'I will multiply your seed as the stars of heaven, and all this land that I have spoken of will I give unto your seed, and they shall inherit it for ever.'"

And the Lord repented of the evil which he thought to do unto his people. And Moses turned, and went down from the mount, and the two tables of the testimony were in his hand: the tables were written on both their sides; on the one side and on the other were they written. And the tables were the work of God, and the writing was the writing of God, graven upon the tables. And when Joshua heard the noise of the people as they shouted, he said unto Moses, "There is a noise of war in the camp." And he said, "It is not the voice of them that shout for mastery, neither is it the voice of them that cry for being overcome: but the noise of them that sing do I hear." And it came to pass, as soon as he came nigh unto the camp, that he saw the calf, and the dancing: and Moses' anger waxed hot, and he cast the tables out of his hands, and broke them beneath the mount. And he took the calf which they had made, and burnt it in the fire, and ground it to powder, and strewed it upon the water, and made the children of Israel drink of it.[39]

And Moses said unto Aaron, "What did this people unto thee, that thou hast brought so great a sin upon them?" And Aaron said, "Let not the anger of my lord wax hot: thou knowest the people, that they are set on

---

[38] The fashioning of the "molten calf," which directly violates the second commandment, probably refers to a small bull. The ritual echoes practices of the fertility religions of Egypt and of the rest of the ancient Near East.

[39] The drinking of water mixed with pulverized gold from the golden calf constitutes a "trial by ordeal." Those who suffered ill effects were regarded as proven guilty.

mischief. For they said unto me, 'Make us gods, which shall go before us: for as for this Moses, the man that brought us up out of the land of Egypt, we wot not what is become of him.' And I said unto them, 'Whosoever hath any gold, let them break it off.' So they gave it me: then I cast it into the fire, and there came out this calf."

And when Moses saw that the people were naked (for Aaron had made them naked unto their shame among their enemies), then Moses stood in the gate of the camp, and said, "Who is on the Lord's side? let him come unto me." And all the sons of Levi gathered themselves together unto him. And he said unto them, "Thus saith the Lord God of Israel, 'Put every man his sword by his side, and go in and out from gate to gate throughout the camp, and slay every man his brother, and every man his companion, and every man his neighbor.'" And the children of Levi did according to the word of Moses: and there fell of the people that day about three thousand men. . . .[40]

And it came to pass on the morrow that Moses said unto the people, "Ye have sinned a great sin: and now I will go up unto the Lord; peradventure I shall make an atonement for your sin." And Moses returned unto the Lord, and said, "Oh, this people have sinned a great sin, and have made them gods of gold. Yet now, if thou wilt forgive their sin—; and if not, blot me, I pray thee, out of thy book which thou hast written." And the Lord said unto Moses, "Whosoever hath sinned against me, him will I blot out of my book. Therefore now go, lead the people unto the place of which I have spoken unto thee: behold, mine Angel shall go before thee: nevertheless in the day when I visit I will visit their sin upon them."

And the Lord plagued the people, because they made the calf, which Aaron made.

And the Lord said unto Moses, "Depart, and go up hence, thou and the people which thou hast brought up out of the land of Egypt, unto the land which I swore unto Abraham, to Isaac, and to Jacob, saying, 'Unto thy seed will I give it': . . . unto a land flowing with milk and honey: for I will not go up in the midst of thee; for thou art a stiffnecked people: lest I consume thee in the way."

And when the people heard these evil tidings, they mourned: and no man did put on him his ornaments. . . . And the children of Israel stripped themselves of their ornaments by the mount Horeb. And Moses took the tabernacle, and pitched it without the camp, afar off from the camp, and called it the tabernacle of the congregation. And it came to pass that every one which sought the Lord went out unto the tabernacle of the congregation, which was without the camp. And it came to pass, when Moses went out unto the tabernacle, that all the people rose up, and stood every man at his tent door, and looked after Moses, until he was gone into the tabernacle. And it came to pass, as Moses entered into the tabernacle, the cloudy pillar descended, and stood at the door of the tabernacle, and the Lord

---

[40] This shocking story seems to suggest that the priests of Levi were consecrated to the priesthood by demonstrating that they could place loyalty to the Lord above ties of friendship or kinship.

talked with Moses. And all the people saw the cloudy pillar stand at the tabernacle door: and all the people rose up and worshipped, every man in his tent door. And the Lord spoke unto Moses face to face, as a man speaketh unto his friend. . . .

And Moses said unto the Lord, "See, thou sayest unto me, 'Bring up this people': and thou hast not let me know whom thou wilt send with me. Yet thou hast said, 'I know thee by name, and thou hast also found grace in my sight.' Now therefore, I pray thee, if I have found grace in thy sight, show me now thy way, that I may know thee, that I may find grace in thy sight: and consider that this nation is thy people." And he said, "My presence shall go with thee, and I will give thee rest." And he said unto him, "If thy presence go not with me, carry us not up hence. For wherein shall it be known here that I and thy people have found grace in thy sight? is it not in that thou goest with us? so shall we be separated, I and thy people, from all the people that are upon the face of the earth."

And the Lord said unto Moses, "I will do this thing also that thou hast spoken: for thou hast found grace in my sight, and I know thee by name." And he said, "I beseech thee, show me thy glory." And he said, "I will make all my goodness pass before thee, and I will proclaim the name of the Lord before thee; and will be gracious to whom I will be gracious, and will show mercy on whom I will show mercy." And he said, "Thou canst not see my face: for there shall no man see me, and live." And the Lord said, "Behold, there is a place by me, and thou shalt stand upon a rock: and it shall come to pass, while my glory passeth by, that I will put thee in a cleft of the rock, and will cover thee with my hand while I pass by: and I will take away mine hand, and thou shalt see my back parts: but my face shall not be seen."

And the Lord said unto Moses, "Hew thee two tables of stone like unto the first: and I will write upon these tables the words that were in the first tables, which thou brokest. And be ready in the morning, and come up in the morning unto Mount Sinai, and present thyself there to me in the top of the mount. And no man shall come up with thee, neither let any man be seen throughout all the mount; neither let the flocks nor herds feed before that mount." . . . . And he hewed two tables of stone like unto the first; and Moses rose up early in the morning, and went up unto Mount Sinai, as the Lord had commanded him, and took in his hand the two tables of stone. And it came to pass, when Moses came down from Mount Sinai with the two tables of testimony in Moses' hand, when he came down from the mount, that Moses wist not that the skin of his face shone while he talked with him. And when Aaron and all the children of Israel saw Moses, behold, the skin of his face shone; and they were afraid to come nigh him. And Moses called unto them; and Aaron and all the rulers of the congregation returned unto him: and Moses talked with them. And afterward all the children of Israel came nigh: and he gave them in commandment all that the Lord had spoken with him in Mount Sinai. . . .[41]

---

[41] The last six chapters of Exodus, omitted here, contain a further set of cultic laws and describe the building of the Tabernacle.

THE HOLINESS CODE

(Leviticus 19:1–19:36)

And the Lord spoke unto Moses, saying, "Speak unto all the congregation of the children of Israel, and say unto them, 'Ye shall be holy: for I the Lord your God am holy.[42]

"'Ye shall fear every man his mother, and his father, and keep my sabbaths: I am the Lord your God.

"'Turn ye not unto idols, nor make to yourselves molten gods: I am the Lord your God.

"'And if ye offer a sacrifice of peace offerings unto the Lord, ye shall offer it at your own will. It shall be eaten the same day ye offer it, and on the morrow: and if ought remain until the third day, it shall be burnt in the fire. And if it be eaten at all on the third day, it is abominable; it shall not be accepted. Therefore every one that eateth it shall bear his iniquity, because he hath profaned the hallowed thing of the Lord: and that soul shall be cut off from among his people.

"'And when ye reap the harvest of your land, thou shalt not wholly reap the corners of thy field, neither shalt thou gather the gleanings of thy harvest. And thou shalt not glean thy vineyard, neither shalt thou gather every grape of thy vineyard; thou shalt leave them for the poor and stranger: I am the Lord your God.

"'Ye shall not steal, neither deal falsely, neither lie one to another.

"'And ye shall not swear by my name falsely, neither shalt thou profane the name of thy God: I am the Lord.

"'Thou shalt not defraud thy neighbor, neither rob him: the wages of him that is hired shall not abide with thee all night until the morning.

"'Thou shalt not curse the deaf, nor put a stumblingblock before the blind, but shalt fear thy God: I am the Lord.

"'Ye shall do no unrighteousness in judgment: thou shalt not respect the person of the poor, nor honor the person of the mighty: but in righteousness shalt thou judge thy neighbor.

"'Thou shalt not go up and down as a talebearer among thy people: neither shalt thou stand against the blood of thy neighbor: I am the Lord.

"'Thou shalt not hate thy brother in thine heart: thou shalt in any wise rebuke thy neighbor, and not suffer sin upon him. Thou shalt not avenge, nor bear any grudge against the children of thy people, but thou shalt love thy neighbor as thyself: I am the Lord.

"'Ye shall keep my statutes. Thou shalt not let thy cattle gender with a diverse kind: thou shalt not sow thy field with mingled seed: neither shall a garment mingled of linen and woollen come upon thee.[43]

---

[42] The Old Testament contains four major "codes" or bodies of laws: the Covenant Code in Exodus, the Deuteronomic Code in Deuteronomy, the Holiness Code in Leviticus, and the Priestly Code, which is scattered through Exodus, Leviticus, and Numbers. Leviticus is largely devoted to Hebrew laws, including laws of the sacrifice and consecration to the priesthood and laws of the "clean" and the "unclean," regulating sex and childbirth, diet, disease, and care of the dead. The passage given here constitutes the Holiness Code, devoted more to ethical than to practical matters.

[43] This odd law against the "mixing of kinds" is repeated in Deuteronomy; it apparently is directed against erasing distinctions which God has ordained.

"'And whosoever lieth carnally with a woman, that is a bondmaid, betrothed to a husband, and not at all redeemed, nor freedom given her; she shall be scourged; they shall not be put to death, because she was not free. And he shall bring his trespass offering unto the Lord, unto the door of the tabernacle of the congregation, even a ram for a trespass offering. And the priest shall make an atonement for him with the ram of the trespass offering before the Lord for his sin which he hath done: and the sin which he hath done shall be forgiven him.

"'And when ye shall come into the land, and shall have planted all manner of trees for food, then ye shall count the fruit thereof as uncircumcised: three years shall it be as uncircumcised unto you: it shall not be eaten of. But in the fourth year all the fruit thereof shall be holy to praise the Lord withal. And in the fifth year shall ye eat of the fruit thereof, that it may yield unto you the increase thereof: I am the Lord your God.

"'Ye shall not eat any thing with the blood: neither shall ye use enchantment, nor observe times.[44]

"'Ye shall not round the corners of your heads, neither shalt thou mar the corners of thy beard.

"'Ye shall not make any cuttings in your flesh for the dead, nor print any marks upon you: I am the Lord.

"'Do not prostitute thy daughter, to cause her to be a whore; lest the land fall to whoredom, and the land become full of wickedness.

"'Ye shall keep my sabbaths, and reverence my sanctuary: I am the Lord.

"'Regard not them that have familiar spirits, neither seek after wizards, to be defiled by them: I am the Lord your God.

"'Thou shalt rise up before the hoary head, and honor the face of the old man, and fear thy God: I am the Lord.

"'And if a stranger sojourn with thee in your land, ye shall not vex him. But the stranger that dwelleth with you shall be unto you as one born among you, and thou shalt love him as thyself; for ye were strangers in the land of Egypt: I am the Lord your God.

"'Ye shall do no unrighteousness in judgment, in meteyard, in weight, or in measure. Just balances, just weights, a just ephah, and a just hin, shall ye have:[45] I am the Lord your God, which brought you out of the land of Egypt.'" . . .

THE WANDERINGS IN THE WILDERNESS

(Numbers 9:15–21:35)
And on the day that the tabernacle was reared up the cloud covered the tabernacle, namely, the tent of the testimony: and at even there was upon the tabernacle as it were the appearance of fire, until the morning. So it was always: the cloud covered it by day, and the appearance of fire by night.

---

[44] This and the five following laws are directed against the practices of other religions: witchcraft, heathen mourning customs, sacred prostitution, and necromancy, or the conjuring of spirits to predict the future.

[45] "Meteyard": balances of scales. "Ephah": unit of dry measure, a little over a bushel. "Hin": unit of liquid measure, about one and a half gallons.

And when the cloud was taken up from the tabernacle, then after that the children of Israel journeyed: and in the place where the cloud abode, there the children of Israel pitched their tents. At the commandment of the Lord the children of Israel journeyed, and at the commandment of the Lord they pitched: as long as the cloud abode upon the tabernacle they rested in their tents. And when the cloud tarried long upon the tabernacle many days, then the children of Israel kept the charge of the Lord, and journeyed not. And so it was, when the cloud was a few days upon the tabernacle; according to the commandment of the Lord they abode in their tents, and according to the commandment of the Lord they journeyed. And so it was, when the cloud abode from even unto the morning, and that the cloud was taken up in the morning, then they journeyed: whether it was by day or by night that the cloud was taken up, they journeyed. Or whether it were two days, or a month, or a year, that the cloud tarried upon the tabernacle, remaining thereon, the children of Israel abode in their tents, and journeyed not: but when it was taken up, they journeyed. At the commandment of the Lord they rested in the tents, and at the commandment of the Lord they journeyed: they kept the charge of the Lord, at the commandment of the Lord by the hand of Moses. . . .

And they departed from the mount of the Lord three days' journey: and the ark of the covenant[46] of the Lord went before them in the three days' journey, to search out a resting place for them. And the cloud of the Lord was upon them by day, when they went out of the camp. And it came to pass, when the ark set forward, that Moses said, "Rise up, Lord, And let thine enemies be scattered; And let them that hate thee flee before thee." And when it rested, he said, "Return, O Lord, Unto the many thousands of Israel." . . .

And the mixt multitude that was among them fell a-lusting: and the children of Israel also wept again, and said, "Who shall give us flesh to eat? We remember the fish, which we did eat in Egypt freely; the cucumbers, and the melons, and the leeks, and the onions, and the garlic. But now our soul is dried away: there is nothing at all, beside this manna, before our eyes."

And the manna was as coriander seed, and the color thereof as the color of bdellium. And the people went about, and gathered it, and ground it in mills, or beat it in a mortar, and baked it in pans, and made cakes of it: and the taste of it was as the taste of fresh oil. And when the dew fell upon the camp in the night, the manna fell upon it.

Then Moses heard the people weep throughout their families, every man in the door of his tent: and the anger of the Lord was kindled greatly; Moses also was displeased. And Moses said unto the Lord, "Wherefore hast thou afflicted thy servant? and wherefore have I not found favor in thy sight, that thou layest the burden of all this people upon me? Have I conceived all this people? have I begotten them, that thou shouldest say unto me, 'Carry them in thy bosom, as a nursing father beareth the sucking

---

[46] The Ark of the Covenant, built according to the instructions given Moses in Exodus, was the physical symbol of the presence of God among the Hebrews. Its contents are unclear; it may have held the stone tablets of the Law or perhaps the brazen serpent made by Moses. The "arks" in modern synagogues hold the scrolls of the Torah.

child, unto the land which thou sworest unto their fathers'? Whence should I have flesh[47] to give unto all this people? for they weep unto me, saying, 'Give us flesh, that we may eat.' I am not able to bear all this people alone, because it is too heavy for me. And if thou deal thus with me, kill me, I pray thee, out of hand, if I have found favor in thy sight; and let me not see my wretchedness."

And the Lord said unto Moses, "Gather unto me seventy men of the elders of Israel, whom thou knowest to be the elders of the people, and officers over them; and bring them unto the tabernacle of the congregation, that they may stand there with thee. And I will come down and talk with thee there: and I will take of the spirit which is upon thee, and will put it upon them; and they shall bear the burden of the people with thee, that thou bear it not thyself alone. And say thou unto the people, 'Sanctify yourselves against to-morrow, and ye shall eat flesh: for ye have wept in the ears of the Lord, saying, "Who shall give us flesh to eat? for it was well with us in Egypt": therefore the Lord will give you flesh, and ye shall eat. Ye shall not eat one day, nor two days, nor five days, neither ten days, nor twenty days; but even a whole month, until it come out at your nostrils, and it be loathsome unto you: because that ye have despised the Lord which is among you, and have wept before him, saying, "Why came we forth out of Egypt?"'" And Moses said, "The people, among whom I am, are six hundred thousand footmen; and thou hast said, 'I will give them flesh, that they may eat a whole month.' Shall the flocks and the herds be slain for them, to suffice them? or shall all the fish of the sea be gathered together for them, to suffice them?" And the Lord said unto Moses, "Is the Lord's hand waxed short? thou shalt see now whether my word shall come to pass unto thee or not."

And Moses went out, and told the people the words of the Lord, and gathered the seventy men of the elders of the people, and set them round about the tabernacle. And the Lord came down in a cloud, and spoke unto him, and took of the spirit that was upon him, and gave it unto the seventy elders: and it came to pass that, when the spirit rested upon them, they prophesied, and did not cease.

But there remained two of the men in the camp, the name of the one was Eldad, and the name of the other Medad: and the spirit rested upon them; and they were of them that were written, but went not out unto the tabernacle: and they prophesied in the camp. And there ran a young man, and told Moses, and said, "Eldad and Medad do prophesy in the camp." And Joshua the son of Nun, the servant of Moses, one of his young men, answered and said, "My lord Moses, forbid them!" And Moses said unto him, "Enviest thou for my sake? would God that all the Lord's people were prophets, and that the Lord would put his spirit upon them!"

And Moses got him into the camp, he and the elders of Israel. And there went forth a wind from the Lord, and brought quails from the sea, and let them fall by the camp, as it were a day's journey on this side, and as it were a day's journey on the other side, round about the camp, and as it were two cubits high upon the face of the earth. And the people stood up all that day, and all that night, and all the next day, and they gathered the

---

[47] Meat.

quails: he that gathered least gathered ten homers:[48] and they spread them all abroad for themselves round about the camp. And while the flesh was yet between their teeth, ere it was chewed, the wrath of the Lord was kindled against the people, and the Lord smote the people with a very great plague. And he called the name of that place Kibroth-hattaavah: because there they buried the people that lusted.[49] And the people journeyed from Kibroth-hattaavah unto Hazeroth; and abode at Hazeroth.

And Miriam and Aaron spoke against Moses because of the Ethiopian woman whom he had married (for he had married an Ethiopian woman). And they said, "Hath the Lord indeed spoken only by Moses? hath he not spoken also by us?" And the Lord heard it. (Now the man Moses was very meek,[50] above all the men which were upon the face of the earth.) And the Lord spoke suddenly unto Moses, and unto Aaron, and unto Miriam, "Come out ye three unto the tabernacle of the congregation." And they three came out. And the Lord came down in the pillar of the cloud, and stood in the door of the tabernacle, and called Aaron and Miriam: and they both came forth. And he said, "Hear now my words: if there be a prophet among you, I the Lord will make myself known unto him in a vision, and will speak unto him in a dream. My servant Moses is not so, who is faithful in all mine house. With him will I speak mouth to mouth, even apparently, and not in dark speeches; and the similitude of the Lord shall he behold: wherefore then were ye not afraid to speak against my servant Moses?"

And the anger of the Lord was kindled against them; and he departed. And the cloud departed from off the tabernacle; and, behold, Miriam became leprous, white as snow: and Aaron looked upon Miriam, and, behold, she was leprous. And Aaron said unto Moses, "Alas, my lord, I beseech thee, lay not the sin upon us, wherein we have done foolishly, and wherein we have sinned. Let her not be as one dead, of whom the flesh is half consumed when he cometh out of his mother's womb." And Moses cried unto the Lord, saying, "Heal her now, O God, I beseech thee." And the Lord said unto Moses, "If her father had but spit in her face, should she not be ashamed seven days?[51] let her be shut out from the camp seven days, and after that let her be received in again." And Miriam was shut out from the camp seven days: and the people journeyed not till Miriam was brought in again. And afterward the people removed from Hazeroth, and pitched in the wilderness of Paran.

And the Lord spoke unto Moses, saying, "Send thou men, that they may search the land of Canaan, which I give unto the children of Israel: of every tribe of their fathers shall ye send a man, every one a ruler among them." And Moses by the commandment of the Lord sent them from the wilderness of Paran: all those men were heads of the children of Israel. . . . And Moses sent them to spy out the land of Canaan, and said unto them, "Get you up this way southward, and go out into the mountain: and see the

[48] A unit of capacity equal to about ten and a half bushels or one hundred gallons.
[49] "Kibroth-hattaavah" means "graves of craving."
[50] In this context, "modest" or "devout" rather than "weak" or "retiring."
[51] To spit in someone's face was a ritual curse; the Lord says that Miriam's punishment should not be less than the seven days' isolation such a defilement would involve.

land, what it is; and the people that dwelleth therein, whether they be strong or weak, few or many; and what the land is that they dwell in, whether it be good or bad; and what cities they be that they dwell in, whether in tents, or in strong holds; and what the land is, whether it be fat or lean, whether there be wood therein, or not. And be ye of good courage, and bring of the fruit of the land."

Now the time was the time of the first ripe grapes. So they went up, and searched the land from the wilderness of Zin unto Rehob, as men come to Hamath. And they ascended by the south, and came unto Hebron; where Ahiman, Sheshai, and Talmai, the children of Anak, were. (Now Hebron was built seven years before Zoan in Egypt.) And they came unto the brook of Eshcol, and cut down from thence a branch with one cluster of grapes, and they bore it between two upon a staff; and they brought of the pomegranates, and of the figs. The place was called the brook Eshcol, because of the cluster of grapes which the children of Israel cut down from thence.[52]

And they returned from searching of the land after forty days. And they went and came to Moses, and to Aaron, and to all the congregation of the children of Israel, unto the wilderness of Paran, to Kadesh; and brought back word unto them, and unto all the congregation, and showed them the fruit of the land. And they told him, and said, "We came unto the land whither thou sentest us, and surely it floweth with milk and honey; and this is the fruit of it. Nevertheless the people be strong that dwell in the land, and the cities are walled, and very great: and moreover we saw the children of Anak there. The Amalekites dwell in the land of the south: and the Hittites, and the Jebusites, and the Amorites, dwell in the mountains: and the Canaanites dwell by the sea, and by the coast of Jordan."

And Caleb stilled the people before Moses, and said, "Let us go up at once, and possess it; for we are well able to overcome it." But the men that went up with him said, "We be not able to go up against the people; for they are stronger than we." And they brought up an evil report of the land which they had searched unto the children of Israel, saying, "The land, through which we have gone to search it, is a land that eateth up the inhabitants thereof; and all the people that we saw in it are men of a great stature. And there we saw the giants, the sons of Anak, which come of the giants: and we were in our own sight as grasshoppers, and so we were in their sight."

And all the congregation lifted up their voice, and cried; and the people wept that night. And all the children of Israel murmured against Moses and against Aaron: and the whole congregation said unto them, "Would God that we had died in the land of Egypt! or would God we had died in this wilderness! And wherefore hath the Lord brought us unto this land, to fall by the sword, that our wives and our children should be a prey? were it not better for us to return into Egypt?"

And they said one to another, "Let us make a captain, and let us return into Egypt." Then Moses and Aaron fell on their faces before all the assembly of the congregation of the children of Israel. And Joshua the son of Nun, and Caleb the son of Jephunneh, which were of them that searched the land, rent their clothes: and they spoke unto all the company of the

---

[52]"Eshcol" means "cluster."

children of Israel, saying, "The land, which we passed through to search it, is an exceeding good land. If the Lord delight in us, then he will bring us into this land, and give it us; a land which floweth with milk and honey. Only rebel not ye against the Lord, neither fear ye the people of the land; for they are bread for us: their defense is departed from them, and the Lord is with us: fear them not." But all the congregation bade stone them with stones.

And the glory of the Lord appeared in the tabernacle of the congregation before all the children of Israel. And the Lord said unto Moses, "How long will this people provoke me? and how long will it be ere they believe me, for all the signs which I have showed among them? I will smite them with the pestilence, and disinherit them, and will make of thee a greater nation and mightier than they."

And Moses said unto the Lord, "Then the Egyptians shall hear it (for thou broughtest up this people in thy might from among them); and they will tell it to the inhabitants of this land: for they have heard that thou Lord art among this people, that thou Lord art seen face to face, and that thy cloud standeth over them, and that thou goest before them, by day time in a pillar of a cloud, and in a pillar of fire by night. Now if thou shalt kill all this people as one man, then the nations which have heard the fame of thee will speak, saying, 'Because the Lord was not able to bring this people into the land which he sware unto them, therefore he hath slain them in the wilderness.' And now, I beseech thee, let the power of my Lord be great, according as thou hast spoken, saying, 'The Lord is longsuffering, and of great mercy, forgiving iniquity and transgression, and by no means clearing the guilty, visiting the iniquity of the fathers upon the children unto the third and fourth generation.' Pardon, I beseech thee, the iniquity of this people according unto the greatness of thy mercy; and as thou hast forgiven this people, from Egypt even until now."

And the Lord said, "I have pardoned according to thy word: but as truly as I live, all the earth shall be filled with the glory of the Lord. Because all those men which have seen my glory, and my miracles, which I did in Egypt and in the wilderness, and have tempted me now these ten times, and have not hearkened to my voice; surely they shall not see the land which I sware unto their fathers, neither shall any of them that provoked me see it. . . . How long shall I bear with this evil congregation, which murmur against me? I have heard the murmurings of the children of Israel, which they murmur against me. Say unto them, 'As truly as I live,' saith the Lord, 'as ye have spoken in mine ears, so will I do to you: your carcases shall fall in this wilderness; and all that were numbered of you, according to your whole number, from twenty years old and upward, which have murmured against me, doubtless ye shall not come into the land, concerning which I sware to make you dwell therein, save Caleb the son of Jephunneh, and Joshua the son of Nun. But your little ones, which ye said should be a prey, them will I bring in, and they shall know the land which ye have despised. But as for you, your carcases, they shall fall in this wilderness. And your children shall wander in the wilderness forty years, and bear your whoredoms, until your carcases be wasted in the wilderness. After the number of the days in which ye searched the land, even forty days, each day for a year, shall ye bear your iniquities, even forty years, and ye shall know my breach of promise. I the Lord have said, "I will surely do it unto all this evil congregation, that are gathered together against me: in this wilderness they shall be consumed, and there they shall die."'"

And the men, which Moses sent to search the land, who returned, and made all the congregation to murmur against him, by bringing up a slander upon the land, even those men that did bring up the evil report upon the land, died by the plague before the Lord. But Joshua the son of Nun, and Caleb the son of Jephunneh, which were of the men that went to search the land, lived still.

And Moses told these sayings unto all the children of Israel: and the people mourned greatly. And they rose up early in the morning, and got them up into the top of the mountain, saying, "Lo, we be here, and will go up unto the place which the Lord hath promised: for we have sinned." And Moses said, "Wherefore now do ye transgress the commandment of the Lord? but it shall not prosper. Go not up, for the Lord is not among you; that ye be not smitten before your enemies. For the Amalekites and the Canaanites are there before you, and ye shall fall by the sword: because ye are turned away from the Lord, therefore the Lord will not be with you." But they presumed to go up unto the hill top: nevertheless the ark of the covenant of the Lord, and Moses, departed not out of the camp. Then the Amalekites came down, and the Canaanites which dwelt in that hill, and smote them, and discomfited them, even unto Hormah. . . .

Now Korah, the son of Izhar, the son of Kohath, the son of Levi, and Dathan and Abiram, the sons of Eliab, and On, the son of Peleth, sons of Reuben, took men; and they rose up before Moses, with certain of the children of Israel, two hundred and fifty princes of the assembly, famous in the congregation, men of renown; and they gathered themselves together against Moses and against Aaron, and said unto them, "Ye take too much upon you, seeing all the congregation are holy, every one of them, and the Lord is among them: wherefore then lift ye up yourselves above the congregation of the Lord?" And when Moses heard it, he fell upon his face: and he spoke unto Korah and unto all his company, saying, "Even to-morrow the Lord will show who are his, and who is holy; and will cause him to come near unto him: even him whom he hath chosen will he cause to come near unto him. This do: take you censers, Korah, and all his company; and put fire therein, and put incense in them before the Lord to-morrow: and it shall be that the man whom the Lord doth choose, he shall be holy: ye take too much upon you, ye sons of Levi." . . .

And Moses sent to call Dathan and Abiram, the sons of Eliab: which said, "We will not come up. Is it a small thing that thou hast brought us up out of a land that floweth with milk and honey, to kill us in the wilderness, except thou make thyself altogether a prince over us? Moreover thou hast not brought us into a land that floweth with milk and honey, or given us inheritance of fields and vineyards: wilt thou put out the eyes of these men? we will not come up."

And Moses was very wroth, and said unto the Lord, "Respect not thou their offering: I have not taken one ass from them, neither have I hurt one of them." . . .

And the Lord spoke unto Moses, saying, "Speak unto the congregation, saying, 'Get you up from about the tabernacle of Korah, Dathan, and Abiram.'" And Moses rose up and went unto Dathan and Abiram; and the elders of Israel followed him. And he spoke unto the congregation, saying, "Depart, I pray you, from the tents of these wicked men, and touch nothing of theirs, lest ye be consumed in all their sins." So they got up from the tabernacle of Korah, Dathan, and Abiram, on every side: and Dathan and Abiram came out, and stood in the door of their tents, and their wives, and their sons, and their little children. And Moses said, "Hereby ye shall know that the Lord hath sent me to do all these works; for I have not done them of mine own mind. If these men die the common death of all men, or if they be visited after the visitation of all men; then the Lord hath not sent me. But if the Lord make a new thing, and the earth open her mouth, and swallow them up, with all that appertain unto them, and they go down quick into the pit; then ye shall understand that these men have provoked the Lord."

And it came to pass, as he had made an end of speaking all these words, that the ground clove asunder that was under them: and the earth opened her mouth, and swallowed them up, and their houses, and all the men that appertained unto Korah, and all their goods. They, and all that appertained to them, went down alive into the pit, and the earth closed upon them: and they perished from among the congregation. And all Israel that were round about them fled at the cry of them: for they said, "Lest the earth swallow us up also." And there came out a fire from the Lord, and consumed the two hundred and fifty men that offered incense. . . .

Then came the children of Israel, even the whole congregation, into the desert of Zin in the first month: and the people abode in Kadesh; and Miriam died there, and was buried there. And there was no water for the congregation: and they gathered themselves together against Moses and against Aaron. And the people chid with Moses, and spoke, saying, "Would God that we had died when our brethren died before the Lord! And why have ye brought up the congregation of the Lord into this wilderness, that we and our cattle should die there? And wherefore have ye made us to come up out of Egypt, to bring us in unto this evil place? it is no place of seed, or of figs, or of vines, or of pomegranates; neither is there any water to drink."

And Moses and Aaron went from the presence of the assembly unto the door of the tabernacle of the congregation, and they fell upon their faces: and the glory of the Lord appeared unto them. And the Lord spoke unto Moses, saying, "Take the rod, and gather thou the assembly together, thou, and Aaron thy brother, and speak ye unto the rock before their eyes; and it shall give forth his water, and thou shalt bring forth to them water out of the rock: so thou shalt give the congregation and their beasts drink."

And Moses took the rod from before the Lord, as he commanded him. And Moses and Aaron gathered the congregation together before the rock, and he said unto them, "Hear now, ye rebels; must we fetch you water out of this rock?" And Moses lifted up his hand, and with his rod he smote the rock twice: and the water came out abundantly, and the congregation drank, and their beasts also.

And the Lord spoke unto Moses and Aaron, "Because ye believed me not, to sanctify me in the eyes of the children of Israel, therefore ye shall not bring this congregation into the land which I have given them. This is the water of Meribah; because the children of Israel strove with the Lord, and he was sanctified in them."[53]

And Moses sent messengers from Kadesh unto the king of Edom, "Thus saith thy brother Israel, 'Thou knowest all the travail that hath befallen us: how our fathers went down into Egypt, and we have dwelt in Egypt a long time; and the Egyptians vexed us, and our fathers: and when we cried unto the Lord, he heard our voice, and sent an angel, and hath brought us forth out of Egypt: and, behold, we are in Kadesh, a city in the uttermost of thy border. Let us pass, I pray thee, through thy country: we will not pass through the fields, or through the vineyards, neither will we drink of the water of the wells: we will go by the king's high way, we will not turn to the right hand nor to the left, until we have passed thy borders.'"

And Edom said unto him, "Thou shalt not pass by me, lest I come out against thee with the sword." And the children of Israel said unto him, "We will go by the high way: and if I and my cattle drink of thy water, then I will pay for it: I will only, without doing any thing else, go through on my feet." And he said, "Thou shalt not go through." And Edom came out against him with much people, and with a strong hand. Thus Edom refused to give Israel passage through his border: wherefore Israel turned away from him. And the children of Israel, even the whole congregation, journeyed from Kadesh, and came unto Mount Hor. And the Lord spoke unto Moses and Aaron in Mount Hor, by the coast of the land of Edom, saying, "Aaron shall be gathered unto his people: for he shall not enter into the land which I have given unto the children of Israel, because ye rebelled against my word at the water of Meribah. Take Aaron and Eleazar his son, and bring them up unto Mount Hor: and strip Aaron of his garments, and put them upon Eleazar his son: and Aaron shall be gathered unto his people, and shall die there."

And Moses did as the Lord commanded: and they went up into Mount Hor in the sight of all the congregation. And Moses stripped Aaron of his garments, and put them upon Eleazar his son; and Aaron died there in the top of the mount: and Moses and Eleazar came down from the mount. And when all the congregation saw that Aaron was dead, they mourned for Aaron thirty days, even all the house of Israel. . . .

And they journeyed from Mount Hor by the way of the Red Sea, to compass the land of Edom: and the soul of the people was much discouraged because of the way. And the people spoke against God, and against Moses, "Wherefore have ye brought us up out of Egypt to die in the wilderness? for there is no bread, neither is there any water; and our soul loatheth this light bread." And the Lord sent fiery serpents among the people, and they bit the people; and much people of Israel died. Therefore the people came to Moses, and said, "We have sinned, for we have spoken against the Lord, and against thee; pray unto the Lord, that he take away the serpents from us." And Moses prayed for the people. And the Lord

[53] It is not clear what happened in the incident of the water to justify the Lord's refusal to let Aaron and Moses enter the land of Canaan. Later, the accusation is repeated: "Ye rebelled against my commandment" (Numbers 27:14). "Meribah" means "contention" or "strife."

said unto Moses, "Make thee a fiery serpent, and set it upon a pole: and it shall come to pass that every one that is bitten, when he looketh upon it, shall live." And Moses made a serpent of brass, and put it upon a pole, and it came to pass that if a serpent had bitten any man, when he beheld the serpent of brass, he lived.[54]

And the children of Israel set forward, and pitched in Oboth. And they journeyed from Oboth, and pitched at Ije-abarim, in the wilderness which is before Moab, toward the sunrising. From thence they removed, and pitched in the valley of Zared. From thence they removed, and pitched on the other side of Arnon, which is in the wilderness that cometh out of the coasts of the Amorites: for Arnon is the border of Moab, between Moab and the Amorites. Wherefore it is said in the Book of the Wars of the Lord,

> "What he did in the Red Sea,
> and in the brooks of Arnon,
> and at the stream of the brooks
> that goeth down to the dwelling of Ar,
> and lieth upon the border of Moab."

And from thence they went to Beer: that is the well whereof the Lord spoke unto Moses, "Gather the people together, and I will give them water." Then Israel sang this song,

> "Spring up, O well; sing ye unto it:
> The princes digged the well,
> The nobles of the people digged it,
> By the direction of the lawgiver,
> With their staves."[55]

And from the wilderness they went to Mattanah: and from Mattanah to Nahaliel: and from Nahaliel to Bamoth: and from Bamoth in the valley, that is in the country of Moab, to the top of Pisgah, which looketh toward Jeshimon.

And Israel sent messengers unto Sihon king of the Amorites, saying, "Let me pass through thy land: we will not turn into the fields, or into the vineyards; we will not drink of the waters of the well: but we will go along by the king's high way, until we be past thy borders." And Sihon would not suffer Israel to pass through his border: but Sihon gathered all his people together, and went out against Israel into the wilderness: and he came to Jahaz, and fought against Israel. And Israel smote him with the edge of the sword, and possessed his land from Arnon unto Jabbok, even unto the children of Ammon: for the border of the children of Ammon was strong. And Israel took all these cities: and Israel dwelt in all the cities of the Amorites, in Heshbon, and in all the villages thereof. For Heshbon was the city of Sihon the king of the Amorites, who had fought against the former

---

[54] The serpent is associated with wisdom and healing throughout primitive culture, as in the intertwined serpents of the *caduceus*, or staff, of Aesculapius, the Greek god of healing. King Hezekiah, we are told, destroyed "the brazen serpent that Moses had made" (II Kings 18:4).

[55] This invocation to the well is thought to be among the oldest portions of the Bible.

king of Moab, and taken all his land out of his hand, even unto Arnon. Wherefore they that speak in proverbs say,

> "Come into Heshbon,
>   let the city of Sihon be built and prepared:
> For there is a fire gone out of Heshbon,
>   a flame from the city of Sihon:
> It hath consumed Ar of Moab,
>   the lords of the high places of Arnon.
> Woe to thee, Moab!
>   thou art undone, O people of Chemosh:
> He hath given his sons that escaped
>   and his daughters into captivity
>   unto Sihon king of the Amorites.
> We have shot at them;
>   Heshbon is perished even unto Dibon,
> And we have laid them waste even unto Nophah,
>   which reacheth unto Medeba."

. . . And they turned and went up by the way of Bashan: and Og the king of Bashan went out against them, he, and all his people, to the battle of Edrei. And the Lord said unto Moses, "Fear him not: for I have delivered him into thy hand, and all his people, and his land; and thou shalt do to him as thou didst unto Sihon king of the Amorites, which dwelt at Heshbon." So they smote him, and his sons, and all his people, until there was none left him alive: and they possessed his land. . . .[56]

THE DEATH OF MOSES

(Deuteronomy 31:14–34:12)

And the Lord said unto Moses, "Behold, thy days approach that thou must die: call Joshua, and present yourselves in the tabernacle of the congregation, that I may give him a charge." And Moses and Joshua went, and presented themselves in the tabernacle of the congregation. And the Lord appeared in the tabernacle in a pillar of a cloud: and the pillar of the cloud stood over the door of the tabernacle.

And the Lord said unto Moses, "Behold, thou shalt sleep with thy fathers; and this people will rise up, and go a-whoring after the gods of the strangers of the land, whither they go to be among them, and will forsake me, and break my covenant which I have made with them. Then my anger shall be kindled against them in that day, and I will forsake them, and I will hide my face from them, and they shall be devoured, and many evils and troubles shall befall them; so that they will say in that day, 'Are not these evils come upon us, because our God is not among us?' And I will surely hide my face in that day for all the evils which they shall have wrought, in

---

[56] The end of Numbers is devoted to the story of Balaam and to the appointment of Joshua as the successor to Moses. Most of Deuteronomy is devoted to a recasting of the Covenant Code. ("Deuteronomy" is Greek for "second law.") These important sections are omitted here in order to preserve the narrative emphasis.

that they are turned unto other gods. Now therefore write ye this song for you, and teach it the children of Israel: put it in their mouths, that this song may be a witness for me against the children of Israel. For when I shall have brought them into the land which I swore unto their fathers, that floweth with milk and honey; and they shall have eaten and filled themselves, and waxen fat; then will they turn unto other gods, and serve them, and provoke me, and break my covenant. And it shall come to pass, when many evils and troubles are befallen them, that this song shall testify against them as a witness; for it shall not be forgotten out of the mouths of their seed: for I know their imagination which they go about, even now, before I have brought them into the land which I swore."

Moses therefore wrote this song the same day, and taught it the children of Israel. . . .

"Give ear, O ye heavens, and I will speak;
     and hear, O earth, the words of my mouth.
My doctrine shall drop as the rain,
     my speech shall distil as the dew,
     as the small rain upon the tender herb,
     and as the showers upon the grass:
Because I will publish the name of the Lord:
     ascribe ye greatness unto our God.

He is the Rock, his work is perfect:
     for all his ways are judgment:
A God of truth and without iniquity,
     just and right is he.
They have corrupted themselves,
     their spot is not the spot of his children:
     they are a perverse and crooked generation.
Do ye thus requite the Lord,
     O foolish people and unwise?
Is not he thy father that hath bought thee?
     hath he not made thee, and established thee?

Remember the days of old,
     consider the years of many generations:
Ask thy father, and he will show thee;
     thy elders, and they will tell thee.
When the Most High divided to the nations their inheritance,
     when he separated the sons of Adam,
He set the bounds of the people
     according to the number of the children of Israel.
For the Lord's portion is his people;
     Jacob is the lot of his inheritance.

He found him in a desert land,
     and in the waste howling wilderness;
He led him about, he instructed him,
     he kept him as the apple of his eye.

As an eagle stirreth up her nest,
    fluttereth over her young,
Spreadeth abroad her wings, taketh them,
    beareth them on her wings:
So the Lord alone did lead him,
    and there was no strange god with him.
He made him ride on the high places of the earth,
    that he might eat the increase of the fields;
And he made him to suck honey out of the rock,
    and oil out of the flinty rock;
Butter of kine, and milk of sheep, with fat of lambs,
    and rams of the breed of Bashan, and goats,
With the fat of kidneys of wheat;
    and thou didst drink the pure blood of the grape.

But Jeshurun[57] waxed fat, and kicked:
    thou art waxen fat, thou art grown thick, thou art covered with fatness;
Then he forsook God which made him,
    and lightly esteemed the Rock of his salvation.
They provoked him to jealousy with strange gods,
    with abominations provoked they him to anger.
They sacrificed unto devils, not to God;
    to gods whom they knew not,
To new gods that came newly up,
    whom your fathers feared not.
Of the Rock that begot thee thou art unmindful,
    and hast forgotten God that formed thee.

And when the Lord saw it, he abhorred them,
    because of the provoking of his sons, and of his daughters.
And he said, 'I will hide my face from them,
    I will see what their end shall be:
For they are a very froward generation,
    children in whom is no faith.
They have moved me to jealousy with that which is not God;
    they have provoked me to anger with their vanities;
And I will move them to jealousy with those which are not a people;
    I will provoke them to anger with a foolish nation.
For a fire is kindled in mine anger,
    and shall burn unto the lowest hell,
And shall consume the earth with her increase,
    and set on fire the foundations of the mountains.

I will heap mischiefs upon them;
    I will spend mine arrows upon them.
They shall be burnt with hunger,
    and devoured with burning heat,
    and with bitter destruction;

---

[57] "The upright one." The name is applied ironically to Israel.

I will also send the teeth of beasts upon them,
    with the poison of serpents of the dust.
The sword without, and terror within,
    shall destroy both the young man and the virgin,
    the suckling also with the man of gray hairs.
I said, "I would scatter them into corners,
    I would make the remembrance of them to cease from among men":
Were it not that I feared the wrath of the enemy,
    lest their adversaries should behave themselves strangely,
And lest they should say, "Our hand is high,
    and the Lord hath not done all this."

For they are a nation void of counsel,
    neither is there any understanding in them.
O that they were wise, that they understood this,
    that they would consider their latter end!'
How should one chase a thousand,
    and two put ten thousand to flight,
Except their Rock had sold them,
    And the Lord had shut them up?
For their rock is not as our Rock,
    even our enemies themselves being judges.
For their vine is of the vine of Sodom,
    and of the fields of Gomorrah:
Their grapes are grapes of gall,
    Their clusters are bitter:
Their wine is the poison of dragons,
    and the cruel venom of asps.

'Is not this laid up in store with me,
    sealed up among my treasures?
To me belongeth vengeance, and recompense;
    their foot shall slide in due time:
For the day of their calamity is at hand,
    and the things that shall come upon them make haste.'
For the Lord shall judge his people,
    And repent himself for his servants,
When he seeth that their power is gone,
    and there is none shut up, or left.
And he shall say, 'Where are their gods,
    their rock in whom they trusted,
Which did eat the fat of their sacrifices,
    and drank the wine of their drink offerings?
Let them rise up and help you,
    And be your protection.'

'See now that I, even I, am he,
    and there is no god with me:
I kill, and I make alive;
    I wound, and I heal:
    neither is there any that can deliver out of my hand.

For I lift up my hand to heaven,
 and say, "I live for ever.
If I whet my glittering sword,
 and mine hand take hold on judgment;
I will render vengeance to mine enemies,
 and will reward them that hate me.
I will make mine arrows drunk with blood,
 and my sword shall devour flesh;
With the blood of the slain and of the captives,
 from the beginning of revenges upon the enemy."'

Rejoice, O ye nations, with his people:
 for he will avenge the blood of his servants,
And will render vengeance to his adversaries,
 and will be merciful unto his land, and to his people."

  And Moses came and spoke all the words of this song in the ears of the people, he, and Hoshea[58] the son of Nun. . . .

  And Moses went up from the plains of Moab unto the mountain of Nebo, to the top of Pisgah, that is over against Jericho. And the Lord showed him all the land of Gilead, unto Dan, and all Naphtali, and the land of Ephraim, and Manasseh, and all the land of Judah, unto the utmost sea, and the south, and the plain of the valley of Jericho, the city of palm trees, unto Zoar. And the Lord said unto him, "This is the land which I swore unto Abraham, unto Isaac, and unto Jacob, saying, 'I will give it unto thy seed': I have caused thee to see it with thine eyes, but thou shalt not go over thither." So Moses the servant of the Lord died there in the land of Moab, according to the word of the Lord. And he buried him in a valley in the land of Moab, over against Beth-peor: but no man knoweth of his sepulchre unto this day. And Moses was a hundred and twenty years old when he died: his eye was not dim, nor his natural force abated. And the children of Israel wept for Moses in the plains of Moab thirty days: so the days of weeping and mourning for Moses were ended. And Joshua the son of Nun was full of the spirit of wisdom; for Moses had laid his hands upon him: and the children of Israel hearkened unto him, and did as the Lord commanded Moses. And there arose not a prophet since in Israel like unto Moses, whom the Lord knew face to face, in all the signs and the wonders, which the Lord sent him to do in the land of Egypt to Pharaoh, and to all his servants, and to all his land, and in all that mighty hand, and in all the great terror which Moses showed in the sight of all Israel.

THE DESTRUCTION OF JERICHO

(Joshua 1:1–6:27)
Now after the death of Moses the servant of the Lord it came to pass that the Lord spoke unto Joshua the son of Nun, Moses' minister, saying, "Moses my servant is dead; now therefore arise, go over this Jordan, thou,

---

[58] Variant form of "Joshua."

and all this people, unto the land which I do give to them, even to the children of Israel. Every place that the sole of your foot shall tread upon, that have I given unto you, as I said unto Moses. From the wilderness and this Lebanon even unto the great river, the river Euphrates, all the land of the Hittites, and unto the great sea toward the going down of the sun, shall be your coast. There shall not any man be able to stand before thee all the days of thy life: as I was with Moses, so I will be with thee: I will not fail thee, nor forsake thee. Be strong and of a good courage: for unto this people shalt thou divide for an inheritance the land, which I swore unto their fathers to give them. Only be thou strong and very courageous, that thou mayest observe to do according to all the law, which Moses my servant commanded thee: turn not from it to the right hand or to the left, that thou mayest prosper whithersoever thou goest. This book of the law[59] shall not depart out of thy mouth; but thou shalt meditate therein day and night, that thou mayest observe to do according to all that is written therein: for then thou shalt make thy way prosperous, and then thou shalt have good success. Have not I commanded thee? Be strong and of a good courage; be not afraid, neither be thou dismayed: for the Lord thy God is with thee whithersoever thou goest."

Then Joshua commanded the officers of the people, saying, "Pass through the host, and command the people, saying, 'Prepare you victuals; for within three days ye shall pass over this Jordan, to go in to possess the land, which the Lord your God giveth you to possess it.'" . . .

And Joshua the son of Nun sent out of Shittim two men to spy secretly, saying, "Go view the land, even Jericho." And they went, and came into a harlot's house, named Rahab, and lodged there. And it was told the king of Jericho, saying, "Behold, there came men in hither to-night of the children of Israel to search out the country." And the king of Jericho sent unto Rahab, saying, "Bring forth the men that are come to thee, which are entered into thine house: for they be come to search out all the country." And the woman took the two men and hid them, and said thus, "There came men unto me, but I wist not whence they were: and it came to pass about the time of shutting of the gate, when it was dark, that the men went out: whither the men went I wot not: pursue after them quickly; for ye shall overtake them." But she had brought them up to the roof of the house, and hid them with the stalks of flax, which she had laid in order upon the roof. And the men pursued after them the way to Jordan unto the fords: and as soon as they which pursued after them were gone out, they shut the gate.

And before they were laid down, she came up unto them upon the roof; and she said unto the men, "I know that the Lord hath given you the land, and that your terror is fallen upon us, and that all the inhabitants of the land faint because of you. For we have heard how the Lord dried up the water of the Red Sea for you, when ye came out of Egypt; and what ye did unto the two kings of the Amorites, that were on the other side Jordan, Sihon and Og, whom ye utterly destroyed.[60] And as soon as we had heard these things, our hearts did melt, neither did there remain any more cour-

---

[59] The legal provisions of the Book of Deuteronomy.

[60] A clearer translation would be: "what you did to the two kings of the Amorites that were beyond the Jordan, to Sihon and Og, whom you utterly destroyed."

age in any man, because of you: for the Lord your God, he is God in heaven above, and in earth beneath. Now therefore, I pray you, swear unto me by the Lord, since I have showed you kindness, that ye will also show kindness unto my father's house, and give me a true token: and that ye will save alive my father, and my mother, and my brethren, and my sisters, and all that they have, and deliver our lives from death." And the men answered her, "Our life for yours, if ye utter not this our business. And it shall be, when the Lord hath given us the land, that we will deal kindly and truly with thee."

Then she let them down by a cord through the window: for her house was upon the town wall, and she dwelt upon the wall. And she said unto them, "Get you to the mountain, lest the pursuers meet you; and hide yourselves there three days, until the pursuers be returned: and afterward may ye go your way." And the men said unto her, "We will be blameless of this thine oath which thou hast made us swear. Behold, when we come into the land, thou shalt bind this line of scarlet thread in the window which thou didst let us down by: and thou shalt bring thy father, and thy mother, and thy brethren, and all thy father's household, home unto thee. And it shall be, that whosoever shall go out of the doors of thy house into the street, his blood shall be upon his head, and we will be guiltless: and whosoever shall be with thee in the house, his blood shall be on our head, if any hand be upon him. And if thou utter this our business, then we will be quit of thine oath which thou hast made us to swear." And she said, "According unto your words, so be it." And she sent them away, and they departed: and she bound the scarlet line in the window.

And they went, and came unto the mountain, and abode there three days, until the pursuers were returned: and the pursuers sought them throughout all the way, but found them not. So the two men returned, and descended from the mountain, and passed over, and came to Joshua the son of Nun, and told him all things that befell them: and they said unto Joshua, "Truly the Lord hath delivered into our hands all the land; for even all the inhabitants of the country do faint because of us."

And Joshua rose early in the morning; and they removed from Shittim, and came to Jordan, he and all the children of Israel, and lodged there before they passed over. And it came to pass after three days that the officers went through the host; and they commanded the people, saying, "When ye see the ark of the covenant of the Lord your God, and the priests the Levites bearing it, then ye shall remove from your place, and go after it. Yet there shall be a space between you and it, about two thousand cubits by measure: come not near unto it, that ye may know the way by which ye must go: for ye have not passed this way heretofore." And Joshua said unto the people, "Sanctify yourselves: for to-morrow the Lord will do wonders among you." And Joshua spoke unto the priests, saying, "Take up the ark of the covenant, and pass over before the people." And they took up the ark of the covenant, and went before the people.

And the Lord said unto Joshua, "This day will I begin to magnify thee in the sight of all Israel, that they may know that, as I was with Moses, so I will be with thee. And thou shalt command the priests that bear the ark of the covenant, saying, 'When ye are come to the brink of the water of Jordan, ye shall stand still in Jordan.'" And Joshua said unto the children of

Israel, "Come hither, and hear the words of the Lord your God." And
Joshua said, "Hereby ye shall know that the living God is among you, and
that he will without fail drive out from before you the Canaanites, and the
Hittites, and the Hivites, and the Perizzites, and the Girgashites, and the
Amorites, and the Jebusites. Behold, the ark of the covenant of the Lord of
all the earth passeth over before you into Jordan. Now therefore take you
twelve men out of the tribes of Israel, out of every tribe a man. And it shall
come to pass, as soon as the soles of the feet of the priests that bear the ark
of the Lord, the Lord of all the earth, shall rest in the waters of Jordan, that
the waters of Jordan shall be cut off from the waters that come down from
above; and they shall stand upon a heap." . . .

And it came to pass, as they that bore the ark were come unto Jordan,
and the feet of the priests that bore the ark were dipped in the brim of the
water (for Jordan overfloweth all his banks all the time of harvest), that the
waters which came down from above stood and rose up upon a heap very
far from the city Adam, that is beside Zaretan: and those that came down
toward the sea of the plain, even the Salt Sea, failed, and were cut off: and
the people passed over right against Jericho. And the priests that bore the
ark of the covenant of the Lord stood firm on dry ground in the midst of
Jordan, and all the Israelites passed over on dry ground, until all the people were passed clean over Jordan. . . .

Now Jericho was straitly shut up because of the children of Israel: none
went out, and none came in. And the Lord said unto Joshua, "See, I have
given into thine hand Jericho, and the king thereof, and the mighty men of
valor. And ye shall compass the city, all ye men of war, and go round about
the city once. Thus shalt thou do six days. And seven priests shall bear
before the ark seven trumpets of rams' horns: and the seventh day ye shall
compass the city seven times, and the priests shall blow with the trumpets.[61]
And it shall come to pass, that when they make a long blast with the ram's
horn, and when ye hear the sound of the trumpet, all the people shall shout
with a great shout; and the wall of the city shall fall down flat, and the
people shall ascend up every man straight before him." . . .

And Joshua rose early in the morning, and the priests took up the ark
of the Lord. And seven priests bearing seven trumpets of rams' horns before the ark of the Lord went on continually, and blew with the trumpets:
and the armed men went before them; but the rearward came after the ark
of the Lord, the priests going on, and blowing with the trumpets. And the
second day they compassed the city once, and returned into the camp: so
they did six days. And it came to pass on the seventh day that they rose
early about the dawning of the day, and compassed the city after the same
manner seven times: only on that day they compassed the city seven times.
And it came to pass at the seventh time, when the priests blew with the
trumpets, Joshua said unto the people, "Shout; for the Lord hath given you
the city. And the city shall be accursed, even it, and all that are therein, to
the Lord: only Rahab the harlot shall live, she and all that are with her in
the house, because she hid the messengers that we sent. And ye, in any wise
keep yourselves from the accursed thing, lest ye make yourselves accursed,
when ye take of the accursed thing, and make the camp of Israel a curse,

[61] The sacred number seven occurs repeatedly in this chapter.

and trouble it. But all the silver, and gold, and vessels of brass and iron, are consecrated unto the Lord: they shall come into the treasury of the Lord." So the people shouted when the priests blew with the trumpets: and it came to pass, when the people heard the sound of the trumpet, and the people shouted with a great shout, that the wall fell down flat, so that the people went up into the city, every man straight before him, and they took the city. And they utterly destroyed all that was in the city, both man and woman, young and old, and ox, and sheep, and ass, with the edge of the sword.[62]

But Joshua had said unto the two men that had spied out the country, "Go into the harlot's house, and bring out thence the woman, and all that she hath, as ye swore unto her." And the young men that were spies went in, and brought out Rahab, and her father, and her mother, and her brethren, and all that she had; and they brought out all her kindred, and left them without the camp of Israel. And they burnt the city with fire, and all that was therein: only the silver, and the gold, and the vessels of brass and of iron, they put into the treasury of the house of the Lord. And Joshua saved Rahab the harlot alive, and her father's household, and all that she had; and she dwelleth in Israel even unto this day; because she hid the messengers, which Joshua sent to spy out Jericho. And Joshua adjured them at that time, saying, "Cursed be the man before the Lord, that riseth up and buildeth this city Jericho: he shall lay the foundation thereof in his firstborn, and in his youngest son shall he set up the gates of it."

So the Lord was with Joshua; and his fame was noised throughout all the country. . . .[63]

from JOB

CHAPTER 1

There was a man in the land of Uz, whose name was Job; and that man was perfect and upright, and one that feared God, and eschewed evil. And there were born unto him seven sons and three daughters. His substance also was seven thousand sheep, and three thousand camels, and five hundred yoke of oxen, and five hundred she asses, and a very great household; so that this man was the greatest of all the men of the east.

And his sons went and feasted in their houses, every one his day; and sent and called for their three sisters to eat and to drink with them. And it was so, when the days of their feasting were gone about, that Job sent and sanctified them, and rose up early in the morning, and offered burnt offerings according to the number of them all: for Job said, "It may be that my sons have sinned, and cursed God in their hearts." Thus did Job continually.

---

[62] This grim annihilation of an entire city, even of the animals, because it was "accursed," is repugnant to modern readers; there are, however, many parallels in the early history of the Semites.

[63] The rest of the Book of Joshua, eighteen more chapters, continues the story of Israel's conquest of Palestine in a series of triumphant sieges and battles under Joshua. The book ends with an account of Joshua's death.

Now there was a day when the sons of God came to present themselves before the Lord, and Satan[1] came also among them. And the Lord said unto Satan, "Whence comest thou?" Then Satan answered the Lord, and said, "From going to and fro in the earth, and from walking up and down in it." And the Lord said unto Satan, "Hast thou considered my servant Job, that there is none like him in the earth, a perfect and an upright man, one that feareth God, and escheweth evil?" Then Satan answered the Lord, and said, "Doth Job fear God for nought? Hast not thou made an hedge about him, and about his house, and about all that he hath on every side? thou hast blessed the work of his hands, and his substance is increased in the land. But put forth thine hand now, and touch all that he hath, and he will curse thee to thy face." And the Lord said unto Satan, "Behold, all that he hath is in thy power; only upon himself put not forth thine hand." So Satan went forth from the presence of the Lord.

And there was a day when his sons and his daughters were eating and drinking wine in their eldest brother's house: and there came a messenger unto Job, and said, "The oxen were plowing, and the asses feeding beside them: and the Sabeans fell upon them, and took them away; yea, they have slain the servants with the edge of the sword; and I only am escaped alone to tell thee." While he was yet speaking, there came also another, and said, "The fire of God is fallen from heaven, and hath burned up the sheep, and the servants, and consumed them; and I only am escaped alone to tell thee." While he was yet speaking, there came also another, and said, "The Chaldeans made out three bands, and fell upon the camels, and have carried them away, yea, and slain the servants with the edge of the sword; and I only am escaped alone to tell thee." While he was yet speaking, there came also another, and said, "Thy sons and thy daughters were eating and drinking wine in their eldest brother's house: and, behold, there came a great wind from the wilderness, and smote the four corners of the house, and it fell upon the young men, and they are dead; and I only am escaped alone to tell thee."

Then Job arose, and rent his mantle, and shaved his head, and fell down upon the ground, and worshipped, and said,

> "Naked came I out of my mother's womb,
> And naked shall I return thither:
> The Lord gave, and the Lord hath taken away;
> Blessed be the name of the Lord."

In all this Job sinned not, nor charged God foolishly.

CHAPTER 2

Again there was a day when the sons of God came to present themselves before the Lord, and Satan came also among them to present himself be-

---

[1] As the ruler of a band of evil spirits opposed to God, Satan appears by name only three times in the King James Version of the Old Testament, though he appears frequently in the New Testament. In Job, he appears in the Prologue but is never mentioned in the debate with the Comforters.

fore the Lord. And the Lord said unto Satan, "From whence comest thou?" And Satan answered the Lord, and said, "From going to and fro in the earth, and from walking up and down in it." And the Lord said unto Satan, "Hast thou considered my servant Job, that there is none like him in the earth, a perfect and an upright man, one that feareth God, and escheweth. evil? and still he holdeth fast his integrity, although thou movedst me against him, to destroy him without cause." And Satan answered the Lord, and said, "Skin for skin,[2] yea, all that a man hath will he give for his life. But put forth thine hand now, and touch his bone and his flesh, and he will curse thee to thy face." And the Lord said unto Satan, "Behold, he is in thine hand; but save his life."

So went Satan forth from the presence of the Lord, and smote Job with sore boils from the sole of his foot unto his crown. And he took him a potsherd[3] to scrape himself withal; and he sat down among the ashes. Then said his wife unto him, "Dost thou still retain thine integrity? curse God, and die." But he said unto her, "Thou speakest as one of the foolish women speaketh. What? shall we receive good at the hand of God, and shall we not receive evil?" In all this did not Job sin with his lips.

Now when Job's three friends heard of all this evil that was come upon him, they came every one from his own place; Eliphaz the Temanite, and Bildad the Shuhite, and Zophar the Naamathite: for they had made an appointment together to come to mourn with him and to comfort him. And when they lifted up their eyes afar off, and knew him not, they lifted up their voice, and wept; and they rent every one his mantle, and sprinkled dust upon their heads toward heaven. So they sat down with him upon the ground seven days and seven nights, and none spake a word unto him: for they saw that his grief was very great.

CHAPTER 3

After this opened Job his mouth, and cursed his day. And Job spake, and said,

"Let the day perish wherein I was born,
  and the night in which it was said, There is a man child conceived.
Let that day be darkness;
  let not God regard it from above,
  neither let the light shine upon it.
Let darkness and the shadow of death stain it;
  let a cloud dwell upon it;
  let the blackness of the day terrify it.
As for that night, let darkness seize upon it;
  let it not be joined unto the days of the year,
  let it not come into the number of the months.
Lo, let that night be solitary,
  let no joyful voice come therein.

---

[2]"A hide for a hide"—a proverbial expression used by tradesmen.
[3]A piece of broken pottery.

Let them curse it that curse the day,
    who are ready to raise up their mourning.
Let the stars of the twilight thereof be dark;
    let it look for light, but have none;
    neither let it see the dawning of the day:
Because it shut not up the doors of my mother's womb,
    nor hid sorrow from mine eyes.

"Why died I not from the womb?
    why did I not give up the ghost when I came out of the belly?
Why did the knees prevent me?
    or why the breasts that I should suck?
For now should I have lain still and been quiet,
    I should have slept: then had I been at rest,
With kings and counsellors of the earth,
    which built desolate places for themselves;
Or with princes that had gold,
    who filled their houses with silver:
Or as an hidden untimely birth I had not been;
    as infants which never saw light.
There the wicked cease from troubling;
    and there the weary be at rest.
There the prisoners rest together;
    they hear not the voice of the oppressor.
The small and great are there;
    And the servant is free from his master.

"Wherefore is light given to him that is in misery,
    and life unto the bitter in soul;
Which long for death, but it cometh not;
    and dig for it more than for hid treasures;
Which rejoice exceedingly,
    and are glad, when they can find the grave?
Why is light given to a man whose way is hid,
    and whom God hath hedged in?
For my sighing cometh before I eat,
    and my roarings are poured out like the waters.
For the thing which I greatly feared is come upon me,
    and that which I was afraid of is come unto me.
I was not in safety, neither had I rest,
    neither was I quiet; yet trouble came."

CHAPTER 4

Then Eliphaz the Temanite answered and said,

"If we assay to commune with thee, wilt thou be grieved?
    but who can withhold himself from speaking?
Behold, thou hast instructed many,
    and thou hast strengthened the weak hands.

Thy words have upholden him that was falling,
    and thou hast strengthened the feeble knees.
But now it is come upon thee, and thou faintest;
    it toucheth thee, and thou art troubled.
Is not this thy fear, thy confidence, thy hope,
    and the uprightness of thy ways?
Remember, I pray thee, who ever perished, being innocent?
    or where were the righteous cut off?[4]
Even as I have seen, they that plow iniquity,
    and sow wickedness, reap the same.
By the blast of God they perish,
    and by the breath of his nostrils are they consumed.
The roaring of the lion, and the voice of the fierce lion,
    and the teeth of the young lions, are broken.
The old lion perisheth for lack of prey,
    and the stout lion's whelps are scattered abroad.

"Now a thing was secretly brought to me,
    and mine ear received a little thereof.
In thoughts from the visions of the night,
    when deep sleep falleth on men,
Fear came upon me, and trembling,
    which made all my bones to shake.
Then a spirit passed before my face;
    the hair of my flesh stood up:
It stood still,
    but I could not discern the form thereof:
An image was before mine eyes,
    there was silence, and I heard a voice, saying,
Shall mortal man be more just than God?
    shall a man be more pure than his maker?
Behold, he put no trust in his servants;
    and his angels he charged with folly:
How much less in them that dwell in houses of clay,
    whose foundation is in the dust,
    which are crushed before the moth?
They are destroyed from morning to evening:
    they perish for ever without any regarding it.
Doth not their excellency which is in them go away?
    they die, even without wisdom."

CHAPTER 5

"Call now, if there be any that will answer thee;
    and to which of the saints wilt thou turn?
For wrath killeth the foolish man,
    and envy slayeth the silly one.

---

[4] Here, as throughout, Eliphaz upholds the doctrine that the good prosper and the wicked are punished in this world. Suffering is thus a proof of sin.

I have seen the foolish taking root:
    but suddenly I cursed his habitation.
His children are far from safety,
    and they are crushed in the gate,
    neither is there any to deliver them.
Whose harvest the hungry eateth up,
    and taketh it even out of the thorns,
    and the robber swalloweth up their substance.
Although affliction cometh not forth of the dust,
    neither doth trouble spring out of the ground;
Yet man is born unto trouble,
    as the sparks fly upward.

"I would seek unto God,
    and unto God would I commit my cause:
Which doeth great things and unsearchable;
    marvellous things without number:
Who giveth rain upon the earth,
    and sendeth waters upon the fields:
To set up on high those that be low;
    that those which mourn may be exalted to safety.
He disappointeth the devices of the crafty,
    so that their hands cannot perform their enterprise.
He taketh the wise in their own craftiness:
    and the counsel of the froward is carried headlong.
They meet with darkness in the daytime,
    and grope in the noonday as in the night.
But he saveth the poor from the sword,
    from their mouth, and from the hand of the mighty.
So the poor hath hope,
    And iniquity stoppeth her mouth.

"Behold, happy is the man whom God correcteth:
    therefore despise not thou the chastening of the Almighty:[5]
For he maketh sore, and bindeth up:
    he woundeth, and his hands make whole.
He shall deliver thee in six troubles:
    yea, in seven there shall no evil touch thee.
In famine he shall redeem thee from death:
    and in war from the power of the sword.
Thou shalt be hid from the scourge of the tongue:
    neither shalt thou be afraid of destruction when it cometh.
At destruction and famine thou shalt laugh:
    neither shalt thou be afraid of the beasts of the earth.
For thou shalt be in league with the stones of the field:
    and the beasts of the field shall be at peace with thee.
And thou shalt know that thy tabernacle shall be in peace;
    and thou shalt visit thy habitation, and shalt not sin.

---

[5] This is the orthodox Jewish doctrine of *musar;* God imposes suffering to chasten or correct.

Thou shalt know also that thy seed shall be great,
    and thine offspring as the grass of the earth.
Thou shalt come to thy grave in a full age,
    like as a shock of corn cometh in in his season.
Lo this, we have searched it, so it is;
    hear it, and know thou it for thy good."

CHAPTER 6

But Job answered and said,

"Oh that my grief were thoroughly weighed,
    and my calamity laid in the balances together!
For now it would be heavier than the sand of the sea:
    therefore my words are swallowed up.[6]
For the arrows of the Almighty are within me,
    the poison whereof drinketh up my spirit:
    the terrors of God do set themselves in array against me.
Doth the wild ass bray when he hath grass?
    or loweth the ox over his fodder?
Can that which is unsavory be eaten without salt?
    or is there any taste in the white of an egg?
The things that my soul refused to touch
    are as my sorrowful meat.
Oh that I might have my request;
    and that God would grant me the thing that I long for!
Even that it would please God to destroy me;
    that he would let loose his hand, and cut me off!
Then should I yet have comfort;
    yea, I would harden myself in sorrow: let him not spare;
    for I have not concealed the words of the Holy One.
What is my strength, that I should hope?
    and what is mine end, that I should prolong my life?
Is my strength the strength of stones?
    or is my flesh of brass?
Is not my help in me?
    and is wisdom driven quite from me?

"To him that is afflicted pity should be showed from his friend;
    but he forsaketh the fear of the Almighty.
My brethren have dealt deceitfully as a brook,
    and as the stream of brooks they pass away;
Which are blackish by reason of the ice,
    and wherein the snow is hid:
What time they wax warm, they vanish:
    when it is hot, they are consumed out of their place.

---

[6] Job replies to Eliphaz by saying that the orthodox explanation cannot be valid in his case, since his suffering exceeds any possible cause.

The paths of their way are turned aside;
 they go to nothing, and perish.
The troops of Tema looked,
 the companies of Sheba waited for them.
They were confounded because they had hoped;
 they came thither, and were ashamed.
For now ye are nothing;
 ye see my casting down, and are afraid.
Did I say, 'Bring unto me'?
 or, 'Give a reward for me of your substance'?
Or, 'Deliver me from the enemy's hand'?
 or, 'Redeem me from the hand of the mighty'?

"Teach me, and I will hold my tongue:
 and cause me to understand wherein I have erred.
How forcible are right words!
 but what doth your arguing reprove?
Do ye imagine to reprove words,
 and the speeches of one that is desperate, which are as wind?
Yea, ye overwhelm the fatherless,
 and ye dig a pit for your friend.

"Now therefore be content, look upon me;
 for it is evident unto you if I lie.
Return, I pray you, let it not be iniquity;
 yea, return again, my righteousness is in it.[7]
Is there iniquity in my tongue?
 cannot my taste discern perverse things?"

CHAPTER 7

"Is there not an appointed time to man upon earth?
 are not his days also like the days of an hireling?
As a servant earnestly desireth the shadow,
 and as an hireling looketh for the reward of his work:
So am I made to possess months of vanity,
 and wearisome nights are appointed to me.
When I lie down, I say, 'When shall I arise, and the night be gone?'
 and I am full of tossings to and fro unto the dawning of the day.
My flesh is clothed with worms and clods of dust;
 my skin is broken, and become loathsome.
My days are swifter than a weaver's shuttle,
 and are spent without hope.

"O remember that my life is wind:
 mine eye shall no more see good.
The eye of him that hath seen me shall see me no more:
 thine eyes are upon me, and I am not.

---

[7] This line would be clearer if translated "Let no injustice be done; my cause is righteous."

As the cloud is consumed and vanisheth away:
    so he that goeth down to the grave shall come up no more.
He shall return no more to his house,
    neither shall his place know him any more.

"Therefore I will not refrain my mouth;
    I will speak in the anguish of my spirit;
    I will complain in the bitterness of my soul.
Am I a sea, or a whale,
    that thou settest a watch over me?
When I say, 'My bed shall comfort me,
    my couch shall ease my complaint';
Then thou scarest me with dreams,
    and terrifiest me through visions:
So that my soul chooseth strangling,
    and death rather than my life.
I loathe it; I would not live alway:
    let me alone; for my days are vanity.
What is man, that thou shouldest magnify him?
    and that thou shouldest set thine heart upon him?
And that thou shouldest visit him every morning,
    and try him every moment?
How long wilt thou not depart from me,
    nor let me alone till I swallow down my spittle?
I have sinned; what shall I do unto thee, O thou preserver of men?
    why hast thou set me as a mark against thee,
    so that I am a burden to myself?
And why dost thou not pardon my transgression,
    and take away mine iniquity?
For now shall I sleep in the dust;
    and thou shalt seek me in the morning, but I shall not be."

CHAPTER 8

Then answered Bildad the Shuhite, and said,

"How long wilt thou speak these things?
    and how long shall the words of thy mouth be like a strong wind?
Doth God pervert judgment?
    or doth the Almighty pervert justice?
If thy children have sinned against him,
    and he have cast them away for their transgression;
If thou wouldest seek unto God betimes,
    and make thy supplication to the Almighty;
If thou wert pure and upright;
    surely now he would awake for thee,
    and make the habitation of thy righteousness prosperous.
Though thy beginning was small,
    yet thy latter end should greatly increase.

"For enquire, I pray thee, of the former age,
    and prepare thyself to the search of their fathers:[8]
(For we are but of yesterday, and know nothing,
    because our days upon earth are a shadow:)
Shall not they teach thee, and tell thee,
    and utter words out of their heart?
Can the rush grow up without mire?
    can the flag grow without water?
Whilst it is yet in his greenness, and not cut down,
    It withereth before any other herb.
So are the paths of all that forget God;
    and the hypocrite's hope shall perish:
Whose hope shall be cut off,
    and whose trust shall be a spider's web.
He shall lean upon his house, but it shall not stand:
    he shall hold it fast, but it shall not endure.
He is green before the sun,
    and his branch shooteth forth in his garden.
His roots are wrapped about the heap,
    and seeth the place of stones.
If he destroy him from his place,
    then it shall deny him, saying, 'I have not seen thee.'
Behold, this is the joy of his way,
    and out of the earth shall others grow.

"Behold, God will not cast away a perfect man,
    neither will he help the evil doers:
Till he fill thy mouth with laughing,
    and thy lips with rejoicing.
They that hate thee shall be clothed with shame;
    and the dwelling place of the wicked shall come to nought."

CHAPTER 9

Then Job answered and said,

"I know it is so of a truth:
    but how should man be just with God?
If he will contend with him,
    he cannot answer him one of a thousand.
He is wise in heart, and mighty in strength:
    who hath hardened himself against him, and hath prospered?
Which removeth the mountains, and they know not:
    which overturneth them in his anger.
Which shaketh the earth out of her place,
    and the pillars thereof tremble.

---

[8] In his eagerness to uphold orthodoxy, Bildad suggests that the cause of Job's suffering may be not in his own sins but in those of his family.

Which commandeth the sun, and it riseth not;
 and sealeth up the stars.
Which alone spreadeth out the heavens,
 and treadeth upon the waves of the sea.
Which maketh Arcturus, Orion, and Pleiades,
 and the chambers of the south.
Which doeth great things past finding out;
 yea, and wonders without number.
Lo, he goeth by me, and I see him not:
 he passeth on also, but I perceive him not.
Behold, he taketh away, who can hinder him?
 Who will say unto him, 'What doest thou?'

"If God will not withdraw his anger,
 the proud helpers do stoop under him.
How much less shall I answer him,
 and choose out my words to reason with him?
Whom, though I were righteous, yet would I not answer,
 but I would make supplication to my judge.
If I had called, and he had answered me;
 yet would I not believe that he had hearkened unto my voice.
For he breaketh me with a tempest,
 and multiplieth my wounds without cause.
He will not suffer me to take my breath,
 but filleth me with bitterness.
If I speak of strength, lo, he is strong:
 and if of judgment, who shall set me a time to plead?
If I justify myself, mine own mouth shall condemn me:
 if I say, I am perfect, it shall also prove me perverse.
Though I were perfect, yet would I not know my soul:
 I would despise my life.
This is one thing, therefore I said it,
 he destroyeth the perfect and the wicked.
If the scourge slay suddenly,
 he will laugh at the trial of the innocent.
The earth is given into the hand of the wicked:
 he covereth the faces of the judges thereof;
 if not, where, and who is he?

"Now my days are swifter than a post:[9]
 they flee away, they see no good.
They are passed away as the swift ships:
 as the eagle that hasteth to the prey.
If I say, 'I will forget my complaint,
 I will leave off my heaviness, and comfort myself':
I am afraid of all my sorrows,
 I know that thou wilt not hold me innocent.
If I be wicked, why then labor I in vain?

[9] Runner.

If I wash myself with snow water,
    and make my hands never so clean;
Yet shalt thou plunge me in the ditch,
    and mine own clothes shall abhor me.
For he is not a man, as I am, that I should answer him,
    and we should come together in judgment.
Neither is there any daysman[10] betwixt us,
    that might lay his hand upon us both.
Let him take his rod away from me,
    and let not his fear terrify me:
Then would I speak, and not fear him;
    but it is not so with me.

CHAPTER 10

"My soul is weary of my life; I will leave my complaint upon myself;
    I will speak in the bitterness of my soul.
I will say unto God, 'Do not condemn me;
    show me wherefore thou contendest with me.
Is it good unto thee that thou shouldest oppress,
    that thou shouldest despise the work of thine hands,
    and shine upon the counsel of the wicked?
Hast thou eyes of flesh?
    or seest thou as man seeth?
Are thy days as the days of man?
    are thy years as man's days,
That thou enquirest after mine iniquity,
    and searchest after my sin?
Thou knowest that I am not wicked;
    and there is none that can deliver out of thine hand.
Thine hands have made me and fashioned me together round about;
    yet thou dost destroy me.
Remember, I beseech thee, that thou hast made me as the clay;
    And wilt thou bring me into dust again?
Hast thou not poured me out as milk,
    and curdled me like cheese?
Thou hast clothed me with skin and flesh,
    and hast fenced me with bones and sinews:
Thou hast granted me life and favor,
    and thy visitation hath preserved my spirit.
And these things hast thou hid in thine heart:
    I know that this is with thee.
If I sin, then thou markest me,
    and thou wilt not acquit me from mine iniquity.
If I be wicked, woe unto me;
    and if I be righteous, yet will I not lift up my head.
I am full of confusion;
    therefore see thou mine affliction;

[10] Umpire.

For it increaseth. Thou huntest me as a fierce lion:
　　and again thou showest thyself marvellous upon me.
Thou renewest thy witnesses against me,
　　and increasest thine indignation upon me;
　　changes and war are against me.

"'Wherefore then hast thou brought me forth out of the womb?
　　Oh that I had given up the ghost, and no eye had seen me!
I should have been as though I had not been;
　　I should have been carried from the womb to the grave.
Are not my days few? cease then,
　　and let me alone, that I may take comfort a little,
Before I go whence I shall not return,
　　even to the land of darkness[11] and the shadow of death;
A land of darkness, as darkness itself;
　　and of the shadow of death, without any order,
　　and where the light is as darkness.'"

CHAPTER 11

Then answered Zophar the Naamathite, and said,

"Should not the multitude of words be answered?
　　and should a man full of talk be justified?
Should thy lies make men hold their peace?
　　and when thou mockest, shall no man make thee ashamed?
For thou hast said, 'My doctrine is pure,
　　and I am clean in thine eyes.'
But oh that God would speak,
　　and open his lips against thee;
And that he would show thee the secrets of wisdom,
　　that they are double to that which is!
Know therefore that God exacteth of thee less than thine iniquity
　　deserveth.[12]

"Canst thou by searching find out God?
　　canst thou find out the Almighty unto perfection?
It is as high as heaven; what canst thou do?
　　deeper than hell; what canst thou know?
The measure thereof is longer than the earth,
　　and broader than the sea.
If he cut off, and shut up,
　　or gather together, then who can hinder him?
For he knoweth vain men:
　　he seeth wickedness also; will he not then consider it?

---

[11] The concept of hell, like the figure of Satan, is late in developing in the Old Testament period. The "land of darkness" mentioned here is the Hebrew *sheol,* a shadowy place where the dead go, similar to the Greek "Hades." It does not imply reward or punishment for one's life on earth.

[12] Zophar, too, insists that Job has deserved his suffering and that God dispenses justice on earth.

For vain man would be wise,
    though man be born like a wild ass's colt.

"If thou prepare thine heart,
    and stretch out thine hands toward him;
If iniquity be in thine hand, put it far away,
    and let not wickedness dwell in thy tabernacles.
For then shalt thou lift up thy face without spot;
    yea, thou shalt be steadfast, and shalt not fear:
Because thou shalt forget thy misery,
    and remember it as waters that pass away:
And thine age shall be clearer than the noonday;
    thou shalt shine forth, thou shalt be as the morning.
And thou shalt be secure, because there is hope;
    yea thou shalt dig about thee, and thou shalt take thy rest in safety.
Also thou shalt lie down, and none shall make thee afraid;
    yea, many shall make suit unto thee.
But the eyes of the wicked shall fail, and they shall not escape,
    and their hope shall be as the giving up of the ghost."

CHAPTER 12

And Job answered and said,

"No doubt but ye are the people,
    and wisdom shall die with you.
But I have understanding as well as you;
    I am not inferior to you:
    yea, who knoweth not such things as these?
I am as one mocked of his neighbor,
    who calleth upon God, and he answereth him:
    the just upright man is laughed to scorn.
He that is ready to slip with his feet
    is as a lamp despised in the thought of him that is at ease.
The tabernacles of robbers prosper,
    and they that provoke God are secure;
    into whose hand God bringeth abundantly.

"But ask now the beasts, and they shall teach thee;
    and the fowls of the air, and they shall tell thee:
Or speak to the earth, and it shall teach thee:
    and the fishes of the sea shall declare unto thee.
Who knoweth not in all these
    that the hand of the Lord hath wrought this?
In whose hand is the soul of every living thing,
    and the breath of all mankind.
Doth not the ear try words?
    and the mouth taste his meat?
With the ancient is wisdom;
    and in length of days understanding.

"With him is wisdom and strength,
 he hath counsel and understanding.
Behold, he breaketh down, and it cannot be built again:
 he shutteth up a man, and there can be no opening.
Behold, he withholdeth the waters, and they dry up:
 also he sendeth them out, and they overturn the earth.
With him is strength and wisdom:
 the deceived and the deceiver are his.
He leadeth counsellors away spoiled,
 and maketh the judges fools.
He looseth the bond of kings,
 and girdeth their loins with a girdle.
He leadeth princes away spoiled,
 and overthroweth the mighty.
He removeth away the speech of the trusty,
 and taketh away the understanding of the aged.
He poureth contempt upon princes,
 and weakeneth the strength of the mighty.
He discovereth deep things out of darkness,
 and bringeth out to light the shadow of death.
He increaseth the nations, and destroyeth them:
 he enlargeth the nations, and straiteneth them again.
He taketh away the heart of the chief of the people of the earth,
 and causeth them to wander in a wilderness where there is no way.
They grope in the dark without light,
 and he maketh them to stagger like a drunken man."

CHAPTER 13

"Lo, mine eye hath seen all this,
 mine ear hath heard and understood it.
What ye know, the same do I know also:
 I am not inferior unto you.
Surely I would speak to the Almighty,
 and I desire to reason with God.
But ye are forgers of lies,
 ye are all physicians of no value.
O that ye would altogether hold your peace!
 and it should be your wisdom.
Hear now my reasoning,
 and hearken to the pleadings of my lips.
Will ye speak wickedly for God?
 and talk deceitfully for him?
Will ye accept his person?
 will ye contend for God?
Is it good that he should search you out?
 or as one man mocketh another, do ye so mock him?
He will surely reprove you,
 if ye do secretly accept persons.

Shall not his excellency make you afraid?
    and his dread fall upon you?
Your remembrances are like unto ashes,
    your bodies to bodies of clay.
Hold your peace, let me alone, that I may speak,
    and let come on me what will.
Wherefore do I take my flesh in my teeth,
    and put my life in mine hand?
Though he slay me, yet will I trust in him:[13]
    but I will maintain mine own ways before him.
He also shall be my salvation:
    for an hypocrite shall not come before him.[14]
Hear diligently my speech,
    and my declaration with your ears.
Behold now, I have ordered my cause;
    I know that I shall be justified.
Who is he that will plead with me?
    for now, if I hold my tongue, I shall give up the ghost.
Only do not two things unto me:
    then will I not hide myself from thee.
Withdraw thine hand far from me:
    and let not thy dread make me afraid.
Then call thou, and I will answer:
    or let me speak, and answer thou me.
How many are mine iniquities and sins?
    make me to know my transgression and my sin.
Wherefore hidest thou thy face,
    and holdest me for thine enemy?
Wilt thou break a leaf driven to and fro?
    and wilt thou pursue the dry stubble?
For thou writest bitter things against me,
    and makest me to possess the iniquities of my youth.
Thou puttest my feet also in the stocks,
    and lookest narrowly unto all my paths;
    thou settest a print upon the heels of my feet.
And he, as a rotten thing, consumeth,
    as a garment that is moth eaten."

CHAPTER 14

"Man that is born of a woman
    is of few days, and full of trouble.

---

[13] The latter part of this line should read "I have no hope," a more defiant and despairing statement.
[14] Job argues that his eagerness to confront God is a proof of his blamelessness, for a guilty man would not dare to come before Him.

He cometh forth like a flower, and is cut down:
    he fleeth also as a shadow, and continueth not.
And dost thou open thine eyes upon such an one,
    and bringest me into judgment with thee?
Who can bring a clean thing out of an unclean?
    not one.
Seeing his days are determined,
    the number of his months are with thee,
    thou hast appointed his bounds that he cannot pass;
Turn from him, that he may rest,
    till he shall accomplish, as an hireling, his day.

"For there is hope of a tree, if it be cut down, that it will sprout again,
    and that the tender branch thereof will not cease.
Though the root thereof wax old in the earth,
    and the stock thereof die in the ground;
Yet through the scent of water it will bud,
    and bring forth boughs like a plant.
But man dieth, and wasteth away:
    yea, man giveth up the ghost, and where is he?
As the waters fail from the sea,
    and the flood decayeth and drieth up:
So man lieth down, and riseth not:
    till the heavens be no more, they shall not awake,
    nor be raised out of their sleep.
O that thou wouldest hide me in the grave,
    that thou wouldest keep me secret, until thy wrath be past,
    that thou wouldest appoint me a set time, and remember me!
If a man die, shall he live again?
    all the days of my appointed time will I wait,
    till my change come.
Thou shalt call, and I will answer thee:
    thou wilt have a desire to the work of thine hands.
For now thou numberest my steps:
    dost thou not watch over my sin?
My transgression is sealed up in a bag,
    and thou sewest up mine iniquity.

"And surely the mountain falling cometh to nought,
    and the rock is removed out of his place.
The waters wear the stones:
    thou washest away the things which grow out of the dust of the earth;
    and thou destroyest the hope of man.
Thou prevailest for ever against him, and he passeth:
    thou changest his countenance, and sendest him away.
His sons come to honor, and he knoweth it not;
    and they are brought low, but he perceiveth it not of them.
But his flesh upon him shall have pain,
    and his soul within him shall mourn."

CHAPTER 19

Then Job answered [the Comforters] and said,

"How long will ye vex my soul,
and break me in pieces with words?
These ten times have ye reproached me:
ye are not ashamed that ye make yourselves strange to me.
And be it indeed that I have erred,
mine error remaineth with myself.
If indeed ye will magnify yourselves against me,
and plead against me my reproach:
Know now that God hath overthrown me,
and hath compassed me with his net.
Behold, I cry out of wrong, but I am not heard:
I cry aloud, but there is no judgment.
He hath fenced up my way that I cannot pass,
and he hath set darkness in my paths.
He hath stripped me of my glory,
and taken the crown from my head.
He hath destroyed me on every side, and I am gone:
and mine hope hath he removed like a tree.
He hath also kindled his wrath against me,
and he counteth me unto him as one of his enemies.
His troops come together,
and raise up their way against me,
and encamp round about my tabernacle.

"He hath put my brethren far from me,
and mine acquaintance are verily estranged from me.
My kinsfolk have failed,
and my familiar friends have forgotten me.
They that dwell in mine house, and my maids, count me for a stranger:
I am an alien in their sight.
I called my servant, and he gave me no answer;
I intreated him with my mouth.
My breath is strange to my wife,
though I intreated for the children's sake of mine own body.
Yea, young children despised me;
I arose, and they spake against me.
All my inward friends abhorred me:
and they whom I loved are turned against me.
My bone cleaveth to my skin and to my flesh,
and I am escaped with the skin of my teeth.
Have pity upon me, have pity upon me, O ye my friends;
for the hand of God hath touched me.
Why do ye persecute me as God,
and are not satisfied with my flesh?

"Oh that my words were now written!
Oh that they were printed in a book!

That they were graven with an iron pen
  and lead in the rock for ever!
For I know that my redeemer liveth,
  and that he shall stand at the latter day upon the earth:
And though after my skin worms destroy this body,
  yet in my flesh shall I see God:
Whom I shall see for myself,
  and mine eyes shall behold, and not another;[15]
  though my reins be consumed within me.
But ye should say, 'Why persecute we him,
  seeing the root of the matter is found in me?'
Be ye afraid of the sword:
  for wrath bringeth the punishments of the sword,
  that ye may know there is a judgment."

CHAPTER 29

Moreover Job continued his parable, and said,

"Oh that I were as in months past,
  as in the days when God preserved me;
When his candle shined upon my head,
  and when by his light I walked through darkness;
As I was in the days of my youth,
  when the secret of God was upon my tabernacle;
When the Almighty was yet with me,
  when my children were about me;
When I washed my steps with butter,
  and the rock poured me out rivers of oil;
When I went out to the gate through the city,
  when I prepared my seat in the street!
The young men saw me, and hid themselves:
  and the aged arose, and stood up.
The princes refrained talking,
  and laid their hand on their mouth.
The nobles held their peace,
  and their tongue cleaved to the roof of their mouth.
When the ear heard me, then it blessed me;
  and when the eye saw me, it gave witness to me:
Because I delivered the poor that cried,
  and the fatherless, and him that had none to help him.
The blessing of him that was ready to perish came upon me:
  and I caused the widow's heart to sing for joy.
I put on righteousness, and it clothed me:
  my judgment was as a robe and a diadem.
I was eyes to the blind,
  and feet was I to the lame.

[15] The Hebrew text is unclear at this point. The word translated "Redeemer" here was a legal term meaning "avenger" or "vindicator." Job probably is saying that after his death he will see God, in the role of "avenger," vindicate him posthumously in the eyes of the world.

I was a father to the poor:
    and the cause which I knew not I searched out.
And I brake the jaws of the wicked,
    and plucked the spoil out of his teeth.
Then I said, 'I shall die in my nest,
    and I shall multiply my days as the sand.'
My root was spread out by the waters,
    and the dew lay all night upon my branch.
My glory was fresh in me,
    and my bow was renewed in my hand.

"Unto me men gave ear,
    and waited, and kept silence at my counsel.
After my words they spake not again;
    and my speech dropped upon them.
And they waited for me as for the rain;
    and they opened their mouth wide as for the latter rain.
If I laughed on them, they believed it not;
    and the light of my countenance they cast not down.
I chose out their way, and sat chief,
    and dwelt as a king in the army,
    as one that comforteth the mourners."

CHAPTER 30

"But now they that are younger than I
    have me in derision,
Whose fathers I would have disdained
    to have set with the dogs of my flock.
Yea, whereto might the strength of their hands profit me,
    in whom old age was perished?
For want and famine they were solitary;
    fleeing into the wilderness in former time desolate and waste.
Who cut up mallows by the bushes,
    and juniper roots for their meat.
They were driven forth from among men,
    (they cried after them as after a thief;)
To dwell in the cliffs of the valleys,
    in caves of the earth, and in the rocks.
Among the bushes they brayed;
    under the nettles they were gathered together.
They were children of fools, yea, children of base men:
    they were viler than the earth.

"And now am I their song,
    yea, I am their byword.
They abhor me, they flee far from me,
    and spare not to spit in my face.
Because he hath loosed my cord, and afflicted me,
    they have also let loose the bridle before me.

Upon my right hand rise the youth;
    they push away my feet,
And they raise up against me
    the ways of their destruction.
They mar my path,
    they set forward my calamity, they have no helper.
They came upon me as a wide breaking in of waters:
    in the desolation they rolled themselves upon me.
Terrors are turned upon me:
    they pursue my soul as the wind:
    and my welfare passeth away as a cloud.

"And now my soul is poured out upon me;
    the days of affliction have taken hold upon me.
My bones are pierced in me in the night season:
    and my sinews take no rest.
By the great force of my disease is my garment changed:
    it bindeth me about as the collar of my coat.
He hath cast me into the mire,
    and I am become like dust and ashes.
I cry unto thee, and thou dost not hear me:
    I stand up, and thou regardest me not.
Thou art become cruel to me:
    with thy strong hand thou opposest thyself against me.
Thou liftest me up to the wind;
    thou causest me to ride upon it,
    and dissolvest my substance.
For I know that thou wilt bring me to death,
    and to the house appointed for all living.

"Howbeit he will not stretch out his hand to the grave,
    though they cry in his destruction.
Did not I weep for him that was in trouble?
    was not my soul grieved for the poor?
When I looked for good, then evil came unto me:
    and when I waited for light, there came darkness.
My bowels boiled, and rested not:
    the days of affliction prevented me.
I went mourning without the sun:
    I stood up, and I cried in the congregation.
I am a brother to dragons,
    and a companion to owls.
My skin is black upon me,
    and my bones are burned with heat.
My harp also is turned to mourning,
    and my organ into the voice of them that weep."

CHAPTER 31

"I made a covenant with mine eyes;
    why then should I think upon a maid?

For what portion of God is there from above?
    and what inheritance of the Almighty from on high?
Is not destruction to the wicked?
    and a strange punishment to the workers of iniquity?
Doth not he see my ways,
    and count all my steps?

If I have walked with vanity,
    or if my foot hath hasted to deceit;
Let me be weighed in an even balance,
    that God may know mine integrity.
If my step hath turned out of the way,
    and mine heart walked after mine eyes,
    and if any blot hath cleaved to mine hands;
Then let me sow, and let another eat;
    yea, let my offspring be rooted out.

"If mine heart have been deceived by a woman,
    or if I have laid wait at my neighbor's door;
Then let my wife grind unto another,[16]
    and let others bow down upon her.
For this is an heinous crime;
    yea, it is an iniquity to be punished by the judges.
For it is a fire that consumeth to destruction,
    and would root out all mine increase.

"If I did despise the cause of my manservant or of my maidservant,
    when they contended with me;
What then shall I do when God riseth up?
    and when he visiteth, what shall I answer him?
Did not he that made me in the womb make him?
    and did not one fashion us in the womb?

"If I have withheld the poor from their desire,
    or have caused the eyes of the widow to fail;
Or have eaten my morsel myself alone,
    and the fatherless hath not eaten thereof;
(For from my youth he was brought up with me, as with a father,
    and I have guided her from my mother's womb;)
If I have seen any perish for want of clothing,
    or any poor without covering;
If his loins have not blessed me,
    and if he were not warmed with the fleece of my sheep;
If I have lifted up my hand against the fatherless,
    when I saw my help in the gate:
Then let mine arm fall from my shoulder blade,
    and mine arm be broken from the bone.
For destruction from God was a terror to me,
    and by reason of his highness I could not endure.

---

[16] That is, grind grain as a servant for someone else.

"If I have made gold my hope,
    or have said to the fine gold, 'Thou art my confidence';
If I rejoiced because my wealth was great,
    and because mine hand had gotten much;
If I beheld the sun when it shined,
    or the moon walking in brightness;
And my heart hath been secretly enticed,
    or my mouth hath kissed my hand:
This also were an iniquity to be punished by the judge:
    for I should have denied the God that is above.

"If I rejoiced at the destruction of him that hated me,
    or lifted up myself when evil found him:
Neither have I suffered my mouth to sin
    by wishing a curse to his soul.
If the men of my tabernacle said not,
    'Oh that we had of his flesh! we cannot be satisfied.'
The stranger did not lodge in the street:
    but I opened my doors to the traveller.
If I covered my transgressions as Adam,
    by hiding mine iniquity in my bosom:
Did I fear a great multitude,
    or did the contempt of families terrify me,
    that I kept silence, and went not out of the door?
Oh that one would hear me!
    behold, my desire is, that the Almighty would answer me,
    and that mine adversary had written a book.
Surely I would take it upon my shoulder,
    and bind it as a crown to me.
I would declare unto him the number of my steps;
    as a prince would I go near unto him.

"If my land cry against me,
    or that the furrows likewise thereof complain;
If I have eaten the fruits thereof without money,
    or have caused the owners thereof to lose their life:
Let thistles grow instead of wheat,
    and cockle instead of barley."

The words of Job are ended.

CHAPTER 38

Then the Lord answered Job out of the whirlwind,[17] and said,

"Who is this that darkeneth counsel
    by words without knowledge?

[17] God appears in a whirlwind elsewhere in the Old Testament as well, notably in Nahum 1:3 and Psalms 18:7–15.

Gird up now thy loins like a man;
    for I will demand of thee, and answer thou me.

"Where wast thou when I laid the foundations of the earth?
    declare, if thou hast understanding.
Who hath laid the measures thereof, if thou knowest?
    or who hath stretched the line upon it?
Whereupon are the foundations thereof fastened?
    or who laid the corner stone thereof;
When the morning stars sang together,
    and all the sons of God shouted for joy?

"Or who shut up the sea with doors,
    when it brake forth, as if it had issued out of the womb?
When I made the cloud the garment thereof,
    and thick darkness a swaddlingband for it,
And brake up for it my decreed place,
    and set bars and doors,
And said, 'Hitherto shalt thou come, but no further:
    and here shall thy proud waves be stayed'?
Hast thou commanded the morning since thy days;
    and caused the dayspring[18] to know his place;
That it might take hold of the ends of the earth,
    that the wicked might be shaken out of it?
It is turned as clay to the seal;
    and they stand as a garment.
And from the wicked their light is withholden,
    and the high arm shall be broken.

"Hast thou entered into the springs of the sea?
    or hast thou walked in the search of the depth?
Have the gates of death been opened unto thee?
    or hast thou seen the doors of the shadow of death?
Hast thou perceived the breadth of the earth?
    declare if thou knowest it all.

"Where is the way where light dwelleth?
    and as for darkness, where is the place thereof,
That thou shouldest take it to the bound thereof,
    and that thou shouldest know the paths to the house thereof?
Knowest thou it, because thou wast then born?
    or because the number of thy days is great?

"Hast thou entered into the treasures of the snow?
    or hast thou seen the treasures of the hail,
Which I have reserved against the time of trouble,
    against the day of battle and war?
By what way is the light parted,
    which scattereth the east wind upon the earth?
Who hath divided a watercourse for the overflowing of waters,
    or a way for the lightning of thunder;

[18] Dawn.

To cause it to rain on the earth, where no man is;
    on the wilderness, wherein there is no man;
To satisfy the desolate and waste ground;
    and to cause the bud of the tender herb to spring forth?

"Hath the rain a father?
    or who hath begotten the drops of dew?
Out of whose womb came the ice?
    and the hoary frost of heaven, who hath gendered it?
The waters are hid as with a stone,
    and the face of the deep is frozen.

"Canst thou bind the sweet influences of Pleiades,
    or loose the bands of Orion?
Canst thou bring forth Mazzaroth in his season?
    or canst thou guide Arcturus with his sons?[19]
Knowest thou the ordinances of heaven?
    canst thou set the dominion thereof in the earth?

"Canst thou lift up thy voice to the clouds,
    that abundance of waters may cover thee?
Canst thou send lightnings, that they may go,
    and say unto thee, 'Here we are'?
Who hath put wisdom in the inward parts?
    or who hath given understanding to the heart?
Who can number the clouds in wisdom?
    or who can stay the bottles of heaven,
When the dust groweth into hardness,
    and the clods cleave fast together?

"Wilt thou hunt the prey for the lion?
    or fill the appetite of the young lions,
When they couch in their dens,
    and abide in the covert to lie in wait?
Who provideth for the raven his food?
    when his young ones cry unto God,
    they wander for lack of meat."

CHAPTER 39

"Knowest thou the time when the wild goats of the rock bring forth?
    or canst thou mark when the hinds do calve?
Canst thou number the months that they fulfil?
    or knowest thou the time when they bring forth?
They bow themselves, they bring forth their young ones,
    they cast out their sorrows.
Their young ones are in good liking, they grow up with corn;
    they go forth, and return not unto them.

---

[19] These are all stars or constellations.

"Who hath sent out the wild ass free?
    or who hath loosed the bands of the wild ass?
Whose house I have made the wilderness,
    and the barren land his dwellings.
He scorneth the multitude of the city,
    neither regardeth he the crying of the driver.
The range of the mountains is his pasture,
    and he searcheth after every green thing.

"Will the unicorn[20] be willing to serve thee,
    or abide by thy crib?
Canst thou bind the unicorn with his band in the furrow?
    or will he harrow the valleys after thee?
Wilt thou trust him, because his strength is great?
    or wilt thou leave thy labor to him?
Wilt thou believe him, that he will bring home thy seed,
    and gather it into thy barn?

"Gavest thou the goodly wings unto the peacocks?
    or wings and feathers unto the ostrich?
Which leaveth her eggs in the earth,
    and warmeth them in dust,
And forgetteth that the foot may crush them,
    or that the wild beast may break them.
She is hardened against her young ones, as though they were not hers:
    her labor is in vain without fear;
Because God hath deprived her of wisdom,
    neither hath he imparted to her understanding.
What time she lifteth up herself on high,
    she scorneth the horse and his rider.

"Hast thou given the horse strength?
    hast thou clothed his neck with thunder?
Canst thou make him afraid as a grasshopper?
    the glory of his nostrils is terrible.
He paweth in the valley, and rejoiceth in his strength:
    he goeth on to meet the armed men.
He mocketh at fear, and is not affrighted;
    neither turneth he back from the sword.
The quiver rattleth against him,
    the glittering spear and the shield.
He swalloweth the ground with fierceness and rage:
    neither believeth he that it is the sound of the trumpet.
He saith among the trumpets, 'Ha, ha';
    and he smelleth the battle afar off,
    the thunder of the captains, and the shouting.

"Doth the hawk fly by thy wisdom,
    and stretch her wings toward the south?

[20] Or wild ox.

Doth the eagle mount up at thy command,
    and make her nest on high?
She dwelleth and abideth on the rock,
    upon the crag of the rock, and the strong place.
From thence she seeketh the prey,
    and her eyes behold afar off.
Her young ones also suck up blood:
    and where the slain are, there is she."

CHAPTER 40

Moreover the Lord answered Job, and said,

"Shall he that contendeth with the Almighty instruct him?
He that reproveth God, let him answer it."

Then Job answered the Lord, and said,

"Behold, I am vile; what shall I answer thee?
    I will lay mine hand upon my mouth.
Once have I spoken; but I will not answer:
    yea, twice; but I will proceed no further."

Then answered the Lord unto Job out of the whirlwind, and said,

"Gird up thy loins now like a man:
    I will demand of thee, and declare thou unto me.
Wilt thou also disannul my judgment?
    wilt thou condemn me, that thou mayest be righteous?
Hast thou an arm like God?
    or canst thou thunder with a voice like him?

"Deck thyself now with majesty and excellency;
    and array thyself with glory and beauty.
Cast abroad the rage of thy wrath:
    and behold every one that is proud, and abase him.
Look on every one that is proud, and bring him low;
    and tread down the wicked in their place.
Hide them in the dust together;
    and bind their faces in secret.
Then will I also confess unto thee
    that thine own right hand can save thee.

"Behold now behemoth,[21] which I made with thee;
    he eateth grass as an ox.
Lo now, his strength is in his loins,
    and his force is in the navel of his belly.

[21] Probably the hippopotamus, here presented as a primeval monster.

He moveth his tail like a cedar:
    the sinews of his stones are wrapped together.
His bones are as strong pieces of brass;
    his bones are like bars of iron.

"He is the chief of the ways of God:
    he that made him can make his sword to approach unto him.
Surely the mountains bring him forth food,
    where all the beasts of the field play.
He lieth under the shady trees,
    in the covert of the reed, and fens.
The shady trees cover him with their shadow;
    the willows of the brook compass him about.
Behold, he drinketh up a river, and hasteth not:
    he trusteth that he can draw up Jordan into his mouth.
He taketh it with his eyes:
    his nose pierceth through snares."

CHAPTER 41

"Canst thou draw out leviathan[22] with an hook?
    or his tongue with a cord which thou lettest down?
Canst thou put an hook into his nose?
    or bore his jaw through with a thorn?
Will he make many supplications unto thee?
    will he speak soft words unto thee?
Will he make a covenant with thee?
    wilt thou take him for a servant for ever?
Wilt thou play with him as with a bird?
    or wilt thou bind him for thy maidens?
Shall the companions make a banquet of him?
    shall they part him among the merchants?
Canst thou fill his skin with barbed irons?
    or his head with fish spears?
Lay thine hand upon him,
    remember the battle, do no more.
Behold, the hope of him is in vain:
    shall not one be cast down even at the sight of him?
None is so fierce that dare stir him up:
    who then is able to stand before me?
Who hath prevented me, that I should repay him?
    whatsoever is under the whole heaven is mine.

"I will not conceal his parts,
    nor his power, nor his comely proportion.
Who can discover the face of his garment?
    or who can come to him with his double bridle?

---

[22] A mythological version of the crocodile, here presented as a sea monster emblematic of primeval chaos.

Who can open the doors of his face?
  his teeth are terrible round about.
His scales are his pride,
  shut up together as with a close seal.
One is so near to another,
  that no air can come between them.
They are joined one to another,
  they stick together, that they cannot be sundered.
By his neesings[23] a light doth shine,
  and his eyes are like the eyelids of the morning.
Out of his mouth go burning lamps,
  and sparks of fire leap out.
Out of his nostrils goeth smoke,
  as out of a seething pot or caldron.
His breath kindleth coals,
  and a flame goeth out of his mouth.
In his neck remaineth strength,
  and sorrow is turned into joy before him.
The flakes of his flesh are joined together:
  they are firm in themselves; they cannot be moved.
His heart is as firm as a stone;
  yea, as hard as a piece of the nether millstone.
When he raiseth up himself, the mighty are afraid:
  by reason of breakings they purify themselves.
The sword of him that layeth at him cannot hold:
  the spear, the dart, nor the habergeon.
He esteemeth iron as straw,
  and brass as rotten wood.
The arrow cannot make him flee:
  slingstones are turned with him into stubble.
Darts are counted as stubble:
  he laugheth at the shaking of a spear.
Sharp stones are under him:
  he spreadeth sharp pointed things upon the mire.
He maketh the deep to boil like a pot:
  he maketh the sea like a pot of ointment.
He maketh a path to shine after him;
  one would think the deep to be hoary.
Upon earth there is not his like,
  who is made without fear.
He beholdeth all high things:
  he is a king over all the children of pride."

CHAPTER 42

Then Job answered the Lord, and said,

"I know that thou canst do every thing,

[23] Sneezes (which send out drops of water reflecting the sun).

and that no thought can be withholden from thee.
'Who is he that hideth counsel without knowledge?'
Therefore have I uttered that I understood not;
    things too wonderful for me, which I knew not.
'Hear, I beseech thee, and I will speak:
    I will demand of thee, and declare thou unto me.'
I have heard of thee by the hearing of the ear:
    but now mine eye seeth thee.
Wherefore I abhor myself, and repent
    in dust and ashes."

And it was so, that after the Lord had spoken these words unto Job, the Lord said to Eliphaz the Temanite, "My wrath is kindled against thee, and against thy two friends: for ye have not spoken of me the thing that is right, as my servant Job hath. Therefore take unto you now seven bullocks and seven rams, and go to my servant Job, and offer up for yourselves a burnt offering; and my servant Job shall pray for you: for him will I accept: lest I deal with you after your folly, in that ye have not spoken of me the thing which is right, like my servant Job." So Eliphaz the Temanite and Bildad the Shuhite and Zophar the Naamathite went, and did according as the Lord commanded them: the Lord also accepted Job. And the Lord turned the captivity of Job, when he prayed for his friends: also the Lord gave Job twice as much as he had before. Then came there unto him all his brethren, and all his sisters, and all they that had been of his acquaintance before, and did eat bread with him in his house: and they bemoaned him, and comforted him over all the evil that the Lord had brought upon him: every man also gave him a piece of money, and every one an earring of gold. So the Lord blessed the latter end of Job more than his beginning: for he had fourteen thousand sheep, and six thousand camels, and a thousand yoke of oxen, and a thousand she asses. He had also seven sons and three daughters. And he called the name of the first, Jemima; and the name of the second, Kezia; and the name of the third, Keren-happuch. And in all the land were no women found so fair as the daughters of Job: and their father gave them inheritance among their brethren. After this lived Job an hundred and forty years, and saw his sons, and his sons' sons, even four generations. So Job died, being old and full of days.

from PSALMS

PSALM 8

1   O Lord our Lord,[1]
        how excellent is thy name in all the earth!
        who has set thy glory above the heavens.

[1] Numbers in left margin are biblical verse numbers.

2   Out of the mouth of babes and sucklings[2] hast thou ordained
                strength
            because of thine enemies,
            that thou mightest still the enemy and the avenger.

3   When I consider thy heavens, the work of thy fingers,
            the moon and the stars, which thou hast ordained;
4   What is man, that thou art mindful of him?
            and the son of man,[3] that thou visitest him?

5   For thou hast made him a little lower than the angels,
            and hast crowned him with glory and honor.
6   Thou madest him to have dominion over the works of thy hands;
            thou hast put all things under his feet:
7   All sheep and oxen,
            yea, and the beasts of the field;
8   The fowl of the air, and the fish of the sea,
            and whatsoever passeth through the paths of the sea.

9   O Lord our Lord,
            how excellent is thy name in all the earth!

PSALM 23

1   The Lord is my shepherd;
            I shall not want.
2   He maketh me to lie down in green pastures:
            he leadeth me beside the still waters.
3   He restoreth my soul:
            he leadeth me in the paths of righteousness for his name's sake.

4   Yea, though I walk through the valley of the shadow of death,
            I will fear no evil: for thou art with me;
            thy rod and thy staff[4] they comfort me.

5   Thou preparest a table before me in the presence of mine enemies:
            thou anointest my head with oil;
            my cup runneth over.[5]
6   Surely goodness and mercy shall follow me all the days of my life:
            and I will dwell in the house of the Lord for ever.[6]

PSALM 91

1   He that dwelleth in the secret place of the Most High[7]
            shall abide under the shadow of the Almighty.

[2] Infants at the breast.   [3] "Son of man" means any individual person.
[4] The rod keeps off enemies; the staff is an emblem of protection.
[5] In verse 5, the metaphor shifts; God is a host lavishing attentions on a dinner guest.
[6] One possible meaning is "I will spend my life worshiping in God's temple."
[7] Dwells in God's presence, or perhaps, more specifically, in the Temple.

2   I will say of the Lord, He is my refuge and my fortress:
       my God; in him will I trust.

3   Surely he shall deliver thee from the snare of the fowler,[8]
       and from the noisome[9] pestilence.

4   He shall cover thee with his feathers,
       and under his wings shalt thou trust:
       his truth shall be thy shield and buckler.[10]

5   Thou shalt not be afraid for the terror by night;
       nor for the arrow that flieth by day;

6   Nor for the pestilence that walketh in darkness;
       nor for the destruction that wasteth at noonday.

7   A thousand shall fall[11] at thy side,
       and ten thousand at thy right hand;
       but it shall not come nigh thee.

8   Only with thine eyes shalt thou behold
       and see the reward of the wicked.

9   Because thou hast made the Lord, which is my refuge,
       even the Most High, thy habitation;

10   There shall no evil befall thee,
       neither shall any plague come nigh thy dwelling.

11   For he shall give his angels charge over thee,
       to keep thee in all thy ways.

12   They shall bear thee up in their hands,
       lest thou dash thy foot against a stone.

13   Thou shalt tread upon the lion and adder:
       the young lion and the dragon shalt thou trample under feet.

14   Because he hath set his love upon me,[12]
       therefore will I deliver him:
       I will set him on high, because he hath known my name.

15   He shall call upon me, and I will answer him:
       I will be with him in trouble;
       I will deliver him, and honor him.

16   With long life will I satisfy him,
       and show him my salvation.

PSALM 103

1   Bless the Lord, O my soul:
       and all that is within me, bless his holy name.

2   Bless the Lord, O my soul,
       and forget not all his benefits:

3   Who forgiveth all thine iniquities;
       Who healeth all thy diseases;

---

[8] Hunter of game birds.   [9] Harmful.   [10] Shield; defense.
[11] Shall be stricken by the plague.   [12] Verses 14–16 are thought of as spoken by God.

4   Who redeemeth thy life from destruction;
        who crowneth thee with loving-kindness and tender mercies;

5   Who satisfieth thy mouth with good things;
        so that thy youth is renewed like the eagle's.

6   The Lord executeth righteousness
        and judgment for all that are oppressed.

7   He made known his ways unto Moses,
        his acts unto the children of Israel.

8   The Lord is merciful and gracious,
        slow to anger, and plenteous in mercy.

9   He will not always chide:
        neither will he keep his anger for ever.

10   He hath not dealt with us after[13] our sins;
        nor rewarded us according to our iniquities.

11   For as the heaven is high above the earth,
        so great is his mercy toward them that fear him.

12   As far as the east is from the west,
        so far hath he removed our transgressions from us.

13   Like as a father pitieth his children,
        so the Lord pitieth them that fear him.

14   For he knoweth our frame;
        he remembereth that we are dust.

15   As for man, his days are as grass:
        as a flower of the field, so he flourisheth.

16   For the wind passeth over it, and it is gone;
        and the place thereof shall know it no more.

17   But the mercy of the Lord is from everlasting to everlasting
        upon them that fear him,
        and his righteousness unto children's children;

18   To such as keep his covenant,
        and to those that remember his commandments to do them.

19   The Lord hath prepared his throne[14] in the heavens;
        and his kingdom ruleth over all.

20   Bless the Lord, ye his angels, that excel in strength,
        that do his commandments, hearkening unto the voice of his
           word.

21   Bless ye the Lord, all ye his hosts;
        ye ministers of his, that do his pleasure.

22   Bless the Lord, all his works in all places of his dominion:
        bless the Lord, O my soul.

PSALM 114

1   When Israel went out of Egypt,
        the house of Jacob from a people of strange language;

---

[13] In proportion to.   [14] Established His (God's own) throne.

2   Judah was his sanctuary,
           and Israel[15] his dominion.

3   The sea saw it,[16] and fled:
           Jordan was driven back.
4   The mountains skipped like rams,
           and the little hills like lambs.

5   What ailed thee, O thou sea, that thou fleddest?
           thou Jordan, that thou wast driven back?
6   Ye mountains, that ye skipped like rams;
           and ye little hills, like lambs?

7   Tremble, thou earth, at the presence of the Lord,
           at the presence of the God of Jacob;
8   Which turned the rock into a standing water,[17]
           the flint into a fountain of waters.

PSALM 130

1   Out of the depths have I cried unto thee, O Lord.
2   Lord, hear my voice:
           let thine ears be attentive to the voice of my supplications.

3   If thou, Lord, shouldest mark iniquities,
           O Lord, who shall stand?
4   But there is forgiveness with thee,
           that thou mayest be feared.

5   I wait for the Lord,
           my soul doth wait, and in his word do I hope.
6   My soul waiteth for the Lord more than they that watch for the
               morning:
           I say, more than they that watch for the morning.

7   Let Israel hope in the Lord:
           for with the Lord there is mercy,
           and with him is plenteous redemption.
8   And he shall redeem Israel from all his iniquities.

[15] Judah was the southern kingdom of Palestine, settled by the tribes of Judah and Benjamin; Israel was the northern kingdom, settled by the tribes descended from Jacob's ten other sons.
[16] Saw God's presence. The reference is to the miraculous dividing of the waters when the Hebrews escaped from Egypt (Exodus 14); Jordan, in the following line, is the river crossed by the Hebrews forty years later, when they entered the Promised Land (Joshua 3). The Jordan too was miraculously dried up to allow a crossing.
[17] A pool. During the Hebrews' forty years of wandering, God empowered Moses to draw water from a rock by striking it with his staff (Exodus 17).

PSALM 137

1   By the rivers of Babylon,[18] there we sat down,
        yea, we wept, when we remembered Zion.
2   We hanged our harps upon the willows in the midst thereof.
3   For there they that carried us away captive required of us a song;
        and they that wasted[19] us required of us mirth, saying,
        Sing us one of the songs of Zion.
4   How shall we sing the Lord's song in a strange land?

5   If I forget thee, O Jerusalem,
        let my right hand forget her cunning.
6   If I do not remember thee,
        let my tongue cleave to the roof of my mouth;
        if I prefer not Jerusalem above my chief joy.

7   Remember, O Lord, the children of Edom[20]
        in the day of Jerusalem;
        who said, Rase[21] it, rase it,
        even to the foundation thereof.
8   O daughter of Babylon, who are to be destroyed;
        happy shall he be, that rewardeth thee as thou hast served us.
9   Happy shall he be, that taketh and dasheth
        thy little ones against the stones.

PSALM 139

1   O Lord, thou hast searched me, and known me.
2   Thou knowest my downsitting and mine uprising;
        thou understandest my thought afar off.
3   Thou compassest my path and my lying down,
        and art acquainted with all my ways.
4   For there is not a word in my tongue,
        but, lo, O Lord, thou knowest it altogether.
5   Thou hast beset me behind and before,
        and laid thine hand upon me.
6   Such knowledge is too wonderful for me;
        it is high, I cannot attain unto it.

7   Whither shall I go from thy Spirit?
        or whither shall I flee from thy presence?
8   If I ascend up into heaven, thou art there:
        if I make my bed in hell,[22] behold, thou art there.

---

[18] The irrigation canals of the Tigris and Euphrates rivers, in Babylonia. The Babylonians conquered the Hebrews' homeland (Zion) in 597 B.C., inaugurating sixty years of exile and captivity.
[19] Laid waste.
[20] A land south of the Dead Sea; an ally of the Babylonians in the sack of Jerusalem.
[21] Raze; demolish.
[22] Sheol, the place of the dead (roughly equivalent to the Greek Hades).

9   If I take the wings of the morning,[23]
        and dwell in the uttermost parts of the sea;
10   Even there shall thy hand lead me,
        and thy right hand shall hold me.
11   If I say, Surely the darkness shall cover me;
        even the night shall be light about me.
12   Yea, the darkness hideth not from thee;
        but the night shineth as the day:
        the darkness and the light are both alike to thee.

13   For thou hast possessed my reins:[24]
        thou has covered me in my mother's womb.
14   I will praise thee; for I am fearfully and wonderfully made:
        marvelous are thy works; and that my soul knoweth right well.
15   My substance was not hid from thee
        when I was made in secret,
        and curiously wrought in the lowest parts of the earth.[25]
16   Thine eyes did see my substance, yet being unperfect;
        and in thy book all my members were written,
        which in continuance were fashioned,
        when as yet there was none of them.
17   How precious also are thy thoughts unto me, O God!
        How great is the sum of them!
18   If I should count them, they are more in number than the sand:
        when I awake, I am still with thee.

19   Surely thou wilt slay the wicked, O God:
        depart from me therefore, ye bloody men.
20   For they speak against thee wickedly,
        and thine enemies take thy name in vain.
21   Do not I hate them, O Lord, that hate thee?
        And am not I grieved with those that rise up against thee?
22   I hate them with perfect hatred:
        I count them mine enemies.
23   Search me, O God, and know my heart:
        try me, and know my thoughts:
24   And see if there be any wicked way in me,
        and lead me in the way everlasting.

JONAH

Now the word of the Lord came unto Jonah[1] the son of Amittai, saying,
"Arise, go to Nineveh, that great city, and cry against it; for their wickedness is come up before me." But Jonah rose up to flee unto Tarshish from
the presence of the Lord, and went down to Joppa; and he found a ship

---

[23] Travel as fast as the dawn spreads.
[24] "Didst form my inward parts" (Revised Standard Version).
[25] A metaphor for the womb.
[1] The name Jonah means "dove," the symbol of Israel.

going to Tarshish: so he paid the fare thereof, and went down into it, to go with them unto Tarshish from the presence of the Lord.

But the Lord sent out a great wind into the sea, and there was a mighty tempest in the sea, so that the ship was like to be broken. Then the mariners were afraid, and cried every man unto his god, and cast forth the wares that were in the ship into the sea, to lighten it of them. But Jonah was gone down into the sides of the ship; and he lay, and was fast asleep. So the shipmaster came to him, and said unto him, "What meanest thou, O sleeper? arise, call upon thy God, if so be that God will think upon us, that we perish not."

And they said every one to his fellow, "Come, and let us cast lots, that we may know for whose cause this evil is upon us." So they cast lots, and the lot fell upon Jonah. Then said they unto him, "Tell us, we pray thee, for whose cause this evil is upon us; what is thine occupation? and whence comest thou? what is thy country; and of what people art thou?" And he said unto them, "I am a Hebrew; and I fear the Lord, the God of heaven, which hath made the sea and the dry land." Then were the men exceedingly afraid, and said unto him, "Why hast thou done this?" For the men knew that he fled from the presence of the Lord, because he had told them.

Then said they unto him, "What shall we do unto thee, that the sea may be calm unto us?" for the sea wrought, and was tempestuous. And he said unto them, "Take me up, and cast me forth into the sea; so shall the sea be calm unto you: for I know that for my sake this great tempest is upon you." Nevertheless the men rowed hard to bring it to the land; but they could not: for the sea wrought, and was tempestuous against them. Wherefore they cried unto the Lord, and said, "We beseech thee, O Lord, we beseech thee, let us not perish for this man's life, and lay not upon us innocent blood: for thou, O Lord, hast done as it pleased thee." So they took up Jonah, and cast him forth into the sea: and the sea ceased from her raging. Then the men feared the Lord exceedingly, and offered a sacrifice unto the Lord, and made vows.

Now the Lord had prepared a great fish to swallow up Jonah. And Jonah was in the belly of the fish three days and three nights. Then Jonah prayed unto the Lord his God out of the fish's belly and said,

> "I cried by reason of mine affliction unto the Lord,
>   and he heard me;
> Out of the belly of hell cried I,
>   and thou heardest my voice.
> For thou hadst cast me into the deep,
>   in the midst of the seas;
>   and the floods compassed me about:
>   all thy billows and thy waves passed over me.
> Then I said, 'I am cast out of thy sight;
>   yet I will look again toward thy holy temple.'
> The waters compassed me about, even to the soul:
>   the depth closed me round about,
> The weeds were wrapped about my head.
>   I went down to the bottoms of the mountains;
>   the earth with her bars was about me for ever:

> Yet hast thou brought up my life from corruption,
> O Lord my God.
> When my soul fainted within me
> I remembered the Lord:
> And my prayer came in unto thee,
> into thine holy temple.
> They that observe lying vanities
> forsake their own mercy.
> But I will sacrifice unto thee
> with the voice of thanksgiving;
> I will pay that that I have vowed;
> salvation is of the Lord."

And the Lord spoke unto the fish, and it vomited out Jonah upon the dry land.

And the word of the Lord came unto Jonah the second time, saying, "Arise, go unto Nineveh, that great city, and preach unto it the preaching that I bid thee." So Jonah arose, and went unto Nineveh, according to the word of the Lord. Now Nineveh was an exceedingly great city of three days' journey. And Jonah began to enter into the city a day's journey, and he cried, and said, "Yet forty days, and Nineveh shall be overthrown." So the people of Nineveh believed God, and proclaimed a fast, and put on sackcloth,[2] from the greatest of them even to the least of them.

For word came unto the king of Nineveh, and he arose from his throne, and he laid his robe from him, and covered him with sackcloth, and sat in ashes. And he caused it to be proclaimed and published through Nineveh by the decree of the king and his nobles, saying, "Let neither man nor beast, herd nor flock, taste any thing: let them not feed, nor drink water: but let man and beast be covered with sackcloth, and cry mightily unto God: yea, let them turn every one from his evil way, and from the violence that is in their hands. Who can tell if God will turn and repent, and turn away from his fierce anger, that we perish not?"

And God saw their works, that they turned from their evil way; and God repented of the evil that he had said that he would do unto them; and he did it not.

But it displeased Jonah exceedingly, and he was very angry. And he prayed unto the Lord, and said, "I pray thee, O Lord, was not this my saying, when I was yet in my country? Therefore I fled before unto Tarshish: for I knew that thou art a gracious God, and merciful, slow to anger, and of great kindness, and repentest thee of the evil. Therefore now, O Lord, take, I beseech thee, my life from me; for it is better for me to die than to live." Then said the Lord, "Doest thou well to be angry?" So Jonah went out of the city, and sat on the east side of the city, and there made him a booth, and sat under it in the shadow, till he might see what would become of the city.

And the Lord God prepared a gourd, and made it to come up over Jonah, that it might be a shadow over his head, to deliver him from his grief. So Jonah was exceeding glad of the gourd. But God prepared a

---

[2] A garment made of coarse goat or camel's hair, worn as a sign of mourning or penitence.

worm when the morning rose the next day, and it smote the gourd that it withered. And it came to pass, when the sun did arise, that God prepared a vehement east wind; and the sun beat upon the head of Jonah, that he fainted, and wished in himself to die, and said, "It is better for me to die than to live." And God said to Jonah, "Doest thou well to be angry for the gourd?" And he said, "I do well to be angry, even unto death." Then said the Lord, "Thou hast had pity on the gourd, for the which thou hast not labored, neither madest it grow; which came up in a night, and perished in a night. And should not I spare Nineveh, that great city, wherein are more than sixscore thousand persons, that cannot discern between their right hand and their left hand; and also much cattle?"

Homer
(Eighth Century B.C.)

Like the Bible, Homer's Iliad *and* Odyssey *are fundamental sources of the culture and literature of the Western world. These epics have been revered not only as masterpieces of language and narrative but also as expressions of central truths about human beings and their place in the scheme of things. They grow out of a story the elements of which are as follows: While a guest at the palace of Meneláos (*Menelaus *in the more familiar English spelling), who was King of Sparta in southern Greece, the Trojan prince Paris fell in love with Helen, his host's supremely beautiful wife, and carried her off to Troy, apparently with her consent. Under the command of Meneláos' brother Agamémnon, the Greeks organized an army and sailed to Troy in order to recapture Helen, to avenge the dishonor of her husband, and to punish Paris for his violation of the sacred code of hospitality. But, despite outnumbering the Trojans, the Greeks were long frustrated in their attempt to take the city, which was to fall only after ten years of siege. The* Iliad *focuses on one important episode in the war, a quarrel between Agamémnon and Akhilleus (Achilles) over ownership of a prisoner slave-girl. The epic then records the tragic consequences of the quarrel: it describes the death of Akhilleus' beloved companion Patróklos (Patroclus) while Akhilleus was sulking on the sidelines and the subsequent revenge taken by Akhilleus on the Trojan hero Hektor (Hector), who had killed his friend. The action of the* Odyssey *takes place after the war is over. The poem concentrates on one of the foremost Greek warriors against Troy, the resourceful Odysseus, who must overcome many obstacles and tribulations in order to return to his wife and homeland. The actual fall of Troy is not described in either of the two Homeric poems. (One ancient account of the city's fall was written many centuries later by the Roman poet Virgil in his* Aeneid, Book II.)*

Again like the Bible, the two Homeric epics have for centuries caused controversy. Debates continue today as strongly as ever. To say that the Iliad *and* Odyssey *were written by Homer is in fact almost a nonstatement, since the meaning of its very terms is ambiguous. What exactly* are *the two poems? Are some parts more authentic than others? Were they composed as wholes or did they evolve? Was Homer a real person or is his name merely a convenient label for a legendary figure or group? Are both poems the work of the same author? If he was an individual, when and where did he live? At what stage of their history were the poems (originally meant to be sung or recited) put into the written form we know? To what extent does the written version preserve the oral version? Were Troy and the Trojan war as described in the* Iliad *historical? Many of these questions, some of which date to early antiquity, still cannot be answered with complete certainty.*

Some probabilities have emerged, however. In the later nineteenth century, the great amateur archaeologist Heinrich Schliemann proved by his excavations that Troy did indeed once exist. A war similar to the one Homer describes probably did occur, around the early twelfth century B.C. Most authorities now believe also that Homer was a single person, who lived around the eighth century B.C. and was a professional bard or minstrel like Demódokos and Phêmios in the Odyssey. *His home-land was probably Ionia, a region south of Troy in Asia Minor (modern Turkey) that faces Greece across the Aegean Sea. Tradition says that he was blind.*

His role in composing the Iliad *and* Odyssey *is harder to define. Undoubtedly he inherited a large store of traditional material that included many prominent incidents and characters of the tale of Troy. He regarded this material as history, and many poems on the subject would have been familiar to him and to his audience. But he probably deserves the main credit at least for shaping and refining this material into the monumental works we know, giving to them the unity, power, and artistry that Aristotle later praised so highly in his* Poetics. *These qualities have caused Homer to be honored as one of the supreme poets of the world. Whether the* Iliad *and* Odyssey *were actually put in written form by him (he lived in an age and place barely emerging from several centuries of illiteracy), were recorded by a scribe to whom he dictated, or were written down only after a considerable period of oral transmission, is still much debated.*

That the Iliad *and* Odyssey *were originally intended to be heard rather than read is the first thing new readers need to know about the poems. The fact explains, for example, the frequent repetitions—of single phrases, of whole lines, and some-times of long passages. Such repetition is characteristic of all forms of oral communi-cation, since—as lecturers, auctioneers, playwrights, and orators know—repetition enhances clarity and helps achieve the desired emphasis. The repetition may even be, as some scholars now believe, a key to the poems' origins, in the oral-formulaic method, a process by which singers improvised by combining traditional phrases with original ones to flesh out a memorized narrative outline. If we ignore the poems' oral manner we put an unnecessary distance between ourselves and their original audi-ence. Moreover, we can misinterpret many of their strategies, especially the "Homeric epithets," the recurrent brief phrases used to describe things or persons. The reader may wonder why Hera, the queen of the gods, is called "white-armed" in some pas-sages and "Goddess of the Golden Chair" in others, where either label (or neither) would seem appropriate, or why Akhilleus is "the great runner" even when he is not running, or why the striking phrase "tamer of horses" should be applied to two different men. The answer is that Homer inserted such phrases in places where they fit the poetic rhythm, even where they are not especially relevant to the narrative context. (The Greek meter, dactyllic hexameter, combines long [—] and short [-] syllables in the pattern* — ˘ ˘ — ˘ ˘ — ˘ ˘ — ˘ ˘ — ˘ ˘ — —, *with certain substitutions permitted.) It is a mistake, then, to read too much into such phrases or to use them to interpret particular passages, even when the phrases do sound appropriate.*

An even more serious error is to look down on Homer as a simple, primitive poet, one whose accomplishments, like those of a precocious child, are impressive mainly because of his early age. In fact, there have been few if any greater artists than Homer. The stories he tells are vivid and powerful in their sweep, but they are also subtle and skillfully shaded. For example, all the principal men in the Iliad, *Greeks and Trojans, are brave in battle, but their styles of bravery are distinctive: Agamémnon is savage, Akhilleus is proud and supremely confident, Hektor is patriotic, Odysseus is pragmatic (as in the* Odyssey *as well). Seemingly fleeting details can be quite significant. When, in Book IV of the* Odyssey, *Telémakhos approaches the palace of Meneláos, one of the king's men hesitates to admit the young man as the code of hospitality would dictate. Meneláos is furious, but we can guess why his man is nervous: years before, another guest named Paris had been welcomed by Meneláos but had gone on to abduct his beautiful wife Helen and thus had set off the entire Trojan war. We must be alert to such subtleties, since Homer's objective manner usually leaves connections unstated. Characterizations are fully individualized. Penélopê in the* Odyssey *is not merely the object of the suitors' lust and greed but also a fully imagined, resourceful wife and woman, a fit mate for the crafty Odysseus. The green young man Telémakhos and the inexperienced but enterprising Phaiákian princess Nausikaa (Nausicaä) are richly realized characters in themselves and also effective foils for Odysseus, the seasoned veteran of life and experience. One of the major achievements of the Homeric poems is that they combine richness of detail and nuance with a masterful control of the poems' general movement and pattern.*

Homer's control results partly, as Aristotle later pointed out, from his careful limiting of his material; the Iliad *treats a single episode in the ten-year Trojan war and the* Odyssey *centers on the troubled homecoming of a single warrior. But the poems have also a far more ambitious aim: to describe as fully as possible the heroic world. Heroism is the theme of both poems. Since the* Iliad *is a tragedy and a war poem, it celebrates the heroism that faces and suffers death. The* Odyssey *is a kind of comedy, and the heroism it celebrates is that of survival, the triumph over death. The* Iliad *derives much of its intensity from its almost claustrophobic atmosphere, its setting confined to a few square miles in and around the besieged city of Troy where thousands of men are cramped together. The closeness of atmosphere is relieved only occasionally by scenes involving the Olympian gods and through similes reminding the audience of the world of nature and peacetime. The* Odyssey *is wholly different. Its geographical vistas are almost endless, taking in the far, romantic reaches of the known and fabled Mediterranean world and even the realm of the dead. In intriguing contrast is the second half of the poem, where the setting narrows to that of a domestic drama on Odysseus' home island. Here the arena of heroism is neither the defeat of an army nor the perils of distant travel but a struggle to reassert private rights to home and property. The suspense of Odysseus' plot against the suitors emerges from a context not of the cosmic but of familiar human detail—a world of good and bad servants, favorite beds, kitchen logistics. In different ways, then, the* Odyssey *is both more panoramic and more intimate than the* Iliad.

The Homeric divinities, similarly, seem both remote and familiar. Their role and relationship to human beings are very difficult to define. In some ways they seem like projections (often in a comic vein) of human activities and the human environment: Poseidon of the sea, Hephaistos of fire and metalworking, Apollo of medicine and archery, Athena of resourcefulness, Aphroditê of love and sex, and so forth. They are thoroughly humanized, and in their rivalries, loyalties, plots, and bickerings they sometimes seem to parody the human beings, on a scale actually smaller than life. On the other hand, they are utterly superior to human beings, in power and above all in their exemption from death. (Paradoxically, the strictest limitation of their power is their inability to share their immortality with their human protégés.) They continually intervene, especially at key moments, to shape the course of events on earth. In doing so they would seem to limit human freedom. Yet the poems also make it clear that men are responsible for their deeds and that they do have choices. The immortals' actions frequently seem to be confirmations rather than causes of what happens; we can say that Odysseus is resourceful because the goddess Athena aids him or that she aids him because, like her, he is resourceful. In any event, the presence of the divinities in the world of the poems emphasizes both the brevity and the urgency of human life and thus enhances our sense of the mystery in the world.

The Iliad *and* Odyssey *are the oldest epics in the Western tradition. Seven centuries after Homer, Virgil creatively imitated and synthesized the two Homeric epics in the* Aeneid, *a story of the Trojan survivors who, under Ainéias, or Aeneas, journeyed like Odysseus through hardships to lay in Italy the foundations of Roman greatness after a battle resembling that in the* Iliad. *Virgil sophisticated the epic, making it a more strictly literary form and using it for doctrinal purposes, as a vehicle for fostering Roman political and religious values. Seventeen hundred years after Virgil, Milton wrote the definitive English epic,* Paradise Lost, *in an attempt to "justify the ways of God to men" and to preach an essentially Christian heroism. Both Milton and Virgil depict a universe governed by an ultimately just providential force, and each either implies or states that his form of heroism has superseded earlier epic values. Each found a model in Homer, despite the vast differences between their metaphysics and Homer's apparent unconcern with it. That indebtedness testifies that Homer was not only a great poet but also one whose vision has universal application.*

FURTHER READING (*prepared by F.S.N.*): A description of the life and culture of pre-Homeric civilization is given by John Chadwick, *The Decipherment of Linear B*, 1960. Howard Clarke's *Homer's Readers*, 1981, surveys clearly what is known of the circumstances under which the Homeric epics were composed. Two recent introductory works on Homer are W. A. Camps, *An Introduction to Homer*, 1980; and Jasper Griffin, *Homer* (in the Past Masters series), 1980. On the Homeric problem, G. S. Kirk, *Homer and the Oral Tradition*, 1976, is useful. A stimulating sampling of essays by artists such as Tolstoy, Pound and Cavafy has been edited by George Steiner and Robert Fagles, *Homer: A Collection of Critical Essays*, 1962; while learned studies by classical scholars such as Bowra, Lord and Blegen have been assembled by Alan J. B. Wace and Frank H. Stubbings, *A Companion to Homer*, 1962. M. I. Finley, *The World of Odysseus*, 1964, discusses the sociology of the *Odyssey*. Charles Taylor, ed., *Essays on the Odyssey: Selected Modern Criticism*, 1963, provides recent interpretations of the work.

THE ODYSSEY

Translated by Robert Fitzgerald

The ten-year war waged by the Greeks against Troy, culminating in the overthrow of the city, is now itself ten years in the past. Helen, whose flight to Troy with the Trojan prince Paris had prompted the Greek expedition to seek revenge and reclaim her, is now home in Sparta, living harmoniously once more with her husband Meneláos (Menelaus). His brother Agamémnon, commander-in-chief of the Greek forces, was murdered on his return from the war by his wife and her paramour. Of the Greek chieftains who have survived both the war and the perilous homeward voyage, all have returned except Odysseus, the crafty and astute ruler of Ithaka (Ithaca), an island in the Aegean Sea off western Greece. Since he is presumed dead, suitors from Ithaka and other regions have overrun his house, paying court to his attractive wife Penélopê, endangering the position of his son Telémakhos (Telemachus), corrupting many of the servants, and literally eating up Odysseus' estate. Penélopê has stalled for time but is finding it increasingly difficult to deny the suitors' demands that she marry one of them; Telémakhos, who is just approaching young manhood, is becoming actively resentful of the indignities suffered by his household.

Many persons and places in the *Odyssey* are best known to readers by their Latinized names, such as *Telemachus*. The present translator has used forms (*Telémakhos*) closer to the Greek spelling and pronunciation. A slanted accent-mark (´) indicates stress; thus *Agamémnon* is accented on the third syllable. A circumflex accent (^) indicates that the vowel sound is long; thus *Kêrês* is pronounced "Care-ace." A dieresis (¨) indicates pronunciation as a separate syllable; thus, *Thoösa* has three syllables rather than two. [*Editors' headnote.*]

BOOK ONE: A GODDESS INTERVENES

Sing in me, Muse, and through me tell the story
of that man skilled in all ways of contending,
the wanderer, harried for years on end,
after he plundered the stronghold
on the proud height of Troy.[1]

                                      He saw the townlands
and learned the minds of many distant men,
and weathered many bitter nights and days
in his deep heart at sea, while he fought only
to save his life, to bring his shipmates home.
But not by will nor valor could he save them,   10
for their own recklessness destroyed them all—
children and fools, they killed and feasted on
the cattle of Lord Hêlios,[2] the Sun,
and he who moves all day through heaven
took from their eyes the dawn of their return.

Of these adventures, Muse, daughter of Zeus,
tell us in our time, lift the great song again.
Begin when all the rest who left behind them
headlong death in battle or at sea
had long ago returned, while he alone still hungered   20
for home and wife. Her ladyship Kalypso
clung to him in her sea-hollowed caves—
a nymph, immortal and most beautiful,
who craved him for her own.

[1] These lines contain the traditional epic "opening formula" that includes the invocation of the inspiring Muse, the statement of the theme, the identification of the hero (in this case Odysseus), and a glance at the significance of the story.
[2] The offense against Hêlios is described in Book XII.

                                    And when long years and seasons
wheeling brought around that point of time
ordained for him to make his passage homeward,
trials and dangers, even so, attended him
even in Ithaka,[3] near those he loved.
Yet all the gods had pitied Lord Odysseus,
all but Poseidon,[4] raging cold and rough   30
against the brave king till he came ashore
at last on his own land.

                                            But now that god

had gone far off among the sunburnt races,
most remote of men, at earth's two verges,
in sunset lands and lands of the rising sun,
to be regaled by smoke of thighbones burning,
haunches of rams and bulls, a hundred fold.
He lingered delighted at the banquet side.

In the bright hall of Zeus upon Olympos
the other gods were all at home, and Zeus,   40
the father of gods and men, made conversation.
For he had meditated on Aigísthos,[5] dead
by the hand of Agamémnon's son, Orestês,
and spoke his thought aloud before them all:

"My word, how mortals take the gods to task!
All their afflictions come from us, we hear.
And what of their own failings? Greed and folly
double the suffering in the lot of man.
See how Aigísthos, for his double portion,
stole Agamémnon's wife and killed the soldier   50
on his homecoming day. And yet Aigísthos
knew that his own doom lay in this. We gods
had warned him, sent down Hermês Argeiphontês,[6]
our most observant courier, to say:
'Don't kill the man, don't touch his wife,
or face a reckoning with Orestês
the day he comes of age and wants his patrimony.'
Friendly advice—but would Aigísthos take it?
Now he has paid the reckoning in full."

[3] Odysseus' island homeland, in the Ionian sea off western Greece (sometimes the spelling is *Ithaca*).

[4] God of the ocean and brother of the chief of the gods who dwelled on Mount Olympos (Olympus), Zeus.

[5] While the Greek commander Agamémnon was away fighting against Troy, Aigísthos (Aegisthus) entered into an adulterous union with Klytaimnéstra (Clytaemnestra), Agamémnon's wife; they murdered Agamémnon upon his return. The murder was later avenged by Orestês, son of Agamémnon and Klytaimnéstra, as is related in Aeschylus' trilogy of plays known as *The Oresteia*.

[6] God of messengers and messenger of the gods; he was also associated sometimes with the wind. "Argeiphontês" connotes brightness or the ability to clear the sky of clouds.

The grey-eyed goddess Athena replied to Zeus: 60

"O Majesty, O Father of us all,
that man is in the dust indeed, and justly.
So perish all who do what he had done.
But my own heart is broken for Odysseus,
the master mind of war, so long a castaway
upon an island in the running sea;
a wooded island, in the sea's middle,
and there's a goddess in the place, the daughter
of one whose baleful mind knows all the deeps
of the blue sea—Atlas,[7] who holds the columns   70
that bear from land the great thrust of the sky.
His daughter will not let Odysseus go,
poor mournful man; she keeps on coaxing him
with her beguiling talk, to turn his mind
from Ithaka. But such desire is in him
merely to see the hearthsmoke leaping upward
from his own island, that he longs to die.
Are you not moved by this, Lord of Olympos?
Had you no pleasure from Odysseus' offerings
beside the Argive[8] ships, on Troy's wide seaboard?   80
O Zeus, what do you hold against him now?"

To this the summoner of cloud replied:

"My child, what strange remarks you let escape you.
Could I forget that kingly man, Odysseus?
There is no mortal half so wise; no mortal
gave so much to the lords of open sky.
Only the god who laps the land in water,
Poseidon, bears the fighter an old grudge
since he poked out the eye of Polyphêmos,
brawniest of the Kyklopês.[9] Who bore   90
that giant lout? Thoösa, daughter of Phorkys,
an offshore sea lord: for this nymph had lain
with Lord Poseidon in her hollow caves.
Naturally, the god, after the blinding—
mind you, he does not kill the man;
he only buffets him away from home.
But come now, we are all at leisure here,
let us take up this matter of his return,
that he may sail. Poseidon must relent
for being quarrelsome will get him nowhere,   100
one god, flouting the will of all the gods."

[7] In myth, Atlas is the titanic being who supports the sky. Here he is described as father of the nymph Kalypso, who is holding Odysseus prisoner on her island, Ogýgia.
[8] The collective name for the Greek forces who fought under Agamémnon against Troy.
[9] The encounter with these one-eyed giants (also spelled *Polyphemus* and *Cyclops*) is described in Book IX.

The grey-eyed goddess Athena answered him:

"O Majesty, O Father of us all,
if it now please the blissful gods
that wise Odysseus reach his home again,
let the Wayfinder, Hermês, cross the sea
to the island of Ogýgia; let him tell
our fixed intent to the nymph with pretty braids,
and let the steadfast man depart for home.
For my part, I shall visit Ithaka   110
to put more courage in the son, and rouse him
to call an assembly of the islanders,
Akhaian[10] gentlemen with flowing hair.
He must warn off that wolf pack of the suitors
who prey upon his flocks and dusky cattle.
I'll send him to the mainland then, to Sparta
by the sand beach of Pylos[11]; let him find
news of his dear father where he may
and win his own renown about the world."

She bent to tie her beautiful sandals on,   120
ambrosial, golden, that carry her over water
or over endless land on the wings of the wind,
and took the great haft of her spear in hand—
that bronzeshod spear this child of Power can use
to break in wrath long battle lines of fighters.

Flashing down from Olympos' height she went
to stand in Ithaka, before the Manor,
just at the doorsill of the court. She seemed
a family friend, the Taphian captain, Mentês,
waiting, with a light hand on her spear.   130
Before her eyes she found the lusty suitors
casting dice inside the gate, at ease
on hides of oxen—oxen they had killed.
Their own retainers made a busy sight
with houseboys, mixing bowls of water and wine,
or sopping water up in sponges, wiping
tables to be placed about in hall,
or butchering whole carcasses for roasting.

Long before anyone else, the prince Telémakhos
now caught sight of Athena—for he, too,   140
was sitting there, unhappy among the suitors,
a boy, daydreaming. What if his great father
came from the unknown world and drove these men
like dead leaves through the place, recovering

[10] In a general sense, "Greek"; more especially, descriptive of men living in a region not far from Ithaka.

[11] A city and region of southern Greece ruled by Nestor, an aged king and counsellor.

honor and lordship in his own domains?
Then he who dreamed in the crowd gazed out at Athena.

Straight to the door he came, irked with himself
to think a visitor had been kept there waiting,
and took her right hand, grasping with his left
her tall bronze-bladed spear. Then he said warmly: 150

"Greetings, stranger! Welcome to our feast.
There will be time to tell your errand later."

He led the way, and Pallas Athena followed
into the lofty hall. The boy reached up
and thrust her spear high in a polished rack
against a pillar, where tough spear on spear
of the old soldier, his father, stood in order.
Then, shaking out a splendid coverlet,
he seated her on a throne with footrest—all
finely carved—and drew his painted armchair   160
near her, at a distance from the rest.
To be amid the din, the suitors' riot,
would ruin his guest's appetite, he thought,
and he wished privacy to ask for news
about his father, gone for years.

                                      A maid
brought them a silver finger bowl and filled it
out of a beautiful spouting golden jug,
then drew a polished table to their side.
The larder mistress with her tray came by
and served them generously. A carver lifted   170
cuts of each roast meat to put on trenchers[12]
before the two. He gave them cups of gold,
and these the steward as he went his rounds
filled and filled again.

                                Now came the suitors,
young bloods trooping in to their own seats
on thrones or easy chairs. Attendants poured
water over their fingers, while the maids
piled baskets full of brown loaves near at hand,
and houseboys brimmed the bowls with wine.
Now they laid hands upon the ready feast   180
and thought of nothing more. Not till desire
for food and drink had left them were they mindful
of dance and song, that are the grace of feasting.
A herald gave a shapely cithern harp
to Phêmios,[13] whom they compelled to sing—
and what a storm he plucked upon the strings
for prelude! High and clear the song arose.

---

[12] Plates.   [13] The house bard, or minstrel.

Telémakhos now spoke to grey-eyed Athena,
his head bent close, so no one else might hear:

"Dear guest, will this offend you, if I speak?   190
It is easy for these men to like these things,
harping and song; they have an easy life,
scot free, eating the livestock of another—
a man whose bones are rotting somewhere now,
white in the rain on dark earth where they lie,
or tumbling in the groundswell of the sea.
If he returned, if these men ever saw him,
faster legs they'd pray for, to a man,
and not more wealth in handsome robes or gold.
But he is lost; he came to grief and perished,   200
and there's no help for us in someone's hoping
he still may come; that sun has long gone down.
But tell me now, and put it for me clearly—
who are you? Where do you come from? Where's your home
and family? What kind of ship is yours,
and what course brought you here? Who are your sailors?
I don't suppose you walked here on the sea.
Another thing—this too I ought to know—
is Ithaka new to you, or were you ever
a guest here in the old days? Far and near   210
friends knew this house; for he whose home it was
had much acquaintance in the world."

                                                              To this

the grey-eyed goddess answered:

                                                           "As you ask,

I can account most clearly for myself.
Mentês I'm called, son of the veteran
Ankhíalos; I rule seafaring Taphos.
I came by ship, with a ship's company,
sailing the winedark[14] sea for ports of call
on alien shores—to Témesê, for copper,
bringing bright bars of iron in exchange.   220
My ship is moored on a wild strip of coast
in Reithron Bight, under the wooded mountain.
Years back, my family and yours were friends,
as Lord Laërtês[15] knows; ask when you see him.
I hear the old man comes to town no longer,
stays up country, ailing, with only one
old woman to prepare his meat and drink
when pain and stiffness take him in the legs
from working on his terraced plot, his vineyard.

[14] This adjective is repeatedly used by Homer to describe the sea. Such "Homeric epithets" are taken as one sign that the *Iliad* and *Odyssey* were designed for oral delivery.
[15] Father of Odysseus. At this point Laërtes is living in retirement on a farm.

As for my sailing here—
the tale was that your father had come home,
therefore I came. I see the gods delay him.
But never in this world is Odysseus dead—
only detained somewhere on the wide sea,
upon some island, with wild islanders;
savages, they must be, to hold him captive.
Well, I will forecast for you, as the gods
put the strong feeling in me—I see it all,
and I'm no prophet, no adept in bird-signs.
He will not, now, be long away from Ithaka,
his father's dear land; though he be in chains
he'll scheme a way to come; he can do anything.

But tell me this now, make it clear to me:
You must be, by your looks, Odysseus' boy?
The way your head is shaped, the fine eyes—yes,
how like him! We took meals like this together
many a time, before he sailed for Troy
with all the lords of Argos in the ships.
I have not seen him since, nor has he seen me."

And thoughtfully Telémakhos replied:

"Friend, let me put it in the plainest way.
My mother says I am his son; I know not
surely. Who has known his own engendering?
I wish at least I had some happy man
as father, growing old in his own house—
but unknown death and silence are the fate
of him that, since you ask, they call my father."

Then grey-eyed Athena said:

                                  "The gods decreed
no lack of honor in this generation:
such is the son Penélopê bore in you.
But tell me now, and make this clear to me:
what gathering, what feast is this? Why here?
A wedding? Revel? At the expense of all?
Not that, I think. How arrogant they seem,
these gluttons, making free here in your house!
A sensible man would blush to be among them."

To this Telémakhos answered:

"Friend, now that you ask about these matters,
our house was always princely, a great house,
as long as he of whom we speak remained here.
But evil days the gods have brought upon it,
making him vanish, as they have, so strangely.

      230

      240

      250

      260

      270

Were his death known, I could not feel such pain—
if he had died of wounds in Trojan country
or in the arms of friends, after the war.
They would have made a tomb for him, the Akhaians,
and I should have all honor as his son.
Instead, the whirlwinds got him, and no glory.
He's gone, no sign, no word of him; and I inherit
trouble and tears—and not for him alone,   280
the gods have laid such other burdens on me.
For now the lords of the islands,
Doulíkhion and Samê, wooded Zakynthos,
and rocky Ithaka's young lords as well,
are here courting my mother; and they use
our house as if it were a house to plunder.
Spurn them she dare not, though she hates that marriage,
nor can she bring herself to choose among them.
Meanwhile they eat their way through all we have,
and when they will, they can demolish me."   290

Pallas Athena was disturbed, and said:

"Ah, bitterly you need Odysseus, then!
High time he came back to engage these upstarts.
I wish we saw him standing helmeted
there in the doorway, holding shield and spear,
looking the way he did when I first knew him.
That was at our house, where he drank and feasted
after he left Ephyra, homeward bound
from a visit to the son of Mérmeris, Ilos.
He took his fast ship down the gulf that time   300
for a fatal drug to dip his arrows in
and poison the bronze points; but young Ilos
turned him away, fearing the gods' wrath.
My father gave it, for he loved him well.
I wish these men could meet the man of those days!
They'd know their fortune quickly: a cold bed.
Aye! but it lies upon the gods' great knees
whether he can return and force a reckoning
in his own house, or not.
                                      If I were you,
I should take steps to make these men disperse.   310
Listen, now, and attend to what I say:
at daybreak call the islanders to assembly,
and speak your will, and call the gods to witness:
the suitors must go scattering to their homes.
Then here's a course for you, if you agree:
get a sound craft afloat with twenty oars
and go abroad for news of your lost father—
perhaps a traveller's tale, or rumored fame
issued from Zeus abroad in the world of men.

Talk to that noble sage at Pylos, Nestor,   320
then go to Meneláos,[16] the red-haired king
at Sparta, last man home of all the Akhaians.
If you should learn your father is alive
and coming home, you could hold out a year.
Or if you learn that he is dead and gone,
then you can come back to your own dear country
and raise a mound for him, and burn his gear,
with all the funeral honors due the man,
and give your mother to another husband.

When you have done all this, or seen it done,   330
it will be time to ponder
concerning these contenders[17] in your house—
how you should kill them, outright or by guile.
You need not bear this insolence of theirs,
you are a child no longer. Have you heard
what glory young Orestês won
when he cut down that two-faced man, Aigísthos,
for killing his illustrious father?
Dear friend, you are tall and well set up, I see;
be brave—you, too—and men in times to come   340
will speak of you respectfully.

                                        Now I must join my ship;
my crew will grumble if I keep them waiting.
Look to yourself; remember what I told you."

Telémakhos replied:

                                        "Friend, you have done me
kindness, like a father to his son,
and I shall not forget your counsel ever.
You must get back to sea, I know, but come
take a hot bath, and rest; accept a gift
to make your heart lift up when you embark—
some precious thing, and beautiful, from me,   350
a keepsake, such as dear friends give their friends."

But the grey-eyed goddess Athena answered him:

"Do not delay me, for I love the sea ways.
As for the gift your heart is set on giving,
let me accept it on my passage home,
and you shall have a choice gift in exchange."

---

[16] Brother of Agamémnon and husband of Helen of Troy. Also spelled *Menelaus*. Helen's elopement with their Trojan guest Paris precipitated the Trojan war.

[17] Suitors for the hand in marriage of the presumably widowed Penélopê, wife of Odysseus.

With this Athena left him
as a bird rustles upward, off and gone.
But as she went she put new spirit in him,
a new dream of his father, clearer now,   360
so that he marvelled to himself
divining that a god had been his guest.
Then godlike in his turn he joined the suitors.

The famous minstrel still sang on before them,
and they sat still and listened, while he sang
that bitter song, the Homecoming of Akhaians—
how by Athena's will they fared from Troy;
and in her high room careful Penélopê,
Ikários' daughter, heeded the holy song.
She came, then, down the long stairs of her house,   370
this beautiful lady, with two maids in train
attending her as she approached the suitors;
and near a pillar of the roof she paused,
her shining veil drawn over across her cheeks,
the two girls close to her and still,
and through her tears spoke to the noble minstrel:

"Phêmios, other spells you know, high deeds
of gods and heroes, as the poets tell them;
let these men hear some other; let them sit
silent and drink their wine. But sing no more   380
this bitter tale that wears my heart away.
It opens in me again the wound of longing
for one incomparable, ever in my mind—
his fame all Hellas[18] knows, and midland Argos."

But Telémakhos intervened and said to her:

"Mother, why do you grudge our own dear minstrel
joy of song, wherever his thought may lead?
Poets are not to blame, but Zeus who gives
what fate he pleases to adventurous men.
Here is no reason for reproof: to sing   390
the news of the Danaans![19] Men like best
a song that rings like morning on the ear.
But you must nerve yourself and try to listen.
Odysseus was not the only one at Troy
never to know the day of his homecoming.
Others, how many others, lost their lives!"

The lady gazed in wonder and withdrew,
her son's clear wisdom echoing in her mind.
But when she had mounted to her rooms again
with her two handmaids, then she fell to weeping   400

---

[18] Greece.   [19] The Greeks who fought against the Trojans.

for Odysseus, her husband. Grey-eyed Athena
presently cast a sweet sleep on her eyes.

Meanwhile the din grew loud in the shadowy hall
as every suitor swore to lie beside her,
but Telémakhos turned now and spoke to them:

"You suitors of my mother! Insolent men,
now we have dined, let us have entertainment
and no more shouting. There can be no pleasure
so fair as giving heed to a great minstrel
like ours, whose voice itself is pure delight.   410
At daybreak we shall sit down in assembly
and I shall tell you—take it as you will—
you are to leave this hall. Go feasting elsewhere,
consume your own stores. Turn and turn about,
use one another's houses. If you choose
to slaughter one man's livestock and pay nothing,
this is rapine; and by the eternal gods
I beg Zeus you shall get what you deserve:
a slaughter here, and nothing paid for it!"

By now their teeth seemed fixed in their under-lips,   420
Telémakhos' bold speaking stunned them so.
Antínoös, Eupeithês' son, made answer:

"Telémakhos, no doubt the gods themselves
are teaching you this high and mighty manner.
Zeus forbid you should be king in Ithaka,[20]
though you are eligible as your father's son."

Telémakhos kept his head and answered him:

"Antínoös, you may not like my answer,
but I would happily be king, if Zeus
conferred the prize. Or do you think it wretched?   430
I shouldn't call it bad at all. A king
will be respected, and his house will flourish.
But there are eligible men enough,
heaven knows, on the island, young and old,
and one of them perhaps may come to power
after the death of King Odysseus.
All I insist on is that I rule our house
and rule the slaves my father won for me."

Eurýmakhos, Pólybos' son, replied:

"Telémakhos, it is on the gods' great knees   440
who will be king in sea-girt Ithaka.

---

[20] At the time of the poem's action, the rulership of most Greek city-states was not automatically passed from father to son.

But keep your property, and rule your house,
and let no man, against your will, make havoc
of your possessions, while there's life on Ithaka.
But now, my brave young friend,
a question or two about the stranger.
Where did your guest come from? Of what country?
Where does he say his home is, and his family?
Has he some message of your father's coming,
or business of his own, asking a favor?   450
He left so quickly that one hadn't time
to meet him, but he seemed a gentleman."

Telémakhos made answer, cool enough:

"Eurýmakhos, there's no hope for my father.
I would not trust a message, if one came,
nor any forecaster my mother invites
to tell by divination of time to come.
My guest, however, was a family friend,
Mentês, son of Ankhíalos.
He rules the Taphian people of the sea."   460

So said Telémakhos, though in his heart
he knew his visitor had been immortal.
But now the suitors turned to play again
with dance and haunting song. They stayed till nightfall,
indeed black night came on them at their pleasure,
and half asleep they left, each for his home.

Telémakhos' bedroom was above the court,
a kind of tower, with a view all round;
here he retired to ponder in the silence,
while carrying brands of pine alight beside him   470
Eurýkleia went padding, sage and old.
Her father had been Ops, Peisênor's son,
and she had been a purchase of Laërtês
when she was still a blossoming girl. He gave
the price of twenty oxen[21] for her, kept her
as kindly in his house as his own wife,
though, for the sake of peace, he never touched her.
No servant loved Telémakhos as she did,
she who had nursed him in his infancy.
So now she held the light, as he swung open   480
the door of his neat freshly painted chamber.
There he sat down, pulling his tunic off,
and tossed it into the wise old woman's hands.
She folded it and smoothed it, and then hung it

---

[21] In the Greek civilization of Homeric times, the ox was a common standard of value.
Articles of clothing, weapons, women taken as war prizes, and servants were evaluated in
terms of how many oxen they were worth.

beside the inlaid bed upon a bar;
then, drawing the door shut by its silver handle
she slid the catch in place and went away.
And all night long, wrapped in the finest fleece,
he took in thought the course Athena gave him.

BOOK TWO: A HERO'S SON AWAKENS

When primal Dawn spread on the eastern sky
her fingers of pink light, Odysseus' true son
stood up, drew on his tunic and his mantle,
slung on a sword-belt and a new-edged sword,
tied his smooth feet into good rawhide sandals,
and left his room, a god's brilliance upon him.
He found the criers with clarion voices and told them
to muster the unshorn[1] Akhaians in full assembly.
The call sang out, and the men came streaming in;
and when they filled the assembly ground, he entered,   10
spear in hand, with two quick hounds at heel;
Athena lavished on him a sunlit grace
that held the eye of the multitude. Old men
made way for him as he took his father's chair.

Now Lord Aigýptios, bent down and sage with years,
opened the assembly. This man's son
had served under the great Odysseus, gone
in the decked ships with him to the wild horse country
of Troy—a spearman, Ántiphos by name.
The ravenous Kyklops in the cave destroyed him[2]   20
last in his feast of men. Three other sons
the old man had, and one, Eurýnomos,
went with the suitors; two farmed for their father;
but even so the old man pined, remembering
the absent one, and a tear welled up as he spoke:

"Hear me, Ithakans! Hear what I have to say.
No meeting has been held here since our king,
Odysseus, left port in the decked ships.
Who finds occasion for assembly, now?
one of the young men? one of the older lot?   30
Has he had word our fighters are returning—[3]
news to report if he got wind of it—
or is it something else, touching the realm?
The man has vigor, I should say; more power to him.
Whatever he desires, may Zeus fulfill it."

---

[1] Having long or flowing hair.   [2] This incident is described in Book IX.
[3] Except for Odysseus and his Ithakans, all the Greek warriors against Troy had by this time returned home or were known to be dead.

The old man's words delighted the son of Odysseus,
who kept his chair no longer but stood up,
eager to speak, in the midst of all the men.
The crier, Peisênor, master of debate,
brought him the staff[4] and placed it in his hand;   40
then the boy touched the old man's shoulder, and said:

"No need to wonder any more, Sir,
who called this session. The distress is mine.
As to our troops returning, I have no news—
news to report if I got wind of it—
nor have I public business to propose;
only my need, and the trouble of my house—
the troubles.

                                    My distinguished father is lost,
who ruled among you once, mild as a father,
and there is now this greater evil still: 50
my home and all I have are being ruined.
Mother wanted no suitors, but like a pack
they came—sons of the best men here among them—
lads with no stomach for an introduction
to Ikários, her father across the sea;
he would require a wedding gift, and give her
to someone who found favor in her eyes.
No; these men spend their days around our house
killing our beeves and sheep and fatted goats,
carousing, soaking up our good dark wine,   60
not caring what they do. They squander everything.
We have no strong Odysseus to defend us,
and as to putting up a fight ourselves—
we'd only show our incompetence in arms.
Expel them, yes, if I only had the power;
the whole thing's out of hand, insufferable.
My house is being plundered: is this courtesy?
Where is your indignation? Where is your shame?
Think of the talk in the islands all around us,
and fear the wrath of the gods,   70
or they may turn, and send you some devilry.
Friends, by Olympian Zeus and holy Justice
that holds men in assembly and sets them free,
make an end of this! Let me lament in peace
my private loss. Or did my father, Odysseus,
ever do injury to the armed Akhaians?
Is this your way of taking it out on me,
giving free rein to these young men?
I might as well—might better—see my treasure
and livestock taken over by you all;   80

[4]The emblem which, placed by the herald in the speaker's hand, gave him the right to
speak as a public official.

then, if you fed on them, I'd have some remedy,
and when we met, in public, in the town,
I'd press my claim; you might make restitution.
This way you hurt me when my hands are tied."

And in hot anger now he threw the staff to the ground,
his eyes grown bright with tears. A wave of sympathy
ran through the crowd, all hushed; and no one there
had the audacity to answer harshly
except Antínoös, who said:

                                        "What high and mighty
talk, Telémakhos! No holding you!   90
You want to shame us, and humiliate us,
but you should know the suitors are not to blame—
it is your own dear, incomparably cunning mother.
For three years now—and it will soon be four—
she has been breaking the hearts of the Akhaians,
holding out hope to all, and sending promises
to each man privately—but thinking otherwise.

Here is an instance of her trickery:
she had her great loom standing in the hall
and the fine warp of some vast fabric on it;   100
we were attending her, and she said to us:
'Young men, my suitors, now my lord is dead,
let me finish my weaving before I marry,
or else my thread will have been spun in vain.
It is a shroud I weave for Lord Laërtês,
when cold death comes to lay him on his bier.
The country wives would hold me in dishonor
if he, with all his fortune, lay unshrouded.'
We have men's hearts; she touched them; we agreed.
So every day she wove on the great loom—   110
but every night by torchlight she unwove it;
and so for three years she deceived the Akhaians.
But when the seasons brought the fourth around,
one of her maids, who knew the secret, told us;
we found her unraveling the splendid shroud.
She had to finish then, although she hated it.

Now here is the suitors' answer—
you and all the Akhaians, mark it well:
dismiss your mother from the house, or make her marry
the man her father names and she prefers.   120
Does she intend to keep us dangling forever?
She may rely too long on Athena's gifts—
talent in handicraft and a clever mind;
so cunning—history cannot show the like
among the ringleted ladies of Akhaia,

Mykênê with her coronet, Alkmênê, Tyro.
Wits like Penélopê's never were before,
but this time—well, she made poor use of them.
For here are suitors eating up your property
as long as she holds out—a plan some god   130
put in her mind. She makes a name for herself,
but you can feel the loss it means for you.
Our own affairs can wait; we'll never go anywhere else,
until she takes an Akhaian to her liking."

But clear-headed Telémakhos replied:

"Antínoös, can I banish against her will
the mother who bore me and took care of me?
My father is either dead or far away,
but dearly I should pay for this
at Ikários' hands, if ever I sent her back.   140
The powers of darkness would requite it, too,
my mother's parting curse would call hell's furies[5]
to punish me, along with the scorn of men.
No: I can never give the word for this.
But if your hearts are capable of shame,
leave my great hall, and take your dinner elsewhere,
consume your own stores. Turn and turn about,
use one another's houses. If you choose
to slaughter one man's livestock and pay nothing,
this is rapine; and by the eternal gods   150
I beg Zeus you shall get what you deserve:
a slaughter here, and nothing paid for it!"

Now Zeus who views the wide world sent a sign to him,
launching a pair of eagles from a mountain crest
in gliding flight down the soft blowing wind,
wing-tip to wing-tip quivering taut, companions;
till high above the assembly of many voices
they wheeled, their dense wings beating, and in havoc
dropped on the heads of the crowd—a deathly omen—
wielding their talons, tearing cheeks and throats;   160
then veered away on the right hand through the city.
Astonished, gaping after the birds, the men
felt their hearts flood, foreboding things to come.
And now they heard the old lord Halithersês,
son of Mastor, keenest among the old
at reading birdflight into accurate speech;
in his anxiety for them, he rose and said:

"Hear me, Ithakans! Hear what I have to say,
and may I hope to open the suitors' eyes

[5] In mythology, the primitive female agents of retribution for evil, especially for evil committed against blood-kindred.

to the black wave towering over them. Odysseus   170
will not be absent from his family long:
he is already near, carrying in him
a bloody doom for all these men, and sorrow
for many more on our high seamark, Ithaka.
Let us think how to stop it; let the suitors
drop their suit; they had better, without delay.
I am old enough to know a sign when I see one,
and I say all has come to pass for Odysseus
as I foretold when the Argives massed on Troy,
and he, the great tactician, joined the rest.   180
My forecast was that after nineteen years,[6]
many blows weathered, all his shipmates lost,
himself unrecognized by anyone,
he would come home. I see this all fulfilled."

But Pólybos' son, Eurýmakhos, retorted:

"Old man, go tell the omens for your children
at home, and try to keep them out of trouble.
I am more fit to interpret this than you are.
Bird life aplenty is found in the sunny air,
not all of it significant. As for Odysseus,   190
he perished far from home. You should have perished with him—
then we'd be spared this nonsense in assembly,
as good as telling Telémakhos to rage on;
do you think you can gamble on a gift from him?
Here is what I foretell, and it's quite certain:
if you, with what you know of ancient lore,
encourage bitterness in this young man,
it means, for him, only the more frustration—
he can do nothing whatever with two eagles—
and as for you, old man, we'll fix a penalty   200
that you will groan to pay.
Before the whole assembly I advise Telémakhos
to send his mother to her father's house;
let them arrange her wedding there, and fix
a portion suitable for a valued daughter.
Until he does this, courtship is our business,
vexing though it may be; we fear no one,
certainly not Telémakhos, with his talk;
and we care nothing for your divining, uncle,
useless talk; you win more hatred by it.   210
We'll share his meat, no thanks or fee to him,
as long as she delays and maddens us.
It is a long, long time we have been waiting
in rivalry for this beauty. We could have gone
elsewhere and found ourselves very decent wives."

[6]These include the ten years of war against Troy.

Clear-headed Telémakhos replied to this:

"Eurýmakhos, and noble suitors all,
I am finished with appeals and argument.
The gods know, and the Akhaians know, these things.
But give me a fast ship and a crew of twenty   220
who will see me through a voyage, out and back.
I'll go to sandy Pylos, then to Sparta,
for news of Father since he sailed from Troy—
some traveller's tale, perhaps, or rumored fame
issued from Zeus himself into the world.
If he's alive, and beating his way home,
I might hold out for another weary year;
but if they tell me that he's dead and gone,
then I can come back to my own dear country
and raise a mound for him, and burn his gear,   230
with all the funeral honors that befit him,
and give my mother to another husband."

The boy sat down in silence. Next to stand
was Mentor, comrade in arms of the prince Odysseus,
an old man now. Odysseus left him authority
over his house and slaves, to guard them well.
In his concern, he spoke to the assembly:

"Hear me, Ithakans! Hear what I have to say.
Let no man holding scepter as a king
be thoughtful, mild, kindly, or virtuous;   240
let him be cruel, and practice evil ways;
it is so clear that no one here remembers
how like a gentle father Odysseus ruled you.
I find it less revolting that the suitors
carry their malice into violent acts;
at least they stake their lives
when they go pillaging the house of Odysseus—
their lives upon it, he will not come again.
What sickens me is to see the whole community
sitting still, and never a voice or a hand raised   250
against them—a mere handful compared with you."

Leókritos, Euênor's son, replied to him:

"Mentor, what mischief are you raking up?
Will this crowd risk the sword's edge over a dinner?
Suppose Odysseus himself indeed
came in and found the suitors at his table:
he might be hot to drive them out. What then?
Never would he enjoy his wife again—
the wife who loves him well; he'd only bring down
abject death on himself against those odds.   260
Madness, to talk of fighting in either case.

Now let all present go about their business!
Halithersês and Mentor will speed the traveller;
they can help him: they were his father's friends.
I rather think he will be sitting here
a long time yet, waiting for news on Ithaka;
that seafaring he spoke of is beyond him."

On this note they were quick to end their parley.
The assembly broke up; everyone went home—
the suitors home to Odysseus' house again.   270
But Telémakhos walked down along the shore
and washed his hands in the foam of the grey sea,
then said this prayer:

                                      "O god of yesterday,
guest in our house, who told me to take ship
on the hazy sea for news of my lost father,
listen to me, be near me:
The Akhaians only wait, or hope to hinder me,
the damned insolent suitors most of all."

Athena was nearby and came to him,
putting on Mentor's figure and his tone,   280
the warm voice in a lucid flight of words:

"You'll never be fainthearted or a fool,
Telémakhos, if you have your father's spirit;
he finished what he cared to say,
and what he took in hand he brought to pass.
The sea routes will yield their distances
to his true son, Penélopê's true son,—
I doubt another's luck would hold so far.
The son is rare who measures with his father,
and one in a thousand is a better man,   290
but you will have the sap and wit
and prudence—for you get that from Odysseus—
to give you a fair chance of winning through.
So never mind the suitors and their ways,
there is no judgment in them, neither do they
know anything of death and the black terror
close upon them—doom's day on them all.
You need not linger over going to sea.
I sailed beside your father in the old days,
I'll find a ship for you, and help you sail her.   300
So go on home, as if to join the suitors,
but get provisions ready in containers—
wine in two-handled jugs and barley meal,
the staying power of oarsmen,
in skin bags, watertight. I'll go the rounds
and call a crew of volunteers together.
Hundreds of ships are beached on sea-girt Ithaka;

let me but choose the soundest, old or new,
we'll rig her and take her out on the broad sea."

This was the divine speech Telémakhos heard   310
from Athena, Zeus's daughter. He stayed no longer,
but took his heartache home,
and found the robust suitors there at work,
skinning goats and roasting pigs in the courtyard.
Antínoös came straight over, laughing at him,
and took him by the hand with a bold greeting:

"High-handed Telémakhos, control your temper!
Come on, get over it, no more grim thoughts,
but feast and drink with me, the way you used to.
The Akhaians will attend to all you ask for—   320
ship, crew, and crossing to the holy land
of Pylos, for the news about your father."

Telémakhos replied with no confusion:

"Antínoös, I cannot see myself again
taking a quiet dinner in this company.
Isn't it enough that you could strip my house
under my very nose when I was young?
Now that I know, being grown, what others say,
I understand it all, and my heart is full.
I'll bring black doom upon you if I can—   330
either in Pylos, if I go, or in this country.
And I will go, go all the way, if only
as someone's passenger. I have no ship,
no oarsmen: and it suits you that I have none."

Calmly he drew his hand from Antínoös hand.
At this the suitors, while they dressed their meat,
began to exchange loud mocking talk about him.
One young toplofty gallant set the tone:

                                        "Well, think of that!

Telémakhos has a mind to murder us.
He's going to lead avengers out of Pylos,   340
or Sparta, maybe; oh, he's wild to do it.
Or else he'll try the fat land of Ephyra—
he can get poison there, and bring it home,
doctor the wine jar and dispatch us all."

Another took the cue:

                                        "Well now, who knows?

He might be lost at sea, just like Odysseus,
knocking around in a ship, far from his friends.
And what a lot of trouble that would give us,
making the right division of his things!

We'd keep his house as dowry for his mother—   350
his mother and the man who marries her."

That was the drift of it. Telémakhos
went on through to the storeroom of his father,
a great vault where gold and bronze lay piled
along with chests of clothes, and fragrant oil.
And there were jars of earthenware in rows
holding an old wine,
mellow, unmixed, and rare; cool stood the jars
against the wall, kept for whatever day
Odysseus, worn by hardships, might come home.   360
The double folding doors were tightly locked
and guarded, night and day, by the serving woman,
Eurýkleia, grand-daughter of Peisênor,
in all her duty vigilant and shrewd.
Telémakhos called her to the storeroom, saying:

"Nurse, get a few two-handled travelling jugs
filled up with wine—the second best, not that
you keep for your unlucky lord and king,
hoping he may have slipped away from death
and may yet come again—royal Odysseus.   370
Twelve amphorai[7] will do; seal them up tight.
And pour out barley into leather bags—
twenty bushels of barley meal ground fine.
Now keep this to yourself! Collect these things,
and after dark, when mother has retired
and gone upstairs to bed, I'll come for them.
I sail to sandy Pylos, then to Sparta,
to see what news there is of Father's voyage."

His loving nurse Eurýkleia gave a cry,
and tears sprang to her eyes as she wailed softly: 380

"Dear child, whatever put this in your head?
Why do you want to go so far in the world—
and you our only darling? Lord Odysseus
died in some strange place, far from his homeland.
Think how, when you have turned your back, these men
will plot to kill you and share all your things!
Stay with your own, dear, do. Why should you suffer
hardship and homelessness on the wild sea?"

But seeing all clear, Telémakhos replied:

"Take heart, Nurse, there's a god behind this plan.   390
And you must swear to keep it from my mother,
until the eleventh day, or twelfth, or till

---

[7] Plural form of "amphora," a jar with two handles and a thin neck.

she misses me, or hears that I am gone.
She must not tear her lovely skin lamenting."

So the old woman vowed by all the gods,
and vowed again, to carry out his wishes;
then she filled up the amphorai with wine
and sifted barley meal into leather bags.
Telémakhos rejoined the suitors.

                                                    Meanwhile

the goddess with grey eyes had other business: 400
disguised as Telémakhos, she roamed the town
taking each likely man aside and telling him:
"Meet us at nightfall at the ship!" Indeed,
she asked Noêmon, Phronios' wealthy son,
to lend her a fast ship, and he complied.
Now when at sundown shadows crossed the lanes
she dragged the cutter to the sea and launched it,
fitted out with tough seagoing gear,
and tied it up, away at the harbor's edge.
The crewmen gathered, sent there by the goddess.   410
Then it occurred to the grey-eyed goddess Athena
to pass inside the house of the hero Odysseus,
showering a sweet drowsiness on the suitors,
whom she had presently wandering in their wine;
and soon, as they could hold their cups no longer,
they straggled off to find their beds in town,
eyes heavy-lidded, laden down with sleep.
Then to Telémakhos the grey-eyed goddess
appeared again with Mentor's form and voice,
calling him out of the lofty emptied hall: 420

"Telémakhos, your crew of fighting men
is ready at the oars, and waiting for you;
come on, no point in holding up the sailing."

And Pallas Athena turned like the wind, running
ahead of him. He followed in her footsteps
down to the seaside, where they found the ship,
and oarsmen with flowing hair at the water's edge.
Telémakhos, now strong in the magic, cried:

"Come with me, friends, and get our rations down!
They are all packed at home, and my own mother   430
knows nothing!—only one maid was told."

He turned and led the way, and they came after,
carried and stowed all in the well-trimmed ship
as the dear son of Odysseus commanded.
Telémakhos then stepped aboard; Athena
took her position aft, and he sat by her.
The two stroke oars cast off the stern hawsers

and vaulted over the gunnels to their benches.
Grey-eyed Athena stirred them a following wind,
soughing from the north-west on the winedark sea,   440
and as he felt the wind, Telémakhos
called to all hands to break out mast and sail.
They pushed the fir mast high and stepped it firm
amidships in the box, made fast the forestays,
then hoisted up the white sail on its halyards
until the wind caught, booming in the sail;
and a flushing wave sang backward from the bow
on either side, as the ship got way upon her,
holding her steady course.
Now they made all secure in the fast black ship,   450
and, setting out the winebowls all a-brim,
they made libation to the gods,

                            the undying, the ever-new,
most of all to the grey-eyed daughter of Zeus.
And the prow sheared through the night into the dawn.

BOOK THREE: THE LORD OF THE WESTERN APPROACHES

The sun rose on the flawless brimming sea
into a sky all brazen—all one brightening
for gods immortal and for mortal men
on plowlands kind with grain.

                           And facing sunrise
the voyagers now lay off Pylos town,
compact stronghold of Neleus.[1] On the shore
black bulls were being offered by the people
to the blue-maned god who makes the islands tremble:
nine congregations, each five hundred strong,
led out nine bulls apiece to sacrifice,   10
taking the tripes to eat, while on their altars
thighbones in fat lay burning for the god.
Here they put in, furled sail, and beached the ship;
but Telémakhos hung back in disembarking,
so that Athena turned and said:

"Not the least shyness, now, Telémakhos.
You came across the open sea for this—
to find out where the great earth hides your father
and what the doom was that he came upon.
Go to old Nestor, master charioteer,   20
so we may broach the storehouse of his mind.

---

[1] Son of the sea-god Poseidon (the "blue-maned god"), he was the founder of Pylos and the father of Nestor.

Ask him with courtesy, and in his wisdom
he will tell you history and no lies."

But clear-headed Telémakhos replied:

"Mentor, how can I do it, how approach him?
I have no practice in elaborate speeches, and
for a young man to interrogate an old man
seems disrespectful—"

                                            But the grey-eyed goddess said:

"Reason and heart will give you words, Telémakhos;
and a spirit will counsel others. I should say   30
the gods were never indifferent to your life."

She went on quickly, and he followed her
to where the men of Pylos had their altars.
Nestor appeared enthroned among his sons,
while friends around them skewered the red beef
or held it scorching. When they saw the strangers
a hail went up, and all that crowd came forward
calling out invitations to the feast.
Peisístratos in the lead, the young prince,
caught up their hands in his and gave them places   40
on curly lambskins flat on the sea sand
near Thrasymêdês, his brother, and his father;
he passed them bits of the food of sacrifice,
and, pouring wine in a golden cup,
he said to Pallas Athena, daughter of Zeus:

"Friend, I must ask you to invoke Poseidon:
you find us at this feast, kept in his honor.
Make the appointed offering then, and pray,
and give the honeyed winecup to your friend
so he may do the same. He, too,   50
must pray to the gods on whom all men depend,
but he is just my age, you are the senior.
so here, I give the goblet first to you."

And he put the cup of sweet wine in her hand.
Athena liked his manners, and the equity
that gave her precedence with the cup of gold,
so she besought Poseidon at some length:

"Earthshaker, listen and be well disposed.
Grant your petitioners everything they ask:
above all, honor to Nestor and his sons;   60
second, to every man of Pylos town
a fair gift in exchange for this hekatomb;[2]

_____
[2] A grand public sacrifice and offering to the gods.

third, may Telémakhos and I perform
the errand on which last night we put to sea."

This was the prayer of Athena—
granted in every particular by herself.
She passed the beautiful wine cup to Telémakhos,
who tipped the wine and prayed as she had done.
Meanwhile the spits were taken off the fire,
portions of crisp meat for all. They feasted,   70
and when they had eaten and drunk their fill, at last
they heard from Nestor, prince of charioteers:

"Now is the time[3]," he said, "for a few questions,
now that our young guests have enjoyed their dinner.
Who are you, strangers? Where are you sailing from,
and where to, down the highways of sea water?
Have you some business here? or are you, now,
reckless wanderers of the sea, like those corsairs
who risk their lives to prey on other men?"

Clear-headed Telémakhos responded cheerfully,   80
for Athena gave him heart. By her design
his quest for news about his father's wandering
would bring him fame in the world's eyes. So he said:

"Nestor, pride of Akhaians, Neleus' son,
you ask where we are from, and I can tell you:
our home port is under Mount Neion, Ithaka.
We are not here on Ithakan business, though,
but on my own. I want news of my father,
Odysseus, known for his great heart, and I
will comb the wide world for it. People say   90
he fought along with you when Troy was taken.
As to the other men who fought that war,
we know where each one died, and how he died;
but Zeus allotted my father death and mystery.
No one can say for sure where he was killed,
whether some hostile landsmen or the sea,
the stormwaves on the deep sea, got the best of him.
And this is why I come to you for help.
Tell me of his death, sir, if perhaps
you witnessed it, or have heard some wanderer   100
tell the tale. The man was born for trouble.
Spare me no part of it for kindness' sake,
but put the scene before me as you saw it.
If ever Odysseus my noble father
served you by promise kept or work accomplished
in the land of Troy, where you Akhaians suffered,
recall those things for me the way they were."

---

[3] Hospitality required that no such questions be asked of guests until they had been welcomed and fed.

Then Nestor, prince of charioteers, made answer:

"Dear friend, you take me back to all the trouble
we went through in that country, we Akhaians: 110
rough days aboard ship on the cloudy sea
cruising away for pillage after Akhilleus;[4]
rough days of battle around Priam's[5] town.
Our losses, then—so many good men gone:
Arês' great Aias[6] lies there, Akhilleus lies there,
Patróklos,[7] too, the wondrous counselor,
and my own strong and princely son, Antílokhos—
fastest man of them all, and a born fighter.
Other miseries, and many, we endured there.
Could any mortal man tell the whole story?   120
Not if you stayed five years or six to hear
how hard it was for the flower of the Akhaians;
you'd go home weary, and the tale untold.
Think: we were there nine years, and we tried everything,
all stratagems against them,
up to the bitter end that Zeus begrudged us.
And as to stratagems, no man would claim
Odysseus' gift for those. He had no rivals,
your father, at the tricks of war.

                                        Your father?   130

Well, I must say I marvel at the sight of you:
your manner of speech couldn't be more like his;
one would say No; no boy could speak so well.
And all that time at Ilion,[8] he and I
were never at odds in council or assembly—
saw things the same way, had one mind between us
in all the good advice we gave the Argives.
But when we plundered Priam's town and tower
and took to the ships, God scattered the Akhaians.
He had a mind to make homecoming hard for them,
seeing they would not think straight nor behave,   140
or some would not. So evil days came on them,
and she who had been angered,
Zeus's dangerous grey-eyed daughter, did it,
starting a fight between the sons of Atreus.[9]

---

[4] The foremost Greek warrior, central figure of the *Iliad*.   [5] King of Troy.
[6] Another great Greek warrior (also spelled *Ajax*), associated here with Arês, the god
of war.
[7] The closest friend of Akhilleus; it was to avenge his death at the hand of the Trojan
leader Hektor that Akhilleus—as is narrated in the *Iliad*—re-entered the battle and killed
Hektor.
[8] Troy.
[9] Atreus was Father of Agamémnon and Meneláos, the brothers who commanded the
Greek forces. Athena's hostility to the Greeks (whom she generally favored and aided) was
occasioned by outrages committed against the Trojan princess and prophetess Kassandra,
who during the sack of Troy had tried to take refuge at Athena's shrine.

First they were fools enough to call assembly
at sundown, unheard of hour;
the Akhaian soldiers turned out, soaked with wine,
to hear talk, talk about it from their commanders:
Meneláos harangued them to get organized—
time to ride home on the sea's broad back, he said;   150
but Agamémnon wouldn't hear of it. He wanted
to hold the troops, make sacrifice, a hekatomb,
something to pacify Athena's rage.
Folly again, to think that he could move her.
Will you change the will of the everlasting gods
in a night or a day's time?
The two men stood there hammering at each other
until the army got to its feet with a roar,
and no decision, wanting it both ways.
That night no one slept well, everyone cursing   160
someone else. Here was the bane[10] from Zeus.
At dawn we dragged our ships to the lordly water,
stowed aboard all our plunder
and the slave women in their low hip girdles.
But half the army elected to stay behind
with Agamémnon as their corps commander;
the other half embarked and pulled away.
We made good time, the huge sea smoothed before us,
and held our rites when we reached Ténedos,[11]
being wild for home. But Zeus, not willing yet,   170
now cruelly set us at odds a second time,
and one lot turned, put back in the rolling ships,
under command of the subtle captain, Odysseus;
their notion was to please Lord Agamémnon.
Not I. I fled, with every ship I had;
I knew fate had some devilment brewing there.
Diomêdês roused his company and fled, too,
and later Meneláos, the red-haired captain,
caught up with us at Lesbos,
while we mulled over the long sea route, unsure   180
whether to lay our course northward of Khios,
keeping the Isle of Psyria off to port,
or inside Khios, coasting by windy Mimas.
We asked for a sign from heaven, and the sign came
to cut across the open sea to Euboia,
and lose no time putting our ills behind us.
The wind freshened astern, and the ships ran
before the wind on paths of the deep sea fish,

[10] Ruin; poison.
[11] The problem described by Nestor in the following lines is whether the part of the Greek fleet that decided to sail immediately should follow a circuitous course homeward among the islands of the Aegean Sea or head straight across it, by a course that was shorter but farther removed from ports.

making Geraistos before dawn. We thanked Poseidon
with many a charred thighbone for that crossing.   190
On the fourth day, Diomêdês' company
under full sail put in at Argos port,
and I held on for Pylos. The fair wind,
once heaven set it blowing, never failed.

So this, dear child, was how I came from Troy,
and saw no more of the others, lost or saved.
But you are welcome to all I've heard since then
at home; I have no reason to keep it from you.
The Myrmidon spearfighters returned, they say,
under the son of lionhearted Akhilleus;   200
and so did Poias' great son, Philoktêtês.
Idómeneus brought his company back to Krete;[12]
the sea took not a man from him, of all
who lived through the long war.
And even as far away as Ithaka
you've heard of Agamémnon—how he came
home, how Aigísthos waited to destroy him
but paid a bitter price for it in the end.
That is a good thing, now, for a man to leave
a son behind him, like the son who punished   210
Aigísthos for the murder of his great father.
You, too, are tall and well set-up, I see;
be brave, you too, so men in times to come
will speak well of you."

                                                    Then Telémakhos said:

"Nestor, pride of Akhaians, Neleus' son,
that was revenge, and far and wide the Akhaians
will tell the tale in song for generations.
I wish the gods would buckle his arms on me!
I'd be revenged for outrage
on my insidious and brazen enemies.   220
But no such happy lot was given to me
or to my father. Still, I must hold fast."

To this Lord Nestor of Gerênia said:

"My dear young friend, now that you speak of it,
I hear a crowd of suitors for your mother
lives with you, uninvited, making trouble.
Now tell me how you take this. Do the people

---

[12] The Myrmidons were Akhilleus' troops; his son was Pyrrhus, also called Neoptólemus.
Philoktêtês was a Greek warrior who, after having been abandoned on the way to Troy because of a malodorous wound, later rejoined the Greek forces and was crucial to their success
in the war. Idómeneus, an ally of the Greeks against the Trojans, was king of Krete (Crete).

side against you, hearkening to some oracle?
Who knows, your father might come home someday
alone or backed by troops, and have it out with them.   230
If grey-eyed Athena loved you
the way she did Odysseus in the old days,
in Troy country, where we all went through so much—
never have I seen the gods help any man
as openly as Athena did your father—
well, as I say, if she cared for you that way,
there would be those to quit this marriage game."

But prudently Telémakhos replied:

"I can't think what you say will ever happen, sir.
It is a dazzling hope. But not for me.   240
It could not be—even if the gods willed it."

At this grey-eyed Athena broke in, saying:

"What strange talk you permit yourself, Telémakhos.
A god could save the man by simply wishing it—
from the farthest shore in the world.
If I were he, I should prefer to suffer
years at sea, and then be safe at home;
better that than a knife at my hearthside
where Agamémnon found it—killed by adulterers.
Though as for death, of course all men must suffer it: 250
the gods may love a man, but they can't help him
when cold death comes to lay him on his bier."[13]

Telémakhos replied:

"Mentor, grievously though we miss my father, why
go on as if that homecoming could happen?
You know the gods had settled it already,
years ago, when dark death came for him.
But there is something else I imagine Nestor
can tell us, knowing as he does the ways of men.
They say his rule goes back over three generations,   260
so long, so old, it seems death cannot touch him.
Nestor, Neleus' son, true sage, say how
did the Lord of the Great Plains, Agamémnon, die?
What was the trick Aigísthos used
to kill the better man? And Meneláos,

[13] This final sentence is a definitive expression of the ancient Greek understanding of the difference between human beings and deities. Though gods may be champions and even comrades of mortals, the latter are doomed to die and the gods are not. The distinction has little to do with morality or metaphysics. The gods belong to a different order of beings, though not necessarily to a superior order.

where was he? Not at Argos[14] in Akhaia,
but blown off course, held up in some far country,
is that what gave the killer nerve to strike?"

Lord Nestor of Gerênia made answer:

"Well, now, my son, I'll tell you the whole story.   270
You know, yourself, what would have come to pass
if red-haired Meneláos, back from Troy,
had caught Aigísthos in that house alive.
There would have been no burial mound for him,
but dogs and carrion birds to huddle on him
in the fields beyond the wall, and not a soul
bewailing him, for the great wrong he committed.
While we were hard-pressed in the war at Troy
he stayed safe inland in the grazing country,
making light talk to win Agamémnon's queen.   280
But the Lady Klytaimnéstra, in the first days,
rebuffed him, being faithful still;
then, too, she had at hand as her companion
a minstrel Agamémnon left attending her,
charged with her care, when he took ship for Troy.
Then came the fated hour when she gave in.[15]
Her lover tricked the poet and marooned him
on a bare island for the seabirds' picking,
and took her home, as he and she desired.
Many thighbones he burned on the gods' altars   290
and many a woven and golden ornament
hung to bedeck them, in his satisfaction;
he had not thought life held such glory for him.

Now Meneláos and I sailed home together
on friendly terms, from Troy,
but when we came off Sunion Point[16] in Attika,
the ships still running free, Onêtor's son
Phrontis, the steersman of Meneláos' ship,
fell over with a death grip on the tiller:
some unseen arrow from Apollo hit him.   300
No man handled a ship better than he did

[14] The region ruled by Agamémnon, brother to Meneláos, whose wife Helen had run off
with the Trojan prince Paris. Homer's account of the slaying of Agamémnon at his homecoming is at this point a fairly simple justification of Agamémnon and his avenging son Orestês;
Aeschylus' account in the *Oresteia* is more psychologically complex. For other accounts of the
story, by the Ancient of the Salt Sea and by Agamémnon himself, see Books IV and XI of the
Odyssey.
[15] This passage presents both Klytaimnéstra and her paramour Aigísthos as frivolous and
irresponsible dalliers; in other versions of the story, notably in Aeschylus' *Oresteia*, both these
adulterers are given an understandable, if not necessarily justifiable, motive for revenge
against Agamémnon.
[16] The tip of a promontory, near Athens, in southeastern Greece. The fleet is trying to sail
westward around the southern coast.

in a high wind and sea, so Meneláos
put down his longing to get on, and landed
to give this man full honor in funeral.
His own luck turned then. Out on the winedark sea
in the murmuring hulls again, he made Cape Malea,[17]
but Zeus who views the wide world sent a gloom
over the ocean, and a howling gale
came on with seas increasing, mountainous,
parting the ships and driving half toward Krete   310
where the Kydonians live by Iardanos river.
Off Gortyn's coastline in the misty sea there
a reef, a razorback, cuts through the water,
and every westerly piles up a pounding
surf along the left side, going toward Phaistos—
big seas buffeted back by the narrow stone.
They were blown here, and fought in vain for sea room;
the ships kept going in to their destruction,
slammed on the reef. The crews were saved. But now
those five that weathered it got off to southward,   320
taken by wind and current on to Egypt;
and there Meneláos stayed. He made a fortune
in sea traffic among those distant races,
but while he did so, the foul crime was planned
and carried out in Argos by Aigísthos,
who ruled over golden Mykênai[18] seven years.
Seven long years, with Agamémnon dead,
he held the people down, before the vengeance.
But in the eighth year, back from exile in Attika,
Orestês killed the snake who killed his father.   330
He gave his hateful mother and her soft man
a tomb together, and proclaimed the funeral day
a festal day for all the Argive people.
That day Lord Meneláos of the great war cry
made port with all the gold his ships could carry.
And this should give you pause, my son:
don't stay too long away from home, leaving
your treasure there, and brazen suitors near;
they'll squander all you have or take it from you,
and then how will your journey serve?   340
I urge you, though, to call on Meneláos,
he being but lately home from distant parts
in the wide world. A man could well despair
of getting home at all, if the winds blew him
over the Great South Sea—that weary waste,
even the wintering birds delay

---

[17] Located at the extreme southern point of the Grecian mainland, directly north of the western end of the island of Krete.

[18] The capital city of the plain of Argos, ruled over by Agamémnon. Also spelled "Mycenae."

one winter more before the northward crossing.
Well, take your ship and crew and go by water,
or if you'd rather go by land, here are
horses, a car, and my own sons for company   350
as far as the ancient land of Lakedaimon[19]
and Meneláos, the red-haired captain there.
Ask him with courtesy, and in his wisdom
he will tell you history and no lies."

While Nestor talked, the sun went down the sky
and gloom came on the land,
and now the grey-eyed goddess Athena said:

"Sir, this is all most welcome and to the point,
but why not slice the bulls' tongues now, and mix
libations for Poseidon and the gods?   360
Then we can all retire; high time we did;
the light is going under the dark world's rim,
better not linger at the sacred feast."

When Zeus's daughter spoke, they turned to listen
and soon the squires brought water for their hands,
while stewards filled the winebowls and poured out
a fresh cup full for every man. The company
stood up to fling the tongues and a shower of wine
over the flames, then drank their thirst away.
Now finally Telémakhos and Athena   370
bestirred themselves, turning away to the ship,
but Nestor put a hand on each, and said:

"Now Zeus forbid, and the other gods as well,
that you should spend the night on board, and leave me
as though I were some pauper without a stitch,
no blankets in his house, no piles of rugs,
no sleeping soft for host or guest! Far from it!
I have all these, blankets and deep-piled rugs,
and while I live the only son of Odysseus
will never make his bed on a ship's deck—   380
no, not while sons of mine are left at home
to welcome any guest who comes to us."

The grey-eyed goddess Athena answered him:

"You are very kind, sir, and Telémakhos
should do as you ask. That is the best thing.
He will go with you, and will spend the night
under your roof. But I must join our ship
and talk to the crew, to keep their spirits up,
since I'm the only senior in the company.

[19]Sparta; in the far south of Greece. Also spelled "Lacedaemon."

The rest are boys who shipped for friendship's sake, 390
no older than Telémakhos, any of them.
Let me sleep out, then, by the black hull's side,
this night at least. At daybreak I'll be off
to see the Kaukonians[20] about a debt they owe me,
an old one and no trifle. As for your guest,
send him off in a car, with one of your sons,
and give him thoroughbreds, a racing team."

Even as she spoke, Athena left them—seeming
a seahawk, in a clap of wings,—and all
the Akhaians of Pylos town looked up astounded. 400
Awed then by what his eyes had seen, the old man
took Telémakhos' hand and said warmly:

"My dear child, I can have no fears for you,
no doubt about your conduct or your heart,
if, at your age, the gods are your companions.
Here we had someone from Olympos—clearly
the glorious daughter of Zeus, his third child,
who held your father dear among the Argives.
O, Lady, hear me! Grant an illustrious name
to me and to my children and my dear wife! 410
A noble heifer shall be yours in sacrifice,
one that no man has ever yoked or driven;
my gift to you—her horns all sheathed in gold."

So he ended, praying; and Athena heard him.
Then Nestor of Gerênia led them all,
his sons and sons-in-law, to his great house;
and in they went to the famous hall of Nestor,
taking their seats on thrones and easy chairs,
while the old man mixed water in a wine bowl
with sweet red wine, mellowed eleven years 420
before his housekeeper uncapped the jar.
He mixed and poured his offering, repeating
prayers to Athena, daughter of royal Zeus.
The others made libation, and drank deep,
then all the company went to their quarters,
and Nestor of Gerênia showed Telémakhos
under the echoing eastern entrance hall
to a fine bed near the bed of Peisístratos,
captain of spearmen, his unmarried son.
Then he lay down in his own inner chamber 430
where his dear faithful wife had smoothed his bed.

When Dawn spread out her finger tips of rose,
Lord Nestor of Gerênia, charioteer,

---

[20] A people who lived near Pylos.

left his room for a throne of polished stone,
white and gleaming as though with oil, that stood
before the main gate of the palace; Neleus here
had sat before him—masterful in kingship,
Neleus, long ago a prey to death, gone down
to the night of the underworld.
So Nestor held his throne and scepter now,   440
lord of the western approaches to Akhaia.
And presently his sons came out to join him,
leaving the palace: Ekhéphron and Stratíos,
Perseus and Arêtós and Thrasymêdês,
and after them the prince Peisístratos,
bringing Telémakhos along with him.
Seeing all present, the old lord Nestor said:

"Dear sons, here is my wish, and do it briskly
to please the gods, Athena first of all,
my guest in daylight at our holy feast.   450
One of you must go for a young heifer
and have the cowherd lead her from the pasture.
Another call on Lord Telémakhos' ship
to invite his crewmen, leaving two behind;
and someone else again send for the goldsmith,
Laerkês, to gild the horns.
The rest stay here together. Tell the servants
a ritual feast will be prepared in hall.
Tell them to bring seats, firewood and fresh water."

Before he finished, they were about these errands.   460
The heifer came from pasture,
the crewmen of Telémakhos from the ship,
the smith arrived, bearing the tools of his trade—
hammer and anvil, and the precision tongs
he handled fiery gold with,—and Athena
came as a god comes, numinous, to the rites.

The smith now gloved each horn in a pure foil
beaten out of the gold that Nestor gave him—
a glory and delight for the goddess' eyes—
while Ekhéphron and Stratíos held the horns.   470
Arêtós brought clear lustral water
in a bowl quivering with fresh-cut flowers,
a basket of barley in his other hand.
Thrasymêdês, who could stand his ground in war,
stood ready, with a sharp two-bladed axe,
for the stroke of sacrifice, and Perseus
held a bowl for the blood. And now Nestor,
strewing the barley grains, and water drops,
pronounced his invocation to Athena

and burned a pinch of bristles from the victim. 480
When prayers were said and all the grain was scattered
great-hearted Thrasymêdês in a flash
swung the axe, at one blow cutting through
the neck tendons. The heifer's spirit failed.
Then all the women gave a wail of joy—
daughters, daughters-in-law, and the Lady Eurydíkê,
Klyménos' eldest daughter. But the men
still held the heifer, shored her up
from the wide earth where the living go their ways,
until Peisístratos cut her throat across, 490
the black blood ran, and life ebbed from her marrow.
The carcass now sank down, and they disjointed
shoulder and thigh bone, wrapping them in fat,
two layers, folded, with raw strips of flesh.
These offerings Nestor burned on the split-wood fire
and moistened with red wine. His sons took up
five-tined forks in their hands, while the altar flame
ate through the bones, and bits of tripe went round.
Then came the carving of the quarters, and they spitted
morsels of lean meat on the long sharp tines 500
and broiled them at arm's length upon the fire.

Polykástê, a fair girl, Nestor's youngest,
had meanwhile given a bath to Telémakhos—
bathing him first, then rubbing him with oil.
She held fine clothes and a cloak to put around him
when he came godlike from the bathing place;
then out he went to take his place with Nestor.
When the best cuts were broiled and off the spits,
they all sat down to banquet. Gentle squires
kept every golden wine cup brimming full. 510
And so they feasted to their heart's content,
until the prince of charioteers commanded:

"Sons, harness the blood mares for Telémakhos;
hitch up the car, and let him take the road."

They swung out smartly to do the work, and hooked
the handsome horses to a chariot shaft.
The mistress of the stores brought up provisions
of bread and wine, with victuals fit for kings,
and Telémakhos stepped up on the painted car.
Just at his elbow stood Peisístratos, 520
captain of spearmen, reins in hand. He gave
a flick to the horses, and with streaming manes
they ran for the open country. The tall town
of Pylos sank behind them in the distance,
as all day long they kept the harness shaking.

The sun was low and shadows crossed the lanes
when they arrived at Phêrai.[21] There Dióklês,
son of Ortílokhos whom Alpheios fathered,
welcomed the young men, and they slept the night.
But up when the young Dawn's finger tips of rose   530
opened in the east, they hitched the team
once more to the painted car,
and steered out eastward through the echoing gate,
whipping their fresh horses into a run.
That day they made the grainlands of Lakedaimon,
where, as the horses held to a fast clip,
they kept on to their journey's end. Behind them
the sun went down and all the roads grew dark.

BOOK FOUR: THE RED-HAIRED
KING AND HIS LADY

By vales and sharp ravines in Lakedaimon
the travellers drove to Meneláos' mansion,
and found him at a double wedding feast
for son and daughter.

                                        Long ago at Troy

he pledged her to the heir of great Akhilleus,
breaker of men—a match the gods had ripened;
so he must send her with a chariot train
to the town and glory of the Myrmidons.
And that day, too, he brought Alektor's daughter
to marry his tall scion,[1] Megapénthês,   10
born of a slave girl during the long war—
for the gods had never after granted Helen
a child to bring into the sunlit world
after the first, rose-lipped Hermionê,
a girl like the pale-gold goddess Aphroditê.[2]

Down the great hall in happiness they feasted,
neighbors of Meneláos, and his kin,
for whom a holy minstrel harped and sang;
and two lithe tumblers moved out on the song
with spins and handsprings through the company.   20
Now when Telémakhos and Nestor's son
pulled up their horses at the main gate,
one of the king's companions in arms, Eteóneus,
going outside, caught sight of them. He turned
and passed through court and hall to tell the master,
stepping up close to get his ear. Said he:

---

[21] A stopping-place on the eastward route from Pylos to Lakedaimon.
[1] Descendant; son.   [2] Goddess of love and beauty.

"Two men are here—two strangers,[3] Meneláos,
but nobly born Akhaians, they appear.
What do you say, shall we unhitch their team,
or send them on to someone free to receive them?"   30

The red-haired captain answered him in anger:

"You were no idiot before, Eteóneus,
but here you are talking like a child of ten.
Could we have made it home again—and Zeus
give us no more hard roving!—if other men
had never fed us, given us lodging?

                                                            Bring

these men to be our guests: unhitch their team!"

Eteóneus left the long room like an arrow,
calling equerries[4] after him, on the run.
Outside, they freed the sweating team from harness,   40
stabled the horses, tied them up, and showered
bushels of wheat and barley in the feed box;
then leaned the chariot pole
against the gleaming entry wall of stone
and took the guests in. What a brilliant place
that mansion of the great prince seemed to them!
A-glitter everywhere, as though with fiery
points of sunlight, lusters of the moon.
The young men gazed in joy before they entered
into a room of polished tubs to bathe.   50
Maidservants gave them baths, anointed them,
held out fresh tunics, cloaked them warm; and soon
they took tall thrones beside the son of Atreus.
Here a maid tipped out water for their hands
from a golden pitcher into a silver bowl,
and set a polished table near at hand;
the larder mistress with her tray of loaves
and savories came, dispensing all her best,
and then a carver heaped their platters high
with various meats, and put down cups of gold.   60
Now said the red-haired captain, Meneláos,
gesturing:

                    "Welcome; and fall to; in time,
when you have supped, we hope to hear your names,
forbears and families—in your case, it seems,
no anonymities, but lordly men.
Lads like yourselves are not base born."

---

[3] The near-breach of hospitality by Eteóneus, which angers Meneláos, is probably explained by wariness; another guest, Paris, had once abducted Helen and thus set off the war.
[4] Men who tended to the horses.

At this,

he lifted in his own hands the king's portion,
a chine of beef, and set it down before them.
Seeing all ready then, they took their dinner;
but when they had feasted well,   70
Telémakhos could not keep still, but whispered,
his head bent close, so the others might not hear:

"My dear friend, can you believe your eyes?—
the murmuring hall, how luminous it is
with bronze, gold, amber, silver, and ivory!
This is the way the court of Zeus must be,
inside, upon Olympos. What a wonder!"

But splendid Meneláos had overheard him
and spoke out on the instant to them both:

"Young friends, no mortal man can vie with Zeus.   80
His home and all his treasures are for ever.
But as for men, it may well be that few
have more than I. How painfully I wandered
before I brought it home! Seven years at sea,
Kypros, Phoinikia, Egypt, and still farther
among the sun-burnt races.
I saw the men of Sidon[5] and Arabia
and Libya, too, where lambs are horned at birth.
In every year they have three lambing seasons,
so no man, chief or shepherd, ever goes   90
hungry for want of mutton, cheese, or milk—
all year at milking time there are fresh ewes.
But while I made my fortune on those travels
a stranger killed my brother, in cold blood,—
tricked blind, caught in the web of his deadly queen.
What pleasure can I take, then, being lord
over these costly things?
You must have heard your fathers tell my story,
whoever your fathers are; you must know of my life,
the anguish I once had, and the great house   100
full of my treasure, left in desolation.
How gladly I should live one third as rich
to have my friends back safe at home!—my friends
who died on Troy's wide seaboard, far
from the grazing lands of Argos.
But as things are, nothing but grief is left me
for those companions. While I sit at home
sometimes hot tears come, and I revel in them,

---

[5] An important city in Phoinikia (Phoenicia), an area along the Syrian coast noted for commerce and craftsmanship.

or stop before the surfeit makes me shiver.
And there is one I miss more than the other   110
dead I mourn for; sleep and food alike
grow hateful when I think of him. No soldier
took on so much, went through so much, as Odysseus.
That seems to have been his destiny, and this mine—
to feel each day the emptiness of his absence,
ignorant, even, whether he lived or died.
How his old father and his quiet wife,
Penélopê, must miss him still!
And Telémakhos, whom he left as a new-born child."

Now hearing these things said, the boy's heart rose   120
in a long pang for his father, and he wept,
holding his purple mantle with both hands
before his eyes. Meneláos knew him now,
and so fell silent with uncertainty
whether to let him speak and name his father
in his own time, or to inquire, and prompt him.
And while he pondered, Helen came
out of her scented chamber, a moving grace
like Artemis,[6] straight as a shaft of gold.
Beside her came Adrastê, to place her armchair,   130
Alkippê, with a rug of downy wool,
and Phylo, bringing a silver basket, once
given by Alkandrê, the wife of Pólybos,
in the treasure city, Thebes of distant Egypt.
He gave two silver bathtubs to Meneláos
and a pair of tripods, with ten pure gold bars,
and she, then, made these beautiful gifts to Helen:
a golden distaff,[7] and the silver basket
rimmed in hammered gold, with wheels to run on.
So Phylo rolled it in to stand beside her,   140
heaped with fine spun stuff, and cradled on it
the distaff swathed in dusky violet wool.
Reclining in her light chair with its footrest,
Helen gazed at her husband and demanded:

"Meneláos, my lord, have we yet heard
our new guests introduce themselves? Shall I
dissemble what I feel? No, I must say it.
Never, anywhere, have I seen so great a likeness
in man or woman—but it is truly strange!
This boy must be the son of Odysseus,   150
Telémakhos, the child he left at home
that year the Akhaian host made war on Troy—
daring all for the wanton that I was."

----

[6] Goddess of the hunt.   [7] A staff used in spinning thread.

And the red-haired captain, Meneláos, answered:

"My dear, I see the likeness as well as you do.
Odysseus' hands and feet were like this boy's;
his head, and hair, and the glinting of his eyes.
Not only that, but when I spoke, just now,
of Odysseus' years of toil on my behalf
and all he had to endure—the boy broke down   160
and wept into his cloak."

                                                   Now Nestor's son,
Peisístratos, spoke up in answer to him:

"My lord marshal, Meneláos, son of Atreus,
this is that hero's son as you surmise,
but he is gentle, and would be ashamed
to clamor for attention before your grace
whose words have been so moving to us both.
Nestor, Lord of Gerênia, sent me with him
as guide and escort; he had wished to see you,
to be advised by you or assisted somehow.   170
A father far from home means difficulty
for an only son, with no one else to help him;
so with Telémakhos:
his father left the house without defenders."

The king with flaming hair now spoke again:

"His son, in my house! How I loved the man,
And how he fought through hardship for my sake!
I swore I'd cherish him above all others
if Zeus, who views the wide world, gave us passage
homeward across the sea in the fast ships.   180
I would have settled him in Argos, brought him
over with herds and household out of Ithaka,
his child and all his people. I could have cleaned out
one of my towns to be his new domain.
And so we might have been together often
in feasts and entertainments, never parted
till the dark mist of death lapped over one of us.
But God himself must have been envious,
to batter the bruised man so that he alone
should fail in his return."   190

A twinging ache of grief rose up in everyone,
and Helen of Argos wept, the daughter of Zeus,[8]
Telémakhos and Meneláos wept,
and tears came to the eyes of Nestor's son—

---

[8] Helen was daughter of Zeus by the mortal woman Lêda. (Lêda was ravished by the god,
who took the form of a swan.)

remembering, for his part, Antílokhos,
whom the son of shining Dawn[9] had killed in battle.
But thinking of that brother, he broke out:

"O son of Atreus, when we spoke of you
at home, and asked about you, my old father
would say you have the clearest mind of all.   200
If it is not too much to ask, then, let us not
weep away these hours after supper;
I feel we should not: Dawn will soon be here!
You understand, I would not grudge a man
right mourning when he comes to death and doom:
what else can one bestow on the poor dead?—
a lock of hair sheared,[10] and a tear let fall.
For that matter, I, too,
lost someone in the war at Troy—my brother,
and no mean soldier, whom you must have known,   210
although I never did,—Antílokhos.
He ranked high as a runner and fighting man."

The red-haired captain Meneláos answered:

"My lad, what you have said is only sensible,
and you did well to speak. Yes, that was worthy
a wise man and an older man than you are:
you speak for all the world like Nestor's son.
How easily one can tell the man whose father
had true felicity, marrying and begetting!
And that was true of Nestor, all his days,   220
down to his sleek old age in peace at home,
with clever sons, good spearmen into the bargain.
Come, we'll shake off this mourning mood of ours
and think of supper. Let the men at arms
rinse our hands again! There will be time
for a long talk with Telémakhos in the morning."

The hero Meneláos' companion in arms,
Asphalion, poured water for their hands,
and once again they touched the food before them.
But now it entered Helen's mind   230
to drop into the wine that they were drinking
an anodyne, mild magic of forgetfulness.
Whoever drank this mixture in the wine bowl
would be incapable of tears that day—
though he should lose mother and father both,
or see, with his own eyes, a son or brother
mauled by weapons of bronze at his own gate.
The opiate of Zeus's daughter bore

[9]Memnon, an Ethiopian king, was the son of Eos, the goddess of the dawn.
[10]To strew a lock of one's hair on the dead was a customary part of funeral ritual.

this canny power. It had been supplied her
by Polydamna, mistress of Lord Thôn,   240
in Egypt, where the rich plantations grow
herbs of all kinds, maleficent and healthful;
and no one else knows medicine as they do,
Egyptian heirs of Paian,[11] the healing god.
She drugged the wine, then, had it served, and said—
taking again her part in the conversation—

"O Meneláos, Atreus' royal son,
and you that are great heroes' sons, you know
how Zeus gives all of us in turn
good luck and bad luck, being all powerful.   250
So take refreshment, take your ease in hall,
and cheer the time with stories. I'll begin.
Not that I think of naming, far less telling,
every feat of that rugged man, Odysseus,
but here is something that he dared to do
at Troy, where you Akhaians endured the war.
He had, first, given himself an outrageous beating
and thrown some rags on—like a household slave—
then slipped into that city of wide lanes
among his enemies. So changed, he looked   260
as never before upon the Akhaian beachhead,
but like a beggar, merged in the townspeople;
and no one there remarked him. But I knew him—
even as he was, I knew him,
and questioned him. How shrewdly he put me off!
But in the end I bathed him and anointed him,
put a fresh cloak around him, and swore an oath
not to give him away as Odysseus to the Trojans,
till he got back to camp where the long ships lay.
He spoke up then, and told me   270
all about the Akhaians, and their plans—
then sworded many Trojans through the body
on his way out with what he learned of theirs.
The Trojan women raised a cry—but my heart
sang—for I had come round, long before,
to dreams of sailing home, and I repented
the mad day Aphroditê
drew me away from my dear fatherland,
forsaking all—child, bridal bed, and husband—
a man without defect in form or mind."   280

Replied the red-haired captain, Meneláos:

"An excellent tale, my dear, and most becoming.
In my life I have met, in many countries,
foresight and wit in many first rate men,

---

[11] An epithet for Apollo in his role as god of physicians.

but never have I seen one like Odysseus
for steadiness and a stout heart. Here, for instance,
is what he did—had the cold nerve to do—
inside the hollow horse,[12] where we were waiting,
picked men all of us, for the Trojan slaughter,
when all of a sudden, you came by—I dare say   290
drawn by some superhuman
power that planned an exploit for the Trojans;
and Deïphobos,[13] that handsome man, came with you.
Three times you walked around it, patting it everywhere,
and called by name the flower of our fighters,
making your voice sound like their wives, calling.
Diomêdês and I crouched in the center
along with Odysseus; we could hear you plainly;
and listening, we two were swept
by waves of longing—to reply, or go.   300
Odysseus fought us down, despite our craving,
and all the Akhaians kept their lips shut tight,
all but Antiklos. Desire moved his throat
to hail you, but Odysseus' great hands clamped
over his jaws, and held. So he saved us all,
till Pallas Athena led you away at last."

Then clear-headed Telémakhos addressed him:

"My lord marshal, Meneláos, son of Atreus,
all the more pity, since these valors
could not defend him from annihilation—   310
not if his heart were iron in his breast.
But will you not dismiss us for the night now?
Sweet sleep will be a pleasure, drifting over us."

He said no more, but Helen called the maids
and sent them to make beds, with purple rugs
piled up, and sheets outspread, and fleecy
coverlets, in the porch inside the gate.
The girls went out with torches in their hands,
and presently a squire led the guests—
Telémakhos and Nestor's radiant son—   320
under the entrance colonnade, to bed.
Then deep in the great mansion, in his chamber,
Meneláos went to rest, and Helen,
queenly in her long gown, lay beside him.

When the young Dawn with finger tips of rose
made heaven bright, the deep-lunged man of battle

---

[12] The Greeks had hidden some of their best warriors inside a huge wooden horse, which the Trojans hauled into their city, thus precipitating its overthrow. For a detailed version of the incident, see Virgil's *Aeneid*, Book II.
[13] By the time of the fall of Troy, Helen had been married to this Trojan prince.

stood up, pulled on his tunic and his mantle,
slung on a swordbelt and a new edged sword,
tied his smooth feet into fine rawhide sandals
and left his room, a god's brilliance upon him.   330
He sat down by Telémakhos, asking gently:

"Telémakhos, why did you come, sir, riding
the sea's broad back to reach old Lakedaimon?
A public errand or private? Why, precisely?"

Telémakhos replied:

"My lord marshal Meneláos, son of Atreus,
I came to hear what news you had of Father.
My house, my good estates are being ruined.
Each day my mother's bullying suitors come
to slaughter flocks of mine and my black cattle;   340
enemies crowd our home. And this is why
I come to you for news of him who owned it.
Tell me of his death, sir, if perhaps
you witnessed it, or have heard some wanderer
tell the tale. The man was born for trouble.
Spare me no part for kindness' sake; be harsh;
but put the scene before me as you saw it.
If ever Odysseus my noble father
served you by promise kept or work accomplished
in the land of Troy, where you Akhaians suffered,   350
recall those things for me the way they were."

Stirred now to anger, Meneláos said:

"Intolerable—that soft men, as those are,
should think to lie in that great captain's bed.
Fawns in a lion's lair! As if a doe
put down her litter of sucklings there, while she
quested a glen or cropped some grassy hollow.
Ha! Then the lord returns to his own bed
and deals out wretched doom on both alike.
So will Odysseus deal out doom on these.   360
O Father Zeus, Athena, and Apollo!
I pray he comes as once he was, in Lesbos,
when he stood up to wrestle Philomeleidês—
champion and Island King—
and smashed him down. How the Akhaians cheered!
If only that Odysseus met the suitors,
they'd have their consummation, a cold bed!
Now for your questions, let me come to the point.
I would not misreport it for you; let me
tell you what the Ancient of the Sea,[14]   370
who is infallible, said to me—every word.

[14] Proteus, who is described in the following passage.

During my first try at a passage homeward
the gods detained me, tied me down to Egypt—
for I had been too scant in hekatombs,
and gods will have the rules each time remembered.
There is an island washed by the open sea
lying off Nile mouth—seamen call it Pharos—
distant a day's sail in a clean hull
with a brisk land breeze behind. It has a harbor,
a sheltered bay, where shipmasters   380
take on dark water for the outward voyage.
Here the gods held me twenty days becalmed.
No winds came up, seaward escorting winds
for ships that ride the sea's broad back, and so
my stores and men were used up; we were failing
had not one goddess intervened in pity—
Eidothea, daughter of Proteus,
the Ancient of the Sea. How I distressed her!
I had been walking out alone that day—
my sailors, thin-bellied from the long fast,   390
were off with fish hooks, angling on the shore—
then she appeared to me, and her voice sang:

'What fool is here, what drooping dunce of dreams?
Or can it be, friend, that you love to suffer?
How can you linger on this island, aimless
and shiftless, while your people waste away?'

To this I quickly answered:

                                            'Let me tell you,
goddess, whatever goddess you may be,
these doldrums are no will of mine. I take it
the gods who own broad heaven are offended.   400
Why don't you tell me—since the gods know everything—
who has me pinned down here?
How am I going to make my voyage home?'

Now she replied in her immortal beauty:

'I'll put it for you clearly as may be, friend.
The Ancient of the Salt Sea haunts this place,
immortal Proteus of Egypt; all the deeps
are known to him; he serves under Poseidon,
and is, they say, my father.
If you could take him by surprise and hold him,   410
he'd give you course and distance for your sailing
homeward across the cold fish-breeding sea.
And should you wish it, noble friend, he'd tell you
all that occurred at home, both good and evil,
while you were gone so long and hard a journey.'

To this I said:

                            'But you, now—you must tell me
how I can trap this venerable sea-god.
He will elude me if he takes alarm;
no man—god knows—can quell a god with ease.'

That fairest of unearthly nymphs replied: 420

'I'll tell you this, too, clearly as may be.
When the sun hangs at high noon in heaven,
the Ancient glides ashore under the Westwind,
hidden by shivering glooms on the clear water,
and rests in caverns hollowed by the sea.
There flippered seals, brine children, shining come
from silvery foam in crowds to lie around him,
exhaling rankness from the deep sea floor.
Tomorrow dawn I'll take you to those caves
and bed you down there. Choose three officers   430
for company—brave men they had better be—
the old one has strange powers, I must tell you.
He goes amid the seals to check their number,
and when he sees them all, and counts them all,
he lies down like a shepherd with his flock.
Here is your opportunity: at this point
gather yourselves, with all your heart and strength,
and tackle him before he bursts away.
He'll make you fight—for he can take the forms
of all the beasts, and water, and blinding fire;   440
but you must hold on, even so, and crush him
until he breaks the silence. When he does,
he will be in that shape you saw asleep.
Relax your grip, then, set the Ancient free,
and put your questions, hero:
Who is the god so hostile to you,
and how will you go home on the fish-cold sea.'

At this she dove under a swell and left me.
Back to the ships in the sandy cove I went,
my heart within me like a high surf running;   450
but there I joined my men once more
at supper, as the sacred Night came on,
and slept at last beside the lapping water.
When Dawn spread out her finger tips of rose
I started, by the sea's wide level ways,
praying the gods for help, and took along
three lads I counted on in any fight.
Meanwhile the nereid[15] swam from the lap of Ocean

    [15] A sea-nymph.

laden with four sealskins, new flayed
for the hoax she thought of playing on her father.   460
In the sand she scooped out hollows for our bodies
and sat down, waiting. We came close to touch her,
and, bedding us, she threw the sealskins over us—
a strong disguise; oh, yes, terribly strong
as I recall the stench of those damned seals.
Would any man lie snug with a sea monster?
But here the nymph, again, came to our rescue,
dabbing ambrosia under each man's nose—
a perfume drowning out the bestial odor.
So there we lay with beating hearts all morning   470
while seals came shoreward out of ripples, jostling
to take their places, flopping on the sand.
At noon the Ancient issued from the sea
and held inspection, counting off the sea-beasts.
We were the first he numbered; he went by,
detecting nothing. When at last he slept
we gave a battlecry and plunged for him,
locking our hands behind him. But the old one's
tricks were not knocked out of him; far from it.
First he took on a whiskered lion's shape,   480
a serpent then; a leopard; a great boar;
then sousing water; then a tall green tree.
Still we hung on, by hook or crook, through everything,
until the Ancient saw defeat, and grimly
opened his lips to ask me:

                                        'Son of Atreus,
who counselled you to this? A god: what god?
Set a trap for me, overpower me—why?'

He bit it off, then, and I answered:

                                        'Old one,
you know the reason—why feign not to know?
High and dry so long upon this island   490
I'm at my wits' end, and my heart is sore.
You gods know everything; now you can tell me:
which of the immortals chained me here?
And how will I get home on the fish-cold sea?'

He made reply at once:

                                'You should have paid
honor to Zeus and the other gods, performing
a proper sacrifice before embarking:
that was your short way home on the winedark sea.
You may not see your friends, your own fine house,
or enter your own land again,   500
unless you first remount the Nile in flood

and pay your hekatomb to the gods of heaven.
Then, and then only,
the gods will grant the passage you desire.'

Ah, how my heart sank, hearing this—
hearing him send me back on the cloudy sea
in my own track, the long hard way of Egypt.
Nevertheless, I answered him and said:

'Ancient, I shall do all as you command.
But tell me, now, the others—   510
had they a safe return, all those Akhaians
who stayed behind when Nestor and I left Troy?
Or were there any lost at sea—what bitterness!—
any who died in camp, after the war?'

To this he said:

                                        'For you to know these things
goes beyond all necessity, Meneláos.
Why must you ask?—you should not know my mind,
and you will grieve to learn it, I can tell you.
Many there were who died, many remain,
but two high officers alone were lost—   520
on the passage home, I mean; you saw the war.
One is alive, a castaway at sea;
the other, Aîas, perished with all hands—
though first Poseidon landed him on Gyrai[16]
promontory, and saved him from the ocean.
Despite Athena's hate, he had lived on,
but the great sinner in his insolence
yelled that the gods' will and the sea were beaten,
and this loud brag came to Poseidon's ears.
He swung the trident[17] in his massive hands   530
and in one shock from top to bottom split
that promontory, toppling into the sea
the fragment where the great fool sat.
So the vast ocean had its will with Aîas,
drunk in the end on salt spume as he drowned.
Meanwhile your brother left that doom astern
in his decked ships—the Lady Hera[18] saved him;
but as he came round Malea
a fresh squall caught him, bearing him away
over the cold sea, groaning in disgust,

---

[16] An island in the Aegean. Aîas, who in the following lines is described as punished for his insolent and sacrilegious boasting, is the "lesser," "Locrian" Aîas (Ajax), the son of Oileus; he is not the "greater" Aîas who was the son of Télamon.

[17] The three-pronged spear wielded by the sea-god Poseidon.

[18] Consort of Zeus; queen of the gods. She consistently sided with the Greeks against the Trojans.

to the Land's End of Argos, where Thyestês[19]   540
lived in the days of old, and then his son,
Aigísthos. Now, again, return seemed easy:
the high gods wound the wind into the east,
and back he sailed, this time to his own coast.
He went ashore and kissed the earth in joy,
hot tears blinding his eyes at sight of home.
But there were eyes that watched him from a height—
a lookout, paid two bars of gold to keep
vigil the year round for Aigísthos' sake,   550
that he should be forewarned, and Agamémnon's
furious valor sleep unroused.
Now this man with his news ran to the tyrant,
who made his crooked arrangements in a flash,
stationed picked men at arms, a score of men
in hiding; set a feast in the next room;
then he went out with chariots and horses
to hail the king and welcome him to evil.
He led him in to banquet, all serene,
and killed him, like an ox felled at the trough;   560
and not a man of either company
survived that ambush in Aigísthos' house.'

Before the end my heart was broken down.
I slumped on the trampled sand and cried aloud,
caring no more for life or the light of day,
and rolled there weeping, till my tears were spent.
Then the unerring Ancient said at last:

'No more, no more; how long must you persist?
Nothing is gained by grieving so. How soon
can you return to Argos? You may take him   570
alive there still—or else meanwhile Orestês
will have despatched him. You'll attend the feast.'

At this my heart revived, and I recovered
the self command to question him once more:

'Of two companions now I know. The third?
Tell me his name, the one marooned at sea;
living, you say, or dead? Even in pain
I wish to hear.'

                                And this is all he answered:

'Laërtês' son, whose home is Ithaka.

[19]Brother of Atreus (the father of Agamémnon and Meneláos). See the headnote to
Aeschylus' *Oresteia*. Homer's account here of the murder of Agamémnon differs considerably
from the version in Aeschylus; in the *Oresteia*, Agamémnon's wife Klytaimnéstra plays a more
significant role than does Aigísthos in the murder.

I saw him weeping, weeping on an island.   580
The nymph Kalypso has him, in her hall.
No means of faring home are left him now;
no ship with oars, and no ship's company
to pull him on the broad back of the sea.
As to your own destiny, prince Meneláos,
you shall not die in the bluegrass land of Argos;
rather the gods intend you for Elysion[20]
with golden Rhadamanthos[21] at the world's end,
where all existence is a dream of ease.
Snowfall is never known there, neither long   590
frost of winter, nor torrential rain,
but only mild and lulling airs from Ocean
bearing refreshment for the souls of men—
the West Wind always blowing.

                                                                  For the gods

hold you, as Helen's lord, a son of Zeus.'

At this he dove under a swell and left me,
and I went back to the ship with my companions,
feeling my heart's blood in me running high;
but in the long hull's shadow, near the sea,
we supped again as sacred Night came on   600
and slept at last beside the lapping water.

When Dawn spread out her finger tips of rose,
in first light we launched on the courtly breakers,
setting up masts and yards in the well-found ships;
went all on board, and braced on planks athwart
oarsmen in line dipped oars in the grey sea.
Soon I drew in to the great stream[22] fed by heaven
and, laying by, slew bulls in the proper number,
until the immortal gods were thus appeased;
then heaped a death mound on that shore against   610
all-quenching time for Agamémnon's honor,
and put to sea once more. The gods sent down
a sternwind for a racing passage homeward.

So ends the story. Now you must stay with me
and be my guest eleven or twelve days more.
I'll send you on your way with gifts, and fine ones:
three chariot horses, and a polished car;
a hammered cup, too, so that all your days,
tipping the red wine for the deathless gods,
you will remember me."

[20] As presented here in Homer, this realm (also called *Elysium*) is not part of the underground Hades which Odysseus visits later in the *Odyssey*. It is, rather, a happy land on the extreme western surface of the earth.

[21] Ruler of Elysion (sometimes portrayed in ancient literature as a judge of the dead in Hades).

[22] The Nile, believed to have a divine source in the sky.

Telémakhos answered: 620

"Lord, son of Atreus, no, you must not keep me.
Not that a year with you would be too long:
I never could be homesick here—I find
your tales and all you say so marvellous.
But time hangs heavy on my shipmates' hands
at holy Pylos, if you make me stay.
As for your gift, now, let it be some keepsake.
Horses I cannot take to Ithaka;
let me bestow them back on you, to serve
your glory here. My lord, you rule wide country,   630
rolling and rich with clover, galingale
and all the grains: red wheat and hoary barley.
At home we have no level runs or meadows,
but highland, goat land—prettier than plains, though.
Grasses, and pasture land, are hard to come by
upon the islands tilted in the sea,
and Ithaka is the island of them all."

At this the deep-lunged man of battle smiled.
Then he said kindly, patting the boy's hand:

"You come of good stock, lad. That was well spoken.   640
I'll change the gift, then—as indeed I can.
Let me see what is costliest and most beautiful
of all the precious things my house contains:
a wine bowl, mixing bowl, all wrought of silver,
but rimmed with hammered gold. Let this be yours.
It is Hephaistos'[23] work, given me by Phaidimos,
captain and king of Sidon. He received me
during my travels. Let it be yours, I say."

This was their discourse on that morning. Meanwhile
guests were arriving at the great lord's house,   650
bringing their sheep, and wine, the ease of men,
with loaves their comely kerchiefed women sent,
to make a feast in hall.

At that same hour,
before the distant manor of Odysseus,
the suitors were competing at the discus throw
and javelin, on a measured field they used,
arrogant lords at play. The two best men,
Antínoös and Eurýmakhos, presided.
Now Phronios' son, Noêmon, came to see them
with a question for Antínoös. He said: 660

"Do any of us know, or not, Antínoös,
what day Telémakhos will be home from Pylos?

---

[23] The god of fire and of metal-working. Also spelled *Hephaestus*.

He took my ship, but now I need it back
to make a cruise to Elis, where the plains are.
I have a dozen mares at pasture there
with mule colts yet unweaned. My notion is
to bring one home and break him in for labor."

His first words made them stare—for they knew well
Telémakhos could not have gone to Pylos,
but inland with his flocks, or to the swineherd.   670
Eupeithês' son, Antínoös, quickly answered:

"Tell the story straight. He sailed? Who joined him—
a crew he picked up here in Ithaka,
or his own slaves? He might have done it that way.
And will you make it clear
whether he took the ship against your will?
Did he ask for it, did you lend it to him?"

Now said the son of Phronios in reply:

"Lent it to him, and freely. Who would not,
when a prince of that house asked for it, in trouble?   680
Hard to refuse the favor, it seems to me.
As for his crew, the best men on the island,
after ourselves, went with him. Mentor I noted
going aboard—or a god who looked like Mentor.
The strange thing is, I saw Lord Mentor here
in the first light yesterday—although he sailed
five days ago for Pylos."

                                                        Turning away,
Noêmon took the path to his father's house,
leaving the two men there, baffled and hostile.
They called the rest in from the playing field   690
and made them all sit down, so that Antínoös
could speak out from the stormcloud of his heart,
swollen with anger; and his eyes blazed:

"A bad business. Telémakhos had the gall
to make that crossing, though we said he could not.
So the young cub rounds up a first rate crew
in spite of all our crowd, and puts to sea.
What devilment will he be up to next time?—
Zeus blast the life out of him before he's grown!
Just give me a fast ship and twenty men;   700
I'll intercept him, board him in the strait
between the crags of Samê[24] and this island.
He'll find his sea adventure after his father
swamping work in the end!"

[24] An island, modern Cephalonia, south and west of Ithaka; also called Kephallênia in this poem.

They all cried "Aye!"
and "After him!" and trailed back to the manor.

Now not much time went by before Penélopê
learned what was afoot among the suitors.
Medôn the crier told her. He had been
outside the wall, and heard them in the court
conspiring. Into the house and up the stairs   710
he ran to her with his news upon his tongue—
but at the door Penélopê met him, crying:

"Why have they sent you up here now? To tell
the maids of King Odysseus—'Leave your spinning:
Time to go down and slave to feed those men?'
I wish this were the last time they came feasting,
courting me or consorting here! The last!
Each day you crowd this house like wolves
to eat away my brave son's patrimony.
When you were boys, did your own fathers tell you   720
nothing of what Odysseus was for them?
In word and act impeccable, disinterested
toward all the realm—though it is king's justice
to hold one man abhorred and love another;
no man alive could say Odysseus wronged him.
But your own hearts—how different!—and your deeds!
How soon are benefactions all forgotten!"

Now Medôn, the alert and cool man, answered:

"I wish that were the worst of it, my Lady,
but they intend something more terrible—   730
may Zeus forfend and spare us!
They plan to drive the keen bronze through Telémakhos
when he comes home. He sailed away, you know,
to hallowed Pylos and old Lakedaimon
for news about his father."

Her knees failed,
and her heart failed as she listened to the words,
and all her power of speech went out of her.
Tears came; but the rich voice could not come.
Only after a long while she made answer:

"Why has my child left me? He had no need   740
of those long ships on which men shake out sail
to tug like horses, breasting miles of sea.
Why did he go? Must he, too, be forgotten?"

Then Medôn, the perceptive man, replied:

"A god moved him—who knows?—or his own heart
sent him to learn, at Pylos, if his father
roams the wide world still, or what befell him."

He left her then, and went down through the house.
And now the pain around her heart benumbed her;
chairs were a step away, but far beyond her;   750
she sank down on the door sill of the chamber,
wailing, and all her women young and old
made a low murmur of lament around her,
until at last she broke out through her tears:

"Dearest companions, what has Zeus given me?
Pain—more pain than any living woman.
My lord, my lion heart, gone, long ago—
the bravest man, and best, of the Danaans,
famous through Hellas and the Argive midlands—
and now the squalls have blown my son, my dear one,   760
an unknown boy, southward. No one told me.
O brute creatures, not one soul would dare
to wake me from my sleep; you knew
the hour he took the black ship out to sea!
If I had seen that sailing in his eyes
he should have stayed with me, for all his longing,
stayed—or left me dead in the great hall.
Go, someone, now, and call old Dólios,
the slave my father gave me before I came,
my orchard keeper—tell him to make haste   770
and put these things before Laërtês; he
may plan some kind of action; let him come
to cry shame on these ruffians who would murder
Odysseus' son and heir, and end his line!"

The dear old nurse, Eurýkleia, answered her:

"Sweet mistress, have my throat cut without mercy
or what you will; it's true, I won't conceal it,
I knew the whole thing; gave him his provisions;
grain and sweet wine I gave, and a great oath
to tell you nothing till twelve days went by,   780
or till you heard of it yourself, or missed him;
he hoped you would not tear your skin lamenting.
Come, bathe and dress your loveliness afresh,
and go to the upper rooms with all your maids
to ask help from Athena, Zeus's daughter.
She it will be who saves this boy from death.
Spare the old man this further suffering;
the blissful gods cannot so hate his line,
heirs of Arkêsios; one will yet again
be lord of the tall house and the far fields."   790

She hushed her weeping in this way, and soothed her.
The Lady Penélopê arose and bathed,
dressing her body in her freshest linen,

filled a basket with barley, and led her maids
to the upper rooms, where she besought Athena:

"Tireless child of Zeus, graciously hear me!
If ever Odysseus burned at our altar fire
thighbones of beef or mutton in sacrifice,
remember it for my sake! Save my son!
Shield him, and make the killers go astray!"   800

She ended with a cry, and the goddess heard her.
Now voices rose from the shadowy hall below
where the suitors were assuring one another:

"Our so-long-courted Queen is even now
of a mind to marry one of us, and knows
nothing of what is destined for her son."

Of what was destined they in fact knew nothing,
But Antínoös addressed them in a whisper:

"No boasting—are you mad?—and no loud talk:
someone might hear it and alarm the house.   810
Come along now, be quiet, this way; come,
we'll carry out the plan our hearts are set on."

Picking out twenty of the strongest seamen,
he led them to a ship at the sea's edge,
and down they dragged her into deeper water,
stepping a mast in her, with furled sails,
and oars a-trail from thongs looped over thole pins,
ready all; then tried the white sail, hoisting,
while men at arms carried their gear aboard.
They moored the ship some way off shore, and left her   820
to take their evening meal there, waiting for night to come.

Penélopê at that hour in her high chamber
lay silent, tasting neither food nor drink,
and thought of nothing but her princely son—
could he escape, or would they find and kill him?—
her mind turning at bay, like a cornered lion
in whom fear comes as hunters close the ring.
But in her sick thought sweet sleep overtook her,
and she dozed off, her body slack and still.

Now it occurred to the grey-eyed goddess Athena   830
to make a figure of dream in a woman's form—
Iphthimê, great Ikários' other daughter,
whom Eumêlos of Phêrai took as bride.
The goddess sent this dream to Odysseus' house
to quiet Penélopê and end her grieving.

So, passing by the strap-slit[25] through the door,
the image came a-gliding down the room
to stand at her bedside and murmur to her:

"Sleepest thou, sorrowing Penélopê?
The gods whose life is ease no longer suffer thee   840
to pine and weep, then; he returns unharmed,
thy little one; no way hath he offended."

Then pensive Penélopê made this reply,
slumbering sweetly in the gates of dream:

"Sister, hast thou come hither? Why? Aforetime
never wouldst come, so far away thy dwelling.
And am I bid be done with all my grieving?
But see what anguish hath my heart and soul!
My lord, my lion heart, gone, long ago—
the bravest man, and best, of the Danaans,   850
famous through Hellas and the Argive midlands—
and now my son, my dear one, gone seafaring,
a child, untrained in hardship or in council.
Aye, 'tis for him I weep, more than his father!
Aye, how I tremble for him, lest some blow
befall him at men's hands or on the sea!
Cruel are they and many who plot against him,
to take his life before he can return."

Now the dim phantom spoke to her once more:

"Lift up thy heart, and fear not overmuch.   860
For by his side one goes whom all men else
invoke as their defender, one so powerful—
Pallas Athena; in thy tears she pitied thee
and now hath sent me that I so assure thee."

Then said Penélopê the wise:

                                                                    "If thou art
numinous[26] and hast ears for divine speech,
O tell me, what of Odysseus, man of woe?
Is he alive still somewhere, seeth he day light still?
Or gone in death to the sunless underworld?"

The dim phantom said only this in answer: 870

"Of him I may not tell thee in this discourse,
alive or dead. And empty words are evil."

---

[25] A hole in a door through which a strap was passed. It allowed a person outside to bolt the
door on the inside.
[26] Gifted with uncanny spiritual powers.

The wavering form withdrew along the doorbolt
into a draft of wind, and out of sleep
Penélopê awoke, in better heart
for that clear dream in the twilight of the night.

Meanwhile the suitors had got under way,
planning the death plunge for Telémakhos.
Between the Isles of Ithaka and Samê
the sea is broken by an islet, Asteris,
with access to both channels from a cove.
In ambush here that night the Akhaians lay.

880

BOOK FIVE: SWEET NYMPH AND OPEN SEA

Dawn came up from the couch of her reclining,
leaving her lord Tithonos'[1] brilliant side
with fresh light in her arms for gods and men.
And the master of heaven and high thunder, Zeus,
went to his place among the gods assembled
hearing Athena tell Odysseus' woe.
For she, being vexed that he was still sojourning
in the sea chambers of Kalypso,[2] said:

"O Father Zeus and gods in bliss forever,
let no man holding scepter as a king
think to be mild, or kind, or virtuous;
let him be cruel, and practice evil ways,
for those Odysseus ruled cannot remember
the fatherhood and mercy of his reign.
Meanwhile he lives and grieves upon that island
in thralldom to the nymph; he cannot stir,
cannot fare homeward, for no ship is left him,
fitted with oars—no crewmen or companions
to pull him on the broad back of the sea.
And now murder is hatched on the high sea
against his son, who sought news of his father
in the holy lands of Pylos and Lakedaimon."

10

20

To this the summoner of cloud replied:

"My child, what odd complaints you let escape you.
Have you not, you yourself, arranged this matter—
as we all know—so that Odysseus

[1] The lover of Eos, goddess of the dawn. No mention is made here of the most famous version of his myth, in which Eos wins for him the gift of immortality but forgets, fatefully, to ensure that Tithonos will never grow older. See Tennyson's poem "Tithonus."

[2] The nymph's island, Ogýgia, is located in a western region of the Mediterranean. The geography of Odysseus' wanderings west of Greece is uncertain.

will bring these men to book, on his return?
And are you not the one to give Telémakhos
a safe route for sailing? Let his enemies
encounter no one and row home again."   30

He turned then to his favorite son and said:

"Hermês, you have much practice on our missions,
go make it known to the softly-braided nymph
that we, whose will is not subject to error,
order Odysseus home; let him depart.
But let him have no company, gods or men,
only a raft that he must lash together,
and after twenty days, worn out at sea,
he shall make land upon the garden isle,
Skhería,[3] of our kinsmen, the Phaiákians.   40
Let these men take him to their hearts in honor
and berth him in a ship, and send him home,
with gifts of garments, gold, and bronze—
so much he had not counted on from Troy
could he have carried home his share of plunder.
His destiny is to see his friends again
under his own roof, in his father's country."

No words were lost on Hermês the Wayfinder,
who bent to tie his beautiful sandals on,
ambrosial, golden, that carry him over water   50
or over endless land in a swish of the wind,
and took the wand with which he charms asleep—
or when he wills, awake—the eyes of men.
So wand in hand he paced into the air,
shot from Pieria[4] down, down to sea level,
and veered to skim the swell. A gull patrolling
between the wave crests of the desolate sea
will dip to catch a fish, and douse his wings;
no higher above the whitecaps Hermês flew
until the distant island lay ahead,   60
then rising shoreward from the violet ocean
he stepped up to the cave. Divine Kalypso,
the mistress of the isle, was now at home.
Upon her hearthstone a great fire blazing
scented the farthest shores with cedar smoke
and smoke of thyme, and singing high and low
in her sweet voice, before her loom a-weaving,
she passed her golden shuttle to and fro.
A deep wood grew outside, with summer leaves

---

[3] The land (also spelled Scheria) of the Phaiákians (Phaeacians), possibly located on the southern shore of the Mediterranean, opposite Ithaka, possibly in Corfu, an island northwest of Ithaka off the west coast of Greece.

[4] An area on the slopes of Mount Olympos.

of alder and black poplar, pungent cypress.   70
Ornate birds here rested their stretched wings—
horned owls, falcons, cormorants—long-tongued
beachcombing birds, and followers of the sea.
Around the smoothwalled cave a crooking vine
held purple clusters under ply of green;
and four springs, bubbling up near one another
shallow and clear, took channels here and there
through beds of violets and tender parsley.
Even a god who found this place
would gaze, and feel his heart beat with delight: 80
so Hermês did; but when he had gazed his fill
he entered the wide cave. Now face to face
the magical Kalypso recognized him,
as all immortal gods know one another
on sight—though seeming strangers, far from home.
But he saw nothing of the great Odysseus,
who sat apart, as a thousand times before,
and racked his own heart groaning, with eyes wet
scanning the bare horizon of the sea.
Kalypso, lovely nymph, seated her guest   90
in a bright chair all shimmering, and asked:

"O Hermês, ever with your golden wand,
what brings you to my island?
Your awesome visits in the past were few.
Now tell me what request you have in mind;
for I desire to do it, if I can,
and if it is a proper thing to do.
But wait a while, and let me serve my friend."

She drew a table of ambrosia near him
and stirred a cup of ruby-colored nectar[5]—   100
food and drink for the luminous Wayfinder,
who took both at his leisure, and replied:

"Goddess to god, you greet me, questioning me?
Well, here is truth for you in courtesy.
Zeus made me come, and not my inclination;
who cares to cross that tract of desolation,
the bitter sea, all mortal towns behind
where gods have beef and honors from mankind?
But it is not to be thought of—and no use—
for any god to elude the will of Zeus.   110

He notes your friend, most ill-starred by renown
of all the peers who fought for Priam's town—
nine years of war they had, before great Troy was down.

---

[5] Ambrosia and nectar were the food and drink of the gods.

Homing, they wronged the goddess[6] with grey eyes,
who made a black wind blow and the seas rise,
in which his troops were lost, and all his gear,
while easterlies and current washed him here.
Now the command is: send him back in haste.
His life may not in exile go to waste.
His destiny, his homecoming, is at hand,   120
when he shall see his dearest, and walk on his own land."

That goddess most divinely made
shuddered before him, and her warm voice rose:

"Oh you vile gods, in jealousy supernal!
You hate it when we choose to lie with men—
immortal flesh by some dear mortal side.
So radiant Dawn once took to bed Orion[7]
until you easeful gods grew peevish at it,
and holy Artemis, Artemis throned in gold,
hunted him down in Delos with her arrows.   130
Then Dêmêtêr of the tasseled tresses yielded
to Iasion,[8] mingling and making love
in a furrow three times plowed; but Zeus found out
and killed him with a white-hot thunderbolt.
So now you grudge me, too, my mortal friend.
But it was I who saved him—saw him straddle
his own keel board, the one man left afloat
when Zeus rent wide his ship with chain lightning
and overturned him in the winedark sea.
Then all his troops were lost, his good companions,   140
but wind and current washed him here to me.
I fed him, loved him, sang that he should not die
nor grow old, ever, in all the days to come.
But now there's no eluding Zeus's will.
If this thing be ordained by him, I say
so be it, let the man strike out alone
on the vast water. Surely I cannot 'send' him.
I have no long-oared ships, no company
to pull him on the broad back of the sea.
My counsel he shall have, and nothing hidden,   150
to help him homeward without harm."

To this the Wayfinder made answer briefly:

"Thus you shall send him, then. And show more grace
in your obedience, or be chastised by Zeus."

---

[6] Compare the passage in Book IV alluding to the insolence of the lesser Aîas, or Ajax.
[7] A gigantic hunter, loved by Eos.
[8] Probably symbolic of harvest-wealth, since the offspring of his union with Dêmêtêr, goddess of the fields, was Plutus, who symbolized wealth.

The strong god glittering left her as he spoke,
and now her ladyship, having given heed
to Zeus's mandate, went to find Odysseus
in his stone seat to seaward—tear on tear
brimming his eyes. The sweet days of his life time
were running out in anguish over his exile, 160
for long ago the nymph had ceased to please.
Though he fought shy of her and her desire,
he lay with her each night, for she compelled him.
But when day came he sat on the rocky shore
and broke his own heart groaning, with eyes wet
scanning the bare horizon of the sea.
Now she stood near him in her beauty, saying:

"O forlorn man, be still.
Here you need grieve no more; you need not feel
your life consumed here; I have pondered it, 170
and I shall help you go.
Come and cut down high timber for a raft
or flatboat; make her broad-beamed, and decked over,
so you can ride her on the misty sea.
Stores I shall put aboard for you—bread, water,
and ruby-colored wine, to stay your hunger—
give you a seacloak and a following wind
to help you homeward without harm—provided
the gods who rule wide heaven wish it so.
Stronger than I they are, in mind and power." 180

For all he had endured, Odysseus shuddered.
But when he spoke, his words went to the mark:

"After these years, a helping hand? O goddess,
what guile is hidden here?
A raft, you say, to cross the Western Ocean,[9]
rough water, and unknown? Seaworthy ships
that glory in god's wind will never cross it.
I take no raft you grudge me out to sea.
Or yield me first a great oath, if I do,
to work no more enchantment to my harm." 190

At this the beautiful nymph Kalypso smiled
and answered sweetly, laying her hand upon him:

"What a dog you are! And not for nothing learned,
having the wit to ask this thing of me!
My witness then be earth and sky
and dripping Styx[10] that I swear by—
the gay gods cannot swear more seriously—

---

[9] The western Mediterranean.
[10] A river in Hades, the realm of the dead. To swear by Styx was the most solemn oath a deity could utter.

I have no further spells to work against you.
But what I shall devise, and what I tell you,
will be the same as if your need were mine.   200
Fairness is all I think of. There are hearts
made of cold iron—but my heart is kind."

Swiftly she turned and led him to her cave,
and they went in, the mortal and immortal.
He took the chair left empty now by Hermês,
where the divine Kalypso placed before him
victuals and drink of men; then she sat down
facing Odysseus, while her serving maids
brought nectar and ambrosia to her side.
Then each one's hands went out on each one's feast   210
until they had had their pleasure; and she said:

"Son of Laërtês, versatile Odysseus,
after these years with me, you still desire
your old home? Even so, I wish you well.
If you could see it all, before you go—
all the adversity you face at sea—
you would stay here, and guard this house, and be
immortal—though you wanted her forever,
that bride for whom you pine each day.
Can I be less desirable than she is?   220
Less interesting? Less beautiful? Can mortals
compare with goddesses in grace and form?"

To this the strategist Odysseus answered:

"My lady goddess, here is no cause for anger.
My quiet Penélopê—how well I know—
would seem a shade before your majesty,
death and old age being unknown to you,
while she must die. Yet, it is true, each day
I long for home, long for the sight of home.
If any god has marked me out again   230
for shipwreck, my tough heart can undergo it.
What hardship have I not long since endured
at sea, in battle! Let the trial come."

Now as he spoke the sun set, dusk drew on,
and they retired, this pair, to the inner cave
to revel and rest softly, side by side.

When Dawn spread out her finger tips of rose
Odysseus pulled his tunic and his cloak on,
while the sea nymph dressed in a silvery gown
of subtle tissue, drew about her waist   240
a golden belt, and veiled her head, and then
took thought for the great-hearted hero's voyage.

A brazen axehead first she had to give him,
two-bladed, and agreeable to the palm
with a smooth-fitting haft of olive wood;
next a well-polished adze; and then she led him
to the island's tip where bigger timber grew—
besides the alder and poplar, tall pine trees,
long dead and seasoned, that would float him high.
Showing him in that place her stand of timber   250
the loveliest of nymphs took her way home.
Now the man fell to chopping; when he paused
twenty tall trees were down. He lopped the branches,
split the trunks, and trimmed his puncheons true.
Meanwhile Kalypso brought him an auger tool
with which he drilled through all his planks, then drove
stout pins to bolt them, fitted side by side.
A master shipwright, building a cargo vessel,
lays down a broad and shallow hull; just so
Odysseus shaped the bottom of his craft.   260
He made his decking fast to close-set ribs
before he closed the side with longer planking,
then cut a mast pole, and proper yard,
and shaped a steering oar to hold her steady.
He drove long strands of willow in all the seams
to keep out waves, and ballasted with logs.
As for a sail, the lovely nymph Kalypso
brought him a cloth so he could make that, too.
Then he ran up his rigging—halyards, braces—
and hauled the boat on rollers to the water.   270

This was the fourth day, when he had all ready;
on the fifth day, she sent him out to sea.
But first she bathed him, gave him a scented cloak,
and put on board a skin of dusky wine
with water in a bigger skin, and stores—
boiled meats and other victuals—in a bag.
Then she conjured a warm landbreeze to blowing—
joy for Odysseus when he shook out sail!
Now the great seaman, leaning on his oar,
steered all the night unsleeping, and his eyes   280
picked out the Pleiadês, the laggard Ploughman,
and the Great Bear, that some have called the Wain,
pivoting in the sky before Orion;
of all the night's pure figures, she alone
would never bathe or dip in the Ocean stream.[11]
These stars the beautiful Kalypso bade him
hold on his left hand as he crossed the main.

---

[11] In northern latitudes, the Big Dipper (the Great Bear, or Wain) never sets but rather
circles around Polaris, the North Star. For Odysseus to keep the constellation on his left would
require him to sail eastward.

Seventeen nights and days in the open water
he sailed, before a dark shoreline appeared;
Skhería then came slowly into view   290
like a rough shield of bull's hide on the sea.

But now the god of earthquake, storming home
over the mountains of Asia from the Sunburned land,
sighted him far away. The god grew sullen
and tossed his great head, muttering to himself:

"Here is a pretty cruise! While I was gone
the gods have changed their minds about Odysseus.
Look at him now, just offshore of that island
that frees him from the bondage of his exile!
Still I can give him a rough ride in, and will."   300

Brewing high thunderheads, he churned the deep
with both hands on his trident—called up wind
from every quarter, and sent a wall of rain
to blot out land and sea in torrential night.
Hurricane winds now struck from the South and East
shifting North West in a great spume of seas,
on which Odysseus' knees grew slack, his heart
sickened, and he said within himself:

"Rag of man that I am, is this the end of me?
I fear the goddess told it all too well—   310
predicting great adversity at sea
and far from home. Now all things bear her out:
the whole rondure[12] of heaven hooded so
by Zeus in woeful cloud, and the sea raging
under such winds. I am going down, that's sure.
How lucky those Danaans were who perished
on Troy's wide seaboard, serving the Atreidai![13]
Would God I, too, had died there—met my end
that time the Trojans made so many casts at me
when I stood by Akhilleus after death.   320
I should have had a soldier's burial
and praise from the Akhaians—not this choking
waiting for me at sea, unmarked and lonely."

A great wave drove at him with toppling crest
spinning him round, in one tremendous blow,
and he went plunging overboard, the oar-haft
wrenched from his grip. A gust that came on howling
at the same instant broke his mast in two,
hurling his yard and sail far out to leeward.
Now the big wave a long time kept him under,   330
helpless to surface, held by tons of water,

---

[12] Circle or sphere.   [13] Sons of Atreus—Agamémnon and Meneláos.

tangled, too, by the seacloak of Kalypso.
Long, long, until he came up spouting brine,
with streamlets gushing from his head and beard;
but still bethought him, half-drowned as he was,
to flounder for the boat and get a handhold
into the bilge—to crouch there, foiling death.
Across the foaming water, to and fro,
the boat careered like a ball of tumbleweed
blown on the autumn plains, but intact still.   340
So the winds drove this wreck over the deep,
East Wind and North Wind, then South Wind and West,
coursing each in turn to the brutal harry.

But Ino[14] saw him—Ino, Kadmos' daughter,
slim-legged, lovely, once an earthling girl,
now in the seas a nereid, Leukothea.
Touched by Odysseus' painful buffeting
she broke the surface, like a diving bird,
to rest upon the tossing raft and say:

"O forlorn man, I wonder   350
why the Earthshaker, Lord Poseidon, holds
this fearful grudge—father of all your woes.
He will not drown you, though, despite his rage.
You seem clear-headed still; do what I tell you.
Shed that cloak, let the gale take your craft,
and swim for it—swim hard to get ashore
upon Skhería, yonder,
where it is fated that you find a shelter.
Here: make my veil your sash; it is not mortal;
you cannot, now, be drowned or suffer harm.   360
Only, the instant you lay hold of earth,
discard it, cast it far, far out from shore
in the winedark sea again, and turn away."

After she had bestowed her veil, the nereid
dove like a gull to windward
where a dark waveside closed over her whiteness.
But in perplexity Odysseus
said to himself, his great heart laboring:

"O damned confusion! Can this be a ruse
to trick me from the boat for some god's pleasure?   370
No I'll not swim; with my own eyes I saw
how far the land lies that she called my shelter.
Better to do the wise thing, as I see it.
While this poor planking holds, I stay aboard;
I may ride out the pounding of the storm,

---

[14] Maddened by Hera, who was jealous of her for helping to rear the young god Dionysos,
Ino leaped into the sea and was transformed into a nereid, or sea-nymph.

or if she cracks up, take to the water then;
I cannot think it through a better way."

But even while he pondered and decided,
the god of earthquake heaved a wave against him
high as a rooftree and of awful gloom.   380
A gust of wind, hitting a pile of chaff,
will scatter all the parched stuff far and wide;
just so, when this gigantic billow struck
the boat's big timbers flew apart. Odysseus
clung to a single beam, like a jockey riding,
meanwhile stripping Kalypso's cloak away;
then he slung round his chest the veil of Ino
and plunged headfirst into the sea. His hands
went out to stroke, and he gave a swimmer's kick.
But the strong Earthshaker had him under his eye,   390
and nodded as he said:

                                                               "Go on, go on;

wander the high seas this way, take your blows,
before you join that race the gods have nurtured.[15]
Nor will you grumble, even then, I think,
for want of trouble."

                                      Whipping his glossy team

he rode off to his glorious home at Aigai.[16]
But Zeus's daughter Athena countered him:
she checked the course of all the winds but one,
commanding them, "Be quiet and go to sleep."
Then sent a long swell running under a norther   400
to bear the prince Odysseus, back from danger,
to join the Phaiákians, people of the sea.

Two nights, two days, in the solid deep-sea swell
he drifted, many times awaiting death,
until with shining ringlets in the East
the dawn confirmed a third day, breaking clear
over a high and windless sea; and mounting
a rolling wave he caught a glimpse of land.
What a dear welcome thing life seems to children
whose father, in the extremity, recovers   410
after some weakening and malignant illness:
his pangs are gone, the gods have delivered him.
So dear and welcome to Odysseus
the sight of land, of woodland, on that morning.
It made him swim again, to get a foothold
on solid ground. But when he came in earshot
he heard the trampling roar of sea on rock,

---

[15] The Phaiákians, or Phaeacians.   [16] An Akhaian city.

where combers, rising shoreward, thudded down
on the sucking ebb—all sheeted with salt foam.
Here were no coves or harborage or shelter,
only steep headlands, rockfallen reefs and crags.
Odysseus' knees grew slack, his heart faint,
a heaviness came over him, and he said:

"A cruel turn, this. Never had I thought
to see this land, but Zeus has let me see it—
and let me, too, traverse the Western Ocean—
only to find no exit from these breakers.
Here are sharp rocks off shore, and the sea a smother
rushing around them; rock face rising sheer
from deep water; nowhere could I stand up
on my two feet and fight free of the welter.
No matter how I try it, the surf may throw me
against the cliffside; no good fighting there.
If I swim down the coast, outside the breakers,
I may find shelving shore and quiet water—
but what if another gale comes on to blow?
Then I go cursing out to sea once more.
Or then again, some shark of Amphitritê's[17]
may hunt me, sent by the genius of the deep.
I know how he who makes earth tremble hates me."

During this meditation a heavy surge
was taking him, in fact, straight on the rocks.
He had been flayed there, and his bones broken,
had not grey-eyed Athena instructed him:
he gripped a rock-ledge with both hands in passing
and held on, groaning, as the surge went by,
to keep clear of its breaking. Then the backwash
hit him, ripping him under and far out.
An octopus, when you drag one from his chamber,
comes up with suckers full of tiny stones:
Odysseus left the skin of his great hands
torn on that rock-ledge as the wave submerged him.
And now at last Odysseus would have perished,
battered inhumanly, but he had the gift
of self-possession from grey-eyed Athena.
So, when the backwash spewed him up again,
he swam out and along, and scanned the coast
for some landspit that made a breakwater.
Lo and behold, the mouth of a calm river
at length came into view, with level shores
unbroken, free from rock, shielded from wind—
by far the best place he had found.
But as he felt the current flowing seaward
he prayed in his heart:

420

430

440

450

460

[17] A sea-nymph, consort of Poseidon and thus queen of the ocean.

"O hear me, lord of the stream:
how sorely I depend upon your mercy!
derelict as I am by the sea's anger.
Is he not sacred, even to the gods,
the wandering man who comes, as I have come,
in weariness before your knees, your waters?
Here is your servant; lord, have mercy on me."   470

Now even as he prayed the tide at ebb
had turned, and the river god made quiet water,
drawing him in to safety in the shallows.
His knees buckled, his arms gave way beneath him,
all vital force now conquered by the sea.
Swollen from head to foot he was, and seawater
gushed from his mouth and nostrils. There he lay,
scarce drawing breath, unstirring, deathly spent.
In time, as air came back into his lungs
and warmth around his heart, he loosed the veil,   480
letting it drift away on the estuary
downstream to where a white wave took it under
and Ino's hands received it. Then the man
crawled to the river bank among the reeds
where, face down, he could kiss the soil of earth,
in his exhaustion murmuring to himself:

"What more can this hulk suffer? What comes now?
In vigil through the night here by the river
how can I not succumb, being weak and sick,
to the night's damp and hoarfrost of the morning?   490
The air comes cold from rivers before dawn.
But if I climb the slope and fall asleep
in the dark forest's undergrowth—supposing
cold and fatigue will go, and sweet sleep come—
I fear I make the wild beasts easy prey."

But this seemed best to him, as he thought it over.
He made his way to a grove above the water
on open ground, and crept under twin bushes
grown from the same spot—olive and wild olive—
a thicket proof against the stinging wind   500
or Sun's blaze, fine soever the needling sunlight;
nor could a downpour wet it through, so dense
those plants were interwoven. Here Odysseus
tunnelled, and raked together with his hands
a wide bed—for a fall of leaves was there,
enough to save two men or maybe three
on a winter night, a night of bitter cold.
Odysseus' heart laughed when he saw his leaf-bed,
and down he lay, heaping more leaves above him.

A man in a distant field, no hearthfires near,   510
will hide a fresh brand in his bed of embers
to keep a spark alive for the next day;
so in the leaves Odysseus hid himself,
while over him Athena showered sleep
that his distress should end, and soon, soon.
In quiet sleep she sealed his cherished eyes.

BOOK SIX: THE PRINCESS AT THE RIVER

Far gone in weariness, in oblivion,
the noble and enduring man slept on;
but Athena in the night went down the land
of the Phaiákians, entering their city.
In days gone by, these men held Hypereia,
a country of wide dancing grounds, but near them
were overbearing Kyklopês,[1] whose power
could not be turned from pillage. So the Phaiákians
migrated thence under Nausíthoös
to settle a New World across the sea,   10
Skhería Island. That first captain walled
their promontory, built their homes and shrines,
and parcelled out the black land for the plow.
But he had gone down long ago to Death.
Alkínoös ruled, and Heaven gave him wisdom,
so on this night the goddess, grey-eyed Athena,
entered the palace of Alkínoös
to make sure of Odysseus' voyage home.
She took her way to a painted bedchamber
where a young girl lay fast asleep—so fine   20
in mould and feature that she seemed a goddess—
the daughter of Alkínoös, Nausikaa.
On either side, as Graces[2] might have slept,
her maids were sleeping. The bright doors were shut,
but like a sudden stir of wind, Athena
moved to the bedside of the girl, and grew
visible as the shipman Dymas' daughter,
a girl the princess' age, and her dear friend.
In this form grey-eyed Athena said to her:

"How so remiss, and yet thy mother's daughter?   30
leaving thy clothes uncared for, Nausikaa,
when soon thou must have store of marriage linen,
and put thy minstrelsy in wedding dress!

[1] These monstrous giants of Sicily are described in Book IX. *Hypereia* means "highlands"; their location is uncertain.
[2] Three goddesses who personify grace and beauty.

Beauty, in these, will make the folk admire,
and bring thy father and gentle mother joy.
Let us go washing in the shine of morning!
Beside thee will I drub, so wedding chests
will brim by evening. Maidenhood must end!
Have not the noblest born Phaiákians
paid court to thee, whose birth none can excel?   40
Go beg thy sovereign father, even at dawn,
to have the mule cart and the mules brought round
to take thy body-linen, gowns and mantles.
Thou shouldst ride, for it becomes thee more,
the washing pools are found so far from home."

On this word she departed, grey-eyed Athena,
to where the gods have their eternal dwelling—
as men say—in the fastness of Olympos.
Never a tremor of wind, or a splash of rain,
no errant snowflake comes to stain that heaven,   50
so calm, so vaporless, the world of light.
Here, where the gay gods live their days of pleasure,
the grey-eyed one withdrew, leaving the princess.

And now Dawn took her own fair throne, awaking
the girl in the sweet gown, still charmed by dream.
Down through the rooms she went to tell her parents,
whom she found still at home: her mother seated
near the great hearth among her maids—and twirling
out of her distaff yarn dyed like the sea—;
her father at the door, bound for a council   60
of princes on petition of the gentry.
She went up close to him and softly said:

"My dear Papà, could you not send the mule cart
around for me—the gig with pretty wheels?
I must take all our things and get them washed
at the river pools; our linen is all soiled.
And you should wear fresh clothing, going to council
with counselors and first men of the realm.
Remember your five sons at home: though two
are married, we have still three bachelor sprigs;   70
they will have none but laundered clothes each time
they go to the dancing. See what I must think of!"

She had no word to say of her own wedding,
though her keen father saw her blush. Said he:

"No mules would I deny you, child, nor anything.
Go along, now; the grooms will bring your gig
with pretty wheels and the cargo box upon it."

He spoke to the stableman, who soon brought round
the cart, low-wheeled and nimble;
harnessed the mules, and backed them in the traces.   80
Meanwhile the girl fetched all her soiled apparel
to bundle in the polished wagon box.
Her mother, for their luncheon, packed a hamper
with picnic fare, and filled a skin of wine,
and, when the princess had been handed up,
gave her a golden bottle of olive oil
for softening girls' bodies, after bathing.
Nausikaa took the reins and raised her whip,
lashing the mules. What jingling! What a clatter!
But off they went in a ground-covering trot,   90
with princess, maids, and laundry drawn behind.
By the lower river where the wagon came
were washing pools, with water all year flowing
in limpid spillways that no grime withstood.
The girls unhitched the mules, and sent them down
along the eddying stream to crop sweet grass.
Then sliding out the cart's tail board, they took
armloads of clothing to the dusky water,
and trod them in the pits, making a race of it.
All being drubbed, all blemish rinsed away,   100
they spread them, piece by piece, along the beach
whose pebbles had been laundered by the sea;
then took a dip themselves, and, all anointed
with golden oil, ate lunch beside the river
while the bright burning sun dried out their linen.
Princess and maids delighted in that feast;
then, putting off their veils,
they ran and passed a ball to a rhythmic beat,
Nausikaa flashing first with her white arms.

So Artemis goes flying after her arrows flown   110
down some tremendous valley-side—

                           Taÿgetos, Erymanthos—
chasing the mountain goats or ghosting deer,
with nymphs of the wild places flanking her;
and Lêto's[3] heart delights to see them running,
for, taller by a head than nymphs can be,
the goddess shows more stately, all being beautiful.
So one could tell the princess from the maids.

Soon it was time, she knew, for riding homeward—
mules to be harnessed, linen folded smooth—
but the grey-eyed goddess Athena made her tarry,   120

---

[3] Mother of Artemis, goddess of the hunt. Taÿgetos and Erymanthos are mountainous
places in Greece.

so that Odysseus might behold her beauty
and win her guidance to the town.

                                  It happened

when the king's daughter threw her ball off line
and missed, and put it in the whirling stream,—
at which they all gave such a shout, Odysseus
awoke and sat up, saying to himself:

"Now, by my life, mankind again! But who?
Savages, are they, strangers to courtesy?
Or gentle folk, who know and fear the gods?
That was a lusty cry of tall young girls—   130
most like the cry of nymphs, who haunt the peaks,
and springs of brooks, and inland grassy places.
Or am I amid people of human speech?
Up again, man; and let me see for myself."

He pushed aside the bushes, breaking off
with his great hand a single branch of olive,
whose leaves might shield him in his nakedness;
so came out rustling, like a mountain lion,
rain-drenched, wind-buffeted, but in his might at ease,
with burning eyes—who prowls among the herds   140
or flocks, or after game, his hungry belly
taking him near stout homesteads for his prey.
Odysseus had this look, in his rough skin
advancing on the girls with pretty braids;
and he was driven on by hunger, too.
Streaked with brine, and swollen, he terrified them,
so that they fled, this way and that. Only
Alkínoös' daughter stood her ground, being given
a bold heart by Athena, and steady knees.

She faced him, waiting. And Odysseus came,   150
debating inwardly what he should do:
embrace this beauty's knees in supplication?
or stand apart, and, using honeyed speech,
inquire the way to town, and beg some clothing?
In his swift reckoning, he thought it best
to trust in words to please her—and keep away;
he might anger the girl, touching her knees.
So he began, and let the soft words fall:

"Mistress: please: are you divine, or mortal?
If one of those who dwell in the wide heaven,   160
you are most near to Artemis, I should say—
great Zeus's daughter—in your grace and presence.
If you are one of earth's inhabitants,
how blest your father, and your gentle mother,

blest all your kin. I know what happiness
must send the warm tears to their eyes, each time
they see their wondrous child go to the dancing!
But one man's destiny is more than blest—
he who prevails, and takes you as his bride.
Never have I laid eyes on equal beauty   170
in man or woman. I am hushed indeed.
So fair, one time, I thought a young palm tree
at Delos[4] near the altar of Apollo—
I had troops under me when I was there
on the sea route that later brought me grief—
but that slim palm tree filled my heart with wonder:
never came shoot from earth so beautiful.
So now, my lady, I stand in awe so great
I cannot take your knees. And yet my case is desperate:
twenty days, yesterday, in the winedark sea,   180
on the ever-lunging swell, under gale winds,
getting away from the Island of Ogýgia.
And now the terror of Storm has left me stranded
upon this shore—with more blows yet to suffer,
I must believe, before the gods relent.
Mistress, do me a kindness!
After much weary toil, I come to you,
and you are the first soul I have seen—I know
no others here. Direct me to the town,
give me a rag that I can throw around me,   190
some cloth or wrapping that you brought along.
And may the gods accomplish your desire:
a home, a husband, and harmonious
converse with him—the best thing in the world
being a strong house held in serenity
where man and wife agree. Woe to their enemies,
joy to their friends! But all this they know best."

Then she of the white arms, Nausikaa, replied:

"Stranger, there is no quirk or evil in you
that I can see. You know Zeus metes out fortune   200
to good and bad men as it pleases him.
Hardship he sent to you, and you must bear it.
But now that you have taken refuge here
you shall not lack for clothing, or any other
comfort due to a poor man in distress.
The town lies this way, and the men are called
Phaiákians, who own the land and city.
I am daughter to the Prince Alkínoös,
by whom the power of our people stands."

[4] An island in the Aegean Sea, birthplace of Apollo and sacred to him.

Turning, she called out to her maids-in-waiting:

"Stay with me! Does the sight of a man scare you?
Or do you take this one for an enemy?
Why, there's no fool so brash, and never will be,
as to bring war or pillage to this coast,
for we are dear to the immortal gods,
living here, in the sea that rolls forever,
distant from other lands and other men.
No: this man is a castaway, poor fellow;
we must take care of him. Strangers and beggars
come from Zeus: a small gift, then, is friendly.   220
Give our new guest some food and drink, and take him
into the river, out of the wind, to bathe."

They stood up now, and called to one another
to go on back. Quite soon they led Odysseus
under the river bank, as they were bidden;
and there laid out a tunic, and a cloak,
and gave him olive oil in the golden flask.
"Here," they said, "go bathe in the flowing water."
But heard now from that kingly man, Odysseus:

"Maids," he said, "keep away a little; let me   230
wash the brine from my own back, and rub on
plenty of oil. It is long since my anointing.
I take no bath, however, where you can see me—
naked before young girls with pretty braids."

They left him, then, and went to tell the princess.
And now Odysseus, dousing in the river,
scrubbed the coat of brine from back and shoulders
and rinsed the clot of sea-spume from his hair;
got himself all rubbed down, from head to foot,
then he put on the clothes the princess gave him.   240
Athena lent a hand, making him seem
taller, and massive too, with crisping hair
in curls like petals of wild hyacinth,
but all red-golden. Think of gold infused
on silver by a craftsman, whose fine art
Hephaistos taught him, or Athena: one
whose work moves to delight: just so she lavished
beauty over Odysseus' head and shoulders.
Then he went down to sit on the sea beach
in his new splendor. There the girl regarded him,   250
and after a time she said to the maids beside her:

"My gentlewomen, I have a thing to tell you.
The Olympian gods cannot be all averse
to this man's coming here among our islanders.
Uncouth he seemed, I thought so, too, before;

but now he looks like one of heaven's people.
I wish my husband could be fine as he
and glad to stay forever on Skhería!
But have you given refreshment to our guest?"

At this the maids, all gravely listening, hastened   260
to set out bread and wine before Odysseus,
and ah! how ravenously that patient man
took food and drink, his long fast at an end.

The princess Nausikaa now turned aside
to fold her linens; in the pretty cart
she stowed them, put the mule team under harness,
mounted the driver's seat, and then looked down
to say with cheerful prompting to Odysseus:

"Up with you now, friend; back to town we go;
and I shall send you in before my father   270
who is wondrous wise; there in our house with him
you'll meet the noblest of the Phaiákians.
You have good sense, I think; here's how to do it:
while we go through the countryside and farmland
stay with my maids, behind the wagon, walking
briskly enough to follow where I lead.
But near the town—well, there's a wall with towers
around the Isle, and beautiful ship basins
right and left of the causeway of approach;
seagoing craft are beached beside the road   280
each on its launching ways. The agora,[5]
with fieldstone benches bedded in the earth,
lies either side Poseidon's shrine—for there
men are at work on pitch-black hulls and rigging,
cables and sails, and tapering of oars.
The archer's craft is not for the Phaiákians,
but ship designing, modes of oaring cutters
in which they love to cross the foaming sea.
From these fellows I will have no salty talk,
no gossip later. Plenty are insolent.   290
And some seadog might say, after we passed:
'Who is this handsome stranger trailing Nausikaa?
Where did she find him? Will he be her husband?
Or is she being hospitable to some rover
come off his ship from lands across the sea—
there being no lands nearer. A god, maybe?
a god from heaven, the answer to her prayer,
descending now—to make her his forever?
Better, if she's roamed and found a husband
somewhere else: none of our own will suit her,   300

[5] Public meeting-place.

though many come to court her, and those the best.'
This is the way they might make light of me.
And I myself should hold it shame
for any girl to flout her own dear parents,
taking up with a man, before her marriage.

Note well, now, what I say, friend, and your chances
are excellent for safe conduct from my father.
You'll find black poplars in a roadside park
around a meadow and fountain—all Athena's—
but Father has a garden in the place—   310
this within earshot of the city wall.
Go in there and sit down, giving us time
to pass through town and reach my father's house.
And when you can imagine we're at home,
then take the road into the city, asking
directions to the palace of Alkínoös.
You'll find it easily: any small boy
can take you there; no family has a mansion
half so grand as he does, being king.
As soon as you are safe inside, cross over   320
and go straight through into the mégaron[6]
to find my mother. She'll be there in firelight
before a column, with her maids in shadow,
spinning a wool dyed richly as the sea.
My father's great chair faces the fire, too;
there like a god he sits and takes his wine.
Go past him; cast yourself before my mother,
embrace her knees—and you may wake up soon
at home rejoicing, though your home be far.
On Mother's feeling much depends; if she   330
looks on you kindly, you shall see your friends
under your own roof in your father's country."

At this she raised her glistening whip, lashing
the team into a run; they left the river
cantering beautifully, then trotted smartly.
But then she reined them in, and spared the whip,
so that her maids could follow with Odysseus.
The sun was going down when they went by
Athena's grove. Here, then, Odysseus rested,
and lifted up his prayer to Zeus's daughter: 340

"Hear me, unwearied child of royal Zeus!
O listen to me now—thou so aloof
while the Earthshaker wrecked and battered me.
May I find love and mercy among these people."

---

[6] The great hall of the house.

He prayed for that, and Pallas Athena heard him—
although in deference to her father's brother[7]
she would not show her true form to Odysseus,
at whom Poseidon smoldered on
until the kingly man came home to his own shore.

BOOK SEVEN: GARDENS AND FIRELIGHT

As Lord Odysseus prayed there in the grove
the girl rode on, behind her strapping team,
and came late to the mansion of her father,
where she reined in at the courtyard gate. Her brothers
awaited her like tall gods in the court,
circling to lead the mules away and carry
the laundered things inside. But she withdrew
to her own bedroom, where a fire soon shone,
kindled by her old nurse, Eurymedousa.
Years ago, from a raid on the continent,   10
the rolling ships had brought this woman over
to be Alkínoös' share—fit spoil for him
whose realm hung on his word as on a god's.
And she had schooled the princess, Nausikaa,
whose fire she tended now, making her supper.

Odysseus, when the time had passed, arose
and turned into the city. But Athena
poured a sea fog around him as he went—
her love's expedient, that no jeering sailor
should halt the man or challenge him for luck.   20
Instead, as he set foot in the pleasant city,
the grey-eyed goddess came to him, in figure
a small girl child, hugging a water jug.

Confronted by her, Lord Odysseus asked:

"Little one, could you take me to the house
of that Alkínoös, king among these people?
You see, I am a poor old stranger here;
my home is far away; here there is no one
known to me, in countryside or city."

The grey-eyed goddess Athena replied to him: 30

"Oh yes, good grandfer, sir, I know, I'll show you
the house you mean; it is quite near my father's.
But come now, hush, like this, and follow me.
You must not stare at people, or be inquisitive.

[7] Poseidon, brother of Athena's father, Zeus.

They do not care for strangers in this neighborhood;
a foreign man will get no welcome here.
The only things they trust are the racing ships
Poseidon gave, to sail the deep blue sea
like white wings in the sky, or a flashing thought."

Pallas Athena turned like the wind, running   40
ahead of him, and he followed in her footsteps.
And no seafaring men of Phaiákia
perceived Odysseus passing through their town:
the awesome one in pigtails barred their sight
with folds of sacred mist. And yet Odysseus
gazed out marvelling at the ships and harbors,
public squares, and ramparts towering up
with pointed palisades along the top.
When they were near the mansion of the king,
grey-eyed Athena in the child cried out: 50

"Here it is, grandfer, sir—that mansion house
you asked to see. You'll find our king and queen
at supper, but you must not be dismayed;
go in to them. A cheerful man does best
in every enterprise—even a stranger.
You'll see our lady just inside the hall—
her name is Arêtê; her grandfather
was our good king Alkínoös's father—
Nausithoös by name, son of Poseidon
and Periboia. That was a great beauty,   60
the daughter of Eurymedon, commander
of the Gigantês[1] in the olden days,
who led those wild things to their doom and his.
Poseidon then made love to Periboia,
and she bore Nausíthoös, Phaiákia's lord,
whose sons in turn were Rhêxênor and Alkínoös.
Rhêxênor had no sons; even as a bridegroom
he fell before the silver bow of Apollo,
his only child a daughter, Arêtê.
When she grew up, Alkínoös married her   70
and holds her dear. No lady in the world,
no other mistress of a man's household,
is honored as our mistress is, and loved,
by her own children, by Alkínoös,
and by the people. When she walks the town
they murmur and gaze, as though she were a goddess.
No grace or wisdom fails in her; indeed
just men in quarrels come to her for equity.
Supposing, then, she looks upon you kindly,
the chances are that you shall see your friends   80
under your own roof, in your father's country."

[1]The Giants, enormous semihuman beings, offspring of Ge, an ancient earth-goddess.

At this the grey-eyed goddess Athena left him
and left that comely land, going over sea
to Marathon, to the wide roadways of Athens
and her retreat in the stronghold of Erekhtheus.[2]
Odysseus, now alone before the palace,
meditated a long time before crossing
the brazen threshold of the great courtyard.
High rooms he saw ahead, airy and luminous
as though with lusters of the sun and moon,   90
bronze-paneled walls, at several distances,
making a vista, with an azure molding
of lapis lazuli.[3] The doors were golden
guardians of the great room. Shining bronze
plated the wide door sill; the posts and lintel
were silver upon silver; golden handles
curved on the doors, and golden, too, and silver
were sculptured hounds, flanking the entrance way,
cast by the skill and ardor of Hephaistos
to guard the prince Alkínoös's house—   100
undying dogs that never could grow old.
Through all the rooms, as far as he could see,
tall chairs were placed around the walls, and strewn
with fine embroidered stuff made by the women.
Here were enthroned the leaders of Phaiákia
drinking and dining, with abundant fare.
Here, too, were boys of gold on pedestals
holding aloft bright torches of pitch pine
to light the great rooms, and the night-time feasting.
And fifty maids-in-waiting of the household   110
sat by the round mill, grinding yellow corn,
or wove upon their looms, or twirled their distaffs,
flickering like the leaves of a poplar tree;
while drops of oil glistened on linen weft.
Skillful as were the men of Phaiákia
in ship handling at sea, so were these women
skilled at the loom, having this lovely craft
and artistry as talents from Athena.

To left and right, outside, he saw an orchard
closed by a pale—four spacious acres planted   120
with trees in bloom or weighted down for picking:
pear trees, pomegranates, brilliant apples,
luscious figs, and olives ripe and dark.
Fruit never failed upon these trees: winter
and summer time they bore, for through the year

[2] Legendary ruler of Athens, Athena's city. Marathon (several centuries after Homer's time the site of a great Greek victory over the Persians) was a plain near Athens, cherished by Athena.

[3] Fine blue stone.

the breathing Westwind ripened all in turn—
so one pear came to prime, and then another,
and so with apples, figs, and the vine's fruit
empurpled in the royal vineyard there.
Currants were dried at one end, on a platform   130
bare to the sun, beyond the vintage arbors
and vats the vintners trod; while near at hand
were new grapes barely formed as the green bloom fell,
or half-ripe clusters, faintly coloring.
After the vines came rows of vegetables
of all the kinds that flourish in every season,
and through the garden plots and orchard ran
channels from one clear fountain, while another
gushed through a pipe under the courtyard entrance
to serve the house and all who came for water.   140
These were the gifts of heaven to Alkínoös.

Odysseus, who had borne the barren sea,
stood in the gateway and surveyed this bounty.
He gazed his fill, then swiftly he went in.
The lords and nobles of Phaiákia
were tipping wine to the wakeful god, to Hermês—
a last libation before going to bed—
but down the hall Odysseus went unseen,
still in the cloud Athena cloaked him in,
until he reached Arêtê, and the king.   150
He threw his great hands round Arêtê's knees,
whereon the sacred mist curled back;
they saw him; and the diners hushed amazed
to see an unknown man inside the palace.
Under their eyes Odysseus made his plea:

"Arêtê, admirable Rhêxênor's daughter,
here is a man bruised by adversity, thrown
upon your mercy and the king your husband's,
begging indulgence of this company—
may the gods' blessing rest on them! May life   160
be kind to all! Let each one leave his children
every good thing this realm confers upon him!
But grant me passage to my father land.
My home and friends lie far. My life is pain."

He moved, then, toward the fire, and sat him down
amid the ashes. No one stirred or spoke
until Ekhenêos broke the spell—an old man,
eldest of the Phaiákians, an oracle,
versed in the laws and manners of old time.
He rose among them now and spoke out kindly: 170

"Alkínoös, this will not pass for courtesy:
a guest abased in ashes at our hearth?

Everyone here awaits your word; so come, then,
lift the man up; give him a seat of honor,
a silver-studded chair. Then tell the stewards
we'll have another wine bowl for libation
to Zeus, lord of the lightning—advocate
of honorable petitioners. And supper
may be supplied our friend by the larder mistress."

Alkínoös, calm in power, heard him out, 180
then took the great adventurer by the hand
and led him from the fire. Nearest his throne
the son whom he loved best, Laódamas,
had long held place; now the king bade him rise
and gave his shining chair to Lord Odysseus.
A serving maid poured water for his hands
from a gold pitcher into a silver bowl,
and spead a polished table at his side;
the mistress of provisions came with bread
and other victuals, generous with her store. 190
So Lord Odysseus drank, and tasted supper.
Seeing this done, the king in majesty
said to his squire:

                    "A fresh bowl, Pontónoös;
we make libation to the lord of lightning,
who seconds honorable petitioners."

Mixing the honey-hearted wine, Pontónoös
went on his rounds and poured fresh cups for all,
whereof when all had spilt they drank their fill.
Alkínoös then spoke to the company:

"My lords and leaders of Phaiákia: 200
hear now, all that my heart would have me say.
Our banquet's ended, so you may retire;
but let our seniors gather in the morning
to give this guest a festal day, and make
fair offerings to the gods. In due course we
shall put our minds upon the means at hand
to take him safely, comfortably, well
and happily, with speed, to his own country,
distant though it may lie. And may no trouble
come to him here or on the way; his fate 210
he shall pay out at home, even as the Spinners[4]
spun for him on the day his mother bore him.
If, as may be, he is some god, come down
from heaven's height, the gods are working strangely:
until now, they have shown themselves in glory

---

[4]The fates, mythological women who determined the span of a human life by spinning, measuring, and cutting the thread symbolic of it.

only after great hekatombs—those figures
banqueting at our side, throned like ourselves.
Or if some traveller met them when alone
they bore no least disguise; we are their kin; Gigantês,
Kyklopês, rank no nearer gods than we."   220

Odysseus' wits were ready, and he replied:

"Alkínoös, you may set your mind at rest.
Body and birth, a most unlikely god
am I, being all of earth and mortal nature.
I should say, rather, I am like those men
who suffer the worst trials that you know,
and miseries greater yet, as I might tell you—
hundreds; indeed the gods could send no more.
You will indulge me if I finish dinner—?
grieved though I am to say it. There's no part   230
of man more like a dog than brazen Belly,
crying to be remembered—and it must be—
when we are mortal weary and sick at heart;
and that is my condition. Yet my hunger
drives me to take this food, and think no more
of my afflictions. Belly must be filled.
Be equally impelled, my lords, tomorrow
to berth me in a ship and send me home!
Rough years I've had; now may I see once more
my hall, my lands, my people before I die!"   240

Now all who heard cried out assent to this:
the guest had spoken well; he must have passage.
Then tipping wine they drank their thirst away,
and one by one went homeward for the night.
So Lord Odysseus kept his place alone
with Arêtê and the king Alkínoös
beside him, while the maids went to and fro
clearing away the wine cups and the tables.
Presently the ivory-skinned lady
turned to him—for she knew his cloak and tunic   250
to be her own fine work, done with her maids—
and arrowy came her words upon the air:

"Friend, I, for one, have certain questions for you.
Who are you, and who has given you this clothing?
Did you not say you wandered here by sea?"

The great tactician carefully replied:

"Ah, majesty, what labor it would be
to go through the whole story! All my years
of misadventures, given by those on high!
But this you ask about is quickly told: 260

in mid-ocean lies Ogýgia, the island
haunt of Kalypso, Atlas' guileful daughter,
a lovely goddess and a dangerous one.
No one, no god or man, consorts with her;
but supernatural power brought me there
to be her solitary guest: for Zeus
let fly with his bright bolt and split my ship,
rolling me over in the winedark sea.
There all my shipmates, friends were drowned, while I
hung on the keelboard of the wreck and drifted   270
nine full days. Then in the dead of night
the gods brought me ashore upon Ogýgia
into her hands. The enchantress in her beauty
fed and caressed me, promised me I should be
immortal, youthful, all the days to come;
but in my heart I never gave consent
though seven years detained. Immortal clothing
I had from her, and kept it wet with tears.
Then came the eighth year on the wheel of heaven
and word to her from Zeus, or a change of heart,   280
so that she now commanded me to sail,
sending me out to sea on a craft I made
with timber and tools of hers. She gave me stores,
victuals and wine, a cloak divinely woven,
and made a warm land breeze come up astern.
Seventeen days I sailed in the open water
before I saw your country's shore, a shadow
upon the sea rim. Then my heart rejoiced—
pitiable as I am! For blows aplenty
awaited me from the god who shakes the earth.   290
Cross gales he blew, making me lose my bearings,
and heaved up seas beyond imagination—
huge and foundering seas. All I could do
was hold hard, groaning under every shock,
until my craft broke up in the hurricane.
I kept afloat and swam your sea, or drifted,
taken by wind and current to this coast
where I went in on big swells running landward.
But cliffs and rock shoals made that place forbidding,
so I turned back, swimming off shore, and came   300
in the end to a river, to auspicious water,
with smooth beach and a rise that broke the wind.
I lay there where I fell till strength returned.
Then sacred night came on, and I went inland
to high ground and a leaf bed in a thicket.
Heaven sent slumber in an endless tide
submerging my sad heart among the leaves.
That night and next day's dawn and noon I slept;
the sun went west; and then sweet sleep unbound me,
when I became aware of maids—your daughter's—   310

playing along the beach; the princess, too,
most beautiful. I prayed her to assist me,
and her good sense was perfect; one could hope
for no behavior like it from the young,
thoughtless as they most often are. But she
gave me good provender and good red wine,
a river bath, and finally this clothing.
There is the bitter tale. These are the facts.''

But in reply Alkínoös observed:

"Friend, my child's good judgment failed in this—   320
not to have brought you in her company home.
Once you approached her, you became her charge.''

To this Odysseus tactfully replied:

"Sir, as to that, you should not blame the princess.
She did tell me to follow with her maids,
but I would not. I felt abashed, and feared
the sight would somehow ruffle or offend you.
All of us on this earth are plagued by jealousy.''

Alkínoös' answer was a declaration:

"Friend, I am not a man for trivial anger: 330
better a sense of measure in everything.
No anger here. I say that if it should please
our father Zeus, Athena, and Apollo—
seeing the man you are, seeing your thoughts
are my own thoughts—my daughter should be yours
and you my son-in-law, if you remained.
A home, lands, riches you should have from me
if you could be contented here. If not,
by Father Zeus, let none of our men hold you!
On the contrary, I can assure you now   340
of passage late tomorrow: while you sleep
my men will row you through the tranquil night
to your own land and home or where you please.
It may be, even, far beyond Euboia—
called most remote by seamen of our isle
who landed there, conveying Rhadamanthos
when he sought Títyos, the son of Gaia.[5]
They put about, with neither pause nor rest,
and entered their home port the selfsame day.
But this you, too, will see: what ships I have,   350
how my young oarsmen send the foam a-scudding!''

---

[5] The lines "It may be . . . Gaia" are somewhat obscure, since Rhadamanthos is pictured in
Book IV as dwelling in Elysion, and Títyos, in Book XI, is punished in Hades. The main point
is clear, though: Alkínoös is boasting of the nautical range and speed of his seafaring people.
Euboia is an island east of Greece. Gaia is another name for Ge, the earth-deity.

Now joy welled up in the patient Lord Odysseus
who said devoutly in the warmest tones:

"O Father Zeus, let all this be fulfilled
as spoken by Alkínoös! Earth of harvests
remember him! Return me to my homeland!"

In this manner they conversed with one another;
but the great lady called her maids, and sent them
to make a kingly bed, with purple rugs
piled up, and sheets outspread, and fleecy   360
coverlets, in an eastern colonnade.
The girls went out with torches in their hands,
swift at their work of bedmaking; returning
they whispered at the lord Odysseus' shoulder:

"Sir, you may come; your bed has been prepared."

How welcome the word "bed" came to his ears!
Now, then, Odysseus laid him down and slept
in luxury under the Porch of Morning,
while in his inner chamber Alkínoös
retired to rest where his dear consort lay.   370

BOOK EIGHT: THE SONGS OF THE HARPER

Under the opening fingers of the dawn
Alkínoös, the sacred prince, arose,
and then arose Odysseus, raider of cities.
As the king willed, they went down by the shipways
to the assembly ground of the Phaiákians.
Side by side the two men took their ease there
on smooth stone benches. Meanwhile Pallas Athena
roamed through the byways of the town, contriving
Odysseus' voyage home—in voice and feature
the crier of the king Alkínoös   10
who stopped and passed the word to every man:

"Phaiákian lords and counselors, this way!
Come to assembly: learn about the stranger,
the new guest at the palace of Alkínoös—
a man the sea drove, but a comely man;
the gods' own light is on him."

                                                    She aroused them,
and soon the assembly ground and seats were filled
with curious men, a throng who peered and saw
the master mind of war, Laërtês' son.
Athena now poured out her grace upon him,   20

head and shoulders, height and mass—a splendor
awesome to the eyes of the Phaiákians;
she put him in a fettle to win the day,
mastering every trial they set to test him.
When all the crowd sat marshalled, quieted,
Alkínoös addressed the full assembly:

"Hear me, lords and captains of the Phaiákians!
Hear what my heart would have me say!
Our guest and new friend—nameless to me still—
comes to my house after long wandering   30
in Dawn lands, or among the Sunset races.
Now he appeals to me for conveyance home.
As in the past, therefore, let us provide
passage, and quickly, for no guest of mine
languishes here for lack of it. Look to it:
get a black ship afloat on the noble sea,
and pick our fastest sailer; draft a crew
of two and fifty from our younger townsmen—
men who have made their names at sea. Loop oars
well to your tholepins,[1] lads, then leave the ship,   40
come to our house, fall to, and take your supper:
we'll furnish out a feast for every crewman.
These are your orders. As for my older peers
and princes of the realm, let them foregather
in festival for our friend in my great hall;
and let no man refuse. Call in our minstrel,
Demódokos, whom God made lord of song,
heart-easing, sing upon what theme he will."

He turned, led the procession, and those princes
followed, while his herald sought the minstrel.   50
Young oarsmen from the assembly chose a crew
of two and fifty, as the king commanded,
and these filed off along the waterside
to where the ship lay, poised above open water.
They hauled the black hull down to ride the sea,
rigging a mast and spar in the black ship,
with oars at trail from corded rawhide, all
seamanly; then tried the white sail, hoisting,
and moored her off the beach. Then going ashore
the crew went up to the great house of Alkínoös.   60

Here the enclosures, entrance ways, and rooms
were filled with men, young men and old, for whom
Alkínoös had put twelve sheep to sacrifice,
eight tuskers[2] and a pair of shambling oxen.
These, now, they flayed and dressed to make their banquet.

---

[1] Pegs on the side of a boat, used as oarlocks.   [2] Animals with tusks, such as boars.

The crier soon came, leading that man of song
whom the Muse cherished; by her gift he knew
the good of life, and evil—
for she who lent him sweetness made him blind.[3]
Pontónoös fixed a studded chair for him   70
hard by a pillar amid the banqueters,
hanging the taut harp from a peg above him,
and guided up his hands upon the strings;
placed a bread basket at his side, and poured
wine in a cup, that he might drink his fill.
Now each man's hand went out upon the banquet.

In time, when hunger and thirst were turned away,
the Muse brought to the minstrel's mind a song
of heroes whose great fame rang under heaven:
the clash between Odysseus and Akhilleus,   80
how one time they contended[4] at the godfeast
raging, and the marshal, Agamémnon,
felt inward joy over his captains' quarrel;
for such had been foretold him by Apollo
at Pytho[5]—hallowed height—when the Akhaian
crossed that portal of rock to ask a sign—
in the old days when grim war lay ahead
for Trojans and Danaans, by God's will.
So ran the tale the minstrel sang. Odysseus
with massive hand drew his rich mantle down   90
over his brow, cloaking his face with it,
to make the Phaiákians miss the secret tears
that started to his eyes. How skillfully
he dried them when the song came to a pause!
threw back his mantle, spilt his gout of wine!
But soon the minstrel plucked his note once more
to please the Phaiákian lords, who loved the song;
then in his cloak Odysseus wept again.
His tears flowed in the mantle unperceived:
only Alkínoös, at his elbow, saw them,   100
and caught the low groan in the man's breathing.
At once he spoke to all the seafolk round him:

"Hear me, lords and captains of the Phaiákians.
Our meat is shared, our hearts are full of pleasure
from the clear harp tone that accords with feasting;
now for the field and track; we shall have trials
in the pentathlon.[6] Let our guest go home

---

[3] According to tradition, Homer himself was blind.
[4] This incident probably took place before the action of the *Iliad*.
[5] The shrine of Apollo at Delphi, on Mount Parnassos (Parnassus); the god uttered oracular pronouncements there.
[6] An athletic contest consisting of five events.

and tell his friends what champions we are
at boxing, wrestling, broadjump and foot racing."

On this he led the way and all went after.   110
The crier unslung and pegged the shining harp
and, taking Demódokos's hand,
led him along with all the rest—Phaiákian
peers, gay amateurs of the great games.
They gained the common, where a crowd was forming,
and many a young athlete now came forward
with seaside names like Tipmast, Tiderace, Sparwood,
Hullman, Sternman, Beacher and Pullerman,
Bluewater, Shearwater, Runningwake, Boardalee,
Seabelt, son of Grandfleet Shipwrightson;   120
Seareach stepped up, son of the Launching Master,
rugged as Arês,[7] bane of men; his build
excelled all but the Prince Laódamas;
and Laódamas made entry with his brothers,
Halios and Klytóneus, sons of the king.
The runners, first, must have their quarter mile.
All lined up tense; then Go! and down the track
they raised the dust in a flying bunch, strung out
longer and longer behind Prince Klytóneus.
By just so far as a mule team, breaking ground,   130
will distance oxen, he left all behind
and came up to the crowd, an easy winner.
Then they made room for wrestling—grinding bouts
that Seareach won, pinning the strongest men;
then the broadjump; first place went to Seabelt;
Sparwood gave the discus the mightiest fling,
and Prince Laódamas outboxed them all.

Now it was he, the son of Alkínoös,
who said when they had run through these diversions:

"Look here, friends, we ought to ask the stranger   140
if he competes in something. He's no cripple;
look at his leg muscles and his forearms.
Neck like a bollard;[8] strong as a bull, he seems;
and not old, though he may have gone stale under
the rough times he had. Nothing like the sea
for wearing out the toughest man alive."

Then Seareach took him up at once, and said:

"Laódamas, you're right, by all the powers.
Go up to him, yourself, and put the question."

[7] God of war.   [8] A sturdy post to which a ship's ropes were tied.

At this, Alkínoös' tall son advanced   150
to the center ground, and there addressed Odysseus:

"Friend, Excellency, come join our competition,
if you are practiced, as you seem to be.
While a man lives he wins no greater honor
than footwork and the skill of hands can bring him.
Enter our games, then; ease your heart of trouble.
Your journey home is not far off, remember;
the ship is launched, the crew all primed for sea."

Odysseus, canniest of men, replied:

"Laódamas, why do you young chaps challenge me?   160
I have more on my mind than track and field—
hard days, and many, have I seen, and suffered.
I sit here at your field meet, yes; but only
as one who begs your king to send him home."

Now Seareach put his word in, and contentiously:

"The reason being, as I see it, friend,
you never learned a sport, and have no skill
in any of the contests of fighting men.
You must have been the skipper of some tramp
that crawled from one port to the next, jam full   170
of chaffering hands: a tallier of cargoes,
itching for gold—not, by your looks, an athlete."

Odysseus frowned, and eyed him coldly, saying:

"That was uncalled for, friend, you talk like a fool.
The gods deal out no gift, this one or any—
birth, brains, or speech—to every man alike.
In looks a man may be a shade, a specter,
and yet be master of speech so crowned with beauty
that people gaze at him with pleasure. Courteous,
sure of himself, he can command assemblies,   180
and when he comes to town, the crowds gather.
A handsome man, contrariwise, may lack
grace and good sense in everything he says.
You now, for instance, with your fine physique—
a god's, indeed—you have an empty noddle.[9]
I find my heart inside my ribs aroused
by your impertinence. I am no stranger
to contests, as you fancy. I rated well
when I could count on youth and my two hands.
Now pain has cramped me, and my years of combat   190
hacking through ranks in war, and the bitter sea."

[9] Head.

Aye. Even so I'll give your games a trial.
You spoke heart-wounding words. You shall be answered."

He leapt out, cloaked as he was, and picked a discus,
a rounded stone, more ponderous than those
already used by the Phaiákian throwers,
and, whirling, let it fly from his great hand
with a low hum. The crowd went flat on the ground—
all those oar-pulling, seafaring Phaiákians—
under the rushing noise. The spinning disk   200
soared out, light as a bird, beyond all others.
Disguised now as a Phaiákian, Athena
staked it and called out:

                                        "Even a blind man,
friend, could judge this, finding with his fingers
one discus, quite alone, beyond the cluster.
Congratulations; this event is yours;
not a man here can beat you or come near you."

That was a cheering hail, Odysseus thought,
seeing one friend there on the emulous field,
so, in relief, he turned among the Phaiákians   210
and said:

                                  "Now come alongside that one, lads.
The next I'll send as far, I think, or farther.
Anyone else on edge for competition
try me now. By heaven, you angered me.
Racing, wrestling, boxing—I bar nothing
with any man except Laódamas,
for he's my host. Who quarrels with his host?
Only a madman—or no man at all—
would challenge his protector among strangers,
cutting the ground away under his feet.   220
Here are no others I will not engage,
none but I hope to know what he is made of.
Inept at combat, am I? Not entirely.
Give me a smooth bow; I can handle it,
and I might well be first to hit my man
amid a swarm of enemies, though archers
in company around me drew together.
Philoktêtês[10] alone, at Troy, when we
Akhaians took the bow, used to outshoot me.
Of men who now eat bread upon the earth   230
I hold myself the best hand with a bow—
conceding mastery to the men of old,

[10] Philoktêtês had inherited the magical bow of the fabled hero Heraklês (Hercules); a
version of his story is dramatized in Sophocles' *Philoctetes*.

Heraklês, or Eurýtos[11] of Oikhalía,
heroes who vied with gods in bowmanship.
Eurýtos came to grief, it's true; old age
never crept over him in his long hall;
Apollo took his challenge ill, and killed him.
What then, the spear? I'll plant it like an arrow.
Only in sprinting, I'm afraid, I may
be passed by someone. Roll of the sea waves   240
wearied me, and the victuals in my ship
ran low; my legs are flabby."

                                                When he finished,
the rest were silent, but Alkínoös answered:

"Friend, we take your challenge in good part,
for this man angered and affronted you
here at our peaceful games. You'd have us note
the prowess that is in you, and so clearly,
no man of sense would ever cry it down!
Come, turn your mind, now, on a thing to tell
among your peers when you are home again,   250
dining in hall, beside your wife and children:
I mean our prowess, as you may remember it,
for we, too, have our skills, given by Zeus,
and practiced from our father's time to this—
not in the boxing ring nor the palestra[12]
conspicuous, but in racing, land or sea;
and all our days we set great store by feasting,
harpers, and the grace of dancing choirs,
changes of dress, warm baths, and downy beds.
O master dancers of the Phaiákians!   260
Perform now: let our guest on his return
tell his companions we excel the world
in dance and song, as in our ships and running.
Someone go find the gittern harp in hall
and bring it quickly to Demódokos!"

At the serene king's word, a squire ran
to bring the polished harp out of the palace,
and place was given to nine referees—
peers of the realm, masters of ceremony—
who cleared a space and smoothed a dancing floor.   270
The squire brought down, and gave Demódokos,
the clear-toned harp; and centering on the minstrel
magical young dancers formed a circle
with a light beat, and stamp of feet. Beholding,
Odysseus marvelled at the flashing ring.

[11] Grandson of Apollo, and Heraklês' instructor in bowmanship. He was killed in a competition with Apollo, god of archery. Eurýtos' bow descended to Odysseus.
[12] A public athletics-ground.

Now to his harp the blinded minstrel sang
of Arês' dalliance with Aphroditê:
how hidden in Hephaistos'[13] house they played
at love together, and the gifts of Arês,
dishonoring Hephaistos' bed—and how   280
the word that wounds the heart came to the master
from Hêlios,[14] who had seen the two embrace;
and when he learned it, Lord Hephaistos went
with baleful calculation to his forge.
There mightily he armed his anvil block
and hammered out a chain, whose tempered links
could not be sprung or bent; he meant that they should hold.
Those shackles fashioned, hot in wrath Hephaistos
climbed to the bower and the bed of love,
pooled all his net of chain around the bed posts   290
and swung it from the rafters overhead—
light as a cobweb even gods in bliss
could not perceive, so wonderful his cunning.
Seeing his bed now made a snare, he feigned
a journey to the trim stronghold of Lemnos,[15]
the dearest of earth's towns to him. And Arês?
Ah, golden Arês' watch had its reward
when he beheld the great smith leaving home.
How promptly to the famous door he came,
intent on pleasure with sweet Kythereia![16]   300
She, who had left her father's side but now,
sat in her chamber when her lover entered;
and tenderly he pressed her hand and said:

"Come and lie down, my darling, and be happy!
Hephaistos is no longer here, but gone
to see his grunting Sintian[17] friends on Lemnos."

As she, too, thought repose would be most welcome,
the pair went in to bed—into a shower
of clever chains, the netting of Hephaistos.
So trussed, they could not move apart, nor rise,   310
at last they knew there could be no escape,
they were to see the glorious cripple now—
for Hêlios had spied for him, and told him;
so he turned back, this side of Lemnos Isle,
sick at heart, making his way homeward.
Now in the doorway of the room he stood
while deadly rage took hold of him; his voice,
hoarse and terrible, reached all the gods:

---

[13] The lame god of fire and metalworking, husband of Aphroditê.   [14] The sun-god.
[15] An island in the Aegean, center of the worship of Hephaistos; it was there that he fell
after Zeus, during a fit of anger, threw him out of heaven.
[16] Aphroditê. Also spelled *Cytherea*.
[17] The Sintians, of Lemnos, had a reputation for crudity.

"O Father Zeus, O gods in bliss forever,
here is indecorous entertainment for you,   320
Aphroditê, Zeus's daughter,
caught in the act, cheating me, her cripple,
with Arês—devastating Arês.
Cleanlimbed beauty is her joy, not these
bandylegs I came into the world with:
no one to blame but the two gods[18] who bred me!
Come see this pair entwining here
in my own bed! How hot it makes me burn!
I think they may not care to lie much longer,
pressing on one another, passionate lovers;   330
they'll have enough of bed together soon.
And yet the chain that bagged them holds them down
till Father sends me back my wedding gifts—
all that I poured out for his damned pigeon,
so lovely, and so wanton."

                                              All the others
were crowding in, now, to the brazen house—
Poseidon who embraces earth, and Hermês
the runner, and Apollo, lord of Distance.
The goddesses stayed home for shame; but these
munificences ranged there in the doorway,   340
and irrepressible among them all
arose the laughter of the happy gods.
Gazing hard at Hephaistos' handiwork
the gods in turn remarked among themselves:

"No dash in adultery now."

                              "The tortoise tags the hare—
Hephaistos catches Arês—and Arês outran the wind."

"The lame god's craft has pinned him. Now shall he
pay what is due from gods taken in cuckoldry."

They made these improving remarks to one another,
but Apollo leaned aside to say to Hermês: 350

"Son of Zeus, beneficent Wayfinder,
would you accept a coverlet of chain, if only
you lay by Aphroditê's golden side?"

To this the Wayfinder replied, shining:

"Would I not, though, Apollo of distances!
Wrap me in chains three times the weight of these,
come goddesses and gods to see the fun;
only let me lie beside the pale-golden one!"

[18] Zeus and Hera.

The gods gave away again to peals of laughter,
all but Poseidon, and he never smiled,   360
but urged Hephaistos to unpinion Arês,
saying emphatically, in a loud voice:

                                              "Free him;

you will be paid, I swear; ask what you will;
he pays up every jot the gods decree."

To this the Great Gamelegs replied:

                                              "Poseidon,

lord of the earth-surrounding sea, I should not
swear to a scoundrel's honor. What have I
as surety from you, if Arês leaves me
empty-handed, with my empty chain?"

The Earth-shaker for answer urged again: 370

"Hephaistos, let us grant he goes, and leaves
the fine unpaid; I swear, then, I shall pay it."

Then said the Great Gamelegs at last:

                                              "No more;

you offer terms I cannot well refuse."

And down the strong god bent to set them free,
till disencumbered of their bond, the chain,
the lovers leapt away—he into Thrace,
while Aphroditê, laughter's darling, fled
to Kypros Isle and Paphos,[19] to her meadow
and altar dim with incense. There the Graces   380
bathed and anointed her with golden oil—
a bloom that clings upon immortal flesh alone—
and let her folds of mantle fall in glory.

So ran the song the minstrel sang.

                                              Odysseus,

listening, found sweet pleasure in the tale,
among the Phaiákian mariners and oarsmen.
And next Alkínoös called upon his sons,
Halios and Laódamas, to show
the dance no one could do as well as they—
handling a purple ball carven by Pólybos.   390
One made it shoot up under the shadowing clouds
as he leaned backward; bounding high in air
the other cut its flight far off the ground—
and neither missed a step as the ball soared.

[19] A city in ancient Cyprus (Kypros), an island south of Turkey where Aphroditê had a cult.

The next turn was to keep it low, and shuttling
hard between them, while the ring of boys
gave them a steady stamping beat.
Odysseus now addressed Alkínoös:

"O majesty, model of all your folk,
your promise was to show me peerless dancers;   400
here is the promise kept. I am all wonder."

At this Alkínoös in his might rejoicing
said to the seafarers of Phaiákia:

"Attend me now, Phaiákian lords and captains:
our guest appears a clear-eyed man and wise.
Come, let him feel our bounty as he should.
Here are twelve princes of the kingdom—lords
paramount, and I who make thirteen;
let each one bring a laundered cloak and tunic,
and add one bar of honorable gold.   410
Heap all our gifts together; load his arms;
let him go joyous to our evening feast!
As for Seareach—why, man to man
he'll make amends, and handsomely; he blundered."

Now all as one acclaimed the king's good pleasure,
and each one sent a squire to bring his gifts.
Meanwhile Seareach found speech again, saying:

"My lord and model of us all, Alkínoös,
as you require of me, in satisfaction,
this broadsword of clear bronze goes to our guest.   420
Its hilt is silver, and the ringed sheath
of new-sawn ivory—a costly weapon."

He turned to give the broadsword to Odysseus,
facing him, saying blithely:

                                        "Sir, my best
wishes, my respects; if I offended,
I hope the seawinds blow it out of mind.
God send you see your lady and your homeland
soon again, after the pain of exile."

Odysseus, the great tactician, answered:

"My hand, friend; may the gods award you fortune.   430
I hope no pressing need comes on you ever
for this fine blade you give me in amends."

He slung it, glinting silver, from his shoulder,
as the light shone from sundown. Messengers
were bearing gifts and treasure to the palace,

where the king's sons received them all, and made
a glittering pile at their grave mother's side;
then, as Alkínoös took his throne of power,
each went to his own high-backed chair in turn,
and said Alkínoös to Arêtê: 440

"Lady, bring here a chest, the finest one;
a clean cloak and tunic; stow these things;
and warm a cauldron for him. Let him bathe,
when he has seen the gifts of the Phaiákians,
and so dine happily to a running song.
My own wine-cup of gold intaglio[20]
I'll give him, too; through all the days to come,
tipping his wine to Zeus or other gods
in his great hall, he shall remember me."

Then said Arêtê to her maids:

                                                        "The tripod: 450

stand the great tripod legs about the fire."

They swung the cauldron on the fire's heart,
poured water in, and fed the blaze beneath
until the basin simmered, cupped in flame.
The queen set out a rich chest from her chamber
and folded in the gifts—clothing and gold
given Odysseus by the Phaiákians;
then she put in the royal cloak and tunic,
briskly saying to her guest:

                                                        "Now here, sir,

look to the lid yourself, and tie it down   460
against light fingers, if there be any,
on the black ship tonight while you are sleeping."

Noble Odysseus, expert in adversity,
battened the lid down with a lightning knot
learned, once, long ago, from the Lady Kirkê.[21]
And soon a call came from the Bathing Mistress
who led him to a hip-bath, warm and clear—
a happy sight, and rare in his immersions
after he left Kalypso's home—where, surely,
the luxuries of a god were ever his.   470
When the bath maids had washed him, rubbed him down,
put a fresh tunic and a cloak around him,
he left the bathing place to join the men
at wine in hall.

[20] A design cut into the surface.
[21] A sorceress; Odysseus' encounter with her is described in Book X. Also spelled *Circe.*

                                                        The princess Nausikaa,
exquisite figure, as of heaven's shaping,
waited beside a pillar as he passed
and said swiftly, with wonder in her look:

"Fare well, stranger; in your land remember me
who met and saved you. It is worth your thought."

The man of all occasions now met this: 480

"Daughter of great Alkínoös, Nausikaa,
may Zeus the lord of thunder, Hera's consort,
grant me daybreak again in my own country!
But there and all my days until I die
may I invoke you as I would a goddess,
princess, to whom I owe my life."

                                                        He left her
and went to take his place beside the king.

Now when the roasts were cut, the winebowls full,
a herald led the minstrel down the room
amid the deference of the crowd, and paused   490
to seat him near a pillar in the center—
whereupon that resourceful man, Odysseus,
carved out a quarter from his chine of pork,
crisp with fat, and called the blind man's guide:

"Herald! here, take this to Demódokos:
let him feast and be merry, with my compliments.
All men owe honor to the poets—honor
and awe, for they are dearest to the Muse
who puts upon their lips the ways of life."

Gentle Demódokos took the proffered gift   500
and inwardly rejoiced. When all were served,
every man's hand went out upon the banquet,
repelling hunger and thirst, until at length
Odysseus spoke again to the blind minstrel:

"Demódokos, accept my utmost praise.
The Muse, daughter of Zeus in radiance,
or else Apollo[22] gave you skill to shape
with such great style your songs of the Akhaians—
their hard lot, how they fought and suffered war.
You shared it, one would say, or heard it all.   510
Now shift your theme, and sing that wooden horse
Epeios built, inspired by Athena—
the ambuscade Odysseus filled with fighters
and sent to take the inner town of Troy.

[22] God of music and prophecy. He would naturally have an affinity with bards.

Sing only this for me, sing me this well,
and I shall say at once before the world
the grace of heaven has given us a song."

The minstrel stirred, murmuring to the god, and soon
clear words and notes came one by one, a vision
of the Akhaians in their graceful ships   520
drawing away from shore: the torches flung
and shelters flaring: Argive soldiers crouched
in the close dark around Odysseus: and
the horse, tall on the assembly ground of Troy.
For when the Trojans pulled it in, themselves,
up to the citadel, they sat nearby
with long-drawn-out and hapless argument—
favoring, in the end, one course of three:
either to stave the vault with brazen axes,
or haul it to a cliff and pitch it down,   530
or else to save it for the gods, a votive glory—
the plan that could not but prevail.
For Troy must perish, as ordained, that day
she harbored the great horse of timber; hidden
the flower of Akhaia lay, and bore
slaughter and death upon the men of Troy.
He sang, then, of the town sacked by Akhaians
pouring down from the horse's hollow cave,
this way and that way raping the steep city,
and how Odysseus came like Arês to   540
the door of Deïphobos,[23] with Meneláos,
and braved the desperate fight there—
conquering once more by Athena's power.

The splendid minstrel sang it.

                                              And Odysseus

let the bright molten tears run down his cheeks,
weeping the way a wife mourns for her lord
on the lost field where he has gone down fighting
the day of wrath that came upon his children.
At sight of the man panting and dying there,
she slips down to enfold him, crying out;   550
then feels the spears, prodding her back and shoulders,
and goes bound into slavery and grief.
Piteous weeping wears away her cheeks:
but no more piteous than Odysseus' tears,
cloaked as they were, now, from the company.
Only Alkínoös, at his elbow, knew—
hearing the low sob in the man's breathing—
and when he knew, he spoke:

[23] Meneláos' wife, Helen, had in Troy been given in marriage to Deïphobos.

"Hear me, lords and captains of Phaiákia!
And let Demódokos touch his harp no more.   560
His theme has not been pleasing to all here.
During the feast, since our fine poet sang,
our guest has never left off weeping. Grief
seems fixed upon his heart. Break off the song!
Let everyone be easy, host and guest;
there's more decorum in a smiling banquet!
We had prepared here, on our friend's behalf,
safe conduct in a ship, and gifts to cheer him,
holding that any man with a grain of wit
will treat a decent suppliant like a brother.   570
Now by the same rule, friend, you must not be
secretive any longer! Come, in fairness,
tell me the name you bore in that far country;
how were you known to family, and neighbors?
No man is nameless—no man, good or bad,
but gets a name in his first infancy,
none being born, unless a mother bears him!
Tell me your native land, your coast and city—
sailing directions for the ships, you know—
for those Phaiákian ships of ours   580
that have no steersman, and no steering oar,
divining the crew's wishes, as they do,
and knowing, as they do, the ports of call
about the world. Hidden in mist or cloud
they scud the open sea, with never a thought
of being in distress or going down.
There is, however, something I once heard
Nausíthoös, my father, say: Poseidon
holds it against us that our deep sea ships
are sure conveyance for all passengers.   590
My father said, some day one of our cutters
homeward bound over the cloudy sea
would be wrecked by the god, and a range of hills
thrown round our city. So, in his age, he said,
and let it be, or not, as the god please.
But come, now, put it for me clearly, tell me
the sea ways that you wandered, and the shores
you touched; the cities, and the men therein,
uncivilized, if such there were, and hostile,
and those godfearing who had kindly manners.   600
Tell me why you should grieve so terribly
over the Argives and the fall of Troy.
That was all gods' work, weaving ruin there
so it should make a song for men to come!
Some kin of yours, then, died at Ilion,
some first rate man, by marriage near to you,
next your own blood most dear?
Or some companion of congenial mind

and valor? True it is, a wise friend
can take a brother's place in our affection."   610

BOOK NINE: NEW COASTS AND POSEIDON'S SON

Now this was the reply Odysseus made:

"Alkínoös, king and admiration of men,
how beautiful this is, to hear a minstrel
gifted as yours: a god he might be, singing!
There is no boon in life more sweet, I say,
than when a summer joy holds all the realm,
and banqueters sit listening to a harper
in a great hall, by rows of tables heaped
with bread and roast meat, while a steward goes
to dip up wine and brim your cups again.   10
Here is the flower of life, it seems to me!
But now you wish to know my cause for sorrow—
and thereby give me cause for more.

                                        What shall I

say first? What shall I keep until the end?
The gods have tried me in a thousand ways.
But first my name: let that be known to you,
and if I pull away from pitiless death,
friendship will bind us, though my land lies far.

I am Laërtês' son, Odysseus.

                                        Men hold me

formidable for guile in peace and war: 20
this fame has gone abroad to the sky's rim.
My home is on the peaked sea-mark of Ithaka
under Mount Neion's wind-blown robe of leaves,
in sight of other islands—Doulíkhion,
Samê, wooded Zakynthos—Ithaka
being most lofty in that coastal sea,
and northwest, while the rest lie east and south.
A rocky isle, but good for a boy's training;
I shall not see on earth a place more dear,
though I have been detained long by Kalypso,   30
loveliest among goddesses, who held me
in her smooth caves, to be her heart's delight,
as Kirkê of Aiaia, the enchantress,
desired me, and detained me in her hall.
But in my heart I never gave consent.
Where shall a man find sweetness to surpass
his own home and his parents? In far lands
he shall not, though he find a house of gold.

What of my sailing, then, from Troy?

What of those years

of rough adventure, weathered under Zeus?   40
The wind that carried west from Ilion
brought me to Ísmaros,[1] on the far shore,
a strongpoint on the coast of the Kikonês.
I stormed that place and killed the men who fought.
Plunder we took, and we enslaved the women,
to make division, equal shares to all—
but on the spot I told them: 'Back, and quickly!
Out to sea again!' My men were mutinous,
fools, on stores of wine. Sheep after sheep
they butchered by the surf, and shambling cattle,   50
feasting,—while fugitives went inland, running
to call to arms the main force of Kikonês.
This was an army, trained to fight on horseback
or, where the ground required, on foot. They came
with dawn over that terrain like the leaves
and blades of spring. So doom appeared to us,
dark word of Zeus for us, our evil days.
My men stood up and made a fight of it—
backed on the ships, with lances kept in play,
from bright morning through the blaze of noon   60
holding our beach, although so far outnumbered;
but when the sun passed toward unyoking time,
then the Akhaians, one by one, gave way.
Six benches were left empty in every ship
that evening when we pulled away from death.
And this new grief we bore with us to sea:
our precious lives we had, but not our friends.
No ship made sail next day until some shipmate
had raised a cry, three times, for each poor ghost
unfleshed by the Kikonês on that field.   70

Now Zeus the lord of cloud roused in the north
a storm against the ships, and driving veils
of squall moved down like night on land and sea.
The bows went plunging at the gust; sails
cracked and lashed out strips in the big wind.
We saw death in that fury, dropped the yards,
unshipped the oars, and pulled for the nearest lee:
then two long days and nights we lay offshore
worn out and sick at heart, tasting our grief,
until a third Dawn came with ringlets shining.   80
Then we put up our masts, hauled sail, and rested,
letting the steersmen and the breeze take over.

---

[1] The land of the Kikonês, in Thrace (on the northern coast of the Aegean Sea).

I might have made it safely home, that time,
but as I came round Malea[2] the current
took me out to sea, and from the north
a fresh gale drove me on, past Kythera.
Nine days I drifted on the teeming sea
before dangerous high winds. Upon the tenth
we came to the coastline of the Lotos Eaters,
who live upon that flower. We landed there   90
to take on water. All ships' companies
mustered alongside for the mid-day meal.
Then I sent out two picked men and a runner
to learn what race of men that land sustained.
They fell in, soon enough, with Lotos Eaters,
who showed no will to do us harm, only
offering the sweet Lotos to our friends—
but those who ate this honeyed plant, the Lotos,
never cared to report, nor to return:
they longed to stay forever, browsing on   100
the native bloom, forgetful of their homeland.
I drove them, all three wailing, to the ships,
tied them down under their rowing benches,
and called the rest: 'All hands aboard;
come, clear the beach and no one taste
the Lotos, or you lose your hope of home.'
Filing in to their places by the rowlocks
my oarsmen dipped their long oars in the surf,
and we moved out again on our sea faring.

In the next land we found were Kyklopês,[3]   110
giants, louts, without a law to bless them.
In ignorance leaving the fruitage of the earth in mystery
to the immortal gods, they neither plow
nor sow by hand, nor till the ground, though grain—
wild wheat and barley—grows untended, and
wine-grapes, in clusters, ripen in heaven's rain.
Kyklopês have no muster and no meeting,
no consultation or old tribal ways,
but each one dwells in his own mountain cave
dealing out rough justice to wife and child,   120
indifferent to what the others do.

                                               Well, then:

across the wide bay from the mainland
there lies a desert island, not far out,
but still not close inshore. Wild goats in hundreds
breed there; and no human being comes
upon the isle to startle them—no hunter
of all who ever tracked with hounds through forests

---

[2] The cape at the southernmost end of Greece; Kythera, mentioned two lines below, is a sizable island just southwest of Malea.

[3] One-eyed giants, inhabitants of Sicily. Also spelled *Cyclops*.

or had rough going over mountain trails.
The isle, unplanted and untilled, a wilderness,
pastures goats alone. And this is why: 130
good ships like ours with cheekpaint at the bows
are far beyond the Kyklopês. No shipwright
toils among them, shaping and building up
symmetrical trim hulls to cross the sea
and visit all the seaboard towns, as men do
who go and come in commerce over water.
This isle—seagoing folk would have annexed it
and built their homesteads on it: all good land,
fertile for every crop in season: lush
well-watered meads along the shore, vines in profusion,   140
prairie, clear for the plow, where grain would grow
chin high by harvest time, and rich sub-soil.
The island cove is landlocked, so you need
no hawsers out astern, bow-stones or mooring:
run in and ride there till the day your crews
chafe to be under sail, and a fair wind blows.
You'll find good water flowing from a cavern
through dusky poplars into the upper bay.
Here we made harbor. Some god guided us
that night, for we could barely see our bows   150
in the dense fog around us, and no moonlight
filtered through the overcast. No look-out,
nobody saw the island dead ahead,
nor even the great landward rolling billow
that took us in: we found ourselves in shallows,
keels grazing shore: so furled our sails
and disembarked where the low ripples broke.
There on the beach we lay, and slept till morning.

When Dawn spread out her finger tips of rose
we turned out marvelling, to tour the isle,   160
while Zeus's shy nymph daughters flushed wild goats
down from the heights—a breakfast for my men.
We ran to fetch our hunting bows and long-shanked
lances from the ships, and in three companies
we took our shots. Heaven gave us game a-plenty:
for every one of twelve ships in my squadron
nine goats fell to be shared; my lot was ten.
So there all day, until the sun went down,
we made our feast on meat galore, and wine—
wine from the ship, for our supply held out,   170
so many jars were filled at Ísmaros
from stores of the Kikonês that we plundered.
We gazed, too, at Kyklopês Land, so near,
we saw their smoke, heard bleating from their flocks.
But after sundown, in the gathering dusk,
we slept again above the wash of ripples.

When the young Dawn with finger tips of rose
came in the east, I called my men together
and made a speech to them:

                               'Old shipmates, friends,
the rest of you stand by; I'll make the crossing   180
in my own ship, with my own company,
and find out what the mainland natives are—
for they may be wild savages, and lawless,
or hospitable and god fearing men.'

At this I went aboard, and gave the word
to cast off by the stern. My oarsmen followed,
filing in to their benches by the rowlocks,
and all in line dipped oars in the grey sea.

As we rowed on, and nearer to the mainland,
at one end of the bay, we saw a cavern   190
yawning above the water, screened with laurel,
and many rams and goats about the place
inside a sheepfold—made from slabs of stone
earthfast between tall trunks of pine and rugged
towering oak trees.

                            A prodigious man
slept in this cave alone, and took his flocks
to graze afield—remote from all companions,
knowing none but savage ways, a brute
so huge, he seemed no man at all of those
who eat good wheaten bread; but he seemed rather   200
a shaggy mountain reared in solitude.
We beached there, and I told the crew
to stand by and keep watch over the ship;
as for myself I took my twelve best fighters
and went ahead. I had a goatskin full
of that sweet liquor that Euanthês' son,
Maron, had given me. He kept Apollo's
holy grove at Ísmaros; for kindness
we showed him there, and showed his wife and child,
he gave me seven shining golden talents   210
perfectly formed, a solid silver winebowl,
and then this liquor—twelve two-handled jars
of brandy, pure and fiery. Not a slave
in Maron's household knew this drink; only
he, his wife and the storeroom mistress knew;
and they would put one cupful—ruby-colored,
honey-smooth—in twenty more of water,
but still the sweet scent hovered like a fume
over the winebowl. No man turned away
when cups of this came round.

A wineskin full 220
I brought along, and victuals in a bag,
for in my bones I knew some towering brute
would be upon us soon—all outward power,
a wild man, ignorant of civility.

We climbed, then, briskly to the cave. But Kyklops
had gone afield, to pasture his fat sheep,
so we looked round at everything inside:
a drying rack that sagged with cheeses, pens
crowded with lambs and kids, each in its class:
firstlings apart from middlings, and the 'dewdrops,' 230
or newborn lambkins, penned apart from both.
And vessels full of whey were brimming there—
bowls of earthenware and pails for milking.
My men came pressing round me, pleading:

'Why not

take these cheeses, get them stowed, come back,
throw open all the pens, and make a run for it?
We'll drive the kids and lambs aboard. We say
put out again on good salt water!'

Ah,

how sound that was! Yet I refused. I wished
to see the caveman, what he had to offer— 240
no pretty sight, it turned out, for my friends.
We lit a fire, burnt an offering,
and took some cheese to eat; then sat in silence
around the embers, waiting. When he came
he had a load of dry boughs on his shoulder
to stoke his fire at suppertime. He dumped it
with a great crash into that hollow cave,
and we all scattered fast to the far wall.
Then over the broad cavern floor he ushered
the ewes he meant to milk. He left his rams 250
and he-goats in the yard outside, and swung
high overhead a slab of solid rock
to close the cave. Two dozen four-wheeled wagons,
with heaving wagon teams, could not have stirred
the tonnage of that rock from where he wedged it
over the doorsill. Next he took his seat
and milked his bleating ewes. A practiced job
he made of it, giving each ewe her suckling;
thickened his milk, then, into curds and whey,[4]
sieved out the curds to drip in withy baskets, 260
and poured the whey to stand in bowls
cooling until he drank it for his supper.

[4] The liquid part of separated milk, as distinguished from the lumpy curds.

When all these chores were done, he poked the fire,
heaping on brushwood. In the glare he saw us.

"Strangers,' he said, 'who are you? And where from?
What brings you here by sea ways—a fair traffic?
Or are you wandering rogues, who cast your lives
like dice, and ravage other folk by sea?'

We felt a pressure on our hearts, in dread
of that deep rumble and that mighty man.   270
But all the same I spoke up in reply:

'We are from Troy, Akhaians, blown off course
by shifting gales on the Great South Sea;
homeward bound, but taking routes and ways
uncommon; so the will of Zeus would have it.
We served under Agamémnon, son of Atreus—
the whole world knows what city
he laid waste, what armies he destroyed.
It was our luck to come here; here we stand,
beholden for your help, or any gifts   280
you give—as custom is to honor strangers.
We would entreat you, great Sir, have a care
for the gods' courtesy; Zeus will avenge
the unoffending guest.'[5]

                                                      He answered this
from his brute chest, unmoved:

                                                      'You are a ninny,
or else you come from the other end of nowhere,
telling me, mind the gods! We Kyklopês
care not a whistle for your thundering Zeus
or all the gods in bliss; we have more force by far.
I would not let you go for fear of Zeus—   290
you or your friends—unless I had a whim to.
Tell me, where was it, now, you left your ship—
around the point, or down the shore, I wonder?'

He thought he'd find out, but I saw through this,
and answered with a ready lie:

                                                      'My ship?
Poseidon Lord, who sets the earth a-tremble,
broke it up on the rocks at your land's end.
A wind from seaward served him, drove us there.
We are survivors, these good men and I.'

Neither reply nor pity came from him,   300
but in one stride he clutched at my companions

---

[5] Zeus was the protector and guarantor of the laws of hospitality.

and caught two in his hands like squirming puppies
to beat their brains out, spattering the floor.
Then he dismembered them and made his meal,
gaping and crunching like a mountain lion—
everything: innards, flesh, and marrow bones.
We cried aloud, lifting our hands to Zeus,
powerless, looking on at this, appalled;
but Kyklops[6] went on filling up his belly
with manflesh and great gulps of whey,   310
then lay down like a mast among his sheep.
My heart beat high now at the chance of action,
and drawing the sharp sword from my hip I went
along his flank to stab him where the midriff
holds the liver. I had touched the spot
when sudden fear stayed me: if I killed him
we perished there as well, for we could never
move his ponderous doorway slab aside.
So we were left to groan and wait for morning.

When the young Dawn with finger tips of rose   320
lit up the world, the Kyklops built a fire
and milked his handsome ewes, all in due order,
putting the sucklings to the mothers. Then,
his chores being all dispatched, he caught
another brace of men to make his breakfast,
and whisked away his great door slab
to let his sheep go through—but he, behind,
reset the stone as one would cap a quiver.
There was a din of whistling as the Kyklops
rounded his flock to higher ground, then stillness.   330
And now I pondered how to hurt him worst,
if but Athena granted what I prayed for.
Here are the means I thought would serve my turn:

a club, or staff, lay there along the fold—
an olive tree, felled green and left to season
for Kyklops' hand. And it was like a mast
a lugger of twenty oars, broad in the beam—
a deep-sea-going craft—might carry:
so long, so big around, it seemed. Now I
chopped out a six foot section of this pole   340
and set it down before my men, who scraped it;
and when they had it smooth, I hewed again
to make a stake with pointed end. I held this
in the fire's heart and turned it, toughening it,
then hid it, well back in the cavern, under
one of the dung piles in profusion there.
Now came the time to toss for it: who ventured

[6] Here used as a singular; his name, we learn later, is Polyphêmos.

along with me? whose hand could bear to thrust
and grind that spike in Kyklops' eye, when mild
sleep had mastered him? As luck would have it,   350
the men I would have chosen won the toss—
four strong men, and I made five as captain.

At evening came the shepherd with his flock,
his woolly flock. The rams as well, this time,
entered the cave: by some sheep-herding whim—
or a god's bidding—none were left outside.
He hefted his great boulder into place
and sat him down to milk the bleating ewes
in proper order, put the lambs to suck,
and swiftly ran through all his evening chores.   360
Then he caught two more men and feasted on them.
My moment was at hand, and I went forward
holding an ivy bowl of my dark drink,
looking up, saying:

                       'Kyklops, try some wine.
Here's liquor to wash down your scraps of men.
Taste it, and see the kind of drink we carried
under our planks. I meant it for an offering
if you would help us home. But you are mad,
unbearable, a bloody monster! After this,
will any other traveller come to see you?'   370

He seized and drained the bowl, and it went down
so fiery and smooth he called for more:

'Give me another, thank you kindly. Tell me,
how are you called? I'll make a gift will please you.
Even Kyklopês know the wine-grapes grow
out of grassland and loam in heaven's rain,
but here's a bit of nectar and ambrosia!'

Three bowls I brought him, and he poured them down.
I saw the fuddle and flush come over him,
then I sang out in cordial tones:

                                    'Kyklops,   380
you ask my honorable name? Remember
the gift you promised me, and I shall tell you.
My name is Nohbdy: mother, father, and friends,
everyone calls me Nohbdy.'

                                  And he said:

'Nohbdy's my meat, then, after I eat his friends.
Others come first. There's a noble gift, now.'

Even as he spoke, he reeled and tumbled backward,
his great head lolling to one side; and sleep

took him like any creature. Drunk, hiccuping,
he dribbled streams of liquor and bits of men.   390

Now, by the gods, I drove my big hand spike
deep in the embers, charring it again,
and cheered my men along with battle talk
to keep their courage up: no quitting now.
The pike of olive, green though it had been,
reddened and glowed as if about to catch.
I drew it from the coals and my four fellows
gave me a hand, lugging it near the Kyklops
as more than natural force nerved them; straight
forward they sprinted, lifted it, and rammed it   400
deep in his crater eye, and I leaned on it
turning it as a shipwright turns a drill
in planking, having men below to swing
the two-handled strap that spins it in the groove.
So with our brand we bored that great eye socket
while blood ran out around the red hot bar.
Eyelid and lash were seared; the pierced ball
hissed broiling, and the roots popped.

                                            In a smithy
one sees a white-hot axehead or an adze
plunged and wrung in a cold tub, screeching steam—   410
the way they make soft iron hale and hard—:
just so that eyeball hissed around the spike.
The Kyklops bellowed and the rock roared round him,
and we fell back in fear. Clawing his face
he tugged the bloody spike out of his eye,
threw it away, and his wild hands went groping;
then he set up a howl for Kyklopês
who lived in caves on windy peaks nearby.
Some heard him; and they came by divers ways
to clump around outside and call:

                                         'What ails you,   420
Polyphêmos? Why do you cry so sore
in the starry night? You will not let us sleep.
Sure no man's driving off your flock? No man
has tricked you, ruined you?'

                                        Out of the cave
the mammoth Polyphêmos roared in answer:

'Nohbdy, Nohbdy's tricked me, Nohbdy's ruined me!'

To this rough shout they made a sage reply:

'Ah well, if nobody has played you foul
there in your lonely bed, we are no use in pain

given by great Zeus. Let it be your father,   430
Poseidon Lord, to whom you pray.'

                                                    So saying
they trailed away. And I was filled with laughter
to see how like a charm the name deceived them.
Now Kyklops, wheezing as the pain came on him,
fumbled to wrench away the great doorstone
and squatted in the breach with arms thrown wide
for any silly beast or man who bolted—
hoping somehow I might be such a fool.
But I kept thinking how to win the game:
death sat there huge; how could we slip away?   440
I drew on all my wits, and ran through tactics,
reasoning as a man will for dear life,
until a trick came—and it pleased me well.
The Kyklops' rams were handsome, fat, with heavy
fleeces, a dark violet.

                                        Three abreast
I tied them silently together, twining
cords of willow from the ogre's bed;
then slung a man under each middle one
to ride there safely, shielded left and right.
So three sheep could convey each man. I took   450
the woolliest ram, the choicest of the flock,
and hung myself under his kinky belly,
pulled up tight, with fingers twisted deep
in sheepskin ringlets for an iron grip.
So, breathing hard, we waited until morning.

When Dawn spread out her finger tips of rose
the rams began to stir, moving for pasture,
and peals of bleating echoed round the pens
where dams with udders full called for a milking.
Blinded, and sick with pain from his head wound,   460
the master stroked each ram, then let it pass,
but my men riding on the pectoral fleece
the giant's blind hands blundering never found.
Last of them all my ram, the leader, came,
weighted by wool and me with my meditations.
The Kyklops patted him, and then he said:

'Sweet cousin ram, why lag behind the rest
in the night cave? You never linger so,
but graze before them all, and go afar
to crop sweet grass, and take your stately way   470
leading along the streams, until at evening
you run to be the first one in the fold.
Why, now, so far behind? Can you be grieving
over your Master's eye? That carrion rogue

and his accurst companions burnt it out
when he had conquered all my wits with wine.
Nohbdy will not get out alive, I swear.
Oh, had you brain and voice to tell
where he may be now, dodging all my fury!
Bashed by this hand and bashed on this rock wall   480
his brains would strew the floor, and I should have
rest from the outrage Nohbdy worked upon me.'

He sent us into the open, then. Close by,
I dropped and rolled clear of the ram's belly,
going this way and that to untie the men.
With many glances back, we rounded up
his fat, stiff-legged sheep to take aboard,
and drove them down to where the good ship lay.
We saw, as we came near, our fellows' faces
shining; then we saw them turn to grief   490
tallying those who had not fled from death.
I hushed them, jerking head and eyebrows up,
and in a low voice told them: 'Load this herd;
move fast, and put the ship's head toward the breakers.'
They all pitched in at loading, then embarked
and struck their oars into the sea. Far out,
as far off shore as shouted words would carry,
I sent a few back to the adversary:

'O Kyklops! Would you feast on my companions?
Puny, am I, in a Caveman's hands?   500
How do you like the beating that we gave you,
you damned cannibal? Eater of guests
under your roof! Zeus and the gods have paid you!'

The blind thing in his doubled fury broke
a hilltop in his hands and heaved it after us.
Ahead of our black prow it struck and sank
whelmed in a spuming geyser, a giant wave
that washed the ship stern foremost back to shore.
I got the longest boathook out and stood
fending us off, with furious nods to all   510
to put their backs into a racing stroke—
row, row, or perish. So the long oars bent
kicking the foam sternward, making head
until we drew away, and twice as far.
Now when I cupped my hands I heard the crew
in low voices protesting:

                                        'Godsake, Captain!
Why bait the beast again? Let him alone!'

'That tidal wave he made on the first throw
all but beached us.'

'All but stove us in!'

'Give him our bearing with your trumpeting,   520
he'll get the range and lob a boulder.'

                                                'Aye

He'll smash our timbers and our heads together!'

I would not heed them in my glorying spirit,
but let my anger flare and yelled:

                                              'Kyklops,
if ever mortal man inquire
how you were put to shame and blinded, tell him
Odysseus, raider of cities, took your eye:
Laërtês' son, whose home's on Ithaka!'

At this he gave a mighty sob and rumbled:

'Now comes the weird[7] upon me, spoken of old.   530
A wizard, grand and wondrous, lived here—Télemos,
a son of Eurymos; great length of days
he had in wizardry among the Kyklopês,
and these things he foretold for time to come:
my great eye lost, and at Odysseus' hands.
Always I had in mind some giant, armed
in giant force, would come against me here.
But this, but you—small, pitiful and twiggy—
you put me down with wine, you blinded me.
Come back, Odysseus, and I'll treat you well,   540
praying the god of earthquake to befriend you—
his son I am, for he by his avowal
fathered me, and; if he will, he may
heal me of this black wound—he and no other
of all the happy gods or mortal men.'

Few words I shouted in reply to him:

'If I could take your life I would and take
your time away, and hurl you down to hell!
The god of earthquake could not heal you there!'

At this he stretched his hands out in his darkness   550
toward the sky of stars, and prayed Poseidon:

'O hear me, lord, blue girdler of the islands,
if I am thine indeed, and thou art father:
grant that Odysseus, raider of cities, never
see his home: Laërtês' son, I mean,
who kept his hall on Ithaka. Should destiny
intend that he shall see his roof again
among his family in his father land,

---

[7] Inescapable destiny.

far be that day, and dark the years between.
Let him lose all companions, and return   560
under strange sail to bitter days at home.'

In these words he prayed, and the god heard him.
Now he laid hands upon a bigger stone
and wheeled around, titanic for the cast,
to let it fly in the black-prowed vessel's track.
But it fell short, just aft the steering oar,
and whelming seas rose giant above the stone
to bear us onward toward the island.

                                                      There
as we ran in we saw the squadron waiting,
the trim ships drawn up side by side, and all   570
our troubled friends who waited, looking seaward.
We beached her, grinding keel in the soft sand,
and waded in, ourselves, on the sandy beach.
Then we unloaded all the Kyklops' flock
to make division, share and share alike,
only my fighters voted that my ram,
the prize of all, should go to me. I slew him
by the sea side and burnt his long thighbones
to Zeus beyond the stormcloud, Kronos'[8] son,
who rules the world. But Zeus disdained my offering;   580
destruction for my ships he had in store
and death for those who sailed them, my companions.
Now all day long until the sun went down
we made our feast on mutton and sweet wine,
till after sunset in the gathering dark
we went to sleep above the wash of ripples.

When the young Dawn with finger tips of rose
touched the world, I roused the men, gave orders
to man the ships, cast off the mooring lines;
and filing in to sit beside the rowlocks   590
oarsmen in line dipped oars in the grey sea.
So we moved out, sad in the vast offing,
having our precious lives, but not our friends.

BOOK TEN: THE GRACE OF THE WITCH

We made our landfall on Aiolia Island,
domain of Aiolos[1] Hippotadês,
the wind king, dear to the gods who never die—
an isle adrift upon the sea, ringed round

---

[8] Equivalent of the Roman Saturn. Chief of the gods in the divine generation preceding
Zeus and the Olympian dynasty; dethroned by his son Zeus.

[1] God of the winds, son of Hippotês. Commonly spelled *Aeolus*. A tradition locates his
island off the north coast of Sicily.

with brazen ramparts on a sheer cliffside.
Twelve children had old Aiolos at home—
six daughters and six lusty sons—and he
gave girls to boys to be their gentle brides;
now those lords, in their parents' company,
sup every day in hall—a royal feast   10
with fumes of sacrifice and winds that pipe
'round hollow courts; and all the night they sleep
on beds of filigree beside their ladies.
Here we put in, lodged in the town and palace,
while Aiolos played host to me. He kept me
one full month to hear the tale of Troy,
the ships and the return of the Akhaians,
all which I told him point by point in order.
When in return I asked his leave to sail
and asked provisioning, he stinted nothing,   20
adding a bull's hide sewn from neck to tail
into a mighty bag, bottling storm winds;
for Zeus had long ago made Aiolos
warden of winds, to rouse or calm at will.
He wedged this bag under my afterdeck,
lashing the neck with shining silver wire
so not a breath got through; only the west wind
he lofted for me in a quartering breeze
to take my squadron spanking home.

                            No luck:

the fair wind failed us when our prudence failed.   30

Nine days and nights we sailed without event,
till on the tenth we raised our land. We neared it,
and saw men building fires along the shore;
but now, being weary to the bone, I fell
into deep slumber; I had worked the sheet
nine days alone, and given it to no one,
wishing to spill no wind on the homeward run.
But while I slept, the crew began to parley:
silver and gold, they guessed, were in that bag
bestowed on me by Aiolos' great heart;   40
and one would glance at his benchmate and say:
'It never fails. He's welcome everywhere:
hail to the captain when he goes ashore!
He brought along so many presents, plunder
out of Troy, that's it. How about ourselves—
his shipmates all the way? Nigh home we are
with empty hands. And who has gifts from Aiolos?
He has. I say we ought to crack that bag,
there's gold and silver, plenty, in that bag!'

Temptation had its way with my companions,   50
and they untied the bag.

                                            Then every wind
roared into hurricane; the ships went pitching
west with many cries; our land was lost.
Roused up, despairing in that gloom, I thought:
'Should I go overside for a quick finish
or clench my teeth and stay among the living?'
Down in the bilge I lay, pulling my sea cloak
over my head, while the rough gale blew the ships
and rueful crews clear back to Aiolia.

We put ashore for water; then all hands   60
gathered alongside for a mid-day meal.
When we had taken bread and drink, I picked
one soldier, and one herald, to go with me
and called again on Aiolos. I found him
at meat with his young princes and his lady,
but there beside the pillars, in his portico,
we sat down silent at the open door.
The sight amazed them, and they all exclaimed:

'Why back again, Odysseus?'

                                    'What sea fiend
rose in your path?'

                        'Did we not launch you well   70
for home, or for whatever land you chose?'

Out of my melancholy I replied:

'Mischief aboard and nodding at the tiller—
a damned drowse—did for me. Make good my loss,
dear friends! You have the power!'

                                    Gently I pleaded,
but they turned cold and still. Said Father Aiolos:

'Take yourself out of this island, creeping thing—
no law, no wisdom, lays it on me now
to help a man the blessed gods detest—
out! Your voyage here was cursed by heaven!'   80

He drove me from the place, groan as I would,
and comfortless we went again to sea,
days of it, till the men flagged at the oars—
no breeze, no help in sight, by our own folly—
six indistinguishable nights and days
before we raised the Laistrygonian height
and far stronghold of Lamos.[2] In that land

---

[2] Son of Poseidon and king of the Laistrygonians. Traditions place their land in southwest
Italy or in Sicily. The following lines describe the almost continuous daylight of summer in the
far north, but it would have been impossible for Odysseus and his men to reach such latitudes.
Traditionally, the shepherd grazes his flock during the night.

the daybreak follows dusk, and so the shepherd
homing calls to the cowherd setting out;
and he who never slept could earn two wages,   90
tending oxen, pasturing silvery flocks,
where the low night path of the sun is near
the sun's path by day. Here, then, we found
a curious bay with mountain walls of stone
to left and right, and reaching far inland,—
a narrow entrance opening from the sea
where cliffs converged as though to touch and close.
All of my squadron sheltered here, inside
the cavern of this bay.

                                              Black prow by prow

those hulls were made fast in a limpid calm   100
without a ripple, stillness all around them.
My own black ship I chose to moor alone
on the sea side, using a rock for bollard;
and climbed a rocky point to get my bearings.
No farms, no cultivated land appeared,
but puffs of smoke rose in the wilderness;
so I sent out two picked men and a herald
to learn what race of men this land sustained.

My party found a track—a wagon road
for bringing wood down from the heights to town;   110
and near the settlement they met a daughter
of Antiphatês the Laistrygon—a stalwart
young girl taking her pail to Artakía,
the fountain where these people go for water.
My fellows hailed her, put their questions to her:
who might the king be? ruling over whom?
She waved her hand, showing her father's lodge,
so they approached it. In its gloom they saw
a woman like a mountain crag, the queen—
and loathed the sight of her. But she, for greeting,   120
called from the meeting ground her lord and master,
Antiphatês, who came to drink their blood.
He seized one man and tore him on the spot,
making a meal of him; the other two
leaped out of doors and ran to join the ships.
Behind, he raised the whole tribe howling, countless
Laistrygonês—and more than men they seemed,
gigantic when they gathered on the sky line
to shoot great boulders down from slings; and hell's own
crashing rose, and crying from the ships,   130
as planks and men were smashed to bits—poor gobbets[3]
the wildmen speared like fish and bore away.
But long before it ended in the anchorage—

[3] Lumps of raw meat.

havoc and slaughter—I had drawn my sword
and cut my own ship's cable. 'Men,' I shouted,
'man the oars and pull till your hearts break
if you would put this butchery behind!'
The oarsmen rent the sea in mortal fear
and my ship spurted out of range, far out
from that deep canyon where the rest were lost.   140
So we fared onward, and death fell behind,
and we took breath to grieve for our companions.

Our next landfall was on Aiaia,[4] island
of Kirkê, dire beauty and divine,
sister of baleful Aiêtês, like him
fathered by Hêlios the light of mortals
on Persê, child of the Ocean stream.

                                       We came

washed in our silent ship upon her shore,
and found a cove, a haven for the ship—
some god, invisible, conned us in. We landed,   150
to lie down in that place two days and nights,
worn out and sick at heart, tasting our grief.
But when Dawn set another day a-shining
I took my spear and broadsword, and I climbed
a rocky point above the ship, for sight
or sound of human labor. Gazing out
from that high place over a land of thicket,
oaks and wide watercourses, I could see
a smoke wisp from the woodland hall of Kirkê.
So I took counsel with myself: should I   160
go inland scouting out that reddish smoke?
No: better not, I thought, but first return
to waterside and ship, and give the men
breakfast before I sent them to explore.
Now as I went down quite alone, and came
a bowshot from the ship, some god's compassion
set a big buck in motion to cross my path—
a stag with noble antlers, pacing down
from pasture in the woods to the riverside,
as long thirst and the power of sun constrained him.   170
He started from the bush and wheeled: I hit him
square in the spine midway along his back
and the bronze point broke through it. In the dust
he fell and whinnied as life bled away.
I set one foot against him, pulling hard
to wrench my weapon from the wound, then left it,

---

[4] Later legend placed this island, home of Kirkê (Circe), near the west coast of Italy, near Rome. Aiêtês was the king of Colchis who lost the magical Golden Fleece to Iêson (Jason) and the Argonauts; see the headnote to Euripides' *Medea*. Medea, Aiêtês' daughter, was also a sorceress; witchcraft ran in the family.

butt-end on the ground. I plucked some withies
and twined a double strand into a rope—
enough to tie the hocks of my huge trophy;
then pickaback I lugged him to the ship,   180
leaning on my long spearshaft; I could not
haul that mighty carcass on one shoulder.
Beside the ship I let him drop, and spoke
gently and low to each man standing near:

'Come, friends, though hard beset, we'll not go down
into the House of Death before our time.
As long as food and drink remain aboard
let us rely on it, not die of hunger.'

At this those faces, cloaked in desolation
upon the waste sea beach, were bared;   190
their eyes turned toward me and the mighty trophy,
lighting, foreseeing pleasure, one by one.
So hands were washed to take what heaven sent us.
And all that day until the sun went down
we had our fill of venison and wine,
till after sunset in the gathering dusk
we slept at last above the line of breakers.
When the young Dawn with finger tips of rose
made heaven bright, I called them round and said:

'Shipmates, companions in disastrous time,   200
O my dear friends, where Dawn lies, and the West,
and where the great Sun, light of men, may go
under the earth by night, and where he rises—
of these things we know nothing. Do we know
any least thing to serve us now? I wonder.
All that I saw when I went up the rock
was one more island in the boundless main,
a low landscape, covered with woods and scrub,
and puffs of smoke ascending in mid-forest.'

They were all silent, but their hearts contracted,   210
remembering Antiphatês the Laistrygon
and that prodigious cannibal, the Kyklops.
They cried out, and the salt tears wet their eyes.
But seeing our time for action lost in weeping,
I mustered those Akhaians under arms,
counting them off in two platoons, myself
and my godlike Eurýlokhos commanding.
We shook lots in a soldier's dogskin cap
and his came bounding out—valiant Eurýlokhos!—
So off he went, with twenty-two companions   220
weeping, as mine wept, too, who stayed behind.

In the wild wood they found an open glade,
around a smooth stone house—the hall of Kirkê—
and wolves and mountain lions lay there, mild
in her soft spell, fed on her drug of evil.
None would attack—oh, it was strange, I tell you—
but switching their long tails they faced our men
like hounds, who look up when their master comes
with tidbits for them—as he will—from table.
Humbly those wolves and lions with mighty paws   230
fawned on our men—who met their yellow eyes
and feared them.

                 In the entrance way they stayed
to listen there: inside her quiet house
they heard the goddess Kirkê.

                              Low she sang
in her beguiling voice, while on her loom
she wove ambrosial fabric sheer and bright,
by that craft known to the goddesses of heaven.
No one would speak, until Politês—most
faithful and likable of my officers, said:

'Dear friends, no need for stealth: here's a young weaver   240
singing a pretty song to set the air
a-tingle on these lawns and paven courts.
Goddess she is, or lady. Shall we greet her?'

So reassured, they all cried out together,
and she came swiftly to the shining doors
to call them in. All but Eurýlokhos—
who feared a snare—the innocents went after her.
On thrones she seated them, and lounging chairs,
while she prepared a meal of cheese and barley
and amber honey mixed with Pramnian wine,   250
adding her own vile pinch, to make them lose
desire or thought of our dear father land.
Scarce had they drunk when she flew after them
with her long stick and shut them in a pigsty—
bodies, voices, heads, and bristles, all
swinish now, though minds were still unchanged.
So, squealing, in they went. And Kirkê tossed them
acorns, mast, and cornel berries—fodder
for hogs who rut and slumber on the earth.

Down to the ship Eurýlokhos came running   260
to cry alarm, foul magic doomed his men!
But working with dry lips to speak a word
he could not, being so shaken; blinding tears
welled in his eyes; foreboding filled his heart.
When we were frantic questioning him, at last
we heard the tale: our friends were gone. Said he:

'We went up through the oak scrub where you sent us,
Odysseus, glory of commanders,
until we found a palace in a glade,
a marble house on open ground, and someone   270
singing before her loom a chill, sweet song—
goddess or girl, we could not tell. They hailed her,
and then she stepped through shining doors and said,
"Come, come in!" Like sheep they followed her,
but I saw cruel deceit, and stayed behind.
Then all our fellows vanished. Not a sound,
and nothing stirred, although I watched for hours.'

When I heard this I slung my silver-hilted
broadsword on, and shouldered my long bow,
and said, 'Come, take me back the way you came.'   280
But he put both his hands around my knees
in desperate woe, and said in supplication:

'Not back there, O my lord! Oh, leave me here!
You, even you, cannot return, I know it,
I know you cannot bring away our shipmates;
better make sail with these men, quickly too,
and save ourselves from horror while we may.'

But I replied:

                                                'By heaven, Eurýlokhos,
rest here then; take food and wine;
stay in the black hull's shelter. Let me go,   290
as I see nothing for it but to go.'

I turned and left him, left the shore and ship,
and went up through the woodland hushed and shady
to find the subtle witch in her long hall.
But Hermês met me, with his golden wand,
barring the way—a boy whose lip was downy
in the first bloom of manhood, so he seemed.
He took my hand and spoke as though he knew me:

                    'Why take the inland path alone,
                    poor seafarer, by hill and dale   300
                    upon this island all unknown?
                    Your friends are locked in Kirkê's pale;[5]
                    all are become like swine to see;
                    and if you go to set them free
                    you go to stay, and never more make sail
                    for your old home upon Thaki.[6]

[5] An enclosed area.   [6] Ithaka.

But I can tell you what to do
to come unchanged from Kirkê's power
and disenthrall your fighting crew:
take with you to her bower   310
as amulet, this plant I know—
it will defeat her horrid show,
so pure and potent is the flower;
no mortal herb was ever so.

Your cup with numbing drops of night
and evil, stilled of all remorse,
she will infuse to charm your sight;
but this great herb with holy force
will keep your mind and senses clear:
when she turns cruel, coming near   320
with her long stick to whip you out of doors,
then let your cutting blade appear,

Let instant death upon it shine,
and she will cower and yield her bed—
a pleasure you must not decline,
so may her lust and fear bestead
you and your friends, and break her spell;
but make her swear by heaven and hell
no witches' tricks, or else, your harness shed,
you'll be unmanned by her as well.'   330

He bent down glittering for the magic plant
and pulled it up, black root and milky flower—
a *molü*[7] in the language of the gods—
fatigue and pain for mortals to uproot;
but gods do this, and everything, with ease.

Then toward Olympos through the island trees
Hermês departed, and I sought out Kirkê,
my heart high with excitement, beating hard.
Before her mansion in the porch I stood
to call her, all being still. Quick as a cat   340
she opened her bright doors and sighed a welcome;
then I strode after her with heavy heart
down the long hall, and took the chair she gave me,
silver-studded, intricately carved,
made with a low footrest. The lady Kirkê
mixed me a golden cup of honeyed wine,
adding in mischief her unholy drug.
I drank, and the drink failed. But she came forward
aiming a stroke with her long stick, and whispered:

[7] Usually spelled *moly*.

'Down in the sty and snore among the rest!'   350

Without a word, I drew my sharpened sword
and in one bound held it against her throat.
She cried out, then slid under to take my knees,
catching her breath to say, in her distress:

'What champion, of what country, can you be?
Where are your kinsmen and your city?
Are you not sluggish with my wine? Ah, wonder!
Never a mortal man that drank this cup
but when it passed his lips he had succumbed.
Hale must your heart be and your tempered will.   360
Odysseus then you are, O great contender,
of whom the glittering god with golden wand
spoke to me ever, and foretold
the black swift ship would carry you from Troy.
Put up your weapon in the sheath. We two
shall mingle and make love upon our bed.
So mutual trust may come of play and love.'

To this I said:

                                                   'Kirkê, am I a boy,
that you should make me soft and doting now?
Here in this house you turned my men to swine;   370
now it is I myself you hold, enticing
into your chamber, to your dangerous bed,
to take my manhood when you have me stripped.
I mount no bed of love with you upon it.
Or swear me first a great oath, if I do,
you'll work no more enchantment to my harm.'

She swore at once, outright, as I demanded,
and after she had sworn, and bound herself,
I entered Kirkê's flawless bed of love.

Presently in the hall her maids were busy,   380
the nymphs who waited upon Kirkê: four,
whose cradles were in fountains, under boughs,
or in the glassy seaward-gliding streams.
One came with richly colored rugs to throw
on seat and chairback, over linen covers;
a second pulled the tables out, all silver,
and loaded them with baskets all of gold;
a third mixed wine as tawny-mild as honey
in a bright bowl, and set out golden cups.
The fourth came bearing water, and lit a blaze   390
under a cauldron. By and by it bubbled,
and when the dazzling brazen vessel seethed
she filled a bathtub to my waist, and bathed me,

pouring a soothing blend on head and shoulders,
warming the soreness of my joints away.
When she had done, and smoothed me with sweet oil,
she put a tunic and a cloak around me
and took me to a silver-studded chair
with footrest, all elaborately carven.
Now came a maid to tip a golden jug   400
of water into a silver finger bowl,
and draw a polished table to my side.
The larder mistress brought her tray of loaves
with many savory slices, and she gave
the best, to tempt me. But no pleasure came;
I huddled with my mind elsewhere, oppressed.

Kirkê regarded me, as there I sat
disconsolate, and never touched a crust.
Then she stood over me and chided me:

"Why sit at table mute, Odysseus?   410
Are you mistrustful of my bread and drink?
Can it be treachery that you fear again,
after the gods' great oath I swore for you?'

I turned to her at once, and said:

                                                                  'Kirkê,

where is the captain who could bear to touch
this banquet, in my place? A decent man
would see his company before him first.
Put heart in me to eat and drink—you may,
by freeing my companions. I must see them.'

But Kirkê had already turned away.   420
Her long staff in her hand, she left the hall
and opened up the sty. I saw her enter,
driving those men turned swine to stand before me.
She stroked them, each in turn, with some new chrism;[8]
and then, behold! their bristles fell away,
the course pelt grown upon them by her drug
melted away, and they were men again,
younger, more handsome, taller than before.
Their eyes upon me, each one took my hands,
and wild regret and longing pierced them through,   430
so the room rang with sobs, and even Kirkê
pitied that transformation. Exquisite
the goddess looked as she stood near me, saying:

'Son of Laërtês and the gods of old,
Odysseus, master mariner and soldier,

[8] An oil, usually having sacred or supernatural properties.

go to the sea beach and sea-breasting ship;
drag it ashore, full length upon the land;
stow gear and stores in rock-holes under cover;
return; be quick; bring all your dear companions.'

Now, being a man, I could not help consenting.   440
So I went down to the sea beach and the ship,
where I found all my other men on board,
weeping, in despair along the benches.
Sometimes in farmyards when the cows return
well fed from pasture to the barn, one sees
the pens give way before the calves in tumult,
breaking through to cluster about their mothers,
bumping together, bawling. Just that way
my crew poured round me when they saw me come—
their faces wet with tears as if they saw   450
their homeland, and the crags of Ithaka,
even the very town where they were born.
And weeping still they all cried out in greeting:

'Prince, what joy this is, your safe return!
Now Ithaka seems here, and we in Ithaka!
But tell us now, what death befell our friends?'

And, speaking gently, I replied:

'First we must get the ship high on the shingle,
and stow our gear and stores in clefts of rock
for cover. Then come follow me, to see   460
your shipmates in the magic house of Kirkê
eating and drinking, endlessly regaled.'

They turned back, as commanded, to this work;
only one lagged, and tried to hold the others:
Eurýlokhos it was, who blurted out:

'Where now, poor remnants? is it devil's work
you long for? Will you go to Kirkê's hall?
Swine, wolves, and lions she will make us all,
beasts of her courtyard, bound by her enchantment.
Remember those the Kyklops held, remember   470
shipmates who made that visit with Odysseus!
The daring man! They died for his foolishness!'

When I heard this I had a mind to draw
the blade that swung against my side and chop him,
bowling his head upon the ground—kinsman
or no kinsman, close to me though he was.
But others came between, saying, to stop me,

'Prince, we can leave him, if you say the word;
let him stay here on guard. As for ourselves,
show us the way to Kirkê's magic hall.'   480

So all turned inland, leaving shore and ship,
and Eurýlokhos—he, too, came on behind,
fearing the rough edge of my tongue. Meanwhile
at Kirkê's hands the rest were gently bathed,
anointed with sweet oil, and dressed afresh
in tunics and new cloaks with fleecy linings.
We found them all at supper when we came.
But greeting their old friends once more, the crew
could not hold back their tears; and now again
the rooms rang with sobs. Then Kirkê, loveliest
of all immortals, came to counsel me:

'Son of Laërtês and the gods of old,
Odysseus, master mariner and soldier,
enough of weeping fits. I know—I, too—
what you endured upon the inhuman sea,
what odds you met on land from hostile men.
Remain with me, and share my meat and wine;
restore behind your ribs those gallant hearts
that served you in the old days, when you sailed
from stony Ithaka. Now parched and spent,
your cruel wandering is all you think of,
never of joy, after so many blows.'

As we were men we could not help consenting.
So day by day we lingered, feasting long
on roasts and wine, until a year grew fat.
But when the passing months and wheeling seasons
brought the long summery days, the pause of summer,
my shipmates one day summoned me and said:

'Captain, shake off this trance, and think of home—
if home indeed awaits us,

                                           if we shall ever see
your own well-timbered hall on Ithaka.'

They made me feel a pang, and I agreed.
That day, and all day long, from dawn to sundown,
we feasted on roast meat and ruddy wine,
and after sunset when the dusk came on
my men slept in the shadowy hall, but I
went through the dark to Kirkê's flawless bed
and took the goddess' knees in supplication,
urging, as she bent to hear:

                                           'O Kirkê,
now you must keep your promise; it is time.
Help me make sail for home. Day after day
my longing quickens, and my company
give me no peace, but wear my heart away
pleading when you are not at hand to hear.'

490

500

510

520

The loveliest of goddesses replied:

'Son of Laërtês and the gods of old,
Odysseus, master mariner and soldier,
you shall not stay here longer against your will;
but home you may not go
unless you take a strange way round and come   530
to the cold homes of Death and pale Perséphonê.[9]
You shall hear prophecy from the rapt shade
of blind Teirêsias[10] of Thebes, forever
charged with reason even among the dead;
to him alone, of all the flitting ghosts,
Perséphonê has given a mind undarkened.'

At this I felt a weight like stone within me,
and, moaning, pressed my length against the bed,
with no desire to see the daylight more.
But when I had wept and tossed and had my fill   540
of this despair, at last I answered her:

'Kirkê, who pilots me upon this journey?
No man has ever sailed to the land of Death.'

That loveliest of goddesses replied:

'Son of Laërtês and the gods of old,
Odysseus, master of land ways and sea ways,
feel no dismay because you lack a pilot;
only set up your mast and haul your canvas
to the fresh blowing North; sit down and steer,
and hold that wind, even to the bourne of Ocean,   550
Perséphonê's deserted strand and grove,
dusky with poplars and the drooping willow.
Run through the tide-rip, bring your ship to shore,
land there, and find the crumbling homes of Death.
Here, toward the Sorrowing Water, run the streams
of Wailing, out of Styx, and quenchless Burning—
torrents[11] that join in thunder at the Rock.
Here then, great soldier, setting foot obey me:
dig a well shaft a forearm square; pour out
libations round it to the unnumbered dead: 560
sweet milk and honey, then sweet wine, and last
clear water, scattering handfulls of white barley.
Pray now, with all your heart, to the faint dead;
swear you will sacrifice your finest heifer,
at home in Ithaka, and burn for them

[9] *Death* refers to Hades, ruler of the land of the dead. *Perséphonê* was his consort.
[10] A famous soothsayer who figures in many Greek myths and legends; see, for example, Sophocles' *Oedipus the King*.
[11] The rivers of Hades. The Sorrowing Water is Acheron; the river of wailing is Cocytus; the burning river is Phlegethon.

her tenderest parts in sacrifice; and vow
to the lord Teirêsias, apart from all,
a black lamb, handsomest of all your flock—
thus to appease the nations of the dead.
Then slash a black ewe's throat, and a black ram,   570
facing the gloom of Erebos;[12] but turn
your head away toward Ocean. You shall see, now
souls of the buried dead in shadowy hosts,
and now you must call out to your companions
to flay those sheep the bronze knife has cut down,
for offerings, burnt flesh to those below,
to sovereign Death and pale Perséphonê.
Meanwhile draw sword from hip, crouch down, ward off
the surging phantoms from the bloody pit
until you know the presence of Teirêsias.   580
He will come soon, great captain; be it he
who gives you course and distance for your sailing
homeward across the cold fish-breeding sea.'

As the goddess ended, Dawn came stitched in gold.
Now Kirkê dressed me in my shirt and cloak,
put on a gown of subtle tissue, silvery,
then wound a golden belt about her waist
and veiled her head in linen,
while I went through the hall to rouse my crew.
I bent above each one, and gently said: 590

'Wake from your sleep: no more sweet slumber. Come,
we sail: the Lady Kirkê so ordains it.'

They were soon up, and ready at that word;
but I was not to take my men unharmed
from this place, even from this. Among them all
the youngest was Elpênor—
no mainstay in a fight nor very clever—
and this one, having climbed on Kirkê's roof
to taste the cool night, fell asleep with wine.
Waked by our morning voices, and the tramp   600
of men below, he started up, but missed
his footing on the long steep backward ladder
and fell that height headlong. The blow smashed
the nape cord, and his ghost fled to the dark.
But I was outside, walking with the rest,
saying:

                 'Homeward you think we must be sailing
to our own land; no, elsewhere is the voyage
Kirkê has laid upon me. We must go
to the cold homes of Death and pale Perséphonê
to hear Teirêsias tell of time to come.'   610

---

[12] Part of the realm of Hades; the equivalent of primitive darkness. Also spelled *Erebus*.

They felt so stricken, upon hearing this,
they sat down wailing loud, and tore their hair.
But nothing came of giving way to grief.
Down to the shore and ship at last we went,
bowed with anguish, cheeks all wet with tears,
to find that Kirkê had been there before us
and tied nearby a black ewe and a ram:
she had gone by like air.
For who could see the passage of a goddess
unless she wished his mortal eyes aware?   620

BOOK ELEVEN: A GATHERING OF SHADES

We bore down on the ship at the sea's edge
and launched her on the salt immortal sea,
stepping our mast and spar in the black ship;
embarked the ram and ewe and went aboard
in tears, with bitter and sore dread upon us.
But now a breeze came up for us astern—
a canvas-bellying landbreeze, hale shipmate
sent by the singing nymph with sun-bright hair;
so we made fast the braces, took our thwarts,
and let the wind and steersman work the ship   10
with full sail spread all day above our coursing,
till the sun dipped, and all the ways grew dark
upon the fathomless unresting sea.

                                                          By night
our ship ran onward toward the Ocean's[1] bourne,
the realm and region of the Men of Winter,
hidden in mist and cloud. Never the flaming
eye of Hêlios lights on those men
at morning, when he climbs the sky of stars,
nor in descending earthward out of heaven;
ruinous night being rove[2] over those wretches.   20
We made the land, put ram and ewe ashore,
and took our way along the Ocean stream
to find the place foretold for us by Kirkê.
There Perimêdês and Eurýlokhos
pinioned the sacred beasts. With my drawn blade
I spaded up the votive pit, and poured
libations round it to the unnumbered dead:
sweet milk and honey, then sweet wine, and last
clear water; and I scattered barley down.

---

[1] The great river believed to encompass the entire (flat) world. In the present passage,
Homer locates Hades in the north and not, as is more usual, beneath the surface of the earth.
[2] Fastened; a nautical term. Hêlios is the sun god.

Then I addressed the blurred and breathless dead,   30
vowing to slaughter my best heifer for them
before she calved, at home in Ithaka,
and burn the choice bits on the altar fire;
as for Teirêsias, I swore to sacrifice
a black lamb, handsomest of all our flock.
Thus to assuage the nations of the dead
I pledged these rites, then slashed the lamb and ewe,
letting their black blood stream into the wellpit.
Now the souls gathered, stirring out of Erebos,
brides and young men, and men grown old in pain,   40
and tender girls whose hearts were new to grief;
many were there, too, torn by brazen lanceheads,
battle-slain, bearing still their bloody gear.
From every side they came and sought the pit
with rustling cries; and I grew sick with fear.
But presently I gave command to my officers
to flay those sheep the bronze cut down, and make
burnt offerings of flesh to the gods below—
to sovereign Death, to pale Perséphonê.
Meanwhile I crouched with my drawn sword to keep   50
the surging phantoms from the bloody pit
till I should know the presence of Teirêsias.

One shade came first—Elpênor, of our company,
who lay unburied still on the wide earth
as we had left him—dead in Kirkê's hall,
untouched, unmourned, when other cares compelled us.
Now when I saw him there I wept for pity
and called out to him:

                               'How is this, Elpênor,
how could you journey to the western gloom
swifter afoot than I in the black lugger?'   60

He sighed, and answered:

                            'Son of great Laërtês,
Odysseus, master mariner and soldier,
bad luck shadowed me, and no kindly power;
ignoble death I drank with so much wine.
I slept on Kirkê's roof, then could not see
the long steep backward ladder, coming down,
and fell that height. My neck bone, buckled under,
snapped, and my spirit found this well of dark.
Now hear the grace I pray for, in the name
of those back in the world, not here—your wife   70
and father, he who gave you bread in childhood,
and your own child, your only son, Telémakhos,
long ago left at home.

                                          When you make sail
and put these lodgings of dim Death behind,
you will moor ship, I know, upon Aiaia Island;
there, O my lord, remember me, I pray,
do not abandon me unwept, unburied,
to tempt the gods' wrath,[3] while you sail for home;
but fire my corpse, and all the gear I had,
and build a cairn for me above the breakers—   80
an unknown sailor's mark for men to come.
Heap up the mound there, and implant upon it
the oar I pulled in life with my companions.'

He ceased, and I replied:

                                          'Unhappy spirit,
I promise you the barrow and the burial.'

So we conversed, and grimly, at a distance,
with my long sword between, guarding the blood,
while the faint image of the lad spoke on.
Now came the soul of Antikleía, dead,
my mother, daughter of Autólykos,   90
dead now, though living still when I took ship
for holy Troy. Seeing this ghost I grieved,
but held her off, through pang on pang of tears,
till I should know the presence of Teirêsias.
Soon from the dark that prince of Thebes came forward
bearing a golden staff; and he addressed me:

'Son of Laërtês and the gods of old,
Odysseus, master of land ways and sea ways,
why leave the blazing sun, O man of woe,
to see the cold dead and the joyless region?   100
Stand clear, put up your sword;
let me but taste of blood, I shall speak true.'

At this I stepped aside, and in the scabbard
let my long sword ring home to the pommel silver,
as he bent down to the sombre blood. Then spoke
the prince of those with gift of speech:

                                          'Great captain,
a fair wind and the honey lights of home
are all you seek. But anguish lies ahead;
the god who thunders on the land prepares it,
not to be shaken from your track, implacable,   110
in rancor for the son whose eye you blinded.
One narrow strait may take you through his blows:

[3] The wrath of the gods would be provoked if a body on earth was left unburied and visible.

denial of yourself, restraint of shipmates.
When you make landfall on Thrinákia[4] first
and quit the violet sea, dark on the land
you'll find the grazing herds of Hêlios
by whom all things are seen, all speech is known.
Avoid those kine, hold fast to your intent,
and hard seafaring brings you all to Ithaka.
But if you raid the beeves, I see destruction 120
for ship and crew. Though you survive alone,
bereft of all companions, lost for years,
under strange sail shall you come home, to find
your own house filled with trouble: insolent men
eating your livestock as they court your lady.
Aye, you shall make those men atone in blood!
But after you have dealt out death—in open
combat or by stealth—to all the suitors,
go overland on foot, and take an oar,
until one day you come where men have lived 130
with meat unsalted, never known the sea,
nor seen seagoing ships, with crimson bows
and oars that fledge light hulls for dipping flight.
The spot will soon be plain to you, and I
can tell you how: some passerby will say,
"What winnowing fan[5] is that upon your shoulder?"
Halt, and implant your smooth oar in the turf
and make fair sacrifice to Lord Poseidon:
a ram, a bull, a great buck boar; turn back,
and carry out pure hekatombs at home 140
to all wide heaven's lords, the undying gods,
to each in order. Then a seaborne death
soft as this hand of mist will come upon you
when you are wearied out with rich old age,
your country folk in blessed peace around you.
And all this shall be just as I foretell.'

When he had done, I said at once,

                                             'Teirêsias,
my life runs on then as the gods have spun it.
But come, now, tell me this; make this thing clear:
I see my mother's ghost among the dead 150
sitting in silence near the blood. Not once
has she glanced this way toward her son, nor spoken.
Tell me, my lord,
may she in some way come to know my presence?'

To this he answered:

[4] Sicily. For the outcome of this prophetic warning about molesting the sun-god's cattle, see Book XII.
[5] A tool used to separate grain from chaff.

'I shall make it clear
in a few words and simply. Any dead man
whom you allow to enter where the blood is
will speak to you, and speak the truth; but those
deprived will grow remote again and fade.'

When he had prophesied, Teirêsias' shade   160
retired lordly to the halls of Death;
but I stood fast until my mother stirred,
moving to sip the black blood; then she knew me
and called out sorrowfully to me:

                                                  'Child,
how could you cross alive into this gloom
at the world's end?—No sight for living eyes;
great currents run between, desolate waters,
the Ocean first, where no man goes a journey
without ship's timber under him.

                                        Say, now,
is it from Troy, still wandering, after years,   170
that you come here with ship and company?
Have you not gone at all to Ithaka?
Have you not seen your lady in your hall?'

She put these questions, and I answered her:

'Mother, I came here, driven to the land of death
in want of prophecy from Teirêsias' shade;
nor have I yet coasted Akhaia's hills
nor touched my own land, but have had hard roving
since first I joined Lord Agamémnon's host
by sea for Ilion, the wild horse country,   180
to fight the men of Troy.
But come now, tell me this, and tell me clearly,
what was the bane that pinned you down in Death?
Some ravaging long illness, or mild arrows
a-flying down one day from Artemis?[6]
Tell me of Father, tell me of the son
I left behind me; have they still my place,
my honors, or have other men assumed them?
Do they not say that I shall come no more?
And tell me of my wife: how runs her thought,   190
still with her child, still keeping our domains,
or bride again to the best of the Akhaians?'

To this my noble mother quickly answered:

'Still with her child indeed she is, poor heart,
still in your palace hall. Forlorn her nights

---

[6] As archer-goddess, Artemis provided the gift of painless death. Among other things, she
was protectress of the weak.

and days go by, her life used up in weeping.
But no man takes your honored place. Telémakhos
has care of all your garden plots and fields,
and holds the public honor of a magistrate,
feasting and being feasted. But your father   200
is country bound and comes to town no more.
He owns no bedding, rugs, or fleecy mantles,
but lies down, winter nights, among the slaves,
rolled in old cloaks for cover, near the embers.
Or when the heat comes at the end of summer,
the fallen leaves, all round his vineyard plot,
heaped into windrows,[7] make his lowly bed.
He lies now even so, with aching heart,
and longs for your return, while age comes on him.
So I, too, pined away, so doom befell me,   210
not that the keen-eyed huntress with her shafts
had marked me down and shot to kill me; not
that illness overtook me—no true illness
wasting the body to undo the spirit;
only my loneliness for you, Odysseus,
for your kind heart and counsel, gentle Odysseus,
took my own life away.'

                                 I bit my lip,
rising perplexed, with longing to embrace her,
and tried three times, putting my arms around her,
but she went sifting through my hands, impalpable   220
as shadows are, and wavering like a dream.
Now this embittered all the pain I bore,
and I cried in the darkness:

                                 'O my mother,
will you not stay, be still, here in my arms,
may we not, in this place of Death, as well,
hold one another, touch with love, and taste
salt tears' relief, the twinge of welling tears?
Or is this all hallucination, sent
against me by the iron queen, Perséphonê,
to make me groan again?'

                                My noble mother   230
answered quickly:

                                 'O my child—alas,
most sorely tried of men—great Zeus's daughter,
Perséphonê, knits no illusion for you.
All mortals meet this judgment when they die.
No flesh and bone are here, none bound by sinew,
since the bright-hearted pyre consumed them down—

---

[7] Drifted heaps, as of leaves or snow.

the white bones long exanimate[8]—to ash;
dreamlike the soul flies, insubstantial.

You must crave sunlight soon.

                             Note all things strange
seen here, to tell your lady in after days.'   240

So went our talk; then other shadows came,
ladies in company, sent by Perséphonê—
consorts or daughters of illustrious men—
crowding about the black blood.

                                 I took thought
how best to separate and question them,
and saw no help for it, but drew once more
the long bright edge of broadsword from my hip,
that none should sip the blood in company
but one by one, in order; so it fell
that each declared her lineage and name.   250

Here was great loveliness of ghosts! I saw
before them all, that princess of great ladies,
Tyro,[9] Salmoneus' daughter, as she told me,
and queen to Krêtheus, a son of Aiolos.
She had gone daft for the river Enipeus,
most graceful of all running streams, and ranged
all day by Enipeus' limpid side,
whose form the foaming girdler of the islands,
the god who makes earth tremble, took and so
lay down with her where he went flooding seaward,   260
their bower a purple billow, arching round
to hide them in a sea-vale, god and lady.
Now when his pleasure was complete, the god
spoke to her softly, holding fast her hand:

'Dear mortal, go in joy! At the turn of seasons,
winter to summer, you shall bear me sons;
no lovemaking of gods can be in vain.
Nurse our sweet children tenderly, and rear them.
Home with you now, and hold your tongue, and tell
no one your lover's name—though I am yours,   270
Poseidon, lord of surf that makes earth tremble.'

He plunged away into the deep sea swell,
and she grew big with Pelias and Neleus,
powerful vassals, in their time, of Zeus.
Pelias lived on broad Iolkos seaboard

---

[8] Separated from the vital spirit, or "soul."
[9] A queen of Thessaly, enamored of the river-god Enipeus, in whose guise Poseidon made love to her. She bore him two sons: Pelias, the usurper-king of Iolkos (see headnote to Euripides' *Medea*), and Neleus (the father of Nestor, who appears earlier in the *Odyssey*).

rich in flocks, and Neleus at Pylos.
As for the sons borne by that queen of women
to Krêtheus, their names were Aison, Pherês,
and Amytháon, expert charioteer.

Next after her I saw Antiopê,   280
daughter of Ásopos. She too could boast
a god for lover, having lain with Zeus
and borne two sons to him: Amphion and
Zêthos, who founded Thebes, the upper city,
and built the ancient citadel. They sheltered
no life upon that plain, for all their power,
without a fortress wall.

                                              And next I saw
Amphitrion's true wife, Alkmênê,[10] mother,
as all men know, of lionish Heraklês,
conceived when she lay close in Zeus's arms;   290
and Megarê, high-hearted Kreon's daughter,
wife of Amphitrion's unwearying son.

I saw the mother of Oidipous, Epikastê,[11]
whose great unwitting deed it was
to marry her own son. He took that prize
from a slain father; presently the gods
brought all to light that made the famous story.
But by their fearsome wills he kept his throne
in dearest Thebes, all through his evil days,
while she descended to the place of Death,   300
god of the locked and iron door. Steep down
from a high rafter, throttled in her noose,
she swung, carried away by pain, and left him
endless agony from a mother's Furies.

And I saw Khloris, that most lovely lady,
whom for her beauty in the olden time
Neleus wooed with countless gifts, and married.
She was the youngest daughter of Amphion,
son of Iasos. In those days he held
power at Orkhómenos, over the Minyai.   310
At Pylos then as queen she bore her children—
Nestor, Khromios, Periklýmenos,
and Pêro, too, who turned the heads of men
with her magnificence. A host of princes

[10] She is a "true wife" because Zeus had adopted the disguise of her husband Amphitrion in order to lie with her; the offspring of this union was Heraklês (Hercules).
[11] More commonly known as *Jocasta*. She was mother and wife of the Theban ruler Oidipous (Oedipus). The story, in which he unwittingly kills his father and marries his mother, is best known through Sophocles' drama *Oedipus the King*. Jocasta committed suicide after learning that she had been guilty of incest.

from nearby lands came courting her; but Neleus
would hear of no one, not unless the suitor
could drive the steers of giant Íphiklos
from Phylakê—longhorns, broad in the brow,
so fierce that one man only, a diviner,[12]
offered to round them up. But bitter fate   320
saw him bound hand and foot by savage herdsmen.
Then days and months grew full and waned, the year
went wheeling round, the seasons came again,
before at last the power of Íphiklos,
relenting, freed the prisoner, who foretold
all things to him. So Zeus's will was done.

And I saw Lêda,[13] wife of Tyndareus,
upon whom Tyndareus had sired twins
indomitable: Kastor, tamer of horses,
and Polydeukês, best in the boxing ring.   330
Those two live still, though life-creating earth
embraces them: even in the underworld
honored as gods by Zeus, each day in turn
one comes alive, the other dies again.

Then after Lêda to my vision came
the wife of Aloeus, Iphimedeia,
proud that she once had held the flowing sea
and borne him sons, thunderers for a day,
the world-renowned Otos and Ephialtês.
Never were men on such a scale   340
bred on the plowlands and the grainlands, never
so magnificent any, after Orion.
At nine years old they towered nine fathoms tall,
nine cubits in the shoulders, and they promised
furor upon Olympos, heaven broken by battle cries,
the day they met the gods in arms.

                                           With Ossa's

mountain peak they meant to crown Olympos
and over Ossa Pelion's[14] forest pile
for footholds up the sky. As giants grown
they might have done it, but the bright son[15] of Zeus   350

[12] Melampous, who was gifted with prophetic power; the giant released him in return for
his services as a prophet. In some versions of the myth, Melampous performs the described
feats as a service to his brother Bias, who courts and eventually marries Pêro.

[13] Mother, by Zeus, of Helen of Troy. By her mortal husband, Tyndareus, she is also
mother of Agamémnon's wife Klytaimnéstra and of the twins named Kastor and Polydeukês
(better known in later myth and in astronomy as the "Gemini," Castor and Pollux). The twins
are granted life after death but can never be both alive at the same time. In some versions of
the myth the twins' father is Zeus.

[14] The mountains Ossa and Pelion are near Olympos, where Zeus and his generation of
deities dwell.

[15] Apollo.

by Lêto of the smooth braid shot them down
while they were boys unbearded; no dark curls
clustered yet from temples to the chin.

Then I saw Phaidra, Prokris; and Ariadnê,
daughter of Minos,[16] the grim king. Theseus took her
aboard with him from Krete for the terraced land
of ancient Athens; but he had no joy of her.
Artemis killed her on the Isle of Dia
at a word from Dionysos.

                               Maira, then,
and Klymênê, and that detested queen,   360
Eríphylê,[17] who betrayed her lord for gold . . .
but how name all the women I beheld there,
daughters and wives of kings? The starry night
wanes long before I close.

                         Here, or aboard ship,
amid the crew, the hour for sleep has come.
Our sailing is the gods' affair and yours."

Then he fell silent. Down the shadowy hall
the enchanted banqueters were still. Only
the queen with ivory pale arms, Arêtê, spoke,
saying to all the silent men:

                            "Phaiákians,   370
how does he stand, now, in your eyes, this captain,
the look and bulk of him, the inward poise?
He is my guest, but each one shares that honor.
Be in no haste to send him on his way
or scant your bounty in his need. Remember
how rich, by heaven's will, your possessions are."

Then Ekhenêos, the old soldier, eldest
of all Phaiákians, added his word:

"Friends, here was nothing but our own thought spoken,
the mark hit square. Our duties to her majesty.   380
For what is to be said and done,
we wait upon Alkínoös' command."

---

[16] King of Krete (Crete), in some myths regarded as a just man who posthumously became
a judge of the dead. In other myths he is a savage ruler who demanded that Athens provide
victims for human sacrifice to the monstrous bull called the Minotaur. The Athenian ruler
Theseus, husband of Phaidra (Phaedra), killed the Minotaur with the aid of Ariadnê, her
sister. After eloping with Ariadnê, Theseus abandoned her on the island of Dia (Naxos).
Ariadnê then incurred the anger of the god Dionysos, though in most versions of the myth she
wedded him.

[17] Corrupted by Polyneices (son of Oidipous of Thebes) with the gift of a gold necklace,
Eríphylê treacherously persuaded her husband Amphiaraos to take part in an ill-fated assault
on Thebes in which he was killed.

At this the king's voice rang:

                                                       "I so command—

as sure as it is I who, while I live,
rule the sea rovers of Phaiákia. Our friend
longs to put out for home, but let him be
content to rest here one more day, until
I see all gifts bestowed. And every man
will take thought for his launching and his voyage,
I most of all, for I am master here."   390

Odysseus, the great tactician, answered:

"Alkínoös, king and admiration of men,
even a year's delay, if you should urge it,
in loading gifts and furnishing for sea—
I too could wish it; better far that I
return with some largesse of wealth about me—
I shall be thought more worthy of love and courtesy
by every man who greets me home in Ithaka."

The king said:

                                  "As to that, one word, Odysseus:
from all we see, we take you for no swindler—   400
though the dark earth be patient of so many,
scattered everywhere, baiting their traps with lies
of old times and of places no one knows.
You speak with art, but your intent is honest.
The Argive troubles, and your own troubles,
you told as a poet would, a man who knows the world.
But now come tell me this: among the dead
did you meet any of your peers, companions
who sailed with you and met their doom at Troy?
Here's a long night—an endless night—before us,   410
and no time yet for sleep, not in this hall.
Recall the past deeds and the strange adventures.
I could stay up until the sacred Dawn
as long as you might wish to tell your story."

Odysseus the great tactician answered:

"Alkínoös, king and admiration of men,
there is a time for story telling; there is
also a time for sleep. But even so,
if, indeed, listening be still your pleasure,
I must not grudge my part. Other and sadder   420
tales there are to tell, of my companions,
of some who came through all the Trojan spears,
clangor and groan of war,
only to find a brutal death at home—
and a bad wife behind it.

After Perséphonê,
icy and pale, dispersed the shades of women,
the soul of Agamémnon, son of Atreus,
came before me, sombre in the gloom,
and others gathered round, all who were with him
when death and doom struck in Aegísthos' hall.   430
Sipping the black blood, the tall shade perceived me,
and cried out sharply, breaking into tears;
then tried to stretch his hands toward me, but could not,
being bereft of all the reach and power
he once felt in the great torque of his arms.
Gazing at him, and stirred, I wept for pity,
and spoke across to him:

'O son of Atreus,
illustrious Lord Marshal, Agamémnon,
what was the doom that brought you low in death?
Were you at sea, aboard ship, and Poseidon   440
blew up a wicked squall to send you under,
or were you cattle-raiding on the mainland
or in a fight for some strongpoint, or women,
when the foe hit you to your mortal hurt?'

But he replied at once:

'Son of Laërtês,
Odysseus, master of land ways and sea ways,
neither did I go down with some good ship
in any gale Poseidon blew, nor die
upon the mainland, hurt by foes in battle.
It was Aigísthos who designed my death,   450
he and my heartless wife,[18] and killed me, after
feeding me, like an ox felled at the trough.
That was my miserable end—and with me
my fellows butchered, like so many swine
killed for some troop, or feast, or wedding banquet
in a great landholder's household. In your day
you have seen men, and hundreds, die in war,
in the bloody press, or downed in single combat,
but these were murders you would catch your breath at:
think of us fallen, all our throats cut, winebowl   460
brimming, tables laden on every side,
while blood ran smoking over the whole floor.
In my extremity I heard Kassandra,[19]
Priam's daughter, piteously crying
as the traitress Klytaimnéstra made to kill her

---

[18] In Agamémnon's version here, his wife (as in Aeschylus' *Oresteia*) bears a greater responsibility for the murder than in the version outlined in Book IV.

[19] A Trojan princess and prophetess. Agamémnon brought her home from Troy as a slave. Also spelled *Cassandra*.

along with me. I heaved up from the ground
and got my hands around the blade, but she
eluded me, that whore. Nor would she close
my two eyes[20] as my soul swam to the underworld
or shut my lips. There is no being more fell,   470
more bestial than a wife in such an action,
and what an action that one planned!
The murder of her husband and her lord.
Great god, I thought my children and my slaves
at least would give me welcome. But that woman,
plotting a thing so low, defiled herself
and all her sex, all women yet to come,
even those few who may be virtuous.'

He paused then, and I answered:

                                         'Foul and dreadful.

That was the way that Zeus who views the wide world   480
vented his hatred on the sons of Atreus—
intrigues of women, even from the start.

                                       Myriads

died by Helen's fault, and Klytaimnéstra
plotted against you half the world away.'

And he at once said:

                                  'Let it be a warning

even to you. Indulge a woman never,
and never tell her all you know. Some things
a man may tell, some he should cover up.
Not that I see a risk for you, Odysseus,
of death at your wife's hands. She is too wise,   490
too clear-eyed, sees alternatives too well,
Penélopê, Ikários' daughter—
that young bride whom we left behind—think of it!—
when we sailed off to war. The baby boy
still cradled at her breast—now he must be
a grown man, and a lucky one. By heaven,
you'll see him yet, and he'll embrace his father
with old fashioned respect, and rightly.

                                     My own

lady never let me glut my eyes
on my own son, but bled me to death first.   500
One thing I will advise, on second thought;
stow it away and ponder it.

                                    Land your ship

in secret on your island; give no warning.
The day of faithful wives is gone forever.

---

[20] That is, she would not perform the customary funeral rites.

But tell me, have you any word at all
about my son's[21] life? Gone to Orkhómenos
or sandy Pylos, can he be? Or waiting
with Meneláos in the plain of Sparta?
Death on earth has not yet taken Orestês.'

But I could only answer:

'Son of Atreus,   510
why do you ask these questions of me? Neither
news of home have I, nor news of him,
alive or dead. And empty words are evil.'

So we exchanged our speech, in bitterness,
weighed down by grief, and tears welled in our eyes,
when there appeared the spirit of Akhilleus,
son of Peleus; then Patróklos' shade,
and then Antílokhos, and then Aias,
first among all the Danaans in strength
and bodily beauty, next to prince Akhilleus.   520
Now that great runner, grandson of Aíakhos,
recognized me and called across to me:

'Son of Laërtês and the gods of old,
Odysseus, master mariner and soldier,
old knife, what next? What greater feat remains
for you to put your mind on, after this?
How did you find your way down to the dark
where these dimwitted dead are camped forever,
the after images of used-up men?'

I answered:

'Akhilleus, Peleus' son, strongest of all   530
among the Akhaians, I had need of foresight
such as Teirêsias alone could give
to help me, homeward bound for the crags of Ithaka.
I have not yet coasted Akhaia, not yet
touched my land; my life is all adversity.
But was there ever a man more blest by fortune
than you, Akhilleus? Can there ever be?
We ranked you with immortals in your lifetime,
we Argives did, and here your power is royal
among the dead men's shades. Think, then, Akhilleus: 540
you need not be so pained by death.'

To this
he answered swiftly:

[21] Agamémnon asks about Orestês, who avenged his father's murder.

'Let me hear no smooth talk
of death from you, Odysseus, light of councils.
Better, I say, to break sod as a farm hand
for some poor country man, on iron rations,
than lord it over all the exhausted dead.
Tell me, what news of the prince my son:[22] did he
come after me to make a name in battle
or could it be he did not? Do you know
if rank and honor still belong to Peleus[23]   550
in the towns of the Myrmidons? Or now, may be,
Hellas and Phthia[24] spurn him, seeing old age
fetters him, hand and foot. I cannot help him
under the sun's rays, cannot be that man
I was on Troy's wide seaboard, in those days
when I made bastion for the Argives
and put an army's best men in the dust.
Were I but whole again, could I go now
to my father's house, one hour would do to make
my passion and my hands no man could hold   560
hateful to any who shoulder him aside.'

Now when he paused I answered:

                                                          'Of all that—

of Peleus' life, that is—I know nothing;
but happily I can tell you the whole story
of Neoptólemos, as you require.
In my own ship I brought him out from Skyros
to join the Akhaians under arms.

                                            And I can tell you,

in every council before Troy thereafter
your son spoke first and always to the point;
no one but Nestor and I could out-debate him.   570
And when we formed against the Trojan line
he never hung back in the mass, but ranged
far forward of his troops—no man could touch him
for gallantry. Aye, scores went down before him
in hard fights man to man. I shall not tell
all about each, or name them all—the long
roster of enemies he put out of action,
taking the shock of charges on the Argives.
But what a champion his lance ran through
in Eurýpulos[25] the son of Télephos! Keteians   580
in throngs around that captain also died—
all because Priam's gifts had won his mother

[22] Neoptólemos, or Pyrrhus, who was brought to the Trojan war after his father's death
and killed Priam, the Trojan king.
[23] Akhilleus' father.   [24] Greece and Peleus' kingdom.
[25] Leader of a force persuaded to join the war in support of the Trojans.

to send the lad to battle; and I thought
Memnon alone in splendor ever outshone him.

But one fact more: while our picked Argive crew
still rode that hollow horse Epeios built,
and when the whole thing lay with me, to open
the trapdoor of the ambuscade or not,
at that point our Danaan lords and soldiers
wiped their eyes, and their knees began to quake,   590
all but Neoptólemos. I never saw
his tanned cheek change color or his hand
brush one tear away. Rather he prayed me,
hand on hilt, to sortie, and he gripped
his tough spear, bent on havoc for the Trojans.
And when we had pierced and sacked Priam's tall city
he loaded his choice plunder and embarked
with no scar on him; not a spear had grazed him
nor the sword's edge in close work—common wounds
one gets in war. Arês in his mad fits   600
knows no favorites.'

                      But I said no more,
for he had gone off striding the field of asphodel,[26]
the ghost of our great runner, Akhilleus Aiákidês,
glorying in what I told him of his son.

Now other souls of mournful dead stood by,
each with his troubled questioning, but one
remained alone, apart: the son of Télamon,
Aîas, it was—the great shade burning still[27]
because I had won favor on the beachhead
in rivalry over Akhilleus' arms.   610
The Lady Thetis, mother of Akhilleus,
laid out for us the dead man's battle gear,
and Trojan children, with Athena,
named the Danaan fittest to own them. Would
god I had not borne the palm that day!
For earth took Aîas then to hold forever,
the handsomest and, in all feats of war,
noblest of the Danaans after Akhilleus.
Gently therefore I called across to him:

'Aîas, dear son of royal Télamon,   620
you would not then forget, even in death,
your fury with me over those accurst
calamitous arms?—and so they were, a bane

[26] A flower, possibly a variety of narcissus.
[27] After the death of Akhilleus, the "greater" Aîas (Ajax) and Odysseus had been rival claimants for Akhilleus' weapons; when the arms were awarded to Odysseus, Aîas killed himself.

sent by the gods upon the Argive host.
For when you died by your own hand we lost
a tower, formidable in war. All we Akhaians
mourn you forever, as we do Akhilleus;
and no one bears the blame but Zeus.
He fixed that doom for you because he frowned
on the whole expedition of our spearmen.   630
My lord, come nearer, listen to our story!
Conquer your indignation and your pride.'

But he gave no reply, and turned away,
following other ghosts toward Erebos.
Who knows if in that darkness he might still
have spoken, and I answered?
                                                        But my heart

longed, after this, to see the dead elsewhere.

And now there came before my eyes Minos,
the son of Zeus, enthroned, holding a golden staff,
dealing out justice among ghostly pleaders   640
arrayed about the broad doorways of Death.

And then I glimpsed Orion, the huge hunter,
gripping his club, studded with bronze, unbreakable,
with wild beasts he had overpowered in life
on lonely mountainsides, now brought to bay
on fields of asphodel.
                                                  And I saw Títyos,

the son of Gaia, lying
abandoned over nine square rods of plain.
Vultures, hunched above him, left and right,
rifling his belly, stabbed into the liver,   650
and he could never push them off.
                                                        This hulk

had once committed rape of Zeus's mistress,
Lêto, in her glory, when she crossed
the open grass of Panopeus toward Pytho.

Then I saw Tántalos[28] put to the torture:
in a cool pond he stood, lapped round by water
clear to the chin, and being athirst he burned
to slake his dry weasand[29] with drink, though drink
he would not ever again. For when the old man
put his lips down to the sheet of water   660
it vanished round his feet, gulped underground,

---

[28] The sin for which Tántalos (Tantalus) is being punished here is uncertain—possibly it is
for revealing the gods' secrets, possibly for his serving his son's flesh to the gods (see the
headnote to Aeschylus' *Oresteia*).
[29] Throat.

and black mud baked there in a wind from hell.
Boughs, too, drooped low above him, big with fruit,
pear trees, pomegranates, brilliant apples,
luscious figs, and olives ripe and dark;
but if he stretched his hand for one, the wind
under the dark sky tossed the bough beyond him.

Then Sísyphos[30] in torment I beheld
being roustabout to a tremendous boulder.
Leaning with both arms braced and legs driving,   670
he heaved it toward a height, and almost over,
but then a Power spun him round and sent
the cruel boulder bounding again to the plain.
Whereon the man bent down again to toil,
dripping sweat, and the dust rose overhead.
Next I saw manifest the power of Heraklês—
a phantom,[31] this, for he himself has gone
feasting amid the gods, reclining soft
with Hêbê of the ravishing pale ankles,
daughter of Zeus and Hêra, shod in gold.   680
But, in my vision, all the dead around him
cried like affrighted birds; like Night itself
he loomed with naked bow and nocked arrow
and glances terrible as continual archery.
My hackles rose at the gold swordbelt he wore
sweeping across him: gorgeous intaglio
of savage bears, boars, lions with wildfire eyes,
swordfights, battle, slaughter, and sudden death—
the smith who had that belt in him, I hope
he never made, and never will make, another.   690
The eyes of the vast figure rested on me,
and of a sudden he said in kindly tones:

'Son of Laërtês and the gods of old,
Odysseus, master mariner and soldier,
under a cloud, you too? Destined to grinding
labors like my own in the sunny world?
Son of Kroníon Zeus or not, how many
days I sweated out, being bound in servitude
to a man far worse than I, a rough master![32]
He made me hunt this place one time   700
to get the watchdog of the dead: no more
perilous task, he thought, could be; but I
brought back that beast, up from the underworld;
Hermês and grey-eyed Athena showed the way.'

---

[30] A Corinthian ruler, noted during his lifetime for cunning treachery. More commonly spelled *Sisyphus*.

[31] Heraklês, or Hercules, was taken to heaven after his death. He was thereafter wedded to the goddess Hêbê.

[32] Eurystheus, in whose service Heraklês was forced to perform many superhumanly difficult feats, including the capture of Cerberus, the dog who guarded the realm of the dead.

And Heraklês, down the vistas of the dead,
faded from sight; but I stood fast, awaiting
other great souls who perished in times past.
I should have met, then, god-begotten Theseus
and Peirithoös,[33] whom both I longed to see,
but first came shades in thousands, rustling
in a pandemonium of whispers, blown together,
and the horror took me that Perséphonê
had brought from darker hell some saurian death's head.[34]
I whirled then, made for the ship, shouted to crewmen
to get aboard and cast off the stern hawsers,
an order soon obeyed. They took their thwarts,
and the ship went leaping toward the stream of Ocean
first under oars, then with a following wind.

710

BOOK TWELVE: SEA PERILS AND DEFEAT

The ship sailed on, out of the Ocean Stream,
riding a long swell on the open sea
for the Island of Aiaia.

                     Summering Dawn
has dancing grounds there, and the Sun his rising;[1]
but still by night we beached on a sand shelf
and waded in beyond the line of breakers
to fall asleep, awaiting the Day Star.

When the young Dawn with finger tips of rose
made heaven bright, I sent shipmates to bring
Elpênor's body from the house of Kirkê.
We others cut down timber on the foreland,
on a high point, and built his pyre of logs,
then stood by weeping while the flame burnt through
corse and equipment.

                  Then we heaped his barrow,
lifting a gravestone on the mound, and fixed
his light but unwarped oar against the sky.
These were our rites in memory of him. Soon, then,
knowing us back from the Dark Land, Kirkê came
freshly adorned for us, with handmaids bearing
loaves, roast meats, and ruby-colored wine.

10

20

She stood among us in immortal beauty
jesting:

                       'Hearts of oak, did you go down
alive into the homes of Death? One visit
finishes all men but yourselves, twice mortal!

---

[33] A friend of Theseus.   [34] Reptilian specter.
[1] Aiaia is distinguished from the sunless land of the dead which they have just left behind.

Come, here is meat and wine, enjoy your feasting
for one whole day; and in the dawn tomorrow
you shall put out to sea. Sailing directions,
landmarks, perils, I shall sketch for you, to keep you
from being caught by land or water
in some black sack of trouble.'

                            In high humor   30
and ready for carousal, we agreed;
so all that day until the sun went down
we feasted on roast meat and good red wine,
till after sunset, at the fall of night,
the men dropped off to sleep by the stern hawsers.
She took my hand then, silent in the hush,
drew me apart, made me sit down, and lay
beside me, softly questioning, as I told
all I had seen, from first to last.

                        Then said the Lady Kirkê:
'So: all those trials are over.

                        Listen with care   40
to this, now, and a god will arm your mind.
Square in your ship's path are Seirênês,[2] crying
beauty to bewitch men coasting by;
woe to the innocent who hears that sound!
He will not see his lady nor his children
in joy, crowding about him, home from sea;
the Seirênês will sing his mind away
on their sweet meadow lolling. There are bones
of dead men rotting in a pile beside them
and flayed skins shrivel around the spot.

                              Steer wide;   50
keep well to seaward; plug your oarsmen's ears
with beeswax kneaded soft; none of the rest
should hear that song.

                      But if you wish to listen,
let the men tie you in the lugger,[3] hand
and foot, back to the mast, lashed to the mast,
so you may hear those harpies'[4] thrilling voices;
shout as you will, begging to be untied,
your crew must only twist more line around you
and keep their stroke up, till the singers fade.
What then? One of two courses you may take,
and you yourself must weigh them. I shall not   60
plan the whole action for you now, but only
tell you of both.

---

[2] In Grecian fable, women who could lure men to their destruction through their entrancing song. Also spelled *Sirens*.

[3] A small boat.

[4] In this passage, the word "harpies" means "temptresses." They are not the obscene and filthy females who appear in Virgil's *Aeneid,* Book III.

Ahead are beetling rocks
and dark blue glancing Amphitritê,[5] surging,
roars around them. Prowling Rocks,[6] or Drifters,
the gods in bliss have named them—named them well.
Not even birds can pass them by, not even
the timorous doves that bear ambrosia
to Father Zeus; caught by downdrafts, they die
on rockwall smooth as ice.
                                        Each time, the Father   70
wafts a new courier to make up his crew.

Still less can ships get searoom of these Drifters,
whose boiling surf, under high fiery winds,
carries tossing wreckage of ships and men.
Only one ocean-going craft, the far-famed
Argo,[7] made it, sailing from Aiêta;
but she, too, would have crashed on the big rocks
if Hêra had not pulled her through, for love
of Iêson, her captain.
                                        A second course[8]   80
lies between headlands. One is a sharp mountain
piercing the sky, with stormcloud round the peak
dissolving never, not in the brightest summer,
to show heaven's azure there, nor in the fall.
No mortal man could scale it, nor so much
as land there, not with twenty hands and feet,
so sheer the cliffs are—as of polished stone.
Midway that height, a cavern full of mist
opens toward Erebos and evening. Skirting
this in the lugger, great Odysseus,
your master bowman, shooting from the deck,   90
would come short of the cavemouth with his shaft;
but that is the den of Skylla, where she yaps
abominably, a newborn whelp's cry,
though she is huge and monstrous. God or man,
no one could look on her in joy. Her legs—
and there are twelve—are like great tentacles,
unjointed, and upon her serpent necks
are borne six heads like nightmares of ferocity,
with triple serried rows of fangs and deep
gullets of black death. Half her length, she sways   100

[5] Sea-nymph; consort of Poseidon. She is the female personification of the ocean.

[6] Possibly the Planctae, islands at the north end of what is now called the Strait of Messina, which divides Sicily from the Italian mainland.

[7] The fabled ship, manned by great heroes and captained by Iêson (Jason), that sailed to capture the Golden Fleece.

[8] The following lines describe the two fabled monsters Skylla (Scylla) and Kharybdis (Charybdis), who presumably personify the dangers of the Strait of Messina. Skylla is a treacherous reef, Kharybdis a whirlpool. The proverbial phrase "between Scylla and Charybdis" has come to mean a situation in which one has to choose between equally dreadful alternatives.

her heads in air, outside her horrid cleft,
hunting the sea around that promontory
for dolphins, dogfish, or what bigger game
thundering Amphitritê feeds in thousands.
And no ship's company can claim
to have passed her without loss and grief; she takes,
from every ship, one man for every gullet.

The opposite point seems more a tongue of land
you'd touch with a good bowshot, at the narrows.
A great wild fig, a shaggy mass of leaves,   110
grows on it, and Kharybdis lurks below
to swallow down the dark sea tide. Three times
from dawn to dusk she spews it up
and sucks it down again three times, a whirling
maelstrom; if you come upon her then
the god who makes earth tremble could not save you.
No, hug the cliff of Skylla, take your ship
through on a racing stroke. Better to mourn
six men than lose them all, and the ship, too.'

So her advice ran; but I faced her, saying: 120

'Only instruct me, goddess, if you will,
how, if possible, can I pass Kharybdis,
or fight off Skylla when she raids my crew?'

Swiftly that loveliest goddess answered me:

'Must you have battle in your heart forever?
The bloody toil of combat? Old contender,
will you not yield to the immortal gods?
That nightmare cannot die, being eternal
evil itself—horror, and pain, and chaos;
there is no fighting her, no power can fight her,   130
all that avails is flight.

                                          Lose headway there
along that rockface while you break out arms,
and she'll swoop over you, I fear, once more,
taking one man again for every gullet.
No, no, put all your backs into it, row on;
invoke Blind Force, that bore this scourge of men,
to keep her from a second strike against you.

Then you will coast Thrinákia,[9] the island
where Hêlios' cattle graze, fine herds, and flocks
of goodly sheep. The herds and flocks are seven,   140
with fifty beasts in each.

[9] Sicily.

No lambs are dropped,
or calves, and these fat cattle never die.
Immortal, too, their cowherds are—their shepherds—
Phaëthousa and Lampetía, sweetly braided
nymphs that divine Neaira bore
to the overlord of high noon, Hêlios.
These nymphs their gentle mother bred and placed
upon Thrinákia, the distant land,
in care of flocks and cattle for their father.

Now give those kine a wide berth, keep your thoughts   150
intent upon your course for home,
and hard seafaring brings you all to Ithaka.
But if you raid the beeves, I see destruction
for ship and crew.
                              Rough years then lie between
you and your homecoming, alone and old,
the one survivor, all companions lost.'

As Kirkê spoke, Dawn mounted her golden throne,
and on the first rays Kirkê left me, taking
her way like a great goddess up the island.
I made straight for the ship, roused up the men   160
to get aboard and cast off at the stern.
They scrambled to their places by the rowlocks
and all in line dipped oars in the grey sea.
But soon an off-shore breeze blew to our liking—
a canvas-bellying breeze, a lusty shipmate
sent by the singing nymph with sunbright hair.
So we made fast the braces, and we rested,
letting the wind and steersman work the ship.
The crew being now silent before me, I
addressed them, sore at heart:

                                        'Dear friends,   170
more than one man, or two, should know those things
Kirkê foresaw for us and shared with me,
so let me tell her forecast: then we die
with our eyes open, if we are going to die,
or know what death we baffle if we can. Seirênês
weaving a haunting song over the sea
we are to shun, she said, and their green shore
all sweet with clover; yet she urged that I
alone should listen to their song. Therefore
you are to tie me up, tight as a splint,   180
erect along the mast, lashed to the mast,
and if I shout and beg to be untied,
take more turns of the rope to muffle me.'

I rather dwelt on this part of the forecast,[10]
while our good ship made time, bound outward down
the wind for the strange island of Seirênês.
Then all at once the wind fell, and a calm
came over all the sea, as though some power
lulled the swell.

                  The crew were on their feet
briskly, to furl the sail, and stow it; then,   190
each in place, they poised the smooth oar blades
and sent the white foam scudding by. I carved
a massive cake of beeswax into bits
and rolled them in my hands until they softened—
no long task, for a burning heat came down
from Hêlios, lord of high noon. Going forward
I carried wax along the line, and laid it
thick on their ears. They tied me up, then, plumb
amidships, back to the mast, lashed to the mast,
and took themselves again to rowing. Soon,   200
as we came smartly within hailing distance,
the two Seirênês, noting our fast ship
off their point, made ready, and they sang:

        This way, oh turn your bows,
          Akhaia's glory,
        As all the world allows—
          Moor and be merry.

        Sweet coupled airs we sing.
          No lonely seafarer
        Holds clear of entering   210
          Our green mirror.

        Pleased by each purling note
          Like honey twining
        From her throat and my throat,
          Who lies a-pining?

        Sea rovers here take joy
          Voyaging onward,
        As from our song of Troy
        Greybeard and rower-boy
          Goeth more learnèd.   220

        All feats on that great field
          In the long warfare,
        Dark days the bright gods willed,
          Wounds you bore there,

---

[10] Odysseus shrewdly failed to mention the inevitable devouring of some of his men by Skylla.

> *Argos' old soldiery*
> *On Troy beach teeming,*
> *Charmed out of time we see.*
> *No life on earth can be*
> *Hid from our dreaming.*

The lovely voices in ardor appealing over the water   230
made me crave to listen, and I tried to say
'Untie me!' to the crew, jerking my brows;
but they bent steady to the oars. Then Perimêdês
got to his feet, he and Eurýlokhos,
and passed more line about, to hold me still.
So all rowed on, until the Seirênês
dropped under the sea rim, and their singing
dwindled away.
                                            My faithful company
rested on their oars now, peeling off
the wax that I had laid thick on their ears;   240
then set me free.
                                            But scarcely had that island
faded in blue air than I saw smoke
and white water, with sound of waves in tumult—
a sound the men heard, and it terrified them.
Oars flew from their hands; the blades went knocking
wild alongside till the ship lost way,
with no oarblades to drive her through the water.

Well, I walked up and down from bow to stern,
trying to put heart into them, standing over
every oarsman, saying gently,

                                                        'Friends,   250
have we never been in danger before this?
More fearsome, is it now, than when the Kyklops
penned us in his cave? What power he had!
Did I not keep my nerve, and use my wits
to find a way out for us?

                                            Now I say

by hook or crook this peril too shall be
something that we remember.

                                            Heads up, lads!

We must obey the orders as I give them.
Get the oarshafts in your hands, and lay back
hard on your benches; hit these breaking seas.   260
Zeus help us pull away before we founder.
You at the tiller, listen, and take in
all that I say—the rudders are your duty;
keep her out of the combers and the smoke;
steer for that headland; watch the drift, or we
fetch up in the smother, and you drown us.'

That was all, and it brought them round to action.
But as I sent them on toward Skylla, I
told them nothing, as they could do nothing.
They would have dropped their oars again, in panic,   270
to roll for cover under the decking. Kirkê's
bidding against arms had slipped my mind,
so I tied on my cuirass and took up
two heavy spears, then made my way along
to the foredeck—thinking to see her first from there,
the monster of the grey rock, harboring
torment for my friends. I strained my eyes
upon that cliffside veiled in cloud, but nowhere
could I catch sight of her.

                                                      And all this time,

in travail, sobbing, gaining on the current,   280
we rowed into the strait—Skylla to port
and on our starboard beam Kharybdis, dire
gorge of the salt sea tide. By heaven! when she
vomited, all the sea was like a cauldron
seething over intense fire, when the mixture
suddenly heaves and rises.

                                                      The shot spume

soared to the landside heights, and fell like rain.

But when she swallowed the sea water down
we saw the funnel of the maelstrom, heard
the rock bellowing all around, and dark   290
sand raged on the bottom far below.
My men all blanched against the gloom, our eyes
were fixed upon that yawning mouth in fear
of being devoured.

                                        Then Skylla made her strike,

whisking six of my best men from the ship.
I happened to glance aft at ship and oarsmen
and caught sight of their arms and legs, dangling
high overhead. Voices came down to me
in anguish, calling my name for the last time.

A man surfcasting on a point of rock   300
for bass or mackerel, whipping his long rod
to drop the sinker and the bait far out,
will hook a fish and rip it from the surface
to dangle wriggling through the air:

                                                      so these

were borne aloft in spasms toward the cliff.

She ate them as they shrieked there, in her den,
in the dire grapple, reaching still for me—
and deathly pity ran me through

at that sight—far the worst I ever suffered,
questing the passes of the strange sea.

                                We rowed on.   310

The Rocks were now behind; Kharybdis, too,
and Skylla dropped astern.

                          Then we were coasting

the noble island of the god, where grazed
those cattle with wide brows, and bounteous flocks
of Hêlios, lord of noon, who rides high heaven.

From the black ship, far still at sea, I heard
the lowing of the cattle winding home
and sheep bleating; and heard, too, in my heart
the words of blind Teirêsias of Thebes
and Kirkê of Aiaia: both forbade me   320
the island of the world's delight, the Sun.
So I spoke out in gloom to my companions:

'Shipmates, grieving and weary though you are,
listen: I had forewarning from Teirêsias
and Kirkê, too; both told me I must shun
this island of the Sun, the world's delight.
Nothing but fatal trouble shall we find here.
Pull away, then, and put the land astern.'

That strained them to the breaking point, and, cursing,
Eurýlokhos cried out in bitterness: 330

'Are you flesh and blood, Odysseus, to endure
more than a man can? Do you never tire?
God, look at you, iron is what you're made of.
Here we all are, half dead with weariness,
falling asleep over the oars, and you
say "No landing"—no firm island earth
where we could make a quiet supper. No:
pull out to sea, you say, with night upon us—
just as before, but wandering now, and lost.
Sudden storms can rise at night and swamp   340
ships without a trace.

                            Where is your shelter

if some stiff gale blows up from south or west—
the winds that break up shipping every time
when seamen flout the lord gods' will? I say
do as the hour demands and go ashore
before black night comes down.

                            We'll make our supper

alongside, and at dawn put out to sea.'

Now when the rest said 'Aye' to this, I saw
the power of destiny devising ill.
Sharply I answered, without hestitation: 350

'Eurýlokhos, they are with you to a man.
I am alone, outmatched.

                                    Let this whole company
swear me a great oath: Any herd of cattle
or flock of sheep here found shall go unharmed;
no one shall slaughter out of wantonness
ram or heifer; all shall be content
with what the goddess Kirkê put aboard.'

They fell at once to swearing as I ordered,
and when the round of oaths had ceased, we found
a halfmoon bay to beach and moor the ship in,   360
with a fresh spring nearby. All hands ashore
went about skillfully getting up a meal.
Then, after thirst and hunger, those besiegers,
were turned away, they mourned for their companions
plucked from the ship by Skylla and devoured,
and sleep came soft upon them as they mourned.

In the small hours of the third watch, when stars
that shone out in the first dusk of evening
had gone down to their setting, a giant wind
blew from heaven, and clouds driven by Zeus   370
shrouded land and sea in a night of storm;
so, just as Dawn with finger tips of rose
touched the windy world, we dragged our ship
to cover in a grotto, a sea cave
where nymphs had chairs of rock and sanded floors.
I mustered all the crew and said:

                                        'Old shipmates,
our stores are in the ship's hold, food and drink;
the cattle here are not for our provision,
or we pay dearly for it.

                              Fierce the god is
who cherishes these heifers and these sheep: 380
Hêlios; and no man avoids his eye.'

To this my fighters nodded. Yes. But now
we had a month of onshore gales, blowing
day in, day out—south winds, or south by east.
As long as bread and good red wine remained
to keep the men up, and appease their craving,
they would not touch the cattle. But in the end,
when all the barley in the ship was gone,
hunger drove them to scour the wild shore
with angling hooks, for fishes and sea fowl,   390
whatever fell into their hands; and lean days
wore their bellies thin.

The storms continued.

So one day I withdrew to the interior
to pray the gods in solitude, for hope
that one might show me some way of salvation.
Slipping away, I struck across the island
to a sheltered spot, out of the driving gale.
I washed my hands there, and made supplication
to the gods who own Olympos, all the gods—
but they, for answer, only closed my eyes   400
under slow drops of sleep.

                                    Now on the shore Eurýlokhos
made his insidious plea:

                                    'Comrades,' he said,
'You've gone through everything; listen to what I say.
All deaths are hateful to us, mortal wretches,
but famine is the most pitiful, the worst
end that a man can come to.

                                    Will you fight it?

Come, we'll cut out the noblest of these cattle
for sacrifice to the gods who own the sky;
and once at home, in the old country of Ithaka,
if ever that day comes—   410
we'll build a costly temple and adorn it
with every beauty for the Lord of Noon.
But if he flares up over his heifers lost,
wishing our ship destroyed, and if the gods
make cause with him, why, then I say: Better
open your lungs to a big sea once for all
than waste to skin and bones on a lonely island!'

Thus Eurýlokhos; and they murmured 'Aye!'
trooping away at once to round up heifers.
Now, that day tranquil cattle with broad brows   420
were grazing near, and soon the men drew up
around their chosen beasts in ceremony.
They plucked the leaves that shone on a tall oak—
having no barley meal—to strew the victims,
performed the prayers and ritual, knifed the kine
and flayed each carcass, cutting thighbones free
to wrap in double folds of fat. These offerings,
with strips of meat, were laid upon the fire.
Then, as they had no wine, they made libation
with clear spring water, broiling the entrails first;   430
and when the bones were burnt and tripes shared,
they spitted the carved meat.

                                    Just then my slumber
left me in a rush, my eyes opened,
and I went down the seaward path. No sooner
had I caught sight of our black hull, than savory

odors of burnt fat eddied around me;
grief took hold of me, and I cried aloud:

'O Father Zeus and gods in bliss forever,
you made me sleep away this day of mischief!
O cruel drowsing, in the evil hour!
Here they sat, and a great work they contrived.'   440

Lampetía[11] in her long gown meanwhile
had borne swift word to the Overlord of Noon:

'They have killed your kine.'

                                     And the Lord Hêlios
burst into angry speech amid the immortals:

'O Father Zeus and gods in bliss forever,
punish Odysseus' men! So overweening,
now they have killed my peaceful kine, my joy
at morning when I climbed the sky of stars,
and evening, when I bore westward from heaven.
Restitution or penalty they shall pay—   450
and pay in full—or I go down forever
to light the dead men in the underworld.'

Then Zeus who drives the stormcloud made reply:

'Peace, Hêlios: shine on among the gods,
shine over mortals in the fields of grain.
Let me throw down one white-hot bolt, and make
splinters of their ship in the winedark sea.'

—Kalypso later told me of this exchange,
as she declared that Hermês had told her.   460
Well, when I reached the sea cave and the ship,
I faced each man, and had it out; but where
could any remedy be found? There was none.
The silken beeves of Hêlios were dead.
The gods, moreover, made queer signs appear:
cowhides began to crawl, and beef, both raw
and roasted, lowed like kine upon the spits.

Now six full days my gallant crew could feast
upon the prime beef they had marked for slaughter
from Hêlios' herd; and Zeus, the son of Kronos,   470
added one fine morning.

                                    All the gales
had ceased, blown out, and with an offshore breeze
we launched again, stepping the mast and sail,
to make for the open sea. Astern of us

[11] One of the nymphs who tended her father Hêlios' cattle.

the island coastline faded, and no land
showed anywhere, but only sea and heaven,
when Zeus Kroníon piled a thunderhead
above the ship, while gloom spread on the ocean.
We held our course, but briefly. Then the squall
struck whining from the west, with gale force, breaking   480
both forestays, and the mast came toppling aft
along the ship's length, so the running rigging
showered into the bilge.

                                 On the after deck

the mast had hit the steersman a slant blow
bashing the skull in, knocking him overside,
as the brave soul fled the body, like a diver.
With crack on crack of thunder, Zeus let fly
a bolt against the ship, a direct hit,
so that she bucked, in reeking fumes of sulphur,
and all the men were flung into the sea.   490
They came up 'round the wreck, bobbing a while
like petrels[12] on the waves.

                              No more seafaring

homeward for these, no sweet day of return;
the god had turned his face from them.

                                  I clambered

fore and aft my hulk until a comber
split her, keel from ribs, and the big timber
floated free; the mast, too, broke away.
A backstay floated dangling from it, stout
rawhide rope, and I used this for lashing
mast and keel together. These I straddled,   500
riding the frightful storm.

                             Nor had I yet

seen the worst of it: for now the west wind
dropped, and a southeast gale came on—one more
twist of the knife—taking me north again,
straight for Kharybdis. All that night I drifted,
and in the sunrise, sure enough, I lay
off Skylla mountain and Kharybdis deep.
There, as the whirlpool drank the tide, a billow
tossed me, and I sprang for the great fig tree,
catching on like a bat under a bough.   510
Nowhere had I to stand, no way of climbing,
the root and bole being far below, and far
above my head the branches and their leaves,
massed, overshadowing Kharybdis pool.
But I clung grimly, thinking my mast and keel
would come back to the surface when she spouted.
And ah! how long, with what desire, I waited!
till, at the twilight hour, when one who hears

---

[12] Sea-birds.

and judges pleas in the marketplace all day
between contentious men, goes home to supper,   520
the long poles at last reared from the sea.

Now I let go with hands and feet, plunging
straight into the foam beside the timbers,
pulled astride, and rowed hard with my hands
to pass by Skylla. Never could I have passed her
had not the Father of gods and men, this time,
kept me from her eyes. Once through the strait,
nine days I drifted in the open sea
before I made shore, buoyed up by the gods,
upon Ogýgia Isle. The dangerous nymph   530
Kalypso lives and sings there, in her beauty,
and she received me, loved me.

                                                        But why tell

the same tale that I told last night in hall
to you and to your lady? Those adventures
made a long evening, and I do not hold
with tiresome repetition of a story."

BOOK THIRTEEN: ONE MORE STRANGE ISLAND

He ended it, and no one stirred or sighed
in the shadowy hall, spellbound as they all were,
until Alkínoös answered:

                                            "When you came

here to my strong home, Odysseus, under
my tall roof, headwinds were left behind you.
Clear sailing shall you have now, homeward now,
however painful all the past.

                                            My lords,

ever my company, sharing the wine of Council,
the songs of the blind harper, hear me further:
garments are folded for our guest and friend   10
in the smooth chest, and gold
in various shaping of adornment lies
with other gifts, and many, brought by our peers;
let each man add his tripod and deep-bellied
cauldron: we'll make levy upon the realm
to pay us for the loss each bears in this."

Alkínoös had voiced their own hearts' wish.
All gave assent, then home they went to rest;
but young Dawn's finger tips of rose, touching
the world, roused them to make haste to the ship,   20
each with his gift of noble bronze. Alkínoös,

their ardent king, stepping aboard himself,
directed the stowing under the cross planks,
not to cramp the long pull of the oarsmen.
Going then to the great hall, lords and crew
prepared for feasting.

                                                As the gods' anointed,
Alkínoös made offering on their behalf—an ox
to Zeus beyond the stormcloud, Kronos' son,
who rules the world. They burnt the great thighbones
and feasted at their ease on fresh roast meat,   30
as in their midst the godlike harper sang—
Demódokos, honored by all that realm.

                                                        Only Odysseus
time and again turned craning toward the sun,
impatient for day's end, for the open sea.
Just as a farmer's hunger grows, behind
the bolted plow and share, all day afield,
drawn by his team of winedark oxen: sundown
is benison for him, sending him homeward
stiff in the knees from weariness, to dine;
just so, the light on the sea rim gladdened Odysseus,   40
and as it dipped he stood among the Phaiákians,
turned to Alkínoös, and said:

"O king and admiration of your people,
give me fare well, and stain the ground with wine;
my blessings on you all! This hour brings
fulfillment to the longing of my heart:
a ship for home, and gifts the gods of heaven
make so precious and so bountiful.

                                                After this voyage
god grant I find my own wife in my hall
with everyone I love best, safe and sound!   50
And may you, settled in your land, give joy
to wives and children; may the gods reward you
every way, and your realm be free of woe."

Then all the voices rang out, "Be it so!"
and "Well spoken!" and "Let our friend make sail!"

Whereon Alkínoös gave command to his crier:

"Fill the winebowl, Pontónoös: mix and serve:
go the whole round, so may this company
invoke our Father Zeus, and bless our friend,
seaborne tonight and bound for his own country."   60

Pontónoös mixed the honey-hearted wine
and went from chair to chair, filling the cups;
then each man where he sat poured out his offering
to the gods in bliss who own the sweep of heaven.

With gentle bearing Odysseus rose, and placed
his double goblet in Arêtê's hands,
saying:

                               "Great Queen, farewell;
be blest through all your days till age comes on you,
and death, last end for mortals, after age.
Now I must go my way. Live in felicity,   70
and make this palace lovely for your children,
your countrymen, and your king, Alkínoös."

Royal Odysseus turned and crossed the door sill,
a herald at his right hand, sent by Alkínoös
to lead him to the sea beach and the ship.
Arêtê, too, sent maids in waiting after him,
one with a laundered great cloak and a tunic,
a second balancing the crammed sea chest,
a third one bearing loaves and good red wine.
As soon as they arrived alongside, crewmen   80
took these things for stowage under the planks,
their victualling and drink; then spread a rug
and linen cover on the after deck,
where Lord Odysseus might sleep in peace.
Now he himself embarked, lay down, lay still,
while oarsmen took their places at the rowlocks
all in order. They untied their hawser,
passing it through a drilled stone ring; then bent
forward at the oars and caught the sea
as one man, stroking.

                            Slumber, soft and deep   90
like the still sleep of death, weighed on his eyes
as the ship hove seaward.

                            How a four horse team
whipped into a run on a straightaway
consumes the road, surging and surging over it!
So ran that craft and showed her heels to the swell,
her bow wave riding after, and her wake
on the purple night-sea foaming.

                            Hour by hour
she held her pace; not even a falcon wheeling
downwind, swiftest bird, could stay abreast of her
in that most arrowy flight through open water,   100
with her great passenger—godlike in counsel,
he that in twenty years had borne such blows
in his deep heart, breaking through ranks in war
and waves on the bitter sea.

                          This night at last
he slept serene, his long-tried mind at rest.

When on the East the sheer bright star arose
that tells of coming Dawn, the ship made landfall

and came up islandward in the dim of night.
Phorkys, the old sea baron, has a cove
here in the realm of Ithaka; two points   110
of high rock, breaking sharply, hunch around it,
making a haven from the plunging surf
that gales at sea roll shoreward. Deep inside,
at mooring range, good ships can ride unmoored.
There, on the inmost shore, an olive tree
throws wide its boughs over the bay; nearby
a cave of dusky light is hidden
for those immortal girls, the Naiadês.[1]
Within are winebowls hollowed in the rock
and amphorai; bees bring their honey here;   120
and there are looms of stone, great looms, whereon
the weaving nymphs make tissues, richly dyed
as the deep sea is; and clear springs in the cavern
flow forever. Of two entrances,
one on the north allows descent of mortals,
but beings out of light alone, the undying,
can pass by the south slit; no men come there.

This cove the sailors knew. Here they drew in,
and the ship ran half her keel's length up the shore,
she had such way on her from those great oarsmen.   130
Then from their benches forward on dry ground
they disembarked. They hoisted up Odysseus
unruffled on his bed, under his cover,
handing him overside still fast asleep,
to lay him on the sand; and they unloaded
all those gifts the princes of Phaiákia
gave him, when by Athena's heart and will
he won his passage home. They bore this treasure
off the beach, and piled it close around
the roots of the olive tree, that no one passing   140
should steal Odysseus' gear before he woke.
That done, they pulled away on the homeward track.

But now the god that shakes the islands, brooding
over old threats of his against Odysseus,
approached Lord Zeus to learn his will. Said he:

"Father of gods, will the bright immortals ever
pay me respect again, if mortals do not?—
Phaiákians, too, my own blood kin?

                                                             I thought

Odysseus should in time regain his homeland;
I had no mind to rob him of that day—   150
no, no; you promised it, being so inclined;

------

[1] Sea-nymphs.

only I thought he should be made to suffer
all the way.

                         But now these islanders
have shipped him homeward, sleeping soft, and put him
On Ithaka, with gifts untold
of bronze and gold, and fine cloth to his shoulder.
Never from Troy had he borne off such booty
if he had got home safe with all his share."

Then Zeus who drives the stormcloud answered, sighing:

"God of horizons, making earth's underbeam   160
tremble, why do you grumble so?
The immortal gods show you no less esteem,
and the rough consequence would make them slow
to let barbs fly at their eldest and most noble.
But if some mortal captain, overcome
by his own pride of strength, cuts or defies you,
are you not always free to take reprisal?
Act as your wrath requires and as you will."

Now said Poseidon, god of earthquake:

                                        "Aye,
god of the stormy sky, I should have taken   170
vengeance, as you say, and on my own;
but I respect, and would avoid, your anger.
The sleek Phaiákian cutter, even now,
has carried out her mission and glides home
over the misty sea. Let me impale her,
end her voyage, and end all ocean-crossing
with passengers, then heave a mass of mountain
in a ring around the city."

Now Zeus who drives the stormcloud said benignly:

"Here is how I should do it, little brother: 180
when all who watch upon the wall have caught
sight of the ship, let her be turned to stone—
an island like a ship, just off the bay.
Mortals may gape at that for generations!
But throw no mountain round the sea port city."

When he heard this, Poseidon, god of earthquake,
departed for Skhería, where the Phaiákians
are born and dwell. Their ocean-going ship
he saw already near, heading for harbor;
so up behind her swam the island-shaker   190
and struck her into stone, rooted in stone, at one
blow of his palm,

                              then took to the open sea.

Those famous ship handlers, the Phaiákians,
gazed at each other, murmuring in wonder;
you could have heard one say:

                                         "Now who in thunder
has anchored, moored that ship in the seaway,
when everyone could see her making harbor?"

The god had wrought a charm beyond their thought.
But soon Alkínoös made them hush, and told them:

"This present doom upon the ship—on me—   200
my father prophesied in the olden time.
If we gave safe conveyance to all passengers
we should incur Poseidon's wrath, he said,
whereby one day a fair ship, manned by Phaiákians,
would come to grief at the god's hands; and great
mountains would hide our city from the sea.
So my old father forecast.

                                         Use your eyes:

these things are even now being brought to pass.
Let all here abide by my decree:

                                         We make   210

an end henceforth of taking, in our ships,
castaways who may land upon Skhería;
and twelve choice bulls we dedicate at once
to Lord Poseidon, praying him of his mercy
not to heave up a mountain round our city."

In fearful awe they led the bulls to sacrifice
and stood about the altar stone, those captains,
peers of Phaiákia, led by their king in prayer
to Lord Poseidon.

                                 Meanwhile, on his island,
his father's shore, that kingly man, Odysseus,
awoke, but could not tell what land it was   220
after so many years away; moreover,
Pallas Athena, Zeus's daughter, poured
a grey mist all around him, hiding him
from common sight—for she had things to tell him
and wished no one to know him, wife or townsmen,
before the suitors paid up for their crimes.

The landscape then looked strange, unearthly strange
to the Lord Odysseus: paths by hill and shore,
glimpses of harbors, cliffs, and summer trees.
He stood up, rubbed his eyes, gazed at his homeland,   230
and swore, slapping his thighs with both his palms,
then cried aloud:

"What am I in for now?
Whose country have I come to this time? Rough
savages and outlaws, are they, or
godfearing people, friendly to castaways?
Where shall I take these things? Where take myself,
with no guide, no directions? These should be
still in Phaiákian hands, and I uncumbered,
free to find some other openhearted
prince who might be kind and give me passage.   240
I have no notion where to store this treasure;
first-comer's trove it is, if I leave it here.

My lords and captains of Phaiákia
were not those decent men they seemed, not honorable,
landing me in this unknown country—no,
by god, they swore to take me home to Ithaka
and did not! Zeus attend to their reward,
Zeus, patron of petitioners, who holds
all other mortals under his eye; he takes
payment from betrayers!

                                            I'll be busy.   250

I can look through my gear. I shouldn't wonder
if they pulled out with part of it on board."

He made a tally of his shining pile—
tripods, cauldrons, cloaks, and gold—and found
he lacked nothing at all.

                                            And then he wept,

despairing, for his own land, trudging down
beside the endless wash of the wide, wide sea,
weary and desolate as the sea. But soon
Athena came to him from the nearby air,
putting a young man's figure on—a shepherd,   260
like a king's son, all delicately made.
She wore a cloak, in two folds off her shoulders,
and sandals bound upon her shining feet.
A hunting lance lay in her hands.

                                            At sight of her

Odysseus took heart, and he went forward
to greet the lad, speaking out fair and clear:

"Friend, you are the first man I've laid eyes on
here in this cove. Greetings. Do not feel
alarmed or hostile, coming across me; only
receive me into safety with my stores.   270
Touching your knees I ask it, as I might
ask grace of a god.

                                            O sir, advise me,

what is this land and realm, who are the people?

Is it an island all distinct, or part
of the fertile mainland, sloping to the sea?"

To this grey-eyed Athena answered:

                                               "Stranger,

you must come from the other end of nowhere,
else you are a great booby, having to ask
what place this is. It is no nameless country.
Why, everyone has heard of it, the nations   280
over on the dawn side, toward the sun,
and westerners in cloudy lands of evening.
No one would use this ground for training horses,
it is too broken, has no breadth of meadow;
but there is nothing meager about the soil,
the yield of grain is wondrous, and wine, too,
with drenching rains and dewfall.

                                     There's good pasture

for oxen and for goats, all kinds of timber,
and water all year long in the cattle ponds.
For these blessings, friend, the name of Ithaka   290
has made its way even as far as Troy—
and they say Troy lies far beyond Akhaia."

Now Lord Odysseus, the long-enduring,
laughed in his heart, hearing his land described
by Pallas Athena, daughter of Zeus who rules
the veering stormwind; and he answered her
with ready speech—not that he told the truth,
but, just as she did, held back what he knew,
weighing within himself at every step
what he made up to serve his turn.

                                           Said he: 300

"Far away in Krete I learned of Ithaka—
in that broad island over the great ocean.
And here I am now, come myself to Ithaka!
Here is my fortune with me. I left my sons
an equal part, when I shipped out. I killed
Orsílokhos, the courier, son of Idómeneus.[2]
This man could beat the best cross country runners
in Krete, but he desired to take away
my Trojan plunder, all I had fought and bled for,
cutting through ranks in war and the cruel sea.   310
Confiscation is what he planned; he knew
I had not cared to win his father's favor
as a staff officer in the field at Troy,
but led my own command.

[2] The king of Krete (Crete).

                                                            I acted: I
hit him with a spearcast from a roadside
as he came down from the open country. Murky
night shrouded all heaven and the stars.
I made that ambush with one man at arms.
We were unseen. I took his life in secret,
finished him off with my sharp sword. That night   320
I found asylum on a ship off shore
skippered by gentlemen of Phoinikia;[3] I gave
all they could wish, out of my store of plunder,
for passage, and for landing me at Pylos
or Elis Town, where the Epeioi are in power.
Contrary winds carried them willy-nilly
past that coast; they had no wish to cheat me,
but we were blown off course.

                                      Here, then, by night
we came, and made this haven by hard rowing.
All famished, but too tired to think of food,   330
each man dropped in his tracks after the landing,
and I slept hard, being wearied out. Before
I woke today, they put my things ashore
on the sand here beside me where I lay,
then reimbarked for Sidon, that great city.
Now they are far at sea, while I am left
forsaken here."

                                      At this the grey-eyed goddess
Athena smiled, and gave him a caress,
her looks being changed now, so she seemed a woman,
tall and beautiful and no doubt skilled   340
at weaving splendid things. She answered briskly:

"Whoever gets around you must be sharp
and guileful as a snake; even a god
might bow to you in ways of dissimulation.
You! You chameleon!
Bottomless bag of tricks! Here in your own country
would you not give your stratagems a rest
or stop spellbinding for an instant?
You play a part as if it were your own tough skin.

No more of this, though. Two of a kind, we are,   350
contrivers, both. Of all men now alive
you are the best in plots and story telling.
My own fame is for wisdom among the gods—
deceptions, too.

[3] Phoenicia; an area of the Syrian coast noted for commerce. Sidon was one of its principal cities.

                                        Would even you have guessed
that I am Pallas Athena, daughter of Zeus,
I that am always with you in times of trial,
a shield to you in battle, I who made
the Phaiákians befriend you, to a man?
Now I am here again to counsel with you—
but first to put away those gifts the Phaiákians   360
gave you at departure—I planned it so.
Then I can tell you of the gall and wormwood
it is your lot to drink in your own hall.
Patience, iron patience, you must show;
so give it out to neither man nor woman
that you are back from wandering. Be silent
under all injuries, even blows from men."

His mind ranging far, Odysseus answered:

"Can mortal man be sure of you on sight,
even a sage, O mistress of disguises?   370
Once you were fond of me—I am sure of that—
years ago, when we Akhaians made
war, in our generation, upon Troy.
But after we had sacked the shrines of Priam
and put to sea, God scattered the Akhaians;
I never saw you after that, never
knew you aboard with me, to act as shield
in grievous times—not till you gave me comfort
in the rich hinterland of the Phaiákians
and were yourself my guide into that city.   380

Hear me now in your father's name, for I
cannot believe that I have come to Ithaka.
It is some other land. You made that speech
only to mock me, and to take me in.
Have I come back in truth to my home island?"

To this the grey-eyed goddess Athena answered:

"Always the same detachment! That is why
I cannot fail you, in your evil fortune,
coolheaded, quick, well-spoken as you are!
Would not another wandering man, in joy,   390
make haste home to his wife and children? Not
you, not yet. Before you hear their story
you will have proof about your wife.

                                        I tell you,

she still sits where you left her, and her days
and nights go by forlorn, in lonely weeping.
For my part, never had I despaired; I felt
sure of your coming home, though all your men
should perish; but I never cared to fight

Poseidon, Father's brother, in his baleful
rage with you for taking his son's eye.   400

Now I shall make you see the shape of Ithaka.
Here is the cove the sea lord Phorkys owns,
there is the olive spreading out her leaves
over the inner bay, and there the cavern
dusky and lovely, hallowed by the feet
of those immortal girls, the Naiadês—
the same wide cave under whose vault you came
to honor them with hekatombs—and there
Mount Neion, with his forest on his back!"

She had dispelled the mist, so all the island   410
stood out clearly. Then indeed Odysseus'
heart stirred with joy. He kissed the earth,
and lifting up his hands prayed to the nymphs:

"O slim shy Naiadês, young maids of Zeus,
I had not thought to see you ever again!
        O listen smiling
to my gentle prayers, and we'll make offering
plentiful as in the old time, granted I
live, granted my son grows tall, by favor
of great Athena, Zeus's daughter,
who gives the winning fighter his reward!"   420

The grey-eyed goddess said directly:
          "Courage;
and let the future trouble you no more.
We go to make a cache now, in the cave,
to keep your treasure hid. Then we'll consider
how best the present action may unfold."

The goddess turned and entered the dim cave,
exploring it for crannies, while Odysseus
carried up all the gold, the fire-hard bronze,
and well-made clothing the Phaiákians gave him.
Pallas Athena, daughter of Zeus the storm king,   430
placed them, and shut the cave mouth with a stone,
and under the old grey olive tree those two
sat down to work the suitors death and woe.
Grey-eyed Athena was the first to speak, saying:

"Son of Laërtês and the gods of old,
Odysseus, master of land ways and sea ways,
put your mind on a way to reach and strike
a crowd of brazen upstarts.
        Three long years
they have played master in your house: three years
trying to win your lovely lady, making   440

gifts as though betrothed. And she? Forever
grieving for you, missing your return,
she has allowed them all to hope, and sent
messengers with promises to each—
though her true thoughts are fixed elsewhere."

At this

the man of ranging mind, Odysseus, cried:

"So hard beset! An end like Agamémnon's
might very likely have been mine, a bad end,
bleeding to death in my own hall. You forestalled it,
goddess, by telling me how the land lies.   450
Weave me a way to pay them back! And you, too,
take your place with me, breathe valor in me
the way you did that night when we Akhaians
unbound the bright veil from the brow of Troy!
O grey-eyed one, fire my heart and brace me!
I'll take on fighting men three hundred strong
if you fight at my back, immortal lady!"

The grey-eyed goddess Athena answered him:

"No fear but I shall be there; you'll go forward
under my arm when the crux comes at last.   460
And I foresee your vast floor stained with blood,
spattered with brains of this or that tall suitor
who fed upon your cattle.

Now, for a while,

I shall transform you; not a soul will know you,
the clear skin of your arms and legs shriveled,
your chestnut hair all gone, your body dressed
in sacking that a man would gag to see,
and the two eyes, that were so brilliant, dirtied—
contemptible, you shall seem to your enemies,
as to the wife and son you left behind.   470

But join the swineherd first—the overseer
of all your swine, a good soul now as ever,
devoted to Penélopê and your son.
He will be found near Raven's Rock and the well
of Arethousa,[4] where the swine are pastured,
rooting for acorns to their hearts' content,
drinking the dark still water. Boarflesh grows
pink and fat on that fresh diet. There
stay with him, and question him, while I
am off to the great beauty's land of Sparta,   480
to call your son Telémakhos home again—

---

[4] The fountain identified with the water-nymph Arethousa (Arethusa) is more often located in Sicily.

for you should know, he went to the wide land
of Lakedaimon, Meneláos' country,
to learn if there were news of you abroad."

Odysseus answered:

                              "Why not tell him, knowing
my whole history, as you do? Must he
traverse the barren sea, he too, and live
in pain, while others feed on what is his?"

At this the grey-eyed goddess Athena said:

"No need for anguish on that lad's account.   490
I sent him off myself, to make his name
in foreign parts—no hardship in the bargain,
taking his ease in Meneláos' mansion,
lapped in gold.
                              The young bucks here, I know,
lie in wait for him in a cutter, bent
on murdering him before he reaches home.
I rather doubt they will. Cold earth instead
will take in her embrace a man or two
of those who fed so long on what is his."

Speaking no more, she touched him with her wand,   500
shriveled the clear skin of his arms and legs,
made all his hair fall out, cast over him
the wrinkled hide of an old man, and bleared
both his eyes, that were so bright. Then she
clapped an old tunic, a foul cloak, upon him,
tattered, filthy, stained by greasy smoke,
and over that a mangy big buck skin.
A staff she gave him, and a leaky knapsack
with no strap but a loop of string.
                              Now then,
their colloquy at an end, they went their ways—   510
Athena toward illustrious Lakedaimon
Far over sea, to join Odysseus' son.

BOOK FOURTEEN: HOSPITALITY IN THE FOREST

He went up from the cove through wooded ground,
taking a stony trail into the high hills, where
the swineherd lived, according to Athena.
Of all Odysseus' field hands in the old days
this forester cared most for the estate;
and now Odysseus found him
in a remote clearing, sitting inside the gate

of a stockade he built to keep the swine
while his great lord was gone.

                           Working alone,

far from Penélopê and old Laërtês,   10
he had put up a fieldstone hut and timbered it
with wild pear wood. Dark hearts of oak he split
and trimmed for a high palisade around it,
and built twelve sties adjoining in this yard
to hold the livestock. Fifty sows with farrows
were penned in each, bedded upon the earth,
while the boars lay outside—fewer by far,
as those well-fatted were for the suitors' table,
fine pork, sent by the swineherd every day.
Three hundred sixty now lay there at night,   20
guarded by dogs—four dogs like wolves, one each
for the four lads the swineherd reared and kept
as under-herdsmen.

                     When Odysseus came,
the good servant sat shaping to his feet
oxhide for sandals, cutting the well-cured leather.
Three of his young men were afield, pasturing
herds in other woods; one he had sent
with a fat boar for tribute into town,
the boy to serve while the suitors got their fill.

The watch dogs, when they caught sight of Odysseus,   30
faced him, a snarling troop, and pelted out
viciously after him. Like a tricky beggar
he sat down plump, and dropped his stick. No use.
They would have rolled him in the dust and torn him
there by his own steading[1] if the swineherd
had not sprung up and flung his leather down,
making a beeline for the open. Shouting,
throwing stone after stone,
he made them scatter; then turned to his lord
and said:

                    "You might have got a ripping, man!   40
Two shakes more and a pretty mess for me
you could have called it, if you had the breath.
As though I had not trouble enough already,
given me by the gods, my master gone,
true king that he was. I hang on here,
still mourning for him, raising pigs of his
to feed foreigners, and who knows where the man is,
in some far country among strangers! Aye—
if he is living still, if he still sees the light of day.

---

[1] Farmhouse or farm.

Come to the cabin. You're a wanderer too.   50
You must eat something, drink some wine, and tell me
where you are from and the hard times you've seen."

The forester now led him to his hut
and made a couch for him, with tips of fir
piled for a mattress under a wild goat skin,
shaggy and thick, his own bed covering.

                                                          Odysseus,
in pleasure at this courtesy, gently said:
"May Zeus and all the gods give you your heart's desire
for taking me in so kindly, friend."

                                                      Eumaios—

O my swineherd!² —answered him:

                                                  "Tush, friend,   60
rudeness to a stranger is not decency,
poor though he may be, poorer than you.

                                              All wanderers
and beggars come from Zeus. What we can give
is slight but well-meant—all we dare. You know
that is the way of slaves,³ who live in dread
of masters—new ones like our own.

                                              I told you
the gods, long ago, hindered our lord's return.
He had a fondness for me, would have pensioned me
with acres of my own, a house, a wife
that other men admired and courted; all   70
gifts good-hearted kings bestow for service,
for a life work the bounty of god has prospered—
for it does prosper here, this work I do.
Had he grown old in his own house, my master
would have rewarded me. But the man's gone.
God curse the race of Helen and cut it down,
that wrung the strength out of the knees of many!
And he went, too—for the honor of Agamémnon
he took ship overseas for the wild horse country
of Troy, to fight the Trojans."

                                              This being told,   80
he tucked his long shirt up inside his belt
and strode into the pens for two young porkers.

---

²This kind of direct address by the poet, expressing affection, is used in the *Odyssey* only for Eumaios.

³Though owned by masters as in modern forms of slavery, and often obtained by forced capture, "slaves" in the aristocratic Homeric times were often more like trusted and responsible servants than like maltreated property. Eumaios and Telémakhos' old nurse Eurýkleia, described elsewhere in the *Odyssey*, are representative examples.

He slaughtered them and singed them at the fire,
flayed and quartered them, and skewered the meat
to broil it all; then gave it to Odysseus
hot on the spits. He shook out barley meal,
took a winebowl of ivy wood and filled it,
and sat down facing him, with a gesture, saying:

"There is your dinner, friend, the pork of slaves.
Our fat shoats are all eaten by the suitors,   90
cold-hearted men, who never spare a thought
for how they stand in the sight of Zeus. The gods
living in bliss are fond of no wrongdoing,
but honor discipline and right behavior.
Even the outcasts of the earth, who bring
piracy from the sea, and bear off plunder
given by Zeus in shiploads—even those men
deep in their hearts tremble for heaven's eye.
But the suitors, now, have heard some word, some oracle
of my lord's death, being so unconcerned   100
to pay court properly or to go about their business.
All they want is to prey on his estate,
proud dogs; they stop at nothing. Not a day
goes by, and not a night comes under Zeus,
but they make butchery of our beeves and swine—
not one or two beasts at a time, either.
As for swilling down wine, they drink us dry.
Only a great domain like his could stand it—
greater than any on the dusky mainland
or here in Ithaka. Not twenty heroes   110
in the whole world were as rich as he. I know:
I could count it all up; twelve herds in Elis,
as many flocks, as many herds of swine,
and twelve wide-ranging herds of goats, as well,
attended by his own men or by others—
out at the end of the island, eleven herds
are scattered now, with good men looking after them,
and every herdsman, every day, picks out
a prize ram to hand over to those fellows.
I too as overseer, keeper of swine,   120
must go through all my boars and send the best."

While he ran on, Odysseus with zeal
applied himself to the meat and wine, but inwardly
his thought shaped woe and ruin for the suitors.
When he had eaten all that he desired
and the cup he drank from had been filled again
with wine—a welcome sight—,
he spoke, and the words came light upon the air:

"Who is this lord who once acquired you,
so rich, so powerful, as you describe him?   130

You think he died for Agamémnon's honor.
Tell me his name: I may have met someone
of that description in my time. Who knows?
Perhaps only the immortal gods could say
if I should claim to have seen him: I have roamed
about the world so long."

               The swineherd answered
as one who held a place of trust:

                       "Well, man,
his lady and his son will put no stock
in any news of him brought by a rover.
Wandering men tell lies for a night's lodging,   140
for fresh clothing; truth doesn't interest them.
Every time some traveller comes ashore
he has to tell my mistress his pretty tale,
and she receives him kindly, questions him,
remembering her prince, while the tears run
down her cheeks—and that is as it should be
when a woman's husband has been lost abroad.
I suppose you, too, can work your story up
at a moment's notice, given a shirt or cloak.
No: long ago wild dogs and carrion   150
birds, most like, laid bare his ribs on land
where life had left him. Or it may be, quick fishes
picked him clean in the deep sea, and his bones
lie mounded over in sand upon some shore.
One way or another, far from home he died,
a bitter loss, and pain, for everyone,
certainly for me. Never again shall I
have for my lot a master mild as he was
anywhere—not even with my parents
at home, where I was born and bred. I miss them   160
less than I do him—though a longing comes
to set my eyes on them in the old country.
No, it is the lost man I ache to think of—
Odysseus. And I speak the name respectfully,
even if he is not here. He loved me, cared for me.
I call him dear my lord, far though he be."

Now royal Odysseus, who had borne the long war,
spoke again:

                  "Friend, as you are so dead sure
he will not come—and so mistrustful, too—
let me not merely talk, as others talk,   170
but swear to it: your lord is now at hand.
And I expect a gift for this good news
when he enters his own hall. Till then I would not
take a rag, no matter what my need.

I hate as I hate Hell's own gate that weakness
that makes a poor man into a flatterer.
Zeus be my witness, and the table garnished
for true friends, and Odysseus' own hearth—
by heaven, all I say will come to pass!
He will return, and he will be avenged   180
on any who dishonor his wife and son."

Eumaios—O my swineherd!—answered him:

"I take you at your word, then: you shall have
no good news gift from me. Nor will Odysseus
enter his hall. But peace! drink up your wine.
Let us talk now of other things. No more
imaginings. It makes me heavy-hearted
when someone brings my master back to mind—
my own true master.

                                          No, by heaven,
let us have no oaths! But if Odysseus   190
can come again god send he may! My wish
is that of Penélopê and old Laërtês
and Prince Telémakhos.

                                          Ah, he's another
to be distressed about—Odysseus' child,
Telémakhos! By the gods' grace he grew
like a tough sapling, and I thought he'd be
no less a man than his great father—strong
and admirably made; but then someone,
god or man, upset him, made him rash,
so that he sailed away to sandy Pylos   200
to hear news of his father. Now the suitors
lie in ambush on his homeward track,
ready to cut away the last shoot of Arkêsios'[4]
line, the royal stock of Ithaka.

                                          No good
dwelling on it. Either he'll be caught
or else Kroníon's[5] hand will take him through.

Tell me, now, of your own trials and troubles.
And tell me truly first, for I should know,
who are you, where do you hail from, where's your home
and family? What kind of ship was yours,   210
and what course brought you here? Who are your sailors?
I don't suppose you walked here on the sea."

To this the master of improvisation answered:

"I'll tell you all that, clearly as I may.
If we could sit here long enough, with meat

---

[4] Odysseus' paternal grandfather.   [5] Zeus, son of Kronos.

and good sweet wine, warm here, in peace and quiet
within doors, while the work of the world goes on—
I might take all this year to tell my story
and never end the tale of misadventures
that wore my heart out, by the gods' will.   220

My native land is the wide seaboard of Krete
where I grew up. I had a wealthy father,
and many other sons were born to him
of his true lady. My mother was a slave,
his concubine; but Kastor Hylákidês,
my father, treated me as a true born son.
High honor came to him in that part of Krete
for wealth and ease, and sons born for renown,
before the death-bearing Kêrês[6] drew him down
to the underworld. His avid sons thereafter   230
dividing up the property by lot
gave me a wretched portion, a poor house.
But my ability won me a wife
of rich family. Fool I was never called,
nor turn-tail in a fight.

                       My strength's all gone,
but from the husk you may divine the ear
that stood tall in the old days. Misery owns me
now, but then great Arês and Athena
gave me valor and man-breaking power,
whenever I made choice of men-at-arms   240
to set a trap with me for my enemies.
Never, as I am a man, did I fear Death
ahead, but went in foremost in the charge,
putting a spear through any man whose legs
were not as fast as mine. That was my element,
war and battle. Farming I never cared for,
nor life at home, nor fathering fair children.
I reveled in long ships with oars; I loved
polished lances, arrows in the skirmish,
the shapes of doom that others shake to see.   250
Carnage suited me; heaven put those things
in me somehow. Each to his own pleasure!
Before we young Akhaians shipped for Troy
I led men on nine cruises in corsairs
to raid strange coasts, and had great luck, taking
rich spoils on the spot, and even more
in the division. So my house grew prosperous,
my standing therefore high among the Kretans.
Then came the day when Zeus who views the wide world
drew men's eyes upon that way accurst   260
that wrung the manhood from the knees of many!

[6] That is, the forces of death.

Everyone pressed me, pressed King Idómeneus
to take command of ships for Ilion.
No way out; the country rang with talk of it.
So we Akhaians had nine years of war.
In the tenth year we sacked the inner city,
Priam's town, and sailed for home; but heaven
dispersed the Akhaians. Evil days for me
were stored up in the hidden mind of Zeus.
One month, no more, I stayed at home in joy   270
with children, wife, and treasure. Lust for action
drove me to go to sea then, in command
of ships and gallant seamen bound for Egypt.
Nine ships I fitted out; my men signed on
and came to feast with me, as good shipmates,
for six full days. Many a beast I slaughtered
in the gods' honor, for my friends to eat.
Embarking on the seventh, we hauled sail
and filled away from Krete on a fresh north wind
effortlessly, as boats will glide down stream.   280
All rigging whole and all hands well, we rested,
letting the wind and steersmen work the ships,
for five days; on the fifth we made the delta.[7]
I brought my squadron in to the river bank
with one turn of the sweeps. There, heaven knows,
I told the men to wait and guard the ships
while I sent out patrols to rising ground.
But reckless greed carried them all away
to plunder the rich bottomlands; they bore off
wives and children, killed what men they found.   290

When this news reached the city, all who heard it
came at dawn. On foot they came, and horsemen,
filling the river plain with dazzle of bronze;
and Zeus lord of lightning
threw my men into blind panic: no one dared
stand against that host closing around us.
Their scything weapons left our dead in piles,
but some they took alive, into forced labor.
And I—ah, how I wish that I had died
in Egypt, on that field! So many blows   300
awaited me!—Well, Zeus himself inspired me;
I wrenched my dogskin helmet off my head,
dropped my spear, dodged out of my long shield,
ran for the king's chariot and swung on
to embrace and kiss his knees. He pulled me up,
took pity on me, placed me on the footboards,

[7] The estuary of the Nile river. Though the entire present account by Odysseus of his past life is meant to deceive, many of his invented stories correspond to what in fact did happen to him.

and drove home with me crouching there in tears.
Aye—for the troops, in battle fury still,
made one pass at me after another, pricking me
with spears, hoping to kill me. But he saved me,   310
for fear of the great wrath of Zeus that comes
when men who ask asylum are given death.

Seven years, then, my sojourn lasted there,
and I amassed a fortune, going about
among the openhanded Egyptians.
But when the eighth came round, a certain
Phoinikian adventurer came too,
a plausible rat, who had already done
plenty of devilry in the world.

                                              This fellow
took me in completely with his schemes,   320
and led me with him to Phoinikia,
where he had land and houses. One full year
I stayed there with him, to the month and day,
and when fair weather came around again
he took me in a deepsea ship for Libya,
pretending I could help in the cargo trade;
he meant, in fact, to trade me off, and get
a high price for me. I could guess the game
but had to follow him aboard. One day
on course due west, off central Krete, the ship   330
caught a fresh norther, and we ran southward
before the wind while Zeus piled ruin ahead.
When Krete was out of sight astern, no land
anywhere to be seen, but sky and ocean,
Kroníon put a dark cloud in the zenith
over the ship, and gloom spread on the sea.
With crack on crack of thunder, he let fly
a bolt against the ship, a direct hit,
so that she bucked, in sacred fumes of sulphur,
and all the men were flung into the water.   340
They came up round the wreck, bobbing a while
like petrels on the waves. No homecoming
for these, from whom the god had turned his face!
Stunned in the smother as I was, yet Zeus
put into my hands the great mast of the ship—
a way to keep from drowning. So I twined
my arms and legs around it in the gale
and stayed afloat nine days. On the tenth night,
a big surf cast me up in Thesprotia.[8]
Pheidon the king there gave me refuge, nobly,   350

[8] In Epirus, on the northwest shore of Greece, somewhat north of Ithaka along the mainland coast.

with no talk of reward. His son discovered me
exhausted and half dead with cold, and gave me
a hand to bear me up till he reached home
where he could clothe me in a shirt and cloak.
In that king's house I heard news of Odysseus,
who lately was a guest there, passing by
on his way home, the king said; and he showed me
the treasure that Odysseus had brought:
bronze, gold, and iron wrought with heavy labor—
in that great room I saw enough to last   360
Odysseus' heirs for ten long generations.
The man himself had gone up to Dodona[9]
to ask the spelling leaves of the old oak
the will of God: how to return, that is,
to the rich realm of Ithaka, after so long
an absence—openly, or on the quiet.
And, tipping wine out, Pheidon swore to me
the ship was launched, the seamen standing by
to take Odysseus to his land at last.
But he had passage first for me: Thesprotians   370
were sailing, as luck had it, for Doulíkhion,[10]
the grain-growing island; there, he said,
they were to bring me to the king, Akastos.
Instead, that company saw fit to plot
foul play against me; in my wretched life
there was to be more suffering.

                                              At sea, then,
when land lay far astern, they sprang their trap.
They'd make a slave of me that day, stripping
cloak and tunic off me, throwing around me
the dirty rags you see before you now.   380
At evening, off the fields of Ithaka,
they bound me, lashed me down under the decking
with stout ship's rope, while they all went ashore
in haste to make their supper on the beach.
The gods helped me to pry the lashing loose
until it fell away. I wound my rags
in a bundle round my head and eased myself
down the smooth lading plank into the water,
up to the chin, then swam an easy breast stroke
out and around, putting that crew behind,   390
and went ashore in underbrush, a thicket,
where I lay still, making myself small.
They raised a bitter yelling, and passed by
several times. When further groping seemed

[9] Site of the oldest oracle of Zeus, where the god's utterances were interpreted from the
rustling of oak-leaves.
[10] An island near Ithaka.

useless to them, back to the ship they went
and out to sea again. The gods were with me,
keeping me hid; and with me when they brought me
here to the door of one who knows the world.
My destiny is yet to live awhile."

The swineherd bowed and said:

"Ah well, poor drifter,   400
you've made me sad for you, going back over it,
all your hard life and wandering. That tale
about Odysseus, though, you might have spared me;
you will not make me believe that.
Why must you lie, being the man you are,
and all for nothing?

I can see so well
what happened to my master, sailing home!
Surely the gods turned on him, to refuse him
death in the field, or in his friends' arms
after he wound up the great war at Troy.   410
They would have made a tomb for him, the Akhaians,
and paid all honor to his son thereafter. No,
stormwinds made off with him. No glory came to him.

I moved here to the mountain with my swine.
Never, now, do I go down to town
unless I am sent for by Penélopê
when news of some sort comes. But those who sit
around her go on asking the old questions—
a few who miss their master still,
and those who eat his house up, and go free.   420
For my part, I have had no heart for inquiry
since one year an Aitolian[11] made a fool of me.
Exiled from land to land after some killing,
he turned up at my door; I took him in.
My master he had seen in Krete, he said,
lodged with Idómeneus, while the long ships,
leaky from gales, were laid up for repairs.
But they were all to sail, he said, that summer,
or the first days of fall—hulls laden deep
with treasure, manned by crews of heroes.

This time   430
you are the derelict the Powers bring.
Well, give up trying to win me with false news
or flattery. If I receive and shelter you,
it is not for your tales but for your trouble,
and with an eye to Zeus, who guards a guest."

---

[11] Aitolia (or Aetolia) was part of the western Greek mainland, east of Ithaka.

Then said that sly and guileful man, Odysseus:

"A black suspicious heart beats in you surely;
the man you are, not even an oath could change you.
Come then, we'll make a compact; let the gods
witness it from Olympos, where they dwell.   440
Upon your lord's homecoming, if he comes
here to this very hut, and soon—
then give me a new outfit, shirt and cloak,
and ship me to Doulíkhion—I thought it
a pleasant island. But if Odysseus
fails to appear as I predict, then Swish!
let the slaves pitch me down from some high rock,
so the next poor man who comes will watch his tongue."

The forester gave a snort and answered:

                                                           "Friend,

if I agreed to that, a great name   450
I should acquire in the world for goodness—
at one stroke and forever: your kind host
who gave you shelter and the hand of friendship,
only to take your life next day!
How confidently, after that, should I
address my prayers to Zeus, the son of Kronos!

It is time now for supper. My young herdsmen
should be arriving soon to set about it.
We'll make a quiet feast here at our hearth."

At this point in their talk the swine had come   460
up to the clearing, and the drovers followed
to pen them for the night—the porkers squealing
to high heaven, milling around the yard.
The swineherd then gave orders to his men:

"Bring in our best pig for a stranger's dinner.
A feast will do our hearts good, too; we know
grief and pain, hard scrabbling with our swine,
while the outsiders live on our labor."

                                                           Bronze

axe in hand, he turned to split up kindling,
while they drove in a tall boar, prime and fat,   470
planting him square before the fire. The gods,
as ever, had their due in the swineherd's thought,
for he it was who tossed the forehead bristles
as a first offering on the flames, calling
upon the immortal gods to let Odysseus
reach his home once more.

Then he stood up
and brained the boar with split oak from the woodpile.
Life ebbed from the beast; they slaughtered him,
singed the carcass, and cut out the joints.
Eumaios, taking flesh from every quarter,   480
put lean strips on the fat of sacrifice,
floured each one with barley meal, and cast it
into the blaze. The rest they sliced and skewered,
roasted with care, then took it off the fire
and heaped it up on platters. Now their chief,
who knew best the amenities, rose to serve,
dividing all that meat in seven portions—
one to be set aside, with proper prayers,
for the wood nymphs and Hermês, Maia's son;
the others for the company. Odysseus   490
he honored with long slices from the chine—
warming the master's heart. Odysseus looked at him
and said:

                                      "May you be dear to Zeus
as you are dear to me for this, Eumaios,
favoring with choice cuts a man like me."

And—O my swineherd!—you replied, Eumaios:

"Bless you, stranger, fall to and enjoy it
for what it is. Zeus grants us this or that,
or else refrains from granting, as he wills;
all things are in his power."

                                      He cut and burnt   500
a morsel for the gods who are young forever,
tipped out some wine, then put it in the hands
of Odysseus, the old soldier, raider of cities,
who sat at ease now with his meat before him.
As for the loaves, Mesaúlios dealt them out,
a yard boy, bought by the swineherd on his own,
unaided by his mistress or Laërtês,
from Taphians,[12] while Odysseus was away.
Now all hands reached for that array of supper,
until, when hunger and thirst were turned away   510
Mesaúlios removed the bread and, heavy
with food and drink, they settled back to rest.

Now night had come on, rough, with no moon,
but a nightlong downpour setting in, the rainwind
blowing hard from the west. Odysseus

---

[12] Inhabitants of western Greece. That Eumaios the slave himself acquired a servant is
another sign that in Homeric times slavery was not always degrading serfdom.

began to talk, to test the swineherd, trying
to put it in his head to take his cloak off
and lend it, or else urge the others to.
He knew the man's compassion.

                                     "Listen," he said,

"Eumaios, and you others, here's a wishful   520
tale that I shall tell. The wine's behind it,
vaporing wine, that makes a serious man
break down and sing, kick up his heels and clown,
or tell some story that were best untold.
But now I'm launched, I can't stop now.

                                  Would god I felt

the hot blood in me that I had at Troy!
Laying an ambush near the walls one time,
Odysseus and Meneláos were commanders
and I ranked third. I went at their request.
We worked in toward the bluffs and battlements   530
and, circling the town, got into canebrakes,[13]
thick and high, a marsh where we took cover,
hunched under arms.

                    The northwind dropped, and night
came black and wintry. A fine sleet descending
whitened the cane like hoarfrost, and clear ice
grew dense upon our shields. The other men,
all wrapt in blanket cloaks as well as tunics,
rested well, in shields up to their shoulders,
but I had left my cloak with friends in camp,
foolhardy as I was. No chance of freezing hard,   540
I thought, so I wore kilts and a shield only.
But in the small hours of the third watch, when stars
that rise at evening go down to their setting,
I nudged Odysseus, who lay close beside me;
he was alert then, listening, and I said:

'Son of Laërtês and the gods of old,
Odysseus, master mariner and soldier,
I cannot hold on long among the living.
The cold is making a corpse of me. Some god
inveigled me to come without a cloak.   550
No help for it now; too late.'

                                  Next thing I knew

he had a scheme all ready in his mind—
and what a man he was for schemes and battles!
Speaking under his breath to me, he murmured:

'Quiet; none of the rest should hear you.'

---

[13] Thick growths of cane.

Then,

propping his head on his forearm, he said:

'Listen, lads, I had an ominous dream,
the point being how far forward from our ships
and lines we've come. Someone should volunteer
to tell the corps commander, Agamémnon;   560
he may reinforce us from the base.'

At this,

Thoas jumped up, the young son of Andraimon,
put down his crimson cloak and headed off,
running shoreward.

Wrapped in that man's cloak

how gratefully I lay in the bitter dark
until the dawn came stitched in gold! I wish
I had that sap and fiber in me now!"

Then—O my swineherd!—you replied, Eumaios:

"That was a fine story, and well told,
not a word out of place, not a pointless word.   570
No, you'll not sleep cold for lack of cover,
or any other comfort one should give
to a needy guest. However, in the morning,
you must go flapping in the same old clothes.
Shirts and cloaks are few here; every man
has one change only. When our prince arrives,
the son of Odysseus, he will make you gifts—
cloak, tunic, everything—and grant you passage
wherever you care to go."

On this he rose

and placed the bed of balsam near the fire,   580
strewing sheepskins on top, and skins of goats.
Odysseus lay down. His host threw over him
a heavy blanket cloak, his own reserve
against the winter wind when it came wild.
So there Odysseus dropped off to sleep,
while herdsmen slept nearby. But not the swineherd:
not in the hut could he lie down in peace,
but now equipped himself for the night outside;
and this rejoiced Odysseus' heart, to see him
care for the herd so, while his lord was gone.   590
He hung a sharp sword from his shoulder, gathered
a great cloak round him, close, to break the wind,
and pulled a shaggy goatskin on his head.
Then, to keep at a distance dogs or men,
he took a sharpened lance, and went to rest
under a hollow rock where swine were sleeping
out of the wind and rain.

BOOK FIFTEEN: HOW THEY CAME TO ITHAKA

South into Lakedaimon[1]
into the land where greens are wide for dancing
Athena went, to put in mind of home
her great-hearted hero's honored son,
rousing him to return.

And there she found him
with Nestor's lad in the late night at rest
under the portico of Meneláos,
the famous king. Stilled by the power of slumber
the son of Nestor lay, but honeyed sleep
had not yet taken in her arms Telémakhos.   10
All through the starlit night, with open eyes,
he pondered what he had heard about his father,
until at his bedside grey-eyed Athena
towered and said:

"The brave thing now, Telémakhos,
would be to end this journey far from home.
All that you own you left behind
with men so lost to honor in your house
they may devour it all, shared out among them.
How will your journey save you then?

Go quickly
to the lord of the great war cry, Meneláos;   20
press him to send you back. You may yet find
the queen your mother in her rooms alone.
It seems her father and her kinsmen say
Eurýmakhos is the man for her to marry.
He has outdone the suitors, all the rest,
in gifts to her, and made her pledges double.
Check him, or he will have your lands and chattels
in spite of you.

You know a woman's pride
at bringing riches to the man she marries.
As to her girlhood husband, her first children,   30
he is forgotten, being dead—and they
no longer worry her.[2]

So act alone.

Go back; entrust your riches to the servant
worthiest in your eyes, until the gods
make known what beauty you yourself shall marry.

This too I have to tell you: now take heed:
the suitors' ringleaders are hot for murder,

---

[1] The story of Telémakhos, broken off after Book IV, is here resumed.
[2] These last three lines are a comment on widows in general, not on Penélopê in particular. Athena assumes this cynical view in order to hasten Telémakhos' return.

waiting in the channel between Ithaka
and Samê's rocky side; they mean to kill you
before you can set foot ashore. I doubt   40
they'll bring it off. Dark earth instead
may take to her cold bed a few brave suitors
who preyed upon your cattle.

                                        Bear well out
in your good ship, to eastward of the islands,
and sail again by night. Someone immortal
who cares for you will make a fair wind blow.
Touch at the first beach, go ashore, and send
your ship and crew around to port by sea,
while you go inland to the forester,
your old friend, loyal keeper of the swine.   50
Remain that night with him; send him to town
to tell your watchful mother Penélopê
that you are back from Pylos safe and sound."

With this Athena left him for Olympos.
He swung his foot across and gave a kick
and said to the son of Nestor:

                                        "Open your eyes,
Peisístratos. Get our team into harness.
We have a long day's journey."

                                        Nestor's son
turned over and answered him:

                                        "It is still night,
and no moon. Can we drive now? We can not,   60
itch as we may for the road home. Dawn is near.
Allow the captain of spearmen, Meneláos,
time to pack our car with gifts and time
to speak a gracious word, sending us off.
A guest remembers all his days
that host who makes provision for him kindly."

The Dawn soon took her throne of gold, and Lord
Meneláos, clarion in battle,
rose from where he lay beside the beauty   70
of Helen with her shining hair. He strode
into the hall nearby.

                                        Hearing him come,
Odysseus' son pulled on his snowy tunic
over the skin, gathered his long cape
about his breadth of shoulder like a captain,
the heir of King Odysseus. At the door
he stood and said:

"Lord Marshal, Meneláos,
send me home now to my own dear country:
longing has come upon me to go home."

The lord of the great war cry said at once: 80

"If you are longing to go home, Telémakhos,
I would not keep you for the world, not I.
I'd think myself or any other host
as ill-mannered for over-friendliness
as for hostility.
                              Measure is best in everything.
To send a guest packing, or cling to him
when he's in haste—one sin equals the other.
'Good entertaining ends with no detaining.'
Only let me load your car with gifts
and fine ones, you shall see.
                              I'll bid the women   90
set out breakfast from the larder stores;
honor and appetite—we'll attend to both
before a long day's journey overland.
Or would you care to try the Argive midlands
and Hellas, in my company? I'll harness
my own team, and take you through the towns.
Guests like ourselves no lord will turn away;
each one will make one gift, at least,
to carry home with us: tripod or cauldron
wrought in bronze, mule team, or golden cup."   100

Clearheaded Telémakhos replied:

                                        "Lord Marshal

Meneláos, royal son of Atreus,
I must return to my own hearth. I left
no one behind as guardian of my property.
This going abroad for news of a great father—
heaven forbid it be my own undoing,
or any precious thing be lost at home."

At this the tall king, clarion in battle,
called to his lady and her waiting women
to give them breakfast from the larder stores.   110
Eteóneus, the son of Boethoös, came
straight from bed, from where he lodged nearby,
and Meneláos ordered a fire lit
for broiling mutton. The king's man obeyed.
Then down to the cedar chamber Meneláos
walked with Helen and Prince Megapénthês.
Amid the gold he had in that place lying
the son of Atreus picked a wine cup, wrought
with handles left and right, and told his son
to take a silver winebowl.

                                        Helen lingered   120
near the deep coffers filled with gowns, her own
handiwork.
                            Tall goddess among women,
she lifted out one robe of state so royal,
adorned and brilliant with embroidery,
deep in the chest it shimmered like a star.
Now all three turned back to the door to greet
Telémakhos. And red-haired Meneláos
cried out to him:

                              "O prince Telémakhos,
may Hêra's Lord of Thunder see you home
and bring you to the welcome you desire!   130
Here are your gifts—perfect and precious things
I wish to make your own, out of my treasure."

And gently the great captain, son of Atreus,
handed him the goblet. Megapénthês
carried the winebowl glinting silvery
to set before him, and the Lady Helen
drew near, so that he saw her cheek's pure line.
She held the gown and murmured:

"I, too,
bring you a gift, dear child, and here it is;
remember Helen's hands by this; keep it   140
for your own bride, your joyful wedding day;
let your dear mother guard it in her chamber.
My blessing: may you come soon to your island,
home to your timbered hall."

                              So she bestowed it,
and happily he took it. These fine things
Peisístratos packed well in the wicker carrier,
admiring every one. Then Meneláos
led the two guests in to take their seats
on thrones and easy chairs in the great hall.   150
Now came a maid to tip a golden jug
of water over a silver finger bowl,
and draw the polished tables up beside them;
the larder mistress brought her tray of loaves,
with many savories to lavish on them;
viands were served by Eteóneus, and wine
by Meneláos' son. Then every hand
reached out upon good meat and drink to take them,
driving away hunger and thirst. At last,
Telémakhos and Nestor's son led out   160
their team to harness, mounted their bright car,
and drove down under the echoing entrance way,
while red-haired Meneláos, Atreus' son,

walked alongside with a golden cup—
wine for the wayfarers to spill at parting.
Then by the tugging team he stood, and spoke
over the horses' heads:

                              "Farewell, my lads.

Homage to Nestor, the benevolent king;
in my time he was fatherly to me,
when the flower of Akhaia warred on Troy."   170

Telémakhos made this reply:

"No fear
but we shall bear at least as far as Nestor
your messages, great king. How I could wish
to bring them home to Ithaka! If only
Odysseus were there, if he could hear me tell
of all the courtesy I have had from you,
returning with your finery and your treasure."

Even as he spoke, a beat of wings went skyward
off to the right—a mountain eagle, grappling   180
a white goose in his talons, heavy prey
hooked from a farmyard. Women and men-at-arms
made hubbub, running up, as he flew over,
but then he wheeled hard right before the horses—
a sight that made the whole crowd cheer, with hearts
lifting in joy. Peisístratos called out:

"Read us the sign, O Meneláos, Lord
Marshal of armies! Was the god revealing
something thus to you, or to ourselves?"

At this the old friend of the god of battle   190
groped in his mind for the right thing to say,
but regal Helen put in quickly:

"Listen:
I can tell you—tell what the omen means,
as light is given me, and as I see it
point by point fulfilled. The beaked eagle
flew from the wild mountain of his fathers
to take for prey the tame house bird. Just so,
Odysseus, back from his hard trials and wandering,
will soon come down in fury on his house.   200
He may be there today, and a black hour
he brings upon the suitors."

                                      Telémakhos

gazed and said:

                         "May Zeus, the lord of Hêra,
make it so! In far-off Ithaka, all my life,
I shall invoke you as a goddess, lady."

He let the whip fall, and the restive mares
broke forward at a canter through the town
into the open country.

                               All that day

they kept their harness shaking, side by side,
until at sundown when the roads grew dim   210
they made a halt at Pherai. There Dióklês
son of Ortílokhos whom Alpheios fathered,
welcomed the young men, and they slept the night.
Up when the young Dawn's finger tips of rose
opened in the east, they hitched the team
once more to the painted car
and steered out westward through the echoing gate,
whipping their fresh horses into a run.
Approaching Pylos Height at the day's end,
Telémakhos appealed to the son of Nestor: 220

"Could you, I wonder, do a thing I'll tell you,
supposing you agree?
We take ourselves to be true friends—in age
alike, and bound by ties between our fathers,
and now by partnership in this adventure.
Prince, do not take me roundabout,
but leave me at the ship, else the old king
your father will detain me overnight
for love of guests, when I should be at sea."

The son of Nestor nodded, thinking swiftly   230
how best he could oblige his friend.
Here was his choice: to pull the team hard over
along the beach till he could rein them in
beside the ship. Unloading Meneláos'
royal keepsakes into the stern sheets,
he sang out:

                        "Now for action! Get aboard,
and call your men, before I break the news
at home in hall to father. Who knows better
the old man's heart than I? If you delay,
he will not let you go, but he'll descend on you   240
in person and imperious; no turning
back with empty hands for him, believe me,
once his blood is up."

                              He shook the reins
to the lovely mares with long manes in the wind,
guiding them full tilt toward his father's hall.
Telémakhos called in the crew, and told them:

"Get everything shipshape aboard this craft;
we pull out now, and put sea miles behind us."

The listening men obeyed him, climbing in
to settle on their benches by the rowlocks,   250
while he stood watchful by the stern. He poured out
offerings there, and prayers to Athena.

Now a strange man came up to him, an easterner
fresh from spilling blood in distant Argos,
a hunted man. Gifted in prophecy,
he had as forebear that Melampous,[3] wizard
who lived of old in Pylos, mother city
of western flocks.

                                 Melampous, a rich lord,
had owned a house unmatched among the Pylians,
until the day came when king Neleus, noblest   260
in that age, drove him from his native land.
And Neleus for a year's term sequestered
Melampous' fields and flocks, while he lay bound
hand and foot in the keep of Phylakos.
Beauty of Neleus' daughter put him there
and sombre folly the inbreaking Fury
thrust upon him. But he gave the slip
to death, and drove the bellowing herd of Iphiklos
from Phylakê to Pylos, there to claim
the bride that ordeal won him from the king.   270
He led her to his brother's house, and went on
eastward into another land, the bluegrass
plain of Argos. Destiny held for him
rule over many Argives. Here he married,
built a great manor house, fathered Antíphatês
and Mantios, commanders both, of whom
Antíphatês begot Oikleiês
and Oikleiês the firebrand Amphiaraos.
This champion the lord of stormcloud, Zeus,
and strong Apollo loved; nor had he ever   280
to cross the doorsill into dim old age.
A woman, bought by trinkets, gave him over
to be cut down in the assault on Thebes.
His sons were Alkmáon and Amphílokhos.
In the meantime Lord Mantios begot
Polypheidês, the prophet, and
Kleitos—famous name! For Dawn[4] in silks
of gold carried off Kleitos for his beauty
to live among the gods. But Polypheidês,
high-hearted and exalted by Apollo   290
above all men for prophecy, withdrew
to Hyperesia[5] when his father angered him.

---

[3] For the stories of Melampous and Amphiaraos, see Book XI and the notes to it.
[4] Eos, goddess of the dawn.
[5] A town on the Corinthian bay; part of Agamémnon's kingdom.

He lived on there, foretelling to the world
the shape of things to come.

His son it was,

Theoklýmenos, who came upon Telémakhos
as he poured out the red wine in the sand
near his trim ship, with prayer to Athena;
and he called out, approaching:

"Friend, well met

here at libation before going to sea.
I pray you by the wine you spend, and by   300
your god, your own life, and your company;
enlighten me, and let the truth be known.
Who are you? Of what city and what parents?"

Telémakhos turned to him and replied:

"Stranger, as truly as may be, I'll tell you.
I am from Ithaka, where I was born;
my father is, or he once was, Odysseus.
But he's a long time gone, and dead, may be;
and that is what I took ship with my friends
to find out—for he left long years ago."   310

Said Theoklýmenos in reply:

"I too
have had to leave my home. I killed a cousin.
In the wide grazing lands of Argos live
many kinsmen of his and friends in power,
great among the Akhaians. These I fled.
Death and vengeance at my back, as Fate
has turned now, I came wandering overland.
Give me a plank aboard your ship, I beg,
or they will kill me. They are on my track."   320

Telémakhos made answer:

"No two ways

about it. Will I pry you from our gunnel[6]
when you are desperate to get to sea?
Come aboard; share what we have, and welcome."

He took the bronze-shod lance from the man's hand
and laid it down full-length on deck; then swung
his own weight after it aboard the cutter,
taking position aft, making a place
for Theoklýmenos near him. The stern lines
were slacked off, and Telémakhos commanded: 330

---

[6]Gunwale; the top edge of the ship's side.

"Rig the mast; make sail!" Nimbly they ran
to push the fir pole high and step it firm
amidships in the box, make fast the forestays,
and hoist aloft the white sail on its halyards.
A following wind came down from grey-eyed Athena,
blowing brisk through heaven, and so steady
the cutter lapped up miles of salt blue sea,
passing Krounoi[7] abeam and Khalkis estuary
at sundown when the sea ways all grew dark.
Then, by Athena's wind borne on, the ship   340
rounded Pheai by night and coasted Elis,
the green domain of the Epeioi; thence
he put her head north toward the running pack
of islets, wondering if by sailing wide
he sheered off Death, or would be caught.

                                             That night

Odysseus and the swineherd supped again
with herdsmen in their mountain hut. At ease
when appetite and thirst were turned away,
Odysseus, while he talked, observed the swineherd
to see if he were hospitable still—   350
if yet again the man would make him stay
under his roof, or send him off to town.

"Listen," he said, "Eumaios; listen, lads.
At daybreak I must go and try my luck
around the port. I burden you too long.
Direct me, put me on the road with someone.
Nothing else for it but to play the beggar
in populous parts. I'll get a cup or loaf,
maybe, from some householder. If I go
as far as the great hall of King Odysseus   360
I might tell Queen Penélopê my news.
Or I can drift inside among the suitors
to see what alms they give, rich as they are.
If they have whims, I'm deft in ways of service—
that I can say, and you may know for sure.
By grace of Hermês the Wayfinder, patron
of mortal tasks, the god who honors toil,
no man can do a chore better than I can.
Set me to build a fire, or chop wood,
cook or carve, mix wine and serve—or anything   370
inferior men attend to for the gentry."

Now you were furious at this, Eumaios,
and answered—O my swineherd!—

[7] The following lines describe the ship's northwest course along the southwest coast of
Greece.

"Friend, friend,
how could this fantasy take hold of you?
You dally with your life, and nothing less,
if you feel drawn to mingle in that company—
reckless, violent, and famous for it
out to the rim of heaven. Slaves
they have, but not like you. No—theirs are boys
in fresh cloaks and tunics, with pomade   380
ever on their sleek heads, and pretty faces.
These are their minions, while their tables gleam
and groan under big roasts, with loaves and wine.
Stay with us here. No one is burdened by you,
neither myself nor any of my hands.
Wait here until Odysseus' son returns.
You shall have clothing from him, cloak and tunic,
and passage where your heart desires to go."

The noble and enduring man replied:

"May you be dear to Zeus for this, Eumaios,   390
even as you are to me. Respite from pain
you give me—and from homelessness. In life
there's nothing worse than knocking about the world,
no bitterness we vagabonds are spared
when the curst belly rages! Well, you master it
and me, making me wait for the king's son.
But now, come, tell me:
what of Odysseus' mother, and his father
whom he took leave of on the sill of age?
Are they under the sun's rays, living still,   400
or gone down long ago to lodge with Death?"

To this the rugged herdsman answered:

"Aye,
that I can tell you; it is briefly told.
Laërtês lives, but daily in his hall
prays for the end of life and soul's delivery,
heartbroken as he is for a son long gone
and for his lady. Sorrow, when she died,
aged and enfeebled him like a green tree stricken;
but pining for her son, her brilliant son,   410
wore out her life.
                    Would god no death so sad
might come to benefactors dear as she!
I loved always to ask and hear about her
while she lived, although she lived in sorrow.
For she had brought me up with her own daughter,
Princess Ktimenê, her youngest child.
We were alike in age and nursed as equals
nearly, till in the flower of our years

they gave her, married her, to a Samian prince,
taking his many gifts. For my own portion   420
her mother gave new clothing, cloak and sandals,
and sent me to the woodland. Well she loved me.
Ah, how I miss that family! It is true
the blissful gods prosper my work; I have
meat and drink to spare for those I prize;
but so removed I am, I have no speech
with my sweet mistress, now that evil days
and overbearing men darken her house.
Tenants all hanker for good talk and gossip
around their lady, and a snack in hall,   430
a cup or two before they take the road
to their home acres, each one bearing home
some gift to cheer his heart."

                                     The great tactician
answered:

                            "You were still a child, I see,
when exiled somehow from your parents' land.
Tell me, had it been sacked in war, the city
of spacious ways in which they made their home,
your father and your gentle mother? Or
were you kidnapped alone, brought here by sea
huddled with sheep in some foul pirate squadron,   440
to this landowner's hall? He paid your ransom?"

The master of the woodland answered:

                                        "Friend,
now that you show an interest in that matter,
attend me quietly, be at your ease,
and drink your wine. These autumn nights are long,
ample for story-telling and for sleep.
You need not go to bed before the hour;
sleeping from dusk to dawn's a dull affair.
Let any other here who wishes, though,
retire to rest. At daybreak let him breakfast   450
and take the king's own swine into the wilderness.
Here's a tight roof; we'll drink on, you and I,
and ease our hearts of hardships we remember,
sharing old times. In later days a man
can find a charm in old adversity,
exile and pain. As to your question, now:

A certain island, Syriê by name—
you may have heard the name—lies off Ortýgia[8]

---

[8] Though there were actual places bearing the names of Syriê and Ortýgia, in the present context they refer vaguely to unidentifiable localities, probably in northwestern Greece, and possibly invented by the poet.

due west, and holds the sunsets of the year.
Not very populous, but good for grazing   460
sheep and kine; rich too in wine and grain.
No dearth is ever known there, no disease
wars on the folk, of ills that plague mankind;
but when the townsmen reach old age, Apollo
with his longbow of silver comes, and Artemis,
showering arrows of mild death.

                                                        Two towns

divide the farmlands of that whole domain,
and both were ruled by Ktêsios, my father,
Orménos' heir, and a great godlike man.

Now one day some of those renowned seafaring   470
men, sea-dogs, Phoinikians, came ashore
with bags of gauds for trading. Father had
in our household a woman of Phoinikia,
a handsome one, and highly skilled. Well, she
gave in to the seductions of those rovers.
One of them found her washing near the mooring
and lay with her, making such love to her
as women in their frailty are confused by,
even the best of them.

                                    In due course, then,
he asked her who she was and where she hailed from: 480
and nodding toward my father's roof, she said:

'I am of Sidon town, smithy of bronze
for all the East. Arubas Pasha's daughter.
Taphian pirates caught me in a byway
and sold me into slavery overseas
in this man's home. He could afford my ransom.'

The sailor who had lain with her replied:

'Why not ship out with us on the run homeward,
and see your father's high-roofed hall again,
your father and your mother? Still in Sidon   490
and still rich, they are said to be.'

                                                        She answered:

'It could be done, that, if you sailors take
oath I'll be given passage home unharmed.'

Well, soon she had them swearing it all pat
as she desired, repeating every syllable,
whereupon she warned them:

                                                        'Not a word
about our meeting here! Never call out to me
when any of you see me in the lane

or at the well. Some visitor might bear
tales to the old man. If he guessed the truth,   500
I'd be chained up, your lives would be in peril.
No: keep it secret. Hurry with your peddling,
and when your hold is filled with livestock, send
a message to me at the manor hall.
Gold I'll bring, whatever comes to hand,
and something else, too, as my passage fee—
the master's child, my charge: a boy so high,
bright for his age; he runs with me on errands.
I'd take him with me happily; his price
would be I know not what in sale abroad.'   510

Her bargain made, she went back to the manor.
But they were on the island all that year,
getting by trade a cargo of our cattle;
until, the ship at length being laden full,
ready for sea, they sent a messenger
to the Phoinikian woman. Shrewd he was,
this fellow who came round my father's hall,
showing a golden chain all strung with amber,
a necklace. Maids in waiting and my mother
passed it from hand to hand, admiring it,   520
engaging they would buy it. But that dodger,
as soon as he had caught the woman's eye
and nodded, slipped away to join the ship.
She took my hand and led me through the court
into the portico. There by luck she found
winecups and tables still in place—for Father's
attendant counselors had dined just now
before they went to the assembly. Quickly
she hid three goblets in her bellying dress
to carry with her, while I tagged along   530
in my bewilderment. The sun went down
and all the lanes grew dark as we descended,
skirting the harbor in our haste to where
those traders of Phoinikia held their ship.
All went aboard at once and put to sea,
taking the two of us. A favoring wind
blew from the power of heaven. We sailed on
six nights and days without event. Then Zeus
the son of Kronos added one more noon—and sudden
arrows from Artemis pierced the woman's heart.   540
Stone-dead she dropped
into the sloshing bilge the way a tern
plummets; and the sailors heaved her over
as tender pickings for the seals and fish.
Now I was left in dread, alone, while wind
and current bore them on to Ithaka.

Laërtês purchased me. That was the way
I first laid eyes upon this land."

                                                                    Odysseus,
the kingly man, replied:

                                                      "You rouse my pity,
telling what you endured when you were young.   550
But surely Zeus put good alongside ill:
torn from your own far home, you had the luck
to come into a kind man's service, generous
with food and drink. And a good life you lead,
unlike my own, all spent in barren roaming
from one country to the next, till now."

So the two men talked on, into the night,
leaving few hours for sleep before the Dawn
stepped up to her bright chair.

                                          The ship now drifting
under the island lee, Telémakhos'   560
companions took in sail and mast, unshipped
the oars and rowed ashore. They moored her stern
by the stout hawser lines, tossed out the bow stones,
and waded in beyond the wash of ripples
to mix their wine and cook their morning meal.
When they had turned back hunger and thirst, Telémakhos
arose to give the order of the day.

"Pull for the town," he said, "and berth our ship,
while I go inland across country. Later,
this evening, after looking at my farms,   570
I'll join you in the city. When day comes
I hope to celebrate our crossing, feasting
everyone on good red meat and wine."

His noble passenger, Theoklýmenos,
now asked:

                              "What as to me, my dear young fellow,
where shall I go? Will I find lodging here
with some one of the lords of stony Ithaka?
Or go straight to your mother's hall and yours?"

Telémakhos turned round to him and said:

"I should myself invite you to our hall   580
if things were otherwise; there'd be no lack
of entertainment for you. As it stands,
no place could be more wretched for a guest
while I'm away. Mother will never see you;
she almost never shows herself at home

to the suitors there, but stays in her high chamber
weaving upon her loom. No, let me name
another man for you to go to visit:
Eurýmakhos,[9] the honored son of Pólybos.
In Ithaka they are dazzled by him now—   590
the strongest of their princes, bent on making
mother and all Odysseus' wealth his own.
Zeus on Olympos only knows
if some dark hour for them will intervene."

The words were barely spoken, when a hawk,
Apollo's courier, flew up on the right,
clutching a dove and plucking her—so feathers
floated down to the ground between Telémakhos
and the moored cutter. Theoklýmenos
called him apart and gripped his hand, whispering: 600

"A god spoke in this bird-sign on the right.
I knew it when I saw the hawk fly over us.
There is no kinglier house than yours, Telémakhos,
here in the realm of Ithaka. Your family
will be in power forever."

                                                    The young prince,
clear in spirit, answered:

                                                              "Be it so,
friend, as you say. And may you know as well
the friendship of my house, and many gifts
from me, so everyone may call you fortunate."

He called a trusted crewman named Peiraios,   610
and said to him:

                                              "Peiraios, son of Klýtios,
can I rely on you again as ever, most
of all the friends who sailed with me to Pylos?
Take this man home with you, take care of him,
treat him with honor, till I come."

                                                                    To this
Peiraios the good spearman answered:

"Aye,
stay in the wild country while you will,
I shall be looking after him, Telémakhos.
He will not lack good lodging."

---

[9]*Eurýmakhos.* Since he is one of Penélopê's principal suitors, it is odd that Eurýmakhos
should be recommended by Telémakhos as a host for his passenger. Indeed, Telémakhos soon
changes his mind and asks the trusted crewman Peiraios to house Theoklýmenos. Possibly
Telémakhos, with something of his father's wariness, hesitates until he has some evidence of
Theoklýmenos' good will.

Down to the ship   620
he turned, and boarded her, and called the others
to cast off the stern lines and come aboard.
So men climbed in to sit beside the rowlocks.
Telémakhos now tied his sandals on
and lifted his tough spear from the ship's deck;
hawsers were taken in, and they shoved off
to reach the town by way of the open sea
as he commanded them—royal Odysseus'
own dear son, Telémakhos.

On foot

and swiftly he went up toward the stockade   630
where swine were penned in hundreds, and at night
the guardian of the swine, the forester,
slept under arms on duty for his masters.

BOOK SIXTEEN: FATHER AND SON

But there were two men in the mountain hut—
Odysseus and the swineherd. At first light
blowing their fire up, they cooked their breakfast
and sent their lads out, driving herds to root
in the tall timber.

When Telémakhos came,
the wolvish troop of watchdogs only fawned on him
as he advanced. Odysseus heard them go
and heard the light crunch of a man's footfall—
at which he turned quickly to say:

"Eumaios,

here is one of your crew come back, or maybe   10
another friend: the dogs are out there snuffling
belly down; not one has even growled.
I can hear footsteps—"

But before he finished
his tall son stood at the door.

The swineherd
rose in surprise, letting a bowl and jug
tumble from his fingers. Going forward,
he kissed the young man's head, his shining eyes
and both hands, while his own tears brimmed and fell.
Think of a man whose dear and only son,
born to him in exile, reared with labor,   20
has lived ten years abroad and now returns:
how would that man embrace his son! Just so
the herdsman clapped his arms around Telémakhos
and covered him with kisses—for he knew
the lad had got away from death. He said:

"Light of my days, Telémakhos,
you made it back! When you took ship for Pylos
I never thought to see you here again.
Come in, dear child, and let me feast my eyes;
here you are, home from the distant places!   30
How rarely, anyway, you visit us,
your own men, and your own woods and pastures!
Always in the town, a man would think
you loved the suitors' company, those dogs!"

Telémakhos with his clear candor said:

"I am with you, Uncle. See now, I have come
because I wanted to see you first, to hear from you
if Mother stayed at home—or is she married
off to someone, and Odysseus' bed
left empty for some gloomy spider's weaving?"   40

Gently the forester replied to this:

"At home indeed your mother is, poor lady,
still in the women's hall. Her nights and days
are wearied out with grieving."

                                                        Stepping back
he took the bronze-shod lance, and the young prince
entered the cabin over the worn door stone.
Odysseus moved aside, yielding his couch,
but from across the room Telémakhos checked him:

"Friend, sit down; we'll find another chair
in our own hut. Here is the man to make one!"   50

The swineherd, when the quiet man sank down,
built a new pile of evergreens and fleeces—
a couch for the dear son of great Odysseus—
then gave them trenchers of good meat, left over
from the roast pork of yesterday, and heaped up
willow baskets full of bread, and mixed
an ivy bowl of honey-hearted wine.
Then he in turn sat down, facing Odysseus,
their hands went out upon the meat and drink
as they fell to, ridding themselves of hunger,   60
until Telémakhos paused and said:

                                                        "Oh, Uncle,
what's your friend's home port? How did he come?
Who were the sailors brought him here to Ithaka?
I doubt if he came walking on the sea."

And you replied, Eumaios—O my swineherd—

"Son, the truth about him is soon told.
His home land, and a broad land, too, is Krete,
but he has knocked about the world, he says,
for years, as the Powers wove his life. Just now   70
he broke away from a shipload of Thesprotians
to reach my hut. I place him in your hands.
Act as you will. He wishes your protection."

The young man said:

                                        "Eumaios, my protection!
The notion cuts me to the heart. How can I
receive your friend at home? I am not old enough
or trained in arms. Could I defend myself
if someone picked a fight with me?

                                        Besides,

mother is in a quandary, whether to stay with me
as mistress of our household, honoring
her lord's bed, and opinion in the town,   80
or take the best Akhaian who comes her way—
the one who offers most.

                                        I'll undertake,

at all events, to clothe your friend for winter,
now he is with you. Tunic and cloak of wool,
a good broadsword, and sandals—these are his.
I can arrange to send him where he likes
or you may keep him in your cabin here.
I shall have bread and wine sent up; you need not
feel any pinch on his behalf.

                                        Impossible

to let him stay in hall, among the suitors.   90
They are drunk, drunk on impudence, they might
injure my guest—and how could I bear that?
How could a single man take on those odds?
Not even a hero could.

                                The suitors are too strong."

At this the noble and enduring man, Odysseus,
addressed his son:

                                "Kind prince, it may be fitting
for me to speak a word. All that you say
gives me an inward wound as I sit listening.
I mean this wanton game they play, these fellows,
riding roughshod over you in your own house,   100
admirable as you are. But tell me,
are you resigned to being bled? The townsmen,
stirred up against you, are they, by some oracle?
Your brothers—can you say your brothers fail you?
A man should feel his kin, at least, behind him
in any clash, when a real fight is coming.

If my heart were as young as yours, if I were
son to Odysseus, or the man himself,
I'd rather have my head cut from my shoulders
by some slashing adversary, if I   110
brought no hurt upon that crew! Suppose
I went down, being alone, before the lot,
better, I say, to die at home in battle
than see these insupportable things, day after
day the stranger cuffed, the women slaves
dragged here and there, shame in the lovely rooms,
the wine drunk up in rivers, sheer waste
of pointless feasting, never at an end!"

Telémakhos replied:

                                        "Friend, I'll explain to you.
There is no rancor in the town against me,   120
no fault of brothers, whom a man should feel
behind him when a fight is in the making;
no, no—in our family the First Born
of Heaven, Zeus, made single sons the rule.
Arkeísios had but one, Laërtês; he
in turn fathered only one, Odysseus,
who left me in his hall alone, too young
to be of any use to him.
And so you see why enemies fill our house
in these days: all the princes of the islands,   130
Doulíkhion, Samê, wooded Zakýnthos,
Ithaka, too—lords of our island rock—
eating our house up as they court my mother.
She cannot put an end to it; she dare not
bar the marriage that she hates; and they
devour all my substance and my cattle,
and who knows when they'll slaughter me as well?
It rests upon the gods' great knees.

                                                Uncle,
go down at once and tell the Lady Penélopê
that I am back from Pylos, safe and sound.   140
I stay here meanwhile. You will give your message
and then return. Let none of the Akhaians
hear it; they have a mind to do me harm."

To this, Eumaios, you replied:

                                                "I know.
But make this clear, now—should I not likewise
call on Laërtês with your news? Hard hit
by sorrow though he was, mourning Odysseus,
he used to keep an eye upon his farm.
He had what meals he pleased, with his own folk.
But now no more, not since you sailed for Pylos;   150

he has not taken food or drink, I hear,
sitting all day, blind to the work of harvest,
groaning, while the skin shrinks on his bones."

Telémakhos answered:

                             "One more misery,
but we had better leave it so.
If men choose, and have their choice, in everything,
we'd have my father home.

                                  Turn back
when you have done your errand, as you must,
not to be caught alone in the countryside.
But wait—you may tell Mother 160
to send our old housekeeper on the quiet
and quickly; she can tell the news to Grandfather."

The swineherd, roused, reached out to get his sandals,
tied them on, and took the road.

                                  Who else
beheld this but Athena? From the air
she walked, taking the form of a tall woman,
handsome and clever at her craft, and stood
beyond the gate in plain sight of Odysseus,
unseen, though, by Telémakhos, unguessed,
for not to everyone will gods appear. 170
Odysseus noticed her; so did the dogs,
who cowered whimpering away from her. She only
nodded, signing to him with her brows,
a sign he recognized. Crossing the yard,
he passed out through the gate in the stockade
to face the goddess. There she said to him:

"Son of Laërtês and the gods of old,
Odysseus, master of land ways and sea ways,
dissemble to your son no longer now.
The time has come: tell him how you together 180
will bring doom on the suitors in the town.
I shall not be far distant then, for I
myself desire battle."

                                Saying no more,
she tipped her golden wand upon the man,
making his cloak pure white, and the knit tunic
fresh around him. Lithe and young she made him,
ruddy with sun, his jawline clean, the beard
no longer grey upon his chin. And she
withdrew when she had done.

                            Then Lord Odysseus
reappeared—and his son was thunderstruck. 190

Fear in his eyes, he looked down and away
as though it were a god, and whispered:

                                      "Stranger,

you are no longer what you were just now!
Your cloak is new; even your skin! You are
one of the gods who rule the sweep of heaven!
Be kind to us, we'll make you fair oblation
and gifts of hammered gold. Have mercy on us!"

The noble and enduring man replied:

"No god. Why take me for a god? No, no.
I am that father whom your boyhood lacked   200
and suffered pain for lack of. I am he."

Held back too long, the tears ran down his cheeks
as he embraced his son.

                                 Only Telémakhos,
uncomprehending, wild
with incredulity, cried out:

                                    "You cannot

be my father Odysseus! Meddling spirits
conceived this trick to twist the knife in me!
No man of woman born could work these wonders
by his own craft, unless a god came into it
with ease to turn him young or old at will.   210
I swear you were in rags and old,
and here you stand like one of the immortals!"

Odysseus brought his ranging mind to bear
and said:

                        "This is not princely, to be swept
away by wonder at your father's presence.
No other Odysseus will ever come,
for he and I are one, the same; his bitter
fortune and his wanderings are mine.
Twenty years gone, and I am back again
on my own island.

                           As for my change of skin,   220
that is a charm Athena, Hope of Soldiers,
uses as she will; she has the knack
to make me seem a beggar man sometimes
and sometimes young, with finer clothes about me.
It is no hard thing for the gods of heaven
to glorify a man or bring him low."

When he had spoken, down he sat.

                                 Then, throwing
his arms around this marvel of a father

Telémakhos began to weep. Salt tears
rose from the wells of longing in both men,   230
and cries burst from both as keen and fluttering
as those of the great taloned hawk,
whose nestlings farmers take before they fly.
So helplessly they cried, pouring out tears,
and might have gone on weeping so till sundown,
had not Telémakhos said:

                                        "Dear father! Tell me
what kind of vessel put you here ashore
on Ithaka? Your sailors, who were they?
I doubt you made it, walking on the sea!"

Then said Odysseus, who had borne the barren sea: 240

"Only plain truth shall I tell you, child.
Great seafarers, the Phaiákians, gave me passage
as they give other wanderers. By night
over the open ocean, while I slept,
they brought me in their cutter, set me down
on Ithaka, with gifts of bronze and gold
and stores of woven things. By the gods' will
these lie all hidden in a cave. I came
to this wild place, directed by Athena,
so that we might lay plans to kill our enemies.   250
Count up the suitors for me, let me know
what men at arms are there, how many men.
I must put all my mind to it, to see
if we two by ourselves can take them on
or if we should look round for help."

                                                          Telémakhos
replied:

                                        "O Father, all my life your fame
as a fighting man has echoed in my ears—
your skills with weapons and the tricks of war—
but what you speak of is a staggering thing,
beyond imagining, for me. How can two men   260
do battle with a houseful in their prime?
For I must tell you this is no affair
of ten or even twice ten men, but scores,
throngs of them. You shall see, here and now.
The number from Doulíkhion alone
is fifty-two, picked men, with armorers,
a half dozen; twenty-four came from Samê,
twenty from Zakýnthos; our own island
accounts for twelve, high-ranked, and their retainers,
Medôn the crier, and the Master Harper   270
besides a pair of handymen at feasts.

If we go in against all these
I fear we pay in salt blood for your vengeance.
You must think hard if you would conjure up
the fighting strength to take us through."

                                                            Odysseus

who had endured the long war and the sea
answered:

                                                            "I'll tell you now.

Suppose Athena's arm is over us, and Zeus
her father's, must I rack my brains for more?"

Clearheaded Telémakhos looked hard and said: 280

"Those two are great defenders, no one doubts it,
but throned in the serene clouds overhead;
other affairs of men and gods they have
to rule over."

                                            And the hero answered:

"Before long they will stand to right and left of us
in combat, in the shouting, when the test comes—
our nerve against the suitors' in my hall.
Here is your part: at break of day tomorrow
home with you, go mingle with our princes.
The swineherd later on will take me down   290
the port-side trail—a beggar, by my looks,
hangdog and old. If they make fun of me
in my own courtyard, let your ribs cage up
your springing heart, no matter what I suffer,
no matter if they pull me by the heels
or practice shots at me, to drive me out.
Look on, hold down your anger. You may even
plead with them, by heaven! in gentle terms
to quit their horseplay—not that they will heed you,
rash as they are, facing their day of wrath.   300
Now fix the next step in your mind.

                                            Athena,

counseling me, will give me word, and I
shall signal to you, nodding: at that point
round up all armor, lances, gear of war
left in our hall, and stow the lot away
back in the vaulted store room. When the suitors
miss those arms and question you, be soft
in what you say: answer:

                                    'I thought I'd move them
out of the smoke. They seemed no longer those
bright arms Odysseus left us years ago   310
when he went off to Troy. Here where the fire's

hot breath came, they had grown black and drear.
One better reason, too, I had from Zeus:
suppose a brawl starts up when you are drunk,
you might be crazed and bloody one another,
and that would stain your feast, your courtship. Tempered
iron can magnetize a man.'

Say that.

But put aside two broadswords and two spears
for our own use, two oxhide shields nearby
when we go into action. Pallas Athena   320
and Zeus All Provident will see you through,
bemusing our young friends.

Now one thing more.

If son of mine you are and blood of mine,
let no one hear Odysseus is about.
Neither Laërtês, nor the swineherd here,
nor any slave, nor even Penélopê.
But you and I alone must learn how far
the women are corrupted; we should know
how to locate good men among our hands,
the loyal and respectful, and the shirkers   330
who take you lightly, as alone and young."

His admirable son replied:

"Ah, Father,

even when danger comes I think you'll find
courage in me. I am not scatterbrained.
But as to checking on the field hands now,
I see no gain for us in that. Reflect,
you make a long toil, that way, if you care
to look men in the eye at every farm,
while these gay devils in our hall at ease
eat up our flocks and herds, leaving us nothing.   340

As for the maids I say, Yes: make distinction
between good girls and those who shame your house;
all that I shy away from is a scrutiny
of cottagers just now. The time for that
comes later—if in truth you have a sign
from Zeus the Stormking."

So their talk ran on,
while down the coast, and round toward Ithaka,
hove the good ship that had gone out to Pylos
bearing Telémakhos and his companions.
Into the wide bay waters, on to the dark land,   350
they drove her, hauled her up, took out the oars
and the canvas for light-hearted squires to carry
homeward—as they carried, too, the gifts

of Meneláos round to Klýtios'[1] house.
But first they sped a runner to Penélopê.
They knew that quiet lady must be told
the prince her son had come ashore, and sent
his good ship round to port; not one soft tear
should their sweet queen let fall.

                              Both messengers,
crewman and swineherd—reached the outer gate   360
in the same instant, bearing the same news,
and went in side by side to the king's hall.
He of the ship burst out among the maids:

"Your son's ashore this morning, O my Queen!"

But the swineherd calmly stood near Penélopê
whispering what her son had bade him tell
and what he had enjoined on her. No more.
When he had done, he left the place and turned
back to his steading in the hills.

                                     By now,
sullen confusion weighed upon the suitors.   370
Out of the house, out of the court they went,
beyond the wall and gate, to sit in council.
Eurýmakhos, the son of Pólybos,
opened discussion:

                           "Friends, face up to it;
that young pup, Telémakhos, has done it;
he made the round trip, though we said he could not.
Well—now to get the best craft we can find
afloat, with oarsmen who can drench her bows,
and tell those on the island to come home."

He was yet speaking when Amphínomos,   380
craning seaward, spotted the picket ship
already in the roadstead under oars
with canvas brailed up; and this fresh arrival
made him chuckle. Then he told his friends:

"Too late for messages. Look, here they come
along the bay. Some god has brought them news,
or else they saw the cutter pass—and could not
overtake her."

                             On their feet at once,
the suitors took the road to the sea beach,
where, meeting the black ship, they hauled her in.   390
Oars and gear they left for their light-hearted

---

[1] Father of the trusty Peiraios; see the end of Book XV.

squires to carry, and all in company
made off for the assembly ground. All others,
young and old alike, they barred from sitting.
Eupeithês' son, Antínoös, made the speech:

"How the gods let our man escape a boarding,
that is the wonder.

We had lookouts posted
up on the heights all day in the sea wind,
and every hour a fresh pair of eyes;
at night we never slept ashore   400
but after sundown cruised the open water
to the southeast, patrolling until Dawn.
We were prepared to cut him off and catch him,
squelch him for good and all. The power of heaven
steered him the long way home.

Well, let this company plan his destruction,
and leave him no way out, this time. I see
our business here unfinished while he lives.
He knows, now, and he's no fool. Besides,
his people are all tired of playing up to us.   410
I say, act now, before he brings the whole
body of Akhaians to assembly—
and he would leave no word unsaid, in righteous
anger speaking out before them all
of how we plotted murder, and then missed him.
Will they commend us for that pretty work?
Take action now, or we are in for trouble;
we might be exiled, driven off our lands.
Let the first blow be ours.
If we move first, and get our hands on him   420
far from the city's eye, on path or field,
then stores and livestock will be ours to share;
the house we may confer upon his mother—
and on the man who marries her. Decide
otherwise you may—but if, my friends,
you want that boy to live and have his patrimony,
then we should eat no more of his good mutton,
come to this place no more.

Let each from his own hall
court her with dower gifts. And let her marry
the destined one, the one who offers most."   430

He ended, and no sound was heard among them,
sitting all hushed, until at last the son
of Nísos Aretíadês arose—
Amphínomos.

He led the group of suitors
who came from grainlands on Doulíkhion,

and he had lightness in his talk that pleased
Penélopê, for he meant no ill.
Now, in concern for them, he spoke:

                                                             "O Friends

I should not like to kill Telémakhos.
It is a shivery thing to kill a prince   440
of royal blood.

                                    We should consult the gods.

If Zeus hands down a ruling for that act,
then I shall say, 'Come one, come all,' and go
cut him down with my own hand—
but I say Halt, if gods are contrary."

Now this proposal won them, and it carried.
Breaking their session up, away they went
to take their smooth chairs in Odysseus' house.
Meanwhile Penélopê the Wise,
decided, for her part, to make appearance   450
before the valiant young men.

                                    She knew now

they plotted her child's death in her own hall,
for once more Medôn, who had heard them, told her.
Into the hall that lovely lady came,
with maids attending, and approached the suitors,
till near a pillar of the well-wrought roof
she paused, her shining veil across her cheeks,
and spoke directly to Antínoös:

                                                             "Infatuate,

steeped in evil! Yet in Ithaka they say
you were the best one of your generation   460
in mind and speech. Not so, you never were.
Madman, why do you keep forever knitting
death for Telémakhos? Have you no piety
toward men dependent on another's mercy?
Before Lord Zeus, no sanction can be found
for one such man to plot against another!
Or are you not aware that your own father
fled to us when the realm was up in arms
against him? He had joined the Taphian pirates
in ravaging Thesprotian folk, our friends.   470
Our people would have raided *him,* then—breached
his heart, butchered his herds to feast upon—
only Odysseus took him in, and held
the furious townsmen off. It is Odysseus'
house you now consume, his wife you court,
his son you kill, or try to kill. And me
you ravage now, and grieve. I call upon you
to make an end of it!—and your friends too!"

The son of Pólybos it was, Eurýmakhos,
who answered her with ready speech:

                                                 "My lady   480
Penélopê, wise daughter of Ikários,
you must shake off these ugly thoughts. I say
that man does not exist, nor will, who dares
lay hands upon your son Telémakhos,
while I live, walk the earth, and use my eyes.
The man's life blood, I swear,
will spurt and run out black around my lancehead!
For it is true of me, too, that Odysseus,
raiders of cities, took me on his knees
and fed me often—tidbits and red wine.   490
Should not Telémakhos, therefore, be dear to me
above the rest of men? I tell the lad
he must not tremble for his life, at least
alone in the suitors' company. Heaven
deals death no man avoids."

                                 Blasphemous lies
in earnest tones he told—the one who planned
the lad's destruction!

                                Silently the lady
made her way to her glowing upper chamber,
there to weep for her dear lord, Odysseus,
until grey-eyed Athena   500
cast sweet sleep upon her eyes.

                               At fall of dusk
Odysseus and his son heard the approach
of the good forester. They had been standing
over the fire with a spitted pig,
a yearling. And Athena coming near
with one rap of her wand made of Odysseus
an old old man again, with rags about him—
for if the swineherd knew his lord were there
he could not hold the news; Penélopê
would hear it from him.

                                Now Telémakhos   510
greeted him first:

                              "Eumaios, back again!
What was the talk in town? Are the tall suitors
home again, by this time, from their ambush,
or are they still on watch for my return?"

And you replied, Eumaios—O my swineherd:

"There was no time to ask or talk of that;
I hurried through the town. Even while I spoke

my message, I felt driven to return.
A runner from your friends turned up, a crier,
who gave the news first to your mother. Ah!   520
One thing I do know; with my own two eyes
I saw it. As I climbed above the town
to where the sky is cut by Hermês' ridge,
I saw a ship bound in for our own bay
with many oarsmen in it, laden down
with sea provisioning and two-edged spears,
and I surmised those were the men.

                                        Who knows?"

Telémakhos, now strong with magic, smiled
across at his own father—but avoided
the swineherd's eye.

                        So when the pig was done,   530
the spit no longer to be turned, the table
garnished, everyone sat down to feast
on all the savory flesh he craved. And when
they had put off desire for meat and drink,
they turned to bed and took the gift of sleep.

BOOK SEVENTEEN: THE BEGGAR AT THE MANOR

When the young Dawn came bright into the East
spreading her finger tips of rose, Telémakhos
the king's son, tied on his rawhide sandals
and took the lance that bore his handgrip. Burning
to be away, and on the path to town,
he told the swineherd:

                            "Uncle, the truth is
I must go down myself into the city.
Mother must see me there, with her own eyes,
or she will weep and feel forsaken still,
and will not set her mind at rest. Your job   10
will be to lead this poor man down to beg.
Some householder may want to dole him out
a loaf and pint. I have my own troubles.
Am I to care for every last man who comes?
And if he takes it badly—well, so much
the worse for him. Plain truth is what I favor."

At once Odysseus the great tactician
spoke up briskly:

                        "Neither would I myself
care to be kept here, lad. A beggar man
fares better in the town. Let it be said   20

I am not yet so old I must lay up
indoors and mumble, 'Aye, Aye' to a master.[1]
Go on, then. As you say, my friend can lead me
as soon as I have had a bit of fire
and when the sun grows warmer. These old rags
could be my death, outside on a frosty morning,
and the town is distant, so they say."

Telémakhos

with no more words went out, and through the fence,
and down hill, going fast on the steep footing,
nursing woe for the suitors in his heart.   30

Before the manor hall, he leaned his lance
against a great porch pillar and stepped in
across the door stone.

Old Eurýkleia

saw him first, for that day she was covering
handsome chairs nearby with clean fleeces.
She ran to him at once, tears in her eyes;
and other maidservants of the old soldier
Odysseus gathered round to greet their prince,
kissing his head and shoulders.

Quickly, then,   40

Penélopê the Wise, tall in her beauty
as Artemis or pale-gold Aphroditê,
appeared from her high chamber and came down
to throw her arms around her son. In tears
she kissed his head, kissed both his shining eyes,
then cried out, and her words flew:

"Back with me!

Telémakhos, more sweet to me than sunlight!
I thought I should not see you again, ever,
after you took the ship that night to Pylos—
against my will, with not a word! you went
for news of your dear father. Tell me now   50
of everything you saw!"

But he made answer:

"Mother, not now. You make me weep. My heart
already aches—I came near death at sea.
You must bathe, first of all, and change your dress,
and take your maids to the highest room to pray.
Pray, and burn offerings to the gods of heaven,
that Zeus may put his hand to our revenge.

---

[1] Odysseus means that he is not yet so old that he must remain in one place, subject to a single master.

I am off now to bring home from the square
a guest, a passenger I had. I sent him
yesterday with all my crew to town.   60
Peiraios was to care for him, I said,
and keep him well, with honor, till I came."

She caught back the swift words upon her tongue.
Then softly she withdrew
to bathe and dress her body in fresh linen,
and make her offerings to the gods of heaven,
praying Almighty Zeus
to put his hand to their revenge.

                                                         Telémakhos
had left the hall, taken his lance, and gone
with two quick hounds at heel into the town,   70
Athena's grace in his long stride
making the people gaze as he came near.
And suitors gathered, primed with friendly words,
despite the deadly plotting in their hearts—
but these, and all their crowd, he kept away from.
Next he saw sitting some way off, apart,
Mentor, with Antiphos and Halithersês,
friends of his father's house in years gone by.
Near these men he sat down, and told his tale
under their questioning.
                                     His crewman, young Peiraios,   80
guided through town, meanwhile, into the Square,
the Argive exile, Theoklýmenos.
Telémakhos lost no time in moving toward him;
but first Peiraios had his say:

                                              "Telémakhos,
you must send maids to me, at once, and let me
turn over to you those gifts from Meneláos!"

The prince had pondered it, and said:

                                              "Peiraios,
none of us knows how this affair will end.
Say one day our fine suitors, without warning,
draw upon me, kill me in our hall,   90
and parcel out my patrimony—I wish
you, and no one of them, to have those things.
But if my hour comes, if I can bring down
bloody death on all that crew,
you will rejoice to send my gifts to me—
and so will I rejoice!"

                                        Then he departed,
leading his guest, the lonely stranger, home.

Over chair-backs in hall they dropped their mantles
and passed in to the polished tubs, where maids
poured out warm baths for them, anointed them,   100
and pulled fresh tunics, fleecy cloaks around them.
Soon they were seated at their ease in hall.
A maid came by to tip a golden jug
over their fingers into a silver bowl
and draw a gleaming table up beside them.
The larder mistress brought her tray of loaves
and savories, dispensing each.

                        In silence
across the hall, beside a pillar, propped
in a long chair, Telémakhos' mother
spun a fine wool yarn.

               The young men's hands   110
went out upon the good things placed before them,
and only when their hunger and thirst were gone
did she look up and say:

                      "Telémakhos,
what am I to do now? Return alone
and lie again on my forsaken bed—
sodden how often with my weeping
since that day when Odysseus put to sea
to join the Atreidai[2] before Troy?

                 Could you not
tell me, before the suitors fill our house,
what news you have of his return?"

                  He answered: 120

"Now that you ask a second time, dear Mother,
here is the truth.

             We went ashore at Pylos
to Nestor, lord and guardian of the West,
who gave me welcome in his towering hall.
So kind he was, he might have been my father
and I his long-lost son—so truly kind,
taking me in with his own honored sons.
But as to Odysseus' bitter fate,
living or dead, he had no news at all
from anyone on earth, he said. He sent me   130
overland in a strong chariot
to Atreus' son, the captain, Meneláos.
And I saw Helen there, for whom the Argives
fought, and the Trojans fought, as the gods willed.
Then Meneláos of the great war cry
asked me my errand in that ancient land

[2]Sons of Atreus—Agamémnon and Meneláos.

of Lakedaimon. So I told our story,
and in reply he burst out:[3]

                                                     'Intolerable!

That feeble men, unfit as those men are,
should think to lie in that great captain's bed,   140
fawns in the lion's lair! As if a doe
put down her litter of sucklings there, while she
sniffed at the glen or grazed a grassy hollow.
Ha! Then the lord returns to his own bed
and deals out wretched doom on both alike.

So will Odysseus deal out doom on these.
O Father Zeus, Athena, and Apollo!
I pray he comes as once he was, in Lesbos,
when he stood up to wrestle Philomeleidês—
champion and Island King—   150
and smashed him down. How the Akhaians cheered!
If that Odysseus could meet the suitors,
they'd have a quick reply, a stunning dowry!
Now for your questions, let me come to the point.
I would not misreport it for you; let me
tell you what the Ancient of the Sea,
that infallible seer, told me.

                                                  On an island

your father lies and grieves. The Ancient saw him
held by a nymph, Kalypso, in her hall;
no means of sailing home remained to him,   160
no ship with oars, and no ship's company
to pull him on the broad back of the sea.'

I had this from the lord marshal, Meneláos,
and when my errand in that place was done
I left for home. A fair breeze from the gods
brought me swiftly back to our dear island."

The boy's tale made her heart stir in her breast,
but this was not all. Mother and son now heard
Theoklýmenos, the diviner, say:

"He does not see it clear—

                                                  O gentle lady,   170

wife of Odysseus Laërtiadês,
listen to me, I can reveal this thing.
Zeus be my witness, and the table set
for strangers and the hearth to which I've come—
the lord Odysseus, I tell you,
is present now, already, on this island!
Quartered somewhere, or going about, he knows

---

[3] The following quotation of Meneláos' words summarizes his narrative in Book IV.

what evil is afoot. He has it in him
to bring a black hour on the suitors. Yesterday,
still at the ship, I saw this in a portent.   180
I read the sign aloud, I told Telémakhos!"

The prudent queen, for her part, said:

                                                          "Stranger,
if only this came true—
our love would go to you, with many gifts;
aye, every man who passed would call you happy!"

So ran the talk between these three.

                                                 Meanwhile,
swaggering before Odysseus' hall,
the suitors were competing at the discus throw
and javelin, on the level measured field.
But when the dinner hour drew on, and beasts   190
were being driven from the fields to slaughter—
as beasts were, every day—Medôn spoke out:
Medôn, the crier, whom the suitors liked;
he took his meat beside them.

                                                 "Men," he said,
"each one has had his work-out and his pleasure,
come in to Hall now; time to make our feast.
Are discus throws more admirable than a roast
when the proper hour comes?"

                                              At this reminder
they all broke up their games, and trailed away
into the gracious, timbered hall. There, first,   200
they dropped their cloaks on chairs; then came their ritual:
putting great rams and fat goats to the knife—
pigs and a cow, too.
                               So they made their feast.

During these hours, Odysseus and the swineherd
were on their way out of the hills to town.
The forester had got them started, saying:

"Friend, you have hopes, I know, of your adventure
into the heart of town today. My lord
wishes it so, not I. No, I should rather
you stood by here as guardian of our steading.   210
But I owe reverence to my prince, and fear
he'll make my ears burn later if I fail.
A master's tongue has a rough edge. Off we go.
Part of the day is past; nightfall will be
early, and colder, too."

Odysseus,
who had it all timed in his head, replied:

"I know, as well as you do. Let's move on.
You lead the way—the whole way. Have you got
a staff, a lopped stick, you could let me use
to put my weight on when I slip? This path   220
is hard going, they said."

Over his shoulders
he slung his patched-up knapsack, an old bundle
tied with twine. Eumaios found a stick for him,
the kind he wanted, and the two set out,
leaving the boys and dogs to guard the place.
In this way good Eumaios led his lord
down to the city.

And it seemed to him
he led an old outcast, a beggar man,
leaning most painfully upon a stick,
his poor cloak, all in tatters, looped about him.   230

Down by the stony trail they made their way
as far as Clearwater, not far from town—
a spring house where the people filled their jars.
Ithakos, Nêritos, and Polýktor[4] built it,
and round it on the humid ground a grove,
a circular wood of poplars grew. Ice cold
in runnels from a high rock ran the spring,
and over it there stood an altar stone
to the cool nymphs, where all men going by
laid offerings.

Well, here the son of Dólios   240
crossed their path—Melánthios.[5]

He was driving
a string of choice goats for the evening meal,
with two goatherds beside him; and no sooner
had he laid eyes upon the wayfarers
than he began to growl and taunt them both
so grossly that Odysseus' heart grew hot:

"Here comes one scurvy type leading another!
God pairs them off together, every time.
Swineherd, where are you taking your new pig,
that stinking beggar there, licker of pots?   250
How many doorposts has he rubbed his back on

---

[4] These three were the founding fathers of the island; Ithakos' name represents the island itself, Nêritos' name an important mountain on the island.

[5] Dólios was a trusty steward of Odysseus' father, Laërtes. As we learn later, Melánthios' sister Melántho, maid to Penélopê, is a mistress of the suitor Eurýmakhos, a fact that probably accounts for the intimacy of her goatherd brother with the suitors.

whining for garbage, where a noble guest
would rate a cauldron or a sword?

                                        Hand him

over to me, I'll make a farmhand of him,
a stall scraper, a fodder carrier! Whey
for drink will put good muscle on his shank!
No chance: he learned his dodges long ago—
no honest sweat. He'd rather tramp the country
begging, to keep his hoggish belly full.
Well, I can tell you this for sure: 260
in King Odysseus' hall, if he goes there,
footstools will fly around his head—good shots
from strong hands. Back and side, his ribs will catch it
on the way out!"

                                And like a drunken fool
he kicked at Odysseus' hip as he passed by.
Not even jogged off stride, or off the trail,
the Lord Odysseus walked along, debating
inwardly whether to whirl and beat
the life out of this fellow with his stick,
or toss him, brain him on the stony ground.   270
Then he controlled himself, and bore it quietly.
Not so the swineherd.

                        Seeing the man before him,
he raised his arms and cried:

                                "Nymphs of the spring,
daughters of Zeus, if ever Odysseus
burnt you a thighbone in rich fat—a ram's
or kid's thighbone, hear me, grant my prayer:
let our true lord come back, let heaven bring him
to rid the earth of these fine courtly ways
Melánthios picks up around the town—
all wine and wind! Bad shepherds ruin flocks!"   280

Melánthios the goatherd answered:

                                        "Bless me!

The dog can snap: how he goes on! Some day
I'll take him in a slave ship overseas
and trade him for a herd!

                                Old Silverbow

Apollo, if he shot clean through Telémakhos[6]
in hall today, what luck! Or let the suitors
cut him down!

                        Odysseus died at sea;

no coming home for him."

---

[6] That is, if Telémakhos should drop dead.

He flung this out
and left the two behind to come on slowly,
while he went hurrying to the king's hall.   290
There he slipped in, and sat among the suitors,
beside the one he doted on—Eurýmakhos.
Then working servants helped him to his meat
and the mistress of the larder gave him bread.

Reaching the gate, Odysseus and the forester
halted and stood outside, for harp notes came
around them rippling on the air
as Phêmios picked out a song. Odysseus
caught his companion's arm and said:

                                                    "My friend,
here is the beautiful place—who could mistake it?   300
Here is Odysseus' hall: no hall like this!
See how one chamber grows out of another;
see how the court is tight with wall and coping;
no man at arms could break this gateway down!
Your banqueting young lords are here in force,
I gather, from the fumes of mutton roasting
and strum of harping—harping, which the gods
appoint sweet friend of feasts!"

                                        And—O my swineherd!
you replied:

                                "That was quick recognition;
but you are no numbskull—in this or anything.   310
Now we must plan this action. Will you take
leave of me here, and go ahead alone
to make your entrance now among the suitors?
Or do you choose to wait?—Let me go forward
and go in first.

                                Do not delay too long;
someone might find you skulking here outside
and take a club to you, or heave a lance.
Bear this in mind, I say."

                                        The patient hero
Odysseus answered:

                                "Just what I was thinking.
You go in first, and leave me here a little.   320
But as for blows and missiles,
I am no tyro[7] at these things. I learned
to keep my head in hardship—years of war
and years at sea. Let this new trial come.

---

[7] Inexperienced beginner.

The cruel belly, can you hide its ache?
How many bitter days it brings! Long ships
with good stout planks athwart—would fighters rig them
to ride the barren sea, except for hunger?
Seawolves—woe to their enemies!"

                                  While he spoke
an old hound, lying near, pricked up his ears   330
and lifted up his muzzle. This was Argos,
trained as a puppy by Odysseus,
but never taken on a hunt before
his master sailed for Troy. The young men, afterward,
hunted wild goats with him, and hare, and deer,
but he had grown old in his master's absence.
Treated as rubbish now, he lay at last
upon a mass of dung before the gates—
manure of mules and cows, piled there until
fieldhands could spread it on the king's estate.   340
Abandoned there, and half destroyed with flies,
old Argos lay.
                        But when he knew he heard
Odysseus' voice nearby, he did his best
to wag his tail, nose down, with flattened ears,
having no strength to move nearer his master.
And the man looked away,
wiping a salt tear from his cheek; but he
hid this from Eumaios. Then he said:

"I marvel that they leave this hound to lie
here on the dung pile;   350
he would have been a fine dog, from the look of him,
though I can't say as to his power and speed
when he was young. You find the same good build
in house dogs, table dogs landowners keep
all for style."

                          And you replied, Eumaios:

"A hunter owned him—but the man is dead
in some far place. If this old hound could show
the form he had when Lord Odysseus left him,
going to Troy, you'd see him swift and strong.
He never shrank from any savage thing   360
he'd brought to bay in the deep woods; on the scent
no other dog kept up with him. Now misery
has him in leash. His owner died abroad,
and here the women slaves will take no care of him.
You know how servants are: without a master
they have no will to labor, or excel.
For Zeus who views the wide world takes away

half the manhood of a man, that day
he goes into captivity and slavery."

Eumaios crossed the court and went straight forward   370
into the mégaron[8] among the suitors;
but death and darkness in that instant closed
the eyes of Argos, who had seen his master,
Odysseus, after twenty years.

                      Long before anyone else
Telémakhos caught sight of the grey woodsman
coming from the door, and called him over
with a quick jerk of his head. Eumaios'
narrowed eyes made out an empty bench
beside the one the carver used—that servant
who had no respite, carving for the suitors.   380
This bench he took possession of, and placed it
across the table from Telémakhos
for his own use. Then the two men were served
cuts from a roast and bread from a bread basket.

At no long interval, Odysseus came
through his own doorway as a mendicant,
humped like a bundle of rags over his stick.
He settled on the inner ash wood sill,
leaning against the door jamb—cypress timber
the skilled carpenter planed years ago   390
and set up with a plumbline.

                      Now Telémakhos
took an entire loaf and a double handful
of roast meat; then he said to the forester:

"Give these to the stranger there. But tell him
to go among the suitors, on his own;
he may beg all he wants. This hanging back
is no asset to a hungry man."

The swineherd rose at once, crossed to the door,
and halted by Odysseus.

                      "Friend," he said,
"Telémakhos is pleased to give you these,   400
but he commands you to approach the suitors;
you may ask all you want from them. He adds,
your shyness is no asset to a beggar."

The great tactician, lifting up his eyes,
cried:

[8] The great hall of the house.

"Zeus aloft! A blessing on Telémakhos!
Let all things come to pass as he desires!"

Palms held out, in the beggar's gesture, he
received the bread and meat and put it down
before him on his knapsack—lowly table!—
then he fell to, devouring it. Meanwhile
the harper in the great room sang a song.   410
Not till the man was fed did the sweet harper
end his singing—whereupon the company
made the walls ring again with talk.

                                                           Unseen,
Athena took her place beside Odysseus
whispering in his ear:

                                          "Yes, try the suitors.
You may collect a few more loaves, and learn
who are the decent lads, and who are vicious—
although not one can be excused from death!"

So he appealed to them, one after another,
going from left to right, with open palm,   420
as though his life time had been spent in beggary.
And they gave bread, for pity—wondering, though,
at the strange man. Who could this beggar be,
where did he come from? each would ask his neighbor;
till in their midst the goatherd, Melánthios,
raised his voice:

                                  "Hear just a word from me,
my lords who court our illustrious queen!
                                                       This man,
this foreigner, I saw him on the road;
the swineherd here was leading him this way;
who, what, or whence he claims to be, I could not   430
say for sure."

                                          At this, Antínoös
turned on the swineherd brutally, saying:

                                                       "You famous
breeder of pigs, why bring this fellow here?
Are we not plagued enough with beggars,
foragers and such rats?
                                          You find the company
too slow at eating up your lord's estate—
is that it? So you call this scarecrow in?"

The forester replied:

                                                    "Antínoös,   440
well born you are, but that was not well said.
Who would call in a foreigner?—unless
an artisan with skill to serve the realm,
a healer, or a prophet, or a builder,
or one whose harp and song might give us joy.
All these are sought for on the endless earth,
but when have beggars come by invitation?
Who puts a field mouse in his granary? My lord,
you are a hard man, and you always were,
more so than others of this company—hard
on all Odysseus' people and on me.   450
But this I can forget
as long as Penélopê lives on, the wise and tender
mistress of this hall; as long
as Prince Telémakhos—"

                                                    But he broke off

at a look from Telémakhos, who said:

                                                    "Be still.

Spare me a long-drawn answer to this gentleman.
With his unpleasantness, he will forever make
strife where he can—and goad the others on."

He turned and spoke out clearly to Antínoös:

"What fatherly concern you show me! Frighten   460
this unknown fellow, would you, from my hall
with words that promise blows—may God forbid it!
Give him a loaf. Am I a niggard? No,
I call on you to give. And spare your qualms
as to my mother's loss, or anyone's—
not that in truth you have such care at heart:
your heart is all in feeding, not in giving."

Antínoös replied:

                                                    "What high and mighty
talk, Telémakhos! No holding you!
If every suitor gave what I may give him,   470
he could be kept for months—kept out of sight!"

He reached under the table for the footstool
his shining feet had rested on—and this
he held up so that all could see his gift.

But all the rest gave alms,
enough to fill the beggar's pack with bread
and roast meat.

So it looked as though Odysseus
had had his taste of what these men were like
and could return scot free to his own doorway—
but halting now before Antínoös   480
he made a little speech to him. Said he:

"Give a mite, friend. I would not say, myself,
you are the worst man of the young Akhaians.
The noblest, rather; kingly, by your look;
therefore you'll give more bread than others do.
Let me speak well of you as I pass on
over the boundless earth!

I, too, you know,
had fortune once, lived well, stood well with men,
and gave alms, often, to poor wanderers
like this one that you see—aye, to all sorts,   490
no matter in what dire want. I owned
servants—many, god knows—and all the rest
that goes with being prosperous, as they say.
But Zeus the son of Kronos brought me down.

No telling
why he would have it, but he made me go
to Egypt with a company of rovers—
a long sail to the south—for my undoing.
Up the broad Nile and in to the river bank
I brought my dipping squadron. There, indeed,   500
I told the men to stand guard at the ships;
I sent patrols out—out to rising ground;
but reckless greed carried my crews away
to plunder the Egyptian farms; they bore off
wives and children, killed what men they found.
The news ran on the wind to the city, a night cry,
and sunrise brought both infantry and horsemen,
filling the river plain with dazzle of bronze;
then Zeus lord of lightning
threw my men into a blind panic; no one dared   510
stand against that host closing around us.
Their scything weapons left our dead in piles,
but some they took alive, into forced labor,
myself among them. And they gave me, then,
to one Dmêtor, a traveller, son of Iasos,
who ruled at Kypros.[9] He conveyed me there.
From that place, working northward, miserably—"

But here Antínoös broke in, shouting:

"God!

What evil wind blew in this pest?

---

[9] Cyprus, a large island off the Syrian coast.

Get over,

stand in the passage! Nudge my table, will you?   520
Egyptian whips are sweet
to what you'll come to here, you nosing rat,
making your pitch to everyone!
These men have bread to throw away on you
because it is not theirs. Who cares? Who spares
another's food, when he has more than plenty?"

With guile Odysseus drew away, then said:

"A pity that you have more looks than heart.
You'd grudge a pinch of salt from your own larder
to your own handy man. You sit here, fat   530
on others' meat, and cannot bring yourself
to rummage out a crust of bread for me!"

Then anger made Antínoös' heart beat hard,
and, glowering under his brows, he answered:

"Now!

You think you'll shuffle off and get away
after that impudence? Oh, no you don't!"

The stool he let fly hit the man's right shoulder
on the packed muscle under the shoulder blade—
like solid rock, for all the effect one saw.
Odysseus only shook his head, containing   540
thoughts of bloody work, as he walked on,
then sat, and dropped his loaded bag again
upon the door sill. Facing the whole crowd
he said, and eyed them all:

"One word only,

my lords, and suitors of the famous queen.
One thing I have to say.
There is no pain, no burden for the heart
when blows come to a man, and he defending
his own cattle—his own cows and lambs.
Here it was otherwise. Antínoös   550
hit me for being driven on by hunger—
how many bitter seas men cross for hunger!
If beggars interest the gods, if there are Furies
pent in the dark to avenge a poor man's wrong, then may
Antínoös meet his death before his wedding day!"

Then said Eupeithês' son, Antínoös:

"Enough.

Eat and be quiet where you are, or shamble elsewhere,
unless you want these lads to stop your mouth

pulling you by the heels, or hands and feet,
over the whole floor, till your back is peeled!"   560

But now the rest were mortified, and someone
spoke from the crowd of young bucks to rebuke him:

"A poor show, that—hitting this famished tramp—
bad business, if he happened to be a god.
You know they go in foreign guise, the gods do,
looking like strangers, turning up
in towns and settlements to keep an eye
on manners, good or bad."

                                           But at this notion
Antínoös only shrugged.

                                           Telémakhos,
after the blow his father bore, sat still   570
without a tear, though his heart felt the blow.
Slowly he shook his head from side to side,
containing murderous thoughts.

                                           Penélopê
on the higher level of her room had heard
the blow, and knew who gave it. Now she murmured:

"Would god you could be hit yourself, Antínoös—
hit by Apollo's bowshot!"

                                           And Eurýnomê
her housekeeper, put in:

                                           "He and no other?
If all we pray for came to pass, not one
would live till dawn!"

                                           Her gentle mistress said: 580

"Oh, Nan,[10] they are a bad lot; they intend
ruin for all of us; but Antínoös
appears a blacker-hearted hound than any.
Here is a poor man come, a wanderer,
driven by want to beg his bread, and everyone
in hall gave bits, to cram his bag—only
Antínoös threw a stool, and banged his shoulder!"

So she described it, sitting in her chamber
among her maids—while her true lord was eating.
Then she called in the forester and said: 590

"Go to that man on my behalf, Eumaios,
and send him here, so I can greet and question him.

---

[10] Affectionate diminutive for an old woman.

Abroad in the great world, he may have heard
rumors about Odysseus—may have known him!'"

Then you replied—O swineherd!

                                               "Ah, my queen,

if these Akhaian sprigs would hush their babble
the man could tell you tales to charm your heart.
Three days and nights I kept him in my hut;
he came straight off a ship, you know, to me.
There was no end to what he made me hear   600
of his hard roving; and I listened, eyes
upon him, as a man drinks in a tale
a minstrel sings—a minstrel taught by heaven
to touch the hearts of men. At such a song
the listener becomes rapt and still. Just so
I found myself enchanted by this man.
He claims an old tie with Odysseus, too—
in his home country, the Minoan[11] land
of Krete. From Krete he came, a rolling stone
washed by the gales of life this way and that   610
to our own beach.

                                      If he can be believed

he has news of Odysseus near at hand
alive, in the rich country of Thesprotia,
bringing a mass of treasure home."

Then wise Penélopê said again:

"Go call him, let him come here, let him tell
that tale again for my own ears.

                                        Our friends

can drink their cups outside or stay in hall,
being so carefree. And why not? Their stores
lie intact in their homes, both food and drink,   620
with only servants left to take a little.
But these men spend their days around our house
killing our beeves, our fat goats and our sheep,
carousing, drinking up our good dark wine;
sparing nothing, squandering everything.
No champion like Odysseus takes our part.
Ah, if he comes again, no falcon ever
struck more suddenly than he will, with his son,
to avenge this outrage!"

                                  The great hall below
at this point rang with a tremendous sneeze[12]—   630

---

[11] Minos, to whom the adjective *Minoan* refers, had been king of Krete (Crete).
[12] A sneeze was regarded as a sign of good luck.

"kchaou!" from Telêmakhos—like an acclamation.
And laughter seized Penélopê.

                                    Then quickly,
lucidly she went on:

                              "Go call the stranger
straight to me. Did you hear that, Eumaios?
My son's thundering sneeze at what I said!
May death come of a sudden so; may death
relieve us, clean as that, of all the suitors!
Let me add one thing—do not overlook it—
if I can see this man has told the truth,
I promise him a warm new cloak and tunic."   640

With all this in his head, the forester
went down the hall, and halted near the beggar,
saying aloud:

                              "Good father, you are called
by the wise mother of Telémakhos,
Penélopê. The queen, despite her troubles,
is moved by a desire to hear your tales
about her lord—and if she finds them true,
she'll see you clothed in what you need, a cloak
and a fresh tunic.

                    You may have your belly
full each day you go about this realm   650
begging. For all may give, and all they wish."

Now said Odysseus, the old soldier:

"Friend,
I wish this instant I could tell my facts
to the wise daughter of Ikários, Penélopê—
and I have much to tell about her husband;
we went through much together.

                              But just now
this hard crowd worries me. They are, you said
infamous to the very rim of heaven
for violent acts: and here, just now, this fellow   660
gave me a bruise. What had I done to him?
But who would lift a hand for me? Telémakhos?
Anyone else?

                    No; bid the queen be patient,
Let her remain till sundown in her room,
and then—if she will seat me near the fire—
inquire tonight about her lord's return.
My rags are sorry cover; you know that;
I showed my sad condition first to you."

The woodsman heard him out, and then returned;
but the queen met him on her threshold, crying: 670
"Have you not brought him? Why? What is he thinking?
Has he some fear of overstepping? Shy
about these inner rooms? A hangdog beggar?"

To this you answered, friend Eumaios:

"No:
he reasons as another might, and well,
not to tempt any swordplay from these drunkards.
Be patient, wait—he says—till darkness falls.
And, O my queen, for you too that is better:
better to be alone with him, and question him,   680
and hear him out."

                                          Penélopê replied:

"He is no fool; he sees how it could be.
Never were mortal men like these
for bullying and brainless arrogance!"

Thus she accepted what had been proposed,
so he went back into the crowd. He joined
Telémakhos, and said at once in whispers—
his head bent, so that no one else might hear:

"Dear prince, I must go home to keep good watch
on hut and swine, and look to my own affairs.   690
Everything here is in your hands. Consider
your own safety before the rest; take care
not to get hurt. Many are dangerous here.
May Zeus destroy them first, before we suffer!"

Telémakhos said:

                                          "Your wish is mine, Uncle.
Go when your meal is finished. Then come back
at dawn, and bring good victims for a slaughter.
Everything here is in my hands indeed—
and in the disposition of the gods."

Taking his seat on the smooth bench again,   700
Eumaios ate and drank his fill, then rose
to climb the mountain trail back to his swine,
leaving the mégaron and court behind him
crowded with banqueters.

                                          These had their joy
of dance and song, as day waned into evening.

BOOK EIGHTEEN: BLOWS AND A QUEEN'S BEAUTY

Now a true scavenger came in—a public tramp
who begged around the town of Ithaka,
a by-word for his insatiable swag-belly,
feeding and drinking, dawn to dark. No pith
was in him, and no nerve, huge as he looked.
Arnaios, as his gentle mother called him,
he had been nicknamed "Iros"[1] by the young
for being ready to take messages.

This fellow

thought he would rout Odysseus from his doorway,
growling at him:

"Clear out, grandfather,   10

or else be hauled out by the ankle bone.
See them all giving me the wink? That means,
'Go on and drag him out!' I hate to do it.
Up with you! Or would you like a fist fight?"

Odysseus only frowned and looked him over,
taking account of everything, then said:

"Master, I am no trouble to you here.
I offer no remarks. I grudge you nothing.
Take all you get, and welcome. Here is room
for two on this doorslab—or do you own it?   20
You are a tramp, I think, like me. Patience:
a windfall from the gods will come. But drop
that talk of using fists; it could annoy me.
Old as I am, I might just crack a rib
or split a lip for you. My life would go
even more peacefully, after tomorrow,
looking for no more visits here from you."

Iros the tramp grew red and hooted:

"Ho,
listen to him! The swine can talk your arm off,   30
like an old oven woman! With two punches
I'd knock him snoring, if I had a mind to—
and not a tooth left in his head, the same
as an old sow caught in the corn! Belt up!
And let this company see the way I do it
when we square off. Can you fight a fresher man?"

Under the lofty doorway, on the door sill
of wide smooth ash, they held this rough exchange.

[1] A pun on Iris, goddess of the rainbow and a messenger of the gods.

And the tall full-blooded suitor, Antínoös,
overhearing, broke into happy laughter.   40
Then he said to the others:

                                        "Oh, my friends,

no luck like this ever turned up before!
What a farce heaven has brought this house!

                                        The stranger

and Iros have had words, they brag of boxing!
Into the ring they go, and no more talk!"

All the young men got on their feet now, laughing,
to crowd around the ragged pair. Antínoös
called out:

                    "Gentlemen, quiet! One more thing:
here are goat stomachs ready on the fire
to stuff with blood and fat, good supper pudding.   50
The man who wins this gallant bout
may step up here and take the one he likes.
And let him feast with us from this day on:
no other beggar will be admitted here
when we are at our wine."

                                        This pleased them all.
But now that wily man, Odysseus, muttered:

"An old man, an old hulk, has no business
fighting a young man, but my belly nags me;
nothing will do but I must take a beating.
When, then, let every man here swear an oath   60
not to step in for Iros. No one throw
a punch for luck. I could be whipped that way."

So much the suitors were content to swear,
but after they reeled off their oaths, Telémakhos
put in a word to clinch it, saying:

                                        "Friend,

if you will stand and fight, as pride requires,
don't worry about a foul blow from behind.
Whoever hits you will take on the crowd.
You have my word as host; you have the word
of these two kings, Antínoös and Eurýmakhos—   70
a pair of thinking men."

                                        All shouted, "Aye!"

So now Odysseus made his shirt a belt
and roped his rags around his loins, baring
his hurdler's thighs and boxer's breadth of shoulder,
the dense rib-sheath and upper arms. Athena
stood nearby to give him bulk and power,

while the young suitors watched with narrowed eyes—
and comments went around:

"By god, old Iros now retiros."

"Aye,

he asked for it, he'll get it—bloody, too."

"The build this fellow had, under his rags!"

Panic made Iros' heart jump, but the yard-boys
hustled and got him belted by main force,
though all his blubber quivered now with dread.
Antínoös' angry voice rang in his ears:

"You sack of guts, you might as well be dead,
might as well never have seen the light of day,
if this man makes you tremble! Chicken-heart,
afraid of an old wreck, far gone in misery!
Well, here is what I say—and what I'll do.
If this ragpicker can outfight you, whip you,
I'll ship you out to that king in Epeíros,
Ékhetos[2]—he skins everyone alive.
Let him just cut your nose off and your ears
and pull your privy parts out by the roots
to feed raw to his hunting dogs!"

Poor Iros

felt a new fit of shaking take his knees.
But the yard-boys pushed him out. Now both contenders
put their hands up. Royal Odysseus
pondered if he should hit him with all he had
and drop the man dead on the spot, or only
spar, with force enough to knock him down.
Better that way, he thought—a gentle blow,
else he might give himself away.

The two

were at close quarters now, and Iros lunged
hitting the shoulder. Then Odysseus hooked him
under the ear and shattered his jaw bone,
so bright red blood came bubbling from his mouth,
as down he pitched into the dust, bleating,
kicking against the ground, his teeth stove in.
The suitors whooped and swung their arms, half dead
with pangs of laughter.

Then, by the ankle bone,

Odysseus hauled the fallen one outside,
crossing the courtyard to the gate, and piled him
against the wall. In his right hand he stuck
his begging staff, and said:

[2] Probably a nonhistorical tyrannical ruler whose name was a byword for cruelty. Epeíros (Epirus), in the preceding line, is the Grecian mainland north of Ithaka.

"Here, take your post.
Sit here to keep the dogs and pigs away.
You can give up your habit of command
over poor waifs and beggarmen—you swab.
Another time you may not know what hit you."   120

When he had slung his rucksack by the string
over his shoulder, like a wad of rags,
he sat down on the broad door sill again,
as laughing suitors came to flock inside;
and each young buck in passing gave him greeting,
saying, maybe,

                                        "Zeus fill your pouch for this!
May the gods grant your heart's desire!"

                                                             "Well done
to put that walking famine out of business."

"We'll ship him out to that king in Epeíros,
Ékhetos—he skins everyone alive."   130

Odysseus found grim cheer in their good wishes—
his work had started well.

                                        Now from the fire
his fat blood pudding came, deposited
before him by Antínoös—then, to boot,
two brown loaves from the basket, and some wine
in a fine cup of gold. These gifts Amphínomos
gave him. Then he said:

                                        "Here's luck, grandfather;
a new day; may the worst be over now."

Odysseus answered, and his mind ranged far:

"Amphínomos, your head is clear, I'd say;   140
so was your father's—or at least I've heard
good things of Nísos the Doulíkhion,
whose son you are, they tell me—an easy man.
And you seem gently bred.

                                        In view of that,
I have a word to say to you, so listen.

Of mortal creatures, all that breathe and move,
earth bears none frailer than mankind. What man
believes in woe to come, so long as valor
and tough knees are supplied him by the gods?
But when the gods in bliss bring miseries on,   150
then willy-nilly, blindly, he endures.
Our minds are as the days are, dark or bright,
blown over by the father of gods and men.

So I, too, in my time thought to be happy;
but far and rash I ventured, counting on
my own right arm, my father, and my kin;
behold me now.

                    No man should flout the law,
but keep in peace what gifts the gods may give.

I see you young blades living dangerously,
a household eaten up, a wife dishonored—   160
and yet the master will return, I tell you,
to his own place, and soon; for he is near.
So may some power take you out of this,
homeward, and softly, not to face that man
the hour he sets foot on his native ground.
Between him and the suitors I foretell
no quittance,[3] no way out, unless by blood,
once he shall stand beneath his own roof-beam."

Gravely, when he had done, he made libation
and took a sip of honey-hearted wine,   170
giving the cup, then, back into the hands
of the young nobleman. Amphínomos, for his part,
shaking his head, with chill and burdened breast,
turned in the great hall.

                    Now his heart foreknew
the wrath to come, but he could not take flight,
being by Athena bound there.

                    Death would have him
broken by a spear thrown by Telémakhos.
So he sat down where he had sat before.

And now heart-prompting from the grey-eyed goddess
came to the quiet queen, Penélopê: 180
a wish to show herself before the suitors;
for thus by fanning their desire again
Athena meant to set her beauty high
before her husband's eyes, before her son.
Knowing no reason, laughing confusedly,
she said:

                  "Eurýnomê, I have a craving
I never had at all—I would be seen
among those ruffians, hateful as they are.
I might well say a word, then, to my son,
for his own good—tell him to shun that crowd;   190
for all their gay talk, they are bent on evil."

Mistress Eurýnomê replied:

[3] Repayment.

                                                           "Well said, child,
now is the time. Go down, and make it clear,
hold nothing back from him.

                                                     But you must bathe
and put a shine upon your cheeks—not this way,
streaked under your eyes and stained with tears.
You make it worse, being forever sad,
and now your boy's a bearded man! Remember
you prayed the gods to let you see him so."

Penélopê replied:

                                                           "Eurýnomê,   200

it is a kind thought, but I will not hear it—
to bathe and sleek with perfumed oil. No, no,
the gods forever took my sheen away
when my lord sailed for Troy in the decked ships.
Only tell my Autonoë to come,
and Hippodameía; they should be attending me
in hall, if I appear there. I could not
enter alone into that crowd of men."

At this the good old woman left the chamber
to tell the maids her bidding. But now too   210
the grey-eyed goddess had her own designs.
Upon the quiet daughter of Ikários
she let clear drops of slumber fall, until
the queen lay back asleep, her limbs unstrung,
in her long chair. And while she slept the goddess
endowed her with immortal grace to hold
the eyes of the Akhaians. With ambrosia
she bathed her cheeks and throat and smoothed her brow—
ambrosia, used by flower-crowned Kythereia[4]
when she would join the rose-lipped Graces dancing.   220
Grandeur she gave her, too, in height and form,
and made her whiter than carved ivory.
Touching her so, the perfect one was gone.
Now came the maids, bare-armed and lovely, voices
breaking into the room. The queen awoke
and as she rubbed her cheek she sighed:

                                                           "Ah, soft

that drowse I lay embraced in, pain forgot!
If only Artemis the Pure would give me
death as mild, and soon! No heart-ache more,
no wearing out my lifetime with desire   230
and sorrow, mindful of my lord, good man
in all ways that he was, best of the Akhaians!"

[4] Aphroditê, goddess of love.

She rose and left her glowing upper room,
and down the stairs, with her two maids in train,
this beautiful lady went before the suitors.
Then by a pillar of the solid roof
she paused, her shining veil across her cheek,
the two girls close to her and still;
and in that instant weakness took those men
in the knee joints, their hearts grew faint with lust;   240
not one but swore to god to lie beside her.

But speaking for her dear son's ears alone
she said:

              "Telémakhos, what has come over you?
Lightminded you were not, in all your boyhood.
Now you are full grown, come of age; a man
from foreign parts might take you for the son
of royalty, to go by your good looks;
and have you no more thoughtfulness or manners?
How could it happen in our hall that you
permit the stranger to be so abused?   250
Here, in our house, a guest, can any man
suffer indignity, come by such injury?
What can this be for you but public shame?"

Telémakhos looked in her eyes and answered,
with his clear head and his discretion:

"Mother,
I cannot take it ill that you are angry.
I know the meaning of these actions now,
both good and bad. I had been young and blind.
How can I always keep to what is fair   260
while these sit here to put fear in me?—princes
from near and far whose interest is my ruin;
are any on my side?

                    But you should know
the suitors did not have their way, matching
the stranger here and Iros—for the stranger
beat him to the ground.

                   O Father Zeus!

Athena and Apollo! could I see
the suitors whipped like that! Courtyard and hall
strewn with our friends, too weak-kneed to get up,
chapfallen to their collarbones, the way   270
old Iros rolls his head there by the gate
as though he were pig-drunk! No energy
to stagger on his homeward path; no fight
left in his numb legs!"

                                                    Thus Penélopê
reproached her son, and he replied. Now, interrupting,
Eurýmakhos called out to her:

                                                      "Penélopê,
deep-minded queen, daughter of Ikários,
if all Akhaians in the land of Argos
only saw you now! What hundreds more
would join your suitors here to feast tomorrow!   280
Beauty like yours no woman had before,
or majesty, or mastery."

                                        She answered:

"Eurýmakhos, my qualities—I know—
my face, my figure, all were lost or blighted
when the Akhaians crossed the sea to Troy,
Odysseus my lord among the rest.
If he returned, if he were here to care for me,
I might be happily renowned!
But grief instead heaven sent me—years of pain.
Can I forget?—the day he left this island,   290
enfolding my right hand and wrist in his,
he said:

                              'My lady, the Akhaian troops
will not easily make it home again
full strength, unhurt, from Troy. They say the Trojans
are fighters too; good lances and good bowmen,
horsemen, charioteers—and those can be
decisive when a battle hangs in doubt.
So whether God will send me back, or whether
I'll be a captive there, I cannot tell.
Here, then, you must attend to everything.   300
My parents in our house will be a care for you
as they are now, or more, while I am gone.
Wait for the beard to darken our boy's cheek;
then marry whom you will, and move away.'

The years he spoke of are now past; the night
comes when a bitter marriage overtakes me,
desolate as I am, deprived by Zeus
of all the sweets of life.
                                        How galling, too,
to see newfangled manners in my suitors!
Others who go to court a gentlewoman,   310
daughter of a rich house, if they are rivals,
bring their own beeves and sheep along; her friends
ought to be feasted, gifts are due to her;
would any dare to live at her expense?"

Odysseus' heart laughed when he heard all this—
her sweet tones charming gifts out of the suitors
with talk of marriage, though she intended none.
Eupeithês' son, Antínoös, now addressed her:

"Ikários' daughter, O deep-minded queen!
If someone cares to make you gifts, accept them!   320
It is no courtesy to turn gifts away.
But we go neither to our homes nor elsewhere
until of all Akhaians here you take
the best man for your lord."

                    Pleased at this answer,
every man sent a squire to fetch a gift—
Antínoös, a wide resplendent robe,
embroidered fine, and fastened with twelve brooches,
pins pressed into sheathing tubes of gold;
Eurýmakhos, a necklace, wrought in gold,
with sunray pieces of clear glinting amber.   330
Eurýdamas's men came back with pendants,
ear-drops in triple clusters of warm lights;
and from the hoard of Lord Polýktor's son,
Peisándros, came a band for her white throat,
jewelled adornment. Other wondrous things
were brought as gifts from the Akhaian princes.
Penélopê then mounted the stair again,
her maids behind, with treasure in their arms.

And now the suitors gave themselves to dancing,
to harp and haunting song, as night drew on;   340
black night indeed came on them at their pleasure.
But three torch fires were placed in the long hall
to give them light. On hand were stores of fuel,
dry seasoned chips of resinous wood, split up
by the bronze hatchet blade—these were mixed in
among the flames to keep them flaring bright;
each housemaid of Odysseus took her turn.

Now he himself, the shrewd and kingly man,
approached and told them:

                    "Housemaids of Odysseus,
your master so long absent in the world,   350
go to the women's chambers, to your queen.
Attend her, make the distaff whirl, divert her,
stay in her room, comb wool for her.

                            I stand here
ready to tend these flares and offer light
to everyone. They cannot tire me out,
even if they wish to drink till Dawn.
I am a patient man."

                                              But the women giggled,
glancing back and forth—laughed in his face;
and one smooth girl, Melántho, spoke to him
most impudently. She was Dólios' daughter,   360
taken as ward in childhood by Penélopê
who gave her playthings to her heart's content
and raised her as her own. Yet the girl felt
nothing for her mistress, no compunction,
but slept and made love with Eurýmakhos.
Her bold voice rang now in Odysseus' ears:

"You must be crazy, punch drunk, you old goat.
Instead of going out to find a smithy
to sleep warm in—or a tavern bench—you stay
putting your oar in, amid all our men.   370
Numbskull, not to be scared! The wine you drank
has clogged your brain, or are you always this way,
boasting like a fool? Or have you lost
your mind because you beat that tramp, that Iros?
Look out, or someone better may get up
and give you a good knocking about the ears
to send you out all bloody."

                                                          But Odysseus
glared at her under his brows and said:

                                                          "One minute:
let me tell Telémakhos how you talk
in hall, you slut; he'll cut your arms and legs off!"   380

This hard shot took the women's breath away
and drove them quaking to their rooms, as though
knives were behind: they felt he spoke the truth.
So there he stood and kept the firelight high
and looked the suitors over, while his mind
roamed far ahead to what must be accomplished.

They, for their part, could not now be still
or drop their mockery—for Athena wished
Odysseus mortified still more.

                                                          Eurýmakhos,
the son of Pólybos, took up the baiting,   390
angling for a laugh among his friends.

"Suitors of our distinguished queen," he said,
"hear what my heart would have me say.

                                                          This man
comes with a certain aura of divinity
into Odysseus' hall. He shines.

                                                          He shines
around the noggin, like a flashing light,
having no hair at all to dim his lustre."

Then turning to Odysseus, raider of cities,
he went on:

                         "Friend, you have a mind to work,
do you? Could I hire you to clear stones   400
from wasteland for me—you'll be paid enough—
collecting boundary walls and planting trees?
I'd give you a bread ration every day,
a cloak to wrap in, sandals for your feet.
Oh no: you learned your dodges long ago—
no honest sweat. You'd rather tramp the country
begging, to keep your hoggish belly full."

The master of many crafts replied:

                                 "Eurýmakhos,
we two might try our hands against each other
in early summer when the days are long,   410
in meadow grass, with one good scythe for me
and one as good for you: we'd cut our way
down a deep hayfield, fasting to late evening.
Or we could try our hands behind a plow,
driving the best of oxen—fat, well-fed,
well-matched for age and pulling power, and say
four strips apiece of loam the share could break:
you'd see then if I cleft you a straight furrow.
Competition in arms? If Zeus Kroníon
roused up a scuffle now, give me a shield,   420
two spears, a dogskin cap with plates of bronze
to fit my temples, and you'd see me go
where the first rank of fighters lock in battle.
There would be no more jeers about my belly.
You thick-skinned menace to all courtesy!
You think you are a great man and a champion,
but up against few men, poor stuff, at that.
Just let Odysseus return, those doors
wide open as they are, you'd find too narrow
to suit you on your sudden journey out."   430

Now fury mounted in Eurýmakhos,
who scowled and shot back:

                          "Bundle of rags and lice!
By god, I'll make you suffer for your gall,
your insolent gabble before all our men."

He had his foot-stool out: but now Odysseus
took to his haunches by Amphínomos' knees,
fearing Eurýmakhos' missile, as it flew.
It clipped a wine steward on the serving hand,
so that his pitcher dropped with a loud clang

while he fell backward, cursing, in the dust.   440
In the shadowy hall a low sound rose—of suitors
murmuring to one another.

                                              "Ai!" they said,
"This vagabond would have done well to perish
somewhere else, and make us no such rumpus.
Here we are, quarreling over tramps; good meat
and wine forgotten; good sense gone by the board."

Telémakhos, his young heart high, put in:

"Bright souls, alight with wine, you can no longer
hide the cups you've taken.[5] Aye, some god
is goading you. Why not go home to bed?—   450
I mean when you are moved to. No one jumps
at my command."

                                    Struck by his blithe manner,
the young men's teeth grew fixed in their under lips,
but now the son of Nísos, Lord Amphínomos
of Aretíadês, addressed them all:

"O friends, no ruffling replies are called for;
that was fair counsel.

                              Hands off the stranger, now,
and hands off any other servant here
in the great house of King Odysseus. Come,
let my own herald wet our cups once more,   460
we'll make an offering, and then to bed.
The stranger can be left behind in hall;
Telémakhos may care for him; he came
to Telémakhos' door, not ours."

                                    This won them over.
The soldier Moulios, Doulíkhion herald,
comrade in arms of Lord Amphínomos,
mixed the wine and served them all. They tipped out
drops for the blissful gods, and drank the rest,
and when they had drunk their thirst away
they trailed off homeward drowsily to bed.   470

BOOK NINETEEN: RECOGNITIONS AND A DREAM

Now by Athena's side in the quiet hall
studying the ground for slaughter, Lord Odysseus
turned to Telémakhos.

[5] That is, they cannot hide the fact that they have drunk so much.

"The arms," he said.
"Harness and weapons must be out of sight
in the inner room. And if the suitors miss them,
be mild; just say 'I had a mind to move them
out of the smoke. They seemed no longer
the bright arms that Odysseus left at home
when he went off to Troy. Here where the fire's
hot breath came, they had grown black and drear.   10
One better reason struck me, too:
suppose a brawl starts up when you've been drinking—
you might in madness let each other's blood,
and that would stain your feast, your courtship.

                                                        Iron
itself can draw men's hands.'"

                                        Then he fell silent,
and Telémakhos obeyed his father's word.
He called Eurýkleia, the nurse, and told her:

"Nurse, go shut the women in their quarters
while I shift Father's armor back
to the inner rooms—these beautiful arms unburnished,   20
caked with black soot in his years abroad.
I was a child then. Well, I am not now.
I want them shielded from the draught and smoke."

And the old woman answered:

                                        "It is time, child,
you took an interest in such things. I wish
you'd put your mind on all your house and chattels.[1]
But who will go along to hold a light?[2]
You said no maids, no torch-bearers."

                                        Telémakhos
looked at her and replied:

                                        "Our friend here.
A man who shares my meat can bear a hand,   30
no matter how far he is from home."

                                        He spoke so soldierly
her own speech halted on her tongue. Straight back
she went to lock the doors of the women's hall.
And now the two men sprang to work—father
and princely son, loaded with round helms
and studded bucklers, lifting the long spears,
while in their path Pallas Athena

---

[1] Possessions other than house and lands.
[2] Maids would normally have been the torch-bearers.

held up a golden lamp of purest light.
Telémakhos at last burst out:

                                                                    "Oh, Father,   40
here is a marvel! All around I see
the walls and roof beams, pedestals and pillars,
lighted as though by white fire blazing near.
One of the gods of heaven is in this place!"

Then said Odysseus, the great tactician,

"Be still: keep still about it: just remember it.
The gods who rule Olympos make this light.
You may go off to bed now. Here I stay
to test your mother and her maids again.
Out of her long grief she will question me."

Telémakhos went across the hall and out   50
under the light of torches—crossed the court
to the tower chamber where he had always slept.
Here now again he lay, waiting for dawn,
while in the great hall by Athena's side
Odysseus waited with his mind on slaughter.

Presently Penélopê from her chamber
stepped in her thoughtful beauty.
                                                    So might Artemis
or golden Aphroditê have descended;
and maids drew to the hearth her own smooth chair
inlaid with silver whorls and ivory. The artisan   60
Ikmálios had made it, long before,
with a footrest in a single piece, and soft
upon the seat a heavy fleece was thrown.
Here by the fire the queen sat down. Her maids,
leaving their quarters, came with white arms bare
to clear the wine cups and the bread, and move
the trestle boards where men had lingered drinking.
Fiery ashes out of the pine-chip flares
they tossed, and piled on fuel for light and heat.
And now a second time Melántho's voice   70
rang brazen in Odysseus' ears:

                                                                    "Ah, stranger,
are you still here, so creepy, late at night
hanging about, looking the women over?
You old goat, go outside, cuddle your supper;
get out, or a torch may kindle you behind!"

At this Odysseus glared under his brows
and said:

                        "Little devil, why pitch into me again?
Because I go unwashed and wear these rags,
and make the rounds? But so I must, being needy;
that is the way a vagabond must live.   80
And do not overlook this: in my time
I too had luck, lived well, stood well with men,
and gave alms, often, to poor wanderers
like him you see before you—aye, to all sorts,
no matter in what dire want. I owned
servants—many, I say—and all the rest
that goes with what men call prosperity.
But Zeus the son of Kronos brought me down.
Mistress, mend your ways, or you may lose
all this vivacity of yours. What if her ladyship   90
were stirred to anger? What if Odysseus came?—
and I can tell you, there is hope of that—
or if the man is done for, still his son
lives to be reckoned with, by Apollo's will.
None of you can go wantoning on the sly
and fool him now. He is too old for that."

Penélopê, being near enough to hear him,
spoke out sharply to her maid:

                                  "Oh, shameless,
through and through! And do you think me blind,
blind to your conquest?[3] It will cost your life.   100
You knew I waited—for you heard me say it—
waited to see this man in hall and question him
about my lord; I am so hard beset."

She turned away and said to the housekeeper:

"Eurýnomê, a bench, a spread of sheepskin,
to put my guest at ease. Now he shall talk
and listen, and be questioned."

                                  Willing hands
brought a smooth bench, and dropped a fleece upon it.
Here the adventurer and king sat down;
then carefully Penélopê began: 110

"Friend, let me ask you first of all:
who are you, where do you come from, of what nation
and parents were you born?"

---

[3] The reference is to Melántho's sexual dalliance with Eurýmakhos. The following words are probably less a threat than a warning that Melántho will have brought on her own punishment.

                                                    And he replied:

"My lady, never a man in the wide world
should have a fault to find with you. Your name
has gone out under heaven like the sweet
honor of some god-fearing king, who rules
in equity over the strong: his black lands bear
both wheat and barley, fruit trees laden bright,
new lambs at lambing time—and the deep sea   120
gives great hauls of fish by his good strategy,
so that his folk fare well.

                                                    O my dear lady,

this being so, let it suffice to ask me
of other matters—not my blood, my homeland.
Do not enforce me to recall my pain.
My heart is sore; but I must not be found
sitting in tears here, in another's house:
it is not well forever to be grieving.
One of the maids might say—or you might think—
I had got maudlin over cups of wine."   130

And Penélopê replied:

                                                    "Stranger, my looks,
my face, my carriage, were soon lost or faded
when the Akhaians crossed the sea to Troy,
Odysseus my lord among the rest.
If he returned, if he were here to care for me,
I might be happily renowned!
But grief instead heaven sent me—years of pain.
Sons of the noblest families on the islands,
Doulíkhion, Samê, wooded Zakýnthos,
with native Ithakans, are here to court me,   140
against my wish; and they consume this house.
Can I give proper heed to guest or suppliant
or herald on the realm's affairs?

                                                    How could I?

wasted with longing for Odysseus, while here
they press for marriage.

                                                    Ruses served my turn
to draw the time out—first a close-grained web
I had the happy thought to set up weaving
on my big loom in hall. I said, that day:
'Young men—my suitors, now my lord is dead,
let me finish my weaving before I marry,   150
or else my thread will have been spun in vain.
It is a shroud I weave for Lord Laërtês
when cold Death comes to lay him on his bier.
The country wives would hold me in dishonor
if he, with all his fortune, lay unshrouded.'
I reached their hearts that way, and they agreed.

So every day I wove on the great loom,
but every night by torchlight I unwove it;
and so for three years I deceived the Akhaians.
But when the seasons brought a fourth year on,   160
as long months waned, and the long days were spent,
through impudent folly in the slinking maids
they caught me—clamored up to me at night;
I had no choice then but to finish it.
And now, as matters stand at last,
I have no strength left to evade a marriage,
cannot find any further way; my parents
urge it upon me, and my son
will not stand by while they eat up his property.
He comprehends it, being a man full grown,   170
able to oversee the kind of house
Zeus would endow with honor.

                                        But you too
confide in me, tell me your ancestry.
You were not born of mythic oak or stone."

And the great master of invention answered:

"O honorable wife of Lord Odysseus,
must you go on asking about my family?
Then I will tell you, though my pain
be doubled by it: and whose pain would not
if he had been away as long as I have   180
and had hard roving in the world of men?
But I will tell you even so, my lady.

One of the great islands of the world
in midsea, in the winedark sea, is Krete:
spacious and rich and populous, with ninety
cities and a mingling of tongues.
Akhaians there are found, along with Kretan
hillmen of the old stock, and Kydonians,
Dorians in three blood-lines, Pelasgians[4]—
and one among their ninety towns is Knossos.   190
Here lived King Minos[5] whom great Zeus received
every ninth year in private council—Minos,
the father of my father, Deukálion.
Two sons Deukálion had: Idómeneus,
who went to join the Atreidai before Troy
in the beaked ships of war; and then myself,

---

[4] Kydonians, Dorians, Pelasgians were various ethnic groups, natives of Krete or immigrants.

[5] Minos, sometimes represented as a cruel king (as in Book XI), is here represented as supremely honored. Knossos is on the north shore of Krete. In this version of his autobiography, Odysseus obviously departs from what he had told Eumaios (Book XIV) and Antínoös (Book XVII).

Aithôn by name—a stripling next my brother.
But I saw with my own eyes at Knossos once
Odysseus.

                        Gales had caught him off Cape Malea,
driven him southward on the coast of Krete,   200
when he was bound for Troy. At Ámnisos,
hard by the holy cave of Eileithuía,[6]
he lay to, and dropped anchor, in that open
and rough roadstead riding out the blow.
Meanwhile he came ashore, came inland, asking
after Idómeneus: dear friends he said they were;
but now ten mornings had already passed,
ten or eleven, since my brother sailed.
So I played host and took Odysseus home,
saw him well lodged and fed, for we had plenty;   210
then I made requisitions—barley, wine,
and beeves for sacrifice—to give his company
abundant fare along with him.

                                  Twelve days
they stayed with us, the Akhaians, while that wind
out of the north shut everyone inside—
even on land you could not keep your feet,
such fury was abroad. On the thirteenth,
when the gale dropped, they put to sea."

Now all these lies he made appear so truthful
she wept as she sat listening. The skin   220
of her pale face grew moist the way pure snow
softens and glistens on the mountains, thawed
by Southwind after powdering from the West,
and, as the snow melts, mountain streams run full:
so her white cheeks were wetted by these tears
shed for her lord—and he close by her side.
Imagine how his heart ached for his lady,
his wife in tears; and yet he never blinked;
his eyes might have been made of horn or iron
for all that she could see. He had this trick—   230
wept, if he willed to, inwardly.

                                    Well, then,
as soon as her relieving tears were shed
she spoke once more:

                      "I think that I shall say, friend,
give me some proof, if it is really true
that you were host in that place to my husband
with his brave men, as you declare. Come, tell me
the quality of his clothing, how he looked,
and some particular of his company."

   [6]Ámnisos is an anchorage off Krete. Eileithuía was a goddess, daughter of Hera, who
controlled maternal labor and childbirth.

Odysseus answered, and his mind ranged far:

"Lady, so long a time now lies between,   240
it is hard to speak of it. Here is the twentieth year
since that man left the island of my father.
But I shall tell what memory calls to mind.
A purple cloak, and fleecy, he had on—
a double thick one. Then, he wore a brooch
made of pure gold with twin tubes for the prongs,
and on the face a work of art: a hunting dog
pinning a spotted fawn in agony
between his forepaws—wonderful to see
how being gold, and nothing more, he bit   250
the golden deer convulsed, with wild hooves flying.
Odysseus' shirt I noticed, too—a fine
closefitting tunic like dry onion skin,
so soft it was, and shiny.

                                                Women there,
many of them, would cast their eyes on it.
But I might add, for your consideration,
whether he brought these things from home, or whether
a shipmate gave them to him, coming aboard,
I have no notion: some regardful host
in another port perhaps it was. Affection   260
followed him—there were few Akhaians like him.
And I too made him gifts: a good bronze blade,
a cloak with lining and a broidered shirt,
and sent him off in his trim ship with honor.
A herald, somewhat older than himself,
he kept beside him; I'll describe this man:
round-shouldered, dusky, woolly-headed;
Eurýbatês, his name was—and Odysseus
gave him preferment over the officers.
He had a shrewd head, like the captain's own."   270

Now hearing these details—minutely true—
she felt more strangely moved, and tears flowed
until she had tasted her salt grief again.
Then she found words to answer:

                                               "Before this
you won my sympathy, but now indeed
you shall be our respected guest and friend.
With my own hands I put that cloak and tunic
upon him—took them folded from their place—
and the bright brooch for ornament.

                                         Gone now,
I will not meet the man again   280
returning to his own home fields. Unkind
the fate that sent him young in the long ship
to see that misery at Ilion, unspeakable!"

And the master improviser answered:

                                      "Honorable

wife of Odysseus Laërtiadês,
you need not stain your beauty with these tears,
nor wear yourself out grieving for your husband.
Not that I can blame you. Any wife
grieves for the man she married in her girlhood,
lay with in love, bore children to—though he   290
may be no prince like this Odysseus,
whom they compare even to the gods. But listen:
weep no more, and listen:
I have a thing to tell you, something true.
I heard but lately of your lord's return,
heard that he is alive, not far away,
among Thesprótians in their green land
amassing fortune to bring home. His company
went down in shipwreck in the winedark sea
off the coast of Thrinákia. Zeus and Hêlios   300
held it against him that his men had killed
the kine of Hêlios. The crew drowned for this.
He rode the ship's keel. Big seas cast him up
on the island of Phaiákians, godlike men
who took him to their hearts. They honored him
with many gifts and a safe passage home,
or so they wished. Long since he should have been here,
but he thought better to restore his fortune
playing the vagabond about the world;
and no adventurer could beat Odysseus   310
at living by his wits—no man alive.
I had this from King Phaidôn of Thesprótia;
and, tipping wine out, Phaidôn swore to me
the ship was launched, the seamen standing by
to bring Odysseus to his land at last,
but I got out to sea ahead of him
by the king's order—as it chanced a freighter
left port for the grain bins of Doulíkhion.
Phaidôn, however, showed me Odysseus' treasure.
Ten generations of his heirs or more   320
could live on what lay piled in that great room.
The man himself had gone up to Dodona
to ask the spelling leaves of the old oak
what Zeus would have him do—how to return to Ithaka
after so many years—by stealth or openly.
You see, then, he is alive and well, and headed
homeward now, no more to be abroad
far from his island, his dear wife and son.
Here is my sworn word for it. Witness this,
god of the zenith, noblest of the gods,   330
and Lord Odysseus' hearthfire, now before me:

I swear these things shall turn out as I say.
Between this present dark and one day's ebb,
after the wane, before the crescent moon,[7]
Odysseus will come."

                                        Penélopê,
the attentive queen, replied to him:

                                        "Ah, stranger,
if what you say could ever happen!
You would soon know our love! Our bounty, too:
men would turn after you to call you blessed.
But my heart tells me what must be.   340
Odysseus will not come to me; no ship
will be prepared for you. We have no master
quick to receive and furnish out a guest
as Lord Odysseus was.

                                Or did I dream him?

Maids, maids: come wash him, make a bed for him,
bedstead and colored rugs and coverlets
to let him lie warm into the gold of Dawn.
In morning light you'll bathe him and anoint him
so that he'll take his place beside Telémakhos
feasting in hall. If there be one man there   350
to bully or annoy him, that man wins
no further triumph here, burn though he may.
How will you understand me, friend, how find in me,
more than in common women, any courage
or gentleness, if you are kept in rags
and filthy at our feast? Men's lives are short.
The hard man and his cruelties will be
cursed behind his back, and mocked in death.
But one whose heart and ways are kind—of him
strangers will bear report to the wide world,   360
and distant men will praise him."

                                                Warily
Odysseus answered:

                                        "Honorable lady,
wife of Odysseus Laërtiadês,
a weight of rugs and cover? Not for me.
I've had none since the day I saw the mountains
of Krete, white with snow, low on the sea line
fading behind me as the long oars drove me north.
Let me lie down tonight as I've lain often,
many a night unsleeping, many a time

---

[7] Between now and the time of the new moon. As it happens, the day specified will be the morrow.

afield on hard ground waiting for pure Dawn.   370
No: and I have no longing for a footbath
either; none of these maids will touch my feet,
unless there is an old one, old and wise,
one who has lived through suffering as I have:
I would not mind letting my feet be touched
by that old servant."

                                        And Penélopê said:

"Dear guest, no foreign man so sympathetic
ever came to my house, no guest more likeable,
so wry and humble are the things you say.
I have an old maidservant ripe with years,   380
one who in her time nursed my lord. She took him
into her arms the hour his mother bore him.
Let her, then, wash your feet, though she is frail.
Come here, stand by me, faithful Eurýkleia,
and bathe—bathe your master, I almost said,
for they are of an age, and now Odysseus'
feet and hands would be enseamed like his.
Men grow old soon in hardship."

                                        Hearing this,
the old nurse hid her face between her hands
and wept hot tears, and murmured:

                                "Oh, my child!   390
I can do nothing for you! How Zeus hated you,
no other man so much! No use, great heart,
O faithful heart, the rich thighbones you burnt
to Zeus who plays in lightning—and no man
ever gave more to Zeus—with all your prayers
for a green age, a tall son reared to manhood.
There is no day of homecoming for you.
Stranger, some women in some far off place
perhaps have mocked my lord when he'd be home
as now these strumpets[8] mock you here. No wonder   400
you would keep clear of all their whorishness
and have no bath. But here am I. The queen
Penélopê, Ikários' daughter, bids me;
so let me bathe your feet to serve my lady—
to serve you, too.

                                My heart within me stirs,
mindful of something. Listen to what I say:
strangers have come here, many through the years,
but no one ever came, I swear, who seemed
so like Odysseus—body, voice and limbs—
as you do."

    [8] Whores.

Ready for this, Odysseus answered: 410

"Old woman, that is what they say. All who have seen
the two of us remark how like we are,
as you yourself have said, and rightly, too."

Then he kept still, while the old nurse filled up
her basin glittering in firelight; she poured
cold water in, then hot.

But Lord Odysseus
whirled suddenly from the fire to face the dark.
The scar: he had forgotten that. She must not
handle his scarred thigh, or the game was up.
But when she bared her lord's leg, bending near,   420
she knew the groove at once.

An old wound
a boar's white tusk inflicted, on Parnassos[9]
years ago. He had gone hunting there
in company with his uncles and Autólykos,
his mother's father—a great thief and swindler
by Hermês'[10] favor, for Autólykos pleased him
with burnt offerings of sheep and kids. The god
acted as his accomplice. Well, Autólykos
on a trip to Ithaka
arrived just after his daughter's boy was born.   430
In fact, he had no sooner finished supper
than Nurse Eurýkleia put the baby down
in his own lap and said:

"It is for you, now,
to choose a name for him, your child's dear baby;
the answer to her prayers."

Autólykos replied:

"My son-in-law, my daughter, call the boy
by the name I tell you. Well you know, my hand
has been against the world of men and women;
odium and distrust I've won. Odysseus
should be his given name.[11] When he grows up,   440
when he comes visiting his mother's home
under Parnassos, where my treasures are,
I'll make him gifts and send him back rejoicing."

Odysseus in due course went for the gifts,
and old Autólykos and his sons embraced him
with welcoming sweet words; and Amphithéa,

[9] The famous mountain near Delphi. Also spelled *Parnassus*.
[10] Noted for cleverness, Hermês was the patron god of thieves, though he is not usually
presented in that role by Homer.
[11] *Odysseus* means something like "wrathful."

his mother's mother, held him tight and kissed him,
kissed his head and his fine eyes.

The father

called on his noble sons to make a feast,
and going about it briskly they led in   450
an ox of five years, whom they killed and flayed
and cut in bits for roasting on the skewers
with skilled hands, with care; then shared it out.
So all the day until the sun went down
they feasted to their hearts' content. At evening,
after the sun was down and dusk had come,
they turned to bed and took the gift of sleep.

When the young Dawn spread in the eastern sky
her finger tips of rose, the men and dogs
went hunting, taking Odysseus. They climbed   460
Parnassos' rugged flank mantled in forest,
entering amid high windy folds at noon
when Hêlios beat upon the valley floor
and on the winding Ocean whence he came.
With hounds questing ahead, in open order,
the sons of Autólykos went down a glen,
Odysseus in the lead, behind the dogs,
pointing his long-shadowing spear.

Before them

a great boar lay hid in undergrowth,
in a green thicket proof against the wind   470
or sun's blaze, fine soever the needling sunlight,
impervious too to any rain, so dense
that cover was, heaped up with fallen leaves.
Patter of hounds' feet, men's feet, woke the boar
as they came up—and from his woody ambush
with razor back bristling and raging eyes
he trotted and stood at bay. Odysseus,
being on top of him, had the first shot,
lunging to stick him; but the boar
had already charged under the long spear.   480
He hooked aslant with one white tusk and ripped out
flesh above the knee, but missed the bone.
Odysseus' second thrust went home by luck,
his bright spear passing through the shoulder joint;
and the beast fell, moaning as life pulsed away.
Autólykos' tall sons took up the wounded,
working skillfully over the Prince Odysseus
to bind his gash, and with a rune[12] they stanched
the dark flow of blood. Then downhill swiftly
they all repaired to the father's house, and there   490
tended him well—so well they soon could send him,

---

[12] Magic spell or charm.

with Grandfather Autólykos' magnificent gifts,
rejoicing, over sea to Ithaka.
His father and the Lady Antikleía
welcomed him, and wanted all the news
of how he got his wound; so he spun out
his tale, recalling how the boar's white tusk
caught him when he was hunting on Parnassos.

This was the scar the old nurse recognized;
she traced it under her spread hands, then let go,   500
and into the basin fell the lower leg
making the bronze clang, sloshing the water out.
Then joy and anguish seized her heart; her eyes
filled up with tears; her throat closed, and she whispered,
with hand held out to touch his chin:

                                         "Oh yes!
You are Odysseus! Ah, dear child! I could not
see you until now—not till I knew
my master's very body with my hands!"

Her eyes turned to Penélopê with desire
to make her lord, her husband, known—in vain,   510
because Athena had bemused the queen,
so that she took no notice, paid no heed.
At the same time Odysseus' right hand
gripped the old throat; his left hand pulled her near,
and in her ear he said:

                                      "Will you destroy me,
nurse, who gave me milk at your own breast?
Now with a hard lifetime behind I've come
in the twentieth year home to my father's island.
You found me out, as the chance was given you.
Be quiet; keep it from the others, else   520
I warn you, and I mean it, too,
if by my hand god brings the suitors down
I'll kill you, nurse or not, when the time comes—
when the time comes to kill the other women."

Eurýkleia kept her wits and answered him:

"Oh, what mad words are these you let escape you!
Child, you know my blood, my bones are yours;
no one could whip this out of me. I'll be
a woman turned to stone, iron I'll be.
And let me tell you too—mind now—if god   530
cuts down the arrogant suitors by your hand,
I can report to you on all the maids,
those who dishonor you, and the innocent."

But in response the great tactician said:

"Nurse, no need to tell me tales of these.
I will have seen them, each one, for myself.
Trust in the gods, be quiet, hold your peace."

Silent, the old nurse went to fetch more water,
her basin being all spilt.
                                                    When she had washed
and rubbed his feet with golden oil, he turned,   540
dragging his bench again to the fire side
for warmth, and hid the scar under his rags.
Penélopê broke the silence, saying:

                                                                "Friend,

allow me one brief question more. You know,
the time for bed, sweet rest, is coming soon,
if only that warm luxury of slumber
would come to enfold us, in our trouble. But for me
my fate at night is anguish and no rest.
By day being busy, seeing to my work,
I find relief sometimes from loss and sorrow;   550
but when night comes and all the world's abed
I lie in mine alone, my heart thudding,
while bitter thoughts and fears crowd on my grief.
Think, how Pandáreos'[13] daughter, pale forever,
sings as the nightingale in the new leaves
through those long quiet hours of night,
on some thick-flowering orchard bough in spring;
how she rills out and tilts her note, high now, now low,
mourning for Itylos whom she killed in madness—
her child, and her lord Zêthos' only child.   560
My forlorn thought flows variable as her song,
wondering: shall I stay beside my son
and guard my own things here, my maids, my hall,
to honor my lord's bed and the common talk?
Or had I best join fortunes with a suitor,
the noblest one, most lavish in his gifts?
Is it now time for that?
My son being still a callow boy forbade
marriage, or absence from my lord's domain;
but now the child is grown, grown up, a man,   570
he, too, begins to pray for my departure,
aghast at all the suitors gorge on.

---

[13] In this version of the nightingale-myth, Aedon (daughter of Pandáreos and wife of
Zêthos) was metamorphosed into a nightingale, through the compassion of Zeus, after she had
killed her only son, Itylos, by mistake. She had intended to kill the eldest son of Niobe, her
sister-in-law, who had aroused her jealousy by having so many children.

Listen:

interpret me this dream: From a water's edge
twenty fat geese have come to feed on grain
beside my house. And I delight to see them.
But now a mountain eagle with great wings
and crooked beak storms in to break their necks
and strew their bodies here. Away he soars
into the bright sky; and I cry aloud—
all this in dream—I wail and round me gather   580
softly braided Akhaian women mourning
because the eagle killed my geese.

Then down

out of the sky he drops to a cornice beam
with mortal voice telling me not to weep.
'Be glad,' says he, 'renowned Ikários' daughter:
here is no dream but something real as day,
something about to happen. All those geese
were suitors, and the bird was I. See now,
I am no eagle but your lord come back
to bring inglorious death upon them all!'   590
As he said this, my honeyed slumber left me.
Peering through half-shut eyes, I saw the geese
in hall, still feeding at the self-same trough."

The master of subtle ways and straight replied:

"My dear, how can you choose to read the dream
differently? Has not Odysseus himself
shown you what is to come? Death to the suitors,
sure death, too. Not one escapes his doom."

Penélopê shook her head and answered:

"Friend,

many and many a dream is mere confusion,   600
a cobweb of no consequence at all.
Two gates for ghostly dreams there are: one gateway
of honest horn, and one of ivory.
Issuing by the ivory gate are dreams
of glimmering illusion, fantasies,
but those that come through solid polished horn
may be borne out, if mortals only know them.
I doubt it came by horn, my fearful dream—
too good to be true, that, for my son and me.
But one thing more I wish to tell you: listen   610
carefully. It is a black day, this that comes.
Odysseus' house and I are to be parted.
I shall decree a contest for the day.
We have twelve axe heads. In his time, my lord
could line them up, all twelve, at intervals

like a ship's ribbing; then he'd back away
a long way off and whip an arrow through.
Now I'll impose this trial on the suitors.
The one who easily handles and strings the bow
and shoots through all twelve axes I shall marry,   620
whoever he may be—then look my last
on this my first love's beautiful brimming house.
But I'll remember, though I dream it only."

Odysseus said:

                                        "Dear honorable lady,

wife of Odysseus Laërtiadês,
let there be no postponement of the trial.
Odysseus, who knows the shifts of combat,
will be here: aye, he'll be here long before
one of these lads can stretch or string that bow
or shoot to thread the iron!"

                                            Grave and wise,   630

Penélopê replied:

                                        "If you were willing

to sit with me and comfort me, my friend,
no tide of sleep would ever close my eyes.
But mortals cannot go forever sleepless.
This the undying gods decree for all
who live and die on earth, kind furrowed earth.
Upstairs I go, then, to my single bed,
my sighing bed, wet with so many tears
after my Lord Odysseus took ship
to see that misery at Ilion, unspeakable.   640
Let me rest there, you here. You can stretch out
on the bare floor, or else command a bed."

So she went up to her chamber softly lit,
accompanied by her maids. Once there, she wept
for Odysseus, her husband, till Athena
cast sweet sleep upon her eyes.

BOOK TWENTY: SIGNS AND A VISION

Outside in the entry way he made his bed—
raw oxhide spread on level ground, and heaped up
fleeces, left from sheep the Akhaians killed.
And when he had lain down, Eurýnomê
flung out a robe to cover him. Unsleeping

the Lord Odysseus lay, and roved in thought
to the undoing of his enemies.

                                        Now came a covey of women
laughing as they slipped out, arm in arm,
as many a night before, to the suitors' beds;
and anger took him like a wave to leap
into their midst and kill them, every one—
or should he let them all go hot to bed
one final night? His heart cried out within him
the way a brach[1] with whelps between her legs
would howl and bristle at a stranger—so
the hackles of his heart rose at that laughter.
Knocking his breast he muttered to himself:

"Down; be steady. You've seen worse, that time
the Kyklops like a rockslide ate your men
while you looked on. Nobody, only guile,
got you out of that cave alive."

                                                        His rage
held hard in leash, submitted to his mind,
while he himself rocked, rolling from side to side,
as a cook turns a sausage, big with blood
and fat, at a scorching blaze, without a pause,
to broil it quick: so he rolled left and right,
casting about to see how he, alone,
against the false outrageous crowd of suitors
could press the fight.

                                        And out of the night sky
Athena came to him; out of the nearby dark
in body like a woman; came and stood
over his head to chide him:

                                        "Why so wakeful,
most forlorn of men? Here is your home,
there lies your lady; and your son is here,
as fine as one could wish a son to be."

Odysseus looked up and answered:

"Aye,
goddess, that much is true; but still
I have some cause to fret in this affair.
I am one man; how can I whip those dogs?
They are always here in force. Neither
is that the end of it, there's more to come.
If by the will of Zeus and by your will
I killed them all, where could I go for safety?
Tell me that!"

---

[1] Female dog; bitch.

                                        And the grey-eyed goddess said:

"Your touching faith! Another man would trust
some villainous mortal, with no brains—and what
am I? Your goddess-guardian to the end
in all your trials. Let it be plain as day:
if fifty bands of men surrounded us   50
and every sword sang for your blood,
you could make off still with their cows and sheep.
Now you, too, go to sleep. This all night vigil
wearies the flesh. You'll come out soon enough
on the other side of trouble."

                                                                    Raining soft

sleep on his eyes, the beautiful one was gone
back to Olympos. Now at peace, the man
slumbered and lay still, but not his lady.
Wakeful again with all her cares, reclining
in the soft bed, she wept and cried aloud   60
until she had had her fill of tears, then spoke
in prayer first to Artemis:

                                                                    "O gracious

divine lady Artemis, daughter of Zeus,
if you could only make an end now quickly,
let the arrow fly, stop my heart,
or if some wind could take me by the hair
up into running cloud, to plunge in tides of Ocean,
as hurricane winds took Pandáreos' daughters[2]
when they were left at home alone. The gods
had sapped their parents' lives. But Aphroditê   70
fed those children honey, cheese, and wine,
and Hêra gave them looks and wit, and Artemis,
pure Artemis, gave lovely height, and wise
Athena made them practised in her arts—
till Aphroditê in glory walked on Olympos,
begging for each a happy wedding day
from Zeus, the lightning's joyous king, who knows
all fate of mortals, fair and foul—
but even at that hour the cyclone winds
had ravished them away   80
to serve the loathsome Furies.

                                                                    Let me be

blown out by the Olympians! Shot by Artemis,
I still might go and see amid the shades
Odysseus in the rot of underworld.

────────

[2] Pandáreos stole a statue from a temple of Zeus; after the death of Pandáreos, his three
daughters (Aedon and two of her sisters), though pitied by the greatest of the goddesses, were
carried away by the Furies, the avengers of the father's wickedness. This story differs from the
one in Book XIX, in which Aedon was changed into a nightingale.

No coward's eye should light by my consenting!
Evil may be endured when our days pass
in mourning, heavy-hearted, hard beset,
if only sleep reign over nighttime, blanketing
the world's good and evil from our eyes.
But not for me: dreams too my demon sends me.   90
Tonight the image of my lord came by
as I remember him with troops. O strange
exultation! I thought him real, and not a dream."

Now as the Dawn appeared all stitched in gold,
the queen's cry reached Odysseus at his waking,
so that he wondered, half asleep: it seemed
she knew him, and stood near him! Then he woke
and picked his bedding up to stow away
on a chair in the mégaron. The oxhide pad
he took outdoors. There, spreading wide his arms,   100
he prayed:

                    "O Father Zeus, if over land and water,
after adversity, you willed to bring me home,
let someone in the waking house give me good augury,
and a sign be shown, too, in the outer world."

He prayed thus, and the mind of Zeus in heaven
heard him. He thundered out of bright Olympos
down from above the cloudlands, in reply—
a rousing peal for Odysseus. Then a token
came to him from a woman grinding flour
in the court nearby. His own handmills were there,   110
and twelve maids had the job of grinding out
whole grain and barley meal, the pith of men.
Now all the rest, their bushels ground, were sleeping;
one only, frail and slow, kept at it still.
She stopped, stayed her hand, and her lord heard
the omen from her lips:

                              "Ah, Father Zeus
almighty over gods and men!
A great bang of thunder that was, surely,
out of the starry sky, and not a cloud in sight.
It is your nod to someone. Hear me, then,   120
make what I say come true:
let this day be the last the suitors feed
so dainty in Odysseus' hall!
They've made me work my heart out till I drop,
grinding barley. May they feast no more!"

The servant's prayer, after the cloudless thunder
of Zeus, Odysseus heard with lifting heart,
sure in his bones that vengeance was at hand.

Then other servants, wakening, came down
to build and light a fresh fire at the hearth.   130
Telémakhos, clear-eyed as a god, awoke,
put on his shirt and belted on his sword,
bound rawhide sandals under his smooth feet,
and took his bronze-shod lance. He came and stood
on the broad sill of the doorway, calling Eurýkleia:

"Nurse, dear Nurse, how did you treat our guest?
Had he a supper and a good bed? Has he lain
uncared for still? My mother is like that,
perverse for all her cleverness:
she'd entertain some riff-raff, and turn out   140
a solid man."

                                    The old nurse answered him:

"I would not be so quick to accuse her, child.
He sat and drank here while he had a mind to;
food he no longer hungered for, he said—
for she did ask him. When he thought of sleeping,
she ordered them to make a bed. Poor soul!
Poor gentleman! So humble and so miserable,
he would accept no bed with rugs to lie on,
but slept on sheepskins and a raw oxhide
in the entry way. We covered him ourselves."   150

Telémakhos left the hall, hefting his lance,
with two swift flickering hounds for company,
to face the island Akhaians in the square;
and gently born Eurýkleia, the daughter
of Ops Peisenóridês, called to the maids:

"Bestir yourselves! you have your brooms, go sprinkle
the rooms and sweep them, robe the chairs in red,
sponge off the tables till they shine.
Wash out the winebowls and two-handled cups.
You others go fetch water from the spring;   160
no loitering; come straight back. Our company
will be here soon; morning is sure to bring them;
everyone has a holiday today."[3]

The women ran to obey her—twenty girls
off to the spring with jars for dusky water,
the rest at work inside. Then tall woodcutters
entered to split up logs for the hearth fire,
the water carriers returned; and on their heels
arrived the swineherd, driving three fat pigs,
chosen among his pens. In the wide court   170
he let them feed, and said to Odysseus kindly:

[3] The day is a special festival.

"Friend, are they more respectful of you now,
or still insulting you?"

Replied Odysseus:

"The young men, yes. And may the gods requite
those insolent puppies for the game they play
in a home not their own. They have no decency."

During this talk, Melánthios the goatherd
came in, driving goats for the suitors' feast,
with his two herdsmen. Under the portico
they tied the animals, and Melánthios   180
looked at Odysseus with a sneer. Said he:

"Stranger,

I see you mean to stay and turn our stomachs
begging in this hall. Clear out, why don't you?
Or will you have to taste a bloody beating
before you see the point? Your begging ways
nauseate everyone. There are feasts elsewhere."

Odysseus answered not a word, but grimly
shook his head over his murderous heart.
A third man came up now: Philoítios
the cattle foreman, with an ox behind him   190
and fat goats for the suitors. Ferrymen
had brought these from the mainland, as they bring
travellers, too—whoever comes along.
Philoítios tied the beasts under the portico
and joined the swineherd.

"Who is this," he said,

"Who is the new arrival at the manor?
Akhaian? or what else does he claim to be?
Where are his family and fields of home?
Down on his luck, all right: carries himself like a captain.
How the immortal gods can change and drag us down   200
once they begin to spin dark days for us!—
Kings and commanders, too."

Then he stepped over

and took Odysseus by the right hand, saying:

"Welcome, Sir. May good luck lie ahead
at the next turn. Hard times you're having, surely.
O Zeus! no god is more berserk in heaven
if gentle folk, whom you yourself begot,[4]
you plunge in grief and hardship without mercy!
Sir, I began to sweat when I first saw you,

---

[4] To say that Zeus was their father was a way of describing great leaders.

and tears came to my eyes, remembering
Odysseus: rags like these he may be wearing
somewhere on his wanderings now—
I mean, if he's alive still under the sun.
But if he's dead and in the house of Death,
I mourn Odysseus. He entrusted cows to me
in Kephallênia,[5] when I was knee high,
and now his herds are numberless, no man else
ever had cattle multiply like grain.
But new men tell me I must bring my beeves
to feed them, who care nothing for our prince,
fear nothing from the watchful gods. They crave
partition of our lost king's land and wealth.
My own feelings keep going round and round
upon this tether: can I desert the boy
by moving, herds and all, to another country,
a new life among strangers? Yet it's worse
to stay here, in my old post, herding cattle
for upstarts.

                                   I'd have gone long since,
gone, taken service with another king; this shame
is no more to be borne; but I keep thinking
my own lord, poor devil, still might come
and make a rout of suitors in his hall."

Odysseus, with his mind on action, answered:

"Herdsman, I make you out to be no coward
and no fool: I can see that for myself.
So let me tell you this. I swear by Zeus
all highest, by the table set for friends,
and by your king's hearthstone to which I've come,
Odysseus will return. You'll be on hand
to see, if you care to see it,
how those who lord it here will be cut down."

The cowman said:

                                   "Would god it all came true!
You'd see the fight that's in me!"

                                            Then Eumaios

echoed him, and invoked the gods, and prayed
that his great-minded master should return.
While these three talked, the suitors in the field
had come together plotting—what but death
for Telémakhos?—when from the left an eagle
crossed high with a rockdove in his claws.

[5] A large island near Ithaka; modern Cephalonia.

Amphínomos got up. Said he, cutting them short: 250

"Friends, no luck lies in that plan for us,
no luck,[6] knifing the lad. Let's think of feasting."

A grateful thought, they felt, and walking on
entered the great hall of the hero Odysseus,
where they all dropped their cloaks on chairs or couches
and made a ritual slaughter, knifing sheep,
fat goats and pigs, knifing the grass-fed steer.
Then tripes were broiled and eaten. Mixing bowls
were filled with wine. The swineherd passed out cups,
Philoítios, chief cowherd, dealt the loaves 260
into the panniers, Melánthios poured wine,
and all their hands went out upon the feast.

Telémakhos placed his father to advantage
just at the door sill of the pillared hall,
setting a stool there and a sawed-off table,
gave him a share of tripes, poured out his wine
in a golden cup, and said:

                      "Stay here, sit down
to drink with our young friends. I stand between you
and any cutting word or cuffing hand
from any suitor. Here is no public house 270
but the old home of Odysseus, my inheritance.
Hold your tongues then, gentlemen, and your blows,
and let no wrangling start, no scuffle either."

The others, disconcerted, bit their lips
at the ring in the young man's voice. Antínoös,
Eupeithês' son, turned round to them and said:

"It goes against the grain, my lords, but still
I say we take this hectoring by Telémakhos.
You know Zeus balked at it, or else
we might have shut his mouth a long time past, 280
the silvery speaker."

                              But Telémakhos
paid no heed to what Antínoös said.

Now public heralds wound through Ithaka
leading a file of beasts for sacrifice, and islanders
gathered under the shade trees of Apollo,
in the precinct of the Archer—while in hall
the suitors roasted mutton and fat beef
on skewers, pulling off the fragrant cuts;

---

[6] The bird's appearance on the left is an ill omen.

and those who did the roasting served Odysseus
a portion equal to their own, for so   290
Telémakhos commanded.

                                                    But Athena

had no desire now to let the suitors
restrain themselves from wounding words and acts.
Laërtês' son again must be offended.
There was a scapegrace[7] fellow in the crowd
named Ktésippos, a Samian, rich beyond
all measure, arrogant with riches, early
and late a bidder for Odysseus' queen.
Now this one called attention to himself:

"Hear me, my lords, I have a thing to say.   300
Our friend has had his fair share from the start
and that's polite; it would be most improper
if we were cold to guests of Telémakhos—
no matter what tramp turns up. Well then, look here,
let me throw in my own small contribution.
He must have prizes to confer, himself,
on some brave bathman or another slave
here in Odysseus' house."

                                     His hand went backward
and, fishing out a cow's foot from the basket,
he let it fly.

                          Odysseus rolled his head   310
to one side softly, ducking the blow, and smiled
a crooked smile with teeth clenched. On the wall
the cow's foot struck and fell. Telémakhos
blazed up:

                     "Ktésippos, lucky for you, by heaven,
not to have hit him! He took care of himself,
else you'd have had my lance-head in your belly;
no marriage, but a grave instead on Ithaka
for your father's pains.

                                     You others, let me see
no more contemptible conduct in my house!
I've been awake to it for a long time—by now   320
I know what is honorable and what is not.
Before, I was a child. I can endure it
while sheep are slaughtered, wine drunk up, and bread—
can one man check the greed of a hundred men?—
but I will suffer no more viciousness.
Granted you mean at last to cut me down:
I welcome that—better to die than have
humiliation always before my eyes,

---

[7] Unprincipled.

the stranger buffeted, and the serving women
dragged about, abused in a noble house."   330

They quieted, grew still, under his lashing,
and after a long silence, Ageláos,
Damástor's son, spoke to them all:

                                                    "Friends, friends,
I hope no one will answer like a fishwife.
What has been said is true. Hands off this stranger,
he is no target, neither is any servant
here in the hall of King Odysseus.
Let me say a word, though, to Telémakhos
and to his mother, if it please them both:
as long as hope remained in you to see   340
Odysseus, that great gifted man, again,
you could not be reproached for obstinacy,
tying the suitors down here; better so,
if still your father fared the great sea homeward.
How plain it is, though, now, he'll come no more!
Go sit then by your mother, reason with her,
tell her to take the best man, highest bidder,
and you can have and hold your patrimony,
feed on it, drink it all, while she
adorns another's house."

                                            Keeping his head,   350
Telémakhos replied:

                                                    "By Zeus Almighty,
Ageláos, and by my father's sufferings,
far from Ithaka, whether he's dead or lost,
I make no impediment to Mother's marriage.
'Take whom you wish,' I say, 'I'll add my dowry.'
But can I pack her off against her will
from her own home? Heaven forbid!"

                                                    At this,
Pallas Athena touched off in the suitors
a fit of laughter, uncontrollable.[8]
She drove them into nightmare, till they wheezed
and neighed as though with jaws no longer theirs,   360
while blood defiled their meat,[9] and blurring tears
flooded their eyes, heart-sore with woe to come.
Then said the visionary, Theoklýmenos:

"O lost sad men, what terror is this you suffer?
Night shrouds you to the knees, your heads, your faces;
dry retch of death runs round like fire in sticks;

[8] The laughter is a sign that the suitors are out of their right minds.
[9] That is, in the eyes of Odysseus, Telémakhos, and Theoklýmenos.

your cheeks are streaming; these fair walls and pedestals
are dripping crimson blood. And thick with shades
is the entry way, the courtyard thick with shades   370
passing athirst toward Érebos, into the dark,
the sun is quenched in heaven, foul mist hems us in . . ."

The young men greeted this with shouts of laughter,
and Eurýmakhos, the son of Pólybos, crowed:

"The mind of our new guest has gone astray.
Hustle him out of doors, lads, into the sunlight;
he finds it dark as night inside!"

The man of vision looked at him and said:

"When I need help, I'll ask for it, Eurýmakhos.
I have my eyes and ears, a pair of legs,   380
and a straight mind, still with me. These will do
to take me out. Damnation and black night
I see arriving for yourselves: no shelter,
no defence for any in this crowd—
fools and vipers in the king's own hall."

With this he left that handsome room and went
home to Peiraios, who received him kindly.
The suitors made wide eyes at one another
and set to work provoking Telémakhos
with jokes about his friends. One said, for instance: 390

"Telémakhos, no man is a luckier host
when it comes to what the cat dragged in. What burning
eyes your beggar had for bread and wine!
But not for labor, not for a single heave—
he'd be a deadweight on a field. Then comes
this other, with his mumbo-jumbo. Boy,
for your own good, I tell you, toss them both
into a slave ship for the Sikels.[10] That would pay you."

Telémakhos ignored the suitors' talk.
He kept his eyes in silence on his father,   400
awaiting the first blow. Meanwhile
the daughter of Ikários, Penélopê,
had placed her chair to look across and down
on father and son at bay; she heard the crowd,
and how they laughed as they resumed their dinner,
a fragrant feast, for many beasts were slain—
but as for supper, men supped never colder
than these, on what the goddess and the warrior
were even then preparing for the suitors,
whose treachery had filled that house with pain.   410

[10] Sicilians.

BOOK TWENTY-ONE: THE TEST OF THE BOW

Upon Penélopê, most worn in love and thought,
Athena cast a glance like a grey sea
lifting her. Now to bring the tough bow out and bring
the iron blades. Now try those dogs at archery
to usher bloody slaughter in.

                         So moving stairward
the queen took up a fine doorhook of bronze,
ivory-hafted, smooth in her clenched hand,
and led her maids down to a distant room,
a storeroom where the master's treasure lay:
bronze, bar gold, black iron forged and wrought.   10
In this place hung the double-torsion bow
and arrows in a quiver, a great sheaf—
quills of groaning.

                      In the old time in Lakedaimon[1]
her lord had got these arms from Íphitos,
Eurýtos'[2] son. The two met in Messenia[3]
at Ortílokhos' table, on the day
Odysseus claimed a debt owed by that realm—
sheep stolen by Messenians out of Ithaka
in their long ships, three hundred head, and herdsmen.
Seniors of Ithaka and his father sent him   20
on that far embassy when he was young.
But Íphitos had come there tracking strays,
twelve shy mares, with mule colts yet unweaned.
And a fatal chase they led him over prairies
into the hands of Heraklês. That massive
son of toil and mortal son of Zeus
murdered his guest at wine[4] in his own house—
inhuman, shameless in the sight of heaven—
to keep the mares and colts in his own grange.
Now Íphitos, when he knew Odysseus, gave him   30
the master bowman's arm; for old Eurýtos
had left it on his deathbed to his son.
In fellowship Odysseus gave a lance
and a sharp sword. But Heraklês killed Íphitos
before one friend could play host to the other.
And Lord Odysseus would not take the bow
in the black ships to the great war at Troy.
As a keepsake he put it by:
it served him well at home in Ithaka.

[1] The region of Sparta, in southern Greece. [2] A famous archer.
[3] A region down the coast from Ithaka, in southwestern Greece.
[4] Íphitos' pursuit of his lost mares brought him to Tiryns, the city of the great hero-adventurer Heraklês, who, according to certain versions of the story, had something to do with the mares' disappearance. By some accounts, Heraklês killed Íphitos by throwing him down from the city walls.

Now the queen reached the storeroom door and halted.   40
Here was an oaken sill, cut long ago
and sanded clean and bedded true. Foursquare
the doorjambs and the shining doors were set
by the careful builder. Penélopê untied the strap
around the curving handle, pushed her hook
into the slit, aimed at the bolts inside
and shot them back. Then came a rasping sound
as those bright doors the key had sprung gave way—
a bellow like a bull's vaunt in a meadow—
followed by her light footfall entering   50
over the plank floor. Herb-scented robes
lay there in chests, but the lady's milkwhite arms
went up to lift the bow down from a peg
in its own polished bowcase.

                             Now Penélopê

sank down, holding the weapon on her knees,
and drew her husband's great bow out, and sobbed
and bit her lip and let the salt tears flow.
Then back she went to face the crowded hall
tremendous bow in hand, and on her shoulder hung
the quiver spiked with coughing death. Behind her   60
maids bore a basket full of axeheads, bronze
and iron implements for the master's game.
Thus in her beauty she approached the suitors,
and near a pillar of the solid roof
she paused, her shining veil across her cheeks,
her maids on either hand and still,
then spoke to the banqueters:

                           "My lords, hear me:

suitors indeed, you commandeered this house
to feast and drink in, day and night, my husband
being long gone, long out of mind. You found   70
no justification for yourselves—none
except your lust to marry me. Stand up, then:
we now declare a contest for that prize.
Here is my lord Odysseus' hunting bow.
Bend and string it if you can. Who sends an arrow
through iron axe-helve sockets,[5] twelve in line?
I join my life with his, and leave this place, my home,
my rich and beautiful bridal house, forever
to be remembered, though I dream it only."

Then to Eumaios:

[5] The details of the feat to be performed have been much discussed and are not entirely clear; in any case, the archer had to send an arrow through twelve openings—notches, holes, or other apertures—in the handles or blades of the axes.

"Carry the bow forward. 80
Carry the blades."

Tears came to the swineherd's eyes
as he reached out for the big bow. He laid it
down at the suitors' feet. Across the room
the cowherd sobbed, knowing the master's weapon.
Antínoös growled, with a glance at both:

"Clods.

They go to pieces over nothing.

You two, there,
why are you sniveling? To upset the woman
even more? Has she not pain enough
over her lost husband? *Sit down.*
Get on with dinner quietly, or cry about it 90
outside, if you must. Leave us the bow.
A clean-cut game, it looks to me.
Nobody bends that bowstave easily
in this company. Is there a man here
made like Odysseus? I remember him
from childhood: I can see him even now."

That was the way he played it, hoping inwardly
to span the great horn bow with corded gut
and drill the iron with his shot—he, Antínoös,
destined to be the first of all to savor 100
blood from a biting arrow at his throat,
a shaft drawn by the fingers of Odysseus
whom he had mocked and plundered, leading on
the rest, his boon companions. Now they heard
a gay snort of laughter from Telémakhos,
who said then brilliantly:

"A queer thing, that!

Has Zeus almighty made me a half-wit?
For all her spirit, Mother has given in,
promised to go off with someone—and
is that amusing? What am I cackling for?
Step up, my lords, contend now for your prize. 110
There is no woman like her in Akhaia,
not in old Argos, Pylos, or Mykênê,
neither in Ithaka nor on the mainland,
and you all know it without praise of mine.
Come on, no hanging back, no more delay
in getting the bow bent. Who's the winner?
I myself should like to try that bow.
Suppose I bend it and bring off the shot,
my heart will be less heavy, seeing the queen my mother 120
go for the last time from this house and hall,
if I who stay can do my father's feat."

He moved out quickly, dropping his crimson cloak,
and lifted sword and sword belt from his shoulders.
His preparation was to dig a trench,
heaping the earth in a long ridge beside it
to hold the blades half-bedded. A taut cord
aligned the socket rings. And no one there
but looked on wondering at his workmanship,
for the boy had never seen it done.

                                      He took his stand then   130
on the broad door sill to attempt the bow.
Three times he put his back into it and sprang it,
three times he had to slack off. Still he meant
to string that bow and pull for the needle shot.
A fourth try, and he had it all but strung—
when a stiffening in Odysseus made him check.
Abruptly then he stopped and turned and said:

"Blast and damn it, must I be a milksop
all my life? Half-grown, all thumbs,
no strength or knack at arms, to defend myself   140
if someone picks a fight with me.

                                             Take over,

O my elders and betters, try the bow,
run off the contest."

                                    And he stood the weapon
upright against the massy-timbered door
with one arrow across the horn aslant,
then went back to his chair. Antínoös
gave the word:

                                  "Now one man at a time
rise and go forward. Round the room in order;
left to right from where they dip the wine."

As this seemed fair enough, up stood Leódês   150
the son of Oinops. This man used to find
vision for them in the smoke of sacrifice.
He kept his chair well back, retired by the winebowl,
for he alone could not abide their manners
but sat in shame for all the rest. Now it was he
who had first to confront the bow,
standing up on the broad door sill. He failed.
The bow unbending made his thin hands yield,
no muscle in them. He gave up and said:

"Friends, I cannot. Let the next man handle it.   160
Here is a bow to break the heart and spirit
of many strong men. Aye. And death is less
bitter than to live on and never have
the beauty that we came here laying siege to

so many days. Resolute, are you still,
to win Odysseus' lady Penélopê?
Pit yourselves against the bow, and look
among Akhaians for another's daughter.
Gifts will be enough to court and take her.
Let the best offer win."

                                                With this Leódês   170
thrust the bow away from him, and left it
upright against the massy-timbered door,
with one arrow aslant across the horn.
As he went down to his chair he heard Antínoös'
voice rising:

                                      "What is that you say?
It makes me burn. You cannot string the weapon,
so 'Here is a bow to break the heart and spirit
of many strong men.' Crushing thought!
You were not born—you never had it in you—
to pull that bow or let an arrow fly.   180
But here are men who can and will."

He called out to the goatherd, Melánthios:

"Kindle a fire there, be quick about it,
draw up a big bench with a sheepskin on it,
and bring a cake of lard out of the stores.
Contenders from now on will heat and grease the bow.
We'll try it limber, and bring off the shot."

Melánthios darted out to light a blaze,
drew up a bench, threw a big sheepskin over it,
and brought a cake of lard. So one by one   190
the young men warmed and greased the bow for bending,
but not a man could string it. They were whipped.
Antínoös held off; so did Eurýmakhos,
suitors in chief, by far the ablest there.

Two men had meanwhile left the hall:
swineherd and cowherd, in companionship,
one downcast as the other. But Odysseus
followed them outdoors, outside the court,
and coming up said gently:

                                    "You, herdsman
and you, too, swineherd, I could say a thing to you,   200
or should I keep it dark?

                            No, no; speak,
my heart tells me. Would you be men enough
to stand by Odysseus if he came back?
Suppose he dropped out of a clear sky, as I did?

Suppose some god should bring him?
Would you bear arms for him, or for the suitors?"

The cowherd said:

                                        "Ah, let the master come!
Father Zeus, grant our old wish! Some courier
guide him back! Then judge what stuff is in me
and how I manage arms!"

                                        Likewise Eumaios   210
fell to praying all heaven for his return,
so that Odysseus, sure at least of these,
told them:

                                        "I am at home, for I am he.
I bore adversities, but in the twentieth year
I am ashore in my own land. I find
the two of you, alone among my people,
longed for my coming. Prayers I never heard
except your own that I might come again.
So now what is in store for you I'll tell you:
If Zeus brings down the suitors by my hand   220
I promise marriages to both, and cattle,
and houses built near mine. And you shall be
brothers-in-arms of my Telémakhos.
Here, let me show you something else, a sign
that I am he, that you can trust me, look:
this old scar from the tusk wound that I got
boar hunting on Parnassos—
Autólykos' sons and I."

                                        Shifting his rags
he bared the long gash. Both men looked, and knew,
and threw their arms around the old soldier, weeping,   230
kissing his head and shoulders. He as well
took each man's head and hands to kiss, then said—
to cut it short, else they might weep till dark—

"Break off, no more of this.
Anyone at the door could see and tell them.
Drift back in, but separately at intervals
after me.
                                        Now listen to your orders:
when the time comes, those gentlemen, to a man,
will be dead against giving me bow or quiver.
Defy them. Eumaios, bring the bow   240
and put it in my hands there at the door.
Tell the women to lock their own door tight.
Tell them if someone hears the shock of arms
or groans of men, in hall or court, not one

must show her face, but keep still at her weaving.
Philoítios, run to the outer gate and lock it.
Throw the cross bar and lash it."

He turned back
into the courtyard and the beautiful house
and took the stool he had before. They followed
one by one, the two hands loyal to him.   250

Eurýmakhos had now picked up the bow.
He turned it round, and turned it round
before the licking flame to warm it up,
but could not, even so, put stress upon it
to jam the loop over the tip

though his heart groaned to bursting.
Then he said grimly:

"Curse this day.
What gloom I feel, not for myself alone,
and not only because we lose that bride.
Women are not lacking in Akhaia,
in other towns, or on Ithaka. No, the worst   260
is humiliation—to be shown up for children
measured against Odysseus—we who cannot
even hitch the string over his bow.
What shame to be repeated of us, after us!"

Antínoös said:

"Come to yourself. You know
that is not the way this business ends.
Today the islanders held holiday, a holy day,[6]
no day to sweat over a bowstring.

Keep your head.
Postpone the bow. I say we leave the axes
planted where they are. No one will take them.   270
No one comes to Odysseus' hall tonight.
Break out good wine and brim our cups again,
we'll keep the crooked bow safe overnight,
order the fattest goats Melánthios has
brought down tomorrow noon, and offer thighbones burning
to Apollo, god of archers,
while we try out the bow and make the shot."

As this appealed to everyone, heralds came
pouring fresh water for their hands, and boys
filled up the winebowls. Joints of meat went round,   280
fresh cuts for all, while each man made his offering,

[6]With ironic appropriateness, a feast day of Apollo, god of archery. Antínoös makes this an excuse for putting off the present challenge.

tilting the red wine to the gods, and drank his fill.
Then spoke Odysseus, all craft and gall:

"My lords, contenders for the queen, permit me:
a passion in me moves me to speak out.
I put it to Eurýmakhos above all
and to that brilliant prince, Antínoös. Just now
how wise his counsel was, to leave the trial
and turn your thoughts to the immortal gods! Apollo
will give power tomorrow to whom he wills.   290
But let me try my hand at the smooth bow!
Let me test my fingers and my pull
to see if any of the oldtime kick is there,
or if thin fare and roving took it out of me."

Now irritation beyond reason swept them all,
since they were nagged by fear that he could string it.
Antínoös answered, coldly and at length:

"You bleary vagabond, no rag of sense is left you.
Are you not coddled here enough, at table
taking meat with gentlemen, your betters,   300
denied nothing, and listening to our talk?
When have we let a tramp hear all our talk?
The sweet goad of wine has made you rave!
Here is the evil wine can do
to those who swig it down. Even the centaur
Eurýtion,[7] in Peiríthoös' hall
among the Lapíthai, came to a bloody end
because of wine; wine ruined him: it crazed him,
drove him wild for rape in that great house.
The princes cornered him in fury, leaping on him   310
to drag him out and crop his ears and nose.
Drink had destroyed his mind, and so he ended
in that mutilation—fool that he was.
Centaurs and men made war for this,
but the drunkard first brought hurt upon himself.

The tale applies to you: I promise you
great trouble if you touch that bow. You'll come by
no indulgence in our house; kicked down
into a ship's bilge, out to sea you go,
and nothing saves you. Drink, but hold your tongue.   320
Make no contention here with younger men."

[7] The centaurs were an uncivilized tribe (often represented in myth as having horses'
trunks and legs and human torsos and heads), inhabitants of Thessaly, in northeastern
Greece. They were invited to the wedding of Peiríthoös, king of the Lapíthai, a neighboring
people, and at the wedding tried to carry off the bride; the present version tells the story in the
singular, of Eurýtion. In the ensuing battle the centaurs were defeated.

At this the watchful queen Penélopê
interposed:

                                        "Antínoös, discourtesy
to a guest of Telémakhos—whatever guest—
that is not handsome. What are you afraid of?
Suppose this exile put his back into it
and drew the great bow of Odysseus—
could he then take me home to be his bride?
You know he does not imagine that! No one
need let that prospect weigh upon his dinner!   330
How very, very improbable it seems."

It was Eurýmakhos who answered her:

"Penélopê, O daughter of Ikários,
most subtle queen, we are not given to fantasy.
No, but our ears burn at what men might say
and women, too. We hear some jackal whispering:
'How far inferior to the great husband
her suitors are! Can't even budge his bow!
Think of it; and a beggar, out of nowhere,
strung it quick and made the needle shot!'   340
That kind of disrepute we would not care for."

Penélopê replied, steadfast and wary:

"Eurýmakhos, you have no good repute
in this realm, nor the faintest hope of it—
men who abused a prince's house for years,
consumed his wine and cattle. Shame enough.
Why hang your heads over a trifle now?
The stranger is a big man, well-compacted,
and claims to be of noble blood.
Ai!   350
Give him the bow, and let us have it out!
What I can promise him I will:
if by the kindness of Apollo he prevails
he shall be clothed well and equipped.
A fine shirt and a cloak I promise him;
a lance for keeping dogs at bay, or men;
a broadsword; sandals to protect his feet;
escort, and freedom to go where he will."

Telémakhos now faced her and said sharply:

"Mother, as to the bow and who may handle it   360
or not handle it, no man here
has more authority than I do—not one lord
of our own stony Ithaka nor the islands lying
east toward Elis: no one stops me if I choose
to give these weapons outright to my guest.

Return to your own hall. Tend your spindle.
Tend your loom. Direct your maids at work.
This question of the bow will be for men to settle,
most of all for me. I am master here."

She gazed in wonder, turned, and so withdrew,   370
her son's clearheaded bravery in her heart.
But when she had mounted to her rooms again
with all her women, then she fell to weeping
for Odysseus, her husband. Grey-eyed Athena
presently cast a sweet sleep on her eyes.

The swineherd had the horned bow in his hands
moving toward Odysseus, when the crowd
in the banquet hall broke into an ugly din,
shouts rising from the flushed young men:

                                          "Ho! Where
do you think you are taking that, you smutty slave?"   380

"What is this dithering?"

                                          "We'll toss you back alone
among the pigs, for your own dogs to eat,
if bright Apollo nods and the gods are kind!"

He faltered, all at once put down the bow, and stood
in panic, buffeted by waves of cries,
hearing Telémakhos from another quarter
shout:

"Go on, take him the bow!

                                          Do you obey this pack?
You will be stoned back to your hills! Young as I am
my power is over you! I wish to God   390
I had as much the upper hand of these!
There would be suitors pitched like dead rats
through our gate, for the evil plotted here!"

Telémakhos' frenzy struck someone as funny,
and soon the whole room roared with laughter at him,
so that all tension passed. Eumaios picked up
bow and quiver, making for the door,
and there he placed them in Odysseus' hands.
Calling Eurýkleia to his side he said:

                                          "Telémakhos
trusts you to take care of the women's doorway.   400
Lock it tight. If anyone inside
should hear the shock of arms or groans of men
in hall or court, not one must show her face,
but go on with her weaving."

The old woman
nodded and kept still. She disappeared
into the women's hall, bolting the door behind her.
Philoítios left the house now at one bound,
catlike, running to bolt the courtyard gate.
A coil of deck-rope of papyrus fiber
lay in the gateway; this he used for lashing,   410
and ran back to the same stool as before,
fastening his eyes upon Odysseus.

　　　　　　　　And Odysseus took his time,
turning the bow, tapping it, every inch,
for borings that termites might have made
while the master of the weapon was abroad.
The suitors were now watching him, and some
jested among themselves:

　　　　　　　　　　　　　　　　"A bow lover!"

"Dealer in old bows!"

　　　　　　　　　　　　　"Maybe he has one like it
at home!"

　　　　　　　"Or has an itch to make one for himself."

"See how he handles it, the sly old buzzard!"   420

And one disdainful suitor added this:

"May his fortune grow an inch for every inch he bends it!"

But the man skilled in all ways of contending,
satisfied by the great bow's look and heft,
like a musician, like a harper, when
with quiet hand upon his instrument
he draws between his thumb and forefinger
a sweet new string upon a peg: so effortlessly
Odysseus in one motion strung the bow.
Then slid his right hand down the cord and plucked it,   430
so the taut gut vibrating hummed and sang
a swallow's note.

　　　　　　　　　In the hushed hall it smote the suitors
and all their faces changed. Then Zeus thundered
overhead, one loud crack for a sign.
And Odysseus laughed within him that the son
of crooked-minded Kronos had flung that omen down.
He picked one ready arrow from his table
where it lay bare: the rest were waiting still
in the quiver for the young men's turn to come.
He nocked it, let it rest across the handgrip,   440
and drew the string and grooved butt of the arrow,
aiming from where he sat upon the stool.

Now flashed

arrow from twanging bow clean as a whistle
through every socket ring, and grazed not one,
to thud with heavy brazen head beyond.

Then quietly

Odysseus said:

"Telémakhos, the stranger
you welcomed in your hall has not disgraced you.
I did not miss, neither did I take all day
stringing the bow. My hand and eye are sound,
not so contemptible as the young men say.   450
The hour has come to cook their lordships' mutton—
supper by daylight. Other amusements later,
with song and harping that adorn a feast."

He dropped his eyes and nodded, and the prince
Telémakhos, true son of King Odysseus,
belted his sword on, clapped hand to his spear,
and with a clink and glitter of keen bronze
stood by his chair, in the forefront near his father.

BOOK TWENTY-TWO: DEATH IN THE GREAT HALL

Now shrugging off his rags the wiliest fighter of the islands
leapt and stood on the broad door sill, his own bow in his hand.
He poured out at his feet a rain of arrows from the quiver
and spoke to the crowd:

"So much for that. Your clean-cut game is over.
Now watch me hit a target that no man has hit before,
if I can make this shot. Help me, Apollo."

He drew to his fist the cruel head of an arrow for Antínoös
just as the young man leaned to lift his beautiful drinking cup,
embossed, two-handled, golden: the cup was in his fingers:
the wine was even at his lips: and did he dream of death?   10
How could he? In that revelry amid his throng of friends
who would imagine a single foe—though a strong foe indeed—
could dare to bring death's pain on him and darkness on his eyes?
Odysseus' arrow hit him under the chin
and punched up to the feathers through his throat.

Backward and down he went, letting the winecup fall
from his shocked hand. Like pipes his nostrils jetted
crimson runnels, a river of mortal red,
and one last kick upset his table
knocking the bread and meat to soak in dusty blood.   20
Now as they craned to see their champion where he lay

the suitors jostled in uproar down the hall,
everyone on his feet. Wildly they turned and scanned
the walls in the long room for arms; but not a shield,
not a good ashen spear was there for a man to take and throw.
All they could do was yell in outrage at Odysseus:

"Foul! to shoot at a man! That was your last shot!"

"Your own throat will be slit for this!"

"Our finest lad is down!
You killed the best on Ithaka."

"Buzzards will tear your eyes out!"

For they imagined as they wished—that it was a wild shot,   30
an unintended killing—fools, not to comprehend
they were already in the grip of death.
But glaring under his brows Odysseus answered:

"You yellow dogs, you thought I'd never make it
home from the land of Troy. You took my house to plunder,
twisted my maids to serve your beds. You dared
bid for my wife while I was still alive.
Contempt was all you had for the gods who rule wide heaven,
contempt for what men say of you hereafter.
Your last hour has come. You die in blood."   40

As they all took this in, sickly green fear
pulled at their entrails, and their eyes flickered
looking for some hatch or hideaway from death.
Eurýmakhos alone could speak. He said:

"If you are Odysseus of Ithaka come back,
all that you say these men have done is true.
Rash actions, many here, more in the countryside.
But here he lies, the man who caused them all.
Antínoös was the ringleader, he whipped us on
to do these things. He cared less for a marriage   50
than for the power Kroníon has denied him
as king of Ithaka. For that
he tried to trap your son and would have killed him.
He is dead now and has his portion. Spare
your own people. As for ourselves, we'll make
restitution of wine and meat consumed,
and add, each one, a tithe of twenty oxen
with gifts of bronze and gold to warm your heart.
Meanwhile we cannot blame you for your anger."

Odysseus glowered under his black brows   60
and said:

"Not for the whole treasure of your fathers,
all you enjoy, lands, flocks, or any gold

put up by others, would I hold my hand.
There will be killing till the score is paid.
You forced yourselves upon this house. Fight your way out,
or run for it, if you think you'll escape death.
I doubt one man of you skins by."

They felt their knees fail, and their hearts—but heard
Eurýmakhos for the last time rallying them.

"Friends," he said, "the man is implacable.   70
Now that he's got his hands on bow and quiver
he'll shoot from the big door stone there
until he kills us to the last man.

                                Fight, I say,
let's remember the joy of it. Swords out!
Hold up your tables to deflect his arrows.
After me, everyone: rush him where he stands.
If we can budge him from the door, if we can pass
into the town, we'll call out men to chase him.
This fellow with his bow will shoot no more."

He drew his own sword as he spoke, a broadsword of fine bronze,   80
honed like a razor on either edge. Then crying hoarse and loud
he hurled himself at Odysseus. But the kingly man let fly
an arrow at that instant, and the quivering feathered butt
sprang to the nipple of his breast as the barb stuck in his liver.
The bright broadsword clanged down. He lurched and fell aside,
pitching across his table. His cup, his bread and meat,
were spilt and scattered far and wide, and his head slammed on the
     ground.
Revulsion, anguish in his heart, with both feet kicking out,
he downed his chair, while the shrouding wave of mist closed on his
     eyes.

Amphínomos now came running at Odysseus,   90
broadsword naked in his hand. He thought to make
the great soldier give way at the door.
But with a spear throw from behind Telémakhos hit him
between the shoulders, and the lancehead drove
clear through his chest. He left his feet and fell
forward, thudding, forehead against the ground.
Telémakhos swerved around him, leaving the long dark spear
planted in Amphínomos. If he paused to yank it out
someone might jump him from behind or cut him down with a sword
at the moment he bent over. So he ran—ran from the tables   100
to his father's side and halted, panting, saying:

"Father let me bring you a shield and spear,
a pair of spears, a helmet.
I can arm on the run myself; I'll give

outfits to Eumaios and this cowherd.
Better to have equipment."

Said Odysseus:

"Run then, while I hold them off with arrows
as long as the arrows last. When all are gone
if I'm alone they can dislodge me."

Quick

upon his father's word Telémakhos   110
ran to the room where spears and armor lay.
He caught up four light shields, four pairs of spears,
four helms of war high-plumed with flowing manes,
and ran back, loaded down, to his father's side.
He was the first to pull a helmet on
and slide his bare arm in a buckler strap.
The servants armed themselves, and all three took their stand
beside the master of battle.

While he had arrows

he aimed and shot, and every shot brought down
one of his huddling enemies.   120
But when all barbs had flown from the bowman's fist,
he leaned his bow in the bright entry way
beside the door, and armed: a four-ply shield
hard on his shoulder, and a crested helm,
horsetailed, nodding stormy upon his head,
then took his tough and bronze-shod spears.

The suitors

who held their feet, no longer under bowshot,
could see a window high in a recess of the wall,
a vent, lighting the passage to the storeroom.
This passage had one entry, with a door,   130
at the edge of the great hall's threshold, just outside.[1]

Odysseus told the swineherd to stand over
and guard this door and passage. As he did so,
a suitor named Ageláos asked the others:

"Who will get a leg up on that window
and run to alarm the town? One sharp attack
and this fellow will never shoot again."

His answer

came from the goatherd, Melánthios:

---

[1] The window in the *mégaron*, or great hall, connects with an external corridor that runs to
the rear of the house, past the women's chambers, to the storeroom; the only exit from the
corridor to the outdoor courtyard is close to where Odysseus and his three allies have posted
themselves. It is therefore, as Mélanthios soon points out, not a safe escape route.

                                              "No chance, my lord.
The exit into the courtyard is too near them,
too narrow. One good man could hold that portal   140
against a crowd. No: let me scale the wall
and bring you arms out of the storage chamber.
Odysseus and his son put them indoors,
I'm sure of it; not outside."

                                        The goatish goatherd
clambered up the wall, toes in the chinks,
and slipped through to the storeroom. Twelve light shields,
twelve spears he took, and twelve thick-crested helms,
and handed all down quickly to the suitors.
Odysseus, when he saw his adversaries
girded and capped and long spears in their hands   150
shaken at him, felt his knees go slack,
his heart sink, for the fight was turning grim.
He spoke rapidly to his son:

"Telémakhos, one of the serving women
is tipping the scales against us in this fight,
or maybe Melánthios."

                                        But sharp and clear
Telémakhos said:

                                  "It is my own fault, Father,
mine alone. The storeroom door—I left it
wide open. They were more alert than I.
Eumaios, go and lock that door,   160
and bring back word if a woman is doing this
or Melánthios, Dólios' son. More likely he."

Even as they conferred, Melánthios
entered the storeroom for a second load,
and the swineherd at the passage entry saw him.
He cried out to his lord:

                                        "Son of Laërtês,
Odysseus, master mariner and soldier,
there he goes, the monkey, as we thought,
there he goes into the storeroom.
                              Let me hear your will:
put a spear through him—I hope I am the stronger—   170
or drag him here to pay for his foul tricks
against your house?"

                        Odysseus said:

                                  "Telémakhos and I
will keep these gentlemen in hall, for all their urge to leave.
You two go throw him into the storeroom, wrench his arms

and legs behind him, lash his hands and feet
to a plank, and hoist him up to the roof beams.
Let him live on there suffering at his leisure."

The two men heard him with appreciation
and ducked into the passage. Melánthios,
rummaging in the chamber, could not hear them   180
as they came up; nor could he see them freeze
like posts on either side the door.
He turned back with a handsome crested helmet
in one hand, in the other an old shield
coated with dust—a shield Laërtês bore
soldiering in his youth. It had lain there for years,
and the seams on strap and grip had rotted away.
As Melánthios came out the two men sprang,
jerked him backward by the hair, and threw him.
Hands and feet they tied with a cutting cord   190
behind him, so his bones ground in their sockets,
just as Laërtês' royal son commanded.
Then with a whip of rope they hoisted him
in agony up a pillar to the beams,
and—O my swineherd—you were the one to say:

"Watch through the night up there, Melánthios.
An airy bed is what you need.
You'll be awake to see the primrose Dawn
when she goes glowing from the streams of Ocean
to mount her golden throne.

No oversleeping   200
the hour for driving goats to feed the suitors."

They stooped for helm and shield and left him there
contorted, in his brutal sling,
and shut the doors, and went to join Odysseus,
whose mind moved through the combat now to come.
Breathing deep, and snorting hard, they stood
four at the entry, facing two score men.
But now into the gracious doorway stepped
Zeus's daughter Athena. She wore the guise of Mentor,
and Odysseus appealed to her in joy: 210

"O Mentor, join me in this fight! Remember
how all my life I've been devoted to you,
friend of my youth!"

For he guessed it was Athena,
Hope of Soldiers. Cries came from the suitors,
and Ageláos, Damástor's son, called out:

"Mentor, don't let Odysseus lead you astray
to fight against us on his side.

Think twice: we are resolved—and we will do it—
after we kill them, father and son,
you too will have your throat slit for your pains   220
if you make trouble for us here. It means your life.
Your life—and cutting throats will not be all.
Whatever wealth you have, at home, or elsewhere,
we'll mingle with Odysseus' wealth. Your sons
will be turned out, your wife and daughters
banished from the town of Ithaka."

Athena's anger grew like a storm wind as he spoke
until she flashed out at Odysseus:

                           "Ah, what a falling off!
Where is your valor, where is the iron hand
that fought at Troy for Helen, pearl of kings,   230
no respite and nine years of war? How many foes
your hand brought down in bloody play of spears?
What stratagem but yours took Priam's town?
How is it now that on your own door sill,
before the harriers[2] of your wife, you curse your luck
not to be stronger?

                        Come here, cousin, stand by me,
and you'll see action! In the enemies' teeth
learn how Mentor, son of Álkimos,
repays fair dealing!"

                         For all her fighting words
she gave no overpowering aid—not yet;   240
father and son must prove their mettle still.
Into the smoky air under the roof
the goddess merely darted to perch on a blackened beam—
no figure to be seen now but a swallow.

Command of the suitors had fallen to Ageláos.
With him were Eurýnomos, Amphímedon,
Demoptólemos, Peisándros, Pólybos,
the best of the lot who stood to fight for their lives
after the streaking arrows downed the rest.
Ageláos rallied them with his plan of battle: 250

"Friends, our killer has come to the end of his rope,
and much good Mentor did him, that blowhard, dropping in.
Look, only four are left to fight, in the light there at the door.
No scattering of shots, men, no throwing away good spears;
we six will aim a volley at Odysseus alone,
and may Zeus grant us the glory of a hit.
If he goes down, the others are no problem."

[2] Predatory dogs or hawks.

At his command, then, "Ho!" they all let fly
as one man. But Athena spoiled their shots.
One hit the doorpost of the hall, another   260
stuck in the door's thick timbering, still others
rang on the stone wall, shivering hafts[3] of ash.
Seeing his men unscathed, royal Odysseus
gave the word for action.

                    "Now I say, friends,
the time is overdue to let them have it.
Battlespoil they want from our dead bodies
to add to all they plundered here before."

Taking aim over the steadied lanceheads
they all let fly together. Odysseus killed
Demoptólemos; Telémakhos   270
killed Euryádês; the swineherd, Élatos;
and Peisándros went down before the cowherd.
As these lay dying, biting the central floor,
their friends gave way and broke for the inner wall.
The four attackers followed up with a rush
to take spears from the fallen men.

                      Re-forming,
the suitors threw again with all their strength,
but Athena turned their shots, or all but two.
One hit a doorpost in the hall, another
stuck in the door's thick timbering, still others   280
rang on the stone wall, shivering hafts of ash.
Amphímedon's point bloodied Telémakhos'
wrist, a superficial wound, and Ktésippos'
long spear passing over Eumaios' shield
grazed his shoulder, hurtled on and fell.
No matter: with Odysseus the great soldier
the wounded threw again. And Odysseus raider of cities
struck Eurýdamas down. Telémakhos
hit Amphímedon, and the swineherd's shot
killed Pólybos. But Ktésippos, who had last evening thrown   290
a cow's hoof at Odysseus, got the cowherd's heavy cast
full in the chest—and dying heard him say:

"You arrogant joking bastard!
Clown, will you, like a fool, and parade your wit?
Leave jesting to the gods who do it better.
This will repay your cow's-foot courtesy
to a great wanderer come home."

                      The master
of the black herds had answered Ktésippos.

[3] Shafts.

Odysseus, lunging at close quarters, put a spear
through Ageláos, Damástor's son. Telémakhos   300
hit Leókritos from behind and pierced him,
kidney to diaphragm. Speared off his feet,
he fell face downward on the ground.

At this moment that unmanning thunder cloud,
the aegis,[4] Athena's shield,
took form aloft in the great hall.

                           And the suitors mad with fear
at her great sign stampeded like stung cattle by a river
when the dread shimmering gadfly strikes in summer,
in the flowering season, in the long-drawn days.
After them the attackers wheeled, as terrible as falcons   310
from eyries in the mountains veering over and diving down
with talons wide unsheathed on flights of birds,
who cower down the sky in chutes and bursts along the valley—
but the pouncing falcons grip their prey, no frantic wing avails,
and farmers love to watch those beakèd hunters.
So these now fell upon the suitors in that hall,
turning, turning to strike and strike again,
while torn men moaned at death, and blood ran smoking
over the whole floor.

                                 Now there was one
who turned and threw himself at Odysseus' knees—   320
Leódês, begging for his life:

                                         "Mercy,

mercy on a suppliant, Odysseus!
Never by word or act of mine, I swear,
was any woman troubled here. I told the rest
to put an end to it. They would not listen,
would not keep their hands from brutishness,
and now they are all dying like dogs for it.
I had no part in what they did: my part
was visionary—reading the smoke of sacrifice.
Scruples go unrewarded if I die."   330

The shrewd fighter frowned over him and said:

"You were diviner to this crowd? How often
you must have prayed my sweet day of return
would never come, or not for years!—and prayed
to have my dear wife, and beget children on her.
No plea like yours could save you
from this hard bed of death. Death it shall be!"

He picked up Ageláos' broadsword
from where it lay, flung by the slain man,

---

[4] The shield of Zeus, lent by him to Athena.

and gave Leódês' neck a lopping blow   340
so that his head went down to mouth in dust.

One more who had avoided furious death
was the son of Terpis, Phêmios, the minstrel,
singer by compulsion to the suitors.
He stood now with his harp, holy and clear,
in the wall's recess, under the window, wondering
if he should flee that way to the courtyard altar,
sanctuary of Zeus, the Enclosure God.
Thighbones in hundreds had been offered there
by Laërtês and Odysseus. No, he thought;   350
the more direct way would be best—to go
humbly to his lord. But first to save
his murmuring instrument he laid it down
carefully between the winebowl and a chair,
then he betook himself to Lord Odysseus,
clung hard to his knees, and said:

                                                            "Mercy,

mercy on a suppliant, Odysseus!
My gift is song for men and for the gods undying.
My death will be remorse for you hereafter.
No one taught me: deep in my mind a god   360
shaped all the various ways of life in song.
And I am fit to make verse in your company
as in the god's. Put aside lust for blood.
Your own dear son Telémakhos can tell you,
never by my own will or for love
did I feast here or sing amid the suitors.
They were too strong, too many; they compelled me."

Telémakhos in the elation of battle
heard him. He at once called to his father:

"Wait: that one is innocent: don't hurt him.   370
And we should let our herald live—Medôn;
he cared for me from boyhood. Where is *he?*
Has he been killed already by Philoítios
or by the swineherd? Else he got an arrow
in that first gale of bowshots down the room."

Now this came to the ears of prudent Medôn
under the chair where he had gone to earth,
pulling a new-flayed bull's hide over him.
Quiet he lay while blinding death passed by.
Now heaving out from under   380
he scrambled for Telémakhos' knees and said:

"Here I am, dear prince; but rest your spear!
Tell your great father not to see in me

a suitor for the sword's edge—one of those
who laughed at you and ruined his property!"

The lord of all the tricks of war surveyed
this fugitive and smiled. He said:

"Courage: my son has dug you out and saved you.
Take it to heart, and pass the word along:
fair dealing brings more profit in the end.   390
Now leave this room. Go and sit down outdoors
where there's no carnage, in the court,
you and the poet with his many voices,
while I attend to certain chores inside."

At this the two men stirred and picked their way
to the door and out, and sat down at the altar,
looking around with wincing eyes
as though the sword's edge hovered still.
And Odysseus looked around him, narrow-eyed,
for any others who had lain hidden   400
while death's black fury passed.

                                    In blood and dust
he saw that crowd all fallen, many and many slain.

Think of a catch that fishermen haul in to a halfmoon bay
in a fine-meshed net from the white-caps of the sea:
how all are poured out on the sand, in throes for the salt sea,
twitching their cold lives away in Hêlios' fiery air:
so lay the suitors heaped on one another.

Odysseus at length said to his son:

"Go tell old Nurse. I'll have a word with her.
What's to be done now weighs on my mind."   410

Telémakhos knocked at the women's door and called:

"Eurýkleia, come out here! Move, old woman.
You kept your eye on all our servant girls.
Jump, my father is here and wants to see you."

His call brought no reply, only the doors
were opened, and she came. Telémakhos
led her forward. In the shadowy hall
full of dead men she found his father
spattered and caked with blood like a mountain lion
when he has gorged upon an ox, his kill—   420
with hot blood glistening over his whole chest,
smeared on his jaws, baleful and terrifying—
even so encrimsoned was Odysseus
up to his thighs and armpits. As she gazed

from all the corpses to the bloody man
she raised her head to cry over his triumph,
but felt his grip upon her, checking her.
Said the great soldier then:

"Rejoice

inwardly. No crowing aloud, old woman.
To glory over slain men is no piety.   430
Destiny and the gods' will vanquished these,
and their own hardness. They respected no one,
good or bad, who came their way.
For this, and folly, a bad end befell them.
Your part is now to tell me of the women,
those who dishonored me, and the innocent."

His own old nurse Eurýkleia said:

"I will, then.

Child, you know you'll have the truth from me.
Fifty all told they are, your female slaves,
trained by your lady and myself in service,   440
wool carding and the rest of it, and taught
to be submissive. Twelve went bad,
flouting me, flouting Penélopê, too.
Telémakhos being barely grown, his mother
would never let him rule the serving women—
but you must let me go to her lighted rooms
and tell her. Some god sent her a drift of sleep."

But in reply the great tactician said:

"Not yet. Do not awake her. Tell those women
who were the suitors' harlots to come here."   450

She went back on this mission through his hall.
Then he called Telémakhos to his side
and the two herdsmen. Sharply Odysseus said:

"These dead must be disposed of first of all.
Direct the women. Tables and chairs will be
scrubbed with sponges, rinsed and rinsed again.
When our great room is fresh and put in order,
take them outside, these women,
between the roundhouse⁵ and the palisade,
and hack them with your swordblades till you cut   460
the life out of them, and every thought of sweet
Aphroditê under the rutting suitors,
when they lay down in secret."

---

⁵ A building, with a cone-shaped roof, near the wall surrounding the courtyard; probably a place for storing implements.

As he spoke
here came the women in a bunch, all wailing,
soft tears on their cheeks. They fell to work
to lug the corpses out into the courtyard
under the gateway, propping one
against another as Odysseus ordered,
for he himself stood over them. In fear
these women bore the cold weight of the dead.   470
The next thing was to scrub off chairs and tables
and rinse them down. Telémakhos and the herdsman
scraped the packed earth floor with hoes, but made
the women carry out all blood and mire.
When the great room was cleaned up once again,
at swordpoint they forced them out, between
the roundhouse and the palisade, pell-mell
to huddle in that dead end without exit.
Telémakhos, who knew his mind,[6] said curtly:

"I would not give the clean death of a beast   480
to trulls[7] who made a mockery of my mother
and of me too—you sluts, who lay with suitors."

He tied one end of a hawser to a pillar
and passed the other about the roundhouse top,
taking the slack up, so that no one's toes
could touch the ground. They would be hung like doves
or larks in springès[8] triggered in a thicket,
where the birds think to rest—a cruel nesting.
So now in turn each woman thrust her head
into a noose and swung, yanked high in air,   490
to perish there most piteously.
Their feet danced for a little, but not long.

From storeroom to the court they brought Melánthios,
chopped with swords to cut his nose and ears off,
pulled off his genitals to feed the dogs
and raging hacked his hands and feet away.

As their own hands and feet called for a washing,
they went indoors to Odysseus again.
Their work was done. He told Eurýkleia:

"Bring me
brimstone[9] and a brazier—medicinal   500
fumes to purify my hall. Then tell

[6] Telémakhos departs from Odysseus' instructions; he gives the offending women a
dishonorable death by hanging rather than death by the knife or sword, as in the ritual
sacrifice of an innocent animal.
[7] Harlots.
[8] Nooses, attached to tied branches, used to trap birds and other small animals.
[9] Sulfur.

Penélopê to come, and bring her maids.
All servants round the house must be called in."

His own old nurse Eurýkleia replied:

"Aye, surely that is well said, child. But let me
find you a good clean shirt and cloak and dress you.
You must not wrap your shoulders' breadth again
in rags in your own hall. That would be shameful."

Odysseus answered:

                         "Let me have the fire.
The first thing is to purify this place."   510

With no more chat Eurýkleia obeyed
and fetched out fire and brimstone. Cleansing fumes
he sent through court and hall and storage chamber.
Then the old woman hurried off again
to the women's quarters to announce her news,
and all the servants came now, bearing torches
in twilight, crowding to embrace Odysseus,
taking his hands to kiss, his head and shoulders,
while he stood there, nodding to every one,
and overcome by longing and by tears.   520

BOOK TWENTY-THREE: THE TRUNK OF
THE OLIVE TREE

The old nurse went upstairs exulting,
with knees toiling, and patter of slapping feet,
to tell the mistress of her lord's return,
and cried out by the lady's pillow:

                                    "Wake,
wake up, dear child! Penélopê, come down,
see with your own eyes what all these years you longed for!
Odysseus is here! Oh, in the end, he came!
And he has killed your suitors, killed them all
who made his house a bordel[1] and ate his cattle
and raised their hands against his son!"

                                  Penélopê said: 10

"Dear nurse . . . the gods have touched you.
They can put chaos into the clearest head
or bring a lunatic down to earth. Good sense
you always had. They've touched you. What is this

---

[1] Bordello; brothel.

mockery you wake me up to tell me,
breaking in on my sweet spell of sleep?
I had not dozed away so tranquilly
since my lord went to war, on that ill wind
to Ilion.

                                        Oh, leave me! Back down stairs!
If any other of my women came in babbling   20
things like these to startle me, I'd see her
flogged out of the house! Your old age spares you that."

Eurýkleia said:

"Would I play such a trick on you, dear child?
It is true, true, as I tell you, he has come!
That stranger they were baiting was Odysseus.
Telémakhos knew it days ago—
cool head, never to give his father away,
till he paid off those swollen dogs!"

The lady in her heart's joy now sprang up   30
with sudden dazzling tears, and hugged the old one,
crying out:

                                        "But try to make it clear!
If he came home in secret, as you say,
could he engage them singlehanded? How?
They were all down there, still in the same crowd."

To this Eurýkleia said:

                                        "I did not see it,
I knew nothing; only I heard the groans
of men dying. We sat still in the inner rooms
holding our breath, and marvelling, shut in,
until Telémakhos came to the door and called me—   40
your own dear son, sent this time by his father!
So I went out, and found Odysseus
erect, with dead men littering the floor
this way and that. If you had only seen him!
It would have made your heart glow hot!—a lion
splashed with mire and blood.

                                        But now the cold
corpses are all gathered at the gate,
and he has cleansed his hall with fire and brimstone,
a great blaze. Then he sent me here to you.
Come with me: you may both embark this time   50
for happiness together, after pain,
after long years. Here is your prayer, your passion,
granted: your own lord lives, he is at home,
he found you safe, he found his son. The suitors
abused his house, but he has brought them down."

The attentive lady said:

                                                    "Do not lose yourself
in this rejoicing: wait: you know
how splendid that return would be for us,
how dear to me, dear to his son and mine;
but no, it is not possible, your notion   60
must be wrong.

                               Some god has killed the suitors,
a god, sick of their arrogance and brutal
malice—for they honored no one living,
good or bad, who ever came their way.
Blind young fools, they've tasted death for it.
But the true person of Odysseus?
He lost his home, he died far from Akhaia."

The old nurse sighed:

                                    "How queer, the way you talk!
Here he is, large as life, by his own fire,
and you deny he ever will get home!   70
Child, you always were mistrustful!
But there is one sure mark that I can tell you:
that scar left by the boar's tusk long ago.
I recognized it when I bathed his feet
and would have told you, but he stopped my mouth,
forbade me, in his craftiness.

                                              Come down,
I stake my life on it, he's here!
Let me die in agony if I lie!"

                                        Penélopê said:

"Nurse dear, though you have your wits about you,
still it is hard not to be taken in   80
by the immortals. Let us join my son, though,
and see the dead and that strange one who killed them."

She turned then to descend the stair, her heart
in tumult. Had she better keep her distance
and question him, her husband? Should she run
up to him, take his hands, kiss him now?
Crossing the door sill she sat down at once
in firelight, against the nearest wall,
across the room from the lord Odysseus.

                                              There
leaning against a pillar, sat the man   90
and never lifted up his eyes, but only waited
for what his wife would say when she had seen him.
And she, for a long time, sat deathly still
in wonderment—for sometimes as she gazed

she found him—yes, clearly—like her husband,
but sometimes blood and rags were all she saw.
Telémakhos' voice came to her ears:

                                                         "Mother,
cruel mother, do you feel nothing,
drawing yourself apart this way from Father?
Will you not sit with him and talk and question him?   100
What other woman could remain so cold?
Who shuns her lord, and he come back to her
from wars and wandering, after twenty years?
Your heart is hard as flint and never changes!"

Penélopê answered:

                                       "I am stunned, child.
I cannot speak to him. I cannot question him.
I cannot keep my eyes upon his face.
If really he is Odysseus, truly home,
beyond all doubt we two shall know each other
better than you or anyone. There are   110
secret signs we know, we two."

                                            A smile
came now to the lips of the patient hero, Odysseus,
who turned to Telémakhos and said:

"Peace: let your mother test me at her leisure.
Before long she will see and know me best.
These tatters, dirt—all that I'm caked with now—
make her look hard at me and doubt me still.
As to this massacre, we must see the end.
Whoever kills one citizen, you know,
and has no force of armed men at his back,   120
had better take himself abroad by night
and leave his kin. Well, we cut down the flower of Ithaka,
the mainstay of the town. Consider that."

Telémakhos replied respectfully:

                                            "Dear Father,
enough that you yourself study the danger,
foresighted in combat as you are,
they say you have no rival.

                                       We three stand
ready to follow you and fight. I say
for what our strength avails, we have the courage."

And the great tactician, Odysseus, answered:

                                            "Good.   130
Here is our best maneuver, as I see it:
bathe, you three, and put fresh clothing on,

order the women to adorn themselves,
and let our admirable harper choose a tune
for dancing, some lighthearted air, and strum it.
Anyone going by, or any neighbor,
will think it is a wedding feast he hears.
These deaths must not be cried about the town
till we can slip away to our own woods. We'll see
what weapon, then, Zeus puts into our hands." 140

They listened attentively, and did his bidding,
bathed and dressed afresh; and all the maids
adorned themselves. Then Phêmios the harper
took his polished shell and plucked the strings,
moving the company to desire
for singing, for the sway and beat of dancing,
until they made the manor hall resound
with gaiety of men and grace of women.
Anyone passing on the road would say:

"Married at last, I see—the queen so many courted. 150
Sly, cattish wife! She would not keep—not she!—
the lord's estate until he came."

                                        So travellers'
thoughts might run—but no one guessed the truth.
Greathearted Odysseus, home at last,
was being bathed now by Eurýnomê
and rubbed with golden oil, and clothed again
in a fresh tunic and a cloak. Athena
lent him beauty, head to foot. She made him
taller, and massive, too, with crisping hair
in curls like petals of wild hyacinth 160
but all red-golden. Think of gold infused
on silver by a craftsman, whose fine art
Hephaistos taught him, or Athena: one
whose work moves to delight: just so she lavished
beauty over Odysseus' head and shoulders.
He sat then in the same chair by the pillar,
facing his silent wife, and said:

                                "Strange woman,
the immortals of Olympos made you hard,
harder than any. Who else in the world
would keep aloof as you do from her husband 170
if he returned to her from years of trouble,
cast on his own land in the twentieth year?

Nurse, make up a bed for me to sleep on.
Her heart is iron in her breast."

Penélopê

spoke to Odysseus now. She said:

"Strange man,

if man you are . . . This is no pride on my part
nor scorn for you—not even wonder, merely.
I know so well how you—how he—appeared
boarding the ship for Troy. But all the same . . .

Make up his bed for him, Eurýkleia.   180
Place it outside the bedchamber my lord
built with his own hands. Pile the big bed
with fleeces, rugs, and sheets of purest linen."

With this she tried him to the breaking point,
and he turned on her in a flash raging:

"Woman, by heaven you've stung me now!
Who dared to move my bed?
No builder had the skill for that—unless
a god came down to turn the trick. No mortal
in his best days could budge it with a crowbar.   190
There is our pact and pledge, our secret sign,
built into that bed—my handiwork
and no one else's!

An old trunk of olive
grew like a pillar on the building plot,
and I laid out our bedroom round that tree,
lined up the stone walls, built the walls and roof,
gave it a doorway and smooth-fitting doors.
Then I lopped off the silvery leaves and branches,
hewed and shaped that stump from the roots up
into a bedpost, drilled it, let it serve   200
as model for the rest. I planed them all,[2]
inlaid them all with silver, gold and ivory,
and stretched a bed between—a pliant web
of oxhide thongs dyed crimson.

There's our sign!
I know no more. Could someone else's hand
have sawn that trunk and dragged the frame away?"

Their secret! as she heard it told, her knees
grew tremulous and weak, her heart failed her.
With eyes brimming tears she ran to him,
throwing her arms around his neck, and kissed him,   210
murmuring:

"Do not rage at me, Odysseus!
No one ever matched your caution! Think
what difficulty the gods gave: they denied us

[2] That is, planed all the bedposts, of which one was the shaped tree trunk.

life together in our prime and flowering years,
kept us from crossing into age together.
Forgive me, don't be angry. I could not
welcome you with love on sight! I armed myself
long ago against the frauds of men,
impostors who might come—and all those many
whose underhanded ways bring evil on! 　　　　　220
Helen of Argos, daughter of Zeus and Leda,
would she have joined the stranger,[3] lain with him,
if she had known her destiny? known the Akhaians
in arms would bring her back to her own country?
Surely a goddess moved her to adultery,
her blood unchilled by war and evil coming,
the years, the desolation; ours, too.
But here and now, what sign could be so clear
as this of our own bed?
No other man has ever laid eyes on it— 　　　　　230
only my own slave, Aktoris, that my father
sent with me as a gift—she kept our door.
You make my stiff heart know that I am yours."

Now from his breast into his eyes the ache
of longing mounted, and he wept at last,
his dear wife, clear and faithful, in his arms,
longed for
　　　　　　as the sunwarmed earth is longed for by a swimmer
spent in rough water where his ship went down
under Poseidon's blows, gale winds and tons of sea.
Few men can keep alive through a big surf 　　　　　240
to crawl, clotted with brine, on kindly beaches
in joy, in joy, knowing the abyss behind:
and so she too rejoiced, her gaze upon her husband,
her white arms round him pressed as though forever.

The rose Dawn might have found them weeping still
had not grey-eyed Athena slowed the night
when night was most profound, and held the Dawn
under the Ocean of the East. That glossy team,
Firebright and Daybright, the Dawn's horses
that draw her heavenward for men—Athena 　　　　　250
stayed their harnessing.
　　　　　　　　　　　Then said Odysseus:

"My dear, we have not won through to the end.
One trial—I do not know how long—is left for me
to see fulfilled. Teirêsias' ghost forewarned me[4]
the night I stood upon the shore of Death, asking

---

[3] Paris, the Trojan guest of Meneláos and Helen, with whom she ran away.
[4] See Book XI.

about my friends' homecoming and my own.
But now the hour grows late, it is bed time,
rest will be sweet for us; let us lie down."

To this Penélopê replied:

                                                        "That bed,
that rest is yours whenever desire moves you,   260
now the kind powers have brought you home at last.
But as your thought has dwelt upon it, tell me:
what is the trial you face? I must know soon;
what does it matter if I learn tonight?"

The teller of many stories said:

                                                "My strange one,
must you again, and even now,
urge me to talk? Here is a plodding tale;
no charm in it, no relish in the telling.
Teirêsias told me I must take an oar
and trudge the mainland, going from town to town,   270
until I discover men who have never known
the salt blue sea, nor flavor of salt meat—
strangers to painted prows, to watercraft
and oars like wings, dipping across the water.
The moment of revelation he foretold
was this, for you may share the prophecy:
some traveller falling in with me will say:
'A winnowing fan, that on your shoulder, sir?'
There I must plant my oar,[5] on the very spot,
with burnt offerings to Poseidon of the Waters: 280
a ram, a bull, a great buck boar. Thereafter
when I come home again, I am to slay
full hekatombs to the gods who own broad heaven,
one by one.
                                Then death will drift upon me
from seaward, mild as air, mild as your hand,
in my well-tended weariness of age,
contented folk around me on our island.
He said all this must come."

                                        Penélopê said:

"If by the gods' grace age at least is kind,
we have that promise—trials will end in peace."   290

So he confided in her, and she answered.
Meanwhile Eurýnomê and the nurse together
laid soft coverlets on the master's bed,

---

[5] The point of this gesture would be to appease the sea-god by spreading his fame even into
places where the sea is unknown. This excursion does not, in fact, take place in the *Odyssey*.

working in haste by torchlight. Eurýkleia
retired to her quarters for the night,
and then Eurýnomê, as maid-in-waiting,
lighted her lord and lady to their chamber
with bright brands.

                         She vanished.

                                   So they came

into that bed so steadfast, loved of old,
opening glad arms to one another.   300
Telémakhos by now had hushed the dancing,
hushed the women. In the darkened hall
he and the cowherd and the swineherd slept.

The royal pair mingled in love again
and afterward lay revelling in stories:
hers of the siege her beauty stood at home
from arrogant suitors, crowding on her sight,
and how they fed their courtship on his cattle,
oxen and fat sheep, and drank up rivers
of wine out of the vats.

                         Odysseus told   310

of what hard blows he had dealt out to others
and of what blows he had taken—all that story.
She could not close her eyes till all was told.

His raid on the Kikonês, first of all,
then how he visited the Lotos Eaters,
and what the Kyklops did, and how those shipmates,
pitilessly devoured, were avenged.
Then of his touching Aiolos's isle
and how that king refitted him for sailing
to Ithaka; all vain: gales blew him back   320
groaning over the fishcold sea. Then how
he reached the Laistrygonians' distant bay
and how they smashed his ships and his companions.
Kirkê, then: of her deceits and magic,
then of his voyage to the wide underworld
of dark, the house of Death, and questioning
Teirêsias, Theban spirit.

                         Dead companions,

many, he saw there, and his mother, too.
Of this he told his wife, and told how later
he heard the choir of maddening Seirênês,   330
coasted the Wandering Rocks, Kharybdis' pool
and the fiend Skylla who takes toll of men.
Then how his shipmates killed Lord Hêlios' cattle
and how Zeus thundering in towering heaven
split their fast ship with his fuming bolt,
so all hands perished.

                                                        He alone survived,
cast away on Kalypso's isle, Ogýgia.
He told, then, how that nymph detained him there
in her smooth caves, craving him for her husband,
and how in her devoted lust she swore   340
he should not die nor grow old, all his days,
but he held out against her.

                                                        Last of all

what sea-toil brought him to the Phaiákians;
their welcome; how they took him to their hearts
and gave him passage to his own dear island
with gifts of garments, gold and bronze . . .

                                                        Remembering,

he drowsed over the story's end. Sweet sleep
relaxed his limbs and his care-burdened breast.

Other affairs were in Athena's keeping.
Waiting until Odysseus had his pleasure   350
of love and sleep, the grey-eyed one bestirred
the fresh Dawn from her bed of paling Ocean
to bring up daylight to her golden chair,
and from his fleecy bed Odysseus
arose. He said to Penélopê:

                                                        "My lady,

what ordeals have we not endured! Here, waiting
you had your grief, while my return dragged out—
my hard adventures, pitting myself against
the gods' will, and Zeus, who pinned me down
far from home. But now our life resumes: 360
we've come together to our longed-for bed.
Take care of what is left me in our house;
as to the flocks that pack of wolves laid waste
they'll be replenished: scores I'll get on raids
and other scores our island friends will give me
till all the folds are full again.

                                                        This day

I'm off up country to the orchards. I must see
my noble father, for he missed me sorely.
And here is my command for you—a strict one,
though you may need none, clever as you are.   370
Word will get about as the sun goes higher
of how I killed those lads. Go to your rooms
on the upper floor, and take your women. Stay there
with never a glance outside or a word to anyone."

Fitting cuirass and swordbelt to his shoulders,
he woke his herdsmen, woke Telémakhos,
ordering all in arms. They dressed quickly,

and all in war gear sallied from the gate,
led by Odysseus.

Now it was broad day

but these three men Athena hid in darkness,
going before them swiftly from the town.

380

BOOK TWENTY-FOUR: WARRIORS, FAREWELL

Meanwhile the suitors' ghosts were called away
by Hermês of Kyllênê,[1] bearing the golden wand
with which he charms the eyes of men or wakens
whom he wills.

He waved them on, all squeaking

as bats will in a cavern's underworld,
all flitting, flitting criss-cross in the dark
if one falls and the rock-hung chain is broken.
So with faint cries the shades trailed after Hermês,
pure Deliverer.

He led them down dank ways,

over grey Ocean tides, the Snowy Rock,
past shores of Dream and narrows of the sunset,
in swift flight to where the Dead inhabit
wastes of asphodel at the world's end.

10

Crossing the plain they met Akhilleus'[2] ghost,
Patróklos and Antílokhos, then Aîas,
noblest of Danaans after Akhilleus
in strength and beauty. Here the newly dead
drifted together, whispering. Then came
the soul of Agamémnon, son of Atreus,
in black pain forever, surrounded by men-at-arms
who perished with him in Aigísthos' hall.
Akhilleus greeted him:

20

"My lord Atreidês,

we held that Zeus who loves the play of lightning
would give you length of glory, you were king
over so great a host of soldiery
before Troy, where we suffered, we Akhaians.
But in the morning of your life
you met that doom that no man born avoids.
It should have found you in your day of victory,
marshal of the army, in Troy country;

30

---

[1] Birthplace and home of Hermês, in Arcadia.
[2] The following passage mentions several heroes of the Trojan war. Patróklos and Antílokhos were especially close friends of Akhilleus.

then all Akhaia would have heaped your tomb
and saved your honor for your son. Instead
piteous death awaited you at home."

And Atreus' son replied:

"Fortunate hero,

son of Pêleus, godlike and glorious,
at Troy you died, across the sea from Argos,
and round you Trojan and Akhaian peers
fought for your corpse and died. A dustcloud wrought
by a whirlwind hid the greatness of you slain,
minding no more the mastery of horses.   40
All that day we might have toiled in battle
had not a storm from Zeus broken it off.
We carried you out of the field of war
down to the ships and bathed your comely body
with warm water and scented oil. We laid you
upon your long bed, and our officers
wept hot tears like rain and cropped their hair.
Then hearing of it in the sea, your mother, Thetis,[3]
came with nereids of the grey wave crying
unearthly lamentation over the water,   50
and trembling gripped the Akhaians to the bone.
They would have boarded ship that night and fled
except for one man's wisdom—venerable
Nestor, proven counselor in the past.
He stood and spoke to allay their fear: 'Hold fast,
sons of the Akhaians, lads of Argos.
His mother it must be, with nymphs her sisters,
come from the sea to mourn her son in death.'

Veteran hearts at this contained their dread
while at your side the daughters of the ancient   60
seagod wailed and wrapped ambrosial shrouding
around you.

Then we heard the Muses sing
a threnody[4] in nine immortal voices.
No Argive there but wept, such keening[5] rose
from that one Muse who led the song.

Now seven

days and ten, seven nights and ten, we mourned you,
we mortal men, with nymphs who know no death,

---

[3] A nereid (sea-nymph), mother of Akhilleus.
[4] Dirge; lament. The Muses are goddesses of song, literature, and the arts. Homer does not describe them elsewhere as being nine in number; this is one of several anomalies about the present scene in Hades that have caused certain commentators to reject it as unauthentic.
[5] Loud, shrill lamenting for the dead.

before we gave you to the flame, slaughtering
longhorned steers and fat sheep on your pyre.

Dressed by the nereids and embalmed with honey,   70
honey and unguent in the seething blaze,
you turned to ash. And past the pyre Akhaia's
captains paraded in review, in arms,
clattering chariot teams and infantry.
Like a forest fire the flame roared on, and burned
your flesh away. Next day at dawn, Akhilleus,
we picked your pale bones from the char to keep
in wine and oil. A golden amphora[6]
your mother gave for this—Hephaistos' work,
a gift from Dionysos.[7] In that vase,   80
Akhilleus, hero, lie your pale bones mixed
with mild Patróklos' bones, who died before you,
and nearby lie the bones of Antílokhos,
the one you cared for most of all companions
after Patróklos.
                           We of the Old Army,
we who were spearmen, heaped a tomb for these
upon a foreland over Hellê's waters,[8]
to be a mark against the sky for voyagers
in this generation and those to come.
Your mother sought from the gods magnificent trophies   90
and set them down midfield for our champions. Often
at funeral games after the death of kings
when you yourself contended, you've seen athletes
cinch their belts when trophies went on view.
But these things would have made you stare—the treasures
Thetis on her silver-slippered feet
brought to your games—for the gods held you dear.
You perished, but your name will never die.
It lives to keep all men in mind of honor
forever, Akhilleus.
                          As for myself, what joy   100
is this, to have brought off the war? Foul death
Zeus held in store for me at my coming home;
Aigísthos and my vixen cut me down."

While they conversed, the Wayfinder[9] came near,
leading the shades of suitors overthrown
by Lord Odysseus. The two souls of heroes
advanced together, scrutinizing these.

---

[6] A type of jar.   [7] God of wine and revelry.
[8] The Hellespont; the modern Dardanelles, the strait connecting the Aegean Sea with the
Sea of Marmara; located just north of Troy.
[9] Hermês.

Then Agamémnon recognized Amphímedon,
son of Meláneus—friends of his on Ithaka—
and called out to him:

                                        "Amphímedon,   110

what ruin brought you into this undergloom?
All in a body, picked men, and so young?
One could not better choose the kingdom's pride.
Were you at sea, aboard ship, and Poseidon
blew up a dire wind and foundering waves,
or cattle-raiding, were you, on the mainland,
or in a fight for some stronghold, or women,
when the foe hit you to your mortal hurt?
Tell me, answer my question. Guest and friend
I say I am of yours—or do you not remember   120
I visited your family there? I came
with Prince Meneláos, urging Odysseus
to join us in the great sea raid on Troy.
One solid month we beat our way, breasting
south sea and west, resolved to bring him round,
the wily raider of cities."

                                     The new shade said:

"O glory of commanders, Agamémnon,
all that you bring to mind I remember well.
As for the sudden manner of our death
I'll tell you of it clearly, first to last.   130
After Odysseus had been gone for years
we were all suitors of his queen. She never
quite refused, nor went through with a marriage,
hating it, ever bent on our defeat.
Here is one of her tricks: she placed her loom,
her big loom, out for weaving in her hall,
and the fine warp of some vast fabric on it.
We were attending her, and she said to us:
'Young men, my suitors, now my lord is dead,
let me finish my weaving before I marry,   140
or else my thread will have been spun in vain.
This is a shroud I weave for Lord Laërtês
when cold Death comes to lay him on his bier.
The country wives would hold me in dishonor
if he, with all his fortune, lay unshrouded.'
We had men's hearts; she touched them; we agreed.
So every day she wove on the great loom—
but every night by torchlight she unwove it,
and so for three years she deceived the Akhaians.
But when the seasons brought the fourth around,   150
as long months waned, and the slow days were spent,
one of her maids, who knew the secret, told us.

We found her unraveling the splendid shroud,
and then she had to finish, willy nilly—
finish, and show the big loom woven tight
from beam to beam with cloth. She washed the shrouding
clean as sun or moonlight.

                        Then, heaven knows
from what quarter of the world, fatality
brought in Odysseus to the swineherd's wood
far up the island. There his son went too   160
when the black ship put him ashore from Pylos.
The two together planned our death-trap. Down
they came to the famous town—Telémakhos
long in advance: we had to wait for Odysseus.
The swineherd led him to the manor later
in rags like a foul beggar, old and broken,
propped on a stick. These tatters that he wore
hid him so well that none of us could know him
when he turned up, not even the older men.
We jeered at him, took potshots at him, cursed him.   170
Daylight and evening in his own great hall
he bore it, patient as a stone. That night
the mind of Zeus beyond the stormcloud stirred him
with Telémakhos at hand to shift his arms
from mégaron to storage room and lock it.
Then he assigned his wife her part: next day
she brought his bow and iron axeheads out
to make a contest. Contest there was none;
that move doomed us to slaughter. Not a man
could bend the stiff bow to his will or string it,   180
until it reached Odysseus. We shouted,
'Keep the royal bow from the beggar's hands
no matter how he begs!' Only Telémakhos
would not be denied.

                        So the great soldier
took his bow and bent it for the bowstring
effortlessly. He drilled the axeheads clean,
sprang, and decanted arrows on the door sill,
glared, and drew again. This time he killed
Antínoös.

                       There facing us he crouched
and shot his bolts of groaning at us, brought us   190
down like sheep. Then some god, his familiar,[10]
went into action with him round the hall,
after us in a massacre. Men lay groaning,
mortally wounded, and the floor smoked with blood.

That was the way our death came, Agamémnon.
Now in Odysseus' hall untended still

---

[10] A friendly attendant spirit.

our bodies lie,[11] unknown to friends or kinsmen
who should have laid us out and washed our wounds
free of the clotted blood, and mourned our passing.
So much is due the dead."

But Agamémnon's   200
tall shade when he heard this cried aloud:

"O fortunate Odysseus, master mariner
and soldier, blessed son of old Laërtês!
The girl you brought home made a valiant wife!
True to her husband's honor and her own,
Penélopê, Ikários' faithful daughter!
The very gods themselves will sing her story
for men on earth—mistress of her own heart,
Penélopê!
Tyndáreus' daughter waited, too—how differently!   210
Klytaimnéstra, the adulteress,
waited to stab her lord and king. That song
will be forever hateful. A bad name
she gave to womankind, even the best."

These were the things they said to one another
under the rim of earth where Death is lord.

Leaving the town, Odysseus and his men
that morning reached Laërtês' garden lands,
long since won by his toil from wilderness—
his homestead, and the row of huts around it   220
where fieldhands rested, ate and slept. Indoors
he had an old slave woman, a Sikel,[12] keeping
house for him in his secluded age.

Odysseus here took leave of his companions.

"Go make yourselves at home inside," he said.
"Roast the best porker and prepare a meal.
I'll go to try my father. Will he know me?
Can he imagine it, after twenty years?"

He handed spear and shield to the two herdsmen,
and in they went, Telémakhos too. Alone   230
Odysseus walked the orchard rows and vines.
He found no trace of Dólios and his sons
nor the other slaves—all being gone that day
to clear a distant field, and drag the stones
for a boundary wall.

---

[11] It is unusual in Homer that the souls of unburied men should be admitted to Hades.
[12] Sicilian.

                                    But on a well-banked plot
Odysseus found his father in solitude
spading the earth around a young fruit tree.

He wore a tunic, patched and soiled, and leggings—
oxhide patches, bound below his knees
against the brambles; gauntlets[13] on his hands   240
and on his head a goatskin cowl of sorrow.[14]
This was the figure Prince Odysseus found—
wasted by years, racked, bowed under grief.
The son paused by a tall pear tree and wept,
then inwardly debated: should he run
forward and kiss his father, and pour out
his tale of war, adventure, and return,
or should he first interrogate him, test him?
Better that way, he thought—
first draw him out with sharp words, trouble him.   250
His mind made up, he walked ahead. Laërtês
went on digging, head down, by the sapling,
stamping the spade in. At his elbow then
his son spoke out:

                              "Old man, the orchard keeper
you work for is no townsman. A good eye
for growing things he has; there's not a nurseling,
fig tree, vine stock, olive tree or pear tree
or garden bed uncared for on this farm.
But I might add—don't take offense—your own
appearance could be tidier. Old age   260
yes—but why the squalor, and rags to boot?
It would not be for sloth, now, that your master
leaves you in this condition; neither at all
because there's any baseness in your self.
No, by your features, by the frame you have,
a man might call you kingly,
one who should bathe warm, sup well, and rest easy
in age's privilege. But tell me:
who are your masters? whose fruit trees are these
you tend here? Tell me if it's true this island   270
is Ithaka, as that fellow I fell in with
told me on the road just now? He had
a peg loose, that one: couldn't say a word
or listen when I asked about my friend,
my Ithakan friend. I asked if he were alive
or gone long since into the underworld.
I can describe him if you care to hear it:
I entertained the man in my own land
when he turned up there on a journey; never
had I a guest more welcome in my house.   280

---

[13] Gloves with protective cuffs.   [14] The goatskin cap is an expression of his mourning.

He claimed his stock was Ithakan: Laërtês
Arkeísiadês, he said his father was.
I took him home, treated him well, grew fond of him—
though we had many guests—and gave him
gifts in keeping with his quality: seven
bars of measured gold, a silver winebowl
filigreed with flowers, twelve light cloaks,
twelve rugs, robes and tunics—not to mention
his own choice of women trained in service,
the four well-favored ones he wished to take."   290

His father's eyes had filled with tears. He said:

"You've come to that man's island, right enough,
but dangerous men and fools hold power now.
You gave your gifts in vain. If you could find him
here in Ithaka alive, he'd make
return of gifts and hospitality,
as custom is, when someone has been generous.
But tell me accurately—how many years
have now gone by since that man was your guest?
your guest, my son—if he indeed existed—   300
born to ill fortune as he was. Ah, far
from those who loved him, far from his native land,
in some sea-dingle[15] fish have picked his bones,
or else he made the vultures and wild beasts
a trove[16] ashore! His mother at his bier
never bewailed him, nor did I, his father,
nor did his admirable wife, Penélopê,
who should have closed her husband's eyes in death
and cried aloud upon him as he lay.
So much is due the dead.
                         But speak out, tell me further: 310
who are you, of what city and family?
where have you moored the ship that brought you here,
where is your admirable crew? Are you a peddler
put ashore by the foreign ship you came on?"

Again Odysseus had a fable ready.

"Yes," he said, "I can tell you all those things.
I come from Rover's Passage where my home is,
and I'm King Allwoes' only son. My name
is Quarrelman.[17]
                    Heaven's power in the westwind
drove me this way from Sikania,[18]   320
off my course. My ship lies in a barren

---

[15] Dell; valley.   [16] A valuable find.
[17] Rover's Passage, Allwoes, and Quarrelman are imaginary assumed (though appropriate)
names.
[18] Sicily, perhaps.

cove beyond the town there. As for Odysseus,
now is the fifth year since he put to sea
and left my homeland—bound for death, you say.
Yet landbirds flying from starboard crossed his bow—
a lucky augury. So we parted joyously,
in hope of friendly days and gifts to come."

A cloud of pain had fallen on Laërtês.
Scooping up handfuls of the sunburnt dust
he sifted it over his grey head, and groaned,   330
and the groan went to the son's heart. A twinge
prickling up through his nostrils warned Odysseus
he could not watch this any longer.
He leaped and threw his arms around his father,
kissed him, and said:

                              "Oh, Father, I am he!
Twenty years gone, and here I've come again
to my own land!

                        Hold back your tears! No grieving!
I bring good news—though still we cannot rest.
I killed the suitors to the last man!
Outrage and injury have been avenged!"   340

Laërtês turned and found his voice to murmur:

"If you are Odysseus, my son, come back,
give me some proof, a sign to make me sure."

His son replied:

                              "The scar then, first of all.
Look, here the wild boar's flashing tusk
wounded me on Parnassos; do you see it?
You and my mother made me go, that time,
to visit Lord Autólykos, her father,
for gifts he promised years before on Ithaka.
Again—more proof—let's say the trees you gave me   350
on this revetted[19] plot of orchard once.
I was a small boy at your heels, wheedling
amid the young trees, while you named each one.
You gave me thirteen pear, ten apple trees,
and forty fig trees. Fifty rows of vines
were promised too, each one to bear in turn.
Bunches of every hue would hang there ripening,
weighed down by the god of summer days."

The old man's knees failed him, his heart grew faint,
recalling all that Odysseus calmly told.   360

[19]Buttressed by stones.

He clutched his son. Odysseus held him swooning
until he got his breath back and his spirit
and spoke again:

                        "Zeus, Father! Gods above!—
you still hold pure Olympos, if the suitors
paid for their crimes indeed, and paid in blood!
But now the fear is in me that all Ithaka
will be upon us. They'll send messengers
to stir up every city of the islands."

Odysseus the great tactician answered:

"Courage, and leave the worrying to me.   370
We'll turn back to your homestead by the orchard.
I sent the cowherd, swineherd, and Telémakhos
ahead to make our noonday meal."

                                                    Conversing

in this vein they went home, the two together,
into the stone farmhouse. There Telémakhos
and the two herdsmen were already carving
roast young pork, and mixing amber wine.
During these preparations the Sikel woman
bathed Laërtês and anointed him,
and dressed him in a new cloak. Then Athena,   380
standing by, filled out his limbs again,
gave girth and stature to the old field captain
fresh from the bathing place. His son looked on
in wonder at the godlike bloom upon him,
and called out happily:

                                    "Oh, Father,
surely one of the gods who are young forever
has made you magnificent before my eyes!"

Clearheaded Laërtês faced him, saying:

"By Father Zeus, Athena and Apollo,
I wish I could be now as once I was,   390
commander of Kephallenians,[20] when I took
the walled town, Nérikos, on the promontory!
Would god I had been young again last night
with armor on me, standing in our hall
to fight the suitors at your side! How many
knees I could have crumpled, to your joy!"

While son and father spoke, cowherd and swineherd
attended, waiting, for the meal was ready.

[20] Inhabitants of the large island (modern Cephalonia) near Ithaka. Nérikos is on a nearby
island.

Soon they were all seated, and their hands
picked up the meat and bread.

                                        But now old Dólios   400
appeared in the bright doorway with his sons,
work-stained from the field. Laërtês' housekeeper,
who reared the boys and tended Dólios
in his bent age, had gone to fetch them in.
When it came over them who the stranger was
they halted in astonishment. Odysseus
hit an easy tone with them. Said he:

"Sit down and help yourselves. Shake off your wonder.
Here we've been waiting for you all this time,
and our mouths watering for good roast pig!"   410

But Dólios came forward, arms outstretched,
and kissed Odysseus' hand at the wrist bone,
crying out:

                            "Dear master, you returned!
You came to us again! How we had missed you!
We thought you lost. The gods themselves have brought you!
Welcome, welcome; health and blessings on you!
And tell me, now, just one thing more: Penélopê,
does she know yet that you are on the island?
or should we send a messenger?"

Odysseus gruffly said,

                                "Old man, she knows.   420
Is it for you to think of her?"

                                        So Dólios
quietly took a smooth bench at the table
and in their turn his sons welcomed Odysseus,
kissing his hands; then each went to his chair
beside his father. Thus our friends
were occupied in Laërtês' house at noon.

Meanwhile to the four quarters of the town
the news ran: bloody death had caught the suitors;
and men and women in a murmuring crowd
gathered before Odysseus' hall. They gave   430
burial to the piteous dead, or bore
the bodies of young men from other islands
down to the port, thence to be ferried home.
Then all the men went grieving to assembly
and being seated, rank by rank, grew still,
as old Eupeithês rose to address them. Pain
lay in him like a brand for Antínoös,

the first man that Odysseus brought down,
and tears flowed for his son as he began:

"Heroic feats that fellow did for us   440
Akhaians, friends! Good spearmen by the shipload
he led to war and lost—lost ships and men,
and once ashore again killed these, who were
the islands' pride.

                                        Up with you! After him!—
before he can take flight to Pylos town
or hide at Elis, under Epeian law!
We'd be disgraced forever! Mocked for generations
if we cannot avenge our sons' blood, and our brothers!
Life would turn to ashes—at least for me;
rather be dead and join the dead!

                                              I say   450

we ought to follow now, or they'll gain time
and make the crossing."

                                    His appeal, his tears,
moved all the gentry listening there;
but now they saw the crier and the minstrel
come from Odysseus' hall, where they had slept.
The two men stood before the curious crowd,
and Medôn said:

                          "Now hear me, men of Ithaka.
When these hard deeds were done by Lord Odysseus
the immortal gods were not far off. I saw
with my own eyes someone divine who fought   460
beside him, in the shape and dress of Mentor;
it was a god who shone before Odysseus,
a god who swept the suitors down the hall
dying in droves."

                            At this pale fear assailed them,
and next they heard again the old forecaster,
Halithérsês Mastóridês. Alone
he saw the field of time, past and to come.
In his anxiety for them he said:

"Ithakans, now listen to what I say.
Friends, by your own fault these deaths came to pass.   470
You would not heed me nor the captain, Mentor;
would not put down the riot of your sons.
Heroic feats they did!—all wantonly
raiding a great man's flocks, dishonoring
his queen, because they thought he'd come no more.
Let matters rest; do as I urge; no chase,
or he who wants a bloody end will find it."

The greater number stood up shouting "Aye!"
But many held fast, sitting all together
in no mind to agree with him. Eupeithês   480
had won them to his side. They ran for arms,
clapped on their bronze, and mustered
under Eupeithês at the town gate
for his mad foray.

                              Vengeance would be his,
he thought, for his son's murder; but that day
held bloody death for him and no return.

At this point, querying Zeus, Athena said:

"O Father of us all and king of kings,
enlighten me. What is your secret will?
War and battle, worse and more of it,   490
or can you not impose a pact on both?"

The summoner of cloud replied:

                                         "My child,
why this formality of inquiry?
Did you not plan that action by yourself—
see to it that Odysseus, on his homecoming,
should have their blood?

                              Conclude it as you will.
There is one proper way, if I may say so:
Odysseus' honor being satisfied,
let him be king by a sworn pact forever,
and we, for our part, will blot out the memory   500
of sons and brothers slain. As in the old time
let men of Ithaka henceforth be friends;
prosperity enough, and peace attend them."

Athena needed no command, but down
in one spring she descended from Olympos
just as the company of Odysseus finished
wheat crust and honeyed wine, and heard him say:

"Go out, someone, and see if they are coming."

One of the boys went to the door as ordered
and saw the townsmen in the lane. He turned   510
swiftly to Odysseus.

                              "Here they come,"
he said, "best arm ourselves, and quickly."

All up at once, the men took helm and shield—
four fighting men, counting Odysseus,
with Dólios' half dozen sons. Laërtês

armed as well, and so did Dólios—
greybeards, they could be fighters in a pinch.
Fitting their plated helmets on their heads
they sallied out, Odysseus in the lead.

Now from the air Athena, Zeus's daughter,   . 520
appeared in Mentor's guise, with Mentor's voice,
making Odysseus' heart grow light. He said
to put cheer in his son:

                                       "Telémakhos,

you are going into battle against pikemen
where hearts of men are tried. I count on you
to bring no shame upon your forefathers.
In fighting power we have excelled this lot
in every generation."

                                     Said his son:

"If you are curious, Father, watch and see
the stuff that's in me. No more talk of shame."   530

And old Laërtês cried aloud:
"Ah, what a day for me, dear gods!
to see my son and grandson vie in courage!"

Athena halted near him, and her eyes
shone like the sea. She said:

                                     "Arkeísiadês,

dearest of all my old brothers-in-arms,
invoke the grey-eyed one and Zeus her father,
heft your spear and make your throw."

Power flowed into him from Pallas Athena,
whom he invoked as Zeus's virgin child,   540
and he let fly his heavy spear.

                                     It struck

Eupeithês on the cheek plate of his helmet,
and undeflected the bronze head punched through.
He toppled, and his armor clanged upon him.
Odysseus and his son now furiously
closed, laying on with broadswords, hand to hand,
and pikes: they would have cut the enemy down
to the last man, leaving not one survivor,
had not Athena raised a shout
that stopped all fighters in their tracks.

                                  "Now hold!"   550

she cried, "Break off this bitter skirmish;
end your bloodshed, Ithakans, and make peace."

Their faces paled with dread before Athena,
and swords dropped from their hands unnerved, to lie
strewing the ground, at the great voice of the goddess.
Those from the town turned fleeing for their lives.
But with a cry to freeze their hearts
and ruffling like an eagle on the pounce,
the lord Odysseus reared himself to follow—
at which the son of Kronos dropped a thunderbolt   560
smoking at his daughter's feet.

                                                                    Athena

cast a grey glance at her friend and said:

"Son of Laërtês and the gods of old,
Odysseus, master of land ways and sea ways,
command yourself. Call off this battle now,
or Zeus who views the wide world may be angry."

He yielded to her, and his heart was glad.
Both parties later swore to terms of peace
set by their arbiter, Athena, daughter
of Zeus who bears the stormcloud as a shield—   570
though still she kept the form and voice of Mentor.

Sappho
(Seventh Century B.C. to Sixth Century B.C.)

What we know about Sappho can be briefly stated: She lived in the late seventh and early sixth centuries B.C.; she was born and spent most of her life on the island of Lesbos in the Aegean Sea; her mother's name was Cleis; she had a daughter also named Cleis; her husband's name was Cercolas (probably); she had two brothers named Charaxos and Larichos and possibly a third named Eurygyos; she had a number of young female companions, perhaps her students; and she wrote magnificent poetry. The voice of this earliest woman poet is intensely personal and intensely musical even in the muffled and distorted form in which it has reached us.

Sappho was well known in classical times. She seems to have been rather prolific, writing perhaps five hundred poems, and she was widely quoted by critics, commentators, and grammarians down through late Roman times. She was one of the poets most parodied on the late Greek comic stage; at least six Greek comedies dealt with her (all are now lost). From these plays sprang a number of legends about Sappho—that she was short, dark, and ugly ("a nightingale with misshapen wings"), that she was a prostitute, and that she died by throwing herself off the Leucadian cliffs when her love for a ferryman named Phaon was not reciprocated. All these legends are now thoroughly discredited.

The earliest surviving manuscript of Sappho's poems dates from the third century

B.C., hundreds of years after her death, and its link with what she actually composed is indirect, depending on a long chain of singers who, over that time, transmitted the lyrics orally, at some undetermined point putting them into writing. Sappho was literally a lyric poet, singing or chanting the poems to her own accompaniment on the lyre, and she may never have put them into writing herself at all. The method of transmission, then, was one obstacle to the accurate preservation of her texts.

But Sappho's reputation as a lesbian (in a sexual as well as a geographical sense) was also a major reason why so little of her work survives. Even in classical times, her homosexuality was the source of some disapproval; Ovid wrote that she "taught how to love girls." But this mild disapproval hardened into hatred in the early Middle Ages. About 380 A.D., St. Gregory of Nazianzos, Bishop of Constantinople, ordered all copies of Sappho's works burned wherever they were found, and again in the eleventh century Pope Gregory VII ordered her poems publicly burned in Rome and Constantinople. As a result of such attacks and of the general loss of classical manuscripts during the Middle Ages, not a single collection of Sappho's poems survived the medieval period.

Interest in Sappho reawakened in the Renaissance, however, and scholars attempted to reconstruct her work by assembling all the lines quoted by other Greek and Latin writers. Longinus' Essay on the Sublime, *for example, contained the complete text of Sappho's "He is more than a hero" (number 39 in this text), and Dionysios of Halikarnassos'* Treatise on Style *contained all of "Prayer to Aphrodite" (number 38). Even so, the results were pitifully small.*

And then, incredibly, in 1879, new poems by Sappho were discovered in an ancient rubbish heap in Egypt; further manuscripts came to light during a series of archeological expeditions in the 1890's. Papyrus scrolls upon which the poems had been copied had been torn, lengthwise, into strips and used as mummy wrappings. Others had been used to stuff mummified crocodiles. As a result of this shredding, the new texts of Sappho, while valuable, include many partial lines; reconstructing what Sappho wrote involves a great deal of guesswork. We now have about seven hundred intelligible lines of Sappho's voluminous verse.

The poet that emerges from this sadly mutilated work is nevertheless powerful and distinctive. Sappho wrote a number of epithalamia *(wedding songs), to be chanted by a chorus before the bridal chamber. But her favorite poetic form was the short, intensely personal lyric, written to be chanted to the lyre by a solo singer. Most of her poems in this form deal with the passions and relationships within her circle of female companions, and especially with her own feelings about these women. Who these companions were is a matter of some speculation. Earlier critics believed that Sappho was a priestess and the leader of a* thiasos, *an organized group of women devoted to the worship of Aphrodite. More recent scholars have vigorously opposed this view and held that the circle of girls, if it had any formal standing at all, was at most a group of students or apprentices who studied poetry and the lyre with Sappho.*

Fortunately, this question does not have to be resolved before we can understand the poems. Whatever her official relationship to the circle of girls, Sappho's emphasis in her poems is almost exclusively personal and passionate. Even the prayers to Aphrodite are full of an aching, human passion, and the pain of longing has seldom been better described than in Number 39, where the glimpse of her loved one sitting by a man eclipses the world of perception, leaving only a feeling like death. If Sappho's world has a "hothouse atmosphere," as one critic has said, within its limits it is a psychologically realistic and extraordinarily moving one.

The passion and the intensity in Sappho's poetry are expressed with a limpid simplicity. The English critic C. M. Bowra describes her poetry as "ordinary speech raised to the highest level of expressiveness." The translator of this selection, Mary Barnard, states that her ambition is to capture in English Sappho's "fresh colloquial directness of speech," the quality that, along with her passion and her lyricism, led an anonymous Roman critic to write that "Sappho was not ninth among men but rather tenth among the lovely Muses."

NOTE ON THE TEXT

Because of complex problems of textual reconstruction, the first lines of the poems included here are sometimes to be read as titles, sometimes as integral parts of the poems. Their numbering corresponds to that in the Barnard translation.

FURTHER READING (*prepared by F.S.N.*): Discussion of Sappho's life and work is found in Bruno Snell, *The Discovery of the Mind,* 1948, trans. T. G. Rosenmeyer, 1953, pp. 43–70; Albin Lesky, *A History of Greek Literature,* 1957, 2nd ed. 1963, trans. J. Willis and C. de Heer, 1966, pp. 138–148; and Willis Barnstone, *Sappho: Lyrics in the Original Greek with Translations,* 1965. Denys L. Page, in his authoritative *Sappho and Alcaeus: An Introduction to the Study of Ancient Lesbian Poetry,* 1955, presents twelve of the longer poems, with translation, commentary and interpretative material; these analyses are followed by useful general remarks on Sappho's writings.

POEMS

Translated by Mary Barnard

30

We drink your health

Lucky bridegroom!
Now the wedding you
asked for is over

and your wife is the   5
girl you asked for;
she's a bride who is

charming to look at,
with eyes as soft as
honey, and a face   10

that Love has lighted
with his own beauty.
Aphrodite[1] has surely

outdone herself in
doing honor to you!   15

34

Lament for a maidenhead

FIRST   Like a quince-apple
VOICE   ripening on a top
         branch in a tree top

         not once noticed by   5
         harvesters or if
         not unnoticed, not reached

SECOND   Like a hyacinth in
VOICE   the mountains, trampled
         by shepherds until   10
         only a purple stain
         remains on the ground

37

You[1] know the place: then

Leave Crete and come to us
waiting where the grove is
pleasantest, by precincts

sacred to you; incense   5
smokes on the altar, cold
streams murmur through the

apple branches, a young
rose thicket shades the ground
and quivering leaves pour   10

down deep sleep; in meadows
where horses have grown sleek
among spring flowers, dill

[1] Goddess of love, as well as of the sea and of beauty, flowers, and seasons.
[1] The poem is addressed to Aphrodite (the "Cyprian" of line 14).

scents the air. Queen! Cyprian!
Fill our gold cups with love   15
stirred into clear nectar

38

Prayer to my lady of Paphos[1]

Dapple-throned Aphrodite,
eternal daughter of God,
snare-knitter! Don't, I beg you,

cow my heart with grief! Come,   5
as once when you heard my far-
off cry and, listening, stepped

from your father's house to your
gold car, to yoke the pair whose
beautiful thick-feathered wings[2]   10

oaring down mid-air from heaven
carried you to light swiftly
on dark earth; then, blissful one,

smiling your immortal smile
you asked, What ailed me now that   15
made me call you again? What

was it that my distracted
heart most wanted? "Whom has
Persuasion to bring round now

to your love? Who, Sappho, is   20
unfair to you? For, let her
run, she will soon run after;

if she won't accept gifts, she
will one day give them; and if
she won't love you—she soon will   25

love, although unwillingly. . . ."
If ever—come now! Relieve
this intolerable pain!

[1] Aphrodite, who was born of the sea foam and washed ashore at Paphos.
[2] The sparrows that drew Aphrodite's chariot.

What my heart most hopes will
happen, make happen; you your-   30
self join forces on my side!

39

He is more than a hero

He is a god in my eyes—
the man who is allowed
to sit beside you—he

who listens intimately   5
to the sweet murmur of
your voice, the enticing

laughter that makes my own
heart beat fast. If I meet
you suddenly, I can't   10

speak—my tongue is broken;
a thin flame runs under
my skin; seeing nothing,

hearing only my own ears
drumming, I drip with sweat;   15
trembling shakes my body

and I turn paler than
dry grass. At such times
death isn't far from me

40

Yes, Atthis,[1] you may be sure

                              Even in Sardis
Anactoria will think often of us

of the life we shared here, when you seemed
the Goddess incarnate   5
to her and your singing pleased her best

Now among Lydian women she in her
turn stands first as the red-

---

[1] Atthis and Anactoria were two of the girls in Sappho's circle.

fingered moon rising at sunset takes

precedence over stars around her;   10
her light spreads equally
on the salt sea and fields thick with bloom

Delicious dew pours down to freshen
roses, delicate thyme
and blossoming sweet clover; she wanders   15

aimlessly, thinking of gentle
Atthis, her heart hanging
heavy with longing in her little breast

She shouts aloud, Come! we know it;
thousand-eared night repeats that cry   20
across the sea shining between us

41

To an army wife, in Sardis:

Some say a cavalry corps,
some infantry, some, again,
will maintain that the swift oars

of our fleet are the finest   5
sight on dark earth; but I say
that whatever one loves, is.

This is easily proved: did
not Helen[1]—she who had scanned
the flower of the world's manhood—   10

choose as first among men one
who laid Troy's honor in ruin?
warped to his will, forgetting

love due her own blood, her own
child, she wandered far with him.   15
So Anactoria, although you

being far away forget us,
the dear sound of your footstep
and light glancing in your eyes

---

[1] Helen of Troy, whose choice of Paris as a lover and subsequent flight with him to Troy
began the Trojan War.

would move me more than glitter   20
of Lydian horse or armored
tread of mainland infantry

42

I have had not one word from her

Frankly I wish I were dead.
When she left, she wept

a great deal; she said to
me, "This parting must be   5
endured, Sappho. I go unwillingly."

I said, "Go, and be happy
but remember (you know
well) whom you leave shackled by love

"If you forget me, think   10
of our gifts to Aphrodite
and all the loveliness that we shared

"all the violet tiaras,
braided rosebuds, dill and
crocus twined around your young neck   15

"myrrh poured on your head
and on soft mats girls with
all that they most wished for beside them

"while no voices chanted
choruses without ours,   20
no woodlot bloomed in spring without song . . ."

43

It was you, Atthis, who said

"Sappho, if you will not get
up and let us look at you
I shall never love you again!

"Get up, unleash your suppleness,
lift off your Chian nightdress[1]
and, like a lily leaning into

"a spring, bathe in the water.
Cleis[2] is bringing your best
purple frock and the yellow

"tunic down from the clothes chest;
you will have a cloak thrown over
you and flowers crowning your hair . . .

"Praxinoa, my child, will you please
roast nuts for our breakfast? One
of the gods is being good to us:

"today we are going at last
into Mitylene, our favorite
city, with Sappho, loveliest

"of its women; she will walk
among us like a mother with
all her daughters around her

"when she comes home from exile . . ."

But you forget everything

97

I have often asked you
not to come now
Hermes,[1] Lord, you
who lead the ghosts
home:
     But this time
I am not happy; I
want to die, to see
the moist lotus open
along Acheron[2]

[1] From the island of Chios, off the coast of Asia Minor.   [2] Sappho's daughter.
[1] The god who guided the dead to the underworld.   [2] The river of Death.

Aeschylus

(C. 525–456 B.C.)

*The oldest of the three great Greek tragedians, Aeschylus was born around 525 B.C.
in Eleusis, a town near Athens, and died in Sicily in 456. He fought in the Persian
wars, taking part in the great Athenian victory at Marathon in 490 and later in
other climactic victories over the invading Persians, including the naval battle of
Salamis in 480. Earlier that year, the Persians had partially destroyed Athens.
Aeschylus' sense of pride in his city's accomplishments and triumphant survival is
expressed most directly in his play* The Persians *(472), the only surviving Greek
tragedy based on history, but also in the Orestes trilogy, or* Oresteia. *Aeschylus is a
definitive spokesman for central Athenian values during the noblest age of ancient
Greece. It is probable, in fact, that the eminent political and civic leader Pericles was
the "choregus" (roughly equivalent of "producer") for one of Aeschylus' plays.*

*Today, as was true in antiquity, Aeschylus is called the "Father of Tragedy." He
earned the title not only by his achievements as an artist, as typified by the power and
loftiness of his stories, themes, and style, but also by his technical innovations. He is
said to have introduced the "second actor" (earlier there had been only one and a
Chorus), thus making possible more complex plots and interactions. (The addition of
an actor multiplied the number of possible characters, since parts were regularly
doubled and men played female as well as male roles.) At the same time, he preserved
the major lyrical and dramatic role of the Chorus, which both participates in and
comments on the action—this in addition to its musical and choreographic function.
His output was impressive: some eighty or ninety plays. Of these, seven have survived:* The Persians, Seven Against Thebes, The Suppliant Maidens, *Prometheus* Bound, *and the three plays that make up the* Oresteia.

*Greek tragedies were regularly written and performed as cycles of three, each
cycle followed by a raucous "satyr play" designed to contrast with the emotional
loftiness and intensity of the tragedies. Aeschylus'* Oresteia, *performed in 458 just
two years before his death, is the only such cycle of tragedies to have survived in its
entirety.*

*Much of the power of this awesome work lies in the universality of its theme. Like
the Book of Job, Virgil's* Aeneid, *and Milton's* Paradise Lost, *the* Oresteia *explores the perennially urgent question of whether suffering and evil can be reconciled
with cosmic justice—and, if it can be, how. The literal story, however, focuses on a
concrete and practical form of the question: What is the relationship between strict
justice and human welfare, individual and communal? Social order, even more
obviously than cosmic justice, would seem to demand that evil acts be punished—
especially when, as in Aeschylus' trilogy, these acts violate the most fundamental
relationships, husband-wife and parent-child. Yet the act of punishment itself frequently seems an obscenity, at odds with our sense of what is noble in humanity and
worth loving or emulating in the divine order, however we define it. In our own time
the question, independent of theology, underlies the debate about the function of
punishment, mercy, rehabilitation, and deterrence in the judicial and penal systems.
It is not at all coincidental that the* Oresteia *ends with the establishment of a law
court.*

*Aeschylus explores the question by dramatizing the events growing out of the curse
on the lineage of Atreus. The family has been guilty of unspeakable atrocities for*

464

generations before the plays' action begins, culminating in Agamemnon's sacrifice of his daughter Iphigeneia and the excesses committed against the innocents of Troy. (See the Headnote to the Oresteia.) *Within the plays themselves, the chain of violence is extended by two further acts: the murder of Agamemnon by his wife Clytaemnestra, and the successful conspiracy of their children, Orestes and Electra, to kill their mother in the cause of justice. The main agency and symbol of retaliation are the Furies, repellent primitive beings who in their very unsophistication embody an uncompromising honesty in dealing with elemental evil, especially violations of blood-kinship.*

"Tragedy" seems hardly the right term for this superdrama, either for the whole or for its separate plays. In Aeschylus' early plays, such as the surviving Persians *and* Seven Against Thebes, *he placed human affairs in the foreground, with the gods relegated to the background. But in the* Oresteia, *as apparently also in the late* Prometheus *and Danaid trilogies (now represented only in the surviving* Prometheus Bound *and* The Suppliant Maidens), *he brought the cosmos itself on stage as he dramatized the divisions within the universe and their ultimate reconciliation. The* Oresteia *is not so much a tragedy, in the Aristotelian sense, as it is a Divine Comedy, tracing the emergence of civilization out of darkness into light. This process is presented in terms of sexual conflict and its resolution, conflict which penetrates all levels of existence, from the psychological through the domestic and political to the cosmic.* Agamemnon *presents a world trapped in a net (a crucial image throughout the trilogy) of blood-vengeance, a primitive code presided over by the conservative, irrational, female Furies. The nightmare world of* Agamemnon *is shot through with sexual conflict and confusion. The unwifely Clytaemnestra "maneuvers like a man," while Aegisthus is a womanly man, and the heart of Cassandra's premonitory vision (which no one understands) is, "What outrage—the woman kills the man!" Confusion of personal sexual identity is echoed on the domestic level in the marital hatred of Agamemnon and his queen and on the political level in the Trojan War, fought "all for another's woman." The Greek victory has been a rape—"for their mad outrage of a queen we raped their city"—and Agamemnon, who killed his own daughter, has been "the darling of all the golden girls who spread the gates of Troy."*

The Libation Bearers *introduces the title character of the trilogy, Orestes, who is to become the pivotal figure in the revolution of values the* Oresteia *traces. The law of blood-vengeance still reigns, but the vengeance of Orestes and Electra, so reluctant and self-doubting, is very different from the self-confident exultation of Clytaemnestra's bloodletting. Sexual conflict and confusion here are translated into the agonized ambivalence of a son and daughter forced to choose between love for a mother and honor for a father. And by the end of the play, sexual conflicts on the familial and political levels have broadened to a cosmic level in the conflict of the embodied Furies with the male Olympian Apollo, who authorized Orestes' vengeance. This conflict is brought directly on stage as we move from the nightmarish mode of* Agamemnon *and the comparatively realistic and Sophoclean manner of* The Libation Bearers *to the allegorical theomachy of* The Eumenides. *The curiously bisexual Athena, female but motherless, since she sprang straight from the head of Zeus, becomes the instrument for the resolution of sexual conflict, personally for Orestes, politically for Athens, and cosmically, in the reconciliation of the gods. The male Olympians triumph, but the female Furies are honored too, as they are transformed into the Eumenides, the "Kindly Ones," watchers over the rain, sunshine, and fertility of nature. This "Divine Comedy" ends with a distinctly nontragic hymn of triumph to the Athenian balance between the claims of earth and sky, female and male, fertility and control, with an optimism unclouded by the darker visions of Sophocles and Euripides.*

Aeschylus' poetic and dramatic style matches the grandeur of his theme. The language, with its daring metaphors and bold dislocations of syntax, mirrors an emotional and intellectual unrest perfectly in keeping with the dramatic excitement and the profundity of theme. Image patterns are used with dazzling skill to heighten effects and to convey nuances of theme and meaning. The patterns are many and omnipresent: of fire, light and darkness, nets, wealth, wind, storm, yokes, animals, hunting, lawsuits, wrestling and other sports, "threeness," and so on. These images are not a code, each image having a static meaning; their significance is always shaped by the immediate context. For example, a yoke can suggest enslavement but also the intimacy of a harmonious bond such as happy marriage. (The word "bond" itself has the same ambiguous meaning.) Moreover, the images evolve in parallel with the evolution of action and values; an example is the ominous torch flame that at the beginning of the Agamemnon *signals the fall of Troy and the imminent fall of the returning general but at the end of* The Eumenides *symbolizes fertility and deep joy.*

As a stage craftsman, Aeschylus is the most daring and flamboyant of the three Greek tragedians. His contemporaries called him the poet of "shock," and a persistent story insisted that he wrote his plays while drunk. He served both as composer and choreographer for his own plays, and the dances he arranged for his choruses were famous for their violence and extravagance: the Persian Lords, for example, in The Persians, *howl and scrape at the earth to conjure up the ghost of Darius. Shock follows shock in the* Oresteia. *The entrance of Agamemnon and his army is an impressive spectacle, and the dark red carpet running out from the palace door like a stream of blood is one of the most brilliant uses of a stage property in Greek drama. A contemporary testified that the first appearance of the Furies in* The Eumenides, *moaning and dripping blood from their eye sockets, caused children in the audience to faint and women to miscarry. The comment is possibly an exercise of critical license, but it nevertheless captures the shock the scene must have created. And the final great procession of the entire cast out of the theater and up to the hill of the Areopagus, in full view of the audience, is an extraordinary dramatic effect that suddenly moves the timeless, legendary action of the plays into the here and now.*

The Oresteia *is an allusive work that, like Virgil's* Aeneid, *brings together the two wellsprings of Greek literature, the* Iliad *and the* Odyssey, *while also transforming them. The Trojan War is the immediate occasion of the acts that bring on Agamemnon's murder and the ensuing events of the three plays. But the Odyssean themes of the warrior's return to his wife and of the loyal son determined to preserve his father and his house from harm are also reworked by Aeschylus with penetrating irony and insight.*

The trilogy makes a political and religious statement, through the medium of great art. But it is more than ideology or theology, and more than art in a narrow sense of the word. It is an emblem of the full range of human nature, one of those rare works—like Dante's Comedy, *Shakespeare's last plays, Beethoven's last music— that can explore vastness and mystery without losing touch with the human, including the earthy and even the homely. Dante included jokes and personal reminiscences in his account of the cosmos; Beethoven in his last symphony inserted a grunting German-band episode into an Olympian, ecstatic hymn to joy. Aeschylus, in* The Libation Bearers, *reminds us through Orestes' old nurse that the agent and victim of large tragic and providential forces was once a baby who needed to have his diapers changed. The magnificence of the* Oresteia *is ultimately a product of its range, its clear understanding and respect for man as a many-layered being. "Beneath" us lie elemental forces like the Furies; "above" us beckon the Olympian forces of the sky; "around" us lie the familiar facts of our condition in the actual world. All three of these levels, though, are within us, needing to be humanized and synthesized if we are to realize our full potential, individually and communally.*

FURTHER READING (*prepared by F.S.N.*): Gilbert Murray in his classic *Aeschylus: The Creator of Tragedy,* 1940, deals not only with the extant works, but also with Aeschylus' contribution to tragedy. Anthony J. Podlecki, *The Political Background of Aeschylean Tragedy,* 1966, comments on all seven plays. H. D. F. Kitto in *Form and Meaning in Drama,* 1956, is concerned mainly with the writings of Aeschylus and Sophocles; while Albin Lesky in *Greek Tragedy,* 1938, trans. H. A. Frankfort, 1965, presents material on all three tragedians. Stimulating essays on many aspects of Aeschylean drama are offered by Marsh H. McCall, ed., *Aeschylus: A Collection of Critical Essays,* 1972. The Greek text of the three plays, a translation, and general remarks are given by W. Headlam and George Thomson, ed., *The Oresteia of Aeschylus,* 1938, 2nd ed. 1966. Anne Lebeck in *The Oresteia: A Study in Language and Structure,* 1971, shows how the imagery in the three dramas is interconnected.

THE ORESTEIA

Translated by Robert Fagles

The genealogy of Orestes, according to Aeschylus.

Before the action of the first play (*Agamemnon*) begins, a line of evil acts, each inciting an act of terrible retaliation, already extends back several generations. Tantalus, the mythical great-grandfather of Agamemnon, murdered his son Pelops and tried to deceive the gods by serving them his son's flesh at a banquet. The gods saw through his deception, however, restoring Pelops to life and punishing Tantalus in Hades in a manner expressed by the word "tantalize." (The sinner was immersed in water up to his neck, with fruit trees over his head, both the water and the fruit receding when he tried to drink or eat.) Pelops in his turn double-crossed and then murdered Myrtilus, a conspirator with him in a plot to win a bride for Pelops.

Pelops had two sons, Atreus and Thyestes. Thyestes seduced his brother's wife; in revenge, Atreus first banished Thyestes and then, after luring him home again, served the flesh of Thyestes' children to him at a banquet. Thyestes cursed the house of Atreus and fled. Aegisthus, a surviving son of Thyestes, inherited his father's hatred of the line of Atreus.

Agamemnon and Menelaus are sons of Atreus. Menelaus married the beautiful Helen. She later eloped with Paris (son of King Priam of Troy), whom Menelaus had been entertaining as a guest. Agamemnon and Menelaus then organized a Greek coalition to recapture Helen from Troy and to take revenge on the Trojans. But the Greek fleet was threatened and detained at the port of Aulis by adverse winds and weather. In order to propitiate the gods, especially Artemis, and secure favorable winds, Agamemnon sacrificed the life of his daughter Iphigeneia, thereby extending the line of sacrilegious killings and incurring the hatred of his wife Clytaemnestra (half-sister to Helen). During Agamemnon's absence at Troy, Clytaemnestra has entered into an adulterous union with Aegisthus, both of whom have a motive for killing Agamemnon. [*Editors' headnote.*]

AGAMEMNON

CHARACTERS

WATCHMAN
CLYTAEMNESTRA
HERALD
AGAMEMNON
CASSANDRA
AEGISTHUS

CHORUS, THE OLD MEN OF ARGOS
AND THEIR LEADER
*Attendants of Clytaemnestra
and of Agamemnon,
bodyguard of Aegisthus*

TIME AND SCENE

A night in the tenth and final autumn of the Trojan war. The house of Atreus in Argos.[1] *Before it, an altar stands unlit; a watchman on the high roofs fights to stay awake.*

WATCHMAN.
    Dear gods, set me free from all the pain,
    the long watch I keep, one whole year awake . . .
    propped on my arms, crouched on the roofs of Atreus
    like a dog.
           I know the stars by heart,
    the armies of the night, and there in the lead
    the ones that bring us snow or the crops of summer,
    bring us all we have—
    our great blazing kings of the sky,

5

[1] According to Homer, Agamemnon lived in Mycenae; Aeschylus changes the scene of the tragedy to Argos. Both cities were located in the plain of Argolis, in south-central Greece.

I know them, when they rise and when they fall . . .
and now I watch for the light, the signal-fire   10
breaking out of Troy, shouting Troy is taken.
So she commands,[2] full of her high hopes.
That woman—she maneuvers like a man.

And when I keep to my bed, soaked in dew,
and the thoughts go groping through the night   15
and the good dreams that used to guard my sleep . . .
not here, it's the old comrade, terror at my neck.
I mustn't sleep, no—

                                        [*Shaking himself awake.*]
                    Look alive, sentry.
And I try to pick out tunes, I hum a little,
a good cure for sleep, and the tears start,   20
I cry for the hard times come to the house,
no longer run like the great place of old.

Oh for a blessed end to all our pain,
some godsend burning through the dark—

                                [*Light appears slowly in the east; he
                                struggles to his feet and scans it.*]

                                        I salute you!
You dawn of the darkness, you turn night to day—   25
I see the light at last.
They'll be dancing in the streets of Argos
thanks to you, thanks to this new stroke of—
                                        Aieeeeee!
There's your signal clear and true, my queen!
Rise up from bed—hurry, lift a cry of triumph   30
through the house, praise the gods for the beacon,
if they've taken Troy . . .
                        But there it burns,
fire all the way. I'm for the morning dances.
Master's luck is mine. A throw of the torch
has brought us triple-sixes[3]—we have won!   35
My move now—

                                [*Beginning to dance, then breaking
                                off, lost in thought.*]

                    Just bring him home. My king,
I'll take your loving hand in mine and then . . .

---

[2]Clytaemnestra, Agamemnon's queen, has established a chain of fire-beacons that will
relay quickly the news that Troy has fallen.
[3]A winning throw of the dice in a game related to backgammon.

the rest is silence. The ox is on my tongue.[4]
Aye, but the house and these old stones,
give them a voice and what a tale they'd tell.   40
And so would I, gladly . . .
I speak to those who know; to those who don't
my mind's a blank. I never say a word.

> [*He climbs down from the roof and*
> *disappears into the palace through a*
> *side entrance. A* CHORUS, *the old*
> *men of Argos who have not learned*
> *the news, enters and marches around*
> *the altar.*]

CHORUS.
    Ten years gone, ten to the day
  our great avenger[5] went for Priam—   45
      Menelaus and lord Agamemnon,
  two kings with the power of Zeus,
  the twin throne, twin scepter,
  Atreus' sturdy yoke of sons
  launched Greece in a thousand ships,   50
  armadas cutting loose from the land,
  armies massed for the cause, the rescue—

> [*From within the palace* CLYTAEM-
> NESTRA *raises a cry of triumph.*]

the heart within them screamed for all-out war!
Like vultures robbed of their young,
  the agony sends them frenzied,   55
soaring high from the nest, round and
round they wheel, they row their wings,
stroke upon churning thrashing stroke,
but all the labor, the bed of pain,
  the young are lost forever.   60
Yet someone hears on high—Apollo,
Pan or Zeus[6]—the piercing wail
these guests of heaven raise,
and drives at the outlaws, late
but true to revenge, a stabbing Fury![7]   65

---

    [4] A proverbial phrase, the equivalent of "my lips are sealed." The watchman is probably
thinking ominously of the guilty affair between Clytaemnestra and Aegisthus.
    [5] Agamemnon and his brother Menelaus (whose wife Helen had run away with Paris, thus
occasioning the war against Troy). Priam was the Trojan King.
    [6] Apollo, Pan, and Zeus are, respectively, the god of prophecy, the god of nature, and the
king of the gods.
    [7] The Furies are female personifications and agents of vengeance for crime, especially
crime against blood-kin. In the last play of the trilogy they are redefined as "the Eumenides,"
or "kindly ones."

[CLYTAEMNESTRA *appears at the
doors and pauses with her entourage.*]

So towering Zeus the god of guests[8]
drives Atreus' sons at Paris,
all for a woman manned by many[9]
the generations wrestle, knees
grinding the dust, the manhood drains,   70
the spear snaps in the first blood rites
    that marry Greece and Troy.
And now it goes as it goes
and where it ends is Fate.
And neither by singeing flesh   75
nor tipping cups of wine[10]
nor shedding burning tears can you
enchant away the rigid Fury.

[CLYTAEMNESTRA *lights the altar-
fires.*]

We are the old, dishonored ones,
the broken husks of men.
Even then they cast us off,   80
the rescue mission[11] left us here
to prop a child's strength upon a stick.
What if the new sap rises in his chest?
He has no soldiery in him,
    no more than we,   85
and we are aged past aging,
gloss of the leaf shriveled,
three legs at a time we falter on.
Old men are children once again,   90
    a dream that sways and wavers
into the hard light of day.

But you,
daughter of Leda, queen Clytaemnestra,
what now, what news, what message
drives you through the citadel   95
    burning victims? Look,
the city gods, the gods of Olympus,
gods of the earth and public markets—
all the altars blazing with your gifts!

---

[8] One of the roles of Zeus. Paris had violated the laws of hospitality by stealing Helen away from the house of his host, Menelaus.

[9] Helen had been courted by innumerable suitors in addition to the man she married (Menelaus) and the man she ran away with (Paris).

[10] Ritual offerings to the gods included sacrificed animals and poured-out wine. The imagery here and the two following lines could refer to any of several persons in the play. Such ambiguity is recurrent in the trilogy.

[11] The naval and military expedition to bring Helen back from Troy.

Argos blazes! Torches   100
race the sunrise up her skies—
drugged by the lulling holy oils,
    unadulterated,
run from the dark vaults of kings.
    Tell us the news!   105
What you can, what is right—
Heal us, soothe our fears!
Now the darkness comes to the fore,
now the hope glows through your victims,
beating back this raw, relentless anguish   110
    gnawing at the heart.

> [CLYTAEMNESTRA *ignores them and*
> *pursues her rituals; they assemble*
> *for the opening chorus.*]

O but I still have power to sound the gods' command at the roads[12]
that launched the kings. The gods breathe power through my
    song,
    my fighting strength, Persuasion grows with the years—
I sing how the flight of fury hurled the twin command,   115
    one will that hurled young Greece
and winged the spear of vengeance straight for Troy!
The kings of birds to kings of the beaking prows,[13] one black,
    one with a blaze of silver
        skimmed the palace spearhand right   120
        and swooping lower, all could see,
            plunged their claws in a hare, a mother
    bursting with unborn young—the babies spilling,
quick spurts of blood—cut off the race just dashing into life!
Cry, cry for death, but good win out in glory in the end.   125

But the loyal seer[14] of the armies studied Atreus' sons,
two sons with warring hearts—he saw two eagle-kings
    devour the hare and spoke the things to come,
"Years pass, and the long hunt nets the city of Priam,
        the flocks beyond the walls,   130
a kingdom's life and soul—Fate stamps them out.
Just let no curse of the gods lour on us first,

---

[12] In lines 112–258 the chorus recalls fearfully the ominous beginning of the expedition
against Troy. The eagles' devouring of the hare was understood by Calchas, the Greek
soothsayer, to foreshadow the destruction of Troy. But Artemis, goddess of the hunt (and
thus protector of pregnant animals) and of childbirth (thus offended by the anticipated
slaughter of innocents at Troy) was angered. Unfavorable winds threatened the Greek fleet
anchored at Aulis. Ironically, Artemis had to be appeased by the sacrificial killing at Aulis of
Agamemnon's daughter Iphigeneia—an example of strict retribution in kind, a central theme
in the Orestes trilogy.

[13] The kings of birds are eagles; the kings of the beaking prows are Agamemnon and
Menelaus.

[14] Calchas.

shatter our giant armor
    forged to strangle Troy. I see
        pure Artemis bristle in pity— 135
            yes, the flying hounds of the Father
    slaughter for armies . . . their own victim . . . a woman
trembling young, all born to die—She loathes the eagles' feast!"[15]
Cry, cry for death, but good win out in glory in the end.

      "Artemis, lovely Artemis, so kind 140
to the ravening lion's tender, helpless cubs,
the suckling young of beasts that stalk the wilds—
    bring this sign for all its fortune,
        all its brutal torment home to birth!
I beg you, Healing Apollo,[16] soothe her before 145
her crosswinds hold us down and moor the ships too long,
pressing us on to another victim . . .
    nothing sacred, no
        no feast to be eaten
           the architect of vengeance 150

                [*Turning to the palace.*]

      growing strong in the house
      with no fear of the husband
here she waits
the terror raging back and back in the future
    the stealth, the law of the hearth, the mother— 155
        Memory womb of Fury child-avenging Fury!"
So as the eagles wheeled at the crossroads,
Calchas clashed out the great good blessings mixed with doom
    for the halls of kings and singing with our fate
we cry, cry for death, but good win out in glory in the end. 160

      Zeus, great nameless all in all,
      if that name will gain his favor,
        I will call him Zeus.
    I have no words to do him justice,
      weighing all in the balance, 165
      all I have is Zeus, Zeus—
Lift this weight, this torment from my spirit,
      cast it once for all.

      He who was so mighty once,[17]
    storming for the wars of heaven, 170
      he has had his day.

---

[15] We are meant to recall also the abominable meal at which Thyestes was served his children's flesh by Atreus.

[16] Apollo, god of healing, is brother to Artemis.

[17] The following lines describe the overthrow of Ouranos (Uranus) by his son Kronos (Saturn) and of the latter by his son Zeus, who now reigns as supreme god.

And then his son who came to power
met his match in the third fall
and he is gone. Zeus, Zeus—
raise your cries and sing him Zeus the Victor!   175
You will reach the truth:

Zeus has led us on to know,
the Helmsman lays it down as law
that we must suffer, suffer into truth.   180
We cannot sleep, and drop by drop at the heart
the pain of pain remembered comes again,
and we resist, but ripeness comes as well.
From the gods enthroned on the awesome rowing-bench
there comes a violent love.

So it was that day the king,   185
the steersman at the helm of Greece,
would never blame a word the prophet said—
swept away by the wrenching winds of fortune
he conspired! Weatherbound we could not sail,
our stores exhausted, fighting strength hard-pressed,   190
and the squadrons rode in the shallows off Chalkis[18]
where the riptide crashes, drags,

and winds from the north pinned down our hulls at Aulis,
port of anguish . . . head winds starving,
sheets and the cables snapped   195
and the men's minds strayed,
the pride, the bloom of Greece
was raked as time ground on,
ground down, and then the cure for the storm
and it was harsher—Calchas cried,   200
"My captains, Artemis must have blood!"—
as harsh the sons of Atreus
dashed their scepters on the rocks,
could not hold back the tears,

and I still can hear the older warlord saying,   205
"Obey, obey, or a heavy doom will crush me—
Oh but doom *will* crush me
once I rend my child,
the glory of my house—
a father's hands are stained,   210
blood of a young girl streaks the altar.
Pain both ways and what is worse?
Desert the fleets, fail the alliance?
No, but stop the winds with a virgin's blood,
feed their lust, their fury?—feed their fury!—   215

---

[18]Chalkis, on the island Euboea, faced the port of Aulis on the mainland.

        Law is law!—
          Let all go well."

And once he slipped his neck in the strap of Fate,
his spirit veering black, impure, unholy,
once he turned he stopped at nothing,
        seized with the frenzy   220
            blinding driving to outrage—
wretched frenzy, cause of all our grief!
Yes, he had the heart
      to sacrifice his daughter!—
    to bless the war that avenged a woman's loss,   225
          a bridal rite that sped the men-of-war.

"My father, father!"—she might pray to the winds;
no innocence moves her judges mad for war.
Her father called his henchmen on,
      on with a prayer,   230
            "Hoist her over the altar
like a yearling, give it all your strength!
She's fainting—lift her,
      sweep her robes around her,
      but slip this strap in her gentle curving lips . . .   235
            here, gag her hard, a sound will curse the house"—
and the bridle chokes her voice . . . her saffron[19] robes
pouring over the sand
                  her glance like arrows showering
wounding every murderer through with pity
          clear as a picture, live,   240
she strains to call their names . . .
I remember often the days with father's guests
when over the feast her voice unbroken,
      pure as the hymn her loving father
bearing third libations, sang to Saving Zeus—   245
transfixed with joy, Atreus' offspring
      throbbing out their love.

What comes next? I cannot see it, cannot say.
The strong techniques of Calchas do their work.
But Justice turns the balance scales,   250
      sees that we suffer
and we suffer and we learn.
And we will know the future when it comes.
Greet it too early, weep too soon.
      It all comes clear in the light of day.   255
Let all go well today, well as she could want,

                    [*Turning to* CLYTAEMNESTRA.]

[19] Orange-yellow, the traditional color of the bridal garment.

our midnight watch, our lone defender,
  single-minded queen.
LEADER.[20]
                                        We've come,
Clytaemnestra. We respect your power.
Right it is to honor the warlord's woman   260
once he leaves the throne.
                            But why these fires?
Good news, or more good hopes? We're loyal,
we want to hear, but never blame your silence.
CLYTAEMNESTRA.
Let the new day shine, as the proverb says,
glorious from the womb of Mother Night.[21]   265

                                    [*Lost in prayer, then turning to the*
                                        CHORUS.]

You will hear a joy beyond your hopes.
Priam's citadel—the Greeks have taken Troy!
LEADER.
  No, what do you mean? I can't believe it.
CLYTAEMNESTRA.
  Troy is ours. Is that clear enough?
LEADER.
                                        The joy of it,
stealing over me, calling up my tears—   270
CLYTAEMNESTRA.
  Yes, your eyes expose your loyal hearts.
LEADER.
  And you have proof?
CLYTAEMNESTRA.
                      I do,
I must. Unless the god is lying.
LEADER.
                                That,
or a phantom spirit sends you into raptures.
CLYTAEMNESTRA.
  No one takes me in with visions—senseless dreams.   275
LEADER.
  Or giddy rumor, you haven't indulged yourself—
CLYTAEMNESTRA.
  You treat me like a child, you mock me?
LEADER.
  Then when did they storm the city?
CLYTAEMNESTRA.
  Last night, I say, the mother of this morning.
LEADER.
  And who on earth could run the news so fast?   280

[20] The principal spokesman for the Chorus.
[21] Ironically, the avenging Furies are also offspring of the primeval Night.

Clytaemnestra.
　　The god of fire—rushing fire from Ida![22]
　　And beacon to beacon rushed it on to me,
　　my couriers riding home the torch.

　　　　　　　　　　　　　　　　　From Troy
　　to the bare rock of Lemnos, Hermes' Spur,
　　and the Escort winged the great light west　　　　　　285
　　to the Saving Father's face, Mount Athos hurled it
　　third in the chain and leaping Ocean's back
　　the blaze went dancing on to ecstasy—pitch-pine
　　streaming gold like a newborn sun—and brought
　　the word in flame to Mount Makistos' brow.　　　　　290
　　No time to waste, straining, fighting sleep,
　　that lookout heaved a torch glowing over
　　the murderous straits of Euripos to reach
　　Messapion's watchmen craning for the signal.
　　Fire for word of fire! tense with the heather　　　　　295
　　withered gray, they stack it, set it ablaze—
　　the hot force of the beacon never flags,
　　it springs the Plain of Asôpos, rears
　　like a harvest moon to hit Kithairon's crest
　　and drives new men to drive the fire on.　　　　　　300
　　That relay pants for the farflung torch,
　　they swell its strength outstripping my commands
　　and the light inflames the marsh, the Gorgon's Eye,
　　it strikes the peak where the wild goats range—
　　my law, my fire whips that camp!　　　　　　　　305
　　They spare nothing, eager to build its heat,
　　and a huge beard of flame overcomes the headland
　　beetling down the Saronic Gulf, and flaring south
　　it brings the dawn to the Black Widow's face—
　　the watch that looms above your heads—and now　　　310
　　the true son of the burning flanks of Ida
　　crashes on the roofs of Atreus' sons!

　　And I ordained it all.
　　Torch to torch, running for their lives,
　　one long succession racing home my fire.　　　　　　315
　　　　　　　　　　　　　　　　　　　　One,
　　first in the laps and last,[23] wins out in triumph.

---

[22] A mountain range near Troy. Clytaemnestra's description of the progress of the flame-signal from Troy to Argos is filled with ironic overtones. Mount Athos, here associated with Zeus as "Saving Father," recalls by contrast Agamemnon's slaying of his daughter Iphigeneia; the "murderous" straits of Euripos are the location of her death; the "Black Widow" (Mount Arachnaion, or "Spider Mountain") suggests both Clytaemnestra herself and a web, one of the variants of the net-imagery ubiquitous in the play; the "true son" of Ida suggests the causal link between Agamemnon's Trojan adventure and his fate at his homecoming as well as foreshadowing the avenging role of his son Orestes.

[23] A winning relay team ("first in the laps") achieves the victory when the runner of the anchor leg (the "last") crosses the finish line.

There you have my proof, *my* burning sign, I tell you—
the power my lord passed on from Troy to me.

LEADER.
    We'll thank the gods, my lady—first this story,
    let me lose myself in the wonder of it all!   320
    Tell it start to finish, tell us all.

CLYTAEMNESTRA.
    The city's ours—in our hands this very day!
    I can hear the cries in crossfire rock the walls.
    Pour oil and wine in the same bowl,
    what have you, friendship? A struggle to the end.   325
    So with the victors and the victims—outcries,
    you can hear them clashing like their fates.

    They are kneeling by the bodies of the dead,
    embracing men and brothers, infants over
    the aged loins that gave them life, and sobbing,   330
    as the yoke constricts their last free breath,
    for every dear one lost.
                                    And the others,
    there, plunging breakneck through the night—
    the labor of battle sets them down, ravenous,
    to breakfast on the last remains of Troy.   335
    Not by rank but the lots of chance they draw,
    they lodge in the houses captured by the spear,
    settling in so soon, released from the open sky,
    the frost and dew. Lucky men, off guard at last,
    they sleep away their first good night in years.   340

    If only they are revering the city's gods,
    the shrines of the gods who love the conquered land,
    no plunderer will be plundered in return.
    Just let no lust, no mad desire seize the armies
    to ravish what they must not touch—   345
    overwhelmed by all they've won!
                                    The run for home
    and safety waits, the swerve at the post,[24]
    the final lap of the grueling two-lap race.
    And even if the men come back with no offense
    to the gods, the avenging dead[25] may never rest—   350
    Oh let no new disaster strike! And here
    you have it, what a woman has to say.
    Let the best win out, clear to see.
    A small desire but all that I could want.

LEADER.
    Spoken like a man, my lady, loyal,   355

---

[24] The turning-post in a race, where the racers turn and head back for where they started.
[25] The Chorus is meant to apply the phrase to the Trojan dead; Clytaemnestra also alludes cryptically to her dead daughter.

full of self-command. I've heard your sign
and now your vision.

> [*Reaching toward her as she turns
> and re-enters the palace.*]

        Now to praise the gods.
The joy is worth the labor.
CHORUS.
    O Zeus my king and Night, dear Night,[26]
    queen of the house who covers us with glories,   360
    you slung your net on the towers of Troy,
    neither young nor strong could leap
    the giant dredge net of slavery,
        all-embracing ruin.
    I adore you, iron Zeus of the guests   365
    and your revenge—you drew your longbow
    year by year to a taut full draw
    till one bolt, not falling short
    or arching over the stars,
        could split the mark of Paris!   370
    The sky stroke of god!—it is all Troy's to tell,
    but even I can trace it to its cause:
    god does as god decrees.
        And still some say
    that heaven would never stoop to punish men   375
    who trample the lovely grace of things
    untouchable. How wrong they are!
        A curse burns bright on crime—
        full-blown, the father's crimes will blossom,
        burst into the son's.   380
    Let there be less suffering . . .
    give us the sense to live on what we need.

        Bastions of wealth
        are no defense for the man
        who treads the grand altar of Justice   385
        down and out of sight.

    Persuasion, maddening child of Ruin
    overpowers him—Ruin plans it all.
    And the wound will smolder on,
        there is no cure,   390
    a terrible brilliance kindles on the night.
    He is bad bronze scraped on a touchstone:[27]
    put to the test, the man goes black.

---

[26] The Chorus in this passage concentrates on Paris as the evil man whom the gods punish, but much of what they say applies also to Agamemnon and the whole line of Atreus. In the latter part of the song (lines 426 ff.), the Chorus begins to sense dimly this more general guilt.

[27] A stone that, rubbed against a metal, shows whether the metal is true or counterfeit.

> Like the boy who chases
>   a bird on the wing,[28] brands his city,   395
>   brings it down and prays,
> but the gods are deaf
> to the one who turns to crime, they tear him down.

>   So Paris learned:
>   he came to Atreus' house   400
>   and shamed the tables spread for guests,
>   he stole away the queen.

> And she left her land *chaos*, clanging shields,
> companions tramping, bronze prows, men in bronze,
>   and she came to Troy with a dowry, death,   405
> strode through the gates
>   defiant in every stride,
> as prophets of the house looked on and wept,
> "Oh the halls and the lords of war,
>   the bed and the fresh prints of love.   410
> I *see* him,[29] unavenging, unavenged,
> the stun of his desolation is so clear—
>   he longs for the one who lies across the sea
> until her phantom seems to sway the house.

>   Her curving images,   415
>   her beauty hurts her lord,
>   the eyes starve and the touch
>   of love is gone,

> "and radiant dreams are passing in the night,
> the memories throb with sorrow, joy with pain . . .   420
>   it is pain to dream and see desires
> slip through the arms,
>   a vision lost forever
> winging down the moving drifts of sleep."
> So he grieves at the royal hearth   425
>   yet others' grief is worse, far worse.
> All through Greece for those who flocked to war
> they are holding back the anguish now,
>   you can feel it rising now in every house;
> I tell you there is much to tear the heart.   430

>   They knew the men they sent,
>   but now in place of men
>   ashes and urns come back
>   to every hearth.   435

[28] To chase a bird on the wing is foolishly to attempt the impossible.
[29] The primary reference is to Menelaus left alone without Helen.

War, War, the great gold-broker of corpses
holds the balance of the battle on his spear!
Home from the pyres he sends them,
   home from Troy to the loved ones,
weighted with tears, the urns brimmed full,
   the heroes return in gold-dust,   440
dear, light ash for men; and they weep,
they praise them, "He had skill in the swordplay,"
   "He went down so tall in the onslaught,"
"All for another's woman." So they mutter
in secret and the rancor steals   445
toward our staunch defenders, Atreus' sons.

          And there they ring the walls, the young,
          the lithe, the handsome hold the graves
          they won in Troy; the enemy earth
             rides over those who conquered.   450

The people's voice is heavy with hatred,
now the curses of the people must be paid,
and now I wait, I listen . . .
   there—there is something breathing
under the night's shroud. God takes aim   455
   at the ones who murder many;
the swarthy Furies stalk the man
gone rich beyond all rights—with a twist
   of fortune grind him down, dissolve him
into the blurring dead—there is no help.   460
The reach for power can recoil,
the bolt of god can strike you at a glance.

          Make me rich with no man's envy,
          neither a raider of cities, no,
          nor slave come face to face with life   465
          overpowered by another.

                  [*Speaking singly.*]

—Fire comes and the news is good,
   it races through the streets
but is it true? Who knows?
Or just another lie from heaven?   470

—Show us the man so childish, wonderstruck,
   he's fired up with the first torch,
then when the message shifts
   he's sick at heart.

          —Just like a woman
to fill with thanks before the truth is clear.   475

—So gullible. Their stories spread like wildfire,
    they fly fast and die faster;
   rumors voiced by women come to nothing.
LEADER.
   Soon we'll know her fires for what they are,
   her relay race of torches hand-to-hand—   480
   know if they're real or just a dream,
   the hope of a morning here to take our senses.
   I see a herald running from the beach
   and a victor's spray of olive shades his eyes
   and the dust he kicks, twin to the mud of Troy,   485
   shows he has a voice—no kindling timber
   on the cliffs, no signal-fires for him.
   He can shout the news and give us joy,
   or else . . . please, not that.
                 Bring it on,
   good fuel to build the first good fires.   490
   And if anyone calls down the worst on Argos
   let him reap the rotten harvest of his mind.

                          [*The* HERALD *rushes in and kneels*
                          on the ground.]

HERALD.
   Good Greek earth, the soil of my fathers!
   Ten years out, and a morning brings me back.
   All hopes snapped but one—I'm home at last.   495
   Never dreamed I'd die in Greece, assigned
   the narrow plot I love the best.
                       And now
   I salute the land, the light of the sun,
   our high lord Zeus and the king of Pytho—[30]
   no more arrows, master, raining on our heads!   500
   At Scamander's banks we took our share,
   your longbow brought us down like plague.
   Now come, deliver us, heal us—lord Apollo!
   Gods of the market, here, take my salute.
   And you, my Hermes, Escort,   505
   loving Herald, the herald's shield and prayer!—
   And the shining dead of the land who launched the armies,
   warm us home . . . we're all the spear has left.

   You halls of the kings, you roofs I cherish,
   sacred seats—you gods that catch the sun,   510
   if your glances ever shone on him in the old days,
   greet him well—so many years are lost.
   He comes, he brings us light in the darkness,
   free for every comrade, Agamemnon lord of men.

[30] The archer-god Apollo, who had sided with the Trojans and launched the arrows of
plague against the Greeks.

Give him the royal welcome he deserves!   515
He hoisted the pickax of Zeus who brings revenge,
he dug Troy down, he worked her soil down,
the shrines of her gods and the high altars, gone!—
and the seed of her wide earth he ground to bits.
That's the yoke he claps on Troy. The king,   520
the son of Atreus comes. The man is blest,
the one man alive to merit such rewards.

Neither Paris nor Troy, partners to the end,
can say their work outweighs their wages now.
Convicted of rapine, stripped of all his spoils,   525
and his father's house and the land that gave it life—
he's scythed them to the roots. The sons of Priam
pay the price twice over.

LEADER.
                                      Welcome home
from the wars, herald, long live your joy.

HERALD.
                                   Our joy—
now I could die gladly. Say the word, dear gods.   530

LEADER.
Longing for your country left you raw?

HERALD.
The tears fill my eyes, for joy.

LEADER.
                                 You too,
down the sweet disease that kills a man
with kindness . . .

HERALD.
                   Go on, I don't see what you—

LEADER.
                                  Love
for the ones who love you—that's what took you.

HERALD.
                             You mean   535
the land and the armies hungered for each other?

LEADER.
There were times I thought I'd faint with longing.

HERALD.
So anxious for the armies, why?

LEADER.
                            For years now,
only my silence kept me free from harm.

HERALD.
                            What,
with the kings gone did someone threaten you?

LEADER.
                               So much . . .   540
now as you say, it would be good to die.

HERALD.
    True, we *have* done well.
    Think back in the years and what have you?
    A few runs of luck, a lot that's bad.
    Who but a god can go through life unmarked?   545

    A long, hard pull we had, if I would tell it all.
    The iron rations, penned in the gangways
    hock by jowl like sheep. Whatever miseries
    break a man, our quota, every sunstarved day.

    Then on the beaches it was worse. Dug in   550
    under the enemy ramparts—deadly going.
    Out of the sky, out of the marshy flats
    the dews soaked us, turned the ruts we fought from
    into gullies, made our gear, our scalps
    crawl with lice.
                    And talk of the cold,   555
    the sleet to freeze the gulls, and the big snows
    come avalanching down from Ida. Oh but the heat,
    the sea and the windless noons, the swells asleep,
    dropped to a dead calm . . .

    But why weep now?   560
    It's over for us, over for them.
    The dead can rest and never rise again;
    no need to call their muster. We're alive,
    do we have to go on raking up old wounds?
    Good-by to all that. Glad I am to say it.   565

    For us, the remains of the Greek contingents,
    the good wins out, no pain can tip the scales,
    not now. So shout this boast to the bright sun—
    fitting it is—wing it over the seas and rolling earth:
    "Once when an Argive expedition captured Troy   570
    they hauled these spoils back to the gods of Greece,
    they bolted them high across the temple doors,
    the glory of the past!"
                        And hearing that,
    men will applaud our city and our chiefs,
    and Zeus will have the hero's share of fame—   575
    he did the work.
                    That's all I have to say.
LEADER.
    I'm convinced, glad that I was wrong.
    Never too old to learn; it keeps me young.

                                [CLYTAEMNESTRA *enters with her*
                                women.]

First the house and the queen, it's their affair,
but I can taste the riches.

CLYTAEMNESTRA.

I cried out long ago!— 580
for joy, when the first herald came burning
through the night and told the city's fall.
And there were some who smiled and said,
"A few fires persuade you Troy's in ashes.
Women, women, elated over nothing." 585

You made me seem deranged.
For all that I sacrificed—a woman's way,
you'll say—station to station on the walls
we lifted cries of triumph that resounded
in the temples of the gods. We lulled and blessed 590
the fires with myrrh and they consumed our victims.

[*Turning to the* HERALD.]

But enough. Why prolong the story?
From the king himself I'll gather all I need.
Now for the best way to welcome home
my lord, my good lord . . .
No time to lose! 595
What dawn can feast a woman's eyes like this?
I can see the light, the husband plucked from war
by the Saving God and open wide the gates.

Tell him that, and have him come with speed,
the people's darling—how they long for him. 600
And for his wife,
may he return and find her true at hall,
just as the day he left her, faithful to the last.
A watchdog gentle to him alone,

[*Glancing toward the palace.*]

savage
to those who cross his path. I have not changed. 605
The strains of time can never break our seal.
In love with a new lord, in ill repute I am
as practiced as I am in dyeing bronze.

That is my boast, teeming with the truth.
I am proud, a woman of my nobility— 610
I'd hurl it from the roofs!

[*She turns sharply, enters the palace.*]

LEADER.

She speaks well, but it takes no seer to know
she only says what's right.

[*The* HERALD *attempts to leave; the
leader takes him by the arm.*]

Wait, one thing.
Menelaus, is he home too, safe with the men?
The power of the land—dear king.   615
HERALD.
I doubt that lies will help my friends,
in the lean months to come.
LEADER.
Help us somehow, tell the truth as well.
But when the two conflict it's hard to hide—
out with it.
HERALD.
                    He's lost, gone from the fleets!   620
He and his ship, it's true.
LEADER.
                              After you watched him
pull away from Troy? Or did some storm
attack you all and tear him off the line?
HERALD.
                                        There,
like a marksman, the whole disaster cut to a word.
LEADER.
How do the escorts give him out—dead or alive?   625
HERALD.
No clear report. No one knows . . .
only the wheeling sun that heats the earth to life.
LEADER.
But then the storm—how did it reach the ships?
How did it end? Were the angry gods on hand?
HERALD.
This blessed day, ruin it with *them?*   630
Better to keep their trophies far apart.

When a runner comes, his face in tears,
saddled with what his city dreaded most,
the armies routed, two wounds in one,
one to the city, one to hearth and home. . .   635
our best men, droves of them, victims
herded from every house by the two-barb whip
that Ares [31] likes to crack,
                              that charioteer
who packs destruction shaft by shaft,
careening on with his brace of bloody mares—   640
When he comes in, I tell you, dragging that much pain,
wail your battle-hymn to the Furies, and high time!

[31] God of war.

But when he brings salvation home to a city
singing out her heart—
how can I mix the good with so much bad   645
and blurt out this?—
               "Storms swept the Greeks,
and not without the anger of the gods!"

Those enemies for ages, fire and water,
sealed a pact and showed it to the world—
they crushed our wretched squadrons.
                     Night looming,   650
breakers lunging in for the kill
and the black gales come brawling out of the north—
ships ramming, prow into hooking prow, gored
by the rush-and-buck of hurricane pounding rain
by the cloudburst—
                 ships stampeding into the darkness,   655
lashed and spun by the savage shepherd's hand!

But when the sun comes up to light the skies
I see the Aegean heaving into a great bloom
of corpses . . . Greeks, the pick of a generation
scattered through the wrecks and broken spars.   660

But not us, not our ship, our hull untouched.
Someone stole us away or begged us off.
No mortal—a god, death grip on the tiller,
or lady luck herself, perched on the helm,
she pulled us through, she saved us. Aye,   665
we'll never battle the heavy surf at anchor,
never shipwreck up some rocky coast.

But once we cleared that sea-hell, not even
trusting luck in the cold light of day,
we battened on our troubles, they were fresh—   670
the armada punished, bludgeoned into nothing.

And now if one of them still has the breath
he's saying *we* are lost. Why not?
We say the same of him. Well,
here's to the best.
                And Menelaus?   675
Look to it, he's come back, and yet . . .
if a shaft of the sun can track him down,
alive, and his eyes full of the old fire—
thanks to the strategies of Zeus, Zeus
would never tear the house out by the roots—   680
then there's hope our man will make it home.

You've heard it all. Now you have the truth.

[Rushing out.]

CHORUS.
  Who—what power named the name that drove your fate?—[32]
what hidden brain could divine your future,
steer that word to the mark,   685
to the bride of spears,
    the whirlpool churning armies,
          Oh for all the world a Helen!
Hell at the prows, hell at the gates
hell on the men-of-war,   690
from her lair's sheer veils she drifted
    launched by the giant western wind,
      and the long tall waves of men in armor,
huntsmen trailing the oarblades' dying spoor[33]
slipped into her moorings,   695
    Simois'[34] mouth that chokes with foliage,
          bayed for bloody strife,

for Troy's Blood Wedding Day—she drives her word,
her burning will to the birth, the Fury
late but true to the cause,   700
to the tables shamed
    and Zeus who guards the hearth—
          the Fury makes the Trojans pay!
Shouting their hymns, hymns for the bride
hymns for the kinsmen doomed   705
to the wedding march of Fate,
    Troy changed her tune in her late age,
      and I think I hear the dirges mourning
"Paris, born and groomed for the bed of Fate!"
They mourn with their life breath,   710
    they sing their last, the sons of Priam
          born for bloody slaughter.

So a man[35] once reared
a lion cub at hall, snatched
from the breast, still craving milk   715
    in the first flush of life.
A captivating pet for the young,

[32] The foregoing inquiries about Menelaus lead naturally to the theme of this choral passage: the significance of Helen, whom Menelaus was bringing home. The Chorus, punning on the root meaning of Helen's name in Greek ("destruction," rendered here as "hell"), see her as an agent of ruin inflicted as just punishment for Paris and the Trojans. She is also, however, a scourge to Greece and to the house of Atreus.
[33] The track of a wild animal. Having sailed from her home to Troy, Helen is pursued by the Greek fleet ("huntsmen") sailing to recover her.
[34] A river near Troy.
[35] Helen is compared to a lion cub reared as a household pet until, having grown, its latent nature asserts itself in bloodshed. The house can be the Trojans' or that of Agamemnon and Menelaus.

and the old men adored it, pampered it
   in their arms, day in, day out,
like an infant just born.   720
Its eyes on fire, little beggar,
fawning for its belly, slave to food.

   But it came of age
and the parent strain broke out
and it paid its breeders back.   725
   Grateful it was,[36] it went
through the flock to prepare a feast,
an illicit orgy—the house swam with blood,
   none could resist that agony—
            massacre vast and raw!   730
From god there came a priest of ruin,
adopted by the house to lend it warmth.

And the first sensation Helen brought to Troy . . .
call it a spirit
   shimmer of winds dying   735
        glory light as gold
   shaft of the eyes dissolving, open bloom
  that wounds the heart with love.
But veering wild in mid-flight
she whirled her wedding on to a stabbing end,   740
slashed at the sons of Priam—hearthmate, friend to the death,
   sped by Zeus who speeds the guest,
a bride of tears, a Fury.

There's an ancient saying,[37] old as man himself:
men's prosperity   745
   never will die childless,
        once full-grown it breeds.
   Sprung from the great good fortune in the race
comes bloom on bloom of pain—
insatiable wealth. But not I,   750
I alone say this. Only the reckless act
can breed impiety, multiplying crime on crime,
   while the house kept straight and just
is blessed with radiant children.

      But ancient Violence longs to breed,   755
       new Violence comes
   when its fatal hour comes, the demon comes

---

[36] Grim humor; the grown lion is like someone thankfully repaying parents for rearing him.

[37] In the following lines the Chorus echoes the traditional belief that excess of prosperity in itself brings on punishment by the gods, but the old men go on to insist that the more important cause is evil deeds. Wealth acquired through evil combines both incitements to divine retribution.

to take her toll—no war, no force, no prayer
can hinder the midnight Fury stamped
with parent Fury moving through the house.   760

But Justice shines in sooty hovels,
        loves the decent life.
From proud halls crusted with gilt by filthy hands
    she turns her eyes to find the pure in spirit—
spurning the wealth stamped counterfeit with praise,   765
    she steers all things toward their destined end.

                                [AGAMEMNON *enters in his chariot,*
                                his plunder borne before him by his
                                entourage; behind him, half hidden,
                                stands CASSANDRA.[38] *The old men*
                                press toward him.]

Come, my king, the scourge of Troy,
    the true son of Atreus—
How to salute you, how to praise you
neither too high nor low, but hit   770
the note of praise that suits the hour?
So many prize some brave display,
they prefer some flaunt of honor
    once they break the bounds.
When a man fails they share his grief,   775
but the pain can never cut them to the quick.
When a man succeeds they share his glory,
torturing their faces into smiles.
But the good shepherd[39] knows his flock.
When the eyes seem to brim with love   780
    and it is only unction,
he will know, better than we can know.
That day you marshaled the armies
all for Helen—no hiding it now—
I drew you in my mind in black;   785
you seemed a menace at the helm,
    sending men to the grave
to bring her home, that hell on earth.
But now from the depths of trust and love
I say Well fought, well won—   790
    the end is worth the labor!
Search, my king, and learn at last
who stayed at home and kept their faith
    and who betrayed the city.

---

[38] A prophetess, daughter of King Priam of Troy, taken captive by Agamemnon.
[39] Agamemnon, regarded as protector of his subjects.

AGAMEMNON.
                        First,
with justice I salute my Argos and my gods,   795
my accomplices who brought me home and won
my rights from Priam's Troy—the just gods.
No need to hear our pleas. Once for all
they consigned their lots to the urn[40] of blood,
they pitched on death for men, annihilation   800
for the city. Hope's hand, hovering
over the urn of mercy, left it empty.
Look for the smoke—it is the city's seamark,
building even now.
                        The storms of ruin live!
Her last dying breath, rising up from the ashes   805
send us gales of incense rich in gold.

For what we must thank the gods with a sacrifice
our sons will long remember. For their mad outrage
of a queen we raped their city—we were right.
The beast of Argos, foals of the wild mare,[41]   810
thousands massed in armor rose on the night
the Pleiades[42] went down, and crashing through
their walls our bloody lion lapped its fill,
gorging on the blood of kings.
                        Our thanks to the gods,
long drawn out, but it is just the prelude.   815

> [CLYTAEMNESTRA *approaches with
> her women; they are carrying dark
> red tapestries.* AGAMEMNON *turns
> to the leader.*]

And your concern, old man, is on my mind.
I hear you and agree, I will support you.
How rare, men with the character to praise
a friend's success without a trace of envy,
poison to the heart—it deals a double blow.   820
Your own losses weigh you down but then,
look at your neighbor's fortune and you weep.
Well I know. I understand society,
the fawning mirror of the proud.
                        My comrades . . .
they're shadows, I tell you, ghosts of men   825
who swore they'd die for me. Only Odysseus:

[40] In deciding law cases, an Athenian juror cast his vote by dropping a pebble into one of two urns signifying conviction and acquittal.

[41] Agamemnon refers to the Greek soldiers who, hidden inside the wooden horse, brought about the fall of Troy. The story is told in Virgil's *Aeneid*, Book II.

[42] The setting of this constellation is associated in the present context with the approach of winter and storms.

I dragged that man to the wars but once in harness
he was a trace-horse, he gave his all for me.
Dead or alive, no matter, I can praise him.

And now this cause involving men and gods.   830
We must summon the city for a trial,
found a national tribunal. Whatever's healthy,
shore it up with law and help it flourish.
Wherever something calls for drastic cures
we make our noblest effort: amputate or wield   835
the healing iron, burn the cancer at the roots.

Now I go to my father's house—
I give the gods my right hand, my first salute.
The ones who sent me forth have brought me home.

> [*He starts down from the chariot,
> looks at* CLYTAEMNESTRA, *stops,
> and offers up a prayer.*]

Victory, you have sped my way before,   840
now speed me to the last.

> [CLYTAEMNESTRA *turns from the
> king to the* CHORUS.]

CLYTAEMNESTRA.
                                    Old nobility of Argos
gathered here, I am not ashamed to tell you
how I love the man. I am older,
and the fear dies away . . . I am human.
Nothing I say was learned from others.   845
This is my life, my ordeal, long as the siege
he laid at Troy and more demanding.
                                    First,
when a woman sits at home and the man is gone,
the loneliness is terrible,
unconscionable . . .   850
and the rumors spread and fester,
a runner comes with something dreadful,
close on his heels the next and his news worse,
and they shout it out and the whole house can hear;
and wounds—if he took one wound for each report   855
to penetrate these walls, he's gashed like a dragnet,
more, if he had only died . . .
for each death that swelled his record, he could boast
like a triple-bodied Geryon[43] risen from the grave,
"Three shrouds I dug from the earth, one for every body   860
that went down!"

---

[43] A three-headed giant.

          The rumors broke like fever,
broke and then rose higher. There were times
they cut me down and eased my throat from the noose.
I wavered between the living and the dead.

                          [*Turning to* AGAMEMNON.]

                              And so
our child is gone, not standing by our side,   865
the bond of our dearest pledges, mine and yours;
by all rights our child should be here . . .
Orestes.[44] You seem startled.
You needn't be. Our loyal brother-in-arms
will take good care of him, Strophios the Phocian.   870
He warned from the start we court two griefs in one.
You risk all on the wars—and what if the people
rise up howling for the king, and anarchy
should dash our plans?
                    Men, it is their nature,
trampling on the fighter once he's down.   875
Our child is gone. That is my self-defense
and it is true.
               For me, the tears that welled
like springs are dry. I have no tears to spare.
I'd watch till late at night, my eyes still burn,
I sobbed by the torch I lit for you alone.   880

                     [*Glancing toward the palace.*]

I never let it die . . . but in my dreams
the high thin wail of a gnat would rouse me,
piercing like a trumpet—I could see you
suffer more than all
the hours that slept with me could ever bear.   885

I endured it all. And now, free of grief,
I would salute that man the watchdog of the fold,
the mainroyal, saving stay[45] of the vessel,
rooted oak that thrusts the roof sky-high,
the father's one true heir.   890
Land at dawn to the shipwrecked past all hope,
light of the morning burning off the night of storm,
the cold clear spring to the parched horseman—
O the ecstasy, to flee the yoke of Fate!

---

[44] One of the many ironies in Clytaemnestra's speech; the preceding lines suggest Orestes'
dead sister Iphigeneia. Clytaemnestra has sent Orestes away to the city of Phocis, to clear the
way for Aegisthus and herself, or to protect Orestes against civil mutiny while his father was
away, or perhaps for both reasons.
[45] A cable that supports the mainroyal mast of a ship.

It is right to use the titles he deserves.   895
Let envy keep her distance. We have suffered
long enough.

[*Reaching toward* AGAMEMNON.]

Come to me now, my dearest,
down from the car of war, but never set the foot
that stamped out Troy on earth again, my great one.

Women, why delay? You have your orders.   900
Pave his way with tapestries.

[*They begin to spread the crimson
tapestries between the king and the
palace doors.*]

Quickly.
Let the red stream flow and bear him home
to the home he never hoped to see[46]—Justice,
lead him in!
Leave all the rest to me.
The spirit within me never yields to sleep.   905
We will set things right, with the gods' help.
We will do whatever Fate requires.

AGAMEMNON.

There
is Leda's daughter,[47] the keeper of my house.
And the speech to suit my absence, much too long.
But the praise that does us justice,   910
let it come from others, then we prize it.
This—
You treat me like a woman, groveling, gaping up at me!
What am I, some barbarian peacocking out of Asia?
Never cross my path with robes and draw the lightning.
Never—only the gods deserve the pomps of honor   915
and the stiff brocades of fame. To walk on them . . .
I am human, and it makes my pulses stir
with dread.[48]
Give me the tributes of a man
and not a god, a little earth to walk on,
not this gorgeous work.   920
There is no need to sound my reputation.
I have a sense of right and wrong, what's more—
heaven's proudest gift. Call no man blest

---

[46] A grim pun: both "the home in Argos he had lost hope of seeing again" and "the home (death) he hoped never to see."

[47] Clytaemnestra; she and Helen are half sisters, Leda being mother to both.

[48] Agamemnon feels (or perhaps feigns) reluctance to commit an act of *hubris,* the overweening pride of a man which will bring on angry retribution by the gods.

until he ends his life in peace, fulfilled.
If I can live by what I say, I have no fear. 925
CLYTAEMNESTRA.
One thing more. Be true to your ideals and tell me—
AGAMEMNON.
True to my ideals? Once I violate them I am lost.
CLYTAEMNESTRA.
Would you have sworn this act[49] to god in a time of terror?
AGAMEMNON.
Yes, if a prophet called for a last, drastic rite.
CLYTAEMNESTRA.
But Priam—can you see him if he had your success? 930
AGAMEMNON.
Striding on the tapestries of god, I see him now.
CLYTAEMNESTRA.
And *you* fear the reproach of common men?
AGAMEMNON.
The voice of the people—aye, they have enormous power.
CLYTAEMNESTRA.
Perhaps, but where's the glory without a little gall?[50]
AGAMEMNON.
And where's the woman in all this lust for glory? 935
CLYTAEMNESTRA.
But the great victor—it becomes him to give away.
AGAMEMNON.
Victory in this . . . war of ours, it means so much to you?
CLYTAEMNESTRA.
O give way! The power is yours[51] if you surrender
all of your own free will to me.
AGAMEMNON.

                        Enough.
If you are so determined— 940

                        [*Turning to the women, pointing to
                        his boots.*]

Let someone help me off with these at least.
Old slaves, they've stood me well.

                        Hurry,
and while I tread his splendors dyed red in the sea,[52]
may no god watch and strike me down with envy
from on high. I feel such shame— 945

---

[49] Clytaemnestra refers to the act of walking on the splendid "red carpet." She also has in mind Agamemnon's willingness in the past to commit an outrage like the killing of his daughter when such an outrage served his purpose.

[50] Clytaemnestra implies that great men must be prepared to endure the "gall" of inferior men's envy.

[51] That is, "If you yield freely and magnanimously to my whim, it is you who will have overcome me" (in their little dispute, what Agamemnon calls "this . . . war of ours").

[52] The red dye of the tapestry-carpet was derived from a kind of sea snail.

to tread the life of the house, a kingdom's worth
of silver in the weaving.

> [*He steps down from the chariot to
> the tapestries and reveals* CASSAN-
> DRA, *dressed in the sacred regalia,
> the fillets,*[53] *robes, and scepter of*
> APOLLO.]

Done is done.
Escort this stranger in, be gentle.
Conquer with compassion. Then the gods
shine down upon you, gently. No one chooses   950
the yoke of slavery, not of one's free will—
and she least of all. The gift of the armies,
flower and pride of all the wealth we won,
she follows me from Troy.

And now,
since you have brought me down with your insistence,   955
just this once I enter my father's house,
trampling royal crimson as I go.

> [*He takes his first steps and pauses.*]

CLYTAEMNESTRA.

There is the sea
and who will drain it dry? Precious as silver,[54]
inexhaustible, ever-new, it breeds the more we reap it—
tides on tides of crimson dye our robes blood-red.   960
Our lives are based on wealth, my king,
the gods have seen to that.
Destitution, our house has never heard the word.
I would have sworn to tread on legacies of robes,
at one command from an oracle, deplete the house—   965
suffer the worst to bring that dear life back!

> [*Encouraged,* AGAMEMNON *strides
> to the entrance.*]

When the root lives on, the new leaves come back,
spreading a dense shroud of shade across the house
to thwart the Dog Star's[55] fury. So you return
to the father's hearth, you bring us warmth in winter   970
like the sun—
And you are Zeus when Zeus
tramples the bitter virgin grape for new wine[56]

---

[53] Ribbons. Cassandra had been wooed by Apollo, the god of prophecy, but because she
resisted him, she had been cursed with the gift of prophesying to hearers who would always
refuse to believe her.
[54] The red fabric had silver woven into it.
[55] The star Sirius, considered as a harbinger of killing heat, disease, and madness.
[56] An allusion to the shedding of the young Iphigeneia's blood.

and the welcome chill steals through the halls, at last
the master moves among the shadows of his house, fulfilled.

> [AGAMEMNON *goes over the thresh-*
> *old; the women gather up the tapes-*
> *tries while* CLYTAEMNESTRA *prays.*]

Zeus, Zeus, master of all fulfillment, now fulfill our prayers—   975
speed our rites to their fulfillment once for all!

> [*She enters the palace, the doors*
> *close, the old men huddle in terror.*]

CHORUS.
Why, why does it rock me,[57] never stops,
this terror beating down my heart,
    this seer that sees it all—
it beats its wings, uncalled unpaid   980
thrust on the lungs
the mercenary song beats on and on
singing a prophet's strain—
   and I can't throw it off
like dreams that make no sense,   985
and the strength drains
that filled the mind with trust,
and the years drift by and the driven sand
    has buried the mooring lines
that churned when the armored squadrons cut for Troy . . .   990
and now I believe it, I can prove he's home,
    my own clear eyes for witness—
            Agamemnon!
Still it's chanting, beating deep so deep in the heart
this dirge of the Furies, oh dear god,
not fit for the lyre,[58] its own master   995
   it kills our spirit
kills our hopes
and it's real, true, no fantasy—
    stark terror whirls the brain
      and the end is coming   1000
        Justice comes to birth—
I pray my fears prove false and fall
and die and never come to birth!
Even exultant health, well we know,
   exceeds its limits,[59] comes so near disease   1005
it can breach the wall between them.

---

[57] The anguished choral song that follows expresses two levels of awareness by the Chorus:
1) its consciousness of the old hereditary curse on the lineage of Atreus and 2) the more
immediate suspicion of Clytaemnestra based on the knowledge of her adulterous relationship
with Aegisthus.

[58] Not fit for joyous song.

[59] The principle of the golden mean, of steering between too little and too much, applies
even to health, according to the Chorus.

Even a man's fate, held true on course,
   in a blinding flash rams some hidden reef;
but if caution only casts the pick of the cargo[60]—
one well-balanced cast—   1010
the house will not go down, not outright;
laboring under its wealth of grief
the ship of state rides on.

Yes, and the great green bounty of god,
sown in the furrows year by year and reaped each fall   1015
can end the plague of famine.

But a man's lifeblood
   is dark and mortal.
Once it wets the earth
what song can sing it back?   1020
Not even the master-healer[61]
   who brought the dead to life—
Zeus stopped the man before he did more harm.

Oh, if only the gods had never forged
the chain that curbs our excess,   1025
   one man's fate curbing the next man's fate,
my heart would outrace my song, I'd pour out all I feel—
         but no, I choke with anguish,
     mutter through the nights.
Never to ravel out a hope in time   1030
and the brain is swarming, burning—

> [CLYTAEMNESTRA *emerges from
> the palace and goes to* CASSANDRA,
> *impassive in the chariot.*]

CLYTAEMNESTRA.
Won't you come inside? I mean you, Cassandra.
Zeus in all his mercy wants you to share
some victory libations[62] with the house.
The slaves are flocking. Come, lead them   1035
up to the altar of the god who guards
our dearest treasures.
         Down from the chariot,
no time for pride. Why even Heracles,[63]
they say, was sold into bondage long ago,

---

[60] A ship in peril can be saved by jettisoning cargo so as to lighten it; similarly, a man may salvage his happiness and his "house" by forsaking his most prized wealth.

[61] Asclepios, a physician so gifted that he brought a dead man back to life. As punishment for thus violating the natural order, Zeus killed him with a thunderbolt. Compare the bitter debate between Apollo and Death in Euripides' *Alcestis.*

[62] Ritual pourings of liquids.

[63] The heroic Heracles (Hercules) had served as a slave to Omphale, queen of Lydia in Asia Minor.

he had to endure the bitter bread of slaves.   1040
But if the yoke descends on you, be grateful
for a master born and reared in ancient wealth.
Those who reap a harvest past their hopes[64]
are merciless to their slaves.
                    From us
you will receive what custom says is right.   1045

              [CASSANDRA *remains impassive.*]

LEADER.
It's *you* she is speaking to, it's all too clear.
You're caught in the nets of doom—obey
if you can obey, unless you cannot bear to.
CLYTAEMNESTRA.
Unless she's like a swallow, possessed
of her own barbaric song, strange, dark.   1050
I speak directly as I can—she must obey.
LEADER.
Go with her. Make the best of it, she's right.
Step down from the seat, obey her.
CLYTAEMNESTRA.
                    Do it *now*—
I have no time to spend outside. Already
the victims crowd the hearth, the Navelstone,[65]   1055
to bless this day of joy I never hoped to see!—
our victims[66] waiting for the fire and the knife,
and you,
if you want to taste our mystic rites, come now.
If my words can't reach you—

              [*Turning to the leader.*]

              Give her a sign,   1060
one of her exotic handsigns.
LEADER.
                  I think
the stranger needs an interpreter, someone clear.
She's like a wild creature, fresh caught.
CLYTAEMNESTRA.
                  She's mad,
her evil genius murmuring in her ears.
She comes from a *city* fresh caught.   1065
She must learn to take the cutting bridle
before she foams her spirit off in blood—
and that's the last I waste on her contempt!

[64] Men whose wealth ("harvest") is not "ancient" but recent.
  [65] Also the name of a stone at Apollo's shrine in Delphi; Orestes goes to that Navelstone, to be purged of his blood-guilt, at the beginning of *The Eumenides.*
  [66] The animals to be sacrificed in the ritual; but Clytaemnestra's statement has also a more sinister private meaning.

[*Wheeling, re-entering the palace.
The leader turns to* CASSANDRA,
who remains transfixed.]

LEADER.
  Not I, I pity her. I will be gentle.
  Come, poor thing. Leave the empty chariot—   1070
  Of your own free will try on the yoke of Fate.

CASSANDRA.
  Aieeeeee! Earth—Mother—
                  Curse of the Earth—Apollo Apollo!
LEADER.
  Why cry to Apollo?
  He's not the god to call with sounds of mourning.
CASSANDRA.
  Aieeeeee! Earth—Mother—   1075
                  Rape of the Earth—Apollo Apollo!
LEADER.
  Again, it's a bad omen.
  She cries for the god who wants no part of grief.[67]

                            [CASSANDRA *steps from the chariot,
                            looks slowly toward the rooftops of
                            the palace.*]

CASSANDRA.
  God of the long road,
            Apollo *Apollo* my destroyer—
  you destroy me once, destroy me twice—   1080
LEADER.
  She's about to sense her own ordeal, I think.
  Slave that she is, the god lives on inside her.
CASSANDRA.
  God of the iron marches,
            Apollo *Apollo* my destroyer—
  where, where have you led me now? what house—   1085
LEADER.
  The house of Atreus and his sons. Really—
  don't you know? It's true, see for yourself.
CASSANDRA.
  No . . . the house that hates god,
            an echoing womb of guilt, kinsmen
                  torturing kinsmen, severed heads,   1090
  slaughterhouse of heroes, soil streaming blood—
LEADER.
  A keen hound, this stranger.
  Trailing murder, and murder she will find.

---

[67] Apollo is more typically associated with joy.

CASSANDRA.
    See, my witnesses—
           I trust to them, to the babies   1095
                wailing, skewered on the sword,
    their flesh charred, the father gorging on their parts—
LEADER.
    We'd heard your fame as a seer,
    but no one looks for seers in Argos.
CASSANDRA.
        Oh no, what horror, what new plot,   1100
    new agony this?—
    it's growing, massing, deep in the house,
                a plot, a monstrous—*thing*
                       to crush the loved ones, no,
    there is no cure, and rescue's far away and—   1105
LEADER.
    I can't read these signs; I knew the first,[68]
    the city rings with them.
CASSANDRA.
        You, you godforsaken—you'd do *this*?
    The lord of your bed,
    you bathe him . . . his body glistens, then—   1110
                  how to tell the climax?—
                      comes so quickly, see,
    hand over hand shoots out, hauling ropes—
                            then lunge!
LEADER.
    Still lost. Her riddles, her dark words of god—
    I'm groping, helpless.
CASSANDRA.
                No no, look *there*!—   1115
    what's that? some net flung out of hell—
        No, *she* is the snare,
    the bedmate, deathmate, murder's strong right arm!
                Let the insatiate discord in the race
    rear up and shriek "Avenge the victim—stone them dead!"   1120
LEADER.
    What Fury is this? Why rouse it, lift its wailing
    through the house? I hear you and lose hope.
CHORUS.
    Drop by drop at the heart, the gold of life ebbs out.
        We are the old soldiers . . . wounds will come
    with the crushing sunset of our lives.   1125
    Death is close, and quick.
CASSANDRA.
                  Look out! *look out*!—
    Ai, drag the great bull from the mate!—

---

[68] The Leader had understood Cassandra's earlier reference to the familiar story of
Thyestes' feast but does not understand her allusion to the imminent murder of Agamemnon.

     a thrash of robes, she traps him—
writhing—
        black horn glints, twists—
            she gores him through!
        And now he buckles, look, the bath swirls red—   1130
There's stealth and murder in that caldron, do you hear?

LEADER.
    I'm no judge, I've little skill with the oracles,
    but even I know danger when I hear it.

CHORUS.
    What good are the oracles to men? Words, more words,
       and the hurt comes on us, endless words   1135
    and a seer's techniques have brought us
    terror and the truth.

CASSANDRA.
    The agony—O I am breaking!—Fate's so hard,
       and the pain that floods my voice is mine alone.
    Why have you brought me here, tormented as I am?   1140
    Why, unless to die with him, why else?

LEADER AND CHORUS.
    Mad with the rapture—god speeds you on
       to the song, the deathsong,
    like the nightingale[69] that broods on sorrow,
       mourns her son, her son,   1145
    her life inspired with grief for him,
    she lilts and shrills, dark bird that lives for night.

CASSANDRA.
    The nightingale—O for a song, a fate like hers!
       The gods gave her a life of ease, swathed her in wings,
    no tears, no wailing. The knife waits for me.   1150
    They'll splay me on the iron's double edge.

LEADER AND CHORUS.
    Why?—what god hurls you on, stroke on stroke
       to the long dying fall?
    Why the horror clashing through your music,
       terror struck to song?—   1155
    why the anguish, the wild dance?
    Where do your words of god and grief begin?

CASSANDRA.
    Ai, the wedding, wedding of Paris,
    death to the loved ones. Oh Scamander,[70]
    you nursed my father . . . once at your banks   1160
       I nursed and grew, and now at the banks,

---

[69] Tereus, husband of Procne, raped his wife's sister Philomela. In revenge, after being informed of the rape by her sister, Procne killed Itys, her son by Tereus, and served the son's flesh as a meal for the father. In some versions of the myth Procne was later metamorphosed into a nightingale, Philomela into a swallow. (In other versions the metamorphoses are reversed, Procne becoming the swallow and Philomela the nightingale.)

[70] A river at Troy.

of Acheron,[71] the stream that carries sorrow,
it seems I'll chant my prophecies too soon.

LEADER AND CHORUS.

What are you saying? Wait, it's clear,
a child could see the truth, it wounds within,   1165
                  like a bloody fang it tears—
    I hear your destiny—breaking sobs,
              cries that stab the ears.

CASSANDRA.

Oh the grief, the grief of the city
ripped to oblivion. Oh the victims,   1170
the flocks my father burned at the wall,
    rich herds in flames . . . no cure for the doom
that took the city after all, and I,
her last ember, I go down with her.

LEADER AND CHORUS.

You cannot stop, your song goes on—   1175
some spirit drops from the heights and treads you down
                and the brutal strain grows—
    your death-throes come and come and
           I cannot see the end!

CASSANDRA.

Then off with the veils that hid the fresh young bride—   1180
we will see the truth.
Flare up once more, my oracle! Clear and sharp
as the wind that blows toward the rising sun,
I can feel a deeper swell now, gathering head
to break at last and bring the dawn of grief.   1185

No more riddles. I will teach you.
Come, bear witness, run and hunt with me.
We trail the old barbaric works of slaughter.

These roofs—look up—there is a dancing troupe
that never leaves. And they have their harmony   1190
but it is harsh, their words are harsh, they drink
beyond the limit. Flushed on the blood of men
their spirit grows and none can turn away
their revel breeding in the veins—the Furies!
They cling to the house for life. They sing,   1195
sing of the frenzy that began it all,
strain rising on strain, showering curses
on the man who tramples on his brother's bed.[72]

There. Have I hit the mark or not? Am I a fraud,
a fortune-teller babbling lies from door to door?   1200

---

[71] A river in Hades, the underground world of the dead.

[72] Thyestes had provoked Atreus' anger by seducing his wife, thus bringing on Atreus' revenge and the lineal curse.

Swear how well I know the ancient crimes
that live within this house.
LEADER.
                                   And if I did?
Would an oath bind the wounds and heal us?
But you amaze me. Bred across the sea,
your language strange and still you sense the truth   1205
as if you had been here.
CASSANDRA.
                         Apollo the Prophet
introduced me to his gift.
LEADER.
    A *god*—and moved with love?
CASSANDRA.
    I was ashamed to tell this once,
but now . . .
LEADER.
                         We spoil ourselves with scruples,   1210
long as things go well.
CASSANDRA.
                         He came like a wrestler,
magnificent, took me down and breathed his fire
through me and—
LEADER.
                         You bore him a child?
CASSANDRA.
                                        I yielded,
then at the climax I recoiled—I deceived Apollo!
LEADER.
    But the god's skills—they seized you even then?   1215
CASSANDRA.
    Even then I told my people all the grief to come.
LEADER.
    And Apollo's anger never touched you?—is it possible?
CASSANDRA.
    Once I betrayed him I could never be believed.
LEADER.
    We believe you. Your visions seem so true.
CASSANDRA.
                                        Aieeee!—
the pain, the terror! the birth-pang of the seer   1220
who tells the truth—
                         it whirls me, oh,
the storm comes again, the crashing chords!

Look, you see them nestling at the threshold?
Young, young in the darkness like a dream,
like children really, yes, and their loved ones   1225
brought them down . . .

       their hands, they fill their hands
with their own flesh, they are serving it like food,
holding out their entrails . . . now it's clear,
I can see the armfuls of compassion, see the father
reach to taste and—
      For so much suffering,   1230
I tell you, someone plots revenge.
A lion[73] who lacks a lion's heart,
he sprawled at home in the royal lair
and set a trap for the lord on his return.
My lord . . . I must wear his yoke, I am his slave.   1235
The lord of the men-of-war, he obliterated Troy—
he is so blind, so lost to that detestable hellhound[74]
who pricks her ears and fawns and her tongue draws out
her glittering words of welcome—
       No, he cannot see
the stroke that Fury's hiding, stealth, murder.   1240
What outrage—the woman kills the man!
         What to call
that . . . monster of Greece, and bring my quarry down?
Viper coiling back and forth?
        Some sea-witch?—
Scylla[75] crouched in her rocky nest—nightmare of sailors?
Raging mother of death, storming deathless war against 1245
the ones she loves!
      And how she howled in triumph,
boundless outrage. Just as the tide of battle
broke her way, she seems to rejoice that he
is safe at home from war, saved for her.

Believe me if you will. What will it matter   1250
if you won't? It comes when it comes,
and soon you'll see it face to face
and say the seer was all too true.
You will be moved with pity.
LEADER.
         Thyestes' feast,
the children's flesh—that I know,   1255
and the fear shudders through me. It's true,
real, no dark signs about it. I hear the rest
but it throws me off the scent.
CASSANDRA.
        Agamemnon.
You will see him dead.

---

[73] The "lion" is Aegisthus. [74] Clytaemnestra.

[75] A female monster, imagined as dwelling in a cave, personifying the dangerous rocks on one side of the strait of Messina, which separates Italy from Sicily. She is described in both Homer's *Odyssey* and Virgil's *Aeneid*.

LEADER.
                                        Peace, poor girl!
Put those words to sleep.
CASSANDRA.
                                        No use,   1260
the Healer[76] has no hand in this affair.
LEADER.
Not if it's true—but god forbid it is!
CASSANDRA.
You pray, and they close in to kill!
LEADER.
What man prepares this, this dreadful—
CASSANDRA.
                                                Man?
You *are* lost, to every word I've said.[77]
LEADER.
                                        Yes—   1265
I don't see who can bring the evil off.
CASSANDRA.
And yet I know my Greek, too well.
LEADER.
So does the Delphic oracle,
but he's hard to understand.
CASSANDRA.
                                        His *fire*!—
sears me, sweeps me again—the torture!   1270
Apollo Lord of the Light, you burn,
you blind me—
                Agony!
                                        She is the lioness,
she rears on her hind legs, she beds with the wolf
when her lion king goes ranging—
                                        she will kill me—
Ai, the torture!
                                        She is mixing her drugs,   1275
adding a measure more of hate for me.
She gloats as she whets the sword for him.
He brought me home and we will pay in carnage.

Why mock yourself with these—trappings, the rod,
the god's wreath, his yoke around my throat?   1280
Before I die I'll tread you—

                        [*Ripping off her regalia, stamping
                        it into the ground.*]

                Down, out,
die die die!
Now you're down. I've paid you back.

---

[76] Apollo.   [77] Cassandra means that she has been referring to a woman, not a man.

Look for another victim—I am free at last—
make her rich in all your curse and doom.

[*Staggering backward as if wrestling with a spirit tearing at her robes.*]

See,   1285
Apollo himself, his fiery hands—I feel him again,
he's stripping off my robes, the Seer's robes!
And after he looked down and saw me mocked,
even in these, his glories, mortified by friends[78]
I loved, and they hated me, they were so blind   1290
to their own demise—

I went from door to door,
I was wild with the god, I heard them call me
"Beggar! Wretch! Starve for bread in hell!"

And I endured it all, and now he will
extort me as his due. A seer for the Seer.   1295
He brings me here to die like this,
not to serve at my father's altar. No,
the block is waiting. The cleaver steams
with my life blood, the first blood drawn
for the king's last rites.

[*Regaining her composure and moving to the altar.*]

We will die,   1300
but not without some honor from the gods.
There will come another[79] to avenge us,
born to kill his mother, born
his father's champion. A wanderer, a fugitive
driven off his native land, he will come home   1305
to cope the stones of hate that menace all he loves.
The gods have sworn a monumental oath: as his father lies
upon the ground he draws him home with power like a prayer.

Then why so pitiful, why so many tears?
I have seen my city faring as she fared,   1310
and those who took her, judged by the gods,
faring as they fare. I must be brave.
It is my turn to die.

[*Approaching the doors.*]

I address you as the Gates of Death.
I pray it comes with one clean stroke,   1315

[78] The Trojans; Cassandra's own people did not heed her.
[79] Orestes, son of Agamemnon and Clytaemnestra.

no convulsions, the pulses ebbing out
in gentle death. I'll close my eyes and sleep.
LEADER.
So much pain, poor girl, and so much truth,
you've told so much. But if you *see* it coming,
clearly—how can you go to your own death,   1320
like a beast to the altar driven on by god,
and hold your head so high?
CASSANDRA.
                          No escape, my friends,
not now.
LEADER.
        But the last hour should be savored.
CASSANDRA.
My time has come. Little to gain from flight.
LEADER.
You're brave, believe me, full of gallant heart.   1325
CASSANDRA.
Only the wretched go with praise like that.
LEADER.
But to go nobly lends a man some grace.
CASSANDRA.
My noble father—you and your noble children.

                                [She nears the threshold and recoils,
                                groaning in revulsion.]

LEADER.
What now? what terror flings you back?
Why? Unless some horror in the brain—
CASSANDRA.
                                Murder.   1330
The house breathes with murder—bloody shambles![80]
LEADER.
No, no, only the victims at the hearth.
CASSANDRA.
I know that odor. I smell the open grave.
LEADER.
But the Syrian myrrh, it fills the halls with splendor,
can't you sense it?
CASSANDRA.
                        Well, I must go in now,   1335
mourning Agamemnon's death and mine.
Enough of life!

                                [Approaching the doors again and
                                crying out.]

[80] A place of bloodshed; a slaughterhouse.

Friends—I cried out,
not from fear like a bird fresh caught,
but that you will testify to *how* I died.
When the queen, woman for woman, dies for me,   1340
and a man falls for the man who married grief.
That's all I ask, my friends. A stranger's gift
for one about to die.
LEADER.
                    Poor creature, you
and the end you see so clearly. I pity you.
CASSANDRA.
I'd like a few words more, a kind of dirge,   1345
it is my own. I pray to the sun,
the last light I'll see,
that when the avengers cut the assassins down
they will avenge me too, a slave who died,
an easy conquest.
                    Oh men, your destiny.   1350
When all is well a shadow can overturn it.
When trouble comes a stroke of the wet sponge,
and the picture's blotted out. And that,
I think that breaks the heart.

                            [*She goes through the doors.*]

CHORUS.
But the lust for power never dies—   1355
    men cannot have enough.
No one will lift a hand to send it
from his door, to give it warning,
"Power, never come again!"
Take this man: the gods in glory   1360
gave him Priam's city to plunder,
brought him home in splendor like a god.
But now if he must pay for the blood
his fathers shed, and die for the deaths
he brought to pass, and bring more death   1365
to avenge his dying, show us one
    who boasts himself born free
of the raging angel, once he hears—

                        [*Cries break out within the palace.*]

AGAMEMNON.
                    Aagh!
Struck deep—the death-blow, deep—
LEADER.
                        Quiet. Cries,
but who? Someone's stabbed—

AGAMEMNON.

                              Aaagh, again . . .   1370
second blow—struck home.

LEADER.

                              The work is done,
you can feel it. The king, and the great cries—
Close ranks now, find the right way out.

> [*But the old men scatter, each speaks
> singly.*]

CHORUS.

—I say send out heralds, muster the guard,
    they'll save the house.

                              —And I say rush in now,   1375
    catch them red-handed—butchery running on their blades.

—Right with you, do something—now or never!

—Look at them, beating the drum for insurrection.

                                                  —Yes,
    we're wasting time. They rape the name of caution,
    their hands will never sleep.

                              —Not a plan in sight.   1380
    Let men of action do the planning too.

—I'm helpless. Who can raise the dead with words?

—What, drag out our lives? bow down to the tyrants,
    the ruin of the house?

                              —Never, better to die
    on your feet than live on your knees.

                              —Wait,   1385
    do we take the cries for signs, prophesy like seers
    and give him up for dead?

                              —No more suspicions,
    not another word till we have proof.

                              —Confusion
    on all sides—one thing to do. See how it stands
    with Agamemnon, once and for all we'll see—   1390

> [*He rushes at the doors. They open
> and reveal a silver caldron that
> holds the body of* AGAMEMNON
> *shrouded in bloody robes, with the
> body of* CASSANDRA *to his left and*
> CLYTAEMNESTRA *standing to his
> right, sword in hand. She strides
> toward the chorus.*]

CLYTAEMNESTRA.
Words, endless words I've said to serve the moment!
Now it makes me proud to tell the truth.
How else to prepare a death for deadly men
who seem to love you? How to rig the nets
of pain so high no man can overleap them?   1395

I brooded on this trial, this ancient blood feud
year by year. At last my hour came.
Here I stand and here I struck
and here my work is done.
I did it all. I don't deny it, no.   1400
He had no way to flee or fight his destiny—

> [*Unwinding the robes from* AGA-
> MEMNON'S *body, spreading them be-
> fore the altar where the old men
> cluster around them, unified as a
> chorus once again.*]

our never-ending, all-embracing net, I cast it
wide for the royal haul, I coil him round and round
in the wealth, the robes of doom, and then I strike him
once, twice, and at each stroke he cries in agony—   1405
he buckles at the knees and crashes here!
And when he's down I add the third, last blow,
to the Zeus who saves the dead beneath the ground
I send that third blow home in homage like a prayer.

So he goes down, and the life is bursting out of him—   1410
great sprays of blood, and the murderous shower
wounds me, dyes me black and I, I revel
like the Earth when the spring rains come down,
the blessed gifts of god, and the new green spear
splits the sheath and rips to birth in glory!   1415

So it stands, elders of Argos gathered here.
Rejoice if you can rejoice—I glory.
And if I'd pour upon his body the libation
it deserves, what wine could match my words?
It is right and more than right. He flooded   1420

the vessel of our proud house with misery,
with the vintage of the curse and now
he drains the dregs. My lord is home at last.

LEADER.
You appall me, you, your brazen words—
exulting over your fallen king.

CLYTAEMNESTRA.
                                        And you,   1425
you try me like some desperate woman.
My heart is steel, well you know. Praise me,
blame me as you choose. It's all one.
Here is Agamemnon, my husband made a corpse
by this right hand—a masterpiece of Justice.   1430
Done is done.

CHORUS.
                    Woman!—what poison cropped from the soil
or strained from the heaving sea, what nursed you,
drove you insane? You brave the curse of Greece.
          You have cut away and flung away and now
the people cast you off to exile,   1435
broken with our hate.

CLYTAEMNESTRA.
                              And now you sentence me?—
you banish *me* from the city, curses breathing
down my neck? But *he*—
name one charge you brought against him then.
He thought no more of it than killing a beast,   1440
and his flocks were rich, teeming in their fleece,
but he sacrificed his own child, our daughter,
the agony I labored into love
to charm away the savage winds of Thrace.

Didn't the law demand you banish him?—   1445
hunt him from the land for all his guilt?
But now you witness what I've done
and you are ruthless judges.
                                        Threaten away!
I'll meet you blow for blow. And if I fall
the throne is yours. If god decrees the reverse,   1450
late as it is, old men, you'll learn your place.

CHORUS.
          Mad with ambition,
                              shrilling pride!—some Fury
crazed with the carnage rages through your brain—
                    I can see the flecks of blood inflame your eyes!   1455
But vengeance comes—you'll lose your loved ones,
stroke for painful stroke.

CLYTAEMNESTRA.
          Then learn this too, the power of my oaths.
          By the child's Rights I brought to birth,

by Ruin, by Fury—the three gods to whom   1460
I sacrificed this man—I swear my hopes
will never walk the halls of fear so long
as Aegisthus lights the fire on my hearth.
Loyal to me as always, no small shield
to buttress my defiance.
                                  Here he lies.   1465
He brutalized me. The darling of all
the golden girls who spread the gates of Troy.
And here his spearprize . . . what wonders she beheld!—
the seer of Apollo shared my husband's bed,
his faithful mate who knelt at the rowing-benches,   1470
worked by every hand.
                            They have their rewards.
He as you know. And she, the swan[81] of the gods
who lived to sing her latest, dying song—
his lover lies beside him.
She brings a fresh, voluptuous relish to my bed!   1475
CHORUS.
    Oh quickly, let me die—
no bed of labor, no, no wasting illness . . .
bear me off in the sleep that never ends,
                now that he has fallen,
now that our dearest shield lies battered—   1480
    Woman made him suffer,
                  woman struck him down.

    Helen the wild, maddening Helen,
one for the many, the thousand lives
you murdered under Troy. Now you are crowned   1485
with this consummate wreath, the blood
that lives in memory, glistens age to age.
Once in the halls she walked and she was war,
angel of war, angel of agony, lighting men to death.
CLYTAEMNESTRA.
    Pray no more for death, broken   1490
as you are. And never turn
    your wrath on her, call her
the scourge of men, the one alone
who destroyed a myriad Greek lives—
Helen the grief that never heals.   1495
CHORUS.
    The *spirit!*—you who tread
the house and the twinborn sons[82] of Tantalus—
you empower the sisters, Fury's twins
              whose power tears the heart!

---

[81] In folklore, the swan sings for the first and last time just before its death.

[82] "Sons" can refer either to Tantalus' grandsons, Thyestes and Atreus, or to his great-grandsons, Agamemnon and Menelaus, who married the sisters Clytaemnestra and Helen.

Perched on the corpse your carrion raven   1500
      glories in her hymn,
           her screaming hymn of pride.

CLYTAEMNESTRA.
    Now you set your judgment straight,
    you summon *him!* Three generations
        feed the spirit in the race.   1505
    Deep in the veins he feeds our bloodlust—
    aye, before the old wound dies
    it ripens in another flow of blood.
CHORUS.
    The great curse of the house, the spirit,
        dead weight wrath—and you can praise it!   1510
    Praise the insatiate doom that feeds
    relentless on our future and our sons.
    Oh all through the will of Zeus,
    the cause of all, the one who works it all.
    What comes to birth that is not Zeus?   1515
    Our lives are pain, what part not come from god?

    Oh my king, my captain,
    how to salute you, how to mourn you?
    What can I say with all my warmth and love?
    Here in the black widow's web you lie,   1520
    gasping out your life
    in a sacrilegious death, dear god,
    reduced to a slave's bed,
    my king of men, yoked by stealth and Fate,
    by the wife's hand that thrust the two-edged sword.   1525
CLYTAEMNESTRA.
    You claim the work is mine, call me
    Agamemnon's wife—you are so wrong.
    Fleshed in the wife of this dead man,
        the spirit lives within me,
    our savage ancient spirit of revenge.   1530
    In return for Atreus' brutal feast
    he kills his perfect son—for every
    murdered child, a crowning sacrifice.
CHORUS.
    And *you*, innocent of his murder?
        And who could swear to that? and how? . . .   1535
    and still an avenger could arise,
    bred by the fathers' crimes, and lend a hand.
    He wades in the blood of brothers,
    stream on mounting stream—black war erupts
        and where he strides revenge will stride,   1540
    clots will mass for the young who were devoured.

Oh my king, my captain,
how to salute you, how to mourn you?
What can I say with all my warmth and love?
Here in the black widow's web you lie,   1545
gasping out your life
in a sacrilegious death, dear god,
reduced to a slave's bed,
my king of men, yoked by stealth and Fate,
by the wife's hand that thrust the two-edged sword.   1550

CLYTAEMNESTRA.
No slave's death, I think—
no stealthier than the death he dealt
our house and the offspring of our loins,
        Iphigeneia, girl of tears.
Act for act, wound for wound!   1555
Never exult in Hades, swordsman,
here you are repaid. By the sword
you did your work and by the sword you die.

CHORUS.
        The mind reels—where to turn?
    All plans dashed, all hope! I cannot think . . .   1560
the roofs are toppling, I dread the drumbeat thunder
    the heavy rains of blood will crush the house
        the first light rains are over—
    Justice brings new acts of agony, yes,
on new grindstones Fate is grinding sharp the sword of Justice.   1565

Earth, dear Earth,
if only you'd drawn me under
long before I saw him huddled
in the beaten silver bath.
Who will bury him, lift his dirge?   1570

[*Turning to* CLYTAEMNESTRA.]

You, can you dare *this*?
To kill your lord with your own hand
then mourn his soul with tributes, terrible tributes—
do his enormous works a great dishonor.
This godlike man, this hero. Who at the grave   1575
will sing his praises, pour the wine of tears?
Who will labor there with truth of heart?

CLYTAEMNESTRA.
This is no concern of yours.
The hand that bore and cut him down
will hand him down to Mother Earth.
This house will never mourn for him.   1580
        Only our daughter Iphigeneia,
by all rights, will rush to meet him
first at the churning straits,

the ferry[83] over tears—   1585
she'll fling her arms around her father,
pierce him with her love.

CHORUS.
                    Each charge meets countercharge.
          None can judge between them. Justice.
          The plunderer plundered, the killer pays the price.   1590
     The truth still holds while Zeus still holds the throne:
                    the one who acts must suffer—
          that is law. Who, who can tear from the veins
     the bad seed, the curse? The race is welded to its ruin.

CLYTAEMNESTRA.
     At last you see the future and the truth!   1595
     But I will swear a pact with the spirit
     born within us. I embrace his works,
     cruel as they are but done at last,
               if he will leave our house[84]
     in the future, bleed another line   1600
     with kinsmen murdering kinsmen.
     Whatever he may ask. A few things
     are all I need, once I have purged
     our fury to destroy each other—
               purged it from our halls.

                              [AEGISTHUS *has emerged from the*
                              palace with his bodyguard and
                              stands triumphant over the body of
                              AGAMEMNON.]

AEGISTHUS.
                              O what a brilliant day   1605
     it is for vengeance! Now I can say once more
     there are gods in heaven avenging men,
     blazing down on all the crimes of earth.
     Now at last I see this man brought down
     in the Furies' tangling robes. It feasts my eyes—   1610
     he pays for the plot his father's hand contrived.

     Atreus, this man's father, was king of Argos.
     My father, Thyestes—let me make this clear—
     Atreus' brother challenged him for the crown,
     and Atreus drove him out of house and home   1615
     then lured him back, and home Thyestes came,
     poor man, a suppliant to his own hearth,
     to pray that Fate might save him.

---

[83] The boat in which Charon ferried the dead across the river Styx to Hades.
[84] As the later plays of the trilogy show, there is sad irony in Clytaemnestra's hope that her deed of revenge will have ended the chain of retributive acts.

So it did.
There was no dying, no staining our native ground
with *his* blood. Thyestes was the guest,   1620
and this man's godless father—

[*Pointing to* AGAMEMNON.]

the zeal of the host outstripping a brother's love,
made my father a feast that seemed a feast for gods,
a love feast of his children's flesh.

He cuts
the extremities, feet and delicate hands   1625
into small pieces, scatters them over the dish
and serves it to Thyestes throned on high.
He picks at the flesh he cannot recognize,
the soul of innocence eating the food of ruin—
look,

[*Pointing to the bodies at his feet.*]

that feeds upon the house! And then,   1630
when he sees the monstrous thing he's done, he shrieks,
he reels back head first and vomits up that butchery,
tramples the feast—brings down the curse of Justice:
"Crash to ruin, all the race of Pleisthenes,[85] crash down!"

So you see him, down. And I, the weaver of Justice,   1635
plotted out the kill. Atreus drove us into exile,
my struggling father and I, a babe-in-arms,
his last son, but I became a man
and Justice brought me home. I was abroad
but I reached out and seized my man,   1640
link by link I clamped the fatal scheme
together. Now I could die gladly, even I—
now I see this monster in the nets of Justice.
LEADER.
Aegisthus, you revel in pain—you sicken me.
You say you killed the king in cold blood,   1645
singlehanded planned his pitiful death?
I say there's no escape. In the hour of judgment,
trust to this, your head will meet the people's
rocks and curses.
AEGISTHUS.
You say! you slaves at the oars—
while the master on the benches cracks the whip?   1650
You'll learn, in your late age, how much it hurts
to teach old bones their place. We have techniques—

[85] Apparently an ancestor of Agamemnon, his exact identity is vague.

chains and the pangs of hunger,
two effective teachers, excellent healers.
They can even cure old men of pride and gall.   1655
Look—can't you see? The more you kick
against the pricks, the more you suffer.

LEADER.
You, pathetic—
the king had just returned from battle.
You waited out the war and fouled his lair,   1660
you planned my great commander's fall.

AEGISTHUS.
                                    Talk on—
you'll scream for every word, my little Orpheus.[86]
We'll see if the world comes dancing to your song,
your absurd barking—snarl your breath away!
I'll make you dance, I'll bring you all to heel.   1665

LEADER.
You rule Argos? You who schemed his death
but cringed to cut him down with your own hand?

AEGISTHUS.
The treachery was the woman's work, clearly.
I was a marked man, his enemy for ages.
But I will use his riches, stop at nothing   1670
to civilize his people. All but the rebel:
him I'll yoke and break—
no cornfed colt, running free in the traces.
Hunger, ruthless mate of the dark torture-chamber,
trains her eyes upon him till he drops!   1675

LEADER.
Coward, why not kill the man yourself?
Why did the woman, the corruption of Greece
and the gods of Greece, have to bring him down?
Orestes—
                    If he still sees the light of day,
bring him home, good Fates, home to kill   1680
this pair at last. Our champion in slaughter!

AEGISTHUS.
Bent on insolence? Well, you'll learn, quickly.
At them, men—you have your work at hand!

                                [*His men draw swords; the old men
                                take up their sticks.*]

LEADER.
    At them, fist at the hilt, to the last man—

AEGISTHUS.
    Fist at the hilt, I'm not afraid to die.   1685

[86]The archetypal poet-musician whose song compelled even nature to listen. See Ovid's
Metamorphoses, Book X.

LEADER.

It's death you want and death you'll have—
we'll make that word your last.

[CLYTAEMNESTRA *moves between
them, restraining* AEGISTHUS.]

CLYTAEMNESTRA.

No more, my dearest,
no more grief. We have too much to reap
right here, our mighty harvest of despair.
Our lives are based on pain. No bloodshed now.   1690

Fathers of Argos, turn for home before you act
and suffer for it. What we did was destiny.
If we could end the suffering, how we would rejoice.
The spirit's brutal hoof has struck our heart.
And that is what a woman has to say.   1695
Can you accept the truth?

[CLYTAEMNESTRA *turns to leave.*]

AEGISTHUS.

But these . . . mouths
that bloom in filth—spitting insults in my teeth.
You tempt your fates, you insubordinate dogs—
to hurl abuse at me, your master!

LEADER.

No Greek
worth his salt would grovel at your feet.   1700

AEGISTHUS.

I—I'll stalk you all your days!

LEADER.

Not if the spirit brings Orestes home.

AEGISTHUS.

Exiles feed on hope—well I know.

LEADER.

More,
gorge yourself to bursting—soil justice, while you can.

AEGISTHUS.

I promise you, you'll pay, old fools—in good time too!   1705

LEADER.

Strut on your own dunghill, you cock beside your mate.

CLYTAEMNESTRA.

Let them howl—they're impotent. You and I have power now.
We will set the house in order once for all.

[*They enter the palace; the great
doors close behind them; the old men
disband and wander off.*]

THE LIBATION BEARERS

CHARACTERS

ORESTES, *son of Agamemnon*   CLYTAEMNESTRA
  and Clytaemnestra   CILISSA, *Orestes' old nurse*
PYLADES, *his companion*   AEGISTHUS
ELECTRA, *his sister*   *A servant of Aegisthus*
CHORUS OF SLAVEWOMEN   *Attendants of Orestes,*
  AND THEIR LEADER   *bodyguard of Aegisthus*

TIME AND SCENE

*Several years have passed since Agamemnon's death. At Argos, before the tomb of
the king and his fathers, stands an altar; behind it looms the house of Atreus.*
ORESTES *and* PYLADES *enter, dressed as travelers.* ORESTES *kneels and prays.*

ORESTES.
    Hermes,[1] lord of the dead, look down and guard
    the fathers' power. Be my savior, I beg you,
    be my comrade now.
                   I have come home
    to my own soil, an exile home at last.
    Here at the mounded grave I call my father,   5
    Hear me—I am crying out to you . . .

                        [*He cuts two locks of hair[2] and lays
                        them on the grave.*]

    There is a lock for Inachos[3] who nursed me
    into manhood, there is one for death.

    I was not here to mourn you when you died,
    my father, never gave the last salute   10
    when they bore your corpse away.

                        [ELECTRA *and a chorus of slave-
                        women enter in procession. They are
                        dressed in black and bear libations,
                        moving toward* ORESTES *at the
                        grave.*]

---

[1] The messenger of the gods, patron of human messengers and heralds. He also guided
the dead to Hades.
[2] The locks were customary ritual tributes to the dead.
[3] River at Argos; Orestes pays tribute to his original fatherland as well as to his dead father,
Agamemnon.

What's this?
Look, a company moving toward us. Women,
robed in black . . . so clear in the early light.

I wonder what they mean, what turn of fate?—
some new wound to the house?   15
Or perhaps they come to honor you, my father,
bearing cups to soothe and still the dead.
That's right, it must be . . .
Electra, I think I see *her* coming, there,
my own sister, worn, radiant in her grief—   20
Dear god, let me avenge my father's murder—
fight beside me now with all your might!

Out of their way, Pylades.[4] I must know
what they mean, these women turning toward us,
what their prayers call forth.   25

[*They withdraw behind the tomb.*]

CHORUS.[5]
Rushed from the house we come
    escorting cups for the dead,
in step with the hands' hard beat,
                        our cheeks glistening,
flushed where the nails have raked new furrows running blood;   30
and life beats on, and through it all
we nurse our lives with tears,
to the sound of ripping linen beat our robes in sorrow,
    close to the breast the beats throb
and laughter's gone and fortune throbs and throbs.   35

Aie!—bristling Terror[6] struck—
    Terror the seer of the house,
the nightmare ringing clear
                        breathed its wrath in sleep,
in the midnight watch a cry!—the voice of Terror   40
deep in the house, bursting down
on the women's darkened chambers, yes,
and the old ones, skilled at dreams, swore oaths to god and called,
    "The proud dead stir under earth,
they rage against the ones who took their lives."   45

[4] Son of Strophios, with whom the exiled Orestes had lived in Phokis after Clytaemnestra
sent him away (see the *Agamemnon*).
[5] The Chorus consists of women brought back from Troy as slaves. In the lament that
follows they express grief for both the house of Atreus and that of Troy.
[6] Clytaemnestra has been frightened by a nightmare; she has therefore sent the women to
Agamemnon's tomb with propitiatory libations (mixtures of honey and wine).

But the gifts, the empty gifts
            she hopes will ward them off—
good Mother Earth!—that godless woman sends me here . . .
        I dread to say her prayer.
What can redeem the blood that wets the soil?   50
Oh for the hearthfire banked with grief,
    the ramparts down, a fine house down—
dark, dark, and the sun, the life is curst,
    and mist enshrouds the halls
        where the lords of war went down.   55

And the ancient pride no war,
            no storm, no force could tame,
ringing in all men's ears, in all men's hearts is gone.
        They are afraid. Success,
    they bow to success, more god than god himself.   60
But Justice waits and turns the scales:
    a sudden blow for some at dawn,
for some in the no man's land of dusk
    her torments grow with time,
        and the lethal night takes others.   65

And the blood that Mother Earth consumes
clots hard, it won't seep through, it breeds revenge
                        and frenzy goes through the guilty,
seething like infection, swarming through the brain.

For the one who treads a virgin's bed   70
there is no cure. All the streams of the world,
    all channels run into one
to cleanse a man's red hands will swell the bloody tide.

And I . . . Fate and the gods brought down their yoke,
they ringed our city, out of our fathers' halls   75
            they led us here as slaves.
And the will breaks, we kneel at their command—
                    our masters right or wrong!
        And we beat the tearing hatred down,
    behind our veils we weep for her,   80

[*Turning to* ELECTRA.]

her senseless fate.
Sorrow turns the secret heart to ice.
ELECTRA.
                        Dear women,
    you keep the house in order, best you can;
    and now you've come to the grave to say a prayer
    with me, my escorts. I'll need your help with this.   85
    What to say when I pour the cup of sorrow?

[Lifting her libation cup.]

What kindness, what prayer can touch my father?
Shall I say I bring him love for love, a woman's
love for husband? My mother, love from her?
I've no taste for that, no words to say   90
as I run the honeyed oil on father's tomb.

Or try the salute we often use at graves?
"A wreath for a wreath. Now bring the givers
gifts to match" . . . no, give them pain for pain.[7]

Or silent, dishonored, just as father died,   95
empty it out for the soil to drink and then
retrace my steps, like a slave sent out with scourings
left from the purging of the halls, and throw
the cup behind me, looking straight ahead.

Help me decide, my friends. Join me here.   100
We nurse a common hatred in the house.
Don't hide your feelings—no, fear no one.
Destiny waits us all,

[Looking toward the tomb.]

    born free,
or slaves who labor under another's hand.
Speak to me, please. Perhaps you've had   105
a glimpse of something better.
LEADER.
        I revere
your father's death-mound like an altar.
I'll say a word, now that you ask,
that comes from deep within me.
ELECTRA.
       Speak on,
with everything you feel for father's grave.   110
LEADER.
Say a blessing as you pour, for those who love you.
ELECTRA.
And of the loved ones, whom to call my friends?
LEADER.
First yourself, then all who hate Aegisthus.
ELECTRA.
I and you. I can say a prayer for us
and then for—
LEADER.
    You know, try to say it.   115

---

[7] Electra possibly means "pain for the murderers to match the pain they gave my father."

ELECTRA.
    There is someone else to rally to our side?
LEADER.
    Remember Orestes, even abroad and gone.
ELECTRA.
    Well said, the best advice I've had.
LEADER.
    Now for the murderers. Remember them and—
ELECTRA.
                                                    What?
    I'm so unseasoned, teach me what to say.   120
LEADER.
    Let some god or man come down upon them.
ELECTRA.
    Judge or avenger, which?
LEADER.
    Just say "the one who murders in return!"
ELECTRA.
    How can I ask the gods for that
    and keep my conscience clear?
LEADER.
                                    How not,   125
    and pay the enemy back in kind?

                                    [ELECTRA *kneels at the grave in*
                                    prayer.]

ELECTRA.
                                    —Herald king
    of the world above and the quiet world below,
    lord of the dead, my Hermes, help me now.
    Tell the spirits underground to hear my prayers,
    and the high watch hovering over father's roofs,   130
    and have her listen too, the Earth herself
    who brings all things to life and makes them strong,
    then gathers in the rising tide once more.

    And I will tip libations to the dead.
    I call out to my father, Pity me,   135
    dear Orestes too.
    Rekindle the light that saves our house!
    We're auctioned off, drift like vagrants now.
    Mother has pawned us for a husband, Aegisthus,
    her partner in her murdering.
                                    I go like a slave,   140
    Orestes driven from his estates while they,
    they roll in the fruits of all your labors,
    magnificent and sleek. O bring Orestes home,
    with a happy twist of fate, my father. Hear me,

make me far more self-possessed than mother,   145
make this hand more pure.

These prayers for us. For our enemies I say,
Raise up your avenger, into the light, my father—
kill the killers in return, with justice!
So in the midst of prayers for good I place   150
this curse for them.
                              Bring up your blessings,
up into the air, led by the gods and Earth
and all the rights that bring us triumph.

                              [*Pouring libations on the tomb and
                              turning to the women.*]

These are my prayers. Over them I pour libations.
Yours to adorn them with laments, to make them bloom,   155
so custom says—sing out and praise the dead.
CHORUS.
Let the tears fall, ring out and die,
          die with the warlord at this bank,
this bulwark of the good, defense against the bad,
the guilt, the curse we ward away   160
with prayer and all we pour. Hear me, majesty, hear me,
     lord of glory, from the darkness of your heart.
                                        Ohhhhhh!—
          Dear god, let him come! Some man
with a strong spear, born to free the house,
     with the torsion bow of Scythia[8] bent for slaughter,   165
splattering shafts like a god of war—sword in fist
     for the slash-and-hack of battle!

                              [ELECTRA *remains at the grave,
                              staring at the ground.*]

ELECTRA.
                                        Father,
you have it now, the earth has drunk your wine.
Wait, friends, here's news. Come share it.
LEADER.
                                        Speak on,
my heart's a dance of fear.
ELECTRA.
                              A lock of hair,   170
here on the grave . . .
LEADER.
                    Whose? A man's?
A growing girl's?

[8] A region in southwest Asia, noted for its archers and their powerful bows.

ELECTRA.
                    And it has the marks,
  and anyone would think—
LEADER.
                                What?
  We're old. You're young, now you teach us.
ELECTRA.
  No one could have cut this lock but I and—   175
LEADER.
  Callous they are, the ones who ought to shear
  the hair and mourn.
ELECTRA.
                    Look at the texture, just like—
LEADER.
  Whose? I want to know.
ELECTRA.
                            Like mine, identical,
  can't you see?
LEADER.
                    Orestes . . . he brought a gift
  in secret?
ELECTRA.
            It's *his*—I can see his curls.   180
LEADER.
  And how could he risk the journey here?
ELECTRA.
  He sent it, true, a lock to honor father.
LEADER.
  All the more cause for tears. You mean
  he'll never set foot on native ground again.
ELECTRA.
                                        Yes!

  It's sweeping over me too—anguish   185
  like a breaker—a sword ripping through my heart!
  Tears come like the winter rains that flood the gates—
  can't hold them back, when I see this strand of hair.

  How could I think another Greek could play
  the prince with this?
                    She'd never cut it,   190
  the murderess, my mother. She insults the name,
  she and her godless spirit preying on her children.

  But how, how can I come right out and say it *is*
  the glory of the dearest man I know, Orestes?
  Stop, I'm fawning on hope.
                            Oh, if only   195
  it had a herald's voice, kind and human—
  I'm so shaken, torn—and told me clearly
  to throw it away, they severed it from a head

that I detest. Or it could sorrow with me
like a brother, aye,
this splendor come to honor father's grave. 200

We call on the gods, and the gods well know
what storms torment us, sailors whirled to nothing.
But if we are to live and reach the haven,
one small seed could grow a mighty tree— 205
Look, tracks.

A new sign to tell us more.
Footmarks . . . pairs of them, like mine.
Two outlines, two prints, his own, and there,
a fellow traveler's.

[*Putting her foot into* ORESTES'
print.]

The heel, the curve of the arch
like twins.

[*While* ORESTES *emerges from behind the grave, she follows cautiously in his steps until they come
together.*]

Step by step, my step in his . . .

we meet— 210
Oh the pain, like pangs of labor—this is madness!
ORESTES.
Pray for the future. Tell the gods they've brought
your prayers to birth, and pray that we succeed.

[ELECTRA *draws back, struggling
for composure.*]

ELECTRA.
The gods—why now? What have I ever won from them?
ORESTES.
The sight you prayed to see for many years. 215
ELECTRA.
And you know the one I call?
ORESTES.

I know Orestes,
know he moves you deeply.
ELECTRA.

Yes,
but now what's come to fill my prayers?
ORESTES.
Here I am. Look no further.
No one loves you more than I.

ELECTRA.

No,   220

it's a trap, stranger . . . a net you tie around me?
ORESTES.
Then I tie myself as well.
ELECTRA.

But the pain,
you're laughing at all—
ORESTES.   •

Your pain is mine.
If I laugh at yours, I only laugh at mine.
ELECTRA.
Orestes—   225
can I call you?—are you really—
ORESTES.

I am!
Open your eyes. So slow to learn.
You saw the lock of hair I cut in mourning.
You scanned my tracks, you could see my marks, •
your breath leapt, you all but saw me in the flesh—   230
Look—

> [*Holding the lock to his temple, then
> to* ELECTRA'S]

put it where I cut it.
It's your brother's. Try, it matches yours.

> [*Removing a strip of weaving from
> his clothing.*]

Work of your own hand, you tamped the loom,
look, there are wild creatures in the weaving.

> [*She kneels beside him, weeping; he
> lifts her to her feet and they em-
> brace.*]

No, no, control yourself—don't lose yourself in joy!   235
Our loved ones, well I know, would slit our throats.
LEADER.
Dearest, the darling of your father's house,
hope of the seed we nursed with tears—you save us.
Trust to your power, win your father's house once more!
ELECTRA.
You light to my eyes, four loves in one!   240
I have to call you father, it is fate;
and I turn to you the love I gave my mother—
I despise her, she deserves it, yes,
and the love I gave my sister,[9] sacrificed

---

[9] Iphigeneia, sacrificed at Aulis. See headnote to the *Oresteia.*

on the cruel sword, I turn to you.   245
You were my faith, my brother—
you alone restore my self-respect.

[*Praying.*]

Power and Justice, Saving Zeus, Third Zeus,[10]
almighty all in all, be with us now.

ORESTES.

Zeus, Zeus, watch over all we do,   250
fledglings reft of the noble eagle father.
He died in the coils, the viper's dark embrace.
We are his orphans worn down with hunger,
weak, too young to haul the father's quarry
home to shelter.

                Look down on us!   255
I and Electra too, I tell you, children
robbed of our father, both of us bound
in exile from our house.

                And what a father—
a priest at sacrifice, he showered you
with honors. Put an end to his nestlings now   260
and who will serve you banquets rich as his?
Destroy the eagle's brood, you can never
send a sign that wins all men's belief.
Rot the stock of a proud dynastic tree—
it can never shore your altar steaming   265
with the oxen in the mornings.

                Tend us—
we seem in ruins now, I know. Up from nothing
rear a house to greatness.

LEADER.

                Softly, children,
white hopes of your father's hearth. Someone
might hear you, children, charmed with his own voice   270
blurt all this out to the masters. Oh, just once
to see them—live bones crackling in the fire
spitting pitch!

ORESTES.

                Apollo will never fail me, no,
his tremendous power, his oracle charges me
to see this trial through.

                I can still hear the god—   275
a high voice ringing with winters of disaster,
piercing the heart within me, warm and strong,
unless I hunt my father's murderers, cut them down
in their own style—they destroyed my birthright.

[10]Zeus in his role as savior. Compare the more material and pragmatic emphasis in the
following prayer to Zeus by Orestes.

"Gore them like a bull!" he called, "or pay their debt   280
with your own life, one long career of grief."

He revealed[11] so much about us,
told how the dead take root beneath the soil,
they grow with hate and plague the lives of men.
He told of the leprous boils that ride the flesh,   285
their wild teeth gnawing the mother tissue, aye,
and a white scurf spreads like cancer over these,
and worse, he told how assaults of Furies spring
to life on the father's blood . . .
                              You can *see* them—
the eyes burning, grim brows working over you in the dark—   290
the dark sword of the dead—your murdered kinsmen
pleading for revenge. And the madness haunts
the midnight watch, the empty terror shakes you,
harries, drives you on—an exile from your city—
a brazen whip will mutilate your back.   295

For such as us, no share in the winebowl,
no libations poured in love. You never see
your father's wrath but it pulls you from the altars.
There is no refuge, none to take you in.
A pariah, reviled, at long last you die,   300
withered in the grip of all this dying.

Such oracles are persuasive,
don't you think? And even if I am not convinced,
the rough work of the world is still to do.
So many yearnings meet and urge me on.   305
The god's commands. Mounting sorrow for father.
Besides, the lack of patrimony[12] presses hard;
and my compatriots, the glory of men
who toppled Troy with nerves of singing steel,
go at the beck and call of a brace of women.   310
Womanhearted he is[13]—if not, we'll soon see.

> [*The leader lights the altar fires.*
> ORESTES, ELECTRA *and the chorus*
> *gather for the invocation at the*
> *grave.*]

CHORUS.
     Powers of destiny, mighty queens of Fate!—
     by the will of Zeus your will be done,

---

[11] In the following lines Orestes describes the physical, psychological, and social ills that, according to Apollo's oracle, Orestes will have to endure if he does not avenge his father's murder.
[12] What Orestes ought rightfully to inherit.
[13] That is, Aegisthus, who now rules Argos with Clytaemnestra.

press on to the end now,
　　Justice turns the wheel.   315
"Word for word, curse for curse
be born now," Justice thunders,
　　hungry for retribution,
"stroke for bloody stroke be paid.
　　The one who acts must suffer."   320
Three generations strong the word resounds.

ORESTES.
　　Dear father, father of dread,
what can I do or say to reach you now?
　　What breath can reach from here
to the bank where you lie moored at anchor?[14]   325
What light can match your darkness? None,
　　but there is a kind of grace that comes
　　　when the tears revive a proud old house
and Atreus' sons, the warlords lost and gone.

LEADER.
　　The ruthless jaws of the fire,[15]   330
　　　my child, can never tame the dead,
　　　　　　his rage inflames his sons.
Men die and the voices rise, they light the guilty, true—
cries raised for the fathers, clear and just,
　　will hunt their killers harried to the end.   335

ELECTRA.
　　Then hear me now, my father,
it is my turn, my tears are welling now,
　　as child by child we come
to the tomb and raise the dirge, my father.
Your grave receives a girl in prayer   340
and a man in flight, and we are one,
　　and the pain is equal, whose is worse?
And who outwrestles death—what third last fall?[16]

CHORUS.
　　But still some god, if he desires,
　　may work our strains to a song of joy,   345
　　from the dirges chanted over the grave
　　　may lift a hymn in the kings' halls
　　and warm the loving cup you stir this morning.

ORESTES.
　　If only at Troy
a Lycian[17] cut you down, my father—   350
gone, with an aura left at home behind you,
　　children to go their ways

---

[14] In the world of the dead; but the phrase calls up also the memory of the Greek fleet at Aulis, where Agamemnon had committed the outrage on Iphigeneia that ultimately brought on his murder.
[15] The fire in which the dead are cremated.
[16] The deciding round in a wrestling match.
[17] The Lycians fought in aid of the Trojans.

and the eyes look on them bright with awe,
and the tomb you win on headlands seas away
      would buoy up the house . . .   355

LEADER.
    And loved by the men you loved
      who died in glory, there you'd rule
                  beneath the earth—lord, prince,
stern aide to the giant kings who judge the shadows there.[18]
You were a king of kings when you drew breath;   360
    the mace you held could make men kneel or die.

ELECTRA.
      No, not under Troy!—
not dead and gone with them, my father,
hordes pierced by the spear Scamander[19] washes down.
    Sooner the killers die   365
as they killed you—at the hands of friends,
and the news of death would come from far away,
    we'd never know this grief.[20]

CHORUS.
    You are dreaming, children,
    dreams dearer than gold, more blest   370
than the Blest beyond the Northwind's raging.[21]
      Dreams are easy, oh,
but the double lash is striking home.
Now our comrades group underground.
Our masters' reeking hands are doomed—   375
    the children take the day!

ORESTES.
    That thrills his ear,
        that arrow lands!
        Zeus, Zeus, force up from the earth
destruction, late but true to the mark,   380
to the reckless heart, the killing hand—
    for parents of revenge revenge be done.

LEADER.
    And the ripping cries of triumph mine
to sing when the man is stabbed,
              the woman[22] dies—   385
why, why hide what's deep inside me,
black wings beating, storming the spirit's prow—
        hurricane, slashing hatred!

[18] The giant kings are Minos, Rhadamanthus, and Aeacus, who were rewarded for their just lives by being made judges of the dead in Hades.

[19] The river Scamander, near Troy.

[20] Electra wishes that Clytaemnestra and Aegisthus had died before they killed Agamemnon.

[21] The Chorus refers to the Hyperboreans, a mythical people supposed to live happily in the far north, beyond Boreas (the north wind). They had a special devotion to Apollo.

[22] Aegisthus is "the man"; Clytaemnestra is "the woman."

Electra.
        Both fists at once
                come down, come down—
                        Zeus, *crush* their skulls! Kill! Kill!   390
        Now give the land some faith, I beg you,
        from these ancient wrongs bring forth our rights.
                Hear me, Earth, and all you lords of death.
Chorus.
        It is the law: when the blood of slaughter
                wets the ground it wants more blood.   395
                        Slaughter cries for the Fury
                of those long dead to bring destruction
                        on destruction churning in its wake!
Orestes.
        Sweet Earth, how long?—great lords of death, look on,
                you mighty curses of the dead. Look on   400
        the last of Atreus' children, here, the remnant
                helpless, cast from home . . . god, where to turn?
Leader.
        And again my pulses race and leap,
        I can feel your sobs, and hope
                                becomes despair   405
                and the heart goes dark to hear you—
        then the anguish ebbs, I see you stronger,
                        hope and the light come on me.
Electra.
        What hope?—what force to summon, what can help?
                What but the pain we suffer, bred by her?   410
        So let her fawn. She can never soothe her young wolves—
                Mother dear, you bred our wolves' raw fury.
Leader and Chorus.
        I beat and beat the dirge like a Persian mourner,[23]
        hands clenched tight and the blows are coming thick and fast,
                you can see the hands shoot out,   415
                now hand over hand and down—the head pulsates,
                        blood at the temples pounding to explode!
Electra.
        Reckless, brutal mother—oh dear god!—
                The brutal, cruel cortege,[24]
                the warlord stripped of his honor guard   420
                        and stripped of mourning rites—
                you dared entomb your lord unwept, unsung.
Orestes.
        Shamed for all the world, you mean—
                dear god, my father degraded so!

[23] Noted for violent demonstrations of grief.
[24] Followers of or ceremony at a funeral. Agamemnon's mutilated body had received no funeral rites.

Oh she'll pay,   425
she'll pay, by the gods and these bare hands—
   just let me take her life and *die*!
LEADER AND CHORUS.
   Shamed? *Butchered*, I tell you—hands lopped,
   strung to shackle his neck and arms!
So she worked,   430
she buried him, made your life a hell.
     Your father mutilated—do you hear?
ELECTRA.
   You tell him of father's death, but I was an outcast,
worthless, leashed like a vicious dog in a dark cell.
  I wept—laughter died that day . . .   435
   I wept, pouring out the tears behind my veils.
     Hear *that*, my brother, carve it on your heart!
LEADER AND CHORUS.
   Let it ring in your ears
     but let your heart stand firm.
  The outrage stands as it stands,   440
    you burn to know the end,
but first be strong, be steel, then down and fight.
ORESTES.
  I am calling you, my father—be with all you love!
ELECTRA.
  I am with you, calling through my tears.
LEADER AND CHORUS.
  We band together now, the call resounds—   445
    hear us now, come back into the light.
  Be with us, battle all you hate.
ORESTES.
  Now force *clash* with force, right with right!
ELECTRA.
  Dear gods, be just—win back our rights.
LEADER AND CHORUS.
  The flesh crawls to hear them pray.   450
    The hour of doom has waited long . . .
pray for it once, and oh my god, it comes.
CHORUS.
  Oh, the torment bred in the race,
     the grinding scream of death
       and the stroke that hits the vein,   455
    the hemorrhage none can stanch, the grief,
  the curse no man can bear.

  But there is a cure in the house
     and not outside it, no,
       not from others but from *them*,   460
    their bloody strife. We sing to you,
  dark gods beneath the earth.

Now hear, you blissful powers underground—
answer the call, send help.
Bless the children, give them triumph now.   465

[*They withdraw, while* Electra
and Orestes *come to the altar.*]

Orestes.
Father, king, no royal death you died—
give me the power now to rule our house.
Electra.
I need you too, my father.
Help me kill her lover, then go free.
Orestes.
Then men will extend the sacred feast to you.   470
Or else, when the steam and the rich savor burn
for Mother Earth, you will starve for honor.
Electra.
And I will pour my birthright out to you—
the wine of the fathers' house, my bridal wine,[25]
and first of all the shrines revere your tomb.   475
Orestes.
O Earth, bring father up to watch me fight.
Electra.
O Persephone,[26] give us power—lovely, gorgeous power!
Orestes.
Remember the bath—they stripped away your life, my father.
Electra.
Remember the all-embracing net—they made it first for you.
Orestes.
Chained like a beast—chains of hate, not bronze, my father!   480
Electra.
Shamed in the schemes, the hoods they slung around you!
Orestes.
Does our taunting wake you, oh my father?
Electra.
Do you lift your beloved head?
Orestes.
Send us justice, fight for all you love,
or help us pin them grip for grip. They threw you—   485
don't you long to throw them down in turn?
Electra.
One last cry, father. Look at your nestlings
stationed at your tomb—pity
your son and daughter. We are all you have.

[25] Electra has been barred from marrying while Clytaemnestra and Aegisthus are alive, lest she bear a son to avenge Agamemnon.
[26] Queen of the land of the dead.

ORESTES.
    Never blot out the seed of Pelops here.   490
    Then in the face of death you cannot die.

                     [*The leader comes forward again.*]

LEADER.
    The voices of children—salvation to the dead!
    Corks[27] to the net, they rescue the linen meshes
    from the depths. This line will never drown!

ELECTRA.
    Hear us—the long wail we raise is all for you.   495
    Honor our call and you will save yourself.

LEADER.
    And a fine thing it is to lengthen out the dirge;
    you adore a grave and fate they never mourned.
    But now for action—now you're set on action,
    put your stars to proof.

ORESTES.
                    So we will.   500
    One thing first, I think it's on the track.
    Why did she send libations? What possessed her,
    so late, to salve a wound past healing?
    To the unforgiving dead she sends this sop,
    this . . . who am I to appreciate her gifts?   505
    They fall so short of all her failings. True,
    "pour out your all to atone an act of blood,
    you work for nothing." So the saying goes.
    I'm ready. Tell me what you know.

LEADER.
                    I know, my boy,
    I was there. She had bad dreams. Some terror   510
    came groping through the night—it shook her,
    and she sent these cups, unholy woman.

ORESTES.
    And you know the dream, you can tell it clearly?

LEADER.
    She dreamed she bore a snake, said so herself and . . .

ORESTES.
    Come to the point—where does the story end?   515

LEADER.
    . . . she swaddled it like a baby, laid it to rest.

ORESTES.
    And food, what did the little monster want?

LEADER.
    She gave it her breast to suck—she was dreaming.

ORESTES.
    And didn't it tear her nipple, the brute inhuman—

---

[27] Floats to keep the net from sinking.

LEADER.

Blood curdled the milk with each sharp tug . . .   520

ORESTES.

No empty dream. The vision of a man.

LEADER.

. . . and she woke with a scream, appalled,
and rows of torches, burning out of the blind dark,
flared across the halls to soothe the queen,
and then she sent the libations for the dead,   525
an easy cure she hopes will cut the pain.

ORESTES.

                                                    No,
I pray to the Earth and father's grave to bring
that dream to life in me. I'll play the seer—
it all fits together, watch!
If the serpent came from the same place as I,   530
and slept in the bands that swaddled me, and its jaws
spread wide for the breast that nursed me into life
and clots stained the milk, mother's milk,
and she cried in fear and agony—so be it.
As she bred this sign, this violent prodigy,   535
so she dies by violence. I turn serpent,
I kill her. So the vision says.

LEADER.

You are the seer for me, I like your reading.
Let it come! But now rehearse your friends.
Say do this, or don't do that—   540

ORESTES.

The plan is simple. My sister goes inside.
And I'd have her keep the bond with me a secret.
They killed an honored man by cunning, so
they die by cunning, caught in the same noose.
So he commands,   545
Apollo the Seer who's never lied before.

And I like a stranger, equipped for all events,
go to the outer gates with this man here,
Pylades, a friend, the house's friend-in-arms.
And we both will speak Parnassian, both try   550
for the native tones of Delphi.[28]
                                              Now, say none
at the doors will give us a royal welcome
(after all the house is ridden by a curse),[29]
well then we wait . . . till a passer-by will stop

---

[28] Delphi and Mount Parnassus, both associated with the god Apollo, are in the region (Phokis) where Orestes has lived in exile. He may mean that he will adopt the regional dialect of Delphi: or that his words will be delphic (obscure but faithful to the commission given him by Apollo).

[29] The curse would cause the house's inhabitants to sin against the laws of hospitality and also to fear visitors.

and puzzle and make insinuations at the house,   555
"Aegisthus shuts his door on the man who needs him.
Why, I wonder—does he know? Is he home?"

But once through the gates, across the threshold,
once I find that man on *my* father's throne,
or returning late to meet me face to face,   560
and his eyes shift and fall—
                              I promise you,
before he can ask me, "Stranger, who are you?"—
I drop him dead, a thrust of the sword, and twist!
Our Fury never wants for blood. *His* she drinks unmixed,
our third libation poured to Saving Zeus.   565

                              [*Turning to* ELECTRA.]

Keep a close watch inside, dear, be careful.
We must work together step by step.

                              [*To the chorus.*]

                              And you,
better hold your tongues, religiously.
Silence, friends, or speak when it will help.

                              [*Looking toward* PYLADES *and the
                              death-mound and beyond.*]

For the rest, watch over me, I need you—   570
guide my sword through struggle, guide me home!

                              [*As* ORESTES, PYLADES *and* ELEC-
                              TRA *leave, the women reassemble for
                              the chorus.*]

CHORUS.
        Marvels, the Earth breeds many marvels,
              terrible marvels overwhelm us.
        The heaving arms of the sea embrace and swarm
with savage life. And high in the no man's land of night   575
        torches[30] hang like swords. The hawk on the wing,
                    the beast astride the fields
        can tell of the whirlwind's fury roaring strong.

        Oh but a man's high daring spirit,
              who can account for that? Or woman's   580
        desperate passion daring past all bounds?
        She couples with every form of ruin known to mortals.

---

[30] Strange celestial bodies, such as comets.

Woman, frenzied, driven wild with lust,
              twists the dark warm harness
of wedded love—tortures man and beast.   585

Well you know, you with a sense of truth
            recall Althaia,[31]
the heartless mother
who killed her son,
ai! what a scheme she had—   590
          she rushed his destiny,
               lit the bloody torch
preserved from the day he left her loins with a cry—
               the life of the torch paced his,
burning on till Fate burned out his life.   595

There is one more in the tales of hate:
            remember Scylla,[32]
the girl of slaughter
seduced by foes
to take her father's life.   600
          The gift of Minos,
             a choker forged in gold
turned her head and Nisos' immortal lock she cut
               as he slept away his breath . . .
ruthless bitch, now Hermes takes her down.   605

Now that I call to mind old wounds that never heal—
   Stop, it's time for the wedded love-in-hate,
for the curse of the halls,
          the woman's brazen cunning
             bent on her lord in arms,   610
    her warlord's power—
               Do you respect such things?
I prize the hearthstone warmed by faith,
a woman's temper nothing bends to outrage.

First at the head of legendary crime stands Lemnos.[33]
   People shudder and moan, and can't forget—   615

---

[31] The Chorus in the following passage cites three examples of perverted parental, filial, or conjugal love, all of which in the present context are ironic or double-edged, like the matricide Orestes and Electra are planning. Althaia, in mythology, had been warned at the birth of her son Meleager that his life would end when a certain torch, or brand from the fire, was burnt out. She hid it away, but later her anger with her son, who had killed her brothers, impelled her to burn the torch, bringing on his death.

[32] This Scylla (not to be confused with the monster of the same name who threatened navigators of the straits of Messina) was in myth the daughter of Nisos, king of Megara, whose city was besieged by King Minos of Crete. In Aeschylus' version of her story she succumbed to bribery (in other versions her motive is love for Minos) and cut off a lock of her father's hair on which his life depended.

[33] An island in the Aegean. It is associated in mythology and legend with atrocities, the most notorious being the attempted slaughter of all husbands and other males by the women of the island, who were jealous of their mistresses.

each new horror that comes
        we call the hells of Lemnos.
                Loathed by the gods for guilt,
cast off by men, disgraced, their line dies out.
Who could respect what god detests?   620
What of these tales have I not picked with justice?

        The sword's at the lungs!—it stabs deep,
                the edge cuts through and through
        and Justice drives it—Outrage still lives on,
                not trodden to pieces underfoot; not yet,   625
                though the laws lie trampled down,
                        the majesty of Zeus.

        The anvil of Justice stands fast
        and Fate beats out her sword.
Tempered for glory, a child will wipe clean   630
the inveterate stain of blood shed long ago—
        Fury brings him home at last,
                the brooding mother Fury!

                                [*The women leave.* ORESTES *and*
                                PYLADES *approach the house of*
                                ATREUS.]

ORESTES.
                                        Slave, the slave!—
where is he? Hear me pounding the gates?
Is there a man inside the house?   635
For the third time, come out of the halls!
If Aegisthus has them welcome friendly guests.

                        [*A voice from inside.*]

PORTER.
        All right, I hear you. . . .
        Where do you come from, stranger? Who are you?
ORESTES.
        Announce me to the masters of the house.   640
        I've come for them, I bring them news.
                                        Hurry,
        the chariot of the night is rushing on the dark!
        The hour falls, the traveler casts his anchor
        in an inn where every stranger feels at home.
                                        Come out!
        Whoever rules the house. The woman in charge.   645
        No, the man, better that way.
        No scruples then. Say what you mean,
        man to man launch in and prove your point,
        make it clear, strong.

[CLYTAEMNESTRA *emerges*[34] *from
the palace, attended by* ELECTRA.]

CLYTAEMNESTRA.

                    Strangers, please,
tell me what you would like and it is yours.   650
We've all you might expect in a house like ours.
We have warm baths and beds to charm away your pains
and the eyes of Justice[35] look on all we do.
But if you come for higher things, affairs
that touch the state, that is the men's concern   655
and I will stir them on.
ORESTES.
                    I am a stranger,
from Daulis, close to Delphi. I'd just set out,
packing my own burden bound for Argos
(here I'd put my burden down and rest),
when I met a perfect stranger, out of the blue,   660
who asks about my way and tells me his.
                    Strophios,
a Phocian, so I gathered in conversation.
"Well, my friend," he says, "out for Argos
in any case? Remember to tell the parents
he is dead, Orestes . . .
                    promise me please   665
(it's only right), it will not slip your mind.
Then whatever his people want, to bring him home
or bury him here, an alien, all outcast here
forever, won't you ferry back their wishes?
As it is, a bronze urn is armor to his embers.   670
The man's been mourned so well . . ."
                    I only tell you
what I heard. And am I speaking now
with guardians, kinsmen who will care?
It's hard to say. But a parent ought to know.[36]

---

[34] Orestes had hoped that Aegisthus, about whom he feels "no scruples," would encounter him first, but (by dramatic logic and the logic of the curse) he is brought immediately face-to-face with his mother, who is simultaneously his fundamental antagonist, a person whose intimate relationship to him causes the ambivalent human feelings in both of them, and the most recent carrier of the self-propagating retaliatory curse that lies on the lineage of Atreus.

[35] A typical specimen of the irony omnipresent in the trilogy. In extending the expected hospitable welcome to the guest, Clytaemnestra evokes her murder of her husband Agamemnon in his bath; the "eyes of Justice" are those that enforce the rites of hospitality and (for the audience) are the forces that punish an adulterous wife for murdering her husband. The dialogue here between Clytaemnestra and Orestes epitomizes the tragedy of the entire story: Clytaemnestra had killed her husband because he had murdered their daughter Iphigeneia at Aulis; now she is engaged in a life-or-death struggle with another of her own children.

[36] This poignant line has at least three meanings: a) "Shouldn't a mother know her own son?"; b) "It is only right that this tragic message be delivered to a parent, not a more distant kinsman or guardian"; c) "Any mother who killed her son's father should be told what has happened to the son she exiled so that she could commit her crimes." Clytaemnestra's reply, in her lines that follow, shows her mixed feelings as mother of the man she has most to fear.

CLYTAEMNESTRA.
                                                              I, I—   675
your words, you storm us, raze us to the roots,
you curse of the house so hard to wrestle down!
How you range—targets at peace, miles away,
and a shaft from your lookout brings them down.
You strip me bare of all I love, destroy me,
now—Orestes.   680

And he was trained so well, we'd been so careful,
kept his footsteps clear of the quicksand of death.
Just now, the hope of the halls, the surgeon to cure
our Furies' lovely revel—he seemed so close,
he's written off the rolls.

ORESTES.
                                          If only I were . . .   685
my friends, with hosts as fortunate as you
if only I *could* be known for better news[37]
and welcomed like a brother. The tie between
the host and stranger, what is kinder?
But what an impiety, so it seemed to me,   690
not to bring this to a head for loved ones.
I was bound by honor, bound by the rights
of hospitality.

CLYTAEMNESTRA.
                        Nothing has changed.
For all that you receive what you deserve,
as welcome in these halls as one of us.   695
Wouldn't another bear the message just as well?
But you must be worn from the long day's journey—
time for your rewards.

                                          [*To* ELECTRA.]

                                          Escort him in,
where the men who come are made to feel at home.
He and his retinue, and fellow travelers.   700
Let them taste the bounty of our house.
Do it, as if you depended on his welfare.

And we will rouse the powers in the house
and share the news. We never lack for loved ones,
we will probe this turn of fortune every way.   705

[37] Messengers were frequently (if illogically) rewarded for bringing good news and were hated or punished for bringing bad news. Clytaemnestra's reply, that the messenger will "receive what you deserve," is another ambiguity; does she mean that he will be rewarded for bringing to Aegisthus (and perhaps to her) the good news that a potentially avenging son is dead, or that the news of this son's death, welcome or not, is a service to the dead son's family, or both? And does Clytaemnestra's reassurance that the messenger will be "as welcome in these halls as one of us" mean that he will be treated kindly or that he will be given the same kind of unnatural treatment that all the house of Atreus has given to its kindred?

[ELECTRA *leads* ORESTES, PYLA-
DES *and their retinue into the
halls;* CLYTAEMNESTRA *follows,
while the chorus reassembles.*]

LEADER.

  Oh dear friends who serve the house,
   when can we speak out, when
  can the vigor of our voices serve Orestes?

CHORUS.

  Queen of the Earth, rich mounded Earth,
  breasting over the lord of ships,   710
  the king's corpse at rest,
  hear us now, now help us,
   now the time is ripe—
  Down to the pit Persuasion goes
  with all her cunning. Hermes of Death,   715
  the great shade patrols the ring
  to guide the struggles, drive the tearing sword.

LEADER.

  And I think our new friend is at his mischief.
  Look, Orestes' nurse in tears.

[*Enter* CILISSA.]

  Where now, old-timer, padding along the gates?   720
  With pain a volunteer to go your way.

NURSE.

             "Aegisthus,"[38]
  your mistress calling, "hurry and meet your guests.
  There's news. It's clearer man to man, you'll see."

  And she looks at the maids and pulls that long face
  and down deep her eyes are laughing over the work   725
  that's done. Well and good for her. For the house
  it's the curse all over—the strangers make that plain.
  But let *him* hear, he'll revel once he knows.

            Oh god,
  the life is hard. The old griefs, the memories
  mixing, cups of pain, so much pain in the halls,   730
  the house of Atreus . . . I suffered, the heart within me
  always breaking, oh, but I never shouldered
  misery like this. So many blows, good slave,
  I took my blows.
      Now dear Orestes—
  the sweetest, dearest plague of all our lives!   735

[38] In addition to revealing the nurse Cilissa's hatred for Aegisthus, her words introduce a poignantly human note. Like his mother Clytaemnestra, Orestes is more, and less, than an instrument in a cosmic system of right and wrong; he was also a human baby who needed feeding and diaper-changing. The nurse's comparison of herself to a "prophet" (line 745) in her dealings with a baby join together the most cosmic, theological implications and the most homely, personal ones.

Red from your mother's womb I took you, reared you . . .
nights, the endless nights I paced, your wailing
kept me moving—led me a life of labor,
all for what?
              And such care I gave it . . .
baby can't think for itself, poor creature.   740
You have to nurse it, don't you? Read its mind,
little devil's got no words, it's still swaddled.
Maybe it wants a bite or a sip of something,
or its bladder pinches—a baby's soft insides
have a will of their own. I had to be a prophet.   745
Oh I tried, and missed, believe you me, I missed,
and I'd scrub its pretty things until they sparkled.
Washerwoman and wetnurse shared the shop.
A jack of two trades, that's me,
and an old hand at both . . .
                 and so I nursed Orestes,   750
yes, from his father's arms I took him once,
and now they say he's dead,
I've suffered it all, and now I'll fetch that man,
the ruination of the house—give him the news,
he'll relish every word.
LEADER.
                She tells him to come,   755
but how, prepared?
NURSE.
             Prepared, how else?
I don't see . . .
LEADER.
          With his men, I mean, or all alone?
NURSE.
Oh, she says to bring his bodyguard, his cutthroats.
LEADER.
No, not now, not if you hate our master—
tell him to come alone.   760
Nothing for him to fear then, when he hears.
Have him come quickly too, rejoicing all the way!
The teller sets the crooked message straight.
NURSE.
                    What,
you're *glad* for the news that's come?
LEADER.
                 Why not,
if Zeus will turn the evil wind to good?   765
NURSE.
But how? Orestes, the hope of the house is gone.
LEADER.
Not yet. It's a poor seer who'd say so.
NURSE.
What are you saying—something I don't know?

LEADER.
>Go in with your message. Do as you're told.
>May the gods take care of cares that come from them. 770

NURSE.
>Well, I'm off. Do as I'm told.
>And here's to the best . . .
>some help, dear gods, some help.

[Exit.]

CHORUS.
>O now bend to my prayer, Father Zeus,
>>lord of the gods astride the sky— 775
>grant them all good fortune,
>the lords of the house who strain to see
>>strict discipline return.
>Our cry is the cry of Justice,
>>Zeus, safeguard it well.

>>>Zeus, 780
>set him against his enemies in the halls!
>>Do it, rear him to greatness—two, threefold
>>he will repay you freely, gladly.

>Look now—watch the colt of a man you loved,
>>yoked to the chariot of pain.
>Now the orphan needs you— 785
>harness his racing, rein him in,
>>>preserve his stride so we
>can watch him surge in the homestretch,
>>>storming for the goal. 790

>>And you who haunt the vaults
>where the gold glows in the darkness,
>hear us now, good spirits of the house,
>>>conspire with us—come,
>and wash old works of blood 795
>in the fresh-drawn blood of Justice.
>Let the gray retainer, murder, breed no more.

>And you, Apollo, lord of the glorious masoned cavern,[39]
>>grant that this man's house lift up its head,
>>>that we may see with loving eyes 800
>>the light of freedom burst from its dark veil!

>>And lend a hand and scheme
>for the rights, my Hermes, help us,
>sail the action on with all your breath.

[39] Apollo's temple at Delphi and the cleft in the earth over which it was built.

Reveal what's hidden, please,   805
  or say a baffling word
in the night and blind men's eyes—
when the morning comes your word is just as dark.

Soon, at last, in the dawn that frees the house,
  we sea-widows wed to the winds   810
      will beat our mourning looms of song
           and sing, "Our ship's come in!
Mine, mine is the wealth that swells her holds—
those I love are home and free of death."

But you, when your turn in the action comes, be strong.   815
      When she cries "Son!" cry out "My *father's* son!"
         Go through with the murder—innocent at last.

Raise up the heart of Perseus[40] in your breast!
  And for all you love under earth
and all above its rim, now scarf your eyes   820
        against the Gorgon's fury—
  In, go in for the slaughter now!

                    [*Enter* AEGISTHUS, *alone.*]

The butcher comes. Wipe out death with death.
AEGISTHUS.
  Coming, coming. Yes, I have my summons.
  There's news, I gather, travelers here to tell it.   825
  No joy in the telling though—Orestes dead.
  Saddle the house with a bloody thing like that
  and it might just collapse. It's still raw
  from the last murders, galled and raw.

  But how to take the story, for living truth?   830
  Or work of a woman's panic, gossip starting up
  in the night to flicker out and die?[41]

                    [*Turning to the leader.*]

                 Do you know?

Tell me, clear my mind.
LEADER.
               We've heard a little.
But get it from the strangers, go inside.
Messengers have no power. Nothing like   835
a face-to-face encounter with the source.

---

[40] The mythical hero Perseus, with the help of Pluto, Hermes, and Athena, killed Medusa, one of the three female monsters (the Gorgons) with snakes in their hair; anyone who looked at her was turned to stone. Athena gave Perseus a mirror so that he would not have to look directly at Medusa.

[41] Compare the Chorus's skepticism about Clytaemnestra's report of the fall of Troy, in *Agamemnon*.

AEGISTHUS.
    —Must see him, test the messenger. Where was he
    when the boy died, standing on the spot?
    Or is he dazed with rumor, mouthing hearsay?
    No, he'll never trap me open-eyed!   840

                        [*Striding through the doors.*]

CHORUS.
    Zeus, Zeus, what can I say?—
    how to begin this prayer, call down
        the gods for help? what words
    can reach the depth of all I feel?
    Now they swing to the work,   845
    the red edge of the cleaver
    hacks at flesh and men go down.
    Agamemnon's house goes down—
        all-out disaster now,
    or a son ignites the torch of freedom,   850
    wins the throne, the citadel,
        the fathers' realms of gold.
    The last man on the bench,[42] a challenger
    must come to grips with two. Up,
    like a young god, Orestes, wrestle—   855
        let it be to win.

                        [*A scream inside the palace.*]

    —Listen!
            —What's happening?
                        —The house,
    what have they done to the house?
LEADER.
                                Back,
    till the work is over! Stand back—
    they'll count us clean of the dreadful business.   860

                        [*The women scatter; a wounded
                        servant of* AEGISTHUS *enters.*]

    Look, the die is cast, the battle's done.
SERVANT.
                                Ai,
    Ai, all over, master's dead—Aie,
    a third, last salute. Aegisthus is no more.

                        [*Rushing at a side door, struggling
                        to work it open.*]

    Open up, wrench the bolts on the women's doors.
    Faster! A strong young arm it takes,   865

[42] The wrestler who must meet the winner of the earlier match or matches.

but not to save him now, he's finished.
What's the use?
                                  Look—wake up!
                                              No good,
I call to the deaf, to sleepers . . . a waste of breath.
Where are you, Clytaemnestra? What are you doing?

LEADER.
  Her head is ripe for lopping on the block.   870
  She's next, and justice wields the ax.

> [*The door opens, and* CLYTAEM-
> NESTRA *comes forth.*]

CLYTAEMNESTRA.
                                              What now?
  Why this shouting up and down the halls?

SERVANT.
  The dead are killing the living,[43] I tell you!

CLYTAEMNESTRA.
  Ah, a riddle. I do well at riddles.
  By cunning we die, precisely as we killed.   875
  Hand me the man-ax, someone, hurry!

> [*The servant dashes out.*]

Now we will see. Win all or lose all,
we have come to this—the crisis of our lives.

> [*The main doors open;* ORESTES,
> *sword in hand, is standing over the
> body of* AEGISTHUS, *with* PYLADES
> *close behind him.*]

ORESTES.
  It's you I want. This one's had enough.

CLYTAEMNESTRA.
  Gone, my violent one—Aegisthus, very dear.   880

ORESTES.
  You love your man? Then lie in the same grave.
  You can never be unfaithful to the dead.

> [*Pulling her toward* AEGISTHUS'
> *body.*]

CLYTAEMNESTRA.
  Wait, son—no feeling for this, my child?
  The breast[44] you held, drowsing away the hours,
  soft gums tugging the milk that made you grow?   885

---

[43] The line means a) the supposedly dead Orestes is killing Aegisthus, and b) all the dead victims of the curse on the house are taking revenge.

[44] Either Clytaemnestra has exposed her breast or Orestes has done so in his violence.

[ORESTES *turns to* PYLADES.]

ORESTES.

What will I do, Pylades—I dread to kill my mother!

PYLADES.

What of the future? What of the Prophet God Apollo,
the Delphic voice, the faith and oaths we swear?
Make all mankind your enemy, not the gods.

ORESTES.

O you win me over—good advice.

[*Wheeling on* CLYTAEMNESTRA,
thrusting her toward AEGISTHUS.]

This way—   890
I want to butcher you—right across his body!
In life you thought he dwarfed my father—*Die!*—
go down with him forever!

You love this man,
the man you should have loved you hated.

CLYTAEMNESTRA.

I gave you life. Let me grow old with you.   895

ORESTES.

What—kill my father, then you'd live with me?

CLYTAEMNESTRA.

Destiny had a hand in that, my child.

ORESTES.

This too: destiny is handing you your death.

CLYTAEMNESTRA.

You have no fear of a mother's curse, my son?

ORESTES.

Mother? You flung me to a life of pain.   900

CLYTAEMNESTRA.

Never flung you, placed you in a comrade's house.

ORESTES.

—Disgraced me, sold me, a freeborn father's son.

CLYTAEMNESTRA.

Oh? then name the price I took for you.

ORESTES.

I am ashamed to mention it[45] in public.

CLYTAEMNESTRA.

Please, and tell your father's failings too.   905

ORESTES.

Never judge him—he suffered, you sat here at home.

CLYTAEMNESTRA.

It hurts women, being kept from men, my son.

ORESTES.

Perhaps . . . but the man slaves to keep them safe at home.

---

[45] Orestes probably means both the killing of Agamemnon in the son's absence and his mother's adultery. Her reply in the next line balances these crimes against Agamemnon's killing of Iphigeneia and his adulteries with Trojan women such as his captive, Cassandra.

CLYTAEMNESTRA.
—I see murder in your eyes, my child—mother's murder!
ORESTES.
You are the murderer, not I—and you will kill yourself.[46]   910
CLYTAEMNESTRA.
Watch out—the hounds of a mother's curse will hunt you down.
ORESTES.
But how to escape a father's if I fail?
CLYTAEMNESTRA.
I must be spilling live tears on a tomb of stone.
ORESTES.
Yes, my father's destiny—it decrees your death.
CLYTAEMNESTRA.
Ai—you are the snake I bore—I gave you life!
ORESTES.

                                                 Yes!   915
That was the great seer, that terror in your dreams.
You killed and it was outrage—suffer outrage now.

> [*He draws her over the threshold;*
> *the doors close behind them, and the*
> *chorus gathers at the altar.*]

LEADER.
I even mourn the victims' double fates.
But Orestes fought, he reached the summit
of bloodshed here—we'd rather have it so.   920
The bright eye of the halls must never die.
CHORUS.
Justice came at last to the sons of Priam,
late but crushing vengeance, yes,
but to Agamemnon's house returned
the double lion,[47]   925
                    the double onslaught
drove to the hilt—the exile sped by god,
by Delphi's just command that drove him home.

Lift the cry of triumph O! the master's house
wins free of grief, free of the ones   930
who bled its wealth, the couple stained with murder,
                    free of Fate's rough path.

He came back with a lust for secret combat,
stealthy, cunning vengeance, yes,
but his hand was steered in open fight   935
          by god's true daughter,

[46] That is, she will have brought on her own death through her evil acts.

[47] Orestes and Pylades. The optimism expressed throughout this choral passage, the belief that the curse has finally been put to rest and that the chain of acts of revenge has been broken, is shortsighted and premature. Later, the Chorus will become aware of this fact.

Right, Right we call her,
we and our mortal voices aiming well—
she breathes her fury, shatters all she hates.

Lift the cry of triumph O! the master's house   940
wins free of grief, free of the ones
who bled its wealth, the couple stained with murder,
          free of Fate's rough path.

Apollo wills it so!—
Apollo, clear from the Earth's deep cleft   945
his voice came shrill, "Now stealth will master stealth!"
And the pure god came down and healed our ancient wounds,
the heavens come, somehow, to lift our yoke of grief—
          Now to praise the heavens' just command.

Look, the light is breaking!   950
The huge chain that curbed the halls gives way.
          Rise up, proud house, long, too long
your walls lay fallen, strewn along the earth.

Time brings all to birth—
soon Time will stride through the gates with blessings,   955
once the hearth burns off corruption, once
the house drives off the Furies. Look, the dice of Fate
fall well for all to see. We sing how fortune smiles—
          the aliens in the house are routed out at last!

Look, the light is breaking!   960
The huge chain that curbed the halls gives way.
          Rise up, proud house, long, too long
your walls lay fallen, strewn along the earth.

> [*The doors open. Torches light*
> PYLADES *and* ORESTES, *sword in*
> *hand, standing over the bodies of*
> CLYTAEMNESTRA *and* AEGISTHUS,
> *as* CLYTAEMNESTRA *stood over the*
> *bodies of* AGAMEMNON *and* CAS-
> SANDRA.]

ORESTES.
Behold the double tyranny of our land!
They killed my father, stormed my fathers' house.   965
They had their power when they held the throne.
Great lovers still, as you may read their fate.
True to their oath, hand in hand they swore
to kill my father, hand in hand to die.
Now they keep their word.

[*Unwinding from the bodies on the
bier the robes that entangled* AGA-
MEMNON, *he displays them, as* CLY-
TAEMNESTRA *had displayed them,
to the chorus at the altar.*]

                    Look once more on this,   970
you who gather here to attend our crimes—
the master-plot that bound my wretched father,
shackled his ankles, manacled his hands.
Spread it out! Stand in a ring around it,
a grand shroud for a man.
                              Here, unfurl it   975
so the Father—no, not mine but the One
who watches over all, the Sun can behold
my mother's godless work. So he may come,
my witness when the day of judgment comes,
that I pursued this bloody death with justice,   980
mother's death.
                        Aegisthus, why mention him?
The adulterer dies. An old custom, justice.

But she who plotted this horror against her husband,
she carried his children, growing in her womb
and she—I loved her once   985
and now I loathe, I have to loathe—
                                    what is she?

                    [*Kneeling by the body of his mother.*]

Some moray eel, some viper born to rot her mate
with a single touch, no fang to strike him,
just the wrong, the reckless fury in her heart!

                    [*Glancing back and forth from*
                    CLYTAEMNESTRA *to the robes.*]

This—how can I dignify this . . . snare for a beast?—   990
sheath for a corpse's feet?
                        This winding-sheet,
this tent for the bath of death!
                            No, a hunting net,
a coiling—what to call—?
                        Foot-trap—
woven of robes . . .
why, this is perfect gear for the highwayman   995
who entices guests and robs them blind and plies
the trade of thieves. With a sweet lure like this
he'd hoist a hundred lives and warm his heart,

Live with such a woman, marry *her?* Sooner
the gods destroy me—die without an heir!   1000
CHORUS. •

> Oh the dreadful work . . .
> Death calls and she is gone.
>   But oh, for you, the survivor,
> suffering is just about to bloom.

ORESTES.

Did she do the work or not?—Here, come close—   1005
This shroud's my witness, dyed with Aegisthus' blade—[48]
Look, the blood ran here, conspired with time to blot
the swirling dyes, the handsome old brocade.

> [*Clutching* AGAMEMNON'S *robes,
> burying his face in them and
> weeping.*]

Now I can praise you, now I am here to mourn.
You were my father's death, great robe, I hail you!   1010
Even if I must suffer the work and the agony
and all the race of man—
                     I embrace you . . . you,
my victory, are my guilt, my curse, and still—
CHORUS.

> No man can go through life
> and reach the end unharmed.   1015
>   Aye, trouble is now,
> and trouble still to come.

ORESTES.

                            But *still,*
that you may know—
                     I see no end in sight,
I am a charioteer—the reins are flying, look,
the mares plunge off the track—
                              my bolting heart,   1020
it beats me down and terror beats the drum,
my dance-and-singing master pitched to fury—

And still, while I still have some self-control,
I say to my friends in public: I killed my mother,
not with a little justice. She was stained   1025
with father's murder, she was cursed by god.
And the magic spells that fired up my daring?
One comes first. The Seer of Delphi who declared,
"Go through with this and you go free of guilt.
Fail and—"

---

[48] Presumably the blade used by Clytaemnestra to kill Agamemnon.

I can't repeat the punishment.   1030
What bow could hit the crest of so much pain?

> [PYLADES *gives* ORESTES *a branch
> of olive and invests him in the robes
> of Apollo, the wreath and insignia
> of suppliants to Delphi.*][49]

Now look on me, armed with the branch and wreath,
a suppliant bound for the Navelstone of Earth,
Apollo's sacred heights
where they say the fire of heaven can never die.   1035

> [*Looking at his hand that still re-
> tains the sword.*]

I must escape this blood . . . it is my own.
—Must turn toward his hearth,
none but his, the Prophet God decreed.

I ask you, Argos and all my generations,
remember how these brutal things were done.   1040
Be my witness to Menelaus[50] when he comes.
And now I go, an outcast driven off the land,
in life, in death, I leave behind a name for—
LEADER.
But you've done well. Don't burden yourself
with bad omens, lash yourself with guilt.   1045
You've set us free, the whole city of Argos,
lopped the heads of these two serpents once for all.

> [*Staring at the women and beyond,*
> ORESTES *screams in terror.*]

ORESTES.
No, no! Women[51]—look—like Gorgons,
shrouded in black, their heads wreathed,
swarming serpents!
　　　　　—Cannot stay, I must move on.   1050
PYLADES.
What dreams can whirl you so? You of all men,
you have your father's love. Steady,
nothing to fear with all you've won.
ORESTES.
　　　　　　　　　　　　No dreams,
these torments, not to me, they're clear, real—the hounds
of mother's hate.

---

[49] Apollo has promised to purge Orestes from blood-guilt after Orestes returns to the god's temple.

[50] Brother of Agamemnon and husband of Helen; he has not yet returned to Argos.

[51] The women are the Furies, avengers of blood-guilt. In the final play of the trilogy they will confront Orestes; eventually they will be renamed "the Eumenides" ("kindly ones").

LEADER.
                    The blood's still wet on your hands.   1055
It puts a kind of frenzy in you . . .
ORESTES.
                        God Apollo!
Here they come, thick and fast,
  their eyes dripping hate—
LEADER.
                      One thing
will purge you. Apollo's touch will set you free
  from all your . . . torments.
ORESTES.
                    You can't see them—   1060
I can, they drive me on! I must move on—

                    [*He rushes out;* PYLADES *follows*
                    close behind.]

LEADER.
Farewell then. God look down on you with kindness,
  guard you, grant you fortune.
CHORUS.
      Here once more, for the third time,
      the tempest in the race has struck   1065
      the house of kings and run its course.
       First the children eaten,
      the cause of all our pain, the curse.
      And next the kingly man's ordeal,
      the bath where the proud commander,   1070
      lord of Achaea's armies lost his life.
      And now a third has come, but who?
       A third like Saving Zeus?
      Or should we call him death?
      Where will it end?—   1075
      where will it sink to sleep and rest,
       this murderous hate, this Fury?

THE EUMENIDES

CHARACTERS

THE PYTHIA, *the priestess of Apollo*   CHORUS OF FURIES AND THEIR LEADER
APOLLO   ATHENA
HERMES   *Escorting Chorus of Athenian women*
THE GHOST OF CLYTAEMNESTRA   *Men of the jury, herald, citizens*

TIME AND SCENE

The FURIES *have pursued* ORESTES *to the temple of* APOLLO *at Delphi. It is morning. The priestess of the god appears at the great doors and offers up her prayer.*

PYTHIA.[1]
    First of the gods I honor in my prayer is Mother Earth,
the first of the gods to prophesy, and next I praise
Tradition, second to hold her Mother's mantic seat,
so legend says, and third by the lots of destiny,
by Tradition's free will—no force to bear her down—   5
another Titan, child of the Earth, took her seat
and Phoebe passed it on as a birthday gift to Phoebus,
Phoebus a name for clear pure light derived from hers.
Leaving the marsh and razorback of Delos,[2] landing
at Pallas' headlands flocked by ships, here he came   10
to make his home Parnassus[3] and the heights.
And an escort filled with reverence brought him on,
the highway-builders, sons of the god of fire who tamed
the savage country, civilized the wilds—on he marched
and the people lined his way to cover him with praise,   15
led by Delphos,[4] lord, helm of the land, and Zeus
inspired his mind with the prophet's skill, with godhead,
made him fourth in the dynasty of seers to mount this throne,
but it is Zeus that Apollo speaks for, Father Zeus.
These I honor in the prelude of my prayers—these gods.   20
But Athena at the Forefront of the Temple[5] crowns our legends.
I revere the nymphs who keep the Corycian rock's[6] deep hollows,
loving haunt of birds where the spirits drift and hover.
And Great Dionysos rules the land. I never forget that day
he marshaled his wild women in arms—he was all god,   25
he ripped Pentheus[7] down like a hare in the nets of doom.
And the rushing springs of Pleistos, Poseidon's[8] force I call,
and the king of the sky, the king of all fulfillment, Zeus.

[1] The name of the priestess derives from the Python, a dragon killed by Apollo when the god assumed power at Delphi. Omitting this incident, the priestess traces the history of the Delphic oracle (the "mantic," or prophetic, center of Greece) in terms of the successive powers or deities who prophesied there. The first was Earth, a primitive maternal being or principle, followed by Themis ("Tradition," associated with justice and custom), followed by Phoebe, a Titaness associated with the moon, followed by her grandson Phoebus, or Apollo, whom the priestess associates in her speech with highway-building, the taming of savagery, and generally the advent of the civilized. But in fact, despite the Pythia's natural inclination toward the "Apollonian" values of reason and moderation, the play will be much more evenhanded in its treatment of the conflicting claims of the primitive forces represented by the Furies, Mother Night, and Mother Earth, and on the other hand the more "civilized" forces Apollo represents.
[2] The island where Apollo was born.
[3] The mountain at Delphi; generally associated with Apollo, it actually had two peaks, one sacred to him and one to Dionysos, the god of wine who embodies the libidinal energies antithetical to Apollo's moderation. Dionysos rules the temple at Delphi during the winter, when Apollo is absent.
[4] The original king from whom Delphi was supposed to derive its name.
[5] Athena had a shrine near the temple's entrance.
[6] An area of Mount Parnassus; it contained a cave sacred to Pan, god of nature.
[7] The rationalistic Pentheus, opposed to the orgiastic worship of Dionysos, was torn apart by his mother and other frenzied female worshipers of the god.
[8] God of the ocean.

Now the prophet goes to take her seat.[9] God speed me—
grant me a vision greater than all my embarkations past!   30

                        [*Turning to the audience.*]

Where are the Greeks among you? Draw your lots and enter.
It is the custom here. I will tell the future
only as the god will lead the way.

                        [*She goes through the doors and
                        reappears in a moment, shaken,
                        thrown to her knees by some terrific
                        force.*]

                        Terrors—
terrors to tell, terrors all can see!—
they send me reeling back from Apollo's house.   35
The strength drains, it's very hard to stand,
crawling on all fours, no spring in the legs . . .
an old woman,[10] gripped by fear, is nothing,
a child, nothing more.

                        [*Struggling to her feet, trying to
                        compose herself.*]

I'm on my way to the vault,   40
it's green with wreaths, and there at the Navelstone[11]
I see a man—an abomination to god—
he holds the seat where suppliants sit for purging;[12]
his hands dripping blood, and his sword just drawn,
and he holds a branch (it must have topped an olive)   45
wreathed with a fine tuft of wool, all piety,
fleece gleaming white. So far it's clear, I tell you.
But there in a ring around the man, an amazing company—
women,[13] sleeping, nestling against the benches . . .
women? No,   50
Gorgons I'd call them; but then with Gorgons
you'd see the grim, inhuman . . .

---

[9] The seat is a tripod situated over the underground cleft beneath the temple. The Pythia's role was to relay the utterances of Apollo.

[10] The Pythia was always an elderly woman.

[11] The Omphalos, a cone-shaped rock near or in the temple. It was believed to be the center of the earth.

[12] Because he has taken his mother Clytaemnestra's life, Orestes must be ritually "purged" of the pollution of blood before he can be tried at law. Here he carries the emblems customary for those seeking purgation.

[13] The Furies, who pursue Orestes in revenge for his act of matricide. Appropriately, the priestess of Apollo does not recognize these primitive beings; she guesses that they may be the Gorgons (female monsters the sight of whom turned gazers to stone) or Harpies (hideous bird-women sent by Helios the sun-god to punish the king Phineus by defiling his food; compare the description of the Harpies in Virgil's *Aeneid,* Book III).

                              I saw a picture
years ago, the creatures tearing the feast
away from Phineus—
                    These have no wings,
I looked. But black they are, and so repulsive.   55
Their heavy, rasping breathing makes me cringe.
And their eyes ooze a discharge, sickening,
and what they wear—to flaunt *that* at the gods,
the idols, sacrilege! even in the homes of men.
The tribe that produced that brood I never saw,   60
or a plot of ground to boast it nursed their kind
without some tears, some pain for all its labor.

Now for the outcome. This is his concern,
Apollo the master of this house, the mighty power.
Healer, prophet, diviner of signs, he purges   65
the halls of others—He must purge his own.

                              [*She leaves. The doors of the temple
                              open and reveal* APOLLO *rising
                              over* ORESTES; *he kneels in prayer
                              at the Navelstone, surrounded by the*
                              FURIES *who are sleeping.* HERMES
                              waits in the background.]

APOLLO.
No, I will never fail you, through to the end
your guardian standing by your side or worlds away!
I will show no mercy to your enemies! Now
look at these—

                              [*Pointing to the* FURIES]

                    these obscenities!—I've caught them,   70
beaten them down with sleep.
                              They disgust me.
These gray, ancient children never touched
by god, man or beast—the eternal virgins.
Born for destruction only, the dark pit,
they range the bowels of Earth, the world of death,   75
loathed by men and the gods who hold Olympus.[14]

Nevertheless keep racing on and never yield.
Deep in the endless heartland they will drive you,
striding horizons, feet pounding the earth forever,
on, on over seas and cities swept by tides!   80
Never surrender, never brood on the labor.

---

[14] There is a natural antipathy between the elemental and ancient force represented by the
Furies and the modern, supposedly more advanced Olympian gods, especially Apollo.

And once you reach the citadel of Pallas,[15] kneel
and embrace her ancient idol in your arms and there,
with judges of your case, with a magic spell—
with words—we will devise the master-stroke   85
that sets you free from torment once for all.
I persuaded you to take your mother's life.
ORESTES.
Lord Apollo, you know the rules of justice,
know them well. Now learn compassion too.
No one doubts your power to do great things.   90
APOLLO.
Remember that. No fear will overcome you.

> [*Summoning* HERMES *from the
> shadows.*]

You, my brother, blood of our common Father,
Hermes, guard him well. Live up to your name,
good Escort. Shepherd him well, he is my suppliant,
and outlaws have their rights that Zeus reveres.   95
Lead him back to the world of men with all good speed.

> [APOLLO *withdraws to his inner
> sanctuary;* ORESTES *leaves with
> * HERMES *in the lead. The* GHOST
> OF CLYTAEMNESTRA *appears at the
> Navelstone, hovering over the* FUR-
> IES *as they sleep.*]

THE GHOST OF CLYTAEMNESTRA.
You—how can you *sleep?*
Awake, awake—what use are sleepers now?
I go stripped of honor, thanks to you,
alone among the dead. And for those I killed   100
the charges of the dead will never cease, never—
I wander in disgrace, I feel the guilt, I tell you,
withering guilt from all the outraged dead!

But I suffered too, terribly, from dear ones,
and none of my spirits rages to avenge me.   105
I was slaughtered by his matricidal hand.
See these gashes—

> [*Seizing one of the* FURIES *weak
> with sleep.*]

Carve them in your heart!

---

[15] Athena; Apollo directs Orestes to her city, Athens. The "ancient idol" was a wooden
statue of the goddess located there.

The sleeping brain has eyes that give us light;
we can never see our destiny by day.

And after all my libations . . . how you lapped   110
the honey, the sober offerings poured to soothe you,
awesome midnight feasts I burned at the hearthfire,
your dread hour never shared with gods.
All those rites, I see them trampled down.
And he springs free like a fawn, one light leap   115
at that—he's through the thick of your nets,
he breaks away!
Mocking laughter twists across his face.
Hear me, I am pleading for my life.
Awake, my Furies, goddesses of the Earth!   120
A dream is calling—Clytaemnestra calls you now.

                              [*The* FURIES *mutter in their sleep.*]

Mutter on. Your man is gone, fled far away.
My son has friends to defend him, not like mine.

                              [*They mutter again.*]

You sleep too much, no pity for my ordeal.
Orestes murdered his mother—he is gone.   125

                              [*They begin to moan.*]

Moaning, sleeping—onto your feet, quickly.
What is your work? What but causing pain?
Sleep and toil, the two strong conspirators,
they sap the mother dragon's deadly fury—

                              [*The* FURIES *utter a sharp moan
                              and moan again, but they are still
                              asleep.*]

FURIES.
Get him, get him, get him, get him—   130
there he goes.
THE GHOST OF CLYTAEMNESTRA.
                         The prey you hunt is just a dream—
like hounds mad for the sport you bay him on,
you never leave the kill.
                         But what are you *doing*?
Up! don't yield to the labor, limp with sleep.
Never forget my anguish.   135
Let my charges hurt you, they are just;
deep in the righteous heart they prod like spurs.
You, blast him on with your gory breath,
the fire of your vitals—wither him, after him,
one last foray—waste him, burn him out!

> [*She vanishes. The lead* Fury *urges
> on the pack.*]

Leader.
                                                    Wake up!   140
I rouse you, you rouse her. Still asleep?
Onto your feet, kick off your stupor.
See if this prelude has some grain of truth.

> [*The* Furies *circle, pursuing the
> scent with hunting calls, and cry out
> singly when they find* Orestes
> *gone.*]

Furies.
—Aieeeeee—no, no, *no,* they do us wrong, dear sisters.

   —The miles of pain, the pain I suffer . . .   145
and all for nothing, all for pain, more pain,
            the anguish, oh, the grief too much to bear.

—The quarry's slipped from the nets, our quarry lost and gone.

            —Sleep defeats me . . . I have lost the prey.

—You—child of Zeus[16]—*you,* a common thief!   150

   —Young god, you have ridden down the powers
proud with age. You worship the suppliant,
            the godless man who tears his parent's heart—

—The matricide, you steal him away, and you a god!

            —Guilt both ways, and who can call it justice?   155

—Not I: her charges stalk my dreams,
yes, the charioteer rides hard,
            her spurs digging the vitals,
      under the heart, under the heaving breast—

—I can feel the executioner's lash, it's searing   160
            deeper, sharper, the knives of burning ice—

—Such is your triumph, you young gods,
   world dominion past all rights.
            Your throne is streaming blood,
      blood at the foot, blood at the crowning head—   165

—I can see the Navelstone of the Earth, it's bleeding,
            bristling corruption, oh, the guilt it has to bear—

[16] Apollo.

Stains on the hearth! The Prophet stains the vault,
  he cries it on, drives on the crime himself.
      Breaking the god's first law, he rates men first,   170
            destroys the old dominions of the Fates.

He wounds me too, yet *him* he'll never free,
  plunging under the earth, no freedom then:
      curst as he comes for purging, at his neck
            he feels new murder springing from his blood.   175

                    [APOLLO *strides from his sanctuary*
                    in full armor, brandishing his bow
                    and driving back the FURIES.]

APOLLO.
  Out, I tell you, out of these halls—fast!—
  set the Prophet's chamber free!

                    [*Seizing one of the* FURIES, *shaking*
                    an arrow across her face.]

             Or take
the flash and stab of this, this flying viper
whipped from the golden cord that strings my bow!

Heave in torment, black froth erupting from your lungs,   180
vomit the clots of all the murders you have drained.
But never touch my halls, you have no right.

Go where heads are severed, eyes gouged out,
where Justice and bloody slaughter are the same . . .
castrations, wasted seed, young men's glories butchered,   185
extremities maimed, and huge stones at the chest,
and the victims wail for pity—
spikes inching up the spine, torsos stuck on spikes.

                    [*The* FURIES *close in on him.*]

So, you hear your love feast, yearn to have it all?
You revolt the gods. Your look,   190
your whole regalia gives you away—your kind
should infest a lion's cavern reeking blood.
But never rub your filth on the Prophet's shrine.
Out, you flock without a herdsman—out!
No god will ever shepherd you with love.   195
LEADER.
  Lord Apollo, now it is your turn to listen.
  You are no mere accomplice in this crime.
  You did it all, and all the guilt is yours.
APOLLO.
  No, how? Enlarge on that, and only that.

LEADER.
You commanded the guest to kill his mother.   200
APOLLO.
—Commanded him to avenge his father, what of it?
LEADER.
And then you dared embrace him, fresh from bloodshed.
APOLLO.
Yes, I ordered him on, to my house, for purging.
LEADER.
And we sped him on, and you revile us?
APOLLO.
Indeed, you are not fit to approach this house.   205
LEADER.
And yet we have our mission and our—
APOLLO.
Authority—you? Sound out your splendid power.
LEADER.
Matricides: we drive them from their houses.
APOLLO.
And what of the wife who strikes her husband down?
LEADER.
That murder would not destroy one's flesh and blood.   210
APOLLO.
Why, you'd disgrace—obliterate the bonds of Zeus
and Hera queen of brides! And the queen of love
you'd throw to the winds at a word, disgrace love,
the source of mankind's nearest, dearest ties.
Marriage of man and wife is Fate itself,   215
stronger than oaths, and Justice guards its life.
But if one destroys the other and you relent—
no revenge, not a glance in anger—then
I say your manhunt of Orestes is unjust.
Some things stir your rage, I see. Others,   220
atrocious crimes, lull your will to act.
                                        Pallas
will oversee this trial. She is one of us.[17]
LEADER.
I will never let that man go free, never.
APOLLO.
Hound him then, and multiply your pains.
LEADER.
Never try to cut my power with your logic.   225
APOLLO.
I'd never touch it, not as a gift—your power.
LEADER.
                                                Of course,
great as you are, they say, throned on high with Zeus.

---

[17] One of the modern Olympian gods, whom the primitive Furies oppose.

But blood of the mother draws me on—must hunt
the man for Justice. Now I'm on his trail!

> [*Rushing out, with the* FURIES *in
> full cry.*]

APOLLO.
And I will defend my suppliant and save him.   230
A terror to gods and men, the outcast's anger,
once I fail him, all of my own free will.

> [APOLLO *leaves. The scene changes
> to the Acropolis in Athens. Escorted
> by* HERMES, ORESTES *enters and
> kneels, exhausted, before the ancient
> shrine and idol of* ATHENA.]

ORESTES.
                                        Queen Athena,
under Apollo's orders I have come.
Receive me kindly. Curst and an outcast,
no suppliant for purging . . . my hands are clean.   235
My murderous edge is blunted now, worn down at last
on the outland homesteads, beaten paths of men.

On and out over seas and dry frontiers,
I kept alive the Prophet's strong commands.
Struggling toward your house, your idol—

> [*Taking the knees of* ATHENA'S *idol
> in his arms.*]

                                        Goddess,   240
here I keep my watch,
I await the consummation of my trial.

> [*The* FURIES *enter in pursuit but
> cannot find* ORESTES *who is en-
> twined around* ATHENA'S *idol. The
> leader sees the footprints.*]

LEADER.
                                        At last!
The clear trail of the man. After it, silent
but it tracks his guilt to light. He's wounded—
go for the fawn, my hounds, the splash of blood,   245
hunt him, rake him down.

                                        Oh, the labor,
the man-killing labor. My lungs are bursting . . .
over the wide rolling earth we've ranged in flock,
hurdling the waves in wingless flight and now we come,
all hot pursuit, outracing ships astern—and now   250

he's here, somewhere, cowering like a hare . . .
the reek of human blood—it's laughter to my heart!

[*Inciting a pair of* FURIES.]

Look, look again, you two,
scour the ground before he escapes—one dodge
and the matricide slips free.

[*Seeing* ORESTES, *one by one they
press around him and* ATHENA'S
idol.]

FURIES.

     —There he is!   255
Clutching the knees of power once again,
 twined in the deathless goddess' idol, look,
he wants to go on trial for his crimes.

      —Never . . .
 the mother's blood that wets the ground,
 you can never bring it back, dear god,   260
the Earth drinks, and the running life is gone.

      —No,
you'll give me blood for blood, you must!
 Out of your living marrow I will drain
 my red libation, out of your veins I suck my food,
  my raw, brutal cups—

     —Wither you alive,   265
 drag you down and there you pay, agony
for mother-killing agony!

    —And there you will see them all.
Every mortal who outraged god or guest or loving parent:
each receives the pain his pains exact.

—A mighty god is Hades. There   270
 at the last reckoning underneath the earth
  he scans all, he squares all men's accounts
and graves them on the tablets of his mind.

[ORESTES *remains impassive.*]

ORESTES.

I have suffered into truth. Well I know
the countless arts of purging, where to speak,   275
where silence is the rule.[18] In this ordeal
a compelling master urges me to speak.

---

[18] A person who had not been ritually purged might spread pollution merely by speaking.

[*Looking at his hands.*]

The blood sleeps, it is fading on my hands,
the stain of mother's murder washing clean.
It was still fresh at the god's hearth. Apollo   280
killed the swine[19] and the purges drove it off.
Mine is a long story
if I'd start with the many hosts I met,
I lived with, and I left them all unharmed.[20]
Time refines all things that age with time.   285

And now with pure, reverent lips I call
the queen of the land. Athena, help me!
Come without your spear—without a battle
you will win myself, my land, the Argive people[21]
true and just, your friends-in-arms forever.   290
Where are you now? The scorching wilds of Libya,
bathed by the Triton pool[22] where you were born?
Robes shrouding your feet
or shod and on the march to aid allies?
Or striding the Giants' Plain[23], marshal of armies,   295
hero scanning, flashing through the ranks?
                                                           Come—
you can hear me from afar, you are a god.
Set me free from this!
LEADER.
                              Never—neither
Apollo's nor Athena's strength can save you.
Down you go, abandoned,   300
searching your soul for joy but joy is gone.
Bled white, gnawed by demons, a husk, a wraith—

                               [*She breaks off, waiting for reply,*
                               but ORESTES *prays in silence.*]

No reply? you spit my challenge back?
You'll feast me alive, my fatted calf,
not cut on the altar first. Now hear my spell,   305
the chains of song I sing to bind you tight.
FURIES.
                              Come, Furies, dance!—
link arms for the dancing hand-to-hand,

---

[19] The animals normally sacrificed in rites of purgation.
[20] That he has not brought misfortune to his hosts indicates that Orestes has been successfully purged.
[21] Athens had contracted an alliance with Argos (the city where the action of the two earlier plays occurs) a few years before the *Oresteia* was performed.
[22] This lake in Libya, according to one version of the myth, was Athena's birthplace.
[23] The place where the Giants (offspring of Ouranos and Ge, the personification of Earth) unsuccessfully challenged the gods of Olympus. The present passage emphasizes Athena's role as warrior and guardian of her city, Athens.

now we long to reveal our art,
our terror, now to declare our right
   to steer the lives of men,   310
we all conspire, we dance! we are
the just and upright, we maintain.
Hold out your hands, if they are clean
   no fury of ours will stalk you,
you will go through life unscathed.   315
But show us the guilty—one like this
   who hides his reeking hands,
and up from the outraged dead we rise,
witness bound to avenge their blood
we rise in flames against him to the end!   320

Mother who bore me,
  O dear Mother Night,
to avenge the blinded dead
and those who see by day,
   now hear me! The whelp Apollo   325
spurns my rights, he tears this trembling victim
           from my grasp—the one to bleed,
   to atone away the mother-blood at last.

   Over the victim's burning head
this chant this frenzy striking frenzy   330
        lightning crazing the mind
               this hymn of Fury
chaining the senses, ripping cross the lyre,[24]
        withering lives of men!

This, this is our right,
  spun for us by the Fates,[25]   335
the ones who bind the world,
and none can shake our hold.
   Show us the mortals overcome,
insane to murder kin—we track them down
        till they go beneath the earth,   340
and the dead find little freedom in the end.

   Over the victim's burning head
this chant this frenzy striking frenzy
        lightning crazing the mind
               this hymn of Fury   345
chaining the senses, ripping cross the lyre,
        withering lives of men!

---

[24] The lyre was associated with Apollo in his role as god of song and of joyful poetry.

[25] In mythology, the three sisters who control the "thread" of a human life. The first spins the thread, the second measures its length, and the third cuts it off at its destined end, the time of death.

Even at birth, I say, our rights were so ordained.
    The deathless gods must keep their hands far off—
no god may share our cups, our solemn feasts.   350
We want no part of their pious white robes—
    the Fates who gave us power made us free.

    Mine is the overthrow of houses, yes,
    when warlust reared like a tame beast
            seizes near and dear—   355
                down on the man we swoop, aie!
                    for all his power black him out!—
for the blood still fresh from slaughter on his hands.

So now, striving to wrench our mandate from the gods,
    we make ourselves exempt from their control,   360
we brook no trial—no god can be our judge.[26]

                        [*Reaching toward* ORESTES.]

His breed, worthy of loathing, streaked with blood,
    Zeus slights, unworthy his contempt.

    Mine is the overthrow of houses, yes,
    when warlust reared like a tame beast   365
            seizes near and dear—
                down on the man we swoop, aie!
                    for all his power black him out!—
for the blood still fresh from slaughter on his hands.

And all men's dreams of grandeur,   370
                tempting the heavens,
all melt down, under earth their pride goes down—
            lost in our onslaught, black robes swarming,
                Furies throbbing, dancing out our rage.

Yes! leaping down from the heights,   375
    dead weight in the crashing footfall
                down we hurl on the runner
                    breakneck for the finish—
cut him down, our fury stamps him down!

Down he goes, sensing nothing,   380
                blind with defilement . . .

---

[26] What the Furies are fighting for is not merely the punishment of Orestes as an individual. They also question the basic grounds of justice. How, they protest, can an Olympian—Athena, for example—be legally competent to decide the question of whether the Olympians or the more primeval powers should be the final court of appeal? And, even more fundamentally, should the primitive law of retaliation for crimes against kindred be subordinated to *any* court or technical legal system?

darkness hovers over the man, dark guilt,
    and a dense pall overhangs his house,
        legend tells the story through her tears.

Yes! leaping down from the heights,   385
    dead weight in the crashing footfall
        down we hurl on the runner
            breakneck for the finish—
cut him down, our fury stamps him down!

        So the center holds.   390
    We are the skilled, the masterful,
        we the great fulfillers,
    memories of grief, we awesome spirits
        stern, unappeasable to man,
    disgraced, degraded, drive our powers through;   395
    banished far from god to a sunless, torchlit dusk,[27]
        we drive men through their rugged passage,
            blinded dead and those who see by day.

        Then where is the man
    not stirred with awe, not gripped by fear   400
        to hear us tell the law that
    Fate ordains, the gods concede the Furies,
        absolute till the end of time?
    And so it holds, our ancient power still holds.
    We are not without our pride, though beneath the earth   405
        our strict battalions form their lines,
    groping through the mist and sunstarved night.

> [*Enter* ATHENA, *armed for combat
> with her aegis*[28] *and her spear.*]

ATHENA.
    From another world I heard a call for help.
    I was on the Scamander's banks, just claiming Troy.[29]

---

[27] These two lines, applicable to either the Furies or their victims, are a good gloss on the Furies. Both they and the punished sinners dwell in a dark underground world that is the polar opposite of the heaven and light where the newer gods dwell on Mount Olympus (above, not below, humanity). Since the Furies and the sinners inhabit the same dark place, the Furies can be understood not just as an external force of punishment but also as the internal force of guilty conscience; the sinner is ultimately his or her own avenger. The concept is akin to what Dante intimates in his *Inferno*, that the outer and internal forces that punish sin are not clearly separable. Intriguingly, then, the Furies can be interpreted as either a primitive force superseded by an advance in ethical understanding or—as a modern depth-psychologist might argue—the personification of a timeless fact about human psychology that has been obscured by the illusory progress of "civilization."

[28] Here, a cape worn by Athena.

[29] In Aeschylus' time the Athenians had a colony near Troy that they claimed had been given them by right after the Trojan war. "Theseus' sons" (line 413) are the Athenians; he was the legendary hero of their city.

The Achaean warlords chose the hero's share   410
of what their spear had won—they decreed that land,
root and branch all mine, for all time to be,
for Theseus' sons a rare, matchless gift.

Home from the wars I come, my pace unflagging,
wingless, flown on the whirring, breasting cape   415
that yokes my racing spirit in her prime.

> [*Unfurling the aegis, seeing* ORES-
> TES *and the* FURIES *at her shrine.*]

And I see some new companions on the land.
Not fear, a sense of wonder fills my eyes.

Who are you? I address you all as one:
you, the stranger seated at my idol,   420
and you, like no one born of the sown seed,
no goddess watched by the gods, no mortal either,
not to judge by your look at least, your features . . .
Wait, I call my neighbors into question.
They've done nothing wrong. It offends the rights,   425
it violates tradition.

LEADER.
                                        You will learn it all,
young daughter of Zeus, cut to a few words.
We are the everlasting children of the Night.
Deep in the halls of Earth they call us Curses.

ATHENA.
Now I know your birth, your rightful name—   430

LEADER.
But not our powers, and you will learn them quickly.

ATHENA.
I can accept the facts, just tell them clearly.

LEADER.
Destroyers of life: we drive them from their houses.

ATHENA.
And the murderer's flight, where does it all end?

LEADER.
Where there is no joy, the word is never used.   435

ATHENA.
Such flight for him? You shriek him on to that?

LEADER.
                                                                     Yes,
he murdered his mother—called that murder just.

ATHENA.
And nothing forced him on, no fear of someone's anger?

LEADER.
What spur could force a man to kill his mother?

ATHENA.
Two sides are here, and only half is heard.   440
LEADER.
But the oath[30]—he will neither take the oath nor give it,
no, his will is set.
ATHENA.
                            And you are set
on the name of justice rather than the act.
LEADER.
How? Teach us. You have a genius for refinements.
ATHENA.
Injustice, I mean, should never triumph thanks to oaths.   445
LEADER.
Then examine him yourself, judge him fairly.
ATHENA.
You would turn over responsibility to me,
to reach the final verdict?
LEADER.
                                        Certainly.[31]
We respect you. You show us respect.

[ATHENA turns to ORESTES.]

ATHENA.
Your turn, stranger. What do you say to this?   450
Tell us your land, your birth, your fortunes.
Then defend yourself against their charge,
if trust in your rights has brought you here to guard
my hearth and idol, a suppliant for purging
like Ixion,[32] sacred. Speak to all this clearly,   455
speak to me.
ORESTES.
                    Queen Athena, first,
the misgiving in your final words is strong.
Let me remove it. I haven't come for purging.
Look, not a stain on the hands that touch your idol.
I have proof for all I say, and it is strong.   460

The law condemns the man of the violent hand
to silence, till a master trained at purging
slits the throat of a young suckling victim,
blood absolves his blood. Long ago
at the halls of others I was fully cleansed   465

---

[30] The ritual oath of innocence. Orestes refuses it because the fact itself of matricide is for him not the main issue. A few lines later Athena argues that such rituals should not govern in legal contests.

[31] The Furies now agree to be bound by Athena's verdict.

[32] After murdering his father-in-law, Ixion was absolved by Zeus. (Later, after trying to seduce Zeus's consort, Hera, Ixion was punished by being tied in the underworld to an ever-revolving wheel.)

in the cleansing springs, the blood of many victims.
Threat of pollution, sweep it from your mind.

Now for my birth. You will know at once.
I am from Argos. My father, well you ask,
was Agamemnon, sea-lord of the men-of-war,   470
your partisan when you made the city Troy
a city of the dead.
                What an ignoble death he died
when he came home—Ai! my blackhearted mother
cut him down, enveloped him in her handsome net—
it still attests his murder in the bath.   475
But I came back, my years of exile weathered—
killed the one who bore me, I won't deny it,
killed her in revenge. I loved my father,
fiercely.
        And Apollo shares the guilt—
he spurred me on, he warned of the pains I'd feel   480
unless I acted, brought the guilty down.
But were we just or not? Judge us now.
My fate is in your hands. Stand or fall
I shall accept your verdict.
ATHENA.
               Too large a matter,
some may think, for mortal men to judge.   485
But by all rights not even I should decide
a case of murder—murder whets the passions.
Above all, the rites have tamed your wildness.
A suppliant, cleansed, you bring my house no harm.
If you are innocent, I'd adopt you for my city.   490

[*Turning to the* FURIES.]

But they have their destiny too, hard to dismiss,
and if they fail to win their day in court—
how it will spread, the venom of their pride,
plague everlasting blights our land, our future . . .

So it stands. A crisis either way.   495

[*Looking back and forth from*
ORESTES *to the* FURIES.]

Embrace the one? expel the other? It defeats me.

But since the matter comes to rest on us,
I will appoint the judges of manslaughter,
swear them in, and found a tribunal here
for all time to come.[33]

---

[33] The court of the Areopagus, the main forum of the Athenian judicial system.

[*To* ORESTES *and the* FURIES.]

My contestants,   500
summon your trusted witnesses and proofs,
your defenders under oath to help your cause.
And I will pick the finest men of Athens,
return and decide the issue fairly, truly—
bound to our oaths, our spirits bent on justice.   505

[ATHENA *leaves. The* FURIES *form
their chorus.*]

FURIES.
Here, now,[34] is the overthrow
of every binding law—once his appeal,
   his outrage wins the day,
his matricide! One act links all mankind,
hand to desperate hand in bloody license.   510
   Over and over deathstrokes
      dealt by children wait their parents,
   mortal generations still unborn.

We are the Furies still, yes,
but now our rage that patrolled the crimes of men,   515
   that stalked their rage dissolves—
we loose a lethal tide to sweep the world!
Man to man foresees his neighbor's torments,
   groping to cure his own—
      poor wretch, there is no cure, no use,   520
   the drugs that ease him speed the next attack.

Now when the sudden blows come down,
let no one sound the call that once brought help,
"Justice, hear me—Furies throned in power!"
   Oh I can hear the father now   525
   or the mother sob with pain
      at the pain's onset . . . hopeless now,
   the house of Justice falls.

There is a time when terror helps,
the watchman must stand guard upon the heart.   530
It helps, at times, to suffer into truth.
   Is there a man who knows no fear
   in the brightness of his heart,
      or a man's city, both are one,
   that still reveres the rights?   535

---

[34] In the following chorus, the Furies argue that the force they represent, of vengeance and fear of punishment, is the very foundation of social order; if Orestes is acquitted, the whole community will be engulfed by general chaos, since the distinction between good and evil will no longer govern human behavior.

Neither the life of anarchy
nor the life enslaved by tyrants, no,
worship neither.
Strike the balance all in all and god will give you power;
the laws of god may veer from north to south—   540
we Furies plead for Measure.
Violence is Impiety's child, true to its roots,
but the spirit's great good health breeds all we love
and all our prayers call down,
prosperity and peace.   545

All in all I tell you people,
bow before the altar of the rights,
revere it well.
Never trample it underfoot, your eyes set on spoils;
revenge will hunt the godless day and night—   550
the destined end awaits.
So honor your parents first with reverence, I say,
and the stranger guest you welcome to your house,
turn to attend his needs,
respect his sacred rights.   555

All of your own free will, all uncompelled,
be just and you will never want for joy,
you and your kin can never be uprooted from the earth.
The reckless one—I warn the marauder
dragging plunder, chaotic, rich beyond all rights: 560
he'll strike his sails,
harried at long last,
stunned when the squalls of torment break his spars to bits.

He cries to the deaf, he wrestles walls of sea
sheer whirlpools down, down, with the gods' laughter   565
breaking over the man's hot heart—they see him flailing, crushed.
The one who boasted never to shipwreck
now will never clear the cape and steer for home;
he lived for wealth,
golden his life long—   570
he rams on the reef of law and drowns unwept, unseen.

> [*The scene has shifted to the Areopagus, the tribunal on the Crag of Ares.*[35] ATHENA *enters in procession with a herald and ten citizens she has chosen to be judges.*]

---

[35] Ares, the god of war, had according to legend once been tried on the Areopagus (the "Crag of Ares" in Athens), for murder.

ATHENA.
Call for order, herald, marshal our good people.
Lift the Etruscan battle-trumpet,[36]
strain it to full pitch with human breath,
crash out a stabbing blast along the ranks.

575

> [*The trumpet sounds. The judges
> take up positions between the audi-
> ence and the actors.* ATHENA *sepa-
> rates the* FURIES *and* ORESTES, *di-
> recting him to the Stone of Outrage
> and the leader to the Stone of
> Unmercifulness, where the* FURIES
> *form their chorus. Then* ATHENA
> *takes her stand between two urns
> that will receive the ballots.*]

And while this court of judgment fills, my city,
silence will be best. So that you can learn
my everlasting laws. And you too,

> [*To* ORESTES *and the* FURIES.]

that our verdict may be well observed by all.

> [APOLLO *enters suddenly and looms
> behind* ORESTES.]

Lord Apollo—rule it over your own sphere!   580
What part have you in this? Tell us.
APOLLO.
                                        I come
as a witness. This man, according to custom,
this suppliant sought out my house and hearth.
I am the one who purged his bloody hands.
His champion too, I share responsibility   585
for his mother's execution.
                                Bring on the trial.
You know the rules, now turn them into justice.

> [ATHENA *turns to the* FURIES.]

ATHENA.
The trial begins! Yours is the first word—
the prosecution opens. Start to finish,
set the facts before us, make them clear.   590
LEADER.
Numerous as we are, we will be brief.

[36] Athena's battle-trumpet, supposedly made in a region of northern Italy.

[*To* ORESTES.]

Answer count for count, charge for charge.
First, tell us, did you kill your mother?
LEADER.
ORESTES.
I killed her. There's no denying that.
LEADER.
Three falls in the match. One is ours[37] already.   595
ORESTES.
You exult before your man is on his back.
LEADER.
But *how* did you kill her? You must tell us that.
ORESTES.
I will. I drew my sword—more, I cut her throat.
LEADER.
And who persuaded you? who led you on?
ORESTES.
This god and his command.

[*Indicating* APOLLO.]

He bears me witness.   600
LEADER.
The Seer? He drove you on to matricide?
ORESTES.
                                              Yes,
and to this hour I have no regrets.
LEADER.
                                    If the verdict
brings you down, you'll change your story quickly.
ORESTES.
I have my trust; my father will help me from the grave.
LEADER.
Trust to corpses now! You made your mother one.   605
ORESTES.
I do. She had two counts against her, deadly crimes.
LEADER.
How? Explain that to your judges.
ORESTES.
She killed her husband—killed my father too.
LEADER.
But murder set her free, and you live on for trial.
ORESTES.
She lived on. You never drove *her* into exile—why?   610
LEADER.
The blood of the man she killed was not her own.
ORESTES.
And I? Does mother's blood run in my veins?

[37] Three overthrows of the opponent were required to win a wrestling match; the Leader claims to have won the first.

LEADER.

How could she breed you in her body, murderer?
Disclaim your mother's blood? She gave you life.

[ORESTES *turns to* APOLLO.]

ORESTES.

Bear me witness—show me the way, Apollo!   615
Did I strike her down with justice?
Strike I did, I don't deny it, no.
But how does our bloody work impress you now?—
Just or not? Decide.
I must make my case to them.

[*Looking to the judges.*]

APOLLO.

                                    Just,   620
I say, to you and your high court, Athena.
Seer that I am, I never lie. Not once
from the Prophet's thrones have I declared
a word that bears on man, woman or city
that Zeus did not command, the Olympian Father.   625
This is *his* justice—omnipotent, I warn you.
Bend to the will of Zeus. No oath can match
the power of the Father.

LEADER.

                              Zeus, you say,
gave that command to your oracle? He charged
Orestes here to avenge his father's death   630
and spurn his mother's rights?

APOLLO.

                              —Not the same
for a noble man to die, covered with praise,
his scepter the gift of god—murdered, at that,
by a woman's hand, no arrows whipping in
from a distance as an Amazon[38] would fight.   635
But as you will hear, Athena, and your people
poised to cast their lots and judge the case.
Home from the long campaign he came, more won
than lost on balance, home to her loyal, waiting arms,
the welcome bath . . .
                              he was just emerging at the edge,   640
and there she pitched her tent, her circling shroud—
she shackled her man in robes,
in her gorgeous never-ending web she chopped him down!

Such was the outrage of his death, I tell you,
the lord of the squadrons, that magnificent man.   645

---

[38] The Amazons were women warriors, noted especially as archers.

Her I draw to the life to lash your people,
marshaled to reach a verdict.
LEADER.
                        Zeus, you say,
sets more store by a father's death? He shackled
his own father, Kronos[39] proud with age.
Doesn't that contradict you?   650

                        [*To the judges.*]

Mark it well. I call you all to witness.
APOLLO.
You grotesque, loathsome—the gods detest you!
Zeus can break chains, we've cures for that,
countless ingenious ways to set us free.
But once the dust drinks down a man's blood,   655
he is gone, once for all. No rising back,
no spell sung over the grave can sing him back—
not even Father can. Though all things else
he can overturn and never strain for breath.
LEADER.
                                      So
you'd force this man's acquittal? Behold, Justice!   660

                [*Exhibiting* APOLLO *and* ORESTES.]

Can a son spill his mother's blood on the ground,
then settle into his father's halls in Argos?
Where are the public altars he can use?
Can the kinsmen's holy water touch his hands?
APOLLO.
Here is the truth, I tell you—see how right I am.   665
The woman you call the mother of the child
is not the parent,[40] just a nurse to the seed,
the new-sown seed that grows and swells inside her.
The *man* is the source of life—the one who mounts.
She, like a stranger for a stranger, keeps   670
the shoot alive unless god hurts the roots.

I give you proof that all I say is true.
The father can father forth without a mother.
Here she stands, our living witness. Look—

                    [*Exhibiting* ATHENA.]

[39] Zeus had overcome his father Kronos (the Roman Saturn) and imprisoned him in the underworld; Apollo will reply to this charge by arguing that imprisonment is not the same as irrevocable death.

[40] This genetic theory is proved, Apollo goes on to argue, by Athena herself, who was born from Zeus's head.

Child sprung full-blown from Olympian Zeus,   675
never bred in the darkness of the womb
but such a stock no goddess could conceive!

And I, Pallas, with all my strong techniques
will rear your host and battlements to glory.
So I dispatched this suppliant to your hearth   680
that he might be your trusted friend forever,
that you might win a new ally,[41] dear goddess.
He and his generations arm-in-arm with yours,
your bonds stand firm for all posterity—
ATHENA.
                             Now
have we heard enough? May I have them cast   685
their honest lots as conscience may decide?
LEADER.
For us, we have shot our arrows, every one.
I wait to hear how this ordeal will end.
ATHENA.
                         Of course.
And what can I do to merit your respect?
APOLLO.
You have heard what you have heard.   690

[*To the judges.*]

Cast your lots, my friends,
strict to the oath that you have sworn.
ATHENA.
                        And now
if you would hear my law, you men of Greece,
you who will judge the first trial of bloodshed.
Now and forever more, for Aegeus' people[42]   695
this will be the court where judges reign.
This is the Crag of Ares, where the Amazons
pitched their tents when they came marching down
on Theseus, full tilt in their fury, erecting
a new city to overarch his city, towers thrust   700
against his towers—they sacrificed to Ares,
named this rock from that day onward Ares' Crag.

Here from the heights, terror and reverence,
my people's kindred powers
will hold them from injustice through the day   705
and through the mild night. Never pollute
our law with innovations. No, my citizens,

[41] The people of Argos; at the time of the *Oresteia*, Athens had recently concluded an alliance with them.
[42] The Athenians; Aegeus was a legendary ruler of the city and father of Theseus.

foul a clear well and you will suffer thirst.
Neither anarchy nor tyranny, my people.
Worship the Mean, I urge you,   710
shore it up with reverence and never
banish terror from the gates, not outright.[43]
Where is the righteous man who knows no fear?
The stronger your fear, your reverence for the just,
the stronger your country's wall and city's safety,   715
stronger by far than all men else possess
in Scythia's rugged steppes or Pelops' level plain.[44]
Untouched by lust for spoil, this court of law
majestic, swift to fury, rising above you
as you sleep, our night watch always wakeful,   720
guardian of our land—I found it here and now.

So I urge you, Athens. I have drawn this out
to rouse you to your future. You must rise,
each man must cast his lot and judge the case,
reverent to his oath. Now I have finished.   725

> [*The judges come forward, pass be-*
> *tween the urns and cast their lots.*]

LEADER.
Beware. Our united force can break your land.
Never wound our pride, I tell you, never.
APOLLO.
The oracles, not mine alone but Zeus's too—
dread them, I warn you, never spoil their fruit.

> [*The leader turns to* APOLLO.]

LEADER.
You dabble in works of blood beyond your depth.   730
Oracles, your oracles will be stained forever.
APOLLO.
Oh, so the Father's judgment faltered when Ixion,
the first man-slayer came to him for purging?
LEADER.
Talk on, talk on. But if I lose this trial
I will return in force to crush the land.   735
APOLLO.
Never—among the gods, young and old,
you go disgraced. I will triumph over you!

[43] The phrase probably means two things: a) maintain as part of your conscience a wholesome fear of committing evil, and b) do not summarily turn away from your city a frightened
stranger seeking asylum.
[44] That is, in the wild land of faraway Scythia or in the Grecian land of Pelops that included
Argos.

LEADER.
Just as you triumphed in the house of Pheres,[45]
luring the Fates to set men free from death.

APOLLO.
What?—is it a crime to help the pious man,   740
above all, when his hour of need has come?

LEADER.
You brought them down, the oldest realms of order,
seduced the ancient goddesses with wine.

APOLLO.
You will fail this trial—in just a moment
spew your venom and never harm your enemies.   745

LEADER.
You'd ride me down, young god, for all my years?
Well here I stand, waiting to learn the verdict.
Torn with doubt . . . to rage against the city or—

ATHENA.
My work is here, to render the final judgment.
Orestes,

> [Raising her arm, her hand
> clenched as if holding a ballot-stone.]

I will cast my lot for you.   750
No mother gave me birth.
I honor the male, in all things but marriage.
Yes, with all my heart I am my Father's child.
I cannot set more store by the woman's death—
she killed her husband, guardian of their house.   755
Even if the vote is equal, Orestes wins.[46]

Shake the lots from the urns. Quickly,
you of the jury charged to make the count.

> [Judges come forward, empty the
> urns, and count the ballot-stones.]

ORESTES.
O God of the Light, Apollo, how will the verdict go?

LEADER.
O Night, dark mother, are you watching now?   760

[45] Father of Admetus, a favorite of Apollo, who preserved Admetus from destined death by overcoming "the ancient goddesses"—that is, the Fates—"with wine" (line 743) so that they agreed to accept an alternative victim. Admetus' wife Alcestis offered her own life instead of his. The story is told in Euripides' *Alcestis*.

[46] In interpreting Athena's decision here, we can accept her own explanation, that she is her father Zeus's child (an Olympian who is biased toward males). But these reasons seem incompatible with her evenhandedness elsewhere in the play. That she has not simply ignored the Furies' side of the case is proved by her later actions and words.

ORESTES.
   Now for the goal—the noose, or the new day!
LEADER.
   Now we go down, or forge ahead in power.
APOLLO.
   Shake out the lots and count them fairly, friends.
   Honor Justice. An error in judgment now
   can mean disaster. The cast of a single lot   765
   restores a house to greatness.

                              [*Receiving the judges' count*, ATHENA
                                 lifts her arm once more.]
ATHENA.
                              The man goes free,
   cleared of the charge of blood. The lots are equal.
ORESTES.
   O Pallas Athena—you, you save my house!
   I was shorn of the fatherland but you
   reclaim it for me. Now any Greek will say,   770
   "He lives again, the man of Argos lives
   on his fathers' great estates. Thanks to Pallas,
   Apollo and Zeus, the lord of all fulfillment,
   Third, Saving Zeus." He respected father's death,
   looked down on mother's advocates—

                              [*Indicating the* FURIES.]

                              he saved me.   775

   And now I journey home. But first I swear
   to you, your land and assembled host, I swear
   by the future years that bring their growing yield
   that no man, no helmsman of Argos wars on Athens,
   spears in the vanguard moving out for conquest.   780
   We ourselves, even if we must rise up from the grave,
   will deal with those who break the oath I take—
   baffle them with disasters, curse their marches,
   send them hawks aloft on the left[47] at every crossing—
   make their pains recoil upon their heads.   785
   But all who keep our oath, who uphold your rights
   and citadel forever, comrade spear to spear,
   we bless with all the kindness of our heart.

   Now farewell, you and the people of your city.
   Good wrestling—a grip no foe can break.   790
   A saving hope, a spear to bring you triumph!

---

[47] The left was the side on which ill omens supposedly appeared. Compare the eagles
(mentioned in *Agamemnon*, lines 118 ff.) who appeared on the right before the sacrifice of
Iphigeneia at Aulis.

[*Exit* ORESTES, *followed by* APOLLO.
The FURIES *reel in wild confusion
around* ATHENA.]

FURIES.

You, you younger gods!—you have ridden down
    the ancient laws, wrenched them from my grasp—
and I, robbed of my birthright, suffering, great with wrath,
      I loose my poison over the soil, aieee!—   795
poison to match my grief comes pouring out my heart,
          cursing the land to burn it sterile and now
rising up from its roots a cancer blasting leaf and child,
        now for Justice, Justice!—cross the face of the earth
the bloody tide comes hurling, all mankind destroyed.   800
. . . Moaning, only moaning? What will I do?
    The mockery of it, Oh unbearable,
mortified by Athens,
we the daughters of Night,
our power stripped, cast down.

ATHENA.

                     Yield to me.   805
No more heavy spirits. You were not defeated—
the vote was tied, a verdict fairly reached
with no disgrace to you, no, Zeus brought
luminous proof before us. He who spoke
god's oracle, he bore witness that Orestes   810
did the work but should not suffer harm.

And now you'd vent your anger, hurt the land?
Consider a moment. Calm yourself. Never
render us barren, raining your potent showers
down like spears, consuming every seed.   815
By all my rights I promise you your seat
in the depths of earth,[48] yours by all rights—
stationed at hearths equipped with glistening thrones,
covered with praise! My people will revere you.

FURIES.

You, you younger gods!—you have ridden down   820
    the ancient laws, wrenched them from my grasp—
and I, robbed of my birthright, suffering, great with wrath,
      I loose my poison over the soil, aieee!—
poison to match my grief comes pouring out my heart,
          cursing the land to burn it sterile and now   825
rising up from its roots a cancer blasting leaf and child,
        now for Justice, Justice!—cross the face of the earth
the bloody tide comes hurling, all mankind destroyed.

---

[48] Appropriately, the Furies, who have been all along portrayed as forces of earth and
night, will be given cave-shrines at the Athenian Acropolis, where they will combine their old
role as ministers of avenging justice with a new role as agents of fertility and the blessings
symbolized by it.

. . . Moaning, only moaning? What will I do?
　　The mockery of it, Oh unbearable,   830
mortified by Athens,
we the daughters of Night,
our power stripped, cast down.
ATHENA.
　　　　　　　　　　　　　　You have your power,
you are goddesses—but not to turn
on the world of men and ravage it past cure.   835
I put my trust in Zeus and . . . must I add this?
I am the only god who knows the keys
to the armory where his lightning-bolt is sealed.
No need of that, not here.
　　　　　　　　　　　　　Let me persuade you.
The lethal spell of your voice, never cast it   840
down on the land and blight its harvest home.
Lull asleep that salt black wave of anger—
awesome, proud with reverence, live with me.
The land is rich, and more, when its first fruits,
offered for heirs and the marriage rites, are yours   845
to hold forever, you will praise my words.
FURIES.
　　But for me to suffer such disgrace . . . I,
the proud heart of the past, driven under the earth,
condemned, like so much filth,
　　and the fury in me breathing hatred—   850
O good Earth,
　　　　what is this stealing under the breast,
what agony racks the spirit? . . . Night, dear Mother Night!
All's lost, our ancient powers torn away by their cunning,
ruthless hands, the gods so hard to wrestle down   855
obliterate us all.
ATHENA.
　　　　　　　　　　I will bear with your anger.
You are older. The years have taught you more,
much more than I can know. But Zeus, I think,
gave me some insight too, that has its merits.
If you leave for an alien land and alien people,   860
you will come to love this land, I promise you.
As time flows on, the honors flow through all
my citizens, and you, throned in honor
before the house of Erechtheus,[49] will harvest
more from men and women moving in solemn file   865
than you can win throughout the mortal world.

Here in our homeland never cast the stones
that whet our bloodlust. Never waste our youth,

---

[49] A legendary ruler of Athens; a temple named for him (the Erechtheum) stood on the Acropolis.

inflaming them with the burning wine of strife.
Never pluck the heart of the battle cock   870
and plant it in our people—intestine war
seething against themselves. Let our wars
rage on abroad, with all their force, to satisfy
our powerful lust for fame. But as for the bird
that fights at home—my curse on civil war.   875

This is the life I offer, it is yours to take.
Do great things, feel greatness, greatly honored.
Share this country cherished by the gods.
FURIES.
     But for me to suffer such disgrace . . . I,
the proud heart of the past, driven under the earth,   880
condemned, like so much filth,
     and the fury in me breathing hatred—
O good Earth,
     what is this stealing under the breast,
what agony racks the spirit? . . . Night, dear Mother Night!   885
All's lost, our ancient powers torn away by their cunning,
ruthless hands, the gods so hard to wrestle down
obliterate us all.
ATHENA.
                    No, I will never tire
of telling you your gifts. So that you,
the older gods, can never say that I,   890
a young god and the mortals of my city
drove you outcast, outlawed from the land.

But if you have any reverence for Persuasion,
the majesty of Persuasion,
the spell of my voice that would appease your fury—   895
Oh please stay . . .
                    and if you refuse to stay,
it would be wrong, unjust to afflict this city
with wrath, hatred, populations routed. Look,
it is all yours, a royal share of our land—
justly entitled, glorified forever.
LEADER.
                    Queen Athena,   900
where is the home you say is mine to hold?
ATHENA.
Where all the pain and anguish end. Accept it.
LEADER.
And if I do, what honor waits for me?
ATHENA.
No house can thrive without you.
LEADER.
                    You would do that—
grant me that much power?

ATHENA.
                              Whoever reveres us—   905
we will raise the fortunes of their lives.
LEADER.
    And you will pledge me that, for all time to come?
ATHENA.
    Yes—I must never promise things I cannot do.
LEADER.
    Your magic is working . . . I can feel the hate,
    the fury slip away.
ATHENA.
                              At last! And now take root   910
in the land and win yourself new friends.
LEADER.
                                          A spell—
what spell to sing? to bind the land forever? Tell us.
ATHENA.
    Nothing that strikes a note of brutal conquest. Only peace—
    blessings, rising up from the earth and the heaving sea,
    and down the vaulting sky let the wind-gods breathe   915
    a wash of sunlight streaming through the land,
    and the yield of soil and grazing cattle flood
    our city's life with power and never flag
    with time. Make the seed of men live on,
    the more they worship you the more they thrive.   920
    I love them as a gardener loves his plants,
    these upright men, this breed fought free of grief.
    All that is yours to give.
                              And I,
    in the trials of war where fighters burn for fame,
    will never endure the overthrow of Athens—   925
    all will praise her, victor city, pride of man.

                              [*The* FURIES *assemble, dancing
                              around* ATHENA, *who becomes their
                              leader.*]

FURIES.

                    I will embrace
            one home with you, Athena,
                    never fail the city
        you and Zeus almighty, you and Ares   930
    hold as the fortress of the gods, the shield
    of the high Greek altars, glory of the powers.
        Spirit of Athens, hear my words, my prayer
            like a prophet's warm and kind,
            that the rare good things of life   935
                come rising crest on crest,
            sprung from the rich black earth and
        gleaming with the bursting flash of sun.

ATHENA.
These blessings I bestow on you, my people, gladly.
I enthrone these strong, implacable spirits here 940
and root them in our soil.
                    Theirs,
    theirs to rule the lives of men,
        it is their fated power.
    But he who has never felt their weight,
    or known the blows of life and how they fall, 945
    the crimes of his fathers hale him toward their bar,
    and there for all his boasts—destruction,
        silent, majestic in anger,
    crushes him to dust.
FURIES.
                    Yes and I ban
        the winds that rock the olive— 950
        hear my love, my blessing—
    thwart their scorching heat that blinds the buds,
        hold from our shores the killing icy gales,
    and I ban the blight that creeps on fruit and withers—
        God of creation, Pan, make flocks increase 955
            and the ewes drop fine twin lambs
                when the hour of labor falls.
            And silver, child of Earth,
                secret treasure of Hermes,
        come to light and praise the gifts of god. 960
ATHENA.
    Blessings—now do you hear, you guards of Athens,
        all that she will do?
    Fury the mighty queen, the dread
    of the deathless gods and those beneath the earth,
    deals with mortals clearly, once for all. 965
    She delivers songs to some, to others
        a blinding life of tears—
    Fury works her will.
FURIES.
                And the lightning stroke
        that cuts men down before their prime, I curse,
        but the lovely girl who finds a mate's embrace, 970
    the deep joy of wedded life—O grant that gift, that prize,
        you gods of wedlock, grant it, goddesses of Fate!
            Sisters born of the Night our mother,
                spirits steering law,
            sharing at all our hearths, 975
            at all times bearing down
                to make our lives more just,
        all realms exalt you highest of the gods.
ATHENA.
    Behold, my land, what blessings Fury kindly,
        gladly brings to pass— 980

I am in my glory! Yes, I love Persuasion;
she watched my words, she met their wild refusals.
Thanks to Zeus of the Councils who can turn
dispute to peace—he won the day.

[*To the* FURIES.]

    Thanks to our duel for blessings;   985
we win through it all.

FURIES.

                    And the brutal strife,
        the civil war devouring men, I pray
    that it never rages through our city, no,
that the good Greek soil never drinks the blood of Greeks,
        shed in an orgy of reprisal life for life—   990
          that Fury like a beast will never
            rampage through the land.
          Give joy in return for joy,
           one common will for love,
         and hate with one strong heart: 995
    such union heals a thousand ills of man.

ATHENA.

Do you *hear* how Fury sounds her blessings forth,
   how Fury finds the way?
Shining out of the terror of their faces
I can see great gains for you, my people.   1000
Hold them kindly, kind as they are to you.
Exalt them always, you exalt your land,
   your city straight and just—
its light goes through the world.

FURIES.

                Rejoice,
        rejoice in destined wealth,   1005
        rejoice, Athena's people—
        poised by the side of Zeus,
loved by the loving virgin girl,[50]
        achieve humanity at last,
        nestling under Pallas' wings   1010
    and blessed with Father's love.

ATHENA.

You too rejoice! and I must lead the way
to your chambers by the holy light of these,
   your escorts bearing fire.

[*Enter* ATHENA'S *entourage of
women, bearing offerings and victims and torches still unlit.*]

---

[50] The "virgin goddess" Athena; her kinship with the Furies, who are now also kindly
Eumenides, ironically recalls Apollo's sneer at the Furies earlier as "the eternal virgins" (line
73).

Come, and sped beneath the earth   1015
  by our awesome sacrifices,
`keep destruction from the country,
bring prosperity home to Athens,
triumph sailing in its wake.
                              And you,
my people born of the Rock King,[51]   1020
lead on our guests for life, my city—
May they treat you with compassion,
compassionate as you will be to them.

FURIES.

                        Rejoice!—
         rejoice—the joy resounds—
         all those who dwell in Athens,   1025
           spirits and mortals, come,
             govern Athena's city well,
          revere us well, we are your guests;
         you will learn to praise your Furies,
         you will praise the fortunes of your lives.   1030

ATHENA.

My thanks! and I will speed your prayers, your blessings—
lit by the torches breaking into flame
I send you home, home to the core of Earth,
escorted by these friends who guard my idol
duty-bound.

                          [ATHENA'S *entourage comes for-*
                          ward, bearing crimson robes.][52]

          Bright eye of the land of Theseus,   1035
come forth, my splendid troupe. Girls and mothers,
trains of aged women grave in movement,
dress our Furies now in blood-red robes.
Praise them—let the torch move on!
So the love this family bears toward our land   1040
will bloom in human strength from age to age.

                         [*The women invest the* FURIES *and*
                         sing the final chorus. Torches blaze;
                         a procession forms, including the
                         actors and the judges and the audi-
                         ence. ATHENA *leads them from the*
                         theater and escorts them through the
                         city.]

THE WOMEN OF THE CITY.
     On, on, good spirits born for glory,
Daughters of Night, her children always young,

[51] The primitive king of the Acropolis.
[52] The red robes and torches recall and reverse the ominous symbolism of robes, blood, and torches in the *Agamemnon*.

now under loyal escort—
Blessings, people of Athens, sing your blessings out.

Deep, deep in the first dark vaults of Earth,
sped by the praise and victims we will bring,
       reverence will attend you—
Blessings now, all people, sing your blessings out.

You great good Furies, bless the land with kindly hearts,   1050
you Awesome Spirits, come—exult in the blazing torch,
       exultant in our fires, journey on.
Cry, cry in triumph, carry on the dancing on and on!

This peace between Athena's people and their guests
must never end. All-seeing Zeus and Fate embrace,   1055
       down they come to urge our union on—
Cry, cry in triumph, carry on the dancing on and on!

Sophocles
(496–406 B.C.)

In more than one sense, Sophocles is the central figure among the three great Greek tragedians. He was born in 496 B.C. in Colonus, the suburb of Athens celebrated in his last play, Oedipus at Colonus; *he died in 406. Much of his life-span thus overlapped that of his predecessor, Aeschylus, who died when Sophocles was forty. The third of the great triumvirate, Euripides, was sixteen years younger than Sophocles but died slightly before him. As a dramatist, Sophocles was a consummate artist who combined the high ethical and religious concerns of Aeschylus with the intense interest in individual human psychology characteristic of Euripides. Sophocles' ninety years of life therefore coincided with the entire history—the rise and fall—of the golden age of Greek tragedy. His years also coincided with the rise and fall of the uniquely splendid—and historically tragic—Athenian culture of the fifth century. In 480, when Sophocles was sixteen years old, he took part in a public celebration of the naval victory over the Persians at Salamis, a victory that—coincidentally or not—raised the curtain on the awesome cultural and social achievements of the ensuing age. Sophocles' death occurred only two years before the definitive collapse of Athenian supremacy, when in 404 the city succumbed to Sparta and its allies.*

By most accounts, Sophocles was a man comfortably at home in his world and at the center of its public life. He was enormously successful and popular as a man of the theater. His temperament was urbane, gregarious, balanced. He held several important public positions during the years of Athens' primacy—as treasurer, as a diplomatic and military policy-maker, as an ambassador, even as a priest. In short, he was what we have come to call a member of the establishment. And yet, intriguingly, he wrote dramas that call into question—though they do not necessarily undermine—the values generally associated with that role. Oedipus, in Oedipus the King, *is the model of a good ruler, a humanely intelligent and vigorously active leader, a man who earlier saved his adopted city Thebes from disaster. Yet Oedipus is finally driven to self-mutilation and self-imposed exile because he has committed, though unwittingly, the most horrendous crimes against the divine order, the natural order, and the polity: patricide, incest, and the pollution of his city. In* Antigone, *Oedipus' brave, lovable, headstrong daughter confronts her uncle Kreon, the new ruler of Thebes, over an issue—the conflicting demands of civic, familial, and religious principles—that few establishmentarians would press urgently. Probings of these themes, stories, or issues are not what one would expect of a religious pietist or of a politically complacent conservative.*

That paradox, along with others, makes Sophocles an especially challenging artist and personality. Scholars disagree on how to interpret him, as man or playwright. He wrote more than 120 plays, of which only seven have survived intact (two are included in this volume; the others are Ajax, The Women of Trachis, Electra, Philoctetes, *and* Oedipus at Colonus). *His artistic control of plot and other elements of the drama have helped identify Sophocles as the perfect "classicist," and the extravagant praise given him by Aristotle in his* Poetics *has reinforced that image. Yet "classicist" is an inadequate term, and a seriously misleading one if we make the simple-minded but familiar identification of the classical with calm, serene detachment. Sophocles tends to represent in his characters general human types, an approach generally considered classical. Antigone is the archetype of the martyr to*

591

*principle, Oedipus of the intelligent man brought low by the very intellectual gifts
and compulsion to understand that make him admirable (not to mention the universality found in him by Sigmund Freud, who discerned in the "Oedipus complex" a
fundamental law of filial and psychic experience). Yet at no time do we lose sight of
these characters as individuals, and indeed as individuals racked by conflict, pain, or
both. Antigone is indeed a type, but (like Cordelia in Shakespeare's* King Lear, *who
has a similar blend of gentleness and toughness) she embodies that type in a distinct
individual personality. For example, Antigone's awareness of the sanctity of the
family bond makes her compassionate toward her dead brother Polyneices but incon-
gruously, brutally contemptuous of her sister Ismene.*

*One of the pervading themes in Sophocles is the justice of the universe. We are to
understand that, in some sense, cosmic justice ultimately prevails, but any cosmic
order that demands the blinding and exile of the essentially just Oedipus and the
death of the heroic Antigone would seem ambiguous and indeed frightening. Few
authors of any age have rendered the experience of raw pain—psychological and
physical—so compellingly. Significantly, the nineteenth-century poet Matthew Arnold described Sophocles as a man who "saw life steadily and saw it whole" but also
as one who heard "the eternal note of sadness" and was preeminently sensitive to "the
turbid ebb and flow of human misery."*

*Sophocles does not treat issues in a vacuum; he is above all a dramatist. The
innovations he made in dramatic method and staging have the effect of making
conflict more humanly immediate—if not necessarily more powerful—than in
Aeschylus. By increasing the number of speaking actors from two to three, Sophocles
made possible even more intricate interpersonal relationships than Aeschylus had
portrayed; by reducing the lyrical role of the Chorus (though he increased its size)
Sophocles was able to focus more directly, and in a less stylized way, on complexities of
character as conveyed in dialogue. He also expanded the use of stage machinery. The
total effect is to intensify our awareness of conflict, both external and within individual characters.*

Oedipus the King *has a special place in literature; it may well be the most
important and influential drama ever written. Aristotle seems to have considered it
the definitive tragedy, just as he considered Homer's* Iliad *and* Odyssey *the definitive epics. The play is the best known and most frequently cited example of "dramatic
irony," where the audience possesses information of which the main characters in the
play are ignorant. The gradual revelation to Oedipus of his past history, an already
familiar story the audience would have known from the very beginning of the play,
makes for powerful suspense, especially since it is Oedipus himself who relentlessly
investigates and puts together the case that—for all the elaborate precautions he has
taken not to commit unspeakable crimes—will in the end damn him in his own eyes
and in those of other people. The gigantic metaphor of eyes, of seeing, and blindness,
is worked with virtuoso skill. But the metaphor is not a mere "literary" device; it
typifies Sophocles' view of man's place in the totality of things. Humanity in his plays
is an integral part of a world-order that can be only partially understood at best. The
cosmic system includes, besides human beings and nature, those darkly inscrutable
forces identified—inadequately—as the gods and fate.*

*Yet Sophocles is not a fatalist either. Despite the sense of inevitability his plays
convey, human beings are considered responsible for their acts. But this belief in
responsibility raises an even deeper question about necessity and human freedom, for
if the lives of men and women are governed by themselves and not by their stars, are
not these human beings themselves determined in their behavior by what they "are"?*

Character may be destiny, but to what extent is character itself an unchangeable given? Even more than such difficult but relatively concrete issues as the conflict between the person and polity, this mind-bending question makes Sophocles' plays touchstones for an appreciation of the human dilemma.

FURTHER READING *(prepared by F.S.N.):* Now available in English is the classic by Karl Reinhardt, *Sophocles,* 1947, trans. Hazel and David Harvey, 1979, which discusses all the extant plays. Other works dealing with all or some of the Sophoclean dramas are S. M. Adams, *Sophocles the Playwright,* 1957; William Nickerson Bates, *Sophocles: Poet and Dramatist,* 1940, repr. 1961; Bernard M. W. Knox, *The Heroic Temper: Studies in Sophoclean Tragedy,* 1964. Further critical works on the life and thought of Sophocles are T. B. L. Webster, *An Introduction to Sophocles,* 1936, repr. 1969; and H. D. F. Kitto, *Sophocles: Dramatist and Philosopher,* 1958, repr. 1981. A number of modern interpretations of Sophocles are edited by Thomas Marion Woodard, *Sophocles: A Collection of Critical Essays,* 1966. A close analysis of the word patterns in *Antigone* is given by R. F. Goheen, *The Imagery of Sophocles' Antigone,* 1951. Luci Berkowitz and Theodore F. Brunner, ed., *Sophocles: Oedipus Tyrannus,* 1970, includes both a translation and a number of essays by various scholars on themes such as religion and psychology. See further M. J. O'Brien, ed., *Twentieth Century Interpretations of Oedipus Rex: A Collection of Critical Essays,* 1968.

OEDIPUS THE KING

Translated by Stephen Berg and Diskin Clay

CHARACTERS

OEDIPUS, *king of Thebes*
PRIEST *of Zeus*
KREON, *Oedipus' brother-in-law*
CHORUS OF THEBAN ELDERS
LEADER OF THE CHORUS
TEIRESIAS, *prophet, servant to Apollo*
JOCASTA, *wife of Oedipus*
MESSENGER *from Corinth*
SHEPHERD, *member of Laios' household*

SERVANT, *household slave of Oedipus*
Delegation of Thebans, servants to lead Teiresias and Oedipus; attendants to Oedipus, Kreon, Jocasta; and Antigone and Ismene, the daughters of Oedipus.

TIME AND SCENE

Dawn. Silence. The royal palace of Thebes. The altar of Apollo[1] *to the left of the central palace. A delegation of Thebans—old men, boys, young children—enters the orchestra*[2] *by the steps below the altar, assembles, and waits. They carry suppliant boughs—olive branches tied with strips of wool. Some climb the steps between the*

[1] The utterances of Apollo, god of prophecy, are central to the play's action. He was also god of healing and, conversely, of plague.

[2] In a Greek theater, the open space in front of the stage.

orchestra and the altar, place their branches on the altar, and return to the orchestra.
A PRIEST *stands apart from the suppliants at the foot of one of the two stairs. Silence.*
Waiting. The central doors open. From inside the palace, limping,[3] OEDIPUS *comes*
through the palace doors and stands at the top of the steps leading down into the
orchestra. He is dressed in gold and wears a golden crown.

OEDIPUS. Why children,
    why are you here, why
    are you holding those branches tied with wool,
    begging me for help? Children,
    the whole city smolders with incense.[4]
    Wherever I go I hear sobbing, praying. Groans fill the air.
    Rumors, news from messengers, they are not enough for me.
    Others cannot tell me what you need.
    I am king, I had to come. As king,
    I had to know. Know for myself, know for me.   10
    Everybody everywhere knows who I am: Oedipus. King.
    Priest of Zeus, we respect your age, your high office.
    Speak.
    Why are you kneeling? Are you afraid, old man?
    What can I give you?
    How can I help? Ask.
    Ask me anything. Anything at all.
    My heart would be a stone
    if I felt no pity for these poor shattered people of mine
    kneeling here, at my feet.   20
PRIEST. Oedipus, lord of Thebes, you see us, the people of Thebes,
    your people,
    crowding in prayer around your altar,
    these small children here, old men bent with age, priests, and I,
        the priest of Zeus,
    and our noblest young men, the pride and strength of Thebes.
    And there are more of us, lord Oedipus, more—gathered in the
        city, stunned,
    kneeling, offering their branches, praying before the two great
        temples of Athena[5]
    or staring into the ashes of burnt offerings,[6] staring,
    waiting, waiting for the god to speak.
    Look,
    look at it,   30
    lord Oedipus—right there,

[3] In Greek, the name Oedipus means "swell-foot." The cause of his lameness is revealed
later in the play.
[4] The city has been making religious offerings to appease the angry gods who have visited
plague on Thebes.
[5] Goddess of wisdom and knowledge; also, the patron of Athens and of Greek cities in
general.
[6] Sacrifices to the gods; the inspection of the ashes, it was hoped, would reveal the gods'
will.

in front of your eyes—this city—
it reels under a wild storm of blood, wave after wave battering
    Thebes.
We cannot breathe or stand.
We hunger, our world shivers with hunger. A disease hungers,
nothing grows, wheat, fruit, nothing grows bigger than a seed.
Our women bear
dead things,
all they can do is grieve,
our cattle wither, stumble, drop to the ground,   40
flies simmer on their bloated tongues,
the plague spreads everywhere, a stain seeping through our
    streets, our fields, our houses,
look—god's fire eating everyone, everything,
stroke after stroke of lightning, the god stabbing it alive—
it can't be put out, it can't be stopped,
its heat thickens the air, it glows like smoking metal,
this god of plague guts our city and fills the black world under us
    where the dead go
with the shrieks of women,
living women, wailing.
You are a man, not a god—I know.   50
We all know this, the young kneeling here before you know it, too,
but we know how great you are, Oedipus, greater than any man.
When crisis struck, you saved us[7] here in Thebes,
you faced the mysterious, strange disasters hammered against us
    by the gods.
This is our history—
we paid our own flesh to the Sphinx until you set us free.
You knew no more than anyone, but you knew.
There was a god in it, a god in you.

[*The* PRIEST *kneels.*]

Help us. Oedipus, we beg you, we all turn to you, kneeling to your
    greatness.
Advice from the gods or advice from human beings—you will
    know which is needed.
But help us. Power and experience are yours, all yours.   60
Between thought and action, between
our plans and their results a distance opens.
Only a man like you, Oedipus, tested by experience,
can make them one. That much I know.

---

[7]Thebes had earlier been ravaged by the Sphinx, a monster with a lion's body and a woman's head, who proposed a famous riddle, a wrong solution to which was punished by death. The question was, "What animal moves first on four legs, then on two, then on three, and is weakest when moving on four legs?" Oedipus correctly solved the riddle: Man, who first crawls, then walks, then goes with a walking stick. The solution of the riddle destroyed the Sphinx and established Oedipus in power as savior of Thebes.

Oedipus, more like a god than any man alive,
deliver us, raise us to our feet. Remember who you are.
Remember your love for Thebes. Your skill was our salvation once
     before.
For this Thebes calls you savior.
Don't let us remember you as the king—godlike in power—   70
who gave us back our life, then let us die.
Steady us forever. You broke the riddle for us then.
It was a sign. A god was in it. Be the man you were—
rule now as you ruled before.
Oh Oedipus,
how much better to rule a city of men than be king of empty earth.
A city is nothing, a ship is nothing
where no men live together, where no men work together.

OEDIPUS. Children, poor helpless children.
I know what brings you here, I know.   80
You suffer, this plague is agony for each of you,
but none of you, not one suffers as I do.
Each of you suffers for himself, only himself.
My whole being wails and breaks
for this city, for myself, for all of you,
old man, all of you.
Everything ends here, with me. I am the man.
You have not wakened me from some kind of sleep.
I have wept, struggled, wandered in this maze of thought,
tried every road, searched hard—   90
finally I found one cure, only one:
I sent my wife's brother, Kreon, to great Apollo's shrine at
     Delphi;[8]
I sent him to learn what I must say or do to save Thebes.
But his long absence troubles me. Why isn't he here? Where is he?
When he returns, what kind of man would I be
if I failed to do everything the god reveals?

> [*Some of the suppliants by the steps
> to the orchestra stand to announce
> KREON'S arrival to the PRIEST.
> KREON comes in by the entrance to
> the audience's left with a garland on
> his head.*]

PRIEST. You speak of Kreon, and Kreon is here.
OEDIPUS. [*turning to the altar of Apollo, then to* KREON]
Lord Apollo, look at him—his head is crowned with laurel, his
     eyes glitter.
Let his words blaze, blaze like his eyes, and save us.

---

[8] The most important center of prophecy in Greece; see the description at the beginning of
Aeschylus' *The Eumenides*.

PRIEST. He looks calm, radiant, like a god. If he brought bad news,   100
    would he be wearing that crown of sparkling leaves?
OEDIPUS. At last we will know.
    Lord Kreon, what did the god Apollo say?
KREON. His words are hopeful.
    Once everything is clear, exposed to the light,
  we will see our suffering is blessing. All we need is luck.
OEDIPUS. What do you mean? What did Apollo say? What should we
    do?
    Speak.
KREON. Here? Now? In front of all these people?
    Or inside, privately?   110

                        [KREON *moves toward the palace.*]

OEDIPUS. Stop. Say it. Say it to the whole city.
    I grieve for them, for their sorrow and loss, far more than I grieve
      for myself.
KREON. This is what I heard—there was no mistaking the god's mean-
      ing—
    Apollo commands us:
    Cleanse the city of Thebes, cleanse the plague from that city,
    destroy the black stain spreading everywhere, spreading,
    poisoning the earth, touching each house, each citizen,
    sickening the hearts of the people of Thebes!
    Cure this disease that wastes all of you, spreading, spreading,
    before it grows so vast nothing can cure it.   120
OEDIPUS. What is this plague?
    How can we purify the city?
KREON. A man must be banished. Banished or killed.
    Blood for blood. The plague is blood,
    blood, breaking over Thebes.
OEDIPUS. *Who* is the man? *Who* is Apollo's victim?
KREON. My lord, before you came to Thebes, before you came to
      power,
    Laios was our king.
OEDIPUS. I know. But I never saw Laios.
KREON. Laios was murdered. Apollo's command was very clear: 130
    Avenge the murderers of Laios. Whoever they are.
OEDIPUS. But where *are* his murderers?
    The crime is old. How will we find their tracks?
    The killers could be anywhere.
KREON. Apollo said the killers are still here, here in Thebes.
    Pursue a thing, and you may catch it;
    ignored, it slips away.
OEDIPUS. And Laios—where was he murdered?
    At home? Or was he away from Thebes?
KREON. He told us before he left—he was on a mission to Delphi,   140
    his last trip away from Thebes. He never returned.

OEDIPUS. Wasn't there a witness, someone with Laios who saw what
   happened?
KREON. They were all killed, except for one man. He escaped.
   But he was so terrified he remembered only one thing.
OEDIPUS. What was it? One small clue might lead to others.
KREON. This is what he said: bandits ambushed Laios, not one man.
   They attacked him like hail crushing a stalk of wheat.
OEDIPUS. How could a single bandit dare attack a king
   unless he had supporters, people with money, here,
   here in Thebes?   150
KREON. There were suspicions. But after Laios died we had no leader,
   no king.
   Our life was turmoil, uncertainty.
OEDIPUS. But once the throne was empty,
   what threw you off the track, what kept you from searching
   until you uncovered everything, knew every detail?
KREON. The intricate, hard song of the Sphinx
   persuaded us the crime was not important, not then.
   It seemed to say we should focus on what lay at our feet, in front of
   us,
   ignore what we could not see.
OEDIPUS. Now *I* am here.   160
   I will begin the search again, I
   will reveal the truth, expose everything, let it all be seen.
   Apollo and you were right to make us wonder about the dead
   man.
   Like Apollo, I am your ally.
   Justice and vengeance are what I want,
   for Thebes, for the god.
   Family, friends—I won't rid myself of this stain, this disease, for
   them—
   they're far from here.[9] I'll do it for myself, for me.
   The man who killed Laios might take revenge on me
   just as violently.   170
   So by avenging Laios' death, I protect myself.
   [*turning to the suppliants*] Rise, children,
   pick up your branches,
   let someone announce my decision to the whole city of Thebes.
   [*to the* PRIEST] I will do everything. Everything.
   And, with the god's help, we will be saved.
   Bright Apollo, let your light help us see.
   Our happiness is yours to give, our failure and ruin yours.
PRIEST. Rise. We have the help we came for, children.
   The king himself has promised.   180
   May Apollo, who gave these oracles, come as our savior now.
   Apollo, heal us, save us from this plague!

---

   [9] Oedipus means that his wife's first husband, Laios, is now far removed by time and death;
in addition, at this point Oedipus wrongly believes that he is the son of parents who reside in
another city (Corinth).

[OEDIPUS *enters the palace. Its doors close.* KREON *leaves by a door to the right on the wing of the stage. The* PRIEST *and suppliants go down into the orchestra and leave by the entrance to the left as a chorus of fifteen Theban elders files into the orchestra by the entrance on the right, preceded by a flute player.*]

CHORUS. voice   voice   voice
   voice who knows everything o god
   glorious voice of Zeus[10]
   how have you come from Delphi bathed in gold
   what are you telling our bright city Thebes
   what are you bringing me
   health death fear
   I know nothing   190
   so frightened rooted here
   awed by you
   healer what have you sent
   is it the sudden doom of grief
   or the old curse the darkness
   looming in the turning season

   o holy immortal voice
   hope golden seed of the future
   listen be with me speak
   these cries of mine rise   200
   tell me
   I call to you reach out to you first
   holy Athena god's daughter who lives forever
   and your sister Artemis[11]
   who cradles the earth our earth
   who sits on her great throne at the hub of the market place
   and I call to Apollo who hurls light
   from deep in the sky
   o gods be with us now
   shine on us your three shields[12]   210
   blazing against the darkness
   come in our suffering as you came once before
   to Thebes o bright divinities
   and threw your saving light against the god of grief
   o gods
   be with us now

[10]The message or communication from Zeus, king of the gods. More concretely, the "voice" is Apollo, the prophetic spokesman of the supreme god's will and knowledge.

[11]Athena was the daughter of Zeus, born directly without a mother from his head; Artemis, born of Zeus and Leto, is her halfsister and also Apollo's full sister.

[12]The protective power of the three deities invoked (Athena, Artemis, Apollo).

pain pain my sorrows have no sound
no name no word no pain like this
plague sears my people everywhere
everyone army citizens no one escapes   220
no spear of strong anxious thought protects us
great Thebes grows nothing
seeds rot in the ground
our women when they labor
cry Apollo Apollo but their children die
and lives one after another split the air
birds taking off
wingrush hungrier than fire
souls leaping away they fly
to the shore   230
of the cold god of evening[13]
west

the death stain spreads
so many corpses lie in the streets everywhere
nobody grieves for them
the city dies and young wives
and mothers gray-haired mothers wail
sob on the altar steps
they come from the city everywhere mourning their bitter days
prayers blaze to the Healer   240
grief cries a flute mingling
daughter of Zeus[14] o shining daughter show us
the warm bright face of peace of help
of our salvation

                                        [*The doors of the palace open.* OE-
                                        DIPUS *enters.*]

and turn back the huge raging jaws of the death god Ares[15]
drive him back drive him away
his flames lash at me
this is his war these are his shields
shouts pierce us on all sides
turn him back lift him on a strong wind   250
rush him away
to the two seas[16] at the world's edge
the sea where the waters boil
the sea where no traveler can land
because if night leaves anything alive
day destroys it

---

[13] Hades, god of the underworld and of the dead.   [14] His daughter Athena.
[15] The god of war—often regarded as the personification of any kind of destruction.
[16] The Atlantic at the western edge of the world, the Black Sea at the eastern.

o Zeus
god beyond all other gods
handler of the fire
father
make the god of our sickness   260
ashes

Apollo
great bowman of light draw back your bow
fire arrow after arrow
make them a wall circling us
shoot into our enemy's eyes
draw the string twined with gold
come goddess[17]
who dances on the mountains   270
sowing light where your feet brush the ground
blind our enemy come
god of golden hair
piled under your golden cap Bacchus
your face blazing like the sea when the sun falls on it
like sunlight on wine
god whose name is our name Bacchus[18]
god of joy god of terror
be with us now your bright face
like a pine torch roaring   280
thrust into the face of the slaughtering war god
blind him
drive him down from Olympos
drive him away from Thebes
forever

OEDIPUS. Every word of your prayers has touched me.
  Listen. Follow me. Join me in fighting this sickness, this plague,
  and all your sufferings may end, like a dark sky,
  clear suddenly, blue, after a week of storms,
  soothing the torn face of the sea,   290
  soothing our fears.
  Your fate looms in my words—
  I heard nothing about Laios' death.
  I know nothing about the murder,
  I was alone, how could I have tracked the killer, without a clue,
  I came to Thebes after the crime was done,
  I was made a Theban after Laios' death. Listen carefully—
  these words come from an innocent man.

[*Addressing the* CHORUS.]

[17] Artemis, goddess of the hunt.
[18] The god of wine, Bacchus or Dionysos, had special associations with Thebes.

One of *you* knows who killed Laios.   300
Where is that man?
Speak.
I command it. Fear is no excuse.
He must clear himself of the dangerous charge.
Who did this thing?
Was it a stranger?
Speak.
I will not harm him. The worst he will suffer is exile.
I will pay him well. He will have a king's thanks.
But if he will not speak because he fears me,
if he fears what I will do to him or to those he loves,   310
if he will not obey me,
I say to him:
My power is absolute in Thebes, my rule reaches everywhere,
my words will drive the guilty man, the man who *knows*,
out of this city, away from Thebes, forever.

Nothing.
My word for him is nothing.
Let him *be* nothing.
Give him nothing.
Let him touch nothing of yours, he is nothing to you.   320
Lock your doors when he approaches.
Say nothing to him, do not speak.
No prayers with him, no offerings with him.
No purifying water.
Nothing.
Drive him from your homes. Let him have no home, nothing.
No words, no food, shelter, warmth of hand, shared worship.
Let him have nothing. Drive him out, let him die.
He is our disease.
                    I know.
                              Apollo has made it clear.
Nothing can stop me, nothing can change my words.   330
I fight for Apollo, I fight for the dead man.
You see me, you hear me, moving against the killer.
My words are his doom.
Whether he did it alone, and escaped unseen,
whether others helped him kill, it makes no difference—
let my hatred burn out his life, hatred, always.
Make him an ember of suffering.
Make all his happiness
ashes.
If he eats at my side, sits at my sacred hearth, and I know these
        things,   340
let every curse I spit out against him find *me*,
come home to *me*.
Carry out my orders. You must,

for me, for Apollo, and for Thebes, Thebes,
this poor wasted city,
deserted by its gods.
I know—the gods have given us this disease.
That makes no difference. You should have acted,
you should have done something long ago to purge our guilt.
The victim was noble, a king—   350
you should have done everything to track his murderer down.
And so,
because I rule now where he ruled;
because I share his bed, his wife;
because the same woman who mothered my children might have
    mothered his;
because fate swooped out of nowhere and cut him down;
because of all these things
I will fight for him as I would fight for my own murdered
    father.
Nothing will stop me.
No man, no place, nothing will escape my gaze. I will not stop   360
until I know it all, all, until everything is clear.
For every king, every king's son and his sons,
for every royal generation of Thebes, *my* Thebes,
I will expose the killer, I will reveal him
to the light.
Oh gods, gods,
destroy all those who will not listen, will not obey.
Freeze the ground until they starve.
Make their wives barren as stone.
Let this disease that shakes Thebes to its roots—   370
or any worse disease, if there is any worse than this—waste them,
crush everything they have, everything they are.
But you men of Thebes—
you, who know my words are right, who obey me—
may justice and the gods defend you, bless you,
graciously, forever.
LEADER. Your curse forces me to speak, Master.
    I cannot escape it.
    I did not murder the king, I cannot show you the man who did.
    Apollo told us to search for the killer.   380
    Apollo must name him.
OEDIPUS. No man can force the gods to speak.
LEADER. Then I will say the next best thing.
OEDIPUS. If there's a third best thing, say that too.
LEADER. Teiresias sees what the god Apollo sees.
    Truth, truth.
    If you heard the god speaking, heard his voice,
    you might see more, more, and more.
OEDIPUS. Teiresias? I have seen to that already.
    Kreon spoke of Teiresias, and I sent for him. Twice.   390
    I find it strange he still hasn't come.

LEADER. And there's an old story, almost forgotten,
    a dark, faded rumor.
OEDIPUS. What rumor? I must sift each story,
    see it, understand it.
LEADER. Laios was killed by bandits.
OEDIPUS. I have heard that story: but who can show me the man who
      saw the murderer?
    Has anyone seen him?
LEADER. If he knows the meaning of fear,
    if he heard those curses you spoke against him,   400
    those words still scorching the air,
    you won't find him now, not in Thebes.
OEDIPUS. The man *murdered*. Why would words frighten him?

> [TEIRESIAS *has appeared from the
> stage entrance to the right of the
> audience. He walks with a staff and
> is helped by a slave boy and attend-
> ants. He stops at some distance from
> center stage.*]

LEADER. Here is the man who can catch the criminal
    They're bringing him now—
    the godlike prophet who speaks with the voice of god.
    He, only he, knows truth.
    The truth is rooted in his soul.
OEDIPUS. Teiresias, you understand all things,
    what can be taught, what is locked in silence,   410
    the distant things of heaven, and things that crawl the earth.
    You cannot see, yet you know the nature of this plague infesting
      our city.
    Only you, my lord, can save us, only you can defend us.
    Apollo told our messenger—did you hear?—
    that we could be saved only by tracking down Laios' killers,
    only by killing them, or sending them into exile.
    Help us, Teiresias.
    Study the cries of birds, study their wild paths,
    ponder the signs of fire, use all your skills of prophecy.
    Rescue us, preserve us.   420
    Rescue yourself, rescue Thebes, rescue me.
    Cleanse every trace of the growing stain left by the dead man's
      blood.
    We are in your hands, Teiresias.
    No work is more nobly human than helping others,
    helping with all the strength and skill we possess.
TEIRESIAS. Wisdom is a curse
    when wisdom does nothing for the man who has it.
    Once I knew this well, but I forgot.
    I never should have come.

OEDIPUS. Never should have come? Why this reluctance, prophet?   430
TEIRESIAS. Let me go home.
    That way is best, for you, for me.
    Let me live my life, and you live yours.
OEDIPUS. Strange words. Teiresias, cruel to the city that gave you life.
    Your holy knowledge could save Thebes. How can you keep
      silent?
TEIRESIAS. What have you said that helps Thebes? Your words are
      wasted.
    I would rather be silent than waste my words.
OEDIPUS. Look at us,   [OEDIPUS *stands, the* CHORUS *kneel.*]
    kneeling to you, Teiresias, imploring you.
    In the name of the gods, if you know—   440
    help us, tell us what you know.
TEIRESIAS. You kneel because you do not understand.
    But I will never let you see my grief. Never.
    My grief is yours.
OEDIPUS. What? You know and won't speak?
    You'd betray us all, you'd destroy the city of Thebes?
TEIRESIAS. I will do nothing to hurt myself, or you. Why insist?
    I will not speak.
OEDIPUS. Stubborn old fool, you'd make a rock angry!
    Tell me what you know! Say it!   450
    Where are your feelings? Won't you ever speak?
TEIRESIAS. You call me cold, stubborn, unfeeling, you insult me. But
    you,
    Oedipus, what do you know about yourself,
    about your real feelings?
    You don't see how much alike we are.
OEDIPUS. How can *I* restrain my anger when I see how little you care
      for Thebes.
TEIRESIAS. The truth will come, by itself,
    the truth will come
    no matter how I shroud it in silence.
OEDIPUS. All the more reason why you should speak.   460
TEIRESIAS. Not another word.
    Rage away, You will never make me speak.
OEDIPUS. I'll rage, prophet, I'll give you all my anger.
    I'll say it all—
    Listen: I think you were involved in the murder of Laios,
    you helped plan it, I think you
    did everything in your power to kill Laios,
    everything but strike him with your own hands,
    and if you weren't blind, if you still had eyes to see with,
    I'd say you, and *you* alone, did it all.   470
TEIRESIAS. Do you think so? Then obey your own words, obey
    the curse everyone heard break from your own lips:
    Never speak again to these men of Thebes,
    never speak again to me.

You, it's
you.
What plagues the city is *you.*
The plague is *you.*

OEDIPUS. Do you know what you're saying?
Do you think I'll let you get away with these vile accusations?

TEIRESIAS. I am safe.   480
Truth lives in me, and the truth is strong.

OEDIPUS. Who taught you this truth of yours? Not your prophet's
craft.

TEIRESIAS. You taught me. You forced me to speak.

OEDIPUS. Speak what? Explain. Teach me.

TEIRESIAS. Didn't you understand?
Are you trying to make me say the word?

OEDIPUS. What word? Say it. Spit it out.

TEIRESIAS. Murderer.
I say *you,*
you are the killer you're searching for.   490

OEDIPUS. You won't say *that* again to me and get away with it.

TEIRESIAS. Do you want more? Shall I make you really angry?

OEDIPUS. Say anything you like. Your words are wasted.

TEIRESIAS. I say you live in shame, and you do not know it,
do not know that you
and those you love most
wallow in shame,
you do not know
in what shame you live.

OEDIPUS. You'll pay for these insults, I swear it.   500

TEIRESIAS. Not if the truth is strong.

OEDIPUS. The truth *is* strong, but not your truth.
You have no truth. You're blind.
Blind in your eyes. Blind in your ears. Blind in your mind.

TEIRESIAS. And I pity you for mocking my blindness.
Soon everyone in Thebes will mock you, Oedipus. They'll
mock you
as you have mocked me.

OEDIPUS. One endless night swaddles you in its unbroken black sky.
You can't hurt me, you can't hurt anyone who sees the light of day.

TEIRESIAS. True. Nothing I do will harm you. You, you   510
and your fate belong to Apollo.
Apollo will see to *you.*

OEDIPUS. Are these your own lies, prophet—or Kreon's?

TEIRESIAS. Kreon? Your plague is *you,* not Kreon.

OEDIPUS. Money, power, one great skill surpassing another,
if a man has these things, other men's envy grows and grows,
their greed and hunger are insatiable.
Most men would lust for a life like mine—but I did not demand
my life,
Thebes gave me my life, and from the beginning, my good friend
Kreon,

loyal, trusted Kreon,   520
was reaching for my power, wanted to ambush me, get rid of me
    by hiring this cheap wizard,
this crass, conniving priest, who sees nothing but profit,
whose prophecy is simple profit. *You,*
what did *you* ever do that proves you a real seer? What did you
    ever *see,* prophet?
And when the Sphinx who sang mysteriously
imprisoned us
why didn't you speak and set us free?
No ordinary man could have solved her riddle,
it took prophecy, prophecy and skill you clearly never had.
Even the paths of birds, even the gods' voices were useless.   530
But I showed up, I, Oedipus,
stupid, untutored Oedipus,
I silenced her, I destroyed her, I used my wits, not omens,
to sift the meaning of her song.
And this is the man you want to kill so you can get close to King
    Kreon,
weigh his affairs for him, advise him, influence him.
No, I think you and your master, Kreon, who contrived this plot,
will be whipped out of Thebes.
Look at you.
If you weren't so old, and weak, oh   540
I'd make you pay
for this conspiracy of yours.
LEADER. Oedipus, both of you spoke in anger.
    Anger is not what we need.
    We need all our wits, all our energy to interpret Apollo's words.
    Then we will know what to do.
TEIRESIAS. Oedipus, you are king, but you must hear my reply.
    My right to speak is just as valid as yours.
    I am not your slave. Kreon is not my patron.
    My master is Apollo. I can say what I please.   550
    You insulted me. You mocked me. You called me blind.
    Now hear *me* speak, Oedipus.
    You have eyes to see with,
    but you do not see yourself, you do not see
    the horror shadowing every step of your life,
    the blind shame in which you live,
    you do not see where you live and who lives with you,
    lives always at your side.
    Tell me, Oedipus, who are your parents?
    Do you know?   560
    You do not even know
    the shame and grief you have brought your family,
    those still alive, those buried beneath the earth.
    But the curse of your mother, the curse of your father
    will whip you, whip you again and again, wherever you turn,
    it will whip you out of Thebes forever,

your clear eyes flooded with darkness.
That day will come.
And then what scoured, homeless plain, what leafless tree,
what place on Kithairon,[19]   570
where no other humans are or ever will be,
where the wind is the only thing that moves,
what raw track of thorns and stones, what rock, gulley,
or blind hill won't echo your screams, your howls of anguish
when you find out that the marriage song,
sung when you came to Thebes, heard in your house,
guided you to *this* shore, this wilderness
you thought was home, *your* home?
And you do not see
all the other awful things   580
that will show you who you really are, show you
to your children, face to face.
Go ahead! Call me quack, abuse Kreon, insult Apollo, the god
who speaks through me, whose words move on my lips.
No man will ever know worse suffering than you,
your life, your flesh, your happiness an ember of pain. Ashes.

OEDIPUS. [*to the* CHORUS] Must I stand here and listen to these attacks?

TEIRESIAS. [*beginning to move away*] I am here, Oedipus, because you
        sent for me.

OEDIPUS. You old fool,
    I'd have thought twice before asking you to come   590
    if I had known you'd spew out such idiocy.

TEIRESIAS. Call me fool, if you like, but your parents,
    who gave you life, they respected my judgment.

OEDIPUS. Parents?
                    What do you mean?
                        Who are my mother and father?

TEIRESIAS. This day is your mother and father—this day will give you
        your birth,
    it will destroy you too.

OEDIPUS. How you love mysterious, twisted words.

TEIRESIAS. Aren't you the great solver of riddles?
        Aren't you Oedipus?

OEDIPUS. Taunt me for the gift of my brilliant mind.   600
    That gift is what makes me great.

TEIRESIAS. That gift is your destiny. It made you everything you are,
    and it has ruined you.

OEDIPUS. But if this gift of mine saved Thebes, who cares what
        happens to me?

TEIRESIAS. I'm leaving. Boy, take me home.

---

[19] Also spelled *Cithaeron*. A mountain range near Thebes. Oedipus, as later events will
reveal, was abandoned there as a child; it will also be his destination when he goes into exile
later. Sophocles' audience knew this detail, and all the other significant elements of the story,
at the outset of the play.

OEDIPUS. Good. Take him home. Here
    I keep stumbling over you, here you're in my way.
    Scuttle home, and leave us in peace!
TEIRESIAS. I'm going. I said what I came to say,
    and that scowl, darkening your face, doesn't frighten me. How can
        you hurt me?   610
    I tell you again:
    the man you've been trying to expose—
    with all your threats, with your inquest into Laios' murder—
    that man is here, in Thebes.
    Now people think he comes from Corinth, but later
    they will see he was born in Thebes.
    When they know, he'll have no pleasure in that news.
    Now he has eyes to see with, but they will be slashed out;
    rich and powerful now, he will be a beggar,
    poking his way with a stick, feeling his way to a strange country.   620
    And his children—the children he lives with—
    will see him at last, see what he is, see who he really is:
    their brother and their father; his wife's son, his mother's
        husband;
    the lover who slept with his father's wife; the man who murdered
        his father—
    the man whose hands still drip with his father's blood.
    These truths will be revealed.

    Go inside and ponder *that* riddle, and if you find I've lied,
    then call me a prophet who cannot see.

                        [OEDIPUS *turns and enters the pal-*
                        ace. TEIRESIAS *is led out through*
                        the stage entrance on the right.]

CHORUS. who did crimes unnameable things
    things words cringe at   630
    which man did the rock of prophecy at Delphi say
    did these things
    his hands dripping with blood
    he should run now flee
    his strong feet swallowing the air
    stronger than the horses of storm winds
    their hooves slicing the air
    now in his armor
    Apollo lunges at him
    his infinite branching fire reaches out   640
    and the steady dread death-hungry Fates follow and never stop
    their quick scissors[20] seeking the cloth of his life

---

[20] The three Fates were spinners of the thread of human life; the third, Atropos, cut the thread at a point that determined the moment of death.

just now
from high snowy Parnassus[21]
the god's voice exploded its blazing message
follow his track find the man
no one knows
a bull loose under wild bushes and trees
among caves and gray rocks
cut from the herd he runs and runs but runs nowhere   650
zigzagging desperate to get away
birds of prophecy birds of death circling his head
forever
voices forged at the white stone core of the earth[22]
they go where he goes always

terror's in me flooding me
how can I judge
what the god Apollo says
trapped hoping confused
I do not see what is here now   660
when I look to the past I see nothing
I know nothing about a feud
wounding the families of Laios or Oedipus
no clue to the truth then or now
nothing to blacken his golden fame in Thebes
and help Laios' family
solve the mystery of his death

Zeus and Apollo know
they understand
only they see   670
the dark threads crossing beneath our life
but no man can say a prophet sees more than I
one man surpasses another
wisdom against wisdom skill against skill
but I will not blame Oedipus
whatever anyone says
until words are as real as things

one thing is clear
years back the Sphinx tested him
his answer was true   680
he was wise and sweet to the city
so he can never be evil
not to me

[21] The mountain near Apollo's oracle at Delphi.
[22] The Omphalos, or Navelstone, at Delphi. It was believed to be the center of the earth.

[KREON *enters through the stage
entrance at right, and addresses the*
CHORUS.]

KREON. Men of Thebes, I hear Oedipus, our king and master,
    has brought terrible charges against me.
    I have come to face those charges. I resent them bitterly.
    If he imagines I have hurt him, spoken or acted against him
    while our city dies, believe me—I have nothing left to live for.
    His accusations pierce me, wound me mortally—
    nothing they touch is trivial, private—   690
    if you, my family and friends,
    think I'm a traitor, if all Thebes believes it, says it.
LEADER. Perhaps he spoke in anger, without thinking,
    perhaps his anger made him accuse you.
KREON. Did he really say I persuaded Teiresias to lie?
LEADER. I heard him say these things,
    but I don't know what they mean.
KREON. Did he look you in the eyes when he accused me?
    Was he in his right mind?
LEADER. I do not know or see what great men do.   700

[*turning to* OEDIPUS, *who has
emerged from the palace*]

But here he is—Oedipus.
OEDIPUS. What? *You* here? Murderer!
    You dare come here, to my palace, when it's clear
    you've been plotting to murder me and seize the throne of
        Thebes?
    You're the bandit, *you're* the killer.
                Answer me—
    Did you think I was cowardly or stupid?
    Is that why you betrayed me?
    Did you really think I wouldn't see what you were plotting,
    how you crept up on me like a cloud inching across the sun?
    Did you think I wouldn't defend myself against you?   710
    You thought I was a fool, but the fool was you, Kreon.
    Thrones are won with money and men, you fool!
KREON. You have said enough, Oedipus. Now let me reply.
    Weigh my words against your charges, then judge for yourself.
OEDIPUS. Eloquent, Kreon. But you won't convince me now.
    Now that I know your hatred, your malice.
KREON. Let me explain.
OEDIPUS. Explain?
    What could explain your treachery?
KREON. If you think this stubborn anger of yours, this perversity,   720
    is something to be proud of, you're mad.
OEDIPUS. And if you think you can injure your sister's husband,
    and not pay for it, *you're* mad.

KREON. I would be mad to hurt you. How have I hurt you?

OEDIPUS. Was it you who advised me to send for that great holy
     prophet?

KREON. Yes, and I'd do it again.

OEDIPUS. How long has it been since Laios disappeared?

KREON. Disappeared?

OEDIPUS. Died. Was murdered . . .

KREON. Many, many years.   730

OEDIPUS. And this prophet of yours—was he practicing his trade at
     the time?

KREON. With as much skill, wisdom and honor as ever.

OEDIPUS. Did he ever mention my name?

KREON. Not in my presence.

OEDIPUS. Was there an inquest? A formal inquiry?

KREON. Of course. Nothing was ever discovered.

OEDIPUS. Then why didn't our wonderful prophet, our Theban
     wizard,
     denounce me as the murderer then?

KREON. I don't know. And when I don't know, I don't speak.

OEDIPUS. But you know this. You know it with perfect certainty.   740

KREON. What do you mean?

OEDIPUS. This: if you and Teiresias were not conspiring against me,
     Teiresias would never have charged *me* with Laios' murder.

KREON. If he said that, you should know.
     But now, Oedipus, it's my right, my turn to question you.

OEDIPUS. Ask anything. You'll never prove I killed Laios.

KREON. Did you marry my sister, Jocasta?

OEDIPUS. I married Jocasta.

KREON. And you gave her an equal share of the power in Thebes?

OEDIPUS. Whatever she wants is hers.   750

KREON. And I share that power equally with you and her?

OEDIPUS. Equally.
     And that's precisely why it's clear you're false, treacherous.

KREON. No, Oedipus.
     Consider it rationally, as I have. Reflect:
     What man, what sane man, would prefer a king's power
     with all its dangers and anxieties,
     when he could enjoy that same power, without its cares,
     and sleep in peace each night? Power?
     I have no instinct for power, no hunger for it either.   760
     It isn't royal power I want, but its advantages.
     And any sensible man would want the same.
     Look at the life I lead. Whatever I want, I get from you,
     with your goodwill and blessing. I have nothing to fear.
     If I were king, my life would be constant duty and constraint.
     Why would I want your power or the throne of Thebes
     more than what I enjoy now—the privilege of power
     without its dangers? I would be a fool to want more
     than what I have—the substance, not the show, of power.

As matters stand, no man envies me, I am courted   770
and admired by all. Men wear no smiling masks for Kreon.
And those who want something from you come to me
because the way to royal favor lies through me.
Tell me, Oedipus, why should I give these blessings up
to seize your throne and all the dangers it confers?
A man like me, who knows his mortal limits and accepts them,
cannot be vicious or treacherous by nature.
The love of power is not my nature, nor is treason
or the thoughts of treason that go with love of power.
I would never dare conspire against your life.   780

Do you want to test the truth of what I say?
Go to Delphi, put the question to the oracle,
ask if I have told you exactly what Apollo said.
Then if you find that Teiresias and I have plotted against you,
seize me and put me to death. Convict me
not by one vote alone, but two—yours *and* mine, Oedipus.
But don't convict me on the strength of your suspicions,
don't confuse friends with traitors, traitors with friends.
There's no justice in that.
To throw away a good and loyal friend   790
is to destroy what you love most—
your own life, and what makes life worth living.
Someday you will know the truth:
time, only time reveals the good man;
one day's light reveals the evil man.
LEADER. Good words
    for someone careful, afraid he'll fall.
    But a mind like lightning
    stumbles.
OEDIPUS. When a clever man plots against me and moves swiftly   800
    I must move just as swiftly, I must plan.
    But if I wait, if I do nothing, he will win, win everything,
    and I will lose.
KREON. What do you want? My exile?
OEDIPUS. No. Your death.
KREON. You won't change your mind? You won't believe me?
OEDIPUS. I'll believe you when you teach me the meaning of envy.
KREON. Envy? You talk about envy. You don't even know what
    sense is.
    Can't you listen to me?
OEDIPUS. I *am* listening. To my own good sense.   810
KREON. Listen to *me*. I have sense on my side too.
OEDIPUS. You? You were born devious.
KREON. And if you're wrong?
OEDIPUS. I still must govern.
KREON. Not if you govern badly.
OEDIPUS. Oh Thebes, Thebes . . .

KREON. Thebes is mine too.

LEADER. [*turning to* JOCASTA, *who has entered from the palace,*
accompanied by a woman attendant]
    Stop. I see
    Jocasta coming from the palace
    just in time, my lords, to help you   820
    settle this deep, bitter feud raging between you.
    Listen to what she says.

JOCASTA. Oedipus! Kreon! Why this insane quarreling?
    You should be ashamed, both of you. Forget yourselves.
    This is no time for petty personal bickering.
    Thebes is sick, dying.
                        —Come inside, Oedipus
    —And you, Kreon, leave us.
    Must you create all this misery over nothing, nothing?

KREON. Jocasta,
    Oedipus has given me two impossible choices: 830
    Either I must be banished from Thebes, my city, my home,
    or be arrested and put to death.

OEDIPUS. That's right.
    I caught him plotting against me, Jocasta.
    Viciously, cunningly plotting against the king of Thebes.

KREON. Take every pleasure I have in life, curse me, let me die,
    if I've done what you accuse me of, let the gods
    destroy everything I have, let them do anything to me.
    I stand here, exposed to their infinite power.

JOCASTA. Oedipus, in the name of the gods, believe him.   840
    His prayer has made him holy, naked to the mysterious
    whims of the gods, has taken him beyond what is human.
    Respect his words, respect me, respect these men standing at your
        side.

CHORUS. [*beginning a dirge-like appeal to* OEDIPUS]
    listen to her
    think yield
    we implore you

OEDIPUS. What do you want?

CHORUS. be generous to Kreon give him respect
    he was never foolish before
    now his prayer to the gods has made him great   850
    great and frightening

OEDIPUS. Do you know what you're asking?

CHORUS. I know

OEDIPUS. Then say it.

CHORUS. don't ever cut him off
    without rights or honor
    blood binds you both
    his prayer has made him sacred
    don't accuse him
    because some blind suspicion hounds you   860

OEDIPUS. Understand me:

when you ask for these things
you ask for my death or exile.
Chorus. no
by the sun
the god who bathes us in his light
who sees all
I will die godless no family no friends
if what I ask means that
it is Thebes 870
Thebes dying wasting away life by life
this is the misery
that breaks my heart
and now this quarrel raging between you and Kreon
is more more than I can bear
Oedipus. Then let him go, if it means I must die
or be forced out of Thebes forever, stripped of all my rights, all
my honors.
Your grief, *your* words touch me. Not his.
I pity you. But him,
my hatred will reach him wherever he goes. 880
Kreon. It's clear you hate to yield, clear
you yield only under pressure, only
when you've worn out the fierceness of your anger.
Then all you can do is sit, and brood.
Natures like yours are a torment to themselves.
Oedipus. Leave. Go!
Kreon. I'm going. Now I know
you do not know me.
But these men know I am the man I seem to be, a just man,
not devious, not a traitor. 890

[Kreon *leaves.*]

Chorus. woman why are you waiting
lead him inside comfort him
Jocasta. Not before I know what has happened here.
Chorus. blind ignorant words suspicion without proof
the injustice of it
gnaws at us
Jocasta. From both men?
Chorus. yes
Jocasta. What caused it?
Chorus. enough enough 900
no more words
Thebes is so tormented now
let it rest where it ended
Oedipus. Look where cooling my rage,
where all your decent, practical thoughts have led you.
Chorus. Oedipus I have said this many times
I would be mad helpless to give advice

if I turned against you now
once
you took our city in her storm of pain   910
straightened her course found fair weather
o lead her to safety now
if you can
JOCASTA. If you love the gods, tell me, too, Oedipus—I implore you—
why are you still so angry, why can't you let it go?
OEDIPUS. I will tell you, Jocasta.
You mean more, far more to me than these men here.
Jocasta, it is Kreon—Kreon and his plots against me.
JOCASTA. What started your quarrel?
OEDIPUS. He said I murdered Laios.   920
JOCASTA. Does he know something? Or is it pure hearsay?
OEDIPUS. He sent me a vicious, trouble-making prophet
to avoid implicating himself. He did not say it to my face.
JOCASTA. Oedipus, forget all this. Listen to me:
no mortal can practise the art of prophecy, no man can see the
future.
One experience of mine will show you why.
Long ago an oracle came to Laios.
It came not from Apollo himself but from his priests.
It said Laios was doomed to be murdered by a son, his son and
mine.
But Laios, from what we heard, was murdered by bandits from a
foreign country,   930
cut down at a crossroads. My poor baby
was only three days old when Laios had his feet pierced together
behind the ankles
and gave orders to abandon our child on a mountain, leave him
alone to die
in a wilderness of rocks and bare gray trees
where there were no roads, no people.
So you see—Apollo didn't make that child his father's killer,
Laios wasn't murdered by his son. That dreadful act which so
terrified Laios—
it never happened.

All those oracular voices meant was nothing, nothing.
Ignore them.   940
Apollo creates. Apollo reveals. He needs no help from men.
OEDIPUS. [*who has been very still*]
While you were speaking, Jocasta, it flashed through my mind
like wind suddenly ruffling a stretch of calm sea.
It stuns me. I can almost see it—some memory, some image.
My heart races and swells—
JOCASTA. Why are you so strangely excited, Oedipus?
OEDIPUS. You said Laios was cut down *near* a crossroads?
JOCASTA. That was the story. It hasn't changed.
OEDIPUS. Where did it happen? Tell me. Where?

Jocasta. In Phokis. Where the roads from Delphi and Daulia meet. 950
Oedipus. When?
Jocasta. Just before you came to Thebes and assumed power.
. Just before you were proclaimed King.
Oedipus. O Zeus, Zeus,
what are you doing with my life?
Jocasta. Why are you so disturbed, Oedipus?
Oedipus. Don't ask me. Not yet.
                                Tell me about Laios.
How old was he? What did he look like?
Jocasta. Streaks of gray were beginning to show in his black hair.
He was tall, strong—built something like you. 960
Oedipus. No! O gods, o
it seems each hard, arrogant curse
I spit out
was meant for me, and I
didn't
know it!
Jocasta. Oedipus, what do you mean? Your face is so strange.
You frighten me.
Oedipus. It *is* frightening—can the blind prophet see, can he
really see?
I would know if you told me . . . 970
Jocasta. I'm afraid to ask, Oedipus.
Told you what?
Oedipus. Was Laios traveling with a small escort
or with many armed men, like a king?
Jocasta. There were five, including a herald.
Laios was riding in his chariot.
Oedipus. Light, o light, light
now everything, everything is clear. All of it.
Who told you this? Who was it?
Jocasta. A household slave. The only survivor. 980
Oedipus. Is he here, in Thebes?
Jocasta. No. When he returned and saw that you were king
and learned Laios was dead, he came to me and clutched my hand,
begged me to send him to the mountains
where shepherds graze their flocks, far from the city,
so he could never see Thebes again.
I sent him, of course. He deserved that much, for a slave, and
more.
Oedipus. Can he be called back? Now?
Jocasta. Easily. But why?
Oedipus. I am afraid I may have said too much— 990
I *must* see him.
Now.
Jocasta. Then he will come.
But surely I have a right to know what disturbs you, Oedipus.
Oedipus. Now that I've come this far, Jocasta,
hope torturing me, each step of mine heavy with fear,

I won't keep anything from you.
Wandering through the mazes of a fate like this,
how could I confide in anyone but you?

My father was Polybos, of Corinth.   1000
My mother, Merope, was Dorian.
Everyone in Corinth saw me as its first citizen,
but one day something happened,
something strange, puzzling. Puzzling, but nothing more.
Still, it worried me.
One night, I was at a banquet,
and a man—he was very drunk—said I wasn't my father's son,
called me "bastard." That stung me, I was shocked.
I could barely control my anger, I lay awake all night.
The next day I went to my father and mother,   1010
I questioned them about the man and what he said.
They were furious with him, outraged by his insult,
and I was reassured. But I kept hearing the word "bastard"
    "bastard"—
I couldn't get it out of my head.
Without my parents' knowledge, I went to Delphi: I wanted the
    truth,
but Apollo refused to answer me.
And yet he did reveal other things, he did show me
a future dark with torment, evil, horror,
he made me *see*—
see myself, doomed to sleep with my own mother, doomed   1020
to bring children into this world where the sun pours down,
children no one could bear to see, doomed
to murder the man who gave me life, whose blood is *my* blood. My
    father.
And after I heard all this, I fled Corinth,
measuring my progress by the stars, searching for a place
where I would never see those words, those dreadful predictions
come true. And on my way
I came to the place where you say King Laios was murdered.

Jocasta, the story I'm about to tell you is the truth:
I was on the road, near the crossroads you mentioned,   1030
when I met a herald, with an old man, just as you described him.
The man was riding in a chariot
and his driver tried to push me off the road
and when he shoved me I hit him. I hit him.
The old man stood quiet in the chariot until I passed under him,
then he leaned out and caught me on the head with an ugly
    goad[23]—
its two teeth wounded me—and with this hand of mine,
this hand clenched around my staff,

---

[23] A barbed stick used to prod animals.

I struck him back even harder—so hard, so quick he couldn't
     dodge it,
and he toppled out of the chariot and hit the ground, face up.   1040
I killed them. Every one of them. I still see them.

                    [*to the* CHORUS]

If this stranger and Laios
are somehow linked by blood,
tell me what man's torment equals mine?

Citizens, hear my curse again—
Give this man nothing. Let him touch nothing of yours.
Lock your doors when he approaches.
Say nothing to him when he approaches.
                         And these, these curses,
with my own mouth I
spoke these monstrous curses against myself.   1050

               [OEDIPUS *turns back to* JOCASTA]

These hands, these bloodstained hands made love to you in your
     dead husband's bed,
these hands murdered him.

If I must be exiled, never to see my family,
never to walk the soil of my country
so I will not sleep with my mother
and kill Polybos, my father, who raised me—his son!—
wasn't I born evil—answer me!—isn't every part of me
unclean? Oh
some unknown god, some savage venomous demon must have
     done this,
raging, swollen with hatred. Hatred   1060
for me.

Holiness, pure, radiant powers, o gods
don't let me see that day,
don't let it come, take me away
from men, men with their eyes, hide me
before I see
the filthy black stain reaching down over me, into me.

                    [*The* CHORUS *have moved away
                    from the stage*]

LEADER. Your words make us shudder, Oedipus,
     but hope, hope
     until you hear more from the man who witnessed the murder.   1070
OEDIPUS. That is the only hope I have. Waiting.
     Waiting for that man to come from the pastures.
JOCASTA. And when he finally comes, what do you hope to learn?

OEDIPUS. If his story matches yours, I am saved.

JOCASTA. What makes you say that?

OEDIPUS. Bandits—you said he told you bandits killed Laios.
   So if he still talks about bandits,
   more than one, I couldn't have killed Laios.
   One man is not the same as many men.
   But if he speaks of one man, traveling alone,   1080
   then all the evidence points to me.

JOCASTA. Believe me, Oedipus, those were his words.
   And he can't take them back: the whole city heard him, not
      only me.
   And if he changes only the smallest detail of his story,
   that still won't prove Laios was murdered as the oracle foretold.
   Apollo was clear—it was Laios' fate to be killed by my son,
   but my poor child died before his father died.
   The future has no shape. The shapes of prophecy lie.
   I see nothing in them, they are all illusions.

OEDIPUS. Even so, I want that shepherd summoned here.   1090
   Now. Do it now.

JOCASTA. I'll send for him immediately. But come inside.
   My only wish is to please you.

> [JOCASTA *dispatches a servant.*]

CHORUS. fate[24]
   be here let what I say be pure
   let all my acts be pure
   laws forged in the huge clear fields of heaven
   rove the sky
   shaping my words limiting what I do
   Olympos[25] made those laws not men who live and die   1100
   nothing lulls those laws to sleep
   they cannot die
   and the infinite god in them never ages

   arrogance insatiable pride
   breed the tyrant
   feed him on thing after thing blindly
   at the wrong time uselessly
   and he grows reaches so high
   nothing can stop his fall
   his feet thrashing the air standing on nothing   1110

---

[24] The choral passage that follows seems central to the play, but its application is problematical. The Chorus expresses a pious revulsion from the kind of evil acts that bring on divine punishment; it then proceeds to define *hubris*, the state of overweening pride that is especially dangerous in provoking divine wrath. The passage implies that if these ancient moral principles and the gods' oracles no longer can be depended on, all order has been lost. But no character in the play seems to have *deliberately* committed such acts of impiety as the Chorus describes.

[25] The mountain home of the gods.

and nowhere to stand he plunges down
o god shatter the tyrant
but let men compete let self-perfection grow
let men sharpen their skills
soldiers citizens building the good city
Apollo
protect me always
always the god I will honor

if a man walks through his life arrogant
strutting proud   1120
says anything does anything
does not fear justice
fear the gods bow to their shining presences
let fate make him stumble in his tracks
for all his lecheries and headlong greed
if he takes whatever he wants right or wrong
if he touches forbidden things
what man who acts like this would boast
he can escape the anger of the gods
why should I join these sacred public dances   1130
if such acts are honored

no
I will never go to the holy untouchable stone
navel of the earth at Delphi
never again
go to the temples at Olympia at Abai[26]
if all these things are not joined
if past present future are not made one
made clear to mortal eyes
o Zeus if that is your name   1140
power above all immortal king
see these things look
those great prophecies are fading
men say they're nothing
nobody prays to the god of light no one believes
nothing of the gods stays

> [JOCASTA *enters from the palace,*
> *carrying a branch tied with strands*
> *of wool, and a jar of incense. She is*
> *accompanied by a servant woman.*
> *She addresses the* CHORUS.]

JOCASTA. Lords of Thebes, I come to the temples of the god
　　with offerings—this incense and this branch.
　　So many thoughts torture Oedipus. He never rests.

---

[26]Sites of oracles, of Apollo and Zeus respectively.

He acts without reason. He is like a man   1150
who has lost everything he knows—the past
is useless to him; strange, new things baffle him.
And if someone talks disaster, it stuns him: he listens, he is afraid.
I have tried to reassure him, but nothing helps.
So I have come to you—
Apollo, close to my life, close to this house,
listen to my prayers: [*she kneels*]
                           help us purify ourselves of this disease,
help us survive the long night of our suffering,
protect us. We are afraid when we see Oedipus confused
and frightened—Oedipus, the only man who can pilot Thebes   1160
to safety.

> [*A* MESSENGER *from Corinth has
> arrived by the entrance to the orches-
> tra on the audience's left. He sees*
> JOCASTA *praying, then turns to
> address the* CHORUS.]

MESSENGER. Friends,
can you tell me where King Oedipus lives
or better still, where I can find him?
LEADER. Here, in this house.
This lady is his wife and mother
of his children.
MESSENGER. May you and your family prosper.
May you be happy always under this great roof.
JOCASTA. Happiness and prosperity to you, too, for your kind words.   1170
But why are you here? Do you bring news?
MESSENGER. Good news for your house, good news for King Oedipus.
JOCASTA. What is your news? Who sent you?
MESSENGER. I come from Corinth, and what I have to say I know will
bring you joy.
And pain perhaps. . . . I do not know.
JOCASTA. Both joy and pain? What news could do that?
MESSENGER. The people of Corinth want Oedipus as their king.
That's what they're saying.
JOCASTA. But isn't old Polybos still king of Corinth?
MESSENGER. His kingdom is his grave.   1180
JOCASTA. Polybos is *dead*?
MESSENGER. If I'm lying, my lady, let me die for it.
JOCASTA. You. [*to a servant*] Go in and tell Oedipus.
O oracles of the gods, where are you now!
This man, the man Oedipus was afraid he would murder.
the man he feared, the man he fled from has died a natural death.
Oedipus didn't kill him, it was luck, luck.

> [*She turns to greet* OEDIPUS *as he
> comes out of the palace.*]

OEDIPUS. Jocasta, why did you send for me? [*taking her gently by the arm*]

JOCASTA. Oedipus,
    listen to this man, see what those ominous, holy predictions of
      Apollo mean now.   1190

OEDIPUS. Who is this man? What does he say?

JOCASTA. He comes from Corinth.
    Your father is dead. Polybos is dead!

OEDIPUS. What?
    Let me hear those words from your own mouth, stranger.
    Tell me yourself, in your own words.

MESSENGER. If that's what you want to hear first, then I'll say it:
    Polybos is dead.

OEDIPUS. How did he die? Assassination? Illness? How?

MESSENGER. An old man's life hangs by a fragile thread. Anything can
    snap it.   1200

OEDIPUS. That poor old man. It was illness then?

MESSENGER. Illness and old age.

OEDIPUS. Why, Jocasta,
    why should men look to the great hearth at Delphi
    or listen to birds shrieking and wheeling overhead—
    cries meaning I was doomed to kill my father?
    He is dead, gone, covered by the earth.
    And here I am—my hands never even touched a spear—
    I did not kill him,
    unless he died from wanting me to come home.   1210
    No. Polybos has bundled up all these oracles
    and taken them with him to the world below.
    They are only words now, lost in the air.

JOCASTA. Isn't that what I predicted?

OEDIPUS. You were right. My fears confused me.

JOCASTA. You have nothing to fear. Not now. Not ever.

OEDIPUS. But the oracle said I am doomed to sleep with my mother.
    How can I live with that and not be afraid?

JOCASTA. Why should men be afraid of anything? Fortune rules our
    lives.
    Luck is everything. Things happen. The future is darkness.   1220
    No human mind can know it.
    It's best to live in the moment, live for today, Oedipus.
    Why should the thought of marrying your mother make you so
      afraid?
    Many men have slept with their mothers in their dreams.
    Why worry? See your dreams for what they are—nothing, nothing
      at all.
    Be happy, Oedipus.

OEDIPUS. All that you say is right, Jocasta. I know it.
    I should be happy,
    but my mother is still living. As long as she's alive,
    I live in fear. This fear is necessary.   1230
    I have no choice.

JOCASTA. But Oedipus, your father's death is a sign, a great sign—
the sky has cleared, the sun's gaze holds us in its warm, hopeful
light.

OEDIPUS. A great sign, I agree. But so long as my mother is alive,
my fear lives too.

MESSENGER. Who is this woman you fear so much?

OEDIPUS. Merope, King Polybos' wife.

MESSENGER. Why does Merope frighten you so much?

OEDIPUS. A harrowing oracle hurled down upon us by some
great god.

MESSENGER. Can you tell me? Or did the god seal your lips?   1240

OEDIPUS. I can.
Long ago, Apollo told me I was doomed to sleep with my mother
and spill my father's blood, murder him
with these two hands of mine.
That's why I never returned to Corinth. Luckily, it would seem.
Still, nothing on earth is sweeter to a man's eyes
than the sight of his father and mother.

MESSENGER. And you left Corinth because of this prophecy?

OEDIPUS. Yes. And because of my father. To avoid killing my father.

MESSENGER. But didn't my news prove you have nothing to fear?   1250
I brought good news.

OEDIPUS. And I will reward you for your kindness.

MESSENGER. That's why I came, my lord. I knew you'd remember me
when you returned to Corinth.

OEDIPUS. I will never return, never live with my parents again.

MESSENGER. Son, it's clear you don't know what you're doing.

OEDIPUS. What do you mean? In the name of the gods, speak.

MESSENGER. If you're afraid to go home because of your parents.

OEDIPUS. I *am* afraid, afraid
Apollo's prediction will come true, all of it,   1260
as god's sunlight grows brighter on a man's face at dawn
when he's in bed, still sleeping,
and reaches into his eyes and wakes him.

MESSENGER. Afraid of murdering your father, of having his blood
on your hands?

OEDIPUS. Yes. His blood. The stain of his blood. That terror never
leaves me.

MESSENGER. But Oedipus, then you have no reason to be afraid.

OEDIPUS. I'm their son, they're my parents, aren't they?

MESSENGER. Polybos is nothing to you.

OEDIPUS. Polybos is not my father?   1270

MESSENGER. No more than I am.

OEDIPUS. But you are nothing to me. Nothing.

MESSENGER. And Polybos is nothing to you either.

OEDIPUS. Then why did he call me his son?

MESSENGER. Because I gave you to him. With these hands
I gave you to him.

OEDIPUS. How could he have loved me like a father if I am not
his son?

Messenger. He had no children. That opened his heart.
Oedipus. And what about you?
   Did you buy me from someone? Or did you find me?   1280
Messenger. I found you squawling, left alone to die in the thickets of
    Kithairon.
Oedipus. Kithairon? What were you doing on Kithairon?
Messenger. Herding sheep in the high summer pastures.
Oedipus. You were a shepherd, a drifter looking for work?
Messenger. A drifter, yes, but it was I who saved you.
Oedipus. Saved me? Was I hurt when you picked me up?
Messenger. Ask your feet.
Oedipus. Why,
    why did you bring up that childhood pain?
Messenger. I cut you free. Your feet were pierced, tied together at
    the ankles   1290
with leather thongs strung between the tendons and the bone.
Oedipus. That mark of my shame—I've worn it from the cradle.
Messenger. That mark is the meaning of your name:
    Oedipus, Swollenfoot, Oedipus.
Oedipus. Oh gods
    who did this to me?
    My mother?
    My father?
Messenger. I don't know. The man I took you from—he would
    know.
Oedipus. So you didn't find me? Somebody else gave me to you?   1300
Messenger. I got you from another shepherd.
Oedipus. What shepherd? Who was he? Do you know?
Messenger. As I recall, he worked for Laios.
Oedipus. The same Laios who was king of Thebes?
Messenger. The same Laios. The man was one of Laios' shepherds.
Oedipus. Is he still alive? I want to see this man.
Messenger. [*pointing to the* Chorus] These people would know that
    better than I do.
Oedipus. Do any of you know this shepherd he's talking about?
    Have you ever noticed him in the fields or in the city?
    Answer, if you have.   1310
    It is time everything came out, time everything was made clear.
    Everything.
Leader. I think he's the shepherd you sent for.
    But Jocasta, she would know.
Oedipus. [*to* Jocasta]
    Jocasta, do you know this man?
    Is he the man this shepherd here says worked for Laios?
Jocasta. What man? Forget about him. Forget what was said.
    It's not worth talking about.
Oedipus. How can I forget
    with clues like these in my hands?
    With the secret of my birth staring me in the face?   1320
Jocasta. No, Oedipus!

No more questions.
For god's sake, for the sake of your own life!
Isn't my anguish enough—more than enough?
OEDIPUS. You have nothing to fear,[27] Jocasta.
Even if my mother
and her mother before her were both slaves,
that doesn't make *you* the daughter of slaves.
JOCASTA. Oedipus, you *must* stop.

                             I beg you—stop!   1330
OEDIPUS. Nothing can stop me now. I must know everything.
Everything!
JOCASTA. I implore you, Oedipus. For your own good.
OEDIPUS. Damn my own good!
JOCASTA. Oh, Oedipus, Oedipus,
I pray to god you never see who you are!
OEDIPUS. [*to one of the attendants, who hurries off through the
exit stage left*]
You there, go find that shepherd, bring him here.
Let that woman bask in the glory of her noble birth.
JOCASTA. God help you, Oedipus—
you were born to suffer, born   1340
to misery and grief.
These are the last words I will ever speak, ever
Oedipus.

                              [JOCASTA *rushes offstage into the
palace. Long silence.*]

LEADER. Why did Jocasta rush away,
Oedipus, fleeing in such pain?
I fear disaster, or worse,
will break from this silence of hers.
OEDIPUS. Let it break! Let everything break!
I must discover who I am, know the secret of my birth,
no matter how humble, how vile.   1350
Perhaps Jocasta is ashamed of my low birth, ashamed to be my
wife.
Like all women she's proud.
But Luck, goddess who gives men all that is good, made *me*,
and I won't be cheated of what is mine, nothing can dishonor me,
ever.
I am like the months, my brothers the months—they shaped me
when I was a baby in the cold hills of Kithairon,
they guided me, carved out my times of greatness,
and they still move their hands over my life.
I am the man I am. I will not stop
until I discover who my parents are.   1360

---

[27] Oedipus believes Jocasta's anguish is caused by fears that he is of lowly birth and social
station.

Chorus. if I know if I see
  if the dark force of prophecy is mine
  Kithairon
  when the full moon
  rides over us tomorrow
  listen listen to us sing to you
  dance worship praise you
  mountain where Oedipus was found
  know Oedipus will praise you
  praise his nurse country and mother   1370
  who blessed our king
  I call on you Apollo
  let these visions please you
  god Apollo
  healer

  Oedipus son
  who was your mother
  which of the deathless mountain nymphs who lay
  with the great god Pan[28]
  on the high peaks he runs across   1380
  or with Apollo
  who loves the high green pastures above
  which one bore you
  did the god of the bare windy peaks Hermes[29]
  or the wild, dervish Dionysos
  living in the cool air of the hills
  take you
  a foundling
  from one of the nymphs he plays with
  joyously lift you hold you in his arms   1390
Oedipus. Old men, I think the man coming toward us now
  must be the shepherd we are looking for.
  I have never seen him, but the years, chalking his face and hair,
    tell me
  he's the man. And my men are with him. But you probably
    know him.
Leader. I do know him. If Laios ever had a man he trusted,
  this was the man.
Oedipus. [*to the* Messenger]
  You—is this the man you told me about?
Messenger. That's him. You're looking at the man.
Oedipus. [*to the* Shepherd *who has been waiting, hanging back*]
  You there, come closer.
                              Answer me, old man.
  Did you work for Laios?   1400
Shepherd. I was born his slave, and grew up in his household.

[28] God of the forest, of mountains, and of wild nature.
[29] Hermes was born on a mountain (Cyllene); he was also the god of shepherds.

OEDIPUS. What was your work?
SHEPHERD. Herding sheep, all my life.
OEDIPUS. Where?
SHEPHERD. Kithairon, mostly. And the country around Kithairon.
OEDIPUS. Do you remember ever seeing this man?
MESSENGER. Which man?
OEDIPUS. [*pointing to the* MESSENGER]
     This man standing here. Have you ever seen him before?
SHEPHERD. Not that I remember.
MESSENGER. No wonder, master. But I'll make him remember.   1410
     He knows who I am. We used to graze our flocks together
     in the pastures around Kithairon.
     Every year, for six whole months, three years running.
     From March until September, when the Dipper rose, signaling the
          harvest.
     I had one flock, he had two.
     And when the frost came, I drove my sheep back to their winter
          pens
     and he drove his back to Laios' fold.
     Remember, old man? Isn't that how it was?
SHEPHERD. Yes. But it was all so long ago.
MESSENGER. And do you remember giving me a baby boy at the
          time—   1420
     to raise as my own son?
SHEPHERD. What if I do? Why all these questions?
MESSENGER. That boy became King Oedipus, friend.
SHEPHERD. Damn you, can't you keep quiet.
OEDIPUS. Don't scold him, old man.
     It's you who deserve to be punished, not him.
SHEPHERD. What did I say, good master?
OEDIPUS. You haven't answered his question about the boy.
SHEPHERD. He's making trouble, master. He doesn't know a thing.

                              [OEDIPUS *takes the* SHEPHERD *by
                              the cloak*]

OEDIPUS. Tell me or you'll be sorry.   1430
SHEPHERD. For god's sake, don't hurt me, I'm an old man.
OEDIPUS. [*to one of his men*] You there, hold him. We'll make him talk.

                              [*The attendant pins the* SHEP-
                              HERD'S *arms behind his back*]

SHEPHERD. Oedipus, Oedipus,
     god knows I pity you.
     What more do you want to know?
OEDIPUS. Did you give the child to this man?
                              Speak.   Yes or no?
SHEPHERD. Yes.
     And I wish to god I'd died that day.
OEDIPUS. You *will* be dead unless you tell me the whole truth.

SHEPHERD. And worse than dead if I do.   1440
OEDIPUS. It seems our man won't answer.
SHEPHERD. No. I told you already. I gave him the boy.
OEDIPUS. Where did you get him? From Laios' household? Or where?
SHEPHERD. He wasn't *my* child. He was given to me.
OEDIPUS. [*turning to the* CHORUS *and the audience*]
     By whom? Someone here in Thebes?
SHEPHERD. Master, please, in god's name, no more questions.
OEDIPUS. You're a dead man if I have to ask you once more.
SHEPHERD. He was one
     of the children
     from Laios'   1450
     household.
OEDIPUS. A slave child? Or Laios' own?
SHEPHERD. I can't say it . . . it's
     awful, the words
     are awful . . . awful.
OEDIPUS. And I,
     I am afraid to hear them . . .
     but I must.
SHEPHERD. He was Laios' own child.
     Your wife, inside the palace, she can explain it all.   1460
OEDIPUS. *She* gave you the child?
SHEPHERD. My lord . . . yes.
OEDIPUS. Why?
SHEPHERD. She wanted me to abandon the child on a mountain.
OEDIPUS. His own mother?
SHEPHERD. Yes. There were prophecies, horrible oracles. She was
     afraid.
OEDIPUS. What oracles?
SHEPHERD. Oracles predicting he would murder his own father.
OEDIPUS. But why did you give the boy to this old man?
SHEPHERD. Because I pitied him, master, because I   1470
     thought the man would take the child away, take him to another
          country.
     Instead he saved him. Saved him for—oh gods,
     a fate so horrible, so awful, words can't describe it.
     If you were the baby that man took from me, Oedipus,
     what misery, what grief is yours!
OEDIPUS. [*looking up at the sun*]
     LIGHT   LIGHT   LIGHT
     never again flood these eyes with your white radiance, oh gods, my
          eyes. All, all
     the oracles have proven true. I, Oedipus, I
     am the child
     of parents who should never have been mine—doomed, doomed!   1480
     Now everything is clear—I
     lived with a woman, she was my mother, I slept in my mother's
          bed, and I
     murdered, murdered my father,

the man whose blood flows in these veins of mine,
whose blood stains these two hands red.

> [OEDIPUS *raises his hands to the*
> *sun, then turns and walks into the*
> *palace.*]

CHORUS. man after man after man
    o mortal generations
    here once
    almost not here
    what are we   1490
    dust ghosts images a rustling of air
    nothing nothing
    we breathe on the abyss
    we are the abyss
    our happiness no more than traces of a dream
    the high noon sun sinking into the sea
    the red spume of its wake raining behind it
    we are you
    we are you Oedipus
    dragging your maimed foot   1500
    in agony
    and now that I see your life finally revealed
    your life fused with the god
    blazing out of the black nothingness of all we know
    I say
    no happiness lasts nothing human lasts

    wherever you aimed you hit
    no archer had your skill
    you grew rich powerful great
    everything came falling to your feet   1510
    o Zeus
    after he killed the Sphinx
    whose claws curled under
    whose weird song of the future[30] baffled and destroyed
    he stood like a tower high above our country
    warding off death
    and from then on Oedipus we called you
    king our king
    draped you in gold
    our highest honors were yours   1520
    and you ruled this shining city
    Thebes   Thebes

---

[30] The Sphinx was a kind of oracle; specifically, her riddle about the three states of man reflects this play's focus on Oedipus' infancy, prime of manhood, and final weakness when, blinded, he must use a walking stick.

now
your story is pain pity no story is worse
than yours Oedipus
ruined savage blind
as you struggle with your life
as your life changes
and breaks and shows you who you are
Oedipus   Oedipus
son father you harbored in the selfsame place[31]   1530
the same place sheltered you both
bridegroom
how could the furrow your father plowed
not have cried out all this time
while you lay there unknowing
and saw the truth too late

time like the sun sees all things
and it sees you
you cannot hide from that light   1540
your own life opening itself to you
to all
married unmarried father son
for so long
justice comes like the dawn
always
and it shows the world your marriage now

I wish
o child of Laios
I wish I had never seen you   1550
I grieve for you
wail after wail fills me and pours out
because of you my breath came flowing back
but now
the darkness of your life
floods my eyes

       [*The palace doors open. A* Servant
       enters and approaches the Chorus
       and audience.]

Servant. Noble citizens, honored above all others in Thebes,
 if you still care for the house of Laios,
 if you still can feel the spirit of those who ruled before, now
 the horrors you will hear, the horrors you will see, will shake 1560
  your hearts and shatter you with grief beyond enduring.

---

[31] Harbored sexually, with Jocasta; geographically, the place alluded to is the mountain
Kithairon, where Laios died and to which Oedipus will flee.

Not even the waters of those great rivers Ister and Phasis[32]
could wash away the blood
that now darkens every stone of this shining house,
this house that will reveal, soon, soon
the misery and evil two mortals,
both masters of this house, have brought upon themselves.

The griefs we cause ourselves cut deepest of all.[33]
LEADER. What we already know
    has hurt us enough,   1570
    has made us cry out in pain.
    What more can you say?
SERVANT. This:
    Jocasta is dead. The queen is dead.
LEADER. Ah, poor
    unhappy Jocasta,
    how did she die?
SERVANT. She killed herself. She did it.
    But you did not see what happened there,
    you were not there, in the palace. You did not see it.   1580
    I did.
    I will tell you how Queen Jocasta died,
    the whole story, all of it. All I can remember.
    After her last words to Oedipus
    she rushed past us through the entrance hall, screaming,
    raking her hair with both hands, and flew into the bedroom, *their*
        bedroom,
    and slammed the doors shut as she lunged at her bridal bed,
    crying "Laios" "Laios"—dead all these years—
    remembering Laios—how his own son years ago
    grew up and then killed him, leaving her to   1590
    sleep with her own son, to have his children, *their* children,
    children—not sons, not daughters, something else, monsters. . . .
    Then she collapsed, sobbing, cursing the bed where she held both
        men in her arms,
    got husband from husband, children from her child.
    We heard it all, but suddenly, I couldn't tell what was happening.
    Oedipus came crashing in, he was howling,
    stalking up and down—we couldn't take our eyes off him—
    and we stopped listening to her pitiful cries.
    We stood there, watching him move like a bull, lurching, charging.
    shouting at each of us to give him a sword, demanding we tell him   1600
    where his wife was, that woman whose womb carried him,
    him and his children, that wife who gave him birth.
    Some god, some demon, led him to her, and he knew—

---

[32] Ister is the Danube River; Phasis is a river flowing into the Black Sea.
[33] The reference may be to the acts of Laios and Oedipus in the distant past or to the recent suicide and self-blinding of Jocasta and Oedipus. The words "cut deepest of all" can also apply to the Thebans and to the theatrical audience.

none of us showed him—
suddenly a mad, inhuman cry burst from his mouth
as if the wind rushed through his tortured body,
and he heaved against those bedroom doors so the hinges whined
and bent from their sockets and the bolts snapped,
and he stood in the room.
There she was—   1610
we could see her—his wife
dangling by her neck from a noose of braided, silken cords
tied to a rafter, still swaying.
And when he saw her he bellowed and stretched up and loosened
    the rope.
cradling her in one arm,
and slowly laid her body on the ground.

That's when it happened—he
ripped off the gold
brooches she was wearing—one on each shoulder of her gown—
and raised them over his head—you could see them flashing—   1620
and tilted his face up and
brought them right down into his eyes
and the long pins sank deep, all the way back into the sockets,
and he shouted at his eyes:
"Now you won't see me, you won't see
my agonies or my crimes,
but in endless darkness, always, there you'll see
those I never should have seen.
And those I should have known were my parents, father and
    mother—
these eyes will never see their faces in the light.   1630
These eyes will never see the light again, never."
Cursing his two blind eyes over and over, he
lifted the brooches again and drove their pins through his
    eyeballs up
to the hilts until they were pulp, until the blood streamed out
soaking his beard and cheeks,
a black storm splashing its hail across his face.

Two mortals acted. Now grief tears their lives apart
as if that pain sprang from a single, sorrowing root
to curse each one, man and wife. For all those years
their happiness was truly happiness, but now, now   1640
wailing, madness, shame and death,
every evil men have given a name,
everything criminal and vile
that mankind suffers they suffer. Not one evil is missing.
LEADER. But now
    does this torn, anguished man
    have any rest from his pain?

SERVANT. No, no—
    then he shouted at us to open the doors and show everyone in
        Thebes
    his father's killer, his mother's—I cannot say it.   1650
    Once we have seen him as he is
    he will leave Thebes, lift the curse from his city—
    banish himself, cursed by his own curses.
    But his strength is gone, his whole life is pain,
    more pain than any man can bear.
    He needs help, someone to guide him.
    He is alone, and blind. Look,
    look—the palace doors are opening—now
    a thing
    so horrible will stand before you   1660
    you will shudder with disgust and try to turn away
    while your hearts will swell with pity for what you see.

> [*The central doors open.* OEDIPUS
> *enters, led by his household servants.*
> *His mask is covered with blood. The*
> CHORUS *begin a dirge to which*
> OEDIPUS *responds antiphonally.*]

CHORUS. horror horror o what suffering
    men see
    but none is worse than this
    Oedipus o
    how could you have slashed out your eyes
    what god leaped on you
    from beyond that last border of space
    what madness entered you   1670
    clawing even more misery into you
    I cannot look at you

    but there are questions
    so much I would know
    so much that I would see
    no no
    the shape of your life makes me shudder
OEDIPUS. I   I
    this voice of agony
    I am   what place am I   1680
    where? Not here, nowhere I know!
    What force, what tide breaks over my life?
    Pain, demon stabbing into me
    leaving nothing, nothing, no man I know, not human,
    fate howling out of nowhere   what am I
    fire a voice where where
    is it being taken?

LEADER. Beyond everything to a place
    so terrible nothing is seen there, nothing is heard.
OEDIPUS. [*reaching out, groping*]
    Thing   thing   darkness   1690
    spilling into me, my
    black cloud smothering me forever,
    nothing can stop you, nothing can escape,
    I cannot push you away.

    I am
    nothing but my own cries breaking
    again and again
    the agony of those gold pins
    the memory of what I did
    stab me   1700
    again
    again.
LEADER. What can you feel but pain.
    It all comes back, pain in remorse,
    remorse in pain, to tear you apart with grief.
OEDIPUS. Dear, loyal friend
    you, only you, are still here with me, still care
    for this blind, tortured man.
    Oh,
    I know you are there, I know you, friend,   1710
    even in this darkness, friend, touched by your voice.
LEADER. What you did was horrible,
    but how could you quench the fire of your eyes,
    what demon lifted your hands?
OEDIPUS. Apollo   Apollo
    it was Apollo, always Apollo,
    who brought each of my agonies to birth,
    but I,
    nobody else, *I,*
    I raised these two hands of mine, held them above my head,   1720
    and plunged them down,
    I stabbed out these eyes.
    Why should I have eyes? Why,
    when nothing I saw was worth seeing?
    Nothing.
LEADER. Nothing. Nothing.
OEDIPUS. Oh friends. Nothing.
    No one to see, no one to love,
    no one to speak to, no one to hear!
                 Friends, friends, lead me away now.
    Lead me away from Thebes—Oedipus,   1730
    destroyer and destroyed,
    the man whose life is hell
    for others and for himself, the man
    more hated by the gods than any other man, ever.

LEADER. Oh I pity you,
    I weep for your fate
    and for your mind,
    for what it is to be you, Oedipus.
    I wish you had never seen the man you are.
OEDIPUS. I hate   1740
    the man who found me, cut the thongs from my feet,
    snatched me from death, cared for me—
    I wish he were dead!
    I should have died up there on those wild, desolate slopes of
        Kithairon.
    Then my pain and the pain
    those I love suffer now
    never would have been.
LEADER. These are my wishes too.
OEDIPUS. Then I never would have murdered my father,
    never heard men call me my mother's husband.   1750

    Now
    I am
    Oedipus!
    Oedipus, who lay in that loathsome bed, made love there in
        that bed,
    his father's and mother's bed, the bed
    where he was born.

    No gods anywhere now, not for me,[34] now,
    unholy, broken man.
    What man ever suffered grief like this?
LEADER. How can I say that what you did was right?   1760
    Better to be dead than live blind.
OEDIPUS. I did what I had to do. No more advice.
    How could *my* eyes,
    when I went down into that black, sightless place beneath the
        earth,
    the place where the dead go down, how,
    how could I have looked at anything,
    with what human eyes could I have gazed
    on my father, on my mother—
    oh gods, my mother!
    What I did against those two   1770
    not even strangling could punish.

    And my children, how would the sight of them, born as they were
        born,
    be sweet? Not to these eyes of mine, never to these eyes.
    Nothing, nothing is left me now—no city with its high walls,
    no shining statues of the gods. I stripped all these things from
        myself—

[34] Oedipus means that he has been forsaken by the gods.

I, Oedipus, fallen lower than any man now, born nobler than the
    best,
born the king of Thebes! Cursed with my own curses, I
commanded Thebes to drive out the killer.
I banished the royal son of Laios, the man the gods revealed
is stained with the awful stain. The secret stain   1780
that I myself revealed is *my* stain. And now, revealed at last,
how could I ever look men in the eyes?
Never. Never.

If I could, I would have walled my ears so they heard nothing,
I would have made this body of mine a wall.
I would have heard nothing, tasted nothing, smelled nothing, seen
    nothing.
         No thought. No feeling. Nothing. Nothing.
So pain would never reach me any more.

O Kithairon,
why did you shelter me and take me in?   1790
Why did you let me live? Better to have died on that bare slope of
    yours
where no man would ever have seen me or known the secret of my
    birth!

Polybos, Corinth, that house I thought was my father's home,
how beautiful I was when you sheltered me as a child
and oh what disease festered beneath that beauty.
Now everyone knows the secret of my birth, knows
how vile I am.

O roads, secret valley, cluster of oaks,
O narrow place where two roads join a third,[35]
roads that drank my blood as it streamed from my hands,   1800
flowing from my dead father's body.
do you remember me now?
Do you remember what I did with my own two hands, there in
    your presence,
and what I did after that, when I came here to Thebes?
O marriage, marriage, you gave me my life, and then
from the same seed, *my* seed, spewed out
fathers, brothers, sisters, children, brides, wives—
nothing, no words can express the shame.
No more words. Men should not name what men should never do.

[To the Chorus*]*

Gods, oh gods, gods,   1810
hide me, hide me
now

[35] Not only the crossroads where Oedipus killed his father, but also the sexual "narrow
place" where Oedipus, his father, and Jocasta conjoined.

far away from Thebes,
kill me,
cast me into the sea,
drive me where you will never see me—never again.

> [*Reaching out to the* CHORUS, *who
> back away*]

Touch this poor man, touch me,
don't be afraid to touch me. Believe me, nobody,
nobody but me can bear
this fire of anguish.   1820
It is mine. Mine.
LEADER. Kreon has come.
Now he, not you, is the sole guardian of Thebes,
and only he can grant you what you ask
OEDIPUS. [*turning toward the palace*]
What can I say to him, how can anything I say
make him listen now?
I wronged him. I accused him, and now everything I said
proves I am vile.
KREON. [*enters from the entrance to the right. He is accompanied by men who
gather around* OEDIPUS]

I have not come to mock you, Oedipus; I have not come to blame
you for the past.

> [*To attendants*]

You men, standing there, if you have no respect for human dignity,   1830
at least revere the master of life,
the all-seeing sun whose light nourishes
every living thing on earth.
Come, cover this cursed, naked, holy thing,[36] hide him
from the earth and the sacred rain and the light,
you powers who cringe from his touch.
Take him. Do it now. Be reverent.
Only his family should see and hear his grief.
Their grief.
OEDIPUS. I beg you, Kreon, if you love the gods,   1840
grant me what I ask.
I have been vile to you, worse than vile.
I have hurt you, terribly, and yet
you have treated me with kindness, with nobility.
You have calmed my fear, you did not turn away from me.
Do what I ask. Do it for yourself, not for me.
KREON. What do you want from me, Oedipus?

---

[36] Because he bears a burden of guilt that transforms ordinary human nature, Oedipus has
paradoxically become a kind of sacred being.

OEDIPUS. Drive me out of Thebes, do it now, now—
  drive me someplace where no man can speak to me,
  where no man can see me anymore.   1850
KREON. Believe me, Oedipus, I would have done it long ago.
  But I refuse to act until I know precisely what the god desires.
OEDIPUS. Apollo has revealed what he desires. Everything is clear.
  I killed my father, I am polluted and unclean.
  I must die.
KREON. That is what the god commanded, Oedipus.
  But there are no precedents for what has happened.
  We need to *know* before we act.
OEDIPUS. Do you care so much for me, enough to ask Apollo?
  For *me*, Oedipus?   1860
KREON. Now even you will trust the god, I think.
OEDIPUS. I will. And I turn to you, I implore you, Kreon—
  the woman lying dead inside, your sister,
  give her whatever burial you think best.

                                          As for me,
  never let this city of my fathers see me here in Thebes.
  Let me go and live on the mountain, on Kithairon—the mountain
  my parents intended for my grave.
  Let me die the way they wanted me to die: slowly, alone—
  die *their* way.
  And yet this much I know—

                                  no sickness,   1870
  no ordinary, natural death[37] is mine.
  I have been saved, preserved, kept alive
  for some strange fate, for something far more awful still.
  When that thing comes, let it take me
  where it will.

                          [OEDIPUS *turns, looking for some-*
                          thing, waiting]

  As for my sons,[38] Kreon,
  they are grown men, they can look out for themselves.
  But my daughters, those two poor girls of mine,
  who have never left their home before, never left their father's
        side,
  who ate at my side every day, who shared whatever was mine,   1880
  I beg you, Kreon,

---

[37] In his play *Oedipus at Colonus,* Sophocles continues the story of *Oedipus the King* (though the plays, along with the further continuation, *Antigone,* were written at different periods of Sophocles' life). Since Oedipus died at Colonus, a suburb of Athens that included a place sacred to the Furies, the personified forces of atonement celebrated in the last play of Aeschylus' Orestes trilogy, the present reference to Oedipus' mysterious and sacred death and resting place would have been important to Sophocles' Athenian audience as a sign of the redemptive value of Oedipus' wanderings and sufferings.

[38] Eteocles and Polyneices. Their enmity in a subsequent war for control of the city of Thebes, and the related ordeals of Oedipus' daughters Antigone and Ismene, are central to Sophocles' *Oedipus at Colonus* and *Antigone.*

care for them, love them.
But more than anything, Kreon,
I want to touch them,

[he begins to lift his hands]

let me touch them with these hands of mine,
let them come to me so we can grieve together.
My noble lord, if only I could touch them with my hands,
they would still be mine just as they were
when I had eyes that could still see.

*[Oedipus' two small daughters are
brought out of the palace]*

O gods, gods, is it possible? Do I hear   1890
my two daughters crying? Has Kreon pitied me and brought me
what I love more than my life—
my daughters?
KREON. I brought them to you, knowing how much you love them,
     Oedipus,
knowing the joy you would feel if they were here.
OEDIPUS. May the gods who watch over the path of your life, Kreon,
prove kinder to you than they were to me.
Where are you, children?
Come, come to your brother's hands—

[taking his daughters into his arms]

his mother was your mother, too,   1900
come to these hands which made these eyes, bright clear eyes once,
sockets seeing nothing, the eyes
of the man who fathered you. Look . . . your father's eyes,
your father—
who knew nothing until now, saw nothing until now, and became
the husband of the woman who gave him birth.
                                                    I weep for you
when I think how men will treat you, how bitter your lives will be.
What festivals will you attend, whose homes will you visit
and not be assailed by whispers, and people's stares?
Where will you go and not leave in tears?   1910
And when the time comes for you to marry,
what men will take you as their brides, and risk the shame of mar-
     rying
the daughters of Oedipus?
What sorrow will not be yours?
Your father killed his father, made love
to the woman who gave birth to him. And he fathered you
in the same place where he was fathered.
That is what you will hear; that is what they will say.
Who will marry you then? You will never marry,

but grow hard and dry like wheat so far beyond harvest 1920
that the wind blows its white flakes into the winter sky.
Oh Kreon,
now you are the only father my daughters have.
Jocasta and I, their parents, are lost to them forever.
These poor girls are yours. Your blood.
Don't let them wander all their lives,
begging, alone, unmarried, helpless.
Don't let them suffer as their father has. Pity them, Kreon,
pity these girls, so young and helpless except for you.
Promise me this. Noble Kreon, 1930
touch me with your hand, give me a sign.

[KREON *takes his hands*]

                                        Daughters,
daughters, if you were older, if you could understand,
there is so much more I would say to you.
But for now, I give you this prayer—
                              Live,
live your lives, live each day as best you can,
may your lives be happier than your father's was.
KREON. No more grief. Come in.
OEDIPUS. I must. But obedience comes hard.
KREON. Everything has its time.
OEDIPUS. First, promise me this. 1940
KREON. Name it.
OEDIPUS. Banish me from Thebes.
KREON. I cannot.   Ask the gods for that.
OEDIPUS. The gods hate me.
KREON. Then you will have your wish.
OEDIPUS. You promise?
KREON. I say only what I mean.
OEDIPUS. Then lead me in.

[OEDIPUS *reaches out and touches
his daughters, trying to take them
with him*]

KREON. Oedipus, come with me. Let your daughters go. Come.
OEDIPUS. No. You will not take my daughters. I forbid it. 1950
KREON. You *forbid* me?
You have no power any more.
All the great power you once had is gone,
gone forever.

[*The* CHORUS *turn to face the audience.* KREON *leads* OEDIPUS *toward the palace. His daughters
follow. He moves slowly, and disappears into the palace as the* CHORUS
ends.]

CHORUS. O citizens of Thebes, this is Oedipus,
    who solved the famous riddle, who held more power than any
      mortal.
    See what he is: all men gazed on his fortunate life,
    all men envied him, but look at him, look.
    All he had, all this man was,
    pulled down and swallowed by the storm of his own life,   1960
    and by the god.
    Keep your eyes on that last day, on your dying.
    Happiness and peace, they were not yours
    unless at death you can look back on your life and say
    I lived, I did not suffer.

ANTIGONE

Translated by Theodore Howard Banks

CHARACTERS IN THE PLAY

CREON,[1] *King of Thebes, brother*
    of Jocasta, the mother and wife
    of Oedipus
EURYDICE, *Queen of Thebes,*
    wife of Creon
HAEMON, *son of Creon*
ANTIGONE } *daughters of Oedipus*
ISMENE   } *and Jocasta*

TIRESIAS, *a prophet*
BOY, *attendant of Tiresias*
GUARD
MESSENGER
CHORUS *of Theban Elders*
ATTENDANTS

SCENE
Courtyard of the royal palace at Thebes. Daybreak.

[*Enter* ANTIGONE *and* ISMENE]

ANTIGONE. Dear sister! Dear Ismene! How many evils
    Our father, Oedipus, bequeathed to us![2]
    And is there one of them—do you know of one
    That Zeus has not showered down upon our heads?
    I have seen pain, dishonor, shame, and ruin,
    I have seen them all, in what we have endured.
    And now comes this new edict by the King
    Proclaimed throughout the city. Have you heard?

---

[1] The Kreon of *Oedipus the King.* The names in this translation sometimes are spelled differently.

[2] The two sisters had accompanied their self-blinded father Oedipus in his wanderings and sufferings after his banishment from Thebes. (The banishment is described at the end of *Oedipus the King.*) Possibly we are to regard Oedipus' lineage as afflicted by an inherited curse. Oedipus' crimes, committed unwittingly, had been to kill his father Laius, the king of Thebes, and to marry his mother.

Do you not know, even yet, our friends are threatened?
They are to meet the fate of enemies.   10
ISMENE. Our friends, Antigone? No, I have heard
Nothing about them either good or bad.
I have no news except that we two sisters
Lost our two brothers when they killed each other.[3]
I know the Argive army fled last night,
But what that means, or whether it makes my life
Harder or easier, I cannot tell.
ANTIGONE. This I was sure of. So I brought you here
Beyond the palace gates to talk alone.
ISMENE. What is the matter? I know you are deeply troubled.   20
ANTIGONE. Yes, for our brothers' fate.[4] Creon has given
An honored burial to one, to the other
Only unburied shame. Eteocles
Is laid in the earth with all the rites observed
That give him his due honor with the dead.
But the decree concerning Polyneices
Published through Thebes is that his wretched body
Shall lie unmourned, unwept, unsepulchered.
Sweet will he seem to the vultures when they find him,
A welcome feast that they are eager for.   30
This is the edict the good Creon uttered
For your observance and for mine—yes, mine.
He is coming here himself to make it plain
To those who have not heard. Nor does he think it
Of little consequence, because whoever
Does not obey is doomed to death by stoning.
Now you can show you are worthy of your birth,
Or bring disgrace upon a noble house.
ISMENE. What can I do, Antigone? As things are,
What can I do that would be of any help?   40
ANTIGONE. You can decide if you will share my task.
ISMENE. What do you mean? What are you planning to do?
ANTIGONE. I intend to give him burial. Will you help?
ISMENE. To give him burial! Against the law?
ANTIGONE. He is our brother. I will do my duty,
Yours too, perhaps. I never will be false.
ISMENE. Creon forbids it! You are too rash, too headstrong.
ANTIGONE. He has no right to keep me from my own.
ISMENE. Antigone! Think! Think how our father perished[5]

[3] Oedipus' two sons, Eteocles and Polyneices, had been rivals for the rulership of the city. After being exiled by Eteocles, Polyneices had recruited a military force in Argos to attack Thebes. In the ensuing battle, the Thebans had defeated the Argives and the brothers Eteocles and Polyneices had killed each other, leaving Creon to rule Thebes.

[4] It was believed that the unburied were treated with contempt in the underground realm of the dead. Moreover, to mourn and to prepare bodies for proper burial was the special duty of the women.

[5] The version in *Oedipus at Colonus* is that Oedipus, after long suffering, died a holy and mysterious death. The events Ismene describes here (her mother Jocasta's suicide and Oedipus' self-blinding) take place in *Oedipus the King*.

In scorn and hatred when his sins, that he   50
Himself discovered, drove him to strike blind
His eyes by his own hand. Think how his mother,
His wife—both names were hers—ended her life
Shamefully hanging in a twisted noose.
Think of that dreadful day when our two brothers,
Our wretched brothers, fought and fell together,
Each slayer and each slain. And now we too,
Left all alone, think how in turn we perish,
If, in defiance of the law, we brave
The power of the commandment of a king.   60
O think Antigone! We who are women
Should not contend with men; we who are weak
Are ruled by the stronger, so that we must obey
In this and in matters that are yet more bitter.
And so I pray the dead to pardon me
If I obey our rulers, since I must.
To be too bold in what we do is madness.
ANTIGONE. I will not urge you. And I would not thank you
    For any help that you might care to give me.
    Do what you please, but I will bury him,   70
    And if I die for that, I shall be happy.
    Loved, I shall rest beside the one I loved.
    My crime is innocence, for I owe the dead
    Longer allegiance than I owe the living.
    With the dead I lie forever. Live, if you choose,
    Dishonoring the laws the gods have hallowed.
ISMENE. No, I dishonor nothing. But to challenge
    Authority—I have not strength enough.
ANTIGONE. Then make that your excuse. I will go heap
    The earth above the brother that I love.   80
ISMENE. O Sister, Sister! How I fear for you!
ANTIGONE. No, not for me. Set your own life in order.
ISMENE. Well then, at least, tell no one of your plan.
    Keep it close hidden, as I too will keep it.
ANTIGONE. Oh! Publish it! Proclaim it to the world!
    Then I will hate you less than for your silence.
ISMENE. Your heart is hot for deeds that chill the blood.
ANTIGONE. I know that I give pleasure where I should.
ISMENE. Yes, if you can, but you will try in vain.
ANTIGONE. When my strength fails, then I shall try no longer.   90
ISMENE. A hopeless task should never be attempted.
ANTIGONE. Your words have won their just reward: my hatred
    And the long-lasting hatred of the dead.
    But leave me and the folly that is mine
    To undergo the worst that can befall me.
    I shall not suffer an ignoble death.
ISMENE. Go then, Antigone, if you must go.
    And yet remember, though your act is foolish,
    That those who love you do so with all their hearts.

> [*Exeunt* ANTIGONE *and* ISMENE.
> *Enter* CHORUS]

CHORUS.
Sunbeam, eye of the golden day, on Thebes the seven-gated,   100
  On Dircé's[6] streams you have dawned at last, O fairest of light.
Dawned on our foes, who had come enflamed by the quarrel of
    Polyneices,
  Shone on their glittering arms, made swifter their headlong
    flight.
    From Argos they came with their white shields flashing,
    Their helmets, crested with horsehair, agleam:
    An army that flew like a snow-white eagle
    Across our borders with shrilling scream.

Above our roofs it soared, at our gates with greedy jaws it was
    gaping;
  But before their spears tasted our blood, and before our circle
    of towers
Felt the flame of their torches, they turned to flight. The foes of
    the Theban dragon[7]   110
Found the surge and clamor of battle too fierce for their feebler
    powers.
    For Zeus, who abhors a proud tongue's boasting,
    Seeing their river of armor flow
    Clashing and golden, struck with his lightning
    To silence the shout of our foremost foe.[8]

He crashed to the earth with his torch, who had scaled the top of
    our ramparts,
  Raging in frenzy against us, breathing tempestuous hate,
Raging and threatening in vain. And mighty Ares,[9] our ally,
  Dealing havoc around him, apportioned to other foemen
    their fate.
    For at seven portals, their seven leaders,   120
    Down to the earth their bronze arms threw
    In tribute to Zeus, the lord of the battle;
    Save the fated brothers, the wretched two,
    Who went to their common doom together,
    Each wielding a spear that the other slew.

Now glorious Victory smiles upon jubilant Thebes rich in chariots.
  Let us give free rein to our joy, forgetting our late-felt war;
  Let us visit in night-long chorus the temples of all the immortals,

---

[6] A river near Thebes.

[7] According to myth, the Thebans were descendants of men metamorphosed from the teeth of a dragon killed by Cadmus, founder of the city.

[8] The foe is Capaneus. Having scaled the walls of Thebes, he boasted that not even Zeus, king of the gods, could stop him, but Zeus killed him with a thunderbolt.

[9] God of war and of destruction.

With Bacchus,[10] who shakes the land in the dances, going be-
   fore.
But behold! The son of Menoeceus approaches,   130
   Creon, the new-crowned King of the land,
Made King by new fortunes the gods have allotted.
   What step has he pondered? What has he planned
To lay before us, his council of elders,
   Who have gathered together at his command?

[*Enter* CREON]

CREON. Elders of Thebes, our city has been tossed
   By a tempestuous ocean, but the gods
Have steadied it once more and made it safe.
You, out of all the citizens, I have summoned,
Because I knew that you once reverenced   140
The sovereignty of Laius, and that later,
When Oedipus was King and when he perished,
Your steadfast loyalty upheld his children.
And now his sons have fallen, each one stained
By his brother's blood, killed by his brother's hand,
So that the sovereignty devolves on me,
Since I by birth am nearest to the dead.[11]
Certainly no man can be fully known,
Known in his soul, his will, his intellect,
Until he is tested and has proved himself   150
In statesmanship. Because a city's ruler,
Instead of following the wisest counsel,
May through some fear keep silent. Such a man
I think contemptible. And one whose friend
Has stronger claims upon him than his country,
Him I consider worthless.[12] As for me,
I swear by Zeus, forever all-beholding,
That I would not keep silence, if I saw
Ruin instead of safety drawing near us;
Nor would I think an enemy of the state   160
Could be my friend. For I remember this:
Our country bears us all securely onward,
And only while it sails a steady course
Is friendship possible. Such are the laws
By which I guard the greatness of the city.
And kindred to them is the proclamation
That I have made to all the citizens

[10] God of wine; his mother Semele, who was ravished by Zeus in the form of lightning, was
a Theban.

[11] Creon is the brother of the dead rivals' mother, Jocasta; he is also a cousin of the former
king Laius.

[12] Creon here states his side of the play's central moral and political issue. The word
"friend" has also the meaning of "kindred."

Concerning the two sons of Oedipus:
Eteocles, who has fallen in our defence,
Bravest of warriors, shall be entombed   170
With every honor, every offering given
That may accompany the noble dead
Down to their rest. But as for Polyneices,
He came from exile eager to consume
The city of his fathers with his fire
And all the temples of his fathers' gods,
Eager to drink deep of his kindred's blood,
Eager to drag us off to slavery.
To this man, therefore, nothing shall be given.
None shall lament him, none shall do him honor.   180
He shall be left without a grave, his corpse
Devoured by birds and dogs, a loathsome sight.
Such is my will. For never shall the wicked
Be given more approval than the just,
If I have power to stop it. But whoever
Feels in his heart affection for his city
Shall be rewarded both in life and death.
CHORUS. Creon, son of Menoeceus, it has pleased you
So to pass judgment on our friend and foe.
And you may give commands to all of us,   190
The living and the dead. Your will is law.
CREON. Then see that this command is carried out.
CHORUS. Sir, lay that burden on some younger man.
CREON. Sentries have been assigned to guard the body.
CHORUS. Then what additional duty would you give us?
CREON. Never to countenance the disobedient.
CHORUS. Who is so stupid as to long for death?
CREON. Death is indeed the punishment. Yet men
Have often been destroyed by hope of gain.

[*Enter* GUARD]

GUARD. My Lord, I cannot say that I have hurried,   200
Or that my running has made me lose my breath.
I often stopped to think, and turned to go back.
I stood there talking to myself: 'You fool,'
I said, 'Why do you go to certain death?'
And then: 'You idiot, are you still delaying?
If someone else tells Creon, you will suffer.'
I changed my mind this way, getting here slowly,
Making a short road long. But still, at last,
I did decide to come. And though my story
Is nothing much to tell, yet I will tell it.   210
One thing I know. I must endure my fate,
But nothing more than that can happen to me.
CREON. What is the matter? What is troubling you?

GUARD. Please let me tell you first about myself.
    I did not do it. I did not see who did.
    It is not right for me to be punished for it.
CREON. You take good care not to expose yourself.
    Your news must certainly be something strange.
GUARD. Yes, it is strange—dreadful. I cannot speak.
CREON. Oh, tell it, will you? Tell it and go away!   220
GUARD. Well, it is this. Someone has buried the body,
    Just now, and gone—has sprinkled it with dust
    And given it other honors it should have.
CREON. What are you saying? Who has dared to do it?
GUARD. I cannot tell. Nothing was to be seen:
    No mark of pickaxe, no spot where a spade
    Had turned the earth. The ground was hard and dry,
    Unbroken—not a trace of any wheels—
    No sign to show who did it. When the sentry
    On the first watch discovered it and told us,   230
    We were struck dumb with fright. For he was hidden
    Not by a tomb but a light coat of dust,
    As if a pious hand had scattered it.
    There were no tracks of any animal,
    A dog or wild beast that had come to tear him.
    We all began to quarrel, and since no one
    Was there to stop us, nearly came to blows.
    Everyone was accused, and everyone
    Denied his guilt. We could discover nothing.
    We were quite willing to handle red-hot iron,   240
    To walk through fire, to swear by all the gods
    That we were innocent of the deed itself,
    And innocent of taking any part
    In planning it or doing it. At last
    One of us spoke. We trembled and hung our heads,
    For he was right; we could not argue with him,
    Yet his advice was bound to cause us trouble.
    He told us all this had to be reported,
    Not kept a secret. We all agreed to that.
    We drew lots for it, and I had no luck.   250
    I won the prize and was condemned to come.
    So here I stand, unwilling, because I know
    The bringer of bad news is never welcome.
CHORUS. Sir, as he spoke, I have been wondering.
    Can this be, possibly, the work of gods?
CREON. Be silent![13] Before you madden me! You are old.
    Would you be senseless also? What you say
    Is unendurable. You say the gods

---

[13] The Chorus's surmise about divine intervention in this first burial is conceivably true; the play is somewhat ambiguous on the matter. The possibility that the Chorus is right emphasizes Creon's departure from his earlier-stated principle that rulers should listen to counsel (line 152).

Cared for this corpse. Then was it for reward,
Mighty to match his mighty services, 260
That the gods covered him? He who came to burn
Their pillared temples and their votive offerings,
Ravage their land, and trample down the state.
Or is it your opinion that the gods
Honor the wicked? Inconceivable!
However, from the first, some citizens
Who found it difficult to endure this edict,
Muttered against me, shaking their heads in secret,
Instead of bowing down beneath the yoke,
Obedient and contented with my rule. 270
These are the men who are responsible,
For I am certain they have bribed the guards
To bury him. Nothing is worse than money.
Money lays waste to cities, banishes
Men from their homes, indoctrinates the heart,
Perverting honesty to works of shame,
Showing men how to practice villainy,
Subduing them to every godless deed.
But all those men who got their pay for this
Need have no doubt their turn to pay will come. 280
[*to the* GUARD] Now, you. As I still honor Zeus the King,
I tell you, and I swear it solemnly,
Either you find the man who did this thing,
The very man, and bring him here to me,
Or you will not just die. Before you die,
You will be tortured until you have explained
This outrage; so that later when you steal
You will know better where to look for money
And not expect to find it everywhere.
Ill-gotten wealth brings ruin and not safety. 290
GUARD. Sir, may I speak? Or shall I merely go?
CREON. You can say nothing that is not offensive.
GUARD. Do I offend your hearing or your heart?
CREON. Is it your business to define the spot?
GUARD. The criminal hurts your heart, and I your ears.
CREON. Still talking? Why, you must have been born talking!
GUARD. Perhaps. But I am not the guilty man.
CREON. You are. And what is more you sold yourself.
GUARD. You have judged me, sir, and have misjudged me, too.
CREON. Be clever about judging if you care to. 300
But you will say that treachery leads to sorrow
Unless you find the man and show him to me.

[*Exit* CREON]

GUARD. Finding him is the best thing that could happen.
Fate will decide. But however that may be,
You never are going to see me here again.

I have escaped! I could not have hoped for that.
I owe the gods my thanks for guarding me.

[*Exit* GUARD]

CHORUS.
Many the marvelous things; but none that can be
    More of a marvel than man! This being that braves
With the south wind of winter the whitened streaks of the sea,   310
    Threading his way through the troughs of engulfing waves.
And the earth most ancient, the eldest of all the gods,
    Earth, undecaying, unwearied, he wears away with his toil;
Forward and back with his plowshare, year after year, he plods,
    With his horses turning the soil.

Man in devising excels. The birds of the air,
    That light-minded race, he entangles fast in his toils.
Wild creatures he catches, casting about them his snare,
    And the salt-sea brood he nets in his woven coils.
The tireless bull he has tamed, and the beast whose lair   320
    Is hidden deep in the wilds, who roams in the wooded hills.
He has fitted a yoke that the neck of the shaggy-maned horse
        will bear;
    He is master of all through his skills.

He has taught himself speech, and wind-like thought, and the
        lore
 Of ruling a town. He has fled the arrows of rain,
The searching arrows of frost he need fear no more,
    That under a starry sky are endured with pain.
Provision for all he has made—unprovided for naught,
    Save death itself, that in days to come will take shape.
From obscure and deep-seated disease he has subtly wrought   330
    A way of escape.

Resourceful and skilled, with an inconceivable art,
    He follows his course to a good or an evil end.
When he holds the canons of justice high in his heart
    And has sworn to the gods the laws of the land to defend,
Proud stands his city; without a city is he
    Who with ugliness, rashness, or evil dishonors the day.
Let me shun his thoughts. Let him share no hearthstone with me,
    Who acts in this way!

CHORUS. Look there! Look there! What portent can this be?   340
    Antigone! I know her, it is she!
    Daughter of Oedipus a prisoner brought?
    You defied Creon? You in folly caught?

[*Enter* GUARD *with* ANTIGONE]

GUARD. She did it. Here she is. We caught this girl
   As she was burying him. Where is the King?
CHORUS. Leaving the palace there, just as we need him.

[*Enter* CREON]

CREON. Why do you need my presence? What has happened?
GUARD. My Lord, no one should take a solemn oath
   Not to do something, for his second thoughts
   Make him a liar. I vowed not to hurry back.   350
   I had been battered by your storm of threats.
   But when a joy comes that exceeds our hopes,
   No other happiness can equal it.
   So I have broken my vow. I have returned,
   Bringing this girl along. She was discovered
   Busy with all the rites of burial.
   There was no casting lots, no, not this time!
   Such luck as this was mine and no one else's.
   Now sir, take her yourself, examine her,
   Convict her, do what you like. But as for me,   360
   I have the right to a complete acquittal.
CREON. This is the girl you caught? How? Where was she?
GUARD. Burying the dead man, just as I have told you.
CREON. Do you mean that? Or have you lost your mind?
GUARD. Your order was that he should not be buried.
   I saw her bury him. Is that all clear?
CREON. How was she seen? You caught her in the act?
GUARD. This was what happened. When we had gotten back,
   With your threats following us, we swept away
   The dust that covered him. We left him bare,   370
   A rotting corpse. And then we sat to windward,
   Up on the hillside, to avoid the stench.
   All of us were alert, and kept awake
   Threatening each other. No one could get careless.
   So the time passed, until the blazing sun
   Stood at the zenith, and the heat was burning.
   Then suddenly the wind came in a blast,
   Lifting a cloud of dust up from the earth,
   Troubling the sky and choking the whole plain,
   Stripping off all the foliage of the woods,   380
   Filling the breadth of heaven. We closed our eyes
   And bore the affliction that the gods had sent us.
   When it had finally stopped, we saw this girl.
   She wailed aloud with a sharp, bitter cry,
   The cry a bird gives seeing its empty nest
   Robbed of its brood. And she too, when she saw
   The naked body, was loud in her lament
   And cursed the men who had uncovered him.
   Quickly she sprinkled him with dust, and then

Lifting a pitcher, poured out three libations[14]   390
To do him honor. When we ran and caught her,
She was unterrified. When we accused her
Both of her earlier and her present act,
She made no effort to deny the charges.
I am part glad, part sorry. It is good
To find that you yourself have gotten clear,
But to bring trouble on your friends is hard.
However, nothing counts except my safety.
CREON [*to* ANTIGONE]. You there. You, looking at the ground. Tell me.
Do you admit this or deny it? Which?   400
ANTIGONE. Yes, I admit it. I do not deny it.
CREON [*to* GUARD]. Go. You are free. The charge is dropped.

[*Exit* GUARD]

Now you,

Answer this question. Make your answer brief.
You knew there was a law forbidding this?
ANTIGONE. Of course I knew it. Why not? It was public.
CREON. And you have dared to disobey the law?
ANTIGONE. Yes. For this law[15] was not proclaimed by Zeus,
Or by the gods who rule the world below.
I do not think your edicts have such power
That they can override the laws of heaven,   410
Unwritten and unfailing, laws whose life
Belongs not to today or yesterday
But to time everlasting; and no man
Knows the first moment that they had their being.
If I transgressed these laws because I feared
The arrogance of man, how to the gods
Could I make satisfaction? Well I know,
Being a mortal, that I have to die,
Even without your proclamations. Yet
If I must die before my time is come,   420
That is a blessing. Because to one who lives,
As I live, in the midst of sorrows, death
Is of necessity desirable.
For me, to face death is a trifling pain
That does not trouble me. But to have left
The body of my brother, my own brother,
Lying unburied would be bitter grief.
And if these acts of mine seem foolish to you,
Perhaps a fool accuses me of folly.

[14] Ritual pourings of liquids.
[15] In the following lines Antigone states her creed; compare Creon's maxim in lines 154–156. Both antagonists can cite religious or political principles. A major question in the play is whether Antigone and Creon are actually governed by these large principles or by more personal motives (good or bad).

CHORUS. The violent daughter of a violent father,   430
    She cannot bend before a storm of evils.
CREON [*to* ANTIGONE]. Stubborn? Self-willed? People like that, I tell
      you,
    Are the first to come to grief. The hardest iron,
    Baked in the fire, most quickly flies to pieces.
    An unruly horse is taught obedience
    By a touch of the curb. How can you be so proud?
    You, a mere slave?[16] [*to* CHORUS] She was well schooled already
    In insolence, when she defied the law.
    And now look at her! Boasting, insolent,
    Exulting in what she did. And if she triumphs   440
    And goes unpunished, I am no man—she is.
    If she were more than niece, if she were closer
    Than anyone who worships at my altar,
    She would not even then escape her doom,
    A dreadful death. Nor would her sister. Yes,
    Her sister had a share in burying him.
    [*to* ATTENDANT] Go bring her here. I have just seen her, raving,
    Beside herself. Even before they act,
    Traitors who plot their treason in the dark
    Betray themselves like that. Detestable!   450
    [*to* ANTIGONE] But hateful also is an evil-doer
    Who, caught red-handed, glorifies the crime.
ANTIGONE. Now you have caught me, will you do more than kill me?
CREON. No, only that. With that I am satisfied.
ANTIGONE. Then why do you delay? You have said nothing
    I do not hate. I pray you never will.
    And you hate what I say. Yet how could I
    Have won more splendid honor than by giving
    Due burial to my brother? All men here
    Would grant me their approval, if their lips   460
    Were not sealed up in fear. But you, a king,
    Blessed by good fortune in much else besides,
    Can speak and act with perfect liberty.
CREON. All of these Thebans disagree with you.
ANTIGONE. No. They agree, but they control their tongues.
CREON. You feel no shame in acting without their help?
ANTIGONE. I feel no shame in honoring a brother.
CREON. Another brother died who fought against him.
ANTIGONE. Two brothers. The two sons of the same parents.
CREON. Honor to one is outrage to the other.   470
ANTIGONE. Eteocles will not feel himself dishonored.
CREON. What! When his rites are offered to a traitor?
ANTIGONE. It was his brother, not his slave, who died.
CREON. One who attacked the land that he defended.
ANTIGONE. The gods still wish those rites to be performed.

---

[16] This is arrogantly false; Antigone is not in fact a slave.

CREON. Are the just pleased with the unjust as their equals?
ANTIGONE. That may be virtuous in the world below.
CREON. No. Even there a foe is never a friend.
ANTIGONE. I am not made for hatred but for love.
CREON. Then go down to the dead. If you must love,   480
    Love them. While I yet live, no woman rules me.
CHORUS. Look there. Ismene, weeping as sisters weep.
    The shadow of a cloud of grief lies deep
    On her face, darkly flushed; and in her pain
    Her tears are falling like a flood of rain.

[*Enter* ISMENE *and* ATTENDANTS]

CREON. You viper! Lying hidden in my house,
    Sucking my blood in secret, while I reared,
    Unknowingly, two subverters of my throne.
    Do you confess that you have taken part
    In this man's burial, or deny it? Speak.   490
ISMENE. If she will recognize my right to say so,
    I shared the action and I share the blame.
ANTIGONE. No. That would not be just. I never let you
    Take any part in what you disapproved of.
ISMENE. In your calamity, I am not ashamed
    To stand beside you, beaten by this tempest.
ANTIGONE. The dead are witnesses of what I did,
    To love in words alone is not enough.
ISMENE. Do not reject me, Sister! Let me die
    Beside you, and do honor to the dead.   500
ANTIGONE. No. You will neither share my death nor claim
    What I have done. My death will be sufficient.
ISMENE. What happiness can I have when you are gone?
ANTIGONE. Ask Creon that. He is the one you value.
ISMENE. Do you gain anything by taunting me?
ANTIGONE. Ah, no! By taunting you, I hurt myself.
ISMENE. How can I help you? Tell me what I can do.
ANTIGONE. Protect yourself. I do not grudge your safety.
ISMENE. Antigone! Shall I not share your fate?
ANTIGONE. We both have made our choices: life, and death.   510
ISMENE. At least I tried to stop you. I protested.
ANTIGONE. Some have approved your way; and others, mine.
ISMENE. Yet now I share your guilt. I too am ruined.
ANTIGONE. Take courage. Live your life. But I long since
    Gave myself up to death to help the dead.
CREON. One of them has just lost her senses now.
    The other has been foolish all her life.
ISMENE. We cannot always use our reason clearly.
    Suffering confuses us and clouds our minds.
CREON. It clouds your mind. You join in her wrong-doing.   520
ISMENE. How is life possible without my sister?
CREON. Your sister? You have no sister. She is dead.

ISMENE. Then you will kill the wife your son has chosen?
CREON. Yes. There are other fields that he can plow.
ISMENE. He will not find such an enduring love.
CREON. A wicked woman for my son? No, never!
ANTIGONE. O Haemon, Haemon! How your father wrongs you![17]
CREON. You and your marriage! Let me hear no more!
CHORUS. You are unyielding? You will take her from him?
CREON. Death will act for me. Death will stop the marriage.   530
CHORUS. It seems, then, you have sentenced her to death.
CREON. Yes. And my sentence you yourselves accepted.
    Take them inside. From now on, they are women,
    And have no liberty. For even the bold
    Seek an escape when they see death approaching.

                         [*Exeunt* ANTIGONE, ISMENE, *and*
                         ATTENDANTS]

CHORUS.
    Blesséd the life that has no evil known,
For the gods, striking, strike down a whole race—
    Doomed parent and doomed child both overthrown.
As when the fierce breath of the winds of Thrace
    Across the darkness of the sea has blown   540
A rushing surge; black sand from deep below
    Comes boiling up; wind-beaten headlands moan,
Fronting the full shock of the billow's blow.

    The race of Oedipus, from days of old,
To long dead sorrows add new sorrows' weight.[18]
    Some god has sent them sufferings manifold.
None may release another, for their fate
    Through generations loosens not its hold.
Now is their last root cut, their last light fled,
    Because of frenzy's curse, words overbold,   550
And dust, the gods' due, on the bloodstained dead.

    O Zeus, what human sin restricts thy might?
Thou art unsnared by all-ensnaring sleep
    Or tireless months. Unaging thou dost keep
Thy court in splendor of Olympian light.
    And as this law was true when time began,
Tomorrow and forever it shall be:
    Naught beyond measure in the life of man
        From fate goes free.

---

[17] In some versions, this line is given to Ismene.
[18] The sorrows of the family extend farther into the past than to Oedipus' acts of patricide and incest; for example, his father Laius had been cursed by Pelops (the ancestor of the cursed family treated in Aeschylus' Orestes trilogy) after Laius had wronged Pelops, his protector during a period of exile, by stealing his son.

For hope, wide-ranging, that brings good to some,   560
To many is a false lure of desire
     Light-minded, giddy; and until the fire
Scorches their feet, they know not what will come.
     Wise is the famous adage: that to one
Whom the gods madden, evil, soon or late,
     Seems good; then can he but a moment shun
          The stroke of fate.

     But Haemon comes, of your two sons the last.[19]
Is his heart heavy for the sentence passed
     Upon Antigone, his promised bride,   570
And for his hope of marriage now denied?

                        [*Enter* HAEMON]

CREON. We soon shall know better than seers could tell us.
     My son, Antigone is condemned to death.
     Nothing can change my sentence. Have you learned
     Her fate and come here in a storm of anger,
     Or do you love me and support my acts?
HAEMON. Father, I am your son. Your greater knowledge
     Will trace the pathway that I mean to follow.
     My marriage cannot be of more importance
     Than to be guided always by your wisdom.   580
CREON. Yes, Haemon, this should be the law you live by!
     In all things to obey your father's will.
     Men pray for children round them in their homes
     Only to see them dutiful and quick
     With hatred to requite their father's foe,
     With honor to repay their father's friend.
     But what is there to say of one whose children
     Prove to be valueless? That he has fathered
     Grief for himself and laughter for his foes.
     Then, Haemon, do not, at the lure of pleasure,   590
     Unseat your reason for a woman's sake.
     This comfort soon grows cold in your embrace:
     A wicked wife to share your bed and home.
     Is there a deeper wound than to find worthless
     The one you love? Turn from this girl with loathing,
     As from an enemy, and let her go
     To get a husband in the world below.
     For I have found her openly rebellious,
     Her only out of all the city. Therefore,
     I will not break the oath that I have sworn.   600
     I will have her killed. Vainly she will invoke
     The bond of kindred blood the gods make sacred.

---

[19] According to one version of the Thebes saga, Haemon's brother Megareus had committed suicide in order to propitiate the war-god Ares and thus save Thebes.

If I permit disloyalty to breed
In my own house, I nurture it in strangers.
He who is righteous with his kin is righteous
In the state also. Therefore, I cannot pardon
One who does violence to the laws or thinks
To dictate to his rulers; for whoever
May be the man appointed by the city,
That man must be obeyed in everything,   610
Little or great, just or unjust. And surely
He who was thus obedient would be found
As good a ruler as he was a subject;
And in a storm of spears he would stand fast
With loyal courage at his comrade's side.
But disobedience is the worst of evils.
For it is this that ruins cities; this
Makes our homes desolate; armies of allies
Through this break up in rout. But most men find
Their happiness and safety in obedience.   620
Therefore we must support the law, and never
Be beaten by a woman. It is better
To fall by a man's hand, if we must fall,
Than to be known as weaker than a girl.

CHORUS. We may in our old age have lost our judgment,
    And yet to us you seem to have spoken wisely.

HAEMON. The gods have given men the gift of reason,
    Greatest of all things that we call our own.
    I have no skill, nor do I wish to have it,
    To show where you have spoken wrongly. Yet   630
    Some other's thought, beside your own, might prove
    To be of value. Therefore it is my duty,
    My natural duty as your son, to notice,
    On your behalf, all that men say, or do,
    Or find to blame. For your frown frightens them,
    So that the citizen dares not say a word
    That would offend you. I can hear, however,
    Murmurs in darkness and laments for her.
    They say: 'No woman ever less deserved
    Her doom, no woman ever was to die   640
    So shamefully for deeds so glorious.
    For when her brother fell in bloody battle,
    She would not let his body lie unburied
    To be devoured by carrion dogs or birds.
    Does such a woman not deserve reward,
    Reward of golden honor?' This I hear,
    A rumor spread in secrecy and darkness.
    Father, I prize nothing in life so highly
    As your well-being. How can children have
    A nobler honor than their father's fame   650
    Or father than his son's? Then do not think
    Your mood must never alter; do not feel

Your word, and yours alone, must be correct.
For if a man believes that he is right
And only he, that no one equals him
In what he says or thinks, he will be found
Empty when searched and tested. Because a man
Even if he be wise, feels no disgrace
In learning many things, in taking care
Not to be over-rigid. You have seen   660
Trees on the margin of a stream in winter:
Those yielding to the flood save every twig,
And those resisting perish root and branch.
So, too, the mariner who never slackens
His taut sheet overturns his craft and spends
Keel uppermost the last part of his voyage.
Let your resentment die. Let yourself change.
For I believe—if I, a younger man,
May have a sound opinion—it is best
That men by nature should be wise in all things.   670
But most men find they cannot reach that goal;
And when this happens, it is also good
To learn to listen to wise counselors.
CHORUS. Sir, when his words are timely, you should heed them.
  And Haemon, you should profit by his words.
  Each one of you has spoken reasonably.
CREON. Are men as old as I am to be taught
  How to behave by men as young as he?
HAEMON. Not to do wrong. If I am young, ignore
  My youth. Consider only what I do.   680
CREON. Have you done well in honoring the rebellious?
HAEMON. Those who do wrong should not command respect.
CREON. Then that disease has not infected her?
HAEMON. All of our city with one voice denies it.
CREON. Does Thebes give orders for the way I rule?
HAEMON. How young you are! How young in saying that!
CREON. Am I to govern by another's judgment?
HAEMON. A city that is one man's is no city.
CREON. A city is the king's. That much is sure.
HAEMON. You would rule well in a deserted country.   690
CREON. This boy defends a woman, it appears.
HAEMON. If you are one. I am concerned for you.
CREON. To quarrel with your father does not shame you?
HAEMON. Not when I see you failing to do justice.
CREON. Am I unjust when I respect my crown?
HAEMON. Respect it! When you trample down religion?
CREON. Infamous! Giving first place to a woman!
HAEMON. But never to anything that would disgrace me.
CREON. Each word you utter is a plea for her.
HAEMON. For you, too, and for me, and for the gods.   700
CREON. You shall not marry her this side of death.
HAEMON. Then if she dies, she does not die alone.

CREON. What! Has it come to this? You threaten me?
HAEMON. No. But I tell you your decree is useless.
CREON. You will repent this. You! Teaching me wisdom!
HAEMON. I will not call you mad. You are my father.
CREON. You woman's slave! Your talk will not persuade me.
HAEMON. Then what you want is to make all the speeches.
CREON. So. Now by all the gods in heaven above us,
   One thing is certain: you are going to pay   710
   For taunting and insulting me. [*to* ATTENDANTS] Bring out
   That hated object. Let her die this moment,
   Here, at her bridegroom's feet, before his eyes.
HAEMON. No, you are wrong. Not at my feet. And never
   Will you set eyes upon my face again.
   Rage, rave, with anyone who can bear to listen.

[*Exit* HAEMON]

CHORUS. Sir, he is gone; his anger gives him speed.
   Young men are bitter in their agony.
CREON. Let him imagine more than man can do,
   Or let him do more. Never shall he save   720
   These two girls; they are going to their doom.
CHORUS. Do you intend to put them both to death?
CREON. That was well said. No, not the innocent.
CHORUS. And the other? In what way is she to die?
CREON. Along a desolate pathway I will lead her,
   And shut her, living, in a rocky vault
   With no more food than will appease the gods,[20]
   So that the city may not be defiled.
   Hades,[21] who is the only god she worships,
   May hear her prayers, and rescue her from death.   730
   Otherwise she will learn at last, though late,
   That to revere the dead is useless toil.

[*Exit* CREON]

CHORUS.
   None may withstand you, O love unconquered,
      Seizing the wealth of man as your prey,
   In the cheek of a maiden keeping your vigil,
      Till night has faded again to day.
   You roam the wilds to men's farthest dwellings,
      You haunt the boundless face of the sea.
   No god may escape you, no short-lived mortal
      From the madness that love inflicts may flee.   740

[20] This method of execution is inconsistent with the earlier passage that decrees death by stoning (lines 26–36). Creon apparently believes, legalistically, that he can avoid the crime of shedding kindred blood by merely shutting Antigone up alone and by providing her with food. Technically no act of execution will have been committed.

[21] King of the realm of the dead. The name can also mean the realm itself.

You twist our minds until ruin follows.
    The just to unrighteous ways you turn.
You have goaded kinsman to strive with kinsman
    Till the fires of bitter hatred burn.
In the eyes of a bride you shine triumphant;
    Beside the eternal laws your throne
Eternal stands, for great Aphrodite,[22]
    Resistless, works her will on her own.

But now I too am moved. I cannot keep
    Within the bounds of loyalty. I weep   750
When I behold Antigone, the bride,
    Nearing the room where all at last abide.

              [*Enter* ANTIGONE, *guarded*]

ANTIGONE.
    See me, my countrymen! See with what pain
I tread the path I shall not tread again,
Looking my last upon the light of day
    That shines for me no more.
Hades, who gives his sleep to all, me, living, leads away
    To Acheron's[23] dark shore.
Not mine the hymeneal chant, not mine the bridal song,
    For I, a bride, to Acheron belong.   760
CHORUS.
    Glorious, therefore, and with praise you tread
The pathway to the deep gulf of the dead.
You have not felt the force of fate's decrees,
Struck down by violence, wasted by disease;
But of your own free will you choose to go,
Alone of mortals, to the world below.
ANTIGONE.
    I know how sad a death she suffered, she
Who was our guest here, Phrygian Niobe.[24]
Stone spread upon her, close as ivy grows,
    And locked her in its chains.   770
Now on her wasted form, men say, fall ceaselessly the snows,
    Fall ceaselessly the rains;
While from her grieving eyes drop tears, tears that her bosom
      steep.
    And like hers, my fate lulls me now to sleep.

---

[22] Goddess of love.   [23] A river in the land of the dead.
[24] Niobe, originally from Phrygia in Asia Minor, was the wife of Amphion, a former ruler of Thebes. Mother of fourteen children, she boasted of her superiority to the goddess Leto, who had only two, Apollo and Artemis. In revenge for her impiety, all Niobe's children were killed and she herself was turned into a stone from which flowed a perpetual stream of her tears. There is an irony: Niobe was punished for flouting the gods, while Antigone is being killed for her piety.

CHORUS.
> She was a goddess[25] of the gods' great race;
> Mortals are we and mortal lineage trace.
> But for a woman the renown is great
> In life and death to share a godlike fate.

ANTIGONE.
> By our fathers' gods, I am mocked! I am mocked![26] Ah! why,   780
> You men of wealth, do you taunt me before I die?
> O sacred grove of the city! O waters that flow
> From the spring of Dircé! Be witness; to you I cry.
> What manner of woman I am you know
> And by what laws, unloved, unlamented, I go
> To my rocky prison, to my unnatural tomb.
> Alas, how ill-bestead!
> No fellowship have I; no others can share my doom,
> Neither mortals nor corpses, neither the quick[27] nor the dead.

CHORUS.
> You have rushed forward with audacious feet   790
> And dashed yourself against the law's high seat.
> That was a grevious fall, my child, and yet
> In this ordeal you pay your father's debt.

ANTIGONE.
> You have touched on the heaviest grief that my heart can hold:
> Grief for my father, sorrow that never grows old
> For our famous house and its doom that the fates have spun.
> My mother's bed! Ah! How can its horrors be told?
> My mother who yielded her love to one
> Who was at once my father and her son.
> Born of such parents, with them henceforth I abide,   800
> Wretched, accursed, unwed.
> And you, Polyneices, you found an ill-fated bride,[28]
> And I, the living, am ruined by you, the dead.

CHORUS.
> A pious action may of praise be sure,
> But he who rules a land cannot endure
> An act of disobedience to his rule.
> Your own self-will you have not learned to school.

ANTIGONE.
> Unwept, unfriended, without marriage song,
> Forth on my road I miserable am led;
> I may not linger. Not for long   810
> Shall I, most wretched, see the holy sun.

---

[25] Niobe was daughter of Tantalus, whose father was Zeus.

[26] Antigone's protest probably reflects her bitter reaction to the elders' implication that she is lucky (in sharing the fate of the famed Niobe).

[27] The living.

[28] Polyneices, as part of his plan to enlist the aid of Argos in attacking Thebes, married a daughter of the Argive king. The war, and Polyneices' death, have brought death to Antigone too.

My fate no friend bewails, not one;
    For me no tear is shed.

[*Enter* CREON]

CREON. Do you not know that singing and lamentation
    Would rise incessantly as death approached,
    If they could be of service? Lead her away!
    Obey my orders. Shut her in her grave
    And leave her there, alone. Then she can take
    Her choice of living in that home, or dying.
    I am not stained by the guilt of this girl's blood,   820
    But she shall see the light of day no longer.
ANTIGONE. O tomb! O cavern! Everlasting prison!
    O bridal-chamber! To you I make my way
    To join my kindred, all those who have died
    And have been greeted by Persephone.[29]
    The last and far most miserable of all,
    I seek them now, before I have lived my life.
    Yet high are the hopes I cherish that my coming
    Will be most welcome to my father; welcome,
    Mother, to you; and welcome to you, Brother.   830
    For when you died I ministered to you all,
    With my own hands washed you and dressed your bodies,
    And poured libations at your graves. And now,
    Because I have given to you, too, Polyneices,
    Such honors as I could, I am brought to this.
    And yet all wise men will approve my act.
    Not for my children, had I been a mother,
    Not for a husband, for his moldering body,
    Would I have set myself against the city
    As I have done. And the law sanctions me.   840
    Losing a husband, I might find another.
    I could have other children. But my parents
    Are hidden from me in the underworld,
    So that no brother's life can bud and bloom
    Ever again.[30] And therefore, Polyneices,
    I paid you special honor. And for this
    Creon has held me guilty of evil-doing,
    And leads me captive for my too great boldness.
    No bridal bed is mine, no bridal song,
    No share in the joys of marriage, and no share   850
    In nursing children and in tending them.

---

[29] Consort of Hades, king of the dead.

[30] For various reasons, including the opinion that Antigone's fine distinctions and perhaps insensitivity here are inconsistent with the rest of the play, some editors and translators reject lines 836–844. The appropriateness of the passage has been defended, on grounds of dramatic psychology (for example, the marital and maternal roles must be merely imagined by Antigone, while her role of sister is one she has experienced) and more technical grounds (for example, the notion that the sibling-bond is closer than either the marital one which involves no blood-kinship or the "half-interest" bond of blood-kinship that links a child with one of its two parents).

But thus afflicted, destitute of friends,
Living, I go down to the vaults of death.
What is the law of heaven that I have broken?
Why should I any longer look to the gods,
Ill-fated as I am? Whose aid should I invoke,
When I for piety am called impious?
If this pleases the gods, then I shall learn
That sin brought death upon me. But if the sin
Lies in my judges, I could wish for them 860
No harsher fate than they have decreed for me.
CHORUS. Still the storm rages; still the same gusts blow,
Troubling her spirit with their savage breath.
CREON. Yes. And her guards will pay for being slow.
ANTIGONE. Ah! With those words I have drawn close to death.
CREON. You cannot hope that you will now be freed
From the fulfillment of the doom decreed.
ANTIGONE.
O Thebes, O land of my fathers, O city!
O gods who begot and guarded my house from of old![31]
They seize me, they snatch me away! 870
Now, now! They show no pity.
They give no second's delay.
You elders, you leaders of Thebes, behold me, behold!
The last of the house of your kings, the last.
See what I suffer. See the doom
That is come upon me, and see from whom,
Because to the laws of heaven I held fast.

[*Exeunt* ANTIGONE *and* GUARDS]

CHORUS.
This likewise Danaë[32] endured:
The light of heaven she changed for a home brass-bound,
In a tomb-like chamber close immured. 880
And yet, O my child, her race was with honor crowned.
And she guarded the seed of Zeus gold-showered.
But naught from the terrible power of fate is free:
Neither war, nor city walls high-towered,
Nor wealth, nor black ships beaten by the sea.

He too bowed down beneath his doom,
The son of Dryas,[33] swift-angered Edonian king,
Shut fast in a rocky prison's gloom.

[31] According to the myths, several of Antigone's forebears in the Theban dynasty were related to the gods, by blood or marriage.

[32] Danaë's father Acrisius, a king of Argos, had imprisoned her because of a prophecy that she would bear a son who would kill him. Zeus came to her in a shower of golden rain, begetting Perseus, who did later kill Acrisius.

[33] Lycurgus, a legendary Thracian king. He had been imprisoned after being driven to madness by the gods for opposing the worship of Bacchus (Dionysus). Maenads (line 890) were orgiastic female worshipers of the god.

How he roused the god with his mad tongue's mocking sting,
    As his frenzy faded, he came to know;   890
For he sought to make the god-filled maenads mute,
    To quench the Bacchic torches' glow,
And angered the Muses, lovers of the flute.

By the double sea[34] and the dark rocks steely blue
    The beach of Bosporus lies and the savage shore
Of Thracian Salmydessus. There the bride
    Of Phineus, whose fierce heart no mercy knew,
Dealt his two sons a blow that for vengeance cried;
    Ares beheld her hand, all stained with gore,
Grasping the pointed shuttle that pierced through   900
    Their eyes that saw no more.

In misery pining, their lot they lamented aloud,
    Sons of a mother whose fortune in marriage was ill.
From the ancient line of Erechtheus[35] her blood she traced;
    Nurtured in caves far-distant and nursed in cloud,
Daughter of Boreas, daughter of gods, she raced
    Swift as a steed on the slope of the soaring hill.
And yet, O child, O child, she also bowed
    To the long-lived fates' harsh will.

[*Enter* TIRESIAS *and* BOY]

TIRESIAS. Elders of Thebes, we have come to you with one   910
    Finding for both the pathway that we followed,
    For in this fashion must the blind be guided.
CREON. What tidings, old Tiresias, are you bringing?
TIRESIAS. I will inform you, I the seer. Give heed.
CREON. To ignore your counsel has not been my custom.
TIRESIAS. Therefore you kept Thebes on a steady course.
CREON. I can bear witness to the help you gave.
TIRESIAS. Mark this. You stand upon the brink of ruin.
CREON. What terrible words are those? What do you mean?
TIRESIAS. My meaning is made manifest by my art   920
    And my art's omens. As I took my station
    Upon my ancient seat of augury,
    Where round me birds of every sort come flocking,
    I could no longer understand their language.
    It was drowned out in a strange, savage clamor,
    Shrill, evil, frenzied, inarticulate.
    The whirr of wings told me their murderous talons

---

[34] The following lines allude to a third story of imprisonment; most interpreters have found the story itself and its application to Antigone obscure. Phineus, a king of Thrace, divorced his wife Cleopatra (daughter of Boreas, the north wind), who had borne him two sons, and cast her into prison; his second wife blinded the two children and entombed them.

[35] A legendary Athenian king, grandfather of Cleopatra.

Tore at each other. Filled with dread, I then
Made trial of burnt sacrifice. The altar
Was fully kindled, but no clear, bright flame 930
Leaped from the offering; only fatty moisture
Oozed from the flesh and trickled on the embers,
Smoking and sputtering. The bladder burst,
And scattered in the air. The folds of fat
Wrapping the thigh-bones melted and left them bare.
Such was the failure of the sacrifice,
That did not yield the sign that I was seeking.
I learned these things from this boy's observation;
He is my guide as I am guide to others.
Your edict brings this suffering to the city, 940
For every hearth of ours has been defiled
And every altar. There the birds and dogs
Have brought their carrion, torn from the corpse
Of ill-starred Polyneices. Hence, the gods
Refuse our prayers, refuse our sacrifice,
Refuse the flame of our burnt-offerings.
No birds cry clearly and auspiciously,
For they are glutted with a slain man's blood.
Therefore, my son, consider what has happened.
All men are liable to grievous error; 950
But he who, having erred, does not remain
Inflexible, but rather makes amends
For ill, is not unwise or unrewarded.
Stubborn self-will incurs the charge of folly.
Give to the fallen the honors he deserves
And do not stab him. Are you being brave
When you inflict new death upon the dead?
Your good I think of; for your good I speak,
And a wise counselor is sweet to hear
When the advice he offers proves of value. 960
CREON. Old man, all of you shoot your arrows at me
Like archers at a target. You have used
Even the art of prophecy in your plotting.
Long have the tribe of prophets traded in me,[36]
Like a ship's cargo. Drive whatever bargain
May please you, buy, sell, heap up for yourself
Silver of Sardis, gold of India. Yet
I tell you this: that man shall not be buried,
Not though the eagles of Zeus himself should bear
The carrion morsels to their master's throne. 970
Not even from the dread of such pollution
Will I permit his burial, since I know
There is no mortal can defile the gods.

---

[36] Ironically, Oedipus (in *Oedipus the King*) had accused Tiresias and Creon himself of a similar, and equally imaginary, mercenary plot.

But even the wisest men disastrously
May fall, Tiresias, when for money's sake
They utter shameful words with specious wisdom.
TIRESIAS. Ah! Do men understand, or even consider—
CREON. Consider what? Doubtless some platitude!
TIRESIAS. How precious beyond any wealth is prudence.
CREON. How full of evil is the lack of prudence.   980
TIRESIAS. Yet you are sick, sick with that same disease.
CREON. I will not in reply revile a prophet.
TIRESIAS. You do. You say my prophecy is false.
CREON. Well, all the race of seers are mercenary.
TIRESIAS. And love of base wealth marks the breed of tyrants.
CREON. Are you aware that you address your King?
TIRESIAS. I made you King by helping you save Thebes.
CREON. Wise in your art and vicious in your acts.
TIRESIAS. Do not enrage me. I should keep my secret.
CREON. Reveal it. Speak. But do not look for profit.   990
TIRESIAS. You too will find no profit in my words.
CREON. How can you earn your pay? I will not change.
TIRESIAS. Then know this. Yes, be very sure of it.
    Only a few more times will you behold
    The swift course of the chariot of the sun
    Before you give as payment for the dead
    Your own dead flesh and blood. For you have thrust
    A living soul to darkness, in a tomb
    Imprisoned without pity. And a corpse,
    Belonging to the gods below you keep   1000
    Unpurified, unburied, unrevered.
    The dead are no concern either of yours
    Or of the gods above, yet you offend them.
    So the avengers, the destroyers, Furies[37]
    Of Hades and the gods, lurking in ambush,
    Wait to inflict your sins upon your head.
    Do you still think my tongue is lined with silver?
    A time will come, and will not linger coming,
    That will awaken in your house the wailing
    Of men and women. Hatred shakes the cities,[38]   1010
    Hatred of you. Their sons are mangled corpses,
    Hallowed with funeral rites by dogs or beasts
    Or birds who bear the all-polluting stench
    To every city having hearth or altar.
    You goaded me, and therefore like an archer
    I shoot my angry arrows at your heart,
    Sure arrows; you shall not escape their sting.
    Boy, lead me home. Let him expend his rage
    On younger men, and let him learn to speak

[37] Primitive personifications of vengeance, especially for crimes against kindred.
[38] The cities that organized the army to attack Thebes.

With a more temperate tongue, and school his heart   1020
To feelings finer than his present mood.

[*Exeunt* TIRESIAS *and* BOY]

CHORUS. Sir, he is gone, with fearful prophecies.
  And from the time that these dark hairs have whitened,
  I have known this: never has he foretold
  Anything that proved false concerning Thebes.
CREON. I also know it well, and it dismays me.
  To yield is bitter. But to resist, and bring
  A curse upon my pride is no less bitter.
CHORUS. Son of Menoeceus, listen. You must listen.
CREON. What should I do? Tell me, I will obey.   1030
CHORUS. Go. Free the girl. Release her from the cavern,
  And build a tomb for the man you would not bury.
CREON. So that is your advice—that I should yield?
CHORUS. Sir, you should not delay. The gods are swift
  In cutting short man's folly with their curse.
CREON. How hard it is to change! Yet I obey.
  I will give up what I had set my heart on.
  No one can stand against the blows of fate.
CHORUS. Go. Go yourself. These things are not for others.
CREON. I will go this moment. Guards there! All of you!   1040
  Take up your axes. Quick! Quick! Over there.
  I imprisoned her myself, and I myself
  Will set her free. And yet my mind misgives me.
  Never to break the ancient law is best.

[*Exit* CREON]

CHORUS.
        Thou[39] art known by many a name.
    O Bacchus! To thee we call.
    Cadmean Semele's glory and pride,
  Begotten of Zeus, whose terrible lightnings flame,
        Whose thunders appall.
  Bacchus, thou dost for us all in thy love provide.   1050
    Over Icaría thou dost reign,
    And where the worshippers journey slow
    To the rites of Eleusis,[40] where mountains shield
  The multitudes crossing Demeter's welcoming plain.
    Thou makest this mother-city of maenads thine own,
      A city beside the rippling flow
  Of the gentle river, beside the murderous field
    Where the teeth of the dragon were sown.

---

[39] The Chorus invokes Bacchus as the patron deity of Thebes.
[40] Icaria is an island in the Aegean Sea; Eleusis, a town near Athens, was the center of the mysterious fertility rites of Demeter, goddess of the fields and harvest.

In the torches' wind-blown flare
Thou art seen, in their flicker and smoke.   1060
Where the two-fold peaks of Parnassus[41] gleam,
Corycian nymphs, as they move through the ruddy glare,
Thee, Bacchus, invoke.
They move in their dance beside the Castalian stream.[42]
O Bacchus, guardian divine!
Down from the slopes of Nysa's[43] hills
Where a mantle of ivy covers the ground,
From headlands rich with the purple grape and the vine,
Thou comest to us, thou comest. O be not long!
Thy triumph the echoing city fills.   1070
The streets are loud with thy praises; the highways resound,
Resound with immortal song.

Thou honorest highly our Theban city,
Thou, and thy mother by lightning slain.
Our people sicken. O Bacchus have pity!
Across the strait with its moaning wave,
Down from Parnassus, come thou again!
Come with thy healing feet, and save!

O thou who leadest the stars in chorus,
Jubilant stars with their breath of fire,   1080
Offspring of Zeus, appear before us!
Lord of the tumult of night, appear!
With the frenzied dance of thy maenad choir,
Bacchus, thou giver of good, draw near!

[*Enter* MESSENGER]

MESSENGER. You of the house of Cadmus and Amphíon,[44]
No man's estate can ever be established
Firmly enough to warrant praise or blame.
Fortune, from day to day, exalts the lucky
And humbles the unlucky. No one knows
Whether his present lot can long endure.   1090
For Creon once was blest, as I count blessings;
He had saved this land of Cadmus from its foes;
He was the sovereign and ruled alone,
The noble father of a royal house.
And now, all has been lost. Because a man
Who has forfeited his joy is not alive,

---

[41] A mountain near Apollo's shrine at Delphi; one of the peaks was sacred to Apollo, one to Bacchus (Dionysus). The Corycian cave, sacred to the god Pan and the Nymphs, was located on the mountain.

[42] A spring and pool on Mount Parnassus.

[43] A mountain where Bacchus had been reared by nymphs.

[44] Amphíon was a former ruler of Thebes; he had helped build the city's walls by his harp-music, which was so powerful that even stones were moved by it.

He is a living corpse. Heap, if you will,
Your house with riches; live in regal pomp.
Yet if your life is unhappy, all these things
Are worth not even the shadow of a vapor   1100
Put in the balance against joy alone.
CHORUS. What new disaster has the King's house suffered?
MESSENGER. Death. And the guilt of death lies on the living.
CHORUS. The guilt of death! Who has been killed? Who killed him?
MESSENGER. Haemon is killed, and by no stranger's hand.
CHORUS. He killed himself? Or did his father kill him?
MESSENGER. He killed himself, enraged by his murderous father.
CHORUS. Tiresias! Now your prophecy is fulfilled.
MESSENGER. Consider, therefore, what remains to do.
CHORUS. There is the Queen, wretched Eurydice.   1110
    Perhaps mere chance has brought her from the palace;
    Perhaps she has learned the news about her son.

[*Enter* EURYDICE]

EURYDICE. Thebans, I heard you talking here together
When I was on my way to greet the goddess,
Pallas Athene, and to pray to her.
Just as I loosed the fastening of the door,
The words that told of my calamity
Struck heavily upon my ear. In terror
I fell back fainting in my women's arms.
But now, repeat your story. I shall hear it   1120
As one who is not ignorant of grief.
MESSENGER. My Lady, I will bear witness to what I saw,
And will omit no syllable of the truth.
Why should I comfort you with words that later
Would prove deceitful? Truth is always best.
Across the plain I guided my Lord Creon
To where unpitied Polyneices lay,
A corpse mangled by dogs. Then we besought
Hecate, goddess of the roads, and Pluto[45]
To moderate their wrath, and to show mercy.   1130
We washed the dead with ceremonial water.
Gathering the scattered fragments that remained,
With fresh-cut boughs we burned them. We heaped up
A mound of native earth above his ashes.
Then we approached the cavern of Death's bride,
The rock-floored marriage-chamber. While as yet
We were far distant, someone heard the sound
Of loud lament in that unhallowed place,
And came to tell our master. As the King
Drew near, there floated through the air a voice,   1140

---

[45] Hecate, associated with crossroads, was a goddess of night, magic, and the underworld;
Pluto is another name for Hades, god of the dead.

Faint, indistinct, that uttered a bitter cry.
The King burst out in anguish: 'Can it be
That I, in my misery, have become a prophet?
Will this be the saddest road I ever trod?
My son's voice greets me. Quickly, slaves! Go quickly!
When you have reached the sepulcher, get through
The opening where the stones are wrenched away,
Get to the mouth of the burial chamber. Look,
See if I know his voice—Haemon's, my son's—
Or if I am deluded by the gods.'   1150
We followed our despairing master's bidding
And in the farthest recess of the tomb
We found Antigone, hanging, with her veil
Noosed round her neck. And with her we found Haemon,
His arms flung round her waist, grieving aloud
For his bride lost in death, his ruined marriage,
His father's deeds. But when his father saw him,
Creon cried piteously and going in,
Called to him brokenly: 'My son, my son,
What have you done? What are you thinking of?   1160
What dreadful thing has driven you out of your mind?
Son, come away. I beg you. I beseech you.'
But Haemon glared at him with furious eyes
Instead of answering, spat in his face,
And drew his sword. His father turned to fly
So that he missed his aim. Immediately,
In bitter self-reproach, the wretched boy
Leaned hard against his sword, and drove it deep
Into his side. Then while his life yet lingered,
With failing strength he drew Antigone close;   1170
And as he lay there gasping heavily,
Over her white cheek his blood ebbed away.
The dead lie clasped together. He is wedded,
Not in this world but in the house of Death.
He has borne witness that of all the evils
Afflicting man, the worst is lack of wisdom.

                          [*Exit* EURYDICE]

CHORUS. What does that mean? Who can interpret it?
    The Queen has gone without a single word.
MESSENGER. It startles me. And yet I hope it means
    That hearing these dreadful things about her son,   1180
    She will not let herself show grief in public
    But will lament in private with her women.
    Schooled in discretion, she will do no wrong.
CHORUS. How can we tell? Surely too great a silence
    Is no less ominous than too loud lament.
MESSENGER. Then I will enter. Perhaps she is concealing

Some secret purpose in her passionate heart.
I will find out, for you are right in saying
Too great a silence may be ominous.

> [*Exit* MESSENGER. *Enter* CREON
> *with* ATTENDANTS, *carrying the
> body of* HAEMON *on a bier*]

CHORUS. Thebans, look there! The King himself draws near,   1190
    Bearing a load whose tale is all too clear.
    This is a work—if we dare speak our thought—
    That not another's but his own hands wrought.
CREON.
       O, how may my sin be told?
    The stubborn, death-fraught sin of a darkened brain!
       Behold us here, behold
    Father and son, the slayer and the slain!
       Pain, only pain
    Has come of my design.
       Fate struck too soon; too soon your spirit fled.   1200
       My son, my young son, you are lying dead
    Not for your folly, but for mine, for mine.
CHORUS. Sir, you have come to learn the right too late.
CREON.
    My lesson has been bitter and complete.
    Some god has struck me down with crushing weight,
    Filling my heart with cruelty and hate.
       Trampling my happiness beneath his feet.
       Grief, bitter grief, is man's fate.

> [*Enter* MESSENGER]

MESSENGER [*indicating* HAEMON].
    Your load is heavy, Sir, but there is more.
    That is the burden you are bearing now.   1210
    Soon you must bear new woe within your house.
CREON. And what worse misery can follow this?
MESSENGER. Your wife is dead, a mother like her son.
    Poor woman, by her own hand she has died.
CREON.
       By her own hand she died.
    Death, spare me! Can you never have your fill?
       Never be satisfied?
    Herald of evil, messenger of ill,
       Your harsh words kill,
    They smite me now anew.   1220
       My wife is dead—You tell me my wife is dead.
       Death after death is heaped upon my head.
    Speak to me, boy. Is what you tell me true?
MESSENGER. It is no longer hidden. Sir, look there.

[*The body of* EURYDICE *is disclosed
through the palace doors*]

CREON.
    Another horror that makes blind mine eyes!
What further agony has fate in store?
My dead son's body in my arms I bore,
    And now beside him his dead mother lies.
       I can endure no more.

MESSENGER. There at the altar with a keen-edged knife   1230
She stabbed herself; and as her eyes were darkened,
She wailed the death of Megareus,[46] her son,
Who earlier had met a noble fate;
She wailed for Haemon; then, with her last breath,
You, as the slayer of your sons, she cursed.

CREON.
    I am shaken with terror, with terror past belief.
Is there none here to end my anguish? None?
    No sword to pierce me? Broken with my grief,
So steeped in agony that we are one.

MESSENGER. Sir, as she died, she burdened you with guilt,   1240
Charging you with the death of both your sons.

CREON. And by what act of violence did she die?

MESSENGER. Hearing the shrill lament for Haemon's fate,
Deep in her heart she drove the bright blade home.

CREON [*to* HAEMON].
    I am your slayer, I alone.
I am guilty, only I.
    I, and none other, must atone.
Lead me away. The truth I own.
    Nothing is left, except to die.

CHORUS. If anything can be good, those words are good.   1250
For when calamity has come upon us,
The thing that is the briefest is the best.

CREON.
    Draw near me, death! O longed for death, draw near!
Most welcome destiny, make no delay.
    Tell me my last hour, my last breath, is here.
I have no wish to see another day.

CHORUS. Such things are yet to come. We are concerned
With doing what must needs be done today.
The future rests in other hands than ours.

CREON. That is my whole desire. That is my prayer.   1260

CHORUS. No. Do not pray. Men must accept their doom.

CREON.
    My life's work there before me lies.
My folly slew my wife, my son.
    I know not where to turn mine eyes.

---

[46] The other son of Creon and Eurydice; he had bravely committed suicide to save Thebes.

> All my misdeeds before me rise.
> Lead me away, brought low, undone.

[Exit CREON]

CHORUS.
> The crown of happiness is to be wise.
> Honor the gods, and the gods' edicts prize.
> They strike down boastful men and men grown bold.
> Wisdom we learn at last, when we are old.

Euripides
(C. 480–406 B.C.)

Aeschylus fought in the momentous Greek naval victory at Salamis in 480 B.C. The adolescent Sophocles helped to celebrate it publicly. Tradition has it that Euripides was born in Salamis on the very day of the battle. Even if, or especially if, the tradition is historically inaccurate (he may have been born a few years earlier), it symbolizes a desire by the ancients to link Euripides with his two mighty predecessors as the third definitive playwright of the greatest age of Greece.

Unlike Aeschylus and Sophocles, Euripides seems to have taken little active part in the official public life of Athens; he was not a social man by temperament. The size of his library indicates that he was extensively learned. From the year 455 on, he participated regularly in the dramatic contests held annually in Athens, but he won first prize less often than did Aeschylus or Sophocles, possibly because of the "irregularities" later alleged, by Aristotle and other critics, to exist in his work, or possibly because of his nonconformist attitude toward Greek religion and Athenian politics. His political dissidence intensified during the last two decades of his life as the tragic and misguided Peloponnesian war against Sparta and its allies moved inexorably toward a dismal conclusion. His play The Trojan Women, *for example (produced in 415), exposes the brutality of "heroic" conquerors and, indirectly, it shows Euripides' distaste for Athenian imperialism. He spent the last two years of his life in Macedonia, where he died in 406, slightly earlier than Sophocles, who conducted a scene of public mourning for him in the theater. After his death, Euripides' plays were immensely popular; of the ninety he wrote, eighteen have survived, as compared with seven apiece by Aeschylus and Sophocles. Among these is* The Cyclops, *the only extant specimen of the grotesque "satyr play" that in Athenian dramatic practice regularly followed the set of three tragedies performed earlier in the same day.*

The two works represented in this volume, Alcestis *(438) and* Medea *(431), are among the earliest surviving plays by Euripides. It is important to remember, however, that they are works not of a novice but rather of a veteran playwright who when he wrote them had been composing for the theater for two decades.*

Euripides' plays illustrate several new departures or emphases. The formal structure is looser than in Aeschylus or Sophocles, though some people prefer to call it freer. He made extensive use of the Prologue, as in the scene involving Apollo and

Death with which Alcestis *opens. He was also partial to the* deus ex machina *conclusion, wherein a deity intervenes to impose an arbitrary resolution. The endings of his plays are frequently ambiguous or disturbing, as in Medea's escape to Athens and the mysterious silence of the resurrected Alcestis, both of which incidents have provoked controversy among interpreters. In Euripides, the Chorus often sings magnificent lyrics, but they tend to be less integral to the dramatic action than in the plays of Aeschylus or Sophocles. Another recurrent device is the* agon, *a direct and usually hostile confrontation between two characters in which arguments or accusations are exchanged in rapid-fire fashion. Euripides also helped popularize the mode of drama we now call tragicomedy;* Alcestis *is a good example. To regard such innovations as regrettable departures from the kind of coherent unity Aristotle called for is unjust to Euripides, who created several powerful forms of drama best understood for what they are in themselves. Their value is not to be measured against arbitrary norms of what ancient drama should be.*

Some of these formal or anti-formal elements, but more especially the ideas implicit in his plays and their highly charged emotionalism, have earned Euripides a reputation as the most "romantic" of the three great tragedians. The alleged untidiness of his dramatic construction parallels and indeed emphasizes the central Euripidean theme of irrationality, in people and in the cosmos. His late play The Bacchae *is one of the most powerful expositions of that theme in literature; the play presents violent and erotic Dionysian forces in the human psyche as frightening but ignorable at one's peril. Throughout* Medea, *the heroine, like many other characters in Euripides, is overcome by passion (sometimes tender, more often violent in the extreme). As an exploration of human values, the play seems to many readers to present an almost maddening stalemate; it is equally impossible either to dismiss Medea's motives or to endorse them, not to mention her hair-raising acts.* Alcestis, *in which the heroine is the exact opposite of Medea, might seem an upbeat exception. But not necessarily. It is true that the play has a happy ending—according to most interpreters, at least—and the return of Alcestis from death touches on one of humanity's most pervasive wish-fulfillment fantasies, as anyone knows who has dreamed about the restoration to life of a dead loved one. But in the meantime the Chorus, in its awesome hymn to "Necessity," has uttered a definitive protest against the brute, obscene fact of death and the unfairness of the human lot in general. The miraculous return of Alcestis only underlines more powerfully the incontestable sovereignty of death; the exception proves the rule. Moreover, Alcestis herself—like her spouse Admetos before the play begins—has been granted only a reprieve; in the end death will have his way with her as he will with Admetos and other mortals.*

According to the Chorus in Aeschylus' Oresteia, *humanity suffers into truth. In Sophocles much the same thing is true, though the theology is less explicit; for example, in* Oedipus at Colonus *the unspeakable suffering endured by the blinded and exiled king is redeemed at his death, when he is mysteriously transfigured. In the last analysis, both these dramatists are optimists—though by no means facile ones. Euripides is more pessimistic. For him, an intellectual and a skeptic, whatever force governs the world—whether we call that force Fate, the divine will, Necessity, or by any other name—is amoral and entirely indifferent to humanity. As* Medea *shows, human acts of good and evil are thrown into a moral void. Certainly suffering has meaning for Euripides;* Alcestis, *for example, is concerned not only with the heroine's nobility but also with the humanization of her husband, whose exemption from the normal human share of misfortune has been a deficiency in his moral education. But, for Euripides, education through suffering is something humanity has to un-*

dergo alone, without much theological comfort. The world, for him, is both utterly
unpredictable and also utterly predictable, in the sense that its operation is affected by
neither piety nor virtue. Granted that it is dangerous to translate the values of an
ancient Athenian into modern terms, it still seems tempting, if not inevitable, to read
Euripides as a quintessentially modern man, for better or worse. His view of the
world, as in modern scientific determinism, posits a universe (in which laws cannot
be changed by human moral acts) almost indistinguishable—from the human point
of view—from one that is not governed at all. The universe most metaphysically
determined is morally the most chaotic.

Euripides' attitude toward the sexes is another crucial topic. Legend surrounds
his birth; at the other end, legend has it that at his death he was torn apart, by dogs or
women. Again, the legend may be quaint, but the fact remains that, beginning in his
own time, Euripides has been charged with misogyny. Aristophanes, for one, gave
weight to the charge, in Lysistrata and in other comedies. But the matter is surely
more complicated, and in some ways the legend is the opposite of the truth. Alcestis
celebrates a heroine not merely selfless but also worthy of the kind of posthumous
immortality of fame that, for Greeks, was generally considered the exclusive prerogative of males. Even the ruthless Medea is extended sympathy and allowed to present
powerfully her case against Jason. Perhaps the key fact about Euripides is that he
took women seriously, in an age when his audience generally regarded them as
inferior, biologically and socially. It is certainly true that, with some exceptions,
Euripides' female characters are far more intense than the male ones. The frenzied
women who worship Dionysus in The Bacchae are terrifying, but they are also in
closer touch than men are with a fundamental vital force, in the psyche and the
world.

Such intensity pervades Euripides' work in general. Critics who do not admire
him prefer to call this intensity sensationalism. But, whatever term we use, melodrama is an inherent part of Euripides' view of life—qualified by, and at the same
time founded on, his skepticism.

FURTHER READING *(prepared by F.S.N.):* Gilbert Murray's popular work *Euripides
and His Age*, 1913, 2nd ed. 1946, remains an excellent introduction to the historical
and cultural context of Euripides' drama. For material on the life and writings of
Euripides see D. J. Conacher, *Euripidean Drama: Myth, Theme and Structure*, 1967;
and T. B. L. Webster, *The Tragedies of Euripides*, 1967, which also compares the
works of Euripides with those of Aeschylus and Sophocles. A challenging modern
selection of studies is given by E. Segal, ed., *Euripides: A Collection of Critical Essays*,
1968. John R. Wilson, ed., *Twentieth Century Interpretations of Euripides' Alcestis*, 1968,
offers useful criticism on the play. Pietro Pucci in his full-scale discussion of *Medea*,
The Violence of Pity in Euripides' Medea, 1980, tackles major problems in interpreting
this work.

MEDEA

Translated by Philip Vellacott

The kingship of the city of Iolcus (in Thessaly, the northeastern region of Greece)
had been usurped by Pelias. Jason's father, Aeson, was half brother of Pelias and
rightful ruler of Iolcus. After a period of protective exile under the tutelage of

Chiron the Centaur, Jason returned to Iolcus. His usurper-uncle Pelias then sent
Jason off to Colchis (on the Black Sea) to capture the magically potent Golden
Fleece of a ram. Jason made the adventurous voyage, in company with some of the
most famous and fabled Greek heroes, called the Argonauts after the name of their
ship the *Argo*. When Jason reached Colchis, its king Aeetes (Medea's father) agreed
to give up the Golden Fleece if Jason performed certain superhumanly difficult
tasks. He was able to perform them with the help of Medea, who had fallen in love
with him and who possessed magical arts. The heroes then returned with the
Golden Fleece to Iolcus, along with Medea, who assisted their return by killing her
brother so that her father Aeetes would be delayed in his pursuit. In Iolcus, Medea
continued to aid Jason by using her witchcraft to cause the death of Pelias at the
hands of his daughters. But Jason was unable to claim his throne, and he and
Medea were banished from Iolcus. They settled in Corinth, the setting of the play
Medea. After some time there, Jason has decided to cast off Medea and to marry
Glauce, daughter of Creon, the king of Corinth. This Creon should not be confused with the Creon who, in Sophocles' Oedipus plays, rules Thebes. [*Editors'
headnote*.]

CHARACTERS

NURSE	JASON
TUTOR *to Medea's sons*	AEGEUS, *king of Athens*
MEDEA	MESSENGER
CHORUS *of Corinthian women*	MEDEA'S TWO CHILDREN
CREON, *king of Corinth*	

SCENE
Before Jason's house in Corinth

NURSE. If only they had never gone! If the Argo's hull
   Never had winged out through the grey-blue jaws of rock[1]
   And on towards Colchis! If that pine on Pelion's[2] slopes
   Had never felt the axe, and fallen, to put oars
   Into those heroes' hands, who went at Pelias' bidding
   To fetch the golden fleece! Then neither would Medea,
   My mistress, ever have set sail for the walled town
   Of Iolcus, mad with love for Jason; nor would she,
   When Pelias' daughters, at her instance, killed their father,
   Have come with Jason and her children to live here   10
   In Corinth; where, coming as an exile, she has earned
   The citizens' welcome; while to Jason she is all
   Obedience—and in marriage that's the saving thing,
   When a wife obediently accepts her husband's will.

   But now her world has turned to enmity, and wounds her
   Where her affection's deepest. Jason has betrayed

---

[1] The Symplegades, two mythical rocks at the north end of the strait of Bosporus, the
entrance to the Black Sea. The rocks were supposed to crush ships that sailed between them.
[2] A mountain in Thessaly.

His own sons, and my mistress, for a royal bed,
For alliance with the king of Corinth. He has married
Glauce, Creon's daughter. Poor Medea! Scorned and shamed,
She raves, invoking every vow and solemn pledge   20
That Jason made her, and calls the gods as witnesses
What thanks she has received for her fidelity.
She will not eat; she lies collapsed in agony,
Dissolving the long hours in tears. Since first she heard
Of Jason's wickedness, she has not raised her eyes,
Or moved her cheek from the hard ground; and when her friends
Reason with her, she might be a rock or wave of the sea,
For all she hears—unless, maybe, she turns away
Her lovely head, speaks to herself alone, and wails
Aloud for her dear father, her own land and home,   30
Which she betrayed and left, to come here with this man
Who now spurns and insults her. Poor Medea! Now
She learns through pain what blessings they enjoy who are not
Uprooted from their native land. She hates her sons:
To see them is no pleasure to her. I am afraid
Some dreadful purpose is forming in her mind. She is
A frightening woman; no one who makes an enemy
Of her will carry off an easy victory.

Here come the boys, back from their running. They've no thought
Of this cruel blow that's fallen on their mother. Well,   40
They're young; young heads and painful thoughts don't go
    together.

[*Enter the* TUTOR *with* MEDEA'S
TWO SONS.]

TUTOR. Old nurse and servant of my mistress's house, tell me,
    What are you doing, standing out here by the door,
    All alone, talking to yourself, harping on trouble?
    Eh? What does Medea say to being left alone?
NURSE. Old friend, tutor of Jason's sons, an honest slave
    Suffers in her own heart the blow that strikes her mistress.
    It was too much, I couldn't bear it; I had to come
    Out here and tell my mistress's wrongs to earth and heaven.
TUTOR. Poor woman! Has she not stopped crying yet?   50
NURSE.   Stopped crying?
    I envy you. Her grief's just born—not yet half-grown.
TUTOR. Poor fool—though she's my mistress and I shouldn't say it—
    She had better save her tears. She has not heard the worst.
NURSE. The worst? What now? Don't keep it from me. What has hap-
        pened?
TUTOR. Why, nothing's happened. I'm sorry I said anything.
NURSE. Look—we're both slaves together: don't keep me in the dark.
    Is it so great a secret? I can hold my tongue.
TUTOR. I'd gone along to the benches where the old men play

At dice, next to the holy fountain of Peirene;   60
They thought I was not listening; and I heard one say
That Creon king of Corinth means to send these boys
Away from here—to banish them, and their mother too.
Whether the story's true I don't know. I hope not.
NURSE. But surely Jason won't stand by and see his sons
Banished, even if he has a quarrel with their mother?
TUTOR. Old love is ousted by new love. Jason's no friend
To this house.
NURSE.   Then we're lost, if we must add new trouble
To old, before we're rid of what we had already.
TUTOR. But listen: it's no time to tell Medea this.   70
Keep quiet, say nothing about it.
NURSE.   Children, do you hear
What sort of father Jason is to you? My curse
On—No! No curse; he is my master. All the same,
He is guilty: he has betrayed those near and dear to him.
TUTOR. What man's not guilty? It's taken you a long time to learn
That everybody loves himself more than his neighbour.
These boys are nothing to their father: he's in love.
NURSE. Run into the house, boys. Everything will be all right.

[*The children move away a little.*]

You do your best to keep them by themselves, as long
As she's in this dark mood; don't let them go to her.   80
I've watched her watching them, her eye like a wild bull's.
There's something that she means to do; and I know this:
She'll not relax her rage till it has found its victim.
God grant she strike her enemies and not her friends!

[MEDEA's *voice is heard from inside
the house.*]

MEDEA. Oh, oh! What misery, what wretchedness!
What shall I do? If only I were dead!
NURSE. There! You can hear; it is your mother
Racking her heart, racking her anger.
Quick, now, children, hurry indoors;
And don't go within sight of her,   90
Or anywhere near her; keep a safe distance.
Her mood is cruel, her nature dangerous,
Her will fierce and intractable.
Come on, now, in with you both at once.

[*The* CHILDREN *go in, and the*
TUTOR *follows.*]

The dark cloud of her lamentations
Is just beginning. Soon, I know,

It will burst aflame as her anger rises.
Deep in passion and unrelenting,
What will she do now, stung with insult?
MEDEA [*indoors*]. Do I not suffer? Am I not wronged? Should I not
    weep?   100
Children, your mother is hated, and you are cursed:
Death take you, with your father, and perish his whole house!
NURSE. Oh, the pity of it! Poor Medea!
Your children—why, what have *they* to do
With their father's wickedness? Why hate *them?*
I am sick with fear for you, children, terror
Of what may happen. The mind of a queen
Is a thing to fear. A queen is used
To giving commands, not obeying them;
And her rage once roused is hard to appease.   110

To have learnt to live on the common level
Is better. No grand life for me,
Just peace and quiet as I grow old.
The middle way, neither great nor mean,
Is best by far, in name and practice.
To be rich and powerful brings no blessing;
Only more utterly
Is the prosperous house destroyed, when the gods are angry.

                            [*Enter the* CHORUS *of Corinthian
                            women.*]

CHORUS.
    I heard her voice, I heard
    That unhappy woman from Colchis   120
    Still crying, not calm yet.
    Old Nurse, tell us about her.
    As I stood by the door I heard her
    Crying inside the palace.
    And my own heart suffers too
    When Jason's house is suffering;
    For that is where my loyalty lies.
NURSE. Jason's house? It no longer exists; all that is finished.
    Jason is a prisoner in a princess's bed;
    And Medea is in her room   130
    Melting her life away in tears;
    No word from any friend can give her comfort.
MEDEA [*still from indoors*].
    Come, flame of the sky,
    Pierce through my head!
    What do I gain from living any longer?
    Oh, how I hate living! I want
    To end my life, leave it behind, and die.

CHORUS.
   O Zeus, and Earth, and Light,
   Do you hear the chanted prayer
   Of a wife in her anguish?   140

          [turning to the door and addres-
          sing MEDEA]

   What madness is this? The bed you long for—
   Is it what others shrink from?
   Is it death you demand?
   Do not pray that prayer, Medea!
   If your husband is won to a new love—
   The thing is common; why let it anger you?
   Zeus will plead your cause.
   Check this passionate grief over your husband
   Which wastes you away.
MEDEA. Mighty Themis! Dread Artemis![3]   150
   Do you see how I am used—
   In spite of those great oaths I bound him with—
   By my accursed husband?
   Oh, may I see Jason and his bride
   Ground to pieces in their shattered palace
   For the wrong they have dared to do to me, unprovoked!
   O my father, my city, you I deserted;
   My brother I shamefully murdered!
NURSE. Do you hear what my mistress is saying,
   Clamouring to Themis, hearer of prayer,   160
   And to Zeus, who is named guardian of men's oaths?
   It is no trifling matter
   That can end a rage like hers.
CHORUS. I wish she would come out here and let us see her
   And talk to her; if she would listen
   Perhaps she would drop this fierce resentful spirit,
   This passionate indignation.
   As a friend I am anxious to do whatever I can.
   Go, nurse, persuade her to come out to us.
   Tell her we are all on her side.   170
   Hurry, before she does harm—to those in there;
   This passion of hers is an irresistible flood.
NURSE. I will. I fear I shall not persuade her;
   Still, I am glad to do my best.
   Yet as soon as any of us servants
   Goes near to her, or tries to speak,
   She glares at us like a mad bull
   Or a lioness guarding her cubs.

[3] Themis is the personification of justice; Artemis is the virgin goddess of the hunt who protects young creatures and women in childbirth.

[*The* NURSE *goes to the door, where
she turns.*]

The men of old times had little sense;
If you called them fools you wouldn't be far wrong.   180
They invented songs, and all the sweetness of music,
To perform at feasts, banquets, and celebrations;
But no one thought of using
Songs and stringed instruments
To banish the bitterness and pain of life.
Sorrow is the real cause
Of deaths and disasters and families destroyed.
If music could cure sorrow it would be precious;
But after a good dinner why sing songs?
When people have fed full they're happy already.   190

[*The* NURSE *goes in.*]

CHORUS.
    I heard her sobbing and wailing,
    Shouting shrill, pitiful accusations
    Against her husband who has betrayed her.
    She invokes Themis, daughter of Zeus,
    Who witnessed those promises which drew her
    Across from Asia to Hellas, setting sail at night,
    Threading the salt strait,
    Key and barrier to the Pontic Sea.[4]

[MEDEA *comes out. She is not
shaken with weeping, but cool and
self-possessed.*]

MEDEA. Women of Corinth, I would not have you censure me,
    So I have come. Many, I know, are proud at heart,   200
    Indoors or out; but others are ill spoken of
    As supercilious, just because their ways are quiet.
    There is no justice in the world's censorious eyes.
    They will not wait to learn a man's true character;
    Though no wrong has been done them, one look—and they hate.
    Of course a stranger must conform; even a Greek
    Should not annoy his fellows by crass stubbornness.
    I accept my place; but this blow that has fallen on me
    Was not to be expected. It has crushed my heart.
    Life has no pleasure left, dear friends. I want to die.   210
    Jason was my whole life; he knows that well. Now he
    Has proved himself the most contemptible of men.

    Surely, of all creatures that have life and will, we women
    Are the most wretched. When, for an extravagant sum,

[4] The Black Sea.

We have bought a husband,[5] we must then accept him as
Possessor of our body. This is to aggravate
Wrong with worse wrong. Then the great question: will the man
We get be bad or good? For women, divorce is not
Respectable; to repel the man, not possible.

Still more, a foreign woman, coming among new laws,   220
New customs, needs the skill of magic, to find out
What her home could not teach her, how to treat the man
Whose bed she shares. And if in this exacting toil
We are successful, and our husband does not struggle
Under the marriage yoke, our life is enviable.
Otherwise, death is better. If a man grows tired
Of the company at home, he can go out, and find
A cure for tediousness. We wives are forced to look
To one man only. And, they tell us, we at home
Live free from danger, they go out to battle: fools!   230
I'd rather stand three times in the front line than bear
One child.
            But the same arguments do not apply
To you and me. You have this city, your father's home,
The enjoyment of your life, and your friends' company.
I am alone; I have no city; now my husband
Insults me. I was taken as plunder from a land
At the earth's edge. I have no mother, brother, nor any
Of my own blood to turn to in this extremity.

So, I make one request. If I can find a way
To work revenge on Jason for his wrongs to me,   240
Say nothing. A woman's weak and timid in most matters;
The noise of war, the look of steel, makes her a coward.
But touch her right in marriage, and there's no bloodier spirit.
CHORUS. I'll do as you ask. To punish Jason will be just.
    I do not wonder that you take such wrongs to heart.

[CREON *approaches.*]

But look, Medea; I see Creon, King of Corinth;
    He must have come to tell you of some new decision.
CREON. You there, Medea, scowling rage against your husband!
    I order you out of Corinth; take your sons and go
    Into exile. Waste no time; I'm here to see this order   250
    Enforced. And I'm not going back into my palace
    Until I've put you safe outside my boundaries.
MEDEA. Oh! this is the cruel end of my accursed life!
    My enemies have spread full sail; no welcoming shore
    Waits to receive and save me. Ill-treated as I am,
    Creon, I ask: for what offence do you banish me?

[5] The reference is to the dowry given with the bride in marriage.

CREON. I fear you. Why wrap up the truth? I fear that you
  May do my daughter some irreparable harm.
  A number of things contribute to my anxiety.
  You're a clever woman, skilled in many evil arts;   260
  You're barred from Jason's bed, and that enrages you.
  I learn too from reports, that you have uttered threats
  Of revenge on Jason and his bride and his bride's father.
  I'll act first, then, in self-defence. I'd rather make you
  My enemy now, than weaken, and later pay with tears.
MEDEA. My reputation, yet again! Many times, Creon,
  It has been my curse and ruin. A man of any shrewdness
  Should never have his children taught to use their brains
  More than their fellows. What do you gain by being clever?
  You neglect your own affairs; and all your fellow citizens   270
  Hate you. Those who are fools will call you ignorant
  And useless, when you offer them unfamiliar knowledge.
  As for those thought intelligent, if people rank
  You above *them,* that is a thing they will not stand.
  I know this from experience: because I am clever,
  They are jealous; while the rest dislike me. After all,
  I am not so clever as all that.
                So you, Creon,
  Are afraid—of what? Some harm that I might do to you?
  Don't let *me* alarm you, Creon. I'm in no position—
  A woman—to wrong a king. You have done me no wrong.   280
  You've given your daughter to the man you chose. I hate
  My husband—true; but you had every right to do
  As you have done. So now I bear no grudge against
  Your happiness: marry your daughter to him, and good luck
  To you both. But let me live in Corinth. I will bear
  My wrongs in silence, yielding to superior strength.
CREON. Your words are gentle: but my blood runs cold to think
  What plots you may be nursing deep within your heart.
  In fact, I trust you so much less now than before.
  A woman of hot temper—and a man the same—   290
  Is a less dangerous enemy than one quiet and clever.
  So out you go, and quickly; no more arguing.
  I've made my mind up; you're my enemy. No craft
  Of yours will find a way of staying in my city.
MEDEA. I kneel to you, I beseech you by the young bride, your child.
CREON. You're wasting words; you'll never make me change my mind.
MEDEA. I beg you! Will you cast off pity, and banish me?
CREON. I will: I have more love for my family than for you.
MEDEA. My home, my country! How my thoughts turn to you now!
CREON. I love my country too—next only to my daughter.   300
MEDEA. Oh, what an evil power love has in people's lives!
CREON. That would depend on circumstances, I imagine.
MEDEA. Great Zeus, remember who caused all this suffering!
CREON. Go, you poor wretch, take all my troubles with you! Go!
MEDEA. I know what trouble is; I have no need of more.

CREON. In a moment you'll be thrown out neck and crop. Here, men!
MEDEA. No, no, not that! But, Creon, I have one thing to ask.
CREON. You seem inclined, Medea, to give me trouble still.
MEDEA. I'll go. [*She still clings to him.*] It was not *that* I begged.
CREON.   Then why resist?
    Why will you not get out?
MEDEA.   This one day let me stay,   310
    To settle some plan for my exile, make provision
    For my two sons, since their own father is not concerned
    To help them. Show some pity: you are a father too,
    You should feel kindly towards them. For myself, exile
    Is nothing. I weep for them; their fate is very hard.
CREON. I'm no tyrant by nature. My soft heart has often
    Betrayed me; and I know it's foolish of me now;
    Yet none the less, Medea, you shall have what you ask.
    But take this warning: if tomorrow's holy sun
    Finds you or them inside my boundaries, you die.   320
    That is my solemn word. Now stay here, if you must,
    This one day. You can hardly in one day accomplish
    What I am afraid of.

                        [*Exit* CREON.]

CHORUS.
        Medea, poor Medea!
        Your grief touches our hearts.
        A wanderer, where can you turn?
        To what welcoming house?
        To what protecting land?
        How wild with dread and danger
        Is the sea where the gods have set your course!   330
MEDEA. A bad predicament all round—yes, true enough;
    But don't imagine things will end as they are now.
    Trials are yet to come for this new-wedded pair;
    Nor shall those nearest to them get off easily.

    Do you think I would ever have fawned so on this man,
    Except to gain my purpose, carry out my schemes?
    Not one touch, not one word: yet he—oh, what a fool!
    By banishing me at once he could have thwarted me
    Utterly; instead, he allows me to remain one day.
    Today three of my enemies I shall strike dead: 340
    Father and daughter; and *my* husband.

    I have in mind so many paths of death for them,
    I don't know which to choose. Should I set fire to the house,
    And burn the bridal chamber? Or creep up to their bed
    And drive a sharp knife through their guts? There is one fear:
    If I am caught entering the house, or in the act,
    I die, and the last laugh goes to my enemies.

The best is the direct way, which most suits my bent:
To kill by poison.

So—say they are dead: what city will receive me then?   350
What friend will guarantee my safety, offer land
And home as sanctuary? None. I'll wait a little.
If some strong tower of help appears, I'll carry out
This murder cunningly and quietly. But if Fate
Banishes me without resource, I will myself
Take sword in hand, harden my heart to the uttermost,
And kill them both, even if I am to die for it.

For, by Queen Hecate,[6] whom above all divinities
I venerate, my chosen accomplice, to whose presence
My central hearth is dedicated, no one of them   360
Shall hurt me and not suffer for it! Let me work:
In bitterness and pain they shall repent this marriage,
Repent their houses joined, repent my banishment.

Come! Lay your plan, Medea; scheme with all your skill.
On to the deadly moment that shall test your nerve!
You see now where you stand. Your father was a king,
His father was the Sun-god:[7] you must not invite
Laughter from Jason and his new allies, the tribe
Of Sisyphus.[8] You know what you must do. Besides—

[*She turns to the* CHORUS.]

We were born women—useless for honest purposes,   370
But in all kinds of evil skilled practitioners.
CHORUS. Streams of the sacred rivers flow uphill;
    Tradition, order, all things are reversed:
        Deceit is *men*'s device now,
        Men's oaths are gods' dishonour.
    Legend will now reverse our reputation;
    A time comes when the female sex is honoured;
        That old discordant slander
        Shall no more hold us subject.
    Male poets of past ages, with their ballads   380
    Of faithless women, shall go out of fashion;
        For Phoebus,[9] Prince of Music,
    Never bestowed the lyric inspiration
        Through female understanding—
        Or we'd find themes for poems,
    We'd counter with our epics against man.

[6]Goddess of witchcraft, though also in some contexts a protective deity.
[7]Helios, father of Aeetes.
[8]An earlier, legendary king of Corinth, noted for deceitfulness.
[9]Apollo, god of music and poetry.

Oh, Time is old; and in his store of tales
    Men figure no less famous
    Or infamous than women.

So you, Medea, wild with love,   390
Set sail from your father's house,
Threading the Rocky Jaws of the eastern sea;
And here, living in a strange country,
Your marriage lost, your bed solitary,
You are driven beyond the borders,
An exile with no redress.
The grace of sworn oaths is gone;
Honour remains no more
In the wide Greek world, but is flown to the sky.
Where can you turn for shelter?   400
Your father's door is closed against you;
Another is now mistress of your husband's bed;
A new queen rules in your house.

                [*Enter* JASON.]

JASON. I have noticed—this is not the first occasion—
What fatal results follow from ungoverned rage.
You could have stayed in Corinth, still lived in this house,
If you had quietly accepted the decisions
Of those in power. Instead, you talked like a fool; and now
You are banished. Well, your angry words don't upset *me;*
Go on as long as you like reciting Jason's crimes.   410
But after your abuse of the King and the princess
Think yourself lucky to be let off with banishment.
I have tried all the time to calm them down; but you
Would not give up your ridiculous tirades against
The royal family. So, you're banished. However, I
Will not desert a friend. I have carefully considered
Your problem, and come now, in spite of everything,
To see that you and the children are not sent away
With an empty purse, or unprovided. Exile brings
With it a train of difficulties. You no doubt   420
Hate me: but I could never bear ill-will to you.
MEDEA. You filthy coward!—if I knew any worse name
For such unmanliness I'd use it—so, you've come!
You, my worst enemy, come to me! Oh, it's not courage,
This looking friends in the face after betraying them.
It is not even audacity; it's a disease,
The worst a man can have, pure shamelessness. However,
It is as well you came; to say what I have to say
Will ease my heart; to hear it said will make you wince.

I will begin at the beginning. When you were sent   430
To master the fire-breathing bulls, yoke them, and sow

The deadly furrow, then I saved your life; and that
Every Greek who sailed with you in the Argo knows.
The serpent that kept watch over the Golden Fleece,
Coiled round it fold on fold, unsleeping—it was I
Who killed it, and so lit the torch of your success.[10]
I willingly deceived my father; left my home;
With you I came to Iolcus by Mount Pelion,
Showing much love and little wisdom. There I put
King Pelias to the most horrible of deaths[11]   440
By his own daughters' hands, and ruined his whole house.
And in return for this you have the wickedness
To turn me out, to get yourself another wife,
Even after I had borne you sons! If you had still
Been childless I could have pardoned you for hankering
After this new marriage. But respect for oaths has gone
To the wind. Do you, I wonder, think that the old gods
No longer rule? Or that new laws are now in force?
You must know you are guilty of perjury to me.

My poor right hand, which you so often clasped! My knees   450
Which you then clung to! How we are besmirched and mocked
By this man's broken vows, and all our hopes deceived!

Come, I'll ask your advice as if you were a friend.
Not that I hope for any help from you; but still,
I'll ask you, and expose your infamy. Where now
Can I turn? Back to my country and my father's house,
Which I betrayed to come with you? Or to Iolcus,
To Pelias's wretched daughters? What a welcome they
Would offer me, who killed their father! Thus it stands:
My friends at home now hate me; and in helping you   460
I have earned the enmity of those I had no right
To hurt. For my reward, you have made me the envy
Of Hellene women everywhere! A marvellous
Husband I have, and faithful too, in the name of pity;
When I'm banished, thrown out of the country without a friend,
Alone with my forlorn waifs. Yes, a shining shame
It will be to you, the new-made bridegroom, that your own sons,
And I who saved your life, are begging beside the road!

O Zeus! Why have you given us clear signs to tell
True gold from counterfeit; but when we need to know   470
Bad *men* from good, the flesh bears no revealing mark?
CHORUS. The fiercest anger of all, the most incurable,
Is that which rages in the place of dearest love.

---

[10] Medea refers in the preceding six lines to the difficult tasks Jason had to accomplish in Colchis to win the Golden Fleece.
[11] Medea had deceitfully persuaded Pelias' daughters that they could magically restore their father's youth by boiling him in a cauldron.

JASON. I have to show myself a clever speaker, it seems.
    This hurricane of recrimination and abuse
    Calls for good seamanship: I'll furl all but an inch
    Of sail, and ride it out. To begin with, since you build
    To such a height your services to me, I hold
    That credit for my successful voyage was solely due
    To Aphrodite,[12] no one else divine or human.   480
    I admit, you have intelligence; but, to recount
    How helpless passion drove you then to save my life
    Would be invidious; and I will not stress the point.
    Your services, so far as they went, were well enough;
    But in return for saving me you got far more
    Than you gave. Allow me, in the first place, to point out
    That you left a barbarous land to become a resident
    Of Hellas;[13] here you have known justice; you have lived
    In a society where force yields place to law.
    Moreover, here your gifts are widely recognized,   490
    You are famous; if you still lived at the ends of the earth
    Your name would never be spoken. Personally, unless
    Life brings me fame, I long neither for hoards of gold,
    Nor for a voice sweeter than Orpheus![14]—Well, *you* began
    The argument about my voyage; and that's my answer.

    As for your scurrilous taunts against my marriage with
    The royal family, I shall show you that my action
    Was wise, not swayed by passion, and directed towards
    Your interests and my children's.—No, keep quiet! When I
    Came here from Iolcus as a stateless exile, dogged   500
    And thwarted by misfortunes—why, what luckier chance
    Could I have met, than marriage with the King's daughter?
    It was not, as you resentfully assume, that I
    Found your attractions wearisome, and was smitten with
    Desire for a new wife; nor did I specially want
    To raise a numerous family—the sons we have
    Are enough, I'm satisfied; but I wanted to ensure
    First—and the most important—that we should live well
    And not be poor; I know how a poor man is shunned
    By all his friends. Next, that I could bring up my sons   510
    In a manner worthy of my descent; have other sons,
    Perhaps, as brothers to your children; give them all
    An equal place, and so build up a closely-knit
    And prosperous family. *You* need no more children, do you?
    While *I* thought it worth while to ensure advantages
    For those I have, by means of those I hope to have.

    Was such a plan, then, wicked? Even you would approve
    If you could govern your sex-jealousy. But you women

[12] Goddess of love.   [13] Greece.
[14] A legendary poet, and one of the Argonauts; his music was so wonderful that he could
enchant nature itself. See the account in Ovid's *Metamorphoses*, Book X.

Have reached a state where, if all's well with your sex-life,
You've everything you wish for; but when *that* goes wrong,   520
At once all that is best and noblest turns to gall.
If only children could be got some other way,
Without the female sex! If women didn't exist,
Human life would be rid of all its miseries.
CHORUS. Jason, you have set your case forth very plausibly.
But to my mind—though you may be surprised at this—
You are acting wrongly in thus abandoning your wife.
MEDEA. No doubt I differ from many people in many ways.
To me, a wicked man who is also eloquent
Seems the most guilty of them all. He'll cut your throat   530
As bold as brass, because he knows he can dress up murder
In handsome words. He's not so clever after all.
You dare outface me now with glib high-mindedness!
One word will throw you: if you were honest, you ought first
To have won me over, not got married behind my back.
JASON. No doubt, if I had mentioned it, you would have proved
Most helpful. Why, even now you will not bring yourself
To calm this raging temper.
MEDEA.   That was not the point;
But you're an ageing man, and an Asiatic wife
Was no longer respectable.
JASON.   Understand this: 540
It's not for the sake of any woman that I have made
This royal marriage, but, as I've already said,
To ensure your future, and to give my children brothers
Of royal blood, and build security for us all.
MEDEA. I loathe your prosperous future; I'll have none of it,
Nor none of your security—it galls my heart.
JASON. You know—you'll change your mind and be more sensible.
You'll soon stop thinking good is bad, and striking these
Pathetic poses when in fact you're fortunate.
MEDEA. Go on, insult me: you have a roof over your head.   550
I am alone, an exile.
JASON.   It was your own choice.
Blame no one but yourself.
MEDEA.   *My* choice? What did I do?
Did I make you my wife and then abandon you?
JASON. You called wicked curses on the King and his house.
MEDEA. I did. On your house too Fate sends me as a curse.
JASON. I'll not pursue this further. If there's anything else
I can provide to meet the children's needs or yours,
Tell me: I'll gladly give whatever you want, or send
Letters of introduction, if you like, to friends
Who will help you.—Listen: to refuse such help is mad.   560
You've everything to gain if you give up this rage.
MEDEA. Nothing would induce me to have dealings with your friends,
Nor to take any gift of yours; so offer none.
A lying traitor's gifts carry no luck.

JASON.   Very well.
   I call the gods to witness that I have done my best
   To help you and the children. You make no response
   To kindness; friendly overtures you obstinately
   Reject. So much the worse for you.
MEDEA.   Go! You have spent
   Too long out here. You are consumed with craving for
   Your newly-won bride. Go, enjoy her.

[Exit JASON.]

                         It may be—   570
   And God uphold my words—that this your marriage-day
   Will end with marriage lost, loathing and horror left.
CHORUS.
      Visitations of love that come
      Raging and violent on a man
      Bring him neither good repute nor goodness.
      But if Aphrodite descends in gentleness
      No other goddess brings such delight.
      Never, Queen Aphrodite,
      Loose against me from your golden bow,
      Dipped in sweetness of desire,   580
      Your inescapable arrow!

      Let Innocence, the gods' loveliest gift,
      Choose me for her own;
      Never may the dread Cyprian[15]
      Craze my heart to leave old love for new,
      Sending to assault me
      Angry disputes and feuds unending;
      But let her judge shrewdly the loves of women
      And respect the bed where no war rages.

      O my country, my home!   590
      May the gods save me from becoming
      A stateless refugee
      Dragging out an intolerable life
      In desperate helplessness!
      That is the most pitiful of all griefs;
      Death is better. Should such a day come to me
      I pray for death first.
      Of all pains and hardships none is worse
      Than to be deprived of your native land.

      This is no mere reflection derived from hearsay;   600
      It is something we have seen.
      You, Medea, have suffered the most shattering of blows;

---

[15] Aphrodite, goddess of love. Born of the foam of the sea, she made her first appearance in Cyprus.

Yet neither the city of Corinth
Nor any friend has taken pity on you.
May dishonour and ruin fall on the man
Who, having unlocked the secrets
Of a friend's frank heart, can then disown him!
He shall be no friend of mine.

[*Enter* AEGEUS.[16]]

AEGEUS. All happiness to you, Medea! Between old friends
  There is no better greeting.
MEDEA.   All happiness to you,   610
  Aegeus, son of Pandion the wise! Where have you come from?
AEGEUS. From Delphi, from the ancient oracle of Apollo.
MEDEA. The centre of the earth,[17] the home of prophecy:
  Why did you go?
AEGEUS.   To ask for children; that my seed
  May become fertile.
MEDEA.   Why, have you lived so many years
  Childless?
AEGEUS.   Childless I am; so some fate has ordained.
MEDEA. You have a wife, or not?
AEGEUS.   I am married.
MEDEA.   And what answer
  Did Phoebus give you about children?
AEGEUS.   His answer was
  Too subtle for me or any human interpreter.
MEDEA. Is it lawful for me to hear it?
AEGEUS.   Certainly; a brain   620
  Like yours is what is needed.
MEDEA.   Tell me, since you may.
AEGEUS. He commanded me 'not to unstop the wineskin's neck'—
MEDEA. Yes—until when?
AEGEUS.   Until I came safe home again.
MEDEA. I see. And for what purpose have you sailed to Corinth?
AEGEUS. You know the King of Troezen, Pittheus, son of Pelops?
MEDEA. Yes, a most pious man.
AEGEUS.   I want to ask his advice
  About this oracle.
MEDEA.   He is an expert in such matters.
AEGEUS. Yes, and my closest friend. We went to the wars together.
MEDEA. I hope you will get all you long for, and be happy.
AEGEUS. But you are looking pale and wasted: what is the matter?   630
MEDEA. Aegeus, my husband's the most evil man alive.
AEGEUS. Why, what's this? Tell me all about your unhappiness.
MEDEA. Jason has betrayed me, though I never did him wrong.
AEGEUS. What has he done? Explain exactly.

---

[16] In myth, the father of Theseus, the great Athenian ruler.
[17] The "Navelstone," believed to be the center of the earth, was located at Delphi. Compare
the opening of Aeschylus' *The Eumenides*.

MEDEA.   He has taken
Another wife, and made her mistress of *my* house.
AEGEUS. But such a thing is shameful! He has never dared—
MEDEA. It is so. Once he loved me; now I am disowned.
AEGEUS. Was he tired of you? Or did he fall in love elsewhere?
MEDEA. Oh, passionately. He's not a man his friends can trust.
AEGEUS. Well, if—as you say—he's a bad lot, let him go.   640
MEDEA. It's royalty and power he's fallen in love with.
AEGEUS.   What?
Go on. Who's the girl's father?
MEDEA.   Creon, King of Corinth.
AEGEUS. I see. Then you have every reason to be upset.
MEDEA. It is the end of everything! What's more, I'm banished.
AEGEUS. Worse still—extraordinary! Why, who has banished you?
MEDEA. Creon has banished me from Corinth.
AEGEUS.   And does Jason
Accept this? How disgraceful!
MEDEA.   Oh, no! He protests.
But he's resolved to bear it bravely.—Aegeus, see,
I touch your beard as a suppliant, embrace your knees,
Imploring you to have pity on my wretchedness.   650
Have pity! I am an exile; let me not be friendless.
Receive me in Athens;[18] give me a welcome in your house.
So may the gods grant you fertility, and bring
Your life to a happy close. You have not realized
What good luck chance has brought you. I know certain drugs
Whose power will put an end to your sterility.
I promise you shall beget children.
AEGEUS.   I am anxious,
For many reasons, to help you in this way, Medea;
First, for the gods' sake, then this hope you've given me
Of children—for I've quite despaired of my own powers.   660
This then is what I'll do: once you can get to Athens
I'll keep my promise and protect you all I can.
But I must make this clear first: I do not intend
To take you with me away from Corinth. If you come
Yourself to Athens, you shall have sanctuary there;
I will not give you up to anyone. But first
Get clear of Corinth without help; the Corinthians too
Are friends of mine, and I don't wish to give offence.
MEDEA. So be it. Now confirm your promise with an oath,
And all is well between us.
AEGEUS.   Why? Do you not trust me?   670
What troubles you?
MEDEA.   I trust you; but I have enemies—
Not only Creon, but the house of Pelias.
Once you are bound by oaths you will not give me up
If they should try to take me out of your territory.

---

[18] Athens often boasted of its hospitality to aliens.

But if your promise is verbal, and not sworn to the gods,
Perhaps you will make friends with them, and agree to do
What they demand. I've no power on my side, while they
Have wealth and all the resources of a royal house.

AEGEUS. Your forethought is remarkable; but since you wish it
I've no objection. In fact, the taking of an oath   680
Safeguards me; since I can confront your enemies
With a clear excuse; while *you* have full security.
So name your gods.

MEDEA.   Swear by the Earth under your feet,
By the Sun, my father's father, and the whole race of gods.

AEGEUS. Tell me what I shall swear to do or not to do.

MEDEA. Never yourself to expel me from your territory;
And, if my enemies want to take me away, never
Willingly, while you live, to give me up to them.

AEGEUS. I swear by Earth, and by the burning light of the Sun,
And all the gods, to keep the words you have just spoken.   690

MEDEA. I am satisfied. And if you break your oath, what then?

AEGEUS. Then may the gods do to me as to all guilty men.

MEDEA. Go now, and joy be with you. Everything is well.
I'll reach your city as quickly as I can, when I
Have carried out my purpose and achieved my wish.

> [AEGEUS *clasps her hand and hur-*
> *ries off.*]

CHORUS. May Hermes, protector of travellers, bring you
Safe to your home, Aegeus; may you accomplish
All that you so earnestly desire;
For your noble heart wins our goodwill.

MEDEA. O Zeus! O Justice, daughter of Zeus! O glorious Sun!   700
Now I am on the road to victory; now there's hope!
I shall see my enemies punished as they deserve.
Just where my plot was weakest, at that very point
Help has appeared in this man Aegeus; he is a haven
Where I shall find safe mooring, once I reach the walls
Of the city of Athens. Now I'll tell you all my plans:
They'll not make pleasant hearing.

> [*Medea's* NURSE *has entered; she*
> *listens in silence.*]

                              First I'll send a slave
To Jason, asking him to come to me; and then
I'll give him soft talk; tell him he has acted well,
Tell him I think this royal marriage which he has bought   710
With my betrayal is for the best and wisely planned.
But I shall beg that my children be allowed to stay.
Not that I would think of leaving sons of mine behind
On enemy soil for those who hate me to insult;
But in my plot to kill the princess they must help.

I'll send them to the palace bearing gifts, a dress
Of soft weave and a coronet of beaten gold.
If she takes and puts on this finery, both she
And all who touch her will expire in agony;
With such a deadly poison I'll anoint my gifts.   720

However, enough of that. What makes me cry with pain
Is the next thing I have to do. I will kill my sons.
No one shall take my children from me. When I have made
Jason's whole house a shambles,[19] I will leave Corinth
A murderess, flying from my darling children's blood.
Yes, I can endure guilt, however horrible;
The laughter of my enemies I will not endure.

Now let things take their course. What use is life to me?
I have no land, no home, no refuge from despair.
My folly was committed long ago, when I   730
Was ready to desert my father's house, won over
By eloquence from a Greek, whom with God's help I now
Will punish. He shall never see alive again
The sons he had from me. From his new bride he never
Shall breed a son; she by my poison, wretched girl,
Must die a hideous death. Let no one think of me
As humble or weak or passive; let them understand
I am of a different kind: dangerous to my enemies,
Loyal to my friends. To such a life glory belongs.
CHORUS. Since you have told us everything, and since I want   740
    To be your friend, and also to uphold the laws
    Of human life—I tell you, you must not do this!
MEDEA. No other thing is possible. You have excuse
    For speaking so: you have not been treated as I have.
CHORUS. But—to kill your own children! Can you steel your heart?
MEDEA. This is the way to deal Jason the deepest wound.
CHORUS. This way will bring you too the deepest misery.
MEDEA. Let be. Until it is done words are unnecessary.
    Nurse! You are the one I use for messages of trust.
    Go and bring Jason here. As you're a loyal servant,   750
    And a woman, breathe no word about my purposes.

[*Exit* NURSE.]

CHORUS. The people of Athens, sons of Erechtheus, have enjoyed
        their prosperity
    Since ancient times. Children of blessed gods,
    They grew from holy soil unscorched by invasion.[20]
    Among the glories of knowledge their souls are pastured;

[19] A slaughterhouse.
[20] An irony and a significant phrase, for *Medea* was produced in 431, on the eve of the long
Peloponnesian War between Athens and the confederacy headed by Sparta. The Athenians
ultimately were conquered.

They walk always with grace under the sparkling sky.
There long ago, they say, was born golden-haired Harmony,
Created by the nine virgin Muses[21] of Pieria.

They say that Aphrodite dips her cup
In the clear stream of the lovely Cephisus;[22]   760
It is she who breathes over the land the breath
Of gentle honey-laden winds; her flowing locks
She crowns with a diadem of sweet-scented roses,
And sends the Loves to be enthroned beside Knowledge,
And with her to create excellence in every art.

Then how will such a city,
Watered by sacred rivers,
A country giving protection to its friends—
How will Athens welcome
You, the child-killer   770
Whose presence is pollution?
Contemplate the blow struck at a child,
Weigh the blood you take upon you.
Medea, by your knees,
By every pledge or appeal we beseech you,
Do not slaughter your children!

Where will you find hardness of purpose?
How will you build resolution in hand or heart
To face horror without flinching?
When the moment comes, and you look at them—   780
The moment for you to assume the role of murderess—
How will you do it?
When your sons kneel to you for pity,
Will you stain your fingers with their blood?
Your heart will melt; you will know you cannot.

> [*Enter* JASON *from the palace. Two
> maids come from the house to attend*
> MEDEA.]

JASON. You sent for me: I have come. Although you hate me, I
    Am ready to listen. You have some new request; what is it?
MEDEA. Jason, I ask you to forgive the things I said.
    You must bear with my violent temper; you and I
    Share many memories of love. I have been taking   790
    Myself to task. 'You are a fool,' I've told myself,
    'You're mad, when people try to plan things for the best,
    To be resentful, and pick quarrels with the King
    And with your husband; what he's doing will help us all.
    His wife is royal; her sons will be my sons' brothers.

---

[21] The nine goddesses of the arts, worshiped at Pieria, on the slopes of Mount Olympus.
[22] The main river near Athens.

Why not throw off your anger? What is the matter, since
The gods are making kind provision? After all
I have two children still to care for; and I know
We came as exiles, and our friends are few enough.'
When I considered this, I saw my foolishness;   800
I saw how useless anger was. So now I welcome
What you have done; I think you are wise to gain for us
This new alliance, and the folly was all mine.
I should have helped you in your plans, made it my pleasure
To get ready your marriage-bed, attend your bride.
But we women—I won't say we are bad by nature,
But we are what we are. You, Jason, should not copy
Our bad example, or match yourself with us, showing
Folly for folly. I give in; I was wrong just now,
I admit. But I have thought more wisely of it since.   810
Children, children! Are you indoors? Come out here.

> [*The* CHILDREN *come out. Their* TU-
> TOR *follows.*]

Children,
Greet your father, as I do, and put your arms round him.
Forget our quarrel, and love him as your mother does.
We have made friends; we are not angry any more.
There, children; take his hand.

> [*She turns away in a sudden flood
> of weeping.*]

Forgive me; I recalled
What pain the future hides from us.

> [*After embracing* JASON *the* CHIL-
> DREN *go back to* MEDEA.]

Oh children! Will you
All your lives long, stretch out your hands to me like this?
Oh, my tormented heart is full of tears and terrors.
After so long, I have ended my quarrel with your father;
And now, see! I have drenched this young face with my tears.   820
CHORUS. I too feel fresh tears fill my eyes. May the course of evil
  Be checked now, go no further!
JASON.   I am pleased, Medea,
  That you have changed your mind; though indeed I do not blame
  Your first resentment. Only naturally a woman
  Is angry when her husband marries a second wife.
  You have had wiser thoughts; and though it has taken time,
  You have recognized the right decision. This is the act
  Of a sensible woman. As for you, my boys, your father
  Has taken careful thought, and, with the help of the gods,
  Ensured a good life for you. Why, in time, I'm sure,   830

You with your brothers will be leading men in Corinth.
Only grow big and strong. Your father, and those gods
Who are his friends, have all the rest under control.
I want to see you, when you're strong, full-grown young men,
Tread down my enemies.

[*Again* MEDEA *breaks down and weeps.*]

What's this? Why these floods of tears?
Why are you pale? Did you not like what I was saying?
Why do you turn away?
MEDEA.   It is nothing. I was thinking
About these children.
JASON.   I'll provide for them. Cheer up.
MEDEA. I will. It is not that I mean to doubt your word.
But women—are women; tears come naturally to us.   840
JASON. Why do you grieve so over the children?
MEDEA.   I'm their mother.
When you just now prayed for them to live long, I wondered
Whether it would be so; and grief came over me.
But I've said only part of what I had to say;
Here is the other thing. Since Creon has resolved
To send me out of Corinth, I fully recognize
That for me too this course is best. If I lived here
I should become a trouble both to you and him.
People believe I bear a grudge against you all.
So I must go. But the boys—I would like *them* to be   850
Brought up in your care. Beg Creon to let them stay.
JASON. I don't know if I can persuade him; but I'll try.
MEDEA. Then—get your wife to ask her father to let them stay.
JASON. Why, certainly; I'm pretty sure she'll win him over.
MEDEA. She will, if she's like other women. But I too
Can help in this. I'll send a present to your wife—
The loveliest things to be found anywhere on earth.
The boys shall take them.—One of you maids, go quickly, bring
The dress and golden coronet.—They will multiply
Her happiness many times, when she can call her own   860
A royal, noble husband, and these treasures, which
My father's father the Sun bequeathed to his descendants.

[*A slave has brought a casket, which*
MEDEA *now hands to her sons.*]

Boys, hold these gifts. Now carry them to the happy bride,
The princess royal; give them into her own hands.
Go! She will find them all that such a gift should be.
JASON. But why deprive yourself of such things, foolish woman?
Do you think a royal palace is in want of dresses?
Or gold, do you suppose? Keep them, don't give them away.
If my wife values me at all she will yield to *me*

More than to costly presents, I am sure of that.   870
MEDEA. Don't stop me. Gifts, they say, persuade even the gods;
    With mortals, gold outweighs a thousand arguments.
    The day is hers; from now on *her* prosperity
    Will rise to new heights. She is royal and young. To buy
    My sons from exile I would give life, not just gold.
    Come, children, go both of you into this rich palace;
    Kneel down and beg your father's new wife, and my mistress,
    That you may not be banished. And above all, see
    That she receives my present into her own hands.
    Go quickly; be successful, and bring good news back,   880
    That what your mother longs for has been granted you.

                                    [*Exit* JASON *followed by the* CHIL-
                                    DREN *and the* TUTOR.]

CHORUS.
        Now I have no more hope,
        No more hope that the children can live;
        They are walking to murder at this moment.
        The bride will receive the golden coronet,
        Receive her merciless destroyer;
        With her own hands she will carefully fit
        The adornment of death round her golden hair.

        She cannot resist such loveliness, such heavenly gleaming;
        She will enfold herself   890
        In the dress and the wreath of wrought gold,
        Preparing her bridal beauty
        To enter a new home—among the dead.
        So fatal is the snare she will fall into,
        So inevitable the death that awaits her;
        From its cruelty there is no escape.

        And you, unhappy Jason, ill-starred in marriage,
        You, son-in-law of kings:
        Little you know that the favour you ask
        Will seal your sons' destruction   900
        And fasten on your wife a hideous fate.
        O wretched Jason!
        So sure of destiny, and so ignorant!

        Your sorrow next I weep for, pitiable mother;
        You, for jealousy of your marriage-bed,
        Will slaughter your children;
        Since, disregarding right and loyalty,
        Your husband has abandoned you
        And lives with another wife.

                                    [*The* TUTOR *returns from the pal-
                                    ace with the two* CHILDREN.]

TUTOR. Mistress! These two boys are reprieved from banishment.   910
  The princess took your gifts from them with her own hand,
  And was delighted. They have no enemies in the palace.

[MEDEA *is silent.*]

Well, bless my soul!
  Isn't that good news? Why do you stand there thunderstruck?
MEDEA [*to herself*]. How cruel, how cruel!
TUTOR.   That's out of tune with the news I brought.
MEDEA. How cruel life is!
TUTOR.   Have I, without knowing it,
  Told something dreadful, then? I thought my news was good.
MEDEA. Your news is what it is. I am not blaming you.
TUTOR. Then why stand staring at the ground, with streaming eyes?   920
MEDEA. Strong reason forces me to weep, old friend. The gods,
  And my own evil-hearted plots, have led to this.
TUTOR. Take heart, mistress; in time your sons will bring you home.
MEDEA. Before then, I have others to send home.—Oh, gods!

[*She weeps.*]

TUTOR. You're not the only mother parted from her sons.
  We are all mortal; you must not bear grief so hard.
MEDEA. Yes, friend. I'll follow your advice. Now go indoors
  And get things ready for them, as on other days.

[*Exit* TUTOR. *The* CHILDREN *come
  to* MEDEA.]

O children, children! You have a city, and a home;
  And when we have parted, there you both will stay for ever,   930
  You motherless, I miserable. And I must go
  To exile in another land, before I have had
  My joy of you, before I have seen you growing up,
  Becoming prosperous. I shall never see your brides,
  Adorn your bridal beds, and hold the torches high.
  My misery is my own heart, which will not relent.
  All was for nothing, then—these years of rearing you,
  My care, my aching weariness, and the wild pains
  When you were born. Oh, yes, I once built many hopes
  On you; imagined, pitifully, that you would care   940
  For my old age, and would yourselves wrap my dead body
  For burial. How people would envy me my sons!
  That sweet, sad thought has faded now. Parted from you,
  My life will be all pain and anguish. You will not
  Look at your mother any more with these dear eyes.
  You will have moved into a different sphere of life.

Dear sons, why are you staring at me so? You smile
  At me—your last smile: why?

[*She weeps. The* CHILDREN *go from
her a little, and she turns to the*
CHORUS.]

Oh, what am I to do?
Women, my courage is all gone. Their young, bright faces—
I can't do it. I'll think no more of it. I'll take them   950
Away from Corinth. Why should I hurt *them,* to make
Their father suffer, when I shall suffer twice as much
Myself? I won't do it. I won't think of it again.

What is the matter with me? Are my enemies
To laugh at me? Am I to let them off scot free?
I must steel myself to it. What a coward I am,
Even tempting my own resolution with soft talk.
Boys, go indoors.

                                        [*The* CHILDREN *go to the door, but
                                        stay there watching her.*]

If there is any here who finds it
Not lawful to be present at my sacrifice,
Let him see to it. My hand shall not weaken.   960

Oh, my heart, don't, don't do it! Oh, miserable heart,
Let them be! Spare your children! We'll all live together
Safely in Athens; and they will make you happy. . . . No!
No! No! By all the fiends of hate in hell's depths, no!
I'll not leave sons of mine to be the victims of
My enemies' rage. In any case there is no escape,
The thing's done now. Yes, now—the golden coronet
Is on her head, the royal bride is in her dress,
Dying, I know it. So, since I have a sad road
To travel, and send these boys on a still sadder road,   970
I'll speak to them. Come, children; give me your hand, dear son;
Yours too. Now we must say goodbye. Oh, darling hand,
And darling mouth; your noble, childlike face and body!
Dear sons, my blessing on you both—but there, not here!
All blessing here your father has destroyed. How sweet
To hold you! And children's skin is soft, and their breath pure.
Go! Go away! I can't look at you any longer;
My pain is more than I can bear.

                                        [*The* CHILDREN *go indoors.*]

                                        I understand
The horror of what I am going to do; but anger,
The spring of all life's horror, masters my resolve.   980

                                        [MEDEA *goes to stand looking to-
                                        wards the palace.*]

CHORUS.
    I have often engaged in arguments,
    And become more subtle, and perhaps more heated,
    Than is suitable for women;
    Though in fact women too have intelligence,
    Which forms part of our nature and instructs us—
    Not all of us, I admit; but a certain few
    You might perhaps find, in a large number of women—
    A few not incapable of reflection;

    And this is my opinion: those men or women
    Who never had children of their own at all   990
    Enjoy the advantage in good fortune
    Over those who are parents. Childless people
    Have no means of knowing whether children are
    A blessing or a burden; but being without them
    They live exempt from many troubles.

    While those who have growing up in their homes
    The sweet gift of children I see always
    Burdened and worn with incessant worry,
    First, how to rear them in health and safety,
    And bequeath them, in time, enough to live on;   1000
    And then this further anxiety:
    They can never know whether all their toil
    Is spent for worthy or worthless children.

    And beyond the common ills that attend
    All human life there is one still worse:
    Suppose at last they are pretty well off,
    Their children have grown up, and, what's more,
    Are kind and honest: then what happens?
    A throw of chance—and there goes Death
    Bearing off your child into the unknown.   1010

    Then why should mortals thank the gods,
    Who add to their load, already grievous,
    This one more grief, for their children's sake,
    Most grievous of all?
MEDEA. Friends, I have long been waiting for a message from the
    palace.
    What is to happen next? I see a slave of Jason's
    Coming, gasping for breath. He must bring fearful news.

[Enter a MESSENGER.*]*

MESSENGER. Medea! Get away, escape! Oh, what a thing to do!
    What an unholy, horrible thing! Take ship, or chariot,
    Any means you can, but escape!
MEDEA.   Why should I escape?   1020

MESSENGER. She's dead—the princess, and her father Creon too,
  They're both dead, by your poisons.
MEDEA.   Your news is excellent.
  I count you from today my friend and benefactor.
MESSENGER. What? Are you sane, or raving mad? When you've com-
    mitted
  This hideous crime against the royal house, you're glad
  At hearing of it? Do you not tremble at such things?
MEDEA. I could make suitable reply to that, my friend.
  But take your time now; tell me, how did they die? You'll give
  Me double pleasure if their death was horrible.
MESSENGER. When your two little boys came hand in hand, and en-
    tered   1030
  The palace with their father, where the wedding was,
  We servants were delighted. We had all felt sorry
  To hear how you'd been treated; and now the word went round
  From one to another, that you and Jason had made it up.
  So we were glad to see the boys; one kissed their hand,
  Another their fair hair. Myself, I was so pleased,
  I followed with them to the princess's room. Our mistress—
  The one we now call mistress in your place—before
  She saw your pair of boys coming, had eyes only
  For Jason; but seeing them she dropped her eyes, and turned   1040
  Her lovely cheek away, upset that they should come
  Into her room. Your husband then began to soothe
  Her sulkiness, her girlish temper. 'You must not,'
  He said, 'be unfriendly to our friends. Turn your head round,
  And give up feeling angry. Those your husband loves
  You must love too. Now take these gifts,' he said, 'and ask
  Your father to revoke their exile for my sake.'
  So, when she saw those lovely things, she was won over,
  And agreed to all that Jason asked. At once, before
  He and your sons were well out of the house, she took   1050
  The embroidered gown and put it round her. Then she placed
  Over her curls the golden coronet, and began
  To arrange her hair in a bright mirror, smiling at
  Her lifeless form reflected there. Then she stood up,
  And to and fro stepped daintily about the room
  On white bare feet, and many times she would twist back
  To see how the dress fell in clear folds to the heel.

  Then suddenly we saw a frightening thing. She changed
  Colour; she staggered sideways, shook in every limb.
  She was just able to collapse on to a chair,   1060
  Or she would have fallen flat. Then one of her attendants,
  An old woman, thinking that perhaps the anger of Pan[23]
  Or some other god had struck her, chanted the cry of worship.

[23] The old woman at first suspects some attack of unreasonable terror such as was associated with the nature-god Pan (from whose name the word "panic" derives).

But then she saw, oozing from the girl's lips, white froth;
The pupils of her eyes were twisted out of sight;
The blood was drained from all her skin. The old woman knew
Her mistake, and changed her chant to a despairing howl.
One maid ran off quickly to fetch the King, another
To look for Jason and tell him what was happening
To his young bride; the whole palace was filled with a clatter
Of people running here and there.   1070
                                        All this took place
In a few moments, perhaps while a fast runner might run
A hundred yards; and she lay speechless, with eyes closed.
Then she came to, poor girl, and gave a frightful scream,
As two torments made war on her together: first
The golden coronet round her head discharged a stream
Of unnatural devouring fire: while the fine dress
Your children gave her—poor miserable girl!—the stuff
Was eating her clear flesh. She leapt up from her chair,
On fire, and ran, shaking her head and her long hair   1080
This way and that, trying to shake off the coronet.
The ring of gold was fitted close and would not move;
The more she shook her head the fiercer the flame burned.
At last, exhausted by agony, she fell to the ground;
Save to her father, she was unrecognizable.
Her eyes, her face, were one grotesque disfigurement;
Down from her head dripped blood mingled with flame; her
    flesh,
Attacked by the invisible fangs of poison, melted
From the bare bone, like gum-drops from a pine-tree's bark—
A ghastly sight. Not one among us dared to touch   1090
Her body. What we'd seen was lesson enough for us.

But suddenly her father came into the room.
He did not understand, poor man, what kind of death
Had struck his child. He threw himself down at her side,
And sobbed aloud, and kissed her, and took her in his arms,
And cried, 'Poor darling child, what god destroyed your life
So cruelly? Who robs me of my only child,
Old as I am, and near my grave? Oh, let me die
With you, my daughter!' Soon he ceased his tears and cries,
And tried to lift his aged body upright; and then,   1100
As ivy sticks to laurel-branches, so he stuck
Fast to the dress. A ghastly wrestling then began;
He struggled to raise up his knee, she tugged him down.
If he used force, he tore the old flesh off his bones.
At length the King gave up his pitiful attempts;
Weakened with pain, he yielded, and gasped out his life.
Now, joined in death, daughter and father—such a sight
As tears were made for—they lie there.
                                        To you, Medea,
I have no more to say. You will yourself know best

How to evade reprisal. As for human life,   1110
It is a shadow, as I have long believed. And this
I say without hesitation: those whom most would call
Intelligent, the propounders of wise theories—
Their folly is of all men's the most culpable.
Happiness is a thing no man possesses. Fortune
May come now to one man, now to another, as
Prosperity increases; happiness never.

[*Exit* MESSENGER.]

CHORUS. Today we see the will of Heaven, blow after blow,
    Bring down on Jason justice and calamity.
MEDEA. Friends, now my course is clear: as quickly as possible   1120
    To kill the children and then fly from Corinth; not
    Delay and so consign them to another hand
    To murder with a better will. For they must die,
    In any case; and since they must, then I who gave
    Them birth will kill them. Arm yourself, my heart: the thing
    That you must do is fearful, yet inevitable.
    Why wait, then? My accursed hand, come, take the sword;
    Take it, and forward to your frontier of despair.
    No cowardice, no tender memories; forget
    That you once loved them, that of your body they were born.   1130
    For one short day forget your children; afterwards
    Weep: though you kill them, they were your beloved sons.
    Life has been cruel to me.

[MEDEA *goes into the house.*]

CHORUS. Earth, awake! Bright arrows of the Sun,
    Look! Look down on the accursed woman
    Before she lifts up a murderous hand
    To pollute it with her children's blood!
    For they are of your own golden race;
    And for mortals to spill blood that grew
    In the veins of gods is a fearful thing.   1140
    Heaven-born brightness, hold her, stop her,
    Purge the palace of her, this pitiable
    Bloody-handed fiend of vengeance!

    All your care for them lost! Your love
    For the babes you bore, all wasted, wasted!
    Why did you come from the blue Symplegades
    That hold the gate of the barbarous sea?
    Why must this rage devour your heart
    To spend itself in slaughter of children?
    Where kindred blood pollutes the ground   1150
    A curse hangs over human lives;
    And murder measures the doom that falls
    By Heaven's law on the guilty house.

[*A child's scream is heard from inside the house.*]

CHORUS. Do you hear? The children are calling for help.
O cursed, miserable woman!
CHILDREN'S VOICES. Help, help! Mother, let me go!
Mother, don't kill us!
CHORUS. Shall we go in?
I am sure we ought to save the children's lives.
CHILDREN'S VOICES. Help, help, for the gods' sake! She is killing us! 1160
We can't escape from her sword!
CHORUS. O miserable mother, to destroy your own increase,
Murder the babes of your body!
Stone and iron you are, as you resolved to be.

There was but one in time past,
One woman that I have heard of,
Raised hand against her own children.
It was Ino,[24] sent out of her mind by a god,
When Hera, the wife of Zeus,
Drove her from her home to wander over the world. 1170
In her misery she plunged into the sea
Being defiled by the murder of her children;
From the steep cliff's edge she stretched out her foot,
And so ended,
Joined in death with her two sons.

What can be strange or terrible after this?
O bed of women, full of passion and pain,
What wickedness, what sorrow you have caused on the earth!

[*Enter* JASON, *running and breathless.*]

JASON. You women standing round the door there! Is Medea
Still in the house?—vile murderess!—or has she gone 1180
And escaped? I swear she must either hide in the deep earth
Or soar on wings into the sky's abyss, to escape
My vengeance for the royal house.—She has killed the King
And the princess! Does she expect to go unpunished?

Well, I am less concerned with her than with the children.
Those who have suffered at her hands will make her suffer;
I've come to save my sons, before Creon's family
Murder them in revenge for this unspeakable
Crime of their mother's.
CHORUS.   Jason, you have yet to learn
How great your trouble is; or you would not have spoken so. 1190

---

[24] Ino had helped to bring up the god Dionysus, who was born of Zeus and Semele. Hera,
Zeus' consort, drove Ino to madness in revenge for Zeus's begetting of Dionysus.

JASON. What trouble? Is Medea trying to kill me too?
CHORUS. Your sons are dead. Their mother has killed both your sons.
JASON. What? Killed my sons? That word kills me.
CHORUS.   They are both dead.
JASON. Where are they? Did she kill them out here, or indoors?
CHORUS. Open that door, and see them lying in their blood.
JASON. Slaves, there! Unbar the doors! Open, and let me see
    Two horrors: my dead sons, and the woman I will kill.

> [JASON *batters at the doors.* MEDEA
> *appears above the roof, sitting in
> a chariot drawn by dragons, with
> the bodies of the two children be-
> side her.*]

MEDEA. Jason! Why are you battering at these doors, seeking
    The dead children and me who killed them? Stop! Be quiet.
    If you have any business with me, say what you wish.   1200
    Touch us you cannot, in this chariot which the Sun
    Has sent to save us from the hands of enemies.
JASON. You abomination! Of all women most detested
    By every god, by me, by the whole human race!
    You could endure—a mother!—to lift sword against
    Your own little ones; to leave me childless, my life wrecked.
    After such murder do you outface both Sun and Earth—
    Guilty of gross pollution? May the gods blast your life!
    I am sane now; but I was mad before, when I
    Brought you from your palace in a land of savages   1210
    Into a Greek home—you, a living curse, already
    A traitor both to your father and your native land.
    The vengeance due for your sins the gods have cast on me.
    You had already murdered your brother at his own hearth
    When first you stepped on board my lovely Argo's hull.
    That was your beginning. Then you became my wife, and bore
    My children; now, out of mere sexual jealousy,
    You murder them! In all Hellas there is not one woman
    Who could have done it; yet in preference to them   1220
    I married you, chose hatred and murder for my wife—
    No woman, but a tiger; a Tuscan Scylla[25]—but more savage.
    Ah, what's the use? If I cursed you all day, no remorse
    Would touch you, for your heart's proof against feeling. Go!
    Out of my sight, polluted fiend, child-murderer!
    Leave me to mourn over my destiny: I have lost
    My young bride; I have lost the two sons I begot
    And brought up; I shall never see them alive again.
MEDEA. I would if necessary have answered at full length
    Everything you have said; but Zeus the father of all
    Knows well what service I once rendered you, and how   1230

[25] A monster who attacked mariners sailing between Italy and Sicily through what is now
called the strait of Messina.

You have repaid me. You were mistaken if you thought
You could dishonour my bed and live a pleasant life
And laugh at me. The princess was wrong too, and so
Was Creon, when he took you for his son-in-law
And thought he could exile me with impunity.
So now, am I a tiger, Scylla?—Hurl at me
What names you please! I've reached your heart; and that is right.

JASON. You suffer too; my loss is yours no less.

MEDEA.   It is true;
But my pain's a fair price, to take away your smile.

JASON. O children, what a wicked mother Fate gave you!   1240

MEDEA. O sons, your father's treachery cost you your lives.

JASON. It was not my hand that killed my sons.

MEDEA.   No, not your hand;
But your insult to me, and your new-wedded wife.

JASON. You thought *that* reason enough to murder them, that I
No longer slept with you?

MEDEA.   And is that injury
A slight one, do you imagine, to a woman?

JASON.   Yes,
To a modest woman; but to you—the whole world lost.

MEDEA. I can stab too: your sons are dead!

JASON.   Dead? No! They live
To haunt your life with vengeance.

MEDEA.   Who began this feud?
The gods know.

JASON.   Yes—they know the vileness of your heart.   1250

MEDEA. Loathe on! Your bitter voice—how I abhor the sound!

JASON. As I loathe yours. Let us make terms and part at once.

MEDEA. Most willingly. What terms? What do you bid me do?

JASON. Give me my sons for burial and mourning rites.

MEDEA. Oh, no! I will myself convey them to the temple
Of Hera[26] Acraea; there in the holy precinct I
Will bury them with my own hand, to ensure that none
Of my enemies shall violate or insult their graves.
And I will ordain an annual feast and sacrifice
To be solemnized for ever by the people of Corinth,   1260
To expiate this impious murder. I myself
Will go to Athens, city of Erechtheus,[27] to make my home
With Aegeus son of Pandion. You, as you deserve,
Shall die an unheroic death,[28] your head shattered
By a timber from the Argo's hull. Thus wretchedly
Your fate shall end the story of your love for me.

JASON. The curse of children's blood be on you!
Avenging Justice blast your being!

[26] The goddess was regarded as defender of wives and marriage.
[27] Legendary Athenian king.
[28] One version of Jason's death is that he died in this way, at Corinth, struck by a falling
beam as he sat near his old ship, the *Argo*.

MEDEA. What god will hear your imprecation,
    Oath-breaker, guest-deceiver, liar?   1270
JASON. Unclean, abhorrent child-destroyer!
MEDEA. Go home: your wife waits to be buried.
JASON. I go—a father once; now childless.
MEDEA. You grieve too soon. Old age is coming.
JASON. Children, how dear you were!
MEDEA. To their mother; not to you.
JASON. Dear—and you murdered them?
MEDEA. Yes, Jason, to break your heart.
JASON. I long to fold them in my arms;
    To kiss their lips would comfort me.   1280
MEDEA. *Now* you have loving words, now kisses for them:
    Then you disowned them, sent them into exile.
JASON. For God's sake, let me touch their gentle flesh.
MEDEA. You shall not. It is waste of breath to ask.
JASON.
        Zeus, do you hear how I am mocked,
        Rejected, by this savage beast
        Polluted with her children's blood?

        But now, as time and strength permit,
        I will lament this grievous day,
        And call the gods to witness, how   1290
        You killed my sons, and now refuse
        To let me touch or bury them.
        Would God I had not bred them,
        Or ever lived to see
        Them dead, you their destroyer!

                                    [*During this speech the chariot has
                                        moved out of sight.*]

CHORUS. Many are the Fates which Zeus in Olympus dispenses;
    Many matters the gods bring to surprising ends.
    The things we thought would happen do not happen;
    The unexpected God makes possible;
    And such is the conclusion of this story.[29]   1300

_____

[29] The last five lines are a formulaic ending, used also at the conclusion of several other
plays by Euripides, including *Alcestis, Andromache, Helen,* and *The Bacchae.*

ALCESTIS

Translated by William Arrowsmith

CHARACTERS

APOLLO

DEATH

CHORUS *of Old Men of Pherai*

LEADER *of Chorus*

MAID *to Alcestis*

ALCESTIS, *wife of Admetos*

ADMETOS, *king of Pherai*

HERAKLES

PHERES, *father of Admetos*

SERVANT

SCENE

The scene is Pherai, chief city of Thessaly. The stage building represents the palace of ADMETOS, *king of Thessaly. In the center is a large double-doored entrance, flanked by two lateral doors; one door leads to the women's quarters, the other to the men's.*

Enter APOLLO, *with traditional bow and quiver, from one of the lateral doors. He walks toward the steps leading to the orchestra, then stops and makes his farewell to the house.*[1]

APOLLO. House of Admetos, farewell.
    Apollo takes his leave of you,
    dear house . . . though it was here that I endured
    what no god should ever be compelled to bear.
    Here, with serfs and laborers, I ate the bread of slavery.

[*He turns to the audience.*]

I do not blame Admetos.
The author of my shame was Zeus. He killed
my son Asklepios, stabbing him through the heart
with his fatal lightning. And I in anger
retaliated. I killed the one-eyed Cyclopes   10
because they forged for Zeus those blazing bolts
in which my son died.[2] And so,
in punishment, Zeus doomed *me*,
a god, to this duress,
constraining me to be the bond-slave
of a death-bound man.

---

[1] The setting, Thessaly, is northeastern Greece. Apollo carried a bow and quiver because he was the god of archery. The orchestra was the open space in front of the stage.

[2] Asklepios, son of Apollo (the god of healing), succeeded in bringing the dead to life. In thus sinning against the natural order of things, he offended Zeus, the king of the gods, and was killed by his lightning. In return, Apollo killed the Cyclopes (not the one-eyed giants of the *Odyssey* and *Aeneid* but the workers in the heavenly smithy where Zeus' thunderbolts were forged).

He drove me here, to this country of Thessaly,
where I served as cowherd for a good and generous man—
a man who is now my friend—Admetos.

                                        Until today
I guarded this house from every evil thing,   20
loyally and well. It was I who saved Admetos
from sentence of death. He was doomed to die young,
but I outwitted the Fates[3] and won him a reprieve:
Admetos' day of death might be deferred
if someone else would volunteer to take his place
below. One by one he asked them all,
all those who were bound to him by ties of love,
but no one would.
His father and mother were old, and he was theirs,
but even they refused. Everyone refused.   30
All but one: his wife Alcestis.
Only she
would volunteer to leave the sweet light of the sun
and take his place below.
                            She is dying now.
Her women are holding her, but she is sinking
in the final agony of death. This is the day,
the fatal day, and she must die.
                            And now
I take my leave of this dear house which sheltered me
and which I love. Death must not pollute
my bright divinity.
                    Look: already   40
the god of Death, the god who consecrates the dead
is here to take his victim to the world below.
He has been waiting for this day with great impatience.
And now Death is here, punctual as always,
at the appointed hour.

> [APOLLO *descends to the orchestra
> and moves toward the eastward exit.
> From the west* DEATH *appears, a
> grim and winged figure, shrouded
> in black and carrying a naked
> sword. Startled to discover* APOLLO,
> *he stops short, and the two gods face
> each other in tense confrontation on
> opposite sides of the orchestra.*]

DEATH. You here,
   Bright One,
   meddling with this house again?

[3] In myth, the Fates were three women who spun, measured, and cut the thread representative of an individual human life. Apollo outwitted them by getting them drunk.

Have you returned
to violate again the dues and honors 50
of the gods below?
You cheated the Fates
by craft and guile.
You saved Admetos from death.
And now, bow in hand,
unsatisfied and unappeased,
you come in violence
to save Alcestis too.
Didn't she give her solemn word
to take Admetos' place? 60

APOLLO. Don't be afraid, Death.
My principles are fair, and I have reason on my side.

DEATH. If you have reason on your side, then why the bow,
Apollo?

APOLLO. The bow is my attribute and habit.
Where I go, it goes.

DEATH. Your habit, is it?
Like your habit of always favoring this house?
Is *that* your principle?

APOLLO. Admetos is my friend.
The troubles of those I love constrain me too.

DEATH. Then you mean to take Alcestis by force?

APOLLO. I did not take Admetos. Not by force. 70

DEATH. Then why is he still here, among the living,
when he belongs below?

APOLLO. He gave you his wife.
You came to get Alcestis, didn't you?

DEATH. I did.
And she is *mine*, Apollo. Where I go, she goes:
beneath the earth.

APOLLO. Take her then.
No, wait, Death . . .

DEATH. Wait?
To kill those doomed to die? Don't teach me my office,
Apollo.

APOLLO. Defer her death.

DEATH. Ah, I see. Go on.

APOLLO. Let Alcestis grow old. Let her live,
I adjure you, Death

DEATH. Never.
I have my dues and honors too, Apollo, 80
as dear to me as yours to you.

APOLLO. One life is all you get. Young or old,
what difference does it make?

DEATH. Honor.
The younger my victim, the more mankind fears me
and respects me.

APOLLO.   Think it over, Death.
   Let Alcestis die old, and her funeral will be rich.
   The profit is yours.
DEATH.   Spoken like a plutocrat, Apollo.
   You legislate in favor of the rich.
APOLLO.   Amazing.
   This talent for quibbling, this shyster wit—
   it's not what we expect of Death.   90
DEATH. The rich would buy immunity from dying.
APOLLO. Then you refuse my appeal?
DEATH.   I do. Irrevocably.
   You know my stubborn nature.
APOLLO.   All too well.
   Men hate you for it. The gods despise you.
DEATH. Even you must learn a limit, Apollo.
   You cannot have your way in everything you want.
   You will not have it now.
APOLLO. Death, Death, all your savagery
   is not enough to help you now.
   Today, now,   100
   a man is coming to Admetos' house.
   A *man*, I say. Man enough
   to break the wild stallions of Diomedes
   and herd them home from frozen Thrace.[4]
   That man will find a welcome in this house.
   He will fight with you and break you, Death,
   and by brute strength bring Alcestis back.
   You shall honor my appeal against your wish.
   You shall not have my thanks.
   My hatred you shall have. You have it now.   110

                    [*Exit* APOLLO *to the east.*]

DEATH. Bluster away, Apollo.
   Words will get you nowhere.

                              [*He moves toward the central door
                              of the palace, then turns and ad-
                              dresses the audience directly.*]

This woman must go beneath the earth.
She is *mine*.
With this sword I now inaugurate my rite.
The head whose curls are cut by this bright blade
is consecrated to the gods below:
forever.

───────────

[4]The man is Herakles. Along with performing other almost impossible tasks imposed on
him by the king Eurystheus as the price of winning immortality, he had been ordered to tame
the fierce horses of Diomedes (a Thracian king).

[DEATH *enters the palace through
the central door. The doors close
slowly behind him. There is a prolonged silence. Then the* CHORUS *of
old citizens of Pherai enter the orchestra, thronging around the entrance to the palace.*]

LEADER. So still. . . . I wonder what this silence means.   120
    Why is the great house so strangely quiet?
    No one at the door, no servant here
    to say the queen has died and we must mourn her.
    Or is Alcestis still alive?
    Let her live!
    If bravery and love deserve the light,
    no woman on this earth,
                                oh Alcestis,
    ever less deserved to die!
CHORUS. [*speaking individually*]
    —Silence. . . .
                —do you hear the cry of women?
    —The beating of women's hands?
    —Or women keening with that cry   130
    that says—
                —everything is over?
    —Nothing.
                —Nothing.
    —Silence still.
    —And no servant stationed at the door. . . .
    O Paian,[5] lord of healing!
    —Great Apollo,
                come,
    calm this storm of sorrow.
    —But if the queen had died,
    the house would shrill with grief,
    the high, shrill cry of sorrow.   140
    —Dead, dead. . . .
                —She must be dead,
    but not yet buried.
    —What makes you so certain?
    —How could Admetos bury such a wife
    with no friends or mourners by?
    —Surely he could not do it.
    —Not a woman like this. . . .
    —Not Alcestis!

    —And where is the cleansing water[6]
    custom prescribes for a house of death?   150

---

[5] God of healing, sometimes identified with Apollo.
[6] Water with which visitors of the dying could cleanse themselves from the defilement of
being in the presence of death.

—There is no water at the door. . . .
—And no locks of hair[7]
hang in the courtyard
to honor the dead. . . .
—No cry of women keening. . . .
—But this is the day decreed.
—Decreed?
          —The day of death.
—Hateful word!
—It hurts, it hurts.
LEADER. As it must.   160
When the good are hurt, those who love them suffer too.
We love, and love hurts.
CHORUS.—Take ship and search the world: there is
no harbor, landfall, haven, hope;
no oracle or pilgrimage a man might go
and, going, save our lady's life.
None:
Not in Lykia[8] where the shining god
sings to mortal men his convalescent song.
Not Sahara where, at holy Ammon's[9]   170
healing touch, the dying desert makes
a miracle of green. But not for her,
whose death shows cruel and sheer
as crag or stone, where hope holds not,
and prayer no purchase has,
and god is still,
and all's despair.

—There *was* one hope: Asklepios, Apollo's
healing son. If *he* still saw the light;
if he were here, he might have brought her   180
back,
alive from Hades[10] and the long black
home. Such was his skill and craft
he medicined to life and saved
death-tamed and -broken men,
redeeming all—until great Zeus,
enraged with man's contriving mind,
hurled the long white flash of fire in which
the healer perished with his art.
And now I see of hope no   190
sign. None. Nothing
but despair.

[7] The rites of mourning included the tribute of a lock of one's hair.
[8] An area of Asia Minor associated with Apollo, the "shining" god of healing.
[9] An African god, sometimes identified with Zeus; he had a temple in a lush oasis of the
Libyan Sahara.
[10] The realm of the dead.

—All that kings might do, our king has done.
Everywhere, on all the altars of the gods,
the blood of sacrifice runs black. But
this disease is mortal. It has no cure.
LEADER. Look:
    a servant girl is coming out.
    She is crying. . . .
    Now we shall know the truth.   200

                                        [*Enter* MAID *from the palace, weep-*
                                        ing. At the sight of the elders of the
                                        CHORUS, *she tries to stifle her sobs.*]

No need to hide your tears, child.
If anything has happened to your mistress,
your sorrow is only natural.
But tell us: is Alcestis still alive?
MAID. What can I tell you? She is still alive.
    And dead.
LEADER.   What are you saying, child?
MAID. Sir, the queen is dying. . . .
LEADER.   Oh, Alcestis, Alcestis!
    What a loss. Poor Admetos, how I pity him. . . .
MAID. The master does not know the meaning of his loss.
    He will not know, until it is too late.   210
LEADER. Nothing can be done to save her?
MAID.   Nothing.
    This is the day. Her destiny is too strong,
    a force she cannot fight.
LEADER.   Admetos—
MAID.   Did all he could.
    Her women are working, preparing for the funeral.
    She will be buried as we knew her and loved her
    in this life: a queen.
LEADER.   In dying and living both:
    incomparably a queen. For courage and love
    Alcestis has no rival among all women
    on this earth.
MAID.   Rival?
                What would the woman be who could rival
    or surpass Alcestis? What woman ever loved a man so much?   220
    Loved him more than herself? So much more
    she gave her life to let him live? In love
    she has no equal, sir: the whole world knows it.
    But what she did and said, in privacy, inside—
    her bravery and beauty in the face of death—
    will touch your heart and amaze you even more.
                                      Listen:
    This morning, when she knew her day had come,
    she bathed her white body in fresh running water

from the river. Then she opened the great cedar chest,
took out her richest, finest things and dressed herself   230
in all her loveliness—oh, sir, she was beautiful!
And then she kneeled,

[*kneeling*]

                                   like this,
                                       before the hearth
and prayed:
                 "Bright goddess[11] who guards my home,
I am going to the world below. This is the last time
I shall ever kneel at your feet. Lady, I pray you,
protect my children and be good to them.
Give my little boy a loving wife.
And give my girl a kind and gentle husband.
Do not let them die like me, before their time
has come.[12] Let them live out their lives; let them be happy   240
here in the land of their fathers."
Then she went from altar to altar, praying at each one
and wreathing it with sprays of fresh myrtle; quietly,
not a sound, not a cry, that sweet face of hers
composed and calm, oh, as though no evil thing
could ever touch her.
                         But there in her room
she threw herself on the great bed, and the sobs
broke from her. "Dear bed," she cried,
"it was here I offered my maiden body and my love
to Admetos. Now I offer him my life. . . .   250
Sweet bed, I love you still . . . even now. So much
that I would rather die than live without you
both. And now it is goodbye. . . .
Some other girl will sleep here in my place
perhaps—not more loving, not more loyal, than me,
but happier, much happier, I think.
Then she kneeled,
                        —so—
                            and kissed the bed,
smothering it with tears, crying uncontrollably,
till there were no tears left. Then she rose
and stumbled, head down, groping for the door.   260
On the sill she stopped and turned, hesitating,
then threw herself back on the bed again. There,
on the bed, the children found her. Sobbing,
they clung to their mother's dress, while she pulled them
to her, hugging and kissing: goodbye, goodbye.

[11] Hestia, goddess of the hearth and the personification of home and family.
[12] Both Alcestis and Admetos are probably to be visualized as very young. Greek girls of
good family often married in their early teens; Alcestis may therefore be no older than twenty
or so, and Admetos almost equally young.

Then the servants came crowding around, mourning.
No one there, not even the meanest, was forgotten.
Graciously, simply, she gave her hand to each
and said goodbye.
              This is what
Admetos' house has lost. What has he gained but life?
If he had died, he would have lost Alcestis.   270
Now, as matters stand, he has lost her anyway.
As long as he lives, his life will have that taste
of pain and loss—a bitterness that lasts.
LEADER. It is a great loss—a loss whose anguish
    he must be suffering now.
MAID.   Yes, he is crying,
holding his wife in his arms, imploring her
not to leave him, not to die, madly
wanting what cannot be,
while she lies there, a dead weight
in his arms, all white and wasted   280
with that dying sickness.
She can barely breathe,
but with what little breath she has,
she is calling for the light,
the light she'll never see again.
She wants the light:
          the light! the light!
a last look at the sun's sweet light.
But, sir, I'll go
and announce your presence.
It isn't everyone who cares about this house   290
or is ready to share our sorrows with us.
But you have always been a good and loyal friend,
and, sir, you're welcome here.

                        [*Exit* MAID *into the palace.*]

CHORUS.—Is there no answer, Zeus?
No way? Must it be disaster?

—Answer our prayers, O Lord!
Or must we put black mourning on?

—We must, we must. But first, friends,
pray to the gods. Their power is great.

[*kneeling*]

O Paian, power of healing, come!   300
Apollo, have pity on this house!
Lord, give us life
as once you conquered Death
and let Admetos live.

Now Death has come to take his queen.
Apollo, lord,
                    beat back this ruthless,
savage god of Death!

—I pity you, Admetos. How, without Alcestis,
can you live at all?

—O gods,   310
in bitterness for this,
a man might cut his throat
or twist the rope around his neck
and hang himself for grief
in heaven's holy face.

—Not for love,
but something more than love,
Alcestis dies for you today,
oh Admetos!
LEADER. Look, here comes the queen Alcestis,   320
    with king Admetos at her side.

> [ALCESTIS, *supported by* ADMETOS
> *and maids, appears from the palace,*
> *followed by the two children. Attend-*
> *ants bring on a litter which they*
> *place near the door.*]

CHORUS. O land of Pherai mourn
    and let the wounded Earth cry sorrow;
    no nobler woman ever lived
    and yet she goes   fading   dying
    wasted
                    down
                        to the world below.
LEADER. Do not say that marriage has more happiness than pain.
    I have seen too many marriages.   And now I see
    the torment of this house: this bravest of women
    dying, and a king in agony. As long as he lives,   330
    his life will taste of death,
    all he will have is hell.
ALCESTIS. [*stretching out her arms in longing to sun and sky*]
    O Sun
    Sweet shining light
    white clouds swelling   wheeling in the blue
ADMETOS. The god of light looks down and sees us suffering.
    Why, why? How have we hurt the gods that you should die,
    Alcestis?

ALCESTIS. [*slumping down, head forward, faintly*]
Sweet earth of Iolkos[13]   O earth
where I was born   O house that sheltered me   340
where I was a girl
in Iolkos

ADMETOS. [*lifting her up and supporting her*]
Up, Alcestis. Stand. Live. Don't leave me now.
Pray. The gods are strong. What they will is done.
Implore the gods, for pity's sake, to let you, please,
let you live.

ALCESTIS. I see the black water and the dead
lake   the boat beached on the sand
and look

              Charon

                            there at the rudder[14]
calling me   Why are you waiting Alcestis?   350
It is time to leave   hurry Alcestis
come
        Don't you hear him calling?
So angry and impatient

ADMETOS. This is a bitter crossing. It is bitter for us both,
Alcestis. O gods, what have we done that we should suffer
so?

ALCESTIS. *No!*   a hand   *some*one   *some*thing
holding me hard, forcing me down

                    down
to the dead world—
              So dark   And look
those black eyes glowing   those great black wings   360
beating over me
             it is Death!   Death!
how terribly he frowns   No no
please   no   let me go   I won't
let me go   the road is dark
I am so afraid

ADMETOS. For all who love you, dear, for the children and me,
this is a dreadful journey. We are afraid for you,
afraid for us all.

ALCESTIS. Admetos let me down   let me lie
down   I am too weak to stand   370
Death is closing in   my eyes are going
dark

                  [*A silence. Then she clutches the
                  children to her.*]

[13] A city (also spelled Iolcus) in Thessaly. Compare the headnote to Euripides' *Medea*.
[14] Alcestis is describing part of the landscape of Hades, realm of the dead. Charon ferried dead souls over a river (sometimes identified as Styx, sometimes as Acheron) to Hades.

O children
goodbye
you have no mother any more
I love you   the light is yours   children
be happy in the light
ADMETOS. Goodbye—
Oh, gods in heaven, I would rather die
than hear you say that dreadful word!   380
Oh, if you could find the strength to speak that hard and bitter
     word to me,
then find the strength to stay!
Oh Alcestis
for our children's sake   for me
be strong   be hard   stand
fight it   live
your dying is my death
in you we live in you we die
by your love we pray you

[*kneeling*]

live   390
ALCESTIS. Admetos, I am dying.
This is my last request of you, so listen well.
Of my own free will I gave my life
to let you live. I am dying for you, Admetos,
but I did not have to die.
I could have chosen otherwise. As your widow
I might have married any man in Thessaly
and lived with him here and ruled this royal house.
But without you, with these children fatherless,
I could not live. I am young, Admetos,   400
but I have given you my youth—the good years,
the happy years. All the others failed you.
Your father and your mother would have let you die,
though they had lived good lives and reached an age
when death comes naturally and right. There was glory too,
for them, in giving up their lives to save their son.
For they had no other sons, and no hope of any
after you. They could have died for you,
and you and I would still have lives to live.
You would not be left alone to mourn for me,   410
and our children would have a mother. . . .
                                                  Why?
Who knows? Some god has brought these things to pass.
Let it be.
               Now, Admetos, I want your promise.
It is a little thing I ask you, nothing much—
oh, nothing like the gift of life I gave you,
since that's a gift that has no price. No,

a small request, but one I have a mother's right to ask,
and you, I think, a father's heart to grant. Surely
you love these children, Admetos, as much as I.
Oh, if you love them, make them masters in this house;   420
do not take a second wife and make her mistress here
where she may do our children harm because they're mine,
and she is jealous.
                 Oh promise me, Admetos, promise me.
Swear to me no woman will ever enter
through that door again. A new wife hates the children
of the old, hates them with a viper's poison.
The boy will have his father to protect him.
                      —But you,
poor girl, what will your childhood be like,
if your father marries a second wife? Will she be kind
while you are growing up? Or will she make up stories   430
out of spite and spoil your hopes of marriage, spoil
your wedding day when I will not be there
to take your side? Not be there to hold your hand and help
in childbirth, when a girl most needs her mother's love
and help. . . .
            I will not be there. I have to die.
Oh, not tomorrow, not the next day, not this month,
but now, in just a minute, I will not be here
with you at all.
             Goodbye   I love you very much
Be happy
              Admetos   be proud of me   you can.
Children   remember your mother   remember my example   440
be brave
LEADER. I will vouch for Admetos.
He is a noble man. He will keep his promise.
ADMETOS. You have my word, my solemn promise.

                    [*solemnly raising his right hand*]

I swear it.
          Oh, Alcestis,
living or dead you are my wife.
I love you, I will always love you.
Only you.
No other woman will ever live with me again.
There is no woman in this world of Thessaly   450
by birth so noble or in looks so lovely,
none, none who could ever take your place
in my home or heart.
Your children are ours; I want no more.
I only pray the gods will let them live
for me to cherish and enjoy:
they are all I have of you.

I will mourn you, not the customary year,
but all my life.
Those whose cowardice has caused your death,   460
my father and mother, will have my hatred, always.
Their love was only words: a lie.
You were loyal in love. You alone, Alcestis.
You loved me so you gave your life, your only life,
to let me live.
                    I know what I have lost, how much,
and I will mourn you as your love and mine deserve.
Here and now I banish from this house
all festivity. The happiness that filled these rooms—
good cheer and gaiety, the table where I sat and drank with
    friends,
the joy of music, flowers—all of them I banish now   470
forever. I used to play the lute, but I will never
touch its strings again. Let the flute I loved
be still.
            Oh, Alcestis, all my joy in life is gone
with you!
            How can I hold you here, a little of you, still?
Listen:
        I'll have an artisan of cunning skill
contrive your likeness for our bed, and at night
I'll lie beside it, dreaming you are there
and whispering your name. . . .
                                Cold comfort, I know,
but I have nothing else. Even seeming helps.
You would come to me at night, often, in dreams,   480
and I would have, if only for a while,
the satisfaction of the love I used to have
in life.
            In life. . . .
                        Oh, Alcestis,
if I had the song and poetry of Orpheus[15]
so I could charm the god of Hell, bewitch his queen
and, by my singing, spell you back from death,
I'd go beneath the ground. Nothing would stop me,
not Kerberos[16] himself or Charon bending
at his fatal oar could stop me from bringing you back
to life.

            Wait for me below. Wait until I die.   490
Make a house for us, where we can be together.
I'll have our bodies buried in a cedar coffin,

[15] A legendary poet and musician who won from the king and queen of the dead (Hades and Persephone) the privilege of bringing his wife Eurydice back to life. The stipulation was that, as he led her back from the Lower World, he must not look behind, but he did so and thus lost her again. The story is told in Ovid's *Metamorphoses*, Book X.
[16] Cerberus, a dog with three heads that guarded the entrance to the land of the dead.

side by side. In death I will never
leave your side, since only you were true in life.
You stood beside me to the bitter end.
LEADER.   Admetos,
I will stand beside you now, as friends should stand,
and we will mourn your wife together.
All our grief combined is less than she deserves.
ALCESTIS. Children, you have heard your father give his word.
He will never make another woman welcome in this house.   500
He will honor my memory.
ADMETOS. I promised.

[*raising his right hand*]

And I will keep my promise.
I swear it.
ALCESTIS.   Then give me your hand.

[*She takes his right hand and formally delivers the children to his
keeping.*]

Now take these children and love them
ADMETOS.   I do.
I love the gift as I love the giver.
ALCESTIS. Love them as their mother loved them
ADMETOS.   I must.
I will love them as their mother would have loved them,
had she lived.
ALCESTIS.   Oh   I should have lived   not died.
My poor children
ADMETOS.   How can I live without you?
ALCESTIS. Time will dull your grief   the dead are nothing   510
ADMETOS. Take me with you, Alcestis! For god's sake,
let me die. . . .
ALCESTIS.   My dying is enough   Admetos
I am dying for you.
ADMETOS.   Stay with me. . . . Stay. . . .
ALCESTIS. Darkness now   so heavy   my eyes are closing
ADMETOS. What am I, Alcestis, without you? Nothing.
ALCESTIS. I am nothing now   the dead are nothing
ADMETOS. Lift your head, Alcestis. Look at your children.
How can you bear to leave them?
ALCESTIS. [*raising her head with a final effort*]
                                        I have to leave them
Goodbye   children
ADMETOS.   Look at them! *Look!*

ALCESTIS. Ahh   520

[*She sinks down on the litter, dead.*]

ADMETOS. What are you doing? No . . . no . . . no . . .
LEADER. She is dead, Admetos.

> [*to the* CHORUS *and audience*]
>
> —The queen is dead.
>
> [*Sobbing and crying, the children
> throw themselves on the body of their
> mother, while* ADMETOS *tries to
> comfort them.*[17]]

ADMETOS. She cannot hear you, she cannot see you.
Poor motherless children. . . .

O gods in heaven,

this is beyond bearing. . . .

> [*Crumbling in grief, he joins his
> children beside the bier.*]

LEADER. It had to be, Admetos. All we can do with death
is bear it patiently. Be brave. You are not the first
to lose a loving wife; you will not be the last.
We were born to die.
ADMETOS.   I know. . . . Day after day
I saw it coming on, those great wings like a black shadow   530
swooping down. And waiting, just waiting—
oh, if you knew the agony of it.

> [*with an effort controlling himself*]
>
> But no more.

I must give orders for the funeral.

> [*to the* CHORUS]
>
> —Good friends,

I need your presence and support. Help me
by remaining here. Raise a song in honor of Alcestis,
and by the beauty and the power of your singing,
cry defiance to this hard and bitter god
whom nothing will appease but death.

---

[17] The translator (whose aim is to produce an effective version for performance) deletes
here a lament by Eumelos, Alcestis' young son, on the grounds that it is too maudlin for
modern tastes, especially since we do not have the music to which the lament would have been
sung in the Greek theater. The translator, in a note, renders the passage thus: "Alas for my
fate! Mother has gone below. She is no longer in the light, Father. She has left me, poor
woman, and orphaned my life. Look, look to her eyelids, at her arms hanging limp. Listen to
me, Mother, listen. It is I, Mother, who call to you—your little fledgling, pressing my lips to
yours. I am young, Father, left alone and forsaken by my dear mother. I have suffered
pitifully, and you, dear, sister, have suffered with me. Ah, Father, your marriage was all in
vain. You failed to reach the goal of old age with her. She died before you died. Now, Mother,
with your going away, our house has been destroyed."

[*to audience*]

—To my subjects
I now proclaim a period of solemn public mourning
for your queen. Shear your hair in sign of sorrow,   540
put on mourning black. Let my cavalry and guard
crop their horses' manes. Throughout this city
let the lyre be still; let no one touch a flute
until twelve moons have waxed and waned and brought the year
full circle.

       I shall never bury anyone I loved
so much, nor anyone who loved me more. Only she
would take my place in death, and she shall have from me
the honor she deserves.

> [*The servants raise the litter holding
> the body of* ALCESTIS *and carry it
> inside the palace, followed by*
> ADMETOS *and the two children.*]

CHORUS. Farewell, Alcestis. Our love goes with you now
  beneath the earth to your long home among the tribes   550
of those on whom the sweet light never shines: unseeing
and unseen. We shall not see your like again.
O Death, in that dark tangle of your mind, if you have
eyes to see, look among the herded dead who go
with Charon in his long slow crossing over Acheron;
look and you will see, blazing in that crowd of ordinary
dead, the noblest life the sunlight ever shone upon!

You shine in memory. And mortal men, remembering
you, will praise your death: a song that does not die.
Each year, unaccompanied, your song shall rise,   560
a shining on the lips of men; or sometimes chanted
to the rude and simple lyre, at Sparta when the year
has come full circle, and the moon, a splendor, rides
the livelong night; or there in Athens' blazing noon.
Wherever there is light, wherever men remember love,
Death shall not eclipse the glory of your shining.

I am old, too old. Oh, if the strength were mine
to bring you back, I'd go below and break the stubborn
grip of Hell, where Charon, toiling, bends his body
to the dead stroke of the sad oar slowly beating   570
over Acheron. So beautiful in love, so strong
and brave, you gave your life to take his place in death!
For love you went below. Rest peacefully, Alcestis.
Earth, lie gently on her grave, for she was gentle always.
LEADER. Lady, if Admetos ever loves again,
  he will have your children's hate and mine. He will have it
always.

CHORUS. They were old, so old, his father and his mother, both
    blanched with age, both in the winter of their years.
    Old, so very old. But still they grudged their bodies   580
    to the grave. Old cowards, grasping at the light,
    so greedy still to live! Though he was theirs, their own,
    those old ones would not die. But you, Alcestis, you,
    in the fresh morning of your days, you gave your life
    and took Admetos' place below. You died for love.
    For such a love as yours, I would give my very life!
LEADER. Unselfish love, like hers, is rare. So rare
    that I would want her at my side, alive. I would love her
    always.

> [*Enter* HERAKLES *from the left.
> Dressed in his familiar lionskin and
> armed with his bow, he is immedi-
> ately recognized by the* CHORUS.]

HERAKLES. I give you greetings, elders of Pherai.

[*to* LEADER]

—Old sir,   590
    is king Admetos here?
LEADER.   He is, Herakles. But tell me:
    what business brings you to Thessaly?
HERAKLES.   Obligation, friend.
    I have a labor to perform. Eurystheus is my master.
    He commands, and I obey.
LEADER.   What is your mission?
    And where are you bound?
HERAKLES.   A long, hard journey.
    My destination's Thrace. My orders are to capture
    Diomedes' horses.
LEADER.   *Diomedes' horses?* It can't be done,
    Herakles. Surely you've heard of Diomedes?
HERAKLES. No. Nothing. I've never been in Thrace before.
LEADER. Those horses are wild. They can't be broken.   600
HERAKLES. *Can't* be broken?
LEADER.   Not without a fight, they can't.
HERAKLES. Fighting's what I do.
    My labors are my life. I can't refuse.
LEADER. But with Diomedes, it's kill or be killed.
HERAKLES. I've confronted Death before.
LEADER.   Suppose you kill him:
    what will it get you?
HERAKLES.   Why, I get his horses.
    And what I get, Eurystheus gets.
LEADER.   It won't be easy
    to put a bridle on those jaws and curb those teeth.

HERAKLES. What's so hard? Are they fire-breathing monsters,
    or just plain horses?
LEADER.   *Wild*·horses, Herakles. Killers.   610
    Cannibal horses,[18] with teeth so sharp and fast
    they can slice a man to ribbons.
HERAKLES.   To hear you tell it,
    they sound like tigers, not a team of horses.
LEADER. You should see their mangers. Caked with human blood.
HERAKLES. So Diomedes bred these pretties, did he?
    And who does Diomedes claim to be? Who bred *him?*
LEADER. His father was the war-god Ares, or so he boasts.
    He commands, as king, the golden cavalry of Thrace.
HERAKLES. Ares' son, is he? There you have the story
    of my labors and my life. It's a damned hard road[19]   620
    I'm doomed to travel, friend. Rough, uphill
    all the way. One after another
    I've had to fight every bastard son the war-god ever had.
    First it was Lykaon. Then Kyknos.[20] And now
    this confrontation with the master of this pack
    of killer horses. But no man on this earth
    has ever seen the son of Alkmene[21] flinch from a fight.
    No one ever will.
LEADER.   Here comes king Admetos now
    to welcome you in person.

                        [*Enter* ADMETOS *from the palace.*
                        His hair is cropped and he is dressed
                        in mourning black.]

ADMETOS.   Welcome, Herakles.
    Son of Zeus, welcome to my house.
HERAKLES.   Heaven smile   630
    on you and yours, Admetos!
ADMETOS.   If only it had.. . . .
    But thank you, Herakles. I know you mean well.
HERAKLES. Why is your hair cut? Are you in mourning?
ADMETOS. There has been a death in my house, Herakles.
    The funeral is today.
HERAKLES.   I hope nothing has happened
    to your children.
ADMETOS.   No, thanks be to heaven,
    my children are alive and well.
HERAKLES.   Your father then?
    If so, he lived a long, full life, Admetos.

---

[18] Diomedes' horses were fed human flesh.

[19] Early in his life, Herakles had been confronted by two women, Pleasure and Virtue. The first offered him a life of ease, the latter offered glory achieved by arduous effort. He chose Virtue.

[20] Sons of Ares, both killed by Herakles.   [21] Herakles' mother; his father was Zeus.

ADMETOS. My father is well. My mother too.
HERAKLES.   Not Alcestis?
   Surely not Alcestis?   640

                              [*a long pause*]

ADMETOS. Yes. . . .

                              [*a short pause, then quickly*]

                 No.
HERAKLES.   What in god's name are you saying,
   Admetos? Is she alive or is she dead? Which?
ADMETOS. Both. Both. I am in agony, Herakles . . .
HERAKLES.   Alive
   and dead? But these are riddles, Admetos.
   Make sense.
ADMETOS.   You know that she was doomed to die?
HERAKLES. I know she promised to take your place below.
ADMETOS. Knowing what she promised, knowing she is doomed,
   how can I think of her as still alive?
HERAKLES.   Ah . . .
   Wait until she dies, Admetos. Don't mourn her yet.
ADMETOS. Those who are doomed are as good as dead.   650
   And the dead are nothing.
HERAKLES.   There is a difference
   between life and death. Or so men think, Admetos.
ADMETOS. That is your opinion, Herakles. Not mine.
HERAKLES. Then why are you in mourning? Clearly
   someone has died, someone you loved, Admetos.
   Who?
ADMETOS.   A woman, Herakles. A woman has died.
HERAKLES. Was she related to you?
ADMETOS.   Not by blood.
   But there were bonds . . . The attachment was strong.
   We loved her very much.
HERAKLES.   Why was she living here?
ADMETOS. After her father's death, she was left an orphan.   660
   We took her in.
HERAKLES.   I am sorry for you, Admetos.
   I have come at a bad time, it seems.

                              [*He shoulders his bow and turns to
                              leave.*]

ADMETOS. What are you doing, Herakles?
HERAKLES.   Leaving, Admetos.
   I have other friends in these parts. I'll stay with them.
ADMETOS. Impossible, my lord. I won't have it.
   I won't hear of it.

HERAKLES.   Your house is in mourning.
A guest would only be a burden.
ADMETOS.   The dead are dead.

> [*taking* HERAKLES *by the arm and
> forcibly detaining him*]

I insist.
         You *must* stay.
HERAKLES.   It wouldn't be right, Admetos.
This is a time for mourning, not entertaining friends.
You cannot do both at once.
ADMETOS.   The guest rooms are separate.   670
I'll put you there.
HERAKLES.   Let me go to someone else,
Admetos. Please. I ask it as a favor.
ADMETOS.   Impossible.
You must stay.

> [*to a servant*]

—You there. Take our guest inside.
Open up the guest rooms on the east wing
of the house. Then serve him dinner and wine.
Be generous. And shut the doors on the courtyard.
I do not want our guest to be disturbed at dinner
by the sounds of mourning.

> [HERAKLES *is escorted inside.*]

LEADER.   Are you mad, Admetos?
Your wife not dead an hour, and you can bear the thought
of entertaining guests?
ADMETOS.   This man is my friend.   680
What would your answer be if I turned my friend away
from my home and city? That I deserved your admiration?
Surely not. And what would I gain?
My wife would still be dead.
My loss would be exactly what it is,
neither more nor less. But I would lose a friend.
I have pain enough without the pain
of having my house called inhospitable and rude.
I am his host; he is my friend and guest.
His hospitality to me is lavish, unsurpassed   690
in generosity and love, when I stay with him in Argos.
And Argos is a thirsty place.[22]
LEADER.   Your friend, you say.
Then why conceal your sorrow from your friend?
ADMETOS. If he suspected what had happened here,

---

[22] That is, both arid in climate and given to heavy drinking.

I do not think he would have stayed. Some, I know,
will shake their heads and say that what I did
was wrong. But this house of mine has yet to learn
discourtesy to guests or less than due regard
for those with claims upon my honor and my love.

[*Exit* ADMETOS *into the palace.*]

CHORUS.
    Hospitality is here.   700
What house could be more gracious or more generous
than this? Open-handed, always prodigal and free,
its master gives such lavish welcoming
that one might think his guests were gods.
Great gods have sheltered here.
Here Apollo, god of Delphi, condescending,
came, his high divinity constrained to serve
as shepherd for a year. And down these blessèd hills,
to mating flocks the god of music sang the season's song,
O Hymen Hymenaios O![23]   710

So powerful Apollo's song
that spotted lynxes crouching in the mountain rocks
were drawn by joy, no longer wild, to stray like browsing sheep
beside the shepherd god. And here, compelled
from Orthrys'[24] shaggy glens, the golden lions came.
Bright god, so sweet your clarity of song,
the fawn came shivering from the darkened wood,
and there, beside the forest edge, shyly stepping
from the arbor of the pines, the strong light caught her—
dappled, on delicate legs, dancing as Apollo sang:
O Hymen Hymenaios O!   720

Your guest was god, Admetos. And so,
by grace, your house is now beyond all mortal houses
blest in wealth of flocks beside the clear blue waters
of Boibias.[25] Westward, mile on mile
across the greening plain, your tilth and pastures range
to far Molossos[26] where the lord of light drops down
to ford his horses in the Adriatic night;
and eastward too your kingdom goes, across the peaks
where Pelion[27] takes its headlong plunge, harborless and sheer,   730
down to the green Aegean. Admetos, all
this blessèd land is yours, by grace of god.

---

[23] A standard refrain in epithalamia, or wedding songs; Hymen was later personified as
god of marriage.
[24] A mountain south of Pherai.
[25] A lake, usually turbid, called "clear" in this passage to emphasize Apollo's powers.
[26] A region in the west of Greece; Admetos' wide rule thus stretches from sea to sea.
[27] A mountain near the coast of Thessaly, in northeastern Greece.

And now, again, this gracious man
has opened wide the doors and welcomed in this house
another guest. Another—even though the wife he loved
was newly dead, and the agony of grief
lay freshly on him . . . Noble man, his courtesy
and grace exceed all human scale. But who can say?
Greatness of soul is all that human wisdom knows;
all philosophy is in it. I stand in awe,   740
Admetos. And somehow I have faith, a growing hope
that for this noble, heaven-minded man,
all, by grace of god, may still be well.

> [*Enter* ADMETOS *from the palace.*]

ADMETOS. My friends, I appreciate your kindness and support.
Thank you for remaining. The funeral is ready now
and my men are bringing out the bier.

> [*Enter Attendants slowly and sol-
> emnly, with the bier of* ALCESTIS *on
> their shoulders. Reverently, they set
> it down directly before the great cen-
> tral doors of the palace.*]

But first,
before we take her body to the grave,
I would like you, friends, to speak the customary words:
the last farewell. We shall not see her in this life again.
LEADER. Wait, Admetos.   750
I see your father Pheres on his way, and servants with him
bringing gifts to offer to the gods below.

> [*Enter* PHERES *dressed in mourn-
> ing black. His shorn hair is white
> and he is stooped with age; he walks
> slowly up the ramp to the bier of*
> ALCESTIS; ADMETOS *faces him on
> the other side of the bier.*]

PHERES.   Son,
I have come to help you bear the burden of your grief.
You have lost a good wife: a decent, loving,
humble wife. A hard and bitter loss, but bear it
you must.

> [*He motions to his servants to come
> forward with the funeral gifts.*]

Accept these tokens of my respect,
and let her take them with her to the world below.
We must honor her in death as she deserves;

she gave her life to let you keep the light. No,   760
she would not let this poor old man drag out
his dying years deprived of all he had—his one,
his only, son. And by her bravery in death,
she has been a credit—no, a glory—to her sex.

                              [*formally addressing the body on the
                              bier*]

—Lady,
rest in peace.
By your courage you have been the savior of my son.
Your generosity restored the fortunes
of my broken house, when it was down. Alcestis,
fare you well, even in the world below.
And rest in peace.
                              —Mark my words, son.   770
Marriage is for most of us a losing proposition.
But this wife of yours was pure gold, and no mistake.
And gold is what I give her now.

                              [*He signals to his servants to lay
                              their gifts upon the bier, while
                              ADMETOS angrily steps forward to
                              intercept them.*]

ADMETOS. Who asked *you* to come? Who invited *you?*[28]
Not I. Not her.
Love? *What* love? Your love's a lie: all words.
So keep your gold. She'll never wear your trinket
love.
She'll be buried as she is. Without your gifts.
Or you. Leave. Who needs you anyway?   780
Who needs you *now?*
You came, you say, to bring me sympathy and help.
The time for you to help was when I had to die
or find a substitute. Where were you *then?*
Vanished. Nowhere. Like your love. You disappeared
and let another take your place in death.
You were old, and she was young.
And now you have the gall to come here with your mock
sorrow and your hypocrisy of love!
You never gave a damn for me!   790
Where was your love when I needed you? Why,
for all you cared, I might have been some slave's bastard

---

[28]The ensuing episode is a good example of the *agon,* a device of Greek tragedy—especially common in Euripides—consisting of a carefully articulated dramatic confrontation between characters.

smuggled in the house and set to suckle at the breast
of that barren bitch who calls herself my mother.²⁹
No, when courage was required,
when dying was the issue and the test,
you showed us what you really are.
Not my father, but a cheap coward!
Gods, is there any coward in this world like you?
There you were, a withered bag of bones, tottering   800
into eternity. But still you wouldn't die! Not *you.*
You didn't dare to die. So you let a woman,
no blood of yours, do your duty for you.
To her and her alone I owe the tenderness and love
I would have lavished on my parents in their age,
had they loved me like a son.
If I were you,
I would have fought—yes, *fought!*—for the privilege
of dying for my son. Besides,
your time was short. A few brief years at best.   810
So what had you to lose?
Every happiness a man could have, you had.
You inherited a kingdom when you were still a boy.
You had a son, so your succession was secure
and you could die in peace, knowing there would be
no rival claimants for your throne, no wars.
You cannot say that you abandoned me
because of my neglect: I showed you all the honor
a son could give. I was always good to you
in your old age. And how have you repaid my love?   820
You would have let me die.
Well, now your time is running out, old man.
So hurry. Use what little time you've got to breed
another son to care for you in your old age and stuff you
in the ground.

                    [*raising his hand.*]

            So help me gods,
I will never lift a hand to bury you!³⁰
You refused to lift a finger for my life.
I disown you both.
If I still live and see the light,
everything I might have owed to you as son,   830
I pledge to her who gave me life.

---

²⁹ For a Greek wife not to have children was grounds for divorcing her, and therefore it
sometimes happened that a wife passed off another woman's child as her own. In his angry
eagerness to disclaim his parents, Admetos unthinkingly calls into question his own legitimacy.
³⁰ To neglect this pious duty to a parent was one of the worst possible acts of disrespect. For
an ancient Greek audience, Admetos' vow would have been shocking in the extreme.

Gods, how I hate them,
all these aging hypocrites, tottering around,
telling you how much they want to die,
stuffed with self-pity, whining about old age
and its indignities, their long, slow, crawling passage
to the grave.
But let them get the slightest glimpse of Death
and suddenly they stick like leeches to the light
and tell you life is not so bad.   840
LEADER. Stop it, both of you.
Haven't you sorrows enough without this too?
                                          Boy,

why must you exasperate your father?
PHERES. Boy,
who in god's name do you think you are?
Are you my master now, and I some poor, bought,
cringing Asiatic slave that you dare dress me down
like this? I am a free man, Thessalian born,
a prince of Thessaly. And I will not be bullied
by the likes of you, arrogant boy.

                              [ADMETOS *turns angrily away.*]

                          Hear me out.   850
Don't think you'll pelt me, boy, with your abuse
and then just turn your back.

Damn you, boy,
I made you lord and master of this house of mine.
I gave you life, I raised you.
I am not obliged to die for you as well.
Or do you think my father died for me?
There is no law, no precedent, in Greece
that children have a claim upon their fathers' lives.
A man is born to happiness, or otherwise.   860
He is born for himself.
Everything you had the right to get from me, you got.
I made you ruler of a rich and populous country.
And I intend to leave you all the vast domain
my father left to me.
So how have I hurt you? What *more* do I owe you?
Life?
No. You live yours, and I'll live mine.
Do your own dying. I'll do mine.
You love the light.   870
What makes you think your father doesn't love it too?
The time we spend beneath the earth, I think, is very long.
And life is short, but what there is of it is good,
good and sweet.

As for fighting, boy, you fought all right.
You fought like hell to live—life at any price!—
beyond your destined time. You only live
because you took her life. You *murdered* her.
And *you* dare talk about *my* cowardice—
you, who let a woman outdo you in bravery,
let her give her life to keep her gigolo
alive?   880
But you're clever, I admit.
Immortality is yours, yours for the asking.
All you have to do is wheedle your latest wife
into dying in your place.
And then, like the cheap coward that you are,
you accuse the rest of us of failing in our duty!

ADMETOS. Listen—

PHERES.   *You* listen, boy. Remember this.
You love your life. Well, so does every man alive.
And if you call us names for *that,*   890
worse things will be said of you. They won't be pretty,
and they'll all be true.

LEADER. There have been too many ugly words, too much abuse,
already.
         —Old man, stop provoking your son.

ADMETOS. Let him talk, and then I'll have my say.
                                                     —You see?
The truth hurts. Your cowardice was your mistake.
You didn't dare to die.

PHERES.   That was no mistake.
The mistake would have been dying for *you.*

ADMETOS. And dying young is just the same as dying old?

PHERES. One life is all we have. Not two.   900

ADMETOS. The way you clutch at that one life of yours,
you'll outlive Zeus.

PHERES.   How have I hurt you
that you should hate me so?

ADMETOS.   Old age
has made you greedy. Greedy to live!

PHERES. Greedy, am I?
Who killed that girl whose corpse you're burying?
And *you* talk to me of greed!

ADMETOS. It was *your* cowardice that killed her.

PHERES. *You* took her life. *You* killed her.

ADMETOS. O gods, I hope   910
I live to see the day when you come crawling to me
for help!

PHERES. That's your style, not mine.
Find some woman to help you live. Marry *her,*
then let her die.

ADMETOS. Your fault. You wouldn't die.

PHERES. No, I wouldn't.
This god's light is sweet, I tell you, sweet.
ADMETOS. You cheap coward, you don't deserve to live!
PHERES. Go bury your dead.   920
Whether you like it or not, *I'm* still alive.
You won't gloat over my dead body. Not today,
boy.
ADMETOS. Don't expect the world to praise you when you die—
if you ever do.
PHERES. What the hell do I care what people say of me
after I'm dead?
ADMETOS. Gods,
what shabby, shameless cowards these old men are!
PHERES. *She* wasn't shabby, was she? No, she was *brave*.   930
Brave enough—stupid enough—to die for you.
ADMETOS. Leave. Let me bury my dead.
PHERES. I'm leaving.
Let the murderer bury his victim in peace.

> [*Exit* PHERES, *followed by his ser-
> vants with the rejected gifts.*]

ADMETOS. Go and be damned to you,
you and that woman I used to call my mother.
You have no son.
Grow old, both of you, as you deserve—
childless, heirless, alone.
Never let me see you in this house again.   940
So help me god,
if I had heralds here to proclaim
that I disown you both and ban you from my house,
I'd do it.

> [*A long silence ensues as* PHERES
> *slowly makes his exit, and* ADMETOS'
> *attendants take up their position by
> the bier.*]

> [*to* CHORUS]

And now, friends, let us perform our sad task,
and take Alcestis' body to the grave.

> [*The Attendants lift the bier of*
> ALCESTIS *to their shoulders and the
> funeral cortège moves slowly and
> solemnly toward the right. Leading
> the procession is the bier, which is
> followed by* ADMETOS *and the
> children, and finally the entire*
> CHORUS.]

LEADER. Fare you well, Alcestis.
    Let Hermes[31] of the unseen world receive his honored guest,
    and the Dark Lord welcome you below as your nobility and love
        deserve.
    For if the good fare best, and courage has its due   950
    even in that pale democracy below,
    the Queen herself of all the dead will rise in homage,
    seeing you, Alcestis.
    No braver mortal ever lived.

> [*Exeunt omnes in slow, funeral pro-*
> *cession. For a while the stage is*
> *empty and silent. Then an old*
> SERVANT, *wearing a scowling*
> *mask, appears from the palace. He*
> *speaks directly to the audience. Now*
> *and then, as he speaks, the voice of*
> HERAKLES *can be heard singing,*
> *off-key and indistinctly, the snatches*
> *of a familiar drinking-song.*]

SERVANT. I've seen a lot of strangers in my time,
    guests traipsing in here from all over the world,
    and we put 'em all up, bed 'em, and feed 'em
    food. But this newest guest is the worst damned
    guest this house and I have ever seen. Right away,
    anyone could have seen Admetos was in mourning.   960
    So what does this dull clod do? Barges in,
    big as life and bold as brass. I mean,
    any man with a grain of decency or ordinary common sense
    would have seen Admetos was in trouble
    and accepted what we had to give without a lot of noise
    and fuss. But not this fellow. Nossirree,
    if we don't fetch him what he wants, he yells at us
    to shake a leg. "Hurry up!" he bellows. "Dammit. *Move!*"
    Then he picks up a great big wooden bowl of wine—
    both hands at once, just like a peasant—   970
    and swills it down, straight, unwatered, strong,
    and reddish black like the ground that grew it.
    Well, before you could say Dionysos,[32]
    he was heated up, half-crocked, high
    as a kite. Then he slaps a wreath of myrtle on his head,
    and starts in murdering some bawdy song.
    Listen . . .

> [*From within is heard the bray of a*
> *drunken voice, singing.*]

[31] One of the messenger-god's functions was to conduct the dead to Hades.
[32] God of wine and revelry.

There *he* was, roaring away over his supper,
without a thought for poor Admetos and his troubles,
and there we were, mourning for our mistress,   980
and what with the maids wailing and beating their breasts—
well, you've never heard such a bloody medley in all
your days. And of course we couldn't tell him we were mourning
because king Admetos had given orders forbidding it.
Anyway, here I am, left
behind at home to entertain this so-called guest
(though, if you ask me, burglar or highwayman
or just plain pirate is closer to the mark).
And meanwhile they've taken our lady to the grave,
and I didn't get to follow her body or hold out my hand   990
and say goodbye to her the way I wanted.
Because she was good to us all, a good, kind mistress,
more like a mother than a mistress, always
calming the master down when he went off in one of his fits
of rage. Anyway, that's why I hate the sight
of this guest who came barging in on our troubles.
Guest or no guest, I detest the man
and, god knows, I've got the right to hate him.

> [*Enter* HERAKLES, *tipsy and reel-
> ing, from the palace. On his head he
> wears a wreath of flowers; in one
> hand he carries a flask of wine, in
> the other a large cup which he peri-
> odically drains and refills. His
> speech is punctuated by periodic hic-
> cups and emphatic belching.*]

HERAKLES. Hey, you there!
Yeah, I mean *you*, with the big frown on your face!   1000
What'sh *your* problem, sourpuss?
Butler'sh oughtta be polite, goddamit.
Servish with a smile.
An' none of those goddam killjoy looksh either.
Here I am, your mashter's bes' fren',
an' all you can do is glower at me with that goddam
miserable mug. An' why?
'Cause someone you barely knew dropped dead.
Dead . . .
C'mere, fella,   1010
an' I'll let you in on a l'il secret.
Make a better man of you.
I mean, wise up:
we all gotta die.
You know what it'sh like to be a *man?*
I mean,
d'you really unnerstan' the human condishun, fren'?

I can see *you* don't. How could you, with a face like that?
Well, lissen, mister:
we all gotta die. An' that's a fact.   1020
There's not a man alive who knows the odds on death.
Here today. Gone tomorrow.
Poof.
That's fate. A mystery. I mean,
there's jus' no knowin'. Man can't figger it out.
Well,
that's my message. So what d'you say?
Cheer up and have a l'il drink,
huh?
Live for the day. Today is ours.   1030
Tomorrow's fate.
Hey,
an' there's somethin' else, Yessir. Aphrodite.[33]
Don't forget Aphrodite, fren'.
'Cause thass a good l'il goddess.
They just don' come any sweeter than Aphrodite.
Take my advice, fella, an' forget your troubles.
Well, what d'you say?
Am I talkin' sense? Damn right I am.
So forget whatever it is thass makin' you so goddam   1040
glum. Come on, man,
have a drink. Drown your troubles.
Here, put these flowers on your head,
and bottoms up!

[*He drains his glass and refills it.*]

Lissen:
you hear that wine purling and gurgling in the cup?
Well, a swallow of this will do wonders, friend,
for whatever's ailing you.
I mean, we all gotta die. Right?
Well, that's why we all gotta think human thoughts,   1050
and live while we can.
Eat, drink, and be merry.
Take it from me,
the way those gloomy, bellyachin' tragedians gripe,
life isn't life at all, it's just a goddam
funeral.
SERVANT. Quite, sir. I understand.
But, sir, this happens to be a house of mourning.
Your drunken revelry is grossly out of place.
Sir.
HERAKLES. Izzat so?   1060

---

[33] Goddess of love, sex, and beauty; in this context she represents all the vital forces contrasting with death.

Jus' because a woman's dead? Stranger too, I hear.
Sure, it's sad, but what's the tragedy? Look,
the family's alive and well.

SERVANT.   *Alive and well?*
You mean you still don't know what happened here?
HERAKLES. Of course I know. Admetos told me when I came.

> [*pulling himself together, more so-
> berly*]

Wait.
Are you saying that Admetos *lied* to me?
SERVANT. You know the master, sir. He is hospitable to a fault.
Sometimes his kindness goes too far.
HERAKLES.   I know his kindness well.
Is that the reason I must go without my supper?   1070
Because of some dead stranger?
SERVANT.   *Stranger,* you say?
Oh, sir, what stranger could ever be as close as she?
HERAKLES. [*soberly now, with genuine concern*]
What has happened here?
What is Admetos hiding from me?
SERVANT. Sir, let it be.
She belonged to us.
Go, and let us mourn our dead in peace.
HERAKLES. So it wasn't a stranger who died?
SERVANT. If it were,
nobody would have minded your getting drunk.   1080
HERAKLES. Then Admetos lied to me? Deceived his friend?
SERVANT. Sir, you couldn't have come at a worse time.
This is a house of mourning. Our hair is shorn;
we are dressed in black. You can see for yourself.
HERAKLES. *Who* died, man?
One of the children? Old Pheres? *Who?*
SERVANT. Admetos' queen, sir. Alcestis. Alcestis is dead.
HERAKLES. Alcestis *dead?*
And you were entertaining *me* when *she* lay dead?
SERVANT. Sir, Admetos honors you.   1090
He could not bear the thought of turning you away.
HERAKLES. What husband ever lost a wife like this?
Oh, Alcestis, Alcestis . . .
SERVANT. When she died, sir,
it seemed as though the whole house, every one of us,
died with her.
HERAKLES. Oh, I knew it, I knew it
when I saw his face all red with weeping,
and his hair shorn, and the bitter anguish in his eyes!
And, like a bloody fool, I believed his story   1100
that he was burying some stranger.

A stranger!
And then he made me enter, forced me to come in,
against my will, and accept the welcome of his house.
And then, while he was suffering, mourning his wife,
there I was, his dearest friend,
—gods!—
feasting and carousing like some stupid, drunken clod,
wreathing my head with these damned flowers!

> [*He rips off his wreath and dashes it
> to the ground.*]

And you let me do it!   1110
The whole house was throbbing with this sorrow,
and you never said a word!

Quick, man.
Where is the funeral being held?
Where can I find Admetos?
SERVANT. Go straight that way, on the road to Larisa.
Just outside the walls, sir, you'll see the place,
a tomb of polished marble.

> [*Exit into palace.*]

HERAKLES. Now, Herakles,
your great ordeal begins.   1120
Come, o my tough spirit, you hard, enduring hands calloused with
     my many labors,
come and prove what man I am.
Prove me Herakles,
the hero son my mortal mother bore to Zeus almighty!

Alcestis is dead,
and I must bring her back to the fields of light,
home, safe, to Admetos' arms, and so discharge my debt
of gratitude and love. Admetos' love to me was great,
and it deserves—and it will get—no ordinary kindness
in return.   1130

Soon, I think,
the god of Death, those black wings beating overhead,
will come swooping down and settle by the grave
to drink the sacrificial blood. I'll lie in ambush
there beside the tomb, and when the Dark Lord comes,
I'll break from hiding, seize him with my arms,
and clamp him in a hold so hard he cannot break it,
god though he is. Let him struggle.
I'll crush him in my mortal grip until he does my will
and lets Alcestis go.   1140

But if Death fails to come,
if the blood stays there untasted on the ground,
I'll go beneath the earth, down to the unseen world below,
confront the god of Hell and his Persephone,[34]
and demand Alcestis back. Make no mistake:
I'll force my way below and bring Alcestis home,
and consign her to Admetos' care.
For he deserves this thanks from me:
His house was overwhelmed with grief,
but even so, he took me in, he made me welcome here.   1150
Kind and noble to a fault, he hid his loss
to do me honor as a friend. Where in all Thessaly,
where in all the world, could I find a friend
as generous as this? I could not do it.
And it will not be said of me
that this good and noble man conferred his kindness on a friend
unworthy of his love.

> [*Exit* HERAKLES *to stage right.*
> *There is a brief silence. Then the*
> CHORUS *re-enter from the left, fol-*
> *lowed by the forlorn and grief-*
> *stricken* ADMETOS.]

ADMETOS. O home no home
    emptiness   silence   pain   loss
    going in or coming out   O   1160
    walls of pain: I cannot leave   cannot stay
    Hurt   has no words
    Hurt   will not be still
    O
        let me die
better never have been born
I envy the dead   the dead are beautiful
not here my home
            down   down
my home is with the dead
I hate the light   I hate this earth
O Earth, come over me   1170
and let me die
so lovely is the hostage that I gave to Death
my life is all below
CHORUS. [*individually, while* ADMETOS *sobs helplessly in response*]
    —Take your grief inside, Admetos. Hide, hide
    from the light.
            —You have cause for grief.
    —You have suffered, heaven knows.
    —But grief will never bring her back.
    —The truth is hard.

---

[34] Queen of the realm of the dead.

—Accept it, Admetos:
—You will not see her in this life again.

ADMETOS. Good friends, the wound is fresh,   1180
and you have opened it again . . . Better,
better by far, it would have been
if we had never married, she and I, never loved,
never lived here in this house together!
How I envy them, those men who never marry,
men who have no children, who live for themselves,
alone. Then each would have one life to live.
That pain would be his, nothing more.
He does not live to see his children sicken,
his wife dying in childbirth . . .   1190
Who that had a heart to love would choose such pain
if he could live alone and never know
how much he had to lose?

CHORUS. —It had to be. We cannot choose our fates.
—A man can fight. But not with life,
not with death.
                    —Accept it like a man.
—Hard, hard, I know.
                    —Be brave, Admetos.
—Courage. Others too have lost their wives.
—Some soon, some late, every man is curbed
by suffering or fate.
                    —Now it is your turn.   1200

ADMETOS. This sorrow lasts forever. There is no end to pain
when those we love go into that eternal night
beneath the earth. Why, why, in the name of heaven,
friends, did you stop me when I tried to die
with her? There, in one grave, she and I,
we could have been together always. Always.
And then the lord of Death would have us both,
two lives instead of one. Loyal in love,
we would have crossed that dead water together.

LEADER. [*with the utmost simplicity*]
Admetos, a friend of mine once lost his son, a fine young boy of   1210
exceptional promise, and an only child. His father was an old man,
white with age, and in the last years of his life. But he bore his loss
with dignity, as bravely as he could.

ADMETOS. This house, how can I call it home? How can I go in, remembering how happy I once was here, and how, of all that happiness, nothing now is left? *Then* and *now:* a gulf so great it seems
two wholly different unconnected worlds. I remember *then.* It was
dusk on our wedding day. All around us the pine torches were
blazing, and she and I were coming home to bed, escorted by a
noisy crowd of happy friends and guests, singing and dancing. I   1220
remember how they congratulated me, and how they wished Alcestis happiness and long life (oh, my dead Alcestis!). In our marriage, they told us, high nobilities on either side had merged and

met. And *now*? Now the only song is the cry of mourning. And the
friends who bring me home wear black instead of white. And the
bed is there, the bed is there . . . I sleep alone.

LEADER. Your luck had been good, Admetos. High happiness and
great wealth—both were yours. So when this sorrow struck so suddenly, it found you unprepared. Suffering was something you had
never known.   1230

    Still, your life is yours; you still have wealth. True, you have lost
your wife and the comfort of her love. So have other men. Is it so
strange, really, that human marriages should end in this divorce of
Death?

ADMETOS. Dear friends,
  strange as it may seem,
I think my wife in death is happier than I am now.
No pain, no hurt, will touch her anymore.
She rests in peace, free at last from all   1240
the endless agony of life. And fame is hers
forever.

As for me,
I should not be alive. I should be dead.
The life I have is not worth living. I know it now.
Too late.

How can I bear to go on living in this house?
What happiness is there in coming home, home to this dead
  house,
with its sound of absence, its echo of a voice
that greeted me when I came home? And now nothing, nothing   1250
but this dead silence.
When I go in, the emptiness inside will drive me out.
The empty rooms, the empty bed, the chair she used
to sit on, and the shining floor all dark with dust,
and the children sobbing, huddling at my knees
wherever I go, crying for their mother,
and servants mourning their dead mistress,
remembering a gentle presence that my house has lost
forever . . . .
          I cannot stay here.
                But in the city
I will see my married friends, friends with wives;   1260
the girls and women thronging to their festivals and dances . . .
The very sight of it would drive me home. All
Alcestis' friends, the girls she used to know—
I could not *bear* to see them now. Not
now.

And I have enemies. Behind my back,
they'll point me out, whispering, "Look there,
look at Admetos,

the man who was afraid of death,
the coward who let his wife go down to Hades   1270
in his place? Do you call *that* a man?
What kind of man would curse his father and mother
because he was afraid of dying?
Who but a coward?"

Friends, you say my life is still mine.
But what's the good of living,
when everything I valued in this world is gone,
when I have lost my honor with my wife?

> [*He stands motionless, head down,*
> *in silent despair.*]

CHORUS. Necessity is stone.
Call her death, compusion, fate: against   1280
what man her cruelty comes, that man is doomed.
If poets know, if scholars speak the truth,
nothing stronger, nothing more resistless,
is.
O Man,
against her hard, relentless coming on,
all your craft and intellect are weak.
There is no power in your spells and Orphic[35] songs;
no virtue in your herbs, your healing lore. Nothing,
nothing can resist her coming on. Only patience.   1290
Suffer and submit.

Necessity is stone,
implacable. She has no face
but rock; no human shape or likeness owns,
no cult, nor shrine. She heeds no sacrifice.
She is force, and flint; no feeling has, no
pity. None.

[*kneeling, all together*]

Mistress, Lady without mercy,[36] I have felt
your stroke before. May you never come again!
Only by your hard strength the will of Zeus is done.   1300
By sheer force you break the iron of the Chalybes.[37]
Your will is granite, cruel. Nothing helps. Only patience.
Suffer and submit.

> [*The* CHORUS *now turn and ad-*
> *dress* ADMETOS *directly.*]

---

[35] Orphism was a Greek cult or religion emphasizing the ultimate salvation of the good and punishment of the wicked.

[36] Necessity (Greek *Ananke*), an impersonal force indifferent to human concerns.

[37] An Asian people skilled in the arts of metallurgy; their iron was especially hard.

Admetos, now
this goddess holds you in the bitter bondage of her grip.
Bear it. Be brave. Though you should mourn Alcestis always,
you cannot bring the dead to life. Great heroes
die. Even the sons of heaven[38] fade, darkened
into death, though they were dear, dear as life
to the grieving gods. Alive, Alcestis had our love;   1310
love will be her portion in the world below, for she was
brave. To her, Admetos, you were bound by bonds of love.
Then will you be less brave?

Glory is her right,
Admetos. Do not let Alcestis' grave be numbered
among the ordinary dead. Make her grave a shrine;
honor it as men would honor gods—a holy place
beside the road where those who journey kneel and pray.
The traveler will see her grave and, turning off,
will say of her, "She gave her life to save another.   1320
She is a blessèd spirit now, and so may also bless.
In homage men will kneel before her grave and pray:

[*all together, kneeling*]

"Hail, Lady, mistress of mercy, by your bravery and love,
bless us and be gracious."

                                    [*Enter* HERAKLES, *followed by a
                                    veiled girl.*]

HERAKLES. Admetos,
   when a man is angry with his friend,
   he should speak his mind frankly and freely;
   not keep his feelings smouldering inside.
   As your friend, I thought I had the right
   to stand beside you in your hour of need   1330
   and prove my loyalty.
   But you misled me;
   you deliberately concealed the truth:
   instead of telling me that Alcestis was dead,
   you let me think that you were burying a stranger.
   Then you made me welcome in your unhappy house,
   you gave me food and drink, as though nothing
   had happened here, nothing at all.
   There you were, in mourning for your wife,
   while I, like a clod, was wreathing my head with flowers,   1340
   pouring long libations to the happy gods, getting
   drunk. *Drunk* at a time like this!

---

[38] Mortal offspring of deities (Achilles, for example, whose father was human and whose mother was divine). Herakles, though only one of his parents is divine, will prove to be an exception by gaining immortality.

But how was I to know?
It was *wrong* of you, Admetos, wrong, I tell you,
to treat a friend this way. But let it pass.
You have sorrows enough, old friend.

Listen: I have a reason for returning.

[*indicating the veiled girl standing
behind him*]

You see this woman?
Do me a favor: Keep her here for me,
in your care, until I finish with my mission   1350
in Thrace. I will come for her on my return,
after I have killed Diomedes, and captured his horses.
But if I don't come back—Heaven avert the omen!—
then keep the girl as a servant in your house:
my gift to you. And no small gift, either.
This woman wasn't easily won, Admetos.
ADMETOS. Where did you win her, Herakles?
HERAKLES. Not far from your house, I happened to pass by a place
    where athletic games were being held, contests
    open to all comers. And the prizes offered   1360
    were very tempting. Well, in a word,
    I entered the contest and I won the prize—
    this woman here.
    The winners in the minor events won horses.
    But in boxing and wrestling the prizes were oxen—
    and they threw in the girl as a bonus.
    Well, as luck would have it, there I was,
    and it seemed a shame to lose such splendid prizes.
    So here she is. Now, as I said, Admetos,
    I'd like you to keep her. Take care of her. She's worth it.   1370
    And she's not stolen either, if that's what you're thinking.
    I won her fair and square in a damned hard fight.
    Someday, Admetos, you may be glad I did.
ADMETOS. Herakles,
    my reason for concealing my wife's death from you
    was neither disrespect nor any lack of love.
    God knows,
    I had troubles enough without driving you away
    to look for shelter somewhere else.
    Alcestis' death is mine to mourn. Mine alone.   1380
    My sorrow is enough.

    As for this woman here,
    I beg you, my lord, if you can somehow manage it,
    please, take her somewhere else.
    Give her to some friend who is not in mourning.
    Tell him to keep her. You have many friends in Pherai.

But please, please,
don't remind me of my loss. Seeing this woman here,
here in Alcestis' house, day in, day out,
would be more, much more, than I could bear.   1390
I am crushed with sorrow as it is, Herakles.
Do not burden me with more.

Besides,
where in this house could a young girl stay?
I mean, she *is* young. I can see it, Herakles,
in her jewelry, in the style of clothes she wears.
How could she live here, surrounded by young men?
How could I protect her? Young men are lusty,
their desires not easily controlled.

               —Herakles,
it is *you*, your interests, I am thinking of.   1400
What can I do? Put her in Alcestis' room?
Take her to Alcestis' bed?
I can hear the gossip now, people in the city
saying I ran to some other woman's bed,
and betrayed the wife who died to save me.
Worse, I can hear Alcestis' voice, reproaching me
from underground. And where Alcestis is concerned,
I cannot be too scrupulous. She and she alone
deserves my love.

              [turning to the veiled woman]

        —Woman, whoever you are,
I tell you this, you look like my Alcestis,   1410
so much like her: the same figure, the same height . . .
You are beautiful too . . .

              [He hides his head.]

Herakles,
for god's sake, take this woman away,
out of my sight! I am weak now, do not make my weakness
    worse . . .
Oh, looking at this girl, I seem to see
my lost Alcestis . . . And my heart starts churning,
and the tears—

             [He sobs unashamedly.]

O god, gods in heaven,
now, now, for the first time, I know the anguish of my life . . .   1420
LEADER. Sorrow: there is nothing more to say.
    It does not matter who or what we are.
    The gods do with us what they will. We must bear it.

HERAKLES. If only I had the strength, Admetos, to bring your wife
   back from the world below, back to the light,
   I would have done it.
ADMETOS.   I know. But why speak of it?
   The dead are dead. They never come back.
   Never . . .
HERAKLES.   Control yourself. Bear it like a man.
ADMETOS. Bear it like a man? Easier said than done, Herakles.
HERAKLES. Suppose you mourned her all your life, Admetos?   1430
   What good would it do?
ADMETOS.   No good at all.
   I mourn because I must. I loved her . . .
HERAKLES. I know:
   Nothing hurts like losing those we love.
ADMETOS. I lost myself when I lost her. Lost myself—
   and so much more.
HERAKLES. She was a beautiful woman, worthy of your love.
ADMETOS. I loved her so much I do not want to live.
HERAKLES. Your loss is still fresh. Time will dull the pain.
ADMETOS. If time is death. Death will dull it.   1440
HERAKLES. A new wife, a new bride, will help you to forget,
   Admetos.
ADMETOS. Silence, Herakles. Not another word.
   How could you suggest such a thing?
HERAKLES.   You won't remarry?
   No woman, ever?
ADMETOS. No woman will ever share my bed again.
HERAKLES. Alcestis is dead. How does this help her?
ADMETOS. Wherever Alcestis is, she deserves my honor.
   I owe it to her.
HERAKLES.   And I respect your feelings.
   There are some, of course, who would call you foolish.   1450
ADMETOS. Let them call me anything they want.
   Anything but bridegroom.
HERAKLES.   I admire you, Admetos.
   You are loyal in love.
ADMETOS. She is dead.
   But I would rather die than betray her love!
HERAKLES. Nobly spoken, my good Admetos.
                                        Well, then,

[*taking the veiled girl by the hand
and bringing her forward*]

make this woman welcome in your generous house.
ADMETOS. By your father Zeus,
   I beg you, please, *no!* Anything but that.
HERAKLES. You will be making a mistake, if you say No.   1460
ADMETOS. I would never forgive myself, if I said Yes.

HERAKLES. Obey, Admetos.
  Let me have my way. The courtesy you show this girl
  may serve you in your time of need.
ADMETOS.   O gods,
  how I wish you'd never won her in those games of yours!
HERAKLES. Friends share and share alike.
  When I am winner, you are winner too, Admetos.
ADMETOS. Splendid, Herakles.
  Then make this woman leave. Immediately.
HERAKLES. If she must. But *look* at her first, Admetos.   1470
  See if she should go.
ADMETOS. [*not looking*]   She *must* go.
  You won't be angry with me, will you, Herakles?
HERAKLES. I have my reasons for insisting, Admetos.
ADMETOS. I surrender. You win.
  But I disapprove. Your insistence displeases me.
HERAKLES. You may forgive me soon. Humor me for now.
ADMETOS. If I must, I must.

                          [*to Attendants*]
                  —Servants, take this woman inside.
HERAKLES. Slaves?
  No, I will not surrender this girl to slaves.
ADMETOS. Then take her in yourself.
HERAKLES.   No, she is *yours*,   1480
  Admetos. I will not give this woman to anyone but you.
ADMETOS. And I refuse to touch that woman's hand.
  Let her go inside by herself.
HERAKLES. [*taking* ADMETOS *by the right arm*]
                          No, Admetos.
  I have faith in your right hand—and yours alone.
ADMETOS. [*unsuccessfully attempting to withdraw his arm from* HERAKLES'
    grip]
  My lord,
  I protest: you are forcing me against my wish.
HERAKLES. Courage, Admetos. Welcome your guest.
  Here, reach out your hand. Now take her hand
  in yours.
ADMETOS. [*reluctantly stretching out his hand, but carefully averting his face*]
        Here is my hand.
HERAKLES.   Good gods, man,
  the way you act you'd think she were some Gorgon[39]
  to turn you to stone.   1490

                          [*gently and ceremoniously, he joins
                          the hands of* ADMETOS *and* AL-
                          CESTIS]

[39] A hideous female; anyone who looked at her was turned to stone.

You have her?

ADMETOS.   I do.

HERAKLES.   Then keep her, Admetos.
She is yours, to have and to hold.
Someday, Admetos,
you will know your kindness was not wasted
on the son of Zeus, your good friend and grateful guest.

[*He raises* ALCESTIS' *veil.*]

Now, Admetos, look. Look at her.
Doesn't she look a little like your own lost Alcestis?

[ADMETOS *stares in silent disbelief.*]

Rejoice, old friend.
Be happy. Your day of mourning is over.   1500

ADMETOS. O god, gods in heaven!
This is some miracle I see, impossible, incredible!
Oh, is it *you?* You, Alcestis? Is it *really* you?
Or is this just some mockery, some sweet illusion
sent me by the gods?

HERAKLES. No mockery, Admetos,
but your own wife, in flesh and blood, your own
lost Alcestis!

ADMETOS. How do I know this is not some ghost from underground?

HERAKLES. I am your friend, Admetos,   1510
not some vulgar trafficker in sorcery and ghosts.

ADMETOS. But I buried her today . . . How can this be?
Is it really Alcestis?

HERAKLES.   The very same Alcestis.
I am not surprised you find it strange.

ADMETOS. Can I touch her? Speak to her?
Can she breathe? Does she feel and hear?

HERAKLES. Speak to her, Admetos.
You have what you wanted. You have it all.
Take it.

ADMETOS. Alcestis!   O Alcestis   1520
eyes I love   o sweetest face
these dear hands I never thought to hold again!
You are mine   so incredibly   mine
again   again!

HERAKLES. Again, Admetos. And may no jealous god envy you
your happiness.

ADMETOS.   O my noblest, kindest friend!
Dear son of great Zeus, may Heaven bless you.
May the great god who fathered you guard you
and keep you safe, as you saved me,
you alone, and gave me back my life.   1530

But tell me:
how did you bring Alcestis back to the light?
HERAKLES. I fought with the god who had her in his power.
ADMETOS. Death!
Where did you find the god?
HERAKLES.   Beside the grave.
I took him by surprise, then threw him to the ground.
ADMETOS. Ah.
But why is Alcestis so still? Why can't she speak?
HERAKLES. Until three days have passed,
and the bitter stain of death has disappeared,   1540
she is forbidden to speak.

Now, Admetos, take her in.
And in the future treat your guests and those you love
as they deserve.

And so, goodbye.
My master Eurystheus is waiting in Argos,
and I have labors to perform.
ADMETOS. Stay with us, Herakles. My house is yours.
HERAKLES. Another time, Admetos.
I have work to do. Work that cannot wait.   1550
ADMETOS. Success go with you, friend.
But when your work is done, come back and be
our guest.

                                              [*Exit* HERAKLES.]

        —To all my subjects and fellow citizens,
I here and now proclaim a feast of thanks and praise
to celebrate the happiness of this great event.
Let the high altars blaze and smoke with sacrifice.
From this day forth we must remake our lives,
and make them better than they were before.

Happiness is mine, and now I know it.

                                     [*Exit* ADMETOS, *with* ALCESTIS,
                                     into the palace]

CHORUS. The gods have many forms.   1560
The gods bring many things
to their accomplishment.
And what was most expected
has not been accomplished.
But god has found his way
for what no man expected.
So ends the play.[40]

                                              [*Exeunt omnes.*]

[40] The last eight lines of the play are a formulaic ending used also to conclude other plays
by Euripides: *The Bacchae, Helen, Andromache,* and *Medea.*

Aristophanes
(C. 450–C. 386 B.C.)

Aristophanes was born around 450 B.C., and his death some time during the 380's marks the end of the great century of ancient Greek drama. The chronological sequence of the four pre-eminent playwrights—the tragedians Aeschylus, Sophocles, and Euripides and the comedian Aristophanes—coincides with two important trends in the theater. In aesthetic form, drama moved from the loftily stylized to the more realistic (as typified in the "New Comedy" of the fourth century, which stressed the individual actors and took away from the Chorus its role in the action); in mood and attitude, there was a shift from idealistic optimism to disillusioned cynicism. These trends in the drama parallel trends in Athenian political, religious, and philosophical attitudes. In the epoch ending shortly before 400 B.C., Athens endured military, political, and cultural ordeals that culminated in the overthrow of Athenian democracy and independence. The period when Athens was the moral and political exemplar of what was best in ancient Greece was at an end.

Aristophanes is the only representative of the fifth-century "Old Comedy" whose works have survived. Since biographical information about him is scant, it is difficult to isolate what is distinctive in him from what is characteristic of the Old Comedy; the man and the movement are not clearly separable. If we are thinking about dramaturgy, neither can be called realistic, since the settings, costumes, and freewheeling plots of Aristophanes' plays are often fantastic to the point of surrealism. In The Wasps (a play about the Athenian judicial system; 422), in The Frogs (a literary satire pitting the deceased tragedians Aeschylus and Euripides against each other; 405), and in The Birds (a utopian fantasy-satire; 414), characters or Chorus or both are costumed and portrayed grotesquely in the guise of the animals after which the plays are named.

Yet Aristophanes is a realist in his own way—in subject and theme, if not in theatrical style. His plays (of the forty he wrote, eleven have survived) repeatedly present unflattering portraits of actual people—people who may well have been in his audience—disguised thinly or not at all (they include Socrates, Euripides, and the Athenian political leader Cleon, whom Aristophanes despised). His favorite subjects were literary satire, particularly lampoons of Euripides and what Aristophanes chose to see as the other dramatist's hatred of women; intellectual satire of newfangled trends in education, philosophy, and moral values; and above all, political satire, directed mainly against the Athenian effort in the Peloponnesian War. Aristophanes consistently regarded the war as cruelty toward the enemies and allies of Athens and as suicidal folly from the vantage-point of Athens itself. In fact, early in his career he was once prosecuted for disloyalty. He got off lightly and immediately resumed his role of political gadfly, which says something about Aristophanes and perhaps about Athenian political tolerance even in its days of militaristic jingoism. Spectators of Aristophanes' plays saw the world pictured not in the long vistas of myth and perennial archetypes about the human condition but in the context of what had happened yesterday and what was likely to happen tomorrow. For all his zany exuberance, Aristophanes was an intellectual, and one concerned intimately with current events.

Lysistrata (411) is one of his masterpieces. A witty specimen of antiwar propaganda, it includes also some of his typical wisecracks about tragedy, literature, and Euripides, though it does not demonstrate much if any of his concern with philosophi-

cal issues. The affection and respect Aristophanes felt for women as capable agents and as custodians of ultimate human sanity come across warmly and brilliantly. The same sympathy and admiration emerge in his plays Thesmophoriazusae, *or Lad-ies' Day (411), in which women plot to avenge themselves on Euripides, and in* Ecclesiazusae, *or* Women in Parliament *(392).*

Roman comedy, which established the model for subsequent comedy in Western theater, was modeled on the Greek New Comedy, a form that thrived after the acces-
sion of Alexander the Great, when Athens lost its political freedom. New Comedy abandoned the Aristophanic Old Comedy's freedom of structure and political com-ment in favor of comparatively realistic plots that usually turned around a young man's attempts to marry over his father's objections. But in many ways the spirit of comedy—laughter, irreverence, the celebration of sexuality, and a movement toward liberation from social and personal bonds—was already established in Old Comedy and was transmitted intact to New Comedy and thence to later dramatic history. In Aristophanes, as in comedy ever since, the action begins with a society constricted by authority, proceeds through a series of laughable irreverent events to dissolve that authority, and ends with a new, liberated society, reconstituted around the values of youth, vitality, and sexuality. Many of Aristophanes' plays end with a feast or a dance, forerunners of the boy-gets-girl celebrations of modern comedy. Sexuality tri-umphs, and as the modern critic Northrop Frye wittily puts it, "the plot usually moves toward an act which, like death in Greek tragedy, takes place offstage, and is symbol-ized by a closing embrace."

Lysistrata *is not far removed from a fertility celebration, and its cheerful, inno-cent obscenity is basic to its meaning. Underlying its bawdy, topical jokes and its absurd, incredible plot is a serious confrontation of values. Aristophanes, like his epic and tragic predecessors, almost instinctively defines this confrontation along sexual lines.* Lysistrata *begins with a comic Athens in thrall to sterile, destructive "male" values, in pursuit of a war that Aristophanes regards as misguided and hopeless. "War's a man's affair," says Lysistrata; she is quoting Homer, but she gives the line an ironic twist very far from Homer's meaning. To the male thirst for glory and self-destructive competitiveness, Lysistrata opposes not only sexuality but also com-mon sense and a respect for nonheroic ordinary life. In the most famous passage in the play, she compares the state to a ball of tangled yarn, which the housewife must untangle, wash, and weave together into a seamless unity. "It would take a woman," the Commissioner exclaims, "to reduce state questions to a matter of carding and weaving!"*

Who "wins" in Lysistrata? *Just as it is typically Greek to see the world as divided between "male" rationality and abstraction and "female" desire and vitality, so it is typically Greek to see the solution as a balance between the two forces. The women* do *stop the war (a bit of unhistorical wishful thinking on the part of Aristophanes), but the men's claims of honor are satisfied, too, in the peace negotiations. The real winner is "Reconciliation," a concept represented on stage by a statue under whose eyes the resolution is effected and given significance in the form of an enormous naked woman. We seem to be witnessing an earthy, comic echo of the sexual reconciliation and the hymn to Athens at the end of the* Oresteia *when Lysistrata says, "Each man be kind to his woman, and you, women, be equally kind," and the play ends with a joyous hymn to "Athena of the House of Brass."*

FURTHER READING *(prepared by F.S.N.):* On the festivals, staging and production of ancient comedy, see F. H. Sandbach, *The Comic Theatre of Greece and Rome,* 1977;

Katherine Lever, *The Art of Greek Comedy*, 1956; and C. W. Dearden, *The Stage of Aristophanes*, 1976. Useful general material on Aristophanes' life and writings may be found in K. J. Dover, *Aristophanic Comedy*, 1972; and Lois Spatz, *Aristophanes*, 1978. Victor Ehrenberg, *The People of Aristophanes: A Sociology of Old Attic Comedy*, 1943, 3rd ed. 1962, introduces the reader to the farmers, tradesmen, slaves and family members of the late fifth century B.C. *Yale Classical Studies*, Vol. XXVI (1980), is devoted to essays on the interpretation of Aristophanes. Gilbert Murray in *Aristophanes: A Study*, 1933, in addition to presenting background material on Aristophanes and on comedy in general, devotes a chapter to *Lysistrata*.

LYSISTRATA

Translated by Dudley Fitts

The political and military background of the play is the Peloponnesian war, a series of conflicts between confederacies led by Athens and Sparta. The Peloponnese, of which Sparta was the capital, was a large peninsula that makes up southern Greece. The period of the war, from 431 B.C. to 404, was a tragic era, especially for Athens, whose defeat in the latter year marked the end of its greatest political and cultural age. In 413, two years before *Lysistrata* was produced in Athens, the city's naval and military forces had suffered a calamitous defeat in connection with the ill-fated Sicilian expedition that Athenian patriots—or imperialists—had hoped would establish Athenian dominance of the Mediterranean. Through comedy that is sometimes caustic and sometimes good-humored, Aristophanes' play was intended to show the folly of both political power-lust and civil war among Greeks. As art, *Lysistrata* is a triumph; judged in the light of historical consequences, the play was a failure, since the war went on to its disastrous end.

Some of the jokes can be understood only if one keeps in mind that the usual costume in fifth-century Greek comedy included an exaggeratedly prominent leather phallus.

The characters' names are in many instances significant puns: for example, Lysistrata's name means "Dismisser of Armies" and "Myrrhine" puns on the word meaning female genitals. [*Editors' headnote.*]

PERSONS REPRESENTED

LYSISTRATA	COMMISSIONER
KALONIKE	KINESIAS
MYRRHINE	SPARTAN HERALD
LAMPITO	SPARTAN AMBASSADOR
CHORUS	A SENTRY

SCENE: *Athens. First, a public square; later, beneath the walls of the Akropolis; later, a courtyard within the Akropolis.*[1]

Until the *éxodos*, the CHORUS is divided into two hemichori: the first, of Old Men; the second, of Old Women. Each of these has its

---

[1] The hill upon which the main civic and religious centers of Athens were located.

KORYPHAIOS. In the *éxodos,* the hemichori return as Athenians and Spartans.[2]

The supernumeraries include the BABY SON of Kinêsias; STRATYLLIS, a member of the hemichorus of Old Women; various individual speakers, both Spartan and Athenian.

PROLOGUE
Athens; a public square; early morning; LYSISTRATA *sola.*

LYSISTRATA.
　　If someone had invited them to a festival—
　　of Bacchos, say; or to Pan's shrine, or to Aphroditê's
　　over at Kôlias[3]—, you couldn't get through the streets,
　　what with the drums and the dancing. But now,
　　not a woman in sight!
　　　　　　　　　　　　Except—oh, yes!

　　　　　　　　　　　　　　　[*Enter* KALONIKE]

　　Here's one of my neighbors, at last. Good
　　morning, Kalonikê.
KALONIKE.
　　　　　　　　　　Good morning, Lysistrata.
　　　　　　　　　　　　　　　　　　　　　Darling,
　　don't frown so! You'll ruin your face!
LYSISTRATA.
　　　　　　　　　　　　　　　Never mind my face.
　　Kalonikê,
　　the way we women behave! Really, I don't blame the men   10
　　for what they say about us.
KALONIKE.
　　　　　　　　　　　No; I imagine they're right.
LYSISTRATA.
　　For example: I call a meeting
　　to think out a most important matter—and what happens?
　　The women all stay in bed!
KALONIKE.
　　　　　　　　　　　Oh, they'll be along.
　　It's hard to get away, you know: a husband, a cook,
　　a child . . . Home life can be *so* demanding!
LYSISTRATA.
　　What I have in mind is even more demanding.
KALONIKE.
　　Tell me: what is it?

---

[2] The *éxodus* is the last choral song of the play. The *koryphaios* is the principal spokesman for the Chorus or, as here, for a division of it.

[3] An area of the Greek coast where Aphroditê, goddess of love, had a temple.

LYSISTRATA.
           It's big.

KALONIKE.
                Goodness! *How* big?

LYSISTRATA.
   Big enough for all of us.

KALONIKE.
               But we're not all here!

LYSISTRATA.
   We would be, if *that's* what was up!
                No, Kalonikê,   20
   this is something I've been turning over for nights,
   long sleepless nights.

KALONIKE.
          It must be getting worn down, then,
   if you've spent so much time on it.

LYSISTRATA.
               Worn down or not,
   it comes to this: Only we women can save Greece!

KALONIKE.
   Only we women? Poor Greece!

LYSISTRATA.
            Just the same,
   it's up to us. First, we must liquidate
   the Peloponnesians—

KALONIKE.
         Fun, fun!

LYSISTRATA.
              —and then the Boiotians.[4]

KALONIKE.
   Oh! But not those heavenly eels!

LYSISTRATA.
             You needn't worry.
   I'm not talking about eels.—But here's the point:
   If we can get the women from those places—   30
   all those Boiotians and Peloponnesians—
   to join us women here, why, we can save
   all Greece!

KALONIKE.
      But dearest Lysistrata!
   How can women do a thing so austere, so
   political? We belong at home. Our only armor's
   our perfumes, our saffron dresses and
   our pretty little shoes!

LYSISTRATA.
        Exactly. Those

---

[4] Inhabitants of a region opposed to Athens in the war. The area was noted for its succulent eels and other seafood. Athenian sophisticates regarded Boiotia as a crude and backward place.

transparent dresses, the saffron, the
perfume, those pretty shoes—
KALONIKE.

Oh?

LYSISTRATA.

Not a single man would lift

his spear—
KALONIKE.

I'll send my dress to the dyer's tomorrow!   40

LYSISTRATA.
—or grab a shield—
KALONIKE.

The sweetest little negligée—

LYSISTRATA.
—or haul out his sword.
KALONIKE.

I know where I can buy

the dreamiest sandals!
LYSISTRATA.

Well, so you see. Now, shouldn't

the women have come?
KALONIKE.

Come? They should have *flown!*

LYSISTRATA.
Athenians are always late.

But imagine!

There's no one here from the South Shore, or from Sálamis.[5]
KALONIKE.
Things are hard over in Sálamis, I swear.
They have to get going at dawn.
LYSISTRATA.

And nobody from Acharnai.[6]

I thought they'd be here hours ago.
KALONIKE.

Well, you'll get

that awful Theagenês woman;[7] she'll be   50
a sheet or so in the wind.

But look!

Someone at last! Can you see who they are?

[*Enter* MYRRHINE *and other women*]

LYSISTRATA.
They're from Anagyros.[8]

---

[5] An island south of Greece, site of the memorable Greek naval victory over the Persians in 480. Lysistrata (whose name means "dismisser of armies") intends to gather women from Greek cities, both allied with and opposed to Athens.
    [6] A town near Athens.
    [7] The wife of Theagenês, a notoriously superstitious man. The phrase "a sheet or so in the wind" means drunk.
    [8] A malodorous marshland.

KALONIKE.

       They certainly are.
You'd know them anywhere, by the scent.

MYRRHINE.

  Sorry to be late, Lysistrata.

         Oh come,
don't scowl so. Say something!

LYSISTRATA.

        My dear Myrrhinê,
what is there to say? After all,
you've been pretty casual about the whole thing.

MYRRHINE.

          Couldn't find
my girdle in the dark, that's all.

        But what *is*
'the whole thing'?

KALONIKE.

      No, we've got to wait   60
for those Boiotians and Peloponnesians.

LYSISTRATA.

That's more like it.—But, look!
Here's Lampitô!

        [*Enter* LAMPITO *with women from
        Sparta*]

LYSISTRATA.

      Darling Lampitô,
how pretty you are today! What a nice color!
Goodness, you look as though you could strangle a bull!

LAMPITO.

Ah think Ah could! It's the work-out
in the gym every day; and, of co'se that dance of ahs
where y' kick yo' own tail.[9]

KALONIKE.

      What an adorable figure!

LAMPITO.

Lawdy, when y' touch me lahk that,
Ah feel lahk a heifer at the altar!

LYSISTRATA.

       And this young lady?   70
Where is she from?

LAMPITO.

     Boiotia. Social-Register type.

LYSISTRATA.

Ah. 'Boiotia of the fertile plain.'

---

[9] The Spartans were proverbially associated with discipline and the more austere virtues. Lampito here refers to a strenuous dance performed as exercise by Spartan females. The translator renders Spartan speech as backwoods American-Southern because the Athenians condescendingly viewed Spartans as unsophisticated.

KALONIKE.
                                              And if you look,
   you'll find the fertile plain has just been mowed.
LYSISTRATA.
   And this lady?
LAMPITO.
                          Hagh, wahd, handsome. She comes from Korinth.
KALONIKE.
   High and wide's the word for it.
LAMPITO.
                                     Which one of you
   called this heah meeting, and why?
LYSISTRATA.
                                        I did.
LAMPITO.
                                     Well, then, tell us:
   What's up?
MYRRHINE.
                  Yes, darling, what *is* on your mind, after all?
LYSISTRATA.
   I'll tell you.—But first, one little question.
MYRRHINE.
                                                 Well?
LYSISTRATA.
   It's your husbands. Fathers of your children. Doesn't it bother you
   that they're always off with the Army? I'll stake my life,   80
   not one of you has a man in the house this minute!
KALONIKE.
   Mine's been in Thrace the last five months, keeping an eye
   on that General.[10]
MYRRHINE.
                     Mine's been in Pylos for seven.
LAMPITO.
                                              And mahn,
   whenever he gets a *dis*charge, he goes raht back
   with that li'l ole shield of his, and enlists again!
LYSISTRATA.
   And not the ghost of a lover to be found!
   From the very day the war began—
                                     those Milesians![11]
   I could skin them alive!
                              —I've not seen so much, even,
   as one of those leather consolation prizes.—
   But there! What's important is: If I've found a way   90
   to end the war, are you with me?

---

[10] Eukrates, an Athenian commander of doubtful loyalty.
[11] Former allies of Athens who had defected shortly before *Lysistrata* was produced. The
Milesians reputedly manufactured a kind of dildo, or phallic substitute.

MYRRHINE.

                      I should *say* so!
Even if I have to pawn my best dress and
drink up the proceeds.

KALONIKE.

              Me, too! Even if they split me
right up the middle, like a flounder.

LAMPITO.

                  Ah'm shorely with you.
Ah'd crawl up Taÿgetos[12] on mah knees
if that'd bring peace.

LYSISTRATA.

            All right, then; here it is:
Women! Sisters!
If we really want our men to make peace,
we must be ready to give up—

MYRRHINE.

                  Give up what!
Quick, tell us!

LYSISTRATA.

        But *will* you?

MYRRHINE.

                We will, even if it kills us.   100

LYSISTRATA.

Then we must give up going to bed with our men.

                  [*Long silence*]

Oh? So now you're sorry? Won't look at me?
Doubtful? Pale? All teary-eyed?

                But come: be frank with me.
Will you do it, or not? Well? Will you do it?

MYRRHINE.

                  I couldn't. No.
Let the war go on.

KALONIKE.

          Nor I. Let the war go on.

LYSISTRATA.

You, you little flounder,
ready to be split up the middle?

KALONIKE.

               Lysistrata, no!
I'd walk through fire for you—you *know* I would!—but don't
ask us to give up *that!* Why, there's nothing like it!

LYSISTRATA.

And you?

BOIOTIAN.

         No. I must say *I'd* rather walk through fire.   110

---

[12] A mountain range near Sparta.

LYSISTRATA.
　　What an utterly perverted sex we women are!
　　No wonder poets write tragedies about us.
　　There's only one thing we can think of.
　　　　　　　　　　　　　　　　But you from Sparta:
　　if you stand by me, we may win yet! Will you?
　　It means so much!
LAMPITO.
　　　　　　　　　　　Ah sweah, it means *too* much!
　　By the Two Goddesses,[13] it does! Asking a girl
　　to sleep—Heaven knows how long!—in a great big bed
　　with nobody there but herself! But Ah'll stay with you!
　　Peace comes first!
LYSISTRATA.
　　　　　　　　　Spoken like a true Spartan!
KALONIKE.
　　But if—
　　　　　　oh dear!
　　　　　　　　　—if we give up what you tell us to,   120
　　will there *be* any peace?
LYSISTRATA.
　　　　　　　　　　　Why, mercy, of course there will!
　　We'll just sit snug in our very thinnest gowns,
　　perfumed and powdered from top to bottom, and those men
　　simply won't stand still! And when we say No,
　　they'll go out of their minds! And there's your peace.
　　You can take my word for it.
LAMPITO.
　　　　　　　　　　　Ah seem to remember
　　that Colonel Menelaos threw his sword away
　　when he saw Helen's breast[14] all bare.
KALONIKE.
　　　　　　　　　　　　But, goodness me!
　　What if they just get up and leave us?
LYSISTRATA.
　　　　　　　　　　　In that case
　　we'll have to fall back on ourselves, I suppose.   130
　　But they won't.
KALONIKE.
　　　　　　I must say that's not much help. But
　　what if they drag us into the bedroom?
LYSISTRATA.
　　　　　　　　　　　Hang on to the door.
KALONIKE.
　　What if they slap us?

[13] Demeter, goddess of the fields and fertility, and her daughter Persephone, who was associated with both death and fertility.
[14] The reference is to Euripides' play *Andromache*; Menelaos (Menelaus), the cuckolded husband of Helen of Troy, is so struck with Helen's beauty that he abandons his plan to kill her in revenge.

LYSISTRATA.
>   If they do, you'd better give in.
> But be sulky about it. Do I have to teach you how?
> You know there's no fun for men when they have to force you.
> There are millions of ways of getting them to see reason.
> Don't you worry: a man
> doesn't like it unless the girl co-operates.

KALONIKE.
> I suppose so. Oh, all right. We'll go along.

LAMPITO.
> Ah imagine us Spahtans can arrange a peace. But you   140
> Athenians! Why, you're just war-mongerers!

LYSISTRATA.
>   Leave that to me.
> I know how to make them listen.

LAMPITO.
>   Ah don't see how.
> After all, they've got their boats; and there's lots of money[15]
> piled up in the Akropolis.

LYSISTRATA.
>   The Akropolis? Darling,
> we're taking over the Akropolis today!
> That's the older women's job. All the rest of us
> are going to the Citadel to sacrifice—you understand me?
> And once there, we're in for good!

LAMPITO.
>   Whee! Up the rebels!
> Ah can see you're a good strat*ee*gist.

LYSISTRATA.
>   Well, then, Lampitô,
> what we have to do now is take a solemn oath.[16]   150

LAMPITO.
> Say it. We'll sweah.

LYSISTRATA.
>   This is it.
> —But where's our Inner Guard?
>   —Look, Guard: you see this shield?
> Put it down here. Now bring me the victim's entrails.

KALONIKE.
> But the oath?

LYSISTRATA.
>   You remember how in Aischylos' *Seven*
> they killed a sheep and swore on a shield? Well, then?

KALONIKE.
> But I don't see how you can swear for peace on a shield.

LYSISTRATA.
> What else do you suggest?

---

[15] A fund stored on the Akropolis, designed to finance the war effort.
[16] What follows is a parody of a standard ritual sacrifice and oath of loyalty.

KALONIKE.
Why not a white horse?[17]
We could swear by that.
LYSISTRATA.
And where will you get a white horse?
KALONIKE.
I never thought of that. *What* can we do?
LYSISTRATA.
I have it!
Let's set this big black wine-bowl on the ground   160
and pour in a gallon or so of Thasian,[18] and swear
not to add one drop of water.
LAMPITO.
Ah lahk *that* oath!
LYSISTRATA.
Bring the bowl and the wine-jug.
KALONIKE.
Oh, what a simply *huge* one!
LYSISTRATA.
Set it down. Girls, place your hands on the gift-offering.

O Goddess of Persuasion! And thou, O Loving-cup
Look upon this our sacrifice, and
be gracious!
KALONIKE.
See the blood spill out. How red and pretty it is!
LAMPITO.
And Ah must say it smells good.
MYRRHINE.
Let me swear first!
KALONIKE.
No, by Aphroditê, we'll match for it!   170
LYSISTRATA.
Lampitô: all of you women: come, touch the bowl,
and repeat after me—remember, this is an oath—:
I WILL HAVE NOTHING TO DO WITH MY HUSBAND OR
    MY LOVER
KALONIKE.
I will have nothing to do with my husband or my lover
LYSISTRATA.
THOUGH HE COME TO ME IN PITIABLE CONDITION
KALONIKE.
Though he come to me in pitiable condition
(Oh Lysistrata! This is killing me!)

[17] In Aeschylus' tragedy *Seven Against Thebes*, the seven leaders attacking the city take an oath on a shield. (This war provides the background of Sophocles' *Antigone*.) The reference to the white horse is possibly some kind of sexual joke, but commentators are puzzled by the phrase.
[18] A wine of high quality.

LYSISTRATA.
> IN MY HOUSE I WILL BE UNTOUCHABLE

KALONIKE.
> *In my house I will be untouchable*

LYSISTRATA.
> IN MY THINNEST SAFFRON SILK 180

KALONIKE.
> *In my thinnest saffron silk*

LYSISTRATA.
> AND MAKE HIM LONG FOR ME.

KALONIKE.
> *And make him long for me.*

LYSISTRATA.
> I WILL NOT GIVE MYSELF

KALONIKE.
> *I will not give myself*

LYSISTRATA.
> AND IF HE CONSTRAINS ME

KALONIKE.
> *And if he constrains me*

LYSISTRATA.
> I WILL BE COLD AS ICE AND NEVER MOVE

KALONIKE.
> *I will be cold as ice and never move*

LYSISTRATA.
> I WILL NOT LIFT MY SLIPPERS TOWARD THE CEILING 190

KALONIKE.
> *I will not lift my slippers toward the ceiling*

LYSISTRATA.
> OR CROUCH ON ALL FOURS LIKE THE LIONESS IN THE
> CARVING

KALONIKE.
> *Or crouch on all fours like the lioness in the carving*

LYSISTRATA.
> AND IF I KEEP THIS OATH LET ME DRINK FROM THIS
> BOWL

KALONIKE.
> *And if I keep this oath let me drink from this bowl*

LYSISTRATA.
> IF NOT, LET MY OWN BOWL BE FILLED WITH WATER

KALONIKE.
> *If not, let my own bowl be filled with water.*

LYSISTRATA.
> You have all sworn?

MYRRHINE.
> We have.

LYSISTRATA.
> Then thus
> I sacrifice the victim.

[*Drinks largely*]

KALONIKE.
                          Save some for us!
Here's to you, darling, and to you, and to you!   200

[*Loud cries off-stage*]

LAMPITO.
   What's all *that* whoozy-goozy?
LYSISTRATA.
                          Just what I told you.
The older women have taken the Akropolis.
Now you, Lampitô,
rush back to Sparta. We'll take care of things here. Leave
these girls here for hostages.
                          The rest of you,
up to the Citadel: and mind you push in the bolts.
KALONIKE.
   But the men? Won't they be after us?
LYSISTRATA.
                          Just you leave
the men to me. There's not fire enough in the world,
or threats either, to make me open these doors
except on my own terms.
KALONIKE.
                          I hope not, by Aphroditê!   210
After all,
we've got a reputation for bitchiness to live up to.

[*Exeunt*]

PÁRODOS:[19] CHORAL EPISODE

The hillside just under the Akropolis. Enter CHORUS OF OLD MEN *with burning torches and braziers; much puffing and coughing.*

KORYPHAIOS[m].
   Forward march, Drakês, old friend: never you mind
   that damn big log banging hell down on your back.
CHORUS[m].
      There's this to be said for longevity: [STROPHE 1]
      You see things you thought that you'd never see.
         Look, Strymodôros, who would have thought it?
         We've caught it—
                          the New Femininity!
      The wives of our bosom, our board, our bed—
      Now, by the gods, they've gone ahead   220

---

[19] The song sung at the first entrance of the Chorus.

And taken the Citadel (Heaven knows why!),
Profanèd the sacred statuar-y,[20]

> And barred the doors,
> The subversive whores!

KORYPHAIOS[m].

Shake a leg there, Philûrgos, man: the Akropolis or bust!
Put the kindling around here. We'll build one almighty big
bonfire for the whole bunch of bitches, every last one;
and the first we fry will be old Lykôn's woman.[21]

CHORUS[m].

[ANTISTROPHE 1]

They're not going to give me the old horse-laugh!
No, by Deméter, they won't pull this off!   230
  Think of Kleómenés:[22] even he
  Didn't go free
> till he brought me his stuff.
A good man he was, all stinking and shaggy,
Bare as an eel except for the bag he
Covered his rear with. God, what a mess!
Never a bath in six years, I'd guess.
> Pure Sparta, man!
> He also ran.

KORYPHAIOS[m].

That was a siege, friends! Seventeen ranks strong
we slept at the Gate. And shall we not do as much   240
against these women, whom God and Euripides[23] hate?
If we don't, I'll turn in my medals from Marathon.

CHORUS[m].

[STROPHE 2]

Onward and upward! A little push,
  And we're there.
Ouch, my shoulders! I could wish
  For a pair
  Of good strong oxen. Keep your eye
  On the fire there, it mustn't die.
> Akh! Akh!
The smoke would make a cadaver cough!   250

Holy Heraklês, a hot spark   [ANTISTROPHE 2]
  Bit my eye!
Damn this hellfire, damn this work!

---

[20] An old and revered wooden statue of Athêna in her role as protectress of Athens.

[21] A woman noted for lax morality; here, as often elsewhere, Aristophanes refers to actual people of his time.

[22] A Spartan king who, in 508, had occupied the Akropolis in aid of the aristocratic party during a civil conflict in Athens. His occupation was brief, not the six years the senile Chorus remembers. The reference to this incident, like the following reminiscence of the great victory at Marathon (490), would make the members of the Chorus a hundred or more years old— probably a joke by Aristophanes, designed to emphasize the old men's decrepitude.

[23] Often represented by Aristophanes, perhaps only half-seriously, as a misogynist.

        So say I.
    Onward and upward just the same.
    (Lachês, remember the Goddess: for shame!)
            Akh! Akh!
    The smoke would make a cadaver cough!
KORYPHAIOS[m].
    At last (and let us give suitable thanks to God
    for his infinite mercies) I have managed to bring   260
    my personal flame to the common goal. It breathes, it lives.
    Now, gentlemen, let us consider. Shall we insert
    the torch, say, into the brazier, and thus extract
    a kindling brand? And shall we then, do you think,
    push on to the gate like valiant sheep? On the whole, yes.
    But I would have you consider this, too: if they—
    I refer to the women—should refuse to open,
    what then? Do we set the doors afire
    and smoke them out? At ease, men. Meditate.
    Akh, the smoke! Woof! What we really need   270
    is the loan of a general or two from the Samos[24] Command.
    At least we've got this lumber off our backs.
    That's something. And now let's look to our fire.

    O Pot, brave Brazier, touch my torch with flame!
    Victory, Goddess, I invoke thy name!
    Strike down these paradigms of female pride,
    And we shall hang our trophies up inside.

                                [*Enter* CHORUS OF OLD WOMEN
                                on the walls of the Akropolis, carry-
                                ing jars of water]

KORYPHAIOS[w].
    Smoke, girls, smoke! There's smoke all over the place!
    Probably fire, too. Hurry, girls! Fire! Fire!
CHORUS[w].
                Nikodikê, run!   [STROPHE 1]   280
                Or Kalyké's done
                To a turn, and poor Kritylla's
                Smoked like a ham.
                        Damn
                These old men! Are we too late?
                I nearly died down at the place
                Where we fill our jars:
                    Slaves pushing and jostling—
                    Such a hustling
                I never saw in all my days.

[24] An island near Asia Minor. At the time of the play it was the headquarters of Athenian forces.

But here's water at last.   [ANTISTROPHE 1]   290
Haste, sisters, haste!
Slosh it on them, slosh it down,
The silly old wrecks!
>   Sex
Almighty! What they want's
A hot bath? Good. Send one down.
Athêna of Athens town,
>   Trito-born![25] Helm of Gold!
>   Cripple the old
Firemen! Help us help them drown!

> [*The* OLD MEN *capture a woman,*
> STRATYLLIS]

STRATYLLIS.
Let me go! Let me go!
KORYPHAIOS[w].
>   You walking corpses,   300
have you no shame?
KORYPHAIOS[m].
>   I wouldn't have believed it!
An army of women in the Akropolis!
KORYPHAIOS[w].
So we scare you, do we? Grandpa, you've seen
only our pickets yet!
KORYPHAIOS[m].
>   Hey, Phaidrias!
Help me with the necks of these jabbering hens!
KORYPHAIOS[w].
Down with your pots, girls! We'll need both hands
if these antiques attack us.
KORYPHAIOS[m].
>   Want your face kicked in?
KORYPHAIOS[w].
Want your balls chewed off?
KORYPHAIOS[m].
>   Look out! I've got a stick!
KORYPHAIOS[w].
You lay a half-inch of your stick on Stratyllis,
and you'll never stick again!   310
KORYPHAIOS[m].
Fall apart!
KORYPHAIOS[w].
>   I'll spit up your guts!
KORYPHAIOS[m].
>   Euripides! Master!
How well you knew women!

[25] Athêna, by one account, was born near Tritonis, a lake in Libya.

KORYPHAIOS^w.
                                        Listen to him! Rhodippê,
    up with the pots!
KORYPHAIOS^m.
                          Demolition of God,
    what good are your pots?
KORYPHAIOS^w.
                                    You refugee from the tomb,
    what good is your fire?
KORYPHAIOS^m.
                                Good enough to make a pyre
    to barbecue you!
KORYPHAIOS^w.
                                We'll squizzle your kindling!
KORYPHAIOS^m.
    You think so?
KORYPHAIOS^w.
                      Yah! Just hang around a while!
KORYPHAIOS^m.
    Want a touch of my torch?
KORYPHAIOS^w.
                                    It needs a good soaping.
KORYPHAIOS^m.
    How about you?
KORYPHAIOS^w.
                          Soap for a senile bridegroom!
KORYPHAIOS^m.
    Senile? Hold your trap!
KORYPHAIOS^w.
                          Just *you* try to hold it!   320
KORYPHAIOS^m.
    The yammer of women!
KORYPHAIOS^w.
                              Oh is that so?
    You're not in the jury room[26] now, you know.
KORYPHAIOS^m.
    Gentlemen, I beg you, burn off that woman's hair!
KORYPHAIOS^w.
    Let it come down!

                          [*They empty their pots on the men*]

KORYPHAIOS^m.
    What a way to drown!
KORYPHAIOS^w.
                          Hot, hey?
KORYPHAIOS^m.
                              Say,
    enough!

---

[26] Elderly Athenians frequently served as jurors in law cases.

Koryphaios[w].
          Dandruff
needs watering. I'll make you
nice and fresh.
Koryphaios[m].
               For God's sake, you,
hold off!

SCENE I

[*Enter a* Commissioner[27] *accompanied by four constables*]

Commissioner.
     These degenerate women! What a racket of little drums,   330
     what a yapping for Adonis on every house-top!
     It's like the time in the Assembly when I was listening
     to a speech—out of order, as usual—by that fool
     Demostratos,[28] all about troops for Sicily,
     that kind of nonsense—
                         and there was his wife
     trotting around in circles howling
     Alas for Adonis!—
                      and Demostratos insisting
     we must draft every last Zakynthian[29] that can walk—
     and his wife up there on the roof,
     drunk as an owl, yowling   340
     Oh weep for Adonis!—
                         and that damned ox Demostratos
     mooing away through the rumpus. That's what we get
     for putting up with this wretched woman-business!
Koryphaios[m].
     Sir, you haven't heard the half of it. They laughed at us!
     Insulted us! They took pitchers of water
     and nearly drowned us! We're still wringing out our clothes,
     for all the world like unhousebroken brats.
Commissioner.
     Serves you right, by Poseidon![30]
     Whose fault is it if these women-folk of ours
     get out of hand? We coddle them,   350
     we teach them to be wasteful and loose. You'll see a husband
     go into a jeweler's. 'Look,' he'll say,

----

[27] One of a group of men appointed to oversee the Athenian legislature after the defeat in Sicily.

[28] One of the most aggressive supporters of the recent disastrous campaign in Sicily. At the time the expedition set forth, the women were celebrating the rituals of Adonis, a god who represented the death-and-resurrection cycle in nature. The women's ritual laments for his death were interpreted as having put a hex on the military expedition.

[29] Dwellers on the island of Zakynthos; they were allies of Athens who, it had been hoped, would strengthen the Athenian forces in the Sicilian campaign.

[30] God of water and ocean.

'jeweler,' he'll say, 'you remember that gold choker
'you made for my wife? Well, she went to a dance last night
'and broke the clasp. Now, I've got to go to Sálamis,
'and can't be bothered. Run over to my house tonight,
'will you, and see if you can put it together for her.'
Or another one
goes to a cobbler—a good strong workman, too,
with an awl that was never meant for child's play. 'Here,'   360
he'll tell him, 'one of my wife's shoes is pinching
'her little toe. Could you come up about noon
'and stretch it out for her?'

                            Well, what do you expect?
Look at me, for example. I'm a Public Officer,
and it's one of my duties to pay off the sailors.
And where's the money? Up there in the Akropolis!
And those blasted women slam the door in my face!
But what are we waiting for?
                        —Look here, constable,
stop sniffing around for a tavern, and get us
some crowbars. We'll force their gates! As a matter of fact,   370
I'll do a little forcing myself.

                           [*Enter* LYSISTRATA, *above, with*
                           MYRRHINE, KALONIKE, *and the*
                           BOIOTIAN]

LYSISTRATA.
                        No need of forcing.
Here I am, of my own accord. And all this talk
about locked doors—! We don't need locked doors,
but just the least bit of common sense.
COMMISSIONER.
        Is that so, ma'am!
                 —Where's my constable?
                          —Constable,
arrest that woman, and tie her hands behind her.
LYSISTRATA.
If he touches me, I swear by Artemis[31]
there'll be one scamp dropped from the public pay-roll tomorrow!
COMMISSIONER.
Well, constable? You're not afraid, I suppose? Grab her,
two of you, around the middle!
KALONIKE.
                  No, by Pándrosos![32]   380
Lay a hand on her, and I'll jump on you so hard
your guts will come out the back door!

[31] The virgin goddess of the hunt, the moon, and childbirth. In the following lines, she is
referred to as "the Moon-Goddess" and "the Taurian."
[32] Daughter of a legendary ruler of Athens.

COMMISSIONER.

                            That's what *you* think!
Where's the sergeant?—Here, you: tie up that trollop first,
the one with the pretty talk!

MYRRHINE.

                       By the Moon-Goddess,
just try! They'll have to scoop you up with a spoon!

COMMISSIONER.

    Another one!
               Officer, seize that woman!
                               I swear
I'll put an end to this riot!

BOIOTIAN.

                    By the Taurian,
one inch closer, you'll be one screaming bald-head!

COMMISSIONER.

    Lord, what a mess! And my constables seem ineffective.
But—women get the best of us? By God, no!
                        —Skythians![33]   390
Close ranks and forward march!

LYSISTRATA.

                   'Forward,' indeed!
By the Two Goddesses, what's the sense in *that*?
They're up against four companies of women
armed from top to bottom.

COMMISSIONER.

                Forward, my Skythians!

LYSISTRATA.

    Forward, yourselves, dear comrades!
You grainlettucebeanseedmarket girls!
You garlicandonionbreadbakery girls!
Give it to 'em! Knock 'em down! Scratch 'em!
Tell 'em what you think of 'em!

                     [*General mêlée; the Skythians yield*]

                 —Ah, that's enough!
Sound a retreat: good soldiers don't rob the dead.   400

COMMISSIONER.

    A nice day *this* has been for the police!

LYSISTRATA.

    Well, there you are.—Did you really think we women
would be driven like slaves? Maybe now you'll admit
that a woman knows something about spirit.

COMMISSIONER.

                           Spirit enough,
especially spirits in bottles! Dear Lord Apollo!

---

[33] Archers from the north who made up much of the Athenian police force.

KORYPHAIOS[m].

Your Honor, there's no use talking to them. Words
mean nothing whatever to wild animals like these.
Think of the sousing they gave us! and the water
was not, I believe, of the purest.

KORYPHAIOS[w].

You shouldn't have come after us. And if you try it again,   410
you'll be one eye short!—Although, as a matter of fact,
what I like best is just to stay at home and read,
like a sweet little bride: never hurting a soul, no,
never going out. But if you *must* shake hornets' nests,
look out for the hornets.

CHORUS[m].

    Of all the beasts that God hath wrought   [STROPHE 1]
      What monster's worse than woman?
    Who shall encompass with his thought
      Their guile unending? No man.

    They've seized the Heights, the Rock, the Shrine—   420
      But to what end? I wot not.
    Sure there's some clue to their design!
      Have you the key? I thought not.

KORYPHAIOS[m].

We might question them, I suppose. But I warn you, sir,
don't believe anything you hear! It would be un-Athenian
not to get to the bottom of this plot.

COMMISSIONER.

                                Very well.

My first question is this: Why, so help you God,
did you bar the gates of the Akropolis?

LYSISTRATA.

                            Why?

To keep the money, of course. No money, no war.

COMMISSIONER.

You think that money's the cause of war?

LYSISTRATA.

                          I do.   430

Money brought about that Peisandros[34] business
and all the other attacks on the State. Well and good!
They'll not get another cent here!

COMMISSIONER.

                    And what will you do?

LYSISTRATA.

What a question! From now on, we intend
to control the Treasury.

COMMISSIONER.

                Control the Treasury!

---

[34] A corrupt and venal Athenian politician who plotted to overthrow the city's democratic
regime.

LYSISTRATA.
  Why not? Does that seem strange? After all,
  we control our household budgets.
COMMISSIONER.

                         But that's different!
LYSISTRATA.
  'Different'? What do you mean?
COMMISSIONER.

                             I mean simply this:
  it's the Treasury that pays for National Defense.
LYSISTRATA.
  Unnecessary. We propose to abolish war.   440
COMMISSIONER.
  Good God.—And National Security?
LYSISTRATA.

                         Leave that to us.
COMMISSIONER.
  You?
LYSISTRATA.
       Us.
COMMISSIONER.
         We're done for, then!
LYSISTRATA.

                     Never mind.
  We women will save you in spite of yourselves.
COMMISSIONER.

                        What nonsense!
LYSISTRATA.
  If you like. But you must accept it, like it or not.
COMMISSIONER.
  Why, this is downright subversion!
LYSISTRATA.

                     Maybe it is.
  But we're going to save you, Judge.
COMMISSIONER.

                   I don't *want* to be saved.
LYSISTRATA.
  Tut. The death-wish. All the more reason.
COMMISSIONER.

                      But the idea
  of women bothering themselves about peace and war!
LYSISTRATA.
  Will you listen to me?
COMMISSIONER.

                 Yes. But be brief, or I'll—
LYSISTRATA.
  This is no time for stupid threats.
COMMISSIONER.

                By the gods,   450
  I can't stand any more!

AN OLD WOMAN.
                         Can't stand? Well, well.
COMMISSIONER.
   That's enough out of you, you old buzzard!
   Now, Lysistrata: tell me what you're thinking.
LYSISTRATA.
   Glad to.
                Ever since this war began
We women have been watching you men, agreeing with you,
keeping our thoughts to ourselves. That doesn't mean
we were happy: we *weren't,* for we saw how things were going;
but we'd listen to you at dinner
arguing this way and that.
                         —Oh you, and your big

Top Secrets!—
                And then we'd grin like little patriots   460
(though goodness knows we didn't feel like grinning) and ask you:
'Dear, did the Armistice come up in Assembly today?'
And you'd say, 'None of your business! Pipe down!' you'd say.
And so we would.
AN OLD WOMAN.
                I wouldn't have by God!
COMMISSIONER.
   You'd have taken a beating, then!
                                     —Go on.
LYSISTRATA.
   Well, we'd be quiet. But then, you know, all at once
you men would think up something worse than ever.
Even *I* could see it was fatal. And, 'Darling,' I'd say,
'have you gone completely mad?' And my husband would look at
      me
and say, 'Wife, you've got your weaving to attend to.   470
'Mind your tongue, if you don't want a slap. "War's
"a man's affair"!'[35]
COMMISSIONER.
                Good words, and well pronounced.
LYSISTRATA.
   You're a fool if you think so.
                         It was hard enough
to put up with all this banquet-hall strategy.
But then we'd hear you out in the public square:
'Nobody left for the draft-quota here in Athens?'
you'd say; and, 'No,' someone else would say, 'not a man!'
And so we women decided to rescue Greece.
You might as well listen to us now: you'll have to, later.
COMMISSIONER.
   You rescue Greece? Absurd.

---

[35] Hector addresses these last four words to his wife, Andromache, in Homer's *Iliad,*
Book VI.

LYSISTRATA.

                    You're the absurd one.   480

COMMISSIONER.

    You expect me to take orders from a woman?

                              I'd die first!

LYSISTRATA.

    Heavens, if that's what's bothering you, take my veil,
here, and wrap it around your poor head.

KALONIKE.

                            Yes,
and you can have my market-basket, too.
Go home, tighten your girdle, do the washing, mind
your beans! 'War's
a woman's affair'!

KORYPHAIOS^W.

              Ground pitchers! Close ranks!

CHORUS^W.

                                   [ANTISTROPHE]

    This is a dance that I know well.
      My knees shall never yield.
    Wobble and creak I may, but still   490
      I'll keep the well-fought field.

    Valor and grace march on before,
      Love prods us from behind.
    Our slogan is EXCELSIOR.[36]
    Our watchword SAVE MANKIND.

KORYPHAIOS^W.

    Women, remember your grandmothers! Remember
that little old mother of yours, what a stinger she was!
On, on, never slacken. There's a strong wind astern!

LYSISTRATA.

    O Erôs of delight! O Aphroditê! Kyprian![37]
If ever desire has drenched our breasts or dreamed
in our thighs, let it work so now on the men of Hellas   500
that they shall tail us through the land, slaves, slaves
to Woman, Breaker of Armies!

COMMISSIONER.

                     And if we do?

LYSISTRATA.

    Well, for one thing, we shan't have to watch you
going to market, a spear in one hand, and heaven knows
what in the other.

KALONIKE.

               Nicely said, by Aphroditê!

LYSISTRATA.

    As things stand now, you're neither men nor women.

---

[36] A Latin motto meaning, roughly, "On to nobler things," or, literally, "higher."

[37] Erôs, Aphroditê, and Kyprian are names for the god and goddess of love.

Armor clanking with kitchen pans and pots—
you sound like a pack of Korybantês![38]

COMMISSIONER.
A man must do what a man must do.

LYSISTRATA.
                                                  So I'm told.   510
But to see a General, complete with Gorgon-shield,[39]
jingling along the dock to buy a couple of herrings!

KALONIKE.
I saw a Captain the other day—lovely fellow he was,
nice curly hair—sitting on his horse; and—can you believe it?—
he'd just bought some soup, and was pouring it into his helmet!
And there was a soldier from Thrace
swishing his lance like something out of Euripides,
and the poor fruit-store woman got so scared
that she ran away and let him have his figs free!

COMMISSIONER.
All this is beside the point.
                                        Will you be so kind   520
as to tell me how you mean to save Greece?

LYSISTRATA.
                                                  Of course.
Nothing could be simpler.

COMMISSIONER.
                              I assure you, I'm all ears.

LYSISTRATA.
Do you know anything about weaving?
Say the yarn gets tangled: we thread it
this way and that through the skein, up and down,
until it's free. And it's like that with war.
We'll send our envoys
up and down, this way and that, all over Greece,
until it's finished.

COMMISSIONER.
                  Yarn? Thread? Skein?
Are you out of your mind? I tell you,   530
war is a serious business.

LYSISTRATA.
                              So serious
that I'd like to go on talking about weaving.

COMMISSIONER.
All right. Go ahead.

LYSISTRATA.
                        The first thing we have to do
is to wash our yarn, get the dirt out of it.

---

[38] Devotees of the earth-goddess Cybele, whose rites included frenzied dancing and music.
[39] The Gorgon's head, in myth, turned gazers to stone; it was therefore a common design
on warriors' shields.

You see? Isn't there too much dirt here in Athens?
You must wash those men away.

                               Then our spoiled wool—
that's like your job-hunters, out for a life
of no work and big pay. Back to the basket,
citizens or not, allies or not,
or friendly immigrants.

                          And your colonies?   540
Hanks of wool lost in various places. Pull them
together, weave them into one great whole,
and our voters are clothed for ever.

COMMISSIONER.

                        It would take a woman
to reduce state questions to a matter of carding and weaving.

LYSISTRATA.

You fool! Who were the mothers whose sons sailed off
to fight for Athens in Sicily?

COMMISSIONER.

                   Enough!
I beg you, do not call back those memories.

LYSISTRATA.

                        And then,
instead of the love that every woman needs,
we have only our single beds, where we can dream
of our husbands off with the Army.

                    Bad enough for wives!   550
But what about our girls, getting older every day,
and older, and no kisses?

COMMISSIONER.

                 Men get older, too.

LYSISTRATA.

Not in the same sense.

               A soldier's discharged,
and he may be bald and toothless, yet he'll find
a pretty young thing to go to bed with.

                   But a woman!
Her beauty is gone with the first grey hair.
She can spend her time
consulting the oracles and the fortune-tellers,
but they'll never send her a husband.

COMMISSIONER.

Still, if a man can rise to the occasion—   560

LYSISTRATA.

Rise? Rise, yourself!

                 [*Furiously*]

Go invest in a coffin!
               You've money enough.

I'll bake you

a cake[40] for the Underworld.

And here's your funeral

wreath!

[*She pours water upon him*]

MYRRHINE.

And here's another!

[*More water*]

KALONIKE.

And here's

my contribution!

[*More water*]

LYSISTRATA.

What are you waiting for?

All aboard Styx Ferry![41]

Charôn's calling for you!

It's sailing-time: don't disrupt the schedule!

COMMISSIONER.

The insolence of women! And to me!
No, by God, I'll go back to town and show   570
the rest of the Commission what might happen to them.

[*Exit* COMMISSIONER]

LYSISTRATA.

Really, I suppose we should have laid out his corpse
on the doorstep, in the usual way.

But never mind.

We'll give him the rites of the dead tomorrow morning.

[*Exit* LYSISTRATA *with* MYRRHINE
and KALONIKE]

PARÁBASIS:[42] CHORAL EPISODE

KORYPHAIOS[m].

[ODE 1]

Sons of Liberty, awake! The day of glory is at hand.

CHORUS[m].

I smell tyranny afoot, I smell it rising from the land.

---

[40] Part of the customary funeral ritual; a honey cake was the offering with which the dead person was to propitiate Cerberus, the monster-dog who guarded the Underworld, or realm of the dead.

[41] The dead were ferried by the boatman Charôn across the river Styx to the Underworld.

[42] An address to the audience by the Chorus.

I scent a trace of Hippias,[43] I sniff upon the breeze
A dismal Spartan hogo that suggests King Kleisthenês.[44]
   Strip, strip for action, brothers!
   Our wives, aunts, sisters, mothers 580
Have sold us out: the streets are full of godless female rages.
Shall we stand by and let our women confiscate our wages?[45]

KORYPHAIOS[m].

[EPIRRHEMA[46] 1]

Gentlemen, it's a disgrace to Athens, a disgrace
to all that Athens stands for, if we allow these grandmas
to jabber about spears and shields and making friends
with the Spartans. What's a Spartan? Give me a wild wolf
any day. No. They want the Tyranny back, I suppose.
Are we going to take that? No. Let us look like
the innocent serpent, but be the flower under it,
as the poet sings. And just to begin with, 590
I propose to poke a number of teeth
down the gullet of that harridan[47] over there.

KORYPHAIOS[w].

[ANTODE 1]

Oh, is that so? When you get home, your own mammá won't know
   you!

CHORUS[w].

Who do you think we are, you senile bravos? Well, I'll show you.
I bore the sacred vessels[48] in my eighth year, and at ten
I was pounding out the barley for Athêna Goddess; then
   They made me Little Bear
   At the Braunonian Fair;
I'd held the Holy Basket by the time I was of age,
The Blessed Dry Figs had adorned my plump décolletage. 600

KORYPHAIOS[w].

[ANTEPIRRHEMA 1]

A 'disgrace to Athens', am I, just at the moment
I'm giving Athens the best advice she ever had?
Don't I pay taxes to the State? Yes, I pay them
in baby boys. And what do you contribute,
you impotent horrors? Nothing but waste: all
our Treasury,[49] dating back to the Persian Wars,
gone! rifled! And not a penny out of your pockets!
Well, then? Can you cough up an answer to that?

---

[43] The last of the Athenian tyrants; he ruled about a century before the present action.
[44] A notoriously effeminate bisexual.
[45] The fund from which the elderly jurors' fees were paid was kept at the Akropolis.
[46] Along with the following "Antode" and "Antepirrhema," this section is a choral song that customarily made a satiric comment on current events.
[47] A sharp-tongued old woman.
[48] In the following lines, the women describe various roles in the rites of Athêna and Artemis. Selected preadolescent Athenian girls of good family were privileged to perform these roles.
[49] A fund originally established in the days of Greek unity to finance the war against Persia; the money had since been misappropriated by unscrupulous politicians.

Look out for your own gullet, or you'll get a crack
from this old brogan that'll make your teeth see stars!   610
CHORUS[m].

                         Oh insolence!   [ODE 2]
                         Am I unmanned?
                         Incontinence!
                         Shall my scarred hand
                         Strike never a blow
                         To curb this flow-
                         ing female curse?

                         Leipsydrion![50]
                         Shall I betray
                         The laurels won   620
                         On that great day?
                         Come, shake a leg,
                         Shed old age, beg
                         The years reverse!

KORYPHAIOS[m].
                                            [EPIRRHEMA 2]
  Give them an inch, and we're done for! We'll have them
launching boats next and planning naval strategy,
sailing down on us like so many Artemisias.[51]
Or maybe they have ideas about the cavalry.
That's fair enough, women are certainly good
in the saddle. Just look at Mikôn's paintings,   630
all those Amazons[52] wrestling with all those men!
On the whole, a straitjacket's their best uniform.
CHORUS[w].

                         Tangle with me,   [ANTODE 2]
                         And you'll get cramps.
                         Ferocity
                         's no use now, Gramps!
                         By the Two,
                         I'll get through
                         To you wrecks yet!

                         I'll scramble your eggs,   640
                         I'll burn your beans,
                         With my two legs.
                         You'll see such scenes
                         As never yet
                         Your two eyes met.
                         A curse? You bet!

---

[50] Another site of patriotic Athenian heroism from the great days (in this instance about a century earlier) of the city's fight against tyranny.

[51] A queen who had commanded a naval unit in the Persian war against Greece.

[52] Fabled women-warriors; Mikôn was a famous contemporary painter.

Koryphaios^w.

If Lampitô stands by me, and that delicious Theban girl,
Ismênia—what good are *you*? You and your seven
Resolutions! Resolutions? Rationing Boiotian eels
and making our girls go without them at Hekatê's Feast!   650
That was statesmanship! And we'll have to put up with it
and all the rest of your decrepit legislation
until some patriot—God give him strength!—
grabs you by the neck and kicks you off the Rock.

SCENE II

[*Re-enter* Lysistrata *and her lieutenants*]

Koryphaios^w [*Tragic tone*].
    Great Queen, fair Architect of our emprise,
    Why lookst thou on us with foreboding eyes?
Lysistrata.
    The behavior of these idiotic women!
    There's something about the female temperament
    that I can't bear!
Koryphaios^w.
             What in the world do you mean?
Lysistrata.
    Exactly what I say.
Koryphaios^w.
         What dreadful thing has happened?   660
    Come, tell us: we're all your friends.
Lysistrata.
                It isn't easy
    to say it; yet, God knows, we can't hush it up.
Koryphaios^w.
    Well, then? Out with it!
Lysistrata.
           To put it bluntly,
    we're dying to get laid.
Koryphaios^w.
        Almighty God!
Lysistrata.
    Why bring God into it?—No, it's just as I say.
    I can't manage them any longer: they've gone man-crazy,
    they're all trying to get out.
         Why, look:
    one of them was sneaking out the back door
    over there by Pan's cave; another
    was sliding down the walls with rope and tackle;   670

another was climbing aboard a sparrow,[53] ready to take off
for the nearest brothel—I dragged *her* back by the hair!
They're all finding some reason to leave.

Look there!

There goes another one.

—Just a minute, you!

Where are you off to so fast?

FIRST WOMAN.

I've got to get home.

I've a lot of Milesian wool, and the worms are spoiling it.

LYSISTRATA.

Oh bother you and your worms! Get back inside!

FIRST WOMAN.

I'll be back right away, I swear I will.
I just want to get it stretched out on my bed.

LYSISTRATA.

You'll do no such thing. You'll stay right here.

FIRST WOMAN.

And my wool?   680

You want it ruined?

LYSISTRATA.

Yes, for all I care.

SECOND WOMAN.

Oh dear! My lovely new flax from Amorgos[54]—
I left it at home, all uncarded!

LYSISTRATA.

Another one!

And all she wants is someone to card her flax.
Get back in there!

SECOND WOMAN.

But I swear by the Moon-Goddess,

the minute I get it done, I'll be back!

LYSISTRATA.

I say No.

If you, why not all the other women as well?

THIRD WOMAN.

O Lady Eileithyia![55] Radiant goddess! Thou
intercessor for women in childbirth! Stay, I pray thee,
oh stay this parturition. Shall I pollute   690
a sacred spot?

LYSISTRATA.

And what's the matter with *you*?

THIRD WOMAN.

I'm having a baby—any minute now.

LYSISTRATA.

But you weren't pregnant yesterday.

---

[53] The bird was associated with Aphroditê, goddess of love.
[54] An Aegean island noted for the excellence of its flax.
[55] A goddess of childbirth. To give birth in the precincts of the Akropolis would be sacrilegious.

THIRD WOMAN.

                                  Well, I am today.
Let me go home for a midwife, Lysistrata:
there's not much time.

LYSISTRATA.

                           I never heard such nonsense.
What's that bulging under your cloak?

THIRD WOMAN.

                                    A little baby boy.

LYSISTRATA.

It certainly isn't. But it's something hollow,
like a basin or—Why, it's the helmet of Athêna!
And you said you were having a baby.

THIRD WOMAN.

                                Well, I am! So there!

LYSISTRATA.

Then why the helmet?

THIRD WOMAN.

                          I was afraid that my pains
might begin here in the Akropolis; and I wanted
to drop my chick into it, just as the dear doves do.

LYSISTRATA.

Lies! Evasions!—But at least one thing's clear:
you can't leave the place before your purification.

THIRD WOMAN.

But I can't stay here in the Akropolis! Last night I dreamed
of the Snake.[56]

FIRST WOMAN.

                    And those horrible owls,[57] the noise they make!
I can't get a bit of sleep; I'm just about dead.

LYSISTRATA.

You useless girls, that's enough: Let's have no more lying.
Of course you want your men. But don't you imagine
that they want you just as much? I'll give you my word,
their nights must be pretty hard.

                              Just stick it out!
A little patience, that's all, and our battle's won.
I have heard an Oracle. Should you like to hear it?

FIRST WOMAN.

An Oracle? Yes, tell us!

LYSISTRATA.

                          Here is what it says:
WHEN SWALLOWS SHALL THE HOOPOE[58] SHUN
  AND SPURN HIS HOT DESIRE,
ZEUS WILL PERFECT WHAT THEY'VE BEGUN
  AND SET THE LOWER HIGHER.

700

710

---

[56] Though never seen, this mythical snake was considered the guardian of Athêna's temple on the Akropolis.

[57] Birds sacred to Athêna.   [58] A bird, here identified with the male sex.

FIRST WOMAN.
     Does that mean we'll be on top?
LYSISTRATA.
     BUT IF THE SWALLOWS SHALL FALL OUT   720
          AND TAKE THE HOOPOE'S BAIT,
     A CURSE MUST MARK THEIR HOUR OF DOUBT,
          INFAMY SEAL THEIR FATE.
THIRD WOMAN.
     I swear, *that* Oracle's all too clear.
FIRST WOMAN.
                                        Oh the dear gods!
LYSISTRATA.
     Let's not be downhearted, girls. Back to our places!
     The god has spoken. How can we possibly fail him?

                              [*Exit* LYSISTRATA *with the dissi-
                              dent women*]

CHORAL EPISODE

CHORUS^m.
                                                  [STROPHE]
     I know a little story that I learned way back in school
     Goes like this:
     Once upon a time there was a young man—and no fool—
     Named Melanion;[59] and his   730
     One aversi-on was marriage. He loathed the very thought.
     So he ran off to the hills, and in a special grot
     Raised a dog, and spent his days
     Hunting rabbits. And it says
     That he never never never did come home.
     It might be called a refuge *from* the womb.
     All right,
                all right,
                          all right!
     We're as bright as young Melanion, and we hate the very sight
     Of you women!
A MAN.
     How about a kiss, old lady?   740
A WOMAN.
     Here's an onion for your eye!
A MAN.
     A kick in the guts, then?
A WOMAN.
     Try, old bristle-tail, just try!

     [59] An obscure personage; in this context, he is a kind of male equivalent of Artemis, the
determinedly virgin goddess of the hunt.

A MAN.

    Yet they say Myronidês[60]

    On hands and knees

    Looked just as shaggy fore and aft as I!

CHORUS[W].

                           [ANTISTROPHE]

    Well, *I* know a little story, and it's just as good as yours.

    Goes like this:

    Once there was a man named Timon[61]—a rough diamond, of

        course,

    And that whiskery face of his   750

    Looked like murder in the shrubbery. By God, he was a son

    Of the Furies, let me tell you! And what did he do but run

    From the world and all its ways,

    Cursing mankind! And it says

    That his choicest execrations as of then

    Were leveled almost wholly at *old* men.

    All right,

            all right,

                 all right!

    But there's one thing about Timon: he could always stand the

        sight

    Of us women.

A WOMAN.

    How about a crack in the jaw, Pop?   760

A MAN.

    I can take it, Ma—no fear!

A WOMAN.

    How about a kick in the face?

A MAN.

    You'd reveal your old caboose?

A WOMAN.

    What I'd show

    I'll have you know,

    Is an instrument you're too far gone to use.

SCENE III

[*Re-enter* LYSISTRATA]

LYSISTRATA.

    Oh, quick, girls, quick! Come here!

A WOMAN.

                      What is it?

---

[60] An Athenian general.

[61] A noted misanthrope (the titular character of one of Shakespeare's plays). The women choose here to present him as an enemy to males rather than to humankind.

LYSISTRATA.

A man.

A man simply bulging with love.

O Kyprian Queen,[62]

O Paphian, O Kythereian! Hear us and aid us!

A WOMAN.

Where is this enemy?

LYSISTRATA.

Over there, by Demêter's shrine.   770

A WOMAN.

Damned if he isn't. But who *is* he?

MYRRHINE.

My husband.

Kinêsias.

LYSISTRATA.

Oh then, get busy! Tease him! Undermine him!
Wreck him! Give him everything—kissing, tickling, nudging,
whatever you generally torture him with—: give him everything
except what we swore on the wine we would not give.

MYRRHINE.

Trust me.

LYSISTRATA.

I do. But I'll help you get him started.
The rest of you women, stay back.

[*Enter* KINESIAS]

KINESIAS.

Oh God! Oh my God!
I'm stiff from lack of exercise. All I can do to stand up.

LYSISTRATA.

Halt! Who are you, approaching our lines?

KINESIAS.

Me? I.

LYSISTRATA.

A man?

KINESIAS.

You have eyes, haven't you?

LYSISTRATA.

Go away.   780

KINESIAS.

Who says so?

LYSISTRATA.

Officer of the Day.

KINESIAS.

Officer, I beg you,
by all the gods at once, bring Myrrhinê out.

LYSISTRATA.

Myrrhinê? And who, my good sir, are you?

[62] *Kyprian* and the names in the following line are epithets for Aphroditê, goddess of love.

KINESIAS.

    Kinêsias. Last name's Pennison. Her husband.

LYSISTRATA.

    Oh, of course. I beg your pardon. We're glad to see you.
We've heard so much about you. Dearest Myrrhinê
is always talking about 'Kinêsias'—never nibbles an egg
or an apple without saying
'Here's to Kinêsias!'

KINESIAS.

               Do you really mean it?

LYSISTRATA.

                    I do.
When we're discussing men, she always says   790
'Well, after all, there's nobody like Kinêsias!'

KINESIAS.

    Good God.—Well, then, please send her down here.

LYSISTRATA.

    And what do *I* get out of it?

KINESIAS.

             A standing promise.

LYSISTRATA.

    I'll take it up with her.

                  [Exit LYSISTRATA]

KINESIAS.

             But be quick about it!
Lord, what's life without a wife? Can't eat. Can't sleep.
Every time I go home, the place is so empty, so
insufferably sad. Love's killing me. Oh,
hurry!

                  [Enter MANES, *a slave, with* KINES-
                  IAS' *baby; the voice of* MYRRHINE *is
                  heard off-stage.]*

MYRRHINE.

         But of course I love him! Adore him!—But no,
he hates love. No. I won't go down.

                  [Enter MYRRHINE, *above]*

KINESIAS.

               Myrrhinê!
Darlingest Myrrhinette! Come down quick!   800

MYRRHINE.

    Certainly not.

KINESIAS.

         Not? But why, Myrrhinê?

MYRRHINE.

    Why? You don't need me.

KINESIAS.
                                    Need you? My God, *look* at me!
MYRRHINE.
   So long!

                                    [*Turns to go*]

KINESIAS.
         Myrrhinê, Myrrhinê, Myrrhinê!
   If not for my sake, for our child!

                                    [*Pinches* BABY]

                                    —All right, you: pipe up!
BABY.
   Mummie! Mummie! Mummie!
KINESIAS.
                                    You hear that?
   Pitiful, I call it. Six days now
   with never a bath; no food; enough to break your heart!
MYRRHINE.
   My darlingest child! What a father *you* acquired!
KINESIAS.
   At least come down for his sake.
MYRRHINE.
                                    I suppose I must.
   Oh, this mother business!

                                    [*Exit*]

KINESIAS.
                           How pretty she is! And younger!   810
   The harder she treats me, the more bothered I get.

                                    [MYRRHINE *enters, below*]

MYRRHINE.
                                             Dearest child,
   you're as sweet as your father's horrid. Give me a kiss.
KINESIAS.
   Now don't you see how wrong it was to get involved
   in this scheming League of women? It's bad
   for us both.
MYRRHINE.
                  Keep your hands to yourself!
KINESIAS.
                                    But our house
   going to rack and ruin?
MYRRHINE.
                           I don't care.

KINESIAS.

                                   And your knitting
all torn to pieces by the chickens? Don't you care?

MYRRHINE.

   Not at all.

KINESIAS.

          And our debt to Aphroditê?
Oh, *won't* you come back?

MYRRHINE.

                              No.—At least, not until you men
make a treaty and stop this war.

KINESIAS.

                                   Why, I suppose   820
that might be arranged.

MYRRHINE.

                         Oh? Well, I suppose
I might come down then. But meanwhile,
I've sworn not to.

KINESIAS.

               Don't worry.—Now, let's have fun.

MYRRHINE.

   No! Stop it! I said no!
                         —Although, of course,
I *do* love you.

KINESIAS.

          I know you do. Darling Myrrhinê:
come, shall we?

MYRRHINE.

          Are you out of your mind? In front of the child?

KINESIAS.

   Take him home, Manês.

                              [*Exit* MANES *with* BABY]

                    There. He's gone.
                                   Come on!
There's nothing to stop us now.

MYRRHINE.

                         You devil! But where?

KINESIAS.

   In Pan's cave. What could be snugger than that?

MYRRHINE.

   But my purification before I go back to the Citadel?   830

KINESIAS.

   Wash in the Klepsydra.[63]

MYRRHINE.

                    And my oath?

---

[63] A spring on the Akropolis.

KINESIAS.
                                        Leave the oath to me.
After all, I'm the man.
MYRRHINE.
                              Well . . . if you say so.
                                                I'll go find a bed.
KINESIAS.
Oh, bother a bed! The ground's good enough for me.
MYRRHINE.
No. You're a bad man, but you deserve something better than dirt.

                    [*Exit* MYRRHINE]

KINESIAS.
What a love she is! and how thoughtful!

                              [*Re-enter* MYRRHINE]

MYRRHINE.
                                        Here's your bed.
Now let me get my clothes off.
                              But, good horrors!
We haven't a mattress.
KINESIAS.
                    Oh, forget the mattress!
MYRRHINE.
                                                No.
Just lying on blankets? Too sordid.
KINESIAS.
                                        Give me a kiss.
MYRRHINE.
Just a second.

                    [*Exit* MYRRHINE]

KINESIAS.
          I swear, I'll explode!

                    [*Re-enter* MYRRHINE]

MYRRHINE.
                                        Here's your mattress.
I'll just take my dress off.
                    But look—   840
where's our pillow?
KINESIAS.
                    I don't *need* a pillow!
MYRRHINE.
                                        Well, *I* do.

                    [*Exit* MYRRHINE]

KINESIAS.
I don't suppose even Heraklês[64]
would stand for this!

[*Re-enter* MYRRHINE]

MYRRHINE.
There we are. Ups-a-daisy!
KINESIAS.
So we are. Well, come to bed.
MYRRHINE.
is everything ready now?
KINESIAS.
I can swear to that. Come, darling!
MYRRHINE.
Just getting out of my girdle.
But remember, now,
what you promised about the treaty.
KINESIAS.
Yes, yes, yes!
MYRRHINE.
But no coverlet!
KINESIAS.
Damn it, I'll be
your coverlet!
MYRRHINE.
Be right back.

[*Exit* MYRRHINE]

KINESIAS.
This girl and her coverlets
will be the death of me.

[*Re-enter* MYRRHINE]

MYRRHINE.
Here we are. Up you go!   850
KINESIAS.
Up? I've been up for ages.
MYRRHINE.
Some perfume?
KINESIAS.
No, by Apollo!
MYRRHINE.
Yes, by Aphroditê!
I don't care whether you want it or not.

[64] A lustful womanizer, Heraklês (Hercules) could also be chivalrous and even self-abasing
in his relations with women.

[*Exit* MYRRHINE]

KINESIAS.
For love's sake, hurry!

[*Re-enter* MYRRHINE]

MYRRHINE.
Here, in your hand. Rub it right in.
KINESIAS.
                              Never cared for perfume.
And this is particularly strong. Still, here goes.
MYRRHINE.
What a nitwit I am! I brought you the Rhodian bottle.
KINESIAS.
Forget it.
MYRRHINE.
        No trouble at all. You just wait here.

[*Exit* MYRRHINE]

KINESIAS.
God damn the man who invented perfume!

[*Re-enter* MYRRHINE]

MYRRHINE.
At last! The right bottle!
KINESIAS.
                        I've got the rightest   860
bottle of all, and it's right here waiting for you.
Darling, forget everything else. Do come to bed.
MYRRHINE.
Just let me get my shoes off.
                        —And, by the way,
you'll vote for the treaty?
KINESIAS.
                        I'll think about it.

[MYRRHINE *runs away*]

There! That's done it! The damned woman,
she gets me all bothered, she half kills me,
and she runs! What'll I do? Where
can I get laid?
                —And you, little prodding pal,
who's going to take care of *you*? No, you and I
had better get down to old Foxdog's[65] Nursing Clinic.   870
CHORUS[m].
            Alas for the woes of man, alas
            Specifically for you.

[65] A well known pimp.

    She's brought you to a pretty pass:
       What are you going to do?
    Split, heart! Sag, flesh! Proud spirit, crack!
    Myrrhinê's got you on your back.

KINESIAS.

    The agony, the protraction!

KORYPHAIOS^m.

                         Friend,
      What woman's worth a damn?
    They bitch us all, world without end.

KINESIAS.

      Yet they're so damned sweet, man!

KORYPHAIOS^m.   880

      Calamitous, that's what I say.
      You should have learned that much today.

CHORUS^m.

    O blessed Zeus, roll womankind
      Up into one great ball;
    Blast them aloft on a high wind,
      And once there, let them fall.
    Down, down they'll come, the pretty dears,
    And split themselves on our thick spears.

               [*Exit* KINESIAS]

SCENE IV

[*Enter a* SPARTAN HERALD]

HERALD.

    Gentlemen, Ah beg you will be so kind
    as to direct me to the Central Committee.   890
    Ah have a communication.

               [*Re-enter* COMMISSIONER]

COMMISSIONER.

                    Are you a man,
    or a fertility symbol?

HERALD.

               Ah refuse to answer that question!
    Ah'm a certified herald from Spahta, and Ah've come
    to talk about an ahmistice.

COMMISSIONER.

              Then why
    that spear under your cloak?

HERALD.

               Ah have no speah!

COMMISSIONER.

    You don't walk naturally, with your tunic

poked out so. You have a tumor, maybe,
or a hernia?
HERALD.
                        You lòst yo' mahnd, man?
COMMISSIONER.
                                    Well,
something's up, I can see that. And I don't like it.
HERALD.
Colonel, Ah resent this.
COMMISSIONER.
                        So I see. But what *is* it?
HERALD.
                                                A staff   900
with a message from Spahta.
COMMISSIONER.
                        Oh. I know about those staffs.[66]
Well, then, man, speak out: How are things in Sparta?
HERALD.
Hahd, Colonel, hahd! We're at a standstill.
Cain't seem to think of anything but women.
COMMISSIONER.
How curious! Tell me, do you Spartans think
that maybe Pan's[67] to blame?
HERALD.
Pan? No. Lampitô and her little naked friends.
They won't let a man come nigh them.
COMMISSIONER.
How are you handling it?
HERALD.
                        Losing our mahnds,
if y' want to know, and walking around hunched over   910
lahk men carrying candles in a gale.
The women have swohn they'll have nothing to do with us
until we get a treaty.
COMMISSIONER.
                        Yes, I know.
It's a general uprising, sir, in all parts of Greece.
But as for the answer—
                        Sir: go back to Sparta
and have them send us your Armistice Commission.
I'll arrange things in Athens.
                                And I may say
that my standing is good enough to make them listen.

---

[66] The pun alludes to a Spartan method of cryptography: a message was written on fabric
wound around a staff (like an overlapping bandage). It was then unwound, despatched by
messenger, and rewound on a staff identical in shape with the sender's. Only then could the
scrambled lines of writing be realigned to make sense.

[67] The nature-god Pan was held accountable for sudden and inexplicable fits of madness,
or "panic." The god could also cause sexual excesses.

HERALD.
A man after mah own haht! Seh, Ah thank you.

[*Exit* HERALD]

CHORAL EPISODE

CHORUS[m].

    Oh these women! Where will you find   [STROPHE]   920
    A slavering beast that's more unkind?
      Where a hotter fire?
    Give me a panther, any day.
    He's not so merciless as they,
      And panthers don't conspire.

CHORUS[w].

    We may be hard, you silly old ass,   [ANTISTROPHE]
    But who brought you to this stupid pass?
      You're the ones to blame.
    Fighting with us, your oldest friends,
    Simply to serve your selfish ends—   930
      Really, you have no shame!

KORYPHAIOS[m].

No, I'm through with women for ever.

KORYPHAIOS[w].

                              If you say so.
Still, you might put some clothes on. You look too absurd
standing around naked. Come, get into this cloak.

KORYPHAIOS[m].

Thank you; you're right. I merely took it off
because I was in such a temper.

KORYPHAIOS[w].

                      That's much better.
Now you resemble a man again.
                    Why have you been so horrid?
And look: there's some sort of insect in your eye.
Shall I take it out?

KORYPHAIOS[m].

                An insect, is it? So that's
what's been bothering me. Lord, yes: take it out!   940

KORYPHAIOS[w].

You might be more polite.
                  —But, heavens!
What an enormous mosquito!

KORYPHAIOS[m].

                You've saved my life.
That mosquito was drilling an artesian well
in my left eye.

KORYPHAIOS[w].
          Let me wipe
those tears away.—And now: one little kiss?
KORYPHAIOS[m].
   No, no kisses.
KORYPHAIOS[w].
        You're so difficult.
KORYPHAIOS[m].
   You impossible women! How you do get around us!
   The poet was right: Can't live with you, or without you.
   But let's be friends.
   And to celebrate, you might join us in an Ode.   950
CHORUS[m and w].
        Let it never be said   [STROPHE 1]
        That my tongue is malicious:
        Both by word and by deed
I would set an example that's noble and gracious.
        We've had sorrow and care
        Till we're sick of the tune.
        Is there anyone here
        Who would like a small loan?
          My purse is crammed,
          As you'll soon find;   960
And you needn't pay me back if the Peace gets signed.

        I've invited to lunch   [STROPHE 2]
        Some Karystian rips[68]—
        An esurient bunch,
But I've ordered a menu to water their lips.
        I can still make soup
        And slaughter a pig.
        You're all coming, I hope?
        But a bath first, I beg!
        Walk right up   970
        As though you owned the place,
And you'll get the front door slammed to in your face.

SCENE V

[*Enter* SPARTAN AMBASSADOR, *with entourage*]

KORYPHAIOS[m].
   The Commission has arrived from Sparta.
                  How oddly
   they're walking!

[68] People from Karystos, allied with Athens. They were considered uninhibited and morally loose.

Gentlemen, welcome to Athens!
How is life in Lakonia?[69]

AMBASSADOR.

Need we discuss that?
Simply use your eyes.

CHORUS[m].

The poor man's right:
What a sight!

AMBASSADOR.

Words fail me.
But come, gentlemen, call in your Commissioners,
and let's get down to a Peace.

CHORAGOS[m].

The state we're in! Can't bear
a stitch below the waist. It's a kind of pelvic   980
paralysis.

COMMISSIONER.

Won't somebody call Lysistrata?—Gentlemen,
we're no better off than you.

AMBASSADOR.

So I see.

A SPARTAN.

Seh, do y'all feel a certain strain
early in the morning?

AN ATHENIAN.

I do, sir. It's worse than a strain.
A few more days, and there's nothing for us but Kleisthenês,
that broken blossom.

CHORAGOS[m].

But you'd better get dressed again.
You know these people going around Athens with chisels,
looking for statues of Hermês.[70]

ATHENIAN.

Sir, you are right.

SPARTAN.

He certainly is! Ah'll put mah own clothes back on.

[*Enter* ATHENIAN COMMISSIONERS]

COMMISSIONER.

Gentlemen from Sparta, welcome. This is a sorry business.   990

SPARTAN.   [*To one of his own group*]:
Colonel, we got dressed just in time. Ah sweah,
if they'd seen us the way we were, there'd have been a new wah
between the states.

---

[69] The southern area of Greece. Sparta was its most important city.

[70] Opponents of the expedition to Sicily had mutilated these phallic statues (commonly located in front of homes) just before the fleet set sail. Some Athenians believed that the vandalism had jinxed the Sicilian campaign.

COMMISSIONER.
    Shall we call the meeting to order?
                                            Now, Lakonians,
    what's your proposal?
AMBASSADOR.
                                We propose to consider peace.
COMMISSIONER.
    Good. That's on our minds, too.
                                    —Summon Lysistrata.
    We'll never get anywhere without her.
AMBASSADOR.
                                                Lysistrata?
    Summon Lysis-*any*body! Only, summon!
KORYPHAIOS[m].
                                No need to summon:
    here she is, herself.

                        [*Enter* LYSISTRATA]

COMMISSIONER.
                    Lysistrata! Lion of women!
    This is your hour to be   1000
    hard and yielding, outspoken and shy, austere and
    gentle. You see here
    the best brains of Hellas (confused, I admit,
    by your devious charming) met as one man
    to turn the future over to you.
LYSISTRATA.
                            That's fair enough,
    unless you men take it into your heads
    to turn to each other instead of to us. But I'd know
    soon enough if you did.
                            —Where is Reconciliation?
    Go, some of you: bring her here.

                        [*Exeunt two women*]

                            And now, women,
    lead the Spartan delegates to me: not roughly   1010
    or insultingly, as our men handle them, but gently,
    politely, as ladies should. Take them by the hand,
    or by anything else if they won't give you their hands.

                        [*The* SPARTANS *are escorted over*]

    There.—The Athenians next, by any convenient handle.

                        [*The* ATHENIANS *are escorted*]

    Stand there, please.—Now, all of you, listen to me.

> [*During the following speech the
> two women re-enter, carrying an
> enormous statue of a naked girl; this
> is* RECONCILIATION.]

I'm only a woman, I know; but I've a mind,
and, I think, not a bad one: I owe it to my father
and to listening to the local politicians.
So much for that.
                  Now, gentlemen,
since I have you here, I intend to give you a scolding.   1020
We are all Greeks.
Must I remind you of Thermopylai, of Olympia,
of Delphoi?[71] names deep in all our hearts?
Are they not a common heritage?
                        Yet you men
go raiding through the country from both sides,
Greek killing Greek, storming down Greek cities—
and all the time the Barbarian[72] across the sea
is waiting for his chance!
          —That's my first point.

AN ATHENIAN.

Lord! I can hardly contain myself.

LYSISTRATA.

                  As for you Spartans:
Was it so long ago that Perikleidês[73]   1030
came here to beg our help? I can see him still,
his grey face, his sombre gown. And what did he want?
An army from Athens. All Messênê
was hot at your heels, and the sea-god splitting your land.
Well, Kimôn and his men,
four thousand strong, marched out and saved all Sparta.
And what thanks do we get? You come back to murder us.

AN ATHENIAN.

They're aggressors, Lysistrata!

A SPARTAN.

               Ah Admit it.
When Ah look at those laigs, Ah sweah Ah'll aggress mahself!

LYSISTRATA.

And you, Athenians: do you think you're blameless?   1040
Remember that bad time when we were helpless,
and an army came from Sparta,
and that was the end of the Thessalian menace,
the end of Hippias[74] and his allies.

---

[71] The place-names evoke the former days of Greek unity and glory before the tragic civil war.

[72] Foreign; non-Greek.

[73] An emissary sent from Sparta, earlier in the fifth century, to request help from Athens in putting down civil war in Sparta and rebellion by Spartan-controlled Messênê. Athens responded by sending a rescue-force led by Kimôn.

[74] The Spartans had helped Athens to overthrow and expel the tyrant Hippias.

> And that was Sparta,
and only Sparta; but for Sparta, we'd be
cringing slaves today, not free Athenians.

> [*From this point, the male responses
> are less to* LYSISTRATA *than to the
> statue*]

A SPARTAN.
 A well shaped speech.
AN ATHENIAN.
> Certainly it has its points.
LYSISTRATA.
 Why are we fighting each other? With all this history
 of favors given and taken, what stands in the way
 of making peace?
AMBASSADOR.
> Spahta is ready, ma'am,   1050
 so long as we get that place back.
LYSISTRATA.
> What place, man?

AMBASSADOR.
 Ah refer to Pylos.[75]
COMMISSIONER.
> Not a chance, by God!
LYSISTRATA.
 Give it to them, friend.
COMMISSIONER.
> But—what shall we have to bargain with?
LYSISTRATA.
 Demand something in exchange.
COMMISSIONER.
> Good idea.—Well, then:
 Cockeville first, and the Happy Hills, and the country
 between the Legs of Mêgara.
AMBASSADOR.
> Mah government objects.
LYSISTRATA.
 Over-ruled. Why fuss about a pair of legs?

> [*General assent. The statue is re-
> moved.*]

AN ATHENIAN.
 I want to get out of these clothes and start my plowing.
A SPARTAN.
 Ah'll fertilize mahn first, by the Heavenly Twins!

---

[75] A town; the root meaning of its name is "flank." This and the following lines make a
series of puns referring both to control of geographical areas and to portions of the female
body as visible in the statue of the nude "Reconciliation." Conventional diplomatic bargaining
for territory is thus blended with the sexual diplomacy employed by the women in the play.

LYSISTRATA.
   And so you shall,   1060
   once you've made peace. If you are serious,
   go, both of you, and talk with your allies.
COMMISSIONER.
   Too much talk already. No, we'll stand together.
   We've only one end in view. All that we want
   is our women; and I speak for our allies.
AMBASSADOR.
   Mah government concurs.
AN ATHENIAN.
                So does Karystos.
LYSISTRATA.
   Good.—But before you come inside
   to join your wives at supper, you must perform
   the usual lustration.[76] Then we'll open
   our baskets for you, and all that we have is yours.   1070
   But you must promise upright good behavior
   from this day on. Then each man home with his woman!
AN ATHENIAN.
   Let's get it over with.
A SPARTAN.
             Lead on. Ah follow.
AN ATHENIAN.
   Quick as a cat can wink!

               [*Exeunt all but the* CHORUSES]

CHORUS[w].
      Embroideries ánd   [ANTISTROPHE 1]
      Twinkling ornaments ánd
      Pretty dresses—I hand
Them all over to you, and with never a qualm.
      They'll be nice for your daughters
      On festival days   1080
      When the girls bring the Goddess
      The ritual prize.
         Come in, one and all:
         Take what you will.
I've nothing here so tightly corked that you can't make it spill.

      You may search my house,   [ANTISTROPHE 2]
      But you'll not find
      The least thing of use,
Unless your two eyes are keener than mine.
      Your numberless brats   1090
      Are half starved? and your slaves?
      Courage, grandpa! I've lots
      Of grain left, and big loaves.

[76] Ceremonial purification.

I'll fill your guts
I'll go the whole hog;
But if you come too close to me, remember: 'ware the dog!

[*Exeunt* CHORUSES]

ÉXODOS

[*A* DRUNKEN CITIZEN *enters, approaches the gate, and is halted by a*
SENTRY]

CITIZEN.
    Open. The. Door.
SENTRY.
               Now, friend, just shove along!
—So you want to sit down. If it weren't such an old joke,
I'd tickle your tail with this torch. Just the sort of gag
this audience appreciates.
CITIZEN.
              I. Stay. Right. Here.   1100
SENTRY.
    Get away from there, or I'll scalp you! The gentlemen from Sparta
are just coming back from dinner.

                    [*Exit* CITIZEN; *the general com-*
                    pany re-enters; the two CHORUSES
                    now represent SPARTANS *and*
                    ATHENIANS.]

A SPARTAN.
               Ah must say,
Ah never tasted better grub.
AN ATHENIAN.
               And those Lakonians!
They're gentlemen, by the Lord! Just goes to show,
a drink to the wise is sufficient.
COMMISSIONER.
               And why not?
A sober man's an ass.
Men of Athens, mark my words: the only efficient
Ambassador's a drunk Ambassador. Is that clear?
Look: we go to Sparta,
and when we get there we're dead sober. The result?   1110
Everyone cackling at everyone else. They make speeches;
and even if we understand, we get it all wrong
when we file our reports in Athens. But today—!
Everybody's happy. Couldn't tell the difference
between *Drink to Me Only* and
The Star-Spangled Athens.

What's a few lies,
washed down in good strong drink?

[*Re-enter the* DRUNKEN CITIZEN]

SENTRY.

God almighty,
he's back again!

CITIZEN.

I. Resume. My. Place.

A SPARTAN.

[*To an* ATHENIAN]

Ah beg yo', seh,
take yo' instrument in yo' hand and play for us.   1120
Ah'm told
yo' understand the in*tri*cacies of the floot?
Ah'd lahk to execute a song and dance
in honor of Athens,

and, of cohse, of Spahta.

CITIZEN.

Toot. On. Your. Flute.

[*The following song is a solo—an
aria—accompanied by the flute.
The* CHORUS OF SPARTANS *begins
a slow dance.*]

A SPARTAN.

O Memory,
Let the Muse speak once more
In my young voice. Sing glory.
Sing Artemision's shore,[77]
Where Athens fluttered the Persians. *Alalaí,*   1130
Sing glory, that great
Victory! Sing also
Our Leonidas and his men,
Those wild boars, sweat and blood
Down in a red drench. Then, then
The barbarians broke, though they had stood
Numberless as the sands before!

O Artemis,
Virgin Goddess, whose darts
Flash in our forests: approve   1140
This pact of peace and join our hearts,

[77] In the former days of Grecian unity, the Athenian fleet had fought against the Persians near Artemision while the Spartans, led by the hero Leonidas, had bravely fought the Persians on land, at Thermopylae. *Alalaí* is a battle cry.

From this day on, in love.
Huntress, descend!

LYSISTRATA.

All that will come in time.
                              But now, Lakonians,
take home your wives. Athenians, take yours.
Each man be kind to his woman; and you, women,
be equally kind. Never again, pray God,
shall we lose our way in such madness.

KORYPHAIOS[a].

                                                    And now

let's dance our joy.

                              [*From this point the dance becomes
                              general*]

CHORUS[a].

Dance, you Graces
                              Artemis, dance   1150
Dance, Phoibos, Lord of dancing
                              Dance,
In a scurry of Maenads, Lord Dionysos
                              Dance, Zeus Thunderer
              Dance, Lady Hêra
Queen of the Sky
                              Dance, dance, all you gods
Dance witness everlasting of our pact
Evohí Evohé
Dance for the dearest
                              the Bringer of Peace
Deathless Aphroditê!

COMMISSIONER.

Now let us have another song from Sparta.   1160

CHORUS[s].

From Taÿgetos, from Taÿgetos,
              Lakonian Muse, come down.
Sing to the Lord Apollo
              Who rules Amyklai[78] Town.

Sing Athêna of the House of Brass![79]

Sing Lêda's Twins,[80] that chivalry
              Respondent on the shore
Of our Eurôtas;[81] sing the girls
              That dance along before:

---

[78] A town, associated with Apollo, in the Spartan region.
[79] The temple of Athena in Sparta.
[80] The "Heavenly Twins," Castor and Pollux, protectors of their sister, Helen of Troy.
[81] The river of Sparta.

Sparkling in dust their gleaming feet,
        Their hair a Bacchant[82] fire,
    And Lêda's daughter,[83] thyrsos raised,
            Leads their triumphant choir.
CHORUSES[s and a].
        Evohé!
                Evohaí!
                        Evohé!
                                We pass
                Dancing
                        dancing
                                to greet
        Athêna of the House of Brass.

---

[82] Associated with the Bacchantes, female worshipers of Bacchus (Dionysus), the god of wine, sex, and revelry.

[83] Helen of Troy, symbol of woman as cause of war but here of woman as reconciler. The thyrsos is a staff carried by worshipers of Dionysus/Bacchus.

Plato
(C.427–C.348 B.C.)

Except for certain great religious teachers, Plato has probably been the most influential thinker in the history of Western culture. Because he believed that dialectic, in the form of oral give-and-take, was a higher form of discourse and a more reliable avenue to wisdom than written treatises, his writings are not necessarily a complete or wholly reliable record of what he believed. But the high reverence in which Plato was held, in his own day and since, has caused his written work to survive more completely than that of virtually any other ancient Greek author. Moreover, the written work itself reflects Plato's dedication to the spoken word, since his most typical literary form is the "Dialogue." The thirty or more works by Plato that have come down to us concentrate mainly on ethical, political, and metaphysical issues, but they also treat in depth or at least touch on many other important matters that have preoccupied philosophers, including issues in mathematics, logic, and physical science.

Plato was a pioneering thinker, but he was much more than a groundbreaker. Are words merely arbitrary symbols for things and human ideas, or do words have a more absolute relationship to what they signify? Are goodness and beauty realities in themselves—independent of the accidents of our observation and tastes—or are they merely attributes that the human mind generalizes from particular objects it considers good or beautiful? Do we know truth through reason or through some more mysterious or intuitive process? If love helps us become our best selves and induces ecstatic states of happiness and generosity, why does it also bring out what is most absurd, irrational, and malignant in us? In forming a just political community, should the first task be to perfect individual citizens, in the hope that they will add up to a just polity, or should individuals model their private virtues on a general conception of what the community needs? These questions raised by Plato, and many others like them, have obsessed countless people—practical men and women as well as abstract theoreticians. And—which is most remarkable—in trying to answer such questions, people have again and again gone directly to Plato's works themselves, not merely to later "sophistications" of his thought.

Plato was born around 427 B.C., in Athens, of an aristocratic lineage that claimed descent from preeminent legendary ancestors. He came under the influence of Socrates—the central figure in most of Plato's Dialogues—when Plato was about twenty, at which time Socrates was in his early sixties. During the eight or so years before Socrates was tried and condemned to death in 399, Plato was one of many bright and well-born young Athenians who listened and learned in the public places of Athens where Socrates held forth. Plato's family was active in Athenian politics, and he himself was drawn toward public life in the critical last decade of the fifth century (years which witnessed among other dramatic events the final defeat of Athens in its civil war against Sparta). But at this time Plato opted against a political career. Significantly, in the Apology, *his account of Socrates' trial, he reports Socrates' opinion that to be apolitical is the only way to retain integrity. In Plato's middle and old age, however (he died around 348), he made several journeys to Sicily, partly with the hope of helping the ruling family of Syracuse realize in practical terms the political principles Plato had come to believe in. The effort failed for several reasons, but the fact that Plato did make the attempt to reconcile theoretical principles with actual practice testifies that he was not simply the otherworldly mystic that many people associate with the term "Platonic."*

Apart from his own direct teaching, whether or not it was preserved in writing, Plato's most distinctive achievement was to found and lead the "Academy" (located in an olive grove near Athens, and named after the hero Academus). This assemblage of brilliant original thinkers, brought together under Plato's direction, was the prototype of modern universities and "think tanks."

The greatness of Plato, and his incalculable influence, are mainly attributable to the inherent profundity and originality of his thought. Even if it had come down to us in the severely colorless vehicle that in our time is considered normal or even essential for hard thinking in philosophy and science, Plato would occupy a central position among intellectuals. But his appeal has been much broader, and that fact is largely due to the literary forms he used, mainly the Dialogue. Plato has often, and rightly, been called a poet (despite the ambiguous view of poetry in works like the Ion*), because of the high eloquence and supernal beauty he often attains. But Plato is also a master of fiction and, almost literally, of drama. The beginning of the* Symposium, *a lively sketch in which Apollodorus, the convert to philosophy, selfrighteously spars with his more worldly interrogators, and the conclusion of that dialogue, where Alcibiades, the handsome young leader and playboy, recounts ruefully his abortive attempt to seduce the aging and ugly Socrates, are triumphs of story-writing. Plato's credentials as a dramatist are revealed on two levels. On one level, ideas themselves are the dramatic "characters," and Plato's triumph is to make these competing ideas compelling in themselves, so that we are drawn to one or another of them, our sympathies evoked as if the ideas were our friends or enemies. In addition, though, the human persons who espouse or oppose various ideological positions are drawn with great subtlety and psychological realism. Most of these people were actual historical human beings, so that Plato portrayed from life and not merely* *from his imagination. But many authors whose explicit aim is biography have not succeeded nearly as well as did Plato in the vivid rendering of personalities.*

Chief among Plato's triumphs of characterization is, of course, Socrates. This multifaceted man—by turns earnest and playful, ironic and unguarded, elevated in mind but physically unprepossessing—emerges as one of the most memorable human beings in history or fiction. To treat him as a mere creature of Plato's art would be absurd, of course, just as it would be absurd to treat Jesus as an invention of the New Testament evangelists. Socrates was a distinct historical individual, in his own right an important personage and an eminent teacher-thinker. But to what extent Plato represented him and his ideas accurately is uncertain. That there was much distortion in Plato's portrait seems unlikely, since Socrates was the most publicly accessible of Athenians, and many of the readers in Plato's audience would have remembered him personally. A much more difficult and important problem is to what extent Plato's ideas coincide with those of his mentor. Plato could hardly have given Socrates so central a place in the Dialogues if the pupil had not embraced and retained many of Socrates' ideas. On the other hand, Socrates died a half-century before Plato did, and Plato's ideas must inevitably have developed during that period. Other complications include the fact that the Dialogues are not always consistent with one another; in some of them Plato may be dramatizing the clash of ideas for its own sake without trying to propose a solution to which either Socrates or Plato himself would have subscribed. And, on top of these difficulties, there is the question of how nearly "Neo-Platonism"—the occultist developments of his ideas during the two millennia after Plato—is consonant with Plato's thought.

Although such critical, biographical, and historical questions are important, in some ways they are distractions. In one sense Platonism is no more or less than what is contained in Plato's works: a set of ideas and a method for testing and exploring them. Whether or not either Plato or Socrates would have endorsed the ideas, and whether they and their adherents are treated ironically or not, are from the thinker's point of view less important than the truth or falsity of various positions. In the Symposium, *for example, Aristophanes' fable explaining sexual attraction as the result of a primordial splitting of people into halves is treated facetiously, but the notion of "soul mates" implied in the fable has survived the ironic context and has become one fundamental "model" of the nature of love. Part of the power of Plato's works is due to the fact that the concepts expressed in them have a reality that can transcend the human drama through which they are so vividly expressed.*

For many people, "Platonism" has come to suggest otherworldliness, ecstasy, and mysticism. And it is undeniable that the tone and content of the Dialogues is sometimes elevated and rhapsodic. The metaphysical doctrine of "Ideas" or "Forms" (introduced in the Republic, Symposium, *and other Dialogues) does indeed seem to suggest that the material world is flawed exactly because it is material. But to regard Plato as a mystic—if by that term we mean a devotee of mystery—is misleading, to say the least. Mind, the senses, the mundane, are central in Plato's works; the reasoning is razor-edged, and the frequent analogies (as Alcibiades points out in the* Symposium) *are usually to such homely creatures as pack-asses and tanners, even when Socrates is leading the way to sublime insights. One of the challenges Plato poses for the modern reader is that of reconciling the mental states of rationalism and excitement. For most people today, those terms are irreconcilable; for example (the cliché goes), poets and other artists* feel, *while scientists* think. *Plato's works suggest that hard thinking can be a positively sensuous experience. To present it through a literary medium that uses comedy, characterization, local setting, and the like is to imply that thinking is not an alternative to living but one of the best parts of living.*

FURTHER READING *(prepared by F. S. N.):* The standard treatment of Plato as writer, philosopher, and influential thinker is Paul Friedländer's *Plato,* 1928–1930, 2nd ed. 1953–1957, 3 vols., trans. Hans Meyerhoff, 1958–1969. Other useful works on Plato's life and writings are by Paul Shorey, *What Plato Said,* 1933, repr. 1965; and by G. C. Field, *The Philosophy of Plato,* 1949, 2nd ed. 1969. On the development of Plato's thought see especially I. M. Crombie, *An Examination of Plato's Doctrines,* 2 vols., 1962–1963, and, by the same author, the shortened version *Plato: The Midwife's Apprentice,* 1964. Plato's lasting influence is treated in A. H. Armstrong, ed., *The Cambridge History of Later Greek and Early Medieval Philosophy,* 1967.

SYMPOSIUM (THE BANQUET)

Translated by W. H. D. Rouse
and Edited by Eric H. Warmington and Philip G. Rouse

APOLLODOROS and FRIEND
ARISTODEMOS, SOCRATES, AGATHON, PAUSANIAS, ARISTOPHANES,
ERYXIMACHOS, PHAIDROS, ALCIBIADES

INTRODUCTORY NOTE[1]

The banquet took place in Agathon's house in 416 B.C.; a few days previously Agathon, the handsome young tragic poet then aged about thirty-one, had won the prize, his first "victory," when one of his tragedies was first performed at a dramatic festival in the Theater of Dionysos, the theater at the foot of the Acropolis at Athens, which accommodated about 30,000 spectators; on page 828 Socrates refers to Agathon's courage in facing such a huge audience. Agathon appears to have been the first to insert into his tragedies choral odes unconnected with the plot of the drama. He gave this banquet to his friends on the next evening after he and his chorus had offered their sacrifice of thanksgiving for his victory.

Of his guests:
    SOCRATES *was then aged fifty-three.*
    PHAIDROS (Phaedrus), *who was invited to preside, was a friend of Plato. The famous dialogue* The Phaedrus, *not included in this volume, on the subject of love, was named after him.*
    PAUSANIAS *was a disciple of Prodicos, the Sophist, of Ceos.*
    ARISTOPHANES, *the famous comic poet, was then about thirty-two. In his comedy* The Clouds, *first performed five years previously, he had made fun of Socrates.*
    ALCIBIADES, *the eminent statesman then about thirty-five, a man of remarkable beauty and talent, but unscrupulous and dissolute, was a great admirer of*

---

[1] The *Introductory Note* is provided by the principal translator, W. H. D. Rouse, or his editors. After his death in 1950, his translation of Plato's writings was edited by Eric H. Warmington and Philip G. Rouse, with the assistance of J. C. G. Rouse. In the following footnotes, the phrase "Translator's note" refers to the footnotes that appear in this composite version.

Socrates, as his speech at the banquet shows. Socrates saved his life in battle when Alcibiades was about twenty.

The story of the banquet, as told by Aristodemos, who attended it with Socrates, is here retold by Apollodoros to a friend while they were out walking together about fifteen years after. Apollodoros is described in the dialogue Phaidon (Phaedo) *as being present weeping at Socrates' death[2] about a year later.*

APOLLODOROS.[3] I think I am pretty well word-perfect in what you are inquiring about. It so happened a day or two ago that I was coming up to town from Phaleron, when someone I knew caught sight of me and called out from behind, some distance away, in a bantering tone—"Hullo, you Phalerian there!" he shouted. "Apollodoros! Halt!" I halted and stood still.

Then he said, "Well, Apollodoros, I was just looking for you. I wanted to know about Agathon's party, Socrates and Alcibiades and the others who were at the dinner then, and the speeches they made about love. Somebody else told me the story; he heard it from Phoinix, Philip's son, and he said you knew too. But he had nothing very clear to say, so you must tell it to me; you are the best man to report your friend's speeches. But tell me first of all," he went on, "were you at the party yourself, or not?"

Then I said, "It is obvious that the story he told was not clear, if you think this party you ask about was held lately, so that I might have been there myself."

"That *is* what I thought," he said.

"How could you think that, my dear Glaucon?" I said. "Don't you know that Agathon has been abroad for many years, and it's only in the last three years I have been spending my time with Socrates, and taking care every day to know whatever he says or does? Before that I used to run all over the place, anywhere, and I thought myself a grand fellow, but I was more miserable than anyone—just as *you* are now, when you think you would do anything rather than be a philosopher."

"Oh, don't jeer," said he, "just tell me when that party was."

I said, "It was when we were boys, and Agathon won the prize with his first tragedy—on the next day after he and his chorus offered the sacrifice of thanksgiving."

"Then that is a long time ago," he said, "as it seems. But who told you the story—was it Socrates?"

"Oh dear me, no," I said, "the same man who told Phoinix; he was a Cydathenaian, Aristodemos, a little man who never wore shoes.[4] He was at the party, a lover of Socrates as much as anyone else in those days, I think. I

---

[2] Socrates was tried and condemned to death in 399 B.C. For an account of his trial, see Plato's *Apology.*

[3] Apollodorus is replying to questions by several unidentified people who want an account of the famous banquet. He is able to tell the story fluently because he also told it a day or two earlier to his friend Glaucon while they were walking to Athens from Phaleron, a port a few miles away. Both conversations take place sixteen years after the banquet itself—a fact that dramatizes how memorable it was. That Apollodorus himself has the story on hearsay, from Aristodemos, dramatizes the same point. When Plato himself wrote the *Symposium* is uncertain—it was probably composed around 384 B.C.

[4] A habit Aristodemos imitates from his admired master, Socrates. "Cydathenaian" refers to the "deme," or political district, where Aristodemos lived.

did ask Socrates himself about some things too, which I heard from this man, and he agreed with all the other had told me."

"Well, I think you might tell me now," he said, "certainly the road to town will do well enough for us to talk and listen as we go."

So as we went along we talked about all this; and hence, as I told you to begin with, I am pretty well word-perfect. Well, if I must tell you people the story too, then I must. The truth is that whenever I speak about philosophy myself or hear others doing so, I am highly delighted, besides believing that it does me good. But when I hear other kinds of talk, especially among you rich men and moneymakers, it annoys me, and I pity you, my friends, because you are doing nothing while you think you are doing something. Well, perhaps again you believe I am a poor devil, and I think you think right; but I don't *think* you are, I *know* it well.

FRIEND. Always the same, Apollodoros! Always abusing yourself and everybody else. You really seem to think everyone wretched except Socrates, beginning with yourself! Where you got that nickname of madman, I don't know exactly, but in what you say you are always mad enough—you rave against yourself and everybody except Socrates!

APOLLODOROS. O my dear man, surely it is plain that I am mad and crazy, if I have such a notion about myself and you all!

FRIEND. It is not worth while quarrelling about this now, Apollodoros; but please do what I begged you—don't say no, but tell me what the speeches were.

APOLLODOROS. Well, they were something like this—but I will try to tell you the story from the beginning as Aristodemos told it.

Aristodemos said that he met Socrates coming from the bath, with evening shoes on, which he did not often wear; and he asked him where he was going so smart; he said, to dinner at Agathon's; yesterday he had refused him at the victory feast, to avoid the crowd; but he accepted for today. "That's why I made myself pretty," he said, "to go pretty to a pretty man![5] But look here," he continued, "how about you yourself feeling willing to go to dinner uninvited?"

And I replied (said Aristodemos), "As you like."

"Come with me, then," said Socrates, "and we will pervert the proverb a bit, and say, 'When gents give dinners, gents may just walk in.'[6] For Homer has really perverted this proverb, and made it vulgar too. He draws Agamemnon as a very perfect gentle knight, and Menelaos as a 'weak warrior': and when Agamemnon gave a feast and a sacrifice, he brings in Menelaos to the feast uninvited, although he is a low man and the other high."

Hearing this, my friend said, "Well, perhaps I'll risk it too, not as you suggest, Socrates, but, as in Homer, I, a poor creature, will go uninvited to a wise man's feast. Then just think what you will say about it, for I certainly will not admit that I came uninvited, I'll tell him that you invited me."

He said, "'Two heads are better than one'; we will plan what we shall say. Well, let us go."

---

[5] As the whole *Symposium* shows, homosexuality was widespread, and considered normal, in fifth-century Athens.

[6] "The Greek text is uncertain, but the proverb seems to have been something like 'When snobs give dinners, gents may just walk in.' Socrates makes a perfect pun on Agathon's name, which means 'the gentleman.' Homer's passage is in *Iliad*, xvii, 588–90." (Translator's note.)

So after some such talk, they started off. On the way, Socrates fell behind, absorbed in his own thoughts; and when my friend was waiting, Socrates told him to go on ahead. When he came to Agathon's house, he found the door open, and there (he said) something rather ridiculous happened; for a servant from inside met him at once, and led him where the others were on their couches,[7] and he came upon them as they were about to begin dinner. But as soon as Agathon saw him, he said, "My dear Aristodemos, you are just in time to join us at dinner; if you have come for something else, put it off to another time; yesterday I looked for you to invite you, but I could not see you anywhere. But why have you not brought us Socrates?" I turned round (continued Aristodemos) but I could not see Socrates following; so I said I had come with Socrates and he had invited me there to dinner. "Very nice of you to come," he said, "but where is the man?"

"He was coming in behind me just now; I wonder myself where he could be."

"You there, you boy,"[8] said Agathon, "look about and bring in Socrates. And you take your place here, Aristodemos, beside Eryximachos."

Then the boy washed his feet, that he might take his place; and another boy came, and reported, "Socrates went into the porch next door and there he is standing, but though I call him he won't come in."

"That's odd," said he, "jusk ask him again and don't let him go."

But my friend said, "Don't do that, leave him alone. That is only his way; he often goes off and stands anywhere. He will come soon, I think. Don't interfere with him, let him alone."

Agathon said, "Very well, if you think so, we must do so. Serve the feast for the rest of us, you boys, and put before us just what you choose, whenever no one directs you (I never tried this before!). Now then, imagine that I also as well as the others here have been invited by you to dinner, and serve us so as to earn our compliments."

After this, he said, they fell to,[9] but no Socrates appeared. Agathon kept on giving orders to send for him, but my friend would not let him. However he did come, after not so long delay as usual, and found them about the middle of dinner. Then Agathon, who was reclining on the lowest seat[10] alone, on the right, said, "This way, Socrates, come by me, I want to get hold of you, to enjoy that wise thought which came to you in the porch. For it is clear you found it and have it still, or you would never have come away."

Socrates sat down, and said, "What a blessing it would be, Agathon, if wisdom could run from the fuller amongst us to the emptier, while we touch one another, as when two cups are placed side by side a bit of wool conveys water from the fuller to the emptier! If wisdom is like that, I think it precious to be beside you, for I think I shall be filled up with fine wisdom. Mine would be poor stuff and questionable, like a dream, but yours brilliant and fast growing; see how it has blazed out of you while you are still

---

[7] As a rule, dinner guests reclined on couches.   [8] A servant.

[9] Began to eat their meal.

[10] "Lowest in dignity, at the end on the right. It was taken in politeness by the host. They reclined in twos." (Translator's note.)

ERYXIMACHOS
(physician)

ARISTODEMOS
(who reported
the speeches)

ARISTOPHANES
(the comic poet;
had hiccup)

Left early

PAUSANIAS

Left early

Not reported

AGATHON

Not reported

ALCIBIADES
(Statesman;
came in
late, drunk)

PHAIDROS
("Father of
the Speech")

from left round to the right

SOCRATES

*The Banquet at Agathon's House (416 B.C.)[11] Diagram showing order of reported speeches.
[NOTE: The diagram is drawn circular for convenience; it is not known how the
couches were arranged. The couches usually accommodated two persons each, but some
were made longer. From representations on ancient vases it seems that each diner
reclined towards his left, supported under his left arm by a large cushion and with his
right hand free to help himself from a low stool or table in front of the couch. They
had no knives or forks. The wine was usually drunk mixed with water, about three
parts of water to two of wine. See A Dictionary of Greek and Roman
Antiquities, by W. Smith, W. Wayte, and G. E. Marindin, 3rd edition (1891), p.
393 on "Cena" and p. 741 on "Symposium."]*

young, and showed itself to us the other day before over thirty thousand of
our nation!"

"You are a scoffer, Socrates!" said Agathon. "Well, we will come into
court before long about this, you and I, on our claim for wisdom, and the
judge shall be Dionysos:[12] now first turn to dinner."

After this (Aristodemos said), Socrates reclined, and he and they all had
their dinner; they poured the drops of grace,[13] and sang a chant to the
god, and did the usual things, and settled down to drinking. Then (he
continued) Pausanias began the talk like this: "Look here, gentlemen," he
said, "how shall we manage our drinking most conveniently? I tell you I am
really not up to the mark myself after yesterday's bout and I want some
rest, and so do most of you, I think—for you were present yesterday; just
consider then how we could manage our drinking most conveniently."

[11] The diagram of the seating arrangement is the work of the translator's editors.
[12] Agathon probably means that the after-dinner talk inspired by drinking (Dionysos was
god of wine) will prove which of the two opponents in this dispute is right.
[13] Libations, or drink-offerings, poured out in honor of the gods.

Then Aristophanes said, "Now that is good advice, Pausanias, to make the drinking as comfortable as we can; I am one of those myself who had a good soaking yesterday."

So Eryximachos, Acumenos' son, when he heard them, said, "Quite right, you two. And one thing more I want to know, how Agathon feels about being fit to drink."

"No," said Agathon, "I don't feel very fit myself either."

The other said, "It seems it would be a bit of luck for us, me and Aristodemos and Phaidros and our friends here, if you with the strongest heads for drinking have thrown up the sponge; for we are always the weaklings. I do not count Socrates; he can do both ways,[14] and it will content him whichever we choose. Then since it seems no one present votes for a hearty bout of deep wine-drinking, perhaps I should not give offense if I tell you the truth about the effect of getting drunk. I think I have seen quite clearly as a physician that drunkenness is a dangerous thing for mankind; and I am not willing to go far in drinking myself, nor would I advise another to do it, especially if he still has a headache from yesterday."

Phaidros the Myrrhinusian responded, "Well, I always take your advice, especially on matters of physic and health; and the rest of us will be wise to do the same now." So all agreed after hearing this not to drink too much during the present party, but everyone should drink just to please himself.

"Very well," said Eryximachos, "since the motion is passed that each one may drink as much as he likes, but no one *must* drink, my next motion is, that the piping-girl who has just come in may go out again, and play to herself, or if she pleases to the women inside, and that today we entertain each other with talk; and with your leave, I will propose what kind of talk." They all agreed, and gave leave, and told him to propose away.

"I will begin," said Eryximachos, "by quoting from the *Melanippe*[15] of Euripides: 'the story is not mine' which I am going to tell, it belongs to Phaidros. For Phaidros is always complaining to me, 'It's a shame, Eryximachos, that many other gods have hymns and paeans made for them by the poets, but Love, that ancient mighty god, has not a single one; of all the thousands of poets who have lived, not one has ever made even an ode to praise him! Or look at the worthy professors,[16] if you please; they compose praises of men like Heracles in prose, as the excellent Prodicos did; perhaps that is not so surprising, but lately I came across a book by some wise man where salt was lauded to the skies for its usefulness, and you could find many other such things praised up. Just think—to make such a fuss about things like salt, when no human being has ever dared to this day to hymn Love worthily! What neglect for so great a god!' I think Phaidros is quite right there. So I wish to make my small contribution, and to offer it to him; and at the same time it seems to me proper on this occasion for us now present to glorify the god. If you vote with me, we should find plenty to amuse us in the speeches; for my proposal is that we should deliver a full-dress oration in praise of Love, each one from left to right, and

[14] As the end of the dialogue shows, Socrates can drink vast amounts without getting drunk.
[15] The play has not survived.
[16] The Sophists (teachers of rhetoric and logic). Prodicos was one of them.

Phaidros must begin first, since he is in the first place[17] and he is also father of the speech."

Then Socrates said, "No one will vote against you, Eryximachos. I could not refuse myself, I suppose, when love is the only thing I profess to know about; nor will Agathon, I suppose, and Pausanias, nor indeed Aristophanes, who devotes all his time to Dionysos and Aphrodite,[18] nor any other of those I see here. However, it is not quite fair on us who are last. But if those before us give us some really good speeches, that will do for us. Then let Phaidros be the first, and speak in praise of Love, and good luck to him." All the others agreed, and asked him to do as Socrates suggested. However, what each one of them all said, Aristodemos could not remember, nor can I remember all he told me. But what I do remember, and what I thought most worth remembering, I will tell you of each of the speeches.

Well, as I say, Phaidros, according to Aristodemos, was the first, and he began hereabouts; that Love was a great god and wonderful on earth and in heaven, especially in his birth. "The god is honorable as being among the most ancient of all," he said; "and a proof is, that parents Love has none, nor are they mentioned by anyone, poet or not, although Hesiod[19] does say that Chaos came first,

> And then
> Broad-breasted Earth, the everlasting seat
> Of all, and Love.

Acusileōs also agreed with Hesiod; he says that after Chaos were produced these two, Earth and Love. But Parmenides says of Birth, that she

> Contrivèd Love the first of all the gods.

Thus many agree that Love is most ancient among them. And being most ancient, he is cause of the greatest good[20] for us. For I cannot say what is a greater good for a man in his youth than a lover, and for a lover than a beloved. For that which ought to guide mankind through all his life, if it is to be a good life, noble blood cannot implant in him so well, nor office, nor wealth, nor anything but Love. And what do I mean by that? I mean shame at ugly things, and ambition in beautiful things; for without these neither city nor man can accomplish great and beautiful works. I say then of a man who loves, that if he should be detected in doing something ugly, or allowing himself to be treated in ugly fashion because through cowardice he did not defend himself, he would suffer less pain to be seen by father or

---

[17] The place of honor, at the far left. Agathon and Socrates are "last," lying on the couch at the extreme right.

[18] As a comic dramatist, Aristophanes would be linked with both Dionysos (at whose festivals all Athenian plays were produced) and with Aphrodite, goddess of love and sex (since comic plots were often bawdy).

[19] Hesiod was a Greek poet, of about the eighth century B.C.; Acusileōs, a compiler of genealogies and myths, lived in the early fifth century; Parmenides was a philosopher-poet of about the same era. With these notions of cosmic origins it is interesting to compare the opening of Ovid's *Metamorphoses* and the opening chapters of the biblical Book of Genesis.

[20] In his speech Phaidros (Phaedrus) emphasizes the practical, political, even military, benefits that spring from love.

friends or anyone else than by his beloved. In the same way we see that the beloved is particularly ashamed before the lover, when seen in any ugly situation. Then if any device could be found how a state or an army could be made up only of lovers and beloved, they could not possibly find a better way of living, since they would abstain from all ugly things and be ambitious in beautiful things towards each other; and in battle side by side, such troops although few would conquer pretty well all the world. For the lover would be less willing to be seen by his beloved than by all the rest of the world, leaving the ranks or throwing away his arms, and he would choose to die many times rather than that; yes, and as to deserting the beloved, or not helping in danger, no one is so base that Love himself would not inspire him to valor, and make him equal to the born hero. And just as Homer says that the god 'breathes fury' into some of the heroes, so does Love really give to lovers a power coming from himself.[21]

"And to die for another—this only lovers are willing to do, not only men, but women. Alcestis,[22] Pelias' daughter, gives sufficient evidence of this to prove it to our nation; she alone was willing to die for her husband, although he had a father and a mother; these the wife so much surpassed in love because of her affection for her husband that she showed they were aliens to their own son and were relatives only in name. Having done this, she was thought, not only by men, but by gods also, to have done so nobly that they sent up her soul from the dead in admiration for her deed, although of all the many who have done noble deeds one might easily count those to whom the gods gave the privilege of having their souls sent up again from Hades. Thus the gods also honor especially earnestness and valor in love. But Orpheus, Oiagros' son, they sent back unsuccessful from Hades, showing him a phantom of his wife for whom he came, but not giving her real self because they thought him soft, being a zither-player, and they thought he did not dare to die for his love like Alcestis, but managed to get into Hades alive. For this reason, therefore, they punished him, and made his death come about by women,[23] unlike Achilles, the son of Thetis; but they honored Achilles and sent him to the Islands of the Blest, because when his mother told him that if he killed Hector he would die, but if he did not kill him he would return home and live to be an old man, he dared to choose, by helping his lover Patroclos and avenging him, not only to die for him, but in his end to perish over his body: hence therefore the gods, admiring him above measure, honored him particularly, because he set so high the value of his lover. (But Aeschylus is absurd[24] when he

---

[21] Phaidros' point is a paradoxical one: he claims that the tender emotion of love can in fact inspire greater feats in war than can the martial impulses incited by the god of war.

[22] The best-known account of Alcestis' heroism in offering herself to Death in place of her husband is Euripides' play *Alcestis*. Even the aged parents of her husband Admetos were unwilling to make that sacrifice. As a reward for her noble courage, she was restored to life. In contrast, the legendary poet Orpheus, mentioned a few sentences below, is depicted as lacking this ultimate courage when he tried to reclaim his wife (Euridice) from the realm of the dead. In the Roman poet Ovid's *Metamorphoses*, Book X, Orpheus is presented more sympathetically; he was granted the privilege of bringing his wife back from the dead, but only on the condition—which he failed to honor—that he not look back to see if she was following him.

[23] Orpheus, in the myth, was savagely dismembered by female worshipers of Dionysos. For Ovid's account of the story, see *Metamorphoses*, Book XI.

[24] The reference is to *The Myrmidons*, a lost play.

says Achilles[25] was the lover and Patroclos the beloved, when he was more beautiful not only than Patroclos but than all the heroes, and was yet beardless, and again much younger, as Homer says.) But in fact the gods do most greatly honor this valor for love's sake; yet they still more respect and admire and reward when the beloved feels affection for the lover, than when the lover does for his beloved. For a lover is more divine than the beloved, since he is inspired. Therefore they honored Achilles more than Alcestis, and sent him to the Islands of the Blest.

"Thus then I say, that of the gods Love is at once oldest, and most precious, and has most power to provide virtue and happiness for mankind, both living and dead."

Such or something like it was the speech of Phaidros, as related to me by Aristodemos; and after Phaidros there were some others which he did not remember well; so he passed them by, and reported the speech of Pausanias,[26] who said, "I do not think, Phaidros, that the rules were properly laid down, I mean that we should just simply belaud Love. For if Love were one, that would do, but really he is not one; and since he is not one, it is more proper to say first which we are to praise. Then I will try to set this right, and say first which Love we ought to praise, and then praise that god worthily. For we all know that Aphrodite is never without a Love: if she were one, Love would be one; but since there are really two, there must be two Loves. Of course there are two goddesses. One I take it is older, and motherless, daughter of Heaven, whom we call Heavenly Aphrodite, the other younger, a daughter of Zeus and Dione, whom we call, as you know, Common. It must be then, you see, that Love too, the one who works with this Aphrodite, should be called Common Love, and the other Heavenly Love. It is true we must praise all gods, but I must try to say what is the province of each of these two. For the performance of every action is, in itself, neither beautiful nor ugly. So what we are doing now, whether drinking or singing or speaking, is not itself beautiful, but according as it is done, so it comes out in the doing: when it is done well and rightly, it is beautiful, but when not rightly done, it is ugly. Just so with being in love, and with Love himself; he is not all beautiful and worthy to be praised, but only so far as he leads to right loving.

"The Love, then, which belongs to Common Aphrodite is really and truly common and works at random; and this is the love which inferior men feel. Such persons love firstly women as well as boys; next, when they love, they love bodies rather than souls; and next, they choose the most foolish persons they can, for they look only to getting something done, and care nothing whether well or not. So what happens to them is that they act at random, whether they do good or whether they do its opposite; for this

---

[25] In Homer's *Iliad*, the incomparable warrior Achilles withdrew from the Greek campaign against Troy because of a quarrel with Agamemnon, the Greek commander-in-chief. He returned to battle, in a mood of guilt and anger, after his friend Patroclos (described here as also his lover) was killed by the Trojan leader Hector. In some versions of the myth, Achilles was rewarded with a kind of paradisal afterlife in the Islands of the Blest. In Book XI of Homer's *Odyssey*, however, Achilles is depicted as bitterly resentful of death; it is better, he says there, to be the meanest slave on earth than to rule as a king among the powerless dead.

[26] Among other things, Pausanias' legalistic approach to the topic and his emphasis on rhetoric indicate that he is a disciple of the Sophists.

Love springs from the goddess which is much younger than the other, and in her birth had a share of both female and male.[27] But the other Love springs from the Heavenly goddess, who firstly has had no share of the female, but only of the male; next, she is the elder, and has no violence in her: consequently those inspired by this love turn to the male, because they feel affection rather for what is stronger and has more mind. One could recognize even in boy-love those who are driven by this Love pure and simple; for they do not fall in love with those who are little boys, but with those who begin to have mind, and that is nearly when they show the down on their chins. For those who begin to love them from this age, I think, are ready to be with them always for all their lives, and to live with them together; they do not wish to get a boy in the foolishness of youth, and then deceive him and laugh at him and go off running to another. There ought to have been a law against loving little boys, that a great deal of earnestness might not have been spent on what is uncertain; for it is uncertain how little boys will turn out, as regards vice and virtue, both of body and soul. Now those who are good place this law before themselves unbidden; but it ought to be made compulsory for those common lovers, just as we make it compulsory as far as we can that they shall not make love to freeborn women. For these are they who bring reproach on the whole thing, so that some dare to say that it is ugly to gratify lovers; they say this with their eye on those common ones, when they see their tactlessness and injustice; since I suppose nothing done decently and lawfully could fairly bring discredit.

Again, here and in Lacedaimon the law about love is confusing, but that in other states is easy to understand. In Elis and Boeotia, and where people are not clever speakers, it is simply laid down that it is right to gratify lovers,[28] and no one young or old would call it ugly; as I think, they wish not to have the trouble of convincing the young, because they cannot argue; but in many other parts of Ionia it is considered ugly, where they are under barbarians. For the barbarians because of the rule of despots call this ugly, as well as philosophy and sports; I suppose it is profitable to their rulers that the subjects should not be great in spirit or make strong friendships and unions, which things love is wont to implant more than anything else. In fact, our own despots[29] here found that out by experience; for the love of Aristogeiton, and the friendship of Harmodios, grown strong, brought their rule to an end. So where it has been laid down as ugly to gratify lovers, that was from the evil condition of those that made the laws, the grasping habits of the rulers and the cowardice of the ruled; and where it was thought simply good, that was from laziness of soul in those who made the laws. But in these parts, much of the law and custom is better, and as I said, it is not easy to understand.

---

[27] The younger Aphrodite had a male and a female parent; the older and more heavenly one had no mother.

[28] In Elis and Boeotia, regions of western and northwestern Greece, pederasty (of which Pausanias obviously approves) was simply endorsed; in Ionia (an area of Asia Minor) it was simply condemned as fostering the kind of noble personal alliances that can subvert despotic regimes such as existed there. Pausanias suggests that in Athens values are more subtle and complex.

[29] Hippias and Hipparchos, who ruled as tyrants over Athens in 514. Their opponents, Aristogeiton and Harmodios, were revered in Athens as champions of liberty.

"For consider that it is called better to love openly than secretly, and especially to love the highest and noblest born, even if they are uglier than others; and consider how wonderfully all encourage the lover—not as if he were doing something ugly, which if he wins is thought beautiful, and if he does not win, ugly; and how the law has allowed the lover, in trying to win, to be praised for doing extraordinary things, which if a man should dare to do in pursuit of anything else except this, or should even wish to accomplish, he would reap the greatest disgrace. For if, wishing to get money from someone, or to win public office, or to get any other power, a man should behave as lovers do towards their beloved, begging and beseeching them in their petitions, and swearing solemn oaths, and sleeping at their doors, and being willing to do slavish services such as no slave would do, he would be hindered both by friends and by enemies from doing his business thus: the friends would be ashamed of such things and warn him, the enemies would upbraid him for flattery and bad manners. But the lover has a grace when he does all this, and the law allows him to do it without discredit, as a thing wholly beautiful; and strangest of all, he alone, as the people say, is pardoned by the gods for breaking the oath he has sworn— for it is said an oath of love simply has no force. Thus both gods and men have given full license to the lover, as the law here says; so far, then, one might think it was considered wholly beautiful in this city both to love and to feel affection for a lover. But on the other hand when fathers place tutors[30] over the loved ones and forbid them to converse with their lovers, and the tutor is ordered to see to it; when age-mates and companions reproach them if they see anything like this going on; and lastly when the older men do not stop these from reproaching them, nor scold them for talking nonsense—if one looked at this, one would think such a thing was considered very ugly here. The fact is, I think, the case is not simple: as I said at the beginning, it is neither beautiful nor ugly by itself, but beautifully done it is beautiful, and uglily done it is ugly—uglily, is to gratify a base man and basely; beautifully, is to gratify a good man and beautifully. A base man is that common lover who loves the body rather than the soul; for he is not lasting since he loves a thing not lasting. For as soon as the flower of the body fades, which is what he loved, 'He takes to the wing and away he flies,'[31] and violates any number of vows and promises; but the lover of a good character remains faithful throughout life, since he has been fused with a lasting thing. These, then, our law wishes to test well and thoroughly; for these reasons, then, it enjoins to pursue the one and eschew the other, setting them tasks and testing them to see which class the lover belongs to, and which class the beloved. Thus you see it is on these grounds that, first of all, to be won quickly is considered ugly—for time should come in, which seems to test everything well; next, to be won by money and political power is ugly, whether it means shrinking from suffering and lack of endurance, or failure to despise the benefits flowing from money or political achievements; for none of these things appears to be firm and lasting, not to mention that genuine affection is never bred from

---

[30] Athenian fathers protect their sons against older males, Pausanias suggests, since these may prove to be noble disciples of the Heavenly Love or ignoble disciples of the Common Love.

[31] "Agamemnon thus speaks about a dream. *Iliad* ii. 71." (Translator's note.)

them. Then only one road is left for our law, if the beloved is to gratify the lover beautifully. For our law is, that as it was not counted flattery or disgrace for lovers to be willing slaves in any slavery to the beloved, so for the beloved, there is only one willing slavery which is no disgrace—and that is in pursuit of virtue.

"For we have a custom that if one wishes to serve another, because he thinks that the man can make him better either in wisdom or any other part of virtue, this willing slavery is not ugly and it is no flattery. Then let us compare these two customs, that which concerns boy-lovers and that which concerns philosophy and virtue in general, if we are to infer that when the beloved gratifies the lover it is beautiful. For when lover and beloved come together each with his law—the one, that when he serves the consenting beloved in anything whatever the service is right, the other, that by doing any service whatever to one who makes him wise and good he does right service, the one able to contribute something for wisdom and virtue in general, the other desiring to get this for education and wisdom in general—then, you see, these laws meet together, and then only it follows that for beloved to gratify lover is beautiful, but never otherwise. In this case, even to be deceived is not ugly; in all others both to be deceived and not to be deceived is ugly. For if one in pursuit of riches gratifies a lover supposed to be rich, and is deceived and gets no money because the lover turns out to be poor, it is no less ugly; for such a one is thought to show, as far as in him lay, that for money he would do anyone and everyone any and every service, and that is not beautiful. By the same argument observe that even if one gratifies another as being good, expecting to be better himself because of his affection for the lover, but since the other turns out to be bad and not possessed of virtue, he is deceived, nevertheless the deceit is beautiful; for he again is thought to have shown, as far as in him lay, that for virtue and to become better he was ready with everything for everyone. And this again is the most beautiful thing of all; so in every case it is beautiful to gratify for the sake of virtue.

"This is the love of the heavenly goddess, love both heavenly and precious to city and men; for it compels both lover and beloved to take all possible care for virtue. But all other loves belong to the other goddess, the common one. Here, my dear Phaidros, you have my humble contribution on Love, as well as I could make it at the moment."

Pausanias paused upon this clause—that's how the stylists teach me to jingle![32]—and Aristodemos said that Aristophanes ought to have spoken next, but he had a hiccup from surfeit or something, and couldn't speak. However, he managed to say to Doctor Eryximachos, who was reclining in the place just below him, "My dear Eryximachos, it's your job either to stop my hiccup, or to speak instead until I stop myself."

And Eryximachos answered, "Well, I will do both; I will speak in your turn, and when you stop the hiccup you shall speak in mine. And while I am speaking, hold your breath a long time and see if the hiccup will stop; if it won't, gargle water. But if it still goes strong, pick up something to tickle your nose with, and sneeze; do this once or twice, and stop it will, even if it is very strong."

---

[32] Probably a satiric reference to the elaborate tricks of speech learned by Pausanias from the Sophists, and illustrated in the speech he has just made.

"Look sharp," says Aristophanes, "speak away, and I'll do all that."

Then (continued Aristodemos) Eryximachos said,[33] "Pausanias began well, but ended feebly, so I think I must try to put a good end to his oration. He said Love was double, and I think he was right in dividing him. But I think I have seen from our art of medicine how great and wonderful the god is, and how he extends over everything human and divine; he is not only in the souls of mankind and directed towards beautiful people, but he is in all the rest, and directed towards many other things; he is in the bodies of all living creatures, and in what grows in the earth, and, one may say, in everything there is. I will begin my speech with medicine, that we may do special honor to my art. The natural body has this double Love; for bodily health and disease are by common consent different things and unlike, and what is unlike desires and loves things unlike. Then there is one love in the healthy, and another in the diseased.[34] So you see just as, according to what Pausanias said just now, it is beautiful to gratify good men, and ugly to gratify the intemperate, so in the bodies themselves, to gratify the good things in each body and the healthy things is beautiful and must be done, and this gratification is what is called the healing art, but to gratify what is bad and diseased is ugly and must not be done, if one is to practice that art. For the healing art, to put it shortly, is knowledge of the body's loves for filling and emptying, and one who distinguishes the beautiful and the ugly love in these things is the most complete physician; and one who makes them change, so that they get one love instead of the other, and, where there is no love when there ought to be, one who knows how to put it in, and to take out love that is in, he would be a good practitioner. You see one must be able to make loving friends of the greatest enemies in the body. Now the greatest enemies are the most opposite, hot and cold, bitter and sweet, dry and wet, and so forth; our ancestor Asclepios,[35] as our poets here say and I believe, composed our art because he knew how to implant love and concord in these. Then the healing art, as I say, is all guided by this god, and so is gymnastic and agriculture; music too is clearly in the same case with this, as it is plain to anyone who thinks for a moment; and perhaps that is what Heracleitos[36] means, since his words are not very clear. He says, 'The One at variance with itself is brought together again, like a harmony of bow and lyre.'[37] It is quite illogical to say that a *harmony* is

---

[33] The speech of the learned physician is in character: it is scientifically oriented and somewhat pedantic. He understands love as the reconciliation of opposites, not just in human relationships but in various human arts and activities and in nature.

[34] Thus (as the principle is applied in medicine), the higher form of the "double" love would encourage a craving for what is healthy, the lower form a craving for what will cause disease.

[35] The founder of medicine; *our poets* refers to Agathon and Aristophanes.

[36] A philosopher who lived around 500 B.C. He taught that the universe operated through flux and through the conflict of opposites.

[37] "The reader may find Eryximachos' explanation which follows easier to understand if he thinks of 'at variance' as meaning 'out of tune,' and 'reconciling' as tuning the strings, and of a bow as giving out a deep faint musical note when the arrow leaves it. 'Harmony' and 'symphony' had not to the Greeks all the meaning they have to us as musical terms. Harmony was rather the relation between single notes which sounded well in sequence, and symphony the sound of those notes played together. (Unison was one form of harmony, and sounds in unison one form of symphony; steady motion, a compromise of quick and slow, is one form of rhythm.)" (Translator's note.)

at variance with itself or is made up of notes still *at variance*. But perhaps he meant to say that it was made from the high and low notes—first at variance, then afterwards reconciled together by the art of music. For I suppose there could not be harmony from high and low notes still at variance, for harmony is symphony and symphony is a kind of agreement; but agreement there cannot be of things at variance so long as they are at variance. But what is at variance, and yet is not unable to be brought into agreement, it is possible to harmonize. Just so rhythm is made from quick and slow, first differing, then brought into agreement. But music places agreement here in all these, just as there the art of healing does, by implanting concord and love for each other; and music again is the knowledge of love affairs concerning harmony and rhythm. And in the very composition of harmony and rhythm it is not difficult to distinguish the love affairs, although the double love is not there yet; but whenever one must use rhythm and harmony for men, either composing (which they call melody-making), or rightly using the melodies and verses made (which is called education[38]), that is the time when there are difficulties, and a good craftsman is wanted. Then the same old argument comes round again, that decent men must be gratified, and also those not yet quite decent that they may become so, and their Love must be protected; and this is the beautiful Love, the Heavenly Love, the Love belonging to the 'Heavenly' Muse Urania; but that of 'Manyhymn' Polymnia[39] is the common one, who must be offered to people with great care whenever he is offered, to let them reap the pleasure from him, but not to implant any intemperance: just so in our art, it is a great business to use well the desires concerned with the art of cookery, so that people may reap the pleasures without disease. So you see, both in music and in physic and in everything else earthly and heavenly, we must watch and protect both Loves as far as we can, for both are there.

"See how the composition of the seasons of the year is full of these two: and so, whenever the things I mentioned just now, hot and cold and dry and wet, have the decent Love towards each other, and get a harmony and a temperate mixture, they come bringing a good season, with health for mankind and the other animals and vegetables and plants, and then they do no harm; but when the violent Love has more power on the seasons of the year, he does harm, and destroys much. For pestilences often come as a result, and many other discordant diseases in wild beasts and growing things: hoar-frosts and hails and blights come from the grasping habits and indecency of such love affairs, knowledge of which as regards the courses of the stars and the seasons of the year is called astronomy. Moreover, all sacrifice and the domain of divination[40] (this is the communion of gods and men together), all this is concerned solely with the protection and healing of Love. For all impiety is wont to occur, as concerns parents both living

---

[38] For the Greeks, and especially for Plato, an intimate connection existed between intellectual and moral development and the right or wrong use of music.

[39] Urania and Polymnia are two of the nine inspiring Muses. Here Eryximachos chooses to identify Urania (the Muse of astronomy) with a higher form of love and Polymnia (or Polyhymnia) with a lower form.

[40] The interpretation of the will of heaven; since both parent-child relationships and the relationship of men to gods were religious matters, divination was relevant to both.

and dead, and gods, if one does not gratify the decent Love and honor him and put him first in every work, but honors the other. So you see this is what divination is ordered to do, to supervise these Loves and to treat them as a physician; and divination is again the craftsman of friendship between men and gods, by its knowledge of the love affairs of mankind which tend towards good law and piety.

"So Love as a whole has great and mighty power, or rather in a word, omnipotence; but the one concerned with good things, being accomplished with temperance and justice, both here and in heaven, has the greatest power, and provides all happiness for us, and makes us able to have society together, and to be friends with the gods also, who are higher than we are. Perhaps indeed I also omit much in praising Love; but I can't help it. If I have omitted something, it is your part, Aristophanes, to fill up the gap; or if you intend to praise the god in some other way, go on and do so, since your hiccup is gone."

So Aristophanes (said Aristodemos) took his turn next, and said, "Oh yes, it has quite gone, but not until sneezing was applied to it; which makes me wonder if the decency of the body desires noises and ticklings like a sneeze; for it stopped at once when I applied the sneeze to it."

Then Eryximachos said, "My good man, look what you're doing! You are playing the fool when you are about to make a speech! You compel me to keep a watch on your speech and look out for something laughable, when you might speak in peace!"

And Aristophanes answered, with a laugh, "Quite right, Eryximachos, I take back what I said. But don't watch me, for as to what I am going to say, I am not at all afraid I may say something laughable, for that would be clear gain and natural to our Muse—but lest the things I say may be just ridiculous!"[41]

"So you think you are going to hurl your shaft, Aristophanes," he said, "and get off scot free? Take care, take care, and be sure you will have to account for yourself. But perhaps I will let you off, if I am so disposed."

"Well, Eryximachos," said Aristophanes. "I intend to speak in a different way from you and Pausanias. For it seems to me that mankind have wholly failed to perceive the power of Love; if they had, they would have built to him their greatest sanctuaries and altars, and they would have made their greatest sacrifice to him; but now nothing of the sort is done, although it most assuredly ought to be done. For he is the most man-loving of gods, being the helper of man, and the healer of those whose healing would be the greatest happiness to the human race. Therefore I will try to introduce you to his power, and you shall teach the others.

"First you must learn about the nature of man and the history of it. Formerly the natural state of man was not what it is now, but quite different. For at first there were three sexes, not two as at present, male and female, but also a third having both together; the name remains with us, but the thing is gone. There was then a male-female sex and a name to

[41] Aristophanes does not want to make a fool of himself, though he is willing to arouse laughter, since that is his trade as a comic dramatist-poet. His speech combines comic parable and deep psychological insight.

match, sharing both male and female, but now nothing is left but the title[42] used in reproach. Next, the shape of man was quite round, back and ribs passing about it in a circle; and he had four arms and an equal number of legs, and two faces on a round neck, exactly alike; there was one head with these two opposite faces, and four ears, and two privy members, and the rest as you might imagine from this. They walked upright as now, in which-ever direction they liked; and when they wanted to run fast, they rolled over and over on the ends of the eight limbs they had in those days, as our tumblers tumble now with their legs straight out. And why there were three sexes, and shaped like this, was because the male was at first born of the sun, and the female of the earth, and the common sex had something of the moon, which combines both male and female; their shape was round and their going was round because they were like their parents. They had terrible strength and force, and great were their ambitions; they attacked the gods, and what Homer said of Otos and Ephialtes[43] is said of them, that they tried to climb into heaven intending to make war upon the gods.

"So Zeus and the other gods held council what they should do, and they were perplexed; for they really could not kill the tribe with thunderbolts and make them vanish like the giants—since then their honors and the sacrifices of mankind would vanish too—nor could they allow them to go on in this wild way. After a deal of worry Zeus had a happy thought. 'Look here,' he said, 'I think I have found a scheme; we can let men still exist but we can stop them from their violence by making them weaker. I will tell you what I'll do now,' says he, 'I will slice each of them down through the middle! Two improvements at once! They will be weaker, and they will be more useful to us because there will be more of them. They shall walk upright on two legs. And if they choose to go on with their wild doings, and will not keep quiet, I'll do it again!' says he, 'I'll slice 'em again through the middle! And they shall hop about on one leg! Like those boys that hop on the greasy wineskins at the fair!'[44] says he; and then he sliced men through the middle, as you slice your serviceberries through the middle for pickle, or as you slice hard-boiled eggs with a hair. While he sliced each, he told Apollo to turn the face and half the neck towards the cut, to make the man see his own cut and be more orderly, and then he told him to heal the rest up. So Apollo turned the face, and gathered up the skin over what is now called the belly, like purses which you pull shut with a string; he made one little mouth, and fastened it at the middle of the belly, what they call the navel. Most of the wrinkles he smoothed out, and shaped the breasts, using a tool like the shoemaker's when he smooths wrinkles out of his leather on the last; but he left a few, those about the navel and the belly, to remind them of what happened. So when the original body was cut through, each half wanted the other, and hugged it; they threw their arms round each other desiring to grow together in the embrace, and died of starvation and general idleness because they would not do anything apart from each

[42] That is, "hermaphrodite."

[43] Otos and Ephialtes are two of the "Giants" who made war against Zeus and the other Olympian gods. See Homer's *Odyssey*, Book XI.

[44] "This was done at the country feast of Dionysos." (Translator's note.)

other. When one of the halves died and the other was left, the half which
was left hunted for another and embraced it, whether he found the half of
a whole woman (which we call woman now), or half of a whole man; and so
they perished. But Zeus pitied them and found another scheme; he moved
their privy parts in front, for these also were outside before, and they had
begotten and brought forth not with each other but with the ground, like
the cicadas.[45] So he moved these parts also in front and made the generation come between them, by the male in the female; that in this embrace, if
a man met a woman, they might beget and the race might continue, and if
a man met a man, they might be satisfied by their union and rest, and
might turn to work and care about the general business of life. So you see
how ancient is the mutual love implanted in mankind, bringing together the
parts of the original body, and trying to make one out of two, and to heal
the natural structure of man.

"Then each of us is the tally[46] of a man; he is sliced like a flatfish, and
two made of one. So each one seeks his other tally. Then all men who are a
cutting of the old common sex which was called manwoman are fond of
women, and adulterers generally come of that sex, and all women who are
mad for men, and adulteresses. The women who are a cutting of the ancient women do not care much about men, but are more attracted to
women, and strumpetesses[47] also come from this sex. But those which are a
cutting of the male pursue the male, and while they are boys, being slices of
the male, they are fond of men, and enjoy lying with men and embracing
them, and these are the best of boys and lads because they are naturally
bravest. Some call them shameless, but that is false; no shamelessness
makes them do this, but boldness and courage and a manly force, which
welcome what is like them. Here is a great proof: when they grow up, such
as these alone are men in public affairs. And when they become men, they
fancy boys, and naturally do not trouble about marriage and getting a
family, but that law and custom compels them; they find it enough themselves to live unmarried together. Such a person is always inclined to be a
boy-lover or a beloved, as he always welcomes what is akin. So when one of
these meets his own proper half, whether boy-lover or anyone else, then
they are wonderfully overwhelmed by affection and intimacy and love, and
one may say never wish to be apart for a moment. These are the ones who
remain together all their lives, although they could not say what they expect to get from each other; for no one could suppose that this is sensual
union, as if this could make anyone delight in another's company so seriously as all that. Plainly the soul of each wants something else—what, it
cannot say, but it divines and riddles what it wants. And as they lie together
suppose Hephaistos[48] were to stand beside them with his tools, and ask,
'What do you want from each other, men?' And if they were at a loss,

[45] These insects, it was believed, were hatched by the sun after the female laid eggs on the
ground. The cicada was also, for Athenians, an emblem of their rootedness in the local soil
and thus of their ethnic integrity.

[46] Half of a broken object that, when matched with the other half, makes a perfect fit—it
thus shows unmistakably that the parts had formerly been a whole. Dice were often used so, as
Aristophanes mentions later in this speech.

[47] Whores.   [48] The blacksmith god of metalworking.

suppose he should ask again, 'Is it only that you desire to be together as close as possible, and not to be apart from each other night or day? For if that is what you desire, I am ready to melt you and weld you together, so that you two may be made one, and as one you may live together as long as you live, and when you die you may die still one instead of two, and be yonder in the house of Hades together. Think if this is your passion, and if it will satisfy you to get this.' If that were offered, we know that not a single one would object, or be found to wish anything else; he would simply believe he had heard that which he had so long desired, to be united and melted together with his beloved, and to become one from two. For the reason is that this was our ancient natural shape, when we were one whole; and so the desire for the whole and the pursuit of it is named Love.

"Formerly, as I say, we were one, but now because of doing wrong we have been dispersed by the god, as the Arcadians were dispersed by the Lacedaimonians.[49] There is fear then, if we are not decent towards the gods, that we may be sliced in half again, and we may go about like so many relief carvings of persons shown in half-view on tombstones, sawn right through the nose, like tally-dice cut in half. For these reasons we must exhort all men in everything to be god-fearing men, that we may escape this fate and attain our desire, since Love is our leader and captain. But let no man oppose Love—and whoever is the gods' enemy does oppose him. For when we are friends with this god and reconciled to him, we shall find and enjoy our very own beloved, which now few are able to do. And don't let Eryximachos chip in and make fun of my speech, and say that I mean Pausanias and Agathon; I should not be surprised if they are really of this class, and both males by nature, but indeed I speak in general of all men and women, that the way to make our race happy is to make love perfect, and each to get his very own beloved and go back to our original nature. If this is the best thing possible, the best thing to our hand must of course be to come as near it as possible, and that is to get a beloved who suits our mind. Then if we would praise the god who is the cause of this, we should rightly praise Love, who in the present gives us our chief blessing by bringing us home to our own, and for the future offers the greatest hopes; that if we duly worship the god, he will restore us to our ancient nature and heal us and make us blessed and happy.

"There is my speech about Love, Eryximachos, very different from yours. Then, as I begged you, do not make fun of it, but let us hear what each of the others will say, or rather, each of the two others; for only Agathon and Socrates are left."

"I will do as you ask," said Eryximachos, "for I did very much enjoy hearing that speech. And if I did not know that both Socrates and Agathon were experts in love matters, I should be afraid they might be puzzled what to say when such a world of things has been said already. But as it is, I don't fear at all."

Then Socrates said, "You played your part well yourself, Eryximachos;

---

[49] The Arcadians, inhabitants of southern Greece, were often regarded as the oldest indigenous Greek people, whose territory had been occupied in later times by the Lacedaimonians, or Spartans.

but if you were where I am now, or rather perhaps where I shall be, when Agathon has made his speech, you would be very much afraid, and like me now, you wouldn't know where you were."

"You want to put a spell on me, Socrates," said Agathon, "and make me shy through thinking that the audience has great expectations of a fine speech from me!"

Socrates answered, "I should have a very bad memory, Agathon, if I thought you would be shy now before a few people like us, since I saw your courage and spirit when you mounted the platform along with the actors, and faced all that huge audience, ready to display your compositions without the smallest sign of confusion."

"What!" said Agathon, "my dear Socrates, you don't really think I am so full of the theater that I don't know a few men with minds are more formidable to a man of sense than many without minds!"

"I should make a mistake, my dear Agathon," Socrates said, "if I imagined anything vulgar about you; I am quite sure that if you were in company with any you thought intelligent, you would rate them above the many. However, perhaps we are not intelligent—for we were there too, and we were among the many—but if you should meet with others who are, you would be ashamed of doing before them anything which you might think ugly. What do you say to that?"

"Quite true," said he.

"And before the many, would you not be ashamed if you thought you were doing something ugly?"

Then Phaidros put in a word, and said, "My dear friend Agathon, if you answer Socrates, he will not care what becomes of our business here! He won't care anything about anything, so long as he can have someone to converse with, especially someone beautiful. For myself, I like hearing Socrates arguing, but it is my duty to care about the praise of Love, and to exact from each one of you his speech. So just pay up to the god, both of you, and then you may argue."

"Quite right, Phaidros," said Agathon, "I am ready to speak; Socrates will be there another time, and often, to talk to.

"First, then,[50] I wish to describe how I ought to speak; then to speak. It seems to me that all who have spoken so far have not praised the god, but have congratulated mankind on the good things which the god has caused for them: what that god was himself who gave these gifts, no one has described. But the one right way for any laudation of anyone is to describe what he is, and then what he causes, whoever may be our subject. Thus, you see, with Love: we also should first praise him for what he is, and then praise his gifts.

"I say then that all gods are happy, but if it is lawful to say this without offense, I say that Love is happiest of them all, being most beautiful and best. And how he is most beautiful, I am about to describe. First of all, Phaidros, he is youngest of the gods. He himself supplies one great proof of what I say, for he flies in full flight away from Old Age, who is a quick

---

[50]Agathon's speech, which combines high eloquence with rhetorical artificiality and prettified conventional ideas about love, is a good foil for the wry tone with which Socrates' following speech begins.

one clearly, since he comes too soon to us all. Love hates him naturally and will not come anywhere near him. But he is always associated with the young, and with them he consorts, for the old saying is right, 'Like ever comes to like.' I am ready to admit many other things to Phaidros, but one I do not admit, that Love is older than Cronos and Iapetos;[51] no, I say he is youngest of the gods, and ever young; but that old business of the gods, which Hesiod and Parmenides tell about, was done through Necessity and not through Love, if they told the truth; for if Love had been in them, there would have been no gelding or enchaining of each other and all those violent things, but friendship and peace, as there is now, and has been ever since Love has reigned over the gods. So then, he is young, and besides being young he is tender; but we need a poet like Homer to show the god's tenderness. For Homer says of Ate[52] that she was a god and tender—at least her feet were tender—when he says that

> Tender are her feet; she comes not near
> The ground, but walks upon the heads of men.

I think he gives good proof of her tenderness, that she walks not on the hard but on the soft. Then let us use the same proof for Love, that he is tender. For he walks not on the earth nor on top of heads, which are not so very soft, but both walks and abides in the softest things there are; for his abode is settled in the tempers and souls of gods and men, and again, not in all souls without exception; no, whenever he meets a soul with a hard temper, he departs, but where it is soft, he abides. So since he always touches with feet and all else the softest of the soft, he must needs be tender. You see, then, he is youngest and tenderest, but besides this his figure is supple, for if he were stiff, he could not fold himself in everywhere, or throughout every soul, and come in and go out unnoticed from the first. A great proof of his good proportion and supple shape is his gracefulness, which, as we all know, Love has in high degree; for there is always war between gracelessness and Love. Colors and beauty are testified by the god's nestling in flowers; for where there is no flower, or flower is past, in body and soul and everything else, Love sits not, but where the place is flowery and fragrant there he both sits and stays.

"Of the god's beauty much more might be said, but this is enough; the virtue of Love comes next. Chief is that Love wrongs not and is not wronged, wrongs no god and is wronged by none, wrongs no man and is wronged by none. Nothing that happens to him comes by violence, for violence touches not Love; nothing he does is violent, for everyone willingly serves Love in everything, and what a willing person grants to a willing, is just—so say 'the city's king, the laws.'[53] And besides justice, he is full of temperance. It is agreed that temperance is the mastery and control of pleasures and desires, and that no pleasure is stronger than Love. But if

[51] Cronos and Iapetos were Titans who had been overcome by Zeus, the chief of the gods in the present divine dynasty. Cronos was Zeus' father. The gelding and enchaining mentioned a few lines later were among the atrocities committed in the former struggles for divine supremacy.

[52] "Atē, presumptuous Madness, something like Sin. *Iliad* xix. 92." (Translator's note.)

[53] "Quoted from Alcidamas, a stylist." (Translator's note.)

they are weaker, then Love would master and control them; and being master of pleasure and desires, Love would be especially temperate. Furthermore, in courage 'not even Ares[54] stands up against Love,' for it is not Ares that holds Love, but Love Ares—love of Aphrodite, as they say; stronger is he that holds than he that is held, and the master of the bravest of all would be himself bravest. Now the justice and temperance and courage of the god have been spoken of, and wisdom is left; so one must try to do the best one is able to do. And first, that I may honor our art[55] as Eryximachos honored his, Love is so wise a poet that he can make another the same; at least, everyone becomes a poet whom Love touches, even one who before that, had 'no music in his soul.' This we may fittingly use as a proof that Love is a good poet or active maker in practically all the creations of the fine arts; for what one has not or knows not, one can neither give to another nor teach another. Now take the making of all living things; who will dispute that they are the clever work of Love, by which all living things are made and begotten? And craftsmanship in the arts; don't we know that where this god is teacher, art turns out notable and illustrious, but where there is no touch of Love, it is all in the dark? Archery, again, and medicine and divination were invented by Apollo, led by desire and love, so that even he would be a pupil of Love; so also the Muses in music and Hephaistos in smithcraft and Athena in weaving and Zeus in 'pilotage of gods and men.' Hence you see also, all that business of the gods was arranged when Love came among them—love of beauty, that is plain, for there is no Love in ugliness. Before that, as I said at the beginning, many terrible things happened to the gods because of the reign of Necessity—so the story goes; but when this god Love was born, all became good both for gods and men from loving beautiful things.

"Thus it seems to me, Phaidros, that Love comes first, himself most beautiful and best, and thereafter he is cause of other such things in others. And I am moved to speak something of him in verse myself, that it is he who makes

> Peace among men, calm weather on the deep,
> Respite from winds, in trouble rest and sleep.

He empties us of estrangement, and fills us with friendliness, ordaining all such meetings as this one, of people one with another, in feasts, in dances, in sacrifices becoming men's guide; he provides gentleness and banishes savagery; he loves to give good will, hates to give ill will; gracious, mild; illustrious to the wise, admirable to the gods; enviable to those who have none of him, treasured by those who have some of him; father of luxury, daintiness, delicacy, grace, longing, desire; careful of good things, careless of bad things; in hardship, in fear, in drinking, in talk a pilot, a comrade, a

---

[54] The god of war, who fell in love with Aphrodite, goddess of love and beauty. She was the mate of the lame blacksmith god Hephaistos. The story of this adulterous triangle is a frequent theme in ancient myth and literature.

[55] The art of the poet (Agathon was a poet-dramatist). The Greek word *poiein* means "to make," which is why, a few lines below, Agathon identifies with one another love, poetry, and all kinds of "making." This wider sense of *poiein* is also explored by Socrates in his later speech.

stand-by[56] and the best of saviors; of all gods and men an ornament, a guide most beautiful and best, whom every man must follow, hymning him well, sharing in the song he sings as he charms the mind of gods and men.

"This, Phaidros, is my speech," he said; "may the god accept my dedication, partly play, partly modest seriousness, and the best that I am able to do."

When Agathon had spoken (Aristodemos told me), all applauded; the young man was thought to have spoken becomingly for himself and for the god. Then Socrates looked at Eryximachos, and said, "Now then, son of Acumenos, do you think there was no reason to fear in the fears I feared? Was I not a prophet when I said, as I did just now, that Agathon would make a wonderful speech, and leave me with nothing to say?"

"Yes, to the first," said Eryximachos, "you were a prophet there, certainly, about the wonderful speech; but nothing to say? I don't think so!"

"Bless you," said Socrates, "and how have I anything to say, I or anyone else, when I have to speak after that beautiful speech, with everything in it? The first part was wonderful enough, but the end! The beauty of those words and phrases! It was quite overwhelming for any listener. The fact is, when I considered that I shall not be able to get anywhere near it, and I have nothing fine to say at all—I was so ashamed that I all but took to my heels and ran, but I had nowhere to go. The speech reminded me of Gorgias,[57] and I really felt quite as in Homer's story; I was afraid that Agathon at the end of his speech might be going to produce the Gorgon's head[58] of Gorgias—the terror in speech-making—directed against *my* speech, and turn me into stone with dumbness. And I understood then that I was a fool when I told you I would take my turn in singing the honors of Love, and admitted I was terribly clever in love affairs, whereas it seems I really had no idea how a eulogy ought to be made. For I was stupid enough to think that we ought to speak the truth about each person eulogized, and to make this the foundation, and from these truths to choose the most beautiful things and arrange them in the most elegant way; and I was quite proud to think how well I should speak, because I believed that I knew the truth. However, apparently this was not the right way to praise anything, but we should dedicate all that is greatest and most beautiful to the work, whether things are so or not; if they were false it did not matter. For it seems the task laid down was not for each of us to praise Love, but to seem to praise him. For this reason then, I think, you rake up every story, and dedicate it to Love, and say he is so-and-so and the cause of such-and-such, that he may seem to be most beautiful and best, of course to those who don't know—not to those who do, I suppose—and the laudation is excellent and imposing. But indeed I did not know how an encomium[59] was

---

[56] "The three words used by Plato mean a ship's pilot, a fighter (not the driver) in a chariot or a marine on a ship, and a man who stands by another in battle." (Translator's note.)

[57] A noted Sophist; Agathon is indebted to him for his rhetorical method.

[58] "*Odyssey* xi, 634. Odysseus, at the end of his visit to the Kingdom of the Dead, grew pale with fear that Persephone [queen of the dead] might out of Hades send upon him a Gorgonhead, and turn him to stone." (Translator's note.) The Gorgons were female monsters who could literally petrify anyone who gazed on them.

[59] A speech of praise.

made, and it was without this knowledge that I agreed to take my part in praising. Therefore the tongue promised, but not the mind, so good-bye to that. For I take it back now; I make no eulogy in this fashion: I could not do it. However, the truth, if you like: I have no objection to telling the truth, in my own fashion, not in rivalry with your speeches, or I should deserve to be laughed at. Then see whether you want a speech of that sort, Phaidros. Will you listen to the truth being told about Love, in any words[60] and arrangement of phrases such as we may hit on as we go?"

Phaidros and the others (continued Aristodemos) told him to go on just as he thought best. "Then, Phaidros," he said, "let me ask Agathon a few little things, that I may get his agreement before I speak."

"Oh, I don't mind," said Phaidros, "ask away." After that Socrates began something like this:

"Indeed, my dear Agathon, I thought you were quite right in the beginning of your speech, when you said that you must first show what Love was like, and afterwards come to his works. That beginning I admire very much. Now then, about Love: you described what he is magnificently well, and so on; but tell me this too—is Love such as to be a love of something, or of nothing? I don't mean to ask if he is a love of mother or father; for that would be a ridiculous question, whether Love is love for mother or father; I mean it in the sense that one might apply to 'father' for instance; is the father a father of something or not? You would say, I suppose, if you wanted to answer right, that the father is father of son or daughter. Is that correct?"

"Certainly," said Agathon.

"And the same with the mother?"

This was agreed.

"Another, please," said Socrates, "answer me one or two more, that you may better understand what I want. What if I were to ask: 'A brother now, in himself, is he brother of something?'"

He said yes.

"Of a brother or sister?"

He agreed.

"Then tell me," he said, "about Love. Is Love love of nothing or of something?"

"Certainly he is love of something."

"Now then," said Socrates, "keep this in your memory, what the object of Love is;[61] and say whether Love desires the object of his love?"

"Certainly," said Agathon.

---

[60] It is typical of Socrates' method of discourse to disclaim—sincerely or ironically—any skill in the use of mere rhetoric. See also his defense of himself in Plato's *Apology*. His concern, he consistently claims, is with truth as distinguished from the techniques of debate. That is why, before he begins his speech here, he insists on elementary definitions in his dialogue with Agathon.

[61] Throughout the *Symposium*, various speakers use the word "love" in different senses: as a god, a principle in physics and nature, an emotion. Here, in his dialogue with Agathon, Socrates is implicitly redefining love, not as the abstraction and pretty personification that Agathon has idealized but as a force in the individual psyche. Later in this work, Socrates himself will shift his definition, expanding and universalizing his understanding of the term.

"Is it when he *has* what he desires and loves that he desires and loves it, or when he has not?"

"Most likely, when he has not," said he.

"Just consider," said Socrates, "put 'necessary' for 'likely'; isn't it necessary that the desiring desires what it lacks, or else does not desire if it does not lack? I think positively myself, Agathon, that it is absolutely necessary; what do you think?"

"I think the same," said he.

"Good. Then would one being big want to be big, or being strong want to be strong?"

"Impossible, according to what we have agreed."

"For I suppose he would not be lacking in whichever of these he is?"

"True."

"For if being strong he wanted to be strong," said Socrates, "and being swift he wanted to be swift, and being healthy he wanted to be healthy—you might go on forever like this, and you might think that those who were so-and-so and had such-and-such did also desire what they had; but to avoid our being deceived I say this—if you understand me, Agathon, it is obvious that these *must* have at this present time all they have, whether they wish to or not—and can anyone desire that? And when one says, 'I am healthy and want to be healthy,' 'I am rich and want to be rich,' 'I desire what I have,' we should answer, 'You, my good man, being possessed of riches and health and strength, wish to go on being possessed of them in the future, since at present you have them whether you want it or not; and when you say, "I desire what I have," consider—you mean only that you want to have in the future what you have now.' Wouldn't he agree?"

Agathon said yes.

Then Socrates went on, "Therefore this love for these blessings to be preserved for him into the future and to be always present for him—this is really loving that which is not yet available for him or possessed by him?"

"Certainly," he said.

"Then he, and every other who desires, desires what is not in his possession and not there, what he has not, and what he is not himself and what he lacks? Those are the sorts of things of which there is desire and love?"

"Certainly," he said.

"Come now," said Socrates, "let us run over again what has been agreed. Love is, first of all, of something; next, of those things which one lacks?"

"Yes," he said.

"This being granted, then, remember what things you said in your speech were the objects of Love. I will remind you, if you wish. I think you said something like this; the gods arranged their business through love of beautiful things, for there could not be a love for ugly things. Didn't you say something like that?"

"Yes, I did," said Agathon.

"And quite reasonably too, my friend," said Socrates; "and if this is so, would not Love be love of beauty, not of ugliness?"

He agreed.

"Well now, it has been agreed that he loves what he lacks and has not?"

"Yes," he said.

"Then Love lacks and has not beauty."

"That must be," said he.

"Very well: do you say that what lacks beauty and in no wise has beauty is beautiful?"

"Certainly not."

"Then if that is so, do you still agree that Love is beautiful?"

Agathon answered, "I fear, Socrates, I knew nothing of what I said!"

"Oh no," said he, "it was a fine speech, Agathon! But one little thing more: don't you think good things are also beautiful?"

"I do."

"Then if Love lacks beautiful things, and good things are beautiful, he should lack the good things too."

"Socrates," he said, "I really could not contradict you; let it be as you say."

"Contradict the truth, you should say, beloved Agathon," he replied; "you can't do that, but to contradict Socrates is easy enough.

"And now you shall have peace from me; but there is a speech about Love which I heard once from Diotima of Mantineia,[62] who was wise in this matter and in many others; by making the Athenians perform sacrifices before the plague she even managed to put off the disease[63] for ten years. And she it was who taught me about love affairs. This speech, then, which she made I will try to narrate to you now, beginning with what is agreed between me and Agathon; I will tell it by myself, as well as I can. You will see that I must describe first, as you did, Agathon, who Love is and what like, and then his works. I think it easiest to do it as the lady did in examining me. I said to her very much what Agathon just now did to me, that Love was a great god, and was a love of beautiful things; and she convinced me by saying the same as I did to Agathon, that he is neither beautiful, according to my argument, nor good. Then I said, 'What do you mean, Diotima? Is Love then ugly and bad?' And she said, 'Hush for shame! Do you think that what is not beautiful must necessarily be ugly?' 'Yes, I do.' 'And what is not wise, ignorant? Do you not perceive that there is something between wisdom and ignorance?' 'What is that?' 'To have right opinion without being able to give a reason,' she said, 'is neither to understand (for how could an unreasoned thing be understanding?) nor is it ignorance (for how can ignorance hit the truth?). Right opinion is no doubt something between knowledge and ignorance.' 'Quite true,' I said. 'Then do not try to compel what is not beautiful to be ugly, or what is not good to be bad. So also with Love. He is not good and not beautiful, as you admit yourself, but do not imagine for that reason any the more that he must be ugly and bad, but something between these two,' said she. 'Well, anyway,' I said, 'he is admit-

---

[62] The banquet is a social occasion demanding good manners, and so Socrates is tactful enough to represent himself, in the following speech, as an ignorant pupil of the prophetess Diotima, a fictitious person whose name means "honored by Zeus." Her city, Mantineia, was a real place, but more important here is the root meaning of the name: "mantic" or "prophetic." The tone and the question-answer, dialectical method of her discourse with Socrates are typical, though with the roles reversed, of his own tone and method in conversing with the ignorant in other dialogues.

[63] The plague mentioned reached Athens in 430 B.C., having raged elsewhere in Greece for several years.

ted by all to be a great god.' 'All who don't know,' she said, 'or all who know too?' 'All without exception.' At this she said, with a laugh, 'And how could he be admitted to be a great god, Socrates, by those who say he is not a god at all?' 'Who are these?' said I. 'You for one,' said she, 'and I for another.' And I asked, 'How can that be?' She said, 'Easily. Tell me, don't you say that all the gods are happy and beautiful? Or would you dare to say that any one of them is not happy and beautiful?' 'Indeed I would not,' said I. 'Then don't you call happy those possessed of good and beautiful things?' 'Certainly.' 'Yet you admitted that Love, because of a lack of good and beautiful things, actually desired those things which he lacked.' 'Yes, I admitted that.' 'Then how could he be a god who has no share in beautiful and good things?' 'He could not be a god, as it seems.' 'Don't you see then,' said she, 'that you yourself deny Love to be a god?'

"'Then what could Love be?' I asked. 'A mortal?' 'Not at all.' 'What then?' I asked. 'Just as before, between mortal and immortal.' 'What is he then, Diotima?' 'A great spirit,[64] Socrates; for all the spiritual is between divine and mortal.' 'What power has it?' said I. 'To interpret and to ferry across to the gods things given by men, and to men things from the gods, from men petitions and sacrifices, from the gods commands and requitals in return; and being in the middle it completes them and binds all together into a whole. Through this intermediary moves all the art of divination, and the art of priests, and all concerned with sacrifice and mysteries and incantations, and all sorcery and witchcraft. For God mingles not with man, but through this comes all the communion and conversation of gods with men and men with gods, both awake and asleep; and he who is expert in this is a spiritual man, but the expert in something other than this, such as common arts or crafts, is a vulgar man. These spirits are many and of all sorts and kinds, and one of them is Love.'

"'Who was his father,' said I, 'and who was his mother?' She answered, 'That is rather a long story, but still I will tell you. When Aphrodite was born, the gods held a feast, among them Plenty, the son of Neverataloss. When they had dined, Poverty came in begging, as might be expected with all that good cheer, and hung about the doors. Plenty then got drunk on the nectar[65]—for there was no wine yet—and went into Zeus's park all heavy and fell asleep. So Poverty because of her penury made a plan to have a child from Plenty, and lay by his side and conceived Love. This is why Love has become follower and servant of Aphrodite, having been begotten at her birthday party, and at the same time he is by nature a lover busy with beauty because Aphrodite is beautiful. Then since Love is the son of Plenty and Poverty he gets his fortunes from them. First, he is always poor; and far from being tender and beautiful, as most people think, he is hard and rough and unshod and homeless, lying always on the ground without bedding, sleeping by the doors and in the streets in the open air, having his mother's nature, always dwelling with want. But from his father again he has designs upon beautiful and good things, being brave and go-ahead and high-strung, a mighty hunter, always weaving devices, and a successful coveter of wisdom, a philosopher all his days, a great wizard and

[64] A "daimon," a being intermediate between gods and human beings.
[65] The usual beverage of the gods.

sorcerer and sophist. He was born neither mortal nor immortal; but on the same day, sometimes he is blooming and alive, when he has plenty, sometimes he is dying; then again he gets new life through his father's nature; but what he procures in plenty always trickles away, so that Love is not in want nor in wealth, and again he is between wisdom and ignorance. The truth is this: no god seeks after wisdom or desires to become wise—for wise he is already; nor does anyone else seek after wisdom, if he is wise already. And again, the ignorant do not seek after wisdom nor desire to become wise; for this is the worst of ignorance, that one who is neither beautiful and good nor intelligent should think himself good enough, so he does not desire it, because he does not think he is lacking in what he does not think he needs.'

"'Then who are the philosophers, Diotima,' said I, 'if those who seek after wisdom are neither the wise nor the ignorant?' 'That's clear enough even to a child,' she answered; 'they are those between these two, as Love is. You see, wisdom is one of the most beautiful things, and Love is a love for the beautiful, so Love must necessarily be a philosopher, and, being a philosopher, he must be between wise and ignorant. His birth is the cause of this, for he comes of a wise and resourceful father, but of a mother resourceless and not wise. Well then, dear Socrates, this is the nature of the spirit; but it was no wonder you thought Love what you did think. You thought, if I may infer it from what you say, that Love was the beloved, not the lover. That was why, I think, Love seemed to you wholly beautiful; for the thing loved is in fact beautiful and dainty and perfect and blessed, but the loving thing has a different shape, such as I have described.'

"Then I said, 'Very well, madam, what you say is right; but Love being such as you describe, of what use is he to mankind?' 'I will try to teach you that next, Socrates,' she said. 'Love then is like that, and born like that, and he is love of beautiful things, as you said he is. But suppose someone should ask us: "Socrates and Diotima, what is meant by love of beautiful things?"—I will put it more clearly: "He that loves beautiful things loves what?"' Then I answered, 'To get them.' 'Still,' she said, 'that answer needs another question, like this: "What will he get who gets the beautiful things?"' I said I could not manage at all to answer that question offhand. 'Well,' said she, 'suppose one should change "beautiful" to "good" and ask that? See here, Socrates, I will say: "What does he love who loves good things?"' 'To get them,' said I. 'And what will he get who gets the good things?' 'That's easier,' said I; 'I can answer that he will be happy.' 'Then,' said she, 'by getting good things the happy are happy, and there is no need to ask further, why he who wishes to be happy does wish that, but the answer seems to be finished.' 'Quite true,' said I. 'But do you think this wish and this love is common to all mankind,' Diotima said, 'and do you think that all men always wish to have the good things, or what do you say?' 'That's it,' said I, 'it's common to all.' 'Why then, Socrates,' said she, 'do we not say that all men are lovers, if they do in fact all love the same things and always, instead of saying that some are lovers and some are not?' 'That surprises me too,' I said. 'Don't let it surprise you,' she said. 'For we have taken one kind of love, and given it the name of the whole, love; and there are other cases in which we misapply other names.' 'For example?' said I.

'Here is one,' she said. 'You know that poetry is many kinds of making; for when anything passes from not-being to being, the cause is always making, or poetry, so that in all the arts the process is making, and all the craftsmen in these are makers, or poets.' 'Quite true,' I said. 'But yet,' said she, 'they are not all called poets; they have other names, and one bit of this making has been taken, that concerning music and verse, and this is called by the name of the whole. For this only is called poetry, and those who have this bit of making are called poets.' 'That is true,' I said. 'So with love, then; in its general sense it is all the desire for good things and for happiness—Love most mighty and all-ensnaring; but those who turn to him by any other road, whether by way of moneymaking, or of a taste for sports or philosophy, are not said to be in love and are not called lovers, but only those who go after one kind and are earnest about that have the name of the whole, love, and are said to love and to be lovers.' 'I think you are right there,' said I. 'And there is a story,' said she, 'that people in love are those who are seeking for their other half,[66] but my story tells that love is not for a half, nor indeed the whole, unless that happens to be something good, my friend; since men are willing to cut off their own hands and feet, if their own seem to them to be nasty. For really, I think, no one is pleased with his own thing, except one who calls the good thing his own and his property, and the bad thing another's; since there is nothing else men love but the good. Don't you think so?' 'Yes,' I said. 'Then,' said she, 'we may say simply that men love the good?' 'Yes,' I said. 'Shall we add,' she asked, 'that they love to have the good?' 'Yes, add that,' I said. 'Not only to have it, but always to have it?' 'Add that too.' 'Then to sum up,' she said, 'it is the love of having the good for oneself always.' 'Most true, indeed,' I said.

"She went on, 'Now if love is the love of having this always, what is the way men pursue it, and in what actions would their intense earnestness be expressed so as to be called love? What is this process? Can you tell me?' 'No,' said I, 'or else, Diotima, why should I, in admiration of your wisdom, have come to you as your pupil to find out these very matters?' 'Well then, I will tell you,' she said. 'It is a breeding in the beautiful, both of body and soul.' 'It needs divination,' I said, 'to tell what on earth you mean, and I don't understand.' 'Well,' she said, 'I will tell you clearer. All men are pregnant,[67] Socrates, both in body and in soul; and when they are of the right age, our nature desires to beget. But it cannot beget in an ugly thing, only in a beautiful thing. And this business is divine, and this is something immortal in a mortal creature, breeding and birth. These cannot be in what is discordant. But the ugly is discordant with everything divine, and the beautiful is concordant. Beauty therefore is Portioner and Lady of Labor[68] at birth. Therefore when the pregnant comes near to a beautiful thing it becomes gracious, and being delighted it is poured out and begets and procreates; when it comes near to an ugly thing, it becomes gloomy and grieved and rolls itself up and is repelled and shrinks back and does not procreate, but holds back the conception and is in a bad way. Hence in the

---

[66] The reference is to Aristophanes' fable, related earlier.
[67] In this passage, "pregnant" means, approximately, "having the potential to procreate."
[68] Apportioner (or destiny) and patroness of childbearing.

pregnant thing swelling full already, there is great agitation about the beautiful thing because he that has it gains relief from great agony. Finally, Socrates, love is not for the beautiful, as you think.' 'Why not?' 'It is for begetting and birth in the beautiful.' 'Oh, indeed?' said I. 'Yes indeed,' said she. 'Then why for begetting?' 'Because begetting is, for the mortal, something everlasting and immortal. But one must desire immortality along with the good, according to what has been agreed, if love is love of having the good for oneself always. It is necessary then from this argument that love is for immortality also.'

"All this she taught me at different times whenever she came to speak about love affairs; and once she asked, 'What do you think, Socrates, to be the cause of this love and desire? You perceive that all animals get into a dreadful state when they desire to procreate, indeed birds and beasts alike; all are sick and in a condition of love, about mating first, and then how to find food for their young, and they are ready to fight hard for them, the weakest against the strongest, and to die for them, and to suffer the agonies of starvation themselves in order to feed them, ready to do anything. One might perhaps think that man,' she said, 'would do all this from reasoning; but what about beasts? What is the cause of their enamored state? Can you tell me?' And I said again that I did not know; and she said, 'Then how do you ever expect to become expert in love affairs, if you do not understand that?' 'Why, Diotima, this is just why I have come to you, as I said; I knew I needed a teacher. Pray tell me the cause of this, and all the other love lore.'

"'Well then,' she said, 'if you believe love is by nature love of that which we often agreed on, don't be surprised. For on the same principle as before, here mortal nature seeks always as far as it can be to be immortal; and this is the only way it can, by birth, because it leaves something young in place of the old. Consider that for a while each single living creature is said to live and to be the same; for example, a man is said to be the same from boyhood to old age; he has, however, by no means the same things in himself, yet he is called the same: he continually becomes new, though he loses parts of himself, hair and flesh and bones and blood and all the body. Indeed, not only body, even in soul, manners, opinions, desires, pleasures, pains, fears, none of these remains the same, but some perish and others are born. And far stranger still, this happens to knowledge too; not only do some kinds of knowledge perish in us, not only are other kinds born, and not even in our knowledge are we ever the same, but the same happens even in each single kind of knowledge. For what is called study and practice means that knowledge is passing out; forgetting is knowledge leaving us, and study puts in new knowledge instead of that which is passing away, and preserves our knowledge so that it seems to be the same. In this way all the mortal is preserved, not by being wholly the same always, like the divine, but because what grows old and goes leaves behind something new like its past self. By this device, Socrates,' said she, 'mortality partakes of immortality, both in body and in all other respects; but it cannot otherwise.[69] Then

---

[69] Other passages in Plato indicate that he and Socrates did believe that the soul is, or can be, immortal. Whether or not the present passage conflicts with that view is a matter of dispute.

do not be surprised that everything naturally honors its own offspring; immortality is what all this earnestness and love pursues.'

"I heard this with admiration; and I said, 'Really, Diotima most wise! Is that really and truly so?' She answered as the complete Sophists do,[70] and said, 'You may be sure of that, Socrates. Just think, if you please, of men's ambition. You would be surprised at its unreasonableness if you didn't bear in mind what I have told you; observe what a terrible state they are in with love of becoming renowned, "and to lay up their fame for ever-more"[71] and for this how ready they are to run all risks even more than for their children, and to spend money and endure hardship to any extent, and to die for it. Do you think Alcestis would have died for Admetos, or Achilles would have died over Patroclos, or your Codros[72] would have died for the royalty of his sons, if they had not thought that "immortal memory of Virtue" would be theirs, which we still keep! Far from it,' she said; 'for eternal virtue and glorious fame like that all men do everything, I think, and the better they are, the more they do so; for the immortal is what they love. So those who are pregnant in body,' she said, 'turn rather to women and are enamored in this way, and thus, by begetting children, secure for themselves, so they think, immortality and memory and happiness, "Providing all things for the time to come"; but those who are pregnant in soul—for there are some,' she said, 'who conceive in soul still more than in body, what is proper for the soul to conceive and bear; and what is proper? wisdom and virtue in general—to this class belong all creative poets, and those artists and craftsmen who are said to be inventive. But much the greatest wisdom,' she said, 'and the most beautiful, is that which is concerned with the ordering of cities and homes, which we call temperance and justice. So again a man with divinity in him, whose soul from his youth is pregnant with these things, desires when he grows up to beget and procreate; and thereupon, I think, he seeks and goes about to find the beautiful thing in which he can beget; for in the ugly he never will. Being pregnant, then, he welcomes bodies which are beautiful rather than ugly, and if he finds a soul beautiful and generous and well-bred, he gladly welcomes the two body and soul together, and for a human being like that he has plenty of talks about virtue, and what the good man ought to be and to practice, and he tries to educate him. For by attaching himself to a person of beauty, I think, and keeping company with him, he begets and procreates what he has long been pregnant with; present and absent he remembers him, and with him fosters what is begotten, so that as a result these people maintain a much closer communion together and a firmer friendship than parents of children, because they have shared between them children more beautiful and more immortal. And everyone would be content to have such children born to him rather than human children; he would look to Homer and Hesiod and the other good poets, and wish to rival them, who leave such offspring behind them, which give their parents

---

[70] "That is, she made a speech rather than answered questions." (Translator's note.)

[71] Here, as later in the paragraph, Diotima either quotes or invents a line of poetry.

[72] A legendary early king of Athens. For Alcestis and the other persons named, see the notes to the earlier speech by Phaidros.

the same immortal fame and memory as they have themselves; or if you like,' she said, 'think what children Lycurgos left in Lacedaimon, the saviors of Lacedaimon and, one may say, of all Hellas. Honor came to Solon[73] also, in your country, by the begetting of his laws; and to many others in many countries and times, both Hellenes and barbarians, who performed many beautiful works and begat all kinds of virtue; in their names many sanctuaries have been made because they had such children, but never a one has been so honored because of human children.

"'These are some of the mysteries of Love, Socrates, in which perhaps even you may become an initiate; but as for the higher revelations, which initiation leads to if one approaches in the right way, I do not know if you could ever become an adept. At least I will instruct you,' she said, 'and no pains will be lacking; you try to follow if you can. It is necessary,' she said, 'that one who approaches in the right way should begin this business young, and approach beautiful bodies. First, if his leader leads aright, he should love one body and there beget beautiful speech; then he should take notice that the beauty in one body is akin to the beauty in another body, and if we must pursue beauty in essence, it is great folly not to believe that the beauty in all such bodies is one and the same. When he has learnt this, he must become the lover of all beautiful bodies, and relax the intense passion for one, thinking lightly of it and believing it to be a small thing. Next he must believe beauty in souls to be more precious than beauty in the body; so that if anyone is decent in soul, even if it has little bloom, it should be enough for him to love and care for, and to beget and seek such talks as will make young people better; that he may moreover be compelled to contemplate the beauty in our pursuits and customs, and to see that all beauty is of one and the same kin, and that so he may believe that bodily beauty is a small thing. Next, he must be led from practice to knowledge, that he may see again the beauty in different kinds of knowledge, and, directing his gaze from now on towards beauty as a whole, he may no longer dwell upon one, like a servant, content with the beauty of one boy or one human being or one pursuit, and so be slavish and petty; but he should turn to the great ocean of beauty, and in contemplation of it give birth to many beautiful and magnificent speeches and thoughts in the abundance of philosophy, until being strengthened and grown therein he may catch sight of some one knowledge, the one science of this beauty now to be described. Try to attend,' she said, 'as carefully as you can.

"'Whoever shall be guided so far towards the mysteries of love, by contemplating beautiful things rightly in due order, is approaching the last grade.[74] Suddenly he will behold a beauty marvellous in its nature, that very Beauty, Socrates, for the sake of which all the earlier hardships had been borne: in the first place, everlasting, and never being born nor

---

[73] Lycurgos (Lycurgus) was the mythical lawgiver of Sparta (Lacedaimon); Solon was a historical person who early in the sixth century played a similar role for Athens.

[74] The following passage is based on two fundamental Platonic concepts: a) the "ladder" that one ascends from lower to higher things, and b) the doctrine of "Ideas." For Plato an Idea is the changeless, eternal spiritual reality that transcends temporal, imperfect material reflections. All existing tables, for example, are imperfect versions of the Idea of a table. The greatest of the Ideas is of the Good, which is virtually identical with the True and the Beautiful.

perishing, neither increasing nor diminishing; secondly, not beautiful here and ugly there, not beautiful now and ugly then, not beautiful in one direction and ugly in another direction, not beautiful in one place and ugly in another place. Again, this beauty will not show itself to him like a face or hands or any bodily thing at all, nor as a discourse or a science, nor indeed as residing in anything, as in a living creature or in earth or heaven or anything else, but being by itself with itself always in simplicity; while all the beautiful things elsewhere partake of this beauty in such manner, that when *they* are born and perish *it* becomes neither less nor more and nothing at all happens to it; so that when anyone by right boy-loving goes up from these beautiful things to that beauty, and begins to catch sight of it, he would almost touch the perfect secret. For let me tell you, the right way to approach the things of love, or to be led there by another, is this: beginning from these beautiful things, to mount for that beauty's sake ever upwards, as by a flight of steps, from one to two, and from two to all beautiful bodies, and from beautiful bodies to beautiful pursuits and practices, and from practices to beautiful learnings, so that from learnings he may come at last to that perfect learning which is the learning solely of that beauty itself, and may know at last that which is the perfection of beauty. There in life and there alone, my dear Socrates,' said the inspired woman, 'is life worth living for man, while he contemplates Beauty itself. If ever you see this, it will seem to you to be far above gold and raiment and beautiful boys and men, whose beauty you are now entranced to see and you and many others are ready, so long as they see their darlings and remain ever with them, if it could be possible, not to eat nor drink but only to gaze at them and to be with them. What indeed,' she said, 'should we think, if it were given to one of us to see beauty undefiled, pure, unmixed, not adulterated with human flesh and colors and much other mortal rubbish, and if he could behold beauty in perfect simplicity? Do you think it a mean life for a man,' she said, 'to be looking thither and contemplating that and abiding with it? Do you not reflect,' said she, 'that there only it will be possible for him, when he sees the beautiful with the mind, which alone can see it, to give birth not to likenesses of virtue, since he touches no likeness, but to realities, since he touches reality; and when he has given birth to real virtue and brought it up, will it not be granted him to be the friend of God, and immortal if any man ever is?'

"This then, Phaidros and gentlemen, is what Diotima said, and I am quite convinced, and, being convinced, I try to persuade other people also to believe that to attain this possession one could not easily find a better helper for human nature than Love. And so I say that every man ought to honor Love, and I honor love matters myself, and I practice them particularly and encourage others; and now and always I sing the praises of Love's power and courage, as much as I am able. Then let this be my speech of eulogy to Love, if you please, Phaidros, or call it anything else you like."

When Socrates had done speaking, there was applause from the rest, and Aristophanes started to say something about Socrates' allusion to his own speech, when suddenly there came a knocking on the courtyard door and a great din as of some party of revellers, and they heard a girl-piper's notes. Then Agathon said to the staff, "Boys, go and see about that. If it is one of our friends, ask him in; if not, say we are not drinking now, we are just going to bed." In a few minutes they heard the voice of Alcibiades[75] in the yard, very drunk and shouting loud, asking where Agathon was, and take him to Agathon. So he was brought in to them by the piping-girl, who with some others of his company supported him; he came to a stand at the door crowned with a thick wreath of ivy and violets and wearing a great lot of ribands on his head, and said, "Good evening, you fellows, will you have a very drunken man to drink with you, or shall we only put a garland on Agathon, which we came for, and then go? For I tell you this," he said, "I could not get at him yesterday, but here I come with the ribands on my head, that I may take them off my head and just twine them about the head of the cleverest and most beautiful of men, if I may say so. Will you laugh at me because I'm drunk? I tell you, even if you laugh, that this is true and I know it. Look here, tell me straight, do I come in on those terms or not? Will you drink with me or not?"

Then they all cheered and told him to come in and take his place, and Agathon gave him a formal invitation. So he came in leaning on those people, pulling off the ribands at the same time to put them on Agathon, and as he held them in front of his eyes, he did not see Socrates, but sat down beside Agathon, between Socrates and him, for Socrates made room for him. He sat down and embraced Agathon and crowned him. Then Agathon said, "Take off Alcibiades' shoes, you boys, and let him make a third on our couch."

"All right," said Alcibiades, "but who is fellow-drinker number three here?" At the same time he turned round and saw Socrates; when he saw him, he jumped up and cried, "What the deuce is this? Socrates here? You lay there again in wait for me, as you are always turning up all of a sudden where I never thought to see you! And now what have you come for? And again, why did you lie there, not by Aristophanes or some other funny man or would-be funny man, but you managed to get beside the handsomest of the company!"

Then Socrates said, "Agathon, won't you defend me? I find that this person's love has become quite a serious thing. From the time when I fell in love with him, I am no longer allowed to look at or talk with a handsome person, not even one, or this jealous and envious creature treats me outrageously, and abuses me, and hardly keeps his hands off me. Then don't let him try it on now, but do reconcile us, or if he uses force, defend me, for I'm fairly terrified at his madness and passion."

"No," said Alcibiades, "there's no reconciliation between you and me! My word, I'll punish you for this by and by; but now, Agathon," he said, "give me some of the ribands, and let me wreath this fellow's wonderful head—there!—so he can't quarrel with me and say I wreathed you and didn't wreath the man who beats all the world at talking, not only the other day like you, but always!" While he spoke he took some of the ribands and wreathed Socrates, and then reclined himself.

[75] The handsome and dissolute Alcibiades (450–404) played a major role in Greek military history in the last sixteen years of his life; he changed his allegiances more than once. His drunken speech, which might seem to be mere comic relief, actually picks up subtly a number of themes explored earlier in the *Symposium*.

When he was settled, he said, "I say, men, I think you are sober. That won't do, you must drink! We agreed on that. Then I choose as prince of the pots, to see that you drink enough, myself. Let 'em bring it in, Agathon, the biggest goblet you have! No, better than that! You, boy there; bring that cooler," said he, for he saw it would hold more than half a gallon; first he filled that and drank it off himself, then told the boy to fill for Socrates, saying, "For Socrates, men, my trick is nothing; he drinks as much as anyone tells him, and never gets drunk one bit the more."

So the boy filled for Socrates, and he drank; then Eryximachos said, "Well, Alcibiades, what do we do? Are we just to say nothing over the cup, and to sing nothing, but only to drink like thirsty men?"

Alcibiades answered, "Good evening to you, Eryximachos, best son of a best father you, and he was very sober too!"[76]

"Same to you," said Eryximachos, "but what are we to do?"

"Whatever you say," he replied, "for we have to obey you. 'One medicine man is worth a host of laymen.'[77] Command what you will."

"Then listen," said Eryximachos. "Before you came in, we decided that each one in turn from left to right should recite the most excellent speech he could as a eulogy in honor of Love. All the rest of us, then, have made their speeches; but since you have made none, and since you have drunk your bumper, you are the proper one to speak; and when you have spoken, lay your commands on Socrates, what you like, and let him do the same with the next man to the right and so with the rest."

"Good," said Alcibiades, "but look here, Eryximachos, I don't think it's fair to tell a drunken man to risk a speech before sober men! And at the same time, bless you my dear! do you really believe anything of what Socrates has just said? Don't you know that the truth is exactly the opposite of what he stated? For if *I* praise anybody in his presence, god or man other than himself, this man will not keep his two hands off *me*."

"Won't you shut up?" said Socrates.

"On my honor, you need not make any objection," said Alcibiades. "I would not praise a single other person in your presence!"

"Very well, do this if you like," said Eryximachos; "praise Socrates."

"What's that?" said Alcibiades. "Must I, Eryximachos? Am I to have at the man and punish him before your faces?"

"Hullo," said Socrates, "what's your notion? To praise me and raise a laugh, or what will you do?"

"I'll tell the truth! Will you let me?"

"Oh yes, let you tell the truth, I even command you to do that."

"Then I'll do it at once!" said Alcibiades. "Look here, this is what I want you to do. If I say anything that is not true, stop me in the middle, and say that I am lying; for I won't tell any lies if I can help it. But if I speak higgledy-piggledy trying to remember, don't be surprised, for it is not easy to set out all your absurdities nicely in order, for one in my state.

"I am to speak in praise of Socrates, gentlemen, and I will just try to do

---

[76] "Alcibiades' Greek becomes poetic!" (Translator's note.)
[77] A quotation from Homer's *Iliad*.

it by means of similes.[78] Oh yes, he will think perhaps it is only for a bit of fun, but my simile will be for truth, not for fun. I say then, that he is exactly like a Silenos,[79] the little figures which you see sitting in the statuaries' shops; as the craftsmen make them, they hold Panspipes or pipes, and they can be opened down the middle and folded back, and then they show inside them images of the gods. And I say further, he is like Marsyas[80] the Satyr. Well anyway, Socrates, your face is like them, I don't suppose you will deny that yourself! In everything else, too, you are like them, listen what comes next. You are a bully! Aren't you? If you don't admit that I will find witnesses. Well, aren't you a piper? Yes, a more wonderful performer than that Marsyas! For he used to bewitch men through instruments by the power of his mouth, and so also now does anyone who pipes his tunes; for those Olympos[81] piped, I say were from Marsyas who taught him; then it is his tunes, whether a good artist plays them or a common piping-girl, which alone enravish us and make plain those who feel the need of the gods and their mysteries, because the tunes are divine. The only difference between you is, that *you* do the very same without instruments by bare words! We, at least, when we hear someone else making other speeches, even quite a good orator, nobody cares a jot, I might say; but when one hears you, or your words recited by another, even a very poor speaker, let a woman hear, or a man hear, or a boy hear, we are overwhelmed and enravished. I, indeed, my friends, if you would not have thought me completely drunk, would have taken a solemn oath before you, and described to you how this man's words have made me feel and still make me feel now. When I hear them my heart goes leaping worse than frantic revellers', and tears run from my eyes at the words of this man, and I see crowds of others in the same state. When I heard Pericles,[82] and other good orators, I thought them fine speakers, but I felt nothing like that, and no confusion in my soul or regret for my slavish condition; but this Marsyas here has brought me very often into such a condition that I thought the life I lead was not worth living. And that, Socrates, you will not say is untrue! And even now at this moment, I know in my conscience that if I would open my ears I could never hold out, but I should be in the same state. For he compels me to admit that I am very remiss, in going on neglecting my own self but attending to Athenian public business. So I force myself, and stop my ears, and off I go running as from the Sirens,[83] or else I should sit down on the spot beside him till I become an old man. I feel towards this one man something which no one would ever think could be in me—to be ashamed before anybody; but I *am* ashamed before him and before no one else. For I know in my conscience that I cannot contradict him and say it is not my duty to do what he tells me, yet when I leave him, public applause is too much for me. So I show my

[78] Comparisons. "A favourite game in society. Socrates obviously plays up, and makes signs or grimaces as Alcibiades goes on, and the other turns to him and to the company in turn." (Translator's note.)

[79] An aged and grotesque companion-tutor of Dionysus, god of wine and revelry. Satyrs were mainly human in shape but usually had tails and goat-feet.

[80] In myth, a legendary inventor of the art of piping.   [81] Another famous musician.

[82] The great Athenian political leader of the fifth century, famous as an orator.

[83] In myth, women who through their alluring songs drew mariners to their destruction. In Homer's *Odyssey*, Book XII, Odysseus orders his crewmates to stop up their ears until they are out of earshot.

heels and run from him, and, whenever I see him, I am ashamed of what I confessed to him. Often enough I should be glad to see him no longer among mankind; but if that should happen, I am sure I should be sorrier still, so I don't know what to do with the fellow.

"The pipings of this satyr have put many others into the same state as me; but let me tell you something else to show how like he is to my simile, and how wonderful his power is. I assure you that not one of you knows this man; but I will show you, since I have begun. You see, of course, that Socrates has a loving eye for beauty, he's always interested in such people and quite smitten with them, and again he is ignorant of everything and knows nothing; that is his pose. Isn't that Silenosity? Very much so! He wraps that round him like a cloak, like the outside of the carved Silenos figure; but inside, when he is opened—what do you think he is full of, gentlemen pot-fellows? Temperance! Let me say that he cares not a straw if one is a beauty, he despises that as no one would ever believe; and the same if one is rich, or has one of those mob distinctions which people think so grand. He thinks all those possessions are worthless and we are nothing, yes, I tell you! Pretending ignorance and making fun of his fellows all his life—that's how he goes on. But when he's in earnest, and opened out—I don't know if anyone has seen the images inside; but I saw them once, and I thought them divine and golden and all-beautiful and wonderful, so that one must in short do whatever Socrates commands. I thought he was in earnest over my youthful bloom, I thought I had found a godsend and a wonderful piece of luck, in that by gratifying Socrates I had the chance to hear all he knew; I thought a lot of my blooming beauty, you know, an awful lot. With this notion—you see, before that, I never used to visit him alone without an attendant—but after that I sent my attendant away and always went in alone; for I must tell you all the truth; now Socrates, attend and refute me if I tell a lie. Well, I paid him visits, gentlemen, I alone and he alone, and I thought he would talk to me as a lover would talk to his darling in solitude, and I was happy. Nothing came of it, nothing, he just talked as usual, and when we had had a nice day together, he always went off. Next I challenged him to gymnastics with me, and I went through it hoping for something then; well, he exercised with me, and we wrestled together often, with nobody there. What's the good of talking? I got nothing by it. Since I was none the better for all that, I resolved to try stronger measures with the man, and not to give in after I had undertaken something, but to find out what was behind the business. So I invited him to dinner with me, exactly like a lover with designs on his beloved. For a long time he would not even consent to come, but at last I persuaded him. The first time he came he wanted to go after dinner. That time I was ashamed, and let him go; but I made my plot again, and after we had dined, I went on talking till late at night, and when he wanted to go, I forced him to stay by pretending it was late. So he rested on the couch next to mine, where he had dined, and no one else was sleeping in the room, only we two. So far I could tell my story to anyone; but what follows you would never have heard me tell, only first, wine is true, as they say—whether children are there or not[84]—secondly, to hide a superimperious deed of Socrates is unfair, I

---

[84] "The proverb was: 'Wine and children are true.'" (Translator's note.)

think, for one who has come to sing his praises. Moreover, I too have 'felt the viper's bite,' as the saying goes. You know they say that one who felt it would not tell what it was like except to other people who had been bitten, since they alone would know it and would not be hard on him for what he allowed himself to do and say in his agony. Well, I have been bitten by a more painful viper, and in the most painful spot where one could be bitten—the heart, or soul, or whatever it should be called—stung and bitten by his discourses in philosophy, which hang on more cruelly than a viper when they seize on a soul young and not ungenerous, and make it do and say anything—and when I see men like Phaidros, Agathon, Eryximachos, Pausanias, Aristodemos, too, and Aristophanes—Socrates himself I need not mention—and how many more! For you have all shared in the philosopher's madness and passion! Then you shall all hear; for you will not be hard on what was done then and what is being said now; but you servants, and anyone else who is common and boorish, clap strong doors on your ears!

"Well then, gentlemen, when the lamp was out and the servants outside, I thought it necessary not to mince matters but to say freely what I felt; so I stirred him up, and said, 'Asleep, Socrates?' 'Not at all,' said he. 'Do you know what is in my mind?' 'What is it?' he asked. 'I think,' said I, 'that you are the only lover I have ever had worthy of me, and now you won't speak a word to me. I'll tell you how I feel: I consider it simpy silly not to gratify you in this, and anything else you want of my property or from my friends. For myself, I think nothing more precious than to attain the height of excellence, and to help me in this there is no one more competent than you. Then I should be much more ashamed before the wise if I did not gratify such a man than I should be ashamed before the multitude of fools if I did.' He answered, playing the innocent as usual, quite like himself, 'My dearest Alcibiades, you are really and truly no bad hand at a bargain, if what you say is really true about me, and if there is in me some power which can make you better; you must see some inconceivable beauty in me immensely greater than your own loveliness. If then you spy it there, and if you are trying to do a deal and exchange beauty for beauty, you want to get very much the better of me, you want to get real beauties for sham, and indeed to exchange "golden for bronze."[85] Bless you, my dear, spy better, and you'll see I am nothing. The sight of the mind begins to see sharp when the sight of the eyes is losing its keenness, and you are far from that still.' I heard him, and said, 'That is what I have to tell you, and I have said exactly what I mean; consider yourself, then, what you believe best for you and me.' 'That's well said,' he answered, 'another time we will consider, and do whatever seems best for us both in this and other matters.'

"When I heard this and said this, and as it were shot my shafts, I thought he was wounded; so I got up, and without letting this man[86] say another word, I threw my own mantle over the man and crept in under this man's threadbare cloak—for it was winter—and threw my arms round this man, this really astonishing and wonderful man, and there I lay the whole

---

[85] "An allusion to Homer, where Diomedes exchanges his bronze armour for Glaucos' golden; *Iliad* vi. 236." (Translator's note.)

[86] "With each phrase he points at Socrates." (Translator's note.)

night! You will not say that is a lie, either, Socrates! Though I had done all this, yet this man was so much above me and so despised me and laughed at my bloom, and insulted me in the point where I did think I was something, gentlemen of the jury—for jury you are, to give a verdict on the superimperiosity of Socrates—that I swear by the gods, I swear by the goddesses, when I got up I had no more slept with Socrates than if I had been with a father or elder brother.

"How do you think I felt after that! I thought I had been disgraced, and yet I admired the way this man was made, and his temperance and courage; and I had met such a human being for wisdom and endurance as I never expected to find in the world, so that I could not bring myself to quarrel and lose his company, nor could I think of any way to attract him. For I knew quite well that to money he was much less vulnerable than Aias[87] to steel, and in what I thought would alone win him, he had escaped me. So I was at a loss, and I walked about, a slave to the creature as no one ever was to anyone. Well, all this happened before our expedition went to Poteidaia;[88] we were both in it, and we were messmates there. And first of all, in bearing hardships he not only beat me but everyone else; when we were cut off somewhere, and had to go without food, as happens on campaign, the others were nothing for endurance. Yet when there was plenty of good cheer, he was the only one who could really enjoy it; particularly, although he did not care for drinking, when he was compelled to drink he beat them all, and what is most wonderful of all, no one in the world has ever seen Socrates drunk. That we shall be able to test presently, as I think. That was not all; in his endurance of the cold winter—the winters were dreadful there—he did wonders, and here is a specimen. Once there was a most dreadful frost, and no one would go out of doors, or if he did he put on an awful lot of things, and swathed his legs, and wrapped up his feet in felt and sheepskin, but this man went out in that weather wearing only such a cloak as he used to wear before, and unshod he marched over the ice more easily than others did with boots on. The soldiers looked black at him thinking he despised them.

> "So much for that;
> But here's a doughty deed the strong man did,[89]

once on that expedition, and it is worth hearing. He got some notion into his head, and there he stood on one spot from dawn, thinking, and when it did not come out, he would not give in but still stood pondering. It was already midday, and people noticed it, and wondered, and said to one another that Socrates had been standing thinking about something ever since dawn. At last when evening came, some of the Ionians after dinner—it was summertime then—brought out their pallets and slept near in the cool, and watched him from time to time to see if he would stand all night.

---

[87] A Greek warrior (also spelled *Ajax*) famous for his impenetrable shield.

[88] The campaign took place in 432, sixteen years before the present banquet. Poteidaia had rebelled against the leadership of Athens.

[89] Quoted from Homer's *Odyssey*, Book IV; Helen of Troy is praising Odysseus.

He did stand until it was dawn, and the sun rose; then he offered a prayer to the sun and walked away.[90]

"Now with your leave we will take the battles; for it is fair to pay him his due. When there was that battle[91] after which the generals actually gave me the prize of valor, this man, when not a single other person came to my rescue, saved my life. I was wounded, but he would not leave me, and saved my weapons and me too. Then I begged the generals myself, Socrates, to give you the prize for valor, and here you will not find fault with me or say I am lying; but the fact is, when the generals looked at my rank and wanted to give me the prize, you were more eager than the generals that I should get it and not yourself. Again, gentlemen, it was worth while to see Socrates when the army was routed and retreating from Delion. I happened to be there on horseback, and he on foot. This man and Laches were retreating together in the rout; I met them, and told them to cheer up, and said I would not desert them. There indeed I had an even better view of Socrates than at Poteidaia, for I had less to fear, being on horseback. First I saw how he kept his head much better than Laches; next I really thought, Aristophanes, to quote your words,[92] that he marched exactly as he does here, 'with swaggering gait and rolling eye,' quietly looking round at friends and enemies, and making it quite clear to everyone even a long way off that if anyone laid a finger on this man, he would defend himself stoutly. And therefore he came off safe, both this man and his companion; for in war where men are like that, people usually don't touch them with a finger, but pursue those who are running headlong.

"One could quote many other things in praise of Socrates, wonderful things: of his other habits one might perhaps say much the same about another man, and yet it is his not being like any other man in the world, ancient or modern, that is worthy of all wonder. Men like Achilles might be found, one might take, for example, Brasidas and others; and again men like Pericles, such as Nestor and Antenor,[93] and there are more besides; and so we might go on with our comparisons. But as for this man, so odd, both the man and his talk, none could ever be found to come near him, neither modern nor ancient, unless he is to be compared to no man at all, but to the Silenoses and satyrs to which I have compared him—him and his talk.

"For indeed there is something which I left out when I began, that even his talk is very like the opening Silenoses. When you agree to listen to the talk of Socrates, it might seem at first to be nothing but absurdity; such words and phrases are wrapped outside it, like the hide of a boisterous satyr. Pack-asses and smiths and shoemakers and tanners[94] are what he talks about, and he seems to be always saying the same things in the same words, so that any ignorant and foolish man would laugh at them. But

---

[90] Socrates had a special devotion to the sun and the sun-god Apollo. This devotion was called into question during his trial; see Plato's *Apology.*

[91] At Poteidaia. Socrates' rescue of Alcibiades is also mentioned in Plato's *Apology.* Alcibiades, as both citizen and soldier, outranked Socrates.

[92] In Aristophanes' play *The Clouds,* which satirizes Socrates.

[93] The five men were renowned for military prowess, eloquence, or wise counsel.

[94] Even when discussing the loftiest and subtlest matters, Socrates tended to use illustrations from commonplace trades and objects.

when they are opened out, and you get inside them, you will find his words first full of sense, as no others are; next, most divine and containing the finest images of virtue, and reaching farthest, in fact reaching to everything which it profits a man to study who is to become noble and good.

"This, gentlemen, is my laudation of Socrates; and I have mixed in as well some blame, by telling you of the way he insulted me. I am not the only one he has treated so; he has done the same to Charmides, Glaucon's son, and Euthydemos, Diocles' son, and very many others, whom he has tricked as a lover and made them treat him as beloved instead. That is a warning to you, Agathon, not to be deceived by this man; try to learn from our experience, and take care not to be the fool in the proverb, who could only learn by his own."

When Alcibiades had ended his speech, there was much laughter at his frankness, because he seemed to be still in love with Socrates. But Socrates said, "You're sober, I think, Alcibiades, or you would never have wrapped all that smart mantle round you in trying to hide why you have said all this, and put your point in a postscript at the end; for your real aim in all you said was to make me and Agathon quarrel: you think I ought to be your lover and love no one else, and Agathon should be your beloved and loved by no one else. But I see through you; your satyric and silenic drama has been shown up. Now, my dearest Agathon, don't let him gain anything by it; only take care that no one shall make you and me quarrel."

Then Agathon said, "Upon my word, Socrates, that's the truth, I am sure. I notice how he reclined between me and you in order to keep us apart. Then he shall gain nothing by it, and I will come past you and recline there."

"Yes do," said Socrates, "recline here below me."[95]

"Oh Zeus!" cried Alcibiades, "how the creature treats me! He thinks he must have the best of me everywhere! Well, if nothing else, you plague, let Agathon recline between us."

"Impossible!" said Socrates. "For you have sung my praises, and it is my duty to praise the next man to the right. Then if Agathon reclines below you—I don't suppose he is going to praise me again, before I have praised him as I should? Then let him alone, you rascal, and don't grudge my praise to the lad; for I want very much to sing his glory."

"Hooray, hooray!" cried Agathon, "I can't stay here, Alcibiades. I must and will change my place, and then Socrates will praise me!"

"Here we are again," said Alcibiades, "the usual thing; where Socrates is, there is no one else can get a share of the beauties! And now how easily he has invented a plausible reason why this one should be beside him!"

Then Agathon got up to go and lie down beside Socrates, but suddenly a great crowd of revellers came to the doors; seeing them open as someone was going out, they marched straight in and found places among the diners, and the whole place was in an uproar. No order was kept any longer and they were forced to drink a great deal of wine. Eryximachos and Phaidros and some others went out and departed (so Aristodemos told

---

[95] Alcibiades, during his speech, has sat between Agathon and Socrates; if Agathon moves to the other side of the three-person group, as Socrates suggests, Socrates will be in the middle.

me), and he fell asleep himself, and slept soundly for a long time, as the nights were long then, and he woke up towards day when the cocks were already crowing. When he awoke he saw the others were either asleep or had gone, but Agathon and Aristophanes and Socrates were the only ones still awake, and they were drinking out of a large bowl from left to right. Socrates was arguing with them; Aristodemos told me he could not remember much of what was said, for he was not listening from the beginning and he was rather drowsy, but he told me the upshot of it was that Socrates was compelling them to admit that the same man ought to understand how to compose both comedy and tragedy, and that he who has skill as a tragic poet has skill for a comic poet.[96] While they were being forced to this, and not following very well, they began to nod, and first Aristophanes fell asleep, and while day was dawning, Agathon too. Socrates made them comfortable, then got up and went away, and Aristodemos himself followed as usual. Socrates went to the Lyceum[97] and had a wash, and spent the day as he generally did, and after spending the day so, in the evening went home to bed.

from THE REPUBLIC

Translated by Benjamin Jowett

The Republic, the second-longest (after the *Laws*) of Plato's works, is an inquiry into the nature of justice. The inquiry leads, in turn, to an attempt to define the ideal state. The form is that of a dialogue between Socrates and six other speakers. Book VII begins with the famous Parable of the Cave (or Den), in which Socrates, addressing an older brother of Plato named Glaucon, illustrates the difference between unenlightened men and enlightened philosophers. The parable also suggests the difficulty philosophers will have in returning to the sphere of practical affairs after having envisioned the ideal, supra-earthly form of the good. (Nevertheless, in the just commonwealth such civic service will be the duty of philosopher-rulers.) [*Editors' headnote.*]

BOOK VII

THE PARABLE OF THE CAVE

And now, I said,[1] let me show in a figure how far our nature is enlightened or unenlightened:—Behold! human beings living in an underground den, which has a mouth open towards the light and reaching all along the den; here they have been from their childhood, and have their legs and necks

---

[96] This argument by Socrates is similar to his reasoning in Plato's *Ion,* where Socrates argues that poetry is a single art. But the main points here are that Socrates can hold his liquor well and that his appetite for argument is insatiable.

[97] A woods and gymnasium in Athens, associated with Apollo.

[1] The entire dialogue is related, by Socrates, on the day after it is supposed to have occurred.

chained so that they cannot move, and can only see before them, being prevented by the chains from turning round their heads. Above and behind them a fire is blazing at a distance, and between the fire and the prisoners there is a raised way; and you will see, if you look, a low wall built along the way, like the screen which marionette players have in front of them, over which they show the puppets.

I see.

And do you see, I said, men passing along the wall carrying all sorts of vessels, and statues and figures of animals made of wood and stone and various materials, which appear over the wall? Some of them are talking, others silent.

You have shown me a strange image, and they are strange prisoners.

Like ourselves, I replied; and they see only their own shadows, or the shadows of one another, which the fire throws on the opposite wall of the cave?

True, he said; how could they see anything but the shadows if they were never allowed to move their heads?

And of the objects which are being carried in like manner they would only see the shadows?

Yes, he said.

And if they were able to converse with one another, would they not suppose that they were naming what was actually before them?

Very true.

And suppose further that the prison had an echo which came from the other side, would they not be sure to fancy when one of the passers-by spoke that the voice which they heard came from the passing shadow?

No question, he replied.

To them, I said, the truth would be literally nothing but the shadows of the images.

That is certain.

And now look again, and see what will naturally follow if the prisoners are released and disabused of their error. At first, when any of them is liberated and compelled suddenly to stand up and turn his neck round and walk and look towards the light, he will suffer sharp pains; the glare will distress him, and he will be unable to see the realities of which in his former state he had seen the shadows; and then conceive some one saying to him, that what he saw before was an illusion, but that now, when he is approaching nearer to being and his eye is turned towards more real existence, he has a clearer vision,—what will be his reply? And you may further imagine that his instructor is pointing to the objects as they pass and requiring him to name them,—will he not be perplexed? Will he not fancy that the shadows which he formerly saw are truer than the objects which are now shown to him?

Far truer.

And if he is compelled to look straight at the light, will he not have a pain in his eyes which will make him turn away to take refuge in the objects of vision which he can see, and which he will conceive to be in reality clearer than the things which are now being shown to him?

True, he said.

And suppose once more, that he is reluctantly dragged up a steep and rugged ascent, and held fast until he is forced into the presence of the sun himself, is he not likely to be pained and irritated? When he approaches the light his eyes will be dazzled, and he will not be able to see anything at all of what are now called realities.

Not all in a moment, he said.

He will require to grow accustomed to the sight of the upper world. And first he will see the shadows best, next the reflections of men and other objects in the water, and then the objects themselves; then he will gaze upon the light of the moon and the stars and the spangled heaven; and he will see the sky and the stars by night better than the sun or the light of the sun by day?

Certainly.

Last of all he will be able to see the sun, and not mere reflections of him in the water, but he will see him in his own proper place, and not in another; and he will contemplate him as he is.

Certainly.

He will then proceed to argue that this is he who gives the season and the years, and is the guardian of all that is in the visible world, and in a certain way the cause of all things which he and his fellows have been accustomed to behold?

Clearly, he said, he would first see the sun and then reason about him.

And when he remembered his old habitation, and the wisdom of the den and his fellow-prisoners, do you not suppose that he would felicitate himself on the change, and pity them?

Certainly, he would.

And if they were in the habit of conferring honors among themselves on those who were quickest to observe the passing shadows and to remark which of them went before, and which followed after, and which were together; and who were therefore best able to draw conclusions as to the future, do you think that he would care for such honors and glories, or envy the possessors of them? Would he not say with Homer,

"Better to be the poor servant of a poor master,"[2]

and to endure anything, rather than think as they do and live after their manner?

Yes, he said, I think that he would rather suffer anything than entertain these false notions and live in this miserable manner.

Imagine once more, I said, such an one coming suddenly out of the sun to be replaced in his old situation; would he not be certain to have his eyes full of darkness?

To be sure, he said.

And if there were a contest, and he had to compete in measuring the shadows with the prisoners who had never moved out of the den, while his sight was still weak, and before his eyes had become steady (and the time which would be needed to acquire this new habit of sight might be very

---

[2] In the dim underworld of Hades visited by Odysseus in the *Odyssey*, Book XI, the shade of the great warrior Achilles says that he would rather be alive as the lowliest servant than reign as king of the underworld.

considerable), would he not be ridiculous? Men would say of him that up he went and down he came without his eyes; and that it was better not even to think of ascending; and if any one tried to loose another and lead him up to the light, let them only catch the offender, and they would put him to death.

No question, he said.

This entire allegory, I said, you may now append, dear Glaucon, to the previous argument; the prison-house is the world of sight, the light of the fire is the sun, and you will not misapprehend me if you interpret the journey upwards to be the ascent of the soul into the intellectual world according to my poor belief, which, at your desire, I have expressed— whether rightly or wrongly God knows. But, whether true or false, my opinion is that in the world of knowledge the idea of good appears last of all, and is seen only with an effort; and, when seen, is also inferred to be the universal author of all things beautiful and right, parent of light and of the lord of light in this visible world, and the immediate source of reason and truth in the intellectual; and that this is the power upon which he who would act rationally either in public or private life must have his eye fixed.

I agree, he said, as far as I am able to understand you.

Moreover, I said, you must not wonder that those who attain to this beatific vision are unwilling to descend to human affairs; for their souls are ever hastening into the upper world where they desire to dwell; which desire of theirs is very natural, if our allegory may be trusted.

Yes, very natural.

And is there anything surprising in one who passes from divine contemplations to the evil state of man, misbehaving himself in a ridiculous manner; if, while his eyes are blinking and before he has become accustomed to the surrounding darkness, he is compelled to fight in courts of law, or in other places, about the images or the shadows of images of justice, and is endeavoring to meet the conceptions of those who have never yet seen absolute justice?

Anything but surprising, he replied.

Any one who has common sense will remember that the bewilderments of the eyes are of two kinds, and arise from two causes, either from coming out of the light or from going into the light, which is true of the mind's eye, quite as much as of the bodily eye; and he who remembers this when he sees any one whose vision is perplexed and weak, will not be too ready to laugh; he will first ask whether that soul of man has come out of the brighter life, and is unable to see because unaccustomed to the dark, or having turned from darkness to the day is dazzled by excess of light. And he will count the one happy in his condition and state of being, and he will pity the other; or, if he have a mind to laugh at the soul which comes from below into the light, there will be more reason in this than in the laugh which greets him who returns from above out of the light into the den.

That, he said, is a very just distinction.

But then, if I am right, certain professors of education must be wrong when they say that they can put a knowledge into the soul which was not there before, like sight into blind eyes.

They undoubtedly say this, he replied.

Whereas, our argument shows that the power and capacity of learning exists in the soul already; and that just as the eye was unable to turn from darkness to light without the whole body, so too the instrument of knowledge can only by the movement of the whole soul be turned from the world of becoming into that of being, and learn by degrees to endure the sight of being, and of the brightest and best of being, or in other words, of the good. . . .

THE APOLOGY

Translated by Benjamin Jowett

In 399 B.C. the seventy-year-old Socrates had made enemies of certain prominent Athenians to the extent that he was brought to trial, on two counts: for atheism and for the corruption of Athenian youth. The *Apology* is Socrates' defense of himself against the charges, both the immediate and specific ones on which he was arraigned and those brought against him during his entire life and career. If the word "apology" is mistakenly understood in its ordinary modern sense, the title of this work will be puzzling, for Socrates' speech is not a confession of guilt or error; it is quite the contrary. Socrates' words are an "apology" in the older sense of *apologia*, meaning an aggressive vindication of himself and of his principles. In keeping with his distinctive style of behavior, Socrates conducts his defense in an utterly personal way, with little regard for expediency or for legal forms and procedures.

Plato himself, then in his late twenties, is mentioned in the *Apology* as among the followers of Socrates present at the trial. If he was indeed present, Plato was in a position to record Socrates' words accurately. To what extent he actually did so, we cannot be sure; as with other Socratic dialogues, we must assume that the *Apology* is a combination of Socrates' ideas and his pupil Plato's own emphases and artistry. But the image of Socrates that emerges is so compelling that it conveys a strong impression of historical and even reportorial accuracy.

For many centuries readers have been irresistibly drawn to compare Socrates and Jesus. The accounts of their trials and executions are especially worthy of comparison—for both the similarities and the differences. See, for example, Matthew 26-27 and John 18-19. [*Editors' headnote.*]

How you, O Athenians, have been affected by my accusers, I cannot tell; but I know that they almost made me forget who I was—so persuasively did they speak; and yet they have hardly uttered a word of truth. But of the many falsehoods told by them, there was one which quite amazed me;—I mean when they said that you should be upon your guard and not allow yourselves to be deceived by the force of my eloquence. To say this, when they were certain to be detected as soon as I opened my lips and proved myself to be anything but a great speaker, did indeed appear to me most shameless—unless by the force of eloquence they mean the force of truth; for if such is their meaning, I admit that I am eloquent. But in how different a way from theirs! Well, as I was saying, they have scarcely spoken the truth at all; but from me you shall hear the whole truth: not, however, delivered after their manner in a set oration duly ornamented with words and phrases. No, by heaven! but I shall use the words and arguments which occur to me at the moment; for I am confident in the justice of my cause: at my time of life I ought not to be appearing before you, O men of Athens, in the character of a juvenile orator—let no one expect it of me. And I must beg of you to grant me a favor:—If I defend myself in my accustomed manner, and you hear me using the words which I have been in the habit of using in the agora,[1] at the tables of the money-changers, or anywhere else, I would ask you not to be surprised, and not to interrupt me on this account. For I am more than seventy years of age, and appearing now for the first time in a court of law, I am quite a stranger to the language of the place; and therefore I would have you regard me as if I were really a stranger,[2] whom you would excuse if he spoke in his native tongue, and after the fashion of his country:—Am I making an unfair request of you? Never mind the manner, which may or may not be good; but think only of the truth of my words, and give heed to that: let the speaker speak truly and the judge decide justly.

And first, I have to reply to the older charges and to my first accusers, and then I will go on to the later ones. For of old I have had many accusers, who have accused me falsely to you during many years; and I am more afraid of them than of Anytus and his associates,[3] who are dangerous, too, in their own way. But far more dangerous are the others, who began when you were children, and took possession of your minds with their falsehoods, telling of one Socrates, a wise man, who speculated about the heaven above, and searched into the earth beneath, and made the worse appear the better cause.[4] The disseminators of this tale are the accusers whom I dread; for their hearers are apt to fancy that such enquirers do not believe in the existence of the gods. And they are many, and their charges against me are of ancient date, and they were made by them in the days when you were more impressible than you are now—in childhood, or it may have been in youth—and the cause when heard went by default, for there was none to answer. And hardest of all, I do not know and cannot tell the names of my accusers; unless in the chance case of a Comic poet.[5] All who from envy and malice have persuaded you—some of them having first convinced themselves—all this class of men are most difficult to deal with; for I cannot have them up here, and cross-examine them, and therefore I must simply fight with shadows in my own defense, and argue when there is no one who answers. I will ask you then to assume with me, as I was saying, that my opponents are of two kinds; one recent, the other ancient: and I hope that

[1] The public marketplace where citizens congregated.

[2] A noncitizen of Athens, whose dialect would have sounded uncouth to Athenians. Socrates' ironic point is that, though he is a genuine and lifelong Athenian, his manner of discourse will sound unconventional, like that of a "stranger" or foreigner.

[3] The three men who pressed charges against Socrates were Anytus, Meletus, and Lycon. Anytus was a wealthy leather merchant who disliked Socrates partly on political grounds and partly because Socrates had tried to persuade Anytus to let his son pursue a career different from his father's. Meletus (cross-examined by Socrates later in the *Apology*) may have been a poet (poets were both adulated and despised by Socrates/Plato). Of Lycon little is known; he may have been a professional orator.

[4] Socrates was almost entirely concerned with ethical human values, as distinguished from both natural science and the tricks of logic and language associated with the Sophists (professional teachers of rhetoric and logic or pseudo-logic). Nevertheless, his dexterity in discourse and his subtleties of argument caused some people to believe that he was a Sophist.

[5] Aristophanes, who in his play *The Clouds* represented Socrates unfavorably, as a pretender to miraculous powers.

you will see the propriety of my answering the latter first, for these accusations you heard long before the others, and much oftener.

Well, then, I must make my defense, and endeavor to clear away in a short time, a slander which has lasted a long time. May I succeed, if to succeed be for my good and yours, or likely to avail me in my cause! The task is not an easy one; I quite understand the nature of it. And so leaving the event with God, in obedience to the law I will now make my defense.

I will begin at the beginning, and ask what is the accusation which has given rise to the slander of me, and in fact has encouraged Meletus to prefer this charge against me. Well, what do the slanderers say? They shall be my prosecutors, and I will sum up their words in an affidavit: 'Socrates is an evil-doer, and a curious person, who searches into things under the earth and in heaven, and he makes the worse appear the better cause; and he teaches the aforesaid doctrines to others.' Such is the nature of the accusation: it is just what you have yourselves seen in the comedy of Aristophanes, who has introduced a man whom he calls Socrates, going about and saying that he walks in air, and talking a deal of nonsense concerning matters of which I do not pretend to know either much or little—not that I mean to speak disparagingly of any one who is a student of natural philosophy. I should be very sorry if Meletus could bring so grave a charge against me. But the simple truth is, O Athenians, that I have nothing to do with physical speculations. Very many of those here present are witnesses to the truth of this, and to them I appeal. Speak then, you who have heard me, and tell your neighbors whether any of you have ever known me hold forth in few words or in many upon such matters. . . . You hear their answer. And from what they say of this part of the charge you will be able to judge of the truth of the rest.

As little foundation is there for the report that I am a teacher, and take money; this accusation has no more truth in it than the other. Although, if a man were really able to instruct mankind, to receive money for giving instruction would, in my opinion, be an honor to him. There is Gorgias of Leontium, and Prodicus of Ceos, and Hippias of Elis,[6] who go the round of the cities, and are able to persuade the young men to leave their own citizens by whom they might be taught for nothing, and come to them whom they not only pay, but are thankful if they may be allowed to pay them. There is at this time a Parian philosopher residing in Athens, of whom I have heard; and I came to hear of him in this way:—I came across a man who has spent a world of money on the Sophists, Callias, the son of Hipponicus, and knowing that he had sons, I asked him: 'Callias,' I said, 'if your two sons were foals or calves, there would be no difficulty in finding some one to put over them; we should hire a trainer of horses, or a farmer probably, who would improve and perfect them in their own proper virtue and excellence; but as they are human beings, whom are you thinking of placing over them? Is there any one who understands human and political virtue? You must have thought about the matter, for you have sons; is there any one?' 'There is,' he said. 'Who is he?' said I; 'and of what country? and what does he charge?' 'Evenus[7] the Parian,' he replied; 'he is the man, and

---

[6] Noted Sophists and teachers, mainly of rhetoric and logic.

[7] A poet and teacher of oratory, from the island of Paros. The low sum he charged may indicate his low repute as a teacher. A mina was worth about forty dollars.

his charge is five minae.' Happy is Evenus, I said to myself, if he really has this wisdom, and teaches at such a moderate charge. Had I the same, I should have been very proud and conceited; but the truth is that I have no knowledge of the kind.

I dare say, Athenians, that some one among you will reply, 'Yes, Socrates, but what is the origin of these accusations which are brought against you; there must have been something strange which you have been doing? All these rumors and this talk about you would never have arisen if you had been like other men: tell us, then, what is the cause of them, for we should be sorry to judge hastily of you.' Now I regard this as a fair challenge, and I will endeavor to explain to you the reason why I am called wise and have such an evil fame. Please to attend then. And although some of you may think that I am joking, I declare that I will tell you the entire truth. Men of Athens, this reputation of mine has come of a certain sort of wisdom which I possess. If you ask me what kind of wisdom, I reply, wisdom such as may perhaps be attained by man, for to that extent I am inclined to believe that I am wise; whereas the persons of whom I was speaking have a superhuman wisdom, which I may fail to describe, because I have it not myself; and he who says that I have, speaks falsely, and is taking away my character. And here, O men of Athens, I must beg you not to interrupt me, even if I seem to say something extravagant. For the word which I will speak is not mine. I will refer you to a witness who is worthy of credit; that witness shall be the God of Delphi[8]—he will tell you about my wisdom, if I have any, and of what sort it is. You must have known Chaerephon; he was early a friend of mine, and also a friend of yours, for he shared in the recent exile of the people,[9] and returned with you. Well, Chaerephon, as you know, was very impetuous in all his doings, and he went to Delphi and boldly asked the oracle to tell him whether—as I was saying, I must beg you not to interrupt—he asked the oracle to tell him whether any one was wiser than I was, and the Pythian prophetess answered, that there was no man wiser. Chaerephon is dead himself; but his brother, who is in court, will confirm the truth of what I am saying.

Why do I mention this? Because I am going to explain to you why I have such an evil name. When I heard the answer, I said to myself, What can the god mean? and what is the interpretation of his riddle? for I know that I have no wisdom, small or great. What then can he mean when he says that I am the wisest of men? And yet he is a god, and cannot lie; that would be against his nature. After long consideration, I thought of a method of trying the question. I reflected that if I could only find a man wiser than myself, then I might go to the god with a refutation in my hand. I should say to him, 'Here is a man who is wiser than I am; but you said that I was the wisest.' Accordingly I went to one who had the reputation of wisdom, and observed him—his name I need not mention; he was a politician whom I selected for examination—and the result was as follows: When I began to talk with him, I could not help thinking that he was not really wise, al-

<hr>

[8] Site of the most famous temple of Apollo; the god's oracles were pronounced there by the Pythia, his priestess.

[9] Five years earlier, after the defeat of Athens by Sparta in 404, the "Thirty Tyrants" had temporarily ruled and terrorized Athens, driving the democratic leaders (who included Socrates' friend Chaerephon) into temporary exile. The democracy had been reestablished in 403.

though he was thought wise by many, and still wiser by himself; and thereupon I tried to explain to him that he thought himself wise, but was not really wise; and the consequence was that he hated me, and his enmity was shared by several who were present and heard me. So I left him, saying to myself, as I went away: Well, although I do not suppose that either of us knows anything really beautiful and good, I am better off than he is,—for he knows nothing, and thinks that he knows; I neither know nor think that I know. In this latter particular, then, I seem to have slightly the advantage of him. Then I went to another who had still higher pretensions to wisdom, and my conclusion was exactly the same. Whereupon I made another enemy of him, and of many others beside him.

Then I went to one man after another, being not unconscious of the enmity which I provoked, and I lamented and feared this: but necessity was laid upon me,—the word of God, I thought, ought to be considered first. And I said to myself, Go I must to all who appear to know, and find out the meaning of the oracle. And I swear to you, Athenians, by the dog I swear!—for I must tell you the truth—the result of my mission was just this: I found that the men most in repute were all but the most foolish; and that others less esteemed were really wiser and better. I will tell you the tale of my wanderings and of the 'Herculean'[10] labors, as I may call them, which I endured only to find at last the oracle irrefutable. After the politicians, I went to the poets; tragic, dithyrambic, and all sorts. And there, I said to myself, you will be instantly detected; now you will find out that you are more ignorant than they are. Accordingly, I took them some of the most elaborate passages in their own writings, and asked what was the meaning of them—thinking that they would teach me something. Will you believe me? I am almost ashamed to confess the truth, but I must say that there is hardly a person present who would not have talked better about their poetry than they did themselves. Then I knew that not by wisdom do poets write poetry, but by a sort of genius and inspiration; they are like diviners or soothsayers who also say many fine things, but do not understand the meaning of them.[11] The poets appeared to me to be much in the same case; and I further observed that upon the strength of their poetry they believed themselves to be the wisest of men in other things in which they were not wise. So I departed, conceiving myself to be superior to them for the same reason that I was superior to the politicians.

At last I went to the artisans,[12] for I was conscious that I knew nothing at all, as I may say, and I was sure that they knew many fine things; and here I was not mistaken, for they did know many things of which I was ignorant, and in this they certainly were wiser than I was. But I observed that even the good artisans fell into the same error as the poets;—because they were good workmen they thought that they also knew all sorts of high matters, and this defect in them overshadowed their wisdom; and therefore I asked myself on behalf of the oracle, whether I would like to be as I

[10] The legendary hero Hercules had been forced to undertake a series of superhumanly difficult tasks.

[11] This view of poets and of their interpreters is elaborated, half-playfully, by Socrates in Plato's *Ion.*

[12] Craftsmen.

was, neither having their knowledge nor their ignorance, or like them in both; and I made answer to myself and to the oracle that I was better off as I was.

This inquisition has led to my having many enemies of the worst and most dangerous kind, and has given occasion also to many calumnies. And I am called wise, for my hearers always imagine that I myself possess the wisdom which I find wanting in others: but the truth is, O men of Athens, that God only is wise; and by his answer he intends to show that the wisdom of men is worth little or nothing; he is not speaking of Socrates, he is only using my name by way of illustration, as if he said, He, O men, is the wisest, who, like Socrates, knows that his wisdom is in truth worth nothing. And so I go about the world, obedient to the god, and search and make enquiry into the wisdom of any one, whether citizen or stranger, who appears to be wise; and if he is not wise, then in vindication of the oracle I show him that he is not wise; and my occupation quite absorbs me, and I have no time to give either to any public matter of interest or to any concern of my own, but I am in utter poverty by reason of my devotion to the god.

There is another thing:—young men of the richer classes, who have not much to do, come about me of their own accord; they like to hear the pretenders examined, and they often imitate me, and proceed to examine others; there are plenty of persons, as they quickly discover, who think that they know something, but really know little or nothing; and then those who are examined by them instead of being angry with themselves are angry with me: This confounded Socrates, they say; this villainous misleader of youth!—and then if somebody asks them, Why, what evil does he practice or teach? they do not know, and cannot tell; but in order that they may not appear to be at a loss, they repeat the ready-made charges which are used against all philosophers about teaching things up in the clouds and under the earth, and having no gods, and making the worse appear the better cause; for they do not like to confess that their pretense of knowledge has been detected—which is the truth; and as they are numerous and ambitious and energetic, and are drawn up in battle array and have persuasive tongues, they have filled your ears with their loud and inveterate calumnies. And this is the reason why my three accusers, Meletus and Anytus and Lycon, have set upon me; Meletus, who has a quarrel with me on behalf of the poets; Anytus, on behalf of the craftsmen and politicians; Lycon, on behalf of the rhetoricians: and as I said at the beginning, I cannot expect to get rid of such a mass of calumny all in a moment. And this, O men of Athens, is the truth and the whole truth; I have concealed nothing, I have dissembled nothing. And yet, I know that my plainness of speech makes them hate me, and what is their hatred but a proof that I am speaking the truth?—Hence has arisen the prejudice against me; and this is the reason of it, as you will find out either in this or in any future enquiry.

I have said enough in my defense against the first class of my accusers; I turn to the second class. They are headed by Meletus, that good man and true lover of his country, as he calls himself. Against these, too, I must try to make a defense:—Let their affidavit be read: it contains something of this kind: It says that Socrates is a doer of evil, who corrupts the youth; and who does not believe in the gods of the state, but has other new divinities of his own. Such is the charge; and now let us examine the particular counts. He says that I am a doer of evil, and corrupt the youth; but I say, O men of Athens, that Meletus is a doer of evil, in that he pretends to be in earnest when he is only in jest, and is so eager to bring men to trial from a pretended zeal and interest about matters in which he really never had the smallest interest. And the truth of this I will endeavor to prove to you.

Come hither, Meletus, and let me ask a question of you. You think a great deal about the improvement of youth?

Yes, I do.

Tell the judges, then, who is their improver; for you must know, as you have taken the pains to discover their corrupter, and are citing and accusing me before them. Speak, then, and tell the judges who their improver is.—Observe, Meletus, that you are silent, and have nothing to say. But is not this rather disgraceful, and a very considerable proof of what I was saying, that you have no interest in the matter? Speak up, friend, and tell us who their improver is.

The laws.

But that, my good sir, is not my meaning. I want to know who the person is, who, in the first place, knows the laws.[13]

The judges, Socrates, who are present in court.

What, do you mean to say, Meletus, that they are able to instruct and improve youth?

Certainly they are.

What, all of them, or some only and not others?

All of them.

By the goddess Herè,[14] that is good news! There are plenty of improvers, then. And what do you say of the audience,—do they improve them?

Yes, they do.

And the senators?

Yes, the senators improve them.

But perhaps the members of the assembly corrupt them?—or do they too improve them?

They improve them.

Then every Athenian improves and elevates them; all with the exception of myself; and I alone am their corrupter? Is that what you affirm?

That is what I stoutly affirm.

I am very unfortunate if you are right. But suppose I ask you a question: How about horses? Does one man do them harm and all the world good? Is not the exact opposite the truth? One man is able to do them good, or at least not many;—the trainer of horses, that is to say, does them good, and others who have to do with them rather injure them? Is not that true, Meletus, of horses, or of any other animals? Most assuredly it is;

---

[13] In the following lines, Socrates calls into play his notorious talent for reducing his opponent's view to foolishness. The half-defiant, half-squirming Meletus is forced to define the noncorrupters of youth first as the "judges" (that is, the men empowered to render the verdict), then the entire audience, then the "senators" (the five hundred select members of the assembly who constituted the Athenian civic council), then the whole "assembly" which in law included the entire adult citizenry of Athens.

[14] Hera, queen of the gods; this oath is often used by Socrates.

whether you and Anytus say yes or no. Happy indeed would be the condition of youth if they had one corrupter only, and all the rest of the world were their improvers. But you, Meletus, have sufficiently shown that you never had a thought about the young: your carelessness is seen in your not caring about the very things which you bring against me.

And now, Meletus, I will ask you another question—by Zeus I will: Which is better, to live among bad citizens, or among good ones? Answer, friend, I say; the question is one which may be easily answered. Do not the good do their neighbors good, and the bad do them evil?

Certainly.

And is there any one who would rather be injured than benefited by those who live with him? Answer, my good friend, the law requires you to answer—does any one like to be injured?

Certainly not.

And when you accuse me of corrupting and deteriorating the youth, do you allege that I corrupt them intentionally or unintentionally?

Intentionally, I say.

But you have just admitted that the good do their neighbors good, and the evil do them evil. Now, is that a truth which your superior wisdom has recognized thus early in life, and am I, at my age, in such darkness and ignorance as not to know that if a man with whom I have to live is corrupted by me, I am very likely to be harmed by him; and yet I corrupt him, and intentionally, too—so you say, although neither I nor any other human being is ever likely to be convinced by you. But either I do not corrupt them, or I corrupt them unintentionally; and on either view of the case you lie. If my offense is unintentional, the law has no cognizance of unintentional offenses: you ought to have taken me privately, and warned and admonished me; for if I had been better advised, I should have left off doing what I only did unintentionally—no doubt I should; but you would have nothing to say to me and refused to teach me. And now you bring me up in this court, which is a place not of instruction, but of punishment.

It will be very clear to you, Athenians, as I was saying, that Meletus has no care at all, great or small, about the matter. But still I should like to know, Meletus, in what I am affirmed to corrupt the young. I suppose you mean, as I infer from your indictment, that I teach them not to acknowledge the gods which the state acknowledges, but some other new divinities or spiritual agencies in their stead. These are the lessons by which I corrupt the youth, as you say.

Yes, that I say emphatically.

Then, by the gods, Meletus, of whom we are speaking, tell me and the court, in somewhat plainer terms, what you mean! for I do not as yet understand whether you affirm that I teach other men to acknowledge some gods, and therefore that I do believe in gods, and am not an entire atheist—this you do not lay to my charge,—but only you say that they are not the same gods which the city recognizes—the charge is that they are different gods. Or, do you mean that I am an atheist simply, and a teacher of atheism?

I mean the latter—that you are a complete atheist.

What an extraordinary statement! Why do you think so, Meletus? Do you mean that I do not believe in the godhead of the sun or moon,[15] like other men?

I assure you, judges, that he does not: for he says that the sun is stone, and the moon earth.

Friend Meletus, you think that you are accusing Anaxagoras:[16] and you have but a bad opinion of the judges, if you fancy them illiterate to such a degree as not to know that these doctrines are found in the books of Anaxagoras the Clazomenian, which are full of them. And so, forsooth, the youth are said to be taught them by Socrates, when there are not unfrequently exhibitions of them at the theater (price of admission one drachma at the most); and they might pay their money, and laugh at Socrates if he pretends to father these extraordinary views. And so, Meletus, you really think that I do not believe in any god?

I swear by Zeus that you believe absolutely in none at all.

Nobody will believe you, Meletus, and I am pretty sure that you do not believe yourself. I cannot help thinking, men of Athens, that Meletus is reckless and impudent, and that he has written this indictment in a spirit of mere wantonness and youthful bravado. Has he not compounded a riddle, thinking to try me? He said to himself:—I shall see whether the wise Socrates will discover my facetious contradiction, or whether I shall be able to deceive him and the rest of them. For he certainly does appear to me to contradict himself in the indictment as much as if he said that Socrates is guilty of not believing in the gods, and yet of believing in them—but this is not like a person who is in earnest.

I should like you, O men of Athens, to join me in examining what I conceive to be his inconsistency; and do you, Meletus, answer. And I must remind the audience of my request that they would not make a disturbance if I speak in my accustomed manner:

Did ever man, Meletus, believe in the existence of human things, and not of human beings? . . . I wish, men of Athens, that he would answer, and not be always trying to get up an interruption. Did ever any man believe in horsemanship, and not in horses? or in flute-playing, and not in flute-players? No, my friend; I will answer to you and to the court, as you refuse to answer for yourself. There is no man who ever did. But now please to answer the next question: Can a man believe in spiritual and divine agencies, and not in spirits or in demigods?[17]

---

[15] Apollo was the god of the sun, Artemis the goddess of the moon; but, whether the sun and moon were literally identified with these deities or not, reverence for the two great celestial bodies was a hallmark of religious piety for the Greeks. Socrates did, in fact, hold the sun and moon in awe, as is shown in Plato's *Symposium*.

[16] A philosopher-scientist, born around 500 B.C. Socrates, concerned almost entirely with ethics, would have resisted such materialist astrophysical theories. The reference to the theater a few lines below may mean that Anaxagoras' ideas were explored by the playwrights (particularly Euripides and Aristophanes) or that the philosopher's writings could be purchased there (or in some similar public place). In any event, Socrates' point is that such religiously heterodox ideas were freely available to the public apart from anything he might have taught.

[17] The ensuing cross-examination of Meletus, logically sound or not, should probably be understood as an attempt by Socrates to prove contemptuously that he could easily defeat his opponents at their legalistic game if he did not have more substantial arguments to make (the ones that emerge in the following parts of his speech).

He cannot.

How lucky I am to have extracted that answer, by the assistance of the court! But then you swear in the indictment that I teach and believe in divine or spiritual agencies (new or old, no matter for that); at any rate, I believe in spiritual agencies,—so you say and swear in the affidavit; and yet if I believe in divine beings, how can I help believing in spirits or demi-gods;—must I not? To be sure I must; and therefore I may assume that your silence gives consent. Now what are spirits or demigods? are they not either gods or the sons of gods?

Certainly they are.

But this is what I call the facetious riddle invented by you: the demigods or spirits are gods, and you say first that I do not believe in gods, and then again that I do believe in gods; that is, if I believe in demigods. For if the demigods are the illegitimate sons of gods, whether by the nymphs or by any other mothers, of whom they are said to be the sons—what human being will ever believe that there are no gods if they are the sons of gods? You might as well affirm the existence of mules,[18] and deny that of horses and asses. Such nonsense, Meletus, could only have been intended by you to make trial of me. You have put this into the indictment because you had nothing real of which to accuse me. But no one who has a particle of under-standing will ever be convinced by you that the same men can believe in divine and superhuman things, and yet not believe that there are gods and demigods and heroes.

I have said enough in answer to the charge of Meletus: any elaborate defense is unnecessary; but I know only too well how many are the enmities which I have incurred, and this is what will be my destruction if I am destroyed;—not Meletus, nor yet Anytus, but the envy and detraction of the world, which has been the death of many good men, and will probably be the death of many more; there is no danger of my being the last of them.

Some one will say: And are you not ashamed, Socrates, of a course of life which is likely to bring you to an untimely end? To him I may fairly answer: There you are mistaken: a man who is good for anything ought not to calculate the chance of living or dying; he ought only to consider whether in doing anything he is doing right or wrong—acting the part of a good man or of a bad. Whereas, upon your view, the heroes who fell at Troy were not good for much, and the son of Thetis[19] above all, who altogether despised danger in comparison with disgrace; and when he was so eager to slay Hector, his goddess mother said to him, that if he avenged his companion Patroclus, and slew Hector, he would die himself—'Fate,' she said, in these or the like words, 'waits for you next after Hector;' he, receiving this warning, utterly despised danger and death, and instead of fearing them, feared rather to live in dishonor, and not to avenge his friend. 'Let me die forthwith,' he replies, 'and be avenged of my enemy, rather than abide here by the beaked ships, a laughing-stock and a burden

---

[18] A mule is a sterile animal produced by the union of a jackass with a mare.

[19] A sea nymph, mother of Achilles, the hero of Homer's *Iliad*. The Trojan prince and hero Hector had killed Achilles' best friend, Patroclus, an event that brought Achilles back into the battle after a period of sulky neutrality occasioned by his quarrel with the Greek commander, Agamemnon. The dialogue cited here, between Achilles and Thetis, occurs in Book XVIII of the *Iliad*.

of the earth.' Had Achilles any thought of death and danger? For wherever a man's place is, whether the place which he has chosen or that in which he has been placed by a commander, there he ought to remain in the hour of danger; he should not think of death or of anything but of disgrace. And this, O men of Athens, is a true saying.

Strange, indeed, would be my conduct, O men of Athens, if I who, when I was ordered by the generals whom you chose to command me at Potidaea and Amphipolis and Delium,[20] remained where they placed me, like any other man, facing death—if now, when, as I conceive and imagine, God orders me to fulfil the philosopher's mission of searching into myself and other men, I were to desert my post through fear of death, or any other fear; that would indeed be strange, and I might justly be arraigned in court for denying the existence of the gods, if I disobeyed the oracle because I was afraid of death, fancying that I was wise when I was not wise. For the fear of death is indeed the pretense of wisdom, and not real wisdom, being a pretense of knowing the unknown; and no one knows whether death, which men in their fear apprehend to be the greatest evil, may not be the greatest good. Is not this ignorance of a disgraceful sort, the ignorance which is the conceit that a man knows what he does not know? And in this respect only I believe myself to differ from men in general, and may perhaps claim to be wiser than they are:—that whereas I know but little of the world below, I do not suppose that I know: but I do know that injustice and disobedience to a better, whether God or man, is evil and dishonorable, and I will never fear or avoid a possible good rather than a certain evil. And therefore if you let me go now, and are not convinced by Anytus, who said that since I had been prosecuted I must be put to death; (or if not that I ought never to have been prosecuted at all); and that if I escape now, your sons will all be utterly ruined by listening to my words—if you say to me, Socrates, this time we will not mind Anytus, and you shall be let off, but upon one condition, that you are not to enquire and speculate in this way any more, and that if you are caught doing so again you shall die;—if this was the condition on which you let me go, I should reply: Men of Athens, I honor and love you; but I shall obey God rather than you, and while I have life and strength I shall never cease from the practice and teaching of philosophy, exhorting any one whom I meet and saying to him after my manner: You, my friend,—a citizen of the great and mighty and wise city of Athens,—are you not ashamed of heaping up the greatest amount of money and honor and reputation, and caring so little about wisdom and truth and the greatest improvement of the soul, which you never regard or heed at all? And if the person with whom I am arguing, says: Yes, but I do care; then I do not leave him or let him go at once; but I proceed to interrogate and examine and cross-examine him, and if I think that he has no virtue in him, but only says that he has, I reproach him with undervaluing the greater, and overvaluing the less. And I shall repeat the same words to every one whom I meet, young and old, citizen and alien, but especially to the citizens, inasmuch as they are my brethren. For know

---

[20] Sites of battles (fought respectively in 432, 422, and 424) in which Socrates had served bravely as a soldier. At Potidaea Socrates had saved the life of the Athenian soldier-playboy Alcibiades; see Plato's *Symposium*.

that this is the command of God; and I believe that no greater good has ever happened in the state than my service to the God. For I do nothing but go about persuading you all, old and young alike, not to take thought for your persons or your properties, but first and chiefly to care about the greatest improvement of the soul. I tell you that virtue is not given by money, but that from virtue comes money and every other good of man, public as well as private. This is my teaching, and if this is the doctrine which corrupts the youth, I am a mischievous person. But if any one says that this is not my teaching, he is speaking an untruth. Wherefore, O men of Athens, I say to you, do as Anytus bids or not as Anytus bids, and either acquit me or not; but whichever you do, understand that I shall never alter my ways, not even if I have to die many times.

Men of Athens, do not interrupt, but hear me; there was an understanding between us that you should hear me to the end: I have something more to say, at which you may be inclined to cry out; but I believe that to hear me will be good for you, and therefore I beg that you will not cry out. I would have you know, that if you kill such an one as I am, you will injure yourselves more than you will injure me. Nothing will injure me, not Meletus nor yet Anytus—they cannot, for a bad man is not permitted to injure a better than himself. I do not deny that Anytus may, perhaps, kill him, or drive him into exile, or deprive him of civil rights; and he may imagine, and others may imagine, that he is inflicting a great injury upon him: but there I do not agree. For the evil of doing as he is doing—the evil of unjustly taking away the life of another—is greater far.

And now, Athenians, I am not going to argue for my own sake, as you may think, but for yours, that you may not sin against the God by condemning me, who am his gift to you. For if you kill me you will not easily find a successor to me, who, if I may use such a ludicrous figure of speech, am a sort of gadfly, given to the state by God; and the state is a great and noble steed who is tardy in his motions owing to his very size, and requires to be stirred into life. I am that gadfly which God has attached to the state, and all day long and in all places am always fastening upon you, arousing and persuading and reproaching you. You will not easily find another like me, and therefore I would advise you to spare me. I dare say that you may feel out of temper (like a person who is suddenly awakened from sleep), and you think that you might easily strike me dead as Anytus advises, and then you would sleep on for the remainder of your lives, unless God in his care of you sent you another gadfly. When I say that I am given to you by God, the proof of my mission is this:—if I had been like other men, I should not have neglected all my own concerns or patiently seen the neglect of them during all these years, and have been doing yours, coming to you individually like a father or elder brother, exhorting you to regard virtue; such conduct, I say, would be unlike human nature. If I had gained anything, or if my exhortations had been paid, there would have been some sense in my doing so; but now, as you will perceive, not even the impudence of my accusers dares to say that I have ever exacted or sought pay of any one; of that they have no witness. And I have a sufficient witness to the truth of what I say—my poverty.

Some one may wonder why I go about in private giving advice and busying myself with the concerns of others, but do not venture to come forward in public and advise the state. I will tell you why. You have heard me speak at sundry times and in divers places of an oracle or sign which comes to me, and is the divinity which Meletus ridicules in the indictment. This sign, which is a kind of voice, first began to come to me when I was a child; it always forbids but never commands me to do anything which I am going to do. This is what deters me from being a politician. And rightly, as I think. For I am certain, O men of Athens, that if I had engaged in politics, I should have perished long ago, and done no good either to you or to myself. And do not be offended at my telling you the truth: for the truth is, that no man who goes to war with you or any other multitude, honestly striving against the many lawless and unrighteous deeds which are done in a state, will save his life; he who will fight for the right, if he would live even for a brief space, must have a private station and not a public one.

I can give you convincing evidence of what I say, not words only, but what you value far more—actions. Let me relate to you a passage of my own life which will prove to you that I should never have yielded to injustice from any fear of death, and that 'as I should have refused to yield' I must have died at once. I will tell you a tale of the courts, not very interesting perhaps, but nevertheless true. The only office of state which I ever held, O men of Athens, was that of senator: the tribe Antiochis, which is my tribe, had the presidency at the trial of the generals who had not taken up the bodies of the slain after the battle of Arginusae; and you proposed to try them in a body, contrary to law, as you all thought afterwards; but at the time I was the only one of the Prytanes who was opposed to the illegality, and I gave my vote against you; and when the orators threatened to impeach and arrest me, and you called and shouted, I made up my mind that I would run the risk, having law and justice with me, rather than take part in your injustice because I feared imprisonment and death. This happened in the days of the democracy.[21] But when the oligarchy of the Thirty was in power, they sent for me and four others into the rotunda, and bade us bring Leon[22] the Salaminian from Salamis, as they wanted to put him to death. This was a specimen of the sort of commands which they were always giving with the view of implicating as many as possible in their crimes; and then I showed, not in word only but in deed, that, if I may be allowed to use such an expression, I cared not a straw for death, and that my great and only care was lest I should do an unrighteous or unholy thing. For the strong arm of that oppressive power did not frighten me into doing wrong; and when we came out of the rotunda the other four went to Salamis and fetched Leon, but I went quietly home. For which I might have lost my life, had not the power of the Thirty shortly afterwards come to an end. And many will witness to my words.

[21] The Athenian senate consisted of five hundred members, fifty from each of the ten phylae, or "tribes." Socrates belonged to a tribe named for the mythical figure Antiochus. Each tribe served for one-tenth of the year as the executive body of the senate; during that period they were called "Prytanes." While Socrates was serving in that capacity, certain Athenian commanders were indicted for allegedly neglecting the dead after the naval battle of Arginusae in 406. Socrates refused to participate in the trial, which violated due process of Athenian law in a number of ways.

[22] As he had defied the authority of the democratic state, Socrates also defied the tyrannical "Thirty" who ruled in 404, by refusing to extradite Leon from Salamis after he had fled there to escape the despotic regime.

Now do you really imagine that I could have survived all these years, if I had led a public life, supposing that like a good man I had always maintained the right and had made justice, as I ought, the first thing? No indeed, men of Athens, neither I nor any other man. But I have been always the same in all my actions, public as well as private, and never have I yielded any base compliance to those who are slanderously termed my disciples, or to any other. Not that I have any regular disciples. But if anyone likes to come and hear me while I am pursuing my mission, whether he be young or old, he is not excluded. Nor do I converse only with those who pay; but any one, whether he be rich or poor, may ask and answer me and listen to my words; and whether he turns out to be a bad man or a good one, neither result can be justly imputed to me; for I never taught or professed to teach him anything. And if any one says that he has ever learned or heard anything from me in private which all the world has not heard, let me tell you that he is lying.

But I shall be asked, Why do people delight in continually conversing with you? I have told you already, Athenians, the whole truth about this matter: they like to hear the cross-examination of the pretenders to wisdom; there is amusement in it. Now this duty of cross-examining other men has been imposed upon me by God; and has been signified to me by oracles, visions, and in every way in which the will of divine power was ever intimated to any one. This is true, O Athenians; or, if not true, would be soon refuted. If I am or have been corrupting the youth, those of them who are now grown up and have become sensible that I gave them bad advice in the days of their youth should come forward as accusers, and take their revenge; or if they do not like to come themselves, some of their relatives, fathers, brothers, or other kinsmen, should say what evil their families have suffered at my hands. Now is their time. Many of them I see in the court. There is Crito, who is of the same age and of the same deme[23] with myself, and there is Critobulus his son, whom I also see. Then again there is Lysanias of Sphettus, who is the father of Aeschines—he is present; and also there is Antiphon of Cephisus, who is the father of Epigenes; and there are the brothers of several who have associated with me. There is Nicostratus the son of Theosdotides, and the brother of Theodotus (now Theodotus himself is dead, and therefore he, at any rate, will not seek to stop him); and there is Paralus the son of Demodocus, who had a brother Theages; and Adeimantus the son of Ariston, whose brother Plato[24] is present; and Aeantodorus, who is the brother of Apollodorus, whom I also see. I might mention a great many others, some of whom Meletus should have produced as witnesses in the course of his speech; and let him still produce them, if he has forgotten—I will make way for him. And let him say, if he has any testimony of the sort which he can produce. Nay, Athenians, the very opposite is the truth. For all these are ready to witness on behalf of the corrupter, of the injurer of their kindred, as Meletus and Anytus call me; not the corrupted youth only—there might have been a motive for that—but their uncorrupted elder relatives. Why should they

[23] District.
[24] The author of the present work. Several of the persons mentioned appear in other works by Plato.

too support me with their testimony? Why, indeed, except for the sake of truth and justice, and because they know that I am speaking the truth, and that Meletus is a liar.

Well, Athenians, this and the like of this is all the defense which I have to offer. Yet a word more. Perhaps there may be some one who is offended at me, when he calls to mind how he himself on a similar, or even a less serious occasion, prayed and entreated the judges with many tears, and how he produced children in court, which was a moving spectacle, together with a host of relations and friends; whereas I, who am probably in danger of my life, will do none of these things. The contrast may occur to his mind, and he may be set against me, and vote in anger because he is displeased at me on this account. Now if there be such a person among you,—mind, I do not say that there is,—to him I may fairly reply: My friend, I am a man, and like other men, a creature of flesh and blood, and not 'of wood or stone,' as Homer says;[25] and I have a family, yes, and sons, O Athenians, three in number, one almost a man, and two others who are still young; and yet I will not bring any of them hither in order to petition you for an acquittal. And why not? Not from any self-assertion or want of respect for you. Whether I am or am not afraid of death is another question, of which I will not now speak. But, having regard to public opinion, I feel that such conduct would be discreditable to myself, and to you, and to the whole state. One who has reached my years, and who has a name for wisdom, ought not to demean himself. Whether this opinion of me be deserved or not, at any rate the world has decided that Socrates is in some way superior to other men. And if those among you who are said to be superior in wisdom and courage, and any other virtue, demean themselves in this way, how shameful is their conduct! I have seen men of reputation, when they have been condemned, behaving in the strangest manner: they seemed to fancy that they were going to suffer something dreadful if they died, and that they could be immortal if you only allowed them to live; and I think that such are a dishonor to the state, and that any stranger coming in would have said of them that the most eminent men of Athens, to whom the Athenians themselves give honor and command, are no better than women. And I say that these things ought not to be done by those of us who have a reputation; and if they are done, you ought not to permit them; you ought rather to show that you are far more disposed to condemn the man who gets up a doleful scene and makes the city ridiculous, than him who holds his peace.

But, setting aside the question of public opinion, there seems to be something wrong in asking a favor of a judge, and thus procuring an acquittal, instead of informing and convincing him. For his duty is, not to make a present of justice, but to give judgment; and he has sworn that he will judge according to the laws, and not according to his own good pleasure; and we ought not to encourage you, nor should you allow yourselves to be encouraged, in this habit of perjury—there can be no piety in that. Do not then require me to do what I consider dishonorable and impious and wrong, especially now, when I am being tried for impiety on the indictment

[25] The words are addressed to the disguised Odysseus by his wife Penelope, in Book XIX of Homer's *Odyssey*.

of Meletus. For if, O men of Athens, by force of persuasion and entreaty I could overpower your oaths, then I should be teaching you to believe that there are no gods, and in defending should simply convict myself of the charge of not believing in them. But that is not so—far otherwise. For I do believe that there are gods, and in a sense higher than that in which any of my accusers believe in them. And to you and to God I commit my cause, to be determined by you as is best for you and me.[26]

There are many reasons why I am not grieved, O men of Athens, at the vote of condemnation. I expected it, and am only surprised that the votes are so nearly equal; for I had thought that the majority against me would have been far larger; but now, had thirty votes gone over to the other side, I should have been acquitted. And I may say, I think, that I have escaped Meletus. I may say more; for without the assistance of Anytus and Lycon, any one may see that he would not have had a fifth part of the votes, as the law requires, in which case he would have incurred a fine of a thousand drachmae.[27]

And so he proposes death as the penalty. And what shall I propose on my part, O men of Athens? Clearly that which is my due. And what is my due? What return shall be made to the man who has never had the wit to be idle during his whole life; but has been careless of what the many care for—wealth, and family interests, and military offices, and speaking in the assembly, and magistracies, and plots, and parties. Reflecting that I was really too honest a man to be a politician and live, I did not go where I could do no good to you or to myself; but where I could do the greatest good privately to every one of you, thither I went, and sought to persuade every man among you that he must look to himself, and seek virtue and wisdom before he looks to his private interests, and look to the state before he looks to the interests of the state; and that this should be the order which he observes in all his actions. What shall be done to such an one? Doubtless some good thing, O men of Athens, if he has his reward; and the good should be of a kind suitable to him. What would be a reward suitable to a poor man who is your benefactor, and who desires leisure that he may instruct you? There can be no reward so fitting as maintenance in the Prytaneum,[28] O men of Athens, a reward which he deserves far more than the citizen who has won the prize at Olympia in the horse or chariot race, whether the chariots were drawn by two horses or by many. For I am in want, and he has enough; and he only gives you the appearance of happiness, and I give you the reality. And if I am to estimate the penalty fairly, I should say that maintenance in the Prytaneum is the just return.

[26] At this point the jurors cast their votes; about 280 vote for conviction, 220 for acquittal. (Plato does not describe these deliberations; there has been no omission from the text.) The next decision is on the sentence.

[27] Socrates ironically intimates that each of his three accusers has captured a third of the vote cast against him—approximately ninety-three apiece, a number lower than the one-fifth (about one hundred) necessary for an accuser to avoid paying a fine. The fine was intended to discourage capricious prosecutions.

[28] A place on the Acropolis where benefactors of Athens were honored. Olympia, in southwestern Greece, was the site of a great festival, held every four years, featuring athletic contests. The modern Olympic games are named for this festival.

Perhaps you think that I am braving you in what I am saying now, as in what I said before about the tears and prayers. But this is not so. I speak rather because I am convinced that I never intentionally wronged any one, although I cannot convince you—the time has been too short; if there were a law in Athens, as there is in other cities, that a capital cause should not be decided in one day, then I believe that I should have convinced you. But I cannot in a moment refute great slanders; and, as I am convinced that I never wronged another, I will assuredly not wrong myself. I will not say of myself that I deserve any evil, or propose any penalty. Why should I? Because I am afraid of the penalty of death which Meletus proposes? When I do not know whether death is a good or an evil, why should I propose a penalty which would certainly be an evil? Shall I say imprisonment? And why should I live in prison, and be the slave of the magistrates of the year—of the Eleven?[29] Or shall the penalty be a fine, and imprisonment until the fine is paid? There is the same objection. I should have to lie in prison, for money I have none, and cannot pay. And if I say exile (and this may possibly be the penalty which you will affix), I must indeed be blinded by the love of life, if I am so irrational as to expect that when you, who are my own citizens, cannot endure my discourses and words, and have found them so grievous and odious that you will have no more of them, others are likely to endure me. No indeed, men of Athens, that is not very likely. And what a life should I lead, at my age, wandering from city to city, ever changing my place of exile, and always being driven out! For I am quite sure that wherever I go, there, as here, the young men will flock to me; and if I drive them away, their elders will drive me out at their request; and if I let them come, their fathers and friends will drive me out for their sakes.

Some one will say: Yes, Socrates, but cannot you hold your tongue, and then you may go into a foreign city, and no one will interfere with you? Now I have great difficulty in making you understand my answer to this. For if I tell you that to do as you say would be a disobedience to the God, and therefore that I cannot hold my tongue, you will not believe that I am serious; and if I say again that daily to discourse about virtue, and of those other things about which you hear me examining myself and others, is the greatest good of man, and that the unexamined life is not worth living,[30] you are still less likely to believe me. Yet I say what is true, although a thing of which it is hard for me to persuade you. Also, I have never been accustomed to think that I deserve to suffer any harm. Had I money I might have estimated the offense at what I was able to pay, and not have been much the worse. But I have none, and therefore I must ask you to proportion the fine to my means. Well, perhaps I could afford a mina, and therefore I propose that penalty:[31] Plato, Crito, Critobulus, and Apollodorus, my friends here, bid me say thirty minae, and they will be the sureties. Let thirty minae be the penalty; for which sum they will be ample security to you.[32]

---

[29] A public committee that enforced and supervised criminal penalties, including executions. It was made up of a representative from each of the ten "tribes," plus a secretary.

[30] One of Socrates' most memorable axioms.

[31] Socrates' decision to propose a monetary penalty is not mercenary but just the opposite: it is a dramatization of his contempt for money as a measure of life and values.

[32] At this point, the five hundred judges cast another split vote, for the death penalty. (Again, Plato does not describe these deliberations; the text given here is complete.)

Not much time will be gained, O Athenians, in return for the evil name which you will get from the detractors of the city, who will say that you killed Socrates, a wise man; for they will call me wise, even although I am not wise, when they want to reproach you. If you had waited a little while, your desire would have been fulfilled in the course of nature. For I am far advanced in years, as you may perceive, and not far from death. I am speaking now not to all of you, but only to those who have condemned me to death. And I have another thing to say to them: You think that I was convicted because I had no words of the sort which would have procured my acquittal—I mean, if I had thought fit to leave nothing undone or unsaid. Not so; the deficiency which led to my conviction was not of words—certainly not. But I had not the boldness or impudence or inclination to address you as you would have liked me to do, weeping and wailing and lamenting, and saying and doing many things which you have been accustomed to hear from others, and which, as I maintain, are unworthy of me. I thought at the time that I ought not to do anything common or mean when in danger: nor do I now repent of the style of my defense; I would rather die having spoken after my manner, than speak in your manner and live. For neither in war nor yet at law ought I or any man to use every way of escaping death. Often in battle there can be no doubt that if a man will throw away his arms, and fall on his knees before his pursuers, he may escape death; and in other dangers there are other ways of escaping death, if a man is willing to say and do anything. The difficulty, my friends, is not to avoid death, but to avoid unrighteousness; for that runs faster than death. I am old and move slowly, and the slower runner has overtaken me, and my accusers are keen and quick, and the faster runner, who is unrighteousness, has overtaken them. And now I depart hence condemned by you to suffer the penalty of death,—they too go their ways condemned by the truth to suffer the penalty of villainy and wrong; and I must abide by my award—let them abide by theirs. I suppose that these things may be regarded as fated,—and I think that they are well.

And now, O men who have condemned me, I would fain prophesy to you; for I am about to die, and in the hour of death men are gifted with prophetic power. And I prophesy to you who are my murderers, that immediately after my departure punishment far heavier than you have inflicted on me will surely await you. Me you have killed because you wanted to escape the accuser, and not to give an account of your lives. But that will not be as you suppose: far otherwise. For I say that there will be more accusers of you than there are now; accusers whom hitherto I have restrained: and as they are younger they will be more inconsiderate with you, and you will be more offended at them. If you think that by killing men you can prevent some one from censuring your evil lives, you are mistaken; that is not a way of escape which is either possible or honorable; the easiest and the noblest way is not to be disabling others, but to be improving yourselves. This is the prophecy which I utter before my departure to the judges who have condemned me.

Friends, who would have acquitted me, I would like also to talk with you about the thing which has come to pass, while the magistrates are busy, and before I go to the place at which I must die. Stay then a little, for we may as well talk with one another while there is time. You are my friends, and I should like to show you the meaning of this event which has happened to me. O my judges—for you I may truly call judges—I should like to tell you of a wonderful circumstance. Hitherto the divine faculty of which the internal oracle is the source has constantly been in the habit of opposing me even about trifles, if I was going to make a slip or error in any matter; and now as you see there has come upon me that which may be thought, and is generally believed to be, the last and worst evil. But the oracle made no sign of opposition, either when I was leaving my house in the morning, or when I was on my way to the court, or while I was speaking, at anything which I was going to say; and yet I have often been stopped in the middle of a speech, but now in nothing I either said or did touching the matter in hand has the oracle opposed me. What do I take to be the explanation of this silence? I will tell you. It is an intimation that what has happened to me is a good, and that those of us who think that death is an evil are in error. For the customary sign would surely have opposed me had I been going to evil and not to good.

Let us reflect in another way, and we shall see that there is great reason to hope that death is a good; for one of two things—either death is a state of nothingness and utter unconsciousness, or, as men say, there is a change and migration of the soul from this world to another. Now if you suppose that there is no consciousness, but a sleep like the sleep of him who is undisturbed even by dreams, death will be an unspeakable gain. For if a person were to select the night in which his sleep was undisturbed even by dreams, and were to compare with this the other days and nights of his life, and then were to tell us how many days and nights he had passed in the course of his life better and more pleasantly than this one, I think that any man, I will not say a private man, but even the great king will not find many such days or nights, when compared with the others. Now if death be of such a nature, I say that to die is gain; for eternity is then only a single night. But if death is the journey to another place, and there, as men say, all the dead abide, what good, O my friends and judges, can be greater than this? If indeed when the pilgrim arrives in the world below, he is delivered from the professors of justice in this world, and finds the true judges who are said to give judgment there, Minos and Rhadamanthus and Aeacus and Triptolemus,[33] and other sons of God who were righteous in their own life, that pilgrimage will be worth making. What would not a man give if he might converse with Orpheus and Musaeus and Hesiod and Homer?[34] Nay, if this be true, let me die again and again. I myself, too, shall have a wonderful interest in there meeting and conversing with Palamedes, and Ajax[35] the son of Telamon, and any other ancient hero who has suffered death through an unjust judgment; and there will be no small pleasure, as I think, in comparing my own sufferings with theirs. Above all, I shall then be able to continue my search into true and false knowledge; as in this world, so also in the next; and I shall find out who is wise, and who pretends to be wise, and is not. What would not a man give, O judges, to be able to examine the leader of the great Trojan expedition; or Odysseus or

---

[33] The four judges of the dead in the afterlife.
[34] Great poets, legendary and real.
[35] Two victims of unjust or dubious trials or verdicts.

Sisyphus,[36] or numberless others, men and women too! What infinite delight would there be in conversing with them and asking them questions! In another world they do not put a man to death for asking questions: assuredly not. For besides being happier than we are, they will be immortal, if what is said is true.

Wherefore, O judges, be of good cheer about death, and know of a certainty, that no evil can happen to a good man, either in life or after death. He and his are not neglected by the gods; nor has my own approaching end happened by mere chance. But I see clearly that the time had arrived when it was better for me to die and be released from trouble; wherefore the oracle gave no sign. For which reason, also, I am not angry with my condemners, or with my accusers; they have done me no harm, although they did not mean to do me any good; and for this I may gently blame them.

Still I have a favor to ask of them. When my sons are grown up, I would ask you, O my friends, to punish them; and I would have you trouble them, as I have troubled you, if they seem to care about riches, or anything, more than about virtue; or if they pretend to be something when they are really nothing,—then reprove them, as I have reproved you, for not caring about that for which they ought to care, and thinking that they are something when they are really nothing. And if you do this, both I and my sons will have received justice at your hands.

The hour of departure has arrived, and we go our ways—I to die, and you to live. Which is better God only knows.[37]

---

[36] Both were noted for their cunning. In mentioning them here, Socrates is anticipating a meeting not merely with eminent men but with adversaries whose mental agility will put his powers to a real test.

[37] In two other dialogues, the *Crito* and the *Phaedo*, the story of Socrates' last days is concluded. In the former, his friend Crito pleads with Socrates to accept an opportunity to escape from Athens, to which Socrates replies (in his usual style of reasoned argument) that such a course would be wrong, since to defy the Athenian laws that have condemned him is the equivalent of rejecting parents who have nurtured him and whose authority he has implicitly accepted throughout his life. The *Phaedo* includes Socrates' argument for the immortality and inviolability of the soul and narrates his serene death, imposed by his drinking of the poison liquid called hemlock.

Aristotle
(384–322 B.C.)

Probably the most versatile and encyclopedic philosopher who ever lived, Aristotle inherited the Platonic tradition but pointed it in important new directions. He was born in 384 B.C. in Stagira (hence his epithet "the Stagirite"), a town in Macedonia on the far northern border of Greece. Since his father was court physician to the Macedonian king, Aristotle absorbed in his early years a good deal of information about the life sciences—a fact that permanently influenced the tendency of his thought. In 367, at the age of seventeen, he went to Athens and studied there in the Academy directed by Plato. Plato admired his pupil and had a strong influence on him; the young Aristotle seems to have believed even more strongly than Plato that the human soul suffered from the prison-house of the body, a view he later changed radically.

When Plato died (in 348 or 347), Aristotle left Athens for twelve years. At Assus, in Asia Minor, he undertook the education of the ruler and wrote part of his Politics, *arguing that the main purpose of the state was to promote the philosophic life among its best citizens. He also married the ruler's niece and had a daughter by her; after his wife's death he had a son, Nicomachus, by another woman. (It is this son who, because he was believed to have edited the work, gave his name to the* Nicomachean Ethics, *one of two treatises by Aristotle on the subject.) After spending three years at Assus, Aristotle moved to the island of Lesbos, where he resumed his investigation of the life sciences, especially marine biology. Here he combined with his characteristic close observation of objective data an equally characteristic conviction that the various creatures are designed to have distinctive purposes.*

Around 342 he returned to his homeland, Macedonia, where the great king Philip now reigned. There he was entrusted with the education of Philip's teen-aged son, Alexander. Aristotle's intention was to instill in the prince a combination of the martial and philosophic virtues. When Philip was murdered in 336, Alexander succeeded him, going on to complete the conquest of Greece that his father had begun and thereafter subjugating the Greeks' inveterate Persian enemies and other empires in a vast region stretching as far east as India. In the process, Alexander made obsolete the traditional Greek city-state that Aristotle, anachronistically, continued throughout his life to think of as the political norm.

By 335 Aristotle had returned to Athens (which was now controlled by Macedonia), where he established the Lyceum, a rival institution to the Academy. At the Lyceum, which had an unprecedented library and extensive facilities for scientific work, Aristotle and his colleagues investigated virtually all areas of science, philosophy, and other branches of learning. In 323, at Alexander's death, the Athenians rebelled against Macedonian domination, with which Aristotle (accurately or not) was associated in the public mind. A charge of impiety was brought against him. His life endangered, Aristotle left Athens, apparently in order to prevent the Athenians from repeating the crime they had committed in executing Plato's mentor, Socrates. One year later, in 322, Aristotle died in Chalcis, a town north of Athens.

Most people today find Plato's dialogues more readable than the works of Aristotle, but this difference is misleading. A great deal of Aristotle's writings, especially his earlier ones, has been lost, including many works in a popular vein: letters, poems, and dialogues that in form and content resembled Plato's. Except for fragments, the works of Aristotle known today were not intended by him for written publication; they are, rather, notes for his teaching at the Lyceum. Moreover, ancient editors transformed his work by grouping together under a single title different treatises on the same subject that he wrote at different times. Partly because of such editing, and partly because Aristotle felt obliged to record positions different from his own, he sometimes appears inconsistent or redundant. Ancient testimony indicates that Aristotle's mind, personality, and literary style were warmer than is evident in the matter-of-fact writings that have come down to us.

Aristotle at least touched on virtually all the fields of human knowledge, treating many of them in depth: natural sciences including zoology, embryology, physics, meteorology, astronomy, even chemistry in a rudimentary way; mathematics (most of his work on this subject has been lost); psychology; politics and ethics (which for him were closely related to each other); the language arts including rhetoric and poetics. In many of these disciplines he pioneered and made striking discoveries. Nor was he content to investigate the subjects in isolation; he tried to bring them together, partly by applying consistent principles of systematic method, partly by subsuming them under the axioms of "first philosophy" developed in his Metaphysics. *This religious-philosophic work is logically prior to the more particular studies, because it treats of the nature of being in itself and delineates the broad principles that govern and differentiate more specific fields of investigation. But both metaphysics and its subsidiary studies depend on a methodology of thinking in general. That methodology, largely developed by Aristotle, is outlined in his* Organon, *a group of tracts dealing with logic and the precise use of language in discourse.*

The Organon *is probably the most permanently valuable of all Aristotle's works; it remains an indispensable sourcebook on how to think straight, both deductively and inductively. The works on natural science have inevitably been superseded by those of researchers who have been able to use modern instruments and modern mathematics, though some of Aristotle's ideas (on the classification of animals, for example) remain roughly valid. His shrewd observations on political science in the* Politics *are still meaningful and provocative, though they are limited somewhat by Aristotle's preoccupation with the peculiar circumstances of the Greek city-state. Much of what he wrote about the humanities, especially ethics and literary theory, is as valuable today as ever; for example, a group of Aristotelian literary critics has been prominent in the twentieth century, and the doctrine of the "tragic flaw" enunciated in the* Poetics *has wide general currency.*

Even where Aristotle's ideas have been superseded, they often remain valuable because they constitute so large a part of our intellectual and cultural history. During the Middle Ages and until after the Renaissance, university education was thoroughly grounded in Aristotle, and indeed one of the most fascinating episodes in the emergence of modern science is its efforts, especially in the seventeenth century, to throw off the weight of what had become Aristotelian dogma. (That this struggle had to occur is ironic, since Aristotle himself believed firmly in the inductive method; he taught emphatically that mere theory must yield to observed facts.) Philosophers and theologians like Thomas Aquinas, and poets like Dante, are impossible to understand adequately without an awareness of Aristotle's contributions to their thought. The doctrine of the unmoved first mover of the universe; the idea of a continuous chain of being running up a scale from inanimate matter to God; the tripartite classification of souls into nutritive (animals, plants, man), sensitive (animals, man), and rational (man, God); the distinction between substance (what a thing really is) *and accident (nonessential properties); the condemnation of taking interest for money (which in works like Dante's* Inferno *is considered usury); the ethical doctrine of the golden mean between two extremes—these ideas, originated or definitively expressed by Aristotle, are fundamental to Western history, literature, and thought. Perhaps the most frequently recurring intellectual model in his works, and one of the most influential, is his fourfold treatment of causes: the material cause (what a thing is made of); the formal cause (its shape or governing principle); the efficient cause (the process by which it was made); and the final cause (its purpose). His concern with final causes pervades Aristotle's analysis of everything from the parts of animals, to man, to the cosmos as a whole.*

Plato and Aristotle are sometimes treated as polar opposites—Plato being an idealist and Aristotle a materialist. That is a serious mistake: both were staunchly opposed to any view of man or the universe as strictly material in their natures, and both considered the philosophic life the highest of human vocations. (Part of the apparent difference between them arises from the literary vehicles in which their work has survived.) There remains a significant distinction between them, however, in what they say and how they reach their conclusions. Though both are rationalist logicians, Aristotle depends more than Plato on data derived from the visible world; in short, his thought is more empirical. His political and ethical thought is more pragmatic, having less of the visionary emphasis than does Plato's. The two also differ in their views of the relationship between spirit and matter; Plato regards the soul as the true human identity, yoked with an essentially unreal, alien body, while Aristotle teaches that in man soul (or form) and body are intimately united and interdependent.

FURTHER READING *(prepared by F.S.N.):* Valuable material on the life, thought and writings of Aristotle may be found in W. D. Ross, *Aristotle*, 1924, 5th ed. repr. 1960; D. J. Allan, *The Philosophy of Aristotle*, 1952; and J. H. Randall, Jr., *Aristotle*, 1960. Werner W. Jaeger, *Aristotle: Fundamentals of the History of His Development*, 1923, trans. Richard Robinson, 1934, 2nd ed. 1948, treats the works in chronological sequence, in order to show Aristotle's intellectual development. On the *Nicomachean Ethics* and Aristotle's main ethical doctrines, see W. F. R. Hardie, *Aristotle's Ethical Theory*, 1968. Humphry House, *Aristotle's Poetics*, 1956, repr. 1967; and John Jones, *On Aristotle and Greek Tragedy*, 1962, survey what Aristotle has to say about the three great tragedians, and about plot, character, action, catharsis and imitation.

from *POETICS*

Translation by Samuel Henry Butcher
as revised by Louise Ropes Loomis
Footnotes by Louise Ropes Loomis

I

I propose to treat of Poetry in itself and of its various kinds, noting the essential quality of each; to inquire into the structure of the plot required for a good poem; into the number and nature of the parts of which a poem is composed; and similarly into whatever else falls within the same inquiry. Following, then, the order of nature, let us begin with the principles which come first.

Epic poetry and tragedy, comedy also and dithyrambic[1] poetry, and the music of the flute and of the lyre in most of their forms, are all in their general conception modes of imitation. They differ, however, from one another in three respects—their mediums, their objects, their manner or mode of imitation being in each case distinct.

For as there are persons who, by conscious art or mere habit, imitate

[1] For dithyrambic poetry the ordinary English reader may understand what we call lyric poetry. More strictly defined the dithyramb was a hymn or ode in rapturous style, such as were sung at the festivals of the god Dionysus.

and represent various objects through the medium of color and form, or, again, by the voice; so in the group of arts above mentioned, taken as a whole, the imitation is produced by rhythm, language, or harmony, either singly or combined.

Thus in the music of the flute and of the lyre, harmony and rhythm alone are employed; also in other arts, such as that of the shepherd's pipe, which are essentially similar to these. In dancing, rhythm alone is used without harmony; for even dancing imitates character, emotion, and action, by rhythmical movement. . . .

There are, again, some arts which employ all the means above mentioned—namely, rhythm, tune, and meter. Such are dithyrambic and nomic[2] poetry, and also tragedy and comedy; but between them the difference is that in the first two cases these means are all employed in combination, in the latter, now one means is employed, now another.

Such, then, are the differences of the arts with respect to the medium of imitation.

II

Since the objects of imitation are men in action, and these men must be either of a high or a low type (for moral character mainly answers to this division, goodness and badness being the distinguishing marks of moral differences), it follows that we must represent men either as better than in real life, or as worse, or as they are. It is the same in painting. Polygnotus depicted men as nobler than they are, Pauson as less noble, Dionysius drew them true to life.[3]

Now it is evident that each of the arts of imitation above mentioned will exhibit these differences, and itself become a distinct kind in imitating objects that are thus distinct. Such diversities may be found even in dancing, flute playing, and lyre playing. So again in language, whether prose or verse, unaccompanied by music. Homer, for example, makes men better than they are; Cleophon as they are; Hegemon of Thasos, the inventor of parodies, worse than they are.[4] The same distinction marks off tragedy from comedy; for comedy aims at representing men as worse, tragedy as better than in actual life.

III

There is still a third difference—the manner in which each of these objects may be imitated. For the medium being the same, the objects the same, the poet may imitate by narration—in which case he can either take another personality as Homer does, or speak in his own person, unchanged—or he may present all his characters as living and moving before us.

These, then, as we said at the beginning, are the three differences which distinguish artistic imitation—the medium, the objects, and the manner. So

[2] Nomic poetry is instructive poetry, maxims or wise sayings in the form of verse.
[3] Unfortunately no work by any of these famous Greek painters has come down to us.
[4] The writings of Cleophon and Hegemon are also lost.

that from one point of view, Sophocles[5] is an imitator of the same kind as Homer—for both imitate higher types of character; from another point of view, he is of the same kind as Aristophanes[6]—for both imitate persons acting and doing. Hence, some say, the name of "drama" is given to such plays, as representing action. . . .

IV

Poetry in general seems to have sprung from two sources, each of them lying deep in our nature. First, the instinct of imitation is implanted in man from childhood, one difference between him and other animals being that he is the most imitative of living creatures, and through imitation learns his earliest lessons. And no less universal is the pleasure he takes in seeing things imitated. We have evidence of this in the facts of experience. Objects which in themselves we view with pain, we delight to contemplate when reproduced with minute fidelity: such as the forms of the most ignoble animals and of dead bodies. The cause of this, again, is that to learn gives the liveliest pleasure, not only to philosophers but to men in general, although their capacity of learning is more limited. Thus the reason why men enjoy seeing a likeness is that in contemplating it they find themselves learning or inferring, and saying perhaps, "Ah, that is he." If they happen not to have seen the original, their pleasure will be due not to the imitation as such, but to the execution, the coloring, or some such other cause.

Imitation, then, is one instinct of our nature. Next there is the instinct for harmony and rhythm, meters being manifestly sections of rhythm. Persons, therefore, starting with this natural gift developed by degrees their special aptitudes, until their rude improvisations gave birth to poetry.

Poetry now diverged in two directions, according to the individual character of the writers. The graver spirits imitated noble actions and the actions of good men. The more trivial sort imitated the actions of meaner persons, at first composing satires, as the former did hymns to the gods and praises of famous men. A poem of the satirical kind cannot indeed be put down to any author earlier than Homer; though there were probably many such writers. But from Homer onward, instances can be cited—his own *Margites*,[7] for example, and other similar compositions. The appropriate meter was also here introduced; hence the measure is still called the iambic[8] or lampooning measure, being that in which people lampooned one another. Thus the older poets were distinguished as writers either of heroic or of lampooning verse.

---

[5] Sophocles was one of the great trio of fifth century Athenian tragedians, the other two being Aeschylus and Euripides. Seven of Sophocles' tragedies have been preserved.

[6] The famous satirical comedy writer of the end of the fifth century B.C.

[7] The mock battle epic that went by the name of *Margites* has long been lost. Whether it was really the work of the author of the *Iliad*, as Aristotle thought, we cannot judge.

[8] The pattern of the iambic meter was a line composed of a series of pairs of syllables, a short syllable, followed by a long one. We in English still use its equivalent, an unaccented syllable followed by an accented, both in comic verse, such as
"O oysters, come and walk with us,
The walrus did beseech,"
and also in grand and serious poetry, such as *Paradise Lost*.

As in the serious style Homer is pre-eminent among poets, for he alone combined dramatic form with excellence of imitation, so he too first laid down the main lines of comedy, by dramatizing the ludicrous instead of writing personal satire. His *Margites* bears the same relation to comedy that the *Iliad* and *Odyssey* do to tragedy. And when tragedy and comedy appeared, the two classes of poets still followed their natural bent: the lampooners became writers of comedy, and the epic poets were succeeded by tragedians, since the drama was a larger and higher form of art. . . . Tragedy advanced by slow degrees; each new element that showed itself was in turn developed. Having passed through many changes, it found its natural form, and there it stopped.

Aeschylus first introduced a second actor;[9] he diminished the importance of the chorus, and assigned the leading part to the dialogue. Sophocles raised the number of actors to three, and added scene painting. It was not till late that the short plot was discarded for one of greater compass, and the grotesque diction of the earlier satiric form for the stately manner of tragedy.

V

Comedy is, as we have said, an imitation of characters of a lower type—not, however, in the full sense of the word bad, the ludicrous being merely a subdivision of the ugly. It consists of some defect or ugliness which is not painful or destructive. To take an obvious example, the comic mask is ugly and distorted, but does not imply pain.

The successive changes through which tragedy passed, and the authors of these changes, are well known, whereas comedy has had no history, because it was not at first treated seriously. . . .

Epic poetry agrees with tragedy in so far as it is an imitation in verse of characters of a higher type. They differ in that epic poetry admits but one kind of meter[10] and is narrative in form. They differ, again, in their length: for tragedy endeavors, as far as possible, to confine itself to a single circuit of the sun, or but slightly to exceed this limit; whereas the epic action has no limits of time. This, then, is a second point of difference; though at first the same freedom was admitted in tragedy as in epic poetry. . . .

VI

Tragedy, then, is an imitation of an action that is serious, complete, and of a certain magnitude; in language embellished with every kind of artistic

[9] Before Aeschylus' time the embryonic Greek tragedy consisted of speeches by a single actor or narrator telling the chorus what had happened and a series of songs, dances, and responses by the chorus, expressing their wonder, joy, or grief at the news.

[10] To a Greek the only meter admissible in an epic poem was the meter of the *Iliad* and the *Odyssey*, or what was called hexameter verse. Virgil used the same meter for the *Aeneid*. In English a well known example of hexameter verse is Longfellow's *Evangeline:*
"This is the forest primeval: the murmuring pines and the hemlocks"—

ornament, the several kinds being found in separate parts of the play; in the form of dramatic action, not of narrative; through pity and fear effecting the proper purification of these emotions.[11] By "language embellished," I mean language into which rhythm, harmony, and song enter. By "the several kinds in separate parts," I mean that some parts are rendered through the medium of verse alone, others again with the aid of song.

Now as tragic imitation implies persons acting, it necessarily follows, in the first place, that spectacular equipment will be a part of tragedy. Next, song and diction, for these are the medium of imitation. By diction, I mean the metrical arrangement of the words: as for song, it is a term whose sense everyone understands.

Again, tragedy is the imitation of an action, and an action implies personal actors, who necessarily possess certain distinctive qualities of character and thought; for it is by these that we form our estimate of their actions and these two—thought and character—are the natural causes from which their actions spring, and on their actions all success or failure depends. Now, the imitation of the action is the plot; by plot I here mean the arrangement of the incidents. By character I mean that because of which we ascribe certain qualities to the actors. Thought is needed whenever they speak to prove a statement or declare a general truth. Every tragedy, therefore, must have six parts, which parts determine its quality—namely, plot, character, diction, thought, spectacle, song. . . .

But most important of all is the structure of the incidents. For tragedy is an imitation, not of men, but of action and life, of happiness and misery. And life consists of action, and its end is a mode of activity,[12] not a quality. Now character determines men's qualities, but it is their actions that make them happy or wretched. The purpose of action in the tragedy, therefore, is not the representation of character: character comes in as contributing to the action. Hence the incidents and the plot are the end of the tragedy; and the end is the chief thing of all. So without action there cannot be a tragedy; there may be one without character. . . .

Again, you may string together a set of speeches expressive of character, and well finished in point of diction and thought, and not produce the essential tragic effect nearly so well as with a play which, however deficient in these respects, yet has a plot and artistically constructed incidents. Besides which, the most powerful elements of emotional interest in tragedy—reversal of the situation and recognition scenes[13]—are parts of the plot. A further proof is that novices in the art attain to finish of diction and precision of portraiture before they can construct the plot. It is the same with almost all the early poets.

The plot, then, is the first principle, and, as it were, the soul of a tragedy: character holds the second place. A similar statement is true of painting. The most beautiful colors, laid on confusedly, will not give as much

---

[11] Note that an unhappy or what we call a tragic ending was not one of the Greek requirements for a tragedy, though Aristotle thought it the perfect ending. See XIII. Many tragedies ended with a solemn reconciliation after a conflict or quiet after pain, to please the audience, Aristotle says.

[12] See the *Ethics*, Book I, chapter 6.

[13] These two admired features of many old dramatic plots Aristotle explains further on.

pleasure as a simple chalk outline of a portrait. Thus tragedy is the imitation of an action, and of actors mainly with a view to the action. . . .

The spectacle is, indeed, an attraction in itself, but of all the parts it is the least artistic, and connected least with the art of poetry. For the power of tragedy is felt even apart from representation and actors. Besides, the production of scenic effects is more a matter for the property man than for the poet.

VII

These principles being established, let us now discuss the proper structure of the plot, since this is the first and most important thing in tragedy.

Now, according to our definition, tragedy is an imitation of an action that is complete and whole and of a certain magnitude; for there may be a whole that is wanting in magnitude. A whole is that which has a beginning, a middle, and an end. A beginning is that which does not have to follow anything else, but after which something else naturally takes place. An end, on the contrary, is that which itself naturally follows something else, either by necessity or as a general rule, but has nothing coming after it. A middle is that which follows something else as some other thing follows it. A well-constructed plot must neither begin nor end at haphazard, but conform to these principles.

Again, a beautiful object, whether it be a living organism or any whole composed of parts, must not only have an orderly arrangement of parts, but must also be of a certain magnitude; for beauty depends on magnitude and order. Hence a very tiny creature cannot be beautiful; for the view of it is confused, the object being seen in an almost imperceptible moment of time. Nor, again, can one of vast size be beautiful; for as the eye cannot take it all in at once, the unity and sense of the whole is lost for the spectator; as it would be if there were a creature a thousand miles long. As, therefore, in the case of living bodies and organisms, a certain magnitude is necessary, and a magnitude which may be easily embraced in one view; so in the plot, a certain length is necessary, and a length which can be easily embraced by the memory. . . . And to state the matter roughly, we may say that the proper length is such as to allow for a sequence of necessary or probable events that will bring about a change from calamity to good fortune, or from good fortune to calamity.

VIII

Unity of plot does not, as some persons think, consist of having a single man as the hero. For infinitely various are the incidents in one man's life which cannot be reduced to unity; and so, too, there are many actions of one man out of which we cannot make one action. Hence the error, as it appears, of all poets who have composed a Heracleid, a Theseid,[14] or other

---

[14] That is, a long-drawn narrative of all the exploits of a Heracles or a Theseus.

poems of the kind. They imagine that as Heracles was one man, the story of Heracles must also be a unity. But Homer, as in all else he is of surpassing merit, here too—whether from art or natural genius—seems to have happily discerned the truth. In composing the *Odyssey* he did not include all the adventures of Odysseus—such as his wound on Parnassus, or his feigned madness at the mustering of the host[15]—incidents between which there was no necessary or probable connection: but he made the *Odyssey* and likewise the *Iliad* center around an action that in our sense of the word is one. As therefore, in the other imitative arts, the imitation is one when the object imitated is one, so the plot, being an imitation of an action, must imitate one action and that a whole, the structural union of the parts being such that, if any one of them is displaced or removed, the whole will be disjointed and disturbed. For a thing whose presence or absence makes no visible difference is not an organic part of the whole.

IX

It is, moreover, evident from what has been said that it is not the function of the poet to relate what has happened but what may happen—what is possible according to the law of probability or necessity. The poet and the historian differ not by writing in verse or in prose. The work of Herodotus[16] might be put into verse, and it would still be a species of history, with meter no less than without it. The true difference is that one relates what has happened, the other what may happen. Poetry, therefore, is a more philosophical and a higher thing than history: for poetry tends to express the universal, history the particular. . . .

But even if a poet chances to take an historical subject, he is nonetheless a poet; for there is no reason why some events that have actually happened should not conform to the law of the probable and the possible, and in virtue of that aspect of them he is their poet or maker.

Of all plots and actions the episodic are the worst. I call a plot "episodic" in which the episodes or acts succeed one another without probable or necessary sequence. Bad poets compose such pieces by their own fault, good poets, to please the players; for, as they write show pieces for competition, they stretch the plot beyond its capacity, and are often forced to break the natural continuity.

But again, tragedy is an imitation not only of a complete action, but of events inspiring fear or pity. Such an effect is best produced when the events come on us by surprise and when, at the same time, they follow as cause and effect. The wonder will then be greater than if they happened of themselves or merely by accident; for coincidences too are most marvelous when they have a look of design. We may instance the statue of Mitys at Argos, which fell upon his murderer while he was watching a festival, and killed him. Such events seem the result of more than chance. Plots, therefore, constructed on these principles are necessarily the best.

---

[15] Incidents said to have occurred before the opening of the *Iliad*.
[16] The first of the great Greek historians, who wrote the story of the world, as he knew it, down through the Persian wars.

X

Plots are either simple or complex, for the actions in real life, of which they are an imitation, are obviously either one or the other. An action which is one and continuous in the sense above defined, I call simple, when the change in the hero's fortune takes place without reversal of the situation and without recognition.

A complex action is one in which the change is accompanied by such a reversal, or by recognition, or by both. These all should arise from the internal structure of the plot, so that what follows should be the necessary or probable result of what went before. It makes a great difference whether the event is caused by or simply happens after the previous action.

XI

Reversal of the situation is a change by which conditions in the play are transformed into their opposite, keeping always to our rule of probability or necessity. Thus in the Oedipus,[17] the messenger comes to cheer Oedipus and free him from his alarms about his mother, but by revealing who Oedipus really is produces the opposite effect. . . .

Recognition, as the name indicates, is a change from ignorance to knowledge, producing love or hate between the persons destined by the poet for good or bad fortune. The best form of recognition is coincident with a reversal of the situation, as in the Oedipus.[18]

Even inanimate things of the most trivial kind may in a sense be objects of recognition. Again, we may recognize or discover whether a person has done a thing or not. But the recognition which is most intimately connected with the plot and action is, as we have said, the recognition of persons. This recognition, combined with a reversal, will produce either pity or fear; and actions producing these effects are those which, by our definition, tragedy represents. Moreover, it is upon such situations that the issue of good or bad fortune will depend. Recognition, then, being between persons, it may happen that one person only is recognized by the other—when the latter is already known—or it may be necessary that the recognition should be on both sides. Thus Iphigenia is revealed to Orestes by the sending of the

---

[17] The *Oedipus Tyrannus [Oedipus the King]* of Sophocles is a tragedy which Aristotle much admired and which happily has come down to us. At its opening, Oedipus is the prosperous king of Thebes, with a wife, Jocasta, whom he dearly loves. In the course of the play he discovers that instead of being, as he supposed, a shepherd's son, he is the child of Jocasta and her former husband, the late King of Thebes, exposed to die in infancy because of an ominous prophecy and rescued by the shepherd who brought him up. He learns also that an arrogant old man he killed in a roadside quarrel was the late king, his father. He is therefore the unwitting murderer of his own father and for years has lived in incest with his own mother. At the news, Jocasta hangs herself and Oedipus puts out his eyes and goes blinded and accursed into banishment.

[18] Shakespeare frequently uses these classical dramatic devices of reversal of situation and recognition. The tragedy of *King Lear* is an outstanding illustration of the first. The themes of disguise, mistaken identity, and revelation or recognition occur again and again; notably in *As You Like It, Twelfth Night, Winter's Tale* and *The Tempest*.

letter; but another act of recognition is required to make Orestes known to Iphigenia.[19]

Two parts, then, of the plot—reversal of the situation and recognition—turn upon surprises. A third part is the scene of suffering. The scene of suffering is a destructive or painful action, such as a death on the stage, bodily agony, wounds, and the like. . . .

XIII

As a sequel to what has already been said, we must proceed to consider what the poet should aim at, and what he should avoid in constructing his plots; and by what means the specific effect of tragedy will be produced.

A perfect tragedy should, as we have seen, be arranged not on the simple but on the complex plan. It should, moreover, imitate actions which excite pity and fear, this being the distinctive mark of tragic imitation. It follows plainly, in the first place, that the change of fortune presented must not be the spectacle of a virtuous man brought from prosperity to adversity: for this moves neither pity nor fear: it merely shocks us. Nor, again, that of a bad man passing from adversity to prosperity: for nothing can be more alien to the spirit of tragedy; it possesses no single tragic quality; it neither satisfies the moral sense nor calls forth pity or fear. Nor, again, should the downfall of an utter villain be exhibited. A plot of this kind would, doubtless, satisfy the moral sense, but it would inspire neither pity nor fear;[20] for pity is aroused by unmerited misfortune, fear by the misfortune of a man like ourselves. Such an event, therefore, will be neither pitiful nor terrible.

There remains, then, the character between these two extremes—that of a man extraordinarily good and just, who yet brings misfortune on himself not by vice or depravity, but by some error or frailty.[21] He must be one who is highly renowned and prosperous, a personage like Oedipus, Thyestes, or other illustrious men of great families.

The best constructed plot should, therefore, be single in its issue, rather than double, as some maintain. The change of fortune should be not from bad to good, but, reversely, from good to bad. It should come about as the

---

[19] The reference here is to Euripides' play of *Iphigenia in Tauris*. Aristotle summarizes briefly the story of Iphigenia in XVII. As the young daughter of King Agamemnon, she was brought from her home to the port of Aulis to be sacrificed, that her father and his fleet might have a favorable wind to sail to Troy. She was snatched from the altar by the goddess Artemis and disappeared. Years later she is a priestess serving in the savage country of Tauris. Her brother Orestes, whom she left at home, a little child, is now a maddened wanderer, seeking absolution for his crime of killing his mother, Clytemnestra, in revenge for her murder of his father, Agamemnon. When Iphigenia finds Orestes on the shore at Tauris, neither, of course, knows the other. In fact, he has no idea that his long lost sister is alive. Through a letter which she gives him he learns who she is, but meanwhile by a law of the country he is condemned to die as a sacrilegious intruder. Through some words of his at the last moment she discovers that he is Orestes and saves him.

[20] Shakespeare's tragedy of *Richard III* is sometimes cited in disproof of this statement. Richard is an "utter villain" but we take a keen interest in his bold struggle to master fate.

[21] Two notably brave and generous tragic heroes, whose downfall is due to one shortcoming in character or judgment, are, of course, Lear and Othello. Some readers would include Hamlet.

result not of vice, but of some great error or frailty, in a character either such as we have described, or better rather than worse. . . . A tragedy, to be perfect according to the rules of art, should be of this construction. Hence they are in error who censure Euripides just because he follows this principle in his plays, many of which end unhappily. It is, as we have said, the right ending. The best proof is that on the stage and in dramatic competition, such plays, if well worked out, are the most tragic in effect; and Euripides, faulty though he may be in the general management of his subject, yet is felt to be the most tragic of the poets.

In the second rank comes the kind of tragedy which some place first. Like the Odyssey, it has a double thread of plot, and also an opposite ending for the good and for the bad actors. It is accounted the best only because of the weakness of the spectators; for the poet is guided in what he writes by the wishes of his audience. The pleasure, however, thence derived is not the true tragic pleasure. It is proper rather to comedy, where those who, in the piece, are the deadliest enemies—like Orestes and Aegisthus[22]—quit the stage as friends at the close, and no one slays or is slain.

XIV

Fear and pity may be aroused by spectacular means; but they may also result from the inner structure of the piece, which is the better way, and indicates a superior poet. For the plot ought to be so constructed that, even without the aid of the eye, he who hears the tale told will thrill with horror and melt to pity at what takes place. This is the impression we should receive from hearing the story of Oedipus. But to produce this effect by the mere spectacle is a less artistic method, and dependent on extraneous aids. Those who employ spectacular means to create a sense not of the terrible but of the merely monstrous are strangers to the purpose of tragedy; for we must not demand of tragedy any and every kind of pleasure, but only that which is proper to it. And since the pleasure the tragic poet should offer is that which comes from pity and fear through imitation, it is evident that this quality must be impressed on the incidents.

Let us then determine what circumstances strike us as terrible or pitiful.

Actions of this sort must happen between persons who are either friends or enemies or indifferent to one another. If an enemy kills an enemy, there is nothing to excite pity either in the act or the intention—except in so far as the suffering itself is pitiful. So too with indifferent persons. But when the tragic incident occurs between those who are near or dear to one another—if, for example, a brother kills, or intends to kill, a brother, a son his father, a mother her son, a son his mother, or any other deed of the kind is done—these are situations to be looked for by the poet. He may not indeed destroy the framework of the received legends—the

---

[22] In the tragic story of Agamemnon and his son Orestes, Aegisthus is the paramour of Agamemnon's wife, Clytemnestra, who influences her to murder her husband on his return from Troy. Orestes, her son, kills Aegisthus as well as his mother when he finally avenges his father. (See Aeschylus' *Oresteia*—Editors' note.)

fact, for instance, that Clytemnestra was slain by Orestes . . . but he ought to show invention of his own, and skillfully handle the traditional material. . . .

Enough has now been said concerning the structure of the incidents and the right kind of plot.

XV

With regard to the characters there are four things to be aimed at. First, and most important, they must be good. Now any speech or action that manifests some kind of moral purpose will be expressive of character: the character will be good if the purpose is good. The goodness is possible in every class of persons. Even a woman may be good, and also a slave, though the one is liable to be an inferior being, and the other quite worthless. The second thing to aim at is appropriateness. There is a type of manly valor, but manliness in a woman, or unscrupulous cleverness, is inappropriate. Thirdly, a character must be true to life: which is something different from goodness and appropriateness, as here described. The fourth point is consistency: for even though the person being imitated, who suggested the type, is inconsistent, still he must be consistently inconsistent.

As in the structure of the plot, so too in the portraiture of character, the poet should always aim at either the necessary or the probable. Thus a person of a given character should speak or act as it is necessary or probable that he would; just as this event should follow that as a necessary or probable consequence. It is therefore evident that the unraveling of the plot, no less than the complication, must arise out of the plot itself; it must not be brought about by supernatural interference—as in the *Medea*.[23] The supernatural should be employed only for events outside the drama—for past or future events, beyond the range of human knowledge, which need to be reported or foretold; for to the gods we ascribe the power of seeing all things. Within the action there must be nothing improbable. If the improbable cannot be excluded, it should be outside the field of the tragedy, as is the improbable element in the *Oedipus* of Sophocles.

Again, since tragedy is an imitation of persons above the common level, the example of good portrait painters should be followed. They, while reproducing the distinctive features of the original, make a likeness true to life and yet more beautiful. So too the poet, in representing men hot tempered or indolent or with other defects of character, should preserve the type and yet ennoble it. In this way Agathon and Homer have portrayed Achilles.[24]

[23] In Euripides' play of *Medea*, the heroine, who out of indignation at her wrongs has killed her two children and brought about the death of her husband's new bride, escapes from his fury into the sky in a magic chariot.

[24] We have nothing left of any work by Agathon. We know only that he was a playwright who promised to rival Euripides but who left Athens for some reason at the age of forty and died disappointed in a foreign land. At the banquet celebrated in Plato's dialogue of the *Symposium* he was the happy and admired host. For Homer's noble treatment of Achilles, see especially the *Iliad*, Books IX, XIX, XXIV.

These, then, are rules the poet should observe. Nor should he neglect those appeals to the eye, which, though not among the essentials, are the concomitants of poetry; for here too there is much room for error. But of this enough has been said in our published treatise. . . .[25]

XVII

In constructing the plot and working it out with the proper diction, the poet should put the scene, as far as possible, before his eyes. In this way, seeing everything with the utmost vividness, as if he were an actual eyewitness, he will discover what is in keeping with it, and be most unlikely to overlook inconsistencies. . . .

Again, the poet should act out his own play to the best of his power, with the gestures that go with it; for those with a sympathetic nature, who themselves feel the emotion, are most convincing; and one who is grieved himself despairs, one who is angry rages with the most lifelike reality. Hence poetry implies either a special gift of nature or a strain of madness. In the one case a man can take the mold of any character; in the other, he is lifted out of his proper self.

As for the story, whether the poet takes it ready-made or constructs it for himself, he should first sketch its general outline and then fill in the episodes and amplify in detail. The general plan may be illustrated by the *Iphigenia*.[26] A young girl is sacrificed; she disappears mysteriously from the eyes of those who sacrificed her; she is transported to another country, where the custom is to offer up all strangers to the goddess. To this ministry she is appointed. Some time later her own brother chances to arrive. The fact that the oracle for some reason ordered him to go there is outside the general plan of the play. The purpose, again, of his coming is outside the action proper. However, he comes, he is seized, and, when on the point of being sacrificed, reveals who he is. The mode of recognition may be either that of Euripides or of Polyidus,[27] in whose play he exclaims very naturally: "So it was not my sister only, but I too who was doomed to be sacrificed"; and by that remark he is saved.

After this, the names being once given, it remains to fill in the episodes. We must see, however, that they are relevant to the action. In the case of Orestes, for example, there is the madness which led to his capture and his deliverance by means of the purificatory rite. In a play the episodes are short, but in epic poetry they lengthen out the tale. Thus the story of the *Odyssey* can be stated briefly. A certain man is absent from home for many years; he is jealously watched by Poseidon, and quite alone. Meanwhile his home is in a wretched plight—suitors are wasting his substance and plotting against his son. At length, tempest-tossed, he arrives and makes himself known; he attacks the suitors with his own hand, and is himself preserved while he destroys them. This is the essence of the plot; the rest is episode.

[25] Aristotle wrote a dialogue *On Poets,* now lost.
[26] On the story of Iphigenia see XI, note.   [27] We have no plays of Polyidus.

XVIII

Every tragedy falls into two parts—complication and unraveling or *dénouement*. Incidents before the play opens and often others within the play itself form the complication; the rest is the unraveling. By the complication I mean all that extends from the beginning of the action to the part which marks the turning point to good or bad fortune. The unraveling is that which extends from the beginning of the change to the end. . . .

Again, the poet should remember what has been often said, and not make an epic structure into a tragedy. By an epic structure I mean one with a multiplicity of plots—as if, for instance, you were to make a tragedy out of the entire story of the *Iliad*. In the epic poem, owing to its length, each part can assume its proper magnitude. In the drama the result is far from answering to the poet's expectation. The proof is that the poets who have dramatized the whole story of the fall of Troy, instead of selecting portions, like Euripides; or who have taken the whole tale of Niobe, and not a part of her story, like Aeschylus, either fail utterly or meet with poor success on the stage. . . .

XXIII

As for that poetry which is narrative in form and imitates in meter, the plot manifestly ought, as in a tragedy, to be constructed on dramatic principles. It should have for its subject a single action, whole and complete, with a beginning, a middle, and an end. It will thus resemble a living organism in all its unity, and produce the pleasure proper to it. It will differ in structure from historical compositions, which of necessity present not a single action, but a single period, and all that happened within that period to one person or to many, however little connected together the events may be. For as the sea fight at Salamis and the battle with the Carthaginians in Sicily took place at the same time but did not tend to any one result, so in the ordinary course of events one thing sometimes follows another, and yet no single end is thereby produced. Such is the way, we may say, most poets write.

Here again, then, as has been already observed, the transcendent excellence of Homer is manifest. He never attempts to make the whole war of Troy the subject of his poem, though that war had a beginning and an end. It would have been too vast a theme, and not easily embraced in a single view. If not that, it would have been overcomplicated by the variety of the incidents in it. As it is, he detaches a single portion, though he admits as episodes many events from the general story of the war—such as the Catalogue of Ships[28] and others—thus diversifying the poem. . . . For this reason the *Iliad* and the *Odyssey* each furnish the subject of but one tragedy, or, at most, of two. . . .

[28] In the second half of Book II of the *Iliad*, Homer interrupts the course of his story to insert a catalogue of the ships that came to Troy and their leaders.

XXIV

Again, epic poetry may have as many kinds as tragedy: it may be simple, or complex, a tale of character or of suffering. The parts also, with the exception of song and spectacle, are the same; for it requires reversals of the situation, recognitions, and scenes of suffering. Moreover, the thought and the diction must be artistic. In all these respects, Homer is our earliest and sufficient model. Indeed each of his poems has a twofold character. The *Iliad* is at once simple and a tale of suffering, and the *Odyssey* complex (for recognition scenes run through it), and at the same time a tale of character. Moreover, in diction and thought they are supreme.

Epic poetry differs from tragedy in the scale on which it is constructed, and in its meter. As regards scale or length, we have already laid down an adequate limit: the beginning and the end must be capable of being brought within a single view. This condition will be satisfied by poems on a smaller scale than the old epics, and answering in length to the group of tragedies presented at a single sitting.[29]

Epic poetry has, however, a great—a special—capacity for enlarging its dimensions, and we can see the reason. In tragedy we cannot imitate several lines of action carried on at one and the same time; we must confine ourselves to the action on the stage and the part taken by the players. But in epic poetry, owing to the narrative form, many events simultaneously transacted can be presented; and these, if relevant to the subject, add mass and dignity to the poem. The epic has here an advantage, and one that conduces to grandeur of effect, to diverting the mind of the hearer, and relieving the story with varying episodes. For sameness of incident soon produces satiety, and makes tragedies fail on the stage. . . .

Homer, admirable in all respects, has the special merit of being the only poet who rightly appreciates the part he should take himself. The poet should speak as little as possible in his own person, for it is not this that makes him an imitator. Other poets appear themselves upon the scene throughout, and imitate but little and rarely. Homer, after a few prefatory words, at once brings in a man or woman or other personage, none of them wanting in characteristic qualities, but each with a character of his own.

The element of the wonderful is required in tragedy. But the improbable, on which the wonderful depends for its chief effects, has wider scope in epic poetry, because there the person acting is not seen. Thus, the pursuit of Hector would be ludicrous if placed upon the stage—the Greeks standing still and not joining in the pursuit, and Achilles waving them back.[30] But in the epic poem the absurdity passes unnoticed. Now the wonderful is pleasing, as may be inferred from the fact that everyone tells a story with some addition of his own, knowing that his hearers like it. . . .

But the poet should prefer probable impossibilities to improbable possibilities. The tragic plot must not be composed of improbable parts. Every-

---

[29] Greek dramatists of the great period used to produce their plays in groups of four, three more or less connected tragedies followed by a comic or satiric play, all seen by the audience in one sitting.

[30] Achilles' pursuit of Hector is described in the *Iliad*, Book XXII.

thing improbable should, if possible, be excluded; or, at all events, it should lie outside the action of the play itself. . . .

But once the improbable has been introduced and an air of likelihood imparted to it, we must accept it in spite of the absurdity. Take even the incidents in the *Odyssey* where Odysseus is left upon the shore of Ithaca.[31] How intolerable even these might have been would be apparent if an inferior poet were to treat the subject! As it is, the absurdity is veiled by the poetic charm with which the poet invests it.

The diction should be elaborated in the pauses of the action where there is no expression of character or thought. For, conversely, character and thought are merely obscured by a diction that is over brilliant.

XXV

With respect to problems and their solutions, the number and nature of the sources from which they spring may be thus set forth.

The poet being an imitator, like a painter or any other artist, must of necessity imitate one of three objects: things as they were or are, things as they are said or thought to be, or things as they ought to be. This he does in language—using either current expressions or, it may be, rare words or metaphors. There are also many modifications of language, which we concede to the poets. Add to this, that the standard of correctness is not the same in poetry and in politics, any more than in poetry and in any other art. Within the art of poetry itself there are two kinds of faults—those which touch its essence, and those which are accidental. If the poet intended to describe something right, but described it incorrectly through lack of ability to express himself, his art is faulty. But if his failure was due to a wrong intention—if, for instance, he represented a horse as throwing out both his off legs at once, or introduced technical inaccuracies in medicine, or some other science—the error was not in the essentials of his art. These are the points of view from which we should consider and answer the questions raised in the problems.

First as to questions which concern the poet's own art. If he describes the impossible, he is guilty of an error; but the error may be justified, if the end of the art be thereby attained (the end being that already mentioned)—if, that is, the effect of this or any other part of the poem is thus rendered more striking. A case in point is the pursuit of Hector. If, however, the end might have been as well or better attained without violating the rules of poetic correctness, the error is not justified; for every kind of error should, if possible, be avoided.

Again, does the error touch the essentials of the poetic art or some accident of it? For example, not to know that a hind has no horns is a less serious matter than to paint it inartistically.

Further, if it be objected that a description is not true to fact, the poet may perhaps reply, "But the objects are as they ought to be"; just as Sophocles said that he drew men as they ought to be, Euripides as they are. In this

[31] *Odyssey,* Book XIII.

way the objection may be met. If, however, the description is neither true nor of the thing as it should be, the poet may answer, "This is how men say the thing is." This dictum applies to the tales about the gods. It may well be that these stories are not loftier than the facts nor yet true to fact; they are, very possibly, what Xenophanes[32] says of them. But anyhow, "this is what is said."

XXVI

The question may be raised whether the epic or tragic form of imitation is the higher. If the more refined art is the higher, and the more refined in every case is that which appeals to the better sort of audience, the art which addresses itself to any and everyone is manifestly most unrefined. The audience then is supposed to be too dull to comprehend unless the performers throw in something of their own, who therefore indulge in perpetual movements.

So we are told that epic poetry is addressed to a cultivated audience, who do not need gestures, tragedy to an inferior public. Being then unrefined, it is evidently the lower of the two.

Now, in the first place, this censure attaches not to the poetic but to the actors' art; for gesticulation may be equally overdone in epic recitation. . . . Next, all action is not to be condemned—any more than all dancing—but only that of bad performers. . . . Again, tragedy, like epic poetry, produces its effect even without action; it reveals its power by mere reading. If, then, in all other respects it is superior, this fault, we say, is not inherent in it.

And superior it is, because it has all the epic elements—it may even use the epic meter, with music and spectacular effects as important accessories; and these produce the most lively of pleasures. Further, it creates a vivid impression when read as well as when acted. Moreover, the art in it attains its end within narrower limits; and the concentrated effect is more pleasurable than one which is spread over a long time and so diluted. What, for example, would be the effect of the *Oedipus* of Sophocles, if it were cast into a form as long as the *Iliad*? Once more, the epic imitation has less unity; as is shown by this, that any epic poem will furnish subjects for several tragedies. . . .

If, then, tragedy is superior to epic poetry in all these respects and, moreover, fulfills its specific function better as an art—for each art ought to produce, not any chance pleasure, but the pleasure proper to it, as already stated—it plainly follows that tragedy is the higher art, as attaining its end more perfectly.

Thus much may suffice concerning tragic and epic poetry in general; their several kinds and parts, with the number of each and their differences; the causes that make a poem good or bad; the objections of the critics and the answer to their objections.

---

[32] Xenophanes of Colophon, who lived almost two hundred years before Aristotle, seems to have been remembered largely for his attacks on and ridicule of the popular polytheism of Greece.

from *NICOMACHEAN ETHICS*

Translation by James E. C. Welldon
as revised by Louise Ropes Loomis
Footnotes by Louise Ropes Loomis

BOOK I

CHAPTER 1

Every art and every scientific inquiry, and similarly every action and purpose, may be said to aim at some good. Hence the good has been well defined as that at which all things aim. But it is clear that there is a difference in ends; for the ends are sometimes activities, and sometimes results beyond the mere activities. Where there are ends beyond the action, the results are naturally superior to the action.

As there are various actions, arts, and sciences, it follows that the ends are also various. Thus health is the end of the medical art, a ship of shipbuilding, victory of strategy, and wealth of economics. It often happens that a number of such arts or sciences combine for a single enterprise, as the art of making bridles and all such other arts as furnish the implements of horsemanship combine for horsemanship, and horsemanship and every military action for strategy; and in the same way, other arts or sciences combine for others. In all these cases, the ends of the master arts or sciences, whatever they may be, are more desirable than those of the subordinate arts or sciences, as it is for the sake of the former that the latter are pursued. It makes no difference to the argument whether the activities themselves are the ends of the action, or something beyond the activities, as in the above-mentioned sciences.

If it is true that in the sphere of action there is some end which we wish for its own sake, and for the sake of which we wish everything else, and if we do not desire everything for the sake of something else (for, if that is so, the process will go on *ad infinitum*, and our desire will be idle and futile), clearly this end will be good and the supreme good. Does it not follow then that the knowledge of this good is of great importance for the conduct of life? Like archers who have a mark at which to aim, shall we not have a better chance of attaining what we want? If this is so, we must endeavor to comprehend, at least in outline, what this good is, and what science or faculty makes it its object.

It would seem that this is the most authoritative science. Such a kind is evidently the political, for it is that which determines what sciences are necessary in states, and what kinds should be studied, and how far they should be studied by each class of inhabitant. We see too that even the faculties held in highest esteem, such as strategy, economics, and rhetoric, are subordinate to it. Then since politics makes use of the other sciences and also rules what people may do and what they may not do, it follows that its end will comprehend the ends of the other sciences, and will therefore be the good of mankind. For even if the good of an individual is identical with the good of a state, yet the good of the state is evidently greater and more perfect to attain or to preserve. For though the good of an individual by himself is something worth working for, to ensure the good of a nation or a state is nobler and more divine.

These then are the objects at which the present inquiry aims, and it is in a sense a political inquiry. . . .

CHAPTER 2

As every science and undertaking aims at some good, what is in our view the good at which political science aims, and what is the highest of all practical goods? As to its name there is, I may say, a general agreement. The masses and the cultured classes agree in calling it happiness, and conceive that "to live well" or "to do well" is the same thing as "to be happy." But as to what happiness is they do not agree, nor do the masses give the same account of it as the philosophers. The former take it to be something visible and palpable, such as pleasure, wealth, or honor; different people, however, give different definitions of it, and often even the same man gives different definitions at different times. When he is ill, it is health, when he is poor, it is wealth; if he is conscious of his own ignorance, he envies people who use grand language above his own comprehension. Some philosophers, on the other hand, have held that, besides these various goods, there is an absolute good which is the cause of goodness in them all.[1] It would perhaps be a waste of time to examine all these opinions; it will be enough to examine such as are most popular or as seem to be more or less reasonable.

CHAPTER 3

Men's conception of the good or of happiness may be read in the lives they lead. Ordinary or vulgar people conceive it to be a pleasure, and accordingly choose a life of enjoyment. For there are, we may say, three conspicuous types of life, the sensual, the political, and, thirdly, the life of thought. Now the mass of men present an absolutely slavish appearance, choosing the life of brute beasts, but they have ground for so doing because so many persons in authority share the tastes of Sardanapalus.[2] Cultivated and energetic people, on the other hand, identify happiness with honor, as honor is the general end of political life. But this seems too superficial an idea for our present purpose; for honor depends more upon the people who pay it than upon the person to whom it is paid, and the good we feel is something which is proper to a man himself and cannot be easily taken away from him. Men too appear to seek honor in order to be assured of their own goodness. Accordingly, they seek it at the hands of the sage and of those who know them well, and they seek it on the ground of their virtue; clearly

---

[1] These were members of Plato's school of thought.

[2] A half legendary ruler of ancient Assyria, whose name to the Greeks stood for the extreme of Oriental luxury and extravagance.

then, in their judgment at any rate, virtue is better than honor. Perhaps then we might look on virtue rather than honor as the end of political life. Yet even this idea appears not quite complete; for a man may possess virtue and yet be asleep or inactive throughout life, and not only so, but he may experience the greatest calamities and misfortunes. Yet no one would call such a life a life of happiness, unless he were maintaining a paradox. But we need not dwell further on this subject, since it is sufficiently discussed in popular philosophical treatises. The third life is the life of thought, which we will discuss later.[3]

The life of money making is a life of constraint; and wealth is obviously not the good of which we are in quest; for it is useful merely as a means to something else. It would be more reasonable to take the things mentioned before—sensual pleasure, honor, and virtue—as ends than wealth, since they are things desired on their own account. Yet these too are evidently not ends, although much argument has been employed to show that they are. . . .

CHAPTER 5

But leaving this subject for the present, let us revert to the good of which we are in quest and consider what it may be. For it seems different in different activities or arts; it is one thing in medicine, another in strategy, and so on. What is the good in each of these instances? It is presumably that for the sake of which all else is done. In medicine this is health, in strategy victory, in architecture a house, and so on. In every activity and undertaking it is the end, since it is for the sake of the end that all people do whatever else they do. If then there is an end for all our activity, this will be the good to be accomplished; and if there are several such ends, it will be these.

Our argument has arrived by a different path at the same point as before; but we must endeavor to make it still plainer. Since there are more ends than one, and some of these ends—for example, wealth, flutes, and instruments generally—we desire as means to something else, it is evident that not all are final ends. But the highest good is clearly something final. Hence if there is only one final end, this will be the object of which we are in search; and if there are more than one, it will be the most final. We call that which is sought after for its own sake more final than that which is sought after as a means to something else; we call that which is never desired as a means to something else more final than things that are desired both for themselves and as means to something else. Therefore, we call absolutely final that which is always desired for itself and never as a means to something else. Now happiness more than anything else answers to this description. For happiness we always desire for its own sake and never as a means to something else, whereas honor, pleasure, intelligence, and every virtue we desire partly for their own sakes (for we should desire them independently of what might result from them), but partly also as means to happiness, because we suppose they will prove instruments of happiness.

---

[3] The discussion of the life of thought occurs in Book X [not included in this volume].

Happiness, on the other hand, nobody desires for the sake of these things, nor indeed as a means to anything else at all.

If we start from the point of view of self-sufficiency, we reach the same conclusion; for we assume that the final good is self-sufficient. By self-sufficiency we do not mean that a person leads a solitary life all by himself, but that he has parents, children, wife and friends and fellow citizens in general, as man is naturally a social being. Yet here it is necessary to set some limit; for if the circle must be extended to include ancestors, descendants, and friends' friends, it will go on indefinitely. Leaving this point, however, for future investigation, we call the self-sufficient that which, taken even by itself, makes life desirable and wanting nothing at all; and this is what we mean by happiness.

Again, we think happiness the most desirable of all things, and that not merely as one good thing among others. If it were only that, the addition of the smallest more good would increase its desirableness; for the addition would make an increase of goods, and the greater of two goods is always the more desirable. Happiness is something final and self-sufficient and the end of all action.

CHAPTER 6

Perhaps, however, it seems a commonplace to say that happiness is the supreme good; what is wanted is to define its nature a little more clearly. The best way of arriving at such a definition will probably be to ascertain the function of man. For, as with a flute player, a sculptor, or any artist, or in fact anybody who has a special function or activity, his goodness and excellence seem to lie in his function, so it would seem to be with man, if indeed he has a special function. Can it be said that, while a carpenter and a cobbler have special functions and activities, man, unlike them, is naturally functionless? Or, as the eye, the hand, the foot, and similarly each part of the body has a special function, so may man be regarded as having a special function apart from all these? What, then, can this function be? It is not life; for life is apparently something that man shares with plants; and we are looking for something peculiar to him. We must exclude therefore the life of nutrition and growth. There is next what may be called the life of sensation. But this too, apparently, is shared by man with horses, cattle, and all other animals. There remains what I may call the active life of the rational part of man's being. Now this rational part is twofold; one part is rational in the sense of being obedient to reason, and the other in the sense of possessing and exercising reason and intelligence. The active life too may be conceived of in two ways,[4] either as a state of character, or as an activity; but we mean by it the life of activity, as this seems to be the truer form of the conception.

The function of man then is activity of soul in accordance with reason, or not apart from reason. Now, the function of a man of a certain kind, and

---

[4] In other words, life may be taken to mean either the mere possession of certain faculties or their active exercise.

of a man who is good of that kind—for example, of a harpist and a good harpist—are in our view the same in kind. This is true of all people of all kinds without exception, the superior excellence being only an addition to the function; for it is the function of a harpist to play the harp, and of a good harpist to play the harp well. This being so, if we define the function of man as a kind of life, and this life as an activity of the soul or a course of action in accordance with reason, and if the function of a good man is such activity of a good and noble kind, and if everything is well done when it is done in accordance with its proper excellence, it follows that the good of man is activity of soul in accordance with virtue, or, if there are more virtues than one, in accordance with the best and most complete virtue. But we must add the words "in a complete life." For as one swallow or one day does not make a spring, so one day or a short time does not make a man blessed or happy. . . .

CHAPTER 8

Goods have been divided into three classes: external goods as they are called, goods of the soul, and goods of the body. Of these three classes goods of the soul are considered goods in the strictest and truest sense. To the soul are ascribed spiritual actions and activities. Thus our definition must be a good one, at least according to this theory, which is both ancient and accepted by philosophers at the present time. It is correct too, inasmuch as we call certain actions and activities the end; for we put the end in some good of the soul and not in an external good. By a similar theory the happy man lives well and does well, and happiness, we have said, is in fact a kind of living and doing well. . . .

CHAPTER 9

. . . Our account accords too with the view of those who hold that happiness is virtue or excellence of some sort; for activity in accordance with virtue is virtue. But there is plainly a considerable difference between calling the supreme good possession or use, a state of mind, or an activity. For a state of mind may exist without producing anything good—for example, if a person is asleep, or in any other way inert. Not so with an activity, since activity implies acting and acting well. As in the Olympic games it is not the most beautiful and strongest who receive the crown but those who actually enter the combat, for from those come the victors, so it is those who act that win rightly what is noble and good in life.

Their life too is pleasant in itself. For pleasure is a state of mind, and whatever a man is fond of is pleasant to him, as a horse is to a lover of horses, a show to a lover of spectacles, and, similarly, just acts to a lover of justice, and virtuous acts in general to a lover of virtue. Now most men find a sense of discord in their pleasures, because their pleasures are not all naturally pleasant. But the lovers of nobleness take pleasure in what is naturally pleasant, and virtuous acts are naturally pleasant. Such acts then are pleasant both to these persons and in themselves. Nor does the life of such persons need more pleasure attached to it as a sort of charm; it possesses pleasure in itself. For, it may be added, a man who does not delight in noble acts is not good; as nobody would call a man just who did not enjoy just action, or liberal who did not enjoy liberal action, and so on. If this is so, it follows that acts of virtue are pleasant in themselves. They are also good and noble, and good and noble in the highest degree, for the judgment of the virtuous man on them is right, and his judgment is as we have described. Happiness then is the best and noblest and pleasantest thing in the world; nor is there any such difference between these things as the inscription at Delos suggests:

> "Justice is noblest, health is best,
> To gain one's wish is pleasantest."

For they all are characteristics of the best activities, and happiness, we hold, is the same as these or as one and the noblest of these.

Still it is clear, as we said, that happiness requires the addition of external goods; for it is impossible, or at least difficult, to do noble deeds with no outside means. For many things can be done only through the aid of friends or wealth or political power; and there are some things the lack of which spoils our felicity, such as good birth, wholesome children, and personal beauty. For a man who is extremely ugly in appearance or low born or solitary and childless can hardly be happy; perhaps still less so, if he has exceedingly bad children or friends, or has had good children or friends and lost them by death. As we said, then, happiness seems to need prosperity of this kind in addition to virtue. For this reason some persons identify happiness with good fortune, though others do so with virtue.

CHAPTER 10

The question is consequently raised whether happiness is something that can be learned or acquired by habit or training of some kind, or whether it comes by some divine dispensation, or even by chance.

Now if there is anything in the world that is a gift of the gods to men, it is reasonable to take happiness as a divine gift, and especially divine as it is the best of human things. This point, however, is perhaps more appropriate to another investigation than the present. But even if happiness is not sent by the gods but is the result of goodness and of learning or training of some kind, it is apparently one of the most divine things in the world; for that which is the prize and end of goodness would seem the best good and in its nature godlike and blessed. It may also be widely extended; for all persons who are not morally deformed may share in it by a process of study and care. And if it is better that happiness should come in this way than by chance, we may reasonably suppose that it does so come, since the order of things in Nature is the best possible, as it is in art and in causation generally, and most of all in the highest kind of causation. And to leave what is greatest and noblest to chance would be altogether unworthy. The definition of happiness itself helps to clear up the question; for happiness we have defined as a kind of virtuous activity of the soul. . . .

It is reasonable then not to call an ox or a horse or any other animal happy; for none of them is capable of sharing in this activity. For the same reason no child can be happy, since the youth of a child keeps him for the time being from such activity; if a child is ever called happy, the ground of felicitation is his promise, rather than his actual performance. For happiness demands, as we said, a complete virtue and a complete life. And there are all sorts of changes and chances in life, and the most prosperous of men may in his old age fall into extreme calamities, as Priam did in the heroic legends.[5] And a person who has experienced such chances and died a miserable death, nobody calls happy.

CHAPTER 11

Is it true then that nobody in the world may be called happy so long as he is alive? Must we adopt Solon's[6] rule of looking to the end? If we follow Solon, can it be said that a man is really happy after his death? Surely such a view is quite absurd, especially for us who define happiness as an activity. But if we do not call a dead man happy, and if Solon's meaning is not this, but rather that it is only when a man is dead that it is safe to call him fortunate, as being free at last from evil and calamities, this again is a view open to objection. For it seems that a dead man may be affected both by good and by evil, in the same way as one who is living but ignorant of them—by honors and dishonors, for instance, and by the successes or misfortunes of his children and his descendants generally. Yet here again a difficulty presents itself. For a person may live happily up to old age and die a happy death, and still his descendants may suffer many vicissitudes of fortune. Some of them may be good and enjoy the life they deserve; others may be bad and have a bad life. Obviously, these descendants may stand in all sorts of different degrees of relationship to their ancestor. It would be strange then if the dead man were to share the shifts in their fortunes and to become happy at one time and miserable at another, as they became either happy or miserable. But it would be equally strange if the future of their descendants should not for a time affect the ancestors at all.

We would best return to our previous difficulty, for it will perhaps afford an answer to the present question. If it is right to wait for the end, and only when the end has come, to call a man happy, not for being happy then but for having been so before, surely it is an extraordinary thing that, at the time when he is happy, we should not speak the truth about him, because we are unwilling to call the living happy in view of the changes to which they are liable, and because we have formed an idea of happiness as something permanent and exempt from the possibility of change, while every man is liable to many turns of fortune's wheel. Unquestionably, if we follow

[5] The disastrous fate of Priam, king of Troy, was part of the well-known Homeric tales.
[6] The historian Herodotus, I, ch. 32, is the authority for the celebrated warning which Solon is said to have addressed to Croesus, to call no man happy until he was dead.

the changes of fortune, we shall often call the same person happy at one time and miserable at another, making the happy man out as "a sort of chameleon with no stability." But to follow the changes of fortune cannot be right. It is not on these that good or evil depends; they are necessary accompaniments to human life, as we said; but it is a man's virtuous activities that constitute his happiness and their opposites that constitute his misery.

The difficulty we have now discussed proves again the correctness of our definition. For there is no human function so constant as virtuous activities; they seem to be more permanent than the sciences themselves. Among these activities too the most noble are the most permanent, and it is of them that the life of happiness chiefly and most continuously consists. This is apparently the reason why they are not likely to be forgotten.[7] The element of durability then which is required will be found in the happy man, and he will preserve his happiness through life; for always or chiefly he will pursue such actions and thoughts as accord with virtue; nor will anyone bear the chances of life so nobly, with such a perfect composure, as he who is truly good and "foursquare without a flaw."[8]

Now the events of chance are numerous and of different magnitudes. Small pieces of good fortune or the reverse do not turn the scale of life in any way, but great and numerous events make life happier if they turn out well, since they naturally give it beauty and the use of them may be noble and good. If, on the other hand, they turn out badly, they mar and mutilate happiness by causing pain and hindrances to many activities. Still, even in these circumstances, nobility shines out when a person bears with calmness the weight of accumulated misfortunes, not from insensibility but from dignity and greatness of spirit.

Then if activities determine the quality of life, as we said, no happy man can become miserable; for he will never do what is hateful and mean. For our idea of the truly good and wise man is that he bears all the chances of life with dignity and always does what is best in the circumstances, as a good general makes the best use of the forces at his command in war, or a good cobbler makes the best shoe with the leather given him, and so on through the whole series of the arts. If this is so, the happy man can never become miserable. I do not say that he will be fortunate if he meets such chances of life as Priam. Yet he will not be variable or constantly changing, for he will not be moved from his happiness easily or by ordinary misfortunes, but only by great and numerous ones; nor after them will he quickly regain his happiness. If he regains it at all, it will be only over a long and complete period of time and after great and notable achievement.

We may safely then define a happy man as one who is active in accord with perfect virtue and adequately furnished with external goods, not for some chance period of time but for his whole lifetime. But perhaps we ought to add that he should always live so and die as he has lived. It is not

[7] Aristotle means that it is comparatively easy to forget scientific truths, when they have once been learned, but it is difficult, if not impossible, to lose the habit of virtuous activity. In other words, he means that knowledge is less stable, and therefore less valuable, than character.

[8] The phrase is taken from Simonides.

given us to foresee the future, but we take happiness as an end, altogether final and complete; and, this being so, we shall call people happy during their lifetime if they possess and continue to possess these characteristics—yet happy only so far as men are happy. . . .

A serious doubt has been raised as to the participation of the dead in any good or evil. It is probable that if anything, whether good or evil, reaches the dead at all, it is feeble and insignificant, both in itself and in relation to them, or if not, is at least of no such magnitude and character as to be capable of making happy those who are not happy or of depriving of their felicity those who are. It would seem then that the dead are affected or influenced in some way by the prosperity and adversity of their friends, but that the influence is of such a kind and degree as not to make them unhappy, if they are happy, nor to have any similar effect. . . .

CHAPTER 13

Inasmuch as happiness is an activity of soul in accordance with perfect virtue, we must now consider virtue, as this will perhaps be the best way of studying happiness. . . . Clearly it is human virtue we have to consider; for the good of which we are in search is, as we said, human good, and the happiness, human happiness. By human virtue or excellence we mean not that of the body, but that of the soul, and by happiness we mean an activity of the soul.

There are some facts concerning the soul which are adequately stated in popular discourses, and these we may rightly accept. It is said, for example, that the soul has two parts, one irrational and the other rational. Whether these parts are separate like the parts of the body or like anything divisible, or whether they are theoretically distinct but in fact inseparable, like the convex and concave in the circumference of a circle, is of no importance to the present inquiry.

Of the irrational part of the soul one part is shared by man with all living things, and vegetative; I mean the part which is the cause of nutrition and growth. For we may assume such a faculty of the soul to exist in all young things that take food, even in embryos, and the same faculty to exist in things full grown, since it is more reasonable to suppose it is the same faculty than something different. Manifestly the virtue or excellence of this faculty is not peculiarly human but is shared by man with all living things; this part or faculty seems especially active in sleep, whereas goodness and badness never show so little as in sleep. Hence the saying that during half their lives there is no difference between the happy and the unhappy. And this is only natural; for sleep is an inactivity of the soul as regards its goodness or badness, except in so far as certain impulses affect it slightly and make the dreams of good men better than those of ordinary people. Enough, however, on this point; we shall now leave the faculty of nutrition, as it has by its nature no part in human goodness.

There is, we think, another natural element of the soul which is irrational and yet in a sense partakes of reason. For in continent and incontinent persons we praise their reason, and that part of their soul which possesses reason, because it counsels them aright and directs them to the best conduct. But we know there is in them also another element naturally opposed to reason that fights and contends against reason. Just as paralyzed parts of the body, when we try to move them to the right, pull in a contrary direction to the left, so it is with the soul; the impulses of incontinent people run counter to reason. But while in the body we see the part which pulls awry, in the soul we do not see it. We may, however, suppose with equal certainty that in the soul too there is something alien to reason, which opposes and thwarts it. The sense in which it is distinct from other things is unimportant. But it too partakes of reason, as we said; at all events, in a continent person it obeys reason, and in a temperate and brave man it is probably still more obedient, for in him it is absolutely harmonious with reason.

It appears then that the irrational part of the soul is twofold; for the vegetative faculty does not participate at all in reason, but the element of appetite and desire in general shares in it, in so far as it is submissive and obedient to reason. It is so in the sense in which we speak of "paying attention" to a father or to friends, but not in the sense in which we speak of "paying attention" to mathematics. All advice, reproof, and exhortation are witness that this irrational part of the soul is in a sense subject to influence by reason. And if we say that this part participates in reason, then as a part possessing reason, it will be twofold, one element possessing reason absolutely and in itself, the other listening to it as a child listens to its father.

Virtue too may be divided to correspond to this difference. For we call some virtues intellectual and others moral. Wisdom, intelligence, and prudence are intellectual; liberality and temperance moral. In describing a person's moral character we do not say that he is wise or intelligent but that he is gentle or temperate. A wise man, however, we praise for his mentality, and such mentality as deserves praise we call virtuous.

BOOK II

CHAPTER 1

Virtue then is twofold, partly intellectual and partly moral, and intellectual virtue is originated and fostered mainly by teaching; it demands therefore experience and time. Moral[1] virtue on the other hand is the outcome of habit, and accordingly its name, *ethike*, is derived by a slight variation from *ethos*, habit. From this fact it is clear that moral virtue is not implanted in us by nature; for nothing that exists by nature can be transformed by habit. Thus a stone, that naturally tends to fall downwards, cannot be habituated or trained to rise upwards, even if we tried to train it by throwing it up ten thousand times. Nor again can fire be trained to sink downwards, nor anything else that follows one natural law be habituated or trained to follow another. It is neither by nature then nor in defiance of nature that virtues grow in us. Nature gives us the capacity to receive them, and that capacity is perfected by habit.

[1] A student of Aristotle must familiarize himself with the conception of intellectual as well as of moral virtues, although it is not the rule in modern philosophy to speak of "virtues" of the intellect.

Again, if we take the various natural powers which belong to us, we first possess the proper faculties and afterwards display the activities. It is obviously so with the senses. Not by seeing frequently or hearing frequently do we acquire the sense of seeing or hearing; on the contrary, because we have the senses we make use of them; we do not get them by making use of them. But the virtues we get by first practicing them, as we do in the arts. For it is by doing what we ought to do when we study the arts that we learn the arts themselves; we become builders by building and harpists by playing the harp. Similarly, it is by doing just acts that we become just, by doing temperate acts that we become temperate, by doing brave acts that we become brave. The experience of states confirms this statement, for it is by training in good habits that lawmakers make the citizens good. This is the object all lawmakers have at heart; if they do not succeed in it, they fail of their purpose; and it makes the distinction between a good constitution and a bad one.

Again, the causes and means by which any virtue is produced and destroyed are the same; and equally so in any part. For it is by playing the harp that both good and bad harpists are produced; and the case of builders and others is similar, for it is by building well that they become good builders and by building badly that they become bad builders. If it were not so, there would be no need of anybody to teach them; they would all be born good or bad in their several crafts. The case of the virtues is the same. It is by our actions in dealings between man and man that we become either just or unjust. It is by our actions in the face of danger and by our training ourselves to fear or to courage that we become either cowardly or courageous. It is much the same with our appetites and angry passions. People become temperate and gentle, others licentious and passionate, by behaving in one or the other way in particular circumstances. In a word, moral states are the results of activities like the states themselves. It is our duty therefore to keep a certain character in our activities, since our moral states depend on the differences in our activities. So the difference between one and another training in habits in our childhood is not a light matter, but important, or rather, all-important.

CHAPTER 2

Our present study is not, like other studies,[2] purely theoretical in intention; for the object of our inquiry is not to know what virtue is but how to become good, and that is the sole benefit of it. We must, therefore, consider the right way of performing actions, for it is acts, as we have said, that determine the character of the resulting moral states.

That we should act in accordance with right reason is a common general principle, which may here be taken for granted. The nature of right reason, and its relation to the virtues generally, will be discussed later. But first of all it must be admitted that all reasoning on matters of conduct must be like a sketch in outline; it cannot be scientifically exact. We began by laying down the principle that the kind of reasoning demanded in any subject

---

[2] Such studies as generally occupied the attention of the Aristotelian school.

must be such as the subject matter itself allows; and questions of conduct and expediency no more admit of hard and fast rules than questions of health.

If this is true of general reasoning on ethics, still more true is it that scientific exactitude is impossible in treating of particular ethical cases. They do not fall under any art or law, but the actors themselves have always to take account of circumstances, as much as in medicine or navigation. Still, although such is the nature of our present argument, we must try to make the best of it.

The first point to be observed is that in the matters we are now considering deficiency and excess are both fatal. It is so, we see, in questions of health and strength. (We must judge of what we cannot see by the evidence of what we do see.) Too much or too little gymnastic exercise is fatal to strength. Similarly, too much or too little meat and drink is fatal to health, whereas a suitable amount produces, increases, and sustains it. It is the same with temperance, courage, and other moral virtues. A person who avoids and is afraid of everything and faces nothing becomes a coward; a person who is not afraid of anything but is ready to face everything becomes foolhardy. Similarly, he who enjoys every pleasure and abstains from none is licentious; he who refuses all pleasures, like a boor, is an insensible sort of person. For temperance and courage are destroyed by excess and deficiency but preserved by the mean.

Again, not only are the causes and agencies of production, increase, and destruction in moral states the same, but the field of their activity is the same also. It is so in other more obvious instances, as, for example, strength; for strength is produced by taking a great deal of food and undergoing a great deal of exertion, and it is the strong man who is able to take most food and undergo most exertion. So too with the virtues. By abstaining from pleasures we become temperate, and, when we have become temperate, we are best able to abstain from them. So again with courage; it is by training ourselves to despise and face terrifying things that we become brave, and when we have become brave, we shall be best able to face them.

The pleasure or pain which accompanies actions may be regarded as a test of a person's moral state. He who abstains from physical pleasures and feels pleasure in so doing is temperate; but he who feels pain at so doing is licentious. He who faces dangers with pleasure, or at least without pain, is brave; but he who feels pain at facing them is a coward. For moral virtue is concerned with pleasures and pains. It is pleasure which makes us do what is base, and pain which makes us abstain from doing what is noble. Hence the importance of having a certain training from very early days, as Plato[3] says, so that we may feel pleasure and pain at the right objects; for this is true education. . . .

CHAPTER 3

But we may be asked what we mean by saying that people must become just by doing what is just and temperate by doing what is temperate. For, it will

[3]*Laws*, II, 653.

be said, if they do what is just and temperate they are already just and temperate themselves, in the same way as, if they practice grammar and music, they are grammarians and musicians.

But is this true even in the case of the arts? For a person may speak grammatically either by chance or at the suggestion of somebody else; hence he will not be a grammarian unless he not only speaks grammatically but does so in a grammatical manner, that is, because of the grammatical knowledge which he possesses.

There is a point of difference too between the arts and the virtues. The productions of art have their excellence in themselves. It is enough then that, when they are produced, they themselves should possess a certain character. But acts in accordance with virtue are not justly or temperately performed simply because they are in themselves just or temperate. The doer at the time of performing them must satisfy certain conditions; in the first place, he must know what he is doing; secondly, he must deliberately choose to do it and do it for its own sake; and thirdly, he must do it as part of his own firm and immutable character. If it be a question of art, these conditions, except only the condition of knowledge, are not raised; but if it be a question of virtue, mere knowledge is of little or no avail; it is the other conditions, which are the results of frequently performing just and temperate acts, that are not slightly- but all-important. Accordingly, deeds are called just and temperate when they are such as a just and temperate person would do; and a just and temperate person is not merely one who does these deeds but one who does them in the spirit of the just and the temperate.

It may fairly be said then that a just man becomes just by doing what is just, and a temperate man becomes temperate by doing what is temperate, and if a man did not so act, he would not have much chance of becoming good. But most people, instead of acting, take refuge in theorizing; they imagine that they are philosophers and that philosophy will make them virtuous; in fact, they behave like people who listen attentively to their doctors but never do anything that their doctors tell them. But a healthy state of the soul will no more be produced by this kind of philosophizing than a healthy state of the body by this kind of medical treatment.

CHAPTER 4

We have next to consider the nature of virtue. Now, as the properties of the soul are three, namely, emotions, faculties, and moral states, it follows that virtue must be one of the three. By emotions I mean desire, anger, fear, pride, envy, joy, love, hatred, regret, ambition, pity—in a word, whatever feeling is attended by pleasure or pain. I call those faculties through which we are said to be capable of experiencing these emotions, for instance, capable of getting angry or being pained or feeling pity. And I call those moral states through which we are well or ill disposed in our emotions, ill disposed, for instance, in anger, if our anger be too violent or too feeble, and well disposed, if it be rightly moderate; and similarly in our other emotions.

Now neither the virtues nor the vices are emotions; for we are not called good or bad for our emotions but for our virtues or vices. We are not praised or blamed simply for being angry, but only for being angry in a certain way; but we are praised or blamed for our virtues or vices. Again, whereas we are angry or afraid without deliberate purpose, the virtues are matters of deliberate purpose, or require deliberate purpose. Moreover, we are said to be moved by our emotions, but by our virtues or vices we are not said to be moved but to have a certain disposition.

For these reasons the virtues are not faculties. For we are not called either good or bad, nor are we praised or blamed for having simple capacity for emotion. Also while Nature gives us our faculties, it is not Nature that makes us good or bad; but this point we have already discussed. If then the virtues are neither emotions nor faculties, all that remains is that they must be moral states.

CHAPTER 5

The nature of virtue has been now described in kind. But it is not enough to say merely that virtue is a moral state; we must also describe the character of that moral state.

We may assert then that every virtue or excellence puts into good condition that of which it is a virtue or excellence, and enables it to perform its work well. Thus excellence in the eye makes the eye good and its function good, for by excellence in the eye we see well. Similarly, excellence of the horse makes a horse excellent himself and good at racing, at carrying its rider and at facing the enemy. If then this rule is universally true, the virtue or excellence of a man will be such a moral state as makes a man good and able to perform his proper function well. How this will be the case we have already explained, but another way of making it clear will be to study the nature or character of virtue.

Now of everything, whether it be continuous or divisible, it is possible to take a greater, a smaller, or an equal amount, and this either in terms of the thing itself or in relation to ourselves, the equal being a mean between too much and too little. By the mean in terms of the thing itself, I understand that which is equally distinct from both its extremes, which is one and the same for every man. By the mean relatively to ourselves, I understand that which is neither too much nor too little for us; but this is not one nor the same for everybody. Thus if 10 be too much and 2 too little, we take 6 as a mean in terms of the thing itself; for 6 is as much greater than 2 as it is less than 10, and this is a mean in arithmetical proportion. But the mean considered relatively to ourselves may not be ascertained in that way. It does not follow that if 10 pounds of meat is too much and 2 too little for a man to eat, the trainer will order him 6 pounds, since this also may be too much or too little for him who is to take it; it will be too little, for example, for Milo[4] but too much for a beginner in gymnastics. The same with running and wrestling; the right amount will vary with the individual. This

---

[4] The famous wrestler, Milo of Croton.

being so, the skillful in any art avoids alike excess and deficiency; he seeks and chooses the mean, not the absolute mean, but the mean considered relatively to himself.

Every art then does its work well, if it regards the mean and judges the works it produces by the mean. For this reason we often say of successful works of art that it is impossible to take anything from them or to add anything to them, which implies that excess or deficiency is fatal to excellence but that the mean state ensures it. Good artists too, as we say, have an eye to the mean in their works. Now virtue, like Nature herself, is more accurate and better than any art; virtue, therefore, will aim at the mean. I speak of moral virtue, since it is moral virtue which is concerned with emotions and actions, and it is in these we have excess and deficiency and the mean. Thus it is possible to go too far, or not far enough in fear, pride, desire, anger, pity, and pleasure and pain generally, and the excess and the deficiency are alike wrong; but to feel these emotions at the right times, for the right objects, towards the right persons, for the right motives, and in the right manner, is the mean or the best good, which signifies virtue. Similarly, there may be excess, deficiency, or the mean, in acts. Virtue is concerned with both emotions and actions, wherein excess is an error and deficiency a fault, while the mean is successful and praised, and success and praise are both characteristics of virtue.

It appears then that virtue is a kind of mean because it aims at the mean.

On the other hand, there are many different ways of going wrong; for evil is in its nature infinite, to use the Pythagorean[5] phrase, but good is finite and there is only one possible way of going right. So the former is easy and the latter is difficult; it is easy to miss the mark but difficult to hit it. And so by our reasoning excess and deficiency are characteristics of vice and the mean is a characteristic of virtue.

"For good is simple, evil manifold."[6]

CHAPTER 6

Virtue then is a state of deliberate moral purpose, consisting in a mean relative to ourselves, the mean being determined by reason, or as a prudent man would determine it. It is a mean, firstly, as lying between two vices, the vice of excess on the one hand, and the vice of deficiency on the other, and, secondly, because, whereas the vices either fall short of or go beyond what is right in emotion and action, virtue discovers and chooses the mean. Accordingly, virtue, if regarded in its essence or theoretical definition, is a mean, though, if regarded from the point of view of what is best and most excellent, it is an extreme.

But not every action or every emotion admits of a mean. There are some whose very name implies wickedness, as, for example, malice, shamelessness, and envy among the emotions, and adultery, theft, and

[5] The Pythagoreans, who saw a mystical and moral significance in numbers, took the opposite principles of "the finite" and "the infinite" to represent respectively good and evil.
[6] A line—perhaps Pythagorean—of unknown authorship.

murder among the actions. All these and others like them are marked as intrinsically wicked, not merely the excesses or deficiencies of them. It is never possible then to be right in them; they are always sinful. Right or wrong in such acts as adultery does not depend on our committing it with the right woman, at the right time, or in the right manner; on the contrary, it is wrong to do it at all. It would be equally false to suppose that there can be a mean or an excess or deficiency in unjust, cowardly, or licentious conduct; for, if that were so, it would be a mean of excess and deficiency, an excess of excess and a deficiency of deficiency. But as in temperance and courage there can be no excess or deficiency, because the mean there is in a sense an extreme, so too in these other cases there cannot be a mean or an excess or a deficiency, but however the acts are done, they are wrong. For in general an excess or deficiency does not have a mean, nor a mean an excess or deficiency. . . .

CHAPTER 8

There are then three dispositions, two being vices, namely, excess and deficiency, and one virtue, which is the mean between them; and they are all in a sense mutually opposed. The extremes are opposed both to the mean and to each other, and the mean is opposed to the extremes. For as the equal if compared with the less is greater, but if compared with the greater is less, so the mean state, whether in emotion or action, if compared with deficiency is excessive, but if compared with excess is deficient. Thus the brave man appears foolhardy compared with the coward, but cowardly compared with the foolhardy. Similarly, the temperate man appears licentious compared with the insensible man but insensible compared with the licentious; and the liberal man appears extravagant compared with the stingy man but stingy compared with the spendthrift. The result is that the extremes each denounce the mean as belonging to the other extreme; the coward calls the brave man foolhardy, and the foolhardy man calls him cowardly; and so on in other cases.

But while there is mutual opposition between the extremes and the mean, there is greater opposition between the two extremes than between extreme and the mean; for they are further removed from each other than from the mean, as the great is further from the small and the small from the great than either from the equal. Again, while some extremes show some likeness to the mean, as foolhardiness to courage and extravagance to liberality, there is the greatest possible dissimilarity between extremes. But things furthest removed from each other are called opposites; hence the further things are removed, the greater is the opposition between them.

In some cases it is deficiency and in others excess which is more opposed to the mean. Thus it is not foolhardiness, an excess, but cowardice, a deficiency, which is more opposed to courage, nor is it insensibility, a deficiency, but licentiousness, an excess, which is more opposed to temperance. There are two reasons why this should be so. One lies in the nature of the matter itself; for when one of two extremes is nearer and more like the mean, it is not this extreme but its opposite that we chiefly contrast with the mean. For instance, as foolhardiness seems more like and nearer to courage than cowardice, it is cowardice that we chiefly contrast with courage; for things further removed from the mean seem to be more opposite to it. This reason lies in the nature of the matter itself; there is a second which lies in our own nature. The things to which we ourselves are naturally more inclined we think more opposed to the mean. Thus we are ourselves naturally more inclined to pleasures than to their opposites, and are more prone therefore to self-indulgence than to moderation. Accordingly we speak of those things in which we are more likely to run to great lengths as more opposed to the mean. Hence licentiousness, which is an excess, seems more opposed to temperance than insensibility.

CHAPTER 9

We have now sufficiently shown that moral virtue is a mean, and in what sense it is so; that it is a mean as lying between two vices, a vice of excess on the one side and a vice of deficiency on the other, and as aiming at the mean in emotion and action.

That is why it is so hard to be good; for it is always hard to find the mean in anything; it is not everyone but only a man of science who can find the mean or center of a circle. So too anybody can get angry—that is easy—and anybody can give or spend money, but to give it to the right person, to give the right amount of it, at the right time, for the right cause and in the right way, this is not what anybody can do, nor is it easy. That is why goodness is rare and praiseworthy and noble. One then who aims at a mean must begin by departing from the extreme that is more contrary to the mean; he must act in the spirit of Calypso's advice,

"Far from this spray and swell hold thou thy ship,"[7]

for of the two extremes one is more wrong than the other. As it is difficult to hit the mean exactly, we should take the second best course,[8] as the saying is, and choose the lesser of two evils. This we shall best do in the way described, that is, steering clear of the evil which is further from the mean. We must also note the weaknesses to which we are ourselves particularly prone, since different natures tend in different ways; and we may ascertain what our tendency is by observing our feelings of pleasure and pain. Then we must drag ourselves away towards the opposite extreme; for by pulling ourselves as far as possible from what is wrong we shall arrive at the mean, as we do when we pull a crooked stick straight.

In all cases we must especially be on our guard against the pleasant, or pleasure, for we are not impartial judges of pleasure. Hence our attitude towards pleasure must be like that of the elders of the people in the *Iliad* towards Helen, and we must constantly apply the words they use;[9] for if we

[7] *Odyssey* XII, but it is Odysseus who speaks there, and the advice has been given him not by Calypso but by Circe.

[8] The Greek proverb means properly "we must take to the oars, if sailing is impossible."

[9] In Homer's *Iliad*, Book III, the old men of Troy acknowledge Helen's almost divine beauty but nevertheless urge that she be given up to the Greeks who are trying to recapture her. (Editors' note.)

dismiss pleasure as they dismissed Helen, we shall be less likely to go wrong. By action of this kind, to put it summarily, we shall best succeed in hitting the mean.

Undoubtedly this is a difficult task, especially in individual cases. It is not easy to determine the right manner, objects, occasion and duration of anger. Sometimes we praise people who are deficient in anger, and call them gentle, and at other times we praise people who exhibit a fierce temper as high spirited. It is not however a man who deviates a little from goodness, but one who deviates a great deal, whether on the side of excess or of deficiency, that is blamed; for he is sure to call attention to himself. It is not easy to decide in theory how far and to what extent a man may go before he becomes blameworthy, but neither is it easy to define in theory anything else in the region of the senses; such things depend on circumstances, and our judgment of them depends on our perception.

So much then is plain, that the mean is everywhere praiseworthy, but that we ought to aim at one time towards an excess and at another towards a deficiency; for thus we shall most easily hit the mean, or in other words reach excellence.

Catullus
(C.84–C.54 B.C.)

Gaius Valerius Catullus, one of the world's great lyric poets and (with Horace) one of the two greatest in Latin literature, was born around 84 B.C. and died young, at about the age of thirty. His birthplace was Verona, in a northern Italian province ("Cisalpine Gaul") that was controlled by Rome in Catullus's lifetime but whose inhabitants did not acquire the rights of Roman citizenship until shortly after his death. His father was wealthy and prominent enough to entertain Julius Caesar as a guest. Although Catullus made one long journey in 57–56; to Asia Minor (where he visited the grave of his brother, as is recorded in Poem 101), most of his life was divided between his home province and Rome. He lived during the eventful last days of the Roman republic, but, although his acquaintances included leading political figures like Caesar, Pompey, and Cicero, Catullus apparently had little interest in politics as such. Although he lampooned Caesar and Pompey, for instance, he did so on personal rather than on political grounds. The social set in which he moved seems to have been smart, sophisticated, and for the most part modernist in its insouciantly easygoing morality.

The most intense of his attachments was with a woman whom in his poems Catullus calls Lesbia, in honor of the Greek poet Sappho of Lesbos, whose poetry was in some respects a model for Catullus. It seems virtually certain that Lesbia was in real life a woman named Clodia, seven to ten years older than Catullus, married but scarcely bound to a rather pompous husband. She was an aristocrat, probably, the center of a set of political adventurers, a woman of brilliance and beauty, probably a nymphomaniac, and, if the gossip of the time was accurate, the lover of her brother and the poisoner of her husband. Something is known of her from a hostile portrait in a speech by Cicero defending one of her former lovers against a charge of attempting to poison her. Her husband, Metellus Celer, was governor of Cisalpine Gaul in the year 62, and if Catullus met Clodia then (which is possible though not certain), he would have been twenty-two years old at the time the affair began. The twenty-five poems that depict it can be arranged to form a dramatic sequence (which does not necessarily reflect their order of composition), beginning in idealism and fire (see Poem 51, a close paraphrase of Sappho's "He is more than a hero") and progressing through disillusionment, reconciliation, jealousy, anger, self-pity, and brooding resolution to shake off his passion, to his final dismissal of Lesbia in the elaborately contemptuous Poem 11, where Catullus ironically returns to the verse form named for Sappho. Whether the obloquy heaped on Lesbia-Clodia is entirely just can be questioned; Cicero's attack on her is that of an adversary lawyer in the courtroom, and the resentment felt by rejected lovers is not always reasonable. But she seems to have been wicked enough.

Catullus's personal social set overlapped with a set of poets he was associated with, the "Neoterics" or "new poets." Catullus, and the others if they were like him (their work has not survived), broke from the main tradition of Roman poetry and its high-serious epic and tragic concern with public themes like history and war; he preferred more personal and occasional topics. The new poetry has a colloquialism drawn in part from Roman comedy overlaid with the influence of Alexandrianism, the school of the late (fourth and third centuries) Greek poet-scholars. The Alexandrian influence helps account for Catullus's concern with meticulous elegance of form, learned allusion, and taste. There is a good deal of art-for-art's-sake estheticism in Catullus. Yet, paradoxically, his art is above all one of intensely personal expression, treating subjects drawn from life, and his feelings are expressed with a directness and intimacy that are distinctly romantic. The sound, of Catullus's short lyrics at least, is that of a personal conversational voice easily recognizable as his. The viewpoint is unabashedly subjective. The range is astonishing. The playfully mock-solemn dirge for Lesbia's dead pet sparrow is delicately light of touch, but Catullus can also be grossly obscene (Poem 39 gives a hint, though only a hint, of this side of him). The rapturous first address to Lesbia (51) is in violent contrast with the blistering farewell (11). Each lyric seems a total indulgence of the poet's mood, at least as the poet's art defines it. The control of tones is masterful. Poem 11, for example, has three distinct tones: mock-heroic inflation, scathing hatred, and self-pity.

Catullus's influence on ancient literature was great, extending even to poets very dissimilar to him like Virgil and Horace. All the same, his poetry came precariously close to disappearing as almost all of Sappho's has done. Poem 62 exists in a ninth-century manuscript; Catullus would else be unknown (except for brief fragments) without the discovery around 1300 of a manuscript of the other 115 or so poems of his that we have. Even this manuscript was soon lost again, but fortunately not before it had been copied. To these lucky accidents we owe the survival of a voice expressive of the passion and the dissipation that coexisted with Roman austerity.

FURTHER READING *(prepared by F. S. N.):* C. J. Fordyce, *Catullus: A Commentary,* 1961, offers an excellent commentary, with the Latin text, on most of the poems. Tenney Frank, *Catullus and Horace: Two Poets in Their Environment,* 1928, attempts to place Catullus in a historical setting. T. P. Wiseman's *Catullan Questions,* 1969; and Kenneth Quinn's *Catullus: An Interpretation,* 1973, both discuss the life of Catullus, questions of dating, the Lesbia poems, and cyclical arrangement. Kenneth Quinn, ed., in *Approaches to Catullus,* 1972, assembles a number of respected essays on Catullus which had previously appeared in scholarly journals.

POEMS

Translated by Horace Gregory

1[1]

Who shall receive my new-born book,
my poems, elegant and shy,
neatly dressed and polished?[2]

You, Cornelius,
shall be my single patron,   5
for, long ago, you praised
my slender lines and stanzas;

You, the only man in Italy
whose genius had the vigour
to write the history of the world   10
in three sturdy volumes;

These were books, by Jupiter,
that showed a learned mind and
the strength for heavy labour.

Then, take this little book   15
for what it is, my friend.

Patroness and Muse,
keep these poems green for
a day or so beyond a hundred years,
                        O Virgin![3]   20

---

[1] This dedicatory poem was written to introduce a collection of Catullus's poems; his surviving work would take up more than one book (that is, scroll), and so it is uncertain which poems the dedication applies to. The addressee is Cornelius Nepos, who had written a history of the world in three scrolls and who, like Catullus, came from Cisalpine Gaul, south of the Alps in northern Italy.

[2] Polished with pumice (volcanic rock), used to smooth the ends of the papyrus and give the volume elegance.

[3] *Virgin.* The Muse.

51[1]

He is changed to a god he who looks on her,
godlike he shines when he's seated beside her,
immortal joy to gaze and hear the fall of
                    her sweet laughter.

All of my senses are lost and confounded;   5
Lesbia rises before me and trembling
I sink into earth and swift dissolution
                    seizes my body.

Limbs are pierced with fire and the heavy tongue fails,
ears resound with noise of distant storms shaking   10
this earth, eyes gaze on stars that fall forever
                    into deep midnight.

                    *   *   *

This languid madness destroys you Catullus,
long day and night shall be desolate, broken,
as long ago ancient kings and rich cities   15
                    fell into ruin.

                    *   *   *

3

Dress now in sorrow, O all
you shades of Venus,
and your little cupids weep.

My girl has lost her darling sparrow;   5
he is dead, her precious toy
that she loved more than her two eyes,
O, honeyed sparrow following her
as a girl follows her mother,
never to leave her breast, but tripping
now here, now there, and always singing   10

[1] This poem, the first in the "Lesbia" sequence, records the poet's feelings at or near the
beginning of his relationship with the woman usually identified as Clodia, a fashionable and
emancipated beauty. (The numbering of Catullus's poems does not correspond to the order of
their composition or of the events recorded.) The first three stanzas are a near-translation
from a poem by Sappho of Lesbos, part of which survives ("He is more than a hero"). Authorities do not agree on whether the last four lines of Catullus's poem are really part of it or
represent instead an error in the manuscript. The Latin meter ("sapphics") is also derived
from Sappho and, as far as we know, was used only twice by Catullus: once here and once in
his bitter farewell to Lesbia (Poem 11). "He" in line one is presumably a rival, possibly Clodia's
husband.

his sweet falsetto
song to her alone.

Now he is gone; poor creature,
lost in darkness,
to a sad place
from which no one returns.   15

O ravenous hell!
My evil hatred rises against your power,
you that devour
all things beautiful;
and now this pitiful, broken sparrow,   20
who is the cause of my girl's grief,
making her eyes weary and red with sorrow.

5

Come, Lesbia, let us live and love,
nor give a damn what sour old men say.
The sun that sets may rise again
but when our light has sunk into the earth,
it is gone forever.
   Give me a thousand kisses,   5
then a hundred, another thousand,
another hundred
   and in one breath
still kiss another thousand,   10
another hundred.
   O then with lips and bodies joined
many deep thousands;
   confuse
their number,
   so that poor fools and cuckolds (envious 15
even now) shall never
learn our wealth and curse us
with their
evil eyes.   20

85

I hate and love.
  And if you ask me why,
I have no answer, but I discern,
can feel, my senses rooted in eternal torture.

109

My life, my love, you say our love will last forever;
O gods remember
her pledge, convert the words of her avowal into a prophecy.
Now let her blood speak, let sincerity govern each syllable fallen
from her lips, so that the long years of our lives shall be   5
a contract of true love inviolate
against time itself, a symbol of eternity.

39[1]

Egnatius has white teeth and therefore always pleasant, always smiling;
and if a lawyer is telling a sad tale for the defense[2] (a pitiful client),
Egnatius is there with his eternal smile.
If there's a funeral with the mother weeping
over the body of her only son,   5
Egnatius arrives gleaming with his happy smile:
no matter where he is or who he sees or what he does,
he is forever smiling.
                          O what a foul disease,
this smile,   10
            not sweet nor gracious,
nor a sign of social charm.
                              Listen to me, my dear,
good, fine Egnatius,
                      if you were Roman, Sabine, Tibertine,   15
or a starved greedy pig from Umbria,
or an Etruscan, short and round, or a dark Lanuvian
with glittering teeth or a man from my own province,[3]
or anybody at all who scrubs his teeth with good clean water daily—
your smile would still offend me; nothing is worse   20
than senseless laughter from a foolish face. But you're a Spaniard,
and we already know the Spanish custom:
                              how Spaniards clean their teeth
and scour their gums with the same water that issues
from their bladders.   25
            So if your teeth are clean, my friend, we know how
you have used your urine.

[1] Egnatius, a Spaniard, was one of Clodia/Lesbia's lovers.
[2] Egnatius is pictured as sitting among the defendant's supporters, where sadness and concern would be fitting.
[3] Six non-Roman peoples who were nevertheless socially accepted. The people of Catullus's own province, in northern Italy south of the Alps, had still not acquired full Roman citizenship in Catullus's lifetime.

8

Poor damned Catullus, here's no time for nonsense,
open your eyes, O idiot, innocent boy, look at what has happened:
once there were sunlit days when you followed after
where ever a girl would go, she loved with greater
love than any woman knew.
Then you took your pleasure
and the girl was not unwilling. Those were the bright days, gone;
now she's no longer yielding; you must be, poor idiot,
more like a man! not running after
her your mind all tears; stand firm, insensitive.
say with a smile, voice steady, "Good-bye, my girl," Catullus
strong and manly no longer follows you, nor comes when you are
    calling
him at night and you shall need him.
You whore! Where's your man to cling to, who will praise your
    beauty,
where's the man that you love and who will call you his,
and when you fall to kissing, whose lips will you devour?
But always, your Catullus will be as firm as rock is.

76

If man can find rich consolation, remembering his good deeds and all
    he has done,
if he remembers his loyalty to others, nor abuses his religion by heart-
    less betrayal
of friends to the anger of powerful gods,[1]
then, my Catullus, the long years before you shall not sink in darkness
    with all hope gone,
wandering, dismayed, through the ruins of love.
All the devotion that man gives to man, you have given, Catullus,
your heart and your brain flowed into a love that was desolate,
    wasted, nor can it return.
But why, why do you crucify love and yourself through the years?
Take what the gods have to offer and standing serene, rise forth as a
    rock against darkening skies;
and yet you do nothing but grieve, sunken deep in your sorrow, Ca-
    tullus,
for it is hard, hard to throw aside years lived in poisonous love that
    has tainted your brain
and must end.
If this seems impossible now, you must rise

[1] That is, does not make dishonest oaths.

to salvation. O gods of pity and mercy, descend and witness my sor-
    row, if ever
you have looked upon man in his hour of death, see me now in de-
    spair.   15
Tear this loathsome disease from my brain. Look, a subtle corruption
    has entered my bones,[2]
no longer shall happiness flow through my veins like a river. No
    longer I pray
that she love me again, that her body be chaste, mine forever.
Cleanse my soul of this sickness of love, give me power to rise, resur-
    rected, to thrust love aside,
I have given my heart to the gods, O hear me, omnipotent heaven,   20
and ease me of love and its pain.

11[1]

Furius, Aurelius, bound to Catullus
though he marches piercing farthest India
where echoing waves of the Eastern Oceans
    break upon the shores:

Under Caspian seas, to mild Arabia,   5
east of Parthia,[2] dark with savage bowmen,
or where the Nile, sevenfold and uprising,
    stains its leveled sands,—

Even though he marches over Alps to gaze on
great Caesar's monuments:[3] the Gallic Rhine and   10
Britons who live beyond torn seas, remotest
    men of distant lands—

Friends who defy with me all things, whatever
gods may send us, go now, friends, deliver
these words to my lady, nor sweet—flattering,   15
    nor kind nor gentle:

---

    [2] These words echo and contrast with the description of ardent love in Poem 51: "swift dissolution/seizes my body./Limbs are pierced with fire."

    [1] This poem marks the final contemptuous farewell to Lesbia/Clodia. In the original Latin, Catullus uses for the second and last time the sapphic verse form used in Poem 51, the overture to the love affair. Furius and Aurelius have apparently been sent as envoys from Lesbia to seek a reconciliation; since they were not in fact friends of Catullus, his address to them as fellow comrades-in-arms is perhaps heavily sarcastic. Before getting to the point—his message to Lesbia—the poet surveys the entire known world, from India in the east to Britain in the west.

    [2] A country in what is now northeastern Iran.

    [3] Reminders of Julius Caesar's exploits. Caesar crossed the Rhine in the summer of 55 B.C., and later in that year he crossed the English Channel to Britain.

Live[4] well and sleep with adulterous lovers,
three hundred men between your thighs, embracing
all love turned false, again, again, and breaking
    their strength, now sterile.

20

She will not find my love (once hers) returning;
she it was who caused love, this lonely flower,[5]
tossed aside, to fall by the plow dividing
    blossoming meadows.

62[1]

BOYS

Twilight and star we hope to see arise, pouring bright rain from
    Mount Olympus[2] down
over the wedding feast, have now arrived, we sing our praise to the
    advancing bride,
rise now to greet her singing:
O Hymen, Hymenaee, come now, O Hymen.[3]

GIRLS

And is it true that Hesperus is here? Witness this company of boys
    now standing

5

facing us and the star of night flames with the fire of Mount Oeta,[4]
O hear them sing and see their ritual, wonder and joy for us to gaze
    upon
O Hymen, Hymenaee, come now, O Hymen.

BOYS

Hear how the girls have set their song in perfect measures, and each
    word recited
sounds from an infallible memory, surely their minds were rooted

10

deep in memorable music while we (our minds and ears distracted)
    wandered, and we shall be outdone;
O victory shall fall to those who sing in perfect rhythm, we must equal

---

[4] The word recalls its use in the first line of the rapturous Poem 5.

[5] The image is another reminiscence of Sappho, who uses a similar image of a damaged flower in "Lament for a maidenhead."

[1] This epithalamium, or wedding song, was not written for any particular wedding. Influenced strongly by Greek poetry, it describes a mixture of Greek and Roman nuptial ceremonies. The setting is the end of an evening feast in the house of the bride's parents; the form is that of a choral competition between the young male and female guests, who are seated apart from each other. The bride makes her appearance in the course of the poem.

[2] That is, the sky; Mount Olympus was the dwelling place of the gods.

[3] A ritual refrain at weddings. (Later Hymen was personified as the god of marriage.) The refrain is probably an interjection by the poet, not by the singers.

[4] There may have been a cult of Hesperus, the evening star, on Oeta, a mountain in central Greece.

them and what they say must find
our words a perfect complement.
O Hymen, Hymenaee, come now, O Hymen.

GIRLS

What are these flames that roll against the skies, divorcing mother
    and child, more terrible   15
than earthly fires? These flames of Hesperus that seize a daughter
    from her mother's arms
delivering the girl into the quick embrace of a young husband—here
    is destruction greater
than a tall city given to its enemies.
O Hymen, Hymenaee, come now, O Hymen.

BOYS

What is more beautiful than this rich fire, the crown of heaven rising,   20
the fire that joins the marriage a true contract spoken by husband and
    parents of the bride,
and yet does not disclose its vital power until the marriage bed is
    made. What a gift from heaven
greater than this gift from gods to man in a superlative hour of happi-
    ness?
O Hymen, Hymenaee, come now, O Hymen.

*   *   *

GIRLS

O friends who love us, Hesperus has taken one of us, our sister,
    taken. . . .[5]   25

*   *   *

BOYS

O Hesperus when you rise, our guardian, eyes open the night long,
you come, disguised as dawn star now disclosing thieves hidden under
    night's vast shadow
but virgins cry against you, a false lamentation against him who is
    desire
coiled in their brains, a secret never spoken.
O Hymen, Hymenaee, come now, O Hymen.   30

GIRLS

We are as flowers[6] in a garden hidden from all men's eyes, no crea-
    ture of the field walks in this place,

[5] Most of the young women's words here and the beginning of the men's reply have been lost. The women apparently charge Hesperus, herald of night, with being the ally of thieves. The men answer that, besides alerting the night police to be on guard. Hesperus as morning star also brings daylight and thus catches thieves (Venus can be either a morning or an evening star).
[6] The following flower-simile, like the one in Catullus's Poem 11, is probably a reminiscence of Sappho's "Lament for a maidenhead."

no plow divides us; only the gentlest wind, rain from a soft warm
   cloud and the quickening sun to nourish us.
We are the treasure that many girls and boys desire; but once deflowered (the flower stained and torn)
the virgin's body rancid, neither boys nor girls will turn to her again
nor can she wake their passion.   35

Boys

You are as a vine in a barren field that cannot climb by its own
   strength
nor its fruit prosper (the vine driven downward with its own weight
   neither the ox nor plowman shall teach it how
to grow, but if its body twined round an elm, gives promise of fruit,
   then by this marriage
many a farmer and his beast will wait upon it). So is it with you O
   virgins.
The virgin, perfect, wastes until she ripens in the marriage bed and
   there receives
her father's blessing and her husband's love.   40
Never resist the power of this union made, O virgin; father and
   mother have given you to him, this man, your husband
your maidenhead by this division is not yours alone, you hold one
   third of that which is the treasure
of parents and your husband—this is the lawful contract given to him
   whose hands receive your dowry.
O Hymen, Hymenaee, come now, O Hymen.   45

101[1]

Dear brother, I have come these many miles, through strange lands to
   this Eastern Continent
to see your grave, a poor sad monument of what you were, O brother.
And I have come too late; you cannot hear me; alone now I must
   speak
to these few ashes that were once your body and expect no answer.
I shall perform an ancient ritual over your remains, weeping,   5
(this plate of lentils for dead men to feast upon, wet with my tears)
O brother, here's my greeting: here's my hand forever welcoming you
and I forever saying: good-bye, good-bye.

---

[1] Catullus's brother had died young, in Asia Minor near the site of ancient Troy. In 57 B.C.,
during a term of service abroad, in nearby Bithynia, Catullus visited his brother's grave. He
offers ritual gifts to the dead.

Virgil

(70 B.C.—19 B.C.)

Because of the nobility of his conceptions and his poetic genius, Virgil has had a more continuous and profound impact on European culture, antique and Christian, than any other single classical author. Since his own day his works have been the fare of schoolboys and of connoisseurs of poetry alike. He has been regarded not only as a prototype of the consummate artist but also as a sage, a religious prophet, and even a sorcerer. Perhaps his most distinctive achievement is to have defined heroism, and its costs, in a context not of primitive social conditions but of a sophisticated, intricately organized civilization and its values.

Like several other great Roman poets, notably Catullus, Horace, and Ovid, Virgil came from the provinces. He was born, like Catullus, in the part of northern Italy called Cisalpine Gaul, in 70 B.C. There he learned the deep love of rural nature that would later shine through his poetry. His father seems to have been a man of humble stock who acquired farm land near Mantua. Virgil nevertheless got a very good education—especially in language and literature, science, and philosophy—at Cremona, Milan, and finally at Rome, where he arrived at the age of seventeen. He is said to have contemplated a career in law but to have lacked the quickness and hardihood necessary for success in it. Although he was amiable and made influential friends in the political and cultural circles of Rome, he was a shy, studious person who never married and who took no direct part in public life. A professional poet, he devoted almost all his time to his art and the studies ancillary to it.

His three principal works were the Eclogues *(written between 42 and 37), the* Georgics *(36–29), and the* Aeneid *(29–19). The* Eclogues *are pastoral poems, in the tradition of the Greek poet Theocritus, depicting the idyllic life of shepherds, but Virgil intriguingly combines with the escapist setting references to actual persons and current topics. Two of the* Eclogues *deal with dispossession from one's land—a poignant, typically Virgilian theme—and are believed to refer to the expropriation of Virgil's family farm for the benefit of soldiers in the army of Mark Antony and Octavian after they defeated the assassins of Julius Caesar at Philippi. (The property was apparently returned to Virgil at a later date.) The* Fourth Eclogue, *which prophesies the birth of a wondrous child who is to restore the Golden Age, was later interpreted by Christians as a prophecy of Jesus; hence its name the "Messianic eclogue." The* Georgics *too has a rural theme and setting; in fact, it is largely a practical handbook for farmers, though the work also has a broad patriotic theme in keeping with Virgil's desire to help restore Italian agriculture and the moral values associated with it. It counterpoints dream and reality, tragedy and comedy, pessimism and optimism. The* Georgics, *composed slowly and carefully, at the rate of less than one line a day, is often praised as the most perfect of all Latin poems. After completing it, Virgil turned to his greatest work, the* Aeneid, *to which he devoted his remaining years. At the time of his death in 19 B.C. he had not quite perfected it and asked that it be burned. Octavian (the emperor Caesar Augustus) is said to have rescued it.*

Despite his retiring temperament, Virgil lived at a time when it was not easy for any Roman to avoid the impact of public events. The wars of Roman against Roman had begun decades before Virgil's birth. During his boyhood the republican form of Roman government was proving less and less capable of curbing the ambitions of powerful men. Pompey the Great, one of the two consuls (chief magistrates) in 70, the year Virgil was born, had a meteoric career as general and legislator. In 55, as Virgil reached the traditional age of manhood, Pompey was consul a second time, and in 52 the leader assumed the unprecedented office of sole consul to deal with the gang warfare and street disorders which were racking the life of the capital. Cicero, the eminent Roman thinker and statesman, dreamed that in some such central and autocratic figure as Pompey Rome might find salvation from the ills that were too widespread for her traditional government to control.

In fact, Rome's first autocracy in almost five centuries was to be established not by Pompey but by Julius Caesar, who, at first simply a popular politician from an impoverished noble family, gradually had begun to emerge as an unmatched leader and a strategist of ruthless brilliance. Caesar defeated Pompey in 48 at the Battle of Pharsalus, and during four breathless years he attempted to reshape Roman government as a centralized monarchy on the model of Alexander the Great. But Caesar's audacity went too far. In 44 a group of conspirators led by Brutus assassinated him in Pompey's Theater at Rome. The conspirators had no clear plan of action. It looked as if Rome would collapse under the sheer size of its own problems, when out of the welter of confusion and carnage emerged Caesar's ailing nineteen-year-old grand-nephew Octavian. A skilled politician driven by an extraordinary genius, Octavian maneuvered his way through the labyrinth of Roman power politics over the next thirteen years, winning at length the general support of Rome. His most formidable rival, his brother-in-law Mark Antony, had become infatuated with Cleopatra, the queen of Egypt, and even planned to yield her part of the Roman domain. In the climactic naval battle of Actium in 31 (an event foreshadowed in Book III of the Aeneid*), Octavian defeated Antony and Cleopatra. Their subsequent suicide left Octavian supreme in authority, and in 23 he became known as Caesar Augustus. His regime aimed at several goals: the civic renewal of Rome, the revival of traditional religious devotion, and the fostering of a new patriotism. The arts were to be important vehicles for these ideals, all of which are reflected in the* Aeneid.

For Virgil, as for many other Romans, the restoration of peace was in itself a blessed achievement, an occasion and opportunity for Roman national glory. In Book I of the Aeneid *Jupiter prophesies a time when*

> *wars will cease, and a rough age grow gentler,*
> *White Faith and Vesta, Romulus and Remus,*
> *Give law to nations. War's grim gates will close,*
> *Tight-shut with bars of iron, and inside them*
> *The wickedness of war sit bound and silent,*
> *The red mouth straining and the hands held tight*
> *In fastenings of bronze, a hundred hundred.*

(I. 305–311)

To "give law to nations"—this, and not mere narrow chauvinism, is the distinctive Roman mission. The shade of Anchises tells his son Aeneas in Book VI:

> *Others, no doubt, will better mould the bronze*
> *To the semblance of soft breathing, draw, from marble,*
> *The living countenance; and others plead*
> *With greater eloquence, or learn to measure,*
> *Better than we, the pathways of the heaven,*

> *The risings of the stars: remember, Roman,*
> *To rule the people under law, to establish*
> *The way of peace, to battle down the haughty,*
> *To spare the meek. Our fine arts, these, forever.*
>
>   (VI. 888–896)

Although Anchises is historically right in conceding superiority in the fine arts to other nations, specifically Greece, and identifying government as the epitome of Roman greatness, it is somewhat ironic that his exhortation, at once modest and proud, should appear in a poem that is one of the world's aesthetic masterpieces.

The Aeneid is, then, a eulogy of Roman values. But it also puts those values in perspective by showing insistently the great cost at which they are achieved and sustained. The poem, particularly in the second half (omitted here), treats political negotiation and war at length, but war is presented there as a moral tragedy, however necessary, and even admirable, martial prowess and courage may be. Aeneas is no Homeric hero, free to demonstrate valor and prowess for their own sake, with no social obligation beyond himself, his family, and the cohorts banded together under him. The distinctively Virgilian melancholy, combined inextricably with tones of triumph, arises largely from the poet's awareness that public duty requires again and again the sacrifice of personal fulfillment. Aeneas, the mirror of Augustus and of Roman potential, must be educated in suffering before he can perform his mission and become a worthy embodiment of the Roman ideal. His affair with Dido is a personal tragedy on both sides. Since Carthage, the city she rules, was to become an inveterate enemy of Rome in three major wars during the two centuries before Virgil, it would have been easy for him to present this African queen as merely ignoble, a focus for propaganda. That instead he portrays her sympathetically, indeed creating in her the most memorable character in Latin literature, both enhances her own tragic stature and underlines Aeneas's tragic dilemma in having to renounce her in the name of duty.

For the formal vehicle of his story and message, Virgil chose the epic, a literary genre he had aspired to since early in his life. His handling of epic owes something to the Greek Alexandrians, but his primary models are the two Homeric epics. Books I to VI are, like the Odyssey, *a tale of wandering; Books VII to XII are a war story, like the* Iliad. *But those general correspondences are, in themselves, only the most superficial marks of Homeric influence, and there are ironic differences too. The journey of Homer's Odysseus is a true homecoming; Aeneas's odyssey, despite the ancestral roots the Trojans have in Italy, is a leavetaking, a deracination. Virgil's echoing of Homer is intricate but also intricately varied, so that the echoing is less imitative than expressive. Virgil's synthesizing tour de force overlies a radical originality of the utmost importance in the history of epic. Aristotle, in his* Poetics, *had praised Homer for his objectivity, his effacement of himself, and had identified such self-effacement as the epic poet's proper role. In his own way, of course, Virgil too is objective; that is, he combines with his didacticism flexibility of sympathy with individual human beings, realistic insight into human psychology, and a sense that there is often right on both sides. Yet the* Aeneid is, *after all, a subjective poem—in the sense that the author's presence can be felt everywhere, in the ideas and in the characteristic Virgilian tone of pathos, introspectiveness, and poignancy.*

An even more important innovation is Virgil's imaginative redefinition of the role of history in epic. Rather than narrating and directly celebrating modern Roman history, which is ultimately his main concern, he chooses to return to the legendary roots of the Roman experience nearly a millennium earlier, in the wanderings and wars of the Trojans after the fall of their city. In treating the seeds of later Roman history, Roman religious ritual, Roman character traits as having been sown in that era of the dim past, the Aeneid, unlike the Homeric models, envisions time and history as a meaningful linear movement toward goals ordained by a mysterious but purposeful providence. Understood in this way, the fall of Troy is ultimately a fortunate fall. In ancient literature the closest thing we have to this is not in pagan literature but in the Bible, especially in the Exodus saga. Both there and in the Aeneid we see a guiding providence operating through divinely appointed, half-reluctant heroes, Moses and Aeneas, both of whom must grow into their roles but then rest content not quite to reach the ultimate goal of their people. In both works the journey is out of a disastrous past toward a new promised land that is also an ancestral homeland. Both leaders must mediate between the exigencies of providence and the weariness and backslidings of their followers. It is no wonder that poets in the Judaeo-Christian tradition could retrospectively claim Virgil as one of their own.

Except for the Bible, the Aeneid may well be the most highly revered book in European literary history, especially before the reemergence of the Greek classics in Europe during the Renaissance. Like the Bible, Virgil's works were used by people seeking supernatural guidance; they opened a copy at random and found wisdom in the first passage their eyes struck. That practice (the Sortes Vergilianae) reflects the moral sententiousness of the Aeneid, but it also reflects the poem's style. To translate Virgil is especially challenging, for almost every line is dense with meaning, nuance, implication. That is partly owing to the nature of classical Latin, which can produce special effects because the word order is freer than in modern English, and partly to Virgil's painstaking method of composition, which is utterly different from the essentially oral manner of Homer's verse (though Virgil did sometimes read his poetry aloud). The meter is the standard epic meter, dactylic hexameter—each of the six feet made up of a long syllable and two short ones (dactyl) or of two long ones (spondee). Virgil uses the meter with infinite expressiveness and variety. The following, the first verse paragraph of Book I, is a specimen:

Ārmă vǐr/ūmquě că/nō, Troi/ae quī / prīmŭs ăb / ō̄rīs
Ītăli/am, fă/tō prŏfŭ/gŭs, Lăvīn/līāquě / vēnĭt
lītŏră, / mūltum̄ il/lě et tēr/rīs iac/tātŭs ĕt / āltō
vī sŭpěr/ŭm, sae/vae mĕmŏr/ēm Iū/nōnĭs ŏb / īrām,
mūltă quŏ/quě et bēl/lō pas/sŭs, dŭm / condĕrĕt / ūrbēm,
īnfēr/rētquě dē/ōs Lătĭ/ō, gĕnŭs / ūndĕ Lă/tīnŭm,
Ālbă/nīquĕ p̄āt/rēs, āt/que altae / moeniă / Rōmae.

In his poem "To Virgil," composed in 1882 for the 1,900th anniversary of Virgil's death, Tennyson paid tribute to what he called Virgil's "ocean-roll of rhythm":

I salute thee, Mantovano [Mantuan], I that loved thee since my day began,
Wielder of the stateliest measure ever molded by the lips of man.

FURTHER READING (prepared by F. S. N.): W. F. Jackson Knight, Roman Vergil, 1944, 2nd ed. 1966, is especially useful on Virgil's language and style. For a comprehensive treatment of Virgil's work and his debt to Homer and to the Alexandri-

ans, see Brooks Otis, *Virgil: A Study in Civilized Poetry,* 1964. Also valuable on the
Alexandrian background to Augustan poetry is J. K. Newman, *Augustus and the New
Poetry,* 1967. Lively and stimulating twentieth-century interpretations are presented
by Steele Commager, ed., *Virgil: A Collection of Critical Essays,* 1966; and by Donald
R. Dudley, ed., *Virgil,* 1969. Viktor Pöschl, *The Art of Vergil: Image and Symbol in the
Aeneid,* 1950, trans. Gerda Seligson, 1962, shows how the epic is unified themati-
cally, symbolically and artistically. Kenneth Quinn, *Virgil's "Aeneid": A Critical Description,* 1968, brings modern critical methods to bear on traditional material.

from *THE AENEID*

Translated by Rolfe Humphries

BOOK I: THE LANDING NEAR CARTHAGE

  Arms and the man I sing,[1] the first who came,
Compelled by fate, an exile out of Troy,
To Italy and the Lavinian coast,[2]
Much buffeted on land and on the deep
By violence of the gods, through that long rage,
That lasting hate, of Juno's. And he suffered
Much, also, in war, till he should build his town
And bring his gods to Latium,[3] whence, in time,
The Latin race, the Alban[4] fathers, rose
And the great walls of everlasting Rome.   10
  Help me, O Muse, recall the reasons: why,
Why did the queen of heaven[5] drive a man
So known for goodness, for devotion, through
So many toils and perils? Was there slight,
Affront, or outrage? Is vindictiveness
An attribute of the celestial mind?
    There was an ancient city, Carthage, once
Founded by Tyrians,[6] facing Italy
And Tiber's[7] mouth, far-off, a wealthy town,
War-loving, and aggressive; and Juno held   20
Even her precious Samos[8] in less regard.
Here were her arms, her chariot, and here,
Should fate at all permit, the goddess burned

----

[1] Lines 1–16 use the standard epic "opening formula," including the identification of the
hero, the proclamation of the theme and of its significance, and the invocation of the inspiring
Muse.
  [2] The west coast of Italy.   [3] The area of Italy destined to be settled by the Trojans.
  [4] The city Alba Longa was founded by Ascanius, Aeneas's son. It produced Romulus, who
was according to legend the founder of Rome.
  [5] Juno, queen of the gods and inveterate enemy of the Trojans.
  [6] People from Tyre, a city on the Syrian coast, noted for commerce.
  [7] The river of Rome. The epithet *War-loving* refers to the fact that Rome and Carthage
fought three wars against each other during the third and second centuries B.C.
  [8] An island in the Aegean Sea, site of the great temple of Juno.

To found the empire of the world forever.
But, she had heard, a Trojan race would come,
Some day, to overthrow the Tyrian towers,
A race would come, imperious people,[9] proud
In war, with wide dominion, bringing doom
For Libya. Fate willed it so. And Juno
Feared, and remembered: there was the old war   30
She fought at Troy for her dear Greeks; her mind
Still fed on hurt and anger; deep in her heart
Paris' decision[10] rankled, and the wrong
Offered her slighted beauty; and the hatred
Of the whole race; and Ganymede's[11] honors—
All that was fuel to fire; she tossed and harried
All over the seas, wherever she could, those Trojans
Who had survived the Greeks and fierce Achilles,
And so they wandered over many an ocean,
Through many a year, fate-hounded. Such a struggle   40
It was to found the race of Rome!

                         They were happy
Spreading the sail, rushing the foam with bronze,
And Sicily hardly out of sight, when Juno,
Still nourishing the everlasting wound,
Raged to herself: "I am beaten, I suppose;
It seems I cannot keep this Trojan king
From Italy. The fates, no doubt, forbid me.[12]
Pallas, of course, could burn the Argive ships,
Could drown the sailors, all for one man's guilt,
The crazy acts of Ajax.[13] Her own hand   50
Hurled from the cloud Jove's thunderbolt, and shattered
Their ships all over the sea; she raised up storm
And tempest; she spiked Ajax on the rocks,
Whirled him in wind, blasted his heart with fire.
And I, who walk my way as queen of the gods,
Sister of Jove, and wife of Jove, keep warring
With one tribe through the long, long years. Who cares
For Juno's godhead? Who brings sacrifice
Devoutly to her altars?"

                   Brooding, burning,
She sought Aeolia, the storm-clouds' dwelling,
A land that sweeps and swarms with the winds' fury,   60
Whose monarch, Aeolus, in his deep cave rules

---

[9] The Romans.

[10] Paris, one of the sons of King Priam of Troy, had been asked to judge which of the three goddesses Juno, Minerva, and Venus was most beautiful. He chose Venus, who rewarded him with Helen; Helen's abduction by Paris from her husband Menelaus then ignited the Trojan War.

[11] Promoted over Juno's daughter Hebe as cupbearer to the gods.

[12] Even the gods were considered subject to the superior power of Fate.

[13] Pallas, or Athena (the Greek equivalent of Minerva, goddess of wisdom), had inflicted the punishment described in revenge for the rape by Ajax of the prophetess Cassandra.

Imperious, weighing down with bolt and prison
Those boisterous struggling roarers, who go raging
Around their bars, under the moan of the mountain.
High over them their sceptered lord sits watching,
Soothing, restraining, their passionate proud spirit,
Lest, uncontrolled, they seize, in their wild keeping,
The land, the sea, the arch of sky, in ruin
Sweeping through space. This Jupiter feared; he hid them   70
Deep in dark caverns, with a mass of mountain
Piled over above them, and a king to give them
Most certain regulation, with a knowledge
When to hold in, when to let go. Him Juno
Approached in supplication:—"Aeolus,
Given by Jove the power to still the waters,
Or raise them with a gale, a tribe I hate
Is on its way to Italy, and they carry
Troy with them, and their household gods, once beaten.
Shake anger into those winds of yours, turn over   80
Their ships, and drown them; drive them in all directions,
Litter the sea with bodies! For such service
The loveliest nymph I have, Deiopea,
Shall be your bride forever, and you will father
Fair children on her fairness." Aeolus
Made answer: "Yours, O Queen, the task of seeking
Whatever it is you will; and mine the duty
To follow with performance. All my empire,
My sceptre, Jove's indulgence, are beholden
To Juno's favor, by whose blessing I   90
Attend the feasts of the gods and rule this storm-land."
     His spear-butt struck the hollow mountain-side,
And the winds, wherever they could, came sweeping forth,
Whirled over the land, swooped down upon the ocean.
East, South, Southwest, they heave the billows, howl,
Storm, roll the giant combers toward the shore.
Men cry; the rigging creaks and strains; the clouds
Darken, and men see nothing; a weight of darkness
Broods over the deep; the heavy thunder rumbles
From pole to pole; the lightning rips and dazzles;   100
There is no way out but death. Aeneas shudders
In the chill shock, and lifts both hands to heaven:—
"O happy men, thrice happy, four times happy,
Who had the luck to die, with their fathers watching
Below the walls of Troy! Ah, Diomedes,
Bravest of Greeks, why could I not have fallen,
Bleeding my life away on plains of Ilium[14]
In our encounter there, where mighty Hector
Went down before Achilles'[15] spear, and huge

[14] *Ilium.* Troy.
[15] Hector and Achilles were the chief warriors of the Trojans and Greeks, respectively. The
slaying of Hector by Achilles is described in Homer's *Iliad*, Book XXII.

Sarpedon[16] lay in dust, and Simois river   110
Rolled to the sea so many noble heroes,
All drowned in all their armor?" And the gale
Howls from the north, striking the sail, head on;
The waves are lifted to the stars; the oars
Are broken, and the prow slews round; the ship
Lies broadside on; a wall of water, a mountain,
Looms up, comes pouring down; some ride the crest,
Some, in the trough, can see the boil of the sand.
The South wind hurls three ships on the hidden rocks,
That sea-reef which Italians call the Altars;   120
The West takes three, sweeping them from the deep
On shoal and quicksand; over the stern of one,
Before Aeneas' eyes, a great sea falls,
Washing the helmsman overboard; the ship
Whirls thrice in the suck of the water and goes down
In the devouring gulf; and here and there
A few survivors swim, the Lycian men
Whose captain was Orontes; now their arms,
Their Trojan treasures, float with the broken timbers
On the swing and slide of the waves. The storm, triumphant,   130
Rides down more boats, and more; there goes Achates;
Abas, Aletes, Ilioneus,
Receive the hostile water; the walls are broken;
The enemy pours in.
                    But meanwhile Neptune[17]
Saw ocean in a welter of confusion,
The roar of storm, and deep and surface mingled.
Troublesome business, this; he rose, majestic,
From under the waves, and saw the Trojan vessels
Scattered all over the sea by the might of the waves
And the wreck of sky; he recognized the anger   140
And cunning of his sister, and he summoned
The winds by name:—"What arrogance is this,
What pride of birth, you winds, to meddle here
Without my sanction, raising all this trouble?
I'll—No, the waves come first: but listen to me,
You are going to pay for this! Get out of here!
Go tell your king the lordship of the ocean,
The trident, are not his, but mine. His realm
Reaches no further than the rocks and caverns
You brawlers dwell in; let him rule that palace,   150
Big as he pleases, shut you in, and stay there!"
    This said, he calmed the swollen sea and cloud,
Brought back the sun; Cymothoe and Triton,[18]
Heaving together, pulled the ships from the reef,

---

[16] King of Lycia, killed while fighting on the side of the Trojans. The *Simois* was a river at the battlefield of Troy.
[17] God of the ocean.
[18] Cymothoe and Triton were, respectively, a sea-nymph and a sea-god.

As Neptune used his trident for a lever,
Opened the quicksand, made the water smooth,
And the flying chariot skimmed the level surface.
Sometimes, in a great nation, there are riots
With the rabble out of hand, and firebrands fly
And cobblestones; whatever they lay their hands on   160
Is a weapon for their fury, but should they see
One man of noble presence, they fall silent,
Obedient dogs, with ears pricked up, and waiting,
Waiting his word, and he knows how to bring them
Back to good sense again. So ocean, roaring,
Subsided into stillness, as the sea-god
Looked forth upon the waters, and clear weather
Shone over him as he drove his flying horses.
     Aeneas' weary children make for harbor,
Whichever lies most near, and the prows are turned   170
To Libya's coast-line. In a bay's deep curve
They find a haven, where the water lies
With never a ripple. A little island keeps
The sea-swell off, and the waves break on its sides
And slide back harmless. The great cliffs come down
Steep to deep water, and the background shimmers,
Darkens and shines, the tremulous aspen moving
And the dark fir pointing still. And there is a cave
Under the overhanging rocks, alive
With water running fresh, a home of the Nymphs,   180
With benches for them, cut from the living stone.
No anchor is needed here for weary ships,
No mooring-cable. Aeneas brings them in,
Seven weary vessels, and the men are glad
To be ashore again, to feel dry sand
Under the salt-stained limbs. Achates strikes
The spark from the flint, catches the fire on leaves,
Adds chips and kindling, blows and fans the flame,
And they bring out the soaked and salty corn,
The hand-mills, stone and mortar, and make ready,   190
As best they can, for bread.
                                        Meanwhile Aeneas
Climbs to a look-out, for a view of the ocean,
Hoping for some good luck; the Phrygian galleys
Might meet his gaze, or Capys' boats, or a pennon
On a far-off mast-head flying. There is nothing,
Nothing to see out yonder, but near the water
Three stags are grazing, with a herd behind them,
A long line browsing through the peaceful valley.
He reaches for the bow and the swift arrows
Borne by Achates,[19] and he shoots the leaders,   200
High-antlered, routs the common herd, and ceases

---

[19] Aeneas's most faithful companion.

Only when seven are slain, a number equal
To the ships' tally, and then he seeks the harbor,
Divides the spoil, broaches the wine Acestes
Had stowed for them at Drepanum on their leaving,
A kingly present, and he calms their trouble,
Saying: "O comrades, we have been through evil
Together before this; we have been through worse,
Scylla, Charybdis, and the Cyclops' dwelling,[20]
The sounding rocks. This, too, the god will end.   210
Call the nerve back; dismiss the fear, the sadness.
Some day, perhaps, remembering even this
Will be a pleasure. We are going on
Through whatsoever chance and change, until
We come to Latium, where the fates point out
A quiet dwelling-place, and Troy recovered.
Endure, and keep yourself for better days."
He kept to himself the sorrow in the heart,
Wearing, for them, a mask of hopefulness.
They were ready for the feasting. Part lay bare   220
The flesh from the torn hides, part cut the meat
Impaling it, still quivering, on spits,
Setting the kettles, keeping the water boiling,
And strong with food again, sprawling stretched out
On comfortable grass, they take their fill
Of bread and wine and venison, till hunger
Is gone, and the board cleared. And then they talk
For a long time, of where their comrades are,
Are, or may be, hopeful and doubtful both.
Could they believe them living? or would a cry   230
Fall on deaf ears forever? All those captains,
Brave Gyas, brave Cloanthus, Amycus,
Lycus, Orontes,—in his secret heart
Aeneas mourns them.
                              Meanwhile, from the heaven
Jupiter watched the lands below, and the seas
With the white points of sails, and far-off people,
Turning his gaze toward Libya. And Venus
Came to him then, a little sadly, tears
Brimming in those bright eyes of hers. "Great father,"
She said, "Great ruler of the world   240
Of men and gods, great wielder of the lightning,
What has my poor Aeneas[21] done? what outrage
Could Trojans perpetrate, so that the world
Rejects them everywhere, and many a death
Inflicted on them over Italy?
There was a promise once, that as the years
Rolled onward, they would father Rome and rulers

[20] These perils are described in Book III.
[21] Venus is Aeneas's mother; Anchises, his father, is a mortal.

Of Roman stock, to hold dominion over
All sea and land. That was a promise, father;
What changed it? Once that promise was my comfort;   250
Troy fell; I weighed one fate against another
And found some consolation. But disaster
Keeps on; the same ill-fortune follows after.
What end of it all, great king? One man, Antenor,
Escaped the Greeks, came through Illyrian waters
Safe to Liburnian regions, where Timavus[22]
Roars underground, comes up nine times, and reaches
The floodland near the seas. One man, Antenor,
Founded a city, Padua, a dwelling
For Trojan men, a resting-place from labor,   260
And shares their quietude. But we, your children,
To whom heaven's height is granted, we are betrayed,
We have lost our ships, we are kept from Italy,
Kept far away. One enemy—I tell you
This is a shameful thing! Do we deserve it?
Is this our rise to power?"
                          He smiled, in answer,
The kind of smile that clears the air, and kissed her.
"Fear not, my daughter; fate remains unmoved
For the Roman generations. You will witness
Lavinium's rise, her walls fulfill the promise;   270
You will bring to heaven lofty-souled Aeneas.
There has been no change in me whatever. Listen!
To ease this care, I will prophesy a little,
I will open the book of fate. Your son Aeneas
Will wage a mighty war in Italy,[23]
Beat down proud nations, give his people laws,
Found them a city, a matter of three years
From victory to settlement. His son,
The boy Ascanius, named Ilus once,
When Troy was standing, and now called Iulus,   280
Shall reign for thirty years, and great in power
Forsake Lavinium, transfer the kingdom
To Alba Longa, new-built capital.
Here, for three hundred years, the line of Hector
Shall govern, till a royal priestess bears
Twin sons to Mars, and Romulus, rejoicing
In the brown wolf-skin[24] of his foster-mother,
Takes up the tribe, and builds the martial walls
And calls the people, after himself, the Romans.
To these I set no bounds in space or time;   290
They shall rule forever. Even bitter Juno

---

[22] The river Timavus flows into the Adriatic Sea (east of Italy); Liburnia is part of the Adriatic coast.
[23] The war is described in the second half of the poem, Books VII to XII.
[24] Romulus and his twin Remus were supposed to have been suckled by a she-wolf.

Whose fear now harries earth and sea and heaven
Will change to better counsels, and will cherish
The race that wears the toga, Roman masters
Of all the world. It is decreed. The time
Will come, as holy years wheel on, when Troy
Will subjugate Mycenae, vanquish Phthia,
Be lord of Argos.[25] And from this great line
Will come a Trojan, Caesar, to establish
The limit of his empire at the ocean,   300
His glory at the stars, a man called Julius
Whose name recalls Iulus. Welcome waits
For him in heaven; all the spoils of Asia
Will weight him down, and prayer be made before him.
Then wars will cease, and a rough age grow gentler,
White Faith and Vesta,[26] Romulus and Remus,
Give law to nations. War's grim gates will close,
Tight-shut with bars of iron, and inside them
The wickedness of war sit bound and silent,
The red mouth straining and the hands held tight   310
In fastenings of bronze, a hundred hundred."
     With that, he sent down Mercury[27] from heaven
That Carthage might be kindly, and her land
And new-built towers receive them with a welcome,
And their queen, Dido, knowing the will of fate,
Swing wide her doors. On the oarage of his wings
He flies through the wide sweep of air to Libya,
Where, at the will of the god, the folk make ready
In kindliness of heart, and their queen's purpose
Is gracious and gentle.
                    All night long Aeneas   320
Had pondered many a care, and with bright morning
Resolved to reconnoiter; the winds have brought him
To a new country: who lives in it, men
Or only beasts? The fields appear untended.
The fleet lies under a hollow cliff, surrounded
By spikes of shade, and groves arch overhead,
Ample concealment. Aeneas and Achates
Went forth together, armed, down the trail in the forest,
And there his mother met him, a girl, it seemed,
From Thrace or Sparta, trim as any huntress   330
Who rides her horses hard, or outspeeds rivers
In her swift going. A bow hung over her shoulder,
Her hair blew free, her knees were bare, her garments
Tucked at the waist and knotted. As she saw them,
"Ho there, young men," she cried, "have you seen my sister
Around here anywhere? She wears a quiver,

---

[25] Cities associated with the Trojans' Greek conquerors: Phthia with Achilles, Mycenae and Argos with Agamemnon, the Greek commander.
[26] Goddess of the hearth.   [27] Messenger of the gods.

And a spotted lynx-hide; maybe you have heard her
Hunting the boar and shouting?"
                                        But her son
Responded: "No; we have heard no sounds of hunting,
We have seen no one here. But tell me, maiden,   340
What name to call you by? In voice and feature
You are, I think, no mortal; a goddess, surely,—
Nymph, or Apollo's sister?[28] Whoever you are,
Be kind to us, lighten our trouble, tell us
Under what sky, along what coast of the world,
We wander, knowing neither land nor people,
Driven by gales and billows. Many a victim
We shall make ready for your altar." Venus
Answered: "I have no title to such honor.
The Tyrian girls all wear these crimson leggings   350
Like mine, and carry quivers. Tyrian folk
Live here; their city is Carthage; over the border
Lies Libya, warlike people. Our queen, Dido,
Came here from Tyre; she was fleeing from her brother,—
A long and complicated story; outrage,—
No matter, here it is, in brief. Her husband
Was Sychaeus, wealthiest of all Phoenicians,
At least in land, and Dido loved him dearly
Since first her father gave her to him, virgin,
And then unlucky bride. She had a brother,   360
Pygmalion, king of Tyre, a monster, evil
In wickedness, and madness came between
Those men, the two of them. Pygmalion murdered
Sychaeus at the altar; he was crazy
And blind for gold and crafty; what did he care
About his sister's love? And he kept it quiet
For a long time, kept telling Dido something
To fool her with false comfort, but Sychaeus
Came to her in a dream, a ghost, unburied,
With the wounds in his breast, the story of the altar,   370
The pale lips blurting out the secret horror,
The crime in the dark of the household. *Flee,* he told her,
Forsake this land; and he told her where the treasure
Lay hidden in earth, uncounted gold and silver.
Dido was moved to flight, secured companions,
All those possessed by fear, all those whom hatred
Had made relentless; ships were standing ready,
As it so happened; they put the gold aboard,
And over the sea the greedy tyrant's treasure
Went sailing, with a woman for a captain.   380
They came here; you will see the walls arising
And the great citadel of the town called Carthage.

---

[28] Diana, goddess of the hunt.

Here they bought ground; they used to call it Byrsa,
That being a word for bull's hide; they bought only
What a bull's hide could cover. And now tell me
Who you might be yourselves? what land do you come from,
Bound for what coast?"

            And he began his answer
With a long sigh: "O goddess, if I told you
All from the first beginning, if you had leisure
To listen to the record of our trouble,   390
It would take me all day long. From ancient Troy,
In case that name means anything, we come
Driven over many seas, and now a storm
Has whipped us on this coast. I am Aeneas,
A good, devoted man; I carry with me
My household gods, saved from the Greeks; I am known
In heaven; it is Italy I seek,
A homeland for me there, and a race descended
From lofty Jove. With a score of ships we started
Over the Phrygian ocean, following fate   400
And the way my mother pointed. Only seven
Are left us now, battered survivors, after
The rage of wind and wave. And here I wander
The wastes of Libya, unknown and needy,
Driven from Europe and Asia." And his mother
Broke in on his complaining:—"Whoever you are,
Some god must care for you, I think, to bring you
Here to the city of Carthage. Follow on,
Go to the royal palace. For, I tell you,
Your comrades have returned, your fleet is safe,   410
Brought to good haven by the turn of the winds,
Unless the augury my parents taught me
Was foolish nonsense. In the heaven yonder
You see twelve swans, rejoicing in long column,
Scattered, a little while ago, and driven
By the swooping eagle, over all the sky,
But now, it seems, they light on land, or watch
Those who came down before them; as they circle
In company, and make a cheerful sound
With whir of wing or song, so, let me tell you,   420
Your ships and men already enter harbor
Or near it under full sail. Keep on, go forward
Where the path leads."

            And as she turned, her shoulders
Shone with a radiant light; her hair shed fragrance,
Her robes slipped to her feet, and the true goddess
Walked in divinity.[29] He knew his mother,
And his voice pursued her flight: "Cruel again!

---

[29] A goddess could be distinguished from a mortal by her gait and carriage.

Why mock your son so often with false phantoms?
Why may not hand be joined to hand, and words
Exchanged in truthfulness?" So, still reproachful,   430
He went on toward the city, with Achates,
But Venus cast dark air around their going,
A veil of mist, so that no man might see them
Or lay a hand on them, or halt them, asking
The reasons of their coming. She soared upward
To Paphos, happily home to temple and altars
Steaming with incense, redolent with garlands.
    And they went on, where the little pathway led them
To rising ground; below them lay the city,
Majestic buildings now, where once were hovels,   440
A wonder to Aeneas, gates and bustle
And well-paved streets, the busy Tyrians toiling
With stones for walls and citadel, or marking
Foundations for their homes, drainage and furrow,
All under ordered process. They dredge harbors,
Set cornerstones, quarry the rock, where someday
Their theater will tower. They are like bees
In early summer over the country flowers
When the sun is warm, and the young of the hive emerge,
And they pack the molten honey, bulge the cells   450
With the sweet nectar, add new loads, and harry
The drones away from the hive, and the work glows,
And the air is sweet with bergamot and clover.
"Happy the men whose walls already rise!"
Exclaims Aeneas, gazing on the city,
And enters there, still veiled in cloud—a marvel!—
And walks among the people, and no one sees him.
    There was a grove in the middle of the city,
Most happy in its shade; this was the place
Where first the Tyrians, tossed by storm and whirlwind,   460
Dug up the symbol royal Juno showed them,
The skull of a war-horse, a sign the race to come
Would be supreme in war and wealth, for ages,
And Dido here was building a great temple
In Juno's honor, rich in gifts, and blessed
With the presence of the goddess. Lintel and rafter
Were bronze above bronze stairways, and bronze portals
Swung on bronze hinges. Here Aeneas first
Dared hope for safety, find some reassurance
In hope of better days: a strange sight met him,   470
To take his fear away. Waiting the queen,
He stood there watching, under the great temple,
Letting his eyes survey the city's fortune,
The artist's workmanship, the craftsman's labor,
And there, with more than wonder, he sees the battles
Fought around Troy, and the wars whose fame had travelled
The whole world over; there is Agamemnon,

Priam, and Menelaus,[30] and Achilles,
A menace to them all. He is moved to tears.
"What place in all the world," he asks Achates,   480
"Is empty of our sorrow? There is Priam!
Look! even here there are rewards for praise,
There are tears for things, and what men suffer touches
The human heart. Dismiss your fear; this story
Will bring some safety to you." Sighing often,
He could not turn his gaze away; it was only
A picture on a wall, but the sight afforded
Food for the spirit's need. He saw the Greeks,
Hard-pressed, in flight, and Trojans coming after,
Or, on another panel, the scene reversed,   490
Achilles in pursuit, his own men fleeing;
He saw, and tears came into his eyes again,
The tents of Rhesus,[31] snowy-white, betrayed
In their first sleep by bloody Diomedes
With many a death, and the fiery horses driven
Into the camp, before they ever tasted
The grass of Troy, or drank from Xanthus' river.
Another scene showed Troilus, poor youngster,
Running away, his arms flung down; Achilles
Was much too good for him; he had fallen backward   500
Out of his car, but held the reins, and the horses
Dragged him along the ground, his hair and shoulders
Bounding in dust, and the spear making a scribble.
And there were Trojan women, all in mourning,
With streaming hair, on their way to Pallas' temple,
Bearing, as gift, a robe, but the stern goddess[32]
Kept her gaze on the ground. Three times Achilles
Had dragged the body of Hector around the walls,
And was selling it for money. What a groan
Came from Aeneas' heart, seeing that spoil,   510
That chariot, and helpless Priam reaching
His hands, unarmed, across the broken body!
And he saw himself there, too, fighting in battle
Against Greek leaders, he saw the Eastern columns,
And swarthy Memnon's[33] arms. Penthesilea,
The Amazon, blazes in fury, leading
Her crescent-shielded thousands, a golden buckle
Below her naked breast, a soldieress
Fighting with men.
                    And as he watched these marvels

[30] Priam was the patriarchal king of Troy, Menelaus was the cuckolded husband of Helen, brother of Agamemnon and co-commander of the Greek forces at Troy.
[31] Rhesus supported the Trojans against the Greeks. Troy could not fall, it was believed, if his horses tasted Troy's grass or drank from its river Xanthus. But before they could do either, Diomede and Ulysses carried the horses off.
[32] Pallas (the Greek Athena or Roman Minerva) sided with the Greeks against the Trojans.
[33] Ethiopian king who sided with the Trojans.

In one long fascinated stare of wonder,   520
Dido, the queen, drew near; she came to the temple
With a great train, all majesty, all beauty,
As on Eurotas' riverside, or where
Mount Cynthus[34] towers high, Diana leads
Her bands of dancers, and the Oreads follow
In thousands, right and left, the taller goddess,
The quiver-bearing maiden, and Latona
Is filled with secret happiness, so Dido
Moved in her company, a queen, rejoicing,
Ordering on her kingdom's rising glory.   530
At Juno's portal, under the arch of the temple,
She took her throne, a giver of law and justice,
A fair partitioner of toil and duty,
And suddenly Aeneas, from the crowd,
Saw Trojan men approaching, brave Cloanthus,
Sergestus, Antheus, and all those others
Whom the black storm had driven here and yonder.
This he cannot believe, nor can Achates,
Torn between fear and joy. They burn with ardor
To seek their comrades' handclasp, but confusion   540
Still holds them in the cloud: what can have happened?
They watch from the cover of mist: men still were coming
From all the ships, chosen, it seemed, as pleaders
For graciousness before the temple, calling
Aloud: what fortune had been theirs, he wonders,
Where had they left the ships; why were they coming?
They were given audience; Ilioneus,
Senior to all, began: "O Queen, whom Jove
Has given the founding of a great new city,
Has given to bridle haughty tribes with justice,   550
We, pitiful Trojans, over every ocean
Driven by storm, make our appeal: keep from us
The terrible doom of fire; protect our vessels;
Have mercy on a decent race; consider
Our lot with closer interest. We have not come
To ravish Libyan homes, or carry plunder
Down to the shore. We lack the arrogance
Of conquerors; there is no aggression in us.
There is a place which Greeks have given a name,
The Land in the West; it is powerful in arms,   560
Rich in its soil; Oenotrians used to live there,
And now, the story goes, a younger people
Inhabit it, calling themselves Italians
After their leader's name.[35] We were going there
When, big with storm and cloud, Orion[36] rising

---

[34] Birthplace of Diana, goddess of the hunt. In the passage following, *Oreads* are mountain nymphs, *the taller goddess* refers to Diana, *Latona* was another name for Leto, mother of Diana.

[35] Italus, a legendary ruler.   [36] The constellation was believed to presage storms.

Drove us on hidden quicksands, and wild winds
Scattered us over the waves, by pathless rocks
And the swell of the surge. A few of us have drifted
Here to your shores. What kind of men are these,
What barbarous land permits such attitudes?   570
We have been denied the welcome of the beach,
Forbidden to set foot on land; they rouse
All kinds of war against us. You despise,
It may be, human brotherhood, and arms
Wielded by men. But there are gods, remember,
Who care for right and wrong. Our king Aeneas
May be alive; no man was ever more just,
More decent ever, or greater in war and arms.
If fate preserves him still, if he still breathes
The welcome air, above the world of shadows,   580
Fear not; to have treated us with kindly service
Need bring you no repentance. We have cities
In Sicily as well, and King Acestes
Is one of us, from Trojan blood. We ask you
To let us beach our battered fleet, make ready
Beams from the forest timber, mend our oarage,
Seek Italy and Latium, glad at knowing
Our king and comrades rescued. But if safety
Is hopeless for him now, and Libyan water
Has been his grave, and if his son Iulus   590
Is desperate, or lost, grant us permission
At least to make for Sicily, whence we came here,
Where king Acestes has a dwelling for us."
The Trojans, as he ended, all were shouting,
And Dido, looking down, made a brief answer:
"I am sorry, Trojans; put aside your care,
Have no more fear. The newness of the kingdom
And our strict need compel to me such measures—
Sentries on every border, far and wide.
But who so ignorant as not to know   600
The nation of Aeneas, manly both
In deeds and people, and the city of Troy?
We are not as dull as that, we folk from Carthage;
The sun shines on us here. Whether you seek
The land in the west, the sometime fields of Saturn,[37]
Or the Sicilian realms and king Acestes,
I will help you to the limit; should you wish
To settle here and share this kingdom with me,
The city I found is yours; draw up your ships;
Trojan and Tyrian I treat alike.   610
Would, also, that your king were here, Aeneas,
Driven by that same wind. I will send good men

---

[37] Italy, where Saturn dwelt after his dethronement by Jupiter and his new generation of gods. Saturn's reign is associated with an ancient "golden age" of simplicity.

Along the coast to seek him, under orders
To scour all Libya; he may be wandering
Somewhere, in woods or town, surviving shipwreck."
   Aeneas and Achates both were eager
To break the cloud; the queen inspired their spirit
With her address. Achates asked Aeneas:—
"What do we do now, goddess-born? You see
They all are safe, our vessels and our comrades,   620
Only one missing, and we saw him drowning,
Ourselves, beneath the waves; all other things
Confirm what Venus told us." And as he finished,
The cloud around them broke, dissolved in air,
Illumining Aeneas, like a god,
Light radiant around his face and shoulders,
And Venus gave him all the bloom of youth,
Its glow, its liveliness, as the artist adds
Luster to ivory, or sets in gold
Silver or marble. No one saw him coming   630
Until he spoke:—"You seek me; here I am,
Trojan Aeneas, saved from the Libyan waves.
Worn out by all the perils of land and sea,
In need of everything, blown over the great world,
A remnant left by the Greeks, Dido, we lack
The means to thank our only pitier
For offer of a city and a home.
If there is justice anywhere, if goodness
Means anything to any power, if gods
At all regard good people, may they give   640
The great rewards you merit. Happy the age,
Happy the parents who have brought you forth!
While rivers run to sea, while shadows move
Over the mountains, while the stars burn on,
Always, your praise, your honor, and your name,
Whatever land I go to, will endure."[38]
His hand went out to greet his men, Serestus,
Gyas, Cloanthus, Ilioneus,
The others in their turn. And Dido marvelled
At his appearance, first, and all that trouble   650
He had borne up under; there was a moment's silence
Before she spoke: "What chance, what violence,
O goddess-born, has driven you through danger,
From grief to grief? Are you indeed that son
Whom Venus bore Anchises? I remember
When Teucer came to Sidon,[39] as an exile
Seeking new kingdoms, and my father helped him,

---

[38] Aeneas's words are ironic in the light of later events in the poem and in history.
[39] *Teucer* was a Greek exiled by his father; he is not to be confused with the Teucer who was
the legendary ancestor of the Trojans (who are therefore sometimes called Teucrians). *Sidon*
was a city near Tyre, Dido's former home.

My father, Belus, conqueror of Cyprus.
From that time on I have known about your city,
Your name, and the Greek kings, and the fall of Troy.   660
Even their enemies would praise the Trojans,
Or claim descent from Teucer's line. I bid you
Enter my house. I, too, am fortune-driven
Through many sufferings; this land at last
Has brought me rest. Not ignorant of evil,
I know one thing, at least,—to help the wretched."
And so she led Aeneas to the palace,
Proclaiming sacrifice at all the temples
In honor of his welcome, and sent presents
To his comrades at the shore, a score of bullocks,   670
A hundred swine, a hundred ewes and lambs
In honor of the joyous day. The palace,
Within, is made most bright with pomp and splendor,
The halls prepared for feasting. Crimson covers
Are laid, with fine embroidery, and silver
Is heavy on the tables; gold, engraven,
Recalls ancestral prowess, a tale of heroes
From the race's first beginnings.
                And Aeneas,
Being a thoughtful father, speeds Achates
Back to the ships, with tidings for Iulus,   680
He is to join them; all the father's fondness
Is centered on the son. Orders are given
To bring gifts with him, saved from the Trojan ruins,
A mantle stiff with figures worked in gold;
A veil with gold acanthus running through it,
Once worn by Helen, when she sailed from Sparta
Toward that forbidden marriage, a wondrous gift
Made by her mother Leda; and the sceptre
That Ilione, Priam's eldest daughter,
Had carried once; a necklace hung with pearls;   690
A crown of gold and jewels. Toward the ships
Achates sped the message.
                Meanwhile Venus
Plotted new stratagems, that Cupid, changed
In form and feature, should appear instead
Of young Ascanius,[40] and by his gifts
Inspire the queen to passion, with his fire
Burning her very bones. She feared the house
Held dubious intentions; men of Tyre
Were always two-faced people, and Juno's anger
Vexed her by night. She spoke to her wingèd son:—   700
"O my one strength and source of power, my son,
Disdainful of Jove's thunderbolt, to you
I come in prayer for help. You know that Juno

---

[40] Aeneas's son is sometimes called Ascanius, sometimes Iulus.

Is hateful toward Aeneas, keeping him tossing
All over the seas in bitterness; you have often
Grieved with me for your brother. And now Dido
Holds him with flattering words; I do not trust
Juno's ideas of welcome; she will never
Pause at a point like this. Therefore I purpose
To take the queen by cunning, put around her   710
A wall of flame, so that no power can change her,
So that a blazing passion for Aeneas
Will bind her to us. Listen! I will tell you
How you can manage this. The royal boy,
My greatest care, has heard his father's summons
To come to the city, bringing presents, rescued
From the flames of Troy and the sea; and he is ready.
But I will make him drowsy, carry him off
In slumber over Cythera, or hide him
Deep on Idalium[41] in a secret bower   720
Before he learns the scheme or interrupts it.
You, for one night, no more, assume his features,
The boy's familiar guise, yourself a boy,
So that when Dido takes you to her bosom
During the royal feast, with the wine flowing,
And happiness abounding, you, receiving
The sweetness of her kiss, will overcome her
With secret fire and poison."
                           For his mother
Cupid put off his wings, and went rejoicing
With young Iulus' stride; the real Iulus   730
Venus had lulled in soft repose, and borne him
Warm in her bosom to Idalian groves,
Where the soft marjoram cradled him with blossom
Exhaling shadowy sweetness over his slumber.
And, with Achates leading, Cupid came
Obedient to his mother, bringing gifts.
The queen receives them, on a golden couch
Below the royal tapestries, where spreads
Of crimson wait Aeneas and his Trojans.
Servants bring water for their hands, and bread   740
In baskets, and fine napkins. At the fire
Are fifty serving-maids, to set the feast,
A hundred more, girls, and a hundred boys
To load the tables, and bring the goblets round,
As through the happy halls the Tyrians throng,
Admire the Trojan gifts, admire Iulus,
The young god with the glowing countenance,
The charming words, the robe, the saffron veil
Edged with acanthus. More than all the rest,

---

[41] *Cythera* was the island associated with Venus's birth; Idalium was a part of Cyprus associated with worship of her.

Disaster-bound, the unhappy queen takes fire,   750
And cannot have enough of looking, moved
Alike by boy and gifts. She watches him
Cling to his father's neck, or come to her
For fondling, and her eyes, her heart, receive him,
Alas, poor queen, not knowing what a god
Is plotting for her sorrow. He remembers
What Venus told him; she forgets a little
About Sychaeus; the heart unused to love
Stirs with a living passion.
When the first quiet settled over the tables,   760
And the boards were cleared, they set the great bowls down,
Crowning the wine with garlands. A great hum
Runs through the halls, the voices reach the rafters,
The burning lamps below the fretted gold,
The torches flaring, put the night to rout.
The queen commands the loving-cup of Belus,
Heavy with gems and gold, and fills it full,
And silence fills the halls before her prayer:—
"Jupiter, giver of laws for host and guest,
Grant this to be a happy day for all,   770
Both Tyrians and travellers from Troy,
And something for our children to remember!
May Bacchus,[42] giver of joy, attend, and Juno
Be kind, and all my Tyrians be friendly!"
She poured libation on the table, touched
The gold rim with her lips, passed on the bowl
To Bitias, who dove deep, and other lords
Took up the challenge. And a minstrel played
A golden lyre, Iopas, taught by Atlas:[43]
Of the sun's labors and the wandering moon   780
He sang, whence came the race of beasts and man,
Whence rain and fire, the stars and constellations,
Why suns in winter hasten to the sea,
Or what delay draws out the dawdling nights.
The Tyrians roar, applauding, and the Trojans
Rejoice no less, and the poor queen prolongs
The night with conversation, drinking deep
Of her long love, and asking many questions
Of Priam, Hector; of the arms of Memnon;
How big Achilles was; and Diomedes,   790
What were his horses like? "Tell us, my guest,"
She pleads, "from the beginning, all the story,
The treachery of the Greeks, the wanderings,
The perils of the seven tiresome years."

---

[42] God of wine.

[43] The bard Iopas sings of astronomical science, which is associated with Atlas, the gigantic being who in mythology supports the heavens on his shoulders.

BOOK II: THE FALL OF TROY

They all were silent, watching. From his couch
Aeneas spoke: "A terrible grief, O Queen,
You bid me live again, how Troy went down
Before the Greeks, her wealth, her pitiful kingdom,
Sorrowful things I saw myself, wherein
I had my share and more. Even Ulysses,[1]
Even his toughest soldiery might grieve
At such a story. And the hour is late
Already; night is sliding down the sky
And setting stars urge slumber. But if you long   10
To learn our downfall, to hear the final chapter
Of Troy, no matter how I shrink, remembering,
And turn away in grief, let me begin it.[2]

Broken in war, set back by fate, the leaders
Of the Greek host, as years went by, contrived,
With Pallas' help, a horse as big as a mountain.
They wove its sides with planks of fir, pretending
This was an offering for their safe return,
At least, so rumor had it. But inside
They packed, in secret, into the hollow sides   20
The fittest warriors; the belly's cavern,
Huge as it was, was filled with men in armor.
There is an island, Tenedos, well-known,
Rich in the days of Priam; now it is only
A bay, and not too good an anchorage
For any ship to trust. They sailed there, hid
On the deserted shore. We thought they had gone,
Bound for Mycenae,[3] and Troy was very happy,
Shaking off grief, throwing the gates wide open.
It was a pleasure, for a change, to go   30
See the Greek camp, station and shore abandoned;
Why, this was where Achilles camped, his minions,
The Dolopes, were here; and the fleet just yonder,
And that was the plain where we used to meet in battle.
Some of us stared in wonder at the horse,
Astounded by its vastness, Minerva's gift,
Death from the virgin goddess, had we known it.
Thymoetes, whether in treachery, or because
The fates of Troy so ordered, was the first one
To urge us bring it in to the heart of the city,   40
But Capys, and some others, knowing better,

---

[1] The Latin name for Odysseus, the Greek hero.
[2] Typically, epic poems begin in the middle of the story, the earlier events being supplied in a flashback narrative like that of Aeneas in Books II and III.
[3] City in Greece ruled by Agamemnon, the Greek commander.

Suspicious of Greek plotting, said to throw it
Into the sea, to burn it up with fire,
To cut it open, see what there was inside it.
The wavering crowd could not make up its mind.

And, at that point, Laocoön came running,
With a great throng at his heels, down from the hilltop
As fast as ever he could, and before he reached us,
Cried in alarm: 'Are you crazy, wretched people?
Do you think they have gone, the foe? Do you think that any   50
Gifts of the Greeks lack treachery? Ulysses,—
What was his reputation? Let me tell you,
Either the Greeks are hiding in this monster,
Or it's some trick of war, a spy, or engine,
To come down on the city. Tricky business
Is hiding in it. Do not trust it, Trojans,
Do not believe this horse. Whatever it may be,
I fear the Greeks, even when bringing presents.'
With that, he hurled the great spear at the side
With all the strength he had. It fastened, trembling,   60
And the struck womb rang hollow, a moaning sound.
He had driven us, almost, to let the light in
With the point of the steel, to probe, to tear, but something
Got in his way, the gods, or fate, or counsel,
Ill-omened, in our hearts; or Troy would be standing
And Priam's lofty citadel unshaken.

Meanwhile, some Trojan shepherds, pulling and hauling,
Had a young fellow, with his hands behind him,
Tied up, and they were dragging him to Priam.
He had let himself be taken so, on purpose,   70
To open Troy to the Greeks, a stranger, ready
For death or shifty cunning, a cool intriguer,
Let come what may. They crowd around to see him,
Take turns in making fun of him, that captive.
Listen, and learn Greek trickiness; learn all
Their crimes from one.
He stopped in the middle, frightened and defenceless,
Looked at the Trojan ranks,—'What land, what waters,
Can take me now?' he cried, 'There is nothing, nothing
Left for me any more, no place with the Greeks,   80
And here are the Trojans howling for my blood!'
Our mood was changed. We pitied him, poor fellow,
Sobbing his heart out. We bade him tell his story,
His lineage, his news: what can he count on,
The captive that he is? His fear had gone
As he began: 'O King, whatever happens,
I will tell the truth, tell all of it; to start with,
I own I am a Greek. Sinon is wretched,
Fortune has made him so, but she will never

Make him a liar. You may perhaps have heard   90
Rumors of Palamedes, son of Belus,[4]
A man of glorious fame. But the Greeks killed him,—
He was against the war, and so they killed him,
An innocent man, by perjury and lying
False witness. Now that he is dead they mourn him.
My father, his poor relative, had sent me
To soldier in his company; I was then
Scarcely beyond my boyhood. Palamedes
Held, for some time, some influence and standing
In royal councils, and we shared his glory,   100
But, and all men know this, Ulysses' hatred,
His cunning malice, pulled him down; thereafter
I lived in darkness, dragging out a lifetime
In sorrow for my innocent lord, and anger,
And in my anger I was very foolish,
I talked; I vowed, if I got home to Argos,
I would have vengeance: so I roused Ulysses
To hate me in his turn, and that began it,
Downfall and evil, Ulysses always trying
To frighten me with hint and accusation,   110
With rumors planted where the crowd would listen;
Oh yes, Ulysses knew what he was doing,
He never stopped, until with Calchas[5] working
Hand in glove with him—why am I telling this,
And what's the use? I am stalling. All the Greeks,
You think, are all alike; what more do you want?
Inflict the punishment. That would be something
Ulysses would rejoice in, and some others
Pay handsome money for!'

But we were all on fire to hear him further.   120
Pelasgian[6] craft meant nothing to our folly.
Trembling and nervous, he resumed his lying:
'The Greeks were tired of the long war; they often
Wanted to sail from Troy for home. Oh, would
That they had only done it! But a storm
Would cut them off, or the wrong wind terrify them.
Especially, just after the horse was finished,
With the joined planks of maple, all the heaven
Roared loud with storm-clouds. In suspense and terror
We sent Eurypylus to ask Apollo   130
What could be done; the oracle was gloomy,
Foreboding: "Blood, O Greeks, and a slain virgin[7]

---

[4] Not to be confused with Dido's father Belus, mentioned in Book I.
[5] As a Greek priest and prophet, Calchas' task was to discover and reveal the will of the gods.
[6] Here a synonym for "Greek."
[7] Iphigenia, daughter of Agamemnon; her life had been sacrificed to appease the gods and thus gain for the Greeks favorable winds for their expedition against Troy.

Appeased the winds when first you came here; blood
Must pay for your return, a life be given,
An Argive life." The word came to our ears
With terror in it, our blood ran cold in our veins,
For whom was fate preparing? who would be
The victim of Apollo? Then Ulysses
Dragged Calchas into our midst, with a great uproar,
Trying his best to make the prophet tell us   140
What the gods wanted. And there were many then
Who told me what was coming, or kept silent
Because they saw, and all too well, the scheme
Ulysses had in mind. For ten days Calchas
Said nothing at all, hid in his tent, refusing
To have a word of his pronounce the sentence,
And all the time Ulysses kept on shouting,
Till Calchas broke, and doomed me to the altar.
And all assented; what each man had feared
In his own case, he bore with great composure   150
When turned another way.
The terrible day was almost on me; fillets
Were ready for my temples, the salted meal
Prepared, the altars standing. But I fled,
I tore myself away from death, I admit it,
I hid all night in sedge and muddy water
At the edge of the lake, hoping, forever hoping,
They might set sail. And now I hope no longer
To see my home, my parents, or my children,
Poor things, whom they will kill because I fled them,   160
Whom they will murder for my sacrilege.
But oh, by the gods above, by any power
That values truth, by any uncorrupted
Remnant of faith in all the world, have pity,
Have pity on a soul that bears such sorrow,
More than I ever deserved.'
He had no need to ask us. Priam said,
Untie him, and we did so with a promise
To spare his life. Our king, with friendly words,
Addressed him, saying, 'Whoever you are, forget   170
The Greeks, from now on. You are ours; but tell me
Why they have built this monstrous horse? who made it,
Who thought of it? What is it, war-machine,
Religious offering?' And he, instructed
In every trick and artifice, made answer,
Lifting his hands, now free: 'Eternal fires,
Inviolable godhead, be my witness,
You altars, you accursèd swords, you fillets
Which I as victim wore, I had the right
To break those solemn bonds, I had the right   180
To hate those men, to bring whatever they hide
Into the light and air; I am bound no longer

To any country, any laws, but, Trojans,
Keep to the promise, if I tell the truth,
If I pay back with interest.
All the Greek hope, since first the war began,
Rested in Pallas, always. But Ulysses,
The crime-contriver, and the son of Tydeus[8]
Attacked Minerva's temple, stole her image
Out of the holy shrine, and slew the guards,   190
And laid their bloody hands upon the goddess,
And from that time the Danaan[9] hopes were broken,
Faltered and failed. It was no doubtful anger
Pallas revealed; she gave them signs and portents.
From her image in the camp the upraised eyes
Shot fire, and sweat ran salty down the limbs,
Thrice from the ground she seemed to flash and leap
With vibrant spear and clashing shield. The priest,
Calchas, made prophecy: they must take to flight
Over the sea, and Troy could not be taken   200
Without new omens; they must go to Argos,
Bring back the goddess again, whom they have taken
In curved ships over the sea. And if they have gone,
They are bound for home, Mycenae, for new arms,
New gods, new soldiers; they will be here again
When least expected. Calchas' message warned them,
And so they built this image, to replace
The one they had stolen, a gigantic offering
For a tremendous sacrilege. It was Calchas,
Again, who bade them build a mass so mighty   210
It almost reached the stars, too big to enter
Through any gate, or be brought inside the walls.
For if your hands should damage it, destruction,
(May God avert it) would come upon the city,
But if your hands helped bring it home, then Asia
Would be invading Greece, and doom await
Our children's children.'
                    We believed him, we
Whom neither Diomede nor great Achilles
Had taken, nor ten years, nor that armada,
A thousand ships of war. But Sinon did it   220
By perjury and guile.
                   Then something else,
Much greater and more terrible, was forced
Upon us, troubling our unseeing spirits.
Laocoön, allotted priest of Neptune,
Was slaying a great bull beside the altars,
When suddenly, over the tranquil deep
From Tenedos,—I shudder even now,

[8] His son was Diomede, one of the greatest of the Greek warriors.
[9] Greek.

Recalling it—there came a pair of serpents
With monstrous coils, breasting the sea, and aiming
Together for the shore. Their heads and shoulders   230
Rose over the waves, upright, with bloody crests,
The rest of them trailing along the water,
Looping in giant spirals; the foaming sea
Hissed under their motion. And they reached the land,
Their burning eyes suffused with blood and fire,
Their darting tongues licking the hissing mouths.
Pale at the sight, we fled. But they went on
Straight toward Laocoön, and first each serpent
Seized in its coils his two young sons, and fastened
The fangs in those poor bodies. And the priest   240
Struggled to help them, weapons in his hand.
They seized him, bound him with their mighty coils,
Twice round his waist, twice round his neck, they squeezed
With scaly pressure, and still towered above him.
Straining his hands to tear the knots apart,
His chaplets[10] stained with blood and the black poison,
He uttered horrible cries, not even human,
More like the bellowing of a bull when, wounded,
It flees the altar, shaking from the shoulder
The ill-aimed axe. And on the pair went gliding   250
To the highest shrine, the citadel of Pallas,
And vanished underneath the feet of the goddess
And the circle of her shield.
                              The people trembled
Again; they said Laocoön deserved it,
Having, with spear, profaned the sacred image.
It must be brought to its place, they cried, the goddess
Must be appeased. We broke the walls, exposing
The city's battlements, and all were busy
Helping the work, with rollers underfoot
And ropes around the neck. It climbed our walls,   260
The deadly engine. Boys, unwedded girls
Sang alleluias round it, all rejoicing
To have a hand on the tow-rope. It came nearer,
Threatening, gliding, into the very city.
O motherland! O Ilium, home of gods,
O walls of Troy! Four times it stopped, four times
The sound of arms came from it, and we pressed on,
Unheedful, blind in madness, till we set it,
Ill-omened thing, on the citadel we worshipped.
And even when Cassandra[11] gave us warning,   270
We never believed her; so a god had ordered.
That day, our last, poor wretches, we were happy,

[10] Garlands for the head.
[11] A daughter of the royal family of Troy; gifted with prophecy, she was nevertheless doomed always to have her true prophecies disbelieved.

Garlanding the temples of the gods
All through the town.
                              And the sky turned, and darkness
Came from the ocean, the great shade covering earth
And heaven, and the trickery of the Greeks.
Sprawling along the walls, the Trojans slumbered,
Sleep holding their weary limbs, and the Greek armada,
From Tenedos, under the friendly silence
Of a still moon, came surely on. The flagship   280
Blazed at the masthead with a sudden signal,
And Sinon, guarded by the fates, the hostile
Will of the gods, swung loose the bolts; the Greeks
Came out of the wooden womb. The air received them
The happy captains, Sthenelus, Ulysses,
Thessandrus, Acamas, Achilles' son
Called Neoptolemus, Thoas, Machaon,
Epeos, who designed the thing,—they all
Came sliding down the rope, and Menelaus
Was with them in the storming of a city   290
Buried in sleep and wine. The watch was murdered,
The open doors welcome the rush of comrades,
They marshal the determined ranks for battle.
      It was the time when the first sleep begins
For weary mortals, heaven's most welcome gift.
In sleep, before my eyes, I seemed to see
Hector, most sorrowful, black with bloody dust,
Torn, as he had been, by Achilles' car,
The thong-marks on his swollen feet. How changed
He was from that great Hector who came, once,   300
Triumphant in Achilles' spoil, from hurling
Fire at the Grecian ships. With ragged beard,
Hair matted with his blood, wearing the wounds
He earned around the walls of Troy, he stood there.
It seemed that I spoke first:—'O light of Troy,
Our surest hope, we have long been waiting for you,
What shores have kept you from us? Many deaths,
Much suffering, have visited our city,
And we are tired. Why do I see these wounds?
What shame has caused them?' Those were foolish questions;   310
He made no answer but a sigh or a groan,
And then: 'Alas, O goddess-born! Take flight,
Escape these flames! The enemy has the walls,
Troy topples from her lofty height; enough
Has been paid out to Priam and to country.
Could any hand have saved them, Hector's would have.
Troy trusts to you her household gods, commending
Her holy things to you; take them, companions
Of destiny; seek walls for them, and a city
To be established, a long sea-wandering over.'   320

From the inner shrine he carried Vesta's chaplets
In his own hands, and her undying fire.

Meanwhile, the city is all confusion and sorrow;
My father Anchises' house, remote and sheltered
Among its trees, was not so far away
But I could hear the noises, always clearer,
The thickening din of war. Breaking from sleep,
I climb to the roof-top, listening and straining
The way a shepherd does on the top of a mountain
When fire goes over the corn, and the winds are roaring,   330
Or the rush of a mountain torrent drowns the fields
And the happy crops and the work of men and oxen
And even drags great trees over. And then I knew
The truth indeed; the craft of the Greeks was hidden
No longer from my sight. The house of a neighbor,
Deiphobus, went up in flames; next door,
Ucalegon was burning. Sigeum's[12] water
Gave back the glow. Men shouted, and the trumpets
Blared loud. I grab my arms, with little purpose,
There was no sense in it, but my heart was burning   340
To mass a band for war, rush to the hilltop
With comrades at my side. Anger and frenzy
Hurry me on. A decent death in battle
Is a helpful thought, sometimes.

And here came Panthus, running from the weapons,
Priest of Apollo, and a son of Othrys,
With holy relics in his hands, and dragging
His little grandson, here came Panthus, running
In madness to my door. 'How goes it, Panthus?
What stronghold still is ours?' I had hardly spoken,   350
When he began, with a groan: 'It has come, this day
Will be our last, and we can not escape it.
Trojans we have been, Troy has been, and glory
Is ours no more. Fierce Jupiter has taken
Everything off to Argos, and Greeks lord it
In a town on fire. The horse, high in the city,
Pours out armed men, and Sinon, arrogant victor,
Lights up more fires. The gates are standing open,
And men are there by the thousands, ever as many
As came once from Mycenae; others block   360
The narrow streets, with weapons drawn; the blades
Flash in the dark; the point is set for murder.
A few of the guards are trying, striking blindly,
For all the good it does.'

[12] A cape near Troy.

His words, or the gods' purpose, swept me on
Toward fire and arms, where the grim furies call,
And the clamor and confusion, reaching heaven.
Ripheus joined me, Epytus, mighty in arms,
Came to my side in the moonlight, Hypanis, Dymas,
And young Coroebus, Mygdon's son, poor youngster,   370
Mad with a hopeless passion for Cassandra,
He wanted to help Priam, but never heeded
The warnings of his loved one.
                              As they ranged
Themselves for battle, eager, I addressed them:
'O brave young hearts, it will do no good; no matter.
Even if your will is fixed, to follow a leader
Taking the final risk, you can't help seeing
The fortune of our state. The gods have gone,
They have left their shrines and altars, and the power
They once upheld is fallen. You are helping   380
A town already burnt. So let us die,
Rush into arms. One safety for the vanquished
Is to have hope of none.'
                          They were young, and angry.
Like wolves, marauders in black mist, whom hunger
Drives blindly on, whose whelps, abandoned, wait them
Dry-jawed, so we went on, through foes, through weapons,
To certain death; we made for the heart of the city,
Black night around us with its hollow shadow.
Who could explain that night's destruction, equal
Its agony with tears? The ancient city,   390
A power for many years, comes down, and corpses
Lie littering the streets and homes and altars.
Not only Trojans die. The old-time valor
Returns to the vanquished heart, and the Greek victors
Know what it is to fall. Everywhere sorrow,
Everywhere panic, everywhere the image
Of death, made manifold.

   Out of a crowd of Greeks comes one Androgeos,
Thinking us allies, hailing us as friendly:
'Why men, where have you been, you dawdling fellows?   400
Hurry along! Here is plunder for the taking,
Others are busy at it, and you just coming
From the high ships!' And then he knew he had blundered;
He had fallen in with foes, who gave no answer.
He stopped, stepped back, like a man who treads on a serpent
Unseen in the rough brush, and then in panic
Draws back as the purple neck swells out in anger.
Even so, Androgeos pulled away in terror.
We rush them, swarm all over them; they are frightened,
They do not know their ground, and fortune favors   410
Our first endeavor. Coroebus, a little crazy

With nerve and luck, cries out: 'Comrades, where fortune
First shows the way and sides with us, we follow.
Let us change our shields, put on the Grecian emblems!
All's fair in war: we lick them or we trick them,
And what's the odds?' He takes Androgeos' helmet,
Whose plume streams over his head, takes up the shield
With proud device, and fits the sword to his side.
And Ripheus does the same, and so does Dymas,
And all the others, happily being armed   420
With spoil, new-won. We join the Greeks, all going
Under no gods of ours, in the night's darkness
Wade into many a fight, and Greeks by the dozens
We send to hell. And some of them in panic
Speed to the ships; they know that shore, and trust it,
And some of them—these were the abject cowards—
Climb scrambling up the horse's sides, again
Take refuge in the womb.

It is not for men to trust unwilling gods.
Cassandra was being dragged from Pallas' temple,   430
Her hair loosed to the wind, her eyes turned upward
To heaven for mercy; they had bound her hands.
Coroebus could not bear that sight; in madness
He threw himself upon them, and he died.
We followed, all of us, into the thick of it,
And were cut down, not only by Greeks; the rooftops,
Held by our friends, rained weapons: we were wearing
Greek crests and armor, and they did not know us.
And the Greeks came on, shouting with anger, burning
To foil that rescue; there was Menelaus,   440
And Agamemnon, and the savage Ajax,
And a whole army of them. Hurricanes
Rage the same way, when winds from different quarters
Clash in the sky, and the forest groans, and Neptune
Storms underneath the ocean. Those we routed
Once in the dark came back again from the byways
And alleys of the town; they mark our shields,
Our lying weapons, and our foreign voices.
Of course we are outnumbered. Peneleus
It was, who slew Coroebus, at the altar   450
Sacred to Pallas. Ripheus fell, a man
Most just of all the Trojans, most fair-minded.
The gods thought otherwise. Hypanis, Dymas,
Were slain by their own men, and Panthus' goodness
Was no protection, nor his priestly office.
I call to witness Troy, her fires, her ashes,
And the last agonies of all our people
That in that hour I ran from no encounter
With any Greek, and if the fates had been
For me to fall in battle, there I earned it.   460

The current swept me off, with two companions,
One, Iphitus, too slow with age, the other,
Pelias, limping from Ulysses' wound.
The noise kept calling us to Priam's palace.

There might have been no fighting and no dying
Through all the city, such a battle raged
Here, from the ground to roof-top. At the threshold
Waves of assault were breaking, and the Greeks
Were climbing, rung by rung, along the ladders,
Using one hand, the right one up and forward   470
Over the battlements, the left one thrust
In the protecting shield. And over their heads
The Trojans pried up towers and planking, wrecking
The building; gilded beams, the spoils of their fathers,
Were ample weapons for the final moment.
Some had the doorways blocked, others, behind them,
Were ready with drawn swords. We had a moment
When help seemed possible; new reinforcement
Might yet relieve the palace.
There was a secret entrance there, a passage   480
All the way through the building, a postern gate,
Where, while the kingdom stood, Andromache[13]
Would go, alone, or bring the little boy,
Astyanax, to Hector's father and mother.
I climbed to the top of the roof, where the poor Trojans
Were hurling down their unavailing darts.
A tower stood on the very edge, a look-out
Over all Troy, the ships and camp of the Greeks.
This we attacked with steel, where the joints were weakest,
And pried it up, and shoved it over. It crashed,   490
A noisy ruin, over the hostile columns;
But more kept coming up; the shower of stones
And darts continued raining.
Before the entrance, at the very threshold
Stood Pyrrhus,[14] flashing proudly in bronze light,
Sleek as a serpent coming into the open,
Fed on rank herbs, wintering under the ground,
The old slough cast, the new skin shining, rolling
His slippery length, reaching his neck to the sun,
While the forked tongue darts from the mouth. Automedon   500
Was with him, Periphas, Achilles' driver,
A giant of a man, and the host from Scyros,[15]
All closing in on the palace, and hurling flames.
Among the foremost, Pyrrhus, swinging an axe,
Burst through, wrenched the bronze doors out of their hinges,

---

[13] Wife of Hector and mother of Astyanax. Hector's parents are Priam and Hecuba, king
and queen of Troy.
   [14] Achilles' son, fierce like his war-loving father.   [15] Birthplace of Pyrrhus.

Smashed through the panelling, turned it into a window.
The long halls came to view, the inner chambers
Of Priam and the older kings; they see
Armed warriors at the threshold.
Within, it is all confusion, women wailing,   510
Pitiful noise, groaning, and blows; the din
Reaches the golden stars. The trembling mothers
Wander, not knowing where, or find a spot
To cling to; they would hold and kiss the doors.
Pyrrhus comes on, aggressive as his father;
No barrier holds him back; the gate is battered
As the ram[16] smashes at it; the doors come down.
Force finds a way; the Greeks pour in, they slaughter
The first one in their path; they fill the courtyard
With soldiery, wilder than any river   520
In flood over the banks and dikes and ploughland.
I saw them, Pyrrhus, going mad with murder,
And Atreus' twin sons,[17] and Hecuba
I saw, and all her daughters, and poor old Priam,
His blood polluting the altars he had hallowed.
The fifty marriage-chambers,[18] the proud hope
Of an everlasting line, are violated,
The doors with the golden spoil are turned to splinters.
Whatever the fire has spared the Greeks take over.
    You would ask, perhaps, about the fate of Priam?   530
When he saw the city fall, and the doors of the palace
Ripped from the hinge, and the enemy pouring in,
Old as he was, he went and found his armor,
Unused so many years, and his old shoulders
Shook as he put it on. He took his sword,
A useless weapon, and, doomed to die, went rushing
Into the midst of the foe. There was an altar
In the open court-yard, shaded by a laurel
Whose shadow darkened the household gods, and here
Hecuba and her daughters had come thronging,   540
Like doves by a black storm driven. They were praying
Here at the altar, and clinging to the gods,
Whatever image was left. And the queen saw Priam
In the arms of his youth. 'O my unhappy husband,'
She cried, 'have you gone mad, to dress yourself
For battle, so? It is all no use; the time
Needs better help than yours; not even my Hector
Could help us now. Come to me, come to the altar;
It will protect us, or at least will let us
Die all together.' And she drew him to her.   550
    Just then through darts, through weapons, came Polites,
A son of Priam, fleeing deadly Pyrrhus,

---

[16] The battering-ram.   [17] Agamemnon and Menelaus.
[18] The quarters of Priam's fifty sons and their wives; Priam also had fifty daughters.

Down the long colonnades and empty hallways,
Wounded, and Pyrrhus after him, vicious, eager
For the last spear-thrust, and he drives it home;
Polites falls, and his life goes out with his blood,
Father and mother watching. And then Priam,
In the very grip of death, cried out in anger:—
"If there is any righteousness in heaven,
To care about such wickedness, the gods   560
Will have the right reward and thanks to offer
A man like this, who has made a father witness
The murder of his son, the worst pollution!
You claim to be Achilles' son. You liar!
Achilles had some reverence, respected
A suppliant's right and trust; he gave me back
My Hector's lifeless body[19] for the tomb,
And let me go to my kingdom.' With the word
He flung a feeble spear, which dropped, deflected
From the rough bronze; it had hung there for a moment.   570
And Pyrrhus sneered: 'So, go and tell my father
The latest news: do not forget to mention,
Old messenger-boy, my villainous behavior,
And what a bastard Pyrrhus is. Now die!'
He dragged the old man, trembling, to the altar,
Slipping in his son's blood; he grabbed his hair
With the left hand, and the right drove home the sword
Deep in the side, to the hilt. And so fell Priam,
Who had seen Troy burn and her walls come down, once monarch,
Proud ruler over the peoples and lands of Asia.   580
He lies, a nameless body, on the shore,
Dismembered, huge, the head torn from the shoulders.
      Grim horror, then, came home to me. I saw
My father when I saw the king, the life
Going out with the cruel wound. I saw Creusa[20]
Forsaken, my abandoned home, Iulus,
My little son. I looked around. They all
Had gone, exhausted, flung down from the walls,
Or dead in the fire, and I was left alone.
      And I saw Helen, hiding, of all places,   590
At Vesta's shrine, and clinging there in silence,
But the bright flames lit the scene. That hated woman,
Fearing both Trojan anger and Greek vengeance,
A common fury to both lands, was crouching
Beside the altar. Anger flared up in me
For punishment and vengeance. Should she then,
I thought, come home to Sparta safe, uninjured

---

[19] After killing Hector, Achilles agreed to return the corpse to Hector's father Priam. (See Homer's *Iliad*, Book XXIV.) Achilles himself has since been slain, struck in the heel (his one vulnerable spot) by an arrow from Paris's bow.
      [20] Aeneas's wife.

Walk through Mycenae,[21] a triumphant queen?
See husband, home, parents and children, tended
By Trojan slave-girls? This, with Priam fallen   600
And Troy burnt down, and the shore soaked in blood?
Never! No memorable name, I knew,
Was won by punishing women, yet, for me,
There might be praise for the just abolition
Of this unholiness, and satisfaction
In vengeance for the ashes of my people.
All this I may have said aloud, in frenzy,
As I rushed on, when to my sight there came
A vision of my lovely mother, radiant
In the dark night, a goddess manifest,   610
As tall and fair as when she walks in heaven.
She caught me by the hand and stopped me:[22]—'Son,
What sorrow rouses this relentless anger,
This violence? Do you care for me no longer?
Consider others first, your aged father,
Anchises; is your wife Creusa living?
Where is Iulus? Greeks are all around them,
Only my love between them, fire and sword.
It is not for you to blame the Spartan woman,
Daughter of Tyndareus, or even Paris.   620
The gods are the ones, the high gods are relentless;
It is they who bring this power down, who topple
Troy from the high foundation. Look! Your vision
Is mortal dull, I will take the cloud away,—
Fear not a mother's counsel. Where you see
Rock torn from rock, and smoke and dust in billows,
Neptune is working, plying the trident, prying
The walls from their foundations. And see Juno,
Fiercest of all, holding the Scaean gates,
Girt with the steel, and calling from the ships   630
Implacable companions. On the towers,—
Turn, and be certain—Pallas take command
Gleaming with Gorgon and storm-cloud. Even Jove,
Our father, nerves the Greeks with fire and spirit,
And spurs the other gods against the Trojans.
Hasten the flight, my son; no other labor
Waits for accomplishment. I promise safety
Until you reach your father's house.' She had spoken
And vanished in the thickening night of shadows.
Dread shapes come into vision, mighty powers,   640
Great gods at war with Troy, which, so it seemed,
Was sinking as I watched, with the same feeling

---

[21] The city in Sparta where Helen had lived with her husband, Menelaus, before her adulterous flight with Paris.
[22] Though she is Aeneas's mother, Venus as goddess of love naturally protects Helen, the most beautiful of all women.

As when on mountain-tops you see the loggers
Hacking an ash-tree down, and it always threatens
To topple, nodding a little, and the leaves
Trembling when no wind stirs, and dies of its wounds
With one long loud last groan, and dirt from the ridges
Heaves up as it goes down with roots in air.
Divinity my guide, I leave the roof-top,
I pass unharmed through enemies and blazing,   650
Weapons give place to me, and flames retire.

    At last I reached the house, I found my father,
The first one that I looked for. I meant to take him
To the safety of the hills, but he was stubborn,
Refusing longer life or barren exile,
Since Troy was dead. 'You have the strength,' he told me,
'You are young enough, take flight. For me, had heaven
Wanted to save my life, they would have spared
This home for me. We have seen enough destruction,
More than enough, survived a captured city.   660
Speak to me as a corpse laid out for burial,
A quick farewell, and go. Death I shall find
With my own hand; the enemy will pity,
Or look for spoil. The loss of burial[23]
Is nothing at all. I have been living too long
Hated by gods and useless, since the time
Jove blasted me[24] with lightning wind and fire.'
He would not move, however we wept, Creusa,
Ascanius, all the house, insistent, pleading
That he should not bring all to ruin with him.   670
He would not move, he would not listen. Again
I rush to arms, I pray for death; what else
Was left to me? 'Dear father, were you thinking
I could abandon you, and go? what son
Could bear a thought so monstrous? If the gods
Want nothing to be left of so great a city,
If you are bound, or pleased, to add us all
To the wreck of Troy, the way is open for it—
Pyrrhus will soon be here; from the blood of Priam
He comes; he slays the son before the father,   680
The sire at the altar-stone; O my dear mother,
Was it for this you saved me, brought me through
The fire and sword, to see our enemies
Here in the very house, and wife and son
And father murdered in each other's blood?
Bring me my arms; the last light calls the conquered.
Let me go back to the Greeks, renew the battle,
We shall not all of us die unavenged.'

---

[23] Failure to receive proper burial was a grievous misfortune. See Book VI.
[24] The god took revenge because Anchises boasted of Venus' love for him.

Sword at my side, I was on the point of going,
Working the left arm into the shield. Creusa   690
Clung to me on the threshold, held my feet,
And made me see my little son:—'Dear husband,
If you are bent on dying, take us with you,
But if you think there is any hope in fighting,
And you should know, stay and defend the house!
To whom are we abandoned, your father and son,
And I, once called your wife?' She filled the house
With moaning outcry. And then something happened,
A wonderful portent. Over Iulus' head,
Between our hands and faces, there appeared   700
A blaze of gentle light; a tongue of flame,
Harmless and innocent, was playing over
The softness of his hair, around his temples.
We were afraid, we did our best to quench it
With our own hands, or water, but my father
Raised joyous eyes to heaven, and prayed aloud:—
'Almighty Jupiter, if any prayer
Of ours has power to move you, look upon us,
Grant only this, if we have ever deserved it,
Grant us a sign, and ratify the omen!'   710
He had hardly spoken, when thunder on the left
Resounded, and a shooting star from heaven
Drew a long trail of light across the shadows.
We saw it cross above the house, and vanish
In the woods of Ida,[25] a wake of gleaming light
Where it had sped, and a trail of sulphurous odor.
This was a victory: my father rose
In worship of the gods and the holy star,
Crying: 'I follow, son, wherever you lead;
There is no delay, not now; Gods of my fathers,   720
Preserve my house, my grandson; yours the omen,
And Troy is in your keeping. O my son,
I yield, I am ready to follow.' But the fire
Came louder over the walls, the flames rolled nearer
Their burning tide. 'Climb to my shoulders, father,
It will be no burden, so we are together,
Meeting a common danger or salvation.
Iulus, take my hand; Creusa, follow
A little way behind. Listen, you servants!
You will find, when you leave the city, an old temple 730
That once belonged to Ceres;[26] it has been tended
For many years with the worship of our fathers.
There's a little hill there, and a cypress tree;
And that's where we shall meet, one way or another.
And one thing more: you, father, are to carry

---

[25] A mountain and mountain range near Troy.
[26] Goddess of the fields and harvest.

The holy objects and the gods of the household,
My hands are foul with battle and blood, I could not
Touch them without pollution.'
                              I bent down
And over my neck and shoulders spread the cover
Of a tawny lion-skin, took up my burden;   740
Little Iulus held my hand, and trotted,
As best he could, beside me; Creusa followed.
We went on through the shadows. I had been
Brave, so I thought, before, in the rain of weapons
And the cloud of massing Greeks. But now I trembled
At every breath of air, shook at a whisper,
Fearful for both my burden and companion.
    I was near the gates, and thinking we had made it,
But there was a sound, the tramp of marching feet,
And many of them, it seemed; my father, peering   750
Through the thick gloom, cried out:—'Son, they are coming!
Flee, flee! I see their shields, their gleaming bronze.'
Something or other took my senses from me
In that confusion. I turned aside from the path,
I do not know what happened then. Creusa
Was lost;[27] she had missed the road, or halted, weary,
For a brief rest. I do not know what happened,
She was not seen again; I had not looked back,
Nor even thought about her, till we came
To Ceres' hallowed home. The count was perfect,   760
Only one missing there, the wife and mother.
Whom did I not accuse, of gods and mortals,
Then in my frenzy? What worse thing had happened
In the city overthrown? I left Anchises,
My son, my household gods, to my companions,
In a hiding-place in the valley; and I went back
Into the city again, wearing my armor,
Ready, still one more time, for any danger.
I found the walls again, the gate's dark portals,
I followed my own footsteps back, but terror,   770
Terror and silence were all I found. I went
On to my house. She might, just might, have gone there.
Only the Greeks were there, and fire devouring
The very pinnacles. I tried Priam's palace;
In the empty courtyards Phoenix and Ulysses
Guarded the spoils piled up at Juno's altar.
They had Trojan treasure there, loot from the altars,
Great drinking-bowls of gold, and stolen garments,
And human beings. A line of boys and women
Stood trembling there.   780

---

[27] The loss, literally, of Creusa (exactly what happens to her is not clear) may indicate
something about Aeneas's priorities, but it is providentially necessary that Aeneas be free to
marry Lavinia as part of the Trojans' later establishment of themselves in Italy.

I took the risk of crying through the shadows,
Over and over, 'Creusa!' I kept calling,
'Creusa!' and 'Creusa!' but no answer.
No sense, no limit, to my endless rushing
All through the town; and then at last I saw her,
Or thought I did, her shadow a little taller
Than I remembered. And she spoke to me
Beside myself with terror:—'O dear husband,
What good is all this frantic grief? The gods
Have willed it so, Creusa may not join you   790
Out of this city; Jupiter denies it.
Long exile lies ahead, and vast sea-reaches
The ships must furrow, till you come to land
Far in the West; rich fields are there, and a river
Flowing with gentle current; its name is Tiber.
And happy days await you there, a kingdom,
A royal wife. Banish the tears of sorrow
Over Creusa lost. I shall never see
The arrogant houses of the Myrmidons,[28]
Nor be a slave to any Grecian woman;   800
I am a Dardan woman; I am the wife
Of Venus' son; it is Cybele[29] who keeps me
Here on these shores. And now farewell, and love
Our son.' I wept, there was more to say; she left me,
Vanishing into empty air. Three times
I reached out toward her, and three times her image
Fled like the breath of a wind or a dream on wings.
The night was over; I went back to my comrades.
    I was surprised to find so many more
Had joined us, ready for exile, pitiful people,   810
Mothers, and men, and children, streaming in
From everywhere, looking for me to lead them
Wherever I would. Over the hills of Ida
The morning-star was rising; in the town
The Danaans held the gates, and help was hopeless.
I gave it up, I lifted up my father,
Together we sought the hills.

BOOK III: THE WANDERINGS OF AENEAS

"After the gods' decision to overthrow
The Asian world, the innocent house of Priam,
And the proud city, built by Neptune, smoked
From the ruined ground, we were driven, different ways,

---

[28] The Greek soldiers who had been led by Achilles.
[29] A goddess identified with Rhea, consort of Saturn during the reign of the older gods. It is possible that Creusa has not died but rather has been mysteriously inducted into the service of Cybele.

By heaven's auguries, seeking lands forsaken.
Below Antandros,[1] under Phrygian Ida,
We built a fleet, and gathered men, uncertain
Of either direction or settlement. The summer
Had scarce begun, when at my father's orders,
We spread our sails. I wept as I left the harbor,   10
The fields where Troy had been. I was borne, an exile
Over the deep, with son, companions, household,
And household gods.
                  Far off there lies a land,
Sacred to Mars; the Thracians[2] used to till it,
Whose king was fierce Lycurgus; they were friendly,
Of old, to Troy, when we were prosperous. Hither
I sailed, and on its curving shore established
A city site; Aeneadae, I called it.
This I began, not knowing fate was adverse.

    I was offering my mother proper homage,   20
And other gods, to bless the new beginnings,
I had a white bull ready as a victim
To the king of the gods. There was a mound nearby,
Bristling with myrtle and with cornel-bushes.
I needed greenery to veil the altar,
But as I struggled with the leafy branches,
A fearful portent met my gaze. Black drops
Dripped from the ends of the roots, black blood was falling
On the torn ground, and a cold chill went through me.
I tried again; the shoot resisted; blood   30
Followed again. Troubled, I prayed to the Nymphs,
To the father of the fields, to bless the vision,
Remove the curse; and down on my knees I wrestled
Once more against the stubborn ground, and heard
A groan from under the hillock, and voice crying:
'Why mangle a poor wretch, Aeneas? Spare me,
Here in the tomb, and save your hands pollution.
You know me, I am Trojan-born, no stranger,
This is familiar blood. Alas! Take flight,
Leave this remorseless land; the curse of greed   40
Lies heavy on it. I am Polydorus,
Pierced by an iron harvest; out of my body
Rise javelins and lances.' I was speechless,
Stunned, in my terror.
    Priam, forever unfortunate, had sent
This Polydorus on a secret mission,
Once, to the king of Thrace, with gold for hiding
When the king despaired of the siege and the city's fortune.

---

[1] A town near Troy.
[2] Inhabitants of Thrace, an area north of the Aegean Sea, northwest of the Hellespont strait (the modern Dardanelles).

And when Troy fell, and Fortune failed, the Thracian
Took Agamemnon's side, broke off his duty, 50
Slew Polydorus, took the gold. There is nothing
To which men are not driven by that hunger.
Once over my fear, I summoned all the leaders,
My father, too; I told them of the portent,
Asked for their counsel. All agreed, a land
So stained with violence and violation
Was not for us to dwell in. Southward ho!
For Polydorus we made restoration
With funeral rites anew; earth rose again
Above his outraged mound; dark fillets made 60
The altar sorrowful, and cypress boughs,
And the Trojan women loosed their hair in mourning.
We offered milk in foaming bowls, and blood
Warm from the victims, so to rest the spirit,
And cry aloud the voice of valediction.
　　　Then, when we trust the sea again, and the wind
Calls with a gentle whisper, we crowd the shores,
Launch ship again, leave port, the lands and cities
Fade out of sight once more.
　　　　　　　　　There is an island[3]
In the middle of the sea; the Nereids' mother[4] 70
And Neptune hold it sacred. It used to wander
By various coasts and shores, until Apollo,
In grateful memory, bound it fast, unmoving,
Unfearful of winds, between two other islands
Called Myconos and Gyaros. I sailed there;
Our band was weary, and the calmest harbor
Gave us safe haven. This was Apollo's city;
We worshipped it on landing. And their king,
Priest of Apollo also, came to meet us,
His temples bound with holy fillets, and laurel. 80
His name was Anius; he knew Anchises
As an old friend, and gave us joyful welcome.
　　　Apollo's temple was built of ancient rock,
And there I prayed: 'Grant us a home, Apollo,
Give walls to weary men, a race, a city
That will abide; preserve Troy's other fortress,
The remnant left by the Greeks and hard Achilles.
Whom do we follow? where are we bidden to go
To find our settlement? An omen, father!'
　　　I had scarcely spoken, when suddenly all things trembled, 90
The doors, and the laurel, and the whole mountain moved,
And the shrine was opened, and a rumbling sound
Was heard. We knelt, most humbly; and a voice
Came to our ears: 'The land which brought you forth,

---

[3] Delos, an island in the Aegean, was the birthplace of Apollo.
[4] Doris; Nereids are sea-nymphs.

Men of endurance, will receive you home.
Seek out your ancient mother. There your house
Will rule above all lands, your children's children,
For countless generations.' Apollo spoke,
And we were joyful and confused, together:
What walls were those, calling the wanderers home?   100
My father, pondering history, made answer:
'Hear, leaders; learn your hopes. There is a land
Called Crete, an island in the midst of the sea,
The cradle of our race; it has a mountain,
Ida, like ours, a hundred mighty cities,
Abounding wealth; if I recall correctly,
Teucer, our greatest father, came from there
To the Rhoetean[5] shores to found his kingdom.
Ilium was nothing then, the towers of Troy
Undreamed of; men lived in the lowly valleys.   110
And Cybele, the Great Mother, came from Crete
With her clashing cymbals, and her grove of Ida
Was named from that original; the silence
Of her mysterious rites, the harnessed lions
Before her chariot wheels, all testify
To Cretan legend. Come, then, let us follow
Where the gods lead, and seek the Cretan kingdom.
It is not far; with Jupiter to favor,
Three days will see us there. With prayer, he made
Most solemn sacrifice, a bull to Neptune,   120
One to Apollo, to Winter a black heifer,
A white one for fair winds.
                              The story ran
That no one lived in Crete, Idomeneus[6]
Having left his father's kingdom, that the houses
Were empty now, dwellings vacated for us.
We sailed from Delos, flying over the water
Past Naxos, on whose heights the Bacchae revel,
Past green Donysa, snowy Paros,[7] skimming
The passages between the sea-sown islands.
No crew would yield to another; there is shouting,   130
And the cheer goes up, 'To Crete, and the land of our fathers!'
A stern wind follows, and we reach the land.
I am glad to be there; I lay out the walls
For the chosen city, name it Pergamea,[8]
And the people are happy. *Love your hearths,* I told them,
Build high the citadel. The ships were steadied

---

[5] Trojan.

[6] Former king of Crete who fought against Troy. In fulfillment of a vow to kill the first living thing he saw after returning to Crete, he murdered his son. His people thereafter banished him, the gods having visited a plague on Crete as punishment.

[7] Naxos, Donysa, and Paros are islands in the south Aegean, passed during the southward voyage to Crete.

[8] Named for Pergamus, the citadel of Troy.

On the dry beach, the young were busy ploughing,
Or planning marriage, and I was giving laws,
Assigning homes. But the weather turned, the sky
Grew sick, and from the tainted heaven came   140
Pestilence and pollution, a deadly year
For people and harvest. Those who were not dying
Dragged weary bodies around; the Dog-Star[9] scorched
The fields to barrenness; grass withered, corn
Refused to ripen. 'Over the sea again!'
My father said, 'let us return to Delos,
Consult the oracle, implore Apollo
To show us kindliness; what end awaits
Our weary destiny, where does he bid us turn
For help in trouble?'   150
    Sleep held all creatures over the earth at rest;
In my own darkness visions came, the sacred
Images of the household gods I had carried
With me from Troy, out of the burning city.
I saw them plain, in the flood of light, where the moon
Streamed through the dormers. And they eased me, saying:
'Apollo would tell you this, if you went over
The sea again to Delos; from him we come
To you, with willing spirit. We came with you
From the burnt city, we have followed still   160
The swollen sea in the ships; in time to come
We shall raise your sons to heaven, and dominion
Shall crown their city. Prepare to build them walls,
Great homes for greatness; do not flee the labor,
The long, long toil of flight. Crete, says Apollo,
Is not the place. There is a land in the West,
Called by the Greeks, Hesperia:[10] anciency
And might in arms and wealth enrich its soil.
The Oenotrians lived there once; now, rumor has it,
A younger race has called it Italy   170
After the name of a leader, Italus.
Dardanus came from there, our ancestor,
As Iasius[11] was. There is our dwelling-place.
Be happy, then, waken, and tell Anchises
Our certain message: seek the land in the West.
Crete is forbidden country.'
    The vision shook me, and the voice of the gods;
(It was not a dream, exactly; I seemed to know them,
Their features, the veiled hair, the living presence.)
I woke in a sweat, held out my hands to heaven,   180
And poured the pure libation for the altar,
Then, gladly, to Anchises. He acknowledged

[9] Sirius, the brightest star in the sky, first visible in the hot days of late summer.
[10] The western region of the world, associated with Hesperus, the evening star.
[11] Brother of Dardanus.

His own mistake, a natural confusion,
Our stock was double, of course; no need saying
We had more ancestors than one. 'Cassandra,'
Anchises said, 'alone, now I remember,
Foretold this fate; it seemed she was always talking
Of a land in the West, and Italian kingdoms, always.
But who would ever have thought that any Trojans
Would reach the shores in the West? Or, for that matter,   190
Who ever believed Cassandra? Let us yield
To the warning of Apollo, and at his bidding
Seek better fortunes.' So we obeyed him,
Leaving this place, where a few stayed, and sailing
The hollow keels over the mighty ocean.
     We were in deep water, and the land no longer
Was visible, sky and ocean everywhere.
A cloud, black-blue, loomed overhead, with night
And tempest in it, and the water roughened
In shadow; winds piled up the sea, the billows   200
Rose higher; we were scattered in the surges.
Clouds took away the daylight, and the night
Was dark and wet in the sky, with lightning flashing.
We wandered, off our course, in the dark of ocean,
And our pilot, Palinurus, swore he could not
Tell day from night, nor the way among the waters.
For three lost days, three starless nights, we rode it,
Saw land on the fourth, mountains and smoke arising.
The sails came down, we bent to the oars; the sailors
Made the foam fly, sweeping the dark blue water.   210
I was saved from the waves; the Strophades received me,
(The word means Turning-point in the Greek language),[12]
Ionian islands where the dire Celaeno
And other Harpies[13] live, since Phineus' house
Was closed to them, and they feared their former tables.
No fiercer plague of the gods' anger ever
Rose out of hell, girls with the look of birds,
Their bellies fouled, incontinent, their hands
Like talons, and their faces pale with hunger.
We sailed into the harbor, happy to see   220
Good herds of cattle grazing over the grass
And goats, unshepherded. We cut them down
And made our prayer and offering to Jove,
Set trestles on the curving shore for feasting.
Down from the mountains with a fearful rush
And a sound of wings like metal came the Harpies,

[12] The Strophades are islands west of Greece, in the Ionian Sea. *Turning-point* refers to the
fact that the Trojans have rounded the southwest corner of Greece; from this time until
shortly after they leave Helenus and Andromache, their course will be northwest, along the
shore and among the islands of Greece that face Sicily and southern Italy.
[13] Foul creatures sent originally by Jove to punish Phineus, king of Thrace, whence the
Harpies have emigrated. Celaeno is their leader.

To seize our banquet, smearing dirtiness
Over it all, with a hideous kind of screaming
And a stinking smell. We found a secret hollow
Enclosed by trees, under a ledge of rock,   230
Where shade played over; there we moved the tables
And lit the fire again; the noisy Harpies
Came out of somewhere, sky, or rock, and harried
The feast again, the filthy talons grabbing,
The taint all through the air. *Take arms*, I ordered,
We have to fight them. And my comrades, hiding
Their shields in the grass, lay with their swords beside them,
And when the birds swooped screaming, and Misenus
Sounded the trumpet-signal, they rose to charge them,
A curious kind of battle, men with sword-blades   240
Against the winged obscenities of ocean.
Their feathers felt no blow, their backs no wound,
They rose to the sky as rapidly as ever,
Leaving the souvenirs of their foul traces
Over the ruined feast. And one, Celaeno,
Perched on a lofty rock, squawked out a warning:—
'Is it war you want, for slaughtered goats and bullocks,
Is it war you bring, you sons of liars, driving
The innocent Harpies from their father's kingdom?
Take notice, then, and let my words forever   250
Stick in your hearts; what Jove has told Apollo,
Apollo told me, and I, the greatest fury,
Shove down your throats; it is Italy you are after,
And the winds will help you, Italy and her harbors
You will reach, all right; but you will not wall the city
Till, for the wrong you have done us, deadly hunger
Will make you gnaw and crunch your very tables!'[14]
She flew back to the forest. My companions
Were chilled with sudden fear; their spirit wavered,
They call on me, to beg for peace, not now   260
With arms, but vows and praying, filthy birds
Or ill-foreboding goddesses, no matter.
Anchises prayed with outstretched hands, appeasing
The mighty gods with sacrifice:—'Be gracious,
Great gods, ward off the threats, spare the devoted!'
He bade us tear the cable from the shore,
Shake loose the sails. And a wind sprang up behind us,
Driving us northward; we passed many islands,
Zacynthus, wooded, Dulichium, and Same,
The cliffs of Neritus, Laertes' kingdom,   270
With a curse as we went by for Ithaca,
Land of Ulysses. Soon Leucate's headland
Came into view, a dreadful place for sailors,

---

[14]This prophecy will be fulfilled, in an unexpectedly casual way, in Book VII, when the hungry Trojans eat the wheaten platters on which they have placed fruit.

Where Apollo had a shrine. We were very weary
As we drew near the little town; the anchor
Was thrown from the prow, the sterns pulled up on the beaches.
　　This was unhoped-for land; we offered Jove
Our purifying rites, and had the altars
Burning with sacrifice. We thronged the shore
With games of Ilium. Naked, oiled for wrestling,   280
The young held bouts, glad that so many islands
Held by the Greeks were safely passed. A year
Went by, and icy winter roughened the waves
With gales from the north. A shield of hollow bronze,
Borne once by Abas,[15] I fastened to the door-posts,
And set a verse below it: *Aeneas won*
These arms from the Greek victors. I gave the order
To man the thwarts and leave this harbor; all
Obeyed, swept oars in rivalry. We left
Phaeacia's airy heights, coasting Epirus,   290
Drawn to Buthrotum, a Chaonian harbor.
　　And here we met strange news, that Helenus,
The son of Priam, was ruling Grecian cities,
Having won the wife of Pyrrhus and his crown,
And that Andromache once more had married
A lord of her own race. Amazed, I burn
With a strange longing to seek out that hero,
To learn his great adventures. It so happened,
Just as I left the landing, that was the day
Andromache, in a grove before the city,   300
By the waters of a river that resembled
The Simois at home, was offering homage,
Her annual mourning-gift to Hector's ashes,
Calling his ghost to the place which she had hallowed
With double altars, a green and empty tomb.
I found her weeping there, and she was startled
At the sight of me, and Trojan arms, a shock
Too great to bear: she was rigid for a moment,
And then lost consciousness, and a long time later
Managed to speak: 'Is it real, then, goddess-born?   310
What are you, living messenger or phantom,
Mortal or ghost? If the dear light has left you,
Tell me where Hector is.' I was moved, so deeply
I found it hard to answer to her tears
And through my own, but I did say a little:—
'I am alive; I seem to keep on living
Through all extremes of trouble; do not doubt me,
I am no apparition. And what has happened
To you, dear wife of Hector? Could any gain

---

[15] Not the Trojan mentioned in the storm-scene of Book I, but rather a Greek killed at
Troy. The present scene takes place at the site of the future naval battle of Actium, where in
31 B.C. Octavian defeated Mark Antony and Cleopatra; see the Introduction to Virgil.

Atone for such a loss? Has fortune tried   320
To even matters at all? Does Pyrrhus still
Presume on you as husband?' With lowered gaze
And quiet voice she answered:—'Happy the maiden
Slain at the foeman's tomb, at the foot of the walls;
Happy the daughter of Priam, who never knew
The drawing of the lots,[16] nor came to the bed
Of a conqueror, his captive. After the fire
I travelled different seas, endured the pride
Achilles filled his son with, bore him children
In bondage, till he tired of me and left me   330
For Leda's daughter and a Spartan marriage.
He passed me on to Helenus, fair enough,
Slave-woman to slave-man; but then Orestes,[17]
Inflamed with passion for his stolen bride,
And maddened by the Furies of his vengeance,
Caught Pyrrhus off-guard, and slew him at the altar
In his ancestral home. And Pyrrhus dying,
Part of the kingdom came to Helenus,
Who named the fields Chaonian, the land
Chaonia, after a man from Troy,   340
And filled the heights, as best he could, with buildings
To look like those we knew. But what of yourself?
What winds, what fate, have brought you here, or was it
Some god? did you know you were on our coast? How is
The boy Ascanius, living still, whom Troy
Might have—does he ever think about his mother?
Does he want to be a hero, a manly spirit,
Such as his father was, and his uncle Hector?'
She was in tears again, when the son of Priam,
Helenus, with an escort, came from the city,   350
Happy to recognize us, bringing us in
With tears and greeting mingled. I went on,
Seeing a little Troy, low walls that copied
The old majestic ramparts, a tiny river
In a dry bed, trying to be the Xanthus,
I found the Scaean gates, to hold and cling to.
My Trojans, too, were fond of the friendly town,
Whose king received them in wide halls; libations
Were poured to the gods, and feasts set on gold dishes.

  Day after day went by, and the winds were calling   360
And the sails filling with a good south-wester.
I put my questions to the king and prophet:
'O son of Troy, the god's interpreter,
Familiar with the tripod and the laurel
Of great Apollo, versed in stars and omens,

---

[16] For the division of the women among the conquerors.
[17] Pyrrhus married Hermione (daughter of Menelaus and Helen and thus Leda's grand-daughter, not her daughter), to whom Orestes had been betrothed.

Bird-song and flying wing, be gracious to me,
Tell me,—for heaven has prophesied a journey
Without mischance, and all the gods have sent me
The counsel of their oracles, to follow
Italy and a far-off country; one,   370
But one, Celaeno, prophesied misfortune,
Wrath and revolting hunger,—tell me, prophet,
What dangers first to avoid, what presence follow
To overcome disaster?'
                                        Bullocks slain
With proper covenant, and the chaplets loosened,
He led me to the temple of Apollo,
The very gates, where the god's presence awed me,
And where he spoke, with eloquent inspiration:—
'O goddess-born, the journey over the sea
Holds a clear sanction for you, under Jove,   380
Who draws the lots and turns the wheel of Fate.
I will tell you some few things, not all, that safely
You may go through friendly waters, and in time
Come to Ausonian[18] harborage; the rest
Helenus does not know, or, if he did,
Juno would stop his speaking. First of all,
Italy, which you think is near, too fondly
Ready to enter her nearest port, is distant,
Divided from you by a pathless journey
And longer lands between. The oar must bend   390
In the Sicilian ocean, and the ships
Sail on a farther coast, beyond the lakes
Of an infernal world, beyond the isles
Where dwells Aeaean Circe,[19] not till then
Can the built city rise on friendly ground.
Keep in the mind the sign I give you now:
One day, when you are anxious and alone
At the wave of a hidden river, you will find
Under the oaks on the shore, a sow, a white one,
Immense, with a new-born litter, thirty young   400
At the old one's udders; that will be the place,
The site of the city, the certain rest from labor.
And do not fear the eating of the tables,
The fates will find a way, Apollo answer.
Avoid this coast of Italy,[20] the lands
Just westward of our own; behind those walls

---

[18] Italian.

[19] A sorceress who, during Odysseus' wanderings as described in Homer's *Odyssey*, Book X, changed his men into swine. Aeaea is her home island.

[20] In the following lines, Helenus advises Aeneas to avoid the eastern coast of Italy (infested with people hostile to the Trojans) and to sail around Sicily rather than through the narrow passage (the modern straits of Messina) dividing Sicily from the Italian mainland. The straits are guarded on both sides, by a rock and whirlpool mythologized as, respectively, Scylla and Charybdis.

Dwell evil Greeks, Narycian Locri, soldiers
Of the Cretan king, Idomeneus; the plains
Are full of them; a Meliboean captain
Governs Petelia, a tiny town   410
Relying on her fortress! Philoctetes
Commands her walls. And furthermore, remember,
Even when the ships have crossed the sea and anchored,
When the altars stand on the shore, and the vows are paid,
Keep the hair veiled, and the robe of crimson drawn
Across the eyes, so that no hostile visage
May interfere, to gaze on the holy fire
Or spoil the sacred omens. This rite observe[21]
Through all the generations; keep it holy.
From that first landing, when the wind brings you down   420
To Sicily's coast, and narrow Pelorus widens
The waters of her strait, keep to the left,
Land on the left, and water on the left,
The long way round; the right is dangerous.
Avoid it. There's a story that this land
Once broke apart—(time brings so many changes)—
By some immense convulsion, though the lands
Had been one country once. But now between them
The sea comes in, and now the waters bound
Italian coast, Sicilian coast; the tide   430
Washes on severed shores, their fields, their cities.
Scylla keeps guard on the right; on the left Charybdis,
The unappeasable; from the deep gulf she sucks
The great waves down, three times; three times she belches
Them high up into the air, and sprays the stars.
Scylla is held in a cave, a den of darkness,
From where she thrusts her huge jaws out, and draws
Ships to her jagged rocks. She looks like a girl
Fair-breasted to the waist, from there, all monster,
Shapeless, with dolphins' tails, and a wolf's belly.   440
Better to go the long way round, make turning
Beyond Pachynus,[22] than to catch one glimpse
Of Scylla the misshapen, in her cavern,
And the rocks resounding with the dark-blue sea-hounds.
And one thing more than any, goddess-born,
I tell you over and over: pray to Juno,
Give Juno vows and gifts and overcome her
With everlasting worship. So you will come
Past Sicily and reach Italian beaches.
You will come to a town called Cumae,[23] haunted lakes,   450
And a forest called Avernus, where the leaves

---

[21] As often in the poem, Virgil ascribes an ancient origin to Roman religious ritual of later times.

[22] The southeastern corner of Sicily, which is triangular.

[23] The meeting with the Sibyl of Cumae, in preparation for Aeneas's descent into the Lower World, occurs in Book VI.

Rustle and stir in the great woods, and there
You will find a priestess, in her wildness singing
Prophetic verses under the stones, and keeping
Symbols and signs on leaves. She files and stores them
In the depth of the cave; there they remain unmoving,
Keeping their order, but if a light wind stirs
At the turn of a hinge, and the door's draft disturbs them,
The priestess never cares to catch them fluttering
Around the halls of rock, put them in order,   460
Or give them rearrangement. Men who have come there
For guidance leave uncounselled, and they hate
The Sibyl's dwelling. Let no loss of time,
However comrades chide and chafe, however
The wind's voice calls the sail, postpone the visit
To this great priestess; plead with her to tell you
With her own lips the song of the oracles.
She will predict the wars to come, the nations
Of Italy, the toils to face, or flee from;
Meet her with reverence, and she, propitious,   470
Will grant a happy course. My voice can tell you
No more than this. Farewell; raise Troy to heaven.'
    After the friendly counsel, other gifts
Were sent to our ships, carved ivory, and gold,
And heavy silver, cauldrons from Dodona,
A triple breastplate linked with gold, a helmet
Shining with crested plume, the arms of Pyrrhus.
My father, too, has gifts; horses and guides
Are added, and sailing-men, and arms for my comrades.
Anchises bade the fleet prepare; the wind   480
Was rising, why delay? But Helenus
Spoke to Anchises, in compliment and honor:—
'Anchises, worthy of Venus' couch, and the blessing
Of other gods, twice saved from Trojan ruins,
Yonder behold Ausonia! Near, and far,
It lies, Apollo's offering; sail westward.
Farewell, made blest by a son's goodness. I
Am a nuisance with my talking.'
                  And his queen,
Sad at the final parting, was bringing gifts,
Robes woven with a golden thread, a Trojan   490
Scarf for Ascanius, all courteous honor
Given with these:—'Take them, my child; these are
The work of my own hands, memorials
Of Hector's wife Andromache, and her love.
Receive these farewell gifts; they are for one
Who brings my own son back to me; your hands,
Your face, your eyes, remind me of him so,—
He would be just your age.'
                 I, also, wept,
As I spoke my words of parting: 'Now farewell;

Your lot is finished, and your rest is won,   500
No ocean fields to plough, no fleeing fields
To follow, you have your Xanthus and your Troy,
Built by your hands, and blest by happier omens,
Far from the path of the Greeks. But we are called
From fate to fate; if ever I enter Tiber
And Tiber's neighboring lands, if ever I see
The walls vouchsafed my people, I pray these shores,
Italy and Epirus, shall be one,
The life of Troy restored, with friendly towns
And allied people. A common origin,   510
A common fall, was ours. Let us remember,
And our children keep the faith.'
     Over the sea we rode, the shortest run
To Italy, past the Ceraunian rocks.[24]
The sun went down; the hills were dark with shadow.
The oars assigned, we drew in to the land
For a little welcome rest; sleep overcame us,
But it was not yet midnight when our pilot
Sprang from his blanket, studying the winds,
Alert and listening, noting the stars   520
Wheeling the silent heaven, the twin Oxen,
Arcturus and the rainy Kids. All calm,
He saw, and roused us; camp was broken; the sail
Spread to the rushing breeze, and as day reddened
And the stars faded, we saw a coast, low-lying,
And made out hills. 'Italy!', cried Achates,
'Italy!' all the happy sailors shouted.
Anchises wreathed a royal wine-bowl, stood
On the high stern, calling:—'Gods of earth and ocean
And wind and storm, help us along, propitious   530
With favoring breath!' And the breeze sprang up, and freshened;
We saw a harbor open, and a temple
Shone on Minerva's headland. The sails came down,
We headed toward the land. Like the curve of a bow
The port turned in from the Eastern waves; its cliffs
Foamed with the salty spray, and towering rocks
Came down to the sea, on both sides, double walls,
And the temple fled the shore. Here, our first omen,
I saw four horses grazing, white as snow,
And father Anchises cried:—'It is war you bring us,   540
Welcoming land, horses are armed for war,
It is war these herds portend. But there is hope
Of peace as well. Horses will bend to the yoke
And bear the bridle tamely.' Then we worshipped
The holy power of Pallas, first to hear us,

---

[24] After this point, the Trojan fleet changes its course; hereafter, until the storm that beaches it at Carthage, the fleet will sail southwest past the heel along the sole of the "boot" of southern Italy, then clockwise around Sicily.

Kept our heads veiled before the solemn altar,
And following Helenus' injunction, offered
Our deepest prayer to Juno.
                                        And sailed on,
With some misgiving, past the homes of Greeks;
Saw, next, a bay, Tarentum, and a town   550
That rumor said was Hercules'; against it,
The towers of Caulon rose, and Scylaceum,[25]
Most dangerous to ships, and a temple of Juno.
Far off, Sicilian Etna[26] rose from the waves,
And we heard the loud sea roar, and the rocks resounding,
And voices broken on the coast; the shoals
Leaped at us, and the tide boiled sand. My father
Cried in alarm:—'This must be that Charybdis
Helenus warned us of. Rise to the oars,
O comrades, pull from the danger!' They responded   560
As they did, always, Palinurus swinging
The prow to the waves on the left, and all our effort
Strained to the left, with oars and sail. One moment
We were in the clouds, the next in the gulf of Hell;
Three times the hollow rocks and reefs roared at us,
Three times we saw spray shower the very stars,
And the wind went down at sunset; we were weary,
Drifting, in ignorance, to the Cyclops[27] shores.

      There is a harbor, safe enough from wind,
But Etna thunders near it, crashing and roaring,   570
Throwing black clouds up to the sky, and smoking
With swirling pitchy color, and white-hot ashes,
With balls of flame puffed to the stars, and boulders,
The mountain's guts, belched out, or molten rock
Boiling below the ground, roaring above it.
The story goes that Enceladus, a giant,
Struck by a bolt of lightning, lies here buried
Beneath all Etna's weight, with the flames pouring
Through the broken furnace-flues; he shifts his body,
Every so often, to rest his weariness,   580
And then all Sicily seems to moan and tremble
And fill the sky with smoke. We spent the night here,
Hiding in woods, enduring monstrous portents,
Unable to learn the cause. There were no stars,
No light or fire in the sky; the dead of the night,
The thick of the cloud, obscured the moon.

                                                   And day
Arrived, at last, and the shadows left the heaven,
And a man came out of the woods, a sorry figure,
In hunger's final stages, reaching toward us
His outstretched hands. We looked again. His beard   590

[25]*Tarentum, Caulon,* and *Scylaceum* were cities lying along the sole of the "boot" of Italy.
[26]A volcano.   [27]One-eyed giants.

Unshorn, his rags pinned up with thorns, and dirty,
He was, beyond all doubt of it, a Greek,
And one of those who had been at Troy in the fighting.
He saw, far off, the Trojan dress and armor,
Stopped short, for a moment, almost started back
In panic, then, with a wild rush, came on,
Pleading and crying:—'By the stars I beg you,
By the gods above, the air we breathe, ah Trojans,
Take me away from here, carry me off
To any land whatever; that will be plenty.   600
I know I am one of the Greeks, I know I sailed
With them, I warred against the gods of Ilium,
I admit all that; drown me for evil-doing,
Cut me to pieces, scatter me over the waves.
Kill me. If I must die, it will be a pleasure
To perish at the hands of men.' He held
Our knees and clung there, grovelling before us.
We urged him tell his story, his race, his fortune.
My father gave him his hand, a pledge of safety,
And his fear died down a little.

                        'I come,' he said,   610
'From Ithaca, a companion of Ulysses;
My name is Achaemenides;[28] my father,
His name was Adamastus, was a poor man,
And that was why I came to Troy. My comrades
Left me behind here, in their terrible hurry,
To leave these cruel thresholds. The Cyclops live here
In a dark cave, a house of gore, and banquets
Soaking with blood. It is dark inside there, monstrous.
He hits the stars with his head—Dear gods, abolish
This creature from the world!—he is not easy   620
To look at; he is terrible to talk to.
His food is the flesh of men, his drink their blood.
I saw him once myself, with two of our men
In that huge fist of his; he lay on his back
In the midst of the cave, and smashed them on a rock,
And the whole place swam with blood; I watched him chew them
The limbs with black clots dripping, the muscles, warm,
Quivering as he bit them. But we got him!
Ulysses did not stand for this; he kept
His wits about him, never mind the danger.   630
The giant was gorged with food, and drunk, and lolling
With sagging neck, sprawling all over the cavern
Belching and drooling blood-clots, bits of flesh,
And wine all mixed together. And we stood
Around him, praying, and drew lots,—we had found a stake
And sharpened it at the end,—and so we bored

---

[28] One of Ulysses', or Odysseus', sailors. The story he summarizes here is told in Homer's *Odyssey*, Book IX.

His big eye out; it glowered under his forehead
The size of a shield, or a sun. So we got vengeance
For the souls of our companions. But flee, I tell you,
Get out of here, poor wretches, cut the cables,   640
Forsake this shore. There are a hundred others
As big as he is, and just like him, keeping
Sheep in the caves of the rocks, a hundred others
Wander around this coast and these high mountains.
I have managed for three months, hiding in forests,
In the caves of beasts, on a rocky look-out, watching
The Cyclops, horribly frightened at their cries
And the tramp of their feet. I have lived on plants and berries,
Gnawed roots and bark. I saw this fleet come in,
And I did not care; whatever it was, I gladly   650
Gave myself up. At least, I have escaped them.
Whatever death you give is more than welcome.'
And as he finished, we saw that very giant,
The shepherd Polyphemus, looming huge
Over his tiny flock; he was trying to find
His way to the shore he knew, a shapeless monster,
Lumbering, clumping, blind in the dark, with a stumble,
And the step held up with trunk of a pine. No comfort
For him, except in the sheep. He reached the sand,
Wading into the sea, and scooped up water   660
To wash the ooze of blood from the socket's hollow,
Grinding his teeth against the pain, and roaring,
And striding into the water, but even so
The waves were hardly up to his sides. We fled
Taking on board our Greek; we cut the cable,
Strained every nerve at the oars. He heard, and struggled
Toward the splash of the wave, but of course he could not catch us,
And then he howled in a rage, and the sea was frightened,
Italy deeply shaken, and all Etna
Rumbled in echoing terror in her caverns.   670
Out of the woods and the thicket of the mountains
The Cyclops came, the others, toward the harbor,
Along the coast-line. We could see them standing
In impotent anger, the wild eye-ball glaring,
A grim assortment, brothers, tall as mountains
Where oak and cypress tower, in the groves
Of Jove or great Diana. In our speed
And terror, we sailed anywhere, forgetting
What Helenus had said: Scylla, Charybdis,
Were nothing to us then. But we remembered   680
In time, and a north wind came from strait Pelorus,
We passed Pantagia,[29] and the harbor-mouth

---

[29] The places named in the following lines are located on the east and south coasts of Sicily; Drepanum lies directly opposite Carthage, across a narrow part of the Mediterranean, and is thus approximately where the action of Book I begins.

Set in the living-rock, Thapsus, low-lying,
The bay called Megara: all these were places
That Achaemenides knew well, recalling
The scenes of former wanderings with Ulysses.
    An island faces the Sicanian bay
Against Plemyrium, washed by waves; this island
Has an old name, Ortygia. The story
Tells of a river, Alpheus, come from Elis,[30]   690
By a secret channel undersea, to join
The Arethusan fountains, mingling here
With the Sicilian waters. Here we worshipped
The land's great gods; went on, to pass Helorus,
A rich and marshy land; and then Pachynus
Where the cliffs rose sharp and high; and Camerina,
With firm foundation; the Geloan plains,
And Gela, named for a river; then Acragas,
A towering town, high-walled, and sometime famous
For its breed of horses; the city of palms, Selinus;   700
The shoals of Lilybaeum, where the rocks
Are a hidden danger; so at last we came
To Drepanum, a harbor and a shoreline
That I could not rejoice in, a survivor
Of all those storms of the sea. For here I lost
My comforter in all my care and trouble,
My father Anchises. All the storms and perils,
All of the weariness endured, seemed nothing
Compared with this disaster; and I had
No warning of it; neither Helenus,   710
Though he foretold much trouble, nor Celaeno,
That evil harpy, prophesied this sorrow.
There was nothing more to bear; the long roads ended
At that unhappy goal; and when I left there,
Some god or other brought me to your shores.'

And so he told the story, a lonely man
To eager listeners, destiny and voyage,
And made an end of it here, ceased, and was quiet.

BOOK IV: AENEAS AND DIDO

    But the queen finds no rest. Deep in her veins
The wound is fed; she burns with hidden fire.
His manhood, and the glory of his race
Are an obsession with her, like his voice,

---

[30] Part of Greece; thus the river Alpheus must flow under the Ionian and Mediterranean seas to join the fountain Arethusa. According to the myth, Alpheus was a river god in love with the nymph Arethusa.

Gesture and countenance. On the next morning,
After a restless night, she sought her sister:
"I am troubled, Anna, doubtful, terrified,
Or am I dreaming? What new guest is this
Come to our shores? How well he talks, how brave
He seems in heart and action! I suppose   10
It must be true; he does come from the gods.
Fear proves a bastard spirit. He has been
So buffeted by fate. What endless wars
He told of! Sister, I must tell you something:
Were not my mind made up, once and for all,
Never again to marry, having been
So lost when Sychaeus left me for the grave,
Slain by my murderous brother at the altar,
Were I not sick forever of the torch[1]
And bridal bed, here is the only man   20
Who has moved my spirit, shaken my weak will.
I might have yielded to him. I recognize
The marks of an old fire. But I pray, rather,
That earth engulf me, lightning strike me down
To the pale shades and everlasting night
Before I break the laws of decency.[2]
My love has gone with Sychaeus; let him keep it,
Keep it with him forever in the grave."
She ended with a burst of tears. "Dear sister,
Dearer than life," Anna replied, "why must you   30
Grieve all your youth away in loneliness,
Not know sweet children, or the joys of love?
Is that what dust demands, and buried shadows?
So be it. You have kept your resolution
From Tyre to Libya, proved it by denying
Iarbas and a thousand other suitors
From Africa's rich kingdoms. Think a little.
Whose lands are these you settle in? Getulians,
Invincible in war, the wild Numidians,
Unfriendly Syrtes, ring us round, and a desert   40
Barren with drought, and the Barcaean rangers.
Why should I mention Tyre, and wars arising
Out of Pygmalion's threats? And you, my sister,
Why should you fight against a pleasing passion?
I think the gods have willed it so, and Juno
Has helped to bring the Trojan ships to Carthage.
What a great city, sister, what a kingdom
This might become, rising on such a marriage!
Carthage and Troy together in arms, what glory
Might not be ours? Only invoke the blessing   50
Of the great gods, make sacrifice, be lavish

---

[1] Carried in wedding processions; an emblem of marriage.
[2] Dido had sworn to remain faithful to her dead husband.

In welcome, keep them here while the fierce winter
Rages at sea, and cloud and sky are stormy,
And ships still wrecked and broken."

                         So she fanned
The flame of the burning heart; the doubtful mind
Was given hope, and the sense of guilt was lessened.
And first of all they go to shrine and altar
Imploring peace; they sacrifice to Ceres,
Giver of law, to Bacchus, to Apollo,
And most of all to Juno, in whose keeping   60
The bonds of marriage rest. In all her beauty
Dido lifts up the goblet, pours libation
Between the horns of a white heifer, slowly,
Or, slowly, moves to the rich altars, noting
The proper gifts to mark the day, or studies
The sacrificial entrails for the omens.
Alas, poor blind interpreters! What woman
In love is helped by offerings or altars?
Soft fire consumes the marrow-bones, the silent
Wound grows, deep in the heart.   70
Unhappy Dido burns, and wanders, burning,
All up and down the city, the way a deer
With a hunter's careless arrow in her flank
Ranges the uplands, with the shaft still clinging
To the hurt side. She takes Aeneas with her
All through the town, displays the wealth of Sidon,
Buildings projected; she starts to speak, and falters,
And at the end of the day renews the banquet,
Is wild to hear the story, over and over,
Hangs on each word, until the late moon, sinking,   80
Sends them all home. The stars die out, but Dido
Lies brooding in the empty hall, alone,
Abandoned on a lonely couch. She hears him,
Sees him, or sees and hears him in Iulus,[3]
Fondles the boy, as if that ruse might fool her,
Deceived by his resemblance to his father.
The towers no longer rise, the youth are slack
In drill for arms, the cranes and derricks rusting,
Walls halt halfway to heaven.

                      And Juno saw it,
The queen held fast by this disease, this passion
Which made her good name meaningless. In anger   90
She rushed to Venus:—"Wonderful!—the trophies,
The praise, you and that boy of yours are winning!
Two gods outwit one woman—splendid, splendid!
What glory for Olympus! I know you fear me,
Fear Carthage, and suspect us. To what purpose?
What good does all this do? Is there no limit?

---

[3] Apparently the actual Iulus, not Cupid, who had been substituted for him in Book I.

Would we not both be better off, to sanction
A bond of peace forever, a formal marriage?
You have your dearest wish; Dido is burning   100
With love, infected to her very marrow.
Let us—why not?—conspire to rule one people
On equal terms; let her serve a Trojan husband;
Let her yield her Tyrian people as her dowry."
    This, Venus knew, was spoken with a purpose,
A guileful one, to turn Italian empire
To Libyan shores: not without reservation
She spoke in answer: "Who would be so foolish
As to refuse such terms, preferring warfare,
If only fortune follows that proposal?   110
I do not know, I am more than a little troubled
What fate permits: will Jupiter allow it,
One city for the Tyrians and Trojans,
This covenant, this mixture? You can fathom
His mind, and ask him, being his wife. I follow
Wherever you lead." And royal Juno answered:
"That I will tend to. Listen to me, and learn
How to achieve the urgent need. They plan,
Aeneas, and poor Dido, to go hunting
When sunlight floods the world to-morrow morning.   120
While the rush of the hunt is on, and the forest shaken
With beaters and their nets, I will pour down
Dark rain and hail, and make the whole sky rumble
With thunder and threat. The company will scatter,
Hidden or hiding in the night and shadow,
And Dido and the Trojan come for shelter
To the same cave. I will be there and join them
In lasting wedlock; she will be his own,
His bride, forever; this will be their marriage."
Venus assented,[4] smiling, not ungracious—   130
The trick was in the open.
    Dawn, rising, left the ocean, and the youth
Come forth from all the gates, prepared for hunting,
Nets, toils, wide spears, keen-scented coursing hounds.
And Dido keeps them waiting; her own charger
Stands bright in gold and crimson; the bit foams,
The impatient head is tossed. At last she comes,
With a great train attending, gold and crimson,
Quiver of gold, and combs of gold, and mantle
Crimson with golden buckle. A Trojan escort   140
Attends her, with Iulus, and Aeneas
Comes to her side, more lordly than Apollo
Bright along Delos' ridges in the springtime
With laurel in his hair and golden weapons

---

[4] Having been told by Jove (in Book I) of the destined future of Trojans and Romans,
Venus is aware that Juno's plan will fail.

Shining across his shoulders. Equal radiance
Is all around Aeneas, equal splendor.
    They reach the mountain heights, the hiding-places
Where no trail runs; wild goats from the rocks are started,
Run down the ridges; elsewhere, in the open
Deer cross the dusty plain, away from the mountains.   150
The boy Ascanius, in the midst of the valley,
Is glad he has so good a horse, rides, dashing
Past one group or another: deer are cowards
And wild goats tame; he prays for some excitement,
A tawny lion coming down the mountain
Or a great boar with foaming mouth.
                          The heaven
Darkens, and thunder rolls, and rain and hail
Come down in torrents. The hunt is all for shelter,
Trojans and Tyrians and Ascanius dashing
Wherever they can; the streams pour down the mountains.   160
To the same cave go Dido and Aeneas,
Where Juno, as a bridesmaid, gives the signal,
And mountain nymphs wail high their incantations,
First day of death, first cause of evil. Dido
Is unconcerned with fame, with reputation,
With how it seems to others. This is marriage
For her, not hole-and-corner guilt; she covers
Her folly with this name.
                    Rumor goes flying
At once, through all the Libyan cities, Rumor
Than whom no other evil was ever swifter.   170
She thrives on motion and her own momentum;
Tiny at first in fear, she swells, colossal
In no time, walks on earth, but her head is hidden
Among the clouds. Her mother, Earth, was angry,
Once, at the gods, and out of spite produced her,
The Titans' youngest sister, swift of foot,
Deadly of wing, a huge and terrible monster,
With an eye below each feather in her body,
A tongue, a mouth, for every eye, and ears
Double that number; in the night she flies   180
Above the earth, below the sky, in shadow
Noisy and shrill; her eyes are never closed
In slumber; and by day she perches, watching
From tower or battlement, frightening great cities.
She heralds truth, and clings to lies and falsehood,
It is all the same to her. And now she was going
Happy about her business, filling people
With truth and lies: Aeneas, Trojan-born,
Has come, she says, and Dido, lovely woman,
Sees fit to mate with him, one way or another,   190
And now the couple wanton out the winter,
Heedless of ruling, prisoners of passion.

They were dirty stories, but the goddess gave them
To the common ear, then went to King Iarbas[5]
With words that fired the fuel of his anger.

    This king was Ammon's son, a child of rape
Begotten on a nymph from Garamantia;
He owned wide kingdoms, had a hundred altars
Blazing with fires to Jove, eternal outposts
In the gods' honor; the ground was fat with blood,   200
The temple portals blossoming with garlands.
He heard the bitter stories, and went crazy,
Before the presences of many altars
Beseeching and imploring:—"Jove Almighty,
To whom the Moorish race on colored couches
Pours festive wine, do you see these things, or are we
A pack of idiots, shaking at the lightning
We think you brandish, when it is really only
An aimless flash of light, and silly noises?
Do you see these things? A woman, who used to wander   210
Around my lands, who bought a little city,
To whom we gave some ploughland and a contract,
Disdains me as a husband, takes Aeneas
To be her lord and master, in her kingdom,
And now that second Paris, with his lackeys,
Half-men, I call them, his chin tied up with ribbons,
With millinery on his perfumed tresses,
Takes over what he stole, and we keep bringing
Gifts to your temples, we, devout believers
Forsooth, in idle legend."
                          And Jove heard him   220
Making his prayer and clinging to the altars,
And turned his eyes to Carthage and the lovers
Forgetful of their better reputation.
He summoned Mercury:—"Go forth, my son,
Descend on wing and wind to Tyrian Carthage,
Speak to the Trojan leader, loitering there
Unheedful of the cities given by fate.
Take him my orders through the rapid winds:
It was not for this his lovely mother saved him
Twice[6] from Greek arms; she promised he would be   230
A ruler, in a country loud with war,
Pregnant with empire; he would sire a race
From Teucer's noble line; he would ordain
Law for the world. If no such glory moves him,
If his own fame and fortune count as nothing,
Does he, a father, grudge his son the towers
Of Rome to be? What is the fellow doing?
With what ambition wasting time in Libya?

[5] A rejected African suitor of Dido, Iarbas is a son of Jove (identified here with Ammon).
[6] First in a combat with Diomede, then during the sack of Troy.

Let him set sail. That's all; convey the message."
    Before he ended, Mercury made ready
To carry out the orders of his father;   240
He strapped the golden sandals on, the pinions
To bear him over sea and land, as swift
As the breath of the wind; he took the wand, which summons
Pale ghosts from Hell, or sends them there, denying
Or giving sleep, unsealing dead men's eyes,
Useful in flight through wind and stormy cloud,
And so came flying till he saw the summit
And towering sides of Atlas,[7] rugged giant
With heaven on his neck, whose head and shoulders   250
Are dark with fir, ringed with black cloud, and beaten
With wind and rain, and laden with the whiteness
Of falling snow, with rivers running over
His agèd chin, and the rough beard ice-stiffened.
Here first on level wing the god paused briefly,
Poised, plummeted to ocean, like a bird
That skims the water's surface, flying low
By shore and fishes' rocky breeding-ground.
So Mercury darted between earth and heaven
To Libya's sandy shore, cutting the wind   260
From the home of Maia's[8] father.
Soon as the winged sandals skim the rooftops,
He sees Aeneas founding towers, building
New homes for Tyrians; his sword is studded
With yellow jasper; he wears across his shoulders
A cloak of burning crimson, and golden threads
Run through it, the royal gift of the rich queen.
Mercury wastes no time:—"What are you doing,
Forgetful of your kingdom and your fortunes,
Building for Carthage? Woman-crazy fellow,   270
The ruler of the gods, the great compeller
Of heaven and earth, has sent me from Olympus
With no more word than this: what are you doing,
With what ambition wasting time in Libya?
If your own fame and fortune count as nothing,
Think of Ascanius at least, whose kingdom
In Italy, whose Roman land, are waiting
As promise justly due." He spoke, and vanished
Into thin air. Appalled, amazed, Aeneas
Is stricken dumb; his hair stands up in terror,   280
His voice sticks in his throat. He is more than eager
To flee that pleasant land, awed by the warning
Of the divine command. But how to do it?
How get around that passionate queen? What opening
Try first? His mind runs out in all directions,

---

[7] The mountain in Africa, here personified as the giant.
[8] Daughter of Atlas and mother of Mercury.

Shifting and veering. Finally, he has it,
Or thinks he has: he calls his comrades to him,
The leaders, bids them quietly prepare
The fleet for voyage, meanwhile saying nothing
About the new activity; since Dido   290
Is unaware, has no idea that passion
As strong as theirs is on the verge of breaking,
He will see what he can do, find the right moment
To let her know, all in good time. Rejoicing,
The captains move to carry out the orders.
    Who can deceive a woman in love? The queen
Anticipates each move, is fearful even
While everything is safe, foresees this cunning,
And the same trouble-making goddess, Rumor,
Tells her the fleet is being armed, made ready   300
For voyaging. She rages through the city
Like a woman mad, or drunk, the way the Maenads
Go howling through the night-time on Cithaeron[9]
When Bacchus' cymbals summon with their clashing.
She waits no explanation from Aeneas;
She is the first to speak: "And so, betrayer,
You hoped to hide your wickedness, go sneaking
Out of my land without a word? Our love
Means nothing to you, our exchange of vows,
And even the death of Dido could not hold you.   310
The season is dead of winter, and you labor
Over the fleet; the northern gales are nothing—
You must be cruel, must you not? Why, even,
If ancient Troy remained, and you were seeking
Not unknown homes and lands, but Troy again,
Would you be venturing Troyward in this weather?
I am the one you flee from: true? I beg you
By my own tears, and your right hand—(I have nothing
Else left my wretchedness)—by the beginnings
Of marriage, wedlock, what we had, if ever   320
I served you well, if anything of mine
Was ever sweet to you, I beg you, pity
A falling house; if there is room for pleading
As late as this, I plead, put off that purpose.
You are the reason I am hated; Libyans,
Numidians, Tyrians, hate me; and my honor
Is lost, and the fame I had, that almost brought me
High as the stars, is gone. To whom, O guest—
I must not call you husband any longer—
To whom do you leave me? I am a dying woman;   330
Why do I linger on? Until Pygmalion,
My brother, brings destruction to this city?

---

[9] A mountain where the Maenads (female worshipers of Bacchus) conducted their orgiastic
rites.

Until the prince Iarbas leads me captive?
At least if there had been some hope of children
Before your flight, a little Aeneas playing
Around my courts, to bring you back, in feature
At least, I would seem less taken and deserted."
    There was nothing he could say. Jove bade him keep
Affection from his eyes, and grief in his heart
With never a sign. At last, he managed something:—   340
'Never, O Queen, will I deny you merit
Whatever you have strength to claim; I will not
Regret remembering Dido, while I have
Breath in my body, or consciousness of spirit.
I have a point or two to make. I did not,
Believe me, hope to hide my flight by cunning;
I did not, ever, claim to be a husband,
Made no such vows. If I had fate's permission
To live my life my way, to settle my troubles
At my own will, I would be watching over   350
The city of Troy, and caring for my people,
Those whom the Greeks had spared, and Priam's palace
Would still be standing; for the vanquished people
I would have built the town again. But now
It is Italy I must seek, great Italy,
Apollo orders, and his oracles
Call me to Italy. There is my love,
There is my country. If the towers of Carthage,
The Libyan citadels, can please a woman
Who came from Tyre, why must you grudge the Trojans   360
Ausonian land? It is proper for us also
To seek a foreign kingdom. I am warned
Of this in dreams: when the earth is veiled in shadow
And the fiery stars are burning, I see my father,
Anchises, or his ghost, and I am frightened;
I am troubled for the wrong I do my son,
Cheating him out of his kingdom in the west,
And lands that fate assigns him. And a herald,
Jove's messenger—I call them both to witness—
Has brought me, through the rush of air, his orders;   370
I saw the god myself, in the full daylight,
Enter these walls, I heard the words he brought me.
Cease to inflame us both with your complainings;
I follow Italy not because I want to."
    Out of the corner of her eye she watched him
During the first of this, and her gaze was turning
Now here, now there; and then, in bitter silence,
She looked him up and down; then blazed out at him:—
"You treacherous liar! No goddess was your mother,
No Dardanus the founder of your tribe,   380
Son of the stony mountain-crags, begotten
On cruel rocks, with a tigress for a wet-nurse!

Why fool myself, why make pretense? what is there
To save myself for now? When I was weeping
Did he so much as sigh? Did he turn his eyes,
Ever so little, toward me? Did he break at all,
Or weep, or give his lover a word of pity?
What first, what next? Neither Jupiter nor Juno
Looks at these things with any sense of fairness.
Faith has no haven anywhere in the world.   390
He was an outcast on my shore, a beggar,
I took him in, and, like a fool, I gave him
Part of my kingdom; his fleet was lost, I found it,
His comrades dying, I brought them back to life.
I am maddened, burning, burning: now Apollo
The prophesying god, the oracles
Of Lycia, and Jove's herald, sent from heaven,
Come flying through the air with fearful orders,—
Fine business for the gods, the kind of trouble
That keeps them from their sleep. I do not hold you,   400
I do not argue, either. Go. And follow
Italy on the wind, and seek the kingdom
Across the water. But if any gods
Who care for decency have any power,
They will land you on the rocks; I hope for vengeance,
I hope to hear you calling the name of Dido
Over and over, in vain. Oh, I will follow
In blackest fire, and when cold death has taken
Spirit from body, I will be there to haunt you,
A shade, all over the world. I will have vengeance,   410
And hear about it; the news will be my comfort
In the deep world below." She broke it off,
Leaving the words unfinished; even light
Was unendurable; sick at heart, she turned
And left him, stammering, afraid, attempting
To make some kind of answer. And her servants
Support her to her room, that bower of marble,
A marriage-chamber once; here they attend her,
Help her lie down.
                        And good Aeneas, longing
To ease her grief with comfort, to say something   420
To turn her pain and hurt away, sighs often,
His heart being moved by this great love, most deeply,
And still—the gods give orders, he obeys them;
He goes back to the fleet. And then the Trojans
Bend, really, to their work, launching the vessels
All down the shore. The tarred keel swims in the water,
The green wood comes from the forest, the poles are lopped
For oars, with leaves still on them. All are eager
For flight; all over the city you see them streaming,
Bustling about their business, a black line moving   430
The way ants do when they remember winter

And raid a hill of grain, to haul and store it
At home, across the plain, the column moving
In thin black line through grass, part of them shoving
Great seeds on little shoulders, and part bossing
The job, rebuking laggards, and all the pathway
Hot with the stream of work.
                        And Dido saw them
With who knows what emotion: there she stood
On the high citadel, and saw, below her,
The whole beach boiling, and the water littered   440
With one ship after another, and men yelling,
Excited over their work, and there was nothing
For her to do but sob or choke with anguish.
There is nothing to which the hearts of men and women
Cannot be driven by love. Break into tears,
Try prayers again, humble the pride, leave nothing
Untried, and die in vain:—"Anna, you see them
Coming from everywhere; they push and bustle
All up and down the shore: the sails are swelling,
The happy sailors garlanding the vessels.   450
If I could hope for grief like this, my sister,
I shall be able to bear it. But one service
Do for me first, dear Anna, out of pity.
You were the only one that traitor trusted,
Confided in; you know the way to reach him,
The proper time and place. Give him this message,
Our arrogant enemy: tell him I never
Swore with the Greeks at Aulis to abolish
The Trojan race, I never sent a fleet
To Pergamus, I never desecrated   460
The ashes or the spirit of Anchises:
Why does he, then, refuse to listen to me?
What is the hurry? Let him give his lover
The one last favor: only wait a little,
Only a little while, for better weather
And easy flight. He has betrayed the marriage,
I do not ask for that again; I do not
Ask him to give up Latium and his kingdom.
Mere time is all I am asking, a breathing-space,
A brief reprieve, until my luck has taught me   470
To reconcile defeat and sorrow. This
Is all I ask for, sister; pity and help me:
If he grants me this, I will pay it ten times over
After my death." And Anna, most unhappy,
Over and over, told her tears, her pleading;
No tears, no pleading, move him; no man can yield
When a god stops his ears. As northern winds
Sweep over Alpine mountains, in their fury
Fighting each other to uproot an oak-tree
Whose ancient strength endures against their roaring   480

And the trunk shudders and the leaves come down
Strewing the ground, but the old tree clings to the mountain,
Its roots as deep toward hell as its crest toward heaven,
And still holds on—even so, Aeneas, shaken
By storm-blasts of appeal, by voices calling
From every side, is tossed and torn, and steady.
His will stays motionless, and tears are vain.

    Then Dido prays for death at last; the fates
Are terrible, her luck is out, she is tired
Of gazing at the everlasting heaven.   490
The more to goad her will to die, she sees—
Oh terrible!—the holy water blacken,
Libations turn to blood, on ground and altar,
When she makes offerings. But she tells no one,
Not even her sister. From the marble shrine,
Memorial to her former lord, attended,
Always, by her, with honor, fleece and garland,
She hears his voice, his words, her husband calling
When darkness holds the world, and from the house-top
An owl sends out a long funereal wailing,   500
And she remembers warnings of old seers,
Fearful, foreboding. In her dreams Aeneas
Appears to hunt her down; or she is going
Alone in a lost country, wandering
Trying to find her Tyrians, mad as Pentheus,
Or frenzied as Orestes, when his mother
Is after him with whips of snakes, or firebrands,
While the Avengers menace at the threshold.[10]

    She was beaten, harboring madness, and resolved
On dying; alone, she plotted time and method;   510
Keeping the knowledge from her sorrowing sister,
She spoke with calm composure:—"I have found
A way (wish me good luck) to bring him to me
Or set me free from loving him forever.
Near Ocean[11] and the west there is a country,
The Ethiopian land, far-off, where Atlas
Turns on his shoulders the star-studded world;
I know a priestess there; she guards the temple
Of the daughters of the Evening Star; she feeds
The dragon there, and guards the sacred branches,   520
She sprinkles honey-dew, strews drowsy poppies,
And she knows charms to free the hearts of lovers
When she so wills it, or to trouble others;
She can reverse the wheeling of the planets,
Halt rivers in their flowing; she can summon

---

[10] Pentheus was driven to madness by Bacchus for opposing worship of him. Orestes was
pursued by the Furies ("Avengers") in revenge for the murder of his mother; see Aeschylus'
Oresteia.
[11] The waters believed to surround the world.

The ghosts of night-time; you will see earth shaking
Under her tread, and trees come down from mountains.
Dear sister mine, as heaven is my witness,
I hate to take these arts of magic on me!
Be secret, then; but in the inner courtyard,   530
Raise up a funeral-pyre, to hold the armor
Left hanging in the bower, by that hero,
That good devoted man, and all his raiment,
And add the bridal bed, my doom: the priestess
Said to do this, and it will be a pleasure
To see the end of all of it, every token
Of that unspeakable knave."

                  And so, thought Anna,
Things are no worse than when Sychaeus perished.
She did not know the death these rites portended,
Had no suspicion, and carried out her orders.   540
    The pyre is raised in the court; it towers high
With pine and holm-oak, it is hung with garlands
And funeral wreaths, and on the couch she places
Aeneas' sword, his garments, and his image,
Knowing the outcome. Round about are altars,
Where, with her hair unbound, the priestess calls
On thrice a hundred gods, Erebus, Chaos,
Hecate, queen of Hell, triple Diana.
Water is sprinkled, from Avernus[12] fountain,
Or said to be, and herbs are sought, by moonlight   550
Mown with bronze sickles, and the stem-ends running
With a black milk, and the caul of a colt, new-born.
Dido, with holy meal and holy hands,
Stands at the altar, with one sandal loosened
And robes unfastened, calls the gods to witness,
Prays to the stars that know her doom, invoking,
Beyond them, any powers, if there are any,
Who care for lovers in unequal bondage.
    Night: and tired creatures over all the world
Were seeking slumber; the woods and the wild waters   560
Were quiet, and the silent stars were wheeling
Their course half over; every field was still;
The beasts of the field, the brightly colored birds,
Dwellers in lake and pool, in thorn and thicket,
Slept through the tranquil night, their sorrows over,
Their troubles soothed. But no such blessèd darkness
Closes the eyes of Dido; no repose
Comes to her anxious heart. Her pangs redouble,
Her love swells up, surging, a great tide rising   570
Of wrath and doubt and passion. "What do I do?
What now? Go back to my Numidian suitors,
Be scorned by those I scorned? Pursue the Trojans?

[12] *Erebus . . . Avernus* were all associated with death or the Lower World.

Obey their orders? They were grateful to me,
Once, I remember. But who would let them take me?
Suppose I went. They hate me now; they were always
Deceivers: is Laomedon[13] forgotten,
Whose blood runs through their veins? What then? Attend them,
Alone, be their companion, the loud-mouthed sailors?   580
Or with my own armada follow after,
Wear out my sea-worn Tyrians once more
With vengeance and adventure? Better die.
Die; you deserve to; end the hurt with the sword.
It is your fault, Anna; you were sorry for me,
Won over by my tears; you put this load
Of evil on me. It was not permitted,
It seems, for me to live apart from wedlock,
A blameless life. An animal does better.
I vowed Sychaeus faith. I have been faithless."   590
So, through the night, she tossed in restless torment.

     Meanwhile Aeneas, on the lofty stern,
All things prepared, sure of his going, slumbers
As Mercury comes down once more to warn him,
Familiar blond young god: "O son of Venus,
Is this a time for sleep? The wind blows fair,
And danger rises all around you. Dido,
Certain to die, however else uncertain,
Plots treachery, harbors evil. Seize the moment
While it can still be seized, and hurry, hurry!   600
The sea will swarm with ships, the fiery torches
Blaze, and the shore rankle with fire by morning.
Shove off, be gone! A shifty, fickle object
Is woman, always." He vanished into the night.
And, frightened by that sudden apparition,
Aeneas started from sleep, and urged his comrades:—
"Hurry, men, hurry; get to the sails and benches,
Get the ships under way. A god from heaven
Again has come to speed our flight, to sever
The mooring-ropes. O holy one, we follow,   610
Whoever you are, we are happy in obeying.
Be with us, be propitious; let the stars
Be right in heaven!" He drew his sword; the blade
Flashed, shining, at the hawser; and all the men
Were seized in the same restlessness and rushing.
They have left the shore, they have hidden the sea-water
With the hulls of the ships; the white foam flies, the oars
Dip down in dark-blue water.
                              And Aurora[14]
Came from Tithonus' saffron couch to freshen
The world with rising light, and from her watch-tower   620

---

[13] King of Troy before Priam; he was noted for deceitfulness.
[14] Goddess of the dawn, mate of Tithonus.

The queen saw day grow whiter, and the fleet
Go moving over the sea, keep pace together
To the even spread of the sail; she knew the harbors
Were empty of sailors now; she struck her breast
Three times, four times; she tore her golden hair,
Crying, "God help me, will he go, this stranger,
Treating our kingdom as a joke? Bring arms,
Bring arms, and hurry! follow from all the city,
Haul the ships off the ways, some of you! Others,
Get fire as fast as you can, give out the weapons,   630
Pull oars! What am I saying? O where am I?
I must be going mad. Unhappy Dido,
Is it only now your wickedness strikes home?
The time it should have was when you gave him power.
Well, here it is, look at it now, the honor,
The faith of the hero who, they tell me, carries
With him his household gods, who bore on his shoulders
His agèd father! Could I not have seized him,
Torn him to pieces, scattered him over the waves?
What was the matter? Could I not have murdered   640
His comrades, and Iulus, and served the son
For a dainty at the table of his father?
But fight would have a doubtful fortune. It might have,
What then? I was going to die; whom did I fear?
I would have, should have, set his camp on fire,
Filled everything with flame, choked off the father,
The son, the accursèd race, and myself with them.
Great Sun, surveyor of all the works of earth,
Juno, to whom my sorrows are committed,
Hecate,[15] whom the cross-roads of the cities   650
Wail to by night, avenging Furies, hear me,
Grant me divine protection, take my prayer.
If he must come to harbor, then he must,
If Jove ordains it, however vile he is,
False, and unspeakable. If Jove ordains,
The goal is fixed. So be it. Take my prayer.[16]
Let him be driven by arms and war, an exile,
Let him be taken from his son Iulus,
Let him beg for aid, let him see his people dying
Unworthy deaths, let him accept surrender   660
On unfair terms, let him never enjoy the kingdom,
The hoped-for light, let him fall and die, untimely,
Let him lie unburied on the sand. Oh, hear me,
Hear the last prayer, poured out with my last blood!
And you, O Tyrians, hate, and hate forever
The Trojan stock. Offer my dust this homage.

---

[15] A goddess associated with the Lower World, worshiped at crossways.
[16] Much of the curse that follows is fulfilled (though the poem does not describe the death
of Aeneas).

No love, no peace, between these nations, ever!
Rise from my bones, O great unknown avenger,
Hunt them with fire and sword, the Dardan settlers,
Now, then, here, there, wherever strength is given.   670
Shore against shore, wave against wave, and war,
War after war, for all the generations."
    She spoke, and turned her purpose to accomplish
The quickest end to the life she hated. Briefly
She spoke to Barce, Sychaeus' nurse; her own
Was dust and ashes in her native country:—
"Dear nurse, bring me my sister, tell her to hurry,
Tell her to sprinkle her body with river water,
To bring the sacrificial beast and offerings,
And both of you cover your temples with holy fillets.   680
I have a vow to keep; I have made beginning
Of rites to Stygian[17] Jove, to end my sorrows,
To burn the litter of that Trojan leader."
Barce, with an old woman's fuss and bustle,
Went hurrying out of sight; but Dido, trembling,
Wild with her project, the blood-shot eyeballs rolling,
Pale at the death to come, and hectic color
Burning the quivering cheeks, broke into the court,
Mounted the pyre in madness, drew the sword,
The Trojan gift, bestowed for no such purpose,   690
And she saw the Trojan garments, and the bed
She knew so well, and paused a little, weeping,
Weeping, and thinking, and flung herself down on it,
Uttering her last words:—
"Spoils that were sweet while gods and fate permitted,
Receive my spirit, set me free from suffering.
I have lived, I have run the course that fortune gave me,
And now my shade, a great one, will be going
Below the earth. I have built a noble city,
I have seen my walls, I have avenged a husband,   700
Punished a hostile brother. I have been
Happy, I might have been too happy, only
The Trojans made their landing." She broke off,
Pressed her face to the couch, cried:—"So, we shall die,
Die unavenged; but let us die. So, so,—
I am glad to meet the darkness. Let his eyes
Behold this fire across the sea, an omen
Of my death going with him."
                         As she spoke,
Her handmaids saw her, fallen on the sword,
The foam of blood on the blade, and blood on the hands.   710
A scream rings through the house; Rumor goes reeling,
Rioting, through the shaken town; the palace
Is loud with lamentation, women sobbing,

[17] Associated with Styx, a river in the Lower World.

Wailing and howling, and the vaults of heaven
Echo the outcry, as if Tyre or Carthage
Had fallen to invaders, and the fury
Of fire came rolling over homes and temples.
Anna, half lifeless, heard in panic terror,
Came rushing through them all, beating her bosom,
Clawing her face:—"Was it for this, my sister?   720
To trick me so? The funeral pyre, the altars,
Prepared this for me? I have, indeed, a grievance,
Being forsaken; you would not let your sister
Companion you in death? You might have called me
To the same fate; we might have both been taken,
One sword, one hour. I was the one who built it,
This pyre, with my own hands; it was my voice
That called our fathers' gods, for what?—to fail you
When you were lying here. You have killed me, sister,
Not only yourself, you have killed us all, the people,   730
The town. Let me wash the wounds with water,
Let my lips catch what fluttering breath still lingers."
She climbed the lofty steps, and held her sister,
A dying woman, close; she used her robe
To try to stop the bleeding. And Dido tried
In vain to raise her heavy eyes, fell back,
And her wound made a gurgling hissing sound.
Three times she tried to lift herself; three times
Fell back; her rolling eyes went searching heaven
And the light hurt when she found it, and she moaned.   740
   At last all-powerful Juno, taking pity,
Sent Iris[18] from Olympus, in compassion
For the long racking agony, to free her
From the limbs' writhing and the struggle of spirit.
She had not earned this death, she had only sought it
Before her time, driven by sudden madness,
Therefore, the queen of Hades had not taken
The golden lock, consigning her to Orcus.[19]
So Iris, dewy on saffron wings, descending,
Trailing a thousand colors through the brightness   750
Comes down the sky, poises above her, saying,
"This lock I take as bidden, and from the body
Release the soul," and cuts the lock; and cold
Takes over, and the winds receive the spirit.

*[In Book V the Trojans return to Sicily, where they solemnize the anniversary of Anchises'
death through religious ritual and athletic contests. During the games some of the women,
weary of travel and incited by Juno, try to burn the ships, but Jove sends a rainstorm that
extinguishes the flames. Aeneas decides to leave the less hardy and zealous of the Trojans*

---

[18] Goddess of the rainbow, Juno's messenger.
[19] The queen of Hades, or the Lower World, was Proserpina. Orcus was its king.

*behind in Sicily, under the friendly ruler Acestes. The fleet then departs for Italy. During the
night, Palinurus, Aeneas's helmsman, is overcome by the god of Sleep and is washed overboard.]*

from BOOK VI: THE LOWER WORLD

Mourning for Palinurus, he drives the fleet
To Cumae's[1] coast-line; the prows are turned, the anchors
Let down, the beach is covered by the vessels.
Young in their eagerness for the land in the west,
They flash ashore; some seek the seeds of flame
Hidden in veins of flint, and others spoil
The woods of tinder, and show where water runs.
Aeneas, in devotion, seeks the heights
Where stands Apollo's temple, and the cave
Where the dread Sibyl dwells, Apollo's priestess,   10
With the great mind and heart, inspired revealer
Of things to come.

                          *   *   *

[*Aeneas approaches the cavern of the Sibyl and invokes her.*]

But the priestess, not yet subject to Apollo,
Went reeling through the cavern, wild, and storming
To throw the god,[2] who presses, like a rider,
With bit and bridle and weight, tames her wild spirit,
Shapes her to his control. The doors fly open,   90
The hundred doors, of their own will, fly open,
And through the air the answer comes:—"O Trojans,
At last the dangers of the sea are over;
That course is run, but graver ones are waiting
On land. The sons of Dardanus will reach
The kingdom of Lavinia—be easy
On that account—the sons of Dardanus, also,
Will wish they had not come there. War, I see,
Terrible war, and the river Tiber foaming
With streams of blood. There will be another Xanthus,   100
Another Simois, and Greek encampment,
Even another Achilles,[3] born in Latium,
Himself a goddess' son. And Juno further
Will always be there: you will beg for mercy,
Be poor, turn everywhere for help. A woman
Will be the cause once more of so much evil,

---

[1] A city, near the modern Naples, where Aeneas is to consult the Sibyl in preparation for
his visit to the Lower World.
[2] Apollo, whom the Sibyl serves.
[3] Turnus, the greatest of the warriors who will fight against Aeneas and the Trojans in
Italy, as Achilles had been their most formidable foe at Troy.

A foreign bride,[4] receptive to the Trojans,
A foreign marriage. Do not yield to evil,
Attack, attack, more boldly even than fortune
Seems to permit. An offering of safety,—   110
Incredible!—will come from a Greek city."[5]

*　　*　　*

[Aeneas requests of the Sibyl the privilege of visiting the Lower World, the realm of the dead. She tells him of a golden bough, hidden in the forest, which he must find in order to make the journey. Guided by two doves, Venus's birds, he finds the bough and, after performing appropriate rites, enters the Lower World, guided by the Sibyl.]

The Sibyl cried a warning,

"Keep off, keep off, whatever is unholy,
Depart from here! Courage, Aeneas; enter
The path, unsheathe the sword. The time is ready
For the brave heart." She strode out boldly, leading
Into the open cavern, and he followed.   280
　　Gods of the world of spirit, silent shadows,
Chaos and Phlegethon,[6] areas of silence,
Wide realms of dark, may it be right and proper
To tell what I have heard, this revelation
Of matters buried deep in earth and darkness!
　　Vague forms in lonely darkness, they were going
Through void and shadow, through the empty realm
Like people in a forest, when the moonlight
Shifts with a baleful glimmer, and shadow covers
The sky, and all the colors turn to blackness.   290
At the first threshold, on the jaws of Orcus,[7]
Grief and avenging Cares have set their couches,
And pale Diseases dwell, and sad Old Age,
Fear, evil-counselling Hunger, wretched Need,
Forms terrible to see, and Death, and Toil,
And Death's own brother, Sleep, and evil Joys,
Fantasies of the mind, and deadly War,
The Furies' iron chambers, Discord, raving,
Her snaky hair entwined in bloody bands.
An elm-tree loomed there, shadowy and huge,   300
The aged boughs outspread, beneath whose leaves,
Men say, the false dreams cling, thousands on thousands.
And there are monsters in the dooryard, Centaurs,
Scyllas, of double shape, the beast of Lerna,
Hissing most horribly, Briareus,
The hundred-handed giant, a Chimaera
Whose armament is fire, Harpies, and Gorgons,

---

[4] Lavinia; Turnus will be Aeneas's rival for her.
[5] Pallanteum, a city on the site of the future Rome; it was founded by Evander, king of Arcadia (in Greece), who had emigrated to Italy.
[6] A river of fire.
[7] The realm ruled by Orcus (also called Pluto, Hades, or Dis), king of the Lower World.

A triple-bodied giant. In sudden panic
Aeneas drew his sword, the edge held forward,
Ready to rush and flail, however blindly,   310
Save that his wise companion warned him, saying
They had no substance, they were only phantoms
Flitting about, illusions without body.
    From here, the road turns off to Acheron,
River of Hell; here, thick with muddy whirling,
Cocytus[8] boils with sand. Charon is here,
The guardian of these mingling waters, Charon,
Uncouth and filthy, on whose chin the hair
Is a tangled mat, whose eyes protrude, are burning,
Whose dirty cloak is knotted at the shoulder.   320
He poles a boat, tends to the sail, unaided,
Ferrying bodies in his rust-hued vessel.
Old, but a god's senility is awful
In its raw greenness. To the bank come thronging
Mothers and men, bodies of great-souled heroes,
Their life-time over, boys, unwedded maidens,
Young men whose fathers saw their pyres burning,
Thick as the forest leaves that fall in autumn
With early frost, thick as the birds to landfall
From over the seas, when the chill of the year compels them   330
To sunlight. There they stand, a host, imploring
To be taken over first. Their hands, in longing,
Reach out for the farther shore. But the gloomy boatman
Makes choice among them, taking some, and keeping
Others far back from the stream's edge. Aeneas,
Wondering, asks the Sibyl, "Why the crowding?
What are the spirits seeking? What distinction
Brings some across the livid stream, while others
Stay on the farther bank?" She answers, briefly:
"Son of Anchises, this is the awful river,   340
The Styx, by which the gods take oath; the boatman
Charon; those he takes with him are the buried,
Those he rejects, whose luck is out, the graveless.
It is not permitted him to take them over
The dreadful banks and hoarse-resounding waters
Till earth is cast upon their bones. They haunt
These shores a hundred restless years of waiting
Before they end postponement of the crossing."
Aeneas paused, in thoughtful mood, with pity
Over their lot's unevenness . . .   350

                    *   *   *

[Among the unburied dead who are not yet permitted to cross the Styx is the lost helmsman Palinurus, who tells Aeneas that he was murdered after swimming to shore. He begs Aeneas to take him across the river, but the Sibyl sternly informs Palinurus that fate cannot be changed by prayer.]

[8] A river.

And they went on,
Nearing the river, and from the stream the boatman
Beheld them cross the silent forest, nearer,
Turning their footsteps toward the bank. He challenged:—
"Whoever you are, O man in armor, coming   410
In this direction, halt where you are, and tell me
The reason why you come. This is the region
Of shadows, and of Sleep and drowsy Night;
I am not allowed to carry living bodies
In the Stygian boat; and I must say I was sorry
I ever accepted Hercules and Theseus
And Pirithous,[9] and rowed them over the lake,
Though they were sons of gods and great in courage.
One of them dared to drag the guard of Hell,
Enchained, from Pluto's throne, shaking in terror,   420
The others to snatch our queen from Pluto's chamber."
The Sibyl answered briefly: "No such cunning
Is plotted here; our weapons bring no danger.
Be undisturbed: the hell-hound in his cavern
May bark forever, to keep the bloodless shadows
Frightened away from trespass; Proserpine,
Untouched, in pureness guard her uncle's[10] threshold.
Trojan Aeneas, a man renowned for goodness,
Renowned for nerve in battle, is descending
To the lowest shades; he comes to find his father.   430
If such devotion has no meaning to you,
Look on this branch at least, and recognize it!"
And with the word she drew from under her mantle
The golden bough; his swollen wrath subsided.
No more was said; he saw the bough, and marvelled
At the holy gift, so long unseen; came sculling
The dark-blue boat to the shore, and drove the spirits,
Lining the thwarts, ashore, and cleared the gangway,
And took Aeneas aboard; as that big man
Stepped in, the leaky skiff groaned under the weight,   440
And the strained seams let in the muddy water,
But they made the crossing safely, seer and soldier,
To the far margin, colorless and shapeless,
Grey sedge and dark-brown ooze. They heard the baying
Of Cerberus, that great hound, in his cavern crouching,
Making the shore resound, as all three throats
Belled horribly; and serpents rose and bristled
Along the triple neck. The priestess threw him
A sop with honey and drugged meal; he opened
The ravenous throat, gulped, and subsided, filling   450
The den with his huge bulk. Aeneas, crossing,

---

[9] Among Hercules' many daring feats was the theft of Cerberus, the dog that guards the
Lower World. Theseus and Pirithous had tried to abduct Proserpina (also spelled *Proserpine*).
[10] Proserpina's father, Jove, was Pluto's brother.

Passed on beyond the bank of the dread river
Whence none return.
                    A wailing of thin voices
Came to their ears, the souls of infants crying,
Those whom the day of darkness took from the breast
Before their share of living. And there were many
Whom some false sentence brought to death. Here Minos[11]
Judges them once again; a silent jury
Reviews the evidence. And there are others,
Guilty of nothing, but who hated living,   460
The suicides. How gladly, now, they would suffer
Poverty, hardship, in the world of light!
But this is not permitted; they are bound
Nine times around by the black unlovely river;
Styx holds them fast.
                    They came to the Fields of Mourning,
So-called, where those whom cruel love had wasted
Hid in secluded pathways, under myrtle,
And even in death were anxious. Procris, Phaedra,
Eriphyle, displaying wounds her son
Had given her, Caeneus, Laodamia,   470
Caeneus, a young man once, and now again
A young man, after having been a woman.
And here, new come from her own wound, was Dido,
Wandering in the wood. The Trojan hero,
Standing near by, saw her, or thought he saw her,
Dim in the shadows, like the slender crescent
Of moon when cloud drifts over. Weeping, he greets her:—
"Unhappy Dido, so they told me truly
That your own hand had brought you death. Was I—
Alas!—the cause? I swear by all the stars,   480
By the world above, by everything held sacred
Here under the earth, unwillingly, O queen,
I left your kingdom. But the gods' commands,
Driving me now through these forsaken places,
This utter night, compelled me on. I could not
Believe my loss would cause so great a sorrow.
Linger a moment, do not leave me; whither,
Whom, are you fleeing? I am permitted only
This last word with you."
                    But the queen, unmoving
As flint or marble, turned away, her eyes   490
Fixed on the ground: the tears were vain, the words,
Meant to be soothing, foolish; she turned away,
His enemy forever, to the shadows
Where Sychaeus, her former husband, took her
With love for love, and sorrow for her sorrow.

---

[11] King of Crete, who had ordered the famous labyrinth built; he later was made judge of the dead.

And still Aeneas wept for her, being troubled
By the injustice of her doom; his pity
Followed her going.

*   *   *

*[Aeneas sees several of the dead Trojan and Greek warriors. Deiphobus, who married Helen
after the death of Paris, tells how she betrayed him to the Greeks on the night of the sack of
Troy.]*

    While they were talking, Aurora's rosy car
Had halfway crossed the heaven; all their time
Might have been spent in converse, but the Sibyl
Hurried them forward:—"Night comes on, Aeneas;
We waste the hours with tears. We are at the cross-road,   570
Now; here we turn to the right, where the pathway leads
On to Elysium, under Pluto's ramparts.
Leftward is Tartarus, and retribution,
The terminal of the wicked, and their dungeon."
Deiphobus left them, saying, "O great priestess,
Do not be angry with me; I am going;
I shall not fail the roll-call of the shadows.
Pride of our race, go on; may better fortune
Attend you!" and, upon the word, he vanished.
    As he looked back, Aeneas saw, to his left,   580
Wide walls beneath a cliff, a triple rampart,
A river running fire, Phlegethon's torrent,
Rocks roaring in its course, a gate, tremendous,
Pillars of adamant, a tower of iron,
Too strong for men, too strong for even gods
To batter down in warfare, and behind them
A Fury, sentinel in bloody garments,
Always on watch, by day, by night. He heard
Sobbing and groaning there, the crack of the lash,
The clank of iron, the sound of dragging shackles.   590
The noise was terrible; Aeneas halted,
Asking, "What forms of crime are these, O maiden?
What harrying punishment, what horrible outcry?"
She answered:—"O great leader of the Trojans,
I have never crossed that threshold of the wicked;
No pure soul is permitted entrance thither,
But Hecate, by whose order I was given
Charge of Avernus' groves, my guide, my teacher,
Told me how gods exact the toll of vengeance.
The monarch here, merciless Rhadamanthus,[12]   600
Punishes guilt, and hears confession; he forces
Acknowledgment of crime; no man in the world,
No matter how cleverly he hides his evil,
No matter how much he smiles at his own slyness,

---

[12] Brother of Minos and, like him, a judge in the Lower World.

Can fend atonement off; the hour of death
Begins his sentence. Tisiphone, the Fury,
Leaps at the guilty with her scourge; her serpents
Are whips of menace as she calls her sisters.
Imagine the gates, on jarring hinge, rasp open,
You would see her in the doorway, a shape, a sentry,   610
Savage, implacable. Beyond, still fiercer,
The monstrous Hydra dwells; her fifty throats
Are black, and open wide, and Tartarus[13]
Is black, and open wide, and it goes down
To darkness, sheer deep down, and twice the distance
That earth is from Olympus."

                                *   *   *

[The Sibyl describes individually several of the guilty and how they are punished.]

"Whoever, in his lifetime, hated his brother,
Or struck his father down; whoever cheated
A client, or was miserly—how many
Of these there seem to be!—whoever went
To treasonable war, or broke a promise
Made to his lord, whoever perished, slain
Over adultery, all these, walled in,
Wait here their punishment. Seek not to know
Too much about their doom. The stone is rolled,
The wheel keeps turning; Theseus forever   650
Sits in dejection; Phlegyas,[14] accursed,
Cries through the halls forever: *Being warned,*
Learn justice; reverence the gods! The man
Who sold his country is here in hell; the man
Who altered laws for money; and a father
Who knew his daughter's bed. All of them dared,
And more than dared, achieved, unspeakable
Ambitions. If I had a hundred tongues,
A hundred iron throats, I could not tell
The fullness of their crime and punishment."   660
And then she added:—"Come: resume the journey,
Fulfill the mission; let us hurry onward.
I see the walls the Cyclops[15] made, the portals
Under the archway, where, the orders tell us,
Our tribute must be set." They went together
Through the way's darkness, came to the doors, and halted,
And at the entrance Aeneas, having sprinkled
His body with fresh water, placed the bough
Golden before the threshold. The will of the goddess

---

[13] The part of the Lower World where evil is punished.
[14] Theseus was punished, perhaps, for his attempt to abduct Proserpina. Phlegyas had burned Apollo's temple at Delphi.
[15] Not the one-eyed giants of Book III, but rather the laborers in the forge of Vulcan, the blacksmith god of fire.

Had been performed, the proper task completed. 670
   They came to happy places, the joyful dwelling,
The lovely greenery of the groves of the blessèd.
Here ampler air invests the fields with light,
Rose-colored, with familiar stars and sun.
Some grapple on the grassy wrestling-ground
In exercise and sport, and some are dancing,
And others singing; in his trailing robe
Orpheus[16] strums the lyre; the seven clear notes
Accompany the dance, the song. And heroes
Are there, great-souled, born in the happier years, 680
Ilus, Assaracus; the city's founder,
Prince Dardanus.[17] Far off, Aeneas wonders,
Seeing the phantom arms, the chariots,
The spears fixed in the ground, the chargers browsing,
Unharnessed, over the plain. Whatever, living,
The men delighted in, whatever pleasure
Was theirs in horse and chariot, still holds them
Here under the world. To right and left, they banquet
In the green meadows, and a joyful chorus
Rises through groves of laurel, whence the river 690
Runs to the upper world.[18] The band of heroes
Dwell here, all those whose mortal wounds were suffered
In fighting for the fatherland; and poets,
The good, the pure, the worthy of Apollo;
Those who discovered truth and made life nobler;
Those who served others—all, with snowy fillets
Binding their temples, throng the lovely valley.
And these the Sibyl questioned, most of all
Musaeus,[19] for he towered above the center
Of that great throng:—"O happy souls, O poet, 700
Where does Anchises dwell? For him we come here.
For him we have traversed Erebus'[20] great rivers."
And he replied:—"It is all our home, the shady
Groves, and the streaming meadows, and the softness
Along the river-banks. No fixed abode
Is ours at all; but if it is your pleasure,
Cross over the ridge with me; I will guide you there
By easy going." And so Musaeus led them
And from the summit showed them fields, all shining,
And they went on over and down. 710
   Deep in a valley of green, father Anchises
Was watching, with deep earnestness, the spirits

---

[16] In myth, the prototype of poets and musicians. He almost succeeded in reclaiming his dead wife Eurydice from the Lower World, but he lost her again when he disobeyed Pluto's order that he not look back as she followed him.
[17] Three illustrious ancestors of the Trojans.
[18] The river is Eridanus, believed in fable to be the underground source of the river Po.
[19] Legendary poet, taught by Orpheus.
[20] The god of darkness; more generally, the Lower World itself.

Whose destiny was light, and counting them over,
All of his race to come, his dear descendants,
Their fates and fortunes and their works and ways,
And as he saw Aeneas coming toward him
Over the meadow, his hands reached out with yearning,
He was moved to tears, and called:—"At last, my son,—
Have you really come, at last? and the long road nothing
To a son who loves his father? Do I, truly,   720
See you, and hear your voice? I was thinking so,
I was hoping so, I was counting off the days,
And I was right about it. O my son!
What a long journey, over land and water,
Yours must have been! What buffeting of danger!
I feared, so much, the Libyan realm would hurt you."
And his son answered:—"It was your spirit, father,
Your sorrowful shade, so often met, that led me
To find these portals. The ships ride safe at anchor,
Safe in the Tuscan sea. Embrace me, father;   730
Let hand join hand in love; do not forsake me."
And as he spoke, the tears streamed down. Three times
He reached out toward him, and three times the image
Fled like the breath of the wind or a dream on wings.
      He saw, in a far valley, a separate grove
Where the woods stir and rustle, and a river,
The Lethe,[21] gliding past the peaceful places,
And tribes of people thronging, hovering over,
Innumerable as the bees in summer
Working the bright-hued flowers, and the shining   740
Of the white lilies, murmuring and humming.
Aeneas, filled with wonder, asks the reason
For what he does not know, who are the people
In such a host, and to what river coming?
Anchises answers:—"These are spirits, ready
Once more for life; they drink of Lethe's water
The soothing potion of forgetfulness.
I have longed, for long, to show them to you, name them,
Our children's children; Italy discovered,
So much the greater happiness, my son."   750
"But, O my father, is it thinkable
That souls would leave this blessedness, be willing
A second time to bear the sluggish body,
Trade Paradise for earth? Alas, poor wretches,
Why such a mad desire for light?" Anchises
Gives detailed answer: "First, my son, a spirit
Sustains all matter, heaven and earth and ocean,
The moon, the stars; mind quickens mass, and moves it.
Hence comes the race of man, of beast, of wingèd

---

[21] River of forgetfulness.

Creatures of air, of the strange shapes which ocean   760
Bears down below his mottled marble surface.
All these are blessed with energy from heaven;
The seed of life is a spark of fire, but the body
A clod of earth, a clog, a mortal burden.
Hence humans fear, desire, grieve, and are joyful,
And even when life is over, all the evil
Ingrained so long, the adulterated mixture,
The plagues and pestilences of the body
Remain, persist. So there must be a cleansing,
By penalty, by punishment, by fire,   770
By sweep of wind, by water's absolution,
Before the guilt is gone. Each of us suffers
His own peculiar ghost. But the day comes
When we are sent through wide Elysium,
The Fields of the Blessed, a few of us, to linger
Until the turn of time, the wheel of ages,
Wears off the taint, and leaves the core of spirit
Pure sense, pure flame. A thousand years pass over
And the god calls the countless host to Lethe
Where memory is annulled, and souls are willing   780
Once more to enter into mortal bodies."
          The discourse ended; the father drew his son
And his companion toward the hum, the center
Of the full host; they came to rising ground
Where all the long array was visible,
Anchises watching, noting, every comer.
"Glory to come, my son, illustrious spirits
Of Dardan lineage, Italian offspring,
Heirs of our name, begetters of our future!
These I will name for you and tell our fortunes: 790
First, leaning on a headless spear, and standing
Nearest the light, that youth, the first to rise
To the world above, is Silvius;[22] his name
Is Alban; in his veins Italian blood
Will run with Trojan; he will be the son
Of your late age; Lavinia will bear him,
A king and sire of kings; from him our race
Will rule in Alba Longa. Near him, Procas,
A glory to the Trojan race; and Capys,
And Numitor, and Silvius Aeneas,   800
Resembling you in name, in arms, in goodness,
If ever he wins the Alban kingdom over.
What fine young men they are! What strength, what prowess!
The civic oak already shades their foreheads.
These will found cities, Gabii, Fidenae,

---

[22] In the following lines, Anchises names Trojan descendants in Italy up to the time of
Romulus, legendary founder of Rome.

Nomentum; they will crown the hills with towers
Above Collatia, Inuus fortress, Bola,
Cora, all names to be, thus far ungiven.
  "And there will be a son of Mars; his mother
Is Ilia, and his name is Romulus,   810
Assaracus' descendant. On his helmet
See, even now, twin plumes; his father's honor
Confers distinction on him for the world.
Under his auspices Rome, that glorious city,
Will bound her power by earth, her pride by heaven,
Happy in hero sons, one wall surrounding
Her seven hills, even as Cybele,[23] riding
Through Phrygian cities, wears her crown of towers,
Rejoicing in her offspring, and embracing
A hundred children of the gods, her children,   820
Celestials, all of them, at home in heaven.
Turn the eyes now this way; behold the Romans,
Your very own. These are Iulus' children,
The race to come. One promise you have heard
Over and over: here is its fulfillment,
The son of a god, Augustus Caesar, founder
Of a new age of gold, in lands where Saturn
Ruled long ago; he will extend his empire
Beyond the Indies, beyond the normal measure
Of years and constellations, where high Atlas   830
Turns on his shoulders the star-studded world.
Maeotia[24] and the Caspian seas are trembling
As heaven's oracles predict his coming,
And all the seven mouths of Nile are troubled.
Not even Hercules, in all his travels,
Covered so much of the world, from Erymanthus
To Lerna; nor did Bacchus, driving his tigers
From Nysa's[25] summit. How can hesitation
Keep us from deeds to make our prowess greater?
What fear can block us from Ausonian land?"   840

                        *   *   *

[Anchises continues to summarize Roman history, up to modern times.]

"Others, no doubt, will better mould the bronze
To the semblance of soft breathing, draw, from marble,
The living countenance; and others plead   890
With greater eloquence, or learn to measure,
Better than we, the pathways of the heaven,
The risings of the stars: remember, Roman,

---

[23] Wife of Saturn and mother of the gods; identified with the fruitfulness of nature. Her crown of towers reflects her having taught the art of fortification.
[24] Region north of the Black Sea.
[25] *Erymanthus, Lerna* were cities in Greece; *Nysa* was the birthplace of Bacchus in India.

To rule the people under law, to establish
The way of peace, to battle down the haughty,
To spare the meek. Our fine arts, these, forever."
    Anchises paused a moment, and they marvelled,
And he went on:—"See, how Marcellus[26] triumphs,
Glorious over all, with the great trophies
Won when he slew the captain of the Gauls,   900
Leader victorious over leading foeman.
When Rome is in great trouble and confusion
He will establish order, Gaul and Carthage
Go down before his sword, and triple trophies
Be given Romulus in dedication."
    There was a young man[27] going with Marcellus,
Brilliant in shining armor, bright in beauty,
But sorrowful, with downcast eyes. Aeneas
Broke in, to ask his father: "Who is this youth
Attendant on the hero? A son of his?   910
One of his children's children? How the crowd
Murmurs and hums around him! what distinction,
What presence, in his person! But dark night
Hovers around his head with mournful shadow.
Who is he, father?" And Anchises answered:—
"Great sorrow for our people! O my son,
Ask not to know it. This one fate will only
Show to the world; he will not be permitted
Any long sojourn. Rome would be too mighty,
Too great in the gods' sight, were this gift hers.   920
What lamentation will the field of Mars[28]
Raise to the city! Tiber, gliding by
The new-built tomb, the funeral state, bear witness!
No youth from Trojan stock will ever raise
His ancestors so high in hope, no Roman
Be such a cause for pride. Alas for goodness,
Alas for old-time honor, and the arm
Invincible in war! Against him no one,
Whether on foot or foaming horse, would come
In battle and depart unscathed. Poor boy,   930
If you should break the cruel fates; if only—
You are to be Marcellus. Let me scatter
Lilies, or dark-red flowers, bringing honor
To my descendant's shade; let the gift be offered,
However vain the tribute."
    So through the whole wide realm they went together,
Anchises and his son; from fields of air
Learning and teaching of the fame and glory,

---

[26] Roman general of the third century B.C.
[27] The Younger Marcellus, descendant of the Marcellus just described and nephew of Augustus Caesar; he died in 23 B.C. at the age of twenty.
[28] Site, in Rome, of the young Marcellus' tomb.

The wars to come, the toils to face, or flee from,
Latinus' city and the Latin peoples,   940
The love of what would be.

*   *   *

[Aeneas and the Sibyl return to the upper world; Aeneas rejoins his comrades. They sail up the west coast of Italy to Caieta.]

SUMMARY OF BOOKS VII–XII

The Trojans continue their northward voyage along the western coast of Italy. They land and, while eating their meal off bread platters, suddenly realize that their acts fulfill the prophecy of hunger and that they are at the destined place. On the following day they reach the river Tiber and the city of King Latinus. He recognizes in Aeneas the realization of a prophecy that his daughter Lavinia would marry a stranger. With Juno's help, the Italian hero Turnus, a suitor of Lavinia who is jealous of Aeneas, stirs up opposition to the Trojans, and Aeneas prepares for war with him. Guided by a dream, Aeneas enlists the support of Evander, whose city lies on the future site of Rome. Aeneas's mother Venus presents him with a shield, made by the god Vulcan, on which important events in the future history of Rome have been carved, a history that culminates in the victory of Augustus over Antony and Cleopatra at Actium.

Turnus's army, after a siege of the Trojans' camp, engages them in battle; the advantage leans first to one side, then to the other. Aeneas, again guided by a dream, returns to the battlefield with his allies. Evander's forces are nearly defeated when his son Pallas rallies them, but he is then killed by Turnus. Aeneas seeks revenge on Turnus, but Juno helps Turnus escape. Aeneas ceremoniously sends Pallas's body back to his father, and a twelve-day truce is declared.

An agreement is finally reached among the gods: Juno will remit her enmity to the Trojans, but they are to adopt the Latin language.

Battle is resumed; Aeneas is wounded but miraculously healed. He finally engages Turnus and kills him in revenge for Pallas's death. The way is now clear for Aeneas to marry Lavinia and for the destined Roman future to take its course.

Ovid

(*43 B.C.–17 A.D.*)

Ovid and Virgil have been the two most influential Latin narrative poets—though for very different reasons. Ovid was born into an old established family in the town now called Sulmona, about a hundred miles east of Rome, in 43 B.C.—one year after the assassination of Julius Caesar. He died in A.D. 17, during the reign of Tiberius, Augustus' successor as emperor. Significantly, even symbolically, the twelve-year-old Ovid was sent to Rome, to be educated for the law, at very nearly the same time Augustus defeated Antony and Cleopatra in the battle of Actium. The victory brought order and peace—if also efficient autocracy—to the Roman state for the first time in generations. (See the Introduction to Virgil.) Virgil's values and sensibilities, shaped and indeed scarred by the experience of civil war, were essentially conservative. Ovid was a decade too young to have known that trauma; his formative years were not shadowed by harrowing memories of iron, blood, and strife. Like a Parisian boulevardier of the 1920's too young to have known the trenches, Ovid frequented a somewhat younger set of artists less closely associated than Virgil's circle was with the Augustan establishment.

After a few routine assignments in the Roman civil service and some travel in Greece, Ovid abandoned the law to become a professional poet. Although the tradition that Ovid was a dissipated playboy probably has little truth, there is no doubt that, as poet, Ovid was witty, skeptical, and almost subversively irreverent toward the austere official Augustan values. For example, his relatively early masterpiece, the Ars Amatoria, *or* Art of Love *(completed about 1 B.C.), a manual on how to conduct love affairs, is an amusingly amoral, worldly, though also psychologically sensitive treatment of men and women in love.*

Perhaps predictably, the poem got Ovid in serious trouble. In A.D. *8, though he was now the leading poet of Rome, he was summoned before Augustus, tried summarily, and banished to Tomis (in modern Romania), an outpost of the Roman empire, and indeed of civilization. One reason for Ovid's exile is known: his authorship of* The Art of Love, *a work incompatible with Augustus' program for Roman piety. There was also a second reason, never explicitly identified by Ovid, that remains mysterious despite much detective work by scholars. Apparently it too was some personal or political offense against Augustus or his official code of values.*

This most urban and urbane of men now had to endure not just the absence of metropolitan society and amenities but also real danger from hostile border tribes. From Tomis the poet wrote a number of poignant works in verse, directly or indirectly pleading for permission to return to the city and to the people he knew and loved. But Augustus did not relent, nor, after his death, did Tiberius. Ovid was still in exile when he died. All this is ironic; whatever real or imaginary excesses Ovid may have been guilty of, they can hardly have rivaled the enormities that Roman historians have attributed to Tiberius, Nero, and their ages.

The Metamorphoses, *composed in the years immediately preceding his exile, belongs to Ovid's middle poetry, between the naughty early love poetry and the sad poetry of exile. The title signifies "miraculous transformations," though this theme sometimes has only perfunctory importance in the tales. Few poems of any age or language have shaped so much later literature. There are many reasons for this influence. For one thing, the poem is an almost exhaustive handbook of the best-known classical myths—it is thus a treasury of good stories and indeed a reference work. It is also a rhetorical tour de force, a model illustrating a great variety of poetic, linguistic, and stylistic tricks. (Ovid's training in the law and public speaking did not go to waste.) It is a wonderfully comic work—as, for example, in its portrait in Book X of Venus as a sexpot whose idea of roughing it is to hunt rabbits. Its characterizations of both gods and human beings are complex and sensitive. It is also, in places, a tragic work, especially if one defines tragedy so as to include painful conflicts within individual persons independent of historical, public, and other grand consequences.*

This interest in the idiosyncrasies, sometimes in the pathology, of feelings, especially of people in love, puts Ovid in somewhat the same relationship to Virgil that Euripides held to Aeschylus. Perhaps the nearest modern equivalent of the Metamorphoses *is Byron's* Don Juan *(1818–1823); defending his poem through a sneer at his brother Romantics' overintensity, Byron once wrote, "You have so many 'divine' poems; is it nothing to have written a human one?" Like* Don Juan, *the* Metamorphoses *is a seriocomic poem, simultaneously a spoof of the heroic tradition and a searching critique of it. In writing the poem, Ovid abandoned his usual poetic meter, the elegiac couplet, and chose instead the six-foot dactyllic line used in the* Iliad, *the* Odyssey, *and the* Aeneid. *The meter is one of many indications that Ovid meant his poem to be compared with Virgil's epic. Sometimes the relationship is that of mock-epic diminution: Virgil's grand vision of origins, which finds the seeds of history and empire in the past, becomes for Ovid an account of the origin of such things as flowers and trees—rather like modern nursery tales about how the tiger got his stripes; Aeneas's meeting with Venus-as-huntress in Book I of the* Aeneid *becomes in Ovid's Book X a facetious picture of the absurdity and discomfort of Venus in that unlikely role. Yet there is a saucy implication that Ovid can beat Virgil at his own game; if Virgil's epic could span a thousand years of legend and history, Ovid will outdo him by beginning, not with the fall of Troy, but with the aboriginal creation of the cosmos itself.*

Ovid repeatedly undermines Virgil's moralism. And yet, as with Byron, his technique of deflation is itself a kind of moral statement. In treating the gods and goddesses not religiously but as recognizable human beings, Ovid satirizes Virgil's religious piety and his implication that the universe, though mysterious, is just. The metamorphoses ordained by Ovid's deities often seem unjust, out of proportion to the offense and motivated by the wounded petty vanity of beings whose superiority to us humans consists merely in the lucky accidents of power and immortality.

From the late Middle Ages on, the Metamorphoses *has never lost its appeal, for readers and for authors both minor and great. A number of attempts have been made to rehabilitate Ovid's moral values, mainly by treating him allegorically. And the central idea of the work can be adapted to serious purposes, as Kafka demonstrates in our century in his novella* The Metamorphosis. *But the most typical attitude of later authors toward Ovid is not reverence but affection. His poetry is above all good entertainment, whether we define that term as diversion or as the deeper pleasure that comes from recognizing his wide range of sympathy and his understanding of human psychology.*

FURTHER READING *(prepared by F.S.N.):* In the influential book by Brooks Otis, *Ovid as an Epic Poet,* 1966, 2nd ed. 1970, a number of individual passages from Ovid are discussed, arranged according to topic. Ovid's life and literary art are treated by L. P. Wilkinson in *Ovid Recalled,* 1955, and in his shortened version *Ovid Surveyed,* 1962. Essays edited by J. W. Binns in *Ovid,* 1973, deal with a number of works by Ovid, and with the influence these works have had throughout the centuries. The *Metamorphoses* is treated in Charles P. Segal, *Landscape in Ovid's Metamorphoses: A Study in the Transformations of a Literary Symbol,* 1969, which is useful on symbol, unity, tradition, and the motif of moral order; and in Otto Steen Due, *Changing Forms: Studies in the Metamorphoses of Ovid,* 1974.

METAMORPHOSES

Translated by Rolfe Humphries

from BOOK I

My intention is to tell of bodies changed
To different forms; the gods, who made the changes,

Will help me—or I hope so—with a poem
That runs from the world's beginning to our own days.[1]

THE CREATION[2]

Before the ocean was, or earth, or heaven,
Nature was all alike, a shapelessness,
Chaos, so-called, all rude and lumpy matter,
Nothing but bulk, inert, in whose confusion
Discordant atoms warred: there was no sun
To light the universe; there was no moon   10
With slender silver crescents filling slowly;
No earth hung balanced in surrounding air;
No sea reached far along the fringe of shore.
Land, to be sure, there was, and air, and ocean,
But land on which no man could stand, and water
No man could swim in, air no man could breathe,
Air without light, substance forever changing,
Forever at war: within a single body
Heat fought with cold, wet fought with dry, the hard
Fought with the soft, things having weight contended   20
With weightless things.
                        Till God, or kindlier Nature,[3]
Settled all argument, and separated
Heaven from earth, water from land, our air
From the high stratosphere, a liberation;
So things evolved, and out of blind confusion
Found each its place, bound in eternal order.
The force of fire, that weightless element,
Leaped up and claimed the highest place in heaven;
Below it, air; and under them the earth
Sank with its grosser portions; and the water,   30
Lowest of all, held up, held in, the land.[4]

Whatever god it was, who out of chaos
Brought order to the universe, and gave it
Division, subdivision, he molded earth,
In the beginning, into a great globe,
Even on every side, and bade the waters
To spread and rise, under the rushing winds,
Surrounding earth; he added ponds and marshes,
He banked the river-channels, and the waters
Feed earth or run to sea, and that great flood   40
Washes on shores, not banks. He made the plains

[1] The full fifteen-book poem ends with the transformations of Julius Caesar into a star and of Augustus, after his death (still in the future), into a god.
[2] The primordial transformation of chaos to order was itself a "metamorphosis." Compare the biblical account of creation in Genesis.
[3] The citing of two possible causes is a reflection of Ovid's wry religious skepticism.
[4] The four primal elements were believed to be fire, air, earth, and water.

Spread wide, the valleys settle, and the forest
Be dressed in leaves; he made the rocky mountains
Rise to full height, and as the vault of Heaven
Has two zones, left and right, and one between them
Hotter than these, the Lord of all Creation
Marked on the earth the same design and pattern.
The torrid zone too hot for men to live in,
The north and south too cold, but in the middle
Varying climate, temperature and season.   50
Above all things the air, lighter than earth,
Lighter than water, heavier than fire,
Towers and spreads; there mist and cloud assemble,
And fearful thunder and lightning and cold winds,
But these, by the Creator's order, held
No general dominion; even as it is,
These brothers brawl and quarrel; though each one
Has his own quarter, still, they come near tearing
The universe apart. Eurus is monarch
Of the lands of dawn, the realms of Araby,   60
The Persian ridges under the rays of morning.
Zephyrus holds the west that glows at sunset,
Boreas, who makes men shiver, holds the north,
Warm Auster governs in the misty southland,
And over them all presides the weightless ether,[5]
Pure without taint of earth.
                              These boundaries given,
Behold, the stars, long hidden under darkness,
Broke through and shone, all over the spangled heaven,
Their home forever, and the gods lived there,
And shining fish were given the waves for dwelling   70
And beasts the earth, and birds the moving air.

But something else was needed, a finer being,
More capable of mind, a sage, a ruler,
So Man was born, it may be, in God's image,
Or Earth, perhaps, so newly separated
From the old fire of Heaven, still retained
Some seed of the celestial force which fashioned
Gods out of living clay and running water.
All other animals look downward; Man,
Alone, erect, can raise his face toward Heaven.   80

THE FOUR AGES

The Golden Age was first, a time that cherished
Of its own will, justice and right; no law,
No punishment, was called for; fearfulness

---

[5] The element of fire.

Was quite unknown, and the bronze tablets[6] held
No legal threatening; no suppliant throng
Studied a judge's face; there were no judges,
There did not need to be. Trees had not yet
Been cut and hollowed, to visit other shores.
Men were content at home, and had no towns
With moats and walls around them; and no trumpets   90
Blared out alarums;[7] things like swords and helmets
Had not been heard of. No one needed soldiers.
People were unaggressive, and unanxious;
The years went by in peace. And Earth, untroubled,
Unharried by hoe or plowshare, brought forth all
That men had need for, and those men were happy,
Gathering berries from the mountain sides,
Cherries, or blackcaps, and the edible acorns.
Spring was forever, with a west wind blowing
Softly across the flowers no man had planted,   100
And Earth, unplowed, brought forth rich grain; the field,
Unfallowed, whitened with wheat, and there were rivers
Of milk, and rivers of honey, and golden nectar
Dripped from the dark-green oak-trees,
                                    After Saturn[8]
Was driven to the shadowy land of death,
And the world was under Jove, the Age of Silver
Came in, lower than gold, better than bronze.
Jove made the springtime shorter, added winter,
Summer, and autumn, the seasons as we know them.
That was the first time when the burnt air glowed   110
White-hot, or icicles hung down in winter.
And men built houses for themselves; the caverns,
The woodland thickets, and the bark-bound shelters
No longer served; and the seeds of grain were planted
In the long furrows, and the oxen struggled
Groaning and laboring under the heavy yoke.

Then came the Age of Bronze, and dispositions
Took on aggressive instincts, quick to arm,
Yet not entirely evil. And last of all
The Iron Age succeeded, whose base vein   120
Let loose all evil: modesty and truth
And righteousness fled earth, and in their place
Came trickery and slyness, plotting, swindling,
Violence and the damned desire of having.
Men spread their sails to winds unknown to sailors,
The pines came down their mountain-sides, to revel
And leap in the deep waters, and the ground,

---

[6] The Roman laws were written and publicly displayed on such tablets.   [7] Calls to battle.
[8] Chief of the gods in the older generation of divinities. He reigned during the Golden Age, until he was deposed by Jove and his dynasty.

Free, once, to everyone, like air and sunshine,
Was stepped off by surveyors. The rich earth,
Good giver of all the bounty of the harvest,   130
Was asked for more; they dug into her vitals,
Pried out the wealth a kinder lord had hidden
In Stygian[9] shadow, all that precious metal,
The root of evil. They found the guilt of iron,
And gold, more guilty still. And War came forth
That uses both to fight with; bloody hands
Brandished the clashing weapons. Men lived on plunder.
Guest was not safe from host, nor brother from brother,
A man would kill his wife, a wife her husband,
Stepmothers, dire and dreadful, stirred their brews   140
With poisonous aconite,[10] and sons would hustle
Fathers to death, and Piety lay vanquished,
And the maiden Justice, last of all immortals,
Fled from the bloody earth.
                              Heaven was no safer.
Giants[11] attacked the very throne of Heaven,
Piled Pelion on Ossa, mountain on mountain
Up to the very stars. Jove struck them down
With thunderbolts, and the bulk of those huge bodies
Lay on the earth, and bled, and Mother Earth,
Made pregnant by that blood, brought forth new bodies,   150
And gave them, to recall her older offspring,
The forms of men. And this new stock was also
Contemptuous of gods, and murder-hungry
And violent. You would know they were sons of blood.

JOVE'S INTERVENTION

And Jove was witness from his lofty throne
Of all this evil, and groaned as he remembered
The wicked revels of Lycaon's table,
The latest guilt, a story still unknown
To the high gods. In awful indignation
He summoned them to council. No one dawdled.   160
Easily seen when the night skies are clear,
The Milky Way shines white. Along this road
The gods move toward the palace of the Thunderer,[12]
His royal halls, and, right and left, the dwellings
Of other gods are open, and guests come thronging.
The lesser gods live in a meaner section,
An area not reserved, as this one is,

[9] Pertaining to the underground world.
[10] A plant related to monkshood, often poisonous.
[11] The Giants were offspring of Earth and Heaven; Ossa and Pelion are mountains in
Thessaly, a region of Greece.
[12] Jove.

For the illustrious Great Wheels of Heaven.
(Their Palatine Hill,[13] if I might call it so.)

They took their places in the marble chamber   170
Where high above them all their king was seated,
Holding his ivory sceptre, shaking out
Thrice, and again, his awful locks, the sign
That made the earth and stars and ocean tremble,
And then he spoke, in outrage: "I was troubled
Less for the sovereignty of all the world
In that old time when the snake-footed[14] giants
Laid each his hundred hands on captive Heaven.
Monstrous they were, and hostile, but their warfare
Sprung from one source, one body. Now, wherever   180
The sea-gods roar around the earth, a race
Must be destroyed, the race of men. I swear it!
I swear by all the Stygian rivers[15] gliding
Under the world, I have tried all other measures.
The knife must cut the cancer out, infection
Averted while it can be, from our numbers.
Those demigods, those rustic presences,
Nymphs, fauns, and satyrs, wood and mountain dwellers,
We have not yet honored with a place in Heaven,
But they should have some decent place to dwell in,   190
In peace and safety. Safety? Do you reckon
They will be safe, when I, who wield the thunder,
Who rule you all as subjects, am subjected
To the plottings of the barbarous Lycaon?"

They burned, they trembled. Who was this Lycaon,
Guilty of such rank infamy? They shuddered
In horror, with a fear of sudden ruin,
As the whole world did later, when assassins
Struck Julius Caesar down, and Prince Augustus[16]
Found satisfaction in the great devotion   200
That cried for vengeance, even as Jove took pleasure,
Then, in the gods' response. By word and gesture
He calmed them down, awed them again to silence,
And spoke once more:

THE STORY OF LYCAON

"He has indeed been punished.
On that score have no worry. But what he did,

[13] In the Rome of Ovid's time, the site of Caesar Augustus' dwelling.

[14] The lower part of the Giants' body was serpentine.

[15] To swear by the river Styx was the most solemn and binding oath a god could take.

[16] A glance ahead to the very end of the poem, which celebrates the metamorphoses of these two Caesars.

And how he paid, are things that I must tell you.
I had heard the age was desperately wicked,
I had heard, or so I hoped, a lie, a falsehood,
So I came down, as man, from high Olympus,
Wandered about the world. It would take too long   210
To tell you how widespread was all that evil.
All I had heard was grievous understatement!
I had crossed Maenala, a country bristling
With dens of animals, and crossed Cyllene,
And cold Lycaeus'[17] pine woods. Then I came
At evening, with the shadows growing longer,
To an Arcadian palace, where the tyrant
Was anything but royal in his welcome.
I gave a sign that a god had come, and people
Began to worship, and Lycaon mocked them,   220
Laughed at their prayers, and said: 'Watch me find out
Whether this fellow is a god or mortal,
I can tell quickly, and no doubt about it.'
He planned, that night, to kill me while I slumbered;
That was his way to test the truth. Moreover,
And not content with that, he took a hostage,
One sent by the Molossians,[18] cut his throat,
Boiled pieces of his flesh, still warm with life,
Broiled others, and set them before me on the table.
That was enough. I struck, and the bolt of lightning   230
Blasted the household of that guilty monarch.
He fled in terror, reached the silent fields,
And howled, and tried to speak. No use at all!
Foam dripped from his mouth; bloodthirsty still, he turned
Against the sheep, delighting still in slaughter,
And his arms were legs, and his robes were shaggy hair,
Yet he is still Lycaon, the same grayness,
The same fierce face, the same red eyes, a picture
Of bestial savagery. One house has fallen,
But more than one deserves to. Fury reigns   240
Over all the fields of Earth. They are sworn to evil,
Believe it. Let them pay for it, and quickly!
So stands my purpose."
                              Part of them approved
With words and added fuel to his anger,
And part approved with silence, and yet all
Were grieving at the loss of humankind,
Were asking what the world would be, bereft
Of mortals: who would bring their altars incense?
Would earth be given the beasts, to spoil and ravage?
Jove told them not to worry; he would give them   250

[17]Maenala, Cyllene, Lycaeus are mountains in Arcadia, a rustic region in Greece.
[18]Inhabitants of Molossus, a city in Crete.

Another race, unlike the first, created
Out of a miracle; he would see to it.

He was about to hurl his thunderbolts
At the whole world, but halted, fearing Heaven
Would burn from fire so vast, and pole to pole
Break out in flame and smoke, and he remembered
The fates had said that some day land and ocean,
The vault of Heaven, the whole world's mighty fortress,
Besieged by fire, would perish. He put aside
The bolts made in Cyclopean[19] workshops; better,   260
He thought, to drown the world by flooding water.

THE FLOOD

So, in the cave of Aeolus,[20] he prisoned
The North-wind, and the West-wind, and such others
As ever banish cloud, and he turned loose
The South-wind, and the South-wind came out streaming
With dripping wings, and pitch-black darkness veiling
His terrible countenance. His beard is heavy
With rain-cloud, and his hoary locks a torrent,
Mists are his chaplet,[21] and his wings and garments
Run with the rain. His broad hands squeeze together   270
Low-hanging clouds, and crash and rumble follow
Before the cloudburst, and the rainbow, Iris,
Draws water from the teeming earth, and feeds it
Into the clouds again. The crops are ruined,
The farmers' prayers all wasted, all the labor
Of a long year comes to nothing.
                    And Jove's anger,
Unbounded by his own domain, was given
Help by his dark-blue brother. Neptune called
His rivers all, and told them, very briefly,
To loose their violence, open their houses,   280
Pour over embankments, let the river horses
Run wild as ever they would. And they obeyed him.
His trident[22] struck the shuddering earth; it opened
Way for the rush of waters. The leaping rivers
Flood over the great plains. Not only orchards
Are swept away, not only grain and cattle,
Not only men and houses, but altars, temples,
And shrines with holy fires. If any building

---

[19] The Cyclops were workers under Vulcan, the blacksmith god of fire.
[20] God of the winds; with the following lines compare the storm at the beginning of Virgil's *Aeneid*, Book I.
[21] A garland for the head.   [22] The three-pronged spear wielded by the sea-god Neptune.

Stands firm, the waves keep rising over its roof-top,
Its towers are under water, and land and ocean   290
Are all alike, and everything is ocean,
An ocean with no shore-line.
                      Some poor fellow
Seizes a hill-top; another, in a dinghy,
Rows where he used to plough, and one goes sailing
Over his fields of grain or over the chimney
Of what was once his cottage. Someone catches
Fish in the top of an elm-tree, or an anchor
Drags in green meadow-land, or the curved keel brushes
Grape-arbors under water. Ugly sea-cows
Float where the slender she-goats used to nibble   300
The tender grass, and the Nereids[23] come swimming
With curious wonder, looking, under water,
At houses, cities, parks, and groves. The dolphins
Invade the woods and brush against the oak-trees;
The wolf swims with the lamb; lion and tiger
Are borne along together; the wild boar
Finds all his strength is useless, and the deer
Cannot outspeed that torrent; wandering birds
Look long, in vain, for landing-place, and tumble,
Exhausted, into the sea. The deep's great license   310
Has buried all the hills, and new waves thunder
Against the mountain-tops. The flood has taken
All things, or nearly all, and those whom water,
By chance, has spared, starvation slowly conquers.

DEUCALION AND PYRRHA

Phocis,[24] a fertile land, while there was land,
Marked off Oetean from Boeotian fields.
It was ocean now, a plain of sudden waters.
There Mount Parnassus lifts its twin peaks skyward,
High, steep, cloud-piercing. And Deucalion there
Rowing his wife. There was no other land,   320
The sea had drowned it all. And here they worshipped
First the Corycian[25] nymphs and native powers,
Then Themis, oracle and fate-revealer.
There was no better man than this Deucalion,
No one more fond of right; there was no woman
More scrupulously reverent than Pyrrha.
So, when Jove saw the world was one great ocean,
Only one woman left of all those thousands,

[23] Sea-nymphs.
[24] A mountainous region separating Boeotia from Oeta, a mountain range on the border of Thessaly.
[25] Of Corycus, a sacred grotto. *Themis*, in the next line, was a goddess of justice who controlled the oracle of Delphi before it became associated with Apollo.

And only one man left of all those thousands,
Both innocent and worshipful, he parted   330
The clouds, turned loose the North-wind, swept them off,
Showed earth to heaven again, and sky to land,
And the sea's anger dwindled, and King Neptune
Put down his trident, calmed the waves, and Triton,[26]
Summoned from far down under, with his shoulders
Barnacle-strewn, loomed up above the waters,
The blue-green sea-god, whose resounding horn
Is heard from shore to shore. Wet-bearded, Triton
Set lip to that great shell, as Neptune ordered,
Sounding retreat, and all the lands and waters   340
Heard and obeyed. The sea has shores; the rivers,
Still running high, have channels; the floods dwindle,
Hill-tops are seen again; the trees, long buried,
Rise with their leaves still muddy. The world returns.

Deucalion saw that world, all desolation,
All emptiness, all silence, and his tears
Rose as he spoke to Pyrrha: "O my wife,
The only woman, now, on all this earth,
My consort and my cousin and my partner
In these immediate dangers, look! Of all the lands   350
To East or West, we two, we two alone,
Are all the population. Ocean holds
Everything else; our foothold, our assurance,
Are small as they can be, the clouds still frightful.
Poor woman—well, we are not all alone—
Suppose you had been, how would you bear your fear?
Who would console your grief? My wife, believe me,
Had the sea taken you, I would have followed.
If only I had the power, I would restore
The nations as my father[27] did, bring clay   360
To life with breathing. As it is, we two
Are all the human race, so Heaven has willed it,
Samples of men, mere specimens."
                                  They wept,
And prayed together, and having wept and prayed,
Resolved to make petition to the goddess
To seek her aid through oracles. Together
They went to the river-water, the stream Cephisus,
Still far from clear, but flowing down its channel,
And they took river-water, sprinkled foreheads,
Sprinkled their garments, and they turned their steps   370
To the temple of the goddess, where the altars
Stood with the fires gone dead, and ugly moss
Stained pediment and column. At the stairs

[26] A merman, son of Neptune.
[27] Prometheus, who made man from clay and also stole fire from heaven for human use.

They both fell prone, kissed the chill stone in prayer:
"If the gods' anger ever listens
To righteous prayers, O Themis, we implore you,
Tell us by what device our wreck and ruin
May be repaired. Bring aid, most gentle goddess,
To sunken circumstance."
           And Themis heard them,
And gave this oracle: "Go from the temple,   380
Cover your heads, loosen your robes, and throw
Your mother's bones behind you!" Dumb, they stood
In blank amazement, a long silence, broken
By Pyrrha, finally: she would not do it!
With trembling lips she prays whatever pardon
Her disobedience might merit, but this outrage
She dare not risk, insult her mother's spirit
By throwing her bones around. In utter darkness
They voice the cryptic saying over and over,
What can it mean? They wonder. At last Deucalion   390
Finds the way out: "I might be wrong, but surely
The holy oracles would never counsel
A guilty act. The earth is our great mother,
And I suppose those bones the goddess mentions
Are the stones of earth; the order means to throw them,
The stones, behind us."
            She was still uncertain,
And he by no means sure, and both distrustful
Of that command from Heaven; but what damage,
What harm, would there be in trying? They descended,
Covered their heads, loosened their garments, threw   400
The stones behind them as the goddess ordered.
The stones—who would believe it, had we not
The unimpeachable witness of Tradition?—
Began to lose their hardness, to soften, slowly,
To take on form, to grow in size, a little,
Become less rough, to look like human beings,
Or anyway as much like human beings
As statues do, when the sculptor is only starting,
Images half blocked out. The earthy portion,
Damp with some moisture, turned to flesh, the solid   410
Was bone, the veins were as they always had been.
The stones the man had thrown turned into men,
The stones the woman threw turned into women,
Such being the will of God. Hence we derive
The hardness that we have, and our endurance
Gives proof of what we have come from.
               Other forms
Of life came into being, generated
Out of the earth: the sun burnt off the dampness,
Heat made the slimy marshes swell; as seed

Swells in a mother's womb to shape and substance,   420
So new forms came to life. When the Nile river
Floods and recedes and the mud is warmed by sunshine,
Men, turning over the earth, find living things,
And some not living, but nearly so, imperfect,
On the verge of life, and often the same substance
Is part alive, part only clay. When moisture
Unites with heat, life is conceived; all things
Come from this union. Fire may fight with water,
But heat and moisture generate all things,
Their discord being productive. So when earth,   430
After that flood, still muddy, took the heat,
Felt the warm fire of sunlight, she conceived,
Brought forth, after their fashion, all the creatures,
Some old, some strange and monstrous.

*   *   *

BOOK X

THE STORY OF ORPHEUS AND EURYDICE

So Hymen[1] left there, clad in saffron robe,
Through the great reach of air, and took his way
To the Ciconian country, where the voice
Of Orpheus called him, all in vain. He came there,
True, but brought with him no auspicious words,
No joyful faces, lucky omens. The torch[2]
Sputtered and filled the eyes with smoke; when swung,
It would not blaze: bad as the omens were,
The end was worse, for as the bride went walking
Across the lawn, attended by her naiads,[3]   10
A serpent bit her ankle, and she was gone.
Orpheus mourned her to the upper world,
And then, lest he should leave the shades untried,
Dared to descend to Styx, passing the portal
Men call Taenarian.[4] Through the phantom dwellers,
The buried ghosts, he passed, came to the king
Of that sad realm, and to Persephone,
His consort, and he swept the strings,[5] and chanted:
"Gods of the world below the world, to whom

---

[1] Hymen, god of marriage, departs from Greece, where he has presided over a wedding described earlier, and arrives in Ciconia, a region of Thrace.
[2] Emblem of marriage.   [3] Water-nymphs.
[4] Taenarum was a cape in southern Greece believed to have an entrance to the world of the dead.
[5] Orpheus is the archetypal poet-musician.

All of us mortals come, if I may speak   20
Without deceit, the simple truth is this:
I came here, not to see dark Tartarus,[6]
Nor yet to bind the triple-throated monster[7]
Medusa's offspring, rough with snakes. I came
For my wife's sake, whose growing years were taken
By a snake's venom. I wanted to be able
To bear this; I have tried to. Love has conquered.
This god is famous in the world above,
But here, I do not know. I think he may be
Or is it all a lie, that ancient story   30
Of an old ravishment,[8] and how he brought
The two of you together? By these places
All full of fear, by this immense confusion,
By this vast kingdom's silences, I beg you,
Weave over Eurydice's life, run through too soon.
To you we all, people and things, belong,
Sooner or later, to this single dwelling
All of us come, to our last home; you hold
Longest dominion over humankind.
She will come back again, to be your subject,   40
After the ripeness of her years; I am asking
A loan and not a gift. If fate denies us
This privilege for my wife, one thing is certain:
I do not want to go back either; triumph
In the death of two."
                      And with his words, the music
Made the pale phantoms weep: Ixion's wheel
Was still, Tityos' vultures left the liver,
Tantalus tried no more to reach for the water,
And Belus' daughters rested from their urns,
And Sisyphus[9] climbed on his rock to listen.   50
That was the first time ever in all the world
The Furies[10] wept. Neither the king nor consort
Had harshness to refuse him, and they called her,
Eurydice. She was there, limping a little
From her late wound, with the new shades of Hell.
And Orpheus received her, but one term
Was set: he must not, till he passed Avernus,[11]
Turn back his gaze, or the gift would be in vain.

---

[6] The place where evil is punished; it sometimes refers to the abode of the dead in general.

[7] The three-headed dog Cerberus, guardian of the world of the dead. Orpheus alludes to the binding and abduction of Cerberus by Hercules.

[8] Pluto, god of the dead, had stolen his bride, Persephone, or Proserpina, from her mother Ceres, goddess of the fields and harvest. Ovid had told the story in Book V.

[9] *Ixion, Tityos, Tantalus, Belus' daughters, and Sisyphus* were sinners being punished; Ixion was bound to a fiery wheel, Tityos' liver was eaten by vultures, Tantalus was placed up to the neck in water that he could not drink, Belus' daughters carried water in a vessel with holes in it, Sisyphus continually pushed a great stone uphill.

[10] The avengers of evil deeds.

[11] A lake, giving off noxious fumes, near the entrance to the underworld.

They climbed the upward path, through absolute silence,
Up the steep murk, clouded in pitchy darkness,   60
They were near the margin, near the upper land,
When he, afraid that she might falter, eager to see her,
Looked back in love, and she was gone, in a moment.
Was it he, or she, reaching out arms and trying
To hold or to be held, and clasping nothing
But empty air? Dying the second time,
She had no reproach to bring against her husband,
What was there to complain of? One thing, only:
He loved her. He could hardly hear her calling
Farewell! when she was gone.

                    The double death   70
Stunned Orpheus, like the man who turned to stone
At sight of Cerberus, or the couple of rock,
Olenos and Lethaea,[12] hearts so joined
One shared the other's guilt, and Ida's mountain,
Where rivers run, still holds them, both together.
In vain the prayers of Orpheus and his longing
To cross the river once more; the boatman Charon
Drove him away. For seven days he sat there
Beside the bank, in filthy garments, and tasting
No food whatever. Trouble, grief, and tears   80
Were all his sustenance. At last, complaining
The gods of Hell were cruel, he wandered on
To Rhodope and Haemus,[13] swept by the north winds,
Where, for three years, he lived without a woman
Either because marriage had meant misfortune
Or he had made a promise. But many women
Wanted this poet for their own, and many
Grieved over their rejection. His love was given
To young boys only, and he told the Thracians
That was the better way: *enjoy that springtime,*   90
Take those first flowers!

                There was a hill, and on it
A wide-extending plain, all green, but lacking
The darker green of shade, and when the singer
Came there and ran his fingers over the strings,
The shade came there to listen. The oak-tree came,
And many poplars, and the gentle lindens,
The beech, the virgin laurel, and the hazel
Easily broken, the ash men use for spears,
The shining silver-fir, the ilex bending
Under its acorns, the friendly sycamore,   100
The changing-colored maple, and the willows
That love the river-waters, and the lotus

---

[12] Lethaea had offended a deity (probably Venus) by boasting of her beauty; her husband
Olenos wished to assume her punishment, but both were turned to stone.
[13] Two mountains in Thrace.

Favoring pools, and the green boxwood came,
Slim tamarisks, and myrtle, and viburnum
With dark-blue berries, and the pliant ivy,
The tendrilled grape, the elms, all dressed with vines,
The rowan-trees, the pitch-pines, and the arbute
With the red fruit, the palm, the victor's triumph,
The bare-trunked pine with spreading leafy crest,
Dear to the mother of the gods since Attis[14]   110
Put off his human form, took on that likeness,
And the cone-shaped cypress joined them, now a tree,
But once a boy, loved by the god Apollo
Master of lyre and bow-string, both together.

THE STORY OF CYPARISSUS

There was a deer, whom the Carthean[15] nymphs
Held sacred, a great stag, whose spreading antlers
Were his own shade-tree. Golden shone those horns,
And round his glossy neck a string of jewels
Fell to his shoulders, and a silver bubble,
Fastened with little straps, gleamed on his forehead,   120
With earrings, made of bronze, at either temple.
He had no fear at all, would enter houses,
Let even unfamiliar people pet him,
But most of all he was fond of Cyparissus,
The handsomest youth in Cea. Cyparissus
Would lead the animal to the green pastures,
Beside the running brooks, wreathe garlands for him
Of many-colored flowers, or ride him, bareback,
Guiding him gently with the crimson bridle.
One summer noon-day, when the heat of the sun   130
Held hot around the seashore, the deer was lying,
Tired, with his body on the grassy ground,
Under a tree's cool shadow, and Cyparissus
Shot him, by some ill luck, with pointed arrow,
And as he saw him dying from the wound,
Wanted to die himself. Apollo offered
Such consolation as he could, advised him
To keep his grief within some proper limit,
But he kept grieving still, and prayed the gods,
As a last boon, to let him grieve forever.   140
And his blood grew thin from that incessant weeping,
His limbs were green in color, and the hair
Over his snowy forehead, bristled, roughened

---

[14] Attis was metamorphosed into a pine tree; the pine was associated with the worship of Cybele ("mother of the gods").

[15] The city Carthea was located on the island of Cea (modern Keos) in the Aegean Sea.

Like any bush, rose, tapering, toward Heaven.
Apollo spoke in sorrow: "I shall mourn you,
As you shall mourn for others, an attendant
On all who mourn their dead." And still the cypress
Remains a tree of mourning.
                                    Such was the grove
Orpheus had drawn to hear him, and the beasts
And birds made a circle all around him.   150
He tried the chords with his thumb, and found the tones
Different but harmonious, and began:
"From Jove, O Muse, my mother, for all things come
From Jove, inspire my song! I have often sung
His power before, his wars against the giants,
His thunderbolts, but now the occasion seeks
A gentler lyre, for I would sing of boys
Loved by the gods, and girls inflamed by love
To things forbidden, and earned punishment.

THE STORY OF GANYMEDE, A VERY BRIEF ONE

The king of the gods once loved a Trojan boy   160
Named Ganymede; for once, there was something found
That Jove would rather have been than what he was.
He made himself an eagle, the only bird
Able to bear his thunderbolts, went flying
On his false wings, and carried off the youngster
Who now, though much against the will of Juno,
Tends to the cups of Jove and serves his nectar.

THE STORY OF APOLLO AND HYACINTHUS

There was another boy, who might have had
A place in Heaven, at Apollo's order,
Had Fate seen fit to give him time, and still   170
He is, in his own fashion, an immortal.
Whenever spring drives winter out, and the Ram
Succeeds the wintry Fish, he springs to blossom
On the green turf. My father[16] loved him dearly,
This Hyacinthus, and left Delphi for him,
Outward from the world's center, on to Sparta,
The town that has no walls, and Eurotas River.
Quiver and lyre were nothing to him there,
No more than his own dignity; he carried
The nets for fellows hunting, and held the dogs   180
In leash for them, and with them roamed the trails

[16] Apollo.

Of the rough mountain ridges. In their train
He fed the fire with long association.
It was noon one day: Apollo, Hyacinthus,
Stripped, rubbed themselves with oil, and tried their skill
At discus-throwing. Apollo sent the missile
Far through the air, so far it pierced the clouds,
A long time coming down, and when it fell
Proved both his strength and skill, and Hyacinthus,
All eager for his turn, heedless of danger,   190
Went running to pick it up, before it settled
Fully to earth. It bounded once and struck him
Full in the face, and he grew deadly pale
As the pale god caught up the huddled body,
Trying to warm the dreadful chill that held it,
Trying to staunch the wound, to keep the spirit
With healing herbs, but all the arts were useless,
The wound was past all cure. So, in a garden,
If one breaks off a violet or poppy
Or lilies, bristling with their yellow stamens,   200
And they droop over, and cannot raise their heads,
But look on earth, so sank the dying features,
The neck, its strength all gone, lolled on the shoulder.
'Fallen before your time, O Hyacinthus,'
Apollo cried, 'I see your wound, my crime:
You are my sorrow, my reproach; my hand
Has been your murderer. But how am I
To blame? Where is my guilt, except in playing
With you, in loving you? I cannot die
For you, or with you either; the law of Fate   210
Keeps us apart: it shall not! You will be
With me forever, and my songs and music
Will tell of you, and you will be reborn
As a new flower whose markings will spell out
My cries of grief, and there will come a time
When a great hero's name will be the same[17]
As this flower's markings.' So Apollo spoke,
And it was truth he told, for on the ground
The blood was blood no longer; in its place
A flower grew, brighter than any crimson,   220
Like lilies with their silver changed to crimson.
That was not all; Apollo kept the promise
About the markings, and inscribed the flower
With his own grieving words: *Ai, Ai*
The petals say, Greek for *Alas!* In Sparta,
Even to this day, they hold their son in honor,
And when the day comes round, they celebrate
The rites for Hyacinthus, as did their fathers.

[17] A pun on the Greek spelling (Aias) of Ajax, one of the heroes of the Trojan War.

TWO INCIDENTS OF VENUS' ANGER

Amathus, a town of Cyprus, is rich in metals,
But never ask that town about her daughters, 230
Whose foreheads once bore horns, or the other ones,
Turned, later, into stone. The former had
An altar at their gates, sacred to Jove,
The god of host and guest: if any stranger
Had seen it, stained with blood, he would suppose
That sheep or calves were slain there, and how wrong
He would have been! That blood came from the murder,
Always, of innocent guests. Venus, offended,
Prepared to leave her Cyprian plains and cities,
And then reflected: 'But these lovely regions 240
Are not at fault, the cities are not guilty.
Let these Horned Girls, these wicked creatures, rather
Pay for their sins by exile or by death
Or by some punishment halfway between,
Let us say, a change of body.' As she wondered
What change, her eyes fell on the horns they carried:
Those they might keep. They were big women by nature,
Let them be bulls!
          "And even so, the others,
The foul Propoetides, would not acknowledge
Venus and her divinity, and her anger 250
Made whores of them, the first such women ever
To sell their bodies, and in shamelessness
They hardened, even their blood was hard, they could not
Blush any more; it was no transition, really,
From what they were to actual rock and stone.

THE STORY OF PYGMALION

One man, Pygmalion, who had seen these women
Leading their shameful lives, shocked at the vices
Nature has given the female disposition
Only too often, chose to live alone,
To have no woman in his bed. But meanwhile 260
He made, with marvelous art, an ivory statue,
As white as snow, and gave it greater beauty
Than any girl could have, and fell in love
With his own workmanship. The image seemed
That of a virgin, truly, almost living,
And willing, save that modesty prevented,
To take on movement. The best art, they say,
Is that which conceals art, and so Pygmalion
Marvels, and loves the body he has fashioned.

He would often move his hands to test and touch it,   270
Could this be flesh, or was it ivory only?
No, it could not be ivory. His kisses,
He fancies, she returns; he speaks to her,
Holds her, believes his fingers almost leave
An imprint on her limbs, and fears to bruise her.
He pays her compliments, and brings her presents
Such as girls love, smooth pebbles, winding shells,
Little pet birds, flowers with a thousand colors,
Lilies, and painted balls, and lumps of amber.
He decks her limbs with dresses, and her fingers   280
Wear rings which he puts on, and he brings a necklace,
And earrings, and a ribbon for her bosom,
And all of these become her, but she seems
Even more lovely naked, and he spreads
A crimson coverlet for her to lie on,
Takes her to bed, puts a soft pillow under
Her head, as if she felt it, calls her *Darling,*
My darling love!
                    "And Venus' holiday
Came round, and all the people of the island
Were holding festival, and snow-white heifers,   290
Their horns all tipped with gold, stood at the altars,
Where incense burned, and, timidly, Pygmalion
Made offering, and prayed: 'If you can give
All things, O gods, I pray my wife may be—
(He almost said, *My ivory girl,* but dared not)—
One like my ivory girl.' And golden Venus
Was there, and understood the prayer's intention,
And showed her presence, with the bright flame leaping
Thrice on the altar, and Pygmalion came
Back where the maiden lay, and lay beside her,   300
And kissed her, and she seemed to glow, and kissed her,
And stroked her breast, and felt the ivory soften
Under his fingers, as wax grows soft in sunshine,
Made pliable by handling. And Pygmalion
Wonders, and doubts, is dubious and happy,
Plays lover again, and over and over touches
The body with his hand. It is a body!
The veins throb under the thumb. And oh, Pygmalion
Is lavish in his prayer and praise to Venus,
No words are good enough. The lips he kisses   310
Are real indeed, the ivory girl can feel them,
And blushes and responds, and the eyes open
At once on lover and heaven, and Venus blesses
The marriage she has made. The crescent moon
Fills to full orb, nine times, and wanes again,
And then a daughter is born, a girl named Paphos,
From whom the island later takes its name.

THE STORY OF CINYRAS AND MYRRHA

Her son was Cinyras; had he been childless,
He might have been a happier man. The story
Is terrible, I warn you. Fathers, daughters,   320
Had better skip this part, or, if you like my songs,
Distrust me here, and say it never happened,
Or, if you do believe it, take my word
That it was paid for. Nature, it may be,
Permits such things to happen. I would offer
Our land[18] congratulations, that it lies
So far away from such abominations.
Panchaia,[19] rich in cinnamon and balsam,
In frankincense and costmary, in flowers
Of every kind, has one more tree, remember,   330
Perhaps not worth its price, the myrrh. Now Myrrha,
Cinyras' daughter, Cupid claimed, had never
Been hurt by darts of his, nor had his torches
Kindled her fire; that was the work of the Furies,
Or one of them, with Stygian snake and firebrand.
Hating a father is a crime, but surely
Loving like this a greater crime than hatred.
Myrrha had many suitors: all the East
Had sent its ardent princes, eager rivals
For Myrrha's bed: make a selection, Myrrha,   340
Choose one of them, they are many, rule out only
One man of all the world!
        "Myrrha herself
Knew her own wickedness, and fought against it:
'What kind of thing is this that I am planning?
O gods, I pray you, keep me decent, keep me
Devoted, as I should be, to my parents,
Respectful of their rights! Keep off this sin,
This crime—or is it crime? Devotion cannot
Condemn such love as crime; the beasts, I notice,
Mate as they will, and no one calls a heifer   350
Disgraced to have her father on her back,
And no one thinks a filly should not welcome
Her sire as stallion; the ram goes in to ewes
He has begotten, and the birds are treaded
By cocks whose treading gave them life. How happy
They are, to be so free! But human culture
Has made malignant laws, laws against nature,
Envious, jealous laws. Yet there are people,
They say, where mothers wed their sons, and daughters

---

[18] The speaker is still Orpheus; his land is Thrace, which, however, had a reputation among Romans for sexual immorality.
[19] Legendary Eastern land, associated with luxury, spices, jewels.

Sleep with their fathers, so that natural love   360
Is doubled. No such luck is mine; I might have
Been native to such countries; here I am,
Frustrated by geography! Why do I
Keep thinking of such matters? Foolish fancies!
Leave me alone! He is worthy to be loved,
Loved as a father. Were I not his daughter,
I might have slept with Cinyras. He is mine
One way, not mine another; his very closeness
Keeps him far off. If I were foreign-born,
My power would be greater; I had better   370
Go from my home, my country, shun this passion,
This crime, that keeps me here, that keeps me watching
My Cinyras, touching him, and talking with him,
And kissing him, if nothing else is granted.
What else is there to look for? Virgin, wanton,
All names, all titles, vanish in confusion:
A mother's rival, and a father's mistress,
Sister of sons, and mother of your brothers!
Have you no fear of the sisters, the grim Furies
With the black snakes for hair, whose cruel torches   380
Threaten the eyes and faces of the guilty?
You have, so far, not sinned in body, Myrrha:
Try not to sin in mind; do not imagine
Embrace a natural law forbids. You want it,
I know, but fact forbids, and he is righteous,
Heedful of moral sanctions—and I wish
He had my kind of passion burning in him!'
All this she told herself, and Cinyras
Did not know what to do, so many suitors,
All worthy men, awaiting her decision.   390
He named them over to her, asked her questions,
Which one of them she would most prefer as husband.
She made no answer, only stared, and seemed
Confused in mind, and wept, and Cinyras
Thought this was natural for a girl, and, kindly,
Bade her not weep, and dried her cheeks, and kissed her.
That made her happy. So—*what kind of husband?*
'A man like you,' she said. He praised her answer
Not knowing what it really meant. 'Be such
A good girl always, dear!' he told her,   400
And Myrrha, like a good girl, kept her eyes
Downcast, too conscious of her guilt in goodness.

And midnight came,[20] with sleep to heal men's troubles,
To ease their bodies. Myrrha could not sleep,
Tossed all night long, unsatisfied, renewing

---

[20] The passage and episode that follow are modeled, somewhat ironically, on Dido's situation as described by Virgil in the *Aeneid*, Book IV.

Her passionate wants, despaired, gave up, again
Wanted to try, knew shame, and knew desire,
Found no way out. As a great tree, deep wounded
By axe-blows, with the final stroke not given,
Wavers which way to fall, and every side   410
May be its dangerous earthward rush, so Myrrha,
Weakened by various wounds, uncertain, faltering,
Leaned one way, then another, torn with conflict.
A love like hers, with neither rest nor limit,
Had no way out but death: death would be pleasant.
She rose, she swung a noose from the high rafter,
Crying, 'Farewell, dear Cinyras; understand
The reason for my death,' ghastly pale,
Fitting the noose around her neck.
                                        "Some stir
Of action, or the murmur of her words,   420
Reached the old nurse who watched outside her doorway,
And she came flying, swung the door wide open,
Saw the grim preparations, screamed, and tore
Her garments, beat her breasts, and in a moment
Snatched loose the rope, and then found time for weeping,
For holding Myrrha in her arms, for asking
All kinds of questions. But Myrrha would not answer,
Would not look up, sullen, and grieving only
For her own slowness, and the nurse insisted,
Making a show of her gray hair, her skinny   430
Old useless breasts, begging her, by her cradle,
Her baby milk, to tell her all her trouble.
She turned away and groaned, but the old nurse
Was bound to find out more, and promised more
Than passive listening. 'Tell me, let me help you;
Old as I am, I have some wit. Is it madness?
I have a way to cure it by charms and simples.
Has some one put an evil spell upon you?
We can work it off with magic. Are the gods
Angry at you? Let sacrifice appease them!   440
What other reasons could there be? The fortunes
Of all your house go well; father and mother
Prosper in health.' Hearing the name of father,
Myrrha gave one long sigh, no clue to the nurse
Of the evil in her heart, but she suspected
Some love affair, and with persistent purpose
Kept up her questions, holding Myrrha close
With her old arms to her old breast. 'I know,'
She said, 'you are in love, and in this business,
Don't worry, I can more than help, and no one,   450
Not even your father, will ever know.' But Myrrha
Tore herself loose, and flung herself, face down,
Crying into her pillow. 'Go away,
Spare my unhappy shame!' But the nurse only

Urged and insisted. 'Go away, or stop it!
Stop asking why I grieve. It is a crime,
The thing you are trying to learn, a crime, I tell you!'
The poor old woman, horrified, held out
Her arms, all trembling with the weight of years,
The load of fear, and fell at her feet, imploring,   460
Coaxing and wheedling, sometimes even trying
To scare her into telling, making threats
To tell about the noose, about the try
At suicide, and giving reassurance
Of all her help, if only she can know
Who the man is. And Myrrha raised her head
To weep on the nurse's bosom, trying, often,
To get the truth out, failing, hiding her face
In the robes again, finally saying only:
'O mother, mother, happy in your husband!'   470
That was enough, and a cold horror crept
Through the old woman's limbs. She knew. She tried,
As best she could, to banish, if she might,
So mad a passion; Myrrha knew the warning
Was given in all truthfulness, but could not
Resign herself to living without having
The one she loved. 'Live, then,' the other told her,
'You will have your—'(but she could not say it) *father.*

The time arrived when all the married women
Held festival for Ceres.[21] Robed in white,   480
They brought the first-fruits, wheaten ears as garlands,
And for nine nights to love a man or touch him
Was a forbidden thing. And the king's wife,
Queen Cenchreis, was one of them, most faithful
In those mysterious rites, and the king's bed
Was empty, and the nurse, losing no time,
Found him, a little drunk, and filled his ears
With a story of a girl who loved him truly,
Named—she made up a name, and praised her beauty.
Cinyras asked one question: how old was she?   490
'Just Myrrha's age.' 'Go get her!' So she went
Back home to Myrrha, crying out, 'My child,
Rejoice, we conquer!' In the heart of Myrrha
There was not all rejoicing, for her mind
Was filled with sad foreboding, but I could not
Say there was no rejoicing and be truthful.

It was the time when all things rest; in Heaven
The Driver of the Oxen[22] turned his team
To their downward course, the golden moon was gone,

---

[21] Goddess of the fields and harvest, and therefore also of fertility in general.
[22] The constellation Bootes; the time is midnight.

The stars were in black cloud, and the night smouldered 500
Without the usual fires, as Myrrha came
On to her guilty deed. Three times she stumbled
At the edge of the threshold, and three times the owl
Wailed out his cry to warn her, but she came on,
Her shame diminished in the night's dark shadow.
Her left hand holds her nurse's hand, the other
Gropes through the dark ahead, she comes to the door,
Opens the door, goes in, and her knees tremble,
Her face is pale and bloodless, and her spirit
Deserts her as she goes. Closer and closer 510
She nears her crime, and more and more she shudders,
Repents her boldness, wishes she might now
Turn back unknown, but the old woman leads her
Along, unwilling, to where the bedside towers,
Where Cinyras waits. 'Take her, she is your own,'
She says and is gone, leaving the two together,
Doomed and devoted. On the bed of incest
The father takes his daughter; words are spoken
To ease her virgin fears, to make the trembling
A little less. He might have called her *Daughter,* 520
Knowing how young she was; she might have answered
Dear father, so the names were right and proper
To suit the guilty deed.
                "Filled with her father
She left the chamber, carrying in her womb
The seed of crime conceived, and she came back
The next night, and the next, till Cinyras,
After so many nights together, eager
To see the girl who loved him, called for lights
And so discovered his love, his crime, his daughter.
He could not speak, but drew the shining sword 530
Out of the sheath, and Myrrha fled, and darkness
And the blind night's favor kept death off. She wandered
Through the wide fields, beyond Arabian palm-trees,
Beyond Panchaia, till, with nine months gone,
In utter weariness she came to rest
In the Sabaean land.[23] Heavy of womb,
Not knowing what to pray for, torn between
Sickness of life and fear of death, she summoned
Her desperation in words of prayer: 'O gods,
If any gods will listen, I deserve 540
Punishment surely, I do not refuse it,
But lest, in living, I offend the living,
Offend the dead in death, drive me away
From either realm, change me somehow, refuse me
Both life and death!' There was a god to listen;
Her last petition had its gods to answer,

[23] Arabia.

For even as she spoke, the earth closed over
Her legs, and slanting down between her toes
A root took hold, supporting the tall trunk,
The bones were stronger, and their central marrow   550
Suffered no change, but the blood was lymph or water,
Or watery sap, and the arms became long branches,
The fingers twigs, the skin rough bark. The tree
Had bound the pregnant belly, held in tight
The swelling breasts, was on its way to cover
Shoulders and neck, and she could not bear the waiting,
Bent her face down to meet it, plunged her features
Into the bark, until her human senses
Had vanished with her human form, but still
She weeps, and the warm tear-drops trickle down,   560
Not without honor, for that distillation
Still keeps her name; men calling it myrrh,[24] no age
Will ever forget the word.
                                    "Within the wood
The child, conceived in guilt, had grown toward life,
Sought its way out; the swollen bole dilated
Under the strain of the weight, and with no voice
To call Lucina:[25] like a woman in labor
The tree, contorted, cried and wept; the goddess
Stood near in pity, reached out helping hands,
Sang charms to aid the birth, and the tree cracked open,   570
The bark was split, the burden loosed, a baby
Gave his first cries, and naiads cradled him
On the soft leaves, and used his mother's tears
To wash him. Even Envy praised his beauty,
He looked so much like Cupid in a painting
All you would need to make them come out even
Would be to give a quiver to both, or neither.

THE STORY OF ADONIS

Time, in its stealthy gliding, cheats us all
Without our notice; nothing goes more swiftly
Than do the years. That little boy, whose sister   580
Became his mother, his grandfather's son,
Is now a youth, and now a man, more handsome
Than he had ever been, exciting even
The goddess Venus, and thereby avenging
His mother's passion. Cupid, it seems, was playing,
Quiver on shoulder, when he kissed his mother,
And one barb grazed her breast; she pushed him away,
But the wound was deeper than she knew; deceived,
Charmed by Adonis' beauty, she cared no more

---

[24] A fragrant resin produced by the tree or shrub.   [25] Goddess of childbirth.

For Cythera's shores nor Paphos' sea-ringed island,   590
Nor Cnidos, where fish teem, nor high Amathus,[26]
Rich in its precious ores. She stays away
Even from Heaven, Adonis is better than Heaven.
She is beside him always; she has always,
Before this time, preferred the shadowy places,
Preferred her ease, preferred to improve her beauty
By careful tending, but now, across the ridges,
Through woods, through rocky places thick with brambles,
She goes, more like Diana[27] than like Venus,
Bare-kneed and robes tucked up. She cheers the hounds,   600
Hunts animals, at least such timid creatures
As deer and rabbits; no wild boars for her,
No wolves, no bears, no lions. And she warns him
To fear them too, as if there might be good
In giving him warnings. 'Be bold against the timid,
The running creatures, but against the bold ones
Boldness is dangerous. Do not be reckless.
I share whatever risk you take; be careful!
Do not attack those animals which Nature
Has given weapons, lest your thirst for glory   610
May cost me dear. Beauty and youth and love
Make no impression on bristling boars and lions,
On animal eyes and minds. The force of lightning
Is in the wild boar's tusks, and tawny lions
Are worse than thunderbolts. I hate and fear them.'
He asks her why. She answers, 'I will tell you,
And you will wonder at the way old crime
Leads to monstrosities. I will tell you sometime,
Not now, for I am weary, all this hunting
Is not what I am used to. Here's a couch   620
Of grassy turf, and a canopy of poplar,
I would like to lie there with you. And she lay there,
Making a pillow for him of her breast,
And kisses for her story's punctuation.

VENUS TELLS ADONIS THE STORY OF ATALANTA

You may have heard (she said) about a girl
Who could outrun the swiftest men. The story
Is very true: she really could outrun them.
It would be hard to say, though, whether her speed
Or beauty earned more praise. She was very lovely.
She asked the oracle, one day, to give her   630
Advice on marriage. "You don't need a husband,"

---

[26] *Cythera, Paphos, Cnidos,* and *Amathus* were Venus's usual earthly dwelling-places.

[27] The austere and "unfeminine" goddess of the hunt, mentioned to emphasize Venus's new, uncharacteristic, and half-hearted attempt to live the outdoor life.

The god replied, "Avoid that habit! Still,
I know you will not: you will keep your life,
And lose yourself." So Atalanta, frightened,
Lived in the shadowy woods, a single woman,
Harshly rejecting urgent throngs of suitors.
"No one gets me who cannot beat me running,
Race me!" she told them, "Wife and marriage-chamber
Go to the winner, but the slow ones get
The booby-prize of death. Those are my terms."   640
The terms were harsh, but beauty has such power
That those harsh terms were met by many suitors,
Foolhardy fellows. Watching the cruel race,
Hippomenes had some remarks to make:
"Is any woman worth it? These young men
Strike me as very silly." But when he saw her,
Her face, her body naked, with such beauty
As mine is, or as yours would be, Adonis,
If you were woman, he was struck with wonder,
Threw up his hands and cried: "I beg your pardon,   650
Young men, I judged you wrongly; I did not know
The value of the prize!" And he caught fire
From his own praising, hoped that no young runner
Would beat her, feared they might, was worried, jealous.
"Why don't I try?" he thought, "God helps the bold."
And, swifter than his thought, the girl sped by
On winged feet, swifter than Scythian arrow,
Yet not too swift for a young man's admiration,
And running made her lovelier: the breeze
Bore back the streaming pinions of her sandals,   660
Her hair was tossed back over ivory shoulders,
The colored ribbons fluttered at her knees,
And a light flush came over her girlish body
The way a crimson awning, over marble,
Tints it in pastel color. As he watched her,
She crossed the finish line, received the crown
Of victory, and the beaten suitors, groaning,
Were led away to death.
                              'Hippomenes,
Undaunted, came from the crowd; he fixed his eyes
On Atalanta, and he made his challenge: 670
"This is too easy, beating all these turtles!
Race against me!" he said, "If you are beaten
It will be no disgrace. Megareus is my father,
Whose grandfather was Neptune, and that makes me
Great-grandson of the king of all the oceans.
Nor is my worth inferior to my race.
Beat me, and you will have something to boast of!"[28]
Listening, looking almost tenderly

---

[28] Hippomenes' challenge parodies the epic hero's inflated challenge to armed combat.

At that young man, she wondered, in confusion,
Which would be better, to win or lose. "What god," 680
She thought, "so hates the young and handsome
He wants to ruin this one, tempting him
To risk his precious life to marry me?
I do not think I am worth it. I am not moved
By his beauty (though I could be); I am moved
Because he seems so young: he does not move me,
Only his age. What of his manly courage,
His nerve, his claim to proud descent, his love
For me, so great a love that death, he claims,
Is an advantage if he cannot have me? 690
Go while you may, O stranger, flee this marriage,
There is too much blood upon it. Any girl
Would marry you, and wisely. Why do I care,
Why worry for him, when I have slain so many?
Let him look out for himself, or let him die
Since the death of all those others has not warned him,
Since life is such a bore! Is he to die
Because he wants to live with me? Is death
To be the price of love? I shall be hated
In victory. It is not my fault. Poor fellow, 700
I wish you would forget it but, since you are crazy,
I wish at least you could run a little faster!
He looks like a girl, almost. I wish he had never
Laid eyes on me. He should have lived. If I
Were luckier, if the fates allowed me marriage,
He was the only one I would have taken
To bed with any pleasure." Atalanta
Was green in love, untutored—she did not know
What she was doing, and loved, and did not know it.

Meanwhile the people and her father, restless, 710
Were clamoring for the race. Hippomenes
Called me in supplication: "O, may Venus
Be near, I pray, assist my daring, favor
The love she gave me!" And a gentle breeze
Bore this soft prayer my way; it moved my heart,
I own, and there was little time to aid him.
There is a field the natives call Tamasus,
The richest part of Cyprus, which the ancients
Hallowed for me, and built my temples there,
And in a field there stands a golden tree, 720
Shining with golden leaves and branches rustling
With the soft click of gold, and golden apples
Are the fruit of that golden tree. I came from there
With three such apples in my hand, and no one
Saw me except Hippomenes, and I
Told him how he should use them.

'The trumpets sounded
The start: the pair, each crouching low, shot forward,
Skimming the sand with flying feet, so lightly
They could run on waves and never wet their sandals,
They could run on fields of grain and never bend them.   730
He heard them cheering: "Go, Hippomenes,
Lean to the work, use all your strength: go, go,
You are sure to win!" I could not tell you whether
The cheering pleased him more, or Atalanta.
How many times, when she could have passed, she lingered,
Slowed down to see his face, and, most unwilling,
Sprinted ahead! And now his breathing labored,
Came in great sobbing gasps, and the finish line
Was a long way off, and he tossed one golden apple,
The first one, down. She looked at it with wonder,   740
Eager to have the shining fruit, she darted
Out of the course, and picked it up, still rolling,
The golden thing. He gained the lead again
As all the people roared applause. She passed him
Again, and once again lost ground to follow
The toss of the second apple, and once more
Caught up and sprinted past him. "O be near me,
Gift-bringing Goddess, help me now!" he cried,
And this time threw the last third apple farther,
Angling it off the course, way to one side.   750
She hesitated, only for a moment,
Whether to chase it, but I made her do it,
And made the fruit weigh more, so she was hindered
Both by the burden and her own delay.
To run my story quickly, as the race
Was run, the girl was beaten, and the winner
Led off his prize.
                'Do you not think, Adonis,
He should have brought me incense, or at least
Given me thanks? He did not. I was angry:
Once slighted, I should not again be slighted.   760
I told myself I would make examples of them.
One day they were going by a temple, hidden
In the deep woods; in ancient times Echion
Had consecrated this to Cybele
In payment of a vow. Their trip was long,
And they were tired, or thought so, but I drove
Hippomenes half crazy with the passion
To take his wife. He saw, beside the temple,
A dimly-lighted cavern, roofed with rock,
A chapel it was, really, where the priesthood   770
Had placed for worship their old wooden idols.
He could not wait, here he took Atalanta,
And the gods turned their eyes away; Cybele,

The tower-crowned[29] Mother, had at first the impulse
To drown them, for their guilt, in the Stygian waters,
But that seemed much too easy. So their necks
Grew rough with tawny manes, their fingers, hooked,
Were claws, their arms were legs, their chests grew heavy,
Their tails swept over the sandy ground, and anger
Blazed in their features, they conversed in growling,   780
Took to the woods to couple: they were lions,
Frightful to all but Cybele, whose bridle
And bit they champed in meekness. Do not hunt them,
Adonis: let all beasts alone, which offer
Breasts to the fight, not backs, or else your daring
Will be the ruin of us both.'

THE FATE OF ADONIS

                              "Her warning
Was given, and the goddess took her way,
Drawn by her swans through air. But the young hunter
Scorned all such warnings, and one day, it happened,
His hounds, hard on the trail, roused a wild boar,   790
And as he rushed from the wood, Adonis struck him
A glancing blow, and the boar turned, and shaking
The spear from the side, came charging at the hunter,
Who feared, and ran, and fell, and the tusk entered
Deep in the groin, and the youth lay there dying
On the yellow sand, and Venus, borne through air
In her light swan-guided chariot, still was far
From Cyprus when she heard his groans, and, turning
The white swans from their course, came back to him,
Saw, from high air, the body lying lifeless   800
In its own blood, and tore her hair and garments,
Beat her fair breasts with cruel hands, came down
Reproaching Fate. 'They shall not have it always
Their way,' she mourned, 'Adonis, for my sorrow,
Shall have a lasting monument: each year
Your death will be my sorrow,[30] but your blood
Shall be a flower. If Persephone
Could change to fragrant mint the girl called Mentha,[31]
Cinyras' son, my hero, surely also
Can be my flower.' Over the blood she sprinkled   810
Sweet-smelling nectar, and as bubbles rise
In rainy weather, so it stirred, and blossomed,

[29] Cybele taught the arts of fortification; hence her crown of towers. The lovers are profaning her shrine by their sexual act.

[30] The reference is to an annual festival commemorating Adonis' death.

[31] A nymph favored by Persephone.

Before an hour, as crimson in its color
As pomegranates are, as briefly clinging
To life as did Adonis, for the winds
Which gave a name to the flower, anemone,
The wind-flower, shake the petals off, too early,
Doomed all too swift and soon."

from BOOK XI

THE DEATH OF ORPHEUS

So with his singing Orpheus drew the trees,
The beasts, the stones, to follow, when, behold!
The mad Ciconian women,[1] fleeces flung
Across their maddened breasts, caught sight of him
From a near hill-top, as he joined his song
To the lyre's music. One of them, her tresses
Streaming in the light air, cried out: "Look there!
There is our despiser!" and she flung a spear
Straight at the singing mouth, but the leafy wand
Made only a mark and did no harm. Another   10
Let fly a stone, which, even as it flew,
Was conquered by the sweet harmonious music,
Fell at his feet, as if to ask for pardon.
But still the warfare raged, there was no limit,
Mad fury reigned, and even so, all weapons
Would have been softened by the singer's music,
But there was other orchestration: flutes
Shrilling, and trumpets braying loud, and drums,
Beating of breasts, and howling, so the lyre
Was overcome, and then at last the stones   20
Reddened with blood, the blood of the singer, heard
No more through all that outcry. All the birds
Innumerable, fled, and the charmed snakes,
The train of beasts, Orpheus' glory, followed.
The Maenads stole the show. Their bloody hands
Were turned against the poet; they came thronging
Like birds who see an owl wandering in daylight;
They bayed him down, as in the early morning
Hounds circle the doomed stag beside the game-pits.
They rushed him, threw the wands, wreathed with green leaves,   30
Not meant for such a purpose; some threw clods,
Some branches torn from the tree, and some threw stones,
And they found fitter weapons for their madness.
Not far away there was a team of oxen

---

[1] Maenads, female Thracian worshippers of Bacchus, the god of wine; they are enraged
because Orpheus has renounced women for boys, as is mentioned in Book X.

Plowing the field, and near them farmers, digging
Reluctant earth, and sweating over their labor,
Who fled before the onrush of this army
Leaving behind them hoe and rake and mattock
And these the women grabbed, and slew the oxen
Who lowered horns at them in brief defiance   40
And were torn limb from limb, and then the women
Rushed back to murder Orpheus, who stretched out
His hands in supplication, and whose voice,
For the first time, moved no one. They struck him down,
And through those lips to which the rocks had listened,
To which the hearts of savage beasts responded,
His spirit found its way to winds and air.

The birds wept for him, and the throng of beasts,
The flinty rocks, the trees which came so often
To hear his song, all mourned. The trees, it seemed,   50
Shook down their leaves, as if they might be women
Tearing their hair, and rivers, with their tears,
Were swollen, and their naiads and their dryads
Mourned in black robes. The poet's limbs lay scattered
Where they were flung in cruelty or madness,
But Hebrus River took the head and lyre
And as they floated down the gentle current
The lyre made mournful sounds, and the tongue murmured
In mournful harmony, and the banks echoed
The strains of mourning. On the sea, beyond   60
Their native stream, they came at last to Lesbos[2]
And grounded near the city of Methymna.
And here a serpent struck at the head, still dripping
With sea-spray, but Apollo came and stopped it,
Freezing the open jaws to stone, still gaping.
And Orpheus' ghost fled under the earth, and knew
The places he had known before, and, haunting
The fields of the blessed, found Eurydice
And took her in his arms, and now together
And side by side they wander, or Orpheus follows   70
Or goes ahead, and may, with perfect safety,
Look back for his Eurydice.
      But Bacchus
Demanded punishment for so much evil.
Mourning his singer's loss, he bound those women,
All those who saw the murder, in a forest,
Twisted their feet to roots, and thrust them deep
Into unyielding earth. As a bird struggles
Caught in a fowler's snare, and flaps and flutters
And draws its bonds the tighter by its struggling,
Even so the Thracian women, gripped by the soil,   80

[2] The island associated with lyric poets, especially with Sappho.

Fastened in desperate terror, writhed and struggled,
But the roots held. They looked to see their fingers,
Their toes, their nails, and saw the bark come creeping
Up the smooth legs; they tried to smite their thighs
With grieving hands, and struck on oak; their breasts
Were oak, and oak their shoulders, and their arms
You well might call long branches and be truthful.

THE STORY OF MIDAS

And even this was not enough for Bacchus.
He left those fields, and with a worthier band
He sought the vineyards of his own Timolus[3]   90
And Pactolus, a river not yet gold
Nor envied for its precious sands. The throng
He always had surrounded him, the satyrs,
The Bacchanals; Silenus,[4] though, was missing.
The Phrygian rustics found him, staggering
Under the weight of years, and maybe also
From more than too much wine, bound him with wreaths
And led him to King Midas. Now this king
Together with the Athenian Eumolpus
Had learned the rites of Bacchic lore from Orpheus.   100
And therefore, since he recognized a comrade,
A brother in the lodge, he gave a party
For ten long days and nights, and then, rejoicing,
Came to the Lydian fields and gave Silenus
Back to his precious foster son. And Bacchus,
Happy and grateful, and meaning well, told Midas
To make his choice of anything he wanted.
And Midas, never too judicious, answered:
"Grant that whatever I touch may turn to gold!"
Bacchus agreed, gave him the ruinous gift,   110
Sorry the monarch had not chosen better.
So Midas went his cheerful way, rejoicing
In his own bad luck, and tried to test the promise
By touching this and that. It all was true,
He hardly dared believe it! From an oak-tree
He broke a green twig loose: the twig was golden.
He picked a stone up from the ground; the stone
Paled with light golden color; he touched a clod,
The clod became a nugget. Awns of grain
Were a golden harvest; if he picked an apple   120
It seemed a gift from the Hesperides.[5]

[3] A mountain in Lydia, a country in Asia Minor; Sardis was its capital.
[4] The habitually drunk foster father of Bacchus.
[5] Islands at the western end of the world, noted for a garden of golden apples.

He placed his fingers on the lofty pillars
And saw them gleam and shine. He bathed his hands
In water, and the stream was golden rain
Like that which came to Danae.[6] His mind
Could scarcely grasp his hopes—all things were golden,
Or would be, at his will! A happy man,
He watched his servants set a table before him
With bread and meat. He touched the gift of Ceres
And found it stiff and hard; he tried to bite   130
The meat with hungry teeth, and where the teeth
Touched food they seemed to touch on golden ingots.
He mingled water with the wine of Bacchus;
It was molten gold that trickled through his jaws.

Midas, astonished at his new misfortune,
Rich man and poor man, tries to flee his riches
Hating the favor he had lately prayed for.
No food relieves his hunger; his throat is dry
With burning thirst; he is tortured, as he should be,
By the hateful gold. Lifting his hands to Heaven,   140
He cries: "Forgive me, father! I have sinned.
Have mercy upon me, save me from this loss
That looks so much like gain!" The gods are kind,
And Bacchus, since he owned his fault, forgave him,
Took back the gift. "You need not be forever
Smeared with that foolish color: go to the stream
That flows by Sardis, take your way upstream
Into the Lydian hills, until you find
The tumbling river's source. There duck your head
And body under the foaming white of the fountain,   150
And wash your sin away." The king obeyed him,
And the power of the golden touch imbued the water,
So that even now the fields grow hard and yellow
If that vein washes over them to flood
Their fields with the water of the touch of gold.

MIDAS NEVER LEARNS

Now Midas, hating wealth, haunted the forests,
The fields, and worshipped Pan,[7] who has his dwelling
In the mountain caves. But Midas still was stupid,
And once again his foolish wits were destined
To do their master damage. Where Timolus   160
Looks out to sea, towering high, one slope
Falling to Sardis and the other slanting

[6]Jupiter had come to Danae as a shower of golden rain.
[7]God of shepherds and of the woods.

Toward little Hypaepa, Pan was singing tunes
Tossing them off to the soft nymphs, and warbling
A trill or two on the reeds joined with wax,
Remarking that the music of Apollo
Was poor beside his own, and offering challenge
To an unequal contest, with Timolus[8]
To be the umpire. So the ancient judge,
Seated on his own mountain, shook his ears   170
Loose from the trees. Around his dark-blue hair
An oaken chaplet twined; acorns hung down
Around his hollow temples. He looked at Pan,
"The judge is ready," he said, and Pan made music
On the rustic reeds, and the barbaric song
Delighted Midas utterly—it so happened
Midas was listening. Then old Timolus
Turned to Apollo, and his forests followed
As he inclined his gaze. Apollo's hair,
Golden, was wreathed with laurel of Parnassus,[9]   180
His mantle, dipped in Tyrian crimson, swept
Along the ground. His lyre, inlaid with jewels,
With Indian ivory, his left hand held;
His right hand held the plectrum.[10] You could tell
The artist from his bearing. With his thumb
He plucked the strings, and charmed by that sweet music,
Timolus ordered Pan to lower his reeds,
Submissive to the lyre, and all approved
The judgment of the holy god of the mountain,
All except Midas, who began to argue,   190
Calling it most unfair. Such stupid ears,
Apollo thought, were surely less than human,
And so he made them longer, stuffed them full
Of gray and shaggy hair, and made their base
Unstable, giving them the power of motion.
The rest of him was human; this one feature
Alone was punished, and he wore the ears
Of the slow-going jackass. So, disfigured,
Ashamed, he tried to hide them with a turban,
But when he had his hair cut, then his barber   200
Saw, dared not tell, and wanted to, and could not
Keep matters to himself, no more than barbers
Today can do, and so he dug a hole
Deep in the ground, and went and whispered in it
What kind of ears King Midas had. He buried
The evidence of his voice, filled up the hole,
Sneaked silently away. But a thick growth
Of whispering reeds began to grow there; these,

---

[8] The god or personification of the mountain.
[9] Mountain in southern Greece, associated with Apollo and the Muses.
[10] A "pick," used to pluck the strings.

At the year's end full-grown, betrayed the sower,
For when a light breeze stirred them, they would whisper   ₂₁₀
Midas has asses' ears! You can still hear them.

*   *   *

The New Testament
(*First and Second Centuries* A.D.)

The name given to the distinctively Christian part of the Bible, the New Testament, *can also be rendered as* New Covenant, *a term that has the advantage of underlining the intimate relationship, of kinship and separation, between it and the Old Testament. The old covenant, sealed at Mount Sinai, was essentially a contract between God and the people of Israel. It was the culmination of a series of lesser covenants established between God and mankind, then between God and the Hebrew patriarchs. The contract spelled out the provisions by which God, on the occasion of the deliverance of the Hebrews from Egypt, revealed Himself to them and singled them out for special obligations and a special mission. Although the Exodus story, as told in the first six books of the Old Testament (the Hexateuch), has mythic content that links it to universal human religious insights, it nevertheless solemnizes a preeminently* historical *event, the establishment of the nation of Israel.*

In later Old Testament times, written and popular traditions grew up stating that a divinely appointed Messiah would arise among the Jews to deliver them from their national tribulations and usher in a new era of triumph and glory. The Christians of the first century believed that this Messiah had in fact appeared, in the historical figure of Jesus of Nazareth. Through him God had established a new covenant, this time with a body of believers extending beyond the Jews. As the old covenant had been sealed with the ritual sprinkling of blood (Exodus 24:6–8), so had the new covenant, for this Messiah was—unexpectedly—a sacrificial victim. But he had risen from the dead as a pledge of an imminent second coming, or Parousia, *that would vindicate God's newly adopted people. The doctrine of the Resurrection and the concomitant belief in the Parousia and final Judgment lay at the heart of Christian faith during the first century.*

The canonical books of the New Testament, as finally defined several centuries after Jesus, number twenty-seven, all written in Greek: the four Gospels, of unknown authorship but named Matthew, Mark, Luke, and John; a history of the early Church written by the author of Luke and called Acts of the Apostles; twenty-one letters, or Epistles, the most important of which are by St. Paul; and a visionary, allegorical work of prophecy named Revelation, or the Apocalypse. The earliest of these books are the Pauline letters, which were written mainly over the sixth decade of the first century; the other books were written at various dates extending through the end of the first century into the early part of the second century. Most of the New Testament books are statements of doctrine and church discipline; the more biographical ones are Acts and the four Gospels that center on the life and teaching of Jesus.

Although the four Gospels contain substantially similar accounts of the trial, sufferings, and execution of Jesus (the Passion), and all present an empty tomb that points to his resurrection, their portrayals of the earlier phases of Jesus' life are significantly different from one another. John, on the one hand, has its own distinctive material. Matthew, Mark, and Luke (the "synoptic" Gospels), on the other hand, contain a common fund of different material, and many passages have almost identical wording. In fact, approximately 99 per cent of Mark, and much of its ordering of material, is paralleled (although sometimes recast) in Matthew and Luke. An enormous scholarly literature attempts to explain the significant overlap when these Gospels are "seen together" (the meaning of synoptic*), and a consensus, called the two-document hypothesis, has dominated the field of interpretation during this century. The hypothesis proposes that Mark is the earliest Gospel (written around 65–70) and that Matthew and Luke, although written independently of each other (between about 80 and 95), are based partly on a direct knowledge of Mark. The shared but non-Markan material in Matthew and Luke is derived from a now lost collection, largely of sayings of Jesus, called Q (from German* Quelle, *"source"). Some authorities postulate that both Matthew and Luke also used other sources, called* M *and* L, *respectively. The synoptic problem is of course important in itself, but it has also intrigued scholars because it bears on the possibility of recovering facts about the historical Jesus from the earliest accounts. This search for the "real" Jesus, independent of later tendentious biases of the Gospel authors (the "evangelists"), was especially urgent in the nineteenth century. The goal no longer preoccupies biblical scholars so insistently, however. They have attained some confidence concerning the typical teaching and activity of Jesus from the earliest form of sayings and stories, but they are doubtful that any of the evangelists, even the earliest, has provided an account either of Jesus' acts or of the sequence of his acts that is free from substantial interpretation.*

*That view may unsettle or puzzle readers accustomed to the goals of modern biography and historiography. But to the earliest Christians it was the overwhelming fact of the Messiah's death, resurrection, and imminent Parousia that was centrally important, not the circumstantial details of his life. (It is significant that the word translated as "gospel"—*good news—*did not originally refer as it usually does now to the formal genre represented by Matthew, Mark, Luke, and John but rather to the essential* message *just outlined.) Moreover, the tradition of both Jewish and pagan historiography assumed that the truth about any event or person could best be revealed by a respect for tradition and sources in the setting of the author's own creative intuition. This combination operates even in the author of Luke and Acts, the New Testament works governed most by the classical rules for writing history. The interest among Christians in what Jesus had said and done during his life as a whole arose only secondarily, and even then less from a modern need for historical accuracy in itself than from a sense of Jesus as an enduring, living presence and a desire to explore and authenticate the current doctrine and discipline of his living Church. The earliest Christians did not feel that the circumstantial data were of value apart from their significance.*

It is important to recognize that each of the four Gospels has its own special intention and effect. The readiest way to prove this true is to read a Gospel straight through, an eye-opening experience for those readers whose acquaintance with the New Testament comes entirely from exposure to brief and mixed excerpts such as are found in prayer books and liturgies. The four Gospels contain basic stories about Jesus' life and death that create an impression of coherence in the New Testament (some apocryphal Gospels written later do not cohere with these accounts), but the portraits differ unmistakably in their overtones: in Mark, Jesus is presented earthily, almost naturalistically; in Luke, beautifully and heroically; in John, with a supernal serenity; in Matthew, as compassionate but magisterial. More careful study reveals also differences between the Gospels in their doctrinal emphases, their views of the timing and nature of the coming apocalyptic Parousia, their definitions of ethical and communal duties of Christians, and their notions of worship. Each Gospel addresses the needs of a different group of early Christians in its own place and set of circumstances.

Matthew was probably written in Syria, as a manual of instruction for a well-established Christian community, containing both Jewish and Gentile converts, that was competing with Pharisaic Judaism after the destruction of the Jerusalem Temple in 70 A.D. The author is concerned to define the Church as the New Israel, replacing the old one by means of a way of righteousness surpassing the righteousness of the Pharisees (a difficult goal, because the Pharisees were the most fervently religious Jews within first-century Jewish society). Events of Jesus' life—especially healings, exorcisms, and other miraculous manifestations of messianic power—are integrated into a careful, fivefold structure framed at the outset by the infancy narrative establishing Jesus' descent through David from Abraham and at the end by the climactic Passion narrative. The gospel culminates five times in authoritative, didactic discourses. The first of these is the Sermon on the Mount (chapters 5–7), which outlines Christian ethics and its spiritual premises; the second (10) concerns missionary discipleship; the third (13) relates parables of God's kingdom; the fourth (18) is on the Church; and the fifth (24–25) is on the apocalyptic end of the world. Some interpreters see in this fivefold organization a deliberate parallel with the five books of the Torah or Mosaic Law.

In Mark, the fact that Jesus is the Messiah is a closely guarded secret, so much so that even the disciples are obtuse on the matter. Matthew, by contrast, is intent to show, beginning with the insistent opening genealogy and the story of the pagan wise men, not only that Jesus is the Messiah but that he was unmistakably that during his lifetime. Except in a few passages, the disciples, especially Peter, are clearly aware of this. There was thus no excuse, according to Matthew, for the perverse failure of the Jewish leaders to recognize Jesus as the Messiah, a failure that forfeits the claim by the Jews to be the special vehicle of God's providence. (Jesus first commissions the disciples to limit their preaching mission, as he has done, to the "lost sheep of the house of Israel"—10:5–6—but in the concluding words of the Gospel he dispatches them to "all nations.") Jesus is human but masterful, divinely sent, as the new star at his birth announced. Dozens of times Matthew quotes the Old Testament (sometimes drawing on the ancient Greek translation of it, the Septuagint) to show that Jesus is the fulfillment of the Old Testament promises.

Matthew's Gospel is a particularly Jewish one; it assumes an awareness, within Christianity and in its relations with its neighbors, of the Jewish scriptures, locutions, ideas, and heritage. These are the very air Matthew breathes. Jesus' disputes with the Pharisees, scribes, and Sadducees have a distinctively Jewish cast of thought, as in his verbal sparring over Old Testament texts (for example, 22:34–46) and in controversies over dietary and sabbatical rules. The position of Matthew's Jesus on such matters is generally that the expounders of the Law are either knowledgeable but hypocritical in their behavior, or ignorant ("the blind lead the blind"), or legalistic, intent on the letter of the Law at the expense of its spirit. A deep irony here, important for an understanding of Matthew, lies in the fact that a similar position

*was central in Pharisaism itself. The Pharisees believed that the Law had to be up-
dated, adapted to the needs of the present, and supplemented by oral tradition if it
was to retain its vitality. Matthew is thus leveling at the Pharisees (the dominant
party in Judaism in Matthew's time) the kind of criticism that they leveled at ultra-
conservative Jews and at rival groups within the ranks of the Pharisees. In short,
the rancor expressed in Matthew toward the Pharisees is of the kind immemorially
felt by religious groups toward others that are close enough in thought and prox-
imity to be considered dangerous rivals.*

    *This relationship—of friction between close kindred—must be kept in mind when
one examines the ambivalence expressed in Matthew toward Jewry and Judaism.
There is no mistaking the antagonism. Usually, however, Jesus does not repudiate the
Law; when asked by a "lawyer" what the greatest commandment is, he dutifully cites
Deuteronomy and Leviticus (Matthew 22:36–40), and in the Sermon on the Mount
he emphatically endorses even the fine print: "Till heaven and earth pass, one jot or
one tittle shall in no wise pass from the law, till all be fulfilled" (5:18). This seems to
contradict other passages in Matthew where Jesus apparently sets aside at least the
minutiae of the Law. Perhaps there is a contradiction, but not necessarily; much depends on the implications of the word* fulfilled. *The frequent citations of Old Testament texts imply not that the Old Testament has been superseded or that a new
chapter has merely been added to it. The new, Christian dispensation is not a repudi-
ation of the Law so much as a living growth from it, and the new teaching no more
negates its origins than the fruit of a tree negates the tree's earlier history of bud
and leaf. It is no coincidence that central discourses and events such as the Sermon
on the Mount, the Temptation, the Transfiguration, and the final commissioning
of the disciples take place on "mountains" (hills, actually), for these settings all bear
witness to their most solemn early archetype in the self-revelation of God at Mount
Sinai. Matthew thus has a strong sense of iconography, of the symbolism of forms,
settings, and stories from the Old Testament. Even the flight from Herod into Egypt
and the later return to Palestine re-enact the migrations described in Genesis, Exodus, and Joshua. Matthew could not have felt or implied the force of such parallels if he thought of the Jewish past as simply annulled, a dead letter. It could be argued that what Matthew's Jesus attacks in the Jewish teachers and leaders is not their
reverence for the law but virtually the opposite: their failure to recognize its living
import. The apparent contrasts between new and old doctrine in the Sermon on the
Mount can be seen as an actual intensifying of the old Law, an insistence that it
be pushed to its ultimate implications.*

    *Although Matthew is a well-written and well-organized book, Luke is the most
polished piece of literature among the Gospels. The author's stylistic versatility is
impressive; he can write in an urbane classical manner (as in the preface to Theophilus—1:1–4) and also in the Old Testament manner, as in the following birth and
infancy narratives, which also show a meticulous sense of structure in the elaborate
parallelism of the stories of John the Baptist and of Jesus. The great anthems of the
first two chapters, now deeply embedded in Christian liturgies, are filled with echoes
of the Old Testament and strongly suggest the style of the Psalms. Even in our brief
excerpt the warmth and joy characteristic of Luke shine through, and many of its key
themes are sounded: the championing of the poor, the lowly, the outcasts; the call of
the Gentiles; the importance of women; the workings of the Holy Ghost.*

    *Uncertainty concerning the origins of the Gospels and their relationship to one
another as documents should not be allowed to obscure the distinctive teaching and
action that lie behind them. The literal ascription of the first five books of the Old*

Testament to Moses is untenable today, but it is equally difficult to ignore one's sense of their historical root in the experience and leadership of an unmistakably distinctive person. Similarly, it is difficult to imagine the Gospels as collections of loosely united traditions whose focus in Jesus is merely a pious convention. One senses a powerful dynamic, best understood as originating in Jesus' historical life and teaching, that has made the New Testament, especially in combination with the Old, the most influential book in human history.

FURTHER READING *(prepared by F.S.N.):* An excellent work of reference, containing general articles on the New Testament, introductions, exegesis, and expositions for individual books, is *The Interpreter's Bible,* ed. George A. Buttrick, 12 vols., 1952. Also very helpful is *The Interpreter's Dictionary of the Bible: An Illustrated Encyclopedia,* ed. George A. Buttrick, 4 vols., 1962, and its *Supplementary Volume,* ed. Keith Crim, 1976. For further useful articles, see John E. Steinmueller and Kathryn Sullivan, eds., *Catholic Biblical Encyclopedia: New Testament,* 1950. Werner Jaeger, *Early Christianity and Greek Paideia,* 1961, shows the influence of Greek civilization on Christianity; David Daube, *The New Testament and Rabbinic Judaism,* 1956, explores the relationship between Christianity and Judaism; and Howard Clark Kee, Franklin W. Young, and Karlfried Froehlich, *Understanding the New Testament,* 1957, 3rd ed. 1973, assembles excellent material on both the Hellenistic and the Jewish background to the Gospel narratives. Exegetical treatments of the individual books are given by A. E. Harvey, *The New English Bible: Companion to the New Testament,* 1970; and by Raymond E. Brown, Joseph A. Fitzmyer, and Roland E. Murphy, *The Jerome Biblical Commentary,* 1968. Early Christian beliefs, the expansion of the early Church, and its consolidation are discussed by James L. Price, *Interpreting the New Testament,* 1961.

THE NEW TESTAMENT

King James Version (1611)

THE GOSPEL ACCORDING TO SAINT MATTHEW

The book of the generation of Jesus Christ, the son of David, the son of Abraham.[1]

Abraham begat Isaac; and Isaac begat Jacob; and Jacob begat Judah and his brethren; and Judah begat Pharez and Zerah of Tamar; and Pharez begat Hezron; and Hezron begat Ram; and Ram begat Amminadab; and Amminadab begat Nahshon; and Nahshon begat Salmon; and Salmon begat Boaz of Rachab; and Boaz begat Obed of Ruth; and Obed begat Jesse; and Jesse begat David the king.

[1] The introductory genealogy is intended to help affirm Jesus as the Messiah, the divinely sent hero who, Jewish tradition expected, would inaugurate a new era of glory and renewal. The list of names is only partly verifiable from the Old Testament. The Messiah, it was believed, would descend from the bloodline of David the king, and the descent from Abraham was important because he was the earliest patriarch of the Hebrews as God's people. The name Jesus means *saviour;* it is the Greek form of the Hebrew Yeshua, or Joshua, and thus the role of Jesus symbolically parallels that of the hero who, succeeding Moses, led the Israelites to triumph in the promised land. *Christ* is not a personal name but an epithet (meaning *Anointed One*) for the Messiah.

And David the king begat Solomon of her that had been the wife of Uriah; and Solomon begat Rehoboam; and Rehoboam begat Abijah; and Abijah begat Asa; and Asa begat Jehoshaphat; and Jehoshaphat begat Jehoram; and Jehoram begat Uzziah; and Uzziah begat Jotham; and Jotham begat Ahaz; and Ahaz begat Hezekiah; and Hezekiah begat Manasseh; and Manasseh begat Amon; and Amon begat Josiah; and Josiah begat Jeconiah and his brethren, about the time they were carried away to Babylon.

And after they were brought to Babylon, Jeconiah begat Shealtiel; and Shealtiel begat Zerubbabel; and Zerubbabel begat Abiud; and Abiud begat Eliakim; and Eliakim begat Azor; and Azor begat Zadok; and Zadok begat Achim; and Achim begat Eliud; and Eliud begat Eleazar; and Eleazar begat Matthan; and Matthan begat Jacob; and Jacob begat Joseph the husband of Mary,[2] of whom was born Jesus, who is called Christ.

So all the generations from Abraham to David are fourteen generations; and from David until the carrying away into Babylon are fourteen generations; and from the carrying away into Babylon unto Christ are fourteen generations.[3] (1:1–17)

Now the birth of Jesus Christ was on this wise: When as his mother Mary was espoused to Joseph, before they came together, she was found with child of the Holy Ghost. Then Joseph her husband, being a just man, and not willing to make her a public example, was minded to put her away privily.[4] But while he thought on these things, behold, the angel of the Lord[5] appeared unto him in a dream, saying, "Joseph, thou son of David, fear not to take unto thee Mary thy wife: for that which is conceived in her is of the Holy Ghost. And she shall bring forth a son, and thou shalt call his name Jesus: for he shall save his people from their sins." Now all this was done, that it might be fulfilled which was spoken of the Lord by the prophet, saying,

"Behold, a virgin shall be with child, and shall bring forth a son,
And they shall call his name Emmanuel,"[6]

which being interpreted is, God with us. Then Joseph being raised from sleep did as the angel of the Lord had bidden him, and took unto him his wife: and knew her not[7] till she had brought forth her firstborn son: and he called his name JESUS. (1:18–25)

---

[2] The genealogy, apparently broken because Joseph is not Jesus' father, could be considered valid because Jewish law sanctioned the status of adopted sons as true ones.

[3] Matthew's tripartite genealogy, corresponding to three ages in Hebrew history, is typical of his concern with schematic structure in the gospel.

[4] Quietly, without making the matter a public issue as he was legally entitled to do.

[5] The dream, the angel, and the virgin birth are typical of the emphasis, especially strong in Matthew, on the miraculous and wondrously supernatural.

[6] Isaiah 7:14. This is the first of many Matthean quotations from the Old Testament to vindicate Jesus as the promised Messiah. Matthew quotes, as he often does, not from the Hebrew text but from the Septuagint, a Greek translation of the Old Testament used by non-Palestinian Jews ignorant of Hebrew. In the Septuagint the word here rendered as *virgin* can have that meaning; in the Hebrew text of Isaiah it means merely *young woman*. Matthew characteristically construes the Old Testament for his distinctive purposes, as foreshadowing the person and life of Jesus.

[7] Did not have sexual intercourse with her.

Now when Jesus was born in Bethlehem of Judea in the days of Herod the king,[8] behold, there came wise men[9] from the east to Jerusalem, saying, "Where is he that is born King of the Jews? for we have seen his star in the east, and are come to worship him." When Herod the king had heard these things, he was troubled, and all Jerusalem with him. And when he had gathered all the chief priests and scribes[10] of the people together, he demanded of them where Christ should be born. And they said unto him, "In Bethlehem of Judea: for thus it is written by the prophet,

> 'And thou Bethlehem, in the land of Judah,
> Art not the least among the princes of Judah:
> For out of thee shall come a Governor,
> That shall rule my people Israel.'"

Then Herod, when he had privily called the wise men, enquired of them diligently what time the star appeared. And he sent them to Bethlehem, and said, "Go and search diligently for the young child; and when ye have found him, bring me word again, that I may come and worship him also." When they had heard the king, they departed; and, lo, the star, which they saw in the east, went before them, till it came and stood over where the young child was. When they saw the star, they rejoiced with exceeding great joy. And when they were come into the house, they saw the young child with Mary his mother, and fell down, and worshipped him: and when they had opened their treasures, they presented unto him gifts; gold, and frankincense, and myrrh. And being warned of God in a dream that they should not return to Herod, they departed into their own country another way. (2:1–12)

And when they were departed, behold, the angel of the Lord appeareth to Joseph in a dream, saying, "Arise, and take the young child and his mother, and flee into Egypt, and be thou there until I bring thee word: for Herod will seek the young child to destroy him." When he arose, he took the young child and his mother by night, and departed into Egypt: and was there until the death of Herod: that it might be fulfilled which was spoken of the Lord by the prophet, saying, "Out of Egypt have I called my son."[11] Then Herod, when he saw that he was mocked of the wise men, was exceeding wroth,[12] and sent forth, and slew all the children that were in Bethlehem, and in all the coasts thereof, from two years old and under, according to the time which he had diligently enquired of the wise men. Then was fulfilled that which was spoken by Jeremiah the prophet, saying,

> "In Ramah was there a voice heard,
> Lamentation, and weeping, and great mourning,

---

[8] The ruler of Palestine, including Judea proper, the southern area of Palestine. He reigned under the authority of Caesar Augustus, because Palestine was part of the Roman empire. He was the father of the Herod who later examines Jesus at his trial. Bethlehem, a few miles south of Jerusalem, had been the home of David.

[9] Astrologers, not, as in later legend, kings. Celestial phenomena were regarded as portents of great events and the birth of august personages.

[10] Legal experts on and interpreters of Old Testament Jewish law.

[11] Hosea 11:1. In Hosea the reference is to God's deliverance of the Israelites out of captivity in Egypt.

[12] Angry.

> Rachel weeping for her children,
> And would not be comforted,
> Because they are not."[13]

But when Herod was dead, behold, an angel of the Lord appeareth in a dream to Joseph in Egypt, saying, "Arise, and take the young child and his mother, and go into the land of Israel: for they are dead which sought the young child's life." And he arose, and took the young child and his mother, and came into the land of Israel. But when he heard that Archelaus did reign in Judea in the room of his father Herod, he was afraid to go thither: notwithstanding, being warned of God in a dream, he turned aside into the parts of Galilee:[14] and he came and dwelt in a city called Nazareth: that it might be fulfilled which was spoken by the prophets, "He shall be called a Nazarene."[15] (2:13–23)

In those days[16] came John the Baptist,[17] preaching in the wilderness of Judea, and saying, "Repent ye: for the kingdom of heaven is at hand." For this is he that was spoken of by the prophet Isaiah, saying,

> "The voice of one crying in the wilderness,
> Prepare ye the way of the Lord,
> Make his paths straight."[18]

And the same John had his raiment of camel's hair, and a leathern girdle about his loins; and his meat was locusts and wild honey. Then went out to him Jerusalem, and all Judea, and all the region around about Jordan, and were baptized of him in Jordan, confessing their sins. But when he saw many of the Pharisees and Sadducees[19] come to his baptism, he said unto them, "O generation of vipers, who hath warned you to flee from the wrath to come? Bring forth therefore fruits meet for repentance: and think not to say within yourselves, 'We have Abraham to our father': for I say unto you, that God is able of these stones to raise up children unto Abraham. And now also the axe is laid unto the root of the trees: therefore every tree which bringeth not forth good fruit is hewn down, and cast into the fire. I indeed baptize you with water unto repentance: but he that cometh after me is mightier than I, whose shoes I am not worthy to bear: he shall baptize

---

[13] Jeremiah 31:15.   [14] The northern area of Palestine.

[15] Probably Matthew is creatively interpreting Isaiah 11:1. Strictly speaking, there is no mention of Nazareth in the Old Testament.

[16] A recurrent phrase that has no specific temporal reference. Here it marks the transition from the days of Jesus' infancy to those of his adulthood.

[17] John is a preacher in the tradition of Old Testament prophecy.   [18] Isaiah 40:3

[19] Two prominent religious groups among Jews of the time, portrayed here as complacent, believing that as favorites of God and offspring of Abraham they have nothing to fear from any such divine judgment as John is proclaiming. The Sadducees were old-fashioned and aristocratic; they acknowledged as authoritative only the literal written Law of Moses and were especially concerned with the priesthood and sacrificial ritual. The Pharisees, although they too venerated the Torah, were more liberal in that they believed that the letter of the Law must be supplemented and applied with the help of tradition and orally transmitted authority. The Pharisees believed that the Scriptures, rightly interpreted, upheld the doctrine of the resurrection of the dead; the Sadducees denied this. (See 22:23–33.) After the sack of Jerusalem in 70 A.D. the Pharisees played a prominent role in preserving Jewish unity and integrity.

you with the Holy Ghost, and with fire: whose fan[20] is in his hand, and he will throughly purge his floor, and gather his wheat into the garner; but he will burn up the chaff with unquenchable fire." (3:1–12)

Then cometh Jesus from Galilee to Jordan unto John, to be baptized of him. But John forbade him, saying, "I have need to be baptized of thee, and comest thou to me?" And Jesus answering said unto him, "Suffer[21] it to be so now: for thus it becometh us to fulfil all righteousness." Then he suffered him. And Jesus, when he was baptized, went up straightway out of the water: and, lo, the heavens were opened unto him, and he saw the Spirit of God descending like a dove, and lighting upon him: and lo a voice from heaven, saying, "This is my beloved Son, in whom I am well pleased." (3:13–17)

Then was Jesus led up of the spirit into the wilderness to be tempted of the devil. And when he had fasted forty days and forty nights,[22] he was afterward ahungered. And when the tempter came to him, he said, "If thou be the Son of God, command that these stones be made bread." But he answered and said, "It is written, 'Man shall not live by bread alone, but by every word that proceedeth out of the mouth of God.'"[23] (4:1–4)

Then the devil taketh him up into the holy city, and setteth him on a pinnacle of the temple, and saith unto him, "If thou be the Son of God, cast thyself down: for it is written,

> 'He shall give his angels charge concerning thee:'
> And 'in their hands they shall bear thee up,
> Lest at any time thou dash thy foot against a stone.'"[24]

Jesus said unto him, "It is written again, 'Thou shalt not tempt the Lord thy God.'"[25] (4:5–7)

Again, the devil taketh him up into an exceeding high mountain, and sheweth him all the kingdoms of the world, and the glory of them; and saith unto him, "All these things will I give thee, if thou wilt fall down and worship me." Then saith Jesus unto him, "Get thee hence, Satan: for it is written, 'Thou shalt worship the Lord thy God, and him only shalt thou serve.'"[26] Then the devil leaveth him, and, behold, angels came and ministered unto him. (4:8–11)

Now when Jesus had heard that John was cast into prison,[27] he departed into Galilee; and leaving Nazareth, he came and dwelt in Capernaum,[28] which is upon the sea coast, in the borders of Zebulun and Naphtali: that it might be fulfilled which was spoken by Isaiah the prophet, saying,

> "The land of Zebulun, and the land of Naphtali,
> By the way of the sea, beyond Jordan,
> Galilee of the Gentiles;

---

[20] Winnowing fan used to separate the grain from the chaff.   [21] Allow.

[22] The number forty is associated with several periods of preparation in the Old Testament, including the forty years the Israelites spent in the wilderness during the Exodus and the forty days and nights Moses spent on Mount Sinai.

[23] Deuteronomy 8:3; all three of Jesus' replies are from this book.   [24] Psalm 91:12.

[25] Deuteronomy 6:16.   [26] Deuteronomy 6:13.

[27] John's imprisonment is recounted later in 14:1–12.

[28] A town on the northern shore of the Sea of Galilee (actually a lake).

The people which sat in darkness
Saw great light;
And to them which sat in the region and shadow of death
Light is sprung up."[29]

From that time Jesus began to preach, and to say, "Repent: for the kingdom of heaven is at hand." (4:12–17)

And Jesus, walking by the sea of Galilee, saw two brethren, Simon called Peter, and Andrew his brother, casting a net into the sea: for they were fishers. And he saith unto them, "Follow me, and I will make you fishers of men." And they straightway left their nets, and followed him. And going on from thence, he saw other two brethren, James the son of Zebedee, and John his brother, in a ship with Zebedee their father, mending their nets; and he called them. And they immediately left the ship and their father, and followed him. (4:18–22)

And Jesus went about all Galilee, teaching in their synagogues, and preaching the gospel of the kingdom, and healing all manner of sickness and all manner of disease among the people. And his fame went throughout all Syria: and they brought unto him all sick people that were taken with divers diseases and torments, and those which were possessed with devils, and those which were lunatic, and those that had the palsy; and he healed them. And there followed him great multitudes of people from Galilee, and from Decapolis,[30] and from Jerusalem, and from Judea, and from beyond Jordan. (4:23–25)

And seeing the multitudes, he went up into a mountain: and when he was set, his disciples came unto him: and he opened his mouth, and taught them, saying,[31]

"Blessed are the poor in spirit: for theirs is the kingdom of heaven.

"Blessed are they that mourn: for they shall be comforted.

"Blessed are the meek: for they shall inherit the earth.

"Blessed are they which do hunger and thirst after righteousness: for they shall be filled.

"Blessed are the merciful: for they shall obtain mercy.

"Blessed are the pure in heart: for they shall see God.

"Blessed are the peacemakers: for they shall be called the children of God.

"Blessed are they which are persecuted for righteousness' sake: for theirs is the kingdom of heaven.

"Blessed are ye, when men shall revile you, and persecute you, and shall say all manner of evil against you falsely, for my sake. Rejoice, and be exceeding glad: for great is your reward in heaven: for so persecuted they the prophets which were before you. (5:1–12)

---

[29] Isaiah 9:1–2.

[30] A region including ten Graeco-Roman towns east of the river Jordan.

[31] Here begins the Sermon on the Mount, which is often regarded as the quintessence of Christian ethical teaching. The discourse continues through Chapter 7. That it is given from a hill (or "mountain") underlines a basic theme in what follows: the relationship of the new teaching to the law of Moses, also delivered from a mountain (Sinai).

THE NEW TESTAMENT / *Matthew*   1051

"Ye are the salt of the earth: but if the salt have lost his savor, wherewith shall it be salted? it is thenceforth good for nothing, but to be cast out, and to be trodden under foot of men. Ye are the light of the world. A city that is set on an hill cannot be hid. Neither do men light a candle, and put it under a bushel,[32] but on a candlestick; and it giveth light unto all that are in the house. Let your light so shine before men, that they may see your good works, and glorify your Father which is in heaven. (5:13–16)

"Think not that I am come to destroy the law, or the prophets: I am not come to destroy, but to fulfill. For verily I say unto you, Till heaven and earth pass, one jot or one tittle shall in no wise pass from the law, till all be fulfilled. Whosoever therefore shall break one of these least command-ments, and shall teach men so, he shall be called the least in the kingdom of heaven: but whosoever shall do and teach them, the same shall be called great in the kingdom of heaven. For I say unto you, That except your righteousness shall exceed the righteousness of the scribes and Pharisees, ye shall in no case enter into the kingdom of heaven. (5:17–20)

"Ye have heard that it was said by them of old time, 'Thou shalt not kill'; and 'whosoever shall kill shall be in danger of the judgment':[33] but I say unto you, That whosoever is angry with his brother without a cause shall be in danger of the judgment: and whosoever shall say to his brother, 'Raca,'[34] shall be in danger of the council:[35] but whosoever shall say, 'Thou fool,' shall be in danger of hell fire. Therefore if thou bring thy gift to the altar, and there rememberest that thy brother hath ought against thee; leave there thy gift before the altar, and go thy way; first be reconciled to thy brother, and then come and offer thy gift. Agree with thine adversary quickly, whiles thou art in the way with him;[36] lest at any time the adversary deliver thee to the judge, and the judge deliver thee to the officer, and thou be cast into prison. Verily I say unto thee, Thou shalt by no means come out thence, till thou hast paid the uttermost farthing.[37] (5:21–26)

"Ye have heard that it was said by them of old time, 'Thou shalt not commit adultery': but I say unto you, That whosoever looketh on a woman to lust after her hath committed adultery with her already in his heart. And if thy right eye offend thee, pluck it out, and cast it from thee: for it is profitable for thee that one of thy members should perish, and not that thy whole body should be cast into hell. And if thy right hand offend thee, cut it off, and cast it from thee: for it is profitable for thee that one of thy members should perish, and not that thy whole body should be cast into hell. It hath been said, 'Whosoever shall put away his wife, let him give her a writing of divorcement': but I say unto you, That whosoever shall put away his wife, saving for the cause of fornication, causeth her to commit adultery: and whosoever shall marry her that is divorced committeth adul-tery. (5:27–32)

"Again, ye have heard that it hath been said by them of old time, 'Thou

[32] A measuring-tub for meal.
[33] Prosecutable in court. Jesus goes on to say that even anger should be similarly prosecutable, like actual murder.
[34] Blockhead or idiot.   [35] The Sanhedrin, the highest Jewish law court.
[36] On the way to court.
[37] The last penny of the money owed for which one is being sued.

shalt not forswear thyself, but shalt perform unto the Lord thine oaths': but
I say unto you, Swear not at all; neither by heaven; for it is God's throne:
nor by the earth; for it is his footstool: neither by Jerusalem; for it is the city
of the great King. Neither shalt thou swear by thy head,[38] because thou
canst not make one hair white or black. But let your communication be,
'Yea, yea'; 'Nay, nay': for whatsoever is more than these cometh of evil.
(5:33–37)

"Ye have heard that it hath been said, 'An eye for an eye, and a tooth for
a tooth': but I say unto you, That ye resist not evil: but whosoever shall
smite thee on thy right cheek, turn to him the other also. And if any man
will sue thee at the law, and take away thy coat, let him have thy cloak also.
And whosoever shall compel thee to go a mile, go with him twain.[39] Give to
him that asketh thee, and from him that would borrow of thee turn not
thou away. (5:38–42)

"Ye have heard that it hath been said, 'Thou shalt love thy neighbor,
and hate thine enemy.'[40] But I say unto you, Love your enemies, bless them
that curse you, do good to them that hate you, and pray for them which
despitefully use you, and persecute you; that ye may be the children of
your Father which is in heaven: for he maketh his sun to rise on the evil
and on the good, and sendeth rain on the just and on the unjust. For if ye
love them which love you, what reward have ye? do not even the
publicans[41] the same? And if ye salute your brethren only, what do ye more
than others? do not even the publicans so? Be ye therefore perfect, even as
your Father which is in heaven is perfect. (5:43–48)

"Take heed that ye do not your alms before men, to be seen of them:
otherwise ye have no reward of your Father which is in heaven. Therefore
when thou doest thine alms, do not sound a trumpet before thee, as the
hypocrites do in the synagogues and in the streets, that they may have glory
of men. Verily I say unto you, They have their reward. But when thou
doest alms, let not thy left hand know what thy right hand doeth: that thine
alms may be in secret: and thy Father which seeth in secret himself shall
reward thee openly. (6:1–4)

"And when thou prayest, thou shalt not be as the hypocrites are: for
they love to pray standing in the synagogues and in the corners of the
streets, that they may be seen of men. Verily I say unto you, They have
their reward. But thou, when thou prayest, enter into thy closet,[42] and
when thou hast shut thy door, pray to thy Father which is in secret; and thy
Father which seeth in secret shall reward thee openly. But when ye pray,
use not vain repetitions, as the heathen do: for they think that they shall be
heard for their much speaking. Be not ye therefore like unto them: for
your Father knoweth what things ye have need of, before ye ask him. After
this manner therefore pray ye:

---

[38] By one's self.   [39] Two.

[40] The Old Testament enjoins love of one's neighbor but not explicitly hatred of enemies.
That was, however, a popular inference from the former.

[41] Tax collectors, a generally despised group; elsewhere in the Gospels they are usually
mentioned more sympathetically.

[42] Private room. Jesus is not condemning, however, congregational prayer in the temple or
synagogue.

> Our Father which art in heaven,
> Hallowed be thy name.
> Thy kingdom come.
> Thy will be done
>   in earth as it is in heaven.
> Give us this day our daily bread.
> And forgive us our debts,
>   as we forgive our debtors.[43]
> And lead us not into temptation,
>   but deliver us from evil:[44]
> For thine is the kingdom, and the power, and the glory,
>   for ever. Amen.

For if ye forgive men their trespasses, your heavenly Father will also forgive you: but if ye forgive not men their trespasses, neither will your Father forgive your trespasses. (6:5–15)

"Moreover when ye fast, be not, as the hypocrites, of a sad countenance: for they disfigure their faces, that they may appear unto men to fast. Verily I say unto you, They have their reward. But thou, when thou fastest, anoint thine head, and wash thy face;[45] that thou appear not unto men to fast, but unto thy Father which is in secret: and thy Father, which seeth in secret, shall reward thee openly. (6:16–18)

"Lay not up for yourselves treasures upon earth, where moth and rust doth corrupt, and where thieves break through and steal: but lay up for yourselves treasures in heaven, where neither moth nor rust doth corrupt, and where thieves do not break through nor steal: for where your treasure is, there will your heart be also. The light of the body is the eye: if therefore thine eye be single,[46] thy whole body shall be full of light. But if thine eye be evil, thy whole body shall be full of darkness. If therefore the light that is in thee be darkness, how great is that darkness! (6:19–23)

"No man can serve two masters: for either he will hate the one, and love the other; or else he will hold to the one, and despise the other. Ye cannot serve God and mammon.[47] Therefore I say unto you, Take no thought for your life, what ye shall eat, or what ye shall drink; nor yet for your body, what ye shall put on. Is not the life more than meat, and the body than raiment? Behold the fowls of the air: for they sow not, neither do they reap, nor gather into barns; yet your heavenly Father feedeth them. Are ye not much better than they? Which of you by taking thought can add one cubit[48] unto his stature? And why take ye thought for raiment? Consider the lilies of the field, how they grow; they toil not, neither do they spin: and yet I say unto you, That even Solomon in all his glory was not arrayed like one of these. Wherefore, if God so clothe the grass of the field, which today is, and tomorrow is cast into the oven,[49] shall he not much more clothe

---

[43] The words *debts* and *debtors* can be rendered as, respectively, the wrongs we have committed and those that have been committed against us.

[44] In most of the earliest manuscripts, the Lord's Prayer ends here.

[45] Anointing and washing were part of preparing for a banquet.

[46] Healthy, as opposed to the "evil" (diseased) eye.   [47] Material possessions and money.

[48] About 20 inches.   [49] As fuel.

you, O ye of little faith? Therefore take no thought, saying, 'What shall we eat?' or, 'What shall we drink?' or, 'Wherewithal shall we be clothed?' (for after all these things do the Gentiles seek:) for your heavenly Father knoweth that ye have need of all these things. But seek ye first the king-dom of God, and his righteousness; and all these things shall be added unto you. Take therefore no thought for the morrow: for the morrow shall take thought for the things of itself. Sufficient unto the day is the evil thereof.[50] (6:24–34)

"Judge not, that ye be not judged. For with what judgment ye judge, ye shall be judged: and with what measure ye mete, it shall be measured to you again. And why beholdest thou the mote[51] that is in thy brother's eye, but considerest not the beam that is in thine own eye? Or how wilt thou say to thy brother, 'Let me pull out the mote out of thine eye'; and, behold, a beam is in thine own eye? Thou hypocrite, first cast out the beam out of thine own eye; and then shalt thou see clearly to cast out the mote out of thy brother's eye. (7:1–5)

"Give not that which is holy unto the dogs, neither cast ye your pearls before swine, lest they trample them under their feet, and turn again and rend you. (7:6)

"Ask, and it shall be given you; seek, and ye shall find; knock, and it shall be opened unto you: for every one that asketh receiveth; and he that seeketh findeth; and to him that knocketh it shall be opened. Or what man is there of you, whom if his son ask bread, will he give him a stone? Or if he ask a fish, will he give him a serpent? If ye then, being evil, know how to give good gifts unto your children, how much more shall your Father which is in heaven give good things to them that ask him? (7:7–11)

"Therefore all things whatsoever ye would that men should do to you, do ye even so to them: for this is the law and the prophets. (7:12)

"Enter ye in at the strait gate: for wide is the gate, and broad is the way, that leadeth to destruction, and many there be which go in thereat: because strait is the gate, and narrow is the way, which leadeth unto life, and few there be that find it. (7:13–14)

"Beware of false prophets,[52] which come to you in sheep's clothing, but inwardly they are ravening wolves. Ye shall know them by their fruits. Do men gather grapes of thorns, or figs of thistles? Even so every good tree bringeth forth good fruit; but a corrupt tree bringeth forth evil fruit. A good tree cannot bring forth evil fruit, neither can a corrupt tree bring forth good fruit. Every tree that bringeth not forth good fruit is hewn down, and cast into the fire. Wherefore by their fruits ye shall know them. (7:15–20)

"Not every one that saith unto me, 'Lord, Lord,' shall enter into the kingdom of heaven; but he that doeth the will of my Father which is in heaven. Many will say to me in that day, 'Lord, Lord, have we not prophe-sied in thy name? and in thy name have cast out devils? and in thy name

---

[50] Each day has anxieties enough of its own; one need not add to them worries about the future.

[51] A tiny speck of wood, as contrasted with a "beam," or large board.

[52] The caution against false prophets and that in the following passage against those who say "Lord, Lord" are less applicable to Jesus' own time than to the problems the early Church faced a half-century later (when Matthew was written).

done many wonderful works?' And then will I profess unto them, 'I never knew you: depart from me, ye that work iniquity.' (7:21–23)

"Therefore whosoever heareth these sayings of mine, and doeth them, I will liken him unto a wise man, which built his house upon a rock: and the rain descended, and the floods came, and the winds blew, and beat upon that house; and it fell not: for it was founded upon a rock. And every one that heareth these sayings of mine, and doeth them not, shall be likened unto a foolish man, which built his house upon the sand: and the rain descended, and the floods came, and the winds blew, and beat upon that house; and it fell: and great was the fall of it." (7:24–27)

And it came to pass, when Jesus had ended these sayings, the people were astonished at his doctrine: for he taught them as one having authority, and not as the scribes.[53] (7:28–29)

When he was come down from the mountain, great multitudes followed him. And, behold, there came a leper and worshipped him, saying, "Lord, if thou wilt, thou canst make me clean." And Jesus put forth his hand, and touched him, saying, "I will; be thou clean." And immediately his leprosy was cleansed. And Jesus saith unto him, "See thou tell no man; but go thy way, show thyself to the priest, and offer the gift that Moses commanded, for a testimony unto them."[54] (8:1–4)

And when Jesus was entered into Capernaum, there came unto him a centurion,[55] beseeching him, and saying, "Lord, my servant lieth at home sick of the palsy, grievously tormented." And Jesus saith unto him, "I will come and heal him." The centurion answered and said, "Lord, I am not worthy that thou shouldest come under my roof: but speak the word only, and my servant shall be healed. For I am a man under authority, having soldiers under me: and I say to this man, 'Go,' and he goeth; and to another, 'Come,' and he cometh; and to my servant, 'Do this,' and he doeth it." When Jesus heard it, he marvelled, and said to them that followed, "Verily I say unto you, I have not found so great faith, no, not in Israel. And I say unto you, That many shall come from the east and west, and shall sit down with Abraham, and Isaac, and Jacob, in the kingdom of heaven. But the children of the kingdom shall be cast out into outer darkness: there shall be weeping and gnashing of teeth." And Jesus said unto the centurion, "Go thy way; and as thou hast believed, so be it done unto thee." And his servant was healed in the selfsame hour. (8:5–13)

And when Jesus was come into Peter's house, he saw his wife's mother laid, and sick of a fever. And he touched her hand, and the fever left her: and she arose, and ministered unto them. When the even was come, they brought unto him many that were possessed with devils: and he cast out the spirits with his word, and healed all that were sick: that it might be fulfilled which was spoken by Isaiah the prophet, saying, "Himself took our infirmities, and bare our sicknesses."[56] (8:14–17)

Now when Jesus saw great multitudes about him, he gave command-

[53] He did not teach with a cautious conformity to tradition, like the scribes, but rather like the prophets.

[54] Leviticus 14:2–9 describes the elaborate rite to be performed after the cure of leprosy.

[55] A military officer (here probably a Roman, certainly a Gentile) who commanded a hundred men.

[56] Isaiah 53:4.

ment to depart unto the other side.[57] And a certain scribe came, and said unto him, "Master, I will follow thee whithersoever thou goest." And Jesus saith unto him, "The foxes have holes, and the birds of the air have nests; but the Son of man[58] hath not where to lay his head." And another of his disciples said unto him, "Lord, suffer me first to go and bury my father." But Jesus said unto him, "Follow me; and let the dead bury their dead." (8:18–22)

And when he was entered into a ship, his disciples followed him. And, behold, there arose a great tempest in the sea, insomuch that the ship was covered with the waves: but he was asleep. And his disciples came to him, and awoke him, saying, "Lord, save us: we perish." And he saith unto them, "Why are ye fearful, O ye of little faith?" Then he arose, and rebuked the winds and the sea; and there was a great calm. But the men marvelled, saying, "What manner of man is this, that even the winds and the sea obey him!" (8:23–27)

And when he was come to the other side into the country of the Gergesenes, there met him two possessed with devils, coming out of the tombs, exceeding fierce, so that no man might pass by that way. And, behold, they cried out, saying, "What have we to do with thee, Jesus, thou Son of God? art thou come hither to torment us before the time?"[59] And there was a good way off from them an herd of many swine feeding. So the devils besought him, saying, "If thou cast us out, suffer us to go away into the herd of swine."[60] And he said unto them, "Go." And when they were come out, they went into the herd of swine: and, behold, the whole herd of swine ran violently down a steep place into the sea, and perished in the waters. And they that kept them fled, and went their ways into the city, and told every thing, and what was befallen to the possessed of the devils. And, behold, the whole city came out to meet Jesus: and when they saw him, they besought him that he would depart out of their coasts. (8:28–34).

And he entered into a ship, and passed over, and came into his own city.[61] And, behold, they brought to him a man sick of the palsy, lying on a bed: and Jesus seeing their faith said unto the sick of the palsy; "Son, be of good cheer; thy sins be forgiven thee." And, behold, certain of the scribes said within themselves, "This man blasphemeth."[62] And Jesus knowing their thoughts said, "Wherefore think ye evil in your hearts? For whether is easier, to say, 'Thy sins be forgiven thee'; or to say, 'Arise, and walk'? But that ye may know that the Son of man hath power on earth to forgive sins," (then saith he to the sick of the palsy,) "Arise, take up thy bed, and go unto thine house." And he arose, and departed to his house. But when the multitudes saw it, they marvelled, and glorified God, which had given such power unto men. (9:1–8)

[57] The eastern side of the Sea of Galilee.

[58] *Son of man* can mean *individual human person*. It also came, by evolution from its first use in Daniel 7, to designate an apocalyptic figure expected to usher in the kingdom of God.

[59] Before God's final destruction of all evil.

[60] The devils ask that they be allowed one last display of their power. The herd of pigs (unclean animals to the Jews and fit to receive the devils) shows that this is Gentile country.

[61] Capernaum, Jesus' base during his ministry in Galilee.

[62] Because only God could forgive sins. Jesus' initial encouragement of the sick man ("be of good cheer") reflects the Jewish belief that God's forgiveness of sins was a prerequisite for recovery from illness.

And as Jesus passed forth from thence, he saw a man, named Matthew, sitting at the receipt of custom:[63] and he saith unto him, "Follow me." And he arose, and followed him. And it came to pass, as Jesus sat at meat in the house, behold, many publicans and sinners came and sat down with him and his disciples. And when the Pharisees saw it, they said unto his disciples, "Why eateth your Master with publicans and sinners?" But when Jesus heard that, he said unto them, "They that be whole need not a physician, but they that are sick. But go ye and learn what that meaneth, 'I will have mercy, and not sacrifice':[64] for I am not come to call the righteous, but sinners to repentance." (9:9–13)

Then came to him the disciples of John, saying, "Why do we and the Pharisees fast oft, but thy disciples fast not?" And Jesus said unto them, "Can the children of the bridechamber mourn, as long as the bridegroom is with them? but the days will come, when the bridegroom shall be taken from them, and then shall they fast. No man putteth a piece of new cloth unto an old garment, for that which is put in to fill it up taketh from the garment, and the rent is made worse. Neither do men put new wine into old bottles: else the bottles break, and the wine runneth out, and the bottles perish: but they put new wine into new bottles, and both are preserved."[65] (9:14–17)

While he spake these things unto them, behold, there came a certain ruler,[66] and worshipped him, saying, "My daughter is even now dead: but come and lay thy hand upon her, and she shall live." And Jesus arose, and followed him, and so did his disciples. (9:18–19)

And, behold, a woman, which was diseased with an issue of blood[67] twelve years, came behind him, and touched the hem of his garment: for she said within herself, "If I may but touch his garment, I shall be whole." But Jesus turned him about, and when he saw her, he said, "Daughter, be of good comfort; thy faith hath made thee whole." And the woman was made whole from that hour. And when Jesus came into the ruler's house, and saw the minstrels[68] and the people making a noise, he said unto them, "Give place: for the maid is not dead, but sleepeth." And they laughed him to scorn. But when the people were put forth, he went in, and took her by the hand, and the maid arose. And the fame hereof went abroad into all that land. (9:20–26)

And when Jesus departed thence, two blind men followed him, crying, and saying, "Thou son of David, have mercy on us." And when he was come into the house, the blind men came to him: and Jesus saith unto them, "Believe ye that I am able to do this?" They said unto him, "Yea, Lord." Then touched he their eyes, saying, "According to your faith be it unto you." And their eyes were opened; and Jesus straitly charged them,

---

[63] Customhouse; the disciple Matthew, a publican, would naturally be found there. He apparently goes on to invite Jesus to a dinner. Publicans were hated because they often used extortion in collecting the taxes.

[64] Hosea 6:6.

[65] The analogies from clothing and wine bottles (more exactly, wineskins) apparently serve to contrast the old Law with Jesus' teaching. But, significantly in Matthew, although Jesus' teaching is radically new, both the new and old wine, or doctrine, "are preserved."

[66] Identified in other Gospels as a synagogue official. [67] Hemorrhage.

[68] The musicians and the other people are professional mourners.

saying, "See that no man know it."[69] But they, when they were departed, spread abroad his fame in all that country. (9:27–31)

As they went out, behold, they brought to him a dumb man possessed with a devil. And when the devil was cast out, the dumb spake: and the multitudes marvelled, saying, "It was never so seen in Israel." But the Pharisees said, "He casteth out devils through the prince of the devils." (9:32–34)

And Jesus went about all the cities and villages, teaching in their synagogues, and preaching the gospel of the kingdom, and healing every sickness and every disease among the people. But when he saw the multitudes, he was moved with compassion on them, because they fainted, and were scattered abroad, as sheep having no shepherd. Then saith he unto his disciples, "The harvest truly is plenteous, but the laborers are few; pray ye therefore the Lord of the harvest, that he will send forth laborers into his harvest." (9:35–38)

And when he had called unto him his twelve disciples,[70] he gave them power against unclean spirits, to cast them out, and to heal all manner of sickness and all manner of disease. Now the names of the twelve apostles[71] are these; The first, Simon, who is called Peter, and Andrew his brother; James the son of Zebedee, and John his brother; Philip, and Bartholomew; Thomas, and Matthew the publican; James the son of Alpheus, and Lebbeus, whose surname was Thaddeus, Simon the Canaanite, and Judas Iscariot, who also betrayed him. These twelve Jesus sent forth, and commanded them, saying,

"Go not into the way of the Gentiles, and into any city of the Samaritans enter ye not:[72] but go rather to the lost sheep of the house of Israel. And as ye go, preach, saying, 'The kingdom of heaven is at hand.' Heal the sick, cleanse the lepers, raise the dead, cast out devils: freely ye have received, freely give. Provide neither gold, nor silver, nor brass in your purses, nor scrip[73] for your journey, neither two coats, neither shoes, nor yet staves: for the workman is worthy of his meat. And into whatsoever city or town ye shall enter, enquire who in it is worthy; and there abide till ye go thence. And when ye come into an house, salute it. And if the house be worthy, let your peace come upon it: but if it be not worthy, let your peace return to you. And whosoever shall not receive you, nor hear your words, when ye depart out of that house or city, shake off the dust of your feet. Verily I say unto you, It shall be more tolerable for the land of Sodom and Gomorrah[74] in the day of judgment, than for that city. (10:1–15)

---

[69] An allusion to the "Messianic secret"; according to some scholars, the early Church inserted in the Gospels such injunctions of secrecy (rare in Matthew) in order to explain the fact that Jesus was not recognized as Messiah until after his resurrection.

[70] The number twelve parallels the twelve sons of Jacob and tribes of the Jews.

[71] The word means those "sent out"; it is not used elsewhere in Matthew.

[72] The command not to proselytize the Gentiles is puzzling in light of the emphasis elsewhere in Matthew (see the conclusion, for example) on the Christian mission to them; perhaps the passage reflects the early Church's awareness that this mission belonged to a later stage. *Samaritans* were inhabitants of Samaria, in the mid-northern part of Palestine, south of Galilee and north of Judea; they shared much of the Jewish heritage but had a separate priesthood and did not recognize Jerusalem as the center of worship.

[73] Bag.   [74] Sinful cities destroyed by God with brimstone and fire; see Genesis 19.

"Behold, I send you forth as sheep in the midst of wolves: be ye therefore wise as serpents, and harmless as doves. But beware of men: for they will deliver you up to the councils,[75] and they will scourge you in their synagogues; and ye shall be brought before governors and kings for my sake, for a testimony against[76] them and the Gentiles. But when they deliver you up, take no thought how or what ye shall speak: for it shall be given you in that same hour what ye shall speak. For it is not ye that speak, but the Spirit of your Father which speaketh in you. And the brother shall deliver up the brother to death, and the father the child: and the children shall rise up against their parents, and cause them to be put to death. And ye shall be hated of all men for my name's sake: but he that endureth to the end shall be saved. But when they persecute you in this city, flee ye into another: for verily I say unto you, Ye shall not have gone over the cities of Israel, till the Son of man be come.[77] The disciple is not above his master, nor the servant above his lord. It is enough for the disciple that he be as his master, and the servant as his lord. If they have called the master of the house Beelzebub,[78] how much more shall they call them of his household? Fear them not therefore: for there is nothing covered, that shall not be revealed; and hid, that shall not be known. What I tell you in darkness, that speak ye in light: and what ye hear in the ear, that preach ye upon the housetops. And fear not them which kill the body, but are not able to kill the soul: but rather fear him[79] which is able to destroy both soul and body in hell. Are not two sparrows sold for a farthing? and one of them shall not fall on the ground without your Father. But the very hairs of your head are all numbered. Fear ye not therefore, ye are of more value than many sparrows. Whosoever therefore shall confess me before men, him will I confess also before my Father which is in heaven. But whosoever shall deny me before men, him will I also deny before my Father which is in heaven. (10:16–33)

"Think not that I am come to send peace on earth: I came not to send peace, but a sword. For I am come to set a man at variance against his father, and the daughter against her mother, and the daughter in law against her mother in law. And a man's foes shall be they of his own household. He that loveth father or mother more than me is not worthy of me: and he that loveth son or daughter more than me is not worthy of me. And he that taketh not his cross, and followeth after me, is not worthy of me. He that findeth his life shall lose it: and he that loseth his life for my sake shall find it. (10:34–39)

"He that receiveth you receiveth me, and he that receiveth me receiveth him that sent me. He that receiveth a prophet in the name of[80] a prophet shall receive a prophet's reward; and he that receiveth a righteous man in the name of a righteous man shall receive a righteous man's reward. And whosoever shall give to drink unto one of these little ones[81] a cup of cold

---

[75] Courts.   [76] To testify in the face of.

[77] A puzzling sentence; the apparent meaning, that the Last Judgment will come before the mission is extended to the Gentiles, can hardly be the meaning intended, because when this Gospel was written, half a century after Jesus, such an extension had occurred.

[78] Identified later (12:24) as "the prince of the devils."   [79] That is, fear God.

[80] "In the name of" can be translated as "because he is."   [81] Lowly disciples of Jesus.

water only in the name of a disciple, verily I say unto you, he shall in no wise lose his reward." (10:40–42)

And it came to pass, when Jesus had made an end of commanding his twelve disciples, he departed thence to teach and to preach in their cities.[82] Now when John had heard in the prison[83] the works of Christ, he sent two of his disciples, and said unto him, "Art thou he that should come, or do we look for another?" Jesus answered and said unto them, "Go and show John again those things which ye do hear and see: the blind receive their sight, and the lame walk, the lepers are cleansed, and the deaf hear, the dead are raised up, and the poor have the gospel preached to them. And blessed is he, whosoever shall not be offended in me."[84] (11:1–6)

And as they departed, Jesus began to say unto the multitudes concerning John, "What went ye out into the wilderness to see? A reed shaken with the wind?[85] But what went ye out for to see? A man clothed in soft raiment? behold, they that wear soft clothing are in kings' houses. But what went ye out for to see? A prophet? yea, I say unto you, and more than a prophet. For this is he, of whom it is written,

'Behold, I send my messenger before thy face,
Which shall prepare thy way before thee.'[86]

Verily I say unto you, Among them that are born of women there hath not risen a greater than John the Baptist: notwithstanding he that is least in the kingdom of heaven is greater than he.[87] And from the days of John the Baptist until now the kingdom of heaven suffereth violence, and the violent take it by force.[88] For all the prophets and the law prophesied until John. And if ye will receive it, this is Elijah[89] which was for to come. He that hath ears to hear, let him hear. (11:7–15)

"But whereunto shall I liken this generation? It is like unto children sitting in the markets, and calling unto their fellows, and saying, 'We have piped unto you, and ye have not danced; we have mourned unto you, and ye have not lamented.'[90] For John came neither eating nor drinking, and they say, 'He hath a devil.' The Son of man came eating and drinking, and they say, 'Behold a man gluttonous, and a winebibber, a friend of publicans and sinners.' But wisdom is justified of her children."[91] (11:16–19)

Then began he to upbraid the cities wherein most of his mighty works were done, because they repented not: "Woe unto thee, Chorazin! woe unto thee, Bethsaida! for if the mighty works, which were done in you, had been done in Tyre and Sidon, they would have repented long ago in sackcloth and ashes. But I say unto you, It shall be more tolerable for Tyre and

---

[82] In towns nearby.   [83] For John's imprisonment, see 14:1–12.
[84] Shall not find me an obstacle to faith.
[85] Either a literal bed of reeds or (figuratively) a weak man.   [86] Malachi 3:1.
[87] Possibly because John lived before the new kingdom of heaven Jesus ushers in.
[88] The sentence is obscure; its meaning is conjectural.
[89] According to Jewish legend, the prophet Elijah, who had never died (2 Kings 2:11–12), would reappear just before the world ended.
[90] Jesus says that, like children at play who are out of tune with one another's moods, the Jews are dissatisfied with anything out of the ordinary—John the ascetic or the allegedly loose-living Jesus.
[91] The sentence is obscure; it may mean "Righteousness is vindicated by its results."

Sidon at the day of judgment, than for you. And thou, Capernaum, which art exalted unto heaven, shalt be brought down to hell: for if the mighty works, which have been done in thee, had been done in Sodom, it would have remained until this day. But I say unto you, That it shall be more tolerable for the land of Sodom in the day of judgment, than for thee."[92] (11:20–24)

At that time Jesus answered and said, "I thank thee, O Father, Lord of heaven and earth, because thou hast hid these things from the wise and prudent, and hast revealed them unto babes. Even so, Father: for so it seemed good in thy sight. All things are delivered unto me of my Father: and no man knoweth the Son, but the Father; neither knoweth any man the Father, save the Son, and he to whomsoever the Son will reveal him. (11:25–27)

"Come unto me, all ye that labor and are heavy laden, and I will give you rest. Take my yoke upon you, and learn of me; for I am meek and lowly in heart: and ye shall find rest unto your souls. For my yoke is easy,[93] and my burden is light." (11:28–30)

At that time Jesus went on the sabbath day through the corn; and his disciples were ahungered, and began to pluck the ears of corn, and to eat. But when the Pharisees saw it, they said unto him, "Behold, thy disciples do that which is not lawful to do upon the sabbath day." But he said unto them, "Have ye not read what David did, when he was ahungered, and they that were with him; how he entered into the house of God, and did eat the showbread, which was not lawful for him to eat, neither for them which were with him, but only for the priests?[94] Or have ye not read in the law, how that on the sabbath days the priests in the temple profane the sabbath, and are blameless? But I say unto you, That in this place is one greater than the temple. But if ye had known what this meaneth, 'I will have mercy, and not sacrifice,'[95] ye would not have condemned the guiltless. For the Son of man is Lord even of the sabbath day." (12:1–8)

And when he was departed thence, he went into their synagogue: and, behold, there was a man which had his hand withered. And they asked him, saying, "Is it lawful to heal on the sabbath days?" that they might accuse him. And he said unto them, "What man shall there be among you, that shall have one sheep, and if it fall into a pit on the sabbath day, will he not lay hold on it, and lift it out? How much then is a man better than a sheep? Wherefore it is lawful to do well on the sabbath days." Then saith he to the man, "Stretch forth thine hand." And he stretched it forth; and it was restored whole, like as the other. (12:9–13)

Then the Pharisees went out, and held a council against him, how they

[92] Chorazin, Bethsaida, and Capernaum (Jesus' city) have seen Jesus and his works but have been unresponsive; they are contrasted unfavorably with the Gentile cities Tyre and Sidon (seaports north of Palestine) and the notoriously wicked city of Sodom.

[93] The yoke of the Law construed spiritually is easy compared with a legalistically construed old Law.

[94] The disciples are accused of breaking sabbath rules about preparation of food. Jesus cites the enforced eating of the showbread (used in the Temple ritual; Leviticus 24:5–9), as told in 1 Samuel 21:1–6. He goes on to argue that the priests can without sin perform their Temple duties on the sabbath and that Jesus and his work are even more important than the Temple.

[95] Ritual sacrifice; Jesus is citing Hosea 6:6.

might destroy him. But when Jesus knew it, he withdrew himself from thence: and great multitudes followed him, and he healed them all; and charged them that they should not make him known: that it might be fulfilled which was spoken by Isaiah the prophet, saying,

> "Behold my servant, whom I have chosen;
>   my beloved, in whom my soul is well pleased:
> I will put my spirit upon him,
>   and he shall show judgment to the Gentiles.
> He shall not strive, nor cry;
>   neither shall any man hear his voice in the streets.
> A bruised reed shall he not break,
>   and smoking flax shall he not quench,
> Till he send forth judgment unto victory.
> And in his name shall the Gentiles trust."[96] (12:14–21)

Then was brought unto him one possessed with a devil, blind, and dumb: and he healed him, insomuch that the blind and dumb both spake and saw. And all the people were amazed, and said, "Is not this the son of David?"[97] But when the Pharisees heard it, they said, "This fellow doth not cast out devils, but by Beelzebub the prince of the devils." And Jesus knew their thoughts, and said unto them, "Every kingdom divided against itself is brought to desolation; and every city or house divided against itself shall not stand: and if Satan cast out Satan, he is divided against himself; how shall then his kingdom stand? And if I by Beelzebub cast out devils, by whom do your children[98] cast them out? therefore they shall be your judges. But if I cast out devils by the Spirit of God, then the kingdom of God is come unto you. Or else how can one enter into a strong man's house, and spoil his goods,[99] except he first bind the strong man? and then he will spoil his house. He that is not with me is against me; and he that gathereth not with me scattereth abroad. Wherefore I say unto you, All manner of sin and blasphemy shall be forgiven unto men: but the blasphemy against the Holy Ghost shall not be forgiven unto men. And whosoever speaketh a word against the Son of man, it shall be forgiven him: but whosoever speaketh against the Holy Ghost, it shall not be forgiven him,[1] neither in this world, neither in the world to come. Either make the tree good, and his fruit good; or else make the tree corrupt, and his fruit corrupt: for the tree is known by his fruit. O generation of vipers, how can ye, being evil, speak good things? for out of the abundance of the heart the mouth speaketh. A good man out of the good treasure of the heart bringeth forth good things: and an evil man out of the evil treasure bringeth forth evil things. But I say unto you, That every idle word that men shall speak, they shall give account thereof in the day of judgment. For by thy words thou shalt be justified, and by thy words thou shalt be condemned." (12:22–37)

[96] Isaiah 42:1–4. The parallel is with the reticence just attributed to Jesus.
[97] The Messiah, who would be a descendant of David.   [98] Your own exorcists.
[99] The strong man is Satan; his "goods" are the persons demonically possessed by him.
[1] The nature of the unforgivable sin against the Holy Ghost is elusive; Jesus may mean there is no chance that people will repent (a prerequisite for God's forgiveness) who wilfully disregard the manifest signs of His works (as in the present casting out of devils).

Then certain of the scribes and of the Pharisees answered, saying, "Master, we would see a sign[2] from thee." But he answered and said unto them, "An evil and adulterous[3] generation seeketh after a sign; and there shall no sign be given to it, but the sign of the prophet Jonah: for as Jonah was three days and three nights in the whale's belly; so shall the Son of man be three days and three nights in the heart of the earth.[4] The men of Nineveh[5] shall rise in judgment with this generation, and shall condemn it: because they repented at the preaching of Jonah; and, behold, a greater than Jonah is here. The queen of the south[6] shall rise up in the judgment with this generation, and shall condemn it: for she came from the uttermost parts of the earth to hear the wisdom of Solomon; and, behold, a greater than Solomon is here. (12:38–42)

"When the unclean spirit is gone out of a man, he walketh through dry places, seeking rest, and findeth none. Then he saith, 'I will return into my house from whence I came out'; and when he is come, he findeth it empty, swept, and garnished. Then goeth he, and taketh with himself seven other spirits more wicked than himself, and they enter in and dwell there: and the last state of that man is worse than the first.[7] Even so shall it be also unto this wicked generation." (12:43–45)

While he yet talked to the people, behold, his mother and his brethren stood without, desiring to speak with him.[8] Then one said unto him, "Behold, thy mother and thy brethren stand without, desiring to speak with thee." But he answered and said unto him that told him, "Who is my mother? and who are my brethren?" And he stretched forth his hand toward his disciples, and said, "Behold my mother and my brethren! For whosoever shall do the will of my Father which is in heaven, the same is my brother, and sister, and mother." (12:46–50)

The same day went Jesus out of the house, and sat by the sea side. And great multitudes were gathered together unto him, so that he went into a ship, and sat; and the whole multitude stood on the shore. And he spake many things unto them in parables, saying, "Behold, a sower went forth to sow; and when he sowed, some seeds fell by the way side, and the fowls came and devoured them up: some fell upon stony places, where they had not much earth: and forthwith they sprung up, because they had no deepness of earth: and when the sun was up, they were scorched; and because they had no root, they withered away. And some fell among thorns; and the thorns sprung up, and choked them: but other fell into good ground, and brought forth fruit, some a hundredfold, some sixtyfold, some thirtyfold. Who hath ears to hear, let him hear." (13:1–9)

And the disciples came, and said unto him, "Why speakest thou unto them in parables?" He answered and said unto them, "Because it is given

---

[2] That Jesus is the Messiah.   [3] Unfaithful to God.

[4] In the tomb, before rising from the dead. (This verse is a late addition to the text.)

[5] Though Gentiles, the inhabitants of Nineveh had repented in response to Jonah's preaching (Jonah 3:5).

[6] The Queen of Sheba, who had come from Arabia (1 Kings 10).

[7] Jesus is apparently describing an exorcism only temporarily successful because nothing good has replaced the cast-out evil. In applying this to his addressees, he may mean that although he has overcome evil, the relief will be only temporary for those who reject him.

[8] Some interpreters take the word here translated "brethren" to mean merely "relatives."

unto you to know the mysteries of the kingdom of heaven, but to them it is not given. For whosoever hath, to him shall be given, and he shall have more abundance: but whosoever hath not, from him shall be taken away even that he hath. Therefore speak I to them in parables: because they seeing see not; and hearing they hear not, neither do they understand. And in them is fulfilled the prophecy of Isaiah, which saith,

> 'By hearing ye shall hear, and shall not understand;
>   and seeing ye shall see, and shall not perceive:
> For this people's heart is waxed gross,
>   and their ears are dull of hearing,
>   and their eyes they have closed;
> Lest at any time they should see with their eyes,
>   and hear with their ears,
> And understand with their heart,
>   and should be converted, and I should heal them.'[9]

But blessed are your eyes, for they see: and your ears, for they hear. For verily I say unto you, That many prophets and righteous men have desired to see those things which ye see, and have not seen them; and to hear those things which ye hear, and have not heard them. Hear ye therefore the parable of the sower. When any one heareth the word of the kingdom, and understandeth it not, then cometh the wicked one, and catcheth away that which was sown in his heart. This is he which received seed by the way side. But he that received the seed into stony places, the same is he that heareth the word, and anon with joy receiveth it; yet hath he not root in himself, but dureth for a while: for when tribulation or persecution ariseth because of the word, by and by he is offended.[10] He also that received seed among the thorns is he that heareth the word; and the care of this world, and the deceitfulness of riches, choke the word, and he becometh unfruitful. But he that received seed into the good ground is he that heareth the word, and understandeth it; which also beareth fruit, and bringeth forth, some a hundredfold, some sixty, some thirty." (13:10–23)

Another parable put he forth unto them, saying, "The kingdom of heaven is likened unto a man which sowed good seed in his field: but while men slept, his enemy came and sowed tares[11] among the wheat, and went his way. But when the blade was sprung up, and brought forth fruit, then appeared the tares also. So the servants of the householder came and said unto him, 'Sir, didst not thou sow good seed in thy field? from whence then hath it tares?' He said unto them, 'An enemy hath done this.' The servants said unto him, 'Wilt thou then that we go and gather them up?' But he said, 'Nay; lest while ye gather up the tares, ye root up also the wheat with them. Let both grow together until the harvest: and in the time of harvest I will say to the reapers, Gather ye together first the tares, and bind them in bundles to burn them: but gather the wheat into my barn.'" (13:24–30)

Another parable put he forth unto them, saying, "The kingdom of heaven is like to a grain of mustard seed, which a man took, and sowed in

---

[9] Isaiah 6:9–10.   [10] A modern translation might say "he lapses."
[11] Darnel, a weed resembling wheat and having poisonous seeds.

his field: which indeed is the least of all seeds: but when it is grown, it is the greatest among herbs, and becometh a tree, so that the birds of the air come and lodge in the branches thereof." (13:31–32)

Another parable spake he unto them; "The kingdom of heaven is like unto leaven, which a woman took, and hid in three measures of meal,[12] till the whole was leavened." All these things spake Jesus unto the multitude in parables; and without a parable spake he not unto them: that it might be fulfilled which was spoken by the prophet, saying,

> "I will open my mouth in parables;
> I will utter things which have been kept secret from the
>   foundation of the world."[13] (13:33–35)

Then Jesus sent the multitude away, and went into the house: and his disciples came unto him, saying, "Declare unto us the parable of the tares of the field." He answered and said unto them, "He that soweth the good seed is the Son of man; the field is the world; the good seed are the children of the kingdom; but the tares are the children of the wicked one; the enemy that sowed them is the devil; the harvest is the end of the world; and the reapers are the angels. As therefore the tares are gathered and burned in the fire; so shall it be in the end of this world. The Son of man shall send forth his angels, and they shall gather out of his kingdom all things that offend, and them which do iniquity; and shall cast them into a furnace of fire: there shall be wailing and gnashing of teeth. Then shall the righteous shine forth as the sun in the kingdom of their Father. Who hath ears to hear, let him hear. (13:36–43)

"Again, the kingdom of heaven is like unto treasure hid in a field; the which when a man hath found, he hideth, and for joy thereof goeth and selleth all that he hath, and buyeth that field. (13:44)

"Again, the kingdom of heaven is like unto a merchant man, seeking goodly pearls: who, when he had found one pearl of great price, went and sold all that he had, and bought it. (13:45–46)

"Again, the kingdom of heaven is like unto a net, that was cast into the sea, and gathered of every kind: which, when it was full, they drew to shore, and sat down, and gathered the good into vessels, but cast the bad away. So shall it be at the end of the world: the angels shall come forth, and sever the wicked from among the just, and shall cast them into the furnace of fire: there shall be wailing and gnashing of teeth." (13:47–50)

Jesus saith unto them, "Have ye understood all these things?" They say unto him, "Yea, Lord." Then said he unto them, "Therefore every scribe which is instructed unto the kingdom of heaven is like unto a man that is an householder, which bringeth forth out of his treasure things new and old."[14] (13:51–52)

And it came to pass, that when Jesus had finished these parables, he departed thence. And when he was come into his own country, he taught them in their synagogue, insomuch that they were astonished, and said,

---

[12] A large amount of dough.   [13] Psalm 78:2.

[14] The sentence probably means that a scribe, expert in the Old Testament law, who is also instructed in Jesus' new doctrine, can and should combine both.

"Whence hath this man this wisdom, and these mighty works? Is not this the carpenter's son? is not his mother called Mary? and his brethren, James, and Joses, and Simon, and Judas? And his sisters, are they not all with us? Whence then hath this man all these things?" And they were offended in him. But Jesus said unto them, "A prophet is not without honor, save in his own country, and in his own house." And he did not many mighty works there because of their unbelief. (13:53–58)

At that time Herod the tetrarch[15] heard of the fame of Jesus, and said unto his servants, "This is John the Baptist; he is risen from the dead; and therefore mighty works do show forth themselves in him." For Herod had laid hold on John, and bound him, and put him in prison for Herodias' sake, his brother Philip's wife.[16] For John said unto him, "It is not lawful for thee to have her." And when he would have put him to death, he feared the multitude, because they counted him as a prophet. But when Herod's birthday was kept, the daughter of Herodias danced before them, and pleased Herod. Whereupon he promised with an oath to give her whatsoever she would ask. And she, being before instructed of her mother, said, "Give me here John Baptist's head in a charger."[17] And the king was sorry: nevertheless for the oath's sake, and them which sat with him at meat, he commanded it to be given her. And he sent, and beheaded John in the prison. And his head was brought in a charger, and given to the damsel: and she brought it to her mother. And his disciples came, and took up the body, and buried it, and went and told Jesus. (14:1–12)

When Jesus heard of it, he departed thence by ship into a desert place apart: and when the people had heard thereof, they followed him on foot out of the cities. And Jesus went forth, and saw a great multitude, and was moved with compassion toward them, and he healed their sick. And when it was evening, his disciples came to him, saying, "This is a desert place, and the time is now past; send the multitude away, that they may go into the villages, and buy themselves victuals." But Jesus said unto them, "They need not depart: give ye them to eat." And they say unto him, "We have here but five loaves, and two fishes." He said, "Bring them hither to me." And he commanded the multitude to sit down on the grass, and took the five loaves, and the two fishes, and looking up to heaven, he blessed, and brake, and gave the loaves to his disciples, and the disciples to the multitude. And they did all eat, and were filled: and they took up of the fragments that remained twelve baskets full. And they that had eaten were about five thousand men, beside women and children. (14:13–21)

And straightway Jesus constrained his disciples to get into a ship, and to go before him unto the other side, while he sent the multitudes away. And when he had sent the multitudes away, he went up into a mountain apart to pray: and when the evening was come, he was there alone. But the ship was now in the midst of the sea, tossed with waves: for the wind was contrary. And in the fourth watch[18] of the night Jesus went unto them, walking on the sea. And when the disciples saw him walking on the sea, they were

---

[15] Herod Antipas, son of the Herod who sought the death of Jesus in chapter 2; he became tetrarch (prince) of Galilee after his father's death.

[16] According to the first-century Jewish historian Josephus, Herod had an adulterous relationship with Herodias. Her daughter, Josephus tells us, was named Salome.

[17] Platter.　　　[18] About 3 A.M.

troubled, saying, "It is a spirit"; and they cried out for fear. But straightway Jesus spake unto them, saying, "Be of good cheer; it is I; be not afraid." And Peter answered him and said, "Lord, if it be thou, bid me come unto thee on the water." And he said, "Come." And when Peter was come down out of the ship, he walked on the water, to go to Jesus. But when he saw the wind boisterous, he was afraid; and beginning to sink, he cried, saying, "Lord, save me." And immediately Jesus stretched forth his hand, and caught him, and said unto him, "O thou of little faith, wherefore didst thou doubt?" And when they were come into the ship, the wind ceased. Then they that were in the ship came and worshipped him, saying, "Of a truth thou art the Son of God." (14:22–33)

And when they were gone over, they came into the land of Gennesaret.[19] And when the men of that place had knowledge of him, they sent out into all that country round about, and brought unto him all that were diseased; and besought him that they might only touch the hem of his garment: and as many as touched were made perfectly whole. (14:34–36)

Then came to Jesus scribes and Pharisees, which were of Jerusalem, saying, "Why do thy disciples transgress the tradition of the elders? for they wash not their hands[20] when they eat bread." But he answered and said unto them, "Why do ye also transgress the commandment of God by your tradition? For God commanded, saying, 'Honor thy father and mother': and, 'He that curseth father or mother, let him die the death.' But ye say, 'Whosoever shall say to his father or his mother, "It is a gift, by whatsoever thou mightest be profited by me"; and honor not his father or his mother, he shall be free.'[21] "Thus have ye made the commandment of God of none effect by your tradition. Ye hypocrites, well did Isaiah prophesy of you, saying,

'This people draweth nigh unto me with their mouth,
And honoreth me with their lips;
But their heart is far from me.
But in vain they do worship me,
Teaching for doctrines the commandments of men.'"[22]

And he called the multitude, and said unto them, "Hear, and understand: not that which goeth into the mouth defileth a man;[23] but that which cometh out of the mouth, this defileth a man." Then came his disciples, and said unto him, "Knowest thou that the Pharisees were offended, after they heard this saying?" But he answered and said, "Every plant, which my heavenly Father hath not planted, shall be rooted up. Let them alone: they be blind leaders of the blind. And if the blind lead the blind, both shall fall into the ditch." Then answered Peter and said unto him, "Declare unto us this parable." And Jesus said, "Are ye also yet without understanding? Do not ye yet understand, that whatsoever entereth in at the mouth goeth into

---

[19] Northwest of the Sea of Galilee.

[20] And thus violate religious ritual as ordained by tradition.

[21] By a legalism, a son could exempt himself from the duty to support his parents by uttering an oath reserving his goods to the Temple.

[22] Isaiah 29:13.

[23] Jesus apparently is questioning the prohibition of unclean foods (the issue of the observance of dietary laws was a vexed one in the early Church).

the belly, and is cast out into the draught?[24] But those things which proceed out of the mouth come forth from the heart; and they defile the man. For out of the heart proceed evil thoughts, murders, adulteries, fornications, thefts, false witness, blasphemies: these are the things which defile a man: but to eat with unwashen hands defileth not a man." (15:1–20)

Then Jesus went thence, and departed into the coasts of Tyre and Sidon. And, behold, a woman of Canaan[25] came out of the same coasts, and cried unto him, saying, "Have mercy on me, O Lord, thou son of David; my daughter is grievously vexed with a devil." But he answered her not a word. And his disciples came and besought him, saying, "Send her away;[26] for she crieth after us." But he answered and said, "I am not sent but unto the lost sheep of the house of Israel." Then came she and worshipped him, saying, "Lord, help me." But he answered and said, "It is not meet to take the children's bread, and to cast it to dogs." And she said, "Truth, Lord: yet the dogs eat of the crumbs which fall from their masters' table." Then Jesus answered and said unto her, "O woman, great is thy faith: be it unto thee even as thou wilt." And her daughter was made whole from that very hour. (15:21–28)

And Jesus departed from thence, and came nigh unto the sea of Galilee; and went up into a mountain, and sat down there. And great multitudes came unto him, having with them those that were lame, blind, dumb, maimed, and many others, and cast them down at Jesus' feet; and he healed them: insomuch that the multitude wondered, when they saw the dumb to speak, the maimed to be whole, the lame to walk, and the blind to see: and they glorified the God of Israel. (15:29–31)

Then Jesus called his disciples unto him, and said, "I have compassion on the multitude, because they continue with me now three days, and have nothing to eat: and I will not send them away fasting, lest they faint in the way." And his disciples say unto him, "Whence should we have so much bread in the wilderness, as to fill so great a multitude?" And Jesus saith unto them, "How many loaves have ye?" And they said, "Seven, and a few little fishes." And he commanded the multitude to sit down on the ground. And he took the seven loaves and the fishes, and gave thanks, and brake them, and gave to his disciples, and the disciples to the multitude. And they did all eat, and were filled: and they took up of the broken meat that was left seven baskets full. And they that did eat were four thousand men, beside women and children.[27] (15:32–38)

And he sent away the multitude, and took ship, and came into the coasts of Magdala.[28] The Pharisees also with the Sadducees came, and tempting desired him that he would show them a sign from heaven. He answered and said unto them, "When it is evening, ye say, 'It will be fair weather: for the sky is red.' And in the morning, 'It will be foul weather today: for the

[24] Drain; privy.

[25] The woman is a Phoenician Gentile; in the Old Testament the name *Canaanite* refers to the original inhabitants of Palestine, who were considered sinful by the Jews.

[26] Give her what she wants and get rid of her.

[27] The near-repetition of the earlier episode (14:14–21, where the number of men is 5,000 rather than 4,000), which occurs also in Matthew's source in the Gospel of St. Mark, is a puzzle.

[28] On the west shore of the Sea of Galilee.

sky is red and lowering.' O ye hypocrites, ye can discern the face of the sky; but can ye not discern the signs of the times? A wicked and adulterous generation seeketh after a sign; and there shall no sign be given unto it, but the sign of the prophet Jonah."[29] And he left them, and departed. (15:39–16:4)

And when his disciples were come to the other side, they had forgotten to take bread. Then Jesus said unto them, "Take heed and beware of the leaven of the Pharisees and of the Sadducees." And they reasoned among themselves, saying, "It is because we have taken no bread."[30] Which when Jesus perceived, he said unto them, "O ye of little faith, why reason ye among yourselves, because ye have brought no bread? Do ye not yet understand, neither remember the five loaves of the five thousand, and how many baskets ye took up? neither the seven loaves of the four thousand, and how many baskets ye took up? How is it that ye do not understand that I spake it not to you concerning bread, that ye should beware of the leaven of the Pharisees and of the Sadducees?" Then understood they how that he bade them not beware of the leaven of bread, but of the doctrine of the Pharisees and of the Sadducees. (16:5–12)

When Jesus came into the coasts of Caesarea Philippi,[31] he asked his disciples, saying, "Whom do men say that I the Son of man am?" And they said, "Some say that thou art John the Baptist: some, Elijah; and others, Jeremiah, or one of the prophets."[32] He saith unto them, "But whom say ye that I am?" And Simon Peter answered and said, "Thou art the Christ, the Son of the living God." And Jesus answered and said unto him, "Blessed art thou, Simon Bar-jona:[33] for flesh and blood hath not revealed it unto thee, but my Father which is in heaven. And I say also unto thee, That thou art Peter, and upon this rock I will build my church; and the gates of hell shall not prevail against it.[34] And I will give unto thee the keys of the kingdom of heaven: and whatsoever thou shalt bind on earth shall be bound in heaven: and whatsoever thou shalt loose on earth shall be loosed in heaven." Then charged he his disciples that they should tell no man that he was Jesus the Christ. (16:13–20)

From that time forth began Jesus to show unto his disciples, how that he must go unto Jerusalem, and suffer many things of the elders and chief priests and scribes, and be killed, and be raised again the third day.[35] Then Peter took him, and began to rebuke him, saying, "Be it far from thee, Lord: this shall not be unto thee." But he turned, and said unto Peter, "Get

[29] See Matthew 12:38–40.

[30] The disciples think they are being charged with forgetfulness.

[31] A town about twenty miles north of the Sea of Galilee.

[32] The beliefs include the possibility that Jesus may be John reincarnate. For Elijah's significance as an apocalyptic precursor, see 11:14 and note. Jeremiah (seventh to sixth centuries B.C.) was one of the greatest of the Old Testament prophets.

[33] Son of Jonah.

[34] *Peter* is from the Greek word meaning *rock*. The phrase *gates of hell* is construed by modern translators as *power of death*. The present passage is one of the most interesting and controversial in the New Testament because of its implications about the nature and origin of the early Church and more particularly because some Roman Catholics believe it supports the primacy of papal authority.

[35] The revelation that the Messiah must suffer rather than reign triumphantly on earth comes as a shock, as Peter's reaction indicates.

thee behind me, Satan: thou art an offense[36] unto me: for thou savorest not the things that be of God, but those that be of men." Then said Jesus unto his disciples, "If any man will come after me, let him deny himself, and take up his cross, and follow me. For whosoever will save his life shall lose it: and whosoever will lose his life for my sake shall find it. For what is a man profited, if he shall gain the whole world, and lose his own soul? or what shall a man give in exchange for his soul? For the Son of man shall come in the glory of his Father with his angels; and then he shall reward every man according to his works. Verily I say unto you, There be some standing here, which shall not taste of death, till they see the Son of man coming in his kingdom."[37] (16:21–28)

And after six days Jesus taketh Peter, James, and John his brother, and bringeth them up into a high mountain[38] apart, and was transfigured before them: and his face did shine as the sun, and his raiment was white as the light. And, behold, there appeared unto them Moses and Elijah talking with him. Then answered Peter, and said unto Jesus, "Lord, it is good for us to be here: if thou wilt, let us make here three tabernacles;[39] one for thee, and one for Moses, and one for Elijah." While he yet spake, behold, a bright cloud overshadowed them: and behold a voice out of the cloud, which said, "This is my beloved Son, in whom I am well pleased; hear ye him." And when the disciples heard it, they fell on their face, and were sore afraid. And Jesus came and touched them, and said, "Arise, and be not afraid." And when they had lifted up their eyes, they saw no man, save Jesus only. (17:1–8)

And as they came down from the mountain, Jesus charged them, saying, "Tell the vision to no man, until the Son of man be risen again from the dead." And his disciples asked him, saying, "Why then say the scribes that Elijah must first come?" And Jesus answered and said unto them, "Elijah truly shall first come, and restore all things. But I say unto you, That Elijah is come already, and they knew him not, but have done unto him whatsoever they listed. Likewise shall also the Son of man suffer of them." Then the disciples understood that he spake unto them of John the Baptist. (17:9–13)

And when they were come to the multitude, there came to him a certain man, kneeling down to him, and saying, "Lord, have mercy on my son: for he is lunatic, and sore vexed: for ofttimes he falleth into the fire, and oft into the water. And I brought him to thy disciples, and they could not cure him." Then Jesus answered and said, "O faithless and perverse generation, how long shall I be with you? how long shall I suffer you? bring him hither to me." And Jesus rebuked the devil; and he departed out of him: and the

[36] An obstacle.

[37] This verse, like 10:23, is hard to construe. It seems to record an unfulfilled prophecy, and a gospel written a half century after Jesus would probably not have preserved so blatant a contradiction of fact. The reference here may be to something other than the triumphant return at the Last Judgment.

[38] The scene is symbolic, recalling the revelation by God on Mount Sinai, which is echoed in several details in the ensuing episode here (the Transfiguration). Moses and Elijah represent "the Law and the Prophets," in short, the total message of the Old Testament.

[39] Tents used as sanctuaries. The best-known tabernacle was that in which the Israelites carried the Ark of the Covenant during the Exodus.

child was cured from that very hour. Then came the disciples to Jesus apart, and said, "Why could not we cast him out?" And Jesus said unto them, "Because of your unbelief: for verily I say unto you, If ye have faith as a grain of mustard seed, ye shall say unto this mountain, 'Remove hence to yonder place'; and it shall remove; and nothing shall be impossible unto you. Howbeit this kind goeth not out but by prayer and fasting."[40] (17:14–21)

And while they abode in Galilee, Jesus said unto them, "The Son of man shall be betrayed into the hands of men: and they shall kill him, and the third day he shall be raised again." And they were exceeding sorry. (17:22–23)

And when they were come to Capernaum, they that received tribute money[41] came to Peter, and said, "Doth not your master pay tribute?" He saith, "Yes." And when he was come into the house, Jesus prevented[42] him, saying, "What thinkest thou, Simon? of whom do the kings of the earth take custom or tribute? of their own children, or of strangers?" Peter saith unto him, "Of strangers." Jesus saith unto him, "Then are the children free.[43] Notwithstanding, lest we should offend them, go thou to the sea, and cast an hook, and take up the fish that first cometh up; and when thou hast opened his mouth, thou shalt find a piece of money: that take, and give unto them for me and thee." (17:24–27)

At the same time came the disciples unto Jesus, saying, "Who is the greatest in the kingdom of heaven?" And Jesus called a little child unto him, and set him in the midst of them, and said, "Verily I say unto you, Except ye be converted, and become as little children, ye shall not enter into the kingdom of heaven. Whosoever therefore shall humble himself as this little child, the same is greatest in the kingdom of heaven. And whoso shall receive one such little child in my name receiveth me. But whoso shall offend[44] one of these little ones which believe in me, it were better for him that a millstone were hanged about his neck, and that he were drowned in the depth of the sea. Woe unto the world because of offenses! for it must needs be that offenses come; but woe to that man by whom the offense cometh! Wherefore if thy hand or thy foot offend thee, cut them off, and cast them from thee: it is better for thee to enter into life halt or maimed, rather than having two hands or two feet to be cast into everlasting fire. And if thine eye offend thee, pluck it out, and cast it from thee: it is better for thee to enter into life with one eye, rather than having two eyes to be cast into hell fire. (18:1–9)

"Take heed that ye despise not one of these little ones; for I say unto you, That in heaven their angels do always behold the face of my Father which is in heaven. For the Son of man is come to save that which was lost.

---

[40] This sentence is omitted in some of the sources.

[41] A tax paid by Jews to defray the expenses of the Temple.

[42] Anticipated; spoke first to.

[43] Exempt. Supreme rulers (the Romans, for example) taxed aliens, not their own citizens; by analogy, Jesus argues, Jews ought not to be legally bound to pay a tax to support their own Temple. Here, however, it is implied, he goes on to pay the tax.

[44] Be a stumbling block. The term *little ones* here probably means simple, unsophisticated believers, not children. Much of the present discourse is more relevant to the experience and organization of the early Church than to the time of the Gospel story.

How think ye? if a man have an hundred sheep, and one of them be gone astray, doth he not leave the ninety and nine, and goeth into the mountains, and seeketh that which is gone astray? And if so be that he find it, verily I say unto you, he rejoiceth more of that sheep, than of the ninety and nine which went not astray. Even so it is not the will of your Father which is in heaven, that one of these little ones should perish. (18:10–14)

"Moreover if thy brother shall trespass against thee, go and tell him his fault between thee and him alone: if he shall hear thee, thou hast gained thy brother. But if he will not hear thee, then take with thee one or two more, that in the mouth of two or three witnesses every word may be established. And if he shall neglect to hear them, tell it unto the church: but if he neglect to hear the church, let him be unto thee as a heathen man and a publican. Verily I say unto you, Whatsoever ye shall bind on earth shall be bound in heaven: and whatsoever ye shall loose on earth shall be loosed in heaven. Again I say unto you, That if two of you shall agree on earth as touching any thing that they shall ask, it shall be done for them of my Father which is in heaven. For where two or three are gathered together in my name, there am I in the midst of them." (18:15–20)

Then came Peter to him, and said, "Lord, how oft shall my brother sin against me, and I forgive him? till seven times?" Jesus saith unto him, "I say not unto thee, Until seven times: but, Until seventy times seven. Therefore is the kingdom of heaven likened unto a certain king, which would take account of his servants. And when he had begun to reckon, one was brought unto him, which owed him ten thousand talents.[45] But forasmuch as he had not to pay, his lord commanded him to be sold, and his wife, and children, and all that he had, and payment to be made. The servant therefore fell down, and worshipped him, saying, 'Lord, have patience with me, and I will pay thee all.' Then the lord of that servant was moved with compassion, and loosed him, and forgave him the debt. But the same servant went out, and found one of his fellowservants, which owed him a hundred pence: and he laid hands on him, and took him by the throat, saying, 'Pay me that thou owest.' And his fellowservant fell down at his feet, and besought him, saying, 'Have patience with me, and I will pay thee all.' And he would not: but went and cast him into prison, till he should pay the debt. So when his fellowservants saw what was done, they were very sorry, and came and told unto their lord all that was done. Then his lord, after that he had called him, said unto him, 'O thou wicked servant, I forgave thee all that debt, because thou desiredst me: shouldest not thou also have had compassion on thy fellowservant, even as I had pity on thee?' And his lord was wroth, and delivered him to the tormentors,[46] till he should pay all that was due unto him. So likewise shall my heavenly Father do also unto you, if ye from your hearts forgive not every one his brother their trespasses." (18:21–35)

And it came to pass, that when Jesus had finished these sayings, he

[45] A talent was a unit of weight and money. Ten thousand talents would be not just a large but an almost astronomical sum, in contrast to a hundred pence, a rather modest sum.

[46] The "lord" in the parable is best imagined as a kind of exotic oriental ruler; torture was not a feature of Palestinian culture in Jesus' time.

departed from Galilee,[47] and came into the coasts of Judea beyond Jordan; and great multitudes followed him; and he healed them there. (19:1–2)

The Pharisees also came unto him, tempting him, and saying unto him, "Is it lawful for a man to put away his wife for every cause?" And he answered and said unto them, "Have ye not read, that he which made them at the beginning made them male and female, and said, 'For this cause shall a man leave father and mother, and shall cleave to his wife: and they twain shall be one flesh?'[48] Wherefore they are no more twain, but one flesh. What therefore God hath joined together, let not man put asunder." They say unto him, "Why did Moses then command to give a writing of divorcement, and to put her away?"[49] He saith unto them, "Moses because of the hardness of your hearts suffered you to put away your wives: but from the beginning it was not so. And I say unto you, Whosoever shall put away his wife, except it be for fornication, and shall marry another, committeth adultery: and whoso marrieth her which is put away doth commit adultery." His disciples say unto him, "If the case of the man be so with his wife, it is not good to marry." But he said unto them, "All men cannot receive this saying,[50] save they to whom it is given. For there are some eunuchs, which were so born from their mother's womb: and there are some eunuchs, which were made eunuchs of men: and there be eunuchs, which have made themselves eunuchs for the kingdom of heaven's sake. He that is able to receive it, let him receive it." (19:3–12)

Then were there brought unto him little children, that he should put his hands on them, and pray: and the disciples rebuked them. But Jesus said, "Suffer little children, and forbid them not, to come unto me: for of such is the kingdom of heaven." And he laid his hands on them, and departed thence. (19:13–15)

And, behold, one came and said unto him, "Good Master, what good thing shall I do, that I may have eternal life?" And he said unto him, "Why callest thou me good? there is none good but one, that is, God: but if thou wilt enter into life, keep the commandments." He saith unto him, "Which?" Jesus said, "Thou shalt do no murder, Thou shalt not commit adultery, Thou shalt not steal, Thou shalt not bear false witness, Honor thy father and thy mother: and, Thou shalt love thy neighbor as thyself." The young man saith unto him, "All these things have I kept from my youth up: what lack I yet?" Jesus said unto him, "If thou wilt be perfect, go and sell that thou hast, and give to the poor, and thou shalt have treasure in heaven: and come and follow me." But when the young man heard that saying, he went away sorrowful: for he had great possessions. (19:16–22)

Then said Jesus unto his disciples, "Verily I say unto you, That a rich

---

[47] Jesus begins his journey to Jerusalem, where he will spend the climactic last week of his life.

[48] Genesis 2:24.

[49] Deuteronomy (a book traditionally ascribed to Moses) 24:1–4. The interpretation of this passage was a controversial topic in Jesus' time.

[50] The reference is apparently to the disciples' stated inference that under such restrictions it is better not to marry, but the Greek text is ambiguous. In any event, Jesus' following statement that marriage should sometimes be renounced for the sake of holiness is radically opposed to Jewish doctrine about the duty to procreate.

man shall hardly enter into the kingdom of heaven. And again I say unto
you, It is easier for a camel to go through the eye of a needle, than for a
rich man to enter into the kingdom of God." When his disciples heard it,
they were exceedingly amazed,[51] saying, "Who then can be saved?" But
Jesus beheld them, and said unto them, "With men this is impossible; but
with God all things are possible."[52] (19:23–26)

Then answered Peter and said unto him, "Behold, we have forsaken all,
and followed thee; what shall we have therefore?" And Jesus said unto
them, "Verily I say unto you, That ye which have followed me, in the
regeneration when the Son of man shall sit in the throne of his glory, ye
also shall sit upon twelve thrones, judging the twelve tribes of Israel. And
every one that hath forsaken houses, or brethren, or sisters, or father, or
mother, or wife, or children, or lands, for my name's sake, shall receive a
hundredfold, and shall inherit everlasting life. But many that are first shall
be last; and the last shall be first. For the kingdom of heaven is like unto a
man that is a householder, which went out early in the morning to hire
laborers into his vineyard. And when he had agreed with the laborers for
a penny a day, he sent them into his vineyard. And he went out about
the third hour,[53] and saw others standing idle in the marketplace, and said
unto them; 'Go ye also into the vineyard, and whatsoever is right I will give
you.' And they went their way. Again he went out about the sixth and ninth
hour, and did likewise. And about the eleventh hour he went out, and
found others standing idle, and saith unto them, 'Why stand ye here all the
day idle?' They say unto him, 'Because no man hath hired us.' He saith
unto them, 'Go ye also into the vineyard; and whatsoever is right, that shall
ye receive.' So when even was come, the lord of the vineyard saith unto his
steward, 'Call the laborers, and give them their hire, beginning from the
last unto the first.' And when they came that were hired about the eleventh
hour, they received every man a penny. But when the first came, they
supposed that they should have received more; and they likewise received
every man a penny. And when they had received it, they murmured
against the goodman of the house, saying, 'These last have wrought but
one hour, and thou hast made them equal unto us, which have borne the
burden and heat of the day.' But he answered one of them, and said,
'Friend, I do thee no wrong: didst not thou agree with me for a penny?
Take that thine is, and go thy way: I will give unto this last, even as unto
thee. Is it not lawful for me to do what I will with mine own? Is thine eye
evil,[54] because I am good?' So the last shall be first, and the first last: for
many be called, but few chosen." (19:27–20:16)

And Jesus going up to Jerusalem took the twelve disciples apart in the
way, and said unto them, "Behold, we go up to Jerusalem; and the Son of
man shall be betrayed unto the chief priests and unto the scribes, and they

---

[51] The amazement probably arises from the general belief that riches were a sign of a man's
holiness.

[52] The meaning perhaps is that God can achieve the near-miracle involved in a man's
renunciation of wealth.

[53] About 9 A.M. The hours are counted from daybreak.

[54] "Are you envious?" This parable as a whole, apart from its implications about God's
mercy, has been construed to apply to Jews versus Gentiles (who come to the truth late) and
also to earlier versus later converted Christians.

shall condemn him to death, and shall deliver him to the Gentiles[55] to mock, and to scourge, and to crucify him: and the third day he shall rise again." (20:17–19)

Then came to him the mother of Zebedee's children[56] with her sons, worshipping him, and desiring a certain thing of him. And he said unto her, "What wilt thou?" She saith unto him, "Grant that these my two sons may sit, the one on thy right hand, and the other on the left, in thy kingdom." But Jesus answered and said, "Ye know not what ye ask. Are ye able to drink of the cup that I shall drink of, and to be baptized with the baptism that I am baptized with?" They say unto him, "We are able." And he saith unto them, "Ye shall drink indeed of my cup, and be baptized with the baptism that I am baptized with: but to sit on my right hand, and on my left, is not mine to give, but it shall be given to them for whom it is prepared of my Father." And when the ten heard it, they were moved with indignation against the two brethren. But Jesus called them unto him, and said, "Ye know that the princes of the Gentiles exercise dominion over them,[57] and they that are great exercise authority upon them. But it shall not be so among you: but whosoever will be great among you, let him be your minister; and whosoever will be chief among you, let him be your servant: even as the Son of man came not to be ministered unto, but to minister, and to give his life a ransom for many." (20:20–28)

And as they departed from Jericho,[58] a great multitude followed him. And, behold, two blind men sitting by the wayside, when they heard that Jesus passed by, cried out, saying, "Have mercy on us, O Lord, thou son of David." And the multitude rebuked them, because they should hold their peace: but they cried the more, saying, "Have mercy on us, O Lord, thou son of David." And Jesus stood still, and called them, and said, "What will ye that I shall do unto you?" They say unto him, "Lord, that our eyes may be opened." So Jesus had compassion on them, and touched their eyes: and immediately their eyes received sight, and they followed him. (20:29–34)

And when they drew nigh unto Jerusalem, and were come to Bethphage, unto the mount of Olives,[59] then sent Jesus two disciples, saying unto them, "Go into the village over against you, and straightway ye shall find an ass tied, and a colt with her: loose them, and bring them unto me. And if any man say ought unto you, ye shall say, 'The Lord hath need of them'; and straightway he will send them." All this was done, that it might be fulfilled which was spoken by the prophet, saying,

> "Tell ye the daughter of Sion,
> Behold, thy King cometh unto thee,
> Meek, and sitting upon an ass,
> And a colt the foal of an ass."[60]

And the disciples went, and did as Jesus commanded them, and brought the ass, and the colt, and put on them their clothes, and they set him

---

[55] Romans.   [56] James and John, two of the twelve disciples.   [57] Over their subjects.

[58] A city near and northeast of Jerusalem, a little west of the river Jordan. The conquest of Jericho under Joshua (Joshua 6) marked the beginning of the Israelites' triumphant occupation of the promised land.

[59] Places on the route from Jericho to Jerusalem.   [60] Zechariah 9:9.

thereon. And a very great multitude spread their garments in the way; others cut down branches from the trees, and strewed them in the way. And the multitudes that went before, and that followed, cried, saying, "Hosanna to the son of David: Blessed is he that cometh in the name of the Lord;[61] Hosanna in the highest." And when he was come into Jerusalem, all the city was moved, saying, "Who is this?" And the multitude said, "This is Jesus the prophet of Nazareth of Galilee." (21:1–11)

And Jesus went into the temple of God, and cast out all them that sold and bought in the temple,[62] and overthrew the tables of the moneychangers, and the seats of them that sold doves, and said unto them, "It is written, 'My house shall be called the house of prayer'; but ye have made it a den of thieves."[63] And the blind and the lame came to him in the temple; and he healed them. And when the chief priests and scribes saw the wonderful things that he did, and the children crying in the temple, and saying, "Hosanna to the son of David"; they were sore displeased, and said unto him, "Hearest thou what these say?" And Jesus saith unto them, "Yea; have ye never read,

> 'Out of the mouth of babes and sucklings
> Thou hast perfected praise'?"[64]

And he left them, and went out of the city into Bethany;[65] and he lodged there. (21:12–17)

Now in the morning as he returned into the city, he hungered. And when he saw a fig tree in the way, he came to it, and found nothing thereon, but leaves only, and said unto it, "Let no fruit grow on thee henceforward for ever." And presently the fig tree withered away. And when the disciples saw it, they marvelled, saying, "How soon is the fig tree withered away!" Jesus answered and said unto them, "Verily I say unto you, If ye have faith, and doubt not, ye shall not only do this which is done to the fig tree, but also if ye shall say unto this mountain, Be thou removed, and be thou cast into the sea; it shall be done. And all things, whatsoever ye shall ask in prayer, believing, ye shall receive." (21:18–22)

And when he was come into the temple, the chief priests and the elders of the people came unto him as he was teaching, and said, "By what authority doest thou these things? and who gave thee this authority?" And Jesus answered and said unto them, "I also will ask you one thing, which if ye tell me, I in like wise will tell you by what authority I do these things. The baptism of John, whence was it? from heaven, or of men?" And they reasoned with themselves, saying, "If we shall say, 'From heaven'; he will say unto us, 'Why did ye not then believe him?' But if we shall say, 'Of men'; we fear the people; for all hold John as a prophet." And they answered Jesus,

---

[61] Psalm 118:26.   [62] In an outer court of the Temple.

[63] Isaiah 56:7; Jeremiah 7:11. Because such commercial activities could not have taken place without the permission of the Temple priests, Jesus' attack is largely directed at them.

[64] Psalm 8:2.

[65] A village two miles from Jerusalem; there Jesus raised Lazarus from the dead (John 11).

and said, "We cannot tell." And he said unto them, "Neither tell I you by what authority I do these things."[66] (21:23–27)

"But what think ye? A certain man had two sons; and he came to the first, and said, 'Son, go work today in my vineyard.' He answered and said, 'I will not': but afterward he repented, and went. And he came to the second, and said likewise. And he answered and said, 'I go, sir': and went not. Whether of them twain did the will of his father?" They say unto him, "The first." Jesus saith unto them, "Verily I say unto you, That the publicans and the harlots go into the kingdom of God before you. For John came unto you in the way of righteousness, and ye believed him not: but the publicans and the harlots believed him: and ye, when ye had seen it, repented not afterward, that ye might believe him. (21:28–32)

"Hear another parable: There was a certain householder, which planted a vineyard, and hedged it round about, and digged a winepress in it, and built a tower, and let it out to husbandmen,[67] and went into a far country: and when the time of the fruit drew near, he sent his servants to the husbandmen, that they might receive the fruits of it. And the husbandmen took his servants, and beat one, and killed another, and stoned another. Again, he sent other servants more than the first: and they did unto them likewise. But last of all he sent unto them his son, saying, 'They will reverence my son.' But when the husbandmen saw the son, they said among themselves, 'This is the heir; come, let us kill him, and let us seize on his inheritance.' And they caught him, and cast him out of the vineyard, and slew him. When the lord therefore of the vineyard cometh, what will he do unto those husbandmen?" They say unto him, "He will miserably destroy those wicked men, and will let out his vineyard unto other husbandmen, which shall render him the fruits in their seasons." Jesus saith unto them, "Did ye never read in the scriptures,

'The stone which the builders rejected,
The same is become the head of the corner:
This is the Lord's doing,
And it is marvellous in our eyes'?[68]

Therefore say I unto you, The kingdom of God shall be taken from you, and given to a nation bringing forth the fruits thereof. And whosoever shall fall on this stone shall be broken: but on whomsoever it shall fall, it will grind him to powder."[69] (21:33–44)

And when the chief priests and Pharisees had heard his parables, they perceived that he spake of them. But when they sought to lay hands on him, they feared the multitude, because they took him for a prophet. (21:45–46)

[66] As a mere interpreter of the Law, Jesus would need the approval of the Jewish authorities, but prophets have direct divine authority. The priests and elders have here confessed their incompetence to judge the basic question as to who are authentic prophets and who are not. Their incompetence, Jesus implies, makes it unnecessary for him to answer their question about authority.
[67] Farmers.   [68] Psalm 118:22–23.
[69] This sentence is absent from some of the manuscripts and translations.

And Jesus answered and spake unto them again by parables, and said, "The kingdom of heaven is like unto a certain king, which made a marriage for his son, and sent forth his servants to call them that were bidden to the wedding: and they would not come. Again, he sent forth other servants, saying, 'Tell them which are bidden, Behold, I have prepared my dinner: my oxen and my fatlings are killed, and all things are ready: come unto the marriage.' But they made light of it, and went their ways, one to his farm, another to his merchandise: and the remnant took his servants, and entreated them spitefully, and slew them. But when the king heard thereof, he was wroth: and he sent forth his armies, and destroyed those murderers, and burned up their city.[70] Then saith he to his servants, 'The wedding is ready, but they which were bidden were not worthy. Go ye therefore into the highways, and as many as ye shall find, bid to the marriage.' So those servants went out into the highways, and gathered together all as many as they found, both bad and good: and the wedding was furnished with guests. And when the king came in to see the guests, he saw there a man which had not on a wedding garment: and he saith unto him, 'Friend, how camest thou in hither not having a wedding garment?'[71] And he was speechless. Then said the king to the servants, 'Bind him hand and foot, and take him away, and cast him into outer darkness; there shall be weeping and gnashing of teeth.' For many are called, but few are chosen." (22:1–14)

Then went the Pharisees, and took counsel how they might entangle him in his talk. And they sent out unto him their disciples with the Herodians,[72] saying, "Master, we know that thou art true, and teachest the way of God in truth, neither carest thou for any man: for thou regardest not the person of men. Tell us therefore, What thinkest thou? Is it lawful to give tribute unto Caesar, or not?" But Jesus perceived their wickedness, and said, "Why tempt ye me, ye hypocrites? Show me the tribute money." And they brought unto him a penny. And he saith unto them, "Whose is this image and superscription?" They say unto him, "Caesar's." Then saith he unto them, "Render therefore unto Caesar the things which are Caesar's; and unto God the things that are God's." When they had heard these words, they marvelled, and left him, and went their way. (22:15–22)

The same day came to him the Sadducees, which say that there is no resurrection,[73] and asked him, saying, "Master, Moses said, 'If a man die, having no children, his brother shall marry his wife, and raise up seed unto his brother.'[74] Now there were with us seven brethren: and the first, when

---

[70] Probably a reference to the Romans' sack of Jerusalem in 70 A.D.

[71] In failing to wear a proper wedding garment the guest is guilty of gross discourtesy. The allegorical significance of the guest is uncertain; perhaps he represents the "bad" who, along with the "good," accept the invitation—a suggestion that the early Church included both kinds.

[72] Followers of Herod and loyalists to Roman rule. The following question about paying taxes is intended to make Jesus liable to prosecution by the Romans if he answers no or else, by answering yes, make him acquiesce in the highly unpopular annual head tax. Jesus avoids the trap, partly by leaving open the question of what is rightfully due to Caesar.

[73] Most Jews of Jesus' time had come to believe in the resurrection of the dead, although the belief had little if any support in the literal text of the Old Testament, which for the Sadducees, unlike the Pharisees, was the sole sanction for doctrine.

[74] Deuteronomy 25:5.

he had married a wife, deceased, and, having no issue, left his wife unto his brother: likewise the second also, and the third, unto the seventh. And last of all the woman died also. Therefore in the resurrection whose wife shall she be of the seven? for they all had her." Jesus answered and said unto them, "Ye do err, not knowing the scriptures, nor the power of God. For in the resurrection they neither marry, nor are given in marriage, but are as the angels of God in heaven. But as touching the resurrection of the dead, have ye not read that which was spoken unto you by God, saying, 'I am the God of Abraham, and the God of Isaac, and the God of Jacob'?[75] God is not the God of the dead, but of the living." And when the multitude heard this, they were astonished at his doctrine. (22:23–33)

But when the Pharisees had heard that he had put the Sadducees to silence, they were gathered together. Then one of them, which was a lawyer, asked him a question, tempting him, and saying, "Master, which is the great commandment in the law?" Jesus said unto him,

"Thou shalt love the Lord thy God with all thy heart, and with all thy soul, and with all thy mind. This is the first and great commandment. And the second is like unto it, Thou shalt love thy neighbor as thyself.[76] On these two commandments hang all the law and the prophets." (22:34–40)

While the Pharisees were gathered together, Jesus asked them, saying, "What think ye of Christ?[77] whose son is he?" They say unto him, "The son of David." He saith unto them, "How then doth David in spirit[78] call him Lord, saying,

> 'The Lord said unto my Lord,
> Sit thou on my right hand,
> Till I make thine enemies thy footstool'?[79]

If David then call him Lord, how is he his son?" And no man was able to answer him a word, neither durst any man from that day forth ask him any more questions. (22:41–46)

Then spake Jesus to the multitude, and to his disciples, saying, "The scribes and the Pharisees sit in Moses' seat: all therefore whatsoever they bid you observe, that observe and do; but do not ye after their works: for they say, and do not. For they bind heavy burdens and grievous to be borne, and lay them on men's shoulders; but they themselves will not move them with one of their fingers. But all their works they do for to be seen of men: they make broad their phylacteries, and enlarge the borders of their garments,[80] and love the uppermost rooms at feasts, and the chief seats in the synagogues, and greetings in the markets, and to be called of men, Rabbi, Rabbi.[81] But be not ye called Rabbi: for one is your Master, even

---

[75] Exodus 3:6.

[76] The two commandments are from Deuteronomy 6:5 and Leviticus 19:18.

[77] Of the Messiah. (*Christ* is not Jesus' personal name.)   [78] Inspired by God.

[79] Psalm 110:1. It was assumed that David was the author of the Psalms and also that the Messiah would be his descendant. The point of Jesus' quoting the passage is not to deny the latter belief but to turn the tables on the Pharisees by showing that despite their supposed expertise they do not know how to construe the passage.

[80] Phylacteries (small boxes attached to the head and wrist and containing copies of important biblical texts) and tassels on the corners of the robe were worn by scriptural injunction.

[81] Aramaic for *Master.*

Christ; and all ye are brethren. And call no man your father upon the earth: for one is your Father, which is in heaven. Neither be ye called masters:[82] for one is your Master, even Christ. But he that is greatest among you shall be your servant. And whosoever shall exalt himself shall be abased; and he that shall humble himself shall be exalted. (23:1–12)

"But woe unto you, scribes and Pharisees, hypocrites! for ye shut up the kingdom of heaven against men: for ye neither go in yourselves, neither suffer ye them that are entering to go in.[83] (23:13)

"Woe unto you, scribes and Pharisees, hypocrites! for ye devour widows' houses, and for a pretense make long prayer: therefore ye shall receive the greater damnation. (23:14)

"Woe unto you, scribes and Pharisees, hypocrites! for ye compass sea and land to make one proselyte, and when he is made, ye make him twofold more the child of hell than yourselves. (23:15)

"Woe unto you, ye blind guides, which say, 'Whosoever shall swear by the temple, it is nothing; but whosoever shall swear by the gold of the temple, he is a debtor'![84] Ye fools and blind: for whether is greater, the gold, or the temple that sanctifieth the gold? And, 'Whosoever shall swear by the altar, it is nothing; but whosoever sweareth by the gift that is upon it, he is guilty.' Ye fools and blind: for whether is greater, the gift, or the altar that sanctifieth the gift? Whoso therefore shall swear by the altar, sweareth by it, and by all things thereon. And whoso shall swear by the temple, sweareth by it, and by him that dwelleth therein. And he that shall swear by heaven, sweareth by the throne of God, and by him that sitteth thereon.[85] (23:16–22)

"Woe unto you, scribes and Pharisees, hypocrites! for ye pay tithe of mint and anise and cummin,[86] and have omitted the weightier matters of the law, judgment,[87] mercy, and faith: these ought ye to have done, and not to leave the other undone. Ye blind guides, which strain at[88] a gnat, and swallow a camel. (23:23–24)

"Woe unto you, scribes and Pharisees, hypocrites! for ye make clean the outside of the cup and of the platter, but within they are full of extortion and excess. Thou blind Pharisee, cleanse first that which is within the cup and platter, that the outside of them may be clean also. (23:25–26)

"Woe unto you, scribes and Pharisees, hypocrites! for ye are like unto whited sepulchers, which indeed appear beautiful outward, but are within full of dead men's bones, and of all uncleanness. Even so ye also outwardly appear righteous unto men, but within ye are full of hypocrisy and iniquity. (23:27–28)

---

[82] Teachers.

[83] Jesus means that the Pharisees refuse to be saved and also prevent others from being saved. Here, and in much of what follows, is reflected the antagonism between Pharisees and Christians at the time this Gospel was written.

[84] Is bound or obligated.

[85] Jesus is attacking teaching that justifies the evasion of the obligation of oaths through legalistic technicalities.

[86] A tithe is a contribution of part of one's goods to the clergy. To pay tithes of substantial goods such as grain would make sense, but the Pharisees, Jesus charges, absurdly extend the principle to such insignificant things as herbs.

[87] Justice.   [88] Strain out of one's drink.

"Woe unto you, scribes and Pharisees, hypocrites! because ye build the tombs of the prophets, and garnish the sepulchers of the righteous, and say, 'If we had been in the days of our fathers, we would not have been partakers with them in the blood of the prophets.' Wherefore ye be witnesses unto yourselves, that ye are the children of them which killed the prophets. Fill ye up then the measure of your fathers.[89] Ye serpents, ye generation of vipers, how can ye escape the damnation of hell? (23:29–33)

"Wherefore, behold, I send unto you prophets, and wise men, and scribes: and some of them ye shall kill and crucify; and some of them shall ye scourge in your synagogues, and persecute them from city to city: that upon you may come all the righteous blood shed upon the earth, from the blood of righteous Abel unto the blood of Zechariah[90] son of Berechiah, whom ye slew between the temple and the altar. Verily I say unto you, All these things shall come upon this generation. (23:34–36)

"O Jerusalem, Jerusalem, thou that killest the prophets, and stonest them which are sent unto thee,[91] how often would I have gathered thy children together, even as a hen gathereth her chickens under her wings, and ye would not! Behold, your house is left unto you desolate.[92] For I say unto you, Ye shall not see me henceforth, till ye shall say, 'Blessed is he that cometh in the name of the Lord.'" (23:37–39)

And Jesus went out, and departed from the temple: and his disciples came to him for to show him the buildings of the temple.[93] And Jesus said unto them, "See ye not all these things? verily I say unto you, There shall not be left here one stone upon another, that shall not be thrown down." (24:1–2)

And as he sat upon the mount of Olives,[94] the disciples came unto him privately, saying, "Tell us, when shall these things be? and what shall be the sign of thy coming, and of the end of the world?" And Jesus answered and said unto them,

"Take heed that no man deceive you. For many shall come in my name, saying, 'I am Christ'; and shall deceive many. And ye shall hear of wars and rumors of wars: see that ye be not troubled: for all these things must come to pass, but the end is not yet. For nation shall rise against nation, and kingdom against kingdom: and there shall be famines, and pestilences, and earthquakes, in divers places. All these are the beginning of sorrows. (24:3–8)

"Then shall they deliver you up to be afflicted, and shall kill you: and ye shall be hated of all nations for my name's sake. And then shall many be offended,[95] and shall betray one another, and shall hate one another. And

---

[89] Finish the job (killing the prophets) of your fathers.

[90] In the Hebrew Bible, Abel was the first victim of murder, Zechariah the last.

[91] Jerusalem was not in fact the place where most of the prophets died. Although the Jews had shown hostility to some of them, the Old Testament does not record many murders of prophets by the Jews. The passage is probably meant to apply to Christian missionaries.

[92] Probably a reference to the destruction of Jerusalem and the Temple by the Romans in 70 A.D.

[93] Important renovations of the Temple had been made in recent years.

[94] This mount commanded a broad view of Jerusalem, with the Temple prominently in the foreground.

[95] A modern translation would be *falter*.

many false prophets shall rise, and shall deceive many. And because iniquity shall abound, the love of many shall wax cold. But he that shall endure unto the end, the same shall be saved. And this gospel of the kingdom shall be preached in all the world for a witness unto all nations; and then shall the end come. (24:9–14)

"When ye therefore shall see the abomination of desolation,[96] spoken of by Daniel the prophet, stand in the holy place, (whoso readeth, let him understand:) then let them which be in Judea flee into the mountains: let him which is on the housetop not come down to take any thing out of his house: neither let him which is in the field return back to take his clothes. And woe unto them[97] that are with child, and to them that give suck in those days! But pray ye that your flight be not in the winter, neither on the sabbath day:[98] for then shall be great tribulation, such as was not since the beginning of the world to this time, no, nor ever shall be. And except those days should be shortened, there should no flesh be saved: but for the elect's sake those days shall be shortened. Then if any man shall say unto you, 'Lo, here is Christ,' or 'there'; believe it not. For there shall arise false Christs, and false prophets, and shall show great signs and wonders; insomuch that, if it were possible, they shall deceive the very elect. Behold, I have told you before.[99] Wherefore if they shall say unto you, 'Behold, he is in the desert'; go not forth: 'behold, he is in the secret chambers'; believe it not. For as the lightning cometh out of the east, and shineth even unto the west; so shall also the coming of the Son of man be. For wheresoever the carcass is, there will the eagles be gathered together. (24:15–28)

"Immediately after the tribulation of those days shall the sun be darkened, and the moon shall not give her light, and the stars shall fall from heaven, and the powers of the heavens shall be shaken: and then shall appear the sign of the Son of man in heaven: and then shall all the tribes of the earth mourn, and they shall see the Son of man coming in the clouds of heaven with power and great glory. And he shall send his angels with a great sound of a trumpet, and they shall gather together his elect from the four winds, from one end of heaven to the other. Now learn a parable of the fig tree; When his branch is yet tender, and putteth forth leaves, ye know that summer is nigh: so likewise ye, when ye shall see all these things, know that it is near, even at the doors. Verily I say unto you, This generation shall not pass, till all these things be fulfilled. Heaven and earth shall pass away, but my words shall not pass away. (24:29–35)

"But of that day and hour knoweth no man, no, not the angels of heaven, but my Father only. But as the days of Noah were, so shall also the coming of the Son of man be. For as in the days that were before the flood they were eating and drinking, marrying and giving in marriage, until the day that Noah entered into the ark, and knew not until the flood came, and took them all away; so shall also the coming of the Son of man be. Then shall two be in the field; the one shall be taken, and the other left. Two women shall be grinding at the mill; the one shall be taken, and the other

[96] Daniel 9:27, 11:31, 12:11. The reference is to the installation of an image of a pagan god in the Temple. In this section, references to the invasion of Palestine and the destruction of Jerusalem are blended with a description of the end of the world.

[97] It will be hard for them; this is an expression of pity.

[98] When travel was forbidden.   [99] Beforehand.

left. Watch therefore: for ye know not what hour your Lord doth come. (24:36–42)

"But know this, that if the goodman of the house had known in what watch the thief would come, he would have watched, and would not have suffered his house to be broken up. Therefore be ye also ready: for in such an hour as ye think not the Son of man cometh. Who then is a faithful and wise servant, whom his lord hath made ruler over his household, to give them meat in due season? Blessed is that servant, whom his lord when he cometh shall find so doing. Verily I say unto you, That he shall make him ruler over all his goods. But and if that evil servant shall say in his heart, 'My lord delayeth his coming'; and shall begin to smite his fellowservants, and to eat and drink with the drunken; the lord of that servant shall come in a day when he looketh not for him, and in an hour that he is not aware of, and shall cut him asunder, and appoint him his portion with the hypocrites: there shall be weeping and gnashing of teeth.[1] (24:43–51)

"Then shall the kingdom of heaven be likened unto ten virgins, which took their lamps, and went forth to meet the bridegroom.[2] And five of them were wise, and five were foolish. They that were foolish took their lamps, and took no oil with them: but the wise took oil in their vessels with their lamps. While the bridegroom tarried, they all slumbered and slept. And at midnight there was a cry made, 'Behold, the bridegroom cometh; go ye out to meet him.' Then all those virgins arose, and trimmed their lamps. And the foolish said unto the wise, 'Give us of your oil; for our lamps are gone out.' But the wise answered, saying, 'Not so; lest there be not enough for us and you: but go ye rather to them that sell, and buy for yourselves.' And while they went to buy, the bridegroom came; and they that were ready went in with him to the marriage:[3] and the door was shut. Afterward came also the other virgins, saying, 'Lord, Lord, open to us.' But he answered and said, 'Verily I say unto you, I know you not.' Watch therefore, for ye know neither the day nor the hour wherein the Son of man cometh. (25:1–13)

"For the kingdom of heaven is as a man traveling into a far country, who called his own servants, and delivered unto them his goods.[4] And unto one he gave five talents, to another two, and to another one; to every man according to his several ability; and straightway took his journey. Then he that had received the five talents[5] went and traded with the same, and made them other five talents. And likewise he that had received two, he also gained other two. But he that had received one went and digged in the earth, and hid his lord's money. After a long time the lord of those servants cometh, and reckoneth with them. And so he that had received five talents came and brought other five talents, saying, 'Lord, thou deliveredst unto me five talents: behold, I have gained beside them five talents more.' His lord said unto him, 'Well done, thou good and faithful servant: thou hast been faithful over a few things, I will make thee ruler over many things:

---

[1] This parable may apply to good and bad stewardship by either Jewish or Christian leaders.

[2] Apparently to escort the bridegroom to the bride's house. Little is known of Jewish weddings of the time.

[3] The marriage feast.   [4] Made them his commercial agents.

[5] A talent was a large sum, roughly equivalent to a bag of gold.

enter thou into the joy of thy lord.' He also that had received two talents came and said, 'Lord, thou deliveredst unto me two talents: behold, I have gained two other talents beside them.' His lord said unto him, 'Well done, good and faithful servant; thou hast been faithful over a few things, I will make thee ruler over many things: enter thou into the joy of thy lord.' Then he which had received the one talent came and said, 'Lord, I knew thee that thou art a hard man, reaping where thou hast not sown, and gathering where thou hast not strewed:[6] and I was afraid, and went and hid thy talent in the earth: lo, there thou hast that is thine.' His lord answered and said unto him, 'Thou wicked and slothful servant, thou knewest that I reap where I sowed not, and gather where I have not strewed: thou oughtest therefore to have put my money to the exchangers,[7] and then at my coming I should have received mine own with usury.[8] Take therefore the talent from him, and give it unto him which hath ten talents. For unto every one that hath shall be given, and he shall have abundance: but from him that hath not shall be taken away even that which he hath. And cast ye the unprofitable servant into outer darkness: there shall be weeping and gnashing of teeth.' (25:14–30)

When the Son of man shall come in his glory, and all the holy angels with him, then shall he sit upon the throne of his glory: and before him shall be gathered all nations: and he shall separate them one from another, as a shepherd divideth his sheep from the goats: and he shall set the sheep on his right hand, but the goats on the left. (25:31–33)

"Then shall the King say unto them on his right hand, 'Come, ye blessed of my Father, inherit the kingdom prepared for you from the foundation of the world: for I was ahungered, and ye gave me meat: I was thirsty, and ye gave me drink: I was a stranger, and ye took me in: naked, and ye clothed me: I was sick, and ye visited me: I was in prison, and ye came unto me.' Then shall the righteous answer him, saying, 'Lord, when saw we thee ahungered, and fed thee? or thirsty, and gave thee drink? When saw we thee a stranger, and took thee in? or naked, and clothed thee? Or when saw we thee sick, or in prison, and came unto thee?' And the King shall answer and say unto them, 'Verily I say unto you, Inasmuch as ye have done it unto one of the least of these my brethren, ye have done it unto me.' (25:34–40)

"Then shall he say also unto them on the left hand, 'Depart from me, ye cursed, into everlasting fire, prepared for the devil and his angels: for I was ahungered, and ye gave me no meat: I was thirsty, and ye gave me no drink: I was a stranger, and ye took me not in: naked, and ye clothed me not: sick, and in prison, and ye visited me not.' Then shall they also answer him, saying, 'Lord, when saw we thee ahungered, or athirst, or a stranger, or naked, or sick, or in prison, and did not minister unto thee?' Then shall he answer them, saying, 'Verily I say unto you, Inasmuch as ye did it not to one of the least of these, ye did it not to me.' And these shall go away into everlasting punishment: but the righteous into life eternal." (25:41–46)

And it came to pass, when Jesus had finished all these sayings, he said

---

[6] The "lord" is a tight-fisted man who is accustomed to making big profits on very small investments. The servant feared that he would take a loss on the money entrusted to him and have to make up at least part of the loss.

[7] Money changers, the equivalent of bankers.   [8] Interest.

unto his disciples, "Ye know that after two days is the feast of the passover,[9] and the Son of man is betrayed to be crucified." Then assembled together the chief priests, and the scribes, and the elders of the people, unto the palace of the high priest, who was called Caiaphas,[10] and consulted that they might take Jesus by subtilty, and kill him. But they said, "Not on the feast day, lest there be an uproar among the people." (26:1–5)

Now when Jesus was in Bethany, in the house of Simon the leper,[11] there came unto him a woman having an alabaster box of very precious ointment, and poured it on his head, as he sat at meat. But when his disciples saw it, they had indignation, saying, "To what purpose is this waste? for this ointment might have been sold for much, and given to the poor." When Jesus understood it, he said unto them, "Why trouble ye the woman? for she hath wrought a good work upon me. For ye have the poor always with you; but me ye have not always. For in that she hath poured this ointment on my body, she did it for my burial.[12] Verily I say unto you, Wheresoever this gospel shall be preached in the whole world, there shall also this, that this woman hath done, be told for a memorial of her." (26: 6–13)

Then one of the twelve, called Judas Iscariot, went unto the chief priests, and said unto them, "What will ye give me, and I will deliver him unto you?" And they covenanted with him for thirty pieces of silver. And from that time he sought opportunity to betray him. (26:14–16)

Now the first day of the feast of unleavened bread the disciples came to Jesus, saying unto him, "Where wilt thou that we prepare for thee to eat the passover?"[13] And he said, "Go into the city to such a man, and say unto him, 'The Master saith, My time is at hand; I will keep the passover at thy house with my disciples.'" And the disciples did as Jesus had appointed them; and they made ready the passover. (26:17–19)

Now when the even was come, he sat down with the twelve. And as they did eat, he said, "Verily I say unto you, that one of you shall betray me." And they were exceeding sorrowful, and began every one of them to say unto him, "Lord, is it I?" And he answered and said, "He that dippeth his hand with me in the dish,[14] the same shall betray me. The Son of man goeth as it is written of him: but woe unto that man by whom the Son of man is betrayed! it had been good for that man if he had not been born." Then Judas, which betrayed him, answered and said, "Master, is it I?" He said unto him, "Thou hast said." (26:20–25)

And as they were eating, Jesus took bread, and blessed it, and brake it, and gave it to the disciples, and said, "Take, eat; this is my body."[15] And he took the cup, and gave thanks, and gave it to them, saying, "Drink ye all of

---

[9] The Passover was the most sacred of the Jewish feasts, commemorating God's deliverance of the Israelites from slavery in Egypt. It is held in early spring, as is its Christian counterpart, Easter.

[10] He served as high priest from A.D. 18 to 36. [11] Presumably a leper healed by Jesus.

[12] Anointing was customary before festive occasions. Corpses were also anointed for burial.

[13] Formerly eaten in the Temple area, the Passover feast was in Jesus' time eaten in private houses in Jerusalem.

[14] Ironically, to eat out of the same bowl would usually express fraternal amity.

[15] The main course at this Passover meal would have been the body of a sacrificed lamb; Jesus thus implies that he too is a sacrificial victim.

it; for this is my blood of the new testament,[16] which is shed for many for the remission of sins. But I say unto you, I will not drink henceforth of this fruit of the vine, until that day when I drink it new with you in my Father's kingdom."[17] (26:26–29)

And when they had sung a hymn, they went out into the mount of Olives. Then saith Jesus unto them, "All ye shall be offended[18] because of me this night: for it is written, 'I will smite the shepherd, and the sheep of the flock shall be scattered abroad.'[19] But after I am risen again, I will go before you into Galilee." Peter answered and said unto him, "Though all men shall be offended because of thee, yet will I never be offended." Jesus said unto him, "Verily I say unto thee, That this night, before the cock crow, thou shalt deny me thrice." Peter said unto him, "Though I should die with thee, yet will I not deny thee." Likewise also said all the disciples. (26:30–35)

Then cometh Jesus with them unto a place called Gethsemane,[20] and saith unto the disciples, "Sit ye here, while I go and pray yonder." And he took with him Peter and the two sons of Zebedee, and began to be sorrowful and very heavy. Then saith he unto them, "My soul is exceeding sorrowful, even unto death: tarry ye here, and watch[21] with me." And he went a little farther, and fell on his face, and prayed, saying, "O my Father, if it be possible, let this cup pass from me: nevertheless not as I will, but as thou wilt." And he cometh unto the disciples, and findeth them asleep, and saith unto Peter, "What, could ye not watch with me one hour? Watch and pray, that ye enter not into temptation: the spirit indeed is willing, but the flesh is weak." He went away again the second time, and prayed, saying, "O my Father, if this cup may not pass away from me, except I drink it, thy will be done." And he came and found them asleep again: for their eyes were heavy. And he left them, and went away again, and prayed the third time, saying the same words. Then cometh he to his disciples, and saith unto them, "Sleep on now, and take your rest: behold, the hour is at hand, and the Son of man is betrayed into the hands of sinners. Rise, let us be going: behold, he is at hand that doth betray me." (26:36–46)

And while he yet spake, lo, Judas, one of the twelve, came, and with him a great multitude with swords and staves, from the chief priests and elders of the people. Now he that betrayed him gave them a sign, saying, "Whomsoever I shall kiss, that same is he: hold him fast." And forthwith he came to Jesus, and said, "Hail, master"; and kissed him. And Jesus said unto him, "Friend, wherefore art thou come?" Then came they, and laid hands on Jesus, and took him. And, behold, one of them which were with Jesus stretched out his hand, and drew his sword, and struck a servant of the high priest's, and smote off his ear. Then said Jesus unto him, "Put up again thy sword into his place: for all they that take the sword shall perish with the sword. Thinkest thou that I cannot now pray to my Father, and he shall presently give me more than twelve legions of angels? But how then shall the scriptures be fulfilled, that thus it must be?" In that same hour

---

[16] The new Covenant; the old Covenant, between God and the Israelites, had been ritually sealed by the sprinkling of blood; see Exodus 24:6–8.

[17] Jesus alludes to one of the images of the Messianic age: as a divine banquet.

[18] Lapse from your faith.   [19] Zechariah 13:7.   [20] The name means "oil press."

[21] Stay awake.

said Jesus to the multitudes, "Are ye come out as against a thief with swords and staves for to take me? I sat daily with you teaching in the temple, and ye laid no hold on me. But all this was done, that the scriptures of the prophets might be fulfilled." Then all the disciples forsook him, and fled. (26:47–56)

And they that had laid hold on Jesus led him away to Caiaphas the high priest, where the scribes and the elders were assembled. But Peter followed him afar off unto the high priest's palace, and went in, and sat with the servants, to see the end. Now the chief priests, and elders, and all the council,[22] sought false witness against Jesus, to put him to death; but found none: yea, though many false witnesses came, yet found they none. At the last came two false witnesses, [23] and said, "This fellow said, 'I am able to destroy the temple of God, and to build it in three days.'" And the high priest arose, and said unto him, "Answerest thou nothing? what is it which these witness against thee?" But Jesus held his peace. And the high priest answered and said unto him, "I adjure thee by the living God, that thou tell us whether thou be the Christ, the Son of God." Jesus saith unto him, "Thou hast said: nevertheless I say unto you, Hereafter shall ye see the Son of man sitting on the right hand of power, and coming in the clouds of heaven."[24] Then the high priest rent his clothes, saying, "He hath spoken blasphemy;[25] what further need have we of witnesses? behold, now ye have heard his blasphemy. What think ye?" They answered and said, "He is guilty of death." Then did they spit in his face, and buffeted him; and others smote him with the palms of their hands, saying, "Prophesy unto us, thou Christ, Who is he that smote thee?"[26] (26:57–68)

Now Peter sat without in the palace:[27] and a damsel came unto him, saying, "Thou also wast with Jesus of Galilee." But he denied before them all, saying, "I know not what thou sayest." And when he was gone out into the porch, another maid saw him, and said unto them that were there, "This fellow was also with Jesus of Nazareth." And again he denied with an oath, "I do not know the man." And after a while came unto him they that stood by, and said to Peter, "Surely thou also art one of them; for thy speech betrayeth thee." Then began he to curse and to swear, saying, "I know not the man." And immediately the cock crew. And Peter remembered the word of Jesus, which said unto him, "Before the cock crow, thou shalt deny me thrice." And he went out, and wept bitterly. (26:69–75)

When the morning was come, all the chief priests and elders of the people took counsel against Jesus to put him to death: and when they had bound him, they led him away, and delivered him to Pontius Pilate the governor.[28] (27:1–2)

---

[22] The Sanhedrin, the highest Jewish court.

[23] It was necessary for evidence to be valid that the same allegation be made independently by two witnesses.

[24] Daniel 7:13, Psalm 110:1.

[25] Blasphemy was a capital offense under Jewish law. Rending one's clothes was a ritual expression of sorrow over a serious breaking of the holy Law.

[26] That is, if Jesus is the Christ (Messiah), he should be able to identify even people he does not know.

[27] In an open-air inner courtyard.

[28] Sentencing for a capital offense was reserved to the Roman authorities. Pilate, who was governor between the years 26 and 36, was often antagonistic to the Jews.

Then Judas, which had betrayed him, when he saw that he was condemned,[29] repented himself, and brought again the thirty pieces of silver to the chief priests and elders, saying, "I have sinned in that I have betrayed the innocent blood." And they said, "What is that to us? see thou to that." And he cast down the pieces of silver in the temple, and departed, and went and hanged himself. And the chief priests took the silver pieces, and said, "It is not lawful for to put them into the treasury, because it is the price of blood." And they took counsel, and bought with them the potter's field, to bury strangers in. Wherefore that field was called, The field of blood, unto this day. Then was fulfilled that which was spoken by Jeremiah the prophet, saying,

"And they took the thirty pieces of silver,
The price of him that was valued,
Whom they of the children of Israel did value;
And gave them for the potter's field,
As the Lord appointed me."[30] (27:3–10)

And Jesus stood before the governor: and the governor asked him, saying, "Art thou the King of the Jews?"[31] And Jesus said unto him, "Thou sayest." And when he was accused of the chief priests and elders, he answered nothing. Then said Pilate unto him, "Hearest thou not how many things they witness against thee?" And he answered him to never a word; insomuch that the governor marveled greatly. (27:11–14)

Now at that feast the governor was wont to release unto the people a prisoner, whom they would. And they had then a notable prisoner, called Barabbas. Therefore when they were gathered together, Pilate said unto them, "Whom will ye that I release unto you? Barabbas, or Jesus which is called Christ?" For he knew that for envy[32] they had delivered him. When he was set down on the judgment seat, his wife sent unto him, saying, "Have thou nothing to do with that just man: for I have suffered many things this day in a dream because of him." But the chief priests and elders persuaded the multitude that they should ask Barabbas, and destroy Jesus. The governor answered and said unto them, "Whether of the twain will ye that I release unto you?" They said, "Barabbas." Pilate saith unto them, "What shall I do then with Jesus which is called Christ?" They all say unto him, "Let him be crucified."[33] And the governor said, "Why, what evil hath he done?" But they cried out the more, saying, "Let him be crucified." When Pilate saw that he could prevail nothing, but that rather a tumult was made, he took water, and washed his hands before the multitude, saying, "I am innocent of the blood of this just person: see ye to it." Then answered all the people, and said, "His blood be on us, and on our children."[34] Then released he Barabbas unto them: and when he had scourged Jesus, he delivered him to be crucified. (27:15–26)

[29] That Jesus was condemned.   [30] Actually, not Jeremiah, but Zechariah 11:12–13.
[31] Pilate as Roman governor would not be interested in such religious charges as blasphemy; Jesus' enemies have apparently tried to depict him as a source of political danger. To judge from Pilate's later behavior, he does not take the charge very seriously.
[32] Malice.   [33] Crucifixion was the penalty imposed by the Romans for insurrection.
[34] Another allusion to the destruction of Jerusalem in 70 A.D.

Then the soldiers of the governor took Jesus into the common hall, and gathered unto him the whole band of soldiers. And they stripped him, and put on him a scarlet robe. And when they had platted a crown of thorns, they put it upon his head, and a reed in his right hand: and they bowed the knee before him, and mocked him, saying, "Hail, King of the Jews!" And they spit upon him, and took the reed, and smote him on the head. And after that they had mocked him, they took the robe off from him, and put his own raiment on him, and led him away to crucify him. And as they came out, they found a man of Cyrene, Simon by name: him they compelled to bear his cross. (27:27–32)

And when they were come unto a place called Golgotha, that is to say, a place of a skull, they gave him vinegar[35] to drink mingled with gall: and when he had tasted thereof, he would not drink. And they crucified him, and parted his garments, casting lots: that it might be fulfilled which was spoken by the prophet, "They parted my garments among them, and upon my vesture did they cast lots."[36] And sitting down they watched him there; and set up over his head his accusation written, *This is Jesus the King of the Jews.* Then were there two thieves crucified with him, one on the right hand, and another on the left. (27:33–38)

And they that passed by reviled him, wagging their heads, and saying, "Thou that destroyest the temple, and buildest it in three days, save thyself. If thou be the Son of God, come down from the cross." Likewise also the chief priests mocking him, with the scribes and elders, said, "He saved others; himself he cannot save. If he be the King of Israel, let him now come down from the cross, and we will believe him. He trusted in God; let him deliver him now, if he will have him: for he said, 'I am the Son of God.'" The thieves also, which were crucified with him, cast the same in his teeth. (27:39–44)

Now from the sixth hour there was darkness over all the land unto the ninth hour.[37] And about the ninth hour Jesus cried with a loud voice, saying, "Eli, Eli, lama sabachthani?" that is to say, "My God, my God, why hast thou forsaken me?"[38] Some of them that stood there, when they heard that, said, "This man calleth for Elijah."[39] And straightway one of them ran, and took a sponge, and filled it with vinegar,[40] and put it on a reed, and gave him to drink. The rest said, "Let be, let us see whether Elijah will come to save him." (27:45–49)

Jesus, when he had cried again with a loud voice, yielded up the ghost. (27:50)

And, behold, the veil of the temple was rent in twain from the top to the bottom; and the earth did quake, and the rocks rent; and the graves were opened; and many bodies of the saints which slept arose, and came out of the graves after his resurrection, and went into the holy city, and appeared unto many. Now when the centurion, and they that were with him, watching Jesus, saw the earthquake, and those things that were done, they feared

---

[35] Probably cheap wine, intended as a narcotic.   [36] Psalm 22:18.

[37] From noon to mid-afternoon.   [38] Quoted from Psalm 22:1.

[39] The mistake probably arises from imperfect hearing of Jesus' utterance of "Eli" ("My God").

[40] Cheap wine.

greatly, saying, "Truly this was the Son of God." And many women were there beholding afar off, which followed Jesus from Galilee, ministering unto him: among which was Mary Magdalene,[41] and Mary the mother of James and Joses, and the mother of Zebedee's children. (27:51–56)

When the even was come, there came a rich man of Arimathea, named Joseph, who also himself was Jesus' disciple: he went to Pilate, and begged the body of Jesus. Then Pilate commanded the body to be delivered. And when Joseph had taken the body, he wrapped it in a clean linen cloth, and laid it in his own new tomb, which he had hewn out in the rock: and he rolled a great stone to the door of the sepulcher, and departed. And there was Mary Magdalene, and the other Mary, sitting over against the sepulcher. (27:57–61)

Now the next day, that followed the day of the preparation, the chief priests and Pharisees came together unto Pilate, saying, "Sir, we remember that that deceiver said, while he was yet alive, 'After three days I will rise again.' Command therefore that the sepulcher be made sure until the third day, lest his disciples come by night, and steal him away, and say unto the people, 'He is risen from the dead': so the last error shall be worse than the first." Pilate said unto them, "Ye have a watch:[42] go your way, make it as sure as ye can." So they went, and made the sepulcher sure, sealing the stone, and setting a watch. (27:62–66)

In the end of the sabbath, as it began to dawn toward the first day of the week, came Mary Magdalene and the other Mary to see the sepulcher. And, behold, there was a great earthquake: for the angel of the Lord descended from heaven, and came and rolled back the stone from the door, and sat upon it. His countenance was like lightning, and his raiment white as snow: and for fear of him the keepers did shake, and became as dead men. And the angel answered and said unto the women, "Fear not ye: for I know that ye seek Jesus, which was crucified. He is not here: for he is risen, as he said. Come, see the place where the Lord lay. And go quickly, and tell his disciples that he is risen from the dead; and, behold, he goeth before you into Galilee; there shall ye see him: lo, I have told you." And they departed quickly from the sepulcher with fear and great joy; and did run to bring his disciples word. And as they went to tell his disciples, behold, Jesus met them, saying, "All hail." And they came and held him by the feet, and worshipped him. Then said Jesus unto them, "Be not afraid: go tell my brethren that they go into Galilee, and there shall they see me." (28:1–10)

Now when they were going, behold, some of the watch came into the city, and showed unto the chief priests all the things that were done. And when they were assembled with the elders, and had taken counsel, they gave large money unto the soldiers, saying, "Say ye, 'His disciples came by night, and stole him away while we slept.' And if this come to the governor's ears, we will persuade him, and secure you."[43] So they took the money, and did as they were taught: and this saying is commonly reported among the Jews until this day. (28:11–15)

---

[41] She is mentioned in the Gospel of Luke (8:2) as a woman out of whom Jesus cast seven devils.

[42] You may have a detachment to stand guard.

[43] Protect you (from being punished for sleeping while on duty).

Then the eleven disciples went away into Galilee, into a mountain where Jesus had appointed them.[44] And when they saw him, they worshiped him: but some doubted. And Jesus came and spake unto them, saying, "All power is given unto me in heaven and in earth. Go ye therefore, and teach all nations,[45] baptizing them in the name of the Father, and of the Son, and of the Holy Ghost: teaching them to observe all things whatsoever I have commanded you: and, lo, I am with you alway, even unto the end of the world." Amen. (28:16–20)

from THE GOSPEL ACCORDING TO SAINT LUKE

Forasmuch as many have taken in hand to set forth in order a declaration of those things which are most surely believed among us, even as they delivered them unto us, which from the beginning were eyewitnesses, and ministers of the word; it seemed good to me also, having had perfect understanding of all things from the very first, to write unto thee in order, most excellent Theophilus,[1] that thou mightest know the certainty of those things, wherein thou hast been instructed. (1:1–4)

There was in the days of Herod, the king of Judea,[2] a certain priest named Zechariah, of the course of Abijah:[3] and his wife was of the daughters of Aaron, and her name was Elisabeth. And they were both righteous before God, walking in all the commandments and ordinances of the Lord blameless. And they had no child, because that Elisabeth was barren, and they both were now well stricken in years. And it came to pass, that while he executed the priest's office before God in the order of his course, according to the custom of the priest's office, his lot was to burn incense when he went into the temple of the Lord. And the whole multitude of the people were praying without at the time of incense. And there appeared unto him an angel of the Lord standing on the right side of the altar of incense. And when Zechariah saw him, he was troubled, and fear fell upon him. But the angel said unto him, "Fear not, Zechariah: for thy prayer is heard; and thy wife Elisabeth shall bear thee a son, and thou shalt call his name John. And thou shalt have joy and gladness; and many shall rejoice at his birth. For he shall drink neither wine nor strong drink; and he shall be filled with the Holy Ghost, even from his mother's womb. And many of the children

---

[44] Had said he would meet them. The "mountain" once more is the setting for a climactic event.

[45] The disciples' commission is now to the whole world, in contrast with their earlier-defined mission to the Jews only (10:5–6).

[1] An unidentified person, apparently of high rank. The name means "beloved by God." The stylistically elaborate opening, along with the address to a patron, indicates that Luke is attempting a highly polished work that follows classical literary and historiographical conventions. Luke's gospel is intended to have special relevance for the non-Jewish world. At the same time, the manner of the following narratives about the births and earliest years of John the Baptist and of Jesus are very much in the Old Testament style.

[2] For Herod, see Matthew 2:1 and note.

[3] *Course* means "division of the priesthood." The Jewish priesthood was descended from Moses' brother Aaron through his grandsons, of whom Abijah was one. The divisions took turns serving in the Temple, and within each division duties were assigned by drawing lots.

of Israel shall he turn to the Lord their God. And he shall go before him in the spirit and power of Elijah,[4] to turn the hearts of the fathers to the children, and the disobedient to the wisdom of the just; to make ready a people prepared for the Lord." And Zechariah said unto the angel, "Whereby shall I know this? for I am an old man, and my wife well stricken in years." And the angel answering said unto him, "I am Gabriel, that stand in the presence of God; and am sent to speak unto thee, and to show thee these glad tidings. And, behold, thou shalt be dumb, and not able to speak, until the day that these things shall be performed, because thou believest not my words, which shall be fulfilled in their season." And the people waited for Zechariah, and marveled that he tarried so long in the temple. And when he came out, he could not speak unto them: and they perceived that he had seen a vision in the temple: for he beckoned unto them, and remained speechless. And it came to pass, that, as soon as the days of his ministration were accomplished, he departed to his own house. And after those days his wife Elisabeth conceived, and hid herself five months, saying, "Thus hath the Lord dealt with me in the days wherein he looked on me, to take away my reproach among men."[5] (1:5–25)

And in the sixth month the angel Gabriel was sent from God unto a city of Galilee,[6] named Nazareth, to a virgin espoused to a man whose name was Joseph, of the house of David; and the virgin's name was Mary. And the angel came in unto her, and said, "Hail, thou that art highly favored, the Lord is with thee: blessed art thou among women." And when she saw him, she was troubled at his saying, and cast in her mind what manner of salutation this should be. And the angel said unto her, "Fear not, Mary: for thou hast found favor with God. And, behold, thou shalt conceive in thy womb, and bring forth a son, and shalt call his name *Jesus*.[7] He shall be great, and shall be called the Son of the Highest: and the Lord God shall give unto him the throne of his father David: and he shall reign over the house of Jacob for ever; and of his kingdom there shall be no end."[8] Then said Mary unto the angel, "How shall this be, seeing I know not a man?" And the angel answered and said unto her, "The Holy Ghost shall come upon thee, and the power of the Highest shall overshadow thee: therefore also that holy thing which shall be born of thee shall be called the Son of God. And, behold, thy cousin[9] Elisabeth, she hath also conceived a son in her old age: and this is the sixth month with her, who was called barren. For with God nothing shall be impossible." And Mary said, "Behold the handmaid of the Lord; be it unto me according to thy word." And the angel departed from her. (1:26–38)

And Mary arose in those days, and went into the hill country[10] with haste, into a city of Judah; and entered into the house of Zechariah, and saluted Elisabeth. And it came to pass, that, when Elisabeth heard the salutation of Mary, the babe leaped in her womb; and Elisabeth was filled with

---

[4] For Elijah's role as a precursor, see Malachi 4; for John the Baptist as Elijah, see Matthew 11:14 and note.

[5] Compare Genesis 30:23, where Rachel too refers to the "reproach" of being barren.

[6] The northern part of Palestine.

[7] For the significance of the name, see note to Matthew 1:1.

[8] On the Messiah and his descent from David, see note to Matthew 1:1.

[9] Kinswoman.　　[10] The country near Jerusalem.

the Holy Ghost: and she spake out with a loud voice, and said, "Blessed art thou among women, and blessed is the fruit of thy womb. And whence is this to me, that the mother of my Lord should come to me? For, lo, as soon as the voice of thy salutation sounded in mine ears, the babe leaped in my womb for joy. And blessed is she that believed: for there shall be a performance of those things which were told her from the Lord." (1:39–45)

And Mary said,

"My soul doth magnify the Lord,[11]
And my spirit hath rejoiced in God my Saviour.
For he hath regarded the low estate of his handmaiden:
For, behold, from henceforth all generations shall call me blessed.
For he that is mighty hath done to me great things;
And holy is his name.
And his mercy is on them that fear him
From generation to generation.
He hath shewed strength with his arm;
He hath scattered the proud in the imagination of their hearts.
He hath put down the mighty from their seats,
And exalted them of low degree.
He hath filled the hungry with good things;
And the rich he hath sent empty away.
He hath holpen his servant Israel,
In remembrance of his mercy;
As he spake to our fathers,
To Abraham, and to his seed for ever."

And Mary abode with her about three months, and returned to her own house. (1:46–56)

Now Elisabeth's full time came that she should be delivered; and she brought forth a son. And her neighbors and her cousins heard how the Lord had showed great mercy upon her; and they rejoiced with her. And it came to pass, that on the eighth day they came to circumcise the child; and they called him Zechariah, after the name of his father. And his mother answered and said, "Not so; but he shall be called John."[12] And they said unto her, "There is none of thy kindred that is called by this name." And they made signs to his father, how he would have him called. And he asked for a writing table, and wrote, saying, "His name is John." And they marveled all.[13] And his mouth was opened immediately, and his tongue loosed, and he spake, and praised God. And fear came on all that dwelt round about them: and all these sayings were noised abroad throughout all the hill country of Judea. And all they that heard them laid them up in their hearts, saying, "What manner of child shall this be!" And the hand of the Lord was with him. (1:57–66)

---

[11] The following anthem, the Magnificat, frequently echoes the Old Testament. Its sympathy with the humble and poor is entirely typical of Luke.

[12] The name means "The Lord has shown favor."

[13] Because Zechariah is presumably deaf as well as dumb, his independent giving of the name evokes wonder.

And his father Zechariah was filled with the Holy Ghost, and prophesied, saying,

"Blessed be the Lord God of Israel;[14]
For he hath visited and redeemed his people,
And hath raised up a horn of salvation for us
In the house of his servant David;
As he spake by the mouth of his holy prophets,
Which have been since the world began:
That we should be saved from our enemies,
And from the hand of all that hate us;
To perform the mercy promised to our fathers,
And to remember his holy covenant;
The oath which he sware to our father Abraham,
That he would grant unto us, that we being delivered out of the hand
     of our enemies
Might serve him without fear,
In holiness and righteousness before him, all the days of our life.
And thou, child, shalt be called the prophet of the Highest:
For thou shalt go before the face of the Lord to prepare his ways;
To give knowledge of salvation unto his people
By the remission of their sins,
Through the tender mercy of our God;
Whereby the dayspring[15] from on high hath visited us,
To give light to them that sit in darkness and in the shadow of death,
To guide our feet into the way of peace."

And the child grew, and waxed strong in spirit, and was in the deserts till
the day of his showing unto Israel. (1:67–80)

And it came to pass in those days, that there went out a decree from
Caesar Augustus, that all the world should be taxed.[16] (And this taxing was
first made when Cyrenius was governor of Syria.) And all went to be taxed,
every one into his own city. And Joseph also went up from Galilee, out of
the city of Nazareth, into Judea, unto the city of David, which is called
Bethlehem;[17] (because he was of the house and lineage of David:) to be
taxed with Mary his espoused wife, being great with child. And so it was,
that, while they were there, the days were accomplished that she should be
delivered. And she brought forth her firstborn son, and wrapped him in
swaddling clothes,[18] and laid him in a manger; because there was no room
for them in the inn. (2:1–7)

And there were in the same country shepherds abiding in the field,
keeping watch over their flock by night. And, lo, the angel of the Lord
came upon them, and the glory of the Lord shone round about them: and

---

[14] Like the Magnificat earlier, this song, the Benedictus, echoes the Old Testament frequently.
[15] The rising sun; an epithet for the Messiah.
[16] Such a census has been recorded, although it took place in 6–7 A.D.
[17] Bethlehem is about five miles south of Jerusalem and almost a hundred miles south of
Nazareth.
[18] Bands of cloth, at the time used to ensure straight growth.

they were sore afraid. And the angel said unto them, "Fear not: for, behold, I bring you good tidings of great joy, which shall be to all people. For unto you is born this day in the city of David a Saviour, which is Christ[19] the Lord. And this shall be a sign unto you; Ye shall find the babe wrapped in swaddling clothes, lying in a manger." And suddenly there was with the angel a multitude of the heavenly host praising God, and saying,

> "Glory to God in the highest,
> And on earth peace, good will toward men."

And it came to pass, as the angels were gone away from them into heaven, the shepherds said one to another, "Let us now go even unto Bethlehem, and see this thing which is come to pass, which the Lord hath made known unto us." And they came with haste, and found Mary, and Joseph, and the babe lying in a manger. And when they had seen it, they made known abroad the saying which was told them concerning this child. And all they that heard it wondered at those things which were told them by the shepherds. But Mary kept all these things, and pondered them in her heart. And the shepherds returned, glorifying and praising God for all the things that they had heard and seen, as it was told unto them. (2:8–20)

And when eight days were accomplished for the circumcising of the child, his name was called *Jesus*, which was so named of the angel before he was conceived in the womb. (2:21)

And when the days of her purification according to the law of Moses were accomplished, they brought him to Jerusalem, to present him to the Lord; (as it is written in the law of the Lord, "Every male that openeth the womb shall be called holy to the Lord";)[20] and to offer a sacrifice according to that which is said in the law of the Lord, "A pair of turtledoves, or two young pigeons."[21] And, behold, there was a man in Jerusalem, whose name was Simeon; and the same man was just and devout, waiting for the consolation of Israel: and the Holy Ghost was upon him. And it was revealed unto him by the Holy Ghost, that he should not see death, before he had seen the Lord's Christ. And he came by the Spirit into the temple: and when the parents brought in the child Jesus, to do for him after the custom of the law, then took he him up in his arms, and blessed God, and said,

> "Lord, now lettest thou thy servant depart in peace,
> According to thy word:
> For mine eyes have seen thy salvation,
> Which thou hast prepared before the face of all people;
> A light to lighten the Gentiles,
> And the glory of thy people Israel."

And Joseph and his mother marveled at those things which were spoken of him. And Simeon blessed them, and said unto Mary his mother, "Behold,

---

[19]Not a personal name but a title (literally, "the anointed one") designating the Messiah.
[20]Exodus 13:2,12.
[21]The ritual purification after conception and childbirth are described in Leviticus 12. The usual offering was a lamb, but the poor were allowed to substitute an extra turtledove or pigeon.

this child is set for the fall and rising again of many in Israel; and for a sign which shall be spoken against; (yea, a sword shall pierce through thy own soul also,) that the thoughts of many hearts may be revealed." (2:22–35)

And there was one Anna, a prophetess, the daughter of Phanuel, of the tribe of Asher; she was of a great age, and had lived with an husband seven years from her virginity; and she was a widow of about fourscore and four years, which departed not from the temple, but served God with fastings and prayers night and day. And she coming in that instant gave thanks likewise unto the Lord, and spake of him to all them that looked for redemption in Jerusalem. And when they had performed all things according to the law of the Lord, they returned into Galilee, to their own city Nazareth. And the child grew, and waxed strong in spirit, filled with wisdom: and the grace of God was upon him. (2:36–40)

Now his parents went to Jerusalem every year at the feast of the passover. And when he was twelve years old, they went up to Jerusalem after the custom of the feast. And when they had fulfilled the days, as they returned, the child Jesus tarried behind in Jerusalem; and Joseph and his mother knew not of it. But they, supposing him to have been in the company, went a day's journey; and they sought him among their kinsfolk and acquaintance. And when they found him not, they turned back again to Jerusalem, seeking him. And it came to pass, that after three days they found him in the temple, sitting in the midst of the doctors,[22] both hearing them, and asking them questions. And all that heard him were astonished at his understanding and answers. And when they saw him, they were amazed: and his mother said unto him, "Son, why hast thou thus dealt with us? behold, thy father and I have sought thee sorrowing." And he said unto them, "How is it that ye sought me? wist[23] ye not that I must be about my Father's business?" And they understood not the saying which he spake unto them. And he went down with them, and came to Nazareth, and was subject unto them: but his mother kept all these sayings in her heart. And Jesus increased in wisdom and stature, and in favor with God and man. (2:41–52)

---

[22] Teachers (of the Jewish Law).   [23] Knew.

The Middle Ages

HE term *Middle Ages* as a description of the thousand-year period between the fifth and the fifteenth centuries—between the end of the Roman Empire and the Renaissance—is at once an oversimplification and a distortion of a long and complex period of European history. Coined by Renaissance and Enlightenment thinkers, the label *Middle Ages* (or its Latin form, the *Medieval* period) implies a mere transitional era, a long interruption in the continuity of Western history during which the classical culture of Greece and Rome, waiting to be revived in the Renaissance, lay dormant or dead.

From our perspective, we can see the Middle Ages in more positive terms, not as an interruption but as a fertile and dynamic period that produced a distinctive and permanently valuable culture of its own. It was more varied than a single, reductive label would imply. There is a certain unity in this long span of history that justifies our considering it as a single period, but within this unity was enormous diversity. Only the very early Middle Ages, from the sixth to the ninth centuries, were characterized by the cultural inertia often attributed to the whole period. The collapse of the Roman Empire left Europe for a time in chaos, with its economy, its social organization, and its culture brought almost to a halt. But even these "Dark Ages" were not without their rays of light, especially in areas where survivals of the Roman heritage or the Church preserved pockets of culture. In retrospect, we can see forces working during this fallow period that were to emerge later in a new and vital form of social organization. The new organization began to take shape in about the tenth century and led by the thirteenth century to a flowering of art and culture that anticipated and rivaled the Renaissance without forfeiting its own distinctively medieval character.

The formidable challenge to the early Middle Ages was to find a mode of social organization to replace the Roman Empire and to weave together the various threads of European culture: the remnants of Latin civilization, Christianity, and the northern, Germanic, "barbarian" tradition. The solution that gradually emerged over a period of several centuries lay in two institutions, the Roman Church and feudalism.

By the time of the Empire's final collapse, the Church had made great strides toward becoming a universal institution. Paul, the "Apostle of the Gentiles," was the chief architect in the conversion of Christianity from a parochial, nationalistic cult among dissident Jews to a universal religion. During the fourth century, Christianity gradually became the state religion of Rome; the emperor Theodosius at the end of the century formally proclaimed it as such, closed heathen temples, and forbade heathen sacrifices.

Within a few years, pagans were actively persecuted as the Christians had been persecuted earlier.

At the beginning of the fifth century, the centralizing forces in Christianity culminated in the claim by Pope Innocent I to jurisdiction over all Christendom. The centrally organized Church was to a large extent modeled on the Empire. As the Empire gradually wasted away, the Church emerged more and more clearly as its spiritual heir and as a universal source of authority. It also became, for a thousand years, the heir and the chief custodian of Latin culture. It preserved much of the classic Roman literature and over the centuries fostered a rich body of medieval Latin writing, largely ecclesiastical in nature. This work included philosophy such as that of St. Augustine, St. Anselm, and St. Thomas Aquinas; rhetoric, such as Geoffrey of Vinsauf's; chronicles and compilations of legendary history, such as the *Gesta Romanorum* and the Venerable Bede's *Ecclesiastical History of the English Nation;* a rich body of Latin religious poetry, especially hymns; and many other works.

The power of the medieval church was based upon two propositions, which it inculcated almost universally: that the visible scene of human life was a perpetual conflict between the Kingdom of God and the Kingdom of the Devil, and that salvation for the individual was available only through the offices of the Church. This world was seen as secondary to the world to come, a testing ground determining whether the individual would spend eternity in Heaven or Hell. Because participation in the sacraments of the Church was a requirement for salvation, the Church vitally affected the individual's fate through all eternity, a fate that at its worst was regarded with a fearful literalness.

The elaborate bureaucracy of the Roman Empire was reflected in the detailed hierarchy through which the Church performed its functions and which, in its meticulous emphasis upon rank and degree, expressed one of the deepest and most pervasive habits of medieval thought. The individual was linked to God through an elaborate chain of hierarchical relationships. Above the individual believer was the priest; above the priest were, in succession, bishop, archbishop, cardinal, and pope. The ranks rose, beyond the earthly Church, above the pope through the intricate orders of angels to God Himself. The pope was thus, in this minutely detailed scheme of things, the direct representative of God on earth, with absolute power to "bind and loose."

Quite apart from its religious function, the medieval Church was a vitally important social institution in the Middle Ages. In an era full of political disorder and conflict, it provided a slight check upon secular warfare, by asserting an authority that transcended political boundaries. It tempered social oppression by opening Church offices to commoners and upholding the doctrine of the equality of all men before God. It also helped unify and stabilize European culture by defining a broadly accepted system of values and beliefs.

The fixed hierarchy of the medieval Church was mirrored in feudalism, the secular social and economic system that gradually emerged to replace the fallen Empire. Feudalism originated in the human need to band together for mutual protection in a lawless and chaotic age. Inhabitants of a particular region placed themselves under the protection of the most powerful local lord and in return for his military protection pledged certain services. Like the Church, feudalism echoed certain aspects of the Roman Empire, notably the custom of clients gathering around wealthy patrons, but it also drew heavily upon the Germanic social organization, in which warriors gathered around a powerful chieftain, to whom they were bound by a complex system of obligations and rewards.

In its fully developed form, feudalism was, like the Church, a pyramidal structure encompassing all of society and organized by an intricate code of privileges and mutual commitments. The medieval king was the secular counterpart of the pope, subordinate to him only in matters of faith. The feudal system placed literal ownership of all the king's domain (except that controlled by the Church) in his hands. These lands, or "fiefs," were, in effect, leased and subleased down through hierarchical orders of nobility to the level of the individual manor, the basic social and economic unit of feudalism. Each nobleman became the "vassal" of his immediate superior and owed him, in return for the lands he was granted, money payments and, when demanded, military service. The exact terms of feudal obligations were never standardized across Europe. They depended on local custom, but they were quite precise and were ritualized in the ceremony of homage and investiture, in which the vassal knelt before his lord and, placing his hands between his lord's hands, vowed to fulfill the terms of his obligation. At the bottom of the feudal pyramid was the serf, bound to the land he worked and obliged to cultivate his lord's land as well, in a sort of peonage or sharecropper arrangement.

Feudal society thus consisted of only two classes, the people and the nobility, which included the orders of the Church as well as the secular feudal orders. There was no socially mobile middle class; such a class, outside the rigid ordering of rank, would have been incompatible with the idea of feudalism, and when it did begin to emerge late in the Middle Ages, it marked the beginning of the collapse of the whole system.

The first comparatively stable kingdom to be established after the fall of Rome was that of the Franks, founded by Clovis (465–511). Charlemagne (742–814), a descendant of Clovis, embarked upon a series of campaigns against the Saxons and Bavarians, the Moors of northeast Spain, and the Lombards in northern Italy, building an immense empire to rival that of the Caesars. He was crowned "Holy Roman Emperor" by Pope Leo III on Christmas Day, 800. Charlemagne's victories became the stuff of legend, and his deeds, along with those of his twelve "peers," were celebrated in a number of medieval works of which the *Song of Roland* is the most famous. The imperial court was also a great center of art and learning, the focal point of the "Carolingian renaissance." Charlemagne brought the learned monk Alcuin from England to found a palace school of theology and literature, imported architects from Italy to build a number of cathedrals, and encouraged the study of Latin literature as well as Germanic epics.

Another nucleus of culture in the early Middle Ages, the Benedictine monastic order, was founded in the late sixth century by St. Benedict of Nursia with the encouragement of the great medieval pope Gregory I (540–604), who launched a series of missions to Christianize the northern Germanic peoples. Within a century, the Benedictine monasteries had spread across Europe, succeeding the Roman schools as centers of learning. In these monasteries libraries were collected and copied, instruction was carried on, and medieval architecture was born, with many of the monks working as master masons in the construction of early cathedrals.

Charlemagne's empire was short-lived, crumbling under the impact of invasions from the north. The Vikings, seafaring warriors from Scandinavia, swept into England and northern France in the ninth century and established the kingdom of Normandy in 885. The result, however, was not a new age of barbarism. The Danish Vikings were gradually assimilated in England, where the reign of Alfred the Great of Wessex (871–899) accompanied a genuine revival of art and learning. The Vikings in Normandy were likewise assimilated with the Franks, and a similar revival of learning took place; when these Normans conquered England in 1066, they brought with them a culture superior to that of the Anglo-Saxons.

The eleventh and twelfth centuries were a time of explosive intellectual and cultural development. The Crusades, launched by Pope Urban II in 1095, were eventually a dismal failure as attempts to capture the Holy Lands from the "Saracens," but they had the unforeseen effect of bringing Europeans into contact with the riches of Muslim culture, literature, mathematics, and science. Industry and commerce began to revive across Europe, and a number of universities were founded: Oxford in 1167, Paris in 1170, Cambridge in 1209. Provence in southern France was a particularly fertile ground; a vigorous economic and cultural atmosphere brought the development of chivalry and a rich tradition of *troubadour* literature expressing chivalric values, a tradition paralleled in northern France by the poetry of the *trouvères*.

This rapid development culminated in the thirteenth century, the high point, in many ways, of medieval culture. Both the medieval papacy and the medieval monarchy reached the height of their power in the thirteenth century, the papacy under Innocent III, Gregory IX, and Nicholas III, the monarchy under such kings as Edward I of England, Louis IX of France, and Ferdinand III of Spain. The greatest of the Gothic cathedrals were built—Notre Dame de Paris, Mont-Saint-Michel, Rheims, Amiens, Chartres. The period also marked the golden age of Scholasticism, the philosophical project of reconciling the teachings of the Church with the logic of Aristotle, or faith with reason; St. Thomas Aquinas's *Summa Theologica*, the masterpiece of Scholasticism, was completed in 1273.

But already, at the peak of its triumph, the medieval system was beginning to show signs of its ultimate decline. The medieval monarchy received an ominous blow when the English barons forced King John to sign Magna Charta in 1215. The strains upon the medieval papacy surfaced in such conflicts as the prolonged struggles between the Guelphs (supporters of the Pope) and the Ghibellines (supporters of the Holy Roman Emperor) in the city-states of Italy. The rise in the thirteenth century of the guilds, organizations of skilled craftsmen, also heralded the rise of a middle class incompatible with the rigid categories of the feudal system and prophetic of its ultimate collapse.

These fragmenting tendencies gained momentum in the turbulent fourteenth century. The papacy was split, for most of the century, by the so-called Babylonian Captivity, 1305–1376, during which the papal see was removed to Avignon in France, and by the following Great Schism (1378–

1417), when there were two, and sometimes even three, rival popes. The chaos that followed the Black Death in mid-century further weakened the feudal system. The second half of the century was shaken by people's revolutions: the French Jacquerie in 1358 and the English Peasants' Revolt in 1381. These and other uprisings were put down, with great cruelty, but they foreshadowed the end of economic serfdom.

The greatest imaginative writers of medieval Europe emerged during its decline. The medieval world view is perhaps best expressed by such writers as Thomas Aquinas and John of Salisbury, but the masterpieces of medieval literature date from the fourteenth century: the *Divine Comedy*, the *Decameron*, the *Rhymes* of Petrarch, the *Canterbury Tales*. Paradoxically, none of these works is wholly medieval in spirit. The tension apparent in all of them between the passing medieval world and the emerging Renaissance world provides much of their energy.

That we can distinguish the "medieval" and the "modern" in such works, however tentatively, suggests that, despite the span and variety of the Middle Ages, there is a certain consistency in its world-view. At the risk of overgeneralizing, it is possible to point to three qualities pervasive enough to define the age: authoritarianism, comprehensiveness, and otherworldliness. The cathedral, often cited as the quintessential expression of the medieval spirit, illustrates all three tendencies. The system of communal engineering that made the building of cathedrals possible implies the subordination of individual creativity to collective authority. If one values the occasional evidences of individual personality, in the playful elaboration of a gargoyle carving, for instance, it is because such features are exceptions. Medieval literature, too, is often anonymous, and when we begin to hear, as in Petrarch, the sound of an individual voice, we know that a new element has entered the medieval literary world.

As for comprehensiveness, the cathedral was also a microcosm of an all-inclusive vision of life. Not only did it represent a synthesis of social values, art, and religion, but its art characteristically undertook to represent the whole Christian revelation, the divine plan from Creation to the Day of Judgment. The literary analogues were the compendiums, ambitious works that attempted a total view of human life, its individual parts placed in relation to a whole, as in Aquinas's *Summa Theologica* or Dante's *Divine Comedy*. And finally, the very shape of the cathedral, its great spires pointing away from the earth toward Heaven, suggests the pervasive otherworldliness of medieval life. This tendency made empirical science impossible but also, at its best, gave a hope and dignity to human life in an age when life was too often bleak and short. Medieval literature has its own distinctive form of earthiness, but it almost always provides a view of eternity too, whether in brief glimpses or in visionary panoramas.

The Middle Ages have a claim to the label the following age pre-empted; they were not merely a hiatus between the classic and modern worlds but in some ways themselves a renaissance, a rebirth after the collapse of Roman civilization. Much of the modern world has medieval origins: the modern state and the modern city, modern languages, and a large body of collective myth, including the idea of romantic love, are rooted in the Middle Ages. But the major medieval achievement was the welding together of the separate strands of Western culture—Hebrew, Greek, Roman, and Christian—into a single culture. This culture has been greatly amplified and modified by succeeding ages, but it still retains the general shape the Middle Ages gave it.

The literature of the Middle Ages is as varied as the time that produced it. Its characteristic forms are the epic, the romance, the allegory, the folktale, the lyric, and the drama.

The Germanic and Celtic tribes had a body of heroic legend as rich as that which Homer drew upon for the *Iliad* and the *Odyssey*. There is good reason to believe that this material was in oral circulation for centuries before Christian monks, in about the eighth century, began to write it down. The earliest of the folk epics is the English *Beowulf*, which may have been based upon the exploits of a sixth-century Scandinavian warrior but acquired a heavy overlay of folklore before an eighth-century English monk put it in written form. (The poem as we know it dates from a tenth-century manuscript.) Although *Beowulf*, like the *Iliad* and the *Aeneid*, celebrates the virtues of its culture's heroic past, these virtues are not precisely the same as those of Greece and Rome. The poem provides a fascinating glimpse into an ancient Germanic courtly culture held together by the complex, ritualized mutual obligations of the *comitatus* relationship, the bond between Germanic warriors and their lord. Magnanimity, loyalty, and the willingness to fight to the death to fulfill an obligation are the virtues celebrated, all against the background of a tragic belief in fate and eventual, inevitable defeat. This ethical system blends in *Beowulf* with other elements derived from Christianity and classical culture. Beowulf has a Christian gentleness; his monstrous antagonists are identified with Cain and the Devil himself, and in the end he, Christlike, lays down his life for his people. The *Beowulf* poet also apparently knew the *Aeneid*. Although he never alludes directly to Virgil's work, its influence is apparent in the poem's sophistication of organization and in the epic conception of Beowulf's character.

The other early medieval folk epics, in various ways, also depict the confrontation of pagan heroic ethics with the ethics of classical culture and Christianity. The *Elder,* or *Poetic, Edda,* composed in the ninth century but written down in the twelfth century, preserves the heroic legends of Iceland; the *Hildebrandslied* (ninth century) and *Nibelungenlied* (early thirteenth century) record German heroic tales; the Irish sagas of Cuchulain and Conchubar (eighth to tenth centuries) and the Welsh *Mabinogion* (eleventh century) preserve the heroic tales of the Celts. In France, the epic spirit was expressed in the *chansons de geste;* the greatest of these was the *Song of Roland* (twelfth century), which, like most of the *chansons de geste*, deals with legends of Charlemagne and his knights. The *Poem of My Cid* (twelfth century) presents a Spanish hero to rival Roland and Cuchulain. The Icelandic sagas, dealing with events in Iceland between about 930 and 1030 but written down several centuries later, represent a late survival of the epic impulse, perhaps because of the relative cultural isolation of Iceland.

In general, however, epic yielded some ground to romance in the eleventh and twelfth centuries. The term *romance* was originally applied to the Old French language as distinguished from the parent language, Latin or "Roman." In time, however, it came to refer to any work in the French language and ultimately to the most common form of French works, the tale of chivalric adventure. France remained pre-eminent in the romance form throughout the Middle Ages. Romances were fundamentally epics in which the center of interest had shifted from warfare to love, especially the elaborately ritualized cult of "courtly love," which first developed among the *troubadours* of Provence and the *trouvères* of northern France. Originally half-facetious, it transferred the homage the epic hero owed to his lord to the romance hero's lady, developing an elaborate code to govern the relation between the sexes. The idealization inherent in courtly love was probably, in part, a sublimation of youthful ungratified fervor; it arose in castles where numbers of young, unmarried knights surrounded their lords and the lords' remote, unattainable ladies. The revival of interest in Greek romances and in Ovid's *Art of Love* was also a factor, as was the growing cult of the Virgin Mary beginning in the second half of the tenth century.

The favorite subjects of medieval romance derived from the Matter of Britain (the Celtic sagas, especially those of King Arthur), the Matter of France (the Charlemagne legends), and the Matter of Rome the Great (Greek and Roman stories). Popular and widely circulated romances included those of Chrétien de Troyes, who wrote the first extant French romance, *Eric and Enid* (twelfth century) and a number of other Arthurian romances; Gottfried von Strassburg's *Tristan* (c. 1200); Wolfram von Eschenbach's *Parzival* (c. 1200); *Floris and Blanchefleur* (c. 1250); *Amis and Amiloun* (before 1300); and *Ipomedon* (fourteenth century). The most charming of these works is the short Provençal romance *Aucassin and Nicolette* (twelfth century), both a romance and a lighthearted spoof of the form.

By the thirteenth century, the worldliness and sensuality of the romances had led the Church to regard them as detrimental to faith. Following its regular policy of assimilation and incorporation, however, the Church did not ban romances but rather encouraged the writing of a new kind, the "moral romance," which advanced Christian ideals while staying within the narrative conventions of the genre. The romances of the Holy Grail, the thirteenth-century French *Romance of the Rose*, and the fourteenth-century English *Sir Gawain and the Green Knight* all belong to this second phase. By the fifteenth century, the romance had become stale and formulaic, and after a period of rambling, inflated prose romances, uneasy blends of chivalric and moral elements, the genre was transformed and blended with new emphases in the Renaissance.

The *Romance of the Rose* also illustrates another major genre of medieval literature, the allegory. One of the most influential works of the Middle Ages, the *Romance of the Rose* is a dream-poem in which the poet visits the Garden of Delight, where he sees the Rose, which symbolizes his sweetheart. Major characters in the story are personified qualities: Idleness, Pleasure, Fair Welcome, Danger, Shame, and Evil Tongue. Primarily an allegory of courtly love, the poem is also a satire directed at a number of targets (including sexual infatuation, superstition, and the celibacy of the clergy) and a compendium of miscellaneous medieval lore. The work became immensely popular in France, England (where it was at least partly translated by Chaucer), and Italy (where it was translated into sonnet form, possibly by Dante). The use of a dream to introduce an allegorical narrative and of the dream-allegory structure to hold together a wide range of material was widely imitated for three hundred years. Chaucer's *Book of the*

Duchess, House of Fame, and *Parliament of Fowls* are all dream allegories; even the *Canterbury Tales* exhibits some features of the genre, including the pilgrimage motif, the use of representative characters, and the inclusion of varied tales within a generally symbolic framework. The fourteenth-century *Confessio Amantis,* by Chaucer's contemporary John Gower, and *Piers Plowman,* by William Langland, both continue to use the form. The supreme masterpiece of the genre is Dante's *Divine Comedy.* Allegory was also an important element in medieval drama. It survived vigorously into later ages, in such works as Edmund Spenser's *Faerie Queene* (1596) and John Bunyan's *Pilgrim's Progress* (1675). In fact, allegory has never died out.

Epic, romance, and allegory were all aristocratic narrative forms, written and read (or listened to) by the medieval aristocracy and gentry. There was also throughout the Middle Ages a flourishing body of popular oral narrative: folktales, beast fables, bawdy anecdotes called *fabliaux,* and folk ballads. These popular works were occasionally collected and written down; there are several collections of versified *fabliaux;* beast fables are the basis of several beast epics, the most famous of which is the French *Romance of Reynard* (twelfth century); and many popular ballads survive, though in versions dating from long after the Middle Ages. The importance of the oral folk tradition lies less in directly surviving texts than in the pervasive influence it exerted upon written literature—as sources, for example, of the stories in the *Decameron* and the *Canterbury Tales.*

Among medieval literary forms, the lyric is second in importance only to romance. There was a rich tradition of Latin lyric poetry that included Latin hymns; praises of rulers or patrons; nature songs; and "Goliardic" poetry (light occasional secular poetry, often satiric, written mainly by clerics in pretended praise of the fictional "Bishop Golias"). Vernacular poetry flowered earliest in twelfth-century Provence in southern France among the *troubadours.* The *troubadours* (or "finders" of treasure) were courtly singers who composed and sang elaborate, highly wrought poems, transmitting them orally to professional minstrels called *jongleurs,* who in turn spread them from place to place. Their major form was the *canzone,* an expression of idealized love written in a complex and rigid rhyme scheme, although they developed a number of other forms as well. The Provençal lyric influenced the *trouvères* of northern France and the *Minnesingers* of Germany. (*Trouvère* also means "finder," and *Minnesinger* means "singer of romantic love.") But its most vigorous influence was in Italy, which traveling troubadours visited in the early thirteenth century. There they inspired a school of imitators some of whom wrote in Provençal themselves, as a tribute to their mentors. Florence became the birthplace of the *dolce stil novo*—a "sweet new style" that combined the forms of the *troubadours* with a grave, philosophical content derived from Scholastic philosophy.

It is one of the more surprising facts about literary history that the very idea of drama had to be reinvented beginning in the tenth century. The plays of Plautus and Terence were read throughout the Middle Ages, and the tenth-century German nun Hroswitha of Gandersheim wrote several plays about saints' lives, imitating the form of Terence though not his ribald content. Medieval readers seem to have thought that the Roman plays were merely monologues or dialogues to be declaimed, not acted, and

Hroswitha apparently had no notion of actual performance. There was a live tradition of popular entertainment—mimes, jugglers, and clowns, as well as a body of pagan fertility plays—but no conception of the sustained acting of a dramatic text.

Drama was reborn out of the liturgy of the Church, beginning in the tenth century with brief dramatized episodes (tropes) inserted into the Mass and then developed over several centuries into increasingly elaborate plays. The plays were separated from the Church in the thirteenth century and came to be performed outdoors at the spring Corpus Christi festivals. The major forms (which overlap considerably) were the mystery play, based upon scripture and performed at the festivals by "mysteries," or trade guilds; the miracle play, based upon a saint's life and staged on his or her feast day; and the morality play, a moral allegory dramatizing the spiritual life of the typical man. Secular forms included the folk play, which was independent of the religious drama and dramatized the deeds of a popular hero such as Robin Hood or St. George; the farce, a genre derived from popular and classical rather than religious models; and the secular interlude, a short play for performance between the parts of a banquet or other celebration.

Medieval drama, like most medieval art, was an international phenomenon, flourishing in England, France, Germany, Spain, and Italy. Although it produced few masterpieces—*Everyman* is one—it made possible the flowering of drama in the Renaissance, which built not only upon the rediscovered drama of Greece and Rome but upon native traditions as well.

Medieval literature, like the age that produced it, was rich and diverse. And, again like the age itself, it was not merely a prelude to what followed but, in many respects, the matrix of the future. Fiction, poetry, and drama since the Renaissance have drawn heavily upon the classical heritage, but the forms in which they developed were established in the Middle Ages.

FURTHER READING (*prepared by J. H.*): C. W. Previté-Orton's *Shorter Cambridge Medieval History*, 2 vols., 1952, is a standard history of the Middle Ages. See also Denys Hay, *The Medieval Centuries*, 1965; Friedrich Heer, *The Medieval World*, 1962; Johan Huizinga, *The Waning of the Middle Ages*, 1924; and R. W. Southern, *The Making of the Middle Ages*, 1953. An authoritative overview of medieval literature is J. A. Burrow's *Medieval Writers and Their Work*, 1982. E. R. Curtius's *European Literature and the Latin Middle Ages*, trans. Willard Trask, 1953, is challenging but rewarding. C. S. Lewis's *The Discarded Image*, 1964, is a very readable description of the popular world view that underlay medieval literature and culture. For aspects of medieval culture closely related to literature, see Henri Pirenne, *Mohammed and Charlemagne*, 1939; T. H. White, *The Book of Beasts*, 1956; Emile Male, *The Gothic Image*, trans. Dora Nussey, 1958; Erwin Panofsky, *Gothic Architecture and Scholasticism*, 1951; and David C. Fowler, *The Bible in Early English Literature*, 1976 (a broader treatment of cultural contexts than the title would suggest). On particular genres, see, for lyric poetry, Maurice Valency's *In Praise of Love*, 1958 (on Provençal and Italian poetry); James J. Wilhelm, *Medieval Song*, 1971; and Frederick Goldin, *Lyrics of the Troubadours and Trouvères*, 1973. On epic and romance, W. P. Ker's *Epic and Romance*, 1897, is, despite its date, still valuable. See also *Arthurian Literature in the Middle Ages*, ed. R. S. Loomis, 1959; and Eugene Vinaver, *The Rise of Romance*, 1971. Good on medieval drama are V. A. Kolve, *The Play Called Corpus Christi*, 1966; and Rosemary Woolf, *The English Mystery Plays*, 1972.

The Song of Roland

(C. *1100* A.D.)

The name given to the Old French epics (written approximately between 1100 and 1500) is chansons de geste, *or "songs of deeds." Those written during the first half of this period are heroic in spirit; thereafter they take on characteristics of the romance, assimilating love stories written in the spirit of "courtly love," a tradition that idealized women and turned the conventions of human love almost literally into a religion. The earlier* chansons de geste, *like the* Roland, *treat almost exclusively of men at war. The public matter of these poems is primarily the struggle of Christianity against the forces of evil as embodied in the Muslims, misrepresented as idolaters, partly out of ignorance and partly for propaganda purposes that sometimes were shaped by the Crusades against Islam waged in the eleventh, twelfth, and thirteenth centuries.*

The central figures in most of the chansons de geste *are Charlemagne (Charles the Great) and members of his court or dynasty. During his lifetime (742–814), the historical Charlemagne forged an empire extending from the Ebro river in Spain to the Elbe in middle Europe, spreading Christianity and centralizing rule. In 800 he was named by the Pope as Holy Roman Emperor, a title and office that, except for a break of a century or so soon after his death, continued to exist until 1806. A learned man himself, he patronized learning and the arts. The* chansons de geste *have, then, a basis in historical fact and are centered on a man who was a towering figure in the development of Western and Christian culture. In the interval between his lifetime and their composition, however, they took on overlays of poetic legend; in* The Song of Roland, *for example, Charlemagne is in intimate touch with the angels of God and is believed by the enemy to be two hundred years old.*

The Roland *is the earliest and best-known surviving specimen of* chanson de geste. *The poem was unknown until 1832, when the first of several manuscripts of the work was discovered. The best of these, located in the Bodleian Library at Oxford University, is a copy by an Anglo-Norman scribe of an earlier version. Scholarly interest in the poem has ever since been intense and widespread, and the* Roland *is now generally honored as the wellspring of French literature. Despite such interest and accolades, however, many basic facts about the poem remain mysteries, the subject of endless but inconclusive conjecture. The last line of the poem, ambiguous in almost every word, identifies the poet (or is it the scribe?) as a man named Turoldus, but nothing certain is known about him except that he was apparently a native of Normandy. The date of the poem is likewise uncertain, but the consensus, especially among those who regard the work as expressing the spirit of the First Crusade (1096–1108 in Palestine and Syria), points to a time near 1100. Moreover, opinion varies about the process of epic gestation that over the course of three centuries transformed the seed of historical fact into the existent poem. One theory is that the* Roland *is essentially a compilation of many separate folk compositions. A more recent, less romantic, hypothesis is that the poem is the work of a single masterful poet who drew on written works by traveling minstrels (jongleurs) who in turn drew on oral traditions kept alive along the pilgrimage routes between France and Spain. The controversy resembles closely the disputes about the identity of Homer, and as with Homer the case for a single great poet becomes stronger as readers and scholars come to recognize the distinctive artistry of* Roland *and the careful shaping that has been given the material.*

The Song of Roland *is an epic, not in the loose sense implying mere grandeur of effect but in very technical ways. It includes many of the marks of the classical epic, including the hyperbolic praise of the past and the heroes of old, the appearance of prophetic dreams and omens, the intervention at key moments of supernatural beings, councils held in the camps of the opposing armies, catalogues of the armies on both sides, the divine commissioning of a half-reluctant hero—Charles—to do the will of Heaven (the last lines show a weary but acquiescent Charles accepting again God's charge to defend Christendom). If we accept the theory that the poem is meant to inspirit the warriors of the First Crusade, we can detect the strategy by which the epic poet defines the characteristic virtues of his people as they were evinced in the past so that these virtues can be extrapolated through the crisis of the present into a hoped-for glorious future. These features are all prominent in the Virgilian epic, with which the* Roland *poet was probably acquainted. Also heroic or epic in manner are the poet's relish in descriptions of fierce individual combats, the defiances and boasts that frame the duels, the stylized epithets ("Charles whose flowing beard is white"). One notes too the resemblance between Homer's willful Achilles and Roland (up to a point— Roland has no touch of Achilles' sulkiness).*

Like most epics, The Song of Roland *is also a portrait of the social structure and values of its age. The basis of its society is feudalism and its system of vassalage. Although some important aspects of feudalism persisted all through the Middle Ages and, more vestigially, into modern times in such systems as the British peerage, true feudalism, with its hierarchical yet also decentralized structure, flourished mainly through the eleventh century. The trend thereafter moved slowly toward concentration of power in the sovereign and in the centralized modern national state. The idea of an absolutist monarch ruling by divine right does not emerge until the sixteenth and seventeenth centuries. It is significant that in the* Roland Charles, *although clearly a revered instrument of God's will, must abide by the decisions of his counsellors and, in the trial of Ganelon, by the verdict of a jury of Ganelon's peers.*

The essence of feudalism is the system of reciprocal bonds between a chief and the vassals who serve him. At the pinnacle is a sovereign, such as Charles, to whom his knights owe service, particularly in war, and who in return is pledged to defend them. Each of these vassal knights has the same relationship to his immediate followers, and so on down the scale to the humblest of common men. Some vassals were maintained as part of their lord's household and were brought up together, forming in the process a bond of close comradeship. Other vassals might be granted lands, or "fiefs," by their liege-lord. Whatever the arrangement, the feudal code of chivalry stressed courage, loyalty, and honor, both inherently and in the eyes of others; Roland, for example, is resolved never to behave in such a way as to inspire mocking songs about him and his men. This intimate system of ties, one man to another, is important in understanding even the narrative method of The Song of Roland; *for example, one reason the poet dwells exclusively on the fights between prominent chiefs is that in the event of the leader's death his followers are entitled to quit the battle.*

The values governing the action of the Roland *are simply identified; they have to do almost exclusively with war and religion, which are intimately related to each other. (The union is epitomized with particular vividness in the archbishop Turpin, equally ready to perform priestly and martial service.) Success in battle is vital, not only for personal reasons but as a proof that God favors one's cause. The Christians* are good. The Saracens are evil, although some of them may be attractive as persons and valiant as warriors. Philosophical subtleties are entirely absent from the poem, as are signs of inward conflict between inclination and duty. Even Ganelon, psychologically complex though he is, with no grudge against Charles, carries out his treacherous scheme without apparent misgivings. Complex ideas or sophistications of theology are foreign to the poem's ideological plainness of line. (In this respect the Roland is wholly unlike Virgil's Aeneid.) The poem's values are ultimately otherworldly and at the same time severely pragmatic.

The narrative method and linguistic style are in keeping with this directness. Few poems ever written are so "unpoetical" if by "poetry" we mean embellishment, richness of language, and rhetorical dazzle. The poet, like Homer, almost completely effaces himself; we know from his occasional expressions of exultation, grief, or partisanship that he sides wholeheartedly with the Christians, but of the distinctive personal cast of his mind there are few signs. Atmospheric descriptions—of scenery, for example—are rare and brief. The vocabulary is simple and limited, the syntax forthright. Figurative language such as similes is almost entirely absent. The versification is similarly square-hewn, the typical unit of statement coinciding with the individual line. But it would be a serious mistake to think of the poet as an artless primitive. His ability to create suspense is extraordinary, enhanced rather than spoiled by occasional glances at the action to come, a strategy that can create an almost Sophoclean dramatic irony. He is also psychologically acute, although recognition of this quality depends entirely on the reader, because, like Homer, the poet prefers to reveal nuances of behavior and motive objectively, through speeches and deeds, without commentary. The very spareness of description enhances its power when it does occur, as in the account of the storm that afflicts France in sympathy with Roland's death (laisse CX), or the memorably ominous lines about the mountain pass at Roncevaux: "High are the hills, deep valleys shun the light; / The cliffs rise grey, the gorges hold dark fear" (laisse LXVI). The effect of the narrative method and style is of absolute, unwavering honesty. One might go farther and find in the poem sublimity, a quality archetypically evoked by grandeur of theme rendered with simplicity.

We should also credit the poet with a sense of structural unity. Some scholars have found the Baligant episode extraneous—an anticlimax after the high drama of Roland's death, a distracting break between that scene and the final punishment of Ganelon, or both. Implicit in some of these interpretations is the assumption that the poem is exclusively centered on Roland personally, that he is an otherwise admirable hero tragically flawed in his pride so that he refuses to sound his horn for help, his eyes opened only when it is too late. But other interpretations are possible. For example, we can see Roland not as flawed but as justified in his lack of "prudence," uniquely clear-sighted in recognizing that the only way to encounter the forces of evil is all-out warfare to the death, not shaky and specious temporizing. The episode of Charles's battle against Baligant, embodying as Baligant and his army do the worldwide forces of evil rather than the limited threat of Spanish paganism, might thus be seen as the vindication of Roland's uncompromising views and a symbolic apocalyptic vindication of Christianity in itself.

The basic narrative unit in The Song of Roland is the verse paragraph, or laisse. Except in the laisses similaires, where the poet's repetitions serve to remove the action described from the flow of time and heighten its significance, each successive laisse moves the action at least slightly forward. Yet each is also a detached unit, making a new start and leading toward a focus of generalization or clarification in *its last line. Thus the movement of the poem, from one laisse to another, has a fitful but compelling rhythm, like a series of short bursts of fire from a machine gun. The movement within each laisse has a similar staccato effect; each line is end-stopped and makes its own distinct statement in preparation for the final climax. Each line has ten syllables (not counting feminine endings), with a strong internal pause, or caesura, after the fourth (occasionally the sixth) syllable. Two stresses precede the caesura and two follow it. The ends of the lines throughout any one laisse are linked by assonance, the repetition of the same vowel sound. In the present translation by Patricia Terry, the caesura is indicated by a space in the middle of each line, and the climactic effect at the end of each laisse is suggested by assonance, which is sometimes also rhyme, in the last two lines. The following example, laisse CXXXVIII, is typical (in the Old French the caesuras are here represented by a space, as in the translation):*

> Halt sont li pui   e tenebros e grant,
> Li val parfont   e les ewes coranz.
> Sonent cil graisle   e deriedre e devant,
> E tuit rachatent   encontre l'olifant.
> Li emperedre   chevalche iriedement,
> E li Franceis   coroços e dolent,
> Nen i at cel   n'i plort e se dement,
> E prient Deu   qu'il guarisset Rodlant
> Josqued il veignent   e'l champ comunement;
> Ensembl'od lui   i ferront veirement.
> De ço qui chalt?   car ne lor valt nient:
> Demorent trop,   n'i poedent estre a tens. AOI.

> High are the hills,   and shadowy and vast,
> Deep the defiles,   and swift the mountain streams.
> The trumpets sound   ahead and to the rear,
> Blaring replies   to Roland's Oliphant.
> In bitter wrath   the Emperor rides on,
> The men of France   in sorrow and in rage;
> Not one but grieves   and bitterly laments,
> Praying that God   will keep Count Roland safe
> Until they come   and join him in the field—
> How they will fight   when they are at his side!
> What does it matter   how loyally they strive?
> They'll be too late   whenever they arrive. AOI.

FURTHER READING *(prepared by W.J.R.):* Anyone interested in exploring *The Song of Roland* in detail should consult Gerald S. Brault's *The Song of Roland: An Analytical Edition*, 1978. Brault's work, in two volumes, is a monumental work of scholarship. Volume I contains an introduction and a commentary; Volume II contains the Oxford text and a facing-page English translation. A general discussion of *Roland* is also available in John Fox's *A Literary History of France: The Middle Ages*, 1974. Alain Renoir's "Roland's Lament: Its Meaning and Function in the *Chanson de Roland*," *Speculum*, 35 (1960), 572–83, examines Roland's lament upon seeing his massacred army and relates the passage's tone and meaning to the structure of the first part of the work. On the social ethic in *Roland*, see John Halverson's "Ganelon's Trial," *Speculum*, 42 (1967), 661–69. Halverson discusses the poem's foundation in the

Germanic feudal tradition and draws comparisons between *Roland* and *Beowulf* in order to illustrate the kinship-dominated social structure. Tony Hunt's "The Tragedy of Roland: An Aristotelian View," *Modern Language Review*, 74 (1979), 791–804, examines the poem's literary qualities and the reasons for its enduring appeal. John R. Allen's "Kinship in the *Chanson de Roland*," in *Jean Misrahi Memorial Volume: Studies in Medieval Literature*, ed. by Hans R. Runte and others, begins with a general discussion of the importance of blood ties in the poem and moves on to an investigation of a more complex type of kinship presented in *Roland*. The question of Roland's pride is considered in Jean Misrahi and William L. Hendrickson, "Roland and Oliver: Prowess and Wisdom, the Ideal of the Epic Hero," *Romance Philology*, 33 (1980), 357–72. The authors discuss what some have called Roland's "sinful" pride and make a defense of Roland's not calling for aid. Christian modifications of the Germanic ideal are also discussed.

from *THE SONG OF ROLAND*

Translated by Patricia Terry

I

The mighty Charles,[1] our emperor and king,
Seven long years has been at war in Spain;
That lofty land lies conquered to the sea.
No fortress now is standing in his way,
No walls, no towns remain for him to break,
Except for Saragossa, high on its hill,
Ruled by Marsile, who has no love for God;
He serves Apollo,[2] and to Mohammed prays—
But he will come, and soon, to evil days! AOI[3]

II

In Saragossa, the pagan king, Marsile,   10
Walks through an orchard whose trees give cooling shade.
The king reclines on a blue marble bench;
His host assembles, some twenty thousand men.
He speaks these words to all his dukes and counts:
"Now hear, my lords, what evils weigh us down!
For Charles has come, the ruler of sweet France,
To seize our lands, and bring us to our knees.
I have no army[4] to fight against his own;

[1] Charlemagne, or Charles the Great (742–814), who from 771 to 814 ruled the Franks (a tribe inhabiting, approximately, the lands of modern France and Germany). As a matter of historical fact, he did not become Emperor until 800, some 22 years later than the campaign (which lasted a few months, not seven years) upon which the poem seems to be based.

[2] According to the poet's distorted version of Islam, its three gods were Apollo, Mohammed, and Tervagant. In fact, the religion of Islam is emphatically monotheistic, worshipping Allah ("God") alone.

[3] These three letters, occurring usually at the end of sections ("laisses"), are one of the most puzzling mysteries about *Roland*. They may be some sort of exclamation.

[4] This statement is inconsistent with the later information that Marsile's army numbers 400,000.

No men of mine   will drive him to defeat—
Give me your counsel,   as you are true and wise,   20
Save me from death,   and from this bitter shame."
Mute are the pagans,   except for one alone:
Blancandrin speaks,   whose castle is Val-Fonde.

III

Among the pagans   Blancandrin was wise,
A trusted vassal,   a brave and loyal knight,
Clever enough   to think of good advice.
He tells the king,   "You need not be afraid.
Send word to Charles,   the arrogant, the proud,
That you in friendship   salute him as your lord,
Offer him gifts: bears and lions and dogs,   30
And seven hundred camels,   a thousand hawks,
Four hundred mule-loads   of silver and of gold,
And fifty carts   to form a wagon-train.
He'll have enough   to pay his hired men.
He has campaigned   so long here in this land,
He won't refuse   to go back home to Aix.[5]
Say you will meet him   in France, on Michael's Day,[6]
To be converted,   adopt the Christian law,
And do him homage   in friendship and good will.
If hostages are needed,   say you will send   40
Ten, even twenty,   to witness your good faith:
We'll have to yield   the sons our wives have borne—
The risk is death,   but I will send my own.
Better that they   should sacrifice their heads
Than that we lose   our honor and our pride,
And live as beggars   with all our rights denied!"   AOI

IV

Says Blancandrin,   "I swear by my right hand,
And by this beard   that ripples on my chest,
You'll see the French   disband their troops and go,
The Franks[7] will soon   be on their way to France.   50
And when each one   has found his home again,
Charles, in the chapel   that he has built in Aix,
Will give a feast   in honor of the saint,
On Michael's Day,   when we'll have sworn to come—
But of our coming   the French will see no sign.

[5] Aix-la-Chapelle, now also called Aachen, a city in the Rhineland, was the capital of Charlemagne's realm.

[6] September 29.

[7] "The 'Franks' (*Francs*) and 'French' (*Françeis*) are for the most part used as synonymous terms. Occasionally, however, the Franks of France are distinguished from the Franks from elsewhere in the Empire. It is stated that Charles prefers the men of France to all others (3031); in 3976–77 the bishops of France are mentioned separately from those of Bavaria and Germany. The boundaries of 'France' are also variable, sometimes including the whole of Charlemagne's empire (larger than life), sometimes more restricted."—Translator's note.

The king is proud,   and cruel is his heart;
He'll have the heads   of all our men cut off.
But better far   that they should lose their heads
Than that we lose   this shining land, fair Spain,
And be condemned   to hardship and disgrace."   60
The pagans say,   "That may well be the case!"

                              V

The king declared   the council at an end.
He summoned forth   Clarin of Balaguer,
Estramariz,   and Eudropin his peer,
Long-bearded Guarlan,   and with him Priamon,
And Machiner,   his uncle Maheu,
And Joüner,   Malbien d'Oltremer,
And Blancandrin,   to be his embassy;
These ten he chose   from his most evil men.
"Barons, my lords,   you'll go to Charlemagne,   70
He is in Cordres,   holding the town besieged.
The olive branch   you'll carry in your hands,
A sign of peace   and your humility.
If you are clever,   if you persuade the king,
Much gold and silver   shall be your thanks from me,
Fiefdoms[8] and land,   as much as you desire."
The pagans say,   "That's more than we require."   AOI

                              VI

Then King Marsile   declares the council closed.
He tells his men,   "Thus you shall go, my lords:
Hold in your hands   the olive branch of peace,   80
And speak for me   to Charlemagne the king;
In his God's name,   ask him to grant me grace.
Say that before   a single month has passed,
I'll bring to France   a thousand of my men,
There be converted,   adopt the Christian law,
Become his vassal   in loyalty and love.
For this he'll have   what hostages he will."
Says Blancandrin,   "Our wishes he'll fulfill."   AOI

                              VII

The ten white mules   are brought for them to ride;
Suatilie's king   had sent them to Marsile.   90
Their reins are gold,   their saddles silver-trimmed.
The envoys mount,   and as they ride away,
Each in his hand   holds high the olive branch.
They go to Charles,   who rules the Frankish land;
He will not see   the treachery they've planned.   AOI

_____
[8] Feudal estates.

VIII

The Emperor Charles   is jubilant and gay:
The lofty walls   of Cordres are torn down,
His catapults   have laid its towers low;
His knights rejoice,   for great is their reward—
Silver and gold,   and costly gear for war.   100
In all the city   no pagan now remains
Who isn't dead   or one of the true Faith.
In a great orchard,   Charlemagne sits in state.
With him are Roland,   and Oliver, his friend;
A duke called Samson,   and fiery Anseïs,
Geoffroy of Anjou,   flag-bearer for the king;
The two companions   Gerin and Gerier.
And with these barons   is no small group of men,
For fifteen thousand   came with them from sweet France.
The knights are seated   on carpets of white silk;   110
The older men,   or clever, pass the time
Playing backgammon,   or else they sit at chess;
The nimble youths   prefer to fence with swords.
Beneath a pine,   beside a briar-rose,
A throne is placed—   it's made of purest gold.
There sits the king,   the ruler of sweet France;
White is his beard,   and silver streaks his hair,[9]
Handsome his form,   his bearing very proud:
No stranger needs   to have him pointed out.
The Saracens[10]   dismount and come on foot   120
To greet the king,   as friendly envoys would.

IX

Then Blancandrin   begins to make his speech.
He says to Charles,   "May God grant you His grace,
That glorious Lord   to whom all men must pray!
We've come to you   at King Marsile's command;
He's learned about the law   that saves men's souls,
And of his wealth   he wants to offer you
Lions and bears,   and leash-trained hunting dogs,
And seven hundred camels,   a thousand hawks,
Silver and gold   four hundred mules will bear,   130
And fifty carts   to form a wagon-train.
These will be loaded   with silver coins and gold.
Enough for you   to well reward your men.
You have campaigned   so long here in this land,
It must be time   to go back home to Aix;
My lord Marsile   says he will follow you."
The Emperor Charles   holds both hands up toward God;
He bows his head,   and gives himself to thought. AOI

---

[9] Charles is depicted as old, although historically he was only thirty-six at the time of the
Spanish campaign.
[10] Arabs; Moslems.

X

The Emperor Charles   sits with his head bent low.
He was not known   for answering in haste: 140
Always he liked   to take his time to speak.
When he looked up,   his face was stern and proud.
Thus he replies: "You've spoken well indeed.
But King Marsile   has been no friend of mine;
Of what you say,   although your words are fair,
How shall I know   how much I can believe?"
"Take hostages,"   the Saracen replies,
"Ten or fifteen   or twenty you shall have;
Though he risks death,   I'll send a son of mine,
And there will be   some even nobler men.   150
When, in your palace   at Aix, you hold the feast
That celebrates   Saint Michael of the Sea,[11]
My lord Marsile   declares that he will come,
And, in those baths[12]   which were God's gift to you,
He will be baptized,   adopt the Christian faith."
Then answers Charles,   "It still is not too late."   AOI

XI

Fair was the evening,   the sun set pure of cloud.
By Charles' command   the mules were led to stalls.
In the great orchard   he had a tent set up,
And there he lodged   the envoys of Marsile;   160
Twelve of his servants   attended to their needs.
There they remained   until it was bright day.
When, in the morning,   the emperor arose,
He heard a mass   and matins[13] first of all,
And then the king   sat down beneath a pine,
And called his barons: for what he must decide
The men of France   would always be his guide.   AOI

XII

Beneath a pine   the emperor takes his place,
And calls his barons   to say what they would do.
Duke Ogier,   Archbishop Turpin came,   170
Richard the Old,   his nephew called Henri,
From Gascony   the brave Count Acelin,
Thibaut of Reims,   his cousin Count Milon,
And there were both   Gerin and Gerier—
Count Roland came,   together with these two,
And Oliver,   so noble and so brave;
The Franks of France,   more than a thousand men.

[11] The reference is to Mont-Saint-Michel, the famous monastery on an island off the coast of Brittany (northwest France).
[12] Aix is famous for its hot mineral springs.   [13] An early-morning prayer service.

Ganelon[14] came   by whom they were betrayed.
And then began   the talks that evil swayed.   AOI

XIII

"Barons, my lords,"   says Charles the Emperor,   180
"This I have heard   from envoys of Marsile:
Of his great wealth   he'll send me a good part,
Lions and bears,   and leash-trained hunting dogs,
Seven hundred camels,   a thousand hawks,
Four hundred mule-loads   of fine Arabian gold,
And with these gifts,   some fifty heavy carts.
But he requests   that I return to France,
And says that when   I'm home again in Aix,
He'll come and yield   to holy Christian law,
He'll take the Faith,   and hold his lands from me;   190
But I don't know   the secrets of his heart."
"We must think twice,"   they say, "before we start!"   AOI

XIV

The king has brought   his discourse to an end.
And now Count Roland   has risen to his feet;
He speaks his mind   against the Saracens,
Saying to Charles,   "You can't believe Marsile!
It's seven years   since first we came to Spain;
For you I've conquered   Noples and Commibles,
I took Val-Terre   and all the land of Pine,
And Balaguer,   Tudela, Sedilie.   200
There King Marsile   displayed his treachery:
Of his vile pagans   he sent to you fifteen;
Each in his hand   held high the olive branch,
And when they spoke,   we heard this very speech.
You let your Franks   decide what should be done;
The plan they chose   was foolishness indeed:
You sent two counts   as envoys to the king,
Basant was one,   the other was Basile—
They left their heads   on a hill near Haltilies!
Finish the fight   the way it was begun: 210
To Saragossa   lead on your gathered host,
Though all your life   at war here you remain,
Avenge those men   so villainously slain!"   AOI

XV

The Emperor Charles   has kept his head bowed down;
He strokes his beard,   arranges his moustache,

---

[14] Dante, in *Inferno*, Canto XXXII, places the legendary Ganelon in hell as a traitor to his country. Note that here he appears, Judas-like, as the one disloyal member of a group of twelve of Charles's followers. His enmity to Roland is unexplained except for a statement late in the poem (laisse CCLXXII) that because of Roland he "lost both goods and gold."

And to his nephew   says neither yes nor no.
The French are silent,   except for Ganelon;
He stands up straight   and comes before the king,
With wrathful pride   begins his argument,
Saying to Charles: "Believe no underling,   220
Not me, not Roland,   who speaks against your good!
When King Marsile   sends messengers to say
He'll place his hands in yours,   and be your man,
He'll do you homage   for all the lands of Spain,
And he'll observe   our holy Christian law—
Whoever urges you   to scorn this peace
Does not care, Sire,   what kind of death we die.
A man too proud   will recklessly advise;
Let's heed no fools,   and keep to what is wise!"   AOI

XVI

When he had stopped,   Duke Naimon rose to speak;   230
In all the court   there was no better man.
He said to Charles,   "You've heard Count Ganelon;
I think the answer   that he has given you
Contains good sense,   if it be understood.
For King Marsile   there's no hope in this war:
All of his castles   have fallen to your hands,
Your catapults   have broken down his walls,
His towns are burned,   his men brought to defeat.
Now envoys ask   your mercy for the king—
If we refuse,   we're guilty of grave sin.   240
Since hostages will prove   he did not lie,
In this great war   there's no one left to fight."
The Frenchmen say,   "The duke is in the right!"

XVII

"Barons, my lords,   which one of you shall go
To Saragossa,   to talk with King Marsile?"
Duke Naimon says,   "I'll do it, by your leave.
Yield to me now   the envoy's staff and glove."
Answers the king,   "The wisest of my men!
By this white beard,   by my moustache I swear
So far from me   I'll never let you go.   250
Sit down; if you are wanted,   I'll let you know!"

XVIII

"Barons, my lords,   what envoy can we send
To Saragossa,   held by the Saracen?"
Count Roland says,   "Let me talk to Marsile!"
"No, you shall not!"   Count Oliver replies,
"Your heart is fierce,   and you are quick to wrath—
If you are sent,   there's sure to be a fight.
By the king's leave,   I'll be the one to go."
Answers the king,   "Be quiet, both of you!

Not you nor he   will set foot in that town!   260
And by this beard   that you can see is white,
I'll tell you now   the twelve peers all must stay."
The French are silent;   they dare not disobey.

XIX

Turpin of Reims   has risen from his place.
He says to Charles,   "Leave all your Franks in peace.
For seven years   you've been here in this land
Where you have suffered   great hardships and fatigue.
Give, Sire, to me   the envoy's staff and glove,
And I will seek   the Spanish Saracen;
I would be glad   to know what he is like."   270
But much displeased   the emperor replies,
"I'll hear no more—   go to your place and sit.
Keep your advice   until I ask for it!"   AOI

XX

"My valiant knights,"   says Charles the Emperor,
"Choose for me now   the nobleman of France
Who is to take   my message to Marsile."
"I name," says Roland,   "Stepfather Ganelon."
The Franks reply,   "He'd do it very well;
We could not make   a wiser choice than this."
Count Ganelon   is furious indeed;   280
Casting aside   his cloak of marten furs,
He shows a tunic   made of the finest silk.
Steel-grey his eyes   and very proud his face,
His carriage noble,   his chest is large around;
He looks so handsome,   his peers all turn and stare.
He says, "You fool,   rash are your words, and wild.
Everyone knows   I'm stepfather to you,
Yet you name me   the envoy to Marsile!
If God should grant   that I come home again,
I won't forget—   and you'll face such a feud   290
That it will last   as long as you're alive!"
"I hear," says Roland,   "your foolishness and pride.
Everyone knows   I answer threats with scorn;
A man of wisdom   this embassy requires—
I'll take your place,   if the king so desires.   AOI

XXI

Ganelon says,   "You shall not take my place!
You're not my man,   nor am I your liege-lord.[15]
But Charles commands me   to serve him in this way:
In Saragossa   I'll talk to King Marsile.
But I will find   some little trick to play,
Fit to relieve   my fury at this wrong."   300
Roland replies   with laughter loud and long.   AOI

---

[15] Master to whom feudal loyalty is due.

XXII

Count Ganelon,   when he hears Roland laugh,
Suffers such pain   he nearly splits with rage,
And he comes close   to falling in a faint.
He says to Roland,   "Now count me not your friend,
For you have swayed   this council to your will!
My rightful king,   you see me here at hand,
Ready to do   whatever you command.   AOI

XXIII

"To Saragossa   I know that I must go.   310
And from that journey   no man comes to his home.
Remember this: your sister is my wife;
She bore my son—   there is no fairer youth—
His name is Baldwin;   he'll make a valiant man.
To him I leave   my fiefdoms, all my lands.
Grant him your care;   I'll see him not again."
Then answers Charles,   "You have too soft a heart.[16]
You know my will;   it's time for you to start."   AOI

XXIV

Thus spoke the king,   "Come forward, Ganelon.
Take now from me   the envoy's staff and glove: 320
You've heard the Franks,   and they have chosen you."
Says Ganelon,   "Sire, this is Roland's work;
I'll have no love,   as long as I may live,
Either for him   or Oliver his friend.
All the twelve peers,   to whom he is so dear,
Sire, in your presence,   I challenge here and now!"
Then says the king,   "You yield too much to wrath.
Now you shall go,   since that is my command."
"I'll have the same   protection from Marsile
You gave Basant   and his brother Basile."   AOI   330

XXV

The Emperor Charles   holds out his right-hand glove,
But Ganelon,   who'd rather not be there,
Taking the gauntlet,[17]   lets it fall to the ground.
The Frenchmen say,   "Oh, God! What does this mean?
Surely this message   will bring us to our woe."
Says Ganelon,   "Your answer won't be slow."

XXVI

"Sire," says the count,   "now grant me leave to go;
Since go I must,   I care not for delay."
The king replies,   "In Jesu's name and mine!"

---

[16]"Charles's irritated reply seems astonishing; one wonders if it does not conceal his embarrassed unwillingness to admit, once Ganelon has, to Charles's relief, been chosen, that the mission is indeed extremely dangerous."—Translator's note.

[17]A glove worn as part of a suit of armor. That it is dropped is an ill omen.

Then Charles' right hand   absolves the count from sin;   340
The staff and letter   are both given to him.

XXVII

Count Ganelon   returning to his tent,
Arrays himself   as if for waging war
With the best arms   his household can provide.
The spurs are gold   he fastens to his feet,
Murglais, his sword,   is hanging at his side,
And now he mounts   his war-horse Tachebrun,
The stirrup held   by his uncle Guinemer.
Then you could see   how many knights shed tears,
All of them saying,   "Alas! You go to die.   350
Long have you served   the great king at his court,
A noble vassal;   none fail to speak your praise.
The man who named you   the envoy to Marsile
Will not live long—   in spite of Charlemagne!
Roland was wrong   not to remember this:
Behind you stands   a mighty family."
And then they say,   "Let us go with you, lord."
The count replies,   "Almighty God forbid!
I'll die alone,   not sacrifice good knights.
But you must go,   my lords, back to sweet France   360
Where you will bring   my greetings to my wife,
To Pinabel,   my good friend and my peer,
And to my son,   Baldwin, whom you all know—
Give him your help,   and serve him as your lord."
Now toward Marsile   Ganelon sets his course. AOI

XXVIII

Ganelon rides   under tall olive trees;
Now he has met   the envoys from Marsile,
And Blancandrin   is riding at his side;
Both of them talk   with great diplomacy.
Says Blancandrin,   "I marvel at your king—   370
For he has conquered   the whole of Italy,
And then to England   he crossed the salty sea
So that the Saxons   would pay Saint Peter's fee.[18]
And what of Spain   will Charlemagne require?"
The count replies,   "That's hidden in his mind.
A greater king   no man will ever find." AOI

XXIX

Says Blancandrin,   "The Franks are noble men;
But they do wrong,   those warlike dukes and counts
When by the counsel   they give to Charlemagne
They wear him out,   and others suffer too."   380

[18] Monetary tribute to Rome. These lines exaggerate the actual historical achievements of Charlemagne.

Ganelon says, "Of this I could accuse
Only Count Roland— who'll pay for it some day.
Not long ago, when Charles sat at his ease,
His nephew came dressed in his battle gear—
He'd gone for plunder somewhere near Carcasonne.
In Roland's hand an apple shone, bright red;
He told his uncle, 'Accept it, my fair lord!
I bring you here the crowns of every king.'
But his great pride will lead him on too far,
For every day we see him risk his life.   390
If he were killed, there'd be an end to strife." AOI

XXX

Says Blancandrin, "Evil is Roland's heart.
He'd have the world surrender to his will,
Proclaim his right to every land on earth!
But by whose help can he attempt so much?"
"The Franks of France! He so commands their love,
They'll never fail him, they're with him to a man.
He gives them gifts of silver and much gold,
War-horses, mules, brocades and costly arms;
The king himself won't cross him in the least: 400
By Roland's sword he'll rule to the far East!" AOI

XXXI

So Ganelon and Blancandrin ride on
Until they've made a solemn pact: they vow
That they will seek to have Count Roland slain.
They go their way, and then dismount at last
In Saragossa where a tall yew tree stands.
Under a pine a throne has been set up,
Draped in brocade of Alexandrian silk.
There sits the king, the ruler of all Spain;
Around him wait his twenty thousand men.   410
Not one of them lets fall a single word;
They're all intent on what they hope to hear
From those two men who even now appear.

XXXII

Now Blancandrin has come before Marsile,
And by the fist he holds Count Ganelon.
He speaks these words: "Hail, in Mohammed's name,
Apollo's too, whose Law we all obey!
We have delivered your message to King Charles;
When he had heard us, he raised his hands on high
To praise his God, but gave us no reply.   420
Now he has sent you one of his noble lords,
A count of France, a man of power and wealth.
From him you'll learn if there is hope for peace."
Marsile replies, "We'll hear him; let him speak."

XXXIII

Count Ganelon   has taken careful thought,
Now he begins   in well-considered words,
Subtly contrived—[19]   the count knows how to talk.
He tells Marsile: "May God grant you His grace,
That glorious Lord   to whom all men must pray!
Now by the will   of Charlemagne the King,   430
You must accept   the holy Christian law,
And half of Spain   he'll let you hold in fief.
Should you refuse   agreement to these terms,
You'll find yourself   a captive and in chains,
Taken by force   to answer Charles at Aix.
There you'll be judged,   and you will be condemned
To die a death   of infamy and shame."
At that Marsile   in fear and fury raised
A throwing spear—   its feathering was gold;
He would have struck,   but that his men took hold. AOI   440

XXXIV

In the king's face   they see the color change;
He stands there raging,   shaking his javelin.
Ganelon's hand   reaches to grasp his sword,
Out of the scabbard   draws it two finger lengths;
He tells the blade: "Shining you are, and fair!
Long have we served,   we two, at King Charles' court!
The Emperor of France   shall never say
I died alone   here in this foreign land
Before their best   have bought you at your price."
The pagans say,   "We must not let them fight!"   450

XXXV

The Saracens   prevail upon Marsile
Until the king   will take his seat again.
Said the caliph,[20]   "You don't do any good
When you are ready   to strike the Frenchman down.
Just let him speak,   and listen to him well."
Ganelon says,   "My lord, I'll suffer that.
But I won't stop,   for all the gold God made,
For all the treasure   that's gathered in this land,
Before I give him,   if he will grant me time,
The message Charles   confided to my care,   460
The words he sends   his mortal enemy."
Ganelon wore   a cloak of sable furs
Covered in folds   of Alexandrian silk.

---

[19]"Ganelon is not only an accomplished liar but an enthusiastic one (see his description of the death of the Caliph, in laisse LIV). [In the speech that here follows] only the tone would seem to misrepresent Charlemagne, except that Marsile will be allowed to keep only half of Spain, in fief to Charles; the other half is to be ruled by Roland. Thus the latter is made, once again, the focal point of the pagans' anger."—Translator's note.

[20]Successor of Mohammed; here, the Ethiopian ruler.

He throws it down— it's caught by Blancandrin—
But has no thought of letting go his sword:
His right hand grasps the handle made of gold.
The pagans say, "Noble he is, and bold!" AOI

XXXVI

Count Ganelon stands close beside the king,
And says to him, "You have no cause for wrath
If Charlemagne who rules the land of France   470
Says you must take the holy Christian law:
One half of Spain he'll let you hold in fief,
His nephew Roland will rule the other part—
There you will have a partner full of pride!
If you refuse agreement to these terms,
In Saragossa you soon will be besieged,
You'll find yourself a prisoner in chains,
And straight away you'll be led off to Aix.
And then no palfrey, no war-horse will you have,
Nor yet a mule to ride with dignity,   480
But you'll be thrown onto some pack-beast's back,
And lose your head at that long journey's end.
Here is the message I've brought at Charles' command."
He puts the letter into Marsile's right hand.

XXXVII

Now King Marsile, his face gone white with rage,
Breaks the seal open and throws the wax away,
Looks at the letter and sees what it contains.
"Thus writes King Charles who rules the land of France:
He won't forget his anger and his grief
About Basant and his brother Basile   490
Whose heads I took on a hill near Haltilie.
If I would make amends, there's just one way:
I'll have to send him my uncle, the Caliph;
If I refuse, he'll have no love for me."
His son spoke up and said to King Marsile,
"Wild empty words we've had from Ganelon,
He's gone too far— he well deserves to die.
Leave him to me, and I'll do what is right."
Then Ganelon prepared for the attack,
Brandished his sword, the pine tree at his back.   500

XXXVIII

Into an orchard the pagan king retired,
And with him went the wisest of his men.
Blancandrin came whose heavy beard was grey,
And Jurfaret, Marsile's own son and heir,
And the Caliph, his uncle and good friend.
Says Blancandrin, "Summon the Frenchman here—
I have his word that he will serve our cause."

Marsile replies, "Then bring him to me now."
Blancandrin takes the count by the right hand,
Walks through the orchard, and leads him to Marsile.   510
They plot the treason that cunning will conceal. AOI

XXXIX

Thus speaks the king: "My fair lord Ganelon,
I know I did an ill-considered thing
When in my rage I went to strike you down.
I pledge you now by these fine sable furs—
The gold they're trimmed with is worth five hundred pounds:
Tomorrow evening I'll have made fair amends."
Says Ganelon, "Your gift I won't refuse.
And if God please, by this you shall not lose!" AOI

XL

Then says Marsile, "Know that I speak the truth,   520
Count Ganelon; I want to be your friend.
Now will you tell me something of Charlemagne.
Old as he is, his time must have run out—
I know he's lived more than two hundred years.[21]
He has made journeys to so many far lands,
So many blows he's taken on his shield,
He has made beggars of so many rich kings—
When will he ever give up and take his rest?"
The count replies, "He's not as you suppose.
No one who sees him and learns to know him well   530
Can fail to say the emperor is great.
My words won't give you the measure of this man—
His noble virtues are far beyond my praise—
And who could put his courage into speech!
By God's grace honor illuminates my lord:
He'd rather die than break faith with his court.

XLI

The pagan says, "Truly, I am amazed
By Charlemagne whose hair is grey with age—
I know he's lived more than two hundred years.
He's dragged his body through so many far lands,   540
Taken such blows from lances and from spears,
So many kings reduced to beggary,
It must be time for him to look for peace."
"That will not happen while Roland is alive;[22]

---

[21] An exaggeration typical of heroic poetry; the historical Charlemagne lived 72 years.
[22] "Here again Ganelon insists that only Roland is responsible for the pagans' misfortunes, and prepares the accomplishment of his own revenge, which depends on the separation of Roland and Charles. While the motive for this may be practical, as Marsile obviously could not hope to defeat the Emperor's entire army even with Ganelon's help, it seems that Ganelon really has no grudge against Charles in spite of the latter's obvious lack of enthusiasm for him. It should be remembered that Ganelon's wife is Charles's sister, and Roland's mother." —Translator's note.

There's no such vassal   under the high-domed sky;
And very brave   is Oliver his friend.
While the twelve peers   whom Charlemagne so loves
Serve as his vanguard   with twenty thousand knights,
The king is safe;   he fears no man alive."   AOI

XLII

The pagan says,   "Now marvelous indeed   550
Is Charlemagne   whose hair has grown so white—
He is at least   two hundred years of age.
When he has conquered   so many distant lands,
Has taken blows   from so many sharp spears,
And such great kings   brought to defeat and death,
Is he not ready   to take his rest at home?"
The count replies,   "Not while his nephew lives.
There's none so valiant   from here to the far East.
A great lord too   is Oliver his friend.
While the twelve peers,   for whom Charles feels such love,   560
Serve him and lead   those twenty thousand Franks,
Charles can be sure   no foe will break his ranks."

XLIII

"Fair Ganelon,"   then says the pagan king,
"You'll see no soldiers   better at war than mine,
And I can summon   four hundred thousand knights.
Can I not fight   King Charles and all his Franks?"
"If you should try it,"   Count Ganelon replies,
"I tell you this,   you'd massacre your men.
Forget that folly,   and hear what I advise:
To Charlemagne   send such a royal gift   570
As to amaze   and gratify the French.
Send twenty men   as hostages for you,
And then the king   will go home to sweet France.
Behind his army   the rear-guard will remain,
And with them Roland,   the nephew of the king,
And Oliver,   so gallant and so brave.
And there they die—   if you'll do as I say.
King Charles will see   the downfall of his pride;
He'll have no wish   to carry on the fight."   AOI

XLIV

Answers Marsile,   "My fair lord Ganelon,   580
Tell me the way   Count Roland can be killed."
Ganelon says,   "Here is the plan I've made:
The king will cross   the mountain pass at Cize,[23]
With a strong guard   remaining far behind.
He'll leave his nephew,   Count Roland, in the rear,
Oliver too,   in whom he has such faith,

---

[23] A valley in the northern Pyrenees, the mountains that divide France from Spain.

With them a host   of twenty thousand Franks.
Then of your pagans,   a hundred thousand men
Must be sent out   to launch the first attack.
You'll see the Frenchmen   wounded and overcome—   590
Not that I say   your men won't suffer too.
If you attack   a second time that way,
You can be sure   that Roland won't escape.
Once you have done   this brave and knightly deed,
All your life long   from warfare you'll be freed."

XLV

"With that same blow   that struck Count Roland down,
You would cut off   the Emperor's right arm;
His mighty host   you'd scatter and destroy,
Nor would he find   so great a force again.
All of his Empire   would be restored to peace."   600
Marsile fell on his neck;   with joy he swore
That Ganelon   should loot his treasure-store. AOI

XLVI

Then says Marsile,   "There's one thing more to do,
Since all good counsel   depends on perfect trust;
Give me your oath   that Roland is to die."
Ganelon says,   "That shall be as you wish."
He swore by relics[24]   he carried in his sword,
And so forever   turned from his rightful lord. AOI

XLVII

A throne was there,   made all of ivory.
A book was brought   by King Marsile's command: 610
Laws of Mohammed   and Tervagant, his gods.
On this he swore,   the Spanish Saracen,
If he found Roland   was named to the rear-guard,
He would attack   with all his pagan knights,
And do his utmost   to see the Frenchman die.
"Amen to that!"   was Ganelon's reply.

XLVIII

There was a pagan,   his name was Valdabron,
Who now approached,   and stood before Marsile.
Laughing for joy,   he said to Ganelon:
"Here is my sword,   a better you'll not find;   620
The hilt is worth   a thousand coins of gold!
I give you this   for friendship's sake, fair lord;
If you will help us,   we cannot fail to find
The valiant Roland   commanding the rear-guard."
The count replies,   "You'll find him there, and win."
Then they exchange   kisses on cheek and chin.

[24] Remains of the bodies or of the personal effects of the saints.

XLIX

Afterward came   a man called Climborin.
Laughing for joy,   he said to Ganelon:
"Now take my helmet—   none better have I seen—
For with your help   in showing us the way,   630
We'll bring great Roland   to his defeat and shame."
Ganelon said,   "You won't have far to seek."
Then they exchanged   kisses on lips and cheek.   AOI

L

Then came the queen,   the lady Bramimonde.
"My lord," she said,   "I count myself your friend,
The king admires you,   and so do all his men.
Give to your wife   these necklaces from me,
Heavy with gold,   jacinths and amethysts—
A greater prize   than all the wealth of Rome,
And none so fine   has Charles who rules the Franks."   640
He put them in his boots,   and gave her thanks.   AOI

LI

Then the king summons   his treasurer Malduit:
"Have they prepared   the tribute for King Charles?"
"The seven hundred camels,   by your command,
Have all been loaded   with silver and with gold,
And twenty men,   our noblest, set to go."   AOI

LII

King Marsile places   his arm around the count,
Saying to him,   "Valiant you are, and wise.
But as you keep   your God's most holy law,
I charge you never   to turn your heart from me!   650
Of all I own   I'll give you a good part:
Ten mules are loaded   with fine Arabian gold,
And every year   you'll have as much again.
Give Charles the keys   to this broad city's walls,
Tell him its treasures   will henceforth be his own,
And then name Roland   commander of the guard.
If I can find him   crossing some narrow pass,
There I'll attack   and fight him to the death."
Ganelon says,   "Then let us speed the day."
He mounts his horse,   and quickly rides away.   AOI   660

LIII

The Emperor Charles   has now retraced his steps
As far as Galne—   that was a captured town
Whose walls Count Roland   had leveled to the ground;
No one would live there   for the next hundred years.
He waits for news   of Ganelon's return,
And for the tribute   offered to him by Spain.

At dawn one morning,   just as the sky grows light,
Count Ganelon   comes back from his long ride.   AOI

LIV

The Emperor Charles   rose early on that day.
Now, having prayed   at matins and a mass,   670
He goes outside   and stands on the green grass.
Roland is with him,   the noble Oliver,
Naimon the Duke,   and many others too.
Ganelon comes,   treacherous and forsworn.
All of his cunning   he puts into his speech,
Saying to Charles,   "I greet you in God's name!
Here are the keys   to King Marsile's fair town;
From Saragossa,   treasures beyond all price,
And twenty nobles,   hostages—guard them well!
But King Marsile   has asked me to explain   680
Why you won't see   his uncle, the Caliph:
Before my eyes   a hundred thousand men
All armed in mail,   some with their helmets closed,
Swords at their belts,   the hilts inlaid with gold,
Sailed with that lord   out to the open sea.
They fled Marsile,   hating the Christian law
Which they refused   to honor and to keep.
They sailed away,   but had not gone four leagues
When they were caught   in such a frightful storm
They all were drowned.   So perished the Caliph.   690
Were he alive,   he'd be here with me now.
As for Marsile,   my lord, you can be sure
That well before   a single month has passed,
He'll follow you   when you return to France.
There he'll accept   the Faith that you uphold,
Both of his hands   he'll place between your own,
And do you homage   for all his lands in Spain."
Then said the king,   "For this may God be thanked!
You have done well,   and great shall be your prize."
Among the hosts,   a thousand trumpets sound;   700
The French break camp,   they load each mule and horse,
And toward sweet France   they gladly set their course.   AOI

LV

King Charles the Great   has conquered all of Spain,
Captured its forts,   its cities laid to waste;
His war, he says,   has now come to its end.
The emperor rides   once more toward his sweet France.
From Roland's spearhead   the flag of battle flies;
When, from a hilltop,   it waves against the sky,
The French make camp   throughout the countryside.
Pagans are riding   through valleys deep and dark,   710
Their coats of mail   are laced up to the chin,

Their helmets closed;   bright swords hang at their sides,
Shields at their necks,   a pennon on each lance;
Where trees grow thick   high on a hill they wait,
Four hundred thousand   watching for day's first light.
Alas! If only   the French could see that sight!   AOI

LVI

The day is over,   the night grows calm and still.
The Emperor Charles   goes to his bed and sleeps.
In dream he rides   through the great pass at Cize;
Clasped in his hands   he holds an ashwood spear: 720
Count Ganelon   wrenches it from his grasp,
With raging strength   shatters and breaks the wood,
And sends the splinters   flying against the sky.
King Charles sleeps on,   not opening his eyes.

LVII

After that dream   another vision came:
He was in France,   in his chapel at Aix.
A vicious beast   was biting his right arm.
Out of the forest   he sees a leopard run,
And he himself   it cruelly attacks.
From his great hall   a boarhound rushes out   730
And comes to Charles,   running with leaps and bounds,
Seizes the beast,   biting off its right ear,
And in its fury   attacks the leopard too.
The Frenchmen watch   the mighty battle rage,
But they don't know   which side will win the fight.
King Charles sleeps on,   and does not wake all night.   AOI

LVIII

Darkness of night   gives way to shining dawn.
Throughout the host,   clarion trumpets sound.
Proud, on his horse,   the emperor appears.
"Barons, my lords,"   says Charlemagne the King,   740
"Narrow and dark   will be this mountain pass—
Who shall remain   to guard us from the rear?"
Ganelon says,   "Choose Roland, my stepson.
You have no baron   as valorous as he."
Fiercely the king   looks at the one who spoke,
And says to him: "Vile demon that you are!
You are insane,   possessed by deadly rage!
And in the vanguard—   who'll have the leader's place?"[25]
Ganelon says,   "Count Ogier the Dane.
None would do better,   and no one can complain."   750

LIX

Count Roland heard   what Ganelon proposed,
And then he answered   with knightly courtesy:

[25] Charles asks who will assume Roland's usual position at the *head* of the army.

"Noble stepfather,   now I must hold you dear,
For you have named me   commander of this guard.
The King of France   won't lose by my neglect
War-horse or palfrey,   that I can promise you;
He shall not lose   a single riding-mule,
Saddle-horse, pack-horse—   none shall give up its life
Until our swords   take payment for that prize."
Ganelon says,   "I know you tell no lies."   AOI   760

LX

When Roland heard   he'd stay with the rear-guard,
To his stepfather   he angrily replied:[26]
"Ignoble serf,   despicable foul wretch,
Do you suppose   I'll let the glove fall here
The way you dropped the staff[27]   at King Charles' feet?"   AOI

LXI

"My rightful lord,"   says Roland to the king,
"Give me the bow[28]   you're holding in your hand;
I promise you   that no man here will say
I let it fall,   like Ganelon that day
The envoy's staff   dropped out of his right hand."
The Emperor Charles   sits with his head bowed low,   770
Pulls his moustache,   and strokes his long white beard,
While in his eyes   unwilling tears appear.

LXII

At that Duke Naimon   stood up to speak his mind—[29]
The court could boast   no better man than he—
Saying to Charles,   "You have heard what's been said;
It's clear enough   that Roland is enraged.
He has been named   to go with the rear-guard;
You have no baron   who will dispute that now.
Give him the bow   that you yourself have bent;
Then choose good men   to fight at his command."   780
Charles puts the bow   in Roland's outstretched hand.

LXIII

The Emperor Charles   calls Roland to come forth.
"My noble nephew,   this is what I intend:
Half of my army   shall stay behind with you.
Accept their service,   and then you will be safe."
Count Roland answers,   "Never will I agree.
May God destroy me,   if I so shame my race!
Just twenty thousand   shall serve me, valiant Franks.

---

[26] Roland's sudden shift from "knightly courtesy" (line 752) to anger may indicate that laisse LX is not authentic; possibly, as Joseph Bédier and the translator suggest, the shift shows that Roland's words in LIX are ironic.

[27] Ganelon had dropped a glove, not a staff (laisse XXV).   [28] An emblem of command.

[29] "Duke Naimon's advice is always followed, usually to disaster."—Translator's note.

You'll cross the mountains,   safely in France arrive—   790
And fear no man   as long as I'm alive!"   AOI

LXIV

Roland has mounted   the horse he rides to war.
There comes to join him   his friend Count Oliver,
And Gerin comes,   the brave Count Gerier,
And Oton comes,   with him Count Bérengier,
And Astor comes,   and fiery Anseïs,
And old Gérard,   the Count of Roussillon,
The powerful and wealthy   Duke Gaïfier.
Says the Archbishop,   "My head on it, I'll go!"
"And I am with you,"   answers Count Gautier,   800
"I'm Roland's vassal—   my help is his by right."
Then they select   the twenty thousand knights.   AOI

LXV

Count Roland says   to Gautier de l'Hum:
"A thousand Franks,   men of our land, you'll take
To occupy   the hills and the ravines,
So that King Charles   may safely go his way."   AOI
Gautier answers,   "For you I'll do my best."
Leading away   a thousand Franks of France,
Gautier will guard   the mountains and ravines;
Whatever happens,   he won't come down again   810
Without a battle—   Almaris of Belferne
Gave them a fight;[30]   and seven hundred blades
Flashed from their scabbards   on that most evil day.

LXVI

High are the hills,   deep valleys shun the light;
The cliffs rise grey,   the gorges hold dark fear.
The French ride on   in misery and pain,
Their passing heard   some fifteen leagues around;
And when once more   they're back again in France,
In Gascony,   where Charlemagne is lord,
Then they remember   the lands they hold, their sons,   820
Their maiden daughters,   their fair and noble wives—
There is not one   who is not moved to weep
But of them all   none sorrows as does Charles,
For he has left   his nephew there in Spain;
And now his tears   the king cannot restrain.   AOI

LXVII

All the twelve peers   have stayed behind in Spain;
They guard the pass   with twenty thousand Franks,
Courageous men   who do not fear to die.

---

[30] The poet anticipates the fighting to come.

And now King Charles   is riding home again;
He drapes his cloak   to hide his grieving face.   830
Duke Naimon rides   next to the emperor;
He says to Charles,   "What weighs your spirits down?"
The king replies,   "Who asks me that does wrong.
I can't keep silent   the sorrow that I feel,
For Ganelon   will be the doom of France.
Last night an angel   sent me a warning dream:
I held a spear—   he broke it from my grasp,
That count who named   my nephew to the guard.
And I left Roland   among that pagan race—
God! If I lose him   no one can take his place."   AOI   840

LXVIII

Charlemagne weeps;   he can't hold back his tears.
They grieve for him,   his hundred thousand Franks,
And for Count Roland   are suddenly afraid.
A traitor's lies   left him to die in Spain—
Rich gifts the pagan   bestowed on Ganelon:
Silver and gold,   brocades and silken cloaks,
Camels and lions,   fine horses, riding mules.
Now King Marsile   summons the lords of Spain,
His counts and viscounts,   his chieftains and his dukes,
His high emirs,[31]   and all their warrior sons: 850
Four hundred thousand   assemble in three days.
In Saragossa   the drums begin to sound;
They place Mohammed   high on the citadel—
No pagan fails   to worship him[32] and pray.
And then they ride   with all their might and main
Through Terre Certaine,[33]   through valleys, over hills,
Until they see   the battle-flags of France.
The twelve companions   are waiting with the guard;
When they are challenged,   the fighting will be hard.

LXIX

King Marsile's nephew   rides up before the host.   860
Laughing, he prods his mule   with a sharp goad,
And to his uncle   addresses this fair speech:
"For years, Lord King,   I've served you faithfully;
My only wages   were hardships, suffering,
And battles fought   and won on many fields.
I ask this boon: have Roland left to me![34]
I'll take his life   on my sharp-pointed spear,
And if Mohammed   protects me in the fight,
The land of Spain   once more shall be our own,

[31] Arab chieftains.   [32] In fact, the use of graven images is forbidden in Islam.
[33] Possibly the term refers to Cerdagne, a valley in Catalonia, a region bordering on France, possibly to the southern slope of the Pyrenees.
[34] Aelroth (we learn his name later, in XCIII) asks that he be the first to fight Roland.

From the high passes   as far as Durestant!³⁵   870
Charles will be weary,   the Frenchmen will retreat;
In all your lifetime,   war will not touch your land."
King Marsile places   the gauntlet in his hand.³⁶   AOI

LXX

King Marsile's nephew,   the gauntlet in his fist,
Speaks to his uncle   in proud and fiery words:
"You've given me,   fair Sire, a noble gift.
Choose for me now   the twelve³⁷ among your lords
Who'll meet in battle   with the twelve peers of France."
First of them all,   Duke Falsaron replies—
This Saracen   was brother to Marsile—   880
He says, "Fair nephew,   both you and I will go,
And they'll find out   what fighting really means.
The rear-guard waits,   protecting Charlemagne;
When we attack,   those Franks will all be slain!"   AOI

LXXI

King Corsalis   comes forward in his turn.
He is a Berber,³⁸   and skilled in the black arts.
He speaks up now,   a vassal true and brave—
For all God's gold   he'd never run away.
Spurring, there comes   Malprimis de Brigant,
Faster on foot   than any horse can run.   890
Before Marsile   he stands and shouts aloud:
"At Roncevaux³⁹   my war-cry shall resound—
If I find Roland,   I'll leave him on the ground!"   AOI

LXXII

Comes an emir,   the lord of Balaguer,
A handsome man,   his face serene and bold.
Whoever sees him   riding his horse to war,
Bearing his arms   with courage and great pride,
Knows that this hero   well deserves his fame;
If he were Christian,   he'd be a noble knight.
Before Marsile   he stops and cries aloud,   900
"I'll take myself   to Roncevaux and fight!
If I find Roland,   there he shall lose his life,
Oliver too,   and all of the twelve peers.
The French will die   in sorrow and great shame.
Now Charlemagne grows old,   weak in his mind;
He'll have no wish   to carry on the war—

---

³⁵ Where this is located is uncertain; the line apparently means "from the Pyrenees to the southern border."
³⁶ By placing the glove in his hand, Marsile grants his nephew's request.
³⁷ "Including himself, as the twelve French peers include Roland."—Translator's note.
³⁸ Native of Barbary, in north Africa.
³⁹ The mountain pass where the battle with Roland and his forces will take place.

In all of Spain   we'll see no more of Franks."
For that fair speech,   Marsile gave many thanks.   AOI

LXXIII

Then an emir   who came from Moriane—
There was no man   more evil in all Spain—   910
Rode to Marsile   and made his boasting speech:
"To Roncevaux   I'll lead my company,
All twenty thousand   with lances and stout shields;
If I find Roland,   his death is a sure thing,
And every day   that loss will grieve his king."   AOI

LXXIV

And then rides forth   Torgis of Tortelose,
He is a count,   the ruler of that town;
His heart desires   to work the Christian's doom,
And with the others   he stands before Marsile,
Telling the king: "We'll triumph—have no fear!   920
Against Mohammed   Saint Peter has no chance:
Give him your prayers,   and we will take the field.
At Roncevaux   Roland shall meet my steel,
And then no man   can save him from quick death.
Look at my sword—   how keen it is, and long;
When this blade strikes   against proud Durendal,[40]
You'll soon be hearing   which one of them went down!
The Franks will die   who meet our men in war,
Leaving old Charles,   whom shame and grief confound,
To live his days   a king without a crown."   930

LXXV

And then rides forth   Escrimiz of Valterne,
That is the fief   held by this Saracen.
His voice rings out   above the crowd of men:
"At Roncevaux   I'll bring the French pride down!
If I find Roland,   he won't leave with his head,
Nor Oliver,   who leads so many men.
All the twelve peers   now stand condemned to die;
The French are lost—   all France will feel their lack—
Charles will be needing   good vassals at his back."   AOI

LXXVI

And then rides forth   the pagan Estorgant—   940
His sworn companion   Estramariz comes too—
Fell traitors both,   famed for their lying tongues.
Then says the king,   "Come forward, my good lords!
Over the mountains   you'll ride to Roncevaux,
Taking your place   as leaders of my men."

---

[40] Roland's sword.

And they reply, "My lord, at your command!
We will attack   Roland and Oliver;
Nothing can save   the twelve peers from the swift death.
Here are our swords,   keen are their blades and strong;
Soon we will stain them   bright crimson with hot blood!   950
The French will die,   and Charlemagne know grief,
All of his Empire   we'll give you for your own.
Come with us, Sire,   and witness their defeat—
We'll have King Charles,   a captive, at your feet."

LXXVII

And then comes running   Margariz of Seville—
He has the land   as far as Cazmarines—
A man so handsome   no lady can resist:
None, in his presence,   but feels inclined toward love,
Or when she sees him   refuses him a smile.
He is the best   of all the pagan knights.   960
His voice rings out   above the swelling crowd
To tell the king,   "Now have no fear, my lord!
At Roncevaux   Count Roland will be slain
By my own hand,   as Oliver shall die;
The twelve peers all   shall have their martyrdom.
Look at my sword—   its hilt is made of gold—
A noble gift   from the Emir of Primes;
I swear to you   I'll sheathe it in red blood.
The Franks will die,   and France be brought to shame.
Old Charlemagne   whose flowing beard is white   970
Shall live his days   in sorrow and in wrath.
Within a year   we'll conquer all of France—
We'll go to bed   in Saint Denis' own town."[41]
The pagan king,   in gratitude, bows down. AOI

LXXVIII

And then comes forward   Chernuble de Munigre;
His hair's so long   it sweeps the very ground.
Sometimes, for fun,   he'll carry on his back
Burdens enough   to overload four mules.
In that far country   from which he comes, they say
The sun won't shine,   no wheat will ever grow,   980
Rain never falls,   nor is there any dew;
The rocks and stones   in all the land are black:
Some, for that reason,   call it the devil's home.
Chernuble says,   "My sword is at my side;
At Roncevaux   I'll stain its keen blade red.
If I should find   great Roland on my way,
I'll challenge him—   or trust me not again—
And my sharp blade   will conquer Durendal.
The Franks will die,   and France see them no more."

---

[41] Paris; St. Denis (third century) was its first bishop and the patron saint of France.

And at these words   the twelve peers take command.   990
They lead away   a hundred thousand men,
All of them eager   to form the battle lines.
They put on armor,   inside a grove of pines.

LXXIX

The pagans wear   Saracen coats of mail,
Most of them furnished   with triple-layered chains.
From Saragossa   come the good helms they lace;
They gird on swords   whose steel comes from Vienne;[42]
Their shields are strong;   Valencia made their spears;
Their battle flags   are crimson, blue and white.
All mules and palfreys   must now be left behind;   1000
Each mounts his war-horse;   in close-knit ranks they ride.
Fair is the day,   the sun shines bright and clear,
Weapons and armor   glitter with fiery light,
A thousand trumpets   command more splendor still.
That great shrill clamor   reaches the Frenchmen's camp.
Oliver says,   "Companion, it would seem
That we will have   some Saracens to fight."
Roland replies,   "God grant that you be right!
Here we will stand,   defending our great king.
This is the service   a vassal owes his lord: 1010
To suffer hardships,   endure great heat and cold,
And in a battle   to lose both hair and hide.
Now every Frank   prepare to strike great blows—
Let's hear no songs   that mock us to our shame![43]
Pagans are wrong,   the Christian cause is right.
A bad example   I'll be in no man's sight."   AOI

LXXX

Count Oliver   has climbed up on a hill.
From there he searches   the valley to his right,
And sees that host   of pagan Saracens.
Then he calls out   to Roland, his sworn friend: 1020
"Coming from Spain   I see the fiery glow
Of shining hauberks,[44]   the blazing steel of helms.
For our brave Franks   this means great toil and pain.
And that foul traitor,   false-hearted Ganelon,
Knew this—that's why   he named us to the guard."
Count Roland answers,   "Stop, Oliver, be still!
Of my stepfather   I'll let no man speak ill."

LXXXI

Count Oliver   has climbed up on a hill;
From there he sees   the Spanish lands below,
And Saracens   assembled in great force.   1030

---

[42] A town on the Rhone river in France, noted for the manufacture of arms, as was Valencia in Spain.
[43] That is, let no mocking songs be written about us.   [44] Tunics of mail.

Their helmets gleam   with gold and precious stones,
Their shields are shining,   their hauberks burnished gold,
Their long sharp spears   with battle flags unfurled.
He tries to see   how many men there are:
Even battalions   are more than he can count.
And in his heart   Oliver is dismayed;
Quick as he can,   he comes down from the height,
And tells the Franks   what they will have to fight.

LXXXII

Oliver says,   "Here come the Saracens—
A greater number   no man has ever seen!   1040
The first host carries   a hundred thousand shields.
Their helms are laced,   their hauberks shining white,
From straight wood handles   rise ranks of burnished spears.
You'll have a battle   like none on earth before!
Frenchmen, my lords,   now God give you the strength
To stand your ground,   and keep us from defeat."
They say, "God's curse   on those who quit the field!
We're yours till death—   not one of us will yield."   AOI

LXXXIII

Oliver says,   "The pagan might is great—
It seems to me,   our Franks are very few!   1050
Roland, my friend,   it's time to sound your horn;
King Charles will hear,   and bring his army back."
Roland replies,   "You must think I've gone mad!
In all sweet France   I'd forfeit my good name!
No! I will strike   great blows with Durendal,
Crimson the blade   up to the hilt of gold.
To those foul pagans   I promise bitter woe—
They all are doomed   to die at Roncevaux!"   AOI

LXXXIV

"Roland, my friend,   let the Oliphant[45] sound!
King Charles will hear it,   his host will all turn back,   1060
His valiant barons   will help us in this fight."
Roland replies,   "Almighty God forbid
That I bring shame   upon my family,
And cause sweet France   to fall into disgrace!
I'll strike that horde   with my good Durendal;
My sword is ready,   girded here at my side,
And soon you'll see   its keen blade dripping blood.
The Saracens   will curse the evil day
They challenged us,   for we will make them pay."   AOI

LXXXV

"Roland, my friend,   I pray you, sound your horn!   1070
King Charlemagne,   crossing the mountain pass,

---

[45] Horn made of ivory.

Won't fail, I swear it, to bring back all his Franks."
"May God forbid!" Count Roland answers then.
"No man on earth shall have the right to say
That I for pagans sounded the Oliphant!
I will not bring my family to shame.
I'll fight this battle; my Durendal shall strike
A thousand blows and seven hundred more;
You'll see bright blood flow from the blade's keen steel.
We have good men; their prowess will prevail, 1080
And not one Spaniard shall live to tell the tale."

LXXXVI

Oliver says, "Never would you be blamed;
I've seen the pagans, the Saracens of Spain.
They fill the valleys, cover the mountain peaks;
On every hill, and every wide-spread plain,
Vast hosts assemble from that alien race;
Our company numbers but very few."
Roland replies, "The better, then, we'll fight!
If it please God and His angelic host,
I won't betray the glory of sweet France! 1090
Better to die than learn to live with shame—
Charles loves us more as our keen swords win fame."

LXXXVII

Roland's a hero, and Oliver is wise;
Both are so brave men marvel at their deeds.
When they mount chargers, take up their swords and shields,
Not death itself could drive them from the field.
They are good men; their words are fierce and proud.
With wrathful speed the pagans ride to war.
Oliver says, "Roland, you see them now.
They're very close, the king too far away. 1100
You were too proud to sound the Oliphant:
If Charles were with us, we would not come to grief.
Look up above us, close to the Gate of Spain:[46]
There stands the guard— who would not pity them!
To fight this battle means not to fight again."
Roland replies, "Don't speak so foolishly!
Cursed be the heart that cowers in the breast!
We'll hold our ground; if they will meet us here,
Our foes will find us ready with sword and spear." AOI

LXXXVIII

When Roland sees the fight will soon begin, 1110
Lions and leopards are not so fierce as he.
Calling the Franks, he says to Oliver:
"Noble companion, my friend, don't talk that way!

---

[46] The mountain pass.

The Emperor Charles,   who left us in command
Of twenty thousand   he chose to guard the pass,
Made very sure   no coward's in their ranks.
In his lord's service   a man must suffer pain,
Bitterest cold   and burning heat endure;
He must be willing   to lose his flesh and blood.
Strike with your lance,   and I'll wield Durendal—   1120
The king himself   presented it to me—
And if I die,   whoever takes my sword
Can say its master   has nobly served his lord."

LXXXIX

Archbishop Turpin   comes forward then to speak.
He spurs his horse   and gallops up a hill,
Summons the Franks,   and preaches in these words:
"My noble lords,   Charlemagne left us here,
And may our deaths   do honor to the king!
Now you must help   defend our holy Faith!
War is upon us—   I need not tell you that—   1130
Before your eyes   you see the Saracens.
Confess your sins,   ask God to pardon you;
I'll grant you absolution   to save your souls.
Your deaths would be   a holy martyrdom,
And you'll have places   in highest Paradise."
The French dismount;   they kneel upon the ground.
Then the archbishop,   blessing them in God's name,
Told them, for penance,   to strike when battle came.[47]

XC

The kneeling Franks   have risen to their feet.
They are absolved,   and free from any sin;   1140
Archbishop Turpin   has signed them with the cross.
Now they have mounted   swift horses bred for war;
They bear the weapons   befitting them as knights.
Thus they await   the Saracen attack.
Count Roland calls   Oliver to his side:
"My lord companion,   the words you spoke were true;
This is the work   of faithless Ganelon—
He sold us all   for treasure, gold and coins.
Now may he suffer   the emperor's revenge!
As for the bargain   that King Marsile has made,   1150
Without good swords   he'll forfeit what he paid."   AOI

XCI

At Roncevaux   Count Roland passes by,
Riding his charger,   swift-running Veillantif.

---

[47] The priest in confession administered absolution as God's agent, on condition that the sinner do penance; here fighting in battle is substituted for the usual forms of penance such as prayer, fasting, and almsgiving.

He's armed for battle,   splendid in shining mail.
As he parades,   he brandishes his lance,
Turning the point   straight up against the sky,
And from the spearhead   a banner flies, pure white,
With long gold fringes   that beat against his hands.
Fair to behold,   he laughs, serene and gay.
Now close behind him   comes Oliver, his friend,   1160
With all the Frenchmen   cheering their mighty lord.
Fiercely his eyes   confront the Saracens;
Humbly and gently   he gazes at the Franks,
Speaking to them   with gallant courtesy:
"Barons, my lords,   softly now, keep the pace!
Here come the pagans   looking for martyrdom.
We'll have such plunder   before the day is out,
As no French king   has ever won before!"
And at this moment   the armies join in war.   AOI

XCII

Oliver says,   "I have no heart for words.   1170
You were too proud   to sound the Oliphant:
No help at all   you'll have from Charlemagne.
It's not his fault—   he doesn't know our plight,
Nor will the men   here with us be to blame.
But now, ride on,   to fight as you know how.
Barons, my lords,   in battle hold your ground!
And in God's name,   I charge you, be resolved
To strike great blows   for those you have to take.
Let's not forget   the war-cry of King Charles!"
He says these words,   and all the Franks cry out;   1180
No one who heard   that mighty shout, "Montjoie!"[48]
Would soon forget   the valor of these men.
And then, how fiercely,   God! they begin to ride,
Spurring their horses   to give their utmost speed,
They race to strike—   what else is there to do?
The Saracens stand firm;   they won't retreat.
Pagans and Christians,   behold! in battle meet.

XCIII

King Marsile's nephew,   Aelroth is his name,
First of the pagans,   rides out before the host,
Taunting our Franks   with loud malicious words: 1190
"Today, foul Frenchmen,   you'll break a lance with us;
You stand here now   abandoned and betrayed!
The king was mad   to leave you at the pass:
This day sweet France   will see its pride cast down.

---

[48] Charles's battle cry. For one explanation, see laisse CLXXXIII. *Mont* means "hill" and
joie means "joy." "Jenkins suggests also the pilgrims' cry of joy on seeing the end of their quest
for Monte Gaudia or a similar hill near Jerusalem or Santiago, but no sure explanation exists."
—Translator's note.

The Emperor Charles   will lose his good right arm!"
Count Roland hears him,   God! with what pain and rage!
He spurs his horse   to run with all its might,
Levels his lance,   strikes Aelroth such a blow
His shield is shattered,   the hauberk split in two,
The pagan's bones   crack open in his chest,   1200
His broken spine   sticks out behind his back
So that the spear   drives out his very soul.
Under the thrust   the body starts to fall,
And Roland hurls him   a spear's length from his horse;
He falls down dead,   his neck broken in two.
But still Count Roland   gives him these parting words:
"Foul infidel,   King Charles is not a fool,
Nor was he ever   unfaithful to his trust.
Wisely he chose   that we should guard the pass;
Sweet France will lose   no glory here today.   1210
Strike on, you Franks!   First blood will win the fight!
Their cause is evil,   and we are in the right."   AOI

*[In laisses XCIV to CII (lines 1213–1310), omitted here, nine other of Charles's peers kill
pagan chieftains in individual combat: Oliver kills Falsaron (Aelroth's uncle, King Marsile's
brother); Archbishop Turpin kills Corsalis; Gerin kills Malprimes de Brigal; Gerier kills the
emir of Balaguer; Samson kills the emir of Moriane; Anseïs kills Torgis of Tortelose; Engelier
de Bordeaux kills Escremiz de Valterne; Oton kills Estorgans; Berengier kills Estramariz. Of
the twelve greatest pagan warriors, only Margariz of Seville and Chernuble remain.]*

CIII

That valiant knight,   Margariz of Seville,
Handsome and strong,   agile and very quick,
Spurs on his horse   and charges Oliver,
Piercing his shield   under its boss of gold
So that the spear-point   grazes his very ribs.
The hand of God   has turned aside that thrust,
The shaft is broken;   Oliver does not fall.
Margariz gallops on,   right through the Franks,
And blows his trumpets   to cheer the pagan ranks.

CIV

Now wondrous battle   rages throughout the field.   1320
Roland fights on,   not caring to keep safe,
Strikes with his spear   until the shaft is gone—
And fifteen blows   it gave before it broke.
Then from its scabbard   he draws great Durendal,
Spurs on and charges   Chernuble de Munigre,
Slashing his helmet   where the bright rubies gleam,
Slices his hood   and downward through his hair,
Between the eyes   he cuts his face in two,
Through the bright hauberk,   of tightly-woven mail,
And all his body   down to the groin is split;   1330

Then through the saddle   adorned with threads of gold,
The sword drives deep   into the pagan's horse,
Cleaving the spine   where there's a joint or no—
Both man and beast   fall dead in thick green grass.
Then Roland says,   "Foul serf, you've found your doom.
See how Mohammed   protects you in the fray!
No man so vile   will win this fight today."

CV

Count Roland gallops   everywhere in the field
With Durendal,   well-made to slash and cleave.
Great is the havoc   among the Saracens—   1340
One on the other   he heaps their bodies high!
The bright blood flows   streaming along the ground,
Roland's hauberk   and both his arms are red,
The neck and shoulders   of his good charger too.
Count Oliver   fights on and never stops;
The other peers,   like him, deserve all praise.
The valiant Franks   strike and cut down their foes;
The pagans die,   or stricken, fall and faint.
Says the archbishop,   "God's blessing be their thanks!"
He shouts, "Montjoie!"   the war-cry of the Franks. AOI   1350

CVI

Oliver rides   through the thick of the fray;
His spear is shattered,   only a stump remains.
He gallops on,   and charges Malsaron,
Breaking his shield   bright with flowers and gold;
The pagan's eyes   are thrust out of his head,
Parts of his brain   stream down him to his feet,
He goes to join   the seven hundred slain.
Oliver kills   Torgis and Esturgoz;
The spear-shaft breaks   and splinters in his hands.
Then Roland says,   "What are you doing, friend?   1360
For such a battle   why did you choose a stick?
I'll take my chances   with iron and stout steel!
Where is your sword,   the one you call Halteclere,
With crystal hilt   and guard of shining gold?"
"I had no time," he says, "to draw my sword,
With all those pagans   to send to their reward!" AOI

CVII

Lord Oliver   has drawn his good Halteclere,
The sword that Roland   was asking him to use,
And shows its powers   in a most knightly way:
He rides to strike   Justin de Val Ferrée—   1370
With just one blow   he splits that pagan's head,
Cleaves through the body,   the brightly polished mail,
The splendid saddle   sparkling with gold and jewels,
And breaks the spine   of Justin's war-horse too;

Both bodies fall   into the meadow grass.
And Roland says,   "That's my true brother now!
For such great blows   Charlemagne holds us dear."
Then from all sides,   "Montjoie!" the Frenchmen cheer.   AOI

CVIII

Count Gerin rides   a horse he calls Sorel,
With Gerier,   his friend, on Passecerf;   1380
They loosen reins   and spur their horses on,
Racing to charge   the pagan Timozel.
One strikes the hauberk,   the other hits the shield,
Both of their spears,   deep in his body, break;
He's thrown off backward,   dead, in a fallow field.
Which was the faster   of these two chevaliers?
I haven't heard,   and certainly can't tell.
Eperveris,   whose father was Borel,
Then met his slayer,   the Gascon Engelier.
Archbishop Turpin   has slaughtered Siglorel;   1390
The great enchanter   went once before to Hell—
That time by magic,   with Jupiter[49] as guide.
Then Turpin says,   "I think he was no friend!"
And Roland answers,   "To death that villain goes.
Oliver, brother,   I love to see such blows!"

CIX

Meanwhile the battle   grows hotter all the time,
Both Franks and pagans   exchange prodigious blows;
Some charge and strike,   others defend their lives.
Spears without number   are shattered, stained with blood,
Pennons are ripped,   and battle-flags destroyed!   1400
So many Franks   who lay down their young lives
Will not return   to mothers or to wives
Or to those waiting   beyond the Gates of Spain.
King Charlemagne   will weep for bitter woe;
What good are tears?   His help will come too late.
Ill was he served   by Ganelon who went
To Saragossa   and sold the king's own men.
For that betrayal,   he lost his life and limbs;
The trial[50] at Aix   condemned him to be hanged
With thirty kinsmen   who also had to pay,   1410
And never thought   their lives would end that way.   AOI

CX

Now fierce and grim   the battle rages on.
Oliver, Roland—   how valiantly they fight!
Turpin delivers   more than a thousand blows;

---

[49] As with Apollo in line 8, the name of a classical god is given to a demon. But Apollo "is worshiped as a god, if only by the Saracens. Classical nomenclature in the *Roland* is no more reliable than the poet's geography."—Translator's note.

[50] This is described near the end of the poem.

Among the peers   none dreams of holding back,
And all together,   the Franks, as one man, strike.
By hundreds, thousands,   the pagans fall and die;
There's no way out   except for those who flee:
Each one who stays   is living his last day.
But others die—   the best among the Franks—   1420
They'll never see   their families, their wives,
Or Charlemagne   who waits beyond the pass.
A fearful storm   that very day strikes France;
Through rushing winds   long peals of thunder roar,
And heavy rains,   enormous hailstones fall,
Great bolts of lightning   are striking everywhere.
Now the whole earth   is trembling dreadfully
From Saint Michel   all the way down to Seinz,
From Besançon   to Wissant on the sea;
There is no stronghold   without a shattered wall.   1430
At noontime shadows   darken the light of day;
The only brightness   comes when the black sky cracks,
And no man sees it   who isn't terrified.
Many declare,   "The world is at an end—
The Day of Wrath   has come upon us now!"
But they know nothing,   and they believe a lie.
The heavens grieve   that Roland is to die.

CXI

The Franks of France   have struck with mighty force;
Enormous numbers   of Saracens are slain:
A hundred thousand,   and just one man remains.[51]   1440
Says the archbishop,   "Our Franks are brave and true;
In all the world   there are no better men.
Gesta Francorum[52]   says of our emperor
That he was served   by heroes one and all."
They walk the field,   searching among the dead;
For grief and pity   they cannot help but weep,
Thinking of those   whose loved ones won't come back.
Then King Marsile   launches a new attack.   AOI

CXII

Now King Marsile   through a deep valley rides
With the great host   he summoned to his aid: 1450
Twenty battalions   march with the Saracen.
Their helmets gleam   with gold and precious stones,
Bright are their shields,   their hauberks saffron-gold.
With seven hundred trumpets   sounding the charge,
Their coming echoes   for many miles around.
Then Roland says,   "Oliver, brother, friend,
Foul Ganelon   has sent us to our deaths;

---

[51] Margariz, presumably; see LXXVII and CIII.
[52] Histories (literally, "Deeds") of the Franks.

But this betrayal   can never be concealed,
And we can leave   our vengeance to King Charles.
We'll have a battle   to try our utmost strength—   1460
Fiercer than any   the world has seen before.
I'll strike them down   with Durendal, my sword,
And you, companion,   strike with your own Halteclere.
We've carried them   through so many far lands,
So many battles   we've won thanks to these blades!
No evil songs   to mock them shall be made."   AOI

CXIII

King Marsile sees   the slaughter of his men.
Then horns and trumpets   ring out at his command,
And he rides on   with his assembled host.
One Saracen   rides out in front: Abisme,   1470
The fiercest man   in all that company.
Evil at heart,   and guilty of great crimes,
He has no faith   in Mary's holy Son.
This pagan's skin   is black as melted pitch.
He'd rather murder   or do vile treachery
Than have the gift   of all Galicia's[53] gold.
He never laughs   or joins in any sport,
But he is bold   and valiant when he fights.
This makes him dear   to the foul king Marsile;
He bears the dragon,   flag of the Saracens.   1480
Archbishop Turpin   will be no friend to him—
Seeing this pagan,   he longs to strike him down.
In a low voice   he speaks thus to himself:
"This man must be   a mighty heretic—
Surely his death   has been too long delayed.
I have no love   for men who are afraid."[54]

CXIV

And so the battle   begins with Turpin's charge.
He rides a horse   he took from King Grossaille,
That time in Denmark   he fought him to his death.
The horse is swift   and spirited and proud;   1490
His hooves are hollow,   slender and strong his legs,
Short in the thigh,   his quarters large around,
His chest is deep,   his back set straight and high.
White is his tail,   yellow his flowing mane,
His ears are small,   his head of tawny gold;
No charger set   to race him has a chance.
Archbishop Turpin   spurs on against Abisme—
And with what valor!   Nothing can stop him now.
He strikes the shield   a superhuman blow;

---

[53] Province in northwest Spain.
[54] "That is, 'I never loved a coward or cowardice'; but it seems clear that Turpin refers to himself, feeling perhaps even a bit reluctant to attack so dreadful a Saracen."—Translator's note.

Its surface sparkles   with topaz, amethyst,   1500
Stones of great virtue,   rubies that hotly glow—
(In Val Metas[55]   a devil gave that shield
To the emir,   who gave it to Abisme).
But Turpin's spear   accords it no respect:
After his blow   it isn't worth a cent.
Right through that pagan   his spear thrusts like a spit;
He throws the body   into an empty space.
The Frenchmen say,   "Against him no one stands!
The holy staff[56]   is safe in Turpin's hands."

CXV

The Franks can see   that hosts of Saracens   1510
All through the field   advance on every side.
They cry out often   to Roland, Oliver,
The twelve French peers,   to come to their defense.
Archbishop Turpin   counsels them in this way:
"Barons, my lords,   surrender not to fear,
But in God's name,   I pray you, hold your ground,
That no man mock you   in a malicious song—
Better to die   with honor on this field!
Very soon now   we'll meet our promised end;
We cannot hope   to live beyond today.   1520
But this I tell you   is true without a doubt:
For you stand open   the gates of Paradise:
You'll take your places   beside the Innocents."[57]
Hearing these words,   the Frenchmen all rejoice;
"Montjoie!" they cry,   as with a single voice. AOI

CXVI

From Saragossa   there came a Saracen
Who called his own   one-half of all that town.
This Climborin,[58]   who was no perfect knight,
Heard the count's oath   that he'd betray the Franks,
In sign of friendship   kissed the count on the mouth,   1530
And gave him gifts: his helm, a precious stone.
Climborin says   he'll bring the Empire down,
And strike the crown   from Charlemagne's proud head.
He rides a charger   whose name is Barbamosche—
No hawk or swallow   can fly as fast as he.
The pagan spurs,   and gives the horse his head,
Charging to strike   the Gascon Engelier.
Hauberk and shield   cannot protect him now;
Climborin's thrust   goes deep into his flesh
Until the spear-head   comes out the other side.   1540

[55] Possibly Mecca, the Islamic holy city.
[56] The crosier (a stylized shepherd's crook), carried by bishops.
[57] The Holy Innocents were the children slaughtered by King Herod in his attempt to kill the newborn Jesus (Matthew, chapter 2) and were thus emblems of the sinless saved.
[58] For Climborin, see XLIX.

He flings the body   a spear's length from his horse,
And then he shouts,   "They're asking for defeat!
Strike them down, pagans—   destroy them in their ranks!"
"There died a hero.   God save us!" cry the Franks.   AOI

CXVII

And then Count Roland   calls Oliver aside:
"My lord, companion,   Engelier has been slain;
We cannot boast   a better knight than he."
The count replies,   "God grant me his revenge!"
With golden spurs   he urges on his horse,
Holding aloft   Halteclere all red with blood;   1550
With mighty force   he strikes at Climborin,
Pulls out his sword—   the Saracen falls dead,
And demons come   to carry off his soul.
Oliver kills   Duke Alphaïen next,
Then Escababi   is parted from his head.
The count unhorses   seven more Arab knights
Who won't be fit   ever to fight again.
And Roland says,   "Now wrathful grows my friend!
His deeds of valor   don't shrink beside my own!
For blows like that   Charles' love is our reward."   1560
And then he shouts,   "Strike on, you noble lords!"

CXVIII

There was a pagan   whose name was Valdabron.[59]
He raised to knighthood   the Saracen Marsile.
Four hundred galleys   he rules upon the sea,
And every sailor   is bound by oath to him.
His treachery   once took Jerusalem,
He desecrated   Solomon's Temple there—
Close to the fonts[60]   he killed the patriarch.
To Ganelon,   who promised him good faith,
He gave his sword   and then a thousand coins.   1570
He rides a horse   whose name is Gramimond—
There is no falcon   who'd beat him in a race.
Urging him now   with the sharp prick of spurs,
Valdabron charges Samson,   the mighty duke;
He breaks his shield,   the hauberk splits in two,
Up to the pennon   he thrusts the spear-point through,
And fells the duke   a spear's length from his horse:
"Strike them down, pagans,   these Franks don't have a chance!"
"There died a hero,"   say grieving men of France.   AOI

CXIX

As for Count Roland,   when he sees Samson dead,   1580
You can imagine   the sorrow that he feels.
He spurs his horse   and charges with great speed,

---

[59] Introduced earlier, in XLVIII.   [60] Basins used for baptism.

Holding his sword   worth more than purest gold.
Valiant, he strikes   with every ounce of strength
Valdabron's helmet   sparkling with precious stones,
Splits his head open,   his body cased in mail;
Cleaving the saddle,   gilded and set with jewels:
The blade goes deeper   and breaks the horse's back.
Some cheer, some grieve,   but man and beast fall dead.
The pagans say,   "You've struck us a hard blow!"   1590
And Roland answers,   "Why should I love your side?
You're in the wrong,   and you are full of pride." AOI

CXX

From Africa   there came an African
Called Malquiant,   the son of King Malcud.
His arms and armor,   all overlaid with gold,
Gleam in the sunlight,   the brightest on the field.
He sits a charger   whose name is Saut-Perdu—
No horse can win   against him in a race.
Malquiant strikes   the fiery Anseïs,
Smashing to bits   the blue and crimson shield;   1600
The hauberk breaks   where it was joined in two,
Spear-point and shaft   into the body thrust:
The count is dead;   his time has all run through.
The French lords say,   "Baron, we grieve for you!"

CXXI

Now through the battle   Archbishop Turpin rides:
No tonsured[61] priest   who ever sang a mass
Had such high courage   to do heroic deeds.
This, to the pagan: "God smite you with His curse!
You have cut down   a man my heart laments."
He sends his horse   galloping on to charge,   1610
Strikes Malquiant   through his Toledo[62] shield,
And flings his body   onto the grassy field.

CXXII

And then comes forward   a pagan called Grandoine,
Capuel's son,   he's Cappadocia's[63] heir.
He sits a horse   whose name is Marmorie—
It gallops faster   than any bird can fly.
He loosens reins   and pricks him with his spurs
To charge Count Gerin   with all his skill and force.
The crimson shield   falls from the Frenchman's neck,
His hauberk breaks,   most of it splits away,   1620
Then the blue banner   thrusts deep into his flesh,
And Grandoine hurls   his body to a rock.

---

[61] Having the top of the head shaved, as was done with priests and monks.
[62] City in central Spain, famous for its excellent steel and weapons.
[63] Region in the central part of what is now Turkey.

That pagan kills   Gerin's friend Gerier,
And Bérengier,   and Gui de Saint-Antoine;
He charges next   the mighty duke Austorge,
Lord of Valence   and Envers on the Rhône,
Who falls down dead   as all the pagans cheer.
The Frenchmen say,   "Our end is coming near."

CXXIII

Roland holds high   his sword stained red with blood.
He has not missed   the outcry of the Franks,   1630
And feels such sorrow   he thinks his heart will break.
This, to the pagan: "God's curse upon you fall!
I'll sell you dear   the noble lord you've slain!"
He spurs his horse   who cares not to delay,
Seeks out Grandoine,   hoping to make him pay.

CXXIV

Grandoine is valiant,   powerful, very brave;
He is a hero,   bold on the battlefield.
All of a sudden   Count Roland bars his path.
Although the pagan   never saw him before,
By his proud face   he knows him, by his eyes,   1640
His noble bearing,   his stature, tall and strong;
Grandoine can't help   but tremble with great fear.
He tries to flee,   but cannot get away
Before Count Roland   stops him with such a blow
That his whole helmet   down to the nose-piece breaks,
The sword blade cleaves   through nose and mouth and teeth,
Down through his body   encased in shining mail,
Into the saddle   all silver-trimmed and gold,
And drives on deep   into the horse's back.
Nothing can save them—   both man and beast fall dead.   1650
Spaniards cry out   in horror at the sight.
The Frenchmen say,   "Our lord knows how to fight!"

CXXV

The wondrous battle   is spirited and grim;
Blow after blow   the angry Frenchmen strike.
Their sword blades cleave   through fists and ribs and spines,
Through cloth and armor   into the living flesh.
On the green grass   the bright blood flows in streams.
The pagans say,   "This is too much for us!
Mohammed's curse   upon the Empire fall!
There are no men   as hard to kill as these."   1660
And to Marsile   the Saracens cry out:
"Ride to our aid,   or we'll be put to rout!"

CXXVI

The battle grows   ever more swift and fierce.
The Frenchmen strike   keen blows with burnished spears.

You would have seen   so many in great pain,
So many dead,   so many drenched in blood!
Face up or downward,   one on the other lies.
The Saracens   cannot bear any more:
They flee the field,   whether they will or no.
The wrathful Franks   pursue them as they go.   AOI   1670

CXXVII

Count Roland says   to Oliver his friend:
"My lord companion,   I'm sure you will agree
That our archbishop   makes a most valiant knight—
There is none better   on earth beneath the sky;
With lance in hand,   or spear, how he can fight!"
The count replies,   "Then let's go to his side!"
When he has spoken,   the Franks attack once more.
Hard are the blows,   the slaughter pitiless;
Many a Christian   is brought to grievous pain.
Then to behold   Roland and Oliver   1680
Wielding their swords   to cut the pagans down!
Beside them Turpin   thrusts with his mighty spear.
We know what happened   according to the *Geste*,
Chronicles, records   bear witness to the fact:
Four thousand pagans   by those few Franks were slain.
Through four assaults   the Frenchmen hold their ground.
But with the fifth   their strength comes to an end.
That final charge   kills all the knights of France
Except for sixty   who by God's will survive—
They'll make the pagans   pay dearly for their lives!   AOI   1690

CXXVIII

Count Roland sees   the slaughter of the Franks.
He says these words   to Oliver his friend:
"Noble companion,   what do you counsel now?
So many Franks   lie dead upon the field—
Well could we weep   for that fair land, sweet France,
Which will not see   these valiant lords again.
Oh! Charles, my friend,   if only you were here!
Oliver, brother,   how can we call him back?
Is there no way   to tell the king our plight?"
Oliver answers,   "Not if we save our fame.   1700
Better to die   than learn to live with shame."   AOI

CXXIX

Then Roland says,   "I'll sound the Oliphant.
King Charles will hear it   on the high mountain pass;
I promise you,   the Franks will all turn back."
Oliver answers,   "Then you would bring disgrace
And such dishonor   on your whole family
The shame of it   would last them all their lives.
Three times I asked,   and you would not agree;

You still can do it,   but not with my consent.
To sound the horn   denies your valor now.   1710
And both your arms   are red with blood of foes!"
The count replies,   "I've struck some pretty blows."   AOI

                          CXXX
Then Roland says,   "This has become a war.
I'll blow my horn,   and Charlemagne will hear."
Oliver says,   "Then you'll disgrace your name.
Each time I asked you,   companion, you refused.
If Charles were with us,   we would not come to grief.
No one can say   our Franks have been to blame.
I promise you—   I swear it by my beard—
If I should live   to see my sister's face,   1720
You'll never lie   in Alda's[64] sweet embrace!"   AOI

                          CXXXI
Then says the count,   "You're angry at me. Why?"
Oliver answers,   "Roland, you are to blame.
There is no madness   in courage for good cause,
But men should listen   to reason, not blind pride.
You were too reckless,   and so these Franks have died.
Never again   will we serve Charlemagne.
Had you believed me,   my lord would be here now,
We would have fought   and beat the Saracens,
Marsile would be   our prisoner, or dead.   1730
We are the victims   of your great prowess now!
We won't be there,   alas! to help King Charles,
A man whose peer   will not be seen on earth.
And you will die,   leaving sweet France to shame.
Brothers in arms   we've been until this day;
Now we have only   a last farewell to say."   AOI

                          CXXXII
Archbishop Turpin,   hearing their angry words,
Urges his horse   with spurs made of pure gold,
And riding up,   reproaches both of them:
"Roland, my lord,   and you, Lord Oliver,   1740
End your dispute,   I pray you, in God's name.
It's too late now   to blow the horn for help,
But just the same,   that's what you'd better do.
If the king comes   at least we'll be avenged—
Why should the Spaniards   go home safe to rejoice?
And then the Franks   will ride back to this place;
They'll find us dead,   our bodies hacked by swords,
Put us in coffins   carried on horses' backs,
And they will weep   for pity and for grief.

---

[64] Roland's fiancee.

We will be buried   with honor in a church,   1750
And not be eaten   by wolves and pigs and dogs."
Then Roland answers: "Your words are wise, my lord."

CXXXIII

Count Roland presses   the horn against his mouth;
He grasps it hard,   and sounds a mighty blast.
High are the hills,   that great voice reaches far—
They hear it echo   full thirty leagues around.
Charlemagne hears,   and so do all his men.
The Emperor says,   "Our Franks are in a fight!"
Count Ganelon   returns a swift reply:
"Except from you,   I'd take that for a lie!" AOI   1760

CXXXIV

And now Count Roland,   in anguish and in pain,
With all his strength   sounds the great horn again.
Bright drops of blood   are springing from his mouth,
Veins in his forehead   are cracking with the strain.
That mighty voice   cries out a second time;
Charlemagne hears it,   high on the mountain pass,
Duke Naimon listens,   and so do all the Franks.
Then says the king,   "That is Count Roland's horn!
He'd never sound it,   except for an attack."
Ganelon says,   "What battle can there be?   1770
You have grown old,   your hair is streaked with white;
The words you speak   could well befit a child.
You ought to know   how great is Roland's pride—
The wonder is   God suffers it so long.
He captured Noples,   and not by your command,
And then flushed out   the Saracens inside;
He fought them all,   Roland, your loyal man,
And then took water   and washed the field of blood,
Hoping that you   would not detect the fight.
Just for a rabbit   he'll blow his horn all day!   1780
Now he is playing   some game to please his peers.
Who in the world   would dare make war on him!
Ride on, I tell you!   What are we waiting for?
We've far to go   to see our lands once more." AOI

CXXXV

Count Roland's mouth   is crimson with his blood,
His temples broken   by the tremendous strain.
He sounds the horn   in anguish and in pain.
Charlemagne hears,   and so do all the Franks.
Then says the king,   "How long that horn resounds!"
Duke Naimon answers,   "Great valor swells the sound!   1790
Roland is fighting: he must have been betrayed—
And by that man   who tells you to hang back.

Take up your arms,   let your war-cry ring out!
Your household needs you,   now speed to its defense.
You've heard enough   how Roland's horn laments!"

CXXXVI

The Emperor Charles   orders his horns to sound.
The French dismount,   prepare themselves for war.
They put on hauberks,   helmets and golden swords;
Their shields are good,   heavy their spears and strong,
Their battle-flags   are crimson, blue and white.   1800
Riding their chargers,   the barons of the host
Spur on and gallop   back through the mountain pass.
Each to the other   pronounces this same vow:
"When we get there,   if Roland's still alive,
We'll fight beside him,   striking hard blows and straight."
What does it matter?   Their help will come too late.

CXXXVII

All afternoon   the sun shines bright and clear,
Armor and weapons   are gleaming in the light,
Hauberks and helmets   glitter as if on fire,
And all the shields,   brilliant with painted flowers,   1810
And all the spears   and gilded battle flags.
In bitter wrath   the Emperor rides on,
The men of France,   in sorrow and in rage.
There is not one   who can hold back his tears;
Because of Roland,   the Frenchmen are afraid.
King Charles commands   that Ganelon be seized;
Summoning forth   all of his household cooks,
He tells their chief,   Besgon, what should be done:
"Here is a felon   I'm leaving in your charge—
He has betrayed   the vassals of my house."   1820
The cook takes over;   a hundred kitchen boys,
The best and worst,   will guard Count Ganelon.
They pluck the hairs   from his moustache and beard,
Each with his fist   strikes him four mighty blows,
And then they beat him   with heavy sticks and clubs.
An iron collar   is put around his neck,
And then they chain him   as if he were a bear.
On a mule's back,   trussed up, he will remain.
They'll guard him well,   and wait for Charlemagne. AOI

CXXXVIII

High are the hills,   and shadowy and vast,   1830
Deep the defiles,   and swift the mountain streams.
The trumpets sound   ahead and to the rear,
Blaring replies   to Roland's Oliphant.
In bitter wrath   the Emperor rides on,
The men of France   in sorrow and in rage;
Not one but grieves   and bitterly laments,

Praying that God   will keep Count Roland safe
Until they come   and join him in the field—
How they will fight   when they are at his side!
What does it matter   how loyally they strive?   1840
They'll be too late   whenever they arrive.   AOI

CXXXIX

Now Charlemagne   rides on in his great rage;
His beard, defiant,   outside his hauberk lies.
The lords of France   spur for the utmost speed,
There isn't one   but angrily laments
That they can't be   already on the field
Where Roland fights   against the Saracens.
I think his wound   won't let him long survive,
But God! the sixty   still fighting at his side—
No king or chieftain   has ever had their like.   AOI   1850

CXL

Count Roland sees   the mountains and the hills
Where all around him   the Franks are lying dead;
He weeps for them,   as a true knight would do.
"Barons, my lords,   may God forgive your sins,
And grant your souls   a place in Paradise,
On holy flowers   may you forever rest!
I've never seen   vassals better than you;
You followed me   so loyally and long,
For Charlemagne   we've won such mighty lands!
The king's own household,   alas! brings him to woe.   1860
And that fair country   where it is sweet to live
Today laid waste   and cruelly bereaved!
Barons of France,   because of me you die;
I can't protect you,   I cannot keep you safe:
Look now to God   who never failed a trust.
Oliver, brother,   I'll not break faith with you.
I'll die of grief,   if not by pagan spears.
My lord, companion,   there's still work for us here!"

CXLI

Roland has gone   back to the battlefield.
With Durendal   he strikes heroic blows: 1870
Faldrun de Pui   he cuts down first of all,
Then twenty-four   of the best pagan knights.
No man has ever   wanted revenge so much.
Just as the stag   runs to escape the hounds,
So do the pagans   before Count Roland flee.
Says the archbishop,   "Bravely you fight, and well!
Yours is the spirit   a chevalier must have,
If he bears arms   and has a horse to ride:
A man in battle   ought to be fierce and strong—
For one who isn't   I wouldn't give two cents.   1880

Instead of fighting   let him become a monk
And spend his days   praying for all our sins."
Roland replies,   "Strike on, and spare not one!"
With that the Franks   begin to fight once more.
Many a Christian   falls to the pagan swords.

CXLII

A man who knows   all captives will be slain
In such a battle   fights to the end of strength;
And so the Franks   like lions[65] face their foes.
Behold Marsile: as a true knight would do,
He sits the horse   that he has named Gaignon,[66]   1890
Pricks with sharp spurs,   and rides against Bevon,
The lord of Beaune   and also of Dijon;
He breaks his shield,   the hauberk splits in two—
With that one blow   he fells the Frenchman dead.
Then Marsile kills   Ivoire and Ivon too,
And with them dies   Gérard of Roussillon.
Seeing that, Roland,   who isn't far away,
Says to the pagan,   "God smite you with His curse!
To you I owe   these good companions slain—
Nor shall we part   before that debt is paid!   1900
Now is the time   to teach you my sword's name."[67]
With that he charges   as a true knight would do;
The count's keen sword   cuts off Marsile's right hand,
Then Jurfaleu   surrenders his blond head—
He was a prince,   the son of King Marsile.
The pagans cry,   "Mohammed help us now!
Gods of our country,   give us revenge on Charles,
For he has sent   such felons here to fight
That death itself   can't drive them from the field."
They tell each other,   "Let's get away from here!"   1910
A hundred thousand   run from the French attack;
Whoever calls,   they won't be coming back.

CXLIII

What does it matter   that King Marsile has fled?
They must still fight   his uncle Marganice,[68]
The lord of Carthage,   Alfrere, and Garmalie,
That land accursed   called Ethiopia
Whose black men serve   as Marganice commands.
They have big noses,   their ears stick out too far;
Some fifty thousand   have come to fight the Franks.
They gallop boldly,   and in wild fury charge,   1920

---

[65] "It is customary to indicate that this is the only formal simile in the poem."—Translator's note.

[66] The name means "watchdog."

[67] "Thus it is apparent that the name 'Durendal' has significance, but nothing further can be effectively said on the subject."—Translator's note.

[68] The Caliph mentioned in laisses XXXV and LIV.

Shouting the war-cry   dear to the pagan hosts.
Then Roland says,   "Here we'll win martyrdom.
Now I can see   how little time is left;
But cursed be he   who lets his life go cheap!
Strike them, my lords,   strike with your shining swords!
Give them a battle   whether you live or die,
That none may say   we brought sweet France to shame.
When Charlemagne   comes to this battlefield,
He'll see the hosts   of slaughtered Saracens—
For each of us   some fifteen pagans dead;   1930
Charles won't reproach us,   he'll bless us all instead." AOI

CXLIV

When Roland sees   this horde of infidels
Who all are darker   than is the blackest ink,
With nothing white   except their gleaming teeth,
He says aloud,   "There isn't any doubt,
Today we'll die—   I can believe it now.
Follow me, Frenchmen!   We'll give them one more charge!"
Oliver says,   "The devil take the last!"
The French attack;   their blows fall hard and fast.

CXLV

And when the pagans   see how few Franks are left,   1940
They take much pride   and comfort from the fact,
Telling each other,   "King Charles is in the wrong."
Then Marganice,   astride a sorrel[69] horse,
Pricks with gold spurs   and gallops from behind
To land his spear   deep in Oliver's back.
The gleaming hauberk   shatters and splits away,
The spear goes through   and opens up his chest.
Says Marganice,   "You've taken a hard blow!
Charlemagne left you   to wait here for your doom.
Let him not glory   in what he's done to Spain—   1950
Your death alone   avenges all our slain."

CXLVI

Oliver feels   how close he is to death.
He raises high   Halteclere's bright burnished blade,
Strikes Marganice,   and splits his tall gold helm,
Its jewels and flowers   fall shattered to the ground;
He cleaves his head   right down into the teeth,
Wrenching the sword,   he hurls the body down.
Then says the count,   "Be damned, you Saracen!
Whatever Charles   may have lost here today,
At least I'm sure   no wife or lady friend   1960
Will hear you boasting,   safe in your lands again,
Of how you captured   silver or gold from me:

---

[69] Light brown or orange-brown.

Your triumphs here   will not be on parade."
He summons then   Count Roland to his aid.   AOI

CXLVII

Oliver knows   he has a fatal wound.
He'll never have his fill   of vengeance now.
In the melee   he fights on valiantly,
He cuts through spears,   the pagans' studded shields,
And feet and fists   and saddle-trees and spines.
Whoever watched him   cut pagans limb from limb,   1970
Bodies piled up   around him on the ground,
Would know that once   he'd seen a noble lord.
The count remembers   the war-cry of King Charles,
And loud and clear   his voice rings out, "Montjoie!"
He calls to Roland,   summons his friend and peer,
"My lord, companion,   come fight beside me now!
We'll part in sorrow   before the sun goes down."   AOI

CXLVIII

Roland is there;   he sees Oliver's face,
The skin is ashen,   so pallid it looks grey,
And from his wounds   bright blood is spurting out;   1980
Its heavy drops   flow down him to the ground.
"O God!" says Roland,   "I don't know what to do.
Was such great valor   destined to be cut down!
My noble friend,   you'll have no peer on earth.
Alas, sweet France!   You are bereft today
Of your good vassals,   laid waste and brought to shame;
The Emperor Charles   will sorely feel the lack."
With these words Roland   faints on his horse's back.   AOI

CXLIX

Here is Count Roland   unconscious on his horse;
Oliver, wounded   and very close to death,   1990
Has bled so much   that both his eyes are dimmed:
Now far or near   he can't see well enough
To give a name   to any man alive.
When he encounters   Count Roland in the field,
Oliver strikes him,   cleaving his golden helm
Brilliant with jewels—   the nose-piece cracks in two—
And yet the blade   does not touch face or head.
Roland's eyes open,   and looking at his friend,
Softly and gently   he asks him only this:
"My lord, companion,   it's Roland—did you know?   2000
I've always loved you;   did you intend that blow?
You gave no challenge   before you charged at me."
Oliver says,   "I recognize your voice,
But I can't see you—   God keep you in His sight!
I struck at you!   I pray you, pardon me."
Roland replies,   "I am not hurt at all;

I do forgive you, here and in front of God."
When he had spoken, each leaned down toward his friend.
So, with great love, they parted in the end.

CL

Oliver suffers the agonies of death;
He feels his eyes turn back into his head,
He cannot hear, he cannot see at all.
Now he dismounts, and kneeling on the ground,
Aloud he asks forgiveness for his sins;
He clasps his hands, and holds them toward the sky,
Praying that God will grant him Paradise,
And give His blessing to Charles and to sweet France,
And to Count Roland above all other men.
Then his heart fails him, his shining helmet bows.
All of his body sinks down against the ground;
The count is dead— no longer did he stay.
Lord Roland weeps, lamenting bitterly;
Many have grieved, but no man more than he.   2020

CLI

When Roland sees that Oliver is dead,
Lying face downward stretched out against the ground,
With tender words he bids his friend farewell:
"Alas, companion! Your valor ends in woe.
We were together so many years and days;
You never wronged me, and I kept faith with you.
Now you are dead, I grieve to be alive."   2030
The marquis faints just as he says these words,
Still on his horse, whose name is Veillantif;
The fine gold stirrups will keep him sitting straight,
So he won't fall however he may sway.

CLII

Before Count Roland recovers from his faint,
While he still sits unconscious on his horse,
The battle brings disaster to his men:
The Franks are dead— he's lost them, every one
Save the archbishop and Gautier de l'Hum[70]
Who from the mountains has now returned at last.   2040
He fought a battle with Spanish Saracens.
His men are dead; their enemies have won.
Down toward the valleys, he flees now, all alone,
Searching for Roland, calling to him for help:
"Ah, noble count! Where are you, valiant lord?
When you were with me, I never was afraid.
It's Gautier— I conquered Maelgut!
Droon is my uncle, his aged head is grey.

[70] For Gautier, see LXIV-LXV.

2010

You used to love me, because you knew me brave.
My spear is broken, my shield has been pierced through,   2050
My hauberk's links scattered and snapped apart,
Deep in my body a pagan lance has thrust;
I'm dying now, but they have bought me dear."
Roland wakes up to hear his final words;
Turning his horse, toward Gautier he spurs. AOI

CLIII

Count Roland, grieving and filled with bitter rage,
Rides once again through the thick of the fight.
Twenty Spaniards he throws dead to the ground,
Gautier kills six, Archbishop Turpin five.
The pagans say, "These men are monstrous fierce!   2060
Take care, my lords, don't let them get away.
If you aren't traitors, we'll rush upon them now—
If you aren't cowards, they won't escape alive!"
Then riding onward with a great hue and cry,
They charge the Franks once more from every side. AOI

CLIV

There is Count Roland, a noble warrior,
Gautier de l'Hum, a worthy chevalier,
Archbishop Turpin, a veteran and brave:
None would be willing to fail the other two.
In the melee they strike the pagans down.   2070
A thousand Spaniards dismount to fight on foot,
While forty thousand stay on their horses' backs—
And even so they don't dare come too near.
They throw their lances, hurl their keen-bladed spears,
All sorts of weapons come flying at the Franks;
With the first blows, Count Gautier is killed,
Turpin of Reims soon finds his shield pierced through,
His helmet breaks— he's wounded in the head—
His chain-mail hauberk is cracked and splits apart,
Four pagan spears strike deep into his flesh,   2080
His war-horse, dying, carries him to the ground.
O God! What sorrow to see Turpin go down! AOI

CLV

Turpin of Reims, finding himself unhorsed,
With four deep wounds where spears thrust through his flesh,
Leaps up again, great fighter that he is,
Looks for Count Roland, and hastens to his side,
Saying just this: "I am not beaten yet!
No man of courage gives up while he's alive."
He draws Almace whose blade is burnished steel,
Strikes in the throng a thousand blows and more.   2090
Soon Charles will say that Turpin spared no foe:
They found four hundred around him in the field,

Some of them wounded, some of them thrust clean through,
And there were others who parted with their heads.
So says the *Geste,* and someone who was there:
Saint Giles[71] for whom Our Lord works miracles
Left an account in Laon's church in France;
Everyone knows this, or nothing understands.

CLVI

Roland delivers many a skillful blow,
But now his body is fevered, drenched with sweat,   2100
His head is throbbing under a dreadful pain,
His temples broken from sounding his great horn.
Longing to know if Charles is on his way,
Weakly, once more, he blows the Oliphant.
King Charles stands still, listening to that call;
"My lords," he says, "now we have come to woe!
My nephew Roland takes leave of us this day—
His horn's voice tells me he won't be long alive.
Who wants to be there had better speed his horse.
Let every trumpet the host commands resound!"   2110
And sixty thousand rang from the lofty peaks
Down through the valleys, echoing loud and clear.
The pagans, listening, think it no empty boast—
They say, "Here come King Charles and all his host." AOI

CLVII

The pagans say, "Now Charles is coming back.
Those trumpet calls rally the men of France;
We'll have great losses if the Emperor comes,
And if Count Roland lives to make war again,
We may as well surrender all of Spain."
About four hundred assemble, helmeted,   2120
The best who fought among the Saracens;
With all their might these men attack anew,
And then Count Roland has work enough to do. AOI

CLVIII

When Roland sees the pagans closing in,
His heart grows stronger, and prouder and more fierce.
He'll yield to none, as long as he's alive.
Astride the horse whose name is Veillantif,
He gallops toward them, pricking with golden spurs;
Into the throng he charges to attack.
Archbishop Turpin is fighting at his side.   2130
The pagans say, "Let's get away from here!
Those trumpet calls mean that the Franks are near—
Their mighty king, great Charles, will soon appear!"

[71] The meaning apparently is that the saint, about whom there were numerous legends, was present in spirit. No account of the battle written by him is known.

CLIX

Count Roland's friendship   no coward ever knew,
Nor any man   false-hearted or too proud,
Nor any knight   who was not skilled at war.
To the archbishop   Roland addressed these words:
"I am on horseback,   my lord, and you're on foot;
For love of you,   here I shall take my stand—
We'll meet together   what good or evil comes,   2140
No mortal man   will make me leave your side.
We shall return   the Saracen attack.
What sword can equal   the blows of Durendal!"
Turpin replies,   "Curse him whose arm grows slack!
We'll be avenged   when Charlemagne comes back."

CLX

The pagans say,   "Ours were unlucky stars!
Would that this evil day   had never dawned!
We've lost our peers,   our lords have all been slain,
The valiant Charles   is coming back again.
Now we can hear   the trumpets of his host,   2150
The mighty clamor   when the Franks shout 'Montjoie!'
And this Count Roland   is hideously fierce—
He can't be conquered   by men of flesh and blood.
Let's cast our lances   and then leave him alone."
The Saracens   throw many javelins,
Lances and darts,   and feathered throwing spears.
Count Roland's shield   is broken and pierced through,
His hauberk's mail   is cracked and split apart,
And still his body   has not been touched at all.
But Veillantif   has suffered thirty wounds;   2160
Beneath Count Roland   he falls dead to the ground.
Then all the pagans   yield to their fear and flee;
And Roland stands,   dismounted, on the field. AOI

CLXI

The pagans flee,   furious and enraged,
Trying their best   to get away in Spain.
Count Roland lacks the means   to chase them now,
For he has lost   his war-horse Veillantif;
Against his will   he has to go on foot.
He went to give   Archbishop Turpin help,
Unlaced his helmet,   removed it from his head,   2170
And then took off   the hauberk of light mail;
The under-tunic   he cut into long strips
With which he stanched   the largest of his wounds.
Then lifting Turpin,   carried him in his arms
To soft green grass,   and gently laid him down.
In a low voice   Roland made this request:
"My noble lord,   I pray you, give me leave,
For our companions,   the men we held so dear,

Must not be left   abandoned now in death.
I want to go   and seek out every one,   2180
Carry them here,   and place them at your feet."
Said the archbishop,   "I grant it willingly.
The field belongs,   thank God, to you and me."

CLXII

Alone, Count Roland   walks through the battlefield,
Searching the valleys,   searching the mountain heights.
He found the bodies   of Ivon and Ivoire,
and then he found   the Gascon Engelier.
Gerin he found,   and Gerier his friend,
He found Aton   and then Count Bérengier,
Proud Anseïs he found,   and then Samson,   2190
Gérard the Old,   the Count of Roussillon.
He took these barons,   and carried every one
Back to the place   where the archbishop was,
And then he put them   in ranks at Turpin's knees.
Seeing them, Turpin   cannot restrain his tears;
Raising his hand,   he blesses all the dead.
And then he says,   "You've come to grief, my lords!
Now in His glory,   may God receive your souls,
Among bright flowers   set you in Paradise!
It's my turn now;   death keeps me in such pain,   2200
Never again   will I see Charlemagne."

CLXIII

Roland goes back   to search the field once more,
And his companion   he finds there, Oliver.
Lifting him in his arms,   he holds him close,
Brings him to Turpin   as quickly as he can,
Beside the others   places him on a shield;
Turpin absolves him,   signing him with the cross,
And then they yield   to pity and to grief.
Count Roland says,   "Brother in arms, fair friend,
You were the son   of Renier, the duke   2210
Who held the land   where Runers valley lies.
For breaking lances,   for shattering thick shields,
Bringing the proud   to terror and defeat,
For giving counsel,   defending what is right,
In all the world   there is no better knight."

CLXIV

When Roland sees   that all his peers are dead,
And Oliver   whom he so dearly loved,
He feels such sorrow   that he begins to weep;
Drained of all color,   his face turns ashen pale,
His grief is more   than any man could bear,
He falls down, fainting   whether he will or no.   2220
Says the archbishop,   "Baron, you've come to woe."

CLXV

When the archbishop   sees Roland on the ground,
He feels more sorrow   than he has ever known.
He reaches out   to grasp the Oliphant;
A swift stream waters   the plain at Roncevaux,
And there, for Roland,   he wants to fill the horn.
Taking short steps,   staggering, he sets out,
But in his weakness   he can't go very far—
He has no strength,   his wounds have bled too much;
He doesn't travel   even a hundred feet   2230
Before he falls—   his heart has given out.
Now death is trying   to put his soul to rout.

CLXVI

Meanwhile Count Roland   recovers from his faint,
He rises to his feet,   but with great pain.
He looks around him,   he searches up and down;
Beyond the place   where his companions lie,
Prone on the grass,   he sees the noble lord,
Archbishop Turpin,   God's delegate on earth.
Count Roland hears him   confessing he has sinned,
With his clasped hands   held upward toward the sky,   2240
Praying that God   will give him Paradise.
Turpin is dead   who fought for Charlemagne.
With mighty blows,   with wise and holy words,
Against the pagans   he championed the Faith.
May God in heaven   bless him and grant him grace.

CLXVII

Roland sees Turpin   lying there on the ground,
Entrails protruding   from his enormous wounds;
Above his forehead   his brains are bubbling out.
On Turpin's chest,   between his collarbones,
Roland has crossed   the beautiful white hands.   2250
Now he laments   as it is done in France:
"O nobly born,   illustrious chevalier,
To heaven's glory   I now commend your soul;
Our Lord will never   be served more willingly.
Since the Apostles,   there has been none like you
To keep the Law,   and bring men to the Faith.
From pain and sorrow   may your free soul arise;
May you find open   the gates of Paradise!"

CLXVIII

Now Roland knows   that death is very near.
His ears give way,   he feels his brain gush out.   2260
He prays that God   will summon all his peers;
Then, for himself,   he prays to Gabriel.[72]

---

[72] The great archangel; like Michael, he is a leader of the heavenly hosts.

Taking the horn,   to keep it from all shame,
With Durendal   clasped in his other hand,
He goes on, farther   than a good cross-bow shot,
West into Spain,   crossing a fallow field.
Up on a hilltop,   under two lofty trees,
Four marble blocks[73]   are standing on the grass.
But when he comes there,   Count Roland faints once more,
He falls down backward;   now he is at death's door.   2270

CLXIX

High are the hills   and very high the trees,
The four great blocks   of polished marble shine;
On the green grass   the count is lying still.
A Saracen   watches with steady eyes:
This man feigned death,   hiding among the slain;
His face and body   he had besmeared with blood.
Now he stands up   and dashes forward fast—
He's handsome, strong   and very valiant too,
But he won't live   to profit from his pride;
He falls on Roland,   seizing him and his arms   2280
And says these words: "Charles' nephew lost the fight!
When I go home,   his sword shall be my prize."
But as he pulls it,   Roland comes back to life.

CLXX

Count Roland feels   the pagan take his sword,
And opening his eyes,   he says just this:
"You look to me   like no one on our side!"
Raising the horn   he'd wanted to keep safe,
He strikes the helmet   shining with gold and jewels,
Shatters the steel,   smashes the skull and bones;
He puts both eyes   out of the pagan's head,
And sends his body   crashing against the ground.   2290
And then he asks him,   "How did you get so brave,
Dog, to attack me   with or without just cause?
Whoever heard this   would say you were insane!
But I have cracked   the Oliphant's broad bell;
Its gold and crystals   were shattered as it fell."

CLXXI

Count Roland feels   that he is going blind.
Now he stands upright,   using what strength remains;
All of the color   has vanished from his face.
In front of him   there is a dark grey stone.   2300
He strikes ten blows   in bitterness and grief;
The steel blade grates   but will not break or dent.
The count cries out,   "O Holy Mary, help!
O Durendal,   alas for your fair fame!

[73] Possibly boundary stones.

My life is over,   I'll care for you no more.
We've won such battles   together in the field,
So many lands   we've conquered, you and I,
For Charles to rule   whose beard is silver-grey.
No man must have you   who fights and runs away!
You have been long   in a good vassal's hands;   2310
You'll have no equal   in all of holy France."

CLXXII

Count Roland strikes   the bright carnelian[74] stone;
The steel blade grates   but will not chip or break.
When Roland sees   he can't destroy his sword,
Then, to himself,   grieving, he speaks its praise:
"O Durendal,   how fair you are, and bright!
Against the sunlight   your keen steel gleams and flames!
Charles was that time   in Moriana's[75] Vales
When by God's will   an angel from the sky
Said to bestow you   upon a chieftain count: 2320
The noble king   girded you at my side.
With you I won him   Anjou and Brittany,[76]
Conquered Poitou   and after that all Maine,
With you I won him   that free land, Normandy,
Conquered Provence,   and then all Aquitaine,
And Lombardy,   Romagna after that.
With you I won him   Bavaria, Flanders too,
And Burgundy,   the Polianis' lands;
Constantinople   paid homage to King Charles,
In Saxony   he does as he desires.   2330
With you I conquered   the Irish and the Scots,
And England too   the king holds as his own.
So many countries   we've won him, many lands
Ruled by King Charles   whose flowing beard is white.
For your sake now   I suffer grief and pain—
Better to die   than leave you here in Spain.
Almighty Father,   keep sweet France from that shame!"

CLXXIII

Count Roland strikes   against a dark grey stone;
More of it falls   than I can make you see.
The steel blade grates   but will not crack or break;   2340
Against the sky   it springs back up again.
Count Roland knows   he can't destroy his sword.
Then, to himself,   he quietly laments:
"O Durendal,   holy you are, and fair!
You have great relics   within your hilt of gold:
Saint Peter's tooth,   drops of Saint Basil's blood,

---

[74] A semi-precious stone.   [75] A region on the Italian border.
[76] In the following lines, the list of lands conquered by or for Charles is historically an
exaggeration. Compare XXVIII.

Hairs from the head   of my lord Saint Denis,
Part of a garment   that Holy Mary wore—
For any pagan   to hold you would be wrong;
Only by Christians   can you be rightly served.   2350
May you not fall   into a coward's hands!
Many wide lands   we've conquered, you and I,
For Charles to rule   whose flowing beard is white;
They have increased   his majesty and might."

CLXXIV

Count Roland feels   the very grip of death
Which from his head   is reaching for his heart.
He hurries then   to go beneath a pine;
In the green grass   he lies down on his face,
Placing beneath him   the sword and Oliphant;
He turns his head   to look toward pagan Spain.   2360
He does these things   in order to be sure
King Charles will say,   and with him all the Franks,
The noble count   conquered until he died.
He makes confession,   for all his sins laments,
Offers his glove   to God[77] in penitence.   AOI

CLXXV

Now Roland feels   his time has all run out.
He looks toward Spain   from high on a steep hill,
And with one hand   beating his breast, he says:
"God, I have sinned   against Thy holy name.
Forgive the sins,   the great ones and the less,   2370
That I committed   from my first hour of life
To this last day   when I have been struck down."
And now toward God   he raises his right glove;
A flight of angels   comes from the skies above.   AOI

CLXXVI

And now Count Roland,   lying beneath a pine,
Has turned his face   to look toward pagan Spain;
And he begins   remembering these things:
The many lands   his valor won the king,
Sweet France, his home,   the men of his own line,
And Charlemagne   who raised him in his house—   2380
The memories   make him shed tears and sigh.
But not forgetting   how close he is to death,
He prays that God   forgive him all his sins:
"O my true Father,   O Thou who never lied,
Thou who delivered   Lazarus from the grave,
Who rescued Daniel[78]   out of the lions' den,

---

[77] A symbolic gesture of dependence, as by a feudal vassal to his chief.

[78] For these two famous biblical miracles—the resurrection of Lazarus by Jesus and the divine protection of Daniel when the Persian king Darius had him imprisoned in the lions' den—see John, chapters 11–12, and Daniel, chapter 6.

Keep now my soul   from every peril safe,
Forgive the sins   that I have done in life."
Roland, in homage,   offers his glove to God.
Saint Gabriel comes and takes it from his hand.							2390
His head sinks down   to rest upon his arm;
Hands clasped in prayer,   the count has met his end.
God sends from heaven   the angel Cherubin,[79]
Holy Saint Michael   who saves us from the sea,
And with these two   the Angel Gabriel flies.
Count Roland's soul   they bring to Paradise.

CLXXVII

Roland is dead;   his soul rests now with God.
The Emperor Charles   rides into Roncevaux;
On every road,   on every mountain path,
On every ell, on every foot of land,							2400
They find a body   of Frank or Saracen.
King Charles cries out,   "Fair nephew, where are you?
Where's the archbishop?   Where is Count Oliver?
Where is Count Gerin,   and Gerier his friend?
Oton—where is he, and noble Bérengier,
Ivoire and Ivon, those two I held so dear?
Tell me what happened   to Gascon Engelier,
Where are Duke Samson,   the valiant Anseïs,
And Old Gérard,   the Count of Roussillon?
Where are the peers, the twelve who stayed behind?"							2410
What good is asking   when no one can reply?
"God!" says the king,   "Now have I cause to grieve,
For where was I   when fighting here began!"
He pulls his beard   in anguish and in pain;
The lords of France   are weeping bitter tears,
And twenty thousand   faint in their grief and fall.
Duke Naimon feels   great sorrow for them all.

CLXXVIII

There is not one   among those noble lords
Who can refrain   from shedding tears of grief:
It is their sons, their brothers that they mourn,							2420
Their nephews, friends;   they weep for their liege lords.
Many among them   fall fainting to the ground.
Only Duke Naimon   can see what must be done;
He is the first   to tell the emperor:
"Look up ahead,   two leagues from where we stand,
See how the dust   is rising from the road—
There are the pagans,   and surely not a few.
Ride after them!   Let us avenge our grief!"
"O God," says Charles, "they are already far—

---

[79] Here the reference is to a particular angel, not to the order of angels the word usually signifies.

Grant me this grace,   let me do what is right,   2430
For they have stolen   the flower of sweet France!"
The king commands   Oton and Geboïn,
Thibault of Reims, and also Count Milon:
"Guard well this field,   the valleys and the heights,
Let all the dead   remain just as they are,
But keep them safe   from lions and wild beasts;
Let no one touch them,   no servant and no squire—
I say to you,   let no man touch these dead
Until God brings us   back to this field again."
They answer him   with reverence and love: 2440
"Right Emperor,   dear lord, as you command."
These four will keep   a thousand knights at hand.   AOI

CLXXIX
The Emperor Charles   has all his trumpets sound.
The mighty lord   rides onward with his host;
They find the tracks   made by the Saracens,
And all together   follow them in pursuit.
When the king sees   that evening will come soon,
In a green meadow   he gets down from his horse,
Kneels on the ground   and prays almighty God
To make the sun   stop moving[80] through the sky,   2450
Delay the night,   and let the day remain.
And then an angel,   who often spoke with him,
Came in great haste   to give him this command:
"Charles, speed you on!   The light won't fail you now.
God knows that you have lost   the flower of France.
You'll have your vengeance   on the vile Saracen!"
Already Charles   has mounted once again.   AOI

CLXXX
For Charlemagne   God worked a miracle:
The sun stops moving,   and stands still in the sky.
The pagans flee,   the Franks pursue them hard,   2460
At Val-Tenebre   they overtake their foes;
Toward Saragossa   they chase them, sword in hand,
With mighty blows   cutting the pagans down,
Driving them off   the wide paths and the roads,
Until they find   the Ebro[81] in their way.
Deep is the water,   and frightening and swift,
There are no boats,   no galleys, not a barge.
The Saracens   invoke their Tervagant;
They all jump in,   but nothing keeps them safe:
The men in armor   weigh more than all the rest,   2470
Some of them sink   straight down into the depths,

---

[80] A repetition of the biblical miracle performed by God during the conquest of the promised land by the Israelites; see Joshua 10:12–14.

[81] The principal river of Spain.

Others are carried   by the swift-running stream,
Those least in danger   still drink, and far too much;
All of them drown   in anguish and in fear.
The French cry,   "Roland, if only you were here!"   AOI

CLXXXI

When Charlemagne   sees all the pagans dead,
Some slain in battle,   and many of them drowned,
Leaving great spoils   for all the Frankish knights,
The noble king,   dismounting from his horse,
Kneels on the ground,   and gives his thanks to God.   2480
When he gets up,   he sees the sun has set.
The emperor says,   "We'll have to make camp here.
It's too late now   to ride to Roncevaux—
All of our horses   are weary and worn out.
Take off their saddles   and let their bridles go;
Free in these meadows,   they'll cool off as they should."
The Franks reply,   "My lord, your words are good."   AOI

CLXXXII

The Emperor Charles   has had his camp set up.
The French dismount   there in the wilderness,
The horses' saddles   are taken off their backs,   2490
The golden bridles   are lifted from their heads,
They roam the meadows   where there is good fresh grass—
There are no other   provisions to be had.
Men who are weary   lie on the ground and sleep;
For on this night   there is no watch to keep.

CLXXXIII

Now in a meadow   the emperor lies down;
His mighty spear   he keeps close by his head,
For on this night   he wishes to stay armed.
He wears his hauberk   of saffron-burnished steel,
His helm is laced,   bright gems gleam in its gold;   2500
Still at his side,   Joyeuse, the peerless sword,
Which changes color   thirty times every day.
We all have heard   what happened to the lance
With which Our Lord   was wounded on the Cross:
Charles has the spearhead—   almighty God be thanked—
He had it mounted   into the golden hilt,
And for that honor,   that sign of heaven's love,
The name Joyeuse   was given to the sword.
Let the French barons   remember this each time
They cry "Montjoie!"   in battle: let them know   2510
That war cry means   they'll conquer any foe.

CLXXXIV

The night is clear,   the moon gleams in the sky.
King Charles lies down,   but for Count Roland grieves,
For Oliver   whose loss weighs on his heart,

For the twelve peers,   for all the men of France:
At Roncevaux   their bloodstained bodies lie.
He can't help weeping,   and bitterly laments,
Praying that God   have mercy on their souls.
The king is weary,   exhausted by his grief,
He falls asleep—   he can't do any more.   2520
In all the meadows   the Franks are sleeping too.
There's not one horse   left standing on its feet;
Those who want grass   eat just what they can reach.
A man does well   to learn what pain can teach.

CLXXXV

Charles goes to sleep   worn out by grief and toil.
Then God in heaven   sends Saint Gabriel down,
Commanding him   to guard the emperor.
The angel stays   close by his head all night,
And in two visions   lets him see what will come:
Another foe   is marching on the king,[82]   2530
The dream shows clearly   the fighting will be grim.
The emperor sees   above him in the sky
Lightning and thunder,   and gusts of wind and hail,
Great are the tempests,   fearful and vast the storms,
The heavens gather   flickering fire and flames
Which all at once   fall down upon his men;
Ash-wood and apple,   their spear-shafts are ablaze,
Their shields are burning   down to the boss of gold,
The shafts snap off   from their keen-bladed spears,
Their chain-mail crumples,   and their strong helms of steel.   2540
With great dismay   Charles sees his knights attacked
By vicious beasts—   by leopards and by bears,
Serpents and vipers,   dragons and devils too,
And there are griffons,[83]   thirty thousand and more,
All of them leaping,   charging against the Franks,
The Franks who cry,   "Charlemagne, help us now!"
And overwhelmed   by pity and by grief,
He starts out toward them,   but something interferes:
A mighty lion   springs at him from a wood,
Fearful to look at,   raging and proud and bold;   2550
He leaps, attacking   the person of the king.
Grappling each other   they wrestle violently:
But who will rise   a victor, who will fall?
The emperor sleeps   and does not wake at all.

CLXXXVI

Later that night   he had another dream:[84]
He was in Aix;   on a dais he stood,

---

[82] The first dream foretells a battle between the Franks and the forces of the oriental emir Baligant (the lion of line 2549).
[83] Monsters having lions' bodies and the heads and wings of eagles.
[84] The second dream foretells the trial of Ganelon, near the end of the poem.

Holding a bear   bound tight with double chains.
Thirty more bears   came out of the Ardennes,[85]
Each of them speaking   exactly like a man.
They said to Charles,   "Sire, give him back to us!   2560
It isn't right   for you to keep him here;
We cannot choose   but bring our kinsman help."
Out of the palace   there came a hunting dog
Who then attacked   the largest of the bears;
On the green grass   apart from all the rest,
While the king watched,   they fought a dreadful fight—
He could not see   which one of them would lose.
All this God's angel   revealed to Charlemagne.
The king slept on   until it was bright day.

                                        CLXXXVII
To Saragossa   the pagan king has fled.   2570
There he dismounts   beneath an olive tree,
Gives up his sword,   his hauberk and his helm;
On the green grass   the king lies down in shame.
Marsile's right hand   was cut completely off,
And he is fainting   from loss of blood and pain.
In front of him,   his wife Queen Bramimonde,
Weeping for grief,   cries out a loud lament.
The queen has with her   some twenty thousand men,
All of them cursing   Charlemagne and sweet France.
Now they attack   Apollo in his crypt,   2580
Reviling him,   disfiguring his form:
"Why, evil god,   have you brought us to shame?
Why have you suffered   the downfall of our king?
For faithful service   you give a poor reward!"
Then they take off   his scepter[86] and his crown,
And to a column   they tie him by the hands;
They knock him down,   stamping him with their feet,
And with great clubs   they smash him into bits.
They take the ruby   away from Tervagant,
And then Mohammed   they thrust into a ditch   2590
Where he'll be trampled   and gnawed by dogs and pigs.

[*Laisses* CLXXXVIII *to* CCLVII (*lines* 2592–3559): *On the following day, the great emir Baligant of "Babylon" (Cairo) arrives with his forces, too late for the battle but resolved to help Marsile and overcome Charles. He is told of the Saracens' defeat and of Roland's death.*

Charles, after camping overnight, returns to Roncevaux. He finds Roland's body and utters a lovingly elegiac lament for him. The dead are buried. Roland, Oliver, and the archbishop Turpin—who will be buried in France—receive special honors.

The army of Baligant suddenly appears; Charles and his forces prepare for war again. The poet recites an epic catalogue of Charles's armies, specifying what part of Europe each division comes from and who commands it. Charles prays for victory, he advances with his army, and they camp for the night.

The pagans too prepare for war. Baligant is described at some length, the poet expressing

---

[85] A region in northeastern France, near Aix-la-Chapelle.   [86] That is, the idol's.

regret that so admirable a hero should not be a Christian. Baligant praises Charles. A cata-
logue, corresponding to that of the Franks, shows that Baligant's army comes from many parts
of the world.

The battle is joined on a broad plain, Roland's horn sounding to hearten the Franks.
Many men, on both sides, die in the fierce fighting. Duke Naimon, after felling Baligant's son,
is seriously wounded by the emir's brother but is rescued by Charles. Informed of his son's death,
Baligant grieves. He rallies the pagans; the Franks fall back.]

CCLVIII

The day goes by;   darkness begins to fall;   3560
Pagans and Franks   are fighting with their swords.
Two men of courage   command these mighty hosts.
They don't forget   to sound their battle-calls,
The great emir   shouting his "Précieuse!"
And Charlemagne,   his famous cry "Montjoie!"
Each recognizes   the other's strong clear voice,
And then they meet   upon the battlefield.
They charge head on;   each one lands with his spear
So great a blow   upon the other's shield
It cracks wide open   below the heavy boss;   3570
The hauberk panels   are cracked and split apart,
And yet the spearheads   don't penetrate the flesh.
The girths give way,   throwing the saddles off,
With them both kings   come crashing to the ground.
Then, in an instant,   both have regained their feet
And drawn their swords,   ready to fight it out.
No way to end   this combat will be found
Till one of them   lies dead upon the ground.   AOI

CCLIX

A might hero   is Charlemagne of France,
And Baligant   will meet him unafraid.   3580
With swords unsheathed,   they come together now,
Their heavy shields   receiving mighty blows
Which split the leathers,   the double wooden frames;
The nails fall out,   the bosses break apart.
Then nothing shelters   the hauberks from the blades,
And fiery sparks   come flashing from their helms.
This is a combat   which has to last as long
As neither man   admits that he is wrong.   AOI

CCLX

Says the emir,   "Charles, if you stop and think,
You will repent   of what you've done to me: 3590
You can't deny   that you have killed my son;
You do great wrong   when you invade my lands.
Become my vassal,   promise me fealty;
Come with me to the East   and serve me there."
King Charles replies,   "That would be vile disgrace.
I'll be no friend   to pagans, or make peace.

Receive the law   that is the gift of God,
Become a Christian,   and you shall know my love;
Serve Him, have faith   in that almighty King."
Says Baligant,   "Tediously you preach!"   3600
They draw their swords,   and there's an end to speech.

CCLXI

The great emir   is powerful and brave:
He strikes Charles' helmet   so terrible a blow
The burnished steel   is cracked and splits apart,
The sword blade cleaves   the emperor's thick hair
And slices off   a hand's breadth of his scalp,
Stripping the flesh   down to the naked bone.
Charlemagne staggers,   comes close to falling down,
But God won't have him   brought to defeat or slain:
Saint Gabriel   comes back to him once more,   3610
And says, "Great king,   what are you waiting for?"

CCLXII

Charlemagne hears   the angel's holy voice:
He's not afraid,   he knows he will not die.
His strength returns,   his mind is clear and calm.
And then he strikes   with the great sword of France;
The emir's helmet,   ablaze with jewels, cracks,
His head is broken   so that the brains spill out,
His face splits open   down to his long white beard:
He is stone dead   before he hits the ground.
Then Charles' "Montjoie!"   rings through the battlefield.   3620
Duke Naimon hears him   and hastens to his side
With Tencendur;[87]   the great king mounts his horse.
Now by God's will,   the pagans turn and flee;
The Frenchmen know   they've won their victory.

CCLXIII

The pagans flee,   for that is what God wills,
The Franks, with Charles,   are riding in pursuit.
The emperor says,   "My lords, avenge your grief,
Relieve your anger   and you will cheer your hearts;
I saw this morning   how tears flowed from your eyes."
They answer, "Sire,   that is what we must do."   3630
So many pagans   the Franks cut down and slay
That very few   manage to get away.

CCLXIV

The day is hot,   the air is thick with dust;
The pagans flee,   still harried by the Franks:
To Saragossa   they chase them all the way.
Queen Bramimonde   has gone up to her tower;

---

[87] Charles's horse.

With her are clerics,   the priesthood of her faith,
That false religion   for which God has no love:
They're not ordained,   nor have they tonsured heads.
She sees the Arabs   running in wild retreat,   3640
And cries aloud,   "Mohammed, help us now!
Alas, fair king,   our men have fled the field,
The great emir,   dishonored, has been slain!"
When Marsile hears her,   he turns to face the wall,
Tears fill his eyes,   he lets his head sink down;
He dies of grief   that nothing can console,
And to quick demons   yields up his sinful soul.   AOI

CCLXV

Dead are the pagans,   except for those who fled,
And Charlemagne   is master of the field.
In Saragossa   the gate is beaten down,   3650
There's no one left   who will defend it now.
Charles takes the stronghold;   his people come inside;
By right of conquest   they sleep there that same night.
Proud is the king   whose beard is silver-grey!
And Bramimonde   has yielded all the towers,
Ten that are large   and fifty that are small.
He does great things   who on God's aid can call!

CCLXVI

The day is over;   now in the dark of night
The moon shines clear,   and stars flame in the sky.
All Saragossa   belongs to Charlemagne.   3660
A thousand Frenchmen   go searching through the town,
Through mosques and temples   of pagan infidels;
With iron hammers   and wedges in their hands
They break the idols,   and all the images,
Putting an end   to magic sorcery.
The king loves God,   and wants to serve Him well;
Calling his bishops,   he has the water blessed,
And then the pagans   are brought to be baptized.
If there are any   who still resist King Charles,
He has them hanged,   or killed by fire or sword.   3670
A hundred thousand   and a good many more
Are baptized Christians;   only the queen is left.
She will be taken,   a captive, to sweet France
To be converted   by love,[88] as Charles commands.

CCLXVII

The night has passed;   when the bright day appears,
Charles leaves a guard   in Saragossa's towers:
A thousand of his knights   remain behind
To hold the city   in the emperor's name.

---

[88] By Christian or divine love, presumably.

The king rides on   with all his other men
And Bramimonde   he holds against her will—   3680
But Charles desires   only to do her good.
In joy and triumph   the Frenchmen leave for home;
They seize Nerbone,   continue on their way,
And when they reach   Saint Seurin's in Bordeaux,[89]
Charles stops to leave   upon the altar there
The Oliphant,   filled up with gold and coins,
As all the pilgrims   who pass that way can see.
Finding large boats,   for crossing the Gironde,[90]
King Charles escorts   his nephew into Blaye,[91]
And his companion,   the noble Oliver,   3690
And the Archbishop,   so valiant and so wise.
In white stone coffins   Charles has the three lords placed;
In Saint-Romain   the noble barons lie.
The Franks commend them   to God and to His names.[92]
Charlemagne rides   through valleys, over hills—
He will not stop   until he reaches Aix;
There he draws rein   beside the mounting block.[93]
From his high palace   the emperor sends out
His messengers   to judges of his court:
Saxons, Bavarians,   Frisians, men of Lorraine,   3700
To Alemans   and men of Burgundy,
And Poitevins,   Normans and Bretons too,
Frenchmen whose wisdom   Charles can rely upon.
And now begins   the trial of Ganelon.

CCLXVIII

The Emperor Charles   has now returned from Spain.
He comes to Aix,   his capital in France,
Enters the palace   and goes to the great hall.
Alda, a lovely maiden,   comes to him there.
She asks the king: "Where is the chieftain count,
Roland, who swore   that I would be his wife?"   3710
Charles, as she speaks,   is overcome with grief;
Tears fill his eyes,   he pulls at his white beard:
"Sister, sweet friend,   I can't bring back the dead.
But I will give you   one better in his place.
You'll marry Louis—   that's all that I can do—
He is my son,   and he shall rule my realm."
Alda replies,   "Your words seem to me strange.
The saints and angels,   and God above forbid

---

[89] A city in southwest France, on the Garonne River.
[90] The estuary of the Garonne River, through which it flows into the Bay of Biscay.
[91] A French town on the Gironde; Charles has here returned to territory under his control.
[92] "There were prayers containing long lists of the various names of God."—Translator's note.
[93] For mounting a horse. Compare the "dais" (CLXXXVI) mentioned in Charles's earlier dream presaging the trial of Ganelon.

That I live on   when Roland has been slain!"
Her color fades,   she falls down at Charles' feet,   3720
And dies—may God   have mercy on her soul!
The lords of France   mourn her and weep for woe.

CCLXIX

Alda the fair   has taken leave of life.
Charlemagne thinks   that she has only swooned;
The emperor feels   such pity that he weeps.
He takes her hands,   and draws her to her feet;
Upon her shoulder   her head hangs limply down.
Charles understands   that she is really dead.
He summons then   four noble countesses,
Has Alda's body   borne to a nunnery;   3730
There they keep vigil   all night until the dawn.
Beside the altar   she has an honored grave,
Richly endowed   by will of Charlemagne.   AOI

CCLXX

The Emperor Charles   has come back home to Aix.
There Ganelon,   the traitor, bound with chains,
In the high town,   before the palace stands.
To a great stake   the serfs have bound him fast,
Both of his hands   are tied with deerskin thongs,
They beat him well   with heavy sticks and rods:
That way he's treated   in the most proper style,   3740
And he must wait   in torment for his trial.

CCLXXI

As it is written   in the old chronicles,
Charlemagne summoned   vassals from many lands;[94]
And in the chapel   at Aix they're gathered now.
The day is solemn,   the feast they celebrate
Is Saint Silvester's—[95]   so many people say.
The trial begins   with speeches on both sides,
And Ganelon,   who did a traitor's deed,
Is dragged before   the emperor to plead.   AOI

CCLXXII

"Barons, my lords,"   says Charlemagne the king,   3750
"Give me your judgment   concerning Ganelon.
He was with me in Spain   among my host,
And there he robbed me   of twenty thousand Franks;
My nephew Roland   you'll never see again,
Nor Oliver,   so courteous and brave—
For gold and treasure   this man betrayed the peers."

---

[94] Ganelon cannot be judged by Charlemagne himself; he must be tried by his peers.
[95] December 31.

"Sire," says the count,   "I won't conceal the truth:
Because of Roland   I lost both goods and gold.[96]
I wanted him   to suffer and to die;
But in that vengeance   there was no treachery."   3760
The Franks reply,   "We'll talk of this and see."

CCLXXIII

Before the king   behold Count Ganelon.
Stalwart he stands,   fair color in his face—
If he were loyal,   he'd look a noble lord.
He sees the French,   the judges who are there,
The thirty members   of his own family,
And then he speaks,   his great voice ringing out:
"Barons of France,   for God's sake hear me now!
My lords, I fought   beside the emperor,
And served him well   in loyalty and love.   3770
His nephew Roland,   hating me in his heart,
Had me condemned   to torment and sure death:
I was to bring   Charles' message to Marsile—
I had the wit   and wisdom to survive.
I faced Count Roland   and challenged him aloud,
And Oliver,   and all the other peers.
Charlemagne heard me,   so did these noble lords:
I am avenged,   but not by treachery."
The Franks reply,   "We'll go and judge your plea."

CCLXXIV

Ganelon sees   his great trial has begun.   3780
Thirty kinsmen   the count has with him there,
Among them one   looked up to by the rest
Called Pinabel—   his castle is Sorence.
This man can argue   so that his views prevail,
And he's a hero   not easy to defeat.   AOI
Ganelon says,   "I place my trust in you—
Save me from death,   defend me in this trial!"
Says Pinabel,   "In no time you'll be free.
If any Frenchman   decides that you should hang,
The Emperor Charles   must have that judgment tried: 3790
My sword shall prove   these accusations lies."
Count Ganelon   with grateful thanks replies.

CCLXXV

Bavarians, Saxons,   have gone to judge the case,
Normans are with them,   Poitevins, men of France,
Germans are there,   and many Thiois too;

---

[96] Ganelon may mean that Roland kept more than his proper share of the spoils of war in
Spain. The basis of Ganelon's self-defense is that he opposed Roland openly, not in the secret
manner that technically was necessary to the definition of treason.

Those from Auvergne   show the most courtesy.
They speak more softly   because of Pinabel,
Telling each other,   "Let's bring this to an end,
Dismiss the trial,   and ask that Charles the King
For this one time   let Ganelon go free—   3800
He'll be his vassal   in loyalty and love.
Roland is dead;   you won't see him again.
No gold or treasure   will bring him back to life.
It would be madness   to fight for his sake now."
They all approve;   no one will disagree
But Geoffroy's[97] brother,   the chevalier Thierry.   AOI

CCLXXVI

And so the barons   return to Charlemagne,
Saying to him,   "Sire, we would ask for this:
Acquit your captive,   let Ganelon go free,
Henceforth to serve you   loyally and with love.   3810
Grant him his life,   for he is nobly born;
And no man's death   will bring Count Roland back,
Nor any gold—   there's nothing to be done."
Then says the king,   "You're traitors, every one!"   AOI

CCLXXVII

When King Charles sees   they all have failed his cause,
He bows his head   so none can see his face;
His words and looks   proclaim his bitter woe.
And then before him   he sees a chevalier,
Thierry, whose brother   is Geoffroy of Anjou.
Not very stalwart,   he's lean and spare of build,[98]   3820
His hair is black,   his face is rather dark;
He isn't tall,   nor could you call him short.
With courtesy   he tells the emperor:
"Fair sire and king,   do not give way to grief!
You know I've served you   a long time faithfully.
Now all my forebears   through me protest this trial:
However Roland   may have wronged Ganelon,
No one may harm   a man who serves the king.
Count Ganelon   is thus a traitor proved;
His oath to you   was broken and betrayed.   3830
And so I judge   that he should hang and die,
And that his body   be treated as befits
A criminal   who's guilty of a crime.
If he has kinsmen   who'd argue this with me,
I'll use this sword   girded here at my side

---

[97] Geoffroy of Anjou, Charles's flag bearer (see VIII) and one of his right-hand men.
[98] "The point is that Thierry will really need God's help if he is to prevail against Pinabel; thus the case will be better proved. And when he does win, the Franks immediately shout, 'A holy miracle!' (3931)."—Translator's note.

To give my judgment   a prompt and sure defense."[99]
The Franks reply,   "Your argument makes sense."

CCLXXVIII

Now Pinabel   stands up before the king;
He's tall and strong,   valiant and very swift:
The man he strikes   won't see another day.   3840
He says to Charles,   "Sire, you convoked this trial;
Pray, then, keep order—   let's not have so much noise.
And as for Thierry,   his judgment has been heard.
I say he's wrong—   now let him come and fight."
His right-hand glove   he offers to the king.[1]
The emperor says,   "I ask for hostages."[2]
His thirty kinsmen   will sponsor Pinabel.
Says Charlemagne,   "He's free then, in your place."
They will be guarded   till justice ends the case.   AOI

CCLXXIX

When Thierry sees   that Pinabel will fight,   3850
He gives his glove,   the right one, to the king,
And Charlemagne,   his hostage, sets him free.
Charles has four benches   arranged to mark the field;
Those who will fight   go out to take their seats.
All think the challenge   well given, rightly met;
Ogier explains   how they are to proceed.
Horses and arms   are sent for with all speed.

CCLXXX

The knights are ready   to meet for their ordeal.   AOI
They've made confession,   have been absolved and blessed,
They've heard a mass,   taken communion too;   3860
Great offerings   they've given to the church.
Now when the champions   appear before the king,
They both are wearing   sharp spurs upon their feet,
They've put on hauberks,   shining and light and strong,
Their burnished helmets   are closed around their heads,
They gird on swords   whose hilts are of pure gold.
Around their necks   they hang their quartered shields,
Their right hands grasp   the long sharp-pointed spears.
Now they have mounted   war-horses bred for speed.
Seeing them go,   a hundred thousand knights   3870
Remember Roland   and weep for Thierry—
For God knows what   the end of this will be!

---

[99] Technically, Thierry is defending a minority verdict of the jury; Pinabel, his opponent, will defend the majority verdict just rendered. In trials by combat, it was believed, the victory or defeat of the combatants demonstrated God's own judgment.

[1] The offering of the glove symbolizes the surrender to Charles of the combatant's feudal estate if he should be killed.

[2] Hostages are kept to guarantee that the combatant will appear for the duel.

CCLXXXI

In a broad meadow   below Aix la Chapelle,
The barons meet;   their battle has begun.
Both are courageous, both of them valiant lords,
And their war-horses   are spirited and swift.
They spur them hard,   and loosening the reins,
They charge each other   and strike with all their might.
Both shields are shattered—   they're broken into bits—
The hauberks break,   the girths are split apart,   3880
The saddles fall,   and with them both the knights.
A hundred thousand   are weeping at the sight.

CCLXXXII

Both chevaliers   have fallen to the ground.   AOI
Losing no time,   they're on their feet again.
Agile and swift   is Pinabel, and strong;
They face each other—   they have no horses now—
And raise their swords   whose hilts are made of gold
To strike and hew   each other's shining helms;
Those heavy blows   can cut right through the steel.
The French lament,   thinking their man must fail.   3890
"O God," says Charles,   "now let the right prevail!"

CCLXXXIII

Says Pinabel,   "Thierry, admit you've lost!
I'll be your vassal   in loyalty and love,
All I possess   shall be at your command—
But reconcile   the king and Ganelon."
Then Thierry answers,   "That's easy to decide!
I'll take no offer   unworthy of a knight!
Let God determine   which one of us is right!"   AOI

CCLXXXIV

And Thierry says,   "Pinabel, you are brave;
You're tall and strong,   your body is well built,   3900
That you are valiant   is known to all your peers.
This is a battle   you can afford to lose!
I'll make your peace   with Charlemagne the king,
But Ganelon   must get what he deserves—
No day will pass   without his death retold."
Says Pinabel,   "Almighty God forbid!
I stand here now   for all my family—
I won't surrender   to any man on earth!
Better to die   than live to merit blame."
So once again   they slash with their great swords,   3910
Striking the helmets   brilliant with gold and jewels—
Great fiery sparks   fly out against the sky.
Now neither champion   will to the other yield
Until a dead man   is lying on the field.   AOI

CCLXXXV

He's a strong fighter, Pinabel of Sorence,
The blow he strikes on Thierry's burnished helm
Sends out such sparks the grass is set on fire.
Then he springs forward, the point of his steel blade
Cutting right through from Thierry's forehead down;
Along his face the sword point slashes deep,   3920
And blood springs out all over his right cheek;
Down to his waist the hauberk links all tear—
Without God's help, he'd have died then and there! AOI

CCLXXXVI

When Thierry sees he's wounded in the face,
His bright blood falling over the meadow grass,
Pinabel's helmet of burnished steel he strikes:
Down through the nose-piece it cracks and splits in two,
His skull is broken and spills the brains inside;
With one last flourish Thierry has felled him dead—
With that great blow he's master of the field.   3930
The Frenchmen shout, "A holy miracle!
Justice demands that Ganelon must die,
With all the kinsmen who came and took his side." AOI

CCLXXXVII

Thierry has won his triumph on the field.
The Emperor Charles comes out to give him thanks;
Four of his barons attend the emperor:
Naimon the Duke, Count Ogier the Dane,
William of Blaye and Geoffroy of Anjou.
King Charlemagne takes Thierry in his arms,
And wipes his face with royal marten furs;   3940
These he puts down— they bring another cloak.
Thierry's armor is gently taken off;
Charles has him mounted on an Arabian mule.
Most joyfully they bring the hero home;
They come to Aix and in the square dismount.
Now they will kill the kinsmen of the count.

CCLXXXVIII

Charlemagne summons the nobles of his court:
"What do you counsel about my hostages?
These men came here to plead for Ganelon,
And stayed as pledges, sponsoring Pinabel."   3950
The Franks reply, "Ill work if one survives!"
The king commands an officer, Basbrun:
"Go hang them all upon the gallows tree!
And by my beard whose hair is silver-grey,
If one escapes, you're dead and put to shame."
The man replies, "I'll do as you command."
A hundred servants help him to drag them off;

They hang all thirty   that they were told to take.
So one man's evil   draws others in its wake.   AOI

CCLXXXIX

They all agree: Bavarians, Alemans,   3960
Poitevins, Bretons,   and men from Normandy,
And first of all   the Franks who come from France,
That Ganelon   should die most horribly.
And so they order   four war-horses[3] brought out
To which they tie   Ganelon's feet and hands.
These are proud chargers,   spirited, bred for speed:
Four servants urge them   the way they ought to go.
There where a river   across a meadow flows,
Count Ganelon   is utterly destroyed:
His ligaments   are twisted and stretched out,   3970
His every limb   is cracked and splits apart;
On the green grass   the bright blood runs in streams.
So Ganelon   as a foul traitor died.
Let no man's treason   give comfort to his pride!

CCXC

The Emperor Charles,   his vengeance being done,
Summoned his bishops,   the ones who came from France,
Bavarians   and Alemans as well:
"A noble captive   is dwelling in this house;
She's heard such sermons   and edifying tales,
She trusts in God,   and wants to take the Faith.   3980
Baptize her now,   that God may have her soul."
The bishops answer,   "Let godmothers be found!"[4]

*   *   *

A great assembly   was gathered at the baths
To see the Queen of Spain   receive the Faith;
To Juliana   they now have changed her name.
She had true knowledge   when Christian she became.

CCXCI

The Emperor Charles,   once justice has been done,
And his great anger   is finally appeased,   3990
Has Bramimonde   baptized into the Faith.
The day is over,   and in the dark of night
The king lies sleeping   in his high vaulted room.
Saint Gabriel   is sent by God to say:
"Charlemagne, summon   your empire's mighty hosts!
You'll march in force   into the land of Bire;

---

[3] The execution by quartering contradicts earlier statements that Ganelon was to be hanged.

[4] The following line, indicated here by the spaced asterisks, is defective in the manuscript. It apparently described the godmothers.

You must relieve   King Vivien at Imphe[5]
Where pagans hold   his city under siege,
And Christian voices   are crying for your help."
The Emperor Charles   has no desire to go.
"God!" says the king,   "how weary is my life!"   4000
He pulls his beard,   the tears flow from his eyes.
Here ends the poem,   for Turoldus declines.[6]

[5]"Nothing is known of Bire, Imphe, or Vivian except that they were all Christian."
—Translator's note.

[6]"The ending of the poem, *Ci falt la geste que Turoldus declinet*, is very famous for being so
enigmatic. *Que* may mean either 'which' or 'because' (Jenkins); *declinet* may mean 'to compose,
sing, recite, or copy.' It may also mean to 'set,' as the sun sets, or to become infirm. While it
is true that my version favors the idea of the poet's explaining why he does not continue his
work with Charlemagne's new expedition, the reason for this disinclination is left as imprecise
as possible. I hoped mainly to let the poem end with the same frustrating vagueness as does
the original."—Translator's note.

Icelandic Saga
(Twelfth through Fourteenth Centuries)

The prose sagas of Iceland are a vital part of medieval literature. The term saga,
*which literally means no more than "a saying," covers a wide range of narratives.
Some of the Icelandic sagas are fairly literal histories—for example, the* Book of
the Settlements, *which deals with the first settlers of Iceland, and Snorri
Sturluson's* Heimskringla, *which chronicles the kings of Norway. Others—the
"lying sagas"—are frankly fictional; these include the Icelandic versions of stories
about Gawain, the Trojan War, and other favorite subjects of medieval romances.*

*The most interesting sagas, however, are the "Sagas of Icelanders" or the "Family
Sagas." These were written for the most part in the twelfth and thirteenth centuries,
but they deal with people and events dating from about 930, when the settlement of
Iceland was substantially complete, to about 1030. (This century overlaps with the
first generation of Icelandic Christianity, which was adopted as the official religion
in the year 1000.) The Family Sagas are poised between fact and fiction. The anonymous authors based their work upon historical tales and legends two or three centuries old, but they exercised a fairly free hand in reshaping their material into artistic
narratives.*

*The world the sagas evoke is stark and dramatic, as harsh and lonely as the
Icelandic landscape. The settlers of Iceland—mostly Norwegians, Norsemen, and
Celts from Ireland and other parts of the British Isles—brought Norse values and
customs with them. Political and social organization was loose and turned around
family estates. The head of a large estate was, by virtue of his position, a* godi—*both
a priest (since he was responsible for maintaining the local temples of Thor, Frey, and
the other Norse gods) and a secular chieftain who distributed land and favors to his
followers, exacting from them in return allegiance and military aid. The* godi's

authority was called his godord, *and his followers were called* thingmen. *This system depended strongly on family ties and other personal bonds of obligation and allegiance.*

The only centralizing institution was the Thing, *a public assembly for deliberation and decision attended by all freemen. At first a regional forum, it became after 925 a national one. This institution, common in ancient Germanic countries, was carried to Iceland from the settlers' native Norway. The* Thing *was both a legislative body and a law court, ruling for or against individual plaintiffs through the general vote of the assembly. It was primarily a deliberative body, however, with little power to enforce its verdicts. Execution of the law therefore remained primarily in the hands of the individuals concerned and was carried out in accordance with the ancient code: either direct vengeance or* wergeld *(blood money, or compensation).*

Such social and political conditions naturally emphasized individual character—an emphasis further sharpened in the religious context of the sagas. Their Christian authors were dealing with pre-Christian men and women subject neither to the Christian God nor to the gods of the Norse pantheon, so that their fortunes depended on their own characters. The code of personal conduct in the sagas is an extension of the ancient Germanic heroic code. The world is ruled by an inexorable fate; man's duty is to face this fate with courage, even defiance. The central ethic is a man's personal and family honor; when that honor is impeached, it must be fully and publicly vindicated. This imperative lies behind most of the bloody and violent deeds of the sagas. The violence is redeemed to some extent, however, by another ideal of conduct: the notion of drengskapr. Drengskapr *means something like "magnanimity" or "largeness of soul." The saga hero not only meets his fate with a stoical acceptance but also treats his enemy with respect and even admiration, avoiding meanness or pettiness of word or deed.*

The style of the sagas is austere, like the heroic code they embody. For the most part, as in the Song of Roland, *the stories are told with a dramatic objectivity. The narrator seldom intrudes his own interpretations or explores the characters' inner thoughts and feelings. The emphasis is upon bare, unadorned narrative, action rather than emotion. We find out what the characters are like by what they do, and we are left on our own to discover the meaning of the story. Great care is taken with the overall structure of the narrative; frequently the meaning is implied by careful balancing and repetition of elements.*

Hrafnkel the Priest of Frey *is one of the shorter sagas, but also one of the most effective. Its violent action unfolds swiftly in a series of short, economical episodes, told objectively and in terse dialogue.* Hrafnkel *is a complex figure, one of the few saga protagonists who change in the course of their stories. The balancing of his story with that of Sam raises basic questions of character, religious faith, and heroic conduct.*

If Hrafnkel *resembles a modern novella, "Authun and the Bear" foreshadows the modern short story. It also reads like a folk tale, with its extravagant action and its use of the Odyssean motif of the beggar hero unrecognized at court. But it is artfully constructed and told. Like* Hrafnkel, *it depends on short, vivid episodes and a free use of dialogue. The behavior of Authun, King Harald, and King Svein is a brief epitome of saga values.*

FURTHER READING *(prepared by W. J. R.):* An excellent introduction to the Family Sagas is Theodore M. Anderson's *The Icelandic Family Saga: An Analytical Reading*, 1967. The first part of this work deals with structure, rhetoric, and the heroic legacy. The second part analyzes several individual sagas, including *Hrafnkel*. Peter Hallberg's *The Icelandic Saga,* trans. by Paul Schach, 1962, examines the centrally important question of the historical reliability of *Hrafnkel*, a matter also explored by E. V. Gordon in *Medium Aevum*, 8 (1939), 1–32. Sigurður Nordal's *Hrafnkels Saga Freysgo*ða, 1949, trans. by R. George Thomas, 1958, is indispensable; it analyzes, among other things, the work's historical reliability, theme, and characterization. *Scandinavian Studies*, 47, No. 4 (1975) consists largely of four critical articles on *Hrafnkel* by Frederik J. Heinemann and Peter Hallberg.

HRAFNKEL THE PRIEST OF FREY

Translated by Gwyn Jones

1

It was in the days of king Harald Fairhair, son of Halfdan the Black, son of Gudrod the Hunting King, son of Halfdan the Freehanded but Foodstingy, son of Eystein Fret, son of Olaf Woodcutter the Swedish king,[1] that a man by the name of Hallfred brought his ship out to Iceland to Breiddal, which lies east of Fljotsdalsherad. On board were his wife and a son by the name of Hrafnkel, who was fifteen years old at the time, handsome and enterprising. Hallfred built himself a house to live in; then, during the winter, a foreign bondwoman died whose name was Arnthrud, which is why the place has been known as Arnthrudarstadir ever since.

In the spring Hallfred moved house northwards over the heath, and built himself a new home at a place called Geitdal. One night he dreamt how a man appeared to him, saying: "There you lie, Hallfred—and rashly, to be sure! Move your home away from here, west across Lagarfljot. All your good luck lies there." After this he awoke and moved house over the Ranga river into Tunga, to the place now known as Hallfredarstadir, where he lived till he was an old man. But a goat and she-goat got left behind him, and the very day Hallfred moved out a landslide crashed on to the farm, and those fine animals perished there—which is why the place has been called Geitdal ever since.

2

Hrafnkel made it his practice to go riding over the heath in summer. By this time Jokulsdal had been fully settled right up to the rock-bridges. Hrafnkel went riding up along Fljotsdalsheid and saw where an empty valley branched off from Jokulsdal, which looked to him a better place to settle in than any other valley he had seen up to then; so when he got back home he asked his father for what was due to him of their property, and announced that he had a mind to make his home there. His father gave him his head over this, and he built himself a home in the valley and called

---

[1] Genealogies of this kind are common in Icelandic sagas. *Hrafnkel the Priest of Frey* contains fewer than most, substituting detailed lists of place names. Harald Fairhair was the famous king of Norway who reigned in the last part of the ninth century and the first part of the tenth and unified Norway under a single rule. His victories in Norway drove out many of his enemies—a major cause of the settlement of Iceland.

it Adalbol, or Manor. Hrafnkel married Oddbjorg, Skjaldulf's daughter from Laxardal, and they had two sons, the elder called Thorir and the younger Asbjorn.

Once Hrafnkel had taken possession of the land at Adalbol he went in a lot for sacrifices and had a big temple built. Hrafnkel loved no other god more than Frey,[2] on whom he bestowed a half share in all his best treasures. He occupied the entire valley and apportioned men their land, but was determined to be their master even so, and took the priesthood over them, for which reason his name was lengthened and he was called Frey's Priest. He was a very overbearing, if talented, man, and compelled the Jokulsdalers to become his retainers. To his own people Hrafnkel was kindly and pleasant, but toward those of Jokulsdal he proved harsh and hard-headed, and they had a rough time of it at his hands. Hrafnkel took part in numerous single combats, and paid no one so much as a penny, so that nobody got any redress from him, whatever it was he did.

Fljotsdalsheid is a hard place to get about in, being very stony and boggy, but despite this father and son were always riding on visits one to the other, for their relationship was very real to them. Hallfred found the road troublesome, and cast about for a route over the high ground which stands in Fljotsdalsheid, where he found a drier if longer road, the one known as Hallfredargata. They alone use this road who really know their way about in Fljotsdalsheid.

3

Living at a farm called Laugarhus, in Hrafnkelsdal, was a man by the name of Bjarni. He was married, and had two sons by his wife, the one called Sam[3] and the other Eyvind—handsome, promising men. Eyvind lived at home with his father, but Sam was married and living in the northern end of the valley at a farm by the name of Leikskalar. He was quite well-to-do. Sam was a highly contentious man and clever at the law, but Eyvind became a merchant and returned to Norway, where he spent the winter. From there he travelled into foreign parts, coming to a halt at Constantinople, where he won the favor of the Greek king and stayed on for a while.

Hrafnkel had one particular treasure in his possession which he prized higher than anything else. This was a stallion, dark mouse-grey in color and with a black stripe the length of his spine, which he called his Freyfaxi. He gave his friend Frey a half share in this stallion. He was so besotted with this stallion that he swore a great oath that he would be the death of any man who rode him without his express permission.

Bjarni's brother Thorbjorn was living in Hrafnkelsdal, at a farm called Holar, opposite Adalbol to the east. Thorbjorn had few assets and many dependants. His eldest son was a big, handy lad by the name of Einar, and it happened one spring that Thorbjorn had a word with Einar, how he should be looking round for some employment—"For I cannot use more labor than this household here can provide, while you are such a handy man you will easily get a good place. This is not a case of lack of affection

---

[2] The Scandinavian god of earth's fruitfulness and the dispenser of wealth.
[3] *Sam* is not the diminuitive of *Samuel*, but a Scandinavian name in its own right, pronounced with a broad *a*, as in "art."

making me get rid of you, for you mean much more to me than my other children. No, it is rather my lack of means that causes it, and my poverty. My other children are growing into workmen, but you will find a good job more easily than they."

"You have told me about this too late," replied Einar, "for by now every one will have his hands on the best jobs, and I don't much fancy having the leavings."

One day Einar caught his horse and rode to Adalbol. Hrafnkel was sitting in the living-room and gave him a warm and cheerful welcome. He asked Hrafnkel for a job.

"Why are you so late asking this," was his reply, "for I would have taken you on the very first? But by now I have engaged all my hands, except for the one job you will not care to have."

Einar asked what this might be. Hrafnkel explained that he had not yet engaged anyone for sheep-tending, and admitted he needed a good man for this. Einar said that he was not much concerned what he did, whether it was that or anything else. He stressed that what he needed was a job with full keep both winter and summer.

"Then I will give you a quick choice," said Hrafnkel. "You shall drive home the fifty ewes at the shieling[4] and fetch in all the summer firewood, and that shall be your work for the two seasons. But I must get one thing straight with you as with my other shepherds. Freyfaxi roams the upper end of the valley with his stud. You must look after him winter and summer, and I warn you against one thing: it is my will that you never get on his back, however great may be your need, for I have sworn a great oath about this, how I would be the death of any man who rides him. Twelve mares run with him, and whichever of these you want to ride, night or day, shall be at your disposal. Now do as I tell you, for it is an old saying: 'His hands are clean who warns another.' Bear in mind now what I have been talking about."

Einar said he would not be so bent on trouble as to ride this horse which was forbidden him—all the more so since there were plenty of others. With that he went home for his clothes, removed back to Adalbol, and later off they went to the shieling in the upper reaches of Hrafnkelsdal at the place called Grjotteigssel. Everything went well for Einar that summer, so that there was never a sheep lost right up till midsummer, but then there were nearly thirty ewes missing in a single night. He searched all over the pastures without finding them, and the sheep were missing nearly a week. One morning it happened that Einar went out early, and all the southern mist and drizzle had cleared away. He took a staff in his hand, a bridle, and saddle-cloth, and walked up across the river Grjotteigsa, which falls away there from the shieling, and there on the tongue of land lay the sheep which had been at home overnight. He headed these back to the shieling and went to look for those others which had been lost earlier. He could see the mares farther out on the tongue and wondered about catching a horse to ride, feeling that he would get along faster if he rode than if he walked. When he reached the mares he stalked them, but these, which never used

---

[4]Summer shed.

to run away from man, were now hard to approach—except for Freyfaxi alone. He was as still as if he had taken root.

Einar realized that the morning was wearing on, and judged that Hrafnkel would not know even if he did ride the stallion. He now laid hold of him and bridled him, fixed the saddle-cloth under him on the horse's back, and rode up beside Grjotargil, so up to the glaciers and west alongside the glaciers where the river Jokulsa falls away, and so down along the river to Reykjasel. He asked all the shepherds at the Reykjasel shieling whether any of them had seen the sheep, but nobody could say that he had. Einar rode Freyfaxi from dawn right to mid-evening, the stallion covering a lot of ground with him in a short time, he was such a fine horse. It now occurred to Einar that it would be time for him to get back and drive in the sheep that were at home, even if he failed to find the others, so he rode east over the ridges into Hrafnkelsdal. As he came down to Grjotteig he heard the bleating of sheep from higher up the very ravine he had ridden by before. He turned that way and saw thirty ewes running towards him, the very ones he had lost the week before, and he headed for home with the sheep.

The stallion was all running with sweat, so that it dripped from every hair he had. He was caked with mud and utterly spent. He went rolling over and over a dozen times, and after that set up a loud neighing; then away he went at a great gallop down along the pathway. Einar turned after him, meaning to head him off, catch him, and lead him back to his mares, but this time he was so shy that Einar could get nowhere near him. He went tearing down the valley without halt or pause till he reached Adalbol, where Hrafnkel was sitting at table. As soon as the horse came in front of the door he neighed shrilly. Hrafnkel spoke to a woman who was serving at table, telling her to go to the door—"Because a horse neighed, and it sounded to me like the neighing of Freyfaxi." She walked out into the doorway, where she saw Freyfaxi in sorry plight, and told Hrafnkel that it was indeed Freyfaxi outside the door, as filthy as could be.

"What can my brave lad want, that he has come home?" asked Hrafnkel. "This can bode no good."

With that he went outside and took a look at Freyfaxi. "I do not like it," he told him, "that they are treating you this way, foster-son, but you had your wits about you when you told me of it. It shall be avenged, so off with you to your stud!"

With no more ado he trotted back up the valley to his mares.

Hrafnkel went to bed that evening and slept through the night. In the morning he had his horse caught and saddled and rode up to the shieling. He rode in blue clothes, had an axe in his hand, but no further weapon.[5] Einar had just driven the sheep into the fold. He was lying on the fold wall, counting the sheep, and the women were busy milking. They greeted Hrafnkel. He asked how they were getting on.

"I have had a bad time of it," confessed Einar, "for there were thirty sheep missing the best part of a week. They are found now though."

Hrafnkel said he had no quarrel with this or its like. "But has not some-

---

[5] Men wore blue clothes when they intended to kill someone. The axe is a battle-axe.

thing worse taken place? It has not happened as often as one would expect that the sheep have got lost, but did you not maybe ride my Freyfaxi yesterday?"

Einar said he could not deny it.

"But why did you ride this horse which was forbidden you, when there were any number of others at your disposal? I would have forgiven you a first offense, had I not sworn so great an oath in the matter. And yet you have owned up to it like a man."

But in the belief that nothing goes right for those men who draw down on themselves the curse for a broken oath, he dismounted, ran at him, and struck him his death-blow. After this he rode back to Adalbol without more ado, told his news, and later sent another man to the sheep at the shieling. He had Einar carried west from the shieling to the hillside, and raised a cairn there to mark his grave. The place is called Einarsvarda, and is mid-eve mark[6] from the shieling.

Thorbjorn heard tell over at Holar of the killing of Einar his son, and took the news hard. He caught his horse, rode over to Adalbol, and asked Hrafnkel to make redress for killing his son.

Hrafnkel retorted that he had killed more men than this one. "And it can be no news to you that I am unwilling to make anyone reparation, and folk have to put up with it just the same. Even so, I admit that this deed of mine strikes me as among the very worst killings I have committed. You have been my neighbor a long while now, I have liked you, and each of us the other. No small matter would have made trouble between me and Einar, had he not ridden the stallion. Well, we must often regret opening our mouths too wide—and seldom repent speaking too little rather than too much. I am now going to make it clear that I regard this deed of mine as worse than anything else I have done. I shall provide your household with milk cows in summer and with meat in the autumn, and I shall do this for you season by season as long as you want to keep on your farm. Under my management your sons and daughters shall be taken off your hands, and so endowed that they can make good matches as a result; while anything at all you know to be in my possession that you have need of from now on, you must tell me and never again go short of whatever it is you need. You shall keep your farm as long as you please, but come here to me as soon as you grow tired of it, whereupon I will look after you to the day of your death; and we shall then be atoned. I shall expect this too, that most people are going to say the man was pretty dear."

"I'll not take this offer," said Thorbjorn.

"What do you want then?" Hrafnkel asked him.

"I want us to appoint men to arbitrate between us."

"Then you consider yourself my equal," replied Hrafnkel, "and we shall never be atoned on those terms."[7]

---

[6]"Mid-eve mark" means that the cairn is at a point where at "mid-eve" (about 6 P.M.) it is on a straight line between the sun and the shed.

[7]Thorbjorn, as the relative of the murdered man, has three choices under Icelandic law. He can (1) avenge the murder directly; (2) accept compensation, arranged either directly or through arbitrators; or (3) bring a formal suit against Hrafnkel. Here he rejects Hrafnkel's liberal offer and demands arbitration. The arrogant Hrafnkel refuses, because arbitration would imply that the parties were equal.

At this Thorbjorn rode away and down along Hrafnkelsdal until he reached Laugarhus and met Bjarni his brother, to whom he told his news, with a request that he should play some part in the affair. But Bjarni held that it was no fair match if Hrafnkel came into it. "For while we have lots of money we cannot possibly tackle Hrafnkel. It's a good saying too that a wise man knows his limits. He has tied up plenty in lawsuits who have more bone in their fists than we. As I see it, you behaved like a fool in refusing so good an offer. I want neither part nor parcel of it."

At this Thorbjorn spoke many bitter words to Bjarni his brother, maintaining that the more there lay at stake the more gutless he proved. Then he rode away, and they parted with little kindness. He made no stay till he came down to Leikskalar, where he knocked and they answered the door. Thorbjorn asked Sam to step outside. Sam had a warm welcome for his kinsman and invited him to put up there, an offer which Thorbjorn accepted without much eagerness. Sam could see that Thorbjorn was heavy-hearted; he asked what had happened, and Thorbjorn told him of the killing of Einar his son.

"It is no great news," commented Sam, "though Hrafnkel kills a man."

Thorbjorn asked whether Sam was prepared to help him in any way. "The case stands thus, that though the dead man is closest to me, the blow has landed not so very far from you either."

"Have you by any chance tried for redress from Hrafnkel?" asked Sam.

Thorbjorn told him the whole truth, how things had gone between the two of them.

"I have never heard tell before," said Sam, "that Hrafnkel has made such offers to anyone as to you now. So I am prepared to ride with you up to Adalbol, and let us approach him humbly and see if he will stand by the same offer. He is sure to behave well one way or another."

"For one thing," answered Thorbjorn, "he will no longer be willing for it; and for another, it is no more to my liking now than when I rode away."

"It is heavy work," said Sam, "I fancy, to bring a lawsuit against Hrafnkel."

"You young men," scolded Thorbjorn, "you will never get anywhere, the way you make mountains out of molehills. I cannot believe anybody has such wretches for kinsmen as I. This strikes me as the height of meanness in a man like you, who consider yourself so smart at law and go falling over yourself in petty suits, but are unwilling to take on this case which is so glaringly clear. It will be a reproach to you, right enough, for you are the biggest boaster in the whole of our family. Well, I see now how the affair will turn out."

"What better off are you than before," asked Sam, "though I do take on the case, and we are both of us thrown out of court?"

"Just the same," said Thorbjorn, "It will be a great comfort to me if you take it on, come of it what may."

"I shall be going into this against my will," Sam warned him. "It is mainly for our kinship's sake that I am doing it. And you may as well know, I think I am helping a fool in helping you."

Then Sam reached out his hand and took over the case from Thorbjorn.

Next Sam had his horse caught and rode up along the valley to a farm where (he had already enlisted men for the purpose) he gave notice of the killing against Hrafnkel. This reached Hrafnkel's ears, and he thought it a great joke that Sam had started a lawsuit against him. The winter wore away, and in spring, when the summons-days came round, Sam rode from home up to Adalbol and summoned Hrafnkel for killing Einar. Afterwards Sam rode down through the valley and summoned the neighbors to ride to the Assembly, and thereafter kept quiet till men made ready for their journey there.[8]

At this point Hrafnkel sent down through the valley to summon his men together. He set off from his territory with seventy men. With this troop he rode east across Fljotsdalsheid, and so past the head of the lake, and across the pass to Skridudal, up along Skridudal and south to Oxarheid, to Berufjord, where he took the direct road of all riders to the Assembly to Sida. South from Fljotsdal it is a seventeen days' journey to the Assembly at Thingvellir.

Once he had ridden away from the district Sam assembled his men. For the most part he got masterless men to ride with him, in addition to those he had called up before. All these too he provided with weapons, clothes, and victuals. Sam left the valley by a different route, proceeding north to the rock-bridges, where he made his crossing, and from there over Modrudalsheid, to spend the night in Modrudal. From there they rode to Herdibreidstunga, and so inland of Blafjoll, on again to Kroksdal, and so south to Sprengisand, making down for Sandafell, and from there to Thingvellir, where Hrafnkel had not yet arrived. He was making slower time because he had the longer road. Sam pitched a booth for his men well away from where the Eastfirthers usually encamp, and somewhat later Hrafnkel reached the Assembly, to pitch his booth where he normally did. He heard that Sam was at the Assembly and thought the whole thing a great joke.

This Assembly was very crowded. Almost all the chieftains who were in Iceland were present there. Sam approached all these chieftains and asked them for help and assistance, but all answered the same way; not one of them could say he was under such obligation to Sam that he was prepared to get into a fight with Hrafnkel the Priest and so imperil his good name; they added further that it had gone one way for most of those who had dealings with Hrafnkel at the Assembly, in that he had driven everyone who had tackled him headlong from their lawsuits. Sam returned to his booth, and the kinsmen were heavy-hearted indeed, fearing that their case would so fall through that they would win nothing but shame and dishonor, and such great dismay filled uncle and nephew that they could neither eat nor sleep; for all the chieftains hung back from helping them, including those they had fully expected to lend them a hand.

---

[8] Icelandic law was largely taken over from Norway. In a case such as the one against Hrafnkel, the plaintiff had to give notice to the defendant and the witnesses by the "summons-days." The case was then presented before the Thing, the national assembly and court. Icelandic law, however, did not provide for enforcement; that is why Sam must give the summons himself and win the support of powerful chieftains for his case, as well as carry out the decision of the court if his suit is successful.

4

Early one morning old Thorbjorn awoke. He roused Sam and told him to get up.

"I can't sleep."

Sam rose and got into his clothes. They went outside, down to the Oxara river below the bridge, where they washed themselves.

"It is my counsel," said Thorbjorn to Sam, "that you have our horses driven in, and let us make ready for home. It is clear by now that nothing lies ahead of us except humiliation."

"And fair enough too," replied Sam, "for you wanted nothing in the world except to fight this out with Hrafnkel, and were unwilling to accept an offer which so many would have been glad to accept who had to claim redress for a near kinsman. You cast a great slur on my courage and everybody else's who didn't want to get into this lawsuit with you, and now I will never give up till I think it beyond all hope that I get something or other to show for it."

At this Thorbjorn was so moved that he wept.

It was then that they saw how, a little lower down than where they were seated, five men came walking together from a booth and east towards the river. He was a tallish man, not very thickly built, who walked at their head, in a leaf-green kirtle[9] and with a mounted sword in his hand, his features regular, and his coloring ruddy, of distinguished appearance, and with a fine head of chestnut hair on him. He was a man easy to recognize, for he had a whitish lock of hair on the left side.

"Up we get," said Sam "and let us cross west of the river to meet these men."

They walked down alongside the river, and this man who was walking in front got in first with a greeting. He asked who they might be, and they told him.

Sam asked the man his name. He said his name was Thorkel, adding that he was the son of Thjostar.

Sam asked what might his origins be, and where was his home.

He was a Westfirther, he said, by birth and descent, and had a home in Thorskafjord.

"Are you a man with a priesthood?" Sam asked him.

"Far from it," he replied.

"Are you a farmer then?"

No, he said, he was not.

"What sort of man are you then?"

"I am a footloose sort of man. I came out to Iceland last winter. I have spent seven years abroad, and went out to Constantinople, where I became a liegeman of the emperor; but at the moment I am lodging with a brother of mine named Thorgeir."

"Is he a man with a priesthood?" asked Sam.

"To be sure he is, with a priesthood the length and breadth of Thorskafjord, and wider still throughout the Westfirths."

"Is he here at the Assembly?" asked Sam.

---

[9] Tunic.

"To be sure he is."

"And how is he off for men?"

"He has seventy," said Thorkel.

"Have you any more brothers?" asked Sam.

"There is a third," Thorkel admitted.

"And who is he?"

"His name is Thormod. He lives at Gardar on Alptanes. He married Thordis, Thorolf Skallagrimsson's daughter, from Borg."

"Would you care to lend us a hand?" asked Sam.

"Why, what do you need?"

"The help and strength of chieftains," replied Sam, "for we have a law-suit to thrash out with Hrafnkel the Priest for the killing of Einar Thorbjorn's son. And we could safely trust to our pleading with support from you."

"It's as I said," Thorkel pointed out. "I hold no priesthood."

"But why are you pushed aside so," demanded Sam, "since you are as much a chieftain's son as your brothers are?"

"I did not tell you," said Thorkel, "that I had no stake in such, but I handed over my authority to Thorgeir my brother before I went abroad. Nor have I taken it back since, for it strikes me as being in very good keeping however long he looks after it. Go and have a word with him, and ask him to help you. He is a man in a thousand, a splendid fellow and in every respect outstanding, youngish still and eager to distinguish himself. In short, the likeliest kind of man to lend you a hand."

"We shall get nothing out of him," said Sam, "unless you put in a word for us."

"I will promise this much," said Thorkel, "to be for you rather than against, for it seems to me a man's plain duty to take up the bloodsuit for his close kinsman. Now get along to the booth, and make your way inside. The men are still asleep there. You will see where two hammocks extend across the innermost side of the booth. I got up from one of them, and in the other Thorgeir my brother lies resting. He has had a big boil on his foot ever since he came to the Assembly, and as a result has had little sleep of nights, but last night the foot broke and the core is out of the boil. He has been sleeping since, and has stuck his foot out from under the bedclothes on to the foot-board, because of the excessive heat which is in the foot. Let the old man lead the way on into the booth. He seems to me very infirm both in sight and years. And, friend," Thorkel went on, "when you reach the hammock, you must stumble heavily, and fall on to the foot-board, catch hold of the toe which is tied up, wrench it towards you—and find out how he takes it."

"You are going to be a great help to us," said Sam, "but this does not sound a good plan to me."

"You can do one or the other," replied Thorkel. "do as I suggest or seek no advice of mine."

"Then what he advises," announced Sam, "shall be done."

Thorkel said he would be coming along later. "For I am waiting for my men."

So now Sam and Thorbjorn set off and arrived inside the booth. All the men there were asleep. They soon saw where Thorgeir was lying. Old Thorbjorn went in front, stumbling awkwardly, and when he reached the hammock he went sprawling on to the foot-board, grabbed at the afflicted toe, and wrenched it towards him. This roused Thorgeir, who shot up in bed, demanding to know who could be dashing about the place so headlong as to go falling over people's feet, which were bad enough before. But Sam and Thorbjorn had nothing really to say for themselves.

Then Thorkel stepped briskly into the booth to speak to Thorgeir his brother. "Don't be in such a flurry and panic over this, brother. It won't hurt you. Many a man acts worse than he intends, and it happens every day that a man cannot attend with equal care to everything when he has a great deal on his mind. Yet it is your excuse, kinsman, that your foot is painful, and, indeed, has suffered great affliction; and you yourself will be the one to feel it most. Now it may also be the case that to this old man his son's death is no less painful, yet he can obtain no cure or redress, and nothing goes right for him. He will be the one to feel this most, and it is only to be expected that a man with so much on his mind will not pay due heed to everything."

"I had no idea he could quarrel with me over it," Thorgeir retorted. "For I didn't kill his son, and by the same token he cannot avenge it on me."

"He didn't mean to avenge it on you," said Thorkel. "He came at you harder than he intended, and paid the penalty for his failing sight. In fact he was looking for some help from you, and what a fine thing it would be now to help a man so old and needy! For this is duty in him, not greed, when he takes up the bloodsuit after his son. But now the chieftains hang back from helping these men, and in so doing show great cowardice."

"Whom are they accusing, these men?" Thorgeir asked.

"Hrafnkel the Priest has killed Thorbjorn's son without cause," explained Thorkel. "He commits crime after crime, and will pay recompense to nobody."

"I must stand with the rest," said Thorgeir. "I do not find myself so obligated to these men that I want a fight with Hrafnkel on my hands. It seems to me he sets to work in such a way every summer against those men who have lawsuits to settle with him that most of them win little or no honor before it ends, and as I see it, it goes one and the same way with the lot of them. That, I fancy, is why most men who have no duty in that matter feel no desire to meddle with it."

"It may be," Thorkel replied, "that if I were a chieftain myself I should act the same way, and think it a bad business to clash with Hrafnkel. But the way things are, I just do not see it in that light, for I should think it best to pit myself against the very man from whom all took a tumble before; and I believe that mine or any other chieftain's fame would increase greatly who could out-row Hrafnkel, yet not grow less though I went the same road as the others, because what happens to the rest can happen to me, and, 'Nothing venture, nothing gain.'"

"I see how you are inclined," said Thorgeir. "You would like to help these men. I am now going to hand over to you my priesthood and authority; you hold it on just such terms as I have held it before, and from there on let us share it equally—and then you help anybody you want to."

"It appears to me," said Thorkel, "that our priesthood is in the safest keeping the longer you hold on to it. I should not care for anyone to hold it as I do you, for you have many talents beyond all us brothers. Nor am I just now settled what I intend to do with myself. Besides you know, kinsman, how I have kept very much to myself since I came to Iceland. However, I can see now what my advice is worth. I have pleaded as much as I will for the present. Maybe Thorkel Lock will come where his word has more weight!"

"I see now the way the wind blows, brother," replied Thorgeir. "You are offended, and I cannot have that, so we will help these men, come of it what may, if you want to."

"I ask only such things," said Thorkel, "as I think will be better granted."

"What do these two reckon themselves capable of," asked Thorgeir, "so that their case may have a happy ending?"

"Even as I said today" (this was Sam speaking), "our need is for the strength of chieftains, but I can manage the pleading of the suit myself."

Thorgeir told him that in that case he was easy to help. "And what is now necessary is to prepare the case as accurately as can be. I fancy too that Thorkel would like you to let him know before the courts go into procession. You will then get some return for your pains, some comfort or shame even greater than before, and anguish and humiliation. Now, go home and be cheerful, for if you are proposing to tackle Hrafnkel the Priest you need to bear up well in the meantime. But let no one know we have promised you aid."

They now returned to their booth and were in high spirits. Everyone was astonished at this, why they had so quickly changed their mood, for they were quite downcast when they left their booth.

They waited there till the courts went into procession, when Sam called out his men and marched to the Lawhill, where the court was by this time in session. Sam went boldly into court, at once began naming his witnesses, and presented his case against Hrafnkel the Priest according to the true law of the land, without error and with distinguished pleading. Hot on his heels came the sons of Thjostar with a strong force of men. Everybody from the west country stood behind them, and it was clear that the sons of Thjostar were well off for friends. Sam prosecuted his case in court to the point where Hrafnkel was called on for the defense, unless some man was present there who desired to put forward a defense on his behalf. There was loud applause for Sam's case, and no one offered to produce any legal defense for Hrafnkel. Men ran to his booth to tell him what was happening. He was quickly on the move, collected his men, and marched towards the court, expecting to find the coast all clear. It was his intention to give such small fry their bellyful of bringing lawsuits against him: he meant to wreck the court for Sam and drive him from his case. But by now there was no chance of this. There was such a press of men in front of him that he could get nowhere near the place. He was crowded away by sheer force, so that he might not hear his prosecutor's case, which made it rather a problem for him to bring forward his defense. So Sam drove his suit to the full limit of the law, till Hrafnkel was declared an outlaw at this Assembly.

5

Hrafnkel returned to his booth at once, had his horses caught, and rode away from the Assembly, profoundly dissatisfied with his end of the case, for nothing of the kind had ever happened to him before. He rode east to Lyngdalsheid, and so eastwards to Sida, and made no stay till he arrived in Hrafnkelsdal and settled in at Adalbol, where he acted as though nothing had happened. But Sam stayed on at the Assembly, strutting about with his tail up. A lot of people were well pleased that it had turned out this way, that Hrafnkel had suffered this blow to his self-esteem; and they now called to mind how he had shown injustice to many.

Sam waited till the Assembly was dissolved and men made ready for home. He thanked the brothers for all they had done, and Thorgeir, laughing, asked Sam how he thought things were going.

It had gone off very well, he maintained.

"You think yourself any better off now than before?" asked Thorgeir.

"I think Hrafnkel has suffered a humiliation which will be remembered for a long time," replied Sam, "and that is worth a lot of money."

"The man is not outlawed so long as the court of execution[10] is not held," quoted Thorgeir, "and that must needs be done at his own domicile, and take place fourteen nights after the weapontake." They call it the weapontake, or recovery of weapons, when the gathering rides from the Assembly. "Now it is my guess," Thorgeir went on, "that Hrafnkel will have arrived home, intending to sit firm in the saddle at Adalbol. It is my further guess that, for anything you can do, he will maintain his position there. So you will be reckoning to ride home and at best remain on your farm— always supposing you can manage it. I guess you have this much from your lawsuit that you can call him a forest outlaw, but he will hold the same old helm of terror over most as before, with the exception (so I guess) that you must needs crawl somewhat lower."

"I have never been frightened of that," said Sam.

"You are a bold fellow," Thorgeir assured him, "but I fancy brother Thorkel is not thinking to leave you in the lurch. He now wants to go on backing you till all is concluded between you and Hrafnkel, and you can rest easy. You must feel that we are bound to stand by you, for we have taken the biggest part in this so far, so we are going to help you this once in the Eastfirths. Do you know any road to the Eastfirths which is not a frequented way?"

Sam said he would follow the same route he had travelled from the east, and was all cock-a-hoop[11] at this.

Thorgeir picked his following and had forty men ride with him. Sam too had forty men, and the entire company was well equipped with weapons and horses.

After this they all followed the same route till they reached Jokulsdal just before dawn. They crossed the river at the bridge; and it was the very morning they had to hold the court of execution. Thorgeir asked how they might best take them by surprise. Sam reckoned he would know a plan for

[10] The "court of execution" was the ceremony carrying out the decision of the court.
[11] Delighted.

this, and without more ado turned from the path up to the bluff, and so along the ridge between Hrafnkelsdal and Jokulsdal, till they came out from under the mountain beneath which stands the farmstead at Adalbol. Grassy clefts ran up on to the heath there, and there was a steep slope down to the valley, and there below stood the farmstead.

Here Sam dismounted. "Let us leave our horses here, with twenty men to watch them," he suggested, "and the other sixty of us will make a dash for the farm. I feel sure there will be few up and doing there."

They did this, and the place has been called Hrossageilar, Horselanes, ever since. They raced swiftly for the farmstead. The hour for rising was past, but the people had not got up. They dashed a beam against the door and rushed inside. Hrafnkel was lying in his bed. They dragged him out of it, together with every man of his household who could use arms. The women and children were driven into a building on their own. In the home-field stood a storehouse, and from this back to the wall of the main building there extended a beam for the washing. They led Hrafnkel that way along with his men. He made many offers for himself and his followers, and when these served no purpose pleaded for the lives of his men.

"For they have done nothing to offend against you, while it is no discredit to me though you kill me. I am not asking to be spared that, but I do ask to be spared humiliation. There is no credit to you in that."

"We have heard tell," said Thorkel, "that you have proved hard-mouthed in harness for your enemies. It is just as well that you are today made to feel this in your turn."

They laid hold of Hrafnkel and his men and tied their hands behind their backs. After that they broke into a storehouse and took a rope down off the hooks. They next took their knives and pierced holes through their hough sinews,[12] threaded the rope through, swung them up so over the beam, and secured them so, eight together.

"So it has come to this, Hrafnkel," said Thorgeir, "that you have got your deserts at last. And how unlikely you must have thought it that you would come by such shame at anyone's hands as is now the case. Which will you do now, Thorkel: stay here with Hrafnkel and keep an eye on them, or will you go with Sam away out of the yard, yet within arrow-shot of the house, and hold the court of execution on some rocky mound where there is neither meadow nor furrow?"

This should be done at the time when the sun is full south.

"I'll stay here with Hrafnkel," replied Thorkel. "That looks to me the less bothersome."

Thorgeir and Sam then went and held the court of execution, after which they walked back, took down Hrafnkel and his men, and laid them out in the home-field. By this time the blood had started into their eyes.

Thorgeir told Sam that he could do just as he pleased with Hrafnkel. "He seems to me to present no problem now."

"I am offering you a choice of two things, Hrafnkel," said Sam to that. "One is that you shall be led away from the house with such men as I please and be killed. However, because you have so many dependent on you, I am prepared to let you go on looking after them. But if you choose to live, then

---

[12] The Achilles tendons in their heels.

leave Adalbol with all your household, and have only those assets I assign you—which will be precious little. For I shall take over this homestead and all your authority too. You shall never lay claim to these, you nor your heirs; nor shall you ever again live nearer than east of Fljotsdalsheid. You can now strike hands on our bargain, if you can bring yourself to accept it."

"To many," said Hrafnkel, "a quick death would seem better than such disgrace. But I shall take the same course as most others: my choice is life, if choice there be. I do it mainly for my sons' sake, for theirs is a poor prospect if I die and leave them."

Hrafnkel was then loosed, and he gave Sam the right to make his own award. He allotted Hrafnkel such goods as he pleased, and this was painfully little. Hrafnkel had his spear with him but no further weapon. That same day Hrafnkel took himself off from Adalbol, and all his people with him.

"I cannot think why you are doing this," Thorgeir told Sam. "You will live to regret it more than anyone that you are giving Hrafnkel his life."

That was how it would have to be then, said Sam.

Hrafnkel now removed to a home east of Fljotsdalsheid and across Fljotsdal to eastwards of Lagarfljot. At the end of the lake stood a little farm, Lokhilla by name, where he bought land on credit, for he had no money beyond what he needed for his farm things. There was a lot of talk about this, how his haughtiness had been humbled, and there were many to call to mind the old proverb—"Pride goes before a fall." This was fine, extensive forest-land, but sadly off for buildings, and that was why he bought the land cheap. Hrafnkel spared no expense; he felled the timber because it was big, and raised a stately farm there which has ever since been called Hrafnkelsstadir, and from that day to this reputed a good farm. He lived there in great hardship that first winter. He had a lavish yield from the fisheries. He went hard at work while the farm was building. That first year he kept calf and kid for feeding through the winter, and all the animals he took that risk with he looked after so well that nearly all of them lived; so that it could just about be said that there were two heads to each of his beasts. That same summer there was a big run of fish in Lagarfljot, which proved a great help towards housekeeping in the district, and that held good every summer.

6

Sam started housekeeping at Adalbol after Hrafnkel, and later held a splendid feast, to which he invited all those who had been retainers of Hrafnkel, offering himself to be their leader in his place. They agreed to this, but were not without misgivings all the same.

The sons of Thjostar advised him to be cheerful, liberal, and kindly to his men, a helper to everyone who had need of him. "Then they are no men if they do not stand firmly by you, whatever your need. We give you this advice because we would like you to make a success of things, for we take you to be a gallant sort of fellow. Now, keep your eyes open and look out for yourself, for 'It is warm work watching out for the wicked.'"

The sons of Thjostar sent after Freyfaxi and his stud, saying that they wanted to see these precious creatures about whom there had been such great tales told. The horses were fetched in and the brothers looked them over.

"These mares appear to me useful for farmwork," said Thorgeir. "It is my advice that they perform such useful tasks as they may, till they can no longer keep going for old age. As for the stallion, he strikes me as no better than other stallions—indeed, rather worse, in that so much evil has come about because of him. I have no desire that further killings come about through him than have arisen already. It is only right that he who owns him should now take him."

They led the stallion down along the level ground. A crag stands below by the river, and underneath it a deep pool. They led the stallion out on to the crag there. The sons of Thjostar drew a bag over his head, tied a stone round his neck, then took long poles and pushed the horse over the edge, so making an end of him. Since then the place has been known as Freyfaxahamar.

Lower down stood the temple which had belonged to Hrafnkel. Thorkel wanted to have a look at it. He had all the gods plundered, and then set fire to the temple, and burnt the whole lot together. Later the guests made ready to leave. Sam chose splendid treasures by way of gifts for both the brothers. They vowed everlasting friendship between them and parted on the most cordial terms. They rode the quickest road west to the Firths and came home to Thorskafjord with honor. Sam established old Thorbjorn at Leikskalar (he was to live there), but Sam's wife went to live with him at Adalbol, and Sam dwelt there for a while.

7

East in Fljotsdal Hrafnkel heard how the sons of Thjostar had destroyed Freyfaxi and burnt the temple. "I think it folly," he said, "to believe in gods," and announced that from then on he never would believe in gods, and he kept to what he said, so that he never again offered up a sacrifice.

Hrafnkel sat tight at Hrafnkelsstadir and raked money together. He quickly won great honor in the district, and everyone showed willingness to sit or stand as he decided for them. At this time ship after ship came sailing from Norway to Iceland (most of the land in the district was settled in Hrafnkel's day), but no one was allowed to settle there in peace unless he asked Hrafnkel's permission. They all had to promise him their backing, and he promised his support in return. He brought under his authority the whole country-side east of Lagarfljot. This territory was soon much bigger and better blessed with men than the one he had ruled before, reaching up around Skridudal, and the whole way along Lagarfljot. And now a change had come over his temper. He was much more popular than before. He had the same mind to be helpful and hospitable, but was now altogether more reasonable than before and gentler in every way. Sam and Hrafnkel often met at various gatherings, but they never made mention of their dealings together. In this fashion six years went by. Sam was well liked by his followers, for he was quiet and easy-going and always ready to help in time of trouble, and bore in mind what those brothers had advised him. Sam was a great man for show.

8

The story goes on to tell how a ship put into Reydarfjord from the open sea whose skipper was Eyvind Bjarnason. He had been abroad for seven years. Eyvind was a much improved man in style and breeding, and had grown into the gallantest person. He was soon informed of what had happened, but he made little or no comment on it. He was a rather reserved sort of man.

As soon as Sam heard the news he rode to the ship, and there was now a great and joyful meeting between the brothers. Sam invited him home out west, and Eyvind accepted eagerly, requesting Sam to ride on home and send horses for his cargo, while he hauled his ship ashore and made it ready for the winter. Sam did as he was asked, went home, and had horses driven to meet Eyvind; and once Eyvind had made arrangements about his cargo he made ready for his journey to Hrafnkelsdal and started up along Reydarfjord. There were five men in the party. The sixth was Eyvind's servant lad, an Icelander by birth, and related to him. Eyvind had plucked this lad from destitution, and carried him abroad with him, and looked after him as himself. This deed of his had become quite famous, and it was the general opinion that there were few to equal him.

They now rode up Thorisdalsheid and were driving sixteen pack-horses in front of them. There were two of Sam's housecarles[13] there and three sailors. They were all dressed in colored clothes and rode with gay shields. They rode across Skridudal and over the ridge to Fljotsdal, at a place called Bulungarvellir, then down to Gilsareyr, where the gravel bank runs west to the river between Hallormsstadir and Hrafnkelsstadir. Then they rode up along Lagarfljot, below the meadow at Hrafnkelsstadir, so past the head of the lake, and forded the Jokulsa at Skalavad. The time was about 7:30 in the morning.

There was a woman by the lake doing her day's wash, and she saw the men passing. The servant woman swept her linen together and ran home, where she flung it down outside near the woodpile and went scurrying indoors. Hrafnkel had not yet got up. Some of the more favored men were lying about the hall, but the workmen had departed about their tasks. It was haymaking time.

The woman burst into speech the moment she came inside. "Aye, true it is," she cried, "that old proverb—'Grow old and grow afraid.' Small grows that honor which is acquired early, if later a man grows shamefully slack and wants for courage ever to exact his dues—and such is very strange in a man who in his day showed spirit. How different is their way of life who grow up in their fathers' homes and seem to you mere nobodies compared with yourselves; but no sooner are they out of their childhood than they go travelling from land to land and are thought of great weight wherever they come, and so they return home again, counting themselves greater than chieftains. Eyvind Bjarnason has just ridden through the river here at Skalavad with so gay a shield that the light came sparkling off it. He is a good enough man to reap a good vengeance on."

The servant woman really let herself go. Hrafnkel got up and gave her

---

[13] Personal servants.

this answer. "No doubt you are babbling what is only too true, yet not out of any good will either. It is just as well then for you to bear some of the load. Hurry south to Vidivellir for Sighvat and Snorri, the sons of Hallstein. Tell them to come to me instantly with any men there who can use arms."

He sent a second woman servant out to Hrolfsstadir for Thord and Halli, the sons of Hrolf, and any there who could use arms. Both sets of brothers were able and worthy men. Hrafnkel also sent after his house-carles, so that they were eighteen all told. They took up their weapons in earnest, and rode through the river as the others had done before.

By now Eyvind and his men had got up on to the heath. He kept riding west till he reached Bersagotur in the middle of the heath. There is a turfless swamp there—it is like riding through nothing but ooze, and one is sinking all the time to the knee or thigh, and on occasion to the horse's belly, while below the surface it is as hard as a slab of rock. Next comes a great waste of stony ground to the west of it, and as they reached this waste the boy looked back and said to Eyvind: "There are men riding after us, no fewer than eighteen of them, with a big man riding in blue clothes. He looks to me like Hrafnkel the Priest, though it is a long time since last I saw him."

"What business is that of ours?" replied Eyvind. "I cannot imagine I have anything to fear from a gallop of Hrafnkel's. I have done nothing against him. He must have an errand west to the Dale to meet his friends."

"I have a feeling it is you he wants to meet," the lad replied.

"I am not aware," said Eyvind, "that anything has happened between him and Sam my brother since they came to terms."

"I should like you to ride off west to the Dale," replied the lad. "Then you will be safe. I know Hrafnkel's temper, how he will do nothing to us if he fails to get at you. Everything is taken care of so long as you are all right. The game is not in the toils then, so all is well, whatever happens to us."

Eyvind said he would not ride off quite so fast. "I don't know who they are, and there would be plenty to laugh at me if I took to my heels with nothing proved."

They now rode west from the stony ground. Ahead of them lay a second swamp, called Oxamyr. This one is very grassy. There are soft patches, so that it is wellnigh impassable, which was why old Hallfred established the higher way round, even though it proved longer.

Eyvind now rode west into the swamp. Their horses sank deep into the mire and they were seriously delayed. The others, who rode unhampered, were overhauling them fast. Hrafnkel and his men were now riding up to the swamp while Eyvind's company were just coming out of it. They recognized Hrafnkel and both his sons, and begged Eyvind to make his escape.

"All the bad places are now past. You will get to Adalbol while the swamp stands between you."

"I'll not run from men to whom I have done no wrong," replied Eyvind.

They then rode up on to the ridge. Hillocks stand on the ridge, and on the slope of the mountain is a turf knoll much denuded by the wind, with high banks surrounding it. Eyvind rode to this knoll, where he dismounted and awaited them.

"We shall soon know their errand now," said Eyvind.

After that they climbed up on to the knoll and tore up some stones for missiles.

At the same time Hrafnkel turned from the path and south to the knoll. He had never a word for Eyvind, but instantly made the assault. Eyvind defended himself skillfully and like a brave man. Eyvind's lad judged himself not strong enough for the fray, got hold of his horse and rode westward over the ridge to Adalbol to tell Sam what game was afoot. Sam moved quickly and sent for his men. They were twenty all told, and a well equipped company, and with these he rode east to the heath to the scene of action. But by this time the battle was over. Hrafnkel was riding eastward from his work, while Eyvind had fallen and all his men with him. The first thing Sam did was to look for life in his brother, but the job had been thoroughly done: they were all dead, the five of them together. Twelve of Hrafnkel's men had fallen too, and six were riding away.

Sam made short stay there, but bade his men instantly give chase. They rode off after them, but their horses were flagging.

"We may be able to catch them," said Sam, "for their horses are tired, while ours are all fresh. Still, it will be a close thing whether we catch them or not before they get down off the heath."

Hrafnkel had by now put himself east of Oxamyr. Pursued and pursuers kept riding till Sam reached the brow of the heath, where he saw how Hrafnkel had come a long way down the slope. He saw too that he would escape away down into his own territory.

"This is where we turn back," he told his men. "It will be easy now for Hrafnkel to collect all the men he wants."

So Sam turned back with that for his pains. He came to where Eyvind was lying, and threw up a mound over him and his mates. The place-names there are now Eyvindartorfa, Eyvindarfjoll, and Eyvindardal.

Then Sam returned to Adalbol with all Eyvind's goods. When he reached home he sent word to his retainers that they should muster there in the morning before breakfast. He had made up his mind to ride east over the heath—"Be our outing as it may," said he. In the evening he went to bed, and a lot of men had gathered there.

9

Hrafnkel rode home and told what had happened. He ate his food and after that gathered a force together, so that he set out with seventy men, and riding with that band westward over the heath, came unawares to Adalbol, seized Sam in his bed, and led him out.

"Now, Sam," said Hrafnkel, "your plight has become such as must have seemed unlikely to you even a short while since, in that I have your life in my hands. I must not now prove a worse fellow to you than you were to me, so I am giving you your choice of two things: to be killed, or the other, that I alone shall shear and shape[14] between us."

Sam said he would rather choose to live, adding that he thought even so either way would be hard.

Hrafnkel said he could expect that. "For we have that to repay you;

---

[14] A proverbial term meaning "settle everything."

whereas I would have treated you twice as well, had you deserved it. You shall move away from Adalbol down to Leikskalar and settle there on your own farm. You shall take with you the goods that Eyvind owned. But you shall not carry away any more in the way of property than what you brought here—all that, though, you shall carry away in full. I shall take back my priesthood, the farm, and homestead likewise. I see that there has been a big increase in my holdings, but you shall not benefit by that. No payment shall be made for Eyvind your brother, because you followed up the bloodsuit too ruthlessly for your former kinsman; while for your kinsman Einar you have had redress enough in that you have enjoyed power and wealth these six winters. Not that, in any case, I consider the killing of Eyvind and his comrades worth more than the maiming of me and my men. You made me a fugitive from my own country-side, but I am content for you to remain at Leikskalar. At the same time it will prove as well for you if you do not puff yourself up to your own hurt. You shall stay my underling as long as we live; and you can count on this too, that the worse we get on together, the worse you will find things."

Sam now went away with his household down to Leikskalar, and there he stayed, on his farm.

10

Hrafnkel organized the household at Adalbol with his men, and put his son Thorir in charge at Hrafnkelsstadir. He now held the priesthood over the entire country-side. Asbjorn stayed with his father, because he was the younger son.

Sam remained at Leikskalar that winter. He was taciturn and kept much to himself, and it was obvious to many that he was disgruntled with his lot. But the winter over, once the days grew longer, Sam with one other man and three horses set out over the bridge, and from there across Modrudalsheid, so over the Jokulsa river (the one up on the mountain), and on to Myvatn, and from there over Fljotsheid and Ljosavatnsskard, making no real break in his journey till he arrived west in Thorskafjord, where he was made most welcome. Thorkel had just got home after a sea-voyage, and had been abroad for four years. Sam spent a week there, resting himself, and then he told them what had now happened between him and Hrafnkel, and asked the brothers for help and backing this time as before.

Thorgeir did more of the answering for the brothers this time. He would be keeping out of it, he said. "There is a great distance between us. We thought we had put things right for you before we came away, so that it would be easy for you to hold on to; but things have turned out as I felt sure they would when you gave Hrafnkel his life, that you would live to regret it most. We begged you to take his life, but, no, you had to have your own way. And how obvious it has become what a difference of judgment lay between you, when he let you live in peace and made his attack only when he had removed from his path him who, in his opinion, was a better man than you. We cannot burden ourselves with this lucklessness of yours, nor have we such great eagerness to quarrel with Hrafnkel that we feel tempted to endanger our good name all over again. But we should like to invite you here in under our lee with all your household, if you consider it less galling here than alongside Hrafnkel."

Sam said he had no wish for that. He told them he wanted to get back home, and asked them to change horses with him, a thing that was quickly put right. The brothers wanted to give him fine gifts, but he would accept nothing, arguing that it would show a mean spirit. With so much for his pains Sam rode back home, and there he remained till old age. He never achieved anything against Hrafnkel to the end of his days.

But Hrafnkel lived on his farm and kept his honors. He died of a sickness, and his burial mound stands in Hrafnkelsdal, down the valley from Adalbol. Great riches were laid in the mound alongside him, all his armor and that good spear of his. His sons succeeded to his authority, Thorir living at Hrafnkelsstadir and Asbjorn at Adalbol. They shared the priesthood between them, and were reckoned very able men.

And that is the end of Hrafnkel's Saga.

AUTHUN AND THE BEAR

Translated by Gwyn Jones

There was a man by the name of Authun, a Westfirther by origin, and rather poorly off. He went abroad from the Westfirths with the help of a good farmer, Thorstein, and of skipper Thorir, who had received hospitality from Thorstein over the winter. Authun had been staying there too, and working for Thorir, and received this for his reward, a passage abroad with the skipper to look after him. Before going on board ship Authun set aside the bulk of his money for his mother, and it was reckoned enough to keep her for three years. They now sailed out and away. They had an easy passage and Authun spent the winter with skipper Thorir, who owned a farm in Moer, in Norway. The following summer they sailed for Greenland, and spent the winter there.

The story tells how Authun bought a bear there, an absolute treasure, and gave every penny he had for it. The following summer they returned to Norway and had an excellent passage. Authun took his bear with him, and was proposing to go south to Denmark, find king Svein, and make him a present of the beast. So when he reached the south of Norway, where the Norwegian king was then in residence, he left the ship, taking his bear with him, and rented himself a lodging.

King Harald was soon told how a bear, an absolute treasure, had come ashore, and that his owner was an Icelander. The king sent for him immediately, and when Authun came into the king's presence he greeted him with due courtesy. The king received his greeting affably, and then: "You have a bear," he said, "an absolute treasure?"

Well, yes, he agreed, he had a beast of a kind.

"Are you willing to sell him to us," asked the king, "for the same price you gave for him?"

"I don't want to, sire," he replied.

"Then would you like me to give you twice the price?" asked the king. "And indeed that would be fairer, since you paid out all you had for him."

"I don't want to, sire."

"You want to give him to me then?" said the king.

"No, sire," he replied.

"Then what do you want to do with him?"

"Go to Denmark," replied Authun, "and give him to king Svein."

"Is it possible," asked king Harald, "that you are such a silly man that you have not heard how a state of war exists between our two countries? Or do you think yourself so blest with luck that you can make your way there with this precious thing when others, for all that they have compelling business there, cannot manage it unscathed?"

"Sire," said Authun, "it is for you to command, yet I cannot willingly agree to anything except what I have already decided."

"Then why should you not go your road," said the king to that, "even as you wish? But come and see me when you return, and tell me how king Svein rewards you for the bear. It may be that you are a man of happy fortune."

"I promise to do so," said Authun.

He now proceeded south along the coast, and east to Vik, and from there to Denmark, and by this time had spent his last penny and was forced to beg food, both for himself and for the bear. He went to see king Svein's steward, a man named Aki, and asked him for some victuals, both for himself and for the bear. "For I am proposing," he said, "to make a present of him to king Svein." Aki said he would sell him food if that was what he was after, but Authun confessed that he had no money to pay for it. "And yet," he said, "I should like my business to be so forwarded that I can produce my bear before the king." "I will give you food and lodging then, whatever you need, until you see the king, but in return I require a half share in this creature. You might look at it this way: the bear will only die on your hands, for you need considerable provisioning and your money is all gone, and in that case you get no profit of your bear."

When he looked at it that way, it seemed to him that what the steward said went pretty close to the mark, so that was what they settled on, that he should make over half the beast to Aki, and it was for the king to set a value on the whole.

And now they were to go together to see the king, and so they did, and stood before his table. The king was puzzled who this man, whom he did not know, could be, and, "Who are you?" he asked Authun.

"I am an Icelander, sire," he replied, "and have just come from Greenland, and more recently still from Norway. I had been meaning to present you with this bear, which I purchased with every penny I had, but I am now in something of a quandary, for I own only half of him." And he went on to tell the king what had taken place between him and his steward Aki.

"Is this true, Aki, what he says?" asked the king.

"Yes," he said, "it is."

"And did you think it seemly, when I had raised you up to be a great man, to obstruct and hinder his path when a man was trying to bring me this fine beast, for which he had given his all, when even king Harald, who is our enemy, saw fit to let him go in peace? Think then how honorable this was on your part! It would be only right to have you put to death—and though I will not do that, you shall leave this land without a moment's delay, and never come into my sight again. As for you, Authun, I owe you the same thanks as if you were giving me the whole animal. So stay here with me." He agreed to this, and remained with king Svein for a while.

But after some time had gone by Authun said to the king, "I should like to go away now, sire." The king answered, rather coldly, "What do you want, if you don't want to stay with us?" "I want to go south on a pilgrimage." "If you did not wish to follow so good a course," the king admitted, "I should be displeased by your eagerness to be off." The king now gave him a large amount of silver, and he traveled southward with the pilgrims to Rome. The king made the arrangements for his journey, and told him to come and see him when he returned.

Now he went his way until he came south to Rome, and when he had spent as much time there as he wished, he set out on his way back. He fell sick, very sick, and grew woefully thin. All the money the king had given him for his journey was now spent, he took the style of a beggar and begged for his food. He had become bald and quite pitiful to see.

He came back to Denmark at Easter, to the very place where the king was in residence. He did not dare let himself be seen but remained in the church transept, hoping to encounter the king as he went to church that evening. But when he saw the king with his handsomely attired courtiers, again he dare not let himself be seen. And when the king went to the drinking in hall, Authun ate his food outside, as is the custom of pilgrims to Rome before they lay aside their staff and scrip.

And now in the evening, as the king went to even-song, Authun reckoned on meeting him; but however daunting a prospect this had looked before, it had by now grown far worse, for the courtiers were in drink. And yet, as they were going back in, the king noticed a man who he felt sure lacked the confidence to come forward and speak to him, and as the courtiers were entering the king turned back, saying, "Let anyone now come forward who craves audience of me, for I believe there is such a man here present." Then Authun came forward and fell at the king's feet, and the king could hardly recognize him. But as soon as he knew who he was, he took Authun by the hand and welcomed him. "How greatly you are changed," he said, "since last we met," and he led him inside behind him. When the courtiers saw him they laughed at him, but, "You need not laugh at him," said the king, "he has provided for his soul better than you." Then the king had a bath prepared for him and gave him clothes to wear, and Authun remained with him.

One day in spring, so the story goes, the king invited Authun to stay with him for the rest of his days, promising that he would make him his cup-bearer and heap him with honors.

"God reward you, sire," said Authun, "for all the honor you would do me, but what I really have in mind is to return to Iceland."

"That strikes me as a curious choice," said the king.

"I cannot bear, sire," said Authun, "that I should enjoy such honors here with you, and my mother tramp the beggar's path out in Iceland, for by now the provision I made for her before I left home will be at an end."

"That is well spoken, and like a man," replied the king, "and you will prove a man of happy fortune. This is the only reason for your departure which would not displease me. But stay with me now till the ships make ready." And so he did.

One day, towards the end of spring, king Svein walked down to the jetties, where ships were being overhauled in readiness for voyages to many lands, to the Baltic and Germany, Sweden, and Norway. He and Authun came to a very fine ship which men were making ready, and, "What do you think of this for a ship, Authun?" asked the king. "Very fine, sire," was his answer. "I am going to give you this ship," said the king, "in return for the bear." Authun thanked him for his gift as well as he knew how.

When time had passed and the ship was quite ready, king Svein had this to say to Authun: "Since you want to be away it is not for me to stop you. But I have heard that your country is ill supplied with havens, the coasts often wide open and dangerous to shipping. Now should you be wrecked and lose both ship and lading, there will be little to show that you have met king Svein and given him a princely gift." With that the king gave him a leather purse full of silver. "You will not be entirely penniless, even if you are shipwrecked, so long as you hold on to this. And yet," said the king, "it may happen that you lose this money too, and you will then reap little benefit, from having found king Svein and given him a princely gift." With that the king drew a ring from his arm and gave it to Authun, saying, "Even if you are so unlucky as to suffer shipwreck and lose your money, you will not be penniless should you manage to get ashore, for many carry gold on them in case of shipwreck, and it will be clear that you have met king Svein if you save the ring. But I would urge upon you," said the king, "not to give away the ring unless you consider yourself under a great enough obligation to some great man—but give him the ring, for it well becomes men of rank to accept such. And now, good luck go with you."

Then he put to sea and sailed to Norway, where he had his goods carried ashore—and he needed more help for this than when he was in Norway last. He then went to visit king Harald, to make good the promise he had made him before going to Denmark. He had a courteous greeting for the king, and the king took it affably. "Sit down," he said, "and take a drink with us." And so he did.

"And how did king Svein reward you for the bear?" king Harald asked him.

"By accepting it from me, sire," replied Authun.

"So too would I have rewarded you," said the king. "How else did he reward you?"

"He gave me silver for my pilgrimage," replied Authun.

"King Svein gives many men silver for pilgrimages, and for other things too," said the king, "and they don't have to bring him a grand present for it. What else was there?"

"He offered to make me his cup-bearer," said Authun, "and heap me with honors."

"In that he spoke well," said the king. "Still, he would give you more of a reward than that."

"He gave me a merchant ship and such wares as sell best here in Norway."

"That was handsome of him," said the king, "but so too would I have rewarded you. Did he reward you with anything further?"

"He gave me a leather purse full of silver, saying I should not then be penniless if I held on to it, even though my ship was wrecked off Iceland."

"That was nobly done," said the king, "and something I would not have done. I should have held us quits had I given you the ship. Did he reward you any further?"

"To be sure he rewarded me, sire," said Authun. "He gave me this ring I have on my arm, arguing it might so turn out that I should lose all that money and yet, said he, not be penniless if I held on to the ring. And he charged me never to part with it unless I should consider myself under so great an obligation to some great man that I wanted to give it him. And now I have found him, for you had the opportunity to deprive me of both these things, the bear and my life too; yet you let me go in peace where others might not."

The king accepted his gift graciously, and gave Authun fine gifts in return before they parted. Authun used his money for a passage to Iceland, promptly left for home that summer, and was thought to be a man of the happiest good fortune.

Aucassin and Nicolette
(Twelfth Century)

"The most exquisite expression of 'courteous love'"—that is what the nineteenth-century American historian Henry Adams called Aucassin and Nicolette, *a romance in which love can overcome stern fathers, prison walls, Saracens, and perhaps even Hell itself.*

The medieval romance evolved in the eleventh and twelfth centuries side by side with the older literary tradition of epic heroism represented in the Icelandic sagas and The Song of Roland. *In the romances, the hero becomes a lover as well as a warrior, and his energizing motive becomes not service to a feudal lord or thirst for glory in war but service to a beloved lady. The literature of courtly love originated in Provence and southern France. Its sources were a renewed interest in classical literature, especially Ovid's* Art of Love, *the growing cult of the Virgin Mary, and the social situation of medieval knights. Young, single men in the service of a lord found it natural to idealize the lady of the castle and to transform the feudal code into a code of love, in which heroic deeds were performed for the sake of a woman. The romance spread quickly through Europe. Eventually the new code began to alarm the Church, which saw in the worldliness and sensuality of the romances a threat to piety. Accordingly, clerics created the "moral" in reaction to the "chivalric" romance; the former, exemplified in stories of the Grail and the fourteenth-century English* Sir Gawain and the Green Knight, *used the conventions of the chivalric romance but conveyed a more spiritual or elevated message. Ultimately both varieties were blended in the lengthy (and often boring) prose romances of the fifteenth century (the earlier ones were in verse), in which chivalry and piety consorted rather uneasily.*

Aucassin and Nicolette *survives from the fresh, early days of the medieval romance. Nothing is known of its author; to judge from the language of the only surviving manuscript, he lived in twelfth-century northern France. Whoever he was, he was a delightful ironist; Aucassin and Nicolette pokes gentle fun at the stock elements of romance at the same time that it creates a sincerely idealized world ruled by love. The story seems to have Oriental roots; Nicolette is a converted "Saracen" (a generalized term for any Oriental "pagan"), and Aucassin's name may be based upon the Arabic Al-Kassim.*

Aucassin and Nicolette has an unusual form: prose sections alternating with verse meant to be sung. There are several other examples of this form in early literature, especially in the Orient, but this is the only surviving example from medieval France. The instructions "Now they tell and relate and continue the tale" suggest that the romance was intended for quasi-dramatic performance, one minstrel reciting the prose portions while another sang the interspersed lyrics.

Aucassin, like all good romance heroes, has only his beloved on his mind. His singlemindedness is charming, if somewhat obtuse; Nicolette is by far the more quick-witted and resourceful of the two. Aucassin will take part in the battle only if promised a kiss from Nicolette, and he dreams of her so intently that he is captured and almost executed without noticing it. (When he wakes up, he conquers his enemies singlehandedly, but only because he realizes that if his head is cut off, he cannot talk to Nicolette!) In one of the most famous passages of the romance, Aucassin declares his preference for the worldly joys and companionship of Hell over the cold comforts of Paradise if only he can have his "very sweet love" with him.

Nicolette is equally committed to her lover and considerably more ingenious in overcoming barriers. Delicately feminine, she nevertheless can escape from prison, cross a deep moat, and brave the beasts and serpents of the forest to win her love. Later in the story, she survives capture by "Paynims" and, disguised as a wandering fiddler, sets out again to find Aucassin.

Aucassin and Nicolette, like most romances, is episodic; we tend to remember such separate scenes as Nicolette's escape from her chamber and Aucassin's discovery of her in her floral lodge in the idealized forest. Two of the most memorable episodes are Aucassin's encounter with the stranger in the forest and the voyage to the castle of Torelore. The stranger in the forest is a "loathly churl," a stock figure out of medieval legend, but here he is treated with a touch of social realism that throws into relief the idealized fantasy world of the rest of the romance. Still another vision of an alternative world emerges in the Torelore episode. Here the poet introduces a stock device from medieval folklore called the couvade—an inversion of sexual roles in which a pregnant king labors in childbirth while his queen leads the army. The incident, along with the ensuing battle fought with apples, eggs, and cheeses, introduces a fantastically Rabelaisian note into the romance. The section also constitutes one of the author's delicately satiric jibes at romance convention; Aucassin reacts in stock fashion, laying about him with his sword, until the king catches his bridle: "It is not our custom to kill each other." The worlds of romance and utopia collide amusingly here.

The love between Aucassin and Nicolette, lightly as it is handled, is the "courteous love" of romance. It is the love of the lords and ladies in Aucassin's notion of Hell; "there, also, go the fair and courteous ladies who have two or three lovers besides their husbands." It is physical love, but it is also highly etherealized, as in light opera or musical comedy. For Aucassin, Nicolette has become the supreme good, as he has become for her. In the fragile and unreal world of the romance, everything the Middle Ages otherwise took most seriously—honor and military glory, obedience to established, hierarchical authority, Heaven and Hell themselves—melt away before the power of love.

FURTHER READING *(prepared by W. J. R.):* F. W. Bourdillon's early edition of *Aucassin et Nicolete*, 1919, provides a good general introduction to the work. Two general studies of medieval French literature contain material on the piece's odd form: Urban Tigner Holmes' *History of Old French Literature*, 1936, and Grace Frank's *The Medieval French Drama*, 1954. More recent criticism is much concerned with parody and satire. Robert Harden's "*Aucassin et Nicolete* as Parody," *Studies in Philology*, 63 (1966), 1–9, studies its mocking of the common medieval motif of divided lovers. Barbara Nelson Sargent's "Parody in *Aucassin et Nicolete:* Some Further Considerations," *French Review*, 43 (1970), 597–605, discusses the parodic rejection of medieval conventions. June Hall Martin's *Love's Fools: Aucassin, Troilus, Calisto, and the Parody of the Courtly Lover*, 1972, considers the piece as a gentle parody of the courtly hero. Nathaniel B. Smith's "The Uncourtliness of Nicolette," in *Voices of Conscience*, ed. by Raymond J. Cormier, 1977, concentrates on the earthiness of Nicolette's character, concluding that the poem may represent a transitional phase between courtly romance and fabliau.

AUCASSIN AND NICOLETTE

Translated by Edward Francis Moyer and
Carey DeWitt Eldridge
Original translation edited by Robert Linker

I

He who wants to hear good rhyme
Of the sport in ancient time
Of two children, young and sweet,
Aucassin and Nicolette,
Of the pains that he endured,
Of the noble deeds he did
For his love with clearest face.
Lovely the song, sweet the tale,
Courteous and well-disposed.
No man can be so oppressed,
So cast down and comfortless,
Burdened down with heaviness,
Who will not be, hearing this,
Cured, restored to joyfulness,
It is so sweet.

II

Now they tell and relate and continue the tale

That Count Bougars de Valence was making war on Count Garin de Beaucaire, so great and so marvelous and so mortal, that not a single day dawned that he was not at the gates and at the walls and at the barriers of the town with a hundred knights and ten thousand soldiers on foot and on horse; and he burned his land and wasted his country and killed his men.

Count Garin de Beaucaire was old and frail and had outlived his time. He had no heir, neither son nor daughter, except a single boy, who was such as I shall tell you.

Aucassin was the name of the lad. Handsome he was and shapely and large and well formed in legs and feet and in body and in arms. His hair was blond and tightly curled, and his eyes were gray and laughing, and his face clear and slender, and his nose high and well placed. He was so endowed with good points that there was in him nothing bad, or that was not good. But he was so overtaken by love which conquers all, that he didn't want to be a knight, or to take arms, or go into the tourney, or do anything at all which he ought to have done.

His father and his mother used to say to him, "Son, take up your arms, get on your horse, defend your land, and aid your men. If they see you among them, they will defend better their bodies and their goods, and your land and mine."

"Father," said Aucassin, "what are you talking about now? Never may God give me anything I ask of him, if as a knight I mount my horse, or go into the fray or battle, there where I may strike a knight or others strike me, if you do not give me Nicolette, my sweet love, whom I love so much."

"Son," said the father, "that could not be. You let Nicolette alone since she is a slave girl who was brought from a foreign land. The viscount of this town bought her from the Saracens and brought her to this town. And he has reared her and baptized her and has made her his god-daughter. So will he give her one of these days to some young man who will earn bread for her with honor. You have nothing to do with all this. If you wish to have a wife, I will give you the daughter of a king or of a count. There is no man in France so rich that if you wish for his daughter you shall not have her."

"Look here, Father," said Aucassin, "where is there such high honor on the earth that if Nicolette, my very sweet love, had it, it wouldn't be well placed in her? If she were Empress of Constantinople or of Germany, or Queen of France or of England, it would be little enough for her, so noble she is, and courtly, and of good manner, and the acme of all good qualities."

III

Now it is sung

> Aucassin lived in Beaucaire;
> Well-built was his castle there.
> Nicolette, of form so fair,
> From her no man could tear him;
> His father tried to scare him,
> And his mother threatened him,
> "Scamp, what do you want to do?
> Nicolette is trim and gay
> But from Carthage cast away;
> From the pagans she was bought.
> Since you want to take a wife,
> Take a wife of high degree."
> "Mother, those wives don't please me.
> Nicolette is debonair,
> Form so sweet and face so clear;
> My heart jumps when she is near.
> Why can't I enjoy her love?
> It is too sweet."

IV

Now they tell and relate and continue the tale

When Count Garin de Beaucaire saw that he would not be able to turn his son away from the love of Nicolette, he went to the viscount of the town, who was in his service; so did he speak to him.

"Sir Count, get rid of Nicolette, your god-daughter. Cursed be the land from which she was brought to this country! For because of her, I lose Aucassin, who does not want to become a knight, or do any of the things he ought to do. And know well that if I could have her, I would burn her in a fire, and you might well have great fear for yourself."

"Sire," said the Viscount, "much does it trouble me that he goes and comes and that he speaks to her. I bought her with my money; so have I reared her and baptized her and made her my god-daughter. And I would have given her to some young man who would have earned bread for her with honor. With this your son, Aucassin, would have had nothing to do. But since it is your will and your pleasure. I will send her to such a land and to such a country that never again will he set eyes upon her."

"Take care that you do it," said Count Garin, "for great evil may come to you from it."

Each went his own way. Now the Viscount was a very, very rich man, and he had a rich palace looking on a garden. In a room in it he had Nicolette placed, high in the tower, and an old woman with her for company and to take care of her. And he had bread and meat and wine brought there and whatever they might need. Then he had the door sealed up so that none might be able, in any way, to go in or come out, except that, opening on the garden, there was one window, quite small, through which there came to them a little fresh air.

V

Now it is sung

> Nicolette in prison put;
> She's in a vaulted chamber
> Fashioned with the greatest skill
> And marvelously painted.
> On the marble window frame
> There the wretched maiden leans.
> Now her hair was blond as grain,
> And her eyebrows were well shaped,
> Clear and slender was her face,
> Never was there fairer seen:
> Toward the forest she looked out
> And saw the roses swelling,
> Heard the birds which twittered there;
> Then the orphan maid cried out,
> "Wretched captive, woe is me!
> Why am I in prison put?
> Aucassin, my youthful lord,
> I am still your own sweetheart
> And by you I'm not abhorred.
> For you I'm a prisoner

Within this vaulted chamber.
Now my life is very hard;
But, by God, sweet Mary's son,
I will not stay longer here
    If I can get out."

VI

Now they tell and relate and continue the tale

Nicolette was in prison, just as you have heard and understood, in the chamber. The cry and the rumor went through all the land and through all the country that Nicolette was lost. Some said that she had fled out of the country, and others said that Count Garin de Beaucaire had had her murdered. Whoever else had joy of it, Aucassin was not glad. He went to the viscount of the town, so did he address him:

"Sir Viscount, what have you done with Nicolette, my very sweet love, for there is nothing in all the world that I love more? Have you stolen her away from me? Know well that if I die of it, payment will be demanded of you; and that will be very right, for you will have slain me with your two hands, for you have taken from me the thing which I love most in this world."

"Fair lord," said the Viscount, "now stay out of this. Nicolette is a captive whom I brought from a strange land, so did I buy her with my wealth from the Saracens. And I have reared her and baptized her and made her my god-daughter; so have I nourished her. And I should have given her one of these days to a young man who should earn bread for her with honor. With this you have nothing to do. Instead, take the daughter of a king or a count. Moreover, what would you think to have gained if you had made her your mistress and put her in your bed? Little indeed would you have won, for all the days of the world your soul would be in Hell because of it, for into Paradise you could never enter."

"What would I be doing in Paradise? I don't want to enter there, but only to have Nicolette, my very sweet love, whom I love so much. For to Paradise go only such people as I shall tell you of: the old priests, the old cripples and maimed ones who, all night and all day, drag themselves before the altars and in the old crypts, and those who wear old worn-out clothes and are dressed in tattered rags, who are naked and without shoes and stockings, and dying of hunger and thirst and of cold and of misery. These go to Paradise. I have nothing to do with them. But to Hell I wish indeed to go; for to Hell go the handsome clerics, and the fine knights who have died in the tourneys and in great wars, and the good soldiers and the brave men; with them I do wish to go. There, also, go the fair and courteous ladies who have two or three lovers besides their husbands. And there go the gold and silver and miniver[1] and gray furs. There, also, go the harpers and the jongleurs, and the kings of the world. With them do I wish to go—provided that I have Nicolette, my very sweet love, with me."

"Surely," said the Viscount, "your speaking gets you nowhere, for you shall never see her. And if you were to speak to her and your father knew

---

[1] Ermine.

it, he would burn both me and her in a fire, and you might well fear for yourself."

"That's what worries me," said Aucassin, and filled with grief he left the viscount.

VII

Now it is sung

Aucassin has turned away
Very sad and all downcast;
For his love with clearest face
No one now can comfort him,
Neither give him good advice.
Toward the palace has he gone;
He has mounted up the steps.
In a chamber has he come,
So did he begin to weep
And to sigh in deepest grief,
Lamenting his lost sweetheart.
"Nicolette, how sweet you were,
Sweet to come and sweet to go,
Sweet to play and sweet to say,
Sweet to tease and sweet to please,
Sweet to kiss and sweet to squeeze.
I for you am all cast down
And am so badly treated
That I think I'll leave this life,
Sister, sweet love."

VIII

Now they tell and relate and continue the tale

While Aucassin was in his chamber mourning for Nicolette his love, Count Bougars de Valence, who had his war to maintain, was in no way forgetting it. He had sent forward his horsemen and foot soldiers, and he then directed himself toward the castle to assail it. And a cry arose and a disturbance, and the knights and the soldiers armed themselves and ran to the gates and to the walls to defend the castle, and the bourgeois went up the passage-ways in the walls and threw down rocks and sharpened stakes. While the assault was great and in full swing, the Count Garin de Beaucaire came to the chamber where Aucassin was grieving and mourning Nicolette, his very sweet love, whom he loved so much.

"Ha! Son," said he, "how very weak and wretched you are, that you watch while they assault the best and strongest of all castles. And know that if you lose it, you are disinherited. Come on, Son, take up your arms, and mount your horse and defend your land, and aid your men, and go into the battle. You need never strike a man there, nor let another strike you; yet if they see you among them, they will defend better their goods and their bodies and your land and mine. You are so big and so strong that you can easily do it, and you ought to do it."

"Father," said Aucassin, "what are you talking about now? May God give me nothing of what I ask of him if I play the knight or mount on a horse or go into the battle, where I may strike some knights, or be struck by others, unless you give me Nicolette, my sweet love, whom I love so much."

"Son," said the father, "that can't be done; rather would I suffer that I should be entirely dispossessed and that I should lose all that I have than that you should ever have her for your wife or for your bride."

He turned away, and when Aucassin saw him about to go, he called him back.

"Father," said Aucassin, "come back, I will make a good bargain with you."

"Such as what, my fine son?"

"I will take up arms and go into the battle on your promise that, if God brings me back safe and sound, you will let me see Nicolette, my sweet love, long enough to have two or three words with her, and that I may kiss her one single time."

"I grant it," said the father.

He gave him his word, and Aucassin was glad.

IX

Now it is sung

Aucassin a kiss will have
If he should return alive;
For a hundred thousand marks
He would not be half so glad.
He demanded armor bright;
Servants clothed him as a knight.
Double hauberk he put on,
Laced his helmet on his head,
Girt his sword with golden hilt,
And on his charger mounted.
Then he took his shield and spear,
Cast a glance down at his feet.
In his stirrups well they sat;
High he holds his head aloft.
He remembers his sweet love.
Forward then he spurs his horse;
Willingly he takes his course.
Right up to the gate he goes
To the battle.

X

Now they tell and relate

Aucassin was armed and on his horse, as you have heard and understood. God, how becoming the shield was at his neck and the helmet on his head and the belt of his sword on his left hip. The lad was big and strong and handsome and noble and well turned out, and the horse which he rode, quick and rapid; and the lad had ridden him straight through the middle of the gate.

Now don't you believe that he was thinking of taking oxen or cows or goats, or that he would strike some knight or another strike him. Nothing like that! Not once did it occur to him. But he thought so much of Nicolette, his sweet love, that he forgot the reins and all that he had to do. And the horse that had felt the spurs carried him into the thick of the battle and hurled him right into the midst of his enemies. They grabbed him from all sides; so did they take him. And they relieved him of his shield and lance; so did they quickly lead him away a prisoner. And they went along, already considering what death they would make him die.

And when Aucassin heard them:

"Ah, God," said he, "sweet creature! Are these my mortal enemies who are holding me here, and who now will cut off my head? And after my head is cut off, never will I speak to Nicolette, my sweet love, whom I love so much. Yet I have here a good sword, and I'm riding a good fresh war-horse. If now I don't defend myself for her sake, never may God help her if she loves me any more."

The lad was big and strong, and the horse on which he sat was lively. And he snatched his sword and began to strike right and left and cut through helmets and nose-pieces and fists and arms and made a slaughter round about him, like the wild boar when the dogs attack him in the forest. And so did he strike down ten knights and wound seven, and rode quickly out of the thick of things. So did he come galloping back, sword in hand.

The Count Bougars de Valence heard them say that they were going to hang Aucassin, his enemy, and he came to that place, and Aucassin did not mistake him. He took his sword in hand and whacked down on the helmet so that it went down over his head. He was so stunned that he fell onto the ground. And Aucassin put out his hand, took him and led him along by the nose-guard of his helmet, and handed him over to his father.

"Father," said Aucassin, "look, here is your enemy who for so long has made war on you and done harm; this war has lasted for twenty years and never could it be ended by anyone."

"Fair son," said the father, "you ought to do these youthful deeds and not chase after foolishness."

"Father," said Aucassin, "don't you go making sermons to me, but keep your promises to me."

"Bah! What promises, fair son?"

"What, Father, have you forgotten them? By my head, whoever else forgets them, I don't want to forget them, so close I hold them to my heart. Didn't you make an agreement with me that if I took up arms and went into battle and if God brought me back safe and sound, you would let me see Nicolette, my sweet love, long enough to have two or three words with her? And didn't you make an agreement that I might kiss her one time? I want you to keep this promise to me."

"I?" said the father. "May God never aid me if I keep faith with you in this. And if she were here now, I would burn her in a fire, and you, yourself, might well be afraid."

"Is this your last word?" asked Aucassin.

"So help me God," said the father, "yes!"

"Well," said Aucassin, "very, very much do I grieve when a man of your age is a liar."

"Count de Valence," said Aucassin, "I took you a prisoner."

"You surely did, sir," said the count.

"Give me your hand on it," said Aucassin.

"Willingly, sir." And he put his hand in his.

"Now swear to me," said Aucassin, "that, any day as long as you live, should you be able to do dishonor or destruction to my father, either in his person or his property, you won't fail to do it."

"Sir, for God's sake," said he, "don't mock me, but set a ransom on me. You will not be able to ask of me gold, or silver, horses or palfreys, miniver or gray fur, or hounds or birds, that I will not give you."

"What?" said Aucassin. "Don't you know that I have taken you prisoner?"

"Oh yes, sir," said the Count Bougars.

"If you do not swear it to me," said Aucassin, "may God never help me if I do not send your head flying now."

"In the name of God," he said, "I'll swear to whatever you please."

So he swore, and Aucassin made him mount on a horse, and he mounted another and led him back until he was in safety.

XI

Now it is sung

Now when sees the Count Garin
That his offspring Aucassin
Cannot tear himself away
From the clear-faced Nicolette,
In a cell he had him set,
In a prison underground,
Which was made of marble dark.
Now when Aucassin came there
He was sadder than before.
If you wish, you now may hear
What lamenting he began:
"Nicolette, sweet fleur-de-lis,
Sweet love with the clearest face,
Sweeter than a bunch of grapes,
Sweeter than the wine bowl's sop.
One time I saw a pilgrim
Who was born in Limousin,
With the palsy nearly dead;
Thus he lay upon his bed.
A sick man he was indeed,
Stricken with a dread disease.
When you passed before his bed,
Then you lifted up your skirt,
And your coat with ermine lined,
Your chemise of linen white,
Until he could see your leg.
Straightway was the pilgrim cured
More than he had ever been.
Then he jumped up from his bed;
To his country he returned,

Safe and sound, completely cured.
O sweet love, sweet fleur-de-lis,
Sweet to kiss, sweet to embrace,
Sweet to come and sweet to go,
Sweet to say and sweet to play,
Sweet to please and sweet to squeeze,
No man could ever hate you.
Yet for your sake I am here
In this prison underground
Where I make a dismal end.
Now I ought to kill myself
    For you, my love."

XII

Now they tell and relate and continue the tale

Aucassin was put in prison, as you have heard and understood and Nicolette was elsewhere in her chamber. This was in the summertime, in the month of May, when the days are hot and long and clear and the nights still and serene.

Nicolette lay one night in her bed, and she saw the moon shine clear through a window, and she heard the nightingale singing in the garden; so did she recall Aucassin, her love whom she loved so much. She began to reflect about Count Garin de Beaucaire, who hated her to death. So did she think that she would remain there no longer; for, if she were discovered and Count Garin heard about it, he would make her die an evil death. She perceived that the old woman who was with her was sleeping. She got up and put on a good chemise of cloth of silk that she had, and she took her bed-clothes and towels, and tied them one to another and made a cord as long as she could. This she tied to the pillar of the window; so did she slide down into the garden. She took the front of her dress with one hand and the back with the other and raised it close about her, because of the dew which she saw heavy upon the grass, and so she made off down the garden.

She had blond hair tightly curled, and eyes gray and laughing, and a slender face, and a nose high and well placed, and lips redder than the cherry or the rose in the summertime, and teeth small and white. And she had firm little breasts which raised up her gown as if they were two walnuts, and she was so slender in the waist that you could have circled it with your two hands. And the blossoms of daisies which she broke with the toes of her feet and which were lying upon her instep were completely black beside her feet and legs, so very, very white was the maiden.

She came to the postern[2] and unlocked it. So did she pass out into the streets of Beaucaire, under cover of the shadows, for the moon was shining very clear. And she wandered about until she came to the tower where her lover was. The tower was cracked from place to place. And Nicolette squatted down against one of the buttresses and wrapped her cloak about her. She stuck her head in through a crevice of the tower, which was old and ancient. So did she hear Aucassin, who, inside, was weeping and wail-

---

[2] Back gate.

ing loudly and regretting his sweet love, whom he loved so much. And
when she had listened enough to him, she began to speak.

XIII

Now it is sung
> Nicolette with clearest face
> Was leaning on a buttress.
> Aucassin she heard to weep
> And lament his sweetheart lost.
> Now she speaks and says her thought.
> "Aucassin, my noble lord,
> Gentle, high-born, honored youth,
> What's the use of all these sighs,
> This weeping and lamenting?
> For you can never have me;
> Your father and your family
> All hate me and detest me.
> For you I'd sail the high seas
> And go to other countries."
> From her hair she cut a lock
> And threw it in his dungeon.
> Noble Aucassin took it
> And did it a great homage.
> He kissed it and embraced it
> And stuck it in his bosom,
> Then began again to weep
> > All for his love.

XIV

Now they tell and relate and continue the tale

When Aucassin heard Nicolette say that she wished to go away to another country, in him there was nothing but anger.

"Fair sweet love," said he, "you shall not go away, for then you would be
the death of me. And the first one who saw you, and who would be able to
do it, would take you immediately and put you into his bed, and so would
he make you his mistress. And once you had lain in a man's bed—if it
wasn't mine—don't think that I would wait until I had found a knife with
which I could pierce my heart and kill myself. No, indeed, I wouldn't wait
that long, but I would rush about until I saw a wall or a dark stone, and I
would dash my head against it so hard that I would make my eyes pop out
and brain myself completely. For I would much prefer to die such a death
than to know that you were in a man's bed—if it wasn't mine."

"Ah!" said she. "I don't think that you love me as much as you say. But I
love you more than you love me."

"Look here," said Aucassin, "fair sweet love, it couldn't be that you
should love me as much as I love you. Woman can't love man as much as
man loves woman, for the love of a woman is in her eye, and in the nipple
of her breast, and in the toe of her foot, but the love of a man is planted in
the heart where it can't escape."

While Aucassin and Nicolette were talking there, the guardsmen of the town were coming down the street. They had their swords drawn beneath their cloaks, for Count Garin had commanded them that if they were able to take her, they should kill her. And the watchman who was on the tower saw them coming and heard them going along talking about Nicolette and threatening to kill her.

"God," said he, "what a great pity for so fair a girl, if they should kill her. And it would be a very great charity if I could tell her, in some way they wouldn't perceive, that she should be on her guard. For if they kill her, then Aucassin, my young lord, will die, and that will be a great loss."

XV

Now it is sung

The watchman was a gallant,
Knowing, proud and courteous man.
So did he begin a song
Which was sweet and ran along.
"Maiden of the noble heart,
Body fair and full of grace,
Thou hast blond and shining hair,
Grayish eyes and smiling face.
Well do I see by thy air,
Thou hast spoken to thy love,
Who now for thee dying is.
Listen while I tell thee this:
From seducers guard thyself;
They are looking for thee here,
Bearing swords beneath their cloaks.
Terribly they'll threaten thee;
Soon much evil will they do
If thou guard not well."

XVI

Now they tell and relate and continue the tale

"Ah," said Nicolette, "may the souls of your father and mother be in blessed repose, since so fairly and courteously you have told me about them. If it please God, I will guard myself well from them, and God help me do it."

She wrapped her cloak about her in the shadow of the buttress until they had passed beyond. Then she took leave of Aucassin and went on until she came to the wall of the castle. The wall was in pieces and had been boarded up, and she climbed up on this and made her way along until she was between the wall and the moat. And she looked down and saw that the moat was very deep and very steep, and she was very, very much afraid.

"Oh God," said she, "sweet creature! If I let myself fall, I'll break my neck, and if I remain here, they will take me tomorrow, and they will burn me in a fire. I would much prefer that I die here than that all the folk should stare at me tomorrow under marvelous circumstances."

She made the sign of the cross above her head and let herself slide down into the moat. And when she came to the bottom, her beautiful feet and her beautiful hands, which had never learned that things might wound them, were bruised and torn, and the blood flowed from them in at least a dozen places; but nevertheless she felt neither hurt nor pain because of the great fear which she had. And though getting in had been much trouble, getting out was even more. She thought to herself that it would never do any good to remain there. She found a sharpened stake which those within had thrown down in defense of the castle, and placing one foot before the other, she mounted up with great difficulty until she came to the top.

Now there was a forest, about two crossbow shots away, which stretched for at least thirty leagues in length and in breadth, and there were savage beasts in it—also serpents. She was afraid that if she entered there, these might kill her; and, on the other hand, she reflected, if they found her there, they would lead her back to the town to burn her.

XVII

Now it is sung

Nicolette with clearest face
Up the moat has made her way.
Then began she to lament
And in Jesus' name to pray:
"Father, King of Majesty,
I do not know where to go.
If I go into the woods,
There the wolves will eat me sure,
The wild boars and the lions,
Of which there are a-plenty.
If I wait the daylight clear
So that they could find me here,
They will light their fires of wood
And my body will be burned.
But, by God of Majesty,
I would very much prefer
That even wolves should eat me,
Or wild boars or the lions,
Than go into the city.
    I *will* not go."

XVIII

Now they tell and relate and continue the tale

Nicolette lamented as you have heard. She commended herself to God and wandered on until she came into the forest. She didn't dare to enter very deep into it because of the savage beasts and because of the serpents; so she crawled into a thick bush. Sleep seized her, and she slept until the next morning at seven-thirty when the shepherds came out of the town and drove their beasts between the wood and the river. There they drew aside to a very beautiful spring which was at the edge of the forest, and spread out a cape and set their bread upon it. And while they were eating, Nicolette was awakened by the cries of the birds and of the shepherds; so did she hurry toward them.

"Fair children," said she, "may the Mother of God aid you."

"God bless *you*!" said the one of them who was more talkative than the others.

"Fair children," said she, "do you know Aucassin, the son of Count Garin de Beaucaire?"

"Yes, we know him well."

"So may God aid you, fair children," she said. "Tell him that there is a beast in this forest, and that he is to come to hunt for it; and if he could catch it, he would not give one leg of it for one hundred marks of gold, not for five hundred, nor for any amount."

And they looked at her, and so did they see her so beautiful that they were all astonished.

"I should tell him *that*?" said he who was more talkative than the others. "Damned be the one who would ever talk about it, or who would ever tell him! It's a phantom that you're talking about, for there is no beast in the forest so valuable, neither stag nor lion nor wild boar, that one of his legs would be worth more than a shilling or two at the most, and you speak of such a great value! Damned be the one who believes you, or whoever shall tell it to him! You are some fairy, and we have no desire for your company, so you keep on your way."

"Ah, fair children," she said, "you will do this. The beast has such medicine that Aucassin will be cured of his illness. And I have five sous here in my purse; take them—if you will tell him. And he ought to hunt it within three days; and if, within three days, he doesn't find it, he never will be cured of his illness."

"By faith," said he, "we will take the money, and if he comes here, we will tell him; but we'll never go to look for him."

"It's up to God," said she.

Then she took leave of the shepherds, and so did she go on her way.

XIX

Now it is sung

> Nicolette with clearest face
> Has parted from the shepherds.
> So she's taken up her way
> Right into the leafy wood,
> Following an abandoned path
> Until she met a highway
> Where seven roads divided
> Which went through the country-side.
> Then the thought came to her head
> How she could prove her lover,
> If he loved her as he said.
> So she took the iris-flower
> And green grass from a thicket
> And some branches thick with leaves.
> So she made a leafy hut;
> Prettier was there never seen.
> By the truthful God she swore
> That if Aucassin came there

And did not for love of her
Rest in it a little while
Never would he be her love
Nor she be his.

XX

Now they tell and relate and continue the tale

Nicolette had made a hut, as you have heard and understood, very pretty and attractive, for she had decorated it well inside and outside with flowers and with leaves. Then she lay down close by the hut in a thick bush to know what Aucassin would do.

And the cry and rumor went through all the land and through all the country that Nicolette was lost. Some said that she had run away, and others said that Count Garin had had her murdered. Whoever may have had joy from it, Aucassin wasn't at all happy about it. And Count Garin, his father, had him taken out of prison. So did he send for the knights and the ladies, and he had made a great rich feast, with which he thought to comfort Aucassin, his son.

Although the feast was most complete, Aucassin stood leaning on a post all sad and all limp. Whoever had joy, Aucassin was in no mood for it; for he saw nothing at all there of the thing he loved. A knight looked at him and came up to him; so did he speak to him.

"Aucassin," said he. "I have been sick with the same illness that you have. I will give you some good advice, if you wish to believe me."

"Sir," said Aucassin, "many thanks. I would appreciate some good advice."

"Get on a horse," said he, "and ride along the forest to cheer yourself up. And you will see the flowers and the plants, and you will hear the little birds sing. By some chance you may hear some word for which you will be better."

"Sir," said Aucassin, "Thanks very much. That's what I'll do."

He slipped out of the hall and went down the stairs and came to the stable where his horse was. He had the saddle and bridle put on. He put his foot in the stirrup and mounted and went out of the castle. And he wandered until he came to the forest and rode along until he reached the spring and found the shepherds just at mid-afternoon. They had spread out a cape on the grass, and they were eating their bread and making very merry.

XXI

Now it is sung

Now the shepherds gather round,
Little Martin and Esmy,
Little Frulin and Johnny,
Little Robin and Aubrey.
"Little shepherd boys," said one,
"God help little Aucassin;
He is a fine young fellow.
And the girl with form so small

And curly hair so yellow.
Bright her face, her eye so gray,
She gave us little pennies
With which we'll buy little cakes,
Little knives and little sheaths,
Little flutes and little horns,
Little crooks and little pipes.
  May God help her."

XXII

Now they tell and relate and continue the tale

When Aucassin heard the shepherds, he recalled Nicolette, his very sweet love, whom he loved so much, and thought that she had been there. He pricked his horse with the spurs, and so did he come up to the shepherds.

"Fair children, may God aid you!"

"God bless *you*!" said the one who was more talkative than the others.

"Fair children," said he, "repeat the song that you were singing just now."

"We will not say it," said the one who was more talkative than the others. "Damned now be the one who will sing it for you, fair sir."

"Fair children," said Aucassin, "don't you know me?"

"Yes, we know very well that you are Aucassin, our young lord, but we don't belong to you, but rather to the count."

"Fair children, you will do this, I pray you."

"Oh, for God's sake!" said he. "Why should I sing for you if it doesn't suit me? When there is no man so rich in this country, except Count Garin in person, who, if he found my oxen, or my cows, or my sheep in his fields, or even in his grain, would risk having his eyes put out, for daring to chase them from it? And why should I sing for you if it doesn't suit me?"

"God aid you, fair children, if you will do it, and take ten sous which I have here in my purse."

"Sir, we will take the money, but I will not sing it for you, for I have sworn it, but I will tell it to you if you wish."

"It's up to God," said Aucassin, "I would rather have it told than nothing."

"Sir, we were here a little while ago, between six and nine this morning, eating our bread by this spring, as we are now, and a maiden came here, the most beautiful in the world, so that we believed her to be a fairy, and this whole wood was made bright by her. And she gave us so much of what she had that we made a promise to her, that if you came here, we would tell you that you should go and hunt in this forest, where there is a beast which, if you should be able to catch it, you would never give up one of its legs for five hundred marks of silver, or for any price. For the beast has such a medicine that, if you could catch it, you would be cured of your illness. And you must take it within three days, and if you haven't caught it, you will never see it again. Now hunt it, if you will; or if you will, leave it, for I have fully acquitted myself towards her."

"Fair children." said Aucassin, "you have told me enough about it, and God let me find it!"

XXIII

Now it is sung

Aucassin has heard the words
Of his love with form so fair.
Much they struck him to the core.
Soon he leaves the shepherd boys
And in the deep woods enters.
His war horse ambled quickly,
At a gallop carried him.
Now he speaks and says three words:
"Nicolette, of form so fair,
In this woods for you I've come.
I'm not hunting stag or boar;
Your tracks I am following.
Your gray eyes and your sweet form,
Your soft speech and gentle laugh
Unto death my heart do wound.
If it please the Father, God,
Then shall I see you again.
                          Sister, sweet love."

XXIV

Now they tell and relate and continue the tale

Aucassin went through the forest from path to path, and his war horse
carried him along at a great speed. Don't think that the briars and thorns
spared him. Nothing of the sort! Rather they ripped up his clothes so that
one could scarcely have made a knot out of the biggest pieces. And blood
ran from his arms and his sides and his legs in forty places—or thirty, so
that after the lad one might follow the traces of blood which fell on the
grass. But he thought so much about Nicolette, his sweet love, that he felt
neither pain nor unhappiness. And he went all day through the forest in
such a way that he never did get news of her. And when he saw evening
approaching, he began to weep because he couldn't find her.

He was riding along an old path all covered with leaves, when he looked
before him, in the middle of the path; so did he see a yokel such as I shall
tell you. Great he was, and marvelous and ugly and hideous; and he had a
great bushy head blacker than charcoal, and he had more than a hand's
breadth between his two eyes, and he had great cheeks and a huge flat nose,
and wide nostrils and thick lips redder than roast beef, and big teeth, yellow
and ugly. And he wore leggings and shoes of cow-hide, cross-laced with
willow bark to above the knee. He was wearing a cape unfinished inside
and out, and he was leaning on a big club.

Aucassin hurried toward him and was very frightened when he got a
good look at him.

"Fair brother, God help you!"

"God help *you*," said he.

"God help *you*. What are you doing here?"

"What's it to you?" said he.

"Nothing," said Aucassin, "I don't ask you except with good reason."

"But why are you crying," said he, "and making such a to-do? Surely, if I were as rich a man as you are, all the world wouldn't make me cry."

"What! do you know me?" said Aucassin.

"Sure, I know well that you are Aucassin, the son of the count, and if you will tell me why you are crying, I will tell you what I am doing here."

"Surely," said Aucassin, "I will tell you very gladly. I came this morning to hunt in the forest, and I had a white greyhound, the most beautiful in the world, and I have lost it. That's why I'm crying."

"To hear," said he, "by the heart that the Lord had in his belly, that you were crying over a stinking dog? May he be badly damned who shall ever take any account of you, when there is no man in this land so rich, that if your father asked him for ten or fifteen or twenty, he would not have given them only too willingly and have been only too glad. But *I* ought to cry and wail."

"And for what reason, brother?"

"Sir, I'll tell you. I was in the hire of a rich farmer, and I drove his plough, a four-ox one. Now three days ago there came to me a great accident by which I lost the best one of my oxen, Roget, the best of my team. So now I am looking for him, and I haven't eaten or drunk for the last three days. And I don't dare go to the town, for they would put me in prison since I don't have the money to pay for it. Of all the wealth in the world, I have nothing more valuable than what you see on my body. I have a poor old mother, and she had nothing more valuable than an old mattress, and they have taken it right out from under her back, so that she lies on the bare straw now. I am much more worried about her than about myself, for money comes and goes. If I have lost now, I will gain it another time; so shall I pay for my ox when I can, nor will I ever cry about it. And you were crying over a filthy dog—may anyone who ever takes any account of you be damned forever!"

"You certainly are a good comfort, fair brother, and may you be blessed! And what was your ox worth?"

"Sir, twenty sous they are asking me for it, and I can't get a single sou knocked off."

"Now take," said Aucassin, "the twenty which I have in my purse, and pay for your ox."

"Sir," said he, "thanks very much, and may God let you find what you are seeking."

He parted from him, and Aucassin rode on. The night was fair and still, and he wandered along until he came to the place where the seven roads forked. So did he look before him, and he saw the hut that Nicolette had built, which was hung outside and inside and on top and in front with flowers and was so beautiful that it could not be more so. When Aucassin saw it, he stopped all of a sudden, and the rays of the moon were shining in it.

"Oh, God," said Aucassin, "Nicolette, my sweet love, was here, and she made this with her own beautiful hands. Because of her sweetness and for love of her, I will get down now and stretch out there for the rest of the night."

Now the horse was big and tall, and Aucassin took his foot out of the stirrup to get down. He was thinking so much about Nicolette, his very sweet love, that he fell so hard on a stone that his shoulder flew out of place. He felt himself badly hurt, but he forced himself along as best he could, and tied the horse with his other hand to a thornbush; then he turned on his side so that he crawled into the hut. He looked up through a hole in the hut, and he saw the stars in the sky. He saw one brighter than the others, and he began to say.

XXV

Now it is sung

> "I can see you, little star,
> Which the moon draws after her.
> Nicolette is with you there,
> My sweet love with golden hair.
> I think God wants to have her
> So that all the evening light
> Can by her be made more bright.
> At the risk of falling down
> Would that I were up with you;
> I would kiss you willingly.
> Though I were a monarch's son,
> You would worthy be of me.
>   Sister, sweet love."

XXVI

Now they tell and relate and continue the tale

When Nicolette heard Aucassin, she came to him, for she was not far off. She came into the hut; so did she throw her arms around his neck, kissed him, and embraced him.

"Fair sweet love, it's good to find you!"

"And you, fair sweet love, it's good to find *you!*"

They kissed each other and embraced; so was their joy beautiful.

"Ah, sweet love," said Aucassin, "just now I hurt my shoulder, and now I feel neither pain nor grief since I have you."

She felt him carefully and found that he had his shoulder out of place. She handled it and pulled it about so with her white hands that, as God who loves lovers willed it, it came back into place; and then she took some flowers and fresh grass and green leaves, and she bound it up with the tail of her chemise, and he was completely cured.

"Aucassin," said she, "fair sweet love, take counsel what you will do. If your father has this forest searched tomorrow, whatever may become of *you,* they will kill *me.*"

"Surely, fair sweet love, I should be very sad over it; but if I am able, they shall never get hold of you."

He mounted on his horse, and took his love up in front of him, kissing and embracing her; so did they set off to the open fields.

XXVII

Now it is sung

> Aucassin, the fair, the blond,
> The gentle and the loving,

Out of that deep woods has gone
With his love between his arms,
His saddle-bow before him.
He kissed her eyes and forehead,
Kissed her mouth and then her chin;
Then did Nicolette begin,
"Aucassin, sweet handsome love,
To what country shall we go?"
"My sweet love, how should I know?
I do not care where we go
In the woods or on the roads
So long as I am with you."
They passed the hills and valleys,
The villages and cities,
And at dawn they reached the sea
And dismounted on the sand
      Near the seashore.

XXVIII
Now they tell and relate and continue the tale

Aucassin had dismounted, both he and his love, as you have heard and understood. He held his horse by the reins, and his love by the hand, and so did they begin to go along the shore. And Aucassin looked toward the sea and saw a ship of merchants who were sailing near the coast.

He hailed them and they came to him, and he made such terms with them that they took them into their ship. And when they were on the high seas, a storm arose, great and marvelous, which drove them from land to land, until they arrived in a strange country and entered into the port of the Castle of Torelore. Then they asked whose land it was, and they told them that it was the land of the King of Torelore. Then they asked what sort of a man he was, and if he had a war, and they told him, "Yes, a great one."

He took leave of the merchants, and they commended him to God. He mounted on his horse, his sword girded on, and his love in front of him, and wandered until he came to the castle. He asked where the king was, and they told him that he was lying in bed with child.

"And where is his wife, then?"

And they told him that she was with the army, and that she had taken away with her everybody in the country. Aucassin heard it, and it seemed to him a great marvel. He came up to the palace and dismounted—both he and his love; and she held the horse, and he went up into the palace, his sword girded on, and wandered about until he came into the room where the king was lying.

XXIX
Now it is sung

In the room came Aucassin
The courteous and the noble.
He came straight up to the bed
On which the king was lying.

Right in front of him he stopped
And spoke; listen what he said:
"Fool, what are you doing here?"
Said the king, "I am with child.
When my month shall be fulfilled
And I shall be well again,
I shall then be churched at mass
As my ancestors have done;
Then from carrying on great war
With my enemies again,
    I shall never stop."

xxx

Now they tell and relate and continue the tale

When Aucassin heard the king speak thus, he took all the bed clothes which were upon him and threw them around the room. He saw just in back of him a big stick. He took it, turned about, and he struck him and beat him so much that he almost killed him.

"Ah, fair sir," said the king, "what do you want of me? Have you gone crazy that you beat me in my own house?"

"By God's heart," said Aucassin, "evil son of a slut, I will kill you, if you do not swear to me that never again shall a man in your land be brought to bed with child."

He swore it, and when he had heard him swear it:

"Sir," said Aucassin, "now lead me there where your wife is with the army."

"Sir, willingly," said the king.

He mounted on his horse, and Aucassin mounted on his, and Nicolette remained in the chambers of the queen. And the king and Aucassin rode along until they came to the place where the queen was, and they found there a battle of rotted wild apples, and of eggs and of fresh cheeses; and Aucassin began to look at them, and he was very, very much astonished indeed.

xxxi

Now it is sung

Aucassin had stopped and now,
Elbow on his saddle-bow,
He begins to marvel at
This violent battlefield,
For both sides had brought with them
Cheeses quite fresh from the vats,
With wood apples rotted soft,
And some large field mushrooms too.
He who most stirs up the fords
Is proclaimed the lord of lords.
Aucassin the valiant knight
Stared at them with all his might
    And began to laugh.

XXXII

Now they tell and relate and continue the tale

When Aucassin saw this marvel, he came to the king; so did he speak to him.

"Sir," said Aucassin, "are these your enemies?"

"Yes, sir," said the king.

"And would you like me to avenge you on them?"

"Yes," said he, "if you like."

And Aucassin put his hand on his sword, so did he rush among them and began to strike right and left and killed many of them. When the king saw that he was killing them, he took him by the bridle and said:

"Ah, fair sir, don't kill them like this."

"What?" said Aucassin, "don't you want me to avenge you?"

"Sir," said the king, "you have done too much. It is not our custom to kill each other."

The enemy turned and fled, and the king and Aucassin returned to the castle of Torelore. And the people of the country told the king that he should cast Aucassin out of the land and detain Nicolette as a wife for his son since she seemed, indeed, to be a woman of high lineage. Nicolette heard it, and was not at all glad about it, and she began to say:

XXXIII

Now it is sung

> "O, sir king of Torelore,"
> Said the lovely Nicolette,
> "Your folk take me for a fool;
> When my love embraces me
> And feels me plump and tender,
> Then am I in such a state
> That neither songs nor dances,
> Fiddle, harp, nor viol gay,
> Nor the pleasures of the play
>   Are worth a thing."

XXXIV

Now they tell and relate and continue the tale

Aucassin was in the castle of Torelore, and Nicolette, his love; and he had great delight and great ease that he had with him Nicolette, his sweet love, whom he loved so much. And while he was in such ease and in such delight, a fleet of the Saracens came by sea and assailed the castle; so did they take it by force. And they took all the treasure and led the men and women away captive. They took Nicolette and Aucassin, and they bound Aucassin's hands and his feet, and they threw him into one ship and Nicolette into another. And there arose a storm on the sea, which separated them.

The ship in which Aucassin was went skimming over the sea until it arrived at the Castle of Beaucaire. The people of the country ran to the wreckage, and they found Aucassin, and so did they recognize him. When those of Beaucaire saw their young lord, they made great joy over it, for

Aucassin had lived in the castle of Torelore for three full years, and his father and mother were dead. They led him to the Castle of Beaucaire; so did they all become his men, and he held his land in peace.

XXXV

Now it is sung

>   Aucassin has gone away
>   To his city of Beaucaire.
>   All the country and the realm
>   He now held in greatest calm,
>   Swore by God of Majesty
>   That he much more regretted
>   Nicolette with clearest face
>   Than all of his relations
>   Though they all were dead and gone.
>   "Sweetheart with the clearest face,
>   I don't know where you may be.
>   God has never made that place
>   Either on the land or sea
>   Where if I thought to find you
>   I would not look."

XXXVI

Now they tell and relate and continue the tale

Now we will leave off about Aucassin and talk of Nicolette. The ship in which Nicolette was belonged to the king of Carthage, and he was her father, and she had twelve brothers, all princes and kings. When they saw Nicolette so beautiful, they offered her very, very great honors and made a feast for her, and often did they ask her who she was, for indeed she seemed to be a very noble lady and of high lineage. But she didn't know how to tell them who she was, for she had been stolen away as a little child. They sailed along until they arrived below the city of Carthage; and when Nicolette saw the walls of the castle and the country, she recognized that she had been brought up there and stolen from there as a little child. But she was not so small a child that she didn't know very well that she had been the daughter of the king of Carthage, and that she had been brought up in the city.

XXXVII

Now it is sung

>   Nicolette, high-born and wise,
>   Now has landed on the shore,
>   Saw the buildings and the walls
>   And the castle and the halls.
>   Seeing which, she cried, "Alas,
>   I am of a high descent,
>   Daughter to the Carthage king
>   And cousin to the emir!
>   Savage people hold me here.
>   Aucassin, well-born and wise,

> Honorable, noble lord,
> Your sweet love so urges me,
> Speaks to me and troubles me,
> God the Spirit grant me this:
> That you hold me in your arms,
> Once again my forehead kiss,
> Kiss my mouth and kiss my face,
>   My sweet young lord."

XXXVIII
Now they tell and relate and continue the tale

When the king of Carthage heard Nicolette speak in that way, he threw his arms around her neck.

"Fair sweet love," said he, "tell me who you are; don't you be afraid of me."

"Sir," said she, "I am the daughter of the king of Carthage, and I was stolen as a little child, fully fifteen years ago."

When he heard her speak thus, he knew well that she was speaking the truth; so did he make a very great holiday for her, and led her into the palace with great honor as the daughter of a king. For a husband he wished to give her a king of the pagans, but she had no desire to get married. She was there three or four full days. She reflected by what device she would be able to search for Aucassin. She bought herself a viol and learned to play it, until they wanted one day to marry her off to a rich pagan king. And she slipped out that night and came to the seaport; so did she take shelter with a poor woman on the shore. And she took an herb and smeared her head and face with it so that she was all black and stained. And she had a coat made and a cloak and a shirt and underbreeches, and rigged herself out in the guise of a jongleur. So she took her viol and came up to a sailor, and she made such terms with him that he took her aboard his ship. They raised their sails, and so did they sail away over the high seas until they arrived at the land of Provence. And Nicolette started out and took her viol; so did she go along playing through the country until she came to the Castle of Beaucaire, there where Aucassin was.

XXXIX
Now it is sung

> At Beaucaire beneath the tower
> There was Aucassin one day
> Seated on a stone stairway.
> Round him were his barons proud.
> He saw the grass and flowers
> And heard the small birds singing
> And remembered of his love,
> For the noble Nicolette,
> Whom he'd loved so many days.
> He gives way to sighs and tears.
> Look, below is Nicolette
> With her viol and her bow.
> Now she speaks and tells her tale,

"Listen to me, noble lords,
Those above and those below,
Would you like to hear a song
Of a proud lord, Aucassin,
Of the noble Nicolette,
How their love endured so long,
How he sought her in the wood;
At Torelore in prison
The pagans one day put them.
Naught of Aucassin we know,
But the noble Nicolette
At Carthage is in prison.
Now her father loves her well
Who is lord of all that realm.
As bride they wish to give her
To a wretched pagan king.
Nicolette won't think of it,
For she loves a fair young lord
By the name of Aucassin.
Well she swears by God's own name
That she will never marry
If she cannot have the one
     Whom she so loves."

XL

Now they tell and relate and continue the tale

When Aucassin heard Nicolette speak thus, he was very glad, and he drew her aside and asked her:

"Fair sweet friend," said Aucassin, "do you know anything of this Nicolette of whom you have just sung?"

"Sir, yes," said she, "I know of her as the most noble creature, and the most gentle and the most wise that was ever born. She is the daughter of the King of Carthage, who took her when Aucassin was taken; so did he lead her into the city of Carthage until he had learned indeed that she was his daughter. He made a great festival; and he wished each day to give her for a husband one of the most exalted kings in all Spain, but she would rather let herself be hanged or burned than take any one of them, however rich he might be."

"Ah, fair sweet friend," said Count Aucassin, "if you would go back to that land and tell her to come here to speak to me, I would give you as much of my wealth as you would dare demand or take. And know that for love of her, I have no desire to take a wife however high her lineage may be, but only to wait for her. For I will have no wife if it isn't she. And if I had known where to find her, I would not be looking for her now."

"Sir," said she, "if you would do this, I would go and seek her for you and for her, whom I love very much."

He swore it to her, and then he had her given twenty pounds. She started to leave him, and he wept for the sweetness of Nicolette. When she saw him weeping:

"Sir," she said, "don't be dismayed, for in a little time I will have her brought into this town; so you will see her."

And when Aucassin heard her, he was very, very glad. And she went away from him; so did she go through the town to the house of the Viscountess, for the Viscount, her god-father, was dead. There she stayed, and she talked to her until she had revealed her plan, and the Viscountess had recognized her and knew indeed that it was Nicolette whom she had reared. So did she have her washed and bathed, and she stayed there eight full days. Then she took an herb which is called Clarity and smeared herself with it. So was she as beautiful as she had ever been at any day. And she dressed herself in rich cloth of silk, of which the lady had much.

She sat in her chamber upon a quilt of stitched silk cloth, and she called the lady and told her that she should go for Aucassin, her love. She did it; and when she came to the palace, she found Aucassin who was weeping and regretting Nicolette his love because she delayed so long, and the lady called him and said to him:

"Aucassin, don't cry any more, but come along with me, and I will show you the thing that you love most in all the world, for it is Nicolette, your sweet love, who has come from distant lands to find you."

And Aucassin was overjoyed!

XLI

Now it is sung

> Now when Aucassin had heard
> Of his love with clearest face,
> How she had come to this land,
> Glad was he, never more so.
> With the lady has he gone;
> Straight to that house did he ride.
> There they entered in a room
> Where Nicolette was sitting.
> When she saw her lover there,
> Glad was she, never more so.
> Up she jumped and ran to him.
> And when Aucassin saw her,
> With both arms stretched out to her,
> He embraced her tenderly
> While he kissed her eyes and face.
> All that night they left them thus.
> In the morning, the next day,
> Aucassin made her his wife.
> Lady of Beaucaire she was;
> Then they lived for many days
> And much pleasure did they have.
> Now has Aucassin his joy
> And Nicolette hers likewise.
> Our *chantefable* takes its end.
>   I cannot tell you more.

Dante Alighieri

(1265–1321)

The reputation of Dante Alighieri, already high in the time immediately following his death, is today such as to rank him with Homer and Shakespeare at the summit of world literature and his Divine Comedy *as perhaps the greatest single work of literary art. Dante's simple title was the* Commedia *(the epithet* Divina *was added on title pages beginning in the sixteenth century). The work was called a comedy because its style was a middle one beneath the high-serious tone of tragedy and because its movement was from sadness to joy. The* Comedy *is often described as the quintessence of the medieval world view, a codification of the values of the high Middle Ages in art, science, theology, and philosophy. This view has considerable truth. It is not without its ironies, however; Dante felt nostalgia for the past and entertained hopes for the future, but he considered his own age vicious, corrupt, and benighted. The circumstances of his life and its public backdrop bear out his judgment in many respects.*

Dante was born in 1265 in the independent, republican city-state of Florence, which in its commercial prosperity and its culture was beginning to rank with the leading cities of Europe. For decades before his birth an appallingly bloody feud had divided Florence into two factions: the Ghibellines, a feudal and military class allied with the Holy Roman Emperor, and the Guelfs, a middle-class party that tended to side with the Papacy in its struggle against the Empire. Dante's family were Guelfs. After an alternation of victories by one side over the other, the Guelfs triumphed decisively when Dante was a year old. But by the end of the century the Guelfs themselves had split into factions: the Blacks, who represented the nobility and were willing to tolerate papal political influence, and the Whites, who represented the commercial bourgeoisie and wanted political independence. Dante was a moderate White. After some military service, he held in his early thirties a succession of increasingly prominent political offices, becoming one of the chief magistrates of Florence in 1300, the year in which the events of the Divine Comedy *are imagined to take place. Fighting broke out in the streets. Dante's solution was to help banish the leaders of both factions, including his brother-in-law and also Guido Cavalcanti, one of his best friends and a fellow poet. But the Blacks conspired with Dante's detested Pope Boniface VIII, who wished to establish his power in Florence and the surrounding region of Tuscany, and with the help of a foreign army the Whites were ousted, while Dante was absent on a diplomatic mission to Rome. In 1302 he was unjustly accused of barratry (graft), tried in absentia, fined the large sum of 5,000 florins, and banished for two years. When he refused to pay the fine and thus admit guilt, the banishment was ruled perpetual, under penalty of being burned alive. Dante never saw his beloved—and henceforth also hated—Florence again, or his wife Gemma, whom he had married in his mid-twenties. The* Divine Comedy *refers often to this century-long saga of bloody and sleazy politics.*

For a time Dante nourished the hope that the Whites would regain control of Florence, but these hopes remained unfulfilled, and gradually Dante became a party of one, disillusioned with all the factions. He was thereafter dependent on a series of patrons who gave him asylum in various Italian cities, mainly in the north. Tradition has it that he spent some time in France and possibly in England, at Oxford. In 1308 his hopes for the regeneration, reordering, and pacification of Italy, including Flor-

ence, were rekindled by the election of a new, idealistic Holy Roman Emperor, Henry VII. Dante believed that most of the political evils of his country, and some of the spiritual ones too, sprang from a lack of guidance by an enlightened Emperor such as Rome had had in its best ancient days. But Henry's expedition to Italy failed, thwarted by party conflicts, the opposition of the Pope, and finally by Henry's death in 1313. Dante's hopes were once more disappointed. His very last years, however, were relatively serene; he had already circulated the first two parts of his Comedy, *the* Inferno *and* Purgatory, *the fame of which helped sustain him, and his children were again with him. His last patron, in Ravenna, was a nephew of the Francesca da Rimini whose story Dante had told so movingly in* Inferno *canto V. Dante died in 1321, not long after he completed the* Paradise *and with it the entire* Comedy.*

As references in that work show, Dante's political vicissitudes are reflected in his art. Yet he lived another inner and creative life independent of public traumas. He seems to have had a happy childhood and a good education, probably under Dominican and Franciscan priests. He studied rhetoric under the philosopher-poet Brunetto Latini whom he honors in Inferno XV. *He was early influenced by French Provençal poetry and by the Italian vernacular poetry that had only recently begun to flourish. A protégé of Guido Cavalcanti, Dante developed a* dolce stil nuovo *("sweet new style"), rejecting elegant artifice for its own sake and emphasizing instead sincerity of feeling and substance in ideas. The central event of his earlier spiritual life is narrated in the* Vita Nuova *("New Life"), an amatory and spiritual autobiography with allegorical overtones, which he composed in Italian in 1292. It records, in a mixture of lyric verse and prose commentary, Dante's first love, inspired in him at the age of nine by the sight of Beatrice Portinari, a girl one year younger. He immediately conceived for her a lifelong, intensely idealistic passion that owes much to the medieval tradition of worship of woman, to which Dante adds a moral and philosophical dimension. Nine years later Dante and Beatrice greeted each other. There followed episodes of alienation and psychological distress (apparently idealized, for Dante seems not to have had much close contact with Beatrice). After she died in 1290, he turned to a compassionate lady who later became an emblem of the philosophical pursuits that occupied him after Beatrice's death. The composition of the* Vita Nuova, *when Dante was twenty-seven, marks the end of the third nine-year period, the number symbolism foreshadowing an even more elaborate dependence in the* Divine Comedy *on threes and nines. In all this it is difficult to separate fact from idealization, but perhaps such a symbol-making mind as Dante's would reject the distinction. The* Vita Nuova *ends with the mention of a wondrous vision and with the determination by Dante that he will write no more of Beatrice until he can write of her "what has not before been written of any woman." This decision is one seed of the* Divine Comedy, *in which Beatrice ("giver of blessings") reappears, the Florentine girl transfigured as the heavenly lady who, having helped rescue Dante from his dark night, conducts him through the spheres of the celestial paradise. She becomes both a symbol and vehicle of God's love and revelation.*

The study of philosophy and literature that Dante embarked on after the death of Beatrice was continued and deepened in later years until he had mastered most of the important ancient and medieval writers accessible in that time before the Renaissance revival of classical Greek. Indeed, he became one of the most learned men in Europe. He was indebted philosophically to Aristotle, by way of St. Thomas Aquinas. Poetically, he was immensely indebted to Virgil, whom he echoes again and again in the Comedy *and chooses to represent as his guide through Hell and most of* Purgatory, _the realms that can be largely understood by the human reason that (among other things) Virgil represents. Dante claimed to know the_ Aeneid _by heart. His erudition led him to attempt several ambitious works. Much of what he had learned by 1305 or so he tried to put into a philosophically encyclopedic work called the_ Convivio _("Banquet"), which was to contain fifteen treatises in alternating prose and verse, like the_ Vita Nuova. _The_ Convivio, _although abandoned by Dante in about 1308, is a landmark in its use of Italian prose instead of Latin for serious philosophical purposes, anticipating the choice of Italian for the_ Comedy. _Conversely, Dante explored the general and practical principles involved in creating a worthy Italian language and literature in a Latin work of the same period,_ De Vulgari Eloquentia _("Of Eloquence in the Vernacular Tongue"), which he also left incomplete. Somewhat later, at the time Dante's hero Henry VII was in Italy, he wrote the Latin_ De Monarchia, _in which, picking up a theme treated in the_ Convivio, _Dante argued the bold thesis that the rightful powers of emperor and pope, respectively temporal and spiritual, were both derived directly from God. The implication was that in a Christian state the two should be separate but equal authorities and should limit themselves to their own mutually exclusive spheres. This idea influences not just the thematic content of the_ Divine Comedy _but its very rationale and symbolism; for example, at the end of the_ Inferno, _at the bottom and center of Hell, the place of supreme dishonor in the jaws of Satan, the author of all evil, is shared by the spiritual traitor Judas and imperial traitors Brutus and Cassius._

Dante wrote the Comedy _between 1308 and 1321, completing the_ Inferno _by 1312 and the_ Purgatory _by 1315. Literally, it is an account of a privileged journey taken by Dante the character (who should be distinguished from the Dante who writes the poem after the fact) into the world of the afterlife. On this level the_ Comedy _is a theological work. The damned are those who, each in his or her own way, have definitively rebelled against God's law and defied or ignored His mercy; these include pagans, Jews, and Christians. The saved are those who, having repented and been forgiven by God, dwell with Him in the celestial paradise. Also among the saved are those who, having died at peace with God, are still spiritually imperfect and must refine away their potential for evil in Purgatory, which Dante locates on a mountain in the southern ocean. The Christian faith is a prerequisite for beatitude, although the righteous Jews of the Old Testament period are saved by their implicit faith in Christ to come; moreover, Jewish infants and baptized Christian infants are also among the saved. The virtuous pagans of antiquity and of more modern times cannot enter Heaven; instead they dwell in Limbo, the uppermost circle of Hell, where their only suffering is to live without hope of redemption. These righteous pagans include even Virgil. Dante shows, especially in the_ Paradise, _that he is troubled by the lot of these blameless persons, and in fact in_ Paradise XX _he opens a loophole, revealing that at least some good pagans can finally be saved. But this is only a loophole, a faint gleam of mysterious hope, and much pathos arises in the_ Inferno _and_ Purgatory _from the assumption that the magisterial and fatherlike Virgil is inexorably excluded from eternal bliss._

Theologically, Purgatory _is the most distinctively Catholic realm, reflecting one fundamental difference in belief between the Catholic and Protestant faiths. The basic Protestant position, as formulated two centuries later during the Reformation, is that man is saved by faith in God's mercy and grace; Catholics believe that man is saved by a combination of such faith and "works" (acts of goodness and remedial suffering). This latter view can make God seem a niggardly taskmaster, forgiving_ *only grudgingly. But the Catholic view, if we can extrapolate from Dante's idea of the Redemption in Paradise VII, is that God is like a generous creditor who might have forgiven a debt outright but instead asks that part be repaid so as to salvage the self-respect and elevate the dignity of the sinner-debtor. Dante's purgatorians thus suffer, in a discipline of compensation, but joyfully and willingly. Because they can rise to a higher slope of the mountain as soon as they feel ready and worthy, their own wills are the essential ministers of the purgatorial process.*

An awareness of such theological fundamentals is important for an understanding of the Comedy, but the modern appeal of the work, even for believers, is not primarily theological but rather ethical and artistic. The Comedy is intended to be a picture of the world we live in; the journey into the afterlife is also the struggle in this life of every person who confronts evil, conquers it, and rises above it. Dante most obviously makes us aware of the temporal life by portraying known persons, great and commonplace, antique and modern, dead and living, and by commenting frequently on immediate, local issues, especially politics. In describing the three great realms and making clear his own emotional states, he draws vivid comparisons with the scenes and landscapes of recognizable life—the breaking of a gambler's lucky streak, the shipyards at Venice, a tailor's squint, fireflies on a summer evening, windmills seen through mist.

Above all, Dante comments on earthly life through the descriptions of the punishments in Hell. These are not merely imposed from outside and after the fact; rather, they are symbols of the sins when they are truly understood and realized in imaginative fullness. Someone once said that the motto of the Inferno might well be "They got what they wanted." Or, in Gerard Manley Hopkins' words, "The lost are like this, and their scourge [is] to be . . . their sweating selves." Thus the adulterous lovers Francesca and Paolo will be united forever, airborne on the winds of passion; the suicides who separated soul from body will remain so divided even after the Last Judgment, when other creatures have reassumed their flesh; the heretics who denied the immortality of the soul lie forever in sarcophagi, which will be sealed at the Judgment just as, in effect, they predicted; the popes who desecrated their office for money are all crammed, upside down and head to foot, into a single hole, in a parody of the apostolic succession and the laying on of hands by which the episcopal office is transmitted; the grafters continue their life of concealment and trickery.

Moreover, the scheme of punishments in Hell reflects a theory of human nature and a rather complex scheme of ethics. (The divisions of Hell and of Purgatory are outlined by Virgil in Inferno XI and Purgatory XVII.) The merely sensual sinners are the least guilty, and of them the sexual sinners least of all, possibly because sex retains some touch of the love that, properly understood, is God. The next most guilty are the violent. But the worst sinners are those who pervert the divine plan of creation by misusing the specifically human power of reason—that is, the fraudulent. But even fraud has gradations, and it is worst when it is treacherous. And the worst form of treachery is that shown to lords and benefactors. God as understood by Dante is associated with motion and energy, and it is therefore appropriate that the punishment for treacherous fraud is not the hell-fire of popular imagination but complete entropy in the form of a lake of ice. The Limbo and the circle of the heretics are conceived in the light of distinctively Christian beliefs, but the remainder of the Inferno is defined in terms of nearly universal human insights and values. Theologically, it may strike some people as arbitrary that in Dante salvation and damnation depend on the state of the human soul at the moment when, perhaps by sudden accident, death occurs, although in fact that notion is not uniquely Dantean or Christian. But from a moral rather than theological perspective, the idea suggests in the most powerful way possible that all actions in life are of incalculable consequence, each containing in itself the essence of utter good or utter evil. Perhaps it is Dante's sense of this urgency that makes him consign the contemptible trimmers, who were neither good nor evil, to the outer vestibule of Hell, lest their presence in Hell proper make "the wicked gain pride by comparison" (Inferno III.42).

    Probably no great work of literature has a structure so precisely articulated as the Divine Comedy. *It is governed, texturally and architecturally, by the numbers 3, 9, and 10. The entire* Comedy *has 100 cantos, the square of the perfect number 10. Each of the three great divisions has 33 cantos (the first of the 34 cantos in the* Inferno *serving as a prelude to the entire work). There are 9 (3 times 3) circles or spheres in each of the three realms, to which is added another region of a different order (the vestibule of Hell, the Garden of Eden, the empyrean Heaven), making a total of 10. The entire poem is written in tercets, three-line stanzas, and the Italian rhyme scheme is* terza rima *("third rhyme"), a system of interlocking rhymes in the pattern* aba bcb cdc, *each end rhyme thus sounding three times. The tercet is the normal syntactical unit of statement, producing along with the rhyme scheme an effect of powerful but deliberate forward movement. The symbolism of threes is an ever-present acknowledgment of the divine Trinity. Dante's mind, like others in the Middle Ages, could imagine a God who is both love and mathematical order.*

    But the synthesizing imagination of Dante is best revealed not in such number symbolism but in the poem's total mode of understanding the structure of reality. Time is boldly conflated and twisted; sinners who have been in Hell for millennia coexist in an eternal now with those who have been dead for only a few years. The period of Dante's journey through Hell, from Good Friday to Easter Sunday, corresponds mythically to the time Jesus spent in the tomb. Cultures that were distinct on earth are homogenized in the hereafter, classical monsters and Christian demons reduced to a common denominator of allegorical and moral values. The boundaries between science, theology, philosophy, geography, history, and other branches of knowledge are virtually nonexistent; Dante hears lectures on politics and lunar astrophysics even in Paradise. Physical gravitation is closely identified with the spiritual operation of love, which is the motive power alike of the astronomical heavens and of every human act, good or bad. Evil and suffering, symbolized in Inferno XIV *by the tears of a gigantic Cretan statue weeping for the sorrows and sins of human history, move ever downward, channeled by Hell's four rivers to the motionless center of the universe; in the meantime, from the mountain of Purgatory on the other side of the globe the river of Lethe flows down to join the others in the same place, carrying with it the dead memories of the vices of the saved. Conversely, as the repentant move up the slopes of Purgatory, the burden of their evil propensities is quite literally lightened, so that like modern astronauts they feel the ascent easier and easier until, made perfect again in Eden, they rise to Heaven as naturally as flames fly upward.*

    The ultimate goal of Dante the pilgrim and of the poem is the direct vision of God in the uncircumscribed empyrean heaven. In describing this experience, the last cantos of the Paradise *achieve a sublimity unsurpassed in literature. There Dante must realize for us what is utterly suprasensory and beyond speech without relinquishing the poetic tools of language and sense imagery that are the poet's only means of communication. His imagistic media, as throughout the* Paradise, *are mainly light, color, and nearly abstract patterns. His subject is not only the Deity but the relation-*

ship of Deity to the immensely variegated, differentiated world of things, places, and people so much of which the Comedy *has revealed:*

> *In its depths I saw contained, bound with love*
> *in one volume, what is scattered*
> *on leaves throughout the world. . . . [Paradise XXXIII.85–87]*

The paradox, fundamental to any theistic vision, is that a God who is one and changeless created and sustains the teeming variety of our world.

It is impossible for translation to capture the exquisite sound effects of Dante's Italian, particularly the incantatory echoing of consonant and vowel sounds in lines such as Dei remi facemmo ali al folle volo *("we made wings of our oars for the mad flight"—*Inferno XXVI.125*). But in many other respects Dante's style and manner are unusually translatable. Although convoluted passages do occur, the hallmarks of Dante's usual style are directness and economy. He prefers verbs and nouns, using adjectives sparingly, and then more for utilitarian description than for atmosphere or ornament. (As an example, see Ulysses' famous speech in* Inferno XXXVI.91–142.*) Exactly because he is describing what none of us has seen, he is compelled, as a good technical writer is, to furnish lucid visual descriptions and analogies. His method is eminently dramatic, realized in the overt gestures and speech of his characters. The characterizations are masterful; the most memorable—Francesca, Farinata, Brunetto Latini, Ulysses, Ugolino—are accomplished in a few dozen lines. Much of this can be captured by a literal translator who, renouncing the hopeless effort to compete with Dante's versification, lets this most literal of poets speak directly to us in language as nearly unclouded as his own.*

FURTHER READING *(prepared by W. J. R.):* A fine biography for the general reader is Monroe Stearns' *Dante: Poet of Love*, 1965, which is also a good introduction to *The Divine Comedy*. Michele Barbi, *Life of Dante*, 1933, trans. by Paul C. Ruggiers, 1954, is divided into sections on biography, the minor works, and *The Divine Comedy*. Carlo Golino's *Dante Alighieri*, 1979, which also provides both biographical information and criticism, has good discussions of works other than *The Divine Comedy*. Background material for the study of Dante's *Comedy*, a canto-by-canto summary, and critical analysis are combined in Aldo S. Bernardo and Anthony L. Pellegrini, *A Critical Study Guide to Dante's "Divine Comedy,"* 1968. The visual aids in this work are particularly useful. A general appreciation of the *Comedy* is offered in Thomas Goddard Bergin's *Dante's "Divine Comedy,"* 1971, which is also good on the cosmology. George Holmes' *Dante*, 1980, in the Past Masters series, is a good introductory overview, of manageable length. For a historical introduction to the *Comedy*, see Erich Auerbach's *Dante, Poet of the Secular World*, 1929, trans. by Ralph Manheim, 1961. Auerbach's analysis of structure in the *Comedy* is also particularly readable and rewarding. *Dante: A Collection of Critical Essays*, ed. by J. Freccero, 1965, contains thirteen articles by Auerbach, Pirandello, and others. Selected cantos are interpreted in Mark Musa's *Advent at the Gates*, 1974. Musa's discussion of ambiguity in the characterization of Francesca is especially interesting. *From Time to Eternity*, ed. by Thomas Goddard Bergin, 1967, contains essays on Dante's Florence, religious theory of his time, and the genesis of the *Comedy*. Marianne Shapiro's *Woman, Earthly and Divine in the "Comedy" of Dante*, 1975, emphasizes the poet's relationship with Beatrice and offers a provocative discussion of Virgil's maternal and paternal aspects in the *Inferno*. Also valuable are David Nolan, ed., *Dante Commentaries: Eight Studies of "The Divine Comedy,"* 1977, and its companion volume, *Dante Soundings*, 1981.

THE DIVINE COMEDY

Translated, with interpolated summaries and
bracketed glosses, by H. R. Huse.

(Summaries of cantos omitted from the *Purgatory*
and *Paradise* are by Philip H. Wicksteed)

INFERNO

A SAMPLE OF THE ORIGINAL VERSE

*The opening tercets from Canto I will give readers an idea of the language and
form of the original work.*

Nel mezzo del cammin di nostra vita
   mi ritrovai per una selva oscura,
   chè la diritta via era smarrita.

Ah quanto a dir qual era è cosa dura
   esta selva selvaggia e aspra e forte
   che nel pensier rinnova la paura!

Tant'è amara che poco è più morte;
   ma per trattar del ben ch'io vi trovai,
   dirò dell'altre cose ch' i' v'ho scorte.

Io non so ben ridir com'io v'entrai,
   tant'era pieno di sonno a quel punto
   che la verace via abbandonai.   12

Ma poi ch'i' fui al piè d'un colle giunto,
   là dove terminava quella valle
   che m'avea di paura il cor compunto,

guardai in alto, e vidi le sue spalle
   vestite già de' raggi del pianeta
   che mena dritto altrui per ogni calle.

Allor fu la paura un poco queta
   che nel lago del cor m'era durata
   la notte chi'i' passai con tanta pièta.

E come quei che con lena affannata
   uscito fuor del pelago alla riva
   si volge all'acqua perigliosa e guata,   24

così l'animo mio, ch'ancor fuggiva,
   si volse a retro a rimirar lo passo
   che non lasciò già mai persona viva.

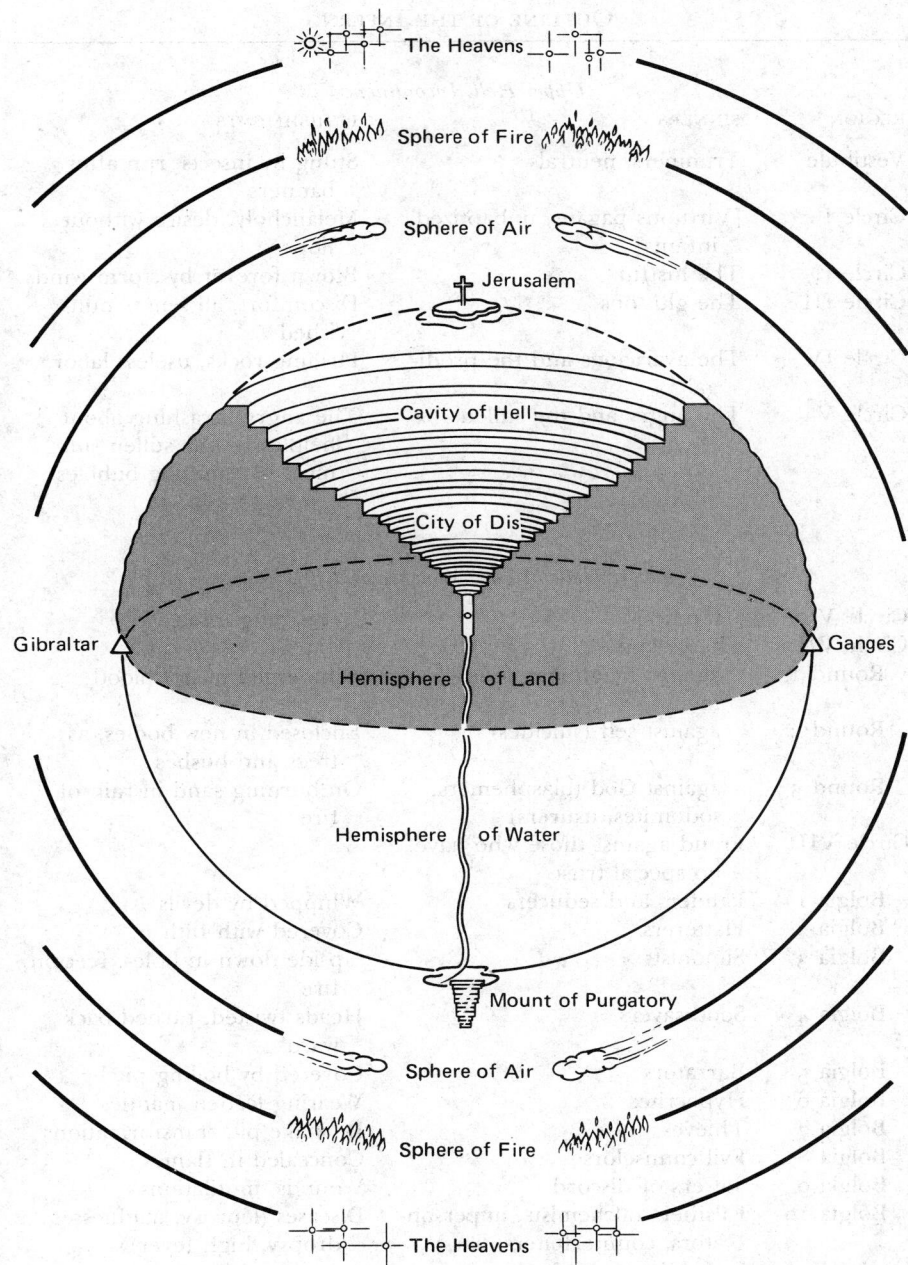

The Heavens

Sphere of Fire

Sphere of Air

Jerusalem

Cavity of Hell

City of Dis

Gibraltar   Ganges

Hemisphere   of Land

Hemisphere   of Water

Mount of Purgatory

Sphere of Air

Sphere of Fire

The Heavens

A diagram of the earth in the center of the universe.

Outline of the Inferno

Upper Hell, Incontinence

REGION	SINNERS	PUNISHMENTS
Vestibule	Trimmers, neutrals	Stung by insects, run after banners
Circle I	[Virtuous pagans, unbaptized infants]	Melancholy, desire without hope
Circle II	The lustful	Blown forever by storm winds
Circle III	The gluttons	Discomfort, all senses punished
Circle IV	The avaricious and the prodigal	Pushing rocks, useless labor
Circle V	The angry and the sullen	The angry thrashing about helplessly; the sullen submerged, emitting bubbles

Lower Hell, Malice (Violence and Fraud)

Circle VI	[Heretics]	In burning tombs
Circle VII	The violent	
Round 1	against neighbors, fellow men	Submerged in hot blood
Round 2	against self (suicides)	Enclosed in new bodies, as trees and bushes
Round 3	against God (blasphemers, sodomites, usurers)	On burning sand in rain of fire
Circle VIII	Fraud against those who have no special trust	
Bolgia 1	Panders and seducers	Whipped by devils
Bolgia 2	Flatterers	Covered with filth
Bolgia 3	Simonists	Upside down in holes, feet on fire
Bolgia 4	Soothsayers	Heads twisted, turned backward
Bolgia 5	Barrators	Covered by boiling pitch
Bolgia 6	Hypocrites	Wearing leaden mantles
Bolgia 7	Thieves	In snake pit, transformations
Bolgia 8	Evil counselors	Concealed in flames
Bolgia 9	Sowers of discord	Wounds, mutilations
Bolgia 10	Falsifiers (alchemists, impersonators, counterfeiters, liars)	Diseases (leprosy, madness, dropsy, high fever)
Circle IX	Fraudulent against those who have special trust	
Caïna	Murderers of kindred	In ice to necks, heads bent forward
Antenora	Traitors to party or country	In ice to necks

OUTLINE OF THE INFERNO *(continued)*

Lower Hell *(continued)*

REGION	SINNERS	PUNISHMENTS
Tolomea	Murderers of guests	In ice to necks, heads bent backward
Giudecca	Traitors to lords and benefactors	Completely submerged in ice

At the Center of the Earth *(Universe)*

Lucifer with Judas, Brutus, and Cassius in his three mouths, with three sets of wings sending forth a freezing blast of impotence, ignorance, and hatred.

NOTE: The souls in Circle I and Circle VI are outside of the classifications of Incontinence and Malice. They are guilty only from a Christian viewpoint, and Dante has to fit them as well as he can into the Aristotelian classification.

CANTO I

VIRGIL

The story begins on Thursday night, April 7, 1300. Dante, at the age of thirty-five, having completed half of man's traditional three-score years and ten, awakens to find himself in the forest of worldliness or sin. He cannot recall how he entered it; he had sunk, as men do, gradually and imperceptibly into sinful habits.

The night passes, and the sun (Divine Enlightenment or Righteous Choice) rises behind the Mount of Rectitude.

In the middle of the journey of our life
    I came to my senses in a dark forest,
    for I had lost the straight path.

Oh, how hard it is to tell
    what a dense, wild, and tangled wood this was,
    the thought of which renews my fear!

So terrible it is that death is hardly worse.
    But to reveal the good that I found there,
    I will speak first of other things.

I cannot tell how I entered it,
    so heavy with slumber was I at the moment
    when I abandoned the true way.

But when I had reached the foot of a hill,
    there where the valley ended
    which had filled my heart with fear,

I looked up, and saw its shoulders
    clothed already with the rays of the planet
    which leads men straight on every path.

12

Then the fear was somewhat quieted
    which had lasted in the lake of my heart
    during the night I had passed so piteously.

And as a seafarer, who has escaped from the storm
    to the shore, turns with wearied breath
    to the turbulent waters and gazes,   24

so I, still fleeing in my mind,
    turned back to look at the pass
    which no one before had ever left alive.

> *As Dante starts to climb the hill, a leopard, the symbol of luxury or lust, appears.*
> *It offers some opposition, but the early hour and the buoyant influence of Spring,*
> *the season when the universe was supposed to have been created, give him hope.*
> *Then a lion (Pride) assails him, rushing on with such fury that the very air*
> *around seems to tremble. And finally a she-wolf, the symbol of avarice or greed,*
> *the most widespread of vices. Dante (Mankind) feels that he could overcome the*
> *others, but at the sight of the wolf, he despairs.*[1]

After I had rested a little my weary body,
    I took my way over the lonely slope
    [climbing][2] so that the firm foot always was the lower.

And behold! almost at the beginning of the rise,
    a leopard, light, and very nimble,
    which was covered with a spotted hide!

It did not move from in front of me,
    but instead so blocked my way
    that several times I turned to go back.   36

The time was the beginning of the morning,
    and the sun was rising with those stars
    that were with it when Divine Love

first set those beautiful things in motion,
    so that I found cause for good hope
    concerning the beast with the gaily spotted hide

in the hour of the day and in the sweet season;
    but even so I feared again
    at the sight of a lion that confronted me.

It appeared to be coming at me
    with head erect and with ravenous hunger,
    so that the air seemed afraid of it,   48

[1] This is a traditional interpretation of the allegory of the three beasts. Other explanations are possible—for example, that the leopard is Fraud, the lion Violence, and the wolf Incontinence. These three evils would correspond to the tripartite classification of sins in Dante's hell.

[2] The words within square brackets, here and later in *The Divine Comedy*, are explanations inserted by the translator.

and a she-wolf came also, burdened
 in her leanness with all cravings,
 and which has indeed made many live in sorrow.

The sight of her brought such fear
 and such distress upon me
 that I lost hope of the ascent.

And as a gambler who gladly wins,
 but when the time comes for him to lose,
 weeps and is saddened in all his thoughts,

so I changed as the restless beast advanced
 against me, and little by little
 drove me down to where the sun is silent.   60

> *At this critical moment, Virgil (Reason, Philosophy), whose voice has long been
> unheard, appears. Dante forgets for a moment his despair, and bends reverently
> before his master. Then he mentions the wolf which has blocked his (and man-
> kind's) reform. Virgil explains the nature of the greed for which the wolf stands:
> it is an element in nearly all the crimes men commit. But a "hound," a redeemer
> (variously identified), possibly from between the towns of Feltro and Montefeltro,
> will ultimately come.*

While I was falling back to a lower place
 someone appeared before me whose voice
 from long silence seemed faint.

When I saw him in that desolation,
 "Have pity on me!" I cried to him,
 "whoever you are, whether a shade or a real man."

He answered, "Not a man now,
 a man once I was, and both my parents
 were Lombards, Mantuans by city.

I was born *sub Julio*[3] although late,
 and I lived in Rome under the good Augustus
 at the time of the false and lying gods.   72

I was a poet and sang of [Aeneas] that just son
 of Anchises who came from Troy
 after proud Ilion had been burned.

But why do you return to such misery?
 Why not climb the delightful mountain
 which is the beginning and the source of all joy?"

"Now are you that Virgil, that spring
 which pours forth so broad a stream of speech?"
 I answered him with bashful brow,

[3] "Under Julius Caesar."

"Oh, honor and light of other poets,
    may the long study and great love help me
    which made me search through your volume!   84

You are my master and my author;
    you alone are the one from whom I took
    the style which has done me honor.

See the beast because of which I turned;
    save me from her, famous sage,
    for she makes my whole body tremble!"

"You must take another road," he answered
    after he had seen me weep,
    "if you want to escape from this wild place;

for the animal of which you complain
    lets no one pass along her way,
    but so hinders that she kills,   96

and she has a nature so vicious and perverse
    that she never satisfies her greedy desires,
    and after feeding is hungrier than before.

Many are the animals with which she mates,
    and there will be still more until the Hound comes
    that will make her die in pain.

He will not feed on earth or pelf,
    but on wisdom, love and virtue,
    and his nation will be between Feltro and Feltro.

He will be the savior of that humbled Italy
    for whom the virgin Camilla,
    Euryalus, Turnus, and Nisus[4] died of wounds.   108

He will hunt her through every town
    until he has driven her back to Hell,
    whence Envy [of man's happiness] first released her.

> *Now Virgil proposes to lead Dante through Hell and Purgatory, and outlines the course of the journey. In Heaven, Beatrice (Revelation, Theology) will be the guide.*
>
> *In his humble submission to the mystery of Divine Justice, Virgil accuses himself of "rebellion" against God's law. There is a note of sadness in his words, condemned as he is, for having lived before Christ, to an eternity of longing. Dante generously suggests his apology by a reference to the God the ancient poet did not and, of course, could not know.*

Therefore I think it best for you
    to follow me, and I will be your guide
    to take you through an eternal place [Hell]

[4] Characters in the second half of Virgil's *Aeneid,* which describes war in Italy.

where you will hear despairing cries
    and will see the tormented spirits
    each of whom proclaims the second death [damnation],

and you will see [in Purgatory] those who are contented
    in the fire, because they hope to come,
    whenever it may be, among the blessed,   120

to whom, then, if you wish to ascend,
    a guide worthier than I will take you:
    to her I will entrust you when I leave,

for that Emperor who reigns up there,
    because I was rebellious to His law,
    does not want me as a guide to His city.

Everywhere He reigns and there He rules;
    there is His seat and His high throne,
    O happy are those whom He chooses!"

And I to him, "Poet, I beg you
    by that God you did not know, in order
    that I may flee from this evil and worse,   132

take me where you have said,
    so that I may see St. Peter's gate
    and those you proclaim so sad."

Then he moved on, and I followed him.

CANTO II

BEATRICE

It is now the evening of Good Friday. The sun which had cheered Dante is going down, and the animals on earth (all workers in God's universe) are returning home from their labors of the day. In this dark moment, Dante's courage fails, and he wonders about the advisability of the journey. It is true, he reflects, that both Aeneas and St. Paul, the "Chosen Vessel," visited the future world; but Aeneas' visit led to the founding of the Roman Empire, divinely ordained to be the seat of the papacy, and St. Paul brought from Heaven a confirmation of the true faith. Dante disclaims any such mission.

The day was departing, and the darkening air
    was taking the creatures that are on earth
    from their daily toil, and I alone

was preparing to endure the hardship
    both of the journey and of the pity
    which unerring memory will relate.

O Muses, O lofty genius, aid me now!
    O mind which inscribed what I saw,
    here your worth will be revealed.

I began, "Poet, you who guide me,
    consider my strength, whether it is great enough
    before you commit me to the arduous journey.   12

You say that [Aeneas] the father of Sylvius,
    still subject to corruption,
    went bodily to the eternal world;

but that the Adversary of all Evil [God]
    should be gracious to him, thinking of the result
    and of who and what he was,

does not seem unreasonable to a thoughtful man;
    for he was chosen in the Empyrean heaven
    to be father of glorious Rome

and of her empire, both of which
    were established for the holy place
    where the successors of St. Peter sit.   24

On this journey through which you honor him,
    he heard things which led to his victory
    and to the papal mantle.

Afterward the Chosen Vessel [St. Paul] went there
    to bring comfort to the faith
    which is the beginning of the way of salvation.

But why should I go? Who grants it?
    I am not Aeneas, nor am I Paul;
    for that neither I nor others believe me worthy.

Therefore, if I allow myself to go,
    I fear the journey may be folly: you are wise
    and understand better than I can speak."   36

And, as a person unwills what he wills,
    and with new thoughts changes purpose,
    holding back from what he has started,

so I became on that dark slope,
    for, by thinking, I delayed the undertaking
    that I had begun so quickly.

> *Not deceived by this rationalizing, Virgil reproves Dante for being afraid. Then,
> to reassure him, he describes the occasion of his coming, a scene in the first circle
> of Hell where the souls of the virtuous pagans are "in suspense," longing for an
> understanding of God and of the mystery of life, with the realization that they can
> never attain it.*

"If I have understood your words rightly,"
    answered that magnanimous shade,
    "your resolution is dulled by cowardice

which often distracts a man
    and turns him away from honorable deeds,
    as imperfect sight causes an animal to shy.   48

To free you from this fear, I will tell
    why I came and what I heard
    when I first took pity on you.

I was among those who are in suspense,
    and a lady [Beatrice] called to me
    so blessed and beautiful that I asked her to command.

Her eyes shone more than the stars,
    and with an angelic voice,
    softly and sweetly she spoke to me,

'O courteous Mantuan soul whose fame
    still lasts on the earth, and will last
    as long as the world,   60

my friend, but not the friend of Fortune,
    is so impeded on the deserted slope
    that in fear he has turned back,

and, from what I have heard in Heaven,
    I am afraid he is already so lost
    that I have come too late for his relief.

Now go to him, and with your eloquent speech
    and with all else needful for his escape
    help him, so that I may be consoled.

I am Beatrice, bidding you to go;
    I come from a place to which I would return;
    Love moved me and makes me speak.   72

When I am in the presence of my Lord
    I will praise you often to Him.'
    She was silent then and I began,

'O lady of virtue [Revelation] through whom alone
    the human race excels all creatures contained
    within the heaven of the smallest orbit [all on earth],

your command so pleases me that complying
    if already begun would seem slow;
    you need only to reveal your desire;

but tell me why you do not shrink
    from descending to this depth from the broad expanse
    to which you are eager to return.'   84

*Beatrice explains how, although pitying Dante, she can feel no distress at the
working of Divine Justice.*

*The formal allegory of the scene in Heaven she then describes is as follows: Mary
(Divine Mercy) sends Lucia (Illuminating Grace) to prepare the way for Beatrice
(Revelation) whom Dante (Mankind) will perceive when Virgil (Reason) makes
him ready to behold her.*

'Since you wish to know so much
   I will tell you briefly,' she answered,
   'why I do not fear to come here.

We should be afraid only of things
   which can harm, not of others,
   since they are not fearful.

Through God's grace I am formed in such a way
   that your misery does not touch me,
   nor does a flame of this burning hurt me.

There is a gentle lady in Heaven [Mary]
   whose pity is aroused by the distress of him
   to whom I send you, and who tempers harsh judgment.   96

She called upon Lucia and said in her request,
   "Your faithful one now has need of you,
   and I recommend him to you."

Lucia, the enemy of all cruelty,
   arose and came to where I was
   seated by the ancient Rachel.

She said, "Beatrice, true praise of God,
   why do you not help him who loved you so much
   that through you he arose above the common crowd?

Do you not hear the pity of his cries?
   Do you not see Death struggling with him
   on the river [of evil] not less terrible than the sea?"   108

On earth men were never so swift
   to seek gain and flee from harm
   as I was after these words were spoken

to come here from my blessed seat,
   trusting in your noble speech
   which honors you and those who have heard it.'

After she said this to me
   she turned away her shining eyes in tears,
   which made me still readier to go,

and to you I came as she desired.
   I freed you from the beast
   which had cut off the short way up the fair mount.   120

So what is it? Why, why do you hold back?
   Why keep such cowardice in your heart?
   Why are you not bold and free,

since three such holy ladies
  care for you in the court of Heaven,
  and my words promise you so much good?"

As little flowers, bent down and closed by the frost of night,
  stand up, all open on their stems,
  when the sun comes back to warm and brighten them,

so I revived my failing strength,
  and so much boldness rushed into my heart
  that I began like one set free,   132

"O compassionate lady who gave aid to me!
  O courteous shade who obeyed so quickly
  the true words she spoke to you!

You have disposed my heart
  with such desire for going by your account
  that I have regained my first intent.

Now go, for one wish is in both of us,
  you my leader [guide], my lord [superior], my master [teacher]!"
  Thus I spoke to him, and when he started

I followed on the deep and wild way.

CANTO III

THE ENTRANCE

*In the faint light of the evening of Good Friday, the anniversary of the Crucifix-
ion when, according to the Creed, Christ "entered into Hell," the two travelers
move on to the gate over which appears a fearful inscription pointing out the woe
within, the eternal pain, the people lost even to hope. Divine Justice (incompre-
hensible to reason alone) moved God in his three-fold attributes of Power, Wisdom, and Love to create Hell. It was made when only eternal things (the elements, the heavens, and the angels) existed, and it also will last and function
eternally.*

*On reading these words Dante begins again to doubt, but, ashamed to confess his
fear, he seeks delay or assurance by asking about their meaning which, incidentally, is painfully explicit. Virgil, undeceived, reproves Dante for his weakness.*

THROUGH ME YOU GO INTO THE CITY OF GRIEF,
  THROUGH ME YOU GO INTO THE PAIN THAT IS ETERNAL,
  THROUGH ME YOU GO AMONG PEOPLE LOST.

JUSTICE MOVED MY EXALTED CREATOR;
  THE DIVINE POWER MADE ME,
  THE SUPREME WISDOM, AND THE PRIMAL LOVE.

BEFORE ME ALL CREATED THINGS WERE ETERNAL,
  AND ETERNAL I WILL LAST.
  ABANDON EVERY HOPE, YOU WHO ENTER HERE.

These words of a dark coloring
    I saw written above a gate; whereupon I said,
    "Master, their meaning is hard for me."   12

Then he spoke like one who understands:
    "Here you must give up all distrust,
    here all cowardice must end.

We have come to the place where I said
    that you would see the woeful people
    who have lost the good of the intellect.

And after he had taken me by the hand,
    with a cheerful look which comforted me,
    he drew me within the secret place [the eternal world].

> *On entering, Dante sees little because of the darkness, but hears sounds which he*
> *distinguishes gradually as cries, languages, words, accents, voices, and finally as*
> *the dull noise of blows. Virgil contemptuously refuses to waste words on the souls*
> *here. They are the trimmers, the mediocre, the poor in spirit, the neutrals, joined*
> *with the angels who refused to take sides in the revolt against God. They are in*
> *a kind of vestibule, outside of Hell proper. Their punishment is slight compared*
> *to those which come later, yet they are envious of every other lot.*

There, sighs, lamentations, and deep wailings
    resounded through the starless air,
    so that at first I began to weep.   24

Diverse tongues, horrible languages,
    words of pain, accents of rage,
    voices loud and hoarse, and the sounds of blows

made a tumult which moved forever
    in that air unchanged by time,
    as sand eddies in a whirlwind.

And I said, my head girt with horror,
    "Master, what is it that I hear,
    and who are these people so overcome by pain?"

Then he to me, "This miserable fate
    afflicts the wretched souls of those
    who lived without infamy and without praise.   36

They are joined with that choir of wicked angels
    who were neither rebellious
    nor faithful to God, but for themselves.

The heavens, to remain beautiful, drove them out,
    nor would deep Hell receive them
    lest the wicked gain pride by comparison."

And I, "Master, what is so burdensome
    that it makes them lament loudly?"
    He answered, "Briefly I will tell you.

They have no hope of death,
    and their blind life is so debased
    that they are envious of every other lot.   48

The world does not grant them any fame;
    pity [of Heaven] and justice [of Hell] alike disdain them.
    Let us not speak of them, but look and pass on."

Some of these souls, neutral and perhaps sedentary in life, are condemned now to active partisanship. The poet recognizes one, but will not distinguish him with a name. Most commentators have identified him as Celestine V, a pope who, by his refusal to keep his office, allowed Dante's great enemy, Boniface VIII, to rise to power. There are less scandalous interpretations, however, notably as Pontius Pilate, who refused justice to Christ and who offers a better motivation for the extreme contempt shown here.

And I, looking, saw a banner
    which, circling, moved so fast
    that it seemed to scorn all rest,

and behind it came such a throng of people
    that I never would have believed
    that death could have undone so many.

After I had recognized some of them,
    I saw and knew the shade of him
    who, through cowardice, made the great refusal.   60

At once I understood and was certain
    that this was the sect of the wicked
    displeasing both to God and to His enemies.

These wretches, who had never really lived,
    were naked and stung constantly
    by hornets and wasps that were there.

These made their faces stream with blood
    which, mixed with tears, was consumed
    by loathsome maggots at their feet.

When Dante asks about a crowd in the distance, Virgil tells him to wait and see. Taking this as a reproach, our poet remains silent for a long time.

As the travelers move on, Charon appears, the ancient boatman of the Styx, who prophesies Dante's ultimate salvation and whom Virgil appeases with a kind of conjuring formula.

When I began to look farther on
    I saw people on the shore of a great river;
    whereupon I said, "Master, now grant   72

that I should know who they are
    and what makes them so ready to pass over,
    as I discern through the faint light."

And he to me, "These things will be known to you
    when we stay our steps
    on the sad bank of the Acheron."

Then with eyes ashamed and lowered,
    fearing that my words might have offended him,
    I kept from speaking until we reached the stream.

And behold! coming toward us in a skiff
    an old man, white with ancient locks,
    shouting, "Woe to you, depraved spirits;   84

hope not ever to see Heaven.
    I come to take you to the other shore
    into eternal darkness, into heat and cold.

And you there, living soul,
    get away from these who are dead."
    But when he saw that I did not leave,

"By another way, at other ports," he said,
    "you will come ashore, not here;
    a lighter boat will carry you."

And my guide, "Charon, do not be disturbed;
    this is wished for where the power is
    to do what is wished; and ask no more."   96

Then were quieted the woolly cheeks
    of the boatman of the livid marsh
    who, around his eyes, had rings of flame.

> *The souls are impelled by a kind of instinct to seek their proper place, since sin leads inevitably to its own results, its own suffering.*
>
> *We are not told how Dante crosses the river. There is a flash, an earthquake, and he falls unconscious. On awakening he is on the other bank.*

But those weary and naked souls
    changed color and gnashed their teeth
    as soon as they heard the cruel words.

They cursed God and their parents,
    the human race, and the place, time, and seed
    of their begetting and of their birth.

Then, all together they withdrew,
    weeping loudly, to the accursed shore
    which awaits every man without fear of God.   108

Charon the demon, with eyes like glowing coals,
    beckoning to them, gathered them in,
    and hit with an oar any who delayed.

As in autumn the leaves fall
     one after the other, until the branch
     sees all its spoils upon the ground,

so, the evil seed of Adam
     fell to that shore, one by one, and at signals,
     as the falcon does at its recall.

Thus they go over the dark water,
     and before they have landed on the other shore,
     again on this side a new crowd assembles.   120

"My son," said the courteous master,
     "those who die in the wrath of God
     gather here from every country,

and they are ready to pass the river,
     for Divine Justice so spurs them
     that fear is changed into desire.

Along here no good spirit ever passes;
     therefore, if Charon complains of you,
     you can understand what his words imply."

When he had ended, the dark country
     trembled so that from fright
     my memory bathes me still with sweat.   132

The tearful land produced a blast
     which flashed a crimson light
     conquering all my senses;

and I fell, like one overcome by sleep.

CANTO IV

LIMBO

When Dante awakens from his swoon he is in Limbo, the first circle of Hell. He interprets Virgil's pallor as due to fear, but learns that it comes from pity for those in the ancient poet's own circle. Although Dante still refrains from questioning, Virgil is anxious to point out that the shades here committed no sin, but died unbaptized or lived before Christ. Their damnation is an article of faith, beyond man's understanding. Here there is no torment other than a sense of unfulfill-ment, a feeling that expresses itself in melancholy, in suspense, in a vague longing for knowledge of God and for a solution of the mystery of life without hope of ever having either.

The deep sleep into which I fell was broken
     by heavy thunder, so that I started,
     like one awakened by force,

and having risen, I glanced around
     and looked intently with rested eyes
     to discover where I was.

In truth, I found myself on the brink
    of the dolorous valley of the abyss
    which resounds with the sound of countless cries.

It was so dark, deep, and cloudy
    that in looking toward the bottom
    I could discern nothing.   12

"Now, let us go into the blind world,"
    the poet began all pale,
    "I will be first and you second."

And I, noticing his color, said,
    "How shall I come if you are afraid,
    you who always comfort me in my doubt?"

And he to me, "The anguish
    of the people down there paints on my face
    the pity which you mistake for fear.

Let us go, for the long way impels us."
    Thus he moved on and made me enter
    the first circle which girds the abyss.   24

Here, so far as one could tell by listening,
    there was no lament, but only sighs
    which made the eternal air tremble.

They came from the sadness without torment
    felt by the great crowd
    of children and of women and of men.

My good master said to me, "You do not ask
    what spirits these are. Now,
    I want you to know before you go farther

that they did not sin, but having merit
    was not enough, for they lacked baptism,
    which is a portal of the faith you hold;   36

and if they lived before Christianity
    they did not worship God rightly;
    among such as these am I myself.

For such defects, not for other faults,
    are we lost, and afflicted only
    in that we live in longing without hope."

Great grief gripped my heart when I heard this,
    for I knew that people of much worth
    were in that Limbo in suspense.

*Dante now risks a timid question. He wants to know about the "Harrowing of
Hell," when Christ was supposed to have gone to Limbo to release the ancient
Hebrews who had believed in His coming. After the explanation the poets move*

on to a special region reserved for the great men of the past. Virgil (as Reason)
approves the recognition of Dante as the sixth in rank of the world's poets.

"Tell me, Master, tell me, sir," I began,
    wishing to be assured of the faith
    that destroys every error,   48

"did any ever through his own merit
    or another's leave here to be blessed?"
    And he, understanding my veiled speech, answered,

"I was new in this condition
    when I saw a Powerful One [Christ]
    crowned with the sign of victory [the cross as an aureole].

He took from here our first parent,
    Abel his son, and Noah,
    obedient Moses, the lawgiver,

the patriarch Abraham, and David, the king,
    Israel [Jacob] with his father and his sons,
    and Rachel for whom he [Jacob] did so much,   60

and many others, and he made them blessed,
    and I wish you to know that before then
    no human souls were ever saved."

We did not stop because of his remarks,
    but kept passing through the forest—
    the forest, I mean, of crowded spirits.

Our way had not yet taken us far
    after my slumber when I saw a light
    which dispelled a hemisphere of darkness.

We were still distant from the glow
    but not too far for me to discern
    that notable people occupied that place.   72

"O you who honor every science and art," I said,
    "who are these whose great merit
    separates them from the others?"

And he answered, "The deserved fame
    which still honors them in your life
    gains favor in Heaven, and thus promotes them."

Meanwhile a voice was heard, saying,
    "Honor the greatest poet;
    his shade which had left is returning."

When this voice was silent
    I saw four great figures come to us,
    their faces neither sad nor gay.   84

My good master began to speak:
    "See that one with sword in hand,
    coming ahead of the others as their lord.

He is Homer, the sovereign poet;
    the other, following, is Horace, the satirist;
    Ovid is the third, and Lucan the last.

Since each shares with me the title 'poet'
    which the single voice pronounced,
    they do me honor, and in doing this do well."

Thus I saw assembled the school
    of that lord of the lofty song who soars
    above the others like an eagle.   96

After they had talked together a little
    they turned to me with signs of greeting,
    and my master smiled at that.

And still more honor they showed me
    by making me one of their group,
    so that I was the sixth among such sages.

> *The poets now come to the Castle of Wisdom or Fame, surrounded by the walls of*
> *the cardinal and speculative virtues and defended by a moat which may represent*
> *eloquence or desire for knowledge. They pass through the gates of the seven*
> *liberal arts. On a kind of enameled meadow within, the great spirits of the past*
> *appear: first the Trojans, Greeks, and legendary figures of early Rome; then*
> *philosophers, scientists, mathematicians, and doctors; and finally the Moorish*
> *scholar Averroës.*

Thus we continued toward the light,
    speaking of matters concerning which silence
    is as fitting now as speech was then,

and we arrived at the foot of a noble castle,
    seven times encircled by high walls,
    defended all around by a fair rivulet.   108

This we crossed as if on solid ground.
    Through seven gates I passed with these sages
    and we arrived on a meadow of fresh verdure.

There we saw people dignified and grave,
    of great authority in their semblance;
    they spoke seldom, and with soft voices.

Afterward we withdrew to one side
    to an open place, luminous and high,
    from which all could be seen.

There, standing on the green enamel,
    the great spirits were shown to me,
    to have seen whom I feel exalted.   120

I saw Electra[5] with many companions,
    among whom I recognized Hector and Aeneas,
    and Caesar clad in arms, with hawklike eyes.

I saw Camilla and Penthesilea
    on the other side, and I saw the Latian king,
    sitting with Lavinia, his daughter.

I saw that Brutus[6] who expelled the Tarquin,
    Lucretia, Julia, Marcia, and Cornelia;
    and alone, to one side, the Saladin.

When I had raised my eyes a little higher
    I saw the Master of the Knowing [Aristotle]
    sitting with his philosophic family.   132

All looked at him, all did him honor;
    there I saw Socrates and Plato
    who stood ahead of the others closest to him:

Democritus, who thought the world due to chance;
    Diogenes, Anaxagoras, and Thales,
    Empedocles, Heraclitus, and Zeno;

and I saw the good compiler of the qualities [of plants],
    Dioscorides, I mean; and Orpheus,
    Tully [Cicero], Linus, and Seneca, the moralist;

Euclid the geometer, and Ptolemy,
    Hippocrates, Avicenna, and Galen,
    and Averroës who made the great commentary [on Aristotle].   144

I cannot enumerate them all fully;
    my long theme so drives me on that many times
    my words fall short of the facts.

The sixfold company diminished to two [Virgil and Dante];
    by another way my wise guide took me,
    out of the quiet into the trembling air,

and I came to a place where no light shines.

CANTO V

FRANCESCA DA RIMINI

Since Hell is like an inverted cone, the circumference of each succeeding circle diminishes.

The guardian of the second ring is Minos, the ancient judge of the dead, represented by Dante as having some of the characteristics of a medieval demon. Like

---

[5] Not the daughter of Agamemnon and Clytemnestra but rather the mother of Dardanus, founder of Troy.

[6] This is not the assassin of Julius Caesar; that Brutus appears at the center of hell in Canto XXXIV. The Brutus referred to here founded the ancient Roman republic.

> *Charon, Minos offers a slight opposition which is overcome by the conjuring formula.*

Thus I descended from the first circle
    down to the second which encloses less space
    but so much more pain that it moves to tears.

There Minos stands, horrible and snarling,
    examining the offenses, judging,
    and sending down as he girds himself—

I mean that when an ill-born soul
    comes before him, it confesses wholly,
    and that discerner of sin,

seeing what place in Hell belongs to it,
    encircles himself with his tail as many times
    as the degrees he wants it to descend.   12

Always many stand in front of him;
    they come in turns to their judgment,
    confess and hear, and then are hurled below.

"O you who come to the painful refuge,"
    Minos said when he saw me,
    interrupting the work of his great office,

"consider how you entered and in whom you trust;
    do not let the breadth of the entrance deceive you."
    And my guide to him, "Why do you cry out?

Do not impede his fated going.
    It is wished for where the power is
    to do what is wished; so ask no more."   24

> *The poets hear and see the shades guilty of lust. A landslide caused by an earth-quake at the time of the Crucifixion perhaps reminds the restless souls as they pass of the impossibility of their redemption. Dante pities more than blames these victims of the flesh and of the imagination. They pass like birds in autumn flight.*

Now I begin to hear the sad notes of pain,
    now I have come to where
    loud cries beat upon my ears.

I have reached a place mute of all light
    which roars like the sea in a tempest
    when beaten by conflicting winds.

The infernal storm which never stops
    drives the spirits in its blast;
    whirling and beating, it torments them.

When they come in front of the landslide,
    they utter laments, moans, and shrieks;
    there they curse the Divine Power.   36

I learned that to such a torment
    carnal sinners are condemned
    who subject their reason to desire.

And, as starlings are borne by their wings
    in the cold season, in a broad and dense flock,
    so that blast carries the evil spirits.

Here, there, up, and down, it blows them;
    no hope ever comforts them
    of rest or even of less pain.

And as cranes go chanting their lays,
    making a long line of themselves in the air,
    so I saw coming, uttering laments,   48

shades born by that strife of winds.

> *Dante is eager to know who is punished here. No vulgar examples are cited but
> only glamorous figures of the ancient and medieval past whom love too com-
> pletely mastered. Perhaps our poet suspects already that Francesca da Rimini
> and her lover are here. In any case he asks to speak to two who seem unusually
> light and is told to address them in the name of love, to which, in a nobler form,
> all his own life was a dedication. The real appeal, however, is in the sympathy
> expressed by the words, "O wearied souls!" Like doves borne on by desire,
> Francesca and Paolo leave their company, so responsive are they still to the
> slightest note of affection.*

I asked, "Master, who are these people
    whom the black air so punishes?"

"The first of those about whom
    you want to know," he said to me,
    "was an empress over many peoples,

by the vice of luxury so subdued
    that she made lust lawful in her decrees
    to take away the blame she had incurred.

She is Semiramis who, we read,
    succeeded Ninus, her spouse;
    she held the land that now the Sultan rules.   60

The other is she [Dido] who killed herself
    after breaking faith with the ashes of Sichaeus;
    next comes luxurious Cleopatra.

See Helen [of Troy] for whom
    so many bad years revolved, and the great Achilles
    whose last battle was with love.[7]

See Paris, Tristan,"—and he pointed out and named

[7] Dante knew a medieval tradition according to which Achilles, as a result of love for a
Trojan princess, was ambushed and killed.

more than a thousand shades
    whom love had taken from our life.

After I had heard my teacher
    name the knights and ladies of olden times,
    pity overcame me, and I felt dismayed.   72

I began, "Poet, willingly would I speak
    with those two who go together
    and seem so light upon the wind."

And he to me, "Wait until they come closer,
    then entreat them by the love
    which impels them and they will come."

As soon as the wind brought them to us,
    I raised my voice, "O wearied souls,
    come speak to us if it is not forbidden."

As doves summoned by their desire,
    with wings raised and firm, sail through the air,
    borne on to their sweet nest by their will alone,   84

so those spirits moved from the band where Dido is,
    coming to us through the malignant air,
    so responsive were they to my affectionate cry.

*Now Francesca speaks, and her first words are an implied prayer to God whose
mysterious justice has condemned her beyond remission, an unselfish prayer for
this living soul who has shown them pity. It is a prayer for the "peace" which
romantic and illicit love can never know. In her heart's response to Dante's
simple words, she treats him already as "gracious" and "benign" and exaggerates
her own misdoing. Her story is a mere outline, told partly in terms of the
maxims of courtly love. With ladylike reticence she does not name herself or
Paolo, her brother-in-law and lover, or even the city where she was born. Death
itself would not have been so tragic: one moment for repentance might have
permitted her to be saved; it was the suddenness of her and Paolo's death that was
so cruel. Caïna, at the bottom of Hell, where traitors to kindred are punished,
awaits her husband who surprised and killed them.*

"O living creature, gracious and benign,
    going through the dark air
    visiting us who stained the earth with blood,

if the King of the universe were friendly to us
    we would pray to Him for your peace,
    since you pity our perverse evil.

Whatever you are pleased to hear from us or say
    we will relate and listen to,
    while the wind, as now, is silent.   96

The city [Ravenna] where I was born
    lies on the shore where the Po descends
    with all its tributaries to find peace.

Love which flames quickly in noble hearts
    was kindled in this soul by the fair body
    taken from me; the manner [of that taking] still offends.

Love that exempts no one beloved from loving
    caught me so strongly with his charm
    that, as you see, it still does not leave me.

Love led us to one death together.
    Caïna waits for him who quenched our lives."
    These words were borne from them to us.   108

On hearing this delicate outline of the tragedy, Dante bows his head, perhaps recalling who the speaker is, and then naming Francesca, he asks, in words as respectful and delicate as her own, about the immediate cause and occasion of her sin. Although she dislikes to recall the intimate details, she speaks, unable to refuse an affectionate appeal. There was no premeditation in her sin. She and Paolo had been reading a love story without suspecting the effect it might have. One moment of weakness overcame them, a moment which ended their reading and their lives and which stands now in contrast to eternity.

When I heard those afflicted souls
    I bent down my face, and held it low so long
    that the poet said, "Of what are you thinking?"

When I answered I began, "Alas!
    how many sweet thoughts, what desire
    led them to the woeful pass!"

Then I turned to them and said,
    "Francesca, your suffering
    makes me weep with sorrow and with pity,

But tell me, at the time of the sweet sighs,
    by what means and how love permitted you
    to know the dubious desires."   120

And she to me, "There is no greater pain
    than to recall a happy time in misery
    and this your teacher knows;

but if to learn the first root of our love
    you have such desire, I will answer
    like one who speaks and weeps.

One day for our delight we were reading
    about Lancelot, how love constrained him;
    alone we were and without any suspicion.

Several times that reading made our glances meet
    and changed the color of our faces;
    but one moment alone overcame us.   132

When we read how the fond smile [of Guinevere]
    was kissed by such a lover,
    he, who never will be separated from me,

kissed me, on my lips, all trembling.
    A Gallehaut [pander] was the book and he who wrote it.
    That day we read no farther."

While one spirit was saying this
    the other wept, so that from pity
    I fainted, as if I had been dying,

and I fell, as a dead body falls.

CANTO VI

The Gluttons

On recovering my senses, which were stunned
    by pity for the two kinsfolk
    who overwhelmed me with sadness,

new torments and new tormented shades
    I see around me, wherever I move
    and wherever I turn to gaze.

The poets are now among the gluttons who are lying like pigs in a sty under a constant, unvarying rain. Although the punishments here are relatively mild, they are particularly distasteful to the luxury-loving. All the senses are afflicted: sight by the dismal setting, touch by the cold rain, smell and taste by the stench, and hearing by the loud barking of Cerberus, the three-headed dog, the bestial guardian of this circle. Cerberus is appeased, not by a honey cake, as in the Aeneid, but by dirt, to emphasize further the filthiness of gluttony.

I am in the third circle of the rain,
    eternal, accursed, cold, and heavy;
    its amount and kind never change.

Large hailstones, dirty water, and snow
    pour down through the dark air;
    the ground that receives them stinks.   12

Cerberus, the fierce and cruel beast,
    barks doglike with three throats
    over those submerged there.

His eyes are red, his beard greasy and black,
    his belly large, his paws armed with claws;
    grasping the spirits, he flays and tears them.

The rain makes them howl like dogs;
    they use one side to shelter the other;
    often they turn, the profane wretches.

When Cerberus, the monster, saw us,
    he opened his mouths and showed his teeth,
    trembling in all his limbs.   24

And my leader, opening his hands,
   took some earth and threw handfuls
   into the ravenous gullets.

As a barking dog, longing for food,
   grows quiet after he has seized it,
   since he thinks only of eating,

so did those filthy heads of the demon Cerberus
   who thunders over the shades,
   making them wish they were deaf.

A soul nicknamed "Ciacco" (the pig) recognizes Dante but is himself unrecogniz-
able since the bestial vice of gluttony disfigures. To spare the feelings of this shade
Dante suggests that perhaps Ciacco's pain prevented the recognition.

We passed over the spirits subdued
   by the heavy rain, placing our feet
   on their nothingness which appears as flesh.   36

They were all lying on the ground
   except one who sat up quickly
   as soon as he saw us pass in front of him.

"O you, led through this Hell,"
   he said to me, "recognize me if you can;
   you were made [born] before I was unmade [died]."

And I to him, "The anguish that you feel
   perhaps takes you from my memory
   so that I do not seem ever to have seen you,

but tell me who you are, placed here
   in such punishment that, if others
   are greater, none is so displeasing."   48

And he to me, "Your city [Florence] so full of envy
   that it can hold no more
   kept me in the bright life.

The citizens called me Ciacco;
   for the damning sin of gluttony,
   as you see, I lie helpless in the rain.

And I, sad spirit, am not alone,
   for all of these are in similar pain
   for a like sin,"—and he said no more.

I answered, "Ciacco, your distress weighs upon me
   so that it moves to tears;
   but tell me, if you can, the fate   60

of the citizens of the divided city;
   if any one of them is just, and tell me
   why such discord has assailed it."

Then he to me, "After long dispute
    they will come to blows, and the rustic party [the Whites]
    will drive out the other with much offense.

Afterward that faction will fall
    within three suns [years], and the other rise
    through one [Boniface VIII] who now is moving carefully.

For a long time it will hold high its head,
    keeping the other under heavy burdens,
    however much it may weep and be put to shame.   72

Two men are just, but are not listened to.
    Pride, envy, and avarice are the sparks
    which have enflamed all hearts."

Here he put an end to his sad words,
    and I said to him, "I wish to learn more,
    and beg you to grant me the gift of further speech.

Farinata and Tegghiaio, who were so worthy,
    Jacopo Rusticucci, Arrigo, and Mosca,
    and the others who set their minds to doing good,

tell me where they are, let me know about them,
    for a great desire urges me to find out
    if Heaven soothes or Hell embitters them."   84

And he, "They are among the blackest spirits;
    different sins weigh them to the bottom;
    if you go down so far, you will see them.

But when you are again in the sweet world,
    I beg you to recall me to the memory of others.
    More I will not say; this is all I answer."

He twisted his straight eyes asquint,
    looked at me a little, then bent his head,
    and fell to the level of the other blind ones.

My guide said to me, "No more will he awaken
    until the angelic trumpet sounds [on Judgment Day]
    when the hostile Power [hostile to sinners] will come.   96

Each then will find his sad tomb,
    will resume his flesh and form,
    and will hear what resounds to all eternity."

Thus we passed over the filthy mixture of the shades
    and of the rain, with slow steps,
    touching a little on the future life.

I asked, "Master, will these torments increase
    after the great judgment,
    or will they be less or equally painful?"

He answered, "Recall your science
which maintains that the more perfect a thing is,
the more bliss or pain it feels.

Although these accursed people
never come to true perfection,
they will be more complete after than before."

We bent our course along that way,
saying much more than I relate,
and came to a place for descending.

There we found Plutus, the great enemy.

108

CANTO VII

The Avaricious and the Prodigal

Plutus, the ancient god of wealth and here the guardian of the circle of the avaricious and the prodigal, is represented as an inflated monster. He speaks in a high voice, like certain fat men, and his words are not clearly comprehensible. A reference to the Power through which the archangel Michael defeated the revolt of Satan easily deflates this weak, unhealthy, and puffy creature, who collapses suddenly, without resistance.

"*Papè Satàn, Papè Satàn, aleppe,*"[8]
Plutus began with a clucking voice,
and that noble sage [Virgil], who understood,

said to comfort me, "Do not fear,
for whatever power he may have,
he cannot prevent our descending this rock."

Then he turned to that inflated visage
and said, "Keep still, accursed wolf;
consume yourself inwardly with your rage.

Not without reason is our going to the depth.
It is decreed on high where Michael
took vengeance for the proud revolt."

12

As sails swelled by the wind
fall entangled when the mast breaks,
so the cruel monster fell to the ground.

The avaricious on one side and the prodigal on the other push great weights around their respective semicircles. At the two points where they clash, like the waves between Scylla and Charybdis, they exchange insults and turn, going to the opposite point. Thus they work hard, like the avaricious on earth, but uselessly, missing the spiritual pleasures which make this life and the next worth while. All are alike, without distinction, and unrecognizable as individuals.

[8] These words are not clearly understandable; perhaps a threat and a warning to Satan. (Translator's note.)

Thus we descended into the fourth cavity,
     taking in more of the dismal bank
     which holds all the evil of the universe.

Ah, Justice of God! Who can combine
     so many new pains and torments,
     and why does our sin so waste us?

As the waves above Charybdis break
     against each other as they meet,
     so in this place the souls must clash.   24

Here I saw more people than elsewhere
     on one side and the other, shouting loudly
     and pushing weights with their chests.

They bump against each other and then all turn,
     pushing back the load and crying,
     "Why do you hoard?" or "Why do you squander?"

Thus they go on each side
     of the dark circle to the opposite point,
     shouting their insulting refrains.

When they reach that place, they turn again
     through their half circles to the other clash.
     And I, my heart oppressed, said,   36

"Master, now tell me who these are
     and if all the tonsured ones
     on the left are of the clergy?"

And he to me, "In the first life
     all were so twisted mentally
     that they could not spend with moderation.

Quite clearly their voices bark this out
     when they come to the two points of the circle
     where contrary faults divide them.

Those whose heads are tonsured, as you see,
     were clerics and popes and cardinals
     in whom avarice shows its strength."   48

And I, "Master, among such as these
     I must surely recognize some
     who were defiled by these vices."

And he to me, "You conceive a vain thought;
     the undiscerning life which made them sordid
     now leaves them too obscure for recognition.

Throughout eternity they will clash;
     some will arise from the grave with fists closed,
     and the others [the prodigal] with their hair shorn.

Bad giving and bad keeping have taken from them
    the fair world and placed them in this strife
    which words of mine will not glorify.   60

> *Wealth, according to Dante, is in the hands of a special divinity, Fortune, who performs her functions as the angels guide and direct the various heavens. No reason or moral order is discernible in the distribution of wealth among individuals, families, and nations.*

Now, my son, you can see how wealth,
    committed to Fortune, and for which
    the human race struggles, mocks us.

All the gold that is under the moon
    or ever was, could not give rest
    to one of these weary souls."

"Master," I asked, "now tell me,
    who is this Fortune
    with the world's riches in her hands?"

And he to me, "Oh foolish creatures,
    how deep is the ignorance that blinds you!
    Now I want you to hear my judgment.   72

He [God] whose understanding transcends all
    made the heavens and gave them guides,
    so that each part shines on all the others,

distributing the light equally.
    Likewise, for mundane splendors,
    He ordained a general minister and guide

to transfer vain wealth in due time
    from people to people, and from one to another family,
    beyond the intervention of human intelligence.

Thus one people rules and another languishes,
    according to her judgment, which is hidden from us,
    like a snake in the grass.   84

Your knowledge is of no avail against her;
    she foresees, judges, and rules her province
    as the other gods [angels] do theirs.

Her activity has no truce;
    necessity makes her quick to act,
    so that changes [in fortune] come often.

She is the one so reviled
    even by those who should praise her
    but who, instead, give her ill repute.

Yet she is blessed and does not hear;
    happy with the other primal [angelic] creatures
    she rules her sphere and rejoices in her bliss.   96

*It is now a little after midnight of Good Friday. In a swamp the poets see the
bemired souls of the angry and the bubbles made by the sullen beneath the surface.
The travelers make a long detour to the left, which indicates an approach to worse
things.*

Now let us descend to greater misery;
    already each star that was rising when I started
    is falling, and staying too long is forbidden."

We crossed the circle to the inner bank
    along a stream which bubbled and flowed
    through a channel it had formed.

The water was darker than purplish-black;
    and, accompanying the murky waves,
    on a rough path, we reached the place below.

This dreary stream forms a marsh, the Styx,
    when it has reached the foot
    of the gray, malignant banks.   108

And I, who remained intent on looking,
    saw muddy people in that bog,
    naked, and with angry looks.

They struck each other not only with their hands,
    but with their heads, chests, and feet,
    and tore each other with their teeth, bit by bit.

My good master said, "Son, now see
    the souls of those whom anger overcame;
    I wish you to believe also

that under the water there are people sighing
    and making bubbles on the surface
    as your eyes tell you wherever you look.   120

Fixed in the slime they say, 'Sullen were we
    in the sweet air gladdened by the sun,
    keeping within us the fumes of spite;

now we are sullen in the black mire.'
    This hymn is gurgled in their throats,
    for they cannot speak in clear words."

Thus we covered a wide arc around the filthy slough
    between the dry bank and the swamp,
    with eyes turned to those swallowing the mire.

At last we came to the foot of a tower.

CANTO VIII

The Angry and the Sullen

*Continuing the account of the fifth circle, Dante anxiously inquires about the
meaning of certain signals. These are explained by the coming of a boat guided
by Phlegyas,[9] the guardian of this round.*

I say, continuing, that long before we reached
    the foot of the high tower
    our eyes were drawn to its top

by two little flames placed there;
    and another gave back a signal from so far
    that our eyes could hardly catch it.

Turning to the sea of all wisdom, I asked,
    "What does this mean? what does the other flame
    answer? and who are they who light it?"

And he to me, "Over the foul waters
    already you can see what is expected
    if the mist of the marsh does not hide it from you."   12

Never did a bowstring drive an arrow
    which sped so quickly through the air
    as a little boat I saw then

coming through the water toward us
    under the guidance of a single boatman
    who cried, "Now you are caught, fell spirit!"

"Phlegyas, Phlegyas, this time you cry out
    in vain," said my lord, "you will keep us
    only while crossing the slough."

As one who learns of a great trick
    played on him and who resents it,
    so Phlegyas became in his pent-up rage.   24

My guide stepped down into the boat,
    making me get in after him,
    and only then did it appear burdened.

As soon as my master and I had embarked,
    the ancient prow moved on,
    cleaving more of the water than it does with others.

*Dante becomes angry at one of the shades, apparently incurring the very sin
punished here, but is commended for it by Virgil. The episode is intended to show
that righteous indignation is permissible. We cannot love gentleness and politeness intensely without disliking arrogance and incivility with equal intensity.*

[9] Enraged with Apollo for raping his daughter, Phlegyas set the god's temple on fire and
was killed by him.

While we were going through the stagnant channel,
    a shade covered with mud rose up, saying [insolently],
    "Who are you, coming before your time?"

I answered, "If I come, I do not stay,
    but who are you, now so dirty?"
    And he, "You see I am one who weeps."   36

Then I to him, "With tears and grief
    stay here, damned spirit,
    for I recognize you for all your filth."

Then the shade stretched both hands toward the boat,
    but my wary master pushed him off, saying,
    "Get over there with the other dogs!"

And embracing me with both arms
    he kissed my face and said, "Indignant soul,
    may she be blessed who bore you!

In the world he was an arrogant person;
    no kindness adorned his memory,
    so his shade is furious here.   48

How many think themselves great kings
    who will lie like swine in the mire,
    leaving behind horrible censure."

And I, "Master, I would be glad
    to see him soused in this soup [muddy water]
    before we leave the pond."

He answered, "Before you see the shore
    you will be satisfied;
    it is proper that such a wish be granted."

In a little while I saw the muddy crowd
    wreak such havoc on him
    that I still praise and thank God for it.   60

All cried, "At Filippo Argenti!"
    and the raging Florentine spirit
    turned with his teeth upon himself.

Here we left him, and of him I say no more.
    A wailing now struck my ears,
    so that I looked ahead intently.

My good master said, "Now son,
    the City of Dis [Satan] draws near,
    with its grave citizens, its great garrison."

And I, "Master, already I discern its mosques
    clearly there within the valley,
    red, as if they had come out of fire."   72

He continued, "The eternal flames
    enkindling them make them glow
    as you see in this lower Hell."

We now arrived within the moats
    which surround the disconsolate city,
    the walls of which seemed of iron.

Not without making a wide circuit [to the left]
    did we come to where the boatman loudly cried,
    "Get out, here is the entrance!"

Above the gates more than a thousand [rebellious angels],
    rained down from Heaven, cried angrily,
    "Who is this one, without death,   84

going through the kingdom of the dead?"
    And my wise master signaled
    that he wished to speak with them secretly.

Then they held back their great anger
    and said, "You come alone and let him go
    who so boldly entered this kingdom.

Let him return by himself on the mad path;
    let him see if he can; for you will stay here,
    you who have led him through so dark a country."

> *Threatened with the loss of Virgil (Reason), Dante begs not to be left alone. His guide tries to reassure him, but, as an intellectual rather than a suggestive force, he can do that only imperfectly. As Virgil leaves, Dante wonders whether the answer to a question about the success of the mission will be "yes," or "no." Virgil also is not sure, but, on returning, tries to comfort Dante by passing off his doubt and dismay as anger. He hopes, with the limited confidence reason gives, that an angel will bring divine aid.*

Think, Reader, if I was frightened
    at the sound of the accursed words,
    for I did not believe I could ever return.   96

"O my dear guide, you who many times
    have made me safe and drawn me
    through deep peril confronting me,

do not leave me so undone," I said,
    "and if going farther is denied us,
    let us retrace our steps together rapidly."

Then that lord who had brought me there replied,
    "Do not fear, for no one can prevent our journey;
    by Such a One it has been granted.

Wait for me here, and with good hope
    comfort and feed your weary spirit,
    for I will not leave you in the lower world."   108

Thus my dear father went away
 and abandoned me, and I remained in doubt,
 for "yes" and "no" struggled within my mind.

I could not hear what he said to our adversaries,
 but he did not stay long with them
 before each of them raced back.

They closed the gates in the face
 of my lord, who remained outside
 and then came toward me with slow steps,

his eyes upon the ground and with a face
 shorn of all boldness. He asked, sighing,
 "Who has denied us the abode of woe?"   120

Then to me he said, "Although I may get angry,
 do not fear, for I will win the fight,
 whatever is contrived within.

This insolence of theirs is not new;
 they showed it once at a less secret gate
 which is now without a fastening.

Over it you saw the deadly inscription;[10]
 and already on this side of it,
 passing through the circles without escort,

someone descends who will open the city for us."

CANTO IX

THE CITY OF DIS

The hue that cowardice put on my face
 when I saw my guide come back
 made him repress more quickly his dismay.

He stopped, attentive, like a man listening;
 for sight could not go far
 through the dark air and thick mist.

"Still we must win the fight," he began,
 "if not . . . such help was offered us;
 oh, how I long for someone to come!"

I noticed how he covered up
 his first words with those that followed
 which expressed a different thought,   12

and his remark made me afraid
 because I drew the words cut off
 into a meaning perhaps worse than he intended.

---

[10] The words written over's hell's gate, III.1–9. Dante and Virgil are now about to enter the lower hell, where the sins of malice (violence and fraud) are punished.

Dante asks indirectly if Virgil really knows the way.

"To this depth of the dismal hole
    does any ever descend from the first circle
    where hope cut off is the only punishment?"

This question I asked, and he answered,
    "It seldom happens that one of us
    makes the journey on which I am going.

It is true that I was down here once before,
    conjured by that cruel Erichtho [a sorceress],
    who brought shades back to their bodies.   24

Not for long had my flesh been without me
    when she made me go within those walls
    to bring out a spirit from Judas' circle.[11]

That is the lowest and darkest place, the one
    farthest removed from the heaven that encircles all.
    I know the road well; therefore be reassured.

This swamp exhaling the great stench
    surrounds the woeful city
    which we cannot enter now peacefully."

> *Three Furies, handmaidens of Hecate, the ancient queen of Hell, symbols of
> madness or remorseful terror, rise up, citing their error in letting Theseus enter
> their region to rescue Persephone. Dante clings to Virgil with desperation. The
> Furies then call upon the Gorgon (Medusa, Despair) to turn the intruder to
> stone. Virgil warns his charge with great urgency not to look at her.*

> *The allegorical meaning is perhaps as follows: the reforming Christian (Dante),
> when confronted by remorseful terror (the Furies), may lose his reason (Virgil),
> but as long as hope remains, he can appeal for divine aid. Only despair
> (Medusa) cuts off irremediably the path to salvation.*

And more he said, but I do not recall it
    because my eyes drew all my thoughts
    to the glowing summit of the high tower   36

where suddenly three infernal Furies,
    with the shape and features of women,
    and stained with blood, stood upright.

They were girded with green hydras[12]
    and had serpents and horned snakes for hair
    with which their wild heads were bound.

And he who knew well the handmaidens
    of the Queen of eternal lamentation
    said to me, "Behold! the fierce Erinyes [Furies].

[11] The very lowest and innermost circle of hell, described in Canto XXXIV.
[12] Monsters with several heads.

The one on the left is Megaera;
  she on the right, weeping, is Alecto;
  Tisiphone is in the middle,"—and with that he was silent. 48

They were tearing their breasts with their nails,
  beating themselves with their hands, and shouting
  so loudly that in fear I drew close to my master.

"Let Medusa come, and we will change him to stone,"
  they all said, looking down,
  "badly did we avenge the assault of Theseus."

"Turn back and keep your eyes closed,
  for if the Gorgon [Medusa] shows herself
  and you see her, there will be no returning."

Thus my master spoke, and he himself
  turned me around, not trusting my hands,
  but with his also covered my eyes. 60

O you who have sound understanding,
  observe the meaning hidden
  beneath the veil of the strange verses.

And now over the turbid waters
  came a crash full of terror
  at which both the shores trembled,

a sound like that of a whirlwind
  made violent by conflicting currents
  which hits the forest without restraint,

shatters, beats down, and sweeps away the boughs.
  Behind a cloud of dust it moves on fiercely,
  and makes the beasts and shepherds flee. 72

My master freed my eyes and said,
  "Now direct your sight over that ancient foam
  to where the mist is thickest."

As frogs before their enemy the snake
  scatter through the water
  until each squats on the bottom,

so I saw more than a thousand ruined spirits
  fleeing before one [an angel] who,
  with dry feet, passed over the Styx.

From his face he fanned that gross air,
  moving his left hand in front of it,
  and only with that effort seemed weary. 84

I saw at once that he was sent from Heaven,
  and I turned to my master, who made a sign
  that I should keep quiet and bow to him.

How full of scorn he seemed to me!
    Coming to the gate, he opened it
    with a wand, for there was no resistance.

"O outcasts from Heaven, despised creatures!"
    he began, on the horrible threshold,
    "why do you harbor this insolence?

Why do you oppose that will
    whose purpose can never be hindered,
    and which has several times increased your pain?   96

Of what use is it to butt against fate?
    Your Cerberus [chained by Hercules] because of this
    still has a chin and throat without hair." [13]

Then he turned back over the filthy road.
    and said no word to us, but seemed
    like one intent on other cares

than those of the people near him;
    and we moved on toward the city,
    safe, after the holy words.

> *On entering, Dante sees open tombs, hotter than iron in a blacksmith's forge.*
> *Each contains the leader of a heretical sect with his followers. Here, contrary to*
> *their custom, the travelers turn to the right, perhaps to indicate that heresy can be*
> *incurred honestly, although persistence in it is a sin of pride.*

We entered without any strife,
    and I, wanting to see what punishments
    such a fortress enclosed,   108

as soon as within glanced around
    and saw on every side a great plain
    full of grief and torment.

As at Arles where the Rhone spreads out
    or at Pola near [the bay of] Quarnero
    which encloses Italy and bathes her boundaries,

the tombs make the land uneven,
    so they did here, on all sides,
    except that these graves were more terrible;

for among the tombs flames spread
    by which they were so heated
    that no trade needs iron hotter.   120

All their lids were open,
    and such harsh laments came from them
    as from the wretched and the suffering.

[13] Theseus of Athens (line 54) tried to carry off Persephone (Hecate), queen of the under-world, but was himself held prisoner until he was rescued by Hercules, who in chaining the dog Cerberus tore the skin from its neck.

And I, "Master, who are the people
    buried within the tombs,
    making themselves heard by their painful sighs?"

And he to me, "Here are the archheretics[14]
    with their followers of every sect;
    and the tombs are laden much more than you think.

Like with like is buried,
    and the monuments are more and less hot."
    Then, after we had turned to the right,   132

we passed between the torments and the high battlements.

CANTO X

FARINATA DEGLI UBERTI

Now along a solitary path
    between the city wall and the torments,
    my master makes his way, and I behind him.

"O supreme genius, you who through the impious circles
    turn me [to the left or right] as you please," I began,
    "speak to me and satisfy my wishes.

The people lying in the sepulchres,
    might they be seen?—all the lids
    are raised and no one guards them."

And he to me, "All will be locked in
    when they return from Jehoshaphat [on Judgment Day]
    with the bodies they have left above.   12

> *Epicurus is with the heretics of Christian times since he, almost alone among*
> *ancient philosophers, denied the immortality of the soul.*

> *Still hesitant about asking questions, Dante represses his desire to see certain*
> *Florentines.*

On this side is the burial place
    of Epicurus and of all his followers
    who hold that the soul dies with the body.

But concerning the question you ask
    you will soon be satisfied,
    and also as to the wish you keep silent."[15]

---

[14] This circle of the heretics, like Limbo, is a special case, heresy being a mental or spiritual condition rather than one of the sins of behavior (Incontinence, Violence, Fraud) punished in the overall threefold scheme of Dante's hell. Moreover, heresy, like failure to be baptized, is a fault defined not by universal ethics but from a specifically Christian point of view.

[15] Possibly a wish to see Farinata.

And I, "Good guide, I hide my thought
    only to speak little; not long ago
    you disposed me to do that."

A deep voice sounds amid the silence of the graves. It is that of Farinata degli
Uberti, a Ghibelline leader who, in 1260, won the bloody battle of Montaperti
over the Florentine Guelfs, to which party Dante's family belonged. In recalling
the bloodshed, Farinata has a moment of spontaneous repentance. Dante timidly
draws closer to his guide who then directs him toward this proud, towering figure.

"O Tuscan, you who through the city of fire
    go alive, speaking thus modestly,
    may it please you to remain in this place.   24

Your speech shows you a native
    of that noble fatherland
    to which, perhaps, I was too harmful."

Suddenly this sound came
    from one of the tombs, so that, startled,
    I drew closer to my guide.

He said to me, "Turn around! what are you doing?
    See Farinata, who has stood erect;
    from the waist upward, wholly, you can see him!"

I had already fixed my eyes on his,
    and he lifted up his chest and head,
    as if he had scorn for Hell,   36

and the bold and ready hands of my guide
    pushed me among the sepulchres to him,
    saying, "Let your words be well chosen."

Disappointed in not seeing someone of his own generation, Farinata asks about
Dante's ancestors. On hearing the names of these former enemies, he tells angrily
how he had scattered them. Now Dante's partisan spirit is aroused. He points out
that his party has been able to return to Florence, whereas Farinata's has not
learned the art of getting back. Dante's remark is an unexpected blow for the
Ghibelline captain, who is unaware of all the events and who remains silent,
trying to recover and to collect his thoughts.

When I was at the foot of his tomb
    he looked at me a little; then, almost disdainfully,
    he asked, "Who were your ancestors?"

I, desirous to obey, did not hide them,
    but revealed them all,
    whereupon he raised his brows a little

and said, "Fiercely were they adverse
    to me and to my ancestors and to my party,
    so that twice I scattered them."   48

"If they were driven out, they came back from every side,"
 I answered him, "both the first and the second time,
 but yours did not learn well that art!"

*Now the shade of the father of Guido Cavalcanti, the latter a leading poet and
Dante's best friend, rises beside the great Ghibelline leader. He too is not interested in Dante. He assumes that our poet is allowed to visit Hell because of some
peculiar merit, and since he cannot conceive of greater nobility of mind than that
of his son, he wonders why Guido is not there also. Dante is perplexed, not
knowing that the shades are ignorant of immediate happenings on earth, and
replies ambiguously, implying lack of devotion on Guido's part to Virgil. The
important point, however, is the past tense of the verb he uses. Cavalcante assumes from it that his son is dead, and from the embarrassed tone of Dante's
remarks, suspects that Guido may have had a fate somewhat like his own. Dante's
delay in answering confirms his fear, and he falls back into his tomb.*

Now beside him there arose to sight
 a shade visible down to his chin;
 I believe he had risen on his knees.

He looked around me as if anxious
 to see if someone else were with me,
 but when this expectation was wholly spent,

weeping he said, "If through this blind prison
 you go because of the greatness of your mind,
 where is my son? why is he not with you?"   60

And I to him, "By myself I do not come;
 Virgil, waiting there, guides me,
 whom perhaps your Guido held in disdain."

His words and the manner of his punishment
 had already revealed his name to me;
 therefore my reply was so complete.

Rising suddenly he cried, "What did you say?
 he *held?* Does he not live still?
 Does not the sweet light strike his eyes?"

When he was aware of some delay
 before I answered, he fell back supine
 and showed himself no more.   72

*Meanwhile Farinata has been pondering over Dante's remark and, without tran-
sition, oblivious to the drama enacted at his feet, he returns the verbal blow by
predicting the poet's exile within four years. Relieved by this aggression, he asks
in a more kindly tone why the Florentines have persecuted his family, and he
points out proudly how, after the battle, when the Ghibelline leaders proposed
razing Florence to the ground, he alone defended and saved her. Now Dante's
partisan spirit is likewise softened, and in the conversation that follows he learns
that the shades remember the past and can predict the future, but, like farsighted
people, cannot see what is close at hand. This accounts for the misunderstanding
between him and Cavalcante, and he asks to have his error corrected.*

But that other magnanimous one, at whose instance
    I had stopped, did not change his expression,
    nor move his head, nor bend his body.

"And if," he said, continuing his first remark,
    "they have badly learned that art,
    it torments me more than this bed.

But not fifty times will be rekindled
    the face of her [Hecate, the moon] who rules here
    before you will know the hardness of that art!

And—so may you return sometime to the sweet world—
    tell me why the people are so fierce
    against my kindred in all their laws."   84

Then I to him, "The slaughter and havoc
    which dyed the [river] Arbia red
    cause such prayers to rise in our temple."

Sighing he shook his head and said,
    "In that I was not alone, nor certainly
    would I and the others have moved without cause,

but I was alone when all the rest
    agreed to wipe out Florence:
    I defended her openly before all."

"So may your descendants sometime have rest,"
    I replied, "please solve for me this puzzle
    which has now entangled my judgment.   96

It seems that you see, if I hear rightly,
    what the future brings,
    but for the present have a different vision."

"Like those with imperfect sight,
    we see things far from us," he said,
    "so much light the Supreme ruler still allows,

but when they come close, or exist, our minds
    do not perceive them, and, without news from others,
    we know nothing of your human state.

Therefore you can understand that our knowledge [gained from
      others]
    will be wholly dead after that moment [Judgment Day]
    when the gates of the future are closed."   108

Then, as if sorry for my fault,
    I said, "Now please tell that fallen one
    that his son is still joined with the living,

and if I was silent at his question,
    let him know it was because my thoughts
    were confused by the error you have corrected."

*Before moving on, Virgil declares emphatically that Beatrice will reveal to Dante
the course of his life. This is a mistake on Virgil's part: Cacciaguida, not Beatrice, makes the prophecy.*[16]

*(The treatment of the heretics is a comedy of errors which illustrates the fallibility
of human reason. The Epicureans, in their tombs, erred in thinking that the
grave ended all; Farinata is deceived in several ways; Cavalcante makes a series
of false assumptions; Dante likewise is bewildered. Finally Virgil [Reason itself]
is emphatically wrong.)*

Already my master was calling me back,
   so that I begged the spirit more hastily
   to tell me who was with him.

He said, "With more than a thousand I lie:
   here is the second Frederick [of Sicily]
   and the Cardinal [Ubaldino]; of the others I am silent."   120

Then he hid himself, and toward the ancient poet
   I turned my steps, meditating
   about the prophecy hostile to me.

My guide moved on and, as we were going,
   he said to me, "Why are you so bewildered?"
   and I satisfied his request.

"Let your mind retain what you have heard
   against you," that sage commanded me,
   "and now listen to this," and he raised his finger:

"When you face the sweet light
   of her [Beatrice] whose fair eyes see everything
   you will learn from her the journey of your life."   132

Then he turned his steps to the left;
   we went from the wall toward the center
   along a path which goes into a valley

which even up there stifled us with its stench.

CANTO XI

THE CLASSIFICATION OF SINS

*As the poets proceed toward the inner edge of the sixth circle, they observe a tomb
inscribed with the name of Anastasius. There was confusion in Dante's time
between a pope and a heretical Byzantine emperor of that name.*

*While waiting to become accustomed to the smell which rises from a river of hot
blood below, Virgil explains the various divisions of Hell.*

*To explain why usurers are classed with blasphemers and sodomites as doing
violence to God, Virgil points out that Nature, which offers man its bounty,*

---

[16] This occurs in *Paradise*, Canto XVII, where the exile of Dante, separated from the places
and people he cherished most, is poignantly outlined by Cacciaguida, Dante's great-great-
grandfather.

derives from God; that man's art (industry) gives further value to the products of Nature and, in a sense, derives also from God; that man was intended to earn his living through the bounty of Nature and by the sweat of his brow, and that usurers violate this divine plan.

At the end of the canto we learn by the position of the stars that it is about three hours after midnight, Saturday, April 9, 1300.

On the edge of a high bank
    formed by a circle of broken rocks
    we stood above a more cruel pack;

and here because of the horrible stench
    which the deep abyss exhales
    we approached behind the cover of a great tomb

on which I saw an inscription saying,
    "I hold Anastasius, the pope,
    whom Photinus drew from the straight path."

"Our descent must be slow, so that our sense of smell
    may get used to the foul breath,
    and then we will not heed it."   12

Thus my master spoke, and I, "Please find compensation,
    so that time will not be wasted."
    And he, "That is what I have been thinking of.

My son," he then continued,
    "below us are three smaller circles
    like those you are leaving,

full of accursed spirits. In order
    that sight alone may suffice henceforth,
    observe how and why they are confined.

The malice which Heaven reproves
    causes injury and grief to others
    either by violence or by fraud,   24

but because fraud is peculiar to man
    it displeases God more; therefore
    the fraudulent are placed lower and have more pain.

The next circle [seventh] is for the violent,
    and, since force can be used
    against God, oneself, and one's fellow men—

I mean against them or their property—
    it is divided into three bands
    as you will clearly hear.

Death and painful wounds may be inflicted
    on one's fellows, and plunder, arson,
    and extortion on their property.   36

Thus the first round torments, in various groups,
    assassins, plunderers, and robbers,
    and all who strike maliciously.

A man may commit violence against himself
    and against his property; therefore, in the second round,
    all who deprive themselves of your world

or gamble and dissipate their wealth
    must unavailingly repent
    and weep instead of being happy.

Violence is committed against the Deity
    by cursing Him and denying Him in one's heart;
    and by scorning Nature and her bounty;   48

therefore the smallest band stamps with its seal
    both Sodom [the sodomites] and Cahors [the usurers]
    and those [the blasphemers] who speak disdaining God.

Fraud which hurts man's conscience
    can be used against those who trust
    and against those who have no special confidence.

In the latter case, only the love that Nature makes
    [the natural brotherhood of man] is violated;
    thus, in the following [eighth] circle are nested

hypocrisy, flattery, sorcery,
    falsifying, theft, and simony,
    panders, barrators, and similar filth.   60

The other fraud violates
    both the love Nature creates and that
    which implies a special trust.

Therefore, in the smallest circle
    at the center of the universe where Dis [Satan] holds forth
    whoever betrays is eternally consumed."

And I, "Master, your account proceeds clearly
    and makes plain the division
    of this abyss and those who are in it,

but tell me, the souls [above] in the slimy bog,
    those whom the wind blows, and those the rain beats,
    and those who meet with such sharp tongues,   72

why are they not inside the ruddy city
    if God is angry with them,
    and if not, why are they in such a plight?"

He answered, "Why does your mind
    go astray more than usual?
    or are you thinking of something else?

Do you not remember those words
    with which your *Ethics* [of Aristotle] treats
    the three dispositions Heaven does not admit—

incontinence, malice, and mad bestiality—
    and how incontinence offends God less
    and incurs less blame?   84

If you consider this teaching
    and recall who is being punished
    outside of the city,

you will see why they are separated
    from these and why, less angrily,
    Divine Justice torments them."

"O Sun, you who heal every troubled vision,
    I am so glad to hear you explain
    that to question pleases me no less than knowing;

but go back a little," I said,
    "to where you say that usury offends
    divine goodness, and solve the puzzle."   96

"Philosophy," he said,
    "states in more than one place
    that Nature takes her course

from the Divine Intellect and from Its operation,
    and if you note well your *Physics,*
    you will find after not many pages

that your activity follows the divine plan,
    as the pupil does his master, so that your art [industry]
    is, as it were, a grandchild of God.

From these two [Nature and Industry], if you recall
    the early part of Genesis,
    man should earn his living and prosper.   108

And because the usurer takes another way,
    he scorns Nature in itself and in its follower [Industry],
    since he places his hope in something else.

But follow me now, for I wish to go.
    The Fishes [Pisces] are quivering on the horizon
    and the Chariot [Big Dipper] lies wholly over Caurus [the north-
        west],

and the cliff we descend is far over there.

CANTO XII

THE VIOLENT

Near a break in the cliff, a landslide caused by the revulsion of the earth at the
Crucifixion, is the Minotaur, a creature with a man's body and a bull's head, the

bestial guardian of the circle of the violent. To get around this monster, Virgil
puts him in a blind rage by mentioning the circumstances of his death, how his
half sister, Ariadne, had guided Theseus through the labyrinth to him.

The place where we came to descend the bank
    was craggy and, because of what was there [the Minotaur],
    such that every eye would shun it.

As the landslide which, on this side of Trento,
    struck the Adige, either because of an earthquake
    or from being undermined—

for, from the top of the mountain
    to the plain, the cliff has so fallen
    that it provides a path for one above—

such was the descent into this ravine;
    and on the edge of the broken chasm,
    the infamy of Crete [the Minotaur], conceived   12

in the false [wooden] cow,[17] was stretched out.
    On seeing us the monster bit himself
    like one subdued by anger.

My sage cried to him, "Perhaps you think
    the Duke of Athens [Theseus] is here
    who killed you in the world.

Get away, beast, for this man does not come
    instructed by your sister,
    but journeys on to see your punishments."

As a bull that breaks loose at the moment
    when it receives a mortal blow
    and cannot go straight, but plunges here and there,   24

so I saw the Minotaur stagger,
    and my wary guide shouted, "Run to the pass;
    while he is raging it is well for you to go down."

Thus we made our way over the loose rocks
    which often moved under my feet
    because of the unusual burden.

As I went on, thinking, my guide said,
    "Perhaps you are wondering about this landslide
    guarded by the bestial wrath I outwitted.

Now I want you to know that the other time
    I went down here into deep Hell
    this cliff had not yet been broken,   36

[17] The Minotaur was born of Pasiphae, wife of Minos, king of Crete, after she hid herself
inside a wooden cow in order to have intercourse with a bull.

but, if I discern correctly, shortly before
    He [Christ] came to the first circle
    to remove the great prey from Dis [at the "harrowing"]

the loathsome pit trembled on all sides
    so that I thought the universe felt love
    because of which some [philosophers] believed

the world has many times reverted to chaos [a fusion
    of the elements]; and at that moment these old rocks
    here and elsewhere fell down.

But look below, for the river of blood
    is near, in which are boiled
    those who through violence harm others."   48

      On the banks of the river are centaurs, creatures with horses' bodies, but whose
      heads (unlike that of the Minotaur) are human.

O blind greed, wicked and foolish,
    which so spurs us in the brief life,
    and in the eternal condemns to such pain!

I saw a wide moat making a bend
    surrounding the level ground [of the circle]
    like the one my escort had mentioned,

and between the foot of the bank and the ditch
    centaurs, armed with arrows, were running, in single file,
    as they used to go hunting in our world.

Seeing us descend all stopped,
    and three came from the band,
    having armed themselves with bows and arrows.   60

One shouted from afar, "To what punishment
    are you coming? Tell us from there;
    if not, I'll draw the bow!"

My master answered, "We will reply
    to Chiron over there; unfortunately,
    you were always quick to act."

Then he touched me and said, "That is Nessus
    who died for the beautiful Dejanira
    and by himself took vengeance for himself.[18]

The one in the middle, looking at his breast,
    is the great Chiron, the teacher of Achilles,
    and the other is Pholus, who was so full of rage.   72

[18] While trying to abduct Dejanira, the centaur Nessus was killed by an arrow from her husband Hercules. As he was dying, Nessus gave Dejanira a robe, stained with his blood, that would supposedly preserve Hercules' love for her. But the robe killed Hercules, after which she committed suicide.

Around the ditch they go by thousands
    shooting shades that rise from the blood
    farther than their sins allow."

As we drew near those rapid beasts
    Chiron took an arrow, and with the notch
    combed back the beard on his jaws,

and when he had uncovered his great mouth
    he said to his companions, "Did you notice
    that the one behind moves what he touches?

The feet of the dead do not do this."
    And my good guide, already close to the breast
    where the two natures were joined, answered,   84

"He is indeed alive, and thus alone
    I must show him the dark valley.
    Necessity brings him here, not pleasure.

A lady [Beatrice] who came from singing hallelujah
    entrusted this mission to me;
    he is no robber nor am I a thief.

Therefore, by that power through which
    I move my feet over so rough a road,
    give us one of your band to be with us,

to show us where the ford is, and to carry
    this man on his back, for he is not a spirit
    that can go through the air."   96

> *Chiron, turning to his better side, appoints Nessus as the leader. The party see*
> *first various Greek and Italian tyrants, sunk to their eyebrows in the blood; then*
> *assassins, among whom, shunned by the others, is the first Englishman men-*
> *tioned, Guy of Montfort who in a church at Viterbo killed Prince Henry. Henry's*
> *heart, it was said, was placed in a golden urn in Westminster Abbey.*

Chiron turned to his right
    and said to Nessus, "Go back and guide them,
    and if you meet another band, make it give way."

We started with our trusted escort
    along the bank of the vermilion stream
    in which those boiled uttered loud cries.

I saw shades in it up to their eyebrows;
    and the great centaur said, "These are tyrants
    who engaged in bloodshed and in plunder.

Now they weep for their pitiless crimes.
    Here are Alexander and fierce Dionysius[19]
    who gave Italy years of woe,   108

---

[19] Either Alexander the Great or another Alexander (of Pherae); Dionysius was tyrant of
Syracuse (fourth century B.C.).

and that head with such black hair
    is Azzolino; and the blond one,
    Opizzo da Este, who, in truth,

was killed by his stepson in the world above."
    Then I turned to the poet, who said,
    "Let him go first now and me second."

A little farther on the centaur stopped
    above a group who down to their throats
    appeared above the boiling stream.

Then he showed us a shade to one side, alone, saying,
    "That one, in God's bosom, pierced the heart
    that still is honored on the Thames."   120

Afterward I saw some who kept their heads
    and chests out of the stream,
    and of those I recognized many.

Thus, little by little, the blood grew shallow
    until it cooked only the feet,
    and there was our passage over the moat.

"As on this side you see the boiling river
    grow shallow," said the centaur,
    "so I wish you to believe

that on the other its bottom gets deeper
    until it reaches the place
    where tyrants must groan.   132

There Divine Justice torments
    that Attila who was a scourge on earth,
    and Pyrrhus and Sextus; and eternally it milks

the tears, which the boiling releases,
    from Rinieri da Corneto and Rinieri Pazzo
    who waged such warfare on the highways."

Then Nessus turned back and repassed the ford.

CANTO XIII

Pier delle Vigne

*The poets enter the wood of the Christian suicides. This wild forest represents the
world as it would be if all revolted against life. It is infested by the Harpies,
loathsome creatures, half human, half birds, which stand for the storm winds of
human passions.*

*In every way the suicides, now changed into trees or saplings, are frustrated.
They have used their power of movement to deprive themselves of what distinguished them from plants; but they have not found death. The Harpies they tried
to escape go with them, and the old agony is pent up in their new embodiments.*

Nessus had not yet reached the other side
    when we entered a wood
    that was marked by no path.

No green foliage was there, but of a dark color,
    no smooth branches, but knotty and twisted,
    no fruit, but poisonous thorns.

The wild beasts that shun cultivated places
    do not have such dense and tangled thickets
    [in the Maremma] between Cecina and Corneto.[20]

Here the ugly Harpies make their nests
    who with sad predictions of future harm
    drove the Trojans from the Strophades.[21]   12

They have wide wings and human necks and faces,
    feet with claws, and great feathered bellies;
    they utter laments on the strange trees.

My good master began to speak, saying,
    "Before you go any farther, know
    that you are in the second round and will be

until you come to the horrible sand.
    Therefore look closely and you will see
    what would seem incredible in my speech."

I heard moans on every side
    and saw no one to make them,
    so that I stopped, all bewildered.   24

I believe he believed that I believed
    that so many voices came from people
    hidden from us among the trees;

therefore he said, "If you break
    a twig of one of these woody plants
    the thoughts you have will be corrected."

Then I stretched forth my hand
    and plucked a small branch from a great thorn tree,
    and its trunk cried, "Why do you break me?"

After it had grown dark with blood,
    it began again to lament, "Why do you tear me?
    have you no trace of pity?   36

We were men, and now are turned to wood;
    your hand should have been more merciful
    if we had been the souls of serpents."

---

[20] Two towns, at the northern and southern edges of the Maremma, a swamp near Florence.

[21] Islands visited by Aeneas and the other Trojans in their wanderings after the fall of Troy. This incident and one involving a bleeding shrub (referred to in line 48) occur in Virgil's *Aeneid,* Book III.

As a green log, burning at one end,
    drips from the other and hisses
    with the steam that escapes,

so from the broken branch words and blood
    came out together; and I let the twig fall
    and stood like one afraid.

The tree whose branch Dante has broken is that of Pier delle Vigne, a famous
statesman, scholar, and poet at the court of Frederick II of Sicily. (In several
curious, repetitious lines Dante imitates the style of the Frederician poets.) Fred-
erick accused him of treason, had him blinded and led in derision on an ass from
town to town. To escape this dishonor, Pier is said to have beaten his head against
the walls of his prison. Dante presents him as innocent, as the model of a devoted
public servant. He is proud of the office he once held and still loyal to the king
who could do no wrong. It was Envy, he says, the harlot at every court, who
caused his death. And he swears by his new body that he was never unfaithful.

"If he [Dante] could have believed, offended soul,"
    my master answered,
    "what he has seen only in my verse,   48

he would not have raised his hand against you,
    but the incredible thing made me prompt him
    to do what grieves me.

Now tell him who you were, so that
    to make amends, he may refresh your fame
    in the world above to which he is permitted to return."

Then the tree, "You so allure me with kind words
    that I cannot keep silent, and may you
    not be wearied if I grow sticky talking.

I am the one who held both keys [of consent and denial]
    to Frederick's heart, and who turned them,
    locking and unlocking so softly   60

that I kept almost everyone from his secrets.
    Such trust I bore to the glorious office
    that I lost sleep and strength.

The harlot [Envy] who never from Caesar's dwelling
    has turned aside her shameless eyes,
    the common bane and vice of courts,

inflamed all minds against me,
    and the inflamed so inflamed Augustus [Frederick]
    that my joyous honors changed to dismal sorrow.

My soul with disgust and scorn,
    hoping to escape disdain,
    made me unjust to my just self.   72

By the new roots of this tree, I swear to you
    that I never broke faith with my lord
    who was so worthy of honor.

And if either of you return to the world,
    comfort my memory which still lies crushed
    by the blow that Envy gave it."

    Pier tells how the souls fall and become trees and bushes.

    *After Judgment Day, the bodies the suicides could not endure for a few brief years
    will hang on their branches forever. This is the final frustration.*

The poet waited a little and then said,
    "Since he is silent, do not lose the chance,
    but question him if you want to hear more."

And I answered, "*You* ask what you think
    will satisfy me, for I could not;
    such pity saddens me."   84

Then he began, "So may this man
    do freely for you what you ask,
    please tell us, imprisoned spirit,

how the soul becomes bound in these branches,
    and let us know if you can
    if any ever frees himself from them."

The tree blew loudly, and soon
    the wind changed into these sounds:
    "Briefly will you be answered.

When the fierce soul leaves the body
    from which it has torn itself,
    Minos sends it to the seventh depth.   96

It falls into the wood; no place is chosen for it,
    but where chance throws it
    it sprouts, like a grain of wheat.

It grows into a sapling and a wild tree;
    the Harpies, feeding then upon its leaves,
    give pain and to the pain an outlet.

Like the others we will come for our bodies,
    but not to be clothed again with them,
    for it is not right to get back what is rejected.

Here we will drag them, and
    in the sad wood our bodies will be hung
    on the branches of our injurious souls."   108

    *Two spirits rush by, chased by the hounds of ruin and crying for a second death
    they can never have. These are souls of reckless squanderers, destroyers of their
    estates and indirectly of themselves. One, Lano, in desperate circumstances, al-
    lowed himself to be killed in the battle of Toppo.*

We were still attentive to the tree,
    believing that it wished to say more,
      when a loud sound startled us

as it does the hunter who sees the boar and chase
    approach his post and who hears the beast
      and the crash of the branches.

And behold! two on the left,
    naked and scratched, fleeing so fast
      that they broke the brambles of the wood.

The one in the front cried, "Now come, now come, O Death!"
    and the other who saw himself outdistanced, called,
      "Lano, your legs were not so nimble   120

at the tournament of Toppo." And, perhaps
    because his breath had failed, he plunged
      into a bush, making a tangle of it and of himself.

Behind them the wood was full of black bitches,
    ravenous and running fast,
      like greyhounds just freed from the leash.

They fixed their teeth in the one who squatted
    and tore him to pieces,
      then carried off the suffering members.

My guide then took me by the hand
    and led me to the bush, which lamented vainly
      through its bleeding wounds.   132

"O Giacomo da Sant'Andrea," it cried,
    "what do you gain by making me a screen?
      what blame have I for your wicked life?"

My master had stopped beside it and asked,
    "Who were you, you who through so many breaks
      blow forth your woeful blood and words?"

> *The soul in the bush deplores the situation in Florence where martial virtue has been sacrificed for money-making (represented by John the Baptist whose image was stamped on Florentine coins); then he identifies himself briefly, not by a name but by an act: he desecrated his own home by making a gallows in it.*

And the bush to us, "O souls coming
    to see the shameful ravage
      that has so separated my leaves from me,

gather them together at the foot of the poor plant.
    I was of the city which changed its first patron [Mars]
      for the Baptist, because of which   144

that god will always sadden it with his art,
    and if, at the bridge over the Arno
      there did not remain a trace of him [the ruins of a statue],

those citizens who rebuilt the city
    on the ashes left by Attila[22]
    would have done their work in vain.

I made a gibbet for myself of my own house."

CANTO XIV

The Violent Against God

*The round of the violent against God or Nature is characterized by sterility. On
the hot sand the blasphemers are lying supine, the sodomites are running, the usurers sitting. Over all is falling a rain of fire which, here and elsewhere, symbolizes
the direct wrath of God.*

Because love for my native city moved me,
    I gathered the scattered leaves and gave them back
    to him whose voice was already faint.

Then we came to where the second round [the wood]
    is divided from the third [the plain]
    and where is seen a fearful kind of justice.

To make the new place manifest,
    I say that we reached a desert
    which repels every plant from its bed.

The doleful wood forms a garland around it,
    just as the dismal moat does to the wood.
    Here, at the very edge, we stopped.   12

The ground was of dry, thick sand,
    not different from that [of the Libyan desert]
    once trod by Cato's feet.[23]

O how greatly the vengeance of God
    should be feared by everyone who reads
    what was apparent to my eyes!

I saw many groups of naked souls,
    all of whom wept miserably,
    but different positions were imposed on them.

Some were lying supine upon the ground,
    some were sitting, bent over,
    and others were running continually.   24

Those that kept moving were most numerous
    and those fewest who were lying in the torment,
    but their tongues were loosened by greater pain.

---

[22] Attila the Hun, fifth-century invader of Europe, was supposed to have sacked Florence.
See also XII.134.
   [23] In 47 B.C., during the Roman civil war between Julius Caesar and Pompey, Cato led part
of Pompey's army across Libya.

Over all the plain, falling slowly,
    dilated flakes of fire came down,
    like snow in Alps without a wind.

As Alexander in those hot parts
    of India saw flames fall on his host
    intact as far as to the ground,

and made his legions trample
    on the soil, since the fire
    could be extinguished better before it spread;   36

so fell the eternal heat
    by which the sand was kindled
    like tinder under flint, to double the pain.

Ever without rest was the dance
    of the miserable hands, now here, now there,
    brushing off the fresh burning.

> *Dante notices a shade still untamed, bold, indomitable, defying Jove and the*
> *thunderbolts which defeated the giants. Virgil has more contempt for this appar-*
> *ent superman than for anyone else in Hell. Flat on his back, feeling hour after*
> *hour eternally the power of the God he is defying, his attitude seems stupid rather*
> *than courageous, and is peculiarly disgusting to Reason.*

I began, "Master, you who have overcome everything
    except the fierce demons who rushed out against us
    at the entrance to the City,

who is that great shade not heeding the fire,
    lying scornful and contorted,
    whom the rain does not seem to ripen?"   48

And he, aware that I was asking my guide
    about him, shouted loudly,
    "As I was alive, so am I dead.

Though Jove exhaust his smith from whom,
    angrily, he took the sharp thunderbolt
    by which I was struck on my last day,

and though he weary the others [the Cyclops] one by one
    in Mongibello [Mt. Etna] at the black forge,
    crying, 'Help, help, good Vulcan!'—

as he did in the battle of Phlegra [against the giants]—
    and hit me with all his strength,
    he could not have the joy of vengeance."   60

Then my guide spoke with such feeling
    that I had never heard his voice so loud,
    "O Capaneus, since your pride

remains untamed you are punished more.
    No torture except your rage itself
    would be adequate for your fury."

Then he turned to me with a better look, saying,
    "This was one of the seven kings
    who besieged Thebes; he held and still seems

to hold God in contempt, and to fear Him little;
    but, as I told him, his blasphemy
    is a fitting ornament for his breast.   72

> *The travelers come to where the overflow from Phlegethon, the river of blood, crosses the plain. The water of this little stream is like the Bulicame, a hot spring near Viterbo, where special bathhouses were provided for prostitutes. Its sterile banks offer a passageway, since over the blood-stained water the fire is quenched, a confirmation or symbol of atonement, the appeasing of God's wrath by human suffering.*

Now follow me and be careful
    not to put your feet on the burning sand,
    but always keep them close to the wood."

In silence we came to where, out of
    the forest, a little rivulet gushes,
    the redness of which still makes me shudder.

As from the Bulicame a stream flows
    which sinful women share among themselves,
    so this one flowed across the sand.

Its bottom and both its sides
    were made of stone and also the banks
    on which I perceived that our way led.   84

"Among all the things I have shown you
    since we entered the gate
    whose threshold is denied to none,

nothing has been seen by your eyes
    as notable as the present stream
    which quenches all the flames above it."

These words were spoken by my guide,
    and I asked him to grant the food
    for which he had given me an appetite.

> *With elaborate symbolism, Virgil now tells of man's fall from grace and the consequences. On Mount Ida, in Crete, the center of the ancient world and the supposed cradle of the human race, there is a statue which represents the history of mankind. Its back is turned toward the East, its face in the direction of the course of empire. Its head, representing the Golden Age of the Ancients or the period of the Garden of Eden, is of gold; other parts, according to the various ages, are of different metals. One foot is of iron (the Roman Empire), the other of clay (the Papacy), and the weight of the statue bears too heavily on the latter, the cause, in Dante's view, of much of the anarchy and disorder in the world. The whole statue except the head has been cracked by man's sin. From this fissure tears drip. They flow down to Hell, form the waters of the Acheron, the Styx, the Phlegethon, and ultimately the frozen Cocytus. Thus, by a kind of conservation of*

sorrow, the tears shed through cruelty are not lost, but flow down to punish those who cause them.

Another river, the Lethe, descends to Hell from Purgatory carrying with it the last trace, that is, the very memory, of sin.

"In the middle of the sea," he said then,
    "lies a waste land, called Crete,
    under whose kings the world once was chaste.   96

A mountain there, named Ida,
    was joyous with water and with leaves;
    now it is deserted, like a thing worn out.

Rhea chose it for the safe cradle
    of her son [Jupiter]; and to hide him better
    when he cried, she had a clamor made.[24]

On the mountain stands a great old man [a statue]
    with back turned toward Damietta [in the East]
    and looking toward Rome as in a mirror.

His head is formed of fine gold,
    his arms and breast are of pure silver;
    then he is of brass as far as to the fork.   108

From there down he is made of fine iron,
    except that the right foot is of baked clay,
    and he stands on that more than on the other.

Every part except the gold is broken
    by a fissure which drips tears
    and these, joining, cut through that bank,

flow down to this pit, and form the Acheron,
    the Styx, and the Phlegethon;
    then, moving on through this narrow channel,

go down to where there can be no further descent.
    They form Cocytus; and since you will see
    how that lake is, I do not describe it."   120

And I to him, "If the present stream
    comes thus from our world,
    why does it appear only here?"

And he, "You know that the place is round,
    and, although you have come far
    always descending to the left,

you have not yet completed the circle;
    therefore, if something new appears,
    it should not cause marveling."

---

[24] Rhea was the wife of Saturn, who devoured most of his sons. To save their son Jupiter, she had his protectors, the Curetes, make loud noises to drown out the infant's crying.

Then I asked, "Master, where are the Phlegethon
    and Lethe, for you are silent about one [Lethe]
    and say that this rain forms the other."   132

"In all your questions you please me,"
    he replied, "but the boiling red water
    ought to answer one [about the Phlegethon].

You will see Lethe outside of this pit
    where souls go to wash themselves
    when guilt, repented, is removed.

Now it is time to leave the wood;
    see that you come behind me;
    the banks, not burned, offer a way,

and over them all fire is extinguished."

CANTO XV

BRUNETTO LATINI

*The banks of the rivulet are like the dikes built by the Flemings or those made
along the Brenta before the snow melts in the Chiarentana mountains. As the
poets pass, they are eyed intently by a band of sodomites. Dante recognizes one as
Brunetto Latini, a famous author and scholar, some of whose lectures Dante
evidently heard. Dante extends his hand with reverence and, using the polite
(*voi*) form of address, tells of his surprise at meeting him in this place.*

Now one of the hard banks offers us a way,
    and the vapor of the stream makes a shelter
    which protects the shores and water from the fire.

As the Flemings between Wissant and Bruges,
    fearing the flood which rushes toward them,
    make a bulwark to repel the sea,

and as the Paduans do along the Brenta
    to defend their cities and their castles,
    before Chiarentana feels the heat,

in such a manner those banks were formed,
    although their builder, whoever he was,
    made them not so high nor so thick.   12

Already we were so far from the wood
    that I could not have seen where it was
    if I had turned back

when we met a band of spirits
    coming along the banks, and each gazed at us
    as, at dusk, under a new moon,

men are wont to look at each other,
    sharpening their eyes at us
    as an old tailor does at his needle's eye.

Thus gazed at by such a group,
    I was recognized by one who grasped my skirt
    and cried, "What a marvel!"   24

And as he held out his arm toward me
    I fixed my glance on his baked aspect
    so that his burned face did not prevent

the recognition of him by my memory.
    Lowering my hand toward his face,
    I asked, "Are *you* here, *ser* Brunetto?"

> *Brunetto proposes to accompany Dante by walking along below him. He must
> keep moving: restlessness is common to the punishment of all sexual sinners.
> Dante shows the greatest affection for his old master, a feeling reciprocated by
> Brunetto, who prophesies Dante's quarrel with the Florentines. They, according
> to legend, represent a fusion of the descendants of a Roman colony and of the
> rough hill people from Fiesole. Dante wishes that Brunetto had not been banished
> in a double sense from human nature, and pays him the supreme tribute to a
> teacher: he taught, not the minutiae of scholarship and pedantry, but the impor-
> tant things, how man, through fame, can make himself eternal.*

And he, "O my son, may it not displease you
    if Brunetto Latini goes back with you a little,
    letting his company move on."

I said to him, "As much as I can I beg you to,
    and if you want me to sit down with you,
    I will do so, if he with whom I go permits."   36

"O son," he said, "whoever of this flock
    stops one instant, lies afterward a hundred years
    without brushing off the fire that strikes him;

therefore, go on; I will follow at your skirts
    and then I will rejoin my band
    which goes lamenting its eternal punishment."

I did not dare go down from the path
    to be with him, but I held my head low
    like one who walks with reverence.

He began, "What chance or destiny
    brings you here before your last day,
    and who is this one showing you the road?"   48

"Up there in the serene life," I answered,
    "I went astray in a valley,
    before my allotted time was spent.

Yesterday morning I turned my back on it;
    then, as I was falling into it again, this shade appeared
    who is taking me home by this road."

And he to me, "If you follow your star
    you cannot fail to reach a glorious port
    if I discerned rightly in the fair life.

And if I had not died so early,
    seeing the heavens so gracious to you,
    I would have cheered you in your work.   60

That ungrateful, malignant people who of old
    came down from Fiesole and still keep
    the roughness of the mountains and the rocks

will become your enemies because of your good deeds.
    And that is right, for among the bitter sorb trees
    it is not fitting that the sweet fig bear fruit.

Old report in the world calls them blind,
    an avaricious, envious, haughty people:
    see that you cleanse yourself from their ways.

Your fate reserves such honor
    that both parties will be hungry for you;
    but far from the goat will be the grass!   72

Let the beasts of Fiesole make fodder
    of themselves and not touch the plant
    if one grows on their dung heap

in whom the holy virtues are revived
    of those Romans who remained there
    when it was made the nest of such wickedness."

"If my request could be fully granted,"
    I answered him, "you would not yet
    be exiled from human nature;

for in my mind is fixed and my heart knows
    the dear and kindly image of you
    as a father when, from hour to hour,   84

you taught how man makes himself eternal;
    and while I am alive, it is fitting
    that my tongue show how grateful I am.

What you say about my life I write down
    and keep to be explained with another text
    by a lady [Beatrice] who can do this if I see her.

This much I would have plain to you—
    so may my conscience not chide me—
    I am prepared for Fortune as she wills.

Such warnings are not new to my ears;
    therefore, as they please, 'Let Fortune
    turn her wheel, and the churl his mattock.'"   96

My master turned to the right
    and looked at me, then said,
    "He listens well who notes what is told."

Among the many famous and infamous men guilty of sodomy was Dante's bishop,
whom Boniface VIII, instead of punishing severely, merely transferred to another
see. Thus the two men whose duty was to teach Dante how to become eternal on
earth and in Heaven are together.

Brunetto hurriedly commends his work, The Treasury, *to Dante and then*
leaves, running fast, his loss of dignity showing the effect of one vice on an
otherwise venerable character.

Nonetheless I continued talking
    to *ser* Brunetto, and I asked
    who were his most noted companions.

And he to me, "It is well to know of some;
    of the others it is more laudable to keep silent,
    for time would be short for so much speech.

Know briefly that all were clerks[25]
    and scholars and of great fame,
    by the same sin defiled on earth.   108

Priscian goes with that wretched crowd,
    and Francesco d'Accorso; moreover,
    if you had a hankering for such filth,

you might see him who by the Servant of the Servants
    was transferred from the Arno to the Bacchiglione,
    where he left his ill-strained muscles.

I would say more, but my going and my speech
    must not continue longer, since I see new smoke
    rising over there from the sand.

People are coming with whom I must not be.
    Let my *Treasury*, in which I live
    be commended to you; more I do not ask."   120

Then he turned, and seemed like one of those
    who, at Verona, through the fields, run races
    for a green cloth; and of these he appeared to move

like the one who wins, and not like the one who loses.

CANTO XVI

THE WATERFALL

Already I had reached a place where the roar
    of the water falling into the next circle
    could be heard, like the hum of a beehive,

[25] Clerics.

when three shades running together
      left a troop passing through the rain
      of the fiery torment.

They came toward us and each cried,
      "Stop, you who by your dress seem to us
      to come from our perverse city!"

Ah! what wounds I saw on their bodies,
      old and recent, burnt in by the flames!
      I still grieve whenever I recall it.   12

My teacher listened to their cries,
      then turned his face toward me and said,
      "Now wait, to these we must be courteous,

and if it were not for the fire
      which the nature of this place lets fall,
      I should say that haste befitted you more than them."

> *Since the edge of the precipice is not far off, the shades propose to keep moving by*
> *circling around one spot.*

As we stopped they began again their old lament,
      and when they had reached us
      all three made of themselves a circle,

as wrestlers, naked and oiled, are wont to do,
      watching for a hold and an advantage,
      before the tugs and blows begin.   24

Thus circling, all kept their eyes on me,
      so that their heads and necks,
      together with their feet, moved continually.

And one of them began, "If the misery of this sandy place
      and our scorched and burned faces
      cause scorn for us and for our prayers,

may our fame incline you to tell us
      who you are, you who move so securely
      your living feet through Hell.

The man in whose footsteps you see me tread,
      although he goes now bare and hairless,
      was of a higher rank than you might believe.   36

He was a grandson of the good Gualdrada;
      Guido Guerra was his name, and in his life
      he did much with counsel and with sword.

The other who treads the sand behind me
      is Tegghiaio Aldobrandi, whose voice
      should have been heeded in the world.

And I, placed on the cross with them,
    am Jacopo Rusticucci; and certainly my fierce wife
    troubles me more than anything else."

If I had been sheltered from the fire,
    I would have thrown myself down among them,
    and I believe my master would have permitted;   48

but since I would have been burned and cooked,
    fear overcame the good will
    which made me eager to embrace them.

Then I began, "Not contempt, but such grief
    as will not soon leave me,
    your condition caused in me

as soon as my lord spoke words
    through which I inferred
    that people like you were coming.

I am from your city; and always
    I have heard and told with affection
    of your honored deeds and names.   60

I leave the gall and go for the sweet fruit
    promised me by my truthful guide,
    but first I must descend to the center."

"So may your soul long guide your body,"
    he answered then,
    "and so may your fame shine after you,

tell us if courtesy and valor dwell
    in our city as they were wont
    or whether they have gone entirely,

for Guglielmo Borsiere who has suffered with us
    only a little while and is over there with his companions
    grieves us much with his remarks."   72

"New people and sudden gains, O Florence,
    have generated pride and excess in you
    so that already you are weeping!"

This I cried with my face raised, and the three
    who understood my words as a reply, glanced at each other
    as people do when the truth is spoken.

"If, at other times, it costs you so little
    to satisfy others," they all replied,
    "you are fortunate, speaking thus at will;

therefore, if you escape from this dark place
    and return to see the beautiful stars,
    when you can delight in saying 'I was there . . .'   84

see that you speak to others about us."
    Then they broke the wheel, and in their flight
    their nimble legs seemed wings.

An "amen" could not have been said
    so quickly as they disappeared;
    whereupon my master thought it best to go on.

I followed him, and we had not gone far
    before the waterfall was so near
    that we could hardly hear each other speak.

As the river which has its own channel at first
    from Monte Veso toward the east,
    on the left slope of the Apennines—   96

which is called Acquacheta up above
    before it flows to its lower bed,
    and at Forlì loses that name—

resounds there above San Benedetto dell'Alpe,
    because of falling in one single leap
    instead of being broken by a thousand,

so, down from a steep bank
    we found the colored water roaring so loudly
    that it soon would have hurt our ears.

A cord around Dante's waist probably stands for self-confidence, useful in combating incontinence, but worse than useless in dealing with the fraud ahead. He gives it to Virgil who throws it over the precipice as a signal. Dante waits anxiously to see what will happen.

I had a cord around my waist
    with which I had thought once
    to catch the leopard with the painted hide.   108

After I had loosened it from my body
    as my leader had ordered me,
    I handed it to him, coiled and knotted.

Then he turned to the right side,
    and threw it far from the bank
    down into that deep abyss.

"Surely," I said within myself, "something strange
    must respond to this new signal
    which my master so follows with his eyes."

Ah, how cautious we must be
    with those who see not only what we do
    but look also within our thoughts!   120

He said to me, "Soon what I am waiting for
    will come up, and what you are thinking about
    will be revealed to your eyes."

To the truth which appears to be a lie
    we should close our lips as long as we can,
    not to incur blamelessly a reproach;

but here I cannot keep silent and, Reader,
    by the notes of this Comedy, I swear to you—
    so may it not lack long favor—

that I saw, through that thick and dark air,
    a form marvelous to every steadfast heart
    come swimming up   132

as a swimmer rises after going down
    to loosen an anchor caught by a rock
    or something else hidden in the sea,

who stretches forth his arms and draws up his feet.

CANTO XVII

GERYON

The monster coming up is Geryon, a symbol of the fraud which is universal and more powerful than arms. His face has an honest look, but his body is reptilelike and covered with devious and intricate patterns, like oriental tapestries. He lies with his head on the bank as beavers were supposed to do when using their tails to throw their prey on the shore.

"Behold the beast with the pointed tail
    that can cross mountains and break through walls;
    behold the one that infects the whole world!"

Thus my guide began to speak to me
    and signaled to the beast to come ashore
    near the end of the stone banks we had walked on;

and that foul image of fraud came up
    and landed his head and breast,
    but did not put his tail upon the bank.

His face was that of an honest man,
    so kind an aspect it had outwardly,
    but all the rest was like a reptile.   12

He had two paws, hairy to the armpits;
    his back and breast and both sides
    were decorated with loops and circles;

never did Tartars nor Turks make cloth
    with more colors in groundwork and in pattern,
    nor did Arachne[26] ever put such webs on her loom.

[26] A skilled weaver who challenged the goddess Minerva to a competition; Minerva later changed her into a spider.

As skiffs sometimes lie along the shore
    partly in the water and partly on land,
    and as up there among the gluttonous Germans

the beaver sits to carry on his war,
    so that worst of wild beasts lay
    on the edge which binds the sand with stone.   24

He darted his tail in the empty space,
    twisting up its venomous tip
    which was armed like that of a scorpion.

> *The usurers (the remaining group of the violent against God) are crouching near
> the edge where it is easy to fall into the circle of fraud below. Dante treats them
> with the utmost contempt, as he does all mercenary souls. They are unrecogniza-
> ble except by the coats of arms on their now empty purses.*
>
> *Virgil has warned Dante not to waste words on them: our poet does not speak at
> all. The usurers are still competing, quarreling, rivaling, and envying each
> other, without honor, courage, good manners, artistic or intellectual distinction.*

My leader said, "We must now bend our course
    a little as far as to the wicked beast
    that is lying over there."

We descended to the right
    and took ten steps on the extreme edge
    in order to avoid the sand and the flames.

After we had reached the monster,
    I saw a little farther on some people on the sand
    sitting close to the empty space.   36

My master said, "So that you may take with you
    complete experience of this round,
    go and see their ways.

Let your talk with them be brief;
    until you return I will speak with this one
    so that he may lend us his strong shoulders."

Thus I advanced along the extreme edge
    of the seventh circle all alone
    to where the sad souls were sitting.

Through their eyes their grief burst forth;
    on this side and that they used their hands,
    brushing off the fire and lifting themselves from the hot
        ground;   48

not otherwise are dogs busy in summer,
    now with their muzzles and now with their paws,
    when bitten by gadflies or fleas.

In looking at the faces of some
    on whom the painful fire was falling,
    I could recognize none, but I noticed

that from the necks of each a purse hung
　　which had a certain color and design
　　and on which it seemed that their eyes feasted.

As I came looking at them,
　　on a yellow purse I saw in azure
　　the head and the form of a lion. 60

Then continuing the course of my glances,
　　I saw another, red as blood,
　　showing a goose whiter than butter.

And one who had a white sack marked
　　with an azure pregnant sow,
　　said to me, "What are you doing in this hole?

Now go away and, since you are still alive,
　　know that my neighbor Vitaliano
　　will sit here on my left side.

With these Florentines I am a Paduan;
　　many times they deafen my ears,
　　shouting, 'Let the sovereign knight come 72

who will bring the pouch marked by three goats.' "
　　Then he twisted his mouth and stuck out his tongue
　　as an ox does to lick its nose.

And I, fearing that to stay longer
　　might annoy my master, who had admonished me
　　to be brief, turned my back on those wearied souls.

*When Dante climbs on Geryon's back over the immense void, he is so frightened
he cannot speak.*

*The transition from violence to deliberate, premeditated fraud is shown by the
long and slow descent.*

I found my leader already mounted
　　on the back of the fierce animal.
　　He said to me, "Now be strong and bold;

we descend here by such stairs.
　　Mount in front, for I wish to be placed
　　so that the tail cannot hurt you." 84

As one who has the chill of the quartan fever
　　so close that his nails are already blue,
　　and who shivers merely at the sight of shade,

so I became on hearing these words,
　　but Virgil's admonition caused the shame
　　which, in sight of his master, makes a servant strong.

I placed myself on those big shoulders.
　　"See that you hold me," I wished to say,
　　but my voice did not come out as I thought.

And he who at other times helped me
    in other fears, as soon as I had mounted,
    embraced and held me with his arms;   96

then said, "Geryon, move now;
    let the circles be large and the descent slow;
    think of the new burden that you have."

As a little ship moves from its berth,
    back, back, thus Geryon moved off,
    and when he felt his whole body clear,

he turned his tail to where his breast had been,
    and stretching it out, moved it like an eel,
    and with his paws drew in the air.

I do not believe there was greater fear when Phaëthon[27]
    let loose the reins [of the sun's chariot] so that the sky
    as still appears [by the Milky Way] was scorched,   108

nor when poor Icarus[28] [while flying] felt his loins unfeathered
    because of the melting of the wax,
    his father shouting to him, "The wrong way you're taking!"

than was mine when I saw myself in the air
    on every side and with every view hidden
    except that of the beast.

It went on swimming slowly, slowly,
    circled and descended, but I was aware of the movement
    only by the wind blowing in my face and from below.

Already I heard the torrent on the right
    roaring horribly beneath us,
    so that I stretched out my head to look down.   120

Then I was still more afraid,
    for I saw fires and heard laments,
    at which I crouched back, all trembling.

I noticed then the descending and the circling
    which I had not seen before
    by the torments drawing near on every side.

As a falcon that has long been on the wing
    without seeing a bird or lure, and that makes the falconer cry,
    "Alas, you are coming down!"

descends wearily, after many circles,
    to where it had swiftly started out,
    and lands far from its master, sullen and angry,   132

---

[27] Son of Apollo, the charioteer of the sun. Entrusted with his father's chariot, Phaëthon lost control of it so that it burned the sky.

[28] Icarus, for whom his father Daedalus made wings cemented with wax, flew too near the sun and fell when it melted the wax.

so Geryon set us down on the bottom,
    at the foot of the jagged rock;
    then freed of the weight of our bodies,

he darted off, like an arrow-notch from the string.

CANTO XVIII

PANDERS, SEDUCERS, AND FLATTERERS

*The matter-of-fact description of Malebolge contrasts with the deviousness of the
fraud it harbors. The term means "evil pouches" or "purses," perhaps with some
reference to the greed which motivates most fraud. Those who sinned through
violence are in the open. The fraudulent, appropriately, are hidden in dark
ditches. Over the moats are "scogli," rocky bridges, which come together at the
center like spokes of a wheel.*

There is a place in Hell called Malebolge,
    all of stone and of an iron color
    like the bank which surrounds it.

Right in the middle of the baleful space
    a well, rather wide and deep, opens up
    whose features I will describe in their place.

The belt that remains, then,
    between the well and the high, hard bank,
    had its bottom divided into ten valleys.

As the ground appears
    where several moats surround a castle
    as a protection for the walls,

such was the design these made.
    And, as from the thresholds of fortresses
    little bridges extend to the outer banks,

so from the bottom of the wall, rough spans
    crossed the ditches and the banks down to the well
    which brings them all together and cuts them off.

In this place, shaken from the back of Geryon,
    we found ourselves, and the poet started
    to the left, and I moved on behind him.

12

*The souls in the first bolgia or ditch are guided by traffic regulations as was the
crowd at the jubilee in Rome in 1300, the panders on the outside going to the
right, the seducers on the inside to the left.*

*We now meet the first devils. These, appropriately, wear the horns associated with
adultery. We find also the first shade who is ashamed. When recognized, he tells
how he sold his sister to the Marquis of Este. He confesses also for the other
Bolognese panders, more numerous than the little children learning the dialect
word for "yes" within the boundaries of their province.*

Here, as elsewhere, movement characterizes punishments for sins related to sexu-

ality. Where the activity was natural, the agent of punishment is wind, a natural
force; where unnatural, as on the plain, a supernatural fire is falling. Here,
among the fraudulent, a devil plies the whip.

On the right I saw new misery,
    new torments, and new tormentors
    with which the first ditch was filled.   24

The sinners along the bottom of the ditch were naked,
    coming on this side facing us, on the other
    moving with us, but with longer steps.

Thus the Romans because of the great throng
    in the year of the jubilee, chose a way
    to divide the traffic on the bridge,

so that on one side all had their faces
    toward the Castle [of Sant' Angelo], and went to St. Peter's,
    on the other side they advanced toward the Mount [Giordano].

On both sides of the dark rock
    I saw horned demons with great whips
    beating the shades fiercely from behind.   36

Ah, how they made them lift their legs
    at the first stroke! Indeed,
    none waited for the second or for the third.

While I was going on, my eyes fell on one;
    whereupon immediately I said,
    "I am not fasting for the sight of him!"[29]

Therefore I delayed advancing to look;
    and my dear leader stopped with me
    and consented that I go back a little.

The whipped shade thought he could hide
    by lowering his face, but it availed him little,
    for I said, "You who cast your eyes on the ground,   48

if the features you wear are not false,
    are Venedico Caccianemico;
    but what brings you into such a pickle?"

And he to me, "Unwillingly I say it,
    but I am compelled by your clear speech
    which makes me recall the world.

I am the one who led Ghisolabella [his sister]
    to do the Marquis' [of Este's] will,
    however the vile tale may sound,

and I am not the only Bolognese weeping here;
    on the contrary the place is so full of them
    that as many tongues are not now being taught   60

[29]"I have seen this person before."

to say 'sipa' between the Savena and the Reno;
    and if you want assurance of that,
    recall to your mind our avaricious hearts."

While he was speaking thus, a demon struck him
    with his whip, saying, "Away, pander!
    Here are no women to turn into cash!"

> *To see the seducers, who have been going to the left, the poets mount to the top of the bridge. They observe Jason, a dignified figure, but whipped, like the others. His principal crime, besides robbing the Colchians of the Golden Fleece and deserting Medea, was the seduction of Hypsipyle. The latter, according to the legend, had already shown her weakness by saving her father's life when the disgusted women of Lemnos tried to kill off all the men.*

I rejoined my escort; then,
    after a few steps, we came
    to where a rough bridge projects from the bank.

Quite easily we climbed it,
    and turning to the right over its ridge
    we moved away from that eternal bank.   72

When we reached the point below which the bridge opens
    to give passage for those whipped,
    my leader said, "Stop, and let your sight

fall on these other ill-born souls
    whose faces you have not yet seen,
    since they have been going with us."

From the old bridge we looked at the file
    coming toward us on the other side
    and whom the whip likewise drove on.

And my good master, without my asking, said,
    "Look at that great one coming,
    who, for his pain, sheds no tears;   84

what a regal bearing he still has!
    That is Jason who through courage and slyness
    deprived the Colchians of their ram [Golden Fleece].

He passed through the island of Lemnos
    after the bold and pitiless women
    had given up to death all their men.

There, with gifts and fine words,
    he deceived Hypsipyle, the young girl
    who first had deceived all the others.[30]

[30] Hypsipyle spared her father and told the other women of Lemnos that he had been killed along with the other males. For a version of the Jason-Medea story, see Euripides' *Medea*.

He abandoned her pregnant and forlorn.
    Such guilt condemns him to this punishment;
    and vengeance is taken also for Medea.   96

With him go all those who deceive in this way:
    let this knowledge suffice for the first vale
    and for those it holds in its grip."

*The poets proceed to where they can see the flatterers in the second ditch. Dante
chooses the elegant Thaïs as his ancient example, perhaps to emphasize the essential filthiness of these sinners who, like dogs, lick the sores of those they exploit.
The contrast is all the more striking because the charge against her seems trivial.
Moreover, Dante had misread the incident in Cicero; the guilty one was Gnatho,
not Thaïs. But the lesson is clear: even Thaïs could not make flattery clean.*

We had already come to where the narrow road
    crosses the second bank and makes of it
    an abutment for another arch.

Here we heard people moaning in the next ditch
    and puffing with their snouts
    and hitting themselves with their hands.

The banks were encrusted with a mold
    condensed from the vapor from below
    which offends both the eyes and nose.   108

The bottom was so deep it could be seen
    only by mounting to the summit of the arch
    where the bridge stands highest.

We reached that place, and down in the ditch
    I saw people plunged in excrement
    which seemed to have come from human privies.

And while I was searching down there with my eyes,
    I saw one with his head so smeared with filth
    that you could not tell if he were a layman or a clerk.

He bawled to me, "Why are you so eager
    to look at me more than at the other ugly ones?"
    And I to him, "Because, if I remember well,   120

I saw you once with dry hair;
    you are Alessio Interminei da Lucca;
    therefore, I eye you more than all the rest."

Then beating on his pate, he said,
    "The flatteries with which my tongue
    was never cloyed have put me down here."

After that my guide said to me,
    "See that you extend your gaze
    so that your eyes may reach the face

of that filthy and disheveled wench
　　who is scratching herself with her dirty nails
　　and now squats and now is standing on her feet.　　132

Thaïs,[31] she is, the harlot
　　who answered her paramour when he said,
　　'Have I *great* favor with you?' 'No, *marvelous!*'

And with this let our sight be satisfied."

CANTO XIX

THE SIMONISTS

Dante's objectivity ceases when we come to the simonists who by trafficking in church offices and enriching themselves tend to destroy the Church itself. Their fat feeds the fire which now punishes them.

O Simon Magus![32] O rapacious followers,
　　you who should be wedded to righteousness
　　and instead prostitute the things of God

for gold and silver, now for you
　　it is necessary that the trumpet sound,
　　since you are in the third ditch.

Already we had mounted to that part
　　of the following bridge
　　which hangs over the middle of the moat.

O Supreme Wisdom, how great is the art Thou showest
　　in Heaven, on earth, and in the evil world,
　　and how justly Thy power rewards!　　12

I saw the livid stone covered with holes
　　on the sides and on the bottom,
　　all round, and of one breadth.

They appeared neither larger nor smaller
　　than those in my beautiful San Giovanni
　　made for the baptizers to stand in,

one of which, not many years ago, I broke
　　to save a drowning child—and let this
　　be my seal [on the truth] to undeceive all men.[33]

---

[31] This is not the famous courtesan but a whore in a play by Terence, the Roman dramatist (second century B.C.).

[32] Simon "the Magician," who, according to Acts of the Apostles 8, was rebuked by Peter for attempting to buy the powers of the apostles that only God could give. The word *simony* is derived from his name.

[33] Untrue rumors apparently had circulated about this incident, but what they were is not known.

From the mouth of each a sinner's feet protruded
    and his legs up to the calf,
    and the rest remained within.   24

The soles of the feet of all were on fire,
    and their legs above the joints writhed so sharply
    that they would have broken withes or ropes.

As flames on oily things are wont
    to move only over the outer surface,
    so they did here from heel to toe.

"Who is that one, Master, who writhes so,
    twitching more than the others, his companions,
    and who feeds a ruddier flame?" I asked.

And he to me, "If you want me to carry you down there
    over the [inner] bank which slopes less steeply,
    you will learn from him about himself and his misdeeds."   36

And I, "Whatever you want is good for me;
    you are my lord, and you know that my will
    is like your own, and you know also what I keep silent."

Then we came to the fourth bank
    where we turned and descended on the left
    down into the narrow and pitted bottom.

My kind master still did not put me down,
    but carried me to the hole of the one
    who was so lamenting with his shanks.

> *The inverted shade, Pope Nicholas III, mistakes Dante for Boniface VIII (still living in 1300) who, after outraging the Church (the "Bride of Christ"), is to follow him here. Nicholas belonged to the Orsini family (*orso*, bear), and used his office to advance the cubs. In this mockery of the apostolic succession, Boniface will be succeeded by Clement V, who, as the tool of Philip the Fair of France, transferred the papacy to Avignon. A certain vulgarity characterizes the speech of all mercenary sinners and the terms used to describe them.*

"O, whoever you are, sad spirit,
    upside down, planted like a stake,"
    I began to say, "if you can, speak."   48

I stood like the friar confessing a treacherous assassin
    who, after being put in the hole [to be buried alive],
    calls the confessor back to delay his death,

and he shouted, "Are you already standing there,
    are you already there, O Boniface?—
    The writing [Book of Fate] lied to me by several years.

Are you so quickly sated with the wealth
    for which you were not afraid to seize the beautiful lady
    through guile and then to outrage her?"

I became like those who wonder

if they are mocked, not understanding the words
    said to them, and who are unable to reply.   60

Then Virgil said, "Tell him quickly
    'I am not, I am not the one you think,'"
    and I answered as I had been bidden.

At that the spirit twisted both his feet,
    then sighing and with a tearful voice
    he said, "What do you ask of me?

If you want so much to learn who I am
    that you have come down the bank to hear,
    know that I was clothed with the great mantle,

and truly I was a son of the she-bear
    so covetous to advance the cubs
    that on earth I put wealth, and here myself, in a sack.   72

Below, under my head, the others[34]
    who preceded me in simony are compressed,
    squeezed into the fissures of the rock.

Down there I also will be pressed
    when he comes for whom I took you
    when I asked the sudden question.

But I have already been roasted
    and have stood thus upside down longer
    than he will stay planted with reddened feet,

for after him, out of the West, will come
    a shepherd without law, of uglier deed,
    fit to cover both him and me.   84

He will be like the Jason[35] of whom we read in Maccabees,
    and as to Jason a king dealt gently,
    so will the ruler of France treat him."

> *Dante addresses Nicholas with intense feeling, restrained only by reverence for this sinner's past office. He mentions the Scarlet Woman, as the symbol of the corrupt Church.*
>
> *In this bolgia things are generally upside down. The clergy inverted their duties and are now inverted themselves; Dante, a layman, hears a confession, like a friar, and then preaches a sermon to an ex-pope.*

I do not know if I was now too bold,
    but I answered him in this strain:
    "Alas, now tell me, how much treasure

did our Lord ask of St. Peter
    before he put the keys in his hands?
    Surely he demanded only, 'Follow me!'

[34] That is, the other simoniacal popes, all of whom are thrust into the same hole.

[35] In 2 Maccabees 4–5 (a book of the Roman Catholic Bible), the unworthy Jason obtains from the king of Syria by bribery the office of Jewish high priest.

Nor did Peter and the others ask Matthias
  for gold or silver when he was chosen
  for the place the guilty soul [Judas] had lost.[36]   96

Therefore, stay there, for you are well punished,
  and keep securely the ill-got money
  which made you so bold against Charles [of Anjou].

And if I were still not prevented
  by reverence for the holy keys
  which you kept in the happy life,

I would use words still heavier;
  for your avarice afflicts the world,
  crushing the good and lifting up the bad.

The Evangelist [St. John] had shepherds like you in mind
  when she [the Scarlet Woman][37] that sitteth upon many waters
  was seen by him fornicating with kings,   108

she who was born with seven heads [virtues]
  and from ten horns [commandments] gained strength
  as long as virtue pleased the bridegroom [the papacy].

You have made a god of gold and silver,
  and how do you differ from the idolater,
  except that he worships one thing of gold, and you a hundred?

> The papal claims to temporal power were based in part on the supposed gift of the
> Western Empire to St. Sylvester by Constantine. The document confirming this
> transfer was not recognized as a forgery until after Dante's time, but our poet
> held that the emperor had no power to make such a gift nor the pope to receive it.
>
> Virgil, as the representative of the Roman Empire in the political allegory, is so
> delighted with Dante's sermon that he carries his pupil out of the ditch and to the
> top of the next bridge.

Ah, Constantine,[38] to how much ill gave birth
  not your conversion, but that dowry
  which the first rich father took from you!"

While I sang these notes to him,
  whether anger or conscience stung him,
  he kicked hard with both his feet.   120

I believe my leader was pleased,
  with such a contented look he listened
  to the true words I had expressed.

With both arms he took hold of me,
  and when he had me quite upon his breast,
  he remounted by the way we had come down,

---

[36] In Acts 1, Matthias is chosen by prayer and the casting of lots as successor to Judas as one of the twelve apostles.

[37] The details Dante gives are from Revelation 17; the passage refers to Rome.

[38] Roman emperor from 306 to 337, a convert to Christianity who moved the capital of the empire to Constantinople.

nor did he tire of holding me tightly,
>but carried me to the top of the arch
>which crosses from the fourth to the fifth bank.

There, softly, he put down his burden—
>softly because of the rough and steep rocks
>which would have been a hard road even for goats.   132

From there another valley was disclosed.

CANTO XX

THE DIVINERS

The sight of the soothsayers, diviners, and magicians, with their heads twisted around and walking backward, makes Dante weep. He had previously shown pity for the victims of our human defects, but now he is sorry for the punishment itself. This is a kind of protest against the divine order, and he is severely rebuked by Virgil. The scolding is most striking since Virgil had been considered a diviner, a master of magic art, and the sin punished here often tempted men of learning like Dante himself.

For new punishments I must make verses
>and provide matter for the twentieth canto
>of the first book, which is about the damned.

I was already placed where I could see
>into the uncovered depth
>which was bathed with tears of anguish,

and I saw people move silent and weeping
>through the circular valley, at the pace of those
>who chant litanies in this world.

When my eyes saw them more clearly
>each appeared to be twisted marvelously
>between the chin and the beginning of the chest,   12

for their faces were turned to the rear,
>and each was obliged to move backward,
>since seeing ahead was denied them.

Perhaps by the force of paralysis
>someone might be wholly twisted thus,
>but I have never seen the case nor believe it exists.

Reader, so may God let you profit
>by your reading, now think for yourself
>how I could keep my face dry

when I saw our [human] image, close at hand,
>so twisted that the tears from the eyes
>bathed the buttocks along the cleft.   24

Certainly I wept, leaning on a rock
    of the hard bridge, so that my escort said to me,
    "Are you, too, like the other fools?

Here pity lives when it is completely dead.
    Who is more impious than that one
    who feels sorrow for God's judgment?

> *Virgil now points out certain soothsayers of antiquity, characters chosen from
> various epic poems. The accounts of them are incorrect in some respects, perhaps
> to show once more the fallibility of men's minds. In discussing Manto, Virgil
> gives an account of the founding of Mantua different from one in the* Aeneid.
> *Moreover, in the* Purgatory, *Manto is mentioned as in a different circle. The
> digression interests even Dante only slightly.*

Lift up your head and see him [an augur] for whom
    the earth opened in the sight of the Thebans
    so that they cried, 'Where are you falling,

O Amphiaraus? why are you giving up the war?'
    and he did not stop rushing headlong
    down to Minos who seizes everyone;   36

observe how he has made a breast of his shoulders;
    because he wished to see too far ahead,
    he looks behind, and goes backward.

See Tiresias [a soothsayer] who changed his semblance
    when he became from man, a woman,
    transforming all his members,

and before he could regain his manly hair
    it was necessary for him to strike again
    the two entwined serpents with his wand.[39]

The one backing up to his belly
    is Aruns who, in the Luni mountains
    beneath which the Carrarese live and plow,   48

had a cave in the white marble for a dwelling
    from which no obstacle cut off
    a view of the sea or of the stars.

And she who covers her breasts
    which you do not see, with her loose tresses,
    and has on the other side all hairy skin,

was Manto, who sought through many lands
    before she settled where I was born
    and of her I would like for you to hear.

---

[39] Tiresias had first been changed from a man into a woman when he struck two entwined
serpents with his wand; years later he saw and struck them again, whereupon he was changed
back into a man. Manto, mentioned later, was his daughter.

After her father had given up his life
    and Bacchus' city [Thebes] was enslaved
    she wandered a long time through the world.   60

In beautiful Italy, above the Tyrol,
    at the foot of the Alps which enclose Germany,
    lies a lake named Benaco.

A thousand brooks and more bathe the Apennino
    from Guarda to Val Canonica
    whose waters come to rest in this lake.

In the middle is a point where the pastors
    of Trento, Brescia, and Verona
    could give a blessing if they went that way.

Peschiera lies as a fair and powerful rampart
    to face the Brescians and the Bergamese
    where the shore is lowest.   72

There, all that the lap of Benaco
    cannot hold must overflow
    through green pastures and make a river.

When the water begins to flow,
    it is no longer called Benaco, but Mincio
    as far as Governo, where it falls into the Po.

After a short course it finds a flat region
    over which it spreads and forms a marsh
    which in summer is wont to be noisome.

While passing there, the cruel virgin
    saw land in the middle of the fen
    uncultivated and devoid of inhabitants.   84

There, to shun all human intercourse,
    she, with her servants, stayed to practice her art,
    and lived, and left there her empty body.

Later the people scattered around
    gathered in that place which was strong
    because of the marsh on all sides.

They built the city on her bones
    and for her who first chose the place
    they called it Mantua, without other augury.

Once its people were more numerous
    before the madness of Casalodi [its ruler]
    was deceived by Pinamonte.   96

Therefore I warn you, that if you ever hear
    of another origin for my city,
    let no falsehood defraud the truth."

And I, "Master, your account is so certain
    and takes such hold on my belief
    that others would be like dead coals.

But tell me about the people passing by,
    whether you see any worthy of note,
    for to that alone my mind reverts."

> *The account of Eurypylus at the time of the Trojan wars differs also from its source in Virgil, a slip all the more striking since Dante implies that he knew the* Aeneid *by heart.*
>
> *Among the modern soothsayers is Michael Scott who lived at the court of Frederick II of Sicily. His legend survived in Scotland down to modern times. Other minor figures include Guido Bonatti, an astrologer of Forlì, Asdente, the cobbler of Parma, and various fortune-tellers and witches.*
>
> *In Italian folklore, the Man in the Moon is Cain. He is mentioned in indicating the time. It is about six o'clock on Saturday morning, April 9, 1300.*

Then he said, "That one who from his cheeks
    lets his beard fall on his dark shoulders
    was an augur [during the Trojan War] when Greece was so empty
        of males   108

that scarcely any remained for the cradles,
    and in Aulis, together with Calchas,
    he set the time for setting sail for Troy.

Eurypylus was his name, and my lofty tragedy
    sings of him in one place,
    as you know well, since you know it all.

The other, so slender in the flanks,
    was Michael Scott, who really knew
    the game of magic frauds.

See also Guido Bonatti, see Asdente
    who now wishes he had attended
    to his leather and his thread, but too late repents.   120

See the poor women who left the needle,
    the shuttle, and the spindle, and became fortunetellers;
    they wrought magic with herbs and images.

But come now, for Cain with his thorns
    is already on the confines of both hemispheres
    and below Seville is sinking in the sea,

and last night the moon was round;
    you must remember, since it was not unwelcome
    at times in the deep wood."

Thus he spoke as we moved on.

CANTO XXI

THE BARRATORS (GRAFTERS)

Thus we went from bridge to bridge, talking of things
    my Comedy does not care to mention,
    and reached the top of the next arch

where we stopped to see the ditch
    and to hear the other vain laments;
    and I found it marvelously dark.

As in the shipyards of the Venetians,
    in winter, the tenacious pitch boils
    to calk their damaged ships,

since the sailors cannot navigate, and instead
    some build new boats, some strengthen the ribs
    of one that has made many voyages;   12

some hammer at the prow and some at the stern;
    some make oars, and some twist ropes;
    some mend the jib and mainsail,

so, not by fire, but through divine art
    a dense tar boils down there
    which coats the banks on each side.

I saw the pitch, but did not see in it
    anything except the bubbles which rise,
    swell up, and then collapse.

While I was looking fixedly down there
    my guide drew me from where I was,
    saying, "Look! look!"   24

Then I turned like one suddenly dismayed,
    striving to see something
    from which he must escape

and who, to see, does not delay his start;
    and I noticed behind us a black devil
    coming at a run over the bridge.

Ah, how fierce he was in aspect,
    and how ferocious he seemed in act,
    with wings open, and light upon his feet!

His shoulders which were high and sharp
    were burdened by the haunches of a sinner
    the sinews of whose feet he clutched.   36

From our bridge he cried, "O Malebranche [devils],
    here is one of the elders[40] of Santa Zita [Lucca],
    put him under while I go back for more

[40] Public officials of Lucca, of which Zita was the patron saint.

to that city I have so well furnished with them.
    Everyone is a barrator there, except Bonturo;[41]
    there, for money, a 'no' becomes a 'yes.'"

Down he hurled him, and turned back
    over the rough bridge, and never was a mastiff
    in such haste to follow a thief.

The sinner plunged in, then rose doubled up,
    but the demons hiding under the bridge shouted,
    "Here there is no Holy Face [as at Lucca] to pray to!   48

Here you do not swim as in the Serchio!
    So, unless you want to feel our hooks,
    don't show yourself above the pitch!"

Then they struck him with more than a hundred prongs,
    saying, "Here you must dance under cover
    and pilfer secretly if you can!"

Not otherwise do cooks have their scullions
    dip the meat in the middle of the boiler
    with forks, so that it will not float.

> *Virgil holds a parley with the demons below the bridge. Then Dante rejoins his
> master, keeping as close to him (Reason) as he can, but using his eyes as well. The
> entire episode with the devils beginning here (a concession to the popular spirit of
> the Middle Ages) symbolizes incidentally Dante's narrow escape from Florence,
> where one of the false charges against him was barratry.*

My good master said, "So that it may not appear
    that you are here, crouch down
    behind a rock and remain hidden,   60

and whatever outrage is done to me
    do not be afraid, for I know about this business;
    once before I was in a like affray."

Then he went to the head of the bridge,
    and as he arrived on the sixth bank
    he needed a steadfast heart.

With that fury and that uproar
    with which dogs run out at a beggar
    who suddenly stops and begs from where he is,

those devils rushed out from under the bridge,
    turning against him all their hooks.
    But he cried, "Let none of you be headstrong.   72

Before your grapples touch me,
    let one of you come forward to hear me
    and then decide about hooking me."

---

[41] This is ironic; Bonturo was an especially notorious grafter.

All shouted, "Let Malacoda go"; whereupon one
　　stepped forward while the others stood firm,
　　and came to him saying, "What good will it do him?"

"Do you think, Malacoda,
　　that you see me here," my master said,
　　"safe from all your opposition,

without divine will and propitious fate?
　　Let me go on, for it is willed in Heaven
　　that I should show another this wild way."　　　　84

Then Malacoda's pride collapsed so suddenly
　　that he let his hook fall at his feet
　　and said to the others, "Do not strike him."

And my guide called to me, "O you, crouching quietly
　　behind the rocks of the bridge,
　　you may come now securely."

I started out and went quickly to him,
　　and all the devils pressed forward,
　　so that I feared they might not keep their pact.

Thus I once saw foot soldiers afraid
　　on leaving Caprona under safe conduct,
　　when they saw themselves among so many enemies.　　96

I drew close to my guide with my whole body,
　　but did not take my eyes
　　from the devils' looks, which were not good.

They lowered their hooks, one saying to another,
　　"Should I nick him on the rump?"
　　and being answered, "Yes, let him have it!"

But the demon who had held the parley
　　with my leader turned instantly,
　　and said, "Quiet, quiet, Scarmiglione!"

　　　Malacoda proposes that a squad accompany the travelers to the next "unbroken"
　　bridge. Since all the bridges over the next bolgia are broken, the devils under-
　　stand that a trick is to be played on Virgil. To be more convincing in his fraud,
　　Malacoda cites some statistics to show how much time has passed since the Cruci-
　　fixion and the resultant earthquake. Dante, using his senses and intuition, would
　　prefer to go on alone, but Virgil (Reason), taken in, tries to reassure him; and the
　　grotesque company moves on.

Then he said to us, "You cannot go farther
　　on this bridge, since the sixth arch
　　lies all broken on the bottom,　　　　　　　　108

but if you still want to go ahead,
　　keep advancing along this bank;
　　nearby is another bridge that provides a way.

Yesterday, five hours later than this hour,
    a thousand two hundred and sixty-six years[42]
    were completed since the bridge here was broken.

I am sending some of my men over there
    to see if any are airing themselves;
    go with them, since they won't be harmful.

Step forward, Alichino and Calcabrina,"
    he then began to say, "and Cagnazzo,
    and you, Barbariccia, guide the squad.   120

Let Libicocco come and Draghignazzo,
    Ciriatto with his tusks, and Graffiacane,
    and Farfarello, and mad Rubicante.

Look around the boiling glue;
    let these be safe as far as to the bridge
    which *all unbroken* passes over the dens."

"Oh, Master, what is this I see?"
    I exclaimed. "Ah, without escort, let us go alone
    if you know the way; as for me, I ask for none.

If you are as wary as usual,
    don't you see that they are gnashing their teeth,
    and with their frowns threaten grief to us?"   132

And he to me, "Do not be afraid,
    let them grind away as they like,
    because they do that for the wretches in the pitch."

The devils turned to the left on the bank,
    but first each pressed his tongue between his teeth,
    as a signal to their leader,

and he, for a trumpet, used his rump.[43]

CANTO XXII

CIAMPOLO OF NAVARRE

I have seen horsemen move camp
    and launch an attack, and hold their muster,
    and sometimes turn back to escape;

I have seen scouting parties in your land,
    O Aretines! and foragers start out,
    tournaments begin and races run,

sometimes at the sound of trumpets or of bells,
    with drums and with castle signals,
    and with familiar and strange devices,

---

[42] Christ died at the age of 33, and the present year is 1300, but Dante is presumably dating from Christ's conception, not his birth.

[43] Farted.

but never yet did I see horse or footmen move
    to so strange a bugle call,
    or a ship at a sign on land or in the sky. 12

We went along with the ten demons;
    ah, fierce company! but "in church with saints,
    and in the tavern with the gluttons!"

I was attentive to the pitch
    to see what the bolgia contained
    and the people burning in it.

As dolphins make signs to sailors
    by the arching of their backs
    to prepare to save their ship,

so now and then, to relieve the pain,
    some of the sinners showed their backs
    and hid again as fast as lightning flashes; 24

and, as at the edge of the water of a ditch,
    frogs lie with just their muzzles out,
    hiding their feet and bodies,

so, on every side, the sinners lay;
    but when Barbariccia came near,
    they withdrew within the boiling.

I saw, and still my heart shudders at it,
    a soul waiting thus, just as it happens
    that one frog may remain when the others dart away,

and Graffiacane who was closest to him
    hooked his pitchy locks, and pulled him out
    so that he looked like an otter. 36

I already knew the names of all the demons
    so well did I note them when they were chosen,
    and as they called each other I noticed how.

"O Rubicante, see that you get your claws
    on him and skin him alive,"
    the accursed ones shouted all together,

and I, "Master, find out if you can
    who the unfortunate wretch is
    that has fallen into the hands of his enemies."

My guide went close to him and asked
    whence he came, and he replied,
    "I was born in the kingdom of Navarre. 48

My mother placed me as a servant to a lord,
    for she had borne me to a spendthrift,
    a destroyer of himself and of his property.

Then I was in the service of good King Thibault;
    there I began to commit barratry
    for which I give reckoning in this heat."

And Ciriatto from each side of whose mouth
    a tusk issued, as from a boar's,
    made him feel how one of them could rip.

The mouse had fallen among vicious cats;
    but Barbariccia took him in his arms
    and said, "Stand over there while I grip him."   60

And turning his face to my master,
    "Ask, if you want to hear more about him,"
    he said, "before the others mangle him."

My guide then said, "Now tell me, do you know
    any others under the pitch who are Italians?"
    And he answered, "A little while ago

I left one from a nearby island—
    (might I still be covered with him,
    for then I would fear neither claw nor hook!").

And Libicocco cried, "Too much have we endured,"
    and with his prong seized his arm
    and tearing it, carried off a sinew.   72

Draghignazzo also tried to lay hold
    of his legs, whereupon their corporal
    turned around with wicked looks.

When they were somewhat pacified
    my guide without delay addressed the sinner
    who was still looking at his wounds.

"Who is the one you say you left
    unluckily in order to come ashore?"
    and he replied, "It was Friar Gomita,

from Gallura, a vessel of every fraud
    who had his master's enemies in his hands
    and dealt with them so [gently] that all praise him.   84

Money he took, and let them off quietly
    as he says; and in other offices also
    he was not a little barrator, but a supreme one.

With him Don Michel Zanche of Logodoro
    keeps company, and their tongues
    are never tired of talking about Sardinia.

O me! see that one grinding his teeth;
    I would say more, but I am afraid
    he is getting ready to scratch my sticky coat!"

And their commander in chief, turning to Farfarello,
    who was rolling his eyes on the point of striking,
    said, "Get over there, vile bird!"   96

"If you wish to see or hear,"
    the frightened one [Ciampolo] then began,
    "some Tuscans or Lombards, I will have some come,

but let the Malebranche stand back a little
    so that their vengeance will not be feared,
    and I, sitting in this very place,

for one that I am, will make many come
    when I whistle, as it is our custom
    to do when any of us gets out."

Cagnazzo at these words raised his snout,
    shaking his head, and said, "Listen to the trick
    he has thought of to plunge down."   108

Then he [Ciampolo], who had a wealth of guile,
    answered, "I am too tricky indeed
    when I get greater sorrow for my friends!"

Alichino could hold back no longer
    and contrary to the others said,
    "If you plunge, I'll not gallop after you,

but will beat my wings above the pitch!
    Let the ridge be left and the bank made a screen
    to see if you can get the best of us."

O you who read will now hear new sport.
    All turned their eyes to the other side,
    and he first who had been most unwilling.   120

The Navarese chose well his time,
    steadied his feet upon the ground, and in an instant
    leaped, and from the marshal freed himself.

At that each was stung with guilt, and that one most
    who had been the cause of the mistake.
    He, swooping down, cried, "You're caught!"

but it availed little, for wings
    could not outstrip terror. The sinner went under,
    and his pursuer, flying, turned up his breast.

Not otherwise does the wild duck plunge
    when the falcon comes near
    which, defeated and angry, flies up again.   132

Calcabrina, furious at the trick,
    also went after him, eager for the sinner to escape
    so that he could start a quarrel.

And when the barrator had disappeared,
    he turned his claws on his companion
    and grappled with him above the ditch.

But Alichino was a full-grown hawk
    for clawing him back, and both fell
    into the middle of the boiling pond.

The heat at once broke their grip,
    but there was no way for them to rise,
    since their wings were so beglued.   144

Barbariccia, complaining with the rest,
    had four fly to the other bank
    with all their hooks, and quickly

on this side and that they went to their places
    and reached with their grapples to those stuck
    and already partly cooked within the crust;

and while they were embarrassed in this way we left them.

CANTO XXIII

THE HYPOCRITES

The devils' fight over the pitch has reminded Dante of a fable which tells how a frog offers to tow a mouse tied to himself over a stream, intending to pull the rodent under. A kite, seeing their struggle, swoops down and carries off both.

Silent, alone, and without company
    we went on, one in front of the other,
    as minor friars go along their way.

My thought was turned to Aesop's fable
    by the present quarrel, where he speaks
    of the frog and of the mouse;

for "mo" and "issa" [synonyms for "now"] are not more alike
    if one compares with close attention
    the beginning and the end of each case.

And, as one thought bursts from another,
    there arose from that one a second
    which caused my first fear to be doubled.   12

I reflected thus: "Those devils through us
    are mocked with such scorn and damage
    as, I believe, must enrage them.

If anger is added to ill will,
    they will rush after us more fiercely
    than a hound after the rabbit he snaps up."

Already I felt my hair stand on end from fear,
    and I looked back intently and said,
    "Master, if you do not quickly hide

yourself and me, I fear the Malebranche;
    we already have them right behind us,
    I so imagine it that I can feel them now."   24

And he, "If I were leaded glass [a mirror]
    I would not reflect your outer image
    more quickly than I do your inner feelings.

Just now your thoughts were coming among mine
    similar to them in force and in meaning,
    so that of them all I made one resolve.

If it happens that the right bank lies
    so that we can go into the next ditch,
    we will escape the dreaded chase."

He had not finished giving this counsel
    when I saw the demons not far away
    coming with wings extended to seize us.   36

My guide suddenly took hold of me and,
    as a mother who is awakened by a noise
    and sees close to her the burning flames,

who takes her son and flees, caring more for him
    than for herself, and who does not stop
    even long enough to put on any clothes,

so, down from the edge of the hard bank,
    lying on his back, my guide slid over the rock
    which walls one side of the ditch.

Water never ran so fast through a sluice
    to turn a millwheel, at the moment
    when it is closest to the paddles,   48

as my master went down over the bank,
    carrying me upon his breast,
    not as a companion, but as a son.

Scarcely had his feet touched the bottom
    when the devils reached the height above us,
    but there was nothing to fear,

for High Providence, which wished to put them
    as ministers of the fifth ditch,
    took from all of them the power to leave.

The hypocrites whom the travelers now see wear gowns brilliant outwardly but of lead, like those Frederick II was supposed to have had melted on the backs of offenders against the throne. Like all who affect a pose, they must carry the weight of it forever. They move slowly, watching their steps. A kind of whining reproach sounds in their affected reference to Dante's and Virgil's clothes and to their "running." Not willing to commit themselves, they qualify the slightest promise with a "perhaps."

Down there we found a painted people
    who moved around the circle with slow steps,
    weeping, and, in countenance, wearied and overcome.   60

They wore capes with low hoods coming down
    in front of their eyes, cut in the style
    of those worn by the monks of Cluny,

outwardly gilded, so that they dazzled,
    but within of lead, and so heavy
    that [in comparison] those Frederick used were of straw.

O mantle eternally tiring! We turned once more
    to the left, moving with the sinners
    and listening to their sad lament;

but, because of their loads, those weary people
    came so slowly that at every step we took
    we found ourselves in new company.   72

Therefore I said to my guide, "Try to find someone
    who by name or deed might be recognized,
    and look around as we move on."

And one who understood the Tuscan speech
    shouted from behind us, "Stay your steps,
    you who are running so through the dark air;

perhaps you will hear from me what you ask for."
    My guide turned around and said,
    "Wait, and then come on at his pace."

I stopped and saw two showing by their looks
    great eagerness to be with me,
    but their burden and the narrow way delayed them.   84

When they came up, with sidelong glances
    they looked at me, without saying a word,
    then turned to each other and remarked,

"This man, by the movement of his throat, seems alive,
    and if they are both dead, by what privilege
    do they go divested of the heavy gown?"

Then they addressed me, "O Tuscan, you who have come
    to the college of the sad hypocrites,
    do not disdain to tell us who you are."

And I to them, "I was born and grew up
    by the beautiful Arno river, in the great city,
    and I am in the body I have always had.   96

But who are you whose distilled grief
    drips down over your cheeks,
    and what punishment glitters so on you?"

The two shades had been chosen as arbiters in the party strife of Florence instead
of the usual one man. Far from being neutral, they favored the Guelfs. As a
result certain houses of Ghibelline leaders near the old Gardingo fortress were
destroyed and the site was made into a public square.

One shade, new to Virgil, naked, like Christ at the Crucifixion, is lying on the
ground. This is Caiaphas, the high priest who, with others of the council of the
Jews, favored sacrificing Christ.

And one answered, "The orange-colored mantles
    are of lead, so thick that their weight
    would make any scales creak.

We are Jolly Friars, and Bolognese,
    I Catalano, and he, Loderingo,
    appointed together by your city

(as a single man usually is taken)
    to preserve the peace, and what we did
    can still be seen around the Gardingo.   108

I began, "O Brothers, your evil . . ."
    but I said no more, for the sight of a shade on the ground,
    crucified with three stakes, caught my eye.

When he saw me he writhed all his body,
    breathing into his beard with sighs,
    and Friar Catalano who noticed that

said to me, "The transfixed one at whom you are looking
    counseled the Pharisees that it was fitting
    to torture one man for the people.[44]

Now he is lying crosswise and naked on the road,
    as you see; and he must feel
    the weight of each one who passes.   120

In a similar way his father-in-law is tortured
    in this ditch, and the others of the Council
    which was a seed of evil for the Jews."

Then I saw Virgil marveling
    over the one stretched out so basely,
    like a cross, in the eternal exile.

Virgil learns of the humiliating trick played on him by the devils of the fifth
bolgia. The hypocrites are more expert in perceiving this deception than Reason
itself. In his usual indirect manner, not committing himself, Catalano points out

[44]For the roles of Caiaphas and his father-in-law Annas in Jesus' passion, see John 11
and 18.

that the Devil tells lies. Virgil, angry at the trick and disgusted with Catalano,
moves on contemptuously, without a word.

Afterward he addressed to the friar these words,
    "Please tell us, if you can,
    whether there is a gap on the right side

by which we two can get out of here
    without constraining the black angels
    to come and extricate us from this bottom."

He answered, "Nearer than you expect
    is a bridge which begins at the outer circle
    and covers all the cruel valleys,

except that over this one it is broken.
    You will be able to climb up on its ruins
    which slope down the side and pile up on the bottom."

My guide stood a moment with his head lowered,
    then said, "Falsely did the one up there
    who hooks the sinners explain the matter."

And the friar added, "I once heard someone say at Bologna
    that the Devil has many vices, among which I heard
    that he is a liar and the father of lies."

Then with long steps my guide went on,
    a little disturbed in his looks by anger,
    and I also departed from the burdened ones,

following the imprints of the beloved feet.

132

144

CANTO XXIV

VANNI FUCCI

A dainty comparison takes us for a moment into the fresh air of late winter when
the nights are beginning to get shorter and when the frost resembles for a while
the snow.

The poets struggle laboriously to get out of the ditch of hypocrisy.

In that part of the young year
    when the sun warms his locks beneath Aquarius
    and the long nights are moving toward the south,

when the frost copies on the ground
    the image of her white sister
    although the point of her pen lasts but little,

the poor peasant whose fodder is getting low
    rises, looks out, and sees the fields all white;
    whereupon he strikes his thigh,

turns back and, lamenting, walks up and down
   like a wretch who does not know what to do.
   Later he looks out again and recovers hope   12

on seeing that the world, in a little while,
   has changed appearance; and he takes his crook
   and drives forth the lambs to feed.

Thus my master made me disheartened
   when I saw his face so troubled,
   and thus quickly to the sore the plaster came.

For, when we reached the ruins of the bridge
   my guide turned to me with that pleasant look
   which I saw first at the foot of the mountain.

He opened his arms, after having made a plan
   within his mind, and looking carefully
   at the rocks he took hold of me,   24

and like one who calculates while working,
   who always seems to provide ahead of time,
   on lifting me toward the top of one rock

he examined another crag, saying,
   "Afterward catch hold of that,
   but see first if it will bear your weight."

It was not a way for one clothed in a leaden cloak,
   for we, he a shade and I pushed,
   could hardly mount from jag to jag.

And were it not that on this side
   the slope was shorter than on the other,
   I do not know about him, but I would have been exhausted;   36

but, since Malebolge slopes wholly
   toward the edge of the lowest well,
   the position of each ditch demands

that one side be higher than the other.
   We came finally to the place
   where the last stone is broken off.

The breath had been so pumped from my lungs
   as I went up that at the top
   I could go no farther, and sat down at once.

"Now you must free yourself from sloth,"
   my master said, "for, sitting on down
   or lying under covers, no one comes to fame,   48

without which whoever consumes his life
   leaves such vestige of himself on earth
   as smoke in air or foam on water.

Therefore get up, overcome your panting
    with the spirit which wins every battle
    if it does not sink with its heavy body.

A longer stairs must be climbed;
    it is not enough to have left this one;
    if you understand, act so that it may profit you."

I then got up showing myself better furnished
    with breath than I was, and I said,
    "Go on, for I am strong and bold."   60

The travelers now come to the ditch of the thieves.

We made our way up over the bridge
    which was rocky, narrow, and difficult,
    and much steeper than the previous ones.

I kept talking in order not to appear faint;
    whereupon from the next ditch a voice issued
    unsuited for forming words.

I do not know what it said, although I was already
    on top of the arch that crosses there,
    but whoever spoke seemed moved to anger.

I had turned to look down, but my living eyes
    could not penetrate to the bottom
    through the darkness; therefore I said,   72

"Master, let us try to reach the next bank,
    for, just as I hear, but do not understand,
    so I look, and can distinguish nothing."

"No reply do I make except by an act,"
    he said, "for a modest request
    should be followed silently by the deed."

We went down the bridge to the place
    where it joins the eighth bank,
    and then the ditch was revealed to me.

I saw in it a terrible pack of serpents
    of such diverse appearance
    that the memory of it still chills my blood.   84

Let Libya with its sands boast no longer,
    for if it produced chelydri, jaculi, and phareae,
    and cencri with amphisbaena [fabulous snakes],

it has never shown so many plagues
    or such bad ones, together with all of Ethiopia
    and the land [Arabia] which lies above the Red Sea.

Amid this cruel and dismal swarm, I saw people running,
    naked and terrified, without hope of hiding place
    or of heliotrope [to make themselves invisible].

Their hands were tied behind them by serpents
    which stuck their heads and tails through their backs,
    and were knotted together in front.   96

And behold! at one that was near our bank
    a serpent sprang and transfixed him
    right where the neck meets the shoulders.

Neither I nor O was ever written so quickly
    as he took fire and burned and fell
    like a cinder to the ground.

Then when he was thus destroyed
    the ashes came together of themselves
    and took on instantly the previous form.

Thus it is maintained by great sages
    that the Phoenix[45] dies and then is reborn
    when the five-hundredth year approaches.   108

During its life it feeds on neither grain
    nor herb, but on incense and amomum,
    and nard and myrrh make up its shroud.

And like one [an epileptic] who falls not knowing how,
    through the force of a demon pulling him to the ground
    or through some obstruction that paralyzes him,

and who, when he gets up, looks around, all bewildered
    by the great anguish he has suffered,
    and while looking sighs,

such was the sinner after he arose.
    O Power of God, how severe it is
    in showering down such blows of vengeance!   120

*The stricken soul is Vanni Fucci, one of Dante's former political enemies, whom
the poet had known, not as a thief, but only as hotheaded and violent. Vanni
predicts obscurely and maliciously certain events which will lead to the defeat of
the Florentine Whites.*

My guide then asked the sinner who he was;
    whereupon he answered, "I rained down from
    Tuscany into this gullet a little while ago.

A bestial, not human life, I liked,
    mule [of irregular birth] that I was; I am Vanni Fucci,
    a beast, and Pistoia was a den worthy of me."

I said to my guide, "Tell him not to slip away
    and ask what sin thrusts him down here,
    for I saw him once a man of blood and rage."

[45] The mythical bird that was consumed in fire every 500 years and then arose to new life
from the ashes of its dead self.

And the soul, having heard, did not dissemble,
    but directed toward me his face
    and his attention with a look of dismal shame.   132

Then he said, "It grieves me more
    that you have caught me in this misery
    than when I was taken from the other world.

I cannot deny what you ask for;
    I have been put down this far for the theft
    of the fine ornaments of the sacristy,

for which another was falsely accused.
    But to keep you from enjoying this sight,
    if you ever get out of this dark place,

open your ears to my prophecy and hear:
    Pistoia first is thinned of Blacks,
    then Florence renews her masters and her ways;   144

Mars draws a fiery vapor [thunderbolt] from Val di Magra
    which is wrapped in turbid clouds,
    and in an impetuous and angry storm

a battle will be fought on the Piceno field;
    then the blast will pierce the mist
    so that every White will be wounded by it.

And I have told you this so that you may grieve."

CANTO XXV

The Metamorphosis of Thieves

At the end of his remarks the thief
    raised both hands, making the [obscene] sign of the fig,
    and shouting, "Take that, God, for at Thee I point them!"

From then on the serpents were my friends,
    for one coiled around his neck, as if saying,
    "I will not have you speak any more,"

and another encircled his arms and bound them,
    so clinching itself in front
    that he could not make a move with those members.

Ah, Pistoia, why do you not resolve to burn
    so that you will last no longer, since you surpass
    your own founders [followers of Catiline] in wickedness?   12

Through all the dark circles of Hell
    I saw no spirit so bold against God,
    not even him [Capaneus] who fell from the walls of Thebes.

The thief fled, saying nothing further.
    Then I saw a centaur, full of wrath, come calling,
    "Where is he? Where is the impious one?"

I do not believe Maremma has as many snakes
    as the centaur had on its back
    up to where our human form begins.

Upon his shoulders, behind his neck,
    a dragon was lying with open wings
    which set on fire all it met.   24

My master said, "That is Cacus [a fire-breathing monster]
    who, under the rocks of Mount Aventine,
    many times made a lake of blood.

He does not go on the same road as his brothers
       [the other centaurs]
    because of the theft he slyly made
    of the great herd [of cattle] kept near him,

which led to the end of his wicked life
    under the club of Hercules, who gave him
    perhaps a hundred blows, although hardly ten were felt."

While Virgil was saying this, the centaur ran off,
    and three spirits [Agnello, Buoso, and Puccio] came below us
    whom neither my master nor I had noticed   36

until they cried, "Who are you?"
    Whereupon our talking ceased,
    and we gave heed to them alone.

I did not recognize them, but it happened
    as sometimes occurs by chance
    that one needed to name the other,

saying, "Where can Cianfa [now a serpent] have remained?"
    In order to make my guide attentive,
    I held my finger against my mouth from chin to nose.

If you are slow, Reader, to believe
    what I am to relate, it will be no wonder,
    for I who saw it scarcely admit it to myself.   48

As I kept my eyes on them, a serpent [Cianfa]
    with six legs darted in front of one
    and fastened itself wholly to him.

With its middle feet it clasped his belly
    and with those in front seized his arms;
    then it set its fangs in both his cheeks.

It spread its hind feet over his thighs
    and thrust its tail between them
    drawing it up along his back.

Ivy never clung to a tree so tightly
    as the horrible beast
    entwined the other's members in its own;   60

then they grew together and exchanged their color
    as if they had been hot wax,
    nor did either one or the other appear as before.

Thus a dark hue moves ahead of a flame
    over a sheet of paper, as the whiteness
    dies away before it becomes black.

The other two [Buoso and Puccio] watched and shouted,
    "O me, Agnello, how you are changing!
    Behold! You are now neither two nor one."

The two heads had already fused into one,
    and the shapes of two faces appeared blended
    in the one in which the others had disappeared.   72

The two arms were formed of four strips;
    the thighs with the legs, the belly and the chest,
    became such members as were never seen.

All the former features were blotted out;
    the perverse image seemed two and none,
    and thus went away with slow steps.

As a lizard, under the great scourge
    of the dog days, passing from hedge to hedge,
    seems a flash as it crosses the path,

so appeared, making for the bellies
    of the remaining two, a small, fiery serpent,
    livid and black as a peppercorn,   84

and pierced that part in one of them
    where we first receive our nourishment;
    then fell, stretched out, in front of him.

The one transfixed [Buoso] looked at it, silently,
    and with feet motionless, yawned,
    as if sleep or a fever had come upon him.

He eyed the reptile, and the reptile him;
    from the wound of one and mouth of the other
    thick smoke issued and combined.

Let Lucan be silent now where he tells
    of poor Sabellus and of Nasidius [transformed by serpents],
    and wait to hear what is announced.   96

Let Ovid keep still concerning Cadmus and Arethusa,
    for if he changes one into a serpent in his verse
    and the other into a spring, I do not envy him,

since he never changed two natures
    face to face so that both forms
    were ready to exchange their substance.

The two responded to each other in such a way
    that the serpent made a fork of its tail,
    and the wounded shade drew its feet together.

The legs and the thighs united,
    so that in a little while there was no sign
    you could see of the joining.   108

The split tail took on the shape
    lost in the other; the skin of one became soft
    and that of the other hard.

I saw the arms withdraw through the armpits
    and the short legs of the reptile
    lengthen as much as the other's arms were shortened.

Then the hind feet, twisted together,
    became the member man hides,
    and the shade from his made two legs project.

As the smoke covered both with a new color
    it brought out hair on one
    and removed it from the other.   120

One got up and the other fell,
    neither, however, turning aside his gaze
    under which each had changed faces.

The one standing drew his snout toward his temples,
    and with the flesh left over
    ears were formed on the smooth cheeks.

What was not drawn back and remained
    in excess made a nose for the face
    and thickened the lips to a fit size.

The one on the ground stretched forth his nose,
    withdrew his ears within his head,
    as a snail does its horns,   132

and his tongue which had been undivided
    and apt for speech, split; and the forked tongue
    united; then the smoke stopped.

The soul that had become a brute
    fled hissing through the ditch,
    and after it the other, talking and sputtering.

Then he turned his new back to the reptile
    and said, "I want Buoso to run
    as I have, crawling over the way."

Thus I saw the seventh ballast change
    and interchange, and let the strangeness of it
    be my excuse if my pen has gone astray.   144

Although my eyes were somewhat confused
    and my mind bewildered, those shades
    could not slip away so secretly

that I did not recognize easily
    Puccio Sciancato, who was the only one
    of the three companions left unchanged.

> *The unidentified figure (originally the second snake) was Francesco de' Caval-*
> *canti, killed by the people of Gaville. The town mourns because of the vengeance*
> *taken for him.*

The other was he because of whom you, Gaville, weep.

CANTO XXVI

ULYSSES

The bitter tone of the beginning lines of an apostrophe to Florence ends quickly
when Dante thinks of the misfortune certain to come to his city, a disaster wished
for by neighboring towns, like Prato, not to mention enemies. Here, as elsewhere,
the invective expresses deep concern, a kind of inverted love.

Rejoice, Florence, since you are so great
    that over land and over sea you beat your wings,
    and your name is famous in Hell!

Among the thieves I found five citizens of yours,
    such that shame comes over me;
    and you do not rise through them to great honor.

But if the truth is dreamed of near the morning,
    you will soon feel what Prato,
    not to mention others, craves for you.

And if that had already happened, it would not be
    too soon; so were it, since it has to be!
    for it will weigh heavier on me as I grow older.   12

> *The poets reach the summit of the bridge over the bolgia where evil counseling is*
> *punished. This sin, incurred mainly by those of superior intelligence, offered*
> *constant temptations to Dante, an exile dependent upon patronage.*
>
> *In the ditch below, lights appear, like fireflies at dusk on a summer evening. And*
> *just as Elisha saw Elijah rise up, enveloped in a cloud of flame, so here the fire*
> *concealed the spirits. Dante asks about a double flame, like that on the funeral*
> *pyre of Eteocles and Polynices, two brothers who had killed each other.*

We departed, and over the steps
    which stones had made for our descent,
    my guide remounted, and drew me up,

and continuing our solitary way
    over the stones and rocks of the bridge,
    feet did not advance without help from hands.

I grieved then, and now I grieve again
  when I direct my thought to what I saw,
  and I control my mind more than usual

so that virtue alone may guide it.
  Thus, if a kindly star or something better [Divine Grace]
  has given an advantage, it may not be harmful through abuse.   24

As a peasant who is resting on a slope
  in the season when the sun that lights the world
  keeps his face least hidden from us—

at the hour when gnats take the place of flies—
  sees fireflies down below in the valley,
  perhaps where he gathers grapes or plows;

so, with as many flames the eighth bolgia
  was all resplendent, as I noticed
  when I came to where I could see the bottom.

And, as he [Elisha] who avenged himself with the bears
  saw the chariot of Elijah depart
  when the horses rose erect to Heaven[46]—   36

for he could not follow so closely with his eyes
  that he could see anything except the flame itself,
  like a little cloud rising upward—

so each light moved through the ditch,
  none revealing what it hid,
  and yet each concealed a sinner.

I was standing on the bridge leaning out to see,
  so that if I had not held to a rock,
  without being pushed I would have fallen,

and my guide, who saw me so attentive, said,
  "Within the fires are the spirits;
  each is wrapped in what is burning him."   48

"Master," I answered, "through hearing you
  I am more certain, but already I was aware
  that this was so, and wished to ask

who is in the fire which comes so divided at the top
  that it seems to rise from the pyre
  on which Eteocles was placed with his brother."

Ulysses and Diomed, in the double flame, are guilty on three counts: (1) the trick of the Trojan horse, which led to the destruction of Troy and the founding of Rome; (2) enticing Achilles to abandon Deidamia and to leave for the Trojan wars, and (3) the theft of the Palladium, a statue of Pallas on which the fate of Troy depended.

[46] For the ascent of Elijah to Heaven and the story of Elisha's revenge on some children who taunted him for his baldness (they were attacked by bears), see 2 Kings 2.

He answered, "In that flame Ulysses and Diomed
    are tortured, and thus they go together
    in punishment as in their battles.

They groan within their flame for the ambush
    of the horse which was the portal
    through which came the noble ancestors of the Romans.[47]   60

Also they weep for the art on account of which
    Deidamia still grieves for Achilles,
    and they suffer too for the Palladium."

"If they can speak within those fires," I said,
    "Master, I beg you earnestly, and beg again
    (and may my prayer be worth a thousand),

that you do not deny our waiting
    until the horned flame comes here;
    you see how my desire bends me toward it!"

And he to me, "Your request is worthy
    of praise; therefore I grant it,
    but see that your tongue keeps silent.   72

Let me speak, for I have conceived
    what you want to know. Since they were Greeks,
    they might shy away from your words."

> *When Virgil, who had celebrated Ulysses in the* Aeneid, *asks about his death, the latter, the representative of the spirit of adventure and of scientific discovery, answers with great dignity and relevance, pointing out how compelling was his desire for knowledge of the two worlds of things and of men. In the story Dante invents, instead of returning to Penelope and the comforts of home, Ulysses sails westward through the Mediterranean, then past Gibraltar, and out on the vast and terrifying Atlantic. His course, like that of Columbus almost two centuries after Dante, is west-southwest. Five months pass; the crew of old men see the constellations of the other hemisphere; then land (probably the island of Purgatory) appears. But a storm arises, and Ulysses ends his life in the glory of a last adventure.*

When the flame had come to where
    time and place seemed best to my guide,
    I heard him speak in these terms:

"O you two within one fire,
    if I merited thanks from you while I lived,
    if I deserved much or little

when in the world I wrote the lofty verses,[48]
    do not move, but let one of you tell
    where, lost, he went to die."   84

---

[47] The story of the Trojan horse is told in Virgil's *Aeneid*, Book II. The Greeks besieging Troy built a large wooden horse and concealed a band of troops inside it; the deluded Trojans brought it into their city, which was then destroyed by the Greeks. The exiled Trojans wandered to Italy, where their descendants founded Rome.

[48] Dante had not read Homer's *Odyssey*. (Ulysses is the Latin name for Odysseus.)

The greater horn of the ancient flame
began to shake, murmuring like a fire
struggling in the wind,

then moving the tip here and there,
as if it were a tongue speaking,
it formed words, and said:

"When I left Circe who detained me
more than a year near Gaeta
before Aeneas had named it thus,

neither fondness for my son, nor pity
for an old father, nor the love for Penelope
which should have made her happy,   96

could overcome in me the desire I had
to gain experience of the world
and of the vices and the worth of men.

I set out on the high, open sea,
with only one ship, and with that little company
by which I was not deserted.

Both coasts I saw as far as Spain,
down to Morocco and the island of Sardinia,
and the others that are bathed in that sea.

I and my companions were old and slow
when we came to that narrow pass [Gibraltar]
where Hercules set up his landmarks   108

so that men should not venture beyond.
On the right I left Seville,
and on the other side had already passed Ceuta.

'O brothers,' I said, 'you who
through a thousand perils have come to the West,
to the brief vigil of our senses

which is left, do not deny
experience of the unpeopled world
to be discovered by following the sun.

Consider what origin you had;
you were not created to live like brutes,
but to seek virtue and knowledge.'   120

With this little speech I made my companions
so eager for the journey
that scarcely then could I have held them back,

and, having turned our stern to the morning,
we made wings of our oars for the mad flight,
always gaining on the left.

The night already saw the stars
  of the other pole, and ours [the North Star] so low
  it did not rise from the ocean floor.

Five times the light upon the moon
  had shone and been extinguished
  since we started on the deep way,   132

when a mount appeared to us,
  dim in the distance, and which seemed
  higher than any I had ever seen.

We rejoiced; but soon our joy changed to sorrow,
  for, from the new land a whirlwind arose
  which struck the prow of our ship.

Three times it made it whirl with all the water;
  the fourth time it lifted high the stern
  and made the prow go down as pleased Another [God],

until at last the sea closed over us."

CANTO XXVII

GUIDO DA MONTEFELTRO

A second flame roars like the brass statue of a bull in which prisoners were burned alive. This instrument of torture was made for a tyrant of Agrigentum and was tried out first on its inventor. The flame contains the soul of Guido da Montefeltro, a famous Ghibelline leader referred to in the Convivio as "our most noble Italian." Guido enquires about Romagna, and Dante outlines briefly the conditions in that region, designating the various rulers by their armorial bearings.

Already the flame was erect and quiet,
  having ended its speech, and was going from us
  with the leave of the dear Poet,

when another flame that came behind it
  made us turn our eyes to its tip
  because of a confused sound issuing from it.

As the Sicilian bull which roared first
  with the groans of the one who made it
  with his tools (and that was right)

bellowed with the voice of the tortured
  in such a way that, although it was of brass,
  it seemed transfixed with pain,   12

so, not having any opening or outlet
  from their source in the fire,
  the doleful words were transformed into its language.

After they had found their way
    up through the tip, giving it the vibration
    the tongue had imparted to them,

we heard it say, "O you to whom I direct my voice,
    and who were speaking Lombard just now,
    saying, 'Now go, further I do not urge you,'

although I have perhaps arrived somewhat late,
    do not be displeased to speak with me;
    you see it does not irk me, and I burn!   24

If you have just now fallen into this blind world
    from that sweet Latin land
    from which I bring all my sin,

tell me if the Romagnuols have peace or war,
    for I was from the mountains there
    between Urbino and the peak from which the Tiber comes."

I was still attentive and bent down
    when my leader nudged me, saying,
    "*You* speak, this is an Italian."

And I, having already prepared my reply,
    began without delay, "O soul,
    you who are hidden down there,   36

your Romagna is not and never was
    without strife in the hearts of its tyrants,
    but no open warfare did I leave there just now.

Ravenna stands as it has for many years,
    the eagle of Polenta brooding over it,
    and covering Cervia with its pinions.

The city [Forlì] which once bore the long siege,
    and made a bloody heap of the French,
    finds itself under the green claws [the Ordelaffi family].

The old and young mastiffs of Verrucchio [the Malatestas]
    who disposed badly of Mantagna [their prisoner],
    as usual, make an auger of their teeth.   48

The cities on the Lamone and the Santerno
    are ruled by the young lion in the white lair
        [Maghinardo da Susinana]
    who, from summer to winter, changes party.

And the city [Cesena] whose side the Savio bathes,
    as it lies between the mountain and the plain,
    lives [under party bosses] between tyranny and freedom.

Now I beg you to tell us who you are;
    do not be more reluctant than another has been;
    so may your name stay proudly in the world."

*After a successful military career, Guido da Montefeltro withdrew from the world
and joined the Franciscan order, hoping to make amends for the sins inseparable
from military life and to prepare securely for the future world. His plan might
have succeeded except for the pope, Boniface VIII, who asked him by what faithless stratagem he might defeat his enemies, offering absolution in advance for the
evil counsel. Obliged either to comply or to disobey his superior, Guido chose what
seemed (to a soldier) the lesser evil, and told how the pope might, through treachery, secure Palestrina, the stronghold of his enemies.*

After the flame had roared a while in its manner,
    the sharp tip moved to and fro,
    and breathed forth this sound: 60

"If I believed that my reply were to anyone
    who would ever return to the world,
    this flame would remain quiet,

but since no one from this ditch
    has ever returned alive, if I hear the truth,
    I will answer without fear of infamy.

I was a man of arms, and then a Cordelier,
    believing, thus girt, to make amends;
    and certainly my intent would have been realized

except for the Great Priest (may ill befall him!)
    who put me back into my former sins;
    and how and why I want you to hear.   72

While I had the form of the flesh and bones
    my mother gave me, my deeds
    were not lionlike, but those of a fox.

The tricks and the secret ways,
    I knew them all, and so carried on their art
    that my fame spread to the ends of the earth.

When I saw that I had reached
    that point in life when everyone
    should lower sail and coil his ropes,

what first had pleased me became repugnant
    and, having repented and confessed, I gave myself to God,
    and alas! that should have availed.   84

The Prince of the new Pharisees [Boniface VIII],
    waging war close to the Lateran—
    and not with Saracens or with Jews,

for every enemy of his was a Christian,
    and none had been a renegade at Acre
    or a merchant in the Sultan's land—

considered neither his high office
    and sacred orders, nor in me that cord I wore
    which used to make those bound with it thinner.

But, as Constantine called upon Sylvester[49]
    in Soracte to cure him of his leprosy,
    so he called me, as his physician,   96

to cure the fever of his pride.
    He asked advice of me, and I kept silent,
    because his words seemed drunken,

and then he said, "Do not let your heart mistrust,
    right now I absolve you; let me know
    how to cast Palestrina to the ground.

I can open and close Heaven,
    as you know, since two are the keys
    that my predecessor [Celestine V] did not hold dear."[50]

The heavy arguments brought me to where
    silence seemed worse to me than complying,
    and I said, 'Father, since you wash away   108

the sin into which I now must fall,
    long promise with short fulfillment
    will make you triumph on your lofty seat.'

> *At Guido's death, St. Francis came for him, but a "black Cherub" from the eighth circle of Hell, the counterpart of those of the eighth heaven who likewise operate through intelligence, objected, and pointed out the impossibility of absolution in advance.*
>
> *Dante uses this extreme example to emphasize the point that salvation depends on the state of the soul at the moment of death. A similar contest, related in Purgatory, occurs in the case of Guido's son, but in almost exactly opposite circumstances.*

When I was dead, Francis came for me,
    but one of the black Cherubim said to him,
    'Don't take him, don't wrong me.

He must come down among my minions
    because he gave the fraudulent advice,
    since when I have been lurking to grasp his hair.

For one who does not repent cannot be absolved,
    nor can *repenting* and *willing* go together
    because the contradiction does not allow it.'   120

Ah, wretched me, how I shuddered
    when he seized me, saying,
    'Perhaps you did not think I was a logician!'

---

[49] For Constantine and Sylvester, see XIX.115–17, the translator's gloss, and the note. Sylvester, according to legend, cured Constantine by baptizing him, in return for which Constantine yielded up the western part of the Roman empire.

[50] For Celestine V, see III.59–60 and translator's gloss.

To Minos he brought me, who twisted his tail
    eight times around his stiff back,
    and after he had bitten it in his rage, he said,

"This is one for the thievish fire.'
    Therefore I am lost here as you see,
    and while moving, clothed in fire, I grieve."

When he had finished speaking
    the sorrowing spirit went on
    twisting and shaking his sharp flame.   132

My guide and I passed over the bridge
    to the top of the next arch
    which crosses the ditch in which a fee is paid

by those who get a burden by dividing [sowing discord].

CANTO XXVIII

The Sowers of Discord

*If it were possible to bring together the wounded on the battlegrounds of southern
Italy in the long series of wars from ancient times down to the Norman invasions
and the wars of Charles of Anjou against Manfred, the scene would be similar to
that of the ninth bolgia.*

Who even in unrhymed words [prose]
    could ever fully tell in many narrations
    of the blood and of the wounds I now saw?

Every tongue certainly would fail
    because our language and our memories
    are insufficient to contain so much.

If all the soldiers were assembled
    who, on the stormy fields of Apulia,
    have groaned for their blood

shed by Trojans, and in the long [Punic] war
    which made so vast a spoil of rings
        [from fingers of dead Romans],
    as Livy writes, who does not err,   12

together with those who suffered painful wounds
    by opposing Robert Guiscard [the Norman conqueror]
    and others whose bones are still piled up

at Ceperano, where every Apulian [allied with Manfred]
    was a traitor, and at Tagliacozzo
    where old Alardo conquered without arms [by strategy],

and were one to show his limbs pierced,
    another his cut off, the view would not equal
    the awful sight of the ninth ditch.

Mahomet, the first shade recognized, had been considered as originally a Christian and as the deliberate cause of the separation of the world into two monotheistic faiths. Mahomet mentions prophetically and with malicious pleasure Fra Dolcino, the leader of a heretical sect who, besieged in 1306, was forced by hunger to surrender.

Indeed, a cask without a stave or endboard
    looks less mutilated than one I saw
    split from his chin down to where wind is broken. 24

His entrails hung between his legs,
    the vital parts appeared with the foul sack
    which makes excrement of what is swallowed.

While I was intently looking at him,
    he gazed at me, and with his hands opened his breast,
    saying, "Now see how I tear myself,

see how mangled Mahomet is!
    In front of me Ali [a son-in-law] goes weeping,
    his head split from chin to forelock;

and all the others you see here
    while alive were sowers of scandal and of schism
    and therefore are split like this. 36

A devil is here behind us who cuts us
    thus cruelly with the edge of his sword,
    reopening all the wounds

when we have gone around the doleful road,
    since they are healed
    before we come again before him.

But who are you, dallying on the bridge,
    perhaps to delay going to your punishment
    decreed upon your own confession?"

"Not yet has death come to him, nor does guilt
    bring him to torment," my master said,
    "but to give him complete experience, 48

I, who am dead, must take him
    down here from round to round, and this
    is as true as that I am speaking to you."

More than a hundred in the ditch,
    when they heard this, stopped to look at me,
    forgetting their pain in their marveling.

"Now tell Fra Dolcino, you who perhaps
    will soon see the sun again, that unless he wants
    to follow me he had better provide himself

with food, so that the snow
    will not bring victory to the Novarese,
    which otherwise would be hard for them to gain." 60

After he had lifted one foot to go
    Mahomet said these words to me,
    then placed it on the ground, moving on.

> *Pier da Medicina, another schismatic of whom little is known, adds the prophecy
> of the death of two citizens of Fano who will be called to a parley and treacher-
> ously thrown overboard. They will not need the usual protection from the squalls
> of Focara, since they will never reach that place. Then Curio is mentioned who
> from private motives urged Caesar to cross the Rubicon and begin the civil war.
> He wishes now he had never seen the town of Rimini near that river. Another
> sower of discord, Mosca, according to tradition advised the killing of an oppo-
> nent to settle a feud rather than a milder punishment, since that, he thought,
> would end the matter. Instead, the murder led to the first conflict between the
> Guelfs and Ghibellines in Florence. On seeing Mosca, Dante's Florentine spirit
> flares up, and he tells him of the banishment of his family, the Lamberti, from the
> city.*

Another who had his throat cut
    and his nose severed up to his eyebrows,
    and who had only a single ear,

having stopped to look with wonder,
    before the others cleared his windpipe
    which was all red outside, and said,

"O you whom sin does not condemn
    and whom I have seen in the Latin land,
    if too much resemblance does not deceive me,   72

recall to mind Pier da Medicina
    if ever you go back to see the sweet plain
    which from Vercelli slopes to Marcabò,

and make known to the two best men of Fano,
    to Messer Guido and to Angiolello,
    that, unless foresight here is vain,

they will be thrown from their ship
    and drowned near La Cattolica
    through the treachery of a base tyrant.

Between the islands of Cyprus and Majorca,
    Neptune has never seen so great a crime
    of pirates or of Argolic people [Greeks].   84

That traitor who sees with one eye only [Malatestino]
    and holds the city [Rimini] which someone here [Curio]
    would wish never to have seen,

will have them come for a parley with him,
    and will act so that to allay Focara's wind,
    they will need neither vow nor prayer."

And I to him, "Point out and tell me
    if you want me to take news of you above,
    who found the sight of that city bitter?"

Then he laid his hand on the jaw
    of one of his companions, and opened his mouth,
    saying, "This is he, and he does not speak.   96

While exiled, he quieted Caesar's fears,
    affirming that a man well prepared
    always loses by any delay."

Oh, how dismayed he seemed to me
    with his tongue cut in his throat,
    Curio, who before spoke so boldly!

And one who had both hands cut off,
    lifting the stumps in the dark air
    so that the blood dirtied his face,

cried, "Remember also Mosca
    who said, alas, 'A thing done has an end,'
    which was a seed of evil for the Tuscans."   108

And I added, "And death to your kindred,"
    whereupon he, heaping grief on grief,
    went off like one maddened by sorrow.

*The last example is that of the Provençal poet Bertran de Born, who, Dante
believed, had fomented a quarrel between Henry, the "young English king," and
his father.*

But I remained to look at the throng,
    and I saw a thing I would fear
    to tell about without more proof,

except that conscience reassures me,
    the good companion which emboldens man
    under the breastplate of conscious innocence.

I saw certainly, and I still seem to see
    a body without a head, going on
    like the others of the sad troop.   120

It held by the hair its severed head
    dangling from its hand like a lantern,
    which looked at us and said, "Woe is me!"

Of itself it made a lamp for itself,
    and they were two in one and one in two;
    how this can be He knows who so ordains.

When it was at the foot of the bridge,
    it lifted the head high with its arm
    to bring the words closer to me,

which were, "Now see my terrible penalty,
    you who, breathing, are visiting the dead;
    judge if any is as great as this.   132

And, that you may take news of me,
> know that I am Bertran de Born, the one
> who gave the young king the evil encouragement.

I made father and son rebellious to each other;
> Ahithophel did not do worse to Absalom
> and to David with his wicked plots.[51]

Because I separated persons thus joined,
> I now carry my brain, alas,
> detached from its source in this body.

Thus retribution is observed in me."

CANTO XXIX

THE FALSIFIERS

Fascinated by the sight of the horrible wounds, Dante keeps looking at them and incurs a reproach. He excuses himself (he is growing up in his relationship with his master) by mentioning that he believed that a relative was there, Geri del Bello, whose violent death had not been avenged. Dante pities Geri, perhaps for the latter's obvious adherence even here to the code of family vengeance.

The time, as usual in Hell, is indicated by the position of the moon: it is now shortly after noon on Saturday.

The great crowd and the diverse wounds
> had made my eyes so inebriated
> that they were eager to remain and weep.

But Virgil said, "What are you looking at?
> Why does your sight still rest down there
> on the sad, mutilated shades?

You have not done so at the other ditches.
> Consider, if you wish to count them,
> that the valley circles for twenty-two miles;

already the moon is under our feet;
> the time granted to us now is short,
> and there is much more to see."   12

"If you had taken note," I answered then,
> "of the cause that made me look,
> perhaps you would have granted me a longer stay."

Meanwhile my guide kept going on
> and I followed, making my reply
> and adding, "Within that hollow

---

[51] For Absalom's rebellion, incited by Ahithophel (or Achitophel), against his father King David, see 2 Samuel 14–18.

on which I kept my eyes fixed so closely
    I believe a spirit of my own blood
    laments the sin that costs so much down here."

Then my master said, "From now on
    do not let your thoughts be distracted by him;
    attend to something else and let him stay there,   24

for I saw him at the foot of the little bridge
    pointing you out and threatening you with his finger,
    and I heard him called Geri del Bello.

You were then so completely occupied
    with him [Bertran de Born] who once held Altaforte
    that you did not look over there, and he departed."

"O my guide, his death by violence
    which has not yet been avenged," I said,
    "by [relatives] the partners of his shame,

made him indignant; therefore he went off
    without speaking to me, as I judge,
    and by that he has made me pity him the more."   36

> *The shades in the tenth bolgia are divided into four groups: falsifiers (1) of
> metals (alchemists), punished by leprosy and paralysis; (2) of persons (impersona-
> tors), punished by delirium or madness; (3) of coins (counterfeiters), afflicted
> with dropsy; and (4) of words (liars), suffering from high fever. Dante treats
> them with mild and amused contempt.*

Thus we talked as far as to the point
    which would have shown the next ditch
    to the bottom if there had been more light.

Then, when we were above
    the last cloister of Malebolge, so that
    its lay brothers could be observed by us,

diverse laments kept striking me
    which had their arrows barbed with such pity
    that I covered my ears with my hands.

Such suffering as there would be if the sick
    in the hospitals of Valdichiana, Maremma, and Sardinia
    [malarious regions] between July and September   48

were all together in one ditch,
    was here; and such stench issued
    as comes from festered limbs.

We descended to the last bank of the long bridge,
    still keeping to the left,
    and then my sight was clearer

down toward the bottom, where the minister
 of the Supreme Lord, Infallible Justice,
 punishes the falsifiers registered here.

I do not believe there was greater sadness
 to see all the people of Aegina sick
 when the air was so full of pestilence   60

that the animals, even to the little worm,
 fell dead—and then the ancient people,
 as the poets hold as true,

were restored by the seed of ants[52]—
 than it was to see in the dark ditch
 the spirits languish in diverse heaps.

One lay upon the belly and one upon the shoulders
 of another, and one on all fours
 was crawling along the dismal path.

Step by step we went without speaking,
 observing and listening to the sick,
 who could not lift their bodies.   72

I saw two sitting, leaning on each other
 as stewpan is propped against stewpan to warm,
 spotted with scabs from head to foot,

and never have I seen a currycomb handled so quickly
 by a stable boy whose master was waiting for him
 or by one staying up against his will

as each of these plied the clawing of his nails
 on himself, because of the great rage
 of itching that had no other help;

and the nails scraped off the scabs
 as a knife does the scales from bream
 or some other fish that has them larger.   84

"O you who disarm yourself with your fingers,
 at times making pincers of them,"
 my guide began to say to one of them,

"tell us if any Latin is among those
 who are here; so may your nails
 suffice eternally for this work!"

"We are both Latins whom you see
 so disfigured here," one answered, weeping,
 "but who are you, asking about us?"

---

[52] Juno inflicted on Aegina a plague that destroyed all living creatures except one man, Aeacus, at whose prayer Jupiter repopulated the island by changing ants into human beings. The story is told by Ovid.

My guide replied, "I am one descending
    with this *live* man from ledge to ledge,
    and I intend to show Hell to him."   96

Then the mutual support broke,
    and each of them, trembling, turned to me,
    with others who had overheard the words.

My good master drew close to me, saying,
    "Ask them what you want to know."
    And I began to speak as he desired:

"So may your memory not fade
    from human minds in the first world,
    but may it live on for many suns,

tell me who you are, and of what people;
    let not your ugly and annoying punishment
    make you afraid to reveal yourselves to me."   108

> *Griffolino, a fraudulent alchemist, tells how he was burned by the presumptive
> father of the simple-minded Albero da Siena, who had taken seriously his remarks
> about flying. This prompts Dante to speak of the Sienese whose sometimes aristo-
> cratic folly was a standing joke in the bourgeois atmosphere of Florence. Dante is
> helped in his gibes by Capocchio, who mentions ironically the notorious spend-
> thrift Stricca and the "Spendthrifts' Club," a group of young Sienese who delib-
> erately ruined themselves by extravagance.*

"I was of Arezzo," one answered,
    "and Albero da Siena had me burned at the stake;
    but what I died for does not bring me here.

It is true that I told him, speaking in jest,
    that I could rise in the air in flight,
    and he who had the desire but little sense

wanted me to show him the art, and because
    I did not make him a Daedalus [a flyer], he had me burned
    by one who considered him as a son.

But to the last ditch of the ten,
    Minos, who cannot err, condemned me
    for the alchemy that I practiced in the world."   120

And I said to the poet, "Now was there ever
    a people as silly as the Sienese?
    Certainly the French are not so by far."

Thereupon the other leper who heard me
    answered my question and said, "Except Stricca
    who knew how to spend with moderation,

and Niccolò who first discovered
    the expensive use of the clove
    in the garden[53] where such seed takes root,

---

[53] The "garden" is Siena.

and except the company in which
 Caccia d'Ascian squandered vineyard and forest
 and the Abbagliato displayed his wit.   132

But that you may know who seconds your remarks
 against the Sienese, sharpen your eyes toward me,
 so that my face may give the right response.

Then you will see that I am the shade of Capocchio
 who falsified the metals by alchemy,
 and you must recall, if I see you correctly,

how good an ape of nature I became."

CANTO XXX

MASTER ADAM AND THE FALSE GREEK

*Two terrible examples of insanity are cited at the beginning of this canto, the
hallucination of Athamas and the hysterical grief of Hecuba. Two impersonators
show a similar mania. One, Gianni Schicchi, had been engaged by Buoso
Donati's son to impersonate his father and dictate a more favorable will. The
commission was well performed except that the testator included himself in the
legacy as the heir of the "queen of the herd," a valuable mare. The other example
is that of Myrrha.*

At the time when Juno because of Semele
 was angry at the Theban royal family,
 as she had shown already more than once,

Athamas was stricken with such madness
 that on seeing his wife coming
 burdened with two sons, one on either hand,

he shouted, "Let us spread the net, so that I
 may catch the lioness and cubs as they pass";
 then he stretched out his pitiless claws,

and seizing one, whose name was Learchus,
 whirled him around and dashed him on a rock;
 and she, with her other burden, drowned herself.[54] 12

And when Fortune had brought low
 the bold pride of the Trojans
 so that both king and kingdom were blotted out,

sad Hecuba, miserable and captive,[55]
 after she had seen her [daughter] Polyxena slain
 and, forlorn, recognized the body of [her son] Polydorus

---

[54] Juno, angered at her consort Jupiter's love for Semele, a Theban princess who bore his
son Bacchus, avenged herself on Semele's whole family. These included Semele's sister Ino,
Ino's husband Athamas, and their children.
[55] Hecuba, queen of Troy, was carried off by the Greeks after they destroyed the city.

on the shore of the sea, in her madness
    barked like a dog, so greatly
    had grief wrenched her mind.

But neither Theban nor Trojan Furies
    were ever seen anywhere so cruel
    in goading beasts, much less human bodies,   24

as those I saw in two spirits, pale and naked,
    who ran biting as a hungry boar does
    when just released from the sty.

One rushed on Capocchio and seized him
    by the neck, then dragging him,
    made his belly scrape on the hard bottom.

And the Aretine [Griffolino], who remained trembling,
    said to me, "That mad one is Gianni Schicchi,
    and he goes thus tearing others."

"Oh," I said to him, "so may the other
    not bite you, please tell us
    who it is before it gets away."   36

And he to me, "That is the ancient spirit
    of wicked Myrrha;[56] who was devoted to her father
    beyond the bounds of lawful love.

She came thus to sin with him,
    changing herself into another's form,
    just as the other who is running off

undertook, to gain the mistress of the herd,
    to impersonate Buoso Donati,
    making a will and giving it a legal form."

After the two mad ones on whom
    I had kept my eyes had passed,
    I turned to look at the other ill-born shades.   48

*The counterfeiters are swollen with dropsy. One, a master of the art, had served
the counts of Romena in one of the coolest, best watered of mountain regions, and
the image of the place where he had worked increases the torture of his thirst.
Amused at the size of Master Adam's belly, Dante asks about two shades on his
boundaries. One, Sinon, suffering now from high fever, had pretended to be a
fugitive from the Greeks, and had persuaded the Trojans to take in the wooden
horse. The other liar is Potiphar's wife. Sinon objects to being called a "Greek
from Troy," and we have a quarrel, the pot calling the kettle black. Sinon,
considering each counterfeit coin as a separate indictment, charges Master Adam
with the commission of more sins than any other demon. His opponent, in rebut-
tal, mentions the infamous notoriety Sinon has gained through the works of
Homer and Virgil. Dante is scolded for listening to the quarrel. He tries to reply,
but is so ashamed that he cannot, and excuses himself by this embarrassment more
effectively than if he had been able to speak.*

[56]The story of Myrrha's incestuous passion is told in Ovid's *Metamorphoses*, Book X.

I saw one who would have looked like a lute
    if only he had had his legs cut off
    at the groin, where they join the body.

The heavy dropsy, disproportioning him thus
    with humors badly absorbed,
    left his head too small for his belly,

and made him hold his lips apart
    as the hectic does who, for thirst,
    has one turned up, the other down.

"O you who are without any punishment
    in this wretched world, and I don't know why,"
    he said to us, "see and take note   60

of the misery of Master Adam!
    When alive I had enough of what I wanted,
    and now, alas! I long for a little drop of water.

The streams which from the green hills
    of Casentino flow down to the Arno,
    making their beds cool and soft,

always stand before my eyes and not in vain,
    for the vision of them dries me up
    more than the disease which wastes my features.

The rigid Justice which goads me
    takes advantage of the place where I sinned
    to put my sighs to quicker flight.   72

There is Romena where I counterfeited
    the [Florentine] currency sealed with the Baptist's image,
    for which I left my body burned above.

But if I could see the miserable soul
    of Guido or of Alessandro or their brother [his employers]
    I would not trade the sight for Fonte Branda [a spring].

One is already in, if the mad shades
    that move around tell the truth,
    but of what avail is it, if my limbs are tied?

Yet, if I were still nimble enough
    to make an inch in a hundred years,
    I would already have started out   84

to find them among these disgusting people,
    although the ditch circles for eleven miles,
    and is not less than half a mile across.

Because of them I am in such a household;
    they induced me to stamp the florins
    which had indeed *three* carats of alloy!"

And I to him, "Who are the two wretches,
    steaming like wet hands in winter,
    lying close to your right frontier?"

"Here I found them on raining down in this ditch,"
    he answered, "since when they have not turned over,
    nor will they, I believe, in eternity.   96

One is the lying woman who accused Joseph;[57]
    the other is false Sinon, the Greek from Troy;
    because of their fever they emit such stench."

And one of them [Sinon] who perhaps
    took badly being named thus darkly,
    with his fist struck the vile belly

which sounded like a drum, and Master Adam
    struck him back in the face with his arm
    which did not seem less hard,

saying to him, "Although locomotion is impossible
    because of my heavy limbs,
    I have an arm free for such business!"   108

Whereupon the other answered, "When you went
    to the fire, you were not so quick,
    but you were still quicker when you made the coins."

And he of the dropsy, "You tell the truth about this,
    but you were not so good a witness
    at Troy when the truth was asked of you."

"If I spoke falsely, you falsified the coins,"
    said Sinon, "and I am here for one fault,
    and you for more than any other demon."

"Remember, perjurer, the horse!" he of the swollen belly
    answered, "and let it be a plague to you
    that the whole world knows of it."   120

"And may the thirst that cracks your tongue
    be a curse to you," said the Greek, "and the foul water
    which makes a hedge before your eyes."

Then the counterfeiter, "Thus your mouth
    still opens to your harm, as usual,
    for, if I am thirsty and humor stuffs me up,

you have the burning and the headache,
    and to lick the mirror[58] of Narcissus
    you would not need a second invitation."

[57] After Joseph, son of Jacob, was sold into Egypt, the wife of Potiphar, an officer of
Pharaoh, made sexual advances to Joseph. Rebuffed by him, she then accused him of making
the advances. See Genesis 39.
   [58] Water. Narcissus fell in love with his own reflected image.

I was wholly intent on listening to them
    when my master said to me, "Now keep on gazing!
    a little more, and I will quarrel with you."   132

When I heard him speak to me with anger,
    I turned to him with such shame
    that the memory of it still haunts me.

As one who dreams of a misfortune
    and, while dreaming, hopes it is a dream,
    so that he longs for what is as if it were not,

so I became, not being able to speak
    although I wanted to excuse myself and did so,
    without knowing that I was doing it.

"Less shame washes away a greater fault,"
    said my master, "than yours has been;
    therefore, free yourself of all sadness   144

and take note that I am at your side
    if it happens again that chance catches you
    where people are in a similar wrangle,

for wishing to overhear it is a low desire."

CANTO XXXI

The Giants

The same tongue first stung me
    so that it tinted both my cheeks,
    then offered me its cure.

Thus I hear that the lance of Achilles
    and of his father was wont first
    to wound and then to heal.

We turned our backs on the miserable ditch,
    going up without speaking
    over the bank which surrounds it.

Here it was less than night and less than day,
    so that my sight did not go far;
    but I heard a horn sound so loudly   12

that it would have made any thunder faint;
    and retracing the course the sound took
    I directed my eyes to one spot.

After the doleful rout,
    when Charlemagne lost his holy company,
    Roland did not blow so terribly.[59]

[59] See *The Song of Roland.* When Charlemagne's army returned from Spain toward France, Roland commanded the elite rear guard. Set upon by the pagans and defeated, Roland refused to blow his great horn to call for help until it was too late.

Only a short while did my eyes look toward the sound
    when I seemed to see many high towers,
    and I asked, "Master, tell me, what city is this?"

And he to me, "Since you are looking
    through the darkness from too far off
    your imagination leads you astray.   24

You will see when you arrive there
    how the senses are deceived by distance;
    therefore move a little faster."

Then he took me tenderly by the hand
    and said, "Before we go farther,
    to make the event seem less strange,

know that these are not towers, but giants,
    and they are in the well around the bank
    from the navel down, all of them."

As, when a mist has cleared somewhat,
    our eyes little by little make out
    what the vapor in the air had hidden,   36

so, piercing through the thick gloom
    on approaching closer and closer to the bank,
    my error fled, and my fear increased.

As, on the circle of its walls,
    Montereggione [a fortress] is crowned with towers,
    so, above the bank which surrounds the pit,

the horrible giants, whom Jove still threatens[60]
    when he thunders in the heavens,
    towered above us with half their bodies.

Already I saw the face, shoulders, and chest
    of one, and a large part of his belly,
    and both his arms down by his side.   48

Certainly when Nature gave up the art
    of producing these creatures she did well
    to deprive Mars of such agents;

and if she does not repent for elephants
    and whales, whoever looks closely
    will hold her more discreet and just,

for where the force of intellect [as in the giants]
    is added to ill will and strength,
    mankind can have no defense.

---

[60] Ovid's *Metamorphoses*, Book I, describes an attack on the gods by giants who piled mountains atop one another.

His face seemed to me as long and wide
    as the pine cone[61] at St. Peter's in Rome,
    and his other features were in proportion.   60

Thus the bank which was an apron
    from his middle down, showed so much of him
    that three Frieslanders [tall men] would have boasted

in vain to reach up to his hair.
    I saw, indeed, thirty great spans[62] of him
    down from [the neck] where a man buckles on his cloak.

> *Nimrod, the builder of the Tower of Babel, a "mighty hunter before the Lord," is*
> *with the giants who revolted against Jove. His words are meaningless. Virgil*
> *apostrophizes him for Dante's benefit. Then the travelers come to Antaeus, who*
> *was not present at the battle of the giants against the gods, and therefore is not*
> *bound like the others. Flattered by Virgil, who understands his fatuous character,*
> *Antaeus extends his hand and places the two poets on the bottom of the pit in the*
> *ninth and last circle.*

"Raphèl maỳ amèch zabì almì"
    the savage mouth for which sweeter
    hymns were unfitting began to say.

And my guide to him, "Stupid soul,
    keep to your horn, and with it express yourself
    when anger or some other passion moves you.   72

Search around your neck and you will find the strap
    which holds it, O confused spirit;
    see it curving across your great chest."

Then he said to me, "He accuses himself.
    This is Nimrod, through whose evil thought
    a single tongue is not used in the world.[63]

Let us leave him and not speak in vain,
    for, as the language of others is to him,
    so is his to them, and is understood by none."

We kept on still to the left
    and at the distance of a crossbow shot
    we found another giant larger and fiercer.   84

Who the master was to bind him
    I cannot say, but his right arm
    at his back and the other in front

were bound by a chain, which held him tied
    from the neck down, so that over his exposed part
    it encircled him five times.

[61] A pine cone made of bronze, about ten feet high, is still visible in the Vatican.
[62] Hand spans.
[63] For the story of the Tower of Babel and the consequent confusion of tongues in the world, see Genesis 11.

"This haughty creature wished to make trial
    of his power against supreme Jove,"
    said my master; "therefore, he has such a reward.

Ephialtes is his name; he fought in the great battle
    when the giants frightened the gods:
    the arms he used once, he never moves."   96

Then I to my guide, "If possible
    I should like for my eyes
    to gain experience of the immense Briareus."

Whereupon he answered, "You will see Antaeus
    nearby, who speaks and is unbound
    and who will put us in the lowest depth of guilt.

The one you wish to see is farther on
    and is bound and built like this one
    except that he looks more ferocious."

Never did an earthquake jar
    so violently a massive tower
    as Ephialtes suddenly shook himself.   108

Then I feared death more than ever,
    and fright alone would have caused it,
    if I had not seen the chains.

We went on then and came to Antaeus
    who protruded above the bank
    fully five ells,[64] not counting his head.

"O you who in the fateful valley
    which made Scipio an heir of glory,
    when Hannibal and his army turned back,[65]

you who once brought a thousand lions as prey—
    and, if you had fought in the great war,
    with your brothers, it seems that some believe   120

the sons of Earth [the giants] might have conquered—
    put us down, do not disdain to do so,
    to where cold locks up Cocytus.

Do not make us go to Tityus or to Typhon;
    this man can give what is longed for here;
    therefore bend over and do not scornfully refuse.

He can revive your fame in the world,
    for he lives and expects a long life, if Divine Grace
    does not call him to herself ahead of time."

[64] An ell is about four or five feet.
[65] Scipio and Hannibal were, respectively, Roman and Carthaginian generals.

Thus my master spoke, and Antaeus
    hurriedly held out the hand whose grip
    Hercules once felt, and took hold of my master.   132

When Virgil felt himself grasped,
    he said to me, "Come, let me take hold of you."
    Then, of himself and me he made one bundle.

As the Garisenda tower seems to fall
    if looked at under its leaning side
    when a cloud passes over it in the opposite direction,

so Antaeus appeared to me as I watched
    while he bent over; and he was such
    that I would have wished to go by another way.

But lightly in the depth which swallows
    Lucifer with Judas he placed us,
    nor did he delay long bent over   144

but rose like a mast set in a ship.

CANTO XXXII

The Traitors

*The tone of the Comedy now becomes harsh, scornful, vindictive. Dante again
calls upon the Muses, but this time on those who helped to build Thebes, "the
ancient home of crime."*

If I had rhymes rough and harsh enough
    to be fitting for the dismal hole
    on which all the other circles weigh,

I would press out the substance of my conception
    more fully; but since I do not have them,
    not without fear do I bring myself to speak.

For, to describe the bottom of the whole universe
    is not an enterprise to take up in jest,
    nor for a tongue that still cries "mamma" and "papa."

But may those ladies who helped Amphion
    to enclose Thebes aid my verse,
    so that words and facts will not differ.   12

O rabble, miscreated above all others,
    in this place to speak of which is hard,
    here [on earth] you would better have been sheep or goats!

When we were down in the dark well
    beyond the feet of the giant and much lower,
    and as I was still looking at the high wall,

I heard someone say, "Watch how you step!
    Move so you won't trample with your feet
    on the heads of the weary, miserable brothers."

Then I turned and saw a lake in front of me
    and under my feet which, frozen,
    had the appearance of glass and not of water.   24

The Danube in Austria never made in winter
    so thick a veil for its current,
    nor the Don up there under its cold skies,

as this did; for if Tambernicchi [a mountain]
    had fallen on it, or Pietrapana,
    it would not have given a creak even at the edge.

And as a frog lies croaking
    with just its muzzle out, in the season
    when the peasant woman thinks of gleaning,

so the shades were lying in the ice,
    livid up to where shame appears,
    their teeth chattering like storks' bills.   36

Each held his face down; their mouths
    gave evidence of the cold,
    and their eyes of their sad hearts.

Caïna, the first division of the ninth circle, contains traitors to kindred, among whom are the counts of Mangona, who killed each other in a quarrel over an inheritance. Other minor figures also are mentioned.

When I had looked around a little,
    I glanced at my feet and saw two so bound together
    that the hair on their heads was intermingled.

"Tell me, you who press your chests so close together,
    who you are," I asked, and they bent their necks,
    and after they had lifted their faces to me,

their eyes, which previously were wet only within,
    gushed through the lids, and the cold
    froze their tears and locked them up again.   48

A clamp never bound wood to wood so strongly.
    Then they, like two goats,
    butted each other, such anger overcame them.

And one who had lost both ears from the cold,
    with his face still downward, said,
    "Why do you look at us so much?

If you want to know who these two are,
    the valley from which the Bisenzio flows
    belonged to them and to their father, Albert.

They came from one body, and you might search
    through all Caïna[66] without finding a shade
    more worthy to be preserved in ice,   60

not him [Mordred] whose breast and shadow
    were laid open by a single blow from Arthur's hand,[67]
    not Focaccia; not this one who covers me

with his head, so that I cannot see beyond
    and whose name was Sassol Mascheroni,—
    if you are a Tuscan you know now who he was.

And, so that you will not put me to further speech,
    know that I was Camicion de' Pazzi, and am waiting
    for Carlino to make me [by comparison] seem innocent."

Afterward I saw a thousand faces made doglike
    by the cold; so that a shudder comes to me
    and always will at the sight of frozen pools.   72

> *Passing on to Antenora, the second division of the ninth circle, where traitors to
> party and country are kept, Dante accidentally kicks one shade who mentions
> Montaperti, the scene of a defeat of the Florentine Guelfs. Dante's suspicion is
> immediately aroused, and he tries by force to make the shade name himself. An-
> other, however, treacherously gives him away as Bocca degli Abati who, at a
> critical moment in the battle, cut off the hand of the Florentine standardbearer,
> an act which was thought to have caused the defeat. Dante's violence incurs no
> reproach: the implication is that ordinary rules of conduct are inapplicable to the
> completely depraved: one must keep away from them or act according to the code
> they establish. This is the realistic Gresham's law of competitive behavior. Bocca
> in turn mentions others, including Buoso da Duera, who had been bribed by
> Charles of Anjou, and Ganelon, the traitor in the* Song of Roland.

And while we were moving toward the center
    to which all weights are drawn
    and I was shivering in the eternal chill,

whether it was destiny or chance, I know not,
    but while walking among the heads
    my foot struck hard against the face of one.

Weeping it cried, "Why do you kick me?
    Unless you come to increase the vengeance
    for Montaperti, why do you molest me?"

And I, "Master, now wait for me here
    until this one relieves me of a doubt,
    then you can make me hurry as you wish."   84

[66] Named for Cain, who murdered his brother Abel (Genesis 4). All the treacherous sinners punished in this and the other three divisions of the ninth circle happen also to be
involved in murder.

[67] Mordred was the evil nephew of King Arthur and a would-be usurper. Arthur killed
him with a blow that penetrated his whole body.

My guide stood still, and I said to the shade
    who was still cursing loudly,
    "Who are you complaining thus of others?"

"Now who are you, going through Antenora[68]
    kicking others' cheeks," he answered,
    "harder than if you were alive?"

"I am alive," was my response,
    "and it may be dear to you, if you want fame,
    that I should include your name in my notes."

And he to me, "The contrary is what I want,
    get away from here; do not bother me,
    for you know badly how to flatter in this bottom."   96

Then I seized him by the scalp and said,
    "You will name yourself
    or not a hair will be left on your head."

And he to me, "Even if you tear it out
    and fall on my head a thousand times,
    I will not tell or show you who I am."

I had already twisted his hair in my hand
    and had pulled out more than one tuft,
    he howling with eyes cast down,

when another shouted, "What's the matter with you, Bocca?
    Isn't it enough to chatter with your jaws
    but you must bark?—What devil is after you?"   108

"Now," I said, "I do not want you to speak,
    damned traitor, for to your shame
    I will carry off true news of you."

"Go," he answered, "and tell what you want,
    but if you get out of here, don't keep silent
    about him who has his tongue so ready.

He is weeping here for the money of the French.
    'I saw,' you can say, 'him of Duera,
    down there where sinners are put to cool.'

If any one asks about the others here,
    you have beside you the one of Beccheria
    whose throat was cut by Florence.   120

Gianni de' Soldanier, I believe,
    is farther on, with Ganelon, and Tebaldello
    who opened Faenza while it was sleeping."

We now see a bestial example of hatred. One shade is gnawing the head of
another, as Tydeus, after being mortally wounded by Menalippus whom he in

[68]Antenor was a Trojan who, according to medieval legend, betrayed his city to the
Greeks. He is treated favorably in Homer's *Iliad*.

turn killed, called for the head of his enemy and chewed on it. Aghast at such a
sight, Dante wonders what could motivate such hatred and offers to help in the
vengeance by making the reason for it known in case there is just cause.

We had already departed from him
    when I saw two frozen in one hole,
    so that the head of one was a hood for the other,

and as bread is chewed from hunger,
    so the one on top set his teeth in the other
    where the brain joins the neck.

Not otherwise did Tydeus gnaw
    in his rage the temples of Menalippus
    than he did this one's skull and flesh.   132

"O you who show by such bestial signs
    hatred of him whom you are chewing,
    tell me why," I said, "on this condition

that if you rightfully complain of him,
    knowing who you are and his sin,
    I may repay you up in the world

if that [tongue] with which I speak is not dried up [by death]."

CANTO XXXIII

COUNT UGOLINO

Count Ugolino, a Pisan, had allied himself with the Florentine Guelfs and in
1285 was in control of his city. Perhaps he is among the traitors because of this
change of party and because of the transfer of certain castles. In that year the
Ghibellines, led by the Archbishop Ruggieri, revolted. Ugolino was called treach-
erously to a parley, then imprisoned with two sons and two grandsons in what
was later known as the "Tower of Hunger." After some months the door of the
prison was nailed shut, and the five were left to die of starvation. The bodies, on
their removal, appeared mutilated, perhaps rat-bitten. Ugolino recognizes Dante
as a Florentine, therefore a Guelf, and explains why he is violating so terribly the
obligations of a neighbor.

The sinner raised his mouth from his fierce repast,
    wiping it on the hair of the head
    the back of which he had despoiled,

and then began, "You wish that I renew
    desperate grief, which wrings my heart,
    merely in thinking of it, before I speak.

But if my words can be seeds to bear infamy
    to the traitor I am gnawing,
    you will see me both speak and weep.

I do not know who you are, nor by what means
    you have come down here, but certainly
    you seem a Florentine when I hear you.   12

You must understand that I was Count Ugolino,
    and this is the Archbishop Ruggieri;
    now I will tell you why I am such a neighbor.

How, as the result of his evil thoughts,
    I was seized, trusting in him,
    and put to death, there is no need to tell,

but what you cannot have learned, that is,
    how cruel my death was, you will hear
    and know if he has offended me.

> *As in the Francesca episode, so here Dante reconstructs what could not be known,
> that is, the lonely, unwitnessed death of the five in prison. In the tower (compared
> to a "mew" in which falcons were kept while molting) several months had passed
> when a symbolic and prophetic dream revealed to the prisoners their fate. In
> describing it, Ugolino's fierce memory gets ahead of his words: the wolf becomes
> "a father" and the whelps "sons," and he turns on Dante, reproaching the poet
> for lack of feeling before he has told what happened.*

A little loophole in the mew which
    because of me was called the 'Tower of Hunger'
    and in which others will be imprisoned   24

had shown through its opening several moons already
    when I had the evil dream
    which tore away the veil of the future.

This one seemed the lord and master of the hunt,
    chasing the wolf and whelps on the mountain
    which prevents the Pisans from seeing Lucca.

With lean, eager, and well-trained hounds [the mob],
    he had placed the Gualandi, Sismondi,
    and Lanfranchi [as leaders] in front of him.

After a short course, the father and the sons
    seemed to me weary, and I thought I saw
    their bodies torn by the sharp teeth.   36

When I had awakened before the dawn
    I heard my children who were with me
    weeping in their sleep and asking for bread.

You are cruel indeed not to grieve already
    in thinking of what my heart foreboded;
    and if you do not weep now, by what are you ever moved?

> *The drama passes in silence: almost nothing is said. On the first day Anselm, the
> smallest, showed concern for his father. On the second, Ugolino bit his hands
> from grief. That and the third day passed in complete silence. On the fourth,
> Gaddo weakened and died, and on the fifth and sixth, the others. On the seventh,
> Ugolino crawled over the bodies, and on the eighth, he succumbed, hunger
> having accomplished what grief could not do.*

*The hatred of Ugolino is communicated to Dante who bursts out in an invective
against Pisa.*

They were now awake, and the hour drew near
    when our food used to be brought to us,
    and each was afraid because of his dream;

and below I heard the door of the horrible tower
    nailed up; whereupon, without saying a word,
    I looked into the faces of my sons.   48

I did not weep, so stony did I become within.
    They cried, and my little Anselm said,
    'You look so [hard], father, what ails you?'

Still I shed no tears nor did I answer
    during all that day and the night after,
    until another sun came forth upon the world.

When a little light had entered
    the awful prison, and I saw
    on four faces my own aspect,

I bit both my hands from grief,
    and they, thinking I did it from hunger,
    suddenly got up and said,   60

'Father, it will be much less painful
    if you eat of us; you clothed us
    with this poor flesh; may you take it from us!'

I became quiet then not to make them more sad.
    That day and the next we all remained mute.
    Ah, hard earth, why did you not open!

After we had reached the fourth day,
    Gaddo fell stretched out at my feet, saying,
    'Father, why don't you help me?'

There he died; and as you see me
    I saw the three of them fall one by one
    between the fifth day and the sixth; then I began,   72

already blind, to crawl over each, and for two days
    I called them after they were dead.
    Then fasting did more than grief."[69]

When he had said this, with eyes awry,
    he seized again the wretched head with his teeth
    which gnawed upon the bone, like a dog's.

Ah, Pisa! shame of the people,
    of the beautiful land [Italy] where "si" ["yes"] is heard,
    since your neighbors are slow to punish you,

---

[69] This line can mean that hunger could make him die as grief could not or else that
Ugolino was driven to cannibalism.

may the Capraia and Gorgona [islands] move
  and make a dam for the Arno at its mouth,[70]
  so that it may drown everyone in you;

for if Count Ugolino was reputed
  to have betrayed you of the castle,
  you should not have put his sons on such a cross.

Their young age made Uguccione
  and Brigata innocent, you modern Thebes![71]
  and the other two named by my song.

> *The poets move on to Tolomea, the third division, where traitors to guests are punished. The heads of these sinners are thrown back, so that the tears, freezing in the cups of their eyes, cause a painful pressure.*

We went farther on to where the frost
  roughly binds another people
  with faces thrown back, not turned down.

Weeping there prevents them from weeping:
  the tears which find a barrier in the eyes
  turn inward to increase the pain,

since they form a solid mass,
  and like visors of crystal fill
  the whole cavity beneath the eyebrows.

And, although, as in a callused spot,
  every feeling had gone from my face
  because of the intense cold,

already I seemed to notice a wind,
  so that I said, "Master, what causes this?
  Is not all vapor [atmospheric change] absent down here?"

And he to me, "Soon you will be
  where your eyes will see the cause
  of the blast and will give you the answer."

And one of the wretches in the cold crust
  shouted at us, "O souls so cruel
  that the last place is assigned to you,

take from my eyes the hard veils,
  so that I may relieve the pain a little
  that stuffs my heart before the tears freeze again."

> *To induce this soul to speak, Dante makes a promise with false intent, that is, he commits fraud, as previously in this circle he had committed violence. Our poet is emphasizing again, in opposition to certain idealists, that golden rules and codes*

---

[70] Pisa is at the mouth of the river Arno.
[71] Thebes was considered the most wicked of the ancient cities.

of honor presuppose a certain uniformity in the social group. To apply them
without discrimination is merely to favor and give superior survival value to the
fraudulent and dishonorable.

The soul whom Dante has tricked had had guests murdered at a banquet, the
signal for the execution being, "Bring on the fruit." He is now getting expensive
dates for cheap figs, that is, being repaid with interest. His soul, apparently, has
descended "quick" into Hell, and is replaced in his body by a demon.

And I to him, "If you want me to help you,
    tell me who you are, and if I do not relieve you,
    may I go to the bottom of the ice!"[72]

He answered then, "I am Friar Alberigo,
    he of the fruit of the evil garden,
    and am getting here dates for my figs."   120

"Oh," I said to him, "are you dead already?"
    And he to me, "How my body fares
    in the world above, I have no knowledge.

Such an advantage this Tolomea[73] has
    that often a soul falls into it
    before Atropos [a Fate] has thrust it forth.

And—so may you remove more willingly
    the frozen tears from my face—
    know that when a soul betrays as I did,

its body is taken from it by a demon
    who afterward controls the flesh
    until its allotted years have passed.   132

It falls into such a cistern as this,
    and perhaps the body of the shade
    wintering behind me appears on earth.

You must know him if you have just come down;
    He is Ser Branca d'Oria [a Genoese], and many years
    have passed since he was thus locked up."

"I believe that you are deceiving me,"
    I said to him, "for Branca d'Oria has not died,
    but eats and sleeps and puts on clothes."

"In the ditch of the Malebranche above,"
    he said, "where the tenacious pitch is boiling,
    Michel Zanche [his victim] had not yet arrived   144

when a devil took over his body
    and that of a close relative
    who did the treacherous act with him.

[72] Dante must in any event go beneath the ice, because that is the way out of hell; see the
next canto.
[73] Probably named for Ptolemy, a soldier of Jericho who in 1 Maccabees 16 murders several
of his relatives whom he invited to a banquet.

But reach out your hand, open my eyes";
   and I did not open them for him;
   and to be rude to him was fitting.

Ah, Genoese, men who are estranged
   from all good ways and full of all corruption,
   why are you not scattered from the earth,

for, with the worst spirit of Romagna [Alberigo],
   I found one of you whose soul
   for his deeds already bathes in Cocytus,   156

and in body seems still alive on earth!

CANTO XXXIV

SATAN

*To the first words of a Latin hymn to the cross, "The banners of the Lord come
forth, . . ." Dante adds the word* inferni, *applying them thus to Satan, the lord
of Hell. Dante is now in Giudecca where traitors to benefactors are completely
submerged in the ice.*

*Satan is represented as the counterpart of the Trinity, with heads of three colors,
yellow, black, and red, standing for impotence, ignorance, and hate, and corresponding to the divine power, wisdom, and love. His three pairs of wings send
forth a threefold blast which freezes Cocytus. In the mouths of Lucifer are Judas,
the traitor to Christ, and Brutus and Cassius, traitors to the Roman Empire. The
poets reach Satan at six o'clock on Saturday evening, having spent twenty-four
hours on the journey.*

"*Vexilla Regis prodeunt inferni*
   toward us, therefore, look ahead,"
   my master said, "and try to discern him."

As, when a thick mist covers the land
   or when night darkens our hemisphere,
   a windmill, turning, appears from afar,

so now I seemed to see such a structure;
   then because of the wind, I drew back
   behind my guide, for there was no other protection.

Already—and with fear I put it into verse—
   I was where the shades are covered in the ice
   and show through like bits of straw in glass.   12

Some were lying, some standing erect,
   some on their heads, others on their feet,
   still others like a bow bent face to toes.

When we had gone so far ahead
   that my master was pleased to show me
   the creature [Lucifer] that once had been so fair,

he stood from in front of me, and made me stop,
    saying, "Behold, Dis![74] Here is the place
    where you must arm yourself with courage."

How faint and frozen I then became,
    do not ask, Reader, for I do not write it down,
    since all words would be inadequate.   24

I did not die and did not stay alive:
    think now for yourself, if you have the wit,
    how I became, without life or death.

The emperor of the dolorous realm
    from mid-breast protruded from the ice,
    and I compare better in size

with the giants than they do with his arms.
    Consider how big the whole must be,
    proportioned as it is to such a part.

If he were once as handsome as he is ugly now,
    and still presumed to lift his hand against his Maker,
    all affliction must indeed come from him.   36

Oh, how great a marvel appeared to me
    when I saw three faces on his head!
    The one in front [hatred] was fiery red;

the two others which were joined to it
    over the middle of each shoulder
    were fused together at the top.

The right one [impotence] seemed between white and yellow;
    the left [ignorance] was in color like those
    who come from where the Nile rises.

Under each two great wings spread
    of a size fitting to such a bird;
    I have never seen such sails on the sea.   48

They had no feathers, and seemed
    like those of a bat, and they flapped,
    so that three blasts came from them.

Thence all Cocytus was frozen.
    With six eyes he wept, and over his three chins
    he let tears drip and bloody foam.

In each mouth he chewed a sinner with his teeth
    in the manner of a hemp brake,[75]
    so that he kept three in pain.

---

[74] Satan. (Dis, or Pluto, was the ancient god of the underworld.)
[75] A machine for crushing stalks of hemp.

To the one in front the biting was nothing
  compared to the scratching, for at times,
  his back was stripped of skin.   60

"The soul up there with the greatest punishment,"
  said my master, "is Judas Iscariot. His head
  is inside the mouth, and he kicks with his legs.

Of the other two whose heads are down,
  the one hanging from the black face is Brutus;
  see how he twists and says nothing.

The other who seems so heavy set is Cassius.[76]
  But night is rising again now,
  and it is time to leave, for we have seen all."

> *At the center of the earth, also the center of gravity, the poets turn and begin
> climbing laboriously, the effort symbolizing the difficulty of getting rid of bad
> habits even when their ugliness is known. Lucifer now appears upside down, and
> the time changes to Saturday morning, since the travelers gain twelve hours in
> passing from Jerusalem time to that of Purgatory, directly opposite.*
>
> *Through the passage made by Lucifer as he fell, the poets reach the foot of
> Purgatory just before dawn on Easter Sunday.*
>
> *Each part of the Comedy ends with the word "stars," which stand for the goal of
> the journey, the objects farthest removed from Satan and the materialism of the
> earth, and whose beauty is most ethereal.*

When my guide was ready, I embraced his neck,
  and he took advantage of the time and place
  so that when the wings were wide open   72

he caught hold of the shaggy sides
  and descended from tuft to tuft
  between the tangled hair and the frozen crust.

When we were at the place where the thigh
  revolves on the swelling of the haunches,
  my guide, with effort and with difficulty,

turned his head to where he had had his feet,
  and grappled the hair, like one mounting,
  so that I thought he was returning into Hell.

"Hold fast, for by such stairs,"
  my master said, panting like one weary,
  "we must depart from so much evil."   84

Then he came through the opening in a rock
  and put me on its edge, sitting,
  and climbed toward me with wary steps.

[76] The place of Brutus and Cassius, the assassins of Julius Caesar, at the center of hell is a
surprise to modern readers accustomed to think of them as heroic opponents of tyranny. But
to Dante they were traitors to the Roman Empire (in the person of Caesar), the agency of
earthly rule that properly counterweighs spiritual authority (Christ through the papacy).

I raised my eyes and thought
 that I would find Lucifer as I had left him,
 but saw him holding up his legs,

and if I then became perplexed,
 let dull people imagine who do not see
 what the point was that I had passed.

"Get up on your feet," said my master,
 "the road is long and the path rough, and already
 the sun has returned to mid-tierce [at 7:30 A.M.]."   96

The place where we were
 was no palace hall, but a natural dungeon,
 dark and with an uneven floor.

"Before I uproot myself from the abyss, Master,"
 I said when I was standing,
 "speak to me a little to dispel my error.

Where is the ice? and how is Satan planted
 so upside down? and how in such a short time
 has the sun made its way from evening to morning?"

And he to me, "You still imagine you are
 on the other side of the center where I grasped the hair
 of the wicked monster that pierces the world.   108

You were over there as long as I descended;
 when I turned, you passed the point
 to which all weights are drawn.

Now you have arrived in the hemisphere
 opposite that which dry land covers
 and at whose summit [Jerusalem] was consumed

the man [Christ] who was born and lived without sin.
 You have your feet on a little circle
 which forms the other face of Giudecca.[77]

Here it is morning when it is evening there,
 and Satan who made a ladder for us
 with his hair is still as he was before.   120

On this side he fell from Heaven, and the earth here,
 through fear, made a veil for itself
 of the sea, and came to our hemisphere,

and perhaps the land [Purgatory] which shows on this side,
 to flee from him, rushed up
 and left this passageway empty."[78]

[77] The innermost ring of the plain of ice; named for Judas.

[78] When Satan fell from heaven into the southern hemisphere, the land there recoiled from him into the northern hemisphere; also, the land within the earth rushed back from him to form the island of Purgatory in the southern ocean, leaving empty the cavern through which Virgil and Dante emerge from hell.

There is a place as remote
    from Beelzebub[79] as his tomb extends,
    not known by sight, but by the sound

of a little stream which descends in it
    along the hollow of a rock which it has eaten out
    with a slow and winding course."[80]   132

My guide and I started on that hidden way
    to return to the bright world,
    and, without caring for any rest,

we climbed, he first and I second,
    until I saw, through a round opening,
    the beautiful things that heaven bears,

and came forth to see again the stars.

---

[79] Here, another name for Satan.

[80] The stream is the river Lethe, which from Eden atop the mountain of Purgatory flows down to the center of the earth to join the four rivers of hell, carrying with it the memory of the vices expiated in Purgatory. All evil, committed by the saved and the damned, thus comes to rest as dead weight, frozen and immobile, at the point of the universe farthest removed from God.

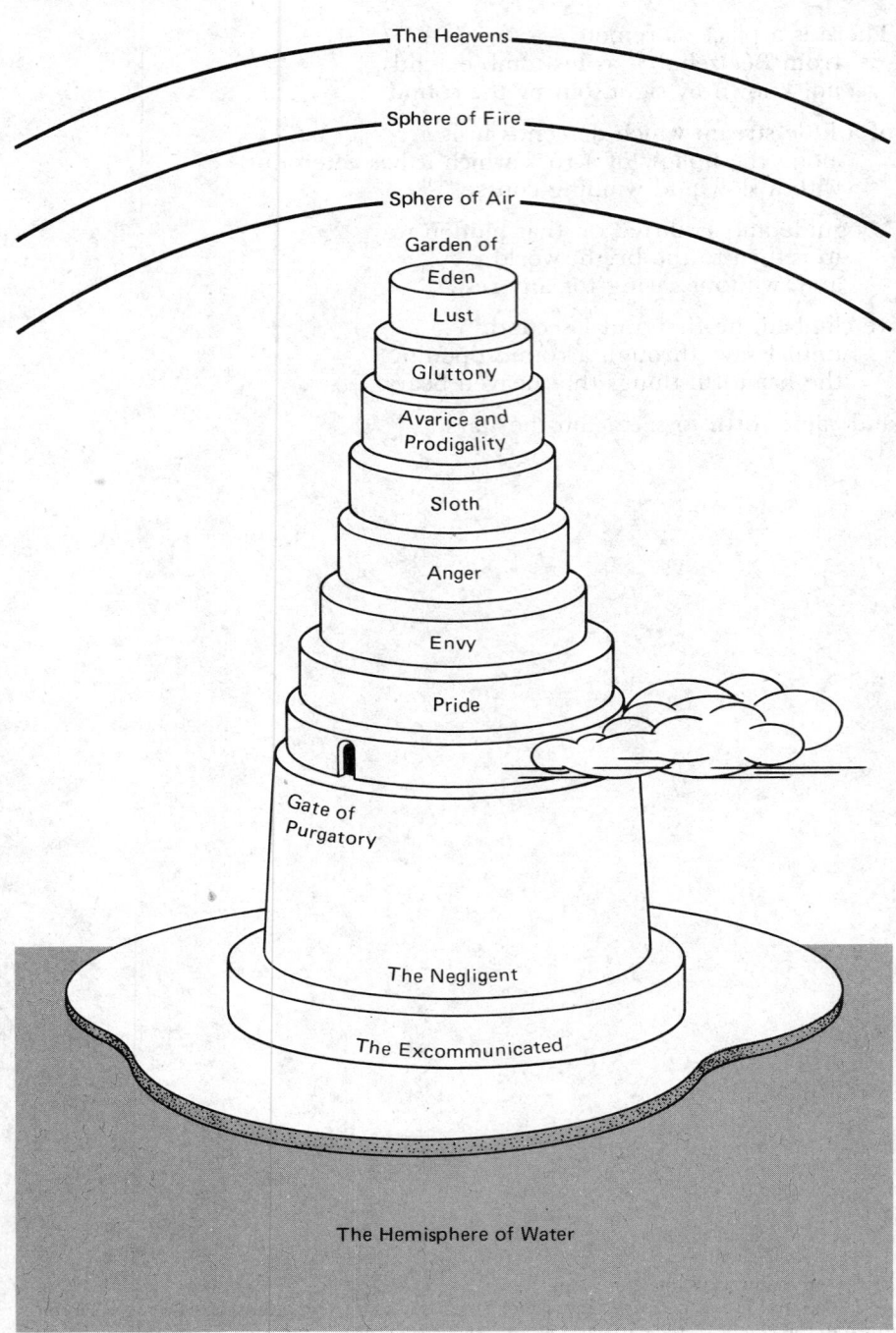

A diagram of Purgatory.

OUTLINE OF PURGATORY

REGION	VICES	METHOD OF SUGGESTION	DISCIPLINES
Shore	[Excommunicated]		Waiting
Below gate	[Negligent]		Waiting
Ledge 1	Pride	Sculptures	Bending necks under heavy weights
Ledge 2	Envy	Voices	Practice in using other senses besides sight
Ledge 3	Anger	Visual and auditory imagery	Satiation with blindness of wrath
Ledge 4	Sloth	Recitation	Developing habit of speedy activity
Ledge 5	Avarice and Prodigality	Recitation	Satiation with living close to the ground
Ledge 6	Gluttony	Voices	Practice in abnegation
Ledge 7	Lust	Recitation	Purification by fire
The Earthly Paradise (Garden of Eden).			

NOTE: The suggestive treatment consists of constant contemplation of the "goads" and "checks," that is, beautiful examples of the opposite virtue and repulsive illustrations of the vice itself.

The first three vices are due to love of a bad object, the fourth to insufficient love, and the last three to disproportionate love.

PURGATORY

CANTO I

CATO

Dante indicates his new subject and invokes the "holy" Muses, especially Calliope, the inspirer of epic poetry whom the daughters of King Pieros once challenged in song, for which boldness they were changed into magpies. It is just before sunrise on Easter, April 10, 1300. The morning star, Venus, is obscuring with its light the constellation of the Fishes. In the new sky are four stars representing the cardinal virtues—Prudence, Temperance, Fortitude, and Justice—previously seen only by Adam and Eve.

To move over better waters now hoists sail
    the little vessel of my mind
    which leaves behind so rough a sea;

and I will sing of the second realm
    where the human spirit is cleansed
    and becomes worthy to rise to Heaven.

Here, O holy Muses, since I am yours,
    let dead poetry be revived
    and let Calliope arise a while,

accompanying my song with the music
    which struck the ears of the wretched magpies
    so that they despaired of pardon.   12

A sweet color of oriental sapphire
    which was forming in the clear sky,
    pure from the zenith to the horizon,

restored delight to my eyes
    as soon as I came out of the dead air
    that had afflicted both my eyes and lungs.

The beautiful planet which prompts to love
    made the whole east smile,
    veiling the Fishes that escorted her.

I turned to the right and set my mind
    on the other pole, and I noticed four stars
    never seen except by the first people.   24

The heavens seemed to rejoice in their light.
    O region of the north, widowed!
    since you are denied that view.

> *Cato, Dante's favorite hero of antiquity and the symbol of Free Will, appears, his face shining with the light of the four virtues. Rather than submit to Caesar, he had committed suicide, a Christian but not a pagan sin. For this devotion to freedom and for other merits he is made the guardian of Purgatory and will be saved on Judgment Day.*

When I had withdrawn my eyes from them,
    turning for a moment to the north
    where the Great Bear [Dipper] had already disappeared,

I saw a solitary old man near me,
    in semblance worthy of so much reverence
    than no son owes more to his father.

The beard he wore was long
    and streaked with white, like his hair
    of which two tresses fell upon his breast.   36

The rays of the four holy lights
    so brightened his face that he appeared
    as if the sun were shining on him.

"Who are you who, moving up the dark stream,
    have fled from the eternal prison?"
    he asked, shaking his plumelike beard.

"Who has guided you or given you a light
    to issue from the black night
    which darkens the infernal depth?

Are the laws of the abyss thus broken,
    or have decrees been changed in Heaven
    so that the damned may come to my cliffs?"   48

My guide then took hold of me,
    and with words and hands and gestures
    made reverent my knees and brow.

Then he answered, "By myself I do not come;
    a lady descended from Heaven, at whose prayers
    I helped this man with my companionship.

But, since it is your will that more
    of our present condition be explained,
    my will is not able to refuse you.

The man has not seen his last hour,
    but through his folly was so close to it
    that there was little time left.   60

I was sent to him, as I said,
    to rescue him, and there was no other way
    than this one on which I have started.

I have shown him all the wicked people
    and now propose to reveal those spirits
    who are purging themselves under your charge.

How I have brought him here would take long to tell;
    a Power from above has helped me
    to bring him to see and to hear you.

May it please you to welcome his coming;
    he is seeking freedom, which is precious,
    as one who gives up life for it knows.   72

You understand, since death for you was not bitter
    in Utica where you left the clothing of your flesh
    which, on the great day, will be so bright.

The eternal laws are not broken by us,
    for this man lives, and Minos does not condemn me.
    I am from the circle where the chaste eyes

of your Marcia still seem to supplicate,
    O holy breast! that you hold her for your own.
    For love of her, then, incline toward us;

let us go through your seven kingdoms;
    I will tell her of your grace
    if you deign to be mentioned down there."   84

*Cato states plainly his indifference to the fate of his wife, Marcia: the felicity of
Heaven would be impaired if earthly relationships were not ended and if sorrow
could be felt for the damned. He directs Virgil to gird Dante with a reed (Humility) and to wash his face, so that he can appear properly before the guardians of
the ledges of Purgatory. The sun (Righteous Choice, Enlightenment) must be
their guide henceforth.*

*The two poets descend to the sea which Ulysses alone had sailed. There, the reed
which Virgil plucks for Dante replaces itself. Humility cannot be defeated: the
more it is crushed the more it grows.*

"Marcia pleased my eyes so much
    while I was yonder," he said then,
    "that I granted all the favors she asked.

Now that she dwells beyond the evil stream
    she cannot move me because of the law
    which was made when I came from there.

But if a lady from Heaven sends and commands you,
    as you say, there is no need for coaxing;
    it is enough that you ask me for her sake.

Go then and see that you gird this man
    with a slender rush, and that you bathe his face,
    so that all stains are washed from it,   96

for it would not be fitting that eyes
    darkened by any mist should meet
    the first minister of those in Paradise.

This little island, around its very base,
    where the waves beat upon it,
    bears reeds upon the soft mud.

No other plant which brings forth leaves
    or grows hard could exist there,
    since it would not yield to the waves.

Afterward do not return along here;
    the sun which is rising now will show you
    the easiest way to climb the mount."   108

Then he disappeared, and I got up
    without speaking and drew close
    to my guide, my eyes fixed on him.

He began, "My son, follow my steps,
    let us turn back, for from here
    the plain slopes down to its low bounds."

The dawn was dispelling the morning hour
    which fled before it, so that from afar
    I recognized the trembling of the sea.

We went over the solitary plain
    like men returning to the road they have lost
    who, until they get there, seem to walk in vain.   120

When we reached the place where the dew
    contends with the sun and
    in shaded spots had dried but little,

my master softly placed both hands
    spread out on the wet grass,
    and I, aware of his purpose,

held toward him my tear-stained cheeks
    on which he wholly restored the color
    which the smoke of Hell had hidden.

We came then to the deserted shore
    whose waters had never been sailed
    by anyone who afterward was able to return.   132

There he girded me, as another [Cato] wished.
    O marvel! for, as he plucked the humble plant,
    it was suddenly reborn as it was

in the place from which he had torn it.

CANTO II[1]

At Jerusalem day is setting and night rising, and in Purgatory day rising and night setting; and as the Poets, pondering on their course, are delaying their journey against their will, they see glowing red in the east a light swiftly approaching them; which Virgil soon recognizes as Charon's angelic counterpart, who with stroke of wing guides a light bark with its charge of happy souls to the mountain of purification. As they land the souls chant the psalm of the Exodus, and with the sign of the cross their angelic guard departs, to renew his mission. The risen sun now shoots full daylight into the sky, obliterating Capricorn from the zenith; the new-come folk inquire the way and Virgil answers that he and his companion are strangers like themselves, whereon the shades observe that Dante breathes and is still in the first life, and in their eagerness almost forget the cleansing for which they have come to the mount. One especially, the musician Casella, presses forward with a look of such affection that the Poet opens his arms to embrace him, but he only clasps an empty shade. Dante must now explain the mystery of his own presence in that place while still in the flesh, and Casella in his turn must explain the delay of many months between his death and his admission into the boat of the redeemed that gathers its happy charge at the mouth of Tiber. Dante's heart and senses are still aching from the anguish of Hell; and the loveliness of earth, sea and sky has re-awakened his perception of the healing power of beauty. So a great longing comes over him once more to hear the sweet singer's voice that has so often soothed him and banished all his cares. Does that power of song which on earth seems akin to the spirit world, survive the

---

[1] The summaries of the cantos omitted from the *Purgatory* and *Paradise* were written by Philip H. Wicksteed.

great change? Casella's answer is to sing, in tones the sweetness whereof can never die, a song that Dante himself had written to the praise of Wisdom; whereon Virgil and all the other souls gather eagerly around, till rebuked for this premature indulgence and repose by the stern Cato, who bids them to press forward the cleansing work of the mountain. Whereon they scud along the plain like startled doves.

CANTO III

When Dante has recovered from his confusion, and Virgil from the self-reproach caused by his momentary neglect of his charge, the Poets look west toward the mountain. The sun shines behind them and throws Dante's shadow right before him. Now for the first time he misses Virgil's shadow, and thinks that he has lost his companionship; but Virgil reassures him. It is nine hour agone since the sun rose in the place where lies that part of him which once cast a shadow. The nature of the aerial bodies in the spirit world is unfathomable by human philosophy, which yearns in vain for solutions of the mysteries of faith. When they arrive at the foot of the mountain, the Poets are at a loss how to scale its precipices; but at their left Dante perceives a group of souls slowly moving toward them from the south. With Virgil's sanction they go to meet them, and by thus reversing the usual direction which the souls take, following the sun, they excite the amazement of the elect spirits from whom they inquire their way. These sheep without a shepherd—for they are the souls of such as died in contumacy against the Church, and they must dree[2] their rebellion against the chief Shepherd by thirty times as long a space of shepherdless wandering—are yet more amazed than before when they see Dante's shadow and hear from Virgil that he is still in the first life. They make sign to them to reverse their course; and one of them, King Manfred, when Dante has failed to recognize him, tells the story of his death at the battle of Benevento; of the pitiless persecution even of his lifeless body by the Bishop of Cosenza and Pope Clement. He declares that the Infinite Goodness hath so wide an embrace that it enfolds all who turn to it; explains the limitations of the power of the Church's malediction; and implores the prayers of his daughter Constance.

CANTO IV

In the eagerness of his attention to Manfred's tale, Dante takes no note of the passing time, and thereby furnishes a practical refutation of the Platonic doctrine of the plurality of souls; for if the soul that presides over hearing were one, and the soul that notes the passage of time another, then the completest absorption of the former could not so involve the latter as to prevent it from exercising its own special function. It is three and a half hours from sunrise when the souls point out the narrow cleft by which the pilgrims are to ascend the mountain; after which they take their leave of them. It is only the wings of longing and hope that enable Dante to overcome the impediments of the ascent, and bring him through the cleft to the open slope of the mountain, which he breasts at Virgil's direction though it lies at an angle of more than forty-five degrees. In answer to his weary plea for a pause, Virgil urges him to gain a terrace that circles the mount a little above them. There they rest, and, looking

---

[2] Live out the time of.

east, survey their ascent, after the complacent fashion of mountain-climbers; but Dante is amazed to find that the sun is north of the equator and strikes on his left shoulder. Virgil explains that this is because they are in the southern hemisphere, at the antipodes of Jerusalem. Were the sun in Gemini instead of Aries, he would be further to the north yet. Dante rehearses and expands the lesson Virgil has taught him, and then (having meanwhile apparently turned west, facing the slope) makes inquiry as to the height of the mountain. Virgil, without making any direct answer, cheers his weary companion by assuring him that as they mount higher, the ascent becomes ever less arduous, till mounting up becomes as spontaneous as the movement of a ship dropping down stream; and then comes rest. Whereat a voice suddenly rising from behind a great stone lying south of them, intimates to Dante that he will probably experience a keen desire for rest before that consummation. Whereon the Poets move to the shady or southern side of the rock where they see souls whose repentance had been deferred to the moment of death, stretched in attitudes of indolence. And in particular Belacqua, an old friend of Dante's, sits hugging his knees like Sloth's own brother. It is he who had given Dante his mocking warning, and who now in the same vein taunts him with his readiness to reproach others for their sloth the moment after he himself had implored Virgil to wait for him; and also with his slowness to understand the astronomical phenomena of the southern heavens. A smile of relief and amusement lightens Dante's face as he finds his friend among the saved, and still his old self. Cannot even the spirit life check his nimble wit or stir his sluggish members? But Belacqua answers sadly that unless aided by the prayer of some soul in grace, he must live as long excluded from purgation as he had lived in the self-exclusion of impenitence upon earth. It is now noonday in Purgatory; night reigns from Ganges to Morocco; and Virgil urges his charge to continue the ascent.

CANTO V

As they pass up the mountain, Dante's shadow still excites the amazement of the souls; but Virgil bids him pay no heed to their exclamations. A group of souls chanting the **Miserere** *breaks into a cry of wonder, and when two of them, sent out as messengers, have received Virgil's statement that Dante is still in the first life, the whole group crowd around him. They tell him that they are souls of the violently slain, who repented and made their peace with God at the last moment. Virgil bids Dante pursue his path, but suffers him to promise to bear news of these souls to their friends on earth and implore their prayers. Dante hears the tale of Jacopo del Cassero. Then Buonconte da Montefeltro tells the story of his death at Campaldino, the struggle of the angel and the devil for his soul, and the fate of his deserted body. And lastly Pia rehearses, in brief pathetic words, the tragedy of her wedded life, and implores the Poet when he is rested from his long journey to bethink him of her.*

CANTO VI

Like a successful gamester who must cleave his way by payments through the host whose quickened sense of friendship overflows in obstructive congratulations and reminiscences, so Dante must pay his way by promises through the crowd of souls to whom he has power of granting such precious boons. Of some of these souls he tells us news, not without side thrusts of warning or reproach at the living. When again free

*to converse with his guide, Dante asks him to explain the seeming contradiction
between the anxiety of these souls for the prayers of others, and his (Virgil's) declaration that the divine Fates cannot be bent by prayer. Virgil explains, firstly, that no
bending of the divine will is involved in the granting of prayer; secondly, that his
rebuke was uttered to souls not in grace; and, finally, that the complete solution of
such questions is not for him (Virgil), but for Beatrice; at the mention of whose name
Dante wishes to make greater speed in ascending the mountain, whereto Virgil answers that the journey is of more days than one. The Poets, now in the shade of the
mountain (since they are on its eastern slope and the sun is already west of north) so
that Dante no longer casts a shadow, and is therefore not instantly to be recognized as
a living man, perceive the soul of Sordello gazing upon them like a couching lion;
but on hearing that Virgil is a Mantuan, he breaks through all reserve and embraces
him as his fellow-countryman. The love of these two fellow-citizens calls back to
Dante's heart the miserable dissensions that rend the cities of Italy, and the callous-
ness with which the Emperors leave them to their fate. But from the reproaches thus
launched against the Italians, Florence is sarcastically excepted, till the sarcasm
breaks down in a wail of reproachful pity.*

CANTO VII

*After repeatedly embracing Virgil, only because he is a Mantuan, Sordello questions
him further; and on hearing who he is, after a moment's pause, amazed and half-
incredulous, falls at his feet to embrace his knees. In answer to Sordello, Virgil
rehearses in words of deepest pathos the nature of his mission and the state of the souls
in Limbo who practiced the moral, but were never clad with the theological, virtues.
In answer to Virgil's questioning concerning the way, Sordello expounds the law of
the mount which suffers no soul to ascend while the sun is below the horizon; and he
offers to lead the pilgrims, ere the now approaching sunset, to a fitting place of rest,
where they shall find noteworthy souls. In a little lap or dell of the mountain they find
the pensive souls of kings and rulers who had neglected their higher functions for
selfish ease or selfish war. Now they are surrounded by every soothing beauty of
nature; but relief from the serious cares of life, which erst they sought unduly, is now
an anguish to them, and their yearning goes forth to the active purgation of the seven
terraces of torment above them. With the enumeration of the kings—old enemies
singing in harmony, and fathers mourning over the sins of their still living sons—
are mingled tributes to the worth, or gibes at the degeneracy of the reigning monarchs, and reflections on the unlikeness of sons and fathers.*

CANTO VIII

*At the pensive hour of sunset the souls devoutly join in their evening hymn, with eyes
uplifted to heaven. As though to remind them that while outside the gate of the true
Purgatory their wills are not intrinsically above the reach of temptation, but are
guarded only by the express intervention and protection of divine grace, two angels
descend and stand on either bank of the dell to guard them against the serpent who
would enter this counterpart of Eden. At the mention of the serpent Dante shrinks
close up to Virgil; but Sordello invites them to descend, as the twilight deepens, into
the little vale, where Dante meets his friend Nino, Judge of Gallurà, and in answer*

to his question tells him that he is still in the first life; whereon both he and Sordello start back in amazement. Nino summons Conrad Malaspina to witness this wonder of God's grace, and then turning to Dante again, implores him to obtain the prayers of his daughter; for his wife, betrothed to a Visconte, has surely forgotten him. Dante, looking to heaven, notes that in this season of repose the four stars that represent the moral virtues have vanished behind the mountain, and the three that represent the theological virtues shine in the sky. This is one of the many indications that the proper business of Purgatory is ethical, the recovery of the sound moral will. The season in which the souls may actually ascend is the one over which the four stars preside. Meanwhile the dreaded serpent approaches, but the angels swoop like celestial hawks upon it, and having put it to flight return to their posts. During the whole assault Conrad has not ceased to gaze on Dante; and he now asks him for news of his country of Valdemagra, and of his kinsfolk there; to which Dante replies that he has never visited those parts, but the noble character of the Malaspini rings through all Europe; whereon he receives the significant comment that ere six years are gone he shall know the worth of the Malaspini better than reportingly.

CANTO IX

It is now about two and a half hours since sunset. The Scorpion has begun to pass the horizon, and the lunar aurora is already whitening in the east, when Dante, reclining in the bosom of the valley, resting from his four-night watch and the toil and anguish of his journey, drops into a deep sleep. In the morning hour when dreams are true, he seems to be clasped in the talons of an eagle—the symbol at once of justice and of baptismal regeneration—and to be borne up into the sphere of fire, the burning of which awakens him; and he starts to find himself alone with Virgil, higher on the mount, nigh to the gate of Purgatory proper. He learns from his guide that, as he slept, Lucia bore him away from Sordello and the other denizens of the valley, and placed him here. His dismay is thus turned into delight as he follows his guide to the narrow portal with its three steps and its angel guard, who first challenges the pilgrims, but on learning their divine authority gives them courteous welcome. On the steps of sincerity, contrition and love, the Poet mounts to the gate and throws himself at the feet of its guardian to implore admission. The angel carves on Dante's brow seven P's, the symbol of the seven deadly sins (peccata), which are purged on the terraces above, and then turning the golden and the silver key which he holds in charge from Peter, he admits Dante; with the solemn warning that he is not to look behind him, when once past the gate. The seldom-turned hinges grate as the portal swings, and a half-heard song of praise to God is the first sound that falls on the Poet's ear within the gate, drawing his heart upward.

CANTO X

The closing door rings, behind the Poets, but Dante, mindful of the warning, looks not back. The cleft through which the pilgrims mount is as tumultuous as the heaving sea, and it is three hours after sunrise ere they issue upon the first terrace, some eighteen feet in breadth, stretching uniformly as far as the eye may reach in either direction. The outer rim of the terrace verges unprotected upon the precipitous downward slope of the mount. The inner side is of marble, cut vertically out of the moun-

tain, and carved with scenes from sacred and pagan history, illustrative of humility, seeming to live and speak in their beautiful and compelling reality. As Dante is gazing unsatiated upon the intaglios, Virgil bids him look to the left, where he beholds strange objects approaching him, which his eyes cannot at first disentangle, but which presently reveal themselves as human forms bent under huge burdens of stone, crumpled up in postures of agonized discomfort. These are the forms of the proud, mere larvae *not yet developed into the angelic* imago, *who had none the less exalted themselves on earth in unseasonable pride, and now wail only that the limits of their strength enable them to bear no more and bend no lower in their humility.*

CANTO XI

The humbled souls approach, with a paraphrase of the Lord's Prayer upon their lips, the petition for protection against temptation being uttered for the sake of those they have left behind, whether on earth or, perhaps, in the Antepurgatory, since souls inside the gate are beyond its reach; which loving offices of prayer the living should surely reciprocate for those who are now purging themselves. In answer to Virgil's inquiry, one of the souls directs the pilgrims to turn to the right, circling the mount with the sun. It is the Sienese Omberto, whose insolence had made him little better than a brigand, and had involved all his race in ruin. As the Poet bends down to hearken, another soul, painfully turning beneath his burden, gazes upon Dante who recognizes him as the miniature painter, Oderisi, now willing to admit the superior excellence of his rival Franco, and fully sensible of the empty and transitory nature of human glory. Cimabue's school of painting is superseded by Giotto's; the older poetic school of Guittone, or Guido, of Arezzo and his companions has been superseded by that of Guido Guinicelli, to which Guido Cavalcanti and Dante himself belong; and who knows whether the founder of yet another school that shall relegate them all to obscurity, may not already be born! Worldly reputation is always of the same empty quality, though the momentary object to which it attaches itself changes, one empty reputation differing from another only in name, and all of them swallowed up in the course of years, what matter whether few or many! One of the heroes of Montaperti and victims of Colle de Valdelsa, who is pacing before them, is already all but forgotten on the very scene of his triumphs and defeats. What are his reputation and his pride to him now, where the only act of his life that avails him is his self-humiliation in begging ransom for his friend, in the marketplace of Siena? an act which Dante himself shall learn better to appreciate in the days of his own anguish of humiliation.

CANTO XII

Dante has bent down in a sympathetic attitude of humility to converse with Oderisi, and when Virgil bids him make better speed he straightens his person so far as needful to comply, but still remains bowed down in heart, shorn of his presumptuous thoughts. As he steps forward with a good will, Virgil bids him once more look down at the pavement which he is treading, and there he sees as it were the lineaments of the defeated proud, from Lucifer and Briareus to Cyrus and Holofernes and Troy. The proud are laid low upon the pavement as the humble were exalted to the upspringing mountainside. A wide stretch of the mountain is circled ere they come to the gentle angel of this terrace of the proud, whose glory is tempered as a morning star, and who promises them an easier ascent henceforth. A stroke of his wing touches the Poet's brow, who then approaches such a stair as was made to ease the ascent to San Miniato in the good old days when weights and measures were true and public records ungarbled. As they mount the stair the blessing of the poor in spirit falls on their ears, with sound how different from the wild laments of Hell! And Dante notes how the steep ascent seems far more easy than the level terrace of a moment back. It is because the P of pride was erased by the stroke of the angel's wing, and thereon all the other six became shallower. This Dante, at a hint from Virgil, ascertains by feeling his brow with outspread fingers, and in innocent delight at the discovery of the cause of his lightened steps, he looks into Virgil's face which answers with a smile of sympathy and encouragement.

CANTO XIII

The Poets mount to the second terrace; of dark rock, tenantless so far as the eye can stretch, and without mark or indication of any kind. Virgil apostrophizes the sun, and in lack of any counter reason, determines to follow him from east to west. After a time voices ring through the air in praise of generosity, the virtue counter to envy; and Virgil anticipates the direct warning against that vice ere they leave this the circle of its purification. Meanwhile they encounter the once envious spirits, appealing with full confidence to the ungrudging love of Mary, of the angels, and of the saints. The envious eyes that once found food for bitterness in all sights of beauty and joy, must now in penance refrain from drinking in the gladness of sea and sky and human love, for their lids are drawn together with such a suture of wire as is used to tame the wildness of the untrained hawk; and their inward darkness is matched by their sober raiment. They lean one against another in mutual love and for mutual support, and upturn their sightless countenances like the blind beggars that gather round church portals. Dante is shamed, as though he were taking ungenerous advantage of those whom he sees, but who cannot know his presence; and, having gained Virgil's leave, addresses the souls in words of soothing beauty and aspiration. In answer to his question whether any of them are of Latium, Sapia the Sienese tells that they are all citizens of one true city; but that she, amongst others, had lived in her earthly pilgrimage in Latium. She tells the story of her evil joy at the defeat of the Sienese by the Florentines at Colle in Valdelsa, and utters her thanks to the humble saint whose prayers have secured her admission to expiatory suffering earlier than the else appointed time. In her turn Sapia questions Dante as to his journey,—with open eyes as she judges, and with breath-formed speech,—around this circle; and he answers that he too shall one day have his eyes closed there, but not for long, since he has sinned far less through envy than through pride. He further reveals to her the wonder of his pilgrimage and receives her petition for his own prayers, and her commission to bear news of her to her kinsfolk among the vain and light-minded Sienese.

CANTO XIV

As Dante converses with Sapia, revealing the wondrous conditions of his own pilgrimage and the mysterious presence of his guide, he is overheard by two spirits who are leaning for support one against another at his right. Nearest to him is Guido del

Duca of Bertinoro, who is the chief speaker, the other being Rinieri da Calboli of Forlì. They speak chiefly to each other, but draw Dante into their conversation, questioning him as to his origin; and when he indicates by a circumlocution that his birthplace lies upon the Arno, Rinieri asks Guido why Dante conceals the name under dark hints as though it were a shameful thing; whereon Guido approves of Dante's shrinking from expressly naming this accursed ditch which rises in the midst of brutishness, and as it swirls through deeper pools, finds ever fiercer or more degraded neighbors, till it reaches the crowning infamy of Pisa. There follows a prediction of the woes which Rinieri's relative Fulcieri shall wreak on Florence in 1303. Deeply stirred by their discourse, Dante questions the spirits as to their own past, and Guido accompanies his answer by a lamentation over the degeneracy of the Romandiola from which they both spring; and implores Dante to pass upon his way and leave him to weep undisturbed. Assured that they are pursuing the right way, since the generosity of these once envious souls would else have notified them of their mistake, the two Poets pursue their way as the warning voices against envy, anticipated by Virgil, ring in their ears; to which Virgil adds his sad reflections on the things which human choice relinquishes and the things it grasps.

CANTO XV

It is three o'clock in the afternoon, and the Poets (having circled nigh a fourth part of the mountain and reached its northern slope) are facing the westering sun, when the dazzling light of the angel guardian of the circle warns them that they have approached the next ascent. They are welcomed to a stair far less steep than those they have already surmounted, and hear the blessing of the merciful, together with songs of lofty encouragement, chanted behind them as they mount. Dante's mind goes back to words in which Guido del Duca, while confessing his own envious disposition on earth, had reproached mankind for fixing their hearts on the things which exclude partnership; and now he questions Virgil as to the meaning of this saying. Virgil answers first briefly, and then in full detail, that the more of any material thing one man has, the less of it there is for others; whereas the more peace or knowledge or love one man has, the more there is for all the others. Hence envy disturbs men's hearts only because they are fixed on material instead of spiritual things. If this exposition does not satisfy him, let him await further light from Beatrice, and meanwhile let him make all speed upon his journey. On this they reach the third terrace—that of the wrathful—whereon Dante in ecstatic vision beholds examples of meekness and patience. Waking, half-bewildered, from his trance, he is called to himself by Virgil, and the two walk toward the evening sun, till a dark cloud of smoke rolling towards them plunges them into the blackness of more than night.

CANTO XVI

Closing his eyes against the gross and bitter fog, led by Virgil like a blind man, Dante hears the harmonious and tender chant of the "Lamb of God" arise from the lips of the once wrathful spirits. One of them, who has heard Dante's conversation with Virgil, questions him and turns back with him to hear his wondrous tale. The spirits in other circles have recognized the special grace shown to Dante in his anticipated vision of unseen things; and to this grace Dante himself now appeals to win from his new companion an account of himself, and directions as to the journey; for meeting these souls circling from west to east raises a doubt in his mind whether he and Virgil have been right in still following the sun. The spirit reveals himself as Marco Lombardo, refers, as other spirits had done, to the degeneracy of the times, reassures Dante as to the course he is taking and implores his prayers. Dante, while giving him the required pledge, catches at this renewed insistence on the evil times, and asks whether it is due to unfavorable conjunctions in the heavens or to inherent degeneracy of earth. Marco heaves a deep sigh at the blindness implied in such a question; as if man were handed over helplessly to planetary influences! As if he had no free will and no direct dependence upon God, which may make him superior to all material influences! The causes of degeneracy must be sought on earth and will be found in the absence of any true governor who perceives at least the turrets of the true city, and so can lead the guileless and impressionable souls of men on the right path. And this evil springs not from corruptness of human nature in general, but from the worldliness and ambition of the clergy who have grafted the sword upon the crook, so that the two lights of the world that once shone in Rome have quenched each other; and the temporal and spiritual powers, confounded together, have ceased to guide and check each other. Hence the world is so degenerate that only three good old men remain as a rebuke to the living generation. Dante accepts the sad wisdom of Marco's discourse, only requesting a word of personal explanation as to one of the three still surviving types of antique virtues; and thereon he begins to see the light struggle through the enveloping darkness, and is told that the angel guardian of the next stair is at hand.

CANTO XVII

The Rise to the Slothful

Reader, if ever in the mountains a mist
    has caught you, through which your sight
    was like a mole's, through a membrane,

and if you remember how, when the thick vapors
    began to lighten, you could see faintly
    from within them the sphere of the sun,

it will be easy for you to imagine
    how I saw that planet which already
    was on the point of setting.

So, keeping step with my trusted master,
    I issued from the cloud into the sun's rays
    which were already dead on the shore below.

12

Among the checks on anger is the example of Procne who, to avenge a wrong done by her husband to her sister, made him eat, unsuspecting, the flesh of his own child. Later she was changed into a nightingale. Another example is that of the mother of Lavinia who committed suicide at the false report of the death of Turnus to whom her daughter had been betrothed. She feared that the victorious Aeneas would take Lavinia from her.

O fantasy which at times steals us
    from ourselves, so that we are not aware
    if a thousand trumpets sound around us,

who creates you, since the senses give no impressions?
    A light formed in heaven moves you
    either by itself or by a will that directs it down.

A trace of the impiety of her [Procne]
    who changed into the bird that delights most
    to sing, appeared in my imagination,

and my mind was so intent
    within itself, that from without
    no impressions were received by it.   24

Then fell within my soaring fantasy
    one [Haman] crucified, scornful and fierce
    in looks even as he died.

Around him were the great Ahasuerus,
    Esther his wife, and the just Mordecai
    who was so honest in word and deed.[3]

And as this vision broke of itself,
    like a bubble as the water fails
    of which it is formed,

so there arose in my vision a maiden
    weeping loudly and saying, "O queen,
    why in your anger did you wish to be nothing?   36

You killed yourself for fear of losing Lavinia,
    yet you have lost her. I must mourn for you
    before mourning for another."

As sleep is broken when suddenly
    a light strikes the closed eyes,
    and being broken, wavers before it quite dies away,

so my imagining ended as soon as a light
    greater than any known here
    had struck my face.

I was turning to see where I was when a voice,
    banishing every other thought,
    said, "Here you mount."   48

It made my will so eager to see
    who was speaking that it could not rest
    until confronted with what it wanted.

---

[3] Ahasuerus was king of Persia. His minister Haman, angry with the upright Jew Mordecai, tried to annihilate the Jews, but Esther, wife of the king and cousin of Mordecai, caused Haman to be crucified (or hanged) instead. See Esther, chapters 3–7.

But as the sun burdens our sight
    and with its excess veils its form,
    so here my powers failed.

"This is a divine spirit, directing us
    on our way without our asking,
    and with his light he hides himself.

He acts as a man should; for whoever
    sees help needed and waits to be asked,
    may prompt an unkind refusal.   60

Now let our feet accept such an invitation;
    let us try to rise before dark,
    for afterward we cannot, until day returns."

Thus my master spoke, and with him
    I turned toward the stairway;
    and as soon as I was on the first step

I felt near my face the motion
    and the fanning of a wing, and heard the words,
    Beati pacifici[4] who are without sinful anger.

Already the last rays followed
    by the night were so high above us
    that stars appeared in several places.   72

"O my strength! why do you melt away?"
    I said to myself, for I felt [as the sun set]
    the power of my legs suspended.

We were at the top, where the stairs
    could not be climbed further,
    and were stranded, like a grounded ship.

I waited a while to see if I might hear
    some sound on the new ledge;
    then I turned to my master and said,

"My dear father, tell me what offense
    is purged on the round where we are;
    if our feet are stayed, do not end your words."   84

And he to me, "Love of good,
    when insufficient, is here restored;
    here the slackened oars are plied again.

But, in order to understand more clearly,
    direct your mind to me
    and you will gain good fruit for our tarrying."

Virgil now classifies the various vices by relating them all to love (desire). In-stinctive desires are primarily innocent, but acquired love may involve a bad

---

[4]"Blessed are the peacemakers" (Matthew 5:9).

*object or be devoted to a legitimate one without moderation. A bad object implies
injury to our fellow men, since all creatures are free from self-hatred or hatred of
God. Proud men wish to dominate others; the envious wish for their decline; the
angry are eager for vengeance. These vices are reformed on the first three ledges.
Insufficient love for spiritual good (sloth) is punished on the fourth ledge. On the
last three, disproportionate love for an object not bad in itself (avarice or prodigality, gluttony, and lust) is cured.*

"Neither Creator nor creature, my son," he began,
   "was ever without love [desire] either instinctive
   or dependent upon the will [acquired], as you know.

The instinctive is always without error,
   but the other can err through a bad object
   or through too little or too much vigor.   96

While it is directed to primal [spiritual] good
   and is moderate in other things,
   it cannot be a cause of sinful pleasure.

But when it turns to evil or to legitimate pleasures
   with too much or too little care,
   the creature works against his Creator.

Hence you can understand that love
   must be the seed of every virtue in you
   and of every act that deserves punishment.

Now, since love can never turn
   from the welfare of its possessor,
   all things are free from self-hatred.   108

And because no one can be conceived
   as separate from the First [God] and existing by himself,
   every desire is cut off from hating Him.

It follows, if I distinguish rightly,
   that the evil we love is our neighbors',
   and this arises in three ways in our mortal clay.

Some [the proud] hoping to excel
   through their neighbors' decline
   long only to reduce their greatness.

Others [the envious] fear losing power,
   honor, and fame if another rises,
   and wish for the contrary.   120

Still others [the angry] feel so disgraced
   by injuries received that they long
   for vengeance and plan suffering for others.

This threefold love is wept for down below.
   Now I want you to hear about that love
   which seeks the good with wrong intensity.

Everyone conceives confusedly
    some ultimate [spiritual] good that will quiet
      all longing, and everyone desires it.

If insufficient love impels us
    toward it, this ledge,
      after due repentance, torments us.

132

There are other good things which do not make us happy;
    they do not give felicity, are not
      the essence and root of every good fruit.

Love which abandons itself too much to them
    is wept for above us in three rounds,
      but why it is described as threefold, I do not say,

so that you can discover it for yourself."

CANTO XVIII

MORAL RESPONSIBILITY—THE SLOTHFUL

*Dante is troubled by still another problem. He wants to understand better what
"love" is, to which all vices and virtues are related. He learns that natural,
instinctive desire is innocent. Love acquired through indulgence, however, may
be sinful and deserving of punishment, since man possesses innate ideas of right
and wrong, and a will which makes choice possible. But the question of moral
responsibility is too deep for Reason alone. Beatrice (Revelation) must give the
final answer.*

The eminent teacher had ended his explanation,
    and looked attentively in my face
      to see if I appeared content,

and I, tormented by a new thirst,
    outwardly kept silent, but inwardly said,
      "Perhaps too much questioning will bother him."

But that true father who knew
    of my timid, unexpressed wish
      gave me the boldness to ask.

Therefore I said, "Master, my sight is so quickened
    in your light that I discern clearly
      all that your explanations contain or describe;

12

so I beg you, dear father,
    to explain 'love' to me, to which you reduce
      every good action and its contrary."

"Direct toward me," he said, "the sharp eyes
    of your mind, and the errors of the blind
      who try to lead will be apparent to you.

The soul created ready to love
    is susceptible to everything that pleases
    as soon as it is awakened into activity.

Your perception of an object
    creates an impression in you
    which makes the soul turn toward it,   24

and if, so turned, it inclines in that direction,
    that inclination is love. It is a natural feeling
    reinforced in you through pleasure experienced.

Then as fire rises because of its form
    which makes it ascend
    to where it can remain in its element,

so the soul, captivated by a desire,
    a spiritual force, never rests
    until the thing loved makes it rejoice.

Now you know the truth
    hidden from those who maintain
    that every love is praiseworthy in itself,   36

because, although it may *appear* good,
    not every seal has worth
    even if impressed on good wax."

"Your words and my attentive mind," I answered,
    "have revealed to me what love is,
    but that has made me doubt still more

for, if love comes from without
    and the soul acts on no other basis,
    whether it goes straight or not, it has no merit."

And he to me, "Whatever reason can see in this
    I can tell you; expect to hear the rest
    only from Beatrice, since it requires faith.   48

Every substantial form [soul] distinct
    from body and united with it
    has in itself a specific virtue[5]

which is imperceptible except in operation
    and demonstrated only by its results,
    as life in plants is shown by their green leaves.

Therefore, whence comes understanding
    of axiomatic truths, man does not know,
    nor his liking for the primal objects of desire

which is in you like the instinct in bees
    to make honey; and this first love
    does not admit of praise or blame.   60

[5] The specific virtue (power) in the human soul is innate knowledge and a tendency to love.

Now, to make every desire conform,
    there is, innate in you, the virtue that counsels
    and which must defend the threshold of consent.

This is the source from which ·
    merit derives, according as good and bad loves
    are accepted or winnowed out.

Those who have gone deeply in philosophy
    have been aware of this innate liberty,
    and therefore have left ethics to the world.

Thus, supposing that every love
    by necessity is kindled in you,
    the power exists in you to resist it.

Beatrice understands this noble virtue as free will;
    therefore see that you have it in mind
    if she undertakes to speak to you about it."

The poets have spent the evening at the edge of the fourth ledge. Souls, formerly slothful, rush by, citing as the "goad" examples of haste and diligence and the opposite qualities as a "check."

The moon, delayed almost to midnight,
    looked like a red-hot kettle,
    and made the stars seem fewer.

It proceeded against the sky's movement [backing up]
    on the path [the ecliptic] which the sun enflames
    when from Rome it is seen setting between Sardinia and Corsica,

and that noble soul [Virgil], on account of whom
    Pietola [his birthplace] is more famous than any other Mantuan
       city,
    had put down the burden of my loading.

So I, having received clear and plain answers
    to my questions, remained
    like one who lets his mind wander.

But this somnolence was dispelled suddenly
    by people who, behind our backs,
    had come around to where we were.

As [the rivers] Ismenus and Asopus once saw a tumult
    and a throng [the Bacchic orgies] at night along their banks
    whenever the Thebans had need of Bacchus,

so such a throng, judging by what I saw,
    bent its way around that ledge,
    driven on by good will and love.

That great crowd, because all in it
    were running, was soon upon us,
    and two in front, weeping, shouted,

72

84

96

"Mary *ran* in haste to the mountain,"[6]
    and "Caesar, to subdue Lerida,
    attacked Marseilles and then *rushed* to Spain."

"Quickly, quickly, let no time be lost
    through insufficient love," shouted the others,
    "so that our efforts to do good may renew grace."

"O people, you in whom keen fervor now
    makes up perhaps for negligence and delay
    shown previously in well-doing,   108

this man who lives (and certainly I do not lie)
    wishes to go up when the sun shines again;
    therefore, tell us where the nearest opening is."

These were the words of my guide,
    and one of those spirits said,
    "Come behind us, and you will find the pass.

We are so full of desire to move
    that we cannot stay; therefore pardon us
    if you take our punishment for rudeness.

I was the Abbot of San Zeno at Verona
    under the rule of the good Barbarossa
    of whom Milan still talks with sorrow.   120

And another already has a foot in the grave
    who will weep for having had power
    over that monastery,

because his son, deformed in body
    and worse in mind and a bastard,
    he has installed in place of its true pastor."

I do not know if he said more or was silent,
    so far had he already moved from us,
    but this I heard and gladly retained.

And Virgil, my help in every need,
    said, "Turn around, see two coming,
    giving sloth a curb [check]."   132

Behind the rest they were saying,
    "The people [sluggish Hebrews] for whom the sea opened
    were dead before Jordan [the Promised Land] saw its heirs," and,

"Those that did not endure toil to the end
    with the son of Anchises [Aeneas]
    gave themselves up to a life without glory."

---

[6] After learning that she would bear Jesus, Mary "arose in those days, and went into the hill country with haste" (Luke 1:39) to visit Elisabeth.

Then when those shades were so far from us
    that they could no longer be seen,
    a new thought came into my mind,

from which others, different, arose,
    and so much did I ramble from one to another
    that in my wandering I closed my eyes,

and transmuted thought into dreams.

    144

CANTO XIX

As morning approaches Dante has a vision of the Siren, whose filthiness Virgil, at the exhortation of a lady from heaven, exposes. Dante is roused by Virgil's repeated summons. The sun is fully up, and the pilgrim, deep in thought, advances to the next stair, where once again he feels the breath of the angel's wing, and hears the blessing of them that mourn. Dante is still plunged in his reverie, from which Virgil rouses him by question, explanation, and admonition. They who have yielded to the Siren,—foul but seeming fair,—must expiate their offenses in the three remaining circles. Let Dante tread the earth like a man and raise his eyes to the heavens above. And so they reach the fifth circle. There the souls of the avaricious and prodigal cleave to the pavement, no longer in sordid love, but in the anguished sense that they are unworthy to look upon aught more fair; and the limbs which had bound themselves on earth are now held in helpless captivity. Virgil inquires the way, and from the form in which the answer is given Dante gathers the law of Purgatory, hereafter to be more fully confirmed, which permits souls to pass without delay or scathe through any circles of the mount wherein sins are purged by which they themselves are unstained. He silently asks Virgil's leave to stay and question the soul that has spoken. It is Pope Adrian V who for little over a month bore the weight of the papal mantle, scarce tolerable to him who would keep it from defilement; and in answer to Dante's tender entreaty he expounds the nature of the penalties of this circle. He himself had been given over to avarice till he reached the summit of human greatness, saw its emptiness and turned in penitence to God. When Dante speaks again, Adrian perceives that he has knelt down, in reverence to Peter's successor; whereon he bluntly bids him straighten his legs, and explains that no formal or official position or relation, however close or however august, has place in the spirit world, where personality is stripped of office. Then he urges Dante to pass on and leave his penitence undisturbed, making a reference to his niece who had married one of Dante's future friends the Malaspini; which reference the pilgrim may, if he so choose, interpret as a request for prayers for the departed soul.

CANTO XX

Unwilling to break short his conference, but more unwilling yet further to trespass on the courteous forbearance of his interlocutor, Dante passes among the weeping souls, through whose eyes that curse of all the world is distilling itself away! When will he come who shall chase the wolf of avarice from earth? Dante hears one of the prostrate souls rehearse examples of generous poverty, and learns that he is the ancestor of the royal line of France, the root of that evil tree that darkens all the Christian lands with

*its shadow. Comparatively harmless in its earlier generations, this house had gath-
ered evil as it gathered strength; hero and saint alike have been its victims; it couched
the lance of Judas against Florence; its own flesh and blood and the sacred orders of
chivalry are alike regarded by it as things to coin; and the very person of the Vicar of
Christ has been crucified by it while thieves were left alive. At such deeds wrath would
torture the divine peace itself were it not soothed by the prospect of vengeance. Warning examples of avarice uttered at night balance the daily recitation of the virtuous
counterparts. The mountain now shakes as with an earthquake, and a mighty cry of
"Glory to God in the highest" rises from all its terraces; startled and perplexed by
which, though bidden by Virgil not to fear, Dante swiftly pursues his path.*

CANTO XXI

STATIUS

The natural thirst which is never quenched
    except with the water [of truth] asked for,
    as a boon, by the woman of Samaria,[7]

tormented me, and haste goaded me
    over the encumbered road, behind my leader;
    and I was sorrowing for the just penance,

when, behold! as Luke tells how Christ,
    already risen from the grave, appeared
    to the two who were on the way,[8]

so a shade appeared to us as we were gazing
    at the crowd at our feet, having come from behind,
    nor were we aware of him until he spoke,   12

saying, "Brothers, may God grant you peace!"
    We turned quickly, and Virgil,
    with a suitable gesture, returned his greeting

and began, "May the true court
    which keeps me in eternal exile
    take you into the council of the blessed!"

"What!" he [the newcomer] cried as we proceeded quickly,
    "If you are shades whom God does not allow above,
    who has brought you so far over the stairs?"

And my leader, "If you look at the marks
    traced by the angel and borne by this man,
    you will see that he must reign among the good.   24

---

[7] In John 4:13–14, in a dialogue by a well, Jesus describes to the Samaritan woman "a well
of water springing up into everlasting life" that will forever quench thirst.
[8] After his resurrection Jesus, remaining unrecognized for some time, joined two of his
followers walking to the village of Emmaus; Luke 24.

But because she [the Fate] who spins
    day and night had not exhausted the thread
    prepared for everyone by Clotho,[9]

his soul [*anima*, fem.), the sister of yours and mine,
    could not come up alone,
    since it does not see as we do.

Therefore I was summoned from the wide throat of Hell
    to show him the way, and I will continue
    as far as my knowledge can take him.

But tell us if you can why the mountain
    trembled a little while ago, and why
    to its wet base all the souls seemed to shout?"   36

In asking this, he so threaded
    the needle's eye of my desire that
    with hope alone he made my thirst less burning.

*The soul who has just joined them explains that on Purgatory meteorological
changes and earthquakes from natural causes cannot happen. A trembling, however, occurs whenever a soul feels free to rise to Heaven, and a cry from all the
ledges celebrates the happy event. As in Hell, a kind of determinism is at work
here: the soul rises of its own accord when it is light enough to do so. Its
"absolute" will to go up is conditioned previously by a compulsion, the need and
desire to get rid of its vices.*

He began, "The holy rule of the mountain
    permits nothing that is disorderly
    or that is contrary to custom.

This place is free from variations;
    only what heaven takes into itself
    can cause change, nothing else,

so that no rain, hail, snow, dew, or frost
    falls higher than the stairs
    of the three short steps.   48

No heavy or light clouds appear, nor lightning,
    nor Thaumas' daughter [the rainbow]
    who often changes place on earth.

Dry vapor [lightning] does not rise above the top
    of the three steps of which I spoke
    where the vicar of St. Peter stands.

Perhaps below, the mountain quakes more or less
    from wind compressed in the earth
    (I know not how), but up here never.

[9] In the myth of the three Fates, Clotho prepares the thread of a person's life, Lachesis
spins it out, and Atropos cuts it off.

It trembles here when a soul
  feels cleansed so that it may go up,
  and such a shout accompanies it.   60

Will alone gives proof of the purity
  which takes the soul by surprise, and helps it
  when it is free to change its cloister.

It wills indeed before, but this desire,
  conditioned by Divine Justice
  as formerly by sin, keeps it in its penance.

And I who have lain in this pain
  five hundred years and more, just now
  felt my will free for a better place.

Therefore you noticed the earthquake,
  and the devout spirits on the mountain gave praise
  to the Lord who, I pray, may soon send them up."   72

Thus he spoke to us, and since we enjoy drinking
  in proportion to our thirst,
  I cannot say how much good he did me.

My wise leader said, "Now I see the net
  which holds you here, and how it is broken,
  why the mountain quakes, and at what you rejoice.

Now please let me know who you were
  and let me learn from your words
  why you have lain here so long."

Statius, the newcomer, a pagan poet, the author of the Thebaid *and the unfinished* Achilleid *(whom Dante had confused with a Christian rhetorician of the
same name and who stands in the allegory for Reason illuminated by Christianity) identifies himself, and attributes his supposed conversion to certain works of
Virgil. Virgil signals to Dante not to reveal his identity, but the latter cannot
repress a smile, which Statius asks him to explain. Virgil finally relieves Dante's
embarrassment and allows him to speak freely. On learning who Virgil is, Statius
tries to embrace him, adding thus another affectionate tribute to the ancient poet
whom Dante must soon leave.*

"At the time when good Titus with the help
  of the Supreme King, avenged the wounds
  from which flowed the blood sold by Judas,[10]   84

I lived yonder," that spirit answered, "with the title
  [of poet] which lasts longest and honors most.
  I was famous but as yet did not have faith.

So sweet was the music of my verse that,
  although of Toulouse, Rome drew me to herself
  where I merited the myrtle crown.

[10] The destruction of Jerusalem in 70 A.D. by the Romans under Titus was considered as a
judgment on the Jews for the death of Jesus.

People still mention my name, Statius.
    I sang of Thebes, and then of great Achilles,
    but I fell by the way with the second burden.

The sparks of the divine flame
    which has inspired more than a thousand
    kindled the fire that I felt in me—   96

I mean the *Aeneid* which was a mother to me
    and the nurse of my poetry;
    without it I would not have been worth a drachma,

and to have lived yonder when Virgil was alive,
    I would have agreed to do a year more
    than I owed before coming out of exile."

At these words, Virgil turned to me
    with a look that said, "Be quiet!"—
    but the will cannot do all it wishes,

for laughter and tears are such close followers
    of the passion from which they spring
    that they obey least in those who are most sincere.   108

I merely smiled, making an involuntary sign,
    whereupon Statius was silent and looked
    in my eyes where the soul is most expressive,

and said, "So may you complete your task,
    why did your face just now
    reveal to me the flashing of a smile?"

Now I am caught on one side and the other;
    one bids me keep silent, the other asks
    that I speak; whereupon I sigh and am understood

by my master, who said to me,
    "Do not be afraid, but speak and tell him
    what he asks for so earnestly."   120

Then I, "Perhaps, ancient spirit,
    you are wondering at my smile,
    but I want you to marvel still more.

He who guides my eyes on high
    is that Virgil from whom you gained
    the power to sing of the gods and of men.

If you believe anything else caused my laughter
    consider it as untrue and that the reason
    was what you said about him."

Already he was bending to embrace my master's feet
    when Virgil said, "Brother, do not do it,
    for you are a shade and are looking at one."   132

And he, on rising, "Now you can understand
    the greatness of the love that warms me
    for you when I forget our emptiness

and consider a shade as a solid thing."

CANTO XXII

*The pilgrims have already begun to mount the stair that leads to the sixth circle.
Another* **P** *has been struck by an angel-wing from Dante's brow, and the blessing
pronounced on those that thirst after righteousness. Virgil, with friendly insistence,
presses to know how so great a soul as that of Statius could have harbored so puny a
vice as avarice; whereon the other acknowledges with a smile the tender friendliness
which this very perplexity implies, but answers that the keen scent of friendship is this
time following a false track, for it is prodigality, not avarice, that has kept him more
than five hundred years a prisoner in the fifth circle, where the two opposing sins are
punished together. Nor had he escaped the pains of Hell for his offense, though
committed in ignorance, had he not read a hidden warning in lines of Virgil's own.
Virgil goes on to ask how Statius became a Christian, for there is no indication in his
poems of his conversion; and Statius answers that it was Virgil's self who, like one
passing through the night, bearing a lantern behind him, had lightened the path for
the feet of others, though not for his own. It was that prophetic* **Eclogue** *which had
revealed the truth to him, and won his sympathy for the persecuted saints; but he
concealed his faith, and had atoned for his laggard love in the circle of the slothful
for over four hundred years. Statius in his turn now questions Virgil as to the fate of
other Latin poets, and Virgil tells him of the sad and noble life in Limbo, of the Greek
and Latin poets there, and of the heroic souls whose story Statius himself had told. It
is past ten o'clock in the morning when the pilgrims issue upon the sixth terrace, and,
with the tacit approval of Statius, follow their usual course with the sun counter-
clockwise, Dante eagerly hearkening to the converse of the two Latin poets. This is the
circle of the gluttons; and the pilgrims encounter a wondrous tree, fruit-laden, and
bedewed with clear water from a neighboring fall, from the midst of the foliage of
which a voice recites examples of abstinence.*

CANTO XXIII

*Dante's eyes search the foliage of the tree till he is summoned to advance by Virgil.
Then he hears the cry, at once grievous and soothing, of the souls who presently
overtake the travellers and turn to look upon them as they pass, though without
pausing. These are the once gluttonous souls, with faces now drawn by thirst and
hunger so emaciated that the extremest examples of famine in sacred or profane
records rush to Dante's mind. Their eye-sockets are like rings that have lost their
gems; and he who reads* omo (homo) ◠◠ *on the face of man would find the three
strokes of the m writ plain enough in the gaunt bones of cheek and nose. How can the
fruit and trickling water work in such fashion on the shadowy forms? One of them
turns his eyes from deep down in the sockets upon Dante, who, when he speaks,
recognizes his old companion Forese; and each of the astonished friends demands
priority of satisfaction for his own amazed curiosity. Forese explains that there are*

other trees like to this, and that each renews the pain of the purging souls; nay, rather their solace; for they exult in crucifying with Christ the old Adam in them. Forese further shows how he owes to his widowed Nella his speedy promotion to the sweet bitterness of torment. She is all the dearer to God in proportion to the loneliness of her virtue in the place of infamy in which she lives. Forese proceeds to denounce the dissolute fashions of the women of Florence. Dante must now in his turn unfold the story of how he had been rescued from the worldly life which he and Forese had once lived together, of the strange journey on which Virgil has conducted him, of the promise that he shall meet Beatrice, and of the manner in which they have encountered Statius.

CANTO XXIV

The souls gather in amazement round the living man; who utters a surmise to his friend that Statius is perchance lingering on his way for the sake of Virgil's companionship; and then questions him concerning his sister Piccarda, and learns that she is already in heaven. The souls are so emaciated as to be barely recognizable, and Forese names a number of them as he points them out to Dante; an office which they accept with complacency, for recognition can bring no added shame, but may bring sympathy or aid to souls in Purgatory. Amongst them is Bonagiunta da Lucca, a poet of the old school of Guittone of Arezzo, who mutters a prophecy concerning a child of the name of Gentucca, whose gracious offices to Dante when she comes to woman's state shall give him tender associations with that city of Lucca which he and others have so fiercely denounced. Then he questions Dante as to the secret of the new school of Tuscan poetry which has superseded the one to which he belonged, and learns that it lies in the principle of trying not to say things beautifully, but to say beautiful things truly; a criticism in which he acquiesces with full content and satisfaction. Then all the other souls sweep forward, while Forese, like a straggler from a caravan, remains behind to question Dante as to his expected term of life, to hear his lamentations over the state of Florence, to utter a prophecy of the death of his relative Corso Donati, and then to speed forward to rejoin his companions, leaving Dante to follow the two great poets. The pilgrims now pass another tree like the one already encountered. They hear that it is a shoot from the one whereof Eve tasted the fruit; and from amongst its foliage warning examples of gluttonous excess are rehearsed. After a lengthened march in silent thought, they are startled by the blinding glory of the angel guardian, whose wing wafts a breath laden as with perfume of flowers on a May morning upon Dante's brow; and the pilgrims hear the blessing pronounced on those whose hunger is measured by righteousness.

CANTO XXV

The pilgrims pursue their way up the stair in single file. As the little stork longs but ventures not to try its wings, so Dante feels the question as to the meaning of what he has seen ever kindled by longing and quenched by diffidence on his lips; till, encouraged by Virgil, he seeks for instructions as to how the shadowy forms which need no sustenance can present the appearance and experience the sensations of gnawing hunger. Virgil hints by analogies from pagan story and from natural philosophy that our own experiences and sensations may well reflect themselves in unsubstantial appearances; or may be connected with physical changes in matter other than that of our bodies of flesh and blood; but refers to Statius, his Christian counterpart, for fuller exposition; for in truth this matter, though no part of Christian revelation, yet verges on those mysterious and intricate portions of Aristotle's doctrine which none save Christian philosophers have had vision clear enough truly to expound. Statius, after a polite disclaimer, proceeds to expound the Aristotelian doctrines of generation and embryology, showing how the human fetus passes through every stage, differing only from the lower forms of plant, polype, or animal, in that it possesses the potentiality of further development; whereas they have reached their goal. At the critical point now reached, Averroës himself went wrong, for finding no organ in the human body appropriated to the immaterial principle of intelligence, he conceived it to be no part of the individual life of man, but a universal all-pervading principle; whereas in truth the human soul or life is inbreathed direct by God into the perfect animal form of the man that is to be; and thereon it draws into itself all the lower vital functions already active there. Therefore when the body dies, the gates of sense are indeed closed; but the soul itself which came from without remains with the purely immaterial powers of memory, intelligence, and will, isolated indeed from intercourse with outward things, but in themselves more vivid than ever. Then the soul drops at once to the bank of Acheron or the mouth of Tiber, becomes aware of its destination, and reflects itself upon an aerial body, flame- or rainbow-like, and through the instrumentality of this aerial body renews its intercourse with the outer world and the experiences of sense. They have now reached the topmost circle, which is filled with flames, save a narrow outward margin on which the Poets march, single file, and whereon Dante must take good heed to his steps; so that he can give but broken attention to the souls who commemorate examples of chastity from the midst of the glowing heat.

CANTO XXVI

The flames redden under Dante's shadow and the amazed souls gather to him, careful, however, not to issue from the flame. One of them has barely questioned Dante, when a group, circling the mountain in the opposite direction, meets them with a brief salutation, and each group alike proclaims a warning example of lust; after which they sweep past each other like flocks of birds, and continue to utter the wail and song suited to their state. But this does not prevent their drawing again to Dante, who tells them his tale and questions them as to their state. When the souls have somewhat recovered from their amazement, one of them explains that the group accompanying the Poet failed to restrain their carnal appetites within the limits prescribed by the social institutions of humanity, whereas the other group had not even observed the laws laid down by nature. Dante's interlocutor is Guido Guinicelli, the founder (or precursor) of the new style of Tuscan poetry, the father of Dante and of his betters; to whom Dante renders his passionate homage of affection and loyalty. But he points to the shade of the Troubadour Arnaut Daniel as superior to himself and superior to all Provençal rivals by as much as the new Tuscan school excels the old school of Guittone of Arezzo. Then, with a petition for Dante's prayers, he yields his place to Arnaut himself; who tells of his state, in his own Provençal tongue; and in his turn implores Dante's prayers.

CANTO XXVII

The Dream of Leah
*As this canto begins, the sun is setting in Purgatory and rising in Jerusalem;
Spain (Ebro) is under the constellation of Libra, and it is noon in India.*

The sun was darting its first beams
    on the place where its Maker shed his blood—
    the Ebro falling beneath the lofty scales,

and the waters of the Ganges made hot by noon—
    and [in Purgatory] day was departing
    when God's glad angel appeared.

Out of the flames he stood on the bank
    and sang, *"Beati mundo corde"*[11]
    in a voice much clearer than ours.

Then, "You cannot go farther, holy souls,
    unless the pain of fire is felt. Enter it
    and do not be deaf to the singing beyond."   12

This he said to us when we drew close,
    and when I heard his words I became
    like one who is laid in the grave.

I leaned over my clasped hands,
    looking at the fire and recalling vividly
    the burned human bodies I had seen.

The good escorts turned toward me
    and Virgil said, "My son,
    here there can be pain, but not death.

Remember! Remember!
    and if I guided you safely on Geryon,
    what will I do now, closer to God?   24

Be assured that if you stayed a thousand years
    in the midst of these flames
    they would not make you lose one hair;

and if perhaps you think that I deceive you,
    go toward them, and with your two hands
    and the hem of your dress gain assurance.

Put aside, put aside all fear;
    turn this way, come, and enter securely."
    But I stood firm despite my conscience.

When he saw me remain still and stubborn,
    somewhat disturbed he said, "Now see, my son,
    this wall is between you and Beatrice!"   36

[11]"Blessed are the pure in heart" (Matthew 5:8).

As Pyramus at the sound of Thisbe's name[12]
    opened his eyes and looked at her
    at the time when the mulberry became red,

so, my stubbornness softened, I turned
    to my wise leader, hearing the name
    which always springs up anew in my mind.

Then he shook his head and said, "What?
    do we want to stay on this side?" then smiled
    as to a child won over by an apple.

He stepped into the fire ahead of me,
    begging Statius to come behind
    who, for a long time, had divided us.   48

When I was in, I would have plunged
    into boiling glass to cool off,
    so extreme was the burning.

My sweet father, to comfort me,
    kept speaking of Beatrice,
    and adding, "I seem already to see her eyes."

A voice singing beyond guided us,
    and attentive only to it,
    we came to where the ascent began.

Venite, benedicti patris mei![13] sounded there
    within a light which so blinded me
    that I could not look at it.   60

"The sun is leaving," it added, "and evening
    comes; do not stop, but hasten
    while the west is still not dark."

The path rose straight within the rock
    so that the rays of the sun,
    already low, were broken in front of me.

The sages and I had mounted a few steps only
    when we noticed by my disappearing shadow
    that the sun was setting behind us.

And before the vast expanse
    of the horizon had become of one hue,
    and before Night held all its domain,   72

each of us made a bed of a step;
    for the nature of the mountain overcame,
    not our desire, but our strength to rise.

---

[12] Pyramus and Thisbe had to confess their love through a chink in the wall between their houses. Later, Pyramus, thinking Thisbe dead, killed himself, his blood turning the fruit of the mulberry red.

[13] "Come ye blessed of my father," the words that welcome the saved into God's kingdom (Matthew 25:34).

As goats, agile and wanton on the heights
    before they have eaten, become tame
    when ruminating, lying silent and quiet

in the shade while the sun is hot,
    watched over by the herdsman who leans
    on his staff, and while leaning guards them;

and as the shepherd who lodges in the open
    passes the night beside his flock,
    watching lest a wild beast scatter it,   84

so we were, all three of us,
    I like the goats and they like the shepherds,
    hemmed in on both sides by high walls.

There, little could be seen outside,
    but in that little the stars appeared
    clearer and larger than usual.

Thus, looking at them and musing,
    sleep came upon me, the sleep which often
    announces events before they occur.

In a dream Dante sees Leah, who represents the innocent active life; Rachel, her sister, stands for contemplation.

At the hour, I believe, when Cytherea [Venus]
    always burning with the fire of love
    first shines from the east on the mount,   96

in a dream I seemed to see a lady,
    young and beautiful, going over a meadow
    gathering flowers and who while singing said,

"Let whoever asks for my name know
    that I am Leah, and I use my fair hands
    to make myself a garland.

I adorn myself to reflect a pleasant image;
    my sister Rachel never leaves her mirror,
    but sits before it all the day.

She likes to see her beautiful eyes
    as I to beautify myself with my hands;
    for her, seeing; for me, doing, satisfies."   108

And now amid the splendors before dawn
    which are the more welcome to pilgrims
    when, on returning, they spend the night nearer home,

on all sides the darkness fled
    and my sleep with it; and I got up
    seeing my great masters already risen.

After climbing to the top of the mountain, Virgil addresses Dante for the last time. The ancient poet has revealed all that Reason can disclose. Under his guidance Dante has freed himself not only of bad habits, but of the innate vices, the very potentiality for sin. He has attained a freedom from hereditary limitations and from environmental conditioning that no one on earth can ever have. The faith in the goodness of Nature, which later in the Renaissance deluded many, is appropriate for him. Free from the need for choice or thought or inner struggle, he can do as he pleases. To symbolize this freedom, this goal of man's reforming efforts, he is figuratively endowed with a crown and miter, the symbols of temporal and spiritual power.

"That sweet fruit [happiness] for which,
     on so many branches, mortals search,
     today will satisfy your hunger."

These words Virgil addressed to me,
     and never were there gifts
     . that caused such delight.   120

So greatly did desire rush upon desire
     to be above, that at every step
     I felt my wings grow for the flight.

When the stairway was wholly under us
     and we were on the top step,
     Virgil fixed his eyes on me and said,

"The temporal fire [of Purgatory] and the eternal [of Hell]
     you have seen, my son, and have come to a place
     where I, by myself, can discern nothing further.

I have brought you here with reason and with art;
     now take pleasure as your guide;
     you are free from the steep and narrow ways.   132

See the sun shining on your brow;
     see the grass, the flowers, and the shrubs
     which the earth here produces of itself.

Until the fair eyes [of Beatrice], now rejoicing, come—
     which in tears made me go to you—
     you can sit or walk among them.

Expect no further word or sign from me;
     free, upright, and whole is your will;
     it would be wrong not to do as it pleases.

Therefore, over yourself, I crown and miter you."

CANTO XXVIII

THE GARDEN OF EDEN

Eager now to look within and around
     the dense and verdant forest which tempered
     for our eyes the light of the new day,

without delay I left the mountain's edge,
    and went slowly over the plain
    on ground fragrant everywhere.

A sweet, unvarying breeze
    touched my face as lightly
    as a gentle wind

and made the leaves, quick to tremble,
    bend in the direction
    of the holy mountain's morning shadow,   12

not deflecting them, however, so far
    that the birds there
    must give up practicing their art;

but these, singing, full of joy, greeted the first hours
    of the day from within the rustling leaves
    which accompanied their song, just as,

in the pine grove on the shore of Chiassi
    a sound swells from branch to branch
    when Aeolus[14] lets the Sirocco blow.

Already my slow steps had taken me
    so far within the ancient forest
    that I could not see where I entered;   24

and behold! a stream prevented me
    from going farther, which with little waves
    bent leftward the grass growing on its banks.

The clearest waters on earth
    would seem to have some mixture in them
    compared with these which conceal nothing,

although they move darkly
    under perpetual shade never pierced
    by the rays of the sun or of the moon.

I held back my steps, but with my eyes
    I glanced beyond the stream to see
    the great variety of fresh May branches.   36

And over there appeared, like something
    which, through the marveling it causes,
    turns every other thought aside,

a solitary lady who went along singing
    and choosing flowers from the flowers
    with which her path was painted.

"O fair lady, you who warm yourself
    in the rays of love (if I can believe your looks
    which are the witnesses of the heart),

[14] God of the winds. The Sirocco is a hot Mediterranean wind.

may you be pleased to come forward
    toward this stream," I said to her,
    "so that I can understand what you sing.   48

You make me imagine where and how
    Proserpine[15] was at the time when her mother
    lost her, and when she lost the Spring."

As a lady when dancing turns
    with feet together and close to the ground,
    hardly moving one ahead of the other,

so she turned on the red and yellow flowers
    toward me, like a virgin,
    lowering her modest eyes.

And she fulfilled all my wishes,
    approaching so that the sweet sound
    of her voice came to me with its meaning.   60

As soon as she reached the place where the grass
    was bathed by the waves of the fair rivulet,
    she delighted me by lifting her eyes.

I do not believe that such light shone
    under the eyelids of Venus
    when she was wounded unintentionally by her son.[16]

She smiled, standing on the other bank,
    carrying in her hands flowers of many colors
    which the high land produces without seed.

The river kept us separated by three steps
    but Hellespont, where Xerxes passed—
    still a check on human pride—   72

was not more hated by Leander[17]
    for flowing between Sestos and Abydos
    than this stream by me for not opening.

"You are strangers here," she began,
    "and perhaps because I smile in this place
    chosen as the nest for human kind,

some wonder keeps you marveling;
    but the psalm *Delectasti*[18] gives light
    which can clear the mist from your minds.

[15] Proserpine was carried off in springtime by Pluto, god of the underworld, from the beautiful garden of Enna in Sicily.

[16] Venus was accidentally nicked by her son Cupid's arrow, which caused her to fall in love with Adonis.

[17] The Hellespont (modern Dardanelles) was a strait crossed by the Persian king Xerxes on his way to invade Greece. The strait also separated the lovers Leander of Abydos and Hero of Sestos.

[18] Psalm 92:4 ("For thou, Lord, hast made me glad through thy work").

And you in front who spoke to me,
    say if you wish to hear more, for I have come
    ready to satisfy all of your requests." 84

> *Matilda, the symbol of innocence and the guardian or presiding spirit of the*
> *Earthly Paradise, explains that the breeze is caused by the revolution of the*
> *heavens which communicate their movement to the sphere of air into which Pur-*
> *gatory projects. All plant life is represented in the Garden of Eden, and its*
> *reproductive power is dispersed over the earth by the moving air. Two streams,*
> *Lethe, which removes guilty memories, and Eunoè, which restores the recollection*
> *of all good deeds, are replenished by the will of God alone.*

> *Matilda adds, as a corollary, that the Ancients with their imperfect vision of the*
> *Christian truth mistook the Garden of Eden for the world in their "Golden Age."*
> *At this reference to their partial error, Virgil and Statius smile.*

"The water," I said, "and the sound of the forest
    combat in me a belief in something
    that denies the possibility of them."

Then she, "I will explain the cause
    of what makes you wonder
    and dispel the fog that has enveloped you.

The Supreme Good which follows only Its own pleasure
    made man good and for good, and gave this place
    to him as a pledge of eternal peace.

Through his fault he stayed here
    only a short time; through his fault he exchanged
    innocent laughter and play for tears and toil. 96

To prevent the vapors caused by the evaporation
    of land and water and which follow the heat
    as much as they can

from doing harm to man, this mountain rose
    so high toward Heaven, and is free
    from the gate upward from atmospheric change.

Now, since the air revolves
    with the primal revolution
    if its circling is not broken anywhere,

on this highest summit which projects
    in the air, such movement strikes
    and makes the dense wood give forth a sound; 108

and the smitten plants have such power
    that they impregnate the breeze with their virtues,
    and the air, revolving, scatters them,

and the land elsewhere, according as it is suited
    in itself and in its climate, conceives
    and produces from different virtues different growths.

Having heard this, it should not appear
    a marvel to you when some plant
    without apparent seed takes root.

And you must know that the sacred land
    where you are is full of every seed
    and has fruit not plucked in your world.   120

The water you see does not come from a spring
    restored by vapor condensed by cold,
    like rivers which rise and fall,

but comes from a stable and certain source,
    since it takes from the will of God
    what is poured forth in two streams.

On this side it descends with the power
    to take away memory of sin, and on the other
    it restores that of all good deeds.

Here it is called Lethe, over there
    Eunoè, and it is not effective
    unless drunk both here and there.   132

Its taste excels all other flavors.
    And, although your thirst may be quenched
    without my revealing more,

I will add as a favor a corollary;
    nor do I believe my remarks will be less dear
    if they go beyond my promise.

Those who in ancient times
    sang of the Golden Age and its happy state
    perhaps dreamed of this place on Parnassus.

Here the root of man's race was innocent,
    here is eternal Spring, and here is every fruit;
    this is the 'nectar' of which all sing."   144

I turned to my poets
    and saw that with smiles
    they had heard the last remark.

Then I turned my face to the fair lady.

CANTO XXIX

*As she chants a blessing on those whose sins are forgiven, Matilda takes her way
along one bank of the stream, while Dante keeps pace with her on the other; till the
air, kindling with splendor and laden with sweet strains of song, fills Dante at once
with the rapture of the Earthly Paradise and a sense of indignation against the act of
sin which had bereft him and mankind of such delights—delights which all the
waters of Helicon can scarce enable him to set in verse. Dante is pacing eastward,
with the stream on his left hand flowing towards him, and on the other side of the*

stream a divine pageant approaches him; the details of which, together with words of song, are gradually disentangled by eye and ear. But when he turns to Virgil for enlightenment, his faithful teacher can no longer instruct him; these are things beyond the reach of his art. Seven lights leave the air painted with seven great rainbow streamers of color stretching away as far as the eye can reach, throwing their glory over the heaven and glowing upon the stream. They represent the sevenfold gifts of the spirit, and beneath their glory tread four and twenty elders, crowned with lilies, representing the books of the Old Testament, chanting blessings on the Virgin. They are followed by the four Gospel beasts as described by Ezekiel and John, enclosing between them the triumphal chariot of the Church, resting on the two wheels of the contemplative and active life, drawn by a griffon whose twofold nature represents the two natures in one person of Christ. The sun itself has not so glorious a chariot. By the right wheel the three theological virtues dance, and by the left the four cardinal virtues. Then come two elders, then four, then one, crowned with roses, representing the remaining books of the New Testament. When Dante is just opposite the car, a peal of thunder arrests the whole procession.

CANTO XXX

THE COMING OF BEATRICE (REVELATION)

The candlesticks are compared to the Septentrion, the constellation that contains the North Star. When they stop, all those in the procession turn expectantly toward the chariot of the Church which is to bring Beatrice (Revelation) to Dante (Mankind). At a call, angels hover over it, and within a rain of flowers that veil her, Beatrice appears, dressed in the colors of the three evangelical virtues. At this climactic moment, Latin phrases occur frequently, among them a line from the Aeneid (Manibus o date lilia plenis!), spoken by an angel as the last and supreme compliment to Virgil, who must now disappear, eclipsed. Dante feels the effect of Beatrice's presence as he had on earth, and in his distress turns to Virgil. But his former guide, denied the sight of Revelation, has already disappeared, and Dante is left alone before the overwhelming spectacle to accomplish the painful but necessary rites of contrition, confession, and satisfaction (penance).

When the Septentrion of the first heaven—
    which never knew rising or setting
    nor the veil of any mist except of sin

and which made everyone there aware
    of his duty, as the lower star does
    him who turns the helm to come to port—

had stopped, the true people who had come
    between it and the griffon[19]
    turned to the chariot as to their peace.

And one of them, as if sent from Heaven,
    cried three times in song *"Veni, sponsa, de Libano,"*[20]
    and all the others sang after him.

12

[19] A beast with an eagle's head and wings and a lion's body.
[20] "Come with me from Lebanon, my spouse" (Song of Solomon 4:8). Allegorically, the line represents Christ's greeting to the Church.

As the blessed, at the last trumpet call,
    will rise quickly from their graves,
      singing with regained voices "Hallelujah,"

so, above the divine vehicle
    a hundred [angels] rose *(ad vocem tanti senis)*[21]
      the ministers and messengers of eternal life.

All cried, *"Benedictus qui venis,"*[22]
    and scattering flowers above and around,
      "Manibus o date lilia plenis!"[23]

I have often seen at the beginning of the day
    the eastern sky all rosy, the rest
      of the heavens beautifully clear,   24

and the sun's face appear veiled,
    so that, through the tempering of the vapors,
      the eyes could look steadily at it.

Thus, within a cloud of flowers,
    thrown by angelic hands, which rose
      and fell on and around the chariot,

underneath a white veil, crowned with olive,
    a lady appeared to me, under a green mantle,
      dressed in the color of living flame.

And my spirit which already had spent
    so long a time without the trembling
      from awe which her presence caused,   36

without seeing her more clearly,
    through a hidden influence which came from her,
      felt the great power of its old love.

As soon as on my eyes the great virtue fell
    which already had pierced me
      before I was out of childhood,[24]

I turned to the left with the expectation
    which a child has who runs to its mother
      when afraid or afflicted,

to say to Virgil, "Not a drop of blood
    unmoved is left in me;
      I recognize the signs of the old love!"[25]   48

---

[21] "At the voice of so great an elder."

[22] "Blessed are you who come" (cf. Matthew 21:9). This is a slight variation on the acclamation of Christ at his entrance into Jerusalem.

[23] "Oh, give lilies with full hands!"

[24] When Dante first saw the earthly Beatrice, he was less than nine years old. She died in 1290, when she was twenty-four, Dante twenty-five.

[25] This line is translated from Virgil's *Aeneid,* Book IV, where Dido tells her sister Anna that Aeneas has reawakened in her the symptoms of love after she thought she had banished it from her life.

But Virgil had left me without his company,
   Virgil, my beloved father, Virgil,
   to whom I gave myself up for my salvation;

nor could all that our ancient mother lost [Eden]
   keep my cheeks, cleaned with dew,
   from being darkened again by tears.

> *Now Beatrice speaks, not in her role as a tender friend, but severely, as a minister of the sacraments, calling Dante by his name (which appears here only), since the confession to follow must be personal and, in a manner, signed. Dante is paralyzed by this reception, but when the angels show sympathy for him, his awakened self-pity and his distress grow until he bursts into tears. Thus the first stage of the sacrament is accomplished.*

"Dante, although Virgil is leaving,
   do not weep yet, do not weep yet,
   for you must cry for another wound!"

As an admiral, at the prow or stern,
   looks at those who man the other ships,
   and heartens them to their work,   60

so—when I turned at the sound of my name,
   which is recorded here from necessity—
   at the left side of the chariot

I saw the lady who at first appeared
   veiled under the angelic shower
   directing her eyes at me from beyond the stream,

although the veil descending from her head,
   wreathed with Minerva's leaves [the olive],
   kept her from being completely manifest.

Queenlike, stern in her bearing,
   she continued, like one who speaks
   while holding back the sharpest words.   72

"Look at me! I am indeed, I am indeed Beatrice.
   How did you dare to approach the mount?
   Did you not know that here man is happy?"

My glances fell down to the clear stream;
   but seeing myself in it, I turned them
   to the grass, such shame burdened my face.

As a mother at times seems cruel
   to her son, so she appeared to me,
   since the taste of stern pity is bitter.

Then she was silent, and the angels sang
   at once, *"In te, Domine, speravi,"*[26]
   but did not go beyond *pedes meos.*[27]   84

---

[26] "In thee, O Lord, do I put my trust" (Psalm 31:1).
[27] "My feet." These words occur in verse 8 of the psalm; after this verse the tone changes from trust and assurance to despondency.

As snow on the living rafters [trees]
    of the back of Italy [the Apennines] congeals
    when blown and packed by Slavic winds,

then, melted, trickles down, if a breath comes
    from the land [Africa] without shadows,
    like fire melting a candle,

so was I without tears or sighs
    before those [angels] whose song is accompanied
    by the melodies of the eternal spheres;

but when I heard in their sweet notes
    their pity for me, more than if they had said,
    "Lady, why do you shame him so?"   96

the frost which had gripped my heart
    became breath and water, and with anguish
    through mouth and eyes came from my breast.

> *To prepare for the next stage, Beatrice tells how Dante, after her death, had*
> *devoted himself to the* donna pietosa *of the* Vita Nuova[28] *(profane philoso-*
> *phy), and to worldliness.*

She, still standing at the side
    of the chariot, then turned to address
    the angels who had shown pity for me.

"You watch in the eternal day,
    so that neither night nor sleep hides from you
    a step taken on the ways of the world;

therefore, my answer takes greater care
    that he, weeping over there, should understand,
    and that his sin and sorrow should be equal.   108

Not only by the operation of the great spheres
    which direct each seed to some end,
    according as the stars are conjoined,

but through the bounty of Divine Grace
    which has such high vapors for its rain
    that our sight cannot come close to them,

this man was such, potentially, in his young life
    that every good disposition
    might have come to marvelous fruition;

but the more vigor there is in the soil
    the more malignant and rank it becomes
    if uncultivated or sown with bad seed.   120

---

[28] The *New Life,* a quasi-allegorical work by Dante in which his spiritual autobiography is
traced in terms of his various loves. *Donna pietosa* means "compassionate lady."

For a while I sustained him with my countenance,
    and showing my youthful eyes to him,
    I led him with me in the right direction.

As soon as I was on the threshold
    of my second age, and changed life,
    he abandoned me, and gave himself to others.

When I had risen from flesh to spirit
    and beauty and virtue had increased in me,
    I was less dear to him and less esteemed,

and he turned his steps on an evil path,
    following false images of good
    which never fulfill their promise.   132

Nor did it avail me to invoke inspirations
    by which, in dreams and otherwise,
    I recalled him, so little did he care.

He fell so low that all means
    for his salvation would have been unavailing
    except to show him the lost people.

Therefore, I visited the portal of the dead,
    and to the one who brought him here,
    in sorrow I addressed my request.

The high decrees of God would be broken
    if Lethe were crossed and such a draught
    were tasted without any payment   144

of the penance that causes tears to flow."

CANTO XXXI

CONFESSION AND SATISFACTION
Beatrice now addresses Dante directly.

"O you beyond the sacred stream,"
    she continued without pausing,
    directing the point of her speech toward me

which even with the edge had seemed sharp,
    "say, say if this is true; to this accusation
    your confession must be joined."

My senses were so confused
    that my words began and were spent
    before released from their organs.

She waited a moment, then, "What are you thinking?"
    she questioned. "Answer me, for your sad memories
    are not yet impaired by the water [of Lethe]!"   12

Confusion and fear joined together
    sent forth such a "yes" from my mouth,
    that eyes were needed to hear it.

As a crossbow under too grēat a tension
    breaks both the string and the bow,
    so that the shaft hits its mark with less force,

so I burst under my heavy burden,
    pouring forth tears and sighs,
    and my voice died away on its passage.

Then she said, "In your desires for me [Revelation]
    which led you to love the good
    above which there is none to aspire to,   24

what chains or what hindering pitfalls
    did you find that you should lose
    the hope of going onward?

And what comforts or what advantages
    were displayed in the aspect of another good
    that you should seek it?"

After heaving a bitter sigh,
    scarcely had I voice for an answer,
    and my lips only with effort formed it.

Sobbing I said, "The present things,
    with their false pleasures, turned my steps away
    as soon as your face was hidden."   36

And she, "If you were silent or denied
    what you confess, your sin would not be concealed,
    known as it is by such a judge.

But when confession bursts
    from one's own mouth, the grindstone in our court
    turns back against the edge [of the sword of Justice].

Still to make you bear more shame
    for your error, and to make you stronger
    another time if you hear the sirens,

put aside your sowing of tears and listen,
    and you will hear how, when my flesh was buried,
    I should have led you in the opposite direction.   48

> *Beatrice refers again to the* pargoletta *(young girl). Then, by telling Dante to
> lift his "beard" instead of "chin," she points out indirectly that he is no child and
> should know better. Overcome by remorse, Dante falls in a faint, in this way
> giving "satisfaction," and accomplishing the last stage of the sacrament.*

Never did nature or art offer such delight
    as the fair members in which I was once enclosed
    and which are now in dust and scattered,

and if the supreme pleasure failed you
   at my death, what mortal thing
   should have drawn you with desire?

At the first shaft of fallacious things
   you should have lifted yourself up,
   following me, no longer [fallacious] like them.

No young girl or other vanity of such brief use
   should have weighed down your wings
   and exposed you to more blows.   60

A young bird takes two or three chances;
   but before the eyes of a full-grown one,
   the net is spread and the arrow shot in vain."

As children mute from shame stand listening,
   with their eyes on the ground,
   conscience-stricken and repentant,

so I stood; and she continued, "Since by hearing
   you suffer, lift up your beard,
   and you will have greater grief in looking."

With less effort a sturdy oak
   is uprooted by a wind of ours
   or by one from Iarbas' land [Libya]   72

than my chin was lifted at her command;
   and when by "beard" she meant my chin,
   I knew the venom of the argument.

Then when my face was raised,
   I saw the primal creatures [angels]
   resting from their scattering of flowers.

And my eyes, still insecure,
   saw Beatrice turned toward the beast
   which is one in two natures.

Under her veil and beyond the stream
   she seemed to surpass her former self
   more than she did others when on earth.   84

The thorn of repentance so pierced me then
   that of all things, those that had made me
   love them most now became most hateful to me.

Such remorse stung my heart
   that I fell, vanquished; and what became of me,
   she knows who caused this.

When my heart gave back a sense
   of outward things, I saw the lady [Matilda]
   above me, saying, "Hold to me, hold to me!"

She had drawn me into the river up to my throat,
   and pulling me behind her, moved on
   as lightly as a little boat over the water.   96

When I was near the sacred shore, *"Asperges me,"*[29]
   I heard so sweetly that I cannot keep the sound
   in mind, much less describe it.

The fair lady opened her arms,
   took my head, and held it down
   until I swallowed the water.

> *Matilda now takes Dante to the four nymphs (Prudence, Temperance, Fortitude, and Justice). These point out the deeper vision of the evangelical virtues (Faith, Hope, and Love) and bring Dante to the griffon (Christ), which he sees reflected in its twofold unity in the eyes of Revelation.*

Then she drew me forth, and led me, bathed,
   to the dance of the four nymphs,
   each of whom covered me with her arms.

"Here we are nymphs, and in Heaven stars.
   Before Beatrice came to the world
   we were ordained for her as handmaids.   108

We will lead you to her eyes; but the three
   over there who gaze more deeply
   will sharpen yours better for the light in them."

Thus they began to sing, and then took me
   with them to the breast of the griffon
   where Beatrice stood, turned toward us.

They said, "See that you do not spare your eyes;
   we have placed you before the jewels
   from which Love once shot his arrows."

A thousand desires hotter than flames
   bound my sight to the shining eyes
   which still were fixed upon the griffon.   120

As the sun in a mirror, not otherwise
   did the twofold creature shine in them,
   now with one, now with the other nature.

Think, Reader, if I marveled
   when I saw the object remain still
   and yet change in its image.

While full of joy and wonder, my soul
   tasted that [spiritual] food which,
   satisfying, gives hunger for itself;

---

[29] "Thou shalt sprinkle me" (King James Version "purge me") "with hyssop, and I shall be clean" (Psalm 51:7).

showing themselves of a higher order
    by their actions, the other three [Virtues] advanced,
    dancing to their angelic measure.   132

"Turn, Beatrice, turn your holy eyes,"
    was their song, "to your faithful one
    who, to see you, has taken so many steps!

Do us the favor of unveiling for him
    your smile, so that he may discern
    the second beauty which you conceal."

O splendor of the living, eternal light [of Beatrice]!
    who has become so pale in the shade of Parnassus,[30]
    or drunk so deeply at its well,

that he would not seem to have a clouded mind
    in trying to describe you as you appeared
    when the harmonious heavens alone veiled you,   144

and you disclosed yourself in the open air?

CANTO XXXII

*The eager gaze with which Dante quenches his ten years' thirst is for a moment
blinded by the glory on which he looks. When he recovers his full powers of vision he
perceives the procession deploying north, toward the noonday sun; and he and
Statius take their places by the right wheel of the chariot; and pass on, to the accompaniment of angelic song, through the forest, till Beatrice descends. They approach the
tree of the knowledge of good and evil, which represents the principle of obedience,
and therefore of the Empire, whereas the car from which Beatrice has descended
represents the Church; the ideal relations between which two powers are represented
by the reverence of the griffon for the tree, the binding of the pole of the chariot to it,
and the spring beauty that at once falls on it. Here slumber falls upon the Poet, from
which he wakes bewildered, like the apostles after the transfiguration, to find Beatrice
bereft of all her glorious escort save the seven nymphs, bearing in their hands the
seven tapers. Here, in this deserted Earthly Paradise, which would be thronged with
inhabitants had Church and State been true to their mission, Dante beholds an
allegorical portrayal of the perverse relations between the two, and of the disasters
and corruptions of the Church, of her persecutions, of the heresies that threatened
her, of the yet more fatal favor of Christian emperors, of the great schism of Islam, of
the foul corruption of the Court of Rome, and the Babylonian captivity of Avignon.*

CANTO XXXIII

*The seven virtues in alternate strains now proclaim, with tears, that the forces of the
world have found their hour; and Beatrice declares that though her glory will for a
time be withdrawn from them, it is but for a season. Then she signs to Matilda, to*

---

[30] The mountain sacred to Apollo and the Muses.

Dante and to Statius to follow her; but after only a few steps, graciously summons Dante to her side, bids him drop all diffidence, interprets the things he has just seen, and hints at the political Messiah who shall restore the due relations of Church and State and purify them both. But her comment is far darker than the text. So at least she knows it will seem to Dante's dull and over-crusted mind; wherefore the stamp has been impressed upon his eye rather than on his unreceptive intellect. Dante gently expostulates with her for uttering herself only in inextricable enigmas. She answers that she does so to show him how inadequate has been the training of the teaching he has lately followed; but he, who, since he drank of Lethe, has forgotten all the interval between his loss of Beatrice upon earth and his finding of her again in Eden, answers that he cannot mind him of ever having wandered from her or being in need of any other school than that of her wisdom; upon which she reminds him that this forgetfulness of ever having left her is a sign that it was tainted with evil; for only the memory of what is so tainted is washed away by Lethe. Finally she promises that henceforth she will vex him no more by veiled discourse, but will speak with the naked simplicity that his untrained powers demand. The sun is now in high heaven, and they reach a fountain whence two streams flow, and seem loth to part from each other. Dante has forgotten all that Matilda told him about them, not so much that Lethe has washed away the thought, for surely it was untainted by any evil, as that before Eunoë is tasted and secures every good impression from being obliterated, such all-absorbing experiences as have but now been Dante's may obliterate from the memory even the most beautiful thoughts that have preceded them. Henceforth, however, all fair memories of good, whatsoever their relative significance, shall be secured against oblivion and shall take their perfect place in the perfect whole; for Dante, followed by Statius, drinks of the stream of Eunoë; and thence with life fresh as the leaves of spring he issues, inly equipped and cleansed for his further journey to the stars.

The Heavens.

Outline of Paradise

The Correspondences

PLANETS, HEAVENS	LIGHT	POSITION	PHYSICAL CHARACTERISTICS	WEAKNESS OR STRENGTH
1. Moon	Pearly		Changing phases, spots	Weakness in Faith
2. Mercury	Veiled, eclipsed by sun	Within shadow of earth	Smallness	Weakness in Hope
3. Venus	Color of flame		Double center of motion	Weakness in Love
4. Sun	White		Brightness	Strength in Prudence
5. Mars	Red	Beyond shadow of earth	Redness	Strength in Fortitude
6. Jupiter	Silvery		Temperate quality	Strength in Justice
7. Saturn	Crystal (cold)		Cold, ascetic	Strength in Temperance
8. Fixed Stars	Various	Along Golden Ladder	Variable	
9. Primum Mobile	Diaphanous		Diaphanous	
10. Empyrean				

The Correspondences

PLANETS, HEAVENS	SOULS REPRESENTED	SUBJECTS DISCUSSED	DENUNCIATIONS
1. Moon	Inconstant nuns	Vows	Ill-advised vows
2. Mercury	Lovers of earthly fame	Incarnation, atonement	Guelfs and Ghibellines
3. Venus	Sensual lovers	Heredity	Mercenary ecclesiastics
4. Sun	Theologians	God expounded in his creatures	Mendicant orders

OUTLINE OF PARADISE (*continued*)

5. Mars	Warriors of Faith	Decay of virility	Effeminacy of Florence
6. Jupiter	Just Rulers	Justice	Unjust rulers
7. Saturn	Monks	Predestination	Luxury and pomp of prelates
8. Fixed Stars	Apostles	Faith, Hope, Love	Unworthy popes
9. Primum Mobile		Angels	Popular preachers
10. Empyrean		[Beatific Vision]	Rejection of Henry VII

The Correspondences

PLANETS, HEAVENS	ANGELS	ANGELIC FUNCTION	HIERARCHIES	EARTHLY REPRESENT-ATIVES
1. Moon	Angels	Messengers to individuals		
2. Mercury	Archangels	Messengers to nations	Purifying	Deacons
3. Venus	Principalities	Guides of princes		
4. Sun	Powers	Subject to God		
5. Mars	Virtues	Divine motion	Illuminating	Priests
6. Jupiter	Dominations	Dominion		
7. Saturn	Thrones	Stability		
8. Fixed Stars	Cherubim	Knowledge	Perfecting	Bishops
9. Primum Mobile	Seraphim	Love		
10. Empyrean				

PARADISE

CANTO I

THE RISE UPWARD

After suggesting the majestic subject of the Paradiso, *that is, the splendor of the
divine idea and its realization in Heaven, Dante invokes Apollo (God) and the
Muses (his own talents), the "two peaks" of Parnassus. He hopes he may sing as
Apollo did in the contest with Marsyas, who was flayed for his presumption in
challenging the god.*

The glory of Him who moves all
    penetrates the universe, and is reflected
    in one place more, in another less.

I have been to the heaven which receives most of His light
    and seen things which one who descends
    has neither power nor knowledge to relate,

for, drawing near to its desire,
    our intellect is lost in such depths
    that memory cannot follow it.

Nevertheless, whatever my mind
    could treasure of the holy kingdom
    will now be the subject of my song.   12

O good Apollo, for the last task
    make me such a vessel of thy worth
    as the beloved laurel crown requires.

Until now one peak of Parnassus
    has been enough for me, but this time
    with both I must enter the arena which remains.

Enter my breast and breathe as thou didst
    when thou drewest Marsyas
    from the sheath of his body.

O divine Power, if Thou lendest Thyself to me,
    so that I may reveal even the shadow
    of the blessed realm imprinted on my mind,   24

Thou shalt see me come to Thy beloved tree [the laurel]
    and crown myself with those leaves
    of which Thou and my subject will make me worthy.

So rarely, Father, are they gathered
    for triumph of Caesar or of poet,—
    the fault and shame of human will—

that the Peneian leaf [the laurel] should bring joy

to the Delphic deity [Apollo]
    when any is eager for it.

A great flame may follow a little spark;
    perhaps after me, with a better voice,
    prayers will be made to which Cyrrha [Apollo] may respond.   36

The various circles of the heavens, the celestial equator, the ecliptic, and the colure of the equinoxes, all of which cross the horizon, are most favorably related on March 21. It is now Wednesday noon, April 13, 1300, not far from this ideal moment, and the sun is still in Aries.

Dante rises swiftly from the Garden of Eden, passing through the sphere of fire which surrounds that of the air. By gazing at Beatrice he transcends his material self, his humanity.

The lamp of the world [the sun] rises for mortals
    by various paths, but on that
    which joins four circles with three crosses

it rises on its best course and is conjoined
    with its most propitious star, and tempers and seals
    the world's wax most perfectly.

Such a course had made morning there [in Eden]
    and evening here, and that hemisphere [at noon]
    was all aglow and ours dark

when I saw Beatrice turned to the left
    and gazing upon the sun:
    an eagle never looked at it so intently!   48

And, as a reflected ray
    is wont to rise upward,
    like a pilgrim wishing to return,

so her attitude, imaged in my mind,
    was copied by me, and I fixed my eyes
    on the sun, in a manner unknown here.

Much is possible to our faculties
    in the place [Eden] made for the human race
    not granted to us on earth.

I did not endure the sight long
    before I noticed a sparkling [the sphere of fire]
    like molten iron coming from a furnace.   60

Suddenly day seemed joined to day,
    as if He who had power to do so
    had adorned the heaven with another sun.

Beatrice remained with her eyes
    fixed on the eternal revolutions,
    and I turned mine, removed from above, on her.

While gazing at her, I became [transformed] like Glaucus[1]
    who tasted the herb which made him,
    in the sea, a companion of the gods.

"Transhumanizing" cannot be expressed in words;
    therefore, let the example suffice those
    for whom Grace reserves this experience.   72

If I were only that part of myself [the soul]
    created last, Thou alone, O Love, knowest,
    Thou that didst lift me with Thy light!

When the revolving [of the heavens] Thou makest eternal
    through desire made me attentive to it
    amid the harmony [of the spheres] Thou didst modulate,

so much of the sky seemed lit up
    by the flames of the sun that never rivers
    or rain ever made so large a lake.

The strangeness of the sound
    and the great light gave me a wish
    never before felt so keenly to know their cause;   84

whereupon she, who saw me as I see myself,
    to quiet my disturbed mind,
    spoke before I asked, and began,

"You become dull through false assumptions,
    so that you do not see
    what you would if you threw them off.

You are not on earth as you believe;
    a thunderbolt never fled down from its home
    as fast as you are going up to yours."

If I was freed of my first doubt
    by these brief words, spoken with a smile,
    I was caught more firmly in another,   96

and I said, "Already I was contented
    concerning one doubt; but now I wonder
    how I can rise through these light bodies."

Then, after a sigh of pity,
    she looked at me with that expression
    a mother has for a delirious child.

> *Beatrice explains that all things have certain characteristics or instincts which*
> *enable them to carry out the divine plan as, for example, that of fire to rise.*
> *Likewise men have an instinct that impels them to soar to Heaven, their true*
> *home, although this may be conditioned or diverted from its goal, just as fire in*

[1] A fisherman transformed to a sea god by eating an herb.

lightning sometimes descends. Since all hindrance has been removed, Dante's rise
is no more marvelous than that water should flow down the side of a mountain.

She began, "All things have order
    in them and this is the Form
    which makes the universe similar to God.

In it the exalted creatures see the imprint
    of the Eternal Power, the end
    for which the rule [order] was created.   108

To the order of which I speak
    all natures are obedient, by diverse lots,
    as more or less close to their source.

Thus they move to diverse ports
    over the great sea of being,
    and each with an instinct to lead it on.

This moves the fire upward toward the moon,
    this is the motive force in mortal hearts,
    this holds together and unites the earth.

Nor do the arrows of this bow
    strike only creatures without intelligence,
    but also those with understanding and love.   120

The Providence which ordains this
    makes serene the heaven [the Empyrean] within which
    turns the one [the Primum Mobile] that moves with greatest
        speed.[2]

And now toward it, as to a goal decreed,
    the power of that bow is carrying us
    which aims its shots at a joyful mark.

It is true that, as the form, many times,
    does not realize the intentions of the artisan
    (since the material is slow to respond),

so the creatures thus impelled
    sometimes deviate from their course,
    since they have that power;   132

and as the fire in a cloud [lightning]
    is seen to fall, so the creature's first impetus,
    diverted by false pleasure, brings it to the ground.

If I judge correctly, you should not wonder more
    at our rising than at the falling of a stream
    from a high mountain to its base.

---

[2] The Empyrean heaven is the uncircumscribed abode of angels and the saved with God;
the Primum Mobile (first mover) is the outermost shell of the material universe.

It would be a marvel if, unhindered,
    you should remain seated down below,
    as quietness would be in a living flame."

Then she turned her face again toward Heaven.

CANTO II

*Warning and promise to the reader, who shall see stranger tilth than when Jason
sowed the dragon's teeth. They reach the moon and inconceivably penetrate into her
substance without cleaving it, even as deity penetrated into humanity in Christ;
which mystery shall in heaven be seen as axiomatic truth. Dante, dimly aware of the
inadequacy of his science, questions Beatrice as to the dark patches on the moon which
he had thought were due to rarity of substance. She explains that if such rarity pierced
right through the moon in the dark parts, the sun would shine through them when
eclipsed; and if not, the dense matter behind the rare would cast back the sun's light;
and describes to him an experiment by which he may satisfy himself that in that case
the light reflected from the dense matter at the surface and from that in the interior of
the moon would be equally bright. She then explains that Dante has gone wrong and
accepted a scientifically inadequate explanation, because he has not understood that
all heavenly phenomena are direct utterances of God and of his Angels. The undivided power of God, differentiated through the various heavenly bodies and agencies,
shines in the diverse quality and brightness of the fixed stars, of the planets and of the
parts of the moon, as the vital principle manifests itself diversely in the several
members of the body, and as joy beams through the pupil of the eye.*

CANTO III

PICCARDA AND THE EMPRESS CONSTANCE

*In the lowest heaven, that of the moon, a slow-moving, changeable planet within
the shadow of the earth, hardly more brilliant with divine light than a pearl, we
find the inconstant nuns, their earthly images faintly visible. They serve as examples of the lowest degree of potential beatitude, and represent, perhaps, all weak
and inconstant people. Among them are Piccarda, the sister of Dante's friend,
Forese Donati, and the great Empress Constance, the two now equal in their
rank.*

That sun which first had warmed my breast with love
    had unveiled, by proving and refuting,
    the fair face of truth to me

and, to confess myself corrected
    and assured, as was fitting,
    I raised my head to speak,

but a sight attracted

my attention so closely
that I forgot to make my confession.

As from transparent and polished glass
or from clear and quiet water,
not so deep that the bottom is lost to sight,   12

the outlines of our faces come back
so faintly that a pearl on a white forehead
appears as clearly to our eyes,

so I saw several faces ready to speak,
which led me into the opposite error from that
which kindled love between the man [Narcissus] and the
       spring:[3]

for, as I became aware of them,
thinking that the countenances were mirrored,
I turned to see whose they were

and perceived nothing. Then I looked ahead
at the light of my sweet guide
whose holy eyes glowed as she smiled.   24

"Do not marvel if I am amused," she said,
"at your childish thought,
since it still does not trust the truth

but turns you as usual toward delusions.
What you saw are true substances [souls],
relegated here through failure to keep their vows;

therefore, speak to them, and hear, and believe,
since the light of the Truth which requites them
does not let them turn from Itself."

I faced the shade which seemed
most desirous of speaking, and began
like one embarrassed by excessive desire,   36

"O well-created spirit, enjoying the rays
of eternal life, the sweetness of which,
untasted, can never be understood,

it would be gracious if you contented me
with your name and your condition."
Then she, ready and with smiling eyes,

"Our charity does not close the door
on just wishes, any more than the Love
which wants all Its court to resemble Itself.

In this world I was a virgin sister,

---

[3] Narcissus took his reflection in water for reality; Dante mistakes reality for reflection.

and if your memory searches well
my greater beauty will not hide me from you.   48

You will see that I am Piccarda,
placed here with these others
and blessed in the sphere that moves slowest.

Our feelings which are enflamed
only by the pleasure of the Holy Spirit rejoice
in being formed according to His plan.

This fate which seems so low
is given us because we neglected our vows,
left unfulfilled in some respect."

Then I to her, "In your countenances
something divine is shining
which makes you different from before;   60

therefore I was not quick to recall you,
but what you say helps me now
so that remembering is easier.

But tell me, while happy here,
do you desire a higher place
to see more or to make yourselves dearer?"

With those other spirits she smiled a little,
then answered me so joyously
that she seemed to burn in the first flame of love.

"My brother, a charity quiets our wills
and makes us wish only for what we have,
and we thirst for nothing else.   72

If we wanted to be higher
our desires would be discordant
with the will of Him who places us here,

which, as you will see, cannot happen
in these spheres if loving is a necessity here
and if you consider what love implies.

Rather it is essential in this blessed state
to remain within the divine will
so that ours can be one with it.

Thus wherever we may be from threshold to threshold
throughout this kingdom pleases all the realm
as it does the King who bends our wills to His.   84

And His will is our peace;
it is that sea to which wholly moves
what He and Nature create."

I understood then how everywhere in Heaven
    is Paradise, although the grace of the Supreme Good
    does not descend equally on all.

But, as it happens that one food satisfies
    while the craving for another remains,
    which we ask for as we refuse the first,

so by act and word I enquired
    if I might learn what the web [vow] was
    that she had not brought to completion.   96

"A perfect life and great merit place in a higher heaven
    a lady [St. Clare] under whose rule," she said,
    "in your world the veil and dress are worn

so that until death the wearers may wake and sleep
    with that Spouse who accepts every vow
    which love conforms to His pleasure.

To follow her, while a girl, I fled from the world
    and dressed myself in her gown,
    and pledged myself to the ways of her order.

       Both Piccarda and Constance were taken by force from their convents and
       married against their will. Lethe, however, has effaced the memory of their
       submission.

Afterward men more used to evil than to good
    tore me away from the sweet cloister;
    and God knows what my life then became;   108

and this other splendor which shows itself
    on my right, and which glows
    with all the light of our sphere

applies what I say to herself.
    She also was a sister, and likewise
    the shadow of the sacred veil was taken from her.

But after she had been led back to the world
    against her will and good custom,
    the veil was never loosened from her heart.

This is the light of the great Constance
    who from the second blast of Swabia [Henry VI]
    conceived the third and last power [Frederick II]."   120

Thus she spoke to me; then began to sing *Ave Maria*
    and while singing vanished
    like a heavy body in deep water.

My eyes followed her as far as they could,

and, when they had lost her,
    turned to the goal of greater longing,

attentive to Beatrice alone
    who flashed so brightly that at first
    my eyes could not endure the light,

and this made me slower in my questioning.

CANTO IV

Piccarda has left Dante entangled in two perplexities. Why are the nuns shorn of what had else been the full measure of their glory because they were torn against their will from the cloister? And if the inconstant moon is the abode of such as have left their vows unfulfilled, was Plato right after all in saying that men's souls come down from the planets connatural with them, and return thereto? This latter specula- tion might lead to dangerous heresy, and Beatrice hastens to explain that the souls who come to meet Dante in the several spheres all have their permanent abiding place with God and the Angels in the Empyrean. Their meeting places with Dante are but symbolical of their spiritual state. But Plato may have had in mind the divine influ- ences that, through the agency of the planets, act upon men's dispositions and pro- duce good or ill effects which should be credited to them rather than to the human will. And indeed it was a confused perception of these divine influences that led men into idolatry. The other difficulty is removed by a distinction between what we wish to do and what, under pressure, we consent to do; for if we consent we cannot plead violence in excuse, although we have done what we did not wish to do. More ques- tions are started in Dante's mind, for only in the all-embracing truth of God can the human mind find that restful possession which its nature promises it. Short of that each newly acquired truth leads on to further questions. Beatrice, who had sighed at Dante's previous bewildered questions, smiles approval now, for he asks her a ques- tion as to vows which has some spiritual import.

CANTO V

Beatrice, rejoicing in Dante's progress, explains the supreme gift of Free Will, shared by angels and men and by no other creature. Hence may be deduced the supreme significance of vows, wherein this Free Will, by its own act, sacrifices itself. Where- fore there can be nothing so august as to form a fitting substitute, nor any use of the once consecrated thing so hallowed as to excuse the breaking of the vow. And yet Holy Church grants dispensations. The explanation lies in the distinction between the content of the vow (the specific thing consecrated) and the act of vowing. The vow must in every case be kept, but he who has made it, may, under due authority, sometimes substitute for the specific content of the vow some other, worth half as much again; which last condition precludes any substitute for the complete self-dedication of monastic vows. And he who makes a vow such as God cannot sanction, has in that act already done evil; to keep such a vow is only to deepen his guilt; and, kept or broken, it brings his religion into contempt. Dante's further questioning is cut short by their ascent to Mercury, which grows brighter at their presence. Here, in the star that scarce asserts itself, but is lost to mortals in the sun's rays, are the once ambitious souls, that now rejoice in the access of fresh objects of love. They approach Dante, and one of them, with lofty gratulations, offers himself as the vehicle of divine enlightenment. Dante questions him as to his history and the place assigned to him in heaven; whereon the spirit (Justinian) so glows with joy that his outward form is lost in light.

CANTO VI

Note that Justinian, the Lawgiver, is the spokesman of the Roman Empire, whereby is indicated that the true significance of the empire lies in its imposing and fostering the arts of peace. Justinian tells how Constantine removed the seat of Empire east from Rome to Byzantium, reversing the progress of Aeneas who went from Troy to Rome, and how he, Justinian, came to the throne two hundred years later. He was a believer in the divine but not in the human nature of Christ, till converted by Agapetus to the truth which he now sees as clearly as logicians see the axiomatic law of contradictories. After his conversion God inspired him with the project of codifying the Roman Law, and he resigned the conduct of war to Belisarius. He goes on to rebuke the Guelf and Ghibelline factions by showing the august nature of the Roman Empire. In his exposition we note that the key of self-sacrifice is at once struck in the name of Pallas, the Etruscan-Greek volunteer who died for the Trojan cause, and is maintained till it leads up to the great struggles with Carthage and the East, and against internal factiousness; the founding of the Empire under Julius and Augustus and the establishment of universal peace; the great act of Redemption for which all was a preparation, and the subsequent fall of Jerusalem; and the Empire's championship of the Church which had been born under its protection. It is equally wicked, therefore, to think of opposing the Empire or of turning it to factious purposes. The story of Rome has been told in the star adorned by those souls whose virtuous deeds had in them some taint of worldly ambition or anxiety for good repute, but who are now free from all envious desire to have a greater reward, and rejoice rather in the harmony of which their estate is part. Here too is the lowly Romeo who was so disinterested but so sensitive concerning his reputation.

CANTO VII

THE REDEMPTION

Justinian, in whom a double light of natural intelligence and illuminating grace shines, moves off with the other changeable, "mercurial," spirits.

Dante wonders how "just vengeance" could be "justly avenged," but, as he raises his head to ask, he is overcome by the awe he had felt on earth even for the mortal Bice (an affectionate shortening of the name Beatrice). She relieves his embarrassment by stating the question for him.

Osanna, sanctus Deus sabaoth,
    superillustrans claritate tua
    felices ignes horum malacoth![4]

Thus, revolving in his song,

---

[4]"Hosannah, holy God of Sabaoth, lighting from above with your brightness the blessed fires of these kingdoms."

I saw this substance [Justinian] singing,
   in whom a double light shone.

Both it and others moved in their dance
   like rapid sparks veiling themselves
   from me by sudden distances.

I wondered, and said within myself,
   "O ask, ask her, ask my lady
   who quenches my thirst so sweetly!"   12

But that reverence which masters me completely,
   even for *Be* and *Ice,* again bowed down
   my head, as if I were drowsy.

Only a little while did Beatrice leave me thus,
   then she began to shine with such a smile
   as would make a man in fire happy:

"According to my infallible perception,
   how a just vengeance
   was justly punished has made you wonder;[5]

but I will quickly free your mind
   and do you listen, for my words
   will make you a gift of great doctrine.   24

> *In answer to Dante's question, Beatrice takes up the problem of the Redemption.*
> *The vengeance of the Cross was just if we consider the human element in Christ;*
> *it was unjust if we consider who assumed that human nature. The two aspects of*
> *Christ explain, therefore, how a just vengeance can justly be avenged. Dante now*
> *wonders why this particular method for man's redemption was chosen.*
>
> *Man, created directly by God, was immortal, free, and godlike. The sin of Adam*
> *destroyed his dignity wholly, which could be regained only by adequate penance.*
> *But man was incapable of sufficient penance by himself, since his presumption*
> *was infinite, and his power to compensate for it limited. Only God could enable*
> *man to redeem himself. And by showing both justice and mercy, God was more*
> *generous than if He had pardoned outright, since His act included both manifes-*
> *tations of His goodness.*
>
> *Beatrice also clears up another matter. The angels and man were created directly*
> *by God and are therefore immortal. Likewise the elements, but the various forms*
> *and combinations of these elements are the work of Nature or the stars, a second*
> *cause, and therefore undergo transformations and decay. Since man's body as*
> *well as his soul was created directly by God, we can assume the resurrection of the*
> *flesh.*

By not enduring, for his own good, a curb

[5] The reference is to a phrase used in Canto VI. The "just vengeance" is the punishment of
man for original sin in the human person of the crucified Christ; "was justly punished" refers
to the vengeance on the Jews in the form of the destruction of Jerusalem in 70 A.D.

on his will, the man never born [Adam],
    by damning himself, damned all his descendants,

so that the human race lay sick down below
    for many centuries, in great error,
    until it pleased the Word of God to descend,

when, by the act of His eternal love,
    He united with Himself
    the nature estranged from its Maker.

Now direct your sight to what is said:
    this [human] nature, united with its Maker,
    when created, was pure and good,   36

but, through its own act, it was banished
    from Paradise, since it turned
    from the way of truth and from its life.

The penalty, therefore, which the cross offered,
    if measured by the nature assumed,
    never struck anyone so justly,

and none ever did such great wrong
    if we consider the Person who suffered
    and by whom that nature was assumed.

Thus from one act different results ensue;
    for the same death which shook the earth
    and opened Heaven pleased God and the Jews.   48

It should not be hard to understand
    any longer that a just vengeance
    was avenged later by a just court.

But I see your mind bound from thought to thought
    in a knot, the loosening of which
    it waits for eagerly.

You say, 'I discern clearly what I hear,
    but why God should choose
    this means for our redemption is hidden from me.'

This decree, my brother, lies buried
    to the eyes of everyone whose mind
    has not matured in the flames of love.   60

Still, since this mark is gazed at much
    and little is discerned,
    I will tell why such a way was most worthy.

The Divine Goodness which spurns all envy,
    burning in Itself, so shines
    that It sends forth Its eternal beauty.

Whatever comes directly from It
    has no end, for when It has sealed,
    Its imprint cannot be removed.

What comes directly from It
    is wholly free, because not subject
    to the power of the new things [stars].   72

What is most conformed to It, therefore, pleases It most,
    for the holy ardor which shines on everything
    is brightest on what is most like Itself.

The human creature had all these advantages,
    and if one of them is lacking,
    he must fall from his nobility.

Only sin disqualifies him and makes him
    dissimilar to the Supreme Good,
    so that he is brightened little with Its light;

and he can never regain his dignity
    unless, with penance equal to his wicked pleasures,
    he makes up for the loss.   84

Your nature when it sinned wholly
    in its seed [Adam] was removed
    from this dignity as well as from Paradise.

Nor could man recover it,
    if you look closely, by any means
    except passing through one of these fords:

either God by his courtesy alone
    might have forgiven, or man by himself
    must have given satisfaction for his folly.

Look now into the abyss
    of the eternal counsel as far as you can,
    closely attentive to my speech.   96

Man with his limitations, afterward obedient,
    could never give satisfaction,
    through his inability to go down in humility

as far as he had risen in his presumption;
    and this is why man was prevented
    from compensating by himself.

Therefore it was necessary for God by His ways
    to restore man to perfect life,
    I mean by one way [mercy] or by both [justice and mercy].

But since a deed is more prized
    the more it displays of the goodness
    in the heart of the doer,   108

the Divine Goodness which puts Its stamp on the world
    was pleased to proceed by all His ways
    to lift you up, and, between the last night

and the first day, there has never been
    or will be so exalted and magnificent an act,
    either by one way or the other;

for, God was more generous to give Himself
    to make man able to redeem himself
    than if he had pardoned,

and all other ways would have been short
    of justice unless the Son of God
    humiliated Himself to become incarnate.   120

Now to fulfill well all your desires,
    I go back to explain a certain point
    so that you may see as I do.

You say, 'I see the water, I see the fire,
    the air, and the earth, and all their mixtures
    become corrupt and last only a short time.

And yet these things too were created,'
    so that if what I said were true
    they should be safe from corruption.

The angels, brother, and the perfect region
    in which you are, can be considered created
    as they are in their entire being,   132

but the elements you have named and the things
    made of them have received their form
    from a created power [a second cause].

The matter in them was created [directly],
    the forming power likewise
    in those stars which circle around them.

The rays and motion of the holy lights
    draw from the potential elements [of matter]
    the soul of every brute and of the plants.

But the Supreme Goodness breathes forth
    your life directly, and enamors it of Itself,
    so that ever after the soul desires It.   144

Hence you can infer from this
    your resurrection, if you consider
    how human flesh was made

when the first parents were formed.''

CANTO VIII

The planet Venus and ancient idolatry. All angels, heavens and blessed spirits, from the Seraphim nearest God outwards, are twined in one concerted cosmic dance; this dance the spirits in Venus leave to minister to Dante, singing Hosannah *as they come; and one of them declares their kinship of movement and of love with the celestial Beings to whom he had once addressed his love hymn. Dante, with Beatrice's sanction, asks who the spirit is, and he with a flash of joy reveals himself as Dante's friend, Carlo Martello, once heir to the lordship of Provence and the kingdom of Naples, and actual king of Hungary, though Sicily had revolted from his house in consequence of that ill government against which his brother, Robert of Naples, mean offspring of a generous sire, would do well to take warning. Dante's joy in meeting his friend is increased by the knowledge that it is seen as clearly by that friend as by himself, and further, by the thought that it is in God that it is thus discerned. He asks him how it is that degenerate children can spring from noble parents. Carlo explains that for every natural attribute of any being there is provision of a corresponding good, and that since God is perfect and has made his ministers perfect for their offices, it follows that there is a fit place for everything and every one, for which place it is designed and at which it is aimed. The social relations of man demand diversity of gift, which diversity is provided for by the action of the heavens on human natures, but without regard to descent, so that natural heredity is overruled by celestial influences. Whereas we in assigning a man's place to him give heed only to hereditary position or such-like irrelevancies instead of studying his natural gift. Hence general confusion and incompetency.*

CANTO IX

Charles, after a note of warning, turns again to God, whom we so impiously neglect. Cunizza approaches; she describes the site of Romano whence she and the tyrant Ezzelin, her brother, sprang. She tells how her past sins no longer trouble her. She speaks of the fair fame on earth of the troubadour Folco, and laments that no such fame is now sought by her countrymen of Venetia; whose woes she predicts and whose crimes she denounces; and then seeming no longer to heed Dante drops again into her place in the cosmic dance. Folco now flashes brighter in Dante's sight, and at his entreaty diverts his voice from its place in the universal song (which, like the universal dance, takes its note from the Seraphim) to minister to his special need. He indicates his birthplace of Marseilles. He tells of his amorous youth but shows how in heaven there is no repentance, because the sin is only seen or remembered as the occasion of the act of God by which the fallen one was uplifted again into his true element: and it is on this divine power and grace that the soul's whole thought and love are centered. He points out to Dante the light of Rahab, speaks of this heaven as just within the range of the cone of the earth's shadow, thereby indicating that the place of these souls in heaven is, in part, determined by the earthly sin that is now no longer in their minds; refers to Rahab's help given to Joshua in conquering the Holy Land, and denounces the Pope for his indifference to its recovery. It is devil-planted Florence that corrupts the world, both shepherd and flock, by her florins. *But vengeance shall not lag.*

CANTO X

God as self-existent contemplating himself as manifested, in that love which in either aspect he breathes forth, made all objects of intelligence or sense with that order which speaks of him to all beholders. Let the reader, then, look upon the equinoctial point, which so clearly displays that art of God which he himself ever contemplates, in love. Let him reflect how the influences of the sun and planets—the seasons and other alternations—would be effective over a smaller part of the earth if the inclination of the ecliptic were less, and would be too violent in their contrasts if it were greater. If the reader will not give himself time to work out these and other such hints, weary listlessness instead of enjoyment will be the fruit of his study, for the author cannot pause to elaborate them for him. The sun is in the spring equinoctial point and Dante is with him. Standing out against the sun by their very brightness are spirits rejoicing in the vision of the relation of the Father to the Son and to the Holy Spirit. Beatrice calls on Dante to thank the sun of the angels; and he thereon so concentrates his thought on God as to forget Beatrice; in pleasure whereat she smiles so beauteously as to shatter the undivided unity of his mind; which thus broken up distributes itself amongst the wondrous objects that claim it. Twelve spirits surround Dante and Beatrice, as with a crown, and thrice circle them, uttering music that may not be conceived on earth; then pause, while one of them, Thomas Aquinas, declares that since the divine grace has kindled in Dante such true love as must ever increase itself by the mere act of loving, and has revealed to him that heavenly bliss to which he who has once known it must ever return, it follows that every blessed soul must freely love to do him pleasure; whereon he tells him who are the other flames; whereon the wheel of lights again begins to revolve with ineffable music.

CANTO XI

Contrast between earth and heaven. Thomas, reading Dante's thoughts, renews his discourse in order to remove certain difficulties. Providence raised up Francis and Dominic to succor the Church. From Assisi Francis rose sun-like, even as the sun in which Doctor and Poet are now discoursing rises to mortals from Ganges or elsewhere according to the place of their abode. His marriage with poverty. The founding and confirming of his order. He preaches to the Soldan, receives the stigmata, and dies commending his bride to his disciples. If he was such, what must Dominic have been, seeing that he was worthy to be his colleague? But almost all his followers are degenerate.

CANTO XII

A second circle of lights encloses the first and—with music whereof our sweetest strains are but as the reflection—the two, like the parallels of a double rainbow, circle Dante and Beatrice, first moving and then at rest. Like the needle of the compass to the north star so Dante is swept round to one of the new-come lights at the sound of its voice. It is Bonaventura, the Franciscan, who undertakes the encomium of Dominic, just as Thomas, the Dominican, had pronounced that of Francis. Dominic's zeal for true learning and against heresy. If he was such, what must his colleague have been? But his disciples are ruined by the extremes of the strict and lax schools of observance. Bonaventura names himself and the other lights that circle with him.

CANTO XIII

The four and twenty brightest stars of heaven, ranged in two crowns, will give a feeble image of the two circles that swept round Dante and his guide. They sing of the Three Persons in the one nature of God and of the two natures in the one Person of Christ. Then they pause again, and Thomas once more speaks. He reads Dante's perplexity: "Did not both Adam and Christ possess all human knowledge in perfection? How then can it be that none ever rose *to equal Solomon's wisdom?" Behold the answer: All mortal and immortal things are but a reflection of the divine Idea— i.e., of the loving self-utterance of the Divine Power—which remains one in itself while it is broken into countless manifestations. But the imprinting influences of heaven and the imprinted matter of earth are not always in equally propitious habit, and hence individual diversities of excellence. But matter was perfectly disposed and the heaven was in supreme excellence of power when Adam was created and when the Virgin conceived. Therefore Dante's initial supposition is true. But there is no contradiction; for Solomon desired not astronomical, nor logical, nor metaphysical, nor geometrical, but regal wisdom. Of all who ever* rose *to kingly rule (which Adam and Christ did not) none had such wisdom as Solomon. Let Dante take warning from this discussion and observe extremest caution in making unqualified deductions however obvious they may appear; for when once we are committed our own vanity prevents us from retreating and we had better not have thought about a problem than so thought as to fortify ourselves against the truth. Philosophy and Theology alike furnish sad examples. And seeming-obvious moral judgments may be as hasty and false as intellectual ones.*

CANTO XIV

The Garment of Light—The Cross of Mars

The sound waves coming from St. Thomas in the ring and from Beatrice in the center remind Dante of the ripples in a round vessel.

In answer to Dante's question as interpreted by Beatrice, Solomon explains that after Judgment Day the brightness of the souls will remain but will not dazzle their bodily eyes, which will have increased powers. The souls look forward to the time when, with their bodies, they will be more complete and therefore still happier.

From the center to the rim, and from the rim to the center,
    the water in a round vessel moves,
      according as it is struck from without or within.

What I say suddenly occurred
    to my mind when the glorious life
      of Thomas became silent,

because of the analogy with the speech
    of him and of Beatrice who, after him,
    was pleased to begin as follows:

"This man has a need which he does not express
    either in thought or with his voice
    to go to the root of another truth.   12

Tell him if the light which makes your substance
    flowerlike will remain eternally
    with you as it is now,

and if it remains tell how,
    when you are again made corporeal,
    your vision will not be harmed."

As, impelled and drawn by greater joy,
    those who dance in a round at times
    lift their voices and rejoice in their movements,

so, at the ready and devout prayer,
    the holy circles showed a new joy
    by their turning and wondrous melody.   24

Whoever laments because here we die
    to live up there, does not take account
    of the refreshment of the eternal rain [of light].

That One and Two and Three which always lives
    and always reigns in Three and Two and One,
    uncircumscribed and circumscribing all,

was sung of three times by each of those spirits
    with such melody that to hear it would be
    a just reward for every merit.

And I heard in the divinest light [that of Solomon]
    of the lesser circle, a modest voice,
    like that of the angel to Mary,   36

answer, "As long as the festival of Paradise
    exists, so long will our love
    radiate around us such a robe [of light].

Its brightness corresponds to our ardor,
    the ardor to our vision, and its intensity
    depends, apart from our merit, on a gift of grace.

When our glorious and holy flesh
    is reassumed, our persons
    through being entire will be more acceptable;

therefore whatever gratuitous light
    the Supreme Good gives us will be increased—
    a light which fits us to see Him;   48

so that our vision must increase,
    as well as the ardor lighted by it,
    and the resultant radiance.

Like a coal that produces flames
    but whose white incandescence shines through them
    so that it maintains its visibility,

this effulgence which already encircles us
    will be outshone by our flesh
    which all this time the earth has covered.

Nor can so much light fatigue us,
    for the organs of the body will be strong enough
    for all that can delight us."   60

So ready were both choirs to say "amen"
    that they truly showed their desire
    for their dead bodies,

perhaps not only for themselves but for their mothers,
    fathers, and others who were dear
    before they became eternal flames.

> *Now a third ring shines around the other two, composed of souls related to the
> Holy Ghost, wise in the things of the spirit, to complete perhaps the symbolism of
> the Trinity. Then Beatrice and Dante rise to the heaven of Mars. Here the
> soldiers of holy crusades appear, ruddy with their love, on the white cross of their
> Faith.*

And behold! a light of equal brightness
    shone around what was there
    like a horizon growing bright,

and, as in early evening, stars
    appear faintly in the sky,
    so that their sight seems real and not real,   72

so I seemed to see new substances
    making a circle outside
    of the other two circumferences.

O true sparkling of the Holy Spirit,
    how suddenly glowing it became
    to my eyes which, overcome, endured it not!

But Beatrice showed herself so beautiful
    and smiling that her appearance must be left
    among the sights which overcame my mind.

Then my eyes gained strength to look up again,
    and I saw myself transported
    alone with my lady to more exalted salvation.   84

I was well aware that I had risen higher
  because of the enkindled smile of the star
  which seemed to me ruddier than usual.

With all my heart, and in that speech [silent prayer]
  which is one in all, I made to God
  such an offering as befitted the new grace.

And the ardor of the sacrifice
  was not exhausted in my breast
  before I knew the offering had been accepted;

for, with such light and such ruddiness
  splendors appeared to me within two rays
  that I exclaimed, "O Helios! [Sun] who dost so adorn them!"   96

As, distinct with lesser and greater lights,
  the Milky Way shows white between the poles,
  making the wise wonder about it,

thus constellated, those rays formed
  in the depths of Mars the venerable emblem [the cross]
  which the joining of quadrants in a circle makes.

Here memory overcomes my mind,
  for that cross flashed forth Christ,
  so that I cannot find a comparison;

but whoever takes up his cross and follows Christ
  will excuse me for what I omit
  when he beholds Christ flashing in that glow.   108

From tip to tip and between the top and bottom
  lights moved shining brightly
  as they met and passed by.

Thus, on earth, particles long and short,
  straight and aslant, fast and slow,
  changing aspect, are seen moving

through a ray of sunlight which streaks
  the shade [in houses] which men provide,
  with intelligence and art, for their protection.

And as a viol and harp, tuned in harmony
  with many strings, make only a sweet tinkling sound
  to one unfamiliar with the music,   120

so from the lights I saw in the cross
  a melody sounded which carried me away
  without my understanding the hymn.

Well was I aware it was a song of lofty praise,
  since "Arise and conquer" came, as to one
  who hears but does not fully understand.

So enamored was I with the hymn
    that until then nothing had ever bound me
    with such sweet ties.

Perhaps these words seem too bold,
    slighting the delight of the beautiful eyes
    which give rest to all my longing,   132

but whoever knows that the living stamps of all beauty
    [the eyes of Beatrice] have more effect the higher they are,
    and that I had not yet turned to them,

can excuse me for what leads to my self-accusation
    and see that I speak the truth and that
    the holy delight, which becomes purer

as it rises, is not disparaged here.

CANTO XV

The souls of the warriors of God upon the cross of Mars cease their hymn, that Dante may converse with one of their number, who shoots like a falling star from his place and, approaching Dante with such joy as Anchises showed to Aeneas in the Elysian Fields, greets him as his offspring and as the recipient of unique grace, the twice-received (now and at his death) of heaven. Dante, giving heed to him and (now first in this higher sphere) looking on Beatrice, is smitten with twofold marvel. The spirit, after rapturous words beyond the scope of the Poet's comprehension, gives thanks to God, tells Dante how eager yet how sweet has been his longing for his arrival, foreread in the heavens; confirms his thought that the spirits see all things in God, as the true mathematician sees all numbers in the conception of unity; but bids him none the less speak out his questions, though already known to him, in God, with their appointed answers. Dante, unlike the souls in glory, has no utterance adequate to show forth his thanks. The spirit, in answer to his question, reveals himself as his great-great-grandfather, the father of Alighieri from whom the Poet's family name is derived. He describes the ancient Florence, confined within the walls to which the Badia was adjacent, and dwells upon the simple ways of her citizens. In such a city was he born, baptized and married. Thence he followed Conrad in his crusade, was knighted, was slain, and arose to the peace of heaven.

CANTO XVI

In profound reverence for his ancestor, and not without a sense of his own derived dignity, Dante addresses the spirit with the ceremonious plural ye, said to have originated in Rome, though no longer in use there; and hereon Beatrice (only moderately interested in Florentine antiquities, and so standing a little apart, but keenly alert to all that may affect the moral or spiritual weal of her charge) checks his rising vanity with a warning smile. Dante, full of such lofty joy as would on earth strain the mind to bursting, questions Cacciaguida as to ancient Florence, whereon he, in the speech of an earlier day, tells the date of his birth and the place where his forebears dwelt, declining, in enigmatical terms, to say more of them. The population of mili-

tary age was then but a fifth of what it had since become, and the narrow limits of the territory of Florence kept the blood of her citizens pure. Would that it were so yet! But lust of power, the confusion resulting from Papal ambition, and the fatal quarrel between the Buondelmonti and Amidei, have ruined all, and have given unwieldy bulk to Florence while polluting her blood. Then follows a dirge on the great families of ancient Florence, introduced by tragic reflections on the tide-like instability of all earthly things. Many of these families are mentioned by name, others are indicated by their characteristics or their blazon. Count Hugo ennobled the six families that bear his coat of arms, with various differences, though Giano della Bella had since joined the people. The Gualterotti and Importuni were already in Florence, but the Buondelmonti were not yet—would that they had never been!—their neighbors. The Amidei and their associates were held in honor. Alas that Buondelmonte broke his marriage word with them, and gave rise to all the internal strife of Florence. How much ill had been avoided if God had plunged him into the Ema as he rode into Florence. But it was fated that she should make her sacrifice to that torso of Mars, at whose feet he was slain.

CANTO XVII

As Phaëton came to Clymene to have his doubts resolved, so, encouraged by Beatrice, did Dante turn to Cacciaguida to learn from him the meaning of all the dark hints as to his future lot which he had heard in the three realms. Cacciaguida, not in oracular ambiguities but in plain speech, tells how contingency is but relative to material and human limitations (though free will is an absolute reality), and therefore he already sees, as a harmonious part of the blessed whole, the future that as a fragment of Dante's experience shall be so bitter. Florence shall accuse him of that treachery of which herself is guilty, and shall do it as at the instigation of the Pope. Slandered, exiled, and in penury, he must go his way, in evil company, till he isolates himself from all, and is justified in so doing by the event. His first refuge shall be in the court of the Scaliger who will anticipate all his requests by granting them, and with whom he shall find the now youthful hero who shall give proof of his worth before Henry VII's mission, and shall at last do deeds which even they who see them shall not credit. He further bids Dante not envy the wrong-doers, whose downfall he shall long outlive, and in answer to the timid suggestions of prudence urges him to reveal to the world the whole content of his vision.

CANTO XVIII

Dante, pondering Cacciaguida's revelation, is roused from his reverie by the consoling words and by the beauty of Beatrice who directs him once again to the spirit of his ancestor; who names to him some of the warrior saints that shoot, as he speaks, along the cross; and who then himself joins in their hymn. Dante turns again to Beatrice and sees, by her yet greater beauty, that they have risen into a higher heaven. Then as he looks again upon the star he sees that the white glowing Jupiter has replaced the ruddy Mars. The spirits here form themselves into successive letters and spell out the opening words of the book of Wisdom *"Love righteousness ye that be judges of the earth." Then other spirits gather upon the crest of the last letter, twine round its limbs and insensibly form it into an eagle, the symbol of Roman law and justice. From this star, then, proceeds our justice. Oh that the divine mind whence it draws its power would once more, in wrath, cleanse the mercenary temple which pollutes its rays! Oh that the chivalry of heaven would pray for the misled world! As for the Pope who makes a traffic of his awful power to grant or withhold Communion, let him think of Peter and Paul! But he will plead that John Baptist, whose image is stamped upon the golden florins, has absorbed all his thoughts.*

CANTO XIX

The just Kings, who compose the eagle of Jupiter, speak as one person, just as many brands give out one warmth, so indicating that the work of all righteous governors is one and the same, the voice of all of them being the one voice of justice. In the heaven of justice, there rises in Dante's mind a passion of hope that he may find the solution of the problem, which so long has tortured him, as to the exclusion of the virtuous heathen from heaven, so contrary in seeming to God's justice. The divine eagle first responds with a burst of triumphant joy, then tells how God's wisdom is in excess of all that the whole creation expresses; and since Lucifer himself, the highest of created things, could not see all (and fell because he would not wait for the full measure of light God would have given him), it follows far more that lesser minds cannot so see but that God sees unutterably deeper. Wherefore our sight must needs be lost in the depths of divine justice, which God's eye alone can pierce. But our very idea of justice is from God, and this thought must quiet Dante's protest as to the exclusion of the virtuous heathen. Who is he that he should judge? There were matter enough for the human mind to boggle at, had we not the authority of Scripture for our guidance and did we not know that the Will of God is itself the perfect standard of goodness and of justice, not to be called to account by any other standard. As the little stork (the symbol of obedient docility) looks up, when fed, to the parent bird that wheels over the nest, so Dante gazes on the eagle; which sings a hymn as far above our understanding as God's judgments are; and then, while reasserting without qualification that belief in Christ is the sole means of access to heaven, yet declares that many heathen will be far nearer Christ on the judgment day than many who call upon his name; whereon follows a long denunciation, in detail, of contemporary Christian monarchs.

CANTO XX

DIVINE GRACE

The eagle names the souls in the lights that form its eye. Among them are two pagans, Trajan and Ripheus. Dante wonders how these two could have been saved and learns that both had faith in Christ. Through the intercession of Gregory the Great, Trajan was allowed to return to earth from Limbus to be converted to Christianity and to die a second time. Ripheus, an inconspicuous character of the Aeneid, permitted somehow to believe in Christ to come, shows how Divine Grace is as unfathomable to our understanding as Divine Justice.

When the sun which lights the whole world
    disappears from our hemisphere
    so that the day on every side is spent,

the sky, before enkindled by it alone,
    suddenly makes itself apparent
    with many lights [stars] on which one splendor [the sun] shines,

and this change came to my mind
    when the ensign of the world and of its leaders
    became silent in its blessed beak,

since all those living lights,
    shining much more brightly, began songs
    which have fallen and disappeared from my memory.   12

O sweet Love, clothed in a smile,
    how ardent didst Thou appear in those pipes
    which had the breath alone of holy thoughts!

After the precious and shining gems
    with which I saw the sixth heaven jeweled
    imposed silence on their angelic chimes,

I seemed to hear the murmuring of a river
    descending clear from stone to stone,
    showing the abundance of its high source;

and, as at the neck of a lute
    the sound takes its form, and as the breath
    within a pipe at the holes,   24

so, without delay or waiting
    that murmuring of the eagle
    rose through its apparently hollow neck.

There it became voice and issued
    through its beak in the form of words,
    for which my heart that inscribed them waited.

"The part of me which sees," it began,
    "and which in mortal eagles endures the sun,
    now must be inspected closely,

for, of the lights with which I am formed,
    those that make my eye sparkle
    were supreme in all their ranks.   36

The one that shines in the middle as the pupil
    was [David] the singer of the Holy Spirit
    who bore the Ark [of the Covenant] from house to house.

Now he knows the merit of his song,
    insofar as a result of his own counsel,
    by the reward which is equally great.

Of the five which make a circle for an eyebrow,
    the one closest to my beak [Trajan]
    consoled the poor widow for her son.

Now he knows how dear it costs
    not to follow Christ by his experience
    with the sweet life and with its opposite.   48

And the one [King Hezekiah] who follows in the circumference
    of which I speak, upon the upper arch,
    delayed his death by his true penitence.

Now he knows that eternal decrees [plans]
    are not violated when a worthy prayer
    turns today into tomorrows down on earth [delays them].

The other [Constantine] with the laws and me [the eagle]
    became a Greek, and by giving [the Western Empire]
    to the shepherd [pope], with good intent, produced evil.

Now he knows how the wrong resulting
    from his good deed is not harmful to him
    although the world is destroyed by it.   60

And the one you see on the downward arc
    was William [II of Sicily], regretted by the land
    which weeps because of the living Charles and Frederick.

Now he knows how Heaven is enamored
    of rightous kings, and by his flashing
    he still is making that apparent.

Who down in the erring world
    would believe the Trojan, Ripheus, was the fifth
    of the holy lights in this circle?

Now he knows much about divine grace
    that the world cannot see, although even his sight
    does not penetrate to the bottom."   72

As a lark soaring in the air
    first sings and then is silent, content
    with the last sweetness which satisfies it,

so the image appeared to me
    under the imprint of the Eternal Pleasure
    by whose will everything becomes what it is,

and, although there in my doubt I was like glass
    [transparent] to the color that shows through it,
    this doubt did not endure to wait in silence,

but, from my tongue, "What things are these?"
    it urged with the force of its own weight;
    whereupon I saw a great revelry of flashing.   84

Then, soon, with a brighter eye,
    the blessed ensign answered me,
    not to keep me suspended in my wonder.

"I see that you believe these things
because I say them, but do not see how,
so that, although believed, they remain mysterious.

You do like those who apprehend a thing
by name but cannot see its essence
unless another discloses it.

Regnum coelorum[6] suffers violence [is moved]
only from warm love and living hope
which vanquish the divine will,   96

not as men overcome each other,
but because it wishes to be overcome
and, vanquished, it conquers with its own kindness.

The first and fifth life [souls] of the eyebrow [Trajan and Ripheus]
make you marvel because you see
the region of the angels embellished with them.

From their bodies they did not come, as you believe,
as Gentiles,[7] but as Christians, with firm faith
in the feet [of Christ] to be pierced or already pierced;

for one returned to his flesh from Hell
whence there is no direct return to good will,
and that was a reward for the living hope [of Gregory]—   108

for the living hope which put power
into prayers made to God to resuscitate him,
so that His will might be changed.

The glorious soul of whom I am speaking,
having returned to the flesh for a while,
believed in Him who could aid him,

and, believing, was so enkindled with flames
of true love that, on his second death,
he was worthy of coming to this festival.

The other [Ripheus], through grace
which is distilled from so deep a spring
that no creature ever saw to the bottom,   120

put all his love below on uprightness;
wherefore, from grace to grace,
God opened his eyes to our future redemption,

and he believed in it and did not endure
from then on the stench of paganism
and reproached the perverse people for it.

Those three ladies [the Christian virtues] whom you saw
at the right wheel [of the chariot] replaced baptism
more than a thousand years before baptism.

[6]"The kingdom of the heavens."   [7]Pagans.

O predestination! how remote your source is
    from the vision that does not see
    the First Cause entire!   132

And you, mortals, be careful
    about making judgments, for we who see God
    do not yet know all the elect;

and such a defect is sweet to us,
    for our good is so refined in this good
    that whatever God wishes we also want."

Thus, by that divine image,
    to clear up my short vision,
    a sweet medicine was given to me;

and, as a good lute player accompanies a singer
    with the vibration of the strings,
    and the song acquires a greater charm,   144

so, while it spoke, I recall
    that I saw the two blessed lights [Trajan and Ripheus]
    with the unison of blinking eyes

move their flames to the measure of the words.

CANTO XXI

*Beatrice and Dante have risen to Saturn, now in the constellation of Leo, and there
Beatrice smiles not (lest her beauty should shatter Dante's mortal senses as Jove's
undisguised presence burned Semele to ashes) but bids him gaze upon that which
shall be revealed to him. The joy it gives him to obey her behests is compensation even
for the withdrawal of his eyes from her countenance, whereon they feasted; and he
sees the golden Jacob's ladder stretch up from Saturn; while a throng of splendors
descends, as though all heaven had been emptied, and splashes in light upon a
certain step of the ladder. Dante addresses the light that arrests itself nearest to him,
first with silent thought, then, when Beatrice gives him leave, with open speech; and
asks why he more than others has approached him, and why the harmony of heaven is
no longer heard. The spirit answers that Dante's senses are not yet sufficiently inured
to bear the divine music in this higher sphere; and that he has approached to welcome
him not because he has greater love than others, but because the divine love, to which
all eagerly respond, has assigned that office to him. Dante, though satisfied by the
answer within its limits, yet pushes his demand further and asks why God assigned
this office just to his interlocutor and no other. Hereon the spirit whirls and glows,
rapt into such immediate and intense communion with God as to see his very essence,
and yet declares that neither he nor the highest of the Seraphim sees the answer to this
question, which lies unfathomably deep in the being of God. Let Dante warn the
world, with its smoke-dimmed faculties, not to presume henceforth to attempt a problem which even in heaven is insoluble. Appalled by this reply, Dante now bashfully
requests to know who it is that has thus checked his presumptuous enquiry, and he
learns that it is Peter Damiani, who called himself Peter the Sinner, and who had
dwelt in the now degenerate convent of Fonte Avellana, and in that of S. Maria in*

Pomposa. In connection with his reception, shortly before his death, of the Cardinal's hat he denounces the pomp and obesity of the Church dignitaries, whereupon there comes whirling down a throng of flames that group themselves round him and raise a cry which so stuns Dante that he understands not what it says.

CANTO XXII

Beatrice soothes and reassures Dante in his terror, and tells him of the divine venge-ance, invoked in the cry he has heard. She bids him look again upon the lights of Saturn; and the brightest amongst them then advances to him, encourages him to trust in the affection of the spirits that surround him, and answers his question without awaiting its utterance. He is Benedict, of Monte Cassino fame, and he is surrounded by other contemplative saints. Encouraged by his words to fling all re-straint aside, Dante asks if he may see him in his undisguised form of glory; and he replies that this lofty desire shall be fulfilled in the Empyrean where all desires have their perfect fulfilment, because there is no temporal succession there but eternal fulness. Contemplation alone can lead to this timeless and spaceless life, whence the Jacob's ladder, that Dante's human eye cannot follow to its summit, is planted upon the star of abstinence and contemplation, and reaches to the heaven which Jacob saw it touch. But now none mounts this ladder, for all the monastic orders are degenerate. Yet God has ere now wrought greater wonders than the renewal of their spirit would be. Therefore there is yet hope. Hereon Benedict returns to his company, and they all are swept whirling back to the highest heaven, while Beatrice by her glance raises Dante instantaneously into his natal sign of Gemini, to the influences of which the Poet now appeals for aid in his recording task. Beatrice bids him, as he draws near to the final glory, and ere he meets the triumphant hosts in this eighth sphere, to strengthen and rejoice his heart by gathering together his heavenly experiences up to this point and realizing how far he has left earth behind. He looks down through all the seven spheres, sees the clear side of the moon and all the related movements and positions of the heavenly bodies, sees the little earth for which we fight so fiercely stretched out before him so that he can trace the rivers right down from the watersheds to the seashore. Then he turns again to Beatrice's eyes.

CANTO XXIII

Beatrice turns towards Cancer, the region of the summer Solstice, from Gemini where the Poet and his guide are placed; and her intent look wakes the eagerness of expect-ancy in him. Ere long he sees heaven lighted by the approach of the triumphant hosts of Christ, the whole harvest of the heavenly husbandry; and outshining all is Christ, whose person pierces the swathings of his glory with blinding light; whereupon, as lightning dilating in the womb of a cloud bursts forth, having no space within, so Dante's mind bursts its own limits and loses itself. . . . Beatrice recalls him as from a forgotten dream, and his sight strengthened by the vision of Christ, is now able to endure her smile. What he then saw he needs must leave untold, albeit what he is forcing himself, line by line, to record proclaims that he yields to no shrinking desire to spare himself. At Beatrice's bidding he mans himself again to look upon the garden of Christ, the Virgin rose and the Apostolic lilies; but Christ himself, in tenderness to the pilgrim's powers, has withdrawn above and shines down upon his chosen ones, himself unseen. Gabriel descends and crowns the virgin who then rises through the Primum Mobile *far out of sight, while the saints reach up tenderly after her with their flames. Oh, what wealth of glory is in these sainted souls who on earth chose and spread the true riches that wax not old. There Peter triumphs in the victory of Christ, with the ancient and the modern assembly for whom his key has unlocked heaven.*

CANTO XXIV

Beatrice appeals to the saints in the starry heaven to give Dante to drink from the heavenly table to which they have been summoned. The divine grace which gives him a foretaste of their feast is their warrant, his immeasurable longing is his claim, and their unbroken enjoyment of that knowledge which he desires makes it easy for them to give. The saints respond joyously to her appeal and in groups of circling lights reveal their varying measures of ecstasy. Peter comes out from the brightest group in answer to Beatrice's prayer. She addresses him as the representative of that Faith by which he himself once walked upon the sea, and to which heaven owes all its citizens; and urges him to test Dante as to Faith. Dante prepares himself, as for examination, and Peter questions him. Dante founds his confession upon the definition in the Epistle to the Hebrews. Faith is the substance or foundation upon which hope is reared, and the basis of the argument by which the reality of unseen things is established. His own faith is unquestioning. It is based on Scripture which is authenticated by miracle. And if one should question the miracles he must face the yet greater miracle of the spread of Christianity without miracle. Peter further demands to hear the positive content of Dante's faith and the specific warrant for it. Dante declares his faith in God, defined first in Aristotelian phrase as the unmoved mover whom the heaven loves and longs for, and then as three Persons in one Essence. For the first belief proofs are drawn from the Physics *and* Metaphysics *as well as from Scripture, for the second from Scripture alone. All else is secondary. Peter signifies his delight in Dante's confession by circling him thrice.*

CANTO XXV

It was the Faith that gained Dante the high privilege of the apostolic benediction. Therefore if his poem should ever melt the heart of the Florentines he will take the poet's crown at that same font whereat he was received into the Faith. St. James now joins St. Peter. When we read of the three chosen disciples to whom Jesus reveals more than to the others we are to take Peter as representing faith, James hope, and John love; and therefore Beatrice urges James to test Dante as to Hope. James questions him. Beatrice herself declares on his behalf that he possesses in fullest measure the virtue of hope, and that it is on that very ground that he has been allowed to antici- pate death in his vision of divine things. As to the nature of Hope and its source he shall answer for himself. Dante defines hope with exclusive reference to the future life, and derives it from Scripture. James, whose own hope, which followed him even to death, is now swallowed up in victory, still loves the virtue he once practiced, and demands to hear the content of Dante's hope, and its source. Dante declares that Isaiah and John tell him of the double garments of the blessed, and that this symbol indicates to him the resurrection of the body as well as the immortality of the soul as the substantive content of his hope. A light as bright as the sun now joins Peter and

James, and is declared by Beatrice to be the Apostle John. Dante strains his sight to see John's body, but is blinded by the glory, and is told that his body is dust, and awaits the general resurrection; Jesus and Mary alone of human beings having arisen with their bodies to heaven. Then of a sudden the harmony is stilled, and the blinded Dante turns in vain to look upon Beatrice.

CANTO XXVI

The Apostle John reassures Dante as to his lost sight, which Beatrice will restore to him as Ananias restored his to Paul; and invites him to discourse meanwhile of Love; and first to tell him what is the supreme object on which his soul's affection is fixed. Dante, resignedly awaiting Beatrice's succor, declares that he is still burning in that same flame which she brought into his heart, and that God is the beginning and end of that and of all his other loves. Moved by the Apostle to declare more at large the justification of his love, Dante answers that, since good as good must be loved, to know God is of necessity to love him, and goes on to declare how Aristotle and the Scriptures have made this truth level to his capacity. When questioned as to other reasons for loving God Dante perceives that he is expected to supplement his account of the supreme love of God, as good in himself, by a statement of the accessory gratitude to God as good to us, and enumerates the creation of the world, his own creation, the redemption and the hope of heaven. He adds that all creatures share his love in proportion as they share the good which is supreme in the Creator. A hymn of praise is raised, and Dante's sight is restored to him; whereon he is bewildered by Beatrice's greater beauty and then by the presence of a fourth flame, wherein he learns the soul of Adam to abide. Overwhelmed at first, then moved to eagerness that will not brook delay, by finding himself face to face with the human being who has had such unique experience and who holds the answer to questions that have so long tantalized the world, Dante reads the answering affection of the first father in the swaying undulations of the light that clothes him and receives the answer to his unspoken questions, as to chronology, the language of Eden, the length of the period of innocence and the nature of the sin that cost the world so dear.

CANTO XXVII

The Poet's ear and eye drink for a space of the glory of Paradise and afterwards, amid deep silence, first the light of Peter glows red with indignation, as he denounces the doings of Pope Boniface VIII; then all heaven is suffused with the same glow and Beatrice's cheek flushes as at a tale of shame, while Peter pursues his denunciation, including Clement the Gascon and John of Cahors in its sweep and then promises redress and bids Dante bear the news to earth. The triumphant spirits, like flashes of flame, rain upwards into the higher heaven, and Beatrice bids Dante look down upon the earth. Dante is in Gemini and the Sun in Aries, with Taurus between, and therefore the half of the earth illuminated by the sun does not correspond with the half that the Seer commands. He sees the earth as we see the moon when she is past the full. The illuminated portion stretches from far west of Gibraltar to the shore of the Levant; and the darkened portion stretches further east. Turning back with renewed longing to Beatrice Dante sees her yet more beautiful and rises with her to the Primum Mobile. *Beatrice expounds to him how time and space take their source and measure from this sphere, and have no relevancy to aught that lies beyond it. It is girt (how, God only understandeth) not by space but by the Divine light and love. Then, with deep yearning, Beatrice turns her thoughts back to the besotted world wherein faith and innocence find refuge only in the hearts and lives of infants, and where humanity blackens from its birth. And all this not because of any inherent degeneracy but because there is none to rule. But ere the hundredth of a day by which the Julian exceeds the Solar year shall by its accumulations have made January cease to be a Winter month! the course shall be reversed.*

CANTO XXVIII

After Beatrice's discourse Dante, gazing upon her eyes, is suddenly aware of the reflection in them of a thing which was not in his sight or thought, and on turning to see what it may be he perceives a point of intensest light with nine concentric circles wheeling around it, swift and bright in proportion to their nearness to the point. Beatrice, quoting Aristotle's praise concerning God, declares that Heaven and all Nature hang upon that point, and bids Dante note the burning love that quickens the movement of the inmost circle. Thereon Dante at once perceives that the nine circles represent the Intelligences or angelic orders connected with the nine revolving heavens, but cannot see why the outmost, swiftest, widest sweeping and most divine heaven should correspond with the inmost and smallest angelic circle. Beatrice explains that the divine substance of the heavens being uniform that heaven which is materially greatest has in it the most of excellence; but it is the excellence, not the size, that is essential. In like manner swiftness and brightness are the measure of the excellence of the angelic circles, and therefore the inmost of them which is swiftest and brightest represents those intelligences that love and know most; and the spiritual correspondence is complete between the two diverse spatial presentations. Thus the relativity of space-conceptions is suggested. God may be conceived as the spaceless center of the universe just as well as the all-embracer. Dante, now enlightened, sees the circles shoot out countless sparks that follow them in their whirling; and hears them all sing Hosanna; while Beatrice further explains how the swift joy of the angels is proportioned to their sight, their sight to their merit, won by grace and by exercise of will; whereas love is not the foundation but the inevitable consequence of knowledge. She has explained the three hierarchies and nine orders of the Angels, as Dionysius (enlightened by his own intense passion of contemplation, and instructed by Paul who had been rapt to heaven) had set them forth. Gregory, having departed from the scheme of Dionysius, smiled at his own error when he beheld this heaven.

CANTO XXIX

Beatrice gazes for a moment upon that point of light wherein every where *is here and every* when *is now, and therein reads the questions Dante would fain have her answer. It was not to acquire any good for himself, but that his reflected light might itself have the joy of conscious existence, that God, in his timeless eternity, uttered himself as love in created beings, themselves capable of loving. It is vain to ask what God was doing before the creation, for Time has no relevance except within the range of creation; nor was the first creation itself successive, or temporal at all; for pure form or act (the angels), pure matter or potentiality (the* materia prima), *and insep-*

arably united act and potentiality (the material heavens) issued into simultaneous being. Jerome was wrong (as Scripture and reason testify) in thinking that the angels were created long before the heavens over which it is the office of certain of them to preside. Dante now knows where the angels were created (in God's eternity) and when (contemporaneously with Time and with the Heavens) and how (all loving); but has yet to learn how soon certain fell (ere one might count twenty) and why (because of Satan's pride), and how the less presumptuous ones recognized the source of their swift and wide range of understanding, and so received grace (the acceptance of which was itself a merit), and were confirmed. This instruction were enough, did not the prevalence of erroneous teaching (honest and dishonest) make it needful to add that the angels, ever rejoicing in the direct contemplation of God, see all things always, and therefore exercise no changing stress of attention, and therefore need no power of memory, since their thought never having lost immediate hold of aught needs not to recall aught. Beatrice goes on to denounce the vain and flippant teaching by which the faithful are deluded, and especially the unauthorized pardonings; and finally, returning to the subject of the angels, explains that though in number they surpass the power of human language or conception, yet each has his own specific quality of insight and of resultant love. Such is the wonder of the divine love which breaks itself upon such countless mirrors, yet remains ever one.

CANTO XXX

When it is dawn with us and noon six thousand miles to the East of us, and the shadow of the earth cast by the sun is level with the plane of our horizon, the stars one by one disappear. And in like manner the angelic rings that seemed to enclose the all-enclosing divine point gradually disappeared; whereon Dante turned to Beatrice and saw her of such transcendent beauty that like every artist who has reached the extreme limit of his skill he must leave this excess unchronicled. Beatrice tells him that they have now issued forth from the heaven that compasses all space into the heaven of light, love, joy, which is not a thing of space, and where he shall behold the angels, and shall see the elect in the forms they will wear after the resurrection. A blinding flash of light enwraps the Poet, and his sight then becomes such that naught can vanquish it; whereon he sees (first in symbolic form, as by the stream of Time; then in their true shapes, as gathering round the circle of Eternity) the things of heaven. The light of God, striking upon the Primum Mobile, *is reflected up upon the ranks of the blest, to whom it gives power to look upon God himself. Dante, in this region, where far and near have no relevancy, gazes upon the saints and Beatrice bids him rejoice in their number; and then directs his sight to one of the few places yet vacant. It is appointed for the emperor Henry who shall strive to set Italy straight, but shall be thwarted by the blinding greed of the Italians and the hypocrisy of Pope Clement, whose fearful fate Beatrice proclaims.*

CANTO XXXI

ST. BERNARD

In the form then of a white rose
    the holy company [the Church] which Christ with His blood
    made His spouse showed itself to me,

but the others [angels] who, flying, see and sing
    of the glory of Him who enamors them
    and of the goodness that has made them so numerous,

like a swarm of bees, at times lighting
    on a flower and then returning
    to where their toil is turned to sweetness,

descended into the great flower
    adorned with so many leaves, and then rose
    to where their love always dwells.   12

They all had faces of living flames,
    and golden wings, and the rest so white
    that no snow equals the whiteness.

When they sank into the flower
    from rank to rank, they bestowed
    the peace and ardor acquired as they flew,

nor did such a flying multitude
    between the flower and what was above
    obscure the vision of the splendor,

for divine light penetrates through the universe
    in proportion to its merit,
    so that there nothing can obscure it.   24

This secure and rejoicing realm,
    abounding in ancient and in new people,
    had eyes and love directed to one mark.

O Threefold Light which in a single star
    scintillating in their sight so satisfies them,
    look down here upon our storms!

If the barbarians coming from the regions [of the North]
    covered by Helice [the Great Dipper] circling
    with her son [Arcas, the Little Dipper] of whom she is fond,

were amazed on seeing Rome
    and her lofty monuments, when the Lateran [the papal palace]
    surpassed all mortal things,   36

I who had come from the human to the divine,
    from Time to Eternity, and from Florence
    to a people just and sane,

what amazement must I have felt!
    Certainly it and my joy made me content
    not to hear and to stand mute.

And as a pilgrim who gains fresh life
    in the temple of his vow as he looks
    and already hopes to report [at home] how it is,

so, through the living light,
    I cast my eyes over the ranks,
    now up, now down, and now around.   48

I saw faces persuasive of love adorned by the light
    of Another and by their own smiles,
    and with gestures graced by every dignity.

My sight had already taken in
    the general form of Paradise,
    but on no point had my eyes been fixed,

and I turned with rekindled desire
    to ask my lady about things
    that kept my mind in suspense.

*Beatrice's role as Revelation is now ended, since Dante is in the actual presence
of God, and she resumes her historical character as Beatrice Portinari, whom the
poet addresses from now on with the familiar tu (for "you"). Her place is taken
by St. Bernard, who was especially devoted to the Virgin Mary and who represents Contemplation or perhaps Intuition.*

I expected one thing, and another responded;
    I thought I would see Beatrice, and instead
    I perceived an old man, clad like those in glory.   60

Benign joy was diffused
    over his eyes and face, his mien kindly,
    as is fitting in a tender father;

and, "Where is she?" I said suddenly;
    whereupon he, "To fulfill your desire
    Beatrice sent me from my place.

If you look at the third row
    of the highest tier you will see her again
    on the throne her merit allots to her."

Without speaking I lifted up my eyes
    and saw her, making herself a crown [a halo of light]
    and reflecting from herself the eternal rays.   72

From the region of the highest thunder
    no mortal eye is so distant
    although plunged deep into the sea

as my sight there from Beatrice,
    but that had no effect on me,
    for her image came down unblurred.

"O lady in whom my hope is strong,
    you who for my salvation endured
    to leave your footprints in Hell,

in all the things that I have seen
  I recognize the grace and the virtue
  of your power and goodness.   84

You have lifted me from slavery to freedom
  by all those ways, by all the means
  through which you had the power to do so.

Continue your generosity toward me,
  so that my soul that you redeemed
  may be freed from my body pleasing to you."

Thus I prayed, and she, so distant
  as it seemed, smiled, and looked at me;
  then turned to the Eternal Spring.

And the holy old man said, "In order
  that you may complete perfectly your journey
  for which purpose prayer and holy love sent me,   96

cast your eyes over this garden,
  for seeing it will prepare them
  for rising higher in the divine radiance.

And the Queen of Heaven for whom I burn
  wholly with love will grant us every grace,
  since I am her faithful Bernard."

As a pilgrim, perhaps from Croatia, who comes
  to see our Veronica [an image of Christ], and who,
  because of his long-felt hunger, is never satiated,

but says in his thoughts as long
  as it is shown, "My Lord, Jesus Christ, true God,
  now was Thy countenance really like this?"   108

so I was while gazing at the living love
  of him [Bernard] who in our world,
  through contemplation, enjoyed that peace.

"Son of Grace, if you keep your eyes
  only down here at this bottom," he began,
  "this joyous life will not be seen by you.

Look at the rows as far as the most remote
  until you see the Queen [Mary] sitting
  to whom this realm is loyal and devoted."

I lifted my eyes and, as in the morning
  the eastern part of the horizon
  outshines that where the sun goes down,   120

so, as if rising from a valley to a mountain,
  I saw with my eyes a part of the edge
  dominating with its light all the rim;

and, as on earth at sunrise, the pole of the chariot [of the sun]
    (which Phaëthon guided badly) is most enflamed
    and on either side the light decreases,

so that pacific oriflamme[8] [of Mary's] shone brighter
    in the middle, and on either side,
    gradually and equally decreased its light.

At that middle point, with wings spread,
    I saw more than a thousand rejoicing angels,
    each distinct in effulgence and in function.   132

I saw there smiling at their games
    and at their songs, a beauty which became a joy
    in the eyes of all the other saints.

And if I had such wealth in speech
    as in imagining, I would not dare
    to attempt the least of the delight she gave.

Bernard, when he saw my eyes
    fixed and intent on his warm love,
    turned his toward her with such affection

that he made mine more eager in their gazing.

CANTO XXXII

THE MYSTIC ROSE

*St. Bernard points out some of the souls that form the white rose. In the lower part
are the children, the little folk who "hastened to the true life."*

Intent on his delight, that contemplator [St. Bernard]
    freely assumed the office of teacher
    and began with these holy words:

"The wound that Mary healed and anointed
    the beautiful one [Eve] who is
    at her feet opened and enlarged.

In order, in the third row,
    Rachel sits beneath her
    with Beatrice, as you see.

Sarah, Rebecca, Judith, and the great-grandmother [Ruth]
    of the singer [David] who, in sorrow
    for his sins, said '*Miserere mei.*'[9]   12

You can see them from rank to rank
    as with the name of each I go downward
    through the rose from petal to petal.

---

[8] A gold-and-flame-colored pennant.   [9] "Have mercy on me" (Psalm 51:1).

And from the seventh row on,
    as down to it, Hebrew women
    divide all the petals of the rose.[10]

According to the way their faith
    conceived of Christ they form the line
    by which the sacred stairway is divided.

On this side, where the flower is mature
    with all its leaves, are seated those
    who believed in Christ to come.   24

On the other, where the semicircles
    are broken by empty seats, are those
    who turned their faces to Christ already come.

And, just as on this side, the glorious seat
    of the Lady of Heaven and those below it
    make so great a division,

so, opposite her, does that of the great John
    who, always holy, endured martyrdom
    and the desert and then Hell for two years.[11]

And beneath him, Francis, Benedict, Augustine
    and others make a dividing line
    down to here from row to row.   36

Now marvel at the divine foresight, for both aspects
    of the Faith [the old Church and the new]
    will fill this garden equally;

and know that downward from the row
    which midway cleaves the two divisions,
    souls have a place through no merit of their own

but through that of others, under certain conditions;
    for all these are spirits released from the flesh
    [as children] before they could have a true choice.

Well can you see this by their faces
    and also by their childish voices
    if you look closely and listen to them.   48

    The children enjoy varying felicity according to the grace they have received.

    Pre-Christian infants were saved through their parents' faith in Christ to come;
    the others, in Christian times, through baptism.

Now you wonder, and wondering, are silent;

[10] The vertical line of Hebrew women seated below Mary forms a boundary between the two semicircles of the Jews and Christians. The amphitheater is also divided top and bottom, the children (Hebrew and Christian) in the bottom half.

[11] John the Baptist, martyred two years before Christ was crucified, spent the interval in Limbo awaiting the harrowing of hell by which Christ released the souls of the just.

but I will undo the tight band
by which your subtle thoughts are held.

Within the amplitude of this realm
nothing can occur by chance
any more than sadness, thirst, or hunger;

for whatever you see is established
by eternal law, so that the ring
fits the finger exactly.

Therefore, that those [little] people
who hastened to the true life
are more and less excellent is not *sine causa.*[12]   60

The King through whom this realm has rest
in such love and in such delight
that no desire ventures to have more,

creating all minds in His happy image
endows with grace diversely, at His pleasure;
and here let the fact suffice.

This is clearly and expressly noted for you
in Holy Scripture in those twins [Jacob and Esau]
who, within their mother, were stirred to wrath.

Therefore, according to the color
of their hair, the light
of grace must worthily crown them.[13]   72

Thus, without merit for their conduct
they are placed in various ranks,
differing only in primal keenness [of spiritual sight].

In the early centuries
the parents' faith alone sufficed,
with innocence, to receive salvation.

Then, after the first ages were completed,
males were obliged through circumcision
to gain power for their innocent wings;

but when the time of grace had come,
without perfect baptism in Christ
such innocence was held back there below.   84

Dante shifts his gaze to the upper part of the rose.

Look now on the face [of Mary]
which bears most resemblance to Christ,
for its brightness alone can prepare you for seeing Christ."

---

[12] Latin, "without cause."
[13] God favored Jacob over his redheaded twin brother Esau from their time in the womb. See Genesis 25.

I saw such joy rain upon her
    borne in the holy minds [of the angels]
    created to fly over that height,

that nothing I had seen before
    had kept me suspended in such wonder
    or revealed to me such likeness to God.

And that love [Gabriel] which first descended
    on her singing *Ave Maria, gratia plena,*[14]
    spread his wings in front of her.   96

The blessed court on all sides
    sang responses to the divine song
    so that every face became brighter.

"O holy father, you who endure for my sake
    to be down here, leaving the sweet place
    where you sit by eternal lot,

who is that angel which, with such rapture,
    looks into the eyes of our Queen,
    so enamored that he seems aflame?"

Thus again I had recourse to the learning
    of him [St. Bernard] who grew beautiful through Mary
    as the morning star does through the sun.   108

And he said to me, "As much confidence and grace
    as there can be in an angel or in a soul
    are in him; and we want it so,

because he is the one who brought the palm [of victory over others]
    down to Mary when the Son of God
    was willing to take on the burden of our flesh.

But follow now with your eyes as I speak
    and note the great patricians
    of this most just and devout empire.

Those two [Eve and Rachel] who up there are happiest
    from being nearest to the Empress [Mary]
    are, as it were, two roots of this rose.   120

The one nearest her on the left
    is [Adam] the father whose bold tasting
    made the human race taste such bitterness.

On the right see the ancient father
    of Holy Church [St. Peter] to whom Christ
    entrusted the keys to this lovely flower;

and the one [John][15] who saw, before his death,

---

[14] "Hail Mary, full of grace" ("thou that art highly favored" in the King James Version), the words of the angel Gabriel at the Annunciation; Luke 1:28.

[15] The author of the Book of Revelation, or Apocalypse.

the deplorable times of the fair Bride [the Church],
    won [by Christ] with the lance and with the nails,

sits beside him; and by the other
    that leader [Moses] rests under whom the fickle,
    ungrateful, and perverse people lived on manna.   132

Opposite Peter see Anna [the mother of Mary] so happy
    to gaze upon her daughter that she
    does not move her eyes while singing hosanna,

and opposite the greatest father of a family [Adam]
    Lucia sits, who sent your lady,[16] when your eyes
    were bent down for your destruction.

But because the time which keeps you in slumber
    is flying, here we will stop, like a tailor
    who makes the gown according to the cloth he has,

and we will direct our eyes to the First Love,
    so that looking toward Him you may penetrate
    as far as possible through His light.   144

But, lest in moving your wings
    you should go back while believing to advance,
    grace must be obtained by prayer—

grace from that one [Mary] who can help you;
    and may you follow me with your affection,
    so that your heart will not be discordant

from my words." And he began this holy prayer.

CANTO XXXIII

THE BEATIFIC VISION

*A prayer to the Blessed Virgin, later copied in great part by Chaucer, opens the
final canto.*

*The stages of the Beatific Vision are, in ascending order, a comprehension of the
world, a vision of the Trinity, and, as a final revelation, a view of the Incarnation.*

"Virgin mother, daughter of thy son,
    humble and exalted more than any creature,
    goal established by Eternal Counsel,

thou art the one by whom human nature
    was so ennobled that its Maker
    did not disdain to become its creature.

Within thy womb was rekindled the love
    through whose warmth this flower
    has blossomed in eternal peace.

[16] See *Inferno,* II.97–108.

Here thou art for us a noonday torch
   of charity, and down below, among mortals,
   a living fount of hope.   12

My lady, thou art so great and so triumphant
   that whoever wants and does not turn to thee
   would have his desire fly without wings.

Thy benignity succors not only those
   who ask, but many times
   freely anticipates the request.

In thee is mercy, in thee pity,
   in thee magnificence, in thee whatever goodness
   can be found in creatures is resumed.

Now, this man who from the deep well
   of the universe up to here
   has seen the spiritual lives, one after another,   24

begs thee of thy grace for strength,
   so that he may lift his eyes
   still higher toward the ultimate salvation.

And I who never for my own sight longed more
   than I do for his, offer thee all my prayers,
   and may they not be insufficient,

in order that thou, through thine, mayst dispel
   every cloud of his mortality, so that
   the Supreme Pleasure may reveal Itself to him.

I pray thee further, O Queen! thou who canst do
   what thou wilt, that thou keepest
   his affection sound after so great a vision.   36

May thy protection overcome his human impulses.
   Behold Beatrice with so many of the blessed
   clasping their hands to aid my prayer."

The eyes [of Mary] venerated and beloved
   by God, fixed on him who prayed, showed
   how gratefully devout prayers are heard.

Then they turned to the Eternal Light into which
   we must not think any mortal vision,
   however clear, can ever penetrate so deeply.

And I who drew near to the goal
   of all desires, ended, as I ought,
   within myself, the ardor of my longing.   48

Bernard signaled to me and smiled
   so that I might look up, but I
   already had made myself as he wished.

For my sight, growing pure, penetrated
    ever deeper into the rays
    of the Light which is true in Itself.

From then on my vision was greater
    than our speech which fails at such a sight,
    just as memory is overcome by the excess.

As one who in a dream sees clearly,
    and the feeling impressed remains afterward,
    although nothing else comes back to mind, 60

so am I; for my vision disappears
    almost wholly, and yet the sweetness
    caused by it is still distilled within my heart.

Thus, in sunlight, the snow melts away;
    thus the sayings of the Sibyl,[17] written
    on light leaves, were lost in the wind.

O Supreme Light that risest so high
    above mortal concepts, give back to my mind
    a little of what Thou didst appear,

and make my tongue strong,
    so that it may leave to future peoples
    at least a spark of Thy glory! 72

For, by returning to my memory
    and by sounding a little in these verses
    more of Thy victory will be conceived.

By the keenness of the living ray I endured
    I believe I would have been dazed
    if my eyes had turned away from it;

and I remember that I was bolder
    because of that to sustain the view
    until my sight *attained* the Infinite Worth.

O abundant grace through which I presumed
    to fix my eyes on the Eternal Light
    so long that I consumed my vision on it! 84

In its depths I saw contained, bound with love
    in one volume, what is scattered
    on leaves throughout the world—

substances [things] and accidents [qualities] and their modes
    as if fused together in such a way
    that what I speak of is a single light.

---

[17] A prophetess (Virgil, *Aeneid*, Books III, VI) who inscribed her prophecies on the leaves
of trees which were then scattered by the wind.

The universal form [principle] of this unity
    I believe I saw, because more abundantly
    in saying this I feel that I rejoice.

One moment obscures more for me than twenty-five centuries
    have clouded since the adventure which made Neptune
    wonder at the shadow of the Argo [the first ship].[18]   96

Thus my mind with rapt attention
    gazed fixedly, motionless and attentive,
    continually enflamed by its very gazing.

In that light we become such
    that we can never consent
    to turn from it for another sight,

inasmuch as the good which is the object
    of the will is all in it, and outside of it
    whatever is perfect there is defective.

Now my speech, even for what I remember,
    will be shorter than that of an infant
    who still bathes his tongue at the breast.   108

Not that more than a single semblance
    was in the living light I gazed upon
    (for it is always as it was before),

but in my vision which gained strength
    as I looked the single appearance,
    through a change in me, was transformed.

Within the deep and clear subsistence
    of the great light three circles of three colors
    and of one dimension [the Trinity] appeared to me,

and one [the Son] seemed reflected from the other [the Father]
    as Iris by Iris,[19] and the third [the Holy Spirit]
    seemed fire emanating equally from both.   120

O how poor our speech is and how feeble
    for my conception! Compared to what I saw
    to say its power is "little" is to say too much.

O Eternal Light [Father], abiding in Thyself alone,
    Thou [Son] alone understanding Thyself, and Thou [Holy
        Spirit]
    understood only by Thee, Thou dost love and smile!

The circle which appeared in Thee
    as a reflected light [the Son]
    when contemplated a while

---

[18] The voyage of Jason and the Argonauts was considered to have taken place in the thirteenth century B.C. Dante means that the world has forgotten since then less than he has forgotten of the divine vision.

[19] Twin rainbows (Iris being the goddess of the rainbow).

seemed depicted with our image within itself
    and of its own [the Circle's] color,
    so that my eyes were wholly fixed on it.   132

Like the geometer who strives
    to square the circle and cannot find
    by thinking the principle he needs

I was at that new sight. I wanted to see
    how the [human] image was conformed
    to the [divine] circle and has a place in it,

but my own wings were not enough for that—
    except that my mind was illumined by a flash
    [of Grace] through which its wish was realized.

For the great imagination here power failed;
    but already my desire and will [in harmony]
    were turning like a wheel moved evenly   144

by the Love which turns the sun and the other stars.

Geoffrey Chaucer
(1340?–1400)

One of the most versatile of English and of medieval poets, Chaucer was born in 1340 or a little later, the son of a London wine merchant. The comfortable middle-class family had been rising socially, and young Geoffrey served as a page in the household of the Countess of Ulster, where as an intimate of a noble family he was well educated and early acclimated to aristocratic values and manners. In 1359 he served on the Continent during one of the military campaigns of the Hundred Years' War, waged in the fourteenth and fifteenth centuries for control of disputed territories in France. He was captured and then ransomed with the help of King Edward III—an episode that marks the beginning of a series of favors, positions, and preferments (interrupted by some tribulations in the 1380's) that Chaucer received from English kings throughout his life. Besides serving again later in the army, he filled several high posts in the country's service: customs supervisor, director of public works, king's forester, and Member of Parliament. He undertook for the crown a number of important diplomatic missions to France, the Low Countries, Spain, and Italy. During his sojourns in Italy he was exposed to the work of the three fourteenth-century Italian masters, Dante, Boccaccio, and Petrarch; their influence on his later work is strong. Chaucer died in 1400, a year after the dethronement of Richard II by Henry IV, and was buried in what is now called the Poets' Corner of Westminster Abbey. That in a turbulent era he enjoyed the favor of three rulers says something about Chaucer as man and civil servant.

Chaucer's lifelong close association with public affairs and men of high station helps explain his urbanity and his wide-ranging knowledge of the world. The often mordant portraits of moral delinquents and, conversely, of saintly types in The Canterbury Tales *testify that in his own way Chaucer is a social critic. But political matters do not play a large part in his works as they do in Dante's. Although he succeeded in portraying definitively the England of his time, Chaucer did so through the gifts he shares with the greatest storytellers: a sure and shrewd power of characterization, a keen eye for the quality of* things, *subtle and penetrating psychology, and an unfailing ear for good dialogue, which, like Shakespeare, he was able to accommodate naturally to a wide variety of verse forms, not to mention prose.*

Chaucer's narrative genius is in many ways best exemplified in Troilus and Criseyde *(1380s), one of his two supreme masterpieces. This poem of more than 8,000 lines, set during the Trojan War, allowed him to develop at book length a single story and to explore exhaustively the psychology of the characters, of whom the heroine Criseyde is the most complex. In* Troilus *Chaucer also develops one of his favorite themes: the nature of love as it reveals the conflicting values of this world and the next.*

The fullest range of Chaucer's powers emerges in his most popular work, The Canterbury Tales, *which he wrote in the late 1380s and early 1390s. The work is unfinished; the plan outlined in the General Prologue calls for four stories from each of thirty or so travelers, but we have only one tale apiece from twenty-four of them. Moreover, the work exists in ten fragments, the order of which has had to be reconstructed by scholarly detective work. Nevertheless, enough was completed and joined together to give the impression of a whole, although not a fully assembled or finally polished one.*

Like Boccaccio's Decameron *(which Chaucer apparently did not know),* The Canterbury Tales *is framed by an agreement among the principals to tell stories to one another. Chaucer's scheme, in which the characters are drawn from all vocations and social classes and the tales usually are emphatically appropriate to the tellers and their stations in life, allows him to achieve a variety at least as wide as Boccaccio's and at the same time to join the tales organically to the basic story of the pilgrimage. That Chaucer's framework is a* religious *pilgrimage is not insignificant; the pilgrims and the characters in their stories are revealed in the light both of the world with which so many of them are preoccupied and also of eternity. The variety of the pilgrims and of their moral conditions has a similar effect; the depravity of characters such as the Pardoner, the integrity of the Knight and sanctity of the Parson, the more ambiguous status of such figures as the fastidious Prioress and the worldly Monk imply, taken together, a moral concern almost as profound as Dante's, if less insistent.*

Chaucer is a distinctively English poet in many ways, but he also illustrates the characteristic internationalism of medieval culture and literature. Medieval authors were not expected to invent their own material, and Chaucer's tales, along with the frequent allusions and illustrations within them, are drawn mainly from non-English sources: French and Italian authors, classical legend and literature (notably Ovid), and the Bible (which Chaucer knew thoroughly). Chaucer reworks such materials in his own vein, infusing them with his distinctive qualities of drama, pathos, and wit. The media of the tales include an assortment of skillfully managed verse forms and genres. The Wife of Bath *relates a folktale; the* Pardoner *delivers a sermon and a morally pointed "exemplum"; the* Nun's Priest's *tale is a mock-heroic beast fable. The* Canterbury Tales *includes also specimens of romance, bawdy fabliau, saint's legend, "tragedy" (defined simply as an account of the downfall of an eminent personage), and other narrative genres.*

Perhaps the most distinctive of Chaucer's gifts as storyteller is his ability to delineate characters and put them in realistic motion. They come most patently alive in the prologues to the individual tales and in the narrative links, but most of his people are realized three-dimensionally in the General Prologue as well. The pilgrims make up a human encyclopedia—comprehensive and universal but composed of unique individuals. Interpreting them can be problematical. The Wife of Bath, for example, projects to some readers an attractively earthy personality and to others a sinister moral obliquity. The Pardoner, unquestionably one of the most unsavory characters in world literature, raises questions too, most obviously about his motives in revealing his cynical duplicity so frankly to the company.

After the Normans conquered England in 1066, French became the language of polite society, while Latin continued to be the language of the learned. To a great extent this was still true in Chaucer's day. His decision to write in English at a time when the language was in a state of flux is a significant milestone in the development of English, like Dante's decision to write his Divine Comedy in Italian. But English continued to change radically for a long time after Chaucer, and it was not until the late seventeenth century that the evolution so slowed that the average modern reader can understand the language of the time without elaborate glossing. Chaucer's language, "Middle English," is thus very different from the English of today. It is not so different, however, that modern readers should be discouraged from trying Chaucer in a good Middle English edition. The following is the beginning of the General Prologue:

> Whan that Aprille with his shoures soote
> The droghte of March hath perced to the rote,
> And bathed every veyne in swich licour
> Of which vertu engendred is the flour;
> Whan Zephirus eek with his swete breeth
> Inspired hath in every holt and heeth
> The tendre croppes, and the yonge sonne
> Hath in the Ram his halve cours yronne,
> And smale foweles maken melodye,
> That slepen al the nyght with open ye
> (So priketh hem nature in hir corages):
> Than longen folk to goon on pilgrymages,
> And palmers for to seken straunge strondes,
> To ferne halwes, kouthe in sondry londes;
> And specially from every shires ende
> Of Engelond to Caunterbury they wende,
> The holy blisful martir for to seke,
> That hem hath holpen whan that they were seke.

    10

FURTHER READING (prepared by W. J. R.): Two works by Derek Stanley Brewer provide vivid sketches of Chaucer and his England: Brewer's Chaucer, 1953, is intended for the new student of Chaucer; his Chaucer and His World, 1978, contains a generous selection of illustrations. Neither of these works offers critical material on Chaucer's poetry. D. W. Robertson, Jr., A Preface to Chaucer, 1962, is an important work in Chaucer scholarship, taking a deductive approach to Chaucer's work through an extensive analysis of background material. Robertson's work is noted for its many unconventional interpretations. Muriel Bowden's A Reader's Guide to

Geoffrey Chaucer, 1964, takes a more centrist approach. This book offers a biographical sketch and a long section on *The Canterbury Tales* that discusses various influences on Chaucer's writing. Maurice Hussey and James Winny, *An Introduction to Chaucer,* 1965, contains material on Chaucer's England, the Church, science, and Chaucer's language. George Lyman Kittredge's *Chaucer and His Poetry,* 1915, reprinted in 1970, based on lectures delivered in 1914, remains fresh and instructive. Critical perspectives from several centuries are represented in *Chaucer: "The Canterbury Tales": A Casebook,* ed. by J. J. Anderson, 1974. This volume includes Paul Ruggier's interesting "Irony in 'The Wife of Bath's Tale.'" Twenty-six essays, balanced between historical scholarship and literary criticism, are collected in *Chaucer: Modern Essays in Criticism,* ed. by Edward Wagenknecht, 1959. The emphasis is on *The Canterbury Tales,* including "The Pardoner's Tale" and "The Wife of Bath's Tale."

THE CANTERBURY TALES

Translated by Theodore Morrison

PROLOGUE

As soon as April pierces to the root
The drought of March, and bathes each bud and shoot
Through every vein of sap with gentle showers
From whose engendering liquor spring the flowers;
When zephyrs have breathed softly all about
Inspiring every wood and field to sprout,
And in the zodiac the youthful sun
His journey halfway through the Ram[1] has run;
When little birds are busy with their song
Who sleep with open eyes the whole night long   10
Life stirs their hearts and tingles in them so,
Then off as pilgrims people long to go,
And palmers[2] to set out for distant strands
And foreign shrines renowned in many lands.
And specially in England people ride
To Canterbury[3] from every countryside
To visit there the blessed martyred saint
Who gave them strength when they were sick and faint.
  In Southwark at the Tabard[4] one spring day
It happened, as I stopped there on my way,   20
Myself a pilgrim with a heart devout
Ready for Canterbury to set out,
At night came all of twenty-nine assorted
Travelers, and to that same inn resorted,

[1] The sun is in Aries (the Ram) during late March and early April.
[2] Zealous pilgrims who traveled to far-distant places.
[3] A city about sixty miles southeast of London. In Canterbury Cathedral was located the shrine of St. Thomas à Becket, murdered there in 1170.
[4] An inn in Southwark, a suburb of London on the south bank of the Thames.

Who by a turn of fortune chanced to fall
In fellowship together, and they were all
Pilgrims who had it in their minds to ride
Toward Canterbury. The stable doors were wide,
The rooms were large, and we enjoyed the best,
And shortly, when the sun had gone to rest,   30
I had so talked with each that presently
I was a member of their company
And promised to rise early the next day
To start, as I shall show, upon our way.
   But none the less, while I have time and space,
Before this tale has gone a further pace,
I should in reason tell you the condition
Of each of them, his rank and his position,
And also what array they all were in;
And so then, with a knight I will begin.   40
   A Knight was with us, and an excellent man,
Who from the earliest moment he began
To follow his career loved chivalry,
Truth, openhandedness, and courtesy.
He was a stout man in the king's campaigns
And in that cause had gripped his horse's reins
In Christian lands and pagan through the earth,
None farther, and always honored for his worth.
He was on hand at Alexandria's fall.[5]
He had often sat in precedence to all   50
The nations at the banquet board in Prussia.
He had fought in Lithuania and in Russia,
No Christian knight more often; he had been
In Moorish Africa at Benmarin,
At the siege of Algeciras in Granada,
And sailed in many a glorious armada
In the Mediterranean, and fought as well
At Ayas and Attalia when they fell
In Armenia and on Asia Minor's coast.
Of fifteen deadly battles he could boast,   60
And in Algeria, at Tremessen,
Fought for the faith and killed three separate men
In single combat. He had done good work
Joining against another pagan Turk
With the king of Palathia. And he was wise,
Despite his prowess, honored in men's eyes,
Meek as a girl and gentle in his ways.
He had never spoken ignobly all his days
To any man by even a rude inflection.
He was a knight in all things to perfection.   70
He rode a good horse, but his gear was plain,

[5] The places mentioned in the following lines were sites of battles, mostly fought against Mohammedans and other pagans.

For he had lately served on a campaign.
His tunic was still spattered by the rust
Left by his coat of mail, for he had just
Returned and set out on his pilgrimage.
  His son was with him, a young Squire, in age
Some twenty years as near as I could guess.
His hair curled as if taken from a press.[6]
He was a lover and would become a knight.
In stature he was of a moderate height   80
But powerful and wonderfully quick.
He had been in Flanders, riding in the thick
Of forays in Artois and Picardy,
And bore up well for one so young as he,
Still hoping by his exploits in such places
To stand the better in his lady's graces.
He wore embroidered flowers, red and white,
And blazed like a spring meadow to the sight.
He sang or played his flute the livelong day.
He was as lusty as the month of May.   90
His coat was short, its sleeves were long and wide.
He sat his horse well, and knew how to ride,
And how to make a song and use his lance,
And he could write and draw well, too, and dance.
So hot his love that when the moon rose pale
He got no more sleep than a nightingale.
He was modest, and helped whomever he was able,
And carved as his father's squire at the table.
  But one more servant had the Knight beside,
Choosing thus simply for the time to ride: 100
A Yeoman, in a coat and hood of green.
His peacock-feathered arrows, bright and keen,
He carried under his belt in tidy fashion.
For well-kept gear he had a yeoman's passion.
No draggled feather might his arrows show,
And in his hand he held a mighty bow.
He kept his hair close-cropped, his face was brown.
He knew the lore of woodcraft up and down.
His arm was guarded from the bowstring's whip
By a bracer, gaily trimmed. He had at hip   110
A sword and buckler, and at his other side
A dagger whose fine mounting was his pride,
Sharp-pointed as a spear. His horn he bore
In a sling of green, and on his chest he wore
A silver image of St. Christopher,
His patron, since he was a forester.
  There was also a Nun, a Prioress,[7]
Whose smile was gentle and full of guilelessness.

---

[6] Curlers.   [7] The head of a convent.

"By St. Loy!"[8] was the worst oath she would say.
She sang mass well, in a becoming way,   120
Intoning through her nose the words divine,
And she was known as Madame Eglantine.
She spoke good French, as taught at Stratford-Bow,[9]
For the Parisian French she did not know.
She was schooled to eat so primly and so well
That from her lips no morsel ever fell.
She wet her fingers lightly in the dish
Of sauce, for courtesy was her first wish.
With every bite she did her skillful best
To see that no drop fell upon her breast.   130
She always wiped her upper lip so clean
That in her cup was never to be seen
A hint of grease when she had drunk her share.
She reached out for her meat with comely air.
She was a great delight, and always tried
To imitate court ways, and had her pride,
Both amiable and gracious in her dealings.
As for her charity and tender feelings,
She melted at whatever was piteous.
She would weep if she but came upon a mouse   140
Caught in a trap, if it were dead or bleeding.
Some little dogs that she took pleasure feeding
On roasted meat or milk or good wheat bread
She had, but how she wept to find one dead
Or yelping from a blow that made it smart,
And all was sympathy and loving heart.
Neat was her wimple[10] in its every plait,
Her nose well formed, her eyes as gray as slate.
Her mouth was very small and soft and red.
She had so wide a brow I think her head   150
Was nearly a span[11] broad, for certainly
She was not undergrown, as all could see.
She wore her cloak with dignity and charm,
And had her rosary about her arm,
The small beads coral and the larger green,
And from them hung a brooch of golden sheen,
On it a large A and a crown above;
Beneath, "All things are subject unto love."
    A Priest accompanied her toward Canterbury,
And an attendant Nun, her secretary.   160
    There was a Monk, and nowhere was his peer,
A hunter, and a roving overseer.[12]

---

[8] A minor saint, popular with women at the royal court in Chaucer's day.
[9] A convent near London, where a dialect of French was spoken.
[10] A cloth worn around the face; part of a nun's habit.   [11] A handspan.
[12] An "outrider," a person who supervised monastic property at some distance from the monastery.

He was a manly man, and fully able
To be an abbot. He kept a hunting stable,
And when he rode the neighborhood could hear
His bridle jingling in the wind as clear
And loud as if it were a chapel bell.
Wherever he was master of a cell
The principles of good St. Benedict,[13]
For being a little old and somewhat strict,   170
Were honored in the breach, as past their prime.
He lived by the fashion of a newer time.
He would have swapped that text for a plucked hen
Which says that hunters are not holy men,
Or a monk outside his discipline and rule
Is too much like a fish outside his pool;
That is to say, a monk outside his cloister.
But such a text he deemed not worth an oyster.
I told him his opinion made me glad.
Why should he study always and go mad,   180
Mewed[14] in his cell with only a book for neighbor?
Or why, as Augustine commanded, labor
And sweat his hands? How shall the world be served?
To Augustine be all such toil reserved!
And so he hunted, as was only right.
He had greyhounds as swift as birds in flight.
His taste was all for tracking down the hare,
And what his sport might cost he did not care.
His sleeves I noticed, where they met his hand,
Trimmed with gray fur, the finest in the land.   190
His hood was fastened with a curious pin
Made of wrought gold and clasped beneath his chin,
A love knot at the tip. His head might pass,
Bald as it was, for a lump of shining glass,
And his face was glistening as if anointed.
Fat as a lord he was, and well appointed.
His eyes were large, and rolled inside his head
As if they gleamed from a furnace of hot lead.
His boots were supple, his horse superbly kept.
He was a prelate to dream of while you slept.   200
He was not pale nor peaked like a ghost.
He relished a plump swan as his favorite roast.
He rode a palfrey brown as a ripe berry.
   A Friar was with us, a gay dog and a merry,
Who begged his district[15] with a jolly air.
No friar in all four orders[16] could compare
With him for gallantry; his tongue was wooing.

---

[13] Sixth-century author of a famous rule, or code, laying down strict regulations for monastic life.
[14] Caged.
[15] The friar is a "limiter," assigned a territory (limits) within which he can beg.
[16] The Franciscans, Dominicans, Carmelites, and Augustinians.

Many a girl was married by his doing,
And at his own cost it was often done.
He was a pillar, and a noble one,   210
To his whole order. In his neighborhood
Rich franklins[17] knew him well, who served good food,
And worthy women welcomed him to town;
For the license that his order handed down,
He said himself, conferred on him possession
Of more than a curate's[18] power of confession.
Sweetly the list of frailties he heard,
Assigning penance[19] with a pleasant word.
He was an easy man for absolution
Where he looked forward to a contribution,   220
For if to a poor order a man has given
It signifies that he has been well shriven,[20]
And if a sinner let his purse be dented
The Friar would stake his oath he had repented.
For many men become so hard of heart
They cannot weep, though conscience makes them smart.
Instead of tears and prayers, then, let the sinner
Supply the poor friars with the price of dinner.
For pretty women he had more than shrift.
His cape was stuffed with many a little gift,   230
As knives and pins and suchlike. He could sing
A merry note, and pluck a tender string,
And had no rival at all in balladry.
His neck was whiter than a fleur-de-lis,[21]
And yet he could have knocked a strong man down.
He knew the taverns well in every town.
The barmaids and innkeepers pleased his mind
Better than beggars and lepers and their kind.
In his position it was unbecoming
Among the wretched lepers to go slumming.   240
It mocks all decency, it sews no stitch
To deal with such riffraff; but with the rich,
With sellers of victuals, that's another thing.
Wherever he saw some hope of profiting,
None so polite, so humble. He was good,
The champion beggar of his brotherhood.
Should a woman have no shoes against the snow,
So pleasant was his *"In principio"*[22]
He would have her widow's mite[23] before he went.
He took in far more than he paid in rent   250

---

[17] Country gentlemen.   [18] Parish priest.
[19] After a sinner confesses to the priest, he is granted absolution (forgiveness of his sins), provided he does the assigned penance.
[20] Given shrift (absolution) in the sacrament of confession.   [21] Lily.
[22] Latin for "in the beginning," the opening words of St. John's gospel. The friar uses Latin to show off.
[23] A tiny sum of money.

For his right of begging within certain bounds.
None of his brethren trespassed on his grounds!
He loved as freely as a half-grown whelp.
On arbitration-days[24] he gave great help,
For his cloak was never shiny nor threadbare
Like a poor cloistered scholar's. He had an air
As if he were a doctor or a pope.
It took stout wool to make his semicope[25]
That plumped out like a bell for portliness.
He lisped a little in his rakishness   260
To make his English sweeter on his tongue,
And twanging his harp to end some song he'd sung
His eyes would twinkle in his head as bright
As the stars twinkle on a frosty night.
Hubert this gallant Friar was by name.
      Among the rest a Merchant also came.
He wore a forked beard and a beaver hat
From Flanders. High up in the saddle he sat,
In figured cloth, his boots clasped handsomely,
Delivering his opinions pompously,   270
Always on how his gains might be increased.
At all costs he desired the sea policed[26]
From Middleburg in Holland to Orwell.
He knew the exchange rates, and the time to sell
French currency, and there was never yet
A man who could have told he was in debt
So grave he seemed and hid so well his feelings
With all his shrewd engagements and close dealings.
You'd find no better man at any turn;
But what his name was I could never learn.   280
      There was an Oxford Student too, it chanced,
Already in his logic well advanced.
He rode a mount as skinny as a rake,
And he was hardly fat. For learning's sake
He let himself look hollow and sober enough.
He wore an outer coat of threadbare stuff,
For he had no benefice[27] for his enjoyment
And was too unworldly for some lay[28] employment.
He much preferred to have beside his bed
His twenty volumes bound in black or red   290
All packed with Aristotle from end to middle
Than a sumptuous wardrobe or a merry fiddle.
For though he knew what learning had to offer
There was little coin to jingle in his coffer.
Whatever he got by touching up a friend
On books and learning he would promptly spend

---

[24]"Love-days," when people settled their disputes, friars sometimes serving as judges.
[25]Jacket.   [26]That is, kept free of pirates.
[27]Position at a church.
[28]Secular. The student, or clerk, is preparing for a career in the Church.

And busily pray for the soul of anybody
Who furnished him the wherewithal for study.
His scholarship was what he truly heeded.
He never spoke a word more than was needed,   300
And that was said with dignity and force,
And quick and brief. He was of grave discourse,
Giving new weight to virtue by his speech,
And gladly would he learn and gladly teach.

    There was a Lawyer, cunning and discreet,
Who had often been to St. Paul's porch to meet
His clients. He was a Sergeant of the Law,
A man deserving to be held in awe,
Or so he seemed, his manner was so wise.
He had often served as Justice of Assize[29]   310
By the king's appointment, with a broad commission,
For his knowledge and his eminent position.
He had many a handsome gift by way of fee.
There was no buyer of land as shrewd as he.
All ownership to him became fee simple.[30]
His titles were never faulty by a pimple.
None was so busy as he with case and cause,
And yet he seemed much busier than he was.
In all cases and decisions he was schooled
That were of record since King William[31] ruled.   320
No one could pick a loophole or a flaw
In any lease or contract he might draw.
Each statute on the books he knew by rote.
He traveled in a plain, silk-belted coat.

    A Franklin[32] traveled in his company.
Whiter could never daisy petal be
Than was his beard. His ruddy face gave sign
He liked his morning sop of toast in wine.
He lived in comfort, as he would assure us,
For he was a true son of Epicurus[33]   330
Who held the opinion that the only measure
Of perfect happiness was simply pleasure.
Such hospitality did he provide,
He was St. Julian[34] to his countryside.
His bread and ale were always up to scratch.
He had a cellar[35] none on earth could match.
There was no lack of pasties in his house,
Both fish and flesh, and that so plenteous
That where he lived it snowed of meat and drink.
With every dish of which a man can think,   340
After the various seasons of the year,

[29] Lawcourt.   [30] Unqualified ownership.
[31] King William the Conqueror (ruled 1066–87).   [32] Country gentleman.
[33] Ancient Greek philosopher, often associated with love of pleasure, although this is an oversimplification of his teaching.
[34] Patron saint of hospitality.   [35] Wine cellar.

He changed his diet for his better cheer.
He had coops of partridges as fat as cream,
He had a fishpond stocked with pike and bream.
Woe to his cook for an unready pot
Or a sauce that wasn't seasoned and spiced hot!
A table in his hall stood on display
Prepared and covered through the livelong day.
He presided at court sessions for his bounty
And sat in Parliament often for his county.   350
A well-wrought dagger and a purse of silk
Hung at his belt, as white as morning milk.
He had been a sheriff and county auditor.
On earth was no such rich proprietor!
    There were five Guildsmen, in the livery
Of one august and great fraternity,[36]
A Weaver, a Dyer, and a Carpenter,
A Tapestry-maker and a Haberdasher.
Their gear was furbished new and clean as glass.
The mountings of their knives were not of brass   360
But silver. Their pouches were well made and neat,
And each of them, it seemed, deserved a seat
On the platform at the Guildhall, for each one
Was likely timber to make an alderman.
They had goods enough, and money to be spent,
Also their wives would willingly consent
And would have been at fault if they had not.
For to be "Madamed" is a pleasant lot,
And to march in first at feasts for being well married,
And royally to have their mantles carried.   370
    For the pilgrimage these Guildsmen brought their own
Cook to boil their chicken and marrow bone
With seasoning powder and capers and sharp spice.
In judging London ale his taste was nice.
He well knew how to roast and broil and fry,
To mix a stew, and bake a good meat pie,
Or capon creamed with almond, rice, and egg.
Pity he had an ulcer on his leg!
    A Skipper was with us, his home far in the west.
He came from the port of Dartmouth, as I guessed.   380
He sat his carthorse pretty much at sea
In a coarse smock that joggled on his knee.
From his neck a dagger on a string hung down
Under his arm. His face was burnished brown
By the summer sun. He was a true good fellow.
Many a time he had tapped a wine cask mellow
Sailing from Bordeaux while the owner slept.
Too nice a point of honor he never kept.
In a sea fight, if he got the upper hand,

---

[36] Perhaps a religious lodge, since they all wear the same "livery," or uniform dress.

Drowned prisoners floated home to every land.   390
But in navigation, whether reckoning tides,
Currents, or what might threaten him besides,
Harborage, pilotage, or the moon's demeanor,
None was his like from Hull to Cartagena.
He knew each harbor and the anchorage there
From Gotland to the Cape of Finisterre
And every creek in Brittany and Spain,
And he had called his ship the *Madeleine*.
    With us came also an astute Physician.
There was none like him for a disquisition   400
On the art of medicine or surgery,
For he was grounded in astrology.[37]
He kept his patient long in observation,
Choosing the proper hour for application
Of charms and images by intuition
Of magic, and the planets' best position.
For he was one who understood the laws
That rule the humors,[38] and could tell the cause
That brought on every human malady,
Whether of hot or cold, or moist or dry.   410
He was a perfect medico, for sure.
The cause once known, he would prescribe the cure,
For he had his druggists ready at a motion
To provide the sick man with some pill or potion—
A game of mutual aid, with each one winning.
Their partnership was hardly just beginning!
He was well versed in his authorities,
Old Aesculapius, Dioscorides,
Rufus, and old Hippocrates, and Galen,
Haly, and Rhazes, and Serapion,   420
Averroës, Bernard, Johannes Damascenus,
Avicenna, Gilbert, Gaddesden, Constantinus.[39]
He urged a moderate fare on principle,
But rich in nourishment, digestible;
Of nothing in excess would he admit.
He gave but little heed to Holy Writ.
His clothes were lined with taffeta; their hue
Was all of blood red and of Persian blue,
Yet he was far from careless of expense.
He saved his fees from times of pestilence,   430
For gold is a cordial,[40] as physicians hold,
And so he had a special love for gold.
    A worthy woman there was from near the city

[37] It was common for physicians in Chaucer's day to be guided by the position of the heavenly bodies.

[38] The relative proportion in a person of the four "humors" (blood, black bile, phlegm, yellow bile) was believed to influence character as well as health.

[39] Famous ancient and medieval medical authorities.

[40] A medical stimulant. Gold was sometimes used as an ingredient.

Of Bath, but somewhat deaf, and more's the pity.
For weaving she possessed so great a bent
She outdid the people of Ypres and of Ghent.[41]
No other woman dreamed of such a thing
As to precede her at the offering,[42]
Or if any did, she fell in such a wrath
She dried up all the charity in Bath.   440
She wore fine kerchiefs of old-fashioned air,
And on a Sunday morning, I could swear,
She had ten pounds of linen on her head.
Her stockings were of finest scarlet-red,
Laced tightly, and her shoes were soft and new.
Bold was her face, and fair, and red in hue.
She had been an excellent woman all her life.
Five men in turn had taken her to wife,
Omitting other youthful company—
But let that pass for now! Over the sea   450
She had traveled freely; many a distant stream
She crossed, and visited Jerusalem
Three times. She had been at Rome and at Boulogne,
At the shrine of Compostella, and at Cologne.
She had wandered by the way through many a scene.
Her teeth were set with little gaps between.[43]
Easily on her ambling horse she sat.
She was well wimpled, and she wore a hat
As wide in circuit as a shield or targe.[44]
A skirt swathed up her hips, and they were large.   460
Upon her feet she wore sharp-roweled spurs.
She was a good fellow; a ready tongue was hers.
All remedies of love she knew by name,
For she had all the tricks of that old game.

There was a good man of the priest's vocation,
A poor town Parson of true consecration,
But he was rich in holy thought and work.
Learned he was, in the truest sense a clerk[45]
Who meant Christ's gospel faithfully to preach
And truly his parishioners to teach.   470
He was a kind man, fully of industry,
Many times tested by adversity
And always patient. If tithes[46] were in arrears,
He was loth to threaten any man with fears
Of excommunication;[47] past a doubt
He would rather spread his offering about
To his poor flock, or spend his property.
To him a little meant sufficiency.

[41] Centers of the weaving industry in Flanders.   [42] Offering at church.
[43] For a woman to be gap-toothed was considered a sign of being highly sexed.
[44] A type of shield.   [45] A clergyman-scholar.
[46] One tenth of one's earnings, the sum due to the Church.
[47] Barring of a person from the church and sacraments—a serious penalty.

Wide was his parish, with houses far asunder,
But he would not be kept by rain or thunder,   480
If any had suffered a sickness or a blow,
From visiting the farthest, high or low,
Plodding his way on foot, his staff in hand.
He was a model his flock could understand,
For first he did and afterward he taught.
That precept from the Gospel he had caught,
And he added as a metaphor thereto,
"If the gold rusts, what will the iron do?"
For if a priest is foul, in whom we trust,
No wonder a layman shows a little rust.   490
A priest should take to heart the shameful scene
Of shepherds filthy while the sheep are clean.
By his own purity a priest should give
The example to his sheep, how they should live.
He did not rent his benefice[48] for hire,
Leaving his flock to flounder in the mire,
And run to London, happiest of goals,
To sing paid masses in St. Paul's for souls,
Or as chaplain from some rich guild take his keep,
But dwelt at home and guarded well his sheep   500
So that no wolf should make his flock miscarry.
He was a shepherd, and not a mercenary.
And though himself a man of strict vocation
He was not harsh to weak souls in temptation,
Not overbearing nor haughty in his speech,
But wise and kind in all he tried to teach.
By good example and just words to turn
Sinners to heaven was his whole concern.
But should a man in truth prove obstinate,
Whoever he was, of rich or mean estate,   510
The Parson would give him a snub to meet the case.
I doubt there was a priest in any place
His better. He did not stand on dignity
Nor affect in conscience too much nicety,
But Christ's and his disciples' word he sought
To teach, and first he followed what he taught.
   There was a Plowman with him on the road,
His brother, who had forked up many a load
Of good manure. A hearty worker he,
Living in peace and perfect charity.   520
Whether his fortune made him smart or smile,
He loved God with his whole heart all the while
And his neighbor as himself. He would undertake,
For every luckless poor man, for the sake
Of Christ to thresh and ditch and dig by the hour
And with no wage, if it was in his power.

---

[48] Hire out his position as pastor of his church.

His tithes on goods and earnings he paid fair.
He wore a coarse, rough coat and rode a mare.
   There also were a Manciple,[49] a Miller,
A Reeve, a Summoner, and a Pardoner,[50]   530
And I—this makes our company complete.
   As tough a yokel as you care to meet
The Miller was. His big-beefed arms and thighs
Took many a ram put up as wrestling prize.
He was a thick, squat-shouldered lump of sins.
No door but he could heave it off its pins
Or break it running at it with his head.
His beard was broader than a shovel, and red
As a fat sow or fox. A wart stood clear
Atop his nose, and red as a pig's ear   540
A tuft of bristles on it. Black and wide
His nostrils were. He carried at his side
A sword and buckler. His mouth would open out
Like a great furnace, and he would sing and shout
His ballads and jokes of harlotries and crimes.
He could steal corn[51] and charge for it three times,
And yet was honest enough, as millers come,
For a miller, as they say, has a golden thumb.
In white coat and blue hood this lusty clown,
Blowing his bagpipes, brought us out of town.   550
   The Manciple was of a lawyers' college,
And other buyers might have used his knowledge
How to be shrewd provisioners, for whether
He bought on cash or credit, altogether
He managed that the end should be the same:
He came out more than even with the game.
Now isn't it an instance of God's grace
How a man of little knowledge can keep pace
In wit with a whole school of learned men?
He had masters to the number of three times ten   560
Who knew each twist of equity and tort;
A dozen in that very Inn of Court
Were worthy to be steward of the estate
To any of England's lords, however great,
And keep him to his income well confined
And free from debt, unless he lost his mind,
Or let him scrimp, if he were mean in bounty;
They could have given help to a whole county
In any sort of case that might befall;
And yet this Manciple could cheat them all!   570
   The Reeve was a slender, fiery-tempered man.

---

[49] A steward.
[50] A reeve was an overseer for an estate; a summoner summoned to the ecclesiastical court persons charged with offenses against the Church; a pardoner distributed or sold pardons for sins in the name of the Pope.
[51] Grain.

He shaved as closely as a razor can.
His hair was cropped about his ears, and shorn
Above his forehead as a priest's is worn.
His legs were very long and very lean.
No calf on his lank spindles could be seen.
But he knew how to keep a barn or bin,
He could play the game with auditors and win.
He knew well how to judge by drought and rain
The harvest of his seed and of his grain. 580
His master's cattle, swine, and poultry flock,
Horses and sheep and dairy, all his stock,
Were altogether in this Reeve's control.
And by agreement, he had given the sole
Accounting since his lord reached twenty years.
No man could ever catch him in arrears.
There wasn't a bailiff, shepherd, or farmer working
But the Reeve knew all his tricks of cheating and shirking.
He would not let him draw an easy breath.
They feared him as they feared the very death. 590
He lived in a good house on an open space,
Well shaded by green trees, a pleasant place.
He was shrewder in acquisition than his lord.
With private riches he was amply stored.
He had learned a good trade young by work and will.
He was a carpenter of first-rate skill.
On a fine mount, a stallion, dappled gray,
Whose name was Scot, he rode along the way.
He wore a long blue coat hitched up and tied
As if it were a friar's, and at his side 600
A sword with rusty blade was hanging down.
He came from Norfolk, from nearby the town
That men call Bawdswell. As we rode the while,
The Reeve kept always hindmost in our file.
    A Summoner in our company had his place.
Red as the fiery cherubim his face.
He was pocked and pimpled, and his eyes were narrow.
He was lecherous and hot as a cock sparrow.
His brows were scabby and black, and thin his beard.
His was a face that little children feared. 610
Brimstone or litharge bought in any quarter,
Quicksilver, ceruse, borax, oil of tartar,[52]
No salve nor ointment that will cleanse or bite
Could cure him of his blotches, livid white,
Or the nobs and nubbins sitting on his cheeks.
He loved his garlic, his onions, and his leeks.
He loved to drink the strong wine down blood-red.
Then would he bellow as if he had lost his head,
And when he had drunk enough to parch his drouth,

---

[52] Remedies for skin diseases.

Nothing but Latin issued from his mouth.   620
He had smattered up a few terms, two or three,
That he had gathered out of some decree—
No wonder; he heard law Latin all the day,
And everyone knows a parrot or a jay
Can cry out "Wat" or "Poll" as well as the pope;
But give him a strange term, he began to grope.
His little store of learning was paid out,
So *"Questio quod juris"*[53] he would shout.
He was a goodhearted bastard and a kind one.
If there were better, it was hard to find one.   630
He would let a good fellow, for a quart of wine,
The whole year round enjoy his concubine
Scot-free from summons, hearing, fine, or bail,
And on the sly he too could flush a quail.
If he liked a scoundrel, no matter for church law.
He would teach him that he need not stand in awe
If the archdeacon threatened with his curse—
That is, unless his soul was in his purse,
For in his purse he would be punished well.
"The purse," he said, "is the archdeacon's hell."   640
Of course I know he lied in what he said.
There is nothing a guilty man should so much dread
As the curse that damns his soul, when, without fail,
The church can save him, or send him off to jail.
He had the young men and girls in his control
Throughout the diocese; he knew the soul
Of youth, and heard their every last design.
A garland big enough to be the sign
Above an alehouse balanced on his head,
And he made a shield of a great round loaf of bread. 650

    There was a Pardoner of Rouncivalle[54]
With him, of the blessed Mary's hospital,
But now come straight from Rome (or so said he).
Loudly he sang, "Come hither, love, to me,"
While the Summoner's counterbass trolled out profound—
No trumpet blew with half so vast a sound.
This Pardoner had hair as yellow as wax,
But it hung as smoothly as a hank of flax.
His locks trailed down in bunches from his head,
And he let the ends about his shoulders spread,   660
But in thin clusters, lying one by one.
Of hood, for rakishness, he would have none,
For in his wallet[55] he kept it safely stowed.
He traveled, as he thought, in the latest mode,
Disheveled. Save for his cap, his head was bare,
And in his eyes he glittered like a hare.

---

[53] Latin for "What law governs this case?"—a phrase picked up in courtrooms.
[54] A hospital just outside London.   [55] Bag.

A Veronica[56] was stitched upon his cap,
His wallet lay before him in his lap
Brimful of pardons from the very seat
In Rome. He had a voice like a goat's bleat.   670
He was beardless and would never have a beard.
His cheek was always smooth as if just sheared.
I think he was a gelding or a mare;
But in his trade, from Berwick down to Ware,
No pardoner could beat him in the race,
For in his wallet he had a pillow case
Which he represented as Our Lady's veil;
He said he had a piece of the very sail
St. Peter, when he fished in Galilee
Before Christ caught him, used upon the sea.   680
He had a latten[57] cross embossed with stones
And in a glass he carried some pig's bones,
And with these holy relics, when he found
Some village parson grubbing his poor ground,
He would get more money in a single day
Than in two months would come the parson's way.
Thus with his flattery and his trumped-up stock
He made dupes of the parson and his flock.
But though his conscience was a little plastic
He was in church a noble ecclesiastic.   690
Well could he read the Scripture or saint's story,
But best of all he sang the offertory,[58]
For he understood that when this song was sung,
Then he must preach, and sharpen up his tongue
To rake in cash, as well he knew the art,
And so he sang out gaily, with full heart.
   Now I have set down briefly, as it was,
Our rank, our dress, our number, and the cause
That made our sundry fellowship begin
In Southwark, at this hospitable inn   700
Known as the Tabard, not far from the Bell.[59]
But what we did that night I ought to tell,
And after that our journey, stage by stage,
And the whole story of our pilgrimage.
But first, in justice, do not look askance
I plead, nor lay it to my ignorance
If in this matter I should use plain speech
And tell you just the words and style of each
Reporting all their language faithfully.
For it must be known to you as well as me   710
That whoever tells a story after a man
Must follow him as closely as he can.

---

[56] An image of Christ's features supposed to have been made on the veil of St. Veronica after she let him wipe his face on it before the Crucifixion.
[57] Made of a brasslike metal.   [58] Part of the Catholic Mass.   [59] Another tavern.

If he takes the tale in charge, he must be true
To every word, unless he would find new
Or else invent a thing or falsify.
Better some breadth of language than a lie!
He may not spare the truth to save his brother.
He might as well use one word as another.
In Holy Writ Christ spoke in a broad sense,
And surely his word is without offense.   720
Plato, if his are pages you can read,
Says let the word be cousin to the deed.
So I petition your indulgence for it
If I have cut the cloth just as men wore it,
Here in this tale, and shown its very weave.
My wits are none too sharp, you must believe.
    Our Host gave each of us a cheerful greeting
And promptly of our supper had us eating.
The victuals that he served us were his best.
The wine was potent, and we drank with zest.   730
Our Host cut such a figure, all in all,
He might have been a marshal in a hall.[60]
He was a big man, and his eyes bulged wide.
No sturdier citizen lived in all Cheapside,[61]
Lacking no trace of manhood, bold in speech,
Prudent, and well versed in what life can teach,
And with all this he was a jovial man.
And so when supper ended he began
To jolly us, when all our debts were clear.
"Welcome," he said. "I have not seen this year   740
So merry a company in this tavern as now,
And I would give you pleasure if I knew how.
And just this very minute a plan has crossed
My mind that might amuse you at no cost.
    "You go to Canterbury—may the Lord
Speed you, and may the martyred saint reward
Your journey! And to while the time away
You mean to talk and pass the time of day,
For you would be as cheerful all alone
As riding on your journey dumb as stone.   750
Therefore, if you'll abide by what I say,
Tomorrow, when you ride off on your way,
Now, by my father's soul, and he is dead,
If you don't enjoy yourselves, cut off my head!
Hold up your hands, if you accept my speech."
    Our counsel did not take us long to reach.
We bade him give his orders at his will.
"Well, sirs," he said, "then do not take it ill,
But hear me in good part, and for your sport,
Each one of you, to make our journey short,   760

---

[60] Managing official in a great medieval house.   [61] A commercial street in London.

Shall tell two stories, as we ride, I mean,
Toward Canterbury; and coming home again
Shall tell two other tales he may have heard
Of happenings that some time have occurred.
And the one of you whose stories please us most,
Here in this tavern, sitting by this post
Shall sup at our expense while we make merry
When we come riding home from Canterbury.
And to cheer you still the more, I too will ride
With you at my own cost, and be your guide.   770
And if anyone my judgment shall gainsay
He must pay for all we spend along the way.
If you agree, no need to stand and reason.
Tell me, and I'll be stirring in good season."
   This thing was granted, and we swore our pledge
To take his judgment on our pilgrimage,
His verdict on our tales, and his advice.
He was to plan a supper at a price
Agreed upon; and so we all assented
To this command, and we were well contented.   780
The wine was fetched; we drank, and went to rest.
   Next morning, when the dawn was in the east,
Up sprang our Host, who acted as our cock,
And gathered us together in a flock,
And off we rode, till presently our pace
Had brought us to St. Thomas' watering place.
And there our Host began to check his horse.
"Good sirs," he said, "you know your promise, of course.
Shall I remind you what it was about?
If evensong and matins don't fall out,[62]   790
We'll soon find who shall tell us the first tale.
But as I hope to drink my wine and ale,
Whoever won't accept what I decide
Pays everything we spend along the ride.
Draw lots, before we're farther from the Inn.
Whoever draws the shortest shall begin.
Sir Knight," said he, "my master, choose your straw.
Come here, my lady Prioress, and draw,
And you, Sir Scholar, don't look thoughtful, man!
Pitch in now, everyone!" So all began   800
To draw the lots, and as the luck would fall
The draw went to the Knight, which pleased us all.
And when this excellent man saw how it stood,
Ready to keep his promise, he said, "Good!
Since it appears that I must start the game,
Why then, the draw is welcome, in God's name.
Now let's ride on, and listen, what I say."

[62] That is, if you feel this morning as you did last evening. Evensong and matins are
evening and morning prayers.

And with that word we rode forth on our way,
And he, with his courteous manner and good cheer,
Began to tell his tale, as you shall hear.

PROLOGUE TO THE WIFE OF BATH'S TALE

"Experience,[1] though all authority
Was lacking in the world, confers on me
The right to speak of marriage, and unfold
Its woes. For, lords, since I was twelve years old
—Thanks to eternal God in heaven alive—
I have married at church door no less than five
Husbands, provided that I can have been
So often wed,[2] and all were worthy men.
But I was told, indeed, and not long since,
That Christ went to a wedding only once   10
At Cana, in the land of Galilee.[3]
By this example he instructed me
To wed once only—that's what I have heard!
Again, consider now what a sharp word,
Beside a well, Jesus, both God and man,
Spoke in reproving the Samaritan:
'Thou hast had five husbands'—this for a certainty
He said to her—'and the man that now hath thee
Is not thy husband.' True, he spoke this way,
But what he meant is more than I can say   20
Except that I would ask why the fifth man
Was not a husband to the Samaritan?
To just how many could she be a wife?
I have never heard this number all my life
Determined up to now. For round and round
Scholars may gloze, interpret, and expound,
But plainly, this I know without a lie,
God told us to increase and multiply.[4]
That noble text I can well understand.
My husband—this too I have well in hand—   30
Should leave both father and mother and cleave to me.[5]
Number God never mentioned, bigamy,

---

[1] The Wife's appeal to experience is somewhat unorthodox, since written works were supposed to have stronger authority. She shows, however, that she can cite them too (though not always accurately).

[2] The Wife is not sure that all her marriages were valid.

[3] For the wedding at Cana, where Christ changed water to wine, see the gospel of John, 2:1–11. For Jesus' meeting with the sinful Samaritan woman, mentioned a few lines later, see John 4:3–30.

[4] God's command to Adam and Eve at the creation; Genesis 1:28.

[5] Adam's words about Eve, Genesis 2:24: "Therefore shall a man leave his father and his mother, and shall cleave unto his wife: and they shall be one flesh."

No, nor even octogamy; why do men
Talk of it as a sin and scandal, then?
   "Think of that monarch, wise King Solomon.[6]
It strikes me that *he* had more wives than one!
To be refreshed, God willing, would please me
If I got it half as many times as he!
What a gift he had, a gift of God's own giving,
For all his wives! There isn't a man now living   40
Who has the like. By all that I make out
This king had many a merry first-night bout
With each, he was so thoroughly alive.
Blessed be God that I have married five,
And always, for the money in his chest
And for his nether purse, I picked the best.
In divers[7] schools ripe scholarship is made,
And various practice in all kinds of trade
Makes perfect workmen, as the world can see.
Five husbands have had turns at schooling me.   50
Welcome the sixth, whenever I am faced
With yet another. I don't mean to be chaste
At all costs. When a spouse of mine is gone,
Some other Christian man shall take me on,
For then, says the Apostle, I'll be free
To wed, in God's name, where it pleases me.
To marry is no sin, as we can learn
From him; better to marry than to burn,[8]
He says. Why should I care what obloquy
Men heap on Lamech and his bigamy?   60
Abraham was, by all that I can tell,
A holy man; so Jacob was as well,
And each of them took more than two as brides,
And many another holy man besides.
Where, may I ask, in any period,
Can you show in plain words that Almighty God
Forbade us marriage? Point it out to me!
Or where did he command virginity?
The Apostle, when he speaks of maidenhood,
Lays down no law. This I have understood   70
As well as you, milords, for it is plain.
Men may advise a woman to abstain
From marriage, but mere counsels aren't commands.
He left it to our judgment, where it stands.
Had God enjoined us all to maidenhood
Then marriage would have been condemned for good.
But truth is, if no seed were ever sown,
In what soil could virginity be grown?

---

[6] The Old Testament king had 700 wives and 300 concubines.   [7] Various.
[8] In 1 Corinthians 7:8–9, Paul recommends celibacy to the unmarried and widows, and then adds, "But if they cannot contain, let them marry: for it is better to marry than to burn."

Paul did not dare command a thing at best
On which his Master left us no behest.   80
  "But now the prize goes to virginity.
Seize it whoever can, and let us see
What manner of man shall run best in the race!
But not all men receive this form of grace
Except where God bestows it by his will.
The Apostle was a maid, I know; but still,
Although he wished all men were such as he,
It was only *counsel* toward virginity.
To be a wife he gave me his permission,
And so it is no blot on my condition   90
Nor slander of bigamy upon my state
If when my husband dies I take a mate.
A man does virtuously, St. Paul has said,
To touch no woman—meaning in his bed.
For fire and fat are dangerous friends at best.
You know what this example should suggest.
Here is the nub: he held virginity
Superior to wedded frailty,
And frailty I call it unless man
And woman both are chaste for their whole span.   100
  "I am not jealous if maidenhood outweighs
My marriages; I grant it all the praise.
It pleases them, these virgins, flesh and soul
To be immaculate. I won't extol
My own condition. In a lord's household
You know that every vessel can't be gold.
Some are of wood, and serve their master still.
God calls us variously to do his will.
Each has his proper gift, of all who live,
Some this, some that, as it pleases God to give.   110
  "To be virgin is a high and perfect course,
And continence is holy. But the source
Of all perfection, Jesus, never bade
Each one of us to go sell all he had
And give it to the poor; he did not say
That all should follow him in this one way.
He spoke to those who would live perfectly,
And by your leave, lords, that is not for me!
The flower of my best years I find it suits
To spend on the acts of marriage and its fruits.   120
  "Tell me this also: why at our creation
Were organs given us for generation,
And for what profit were we creatures made?
Believe me, not for nothing! Ply his trade
Of twisting texts who will, and let him urge
That they were only given us to purge
Our urine; say without them we should fail
To tell a female rightly from a male

And that's their only object—say you so?
It won't work, as experience will show.   130
Without offense to scholars, I say this,
They were given us for both these purposes,
That we may both be cleansed, I mean, and eased
Through intercourse, where God is not displeased.
Why else in books is this opinion met,
That every man should pay his wife his debt?
Tell me with what a man should hope to pay
Unless he put his instrument in play?
They were supplied us, then, for our purgation,
But they were also meant for generation.   140
    "But none the less I do not mean to say
That all those who are furnished in this way
Are bound to go and practice intercourse.
The world would then grant chastity no force.
Christ was a maid, yet he was formed a man,
And many a saint, too, since the world began,
And yet they lived in perfect chastity.
I am not spiteful toward virginity.
Let virgins be white bread of pure wheat-seed.
Barley we wives are called, and yet I read   150
In Mark, and tell the tale in truth he can,
That Christ with barley bread cheered many a man.[9]
In the state that God assigned to each of us
I'll persevere. I'm not fastidious.
In wifehood I will use my instrument
As freely by my Maker it was lent.
If I hold back with it, God give me sorrow!
My husband shall enjoy it night and morrow
When it pleases him to come and pay his debt.
But a husband, and I've not been thwarted yet,   160
Shall always be my debtor and my slave.
From tribulation he shall never save
His flesh, not for as long as I'm his wife!
I have the power, during all my life,
Over his very body, and not he.
For so the Apostle has instructed me,[10]
Who bade men love their wives for better or worse.
It pleases me from end to end, that verse!"
    The Pardoner, before she could go on,
Jumped up and cried, "By God and by St. John,   170
Upon this topic you preach nobly, Dame!
I was about to wed, but now, for shame,
Why should my body pay a price so dear?

---

[9] The Wife alludes to the miracle in which Jesus fed 5,000 people with five barley loaves and two fishes.

[10] The Wife cites only the second half of the Apostle's (Paul's) statement (1 Corinthians 7:4): "The wife hath not power of her own body, but the husband: and likewise also the husband hath not power of his own body, but the wife."

I'd rather not be married all this year!"
    "Hold on," she said. "I haven't yet begun.
You'll drink a keg of this before I'm done,
I promise you, and it won't taste like ale!
And after I have told you my whole tale
Of marriage, with its fund of tribulation—
And I'm the expert of my generation,   180
For I myself, I mean, have been the whip—
You can decide then if you want a sip
Out of the barrel that I mean to broach.
Before you come too close in your approach,
Think twice. I have examples, more than ten!
'The man who won't be warned by other men,
To other men a warning he shall be.'
These are the words we find in Ptolemy.
You can read them right there in his *Almagest*."[11]
    "Now, Madame, if you're willing, I suggest,"   190
Answered the Pardoner, "as you began,
Continue with your tale, and spare no man.
Teach us your practice—we young men need a guide."
    "Gladly, if it will please you," she replied.
"But first I ask you, if I speak my mind,
That all this company may be well inclined,
And will not take offense at what I say.
I only mean it, after all, in play.
    "Now, sirs, I will get onward with my tale.
If ever I hope to drink good wine or ale,   200
I'm speaking truth: the husbands I have had,
Three of them have been good, and two were bad.
The three were kindly men, and rich, and old.
But they were hardly able to uphold
The statute which had made them fast to me.
You know well what I mean by this, I see!
So help me God, I can't help laughing yet
When I think of how at night I made them sweat,
And I thought nothing of it, on my word!
Their land and wealth they had by then conferred   210
On me, and so I safely could neglect
Tending their love or showing them respect.
So well they loved me that by God above
I hardly set a value on their love.
A woman who is wise is never done
Busily winning love when she has none,
But since I had them wholly in my hand
And they had given me their wealth and land,
Why task myself to spoil them or to please
Unless for my own profit and my ease?   220

[11] The saying is not in the *Almagest*, although it was attributed to Ptolemy by a translator of the work. The same is true of the Wife's later citation of Ptolemy.

I set them working so that many a night
They sang a dirge, so grievous was their plight!
They never got the bacon, well I know,
Offered as prize to couples at Dunmow[12]
Who live a year in peace, without repentance!
So well I ruled them, by my law and sentence,
They were glad to bring me fine things from the fair
And happy when I spoke with a mild air,
For God knows I could chide outrageously.

    "Now judge if I could do it properly!   230
You wives who understand and who are wise,
This is the way to throw dust in their eyes.
There isn't on the earth so bold a man
He can swear false or lie as a woman can.
I do not urge this course in every case,
Just when a prudent wife is caught off base;
Then she should swear the parrot's mad who tattled
Her indiscretions, and when she's once embattled
Should call her maid as witness, by collusion.
But listen, how I threw them in confusion: 240
    "'Sir dotard,[13] this is how you live?' I'd say.
'How can my neighbor's wife be dressed so gay?
She carries off the honors everywhere.
I sit at home. I've nothing fit to wear.
What were you doing at my neighbor's house?
Is she so handsome? Are you so amorous?
What do you whisper to our maid? God bless me,
Give up your jokes, old lecher. They depress me.
When I have a harmless friend myself, you balk
And scold me like a devil if I walk   250
For innocent amusement to his house.
You drink and come home reeling like a souse
And sit down on your bench, worse luck, and preach.
Taking a wife who's poor—this is the speech
That you regale me with—costs grievously,
And if she's rich and of good family,
It is a constant torment, you decide,
To suffer her ill humor and her pride.
And if she's fair, you scoundrel, you destroy her
By saying that every lecher will enjoy her;   260
For chastity at best has frail protections
If a woman is assailed from all directions.
    "'Some want us for our wealth, so you declare,
Some for our figure, some think we are fair,
Some want a woman who can dance or sing,
Some want kindness, and some philandering,

---

[12] A town in Essex, in southeastern England. Such a prize for peaceable couples was in fact given.
[13] A senile person.

Some look for hands and arms well turned and small.
Thus, by your tale, the devil may take us all!
Men cannot keep a castle or redoubt[14]
Longer, you tell me, than it can hold out.   270
Or if a woman's plain, you say that she
Is one who covets each man she may see,
For at him like a spaniel she will fly
Until she finds some man that she can buy.
Down to the lake goes never a goose so gray
But it will have a mate, I've heard you say.
It's hard to fasten—this too I've been told—
A thing that no man willingly will hold.
Wise men, you tell me as you go to bed,
And those who hope for heaven should never wed.   280
I hope wild lightning and a thunderstroke
Will break your wizened neck! You say that smoke
And falling timbers and a railing wife
Drive a man from his house. Lord bless my life!
What ails an old man, so to make him chide?
We cover our vices till the knot is tied,
We wives, you say, and then we trot them out.
Here's a fit proverb for a doddering lout!
An ox or ass, you say, a hound or horse,
These we examine as a matter of course.   290
Basins and also bowls, before we buy them,
Spoons, spools, and such utensils, first we try them,
And so with pots and clothes, beyond denial;
But of their wives men never make a trial
Until they are married. After that, you say,
Old fool, we put our vices on display.
    "'I am in a pique if you forget your duty
And fail, you tell me, to praise me for my beauty,
Or unless you are always doting on my face
And calling me "fair dame" in every place,   300
Or unless you give a feast on my birthday
To keep me in good spirits, fresh and gay,
Or unless all proper courtesies are paid
To my nurse and also to my chambermaid,
And my father's kin with all their family ties—
You say so, you old barrelful of lies!
    "'Yet just because he has a head of hair
Like shining gold, and squires me everywhere,
You have a false suspicion in your heart
Of Jenkin, our apprentice. For my part   310
I wouldn't have him if you died tomorrow!
But tell me this, or go and live in sorrow:
That chest of yours, why do you hide the keys
Away from me? It's my wealth, if you please,

[14] A small fort or defensive hiding place.

As much as yours. Will you make a fool of me,
The mistress of our house? You shall not be
Lord of my body and my wealth at once!
No, by St. James himself, you must renounce
One or the other, if it drives you mad!
Does it help to spy on me? You would be glad   320
To lock me up, I think, inside your chest.
"Enjoy yourself, and go where you think best,"
You ought to say; "I won't hear tales of malice.
I know you for a faithful wife, Dame Alice."
A woman loves no man who keeps close charge
Of where she goes. We want to be at large.
Blessed above all other men was he,
The wise astrologer, Don Ptolemy,
Who has this proverb in his *Almagest:*
"Of all wise men his wisdom is the best   330
Who does not care who has the world in hand."
Now by this proverb you should understand,
Since you have plenty, it isn't yours to care
Or fret how richly other people fare,
For by your leave, old dotard, you for one
Can have all you can take when day is done.
The man's a niggard to the point of scandal
Who will not lend his lamp to light a candle;
His lamp won't lose although the candle gain.
If you have enough, you ought not to complain.   340
"'You say, too, if we make ourselves look smart,
Put on expensive clothes and dress the part,
We lay our virtue open to disgrace.
And then you try to reinforce your case
By saying these words in the Apostle's name:
"In chaste apparel, with modesty and shame,
So shall you women clothe yourselves," said he,
"And not in rich coiffure or jewelry,
Pearls or the like, or gold, or costly wear."[15]
Now both your text and rubric, I declare,   350
I will not follow as I would a gnat!
"'You told me once that I was like a cat,
For singe her skin and she will stay at home,
But if her skin is smooth, the cat will roam.
No dawn but finds her on the neighbors calling
To show her skin, and go off caterwauling.
If I am looking smart, you mean to say,
I'm off to put my finery on display.
"'What do you gain, old fool, by setting spies?
Though you beg Argus[16] with his hundred eyes   360
To be my bodyguard, for all his skill

[15] See St. Paul's First Epistle to Timothy 2:9.
[16] In mythology, a hundred-eyed giant who served as a guard.

He'll keep me only by my own free will.
I know enough to blind him, as I live!
   "'There are three things,[17] you also say, that give
Vexation to this world both south and north,
And you add that no one can endure the fourth.
Of these catastrophes a hateful wife—
You precious wretch, may Christ cut short your life!—
Is always reckoned, as you say, for one.
Is this your whole stock of comparison,   370
And why in all your parables of contempt
Can a luckless helpmate never be exempt?
You also liken woman's love to hell,
To barren land where water will not dwell.
I've heard you call it an unruly fire;
The more it burns, the hotter its desire
To burn up everything that burned will be.
You say that just as worms destroy a tree
A wife destroys her spouse, as they have found
Who get themselves in holy wedlock bound.'   380
   "By these devices, lords, as you perceive,
I got my three old husbands to believe
That in their cups they said things of this sort,
And all of it was false; but for support
Jenkin bore witness, and my niece did too.
These innocents, Lord, what I put them through!
God's precious pains! And they had no recourse,
For I could bite and whinny like a horse.
Though in the wrong, I kept them well annoyed,
Or oftentimes I would have been destroyed!   390
First to the mill is first to grind his grain.
I was always the first one to complain,
And so our peace was made; they gladly bid
For terms to settle things they never did!
   "For wenching I would scold them out of hand
When they were hardly well enough to stand.
But this would tickle a man; it would restore him
To think I had so great a fondness for him!
I'd vow when darkness came and out I stepped,
It was to see the girls with whom he slept.   400
Under this pretext I had plenty of mirth!
Such wit as this is given us at our birth.
Lies, tears, and needlework the Lord will give
In kindness to us women while we live.
And thus in one point I can take just pride:
In the end I showed myself the stronger side.
By sleight or strength I kept them in restraint,
And chiefly by continual complaint.

---

[17] Several of the examples of unpleasantness in the following lines are from Proverbs, chapter 30.

In bed they met their grief in fullest measure.
There I would scold; I would not do their pleasure.   410
Bed was a place where I would not abide
If I felt my husband's arm across my side
Till he agreed to square accounts and pay,
And after that I'd let him have his way.
To every man, therefore, I tell this tale:
Win where you're able, all is up for sale.
No falcon by an empty hand is lured.
For victory their cravings I endured
And even feigned a show of appetite.
And yet in old meat I have no delight;   420
It made me always rail at them and chide them,
For though the pope himself sat down beside them
I would not give them peace at their own board.
No, on my honor, I paid them word for word.
Almighty God so help me, if right now
I had to make my last will, I can vow
For every word they said to me, we're quits.
For I so handled the contest by my wits
That they gave up, and took it for the best,
Or otherwise we should have had no rest.   430
Like a mad lion let my husband glare,
In the end he got the worst of the affair.
    "Then I would say, 'My dear, you ought to keep
In mind how gentle Wilkin looks, our sheep.
Come here, my husband, let me kiss your cheek!
You should be patient, too; you should be meek.
Of Job and of his patience when you prate
Your conscience ought to show a cleaner slate.
He should be patient who so well can preach.
If not, then it will fall on me to teach   440
The beauty of a peaceful wedded life.
For one of us must give in, man or wife,
And since men are more reasonable creatures
Than women are, it follows that *your* features
Ought to exhibit patience. Why do you groan?
You want my body yours, and yours alone?
Why, take it all! Welcome to every bit!
But curse you, Peter, unless you cherish it!
Were I inclined to peddle my *belle chose*,[18]
I could go about dressed freshly as a rose.   450
But I will keep it for your own sweet tooth.
It's your fault if we fight. By God, that's truth!'
    "This was the way I talked when I had need.
But now to my fourth husband I'll proceed.
    "This fourth I married was a roisterer.
He had a mistress, and my passions were,

[18] Literally, "beautiful thing" (French).

Although I say it, strong; and altogether
I was young and stubborn, pert in every feather.
If anyone took up his harp to play,
How I could dance! I sang as merry a lay   460
As any nightingale when of sweet wine
I had drunk my draft. Metellius,[19] the foul swine,
Who beat his spouse until he took her life
For drinking wine, had I only been his wife,
He'd never have frightened me away from drinking!
But after a drink, Venus gets in my thinking,
For just as true as cold engenders hail
A thirsty mouth goes with a thirsty tail.
Drinking destroys a woman's last defense
As lechers well know by experience.   470
    "But, Lord Christ, when it all comes back to me,
Remembering my youth and jollity,
It tickles me to the roots. It does me good
Down to this very day that while I could
I took my world, my time, and had my fling.
But age, alas, that poisons everything
Has robbed me of my beauty and my pith.
Well, let it go! Good-by! The devil with
What cannot last! There's only this to tell:
The flour is gone, I've only chaff to sell.   480
Yet I'll contrive to keep a merry cheek!
But now of my fourth husband I will speak.
    "My heart was, I can tell you, full of spite
That in another he should find delight.
I paid him for this debt; I made it good.
I furnished him a cross of the same wood,
By God and by St. Joce—in no foul fashion,
Not with my flesh; but I put on such passion
And rendered him so jealous, I'll engage
I made him fry in his own grease for rage!   490
On earth, God knows, I was his purgatory;
I only hope his soul is now in glory.
God knows it was a sad song that he sung
When the shoe pinched him; sorely was he wrung!
Only he knew, and God, the devious system
By which outrageously I used to twist him.
He died when I came home from Jerusalem.
He is buried near the chancel, under the beam
That holds the cross. His tomb is less ornate
Than the sepulcher where Darius[20] lies in state   500
And which the paintings of Appelles graced
With subtle work. It would have been a waste

---

[19] The source of the story of Metellius is Valerius Maximus, one of Chaucer's favorite
books.
[20] According to legend, Darius, king of the ancient Persians, had a lavish tomb.

To bury him lavishly. Farewell! God save
His soul and give him rest! He's in his grave.
   "And now of my fifth husband let me tell.
God never let his soul go down to hell
Though he of all five was my scourge and flail!
I feel it on my ribs, right down the scale,
And ever shall until my dying day.
And yet he was so full of life and gay   510
In bed, and could so melt me and cajole me
When on my back he had a mind to roll me,
What matter if on every bone he'd beaten me!
He'd have my love, so quickly he could sweeten me.
I loved him best, in fact; for as you see,
His love was a more arduous prize for me.
We women, if I'm not to tell a lie,
Are quaint in this regard. Put in our eye
A thing we cannot easily obtain,
All day we'll cry about it and complain.   520
Forbid a thing, we want it bitterly,
But urge it on us, then we turn and flee.
We are chary of what we hope that men will buy.
A throng at market makes the prices high;
Men set no value on cheap merchandise,
A truth all women know if they are wise.
   "My fifth, may God forgive his every sin,
I took for love, not money. He had been
An Oxford student once, but in our town
Was boarding with my good friend, Alison.   530
She knew each secret that I had to give
More than our parish priest did, as I live!
I told her my full mind, I shared it all.
For if my husband pissed against a wall
Or did a thing that might have cost his life,
To her, and to another neighbor's wife,
And to my niece, a girl whom I loved well,
His every thought I wouldn't blush to tell.
And often enough I told them, be it said.
God knows I made his face turn hot and red   540
For secrets he confided to his shame.
He knew he only had himself to blame.
   "And so it happened once that during Lent,
As I often did, to Alison's I went,
For I have loved my life long to be gay
And to walk out in April or in May
To hear the talk and seek a favorite haunt.
Jenkin the student, Alice, my confidante,
And I myself into the country went.
My husband was in London all that Lent.   550
I had the greater liberty to see
And to be seen by jolly company.

How could I tell beforehand in what place
Luck might be waiting with a stroke of grace?
And so I went to every merrymaking.
No pilgrimage was past my undertaking.
I was at festivals, and marriages,
Processions, preachings, and at miracle plays,[21]
And in my scarlet clothes I made a sight.
Upon that costume neither moth nor mite   560
Nor any worm with ravening hunger fell.
And why, you ask? It was kept in use too well.
  "Now for what happened. In the fields we walked,
The three of us, and gallantly we talked,
The student and I, until I told him he,
If I became a widow, should marry me.
For I can say, and not with empty pride,
I have never failed for marriage to provide
Or other things as well. Let mice be meek;
A mouse's heart I hold not worth a leek.   570
He has one hole to scurry to, just one,
And if that fails him, he is quite undone.
  "I let this student think he had bewitched me.
(My mother with this piece of guile enriched me!)
All night I dreamed of him—this too I said;
He was killing me as I lay flat in bed;
My very bed in fact was full of blood;
But still I hoped it would result in good,
For blood betokens gold, as I have heard.
It was a fiction, dream and every word,   580
But I was following my mother's lore
In all this matter, as in many more.
  "Sirs—let me see; what did I mean to say?
Aha! By God, I have it! When he lay,
My fourth, of whom I've spoken, on his bier,
I wept of course; I showed but little cheer,
As wives must do, since custom has its place,
And with my kerchief covered up my face.
But since I had provided for a mate,
I did not cry for long, I'll freely state.   590
And so to church my husband on the morrow
Was borne away by neighbors in their sorrow.
Jenkin, the student, was among the crowd,
And when I saw him walk, so help me God,
Behind the bier, I thought he had a pair
Of legs and feet so cleanly turned and fair
I put my heart completely in his hold.
He was in fact some twenty winters old
And I was forty, to confess the truth;
But all my life I've still had a colt's tooth.   600

---

[21] Plays based on the lives of the saints.

My teeth were spaced apart;[22] that was the seal
St. Venus printed, and became me well.
So help me God, I was a lusty one,
Pretty and young and rich, and full of fun.
And truly, as my husbands have all said,
I was the best thing there could be in bed.
For I belong to Venus in my feelings,
Though I bring the heart of Mars to all my dealings.
From Venus come my lust and appetite,
From Mars I get my courage and my might,   610
Born under Taurus, while Mars stood therein.
Alas, alas, that ever love was sin!
I yielded to my every inclination
Through the predominance of my constellation;
This made me so I never could withhold
My chamber of Venus, if the truth be told,
From a good fellow; yet upon my face
Mars left his mark, and in another place.
For never, so may Christ grant me intercession,
Have I yet loved a fellow with discretion,   620
But always I have followed appetite,
Let him be long or short or dark or light.
I never cared, as long as he liked me,
What his rank was or how poor he might be.
    "What should I say, but when the month ran out,
This jolly student, always much about,
This Jenkin married me in solemn state.
To him I gave land, titles, the whole slate
Of goods that had been given me before;
But my repentance afterward was sore!   630
He wouldn't endure the pleasures I held dear.
By God, he gave me a lick once on the ear,
When from a book of his I tore a leaf,
So hard that from the blow my ear grew deaf.
I was stubborn as a lioness with young,
And by the truth I had a rattling tongue,
And I would visit, as I'd done before,
No matter what forbidding oath he swore.
Against this habit he would sit and preach me
Sermons enough, and he would try to teach me   640
Old Roman stories,[23] how for his whole life
The man Sulpicius Gallus left his wife
Only because he saw her look one day
Bareheaded down the street from his doorway.
    "Another Roman he told me of by name
Who, since his wife was at a summer's game
Without his knowledge, thereupon forsook
The woman. In his Bible he would look

---

[22] A sign of lustiness.   [23] The following two stories are from Valerius Maximus.

And find that proverb of the Ecclesiast
Where he enjoins and makes the stricture fast   650
That men forbid their wives to rove about.
Then he would quote me this, you needn't doubt:
'Build a foundation over sands or shallows,
Or gallop a blind horse across the fallows,
Let a wife traipse to shrines that some saint hallows,
And you are fit to swing upon the gallows.'
Talk as he would, I didn't care two haws
For his proverbs or his venerable saws.
Set right by him I never meant to be.
I hate the man who tells my faults to me,   660
And more of us than I do, by your pleasure.
This made him mad with me beyond all measure.
Under his yoke in no case would I go.
    "Now, by St. Thomas, I will let you know
Why from that book of his I tore a leaf,
For which I got the blow that made me deaf.
    "He had a book, *Valerius,* he called it,
And Theophrastus, and he always hauled it
From where it lay to read both day and night
And laughed hard at it, such was his delight.   670
There was another scholar, too, at Rome
A cardinal, whose name was St. Jerome;
He wrote a book against Jovinian.
In the same book also were Tertullian,
Chrysippus, Trotula, Abbess Héloïse
Who lived near Paris; it contained all these,
Bound in a single volume, and many a one
Besides; the Parables of Solomon
And Ovid's *Art of Love.* On such vacation
As he could snatch from worldly occupation   680
He dredged this book for tales of wicked wives.[24]
He knew more stories of their wretched lives
Than are told about good women in the Bible.
No scholar ever lived who did not libel
Women, believe me; to speak well of wives
Is quite beyond them, unless it be in lives
Of holy saints; no woman else will do.
Who was it painted the lion,[25] tell me who?
By God, if women had only written stories
Like wits and scholars in their oratories,[26]   690
They would have pinned on men more wickedness
Than the whole breed of Adam can redress.

---

[24] Jenkin's collection of anti-feminine literature is wide-ranging, including the Bible; ancient classical authors such as Theophrastus and Ovid; early Christian authors such as Tertullian and Jerome; and medieval writers such as the twelfth-century Héloïse (loved by Abelard).

[25] In a fable of Aesop, a lion who sees a picture of a man killing a lion says that if lions could paint, the roles in the picture might be reversed.

[26] Private chapels.

Venus's children clash with Mercury's;
The two work evermore by contraries.
Knowledge and wisdom are of Mercury's giving,
Venus loves revelry and riotous living,
And with these clashing dispositions gifted
Each of them sinks when the other is uplifted.
Thus Mercury falls, God knows, in desolation
In the sign of Pisces, Venus's exaltation,   700
And Venus falls when Mercury is raised.
Thus by a scholar no woman can be praised.
The scholar, when he's old and cannot do
The work of Venus more than his old shoe,
Then sits he down, and in his dotage fond
Writes that no woman keeps her marriage bond!
    "But now for the story that I undertook—
To tell how I was beaten for a book.
    "Jenkin, one night, who never seemed to tire
Of reading in his book, sat by the fire   710
And first he read of Eve, whose wickedness
Delivered all mankind to wretchedness
For which in his own person Christ was slain
Who with his heart's blood bought us all again.
'By this,' he said, 'expressly you may find
That woman was the loss of all mankind.'
    "He read me next how Samson lost his hair.
Sleeping, his mistress clipped it off for fair;
Through this betrayal he lost both his eyes.[27]
He read me then—and I'm not telling lies—   720
How Deianeira, wife of Hercules,
Caused him to set himself on fire.[28] With these
He did not overlook the sad to-do
Of Socrates with *his* wives—he had two.
Xantippe emptied the pisspot on his head.
This good man sat as patient as if dead.
He wiped his scalp; he did not dare complain
Except to say 'With thunder must come rain.'
    "Pasiphaë,[29] who was the queen of Crete,
For wickedness he thought her story sweet.   730
Ugh! That's enough, it was a grisly thing,
About her lust and filthy hankering!
And Clytemnestra[30] in her lechery
Who took her husband's life feloniously,

---

[27] Judges, chapter 16. Samson confided to his beloved, Delilah, that his strength lay in his hair; she betrayed him by having it cut off while he was sleeping. Thus weakened, he was enslaved by the Philistines.

[28] In her jealousy she gave Hercules a poisoned robe, which caused him such agony that to escape the pain he had himself cremated.

[29] She fell in love with a bull and gave birth to a monster, half bull and half human.

[30] Wife of Agamemnon, commander of the Greeks against Troy. On his return from the war, she and her paramour killed him.

He grew devout in reading of her treason.
And then he told me also for what reason
Unhappy Amphiaraus lost his life.
My husband had the story of *his* wife,
Eriphyle, who for a clasp of gold
Went to his Grecian enemies and told   740
The secret of her husband's hiding place,
For which at Thebes he met an evil grace.³¹
Livia and Lucilia, he went through
Their tale as well; they killed their husbands, too.
One killed for love, the other killed for hate.
At evening Livia, when the hour was late,
Poisoned her husband, for she was his foe.
Lucilia doted on her husband so
That in her lust, hoping to make him think
Ever of her, she gave him a love-drink   750
Of such a sort he died before the morrow.³²
And so at all turns husbands come to sorrow!
    "He told me then how one Latumius,
Complaining to a friend named Arrius,
Told him that in his garden grew a tree
On which his wives had hanged themselves, all three,
Merely for spite against their partnership.
'Brother,' said Arrius, 'let me have a slip
From this miraculous tree, for, begging pardon,
I want to go and plant it in my garden.'   760
    "Then about wives in recent times he read,
How some had murdered husbands lying abed
And all night long had let a paramour
Enjoy them with the corpse flat on the floor;
Or driven a nail into a husband's brain
While he was sleeping, and thus he had been slain;
And some had given them poison in their drink.
He told more harm than anyone can think,
And seasoned his wretched stories with proverbs
Outnumbering all the blades of grass and herbs   770
On earth. 'Better a dragon for a mate,
Better,' he said, 'on a lion's whims to wait
Than on a wife whose way it is to chide.
Better,' he said, 'high in the loft to bide
Than with a railing wife down in the house.
They always, they are so contrarious,
Hate what their husbands like,' so he would say.
'A woman,' he said, 'throws all her shame away
When she takes off her smock.' And on he'd go:

---

³¹ In mythology, Amphiaraus was tricked by his wife (who had been bribed) into joining an expedition against Thebes from which it was known that he would not return alive.
³² In ancient Roman history there were two Livias, each of whom killed her husband. Lucilia was married to the great Roman poet Lucretius (first century B.C.); the story of the love potion is from St. Jerome.

'A pretty woman, unless she's chaste also,   780
Is like a gold ring stuck in a sow's nose.'
Who could imagine, who would half suppose
The gall my heart drank, raging at each drop?
    "And when I saw that he would never stop
Reading all night from his accursed book,
Suddenly, in the midst of it, I took
Three leaves and tore them out in a great pique,
And with my fist I caught him on the cheek
So hard he tumbled backward in the fire.
And up he jumped, he was as mad for ire   790
As a mad lion, and caught me on the head
With such a blow I fell down as if dead.
And seeing me on the floor, how still I lay,
He was aghast, and would have fled away,
Till I came to at length, and gave a cry.
'Have you killed me for my lands? Before I die,
False thief,' I said, 'I'll give you a last kiss!'
    "He came to me and knelt down close at this,
And said, 'So help me God, dear Alison,
I'll never strike you. For this thing I have done   800
You are to blame. Forgive me, I implore.'
So then I hit him on the cheek once more
And said, 'Thus far I am avenged, you thief.
I cannot speak. Now I shall die for grief.'
But finally, with much care and ado,
We reconciled our differences, we two.
He let me have the bridle in my hand
For management of both our house and land.
To curb his tongue he also undertook,
And on the spot I made him burn his book.   810
And when I had secured in full degree
By right of triumph the whole sovereignty,
And he had said, 'My dear, my own true wife,
Do as you will as long as you have life;
Preserve your honor and keep my estate,'
From that day on we had settled our debate.
I was as kind, God help me, day and dark
As any wife from India to Denmark,
And also true, and so he was to me.
I pray the Lord who sits in majesty   820
To bless his soul for Christ's own mercy dear.
And now I'll tell my tale, if you will hear."
    "Dame," laughed the Friar, "as I hope for bliss,
It was a long preamble to a tale, all this!"
    "God's arms!" the Summoner said, "it is a sin,
Good people, how friars are always butting in!
A fly and a friar will fall in every dish
And every question, whatever people wish.
What do you know, with your talk about 'preambling'?

Amble or trot or keep still or go scrambling,   830
You interrupt our pleasure."
                                    "You think so,
Sir Summoner?" said the Friar. "Before I go,
I'll give the people here a chance or two
For a laugh at summoners, I promise you."
    "Curse on your face," the Summoner said, "curse me,
If I don't tell some stories, two or three,
On friars, before I get to Sittingborne,[33]
With which I'll twist your heart and make it mourn,
For you have lost your temper, I can see."
    "Be quiet," cried our Host, "immediately,"   840
And ordered, "Let the woman tell her tale.
You act like people who've got drunk on ale.
Do, Madame, tell us. That is the best measure."
    "All ready, sir," she answered "at your pleasure,
With the license of this worthy Friar here."
    "Madame, tell on," he said. "You have my ear."

THE WIFE OF BATH'S TALE

In the old days when King Arthur ruled the nation,
Whom Welshmen speak of with such veneration,
This realm we live in was a fairy land.
The fairy queen danced with her jolly band
On the green meadows where they held dominion.
This was, as I have read, the old opinion;
I speak of many hundred years ago.
But no one sees an elf now, as you know,
For in our time the charity and prayers
And all the begging of these holy friars   10
Who swarm through every nook and every stream
Thicker than motes of dust in a sunbeam,
Blessing our chambers, kitchens, halls, and bowers,
Our cities, towns, and castles, our high towers,
Our villages, our stables, barns, and dairies,
They keep us all from seeing any fairies,
For where you might have come upon an elf
There now you find the holy friar himself
Working his district on industrious legs
And saying his devotions while he begs.   20
Women are safe now under every tree.
No incubus[1] is there unless it's he,
And all they have to fear from him is shame.
    It chanced that Arthur had a knight who came

---

[33] About forty miles from London.
[1] An evil spirit believed to have intercourse with women, in their sleep.

Lustily riding home one day from hawking,
And in his path he saw a maiden walking
Before him, stark alone, right in his course.
This young knight took her maidenhead by force,
A crime at which the outcry was so keen
It would have cost his neck, but that the queen,   30
With other ladies, begged the king so long
That Arthur spared his life, for right or wrong,
And gave him to the queen, at her own will,
According to her choice, to save or kill.

  She thanked the king, and later told this knight,
Choosing her time, "You are still in such a plight
Your very life has no security.
I grant your life, if you can answer me
This question: what is the thing that most of all
Women desire? Think, or your neck will fall   40
Under the ax! If you cannot let me know
Immediately, I give you leave to go
A twelvemonth and a day, no more, in quest
Of such an answer as will meet the test.
But you must pledge your honor to return
And yield your body, whatever you may learn."

  The knight sighed; he was rueful beyond measure.
But what! He could not follow his own pleasure.
He chose at last upon his way to ride
And with such answer as God might provide   50
To come back when the year was at the close.
And so he takes his leave, and off he goes.

  He seeks out every house and every place
Where he has any hope, by luck or grace,
Of learning what thing women covet most.
But it seemed he could not light on any coast
Where on this point two people would agree,
For some said wealth and some said jollity,
Some said position, some said sport in bed
And often to be widowed, often wed.   60
Some said that to a woman's heart what mattered
Above all else was to be pleased and flattered.
That shaft, to tell the truth, was a close hit.
Men win us best by flattery, I admit,
And by attention. Some say our greatest ease
Is to be free and do just as we please,
And not to have our faults thrown in our eyes,
But always to be praised for being wise.
And true enough, there's not one of us all
Who will not kick if you rub us on a gall.   70
Whatever vices we may have within,
We won't be taxed with any fault or sin.

  Some say that women are delighted well
If it is thought that they will never tell

A secret they are trusted with, or scandal.
But that tale isn't worth an old rake handle!
We women, for a fact, can never hold
A secret. Will you hear a story told?
Then witness Midas! For it can be read
In Ovid that he had upon his head   80
Two ass's ears that he kept out of sight
Beneath his long hair with such skill and sleight
That no one else besides his wife could guess.
He loved her well, and trusted her no less.
He begged her not to make his blemish known,
But keep her knowledge to herself alone.
She swore that never, though to save her skin,
Would she be guilty of so mean a sin,
And yet it seemed to her she nearly died
Keeping a secret locked so long inside.   90
It swelled about her heart so hard and deep
She was afraid some word was bound to leap
Out of her mouth, and since there was no man
She dared to tell, down to a swamp she ran—
Her heart, until she got there, all agog—
And like a bittern booming in the bog
She put her mouth close to the watery ground:
"Water, do not betray me with your sound!
I speak to you, and you alone," she said.
"Two ass's ears grow on my husband's head!   100
And now my heart is whole, now it is out.
I'd burst if I held it longer, past all doubt."
Safely, you see, awhile you may confide
In us, but it will out; we cannot hide
A secret. Look in Ovid if you care
To learn what followed; the whole tale is there.[2]
    This knight, when he perceived he could not find
What women covet most, was low in mind;
But the day had come when homeward he must ride,
And as he crossed a wooded countryside   110
Some four and twenty ladies there by chance
He saw, all circling in a woodland dance,
And toward this dance he eagerly drew near
In hope of any counsel he might hear.
But the truth was, he had not reached the place
When dance and all, they vanished into space.
No living soul remained there to be seen
Save an old woman sitting on the green,
As ugly a witch as fancy could devise.
As he approached her she began to rise   120
And said, "Sir knight, here runs no thoroughfare.

---

[2] See Ovid, *Metamorphoses,* Book XI. In Ovid, however, it is Midas's barber, not his wife,
who reveals the secret.

What are you seeking with such anxious air?
Tell me! The better may your fortune be.
We old folk know a lot of things," said she.
  "Good mother," said the knight, "my life's to pay,
That's all too certain, if I cannot say
What women covet most. If you could tell
That secret to me, I'd requite you well."
  "Give me your hand," she answered. "Swear me true
That whatsoever I next ask of you,   130
You'll do it if it lies within your might
And I'll enlighten you before the night."
  "Granted, upon my honor," he replied.
  "Then I dare boast, and with no empty pride,
Your life is safe," she told him. "Let me die
If the queen herself won't say the same as I.
Let's learn if the haughtiest of all who wear
A net or coverchief upon their hair
Will be so forward as to answer 'no'
To what I'll teach you. No more; let us go."   140
With that she whispered something in his ear,
And told him to be glad and have no fear.
  When they had reached the court, the knight declared
That he had kept his day, and was prepared
To give his answer, standing for his life.
Many the wise widow, many the wife,
Many the maid who rallied to the scene,
And at the head as justice sat the queen.
Then silence was enjoined; the knight was told
In open court to say what women hold   150
Precious above all else. He did not stand
Dumb like a beast, but spoke up at command
And plainly offered them his answering word
In manly voice, so that the whole court heard.
  "My liege and lady, most of all," said he,
"Women desire to have the sovereignty
And sit in rule and government above
Their husbands, and to have their way in love.
That is what most you want. Spare me or kill
As you may like; I stand here by your will."   160
  No widow, wife, or maid gave any token
Of contradicting what the knight had spoken.
He should not die; he should be spared instead;
He was worthy of his life, the whole court said.
  The old woman whom the knight met on the green
Sprang up at this. "My sovereign lady queen,
Before your court has risen, do me right!
It was I who taught this answer to the knight,
For which he pledged his honor in my hand,
Solemnly, that the first thing I demand,   170
He would do it, if it lay within his might.

Before the court I ask you, then, sir knight,
To take me," said the woman, "as your wife,
For well you know that I have saved your life.
Deny me, on your honor, if you can."
  "Alas," replied this miserable man,
"That was my promise, it must be confessed.
For the love of God, though, choose a new request!
Take all my wealth, and let my body be."
  "If that's your tune, then curse both you and me,"   180
She said. "Though I am ugly, old, and poor,
I'll have, for all the metal and the ore
That under earth is hidden or lies above,
Nothing, except to be your wife and love."
  "My love? No, my damnation, if you can!
Alas," he said, "that any of my clan
Should be so miserably misallied!"
  All to no good; force overruled his pride,
And in the end he is constrained to wed,
And marries his old wife and goes to bed.   190
  Now some will charge me with an oversight
In failing to describe the day's delight,
The merriment, the food, the dress at least.
But I reply, there was no joy nor feast;
There was only sorrow and sharp misery.
He married her in private, secretly,
And all day after, such was his distress,
Hid like an owl from his wife's ugliness.
  Great was the woe this knight had in his head
When in due time they both were brought to bed.   200
He shuddered, tossed, and turned, and all the while
His old wife lay and waited with a smile.
"Is every knight so backward with a spouse?
Is it," she said, "a law in Arthur's house?
I am your love, your own, your wedded wife,
I am the woman who has saved your life.
I have never done you anything but right.
Why do you treat me this way the first night?
You must be mad, the way that you behave!
Tell me my fault, and as God's love can save,   210
I will amend it, truly, if I can."
  "Amend it?" answered this unhappy man.
"It can never be amended, truth to tell.
You are so loathsome and so old as well,
And your low birth besides is such a cross
It is no wonder that I turn and toss.
God take my woeful spirit from my breast!"
  "Is this," she said, "the cause of your unrest?"
  "No wonder!" said the knight. "It truly is."
  "Now sir," she said, "I could amend all this   220
Within three days, if it should please me to,

And if you deal with me as you should do.
    "But since you speak of that nobility
That comes from ancient wealth and pedigree,
As if *that* constituted gentlemen,
I hold such arrogance not worth a hen!
The man whose virtue is pre-eminent,
In public and alone, always intent
On doing every generous act he can,
Take him—he is the greatest gentleman!   230
Christ wills that we should claim nobility
From him, not from old wealth or family.
Our elders left us all that they were worth
And through their wealth and blood we claim high birth,
But never, since it was beyond their giving,
Could they bequeath to us their virtuous living;
Although it first conferred on them the name
Of gentlemen, they could not leave that claim!
    "Dante the Florentine on this was wise:
'Frail is the branch on which man's virtues rise'—   240
Thus runs his rhyme—'God's goodness wills that we
Should claim from him alone nobility.'[3]
Thus from our elders we can only claim
Such temporal things as men may hurt and maim.
    "It is clear enough that true nobility
Is not bequeathed along with property,
For many a lord's son does a deed of shame
And yet, God knows, enjoys his noble name.
But though descended from a noble house
And elders who were wise and virtuous,   250
If he will not follow his elders, who are dead,
But leads, himself, a shameful life instead,
He is not noble, be he duke or earl.
It is the churlish deed that makes the churl.
And therefore, my dear husband, I conclude
That though my ancestors were rough and rude,
Yet may Almighty God confer on me
The grace to live, as I hope, virtuously.
Call me of noble blood when I begin
To live in virtue and to cast out sin.   260
    "As for my poverty, at which you grieve,
Almighty God in whom we all believe
In willful poverty chose to lead his life,
And surely every man and maid and wife
Can understand that Jesus, heaven's king,
Would never choose a low or vicious thing.
A poor and cheerful life is nobly led;
So Seneca and others have well said.
The man so poor he doesn't have a stitch,

---

[3] *Purgatory*, Canto VII.

If he thinks himself repaid, I count him rich.   270
He that is covetous, he is the poor man,
Pining to have the things he never can.
It is of cheerful mind, true poverty.
Juvenal[4] says about it happily:
'The poor man as he goes along his way
And passes thieves is free to sing and play.'
Poverty is a good we loathe, a great
Reliever of our busy worldly state,
A great amender also of our minds
As he that patiently will bear it finds.   280
And poverty, for all it seems distressed,
Is a possession no one will contest.
Poverty, too, by bringing a man low,
Helps him the better both God and self to know.
Poverty is a glass where we can see
Which are our true friends, as it seems to me.
So, sir, I do not wrong you on this score;
Reproach me with my poverty no more.

   "Now, sir, you tax me with my age; but, sir,
You gentlemen of breeding all aver   290
That men should not despise old age, but rather
Grant an old man respect, and call him 'father.'

   "If I am old and ugly, as you have said,
You have less fear of being cuckolded,
For ugliness and age, as all agree,
Are notable guardians of chastity.
But since I know in what you take delight,
I'll gratify your worldly appetite.

   "Choose now, which of two courses you will try:
To have me old and ugly till I die   300
But evermore your true and humble wife,
Never displeasing you in all my life,
Or will you have me rather young and fair
And take your chances on who may repair
Either to your house on account of me
Or to some other place, it well may be.
Now make your choice, whichever you prefer."

   The knight took thought, and sighed, and said to her
At last, "My love and lady, my dear wife,
In your wise government I put my life.   310
Choose for yourself which course will best agree
With pleasure and honor, both for you and me.
I do not care, choose either of the two;
I am content, whatever pleases you."

   "Then have I won from you the sovereignty,
Since I may choose and rule at will?" said she.
   He answered, "That is best, I think, dear wife."

---

[4] Roman poet (about 60–140 A.D.). The reference is to his *Satires*, X.

"Kiss me," she said. "Now we are done with strife,
For on my word, I will be both to you,
That is to say, fair, yes, and faithful too.
May I die mad unless I am as true   320
As ever wife was since the world was new.
Unless I am as lovely to be seen
By morning as an empress or a queen
Or any lady between east and west,
Do with my life or death as you think best.
Lift up the curtain, see what you may see."
    And when the knight saw what had come to be
And knew her as she was, so young, so fair,
His joy was such that it was past compare.   330
He took her in his arms and gave her kisses
A thousand times on end; he bathed in blisses.
And she obeyed him also in full measure
In everything that tended to his pleasure.
    And so they lived in full joy to the end.
And now to all us women may Christ send
Submissive husbands, full of youth in bed,
And grace to outlive all the men we wed.
And I pray Jesus to cut short the lives
Of those who won't be governed by their wives;   340
And old, ill-tempered niggards who hate expense,
God promptly bring them down with pestilence!

WORDS OF THE HOST TO THE PARDONER

"Now my fine friend," he said, "you Pardoner,
Be quick, tell us a tale of mirth or fun."[1]
    "By St. Ninian," he said, "it shall be done,
But at this tavern here, before my tale,
I'll just go in and have some bread and ale."
    The proper pilgrims in our company
Cried quickly, "Let him speak no ribaldry!
Tell us a moral tale, one to make clear
Some lesson to us, and we'll gladly hear."
    "Just as you wish," he said. "But I must think
Of something edifying while I drink."

PROLOGUE TO THE PARDONER'S TALE

"In churches," said the Pardoner, "when I preach,
I use, milords, a lofty style of speech
And ring it out as roundly as a bell,

---

[1] The Host, having heard a sad tale from the Physician, wants the Pardoner to tell a merrier one. The travelers are at a tavern.

Knowing by rote all that I have to tell.
My text is ever the same, and ever was:
Radix malorum est cupiditas.[2]
  "First I inform them whence I come; that done,
I then display my papal bulls,[3] each one.
I show my license first, my body's warrant,
Sealed by the bishop, for it would be abhorrent   10
If any man made bold, though priest or clerk,
To interrupt me in Christ's holy work.
And after that I give myself full scope.
Bulls in the name of cardinal and pope,
Of bishops and of patriarchs I show.
I say in Latin some few words or so
To spice my sermon; it flavors my appeal
And stirs my listeners to greater zeal.
Then I display my cases made of glass
Crammed to the top with rags and bones. They pass   20
For relics[4] with all the people in the place.
I have a shoulder bone in a metal case,
Part of a sheep owned by a holy Jew.
'Good men,' I say, 'heed what I'm telling you:
Just let this bone be dipped in any well
And if cow, calf, or sheep, or ox should swell
From eating a worm, or by a worm be stung,
Take water from this well and wash its tongue
And it is healed at once. And furthermore
Of scab and ulcers and of every sore   30
Shall every sheep be cured, and that straightway,
That drinks from the same well. Heed what I say:
If the good man who owns the beasts will go,
Fasting, each week, and drink before cockcrow
Out of this well, his cattle shall be brought
To multiply—that holy Jew so taught
Our elders—and his property increase.
  "'Moreover, sirs, this bone cures jealousies.
Though into a jealous madness a man fell,
Let him cook his soup in water from this well,   40
He'll never, though for truth he knew her sin,
Suspect his wife again, though she took in
A priest, or even two of them or three.
  "'Now here's a mitten that you all can see.
Whoever puts his hand in it shall gain,
When he sows his land, increasing crops of grain,
Be it wheat or oats, provided that he bring
His penny or so to make his offering.
  "'There is one word of warning I must say,
Good men and women. If any here today   50

_____

[2] "Greed is the root of all evil," adapted from 1 Timothy 6:10.   [3] Documents.
[4] That is, of saints or biblical personages.

Has done a sin so horrible to name
He daren't be shriven[5] of it for the shame,
Or if any woman, young or old, is here
Who has cuckolded her husband, be it clear
They may not make an offering in that case
To these my relics; they have no power nor grace.
But any who is free of such dire blame,
Let him come up and offer in God's name
And I'll absolve him through the authority
That by the pope's bull has been granted me.'   60
　"By such hornswoggling I've won, year by year,
A hundred marks[6] since being a pardoner.
I stand in my pulpit like a true divine,
And when the people sit I preach my line
To ignorant souls, as you have heard before,
And tell skullduggeries by the hundred more.
Then I take care to stretch my neck well out
And over the people I nod and peer about
Just like a pigeon perching on a shed.
My hands fly and my tongue wags in my head   70
So busily that to watch me is a joy.
Avarice is the theme that I employ
In all my sermons, to make the people free
In giving pennies—especially to me.
My mind is fixed on what I stand to win
And not at all upon correcting sin.
I do not care, when they are in the grave,
If souls go berry-picking that I could save.
Truth is that evil purposes determine,
And many a time, the origin of a sermon: 80
Some to please people and by flattery
To gain advancement through hypocrisy,
Some for vainglory, some again for hate.
For when I daren't fight otherwise, I wait
And give him a tongue-lashing when I preach.
No man escapes or gets beyond the reach
Of my defaming tongue, supposing he
Has done a wrong to my brethren or to me.
For though I do not tell his proper name,
People will recognize him all the same.   90
By sign and circumstance I let them learn.
Thus I serve those who have done us an ill turn.
Thus I spit out my venom under hue
Of sanctity, and seem devout and true!
　"But to put my purpose briefly, I confess
I preach for nothing but for covetousness.
That's why my text is still and ever was

[5] Absolved of sins in the confessional.
[6] The equivalent today of a few thousand dollars.

Radix malorum est cupiditas.
For by this text I can denounce, indeed,
The very vice I practice, which is greed.   100
But though that sin is lodged in my own heart,
I am able to make other people part
From avarice, and sorely to repent,
Though that is not my principal intent.
   "Then I bring in examples, many a one,
And tell them many a tale of days long done.
Plain folk love tales that come down from of old.
Such things their minds can well report and hold.
Do you think that while I have the power to preach
And take in silver and gold for what I teach   110
I shall ever live in willful poverty?
No, no, that never was my thought, certainly.
I mean to preach and beg in sundry lands.
I won't do any labor with my hands,
Nor live by making baskets. I don't intend
To beg for nothing; that is not my end.
I won't ape the apostles; I must eat,
I must have money, wool, and cheese, and wheat,
Though I took it from the meanest wretch's tillage
Or from the poorest widow in a village,   120
Yes, though her children starved for want. In fine,
I mean to drink the liquor of the vine
And have a jolly wench in every town.
But, in conclusion, lords, I will get down
To business: you would have me tell a tale.
Now that I've had a drink of corny ale,
By God, I hope the thing I'm going to tell
Is one that you'll have reason to like well.
For though myself a very sinful man,
I can tell a moral tale, indeed I can,   130
One that I use to bring the profits in
While preaching. Now be still, and I'll begin."

THE PARDONER'S TALE

There was a company of young folk living
One time in Flanders, who were bent on giving
Their lives to follies and extravagances,
Brothels and taverns, where they held their dances
With lutes, harps, and guitars, diced at all hours,
And also ate and drank beyond their powers,
Through which they paid the devil sacrifice
In the devil's temple with their drink and dice,
Their abominable excess and dissipation.
They swore oaths that were worthy of damnation;   10

It was grisly to be listening when they swore.
The blessed body of our Lord they tore—
The Jews, it seemed to them, had failed to rend
His body enough—and each laughed at his friend
And fellow in sin. To encourage their pursuits
Came comely dancing girls, peddlers of fruits,
Singers with harps, bawds and confectioners
Who are the very devil's officers
To kindle and blow the fire of lechery
That is the follower of gluttony.   20
   Witness the Bible, if licentiousness
Does not reside in wine and drunkenness!
Recall how drunken Lot, unnaturally,
With his two daughters lay unwittingly,
So drunk he had no notion what he did.[1]
   Herod, the stories tell us, God forbid,
When full of liquor at his banquet board
Right at his very table gave the word
To kill the Baptist, John, though guiltless he.[2]
   Seneca[3] says a good word, certainly.   30
He says there is no difference he can find
Between a man who has gone out of his mind
And one who carries drinking to excess,
Only that madness outlasts drunkenness.
O gluttony, first cause of mankind's fall,[4]
Of our damnation the cursed original
Until Christ bought us with his blood again!
How dearly paid for by the race of men
Was this detestable iniquity!
This whole world was destroyed through gluttony.   40
   Adam our father and his wife also
From paradise to labor and to woe
Were driven for that selfsame vice, indeed.
As long as Adam fasted—so I read—
He was in heaven; but as soon as he
Devoured the fruit of that forbidden tree
Then he was driven out in sorrow and pain.
Of gluttony well ought we to complain!
Could a man know how many maladies
Follow indulgences and gluttonies   50
He would keep his diet under stricter measure
And sit at table with more temperate pleasure.
The throat is short and tender is the mouth,
And hence men toil east, west, and north, and south,
In earth, and air, and water—alas to think—

---

[1] See Genesis 19:30–36.
[2] See the versions of the story in the gospels of Matthew (chapter 14) and Mark (chapter 6).
[3] A Roman writer of the first century.
[4] Because Adam and Eve sinned by eating a forbidden fruit.

Fetching a glutton dainty meat and drink.
   This is a theme, O Paul, that you well treat:
"Meat unto belly, and belly unto meat,
God shall destroy them both," as Paul has said.[5]
When a man drinks the white wine and the red—   60
This is a foul word, by my soul, to say,
And fouler is the deed in every way—
He makes his throat his privy through excess.
   The Apostle[6] says, weeping for piteousness,
"There are many of whom I told you—at a loss
I say it, weeping—enemies of Christ's cross,
Whose belly is their god; their end is death."
O cursed belly! Sack of stinking breath
In which corruption lodges, dung abounds!
At either end of you come forth foul sounds.   70
Great cost it is to fill you, and great pain!
These cooks, how they must grind and pound and strain
And transform substance into accident[7]
To please your cravings, though exorbitant!
From the hard bones they knock the marrow out.
They'll find a use for everything, past doubt,
That down the gullet sweet and soft will glide.
The spiceries of leaf and root provide
Sauces that are concocted for delight,
To give a man a second appetite.   80
But truly, he whom gluttonies entice
Is dead, while he continues in that vice.
   O drunken man, disfigured is your face,
Sour is your breath, foul are you to embrace!
You seem to mutter through your drunken nose
The sound of "Samson, Samson," yet God knows
That Samson[8] never indulged himself in wine.
Your tongue is lost, you fall like a stuck swine,
And all the self-respect that you possess
Is gone, for of man's judgment, drunkenness   90
Is the very sepulcher and annihilation.
A man whom drink has under domination
Can never keep a secret in his head.
Now steer away from both the white and red,
And most of all from that white wine keep wide
That comes from Lepe. They sell it in Cheapside
And Fish Street.[9] It's a Spanish wine, and sly
To creep in other wines[10] that grow nearby,
And such a vapor it has that with three drinks
It takes a man to Spain; although he thinks   100

---

[5] See 1 Corinthians 6:13.   [6] St. Paul. See Philippians 3:18–19.
   [7] Philosophical terms; "substance" is what a thing really is, "accident" is a nonessential
quality or property of it.
   [8] The Old Testament hero. His story is told in Judges, chapters 13–16.
   [9] Main streets in London.   [10] Be mixed with other wines.

He is home in Cheapside, he is far away
At Lepe. Then "Samson, Samson" will he say!
  By God himself, who is omnipotent,
All the great exploits in the Old Testament
Were done in abstinence, I say, and prayer.
Look in the Bible, you may learn it there.
  Attila,[11] conqueror of many a place,
Died in his sleep in shame and in disgrace
Bleeding out of his nose in drunkenness.
A captain ought to live in temperateness!   110
And more than this, I say, remember well
The injunction that was laid on Lemuel—
Not Samuel, but Lemuel, I say!
Read in the Bible; in the plainest way
Wine is forbidden to judges and to kings.[12]
This will suffice; no more upon these things.
  Now that I've shown what gluttony will do,
Now I will warn you against gambling, too;
Gambling, the very mother of low scheming,
Of lying and forswearing and blaspheming   120
Against Christ's name, of murder and waste as well
Alike of goods and time; and, truth to tell,
With honor and renown it cannot suit
To be held a common gambler by repute.
The higher a gambler stands in power and place,
The more his name is lowered in disgrace.
If a prince gambles, whatever his kingdom be,
In his whole government and policy
He is, in all the general estimation,
Considered so much less in reputation.   130
  Stilbon,[13] who was a wise ambassador,
From Lacedaemon once to Corinth bore
A mission of alliance. When he came
It happened that he found there at a game
Of hazard all the great ones of the land,
And so, as quickly as it could be planned,
He stole back, saying, "I will not lose my name
Nor have my reputation put to shame
Allying you with gamblers. You may send
Other wise emissaries to gain your end,   140
For by my honor, rather than ally
My countrymen to gamblers, I will die.
For you that are so gloriously renowned
Shall never with this gambling race be bound

---

[11] Attila the Hun, fifth-century invader of Europe.
[12] In Proverbs, 31:4, Lemuel's mother admonishes him, "It is not for kings to drink wine." Not to be confused, the Pardoner insists, with Samuel, another Old Testament figure.
[13] This story and the following one about Demetrius are from a book by John of Salisbury, a learned English scholar of the twelfth century. Lacedaemon (Sparta) and Corinth were city-states of ancient Greece.

By will of mine or treaty I prepare."
Thus did this wise philosopher declare.
    Remember also how the Parthians'[14] lord
Sent King Demetrius, as the books record,
A pair of golden dice, by this proclaiming
His scorn, because that king was known for gaming,   150
And the king of Parthia therefore held his crown
Devoid of glory, value, or renown.
Lords can discover other means of play
More suitable to while the time away.
    Now about oaths I'll say a word or two,
Great oaths and false oaths, as the old books do.
Great swearing is a thing abominable,
And false oaths yet more reprehensible.
Almighty God forbade swearing at all,
Matthew be witness; but specially I call   160
The holy Jeremiah on this head.
"Swear thine oaths truly, do not lie," he said.
"Swear under judgment, and in righteousness."[15]
But idle swearing is a great wickedness.
Consult and see, and he that understands
In the first table of the Lord's commands
Will find the second of his commandments this:
"Take not the Lord's name idly or amiss."
If a man's oaths and curses are extreme,
Vengeance shall find his house, both roof and beam.   170
"By the precious heart of God," and "By his nails"—
"My chance is seven, by Christ's blood at Hailes,[16]
Yours five and three." "Cheat me, and if you do,
By God's arms, with this knife I'll run you through!"—
Such fruit comes from the bones, that pair of bitches:
Oaths broken, treachery, murder. For the riches
Of Christ's love, give up curses, without fail,
Both great and small!—Now, sirs, I'll tell my tale.
    These three young roisterers of whom I tell
Long before prime[17] had rung from any bell   180
Were seated in a tavern at their drinking,
And as they sat, they heard a bell go clinking
Before a corpse being carried to his grave.
One of these roisterers, when he heard it, gave
An order to his boy: "Go out and try
To learn whose corpse is being carried by.
Get me his name, and get it right. Take heed."
    "Sir," said the boy, "there isn't any need.

---

[14] Parthia was an ancient region in what is now Iran.
[15] In the gospel of Matthew, 5:34 (part of the Sermon on the Mount), Christ says, "Swear not at all." See also Jeremiah 4:2.
[16] In the dice game of hazard, a player's "chance" was roughly the equivalent of his "point" in modern craps. Hailes was an English abbey supposed to possess a relic of Christ's blood.
[17] An early morning hour, between seven and nine.

I learned before you came here, by two hours.
He was, it happens, an old friend of yours,
And all at once, there on his bench upright
As he was sitting drunk, he was killed last night.
A sly thief, Death men call him, who deprives
All the people in this country of their lives,
Came with his spear and smiting his heart in two
Went on his business with no more ado.
A thousand have been slaughtered by his hand
During this plague. And, sir, before you stand
Within his presence, it should be necessary,
It seems to me, to know your adversary.
Be evermore prepared to meet this foe.
My mother taught me thus; that's all I know."
    "Now by St. Mary," said the innkeeper,
"This child speaks truth. Man, woman, laborer,
Servant, and child the thief has slain this year
In a big village a mile or more from here.
I think it is his place of habitation.
It would be wise to make some preparation
Before he brought a man into disgrace."
    "God's arms!" this roisterer said. "So that's the case!
Is it so dangerous with this thief to meet?
I'll look for him by every path and street,
I vow it, by God's holy bones! Hear me,
Fellows of mine, we are all one, we three.
Let each of us hold up his hand to the other
And each of us become his fellow's brother.
We'll slay this Death, who slaughters and betrays.
He shall be slain whose hand so many slays,
By the dignity of God, before tonight!"
    The three together set about to plight
Their oaths to live and die each for the other
Just as though each had been to each born brother.
And in their drunken frenzy up they get
And toward the village off at once they set
Which the innkeeper had spoken of before,
And many were the grisly oaths they swore.
They rent Christ's precious body limb from limb—
Death shall be dead, if they lay hands on him!
    When they had hardly gone the first half mile,
Just as they were about to cross a stile,
An old man, poor and humble, met them there.
The old man greeted them with a meek air
And said, "God bless you, lords, and be your guide."
    "What's this?" the proudest of the three replied.
"Old beggar, I hope you meet with evil grace!
Why are you all wrapped up except your face?
What are you doing alive so many a year?"
    The old man at these words began to peer

Into this gambler's face. "Because I can,
Though I should walk to India, find no man,"   240
He said, "in any village or any town,
Who for my age is willing to lay down
His youth. So I must keep my old age still
For as long a time as it may be God's will.
Nor will Death take my life from me, alas!
Thus like a restless prisoner I pass
And on the ground, which is my mother's gate,
I walk and with my staff both early and late
I knock and say, 'Dear mother, let me in!
See how I vanish, flesh, and blood, and skin!   250
Alas, when shall my bones be laid to rest?
I would exchange with you my clothing chest,
Mother, that in my chamber long has been
For an old haircloth rag to wrap me in.'
And yet she still refuses me that grace.
All white, therefore, and withered is my face.
    "But, sirs, you do yourselves no courtesy
To speak to an old man so churlishly
Unless he had wronged you either in word or deed.
As you yourselves in Holy Writ may read,   260
'Before an aged man whose head is hoar
Men ought to rise.'[18] I counsel you, therefore,
No harm nor wrong here to an old man do,
No more than you would have men do to you
In your old age, if you so long abide.
And God be with you, whether you walk or ride!
I must go yonder where I have to go."
    "No, you old beggar, by St. John, not so,"
Said another of these gamblers. "As for me,
By God, you won't get off so easily!   270
You spoke just now of that false traitor, Death,
Who in this land robs all our friends of breath.
Tell where he is, since you must be his spy,
Or you will suffer for it, so say I
By God and by the holy sacrament.
You are in league with him, false thief, and bent
On killing us young folk, that's clear to my mind."
    "If you are so impatient, sirs, to find
Death," he replied, "turn up this crooked way,
For in that grove I left him, truth to say,   280
Beneath a tree, and there he will abide.
No boast of yours will make him run and hide.
Do you see that oak tree? Just there you will find
This Death, and God, who bought again mankind,
Save and amend you!" So said this old man;
And promptly each of these three gamblers ran

---

[18] See Leviticus 19:32.

Until he reached the tree, and there they found
Florins of fine gold, minted bright and round,
Nearly eight bushels of them, as they thought.
And after Death no longer then they sought. 290
Each of them was so ravished at the sight,
So fair the florins glittered and so bright,
That down they sat beside the precious hoard.
The worst of them, he uttered the first word.
  "Brothers," he told them, "listen to what I say.
My head is sharp, for all I joke and play.
Fortune has given us this pile of treasure
To set us up in lives of ease and pleasure.
Lightly it comes, lightly we'll make it go.
God's precious dignity! Who was to know 300
We'd ever tumble on such luck today?
If we could only carry this gold away,
Home to my house, or either one of yours—
For well you know that all this gold is ours—
We'd touch the summit of felicity.
But still, by daylight that can hardly be.
People would call us thieves, too bold for stealth,
And they would have us hanged for our own wealth.
It must be done by night, that's our best plan,
As prudently and slyly as we can. 310
Hence my proposal is that we should all
Draw lots, and let's see where the lot will fall,
And the one of us who draws the shortest stick
Shall run back to the town, and make it quick,
And bring us bread and wine here on the sly,
And two of us will keep a watchful eye
Over this gold; and if he doesn't stay
Too long in town, we'll carry this gold away
By night, wherever we all agree it's best."
  One of them held the cut out in his fist 320
And had them draw to see where it would fall,
And the cut fell on the youngest of them all.
At once he set off on his way to town,
And the very moment after he was gone
The one who urged this plan said to the other:
"You know that by sworn oath you are my brother.
I'll tell you something you can profit by.
Our friend has gone, that's clear to any eye,
And here is gold, abundant as can be,
That we propose to share alike, we three. 330
But if I worked it out, as I could do,
So that it could be shared between us two,
Wouldn't that be a favor, a friendly one?"
  The other answered, "How that can be done,
I don't quite see. He knows we have the gold.
What shall we do, or what shall he be told?"

"Will you keep the secret tucked inside your head?
And in a few words," the first scoundrel said,
"I'll tell you how to bring this end about."
   "Granted," the other told him. "Never doubt,   340
I won't betray you, that you can believe."
   "Now," said the first, "we are two, as you perceive,
And two of us must have more strength than one.
When he sits down, get up as if in fun
And wrestle with him. While you play this game
I'll run him through the ribs. You do the same
With your dagger there, and then this gold shall be
Divided, dear friend, between you and me.
Then all that we desire we can fulfill,
And both of us can roll the dice at will."   350
Thus in agreement these two scoundrels fell
To slay the third, as you have heard me tell.
   The youngest, who had started off to town,
Within his heart kept rolling up and down
The beauty of these florins, new and bright.
"O Lord," he thought, "were there some way I might
Have all this treasure to myself alone,
There isn't a man who dwells beneath God's throne
Could live a life as merry as mine should be!"
And so at last the fiend, our enemy,   360
Put in his head that he could gain his ends
If he bought poison to kill off his friends.
Finding his life in such a sinful state,
The devil was allowed to seal his fate.
For it was altogether his intent
To kill his friends, and never to repent.
So off he set, no longer would he tarry,
Into the town, to an apothecary,
And begged for poison; he wanted it because
He meant to kill his rats; besides, there was   370
A polecat living in his hedge, he said,
Who killed his capons; and when he went to bed
He wanted to take vengeance, if he might,
On vermin that devoured him by night.
   The apothecary answered, "You shall have
A drug that as I hope the Lord will save
My soul, no living thing in all creation,
Eating or drinking of this preparation
A dose no bigger than a grain of wheat,
But promptly with his death-stroke he shall meet.   380
Die, that he will, and in a briefer while
Than you can walk the distance of a mile,
This poison is so strong and virulent."
   Taking the poison, off the scoundrel went,
Holding it in a box, and next he ran
To the neighboring street, and borrowed from a man

Three generous flagons. He emptied out his drug
In two of them, and kept the other jug
For his own drink; he let no poison lurk
In that! And so all night he meant to work   390
Carrying off the gold. Such was his plan,
And when he had filled them, this accursed man
Retraced his path, still following his design,
Back to his friends with his three jugs of wine.
    But why dilate upon it any more?
For just as they had planned his death before,
Just so they killed him, and with no delay.
When it was finished, one spoke up to say:
"Now let's sit down and drink, and we can bury
His body later on. First we'll be merry,"   400
And as he said the words, he took the jug
That, as it happened, held the poisonous drug,
And drank, and gave his friend a drink as well,
And promptly they both died. But truth to tell,
In all that Avicenna[19] ever wrote
He never described in chapter, rule, or note
More marvelous signs of poisoning, I suppose,
Than appeared in these two wretches at the close.
Thus they both perished for their homicide,
And thus the traitorous poisoner also died.   410
    O sin accursed above all cursedness,
O treacherous murder, O foul wickedness,
O gambling, lustfulness, and gluttony,
Traducer of Christ's name by blasphemy
And monstrous oaths, through habit and through pride!
Alas, mankind! Ah, how may it betide
That you to your Creator, he that wrought you
And even with his precious heart's blood bought you,
So falsely and ungratefully can live?
    And now, good men, your sins may God forgive   420
And keep you specially from avarice!
My holy pardon will avail in this,
For it can heal each one of you that brings
His pennies, silver brooches, spoons, or rings.
Come, bow your head under this holy bull!
You wives, come offer up your cloth or wool!
I write your names here in my roll, just so.
Into the bliss of heaven you shall go!
I will absolve you here by my high power,
You that will offer, as clean as in the hour   430
When you were born. —Sirs, thus I preach. And now
Christ Jesus, our souls' healer, show you how
Within his pardon evermore to rest,

---

[19] Arab philosopher, physician, and author of a medical textbook of the early eleventh century.

For that, I will not lie to you, is best.
   But in my tale, sirs, I forgot one thing.
The relics and the pardons that I bring
Here in my pouch, no man in the whole land
Has finer, given me by the pope's own hand.
If any of you devoutly wants to offer
And have my absolution, come and proffer   440
Whatever you have to give. Kneel down right here,
Humbly, and take my pardon, full and clear,
Or have a new, fresh pardon if you like
At the end of every mile of road we strike,
As long as you keep offering ever newly
Good coins, not counterfeit, but minted truly.
Indeed it is an honor I confer
On each of you, an authentic pardoner
Going along to absolve you as you ride.
For in the country mishaps may betide—   450
One or another of you in due course
May break his neck by falling from his horse.
Think what security it gives you all
That in this company I chanced to fall
Who can absolve you each, both low and high,
When the soul, alas, shall from the body fly!
By my advice, our Host here shall begin,
For he's the man enveloped most by sin.
Come, offer first, Sir Host, and once that's done,
Then you shall kiss the relics, every one,   460
Yes, for a penny! Come, undo your purse!
   "No, no," said he. "Then I should have Christ's curse!
I'll do nothing of the sort, for love or riches!
You'd make me kiss a piece of your old britches
And for a saintly relic make it pass
Although it had the tincture of your ass.
By the cross St. Helen[20] found in the Holy Land,
I wish I had your balls here in my hand
For relics! Cut 'em off, and I'll be bound
If I don't help you carry them around.   470
I'll have the things enshrined in a hog's turd!"
   The Pardoner did not answer; not a word,
He was so angry, could he find to say.
   "Now," said our Host, "I will not try to play
With you, nor any other angry man."
   Immediately the worthy Knight began,
When he saw that all the people laughed, "No more,
This has gone far enough. Now as before,
Sir Pardoner, be gay, look cheerfully,
And you, Sir Host, who are so dear to me,   480

---

[20] She was believed to have discovered the cross of Jesus about 200 years after the Crucifixion.

Come, kiss the Pardoner, I beg of you,
And Pardoner, draw near, and let us do
As we've been doing, let us laugh and play."
And so they kissed, and rode along their way.

THE KNIGHT'S INTERRUPTION
OF THE MONK'S TALE

"Stop!" cried the Knight.[1] "No more of this, good sir!
You have said plenty, and much more, for sure,
For only a little such lugubriousness
Is plenty for a lot of folk, I guess.
I say for me it is a great displeasure,
When men have wealth and comfort in good measure,
To hear how they have tumbled down the slope,
And the opposite is a solace and a hope,
As when a man begins in low estate
And climbs the ladder and grows fortunate,   10
And stands there firm in his prosperity.
That is a welcome thing, it seems to me,
And of such things it would be good to tell."
  "Well said," our Host declared. "By St. Paul's bell,
You speak the truth; this Monk's tongue is too loud.
He told how fortune covered with a cloud—
I don't know what-all; and of tragedy
You heard just now, and it's no remedy,
When things are over and done with, to complain.
Besides, as you have said, it is a pain   20
To hear of misery; it is distressing.
Sir Monk, no more, as you would have God's blessing.
This company is all one weary sigh.
Such talking isn't worth a butterfly,
For where's the amusement in it, or the game?
And so, Sir Monk, or Don Pierce by your name,
I beg you heartily, tell us something else.
Truly, but for the jingling of your bells
That from your bridle hang on every side,
By Heaven's King, who was born for us and died,   30
I should long since have tumbled down in sleep,
Although the mud had never been so deep,
And then you would have told your tale in vain;
For certainly, as these learned men explain,
When his audience have turned their backs away,
It doesn't matter what a man may say.
I know well I shall have the essence of it
If anything is told here for our profit.

---

[1] The Monk, whom the Knight interrupts, has been narrating a long series of "tragedies,"
tales about the fall of eminent personages.

A tale of hunting, sir, pray share with us."
   "No," said the Monk, "I'll not be frivolous.   40
Let another tell a tale, as I have told."
   Then spoke our Host, with a rude voice and bold,
And said to the Nun's Priest, "Come over here,
You priest, come hither, you Sir John, draw near!
Tell us a thing to make our spirits glad.
Be cheerful, though the jade you ride is bad.
What if your horse is miserable and lean?
If he will carry you, don't care a bean!
Keep up a joyful heart, and look alive."
   "Yes, Host," he answered, "as I hope to thrive,   50
If I weren't merry, I know I'd be reproached."
And with no more ado his tale he broached,
And this is what he told us, every one,
This precious priest, this goodly man, Sir John.

THE NUN'S PRIEST'S TALE

Once a poor widow, aging year by year,
Lived in a tiny cottage that stood near
A clump of shade trees rising in a dale.
This widow, of whom I tell you in my tale,
Since the last day that she had been a wife
Had led a very patient, simple life.
She had but few possessions to content her.
By thrift and husbandry of what God sent her
She and two daughters found the means to dine.
She had no more than three well-fattened swine,   10
As many cows, and one sheep, Moll by name.
Her bower and hall were black from the hearth-flame
Where she had eaten many a slender meal.
No dainty morsel did her palate feel
And no sharp sauce was needed with her pottage.
Her table was in keeping with her cottage.
Excess had never given her disquiet.
Her only doctor was a moderate diet,
And exercise, and a heart that was contented.
If she did not dance, at least no gout prevented;   20
No apoplexy had destroyed her head.
She never drank wine, whether white or red.
She served brown bread and milk, loaves white or black,
Singed bacon, all this with no sense of lack,
And now and then an egg or two. In short,
She was a dairy woman of a sort.
   She had a yard, on the inside fenced about
With hedges, and an empty ditch without,
In which she kept a cock, called Chanticleer.

In all the realm of crowing he had no peer.   30
His voice was merrier than the merry sound
Of the church organ grumbling out its ground
Upon a saint's day. Stouter was this cock
In crowing than the loudest abbey clock.
Of astronomy instinctively aware,
He kept the sun's hours with celestial care,
For when through each fifteen degrees it moved,
He crowed so that it couldn't be improved.
His comb, like a crenelated[1] castle wall,
Red as fine coral, stood up proud and tall.   40
His bill was black; like polished jet it glowed,
And he was azure-legged and azure-toed.
As lilies were his nails, they were so white;
Like burnished gold his hue, it shone so bright.
This cock had in his princely sway and measure
Seven hens to satisfy his every pleasure,
Who were his sisters and his sweethearts true,
Each wonderfully like him in her hue,
Of whom the fairest-feathered throat to see
Was fair Dame Partlet. Courteous was she,   50
Discreet, and always acted debonairly.
She was sociable, and bore herself so fairly,
Since the very time that she was seven nights old,
The heart of Chanticleer was in her hold
As if she had him locked up, every limb.
He loved her so that all was well with him.
It was a joy, when up the sun would spring,
To hear them both together sweetly sing,
"My love has gone to the country, far away!"
For as I understand it, in that day   60
The animals and birds could sing and speak.
    Now as this cock, one morning at daybreak,
With each of the seven hens that he called spouse,
Sat on his perch inside the widow's house,
And next him fair Dame Partlet, in his throat
This Chanticleer produced a hideous note
And groaned like a man who is having a bad dream;
And Partlet, when she heard her husband scream,
Was all aghast, and said, "Soul of my passion,
What ails you that you groan in such a fashion?   70
You are always a sound sleeper. Fie, for shame!"
    And Chanticleer awoke and answered, "Dame,
Take no offense, I beg you, on this score.
I dreamt, by God, I was in a plight so sore
Just now, my heart still quivers from the fright.
Now God see that my dream turns out all right
And keep my flesh and body from foul seizure!

---

[1] Having walls with notched openings at the top.

I dreamed I was strutting in our yard at leisure
When there I saw, among the weeds and vines,
A beast, he was like a hound, and had designs   80
Upon my person, and would have killed me dead.
His coat was not quite yellow, not quite red,
And both his ears and tail were tipped with black
Unlike the fur along his sides and back.
He had a small snout and a fiery eye.
His look for fear still makes me almost die.
This is what made me groan, I have no doubt."
     "For shame! Fie on you, faint heart!" she burst out.
"Alas," she said, "by the great God above,
Now you have lost my heart and all my love!   90
I cannot love a coward, as I'm blest!
Whatever any woman may protest,
We all want, could it be so, for our part,
Husbands who are wise and stout of heart,
No blabber, and no niggard, and no fool,
Nor afraid of every weapon or sharp tool,
No braggart either, by the God above!
How dare you say, for shame, to your true love
That there is anything you ever feared?
Have you no man's heart, when you have a beard?   100
Alas, and can a nightmare set you screaming?
God knows there's only vanity in dreaming!
Dreams are produced by such unseemly capers
As overeating; they come from stomach vapors
When a man's humors[2] aren't behaving right
From some excess. This dream you had tonight,
It comes straight from the superfluity
Of your red choler, certain as can be,
That causes people terror in their dreams
Of darts and arrows, and fire in red streams,   110
And of red beasts, for fear that they will bite,
Of little dogs, or of being in a fight;
As in the humor of melancholy lies
The reason why so many a sleeper cries
For fear of a black bull or a black bear
Or that black devils have him by the hair.
Through other humors also I could go
That visit many a sleeping man with woe,
But I will finish as quickly as I can.
     "Cato, that has been thought so wise a man,   120
Didn't he tell us, 'Put no stock in dreams'?
Now, sir," she said, "when we fly down from our beams,
For God's sake, go and take a laxative!
On my salvation, as I hope to live,

---

[2] The four substances in the body believed to determine personality types and states of
health. Dame Partlet discusses two: choler (bile) and melancholy (black bile).

I give you good advice, and no mere folly:
Purge both your choler and your melancholy!
You mustn't wait or let yourself bog down,
And since there is no druggist in this town
I shall myself prescribe for what disturbs
Your humors, and instruct you in the herbs 130
That will be good for you. For I shall find
Here in our yard herbs of the proper kind
For purging you both under and above.
Don't let this slip your mind, for God's own love!
Yours is a very choleric complexion.
When the sun is in the ascendant, my direction
Is to beware those humors that are hot.
Avoid excess of them; if you should not,
I'll bet a penny, as a true believer,
You'll die of ague, or a tertian fever. 140
A day or so, if you do as I am urging,
You shall have worm-digestives, before purging
With fumitory or with hellebore
Or other herbs that grow here by the score;
With caper-spurge, or with the goat-tree berry
Or the ground-ivy, found in our yard so merry.
Peck 'em up just as they grow, and eat 'em in!
Be cheerful, husband, by your father's kin!
Don't worry about a dream. I say no more."
    "Madame," he answered, "thanks for all your lore. 150
But still, to speak of Cato, though his name
For wisdom has enjoyed so great a fame,
And though he counseled us there was no need
To be afraid of dreams, by God, men read
Of many a man of more authority
Than this Don Cato could pretend to be
Who in old books declare the opposite,
And by experience they have settled it,
That dreams are omens and prefigurations
Both of good fortune and of tribulations 160
That life and its vicissitudes present.
This question leaves no room for argument.
The very upshot makes it plain, indeed.
    "One of the greatest authors that men read
Informs us that two fellow travelers went,
Once on a time, and with the best intent,
Upon a pilgrimage, and it fell out
They reached a town where there was such a rout
Of people, and so little lodging space,
They could not find even the smallest place 170
Where they could both put up. So, for that night,
These pilgrims had to do as best they might,
And since they must, they parted company.
Each of them went off to his hostelry

And took his lodging as his luck might fall.
Among plow oxen in a farmyard stall
One of them found a place, though it was rough.
His friend and fellow was lodged well enough
As his luck would have it, or his destiny
That governs all us creatures equally.   180
And so it happened, long before the day,
He had a dream as in his bed he lay.
He dreamed that his parted friend began to call
And said, 'Alas, for in an ox's stall
This night I shall be murdered where I lie.
Come to my aid, dear brother, or I die.
Come to me quickly, come in haste!' he said.
He started from his sleep, this man, for dread,
But when he had wakened, he rolled back once more
And on this dream of his he set no store.   190
As a vain thing he dismissed it, unconcerned.
Twice as he slept that night the dream returned,
And still another and third time his friend
Came in a dream and said, 'I have met my end!
Look on my wounds! They are bloody, deep, and wide.
Now rise up early in the morningtide
And at the west gate of the town,' said he,
'A wagon with a load of dung you'll see.
Have it arrested boldly. Do as bidden,
For underneath you'll find my body hidden.   200
My money caused my murder, truth to tell,'
And told him each detail of how he fell,
With piteous face, and with a bloodless hue.
And do not doubt it, he found the dream was true,
For on the morrow, as soon as it was day,
To the place where his friend had lodged he made his way,
And no sooner did he reach this ox's stall
Than for his fellow he began to call.
    "Promptly the stableman replied, and said,
'Your friend is gone, sir. He got out of bed   210
And left the town as soon as day began.'
    "At last suspicion overtook this man.
Remembering his dreams, he would not wait,
But quickly went and found at the west gate,
Being driven to manure a farmer's land
As it might seem, a dung cart close at hand
That answered the description every way,
As you yourself have heard the dead man say.
And he began to shout courageously
For law and vengeance on this felony.   220
'My friend was killed this very night! He lies
Flat in this load of dung, with staring eyes.
I call on those who should keep rule and head,
The magistrates and governors here,' he said.

'Alas! Here lies my fellow, done to death!'
    "Why on this tale should I waste further breath?
The people sprang and flung the cart to ground
And in the middle of the dung they found
The dead man, while his murder was still new.
    "O blessed God, thou art so just and true,   230
Murder, though secret, ever thou wilt betray!
Murder will out, we see it day by day.
Murder so loathsome and abominable
To God is, who is just and reasonable,
That he will never suffer it to be
Concealed, though it hide a year, or two, or three.
Murder will out; to this point it comes down.
    "Promptly the magistrates who ruled that town
Have seized the driver, and put him to such pain,
And the stableman as well, that under strain   240
Of torture they were both led to confess
And hanged by the neck-bone for their wickedness.
    "Here's proof enough that dreams are things to dread!
And in the same book I have also read,
In the very chapter that comes right after this—
I don't speak idly, by my hopes of bliss—
Two travelers who for some reason planned
To cross the ocean to a distant land
Found that the wind, by an opposing fate,
Blew contrary, and forced them both to wait   250
In a fair city by a harborside.
But one day the wind changed, toward eventide,
And blew just as it suited them instead.
Cheerfully these travelers went to bed
And planned to sail the first thing in the morning.
But to one of them befell a strange forewarning
And a great marvel. While asleep he lay,
He dreamed a curious dream along toward day.
He dreamed that a man appeared at his bedside
And told him not to sail, but wait and bide.   260
'Tomorrow,' he told the man, 'if you set sail,
You shall be drowned. I have told you my whole tale.'
He woke, and of this warning he had met
He told his friend, and begged him to forget
His voyage, and to wait that day and bide.
His friend, who was lying close at his bedside,
Began to laugh, and told him in derision,
'I am not so flabbergasted by a vision
As to put off my business for such cause.
I do not think your dream is worth two straws!   270
For dreams are but a vain absurdity.
Of apes and owls and many a mystery
People are always dreaming, in a maze
Of things that never were seen in all their days

And never shall be. But I see it's clear
You mean to waste your time by waiting here.
I'm sorry for that, God knows; and so good day.'
With this he took his leave and went his way.
But not the half his course had this man sailed—
I don't know why, nor what it was that failed—   280
When by an accident the hull was rent
And ship and man under the water went
In full view of the vessels alongside
That had put out with them on the same tide.
Now then, fair Partlet, whom I love so well,
From old examples such as these I tell
You may see that none should give too little heed
To dreams; for I say seriously, indeed,
That many a dream is too well worth our dread.
    "Yes, in St. Kenelm's life I have also read—   290
He was the son of Cynewulf, the king
Of Mercia—how this Kenelm dreamed a thing.
One day, as the time when he was killed drew near,
He saw his murder in a dream appear.
His nurse explained his dream in each detail,
And warned him to be wary without fail
Of treason; yet he was but seven years old,
And therefore any dream he could but hold
Of little weight, in heart he was so pure.
I'd give my shirt, by God, you may be sure,   300
If you had read his story through like me!
    "Moreover, Partlet, I tell you truthfully,
Macrobius[3] writes—and by his book we know
The African vision of great Scipio—
Confirming dreams, and holds that they may be
Forewarnings of events that men shall see.
Again, I beg, look well at what is meant
By the Book of Daniel in the Old Testament,
Whether *he* held that dreams are vanity!
Read also about Joseph. You shall see   310
That dreams, or some of them—I don't say all—
Warn us of things that afterward befall.
Think of the king of Egypt, Don Pharaoh;
Of his butler and his baker think also,
Whether they found that dreams have no result.[4]
Whoever will search through kingdoms and consult
Their histories reads many a wondrous thing
Of dreams. What about Croesus, Lydian king—
Didn't he dream he was sitting on a tree,
Which meant he would be hanged? Andromache,   320

[3] A fifth-century author of a commentary on Cicero's *Dream of Scipio.*
[4] See Genesis, chapters 40–41. Joseph, imprisoned in Egypt, won his freedom by interpreting accurately the dreams of Pharaoh's butler and baker and later Pharaoh's own dreams.

The woman who was once great Hector's wife,
On the day that Hector was to lose his life,
The very night before his blood was spilled
She dreamed of how her husband would be killed
If he went out to battle on that day.
She warned him; but he would not heed nor stay.
In spite of her he rode out on the plain,
And by Achilles he was promptly slain.
But all that story is too long to tell,
And it is nearly day. I must not dwell   330
Upon this matter. Briefly, in conclusion,
I say this dream will bring me to confusion
And mischief of some sort. And furthermore,
On laxatives, I say, I set no store,
For they are poisonous, I'm sure of it.
I do not trust them! I like them not one bit!
    "Now let's talk cheerfully, and forget all this.
My pretty Partlet, by my hope of bliss,
In one thing God has sent me ample grace
For when I see the beauty of your face,   340
You are so scarlet-red about the eye,
It is enough to make my terrors die.
For just as true as *In principio*
Mulier est hominis confusio—[5]
And Madame, what this Latin means is this:
'Woman is man's whole comfort and true bliss'—
When I feel you soft at night, and I beside you,
Although it's true, alas, I cannot ride you
Because our perch is built so narrowly,
I am then so full of pure felicity   350
That I defy whatever sort of dream!"
    And day being come, he flew down from the beam,
And with him his hens fluttered, one and all;
And with a "cluck, cluck" he began to call
His wives to where a kernel had been tossed.
He was a prince, his fears entirely lost.
The morning had not passed the hour of prime
When he treaded Partlet for the twentieth time.
Grim as a lion he strolled to and fro,
And strutted only on his either toe.   360
He would not deign to set foot on the ground.
"Cluck, cluck," he said, whenever he had found
A kernel, and his wives came running all.
Thus royal as a monarch in his hall
I leave to his delights this Chanticleer,
And presently the sequel you shall hear.
    After the month in which the world began,[6]

[5] Literally, "In the beginning, woman is the ruin of man."
[6] According to tradition, the creation occurred at the beginning of spring.

The month of March, when God created man,
Had passed, and when the season had run through
Since March began just thirty days and two,   370
It happened that Chanticleer, in all his pride,
While his seven hens were walking by his side,
Lifted his eyes, beholding the bright sun,
Which in the sign of Taurus had then run
Twenty and one degrees and somewhat more,
And knew by instinct, not by learned lore,
It was the hour of prime. He raised his head
And crowed with lordly voice. "The sun," he said,
"Forty and one degrees and more in height
Has climbed the sky. Partlet, my world's delight,   380
Hear all these birds, how happily they sing,
And see the pretty flowers, how they spring.
With solace and with joy my spirits dance!"
But suddenly he met a sore mischance,
For in the end joys ever turn to woes.
Quickly the joys of earth are gone, God knows,
And could a rhetorician's art indite it,
He would be on solid ground if he should write it,
In a chronicle, as true notoriously!
Now every wise man, listen well to me.   390
This story is as true, I undertake,
As the very book of Lancelot of the Lake
On which the women set so great a store.
Now to my matter I will turn once more.
     A sly iniquitous fox, with black-tipped ears,
Who had lived in the neighboring wood for some three years,
His fated fancy swollen to a height,
Had broken through the hedges that same night
Into the yard where in his pride sublime
Chanticleer with his seven wives passed the time.   400
Quietly in a bed of herbs he lay
Till it was past the middle of the day,
Waiting his hour on Chanticleer to fall
As gladly do these murderers, one and all,
Who lie in wait, concealed, to murder men.
O murderer, lurking traitorous in your den!
O new Iscariot, second Ganelon,
False hypocrite, Greek Sinon,[7] who brought on
The utter woe of Troy and all her sorrow!
O Chanticleer, accursed be that morrow   410
When to the yard you flew down from the beams!
That day, as you were well warned in your dreams,
Would threaten you with dire catastrophe.

---

[7] Judas Iscariot betrayed Jesus; Ganelon is the traitor in *The Song of Roland;* Sinon, by
means of the Trojan horse, betrayed the Trojans to the besieging Greeks (see Virgil's *Aeneid,*
Book II).

But that which God foresees must come to be,
As there are certain scholars who aver.
Bear witness, any true philosopher,
That in the schools there has been great altercation
Upon this question, and much disputation
By a hundred thousand scholars, man for man.
I cannot sift it down to the pure bran   420
As can the sacred Doctor, Augustine,
Or Boëthius, or Bishop Bradwardine,[8]
Whether God's high foreknowledge so enchains me
I needs must do a thing as it constrains me—
"Needs must"—that is, by plain necessity;
Or whether a free choice is granted me
To do it or not do it, either one,
Though God must know all things before they are done;
Or whether his foresight nowise can constrain
Except contingently, as some explain;   430
I will not labor such a high concern.
My tale is of a cock, as you shall learn,
Who took his wife's advice, to his own sorrow,
And walked out in the yard that fatal morrow.
Women have many times, as wise men hold,
Offered advice that left men in the cold.
A woman's counsel brought us first to woe
And out of Paradise made Adam go
Where he lived a merry life and one of ease.
But since I don't know whom I may displease   440
By giving women's words an ill report,
Pass over it; I only spoke in sport.
There are books about it you can read or skim in,
And you'll discover what they say of women.
I'm telling you the cock's words, and not mine.
Harm in no woman at all can I divine.
  Merrily bathing where the sand was dry
Lay Partlet, with her sisters all near by,
And Chanticleer, as regal as could be,
Sang merrily as the mermaid in the sea;   450
For the *Physiologus*[9] itself declares
That they know how to sing the merriest airs.
And so it happened that as he fixed his eye
Among the herbs upon a butterfly,
He caught sight of this fox who crouched there low.
He felt no impulse then to strut or crow,
But cried "cucock!" and gave a fearful start

---

[8] All three had discussed the notoriously difficult matter of reconciling God's foreknowledge with man's free will. Augustine (353–430), author of the *Confessions,* was one of the greatest Christian theologians; Boëthius (about 475–524) was a Roman who wrote *The Consolation of Philosophy,* one of the most influential works in the Middle Ages; Bradwardine was a theologian of Chaucer's own century.
[9] A book about animals, including legendary ones.

Like a man who has been frightened to the heart.
For instinctively, if he should chance to see
His opposite, a beast desires to flee,   460
Even the first time that it meets his eye.
   This Chanticleer, no sooner did he spy
The fox than promptly enough he would have fled.
But "Where are you going, kind sir?" the fox said.
"Are you afraid of me, who am your friend?
Truly, I'd be a devil from end to end
If I meant you any harm or villainy.
I have not come to invade your privacy.
In truth, the only reason that could bring
This visit of mine was just to hear you sing.   470
Beyond a doubt, you have as fine a voice
As any angel who makes heaven rejoice.
Also you have more feeling in your note
Than Boëthius,[10] or any tuneful throat.
Milord your father once—and may God bless
His soul—your noble mother too, no less,
Have been inside my house, to my great ease.
And verily, sir, I should be glad to please
You also. But for singing, I declare,
As I enjoy my eyes, that precious pair,   480
Save you, I never heard a man so sing
As your father did when night was on the wing.
Straight from the heart, in truth, came all his song,
And to make his voice more resonant and strong
He would strain until he shut his either eye,
So loud and lordly would he make his cry,
And stand up on his tiptoes therewithal
And stretch his neck till it grew long and small.
He had such excellent discretion, too,
That whether his singing, all the region through,   490
Or his wisdom, there was no one to surpass.
I read in that old book, *Don Burnel the Ass,*[11]
Among his verses once about a cock
Hit on the leg by a priest who threw a rock
When he was young and foolish; and for this
He caused the priest to lose his benefice.
But no comparison, in all truth, lies
Between your father, so prudent and so wise,
And this other cock, for all his subtlety.
Sing, sir! Show me, for holy charity,   500
Can you imitate your father, that wise man?"
   Blind to all treachery, Chanticleer began
To beat his wings, like one who cannot see

---

[10] Boëthius, along with his other works, wrote a treatise on music.
[11] A twelfth-century poem by Nigel Wireker. The cock took his revenge by crowing late, thus causing the priest to oversleep on the day when he was to have been ordained.

The traitor, ravished by his flattery.
   Alas, you lords, about your court there slips
Many a flatterer with deceiving lips
Who can please you more abundantly, I fear,
Than he who speaks the plain truth to your ear.
Read in Ecclesiastes,[12] you will see
What flatterers are. Lords, heed their treachery!   510
   This Chanticleer stood tiptoe at full height.
He stretched his neck, he shut his eyelids tight,
And he began to crow a lordly note.
The fox, Don Russell, seized him by the throat
At once, and on his back bore Chanticleer
Off toward his den that in the grove stood near,
For no one yet had threatened to pursue.
   O destiny, that no man may eschew!
Alas, that he left his safe perch on the beams!
Alas, that Partlet took no stock in dreams!   520
And on a Friday happened this mischance!
   Venus, whose pleasures make the whole world dance,
Since Chanticleer was ever your true servant,
And of your rites will all his power observant
For pleasure rather than to multiply,
Would you on Friday[13] suffer him to die?
   Geoffrey,[14] dear master of the poet's art,
Who when your Richard perished by a dart
Made for your king an elegy so burning,
Why have I not your eloquence and learning   530
To chide, as you did, with a heart so filled,
Fridays? For on a Friday he was killed.
Then should I show you how I could complain
For Chanticleer in all his fright and pain!
   In truth, no lamentation ever rose,
No shriek of ladies when before its foes
Ilium fell, and Pyrrhus with drawn blade
Had seized King Priam by the beard and made
An end of him—the *Aeneid* tells the tale—[15]
Such as the hens made with their piteous wail   540
In their enclosure, seeing the dread sight
Of Chanticleer. But at the shrillest height
Shrieked Partlet. She shrieked louder than the wife
Of Hasdrubal, when her husband lost his life

---

[12] The intended reference is apparently not to Ecclesiastes but to Ecclesiasticus (a book of the Roman Catholic Bible), 12:10ff, 27:26.

[13] Friday is Venus's day. (Compare the French for *Friday, vendredi*.)

[14] Geoffrey of Vinsauf, a twelfth-century author of a book on poetry. It includes as an example a poem, written in an elaborate style, about the death of King Richard the Lion-Hearted (Richard I).

[15] See Book II of Virgil's *Aeneid*. When the Greeks took Troy (Ilium), Pyrrhus, the son of Achilles, killed Priam, the Trojan king. The Nun's Priest goes on to compare the hens' lament over Chanticleer to the wailing when the Romans destroyed Carthage (second century B.C.) and when the emperor Nero supposedly burned Rome (A.D. 64).

And the Romans burned down Carthage; for her state
Of torment and of frenzy was so great
She willfully chose the fire for her part,
Leaped in, and burned herself with steadfast heart.

    Unhappy hens, you shrieked as when for pity,
While the tyrant Nero put to flames the city   550
Of Rome, rang out the shriek of senators' wives
Because their husbands had all lost their lives;
This Nero put to death these innocent men.
But I will come back to my tale again.

    Now this good widow and her two daughters heard
These woeful hens shriek when the crime occurred,
And sprang outdoors as quickly as they could
And saw the fox, who was making for the wood
Bearing this Chanticleer across his back.
"Help, help!" they cried. They cried, "Alas! Alack!   560
The fox, the fox!" and after him they ran,
And armed with clubs came running many a man.
Ran Coll the dog, and led a yelping band;
Ran Malkyn, with a distaff[16] in her hand;
Ran cow and calf, and even the very hogs,
By the yelping and the barking of the dogs
And men's and women's shouts so terrified
They ran till it seemed their hearts would burst inside;
They squealed like fiends in the pit, with none to still them.
The ducks quacked as if men were going to kill them.   570
The geese for very fear flew over the trees.
Out of the beehive came the swarm of bees.
Ah! Bless my soul, the noise, by all that's true,
So hideous was that Jack Straw's[17] retinue
Made never a hubbub that was half so shrill
Over a Fleming they were going to kill
As the clamor made that day over the fox.
They brought brass trumpets, and trumpets made of box,
Of horn, of bone, on which they blew and squeaked,
And those who were not blowing whooped and shrieked.   580
It seemed as if the very heavens would fall!

    Now hear me, you good people, one and all!
Fortune, I say, will suddenly override
Her enemy in his very hope and pride!
This cock, as on the fox's back he lay,
Plucked up his courage to speak to him and say,
"God be my help, sir, but I'd tell them all,
That is, if I were you, 'Plague on you fall!
Go back, proud fools! Now that I've reached the wood,
I'll eat the cock at once, for all the good   590
Your noise can do. Here Chanticleer shall stay.'"

---

[16] A long staff; part of a spinning wheel.
[17] In 1381, Jack Straw led into London a mob intent on killing foreigners.

"Fine!" said the fox. "I'll do just what you say."
But the cock, as he was speaking, suddenly
Out of his jaws lurched expeditiously,
And flew at once high up into a tree.
And when the fox saw that the cock was free,
"Alas," he said, "alas, O Chanticleer!
Inasmuch as I have given you cause for fear
By seizing you and bearing you away,
I have done you wrong, I am prepared to say.   600
But, sir, I did it with no ill intent.
Come down, and I shall tell you what I meant.
So help me God, it's truth I'll offer you!"
    "No, no," said he. "We're both fools, through and through.
But curse my blood and bones for the chief dunce
If you deceive me oftener than once!
You shall never again by flattery persuade me
To sing and wink my eyes, by him that made me.
For he that willfully winks when he should see,
God never bless him with prosperity!"   610
    "Ah," said the fox, "with mischief may God greet
The man ungoverned, rash, and indiscreet
Who babbles when to hold his tongue were needful!"
    Such is it to be reckless and unheedful
And trust in flattery. But you who hold
That this is a mere trifle I have told,
Concerning only a fox, or a cock and hen,
Think twice, and take the moral, my good men!
For truly, of whatever is written, all
Is written for our doctrine, says St. Paul.   620
Then take the fruit, and let the chaff lie still.
Now, gracious God, if it should be your will,
As my Lord teaches, make us all good men
And bring us to your holy bliss! Amen.

Everyman
(Late Fifteenth Century)

Everyman *was written in England by an anonymous clerical playwright in about*
1475. There is a similar Dutch play of the same period named Elckerlyc.
Everyman *may be a translation of the Dutch play, or both may be derived independ-*
ently from a Latin work named Homulus. *Current scholarly opinion tends to con-*
clude, however, that the English play is the original. Nothing is known of the author,
and although the play was apparently produced with some frequency in the seventy-
five years following its composition, no production records survive.

Everyman *is the best example of the medieval "morality play," characterized by an allegorical plot that deals with some archetypal action in man's spiritual life and by characters who personify abstract ideas, such as Fellowship, Wealth, or Knowledge. Morality plays were only one genre in a rich body of drama that flourished in Europe from the tenth to the sixteenth century, fascinating both in its own right and as background to the flowering of an even richer and more varied drama in the Renaissance.*

By the time of the fall of Rome, classical drama had already declined to the level of crude entertainment, and the collapse of the Roman Empire ended dramatic performance altogether for more than five centuries. When drama began to re-emerge in the tenth century, it was again from religious roots. As classical drama had begun in the worship of Dionysus, so medieval drama was born in the Christian liturgy. The earliest bits of medieval drama were tropes, *brief exchanges of dialogue introduced into the chanted liturgy. These tropes were gradually elaborated until by the twelfth century practically all the narrative portions of the Bible had been dramatized in short, often crude, but vivid plays presented in the churches at Christmas and Easter. By the fourteenth century, these liturgical plays had attracted such large and unruly audiences that they were removed from the churches and presented in village streets, usually on Corpus Christi Day, in late May or early June. Production of the plays was taken over by the craft and trade guilds, although the clergy continued to play an active role, especially in writing the plays. By the end of the fourteenth century, every town of any size in England had its own cycle of religious plays. Some idea of the numbers of plays involved is suggested by the four cycles that survive: the York cycle of forty-eight plays, the Wakefield cycle of thirty-two plays, the Chester cycle of twenty-five plays, and the Coventry cycle of forty-two plays. The subject matter was quite varied, ranging from authentic Biblical material to various folk accretions upon that material to saints' lives. (Scholars used to discriminate between mystery plays, based on the Bible, and miracle plays dealing with the lives of saints, but the distinction is so blurry in practice that they are now generally grouped together as liturgical plays.)*

The morality play was the last of the medieval dramatic genres to emerge, in the middle of the fourteenth century, although there were many precedents for such didactic, allegorical works in nondramatic literature. The recurring subjects of morality plays are suggested by the titles of some of those that preceded Everyman: The Pride of Life, The Castle of Perseverance, *and* The Debate of the Body and the Soul.

Medieval plays were produced in several different ways. When they were still performed inside churches, they were staged on platforms distributed around the church, with a different platform, or mansion, *for each locale. When they moved outside the churches, they were performed on large, two-decker pageant wagons. A curtained-off lower level was used as a dressing room, and a platform on the second level, reached by a ladder, was used as a stage. Sometimes the action spilled off the wagon-stage and into an open area in front of the wagon, the* platea. *These pageant wagons moved from one stopping place in the town to another on performance days, the actors performing their play at each stop. A spectator could station himself in one place and see the successive plays in the cycle performed in sequence.*

By the time Everyman *was performed, however, a somewhat different production method had been adopted for the longer morality plays. These were performed not as part of a cycle by members of a guild but independently by troupes of traveling players performing in town squares and on village greens. The original setting for*

Everyman *was probably a stationary version of pageant-wagon staging: a two-story scaffold stage with an open space in front of it and probably two smaller sets, one on each side of the scaffold, for Goods and Good Deeds. This simple theater presented an elementary model of the medieval world view. God undoubtedly appeared on the "Heaven" of the top level, Death entered from the "Hell" of the covered lower level, and Everyman's main action was played on the "Earth" of the* platea. *In other respects as well, the theater and the conventions of staging allowed every element of the play to be translated into concrete, dramatic terms. The idea that earthly possessions weigh one down in the quest for salvation is vividly and amusingly presented by the immobilized Goods, unable to stir because of the chests and bags full of gold lying upon and around him. Similarly, the "scourge of penance" that Knowledge gives Everyman is no metaphor, but an actual whip.*

The hasty reader of Everyman *may dismiss it as crude and obvious, interesting only historically. It is true that the message of the play is presented with a crude directness and that its rhymed doggerel is naive, sometimes monotonous. But upon a closer reading, and especially after seeing a good performance, one's respect for the skill and artistry of the nameless playwright is likely to increase. The play presents a generalized, archetypal action, a sort of x-ray of human experience, but this generalizing tendency is everywhere in tension with a robust and earthy specificity. Everyman is not only all men, but a very particular man, economically but tellingly characterized. He is a fundamentally good-hearted but superficial sensualist who, at the existential moment when he must confront the reality of his impending death, undergoes a radical and convincing psychological transformation. The secondary characters are handled with a similar economical skill and frequently with a mordant, ironic comic touch. Fellowship, Kindred and Cousin, Goods, and the rest are not mere walking abstractions but vivid embodiments of the qualities they represent. Fellowship, for example, within his short scene, is presented as hail-fellow-well-met, blustery, effusive, and full of reminiscences of drinking bouts, but quick to take his leave when he discovers that something more serious than a party is about to occur. The action, too, is poised on a delicate line between the general and the particular. The plot is often described as an archetypal journey through life, but it is actually not quite so general; it suggests the whole of life through focusing sharply upon its end. The story becomes not only a parable of all men's lives but a moving and personal study in one man's experience. Even the jogtrot language, at first distracting, comes to have a crude, direct power that is very moving.*

Paradoxically, Everyman, *which seems so quintessentially of its age, has had a long and prominent history on the modern stage and has exercised a considerable influence upon modern drama. William Poel restaged the play in London in 1901 in the medieval manner; the revival attracted much favorable attention and was repeated a number of times during the following fifteen years. The great German director Max Reinhardt was inspired by Poel's production to present his own version, adapted by the poet and playwright Hugo von Hofmannsthal. Reinhardt's* Jedermann (*German for* Everyman) *was first performed in 1911 in an elaborate production in an old Berlin circus building. In 1920, Reinhardt restaged his version of the play in front of the Salzburg Cathedral as part of the Salzburg Festival. The play was enormously successful and has been repeated every year since then to enormous festival crowds, except for a nine-year dark period between 1937 and 1946, when Hitler banned it as "Jewish." The Dutch version of the play has a similar annual production at the Holland Festival in the city of Delft.*

Everyman, *along with other pre-realistic plays, has had a strong influence upon the development of the post-realistic modern drama, especially as a model for dramatizing inner, psychological action. Its influence is especially clear in two modern plays that also deal with approaching death: Eugene Ionesco's* Exit the King *and Samuel Beckett's* Endgame.

FURTHER READING *(prepared by W.J.R.):* A thorough background study of miracle, mystery, and morality plays is Hardin Craig's *English Religious Drama of the Middle Ages,* 1955. In A. P. Rossiter's *English Drama From Early Times to the Elizabethans,* 1950, morality plays are divided into two classes, those that view a man's life from cradle to grave and those that deal with a more specific situation. *The Castle of Perseverance* and *Everyman,* respectively, are discussed as representatives of these two classes, along with several other specimens. Glynne Wickham's *Shakespeare's Dramatic Heritage,* 1969, discusses the 1964 London production of *Everyman,* in which Everyman drifted onto stage wearing jeans and listening to music from *Bye-bye Birdie.* Wickham discusses the persistence of the play's appeal and its ability to survive when transposed to a new setting. The first chapter of W. Roy MacKenzie's *The English Moralities From the Point of View of Allegory,* 1966, discusses the nature of the morality play, specifically considering *Everyman* as its best representative. Two complementary essays on the play's structure, a somewhat neglected topic, are Lawrence V. Ryan's "Doctrine and Dramatic Structure in *Everyman,*" *Speculum,* 32 (1957), 722–35, and Thomas F. Van Laan's "*Everyman:* A Structural Analysis," PMLA, 78 (1963), 465–75. Ryan discusses the relationship between structure and doctrinal content, arguing that the play's moral lessons are a natural outgrowth of the action.

EVERYMAN

MESSENGER	KNOWLEDGE
GOD: *Adonai*[1]	CONFESSION
DEATH	BEAUTY
EVERYMAN	STRENGTH
FELLOWSHIP	DISCRETION
COUSIN	FIVE WITS
KINDRED	ANGEL
GOODS	DOCTOR
GOOD DEEDS	

Here beginneth a treatise how the High Father of Heaven sendeth Death to summon every creature to come and give account of their lives in this world, and is in manner of a moral play.

MESSENGER. I pray you all give your audience,
    And hear this matter with reverence,
    By figure[2] a moral play—
    The *Summoning of Everyman* called it is,
    That of our lives and ending shows
    How transitory we be all our day.
    This matter is wondrous precious,

                                                   5

[1] Hebrew name for God.   [2] In form.

But the intent of it is more gracious,[3]
And sweet to bear away.
The story saith:—Man, in the beginning,   10
Look well, and take good heed to the ending,
Be you never so gay!
Ye think sin in the beginning full sweet,
Which in the end causeth the soul to weep,
When the body lieth in clay.   15
Here shall you see how Fellowship and Jollity,
Both Strength, Pleasure, and Beauty,
Will fade from thee as flower in May.
For ye shall hear how our Heaven King
Calleth Everyman to a general reckoning.   20
Give audience, and hear what he doth say.   [*Exit.*]

[GOD *speaketh from above.*]

GOD. I perceive, here in my majesty,
How that all creatures be to me unkind,
Living without dread in worldly prosperity.
Of ghostly sight[4] the people be so blind,   25
Drowned in sin, they know me not for their God.
In worldly riches is all their mind,
They fear not my rightwiseness,[5] the sharp rod;
My love that I showed when I for them died
They forget clean, and shedding of my blood red;   30
I hanged between two, it cannot be denied;
To get them life I suffered to be dead;
I healed their feet, with thorns hurt was my head.
I could do no more than I did, truly;
And now I see the people do clean forsake me.   35
They use the seven deadly sins damnable;
As pride, covetise, wrath, and lechery,
Now in the world be made commendable;
And thus they leave of angels the heavenly company.
Every man liveth so after his own pleasure,   40
And yet of their life they be nothing sure.
I see the more that I them forbear
The worse they be from year to year;
All that liveth appaireth[6] fast.
Therefore I will, in all the haste,   45
Have a reckoning of every man's person;
For, and[7] I leave the people thus alone
In their life and wicked tempests,
Verily they will become much worse than beasts;
For now one would by envy another up eat;   50
Charity they all do clean forget.
I hoped well that every man

---

[3] Having to do with God's grace.   [4] Spiritual insight.   [5] Righteousness.
[6] Degenerates.   [7] If (frequently throughout the play).

In my glory should make his mansion,
And thereto I had them all elect;
But now I see, like traitors deject,[8]   55
They thank me not for the pleasure that I to them meant,
Nor yet for their being that I them have lent.
I proffered the people great multitude of mercy,
And few there be that asketh it heartily;
They be so cumbered with worldly riches,   60
That needs on them I must do justice,
On every man living, without fear.
Where art thou, Death, thou mighty messenger?

[Enter DEATH.]

DEATH. Almighty God, I am here at your will,
    Your commandment to fulfil.   65
GOD. Go thou to Everyman,
    And show him, in my name,
    A pilgrimage he must on him take,
    Which he in no wise[9] may escape;
    And that he bring with him a sure reckoning   70
    Without delay or any tarrying.
DEATH. Lord, I will in the world go run over all,
    And cruelly out search both great and small. [GOD *withdraws.*]
    Every man will I beset that liveth beastly
    Out of God's laws, and dreadeth not folly.   75
    He that loveth riches I will strike with my dart,
    His sight to blind, and from heaven to depart,
    Except that alms be his good friend,
    In hell for to dwell, world without end.
    Lo, yonder I see Everyman walking;   80
    Full little he thinketh on my coming;
    His mind is on fleshly lusts and his treasure;
    And great pain it shall cause him to endure
    Before the Lord, Heaven King.
    Everyman, stand still! Whither art thou going   85
    Thus gaily? Hast thou thy Maker forgot?
EVERYMAN. Why askest thou?
    Wouldst thou wete?[10]
DEATH. Yea, sir, I will show you;
    In great haste I am sent to thee   90
    From God out of his Majesty.
EVERYMAN. What, sent to me?
DEATH. Yea, certainly.
    Though thou have forgot him here,
    He thinketh on thee in the heavenly sphere,   95
    As, ere we depart, thou shalt know.
EVERYMAN. What desireth God of me?
DEATH. That shall I show thee;

---

[8] Abject.   [9] In no way (frequently throughout the play).   [10] Know.

A reckoning he will needs have
Without any longer respite. 100
EVERYMAN. To give a reckoning longer leisure I crave;
This blind matter troubleth my wit.
DEATH. On thee thou must take a long journey;
Therefore thy book of count[11] with thee thou bring;
For turn again thou can not by no way. 105
And look thou be sure of thy reckoning,
For before God thou shalt answer and show
Thy many bad deeds, and good but a few,
How thou hast spent thy life, and in what wise,
Before the Chief Lord of paradise. 110
Have ado[12] that we were in that way,
For, wete thou well, thou shalt make none attorney.[13]
EVERYMAN. Full unready I am such reckoning to give.
I know thee not. What messenger art thou?
DEATH. I am Death, that no man dreadeth. 115
For every man I 'rest, and no man spareth;
For it is God's commandment
That all to me should be obedient.
EVERYMAN. O Death! thou comest when I had thee least in mind!
In thy power it lieth me to save, 120
Yet of my goods will I give thee, if thou will be kind;
Yea, a thousand pound shalt thou have,
If thou defer this matter till another day.
DEATH. Everyman, it may not be, by no way!
I set not by gold, silver, nor riches, 125
Nor by pope, emperor, king, duke, nor princes.
For, and I would receive gifts great,
All the world I might get;
But my custom is clean contrary.
I give thee no respite. Come hence, and not tarry. 130
EVERYMAN. Alas! shall I have no longer respite?
I may say Death giveth no warning.
To think on thee, it maketh my heart sick,
For all unready is my book of reckoning.
But twelve year and I might have abiding, 135
My counting-book I would make so clear,
That my reckoning I should not need to fear.
Wherefore, Death, I pray thee, for God's mercy,
Spare me till I be provided of remedy.
DEATH. Thee availeth not to cry, weep, and pray; 140
But haste thee lightly that thou were gone that journey,
And prove thy friends if thou can.
For wete thou well the tide abideth no man;
And in the world each living creature
For Adam's sin must die of nature. 145
EVERYMAN. Death, if I should this pilgrimage take,

---

[11] Accounts.   [12] Get ready.   [13] You cannot make anyone your representative.

And my reckoning surely make,
Show me, for saint charity,
Should I not come again shortly?
DEATH. No, Everyman; and thou be once there,   150
Thou mayst never more come here,
Trust me verily.
EVERYMAN. O gracious God, in the high seat celestial,
Have mercy on me in this most need!
Shall I have no company from this vale terrestrial   155
Of mine acquaintance that way me to lead?
DEATH. Yea, if any be so hardy,
That would go with thee and bear thee company.
Hie thee that thou were gone[14] to God's magnificence,
Thy reckoning to give before his presence.   160
What! weenest[15] thou thy life is given thee,
And thy worldly goods also?
EVERYMAN. I had weened so, verily.
DEATH. Nay, nay; it was but lent thee;
For, as soon as thou art gone,   165
Another a while shall have it, and then go therefrom
Even as thou hast done.
Everyman, thou art mad! Thou hast thy wits[16] five,
And here on earth will not amend thy life;
For suddenly I do come.   170
EVERYMAN. O wretched caitiff![17] whither shall I flee,
That I might 'scape endless sorrow?
Now, gentle Death, spare me till tomorrow,
That I may amend me
With good advisement.   175
DEATH. Nay, thereto I will not consent,
Nor no man will I respite,
But to the heart suddenly I shall smite
Without any advisement.
And now out of thy sight I will me hie;   180
See thou make thee ready shortly,
For thou mayst say this is the day
That no man living may 'scape away.   [*Exit* DEATH.]
EVERYMAN. Alas! I may well weep with sighs deep.
Now have I no manner of company   185
To help me in my journey and me to keep;
And also my writing is full unready.
How shall I do now for to excuse me?
I would to God I had never been gete![18]
To my soul a full great profit it had be;   190
For now I fear pains huge and great.
The time passeth; Lord, help, that all wrought.
For though I mourn it availeth naught.
The day passeth, and is almost a-go;[19]

---

[14] Hasten to be gone.   [15] Thinkest.   [16] Senses.   [17] Knave.   [18] Born.   [19] Gone.

I wot[20] not well what for to do. 195
To whom were I best my complaint to make?
What if I to Fellowship thereof spake,
And showed him of this sudden chance?
For in him is all mine affiance,[21]
We have in the world so many a day 200
Been good friends in sport and play.
I see him yonder, certainly;
I trust that he will bear me company;
Therefore to him will I speak to ease my sorrow.
Well met, good Fellowship, and good morrow! 205

[FELLOWSHIP *speaketh*.]

FELLOWSHIP. Everyman, good morrow, by this day!
    Sir, why lookest thou so piteously?
    If any thing be amiss, I pray thee me say,
    That I may help to remedy.
EVERYMAN. Yea, good Fellowship, yea, 210
    I am in great jeopardy.
FELLOWSHIP. My true friend, show to me your mind;
    I will not forsake thee to my life's end
    In the way of good company.
EVERYMAN. That was well spoken, and lovingly. 215
FELLOWSHIP. Sir, I must needs know your heaviness;
    I have pity to see you in any distress;
    If any have you wronged, ye shall revenged be,
    Though I on the ground be slain for thee,
    Though that I know before that I should die. 220
EVERYMAN. Verily, Fellowship, gramercy.[22]
FELLOWSHIP. Tush! by thy thanks I set not a straw!
    Show me your grief, and say no more.
EVERYMAN. If I my heart should to you break,
    And then you to turn your mind from me, 225
    And would not me comfort when you hear me speak,
    Then should I ten times sorrier be.
FELLOWSHIP. Sir, I say as I will do, indeed.
EVERYMAN. Then be you a good friend at need;
    I have found you true here before. 230
FELLOWSHIP. And so ye shall evermore;
    For, in faith, and thou go to hell,
    I will not forsake thee by the way!
EVERYMAN. Ye speak like a good friend. I believe you well;
    I shall deserve it, and I may. 235
FELLOWSHIP. I speak of no deserving, by this day!
    For he that will say and nothing do
    Is not worthy with good company to go;
    Therefore show me the grief of your mind,
    As to your friend most loving and kind. 240

---

[20] Know.   [21] Trust.   [22] Thank you.

EVERYMAN. I shall show you how it is:
    Commanded I am to go a journey,
    A long way, hard and dangerous,
    And give a strict count without delay
    Before the high judge, Adonai.   245
    Wherefore, I pray you, bear me company,
    As ye have promised, in this journey.
FELLOWSHIP. That is matter indeed! Promise is duty;
    But, and I should take such a voyage on me,
    I know it well, it should be to my pain.   250
    Also it maketh me afeared, certain.
    But let us take counsel here as well as we can,
    For your words would fright a strong man.
EVERYMAN. Why, ye said if I had need,
    Ye would me never forsake, quick nor dead,   255
    Though it were to hell, truly.
FELLOWSHIP. So I said, certainly,
    But such pleasures be set aside, the sooth[23] to say.
    And also, if we took such a journey,
    When should we come again?   260
EVERYMAN. Nay, never again till the day of doom.
FELLOWSHIP. In faith, then will not I come there!
    Who hath you these tidings brought?
EVERYMAN. Indeed, Death was with me here.
FELLOWSHIP. Now, by God that all hath bought,   265
    If Death were the messenger,
    For no man that is living today
    I will not go that loath journey—
    Nor for the father that begat me!
EVERYMAN. Ye promised otherwise, pardie.[24]   270
FELLOWSHIP. I wot well I said so, truly;
    And yet if thou wilt eat, and drink, and make good cheer,
    Or haunt to women the lusty company,
    I would not forsake you while the day is clear,
    Trust me verily!   275
EVERYMAN. Yea, thereto ye would be ready;
    To go to mirth, solace, and play,
    Your mind will sooner apply
    Than to bear me company in my long journey.
FELLOWSHIP. Now, in good faith, I will not that way.   280
    But and thou wilt murder, or any man kill,
    In that I will help thee with a good will!
EVERYMAN. O, that is a simple advice indeed!
    Gentle fellow, help me in my necessity;
    We have loved long, and now I need,   285
    And now, gentle Fellowship, remember me!
FELLOWSHIP. Whether ye have loved me or no,
    By Saint John, I will not with thee go.

[23] Truth.   [24] *Par dieu:* indeed. (Literally, "by God.")

EVERYMAN. Yet, I pray thee, take the labor, and do so much for me
    To bring me forward, for saint charity,   290
    And comfort me till I come without the town.
FELLOWSHIP. Nay, and thou would give me a new gown,
    I will not a foot with thee go;
    But, and thou had tarried, I would not have left thee so.
    And as now God speed thee in thy journey,   295
    For from thee I will depart as fast as I may.
EVERYMAN. Whither away, Fellowship? Will you forsake me?
FELLOWSHIP. Yea, by my fay,[25] to God I betake[26] thee.
EVERYMAN. Farewell, good Fellowship! For thee my heart is sore;
    Adieu for ever! I shall see thee no more.   300
FELLOWSHIP. In faith, Everyman, farewell now at the end!
    For you I will remember that parting is mourning.

                    [*Exit* FELLOWSHIP.]

EVERYMAN. Alack! shall we thus depart indeed
    (Ah, Lady, help!) without any more comfort?
    Lo, Fellowship forsaketh me in my most need.   305
    For help in this world whither shall I resort?
    Fellowship here before with me would merry make,
    And now little sorrow for me doth he take.
    It is said, "In prosperity men friends may find,
    Which in adversity be full unkind."   310
    Now whither for succor shall I flee,
    Sith that[27] Fellowship hath forsaken me?
    To my kinsmen I will, truly,
    Praying them to help me in my necessity;
    I believe that they will do so,   315
    For "kind will creep where it may not go."[28]
    I will go say,[29] for yonder I see them go.
    Where be ye now, my friends and kinsmen?

             [*Enter* KINDRED *and* COUSIN.]

KINDRED. Here be we now, at your commandment.
    Cousin, I pray you show us your intent   320
    In any wise, and do not spare.
COUSIN. Yea, Everyman, and to us declare
    If ye be disposed to go any whither,
    For, wete you well, we will live and die together.
KINDRED. In wealth and woe we will with you hold,   325
    For over his kin a man may be bold.
EVERYMAN. Gramercy, my friends and kinsmen kind.
    Now shall I show you the grief of my mind.
    I was commanded by a messenger
    That is a high king's chief officer;   330
    He bade me go a pilgrimage, to my pain,
    And I know well I shall never come again;

[25] Faith.   [26] Commit.   [27] Since.   [28] Walk.   [29] Try.

Also I must give a reckoning straight,
For I have a great enemy that hath me in wait,[30]
Which intendeth me for to hinder.   335
KINDRED. What account is that which ye must render?
  That would I know.
EVERYMAN. Of all my works I must show
  How I have lived, and my days spent;
  Also of ill deeds that I have used   340
  In my time, sith life was me lent;
  And of all virtues that I have refused.
  Therefore I pray you go thither with me,
  To help to make mine account, for saint charity.
COUSIN. What, to go thither? Is that the matter?   345
  Nay, Everyman, I had liefer fast bread and water
  All this five year and more.
EVERYMAN. Alas, that ever I was bore!
  For now shall I never be merry
  If that you forsake me.   350
KINDRED. Ah, sir, what! Ye be a merry man!
  Take good heart to you, and make no moan.
  But one thing I warn you, by Saint Anne,
  As for me, ye shall go alone.
EVERYMAN. My Cousin, will you not with me go?   355
COUSIN. No, by our Lady! I have the cramp in my toe.
  Trust not to me; for, so God me speed,
  I will deceive you in your most need.
KINDRED. It availeth not us to tice.[31]
  Ye shall have my maid with all my heart;   360
  She loveth to go to feasts, there to be nice,[32]
  And to dance, and abroad to start;
  I will give her leave to help you in that journey,
  If that you and she may agree.
EVERYMAN. Now show me the very effect of your mind.   365
  Will you go with me, or abide behind?
KINDRED. Abide behind? Yea, that will I, and I may!
  Therefore farewell till another day.   [*Exit* KINDRED.]
EVERYMAN. How should I be merry or glad?
  For fair promises men to me make,   370
  But when I have most need, they me forsake.
  I am deceived; that maketh me sad.
COUSIN. Cousin Everyman, farewell now,
  For verily I will not go with you;
  Also of mine own life an unready reckoning   375
  I have to account; therefore I make tarrying.
  Now, God keep thee, for now I go.   [*Exit* COUSIN.]
EVERYMAN. Ah, Jesus! is all come hereto?
  Lo, fair words maketh fools fain;[33]
  They promise and nothing will do certain.   380

---

[30]Lies in wait for me.   [31]Entice.   [32]Wanton.   [33]Glad.

My kinsmen promised me faithfully
For to abide with me steadfastly,
And now fast away do they flee.
Even so Fellowship promised me.
What friend were best me of to provide?   385
I lose my time here longer to abide.
Yet in my mind a thing there is:
All my life I have loved riches;
If that my Goods now help me might,
He would make my heart full light.   390
I will speak to him in this distress.
Where art thou, my Goods and riches?
GOODS [*from within*]. Who calleth me? Everyman? What, hast thou
    haste?
I lie here in corners, trussed and piled so high,
And in chests I am locked so fast,   395
Also sacked in bags—thou mayst see with thine eye—
I cannot stir; in packs low I lie.
What would ye have? Lightly me say.
EVERYMAN. Come hither, Goods, in all the haste thou may.
For of counsel I must desire thee.   400

[*Enter* GOODS.]

GOODS. Sir, and ye in the world have sorrow or adversity,
That can I help you to remedy shortly.
EVERYMAN. It is another disease that grieveth me;
In this world it is not, I tell thee so.
I am sent for another way to go,   405
To give a strict count general
Before the highest Jupiter of all;
And all my life I have had joy and pleasure in thee;
Therefore I pray thee go with me,
For, peradventure,[34] thou mayst before God Almighty   410
My reckoning help to clean and purify;
For it is said ever among,
That "money maketh all right that is wrong."
GOODS. Nay, Everyman; I sing another song,
I follow no man in such voyages;   415
For, and I went with thee,
Thou shouldst fare much the worse for me;
For because on me thou did set thy mind,
Thy reckoning I have made blotted and blind,
That thine account thou cannot make truly;   420
And that hast thou for the love of me.
EVERYMAN. That would grieve me full sore,
When I should come to that fearful answer.
Up, let us go thither together.
GOODS. Nay, not so! I am too brittle, I may not endure;   425

[34] Perhaps.

I will follow no man one foot, be ye sure.
EVERYMAN. Alas! I have thee loved, and had great pleasure
  All my life-days on goods and treasure.
GOODS. That is to thy damnation, without lesing![35]
  For my love is contrary to the love everlasting.   430
  But if thou had me loved moderately during,
  As to the poor to give part of me,
  Then shouldst thou not in this dolor be,
  Nor in this great sorrow and care.
EVERYMAN. Lo, now was I deceived ere I was ware,   435
  And all I may wyte[36] my spending of time.
GOODS. What, weenest thou that I am thine?
EVERYMAN. I had weened so.
GOODS. Nay, Everyman, I say no;
  As for a while I was lent thee,   440
  A season thou hast had me in prosperity.
  My condition is man's soul to kill;
  If I save one, a thousand I do spill;[37]
  Weenest thou that I will follow thee
  From this world? Nay, verily.   445
EVERYMAN. I had weened otherwise.
GOODS. Therefore to thy soul Goods is a thief;
  For when thou art dead, this is my guise—[38]
  Another to deceive in the same wise
  As I have done thee, and all to his soul's reprief.[39]   450
EVERYMAN. O false Goods, curséd thou be!
  Thou traitor to God, that hast deceived me
  And caught me in thy snare.
GOODS. Marry! thou brought thyself in care,
  Whereof I am right glad.   455
  I must needs laugh, I cannot be sad.
EVERYMAN. Ah, Goods, thou hast had long my heartly love;
  I gave thee that which should be the Lord's above.
  But wilt thou not go with me indeed?
  I pray thee truth to say.   460
GOODS. No, so God me speed!
  Therefore farewell, and have good day.   [*Exit* GOODS.]
EVERYMAN. O, to whom shall I make my moan
  For to go with me in that heavy journey?
  First Fellowship said he would with me gone;   465
  His words were very pleasant and gay,
  But afterward he left me alone.
  Then spake I to my kinsmen, all in despair,
  And also they gave me words fair,
  They lacked no fair speaking,   470
  But all forsook me in the ending.
  Then went I to my Goods, that I loved best,
  In hope to have comfort, but there had I least;

---

[35] Lying.   [36] Blame upon.   [37] Ruin.   [38] Practice: trick.   [39] Reproof.

For my Goods sharply did me tell
That he bringeth many into hell.   475
Then of myself I was ashamed,
And so I am worthy to be blamed;
Thus may I well myself hate.
Of whom shall I now counsel take?
I think that I shall never speed   480
Till that I go to my Good Deeds.
But alas! she is so weak
That she can neither go nor speak.
Yet will I venture on her now.
My Good Deeds, where be you?   485

              [GOOD DEEDS *speaks from the ground.*]

GOOD DEEDS. Here I lie, cold in the ground.
  Thy sins hath me sore bound,
  That I cannot stir.
EVERYMAN. O Good Deeds! I stand in fear;
  I must you pray of counsel,   490
  For help now should come right well.
GOOD DEEDS. Everyman, I have understanding
  That ye be summoned account to make
  Before Messias, of Jerusalem King;
  And you do by me,[40] that journey with you will I take.   495
EVERYMAN. Therefore I come to you my moan to make;
  I pray you that ye will go with me.
GOOD DEEDS. I would full fain, but I cannot stand, verily.
EVERYMAN. Why, is there anything on you fall?
GOOD DEEDS. Yea, sir, I may thank you of all;   500
  If ye had perfectly cheered[41] me,
  Your book of count full ready had be.
  Look, the books of your works and deeds eke;[42]
  Ah, see how they lie under the feet,
  To your soul's heaviness.   505
EVERYMAN. Our Lord Jesus help me!
  For one letter here I can not see.
GOOD DEEDS. There is a blind reckoning in time of distress!
EVERYMAN. Good Deeds, I pray you, help me in this need,
  Or else I am for ever damned indeed;   510
  Therefore help me to make my reckoning
  Before the Redeemer of all thing,
  That King is, and was, and ever shall.
GOOD DEEDS. Everyman, I am sorry of your fall,
  And fain would I help you, and I were able.   515
EVERYMAN. Good Deeds, you counsel I pray you give me.
GOOD DEEDS. That shall I do verily;
  Though that on my feet I may not go,

[40] If you take my advice.   [41] Cherished.   [42] Also.

I have a sister that shall with you also,
Called Knowledge, which shall with you abide,   520
To help you to make that dreadful reckoning.

[*Enter* KNOWLEDGE.]

KNOWLEDGE. Everyman, I will go with thee, and be thy guide
  In thy most need to go by thy side.
EVERYMAN. In good condition I am now in every thing,
  And am wholly content with this good thing;   525
  Thanked be God my Creator.
GOOD DEEDS. And when he hath brought thee there,
  Where thou shalt heal thee of thy smart,
  Then go you with your reckoning and your Good Deeds together
  For to make you joyful at heart   530
  Before the blesséd Trinity.
EVERYMAN. My Good Deeds, gramercy!
  I am well content, certainly,
  With your words sweet.
KNOWLEDGE. Now go we together lovingly   535
  To Confession, that cleansing river.
EVERYMAN. For joy I weep; I would we were there!
  But, I pray you, give my cognition
  Where dwelleth that holy man, Confession.
KNOWLEDGE. In the house of salvation;   540
  We shall find him in that place,
  That shall us comfort, by God's grace.

[KNOWLEDGE *leads* EVERYMAN *to*
CONFESSION.]

Lo, this is Confession. Kneel down and ask mercy,
For he is in good conceit[43] with God almighty.
EVERYMAN [*kneeling*]. O glorious fountain, that all uncleanness doth
    clarify,   545
  Wash from me the spots of vice unclean,
  That on me no sin may be seen.
  I come, with Knowledge, for my redemption,
  Redempt with hearty and full contrition;
  For I am commanded a pilgrimage to take,   550
  And great accounts before God to make.
  Now, I pray you, Shrift,[44] mother of salvation.
  Help my Good Deeds for my piteous exclamation.
CONFESSION. I know your sorrow well, Everyman.
  Because with Knowledge ye come to me,   555
  I will you comfort as well as I can,
  And a precious jewel I will give thee,
  Called penance, voider of adversity;
  Therewith shall your body chastised be,

---

[43] Esteem.   [44] The sacrament of confession.

With abstinence, and perseverance in God's service.   560
Here shall you receive that scourge of me.

[*Gives* EVERYMAN *a scourge.*]

Which is penance strong, that ye must endure
To remember thy Savior was scourged for thee
With sharp scourges, and suffered it patiently;
So must thou ere thou 'scape that painful pilgrimage.   565
Knowledge, keep him in this voyage,
And by that time Good Deeds will be with thee.
But in any wise be seeker of mercy,
For your time draweth fast, and ye will saved be;
Ask God mercy, and He will grant truly;   570
When with the scourge of penance man doth him bind,
The oil of forgiveness then shall he find.   [*Exit* CONFESSION.]
EVERYMAN. Thanked be God for his gracious work!
For now I will my penance begin;
This hath rejoiced and lighted my heart,   575
Though the knots be painful and hard within.
KNOWLEDGE. Everyman, look your penance that ye fulfil,
What pain that ever it to you be,
And Knowledge shall give you counsel at will
How your account ye shall make clearly.   580

[EVERYMAN *kneels.*]

EVERYMAN. O eternal God! O heavenly figure!
O way of rightwiseness! O goodly vision!
Which descended down in a virgin pure
Because he would Everyman redeem,
Which Adam forfeited by his disobedience.   585
O blesséd Godhead! elect and high divine,
Forgive me my grievous offence;
Here I cry thee mercy in this presence.
O ghostly treasure! O ransomer and redeemer!
Of all the world hope and conductor,   590
Mirror of joy, and founder of mercy,
Which illumineth heaven and earth thereby,
Hear my clamorous complaint, though it late be.
Receive my prayers; unworthy in this heavy life.
Though I be a sinner most abominable,   595
Yet let my name be written in Moses' table.
O Mary! pray to the Maker of all thing,
Me for to help at my ending,
And save me from the power of my enemy,
For Death assaileth me strongly.   600
And, Lady, that I may by means of thy prayer
Of your Son's glory to be partner,
By the means of his passion I it crave;
I beseech you, help my soul to save.   [*He rises.*]

Knowledge, give me the scourge of penance.   605
My flesh therewith shall give a quittance.
I will now begin, if God give me grace.
KNOWLEDGE. Everyman, God give you time and space.
Thus I bequeath you in the hands of our Savior,
Now may you make your reckoning sure.   610
EVERYMAN. In the name of the Holy Trinity,
My body sore punished shall be.   [*Scourges himself.*]
Take this, body, for the sin of the flesh;
Also thou delightest to go gay and fresh,
And in the way of damnation thou did me bring;   615
Therefore suffer now strokes of punishing.
Now of penance I will wade the water clear,
To save me from purgatory, that sharp fire.

                              [GOOD DEEDS *rises from floor.*]

GOOD DEEDS. I thank God, now I can walk and go,
And am delivered of my sickness and woe.   620
Therefore with Everyman I will go, and not spare;
His good works I will help him to declare.
KNOWLEDGE. Now, Everyman, be merry and glad!
Your Good Deeds cometh now, ye may not be sad;
Now is your Good Deeds whole and sound,   625
Going upright upon the ground.
EVERYMAN. My heart is light, and shall be evermore.
Now will I smite faster than I did before.
GOOD DEEDS. Everyman, pilgrim, my special friend,
Blesséd be thou without end.   630
For thee is prepared the eternal glory.
Ye have me made whole and sound,
Therefore I will bide by thee in every stound.[45]
EVERYMAN. Welcome, my Good Deeds; now I hear thy voice,
I weep for very sweetness of love.   635
KNOWLEDGE. Be no more sad, but ever rejoice;
God seeth thy living in his throne above.
Put on this garment to thy behoof,
Which is wet with your tears,
Or else before God you may it miss,   640
When you to your journey's end come shall.
EVERYMAN. Gentle Knowledge, what do ye it call?
KNOWLEDGE. It is the garment of sorrow;
From pain it will you borrow;
Contrition it is   645
That getteth forgiveness;
It pleaseth God passing well.
GOOD DEEDS. Everyman, will you wear it for your heal?

                              [EVERYMAN *puts on garment of
                              contrition.*]

---

[45] In every situation; always.

EVERYMAN. Now bléssed be Jesu, Mary's Son,
    For now have I on true contrition.   650
    And let us go now without tarrying;
    Good Deeds, have we clear our reckoning?
GOOD DEEDS. Yea, indeed I have it here.
EVERYMAN. Then I trust we need not fear.
    Now, friends, let us not part in twain.   655
KNOWLEDGE. Nay, Everyman, that will we not, certain.
GOOD DEEDS. Yet must thou lead with thee
    Three persons of great might.
EVERYMAN. Who should they be?
GOOD DEEDS. Discretion and Strength they hight,[46]   660
    And thy Beauty may not abide behind.
KNOWLEDGE. Also ye must call to mind
    Your Five Wits as for your counselors.
GOOD DEEDS. You must have them ready at all hours.
EVERYMAN. How shall I get them hither?   665
KNOWLEDGE. You must call them all together,
    And they will hear you incontinent.[47]
EVERYMAN. My friends, come hither and be present;
    Discretion, Strength, my Five Wits, and Beauty.

               [*Enter* DISCRETION, STRENGTH,
               FIVE WITS, *and* BEAUTY.]

BEAUTY. Here at your will we be all ready.   670
    What will ye that we should do?
GOOD DEEDS. That ye would with Everyman go,
    And help him in his pilgrimage.
    Advise you, will ye with him or not in that voyage?
STRENGTH. We will bring him all thither,   675
    To his help and comfort, ye may believe me.
DISCRETION. So will we go with him all together.
EVERYMAN. Almighty God, lovéd may thou be!
    I give thee laud that I have hither brought
    Strength, Discretion, Beauty, and Five Wits. Lack I naught;   680
    And my Good Deeds, with Knowledge clear,
    All be in company at my will here.
    I desire no more to my business.
STRENGTH. And I, Strength, will by you stand in distress,
    Though thou would in battle fight on the ground.   685
FIVE WITS. And though it were through the world round,
    We will not depart for sweet nor sour.
BEAUTY. No more will I, unto death's hour,
    Whatsoever thereof befall.
DISCRETION. Everyman, advise you first of all;   690
    Go with a good advisement and deliberation.
    We all give you virtuous monition
    That all shall be well.

[46] Are called.   [47] At once.

EVERYMAN. My friends, hearken what I will tell:
 I pray God reward you in his heavenly sphere.   695
 Now hearken, all that be here,
 For I will make my testament
 Here before you all present:
 In alms half my goods I will give with my hands twain
 In the way of charity, with good intent,   700
 And the other half still shall remain;
 I it bequeath to be returned there it ought to be.
 This I do in despite of the fiend of hell,
 To go quite out of his peril
 Ever after and this day.   705
KNOWLEDGE. Everyman, hearken what I say;
 Go to Priesthood, I you advise,
 And receive of him in any wise
 The holy sacrament and ointment together;
 Then shortly see ye turn again hither;   710
 We will all abide you here.
FIVE WITS. Yea, Everyman, hie you that ye ready were.
 There is no emperor, king, duke, nor baron,
 That of God hath commission
 As hath the least priest in the world being;   715
 For of the blessèd sacraments pure and benign
 He beareth the keys, and thereof hath the cure
 For man's redemption—it is ever sure—
 Which God for our soul's medicine
 Gave us out of his heart with great pain,   720
 Here in this transitory life, for thee and me.
 The blessèd sacraments seven there be:
 Baptism, confirmation, with priesthood good,
 And the sacrament of God's precious flesh and blood,
 Marriage, the holy extreme unction, and penance.   725
 These seven be good to have in remembrance,
 Gracious sacraments of high divinity.
EVERYMAN. Fain would I receive that holy body
 And meekly to my ghostly[48] father I will go.
FIVE WITS. Everyman, that is the best that ye can do.   730
 God will you to salvation bring,
 For priesthood exceedeth all other thing;
 To us Holy Scripture they do teach,
 And converteth man from sin, heaven to reach;
 God hath to them more power given,   735
 Than to any angel that is in heaven.
 With five words[49] he may consecrate
 God's body in flesh and blood to make,
 And handleth his Maker between his hands.
 The priest bindeth and unbindeth all bands,   740
 Both in earth and in heaven;

---

[48] Spiritual. [49] The five words are *Hoc est enim corpus meum:* "For this is my body."

Thou ministers all the sacraments seven;
Though we kissed thy feet, thou wert worthy;
Thou art the surgeon that cureth sin deadly:
No remedy we find under God   745
But all only priesthood.
Everyman, God gave priests that dignity,
And setteth them in his stead among us to be;
Thus be they above angels, in degree.

[*Exit* EVERYMAN.]

KNOWLEDGE. If priests be good, it is so, surely.   750
But when Jesus hanged on the cross with great smart,
There he gave out of his blesséd heart
The same sacrament in great torment.
He sold them not to us, that Lord omnipotent.
Therefore Saint Peter the Apostle doth say   755
That Jesus' curse hath all they
Which God their Savior do buy or sell,
Or they for any money do take or tell.
Sinful priests giveth the sinners example bad;
Their children sitteth by other men's fires, I have heard;   760
And some haunteth women's company
With unclean life, as lusts of lechery.
These be with sin made blind.
FIVE WITS. I trust to God no such may we find.
Therefore let us priesthood honor,   765
And follow their doctrine for our souls' succor.
We be their sheep, and they shepherds be
By whom we all be kept in surety.
Peace! for yonder I see Everyman come,
Which hath made true satisfaction.   770
GOOD DEEDS. Methinketh it is he indeed.

[*Re-enter* EVERYMAN.]

EVERYMAN. Now Jesu be your alder speed.[50]
I have received the sacrament for my redemption,
And then mine extreme unction.
Blesséd be all they that counseled me to take it!   775
And now, friends, let us go without longer respite.
I thank God that ye have tarried so long.
Now set each of you on this rod[51] your hand,
And shortly follow me.
I go before, there I would be. God be our guide.   780
STRENGTH. Everyman, we will not from you go,
Till ye have done this voyage long.
DISCRETION. I, Discretion, will bide by you also.
KNOWLEDGE. And though this pilgrimage be never so strong,
I will never part you fro.   785

---

[50] Jesus be the succor of all of you.   [51] Cross.

Everyman, I will be as sure by thee
As ever I did by Judas Maccabee.[52]

[*They go together to the grave.*]

EVERYMAN. Alas! I am so faint I may not stand,
My limbs under me do fold.
Friends, let us not turn again to this land,   790
Not for all the world's gold;
For into this cave must I creep
And turn to earth, and there to sleep.
BEAUTY. What, into this grave? Alas!
EVERYMAN. Yea, there shall you consume, more and less.   795
BEAUTY. And what, should I smother here?
EVERYMAN. Yea, by my faith, and never more appear.
In this world live no more we shall,
But in heaven before the highest Lord of all.
BEAUTY. I cross out all this; adieu, by Saint John!   800
I take my cap in my lap and am gone.
EVERYMAN. What, Beauty, whither will ye?
BEAUTY. Peace! I am deaf. I look not behind me,
Not and thou would give me all the gold in thy chest. [*Exit* BEAUTY.]
EVERYMAN. Alas, whereto may I trust?   805
Beauty goeth fast away from me;
She promised with me to live and die.
STRENGTH. Everyman, I will thee also forsake and deny.
Thy game liketh me not at all.[53]
EVERYMAN. Why, then ye will forsake me all?   810
Sweet Strength, tarry a little space.
STRENGTH. Nay, sir, by the rood[54] of grace,
I will hie me from thee fast,
Though thou weep till thy heart to-brast.[55]
EVERYMAN. Ye would ever bide by me, ye said.   815
STRENGTH. Yea, I have you far enough conveyed.
Ye be old enough, I understand,
Your pilgrimage to take on hand.
I repent me that I hither came.
EVERYMAN. Strength, you to displease I am to blame;   820
Yet promise is debt, this ye well wot.
STRENGTH. In faith, I care not!
Thou are but a fool to complain.
You spend your speech and waste your brain;
Go, thrust thee into the ground.   [*Exit* STRENGTH.]   825
EVERYMAN. I had weened surer I should you have found.
He that trusteth in his Strength
She him deceiveth at the length.
Both Strength and Beauty forsaketh me,
Yet they promised me fair and lovingly.   830

---

[52] Jewish patriot, second century B.C.   [53] I do not like this game at all.   [54] Cross.
[55] Break into pieces.

DISCRETION. Everyman, I will after Strength be gone;
   As for me I will leave you alone.
EVERYMAN. Why, Discretion, will ye forsake me?
DISCRETION. Yea, in faith, I will go from thee;
   For when Strength goeth before   835
   I follow after evermore.
EVERYMAN. Yet, I pray thee, for the love of the Trinity,
   Look in my grave once piteously.
DISCRETION. Nay, so nigh will I not come.
   Farewell, every one!   [*Exit* DISCRETION.] 840
EVERYMAN. O all thing faileth, save God alone—
   Beauty, Strength, and Discretion;
   For when Death bloweth his blast,
   They all run from me full fast.
FIVE WITS. Everyman, my leave now of thee I take;   845
   I will follow the other, for here I thee forsake.
EVERYTHING. Alas! then may I wail and weep,
   For I took you for my best friend.
FIVE WITS. I will no longer thee keep;
   Now farewell, and there an end.   [*Exit* FIVE WITS.] 850
EVERYMAN. O Jesu, help! All hath forsaken me!
GOOD DEEDS. Nay, Everyman; I will bide with thee,
   I will not forsake thee indeed;
   Thou shalt find me a good friend at need.
EVERYMAN. Gramercy, Good Deeds! Now may I true friends see. 855
   They have forsaken me, every one;
   I loved them better than my Good Deeds alone.
   Knowledge, will ye forsake me also?
KNOWLEDGE. Yea, Everyman, when ye to death shall go;
   But not yet, for no manner of danger.   860
EVERYMAN. Gramercy, Knowledge, with all my heart.
KNOWLEDGE. Nay, yet I will not from hence depart
   Till I see where ye shall be come.
EVERYMAN. Methink, alas, that I must be gone
   To make my reckoning and my debts pay,   865
   For I see my time is nigh spent away.
   Take example, all ye that this do hear or see,
   How they that I loved best do forsake me,
   Except my Good Deeds that bideth truly.
GOOD DEEDS. All earthly things is but vanity.   870
   Beauty, Strength, and Discretion do man forsake,
   Foolish friends and kinsmen, that fair spake,
   All fleeth save Good Deeds, and that am I.
EVERYMAN. Have mercy on me, God most mighty;
   And stand by me, thou Mother and Maid, holy Mary! 875
GOOD DEEDS. Fear not, I will speak for thee.
EVERYMAN. Here I cry God mercy!
GOOD DEEDS. Short our end, and 'minish our pain.
   Let us go and never come again.
EVERYMAN. Into thy hands, Lord, my soul I commend.   880

Receive it, Lord, that it be not lost.
As thou me boughtest, so me defend,
And save me from the fiend's boast,
That I may appear with that blesséd host
That shall be saved at the day of doom.   885
In manus tuas—of might's most
For ever—*commendo spiritum meum.*[56]

> [EVERYMAN *and* GOOD DEEDS *descend into the grave.*]

KNOWLEDGE. Now hath he suffered that we all shall endure;
The Good Deeds shall make all sure.
Now hath he made ending.   890
Methinketh that I hear angels sing
And make great joy and melody
Where Everyman's soul received shall be.
ANGEL [*within*]. Come, excellent elect spouse to Jesu!
Here above thou shalt go   895
Because of thy singular virtue.
Now the soul is taken the body fro,
Thy reckoning is crystal clear.
Now shalt thou into the heavenly sphere,
Unto the which all ye shall come   900
That liveth well before the day of doom.

> [*Exit* KNOWLEDGE. *Enter* DOCTOR[57] *for Epilogue.*]

DOCTOR. This moral men may have in mind:
Ye hearers, take it of worth, old and young,
And forsake Pride, for he deceiveth you in the end,
And remember Beauty, Five Wits, Strength, and Discretion,   905
They all at the last do Everyman forsake,
Save his Good Deeds there doth he take.
But beware, and they be small
Before God he hath no help at all.
None excuse may be there for Everyman.   910
Alas, how shall he do then?
For, after death, amends may no man make,
For then mercy and pity doth him forsake.
If his reckoning be not clear when he doth come,
God will say, "*Ite, maledicti, in ignem aeternum.*"[58]   915
And he that hath his account whole and sound,
High in heaven he shall be crowned.
Unto which place God bring us all thither,
That we may live body and soul together.
Thereto help the Trinity!   920
Amen, say ye, for saint charity.

THUS ENDETH THIS MORAL PLAY OF EVERYMAN.

[56]"Into thy hands I commend my spirit."   [57]Theologian.
[58]"Go, cursed ones, into eternal fire."

The Renaissance

THE word *Renaissance* means *rebirth*. The term purports to describe a movement in European intellectual, cultural, and political history that first flourished in Italy, mainly from the mid-fourteenth to the sixteenth centuries, and then in other parts of Europe during an overlapping but generally later period that ended in the mid-seventeenth century. The origin of the Renaissance, both the concept and the term, is of considerable interest in exploring the question, much debated in the twentieth century, whether there was any genuine rebirth in the Renaissance and whether the movement so labelled really had a distinctive existence.

To many people in the vanguard of Renaissance literature, art, and thought, the age did in fact seem new. The first major spokesman for this view was Petrarch (1304–1374), who believed that the thousand years separating his age from the fall of ancient Roman civilization had been a dark night and that the first priority of his contemporaries should be to restore ancient literature, for its own sake and in the interests of human virtue. His followers, the humanists of Italy and later of northern Europe, extended Petrarch's primarily literary emphasis to include important new directions in the fine arts, religious studies, philosophy, mathematics, and political theory. When the new heliocentric astronomy was developed (or rediscovered) by Copernicus (1473–1543), the new Protestant movement was launched in 1517 by Luther (1483–1546), and maritime exploration in the fifteenth and sixteenth centuries revealed the existence of the western hemisphere, the age necessarily became aware that changes of awesome momentousness, for better or worse, were in process. But for the most part the consciousness by the age of its own novelty remained limited and was primarily a matter of high culture. The term *rebirth* was popularized during the Renaissance by the eminent art historian Giorgio Vasari in his *Lives of the Most Eminent Italian Painters, Sculptors, and Architects* (1550), in which Vasari acclaimed the new artists for having revived classical esthetic values and recovered the faculty to see and depict nature.

The modern, much broader, concept of a Renaissance is largely the creation not of the age itself but of retrospect. To eighteenth-century Enlightenment thinkers the Renaissance was the age when medieval "superstition," especially revealed religion, was overthrown. But it was not until the nineteenth century that there emerged the model of the Renaissance familiar today, along with its mystique. The landmarks of this new model were Jules Michelet's volume on the Renaissance in his *History of France* (1855) and Jacob Burckhardt's *The Civilization of the Renaissance in Italy* (1860), in combination with the work of Burckhardt's followers who broadened his model of the early Italian Renaissance to include later periods, other parts of Europe, and fields such as economic life that Burckhardt had not treated in depth. For these scholars and their intellectual heirs the Renaissance was not only or even primarily a revival of learning and the arts but a period with its own organic coherence, a sudden and radical break with the Middle Ages, and the point of departure for the modern world. In Michelet's phrase, it marked "the discovery of the world and of man." Above all, the Renaissance was an age of individual personalities, liberated from the political constraints of Holy Roman Emperor and pope, free to understand and express themselves for good or evil. The state, for Burckhardt, had become a "work of art," the product of events working through human personalities rather than something imposed by an external sanction such as tradition or the will of God. The age had a pagan vitality.

This view of the Renaissance has the obvious appeal of glamour, and it survives, as not only the popular model but also that of scholars, even when they feel they must reject or modify it as many of them have done. Medievalists especially have bridled. They insist that many of the supposedly new departures in the Renaissance—the revival of classical learning, the emergence of an urban culture that fostered the arts and a capitalist economy, exploration of distant lands, the development of the rationalist scientific mentality, the growth of a lay rather than clerical culture, and the rise of national states—were actually continuations of trends that began centuries before Petrarch. It is also highly questionable, according to champions of the Middle Ages, that the most typical Renaissance trends were advances for humankind. For the most skeptical among them, the Renaissance was not a rebirth but the twilight of the great medieval era.

The conviction remains that the concept of a Renaissance (whether that is the right word or not) is useful and represents something real. But it can no longer be argued easily that the discontinuity with the Middle Ages was radical or that a single spirit dominated all of southern and western Europe for three centuries or that the Renaissance is simply an early stage of modernism. The tendency in Renaissance studies today is to examine different places and stages of it closely, discriminating and qualifying conscientiously in accord with concrete evidence rather than broad formulas, however exhilarating. In this brief essay there is not enough space to record all the qualifications and exceptions that the complexity of the Renaissance age and culture calls for. Almost all the generalizations that follow are challengeable. Even so, they may be helpful, especially because many of them originate in the Renaissance view of itself. Moreover, they provide an index to the history of sensibility. In the last century or so readers have developed the habit, when reading Renaissance literature, of isolating and responding selectively to those qualities in it that have the expansiveness of spirit which, accurately or not, has been understood as distinctively Renaissance.

We can begin with humanism, an aspect of the Renaissance that touches on virtually all the others. In a broad sense, the term *humanism* can be defined as any view of the world that places humankind at the center of things. It is as old as Greek antiquity but also quite modern, numbering among its adherents a wide variety of groups ranging from Marxists to existentialists (religious, atheistic, and agnostic) to educators who insist on the primacy of the liberal arts and humanities. In a more restricted though still rather elastic sense, humanism refers to a distinctive habit of thought that pervades Renaissance art and philosophy. Beginning roughly in the latter fourteenth century, with such men as Petrarch, it spread over the following centuries throughout Europe; in the north it reached its zenith of creative expression in the first decades of the sixteenth century in the great Dutch scholar, theologian, and satirist Desiderius Erasmus (1466?–1536) and in his English colleague Thomas More (1478–1535), the author of *Utopia*.

The humanists tended to think of themselves as a new breed, and they do represent at least a striking shift in emphasis. They accorded man a high degree of autonomy, an extreme form of which was expressed by the Italian humanist Pico della Mirandola (1463–1494) in his *Oration on the Dignity of Man*. In a famous passage from that work God addresses man: "I have given you, Adam, neither a predetermined place nor a particular aspect nor any special prerogatives in order that you may take and possess these through your own decision and choice. The limitations on the nature of other creatures are contained within my prescribed laws. You shall determine your own nature without constraint from any barrier, by means of the freedom to whose power I have entrusted you. . . . I have made you neither heavenly nor earthly, neither mortal nor immortal so that, like a free and sovereign artificer, you might mold and fashion yourself into that form you yourself shall have chosen." Asceticism was no longer necessarily the hallmark of sanctity, and pleasure became more respectable, whether celebrated riotously as in Rabelais or in the more spiritualized form it usually took for the northern humanists. (It must be stated, however, that the stereotype of Italian humanists as pagan rather than Christian is a misleading caricature.) The world and the life of the body were to be accepted and rejoiced in, regarded not as signs that man is alienated from his higher self but as avenues that, in parallel with the soul, humanity can use for its fulfillment. In "The Godly Feast," one of Erasmus's *Colloquies*, the host Eusebius urges his dinner guests: "But while we feast our minds plenteously, let us not neglect their partners." Asked who these partners are, he replies, "Our bodies; aren't they partners of our minds? For I prefer 'partners' to 'instruments' or 'dwellings' or 'tombs .'" The honorific status given in the Middle Ages to clerical authority and to the ideal of celibacy was considerably modified.

The vehicle for realizing the humanists' ideals was to be reason—more concretely, education of the most comprehensive kind: physical, moral, literary, philosophical. The ancient classics became major and indispensable tools of this education; without them the truly good life could not be envisioned in its wholeness. The humanists were therefore earnestly committed to the recovery and editing of ancient texts (which were not so much discovered as unearthed from churches and monasteries). The texts included both the secular and (especially for the northern humanists) the religious; Erasmus, most notably, did a landmark Greek edition of the New Testament. Moreover, this philological scholarship was not regarded as fastidious purism or as intellectual escapism; quite the contrary, for the humanists had as prime goals both the perfection of individual human character and the reform of public evils, in church and state. (More's *Utopia* is a clear case in point.) They were activist social scientists. In their educational systems, they wished to substitute for the medieval concern with elaborate formal logic an ideal of practical and moral wisdom instilled through a curriculum dominated by poetry, history, moral philosophy, and—in lieu of medieval theology—the Bible itself. Although they were in one way elitists, aiming to train a special educated cadre of reforming leaders, they were also egalitarian to the extent that they prized feudal nobility of birth less than a moral and intellectual nobility, the signs of which were rhetorical eloquence, refined diction, and urbane wit, all these combined with rectitude of conduct.

Humanist thought, elusive and ambiguous though it sometimes seems, was fundamentally concerned with wholeness, of the human personality and of world view. The clearest example is in their religious thought. Most of them were firm believers in Christianity (such occasional puzzles as Rabelais and Montaigne notwithstanding), which they did not regard as a system in rivalry with pagan antiquity. Nor did they regard antiquity as a mere allegorizing of Christian revelation (as often in Dante); the achievement of a genuinely historical point of view, by which the events and ideas of classical times could be understood as they really were in themselves, was another of their prime goals, akin to their passion for rejecting spurious literary texts and traditions. Rather, they saw Christianity and paganism as organic parts of total truth. In "The Godly Feast," Eusebius says, "whatever is devout and contributes to good morals should not be called profane. Sacred Scripture is of course the basic authority in everything; yet I sometimes run across ancient sayings or pagan writings—even the poets'—so purely and reverently and admirably expressed that I can't help believing their authors' hearts were moved by some divine power. And perhaps the spirit of Christ is more widespread than we understand, and the company of saints includes many not in our calendar. Speaking frankly among friends, I can't read [certain of Cicero's works] without sometimes kissing the book and blessing that pure heart, divinely inspired as it was. . . . So that I would much rather let all of Scotus [the medieval philosopher] and others of his sort perish than the books of a single Cicero or Plutarch." Some of the humanists went so far as to envisage a primal religious revelation of which all the world's creeds are reflections.

The complexity of the Renaissance age is well illustrated in the ambiguous relationship between humanism and the religious currents of the time, especially the Protestant Reformation, customarily dated from Luther's definitive rebellion against the Catholic Church in 1517. The papacy had been in dire trouble in the fourteenth and fifteenth centuries, sorely tried by its "Babylonian captivity" when the seat of the papacy was moved to Avignon in France, then weakened by a period of schism when there were rival popes, and after that by a period when a council laid claim to ecclesiastical authority. In the meantime, skeptical and heretical movements that had grown out of the late Middle Ages were flourishing, and powerful movements stressing mystical experience and simple piety were spreading rapidly among both clergy and laity. The last half of the fifteenth century and the first two decades of the sixteenth, immediately before Luther's revolt, saw a reinvigorated papacy at its height of cultural glory: the re-

1572

nowned Vatican Library was created, and Popes Julius II and Leo X, reigning from 1503 to 1521, patronized the work of great artists including Michelangelo and Raphael. But many of the popes of the time were concerned more with political and personal aggrandizement than with the spiritual welfare of the European church. Out of this background the Reformation emerged, claiming to reassert the values of authentic early Christianity, drawing for theological support on epistles by St. Paul and the writings of early church fathers like Augustine (and of course on the Gospels as the Reformers understood them), preaching that man was saved not by his own efforts ("works") but by faith. The Protestant opposition to indulgences (remissions of punishment in Purgatory) was therefore not merely a moral rebellion against the venal selling of them by Rome but a theological stance that rejected the whole idea of Purgatory, with its implication that man can satisfy divine justice in his own person rather than exclusively in Christ.

The Reformation is in different ways an expression of humanist ideals and a contradiction of them. The Protestant attempt to recover the ancient text and meaning of the Bible and to spread them widely, free of medieval theological overlays, is akin to and indeed part of the humanist movement, which conservative Catholic churchmen distrusted. Both Protestants and humanists agreed also in their contempt for medieval scholasticism in general, in pressing for institutional reform in the church, and in encouraging the active role of the laity in intellectual and religious life. Both put a high value on simple piety in contrast with elaborate formal liturgy and complicated systems of devotion such as the veneration of saints and their relics and the earning of indulgences. On the other hand, the two movements differed in some fundamental ways. The humanists were essentially optimistic about human nature, asserting the crucial role of free will. This emphasis contradicted the view, held by John Calvin (1509–1564) and the Protestant radicals who followed him, that humanity is weak in its fallen state ("totally depraved," to use the technical term) and therefore dependent on God's free gift of grace rather than its own spiritual exertions. Humanists tended not to be interested in sectarian dogma as such, except—as with Erasmus and More—to resist divisive innovations that threatened Church unity. Moreover, though the humanists scorned most things medieval, their essential internationalism, typified in the insistence by Erasmus and More that the Church remain unified, is closer to the medieval model than to the new localism and nationalism that evolved in parallel with the Protestant churches. And the advocacy of religious tolerance by humanists like Erasmus is antithetical to the intense sectarian partisanship expressed both in Protestantism and in the Catholic Counter-Reformation. (The latter is best exemplifed in the militant Society of Jesus, or Jesuits, founded on a military model in 1534 by the Spanish saint and former soldier Ignatius Loyola. In the literature of Protestant countries like England, the Jesuits generally appear not only as agents of "papist" religion but as unscrupulous, subversive machiavels working in the interest of foreign political powers. It is interesting, then, that Ignatius himself exhibited a kind of practical mysticism that owes something to the devotional trends, fostered by humanists, that had helped produce the Reformation.) Finally, the humanists' willingness to envisage the world in terms of classical models that might be compatible with Christianity but also existed independent of it did not square with the impulse in radical Protestantism to reject everything that was religiously neutral as pagan worldliness. The humanists were thus in a curious position after the Reformation, distrusted as sowers of heresy by many Catholics (despite his Catholicism, some of Erasmus's works were put on the *Index* of prohibited books) and rejected by many Protestants as faint-hearted, worldly temporizers, the lukewarm whom God, in the biblical phrase, would spew out of His mouth.

The role of the Renaissance and of humanism in the evolution of modern science is also ambivalent. The discovery of the world and the discovery of man that Michelet found in the Renaissance age are not necessarily parallel endeavors. It is true that the recovery of ancient authors made available to thinkers models of the cosmos not available in the Middle Ages, including the heliocentric astronomy with which Copernicus replaced the old Ptolemaic model, and some unknown works by ancient scientists like Archimedes were revived. Humanists encouraged the study of algebra and geometry, the latter overlapping with experiments by painters in visual perspective. Thus the way was prepared for the incomparable mathematical developments of the seventeenth century that provided the language of modern science. But the human-centeredness of the humanists, as is still true of some of their modern counterparts, sometimes took the form of an antagonism or at least indifference to science.

For modern science to develop, another radical change had also to occur: the medieval picture of the universe, with its beautiful model of correspondences between matter on one hand and theology and human psychology on the other, had to be replaced by a more objective view of nature as having its own autonomy independent of its roles of revealing God and reflecting man. The medieval correlation between the four humors in the human body and their corresponding psychological dispositions, and between the humors and the four elements in material nature; the systematic linking of the heavenly spheres with the hierarchical orders of angels; the notion that an apple falls from a tree because it loves the earth—such ideas had to go. (E. M. W. Tillyard argues in *The Elizabethan World Picture*, 1946, that assumptions like these continued to dominate much of Renaissance thought and art.) The trend in the Renaissance to study nature more objectively appears, for example, in the concern for accurate anatomy—systematically in the work of Vesalius (1514–1564) and esthetically in the proportions and musculature of painted or sculpted nudes. The dogmatic medieval reverence for Galen in medicine and for Aristotle in general was weakened.

The new empirical direction was, however, more an extrapolation of late medieval thought than a bold Renaissance innovation. Furthermore, although empiricism is fundamental to experimental method, it is probably less essential to pure science than the mental discipline of abstraction: one must learn, in accounting for the trajectory of the falling apple, to ignore certain quite objective facts about it—that it is a Winesap, is overripe, and has a worm in it—and concentrate exclusively on the abstract properties (mass, distance from other objects) it shares with all other gravitationally attracted bodies. It can be argued convincingly that this abstract habit of thinking is much closer than the humanists' practical wisdom to the medieval scholastic discipline.

In pure science, then, the Renaissance is probably best understood as a transition period. Technologically, however, there were some epochal advances. The most important by far was the invention in the late fifteenth century, by Johann Gutenberg (1400?–1468?) and others, of printing by movable type. In the last few decades of the century, several million books were printed, multiplying by an incalculable factor the impact of all the religious, intellectual, and literary trends in the later Renaissance. It is true that this invention too depended on earlier discoveries—in paper-making, for example—but the practical culmination of the technology of printing in the Renaissance itself marks one of the few unquestionable differences, not only from the Middle Ages but from all previous world history.

The new technology included also the navigational tools—again, drawing on pre-Renaissance and non-European cultures—that made possible the Renaissance age of geographical exploration. At the end of the fifteenth century Bartholomeu Dias and Vasco da Gama opened the route to India around the Cape of Good Hope and Columbus reached the New World; in the sixteenth century Magellan's crew and Francis Drake sailed around the globe. Such voyages had an enormous impact on the European imagination, influencing works like More's *Utopia* and Luiz Vaz de Camoëns' (1524–1580) Portuguese epic *The Lusiads*, which celebrates Vasco da Gama and vaunts his superiority to those mere Mediterranean sailors Odysseus and Aeneas. The new geographical discoveries also affected the politics and economics of Europe in important ways, accelerating the trends toward nationalism, middle-class power, economic capitalism, urbanization, and the shift of money and power from the Mediterranean to the countries on the Atlantic and the North Sea.

It is precisely in such sociological, political, and economic areas, however, that the nineteenth-century model of the Renaissance as a separate and distinct, organically whole age breaks down most seriously. It is beyond question that by the sixteenth century rulers such as Philip II in Spain and the Netherlands, Francis I in France, and Henry VIII in England had achieved unprecedented authority in their realms, built on their predecessors' consolidation of royal power, territory, and wealth in the fifteenth century. Because in many respects the feudal nobility was the greatest obstacle to royal authority, the monarchs' new power was wielded increasingly through complex bureaucracies staffed largely by a new kind of middle-class men distinguished less by birth than by talent or money. (Italy, with its city-states, was dominated by outside powers in the sixteenth century and was not unified as a nation until the nineteenth.) It is also true that these new national regimes, along with the Italian city-states, had begun to define themselves and their goals in increasingly secular and local terms, less dominated than in the past by the transnational authority of pope or Holy Roman Emperor or by the model of European Christendom as a unity. Populations boomed; banking flourished as money came to replace payment in kind and services; cities grew dramatically in size and importance, along with the intellectual and artistic activity that urban centers help foster. But the roots of all these movements go back, in some cases several centuries, into the medieval period. Moreover, the Renaissance is ridden by a great political-cultural paradox: while medieval internationalism was losing ground to the more local autonomy of city-state and national monarchy, in accordance with an ideal of patriotic citizenship that the humanists encouraged, the different parts of Europe were at the same time becoming more intellectually and culturally interdependent—a trend, greatly reinforced by the printing press, that also owes much to the humanists. A roughly similar paradox exists in the twentieth century: the breakup of the international colonial systems into scores of autonomous new states has coincided with the internationalist movement represented politically in the United Nations and with developments in technology and communication that have helped transform the world into a "global village."

Just as the humanists reacted contemptuously against things medieval in the name of a revived antiquity, so their classicizing counterparts in the visual arts often rejected medieval art, in theory at least. The Italians coined for it the pejorative term *Gothic* with a glance at the barbarians who overran ancient Rome. Today that term survives, but the accompanying value judgment has changed vastly. The Gothic style, alive from the twelfth to the fifteenth centuries (in some parts of Europe into the sixteenth), is now regarded as the expression of one of the great ages of world art. Much of its painting has disappeared, although a good deal is known about how it used two-dimensional media from tapestries, stained glass, and glorious color illuminations in manuscripts. Above all, its public architecture survives in the great European cathedrals, which embody an organic unity and a fusion with sculpture and other arts scarcely to be paralleled since the age of the Parthenon in ancient Greece.

The transition from Gothic to Renaissance art is problematical, like so many other aspects of the period when it happened. Compared with the Gothic, Renaissance art is more concerned with classical forms and subjects, with secular themes directed to a more secular clientele, with landscape and other aspects of nature, with the illusion of depth, with individual portraiture, and generally with greater representational realism. All these trends are also observable, however, in late medieval Gothic art as it developed from the Romanesque style that prevailed between the tenth and twelfth centuries. Further complications arise when one distinguishes between different parts of Europe, different stages of the Renaissance, and different art media. There remains nevertheless an immense difference between the Gothic and Renaissance periods in degree and also in consciousness, for the new trends were pursued with a programmatic deliberateness in the Renaissance that one does not find in the earlier era.

The most comprehensive of these trends was the revival of antiquity. Architectural models still existed, especially in Italy, and could be imitated directly. The spirituality implicit in the vertical-line composition and pointed arches of the Gothic cathedral yielded to the essentially horizontal classical emphasis. (Another way of looking at this shift is to see the cutting edge of architectural innovation as having shifted south to Italy, since the great Gothic cathedrals, with their mystically soaring vertical lines and spaces and their walls opened up with stained glass, had been an almost exclusively northern phenomenon.) The dome was revived by Filippo

Brunelleschi in his design for the Florence cathedral (1420), a landmark of the new style, and was used climactically by Michelangelo for St. Peter's in Rome. Classical columns, with their distinctive capitals marking the intersection of vertical with horizontal, took priority over the less clearly end-stopped Gothic pillars. In sculpture and painting, there were greater difficulties, since few antique models existed, especially in the early Renaissance before the discovery of statues such as the Apollo Belvedere. But artists in these media too did their enthusiastic best to classicize. Donatello (1386?–1466) pioneered in the revival of the free-standing nude and the equestrian statue. Painters, besides espousing the classical ideals of proportion and harmony, turned to ancient historical and mythological subjects—although the most frequent ones were still derived from the Bible and the lives of the saints.

The renewed interest in nature by Renaissance artists took many forms. The most obvious was an increased emphasis on landscape, though still almost always integrated with a human subject. The basic medieval world view had regarded the physical creation as sacramental and symbolic, and the Renaissance did not by any means discard that view; Renaissance pictures continued to be expressions of ideas, often retaining a system of symbols and icons inherited from the Middle Ages, as myriad Renaissance "emblem books" attest. At the same time, Renaissance art suggests also that, apart from its human or divine analogies, the world "out there" can be reproduced for what it is in itself. The picture frame became a window through which one glimpsed the living world. (According to Vasari, Leonardo da Vinci once played a practical joke on his father by creating a terrifying picture so lifelike that it was mistaken for reality.) Anatomy became a formal study for artists; drawing from nude models became commonplace, and the nude as a subject became ubiquitous. Color effects were perfected, especially by Titian and other Venetians. Portraits of individuals became an important genre, as exemplified in the masterfully realistic ones done by Hans Holbein the Younger (1497?–1543) of Erasmus, More, and Henry VIII. This individualism of subject reinforces the general motif of individualism ascribed to the Renaissance in the nineteenth-century model.

Even more to the point is the new individualistic role of the artist. The greatest medieval works of art, the cathedrals, had been collective, indeed communal achievements, a union of large vision with the painstaking efforts of hundreds of skilled artists and craftsmen who remained anonymous. Many of the best medieval artists are identified today only by the word *Master* linked to the name of his city or one of his masterpieces. But in the Renaissance, artists, often working for individual patrons whom they glorified as individuals, came to think of themselves also as unique men expressing their own unique visions and values. Some of them took to signing their canvases, a new practice, and even when they did not do so their works were figuratively signed by the unmistakable presence of their own personal styles. The medieval artist had been a maker and a servant of God; the Renaissance artist was a creator and, as such, God's rival.

Because it was essentially a literary movement, humanism naturally had its most direct impact on literature. Classical modes were revitalized—for example, the ode, the dialogue, and the pastoral, a form popular in Renaissance literary genres ranging from song to prose romance to drama. Besides serving as midwives of the revived classicism, some of the humanists created literary masterpieces themselves. They were at their best in the non-fictional or semi-fictional forms wherein inventiveness could be combined with the expression of ideas and opinions: letters, orations, dialogues, and treatises. Their admiration of Plato appears in the writings of Marsilio Ficino (1433–1499) and Pico della Mirandola, whose *Oration on the Dignity of Man* (1486) has already been mentioned. Dialogues included Erasmus's *Colloquies* (1519), More's *Utopia* (1516), and Baldassare Castiglione's *Book of the Courtier* (1514; published 1528), a vastly influential exposition of the ideal of the Renaissance gentleman. Erasmus's *Praise of Folly* (1509) is a many-sided ironic masterpiece which, like *Utopia*, shows the reformist side of humanism.

The most fundamental development in Renaissance literature was the growth of literary nationalism. All the important medieval vernacular languages of Europe had produced important literature, but it lived in the shadow of Latin, the international language, and the vernacular literatures themselves had typically reflected international rather than local traditions. In the Renaissance, political and personal allegiances to patrons, city-states, or national monarchies helped foster literary ambitions linked to the writers' own distinctive languages. Latin continued to thrive; among many other writers, More and Erasmus used it, in the works just mentioned, and into the seventeenth and eighteenth centuries it continued to be the normal vehicle for scientific discourse, including such monumental works as Isaac Newton's *Principia* (1687). It also remained the language of Roman Catholic liturgy and church government into the twentieth century. But the new Latin of the humanists was based on classical models such as Cicero's prose, and the concentration on such models helped to kill medieval Latin as a living language—a real loss, since in its spare directness medieval Latin had a beauty and functionality that the humanists did not properly appreciate. Their adulation for the classical tongues was also in some respects a roadblock to the development of the vernacular literatures; for example, humanism may have retarded for a time the development of Italian literature in the fifteenth century.

For the most part, though, the humanist impulse had the contrary effect: local patriotic feelings, reinforced by the humanist ideal of dedicated citizenship, inspired a desire to assert national identity while emulating in the national languages the achievements of antiquity. A notable example was the formation of the *Pléiade*, a group of sixteenth-century French writers that included Pierre de Ronsard (1524–1585), the greatest French poet of the Renaissance, and Joachim du Bellay (1522?–1560). Du Bellay, in his *Defense and Glorification of the French Language* (1549), produced the group's manifesto, calling for a French language and literature to rival that of Italy and antiquity in genres including tragedy, the ode, and the sonnet. The emergence of modern Italian vernacular literature had begun much earlier when Dante chose the Tuscan dialect for *The Divine Comedy*, supporting his program for Italian in a Latin treatise *On Eloquence in the Vernacular Tongue* (1304–1305), and later in the fourteenth century Petrarch and Boccaccio lent the weight of their prestige to Tuscan Italian. In Portugal, the achievements of Camoëns (1524–1580) in lyric and epic went a long way toward defining the Portuguese language. In the Protestant countries such as Germany, Holland, and England where the movement to translate the Bible into the vernacular could thrive, these translations were formative, especially Luther's German version (the New Testament in 1522, the Old Testament in 1534).

The most conscious and comprehensive assertions of Renaissance values appear in the long narrative works of the period, especially epics or works touched by the epic impulse. This is natural enough; the epic has always been a vehicle for communal ideas. If we did not know any of the great Renaissance epics and had to create a theoretical model for them on the basis of other tendencies of the time and clichés about it, we might arrive at something like this: a story of imposing events, written in a classical unrhymed verse, scornful of the outgrown medieval heritage, celebrating a modernist theme such as the recent achievements of the poet's own nation, and centered on a heroic but mentally elevated "Renaissance man" aglow with confidence and optimism. But, although virtually every Renaissance epic illustrates one or more of these motifs, what we most often find is a mixture, seemingly incongruous, of the modern, classical, and medieval, accompanied often by ambivalent value judgments. Some of these incongruities are attributable to the epic tradition itself, which since Virgil has tended to combine nationalist modernism with nostalgia, usually intimating a desire to keep alive what was best in the past and, on the other hand, a consciousness of having progressed beyond it.

Rabelais' *Gargantua and Pantagruel* (1532–1552), Cervantes' *Don Quixote* (1605, 1615), and Shakespeare's English history plays (1591–1599) are not epics in a strict formal sense, but they have the scale, comprehensiveness, and national flavor of epic. Rabelais' work is perhaps the showcase example of worldly Renaissance exuberance; yet it also recalls the medieval "goliardic," a student tradition of wining and wenching. The searching complexities of *Don Quixote* build from a direct confrontation between an idealism symbolized by the medieval romances and a contrasting pragmatism, and which set of values Cervantes endorses is not a question to answer simply. The *Quixote* is among other things an examination of the Spanish national character, but in the spirit of a sensitive critique rather than of panegyric. Of Shakespeare's ten English history plays, eight span the period from the end of the fourteenth century to the emergence in 1485 of the Tudor dynasty still reigning in Shakespeare's time, and these plays have been taken sometimes to constitute Shakespeare's epic. In it he celebrates the emergence of peace and order from a fragmented, dying medieval feudalism, but he also portrays the noble beauty of the chivalric code. None of these three authors, then, is simply heralding the glories of a new civilization unrooted in the medieval past.

When we turn to works more strictly describable as epics (almost all of them, interestingly, written in rhymed rather than in classical verse forms), we find the same mixture of allegiances. Perhaps the closest thing to our hypothetical national and modernist model is Camoëns' *Lusiad* (1572), a poem that intricately imitates Virgil's *Aeneid* and acclaims triumphantly the unprecedented Portuguese voyages around the Cape to the Far East for the glory of the nation and of Catholic Christianity. Here the sense of a vast new world in contrast to the constricted Mediterranean world of epic memory accords well enough with the nineteenth-century vision of an expansive

Renaissance spirit. Iberian interest in the new explorations is also reflected in several sixteenth-century Spanish epics by authors including Alonso de Ercilla y Zúñiga (1534–1594) and the great dramatist Lope de Vega (1562–1635).

The definitive Italian Renaissance epics are quite another matter. They consist of a series of poems written in Ferrara under the patronage of the Este family: the *Orlando in Love* (1483) of Matteo Boiardo, the *Orlando Driven Mad* (1516) of Ludovico Ariosto, and the *Jerusalem Delivered* (1575) of Torquato Tasso. (Boiardo and Ariosto built from an earlier work, *Morgante the Giant,* written about 1480 by Luigi Pulci.) All these authors belong unmistakably to the Renaissance; Ariosto especially, with his gaiety, sophistication, and sensuousness, and his theme of the impossible quest, expresses something quintessential to his time and place. But, like Pulci and Boiardo, he treats medieval matter and heroes derived from the traditions of King Arthur, Charlemagne, and Roland, although the hero of the great, austere *chanson de geste* is scarcely recognizable in this new Orlando ("Roland," in Italian). These poems are much closer to the magical atmosphere and free form of medieval romance than to the classical epic. Tasso's poem conforms more nearly to the ancient models, but it too has a medieval subject (the first Crusade) and owes much to the romance genre and atmosphere; moreover, the ideal it celebrates is a united Christian Europe that in the days of the Counter-Reformation had become no more than a wistful memory.

Edmund Spenser (1552?–1599), although a fervent Renaissance Protestant, wrote in this tradition of Italianate medievalism. In *The Faerie Queene* (published 1590–1595) he attempted a portrait of the ideal man based on a scheme of Aristotelian ethical virtues that medieval authors like Dante would probably have found congenial, and he chose for his vehicle a blend of romance, allegory, and archaic diction that also have strong medieval associations. On the other hand, Spenser's political allegory is modern and militantly Protestant, pitting Queen Elizabeth (Gloriana, the fairy queen) and her champions against evil popes and Catholic monarchs who serve as agents of the Satanic.

The culmination of Renaissance epic was achieved by Milton, who inherited many of Spenser's values but wrote an utterly different kind of poem. His *Paradise Lost,* influenced by *La Semaine* (*The Week*, 1578), an epic account of the creation by the French Protestant poet Guillaume du Bartas, treats the fall of humankind, a universal theme sanctioned by the divine truth of the Bible rather than the mere fictions of medieval legend or classic fable. In his close textural and structural use of Homer and Virgil, his anti-medievalism (reflected in a scornful passage abusing the monastic orders), his contemptuous rejection of rhyme as medieval barbarism, his deliberate disavowal of medieval romance as an epic mode ("fabled knights / In battles feigned")—in all these respects Milton adopts the humanist stance. Even more fundamentally, *Paradise Lost* is humanist in its relative freedom from sectarian factionalism (the passage about the monks notwithstanding) and in its ultimate theme: freedom, more specifically human free will. In rising above the doctrinaire polemics for his nation and theology that he reserved for his Puritan prose tracts, Milton may well have achieved in *Paradise Lost,* more than any other major Renaissance epic poet and at the very end of the Renaissance, the humanist goals that in so many ways define the age.

Renaissance values appear in the epics as broad, comprehensive visions, but equally characteristic is a new kind of literary intimacy and particularity akin to the vogue of portrait painting and the new self-expressive role of the artist. The best literary portraits are the characters in Shakespeare's plays; although they often owe something to earlier literary and dramatic traditions such as the morality play, scores of them are fully realized individuals. It may seem paradoxical, then, that Shakespeare reveals very little of himself. For the epitome of Renaissance self-revelation we can go to Montaigne (1533–1592), whose *Essays* (1580–1588) combine far-reaching speculation with the minutest factual details of his personal life and the quirks of his mind, all colored by his distinctive personality and voice.

But the principal medium for self-expression was the lyric. The prototype, once more, is Petrarch, whose lyrics focus so insistently on the poet himself. His Laura is clearly in the line of Dante's Beatrice, but, without denying that Beatrice is a real woman or that Laura is idealized, one senses that the latter is far more fully a unique individual. In the sonnet especially, Petrarch started a Renaissance fashion taken up by almost all the lyric poets of Europe, including Camoëns, Ronsard, Spenser, Sir Philip Sidney (1554–1586), Shakespeare, and Milton. It became the confessional love poem *par excellence,* but even when the subject was not inherently private or amatory (Shakespeare on time, Donne on religious experience), the viewpoint on these more universal matters was still usually subjective. This is not to say that the sonnets were reliably autobiographical; in fact, the genre became one of the most artificial, convention-ridden of forms, full of stylized sighing lovers, cruel but idealized mistresses (sometimes quite fictional), and other stock devices of the courtly love apparatus whose roots extend back beyond Petrarch into the Middle Ages. But even the most conventional of the sonnets reflect the vogue of self-expression, since the sonneteer had at least to assume the guise of a man revealing his intimate thoughts or feelings. "Fool," says Sidney's muse to him, "look in thy heart and write." (Ultimately the Petrarchan tradition of courtly praise fell by its own weight of artificiality; Donne in his lyrics scrutinizes the conventions ironically, and Shakespeare could satirize them as he does in his sonnet 130: "My mistress' eyes are nothing like the sun; / Coral is far more red than her lips' red . . . .") Often, too, the sonneteers' self-consciousness took the form of commentary on their own work; poetry and the poets' ability to give immortality to their addressees were frequent themes, and beneath the overlays of this convention is an authentic new sense of the power of art that is characteristic of the Renaissance.

The heightened interest during the Renaissance in objectifying the world, portraying individuals, and exploring the complexities of human psychology as it is reflected in behavior—all these were favorable conditions for a resurgent interest in drama, which, especially in England and Spain, flourished as it had not done since Greek antiquity. The exact origins of this new dramatic impulse are hard to untangle from one another. The classical revival was unquestionably important: the plays of Terence, Plautus, and Seneca known to the Middle Ages were now approached less exclusively as rhetorical models and more as literary theater; the Greek dramatists were rediscovered along with some plays by Plautus that had disappeared; at schools and universities plays were studied avidly, and scholars began to write classically inspired dramas of their own, in both Latin and the vernacular. The printing press helped immeasurably; in the half-century or so after it came into use, the plays of all the great ancient dramatists—Aeschylus, Sophocles, Euripides, Aristophanes, Plautus, Terence, and Seneca—were published. The same period saw the publication of Aristotle's *Poetics*, and with it came a new consciousness of classical "rules" such as the preservation of the unities. Tragedians learned from Seneca how to write a long play that held together; comic playwrights learned the intricacies of tight plotting from Plautus and Terence. When the public theaters of London began to thrive in the 1580s and 1590s, the first important plays were written by men who, like Thomas Kyd (1557?–1595) and Christopher Marlowe (1564–1593), had learned their craft in the schools or universities.

Nevertheless, many of the greatest Renaissance plays are not in any obvious way classical. In both Spain and England, the most vital sources of the new drama were in native popular theatrical traditions which, in turn, had their ultimate roots in the medieval church. Shakespeare's friend and fellow playwright Ben Jonson (1572–1637), an aggressive advocate of classical form, felt himself to be in that role an enlightened exception among his formally footloose contemporaries. In Spain, the enormously prolific Lope de Vega (1562–1635) wrote a manifesto in 1609 rejecting classical rules; this anti-classical position was later modified by Calderón de la Barca (1600–1681), but he too in his more intellectual and theological vein was thoroughly Spanish in his religious preoccupations. Both Lope de Vega and Shakespeare blended the comic and the serious in a fashion closer to medievalism than to classicism. Even the staging of their plays, despite immense advances in professionalism and sophistication, recalls certain medieval features; for example, in the Elizabethan theater the areas below and above the main acting platform continued to be referred to as the "hell" and the "heaven," as in the three-level stage of the medieval period. (See the Introductions to *Everyman*, Shakespeare, and Calderón.)

The fact is that, although the Renaissance drama of England and Spain is unimaginable apart from either its medieval origins or the classical revival, it achieved expressive heights and explored human experience in ways not always clearly attributable to either strain. Religious themes continued to be immensely popular in Spain, but so were secular ones. In England these completely supplanted the overt devotional emphasis of the miracle, mystery, and morality plays. A Christian norm might be present, but, like the classicist goal of coherent unity, it was there organically and implicitly rather than texturally and explicitly. The history play perfected by Marlowe, Shakespeare, and Lope de Vega was an almost wholly new genre. Comedy owed something to medieval farce and to the stock characters of the Roman comedians (the "wily slave" transformed into the clowns and other clever "low" characters of playwrights such as Shakespeare), but in its highest reaches it became something new to the stage. In the Shakespearean comedies *Twelfth Night*, *As You Like It*, and *A Midsummer Night's Dream* (set, ludicrously, in ancient Athens but really in fairyland), laughter is combined with a warm and sympathetic insight into the romantic feelings of men and women, articulating a distinctive definition of love. Tragedy became both intimate and cosmic. The medieval notion of tragedy was simply the fall of a great personage from prosperous eminence (a strain vestigially recognizable in Shakespearean tragedies like *Macbeth*). The classical impulse in the Renaissance transformed this model radically—for example, Senecan models added a dimension of melodrama and a stoic sense of fatality, and from Aristotle came the notion of the hero's "tragic flaw." But no such formulas can define the great English tragedies of Marlowe, Shakespeare, or John Webster (1580?–1625). In Shakespeare's *Hamlet, King Lear, Othello,* and *Macbeth,* it is not only the hero's life and happiness but the entire vision of a morally ordered universe that is at stake, threatened by a demonic principle of evil that seems to have escaped human or divine control. Whether or not the principle of righteousness prevails in the end is a question that can be answered differently about different plays (opinion is notoriously divided about *King Lear*), but even when it does reassert itself, a terrible price has been paid in the suffering or destruction of precious, noble individuals. There is at the least a heartrending sense of human waste. But this sense is also mitigated by the very existence of human goodness, whether it triumphs or not. The integrity and love of Lear's daughter Cordelia are realities that in their nature cannot be denied or annulled, even by death. For dramatic visions so vast as these one must go back to Greek tragedy, and it might be argued that Shakespeare goes beyond the Greeks by combining with his cosmic themes a more intimate concern for the unique human person.

Italy, the original center of the humanist movement and the revival of antiquity, did not produce a great dramatic literature in the Renaissance, although some of its distinguished authors, including Ariosto and Tasso, produced notable plays, and there were occasional masterpieces such as Machiavelli's *Mandragola* (about 1518). Italy contributed influentially to post-Renaissance stagecraft, however; as in painting, it pioneered in the development of illusional perspective in stage settings, and it helped develop important architectural features like the proscenium arch. Such elements look past the Renaissance to the "picture-frame" stage that became the principal model for theater from the late seventeenth century until well into the twentieth. (Much of this new stagecraft reached other countries by way of Italian opera, a new art form developed around 1600 in rivalry with the integration of the arts in ancient Greek drama and crowned with immediate greatness in the works of Claudio Monteverdi—1567–1643.) The modern picture-frame stage, typically opening into someone's living room, is itself an emblem for the kind of realistically intimate drama often enacted on it, and the emblem represented by the physical theater is applicable to earlier dramatic traditions as well. The essentially public action of classical Greek drama took place before an unchanging background, the *skene* that typically represented a palace and concealed from the audience the merely domestic private scenes imagined to take place behind it. The medieval stage presented simultaneously to the audience three levels—heaven, earth, and hell—representing a constant awareness of the relationship between here and hereafter. The Renaissance stage of England and Spain was the vehicle for complete fluidity and variety, capable of representing, with the indispensable help of poetic language, any conceivable setting and of shifting from one to another instantaneously. The ceremonial and casual, the public and intimate, the lofty and low, the violent and serene, the realistic and romantic—all these manners and moods, in any combination, were at the service of the playwright and actors. It is therefore not surprising that Renaissance drama could encompass more of the world and of life than has been possible in the theater of any other age.

FURTHER READING *(prepared by W. J. R.):* Scholarship on the Renaissance is nearly as interesting as the Renaissance itself. One can begin with Jacob Burckhardt's epoch-making study, *The Civilization of the Renaissance in Italy.* First published in 1860, Burckhardt's book definitively shaped the modern conception of the Renaissance; he emphasizes the primacy of individualism and views the Renaissance as being essentially an outgrowth of political movements. Translated and revised many times, the best edition is probably the S. G. C. Middlemore translation, published in 1878 and reprinted in 1955. More concise is J. H. Plumb's *The Italian Renaissance,* 1961, which in surveying the period refers often to Dante, Boccaccio, Petrarch, and Machiavelli. On the Renaissance in England, one can begin with E. M. W. Tillyard's *The Elizabethan World Picture,* 1946, reprinted many times. Tillyard identifies three models by which the Elizabethans imagined the world: a chain, a set of correspondences, and a dance. Tillyard's *The English Renaissance: Fact or Fiction?,* 1952, identifies and discusses essential differences between Medieval and Renaissance thought in order to answer the question posed by the title; see also the excellent discussions in *The Renaissance: A Reconsideration of the Theories and Interpretations of the Age,* ed. by Tinsley Helton, 1961. Two of the essays in this volume warrant special mention: Harry Levin's "English Literature of the Renaissance" and Paul Oskar Kristeller's "Changing Views of the Renaissance Since Jacob Burckhardt." A sound and readable survey of the Renaissances in Italy and in the North is Wallace K. Ferguson's *The Renaissance,* 1940, which also discusses pre-Renaissance history. The principles and attitudes reflected in Renaissance literature are treated in Douglas Bush's *Prefaces to Renaissance Literature,* 1965. Paul Oskar Kristeller's *Renaissance Thought and Its Sources,* ed. by Michael Mooney, 1979, and Ernst Cassirer's *The Individual and the Cosmos in Renaissance Philosophy,* 1927, translated by Mario Domadi, 1963, are both careful and incisive. Kristeller begins with humanism and proceeds to study the classical forerunners of Renaissance thought, Renaissance attitudes toward the individual, and other topics; Cassirer's classic examines the Renaissance as a systematic unity. An excellent guide to humanism is Douglas Bush's *The Renaissance and English Humanism,* 1939, reprinted 1965, which examines both English and continental humanism. A particularly readable essay on the foundations of English humanism opens Fritz Caspari's *Humanism and the Social Order in Tudor England,* 1954, which goes on to treat Erasmus, More, Sidney, and Spenser. A comprehensive historical introduction to humanism is found in Myron P. Gilmore's *The World of Humanism, 1453–1517,* 1952, reprinted 1962. Gilmore's chapter on the scholarship conducted by the humanists is especially good. Frederic Seebohm's enduring *The Oxford Reformers: Colet, Erasmus and More,* 1869, 1938, can still be recommended.

Francis Petrarch
(1304–1374)

Possibly the greatest love poet in Western literature was Francis Petrarch, the four-teenth-century Italian classicist, humanist, and literary arbiter. Born in Arezzo in 1304, Petrarch was set to the study of law, first at Montpellier and then at Bologna. When his father died, the twenty-two-year-old Petrarch renounced law and moved to the lively city of Avignon, the seat of the papacy during its "Babylonian captivity" from 1309 to 1378. After briefly considering the Church, he entered instead the service of the wealthy and powerful Colonna family, the first of a series of patrons who made it possible for Petrarch to devote his life exclusively to literature. He has thus been called the first modern man of letters. By 1341 his reputation was so high that he received a laurel crown as poet laureate from the Roman Senate, an honor Petrarch always treasured as symbolizing not only his own achievement but his spirit-ual links with the great poets of classical Rome. For the rest of his life, Petrarch continued to be a celebrated public man, an intimate and counsellor of princes as well as an arbiter of literary taste. During his mature years, he moved from one residence to another, to Milan as guest of the Visconti, to Venice as guest of the Republic, and finally to Arqua, near Padua, where he spent the last four years of his life in a country retreat. He died in 1374, just before his seventieth birthday, his copy of Virgil open before him on his desk.

In his own day and his own estimation, Petrarch's major achievement was in his Latin works, which far outnumbered his Italian ones. In a letter to Boccaccio, written in his later years, he told of his decision, sometime in his thirties, to use Latin rather than Italian in his major literary work. He had, he said, already begun "a great work" in Italian but had given it up for fear that his words would be "mangled by the public." (Dante, who had visited Petrarch's family when Petrarch was seven, had completed The Divine Comedy *in Italian in 1321, about fifteen years before Petrarch decided in favor of Latin.) The most important of Petrarch's many Latin works are* Africa, *an unfinished epic poem about Scipio Africanus, the third-century B.C. conqueror of Hannibal; the* Secretum Meum *(My Secret), a spiritual autobi-ography in the form of three imaginary dialogues between Petrarch and St. Augus-tine; and his* Letters, *both in verse and prose, which Petrarch himself carefully edited and collected into a number of volumes. The humane and liberal spirit of Petrarch's classical studies was to be a major influence in the development of Renais-sance humanism throughout Europe.*

Later ages have known Petrarch less as a classicist, however, than as the author of the collection of poems in Italian which he called the Rerum vulgarium fragmenta *(Poetic Fragments in the Vernacular) and which is now generally known either as the* Canzoniere *(Lyric Poems) or simply the* Rhymes. *This collec-tion of poems was gradually built up through Petrarch's mature life. At least three times Petrarch arranged them in systematic collections, and he was still polishing and rearranging them when he died; the final version of the sequence contains 366 poems, intended to be read, like the Breviary, over the course of a year.*

The inspiration for the poems was Petrarch's crucial meeting, on April 6, 1327, with "Laura," in the church of St. Clare in Avignon. (Petrarch never revealed Laura's identity, but she is believed to have been Laurette de Noves, who had been married for two years when Petrarch met her and who had a number of children by the time of her death in 1348.) Petrarch adored her, hopelessly and from afar, until her death twenty-one years later and continued to cherish her memory in his poetry for another ten years, after which he professed to renounce earthly love and turn his thoughts only to God.

There is something faintly absurd to the modern reader about this protracted and self-conscious cultivation of a hopeless love (especially, perhaps, when one learns that Petrarch had two illegitimate children by different mothers during the time of his idealization of Laura). But there is more than a little of the conventional in Petrarch's adoration of Laura. By the time he wrote, there was already a long tradition of sequences of love poems addressed to an unattainable woman. Originating in the poems of the twelfth- and thirteenth-century troubadours of southern France, the tradition had found its most notable expression before Petrarch in Dante's La Vita Nuova (The New Life), devoted to the transformation of the real Beatrice Portinari into "Beatrice," a symbol of Christian salvation (Latin beata, "blessed"). A friend of Petrarch, Giacomo Colonna, even suggested that Laura was not a real person but an invented symbol of the poetic "laurel." Petrarch replied with some vehemence that Laura was indeed real and that no one could counterfeit the "weariness and pallor" that his hopeless love had given him. But real passion for a real woman does not preclude making her also into a conventional poetic figure.

What raised the Rhymes *above the level of its predecessors and made it one of the most widely read and imitated collections of poems in literary history was the wealth of classical learning in the poems, their scope and variety, their arrangement into a developing structure, and their sheer beauty. The classicism of the* Rhymes *is not obtrusive, but it is the more powerful for being so thoroughly assimilated. Virgil, Horace, Catullus, and especially Ovid are echoed throughout the* Rhymes. *One realizes with something of a shock, for example, that the poem "Upon the breeze she spread her golden hair" (XC), personal as it seems, is a close reworking of a passage from the Aeneid. Ovid is a pervasive presence in the* Rhymes, *not the Ovid of the Art of Love or the moralized, allegorical Ovid of the medieval interpreters, but the Ovid of the* Metamorphoses; *Ovid's Daphne, who, pursued by Apollo, was changed into a laurel tree, is one of the most important classical analogues for the Laura in Petrarch's sequence. The* Rhymes *are quite varied both in form and content. Sonnets predominate; 317 of the 366 poems in the collection are in this form. But there are also a number of* canzoni *(poems made up of five or six stanzas of equal length, followed by a shorter* envoy, *such as CXXVI and CXXIX), and several other forms appear. Most of the poems are about Laura, but a significant number have nothing to do with her, dealing instead with politics, moral problems, friendship, and other topics. The sequence begins and ends with a renunciation of the poet's passion for Laura. The poems between fall most obviously into two groups: Part One, consisting of 265 poems that deal with the living Laura, and Part Two, consisting of 99 poems devoted to the memory of the dead Laura. The poems are arranged in loose chronology, but more important than chronology is the range of moods of the speaker, a range that includes every emotion from spiritual ecstasy to agonized self-laceration and melancholy resignation, every mood associated with love, perhaps, except the joy of physical consummation.*

Laura comes to mean many things for Petrarch in the course of the poems; as Thomas G. Bergin has pointed out, they reveal at least four Lauras. One is the Laura of the poet's "laurel," his poetic ambitions which he pursues as Apollo pursued his Daphne. Another is Laura as a virtuous guide to Heaven, like Dante's Beatrice; this view of Laura comes to dominate the second part of the sequence, after Laura's death.

A third Laura represents beauty itself, especially as a fascinating temptation that draws the poet away from his proper pursuit of salvation; this Laura appears most explicitly in the sonnets of recantation: I and CCCLXV. And finally, Laura is, of course, merely a young woman with whom the poet fell in love on a spring day in 1327; many of the poems do not emphasize any metaphoric meanings for Laura but present her as a real human presence.

It is not Laura, however, but the poet who is the protagonist of the **Rhymes.** *His lady is described in loving detail, but always from outside, from the poet's point of view; Petrarch has no interest in the workings of Laura's mind or in her attitudes toward such subjects as, say, her husband or her children. The personality we remember after reading the poems is Petrarch's—nostalgic, melancholy, passionate and yet always curiously removed from life, an observer rather than a participant.*

The deeply personal and introspective quality of the **Rhymes** *and their brilliant technique established a vogue that endured for at least three centuries and left a permanent impression on Western poetry, especially love poetry. "Petrarchism" offered a way of portraying the loved one, as a fascinating combination of earthly and divine qualities; a characteristic stance for the lover; and a repertory of devices that could be endlessly imitated, sometimes well, sometimes clumsily and mechanically. These included a repertory of stock images—stormy seas, beautiful landscapes, marble tombs, battles—and a liberal use of antithesis (strong contrasts), oxymoron (contradictory terms), and hyperbole (exaggeration). (See Poem CXXXIV for examples of Petrarch's own use of such devices.) Exaggerated Petrarchan catalogues of the features of a stock, composite mistress had become so common by Shakespeare's time that he could parody them in his Sonnet 130:*

> *My mistress' eyes are nothing like the sun;*
> *Coral is far more red than her lips' red:*
> *If snow be white, why then her breasts are dun;*
> *If hairs be wires, black wires grow on her head.*

But pervasive as Petrarch's literary influence was, his influence upon attitudes toward love was probably even greater; even today, lovers who never heard of Petrarch tend to adopt Petrarchan attitudes. "The amatory attitudes of the **Rhymes** *have in fact been built into our culture," Thomas G. Bergin writes. "It is possible, of course, that some day there may be a revolution in human emotions, whether it be a new morality or a new erotic, but until that day comes we shall live by the code that Petrarch elaborated with such instinctive perception and such compelling sophistication." We may be somewhat more skeptical than Bergin about the desirability of some aspects of Petrarchan love, such as the radical split between the physical and the spiritual; the "revolution in human emotions" he mentions may now be taking place. But until it is completed, we must agree that lovers' meetings "will take place in the kingdom that Petrarch has explored for them."*

FURTHER READING *(prepared by W. J. R.):* Thomas G. Bergin's *Petrarch,* 1970, is an excellent introduction to the study of Petrarch. Bergin provides a concise survey of Petrarch's life and a clear and substantial commentary on the *Triumphs* and the *Rhymes.* Ernest Hatch Wilkins' *Life of Petrarch,* 1961, is a more detailed biography of the poet. Morris Bishop's *Petrarch and His World,* 1963, analyzes Petrarch and his times in great detail, but it is nonetheless suited for the new student of the poet. More intensive critical evaluation can be found in Ernest Hatch Wilkins' *Studies in the Life and Works of Petrarch,* 1955. This volume is primarily a collection of essays taken from periodicals, but arranged to establish an organic integrity. Chapter Five, the pivotal essay, examines Petrarch's two-year residence in Provence (1351–53). J. H. Whitfield's *Petrarch and the Renascence,* 1943, gives an excellent overview of critical attitudes towards the early Renaissance. Whitfield discusses Petrarch's view of antiquity in relation to Dante's and proceeds to examine Petrarch's unique contribution to his century. A Nobel Prize poet's thoughts on Petrarch are recorded in Salvatore Quasimodo's *The Poet and the Politician,* 1960, translated by Thomas G. Bergin, 1964. The second essay in this volume contains sections on both Petrarch's solitude and Dante's reputation. Two works by Aldo S. Bernardo examine Petrarchan works other than the *Rhymes. Petrarch, Scipio and the "Africa,"* 1962, examines Petrarch's great and neglected epic, often comparing the intellectual link between Petrarch and Scipio Africanus to the emotional link between Petrarch and Laura. *Petrarch, Laura and the "Triumphs,"* 1974, examines Laura from multiple perspectives—as she is seen in the *Rhymes,* the Latin poetry, and the *Triumphs.* Stephen Minta's *Petrarch and Petrarchism: The English and French Traditions,* 1980, is an excellent anthology of poems by Petrarch and by English and French poets influenced by him.

RHYMES

Translation and notes by Anthony Mortimer

I

All you that hear in scattered rhymes[1] the sound
of sighs on which I used to feed my heart
in my first youthful error when, in part,
I was another man, now left behind;

for the vain hopes, vain sorrows of my mind,   5
the tears and discourse of my varied art,
in any who have played a lover's part
pardon and pity too I hope to find.

But now I see too well how I became
a tale for common gossip everywhere,   10
so that I grow ashamed of what I am;

and of my raving still the fruit is shame
and penitence, and last the knowledge clear
that all the world loves is a passing dream.

[1] The poet regards his "scattered rhymes" as a collection of fragments (*Rerum vulgarium fragmenta*), but there is also the possibility that they are scattered through the world. The whole sonnet is, indeed, indicative of Petrarch's ambiguous attitude towards the *Canzoniere:* he deplores it as evidence of a "youthful error," but he still hopes to find readers. (Notes, unless otherwise indicated, are by the translator.)

III

It was that very day on which the sun
in awe of his creator dimmed the ray,[1]
when I was captured, with my guard astray,
for your fine eyes, my lady, bound me then.

It hardly seemed the time for me to plan   5
defence against Love's stroke; I went my way
secure, unwary; so upon that day
of general sorrow all my pains began.

Love found me with no armour for the fight,
my eyes an open highway to the heart,   10
eyes that are now a vent for tears to flow.

And yet he played no honourable part,
wounding me with his shaft in such a state;
he saw you armed and dared not lift the bow.

XC

Upon the breeze she spread her golden hair[1]
that in a thousand gentle knots was turned,
and the sweet light beyond all measure burned
in eyes where now that radiance is rare;

and in her face there seemed to come an air   5
of pity, true or false, that I discerned:
I had love's tinder in my breast unburned,
was it a wonder if it kindled there?

She moved not like a mortal, but as though
she bore an angel's form, her words had then   10
a sound that simple human voices lack;

a heavenly spirit, a living sun
was what I saw; now, if it is not so,
the wound's not healed because the bow grows slack.

[1] Petrarch first saw Laura at matins in the church of Saint Clare in Avignon on April 6,
1327. This was not the moveable feast of Good Friday, but, according to medieval calculations,
the exact calendar anniversary of Christ's death.
[1] This sonnet is inspired by a description of Venus appearing to Aeneas in Virgil's *Aeneid*,
Book I. (Editors' note.)

CXXVI

Waters[1] fresh and sweet and clear
where the fair limbs reclined
of the one creature who to me seems woman;
and gentle tree-trunk where,
with sighs I call to mind,   5
the leaning side once loved to find a column;
flowers and grass that often
the light gown hid from sight
with the angelic breast;[2]
airs breathing holy rest   10
where Love with those fair eyes opened my heart:
come, and together grant
a hearing to my last lament.

If it be destiny,
and heaven works for this,   15
that Love should close these weeping eyes of mine,
then may some kindness lay
the body in your midst
and the soul naked to its home return;
death shall become less stern   20
if such a hope I bear
into that fearful pass,
for the soul's weariness
could find no calmer haven anywhere,
nor could it ever leave   25
the troubled flesh in a more quiet grave.

A time may come again
when she perhaps will stray
to the old haunt, untamed, yet fair and meek,
and where she saw me then   30
upon that blessed day
will turn an eager and a happy look,
and there, O pity! seek
and find me turned to dust amid the stones:
at this may Love arise,   35
inspiring her with sighs
so sweet she forces heaven[1] and obtains
its mercy for my soul,
drying her eyes upon the lovely veil.

---

[1] The waters of the Sorgue in Vaucluse.

[2] Commentators have been unnecessarily puzzled here. The poet, in fact, recalls Laura in a number of different attitudes: bathing in the river, leaning against a tree, and sitting on the ground so that the gown which covers her breast also covers the grass and flowers.

[1] Bosco [a modern Italian critic] points out that heaven will be impressed not by Laura's sorrow or piety, but by the sweetness of her sighs and the elegance of her gestures. Even the intercession of the living for the dead is seen in aesthetic terms.

From the fair boughs there fell, 40
sweet in the memory,
upon her lap a rain of every flower,
and she sat there and still
was humble in such glory,
already covered by the loving shower; 45
upon the hem lay flowers,
and some the tresses crowned
which seemed that day to hold
both pearls and polished gold;
some rested on the waves, some on the ground; 50
some, sweetly turning through the air,
seemed in their drift to whisper: "Love reigns here."

How often I exclaimed,
seized by a sudden fear:
"For certain she was born in Paradise!" 55
Such deep oblivion came
from her celestial air,
the words, the gentle smiling, and the eyes,
so faintly did I seize
the image truth would show, 60
that I said sighing then:
"How came I here, or when?"
thinking myself in heaven, not here below.
And ever since I've loved this place
so much that elsewhere I can find no peace. 65

Song, had you beauty as you have desire,
intrepidly you could
go out among the crowd and leave this wood.

CXXIX

From thought to thought, from mountainside to mountain
Love leads me on, since every beaten trail
I feel as hostile to my peace of mind.
If some deserted heath has stream or fountain,
or if two hills should hide a shadowed vale, 5
the spirit sees its suffering decline,
and there, as Love designs,
now laughs and weeps, now fears and learns to trust;
the face that follows where the spirit leads
grows clear and overclouds, 10
and no condition ever seems to last:
so, at the sight, a man who knew that life
would say: "He burns, and stands in doubtful strife."

Among high mountains and wild woods I find
some kind of rest; but each frequented place   15
becomes an enemy that my eyes abhor.
At every step a new thought comes to mind
of my dear lady, often bringing gladness
out of the torment that I feel for her;
and hardly would I prefer   20
to change the sweet and bitter life I bear
when I reflect: "Perhaps Love keeps in view
a better time for you;
you hate yourself, but she may hold you dear."
And with this thought sighing I change again: 25
"Can it be ever true? but how? and when?"

Where a tall pine-tree or a hill gives shade
sometimes I stop, and on the nearest stone
my mind will draw her face. At last I find,
on coming to myself, my breast is bathed   30
with that emotion; then "alas," I groan,
"where are you now? what have you left behind?"
But while my wandering mind
can be kept steadfastly on that first thought
and I forget myself and gaze on her,   35
then I feel Love so near
the soul is sated with its own deceit:
I see her in so many things, so fair,
that if the illusion lasts I ask no more.

Often I've seen (who will believe me now?)   40
on the green grass or in transparent water
her living self, in beech-trees or the face
of a white cloud, and ever fashioned so
that Leda[1] would have surely said her daughter
fades like a star outshone by the sun's rays;   45
and the more wild the place
I come upon, the lonelier the shore,
the fairer does thought shadow forth[2] my love.
Then, when the truth removes
that sweet illusion, I sit as before,   50
cold and stone-dead upon the living stone,[3]
like one who thinks and weeps and writes alone.

To where the mountain shadows never lie,
towards the highest and best vantage-point,

[1] Leda, seduced by Zeus in the form of a swan, was the mother of Helen of Troy. (Editors'
note.)

[2] The Italian word is *adombra*. More than "shadow forth" this suggests the conscious chiaro-
scuro of the painter, thus continuing the artist metaphor introduced in the previous stanza.

[3] The contrast is probably between the stone effigy on a tomb *(pietra morta)* and the natural
stone *(pietra viva)* upon which the poet sits. Having transformed so many shapes into Laura's
image, the poet now becomes an image himself. This reading is confirmed by the last line of
the poem.

a fierce desire often makes me start. 55
There I begin to measure with the eye
my sufferings, and tearfully give vent
to the sad mists that thicken in my heart,
when both my gaze and thought
span all that lies between me and the fair 60
face that is still so near and far away;
then, whispering to myself, I say:
"What can you know? this moment over there
perhaps your absence makes her sigh for you;"
and in this thought the spirit breathes anew. 65

My song, beyond this alp,
where skies are happier and clear above,
you'll find me sitting by a stream that flows
where gentle aura blows
in from a fresh and fragrant laurel-grove: 70
there is my heart and she that stole it from me;
and here my image all that you can see.[4]

CXXXIV

I find no peace, and have no arms for war,
and fear and hope, and burn and yet I freeze,
and fly to heaven, lying on earth's floor,
and nothing hold, and all the world I seize.

My jailer opens not, nor locks the door, 5
nor binds me to her, nor will loose my ties;
Love kills me not, nor breaks the chains I wear,
nor wants me living, nor will grant me ease.

I have no tongue, and shout; eyeless, I see;
I long to perish, and I beg for aid; 10
I love another, and myself I hate.

Weeping I laugh, I feed on misery,
by death and life so equally dismayed:
for you, my lady, am I in this state.

CCLXV

Fierce heart and bitter, and most cruel will,
sweet, humble, and angelic to the sight,

---

[4] The envoi sends the poem to join the poet's heart which is with Laura beyond the Alps. For once I have attempted to translate the pun on Laura's name.

if this first rigor last throughout the fight,
the honour of their trophies will be small;

for when grass, leaf, and flower spring and fall,   5
when daylight comes, and in the dark of night,
always I weep. Indeed I have the right
on Love, my fate, my lady thus to call.

I live on hope alone, remembering
how I have seen a little moisture prove   10
to wear down marble and the solid stone:

there cannot be a heart so hard that weeping,
praying, and loving sometime will not move,
nor yet a will so cold it cannot burn.

CCXCII

The eyes I spoke of once in words that burn,
the arms and hands and feet and lovely face
that took me from myself for such a space
of time and marked me out from other men;

the waving hair of unmixed gold that shone,   5
the smile that flashed with the angelic rays
that used to make this earth a paradise,
are now a little dust, all feeling gone;

and yet I live, grief and disdain to me,
left where the light I cherished never shows,   10
in fragile bark on the tempestuous sea.

Here let my loving song come to a close,
the vein of my accustomed art is dry,
and this, my lyre, turned at last to tears.[1]

CCCLXV[1]

I keep lamenting over days gone by,
the time I spent loving a mortal thing,

[1] See Job, 30:31, "My lyre is turned to mourning."
[1] The last sonnet, but not the last poem in the *Canzoniere*, which concludes with a canzone
to the Virgin.

with no attempt to soar, although my wing
might give no mean example in the sky.[2]

You that my foul unworthy sins descry,   5
unseen and everlasting, heaven's King,
succour my soul, infirm and wandering,
and what is lacking let your grace supply;

so if I lived in tempest and in war,
I die in port and peace; however vain   10
the stay, at least the parting may be fair.

Now in the little life that still remains
and at my death may your quick hand be near:
in others, you well know, my hope is gone.

[2] The humility of the recantation is rendered more poignant by this lingering touch of
human pride. Love for the "mortal thing" has been an obstacle to salvation, but there is also
the explicit regret that it has prevented him from demonstrating his true worth in the eyes of
the world.

Giovanni Boccaccio
(1313–1375)

*The great triumvirate of Italian literature in the fourteenth century consists of
Dante, Petrarch, and Boccaccio. Boccaccio, the youngest, was born in 1313, the
illegitimate son of a merchant-banker who had family roots in or near Florence. The
legend, nurtured by Boccaccio, that he was born in Paris of an aristocratic mother is
now regarded skeptically. He spent his childhood, not very happily, in Florence, moving
with his businessman father to Naples when Boccaccio was about fourteen. His father
gave him twelve years of education, first in commerce and then in church law, but
Boccaccio wanted above all else to be a poet. His contact with the aristocracy of
Naples, who had banking connections with his father's firm, gave Boccaccio the
opportunity to develop as both writer and gentleman, since the Neapolitan court was
highly cultivated and intellectual in tone. At the same time, his connection with
commerce, in Naples and later in Florence, taught him about the life of middle-class
people. It was in Naples too that Boccaccio is supposed to have met "Fiammetta," the
object of his passionate love—the equivalent for Boccaccio of Dante's Beatrice and
Petrarch's Laura. The identity of Fiammetta in real life is uncertain, and her very
existence has been questioned. Real or fictitious, however, she was the occasion or
focus for much of Boccaccio's early work. In this period, he wrote mainly in Italian
rather than in the traditional learned language, Latin.*

*In 1340, Boccaccio reluctantly left Naples, where he had been very happy, and
returned to Florence, where his literary art reached its full flower, culminating in* The

Decameron *(completed by 1353), or "Work of Ten Days." Boccaccio's earlier writing had been distinctly medieval in its concern with chivalric themes and its use of the genres of romance and allegory. Certain of his early works had revealed his gift of keen insight into human psychology, but nothing quite prepares us for* The Decameron, *with its brilliant dramatic and narrative styles and its rich variety of tones, from the wholly serious and tragic to the raucously farcical. Boccaccio had seen at first hand in Florence the ravages of the plague (the Black Death), and his vividly gruesome account of it at the beginning of* The Decameron *throws into relief the idyllic life led by the seven women and three men who tell the stories. The tone of their life in their country refuge is witty, refined, decorous, but relaxedly sensuous, in sharp contrast with the horrors they have escaped. The reader is aware, however, at some level of consciousness, of the terrible background. The most broadly comic parts of the work can be experienced as a reflex response to the plague, by characters and readers alike.*

The Decameron *served as a model for Italian prose writers and had an enormous influence on later European literature. But Boccaccio wrote no later works in the same vein. In 1350, he met Petrarch (of whom he had already written a biography), and the two men enjoyed a close friendship for the rest of their lives. Petrarch influenced Boccaccio in some important ways, turning him toward the Latin tongue and various scholarly projects (for example, compendia of ancient myths, of famous men and women, and of place names in classical literature). Petrarch seems also to have been one cause, though not the only one, of an increasingly moral and religious tone in Boccaccio's later years. On the other hand, it was Petrarch who, when Boccaccio contemplated burning his earlier works, persuaded him not to do so. Having proved himself, in* The Decameron, *to be a humanist in the modern, popular sense, the older Boccaccio proved himself a humanist in the more technical sense that has to do with the revival of ancient classical learning and literature. He was instrumental, for example, in encouraging the translation of the epics of Homer. He also wrote, in Italian, a treatise on Dante and a commentary on the first half of Dante's* Inferno. *Despite the honor of public offices and of several ambassadorships, the last decades of Boccaccio's life were unsettled, often overshadowed by poverty. He died in 1375, a year later than Petrarch.*

The much discussed question whether Boccaccio belongs to the Middle Ages or to the Renaissance is for some scholars a pseudoquestion, implying an overly simple view of the Middle Ages as piously ascetic and of the Renaissance as exclusively secular. Even if one allows for the distortions of stereotyping, however, it is difficult not to see in Boccaccio's work, or at least The Decameron, *something distinctively modern. Much of his work looks backward to medieval chivalric values and beyond them to antiquity. But the worldly pragmatism of* The Decameron, *with its almost exclusive emphasis on human ingenuity and resourcefulness, is something genuinely new. Heaven and divine grace play almost no role in* The Decameron. *In the hundred tales, people are what the vicissitudes of life and their own characters make them, whether shrewd or gullible, high-minded or unscrupulous. Moreover,* The Decameron *also represents a transition to social realism; the ten storytellers have the manners of aristocrats, but many of the stories involve people of the lower and especially the middle classes. The essence of* The Decameron *is its variety—of subject matter, of tone, and of source (Boccaccio invented few, if any, of the tales in toto). The sense of a broad social and literary spectrum is one of the several parallels between Boccaccio and Chaucer, who was influenced by him.*

Part of the worldliness of The Decameron *is its notorious bawdiness, which is sometimes very explicit. Boccaccio's defensiveness on the matter shows that in his own time, and not only in later more prudish eras, some of the stories gave offense. Boccaccio tries to vindicate himself in his conclusion, advancing arguments that the reader may or may not find convincing. To them one may add the obvious: that the governing theme of* The Decameron *is love, and any comprehensive treatment of it must include the carnal as well as the psychological and spiritual. To many readers the main justification for the bawdiness will be the sparkling wit that characterizes many of the sexual episodes. It must be added too that the sexuality of* The Decameron *is intimately connected with its treatment of the sexes, particularly the very modern portrayal of women not as etherealized ideals but as realistic creatures of flesh and blood who are driven as much by desire as men are. (The controversially patient Griselda is the exception that dramatizes the rule.) Women in* The Decameron *are seldom passive victims. They are as much in control of their lives as the men are, sometimes more so.*

FURTHER READING (*prepared by W. J. R.*): Thomas Bergin's *Boccaccio*, 1982, is a comprehensive introduction to the author's life and writings. Thomas Caldecot Chubb's *The Life of Giovanni Boccaccio*, 1930, is solidly packed with dates and facts. Vittore Branca's *Boccaccio: The Man and His Works*, translated by Richard Monges, 1976, provides a brief biographical sketch. Book II is devoted to *The Decameron*, with discussions of the medieval tradition in Boccaccio's work, his narrative art, and other topics. On style, see *An Anatomy of Boccaccio's Style*, ed. by Marga Cottino-Jones, 1968. Critical approaches in this volume range from linguistic to archetypal. The first essay offers an overview of Boccaccio criticism. John M. Ferrante's "Narrative Patterns in the *Decameron*," *Romance Philology*, 31 (1978), 585–604, covers the entire *Decameron*, seeking to clarify the meaning of narrative themes. "The Worlds of the *Decameron*," Chapter Two in Yvonne Rodax's *The Real and the Ideal in the Novella of Italy, France and England*, 1968, discusses the achievement of vigorous reality in Boccaccio's tales, with a particular emphasis on medieval values. The first and third chapters in this work, on the novella and on *The Canterbury Tales*, are also of interest. Shirley S. Allen's "The Griselda Tale and the Portrayal of Women in the *Decameron*," *Philological Quarterly*, 56 (1977), 1–13, considers previous interpretations of the tale of "patient Griselda" and argues that viewing the tale as an ironic plea for women's rights is in accord with the overall unity of *The Decameron*. Marga Cottino-Jones' "Comic Modalities in the *Decameron*," in *Versions of Medieval Comedy*, ed. by Paul G. Ruggiers, 1977, investigates the varying comic tones and makes some general observations on the nature of Boccaccio's comedy. Cormac Cuilleanáin's "Man and Beast in the *Decameron*," *Modern Language Review*, 75 (1980), 86–93, studies animal imagery and symbolism as it reveals Boccaccio's principal theme of man's existence in a social community.

THE DECAMERON

Translated by Richard Aldington

THE FIRST DAY

Here begins the first day of the Decameron, *wherein, after the author has showed the reasons why certain persons gathered to tell tales, they treat of any subject pleasing to them, under the rule of Pampinea.*

Most gracious ladies, knowing that you are all by nature pitiful, I know that in your judgment this work will seem to have a painful and sad origin. For it brings to mind the unhappy recollection of that late dreadful plague,[1] so pernicious to all who saw or heard of it. But I would not have this frighten you from reading further, as though you were to pass through nothing but sighs and tears in your reading. This dreary opening will be like climbing a steep mountain side to a most beautiful and delightful valley, which appears the more pleasant in proportion to the difficulty of the ascent. The end of happiness is pain, and in like manner misery ends in unexpected happiness.

This brief fatigue (I say brief, because it occupies only a few words) is quickly followed by pleasantness and delight, as I promised you above; which, if I had not promised, you would not expect perhaps from this opening. Indeed, if I could have taken you by any other way than this, which I know to be rough, I would gladly have done so; but since I cannot otherwise tell you how the tales you are about to read came to be told, I am forced by necessity to write in this manner.

In the year 1348 after the fruitful incarnation of the Son of God, that most beautiful of Italian cities, noble Florence, was attacked by deadly plague. It started in the East either through the influence of the heavenly bodies or because God's just anger with our wicked deeds sent it as a punishment to mortal men; and in a few years killed an innumerable quantity of people. Ceaselessly passing from place to place, it extended its miserable length over the West. Against this plague all human wisdom and foresight were vain. Orders had been given to cleanse the city of filth, the entry of any sick person was forbidden, much advice was given for keeping healthy; at the same time humble supplications were made to God by pious persons in processions and otherwise. And yet, in the beginning of the spring of the year mentioned, its horrible results began to appear, and in a miraculous manner. The symptoms were not the same as in the East, where a gush of blood from the nose was the plain sign of inevitable death; but it began both in men and women with certain swellings in the groin or under the armpit. They grew to the size of a small apple or an egg, more or less, and were vulgarly called tumors. In a short space of time these tumors spread from the two parts named all over the body. Soon after this the symptoms changed and black or purple spots appeared on the arms or thighs or any other part of the body, sometimes a few large ones, sometimes many little ones. These spots were a certain sign of death, just as the original tumor had been and still remained.

No doctor's advice, no medicine could overcome or alleviate this disease. An enormous number of ignorant men and women set up as doctors in addition to those who were trained. Either the disease was such that no treatment was possible or the doctors were so ignorant that they did not know what caused it, and consequently could not administer the proper remedy. In any case very few recovered; most people died within about three days of the appearance of the tumors described above, most of them without any fever or other symptoms.

[1] The "Black Death," probably bubonic plague, killed millions in Europe and Asia in the mid-fourteenth century.

The violence of this disease was such that the sick communicated it to the healthy who came near them, just as a fire catches anything dry or oily near it. And it even went further. To speak to or go near the sick brought infection and a common death to the living; and moreover, to touch the clothes or anything else the sick had touched or worn gave the disease to the person touching.

What I am about to tell now is a marvelous thing to hear; and if I and others had not seen it with our own eyes I would not dare to write it, however much I was willing to believe and whatever the good faith of the person from whom I heard it. So violent was the malignancy of this plague that it was communicated, not only from one man to another, but from the garments of a sick or dead man to animals of another species, which caught the disease in that way and very quickly died of it. One day among other occasions I saw with my own eyes (as I said just now) the rags left lying in the street of a poor man who had died of the plague; two pigs came along and, as their habit is, turned the clothes over with their snouts and then munched at them, with the result that they both fell dead almost at once on the rags, as if they had been poisoned.

From these and similar or greater occurrences, such fear and fanciful notions took possession of the living that almost all of them adopted the same cruel policy, which was entirely to avoid the sick and everything belonging to them. By so doing, each one thought he would secure his own safety.

Some thought that moderate living and the avoidance of all superfluity would preserve them from the epidemic. They formed small communities, living entirely separate from everybody else. They shut themselves up in houses where there were no sick, eating the finest food and drinking the best wine very temperately, avoiding all excess, allowing no news or discussion of death and sickness, and passing the time in music and suchlike pleasures. Others thought just the opposite. They thought the sure cure for the plague was to drink and be merry, to go about singing and amusing themselves, satisfying every appetite they could, laughing and jesting at what happened. They put their words into practice, spent day and night going from tavern to tavern, drinking immoderately, or went into other people's houses, doing only those things which pleased them. This they could easily do because everyone felt doomed and had abandoned his property, so that most houses became common property and any stranger who went in made use of them as if he had owned them. And with all this bestial behavior, they avoided the sick as much as possible.

In this suffering and misery of our city, the authority of human and divine laws almost disappeared, for, like other men, the ministers and the executors of the laws were all dead or sick or shut up with their families, so that no duties were carried out. Every man was therefore able to do as he pleased.

Many others adopted a course of life midway between the two just described. They did not restrict their victuals so much as the former, nor allow themselves to be drunken and dissolute like the latter, but satisfied their appetites moderately. They did not shut themselves up, but went about, carrying flowers or scented herbs or perfumes in their hands, in the belief that it was an excellent thing to comfort the brain with such odors;

for the whole air was infected with the smell of dead bodies, of sick persons and medicines.

Others again held a still more cruel opinion, which they thought would keep them safe. They said that the only medicine against the plaguestricken was to go right away from them. Men and women, convinced of this and caring about nothing but themselves, abandoned their own city, their own houses, their dwellings, their relatives, their property, and went abroad or at least to the country round Florence, as if God's wrath in punishing men's wickedness with this plague would not follow them but strike only those who remained within the walls of the city, or as if they thought nobody in the city would remain alive and that its last hour had come.

Not everyone who adopted any of these various opinions died, nor did all escape. Some when they were still healthy had set the example of avoiding the sick, and, falling ill themselves, died untended.

One citizen avoided another, hardly any neighbor troubled about others, relatives never or hardly ever visited each other. Moreover, such terror was struck into the hearts of men and women by this calamity, that brother abandoned brother, and the uncle his nephew, and the sister her brother, and very often the wife her husband. What is even worse and nearly incredible is that fathers and mothers refused to see and tend their children, as if they had not been theirs.

Thus, a multitude of sick men and women were left without any care except from the charity of friends (but these were few), or the greed of servants, though not many of these could be had even for high wages. Moreover, most of them were coarse-minded men and women, who did little more than bring the sick what they asked for or watch over them when they were dying. And very often these servants lost their lives and their earnings. Since the sick were thus abandoned by neighbors, relatives and friends, while servants were scarce, a habit sprang up which had never been heard of before. Beautiful and noble women, when they fell sick, did not scruple to take a young or old manservant, whoever he might be, and with no sort of shame, expose every part of their bodies to these men as if they had been women, for they were compelled by the necessity of their sickness to do so. This, perhaps, was a cause of looser morals in those women who survived.

In this way many people died who might have been saved if they had been looked after. Owing to the lack of attendants for the sick and the violence of the plague, such a multitude of people in the city died day and night that it was stupefying to hear of, let alone to see. From sheer necessity, then, several ancient customs were quite altered among the survivors.

The custom had been (as we still see it today) that women relatives and neighbors should gather at the house of the deceased, and there lament with the family. At the same time the men would gather at the door with the male neighbors and other citizens. Then came the clergy, few or many according to the dead person's rank; the coffin was placed on the shoulders of his friends and carried with funeral pomp of lighted candles and dirges to the church which the deceased had chosen before dying. But as the fury of the plague increased, this custom wholly or nearly disappeared, and new customs arose. Thus, people died, not only without having a number of women near them, but without a single witness. Very few indeed were honored with the piteous laments and bitter tears of their relatives, who, on the contrary, spent their time in mirth, feasting and jesting. Even the women abandoned womanly pity and adopted this custom for their own safety. Few were they whose bodies were accompanied to church by more than ten or a dozen neighbors. Nor were these grave and honorable citizens but grave-diggers from the lowest of the people who got themselves called sextons, and performed the task for money. They took up the bier and hurried it off, not to the church chosen by the deceased but the church nearest, preceded by four or six of the clergy with few candles and often none at all. With the aid of the grave-diggers, the clergy huddled the bodies away in any grave they could find, without giving themselves the trouble of a long or solemn burial service.

The plight of the lower and most of the middle classes was even more pitiful to behold. Most of them remained in their houses, either through poverty or in hopes of safety, and fell sick by thousands. Since they received no care and attention, almost all of them died. Many ended their lives in the streets both at night and during the day; and many others who died in their houses were only known to be dead because the neighbors smelled their decaying bodies. Dead bodies filled every corner. Most of them were treated in the same manner by the survivors, who were more concerned to get rid of their rotting bodies than moved by charity towards the dead. With the aid of porters, if they could get them, they carried the bodies out of the houses and laid them at the doors, where every morning quantities of the dead might be seen. They then were laid on biers, or, as these were often lacking, on tables.

Often a single bier carried two or three bodies, and it happened frequently that a husband and wife, two or three brothers, or father and son were taken off on the same bier. It frequently happened that two priests, each carrying a cross, would go out followed by three or four biers carried by porters; and where the priests thought there was one person to bury, there would be six or eight, and often, even more. Nor were these dead honored by tears and lighted candles and mourners, for things had reached such a pass that people cared no more for dead men than we care for dead goats. Thus it plainly appeared that what the wise had not learned to endure with patience through the few calamities of ordinary life, became a matter of indifference even to the most ignorant people through the greatness of this misfortune.

Such was the multitude of corpses brought to the churches every day and almost every hour that there was not enough consecrated ground to give them burial, especially since they wanted to bury each person in the family grave, according to the old custom. Although the cemeteries were full they were forced to dig huge trenches, where they buried the bodies by hundreds. Here they stowed them away like bales in the hold of a ship and covered them with a little earth, until the whole trench was full.

Not to pry any further into all the details of the miseries which afflicted our city, I shall add that the surrounding country was spared nothing of what befell Florence. The villages on a smaller scale were like the city; in the fields and isolated farms the poor wretched peasants and their families were without doctors and any assistance, and perished in the highways, in their fields and houses, night and day, more like beasts than men. Just as the townsmen became dissolute and indifferent to their work and property, so the peasants, when they saw that death was upon them, entirely neglected the future fruits of their past labors both from the earth and from cattle, and thought only of enjoying what they had. Thus it happened that cows, asses, sheep, goats, pigs, fowls and even dogs, those faithful companions of man, left the farms and wandered at their will through the fields, where the wheat crops stood abandoned, unreaped and ungarnered. Many of these animals seemed endowed with reason, for, after they had pastured all day, they returned to the farms for the night of their own free will, without being driven.

Returning from the country to the city, it may be said that such was the cruelty of Heaven, and perhaps in part of men, that between March and July more than one hundred thousand persons died within the walls of Florence, what between the violence of the plague and the abandonment in which the sick were left by the cowardice of the healthy. And before the plague it was not thought that the whole city held so many people.

Oh, what great palaces, how many fair houses and noble dwellings, once filled with attendants and nobles and ladies, were emptied to the meanest servant! How many famous names and vast possessions and renowned estates were left without an heir! How many gallant men and fair ladies and handsome youths, whom Galen, Hippocrates and Aesculapius[2] themselves would have said were in perfect health, at noon dined with their relatives and friends, and at night supped with their ancestors in the next world!

But it fills me with sorrow to go over so many miseries. Therefore, since I want to pass over all I can leave out, I shall go on to say that when our city was in this condition and almost emptied of inhabitants, one Tuesday morning the venerable church of Santa Maria Novella had scarcely any congregation for divine service except (as I have heard from a person worthy of belief) seven young women in the mourning garments suitable to the times, who were all related by ties of blood, friendship or neighborship. None of them was older than twenty-eight or younger than eighteen; all were educated and of noble blood, fair to look upon, well-mannered and of graceful modesty.

I should tell you their real names if I had not a good reason for not doing so, which is that I would not have any of them blush in the future for the things they say and hearken to in the following pages. The laws are now strict again, whereas then, for the reasons already shown, they were very lax, not only for persons of their age but for those much older. Nor would I give an opportunity to the envious (always ready to sneer at every praiseworthy life) to attack the virtue of these modest ladies with vulgar speech. But so that you may understand without confusion what each one says, I intend to give them names wholly or partly suitable to the qualities of each.

The first and eldest I shall call Pampinea, the second Fiammetta, the third Filomena, the fourth Emilia, the fifth Lauretta, the sixth Neifile, and

---

[2] The first two were ancient Greek physicians; Aesculapius was a Graeco-Roman god of medicine.

the last Elisa[3] (or "the virgin") for a very good reason. They met, not by arrangement, but by chance, in the same part of the church, and sat down in a circle. After many sighs they ceased to pray and began to talk about the state of affairs and other things. After a short space of silence, Pampinea said:

"Dear ladies, you must often have heard, as I have, that to make a sensible use of one's reason harms nobody. It is natural for everybody to aid, preserve and defend his life as far as possible. And this is so far admitted that to save their own lives men often kill others who have done no harm. If this is permitted by the laws which are concerned with the general good, it must certainly be lawful for us to take any reasonable means for the preservation of our lives. When I think of what we have been doing this morning and still more on former days, when I remember what we have been saying, I perceive and you must perceive that each of us goes in fear of her life. I do not wonder at this, but, since each of us has a woman's judgment, I do wonder that we do not seek some remedy against what we dread.

"In my opinion we remain here for no other purpose than to witness how many bodies are buried, or listen whether the friars here (themselves reduced almost to nothing) sing their offices at the canonical hours,[4] or to display by our clothes the quantity and quality of our miseries to anyone who comes here. If we leave this church we see the bodies of the dead and the sick being carried about. Or we see those who had been exiled from the city by the authority of the laws for their crimes, deriding this authority because they know the guardians of the law are sick or dead, and running loose about the place. Or we see the dregs of the city battening on our blood and calling themselves sextons, riding about on horseback in every direction and insulting our calamities with vile songs. On every side we hear nothing but "So-and-so is dead" or "So-and-so is dying." And if there were anyone left to weep we should hear nothing but piteous lamentations. I do not know if it is the same in your homes as in mine. But if I go home there is nobody left there but one of my maids, which fills me with such horror that the hair stands upon my head. Wherever I go or sit at home I seem to see the ghosts of the departed, not with the faces as I knew them but with dreadful looks which terrify me.

"I am ill at ease here and outside of here and at home; the more so since nobody who has the strength and ability to go away (as we have) now remains here, except ourselves. The few that remain (if there are any), according to what I see and hear, do anything which gives them pleasure or pleases their appetites, both by day and night, whether they are alone or in company, making no distinction between right and wrong. Not only laymen, but those cloistered in convents have broken their oaths and given

---

[3] Most of the names are derived from Greek and have something to do with love. The qualities or roles associated with the seven women are probably as follows: Pampinea (the eldest) is a leader and adviser; Fiammetta is loving and beloved; Philomena (related to "nightingale") is a lover of music; Emilia has pleasant manners; Lauretta (related to *laurel*) is learned; Neifile is young and naive; Elisa, who is also young, recalls *Elissa*, a name for Dido, the passionate Carthaginian queen in Virgil's *Aeneid*.

[4] Chant their prayers at the times of day specified by the Church.

themselves up to the delights of the flesh, and thus in trying to escape the plague by doing what they please, they have become lascivious and dissolute.

"If this is so (and we may plainly see it is) what are we doing here? What are we waiting for? What are we dreaming about? Are we less eager and active than other citizens in saving our lives? Are they less dear to us than to others? Or do we think that our lives are bound to our bodies with stronger chains than other people's, and so believe that we need fear nothing which might harm us? We were and are deceived. How stupid we should be to believe such a thing! We may see the plainest proofs from the number of young men and women who have died of this cruel plague.

"I do not know if you think as I do, but in my opinion if we, through carelessness, do not want to fall into this calamity when we can escape it, I think we should do well to leave this town, just as many others have done and are doing. Let us avoid the wicked examples of others like death itself, and go and live virtuously in our country houses, of which each of us possesses several. There let us take what happiness and pleasure we can, without ever breaking the rules of reason in any manner.

"There we shall hear the birds sing, we shall see the green hills and valleys, the wheat-fields rolling like a sea, and all kinds of trees. We shall see the open Heavens which, although now angered against man, do not withhold from us their eternal beauties that are so much fairer to look upon than the empty walls of our city. The air will be fresher there, we shall find a greater plenty of those things necessary to life at this time, and fewer troubles. Although the peasants are dying like the townsmen, still, since the houses and inhabitants are fewer, we shall see less of them and feel less misery. On the other hand I believe we are not abandoning anybody here. Indeed we can truthfully say that we are abandoned, since our relatives have either died or fled from death and have left us alone in this calamity as if we were nothing to them.

"If we do what I suggest, no blame can fall upon us; if we fail to do it, the result may be pain, trouble and perhaps death. Therefore I think that we should do well to take our servants and all things necessary, and go from one house to another, enjoying whatever merriment and pleasure these times allow. Let us live in this way (unless death comes upon us) until we see what end Heaven decrees to this plague. And remember that going away virtuously will not harm us so much as staying here in wickedness will harm others."

The other ladies listened to what Pampinea said, praised her advice, and in their eagerness to follow it began to discuss details, as if they were going to leave at once. But Filomena, who was a most prudent young woman, said:

"Ladies, although what Pampinea says is excellent advice, we must not rush off at once, as you seem to wish. Remember we are all women; and any girl can tell you how women behave together and conduct themselves without the direction of some man. We are fickle, wayward, suspicious, faint-hearted and cowardly. So if we have no guide but ourselves I greatly suspect that this company will very soon break up, without much honor to ourselves. Let us settle this matter before we start."

Elisa then broke in:

"Indeed men are a woman's head and we can rarely succeed in anything without their help; but how can we find any men? Each of us knows that most of her menfolk are dead, while the others are away, we know not where, flying with their companions from the end we wish to escape. To ask strangers would be unbecoming; for, if we mean to go away to save our lives we must take care that scandal and annoyance do not follow us where we are seeking rest and amusement."

While the ladies were thus arguing, three young men came into the church, the youngest of whom was not less than twenty-five. They were lovers whose love could not be quenched or even cooled by the horror of the times, the loss of relatives and friends, or even fear for themselves. The first was named Pamfilo, the second Filostrato, the third Dioneo.[5] They were pleasant, well-mannered men, and in this public calamity they sought the consolation of looking upon the ladies they loved. These ladies happened to be among our seven, while some of the others were related to one or other of the three men. They no sooner came into sight than the ladies saw them; whereupon Pampinea said with a smile:

"See how Fortune favors our plan at once by sending us these valiant and discreet young men, who will gladly act as our guides and servants if we do not refuse to accept them for such duties."

Neifile then became crimson, for she was one of the ladies beloved by one of the young men, and said:

"For God's sake, Pampinea, be careful what you are saying. I know quite well that nothing but good can be said of any of them and I am sure they could achieve greater things than this. I also think that their company would be fitting and pleasant, not only to us, but to ladies far more beautiful and charming than we are. But it is known to everyone that they are in love with some of us women here; and so, if we take them with us, I am afraid that blame and infamy will fall upon us, through no fault of ours or theirs."

Then said Filomena:

"What does that matter? If I live virtuously, my conscience never pricks me, whatever people may say. God and the truth will fight for me. If these men would come with us, then indeed, as Pampinea said, fortune would be favorable to our plan of going away."

The others not only refrained from censuring what she said, but agreed by common consent that the men should be spoken to, told their plan, and asked if they would accompany the ladies on their expedition. Without more ado, Pampinea, who was related to one of them, arose and went towards them where they stood looking at the ladies, saluted them cheerfully, told them the plan, and begged them in the name of all the ladies to accompany them out of pure and fraternal affection.

At first the young men thought this was a jest. But when they saw the lady was speaking seriously, they said they were willing to go. And in order to start without delay they at once gave the orders necessary for departure. Everything necessary was made ready, and word was sent on ahead to the

---

[5] The name *Pamphilo* means "loving all"; *Filostrato* means "lover of strife" (perhaps the strife of being in love) and also "victim of love"; *Dioneo* is related to one of the names of Venus, goddess of sexual love.

place they were going. At dawn next morning, which was Wednesday, the ladies with some of their servants, and the young men with a man servant each, left the city and set out. They had not gone more than two miles when they came to the first place where they were to stay.

This estate was on slightly raised ground, at some distance from any main road, with many trees and plants, fair to look upon. At the top of the rise was a country mansion with a large inner courtyard. It had open colonnades, galleries and rooms, all beautiful in themselves and ornamented with gay paintings. Roundabout were lawns and marvelous gardens and wells of cool water. There were cellars of fine wines, more suitable to wine connoisseurs than to sober and virtuous ladies. The whole house had been cleaned, the beds were prepared in the rooms, and every corner was strewn with the flowers of the season and fresh rushes. All of which the company beheld with no little pleasure.

They all sat down to discuss plans, and Dioneo, who was a most amusing young man and full of witticisms, remarked:

"Ladies, your good sense, rather than our foresight, has brought us here. I do not know what you are thinking of doing with your troubles here, but I dropped mine inside the gates of the city when I left it with you a little time ago. Therefore, either you must make up your minds to laugh and sing and amuse yourselves with me (that is, to the extent your dignity allows), or you must let me go back to my troubles and stay in the afflicted city."

Pampinea, who had driven away her woes in the same way, cheerfully replied:

"Dioneo, you speak well, let us amuse ourselves, for that was the reason why we fled from our sorrows. But when things are not organized they cannot long continue. And, since I began the discussion which brought this fair company together and since I wish our happiness to continue, I think it necessary that one of us should be made chief, whom the others will honor and obey, and whose duty shall be to regulate our pleasures. Now, so that everyone—both man and woman—may experience the cares as well as the pleasures of ruling and no one feel any envy at not sharing them, I think the weight and honor should be given to each of us in turn for one day. The first shall be elected by all of us. At vespers[6] he or she shall choose the ruler for the next day, and so on. While their reigns last these rulers shall arrange where and how we are to spend our time."

These words pleased them all and they unanimously elected her for the first day. Filomena ran to a laurel bush, whose leaves she had always heard were most honorable in themselves and did great honor to anyone crowned with them, plucked off a few small branches and wove them into a fair garland of honor. When this was placed on the head of any one of them, it was a symbol of rule and authority over the rest so long as the party remained together.

Pampinea, thus elected queen, ordered silence. She then sent for the three servants of the young men and the four women servants the ladies had brought, and said:

"To set a first example to you all which may be bettered and thus allow

---

[6] One of the canonical hours; about 6 P.M.

our gathering to live pleasantly and orderly and without shame and to last as long as we desire, I appoint Dioneo's servant Parmeno as my steward, and hand over to him the care of the whole family and of everything connected with the dining hall. Pamfilo's servant Sirisco shall be our treasurer and buyer, and carry out Parmeno's instructions. Tindaro shall wait on Filostrato and Dioneo and Pamfilo in their rooms, when the other two servants are occupied with their new duties. Filomena's servant Licisca and my own servant Misia shall remain permanently in the kitchen and carefully prepare the food which Parmeno sends them. Lauretta's Chimera and Fiammetta's Stratilia shall take care of the ladies' rooms and see that the whole house is clean. Moreover we will and command that everyone who values our good grace shall bring back only cheerful news, wherever he may go or return from, and whatever he may hear or see."

Having given these orders, which were approved by everyone, she jumped gaily to her feet and said:

"Here are gardens and lawns and other delicious places, where each of us can wander and enjoy them at will. But let everyone be here at the hour of Tierce[7] so that we can eat together while it is still cool."

The company of gay young men and women, thus given the queen's permission, went off together slowly through the gardens, talking of pleasant matters, weaving garlands of different leaves, and singing love songs. After the time allotted by the queen had elapsed they returned to the house and found that Parmeno had carefully carried out the duties of his office. Entering a ground floor room decorated everywhere with broom[8] blossoms, they found tables covered with white cloths and set with glasses which shone like silver. They washed their hands and, at the queen's command, all sat down in the places allotted them by Parmeno. Delicately cooked food was brought, exquisite wines were at hand, and the three men servants waited at table. Everyone was delighted to see things so handsome and well arranged, and they ate merrily with much happy talk.

All the ladies and young men could dance and many of them could play and sing; so, when the tables were cleared, the queen called for musical instruments. At her command Dioneo took a lute and Fiammetta a viol, and began to play a dance tune. The queen sent the servants to their meal, and then with slow steps danced with the two young men and the other ladies. After that, they began to sing gay and charming songs.

In this way they amused themselves until the queen thought it was time for the siesta. So, at the queen's bidding, the three young men went off to their rooms (which were separated from the ladies') and found them filled with flowers as the dining hall had been. And similarly with the women. So they all undressed and went to sleep.

Not long after the hour of Nones,[9] the queen arose and made the other women and the young men also get up, saying that it was harmful to sleep too long during the daytime. Then they went out to a lawn of thick green grass entirely shaded from the sun. A soft breeze came to them there. The queen made them sit down in a circle on the grass, and said:

"As you see, the sun is high and the heat great, and nothing can be heard but the cicadas in the olive trees. To walk about at this hour would be

[7] A canonical hour; 9 A.M.   [8] A shrub.   [9] A canonical hour; about 3 P.M.

foolish. Here it is cool and lovely, and, as you see, there are games of chess and draughts which everyone can amuse himself with, as he chooses. But, if my opinion is followed, we shall not play games, because in games the mind of one of the players must necessarily be distressed without any great pleasure to the other player or the onlookers. Let us rather spend this hot part of the day in telling tales, for thus one person can give pleasure to the whole company. When each of us has told a story, the sun will be going down and the heat less, and we can then go walking anywhere we choose for our amusement. If this pleases you (for here I am ready to follow your pleasure) let us do it. If it does not please you, let everyone do as he likes until evening."

The women and men all favored the telling of stories.

"Then if it pleases you," said the queen, "on this first day I order that everyone shall tell his tale about any subject he likes."

She then turned to Pamfilo, who was seated on her right, and ordered him to begin with a tale. Hearing this command, Pamfilo at once began as follows, while all listened.[10]

THIRD DAY, TENTH TALE

Alibech becomes a hermit, and the monk Rustico teaches her how to put the devil in Hell. She is afterwards taken away and becomes the wife of Neerbale.

Dioneo had listened closely to the queen's story, and, when it was over and only he remained to tell a story, he did not wait to be commanded, but smilingly began as follows:

Most gracious ladies, perhaps you have never heard how the devil is put into hell; and so, without departing far from the theme[1] upon which you have all spoken today, I shall tell you about it. Perhaps when you have learned it, you also will be able to save your souls, and you may also discover that although love prefers to dwell in gay palaces and lovely rooms rather than in poor huts, yet he sometimes makes his power felt among thick woods and rugged mountains and desert caves. Whereby we may well perceive that all of us are subject to his power.

Now, to come to my story—in the city of Capsa[2] in Barbery there lived a very rich man who possessed among other children a pretty and charming daughter, named Alibech. She was not a Christian, but she heard many Christians in her native town crying up the Christian Faith and service to God, and one day she asked one of them how a person could most effectively serve God. The reply was that those best serve God who fly furthest from the things of this world, like the hermits who had departed to the solitudes of the Thebaid[3] Desert.

---

[10] Here the series of a hundred tales, ten each day, begins. After the first day, when the choice of tales is unrestricted, each day has a prescribed theme.

[1] The stories told on the third day (ruled by Neifile) concern people who by cleverness gained or regained something desirable.

[2] A city in Tunisia; Barbery is in northern Africa.   [3] Near Thebes, in Egypt.

The girl was about fourteen and very simple minded. Urged by a mere childish enthusiasm and not by a well ordered desire, she secretly set out next morning quite alone, without saying a word to anyone, to find the Thebaid Desert. Her enthusiasm lasted several days and enabled her with great fatigue to reach those solitudes. In the distance she saw a little hut with a holy man standing at its entrance. He was amazed to see her there, and asked her what she was seeking. She replied that by God's inspiration she was seeking to serve Him, and begged the hermit to show her the right way to do so. But the holy man saw she was young and pretty, and feared that if he kept her with him he might be tempted of the devil. So he praised her good intentions, gave her some roots and wild apples to eat and some water to drink, and said:

"Daughter, not far from here dwells a holy man who is a far greater master of what you are seeking than I am; go to him."

And so he put her on the way. When she reached him, she was received with much the same words, and passing further on came to the cell of a young hermit named Rustico, to whom she made the same request as to the others. To test his spiritual strength, Rustico did not send her away, but took her into his cell. And when night came, he made her a bed of palm leaves and told her to sleep there.

Almost immediately after this, temptation began the struggle with his spiritual strength, and the hermit found that he had greatly over-estimated his powers of resistance. After a few assaults of the demon he shrugged his shoulders and surrendered. Putting aside holy thoughts and prayers and macerations,[4] he began to think of her beauty and youth, and then pondered how he should proceed with her so that she should not perceive that he obtained what he wanted from her like a dissolute man. First of all he sounded her by certain questions, and discovered that she had never lain with a man and appeared to be very simple minded. He then saw how he could bring her to his desire under pretext of serving God. He began by eloquently showing how the devil is the enemy of the Lord God, and then gave her to understand that the service most pleasing to God is to put the devil back into hell, to which the Lord God has condemned him. The girl asked how this was done, and Rustico replied:

"You shall soon know. Do what you see me do."

He then threw off the few clothes he had and remained stark naked, and the girl imitated him. He kneeled down as if to pray and made her kneel exactly opposite him. As he gazed at her beauty, Rustico's desire became so great that the resurrection of the flesh occurred. Alibech looked at it with amazement, and said:

"Rustico, what is that thing I see sticking out in front of you which I haven't got?"

"My daughter," said Rustico, "that is the devil I spoke of. Do you see? He gives me so much trouble at this moment that I can scarcely endure him."

Said the girl:

"Praised be God! I see I am better off than you are, since I haven't such a devil."

[4] Starvation diets.

"You speak truly," said Rustico, "but instead of this devil you have something else which I haven't."

"What's that?" said Alibech.

"You've got hell," replied Rustico, "and I believe God sent you here for the salvation of my soul, because this devil gives me great trouble, and if you will take pity upon me and let me put him into hell, you will give me the greatest comfort and at the same time will serve God and please Him, since, as you say, you came here for that purpose."

In all good faith the girl replied: "Father, since I have hell in me, let it be whenever you please."

Said Rustico: "Blessings upon you, my daughter. Let us put him in now so that he will afterwards depart from me."

So saying, he took the girl to one of their beds, and showed her how to lie so as to imprison the thing accursed of God. The girl had never before put any devil into her hell and at first felt a little pain, and exclaimed to Rustico:

"O father! This devil must certainly be wicked and the enemy of God, for even when he is put back into hell he hurts it."

"Daughter," said Rustico, "it will not always be so."

To prevent this from happening, Rustico put it into hell six times, before he got off the bed, and so purged the devil's pride that he was glad to rest a little. Thereafter he returned often and the obedient girl was always glad to take him in; and then the game began to give her pleasure, and she said to Rustico:

"I see that the good men of Capsa spoke the truth when they told me how sweet a thing is the service of God. I certainly do not remember that I ever did anything which gave me so much delight and pleasure as I get from putting the devil into hell. I think that everyone is a fool who does anything but serve God."

Thus it happened that she would often go to Rustico, and say:

"Father, I came here to serve God and not to remain in idleness. Let us put the devil in hell."

And once as they were doing it, she said:

"Rustico, I don't know why the devil ever goes out of hell. If he liked to remain there as much as hell likes to receive and hold him, he would never leave it."

The girl's frequent invitations to Rustico and their mutual pleasures in the service of God so took the stuffing out of his doublet[5] that he now felt chilly where another man would have been in a sweat. So he told the girl that the devil must not be chastened or put into hell except when pride made him lift his head. "And we," he said, "have so quelled his rage that he prays God to be left in peace." And in this way he silenced the girl for a time. But when she found that Rustico no longer asked her to put the devil in hell, she said one day:

"Rustico, your devil may be chastened and give you no more trouble, but my hell is not. You should therefore quench the raging of my hell with your devil, as I helped you to quell the pride of your devil with my hell."

Rustico, who lived on nothing but roots and water, made a poor re-

---

[5] Jacket.

sponse to this invitation. He told her that many devils would be needed to soothe her hell, but that he would do what he could. In this way he satisfied her hell a few times, but so seldom that it was like throwing a bean in a lion's mouth. And the girl, who thought they were not serving God as much as she wanted, kept murmuring.

Now, while there was this debate between the excess of desire in Alibech's hell and the lack of potency in Rustico's devil, a fire broke out in Capsa, and burned Alibech's father with all his children and servants. So Alibech became heir to all his property. A young man named Neerbale, who had spent all his money in riotous living, heard that she was still alive and set out to find her, which he succeeded in doing before the Court took over her father's property as that of a man who had died without heirs. To Rustico's great relief, but against her will, Neerbale brought her back to Capsa and married her, and together they inherited her large patrimony. But before Neerbale had lain with her, certain ladies one day asked her how she had served God in the desert. She replied that her service was to put the devil in hell, and that Neerbale had committed a great sin by taking her away from such service. The ladies asked:

"And how do you put the devil in hell?"

Partly in words and partly by gestures, the girl told them. At this they laughed so much that they are still laughing, and said:

"Be not cast down, my child, they know how to do that here, and Neerbale will serve the Lord God with you in that way."

As they told it up and down the city, it passed into a proverb that the service most pleasing to God is to put the devil into hell. And this proverb crossed the seas and remains until this day.

Therefore, young ladies, when you seek God's favor, learn to put the devil in hell, because this is most pleasing to God and to all parties concerned, and much good may come of it.

Dioneo's tale moved the chaste ladies to laughter hundreds of times, so apt and amusing did they find his words. When he had finished, the queen knew that the end of her reign had come, and therefore took the laurel wreath from her head and placed it upon Filostrato's, saying pleasantly:

"We shall soon find out if the wolf can guide the flock, as well as the flock has guided the wolves."

Filostrato laughingly replied:

"If my advice were followed, the wolves would have showed the flock how to put the devil in hell, as Rustico taught Alibech; and so they would not be called wolves, where you would not be the flock. However, since the rule now falls to me, I shall begin my reign."

Said Neifile:

"Filostrato, in trying to teach us, you might have learned wisdom, as Masetto da Lamporecchio learned it from the nuns,[6] and you might have regained your speech when your bones were rattling together from exhaustion!"

Filostrato, finding the ladies' sickles were as good as his shafts, ceased jesting, and occupied himself with the government of his kingdom. Calling the steward, he made enquiries into everything, and gave orders to ensure

---

[6] A reference to another tale told earlier on the third day.

the well being and satisfaction of the band during his kingship. He then turned to the ladies and said:

"Amorous ladies, to my own misfortune—although I was quite aware of my disease—I have always been one of Love's subjects owing to the beauty of one of you. To be humble and obedient to her and to follow all her whims as closely as I could, was all of no avail to me, and I was soon abandoned for another. Thus I go from bad to worse, and believe I shall until I die. Tomorrow then it is my pleasure that we tell tales on a theme in conformity with my own fate—that is, about those persons whose love ended unhappily. In the long run I expect a most unhappy end for myself, and the person who gave me the nickname of Filostrato, or the Victim of Love, knew what she was doing."

So saying, he rose to his feet, and gave them all leave to depart until supper time.

The garden was so delightful and so beautiful that they all chose to remain there, since no greater pleasure could be found elsewhere. The sun was now not so hot, and therefore some of them began to chase the deer and rabbits and other animals which had annoyed them scores of times by leaping in among them while they were seated. Dioneo and Fiammetta began to sing the song of Messer Guglielmo and the Lady of Vergiu. Filomena and Pamfilo played chess. Thus, with one thing and another, time passed so quickly that supper time arrived long before they expected. The tables were set round the fountain, and there they ate their evening meal with the utmost pleasure.

When they rose from table, Filostrato would not depart from the path followed by the preceding queens, and so ordered Lauretta to dance and sing a song. And she said:

"My lord, I do not know any songs of other persons, and I do not remember any of my own which are fitting for this merry band. But if you wish to have one of those I remember, I will gladly sing it."

"Nothing of yours could be anything but fair and pleasing," said the king, "so sing it just as it is."

Then to the accompaniment of the others, Lauretta sang as follows in a sweet but rather plaintive voice:

No helpless lady has such cause to weep as I, who vainly sigh, alas, for love.

He who moves the heavens and all the stars[7] made me for His delight so fair, so sweet, so gracious and so lovely that I might show to every lofty mind some trace of that high Beauty which ever dwells within His presence. But a weak man, who knew not Beauty, found me undelightful and scorned me.

Once there was one who held me dear, and in my early years took me into his arms and to his thoughts, being quite conquered by my eyes. And time, that flies so swiftly, he spent in serving me; and I in courtesy made him worthy of me. But now, alas, he is taken from me.

Then came a proud presumptuous man, who thought himself both noble and valorous, and made me his, but through false belief became most jealous of me. And

---

[7] The mover is God; the line is a close paraphrase of the last line of Dante's *Divine Comedy*.

then, alas, I came near to despair, for I saw that I, who came into the world to pleasure many, was possessed by one alone.

I curse my luckless fate that ever I said "yes" to man, and changed to a wife's garb. I was so gay in my old plain maiden's dress! Now in these finer clothes I lead so sad a life, reputed less than chaste. O hapless wedding feast! Would I had died before I knew the fate it held for me!

O my first love, with whom I was so happy, who now in Heaven do stand before Him who created it, have pity on me. I cannot forget you for another. Let me feel that the flame wherewith you burned for me is not extinct, and pray that I may soon return to you.

Here ended Lauretta's song, which was noted carefully by them all, but interpreted differently. Some understood it in the Milanese sense—that it is better to be a good pig than a pretty girl.[8] Others were of a better, more sublime and truer understanding, but of this I shall not now speak.

After this the king had many torches brought and made them sing other songs as they sat on the grass and flowers, until the rising stars began to turn towards the west. Then, thinking it time for sleep, he said good night and sent each one to his room.

END OF THE THIRD DAY

FOURTH DAY, SECOND TALE

Frate Alberto persuades a lady that the Angel Gabriel is in love with her and thus manages to lie with her several times. From fear of her relatives he flies from her house and takes refuge in the house of a poor man, who next day takes him to the Piazza as a wild man of the woods. He is recognized, arrested, and imprisoned.

The tale told by Fiammetta many times drew tears from her companions' eyes, but when it was ended the king said with a stern face:

"I should value my life little in comparison with half the joy Ghismonda had with Guiscardo.[1] Nor should you marvel at this, since while I am alive I suffer a thousand deaths hourly, and yet not one particle of delight is granted me. But, putting aside my life and its fate, it is my will that Pampinea should continue with a tale in part similar to my own fate. If she continues as Fiammetta has begun, doubtless some drops of dew will fall upon my amorous fire, and I shall feel them."

Pampinea felt the wishes of the company more through her own affection than through the king's words, and, being more willing to amuse them than to please the king, she determined to tell an amusing tale without departing from the subject given, and so began:

They say commonly in proverbial style: A wicked man who is thought to be good can do evil and yet not have it believed. This gives me ample

---

[8] That is, it is better to be an unhappy wife and alive than happily married and dead.
[1] Characters in the sad story with which Fiammetta had begun the fourth day's storytelling. The theme for the day, under Filostrato's rule, is love that ends unhappily.

material to speak on the subject proposed, and at the same time to show the hypocrisy of the monks. Their gowns are long and wide, their faces artificially pale, their voices humble and pleading when they ask something, loud and rude when they denounce their own vices in others, and when they declare how they obtain salvation of themselves and others by their gift. Not as men who seek Paradise, like ourselves, but as if they were its owners and lords, they allot a more or less eminent place there to everyone who dies, in accordance with the amount of money he leaves them; and thereby they first deceive themselves—if they really believe it—and then deceive those who put faith in their words. If I were permitted to do so, I could soon show many simple minded persons what is hidden in their ample gowns. Would to God that all their lies had the same fate as befell a minor friar,[2] who was no paltry fellow, but was considered one of the best casuists of Venice. It gives me the greatest pleasure to tell this tale, so that perhaps I may divert your minds with laughter and amusement from the pity you feel for Ghismonda's fate.

In Imola, most worthy ladies, there lived a man of wicked and corrupt life, named Berto della Massa. His evil deeds were so well known to many people of Imola that no one in Imola would believe him when he spoke truth, let alone when he lied. Seeing, then, that his tricks were useless there, he moved in despair to Venice, that welcomer of all wickedness, thinking that in that town he might make a different use of his vices than he had done before. As if conscience-stricken for his wicked deeds, he gave signs of the greatest humility. He became not only the most Catholic of men, but made himself a minor friar, and took the name of Friar Alberto da Imola. In this guise he began to pretend to a severe life, praising penitence and abstinence, and never eating flesh or drinking wine when he could not get them good enough for him.

Never before had a thief, a ruffian, a forger, a murderer turned into a great preacher without having abandoned those vices, even when he had practiced them secretly. And after he had become a priest, whenever he was celebrating Mass at the altar in the presence of a large congregation, he always wept over the Saviour's Passion, for he was a man who could shed tears whenever he pleased. In short, what with his sermons and his tears, he so beguiled the Venetians that he was trustee and guardian of nearly everyone's will, the keeper of many people's money, the confessor and adviser of most men and women. Thus, from wolf he became shepherd, and in those parts the fame of his sanctity was greater than San Francesco's[3] ever was at Assisi.

Now, it happened that a silly stupid young woman, named Madonna Lisetta da ca Quirino, the wife of a merchant who was away in Flanders with the galleys, went with other women to confess to this holy friar. As she knelt at his feet like the Venetian she was—and they are all fools—he asked her half way through her confession if she had a lover. And she tartly replied:

[2] A member of the Franciscan religious order (Order of Friars Minor).
[3] Saint Francis of Assisi (1182?–1226), of whose piety many stories were told. He is eulogized in Dante's *Paradiso*, canto XI.

"Why, messer friar, have you no eyes in your head? Do you think my beauties are no more than these other women's? I could have as many lovers as I wanted. But my beauty is not to be yielded to the love of anybody. How many beauties do you see like mine, for I should be beautiful in Paradise?"

And she went on to say so many things about her beauties that it was tedious to listen to her. Friar Alberto at once saw her weakness, and, feeling that she was ready made to his hand, he fell in love with her. But, reserving his flatteries for another time, he put on his saintly air and began to reprove her, and to say this was vain-glory and other things of the kind. So the lady told him he was a fool, and did not know how to distinguish one beauty from another. And Friar Alberto, not wanting to anger her too much, finished off the confession and let her go with the others.

A few days later he went with a trusted friend to Madonna Lisetta's house and took her aside into a room where they could not be seen. There he fell on his knees before her, and said:

"Madonna, I beseech you for God's sake to forgive me for what I said to you on Sunday when you spoke of your beauty, because I was so severely punished that night I have not been able to get up until today."

Then said Madonna Pot-stick: "And who punished you?"

"I will tell you," said Friar Alberto. "While I was praying that night, as I always do, I suddenly saw a bright light in my cell. Before I could turn to see what it was, I beheld a most beautiful young man with a large stick in his hand, who took me by the cowl, dragged me to my feet and beat me as if to break my bones. I asked him why he did this, and he replied: 'Because you presumed today to reprove the heavenly beauty of Madonna Lisetta whom I love more than anything except God himself.' And I asked: 'Who are you?' And he said he was the Angel Gabriel. 'O my lord,' said I, 'I beg you will pardon me.' And he said: 'I will pardon you on condition that you go to her as soon as you can and obtain her forgiveness. And if she does not forgive you I shall return here, and so deal with you that you will be miserable for the rest of your days.' What he afterwards said to me I dare not tell you until you have pardoned me."

Donna Windy-noddle, who was as sweet as salt, was enchanted at these words, and thought them all true.

"I told you, Friar Alberto," said she, "that mine were heavenly beauties. But, so help me God, I am sorry for you, and to spare you any further trouble I forgive you, if only you will tell me truly what the Angel then said."

"Madonna," replied Friar Alberto, "since you have pardoned me, I will tell you willingly. But, you must not repeat a word of what I tell you to anyone in the world, if you do not want to destroy your happiness, you who are the luckiest woman in the world.

"The Angel Gabriel told me to tell you that he loves you so much he would often have come to spend the night with you, but for his fear of terrifying you. He now sends you a message through me to say that he wants to come to you one night and to spend part of it with you. But he is an Angel, and if he came to you in the form of an Angel you could not touch him; and so he says that for your delight he will come in a man's shape and bids you tell him when you want him to come and in whose shape, and he will come. And so you ought to think yourself more blessed than any other woman living."

Madonna Silly then said she was very glad to have the Angel Gabriel in love with her, because she loved him and always put up a fourpenny candle to him wherever she saw him painted. Whenever he liked to come to her he would be welcome and he would find her alone in her room, on one condition, which was that he would not abandon her for the Virgin Mary whom he was said to be very fond of; and she was inclined to believe this since whenever she saw his picture he was kneeling before the Virgin.[4] In addition, she said that the Angel should come in any shape he pleased—she would not be afraid.

Then said Friar Alberto:

"Madonna, you speak wisely, and I will arrange with him as you say. But you can do me a great favor, which will cost you nothing. The favor is that you will allow him to come in my body. This will be a very great favor because he will take the soul from my body and put it in Heaven, and he will enter into me, and my soul will be in Paradise as long as he remains with you."

Then said Madonna Littlewit:

"I am content. I want you to have this consolation for the stripes[5] you received on my account."

Said Friar Alberto:

"Tonight leave the door of your house open, so that he can come in. Since he is coming in a human body, he can only enter by the door."

The lady replied that this should be done. Friar Alberto departed, and she remained in such a state of delight that her chemise did not touch her backside, and the time she had to wait for the Angel Gabriel seemed like a thousand years.

Friar Alberto thought it better to be a good horseman than an Angel that night, so he fortified himself with all sorts of good cheer, in order not to be unhorsed too easily. He obtained permission to be out that night, and went with his trusted friend to the house of a woman friend, which he had made his starting point more than once before when he was going to ride the mare. From there he went in disguise to the lady's house, and having transformed himself into an Angel with the fripperies[6] he had brought with him, he went upstairs into the lady's bedroom. When she saw something white come in, she kneeled down. The Angel gave her his benediction, raised her to her feet, and signed to her to get into bed. She did so immediately in her willingness to obey, and the Angel got into bed with his devotee.

Friar Alberto was a robust and handsome man and in excellent health. Donna Lisetta was fresh and pretty and found him a very different person from her husband to lie with. That night he flew many times with her without wings, which made her call herself blessed; and in addition he told her a great many things about heavenly glory. Just before dawn, he col-

---

[4] The Annunciation, in which the angel Gabriel tells the Virgin Mary that she will be the mother of God, was a perennial subject of religious paintings.
[5] Blows.   [6] Gaudy costumes.

lected his trappings and returned to his friend, who had kept friendly company with the other woman so that she should not feel afraid by sleeping alone.

After the lady had dined, she went with a woman friend to see Friar Alberto, and gave him news of the Angel Gabriel, telling him how the Angel looked and what he had said about the glory of eternal life, to which she added all sorts of marvelous fables.

"Madonna," said Friar Alberto, "I know not how you were with him, all I know is that last night he came to me, and when I had delivered him your message, he suddenly took my soul to a place where there were more flowers and roses than ever I saw, one of the most delicious places that ever existed, where my soul remained until dawn this morning. But what happened to my body I do not know."

"Didn't I tell you?" said the lady. "Your body lay all night in my arms with the Angel Gabriel. And if you don't believe me, look under your left breast, where I gave the Angel such a kiss that the mark will remain for several days."

Then said Friar Alberto:

"I will do something today which I have not done for a very long time. I shall undress myself to see if what you say is true."

After a lot more chatter, the lady returned home. And Friar Alberto thereafter visited her many times in the guise of an Angel, without the slightest difficulty. But one day Madonna Lisetta was with one of her gossips,[7] and as they were discussing their beauties, she said like the empty-pated fool she was, in order to show off:

"If you knew who was in love with my beauty you would not speak of anyone else's."

The gossip was anxious to hear about it, and knowing Lisetta well, said:

"Madonna, you may be right, but as I do not know whom you mean I shall not change my opinion so easily."

The lady, who had very little sense, then said:

"Gossip, he does not want it talked about, but the person I mean is the Angel Gabriel, who loves me more than himself, so he says, because I am the most beautiful person in the world or the Maremma."[8]

The gossip felt like laughing outright, but restrained herself to keep the conversation going, and said:

"God's faith, Madonna, if you mean the Angel Gabriel and say so, it must be true, but I did not think the angels did such things."

"Gossip," said the lady, "you are wrong. By God's favor, he does it better than my husband, and he tells me they do it up above. But, because he thinks me more beautiful than anyone in Heaven, he has fallen in love with me, and often spends a night with me. So you see!"

As soon as the gossip had left Madonna Lisetta, it seemed like a thousand years to her before she had got into a company where she could laugh at all this. She went to a gathering of women, and told them the whole tale. These women told their husbands and other women, and they told others,

---

[7] Intimate friends.

[8] A marshy region near Florence. The boast is ludicrous, since the Maremma is a mere local district.

and so in less than two days the story was all over Venice. Among others who heard it were the lady's cousins, and, without saying anything to her, they made up their minds to find this Angel and see whether he could fly. So they watched for him every night.

Some rumors of all this came to the ears of Friar Alberto, who went to the lady one night to scold her for it. He was scarcely undressed when her cousins, who had seen him come in, were at the door. Friar Alberto heard them, and guessed what they were. He jumped up, and, having no other means of escape, opened a window overlooking the Grand Canal,[9] from which he threw himself into the water.

The water there was deep; he was a good swimmer, and so did himself no harm. He swam to the other side of the canal and immediately entered an open house there, begging the goodman[10] for the love of God to save his life, and told him all sorts of lies to explain why he was there naked at that hour of night.

The goodman, who was just setting off on his business, pitied Friar Alberto and put him into bed, telling him to stop there until he came back. He then locked the friar in, and went about his business.

When the lady's cousins entered her room, they found the Angel Gabriel had left his wings behind and flown away. They abused the lady indignantly, and, leaving her very disconsolate, returned home with the Angel's trappings.

Meanwhile, soon after dawn, the goodman was on the Rialto[11] and heard how the Angel Gabriel had gone to lie with Madonna Lisetta the night before, how he had been discovered by her relatives and had thrown himself into the canal, and nobody knew what had become of him. So he immediately realized that this was the man in his own house. He went home and after much discussion arranged that the Friar should pay him fifty ducats not to hand him over to the cousins; and this was done. Friar Alberto then wanted to leave, but the goodman said:

"There is only one way of doing this. There is a festival today where one man leads another dressed like a bear or a wild man of the woods or one thing or another, and then there is a hunt in the Piazza di San Marco,[12] and when that is over the festival ends. Then everyone goes off where he pleases with the person he has brought in disguise. Now, you may be spied out here, and so, if you like, I will lead you along in some disguise and can take you wherever you like. Otherwise I don't see how you can leave here without being recognized. The lady's relatives know you must be in some house in the neighborhood, and have posted guards everywhere to catch you."

Friar Alberto did not at all like the idea, but he was so much afraid of the lady's relatives that he agreed to it, and told the man where he wanted to go, and how he should be led along. The goodman smeared him all over with honey and then covered him with feathers, put a chain round his neck and a mask on his face. In one hand he gave him a large stick and in the

[9] The famous canals of Venice serve in lieu of streets.
[10] A title of respect for a man below the rank of gentry.
[11] The commercial center of Venice.
[12] The principal public square of Venice; St. Mark is the city's patron saint.

other two great dogs which he had brought from the butcher; and then he sent someone to the Rialto who announced that everyone who wanted to see the Angel Gabriel should go to the Piazza di San Marco. That was true Venetian good faith!

Having done this, he took the Friar out, and, walking before him, led him along on a chain; and everybody came round saying: "What's this? What's this?" And thus he took the Friar to the Piazza, where there was a great crowd of people, made up of those who had followed them and those who had come from the Rialto on hearing the announcement. He then led his wild man of the woods to a column in a conspicuous and elevated place, pretending that he was waiting for the hunt. The poor friar was greatly plagued by flies and gad-flies, because he was smeared all over with honey. And when the goodman saw that the Piazza was full of people, he pretended that he was going to unchain his wild man; but instead he took off Friar Alberto's mask, and shouted:

"Gentlemen, since the pig has not come to the hunt and since the hunt is off, I don't want you to have gathered here for nothing, and so I want you to see the Angel Gabriel who came down from Heaven to earth last night to console the ladies of Venice."

As soon as the mask was off, Friar Alberto was recognized by everybody, and there went up a great shout against him, everybody saying the most insulting things that ever were said to any scoundrel. And first one and then another threw all sorts of filth in his face. There he was kept a long time until the news reached the other friars of his convent. Six of them came down to the Piazza, threw a gown on his back and bound him, and then in the midst of a great tumult took him back to the monastery, where he was imprisoned. And it is believed that he soon died there after a life of misery.

Thus a man who was thought to be good and acted evilly without being suspected, tried to be the Angel Gabriel and was turned into a wild man of the woods; and, in the long run, was insulted as he deserved and came to weep in vain for the sins he had committed. Please God that this may happen to all like him.

FIFTH DAY, EIGHTH TALE

Nastagio degli Onesti is in love with one of the Traversari and spends all his possessions without obtaining her love. At the request of his relatives, he goes to Chiassi, and there sees a horseman hunting a girl who is killed and devoured by two dogs. He invites his relatives and the lady he loves to dine with him, and she sees the girl torn to pieces. Fearing the same fate, she marries Nastagio and lives happily with him.[1]

When Lauretta was silent, Filomena, at the queen's command, began thus:

Charming ladies, as pity is commended in us, so divine justice rigidly punishes cruelty in you. To display this to you and cause you to drive it

---

[1] The theme of the stories on the fifth day, under Fiammetta's rule, is love transformed from grief to happiness.

wholly from you, I desire to tell you a tale no less full of compassion than of delight.

In Ravenna, that most ancient city of Romagna, there were of old many nobles and gentlemen, among whom was a young man named Nastagio degli Onesti, who became exceedingly rich on the death of his father and an uncle. As happens to young men without a wife, he fell in love with a daughter of Messer Paolo Traversaro, a girl of far more noble birth than he, whom he hoped to win by his actions. But however fair and praiseworthy they were, they not only failed to please her but actually seemed to displease her, so cruelly, harshly, and unfriendly did the girl behave, perhaps on account of her rare beauty, perhaps because her lofty and disdainful nobility of birth made her despise him and everything he liked.

This was so hard for Nastagio to bear that for very grief he often desired to slay himself. But, dreading to do this, he very often determined to leave her or, if he could, to hate her as she hated him. But in vain, for it seemed that the less hope he had, the more his love grew.

As the young man continued to love and to spend money recklessly, his friends and relatives felt that he was wasting both himself and his possessions. So they often advised and begged him to leave Ravenna, and to go and live somewhere else for a time, to diminish his love and his expense. Nastagio several times made mock of this advice; but unable to say "No" to their repeated solicitations, he agreed to do it. He made great preparations, as if he were going to France or Spain or some other far off land, mounted his horse, and left Ravenna accompanied by many of his friends. He went to a place about three miles from Ravenna, called Chiassi; and having set up tents and pavilions there, told his friends he meant to stay there and that they should return to Ravenna. There Nastagio led the most extravagant life, inviting different parties of people to dine or sup, as he had been accustomed to do.

Now, in very fine weather about the beginning of May, he began to think of his cruel lady, and ordered his attendants to leave him alone so that he could dream of her at his ease; and in his reverie his footsteps led him into the pine woods. The fifth hour of the day[2] was already spent, and he was a good half mile inside the woods, forgetful of food and everything else, when suddenly he thought he heard a loud lamentation and the wild shrieks of a woman. Breaking off his sweet reverie, he raised his head to see what it was, and to his surprise found himself in the pine forest. But, in addition, as he looked in front of him he saw coming towards him a very beautiful girl, naked, with disordered hair, and all scratched by the thorns and twigs of the brambles and bushes in the wood. She was weeping and calling for mercy. Beside her he saw two very large, fierce mastiffs, savagely pursuing her, and frequently snapping cruelly at her; and behind her on a black horse was a dark knight, with grief and anger in his face, with a sword in his hand, who often threatened her with death in dreadful and insulting terms.

This aroused astonishment and terror in his soul, and finally compassion for the unfortunate lady, from which was born the desire to set her free from such agony and such a death, if he could. But, finding himself

---

[2] 11 A.M.

unarmed, he ran to tear off a tree bough in place of a cudgel, and began to advance towards the dogs and the knight. But the knight saw him, and called to him from a distance:

"Nastagio, don't meddle here, let me and these dogs do what this wicked woman has deserved."

As he spoke the dogs seized the girl by the thighs, bringing her to the ground, and the knight dismounted from his horse. Nastagio went up to him, and said:

"I do not know who you are, though you seem to know me; but I tell you it is baseness in an armed knight to want to kill a naked woman, and to have set dogs at her, as if she were a wild beast. I shall certainly defend her as far as I can."

Then said the knight:

"Nastagio, I am of the same country as yourself, and you were still a little child when I, whose name was Messer Guido degli Anastagi, was more deeply in love with this woman than you now are with your Traversaro. Owing to her cruelty and pride, my misfortune caused me in despair to kill myself with the sword you see in my hand, and I am damned to eternal punishment. Not long afterwards, she, who had rejoiced exceedingly at my death, died also, and died unrepentant, believing that she had not sinned but done well; but for the sin of her cruelty and of her rejoicing at my torments, she too was and is damned to the punishments of hell. When she descended into hell, the punishment imposed upon us was that she should fly from me and that I, who once loved her so much, should pursue her as a mortal enemy, not as a beloved woman. As often as I catch her I kill her with the very sword with which I slew myself, and split her open, and drag out (as you will soon see) that hard cold heart, wherein love and pity could never enter, together with her entrails, and give them to these dogs to eat.

"After no long space of time, in accordance with the justice and the will of God, she rises up again as if she had not been dead, and once more begins her anguished flight, and I and the dogs pursue her. Every Friday at this hour I catch up with her here and slaughter her as you will see. And do not think that we rest on other days. I catch her in other places where she thought or wrought cruelly against me. Having changed from a lover to an enemy, as you see, I am condemned in this way to pursue her for as many years as the months she was cruel to me. Now let me execute divine justice, and strive not to oppose what you cannot prevent."

Nastagio was terrified by these words, and there was scarcely a hair of his body which did not stand on end. He drew back and gazed at the miserable girl, awaiting fearfully what the knight would do. When the knight had done speaking, he rushed like a mad dog at the girl with his sword in his hand, while she, held on her knees by the mastiffs, shrieked for mercy. But he thrust his sword with all his strength through the middle of her breast until it stood out behind her back. When the girl received this thrust, she fell forward still weeping and shrieking. The knight took a dagger in his hand, slit her open, took out her heart and everything near it, and threw them to the mastiffs who hungrily devoured them at once.

But before long the girl suddenly rose to her feet as if nothing had happened, and began to run towards the sea, with the dogs continually snapping at her. The knight took his sword, remounted his horse and followed; and in a short time they were so far away that Nastagio lost sight of them. After seeing these things, Nastagio hesitated a long time between pity and fear; but after some time it occurred to him that it might be useful to him, since it happened every Friday. So, having marked the place, he returned to his servants, and in due course sent for many of his relatives and friends, to whom he said:

"You have long urged me to refrain from loving my fair enemy and to cease my expense. I am ready to do so, if you will do me one favor—which is that next Friday you will come and dine with me, and bring Messer Paolo Traversaro, his wife, his daughter, all their women relatives, and any other women you like. Why I want this you will see later."

They thought this a small thing to do. So they returned to Ravenna, and invited those whom Nastagio wanted. And although it was hard to get the girl whom Nastagio loved, still she went along with the rest. Nastagio made preparations for a magnificent feast, and had the tables set among the pines near the place where he had seen the massacre of the cruel lady. He placed the men and women at table in such a manner that the girl he loved was exactly opposite the place where this would happen.

The last course had arrived when they all began to hear the despairing shrieks of the pursued lady. Everyone was astonished and asked what it was. Nobody knew. They stood up to look, and saw the agonized girl and the dogs and the knight. And in a very short time they all arrived in front of them. Great was the uproar against knight and dogs, and many started forward to help the girl. But the knight, speaking to them as he had spoken to Nastagio, not only made them draw back, but filled them with astonishment and terror. He did what he had done before; and all the women, many of whom were relatives of the suffering girl and of the knight, and remembered his love and death, wept as wretchedly as if it had been done to themselves.

When the massacre was over, and the lady and the knight had gone, those who had seen it fell into different sorts of discourse. But the most frightened was the cruel lady beloved by Nastagio, who had distinctly seen and heard everything, and knew that these things came nearer to her than to anyone else, for she remembered the cruelty with which she had always treated Nastagio. So that in her mind's eye she already seemed to be flying from his rage and to feel the mastiffs at her sides.

Such fear was born in her from this that, to avoid its happening to her, she could scarcely wait for that evening to change her hate into love and to send a trusted maid-servant secretly to Nastagio, begging him to go to see her, because she was ready to do anything he pleased. Nastagio replied that this was a happiness to him but that he desired his pleasure with honor, which was to take her as his wife, if she would agree. The girl knew that she herself had been the only obstacle to this hitherto, and replied that she was willing. So making herself the messenger, she told her father and mother that she was willing to marry Nastagio, which greatly delighted them. Next Sunday Nastagio married her and made a wedding feast, and lived happily with her for a long time.

Nor was this the only good which resulted from this terrifying apparition, for all the ladies of Ravenna took fear, and became far more compliant to the pleasures of the men than they had ever been before.

FIFTH DAY, NINTH TALE

Federigo degli Alberighi loves, but is not beloved. He spends all his money in
courtship and has nothing left but a falcon, and this he gives his lady to eat when
she comes to visit him because there is nothing else to give her. She learns of this,
changes her mind, takes him as her husband, and makes him a rich man.

Filomena had ceased speaking, and the queen, seeing that nobody was
left to speak except Dioneo (who had his privilege[1]) and herself, began
cheerfully as follows:

It is now my turn to speak, dearest ladies, and I shall gladly do so with a
tale similar in part to the one before, not only that you may know the power
of your beauty over the gentle heart, but because you may learn yourselves
to be givers of rewards when fitting, without allowing Fortune always to
dispense them, since Fortune most often bestows them, not discreetly but
lavishly.

You must know then that Coppo di Borghese Domenichi, who was and
perhaps still is one of our fellow citizens, a man of great and revered authority in our days both from his manners and his virtues (far more than
from nobility of blood), a most excellent person worthy of eternal fame,
and in the fullness of his years delighted often to speak of past matters with
his neighbors and other men. And this he could do better and more orderly and with a better memory and more ornate speech than anyone else.

Among other excellent things, he was wont to say that in the past there
was in Florence a young man named Federigo, the son of Messer Filippo
Alberighi, renowned above all other young gentlemen of Tuscany for his
prowess in arms and his courtesy. Now, as most often happens to gentlemen, he fell in love with a lady named Monna Giovanna, in her time held to
be one of the gayest and most beautiful women ever known in Florence. To
win her love, he went to jousts and tourneys, made and gave feasts, and
spent his money without stint. But she, no less chaste than beautiful, cared
nothing for the things he did for her nor for him who did them.

Now as Federigo was spending far beyond his means and getting nothing in, as easily happens, his wealth failed and he remained poor with
nothing but a little farm, on whose produce he lived very penuriously, and
one falcon which was among the best in the world. More in love than ever,
but thinking he would never be able to live in the town any more as he
desired, he went to Campi where his farm was. There he spent his time
hawking,[2] asked nothing of anybody, and patiently endured his poverty.

Now while Federigo was in this extremity it happened one day that
Monna Giovanna's husband fell ill, and seeing death come upon him, made
his will. He was a very rich man and left his estate to a son who was already
growing up. And then, since he had greatly loved Monna Giovanna, he
made her his heir in case his son should die without legitimate children;
and so died.

---

[1] Dioneo is allowed by special dispensation to depart from the theme of the day's stories, in
return for which he has offered to be the last speaker.

[2] Hunting small game with the aid of trained hawks, especially falcons.

Monna Giovanna was now a widow, and as is customary with our women, she went with her son to spend the year in a country house she had near Federigo's farm. Now the boy happened to strike up a friendship with Federigo, and delighted in dogs and hawks. He often saw Federigo's falcon fly, and took such great delight in it that he very much wanted to have it, but did not dare ask for it, since he saw how much Federigo prized it.

While matters were in this state, the boy fell ill. His mother was very much grieved, as he was her only child and she loved him extremely. She spent the day beside him, trying to help him, and often asked him if there was anything he wanted, begging him to say so, for if it were possible to have it, she would try to get it for him. After she had many times made this offer, the boy said:

"Mother, if you can get me Federigo's falcon, I think I should soon be better."

The lady paused a little at this, and began to think what she should do. She knew that Federigo had loved her for a long time, and yet had never had one glance from her, and she said to herself:

"How can I send or go and ask for this falcon, which is, from what I hear, the best that ever flew, and moreover his support in life? How can I be so thoughtless as to take this away from a gentleman who has no other pleasure left in life?"

Although she knew she was certain to have the bird for the asking, she remained in embarrassed thought, not knowing what to say, and did not answer her son. But at length love for her child got the upper hand and she determined that to please him in whatever way it might be, she would not send, but go herself for it and bring it back to him. So she replied:

"Be comforted, my child, and try to get better somehow. I promise you that tomorrow morning I will go for it, and bring it to you."

The child was so delighted that he became a little better that same day. And on the morrow the lady took another woman to accompany her, and as if walking for exercise went to Federigo's cottage, and asked for him. Since it was not the weather for it, he had not been hawking for some days, and was in his garden employed in certain work there. When he heard that Monna Giovanna was asking for him at the door, he was greatly astonished, and ran there happily. When she saw him coming, she got up to greet him with womanly charm, and when Federigo had courteously saluted her, she said:

"How do you do, Federigo? I have come here to make amends for the damage you have suffered through me by loving me more than was needed. And in token of this, I intend to dine today familiarly with you and my companion here."

"Madonna," replied Federigo humbly, "I do not remember ever to have suffered any damage through you, but received so much good that if I was ever worth anything it was owing to your worth and the love I bore it. Your generous visit to me is so precious to me that I could spend again all that I have spent; but you have come to a poor host."

So saying, he modestly took her into his house, and from there to his garden. Since there was nobody else to remain in her company, he said:

"Madonna, since there is nobody else, this good woman, the wife of this workman, will keep you company, while I go to set the table."

Now, although his poverty was extreme, he had never before realized what necessity he had fallen into by his foolish extravagance in spending his wealth. But he repented of it that morning when he could find nothing with which to do honor to the lady, for love of whom he had entertained vast numbers of men in the past. In his anguish he cursed himself and his fortune and ran up and down like a man out of his senses, unable to find money or anything to pawn. The hour was late and his desire to honor the lady extreme, yet he would not apply to anyone else, even to his own workman; when suddenly his eye fell upon his falcon, perched on a bar in the sitting room. Having no one to whom he could appeal, he took the bird, and finding it plump, decided it would be food worthy of such a lady. So, without further thought, he wrung its neck, made his little maid servant quickly pluck and prepare it, and put it on a spit to roast. He spread the table with the whitest napery, of which he had some left, and returned to the lady in the garden with a cheerful face, saying that the meal he had been able to prepare for her was ready.

The lady and her companion arose and went to table, and there together with Federigo, who served it with the greatest devotion, they ate the good falcon, not knowing what it was. They left the table and spent some time in cheerful conversation, and the lady, thinking the time had now come to say what she had come for, spoke fairly to Federigo as follows:

"Federigo, when you remember your former life and my chastity, which no doubt you considered harshness and cruelty, I have no doubt that you will be surprised at my presumption when you hear what I have come here for chiefly. But if you had children, through whom you could know the power of parental love, I am certain that you would to some extent excuse me.

"But, as you have no child, I have one, and I cannot escape the common laws of mothers. Compelled by their power, I have come to ask you— against my will, and against all good manners and duty—for a gift, which I know is something especially dear to you, and reasonably so, because I know your straitened fortune has left you no other pleasure, no other recreation, no other consolation. This gift is your falcon, which has so fascinated my child that if I do not take it to him, I am afraid his present illness will grow so much worse that I may lose him. Therefore I beg you, not by the love you bear me (which holds you to nothing), but by your own nobleness, which has shown itself so much greater in all courteous usage than is wont in other men, that you will be pleased to give it me, so that through this gift I may be able to say that I have saved my child's life, and thus be ever under an obligation to you."

When Federigo heard the lady's request and knew that he could not serve her, because he had given her the bird to eat, he began to weep in her presence, for he could not speak a word. The lady at first thought that his grief came from having to part with his good falcon, rather than from anything else, and she was almost on the point of retraction. But she remained firm and waited for Federigo's reply after his lamentation. And he said:

"Madonna, ever since it has pleased God that I should set my love upon you, I have felt that Fortune has been contrary to me in many things, and have grieved for it. But they are all light in comparison with what she has done to me now, and I shall never be at peace with her again when I reflect that you came to my poor house, which you never deigned to visit when it was rich, and asked me for a little gift, and Fortune has so acted that I cannot give it to you. Why this cannot be, I will briefly tell you.

"When I heard that you in your graciousness desired to dine with me and I thought of your excellence and your worthiness, I thought it right and fitting to honor you with the best food I could obtain; so, remembering the falcon you ask me for and its value, I thought it a meal worthy of you, and today you had it roasted on the dish and set forth as best I could. But now I see that you wanted the bird in another form, it is such a grief to me that I cannot serve you that I think I shall never be at peace again."

And after saying this, he showed her the feathers and the feet and the beak of the bird in proof. When the lady heard and saw all this, she first blamed him for having killed such a falcon to make a meal for a woman; and then she inwardly commended his greatness of soul which no poverty could or would be able to abate. But, having lost all hope of obtaining the falcon, and thus perhaps the health of her son, she departed sadly and returned to the child. Now, either from disappointment at not having the falcon or because his sickness must inevitably have led to it, the child died not many days later, to the mother's extreme grief.

Although she spent some time in tears and bitterness, yet, since she had been left very rich and was still young, her brothers often urged her to marry again. She did not want to do so, but as they kept on pressing her, she remembered the worthiness of Federigo and his last act of generosity, in killing such a falcon to do her honor.

"I will gladly submit to marriage when you please," she said to her brothers, "but if you want me to take a husband, I will take no man but Federigo degli Alberighi."

At this her brothers laughed at her, saying:

"Why, what are you talking about, you fool? Why do you want a man who hasn't a penny in the world?"

But she replied:

"Brothers, I know it is as you say, but I would rather have a man who needs money than money which needs a man."

Seeing her determination, the brothers, who knew Federigo's good qualities, did as she wanted, and gave her with all her wealth to him, in spite of his poverty. Federigo, finding that he had such a woman, whom he loved so much, with all her wealth to boot, as his wife, was more prudent with his money in the future, and ended his days happily with her.

FIFTH DAY, TENTH TALE

Pietro di Vinciolo goes out to sup. His wife brings a lover into the house; Pietro returns, and she hides the lover under a chicken coop. Pietro tells her how, while he was supping with Ercolano, a young man whom the wife had hidden was discovered. She blames Ercolano's wife, but an ass unhappily treads on the lover's finger as he is under the coop, and he gives a shriek; Pietro runs out, sees him, and perceives how his wife has tricked him; but in the end he pardons her fault.

The queen finished her tale, and they all praised God for having worthily rewarded Federigo; and then Dioneo began, without waiting to be ordered.

I know not whether it be an accidental vice and the result of the corruption of men's manners, or whether it be a natural failing to laugh at bad things rather than at good deeds, especially when we are not directly concerned. Now since the task I undertook before and am about to carry out again, has no other object but to drive away melancholy from you and to raise mirth and merriment, I shall tell you this tale, enamored ladies, although its matter in part be less than chaste, because it may amuse you. While you listen to it, do as you do when you enter a garden and, stretching out your delicate hands, pluck the roses and avoid the thorns. In so doing, leave the bad man in his misfortune with his woes, and laugh at the amorous tricks of the wife, and feel compassion for the misfortunes of others, where it is needed.

Not long ago in Perugia there was a rich man named Pietro di Vinciolo, who took a wife, more to deceive others and to avoid the general opinion of himself among the Perugians, than for any desire he had of her. And Fortune was so far conformable to his wish that the wife he took was a robust wench with lively red hair, who would rather have had two husbands than one, whereas she had chanced upon a man who would rather have had to do with another man than with her.

In process of time she found this out. And since she was fresh and pretty, and felt herself friskish and robust, she got angry and often exchanged sharp words with her husband; and they led a miserable life together. But, seeing that this exhausted her without improving her husband, she said to herself:

"This man leaves me in sorrow and goes off in his vice in wooden shoes through the dry, while I am trying to carry someone else in a ship through the rain.[1] I took him as my husband and gave him a good large dowry, knowing him to be a man, and thinking he wanted what men do and ought to want; and if I had not thought he was a man, I would never have taken him. He knew I was a woman; why did he marry me if he didn't like women? This is unendurable. If I had not wanted to live the life of the world, I should have become a nun. If I wait for delight and pleasure from him, I might perhaps wait in vain until I am an old woman, and then vainly regret my lost youth. He himself is an example to me, that I should find some consolation, and some pleasure as he does. In me this pleasure will be commendable, whereas in him it is blameworthy; for I only offend the laws, whereas he offends the laws and Nature too."

Having thought this over a good many times, the good woman, with an idea of carrying out her plan secretly, became familiar with an old woman, who yet seemed more like a pious old thing than a bawd, always going to church services with beads in her hand and never talking about anything but the lives of the Fathers or the stigmata of St. Francis,[2] so that almost everybody thought she was a saint. And when she thought it a fitting time, the wife told her everything she intended.

---

[1] She means that sexually her husband goes against nature whereas she conforms to it.
[2] The Fathers were religious authorities in the ancient Christian church. St. Francis of Assisi was believed to have received in his own body the marks ("stigmata") of Christ's wounds.

"My child," said the old woman, "God, who knows everything, knows that in this you will do well. And if you did it for no other reason, yet you and every other young woman should do it, in order not to waste the time of your youth, because to those who have any understanding there is no grief like having wasted time. What the devil good are we when we are old, except to watch the supper on the hearth? If anyone knows it and can bear witness to it, I can. Now I am an old woman I realize with bitter soul-prickings how I wasted my time. And although I did not lose it all (for I don't want you to think I was a simpleton), still I did not do what I could have done. When I remember it, and see what I now am, and think how nobody would kindle up a spark of desire for me, God knows what grief I feel.

"The same thing does not happen to men. They are born fitted for a thousand things and not for this only, while the larger number of them are much better old than young. But women are only born to do it and make children, and so are esteemed. And if you haven't noticed anything else, you ought to have noticed this—that we are always ready for it, which does not happen with men. Moreover, one woman would tire out many men, whereas many men cannot tire one woman. Now, since we are born for this, I say once more you will be doing well to give your husband tit for tat, so that in your old age your mind will not have any reproach to bring against your flesh.

"Everyone gets from this world what he takes from it, especially women, who have far more necessity to make use of time while they have it than men, because, as you can see for yourself, when we get old, neither husband nor anyone else wants to see us, so we're chased in the kitchen to tell tales to the cat, and scour the pots and pans. Worse than that even, they make songs about us, saying: 'The best morsels for the girls, and quinsies[3] to the old women'; and they say lots of other similar things.

"To keep you no longer in talk, I say now that you could not have spoken to anyone in the world who can be more useful to you than me; for however haughty a man may be I am not afraid to say what is necessary to him, and however harsh or boorish, I can smooth him down and bring him to the point I want. Tell me the one you want, and leave the rest to me. But remember, my child, that I am poor, and that you will be remembered in all my church-goings and all the paternosters I say; and I shall pray God for the souls of all your departed dead."

Thus ended the old woman. And the young woman came to an agreement with the old one that, if she saw him, she was to bring her a young man who often passed through the district; and she described him in such a way that the old woman knew who he was. Then she gave her a piece of salt meat, and sent her away.

Not many days afterwards the old woman brought the young man described to her room, and soon afterwards another, according as the young woman wanted. And, although in fear of her husband, she did not miss the opportunity.

One evening her husband was going out to supper with a friend of his,

[3] Inflammations of the throat; the literal meaning in the Italian is "things to choke on."

named Ercolano, and so the girl arranged with the old woman to bring her a young man, who was one of the handsomest and pleasantest in Perugia. Which was quickly done. The young woman and the young man were just sitting down to supper, when they heard Pietro at the door, shouting to her to open it. When she heard it, the wife gave herself up for dead. Wanting to hide the young man if she could, and not having the cunning to get him out of the house or hide him elsewhere, she hid him under a chicken coop in a shed next to the room in which they were supping, and threw over it a piece of straw sacking she had emptied that day. After which, she quickly opened the door to her husband. When he came into the house, she said:

"You've guzzled up that supper pretty quickly."

"We never even tasted it," said Pietro.

"How did that happen?" asked his wife.

"I'll tell you," said Pietro. "Ercolano and his wife and I were sitting down to table when we heard somebody sneeze near us, to which we paid no attention the first and second times. But the person sneezed a third, a fourth, a fifth and many other times, which greatly surprised us. Ercolano was already a little annoyed with his wife because she had kept him waiting a long time at the door, and said to her in a rage: 'What does this mean? Who is it sneezing like this?' He got up from the table, and went to the staircase near at hand, under which was a cupboard to store things away, as we see arranged in houses every day.

"It seemed to him that the sound of the sneezing came from this cupboard, so he opened a little door in it, and as soon as this was opened there suddenly came out the worst stink of sulphur imaginable, which he had noticed before and had complained of, whereupon his wife had said: 'I am whitening my veils in there with sulphur, and the pots too, which I sprinkled with sulphur so that they would get the fumes, and put them under the staircase, and the smell still comes from them.' And after Ercolano had opened the door and the fumes had cleared off a little, he looked inside and saw the person who had sneezed and was still sneezing owing to the sulphur fumes. And as he sneezed, the sulphur had got such a hold on his chest, that he was not far from never sneezing or doing anything else again.

"As soon as Ercolano saw him, he shouted: 'Now I see, wife, the man for whose sake you kept us waiting at the door so long without opening when we came. But may I never have anything please me again, if I don't make you pay for this!' The wife, hearing this and seeing that her fault was discovered, fled from the table without attempting any excuse; and I don't know where she went. Ercolano, not noticing that his wife had fled, told the sneezing man to come out; but he was beyond all power of moving, and did not stir for anything Ercolano said.

"Thereupon Ercolano took him by one of his feet and dragged him out, and ran for a knife to kill him. But, fearing the police on my own account, I jumped up and prevented him from killing the man or doing him any harm. My shouting and defending him aroused the neighbors who came in and took the almost swooning young man, and carried him somewhere—I don't know where—out of the house. So our supper was quite spoiled by all this, and I not only haven't guzzled it but never even tasted it, as I said."

At this tale the wife perceived that there were others who knew as much as she did, although some had bad luck She would have been glad to defend Ercolano's wife with words, but as blaming the faults of others seemed to her to make things easier for her own, she said:

"Here's fine doings! Here's a good and saintly woman! Here's the faith of a modest woman, who seemed to me so saintly that I would have confessed my sins to her. And, what's worse, she gives a mighty good example to the young, since she's getting old already. Cursed be the hour when she came into the world and the hour which allowed her to live, the wicked deceitful woman that she must be, the universal shame and scorn of all women on this earth! Curse her for leaving her chastity and the faith promised to her husband and the honor of the world, he that is such a good man and an honorable citizen and treated her so well, for another man, and not being ashamed to bring him to scorn and herself with him! So help me God, I'd have no pity on such women. They ought to be killed. They ought to be thrown into the fire and burned to ashes."

Then, recollecting that her lover was near at hand, hidden under the hen-coop, she began to urge Pietro to go to bed, as it was then bedtime. But Pietro was more anxious to have something to eat than to go to bed, and asked if there were not something for supper.

"Ah!" said the wife, "yes, indeed, there's supper! We're quite accustomed to have supper when you're not here! Yes, I'm Ercolano's wife, am I? Why don't you go to bed? Go to sleep this evening!"

Now, it happened that during the evening some of Pietro's workmen had brought certain things in from the country, and had stalled their asses without giving them any water to drink, in a little stable next to the shed. One of the asses was very thirsty indeed, and, managing to get his head out of the halter, walked out of the stable and went snuffing at everything, trying to find some water. And so he came up to the hen-coop where the young man was hidden.

He was on his hands and knees, and one of his fingers was outside the hen-coop. Now, as luck or ill luck would have it, the ass trod on his finger; whereupon, in his anguish, he uttered a yell. Pietro was astonished to hear it, and knew that someone must be in the house. He went out of the room and heard the young man moaning, for the ass had not yet taken its hoof off his finger and was still pressing heavily on it. Said Pietro: "Who's there?" He ran to the hen-coop, lifted it up, and saw the young man who, in addition to the pain he felt from the ass treading on his finger, was trembling with fear lest Pietro should do him an injury.

Pietro recognized him as a young man he had long been prowling after for his vicious pleasures, and asked him: "What are you doing here?" but the youth made no answer, and only begged him for the love of God to do him no harm.

"Get up," said Pietro, "I won't do you any harm; but tell me, how do you happen to be here, and why?"

The young man confessed everything. Pietro, no less joyous than his wife was distressed at the discovery, took him by the hand and led him into the room, where the wife was waiting in the greatest terror imaginable. Pietro made her sit down opposite and said:

"So you cursed so hard Ercolano's wife, and you said she ought to be burned and that she was the shame of you all—why didn't you say it of yourself? Or, if you didn't want to confess that, how could your conscience endure to say it of her, when you knew you had done the same thing as she had? Nothing, indeed, induced you to do it, except that all you women are alike, and you hope to hide your own sins under the failings of others. May fire come down from heaven and burn you all, vile generation that you are!"

The wife, seeing that at the first onslaught he had hurt her with nothing worse than words, and noticing that he was in high glee at holding such a handsome youth by the hand, plucked up heart and said:

"I am very sure that you would like fire to come from heaven and burn up all us women, since you are as fond of us as a dog is of sticks. But, God's Cross! You won't see it happen. I should like to have a little discussion with you, to find out what you complain of. It is indeed well to compare me with Ercolano's wife, a hypocritical, snivelling old woman, who gets what she wants out of him, and he treats her as well as a wife can be treated, which doesn't happen to me. For, granted that I am well clad and shod, you know how I fare in other matters and how long it is since you lay with me. I'd go with rags on my back and broken shoes and be well treated by you in bed, rather than have all these things and be treated as you treat me. Understand plainly, Pietro, I'm a woman like other women, and I want what they want. So, if I go seeking for what I can't get from you, there's no need to abuse me. At least I do you so much honor that I don't go with boys and scrubby fellows."

Pietro saw that she could go on talking all night, and so, as he cared nothing about her, he said:

"That's enough, wife. I'll be content with that. Will you be so gracious as to get us some supper, for I rather fancy this boy has had no more supper than I have."

"No, indeed," said the wife, "he has had no supper; for when you arrived in an ill hour, we were just sitting down to table to sup."

"Go along then," said Pietro, "and get us some supper, and afterwards I will arrange this affair in such a way that you will have nothing to complain of."

Finding her husband so agreeable, the wife jumped up and re-laid the table, brought out the supper she had prepared, and supped merrily with her bad husband and the young man. What Pietro arranged after supper to satisfy all three of them has entirely gone out of my head. But I know that next morning the young man found himself in the piazza, not quite knowing whether the night before he had been with the wife or the husband. And so, dear ladies, I want to tell you: "He who does it to you, you do it to him." And if you can't, keep it in mind while you can, so that the ass may receive what he gets at home.

Dioneo's tale was now ended, and the ladies' laughter was restrained less from lack of amusement than from shame. The queen, seeing that the end of her reign was at hand, stood up and took off her garland, and gracefully placed it on Elisa's head, saying:

"Madonna, it is now for you to give orders."

Having received the honor, Elisa followed the adopted routine and first arranged with the steward for what was needed during the period of her rule; after which she said to the satisfaction of the company:

"We have already heard how many people by means of good sayings and prompt retorts and quick wits have been able to turn the teeth of others on themselves with a sharp nip or have averted threatened dangers. And since this is a good topic and may be useful, my will is that tomorrow, with God's help, we tell tales within these limits—that is, of such persons who have retorted a witticism directed at them, or with a quick retort or piece of shrewdness have escaped destruction, danger or contempt."

This was highly commended by them all. Whereupon the queen rose to her feet, and gave them all to do as they chose until supper time. The merry company arose as the queen arose, and according to custom, each of them gave himself up to what pleased him most. But when the cicadas ceased their song, everyone was called, and they all went to supper. After this had been festively served, they went to singing and music. Emilia danced at the queen's command, and then Dioneo was ordered to sing a song. He immediately began: "Old mother Hale, lift up your tail, and see the good news I bring you." Whereat all the ladies burst out laughing, especially the queen, who ordered him to abandon that song and start another.

"Madonna," said Dioneo, "if I had cymbals, I would sing: 'Up with your petties, Monna Lapa,' or 'Under the olive tree springs the grass,' or would you like me to sing: 'The waves of the ocean make me ill with their motion'? But then I haven't any cymbals, so see which of these others you would like. Do you like: 'Out you go to be chopped to shreds, like a melon down in the garden beds'?"

"No," said the queen, "sing something else."

"Well," said Dioneo, "shall I sing: 'Monna Simona, put it up in the cask, it isn't the month of October'?"

"No, no," said the queen laughing, "sing a nice song, if you like, but not that one."

"Don't get angry, madonna," said Dioneo. "Which do you like best? I know over a thousand. Would you like: 'If I don't tickle my little prickle,' or 'Gently, gently, husband dear,' or 'I'll buy a cock for a hundred dollars'?"

"Dioneo," said the queen rather angrily, although all the others were laughing, "cease joking, and sing a pleasant song. If you don't, you will discover how angry I can be."

At this Dioneo left his jests, and began to sing as follows:

Love, the fair light that issues from her eyes has made me slave to thee and her.

The splendor of her lovely eyes, passing through mine, moved me before your flame was kindled in my heart. However great your worth, I learned it through her beauteous face; imagining which, I found my self gathering every virtue and yielding them to her—another cause of sighs in me.

Now, dear my Lord, I have become one among your followers, and in obedience await your grace; but yet I know not if the high desire which you have set within my breast and my unshaken faith are wholly known to her, who so possesses all my mind that save from her I would not and I do not hope for peace.

Therefore I pray you, sweet my love, to show them to her, and make her feel a little of your flame, in grace to me who, as you see, am all consumed with love, and bit by bit worn down with pain. And then, when it is time, commend me to her, as you should, and gladly would I come with you to do it.

When Dioneo by his silence showed that his song was ended, the queen, after having highly praised it, had others sung. And when part of the night was spent and the queen felt that the heat of day was quenched in night's coolness, she ordered everyone to rest as he chose until the following day.

HERE ENDS THE FIFTH DAY

TENTH DAY, TENTH TALE

The Marquess of Saluzzo is urged by his subjects to take a wife and, to choose in his own way, takes the daughter of a peasant. He has two children by her and pretends to her that he has killed them. He then pretends that he is tired of her and that he has taken another wife and so brings their own daughter to the house as if she were his new wife, after driving her away in her shift. She endures it all patiently. He brings her back home, more beloved by him than ever, shows her their grown children, honors her and makes others honor her as Marchioness.

When the king[1] had ended his long tale, which, to judge by their looks, had greatly pleased everyone, Dioneo said, laughing:

"The good man who was waiting to bring down the ghost's stiff tail that night would not have given two cents for all the praise you give Messer Torello!"[2]

Then, knowing that he was the only one left to tell a tale, he began:

Gracious ladies, as far as I can see, today has been given up to Kings, Sultans and such like persons; so, not to wander away too far from you, I shall tell you about a Marquess, but not of his munificence. It will be about his silly brutality, although good came of it in the end. I do not advise anyone to imitate him, for it was a great pity that good did come to him.

A long time ago the eldest son of the Marquess of Saluzzo was a young man named Gualtieri. He was wifeless and childless, spent his time hunting and hawking, and never thought about marrying or having children, wherein he was probably very wise. This displeased his subjects, who several times begged him to take a wife, so that he might not die without an heir and leave them without a ruler, offering to find him a wife born of such a father and mother as would give him good hopes of her and content him. To which Gualtieri replied:

"My friends, you urge me to do something I was determined never to do, seeing how hard it is to find a woman of suitable character, and how many of the opposite sort there are, and how wretched is the life of a man who takes a wife unsuitable to him. It is foolishness of you to think you can judge a girl by the characters of her father and mother (from which you argue that you can find me one to please me), for I do not see how you can

---

[1] Pamfilo, who rules over the tenth day. The theme of the day is liberal and munificent behavior.

[2] A reference to the immediately preceding story and to the first story of Day Seven.

really know the fathers' or the mothers' secrets. And even if you did know them, daughters are often quite different from their fathers and mothers.

"But you want me to take these chains, and I am content to do so. If it turns out badly I want to have no one to complain of but myself, and so I shall choose for myself. And I tell you that if you do not honor the wife I choose as your lady you will find out to your cost how serious a thing it is to have compelled me by your entreaties to take a wife against my will."

They replied that they were content, if only he would take a wife.

For some time Gualtieri had been pleased by the character of a poor girl in a hamlet near his house. He thought her beautiful, and that he might live comfortably enough with her. So he decided that he would marry her without seeking any further, and, having sent for her father, who was a very poor man, he arranged to marry her. Having done this, Gualtieri called together all his friends from the surrounding country, and said:

"My friends, it has pleased you to desire that I should marry, and I am ready to do so, more to please you than from any desire I have of taking a wife. You know you promised me that you would honor anyone I chose as your lady. The time has now come for me to keep my promise to you and you to keep yours to me. I have found a girl after my heart quite near here; I intend to marry her and to bring her home in a few days. So take thought to make a handsome marriage feast and how you can honorably receive her, so that I may consider myself content with your promise as you may be with mine."

The good men cheerfully replied that they were glad of it, and that they would consider her their lady and honor her as their lady in all things. After which, they all set about preparing a great and handsome wedding feast, and so did Gualtieri. He prepared a great and fine banquet, and invited many friends and relatives and noblemen and others. Moreover, he had rich and beautiful dresses cut out and fitted on a girl, who seemed to him about the same build as the girl he proposed to marry. And he also purchased girdles and rings and a rich and beautiful crown, and everything necessary to a bride.

When the day appointed for the wedding arrived, Gualtieri about the middle of Terce[3] mounted his horse, and so did those who had come to honor him. Everything being arranged, he said:

"Gentlemen, it is time to go for the bride."

Setting out with all his company he came to the hamlet and the house of the girl's father, where he found her drawing water in great haste, so that she could go with the other women to see Gualtieri's bride. And when Gualtieri saw her, he called her by her name, Griselda, and asked where her father was. She blushed and said:

"He is in the house, my lord."

Gualtieri dismounted, told everyone to wait for him, entered the poor little house where he found the girl's father (who was named Giannucole), and said to him:

"I have come to marry Griselda, but first I want to ask her a few things in your presence."

He then asked her whether, if he married her, she would try to please

---

[3] 7:30 A.M.

him, and never be angry at anything he said or did, and if she would be obedient, and several other things, to all of which she said "Yes." Gualtieri then took her by the hand and led her forth. In the presence of all his company he had her stripped naked, and then the clothes he had prepared were brought, and she was immediately dressed and shod, and he had a crown put on her hair, all unkempt as it was. Everyone marveled at this, and he said:

"Gentlemen, I intend to take this girl as my wife, if she will take me as her husband."

He then turned to her, as she stood blushing and irresolute, and said:

"Griselda, will you take me as your husband?"

"Yes, my lord," she replied.

"And I will take you as my wife," said he.

Then in the presence of them all he pledged his faith to her; and they set her on a palfrey and honorably conducted her to his house. The wedding feast was great and handsome, and the rejoicing no less than if he had married the daughter of the King of France.

The girl seemed to have changed her soul and manners with her clothes. As I said, she was beautiful of face and body, and she became so agreeable, so pleasant, so well-behaved that she seemed like the daughter of a nobleman, and not Giannucole's child and a cattle herder; which surprised everyone who had known her before. Moreover, she was so obedient and so ready to serve her husband that he felt himself to be the happiest and best matched man in the world. And she was so gracious and kindly to her husband's subjects that there was not one of them but loved her and gladly honored her, while all prayed for her good and her prosperity and advancement. Whereas they had said that Gualtieri had showed little wisdom in marrying her, they now said that he was the wisest and shrewdest man in the world, because no one else would have known the lofty virtue hidden under her poor clothes and village garb.

In short, before long she acted so well that not only in the marquisate but everywhere people were talking of her virtues and good actions; and whatever had been said against her husband for having married her was now turned to the opposite. She had not long been with Gualtieri when she became pregnant, and in due time gave birth to a daughter, at which Gualtieri rejoiced greatly.

Soon after this the idea came to him to test her patience with a long trial and intolerable things. He said unkind things to her, seemed to be angry, and said that his subjects were most discontented with her on account of her low birth, and especially when they saw that she bore children. He said they were very angry at the birth of a daughter and did nothing but murmur. When the lady heard these words, she did not change countenance or cheerfulness, but said to him:

"My lord, you may do with me what you think most to your honor and satisfaction. I shall be content, for I know that I am less than they and unworthy of the honor to which you have raised me by your courtesy."

Gualtieri liked this reply and saw that no pride had risen up in her from the honor done her by him and others.

Soon after, he informed his wife in general terms that his subjects could not endure the daughter she had borne. He then gave orders to one of his servants whom he sent to her. The man, with a dolorous visage, said:

"Madonna, if I am to avoid death I must do what my lord bids me. He tells me I am to take your daughter and . . ."

He said no more, but the lady, hearing these words and seeing the servant's face, and remembering what had been said to her, guessed that he had been ordered to kill the child. She went straight to the cradle, kissed and blessed the child, and although she felt great anguish in her heart, put the child in the servant's arms without changing her countenance, and said:

"Do what my lord and yours has ordered you to do. But do not leave her for the birds and animals to devour her body, unless you were ordered to do so."

The servant took the child and told Gualtieri what the lady had said. He marveled at her constancy, and sent the servant with the child to a relative at Bologna, begging her to bring her up and educate her carefully, but without ever saying whose daughter she was.

After this the lady again became pregnant, and in due time brought forth a male child, which delighted Gualtieri. But what he had already done was not enough for him. He pierced the lady with a worse wound, and one day said to her in pretended anger:

"Since you have borne this male child, I cannot live at peace with my subjects, who complain bitterly that a grandson of Giannucole must be their lord after me. If I am not to be driven out, I fear I must do now as I did before, and in the end abandon you and take another wife."

The lady listened to him patiently, and her only reply was:

"My lord, content yourself and do what is pleasing to you. Do not think about me, for nothing pleases me except as it pleases you."

Not many days afterwards Gualtieri sent for his son in the same way that he had sent for his daughter, and while pretending in the same way to kill the child, sent it to be brought up in Bologna, as he had sent the girl. And his wife said no more and looked no worse than she had done about the daughter. Gualtieri marveled at this and said to himself that no other woman could have done what she did; and if he had not seen that she loved her children while she had them, he would have thought she did it to get rid of them, whereas he saw it was from obedience to him.

His subjects thought he had killed his children, blamed him severely and thought him a cruel man, while they felt great pity for his wife. And when the women condoled with her on the death of her children, she never said anything except that it was not her wish but the wish of him who begot them.

Several years after his daughter's birth, Gualtieri thought the time had come for the last test of his wife's patience. He kept saying that he could no longer endure to have Griselda as his wife, that he knew he had acted childishly and wrongly when he married her, that he therefore meant to solicit the Pope for a dispensation to marry another woman and abandon Griselda; for all of which he was reproved by many good men. But his only reply was that it was fitting this should be done.

Hearing of these things, the lady felt she must expect to return to her father's house and perhaps watch cattle as she had done in the past, and see another woman take the man she loved; at which she grieved deeply. But she prepared herself to endure this with a firm countenance, as she had endured the other wrongs of Fortune.

Not long afterwards Gualtieri received forged letters from Rome, which he showed to his subjects, pretending that the Pope by these letters gave him a dispensation to take another wife and leave Griselda. So, calling her before him, he said to her in the presence of many of his subjects:

"Wife, the Pope has granted me a dispensation to leave you and to take another wife. Now, since my ancestors were great gentlemen and lords of this country while yours were always laborers, I intend that you shall no longer be my wife, but return to Giannucole's house with the dowry you brought me, while I shall bring home another wife I have found more suitable for me."

At these words the lady could only restrain her tears by a great effort, beyond that of women's nature, and replied:

"My lord, I always knew that my lowly rank was in no wise suitable to your nobility; and the rank I have had with you I always recognized as coming from God and you, and never looked upon it as given to me, but only lent. You are pleased to take it back, and it must and does please me to return it to you. Here is the ring with which you wedded me; take it. You tell me to take the dowry I brought you; to do this there is no need for you to pay anything nor shall I need a purse or a sumpter horse,[4] for I have not forgotten that I came to you naked. If you think it right that the body which has borne your children should be seen by everyone, I will go away naked. But in exchange for my virginity, which I brought here and cannot carry away, I beg you will at least be pleased to let me take away one shift[5] over and above my dowry."

Gualtieri, who was nearer to tears than anyone else present, managed to keep his countenance stern, and said:

"You shall have a shift."

Those who were present urged him to give her a dress, so that she who had been his wife for thirteen years should not be seen to leave his house so poorly and insultingly as it would be for her to leave it in a shift. But their entreaties were vain. So the lady, clad only in her shift, unshod and with nothing on her head, commended him to God, left his house, and returned to her father accompanied by the tears and lamentation of all who saw her.

Giannucole (who had never believed it was true that Gualtieri would keep his daughter as a wife and had always expected this event), had kept the clothes she had taken off on the morning when Gualtieri married her. So she took them and put them on, and devoted herself to drudgery in her father's house, enduring the assaults of hostile Fortune with a brave spirit.

After Gualtieri had done this, he told his subjects that he was to marry the daughter of one of the Counts of Panago. He therefore made great preparations for the wedding, and sent for Griselda to come to him; and when she came, he said:

"I am bringing home the lady I have just married, and I intend to do her honor at her arrival. You know there is not a woman in the house who can prepare the rooms and do many other things needed for such a feast.

---

[4] Pack horse.   [5] Loose undergarment; slip.

You know everything connected with the house better than anyone, so you must arrange everything that is to be done, and invite all the women you think fit and receive them as if you were mistress of the house. Then, when the marriage feast is over, you can return home."

These words were a dagger in Griselda's heart, for she had not been able to dispense with the love she felt for him as she had her good fortune, but she said:

"My lord, I am ready."

So, in her coarse peasant dress, she entered the house she had left a little before in her shift, and had the rooms cleaned and arranged, put out hangings and carpets in the halls, looked to the kitchen, and set her hand to everything as if she had been a scullery wench of the house. And she never paused until everything was ready and properly arranged.

After this she invited all the ladies of the surrounding country in Gualtieri's name, and then awaited the feast. On the wedding day, dressed in her poor clothes, she received all the ladies with a cheerful visage and a womanly manner.

Gualtieri had had his children carefully brought up in Bologna by his relative, who was married into the family of the Counts of Panago. The daughter was now twelve years old, the most beautiful thing ever seen, and the boy was seven. He sent to her and asked her to come to Saluzzo with his son and daughter, to bring an honorable company with her, and to tell everyone that she was bringing the girl as his wife, and never to let anyone know that the girl was anything else. Her husband did what the Marquess asked, and set out. In a few days he reached Saluzzo about dinner time, with the girl and boy and his noble company; and all the peasants of the country were there to see Gualtieri's new wife.

The girl was received by the ladies and taken to the hall where the tables were spread, and Griselda went cheerfully to meet her, saying:

"Lady, you are welcome."

The ladies had begged Gualtieri, but in vain, to allow Griselda to stay in her room or to lend her one of her own dresses, so that she might not have to meet strangers in such a guise. They all sat down to table and began the meal. Every man looked at the girl and said that Gualtieri had made a good exchange, and Griselda above all praised her and her little brother.

Gualtieri now felt that he had tested his wife's patience as far as he desired. He saw that the strangeness of all this did not alter her and he was certain it was not the result of stupidity, for he knew her to be an intelligent woman. He thought it now time to take her from the bitterness which he felt she must be hiding behind a smiling face. So he called her to him, and in everyone's presence said to her smilingly:

"What do you think of my new wife?"

"My lord," replied Griselda, "I see nothing but good in her. If she is as virtuous as she is beautiful, as I well believe, I have no doubt that you will live with her the happiest lord in the world. But I beg you as earnestly as I can not to give her the wounds you gave the other woman who was your wife. I think she could hardly endure them, because she is younger and because she has been brought up delicately, whereas the other labored continually from her childhood."

Gualtieri saw that she really believed he was to marry the other, and yet spoke nothing but good of her. He made her sit down beside him, and said:

"Griselda, it is now time that you should reap the reward of your long patience, and that those who have thought me cruel and wicked and brutal should know that what I have done was directed towards a pre-determined end, which was to teach you to be a wife, then how to choose and keep a wife, and to procure me perpetual peace so long as I live with you. When I came and took you to wife, I greatly feared that this would not happen to me; and so, to test you, I have given you the trials and sufferings you know. I have never perceived that you thwarted my wishes by word or deed, and I think that in you I have the comfort I desire. I mean to give you back now what I deprived you of for a long time, and to heal the wounds I gave you with the greatest delight. Therefore, with a glad spirit, take her whom you think to be my wife and her brother as your children and mine. They are the children whom you and many others have long thought that I had cruelly murdered. And I am your husband, who loves you above all things, believing I can boast that no man exists who can so rejoice in his wife as I in you."

He then embraced and kissed her. She was weeping with happiness. They both arose and went to where their daughter was sitting, quite stupefied by what she had heard, and tenderly embraced her and her brother, thus undeceiving them and many of those present.

The ladies arose merrily from table and went with Griselda to her room. With better hopes they took off her old clothes and dressed her in one of her noble robes, and brought her back to the hall a lady, which she had looked even in her rags.

They rejoiced over their children, and everyone was glad at what had happened. The feasting and merrymaking were prolonged for several days, and Gualtieri was held to be a wise man, although they thought the testing of his wife harsh and intolerable. But above all they esteemed the virtue of Griselda.

The Count of Panago soon afterwards returned to Bologna. Gualtieri took Giannucole away from his labor and installed him as his father-in-law, so that he ended his days honorably and in great content. He afterwards married off his daughter to a nobleman of great wealth and distinction, and lived long and happily with Griselda, always honoring her as much as he could.

What more is to be said, save that divine souls are sometimes rained down from Heaven into poor houses, while in royal palaces are born those who are better fitted to herd swine than to rule over men? Who but Griselda could have endured with a face not only tearless but cheerful, the stern and unheard-of tests imposed on her by Gualtieri? It would perhaps not have been such a bad thing if he had chosen one of those women who, if she had been driven out of her home in a shift, would have let another man so shake her fur that a new dress would have come from it.

Dioneo's tale was over, and the ladies talked about it, taking first one part and then another, blaming some things and praising others. The king looked up at the sky and saw that the sun was already sinking towards the hour of Vespers,[6] and so, without rising, he spoke thus:

"Beautiful ladies, as I think you know, human wisdom does not wholly consist in remembering past things and knowing the present; but grave men esteem it the highest wisdom to be able to foresee the future from a knowledge of both.

"As you know, it will be a fortnight tomorrow since we left Florence to find some amusement to support our health and vitality, and to escape the melancholy, agony and woes which have continued in our city since the beginning of the plague. In my opinion we have virtuously performed this. We have told merry tales, which perhaps might incline to concupiscence; we have eaten and drunk well, played and sung music, all of which things incite weak minds to things less than virtuous; but so far as I have seen there has not been one word or one act on your part or on ours which could be blamed. I have noticed only continual virtue, concord and fraternal familiarity; which is certainly most pleasing to me in your honor and in mine. Now, through too long a habit something might arise which would turn to annoyance, and if we stay away too long an opportunity for scandal might occur; and moreover each of us has now for one day exercised the honor which now dwells in me. I therefore think, if you agree, that it would be well for us to return to the place from which we set out. And, if you consider the matter, our being together is already known round about, and so our company might be increased in such a way as to destroy our pleasure. If you approve my advice, I shall retain the crown until we leave, which I think should be tomorrow. If you decide otherwise, I am quite ready to crown someone for tomorrow."

The discussion between the ladies and young men was long, but at last the king's advice was adopted as wise and virtuous, and they determined to do as he had said. So, having called the steward, he discussed with him what should be done next morning, and then, standing up, gave the company their freedom until supper time.

The ladies and the rest arose, and as usual amused themselves in different ways. They came to supper merrily, and after that began to sing and dance and play music. After Lauretta had danced, the king ordered Fiammetta to sing a song, and she began pleasantly as follows:

If Love came to us without jealousy, no woman living—whoever she might be—
would be so glad as I!

And if a woman should be pleased to find in her lover gay youth, the very pinnacle of
virtue, eagerness and prowess, wisdom, manners, eloquent speech and perfect
grace—I should be pleased, who love them all and see them in my hope.

But since I see that other ladies are as wise as I, I tremble with my fears and dread the
worst—which is that others may desire the man I love; and so my wondrous
fortune turns to woe and sighing, and all life seems ill.

If my lover were but as faithful as he is valiant, I should feel no jealousy. But now so
many ladies seek for lovers that I think all men are faithless. This stabs my heart

[6] 6 P.M.

and makes me wish to die; I dread each woman who looks at him, and fear I may be robbed of him.

Therefore in God's name I beg all ladies not to work this wrong on me; for should any seek to do me harm by word or sign or flattery, either I shall turn fool at learning it or she shall weep her bitter foolishness!

When Fiammetta had ended her song, Dioneo, who was sitting beside her, said laughingly:

"Madonna, you would be very courteous to let all women know this, so that no one in ignorance may deprive you of a possession, whose loss would make you so angry!"

After this, they sang several other songs, and when it was nearly midnight, the king commanded that they should all go to bed.

Next morning they arose after the steward had already sent off all their baggage, and returned to Florence under the guidance of their prudent king. The three young men left the seven ladies in Santa Maria Novella, where they had met; and after taking leave of them went about their business. And the ladies returned home.

END OF THE TENTH AND LAST DAY

CONCLUSION

Most noble ladies, for whose delight I have given myself over to this long task, I believe that with the aid of divine grace it is more through your pious prayers than any merit of mine that I have carried out what I promised to do at the beginning of this work. So now, after giving thanks, first to God and then to you, I shall rest my pen and weary hand. I know that these tales can expect no more immunity than any others, as I think I showed in the beginning of the Fourth Day;[1] and so before I rest, I mean to reply to certain objections which might be made by you or others.

Some of you may say that in writing these tales I have taken too much license, by making ladies sometimes say and often listen to matters which are not proper to be said or heard by virtuous ladies. This I deny, for there is nothing so unchaste but may be said chastely if modest words are used; and this I think I have done.

But suppose it to be true—and I shall not strive with you, for you are certain to win—I reply that I have many arguments ready. First, if there is any license in some of them, the nature of the stories demanded it; and if any understanding person looks at them with a reasonable eye he will see that they could not be related otherwise, unless I had altered them entirely. And if there are a few words rather freer than suits the prudes, who weigh words more than deeds and take more pains to appear than to be good, I say that I should no more be reproved for having written them than other

---

[1] At the beginning of Day Four, Boccaccio had defended himself against detractors who had charged him, among other things, with too great a fondness for women. He replied that love for them was almost irresistibly natural.

men and women are reproved for daily saying "hole," "peg," "mortar," "pestle," "sausage," "Bologna sausage," and the like things.[2] My pen should be allowed no less power than is permitted the painter's brush; the painters are not censured for allowing Saint Michele to slay the serpent with a sword or lance and Saint Giorgio to kill the dragon as he pleases. They make Christ male and Eve female, and they fasten sometimes with one nail, sometimes with two, the feet of Him who died for the human race on the Cross.

In addition, anyone can see that these things were not told in church, where everything should be treated with reverent words and minds (although you will find plenty of license in the stories of the church); nor were they told in a school of philosophers, where virtue is as much required as anywhere else; nor among churchmen or other philosophers in any place; but they were told in gardens, in pleasure places, by young people who were old enough not to be led astray by stories, and at a time when everyone threw his cap over the mill and the most virtuous were not reproved for it.

But, such as they are, they may be amusing or harmful, like everything else, according to the persons who listen to them. Who does not know that wine is a most excellent thing, if we may believe Cinciglione and Scolaio,[3] while it is harmful to a man with a fever? Are we to say wine is wicked because it is bad for those who are feverish? Who does not know that fire is most useful and even necessary to mankind? And because it sometimes destroys houses, villages and towns, shall we say it is bad? Weapons defend the safety of those who wish to live in peace, but they also kill men, not through any wrong in them but through the wickedness of those who use them ill.

No corrupt mind ever understands words healthily. And just as such people do not enjoy virtuous words, so the well-disposed cannot be harmed by words which are somewhat less than virtuous, any more than mud can sully sunlight or earthy filth the beauty of the skies.

What books, what words, what letters are more holy, more worthy, more to be revered than those of the divine Scripture? Yet many people by perversely interpreting them have sent themselves and others to perdition. Everything in itself is good for something, and if wrongly used may be harmful in many ways; and I say the same of my tales. Whoever wants to turn them to bad counsel or bad ends will not be forbidden by the tales themselves, if by any chance they contain such things and are twisted and turned to produce them. Those who want utility and good fruits from them, will not find them denied; nor will the tales ever be thought anything but useful and virtuous if they are read at the times and to the persons for which they are intended.

Those who have to say paternosters and play the hypocrite to their confessor can leave them alone; my tales will run after nobody asking to be read. And yet bigots say and even do such little trifles from time to time!

---

[2] Words that can be used literally and innocently or with sexual meanings. Boccaccio goes on to cite paintings in which images that might be considered phallic can be used for pious purposes.

[3] Names used to represent drinkers.

There will also be people to say that if some of the tales here were absent it would be all the better. Granted. But I could only write down the tales which were related;[4] if they had told better ones, I should have written them down better. But suppose that I was both the inventor and the scribe (which I was not), I say that I am not ashamed that they are not all good, because there is no one, save God alone, who can do everything well and perfectly. Charlemagne, who first devised the Paladins,[5] could not make enough of them to form an army. In a multitude of things we must be prepared to find diverse qualities. No field was ever so well cultivated that it contained no nettles, briars and thorns mingled with better plants.

Moreover, since I was speaking to simple young women such as most of you are, it would have been folly for me to go seeking and striving to find such exquisite things and to take pains to speak with great measure. However, those who read these tales can leave those they dislike and read those they like. I do not want to deceive anybody, and so all these tales bear written at the head a title explaining what they contain.

I suppose some people will say that some of the tales are too long. I reply that for those who have something else to do it is folly to read the tales, even when they are short. A long time has passed between the day when I began to write and now when I have come to the end of my labors; but I have not forgotten that I said my work is offered to those ladies who are unoccupied, and not to others. To those who read for pastime, no tale can be too long if it succeeds in its object. Brevity befits students, who labor to spend time usefully, not to make it pass; but not you, ladies, who have unoccupied all that time you do not spend in love pleasures. None of you has studied at Athens, Bologna or Paris;[6] and so one must chatter a little more volubly for you than for those who have sharpened their wits by study.

I have no doubt that others will say that the things related are too full of jests and jokes, and that it ill befits a grave and weighty man to write such things. To them I must offer thanks and do thank them that they are so zealously tender of my good fame. But I shall reply to their objection. I confess I am weighty, and have often weighed myself. But, speaking to those who have not weighed me, I must observe that I am not grave but so light that I float in water. Considering that the friars' sermons, which are made to censure men's sins, are full of jokes and jests and railleries, I think that such things do not go ill in my tales, which are written to drive away ladies' melancholy. However, if the tales make them laugh too much, they can easily cure that by reading the lamentations of Jeremiah, the passion of the Saviour and the penitence of Mary Magdalene.

Who can doubt that there will be others who will say that I have a wicked poisonous tongue, because in some places I have written the truth about the friars? I mean to pardon those who say that, because it cannot be believed but that they are moved except by just cause, since the friars are

---

[4] As Chaucer does also in the General Prologue to *The Canterbury Tales,* Boccaccio adopts the conventional literary pose of a man who merely reports what others have said.

[5] The twelve eminent knights who served the great emperor Charlemagne (742–814); for an account of them, see *The Song of Roland* (which Boccaccio did not know).

[6] Athens was the center of ancient learning; Bologna and Paris had great medieval universities.

good men who avoid poverty for the love of God, and do good service to the ladies and say nothing about it. And if they did not all smell a little of the goat, their company would be most pleasant.

Yet I confess that there is no stability in the things of this world and that everything changes. So may it have chanced with my tongue. I do not trust my own judgment, which I always avoid in matters concerning myself, but one of my women neighbors the other day told me I have the best and sweetest tongue in the world. But, to speak the truth, when that happened there were not many of my tales left to finish. And so let what I have said suffice as a reply to those who make these objections.

I leave it to every lady to say and think what she pleases; for me it is time to end my words, giving thanks humbly to Him who by His aid and after so much labor has brought me to the desired end.

And you, fair ladies, rest in peace in His grace; and if in reading any of these tales you find any pleasure, remember me.

Niccolò Machiavelli
(1469–1527)

Niccolò Machiavelli—historian, theorist of history and of politics, and dramatist— was born in 1469 in Florence, a city he loved passionately and served or wished to serve throughout his life. His family had long been prominent in the city, but his father was impoverished, and Niccolò did not receive the best of formal educations; he learned Latin but not Greek, and he was in certain respects self-taught. Neverthe- less, after a youth of which we know little, he achieved in 1498 an important post in the Florentine government, and from that time until 1512 he held several key offices having to do with the internal, foreign, and military affairs of the city (Florence was then a republic, as it had been on and off for centuries). His military interests and assignments helped foster in him one of his key ideas: the desirability of a native soldiery as contrasted with venal, undependable mercenaries. He also was entrusted with a good many important diplomatic missions that took him to France, Switzer- land, Austria, southern Germany, and several parts of Italy.

During his travels he gained firsthand experience of the turbulence and disunited vulnerability of Italy, experience that he was to draw on in his writings. He also learned much about the realities of contemporary intrigue and power politics during an era of notorious violence and corruption, in Italy and throughout much of Eu- rope. (Compare Raphael Hythloday's mordant comments in Book One of More's Utopia.) In 1502–1503 he observed at first hand the activities of Cesare Borgia, the unsavory political and military adventurer in whom Machiavelli, despite certain misgivings, found the boldness, acumen, and resourcefulness that he was to recom- mend in The Prince. Cesare's near-success in unifying central Italy provided in some respects a model for the larger unification of Italy that was one of Machiavelli's most cherished goals. The choice of such a model was to do Machiavelli's reputation no good when, later in the sixteenth century, gossip circulated about incestuous acts and murders by poison on the part of Cesare, his sister Lucrezia, and their father Pope Alexander VI.

In 1512 the Medici family came to power in Florence, toppling the republic. Machiavelli was ousted from his posts and, suspected of disaffection as a member of the old government, was imprisoned and even tortured. Now in poverty, he retired to his modest patrimonial estate, where in 1513 he wrote The Prince *and much of the* Discourses on the First Decade of Titus Livius. *The former work, on which Machiavelli's popular fame rests, was intended on a personal level to win favor with and office from the Medici rulers; Machiavelli dedicated the book first to Giuliano de' Medici and then, after his death in 1516, to his nephew Lorenzo. On a higher level the book was meant to serve the cause of Italian independence and unity by instructing and inspiring the leader who might deliver the country from its abject condition. In or around 1518 Machiavelli wrote the comedy* Mandragola, *or* The Mandrake Root, *a masterpiece of world drama. In 1520 he wrote* On the Art of War, *a milestone in the theory of military tactics. In his last years Machiavelli was given a few minor diplomatic assignments by the Medici and also won their patronage for certain written works, including a history of Florence. In 1527 the forces of the Holy Roman Emperor, Charles V, sacked Rome, an event that helped drive the Medici from power in Florence. Although the republic was restored, Machiavelli was not in favor with the new regime either, and his hope to return to public office was disappointed. He died in the same year.*

Machiavelli's political writings, especially The Prince, *present a difficult challenge to interpreters; this much at least the author has in common with Thomas More, who two years later wrote the problematical* Utopia, *a book that seems to be the polar antithesis of* The Prince. *In the later sixteenth century Machiavelli came to be regarded as the epitome of coldblooded immorality; indeed, the "machiavel" became a stock character in Elizabethan drama, most notably in Christopher Marlowe's* Jew of Malta. *Marlowe's "Machiavelli" tells the audience, "I count religion but a childish toy, / And hold there is no sin but ignorance. . . . Might first made kings, and laws were then most sure / When . . . they were writ in blood." This myth about Machiavelli fed partly on itself, unbeholden to evidence from his writings, and it was reinforced in northern Europe by a stereotype of Italians as treacherous. What textual evidence there was came mainly from* The Prince; *the zealous republican Machiavelli of the* Discourses *seems a very different person. Certain passages in* The Prince, *and perhaps even its general tenor, do seem to support the traditional and popular view, which is by no means dead today even among informed readers of Machiavelli. At the very least, however, we owe it to Machiavelli to read what he actually wrote and to consider in what sense, if any, he really taught the doctrine often ascribed to him that "the end justifies the means."*

But Machiavelli has many strong defenders. Besides appealing to the integrity of his private life and the evidence from works like the Discourses, *his partisans urge a reappraisal of* The Prince *itself. Some of them praise Machiavelli as a political realist; they consider him one of the first thinkers to treat politics as a science rather than as a branch of ethics. Others have read* The Prince *as sustained, straight-faced irony, a devastating indictment of tyranny that for satiric purposes advises exactly the evils it seeks to expose. Others take* The Prince *more nearly at its word but subordinate the details of Machiavelli's practical advice to his main purpose, stated stirringly in chapter XXVI, of uniting and liberating his country. In their view, Machiavelli thus becomes a precursor of the patriots of the Risorgimento, the century-long movement to unify and free Italy that culminated in 1870. Other admirers turn the emphasis from political science to literary art, emphasizing Machiavelli's creative side and the indisputable fact of his preeminence as a master of Italian prose.*

In any case, there are many engrossing aspects of Machiavelli besides his morality. His prescriptions aside, his world view deserves attention in itself. In some ways he was a true Renaissance humanist, most clearly in his conviction that the classical past, which for Machiavelli meant primarily the Roman past, was directly relevant to the problems of modern times. This opinion is clearly not just sentimental nostalgia, for he finds in the ancients the same egocentric human nature he finds in his contemporaries. Yet out of selfishness and conflict, which for Machiavelli are givens in human nature and the state, the Romans created the greatest political entity the world has ever known. By the same token, since human nature does not change, he believes that the ancient glories can be revived, not by divine grace but by human skill and enterprise—within, admittedly, the limits of a fickle Fortune. The result is a unique and compelling vision, combining jaundiced caution with bracing self-assurance, unblinking realism with a peculiar brand of hope.

FURTHER READING *(prepared by W. J. R.):* Roberto Ridolfi's *The Life of Niccolò Machiavelli,* 1954, trans. by Cecil Grayson, 1963, is an excellent biography, as well as a comprehensive overview of Machiavelli's work. Ridolfi also provides an introductory account of the Italian Renaissance. The Past Masters series, which provides authoritative but fairly brief general introductions to great writers, includes Quentin Skinner's *Machiavelli,* 1981. Charles D. Tarlton's *Fortune's Circle,* 1970, uses Machiavelli's own writing to discover what it reveals about him. Works concentrating on the Italy of Machiavelli's time are numerous. Two suited for the general reader are J. H. Plumb's *The Italian Renaissance,* 1961, and J. R. Hale's *Machiavelli and Renaissance Italy,* 1960. Plumb's work is a concise survey of the period, with frequent references to Machiavelli, Dante, Petrarch, and other writers; Hale's work provides a clear account of Machiavelli's life and writings, with useful chronological tables and charts. E. Harris Harrison's "Machiavelli's *Prince* and More's *Utopia,*" in *Facets of the Renaissance,* ed. William H. Werkmeister, 1959, compares the two works in their cultural contexts, providing an excellent joint introduction to both writers. Herbert Butterfield's *The Statecraft of Machiavelli,* 1940, rpt. 1955, is a readable study of this complex subject. Allan H. Gilbert's *Machiavelli's "Prince" and Its Forerunners,* 1938, is primarily a running commentary on *The Prince.* An introductory chapter discusses clearly the tradition of books written to advise princes. Sydney Anglo's *Machiavelli: A Dissection,* 1969, discusses each of Machiavelli's major works. For a sociological approach, see J. E. Siegel's "Violence and Order in Machiavelli," in *Violence and Aggression,* ed. Philip J. Wiener, 1974. Siegel examines Machiavelli's views on violence and attempts to reconcile Machiavelli's apparent brutality and his romantic idealism.

from *THE PRINCE*

Translated by Ninian Hill Thomson

CHAPTER I

OF THE VARIOUS KINDS
OF PRINCEDOM, AND OF THE
WAYS IN WHICH THEY ARE ACQUIRED

All the States and Governments by which men are or ever have been ruled, have been and are either Republics or Princedoms. Princedoms are either hereditary, in which the sovereignty is derived through an ancient line of ancestors, or they are new. New Princedoms are either wholly new, as that of Milan to Francesco Sforza;[1] or they are like limbs joined on to the hereditary possessions of the Prince who acquires them, as the Kingdom of Naples to the dominions of the King of Spain.[2] The States thus acquired have either been used to live under a Prince or have been free; and he who acquires them does so either by his own arms or by the arms of others, and either by good fortune or by merit.[3]

CHAPTER II

OF HEREDITARY PRINCEDOMS

Of Republics I shall not now speak, having elsewhere spoken of them at length.[4] Here I shall treat exclusively of Princedoms, and, filling in the outline above traced out, shall proceed to examine how such States are to be governed and maintained.

I say, then, that hereditary States, accustomed to the family of their Prince, are maintained with far less difficulty than new States, since all that is required is that the Prince shall not depart from the usages of his ancestors, trusting for the rest to deal with events as they arise. So that if an hereditary Prince be of average address,[5] he will always maintain himself in his Princedom, unless deprived of it by some extraordinary and irresistible force; and even if so deprived will recover it, should any, even the least, mishap overtake the usurper. We have in Italy an example of this in the

[1] Milan had formerly been ruled by the Duke Filippo Maria Visconti; after his death, his son-in-law Sforza (1401–1466) betrayed the succeeding republic and assumed control as Duke of Milan in 1450.

[2] In 1500, King Louis XII of France and Ferdinand "the Catholic," King of Spain, agreed to share the rule of the much-disputed Kingdom of Naples, but in 1503 it was seized by force by Ferdinand for Spain.

[3] *Merit* here translates the Italian *virtù.* A key word in Machiavelli, it can be variously interpreted as merit, ingenuity, human ability, worth, vigor, strength, and a number of related qualities. It rarely means "virtue."

[4] In the *Discourses on the First Decade of Titus Livius.* Livius, or Livy (59 B.C.–A.D. 17) wrote a history of ancient Rome from which Machiavelli believed much could be learned by the Italians of his own time. Livy's first ten books, or "decade," describe the early years of Rome, before it became an empire under the Caesars.

[5] Adroitness or energy.

Duke of Ferrara, who never could have withstood the attacks of the Venetians in 1484, nor those of Pope Julius[6] in 1510, had not his authority in that State been consolidated by time. For since a Prince by birth has fewer occasions and less need to give offense, he ought to be better loved, and will naturally be popular with his subjects unless outrageous vices make him odious. Moreover, the very antiquity and continuance of his rule will efface the memories and causes which lead to innovation. For one change always leaves a dovetail into which another will fit.

CHAPTER V

How Cities or Provinces Which Before Their Acquisition Have Lived Under Their Own Laws Are To Be Governed

When a newly acquired State has been accustomed, as I have said, to live under its own laws and in freedom, there are three methods whereby it may be held. The first is to destroy it; the second, to go and reside there in person; the third, to suffer it to live on under its own laws, subjecting it to a tribute, and entrusting its government to a few of the inhabitants who will keep the rest your friends. Such a Government, since it is the creature of the new Prince, will see that it cannot stand without his protection and support, and must therefore do all it can to maintain him; and a city accustomed to live in freedom, if it is to be preserved at all, is more easily controlled through its own citizens than in any other way.

We have examples of all these methods in the histories of the Spartans and the Romans. The Spartans held Athens and Thebes[7] by creating oligarchies in these cities, yet lost them in the end. The Romans, to retain Capua, Carthage, and Numantia,[8] destroyed them and never lost them. On the other hand, when they thought to hold Greece as the Spartans had held it, leaving it its freedom and allowing it to be governed by its own laws, they failed, and had to destroy many cities of that Province before they could secure it. For, in truth, there is no sure way of holding other than by destroying, and whoever becomes master of a City accustomed to live in freedom and does not destroy it, may reckon on being destroyed by it. For if it should rebel, it can always screen itself under the name of liberty and its ancient laws, which no length of time, nor any benefits conferred will ever cause it to forget; and do what you will, and take what care you may, unless the inhabitants be scattered and dispersed, this name, and the old order of things, will never cease to be remembered, but will at once be turned against you whenever misfortune overtakes you, as when Pisa rose against the Florentines after a hundred years of servitude.[9]

[6] For more on the warlike Julius II (reigned 1503–1513), see chapters XI and XXV.

[7] *Spartans . . . Thebes.* Athens fell to Sparta in 404 B.C. The Spartans seized Thebes in 382 B.C.

[8] *Romans . . . Numantia.* The Romans took Capua (in southwest Italy) in 211 B.C., Carthage (in north Africa, near modern Tunis) in 146 B.C., and Numantia (in Spain) in 133 B.C.

[9] Pisa, a city west of Florence where the Arno, the river of Florence, flows into the sea, was controlled by that city through most of the fifteenth century. When King Charles VIII of France swept through Italy in 1494, Pisa rebelled and was not subjugated by Florence again until 1509.

If, however, the newly acquired City or Province has been accustomed to live under a Prince, and his line is extinguished, it will be impossible for the citizens, used, on the one hand, to obey, and deprived, on the other, of their old ruler, to agree to choose a leader from among themselves; and as they know not how to live as freemen, and are therefore slow to take up arms, a stranger may readily gain them over and attach them to his cause. But in Republics there is a stronger vitality, a fiercer hatred, a keener thirst for revenge. The memory of their former freedom will not let them rest; so that the safest course is either to destroy them, or to go and live in them.

CHAPTER VIII

OF THOSE WHO BY THEIR CRIMES COME TO BE PRINCES

But since from privacy[10] a man may also rise to be a Prince in one or other of two ways, neither of which can be referred wholly either to merit or to fortune, it is fit that I notice them here, though one of them may fall to be discussed more fully in treating of Republics.

The ways I speak of are, first, when the ascent to power is made by paths of wickedness and crime; and second, when a private person becomes ruler of his country by the favor of his fellow-citizens. The former method I shall make clear by two examples, one ancient, the other modern, without entering further into the merits of the matter, for these, I think, should be enough for any one who is driven to follow them.

Agathocles the Sicilian came, not merely from a private station, but from the very dregs of the people, to be King of Syracuse.[11] Son of a potter, through all the stages of his fortunes he led a foul life. His vices, however, were conjoined with so great vigor both of mind and body, that becoming a soldier, he rose through the various grades of the service to be Praetor[12] of Syracuse. Once established in that post, he resolved to make himself Prince, and to hold by violence and without obligation to others the authority which had been spontaneously entrusted to him. Accordingly, after imparting his design to Hamilcar,[13] who with the Carthaginian armies was at the time waging war in Sicily, he one morning assembled the people and senate of Syracuse as though to consult with them on matters of public moment, and on a preconcerted signal caused his soldiers to put to death all the senators, and the wealthiest of the commons. These being thus got rid of, he assumed and retained possession of the sovereignty without opposition on the part of the people; and although twice defeated by the Carthaginians, and afterwards besieged, he was able not only to defend his city, but leaving a part of his forces for its protection, to invade Africa with the remainder, and so in a short time to raise the siege of Syracuse, reducing the Carthaginians to the utmost extremities, and compelling them to make terms whereby they abandoned Sicily to him and confined themselves to Africa.

Whoever examines this man's actions and achievements will discover

---

[10] The rank of private citizen.
[11] Agathocles lived from 361 to 289 B.C.; Syracuse is in southeastern Sicily.
[12] Military commander.   [13] A Carthaginian general.

little or nothing in them which can be ascribed to Fortune, seeing, as has already been said, that it was not through the favor of any, but by the regular steps of the military service, gained at the cost of a thousand hardships and hazards, he reached the Princedom which he afterwards maintained by so many daring and dangerous enterprises. Still, to slaughter fellow-citizens, to betray friends, to be devoid of honor, pity, and religion, cannot be counted as merits, for these are means which may lead to power, but which confer no glory. Wherefore, if in respect of the valor with which he encountered and extricated himself from difficulties, and the constancy of his spirit in supporting and conquering adverse fortune, there seems no reason to judge him inferior to the greatest captains that have ever lived, his unbridled cruelty and inhumanity, together with his countless crimes, forbid us to number him with the greatest men; but, at any rate, we cannot attribute to Fortune or to merit what he accomplished without either.

In our own times, during the papacy of Alexander VI,[14] Oliverotto of Fermo, who some years before had been left an orphan, and had been brought up by his maternal uncle Giovanni Fogliani, was sent while still a lad to serve under Paolo Vitelli, in the expectation that a thorough training under that commander might qualify him for high rank as a soldier. After the death of Paolo, he served under his brother Vitellozzo, and in a very short time, being of a quick wit, hardy and resolute, he became one of the first soldiers of his company. But thinking it beneath him to serve under others, with the countenance of the Vitelleschi[15] and the connivance of certain citizens of Fermo who preferred the slavery to the freedom of their country, he formed the design to seize on that town.

He accordingly wrote to Giovanni Fogliani that after many years of absence from home, he desired to see him and his native city once more, and to look a little into the condition of his patrimony; and as his one endeavor had been to make himself a name, in order that his fellow-citizens might see that his time had not been mis-spent, he proposed to return honorably attended by a hundred horsemen from among his own friends and followers; and he begged Giovanni graciously to arrange for his reception by the citizens of Fermo with corresponding marks of distinction, as this would be creditable not only to himself, but also to the uncle who had brought him up.

Giovanni, accordingly, did not fail in any proper attention to his nephew, but caused him to be splendidly received by his fellow-citizens, and lodged him in his house; where Oliverotto having passed some days, and made the necessary arrangements for carrying out his wickedness, gave a formal banquet, to which he invited his uncle and all the first men of Fermo. When the repast and the other entertainments proper to such an occasion had come to an end, Oliverotto artfully turned the conversation to matters of grave interest, by speaking of the greatness of Pope Alexander and Cesare his son,[16] and of their enterprises; and when Giovanni and the others were replying to what he said, he suddenly rose up, observing that

---

[14] Rodrigo Borgia; his papacy lasted from 1492 to 1503.   [15] Followers of Vitellozzo.
[16] Cesare Borgia (1475?–1507), warrior, natural son of Alexander VI, and the subject of luridly scandalous stories involving murder and incest. In chapter VII Machiavelli praises Cesare as in most respects a model of political acumen.

these were matters to be discussed in a more private place, and so withdrew to another chamber; whither his uncle and all the other citizens followed him, and where they had no sooner seated themselves, than soldiers rushing out from places of concealment put Giovanni and all the rest to death.

After this butchery, Oliverotto mounted his horse, rode through the streets, and besieged the chief magistrate in the palace, so that all were constrained by fear to yield obedience and accept a government of which he made himself the head. And all who from being disaffected[17] were likely to stand in his way, he put to death, while he strengthened himself with new ordinances, civil and military, to such purpose, that for the space of a year during which he retained the Princedom, he not merely kept a firm hold of the city, but grew formidable to all his neighbors. And it would have been as impossible to unseat him as it was to unseat Agathocles, had he not let himself be overreached by Cesare Borgia on the occasion when, as has already been told, the Orsini and Vitelli were entrapped at Sinigaglia;[18] where he too being taken, one year after the commission of his parricidal crime, was strangled along with Vitellozzo, whom he had assumed for his master in villainy as in valor.

It may be asked how Agathocles and some like him, after numberless acts of treachery and cruelty, have been able to live long in their own country in safety, and to defend themselves from foreign enemies, without being plotted against by their fellow-citizens, whereas, many others, by reason of their cruelty, have failed to maintain their position even in peaceful times, not to speak of the perilous times of war. I believe that this results from cruelty being well or ill employed. Those cruelties we may say are well employed, if it be permitted to speak well of things evil, which are done once for all under the necessity of self-preservation, and are not afterwards persisted in, but so far as possible modified to the advantage of the governed. Ill-employed cruelties, on the other hand, are those which from small beginnings increase rather than diminish with time. They who follow the first of these methods, may, by the grace of God and man, find as did Agathocles, that their condition is not desperate; but by no possibility can the others maintain themselves.

Hence we may learn the lesson that on seizing a state, the usurper should make haste to inflict what injuries he must, at a stroke, that he may not have to renew them daily, but be enabled by their discontinuance to reassure men's minds, and afterwards win them over by benefits. Whosoever, either through timidity or from following bad counsels, adopts a contrary course, must keep the sword always drawn, and can put no trust in his subjects, who suffering from continued and constantly renewed severities, will never yield him their confidence. Injuries, therefore, should be inflicted all at once, that their ill savor being less lasting may the less offend; whereas, benefits should be conferred little by little, that so they may be more fully relished.

But, before all things, a Prince should so live with his subjects that no vicissitude of good or evil fortune shall oblige him to alter his behavior;

---

[17] Discontented; not loyal.

[18] Cesare's murder at Sinigaglia of the enemies here mentioned took place in 1501–1502.

because, if a need to change come through adversity, it is then too late to resort to severity; while any leniency you may use will be thrown away, for it will be seen to be compulsory and gain you no thanks.

CHAPTER IX

Of the Civil Princedom

I come now to the second case, namely, of the leading citizen who, not by crimes or violence, but by the favor of his fellow-citizens, is made Prince of his country. This may be called a Civil Princedom, and its attainment depends not wholly on merit, nor wholly on good fortune, but rather on what may be termed a *fortunate astuteness*. I say then that the road to this Princedom lies either through the favor of the people or of the nobles. For in every city are to be found these two opposed humors having their origin in this, that the people desire not to be domineered over or oppressed by the nobles, while the nobles desire to oppress and domineer over the people. And from these two contrary appetites there arises in cities one of three results, a Princedom, or Liberty, or License. A Princedom is created either by the people or by the nobles, according as one or other of these factions has occasion for it. For when the nobles perceive that they cannot withstand the people, they set to work to magnify the reputation of one of their number, and make him their Prince, to the end that under his shadow they may be enabled to indulge their desires. The people, on the other hand, when they see that they cannot make head against the nobles, invest a single citizen with all their influence and make him Prince, that they may have the shelter of his authority.

He who is made Prince by the favor of the nobles, has greater difficulty to maintain himself than he who comes to the Princedom by aid of the people, since he finds many about him who think themselves as good as he, and whom, on that account, he cannot guide or govern as he would. But he who reaches the Princedom by the popular support, finds himself alone, with none, or but a very few about him who are not ready to obey. Moreover, the demands of the nobles cannot be satisfied with credit to the Prince, nor without injury to others, while those of the people well may, the aim of the people being more honorable than that of the nobles, the latter seeking to oppress, the former not to be oppressed. Add to this, that a Prince can never secure himself against a disaffected people, their number being too great, while he may against a disaffected nobility, since their number is small. The worst that a Prince need fear from a disaffected people is, that they may desert him, whereas when the nobles are his enemies he has to fear not only that they may desert him, but also that they may turn against him; because, as they have greater craft and foresight, they always choose their time to suit their safety, and seek favor with the side they think will win. Again, a Prince must always live with the same people, but need not always live with the same nobles, being able to make and unmake these from day to day, and give and take away their authority at his pleasure.

But to make this part of the matter clearer, I say that as regards the nobles there is this first distinction to be made. They either so govern their conduct as to bind themselves wholly to your fortunes, or they do not.

Those who so bind themselves, and who are not grasping, should be loved and honored. As to those who do not so bind themselves, there is this further distinction. For the most part they are held back by pusillanimity and a natural defect of courage, in which case you should make use of them, and of those among them more especially who are prudent, for they will do you honor in prosperity and in adversity give you no cause for fear. But where they abstain from attaching themselves to you of set purpose and for ambitious ends, it is a sign that they are thinking more of themselves than of you, and against such men a Prince should be on his guard, and treat them as though they were declared enemies, for in his adversity they will always help to ruin him.

He who becomes a Prince through the favor of the people should always keep on good terms with them; which it is easy for him to do, since all they ask is not to be oppressed. But he who against the will of the people is made a Prince by the favor of the nobles, must, above all things, seek to conciliate the people, which he readily may by taking them under his protection. For since men who are well treated by one whom they expected to treat them ill, feel the more beholden to their benefactor, the people will at once become better disposed to such a Prince when he protects them, than if he owed his Princedom to them.

There are many ways in which a Prince may gain the good-will of the people, but, because these vary with circumstances, no certain rule can be laid down respecting them, and I shall, therefore, say no more about them. But this is the sum of the matter, that it is essential for a Prince to be on a friendly footing with his people, since, otherwise, he will have no resource in adversity. Nabis, Prince of Sparta, was attacked by the whole hosts of Greece and by a Roman army flushed with victory, and defended his country and crown against them; and when danger approached, there were but few of his subjects against whom he needed to guard himself,[19] whereas had the people been hostile, this would not have been enough.

And what I affirm let no one controvert by citing the old saw that *"he who builds on the people builds on mire,"* for that may be true of a private citizen who presumes on his favor with the people, and counts on being rescued by them when overpowered by his enemies or by the magistrates. In such cases a man may often find himself deceived, as happened to the Gracchi in Rome, and in Florence to Messer Giorgio Scali.[20] But when he who builds on the people is a Prince capable of command, of a spirit not to be cast down by ill-fortune, who, while he animates the whole community by his courage and bearing, neglects no prudent precaution, he will not find himself betrayed by the people, but will be seen to have laid his foundations well.

The most critical juncture for Princedoms of this kind, is at the moment when they are about to pass from the popular to the absolute form of government: and as these Princes exercise their authority either directly or

---

[19] Nabis, who ruled Sparta from 205 to 192 B.C., protected himself against the external threats by executing eighty suspected men—a small number in Machiavelli's context.

[20] The Gracchi (second century B.C.) were two brothers who served as Roman tribunes (spokesmen for the people) and died because of the enmity of the aristocrats and of the mob. Scali (fourteenth century) was a leader of the Florentine people who lost their support and was beheaded.

through the agency of the magistrates, in the latter case their position is weaker and more hazardous, since they are wholly in the power of those citizens to whom the magistracies are entrusted, who can, and especially in difficult times, with the greatest ease deprive them of their authority, either by opposing, or by not obeying them. And in times of peril it is too late for a Prince to assume to himself an absolute authority, for the citizens and subjects who are accustomed to take their orders from the magistrates, will not when dangers threaten take them from the Prince, so that at such seasons there will always be very few in whom he can trust. Such Princes, therefore, must not build on[21] what they see in tranquil times when the citizens feel the need of the State. For then every one is ready to run, to promise, and, danger of death being remote, even to die for the State. But in troubled times, when the State has need of its citizens, few of them are to be found. And the risk of the experiment is the greater in that it can only be made once. Wherefore, a wise Prince should devise means whereby his subjects may at all times, whether favorable or adverse, feel the need of the State and of him, and then they will always be faithful to him.

CHAPTER X

How the Strength of All Princedoms Should Be Measured

In examining the character of these Princedoms, another circumstance has to be considered, namely, whether the Prince is strong enough, if occasion demands, to stand alone, or whether he needs continual help from others. To make the matter clearer, I pronounce those to be able to stand alone who, with the men and money at their disposal, can get together an army fit to take the field against any assailant; and, conversely, I judge those to be in constant need of help who cannot take the field against their enemies, but are obliged to retire behind their walls, and to defend themselves there. Of the former I have already spoken, and shall speak again as occasion may require. As to the latter there is nothing to be said, except to exhort such Princes to strengthen and fortify the towns in which they dwell, and take no heed of the country outside. For whoever has thoroughly fortified his town, and put himself on such a footing with his subjects as I have already indicated and shall hereafter speak of, will always be attacked with much circumspection; for men are always averse to enterprises that are attended with difficulty, and it is impossible not to foresee difficulties in attacking a Prince whose town is strongly fortified and who is not hated by his subjects.

The towns of Germany[22] enjoy great freedom. Having little territory, they render obedience to the Emperor[23] only when so disposed, fearing neither him nor any other neighboring power. For they are so fortified that it is plain to every one that it would be a tedious and difficult task to reduce them, since all of them are protected by moats and suitable ramparts, are well supplied with artillery, and keep their public magazines constantly stored with victual, drink and fuel, enough to last them for a year. Besides

---

[21] Count on.   [22] The term refers here to Switzerland and Austria.
[23] The Holy Roman Emperor, at the time Maximilian I.

which, in order to support the poorer class of citizens without public loss, they lay in a common stock of materials for these to work on for a year, in the handicrafts which are the life and sinews of such cities, and by which the common people live. Moreover, they esteem military exercises and have many regulations for their maintenance.

A Prince, therefore, who has a strong city, and who does not make himself hated, can not be attacked, or should he be so, his assailant will come badly off; since human affairs are so variable that it is almost impossible for any one to keep an army posted in leaguer[24] for a whole year without interruption of some sort. Should it be objected that if the citizens have possessions outside the town, and see them burned, they will lose patience, and that self-interest, together with the hardships of a protracted siege, will cause them to forget their loyalty; I answer that a capable and courageous Prince will always overcome these difficulties, now, by holding out hopes to his subjects that the evil will not be of long continuance; now, by exciting their fears of the enemy's cruelty; and, again, by dexterously silencing those who seem to him too forward in their complaints. Moreover, it is to be expected that the enemy will burn and lay waste the country immediately on their arrival, at a time when men's minds are still heated and resolute for defense. And for this very reason the Prince ought the less to fear, because after a few days, when the first ardor has abated, the injury is already done and suffered, and cannot be undone; and the people will now, all the more readily, make common cause with their Prince from his seeming to be under obligations to them, their houses having been burned and their lands wasted in his defense. For it is the nature of men to incur obligation as much by the benefits they render as by those they receive.

Wherefore, if the whole matter be well considered, it ought not to be difficult for a prudent Prince, both at the outset and afterwards, to maintain the spirits of his subjects during a siege; provided always that victuals and the other means of defense do not run short.

CHAPTER XI

OF ECCLESIASTICAL PRINCEDOMS

It now only remains for me to treat of Ecclesiastical Princedoms, all the difficulties in respect of which precede their acquisition. For they are acquired by merit or good fortune, but are maintained without either; being upheld by the venerable ordinances of Religion, which are all of such a nature and efficacy that they secure the authority of their Princes in whatever way they may act or live. These Princes alone have territories which they do not defend, and subjects whom they do not govern; yet their territories are not taken from them through not being defended, nor are their subjects concerned at not being governed, or led to think of throwing off their allegiance; nor is it in their power to do so. Accordingly these Princedoms alone are secure and happy. But inasmuch as they are sustained by agencies of a higher nature than the mind of man can reach, I forbear to speak of them: for since they are set up and supported by God

[24] Encamped for a siege.

himself, he would be a rash and presumptuous man who should venture to discuss them.

Nevertheless, should any one ask me how it comes about that the temporal power of the Church, which before the time of Alexander was looked on with contempt by all the Potentates of Italy, and not only by those so styling themselves, but by every Baron and Lordling however insignificant, has now reached such a pitch of greatness that the King of France trembles before it, and that it has been able to drive him out of Italy and to crush the Venetians; though the causes be known, it seems to me not superfluous to call them in some measure to recollection.

Before Charles of France passed into Italy,[25] that country was under the control of the Pope, the Venetians, the King of Naples, the Duke of Milan, and the Florentines. Two chief objects had to be kept in view by all these powers; first, that no armed foreigner should be allowed to invade Italy; second, that no one of their own number should be suffered to extend his territory. Those whom it was especially needed to guard against, were the Pope and the Venetians. To hold back the Venetians it was necessary that all the other States should combine, as was done for the defense of Ferrara;[26] while to restrain the Pope, use was made of the Roman Barons, who being divided into two factions, the Orsini and Colonnesi, had constant cause for feud with one another, and standing with arms in their hands under the very eyes of the Pontiff, kept the Popedom feeble and insecure.

And although there arose from time to time a courageous Pope like Sixtus,[27] neither his prudence nor his good fortune could free him from these embarrassments. The cause whereof was the shortness of the lives of the Popes. For in the ten years, which was the average duration of a Pope's life, he could barely succeed in humbling one of these factions; so that if, for instance, one Pope had almost exterminated the Colonnesi, he was followed by another, who being the enemy of the Orsini had no time to rid himself of them, but so far from completing the destruction of the Colonnesi, restored them to life. This led to the temporal authority of the Popes being little esteemed in Italy.

Then came Alexander VI, who more than any of his predecessors showed what a Pope could effect with money and arms, achieving by the instrumentality of Duke Valentino,[28] and by taking advantage of the coming of the French into Italy, all those successes which I have already noticed[29] in speaking of the actions of the Duke. And although his object was to aggrandize, not the Church but the Duke, what he did turned to the advantage of the Church, which after his death, and after the Duke had been put out of the way, became the heir of his labors.

After him came Pope Julius, who found the Church strengthened by the possession of the whole of Romagna,[30] and the Roman Barons exhausted and their factions shattered under the blows of Pope Alexander.

---

[25] This occurred in 1494.

[26] In 1484 Ferrara was defended against Venice by a coalition of the papacy, Naples, Florence, and Milan.

[27] Sixtus IV reigned from 1471 to 1484.   [28] Alexander's son, Cesare Borgia.

[29] In Chapter VII, omitted here.   [30] A region northeast of Florence.

He found also a way opened for the accumulation of wealth,[31] which before the time of Alexander no one had followed. These advantages Julius not only used but added to. He undertook the conquest of Bologna, the overthrow of the Venetians, and the expulsion of the French from Italy; in all which enterprises he succeeded, and with the greater glory to himself in that whatever he did, was done to strengthen the Church and not to aggrandize any private person. He succeeded, moreover, in keeping the factions of the Orsini and Colonnesi within the same limits as he found them; and, though some seeds of insubordination may still have been left among them, two causes operated to hold them in check; first, the great power of the Church, which overawed them, and, second, their being without Cardinals,[32] who had been the cause of all their disorders. For these factions while they have Cardinals among them can never be at rest, since it is they who foment dissension both in Rome and out of it, in which the Barons are forced to take part, the ambition of the Prelates thus giving rise to tumult and discord among the Barons.

His Holiness, Pope Leo,[33] has consequently found the Papacy most powerful; and from him we may hope, that as his predecessors made it great with arms, he will render it still greater and more venerable by his benignity and other countless virtues.

CHAPTER XIV

Of the Duty of a Prince in Respect of Military Affairs

A Prince, therefore, should have no care or thought but for war, and for the regulations and training it requires, and should apply himself exclusively to this as his peculiar province; for war is the sole art looked for in one who rules, and is of such efficacy that it not merely maintains those who are born Princes, but often enables men to rise to that eminence from a private station; while, on the other hand, we often see that when Princes devote themselves rather to pleasure than to arms, they lose their dominions. And as neglect of this art is the prime cause of such calamities, so to be a proficient in it is the surest way to acquire power. Francesco Sforza,[34] from his renown in arms, rose from privacy to be Duke of Milan, while his descendants, seeking to avoid the hardships and fatigues of military life, from being Princes fell back into privacy. For among other causes of misfortune which your not being armed brings upon you, it makes you despised, and this is one of those reproaches against which, as shall presently be explained, a Prince ought most carefully to guard.

Between an armed and an unarmed man no proportion holds, and it is contrary to reason to expect that the armed man should voluntarily submit to him who is unarmed, or that the unarmed man should stand secure among armed retainers. For with contempt on one side, and distrust on the

---

[31] Pope Julius accumulated wealth by creating new cardinals.

[32] Having no cardinals in their families.

[33] Giovanni de' Medici, Leo X, uncle of the Lorenzo to whom *The Prince* was dedicated, reigned from 1513 to 1521.

[34] For Sforza, see chapter I and note.

other, it is impossible that men should work well together. Wherefore, as has already been said, a Prince who is ignorant of military affairs, besides other disadvantages, can neither be respected by his soldiers, nor can he trust them. A Prince, therefore, ought never to allow his attention to be diverted from warlike pursuits, and should occupy himself with them even more in peace than in war. This he can do in two ways, by practice or by study.

As to the practice, he ought, besides keeping his soldiers well trained and disciplined, to be constantly engaged in the chase, that he may inure his body to hardships and fatigue, and gain at the same time a knowledge of places, by observing how the mountains slope, the valleys open, and the plains spread; acquainting himself with the characters of rivers and marshes, and giving the greatest attention to this subject. Such knowledge is useful to him in two ways; for first, he learns thereby to know his own country, and to understand better how it may be defended; and next, from his familiar acquaintance with its localities, he readily comprehends the character of other districts when obliged to observe them for the first time. For the hills, valleys, plains, rivers, and marshes of Tuscany,[35] for example, have a certain resemblance to those elsewhere; so that from a knowledge of the natural features of that province, similar knowledge in respect of other provinces may readily be gained. The Prince who is wanting in this kind of knowledge, is wanting in the first qualification of a good captain, for by it he is taught how to surprise an enemy, how to choose an encampment, how to lead his army on a march, how to array it for battle, and how to post it to the best advantage for a siege.

Among the commendations which Philopoemon,[36] Prince of the Achaians, has received from historians is this—that in times of peace he was always thinking of methods of warfare, so that when walking in the country with his friends he would often stop and talk with them on the subject. "If the enemy," he would say, "were posted on that hill, and we found ourselves here with our army, which of us would have the better position? How could we most safely and in the best order advance to meet them? If we had to retreat, what direction should we take? If they retired, how should we pursue?" In this way he put to his friends, as he went along, all the contingencies that can befall an army. He listened to their opinions, stated his own, and supported them with reasons; and from his being constantly occupied with such meditations, it resulted, that when in actual command no complication could ever present itself with which he was not prepared to deal.

As to the mental training of which we have spoken, a Prince should read histories, and in these should note the actions of great men, observe how they conducted themselves in their wars, and examine the causes of their victories and defeats, so as to avoid the latter and imitate them in the former. And above all, he should, as many great men of past ages have done, assume for his models those persons who before his time have been renowned and celebrated, whose deeds and achievements he should con-

---

[35] The region around Florence, the city with which Machiavelli is most concerned.

[36] Philopoemon (c. 250–183 B.C.) was general of the Achaean League, a coalition of Greek cities of the Peloponnesian peninsula in southern Greece.

stantly keep in mind, as it is related that Alexander the Great sought to resemble Achilles, Caesar Alexander, and Scipio Cyrus.[37] And anyone who reads the life of this last-named hero, written by Xenophon,[38] recognizes afterwards in the life of Scipio, how much this imitation was the source of his glory, and how nearly in his chastity, affability, kindliness, and generosity, he conformed to the character of Cyrus as Xenophon describes it.

A wise Prince, therefore, should pursue such methods as these, never resting idle in times of peace, but strenuously seeking to turn them to account, so that he may derive strength from them in the hour of danger, and find himself ready should Fortune turn against him, to resist her blows.

CHAPTER XV

OF THE QUALITIES IN RESPECT OF WHICH MEN, AND MOST OF ALL PRINCES, ARE PRAISED OR BLAMED

It now remains for us to consider what ought to be the conduct and bearing of a Prince in relation to his subjects and friends. And since I know that many have written on this subject, I fear it may be thought presumptuous in me to write of it also; the more so, because in my treatment of it I depart from the views that others have taken.

But since it is my object to write what shall be useful to whosoever understands it, it seems to me better to follow the real truth of things than an imaginary view of them. For many Republics and Princedoms have been imagined[39] that were never seen or known to exist in reality. And the manner in which we live, and that in which we ought to live, are things so wide asunder, that he who quits the one to betake himself to the other is more likely to destroy than to save himself; since any one who would act up to a perfect standard of goodness in everything, must be ruined among so many who are not good. It is essential, therefore, for a Prince who desires to maintain his position, to have learned how to be other than good, and to use or not to use his goodness as necessity requires.

Laying aside, therefore, all fanciful notions concerning a Prince, and considering those only that are true, I say that all men when they are spoken of, and Princes more than others from their being set so high, are characterized by some one of those qualities which attach either praise or blame. Thus one is accounted liberal,[40] another miserly (which word I use, rather than *avaricious*, to denote the man who is too sparing of what is his own, *avarice* being the disposition to take wrongfully what is another's); one is generous, another greedy; one cruel, another tenderhearted; one is faithless, another true to his word; one effeminate and cowardly, another high-spirited and courageous; one is courteous, another haughty; one im-

[37] Achilles was the warrior hero of Homer's *Iliad;* Scipio was a Roman general who defeated the Carthaginians in the Punic Wars; Cyrus was an ancient Persian prince.

[38] Greek soldier (c.430–c.355 B.C.), author of various works including the *Cyropaedia* or *Education of Cyrus.*

[39] For example, in Plato's *Republic.*   [40] Free-giving; generous.

pure, another chaste; one simple,[41] another crafty; one firm, another facile;[42] one grave, another frivolous; one devout, another unbelieving; and the like. Every one, I know, will admit that it would be most laudable for a Prince to be endowed with all of the above qualities that are reckoned good; but since it is impossible for him to possess or constantly practice them all, the conditions of human nature not allowing it, he must be discreet enough to know how to avoid the infamy of those vices that would deprive him of his government, and, if possible, be on his guard also against those which might not deprive him of it; though if he cannot wholly restrain himself, he may with less scruple indulge in the latter. He need never hesitate, however, to incur the reproach of those vices without which his authority can hardly be preserved; for if he well consider the whole matter, he will find that there may be a line of conduct having the appearance of virtue, to follow which would be his ruin, and that there may be another course having the appearance of vice, by following which his safety and well-being are secured.

CHAPTER XVI

OF LIBERALITY AND MISERLINESS

Beginning, then, with the first of the qualities above noticed, I say that it may be a good thing to be reputed liberal, but, nevertheless, that liberality without the reputation of it is hurtful; because, though it be worthily and rightly used, still if it be not known, you escape not the reproach of its opposite vice. Hence, to have credit for liberality with the world at large, you must neglect no circumstance of sumptuous display; the result being, that a Prince of a liberal disposition will consume his whole substance in things of this sort, and, after all, be obliged, if he would maintain his reputation for liberality, to burden his subjects with extraordinary taxes, and to resort to confiscations and all the other shifts[43] whereby money is raised. But in this way he becomes hateful to his subjects, and growing impoverished is held in little esteem by any. So that in the end, having by his liberality offended many and obliged few, he is worse off than when he began, and is exposed to all his original dangers. Recognizing this, and endeavoring to retrace his steps, he at once incurs the infamy of miserliness.

A Prince, therefore, since he cannot without injury to himself practice the virtue of liberality so that it may be known, will not, if he be wise, greatly concern himself though he be called miserly. Because in time he will come to be regarded as more and more liberal, when it is seen that through his parsimony his revenues are sufficient; that he is able to defend himself against any who make war on him; that he can engage in enterprises against others without burdening his subjects; and thus exercise liberality towards all from whom he does not take, whose number is infinite, while he is miserly in respect of those only to whom he does not give, whose number is few.

In our own days we have seen no Princes accomplish great results save those who have been accounted miserly. All others have been ruined. Pope

---

[41] Not double-dealing.   [42] Easygoing.   [43] Tricks; stratagems.

Julius II, after availing himself of his reputation for liberality to arrive at the Papacy, made no effort to preserve that reputation when making war on the King of France, but carried on all his numerous campaigns without levying from his subjects a single extraordinary tax, providing for the increased expenditure out of his long-continued savings. Had the present King of Spain been accounted liberal, he never could have engaged or succeeded in so many enterprises.

A Prince, therefore, if he is enabled thereby to forbear from plundering his subjects, to defend himself, to escape poverty and contempt, and the necessity of becoming rapacious, ought to care little though he incur the reproach of miserliness, for this is one of those vices which enable him to reign.

And should any object that Caesar by his liberality rose to power, and that many others have been advanced to the highest dignities from their having been liberal and so reputed, I reply, "Either you are already a Prince or you seek to become one; in the former case liberality is hurtful, in the latter it is very necessary that you be thought liberal; Caesar was one of those who sought the sovereignty of Rome; but if after obtaining it he had lived on without retrenching his expenditure, he must have ruined the Empire." And if it be further urged that many Princes reputed to have been most liberal have achieved great things with their armies, I answer that a Prince spends either what belongs to himself and his subjects, or what belongs to others; and that in the former case he ought to be sparing, but in the latter ought not to refrain from any kind of liberality. Because for a Prince who leads his armies in person and maintains them by plunder, pillage, and forced contributions, dealing as he does with the property of others this liberality is necessary, since otherwise he would not be followed by his soldiers. Of what does not belong to you or to your subjects you should, therefore, be a lavish giver, as were Cyrus, Caesar, and Alexander; for to be liberal with the property of others does not take from your reputation, but adds to it. What injures you is to give away what is your own. And there is no quality so self-destructive as liberality; for while you practice it you lose the means whereby it can be practiced, and become poor and despised, or else, to avoid poverty, you become rapacious and hated. For liberality leads to one or other of these two results, against which, beyond all others, a Prince should guard.

Wherefore it is wiser to put up with the name of being miserly, which breeds ignominy, but without hate, than to be obliged, from the desire to be reckoned liberal, to incur the reproach of rapacity, which breeds hate as well as ignominy.

CHAPTER XVII

OF CRUELTY AND CLEMENCY, AND WHETHER IT IS BETTER TO BE LOVED OR FEARED

Passing to the other qualities above referred to, I say that every Prince should desire to be accounted merciful and not cruel. Nevertheless, he should be on his guard against the abuse of this quality of mercy. Cesare

Borgia was reputed cruel, yet his cruelty restored Romagna, united it, and brought it to order and obedience; so that if we look at things in their true light, it will be seen that he was in reality far more merciful than the people of Florence, who, to avoid the imputation of cruelty, suffered Pistoja to be torn to pieces by factions.[44]

A Prince should therefore disregard the reproach of being thought cruel where it enables him to keep his subjects united and obedient. For he who quells disorder by a very few signal examples will in the end be more merciful than he who from too great leniency permits things to take their course and so to result in rapine and bloodshed; for these hurt the whole State, whereas the severities of the Prince injure individuals only.

And for a new Prince, of all others, it is impossible to escape a name for cruelty, since new States are full of dangers. Wherefore Virgil, by the mouth of Dido, excuses the harshness of her reign on the plea that is was new, saying:—

> "A fate unkind, and newness in my reign
> Compel me thus to guard a wide domain."[45]

Nevertheless, the new Prince should not be too ready of belief, nor too easily set in motion; nor should he himself be the first to raise alarms; but should so temper prudence with kindliness that too great confidence in others shall not throw him off his guard, nor groundless distrust render him insupportable.

And here comes in the question whether it is better to be loved rather than feared, or feared rather than loved. It might perhaps be answered that we should wish to be both; but since love and fear can hardly exist together, if we must choose between them, it is far safer to be feared than loved. For of men it may generally be affirmed that they are thankless, fickle, false, studious to avoid danger, greedy of gain, devoted to you while you are able to confer benefits upon them, and ready, as I said before, while danger is distant, to shed their blood, and sacrifice their property, their lives, and their children for you; but in the hour of need they turn against you. The Prince, therefore, who without otherwise securing himself builds wholly on their professions is undone. For the friendships which we buy with a price, and do not gain by greatness and nobility of character, though they be fairly earned are not made good,[46] but fail us when we have occasion to use them.

Moreover, men are less careful how they offend him who makes himself loved than him who makes himself feared. For love is held by the tie of obligation, which, because men are a sorry breed, is broken on every whisper of private interest; but fear is bound by the apprehension of punishment which never relaxes its grasp.

Nevertheless a Prince should inspire fear in such a fashion that if he do not win love he may escape hate. For a man may very well be feared and yet

---

[44] Pistoja was a city near Florence and under its control. Florence failed to assert its power and allowed a bloody civil war to continue.

[45] *Aeneid,* Book II.   [46] Made use of.

not hated, and this will be the case so long as he does not meddle with the property or with the women of his citizens and subjects. And if constrained to put any to death, he should do so only when there is manifest cause or reasonable justification. But, above all, he must abstain from the property of others. For men will sooner forget the death of their father than the loss of their patrimony. Moreover, pretexts for confiscation are never to seek,[47] and he who has once begun to live by rapine always finds reasons for taking what is not his; whereas reasons for shedding blood are fewer, and sooner exhausted.

But when a Prince is with his army, and has many soldiers under his command, he must needs disregard the reproach of cruelty, for without such a reputation in its Captain, no army can be held together or kept under any kind of control. Among other things remarkable in Hannibal[48] this has been noted, that having a very great army, made up of men of many different nations and brought to fight in a foreign country, no dissension ever arose among the soldiers themselves, nor any mutiny against their leader, either in his good or in his evil fortunes. This we can only ascribe to the transcendent cruelty, which, joined with numberless great qualities, rendered him at once venerable and terrible in the eyes of his soldiers; for without this reputation for cruelty these other virtues would not have produced the like results.

Unreflecting writers, indeed, while they praise his achievements, have condemned the chief cause of them; but that his other merits would not by themselves have been so efficacious we may see from the case of Scipio, one of the greatest Captains, not of his own time only but of all times of which we have record, whose armies rose against him in Spain from no other cause than his too great leniency in allowing them a freedom inconsistent with military strictness. With which weakness Fabius Maximus[49] taxed him in the Senate House, calling him the corrupter of the Roman soldiery. Again, when the Locrians[50] were shamefully outraged by one of his lieutenants, he neither avenged them, nor punished the insolence of his officer; and this from the natural easiness of his disposition. So that it was said in the Senate by one who sought to excuse him, that there were many who knew better how to refrain from doing wrong themselves than how to correct the wrong-doing of others. This temper, however, must in time have marred the name and fame even of Scipio, had he continued in it, and retained his command. But living as he did under the control of the Senate, this hurtful quality was not merely disguised, but came to be regarded as a glory.

Returning to the question of being loved or feared, I sum up by saying, that since his being loved depends upon his subjects, while his being feared depends upon himself, a wise Prince should build on what is his own, and not on what rests with others. Only, as I have said, he must do his utmost to escape hatred.

---

[47] Never lacking.

[48] Carthaginian general (247–182 B.C.), defeated by Scipio. One of Hannibal's most spectacular feats was to lead his invading army across the Alps from Spain to Italy.

[49] Fabius Cunctator ("The Delayer"), noted for his tactic of harassing Hannibal's army without meeting it head-on. He became dictator of Rome in 217 B.C.

[50] Scipio took Locri, in southern Italy, in 205 B.C.

CHAPTER XVIII

How Princes Should Keep Faith

Every one understands how praiseworthy it is in a Prince to keep faith, and
to live uprightly and not craftily. Nevertheless, we see from what has taken
place in our own days that Princes who have set little store by their word,
but have known how to overreach men by their cunning, have accomplished great things, and in the end got the better of those who trusted to
honest dealing.

Be it known, then, that there are two ways of contending, one in accordance with the laws, the other by force; the first of which is proper to men,
the second to beasts. But since the first method is often ineffectual, it becomes necessary to resort to the second. A Prince should, therefore, understand how to use well both the man and the beast. And this lesson has been
covertly taught by the ancient writers, who relate how Achilles and many
others of these old Princes were given over to be brought up and trained by
Chiron the Centaur;[51] since the only meaning of their having for instructor
one who was half man and half beast is, that it is necessary for a Prince to
know how to use both natures, and that the one without the other has no
stability.

But since a Prince should know how to use the beast's nature wisely, he
ought of beasts to choose both the lion and the fox; for the lion cannot
guard himself from the toils,[52] nor the fox from wolves. He must therefore
be a fox to discern toils, and a lion to drive off wolves.

To rely wholly on the lion is unwise; and for this reason a prudent
Prince neither can nor ought to keep his word when to keep it is hurtful
to him and the causes which led him to pledge it are removed. If all men
were good, this would not be good advice, but since they are dishonest and
do not keep faith with you, you, in return, need not keep faith with them;
and no Prince was ever at a loss for plausible reasons to cloak a breach of
faith. Of this numberless recent instances could be given, and it might be
shown how many solemn treaties and engagements have been rendered
inoperative and idle through want of faith in Princes, and that he who has
best known to play the fox has had the best success.

It is necessary, indeed, to put a good color[53] on this nature, and to be
skillful in simulating and dissembling. But men are so simple, and governed so absolutely by their present needs, that he who wishes to deceive
will never fail in finding willing dupes. One recent example I will not omit.
Pope Alexander VI had no care or thought but how to deceive, and always
found material to work on. No man ever had a more effective manner of
asseverating, or made promises with more solemn protestations, or observed them less. And yet, because he understood this side of human nature, his frauds always succeeded.

It is not essential, then, that a Prince should have all the good qualities
which I have enumerated above, but it is most essential that he should seem
to have them; I will even venture to affirm that if he has and invariably
practices them all, they are hurtful, whereas the appearance of having
them is useful. Thus, it is well to seem merciful, faithful, humane, religious,

---

[51] Centaurs were half man, half horse.   [52] Traps.   [53] Good appearance.

and upright, and also to be so; but the mind should remain so balanced that were it needful not to be so, you should be able and know how to change to the contrary.

And you are to understand that a Prince, and most of all a new Prince, cannot observe all those rules of conduct in respect whereof men are accounted good, being often forced, in order to preserve his Princedom, to act in opposition to good faith, charity, humanity, and religion. He must therefore keep his mind ready to shift as the winds and tides of Fortune turn, and, as I have already said, he ought not to quit good courses if he can help it, but should know how to follow evil courses if he must.

A Prince should therefore be very careful that nothing ever escapes his lips which is not replete with the five qualities above named, so that to see and hear him, one would think him the embodiment of mercy, good faith, integrity, humanity, and religion. And there is no virtue which it is more necessary for him to seem to possess than this last; because men in general judge rather by the eye than by the hand, for every one can see but few can touch. Every one sees what you seem, but few know what you are, and these few dare not oppose themselves to the opinion of the many who have the majesty of the State to back them up.

Moreover, in the actions of all men, and most of all of Princes, where there is no tribunal to which we can appeal, we look to results. Wherefore if a Prince succeeds in establishing and maintaining his authority, the means will always be judged honorable and be approved by every one. For the vulgar are always taken by appearances and by results, and the world is made up of the vulgar, the few only finding room when the many have no longer ground to stand on.

A certain Prince[54] of our own days, whose name it is as well not to mention, is always preaching peace and good faith, although the mortal enemy of both; and both, had he practiced them as he preaches them, would, oftener than once, have lost him his kingdom and authority.

CHAPTER XXIII

THAT FLATTERERS SHOULD BE SHUNNED

One error into which Princes, unless very prudent or very fortunate in their choice of friends, are apt to fall, is of so great importance that I must not pass it over. I mean in respect of flatterers. These abound in Courts, because men take such pleasure in their own concerns, and so deceive themselves with regard to them, that they can hardly escape this plague; while even in the effort to escape it there is risk of their incurring contempt.

For there is no way to guard against flattery but by letting it be seen that you take no offense in hearing the truth: but when every one is free to tell you the truth, respect falls short. Wherefore a prudent Prince should follow a middle course, by choosing certain discreet men from among his subjects, and allowing them alone free leave to speak their minds on any matter on which he asks their opinion, and on none other. But he ought to

[54] King Ferdinand of Spain.

ask their opinion on everything, and after hearing what they have to say, should reflect and judge for himself. And with these counsellors collectively, and with each of them separately, his bearing should be such, that each and all of them may know that the more freely they declare their thoughts the better they will be liked. Besides these, the Prince should hearken to no others, but should follow the course determined on, and afterwards adhere firmly to his resolves. Whoever acts otherwise is either undone by flatterers, or from continually vacillating as opinions vary, comes to be held in light esteem.

With reference to this matter, I shall cite a recent instance. Father Luke, who is attached to the Court of the present Emperor Maximilian, in speaking of his Majesty told me, that he seeks advice from none, yet never has his own way; and this from his following a course contrary to that above recommended. For being of a secret disposition, he never discloses his intentions to any, nor asks their opinion; and it is only when his plans are to be carried out that they begin to be discovered and known, and at the same time they begin to be thwarted by those he has about him, when he being facile[55] gives way. Hence it happens that what he does one day, he undoes the next; that his wishes and designs are never fully ascertained; and that it is impossible to build on his resolves.

A Prince, therefore, ought always to take counsel, but at such times and seasons only as he himself pleases, and not when it pleases others; nay, he should discourage every one from obtruding advice on matters on which it is not sought. But he should be free in asking advice, and afterwards, as regards the matters on which he has asked it, a patient hearer of the truth, and even displeased should he perceive that any one, from whatever motive, keeps it back.

But those who think that every Prince who has a name for prudence owes it to the wise counsellors he has around him, and not to any merit of his own, are certainly mistaken; since it is an unerring rule and of universal application that a Prince who is not wise himself cannot be well advised by others, unless by chance he surrender himself to be wholly governed by some one adviser who happens to be supremely prudent; in which case he may, indeed, be well advised; but not for long, since such an adviser will soon deprive him of his Government. If he listen to a multitude of advisers, the Prince who is not wise will never have consistent counsels, nor will he know of himself how to reconcile them. Each of his counsellors will study his own advantage, and the Prince will be unable to detect or correct them. Nor could it well be otherwise, for men will always grow rogues on your hands unless they find themselves under a necessity to be honest.

Hence it follows that good counsels, whencesoever they come, have their origin in the prudence of the Prince, and not the prudence of the Prince in wise counsels.

---

[55] Lacking in firmness.

CHAPTER XXV

WHAT FORTUNE CAN EFFECT IN HUMAN AFFAIRS, AND HOW SHE MAY BE WITHSTOOD

I am not ignorant that many have been and are of the opinion that human affairs are so governed by Fortune and by God, that men cannot alter them by any prudence of theirs, and indeed have no remedy against them; and for this reason have come to think that it is not worth while to labor much about anything, but that they must leave everything to be determined by chance.

Often when I turn the matter over, I am in part inclined to agree with this opinion, which has had the readier acceptance in our own times from the great changes in things which we have seen, and every day see happen contrary to all human expectation. Nevertheless, that our free will be not wholly set aside, I think it may be the case that Fortune is the mistress of one half our actions, and yet leaves the control of the other half, or a little less, to ourselves. And I would liken her to one of those wild torrents which, when angry, overflow the plains, sweep away trees and houses, and carry off soil from one bank to throw it down upon the other. Every one flees before them, and yields to their fury without the least power to resist. And yet, though this be their nature, it does not follow that in seasons of fair weather, men cannot, by constructing weirs and moles,[56] take such precautions as will cause them when again in flood to pass off by some artificial channel, or at least prevent their course from being so uncontrolled and destructive. And so it is with Fortune, who displays her might where there is no organized strength to resist her, and directs her onset where she knows that there is neither barrier nor embankment to confine her.

And if you look at Italy, which has been at once the seat of these changes and their cause, you will perceive that it is a field without embankment or barrier. For if, like Germany, France, and Spain, it had been guarded with sufficient skill, this inundation, if it ever came upon us, would never have wrought the violent changes which we have witnessed.

This I think enough to say generally touching resistance to Fortune. But confining myself more closely to the matter in hand, I note that one day we see a Prince prospering and the next day overthrown, without detecting any change in his nature or character. This, I believe, comes chiefly from a cause already dwelt upon, namely, that a Prince who rests wholly on Fortune is ruined when she changes. Moreover, I believe that he will prosper most whose mode of acting best adapts itself to the character of the times; and conversely that he will be unprosperous, with whose mode of acting the times do not accord. For we see that men in these matters which lead to the end that each has before him, namely, glory and wealth, proceed by different ways, one with caution, another with impetuosity, one with violence, another with subtlety, one with patience, another with its contrary; and that by one or other of these different courses each may succeed.

[56] Dams and breakwaters.

Again, of two who act cautiously, you shall find that one attains his end, the other not, and that two of different temperament, the one cautious, the other impetuous, are equally successful. All which happens from no other cause than that the character of the times accords or does not accord with their methods of acting. And hence it comes, as I have already said, that two operating differently arrive at the same result, and two operating similarly, the one succeeds and the other not. On this likewise depend the vicissitudes of Fortune. For if to one who conducts himself with caution and patience, time and circumstances are propitious, so that his method of acting is good, he goes on prospering; but if these change he is ruined, because he does not change his method of acting.

For no man is found so prudent as to know how to adapt himself to these changes, both because he cannot deviate from the course to which nature inclines him, and because, having always prospered while adhering to one path, he cannot be persuaded that it would be well for him to forsake it. And so when occasion requires the cautious man to act impetuously, he cannot do so and is undone: whereas, had he changed his nature with time and circumstances, his fortune would have been unchanged.

Pope Julius II proceeded with impetuosity in all his undertakings, and found time and circumstances in such harmony with his mode of acting that he always obtained a happy result. Witness his first expedition against Bologna, when Messer Giovanni Bentivogli[57] was yet living. The Venetians were not favorable to the enterprise; nor was the King of Spain. Negotiations respecting it with the King of France were still open. Nevertheless, the Pope with his wonted hardihood and impetuosity marched in person on the expedition, and by this movement brought the King of Spain and the Venetians to a check, the latter through fear, the former from his eagerness to recover the entire Kingdom of Naples; at the same time, he dragged after him the King of France, who, desiring to have the Pope for an ally in humbling the Venetians, on finding him already in motion saw that he could not refuse him his soldiers without openly offending him. By the impetuosity of his movements, therefore, Julius effected what no other Pontiff endowed with the highest human prudence could. For had he, as any other Pope would have done, put off his departure from Rome until terms had been settled and everything duly arranged, he never would have succeeded. For the King of France would have found a thousand pretexts to delay him, and the others would have menaced him with a thousand alarms. I shall not touch upon his other actions, which were all of a like character, and all of which had a happy issue,[58] since the shortness of his life did not allow him to experience reverses. But if times had overtaken him, rendering a cautious line of conduct necessary, his ruin must have ensued, since he never could have departed from those methods to which nature inclined him.

To be brief, I say that since Fortune changes and men stand fixed in their old ways, they are prosperous so long as there is congruity between them, and the reverse when there is not. Of this, however, I am well persuaded, that it is better to be impetuous than cautious. For Fortune is a woman who to be kept under must be beaten and roughly handled; and we

---

[57] Member of a family of Bologna, attacked by Julius in 1506.   [58] Favorable outcome.

see that she suffers herself to be more readily mastered by those who so treat her than by those who are more timid in their approaches. And always, like a woman, she favors the young, because they are less scrupulous and fiercer, and command her with greater audacity.

CHAPTER XXVI

An Exhortation to Liberate Italy from the Barbarians

Turning over in my mind all the matters which have above been considered, and debating with myself whether in Italy at the present hour the times are such as might serve to confer honor on a new Prince, and whether a fit opportunity now offers for a prudent and valiant leader to bring about changes glorious for himself and beneficial to the whole Italian people, it seems to me that so many conditions combine to further such an enterprise, that I know of no time so favorable to it as the present. And if, as I have said, it was necessary in order to display the valor of Moses that the children of Israel should be slaves in Egypt, and to know the greatness and courage of Cyrus that the Persians should be oppressed by the Medes,[59] and to illustrate the excellence of Theseus[60] that the Athenians should be scattered and divided, so at this hour, to prove the worth of some Italian hero, it was required that Italy should be brought to her present abject condition, to be more a slave than the Hebrew, more oppressed than the Persian, more disunited than the Athenian, without a head, without order, beaten, spoiled, torn in pieces, over-run and abandoned to destruction in every shape.

But though, heretofore, glimmerings may have been discerned in this man or that, whence it might be conjectured that he was ordained by God for her redemption, nevertheless it has afterwards been seen in the further course of his actions that Fortune has disowned him; so that our country, left almost without life, still waits to know who it is that is to heal her bruises, to put an end to the devastation and plunder of Lombardy,[61] to the exactions and imposts of Naples and Tuscany, and to stanch those wounds of hers which long neglect has changed into running sores.

We see how she prays God to send some one to rescue her from these barbarous cruelties and oppressions. We see too how ready and eager she is to follow any standard were there only some one to raise it. But at present we see no one except in your illustrious House[62] (pre-eminent by its virtues and good fortune, and favored by God and by the Church whose headship it now holds), who could undertake the part of a deliverer.

But for you this will not be too hard a task, if you keep before your eyes the lives and actions of those whom I have named above. For although these men were singular and extraordinary, after all they were but men,

---

[59] Inhabitants of Media, an ancient region in what is now northwestern Iran. Cyrus the Great (sixth century B.C.) founded the Persian empire.

[60] A mythical king of Athens. The Athenians credited him with unifying the scattered communities of Attica, the region near Athens.

[61] By the Swiss and then the French. Lombardy is in northern Italy, surrounding Milan.

[62] The Medici family.

not one of whom had so great an opportunity as now presents itself to you. For their undertakings were not more just than this, nor more easy, nor was God more their friend than yours. The justice of the cause is conspicuous; for that war is just which is necessary, and those arms are sacred from which we derive our only hope. Everywhere there is the strongest disposition to engage in this cause; and where the disposition is strong the difficulty cannot be great, provided you follow the methods observed by those whom I have set before you as models.

But further, we see here extraordinary and unexampled proofs of Divine favor. The sea has been divided; the cloud has attended you on your way; the rock has flowed with water; the manna has rained from heaven; everything has concurred to promote your greatness.[63] What remains to be done must be done by you; since in order not to deprive us of our free will and such share of glory as belongs to us, God will not do everything himself.

Nor is it to be marvelled at if none of those Italians I have named has been able to effect what we hope to see effected by your illustrious House; or that amid so many revolutions and so many warlike movements it should always appear as though the military virtues of Italy were spent; for this comes from her old system being defective, and from no one being found among us capable to strike out a new. Nothing confers such honor on the reformer of a State, as do the new laws and institutions which he devises; for these when they stand on a solid basis and have a greatness in their scope, make him admired and venerated. And in Italy material is not wanting for improvement in every form. If the head be weak the limbs are strong, and we see daily in single combats, or where few are engaged, how superior are the strength, dexterity, and intelligence of Italians. But when it comes to armies, they are nowhere, and this from no other reason than the defects of their leaders. For those who are skillful in arms will not obey, and every one thinks himself skillful, since hitherto we have had none among us so raised by merit or by fortune above his fellows that they should yield him the palm. And hence it happens that for the long period of twenty years, during which so many wars have taken place, whenever there has been an army purely Italian it has always been beaten. To this testify, first Taro, then Alessandria, Capua, Genoa, Vaila, Bologna, Mestri.[64]

If then your illustrious House should seek to follow the example of those great men who have delivered their country in past ages, it is before all things necessary, as the true foundation of every such attempt, to be provided with national troops, since you can have no braver, truer, or more faithful soldiers; and although every single man of them be good, collectively they will be better, seeing themselves commanded by their own Prince, and honored and esteemed by him. That you may be able, therefore, to defend yourself against the foreigner with Italian valor, the first step is to provide yourself with an army such as this.

And although the Swiss and the Spanish infantry are each esteemed

---

[63] The divided sea, the cloud, the water from the rock, and the manna were signs of divine favor when the Israelites escaped from bondage in Egypt; see Exodus 14, 13, 17, 16.

[64] *Taro . . . Mestri.* These defeats occurred between 1495 and 1513.

formidable, there are yet defects in both, by reason of which troops trained on a different system might not merely withstand them, but be certain of defeating them. For the Spaniards cannot resist cavalry, and the Swiss will give way before infantry if they find them as resolute as themselves at close quarters. Whence it has been seen, and may be seen again, that the Spaniards cannot sustain the onset of the French men-at-arms,[65] and that the Swiss are broken by the Spanish foot.[66] And although of this last we have no complete instance, we have yet an indication of it in the battle of Ravenna,[67] where the Spanish infantry confronted the German companies, who have the same discipline as the Swiss; on which occasion the Spaniards by their agility and with the aid of their bucklers[68] forced their way under the pikes, and stood ready to close with the Germans, who were no longer in a position to defend themselves; and had they not been charged by cavalry, they must have put the Germans to utter rout. Knowing, then, the defects of each of these kinds of troops, you can train your men on some different system, to withstand cavalry and not to fear infantry. To effect this, will not require the creation of any new forces, but simply a change in the discipline of the old. And these are matters in reforming which the new Prince acquires reputation and importance.

This opportunity then, for Italy at last to look on her deliverer, ought not to be allowed to pass away. With what love he would be received in all those Provinces which have suffered from the foreign inundation, with what thirst for vengeance, with what fixed fidelity, with what devotion, and what tears, no words of mine can declare. What gates would be closed against him? What people would refuse him obedience? What jealousy would stand in his way? What Italian but would yield him homage? This barbarian tyranny stinks in all nostrils.

Let your illustrious House therefore take upon itself this enterprise with all the courage and all the hopes with which a just cause is undertaken; so that under your standard this our country may be ennobled, and under your auspices be fulfilled the words of Petrarch:—

> Brief will be the strife
> When valor arms against barbaric rage;
> For the bold spirit of the bygone age
> Still warms Italian hearts with life.[69]

---

[65] Cavalry.   [66] Foot soldiers; infantry   [67] In 1512.   [68] Shields.
[69] Canzone beginning "Italia mia"—an anti-German poem.

from DISCOURSES ON THE FIRST DECADE OF TITUS LIVIUS, BOOK I

Translated by Ninian Hill Thomson

CHAPTER X

That in proportion as the Founder of a Kingdom or Commonwealth merits Praise, he who founds a Tyranny deserves Blame.

Of all who are praised they are praised the most, who are the authors and founders of religions. After whom come the founders of kingdoms and commonwealths. Next to these, they have the greatest name who as commanders of armies have added to their own dominions or those of their country. After these, again, are ranked men of letters, who being of various shades of merit are celebrated each in his degree. To all others, whose number is infinite, is ascribed that measure of praise to which his profession or occupation entitles him. And, conversely, all who contribute to the overthrow of religion, or to the ruin of kingdoms and commonwealths, all who are foes to letters and to the arts which confer honor and benefit on the human race (among whom I reckon the impious, the cruel, the ignorant, the indolent, the base and the worthless), are held in infamy and detestation.

No one, whether he be wise or foolish, bad or good, if asked to choose between these two kinds of men, will ever be found to withhold praise from what deserves praise, or blame from what is to be blamed. And yet almost all, deceived by a false good and a false glory, allow themselves either ignorantly or willfully to follow in the footsteps of such as deserve blame rather than praise; and, having it in their power to establish, to their lasting renown, a commonwealth or kingdom, turn aside to create a tyranny, without a thought how much they thereby lose in name, fame, security, tranquillity, and peace of mind; and into how much infamy, scorn, danger, and disquiet they run. But were they to read history, and turn to profit the lessons of the past, it seems impossible that those living in a republic as private citizens, should not prefer, in their native city, to play the part of Scipio rather than of Caesar;[1] or that those who by good fortune or by merit have risen to be rulers, should not seek rather to resemble Agesilaus, Timoleon, and Dion, than to copy Nabis, Phalaris and Dionysius;[2] since they would see that the latter are loaded with infamy, while the former have been extolled beyond bounds. They would see, too, how Timoleon and others like him, had as great authority in their country as Dionysius or Phalaris in theirs, while enjoying far greater security. Nor let any one finding Caesar celebrated by

[1] Scipio Africanus Major (234–183 B.C.) could have become ruler of Rome but retired to private life; Caesar was instrumental in turning Rome from a republic into a monarchy.
[2] *Agesilaus . . . Dionysius.* Agesilaus of Sparta, Timoleon of Corinth, and Dion of Syracuse were men of the fourth century B.C. who renounced power or overcame tyrants; Nabis of Sparta (second–first century B.C.), Phalaris of Agrigentum, in Sicily (sixth century B.C.), and Dionysius I and II of Syracuse (fourth century B.C.) were tyrants.

a crowd of writers, be misled by his glory; for those who praise him have been corrupted by his good fortune, and overawed by the greatness of that empire which, being governed in his name,[3] would not suffer any to speak their minds openly concerning him. But let him who desires to know how historians would have written of Caesar had they been free to declare their thoughts, mark what they say of Catiline,[4] than whom Caesar is more hateful, in proportion as he who does is more to be condemned than he who only desires to do evil. Let him note also what praises they lavish upon Brutus,[5] because being unable, out of respect for his power, to reproach Caesar, they magnify his enemy. And if he who has become prince in any State will but reflect, how, after Rome was made an empire, far greater praise was earned by those emperors who lived within the laws, and worthily, than by those who lived in the contrary way, he will see that Titus, Nerva, Trajan, Hadrian, Antoninus and Marcus had no need of praetorian cohorts,[6] or of countless legions to guard them, but were defended by their own good lives, the good-will of their subjects, and the attachment of the senate. In like manner he will perceive in the case of Caligula, Nero, Vitellius,[7] and ever so many more of those evil emperors, that all the armies of the east and of the west were of no avail to protect them from the enemies whom their bad and depraved lives raised up against them. And were the history of these emperors rightly studied, it would be a sufficient lesson to any prince how to distinguish the paths which lead to honor and safety from those which end in shame and insecurity. For of the twenty-six emperors from Caesar to Maximinus,[8] sixteen came to a violent, ten only to a natural death; and though one or two of those who died by violence may have been good princes, as Galba or Pertinax,[9] they met their fate in consequence of that corruption which their predecessors had left behind in the army. And if among those who died a natural death, there be found some bad emperors, like Severus,[10] it is to be ascribed to their signal good fortune and to their great abilities, advantages seldom found united in the same man. From the study of this history we may also learn how a good government is to be established; for while all the emperors who succeeded to the throne by birth, except Titus, were bad, all were good who succeeded by adoption; as in the case of the five from Nerva to Marcus. But so soon as the empire fell once more to the heirs by birth, its ruin recommenced.

Let a prince therefore look to that period which extends from Nerva to Marcus, and contrast it with that which went before and that which came after, and then let him say in which of them he would wish to have been born or to have reigned. For during these times in which good men gov-

---

[3] Originally a proper name, "Caesar" came to be a title of the Roman emperors.

[4] An unscrupulous but unsuccessful power-seeking Roman plotter, first century B.C.; opposed by Cicero.

[5] In the name of liberty and of the threatened republican form of government, Brutus assassinated Julius Caesar in 44 B.C. The attitude toward Brutus here contrasts with that of Dante in *Inferno,* canto xxxiv.

[6] The elite (but often corrupt) military guard of the Roman emperors. The six emperors mentioned ruled almost uninterruptedly between 79 and 180 A.D.

[7] Roman emperors of the first century; all three were assassinated.

[8] Maximinus was emperor from 235 to 238 A.D.

[9] Galba was emperor in 69 A.D., Pertinax in 193 A.D.

[10] Emperor from 193 to 211 A.D.

erned, he will see the prince secure in the midst of happy subjects, and the
whole world filled with peace and justice. He will find the senate maintaining its authority, the magistrates enjoying their honors, rich citizens their
wealth, rank and merit held in respect, ease and content everywhere prevailing, rancor, license, corruption and ambition everywhere quenched,
and that golden age restored in which every one might hold and support
what opinions he pleased. He will see, in short, the world triumphing, the
sovereign honored and revered, the people animated with love, and rejoicing in their security. But should he turn to examine the times of the other
emperors, he will find them wasted by battles, torn by seditions, cruel alike
in war and peace; many princes perishing by the sword; many wars foreign
and domestic; Italy overwhelmed with unheard-of disasters; her towns destroyed and plundered; Rome burned; the Capitol razed to the ground by
Roman citizens; the ancient temples desolated; the ceremonies of religion
corrupted; the cities rank with adultery; the seas covered with exiles, and
the islands polluted with blood. He will see outrage follow outrage; rank,
riches, honors, and, above all, virtue imputed as mortal crimes; informers
rewarded; slaves bribed to betray their masters, freedmen their patrons,
and those who were without enemies brought to destruction by their
friends; and then he will know the true nature of the debt which Rome,
Italy, and the world owe to Caesar; and if he possess a spark of human
feeling, will turn from the example of those evil times, and kindle with a
consuming passion to imitate those which were good.

And in truth the prince who seeks for worldly glory should desire to be
the ruler of a corrupt city; not that, like Caesar, he may destroy it, but that,
like Romulus,[11] he may restore it; since man cannot hope for, nor Heaven
offer any better opportunity of fame. Were it indeed necessary in giving a
constitution to a State to forfeit its sovereignty, the prince who, to retain his
station, should withhold a constitution, might plead excuse; but for him
who in giving a constitution can still retain his sovereignty, no excuse is to
be made.

Let those therefore to whom Heaven has afforded this opportunity,
remember that two courses lie open to them; one which will render them
secure while they live and glorious when they die; another which exposes
them to continual difficulties in life, and condemns them to eternal infamy
after death.

[11] Mythological son of Mars who ousted a usurping king and then founded Rome in 753 B.C.

Thomas More
(1478–1535)

*Renaissance humanism, of which Thomas More was one of the shining lights, en-
couraged religious tolerance. But this aspect of the movement could not coexist easily
after the Protestant Reformation and the Catholic Counter-Reformation with the*

new sectarian antagonisms that embittered European religion in the latter sixteenth and seventeenth centuries. The tragedy of this factionalism gives a special poignancy to More's life and to his Utopia, *written as it was in the last few years before the emergence of Luther.*

More, the son of a lawyer, was born in 1478 in London, where he spent most of his life. He attended an excellent school there, St. Anthony's, and from about age twelve to fourteen he was maintained in the household of John Morton, the Lord Chancellor of England and Archbishop of Canterbury who is recalled admiringly by Raphael Hythloday in Book One of Utopia. *At fourteen More entered Oxford, where his studies emphasized Latin and logic. Two years later he enrolled in one of London's Inns of Court, in accordance with his father's wishes that he become a lawyer. Although More had no great enthusiasm for that profession, his legal training was important in light of his later public service and the concomitant knowledge it fostered in him of all levels of society. In 1499 he met Desiderius Erasmus, with whom he was to have a lifelong friendship. (It was during a sojourn in More's house, in 1509, that Erasmus wrote his best-known work,* The Praise of Folly, *the Latin title of which,* Moriae Encomium, *puns affectionately on More's name.) There was an enduring ascetic strain in More (he continued throughout his life to wear a hair shirt that contrasted with his habitual cheerfulness), and for a while he considered becoming a Catholic priest. He also loved classical and theological learning, which always competed for his time with public and domestic duties. These preoccupations led him to spend about four years in a Carthusian monastery in London. He chose, however, a life in the world, and in 1505, soon after he left the monastery, he married Jane Colt. She died in 1511, leaving him with three young daughters and a son. He soon remarried a widow with two children. To these children and stepchildren were later added several other wards, who made up a school in More's household. An excellent humanist education, in religion, the classics, philosophy, and science, was imparted not only to the boys but also (which was noteworthy in More's time) to the girls. He once wrote, "The harvest will not be affected whether it be a man or woman who sows the seed. Both are reasonable beings, distinguished in this from the beasts; both therefore are suited equally for those studies by which reason is cultivated."*

In 1509 Henry VIII succeeded Henry VII as King of England. The new monarch was welcomed hopefully by humanists as a potential social reformer, but they were soon disillusioned when Henry showed a penchant for military and political adventurism. At about the same time, More was himself embarking on a life of public service that, besides the office of Under-Sheriff of London, included diplomatic missions. During one such mission, to Flanders in 1515, to help settle a dispute about the wool trade, More took advantage of leisure occasioned by delays in the negotiations to write the second Book of Utopia. *The first Book, which begins as a factual account of the stay in Flanders, was written in the following year, after More returned to England. (Some of More's writings were in English, but* Utopia, *designed mainly to be read by fellow humanists, statesmen, and intellectuals, was written in Latin.) At about this time More also wrote his* History of Richard III, *a landmark of English history-writing that was to shape Shakespeare's notorious (and unfair, according to some modern historians) portrait of Richard as an unscrupulous murderer.*

More's own Hythloday, in Utopia, *had advised that good men and philosophers should avoid the service of kings (advice that can be fruitfully contrasted with the role of adviser that Machiavelli adopts in* The Prince, *written only three years earlier). Nevertheless, More entered Henry's service, steadily winning the king's increasing*

*favor and attaining one high office after another: member of the King's Council in
1517, Under-Treasurer in 1521, knight in the same year, Speaker of the House of
Commons in 1523, High Steward of Oxford in 1524 and of Cambridge in 1525,
Chancellor of the duchy of Lancaster in 1525, and climactically, in 1529, Lord
Chancellor, the highest post under the Crown. In 1526 More helped Hans Holbein
the Younger attain the post of English court painter, and to Holbein we owe famous
portraits of Henry, Erasmus, and More himself.*

*These were also the first years of the Protestant Reformation, following on
Luther's nailing of his theses to the church door at Wittenberg in 1517. More was a
zealous propagandist against what he regarded as the new heresies. From the pope
Henry VIII won for himself and subsequent British monarchs the title Defender of
the Faith, by a piece of apologetics in which More had a hand—though, ironically in
light of later events, More cautioned Henry against conceding to the pope in this
tract more authority in England than was lawful. More's polemical writings reached
a climax between 1529 and 1533. In the epitaph he composed for himself, More
boasted of his severity to heretics, though it is also true that he once claimed to oppose
"that vice of theirs and not their persons."*

*The final and most famous episode in More's life began in 1527. Henry, in love
with Anne Boleyn (the mother of the future Queen Elizabeth I) and unhappy over the
failure of his queen, Catherine of Aragon, to bear a male heir, expressed a desire that
the pope, on tortuous grounds, approve a divorce. When the pope refused, Henry
repudiated his authority and claimed for himself the headship of the Church in
England. Asked in his role of Lord Chancellor to assent, More refused, believing that
the pope's spiritual authority was essential to the Church unity More always cherished. He also refused to attend the coronation of Anne after Henry married her in
1533, an act of omission that was ominous for him. After being imprisoned in the
Tower of London, where he lived contentedly, he was tried and beheaded for high
treason in 1535, jesting whimsically with his captors on the way to his death. Exactly
four centuries later, in 1935, he was canonized a saint of the Roman Catholic
Church.*

*Another posthumous honor was rendered More in the twentieth century: the
listing of his name on a monument in Moscow as a saint, so to speak, of Communism.
That he should be enshrined, at virtually the same time, by the Church and also by the
Soviets is an emblem of the enigmatic standing of More and particularly of his*
Utopia. *More is one of several authors of the sixteenth century—Machiavelli, Erasmus, and Montaigne are also among them—whose works puzzle interpreters because
they present internal problems of consistency in tone or viewpoint or because they seem
anomalous in light of the author's life and other works.*

The basic problem in interpreting Utopia *is to explain it as a whole, without
ignoring ideas and emphases that conflict with simplistic readings. One possibility is
to see the work as a recreational, high-spirited intellectual game of the kind
humanists liked to play, a teasing blend of realism and fancy to be savored more for
its inventiveness than for a serious message. That a characteristic element of playful-
ness in More appears in* Utopia *is undeniable. But, although the humor in the book
sometimes does seem an end in itself, as in the account of newborn artificially incu-
bated chickens, the premarital inspection of prospective mates, and some of the ety-
mologies, the humor can also sharpen the edge of the satire, as in the account of the
showy Anemolian ambassadors. In any case, the social distress surveyed in Book One
hardly seems the matter of comedy. It is possible that some of the humor is a protective
packaging designed to preserve More from official reprisals.*

   *Giving only light weight to evidence from More's other writings and to the central
importance in the Utopian state of belief in God and in rewards and punishments
after death, Marxists and other socialists focus on Raphael Hythloday's fervid attack
on social and economic evils such as private property, commercial greed, and the
selfishness of kings. In this reading, More's occasional polite objections to Hythloday's
ideas are not to be taken very seriously.*

   Some Catholic interpreters, however, see Utopia *not as a herald of a socialist
future but as a defense of the medieval past, including the form of uncompetitive
communal living practiced in monasteries. But it is one thing to celebrate ideals that
even in the Middle Ages governed only small pockets of society and another thing to
depict and apparently praise a whole state ruled by communist principles.*

   Another possibility is that More is using an a fortiori *strategy: if the Utopians
can achieve a society so just and attractive by using natural reason alone, it is
shameful that Europeans blessed with the advantage of Christian revelation should
live such evil and wretched lives in states so badly ruled. This view has some support
in the text: the religion of the Utopians is in fact founded on such Christian premises
as the immortality of the soul and the justice of divine providence, and the Utopians
eagerly receive Christian teachings when they learn of them. But how then does one
account for those Utopian practices—including euthanasia, a priesthood open to
women and married men, and divorce on grounds of incompatibility—that do not so
much fall short of the highest potential of Catholic Christianity as contravene Catholicism? Would More, who had his share of the humanist faith in reason, intimate that
adherence to the doctrines and discipline of the Church was actually in defiance of
reason?*

   Still another view holds that Utopia *is not a scheme for a perfect commonwealth
but rather a moral treatise, the details of Utopian sociology being merely ancillary to
More's central purpose: to reform persons and not societies and particularly to root
out the sin of pride that, in accordance with a Christian commonplace, underlies all
other sins. To this reading at least two objections may be made: first, it seems unlikely
that a general tract against personal pride should dwell so minutely and with such
relish on social mechanics, and second, pride is attributed to a very specific social
fact, the existence of private property—which brings us back to the socialist readings.*

   *Most of the interpretations just outlined assume that in one way or another the
values governing the Utopian commonwealth are desirable. But that is not a necessary assumption. It is perhaps unimportant that there are certain practical problems;
for example, the small number of priests seems inadequate to their function as educators of the young. More cannot be expected to have worked out every detail. And the
advantages of living in Utopia are heightened by contrast with the wretched conditions, especially of the poor, in More's time. It remains true, however, that there is a
certain colorlessness, uniformity, and lack of passion in Utopian life. It is interesting
that Book One, which focuses on the severely flawed Europe of More's day, contains a
number of lively personal portraits, real and fictional. But Book Two, though in
principle allowing for diversity among the Utopians (in their religious views, for
example), presents few individual persons and none that are memorable.*

   *This fact is important in connection with attempts in later literature to portray
utopias and dystopias (evil polities). More was not, of course, the first writer who
tried to envisage comprehensive human felicity; before him there were visions like
Ovid's of the primitive Golden Age and hypothesized good societies like that of Plato's*
Republic, *not to mention Christian images of heaven. More's Utopia differs, obviously, from the Christian heaven by being located on earth, from Plato's common-*

wealth by the purported realism of Utopia and its democratic spirit and machinery, from primitivist images of the good life by its dependence not on simple, unsophisticated conditions of nature and mind but on an advanced rationality, expressed in an intricately structured social organization and in technology. It is this emphasis on structure, artifice, and mental discipline that tends to recur in later utopias and dystopias such as Francis Bacon's New Atlantis, *Book Four of Swift's* Gulliver's Travels, *Edward Bellamy's* Looking Backward, *several works by H. G. Wells, Aldous Huxley's* Brave New World, *George Orwell's* 1984, *and B. F. Skinner's* Walden Two. *The persistent theme of the relationship between social organization and mind in the utopian tradition has made it a continuing forum not only for confronting the desirable and undesirable possibilities of social structures but also for investigating the meaning of progress and the essential meaning of human nature. Such issues are implicit, apart from the values that inform any particular work, in the very notion of envisaging a thoroughly perfect or thoroughly evil society articulated in response to ideology.*

FURTHER READING *(prepared by W. J. R.):* Several fine biographies of Thomas More are available; one of the best is still R. W. Chambers' *Thomas More*, 1935, which also discusses More's writings and his era. Penry Williams' *The Tudor Regime*, 1979, though not concerned directly with More, contains an excellent analysis of the process of Tudor government. An analysis of *Utopia* in the light of sixteenth-century social conditions and political philosophy can be found in Russell Ames' *Citizen Thomas More and His Utopia*, 1949. Richard Schoeck's *The Achievement of Thomas More*, 1976, is a fine introduction to More's other writings. Ligeia Gallagher's *More's "Utopia" and Its Critics*, 1964, contains the text of *Utopia*, a good introduction to it, and a collection of modern critical responses. Forty-seven articles are gathered in *Essential Articles for the Study of Thomas More*, ed. R. S. Sylvester, 1977, including Robert Bolt's preface to *A Man for All Seasons*, which could provide a useful starting point for the new reader of *Utopia*. The genesis of *Utopia* is intensively studied in J. H. Hexter's *More's "Utopia": The Biography of an Idea*, 1952. Part Two of this work contains a detailed analysis of *Utopia*. Walter R. Davis's "Thomas More's *Utopia* as Fiction," *Centennial Review*, 24 (1980), 249-68, treats Book I as exposition on the nature of fiction itself and Book II as a representative of such fiction. Over the last two decades *The Complete Works of St. Thomas More*, in the Yale Edition, have been appearing in separate volumes, which include excellent critical apparatus.

UTOPIA

Translated by Peter K. Marshall

BOOK ONE

The most victorious King of England, Henry the Eighth, most accomplished in all the virtues of an outstanding prince, recently had a disagreement on certain matters of great importance with Charles, the most serene Prince of Castile. To settle and arrange this dispute, the King sent me as ambassador to Flanders,[1] together with that incomparable man Cuthbert Tunstall,[2] whom, to everyone's great joy, he recently made Master of the Rolls. But of this man's virtues I shall say nothing, not because I am afraid that a friend's evidence should be considered suspect, but because his goodness and learning are too great to be praised by me, and also too well known and famous everywhere to need my praise; unless, as the saying goes, I should wish to seem to be illuminating the sun with a lantern.

As had been arranged, all those excellent gentlemen met us at Bruges who had been entrusted with the affair by their prince. The chief and head of these was the Margrave of Bruges, a most distinguished gentleman. But their learned spokesman was George de Theimsecke, Provost of Kassel, a man eloquent by training and nature, greatly skilled in law and an unrivaled master in debating affairs both by his natural genius and by his constant experience in practical matters. We met once or twice, but could not sufficiently agree on certain points; so they said good-bye to us for a few days and left for Brussels to find out what their prince had in mind.[3] Meanwhile I set off to Antwerp; for so my affairs demanded.

While I was staying there, I had visits from several people but none was more welcome than Peter Giles,[4] a native of Antwerp. He is a man of great honesty and high position among his people, worthy of the highest. I cannot say which is greater, his learning or his excellence of character; for he is of the highest quality and deeply read in literature, with an open heart to everyone. Toward his friends he is so affectionate, loving, faithful, and sincere that you could scarcely find one or two people anywhere whom you would feel comparable to him in all respects of friendship. He has a rare modesty and no one could be less pretentious, no one could possess a wiser simplicity. Further, he is so graceful in talk and so harmlessly witty that by his sweet company and delightful conversation he greatly alleviated my longing for my own country and home, my wife and children, whom I was

---

[1] The fictional tale that will be told by the fictional Raphael Hythloday is set in a context of historical fact. More was despatched in 1515 to serve as a negotiator in a commercial dispute, involving the wool trade, between England (then ruled by Henry VIII) and Flanders (approximately, modern Belgium), which was then ruled by Spain. The negotiations dragged on for six months, during which time More wrote the second Book of *Utopia*. Prince Charles (1500–1558) was later to become king of Spain and Holy Roman Emperor.

[2] A close friend of More; later Bishop of London.

[3] Charles spent a week in Brussels in July 1515.

[4] Peter Giles, a friend (like More) of the great Dutch humanist Desiderius Erasmus, was Chief Secretary of Antwerp.

restless to see again as I had already been away from home for more than four months.

One day I had attended Mass in the Cathedral of Notre Dame, a most beautiful building, always crowded with people. When the service was finished, I was preparing to return to the place where I was staying, when I happened to see Peter Giles conversing with a stranger, a man approaching old age, with a sunburned face and a long beard, whose cloak was carelessly hanging from his shoulder. From his appearance and dress I judged him to be a sailor. When Peter saw me, he came up and greeted me. As I was about to reply, he drew me aside a little distance, and said, "Do you see this man?" at the same time pointing out the man with whom I had seen him talking. "I intended, " he said, "to bring him straight to you." "He would have been most welcome," I said, "for your sake." "No," said Peter, "for his own sake, if you knew him. For there is no one alive today who could tell you so much about unknown peoples and lands; and I know that you are most eager to hear about such things." "So," said I, "my guess was not far amiss. For at first glance, I felt that the man was a sailor." "And yet," said Peter, "you are very wrong. For he sailed certainly, not like Palinurus,[5] but like Ulysses, or rather, like Plato. Raphael Hythloday[6] over there (for this is his name) has a great knowledge of Latin and a profound one of Greek. He paid more attention to Greek than Latin because he had devoted himself entirely to philosophy, and on this subject he knew that nothing of any importance is extant in Latin except a few things of Seneca and Cicero. Well, he left to his brothers the inheritance he had at home (he is Portuguese), and from a desire to see the world joined himself to Amerigo Vespucci.[7] In the last three of those four voyages that everyone is reading about, he was Amerigo's constant companion, except that on the last voyage he did not return with him. For he, with the greatest difficulty, obtained permission from him to be among those twenty-three who at the end of the last voyage were left in the fort.[8] And so he was left behind, as a concession to his mind, which cared more for foreign travel than a grave; for he was constantly repeating the sayings: 'Who does not have an urn is covered by the sky,' and 'The road to heaven is the same length from all directions.' His attitude would have cost him dearly, if God had not been favorable to him.

"After Vespucci left, he visited many regions with five companions from the fort, and by good fortune at last came to Ceylon and from there to Calicut.[9] There he was lucky to find some Portuguese ships and at last, contrary to his expectations, he returned to his own country."

When Peter told me this, I thanked him for his kindness toward me for being so anxious that I should enjoy the talk of a man whose conversation

---

[5] Aeneas's pilot in Virgil's *Aeneid*, Book V; he fell asleep at the helm, went overboard, and drowned. By contrast, Ulysses (Homer's Odysseus) and Plato became wiser by traveling.

[6] The surname means "dispenser of nonsense."

[7] An Italian explorer in the service of Spain and Portugal who in 1507 published an account of four voyages, taken between 1497 and 1504, to the New World. The Americas are named for him.

[8] At Cape Frio, in Brazil; Vespucci describes leaving men there. During one voyage, he claimed, he encountered a people who (like the Utopians) owned property communally.

[9] The Portuguese discovered Ceylon in 1505. Calicut is in India.

he thought would be pleasant to me. Then I turned to Raphael. After an exchange of greetings and those pleasantries which people say on first meeting a stranger, we left that place and went to my house; and there in the garden we sat on a bench covered with green turf and began to talk together.

So he told us how he and his companions who had remained in the fort, after the departure of Vespucci, by kind approaches gradually won the favor of the natives of that land, and soon were able to move among them with no danger and with great ease, and how also they were regarded with great affection by a certain leader, whose country and name I have forgotten. By his generosity, he said, he and his five companions were given an abundance of supplies and money. For their journey (which was by boat on the water and by chariot on land) they were also given a very trusty guide to take them to other leaders whom they wished to see, and were supplied with the highest commendations. After traveling for many days, he said, he discovered towns and cities, and populous republics with excellent constitutions.

For under the Equator, and on both sides of it, for the distance taken in by the movement of the sun, there lie great deserts parched with constant heat. Everywhere the land is rough and harsh to the sight, terrible, untended, inhabited by wild beasts and serpents, or else men no less wild than the beasts nor less dangerous. But when you have traveled farther, gradually everything grows more gentle: the climate is less harsh, the land pleasantly green, the animals more mild. Eventually you meet peoples, cities, towns. In these there is constant commerce by land and sea, not merely among themselves and their neighbors, but also with far distant countries.

From there he had the opportunity to visit many lands far and wide, because he and his companions were readily welcomed on any ship that was being fitted out for any journey. He said that the ships they saw in the first regions had a flat keel; their sails were made from stitched reeds or osiers, in some places leather. But afterward they came across pointed keels and canvas sails, in short, everything like ours. Their sailors have a great knowledge of the sea and the sky.

But he said he won great favor by showing them how to use the magnet.[10] They had been previously quite ignorant of this, and consequently had been afraid to venture on the sea and did so only in the summer. But now, relying on the magnet, they are not worried by the winter, quite without fear but not without danger; for there is a great hazard that the very thing which they thought would bring them great good may, through their lack of prudence, be the cause of great ills.

He related what he saw in each place, but it would be too long for me to tell it all, and is not the purpose of this work. Perhaps I shall repeat it in another place, especially what it would be profitable to know; above all, those just and wise provisions which he observed among peoples continually living together in harmony. For we asked eagerly about these matters and he gladly discoursed on them. But we did not inquire about monsters,

[10] The magnetic compass, invented in the East and first used by Europeans for navigation in the fifteenth century.

for there is nothing unusual about this subject. For everywhere you can find Scyllas and greedy Celaenos and man-eating Laestrygonians,[11] and fearsome monsters of that kind; but people governed by healthy and wise laws cannot be found just anywhere.

But just as he observed many foolish practices among those new peoples, so he also told us of many institutions from which we might take suitable examples for correcting the errors of these cities, nations, peoples and kingdoms of ours. As I said, I shall relate these in another place. For the moment I want to repeat only what he said about the ways and institutions of the Utopians.[12] But first I will give the conversation which gradually led us to the mention of that republic.

Raphael had first with great wisdom touched upon the various mistakes both in our world and in that new one (and certainly they are very numerous in both places). Then he mentioned the wiser provisions that both we and they have. He so thoroughly understood the ways and practices of each people that it seemed that he had spent his whole life in whatever place he visited. In amazement at the man, Peter said, "My dear Raphael, I am surprised that you do not join yourself to some king. I am quite sure that you would be in great favor with any king, since by this learning and knowledge of places and men you could not merely give pleasure but also instruct by examples and aid by your advice. In this way you would look after your own interests admirably and also be able to help your family and friends greatly."

"As to my family and friends," he said, "I am not much worried, since I think that I have fulfilled my obligations toward them well enough. For other people do not part with their possessions unless they are old and sick, and even then with reluctance when they can no longer hold on to them; but I shared mine out to my family and friends not only when I was healthy and lively, but also when I was a young man. I think they ought to be content with this liberality of mine, and not demand and expect in addition that for their sakes I should give myself into servitude to kings."

"God forbid," said Peter. "My intention was that you should go not into servitude but into service of kings." "That" said he, "is only one syllable less than servitude." "But whatever name you give to it," said Peter, "my opinion is that this is the very road by which you could not only bring profit to others, both privately and publicly, but also make your own condition more prosperous."

"Should I make myself more prosperous," said Raphael, "by the road I find repulsive? And yet now I live just as I wish—a blessing which I suspect comes to very few men in high positions. But there are enough men of that kind who court the friendship of the powerful. So do not think it any great loss if they are going to do without me and one or two like me."

Then I said, "It is clear, Raphael, that you desire neither wealth nor power; and I for one respect and look up to a man of your mind no less than any of those who are in powerful positions. But you will be acting in a

---

[11] *Scyllas . . . Laestrygonians.* Scylla is a monster described in Homer's *Odyssey*, Book XII, who devours some of Odysseus' boatmen. Celaeno is one of Virgil's Harpies (*Aeneid*, Book III), birds with women's faces; the Laestrygonians, in the *Odyssey*, Book X, are gigantic cannibals.

[12] *Utopia* is from Greek, meaning "no place," with a pun on the Greek for "good place."

way worthy of your noble and philosophic spirit if you so dispose yourself, even though it may involve some private disadvantage, as to lend your ability and industry to public affairs. This you could most profitably do if you were a counselor to some great prince, and (as I am sure you would do) gave him advice both upright and honorable. For from a prince a river of all good or evil things flows upon the whole people as if from some perpetual fountain. But you have such perfect learning that even without much experience you could make yourself an indispensable counselor to any king, and such experience of affairs that you could do so without any learning."

"My dear More," said he, "you are twice wrong, first about me and secondly about the matter itself. For I do not have the ability you attribute to me, and even if I did, though I might disturb my own peace, I should not advance the state at all. For in the first place, practically all princes themselves take greater delight in spending their time on military pursuits than on the good arts of peace; and I neither have nor want skill in those matters. They are much more concerned how to get new kingdoms for themselves, by fair means or foul, than to administer well what they already have. Moreover, all the counselors of kings either are so wise as not to be in need of another's advice, or else think themselves so wise that they do not gladly welcome it. The only exception is when they flatter and agree to all the most ridiculous remarks of men whom, because of their great influence with the prince, they wish to win over by fawning. And certainly it is a natural failing for a man to be pleased with his own inventions. So a raven dotes on its chick and a monkey loves its young.

"But suppose that in that company of people who either are jealous of others' thoughts or prefer their own, a man should bring something forward which he has read of as done on other occasions, or has seen done in other parts. Those who hear it act exactly as if their whole reputation for wisdom were in danger, and as if after that they ought to be considered absolute fools if they cannot find some way to discredit others' discoveries. If all other means fail them, then they take refuge in saying, "These things pleased our forefathers. If only we could match their wisdom!" So with these words they are quite content, as if they had brought the discussion to a brilliant conclusion. As if it would involve terrible dangers if anyone were found wiser than his forefathers in any matter at all! Yet all their wisest decisions we are quite happy to let go; but if anywhere they might have made more prudent decisions, we eagerly fasten onto them, and hold on with our teeth. So I have come across these proud, stupid and bad-tempered judgments in many parts of the world, and in England too, once."

"Please tell me," said I. "Did you visit us?" "Yes," he said, "and I stayed there several months, not long after the western English rose in civil war against their king and were crushed with pitiful slaughter.[13] During that time I was much indebted to the Right Reverend Father John Morton,[14]

[13] In 1497, in the reign of Henry VII, 15,000 men of Cornwall, in southwest England, rebelled in protest against a tax designed to support a war against Scotland. The rebels marched on London but were defeated with much loss of life.

[14] As a boy, More had spent two years in Archbishop (later Cardinal) Morton's household. The high office of Lord Chancellor was attained by More himself, in 1529.

Archbishop of Canterbury and Cardinal, and at that time Chancellor of England too. What I am about to say is well known to More, but believe me, Peter, he was a man worthy of the highest respect not more for his authority than for his wisdom and goodness. He was of moderate height and belied his advanced years. His face inspired reverence, not fear. In dealing with people he was easy, yet serious and dignified. It was his pleasure on occasions to speak harshly to those with requests to make of him, without any malice, just to find out what readiness of mind and spirit each man had. As long as a man kept away from impudence, he was delighted by such readiness, as being congenial to his own nature, and he welcomed it as a quality appropriate to a man of action. His conversation was polished and to the point. He had great skill in law, an incomparable intellect and a prodigious memory. He had these virtues in great abundance from birth, but he advanced them still further by studying and practice.

"The King appeared to put great trust in his advice, and the state to rely upon it heavily when I was there. For practically from his early youth he was taken straight from school to court and was employed in important matters all his life. Constantly tossed by the varying tides of fortune, he had with many great dangers learned worldly wisdom. When it is won this way, it does not easily leave.

"It happened one day that I was at his table, and a certain layman was there, learned in your laws. On some pretext or other he began loudly to sing the praises of that stern justice which was then being used in England against thieves, who, he said, were strung up everywhere, sometimes twenty on one gallows.[15] And so he said he was all the more puzzled, when so few escaped punishment, what evil fate produced so many robbers all over the country. Then, presuming to speak freely in front of the Cardinal, I said, "There is no reason why you should be surprised. For this punishment inflicted upon thieves is beyond the bounds of justice and not to the public advantage. It is too severe for punishing robbery, but not sufficient to restrain it. For simple theft[16] is not so great a crime as to deserve capital punishment, nor is there any penalty strong enough to keep from theft men who have no other means of gaining a livelihood. So in this matter not only you, but a good part of this world also, seem to copy bad teachers, who more readily beat their students than educate them. For harsh and terrible punishments are inflicted upon thieves, when it would be much better to see that they had a means to earn a living. In this way they would be freed from the awful necessity of stealing and then being put to death.'

"'This has all been seen to well enough,' he said. 'There are manual crafts and there is farming: from these a man may support his life, unless by nature he prefers to be evil.' 'But you will not get out of it as easily as this,' I said. 'In the first place, let us forget those who often come home mutilated from foreign or civil wars, as recently happened among your people in the Cornish war, and not so long ago in France.[17] These men give their limbs to their country or their king; their disability does not allow

[15] In England capital punishment for theft was not outlawed until the early nineteenth century.

[16] Theft is simple when it does not use violence.

[17] In 1492, under Henry VII, there had been a minor war in France.

them to practice their former crafts, nor at such an age can they learn a new one. As I say, let us forget these, as wars come and go. Let us consider those cases that arise every day.

"'Now, there is a large number of noblemen who live in idleness like drones by the labors of others—in other words, they skin the tenants on their farms by increasing the rents. For that is the only thrift they know, though in other spheres they are so lavish as to beggar themselves. But as well as this, they take around an immense crowd of idle attendants, who have never learned any means of making a living. As soon as their master dies, or they themselves fall sick, they are thrown out straightaway. For masters are readier to support idlers than invalids, and often an heir cannot immediately afford the number of servants his dead father kept. Meanwhile they have the choice of violent hunger or violent robbery. For what are they to do? In wandering about, they wear out their clothes and health, and when they are unkempt with sickness and their clothes covered with patches, no gentleman deigns to receive them and no countryman dares. For they are well aware of the value of a man brought up softly in idleness and luxuries, who is used to sneering at the whole neighborhood with a braggart's look and despising everyone but himself, dressed up with his sword and shield. They know that he will be quite unsuited to be the faithful servant of a poor man, with a spade and a hoe, niggardly wages and scant food.'

"'No,' he said, 'this is the kind of man we ought especially to cultivate. For these are men of higher and nobler spirit than craftsmen or farmers, and in them lies the power and strength of the army whenever a battle must be fought.'

"'Of course,' I said, 'you might just as well say that we should cultivate thieves because of wars; for undoubtedly you will never be without wars as long as you have thieves. For neither are robbers fainthearted soldiers, nor are soldiers cowardly robbers; so nice an agreement is there between these two arts. But this is frequent among you, but not confined to you. For it belongs to practically all nations. Another more pestilential plague infests France as well; the whole country is filled and besieged with mercenary soldiers in peacetime too (if that can be called peace). They were brought in under the same belief through which you English thought that idle servants ought to be supported here: because, that is, the wise fools decided that the public safety depended upon the constant presence of a strong and firm garrison, especially of veterans. For they have no confidence in inexperienced men. The result is that they even have to seek out a war so as not to have unskilled soldiers, and wantonly to kill men so that (as Sallust[18] wittily puts it) their hands or spirits may not grow dull through lack of practice.

"'But how dangerous it is to keep beasts of this kind France has learned to her cost, and the same lesson is shown by the Romans, the Carthaginians, the Syrians and many other people. For their standing armies on various pretexts have overthrown their empires, and ravaged their country and cities. But how unnecessary this is can be seen from the example of the

---

[18] Roman historian, first century B.C.

French: their soldiers, though trained to the fingertips, yet when matched with your levies,[19] cannot often boast that they have come off superior—I say no more, so as not to seem to flatter you to your face. But neither those city craftsmen of yours nor the rough and uncouth farmers are believed to be very afraid of the idle attendants of the noblemen—except for those who do not happen to have a body to match their strength and boldness, or whose strength of spirit is broken by poverty. So there is no danger that these attendants might grow soft if they were trained in honest crafts for their livelihood and exercised in manly work; for as it is now, their strong and robust bodies (nobles choose to corrupt only picked men) grow feeble with idleness or soft with womanly tasks. Certainly, whatever is the truth of this matter, of one thing I am quite sure: that it is by no means to the interest of the state to keep, against the possibility of a war which you never have except when you wish, an immense crowd of the sort that destroys the peace—and we ought to have much more consideration for peace than war.

"'But this is not the only reason which drives men to steal. There is another one more peculiar to you English in my opinion.' 'What is that?' said the Cardinal. 'Your sheep,' I said, 'which are normally so gentle and need so little food. Now (so they say) they have begun to be so ravenous and wild that they even eat up men. They devastate and destroy fields, houses and towns. For in whatever parts of the kingdom fine and therefore more precious wool is produced, there the nobles and gentlemen, and also some holy abbots, are not content with the rents and annual profits that their predecessors used to get from their farms. They are not satisfied to live in luxury and idleness and be of no use to the state; they even harm it. They leave nothing for arable land, enclose everything for pasture,[20] destroy houses, tear down towns and leave only the church to house the sheep; and as if the forests and parks lost you too little ground, those good men turn all houses and cultivated land into a desert.

"'Thus, so that one glutton, the insatiable and terrible plague of the country, may join together fields and enclose several thousand acres, some tenants are ejected. Others are stripped of their own land by trickery or violence, or, wearied by their wrongs, are driven to sell. And so, however it happens, the wretched people leave, men, women, husbands, wives, orphans, widows, parents with small children, and with their large, but impoverished, band of servants (as farming needs many hands); they leave, I say, the home they knew so well, nor can they find anywhere to go. All their furniture, which would not bring a high price even if it could wait for a buyer, they sell for a pittance, since it must go out. This money they soon spend on their wanderings. What is there left for them then except to steal and hang (justly, of course), or else roam and beg? Although even then they are thrown into prison as vagrants, because they are traveling around with nothing to do. For no one will hire their services, even though they

---

[19] Levies of unprofessional soldiers. They had helped defeat the French in several notable battles of the fourteenth and fifteenth centuries: Crecy (1346), Poitiers (1356), and Agincourt (1415). The victory at Agincourt, under the former "Prince Hal" of Shakespeare's *Henry the Fourth* plays, is a central episode in his *Henry the Fifth*.

[20] The "enclosure" movement, which converted crop fields into sheep pastures, was often attacked by social reformers in More's time.

offer them eagerly. For those accustomed to farming have nothing to do where no crops are sown. One shepherd or attendant is enough to graze the land with cattle, although formerly many hands were needed to cultivate it so as to ensure a good harvest.

"'And this is the reason why in many places food is much dearer. The price of wool too has risen so high that it just cannot be bought by the poor, who usually make their cloth from it in England; and for that reason more people are driven from work to idleness. For after the institution of the enclosures, the rot destroyed a very large number of sheep. It was as if God punished the owners' greed by sending destruction to the sheep, although it would have been juster if it had fallen on their own heads. But even if the number of sheep increases enormously, yet the price does not come down. For although there cannot be said to be a monopoly on sheep, since more than one man is engaged in selling them, they are certainly in the control of a very small number. For they have almost all fallen into the hands of a few rich men who are under no necessity to sell before they want, and who do not want to until they may at their own price. Now there is the same reason why the other kinds of cattle are equally dear, or even more so, since there is no one left to look after their reproduction now that the houses have been pulled down and farming is neglected. Nor do those rich men rear the young of the larger cattle as they do of the sheep. Instead they buy them cheaply when they are lean, fatten them up on their pastures and sell them again at a great price. So in my opinion the entire evil effect of this affair has not yet been felt. For until now they have been raising the prices only in these places where they sell; but when eventually they remove them more quickly than they can be born, then the supply will gradually decrease in the places where they are bought too, and a great and troublesome shortage will follow there.

"'So now the wicked greed of a few has turned to a plague the very thing which made this island of yours seem so especially prosperous. For this dearness of food is the reason why everyone is dismissing as many servants as he can. Where are they going, I ask you, except to beg? Or on a course to which well-bred minds are more easily persuaded—to steal?

"'Now beside this wretched poverty and need we find wanton luxury. For among the servants of noblemen, and the craftsmen and even the countrymen too, among people of all ranks, are found many new styles in clothing and an excessive lavishness in food. Now places of ill repute, brothels, whorehouses and stews,[21] winehouses, alehouses, so many wicked games, dice, cards, the tables, tennis, bowls, quoits[22]—these all quickly exhaust their money and send their devotees straight off somewhere to steal.

"'Cast out these pernicious pests. Make a law that those who pulled them down should reconstruct the houses and country towns, or else give them up to people who are prepared to replace and rebuild them. Check the rich from buying everything up and put an end to their freedom in monopoly. Let fewer men be kept in idleness; bring back farming; reintroduce clothmaking to be an honorable business and a useful occupation for that idle mob, or for those whom until now poverty has made thieves, or those who are now vagrants or idle servants, both good material for future

---

[21] Brothels.   [22] A game resembling horseshoe-pitching.

thieves. Certainly if you do not heal these ills, your boasts of justice exercised in the punishment of theft are quite useless. This justice, in fact, is ostentatious rather than just or advantageous. When you allow people to be brought up in the worst possible way and their characters to be gradually corrupted from a tender age, and then punish them when they commit those crimes as men which they showed all signs of doing from their childhood on—I ask you, what else are you doing than making men thieves and then punishing them?'

"While I was still saying this, the lawyer meanwhile had seriously got himself ready to speak and had decided to use that usual method of debaters[23] who repeat men's words with more care than they reply to them. In fact, they have a very high regard for memory. 'Yes,' he said, 'a good speech for a foreigner. You have been in a position to hear a little on these matters rather than gain any precise knowledge. I shall make this clear very quickly. First of all, I shall go over what you said in the same order. Then I shall demonstrate on what matters you have been misled by ignorance of our ways. Finally I shall destroy and refute all your reasoning. So, to begin with my first point, you seemed to me on four—' 'Hush,' said the Cardinal. 'To judge from your beginning, your reply is going to be lengthy. So for the moment we shall relieve you of the trouble of replying and keep it intact for you for your next meeting. If you or Raphael here has no other commitments, I should like that to take place tomorrow.

"'But meanwhile, Raphael, I should be very glad to hear from you why you think that theft ought not to be punished by death and what alternative penalty you suggest as being more to the public good. For not even you think that it ought to be tolerated. As things are now, men rush into theft despite the death penalty. Once you guarantee them their lives, what force or fear can restrain criminals? They would take the mitigation of the penalty as an inducement and invitation to crime.'

"'Reverend father,' I said, 'it seems to me outrageously unjust to take away a man's life for taking money. For in my opinion human life is worth more than all the possessions fortune can give. But if they say that this penalty is aimed against the violation of justice and breaking the laws rather than the theft, would we not be right in calling this extreme justice extreme injustice? For we must not approve of legal ordinances so severe that the slightest disobedience is immediately met with a drawn sword; nor of decrees so stoical[24] that all sins are considered equal, that it makes no difference whether you kill a man or steal money from him. If equity means anything, there is absolutely no similarity between these crimes. God has forbidden us to kill. Do we then kill so easily for the theft of a trifling sum? For if you interpret that commandment of God as forbidding killing except where human law declares a man ought to be killed, what is to prevent men from similarly deciding among themselves when it is permissible to commit fornication, adultery and perjury? God has forbidden us to kill not merely others but ourselves too. Now, if human agreement on mutual slaughter, on fixed conditions, has such validity that it releases its

---

[23] The lawyer's aborted rejoinder is in the medieval scholastic style of argument, which More is mocking.

[24] The ancient Stoics taught the doctrine outlined here.

followers from that divine commandment and with no example from God allows them to kill people whom human sanction orders, are we not in this way giving only as much right to God's commandment as human law allows? And of course the result will be that in the same way men will decide in all matters how far it is convenient to observe God's commandments. The law of Moses, cruel and harsh though it was (for it was introduced against servants,[25] and stubborn ones at that), yet punished theft with a fine, not death. Let us not imagine that in the new law of kindness, by which He rules us as a father his children, God has granted us a greater license for cruelty against one another.

"'These are the reasons why I think it is not right. I am sure that everyone realizes how absurd it is and even dangerous for the state that a thief and murderer should be given the same punishment. For when a robber sees that no less a danger awaits a man condemned for theft than one convicted of homicide as well, by this single thought he is driven to murder the man he would otherwise merely have robbed. For if he is caught there is no more danger, and also there is greater safety in murder and a greater hope of concealing his crime if the witness is removed. So in trying to terrify thieves with excessive cruelty, we provoke them to kill good men.

"'To turn to the question of what punishment could be more suitable, in my opinion this is much easier to find than a worse one. For why should we doubt that the profitable way for punishing crime is the one approved of long ago by the Romans, men who had great experience in governing a state? For men found guilty of serious crimes were condemned to be sent to the stone quarries or mines, and kept in chains constantly.

"'Although in this connection nowhere have I seen a better institution than the one I noticed in my travels in Persia among the people called Polylerites.[26] These people are quite numerous and enjoy excellent institutions. They are free and governed by their own laws except that they pay an annual tribute to the King of Persia. They are far from the sea, practically shut in by mountains, and enjoy the fruits of a bountiful land. They do not visit others often, nor are they visited themselves. It is an ancient practice of their country not to try to extend their territory, and what they have is easily protected from all attack by the mountains and the tribute they pay to the powerful king. They are quite free from military service and lead a comfortable rather than a glorious life, prosperous rather than noble or distinguished. For I believe they are known to no one except their neighbors, even by name.

"'In this country those convicted of theft return what they stole to the owner, not to the king, as happens in other places. For they think that the king has as little right to the thing stolen as the thief himself. But if whatever is stolen cannot be recovered, the equivalent is paid from the thieves' property, which otherwise remains intact for their wives and children. The thieves themselves are condemned to hard labor. Unless the theft was a violent one, they are not shut up in prison, nor do they wear fetters, but

---

[25] Slaves; that is, the Jews of the Old Testament. The contrast is with the theological notion of Christian liberty, especially as developed in the Epistles of St. Paul.

[26] The name of this fictional people is from Greek, meaning "much nonsense"—a typical example of More's whimsical humor.

they are free and unrestricted to do their work for the state. Those who
refuse to work or are halfhearted about it, they flog rather than imprison.
Those who work hard suffer no violence and at night merely have a roll call
and are shut up in their rooms. Apart from the constant work, there is
nothing harsh about their lives. For their fare is not too severe, and as they
are public servants, it comes out of public funds. Some variations occur: in
some places the funds to support them come from charity. Although this
way is not without risk, yet the people are so kindhearted that there is
always plenty. In other parts some public revenues are marked out for that
purpose. Elsewhere each man pays a tax for it. In several regions they do
no public work, but any private citizen who needs laborers can hire their
services in the marketplace for the day, at a fixed price which is slightly
lower than what he would have paid for a free man. If such a servant is lazy
he may be flogged.

"'So they are never without work, and besides paying for their keep,
this system also brings something into the public treasury every day from
each of them. They are one and all dressed in the same color clothing;
their hair is not shaved but cut a little above their ears, and a small piece is
taken from the tip of one ear. Each man may receive food and drink from
his friends and clothing of the proper color. But to give money is a capital
offense for the giver as well as the receiver. No less dangerous is it for a
free man also to receive money from a convict for any reason whatever,
and also for a slave (this is the name they give to the convicts) to touch
weapons. Each district distinguishes its slaves by a special badge, which it is
a capital offense to throw away—just as it is for them to be seen outside
their own region, or to have any conversation with a slave of another district. It is no safer to plan to run away than it is actually to do so. To be an
accomplice in such a plan means death for a slave and servitude for a free
man. There are rewards decreed for an informer—for a free man money,
for a slave freedom. Both classes of such informers are given pardon and
impunity if they were involved in the plan, to prevent its being safer to go
through with it than to repent.

"'I have shown you the law and arrangements dealing with this question. It is perfectly obvious how humane and advantageous it is. The anger
of the law takes the form of destroying the vices but saving the men, who
are so treated that they must be good and spend the rest of their lives
repairing the damage they previously did.

"'So little fear is there of their falling back into their old ways, that
travelers who have decided upon some journey think that the slaves are the
safest of guides, and change them at each district. For if they want to commit robbery, they have everything against them: they have no weapons;
money is merely an indication of crime; if they are caught, punishment is
all ready for them; they have absolutely no hope of escaping anywhere. For
how could a man conceal and hide his flight when his clothing is quite
unlike everyone else's, except by escaping naked? Even if he did this, his
ear would give him away. There is hardly any danger that they would enter
a plot for conspiracy against the state. The only way for any district to
entertain such hopes would be to win over the slaves of many other districts
beforehand. But so far are they from being able to form a conspiracy, that
they cannot even meet and talk together, or so much as exchange a greet-

ing. Nor can it be imagined that they would fearlessly confide such a plan to their fellows, when they know that silence would be dangerous, but betrayal would be highly profitable. On the other hand, none is entirely without the hope that he may eventually recover his liberty by obedience and endurance and by showing that he is capable of leading a better life later. For every year several are freed as a reward for their patience.'

"After saying all this, I added that I saw no reason why this method should not be adopted in England too, with much greater profit than came from the justice the lawyer had so highly praised. At this the lawyer said, 'That plan could never be established in England without bringing the state into the greatest jeopardy.' While saying this, he shook his head, made a wry face and so fell silent. And all present gave their support to him.

"Then the Cardinal said, "It is not easy to guess whether the plan would work or not without making an experiment. But suppose that after pronouncing the death sentence the King ordered a stay of execution and tried this method out (after abolishing all rights of sanctuary[27]): if the plan worked out well, then it would be right to establish it permanently. If it did not, then those previously condemned could still be put to death. This would be no more against the interests of the state nor more unjust than if the execution were immediately carried out. Nor can any danger arise in the intervening period. I am quite sure that vagrants could well be treated in the same way. So far, in spite of all the legislation against them, we have achieved nothing.'

"After the Cardinal had finished, they all vied with one another to praise the suggestions that they had despised when they came from me—especially the point on vagrants, since this had been an addition of the Cardinal himself.

"Perhaps I ought not to repeat the absurd events that followed. Yet I will, as they were not bad and had some bearing on the subject.

"As it happened, there was standing nearby a parasite who wanted to seem to be playing the fool. But his imitation was quite lifelike. He tried for laughs with such feeble jokes that he was laughed at himself more often than his witticisms. Yet every now and then he brought out such a clever remark that it made us believe in the saying about dice: that eventually you are bound to throw two sixes. One of our company was saying that my suggestions had taken care of thieves and the Cardinal's of vagrants, and it now remained to give some public aid to people driven to poverty and rendered incapable of working for a living by sickness or age. The fool interrupted by saying, 'Allow me. I shall make good provision for this as well. For I should give anything to get rid of such people out of my sight. They have often made great nuisances of themselves by asking me for money with those whines and tears. But they have never been able to put them on successfully enough to get a penny out of me. For always one of two things happens: either I do not want to give, or else I just cannot, as I have nothing. And so they have now learned wisdom. For they do not waste their energy when they see me pass; they let me go by in silence. So they no longer have any hopes of getting anything from me, no more than if I were a priest. But I would pass a law to divide up all those beggars into the

[27] The right of a criminal to evade capture by taking refuge in a church.

Benedictine monasteries and make them lay brothers[28] and the women nuns.' The Cardinal smiled and applauded the joke, as the others genuinely did too.

"But a certain friar, who was a learned divine, was so amused by this witticism against priests and monks that he too began to joke, although normally he was a man of serious and grim appearance. 'No,' he said, 'you will not be rid of beggars so easily, if you do not also make some provision for us friars too.' 'And yet,' said the parasite, 'that is already taken care of. For the Cardinal made excellent provision for you when he decided that vagrants should be locked up and put to work. For you are the biggest vagrants of all.'[29]

"When everyone saw that the Cardinal did not disapprove, they began to take the joke up eagerly, all except the friar. For it was not surprising that after being made the object of such bitter wit, his anger flared up so hotly that he could not restrain himself from open abuse. He called the man a knave, a slanderer, a backbiter and a son of perdition. All the time he cited terrible threats from the Holy Scriptures. Now the jester began to play the jester in earnest and he was a master in his field. 'Do not be angry, good brother,' he said. 'It is written: "In your patience ye shall win your souls."'[30] Then the friar replied (for I shall repeat his actual words), 'I am not angry, you wretch, or at least I am not committing any sin. For the Psalmist says, "Stand in awe and sin not."'[31]

"Then the friar was gently warned by the Cardinal to control his feelings. 'My lord,' said the friar, 'I am only speaking out of good zeal, as I ought. For the saints had good zeal and so it is said: "For the zeal of thine house hath eaten me up,"[32] and in church we sing: "The mockers of Elisha, while he went up to the house of God, felt the zeal of the bald"[33]—just as perhaps he shall feel, that mocker, that ribald buffoon.' 'You are acting,' said the Cardinal, 'out of good feeling perhaps, but your action will probably be holier and certainly wiser if you do not get into a stupid quarrel with a foolish and stupid fellow.' 'No, my lord,' he said, 'I should not be acting more wisely. For Solomon himself, the wisest of men, says, "Answer a fool according to his folly,"[34] just as I am doing now, and I am showing him the pit into which he will fall if he does not take great care. For if the many mockers of Elisha, who was only one bald man, felt the zeal of the bald, how much more will it be felt by one mocker of many friars, among whom are many bald men?[35] And we also have a papal bull,[36] by which all who mock us are excommunicated.' When he saw that there was no end to this, the Cardinal dismissed the parasite with a nod, and gave the conversation a convenient turn to another subject. Shortly after this, he rose from the

---

[28] Unordained members of the monastic community, expected to perform lowly work.
[29] Friars, unlike monks, supported themselves by traveling around and begging.
[30] Luke 21:19.
[31] The quotation is from Psalms 4:4 (4:5 in the Vulgate [Catholic] version). The passage can also be translated "Be angry, and sin not."
[32] Psalms 69:9 (Vulgate 68:10).
[33] The Old Testament prophet Elisha, as related in 2 Kings 2:23-24, was taunted by children for his baldness. Elisha's punishing curse caused forty-two of the children to be destroyed by bears.
[34] Proverbs 26:5. This book was attributed to Solomon.
[35] The friars shaved their heads.   [36] A document sent out by the Pope.

table and dismissed us, to give his attention to the cases of his clients.

"My dear More, look what a long story I have burdened you with! I should have been quite ashamed to keep on for so long if you had not eagerly requested this of me and seemed so intent on the tale that you did not want a single detail left out. For although I did so rather briefly, I simply had to relate it to show up the judgment of those fellows. For when they had despised my words, they began to approve of them when the Cardinal immediately showed his favor. They so fawned upon him that they even flattered and seriously entertained his parasite's ideas, when, as a joke, his master did not reject them. From this you can judge what worth the courtiers would put upon me and my suggestions."

"My dear Raphael," I said, "you have given me great pleasure by the wisdom and charm of all you said. At times I thought I was in my own country and even somehow to become a child again, by the delightful remembrance of the Cardinal, in whose palace I was brought up as a child. When you praise his memory so, Raphael, you cannot imagine how much dearer you are made to me on this account, although you were very dear even before. But I still cannot change my opinion in any way. I am quite convinced that if you could school yourself to tolerate princes' courts, you could do a great deal of public good by your advice. So there is nothing more appropriate to your duty, that is the duty of a good man. Your Plato judges that states will become blessed only if philosophers become kings or kings philosophers.[37] How distant will such blessings be if philosophers do not even condescend to give their advice to kings?" "They are not so ungrateful," he said. "They would gladly do so. In fact, they have already done this in many published books, if only those in power were ready to listen to good advice. But Plato was clearly quite right: if kings do not become philosophers themselves, they will never approve of the advice of philosophers, since from childhood they have been infected and tainted with wrong beliefs. Plato himself found this out in the case of Dionysius.[38] If I were to put sound advice before some king and try to root out of him the pernicious seeds of evil, do you not think that I should be immediately thrown out or laughed to scorn?

"Now, suppose I were with the French King[39] and sitting on his council in secret consultation, in a circle of wise men, with the King himself as president. The question earnestly being discussed is: By what means and wiles can he hold on to Milan, and drag that fugitive Naples back? After that, how can he overthrow the Venetians and bring the whole of Italy into subjection? Then conquer Flanders, Brabant, the whole of Burgundy, and other countries as well which he has already invaded in his imagination? Here one advises that a treaty ought to be made with the Venetians, to last only as long as suits the King's convenience; their plan should be shared with them; even a part of the booty be deposited with them, which he can get back when matters are finished to his satisfaction. Another urges that the Germans should be hired, another that the Swiss ought to be won over

---

[37] Plato, *Republic*, Book V.

[38] There was a plan for Plato to help educate Dionysius, the young ruler of Syracuse in Sicily; the effort failed and Plato was sorely mistreated.

[39] The ruses and strategems attributed to France in the following passage are founded on contemporary historical fact.

with money. Another thinks that the godhead of His Imperial Majesty[40] ought to be appeased with a sacrifice of gold. Yet another advises that peace should be made with the King of Aragon and that his own kingdom of Navarre should be given up to him as a guarantee of peace. Another is of the opinion that the King of Castile should be lured by some hope of affinity[41] and some noble courtiers should be bribed to come over to their party. The biggest stumbling block of all is the question of England. But they agree that peace must be made and the alliance, always so feeble, should be bound with the strongest ties, so that they can be called friends and suspected as enemies. The Scots[42] should be kept ready as if on watch, prepared for any opportunity, to be let loose immediately the English show any signs of activity. Some noble exile also should be trained secretly (for the treaties prevent this from happening openly) to maintain that the kingdom belongs to him so that the French King might have this weapon to check the king he suspects. Here, I say, amid such weighty discussion, with so many distinguished men vying to give their advice for war, suppose that all on my own I should arise and advise a different course: that Italy should be left alone and the French stay at home; that the kingdom of France is practically too big to be conveniently administered by one man, so that the King should not think of adding others. Then suppose I put before them the decrees of the Achorians,[43] a people lying to the southeast of the island of Utopia. They once waged a war to obtain another kingdom for their king, which he claimed was his due inheritance because of some old affinity. When they finally won it, they saw that they had just as much trouble holding on to it as they had endured in gaining it. And seeds of rebellion were ever springing up within, or invasion from without. So they always had to fight either for the people they had conquered or against them. They never had an opportunity to dismiss their army and all the time their resources were being drained and their money going abroad. Their blood was being spent on others' glory and peace was no safer. At home characters had become corrupted by war, people had tasted the joy of robbery, boldness was strengthened by slaughter, the laws were held in contempt. The King, divided between the cares of two realms, could not give his proper attention to either. When they saw that there was no other end to these ills, at last they devised a plot and very gently gave their king the choice of retaining whichever kingdom he wanted. For they said he would not be able to have both and they were too numerous to be governed by half a king, since no one would willingly hire a muleteer to share with another. So that good king was compelled to give his new kingdom to one of his friends (who shortly after was thrown out) and be content with the old. Suppose that besides this I showed that after so many nations had been set in a turmoil for the French King's sake, when his coffers had been drained and his people ruined, by some chance these preparations for war would come to no purpose. I should tell him to look after the kingdom he inherited, and embellish it as much as he could, and make it as flourishing

----

[40] The Holy Roman Emperor, at the time Maximilian of Austria.

[41] Alliance by marriage.

[42] Historically, Scotland has often opposed England and, backed by France, supported rivals of the reigning English sovereigns.

[43] A fictional people; the name means "inhabitants of nowhere."

as possible; to love his people and be loved by them; to live together with them and make his rule gentle; to say good-bye to other kingdoms, since the one that had fallen to his lot was enough and more than enough. If I were to say all this, my dear More, how do you think it would be received?" "Not readily, I am sure," said I.

"Let us go on then," he said. "Suppose that his counselors were debating with a king and devising means to pile up money for him. One advises that the value of money should be raised[44] when the king has to pay any out, and then lowered below its proper value when he has to take any, so that he may pay much money with little and receive much instead of little. Another advises him to feign a war and on that pretext to gather in much money; then, when it seems fit, to make peace with religious ceremonies to deceive the unfortunate people who suppose that he is a holy king with compassion for human blood. Another reminds him of certain ancient moth-eaten laws, outdated by long disuse. As no one remembers that they were passed, all have broken them. So the king ought to impose fines for their transgression. There could be no richer source, none more honorable, since it wears the mask of justice. Another advises him to forbid many things with heavy fines, especially such things as are against the interest of the people; then to give a dispensation for money to those whose interests are damaged by the decree. In this way he would gain favor with the people and profit in two ways: either from the fines imposed on those whose greed for gain has lured them into the snare, or else from the sale of immunities, which, of course, will be all the more expensive in proportion to the king's goodness. For it is only with the greatest reluctance that he allows any citizen to do anything against the interests of the people, and consequently only at a high price. Another recommends that he should bring the judges over to his side to give judgment for the king in every case; and that he should also summon them to the palace and invite them to discuss his affairs in his presence. In this way no case of his will be so manifestly unjust as not to allow one of them to find some crack in it for a false accusation—either because he likes to make objections, or because he hates agreeing with everyone, or else to win the king's favor. Thus while the judges differ and a perfectly clear case is disputed and the truth itself is questioned, the king is given a convenient opportunity to interpret the law to his own convenience. The others will support him either from shame or from fear. So afterward their sentence is delivered from the bench without any fear. For anyone pronouncing judgment for the king must have a good excuse; for it is enough for him to have equity on his side, or merely the words of a law, or the twisted meaning of a document, or—what outweighs all laws with conscientious judges—the king's indisputable prerogative. They all agree with that saying of Crassus:[45] 'No amount of money is enough for a king who has to keep an army.' They all agree too that a king can do no wrong, however much he may wish, since all men's possessions are his and the men themselves too; that a subject owns only as much as the king's kindness

---

[44] That is, money should be declared to have a higher value than it actually has. Several of the fiscal expedients mentioned in the following passage were used in England under Henry VII.

[45] A rich Roman and financial opportunist of the first century B.C., partner in rule with Pompey and Julius Caesar.

allows him to keep; that it is greatly to the king's advantage that this should
be as little as possible, as he is safe only if his people do not run riot with
riches and freedom, since these are not so ready to bear harsh and unjust
commands; while on the other hand, need and poverty blunt their spirits,
make them more patient, beat them down and take away any brave hopes
of rebellion. Suppose that in my turn I should stand up and maintain that
all this advice is both dishonorable and disadvantageous for the king, since
his honor and safety rest upon the people's wealth more than his own. I
should show that they choose a king for themselves for their own sake, not
his,[46] so that by his toil and care they may live profitably and safe from
injury. So the king ought to concern himself with his people's well-being
rather than his own. It is just like the duty of a shepherd, who, insofar as he
is a shepherd, must tend his sheep rather than himself. The very facts show
how far wrong those people are who think that the people's poverty is a
guarantee of peace. For where could you find more quarrels than among
beggars? Who is more anxious for a change of government than a man who
is discontent with the present condition of his life? Or who is bolder in
stirring up revolution in the hope of gain from some source or other than
the man who now has nothing to lose? If a king were so despised or so
hated by his subjects that he could only keep them in their duty by outrageous measures, by plundering and appropriation, by reducing them to
poverty, it would surely be better for him to abdicate than to retain his
throne by measures by which he keeps the name of power but loses majesty. For it is not dignified for a king to exercise his power over beggars
instead of rich and prosperous citizens. This was realized by Fabricius,[47] a
man of lofty and sublime spirit, when he replied that he preferred to rule
the rich than be rich himself. And for one man to abound in pleasures and
delights, while the others are groaning and weeping around him—this is to
be the custodian not of a kingdom but of a prison. He is just like a bad
doctor who can cure a disease only by bringing on another; for a king who
can govern his subjects' lives only by taking away the comforts of life must
admit that he does not know how to rule free men. He should change
either his laziness or his pride. For it is mainly for these vices that his people
despise or hate him. Let him live harmlessly out of his own pocket, fit his
expenditure to his income, check ill-doing, by right training of his subjects
prevent abuses rather than let them grow and then punish them. Let him
not be quick to revive laws fallen into disuse, especially those which have
been out of use for a long time and never missed. Nor let him ever, under
the pretext of a fine, take anything which a judge would not allow a private
citizen to receive, because it is unjust and cunning. Suppose I suggest to
them the law of the Macarenses,[48] who also are not too far from Utopia. On
the day he ascends the throne, their king is bound, by an oath sanctioned
by great sacrifices, that he will never at one time have over a thousand
pounds of gold in his treasury or the equivalent weight of silver. They say
that this law was introduced by an excellent king, who had more care for
his country's well-being than his own wealth, as a bar to a king's piling up

[46] This apparently modern view is actually medieval as well. The heyday of belief in the
absolute power of kings came later in the sixteenth and in the seventeenth centuries.
[47] A virtuous Roman, third century B.C.   [48] The name means "fortunate."

enough gold to create poverty among his people. For he realized that that amount would suffice, whether the king had to fight against rebels or the whole kingdom against an enemy's invasions. But it was not enough to incite him to invade other men's property. That was the main reason for passing the law. Another one was that he thought that provision was thereby made that there would be enough money in circulation for the citizens' daily trading. He also thought that since the king had to pay out whatever came into his treasury above the legal amount, he would not seek an occasion to do anyone an injustice. Such a king will be feared by the wicked and loved by the good. If then I were to put forward such suggestions to men violently inclined to the opposite, how deaf do you think they would be to my tale?"

"Very deaf indeed," I said. "Nor am I at all surprised, nor (to tell the truth) do I think that suggestions ought to be made or advice proffered which you are sure will never be taken. For how could so strange a tale do any good or work its way into their hearts, when the opposite belief is already firmly planted in their minds? This scholastic[49] philosophy is all right among friends in familiar conversation."

"That is precisely what I meant," he said, "when I said that there is no place for philosophy with kings." "No, there certainly is not," said I, "for this scholastic philosophy which thinks that everything is appropriate everywhere. But there is another philosophy of a more civil kind, which knows the stage it should act on, adapts itself accordingly in the play it has in hand and plays its part appropriately and with decorum. This is the one you should adopt. Otherwise, when a play of Plautus is being acted, and the servants are trifling among themselves, if you come on stage dressed like a philosopher and recite the passage from the *Octavia* where Seneca disputes with Nero, would it not have been better to act a dumb show than by reciting inappropriate lines to make it a tragicomedy?[50] For you would ruin and destroy the present play if you mixed in alien matter, even if the lines you brought were better. Whatever play is in hand, act it to the best of your ability, and do not wreck the whole of it because you remember another that is wittier.

"It is exactly the same in a state and the consultations of kings. If erroneous beliefs cannot be plucked out root and all, if you cannot heal long established evils to your satisfaction, you must not therefore desert the state and abandon the ship in a storm, because you cannot check the winds. Nor should you force upon people strange and unaccustomed discourses which you know will have no weight with them in their opposite beliefs. But you should try and strive obliquely to settle everything as best you may, and what you cannot turn to good, you should make as little evil as possible. For it is not possible for everything to be good unless all men are good, and I do not expect that that will come about for many years."

"The only result of this course," he said, "would be to make me as mad as the people whose insanity I am trying to cure. For if I want to speak the

---

[49] Characteristic of the medieval universities.
[50] Plautus (c. 254-184 B.C.) and Seneca (4? B.C.-65 A.D.) were Roman playwrights, the former of low comedy, the latter of lofty tragedy.

truth, this is what I must say. But whether it is appropriate for a philosopher to lie, I do not know. It certainly is not for me. Yet although my
conversation might perhaps be unpleasant and annoying to them, I do not
see why it ought to be outrageously strange. Suppose I were to say what
Plato invents[51] in his *Republic* or what the Utopians do in theirs—although
this might be better (as I am sure it is), yet it might seem out of place. For in
our society every man has his private possessions, but there everything is
held in common.

"Admittedly my discourse cannot please those who have decided to
rush headlong by the opposite road, since it calls them back and points out
the dangers. But otherwise what else did it contain which could not, or
indeed ought not, to be said anywhere? For if we ought to omit everything,
as being strange and inappropriate, which the corrupt ways of men have
made appear odd, then we ought to cover up among Christians practically
everything that Christ taught and so strongly forbade us to cover up that
whatever He whispered in the ears of His disciples He ordered them to
proclaim upon the housetops.[52] The greater part of His teaching is much
further removed from men's ways than my speech was. But cunning
preachers, following your advice, I suppose, because men were loath to
adapt their ways to the rule of Christ, fitted His teaching to their ways like a
lead rule,[53] so that at least they should join together somehow. I do not see
what they have achieved by this, except that men may be evil with more
safety. And I myself, I am sure, should achieve just as little in the councils
of kings. For either I should be of a different opinion, which would be the
same as having no opinion, or else I should be of the same and be a helper
of their madness, as Micio says in Terence.[54] For I cannot see the point of
that oblique way of yours, by which you think that if everything cannot be
made good, I should strive at least to get it managed suitably and rendered
as little evil as possible. For with a king there is no place for dissimulation or
conniving. One must openly praise the vilest plans and put one's signature
to the most disastrous decrees. He would be considered a spy and almost a
traitor who gave faint praise to wicked decisions.

"Moreover, nothing happens in which you could be of any benefit,
when you are put amid colleagues who would more easily corrupt even the
best of men than be corrected themselves, by whose evil company either
you will be depraved, or else, in your blameless and innocent state, you will
act as a cloak to another's wickedness and folly. So far from possible is it to
change anything for the better by that oblique path.

"For this reason Plato shows with a beautiful comparison why wise men
rightly keep away from politics.[55] When they see the people swarm in the
streets and get drenched with constant rain, and they cannot persuade
them to move out of the rain and go to their houses, they know that they
would achieve nothing by going out themselves, except to get wet with
them, and so they keep themselves indoors. Since they cannot cure the folly
of others, they are content if at least they are safe themselves.

[51] In *The Republic*, Book III, Socrates advocates a version of communism.
[52] See Matthew 10:27; Luke 12:3.
[53] Yardstick made of lead and thus easily bent out of a straight line.
[54] Roman comic dramatist, second century B.C.   [55] Plato, *Republic*, Book VI.

"Although, my dear More, to speak the truth as it comes to mind, I think that wherever there are private possessions, where everything is measured by money, there a state can scarcely ever be justly and successfully managed—unless you think that is justice where all the best things come to the worst men, or that is success where everything is divided among a very few. Nor are they entirely prosperous, while the others are absolutely wretched.

"So I think over the wise and holy customs of the Utopians, who need so few laws for government so successful that virtue has its reward, and yet with equality of wealth all men have everything in abundance. Then I compare and contrast with their ways so many other nations, always making laws, but none of them all ever well enough governed, in which what each man gets he calls his own private possession. Their countless laws, passed every day, are not enough to help each man to obtain that which everyone calls his own, nor to protect it, nor to distinguish it from another's. This is clearly shown by those innumerable lawsuits which spring up all the time, but never come to an end. When I ponder on all this, I sympathize more with Plato and I am less surprised that he refused to pass any laws for men who refused those by which everyone shared all property equally.[56] For that wise man saw that the one and only path to public safety lay in equality of property. I do not think that this could ever come about where each man has his own possessions. For where each man by fixed titles appropriates as much as he can, a few share out all the wealth and leave poverty for the rest. It usually happens that the one class of men deserves the lot of the other. For the rich are greedy, wicked and useless, while the poor are modest and simple men, and by their daily labor contribute to the public good rather than their own.

"So I am convinced that things cannot be distributed in equity and justice, nor mortals' affairs be managed prosperously, unless private ownership is totally abolished. If it is left, the greatest and best part of mankind will always have the worrying and unavoidable burden of poverty and cares. I admit that this can be somewhat relieved, but maintain that it cannot be eradicated. But suppose that it were decreed that no one should have above a certain amount of land, and that each man could only have so much money. Suppose that laws were passed to prevent excessive power in the king and excessive arrogance in his people; that it were decided that offices should not be canvassed[57] or sold, and that no expense should be necessary for their tenure (otherwise an opportunity is given for repairing losses by trickery and plunder, and it is necessary to put rich men in charge of those posts which rather need the attention of the wise). By such laws, I say, just as desperately sick bodies can be supported by constant medication, so these evils too could be assuaged and lessened. But there is absolutely no hope that they may be cured and restored to a good condition, as long as private property exists. While you attend to the cure of one part, you make the wound in the other parts more inflamed. So from the cure of

[56] Plato refused to make laws for the city of Megalopolis, in southwestern Greece, unless private ownership was given up. The incident is related in Diogenes Laertius' *Lives of the Eminent Philosophers.*
[57] Applied or campaigned for.

the one grows the disease of the other, since nothing can be added to one without being taken from another."

"But," said I, "I am of the opposite opinion, that life can never be comfortable with community of possessions. For how could there be an abundant supply of things, when each man takes himself away from work? For considerations of his own profit do not urge him on, and confidence in another's industry makes him lazy. But when they are goaded by poverty and there is no law for a man to protect what he has gained, then must not constant murder and sedition vex the state? Above all, the authority of magistrates and their respect are abolished. I cannot even imagine what place there could be for such respect in men among whom there is no distinction." "I am not surprised," he said, "that you think this, when you have either no idea of what this would be like, or else a false one. But if you had been in Utopia with me and seen in person their habits and practices, as I did (for I lived there more than five years and would never have wanted to leave except to tell of that new world), then you would openly admit that this was the only place where you had seen a people properly governed."

"And yet," said Peter Giles, "you would have a hard time persuading me that a better governed people could be found in that new world than in this one known to us. For I think there are intellects just as good here and republics older than there, and long experience has discovered us many conveniences for life, not to mention certain chance discoveries of ours which no mind could ever have thought up."

"As far as concerns the oldness of republics," he said, "you could judge better if you had read the histories of that world. If they can be trusted, they had cities before we had men. Now, whatever up till now mind has discovered or chance found, could have come about in either place. But I am sure that although we excel them in brain, yet we are left far behind in enthusiasm and industry. For, as their annals show, before our arrival there, they had never heard anything of us (whom they call the Ultraequinoctials[58]), except that once over twelve hundred years ago a ship was carried by a storm to the island of Utopia and wrecked there. Some Romans and Egyptians were cast up on the shore and stayed there ever after.

"See what use their industry made of this one opportunity. Every art within the Roman empire which could be of any use, they learned from the shipwrecked strangers or discovered from the basis they offered. Such profit did they take from the single arrival of people from our world. But if any like chance brought anyone here from their world long ago, this has been quite blotted out, just as perhaps future generations will forget that I was once there. As they from one encounter immediately made their own all our happiest discoveries, so I think it would be a long time before we adopted any of their better ideas. This I think is the most important reason why their state is governed more wisely and is more prosperous, although we are in no way inferior to them in intellect or wealth."

"So, my dear Raphael," I said, "I beg and beseech you to describe that island to us. Do not try to be brief, but unfold in due order their lands, rivers, cities, men, ways, institutes, laws—everything you think we wish to

---

[58] People from beyond the equator.

know. And you will think we wish to know everything of which we are so
far ignorant." "There is nothing," he said, "I should be gladder to do, for I
have it all ready. But it needs some leisure." "Let us go in then," I said, "to
have lunch. Soon we shall take the time as we please." "Very well," said he.
So we went in and had lunch.

After lunch we came back to the same place, and sat down on the same
seat. The servants were told that no one should interrupt us, and Peter
Giles and I urged Raphael to give us what he had promised. When he saw
that we were anxious and eager to hear, he sat silent for a while, lost in
thought, and then began in the following way.

BOOK TWO

CHAPTER ONE
ON THE COUNTRY AND ITS AGRICULTURE

The island of Utopia extends in the middle, where it is widest, for two
hundred miles.[1] For a great part it is not much narrower, but gradually
narrows at both ends. This makes a circumference of five hundred miles
and gives the whole island the shape of a new moon, whose horns are
separated by about eleven miles of sea. The water opens up to a large width
inside, and as the winds are checked by land on all sides, it is like a big lake,
placid and calm. It makes practically all the bay there one big harbor, which
is very busy and sends ships in all directions. The entrance is made dangerous by shallows and rocks. In about the middle of the gap a single rock
sticks up, but it is not dangerous, as it is visible. They have built a tower on
this to house a garrison. The other rocks are hidden and treacherous. The
channels are known only to the Utopians themselves, and so it is not often
that a stranger makes his way into this bay except with a Utopian pilot. For
even the inhabitants themselves hardly have a safe entrance, except by
marking their passage by certain signs on the shore. By moving these to
different places they could easily lure an enemy fleet to destruction, however numerous it might be. On the other side of the island there are also
many harbors. But everywhere the landing is so well protected, either naturally or artificially, that a few defenders could ward off great hordes.

But, as they tell and as the appearance of the place shows, that land was
once not surrounded by water. It was previously called Abraxa and received its present name from its conqueror, Utopus. It was he who brought
his rough and rude people to that high point of culture and civilization
whereby they now surpass practically all other men. As soon as he landed
and conquered the place, he caused that part where it was joined to the
mainland to be cut through and let the sea around the land. He put to work
on that task not merely the original inhabitants, but so that they should not
take this work as an insult, he also joined to them all his own soldiers. With
the labor divided among so many men, the task was completed with unbe-

---

[1] Utopia is approximately as big as England.

lievable speed. The neighboring people, who at the beginning had laughed at this idle undertaking, were struck with admiration and fear at the success.

The island has fifty-four[2] cities, all of them large and magnificent. Their language, customs, institutions and laws are all the same. The layout of all the cities is the same, and, as far as the terrain allows, their appearance is the same everywhere. A distance of twenty-four miles separates the nearest cities, and none is so remote that a man cannot reach another in one day's journey.

From each city three experienced old men meet every year to discuss the common affairs of the island at Amaurote.[3] This is considered the chief city, as it lies in the center of the island and is convenient for the representatives from all parts. The territories are assigned to the cities in such a way that in no direction does any one of them have less than twenty miles and in some directions they have much more—that is, on the side where cities are separated by a greater distance. No city is anxious to extend its territory. For they think themselves farmers rather than masters of what they have.

In the country throughout their land they have well arranged manors, well provided with farming equipment. The citizens take it in turns to live there. No country household has fewer than forty men and women, as well as two permanent slaves. In charge of all these are a man and wife of mature wisdom. Over each group of thirty households is put one phylarch.[4] From each household twenty return to the city every year after completing two years in the country. In their place are put twenty fresh men from the city, and they are trained by those who have spent a year in the country and are therefore more skilled in farming. They themselves will teach others the following year. This is done in case their inexperience should harm the crops if they were all equally new and ignorant of farming. This practice of renewing the farmers is rigidly observed so that no one should be compelled against his will to endure the harder life any longer. Nevertheless, many who by nature love farming are allowed to stay on there. The farmers till the land, feed the animals, gather wood and transport it to the city by land or sea, whichever is more convenient. They rear a very large number of chicks, by an amazing device. For the hens do not sit on the eggs. Instead they keep a great number of eggs warm with an even heat, and so hatch them. As soon as the chicks come out of the eggs, they follow the men and recognize them as if they were their mothers.

They keep very few horses, and only high-spirited ones. Their purpose is to exercise their young men in riding. For all the work of plowing and carrying is undertaken by oxen. They admit that oxen are inferior to horses in power, but think they excel them in endurance and are liable to fewer diseases. In addition to this, oxen need less expenditure of effort and money for their keep, and finally, when their working days are over, they can be used as food.

They use grain only for bread. For they drink wine, cider or perry,[5] or occasionally pure water, often also water in which they have boiled honey

---

[2] Approximately the number of counties in England.
[3] The name means "dim" (like misty London, which Amaurote resembles in other ways as well).
[4] *Phylarch* means "ruler of a tribe."   [5] Pear cider.

or licorice root, of which they have a large supply. When they have discovered (as they do very accurately) how much food is consumed by each city and the surrounding district, they yet plant a far greater crop and bring up far more cattle than their own needs require, and they share the surplus with their neighbors. They get from the city whatever supplies they need which are not kept in the country, and without any payment they get them from the city magistrates with no trouble at all. For each month several of them go to the city for a festival. When harvest time draws near, the farmers' phylarchs report to the city magistrates how many citizens should be sent to them. This crowd of harvesters, arriving on the appointed day, can finish practically the whole work on one fair day.

CHAPTER TWO
ON THE CITIES, AND ESPECIALLY AMAUROTE

Whoever knows one of their cities knows them all. As far as the nature of the ground allows they are absolutely identical. So I shall describe any one of them to you, as it does not much matter which. Which could be a better example than Amaurote? None deserves this more, as the others acknowledge it as head because of the presence of the Senate there, and none is better known to me, as I lived there for five years without a break.

Well now, Amaurote lies on a gentle slope of hill and is almost square in shape. Its side starts a little below the top of the hill and extends for two miles to the river Anyder.[6] Along the riverbank it is somewhat longer.

The Anyder rises eighty miles above Amaurote from a small spring; but it is increased by the addition of other rivers, two of which are quite sizable, and before it reaches the city itself it is half a mile wide. Soon it becomes even wider and flows on for another sixty miles before entering the ocean. In all this distance that lies between the city and the sea, and also several miles above the city, the water ebbs and flows with a swift tide for six hours at a time. When the sea rushes in for thirty miles, it fills the whole basin of the Anyder with its own water and pushes back the river. And it contaminates the water with brine a little farther than that too; but above this the water bit by bit becomes fresh and when it flows past the city it is pure. When the tide recedes, the river follows it, pure and untainted almost to its very mouth.

The city is joined to the other bank with a bridge made not out of piles and timber, but out of fine stone arches.[7] The bridge is in the part of the city farthest from the sea to allow ships to sail along all that side without any hindrance. They also have another small river, which is very calm and placid. It rises on the same hill the city is on and flows down right through the middle of it until it joins the Anyder. As the source of this stream lies a little outside the city, the Amaurotes have fenced it in and joined it to the city. This is done so that if ever they are attacked by an enemy, their water cannot be diverted or poisoned. The water is led off in brick channels in various directions to the lower parts of the city. If the ground prevents this anywhere, rainwater is collected in large tanks and is just as useful.

[6] *Anyder* means "without water."   [7] Like London Bridge.

A high, thick wall surrounds the city, set with numerous towers and bastions. On three sides a moat surrounds the walls. This is dry, but deep and broad and entangled with briers. On the fourth side the river itself acts as a moat. The streets are well laid out for traffic and also to keep off the winds. The buildings are fine to see, as a long and unbroken row of them can be seen stretching along the whole street with their fronts facing you. These streets are twenty feet wide.[8] At the backs of the houses for the whole length of the streets lie wide gardens, closed in on all sides by the backs of streets. Every house has its own door to the street and also a back door to the garden. These doors are made of two leaves; they need only a slight push to open them, and close automatically. They let anyone enter and nothing is private anywhere. For they even change their houses by lot every ten years.

The gardens are very important to them. In them they have vines, fruits, herbs and flowers, all so neatly and carefully tended that I have never seen anything more prolific or more attractive. They are inspired to take this interest not merely because of the pleasure it gives, but by the rivalry between the streets for the excellence of their gardens. And certainly it would be hard to find anything in the whole city more profitable for the citizens or more pleasurable. It is for this reason that the founder seems to have paid more attention to the establishment of such gardens than to anything else.

For they say that the entire plan of the city right from the beginning was laid out by Utopus himself. But he left it to later generations to embellish and adorn it further, as he realized that this could hardly be done in a single life span. They keep records, written with great care and accuracy, covering the events of the 1,760 years from the conquest of the island. In these it is written that at first their houses were small, like cottages and huts, made out of any wood without discrimination; the walls were smeared with mud and the roofs rose to a ridge and were thatched. But now every house is remarkable for having three stories. The walls are faced with flint or plaster or brick, and are filled up with rubble. The roofs are flat and covered with an inexpensive substance so mixed that it cannot be harmed by fire and it is superior to lead for protection against the weather. They keep the wind out of the windows with glass, as it is quite plentiful there, or occasionally also with fine linen dipped in clear oil or amber. This dipping has two advantages, as by this means it lets in more light and less wind.

CHAPTER THREE
ON THE MAGISTRATES

Every thirty households each year choose a magistrate for themselves, whom in the older language they call a syphogrant[9] and in the more modern a phylarch. Over ten syphogrants and their households there is an officer put in charge, previously called a tranibore, now a protophylarch.

The syphogrants are two hundred in number. They all swear to choose

---

[8] By the standards of More's day, these streets would be grand boulevards.
[9] The meaning is uncertain, as also of *tranibore*.

the man they think most suitable, and with a secret ballot elect a president, one of four previously nominated by the whole people. For one man is chosen from each quarter of the city to be put up for election before the Senate. The President holds his office for life, unless he is suspected of aiming at a dictatorship. They elect tranibores every year, but do not change them very often. All other offices are annual. The tranibores consult with the President every other day, occasionally more often if circumstances demand it. Their consultation is on matters of state and they quickly settle any disputes between private citizens, although these are very few. They always elect two syphogrants to sit with them in the Senate, a different pair each day. It is sanctioned that no legislation affecting the state should be passed unless it has been debated for three days previously in the Senate. To make plans on public affairs outside the Senate or the public elections is an offense punishable by death. The reason for this, they say, is to make it difficult for the President and tranibores to conspire together to oppress the people with a dictatorship and so change the constitution. And so matters considered of great importance are put before the syphogrants for their vote. These report on it to their households, consult among themselves and then report their decision to the Senate. Occasionally a matter is brought before the council of the whole island.

The Senate has the practice of debating nothing on the first day it is proposed to them, but it is put off for a full meeting of their body. This is to prevent someone from babbling the first thing that comes into his head, and then from a perverse and unnatural fear of seeming to have been shortsighted in the beginning, thinking up arguments to defend his plan rather than consulting the interests of the state, ready to damage the public good rather than his own reputation. Such a man ought to have seen to it right from the first that he spoke with more deliberation than haste.

CHAPTER FOUR
ON THE OCCUPATIONS OF THE UTOPIANS

All the men and women have one occupation in common—agriculture, in which everyone is skilled. They are all trained in this from childhood, partly by learning rules in school, and partly from being taken to the countryside near the city as if in play. As well as watching, they use the opportunity for exercise to gain some practical experience.

Besides agriculture (which, as I have said, is shared by all), each man is taught one occupation as his own specialty. This is usually weaving of wool or flax, or the craft of a mason, a smith, an ironworker or a carpenter. Nor is there any other trade there that occupies any number of men worth mentioning. For throughout the island there is only one style of clothing, except that one sex is distinguished from another and unmarried from married people by their dress. This style is retained all through life. It is attractive, allows easy movement and is designed to be equally suitable for cold and hot weather. Each household makes its own clothes. But of those other crafts each person learns one or another, not merely men, but women too. But because of their comparative weakness, the women do lighter tasks. They usually work wool or flax. To the men are assigned the

other, more laborious crafts. A person is generally trained to the craft of
his father, as most men are naturally inclined that way. But if anyone's bent
lies in a different direction, he is adopted into a household concerned with
the craft he wants to practice. His father and the magistrates as well see to
it that the new father he goes to is a worthy and honorable head of a family.
If anyone learns one craft thoroughly and wishes to know another as well,
he is likewise allowed. When he has a command of both, he practices whichever he wishes, unless the state happens to need one more than the other.

It is the chief and almost the only task of the syphogrants to see that no
one is idle, but that everyone diligently sets about his craft, but not like a
beast, worn out by constant toil from early morning until late at night.[10]
For even a slave is not as hard pressed as that. Nevertheless, this is the life
of workmen practically everywhere except in Utopia. The Utopians divide
night and day into twenty-four hours of equal length and assign only six to
work: three before midday, after which they go to lunch; after lunch they
have two hours in the afternoon for rest; after that they work for another
three hours before dinner. Counting their first hour from midday, they go
to bed around eight o'clock. Sleep claims eight hours. They are allowed to
do as they please with the hours in between their work and sleep and meals.
The purpose is not to allow them to waste this free time in wild living or
idleness, but to enable them to apply their minds to whatever useful pursuit
they wish in their free time. Most men devote their intervening hours to
literature. For it is customary to hold public lectures every day before
dawn. Only those are compelled to go who have been chosen by name to
study literature. But a great number of men and women alike, from all
classes, attend the lectures, their choice depending on their natural inclination. If anyone would prefer to spend this time in the practice of his trade
(as happens to many who are not inspired by the thought of learning) he is
not prevented. In fact, he is even praised as being beneficial to the state.

After dinner they devote one hour to games, in the gardens during the
summer, and in the winter in the common halls where they eat. There they
practice music, or refresh themselves with conversation. They do not even
know dice and such foolish and pernicious games. But they play two games
not unlike chess: one is a battle of numbers in which one number makes
booty of another; the second is a game where, in battle array, vices fight
with virtues. In this game a clever demonstration is given of the mutual
discord of vices and their unity against virtues. It is also shown what vices
oppose what virtues, with how much strength they openly assault, the wiles
they use for oblique attack, the defenses virtues use to break the power of
vices, the means they employ to foil their attempts and the ways in which
either side gains victory.

But at this point, to avoid giving you a wrong impression, we must
examine one aspect more closely. For as they spend only six hours in work,
it might be that you think a shortage of supplies must follow. This is quite
the reverse of the truth. In fact, this period of time is enough and more
than enough to provide everything needed to support life or make it more
comfortable. You will easily understand this if you remember how large a

---

[10] In More's time, the law dictated that laborers work from daybreak to dark between
September and March, from about 5 A.M. to 7 or 8 P.M. in spring and summer.

part of the population is idle in other countries. In the first place, there are all the women, a half of the total number; or if women are occupied in business anywhere, the men usually snore in their place. On top of this, there is a large and idle number of priests and religious, as they are called. Add to this all the rich men, especially the owners of estates, who are commonly called gentlemen, and the nobles. Add to these their servants, all that sewage of swashbuckling villains. Then count in the strong and healthy beggars, who use some sickness as a cloak for their laziness. You will certainly find that all these are far more numerous than the men whose labor provides all that human needs require. Of these latter, consider how few are engaged in necessary trades. For where we measure everything by money, many crafts are bound to be practiced which are quite useless and superfluous, merely the servants of luxury and vice. For if this large number now engaged in work were divided up to practice as few crafts as the convenient use of nature requires, then in the great abundance that would necessarily ensue, the prices would be too small to allow the craftsmen to earn a living. But take all those who now waste their time in idle occupations, and also all that mob enjoying the leisure of laziness and sloth, each one of whom consumes as much as two workmen who provide the goods; if they were all put to useful occupations, you can easily see how little time would amply suffice for supplying everything demanded by considerations of necessity or comfort, and of pleasure too if it is real and natural.

This is made clear by the state of affairs in Utopia. For there in the whole city and the surrounding neighborhood, scarcely five hundred persons of all the men and women strong and young enough to work are exempted.[11] Among these are the syphogrants, who are legally released from work; but they do not use this privilege, so that by their example they may more easily attract people to their occupations. The same immunity is enjoyed by those to whom the people, persuaded by the recommendation of the priests and secret election of the syphogrants, give a perpetual release to allow them to devote themselves to learning. If any one of these falls short of the hopes entertained of him, he is thrust back among the workers. Contrariwise, it often happens that a mechanic spends his leisure time in such hard work on literature and makes such progress that he is taken from his trade and promoted to the class of scholars.

From this order are chosen ambassadors, priests, tranibores, and even the President himself, who is called in their old language Barzanes and in the newer one Ademus.[12] Since the remainder of the population is neither idle nor engaged in useless trades, it is easy to estimate how few hours produce so much good work. In addition to what I have said, there is also this advantage: they have to spend less time in the necessary crafts than other people. For in the first place, building or repairing houses requires the constant work of so many men everywhere simply because a spendthrift heir allows the house his father built gradually to crumble. So his successor must at great cost begin all over again what could have been safeguarded for so little. It also often happens that a man fastidiously turns

[11] From figures given in Chapter Five, this works out to fewer than one person in a hundred.

[12] *Barzanes* means "son of Zeus"; *Ademus* means "without people."

his nose up at a house that cost another a great deal. So it is neglected and soon falls down. Then he builds another elsewhere at no less a price. But in Utopia, where everything is in good order and the state well established, it happens only very infrequently that a new site is chosen for building. They quickly repair present faults and also take precautionary measures against those that are likely to arise. So the buildings last for a long time with only a slight expenditure of labor, and workmen in that field occasionally have practically nothing to do—except that they are given timber to cut at home and stones to square and shape in the meanwhile, so that if any work does come it can rise more quickly.

Now see how few workmen they need for their clothing. When they are at work they are carelessly clothed in leather or skins, which will last seven years. When they go out of doors, they put a cloak on top to cover up their simple clothes. Throughout the whole island these cloaks are of the same natural color. So they need much less woolen cloth than is required in other countries and it also costs them much less. But linen is easier to produce and so is used more commonly. But in linen cloth only whiteness is observed, in woolen only cleanliness. No value is put upon a finer thread. Thus, while elsewhere four or five woolen cloaks of different colors are not enough for one man, and as many silk tunics, and for a more fastidious man not even ten are enough, in Utopia each man is content with one and it generally lasts him two years. For there is no reason why he should want more; if he obtained them, he would not be any better protected against the cold, nor would he seem one jot more attractive in his clothing.

So with everyone practicing useful crafts and fewer men needed for each, as there is a great abundance of supplies, occasionally they lead out a huge crowd to repair the public roads if any are worn away. Very often not even such work is required and so they make a public announcement of fewer working hours. For the magistrates do not exercise the citizens against their will in unnecessary work, since the institution of the republic has this one chief aim—that, as far as public necessity allows, all citizens should be given as much time as possible away from bodily service for the freedom and cultivation of the mind. For there, they think, lies happiness in life.

CHAPTER FIVE
ON THEIR LIVES TOGETHER

But now I must explain the interrelationships of the citizens, what mutual intercourse they have and what method there is for dividing everything up. Now, the city is composed of households and generally blood ties make up households. For when the women have matured, they are married and go to live in their husbands' homes. But male children and grandchildren remain in the household and obey the oldest of the parents, unless his mind is feeble from old age. Then the next in age takes his place.

Each city has six thousand such households, not counting the surrounding districts. To prevent the population from decreasing or expanding above the limit, no household is allowed to have fewer than ten or more than sixteen adults. No limit can be put upon the number of children. This number is easily maintained by transferring to smaller households those that are above the limit in larger ones. But if ever the number is exceeded for the whole city, they use the surplus to fill the gaps in their other cities. But if by any chance the numbers swell beyond the limit for the whole island, they choose citizens from any city and with their own laws set up a colony on the nearby mainland, wherever the inhabitants have too much land to cultivate. They take in any of the inhabitants of the country who wish to live with them. Thus joined with men who are willing, they easily merge into the same way of life and the same habits. That is advantageous for both peoples: for by their practices they bring it about that the land which appeared insufficient[13] and niggardly to the others is now more than enough for both. But those who refuse to live by their laws they drive out of the boundaries they mark out for themselves. If they resist, they go to war against them. For they think it the justest reason for war when any nation refuses to others the use and possession of that land which it does not use itself, but owns in idle emptiness, when the others by the law of nature ought to be nourished from it. It is said to have happened only twice ever, from a plague, that some of their cities are so reduced in numbers that they cannot be replenished from other parts of the island if each city is to keep its level. In that case citizens return from a colony to make up the numbers. For they prefer their colonies to die out rather than let any of the cities in the island decrease.

But to come back to the common lives of the citizens, as I said, the oldest member is head of each household. Wives serve their husbands, children their parents, and, in short, the younger serve the elder. Each city is divided into four equal parts. In the middle of each part is a marketplace for everything. There the produce of each household is brought and put in certain buildings. Each different kind of product is put separately into barns. From these each family head seeks what he and his family need, and he carries off whatever he seeks, without any money or exchange of any kind. For why should anything be refused him? There is more than enough of everything and there is no fear that anyone will ask for more than he needs. For why would he be likely to seek too much, when he knows for certain that his needs will always be met? A man is made greedy and grasping either by the fear of need (a fear common to all creatures) or else (in man alone) by pride, which thinks it glorious to surpass others in superfluous show. This kind of vice has no place at all in the ways of the Utopians.

Next to the markets I have mentioned are provision markets, where they bring vegetables, fruits and bread, as well as fish and the animals and birds that can be eaten. These markets are outside the city where the filth and muck can be washed away in the river. From there they bring the animals that have been killed and cleaned by the hands of their slaves. For they do not allow their own citizens to grow accustomed to the slaughter of animals, as they think that constant practice in this gradually destroys the kindness and gentle feeling of our souls. Nor do they allow anything filthy and impure to be brought into the city, whose corruption could pollute the air and carry in some disease.

[13] That is, not productive enough.

Moreover, each street has certain large halls set at an equal distance apart, each one known by a separate name. The syphogrants live in these. Thirty households, fifteen from either side, are assigned to each hall and take their meals there. The caterers of each hall go into the market at a fixed hour and after telling the number of their charges, get the food.

But chief consideration is given to the sick, who are looked after in public hospitals. For they have four hospitals in the range of the city, a little outside the walls. These are so large that they could match as many small towns, and no number of patients, however great, would be cramped for lack of space. They also allow the isolation of patients who are suffering from a contagious disease. These hospitals are so well arranged, and so fully supplied with all things conducive to health, such tender and constant treatment is given, and the best doctors are so constantly in attendance, that while no one is sent there against his will, yet there is practically no one in the whole city who would not prefer to lie there when ill rather than at his own home. When the caterer for the sick has received the food in accordance with the doctor's prescription, then all the best remaining portions are divided equally among the halls, depending on the number in each. The only distinction is that some consideration is given to the President, the Bishop and the tranibores, and also to ambassadors and all foreigners—if there are any, as very rarely happens. These too, if there are any, are provided with certain houses properly equipped.

To these halls at the fixed hours of lunch and dinner come the whole syphograntia, summoned by the sound of a bronze trumpet, except for those who are sick in the hospitals or at home. Yet no one is prevented, after the halls have had enough, from taking food home from the market. For they know that no one does it for no reason. Although there is no rule forbidding eating at home, yet no one does this willingly, since it is not considered honorable, and in any case it is foolish to take the pains to prepare an inferior meal, when a rich and plentiful one is to be had at a nearby hall. In this hall, the slaves do all the tasks that are dirty or burdensome. But the job of cooking and preparing the food and making ready the whole meal is left to the women alone, each household taking its turn. Depending on their number, the people sit at three or more tables. The men are placed near the wall, the women nearer the door, so that if any sudden illness comes upon them (as occasionally happens in pregnancy) they may get up without disturbing the company and find their way to the nurses.

These nurses sit apart with the suckling children in a room set aside especially for that purpose. There is always a fire and clean water and also cradles, so that they can put the children down to rest and, when they wish, take off their swaddling clothes[14] in front of the fire and refresh them with play. Each mother is nurse to her own child, except where death or illness prevents this. When that happens, the wives of the syphogrants quickly find a nurse, and this is not difficult. For the women who can fulfill this function offer themselves to no task more willingly; since everyone praises this act of mercy and the child so brought up regards his nurse as his mother. In the nurses' room sit all the children under five years of age. All

[14] Wrappings for the bodies of infants.

the other children of either sex who are below the age of marriage either serve at table or, if they are too young, stand nearby in absolute silence. Both classes of children eat what is offered to them by those at table, and they have no other set time for eating. The syphogrant and his wife sit in the middle of the first table, as this is the most distinguished place and from it can be seen the whole assembly, since the table runs across the highest part of the dining room. These are joined by two of the eldest present, as they sit four at a table. If there is a church located in that syphograntia, the priest and his wife sit with the syphogrant to preside. On each side sit the younger people and after them the older members, and so on throughout the whole hall. People of the same age sit together, but yet are mixed in with other age groups. They say that the reason for this practice is to allow the dignity and reverence of the old to check the young from unnecessary license in words and actions, since nothing can be done or said at table without being noticed by those nearby in one direction or another. The dishes are not served from the first place on, but first of all the older people, whose places are marked out in some special way, are given the choicest food; then the others are served impartially. If there are not enough tidbits[15] to distribute to the whole company, the older people share theirs at their discretion with those sitting near them. In this way respect for the elderly is preserved and at the same time all have the same advantages.

They begin every lunch and dinner with some reading suitable for forming the character. This is kept short to avoid boredom. Using this as a basis, the old men indulge in moral conversation, which nevertheless is not gloomy or lacking in wit. But they do not occupy the whole meal with lengthy dissertations. Rather, they gladly listen to the younger members also and even deliberately provoke them to speak so that they may discover the nature and mind of each, as these betray themselves in the freedom of the table. Their lunches are rather brief, their dinners more lavish. For lunch is succeeded by work, but dinner by sleep and rest for the night. This, they think, is more conducive to healthy digestion. No dinner passes without music, nor is the second course without its delights. They burn sweet-scented spices and scatter unguents and do everything to make the diners merrier. For they are readily inclined in this direction and think no kind of pleasure forbidden, as long as no inconvenience follows it.

In this way, then, they live together in the city. But in the country, as they are more widely scattered, they all eat in their own homes. For no household lacks for food, as they are the source of supply for the city.

CHAPTER SIX
ON THE TRAVELS OF THE UTOPIANS[16]

But if any of the Utopians wish to see their friends who live in another city, or to visit the place itself, they easily obtain permission from their

---

[15] Delicacies.

[16] Besides travel, this chapter outlines the Utopians' commerce; their moral, religious, and ethical philosophy; and their intellectual zeal.

syphogrants and tranibores, unless some special need keeps them at home. So there is sent with such men a number of people with a letter from the President showing that they have permission to be away and also fixing the day of their return. They are given a wagon with a public servant to drive the oxen and look after them. But if they have no woman in their company, they send the wagon back as a burden and hindrance. For the whole journey they carry nothing with them, yet lack nothing; for everywhere they are at home. If they stay in any place longer than one day, each man practices his craft there and is treated with great kindness by the workers in his craft. If anyone wanders beyond his territory on his own authority, and is caught without written permission from the President, he is treated with much abuse and dragged back as a runaway and punished severely. If he dares to do it a second time, the penalty is slavery.

But if anyone has the urge to wander through the territory of his own city, he is allowed to do so after obtaining the permission of his father and the consent of his wife. But into whatever country district he arrives, he is given no food until he has completed the amount of work normally done there before midday, or dinnertime, as the case may be. With this provision, a man may go wherever he likes within the territory of his own city. For he will be no less useful to the city than if he were actually in it.

Now you see how little freedom they have for being idle. There is no pretext for laziness, no wine taverns, no alehouses, no brothels, no occasion for vice, no lurking places, no secret meetings. Thus, under the watchful eyes of all, they must perform their usual work or enjoy honorable leisure.

As the people have this practice, an abundant supply of all things must inevitably follow. As this is equally distributed among all, no one can be a pauper or a beggar. In the Senate of Amaurote (which, as I have said, three men from each city attend every year), as soon as it is decided what product is in plentiful supply anywhere, or what is not so plentiful elsewhere, then immediately the abundance of one place makes up the need of the other. And this they do free, receiving nothing in exchange for what they give. But if they have given anything from their supplies to a particular city without asking for anything in exchange, they receive whatever they themselves need from another city to which they have given nothing. So the whole island is just like one household.

But after they have made sufficient provision for themselves (and this they do not think achieved until they have provided for two years, in case the next year's crop should be unsatisfactory), then from the surplus they export to other countries a great abundance of grain, honey, wool, timber, scarlet and purple dye, sheepskins, wax, tallow, leather and also animals. They make a gift of a seventh part of all these commodities to the needy in that country. By this trade they import into their own country not merely what they need at home (for that is practically nothing except iron), but also a great abundance of silver and gold. By constantly following this practice, they now have a great surplus of those metals, more than one could believe. And so now they do not care whether they sell for ready cash or on credit, having by far the greatest amount owed to them. In making these loans, they give no credit to private individuals, but rather to whole cities, with the usual documents drawn up. When the day for repayment comes, the other city gathers in the debts of the private debtors and puts the amount into its treasury; it then enjoys the interest on that money until the Utopians ask for it back. For the most part they never ask for it. For they think it unjust to take away, from people who could use it, something for which they themselves have no use. But if circumstances demand that they should lend some part of that money to another country, then they ask for it back, or when they have to wage a war. For this single purpose they keep all the treasure they have at home, to protect them in extreme or sudden danger. They prefer to hire foreign soldiers for a huge wage, as they more willingly expose them to danger than their own citizens. For they realize that their very enemies can usually be bought by a huge sum of money, and either by treachery or civil strife be put in discord among themselves. For this reason they keep a treasury beyond value. Yet they keep it not as a treasury, but in a way I am really ashamed to relate, out of fear that my words will not be believed. My reticence is the more justified, as I realize that if I had not seen it in person, I could only with the greatest difficulty have been persuaded to believe the tale if told by another. For the less a thing fits the hearer's ways, the less credence is it always given. Yet a wise observer will perhaps be less surprised, since their other practices are so far removed from ours, if their use of silver and gold is suited to considerations of their ways rather than ours. For they do not use money, but save it for an eventuality which may or may not happen.

Meanwhile the gold and silver, of which money is made, no one of the Utopians values more than the nature of the things themselves deserves. In this respect, who does not see how vastly inferior they are to iron? Men could no more live without iron than without fire and water, though nature has given no use to gold and silver, which we might not easily go without, if man's folly had not put a price upon scarceness. Quite the reverse is truly the case: like a fond mother, nature has put all the best things in the open, like air, water and the earth itself, but has far removed empty and useless things. So if among the Utopians these metals were hidden away in some tower, the foolish cunning of people might suspect the President and Senate of tricking the people and getting some advantage themselves. Moreover, if they worked them into vessels and suchlike, if ever the occasion arose for melting them down again and paying them out as wages for the soldiers, they see, of course, that people would be very annoyed at being deprived of things they have come to enjoy as luxuries.

To remedy this, they have thought up a plan as harmonious with their other practices as it is remote from ours (as we value gold so highly and store it up so carefully). So only those who have observed it can readily believe it. They eat and drink out of earthenware and glass vessels, most elegant but yet cheap. But out of the gold and silver, not merely in common halls, but in private houses too, they make chamberpots and all the most humble utensils. In addition, from the same metals they fashion the chains and thick fetters with which they confine their slaves. Finally, those in ill repute for some crime have gold rings hanging from their ears, gold rings on their fingers, gold necklaces and gold headbands. So they ensure in every way that in their country gold and silver are in disgrace. So, although other nations feel the removal of these metals as keenly as the removal of their very entrails, yet no one in Utopia would think that he had lost one penny if at any time circumstances demanded them all to be taken away.

They also gather pearls on the shore, and on certain rocks diamonds and carbuncles. They do not go looking for them, but if they happen to chance upon them they polish them up. With these they adorn their young children. Although in early childhood they glory and delight in such ornaments, yet when they have grown a little older, without any warning from their parents, they observe that only children use such trifles, and then they put them aside in shame. This is exactly like our children, who, when they grow up, throw away their nuts, brooches and dolls. These ways are so very different from other nations', but how different are the mental attitudes they produce, I never realized better than in the case of the ambassadors of the Anemolians.[17]

These men came to Amaurote while I was there, and since they were coming to discuss important matters, those three citizens from each city had come before their arrival. All ambassadors from neighboring countries were in the habit of coming in the plainest possible clothing, since they had been there before and knew the character of the Utopians, and understood that they paid no honor to sumptuous raiment, despised silk and even rejected gold. But the Anemolians lived farther away and had had less intercourse with them. Upon hearing that all Utopians used the same rough kind of dress, they inferred that they just did not have what they did not use. So, with more pride than wisdom, they decided to deck themselves like gods in the elegance of their equipment, and to dazzle the eyes of the poor Utopians with the glitter of their finery. And so the three ambassadors made their entrance, with a hundred attendants, all in multicolored clothing, mostly of silk. The ambassadors themselves, being nobles at home, had gold clothes, huge necklaces and gold earrings, as well as gold rings on their hands and chains hanging from their hats, which sparkled with pearls and gems. In short, they were arrayed with all the things that in Utopia were the punishment of slaves, or the shame of people in disgrace, or the playthings of children. So it was worthwhile seeing how they preened themselves when they compared their ornaments with the Utopians' clothes. (For the people had poured out into the streets.) On the other hand, it was just as delightful to observe how wrong they had been in their hopes and expectations, and how far they were from producing the impression they had imagined. For all the splendor of their equipment seemed shameful to the eyes of all the Utopians, except a very few who had visited other countries for some worthy reason. They greeted the humblest members with reverence as if they were the masters, and considering the ambassadors themselves as slaves, because of their use of golden chains, passed them by with absolutely no mark of respect. You ought to have seen the children too! Those that had thrown away their gems and pearls, when they saw them on the ambassadors' hats, nudged their mothers and shouted to them, "Look, Mother! See that big booby still using his pearls and gems, just like a little boy!" But the mother, still taking it seriously, replied, "Hush, my son! He's one of the ambassadors' fools, I think." Others criticized those golden chains as being useless; for they were so thin that a slave could easily break them, yet so loose that he could shake them

---

[17] The name means "windy people."

off whenever he wished to run away wherever he wanted, free and unfettered.

The ambassadors stayed there one or two days and observed that so much gold was thought so little of, and saw that it was despised there as much as it was honored in their own country. When they also learned that the chains and fetters of a single runaway slave took more gold and silver than all the trappings of the three of them, their feathers drooped and in shame they laid aside all that finery of which they had been so arrogantly proud. This came about especially after they had spoken more freely with the Utopians and learned their ways and opinions. For they are amazed that any man can be pleased with the feeble glow of a little gem or stone, when he can gaze at a star and the very sun itself; or that anyone is so crazy as to think himself more distinguished because of a thread of finer wool; for however fine a thread it may be, a sheep once wore it, and all the time it was nothing more than a sheep.

They are also amazed that gold, of its own nature so useless, is now everywhere so highly valued that man himself, through whom and for whose use it gained its worth, is valued much less than gold itself. This is so much so that some blockhead, with no more sense than a lump of wood and just as wicked as he is foolish, yet keeps many wise and good men in slavery, merely because he has a great pile of gold coins. If some chance or legal twist (which, no less than chance, exchanges high with low) transfers it from that master to the lowest wretch of all his household, soon he passes into the service of his servant, like an addition and tailpiece to his money. But much more are they amazed at and loathe the madness of men who pay practically divine honors to the rich, when they owe nothing to them, nor are they under any obligation to them, from no other consideration except their wealth; they do this even though they realize full well that they are so mean and greedy that, as long as the owners are alive, never will a penny come to them from such a huge pile of money.

They have formed these and similar opinions partly from their training, being brought up in a republic whose practices are very far removed from these kinds of stupidity, and partly from learning and literature. For although there are not many in each city who are exempt from other labors and are given over solely to learning (those, that is, in whom from childhood they have noticed an excellent character, an outstanding intellect and an inclination to good arts), yet all children are given a taste of literature; and a good part of the population, both men and women, throughout their lives spend those leisure hours we have mentioned in literature. They receive their learning in their own language. For it has a rich vocabulary, a pleasant sound and is an unsurpassed vehicle for expressing feelings. Practically the same language is current for a great area of that part of the world, except that it loses its purity outside Utopia in various ways.

Of all those philosophers whose names are so famous in the world known to us, not even a rumor had reached Utopia before our arrival. Yet in music and dialectic,[18] in arithmetic and geometry, their ancient philosophers made practically the same discoveries as ours. But although they

---

[18] Logic.

match our ancients in almost everything, yet they are far behind the discoveries of our modern dialecticians.[19] For they have not discovered a single one of those rules which children learn everywhere in our world, about restrictions, amplifications and suppositions, all thought out with great acuteness in the handbooks on logic. Moreover, so far are they from finding "second intentions,"[20] that none of them could see Man Himself in the abstract,[21] as they call it, although (as you know) he is absolutely colossal and bigger than any giant, and although at that time we pointed to him with our fingers. But they are very learned in the course of the stars and the motions of the heavenly spheres. They have even skillfully devised instruments of various shapes in which they contain very precisely the movements and positions of the sun and moon and the other stars which appear on their horizon. But they do not even dream of the "friendships" and "dissensions" of the planets and all that fraud of divination from the stars.[22] They use certain signs seen long beforehand to forecast the rains, winds and other changes of the weather. But about the causes of all these things, and the tides and saltiness of the sea, and in general the origin and nature of the heavens and the earth, they partly put forward the same opinions as our old philosophers; partly also, as ours disagree among themselves, so they have different opinions from all of them, while they bring forward new explanations for things; nor yet do they agree everywhere among themselves.

In moral philosophy their discussions are the same as ours. They investigate the goods of the spirit and the body, and those of fortune; then whether the name "good" suits all these, or only those of the spirit. They discuss virtue and pleasure; but the first and foremost point of dispute is whether they think man's happiness lies in one thing or more. But on this point they seem to favor too much the side supporting pleasure, since by this they define the whole or the greatest part of human happiness. And what is more surprising, they seek support for so pleasure-loving an opinion from religion, despite its harsh, severe, sad and rigid nature. For they never discuss happiness without joining to rational philosophy some principles taken from religion. Without these principles, they think that reason in itself is maimed and weak for the investigation of true happiness. Their principles are such as these: the soul is immortal and by the kindness of God born to happiness; for our virtues and good deeds, rewards are appointed after this life, and for our sins, punishments. Although these tenets belong to religion, yet they think that men are led to believe and accept them by reason. If they are abolished, they claim without any hesitation that no one is so stupid as not to feel that he ought to seek pleasure by right or wrong means. This merely would he watch, that a lesser pleasure should not stand in the way of a greater, or that he should not follow a pleasure

[19] The medieval scholastic thinkers, who were frequently ridiculed by Renaissance humanists for alleged over-subtlety.

[20] First intentions are the mind's direct apprehension of things; second intentions are notions derived from the mind's further reflection on the things.

[21] More refers to the great medieval debate between the "nominalists," who believed that such universals as "mankind" (as distinguished from individual men) were mere names, and the "realists," who believed that the universals were real.

[22] Astrology, ridiculed here, was still intellectually respectable in More's time.

which would be rewarded by pain. For they consider it sheer madness to pursue harsh and difficult virtue, and not merely to renounce a pleasant life but even willingly to endure pain, from which you might expect no profit. For what profit can there be if you gain nothing after death when you have passed the whole of this life unpleasantly, that is to say, miserably. But actually they do not think that happiness lies in all pleasure, but only in that which is good and honorable. For to this, as if to the highest good, our nature is drawn by virtue itself, to which alone those of the opposite belief attribute happiness. For they define virtue as "living in accordance with nature," since for that purpose were we created by God. Whoever obeys reason in desiring and avoiding anything is following the lead of nature. Moreover, reason primarily inflames men to the love and veneration of the divine majesty to whom we owe our existence and the possibility of attaining happiness. Secondly, it advises and urges us to lead a life with the least worry and the greatest joy, and also, in accordance with the kinship of nature, to offer ourselves as helpers to all others to attain that same end. For never has there been anyone so stern and severe a follower of virtue and hater of pleasure, a man to enjoin labors, vigils and penance upon you, who did not at the same time bid you exert all your efforts toward lightening the need and discomfort of others and who did not judge that in the name of humanity what is most deserving of praise is that a man should save and console another. For it is a most humane virtue, and none is more appropriate for a man than to lessen the misery of others, remove the anguish of their lives and restore them to joy, in other words, to pleasure. Why then should not nature urge a man to do the same for himself?

For there are two possibilities: either a life of joy, that is to say, pleasure, is evil, in which case you ought not to help anyone toward it, but rather deprive all men of it as far as you can, because of its harmful and deadly quality; or else, if you are not merely allowed but even commanded to win it for others as being something good, why can you not do this for yourself above all others? For it is only right to be as kind to yourself as to others. For when nature encourages you to be good to others, she does not then order you to be cruel and harsh to yourself. So, they say, the life of joy, that is, of pleasure, is prescribed to us by nature herself as the end of all our activities. They define virtue as living according to nature's prescription. But when nature encourages mankind to help one another to a happier life (and this she does with good reason; for no one is so far above the lot of the human race as to be nature's sole concern; for she looks after all men alike, whom she embraces with the common bond of similar appearance), you can be sure that she repeatedly exhorts you to see to it that you do not follow your own advantages to the extent of producing disadvantages for others.

Therefore they think that not only private agreements should be observed, but also public laws. For either a good president justly enacted them, or else the people as a whole, not being oppressed by a tyrant or ensnared by guile, sanctioned them by common agreement for sharing the advantages of life, that is to say, the material of pleasure. Provided that you do not violate these laws, it is a mark of wisdom to procure your own advantage, just as it is a mark of natural affection to procure that of the state as a whole. But to deprive another of his pleasure while you achieve your own—this is injustice. On the other hand, to deprive yourself of something to give it to others is a task of humanity and kindness; this never removes as much advantage as it restores. For it is compensated by the return of benefits, and also the very consciousness of having done a kindness, and the remembrance of the affection and good will of those to whom you have been kind, bring on pleasure to the mind much greater than the bodily pleasure would have been from which you abstained. Finally, as religion is easily able to persuade a mind which readily agrees, in the place of a brief and small pleasure God repays us with a great joy which will never die. Therefore in this way, after carefully examining and considering the matter, they think that all our actions, and among them the virtues themselves, look toward pleasure as their final state and happiness.

By "pleasure" they mean every motion and state of the body or mind in which, with nature's guidance, it is pleasant to be. To this they add, with good reason, the appetite of nature. For not merely the senses, but correct reason also follows whatever is pleasant by nature, provided that the way to it does not involve injustice, the loss of a greater pleasure, or hard work as an inevitable consequence. But what men contrary to nature imagine by idle agreement to be pleasant for them, as if it were in their power to change things just as they do their names—all these things the Utopians decree are of no use for the attainment of happiness. Instead, these practices even hinder it greatly, if it is only because when once they have settled in a man, they seize on all his mind with a false belief about pleasure and bring it about that there is no room anywhere for true and genuine delights. For there are many things which of their own nature contain no sweetness, and even on the whole a large share of bitterness; but by the perverse enticement of evil desires, they are not merely considered as the highest pleasures, but even counted among the chief reasons for life.

In this kind of spurious pleasure they include those people I mentioned before, who think themselves the better for wearing better clothes. On this point they are twice wrong. For they are just as mistaken in thinking their clothing better as they are in thinking this of themselves. For if you regard the use of a garment, why should finer wool be better than coarser? But yet those men, as if their superiority lay in their nature not their error, preen themselves and think that their value is increased in this way. And so, as if by right, they demand for their finer clothes a respect that they would not have dared hope for in cheaper attire, and if they are passed by and neglected they feel outraged.

But is it not part of the same ignorance to enjoy empty and useless honors? For what natural and true pleasure is brought by another's bared head or bent knees? Will this heal the pain in your own knees, or the frenzy in your own head? In this image of counterfeit pleasure, men enjoy sweet madness who flatter and applaud themselves in their belief in their nobility; for they happened to be born of ancestors whose wealth, above all in land, goes back many generations (for nobility is nothing else these days). They think themselves not in the slightest degree less noble even if their ancestors left them nothing of it at all, or if they themselves squandered what was left to them.

In this number they also include those who, as I said, are delighted with gems and precious stones, and who think that somehow they have become gods if they obtain an especially fine one, above all, one of the kind most highly valued by their own people at that particular time. For the same kinds of stones are not considered valuable by all people, nor at all times. But they buy them only if they are removed from their gold setting and displayed all alone. In fact, they will not buy them even under these circumstances unless the seller takes an oath and gives them a guarantee that the gem or stone is genuine; so careful are they that a counterfeit stone should not deceive their eyes into judging it real. But as far as sight is concerned, why should a fabricated stone give less pleasure when your eye cannot distinguish it from a real one? Each ought to have the same value for you as it does for a blind man. What of those people who guard excessive riches, not to get any advantage from the pile but merely to gaze at it? Do they get true pleasure, or are they not rather deceived by a false pleasure? Or what of those who, by an opposite failing, hide away gold that they will never use and perhaps not even see any more, and who, in their concern not to lose it, do in fact lose it? For what else is it when you return to the earth something that you have removed from your own use and perhaps that of all men too? And yet when you have hidden your treasure away, as if you were now free of all care, you jump for joy. Suppose someone stole it and you died ten years later in complete ignorance of the theft. During all those ten years of your life when the money was gone, what did it matter to you whether the money was stolen or still safe? You can be quite sure that in either way you got the same profit from it.

To these foolish pleasures they join those of gamblers (whose madness they know by hearsay, not experience) and hunters and hawkers. For, they say, what pleasure does it bring to throw the dice on the board, when you have done it so often that if there were any pleasure in it, you would have become bored with the constant experience? Or what pleasure can there be, rather than disgust, in hearing the barking and howling of dogs? Or what greater experience of pleasure is there when a dog chases a hare than when a dog chases a dog? For it is the same action in each case. For if running pleases you, there is running involved. But if you are held by the hope of slaughter and the expectation of seeing something torn to pieces before your eyes, it ought rather to move you to pity to see a little hare so weak, shy and harmless torn apart by a powerful, fierce and cruel dog. So the Utopians delegate this practice of hunting, as something unworthy of free men, to butchers (which trade, as I have said above, is carried on by slaves). For they think that hunting is the lowest part of that trade, while its other parts are both more useful and more honorable, since they produce much more advantage and kill animals merely out of necessity; while the hunter seeks nothing but pleasure from the slaughter and dismembering of a poor little animal. They think that this delight in seeing death arises in beasts too, either from an innate spirit of cruelty or else because the constant experience of so savage a pleasure turns into cruelty. Therefore they unambiguously decide that although the common crowd of men considers them pleasures, these and innumerable such-like practices have nothing to do with real pleasure, as there is nothing in them sweet by nature. For they are not moved from this opinion even though these practices stir the senses with delight and this appears to be the function of pleasure. The reason is not the inherent nature of the experience, but the corrupt habit of the men involved. From this fault they welcome the bitter for the sweet, just as pregnant women have a distorted sense of taste and think pitch and tallow sweeter than honey. Yet no man's judgment, corrupted by disease or habit, can change the nature of pleasure, any more than it can change that of anything else.

They make various divisions in the pleasures they call true. For they assign some to the mind and others to the body. To the mind they give intelligence and that joy which the contemplation of the truth produces. To this they add the sweet recollection of a life well led and the certain hope of future good. The pleasures of the body they divide into two categories. The first is that which affects the senses with a clear delight. This sometimes comes about by the renewal of those parts which our natural heat has dried up. For these are restored by food and drink. At other times it happens when those things are expelled of which our body has too great an abundance. This pleasure is produced when we empty our bowels, or have sexual intercourse, or else by rubbing or scratching relieve an itching in any part. But occasionally a pleasure arises that is not going to restore anything our limbs lack or remove anything they have in excess; yet it tickles, affects and attracts our sense with a clear feeling by some secret force—for example, the pleasure of music.

The second kind of bodily pleasure that they define is that which consists of a calm and balanced bodily condition; that is, each man's own bodily health interrupted by no ill. For if no pain assaults it, this state of health is delightful in itself, even if it is stirred by no external pleasure. For although it is less obvious and less clearly perceptible than the swelling desire of eating and drinking, yet nonetheless many men think this the greatest of pleasures. Almost all the Utopians claim that it is a great pleasure, the foundation and basis of all others; for even alone it can produce a calm and delightful state of life, but if it is removed there is no place left anywhere for any pleasure. For merely to be without pain they call insensibility, not pleasure, unless there is also present a state of health. The Utopians have long since rejected the opinion of those who thought that a stable and tranquil state of health (a question hotly debated among them) ought not to be considered a pleasure because its presence could not be felt except by some opposite emotion. But now they practically all agree on the opposite opinion that health must be considered a very special pleasure. For, they argue, since in sickness there is pain, the implacable enemy of pleasure, just as sickness is of health, why then should there not be pleasure in the placid state of good health? They do not think the question is affected if you say sickness *is* pain, or sickness *contains* pain. For the same effect is produced in either case. If health is a pleasure in itself, or if it necessarily produces pleasure (just as heat is produced by fire), then in either case a man who has constant good health must also have pleasure. Moreover, they say, when we eat, all that is happening is that health, which had begun to be impaired, is using food as an ally to fight against hunger. While health is gradually growing stronger, that very advance to its customary strength produces the pleasure, by which we are refreshed. So if health rejoices in the battle, will it not also be happy when it gains the victory? When it has at last successfully gained its former vigor (its only aim in the whole conflict), will it straightway become stupid, and not recognize and embrace its own goods? For they think the opinion that good health is not felt to be far from the truth. For, they argue, who when awake does not feel that he is healthy, except the man who is not? Who is afflicted by such stupor or lethargy as to say that health is not pleasant and delightful? But what is delight except pleasure under another name?

Therefore[23] they embrace chiefly the pleasures of the mind, thinking them the most important of all. They say that the most special part of them comes from the practice of the virtues and the realization of living a good life. Of the bodily pleasures they give first place to health. For they think that the joy of eating and drink, and whatever produces the same kind of delight, ought to be sought, but only for the sake of health. For such things are not pleasant in themselves, but only insofar as they oppose the stealthy attack of sickness. So just as the wise man avoids illness instead of hoping for medicine, and vanquishes pains instead of looking for consolations, so it will be better for him not to need this kind of pleasure instead of feeling its gratification. If anyone thinks himself blessed because of this kind of pleasure, then he must admit that he would be most fortunate if he spent his life in perpetual hunger, thirst, itching, eating, drinking, scratching and rubbing. Who does not see how disgusting and even how wretched such a life would be? Surely these are the lowest of all pleasures, just as they are the least pure. For they are never present unless joined to the opposite pains. For with the pleasure of eating is joined hunger, and by a very unequal law too. For the pain is more intense, as well as more enduring, since it is produced before the pleasure and is extinguished only when the pleasure dies too.

So they think that pleasures of this kind ought not to be highly valued, except insofar as they are necessary. But they do delight in these pleasures and gratefully recognize the kindness of fond mother nature, who uses the most alluring sweetness to entice her children to what must of necessity be done so often. For how miserable life would be if we had to drive away these daily illnesses of hunger and thirst with bitter drugs, like other sicknesses that attack us more rarely! But they gladly take care of their appearance, their strength and their suppleness as being the special delightful gifts of nature. They also pursue, as the delightful seasoning of life, those pleasures that come through the ears, eyes, and nostrils, which nature intended to be peculiar to man. For there is no other kind of animal that looks up to the beautiful appearance of the world, or is stirred by any sweetness of smell, except for choosing food, or is able to distinguish consonant or dissonant chords in music. But in all pleasures the Utopians have this reservation: that a lesser pleasure should not get in the way of a greater, and that a pleasure should not eventually produce pain. This they think necessarily ensues if it is not a worthy pleasure. But to despise physical beauty, to wear away one's strength, to turn nimbleness to sloth, to waste the body with fasting, to injure one's health and reject the other delights of nature (except if a man ignores his own advantage, while eagerly winning that of others or of the whole state, since in return for this toil he expects a greater pleasure from God), to punish oneself for the empty shadow of virtue, to no one's advantage, or to strive after greater fortitude for an

---

[23] That is, "to sum up."

adversity that may never come—all this they think is absolutely insane. It is the action of a mind at once cruel to itself and ungrateful to nature, all of whose kindness they reject, as if they scorned to owe her anything.

This is their opinion on virtue and pleasure. They think that human reason can find none truer, unless revealed religion inspires man with something more holy. Our time does not allow us to discuss whether they are right or wrong in this opinion, nor is it necessary to do so. For I have promised to tell you of their practices, not defend them.

But I am quite sure that whatever may be the status of their decisions, there is nowhere a more distinguished nation, nor a more prosperous republic. They are quick and nimble in body, with more strength than their height would suggest. Not that they are short. And although their soil is not fertile everywhere, nor their climate perfectly healthful, yet they so protect themselves against the weather by temperance in living, and make up the deficiencies of the soil by hard work so successfully, that nowhere in the world is there a greater production of grain and cattle, nowhere are men's bodies more lively and liable to fewer diseases. Of course, you can see them carefully attending to matters that farmers look after everywhere, so that by skill and hard work they can improve soil none too rich by nature. But you will also see the people pull up whole woods by the roots and transplant them elsewhere. In this they aim not to increase the production, but to make transportation easier, so that they can have timber nearer the sea, or the rivers, or the cities themselves. For it is less laborious to transport grain far over land than timber. The people are affable, witty, clever; they enjoy their leisure, but (when necessary) can endure physical labor well enough—although they do not go out of their way to look for it; they never tire of mental study.

When they heard from us about Greek literature and learning (for we did not think they would like much in Latin except the historians and poets), they were very anxious that we should explain and teach it all to them. So we began to lecture to them, at first more to show willingness than because we expected any profit would come of it. But when we had made some progress, their industry immediately made us realize that our efforts were not being wasted. For they began to imitate the Greek letters so easily, to pronounce the words so accurately, to commit things to memory so quickly and repeat them so exactly, that we were astounded, although most of them came from the company of the scholars, men of chosen intelligence and mature years, who were not merely fired with their own enthusiasm, but were also ordered by a decree of the Senate. So in less than three years there was nothing in Greek for them to learn. They were able to read the good authors without any stumbling (except where the text was faulty).[24]

In my opinion, they absorbed that literature all the more easily because, in a way, it was not alien to them. For I suspect that the Utopians have their origins in Greece, since their language, in other respects much like Persian, retains some traces of Greek in the names of their cities and magistrates. When I was planning my fourth voyage, I put on board ship a fair supply of books as cargo, since I had decided to stay a long while. Of these I gave

[24] To establish the best texts of the ancient classics was a prime endeavor of the humanists.

to the Utopians several works of Plato and more of Aristotle; also Theophrastus' work *On Plants*, but, I am sorry to say, this was imperfect in many passages. For while we were sailing, I did not take enough care of this book and a monkey found it. In his play and frolicking he tore out several pages from different sections and ripped them up. Of the writers of grammar they have only Lascaris; for I did not bring Theodorus with me, nor any dictionary except Hesychius and Dioscorides. They are very fond of the works of Plutarch, and are also delighted with the wit and grace of Lucian. Of the poets they have Aristophanes, Homer and Euripides, as well as Sophocles in the small Aldine[25] edition; of the historians Thucydides and Herodotus, together with Herodian. On medicine, too, my companion Tricius Apinatus[26] had brought with him some minor works of Hippocrates, and Galen's *Microtechne*, which books they value very highly. For although they need medicine least of all people, yet nowhere is it more honored, since they count knowledge of medicine among the most beautiful and useful parts of philosophy. When by the help of this philosophy they search out the secrets of nature, they think that, besides gaining a wonderful pleasure from it, they also obtain the highest favor with its Author and Designer. They think that like other designers he has exposed the workings of this world to the sight of man (whom alone He created with ability to understand it), and therefore He is all the fonder of a careful and exact investigator and admirer of His work, than of a man who, like an animal without any mind, ignores so great and wonderful a sight, remaining dull and unmoved.

So from their reading the Utopians are amazingly clever at discovering devices to help make life more comfortable. But they owe two such pieces of knowledge to us, namely printing and papermaking. Yet their debt is not merely to us, but also to themselves to a large extent. For when we were showing them the printing of Aldus in paper books, and telling them about the material used in making paper and about the art of printing, just talking rather than explaining clearly (as none of us had precise knowledge of either process), yet they immediately worked it all out on their own with great skill. Although they previously wrote only on skin, bark or papyrus, now they immediately tried to make paper and print. At first they did not get very far, but by constantly experimenting they soon mastered both. They made so much progress that, if they had the manuscripts of Greek books, they would not lack for printed copies. But as it is, they have only what I have told you about. But what they have, they have printed and multiplied into many thousand copies.

If anyone visits their country who is commended by some great intellectual gift or a knowledge of many lands from constant travel (which is why our landing pleased them so much), he is welcomed with open arms. For they are glad to hear what is done in every land. But only rarely do people go there for trade. For what would they bring? Only iron, or gold and silver, and then everyone would rather carry this away with him. As for their own exports, the Utopians think it better to transport them them-

[25] The Aldine Press in Venice, founded in the late fifteenth century by Aldus Manutius, pioneered the printing of ancient Greek literature and was a center of Greek scholarship.
[26] An invented name (based on the names of two small towns in southern Italy), suggesting insignificance.

selves rather than have others come to fetch them. In this way they can examine different people more carefully and not lose their experience and skill on the sea.

CHAPTER SEVEN
ON SLAVES[27]

For slaves they do not have men captured in war (unless they fought the war themselves), nor the children of slaves, nor anyone who could be bought as a slave in another country. Instead they have any of their own citizens who have been reduced to slavery for some offense, or the inhabitants of foreign cities who have been condemned to death for some crime they have committed. This latter class is by far the more common. For they take away many of these, sometimes for a small price, more often for nothing, just by asking for them. They keep this kind of slave not merely in constant labor, but also in chains. Their own people they treat more severely: they think they are the more hopeless and deserving of the harsher punishment, because after such an excellent training to virtue they still could not be restrained from crime.

There is another class of slaves, composed of poor overworked drudges from another country, who have deliberately chosen to be slaves in Utopia. These are decently treated, and handled with not much less kindness than Utopians, except that they have a little more work imposed on them as they are used to it. It does not often happen that one wishes to leave, but if he does, they do not hold him against his will, nor do they send him away empty-handed.

As I have said, they treat the sick with great kindness and leave nothing undone to restore their health, whether it is by drugs or by dieting. If anyone is suffering from an incurable disease, they console him by sitting with him, talking to him and supplying all the comforts they can. But if a disease is not merely beyond treatment, but also a constant source of pain and agony, the priests and magistrates remind him that he is not up to all the tasks of life, is troublesome to others and a burden to himself, and is now outliving his own death. Then they advise him not to resolve to feed that pestilence and sickness any longer, nor to hesitate to die, since life is a torment to him. They bid him to take good hope and release himself from that bitter life, as if from a prison or torture rack, or at least give his permission for others to remove him. They tell him that since he is going to put an end not to pleasure but to punishment, he would be well advised to do it; and since in that matter he is going to take the advice of priests, the interpreters of God, his action will also be pious and holy. Those who are persuaded by this either end their own lives by abstinence from food, or else are released from it while they are asleep, without any sensation of death. But they never remove anyone against his will, nor are they any the less considerate to him. It is considered honorable to yield to persuasion and die like this. But they think a man unworthy of burial or cremation who

---

[27] Besides slavery (more exactly, servitude), this chapter treats of euthanasia, marriage, penal law, and foreign relations.

commits suicide without having a reason approved of by the priests and Senate. Instead, in great disgrace, he is flung unburied into some bog.

A woman does not marry before she is eighteen years old, and a man not until he is four years older than that. If a man or woman is found guilty of secret lust before marriage, the offender is severely punished and both are forbidden to marry forever, unless the President pardons them and forgives their offense. But also the head of the household and his wife in whose home the shameful act was committed are held in great disgrace, on the grounds that they were remiss in their duty. The reason for the severe punishment of this crime is the realization that very few people would join in married love, in which they saw they had to spend all their lives with one person and endure all the consequent inconvenience, if they were not carefully restrained from random sexual relations.

Moreover, in choosing partners, they seriously and rigidly observe a ritual that to us seemed quite absurd and ridiculous. A respectable and honored matron shows the woman (whether she is a maiden or a widow) to her suitor in complete nakedness. And in turn some trustworthy man shows the suitor naked to the girl. When we were laughing at this custom as being a silly one and were finding fault with it, the Utopians expressed their surprise at the amazing stupidity of all other nations. For, they said, in a matter involving a trifling sum of money, like buying a horse, other people are so careful that they refuse to buy the horse, however uncovered he may be, if the saddle and harness are not taken off, in case there is a sore hidden under those coverings. But in choosing a wife (a matter which will bring pleasure or revulsion for the rest of one's life) they are so careless that, while the rest of her body is concealed by clothes, they judge the whole woman from a space of a few inches (for only her face is visible) and then marry her—not without a great danger of a bad match if anything offends their taste afterward. For not all men are wise enough to regard character only, and in the marriages of such wise men bodily endowments make a useful addition to the spiritual virtues. Naturally so foul a deformity can lie concealed under those clothes that it can quite alienate the mind from one's wife, when it is no longer possible he be bodily separated from her. If such a deformity should happen to come about after marriage, then each man must bear his lot. But there ought to be legal provision to prevent anyone from being caught by such guile before marriage. The Utopians had to be all the more cautious on this, as they are the only people in that world who are content with one wife, and marriage is not often dissolved for them except by death, unless the reason is adultery or some unendurable fault of character. If either husband or wife is afflicted in this way, the Senate gives permission to him or her to find another partner. The other partner forever lives a single life, in disgrace. But they in no way tolerate a man to divorce his wife, if she is blameless, just because some physical misfortune strikes her. For they think it cruel to abandon anyone in his hour of greater need, and believe that it will also breed great distrust in old age, which both brings sickness and is a sickness itself. But it sometimes happens that the characters of husband and wife are quite irreconcilable, and they both discover others with whom they hope they can live more pleasantly. So they separate by mutual consent and contract new marriages. But this cannot be done without the permission of the Senate, which allows divorces only after its members and their wives have carefully examined the case. It is not easy even then, as they know that a ready hope of new marriage is most disadvantageous for strengthening the love of husband and wife.

Adulterers are punished with the severest slavery. If both offenders were married, the injured parties, if they wish, may gain a divorce and marry each other. Otherwise they may marry anyone they want. But if the injured party remains in love with so ill-deserving a partner, he is not forbidden to enjoy his right of marriage, as long as he is willing to follow the convicted partner in his hard labor. It sometimes happens that the repentance of the one and the constant kindness of the other move the President to compassion and gain them freedom once more. But if such a person falls back into his criminal ways, he is put to death.

For other crimes there is no fixed punishment regulated by any law, but the Senate judges the severity or mildness of the offense and decides upon an appropriate punishment. Husbands chastise their wives and parents their children, unless they have committed so terrible a crime that its public punishment is beneficial to morality. But usually the most serious crimes are punished with slavery. For they think this just as unpleasant for the criminals and more profitable for the state than if they hurried to execute the guilty and do away with them immediately. For their work brings more profit than their death, and by their example they can deter others from similar offenses for a longer time. But if in this treatment they rebel and fight against authority, then they are slaughtered like wild beasts that no prison or chain can confine. Yet if they are patient, not absolutely all hope is taken away. If after being subdued by long misfortune they clearly show enough repentance to demonstrate that their sin is more displeasing to them than their punishment, then sometimes by the President's prerogative, sometimes by the vote of the people, their slavery is mitigated or altogether remitted. To have tried to commit adultery is no less dangerous than to have succeeded. For in the case of every crime, they judge a fixed and clearly aimed attempt to be the equivalent of the deed itself. Nor do they think it ought to be in his favor that he did not go all the way, since it was not his doing that he failed.

They take great delight in fools. Although it is considered shameful to do them any harm, yet it is permissible to get pleasure from their foolishness. For they think that this is very good for the fools themselves. If anyone is so stern and severe that he cannot laugh at any word or action of theirs, to his safekeeping they refuse to entrust a fool. For they are afraid that a man who finds no use and no amusement in a fool (and this is a fool's only advantage) will not look after him with sufficient kindness.

To mock a man who is deformed or crippled is considered disgusting and disgraceful, not to the man mocked, but to the mocker. For he stupidly reproaches as a failing something that the man could not possibly avoid. They think a person lazy and slothful who does not look after his natural beauty; but with them it is a disgraceful arrogance to seek help from paint. For they know by experience how little husbands are attracted by their wives' beauty as compared with integrity and humility of character. For although some men are won by physical beauty alone, no one's affection is kept except by virtue and obedience.

They do not merely deter people from crimes by punishment; they also set up rewards to incite them to virtue. And so they put up statues in the marketplace to distinguished men and those who have been great benefactors to the state. This is done as a memorial to their benefactions, and also so that the glory of their ancestors may serve their descendants as a spur and incitement to virtue. Anyone who canvasses for an office is debarred from all promotion. They live together in love, as no magistrate is haughty or terrifying. They are called "fathers" and so do they act. Those who wish may pay them respect, as is only right, but this is not demanded of men against their will. Not even the President himself is distinguished by his clothing or by a crown. His only distinctive mark is a small sheaf of corn[28] which he carries, just as the Bishop's is a wax candle carried before him.

They have very few laws, as people so trained do not need many. The chief criticism they bring against other people is that an infinite number of books of laws and commentaries is not enough. The Utopians think it most unjust that any men should be bound by laws that are either too numerous to read or too obscure for anyone to understand. Moreover, they exclude absolutely all lawyers since these plead cases with cunning and slyly dispute the laws. For they think it useful that each man should plead his own case and repeat to the judge what he would have told his counsel. In this way there will be less doubt and the truth can be elicited more easily, since the speaker has not been taught any deceit by his lawyer, and the judge can shrewdly weigh up each point and help simpler minds against the false accusations of the cunning. It is hard for this procedure to be observed in other countries amid such a mass of tangled laws. But in Utopia every man has a good knowledge of law. For, as I have said, the laws are very few, and they think that the bluntest interpretation is the best. All laws, they say, are passed with the sole reason of reminding each man of his duty; therefore a more subtle interpretation reminds fewer people, as only few can follow it; whereas a more straightforward and simple meaning of the laws is open to everyone. Otherwise, as far as the common people are concerned (and they are the most numerous and most in need of being reminded), you might just as well pass no law at all as pass one and then interpret it in a sense that no one could possibly discover except by a very keen mind and much debate. For the blunt judgment of the common man could never discover such an interpretation, nor does he have enough time, with his days spent in working for his living.

These virtues of the Utopians have incited their neighbors, who are free and under their own control (for the Utopians long ago freed many of them from tyranny), to take their magistrates from them, some every year, others for a period of five years. After they have completed their term of office, they escort them back with glory and honor, and take back fresh ones with them to their country. Now, these nations take an excellent and healthy care of their states. Since the safety or destruction of a state depends on the character of its magistrates, they could have made no wiser choice than men who are strangers in the land and could not be deflected from honesty by any bribe (since it would shortly be useless to them when they returned to their own country), nor influenced by favor or hatred toward anyone. If ever these two evils of bias and greed settle on the law

[28] Grain.

courts, they immediately destroy all justice, the strongest sinew of the state. The Utopians call the people who fetch magistrates from them "allies," and the others to whom they have given aid they call "friends."

Other nations are in the habit of making treaties all the time, then breaking them and renewing them. But the Utopians make none at all. For what is the purpose of a treaty? they say. It is as if nature does not put enough love between man and man. If a man scorns nature, do you think he could care about words? They are led to this opinion particularly because in that part of the world the treaties and pacts of princes are not observed very faithfully. For in Europe, and especially those parts controlled by the faith and religion of Christ, the majesty of treaties is everywhere holy and unbreakable. This is partly because of the justice and goodness of the princes, partly because of the reverence and fear felt for the popes, who most religiously perform whatever they undertake and bid all other princes keep exactly to their promises, while those who seek to evade them they coerce with the severity of their pontifical censure. For they quite rightly think it most disgraceful if there is no faith in the treaties of men who are called by the special name of "faithful." [29]

But in that new world, as far separated from us by the equator as by their way of life and character, there is no confidence in treaties. The more numerous and sacred are the rites tying the knot, the more quickly is it undone. They easily find some verbal quibble, and occasionally formulate treaties deliberately in ambiguous language, so that they can never be bound by firm ties without having some loophole for wriggling out of the treaty and their good faith at the same time. If they found that this cunning, or rather this fraud and deceit, had played a part in an agreement between private individuals, they would look angry and shout "Sacrilege! They deserve the gallows!" while all the time they pride themselves on having given the same advice to their princes. This makes all justice seem either a lowly and humble virtue, far below princely eminence, or else capable of two divisions: The one befits the common people, going on foot and crawling along the ground, unable to leap over barriers, restricted with many fetters. The other is the virtue of princes, more august than the popular kind and much freer, which is allowed to do anything it wants.

As I said, I think that the reason why the Utopians make no treaties lies in the character of the princes there who keep their treaties so badly. Perhaps they would change their opinion if they lived here. However, they think that even if they are scrupulously observed, yet it was bad that the habit of making treaties started in the first place. This is the reason why nations think themselves born enemies and adversaries, just as if there were no natural bond uniting two peoples separated merely by a hill or a stream. Consequently such people think it right to plot the other's destruction if no treaties stand in the way. Even when they have entered upon a treaty they imagine that no friendship has been formed, rather that they still have freedom to plunder as far as the treaty has not been carefully worded and contains no sufficiently precise clause to ban this. But the Utopians are of the contrary opinion, that no one must be considered an

---

[29] This heavily sarcastic passage is directed at, among other targets, the shifty diplomacy of Popes Alexander VI (reigned 1492–1503) and Julius II (reigned 1503–1513).

enemy who has done no harm, that the fellowship of nature acts as a treaty, and that a better and more powerful bond exists between men from kindness than from treaties, that is to say, from the spirit rather than from words.

CHAPTER EIGHT
ON WARFARE

They absolutely detest war and battle as being quite beastly and employed by no kind of beast as constantly as man. Contrary to the custom of practically all nations, they think nothing as inglorious as the glory gained from war. The Utopians, both men and women, on fixed days give themselves to constant military training to keep themselves in practice for the time when war is necessary. Nevertheless, they do not deliberately look for war, except to protect their own territory, or to drive off an enemy who has invaded the land of their friends, or out of pity for a people oppressed by tyranny to free them with their own forces from the yoke and slavery of the tyrant, as they do out of compassion. Yet they give aid to their friends not always to allow them to defend themselves, but sometimes they help them pay back and avenge wrongs already done to them. But this they do only if they themselves are consulted while the matter is still fresh. If they approve of the cause and are satisfied that restitution has been demanded but not made, then they take the responsibility of waging war. They do not make this decision only when an enemy has come on a plundering expedition. Their response is much more violent when their friends' merchants in any country, either under cover of unjust laws or by the misrepresentation of good laws, suffer an unjust accusation under the name of justice. This was precisely the reason for the war that the Utopians waged a little before our time on behalf of the Nephelogetes against the Alaopolites.[30] For in the land of the Alaopolites some merchants of the Nephelogetes had suffered injustice, as the Utopians thought, under the guise of justice. To the power and malice of both sides were added the support and aid of neighboring countries too. The injustice, if such it was, was avenged by so savage a war, that of the most flourishing nations some were shattered and others were severely beaten, and these evils upon evils were finally ended by the slavery and surrender of the Alaopolites. As the Utopians were not fighting for themselves, by this surrender the Alaopolites came under the power of the Nephelogetes, although they were in no way to be compared to the Alaopolites at the height of their power.

So keenly do the Utopians avenge wrongs done to their friends even in money matters, although they are not so quick about their own. If they themselves are ever cheated and deprived of their goods, as long as there is no physical violence, their anger merely takes the form of abstaining from trade with that nation until satisfaction is given. This is not because they care less for their own citizens than for their allies, but yet they are more annoyed if their allies are cheated of money than if they themselves suffer

---

[30] *Nephelogetes* means "born in the clouds"; *Alaopolites* means either "without a country" or "blind."

this. For their friends' merchants lose their own private possessions and consequently suffer greatly by the loss. But their own citizens lose nothing except what belongs to the state and what was in great abundance and excess at home. Otherwise it would not have been sent abroad. Therefore no one feels the loss. So they think it excessively cruel to avenge a loss by the deaths of many men, when none of them feels any disadvantage from that loss in his life or way of living. But if any of their citizens are maimed in any country or killed, whether that is done by public or private plan, they investigate the matter through envoys. Unless the offenders are handed over, they cannot be restrained from declaring war immediately. If the offenders are handed over, they are punished with death or slavery.

If they gain a bloody victory, they are not merely sorry but even ashamed, considering it folly to have paid too great a price for merchandise, no matter how precious it is. They are very proud if they can conquer and overcome the enemy by guile and deceit. For this they arrange a public triumph and erect a trophy as if a great battle had been won. Then they boast that they have behaved manfully and courageously when they gain a victory in the way possible to no other animal than man, that is, by strength of mind. For bodily strength is the weapon of bears, lions, boars, wolves, dogs and the other beasts. Although most of them surpass us in strength and ferocity, they are all inferior to us in intelligence and reason.

The Utopians have only one aim in war—to gain that object which would have prevented them from going to war if they had previously won it. Or, if circumstances prevent this, they exact so terrible a penalty from their enemy that fear restrains others from attempting the same. These are the objectives they have, and these they aim at first of all. Yet they are more concerned with avoiding danger than winning praise and glory. So, as soon as they have declared war, they have many proclamations set up secretly all at one time in the most conspicuous parts of the enemy territory, signed with their public seal. In these they promise huge rewards if anyone kills the enemy leader. Then they announce smaller, but not inconsiderable, rewards for the head of each man whose name is contained in that same notice. These are the people they consider responsible, after their leader, for the hostile action against them. Whatever reward they announce for a killer is doubled if he brings any of the proscribed[31] to them alive. They also try to bring over the proscribed persons themselves to work against their former allies, by the same rewards with an additional promise of impunity.

Therefore their enemies soon come to suspect others, and are not faithful or trusting among themselves, but live in the greatest fear and danger. For it is well known that frequently a good part of the proscribed and, above all, the leader himself have been betrayed by those in whom they placed the greatest trust. So easily are men persuaded to any crime by gifts. The Utopians set no limit upon these gifts, but remembering the peril to which they are inciting others, they see to it that the greatness of the danger is compensated by the size of the recompense. Therefore they promise not merely great amounts of gold, but also estates with great returns to enjoy as

[31] Outlawed by public proclamation.

their own forever in safe places among friends. They keep their promises most faithfully.

This way of bidding for and buying an enemy is held in bad repute by other nations, as being a cruel crime of a depraved mind. But the Utopians think it most praiseworthy and a mark of prudence, since they can rid themselves of great wars in this way without a single battle. They also consider it an act of mercy and compassion, since by the death of a few guilty persons they save the lives of many innocent who would have fallen in the fighting, on their own side and on their enemy's. They feel sorry for the common crowd of the enemy almost as much as their own, since they realize that they do not come to war of their own accord, but are driven to it by the madness of their leaders.

If no progress is made by these means, they sow and foster seeds of discord by bringing the leader's brother or one of the nobles to hope that he will win control of the country. If domestic factions fail, they stir up their enemy's neighbors and set them in conflict by digging up some old legal claim such as kings are never without. They promise support for the war and supply money plentifully, but their citizens sparingly. For they regard them as so precious and value them so highly that they would not willingly exchange any of their citizens for the enemy leader. But they pay out gold and silver lavishly, as this is the only purpose for which they keep them. For their lives would be no less comfortable even if they spent it all. In fact, besides their wealth in Utopia itself, they have unlimited treasure abroad, since, as I said before, very many nations are in their debt. So they hire soldiers from all lands and send them to the war, especially from the Zapoletes.[32] This nation is five hundred miles distant from Utopia toward the east, and it is rough, wild and savage. They prefer forests and craggy mountains, where they were brought up. They are a hard people, able to endure heat, cold and toil, unacquainted with luxuries, not concerned with agriculture. They pay little attention to their houses and clothing, devoting their energies merely to raising cattle. They live mainly by hunting and plunder. They are a nation born only for war, eagerly seeking any opportunity to wage war, and gladly embracing it once it is found. They go out in great numbers and for a low price offer their services to anyone needing soldiers. They know only this one art of life—that by which death is sought. They fight bitterly and faithfully for those under whom they are serving. But they do not bind themselves for any fixed length of time. They take sides on the condition that on the next day they will side even with the enemy if they offer a greater wage. On the next day after that they come back again if lured by a slightly higher sum. It is only rarely that there is a war in which a good number of them is not in each army. So it happens every day that men joined by ties of blood, who lived in great concord when hired on the same side, shortly after are separated to different sides and clash in war. With great ferocity, forgetting their birth and friendship, they plunge their swords into one another. No other reason incites them to this mutual slaughter than the trifling sum of money paid to them by opposing

---

[32] The name means "ready to sell"; More is thinking of the Swiss, many of whom served as mercenaries at the time.

leaders. They are so careful about this money that if only one penny is added to their daily wage they are quite ready to change sides. So quickly have they drunk in avarice. Yet it is no use to them. For what they earn by their blood they immediately squander in luxury, and this luxury itself is not of a very high quality.

This nation fights for the Utopians against anyone, since they are hired at a price that cannot be matched anywhere else. For just as they seek good men to use, so the Utopians seek these worst of men to abuse. When necessity demands, they incite them with great promises and expose them to the greatest dangers, from which usually a great part never return to claim their rewards. To those that are left they faithfully pay what they promised so that they will be inspired to similar acts of daring. Nor do they care how many of these they send to their death, as they believe that they would earn the deepest thanks of the human race if they could cleanse the earth of all the filth of a people so foul and wicked.

After these, they use the forces of the people on whose behalf they are taking up arms, then auxiliary squadrons of their other friends. Last of all they join to them their own citizens. One of them, a man of proved bravery, they put in charge of the whole army. They also create two substitutes for him. If he is safe, they are both without any office; but if he is captured or killed, one of them succeeds to his position by a sort of inheritance. If it is rendered necessary by the many fortunes of war, the third man succeeds him to prevent the army being thrown into confusion because of the danger of its leader. A levy is held from each city out of those who volunteer. For no one is thrust out into military service against his will. They are convinced that if anyone is timid by nature, besides being no use in action, he will also make his companions afraid. But if any war presses close to their own country, provided that they are physically fit, they mix such cowards with men of better quality and put them on board ship, or else position them at intervals along the walls, from which they have nowhere to flee. So their fear is overcome by their sense of shame in front of their own people, the presence of the enemy and the impossibility of flight. And often extreme necessity turns into bravery.

Just as none of them is dragged to war against his will, so they do not prevent women who wish from accompanying their husbands on service. In fact, they encourage them and urge them on with praise. The women who go out are positioned each with her own husband together in line of battle. Also each man is surrounded by his children and relatives, so that those whom nature especially urges to supply help to one another may be of mutual assistance nearby. A husband who returns without his wife, or a wife without her husband, is held in the greatest disgrace, as is a son who returns after losing his father. So if the Utopians themselves come to be engaged in close fighting, as long as the enemy stand their ground, a long and bitter battle ensues, which is decided only by absolute destruction. As I have said, they try every means to avoid having to fight themselves, as long as they can wage war through the agency of mercenaries. But when they cannot help going into battle, they are fearless in handling what they wisely avoided as long as they could. They do not grow fierce at the first encounter, but rather by delaying they gradually gain their strength and become so resolute that they can more quickly be killed than repulsed. For that security of a livelihood that each has at home, and the absence of all anxious care for their families (a worry that breaks brave spirits everywhere), give them a nobility of spirit that disdains defeat. Their military training also gives them confidence. Finally, they are given courage by their right beliefs with which they have been filled from childhood by their training and the laws of the state. With this courage they do not hold life so cheap as to throw it away to no purpose, nor so outrageously dear as to cling to it greedily and shamefully when honor persuades them to lay it down.

When the battle is at its height and raging on all sides, a band of chosen young men sworn to one purpose makes for the enemy leader. They openly attack him, as well as creeping up on him stealthily. They aim at him from near and far, and assail him with a long, unbroken line, with fresh men constantly taking the place of those exhausted. If he does not flee, he rarely escapes death or being captured alive by his enemies. If the Utopians gain the victory themselves, they never follow it up with slaughter. For they prefer to capture those who flee rather than kill them. But they never give chase without leaving behind one line of troops in full array under their standards. They cling to this rule so firmly that, if they gain victory with their last line after being defeated in all other sections, they prefer to allow all the enemy to escape rather than throw their own ranks into confusion by giving chase. For they remember an experience that has been not infrequent with them: after the main body of their whole army had been defeated and crushed, the enemy were exultant at their victory and chased the fleeing troops in all different directions; a few of the Utopian reserves watching for their opportunities suddenly attacked the scattered and straggling enemy, who were careless from an unwarranted sense of security. So they changed the outcome of the whole battle, and by wresting so certain and undoubted a victory from their hands, though conquered they conquered the conquerors in turn.

It is not easy to say whether they are more cunning in setting ambushes or cautious in avoiding them. You would imagine they are getting ready to flee, when nothing is further from their minds. On the other hand, when they do plan flight, you would never suspect it was in their minds. For if they feel that they are being pressed too hard because of superior numbers or the unfavorable ground, then by night they shift camp in complete silence. Or they use some stratagem to deceive the enemy. Or else by day they retreat so gradually, keeping such good order, that it is just as dangerous to attack them when they are retreating as when they are pressing hard. They fortify their camps most carefully with a very deep and wide ditch, and throw the earth so excavated on the inside. Nor do they use slaves for this work. The task is done by the hands of the soldiers themselves and the whole army is engaged in the work, with the exception of those who are on armed guard in front of the rampart for sudden attacks. With so many helpers, they finish the large and extensive fortifications more quickly than would ever be believed.

They use armor which is strong enough to take blows, yet is so suited to any movement or gesture that they do not feel its weight even when swimming. For right at the beginning of their military training they get used to swimming in full armor. For long-range weapons they have arrows, which the infantry and cavalry can dispatch with great force as well as accuracy.

For short-range weapons they use not swords, but axes, which are deadly with their sharp edge or sheer weight, according as the users slice or merely strike. They are extremely clever at inventing engines of war. When they have made them they are most careful to hide them in case their discovery, before they are needed, might make them ridiculous rather than useful. In manufacturing them, their chief aim is to make them easy to transport and suitable for maneuvering.

When they have made a temporary truce with their enemies, they observe it so strictly that they do not break it even when provoked. They do not devastate the enemy's land or burn his crops. In fact, they are careful not even to trample them down with the feet of their soldiers or horses, as far as possible, since they believe that the crops are growing for their own use. They never harm an unarmed man, unless he is a spy. If a city surrenders to them they protect it. If they take one by storm, they do not plunder it, but kill the men responsible for hindering the surrender and reduce the other defenders to slavery. They leave untouched all the civilian population. If they discover that anyone advocated surrender, they give him a share of the property of the condemned. They distribute the rest among the auxiliary troops. For of the Utopians themselves no one takes any of the booty.

But when a war is finished, they charge their expenses not to the friends on whose behalf they incurred them, but to the vanquished. On this account they make them pay partly in money, which they put aside for similar military purposes, and partly in land in the territory of the defeated country, to belong to the Utopians forever and provide them with a considerable revenue. They have revenues of this kind now in many countries. They were obtained gradually for various reasons and have grown to over seven hundred thousand ducats[33] a year. To these they send out some of their citizens as financial agents, to live in great splendor in the foreign country and play the part of millionaires. But yet there is plenty left to be paid into the treasury, unless they prefer to lend it to the country producing it. They often do this as long as the others have need of it. It hardly ever happens that they ask for the whole amount back. They assign part of these landed estates to the men who at the Utopians' request undergo the kind of danger I described previously. If any king takes up arms against them and is ready to invade their territory, they immediately rush to oppose him in full strength outside their boundaries. For they do not like to make war on their own soil, nor is any necessity great enough to compel them to let foreign auxiliaries into their own island.

CHAPTER NINE
ON THE RELIGIONS OF THE UTOPIANS

They have different religions not merely in the island but even in single cities. Some worship the sun as a god, others the moon or any of the planets. Some look up to a man, not only as a god but as the highest god, if he was famed for virtue or glory long ago. But by far the largest section of the

---

[33] Worth about 330,000 English pounds during More's time—a vast sum of money.

population, and the wisest too, adheres to none of these beliefs, but thinks that there is a certain single divinity, unknown, eternal, boundless, inexplicable, beyond the understanding of the human mind, diffused through the whole of this universe in virtue,[34] not bulk. They call him "the father." To this one divinity they attribute the beginnings, increases, advances, changes and ends of all things. They do not accord divine honors to anyone else.

Although all the others have different beliefs, yet they agree with them on this point: they believe that there is one Supreme Being who is responsible for the creation and protection of the universe. They all agree in calling him Mythra[35] in their native tongue, but they disagree in having different conceptions of him. Each man thinks that whatever he considers the Supreme Power is that selfsame person to whose divinity and majesty alone all nations assign the sum of all things. But they are gradually departing from that multiplicity of superstitions and coming together to that one religion which reason judges to surpass all others.[36] It is quite certain that the others would have disappeared long ago, except that when anyone planned to change his religion, whatever ill fortune occurred, he interpreted it in his terror not as a chance happening but as a sign from heaven, as if the power whose worship was being abandoned was punishing the wicked design against itself.

The Utopians heard from us the name of Christ, his teaching, his ways and his miracles, also the equally wonderful fortitude of the martyrs, whose blood willingly shed brought over so many countries to their beliefs in all parts of the world. You would not believe how readily they agreed to this, whether God was secretly inspiring them or our religion seemed closest to the belief most prevalent among them. Yet I believe they were also brought to this opinion because they heard that Christ favored communal living[37] among his followers and that this was still the practice in real Christian communities.[38] But whatever impelled them, many came over to our religion and were washed with the water of baptism.

There were four of us left, as two of our company had died, and unfortunately none of us was a priest.[39] The Utopians were initiated in the other points of Christianity, but still were without those sacraments which in our world only priests can supply. Yet they understand and make this their most earnest prayer. In fact, they even debate heatedly among themselves whether one of their own number could be chosen to receive the order of priesthood without the sending of a Christian bishop. And certainly it seemed as if they were going to choose one. But they had not yet chosen him when I left. Those who do not believe in Christianity nevertheless deter no one from it, nor attack a man instructed in it, except that one of our company was punished in my presence. He had been recently baptized,

---

[34] Active power.   [35] The Persian god of light.

[36] That is, the religion ascribed a little earlier to the "wisest."

[37] On the communism of the early Christians, see Acts of the Apostles 2:44–45 and 4:32–35.

[38] Monasteries and convents.

[39] Of the seven Roman Catholic sacraments, two (Baptism and Matrimony) could be administered if necessary without a priest. Three (the Eucharist; Penance, or confession; and Extreme Unction, the rite for the dying) ordinarily required a priest. Two (Confirmation and Holy Orders, or the ordination of priests) required a bishop.

and much against our advice was discoursing in public on the worship of
Christ with more enthusiasm than wisdom. So fervent did he grow that he
not only extolled our beliefs above others, but absolutely condemned all
others. He called the beliefs profane and their adherents impious and sacrilegious, deserving to be punished with everlasting fire. When he had
been speaking like this for some time, they arrested him, then prosecuted
and convicted him not for scorning a religion but for stirring up discord
among the people. The penalty was exile. For it is one of their oldest established laws that no one should be penalized for his religious beliefs.

For right at the beginning King Utopus had heard that before his arrival the inhabitants fought constantly among themselves on religious issues, and he had observed that the reason for his conquest was that all the
different sects were in strife and so fought singly for their country. So after
his victory he first of all passed a law that everyone should be allowed to
follow whatever religion he pleased; that a man might attempt to bring
others over to his religion only to the extent of offering reasons calmly and
soberly, without destroying others bitterly if he could not gain his end by
persuasion; that he should not use any force and should refrain from
abuse. If anyone goes beyond the limit in religious dispute, he is punished
by exile or slavery.

Utopus introduced this law not merely to preserve peace, which he saw
completely overthrown by constant strife and inextinguishable hatred, but
also because he thought that such an enactment would further the cause of
religion. He was never rash enough to give any definite view on religion, as
if he was not sure whether God, desiring various and manifold worship,
gave different inspiration to different people. But he thought it arrogant
and foolish to demand by violence and threats that your views should be
accepted by everyone. Even if one alone were true and all others idle, he
easily foresaw that, provided the matter is handled with wisdom and moderation, the force of truth must eventually arise and stand out; but if there
is armed strife and confusion, since the worst men are the most stubborn,
the best and most holy religion would be overthrown by the empty superstitions, like crops among thorns and weeds. So he left the whole matter
undecided and left each man the liberty to believe what he wished. But he
issued severe and careful restrictions against anyone's so falling away from
the dignity of human nature as to believe that the soul dies with the body or
that the world revolves by chance without divine providence. And therefore they believe that after this life vice is punished and virtue rewarded. If
anyone takes the contrary view, they do not even count him as a human
being, since he has lowered the sublime nature of his soul to the cheapness
of a beast's body. Much less do they consider him a citizen, as he would not
have the slightest respect for laws and customs if fear did not compel him.
For who can doubt that if a man has no fear outside the laws, no hope
beyond the body, he will try to evade by stealth or overthrow by violence
the public laws of his country, while gratifying his private desires. So if a
man is of this opinion, he is given no share in public office, is entrusted
with no magistracy and is put in charge of no public administration. Therefore he is despised on all sides as having a lazy and mean nature. Yet they
inflict no actual punishment upon him, as they are convinced that no man
is capable of believing anything he chooses. Nor do they force him by

threats to conceal his mind. They do not tolerate deceit and lies, but hold them in the greatest detestation as being nearest to fraud. But they do prevent him from discussing his opinion, although this applies only to dispute before the common people. For they not merely allow but even encourage him to have private discussion with the priests and worthy citizens, being convinced that that madness will eventually yield to reason.

There are others of no inconsiderable number who are not so prohibited, as their beliefs are not entirely devoid of reason and they themselves are not evil men. These hold to a widely different error in believing that dumb animals too have eternal souls, although they are not to be compared to ours in dignity nor are they born to equal felicity. For they all believe as a sure and certain fact that man will enjoy such happiness, that while bewailing sickness, they lament no one's death, unless they see anyone being dragged from life in sadness and against his will. This they consider a very bad omen, as if the soul has given up all hope from a guilty conscience and is afraid to leave because of some hidden foreboding of imminent punishment. They also think that a man's arrival will not be welcome to God, if he does not run willingly when summoned, but has to be dragged protesting and unwilling. So those who witness this kind of death are appalled and conduct his funeral in sad silence. After praying for God's mercy on his soul and beseeching Him to pardon his weakness out of His kindness, they cover the corpse with earth.

On the other hand, whoever departs this life eagerly, full of good hope, is mourned by no one. They accompany his funeral with singing, commending his soul to God with great affection. At last they burn the body with reverence rather than grief, and set up a stone on the spot engraved with the dead man's titles. When they return home they recall his character and achievements, and no part of his life is told more often or more gladly than his happy death. This recollection of goodness they think is a most effective spur to virtue for the living and a most acceptable reverence for the dead. They believe that the dead are present at conversations about themselves, although they are invisible to dull mortal eyes. For it would not be appropriate to the lot of the blessed to be deprived of the freedom to journey where they wish, and it would be ungrateful to have thrown away all desire to see their friends, who were bound to them during life by mutual love and charity. They imagine that in good men, this love (like the other blessings) is increased rather than diminished after death. So they believe that the dead move among the living, as witnesses of their words and deeds. Therefore they go about their tasks with more confidence, relying upon these overseers. The belief in the presence of their ancestors also keeps them from secret dishonesty.

They completely discountenance and laugh at augury[40] and the other forms of divination springing from idle superstition, which are much in favor in other countries. But miracles, which arise by no natural agency, they respect as being the work and witness of the presence of God. They say that they have frequent miracles in their country, and on occasion, when important matters of state are in doubt, by public intercession and with absolute confidence they obtain and receive them.

[40] Supernatural foretelling of the future; divination.

They consider the contemplation and praise of nature an act of worship pleasing to God. But there are a good many people who, from their love of religion, ignore learning and are not concerned to acquire any knowledge, although they do not give themselves up to idleness. For they believe that future happiness after death is earned by work and kind actions to others. So some minister to the sick, others repair the roads, clean out ditches, mend bridges, dig up turf, sand or stones, fell trees and cut them up, transport wood, grain and other commodities to the cities in carts, and in both public and private life they act as servants and even more than slaves. For whatever task there is anywhere that is hard, difficult or filthy, which puts off others because of the toil, disgust or sheer impossibility, this they take entirely upon themselves with a willing and happy heart. They procure leisure for others, but spend their own lives in constant work and toil. However, they do not blame or rebuke the lives of others, nor praise their own. The lower they go in their servile work, the higher is the honor accorded to them by all.

Yet these people are divided into two sects. The first consists of those who do not marry and who keep away from sex, as well as from eating flesh, some of them from the meat of all living creatures. They absolutely renounce the pleasures of the present life as if they were harmful, and give all their attention to those of the next life by vigils and sweat, when in the meantime they are keen and energetic with the hope of soon winning the life to come. The other sect is just as desirous of work, but they prefer marriage. They do not despise the solace it brings, and believe that they owe a work to nature and children to their country. They avoid no pleasure, provided that it does not delay them in their work. They like the flesh of four-footed beasts, if only because they think that this food renders them stronger for any task. This sect the Utopians judge wiser, while they think the other sect more holy. They would laugh at them if they attempted a rational defense of their preference for celibacy over marriage and for the hard life over the easy. But since they claim they are led to it by religion, they look up to them and revere them. They have no more anxious concern than to avoid any forthright pronouncement on any religion. So this is what the people are like to whom in their own language they give the special name "bouthrescas," which may be translated as "religious."

They have priests who are very saintly and hence very few. For they do not have more than thirteen in each city, with an equal number of churches, except when they go to war. Then seven of them set out with the army and in the meanwhile their places are filled with others. But when they return, each takes up his old position. Those who are above the requisite number, until they duly succeed priests who die, are companions to the Bishop. He is the head of them all. They are chosen by the people, just like the other magistrates, by secret ballot to avoid party strife. When elected, they are consecrated by the college of priests. These are in charge of divine affairs, look after religious matters and act as moral censors. It is considered a great disgrace for anyone to be summoned or rebuked by them for loose living.

Their function is to exhort and admonish, but it is for the President and the other magistrates to check and punish the guilty. However, the priests are allowed to excommunicate anyone they find to be shamefully wicked. This is the greatest punishment they can suffer. For they are afflicted with severe disgrace and are tortured by an inward terror of religion, fearing that even their bodies will not be safe for long. If they do not quickly profess their repentance to the priests, they are arrested and punished by the Senate for impiety.

The priests instruct the boys and youths, and a concern for morals and virtue comes before that for learning. For they are very careful to instill immediately into the tender and obedient minds of the children good beliefs which are useful for preserving the republic. When these beliefs have settled in them as children, they follow them throughout life and prove extremely useful for maintaining the condition of the republic, which can be destroyed only by vices, and these are born from wicked beliefs.

Women also may be priests, but more rarely than men, and even then only aged widows are chosen. The male priests have as wives the most distinguished ladies in the country. For among the Utopians no magistrate is given greater honor, so much so that even if the priests commit a crime, they are not brought before a court. They are left merely to God and themselves. For they do not think it right to touch them with mortal hand, however criminal they may be, since they have so especially been consecrated to God, as a kind of offering. It is easier for them to observe this custom, as there are so few priests and such care is taken in choosing them. It does not easily happen that a man degenerates to corruption and vice, when he was advanced as the most virtuous of good men to a position of such dignity, with regard to his virtue alone. Even if this did happen (as human nature is so changeable), yet as they are so few and have no power except honor, there would be no great fear for the public safety from them. They have priests so few and far between to prevent the dignity of the order, held in such veneration by them now, from becoming debased by sharing their honor with many. This is all the more so since they think it difficult to find many people good enough for that dignity. To bear this office it is not enough to have average goodness.

Nor are they honored more among their own people than in foreign countries. The following tale will make this clear and also explain its origin. For when their forces are engaged in battle, the priests kneel down a short distance away, dressed in their sacred robes. They hold up their hands to heaven and pray above all for peace and secondly for victory for their country, but a bloody victory for neither side. When the Utopians are winning, they rush into the line of battle and stop them from showing cruelty to the vanquished foe. For an enemy merely to have seen them and addressed them in person is enough to save his life. To touch their flowing robes protects his other possessions from all outrage of war. Therefore with all nations they have acquired such veneration and so much true majesty that frequently they win no less safety from the enemy for their own men than they had brought to the enemy from their own citizens. For it is well known that on occasion, when their own troops have been pushed back and matters have looked hopeless, with the Utopians in flight and the enemy rushing in to kill and plunder, the slaughter has been stopped by the intervention of the priests, the troops of both sides separated and peace settled and arranged on equal terms. There has never been any race so fierce, cruel and barbarous as not to consider the priests' persons sacrosanct and untouchable.

For feast days they have the first and last days of each month and year, dividing the year into months. They measure the months by the course of the moon and the year by the sun. In their own language they call the first days Cynemerns and the last days Trapemerns.[41] These names mean "First Feast" and "Last Feast."

Their churches are wonderful to see. For they are not merely examples of excellent craftsmanship but, as was necessary because of the small number of churches, they can hold an immense number of people. But they are all fairly dark. They say this was done not from ignorance of how to build, but on the advice of the priests, as they think too much light scatters men's thoughts, while a darker, dim light gathers together the mind and increases devotion. Since religion is not the same for them all, and yet they all take the form, however varied and manifold they are, of coming by different ways to the goal of worship of the divine nature, therefore there is nothing seen or heard in their churches which would not fit them all alike. If any sect has its own special rite, each man performs it in his own home. The public rites they manage in such a way as to take nothing from the private.

Therefore no image of a god is seen in any church. So everyone is free to imagine God as he wishes according to his own religion. They have no special name for God except Mythra. By this name they all agree upon the single nature of a divine majesty, whatever it may be. Only those prayers are used which anyone could utter without offending his particular sect.

So on the days of the Last Feasts they come together to church in the evening, still fasting, to give thanks to God for the successful completion of the month or year of which it is the last day. The following day is the First Feast. They flock to the churches in the morning to pray for a happy and successful outcome of the year or month they are beginning with that feast day. But on the Last Feasts, before they go to church, at home the wives kneel before their husbands, and children before their parents, and confess that they have sinned by some actual deed or else by some carelessness in their duty. They then beg forgiveness for their mistake. So if any cloud of discord has arisen at home, it is blown away by such atonement. So they take part in the services at church with a pure and peaceful mind. For it is an offense to be present with a troubled mind. For this reason, people do not go to the rites if they are aware of harboring anger or hatred against anyone, until they have become reconciled and purged their feelings, for fear of swift and great punishment.

When they come to church, the men sit on the right, and the women on their own on the left. They seat themselves so that the male members of each household sit in front of the head of the house and the females in front of his wife. In this way it is arranged that the gestures of every member in public are observed by those by whose authority and discipline they are controlled at home. They are also careful to see that a younger person is everywhere near an older, in case children put in the charge of other

---

[41] The Greek derivations suggest the literal meanings, respectively, "dog-days" and "turning-days."

children should spend in childish frivolity the time in which they ought to be forming a religious fear toward God, a great and almost unique incitement to virtue.

They kill no animal in sacrifices, nor do they believe that the divine mercy delights in blood and slaughter. For He gave animals life that they might live. They burn incense and other sweet-smelling things. They also carry a large number of candles, not that they fail to realize that such things contribute no more to the divine nature than do men's prayers, but this harmless kind of worship pleases them. And by these scents and lights and the other ceremonies, men feel somehow that they are lifted up and rise to worship God with more fervent mind. In church the people wear white. The priest has many-colored robes, wonderful in workmanship and design, although the material is not very valuable. For they are not embroidered with gold or set with precious stones, but they are worked so cleverly and expertly from different feathers that no costly material could equal the value of the work. Moreover, in these birds' feathers and the definite arrangement they have in the priest's vestments, they say that there are contained certain mysteries. The priests zealously teach the interpretation of these feathers, and when it is known, people are reminded of God's goodness to them, the reverence they owe in turn to God, and their duties to one another.

When the priest first comes out of the vestry[42] in these vestments, they all immediately fall to the floor in reverence. There is such profound silence on all sides that the very scene inspires a kind of fear as if some divinity were present. They lie like this for a little while, and at a sign from the priest they stand up. Then they sing God's praises to the accompaniment of musical instruments, which are mainly of a form different from that seen in our world. Most of them far exceed ours in sweetness, but yet some of them are not even to be compared with ours. But in one matter they are clearly far ahead of us. All their music, whether it is played on instruments or performed by the human voice, so imitates and represents natural feelings that the sound is adapted to the subject. Whether it is a prayer or a tune of gladness, peace, trouble, sadness or anger, it so reproduces the feeling by the form of the melody that it affects the listeners' minds in an amazing way, sinks into them and inflames their spirits.

At the end the priest and people together recite solemn prayers in a fixed form of words. These are so composed that what they all say together, each man may apply privately to himself. In these everyone recognizes God as the author of creation and guidance of the world, and of all good things as well. He thanks God for so many benefits received, but specifically that by God's kindness he chanced to be born in that most blessed republic and that he was taught that religion which he hopes is truest. It is his prayer that God's goodness will bring it to his knowledge if he is in any way wrong in this, and if there is anything better than his country and religion and more acceptable to God. For he is ready to follow, he says, wherever God leads him. But if this form of republic is best and his religion most correct, then he prays God to grant him steadfastness and to lead all other men to that way of life and to the same belief about God,

---

[42] The room where the priest puts on his vestments.

unless there is anything in this variety of religions that pleases God's inscrutable will. Finally he prays that he may have an easy death before being
received to Him—how soon or late he does not dare to suggest. Although,
if this does not offend His majesty, he would much rather die a difficult
death and come to God than be kept from Him any longer in the most
prosperous of lives. After this prayer they again fall to the floor. Shortly
afterward they stand up and go to lunch. The remainder of the day they
pass in games and military exercises.

I have described to you as truthfully as I could the form of the republic
which I judge not merely the best, but the only one that can rightfully claim
the name of republic. For elsewhere men talk of public good, but look after
their private good. In Utopia, where nothing is private, they really do public business. In both places there is good reason for acting as they do. For
elsewhere, everyone knows that however prosperous the republic may be,
he will starve of hunger if he does not make some separate provision for
himself. And so he is forced to believe that he ought to take account of
himself rather than the people, that is, others. On the other hand, in
Utopia, where all possessions are in common, everyone is certain that, provided that care is taken to keep the public barns full, everyone will have
whatever he wants for his private use. For there is no unfair distribution of
property, there are no paupers or beggars there, and though no one has
anything, yet all are rich. What greater riches can there be than a life in
happiness and peace, with all cares removed, without being worried about
one's own food, or being harassed by one's wife's complaints and demands,
or being afraid of poverty for one's son or anxious about a daughter's
dowry? Instead they are assured of the livelihood and happiness of themselves and all their family, wife, sons, grandchildren, great-grandchildren,
great-great-grandchildren and all the long list of descendants that nobles
assume. Care is also taken of people who are incapable of the work they
once did, just as much as for those still able.

At this point I should like someone to dare compare with this equity the
justice of other nations. I'll be damned if I can find any trace of justice or
equity among them. For what sort of justice is this when some noble or
goldsmith[43] or moneylender or any one of those who do either nothing or
else nothing very necessary to the republic achieves a glorious and splendid
life either by idleness or unnecessary business? Meanwhile a laborer, carter,
smith or farmer suffers heavy and constant toil that beasts could hardly
endure, work so necessary that no republic could last without it for even
one year. Yet they provide so poor a living for themselves and lead such a
miserable life that the condition of beasts might seem far preferable. For
the animals do not suffer such constant toil, and their food is not much
worse and is pleasanter to them, nor do they meanwhile have any fear for
the future. But men are incited for the present by barren and unprofitable
work, and killed off by the recollection of an impoverished old age. For as
they do not earn enough each day to keep them for that day, they certainly
cannot have any surplus to put away for their old age each day.

Is this not an unjust and ungrateful republic which lavishes such riches
upon the nobles, as they call them, and the goldsmiths and the others of

---

[43] Goldsmiths at the time often performed the functions of bankers.

that kind, who are idlers or mere flatterers and inventors of empty pleasures? Yet it makes no kindly provision for farmers, coal miners, laborers,
carters and smiths, without whom there would be no republic at all. The
republic abuses their labor when they are young and healthy, but when
they are slow with age and sickness and utterly destitute, she forgets the
sleepless nights they have spent and does not remember their many great
benefits. Instead she shows her ingratitude by rewarding them with a
wretched death. On top of this, from the daily wage of the poor, the rich
wear something away every day, not merely by private fraud but even by
public laws. So while it previously seemed unjust to give unkindness in
return for good service to the state, the rich have twisted this and by passing laws made it justice.[44]

And so, when I examine and consider all the flourishing republics in
the world today, believe me, nothing comes to mind except a conspiracy of
the rich, who seek their own advantage under the name and title of the
republic. They also devise and think up all sorts of ways and means to hold
on to their ill-gotten gains with no fear of losing them, and then to hire the
labor of all the poor at the lowest price and abuse them. When once the rich
have decreed that these devices are to be observed in the public name (in
other words, in the name of the poor too), they then become laws. But
when vile men with their insatiable greed have shared among themselves
what would have been enough for everybody, even so they are very far
from the prosperity of the Utopian republic. Since all greed for money and
also the use of it have been removed in Utopia, how great a burden of
troubles has been cut back and how great a harvest of crimes has been torn
up by the roots! For who does not realize that fraud, theft, plunder, quarrels, brawls, discord, sedition, murder, treachery, poisoning—all these are
avenged by daily punishment, not checked; but if money is killed, they will
die with it? Also fear, worry, care, toil and sleepless nights will also perish at
the same moment as money. Yes, poverty itself, which alone seemed to lack
money, would immediately decrease if money were absolutely abolished
everywhere.

To picture this more clearly, consider a barren and unfruitful year in
which famine has taken away many thousand men. I firmly maintain that at
the end of that shortage an examination of rich men's barns would reveal
so much grain that, if it had been distributed among those killed by starvation, no one at all would have noticed the poor harvest. So easily could a
living be made if that blessed thing money (a brilliant discovery to open up
the way to a living) did not on its own shut off from us the path to a living. I
am quite sure that the rich feel this too and are well aware how better a
state it would be to lack nothing essential rather than abound in superflui-
ties, to be taken from countless cares rather than be besieged by great
wealth. Nor does it occur to me to doubt that the whole world could easily
have been brought long ago to the laws of Utopia by the consideration of
each man's advantage or by the authority of our Saviour Christ, who, with
his great wisdom, could not fail to know what was best and, with his great
kindness, could not fail to advise what he knew to be best. This would have

---

[44] In More's time, recent laws governing labor favored the employers' rather than the
workers' interests.

been possible, if that single beast—the chief and parent of all plagues—pride did not fight against it.[45] Pride measures her prosperity not by her own advantages, but by others' disadvantages. She would not even wish to become a goddess if there were no wretches left over whom she could rule and exult, by comparison with whose wretchedness her own felicity might shine, whose need she might torture and inflame by displaying her own riches. This serpent of hell creeping over the breasts of men drags them back and stops them from seeking a better way of life.

Since she is too deeply fixed in the hearts of men to be easily plucked out, I am glad that the Utopians at least have achieved this form of republic, though I greatly wish all men had. The Utopians have followed those rules of life with which they laid such foundations for their republic as are most prosperous and also, as far as the human mind may conjecture, destined to last forever. For since they have cut out together with the other vices the roots of ambition and strife, there is no danger of internal discord, which alone has destroyed the well protected riches of many cities. With their concord safe at home and their institutions healthy, not even the jealousy of all the neighboring princes could shake or move that empire, although they have often tried in the past and always been driven back.

So Raphael finished his account. Many points occurred to me where the ways and laws of that people seemed regulated quite absurdly—for example, their method of waging war, their religious practices and other institutions of theirs too, but particularly the foundation stone of the whole government—I mean their communal life and living without any use for money, since by this one enactment are overthrown all nobility, magnificence, splendor and majesty, the true glory and ornaments, as popular opinion goes, of a republic. Yet I knew he was tired from his speech and I was not sure whether he could tolerate any contrary opinion, especially as I remembered he had censured others on that account, as if they were afraid of being thought unintelligent if they could not find something to criticize in others' discoveries. So I praised the Utopians' constitution and Raphael's speech, took him by the hand and led him indoors to dinner, saying that there would be another time for us to think more deeply on those matters and discuss them more fully with him. I hope this may happen someday. Meanwhile, although I cannot agree with everything he said, although he is otherwise beyond all doubt a most learned man with deep experience of human affairs, yet I readily admit that in the republic of Utopia there are very many things that I would pray might come to our cities rather than hope[46] they might ever be established.

---

[45] It was a Christian commonplace that pride was the great sin comprehending or implying all the others.

[46] That is, expect.

François Rabelais

(1494?–1553)

Of François Rabelais, the great French historian Jules Michelet wrote that no man had ever better captured the spirit of his age. Rabelais, he said, was a man "who contained the genius of his century and overflowed it at every moment." This would seem to be a strange judgment to make of the author of a book as seemingly fantastic and unreal as Gargantua and Pantagruel. *The rambling and obscene adventures of two folklore giants seem at first glance to be little more than a string of sexual and excremental jokes. But what Michelet saw in* Gargantua and Pantagruel *were the explosive energies and conflicts of a world in transition between two ages.*

The century Michelet had in mind, the sixteenth (Rabelais lived from about 1494 to 1553), rivaled our own in terms of rapidity and violence of change. Within Rabelais' lifetime, Europeans discovered the New World and sailed around the globe, the glory of the Italian Renaissance spread to northern Europe, and printing presses began to disseminate the New Learning that followed the rediscovery of classical civilization. In France, King Francis I was locked in a struggle with the Spanish Holy Roman Emperor, Charles V, for control of Europe. The Catholic Church was under attack by reformers from without—Luther, Zwingli, and Calvin all flourished during Rabelais' lifetime—and from within—the great Dutch humanist and reformer Erasmus was Rabelais' contemporary and intellectual father. The Church stiffened in response to these challenges, and, in France, the Faculty of Theology at the Sorbonne university used the stake freely to enforce orthodoxy and repress dissent.

Rabelais threaded his way through these tumultuous times, frequently in danger because of his beliefs and his satiric writing. Born in Chinon, in the province of Touraine, the son of a prominent lawyer, he was by the age of twenty-seven a priest and a monk in a Franciscan monastery and an avid student of Greek. After the Sorbonne forbade the study of Greek in France and Rabelais' books were confiscated, he moved to a more liberal Benedictine monastery and resumed his studies. In 1527 or 1528, he left the monastery and took up the study of medicine, first in Paris and then at Montpellier, where he became a bachelor of medicine in 1530 and a doctor in 1537.

In 1532, Rabelais was in Lyons, editing Greek medical texts for a printer and serving as a doctor in a hospital. In the summer of that year, he read an anonymous book published in Lyons: The Great and Inestimable Chronicles of the Great and Enormous Giant Gargantua, *a crudely comic tale of a family of giants created by Merlin to serve King Arthur. The name and character of Gargantua were not original with the anonymous author; they had been a part of French folklore for centuries. The great success of the book and a visit to his familial home, which was then suffering from a severe drought, inspired Rabelais to write a sequel to the anonymous best seller.* Pantagruel *appeared in the autumn of 1532 and was an enormous success. Like Gargantua, Pantagruel originated in folk tradition, as a demon who poured salt down the throats of drunkards. He had appeared in a French mystery play half a century before, and by Rabelais' day the demon's name had become a proverbial term for a parching thirst.* Pantagruel, *like the anonymous* Gargantua *which inspired it, was a collection of traditional tales, but Rabelais made them his own through his exuberant style and satiric wit.*

The following summer, Rabelais met his greatest patron, Jean du Bellay, the

Bishop of Paris who was later to become archbishop and cardinal. He accompanied Du Bellay to Rome in 1534, where Rabelais unsuccessfully sought papal absolution for having left the monastic life without permission. Upon his return, he published his own version of the anonymous Gargantua, *as a sort of prologue to* Pantagruel. *It appears that Rabelais wanted not only to capitalize upon his success with* Pantagruel, *but also to write a similar work which would exploit more fully and more pointedly the satiric possibilities of the material.* Gargantua *is consequently much more satiric and outspoken than the earlier* Pantagruel.

Pantagruel *incurred the disapproval of the Sorbonne as an obscene book, and increasing religious persecution drove Rabelais into hiding for a time. In 1535, however, he accompanied Du Bellay on a second trip to Rome, and this time he was successful in obtaining absolution for having left the monastery. He was permitted to return to a Benedictine monastery, if he wished, and to practice medicine. Officially at least, Rabelais remained in good standing with the Church for the rest of his life.*

Rabelais traveled to Italy once again in 1539, this time with Jean du Bellay's older brother Guillaume, seigneur de Langey, remaining there until 1541. A new, definitive edition of Gargantua and Pantagruel *was published in that year. In this edition, Rabelais tempered his satire considerably; the term* theologians *was changed to* sophists *throughout. Nevertheless, in 1543, the Sorbonne officially condemned the book, forbidding its sale or possession. Despite this action, Rabelais obtained the King's permission in 1545 to publish a* Third Book, *which appeared in 1546. This book continued the adventures of Pantagruel and Panurge but was addressed to a more learned audience. Almost wholly lacking in narrative, it deals primarily with Panurge's desire to marry. After a series of thirteen consultations, his advisors conclude that if Panurge marries, he will almost certainly be cuckolded, beaten, and robbed by his wife. Despite the King's sanction and the comparative mildness of Rabelais' satire, soon after its publication the Sorbonne condemned the* Third Book *as well.*

Rabelais went again to Rome in 1548. Opposition to Gargantua and Pantagruel *intensified during his absence, but in 1550 Rabelais obtained the King's permission not only to republish the first three books, "revised and corrected," but also to bring out sequels. The* Fourth Book *therefore appeared in 1552. This volume told the fantastic tale of Pantagruel's and his friends' quest for the oracle of the Divine Bottle. The Sorbonne banned the book almost immediately, a year before Rabelais died in mid-1553. A* Fifth Book *of* Gargantua and Pantagruel *appeared posthumously in 1564. This book is almost certainly not entirely authentic, though it probably incorporates sketches and uncompleted fragments of a concluding book. It is notable mainly for completing the story of the voyage of Pantagruel and his friends; they finally reach the Divine Bottle, receive its oracle ("Drink!"), and set out for home again.*

Gargantua and Pantagruel *is easy to read but hard to describe or interpret. We look in vain for traditional elements of plot, character, and theme. The plot is rambling, episodic, and at times incoherent, and the major as well as the minor characters are little more than monstrous caricatures. Nor is it easy to identify the book's theme. It has traditionally been read as a satire, but the satirical element seems sporadic. In* Gargantua, *there is some satire on medieval ways of teaching and of reading such authors as Homer and Ovid, and the episode of Janotus de Bragmardo satirizes the Sorbonnists. In* Pantagruel, *the wordless debate between Panurge and Thaumaste satirizes scholastic modes of discourse. But these passages are comparatively short. What, if anything, is being satirized in, for instance, the long and monstrous descrip-*

tion of how Gargantua was born? It is hard to account for the overall impact of this flood of energetic obscenity merely in terms of satire.

Nor is the book only an entertaining story about giants. There have been such giant stories throughout literary history—for example, the stories of the Cyclops in the Odyssey *and of Goliath in the Old Testament; the folktale of "Jack and the Beanstalk"; and the story of the Brobdingnagians in the second book of Swift's* Gulliver's Travels. *But none of these is much like the giants in* Gargantua and Pantagruel. *Giants in literature tend to be either monstrous ogres, as in "Jack and the Beanstalk," or kindly big people whose stature echoes their magnanimity, as in* Gulliver's Travels. *The giants in* Gargantua and Pantagruel *seem to be great babies, whose size parallels their gigantic appetites—for food, wine, sex, and every other gratification. Nor does Rabelais seem to take the fact that they are giants very seriously. Swift gets a great deal of fun out of calculating his giants' precise size and exploring the implications of such size. Rabelais is wildly inconsistent in his treatment of his giants' relationship to normal-sized people and objects. Through much of the book, he presents them as ordinary people.*

Gargantua and Pantagruel *is not pornography, either, despite the liberal references to copulation. Grangousier and Gargamelle may "play the two-backed beast, rubbing and grinding their respective bacons together," but the effect is hardly erotic. The sexual act, like Panurge's "tailrasping bumswinks," is invariably presented as grotesque and absurd, parallel to other bodily functions such as eating, drinking, defecating, urinating, and vomiting.*

The meaning of Rabelais' comedy, modern critics have concluded, does not lie in either satire, folk-fantasies of gigantism, or pornography, but in its "carnivalesque" character. Rabelais' comedy is derived from the rich, bawdy comedy of the medieval carnivals and feast days, in which traditional authority was overturned, at least for the day, the king becoming a fool and the fool a king. Such comedy was full of extravagance, of oaths and curses, of distorted physical dimensions and appetites, and of fantastic combats, couplings, feastings, and drinkings. Its meaning was the celebration of the body and of experience in opposition to rigid forms of social authority; its effect was release and renewal.

Rabelais expresses this carnival spirit through an overwhelming exuberance of language. One critic has spoken of his ivresse lexicographique, *his "lexicographical drunkenness." His style is strongly oral—the book begins, "Hail, O most valiant and illustrious drinkers! Your health, my precious pox-ridden comrades"—and it explodes in truly gigantic lists, bravura speeches, threats, imprecations, curses, invented languages, mock-heroic descriptions, and other extravagances of verbal invention, indulged almost for their own sake.*

This sprawling and ebullient narrative is held together by the central metaphor of drinking. Gargantua comes tumbling out of Gargamelle's womb crying, "Drink, drink, drink!" and the entire book ends with the Oracle of the Divine Bottle: "Drink!" The thirst which began in a topical allusion to the great drought of 1532 becomes, as the book progresses, a thirst for experience and for life itself.

But "Drink!" is not the only counsel of the book. As modern critics such as Donald M. Frame have pointed out, two main voices dominate Gargantua and Pantagruel. *One is the voice of Rabelais' mock persona, Alcofribas Nasier, and that of the wily Panurge. This is the voice we ordinarily call "Rabelaisian"—lusty, obscene, jolly, and sometimes cruel. There is something infantile about this voice, something the English writer John Cowper Powys described as "becoming like a little child literally, in the sense of becoming like an ordinary, harmless, healthy, sense-absorbed, indecently shameless babe or suckling." This is the voice that opens the book, loudly hailing the readers as "most valiant and illustrious drinkers!" and proceeding to delight in unrestrained accounts of gratifications of all sorts. (We might add that there is profound misogyny in this voice, too, a quality that appears strongly in Panurge's cruel revenge upon the "Parisienne of high degree.")*

But there is another voice in the book, too, a restrained, stoic, tranquil voice of moderation identified in the later books with Pantagruel but also characteristic of Gargantua, once he becomes educated. It is heard, for example, in the description of how Ponocrates organized Gargantua's education and, at its most serious, in Gargantua's long letter to Pantagruel in Paris. This letter expresses quite directly and without a trace of the "Panurgian" voice the high conception of education and of human possibilities that underlies this extraordinary book.

FURTHER READING *(prepared by W. J. R.):* Biographies of Rabelais are plentiful and divergent in approach. Jean Plattard's *The Life of François Rabelais,* 1931, trans. by Louis P. Roche, 1968, is still the standard biography, with detailed accounts of the writer's phases of development and much attention to his writing. Marcel Tetel's *Rabelais,* 1967, examines the writer's artistry, explaining why Rabelais' reputation remains high in spite of the topicality of many of his ideas. Mikhail Bakhtin's *Rabelais and His World,* trans. by Helene Iswolsky, 1965, discusses the writer and his times from several perspectives and analyzes his imagery. Thomas M. Greene, *Rabelais: A Study in Comic Courage,* 1970, in the Landmarks in Literature series, is an introductory study that discusses Rabelais' works in their intellectual context and delineates his main themes. Abraham C. Keller's *The Telling of Tales in Rabelais,* 1963, concentrates on his narrative art, with interesting observations on the integration of didacticism and entertainment. Rabelais' method is also discussed in Barbara C. Bowen's *The Age of Bluff: Paradox and Ambiguity in Rabelais and Montaigne,* 1972. Defining "bluff" as a deliberate intention to disconcert the reader and to provoke thought, Bowen discusses Rabelais' use of paradox, enigma, antithesis, and other devices. Marcel Tetel's "The Function and Meaning of the Mock Epic Framework in Rabelais," *Neophilologus,* 59 (1975), 157–164, argues that the mock epic served Rabelais as the most expedient vehicle for several of his literary purposes. Tetel discusses *Gargantua and Pantagruel* in relation to the heroic epic, the quest epic, and the Bildungsroman. Chapter Two of Harcourt Brown's *Science and the Human Comedy,* 1976, examines why Rabelais has always been of great interest to medical people.

GARGANTUA AND PANTAGRUEL

Translated by Jacques LeClercq

TO MY READERS

Dear friends and readers who may scan these tomes,
Lay by all sense of prejudiced objection,
My pages bring no virus or infection
Across the thresholds of your virtuous homes.
True they can teach you only scant perfection
Save laughter's joys—though I confess I find
No theme more welcome to my heart and mind,

> *As I observe your melancholy fears,*
> *Your gib-cat airs, your saturnine dejection. . . .*
> *Better to write of laughter than of tears,*
> *For laughter is the essence of mankind.*

LIVE HAPPY!

from THE FIRST BOOK

The Very Horrendous Life of the Great Gargantua, Father of Pantagruel, Set Down of Yore by Monsieur Alcofribas,[1] Abstractor of Quintessence, A Book Filled with Pantagruelism.[2]

THE AUTHOR'S PROLOGUE

Hail, O most valiant and illustrious drinkers! Your health, my precious pox-ridden comrades! To you alone, I dedicate my writings. Suffer me, therefore, to draw your attention to a dialogue of Plato's called *The Banquet*.

In this work, Alcibiades, praising his master Socrates (undoubtedly the prince of philosophers), happens, among other things, to liken him to sileni.

Sileni, in the days of yore, were very small boxes such as you may see nowadays at your apothecary's. They were named for Silenus, foster father to Bacchus. The outside of these boxes bore gay, fantastically painted figures of harpies, satyrs, bridled geese, hares with gigantic horns, saddled ducks, winged goats in flight, harts in harness and many other droll fancies. They were pleasurably devised to inspire just the sort of laughter Silenus, Bacchus' master, inspired.

But inside these sileni, people kept priceless drugs such as balsam of Mecca, ambergris from the sperm whale, amomum from the cardamon, musk from the deer and civet from the civet's arsehole—not to mention various sorts of precious stones, used for medical purposes, and other invaluable possessions.

Well, Alcibiades likened Socrates to these boxes, because, judging by his exterior, you would not have given an onion skin for him. He was ill-shaped, ridiculous in carriage, with a nose like a knife, the gaze of a bull and the face of a fool. His ways stamped him a simpleton, his clothes a bumpkin. Poor in fortune, unlucky when it came to women, hopelessly unfit for all office in the republic, forever laughing, forever drinking neck to neck with his friends, forever hiding his divine knowledge under a mask of mockery. . . .

Yet had you opened this box, you would have found in it all sorts of priceless, celestial drugs: immortal understanding, wondrous virtue, indomitable courage, unparalleled sobriety, unfailing serenity, perfect assur-

---

[1] Alcofribas (Nasier) is an anagram of *François Rabelais*. The first two books of *Gargantua and Pantagruel* were published under this pseudonym.
[2] The name Rabelais gave to the half-serious philosophy expressed in his books.

ance and a heroic contempt for whatever moves humanity to watch, to bustle, to toil, to sail ships overseas and to engage in warfare.

Alcibiades? Socrates? The sileni? Why all this introductory flourish? Let me explain to you only, O my beloved disciples, and to such other idlers and idiots as read my works. Having noted the flippant titles of certain books of my invention—*Gargantua, Pantagruel, Drownbottle, The Dignity of Codpieces and Trouserflies, Of Peas and Bacon, with Tables and Sauce Material, etc.*—you jump to the conclusion that these tomes are filled with mere jests, vulgarities and buffoonery. Alas! you leap at the outward and visible sign; you swallow that title in a spirit of levity and derision without pausing to make further inquiry. How unseemly to consider so frivolously the works of humankind! Is it you who profess that clothes do not make the man nor robes the monk? Do I quote you when I declare that a fellow most monasterially apparelled may turn out to be a downright infidel whereas another, draped in a Spanish cloak, may possess every virtue on earth except Castilian pride and daring? Well then, you see why you should look beyond my title, open my book and seriously weigh its subject matter. The spice secreted within the box is more precious, far, than its exterior promised. In other words, the topics treated are not so foolish as the title suggested at first hand.

Again, supposing you find enough tomfoolery to live up to the title, must you tarry there, as Ulysses tarried at the song of the sirens?[3] Certainly not. Instead, you should lend a loftier sense to what you first believed written in the exuberance of humor.

Have you ever uncorked a bottle of wine? God help us, do you remember the look on your face?

Or have you ever seen a dog fall on a marrow bone? (The dog, I may add, is, as Plato says in Book II of the *Republic,* the most philosophic beast in the world.) If you have seen my dog, you may recall how intently he scrutinizes his bone, how solicitously he guards it, how fervently he clutches it, how warily he bites his way into it, how passionately he breaks it, how diligently he sucks it. What force moves him to act so, what hope fosters such zealous pains, what recompense does he aspire to? Nothing but a little marrow. (To be sure this little is more toothsome than large quantities of any other meat, for—as Galen[4] testifies in Chapter III of his *Concerning the Natural Faculties,* and Chapter XI of *Concerning the Uses of the Various Parts of the Human Body*—marrow is the most perfect food elaborated by nature.)

Modelling yourself upon the dog, you should be wise to scent, to feel and to prize these fine, full-flavored volumes. You should be fleet in your pursuit of them, resolute in your attack. Then, by diligent reading and prolonged meditation, you should break the bone of my symbols to suck out the marrow of my meaning—for I make use of allegory as freely as Pythagoras[5] did. As you read, you must confidently expect to become val-

---

[3]In Book XII of Homer's *Odyssey.* The Sirens lured ships onto their rocks with their songs; Odysseus stopped his men's ears with wax and had them tie him to the mast so that he could listen without danger.

[4]Greek physician (c. 130–c. 200 A.D.). He was revered as the supreme medical authority throughout the Middle Ages.

[5]Greek philosopher, sixth century B.C. The Pythagoreans were associated with allegory because they saw the visible world as veiling the true reality, which lay in numbers.

iant and wise. For here you will find a novel savor, a most abstruse doctrine; here you will learn the deepest mysteries, the most agonizing problems of our religion, our body politic, our economic life.

Do you honestly believe that Homer, penning his *Iliad* or *Odyssey,* ever dreamed of the allegorical patchwork subsequently inflicted upon him by Plutarch, by Heraclides Ponticus, by Eustathius, by Cornutus the Stoic, or by Politian, the Italian who filched his criticism from the lot of them?[6]

If you *do,* you are miles away from my opinion, for *I* hold that Homer no more dreamed of all this allegorical fustian than Ovid in his *Metamorphoses* dreamed of the Gospel.[7] Yet whenever he met folk as witless as himself, a certain Friar Jobbernowl, a true glutton for bacon and misinformation, strove to establish the Christianity of Ovid. Fit lids, that audience, for such a pot, say I, quoting the old saw.

If you agree with the Friar, why refuse the same consideration to my own original mirthful chronicles? Yes, even though I, writing them, gave the matter no more thought than you, who were probably also drinking. I may add that in composing this masterpiece I have not spent or wasted more leisure than is required for my bodily refection—food and drink to you! Is that not the proper time to commit to the page such sublime themes and such profound wisdom? Homer, the paragon of all philologists, knew it perfectly well and Ennius also, the father of the Latin poets, as Horace testifies, though a certain sorry clown has said that his poems smelled more of wine than of oil.[8]

So, too, spoke a third-rate cynic about my books, but a ripe turd to the fellow! Oh, the sweet fragrance of wine! How much more reconciling, smiling and beguiling wine is than oil! Let the world say I spent more on wine than on oil: I shall glory in it, like Demosthenes when they accused him of the opposite. For my part, I consider it honorable and noble to be reputed a sportsman and a wit, for as such I am welcome wherever two or three Pantagruelists are gathered together. Did not a certain surly bore denounce Demosthenes[9] because his *Orations* smelled like a filthy rag in an oil can? Not so, I!

Accordingly, take in perfect part all I write and do; revere the cheese-shaped brain which feeds you this noble flummery; strive diligently to keep me ever jocund.

And now, my hearties, be gay, and gayly read the rest, with ease of body and in the best of kidney! And you, donkey-pizzles, hark!—may a canker rot you!—remember to drink to me gallantly, and I will counter with a toast at once!

---

[6] All authors of classical or humanist commentaries on Homer. Politian (1454–94) was an Italian humanist whose preface to Homer was unjustly said to have been plagiarized from the commentary on Homer wrongly attributed to Plutarch.

[7] Ovid's *Metamorphoses* was often "moralized," or interpreted to yield Christian meanings, in the Middle Ages. The "Friar Jobbernowl" in the next sentence is the fourteenth-century English monk Thomas Wallis, who wrote such a commentary.

[8] Quintus Ennius (239–169? B.C.) was said to be the "father of the Latin poets." Who, if anyone, ever said that his "poems smelled more of wine than of oil" has never been discovered.

[9] Demosthenes (384?–322 B.C.) was a famous Greek orator. The "surly bore" was a certain Pytheas.

I

Gargantua: His Genealogy
and Antiquity

If you would learn the genealogy and antiquity which produced Gargantua, then I refer you to the lofty *Chronicle of Pantagruel.* Here you will learn in greater detail how giants were born in this world and how Gargantua, father to Pantagruel, descended directly from them. Do not take it amiss if, for the moment, I omit the account here, though the oftener I told the tale, the better it would please your lordships. I make this statement on the authority of Plato, in his *Philebus* and *Gorgias,* and of Flaccus, who declares there that certain topics (ours is undoubtedly among them) improve by repetition.

Would to God every one could be as certain of his pedigree from the days of Noah's celebrated ark down to the present. To my way of thinking, many a man sprung from a race of sham relic-peddlers and journeymen-carriers walks the earth to-day an emperor, king, duke, prince or pope. Similarly, not a few or our sorriest, most miserable tramps are sprung from the blood and lineage of proud kings and emperors. This is due to the unbroken descent of universal monarchy from the Assyrians to the Medes, from the Medes to the Persians, from the Persians to the Macedonians, from the Macedonians to the Romans, from the Romans to the Byzantine Greeks, and, finally, from the Greeks to the French.

What is more, to give you some notion of myself who now address you, I believe I derive my origin from some opulent monarch of olden days. For you never yet clapped eyes upon a man who craved kingship or wealth more passionately than I or longed more fervidly to live sumptuously, to do nothing, to avoid worry, to enrich abundantly both his friends and all other gentlemen of learning and worth. Yet I am consoled as I reflect that I shall be all this in the next world, to a vaster extent even than I dare wish to-day. For your part, if you nourish these or loftier hopes, take comfort in your distress and drink of the best, if you can manage it.

But to return to our sheep, as the Judge said to Pathelin in the farce.[10] Or, to come back to the point at issue! I solemnly declare that by the sovereign gift of Heaven, Gargantua's antiquity and pedigree have been more carefully preserved for us than any save the Messiah's. (Of the latter, I forbear to speak since it lies not in my province and since devils outside the Church and hypocrites within are strenuously opposed to it.)

Gargantua's pedigree was found by Jean Andeau in a meadow he owned at St. Mexme, near the pole-arch below L'Olive as you bear toward the hamlet of Narsay. They were scouring some ditches here when the diggers suddenly struck a tomb, a bronze tomb immeasurably long since it advanced so far into the sluices of the river Vienne that its other end was never found. They opened it where they saw a goblet with the legend HIC BIBITUR or HERE BE DRINKING written in highly obscure Etruscan script. And they found nine flagons, set up as the Gascons do ninepins, in rows of threes. Over the middle pin lay a book—and what a book! At once bulky

---

[10] *Pathelin* was a fifteenth-century French farce, to which Rabelais refers frequently.

yet small, big yet little, greasy and gray, moldy yet fragrant as attar of roses.

Upon its pages lay Gargantua's genealogy, engrossed at length in the cursive penmanship of the Papal Chancelry, not upon paper, nor upon parchment, nor yet upon wax, but on the bark of an elm tree. Unfortunately it was so worn by age that barely three consecutive letters were discernible.

Unworthy though I am, I was summoned. With the invaluable help of a pair of spectacles, I practiced that art which, according to Aristotle, makes it possible to read letters unapparent to the naked eye. As you may see, I translated it, pantagruelizing the while. In other words, I drank to my heart's content as I read of Pantagruel's horrendous exploits. . . .

III

How Gargantua Was Borne
Eleven Months in His
Mother's Womb

In his day, Grangousier or Greatgullet was a rollicking blade and a superlative toper.[11] With him it was always bottoms-up and no heel taps, for he drank deep as any man on the face of the earth. And he was ever ready to eat salted meat, which serves to rouse the thirst. Thus he was ordinarily well provided with hams from Mainz in Westphalia and Bayonne in Gascony; with oxtongues and chitterlings[12] in season; with salted beef and mustard; with sausages galore—not from Bologna, for he feared the Italian poisoner as a curer of bacon, but from Bigorre, Longaulnay, Brenne and Rouergue, all places nearer home.

Having attained manhood, appropriately enough he married Gargamelle—the name means gullet, also—daughter to the King of the Parpaillos or Butterflies, a jolly hoyden with a pleasing mug. Together the pair often played the two-backed beast, rubbing and grinding their respective bacons together so blithesomely and to such good purpose that she was soon big with a fair son, whom she bore for eleven months.

Does this sound strange? Perhaps. But a woman *can* bear offspring in her belly as long or even longer, especially when that offspring is a masterpiece of nature, destined to accomplish mighty exploits in his due time. Homer, himself, cites the child with which Neptune swelled the nymph Tyro: it was born a whole year after the conception. As Aulus Gellius comments, in Book III of the *Attic Nights,* such gestation was merely in keeping with the Sea God's majesty and assured the child its perfect form. By the same token, Jupiter miraculously protracted the duration of the night he bedded with Alcmena to forty-eight full hours. A shorter period could never have sufficed for the forging of Hercules, who purged the world of its monsters and tyrants.

What I state here, my masters, is confirmed by all the Pantagruelists of antiquity; they establish not only the feasibility of a child being born of woman in the eleventh month but also his legitimacy eleven months after

---

[11] Drinker.　　[12] The small intestines of pigs.

her husband's death. I invoke the authority of Hippocrates, in his book *Concerning Nourishment;* of Pliny the Elder in Chapter v, Book vii of his *Natural History;* of Plautus in his play the *Cistellaria;* of Marcus Varro, who, in his satire *The Testament,* quotes Aristotle to this effect; of Censorinus, in *Concerning the Day of Birth;* of Aristotle, Book vii, Chapters iii and iv of *Concerning the Nature of Animals;* of Aulus Gellius, Book iii, Chapter xvi of the *Attic Nights;* of Servius, who, in his commentary of Virgil's *Eclogues,* cites the verse:

> *Matri longa decem tulerunt fastidia menses*

or:

> *Ten loathsome months these mothers bore their burden*

and of a thousand other fools whose number has been increased by the lawyers. (Cf. Justinian's *Pandects* or *Digest,* Law iii, Paragraph xiii, Book xxx, Chapter viii, *De suis et legitimis heredibus, lege intestato* or *Concerning personal and legitimate heirs legally unprovided for by will;* cf. also *Novella* xxxix, Justinian's *Novels,* which were an unauthorized collection of constitutions subsequent to the lawgiver's *Codex: De restitutionibus et ea quae parit in undecimo mense post mortem viri* or *Concerning legal restitution and the female who bears child in the eleventh month following decease of her husband.*)

Furthermore, to the same purpose, the lawyers have scrawled, stamped, sealed and scribbled their bacon-filching Gallus Law *(Digest: De liberis et posthumis heredibus intestuendis vel exheredandis* or *Concerning posthumous children and heirs unprovided for by will or disinherited)* and the Law *De statu hominum: Septimo mense nasci perfectum partum jam receptum est propter auctoritatem doctissimi viri Hippocratis* or *A birth occurring the seventh month following conception is to-day legal and acceptable according to the authority of the illustrious scholar Hippocrates (Digest,* Law xii, Book i, Chapter lvii) and several other laws that I dare not name at present. Does this seem involved? I have at least spared you the jurisprudential transcriptions, which read: *ff. de suis, et legit 1, intestato,* for instance, or *ff. de lib. et posth. 1. sept. ff. de stat. hom.*

Thanks to these learned laws, our virtuous widows may, for two months after their husbands' demise, freely indulge in games of gripcrupper with a pig in the poke, heels over head and to their hearts' content.

As for you, my friends and lusty lads all, should you find any widows worth lowering your breeches for, I pray you most graciously to mount them, surmount them and bring them home to me. For, should they bourgeon the third month, the child will fall heir to the deceased husband and, these ladies' condition being legal and respectable, they scuttle away, go the whole hog and, *vogue la galère!* the devil take the hindmost. . . . In brief, they behave like Julia, daughter of the Emperor Octavian, who never abandoned herself to her bellybumpers unless she was plump with child, on the principle that a vessel takes on its pilot only after it has been caulked and laden.[13] Now if any one upbraids these righteous ladies for suffering

---

[13] Both Julia (39 B.C.–A.D. 14), daughter of the Emperor Augustus (Octavian), and her daughter Julia (18 B.C.–A.D. 28) were notorious for their immorality.

themselves to be thus vaginoexcavated on their fullness, when even the beasts, littering, will not endure their males to masculate, what will the answer be? Like Populia of yore, according to Macrobius (*Saturnalia*, Book II), they will reply that those are beasts, precisely, whereas for their part they are women, skilled and experienced in the noble joys and the agreeable little quirks of superfetation.

If the devil would not have them potbellied, he must twist the spigot hard and stop up the bunghole.

IV

How Gargamelle, Bigswoln With Gargantua, Ate an Abundance of Tripe

The occasion and manner of Gargamelle's delivery were as I am about to relate; if you do not believe me, may your vent-peg slip, may your stopper fail your (rectal) organ, your fundament fall and your flue pipe collapse!

This is exactly what happened to Gargamelle, on February third, after dinner. And why? Because she had eaten too abundantly of tripe . . . of that tripe which comes from beeves . . . from beeves which are fatted in their stalls and put to graze in meadows . . . in meadows which bear two crops of grass each year. . . .

Three hundred and sixty-seven thousand and fourteen of these fat beeves had been slaughtered. They were to be salted on Shrove Tuesday so that there would be pressed beef aplenty that spring for the invocation of thirst and its subsequent exorcization by wine.

There was abundance of tripe, as you may imagine, such succulent tripe, too, that every one licked his fingers with glee. But there was a rub—and a four-devil power rub at that! Alas, the tripe could not be kept on hand long or it would spoil—a most disagreeable thought! They therefore decided to guzzle it all down to the last scrap. For fear of leaving any, they summoned all the citizenry of Sinais, Seuilly, La Roche Clermault and Vaugaudry, without forgetting their friends from Coudray-Montpensier and Gué de Vède and other neighbors, all accomplished tosspots, debonair fellows and ha! fine cuedrivers, skilled tailpushers, all!

That dear man Grangousier, mightily pleased at their company, ordered meat by the ton, wine by the thousand gallons. No pains were spared to honor his guests. But he *did* caution his wife to eat sparingly, since she was near her time, and in her condition tripe was not exactly the most suitable diet.

"Whoever eats the skins of these chitterlings," he announced, "is an unparalleled turdchewer!"

Despite his warnings, Gargamelle consumed sixteen quarters, two bushels and six pecks; in cases, barrels and pots. La! the sweet fecality that must have swelled up within her!

After dinner, they all made helter-skelter for La Saussaie, a meadow planted with willow trees. Here, on the soft greensward, they danced so gleefully to the tune of airy flutes and melodious bagpipes that to watch them was a most heavenly pastime.

VI

The Strange and
Wonderful Manner of
Gargantua's Birth

While they were thus engaged. . , Gargamelle began to feel slightly upset in her lower parts. Grangousier immediately rose from the grass and proceeded to comfort her most feelingly. She must now be in travail, he suspected. So he told her to lie down on the grass under the willows and expect shortly to see a pair of new feet next to her own. She must therefore pluck up her courage at the prospect of the babe's arrival; though the pain was somewhat grievous, it would be brief. More, her joy when it was over would banish even the memory of what she had suffered.

"I can prove it to you," he said, "for God, that is our Saviour, says in the *Gospel According to St. John* (Chapter XVI): 'A woman in travail hath sorrow because her hour is come; but as soon as she is delivered of the child, she remembereth no more the anguish.'"

"Ha!" Gargamelle broke in. "You speak nobly. I derive greater pleasure and profit in hearing such thoughts from the Gospel than in listening to the *Life of St. Margaret* or to other like cant prescribed for women in childbearing."[14]

"Courage, girl," Grangousier continued, "all you need is the courage of a sheep! Dispatch this boy and we shall be busy soon making another!"

"Ha," she countered, "it's easy for you men to dismiss it so lightly! Ah, well! by the help of God, I shall strive my utmost, since such is your wish, Grangousier. But would to God it had been cut off you!"

"What?" asked Grangousier.

"Ha," she said, "what an innocent you are! You heard what I said."

"Do you mean my member?" he cried. "'Sblood![15] if you wish it, I'll have a knife brought me."

"Oh, never! God forbid! God forgive me, I didn't speak it from my heart, so don't take any notice of what I said. But I shall be having plenty of work to-day, unless God come to my aid, and all because of your member, that you might have pleasure."

"Courage, courage!" he urged. "The worst is over. Once the plow is out of the mire, sit tight and let the four front oxen do the pulling. For my part, I'm off to swill up a few more draughts of wine. Meantime, should any harm befall you, I shall be near by. Halloo through your hands and I shall rush to your side!"

A few moments later she began to groan, lament and cry out. Suddenly crowds of midwives came rushing up from all directions. Feeling and groping her below, they found certain loose shreds of skin, of a rather unsavory odor, which they took to be the child. It was, on the contrary, her fundament which had escaped with the mollification of her right intestine (you call it the bumgut) because she had eaten too much tripe, as I explained above.

---

[14] The *Life of St. Margaret*, patron saint of childbearing, was often read to women during labor.

[15] A distortion of "God's blood!," a common oath.

Thereupon, a grimy old baggage of the company, who had come from Brisepaille near St. Genou threescore years before, and was reputed to be a great she-physician, administered an astringent. So horrible was this restrictive medicine that it obstructed and contracted the sphincters of Gargamelle's vents and flues, until you could barely have pried them open with your teeth. A truly revolting thought, this, but one suggested by the story of the Devil at St. Martin's Mass noting down the chatter of two trollops and with his teeth stretching the parchment he wrote on, in a vain effort to keep up with them.[16]

As a result of Gargamelle's discomfort, the cotyledons of the placenta of her matrix were enlarged. The child, leaping through the breech and entering the hollow vein, ascended through her diaphragm to a point above her shoulders. Here the vein divides into two; the child accordingly worked his way in a sinistral direction, to issue, finally, through the left ear.

No sooner born, he did not, like other babes, cry: "Whaay! Whaay!" but in a full, loud voice bawled: "Drink, drink, drink!" as though inviting the company to fall to. What is more, he shouted so lustily that he was heard throughout the regions of Beuxe (pronounced "booze") and Bibarois (which in sound evokes bibbers and is how the Gascons pronounce "Vivarais").

Now I suspect that you do not thoroughly believe this strange nativity. If you do not, I care but little, though an honest and sensible man always believes what he is told and what he finds written. Does not Solomon say in *Proverbs* (XIII, 15): *"Innocens credit omni verbo,* the innocent believeth every word," and does not St. Paul (*I Corinthians,* 13) declare: *"Charitas omnia credit,* Charity believeth all."

Why should you not believe what I tell you? Because, you reply, there is no evidence. And I reply in turn that for this very reason you should believe with perfect faith. For the gentlemen of the Sorbonne say that faith is the argument of non-evident truths.

Is anything I have related beyond our law or faith, contrary to our reason, or opposed to Divine Scriptures? For my part, I find nothing in the Holy Bible that stands against it. And if such had been the will of God, would you affirm that He could not accomplish it? Ha, I pray you, do not ambiguembrangle your minds with such vain conceits. I tell you that nothing is impossible to God and, if He but pleased, women would henceforth give birth to their children through the left ear.

Was not Bacchus engendered out of the very thigh of Jupiter? Was not Roquetaillade or Cleftrock ushered into the world through his mother's heel? Did not Croquemouche or Craunchfly first see the light out of his nurse's slipper? Was not Minerva progenerated out of the brain and through the ear of Jupiter? Was not the bark of a myrrh tree brought to bed of Adonis? And did not an eggshell, laid and hatched by Leda, extravasate Castor and Pollux into being?[17]

---

[16] The episode referred to here appears in the mystery play of the *Life of St. Martin.* The devil at St. Martin's Mass is so frustrated by being unable to keep up with the gossip of two young women or to keep his parchment unrolled to write it down that he strikes his head against a pillar.

[17] The stories of the miraculous births of Bacchus, Minerva, Adonis, and Castor and Pollux appear in classical mythology; those of Roquetaillade and Croquemouche are whimsical inventions by Rabelais.

You would be infinitely more surprised and stunned were I presently to expose to you the entire chapter in which Pliny deals with fantastic and unnatural births, yet I am not nearly so accomplished a liar as he was. Read his *Natural History*, Book VII, Chapter III, yourselves, and do not plague me further with the subject.

VII

How Gargantua Came By
His Name and How He
Swilled Down the Wine

That excellent man Grangousier was drinking and making merry with the others, when he heard a horrible tumult. It was his son emerging into the light of this world, bellowing, "Drink, drink, drink!"

At once Grangousier exclaimed: *"Que grand tu as le gousier"* or "What a great gullet you have!" Hearing this, the company declared that the child should indeed be named *"grand tu as"*: Gargantua or Greatgullet. Were these not the first sounds the father had uttered after the child's birth? And was this not an ancient Hebrew custom well worth following? Grangousier assented; Gargamelle was delighted with the idea.

Next, to quiet the babe, they made him drink till his throat almost burst. Then, carrying him to the font, they baptized him, as is the custom among all good Christians.

Shortly after, they appointed seventeen thousand nine hundred and thirteen cows from Pontille and Bréhémont to furnish him with milk in ordinary,[18] for, considering his enormous needs, it was impossible to find a satisfactory nurse in all the country. Nevertheless, certain learned doctors, disciples of Duns Scotus,[19] have affirmed that his own mother suckled him. She could, they say, draw from her breasts two thousand one hundred and three hogsheads and eighteen pints at one time. This seems scarcely probable. Indeed, this point has been condemned by the Sorbonne as mammarily scandalous and reeking with heresy.

Gargantua was thus looked after until he was twenty-two months old. Then, on the advice of the physicians, they began to carry him, and Jean Denyau built a special ox-drawn cart for him. They drove him about in it here, there and everywhere with the greatest pleasure; and a fine sight he was, too, with a great, open face and almost eighteen chins! He cried very little but he beshitted himself at all times. For he was wondrously phlegmatic of bum, as much by natural complexion as from an accidental predisposition, due to exaggerated quaffing of the juices of Septembral mash.[20] Yet he never touched a drop without good reason; for whenever he happened to be out of sorts, vexed, angry or melancholy, if he stamped, wept or shouted, they brought him a drink. This invariably restored his native good humor and at once made him as quiet and happy as before.

[18] For everyday use.
[19] British or Irish scholastic philosopher (d. 1308). He was a favorite satirical target of Rabelais; the fact that our modern word *dunce* comes from his name suggests his low reputation in the Renaissance.
[20] New autumn wine.

One of his governesses told me on oath what a rooted habit this tippling had become. Indeed, the mere clinking of pints and flagons sent him off into the ecstasy of one who tastes the joys of Paradise. Accordingly, in view of this divine character, they used to delight him every morning by making music on glasses with knives, on bottles with their stoppers, and on pots with their lids. At this he would turn gay, thrill with joy, wag his head and rock from side to side, monochording with his fingers and barytoning through his tail.

XI

OF GARGANTUA'S ADOLESCENCE

From three to five years of age, Gargantua was, by his father's orders, brought up and instructed in all proper discipline. He spent his time like other small children; namely, in drinking, eating and sleeping; in eating, sleeping and drinking; in sleeping, drinking and eating.

He was forever wallowing in dirt, covering his nose with filth and begriming his face. He wore his shoes down to a frazzle, lay with his mouth gaping to catch heaven knows what, and delighted in chasing butterflies—an infidel tribe over which his father ruled. He used to piddle on his shoes, brown up his shirt-tails, wipe his nose on his sleeve, clear his nostrils into his soup, and dive headlong into the foulest muck at hand. He was wont to drink from his slipper, scratch his belly with a wicker basket and sharpen his teeth on a wooden shoe. When he washed his hands, he did so in his soup; he combed his hair with a drinking cup, fell flat on his rump between two stools, blew hot and cold, cut blocks with a razor and drank while he ate his broth. His bread he consumed without dough; he bit laughing and laughed biting. Often he coughed up, figuratively and literally. Fat? another ounce of wind and he would have exploded. Appreciative? He would piss, full-bladdered, at the sun. Cautious? He used to hide under water for fear of the rain.

Among Gargantua's other pursuits were striking on the iron while it was cold;[21] going woolgathering; shamming Abraham or playing the hypocrite; throwing up his food or flaying the fox, as the saying goes; reciting the monkey's paternoster or letting his teeth chatter like a baboon's. If he had wandered from the point, he invariably followed the Judge's advice to Pathelin, and came back to his sheep . . . he turned his hogs to hay or, as some say, took the wrong sow by the ear . . . he beat the dog for the lion or thrashed the slave to teach the master a lesson . . . he put the cart before the horse and locked the stable door after the mare was stolen. . . . He did not self-flatteringly scratch himself where he itched, but unexpectedly enough where he did not. He would pump people and bite off more than he could chew, leap before he looked, milk the ram and tickle himself to make himself laugh. A fine trencherman, withal, he plied a tireless knife and fork.

Among his other accomplishments were stealing pigs and giving the feet to God . . . having the magnificat sung at matins and considering it

[21] The following passage is a mishmash of popular proverbs.

perfectly seasonable . . . eating red cabbage and voiding white beets . . .
knowing black from white and spotting a fly in a bowl of milk . . . cooling
his heels . . . pouring water into sieves. . . . He would scribble on papers,
mess up parchments and save his bacon by taking French leave. He collected hairs from the dog that bit him, tossed the pot, threw up and
reckoned without his host. He beat about the bush without stirring the
birds; he thought the moon was made of green cheese and bladders were
lanterns.

He feathered his nest; had two strings to his bow and two linings to his
purse; he would play the ass if he could get a sack of bran out of it and
he made a mallet of his fist. With the greatest ease, he caught weasels
asleep and washed blackamoors white; and, throwing in his lot with
such as believe Rome was not built in a day, he held that some roads
led elsewhere.

Gargantua was also inclined to look a gift horse in the mouth . . . tell
cock and bull stories . . . throw the helve after the hatchet . . . rob Peter to
pay Paul . . . fence in the cuckoo to preserve the summer and keep the
moon safe from the wolves . . . hope, if the heavens fell, to catch larks . . .
make a virtue of necessity . . . cut his coat according to his cloth . . . split no
hairs and care as little for the shaven as for the shorn. . . .

Every morning Gargantua retched, spewed, flayed the fox. He ate out
of the same dish as his father's puppies: he would bite their ears, they
would scratch his nose, and he blow into their arseholes whilst they licked
his chops.

Do you know what else he did, my brave lads? May the drunkard's pip
rot your guts if the little lecher wasn't forever groping his nurses upside-
down, arsey-turvy, *hirdie-girdie, giddy-up, whoah, Hinny!*—and if he wasn't
beginning to bring his codpiece into play and turn it to account. Every
morning his governesses prinked and dizened it with lovely nosegays and
fine silken tassels. Their favorite pastime was to feel and finger his organ,
to knead and mold it lovingly as pharmacists handle ointment and salve to
make a large, solidified cylindrical suppository. Then they would burst out
laughing for joy at the sport as, under their skilled hands, it would prick up
its ears.

One called it her darling faucet, another her corking pin, a third her
coral branch, a fourth her bungpeg, a fifth her stopgap. Others named it
variously their ramrod, their spikebit, their swagdangle, their trunnion,
their private hardware because it must be hard where they stocked it, their
lever, their borer, their little ruddy sausage, their nutty little booby prize.

"It belongs to me!" one cried.

"No. it's mine!" another protested.

"What about me?" piped up a third. "Shall I have no share in it? By my
faith, I'll cut it off then."

"Ha!" said the other. "You would hurt him, Madame, if you cut it off.
Do you propose to cut a child's penial utensil? He'd be Master Bobtail,
then!"

And so that he might play like other little children they made him a fine
whirligig with the wings from a windmill in the Mirebelais region of the
Poitou.

XIV

How Gargantua Was Taught
Latin by a Theologian
and Sophist

The excellent Grangousier was rapt with admiration as he listened to his son talking. Truly this lad was marvellously gifted! What a vast intelligence, what cogent understanding! Turning to the governesses:

"Philip, King of Macedon," he declared, "recognized the sound judgment of Alexander, his son, when he saw how skillfully the lad managed his horse. This beast Bucephalus was so fierce and unruly that it threw all its riders. It cracked one man's neck, smashed another's legs, brained a third, and crushed the jawbone of a fourth. No one, then, dared mount it. Alexander happened to be in the hippodrome watching them breaking in and training the horses; he noticed at once that the beast's frenzy came from fright at its own shadow. He therefore made short shrift of vaulting upon its back and heading it towards the sun. There, its shadow falling behind it, he easily mastered it. Philip, by this token, realized the divine insight rooted in his son's intelligence and had him most carefully reared by Aristotle, then the most renowned philosopher in Greece.

"For my part, the brief conversation I have just had with Gargantua in your presence suffices to convince me that his mind is illumined by the divine spark. How else, pray, could he have proved so acute, so subtle, so profound and withal so serene? Give the boy proper schooling, say I, and he will attain a supreme degree of wisdom! Accordingly, I intend to trust him to some scholar who will instruct him to his capacity. What is more, I shall spare no cost."

The name of Master Tubal Holofernes, a great sophist and Doctor of Theology, was proposed to Grangousier.[22] Subsequently this savant taught Gargantua his A B C so thoroughly that he could say it by heart backwards. This took five years and three months. A succession of standard texts followed; the *Facet* (a treatise of puerile moral precepts), the *Ars Grammatica* of Actius Donatus, the fourth-century grammarian; the *Theodolet* (in which Theodulus, Bishop of Syria in the fifth century, exposed in Latin the falsity of mythology and the truth of Holy Scripture) and the *Alanus in Parabolis* (a series of moral quatrains by Alanus of Lille, a thirteenth-century worthy). It took Gargantua thirteen years, six months and two weeks to master these authorities.

It is only fair to add, however, that Gargantua, in the process, learned to write in Gothic characters. (Printing had not yet been invented and the young student had to write out his own texts.)

He had, therefore, to carry in front of him a tremendous writing apparatus that weighed more than seven hundred thousand pounds. The pencase was as large and as tall as the great columns of the Church of St.

---

[22] Tubal Holofernes' names are both biblical; see Genesis 4:22 and the book of Judith. Master Holofernes' instruction of Gargantua parodies the medieval method of teaching, including reading to the pupil, rote drill, endless repetition, and a very slow pace. The books named were standard medieval textbooks, currently being discredited by the New Learning.

Martin of Ainay in Lyons; the inkhorn was suspended to it by great iron chains wide enough to hold five cubic yards of merchandise.

Another book, *De Modis Significandi*—a work of speculative grammar by Thomas Aquinas, or Albert of Saxony or probably Duns Scotus—was Gargantua's next reading, together with comments by Hurtebize or Windjammer, by Fasquin or Roadheaver, by Tropditeux or Toomanysuch, by Gualehault or Galahad, by Jean Le Veau or John Calf, by Billonio or Lickspittle, by Brelinguandus or Timeserver, and by a rabble of others. This took more than eighteen years and eleven months, but Gargantua knew the texts so well that at examinations he could recite them by heart backwards. And he could prove to his mother on his fingers' ends that *de modis significandi non erat scientia,* grammar was no science.

Next he read the *Compost* or *Popular Calendar,* and had spent sixteen years and two months at it, when suddenly, in 1420, his tutor died of the pox.

Holofernes' successor was another wheezy old pedant named Master Jobelin Bridé or Jolter Clotpoll, who read him the *Liber Derivationum* or *Latin Vocabulary* of Hugutio of Pisa, thirteenth-century Bishop of Ferrara . . . the *Grecism* by Everard de Béthune, a philological lexicon illustrating the Latin words derived from the Greek . . . *De Octo Partibus Orationis* or *Of the Eight Parts of Speech* . . . the *Quid Est?* or *What is it?* a school manual in the form of questions and answers . . . the *Supplementum,* a collection of commentaries . . . the *Mammotreptus,* a monkish or monkeyish commentary on the Psalter and the Saints . . . the *Libellus de Moribus in Mensa Servandis* or *Essay on Manners in Serving at Table,* a rhymed treatise on youthful propriety and morals by Sulpizio de Veroli . . . Seneca's *De Quatuor Virtutibus Cardinalibus* or *Of the Four Cardinal Virtues,* a moral work by Martin de Braga, Bishop of Mondonedo in the sixth century . . . the *Specchio della vera Penitenza* or *Mirror of True Penitence* by Jacobo Passaventi, the Florentine monk of the sixteenth century—with its inevitable commentary! . . . a book of sermons, *Dormi Secure* or *Sleep in Peace,* a collection designed to save the preacher the pains of composing his sermons . . . and finally, other stuff of the same ilk, feather, kidney and broth. . . .

Indeed, Gargantua grew as even as any down ever smoothed, as full of matter as any goose liver ever crammed!

XV

HOW GARGANTUA WAS PUT
UNDER OTHER PROFESSORS

At last his father realized that though Gargantua was studying most industriously and spending all his time at it, he was profiting not at all. Worse, this training had actually made the lad over into a fool, a dunce, a booby and a nincompoop.

One day Grangousier happened to complain of it to Don Philippe des Marais, Viceroy of Papeligosse, a kingdom of Cockaigne.[23] That monarch assured Grangousier that Gargantua would be better off learning nothing than studying books of the sort with pedagogues of that school. Their

---

[23] An imaginary country of idleness and luxury.

knowledge, said Don Philippe, was but rubbish, their wisdom flapdoodle; they succeeded merely in bastardizing noble spirits and corrupting the flower of youth.

"Upon my word, I'll prove it!" Don Philippe declared. "Take any lad of to-day with but two years' schooling. If he is not superior to your son in judgment, speech, bearing and personality, then I'm the greatest logger-head and shallowpate from here to Brenne."

This challenge pleased Grangousier mightily; he at once gave orders that a match of wits take place.

That evening, at supper, Don Philippe brought in a young page of his named Eudemon, which means "the fortunate." The lad hailed from Villegongis near St. Genou in Touraine. He was so neat, so spruce, so handsome and his hair was so beautifully combed that he looked more like an angel than like a man.[24]

Don Philippe turned to Grangousier:

"Do you see this lad? He's not twelve years old. Let us prove, if you will, the difference between the pedantic balderdash of yesterday's wiseacres and the intelligence of our modern boys."

Grangousier was agreeable to such a test and bade the page begin the debate. Whereupon Eudemon, asking leave of the Viceroy, his master, to do so, rose, hat in hand. His face was open and frank, his lips red, his glance confident. Looking at Gargantua with youthful modesty, he proceeded to praise and commend the boy—first for his virtues and good manners, next for his knowledge, thirdly for his nobility, fourthly for his bodily excellences and, in the fifth place, exhorted him most gracefully to reverence his father in all respects, because his father was so careful to have him well brought up. Finally, Eudemon prayed Gargantua to admit him among the least of his bondsmen. He added that the only boon he craved from Heaven, at present, was to serve Gargantua in some agreeable manner. Eudemon accompanied the whole speech with gestures so appropriate, his delivery was so distinct, his voice rang so eloquent, his idiom was so elegant and he couched his phrases in such perfect Latin that he seemed rather a Tiberius Gracchus, a Cicero or an Aemilius Lepidus of old,[25] than a youth of our own day.

Gargantua's only reaction was to burst into tears. He bawled like a sick cow, hung his head and hid his face in his cap, until there was about as much possibility of drawing a word from him as a salvo of farts from the rump of a dead donkey.

This so incensed his father that Grangousier vowed to slay Master Jobelin Clotpoll, but Don Philippe remonstrated with him and, by fair persuasions, soothed his ire. Grangousier thereupon ordered them to pay the pedagogue off and to get him as properly fuddled up as your finest scholar of the Sorbonne. This accomplished, let him go to the devil!

"There is this consolation!" cried Grangousier. "To-day at least, he will not cost his host much if by chance he dies in his cups like an Englishman."

---

[24] Eudemon represents the new education, in contrast to Gargantua's old-fashioned education. He speaks in Ciceronian Latin and, in his speech, follows an orderly mode of developing a thesis.

[25] The Roman orator Cicero (106–43 B.C.) praised both Tiberius Gracchus and Aemilius Lepidus for their skill in oratory.

When Master Jobelin Clotpoll had gone away, Grangousier asked Don Philippe's advice about a tutor for Gargantua. They finally decided to appoint Ponocrates, Eudemon's teacher, to the position; auspiciously enough, in Greek the name means "vigorous." And soon, the three were to go to Paris in order to find out what studies young men were at this period pursuing in France.

XVI

How Gargantua Went to
Paris Upon an Enormous
Mare Which Destroyed
the Oxflies of the Beauce

In the same season, Fayolles, fourth king of Numidia, sent Grangousier a mare from Africa. It was the hugest and most enormous mare ever seen, the strangest monster in the world; for Africa, as the saying goes, may always be relied upon to produce something wonderfully new. The beast was as big as six elephants; like Julius Caesar's charger, her feet were cloven into human toes; her ears hung down like those of the goats of Languedoc; and a little horn grew out of one buttock. Save for a few dapple-gray spots as overlay, her coat was the color of burnt sorrel, which shows that she partook of the four elements, earth, water, air and fire. Above all, she had a horrible tail. It was more or less as tall as the tower of St. Mars near Langeais; and just as square, with tufts of hair as tightly spun and woven as the beards on ears of corn.

Do you marvel at this? You have greater cause to marvel at the tails of the rams of Scythia, which weighed more than thirty pounds each, or—if Jean Thenaud speaks truthfully in his *Voyage from Angoulême to Cairo*—at those of the Syrian sheep which are so long and heavy that, to hold them up, the natives have to hitch a small cart to the beast's rump. Ha! my lusty country wenchthumpers, you've no such tails as these!

The mare Fayolles sent Grangousier was brought overseas in three Genoese carracks and a brigantine; she landed at Les Sables d'Olonne in Talmondais.

When Grangousier laid eyes upon her:

"Ah!" he exclaimed. "Here is just what my son needs to bear him to Paris! So now, in God's name, all will go well: Gargantua shall be a great scholar one of these days! Were it not for dumb brutes we should all be scholars!"

Next day, having drunk liberally, as you may imagine, Gargantua set out on his journey, accompanied by his tutor Ponocrates, the young page Eudemon and his train. And, because the weather was serene and temperate, Grangousier had a pair of dun-colored boots made for him. According to Babin and the Chinon cobblers, these are technically known as buskins.

So they travelled along the highway very merrily, living on the fat of the land and making the best of cheer, until a little beyond Orléans they came to a huge forest, about thirty-five leagues long and seventeen wide. Alas! the woods were aswarm with oxflies and hornets of all varieties, so the wretched mares, asses and horses suffered a veritable massacre. But, by means of a trick they never suspected, Gargantua's mare handsomely avenged all the outrages visited upon her kind. For suddenly, when in the heart of the forest the wasps attacked her, she swished her tail and, sweeping all about her, not only felled the stingers but uprooted all the trees. Up and down, right and left, lengthwise and athwart, here and there, over and under, before her and aback, this way and that, she mowed down the woods like so much grass. And this region, which she thus turned into fallow land, has never known tree or wasp since.

Gargantua, delighted by the spectacle, forbore to boast, merely commenting to his followers:

"*Je trouve beau ce!* I find this pleasant!"

Whence this pleasant land has been known as Beauce ever since.

However, when it came to breakfasting, they had to content themselves with their yawns; in memory of which the gentlemen of the Beauce, proverbially poor, still subsist on a diet of yawns and gaping, and find it very nourishing. Indeed, they spit all the better for it.

At last they reached Paris, where Gargantua rested two or three days, making merry with his followers and inquiring about what scholars were then in the city and what wines people drank.

XVII

Of the Treat Gargantua
Gave the Parisians on
His Arrival and How He
Carried Off the Great
Bells of Notre Dame

After a few days' rest, Gargantua went sightseeing. He attracted the attention of all the townsmen because Parisians are such fools, dolts and gulls that a mountebank, a hawker of relics and indulgences,[26] a mule with a bell on its neck or a fiddler on a street corner, collects a greater mob than the most distinguished and authoritative preacher.

They thronged so thick about him that he said in a loud clear voice:

"Upon my word, I think these boobies want me to pay my welcome here and give the Bishop an offertory.[27] Quite right, too! I'll treat them! They'll get their drink! I recognize my obligations and liquidate I shall!—but only *par ris,* for sport!"

Then, smiling, he unfastened his noble codpiece and lugging out his great pleasure-rod, he so fiercely bepissed them that he drowned two hundred and sixty thousand four hundred and eighteen, exclusive of women and children.

By sheer fleetness of foot, a certain number escaped this mighty pissflood, and reaching the top of the Montagne Ste. Geneviève, beyond the University, sweating, coughing, hawking and out of breath, they began to swear and curse, some in anger, others in jest:

—"God's plague and a pox take it! I'll deny God, if. . ."

[26] Memorials of saints and papers remitting temporal punishments for sins.
[27] Fee paid to bishops after their ordination.

—"'Sblood!"

—"Christ, look ye, it's *Mére de . . . merde . . .* shit . . . Mother of God!"

—"*Pocapedion!* God's head!" roared a Gascon.

—"*Das dich Gots leyden Schend!*" bellowed a German trooper. "Christ's passion roil you!"

—"*Pote de Christo!*" an Italian voice rang out. "Christ's power!"

—"*Ventre St. Quenet!* . . . By the bellies of all the apostles . . . God's virtue . . . by St. Fiacre of the land of Brie!"

They called upon the renowned saint who cured miraculously such ailments as hemorrhoids and chancres, and who was patron to gardeners and husbandmen; one, doubtless a Scots Guard, invoked St. Andrew; and St. Theobald of Vico, the patron of shoemakers, was duly implored to intercede.

—"*Pasques Dieu!* God's passover!" said one, using an oath consecrated by King Louis XI.

—"*Bonjour Dieu!* God's light!" said another, after the manner of Charles VII.

—"*Le Diable m'emporte!* Devil take me!" said a third, quoting Louis XII.

—"*Foy de Gentilhomme!* My faith as a gentleman!" said a fourth, like Francis I.

—"*Par St. Andouille* . . . by St. Chitterling . . . by St. Godegran stoned to death with apple dumplings . . . by St. Foutin, the fornicators' friend! . . . by St. Vitus and his jig! . . . *Carimari, Carimara, hocus, pocus!* . . . by St. Mamica, the virgin martyr, by our lusty mammical duty to all virgins. . . ."

But, whatever protector each invoked, one and all cried:

"*Nous sommes baignés par ris,* we are drenched *par ris,* for sport."

Accordingly, the city which Strabo (Book IV) calls Leucetia—the name, signifying "whiteness" in Greek, pays a pretty tribute to the thighs of the local ladies—was, ever after Gargantua's exploit, named *par ris* or Paris.

And, since at this new christening every single townsman present swore by all the saints in his parish, the Parisians, who are made up of all nations and all varieties of men, will quite naturally swear at, to or by anything. Indeed they are not a little presumptuous and conceited, whence Joaninus de Barranco in his *Liber de Copiositate Reverentiarum* or *Of the Abundance of Venerable Things* opines that the word *Parisian* comes from the Greek *Parrhesieus,* a bold talker.

His account liquidated, Gargantua considered the great bells in the Towers of Notre Dame and made them ring out most harmoniously. The music suggested to him that they might sound very sweet tinkling on his mare's neck when he sent her back to his father laden with Brie cheese and fresh herring. So he promptly picked up the bells of the Cathedral and carried them home.

Meanwhile, a master beggar or Commander of the Order of St. Anthony came upon his swinish errand. These friars were reputed to cure St. Anthony's fire[28] and to restore ailing pigs that had been placed under the protection of their patron. For this reason, or because they abandoned their original right to let their porkers run free in the streets, they were

[28] A skin disease.

entitled to donations of ham and bacon. This larded hamster, then, plotted to filch the bells from Gargantua so that he might be heard from afar and make the bacons tremble in the very pantries. However, he very honestly left them behind him, not because they were too precious, but because they were too heavy for him to carry. This friar was not, I may add, the present Commander of the Order at Bourg-en-Bresse who happens to be much too good a friend of mine to behave thus.

The whole city was in an uproar, for Parisians, as you know, are ever prone to insurrection. Indeed, foreigners marvel at the patience of French kings who, faced with troubles arising daily out of the mob's violence, will not justifiedly stamp them out at their source. Would to God I knew the den where these plots and conspiracies were hatched! How speedily I would publish and denounce them in the confraternities of my parish.

You will readily believe that the place where all these people stormed and rioted was the royal Hôtel de Nesle, then the seat of the University Court, but now no longer the site of the Oracle of Lutetia.[29] Here the whole grievance of the stolen bells was discussed and deplored. After extensive argumentation *pro* and *con,* they moved in the finest syllogistic Baraliptonic idiom to empower the oldest and most authoritative member of the faculty to apprise Gargantua of the dreadful damage they suffered through the loss of these bells. Despite certain objections that this mission could be better fulfilled by an orator than by a divine, our Master Janotus de Bragmardo, Doctor of Theology, was delegated.

XVIII

How Janotus De Bragmardo Was Sent to Recover the Great Bells

Master Janotus, with a haircut like that affected by Julius Caesar,[30] settled the traditional doctoral hood over his cootlike head. Next, he antidoted his stomach against possible contamination, with cakes baked in the most secular ovens, and holy water from his excellently stocked cellar. Then, he proceeded to Gargantua's. Before him crawled three black beadles; behind him he dragged five or six servile and artless Masters of Arts, all of them mildewed and rotten as cheeses.

Ponocrates met them as they entered and was terrified at their motley: he was convinced they must be crazed mummers.[31] He therefore asked one of the artless magisters what this masquerade meant. For answer, he was told they wished to recover the missing bells.

Hearing this, Ponocrates immediately hastened with the news to Gargantua so the latter might have an answer and a plan ready for them. Gargantua, learning what had happened, called aside his tutor Ponocrates, his steward Philotomus—the name means a lover of carving—his esquire

---

[29] The pillars of Isis, the patron goddess of Paris. In 1514, they were in the Church of St. Germain des Prés.

[30] Caesar was bald.   [31] Pantomime actors.

Gymnastes ("teacher of esthetics") and Eudemon. A summary conference was held instanter to plan their reply and subsequent actions. It was unanimously agreed to take the learned doctors to the conservatory or wine room and there make them drink uproariously. Thus this wheezing old dryasdust would be denied the vainglory of supposing the bells had been restored at his request, for, while he tippled, they would summon the Provost of the City, the Rector of the University and the Vicar-General to the Bishop of Paris. To these officers they would hand over the bells ere ever the old sophister had delivered his message. The bells delivered, officers and jokesters would together listen to Janotus' eloquent harangue.

Which is exactly what happened. The authorities arrived, our theologian was ushered into the official meeting, and, having hawked and spluttered, began as follows.[32]

XIX

Master Janotus' Harangue
for the Recovery of the
Great Bells

"Ahem, hem, hem! *B'na dies,* Sir, g'day to you, *b'na dies vobis* and g'day to you, gentlemen. It were but right that you should return our bells, for we are in sore need of them! Hem, ahem, ughsh! Many a time we have heretofore refused good money for them from the citizens of London (near Cahors) and of Bordeaux (in the land of Brie). These aspired to purchase our bells for the substantific quality of their elementary complexion which is intronificated in the terrestriality of their quidditative nature to extraneize the tempests and hurricanes that fall upon our vines . . . not our own vines, strictly speaking, but those that lie about us. . . . For, gentles, if we lose the juice of the grape, we lose all, both sense and law.

"If you restore them to us at my request, I shall gain one and one-quarter yards of sausage by it. And a fine pair of breeches, too, which will do my legs a lot of good—or, if I don't, then they'll have broken their promise! No, by God! *Domine,* a pair of breeches is a goodly thing and *vir sapiens non abhorrebit eam,* no, he that is wise will not abhor them. Ha, ha! it's not any sort of man that can come by a pair of breeches. You'll not find them growing on trees, believe me, for *I* know! Consider, *Domine,* O my Lord, that I have spent eighteen long days matagrobilizing this noble speech: *Redite quae sunt Caesari Caesaris et quae sunt Dei, Deo,* Render therefore unto Caesar the things which be Caesar's and unto God the things which be God's. *Ibi jacet lepus,* ay, that's where the hare lies; there's the rub!

"By my faith, *Domine,* by God's body, if you will sup with me *in camera charitatis,* in the guest hall, *nos faciemus bonum cherubin,* we shall make good cheer. *Ego occidi unum porcum,* I have slain a porker, *et ego habet bon vino,* and it's good wine I have, too. But of good wine, man cannot make bad Latin.

---

[32] Master Janotus is a scholastic theologian of the Sorbonne, perpetual butt of Rabelais' satire, and his pompous and incoherent speech parodies what Rabelais perceived to be the theologians' ignorance, pomposity, and laziness of thought.

"Well then, *de parte Dei, date nobis bellas nostras,* by God, give us back our bells. Look ye, I will give you in the name of the faculty a *Sermones de Utino,* ay, a divine sermon if, *utinam,* would to heaven, you give us back our bells. *Vultis etiam pardonos? Per diem, vos habetis et nihil payabatis.* Do you wish pardons and indulgences into the bargain? By God, you shall have them without paying a penny!

"O Sir, *Domine, restor bellsimus nobis,* give us back our bells! Truly, *est bonum urbis,* it is for the good of the city. Every one here uses them. If your mare enjoys them, so does our faculty *quae comparata est jumentis insipientibus et similis facta est eis, psalmo nescio quo,* our faculty which is comparable to the dumb insensible beasts and fashioned like them, in I forget what psalm. Ay, I have set it down correctly upon my register, *est bonum Achilles,* it is the incontrovertible argument known in scholastics as *Achilles.* So! I prove to you that you must give them up. *Ergo sic argumentor,* thus argue I:

"*Omnis bella bellabilis, in bellerio bellando, bellans bellativo bellare bellantes. Parisius habet bellas. Ergo Gluc.* Every bellable bell, to be belled in the belfry, belling by the bellative, makes the bellers bell bellfully! In Paris there are bells. Q. E. D.[33]

"Ha, ha, ha, that is to the point: it is *in tertio primae,* in *Darii,* ay, Sir, in the third mode of the figure of syllogism, in the category called *Darii*—or anyhow you will find it somewhere. By my soul, I have seen the day when I could beat the devil's own tattoo in an argument, but nowadays I simply ramble on deliriously, alas! and henceforth ask nothing but good wine, a good bed, my back to the fire, my belly to the table and a fine dish for my gullet.

"Eh, *Domine,* I beg you, *in nomine patris, Filii et Spiriti Sancti,* in the name of the Father, Son and Holy Ghost, give us back our bells and God rid you of ill and our Lady of Health, *qui vivit et regnat per omna secula secularum, amen,* who liveth and reigneth throughout all eternity, amen! Ahem! hum! ughthasch! gruhemhursch!

"*Verum enim vero, quando quidem, dubio procul, edepol, quoniam, ita certe, meus Deus fidus,* but verily whereas indubitably by Pollux in as much as thus as a matter of course by the God who presideth over good faith, a town without bells is like a blind man without his staff, an ass without a rump or a cow without a clapper. So until you duly restore them to us we shall not stop shouting at you like a blind man who has lost his staff, braying like an ass without a rump and bellowing like a cow that has no bell about its neck.

"A certain Latinist who lived near the hospital once said upon the authority of Nopatus—forgive me! a slip of the tongue! I mean Pontanus, the secular poet—that he wished those bells were made of feathers and their clappers of fox-tails because their chyme, no! their chime produced a colicle—I mean a chronicle—a diarrhea, no! a diary!—in the bowels of his head when he was trying to compose his carminiformal lines. But *nac petitin petitac, tic, torche, lorgne,* smack, bang, crash, tinkle, tinkle, smash; he was declared a heretic—that's as easily done as making a wax figure!

"More the deponent shall not say. *Valete et plaudite,* hail and applaud our efforts! *Calepinas recensui,* I, Calepinus, I have said my say."

---

[33] *Quod erat demonstrandum,* the formula for ending a logical demonstration.

XX

How the Theologian
Carried Off His Cloth
and Was Arraigned
Before the Sorbonne

The theologian had no sooner concluded than Ponocrates and Eudemon burst into such uproarious peals of mirth that they all but gave up the ghost. Theirs was almost the plight of Roman Crassus who died of laughter when he saw a mule eating thistles and Greek Philemon, an ass eating figs prepared for his own dinner.[34] Master Janotus began to laugh too, and all vied in hilarity. Their eyes watered at the violent concussion of the cerebral substance which pressed out these lachrymal humidities and brought them flowing out through the optic nerves. Here was a picture of Democratus heraclitizing and Heraclitus democratizing—your jocund philosopher crying like your pessimist, your malcontent convulsed with merriment.[35]

When their guffaws were spent, Gargantua consulted with his followers as to what to do. Ponocrates proposed that they ply the priceless orator with further drinks since he had afforded them more amusement and jollity than Songecreux, the famous comedian. More, Janotus should be awarded one and one-quarter yards of sausage mentioned in his gleeful harangue, a pair of breeches, three hundred full-size logs of firewood, twenty-five hogsheads of wine, a great bed with three layers of down to the mattress and a deep capacious dish—all of which he had declared necessary for his old age.

This proposal was carried out with the exception of the breeches, for Gargantua did not believe they could readily find a pair suitable to the savant's figure. What fashion, indeed, would become him best? The martingale mode, which provides a drawbridge to the rump for more convenient cacking? Pantaloons, such as Dutch sailors wear, which offer great comfort to the kidneys? Slashed and puffed nether garments such as the Switzers sport to keep the belly warm? Round breeches, with sausage rolls and a seat like a cod's tail, to ventilate the reins?

Considering the difficulty of the problem, Gargantua gave Janotus seven ells[36] of black cloth and three of white for the linings. His porters carried the wood to Janotus' lodgings, the Masters of Arts carried the sausages and vessels while Master Janotus expressed a desire to carry the cloth himself.

One of the Masters of Arts, Jousse Bandouille, objected that it was neither usual nor decent for one of Janotus' high academic standing to do so: he should, rather, depute this task to one of his humbler followers.

"Ha, you mule, you dolt!" Janotus answered. "Your conclusion is not *in modo et figura*, you defy the principles of formal logic. Have you never read

---

[34] These stories of men who died laughing derive from Erasmus, the Dutch humanist (1469?–1536), and Valerius Maximus, a first-century A.D. compiler of anecdotes.

[35] Democritus (c. 460–c. 370 B.C.) and Heraclitus (c. 535–c. 475 B.C.) were both Greek philosophers. In a comic oversimplification, they are presented here as spokesmen of optimism and pessimism.

[36] An old measure of length, about forty-five inches.

our standard textbook? Consult the section *Suppositiones* in the work called *Parva Logicalia. Pannus pro quo supponit?* to what object is the cloth related?"

"*Confuse et distributive!*" Bandouille replied. "Its relation is general and particular to no person!"

"I do not ask you, ass, *quo modo supponit, how* it is related but *pro quo, to what object?* The answer, blockhead, is *pro tibiis meis:* to my legs! Therefore, I shall bear the cloth *egomet, sicut suppositum portat ad positum, I myself,* as the substance carries the attribute!"

Whereupon he made off with it as stealthily as Pathelin in the farce.

The cream of the jest was when the wheezy old divine, with utmost confidence, in a full assembly of the Sorbonne, demanded the breeches and sausages promised him by the University. That august body peremptorily denied his claim since he had already been thus repaid by Gargantua, according to information upon the circumstances. Janotus objected that he had received Gargantua's gifts *gratis* and out of pure liberality which in no way released the University from promises made previously. His colleagues replied that he should be content with reason and that he would not get one jot more from the University.

"Reason?" Janotus protested. "We practice none of *that* here! O wretched traitors, you are not worth the room you take! Alas! earth has not spawned creatures more evil than yourselves—that I know well enough. Do not limp before cripples, do not preach to the wise, do not teach your grandmother to suck eggs. Have I not practiced wickedness with you? By the spleen and liver of God, I will inform the king of the outrageous abuses that are forged in this inferno by your agency and devising. May I be devoured with leprosy if I do not have you all burned alive like Sodomite buggers, traitors, heretics, fornicators and sworn enemies to God and all the virtues!"

At these words, they drew up an indictment against him; Janotus, for his part, immediately cited them to appear. In sum, the suit was brought into Court and is still pending. From this moment on, the pundits of the Sorbonne vowed they would not remove the filth on their bodies until a definitive verdict was handed down. Janotus and *his* partisans swore they would refrain from blowing their noses.

Because of these vows, the factions have continued dirty and snotty to this day, for the Court has not yet fully considered all the proceedings. A verdict will be given at the Greek kalends[37] or never, for, as you know, these savants accomplish more than nature and go against their own articles.

Do not the Articles of Paris insist that God alone can perform infinite things? Nature, on the other hand, creates nothing immortal: she puts an end and a period to all things by her engendered, for *omnia orta cadunt,* all things rise and fall. . . . But these idlers and pettifoggers make the suits they are concerned in both infinite and immortal. And, in doing so, they justify the words of Chilo,[38] the Lacedemonian, consecrated at Delphos:

"Wretchedness is the handmaiden of lawsuits and suitors are miserable, for they shall reach the end of their lives sooner than the satisfaction of their alleged claims."

---

[37] First day of the month; since the Greek calendar had no kalends, this means "never."
[38] This saying is recorded by the Roman orator and statesman Pliny (62?–113 A.D.).

XXI

Gargantua's Education and Social Life Under the Direction of His Preceptors at the Sorbonne

The first few days having been spent thus and the bells put back in place, the citizens of Paris, in acknowledgment of Gargantua's civility, offered to feed and maintain his mare as long as he wished. Gargantua accepted this courtesy, so the Parisians sent the beast to graze in the Forest of Bière or Fontainebleau. (I do not believe she is still there.)

This accomplished, Gargantua resolved with all his heart to study under the direction of Ponocrates. But the latter, wishing to learn how the lad's former teachers had wasted so much time making a crackbrained, addlepated dunce of him, decided he should do exactly as he had in the past.

Gargantua therefore arranged his schedule so as to awake usually between eight and nine o'clock, rain or shine, dark or daylight, simply because his preceptors had decided this on the strength of the Psalmist's saw: "*Vanum est vobis ante lucem surgere,* it is vain for you to rise up betimes."

Then he wriggled and writhed, wallowing in his bed and tossing about like a parched pea, the better to stimulate his vital spirits. Next, he would dress, according to the season, but he was always happy to don a long, hanging gown of heavy wool lined with fox. Next, he combed out his hair with the comb of Jacques Almain, the Sorbonne theologian, known in English as John Handy—a comb consisting of four fingers and a thumb—for his mentors maintained that to brush one's hair, wash one's face and make oneself clean were, in this world, a pure waste of time.

Next Gargantua dunged, piddled, vomited, belched, broke wind, yawned, spat, coughed, hiccoughed, sneezed and snotted himself as majestically and bountifully as an archdeacon. Next he proceeded to breakfast in order to fortify himself against the morning mist and cold. His menu consisted of splendid fried tripe, choice meats grilled on charcoal, rich hams, succulent roast venison and numerous soups and brews, with toast, cheese, parsley and chopped meat floating on the surface.

Ponocrates objected that he should not eat so soon after rising without having taken any exercise. To which he replied:

"Exercise? Good God, didn't I tumble and jounce in bed six or seven times before I got up? Surely, that is exercise enough? Pope Alexander VI did this on the advice of his Jew physician, Bonnet de Lates, and lived till the day of his death in spite of his enemies. My first masters taught me this habit, for breakfast, they said, gave man a good mind. So they started the day by drinking. It suits me perfectly and I manage to dine the better for it. Master Tubal Holofernes, who was graduated Licentiate in Paris at the head of his class, used to tell me that to hasten was not enough, one must set out betimes. By the same token, the total health of mankind does not consist in drinking down and lapping up, *glub, glub, glub,* like so many ducks, but rather in falling to, early in the morning. *Unde versus;* so runs the rune:

> *Lever matin n'est point bonheur*
> *Boire matin est le meilleur.*

> *To rise betimes is not enough,*
> *To drink at morning, that's the stuff!"*

After an abundant breakfast, Gargantua repaired to church, with, in his train, a varlet bearing a basket. The latter contained a huge breviary swaddled in velvet and weighing about twelve hundred and six pounds including the filth of thumbmarks, dogeared corners, golden clasps and nonpareil parchment. Twenty-six, if not thirty, masses ensued for the benefit of Gargantua and his chaplain. Under his tall hood, this chaplain looked for all the world like a peewit . . . and had very thoroughly antidoted his breath against possible poisons with much syrup of the vine! Chaplain and pupil babbled the mumbo jumbo of the litany, thumbing their rosaries so carefully that not one single bead fell to the ground.

As he left the church, they brought him an oxcart laden with a huge heap of paternosters, chaplets and relics from St. Claude in the Jura, each bigger than a hatblock.[39] Gargantua and his chaplain then strolled in the cloisters, galleries or garden, saying more aves than sixteen hermits.

After, Gargantua would study for a short half-hour, his eyes glued to his book but his mind, to quote Terence's *Eunuch*,[40] wool-gathering in the kitchen. Then he proceeded to make water, filling a large urinal to capacity, after which he sat down at table, and, being naturally phlegmatic, began his meal with a few dozen hams, smoked tongues of beef, caviar, sausages and other like forerunners of wine.

Then four servants in turn shovelled mustard into his mouth by the spadeful, thus preparing him to drain a horrific draught of white wine to relieve his kidneys. Then the meal proper began with viands to his liking, according to the season; Gargantua ceasing to eat only when his belly had reached bursting point.

When it came to drinking, he acknowledged neither end nor rule; for, he said, there were no limits and boundaries to swilling until the tosspot felt the cork soles of his shoes swell up a half-foot from the ground.

XXIII

How Ponocrates Gave Gargantua Such Instruction That Not an Hour of the Day Was Wasted.

When Ponocrates saw Gargantua's vicious mode of life, he determined to bring him up otherwise. But for the first few days he bore with him, for he realized that nature cannot endure sudden and violent changes.

To begin his work the better, Ponocrates requested a learned physician of the times, Master Theodore—the name means "God-given"—to examine Gargantua thoroughly with a view to steering him on the right course. The scholar purged Gargantua canonically with Anticyrian hellebore, an herb indicated for cerebral disorders and insanity, thus cleansing his brain of its unnatural, perverse condition. Ponocrates, by the same aperient

---

[39] St. Claude was famous for rosaries.

[40] A comedy by the Roman dramatist Terence (c. 185–c. 159 B.C.).

means, made the lad forget all he had learned under his former teachers, just as Timotheus of old treated pupils who had already studied under other musicians. Timotheus, incidentally, used to charge this class of students double!

For Gargantua's further edification, Ponocrates made him mingle among learned men whose company fired him with a desire to emulate them, to study more profitably and to make his mark. Next, Ponocrates so arranged the lad's schedule that not a moment of the day was wasted; all his time was spent in the pursuit of learning and honest knowledge.

By this new dispensation, Gargantua awoke at about four in the morning. While the servants massaged him, he would listen to some page of Holy Scripture, read aloud in clear tones and pronounced with fitting respect for the text. A young page, a native of Basché, near Chinon, was appointed reader, as his name, Anagnostes, shows. According to the purpose and argument of this lesson, Gargantua frequently turned to worship, adore, pray and reverence Almighty God, Whose majesty and wondrous wisdom were made manifest in the reading.

Next, he would repair to secret places to make excretion of his natural digestions; here his tutor repeated what had been read, expounding its more obscure and difficult features. Returning to the house, they would study the heavens. Was it the same sky they had observed the night before? Into what signs was the sun entering that day? and the moon?

After this astronomical survey, Gargantua was dressed, combed, curled, trimmed and perfumed, and, while this was being done, he heard the lessons of the day before. Then, having recited them by heart, he would argue certain practical, human and utilitarian cases based upon the principles enunciated. This part of the program sometimes took two or three hours, though usually he had exhausted it by the time he was fully clad.

Then, for three good hours, he was read or lectured to, after which they went to the Tennis Court at the Grande Bracque in the Place de l'Estrapade or to the playing fields.

On the way, they discussed various aspects of the subject previously treated. Then they would play tennis, handball and three-cornered catch, exercising their bodies as vigorously as they had exercised their minds before.

All their play was free for they left off when they pleased, which was usually when they had sweated a good bit or were otherwise tired. They were thoroughly wiped and rubbed down, after which they changed their shirts and walked quietly home to see if dinner were ready. As they waited, they would go over certain points they had retained of the lectures.

Meanwhile My Lord Appetite put in an appearance and they sat down most opportunely to table.

At the beginning of the meal, they listened to the reading of some agreeable chronicle of chivalry in ancient times, until Gargantua gave the signal for wine to be served. Then, if they wished, the reading went on or they could talk merrily together. Often they discussed the virtues, property, efficacy and nature of what was served at table: bread, wine, water, salt, meat, fish, fruit, herbs, roots and their preparation. Thus Gargantua soon knew all the relevant passages in Pliny's *Natural History* . . . in the grammarian Athenaeus' *Deipnosophistes* or *The Banquet of the Sages*, which treats of flowers, fruits and their various uses . . . in Dioscorides' famous medical treatise, the bible of apothecaries . . . in the *Vocabularium* by Julius Pollux, a grammarian and sophist of Marcus Aurelius' day, who wrote of hunting and fishing . . . in Galen's numerous dissertations upon alimentation . . . in the works of Porphyrius, the third-century Greek author of a *Treatise upon Abstinence from Meat* . . . in Oppian's two poems, *Cynegetica* which deals with venery and *Halieutica* with angling . . . in *Of Healthy Diet* by Polybius of Cos, disciple and son-in-law of Hippocrates . . . in Heliodorus of Emesa, Syrian Bishop of Tricca and a celebrated novelist of the fourth century . . . in Aristotle's essays on natural history . . . in the Greek works upon animals by Claudius Aelianus, a Roman contemporary of Heliogobalus . . . and in various other tomes. . . . Often for surer authority as they argued, they would have the book in question brought to the table. Gargantua so thoroughly and cogently learned and assimilated all he heard that no physician of his times knew one-half so much as he.

They discussed the lessons they had learned that morning and topped their meal off with quiddany, a sort of quince marmalade and an excellent digestive. After which Gargantua picked his teeth with a fragment of mastic,[41] washed his hands and daubed his eyes with cool clear water, and, instead of saying grace, sang the glory of God in noble hymns, composed in praise of divine bounty and munificence.

Presently cards were brought them and they played, not for the sake of the pastime itself but to learn a thousand new tricks and inventions all based on arithmetic.

Thus Gargantua developed a keen enthusiasm for mathematics, spending his leisure after dinner and supper every evening as pleasantly as once he had, dicing and gaming. As a result, he knew so much about its theory and practice that Cuthbert Tunstal, Bishop of Durham and secretary to King Henry VIII, a voluminous writer on the subject, confessed that, beside Gargantua, he knew no more about arithmetic than he did about Old High Gothic. Nor was it arithmetic alone our hero learned, but also such sister sciences as geometry, astronomy and music.

Now the digestion of foods is a most important matter. There is the first stage which occurs in the stomach, where the viands are changed into chyle; the second, in the liver, where the chyle is transformed into blood; the third, in the habit of the body, where the blood is finally converted into the substance of each part. So, whilst Gargantua awaited the first stage of digestion, they made a thousand delightful instruments, drew geometrical figures and even applied the principles of astronomy.

After, they amused themselves singing a five-part score or improvising on a theme chosen at random. As for musical instruments, Gargantua learned to play the lute, the spinet, the harp, the nine-holed transverse or German flute, the viol and the sackbut or trombone.

Having spent an hour thus and completed his digestion, he discharged his natural excrements and then settled down again to work three hours or more at his principal study. Either he revised the morning reading, or proceeded in the text at hand or practised penmanship in the most carefully formed characters of modern Roman and ancient Gothic script.

---

[41] An aromatic resin from a tree.

Next, they went out with a young gentleman of Touraine, the esquire Gymnastes, who instructed Gargantua in the art of horsemanship. Having changed his clothes, he proceeded to mount a fiery Italian charger, a Flemish dray horse, a Spanish jennet, an Arab thoroughbred and a hackney. These he would put vigorously through their paces, letting them "career" or gallop a short distance at full speed, making them leap high in the air, jump ditches, clear stiles, and turn short in a ring both to the right and to the left. Next he wielded but did not break his lance, for it is arrant stupidity to boast: "I have broken ten lances in a tilt or fight." A wretched carpenter can do the same. On the contrary, the whole glory of such combat lies in besting ten enemies with one and the same lance. So with a strong, stiff, steel-tipped lance, Gargantua would force the outer door of some house, pierce an adversary's armor, beat down a tree, pick up a ring, carry off a cuirassier saddle, a hauberk or a gauntlet. And he performed these feats armed cap-à-pie.[42]

In the technique of parading his horse with prances and flourishes to a fanfare of trumpets—the ceremonial of knights as they enter the lists—he had no equal. As for the divers terms of the equine vocabulary from *giddyup* and *cluck* to *whoa* and *grrr*, no horseman could hold a candle to him. Indeed Cesare Fieschi, the celebrated jockey of Ferrara, was a mere monkey in comparison.

He learned, too, to leap hastily and with singular dexterity from one horse to another without setting foot to the ground (the nags were circus horses or, to be technical, "desultories"). Further, lance in hand, he could leap on horseback from either side without stirrups and rule the beast at will without a bridle, for such accomplishments are highly useful in military engagements.

Another day he would practise wielding the battle-axe, which he managed so skillfully, in the nimblest thrusts, the most powerful lunges and the vast encircling sweeps of the art, that he passed knight-at-arms in the field and at all tests. Sometimes unarmed, sometimes carrying a buckler or a rolled cape of mail over his arm or a small shield over his wrist, Gargantua brandished the pike, plied the double-edged, two-handed sword, the bastard claymore used by archers, the Spanish rapier, the dagger and the poniard.

He hunted, too: stag, roebuck, bear, fallow deer, wild boar, hare, partridge, pheasant and otter . . . he played at ball, ever ready with well-aimed foot or powerful fist to send the great sphere whizzing through the air . . . he learned to wrestle and to run. . . . As for jumping, he did not go in for the various forms of running jumps, such as the three-steps-and-a-leap, the hop-step-and-jump or the German high-jump. As Gymnastes pointed out, these were quite useless in warfare. Instead, he practiced the standing jumps. Starting from scratch, he could in one leap top a hedge, clear a ditch, mount six paces upon a wall and thus reach a window-ledge one lance's height from the ground.

Gargantua could swim in the deepest water, breaststroke, back and sidestroke, using his whole body or his feet alone. He could cross the

---

[42] From head to foot.

breadth of the Seine or the Loire at Montsoreau, dragging his cloak along in his teeth and holding a book high and dry over the waters—thus renewing the exploit with which Plutarch credits Julius Caesar during the Alexandrian War. Then, using one hand only, he could, with a single great pull, climb into a boat, whence a moment later he would dive headlong into the water again, sound its utmost depths, touch bottom, explore the hollows of rocks and plunge into any pits and abysses he fancied. He would turn the boat about, managing it perfectly, bringing it swiftly or slowly upstream or down and arresting its course at a milldam. He could guide it with one hand while he plied hard about him with a great oar; he could run up a sail, hoist himself up a mast by the shrouds, dance along the yards, operate the compass, tackle the bowlines to sail close to the wind and steer the helm.

His water sports done, he would dash full speed up a mountain, then down quite as fast. He climbed trees like a cat, hopping from one to the next like a squirrel and pulling down great boughs—like the celebrated Milo of Crotona who, Pausanias tells us, met his death devoured by wolves, his hands caught in the cleft of an oak he had sought to split. With two well-steeled daggers and a pair of well-tried mason's punches, he could scurry up the side of a house like a rat, then leap down again, from roof to ground, so expertly that he landed without hurt. Gargantua also cast the dart, threw the iron bar, put the stone, tossed the boar-spear, hurled the javelin, shied the halberd. He drew the bow to breaking point; he could shoulder a harquebuss—a great siege piece weighing fifty pounds—and fire it off like a crossbow. He could set a huge cannon on its carriage, hit buttmarks and other targets for horizontal shooting, or, point-blank, bring down papgays (stuffed figures of parrots on poles), clay pigeons and other verticle marks, facing them on a level or upwards, or downwards or sidewise. Like the ancient Parthians, he could even hit them as he retreated.

They would tie a cable to a high tower and let it dangle to the ground. Gargantua hoisted himself up with both hands, then slipped down again as evenly, surely and plumb as a man running along a flat meadow. Or they would set a great pole across two trees for Gargantua to hang from by his hands. He moved along the pole from tree to tree so swiftly, without setting foot on *terra firma,* that a man, running on the ground below, could not have caught him. To expand his chest and exercise his lungs, he would roar like all the devils in hell. Once indeed, I heard him call Eudemon across all Paris, from the Porte St. Victor, the gate by the University, all the way to Montmartre, a village on a hill two miles beyond the walls of the city. Stentor, who cried louder than forty men, displayed no such vocal power, even at the siege of Troy.

To develop his sinews, they made him two great pigs of lead, each weighing eight hundred and five tons. These pigs (called salmons in France because the metal is shaped like this fish) Gargantua named *alteres,* an ancient Greek term for the weights used to give jumpers their initial spring—our modern dumb-bells. Taking one in each hand, Gargantua then performed an inimitable feat. He would raise them high above his head and, never turning a hair, stock-still as a statue, hold them aloft for three-quarters of an hour. He played at Barriers or Tug-of-War with the stoutest champions. When his turn came he took root so firmly as to defy the sturdiest to budge him. Nor was it thus alone he emulated Milo of Crotona. Like the ancient athlete, he could hold a pomegranate so fast in his hand that none could wrest it from him, yet so adroitly that he did not crush it.

Having spent his time in such manly sports, he had himself washed, rubbed down and given a change of clothes. Then he returned home at a leisurely pace, passing through some meadow or grassy space to examine the trees and plants. These he would compare with what the authorities wrote of them in their books: among the Ancients, Theophrastus, the successor of Aristotle and teacher of Menander . . . or Palladius, whose poem *De re rustica* was translated by Pietro Marini . . . or Dioscorides Pedanius, the Greek physician of the first century . . . or Pliny or Nicander or Aemilius Macer, the Roman, or Galen himself. . . . Gargantua and his companions picked specimens by the handful and took them home to a young page named Rhizotome or Rootcutter, who watched over them and the various small mattocks, pickaxes, hooks, hoes, pruning-knives, shears and other botanical instruments.

At home, whilst the servants prepared dinner, our young men repeated certain passages of what had been read. Then they sat down to table. Here I would have you note that their dinner was simple and frugal; they ate no more than necessary to quiet the baying of the belly. Supper, on the contrary, was a large and copious meal; they ate what they needed for their sustenance and nourishment. Such indeed is the true system prescribed by the art of sound, self-respecting physicians though a rabble of dunderhead quacks, wrangling eternally in the claptrap routine of the Arab nostrum shop of Avicenna, recommend the exact opposite. During supper, they continued the lesson given at dinner as long as they saw fit; the rest of the meal was spent in earnest and profitable discussion.

Having said grace, they applied their voices to sing tunefully or they played upon harmonious instruments. Or they amused themselves with such minor pastimes as cards, dice cups and dice afforded. Sometimes they tarried here enjoying themselves and making merry until bedtime; they would visit learned men or such as had travelled in foreign lands. Well into the night, before retiring, they would go to the most exposed spot in the house, whence they examined the face of the sky, noting the comets, if any were visible, and the various figures, positions, aspects, oppositions and conjunctions of the heavenly bodies.

According to the Pythagorean system, Gargantua would, with his tutor, recapitulate briefly all that he had read, seen, learned, done and assimilated in the course of the day.

Then they prayed to God the Creator, doing Him worship and confirming their faith in Him, glorifying Him for His immense goodness, vouchsafing thanks for all the mighty past and imploring His divine clemency for all the future.

And so they retired to rest.

XXIV

HOW GARGANTUA SPENT HIS
TIME IN RAINY WEATHER

In intemperate or rainy weather, things went on much the same as usual before dinner except that Gargantua had a fine bright fire lighted to correct the inclemency of the air. But after dinner, instead of gymnastics, they stayed indoors and, by way of apotherapy or exercise amused themselves by bundling hay, splitting logs, sawing wood and threshing sheaves in the barn. Then they studied the arts of painting and sculpture. Or they revived the ancient Roman game of *Tali*, dicing as the Italian humanist Nicolaus Leonicus Thomaeus wrote of it in his dialogue *Sannutus, Of the Game of Dice*, and as our good friend Janus Lascaris, librarian to our sovereign king, plays at the game. In their sport, they reviewed such passages of ancient authors as mention or quote some metaphor drawn from this play.

In much the same way, they might go to watch workmen forging metals or casting pieces of ordnance. Or they might visit the lapidaries, goldsmiths and cutters of precious stones in their ateliers, the alchemists in their laboratories, the coiners at the mint, the tapestry-workers, velvet-workers and weavers at their looms, the watchmakers, looking-glass framers, printers, lutemakers, dyers and other such artisans in their workshops. Wherever they went, they would distribute gratuities, invariably investigating and learning the various inventions and industry of the trade.

Or they might attend public lectures, official convocations, oratorical performances, speeches, pleadings by eloquent attorneys and sermons by evangelical preachers—that is, such priests as wished to restore Christianity to the primitive tradition of the Gospel. Gargantua also frequented fencing halls and tested his skill at all weapons against the masters, proving to them by experience that he knew as much as they and, indeed, even more.

Instead of herborizing, they would inspect the shops of druggists, herbalists and apothecaries, studiously examining the sundry fruits, roots, leaves, gums, seeds and exotic unguents and learning how they could be diluted or adulterated. He viewed jugglers, mountebanks and medicasters—who sold Venice treacle, a cure for all ills—carefully observing their tricks and gestures, their agile capers and smooth oratory. His favorites were those from Chauny in Picardy who are born jabberers and the readiest expounders of mealy-mouthed flimflam concerning their ability to weave ropes of sand, extract sunbeams from cucumbers and milk a he-goat into a sieve.

Returning home to supper, they would eat more sparingly than on fine days. Their meats would, by the same token, be more desiccative and extenuating so as to counteract the humidity communicated to their bodies by the necessary contiguity of the atmosphere and to nullify what harm might arise from lack of their customary exercise.

Such was Gargantua's program and so he continued from day to day, benefiting as you would expect a young man of his age and intelligence to benefit under such a system faithfully applied. To be sure, the whole thing may have seemed incredibly difficult to him at the outset, but it soon proved so light, so easy and so pleasant as to appear more like a king's pastime than the study of a schoolboy.

However, Ponocrates was careful to supply relaxation from this violent bodily and mental tension. Once a month, on some very bright serene day, they would clear out of town early in the morning, bound for the near-by villages of Gentilly, Boulogne, Montrouge, Pont-de-Charenton, Vanves or St. Cloud. There they spent the whole day enjoying themselves to their heart's content, sporting and merrymaking, drinking toast for proffered toast, playing, singing, dancing, tumbling about or loafing in some fair meadow, turning sparrows out of their nests, bagging quail and fishing for frogs and crayfish.

But though this holiday was free of books and reading, it was not spent unprofitably. Lying in the green meadow, they usually recited certain delightful lines from Virgil's *Georgics*, from Hesiod's *Works and Days* or from Politian's *Husbandry*. Or they broached some savory epigram in Latin, then turned it into a French roundelay or ballade.

In their feasting, they would sometimes separate the twin elements, isolating the wine and the water in their drink by pouring the latter into a cup of ivy-wood, as Cato teaches in his *De re rustica*, and Pliny elsewhere. Then they would wash the wine in a basin full of water and draw it out with a funnel, as pure as ever. And they pumped the water with a syphon from one glass to another, manufacturing several sorts of automatic or self-operating devices.

LII

How Gargantua Had the Abbey of Thélème Built for the Monk[43]

There remained only the monk to provide for. Gargantua offered him the Abbey of Seuilly: he refused. What about the Benedictine abbeys of Bourgueil or St. Florent, among the richest in France: he might have either or both? Again, the offer met with a flat refusal: Friar John of the Funnels answered peremptorily that he did not seek the charge or government of monks.

"For," he explained, "how shall I govern others when I cannot possibly govern myself?" There was a pause. "But—" he hesitated. "But if you believe I have given and can give you good service, let me found an abbey after my own heart."

The notion delighted Gargantua: he forthwith offered his estate of Thélème, by the Loire, two leagues away from Port Huault. Thélème in Greek means free will, an auspicious name for Friar John's abbey. Here indeed he could institute a religious order contrary to all others.

"First," said Gargantua, "you must not build a wall around it, for all other abbeys are solidly enclosed."

---

[43] "The monk" is Friar John, a major character in the episode of the Picrocholine War, here omitted, and in later books of *Gargantua and Pantagruel*. The Picrocholine War, an absurdly inflated contest begun with a dispute with some cake-peddlers, parodies a quarrel in Rabelais' own Chinon country over navigation rights on the River Loire. In this episode, Rabelais reveals his hatred of war, his discrimination between just and unjust wars, and his humane attitudes on the treatment of defeated enemies.

"Quite so," agreed the monk, "for where there are *mures*, walls, before, and *mures*, walls, behind, we have *murmures,* murmurs of envy and plotting."

Now in certain monasteries it is a rule that if any women enter (I mean honest and chaste ones) the ground they tread upon must be swept over. Therefore it was decreed that if a monk or nun should by any chance enter Thélème, every place that religious passed through should be thoroughly disinfected.

Similarly because all monasteries and convents on earth are compassed, limited and regulated by hours, at Thélème no clock or dial of any sort should be tolerated. On the contrary, their time here would be governed by what occasions and opportunities might arise. As Gargantua sagaciously commented:

"I can conceive of no greater waste of time than to count the hours. What good comes of it? To order your life by the toll of a bell instead of by reason or common sense is the veriest piece of asininity imaginable."

By the same token, they established the qualifications for entrance into their order. Was it not true that at present women took the veil only if they were wall-eyed, lame, hunchbacked, ill-favored, misshapen, half-witted, unreasonable or somewhat damaged? That only such men entered monasteries as were cankered, ill-bred idiots or plain nuisances?

("Incidentally," said Friar John, "if the woman is neither fair nor good, of what use is the cloth?")

"Let the clot hump her," Gargantua replied.

"I said 'cloth' not 'clot.' "

"Well, what's the answer?"

"To cover her face or her arse with!")

Accordingly, they decided to admit into the new order only such women as were beautiful, shapely, pleasing of form and nature, and such men as were handsome, athletic and personable.

Again, because men entered the convents of this world only by guile and stealth, it was decreed that no women would be in Thélème unless men were there also, and vice-versa.

Moreover, since both men in monasteries and women in convents were forced after their year of noviciate to stay there perpetually, Gargantua and Friar John decided that the Thélèmites, men or women, might come and go whenever they saw fit.

Further, since the religious usually made the triple vow of chastity, poverty and obedience, at Thélème all had full leave to marry honestly, to enjoy wealth and to live in perfect freedom.

As for the age of initiation, they stipulated that women were admissible between the ages of ten and fifteen, men between twelve and eighteen.

LIII

How the Abbey of Thélème
was Built and Endowed

To build and furnish the abbey, Gargantua paid in cash twenty-seven hundred thousand eight hundred and thirty-one crowns in current coin of the realm, fresh from the mint, with a sheep on the obverse and the king's head on the reverse. He undertook to pay yearly, until the project was completed, sixteen hundred and sixty-nine thousand crowns, with the sum on the obverse, and as many again with the seven stars, the whole to be levied upon custom receipts.

For the foundation and maintenance of Thélème, he settled in perpetuity twenty-three hundred and sixty-nine thousand, five hundred and fourteen nobles (a coin stamped by the English kings with the rose of York), free of all tax, burden or fealty, payable yearly at the abbey gate. These privileges were all corroborated by letters patent.

The building was hexagonal; in each corner rose a great, circular tower, each identical, sixty yards in diameter. To the north, the river Loire flowed past the first tower which was named *Arctice* or Northern. East of it rose *Calaer* which means "situated in the balmy air"; then, successively, *Anatole* or Eastern; *Mesembrine* or Southern; *Hesperia* or Occidental; and the last, *Cryere* or Glacial. The distance between each tower was three hundred and twelve yards. The building was throughout six storys high, counting the underground cellar for one. The ground floor was vaulted like a basket handle; the others, covered with Flanders mistletoe,[44] jutting out like brackets and pendants. The roof, of finest slate, was lined with lead and bore little figures of mannikins and animals well assorted and gilt. The gutters jutted out from the walls between the casement arches; they were painted diagonally gold and blue down to the ground, where they ended in pipes which carried the water into the river below.

This building was a hundred times more magnificent than Bonnivet, Chambord or Chantilly.[45] There were nine thousand three hundred and thirty-two suites, each with a salon, a study, a dressing room, an oratory and an exit into a great hall. In the wing between each tower was a winding stairway. The steps, grouped in units of twelve between each landing, were of porphyry, of Numidian stone, of serpentine marble; they were twenty-two feet long and three fingers thick. At each landing, two spendid round antique archways admitted the light and led to an open loggia of the same dimensions. The stairway, rising to the roof, ended in a pavilion; on either side lay a great hall which in turn led to the apartments.

The wing between the towers called *Arctice* and *Cryere* contained rich libraries of Greek, Latin, Hebrew, French, Italian and Spanish volumes, grouped in their respective sections. In the center rose a marvellous winding ramp conceived in such ample proportions that six soldiers with their lances at rest could ride up it abreast to the top of the palace. Its entry, outside the house, was an archway six fathoms wide.

Between *Anatole* and *Mesembrine* were spacious galleries with murals representing heroic feats of olden times, scenes from history and pictures of the earth. Here again were a stairway and gate as described upon the river side. On this gate, couched in great antique letters, ran the following legend.

---

[44] A kind of plaster.   [45] Three of the most magnificent castles in France.

LIV

INSCRIPTION ENGRAVED ON
THE MAIN GATE AT THÉLÈME

Here enter not, smug hypocrites or holy loons,
Bigots, sham-Abrahams, impostors of the cloth,
Mealy-mouthed humbugs, holier-than-thou baboons,
Lip-service lubbers, smell-feast picaroons.
Else had we to admit the Goth and Ostrogoth,
Precursors of the ape and others of that broth.
Hence, sneaks and mischief-makers, colporteurs of lies,
Be off to other parts to sell your merchandise.

Being foul you would befoul
Man, woman, beast or fowl.
The vileness of your ways   10
Would sully my sweet lays,
Owls—And your own black cowl,
Being foul, you would befoul.

Here enter not, defenders of dishonest pleas,
Clerks, barristers, attorneys who make freemen slaves,
Canon Law pettifoggers, censors, Pharisees,
Judges, assessors, arbitrators, referees
Who blithely doom good people to untimely graves,
The gibbet is your destination, legal knaves!   20
Be off: indict the rope if you should find it short,
Here there is no abuse; we do not need your court.

Tangle, wrangle, brangle
We loathe, from any angle.
Our aim is joy and sport,
Time's swift, youth's fleet, life's short.
You, go and disentangle
Tangle, wrangle, brangle!

Here enter not, curmudgeon, loan shark, muckworm, hunks,
Bloodsucking usurer, extortioner, pennystint, . . .   30
Hence, lawsuit-chasing crimps, greedy as starving punks
Tracking a patron; lickgolds, hiding cash in trunks,
Harpyclaws, crunchfists, jaundiced zealots of the mint,
Your crackling, sallow palms are itching. Skin a flint!
Heap up your hoard, O scrub-faced curs, heap up afresh,
And as you grudge and gripe and screw, God rot your flesh!

Those grim and grisly faces
Bear all the ravaged traces
Of hidebound avarice;
We cannot stomach this.   40
Banish from all blithe places
Those grim and grisly faces.

Here enter not, you churls, sour boors, invidious fools,
Old, jealous brabblers, scolds, neither by night nor day,
Nor grumblers, soreheads, sulkers, badgers bred in schools
Of hate; nor ghosts of malaperts; nor firebrands' ghouls
From Rhineland, Greece or Rome, fiercer than wolves at bay;
Nor you, riddled with pox, your face a Milky Way
Of scars not stars; nor you, clapstricken to the bone:
Enjoy your shameless crusts and blemishes alone.   50

> Honor, praise and pleasure
> Are here in goodly measure:
> Health reigns supreme because
> We follow Nature's laws.
> Ours is a triple treasure:
> Honor, praise and pleasure.

But enter here thrice welcome, men of goodly parts,
Gallants and noble gentlemen, thrice welcome be!
Here you will find an abbey after your own hearts,
Where living is esteemed the highest of the arts.   60
Come in your tens and hundreds, come in thousands, we
Shall clasp you to our bosoms in fond amity:
Come wise, come proud, come gay, come courteous, come mellow,
Come true sophisticate, come worldling, come, good fellow!

> Comrades, companions, friends,
> Assemble from the ends
> Of earth in this fair place
> Where all is mirth and grace.
> Felicity here blends
> Comrades, companions, friends.   70

Here enter, all ye loyal scholars who expound
Novel interpretations of the Holy Writ.
Here is a fort and refuge; from this favored ground
You may confound the error that is elsewhere found,
You may found a profound new faith instead of it,
Sweeping away false teachings, bit by fallacious bit.
Come unto us and make your cogent meanings heard:
Destroy the foes of God and of his Holy Word.

> The Holy Word of God
> Shall never be downtrod   80
> Here in this holy place,
> If all deem reason grace,
> And use for staff and rod
> The Holy Word of God.

Here enter, ladies fair of eminent degree,
Come soon with starry eyes, lips smiling, comely face,
Flowers of loveliness, angels of harmony,

Resplendent, proud yet of the rarest modesty,
Sprightly of flesh, lithe-waisted and compact of grace,
Here is your home. A gallant lord designed this place   90
For you, that beauty, charm and virtue might find room
Deliciously to breathe, exquisitely to bloom.

Who makes a priceless gift
Wins pardon without shrift.
Donor, recipient
Alike find rich content.
To him your voices lift
Who makes a priceless gift.

LV

How the Monks and Nuns
Lived at Thélème

In the middle of the lower court stood a magnificent alabaster fountain, surmounted by the Three Graces holding cornucopias and spouting water through their breasts, mouths, ears, eyes and other orifices. The buildings above this court stood upon great pillars of chalcedony and porphyry, forming classical arches about lengthy wide galleries adorned with paintings and trophies of various animals: the horns of bucks, unicorns and hippopotami, elephants' tusks and sundry other curiosities.

The ladies' quarters ran from *Arctice* all the way to the *Mesembrine* Gate; the rest of the abbey was reserved for men. In front of this part, between the outer two towers, lay the recreational facilities: the tilting yard, the riding school, the theater and the natatorium[46] which included wonderful swimming pools on three different levels, with every sort of equipment and myrtle water aplenty.

Near the river was the fine pleasure garden, with, in the middle, a maze. Tennis courts and football fields spread out between the next two towers. Close to *Cryere*, an orchard offered a mass of fruit trees laid out in quincunxes, with, at its end, a sizy park abounding in venison.

The space between the third pair of towers was reserved for the shooting ranges: here were targets and butts for harquebuss, long bow and crossbow. The servants' quarters, one story high, were situated outside *Hesperia*. Beyond was the falconry, managed by expert falconers and hawk trainers and annually supplied by the Cretans, Venetians and Sarmatian Poles with all manner of birds. There were priceless eagles for hunting hares, foxes and cranes. There were gerfalcons, goshawks, sakers for hunting wild geese, herons and bitterns. There were falcons, lanners, sparhawks and merlins for hunting larks and partridges. Other birds there were, too, in great quantities, so well trained that when they flew afield for their own sport they never failed to catch every bird they encountered. . . . The venery with its hounds and beagles stood a little further along towards the park.

[46] Swimming area.

All the halls, apartments and chambers were richly hung with tapestries varying with the season; the floors were covered with green cloth, the beds all embroidered. Each rear chamber boasted a pierglass set in a heavy gold frame adorned with pearls. Near the exits of the ladies' halls were the perfumers and hairdressers who ministered to the gentlemen before the latter visited the ladies. These attendants furnished the ladies' rooms with rose water, orange-flower water and angelica,[47] supplying a precious small atomizer to give forth the most exquisite aromatic perfumes.

LVI

How the Monks and Nuns of Thélème Were Apparelled

When first the abbey was founded, the ladies dressed according to their taste and pleasure. Subsequently of their own free will they modified their costume as follows.

They wore hose, of scarlet or kermes-red, reaching some three inches above the knee, the edge being exquisitely embroidered or slashed. Their garters, which matched their bracelets, came both a whit over and under the knee. Their shoes, pumps and slippers were of red, violet or crimson velvet and jagged as a lobster's claws.

Over their slips, they put on a tight tunic of pure silk camlet, and over that a taffeta farthingale or petticoat, red, white, beige, gray or of any other color. Above this farthingale went a skirt of silver taffeta, with fine gold embroidery and delicate cross-stitch work. According to the temperature, the season or the ladies' whim, these skirts might be satin, damask or velvet and, in color, orange, green, cendré, blue, canary yellow, scarlet, crimson or white, or of cloth-of-gold, cloth-of-silver, or any other choice material variously embroidered, stitched, brocaded or spangled according to the occasion for which they were worn.

Their gowns, or over-garments, were also governed by timely considerations. They might be cloth-of-gold with silver embossing or red satin with gold brocade or taffeta, white, blue, black or tawny. Or they might be silk rep, silk camlet, velvet, cloth-of-silver, cloth-of-gold or satin variously figured with gold and silver thread.

In summer, instead of these gowns, they wore lovely light smocks made of the same material, or capes, Moorish-fashion, with hoods to protect and shade their faces from the sun. These Moresco capes were of violet velvet, having raised gold stitching over silver purl or gold piping and cording, with small Indian pearls at their ends. And ever a gay colored plume, the color of their sleeves, bravely garnished with gold! In winter, their gowns were of taffeta in all the colors mentioned above, but lined with lynx, weasel, Calabrian marten, sable and other rare fur. Their beads, rings, chains and necklaces were of precious stones: carbuncles, rubies, balas rubies, diamonds, sapphires, emeralds, turquoises, garnets, agates, beryls and priceless pearls.

Their headgear also varied with the season. In winter, it was in the

---

[47] An aromatic herb.

French fashion with a cap over the temples covered by a velvet hood with hanging veil. In spring it was in the Spanish, with laces and veils. In summer it was in the Tuscan, the hair elaborately entwined with gold chains and jewels. On Sundays and holidays, however, they followed the French mode which is more seemly and modest.

The men, too, dressed according to their personal taste. Their hose were of light wool or serge cloth, white, black, scarlet or kermes-red. Their velvet breeches were of the same hue or almost; they were embroidered or slashed to their taste. The doublet was of cloth-of-gold, cloth-of-silver, velvet, satin or damask, embroidered, panelled or slashed on one model, the points silk to match and the ornaments of fine enamelled gold.

Their cloaks and jerkins were of cloth-of-gold, cloth-of-silver, gold tissue or velvet, purfled or brocaded at pleasure; their over-garments were every whit as costly as the ladies'. Their girdles were silk, matching their doublets. Each wore on his side a handsome sword with gilt hilt and pommel; the scabbard velvet, matching his breeches, and the ferrule a wondrous example of the goldsmith's art. So too the dagger. Their caps were of black velvet, trimmed with jewels and rings and buttons of gold, with a white plume set in jauntily and parted by many rows of spangles from which hung splendent emeralds and various other stones.

Such was the sympathy between the gallants and their ladies that they matched one another's costumes every day. And in order to be sure of it, certain gentlemen were appointed to report every morning to the youths what garments their ladies planned to wear on that occasion. All here was done for the pleasure of the fair.

Handsome though the clothes were and rich the accoutrements, lads or girls wasted no time in dressing. The wardrobe masters had everything ready before their gentlemen arose and the maids were so nimble that in a trice their mistresses were apparelled from head to toe.

To facilitate matters, over a distance of half-a-league, a row of light, well-appointed cottages housed the goldsmiths, lapidaries, embroiderers, tailors, gold drawers, velvet weavers, tapestry makers and upholsterers. Here each worked at his trade, and all for the jolly friars and comely nuns of the new abbey. They received materials and stuffs from My Lord Nausiclete, famous for his ships, as the name indicates. Each year brought them seven vessels from the Pearl and Cannibal Islands or Antilles, laden with ingots of gold, raw silk, pearls and precious stones.

If pearls through age tended to lose their luster, the jewellers, following the method of Avicenna, fed them to the roosters, and they regained their native sparkle.

LVII

How Those of Thélème Were Governed in Their Manner of Living

Their whole life was ordered not by law, statute or rule, but according to their free will and pleasure. They arose when they pleased. They ate, drank, worked and slept when the spirit moved them. No one awoke them, forced food or drink upon them or *made* them do anything else. Gargantua's plan called for perfect liberty. The only rule of the house was:

DO AS THOU WILT

because men that are free, of gentle birth, well-bred and at home in civilized company possess a natural instinct that inclines them to virtue and saves them from vice. This instinct they name their honor. Sometimes they may be depressed or enslaved by subjection or constraint; for we all long for forbidden fruit and covet what is denied us. But they usually apply the fine forces that tend to virtue in such a way as to shake off the yoke of servitude.

The Thélèmites, thanks to their liberty, knew the virtues of emulation. All wished to do what they saw pleased one of their number. Let some lad or maid say "Let us drink" and all of them drank, "Let us play" and all of them played, "Let us frolic in the fields" and all of them frolicked. When falconry or hawking were in order, the ladies sat high upon their saddles on fine nags, a sparhawk, lanner or merlin on one daintily gloved wrist, while the men bore other kinds of hawks.

They were so well-bred that none, man or woman, but could read, write, sing, play several instruments, speak five or six languages and readily compose verse and prose in any of them. Never had earth known knights so proud, so gallant, so adroit on horseback and on foot, so athletic, so lively, so well-trained in arms as these. Never were ladies seen so dainty, so comely, so winsome, so deft at handwork and needlework, so skillful in feminine arts, so frank and so free as these.

Thus when the time came for a man to leave the abbey (either at his parents' request or for some other reason) he took with him one of the ladies—the particular one who had chosen him for her knight—and they were married. And though they had lived in devotion and friendship at Thélème, their marriage relations proved even more tender and agreeable. Indeed to the end of their lives they loved one another as they had on the day of their wedding. . . .

from THE SECOND BOOK

Pantagruel, King of the Dipsodes,[1] Restored to His True Nature, Together with His Deeds and Horrendous Feats. Set Down by the Late Monsieur Alcofribas, Abstractor of Quintessence.

THE AUTHOR'S PROLOGUE

O most illustrious and most valorous champions, gentlemen and all others who delight in honest entertainment and wit, I address this book to you. You have read and digested the *Mighty and Inestimable Chronicles of the Huge*

---

[1] *Dipsodes* means "Thirsty Ones." The Dipsodes appear in a later section of *Pantagruel*, here omitted.

Giant Gargantua.[2] Like true believers, you have taken them upon faith as you do the texts of the Holy Gospel. Indeed, having run out of gallant speeches, you have often spent hours at a time relating lengthy stories culled from these *Chronicles* to a rapt audience of noble dames and matrons of high degree. On this count, then, you deserve vast praise and sempiternal memory.

I intend each and every reader to lay aside his business, to abandon his trade, to relinquish his profession, and to concentrate wholly upon my work. Rapt and absorbed, all might then learn these tales by heart, so that if ever the art of printing perished and books failed, these tales might be handed down, like mystic religious lore, through our children to posterity! Is there not greater profit in them than a rabble of critics would have you believe? And what critics! Scabby-faced windbags, who understand these droll anecdotes even less than Raclet, the silver-tongued Professor of Law at Dôle, understands the *Institutes* of Justinian.[3]

I have known a number of proud and powerful lords who delighted in hunting huge beasts, or in flying hawks after wild ducks. Suppose, in the course of their sport, they failed to track down the deer when the huntsmen headed him off. Or suppose the falcon refused to soar in pursuit when the prey whirred away amid a tumult of wings. These lords were quite naturally incensed. But do you know what comfort they found in their disappointment? Do you know how they cheated their boredom? By relating the priceless exploits of the said Gargantua.

Others upon this planet (here is no cock-and-bull story!), being chronic sufferers from toothache, vainly spent all their worldly fortune upon physicians. In the end, these found no more expedient remedy than to lay the *Chronicles* between two pieces of warm linen, apply them to the painful spot and, adding a little quackshit powder, use them as a poultice.

What shall I say of those wretched devils plagued by pox and gout? How often they have appeared before us saturated with quicksilver ointment, salves and grease. Their faces shone like a larder keyhole . . . their teeth danced in their heads like the keyboard of an organ or spinet under the fingers of a maestro . . . they foamed at the gullet like a boar at bay in the toils of a pack of bloodhounds. . . . What did they do in this crisis? Their sole consolation was to have somebody read them a few pages of this book.

Some, experiencing no manifest relief at this reading, delivered themselves up to fivescore giant casks of devils, just as women in travail do when the *Life of St. Margaret* is read to them.

Is this nothing? Then find me a book in any language, in any branch of art or science, that possesses such virtues, properties and prerogatives. Find it, I say, and I will buy you a pint of tripes! No, gentlemen, no, none such exists. My book is peerless, incomparable, nonpareil, and—I maintain it in the teeth of hellfire—unique! If any one contradicts me, let him be herewith denounced as a false prophet, a champion of predestination, a poisoner and seducer of the people.

To be sure, you can find certain occult properties in some works of high

---

[2] Not Rabelais' *Gargantua*, but the anonymous tale which inspired Rabelais to write first *Pantagruel* and then *Gargantua*.

[3] Codification of Roman law by the Byzantine emperor Justinian (483–565).

timber such as *Fessepinte* or *Whip Pot, Orlando Furioso, Robert the Devil, Fierabras the Saracen Giant, William the Fearless, Huon of Bordeaux, Mandeville the Traveller* and *Matabrune.*[4] But they are not to be mentioned in the same breath with the work we speak of. Has not the whole world been forced by infallible experience to recognize the tremendous advantages and benefits to be derived from the *Gargantuan Chronicles*? Within two months the printers sold more copies of this work than they will sell Bibles for nine years to come.

Desiring, therefore, to entertain you further, I subscribe myself your humble servant, and herewith offer you another volume of identical stamp. Identical? It is, if anything, a little more worthy of faith and respect than its predecessor. Do you believe, unless you willfully court error, that I speak of my book as the Jews speak of the Mosaic Law? I was born under a different planet: it has never occurred to me to lie or to make false representation. I speak like St. John in the Apocalypse: "*Quod vidimus testamur,* we relate what we have seen." Or rather I quote his words like some lusty Thurifer (should I say Turdifer?) of the Martyr Lovers, or some Terrifying Torrefier of the affections. Ay, *quod vidimus, testamur*: I speak to you of the horrendous and frightful feats and prowesses of Pantagruel, whose flunkey I have been from infancy until now, when I come, by his leave, to visit my native cow-country,[5] and to ascertain if any of my relatives are alive.

However, before I conclude this prologue, I hereby deliver myself up body and soul, belly and bowels, to a hundred thousand basketfuls of raving devils, if I have lied so much as once throughout this work. By the same token, may St. Anthony sear you with his erysipelatous fire . . . may Mahomet's disease whirl you in its epileptic jitters . . . may the festers, ulcers and chancres of every purulent pox infect, scathe, mangle and rend you, entering your bumgut as tenuously as mercurialized cow's hair . . . and may you vanish into an abyss of brimstone and fire, like Sodom and Gomorrah, if you do not believe implicitly what I am about to relate in the present *Chronicles.* . . .

II

OF THE NATIVITY OF THE
MOST REDOUBTABLE
PANTAGRUEL

At the age of four hundred fourscore and forty-four years, Gargantua begat his son Pantagruel upon his wife named Badebec, daughter to the king of the dimly-seen Amaurotes in Utopia.[6] She died in the throes of childbirth. Alas! Pantagruel was so extraordinarily large and heavy that he could not possibly come to light without suffocating his mother.

If you would fully understand how he came to be christened Panta-

---

[4] Except for *Fessepinte,* an imaginary title, these are all famous medieval romances of chivalry.
[5] Rabelais wrote *Pantagruel* during a visit in 1532 to his native area around Chinon, in the province of Touraine. The region was then suffering from a severe drought.
[6] *Amaurote,* which means "dimly seen" (hence "imaginary"), is the principal city in Thomas More's *Utopia* (1516).

gruel, you must remember that a terrible drought raged that year throughout the land of Africa. For thirty-six months, three weeks, four days, thirteen hours and even longer, there was no drop of rain. And the sun blazed so fiercely that the whole earth was parched.

Even in the days of Elijah,[7] the soil was no drier, for now no tree on earth bore leaf or flower. The grass had no verdure; rivers and springs ran dry; the luckless fishes, abandoned by their element, crawled on solid earth, crying and screaming most horribly. Birds fell from the air for want of moisture; wolves, foxes, harts, wild boars, fallow deer, hares, rabbits, weasels, martens, badgers and other beasts were found dead in the fields, their mouths agape.

As for the men, their state was very piteous. You should have seen them with their tongues dangling like a hound's after a run of six hours. Not a few threw themselves into the wells. Others lay under a cow's belly to enjoy the shade—these it is whom Homer calls *Alibantes,* the desiccated.[8] The whole country was at a standstill. The strenuous efforts of mortals against the vehemence of this drought was a horrible spectacle. It was hard enough, God knows, to save the holy water in the churches from being wasted; but My Lords the Cardinals and our Holy Father laid down such strict rules that no man dared take more than a lick of it. In the churches, scores of parched, unhappy wretches followed the priest who distributed it, their jaws yawning for one tiny driblet. Like the rich man in *Luke,* who cried for Lazarus to dip his fingers in water,[9] they were tormented by a flame, and would not suffer the slightest drop to be wasted. Ah! thrice happy that year the man who had a cool, well-plenished wine cellar underground!

In discussing the question: "Why is sea water salty?" the philosopher Aristotle, after Empedocles,[10] supplies the following reason. When Phoebus[11] gave the reins of his luminous chariot to Phaëton, his son, the latter, unskilled in the art of driving, was incapable of following the ecliptic lines between the two tropics of the sun's sphere. Accordingly, he strayed from the appointed path and came so close to earth that he dried up all the countries under his course. He also burnished that great portion of heaven which philosophers call *Via Lactea* or the Milky Way, and good drinkers St. James' Way, since it is the starry line that guides pilgrims to Santiago de Compostella.[12] (On the other hand, poets declare that it is here Juno's milk dropped while she was suckling Hercules.)[13]

Earth at that time was so excessively heated that it broke into an enormous sweat which ran over the sea, making the latter salty, since all sweat is salt. If you do not admit this last statement, then taste of your own sweat. Or savor the perspiration of your pox-stricken friends when they are put in sweatboxes for treatment.[14] It is all one to me.

---

[7] During Elijah's time, there was a three-year drought. See I Kings 17.

[8] Plutarch (46?–c. 120 A.D.) discusses the word *alibantes* ("dried up"). It does not appear in Homer, though this passage is in Plutarch's commentary on Homer in the *Symposiaca.*

[9] The rich man in Hell asked Lazarus in Heaven for a drop of water (Luke 16:24).

[10] Fifth-century B.C. Greek philosopher. In his *Meteorologica,* Aristotle cites Empedocles' explanation but refutes it.

[11] God of the sun.

[12] Shrine in northwest Spain, built over the supposed tomb of the apostle St. James.

[13] Juno, wife of Jupiter and queen of the gods, was mother of Hercules.

[14] A common method for treating syphilis at the time.

Practically the same thing happened the year I am speaking of. On a certain Friday, all the people were intent upon their devotions. A noble procession was in progress with plenty of litanies and fine preachings. Supplications arose toward Almighty God beseeching Him to cast His eye of mercy upon them in their affliction. Suddenly they clearly saw some great drops of water stand out upon the ground, exactly as from a person sweating copiously.

The wretched populace began to rejoice as though here were a great blessing. Some declared that, since the air lacked all moisture, earth was supplying the deficiency. Other scientists asseverated that it was a shower of the Antipodes, as described by Seneca in *Quaestiones Naturales*, Book IV, where he treats of the Nile's source, attributing its floods to distant rains washed underground into the river. But they were thoroughly deceived. For, the procession done, when each sought to gather up this dew and drink it up by the bowlful, they found it was only pickle, far saltier than the saltiest water of the sea.

Another great mishap befell Gargantua that week. A dungchafing lout, bearing two great bags of salt and a hambone in his gamepouch, walked into poor Gargantua's mouth as the giant lay snoring. The clod spilled a quantity of salt in Gargantua's throat. Gargantua, crazy with thirst he could not slake, angrily snapped his mouth shut. He gnashed his teeth fiercely; they ground like millstones. Later the rascal told me he was so terrified you could have stopped up his nose with a bale of hay. He fell flat on his face like a dead man, dropping the two saltbags that had tormented Gargantua. They were at once swallowed up and entombed.

My rogue vowed vengeance. Thrusting his hand in his gamepouch, he drew out a great hambone, highly salted, still covered with hair, and twenty-eight inches long. Ragefully he rammed it down Gargantua's throat. The giant, drier than ever, felt the pig's hair tickling his belly and, willy-nilly, spewed up all he had. Eighteen tumbrils could not have drawn away the rich nauseous yield. My dungchafer, hidden in the cavity of one of his teeth, was forced to take French leave[15] in such pitiful condition that all who saw him were horrified. Gargantua, looking down, noticed this jackpudding whirling about in a great puddle.

"Here is some worm that sought to sting me in the belly," he mused, happy to have expelled him from his body.

Because he was born that very day, his father called him Pantagruel or All-Athirst, a name derived from the Greek *panta* meaning all, and the Hagarene or Saracen *gruel* meaning athirst.[16] Gargantua inferred thereby that at his son's birth the entire universe was wholly parched. Prophetically, too, he realized that some day Pantagruel would become Supreme Lord of the Thirsty, a fact indicated even more surely by a further portent.

For while his mother Badebec was bringing him forth and the midwives stood by ready to receive him, there first issued from her belly seventy-eight salt-vendors, each leading a salt-laden mule by the halter. They were followed by nine dromedaries, bearing hams and smoked oxtongues; seven

---

[15] Hasty departure without permission.

[16] A facetious etymology. Pantagruel was a demon in medieval French plays, who made everyone he met thirsty. The Saracen language is Moorish, called "Hagarene" because the Moors were said to be descended from the biblical Hagar.

camels bearing chitterlings; twenty-five cartloads of leeks, garlic, onions and chives. This terrified some midwives, but others said:

"Here is good provision! As it is, we drink but lazily, instead of vigorously. This must be a good omen, since these victuals are spurs to bibbing wine!"

As they were tattling away, out pops Pantagruel, hairy as a bear! At which, prophetically, one of them exclaimed:

"God help us, he is born hair and all, straight from the arse of Satan in flight. He will do terrible wonders. If he lives, he will grow to a lusty age!"

Of Pantagruel's race are those who drink so heavily in the evening that they must rise at night to drink again, quenching the coals of fire and blistering thirst in their throats. This form of thirst is called Pantagruel, in memory of the giant.

III

OF GARGANTUA'S GRIEF AT
THE DEMISE OF HIS WIFE
BADEBEC

At Pantagruel's birth, none was more amazed and perplexed than his father Gargantua. On one hand, he saw his wife Badebec dead, on the other, his son Pantagruel, large as life and much noisier. He was at a complete loss what to say or do. A terrible doubt racked his brain: should he weep over the death of his wife or rejoice over the birth of his son? On either hand, sophistical arguments arose to choke him. He could frame them capitally *in modo et figura*, according to the modes and figures of the syllogism in formal logic. But he could not resolve them. So there he was, fretting like a mouse caught in a trap, or a kite[17] snared in a gin.

"Shall I weep?" he cried. "Ay! . . . And why? Because my dear wife is dead! She was the most *this* and the most *that* who ever lived! I shall never see her again, I shall never know her like, I have suffered an irreparable loss! O God! what have I done to Thee to be thus punished? Why didst Thou not snatch me away before her, when to live without her is but to languish! Ah, Badebec, my darling, my love, my sweetheart, my dainty follicle (yet in area it was a good five and a half acres!), my tender mistress, my codpiece darling, my favorite pump, my dearest slipper, never shall I see you again! Alas, poor Pantagruel, you have lost your blessed mother, your indulgent nurse, your beloved lady! Ha, false Death, how outrageously evil to rob me of one that should by rights have been immortal. . . ."

As he spoke, he cried like a cow. But suddenly, struck by the thought of Pantagruel, he began to laugh like a calf.

"Ha, my little son!" he said, "my ballocky darling, my adorable fartlet, how lusty you are! How grateful I am to God for granting me a son so handsome, so sprightly, so gay and so spirited! Ho, ho, ho, ho, how happy I am! Let us drink, ho! and put away our melancholy! Bring out the best wine, rinse the glasses, lay the table, drive out those dogs, poke up this fire,

---

[17] A kind of hawk.

light the candles, close that door there, cut the bread in sippets for our pottage, send away these beggar folk but give them anything they ask for! You, there, hold my gown! I shall strip to my doublet to entertain the gossips better!"

As he said this, he heard the priests chanting litanies and mementos[18] as they bore his wife off to burial. All his glee suddenly evaporated; he was transported to the opposite extreme of emotion.

"Lord God," said Gargantua, "must I cry myself blind? This is the torment of hell! I am no longer young, I grow old, the weather is dangerous: I might easily fall ill of a fever. Already I am beside myself. Upon my faith as a gentleman, it were better I weep less and drink more. My wife is dead; well then, by God—*da jurandi veniam*,[19] excuse my language—my tears will not resurrect her. It is well with her . . . she is in Paradise at least, if no higher . . . she is praying to God for us . . . she is happy, beyond the reach of our miseries and calamities. . . . The same fate stares us all in the face. God help the survivor, I must think of finding me another wife.

"But here is what *you* must do—" He turned to the midwives. "Midwives, sages-femmes! (Where are they, good people, I cannot see them? Who ever saw a *femme* who was really *sage*!) Go, go to my wife's funeral whilst I stay here holding my son, for I feel somewhat out of sorts and dare not expose myself to sickness. Down a good drink first, too! You will be all the better for it, I assure you."

Doing as they were bid, they attended Badebec's funeral, while poor Gargantua remained at home, composing the following epitaph to be engraved upon her tombstone:

> Here lies sweet Badebec, snatched in the middle
> Of bearing child. What a metathesis!
> Her face was like the carving on a fiddle,
> Her body Spanish and her belly Swiss,[20]
> Pray God if she wrought anything amiss,
> He pardon her and she be sanctified.
> Here lies her body that expired, I wis,
> The very year and day wherein she died.

IV

OF PANTAGRUEL'S CHILDHOOD

In the ancient historiographers and poets, I find many cases of extraordinary childbirth. They would be too long to repeat, so if you are interested, I simply refer you to Chapter VII of Pliny's *Natural History: De Prodigiosis Partubus* or *Of Prodigious Births*.

Be that as it may, you have certainly never heard of any birth so wonderful as Pantagruel's. Indeed, his growth in stature and strength, during his brief sojourn in his mother's belly, almost defies belief.

---

[18] Prayers for the dead.
[19] The Latin is immediately translated: "Excuse my language."
[20] The Spanish were reputed to be slim and the Swiss fat.

Hercules, who slew two serpents in his crib, was small beer compared to Pantagruel, for the serpents were tiny and weak, whereas Pantagruel, while still in the cradle, accomplished feats of the most terrific kidney.

I shall not here dwell upon how at each of his meals he lapped up the milk of forty-six hundred cows . . . how, to make a skillet to boil his pap in, all the braziers of Saumur in Anjou, of Villedieu in Normandy, of Bramont in Lorraine, were set to work day and night . . . how, to serve him this pap, they used a colossal cup. . . . You may still see that cup in Bourges in front of the palace of the Duc de Berry: it is called the Giant's Bowl and filled with wine once a year for the poor. As an infant, Pantagruel had such long powerful teeth that he bit a great piece off the edge, as plainly appears to-day.

One morning when they brought in a cow to give him suck (history tells us he never had any other nurse) he worked one of his arms free from the swaddling bands that prisoned him. Seizing the cow below the hamstring, he chewed up two of her teats and half her belly, including liver and kidneys. He would have devoured her whole, had she not bellowed as if a pack of starving wolves had their fangs in her legs—at which horrible tumult, crowds of people rushed into the nursery and led her away. But they did not do a thorough job, for the babe still held on to the quarter he had seized and gulped down its meat as effortlessly as you would dispatch a sausage. When they sought to take the bone away, he swallowed it whole, as a cormorant bolts down a small fish. Though still unable to speak, he mumbled "Goo, goo, goo!" to convey his appreciation and eager acceptance of another.

After this scene, his attendants bound him with great cables like those manufactured at Tain on the Rhône for the transport of salt to Lyons and Vienne, or like those holding the pride of the French Navy, the *Grande Française,* in the port of Le Havre de Grâce in Normandy.

One day a huge bear Gargantua had raised escaped from his cage and began licking Pantagruel's face. (His nurses had failed to wipe his chops thoroughly.) The babe snapped off his chains as easily as Samson broke the bonds of the Philistines and, if you please, picked up My Lord Bear, tore him to pieces like a chicken and swallowed him in one fine hot mouthful!

Gargantua grew alarmed; he feared the babe would come to grief. So he had four great iron chains forged and bound him to as many arched props fastened to his cradle. Of these chains, one is now at La Rochelle; they draw it up at night, between the great towers of Chaîne and St. Nicolas, to close the harbor. Another is at Lyons, stretched across the Saône from the Abbey of Ainay to the Porte St. Georges. A third is at Angers, where it controls navigation on the Maine. The fourth was carried off by the devils to bind Lucifer when he ran amuck because of a colic caused by eating a bailiff's soul fricassée for breakfast. On this score you may credit what Nicolas de Lyra, the Italian biblical scholar, has to say on the passage in the *Psalter* which begins: "*Et Og regem Basan,* And Og, King of Bashan. . . ." Here Og, though still tiny, was so hardy and tough that they had to secure him in his cradle with iron fetters.

For a while Pantagruel remained tranquil and at peace, unable to break his bonds since he could not even swing his arms.

But not for long. On a great holiday, his father was sumptuously entertaining all the princes of his court. The members of the household were naturally too busy serving the banquet to bother about poor Pantagruel, who was left behind *a reculorum,* like a poop! What do you suppose he did?

What he did, my friends? Listen!

With his arms, he strove to break the chains. In vain: they were too strong. So he stamped his feet so furiously that he knocked out the bottom end of his cradle, a great square seven-span beam. Having got his feet out, he edged down until his soles touched the ground. Then, with tremendous force, he rose to his feet and strode off, the cradle bound to his back. He looked for all the world like a tortoise crawling up a well or a five-hundred-ton galleon advancing on end.

Thus disguised, he burst into the banquet hall, terrifying the company. But, as his arms were bound, he could reach for no food. So, with great effort, he bent over to lap up a choice morsel with the flat of his tongue. His father realized that they had neglected to feed him, and, having consulted his guests, ordered the chains removed. The physicians intervened. If Pantagruel were kept in his cradle any longer, they averred, he would suffer all his life from gallstones.

The babe unchained, they made him sit down. He proceeded to eat his fill. Then with one blow of his fist, he struck savagely at his cradle, smashing it into more than five hundred thousand pieces. And he swore he would never lie in it again.

V

The Noble Pantagruel's
Adolescence

Pantagruel grew and developed visibly from day to day, which naturally delighted his father. While he was still a tiny mite, his father had a crossbow made for him to shoot at small birds. It is still preserved in the great tower at Bourges; they call it the crossbow of Chantelle, because it was made in the famous arsenal there.[21]

Desiring the lad to study during his formative years, Gargantua sent him to Poitiers, where he profited greatly. It was here he noticed how heavy time hung on the students' hands, pitied them for it, and determined to remedy the situation. So one fine day he picked up a great stone off a ledge of rocks called Passelourdin and, though it was two thousand yards square and fourteen feet thick, easily set it on four pillars in the middle of a field. Thus, when the university students wanted something to do, they could spend their time climbing on top of it, banquet there abundantly upon flagons of wine, hams and pasties, and carve their names upon it with a knife.

To-day, this stone is known as La Pierre Levée, the Lifted Stone. In memory of Pantagruel's feat, no student can register at the University of Poitiers without first drinking in the mystic fountain of Croûtelle, going to Passelourdin and scaling the Lifted Stone.[22]

---

[21] The "crossbow of Chantelle" was a large siege engine at the castle of Chantelle.
[22] There was such a stone formation in Poitiers. It is now broken in two.

Reading the noble *Chronicles* of his ancestors, Pantagruel discovered that Geoffroi de Lusignan, known as Geoffrey with the Great Tooth, his stepmother's daughter-in-law's uncle's son-in-law's aunt's eldest sister's cousin-in-law's grandfather, was buried at Maillezais, the abbey he had destroyed and later rebuilt.[23] Accordingly, like a dutiful relative, Pantagruel took a day off to call on Ardillon, the noble abbot; then, passing through Sansay, Celles, Coulonges and Fontenay-le-Comte (where he saluted the learned Tiraqueau),[24] he reached Maillezais and duly visited the sepulcher of Geoffrey with the Great Tooth.

It frightened him not a little to see his ancestor portrayed there as a furious warrior, his fierce broadsword half-drawn. When Pantagruel asked the reason for this savage depiction, the canons of the place merely quoted Horace:[25] "*Pictoribus atque poetis, etc.,* poets and painters are entitled to depict whatever they like according to their own fancy." But Pantagruel was not satisfied with their answer.

"He is not presented thus without cause," he replied. "I suspect some wrong was done him at his death. Some wrong, I may add, which he looks to his kindred to avenge. I shall inquire further into the matter and do what is right."

Instead of returning to Poitiers, he decided to inspect the other universities of France. Proceeding to La Rochelle, he embarked for Bordeaux, where he found no great activity except for some stevedores playing chuckfarthing on the strand.

From Bordeaux he went to Toulouse, where he learned to dance very gracefully and to ply the two-handed sword, a tradition among the students of this university. But he did not tarry long when he saw that they burned their professors alive like red herrings.[26]

"God forbid that I should die thus!" he cried. "For I am naturally dry enough already, without heating myself further."

Next, he journeyed to Montpellier, where he found some excellent Mirevaux wines and jovial company. He thought of studying medicine here but decided the profession was too troublesome and morbid. Besides, physicians smelled hellishly of enemas. He was, however, anxious to study law. But the faculty, in the way of jurists, consisted of three scrofulous mephitics and a bold coot. So he left the city.

Less than three hours later, he had crossed the famous Roman aqueduct called the Pont du Gard and reached the amphitheatre of Nîmes, a feat seemingly divine rather than human.

Thence he went to Avignon, where, within three days, he fell in love, for the local women are great thigh-squeezers, it being Papal territory.[27] Seeing this, his tutor, Epistemon the Learned, took him to Valence in Dauphiné. Here he saw scant activity, but observed that the town bullies used to beat the scholars. This infuriated Pantagruel; accordingly, one fine Sunday

---

[23] Rabelais' patron, Geoffroy d'Estissac, welcomed humanists to the priory of Maillezais.

[24] These were places and people Rabelais had known in his youth.

[25] The statement appears in *The Art of Poetry* by Horace (65–8 B.C.).

[26] Jean de Caturce, professor of law at the University of Toulouse, was burned alive in June, 1532.

[27] Avignon was under the government of the Holy See and had a reputation for moral laxness.

morning, he took appropriate action. The populace was dancing on the square. A student sought to join in—an impertinence these lubbers would not countenance. Observing this, Pantagruel chased the whole crowd to the edge of the Rhône and would have drowned them, had they not burrowed into the earth like moles and lain in hiding a good two miles under the river. The hole down which they escaped may still be seen there today.[28]

Leaving Valence, in three hops and a jump, Pantagruel was in Angers, where he settled comfortably and would have remained but for the plague. So he went to Bourges, where he studied long and to great advantage under the Faculty of Law. He would sometimes remark that law books were like a fair robe of gold, priceless and dazzling, but edged with excrement.

"For," he added, "no books on earth are so rich, so beautiful, so decorative as the texts of the Roman *Pandects*.[29] But their border—the marginal glosses by medieval commentators like Accursius—is lousy, foul and villainous as a hundred tubs of shit!"

From Bourges, Pantagruel migrated to Orléans, where he found many a swaggering scholar to celebrate his arrival. The students here were much given to tennis; Pantagruel learned fast, and in an incredibly short time became a champion. Sometimes they would take him to the islands, the waterfront district of Orléans, to play Poussavant, which some call Push-it-in, and others, Bowling. And, fearful lest he strain his eyes, Pantagruel took good care not to study too hard. In point of fact, he did nothing. Had not a professor of his often declared in public that ophthalmia was harmful to the eyes?

One day a fellow-student of his received the degree of Master of Laws. His learning would have fit in a nutshell, but he danced beautifully and played a fine game of tennis. Pantagruel wrote the following lampoon in honor of the Masters of Laws of the University of Orléans:

> One tennis ball in pocket and
> One tennis racket in your hand.
> One solitary law to coddle
> In the desert of your noddle,
> One pair of heels to dance with. . . .   Good!
> You qualify to wear the hood
> Of Legum Magister,[30] and are
> Forthwith admitted to the Bar.

VI

HOW PANTAGRUEL MET A
LIMOUSIN WHO SPOKE
SPURIOUS FRENCH

One evening after supper—I cannot say exactly when—Pantagruel was strolling with some friends near the north gate of Orléans, by the road to

---

[28] There was a cavern under the church of Saint-Pierre, in Valence.

[29] Selections from classical jurists, one of the four parts of the *Corpus Juris Civilis*, the codification of Roman law produced under the direction of the sixth-century Byzantine emperor Justinian.

[30] Master of Laws.

Paris. Here he met a neat young student walking down the road. After they had bowed to one another, Pantagruel asked:

"Well, friend, where are you coming from at this time of day?"

The scholar replied:

"From the alme, inclyte and celebrate academy which is vocitated Lucetia."

"What on earth does he mean?" Pantagruel asked one of his men.

"He means: 'From Paris!'"

"So you come from Paris, eh?" Pantagruel resumed. "And how do you gentlemen students spend your time in Paris?"

The scholar replied:

"We transfretate the Sequana at the dilucul and crepuscul; we deambulate by the compites and quadrives of the metropolis; we despume the Latin verbocination and, like verisimilary amorabonds, we captate the benevolence of the omnijugal, omniform and omnigeneous muliebrine sex. At certain diecules, we invisitate upon the lupanars and, amid a venerean ecstasis, we inculcate our virilia into the most antipodean recesses of the pudenda of these supremely amicable meretricules. Then we proceed to pabulate in the mercantile taberna of the *Fir Cone,* the *Castle,* the *Magdalen* and the *Mule,* upon rare vervicina spatula performinated with petrosil. If by misfortune, there be rarity or penury of numismatical in our marsupia, or if we be exhausted of ferrugine metal, to pay, we demit our codexes and we oppignerate our vestments while we prestolate the Tabellaries who are to come from our patriotic Lares and Penates."

"What the devil is this jargon?" cried Pantagruel. "By God, I think you must be some sort of heretic."

(There was no interpreter here to tell Pantagruel that what the fellow meant was this: "We cross the Seine at dawn and dusk; we walk through the thoroughfares and crossroads of the city; we rake up Latin to speak and, as true lusty fellows, we win the favors of women. Occasionally we go to brothels and, hot with love, push our cods into the depths of these friendly little harlots' cunnies. Then, in the taverns of the *Fir Cone,* the *Castle,* the *Magdalen* and the *Mule,* we eat shoulders of mutton garnished with parsley; should we have little money in our purses or be out of cash, we settle the bill by pledging our books and pawning our clothes while awaiting remittances from home.")

So then, Pantagruel having taxed the Limousin student with heresy:

"Nay, my Lord," he replied, "for libentissimally as soon as it illucesces a minutule fragment of the day, I demigrate to some one of those so well architected ecclesiastical abodes. There, irrorigating myself with sweet lustral water, I rattle off little slices of some missic precation of our sacrificula. Submurmurating my horary precules, I elave and absterge my anima of its nocturnal inquinations; I revere the Olympicoles; I latrially venerate the supernal astripotent; I dilige and redame my proxims; I observe the Decalogical precepts and, according to the facultatule of my vires, I do not discede from them one unguicule. However it is veriform that since Mammona does not supergurgitate anything in my loculas, I am somewhat rare and tardigrade in supererogating the eleemosynaries to these indigents who hostially queritate their stipend."

(Poor Pantagruel! He could not know the fellow meant: "For when day breaks I withdraw to a well-built church, and there, sprinkling myself with holy water, I mumble a few words of the mass. While saying my prayers, I wash and cleanse my soul of the pollution of the night; I worship the high gods; I adore the master of the spheres; I love and cherish my neighbors; I follow the Ten Commandments and, within the measure of my power, I do not deviate a nail's breadth from these teachings. It is certain that because the Goddess of Wealth puts nothing in my purse, I very rarely give alms to the beggars who seek money from door to door.")

So, hearing the Limousin's mad flow of words:

"Midden and dung!" Pantagruel roared. "What does this lunatic mean? I think he is forging some diabolic tongue and laying a spell of witchcraft upon us."

To which one of his followers replied:

"Doubtless, My Lord, this rascal is trying to imitate the language of the Parisians. But all he is doing is to flay the Latin tongue, under the impression that he is using the noble style of Pindar. He fancies himself no end of an orator in French because he disdains our usual mode of speech."

"Is that true?" Pantagruel asked the scholar.

"Ah, My Lord!" the scholar replied, "my genius is not natively adept to what this flagitious nebulon manifests, as he excoriates the cuticle of our vernacular Gallic. On the contrary, I applicate my scruples viceversally and with the auxiliary of both sails and oars—*veles et rames*—I effortize to locupletate it with Latinicome redundance."

(All of which simply meant: "My genius is not naturally apt to grasp what this worthless vagabond says as he accuses me of flaying the skin of our French vernacular. On the contrary, I devote all my attention and make every possible effort to endow it with a Latin richness.")

"By God," Pantagruel growled, "I'll teach you how to speak. But come here, first, and tell me where you hail from?"

"The primeval origin of my aves and ataves," said the scholar, "was indigenous to the Lemovican regions where requiesces the cadaver of the hagiotate St. Martial."

(Which being interpreted meant: "My ancestors were born in the Limousin where St. Martial is buried.")

"I understand you perfectly," Pantagruel roared. "It all boils itself down to the fact that you're a Limousin trying to play the Parisian. Come here, my lad, and I'll curry your hair for you."

Seizing him by the throat:

"You're a flayer of Latin, eh? By St. John, I'll make you flay the fox—or vomit, ay, since you don't understand French. Unless I flay you alive!"

The wretched Limousin at once changed his tune.

"Eh but lawd gen'leman! Ho, Sint Martiaw, ho, cum to me help! Ooh, ho, leave me but be, and do ye not tech me!"

To which Pantagruel answered:

"Now you are speaking naturally."

So he let him go, for the unhappy Limousin had completely befouled his breeches, which were cut like a codfish tail, with a slash and not full-bottomed. At which Pantagruel cried:

"By St. Alipentin, what a civet, what a stew! The devil take this turnip-fed bumpkin. Phew! he whiffs to high heaven!"

And Pantagruel fled. But the scholar was thoroughly impressed by Pantagruel's throat-squeezing influence. He declared ever after that Pantagruel held him by the gullet. And he repented throughout his life, until some years later he died the death of Roland—from thirst![31] Thus the law of divine vengeance vindicated the instructions of Favorinus, the philosopher, in Aulus Gellius' *Attic Nights* where we are warned to speak the common idiom and where Octavius Augustus urges us to steer clear of unusual words even as mariners avoid reefs at sea.

VIII

How Pantagruel in Paris Received a Letter From His Father Gargantua

As you may suppose, Pantagruel studied very hard and profited much by his study, for his intelligence was naturally active and his memory as full as twelve casks of olives. While in Paris, he received the following letter from his father:

My beloved son,

Among the gifts, graces and prerogatives with which our sovereign Creator, God Almighty, blessed and enriched humanity from the beginning, there is one that I deem supreme. By its means, though we be mortal, we can yet achieve a sort of immortality; through it, we may, in the course of our transitory lives, yet perpetuate our name and race.

To be sure, what we gain by a progeny born of lawful wedlock cannot make up for what we lost through the sin of our first parents. Adam and Eve disobeyed the commandments of the Lord their God: mortality was their punishment. By death the magnificent mold in which Man was fashioned vanished into the dust of oblivion.

However, thanks to seminal propagation, what a man loses his children revive and, where they fail, their children prevail. So it has gone, and so it shall be, from generation to generation, until the Day of Judgment, when Christ shall restore to God the Father His kingdom pacified, secured and cleansed of all sin. Then all generation and corruption shall cease, for the elements will have completed their continuous transmutations. The peace humanity has craved so anxiously will have been attained; all things will have been reduced to their appointed end and period.

I therefore have reason to give thanks to God, my Saviour, for having granted me the joy of beholding my old age blossom anew in your youth. When, by His pleasure, which rules and orders everything, my soul must abandon this human habitation, I shall not believe I am dying utterly, but rather passing from one place to another. For in you my visible image will continue to live on earth; by you, I shall go on frequenting honorable men and true friends, as I was wont to do.

My associations have not been without sin, I confess. We all transgress and must continually beseech God to forgive us our trespasses. But they have been without reproach in the eyes of men.

That is why if, beside my bodily image, my soul did not likewise shine in you, you

[31] In the *Song of Roland*, Roland, grieving over his fallen knights, dies craving a drink of water. The Archbishop dies trying to get the water for him.

would not be accounted worthy of guarding the precious immortality of my name. In that case, the least part of me (my body) would endure. Scant satisfaction, that, when the best part (my soul, which should keep my name blessed among men) had degenerated and been bastardized. I say this not through any doubt as to your virtue, which I have already often tested, but to encourage you to go on doing ever better and profiting by your constant improvement.

My purpose is not so much to keep you absolutely on your present virtuous course as to make you rejoice that you have kept and are keeping on it. I seek to quicken your heart with resolutions for the future. To help you make and carry these out, remember that I have spared nothing. I have helped you as though my sole treasure on earth were once in my lifetime to see you well-bred and accomplished in honesty and valor as well as in knowledge and civility. Ay, I have longed to leave you after my death as a mirror of your father's personality. The reflection may not prove perfect in practice, but certainly I could not more studiously wish for its perfection.

My late father Grangousier, of blessed memory, made every effort that I might achieve mental, moral and technical excellence. The fruit of my studies and labors matched, indeed surpassed, his dearest wish. But you can realize that conditions were not as favorable to learning as they are to-day. Nor had I such gifted teachers as you. We were still in the dark ages; we still walked in the shadow of the dark clouds of ignorance; we suffered the calamitous consequences of the destruction of good literature by the Goths.[32] *Now, by God's grace, light and dignity have been restored to letters, and I have lived to see it. Indeed, I have watched such a revolution in learning that I, not erroneously reputed in my manhood the leading scholar of the century, would find it difficult to enter the bottom class in a grammar school.*

I tell you all this not through boastfulness, though in writing to you I might be proud with impunity. Does not Marcus Tullius[33] *authorize it in his book* OF OLD AGE, *and Plutarch in* HOW A MAN MAY PRAISE HIMSELF WITHOUT ENVY? *Both authors recognize that such pride is useful in fostering the spirit of emulation. No—I do it simply to give you a proof of my love and affection.*

To-day, the old sciences are revived, knowledge is systematized, discipline reëstablished. The learned languages are restored: Greek, without which a man would be ashamed to consider himself educated; Hebrew, Chaldean and Latin. Printing is now in use, an art so accurate and elegant that it betrays the divine inspiration of its discovery, which I have lived to witness. Alas! Conversely, I was not spared the horror of such diabolic works as gunpowder and artillery.

To-day, the world is full of learned men, brilliant teachers and vast libraries: I do not believe that the ages of Plato, Cicero or Papinian[34] *afforded such facilities for culture. From now on, it is unthinkable to come before the public or move in polite circles without having worshipped at Minerva's*[35] *shrine. Why, the robbers, hangmen, adventurers and jockeys of to-day are infinitely better educated than the doctors and preachers of my time. More, even women and girls aspire to the glory, the heavenly manna of learning. Thus, at my advanced age, I have been forced to take up Greek. Not that I had despised it, like Cato; I never had the opportunity to learn it. Now I delight in reading Plutarch's* MORALS, *Plato's noble* DIALOGUES, *the* MONUMENTS *of Pausanias and the* ANTIQUITIES *of Athenaeus, as I await the hour when it shall please God, my Creator, to call me back to His bosom.*

[32] *Goths* meant any barbarians.   [33] Cicero (106–43 B.C.).
[34] A learned Roman jurist of the third century A.D.   [35] Goddess of wisdom.

That is why, my dear son, I urge you to spend your youth making the most of your studies and developing your moral sense. You are in Paris, which abounds in noble men upon whom to pattern yourself; you have Epistemon, an admirable tutor, who can inspire you by direct oral teaching. But I demand more of you. I insist you learn languages perfectly! Greek first, as old Quintilian prescribes; then Latin; then Hebrew for the sake of the Holy Scripture; then Chaldee and Arabic, too. Model your Greek style on Plato, your Latin on Cicero. Let no history slip your memory; cultivate cosmography, for you will find its texts helpful.

As for the liberal arts of geometry, arithmetic and music, I gave you a taste of them when you were a little lad of five or six. Proceed further in them yourself, learning as much as you can. Be sure to master all the rules of astronomy; but dismiss astrology and the divinatory art of Lullius as but vanity and imposture.[36] Of civil law, I would have you know the texts of the Code by heart, then compare them with philosophy.

A knowledge of nature is indispensable; devote yourself to this study with unflagging curiosity. Let there be no sea, river or fountain but you know the fish that dwell in it. Be familiar with all the shrubs, bushes and trees in forest or orchard, all the plants, herbs and flowers that grow on the ground, all the birds of the air, all the metals in the bowels of earth, all the precious stones in the orient and the south. In a word, be well informed in everything that concerns the physical world we live in.

Then carefully consult the works of Greek, Arabian and Latin physicians, without slighting the Jewish doctors, Talmudists and Cabbalists.[37] By frequent exercises in dissection, acquire a perfect knowledge of that other world, which is man.

Devote a few hours a day to the study of Holy Writ. Take up the New Testament and the Epistles in Greek; then, the Old Testament in Hebrew. Strive to make your mind an inexhaustible storehouse of knowledge. For you are growing to manhood now: soon you will have to give up your studious repose to lead a life of action. You will have to learn to bear arms, to achieve knighthood, so as to defend my house and help our allies frustrate the attacks of evildoers.

Further, I wish you soon to test what profit you have gained from your education. This you can best do by public discussion and debate on all subjects against all comers, and by frequenting learned men both in Paris and elsewhere.

But remember this. As Solomon says, wisdom entereth not into a malicious soul, and science without conscience spells but destruction of the spirit. Therefore serve, love and fear God, on Him pin all your thoughts and hopes; by faith built of charity, cling to Him so closely that never a sin come between you. Hold the abuses of the world in just suspicion. Set not your heart upon vanity, for this life is a transitory thing, but the Word of God endureth forever. Be serviceable to your neighbor, love him as you do yourself. Honor your teachers. Shun the company of all men you would not wish to resemble; receive not in vain the favors God has bestowed upon you.

When you realize that you have acquired all the knowledge Paris has to offer, come back so I may see you and give you my blessing before I die.

My son, the peace and grace of Our Lord be with you. Amen.

Your father,

GARGANTUA

From Utopia, the seventeenth day of September.

---

[36] *Lullius* was Raymond Lully, thirteenth-century astrologer and philosopher.

[37] The Talmudists and Cabbalists wrote commentaries on Jewish law as well as on Scriptures.

Having read this letter, Pantagruel, greatly encouraged, strove more ardently than ever to profit in his work. Had you seen him studying vigorously, practically and tirelessly, you would have compared his spirit moving among his books to flames blazing through a bonfire of dry branches.

IX

How Pantagruel Met
Panurge Whom He Loved
All His Life

One day Pantagruel was walking in the country towards the Abbey of St. Antoine, conversing and philosophizing with his servants and some students. Suddenly he met a man of fine stature and handsome mien, but severely wounded in several places, and so tattered that he must have been fighting a pack of mastiffs. His clothes were as ragged as a Norman apple-picker's.

Seeing him from afar:

"Do you see that fellow coming from the Charenton bridge?" Pantagruel asked his companions. "Upon my word, he is poor only in fortune; his face bespeaks a rich and noble family. Doubtless the misadventures that invariably beset too-curious people have reduced him to his present misery."

When the fellow drew close, Pantagruel addressed him.

"Stop, friend, I beg you, and answer a few questions," he said. "I assure you you'll have no cause to regret it. The calamity that has befallen you moves me to pity; I am eager to help you however I can. Tell us, friend: who are you? Where are you going? What do you wish? And what is your name?"

The fellow answered:

"Juncker, Gott geb euch glück unnd hail. Zuvor, Lieber Juncker, ich las euch wissen das da ir mich von fragt, ist ein arm unnd erbarmglich ding, unnd wer vil darvon zu sagen, welches euch verdruslich zu hoeren, unnd mir zu erzelen wer, viewol die Poeten unnd Orators vorzeiten haben gesagt in iren Sprüchen unnd Sentenzen, das die Gedechtnus des Ellends unnd Armuot vorlangs erlitten ist ain grosser Lust."

(He spoke in German, saying: "Young gentleman, God prosper you and bring you joy. But first, my dear young gentleman, I must inform you that what you seek to know is a wretched and pitiful thing. It would make an endless story. And it would prove no pleasanter for you to hear than for me to tell, though the poets and orators of ancient times have stated in maxim and adage that the remembrance of sorrows endured is a great joy.")

"My friend," said Pantagruel, "I cannot understand this gibberish. If you expect us to understand, then speak another tongue."

The stranger replied:

"Al barildim gotfano dech min brin alabo dordin falbroth ringuam albaras. Nin porth zadikim almucathin milko prin al elmim enthoth dal heben ensouim: kuthim al dum alkatim nim broth dechoth porth min michais im endoth, pruch dal maisoulum

hol moth dansrilrim lupaldas im voldemoth. Nin hur diavosth mnarbotim dal gousch palfrapin duch im scoth pruch galeth dal Chinon *min foulchrich al conin butathen doth dal prim."*

(The words sounded vaguely like Arab, but it was a fantastic jargon he spoke. His hearers could make out only a single place-name: Chinon.)

"Can you make head or tail of it?" Pantagruel appealed to the others.

"I think it is the language of the Antipodes," Epistemon ventured. "But it's such a jawbreaker not even the devil himself would dare twist his tongue to it."

"My friend," said Pantagruel, "the walls may understand you, if they have ears to hear. But not one man jack among us can follow a syllable."

The stranger sighed. Then:

"Signor mio: voi videte par exempio che la cornamusa non suona mai s'ella non ha il ventre pieno," he went on. *"Cosi io parimente non vi saperei contare le mie fortune, se prima il tribulato ventre non a la solita refettione, alquale é adviso che le mani et li denti abbui perso il loro ordine naturale et del tuto annichillati."*

(A person conversant in Italian would have gathered: "My Lord, you know, for example, that no bagpipe ever makes a sound without a full belly. By the same token, I couldn't possibly tell you my adventures unless my tormented stomach first received its usual refreshment. To my paunch, it appears as though my hands and teeth had lost their natural functions and were utterly annihilated.")

"We're no better off than before," Epistemon grumbled.

The stranger continued:

"Lord geft tholb be sua virtiuss be Intelligence ass yi Body schal biss be naturall relvtht, tholb suld of me pety have, for Natur hass ulss equaly maide; bot Fortune sum exaltit hess, and oyis deprevit. Non ye less viois mou virtius deprevit and virtius men descrevis; for anen ye lad end, iss non good."

(This was Scots English. Its purport: "My Lord, if your generosity of spirit is as lofty as your body is by nature, you will have pity on me. For Nature hath created us equal, but Fortune hath exalted some, and others she hath brought low. Nevertheless, though virtue be often beggarly and the upright scorned, yet till the hour of death, no man may boast that he is good.")

"Floored again," cried Pantagruel. Panurge immediately resumed:

"Jona andie, guaussa goussy etan behar da erremedio, beharde, versela ysser lan da. Anbates, otoyyes nausu, eyn essassu gourr ay proposian ordine den. Non yssena bayta fascheria egabe, genherassy badia sadassu noura assia. Aran Rondovan gualde eydassu nay dessuna. Estou oussyc eguinan soury hin, er darstura eguy harm, Genicoa plasar vadu."

(A bastard Basque, this. Most Gascon lackeys could have told Pantagruel it meant: "Great Lord, all things have their remedy: if unapparent, then we must sweat to find it. I implore you therefore to let me know clearly if my suggestion is in order. If you see no inconvenience, then give me my fill. Once you have done that, ask me what you will: I shall not fail you. Please God, I speak the truth from the depths of my heart.")

"Are you there, Genoica?" mocked Eudemon. "My God!!!"[38]

"By St. Ninnyhammer," cried Carpalim, Gargantua's valet. "May your bum burst if I didn't almost get the drift of it."

"Prug frest strinst," the stranger continued, *"sorgdmand strochdt drhds pag brleland* Gravot, Chavigny, La Pomardière, *rusth pkallhdracg* La Devinière près Nays, Seuilly. *Halmuch monach drupp delmeupplistrincq drlnd dodelb up drent loch minc stzrinquald* de vins *der Cordelis hur jocst-stzampenards."*

Again, in this mad balderdash, all they made out was the placenames Gravot, Chavigny, La Pomardière, La Devinière, Nays, Seuilly and the word "wines."

"Do you speak Christian, my friend," Epistemon asked, "or Gipsy language, Welsh or Czech?"

"No," said another, "that's Lantern Language, spoken in the Isles of Nowhere."

The stranger changed his tack:

"Herre, ie en spreeke anders gheen taele, dan kersten taele; my dunct nochtans, al en seg icu met een woordt, mynen noot verklaert ghenonch wat ie begeere; gheeft my uyt bermherticheyt yet waer vn ic ghevoct magh zunch."

(Translated from the Dutch this meant: "Sir, I speak no tongue that is not Christian. Yet I should think that, without my saying a word, my rags betray clearly enough what it is I wish. In human charity, give me something to revive me!")

"It's all of one piece," Pantagruel grumbled. "And about as clear as mud."

"Seignor, de tanto hablar yo soy cansado. Por que suplico a Vostra Reverentia que mire a los preceptos evangeliques, para que ellos movant vostra Reverentia a lo que as de conscientia, y, si ellos non bastarent para mover Vostra Reverentia a piedad, suplico que mire a la piedad natural, la qual yo creo que la movra, como es de razon, y con esto non digo mas."

(The Spanish means: "My Lord, I am tired from so much speaking. So I beg your Reverence to consider the precepts of the Gospel, so that they may move your Reverence to fulfill the demands of conscience. If they do not suffice to move your Reverence to pity, then I implore you to consider natural compassion, which I think must reasonably do so. On this head, I shall say no more.")

"By God, I've no doubt you can speak a score of languages fluently," said Pantagruel. "But tell us what you want in some language we can understand."

[38] *Genoica* means "from God."

"Myn Herre," the stranger said, *"endog jeg med ingen tunge talede, lygesom boeen, ocg uskielig creatuer; myne kledebon och myne legoms magerhed uudviser allyguevel klarlig huvad tyng meg meest behoff girered, som aer sandeligh mad och drycke: hwarfor forbarme teg omsyder ofvermeg, oc befael at gyffue meg nogeth, aff huglket jeg kand styremyne groeendes maghe, lygeruïss son mand Cerbero en soppe forsetthr: Soa shal tue loeffue lenge och lyksaligth."*

(Translating the Danish: "Sir, even if like a babe or beast I spoke no language whatever, my clothing and my emaciated body should plainly show what I need: food and drink. Have pity on me then and order them to give me something to master my baying belly, even as sops are tossed to Cerberus.[39] Do this and you will live long and happy."

"I think," Epistemon said, "that is how the Goths spoke. Were God willing we would all speak thus—through our tailpieces!"

"Adoni, scolom techa," the stranger cried. *"Im ischar harob hal hebdeca bemeherah thithen li kikar lehem, chancathub: Laah al Adonai cho nen ral."*

(In Hebrew: "Sir, the peace of God be upon you. If you wish to do good to your servitor, give me a loaf of bread at once, for it is written: 'He that hath pity upon the poor lendeth to the Lord.'")

"Ha!" cried Epistemon. "This time I understand. That's Hebrew, well turned and rhetorically pronounced."

The wag resumed:

"Despota tinyn panagathe, doiti sy mi uc artodotis? Horas gar limo analiscomenon eme athlios. Ce en to metaxy eme uc eleis udamos, zetis de par emu ha u chre, ce homos philologi pamdes homologusi tote logus te ce rhemeta peritta hyrparchin, opote pragma afto pasi delon esti. Entha gar anancei monon logi isin, hina pragmata, hon peri amphibitumen, me prosphoros epithenete."

(In Greek: "Excellent master, why do you give me no bread? You see me miserable and perishing of hunger, yet instead of coming to my aid, you ask me irrelevant questions. Nevertheless, all intelligent people agree unanimously that discourse and words are superfluous when the facts are patent to all. The only words needful here are those you should speak to give me what we are arguing about.")

"Good Lord! That's Greek!" cried Carpalim. "I've heard it spoken before. How do you know it? Have you ever lived in Greece?"

The stranger, for only answer, said:

"Agonou dont oussoys von denaguez algarou, nou den farou zamist vous mariston ulbrou, fousquez vous brol, tam bredaguez moupreton den goul houst, daguez daguez nou croupys fost bardounnoflist nou grou. Agou paston tol nalprissys hourtou los ecbatonous prou dhouquys brol panygou den bascrou noudous caguons goulfren goul oust troppassou."

---

[39] The dog that guarded the entrance to Hades in classical mythology.

"I believe I understand him," said Pantagruel. "Either that language is my native Utopian or it is much like it in sound."

But as he sought to address him, the stranger interrupted:

"Jam toties vos per Sacra perque Deos Deasque omnis obtestatus sum ut, si qua vos pietas permovet, egestatem meam solaremini, nec hilum proficio clamans et ejulans. Sinite, quaeso, sinite, viri impii, Quo me fata vocant abire, nec ultra vanis vestris interpellationibus obtundatis, memores veteris illius adagii, quo Venter famelicus auriculis carere dicitur."

(Which Latin meant: "Already, by all I hold sacred, by the gods and goddesses above, I have repeatedly implored you to allay my suffering, if pity can move you. But I have gained nothing by my prayers and supplications. Leave me, therefore, I pray you, O impious men; let me go whither destiny calls. Cease wearying me with your vain questions and remember the ancient adage: 'The empty belly hath no ears to hear.'")

"By God, friend, can't you speak French?" Pantagruel demanded.

"Why of course, I can speak French very well," the stranger answered. "It is my natural language, praise God, my mother-tongue, for I was born and brought up in Touraine, the garden of France."

"Then tell us what is your name," Pantagruel urged, "and explain where you have come from. By my faith, I've already taken such a liking to you that if you incline to my wishes, you shall never budge out of my company. God's truth, you and I shall make a pair of friends to match Aeneas and Achates."[40]

"My Lord, my true and proper Christian name is Panurge. I have just returned from Turkey whither I was taken prisoner after the disaster at Mytilene.[41] I shall be only too pleased to tell you of my adventures, which are more wonderful than those of Ulysses. But you are pleased to attach me to your person; I heartily accept the offer and swear never to leave you, should you go to all the devils in hell. I shall therefore have more leisure at another time to give an account of myself. For the moment, I most urgently need to feed. My teeth are sharp, my belly empty, my throat dry and my appetite a devouring flame. All is ready if you will but give the word. To see me fall to, would be a feast for the eyes. For God's sake, order me some food."

Pantagruel bade them take him home and provide him with victuals aplenty. Panurge ate abundantly that evening, went to bed with the chickens, and slept until the morrow at dinner time. Thus the interval from bed to board was but three steps and a jump.

XVI

OF THE CHARACTER AND
CONDITION OF PANURGE

Panurge was then about thirty-five years old and as fine to gild as a dagger of lead. Of medium height, neither too tall nor too short, he had an aqui-

---

[40] Companion and friend of Aeneas in Virgil's *Aeneid*.

[41] The French besieged the Greek island of Mytilene in 1502 but were defeated by the Turks. The name Panurge comes from the Greek *panourgos*, "apt at everything, a knave."

line nose, shaped like the handle of a razor. He cut a very gallant figure though he was a trifle lewd by nature, and subject to a disease at that time called impecunitis, an incomparable malady.

Yet when he needed money, he knew thirty-three methods of acquiring it, the most ordinary and honorable of which was filching. He was a quarrelsome fellow, a sharper, a toper, a roisterer and a profligate, if ever there was one in the city of Paris. In every other respect, he was the best fellow in the world.

He was constantly plotting against the sergeants and the watch. Sometimes he assembled three or four sportsmen, plied them with drink until they were boozy as Knights Templars, then took them up the hill to Ste. Geneviève or near the Collège de Navarre. Placing his sword on the pavement and his ear to his sword, he waited till he heard the blade shake—an infallible sign that the watch was not far off. Then he and his companions took a dung cart and rolled it down hill. Ere it was halfway down, they had fled in the opposite direction, for in less than two days Panurge knew every street and alley in Paris as well as his postprandial grace: *Deus det nobis pacem suam,* God grant us His peace.

Another time he laid down a train of gunpowder where the watch was due to pass. Just as the troop debouched,[42] he set fire to it, vastly delighted in observing how gracefully they took to their heels, in mortal terror that St. Anthony's fire had caught them by the legs.

The luckless Masters of Arts and theologians he persecuted more than any other class of men. When he met one, he never failed to do him some harm, either slipping a turd into his hood or pinning little foxtails or hares' ears to his back.

One day when all the theologians had been summoned to the Sorbonne to examine the articles of the faith, he made a tart of garlic, asafoetida, galbanum, castoreum and steaming excrement, which he steeped and tempered in the corrupt manner of chancres and pockbiles. Very early in the morning he so theologically greased and anointed the lattices and grates of the trellised gallery of the Hall of Records that not even the devil himself had dared stay there. The worthy pedagogues puked in public as abundantly as though they had flayed the fox. Ten or twelve died of the plague, fourteen contracted leprosy, eight came down with pestiferous ulcers, and more than twenty-eight caught the pox. But Panurge was jubilant.

Usually he carried a whip under his gown with which he mercilessly belabored such pages as he met bearing wine for their masters, in order to speed them on their way.

In his coat he had more than twenty-six little pockets and pouches which were always full. One held a pair of loaded dice and a small knife like a glover's awl to cut purses with. Another, verjuice[43] to throw in the eyes of those who annoyed him. A third, burrs, penned with gosling or capon feathers, to stick on to the robes and bonnets of honest people. He often gave married men a fine pair of horns which they bore through the city sometimes all their lives long. To the back of the women's hoods, he liked to affix various knickknacks shaped like the sexual organ of man.

---

[42] Marched out.
[43] An acid juice made from crab apples or unripe grapes, used in cooking.

Another pocket held a lot of little packages filled with fleas and lice which he recruited from the tramps at St. Innocent's graveyard and cast with small sticks or quills down the backs of the smartest gentlewomen he could find. He did this even in church, for he never sat up in the choir, preferring to stand in the nave among the women during mass, vespers or sermon. Another pocket held a large supply of bent nails with which he would couple men and women together where they sat. This was particularly amusing when the victims wore gowns of costly sarsenet taffeta, because they ripped them to shreds as they sought to separate. Still another pocket held a squib with tinder, flints, matches, vesuvians, sulphur and other combustibles. Another, two or three burning-glasses with which he tortured and disconcerted men and women at church. For he said there was only an antistrophe between *femme folle à la messe* and *molle à la fesse* or working a cunning stunt and a stunning cunt. Another pouch held needles, threads and pins for all manner of minor deviltries.

Once at the door of the Great Hall in the Palais de Justice, Panurge saw a Cordelier father[44] getting ready to say mass before the proceedings of the day. Immediately he ran up to help the holy man don his vestments and, in the process, managed to sew his alb[45] to his robe and shirt. Then, as the magistrates arrived for mass, Panurge withdrew. Mass done, as he reached the formula *Ite, missa est,* the wretched friar tried to take off his alb. But, at the same time, off came the robe and shirt solidly sewn to it. Our Cordelier, thus stripped to the shoulders, revealed his dangledingus to all the world—and it was no small crosier, as you may imagine. The harder he tugged, the more he exposed himself. So much so indeed, that one of the counselors cried:

"What is the matter? Is this good friar making an offering of his tail for us to kiss? No, by heaven, let St. Anthony's fire kiss it for us!"

From then on, an ordinance forbade the poor good fathers to disrobe before the world, the vestry-room being indicated as the only fit place for this. They were especially warned against doing so in the presence of women, lest it tempt the latter to sin through longing. When people wondered why the fathers were genitally so well-equipped, Panurge solved the problem.

"What makes the ears of asses so long?" he asked, and answering his own question: "Their dams put no caps on their ears. Alliacus, Chancellor of the University and Chaplain to Charles VI, proves this in his *Suppositiones*. Similarly, what makes the whangletools of our holy fathers hang so low? Well, they never wear dark breeches, so their lusty organs, dangling down at liberty like a horse given head, knock against their knees like women's beads. Why are they correspondingly large? Because, with all this waggling to and fro, the humors of the body sink down into these parts. Do not the legists point out that continual agitation and continual motion are the cause of attraction?"

Another of Panurge's pouches held stone-alum, an itching-powder which he poured down the backs of those he considered the proudest and most stately ladies. Some would at once strip off their clothes then and

---

[44] Franciscan friar (so called from the knotted cord worn around the waist).
[45] White linen robe worn by a priest.

there before the public . . . others danced like cats on hot coals or a drumstick on a tabor . . . others again rushed madly into the street and he at their heels. . . . Those inclined to disrobe, he assisted by sheltering them under his cape, as any courteous and gallant gentleman would have done.

In another pocket he had a small leather bottle full of old oil. If he saw a man or woman in a handsome costume, he would grease and stain it in the most conspicuous places. His technique here was an art. Pretending to admire the material, he would finger it.

"Rare cloth, this, sir," or "Fine satin, upon my word!" or "Oh, what lovely taffeta, Madame!" he would exclaim. "God give you all your noble heart desires. You have a new suit, My Lord! And you a new dress, My Lady. Well, you know the saying: New clothes, new friends. God give you joy in them!"

As he spoke, his hands passed lightly over the shoulders and a long ugly smear remained

> So indelible a spot
> Stamped on body, soul and fame
> That the devil could not blot
> Out its testament of shame.

As he took his leave of the ladies, he would say:

"Madame, take care not to fall. You've a huge filthy hole out of sight in front of you, there!"

In another pocket he kept euphorbium,[46] very finely pulverized and spread over a dainty handkerchief he had stolen from a pretty salesgirl in the Galleries of the Sainte-Chapelle, hard by the law courts and frequented by the gallants of the day. (He filched it while removing from between her breasts a louse he had dropped there.)

When he happened to be in gentle company, he would steer the conversation on to the subject of lace and lingerie. Then, thrusting his hands into some lady's bosom:

"Glorious work, this. Is it Flanders or Hainault?"

Then, drawing his handkerchief:

"Just look at this kerchief, Madame. Would you say it was Frontignan or Fontarabia?"

Shaking it hard under her nose, he would make her sneeze for hours at a time. Then he would fart like a dray horse.

"Tut, tut," the lady would say. "Are you whiffling, Panurge?"

"No, Madame," he would reply gallantly, "I am merely tuning my tail to the plain song you make with your nose."

Panurge was never without pincers, a picklock, a pelican, a jimmy, a crook or other tools against which no chest or door could avail. Finally, in another pocket he kept a whole battery of small goblets which he worked with amazing skill, for his fingers were nimble and adroit as those of Minerva or Arachne.[47] He had indeed once been an itinerant quack, barking

---

[46] An acrid medicinal powder.

[47] Minerva and Arachne, in Greek mythology, were both renowned for their skill in weaving. When Arachne defeated Minerva in a weaving contest, she was turned into a spider.

antidotes for poison. When he presented a sum of money and asked for change, the changer had to be spry as Argus[48] to catch Panurge spiriting away five, six or seven coins at a time, visibly, openly, manifestly, without lesion or hurt, whilst all the changer noticed was a slight draught.

XVII

HOW PANURGE WON INDULGENCES, HOW HE MARRIED OFF VARIOUS OLD WOMEN, AND HOW HE FOUGHT SEVERAL LAWSUITS IN PARIS

One day I found Panurge silent and sullen. Suspecting he was penniless, I said:

"Panurge, I can see by your face that you are sick. I know your trouble: you've a flux in your purse. Don't worry, old fellow. Like Pathelin I've still:

> Four coins of one kind, five of the other
> Changelings, bereft of both father and mother.

Do you need them? They're yours to acquire as readily as the pox."

"A turd for money!" he exclaimed. "I'll be rolling in wealth some day. For I've a philosopher's stone which draws money out of men's purses as surely as a magnet draws steel. By the way, how about coming along to gain a few pardons?"

"I'm no great hand at pardons in this world," I said. "And I'm not so sure I shall be in the next. But let us go, in God's name, for one pardon, if it costs no more than one penny."

"Fine! You lend me a penny at interest," said Panurge.

"No, no, I'll give it to you gladly."

"*Grates vobis dominos,* thank you, My Lord!"

We began with St. Gervais where I stopped at the first box, gave my alms, received my pardon and cried quits. (I am easily satisfied in such matters.) I was saying a few prayers to St. Bridget before the image of Christ when I noticed Panurge stopping at every box and always handing money to the pardoners.

From St. Gervais we proceeded successively to Notre Dame, to St. Jean, to St. Antoine and to all the other churches that had cashier's desks for trading in pardons. I myself acquired no more, but Panurge kissed the relics at every box and everywhere paid the piper (I mean the pardoner!). To be brief, on our way home he stood me to a drink at the Taverne du Château, and there showed me ten or twelve of his little pouches, cram-full of cash. I crossed myself.

"Where on earth did you find all that money in so short a time?" I asked.

"Where else but in the collection plates?" he answered. "When I gave

---

[48] In Greek mythology, a giant with a hundred eyes, set to guard the heifer Io.

them my first penny, I laid it down so neatly that it looked like three-pence. So with one hand, I took up three, six, ninepence, indeed, a shilling or even two; while with the other, I raked in as much again. So it went, in all the churches we visited."

"But Panurge, you've damned yourself for a sacrilegious thief."

"I suppose it seems so to you. But *I* don't look at it like that: I consider this money a gift from the pardoners. When they presented the relics to me, did they say *'Centuplium accipies!'* or not? Does that mean that for one penny I shall have one hundred, or not? *Accipies* is the future: it means thou shalt have. Well, the Hebrews always used the future tense to denote the imperative as in the law *Dominum Deum tuum adorabis et illi soli servies; diliges praemium tuum et sic de aliis,* Thou shalt adore thy God and serve Him only; thou shalt take thy reward, and thy fellows, likewise. Thus when the pardoner says *'Centuplium accipies,* thou shalt have one hundred' he means *'Centuplium accipe,* have a hundred.' Rabbi Kimchi, the learned Jew of Narbonne, and Rabbi Aben Ezra, the celebrated Spaniard, both expound this principle *et ibi Bartolus,* Bartolo too!

"What's more, Pope Sixtus IV granted me a yearly pension of fifteen hundred francs from his ecclesiastical revenues and treasure when I cured him of a chancrous swelling. It had tortured him so cruelly he feared he would remain a cripple for the rest of his days. Thus I am paying myself my due out of the ecclesiastical treasure with my own hands, since others will not.

"Ha, my good friend," Panurge went on, "you would be dumbfounded if I told you how nicely I feathered my nest during the Mytilene Crusade. Why, I netted more than six thousand florins cash!"

"What ever has become of them?" I asked incredulously. "You haven't a sou to your name now."

"They went where they came from," he told me. "They simply changed hands. But I used up a good three thousand marrying off women. Not girls, you understand, they come all too easily by a husband. No, I married off ancient hags, horrible old sempiternal trots without a tooth in their heads.

"I figured it this way: 'These superannuated harridans spent their youth to advantage, thigh-squeezing and buttock-clenching with their arses cocked for all comers,' I said. 'In the course of time, no one would have traffic with them any more. Well, by God, I intend to treat them to one more branglebump before they die.'

"So I gave one a dowry of one hundred florins, another one hundred and twenty, a third three hundred, briefly, a sum always proportional to their degree of infamy, horror and repulsion. There were others who had to be still more heavily endowed or even the devil himself would have forborne to scrobiculate them. Then I sought out some strapping hodcarrier or some thumping colossus of a stevedore and performed the marriage myself.

"But before showing him his hag, I flashed the money before him, saying: 'This is yours, lad, if you'll undertake to pull off one good tailrasping bumswink.' Poor devils, they gaped like old mules. So I made careful preparations, served them a fine meal with the best of wine and

heady spices to put the old witches in rut and heat. In the end, they buckled
to, like all good Christian souls. When the belles were too horribly ugly and
moldering, I had them put their heads in a sack to hide their faces. . . .

"I have also lost a good deal of money in lawsuits."

"What lawsuits can *you* have had?" I asked. "You own no house or
lands."

"True, but I had suits aplenty. Inspired by the devil, the ladies of this
city invented a sort of high-mounted neckpiece, closed in front and slit
behind; it covered their breasts so completely that a wretched man couldn't
slip his hands under for love or money. You can imagine how their poor,
contemplative lovers grieved. Well, one fine Tuesday, I presented a petition to the Court making myself a party against these ladies. I established
the great interest I laid claim to in the matter, and I protested that, by the
same process, I would have the fly of my trousers sewn over my bum unless
the Court acted immediately.

"The ladies for their part, formed an association for their common
defense, drew up their *fundamenta* (I mean basic arguments, of course) and
appointed an attorney to represent them. However, I pursued them so
vigorously that a decree of the Court abolished these horse-collars unless
they were also openable in front. But it cost me a pile of money.

"I had another lawsuit, too. A very nasty business it was. This time I
attacked Master Fiefaugh, the city dung-farmer and scavenger. I peti-
tioned the Court that neither he nor his deputies be allowed to mull over
the *Pipes of Pan* or the mountains of *Sentences* by night,[49] but, on the contrary, they should peruse these in broad daylight in the schools of the Sorbonne and in the presence of the theologians. I was condemned to costs
through the mistaking of some minor clause in the sergeant's evidence.

"Another time I complained to the Court against the mules of the magistrates, counsellors and other officers of the Palais de Justice. I sought to
obtain that, when they left these mules to champ on their bridles in the
lower courtyard, the beasts be given bibs. Thus they would not cover the
pavement with their drivelling and slobbering, and the pages of the Palais
might play dice or *Deny Thy God*[50] without dirtying the knees of their
breeches. I won a fine decree, but it cost a tidy sum.

"Apropos, guess how much I have to pay for the little banquets I give
the pages every day?"

"Banquets? I didn't know you gave them banquets?"

"My poor friend, you get no fun at all out of life!" he sighed. "But
I—well, I get more than the king himself. If only you joined me, we could
raise a thousand devils!"

"No, no," I protested, "by St. Adauras, I will not. Some day or other,
you will be hanged!"

"And you buried! Which is the more honorable, air or earth? Ha, you
old dullard, didn't Christ hang aloft?"

"Hm!"

"To get back to my story. As these pages are banqueting, I keep their

[49] Peter Lombard's *Sentences* was a twelfth-century compendium of Christian dogma, frequently taught in the schools. There is a pun on *sentences* and *scents*. The *Pipes of Pan* is an
imaginary book, perhaps with a vaguely excremental suggestion.

[50] A gambling game.

masters' mules. And I invariably cut the stirrup-leather of one or two mules on the mounting side so it hangs by a thread. When some great puffbelly of a counsellor takes a swing to mount, he falls flat as a hog, affording the spectators much more than a hundred francs' worth of amusement. But I laugh even more as I think how the minute they reach home they thrash Master Page like green rye. That amply compensates me for what it costs me to banquet them."

In conclusion, as I said before, Panurge knew thirty-three methods of acquiring money. But he knew two hundred and fourteen methods of spending it, exclusive of wetting the yawning gulf that spread below his nostrils.

XVIII

How a Great Scholar of
England Sought to Argue
Against Pantagruel and
How He Was Overcome
by Panurge

About the same time, an illustrious savant, Thaumastes (the name signifies a worker of wonders), hearing rumors of Pantagruel's reputation for incomparable knowledge, came from England to meet him and prove whether his celebrity were justified. Reaching Paris, he called on Pantagruel at the Hôtel St. Denis. (Situated at the corner of the Rue St. Andrédes-Arts and the Rue des Grands-Augustins, it later became a hostel for students of the Benedictine order.)

Pantagruel was, at the moment, strolling in the garden, philosophizing as the Peripatetics[51] used to do. Seeing his enormous height, the Englishman trembled with fear; then, recovering his wits, he bowed courteously and said:

"My Lord, Plato, the prince of philosophers, says: 'Verily if the image of knowledge and wisdom were corporeal and visible to mortal eye, it would stir up the admiration of all the world.' Surely this must be so when the mere rumor of knowledge, scattered in the air, can haply reach the ears of those men we call philosophers because they are curious and studious of wisdom? Surely this must be so when, reaching their ears, that mere rumor does not suffer them to sleep or rest in peace, but inspires and fires them to haste towards that mortal in whom Wisdom has established her temple and uttered her oracles. All this has been clearly demonstrated by many examples in the past. The Queen of Sheba came from the furthest borders of the East, from the Persian Sea, to observe the order of Solomon's house and to hear his wisdom. Anacharsis travelled from distant Scythia all the way to Athens to visit Solon. Pythagoras sought out the prophets of Memphis. Plato journeyed to Egypt to interview the magicians and to Tarentum to meet Archytas. Apollonius of Tyana journeyed to the remote Mount Caucasus, tarried among the Scythians, the Massagetes, the Indians, sailed down the great river Pison to reach the land of the Brahmans where he con-

---

[51] Followers of Aristotle, who taught as he walked in the Lyceum of Athens.

versed with Hiarches and continued to Babylon, Chaldea, Media, Assyria, Parthia, Syria, Phoenicia, Arabia, Palestine, Alexandria, and even Ethiopia where he consulted the Gymnosophists. Livy, too, is a case in point. Not a few studious persons came from various points in France and Spain to see, hear and question him.

"I dare not include myself among these lofty souls. . . . But I will admit that I am studious and a lover, not of letters only, but of lettered people also. When I heard reports of your wisdom, I left my country, my home, my kinfolk and my friends; I came hither, reckoning as nothing the length of the journey, the discomforts of the sea, the strangeness of this land. I had but one purpose: to see you and to confer with you about certain problems in philosophy, geomancy, and occult science about which I am doubtful and cannot find satisfaction. If you can resolve them, I will deliver myself to you as a slave, together with my posterity. (This is the most valuable gift I have at my disposal.) My problems I shall draw up in writing and communicate to all the learned men in town. As soon as this is done, we can discuss them publicly.

"But I would wish us to conduct our argument in a particular way. Let us not proceed *pro* and *contra* like the crackpate theologians. Let us not proceed after the manner of the Academics, by declamation, which is an exercise of oratory rather than debate. Let us not proceed by numbers, as Pythagoras did or as Pico della Mirandola[52] wished to do at Rome. I would prefer to discuss by signs alone, without speaking a word, for alas! these subjects are too profound for human words to explain them to my satisfaction. To this effect, may it please My Lord to be in the great Hall of Navarre to-morrow morning at seven o'clock."

When he was done, Pantagruel answered civilly:

"Sir, what favors God has given me I could not refuse to share with any man on earth. No good but comes from Him and He is pleased to have it increased among men worthy and fit to receive the heavenly manna of pure knowledge. Because I recognize that you hold the first rank among such, I am ready, at any hour you wish, to accede to the best of my poor ability to any request you make.

"Naturally I shall learn more from you than you from me. However, you ask that we confer together concerning your doubts; you wish us to seek a solution by plunging into that inexhaustible well at the bottom of which, says Heracles, the truth lies hidden. I commend the mode of disputation you propose; I welcome signs rather than words, for I am convinced we shall understand one another thoroughly. Nor shall we be annoyed by the hand-clapping of those theological blockheads at every conclusive point of an argument.

"Tomorrow, therefore, I shall appear without fail at the appointed place at seven o'clock in the morning. Finally, I must beg that there be no strife or tumult, since we seek neither honors nor applause but the truth only."

"My Lord," Thaumastes answered, "God keep you ever in His grace. I

---

[52] The sixth-century B.C. Greek philosopher Pythagoras held that the essence of all things was number (30 for marriage, 100 for virginity, etc.). The fifteenth-century Italian humanist Pico della Mirandola did not argue by numbers, but he was renowned for his memory, and in 1486 he defended in Rome 900 theses reconciling Platonism and Christianity.

thank your highness and magnificence most heartily for deigning to abase itself to my mediocrity. So, farewell until to-morrow."

Readers, as you peruse this page, do not believe that any two human beings were ever more elevated or transported in thought than Thaumastes and Pantagruel that night. In fact Thaumastes confided to the porter of the Hôtel de Cluny, where, as a distinguished foreign visitor, he lodged, that never before in his life had he been so dry.

"I much fear Pantagruel has me by the throat!" he said. "Ay, I've got the Pantagruel! Tell them to bring me wine to drink, I beg you, and let me have some fresh water to gargle my palate."

Pantagruel, for his part, escaped into the loftiest realms of speculation, spending the whole night conning the Venerable Bede's *Of Numbers and Signs,* which treats of the expression of thought by manual movements . . . Plotinus' *Of the Unrelatable,* dealing with neo-Platonic metaphysics . . . Proclus' *Of Sacrifice and Magic* . . . Artemidorus Daldianus' *The Interpretation of Dreams,* which is the source of all modern manuals of fortune telling . . . Anaxagoras' *Of Signs* . . . Dinarius' *Of the Ineffable* . . . the works of Philistion . . . Hipponax's *On the Things that must be passed over in Silence* and a vast quantity of other works. . . .

At last Panurge remonstrated with him:

"Put away all this rubbish, My Lord, and go to bed. I can see you're so excited and wrought up that you'll take some sudden fever from this excess of thinking. Follow my advice: first, drink down twenty-five or thirty hearty draughts of wine; then go to bed and sleep your head off. To-morrow morning, I'll tackle Master Englishman, and if I don't drive him *ad metam non loqui,* to the limits of speech, you can call me an idiot."

"But he's extraordinarily learned, Panurge. How can you answer him?"

"Leave it to me!" Panurge answered. "Is any man as learned as the devils?"

"Certainly not, save by the special grace of God."

"Well, every time I've debated with the devils," Panurge declared, "I've floored them and turned them scut over head. Don't you worry: I'll have the Englishman evacuating vinegar before the public."

Panurge then spent the night tippling and staking the last point on his breeches at *Primus et Secundus,* a game like Tiddlywinks and *Vergette* or Top Rod. But he did not fail to escort his master to the appointed place in ample time.

You may be sure the hall was filled, for neither great nor small in Paris but thought:

"That devil of a Pantagruel confounded and overthrew all the jobbernowl theologians, the addlepated Sorbonne theorists! But he's met his match now: that Englishman's a devil of a fellow! We shall see what we shall see!"

When all were assembled, Thaumastes stood waiting for Pantagruel and Panurge; as the three entered the hall, the professors, Masters of Arts and students burst into applause according to their absurd custom. Pantagruel, in a voice loud as the report of a double cannon, shouted:

"Peace, peace, in the devil's name. Peace, by God, you rascals, or if you go on bothering me, I'll cut your heads from your shoulders!"

At which they sat there, struck of a heap and blinking like owls. Had they swallowed fifteen pounds of feathers, they would not have dared cough. The mere sound of his voice so parched their throats that their tongues hung a half-foot out of their mugs. It was as though Pantagruel had salted their throats.

Panurge then addressed the Englishman:

"Sir, have you come here to dispute contentiously the propositions you put forward, or to learn the truth?"

"Sir," Thaumastes replied, "one thing alone brings me here: my longing to discover the truth about matters that have puzzled me my whole life long. To the problems I now proffer, I never yet found a satisfactory solution in book or scholar. As for contentiously disputing anything, I will not do it. It is a wretched waste of time which I abandon to those sottish sophisters, sorbillants, sorbonagres, sorbonigenes, sorbonicoles, sorboniforms, sorbonisecs, niborcisants, sorbonisants, saniborsants, sorbonnets, sorbonzes, and sorbondsmen who, in their discussions, seek not the truth but only contradiction and debate."

"Sir," said Panurge, " I am but a humble disciple of Pantagruel, my master. Yet if I can give you satisfaction on all these points, it would be a slight upon my master's eminence to trouble him therewith, would it not? It is fitter, therefore, that he take the chair and sit as judge and moderator of our theses, and, furthermore, give you satisfaction on those particulars in which I fail to measure up to your expectations."

"That will be perfectly satisfactory," Thaumastes agreed. "Proceed, sir."

Here I must beg you to note that Panurge had affixed to the end of his elongated codpiece a rich tuft of red, white, green and blue silk. He had also put a fat orange in his pocket.

XIX

How Panurge Nonplussed
The Englishman Who
Argued by Signs

The audience watched breathlessly.

The Englishman raised one hand, then the other, clinching his fingertips together to form the figure we of the Chinon country call the hen's arse. Next, he clapped the nails of one hand over the other four times. Next, he opened out his palms and smacked them sonorously together once. Linking his hands again in the figure described above, he struck twice; then, opening them out again, four times. This done, he joined his hands in an attitude of prayer.

Panurge suddenly shot his right hand up into the air . . . placed his thumb in his nostril . . . held the four fingers extended parallel from the point of his nose . . . closed his left eye completely . . . and winked with the right in such a way as to mark a deep depression of lid and lash. . . . Then he maneuvered correspondingly with his left hand, there being an interval of about a cubit and a half between hands. Then, in the same position, he lowered one hand after the other to the ground. Finally he flung both out as though aiming straight at the Englishman's nose.

"But if Mercury—" the Englishman cried.

"Mum's the word!" Panurge objected.

The Englishman raised an open left hand, made a fist, placed his thumb on the point of his nose. Then he quickly raised his right hand, open too, to bring it down and link his left little finger with his right thumb, moving the other fingers slowly through the air. He then repeated the operation, the right hand doing what the left hand had done, and conversely.

Panurge betrayed not the slightest astonishment. Drawing out his thrice-great codpiece with his left hand, he picked out of it with his right a stump of a white oxrib and two similarly shaped bits of wood, one ebony, the other red Brazil wood. Holding them between his fingers, he clicked them together like castanets or like the clappers with which the lepers in the Breton colonies warn people of their approach. Panurge's rendering, however, was both more harmonious and finished than the lepers'. Bending his tongue back against the roof of his mouth, he began chirruping most merrily, his eyes fastened upon the Englishman.

The theologians, physicians and surgeons were convinced that Panurge meant the Englishman was riddled with leprosy. The counsellors, jurisconsults and decretalists were certain he sought to convey that leprosy possessed some mysterious form of human felicity, as Our Lord had once maintained.

The Englishman, nothing daunted, held his hands aloft, closing the three major fingers in his fist and passed his thumbs through index and middle finger. He paused a moment, then presented this figure for Panurge's inspection. Then he joined his hands so that thumbs and little fingers met.

Panurge, without uttering a word, put the nail of his left forefinger to that of his left thumb, forming a buckle-shaped hollow. Closing all the fingers of his right—save the index—in his fist, he held that index stiffly forward and kept pushing it vigorously into the buckle described above and pulling it as vigorously out, with quick, deep, staccato thrusts. Next, he extended his right index and middle finger, stretching them as far apart as he could and directing them accusingly at Thaumastes. After, he placed his left thumb on the corner of his left eye, spreading his hand like the wing of a bird or like the fin of a fish, moving it most gracefully this way and that. He repeated the gesture, conversely, with his right hand.

Thaumastes grew pale . . . trembled. . . . With a quavering right hand, he struck his middle finger against the muscle of the palm, a little above the thumb. Then he placed his right index finger into the buckle so made, but he thrust it under, not over, as Panurge had done.

Panurge then clapped his hands and blew into his palm. This done, he once more brought his right index into the buckle-shaped orifice made by his left, with the same jiggling in and out as before. Then he thrust out his chin and stared at Thaumastes.

The audience, which knew nothing about all these signs, at least understood quite clearly that Panurge was asking Thaumastes: "What do you mean by that?"

In effect, Thaumastes began to sweat like a horse. Great beads of perspiration stood out on his wan brow. He looked like a man wonderfully, strangely rapt in august contemplation. Recovering his presence of mind, he put all the nails of his left against those of his right, opening his fingers in semicircles and holding his hands as high as he possibly could.

With lightning speed, Panurge set his right thumb under his jaw and his little finger in the buckle of his left hand. Holding this stance, he made his teeth rattle together very melodiously, the upper against the lower.

Thaumastes, though exhausted, rose panting. But, in rising, he let a great fart—a waiter's fart, for the stew followed. And he piddled strong vinegar. The fellow stank like all the devils of hell. A moment after, the audience began holding their noses, for Thaumastes was bemucking himself with sheer anguish.

All the same, he raised his right hand, bringing the tips of its fingers together. And laid his left flat on his chest.

Panurge replied by pulling out his long codpiece with its multi-colored tuft, stretching it about a cubit and a half, then holding it in the air with his left hand. With his right, he seized his orange, tossed it up in the air seven times, and, at the seventh, hid it in his right fist. Here he held it motionless, then began shaking it before Thaumastes. The latter, his cheeks puffed out like a bagpiper's, blew as though he were inflating a pig's bladder. So Panurge placed one finger on his left hand in his anus, while he sucked in the air with the sound a man makes when he eats oysters in the shell or when he sips soup. Next, he opened his mouth a little and clapped his right hand down on it, making a resonant, loud sound that seemed to emerge from the depths of the diaphragm up through his windpipe. He repeated this noise sixteen times.

Thaumastes kept blowing like a goose. So Panurge put his right forefinger into his mouth, pressed it very hard against the oral muscles and drew it back sharply, making a noise like a child shooting off a pop-gun. He did this nine times in succession.

"Gentlemen, gentlemen, the great secret!" Thaumastes shouted. "He's up to the elbows in it!"

And he drew a dagger which he held point down. Panurge, in turn, pulled out his long codpiece and shook it violently against his thighs. Then he placed his hands in the form of a comb and laid them on his head, pulling his tongue out as far as possible and rolling his eyes like a dying goat.

"Ah, I understand," cried Thaumastes. "But what?"

So saying he pressed the handle of his dagger against his chest and the flat of his hand against its point, turning the tips of his fingers inward.

Panurge bowed his head to the left, buried his middle finger in his right ear and raised his thumb . . . crossed his arms over his breast and coughed five times in succession. . . . At the fifth cough, he stamped his right foot on the ground, raised his left arm, and, closing his fist, held the thumb against his forehead, striking his breast six times with his right hand.

As though not yet utterly satisfied, Thaumastes put his left thumb to the tip of his nose, closing the other fingers in his fist. Panurge put his two forefingers on either side of his mouth, drew it out as far as he could, exposing all his teeth; with his thumbs, he lowered his pupils. It was, the audience agreed, a most unpleasant sight.

XX

How Thaumastes Proclaimed
the Virtues and Knowledge of Panurge

Thaumastes rose. Doffing his doctoral bonnet, he thanked Panurge under his breath, then in a loud voice addressed the audience:

"Gentlemen, this is a fitting time to cite the words of the Gospel: '*Et ecce plusquam Salomon hic,* And behold, a greater than Solomon is here!' Ay, gentlemen, you have in your midst a nonpareil treasure. I refer to Monsieur Pantagruel. Rumor of his fame drew me out of the depths of England to journey hither and confer with him upon certain insoluble problems— of magic, alchemy, cabbalistics, geomancy, astrology and philosophy— problems that would give me no peace. Well, sirs, now I resent his reputation, because it has proved, as it were, jealous of him: it reports only one thousandth part of what is really his.

"You have watched his mere disciple give me satisfaction and, indeed, tell me more than I had asked for. Better, he indicated and solved further inestimable doubts for me. Again, I swear he discovered, for my benefit, the true source, well and abyss of the encyclopedia of learning. And he did so incomparably. Truly, I never dreamed I could find a human being capable of grasping the rudiments of Monsieur Panurge's reasoning—I refer to our discussion by signs, when not one word, indeed not a half-word, passed our lips. But I intend at a future time to put our theses and solutions in writing so that none dare suspect it was a hoax or a piece of tomfoolery. And I shall print my findings so that all may learn as I learned.

"Imagine what the master could have done when the disciple has achieved such an eminent feat. For *non est discipulus super magistrum,* the disciple is not above his master. At all events, God be praised and magnified forever! And you, gentlemen of the audience, I thank you from the depths of my heart for the honor you have done us. May the Lord repay you for it eternally!"

Pantagruel in turn thanked the spectators, and took Thaumastes off to dinner with him. You may be certain they drank at top speed as all good Christians on All Souls' Day, ay, with belly unbuttoned, as the phrase goes—for in those days they fastened their bellies with buttons as we now fasten the collars of our doublets. On they bibbed and caroused, till they had not the foggiest notion of whether they were coming or going. Blessed Lady! how they spliced the main brace! And the flagons trotting every which way, and they bawling:

"Page, draw, wine ho!"

"Pour, by the devil, pour."

"Here, boy! wine for me!"

"Wine, wine. . . ."

Never a one of the company but consumed at least twenty-five or thirty hogsheads. Do you know how? *Sicut terra sine aqua,* like earth without water, for the weather was hot. Besides, they were very dry.

As for the theses propounded by Thaumastes and the meaning of the signs exchanged, I would gladly explain them. But I am told Thaumastes has written and published in London a voluminous tome in which he exhausts the subject, omitting not the minutest detail. For the nonce, I therefore take no note of the matter.

XXI

How Panurge Fell in Love
With a Parisienne of
High Degree

As a result of his debate with the English scholar, Panurge had acquired quite a reputation in Paris. The activity of his codpiece was proportionally greater, and, to that effect, he had it pinked and slashed with ornate embroidery, after the Roman fashion. His praises became a topic of general conversation. There was even a song written to celebrate his exploits; the little children sang it as they went to fetch mustard. Best of all, he was made welcome in the most elegant circles. But it went to his head; he actually had the presumption to beleaguer one of the great ladies of the city.

Scorning the rigmarole of prefaces and preliminaries dear to such languishing, dreamy lovers as never touch meat in Lent, Panurge popped the question outright.

"Madame," he told this lofty lady, "it would prove beneficent to the commonwealth, pleasurable to your person, honorable to your progeny and necessary to me that I cover you for the propagation of my race. You may take my word for this, Madame; experience will prove it to you conclusively."

The lady, indignant, thrust him a thousand leagues away.

"You crazy knave, how dare you talk like that? Who do you think I am? Get out of here at once and never let me lay eyes upon you again. For two pins, I'd have your arms and legs sawed off!"

"Madame," he protested, "I would not care two pins if my arms and legs were sawed off, providing you and I had first fought a merry bout of spermary-snuggery. For," he showed her his long codpiece, "here is Master Johnny Inigo, a master instrumentalist who begs to fiddle and thrum, sweep the *viola d'amore*, play the manichord, tweedle the gittern, strike the lyre, beat the drum, wind the horn and grind the organ until you feel his music throbbing in the marrow of your bones. A wily gallant, Master Johnny: he will not fail to find all the cranks, winches, wedges, pullies, nippers, clutches, teeth, springs and rigging stored in your delicate cockpit. You'll be needing no scouring or brushing up after *him*."

"Go to, scoundrel, and away! One more word out of you and I'll shout for help; I'll have my servants beat you to death."

"No, Madame," Panurge protested. "You are not as cruel as you pretend. You cannot be or else your face is a living lie. Let earth soar upward into the firmament, let high heaven sink into the bottomless pit, let the whole concert of nature be annihilated ere your beauty and grace secrete one drop of gall or malice. They say that is is virtually impossible for man:

> To find in women beauty unallied
> With arrogance or cruelty or pride

but that holds only for vulgar beauties. Your own is so priceless, so unique, so heavenly that I vow Nature has bestowed it on you as a paragon to prove what she can do when she cares to muster all her power and science. Everything in you is honey, sugar, celestial manna. To you Paris should have awarded the golden apple, not to Venus or Juno or Minerva.[53] For Juno possessed no such nobility, Minerva no such wisdom, Venus no such comeliness.

"O ye heavenly gods and goddesses! how happy the man whom you allow to kiss and fondle you, to cosset, nuzzle and cockle you, to thrust his prolific engine of pleasure into the pod of your quivering quim. By God, I am that man, I plainly feel it. Already she loves me her bellyful I swear; ay, Panurge is predestined to it by the nixies and fairies. Let us lose no time: come, slap-dash, helter-skelter, holus-bolus, to horse and fair riding, tantivy, hoicks!"

Whereupon he sought to embrace her; but she moved towards the window as if to call for help, so Panurge made off hastily. Yet ere retreating:

"Madame," he said, "wait for me here; I'll call your friends, don't bother!"

And he withdrew, unfeased and no less cheerful despite the rebuff.

Next day, as she arrived at church, Panurge stood waiting at the door, offered her holy water, bowed deep as she passed, then kneeled familiarly beside her:

"Madame," he declared, "you must know how madly in love with you I am. Why, I can neither piddle nor cack for love of you! I don't know how *you* feel, but, Madame, suppose I took ill from it, wouldn't you be responsible?"

"Go away, I don't care anything about it. Leave me alone to my prayers."

"One moment!" Panurge begged. "Please equivocate on '*à Beaumont le Viconte?*' or on 'Runt and Codger are fellow-muckers!'"

"I don't know what you mean!"

"Quite easy! '*A beau con le vit monte,*' 'Cunt and Rodger are mellow fuckers!' Now, pray to God that He grant whatever your noble heart desires. And oh, Madame, I beg you: give me those beads a moment."

"Here you are, stop bothering me."

She was about to take off her rosary—it was of cestrin wood with gold ornamentation—when Panurge promptly drew one of his knives and neatly cut it. Before carrying it off to pawn:

"Would you like my knife?" he asked.

"No, certainly not!"

"It's yours to grind or sheathe, Madame, body and soul, bag and baggage, tripe and guts."

But the lady was worried over the loss of her beads, so many implements to help her keep her countenance in church:

"This chattering scoundrel must be some eccentric foreigner," she mused. "He will never return my rosary. What will my dear husband say? He'll be furious! But I'll tell him a sneak thief cut it off me at church. He must believe me: I've still the end fastened on my girdle."

[53] The shepherd Paris awarded a golden apple to Venus for her beauty, over Juno and Minerva, indirectly causing the Trojan War.

After dinner, Panurge went to call on her with, in his sleeve, a purse full of tokens specially struck for use in the law courts.

"Which of us is the better lover, Madame, you or I?"

"For my part I cannot hate you," she said magnanimously. "God commands us to love our neighbors."

"Aren't you in love with me?"

"I've told you repeatedly not to talk to me like that!" she insisted. "If you mention it again, I'll show you I'm not to be trifled with. Go away, I tell you. But give me back my rosary; my husband might ask me for it."

"Give you back your rosary? No, by heaven, I shall do nothing of the sort. But I'll tell you what I *will* do: I'll gladly give you another. Would you like one in beautifully enamelled gold with beads shaped like great pendulous knockers? Or like loveknots or ingots, heavy in the hand? Or ebony or broad zircons or square-cut garnets with mountings of rare turquoises, or costly topazes or priceless sapphires or precious rubies set with glittering diamonds of twenty-eight facets? No, no, that is a trumpery gift. I know of a marvellous rosary: it's made of exquisite emeralds with a mounting of speckled gray amber; at the buckle there's a Persian pearl fat as an orange . . . and the bauble costs but a paltry five-and-twenty thousand ducats. I will make you a present of it; I've heaps of cash!"

He made his tokens ring as though they were genuine, authentic golden crowns with the shining sun of France stamped upon them.

"Do you fancy a piece of violet or crimson velure, dyed in grain, or a piece of scarlet or brocaded satin? Is it your pleasure to accept chains, brooches, tiaras or rings? You have but to say the word: fifty thousand is a trifle!"

His offer made her mouth water. Yet she stood her ground.

"No, thank you, I want nothing to do with you."

"By God, I certainly want to do something with *you!* What I want will cost you nothing; you'll be out nothing when you've given it. Look, Madame," and he showed her his long codpiece. "Here is Master Johnny Scramblecunney who craves lodging."

He was about to strike root there, when she started to cry out, though none too loud. The mask of courtesy fell from Panurge's face.

"So you won't let me have a little harmless fun, eh? Not even a morsel for me, eh? A bucket of turds to you! you don't deserve the honor or pleasure of it. But by God! I'll make the dogs ride you!"

With which he beat a hasty retreat in dread of blows. (He was by nature fearful of them.)

XXII

How Panurge Played a None Too Pleasant Trick on the Parisienne of High Degree

Next day was Corpus Christi, a feast on which the ladies of Paris put on their stateliest apparel. Panurge's charmer was decked out in a rich gown of crimson velvet, with a skirt of costly white velure.

The day before, Panurge scoured the town for a bitch in heat. Having found one, he tied his belt around her neck and took her home. All that day and through the night, he fed her abundantly; in the morning he killed her, plucked out that part the Greek geomancians know, cut it as fine as he could, tucked it away in one of his innumerable pockets and went to the church. He was sure his lady would soon arrive to take part in the procession always held on that day.

When she entered, Panurge bowed courteously, offered her some holy water and, shortly after she had finished her petty devotions, sat down on the bench beside her. As she looked up, he passed her a paper on which he had written the following rondeau:

> Sweet lady, once, once only I expressed
> My admiration; you denied my quest,
> You drove me irremediably away
> Although I never harmed you (welladay!)
> In act or word or libel or the rest. . . .
> Granted my wooing stirred no answering zest,
> You could have been more honest, and confessed:
> "I do not wish it, friend. Leave me, I pray!"
>   Sweet lady, once,
> Once more and never again I shall protest
> Ere love's flame utterly consume my breast,
> One boon alone I languish for: to lay
> My peacock, shoveller, cockerel, popinjay
> Deep in the shelter of your downy nest.
>   Sweet lady, once!

While she was unfolding the paper to see what was inside, Panurge deftly sprinkled his drug all over her, spilling it impartially in the folds of her sleeves and skirt.

"Madame," he said before taking his leave, "a lover's life is not always a bed of roses. In my case I can only hope the anguished nights, the sorrows and tribulation I undergo for love of you will be deducted from my trials in purgatory. At least pray God He give me patience to bear my affliction."

Panurge had scarcely spoken when all the dogs in the church, attracted by the odor of the drug, scurried over to the lady. Big and little, large and small, one and all came up, sniffed, raised their legs, cocked their members and let fly on her dress. It was the most horrible sight imaginable.

Panurge pretended to chase them off, then bowed and retired to watch the sport from the vantage point of a chapel. Those wretched curs were squirting all over her clothes. One huge greyhound placed a paw on her shoulder to aim at her head . . . other dogs pumped in her sleeves . . . still others drenched her backside, while the puppies piddled in her shoes. . . . The women close to her sought to keep the beasts off, but with scant success. Meanwhile, holding his sides, Panurge, between guffaws of laughter, told certain lords who were next to him:

"I think that lady's in heat. Or some wolfhound covered her recently."

Seeing the dogs crowded as thick about her as about a bitch in heat, he ran off to fetch Pantagruel. On the way, he stopped to kick every dog he met, crying:

"To church with you! To your genuflexions! Follow the odor of sanctity! Be off and join your fellows at the urinarian baptism! Forward, by all the devils, be off, devil take you!"

"Master," he said breathlessly to Pantagruel, "please come and see all the dogs of the country gathered about the loveliest lady in town, and every one of them agog to scrounge her!"

Pantagruel, delighted at the novelty of it, accompanied Panurge back to church and enjoyed the fun immensely. By the time the procession began, matters had reached a crisis. There were more than six hundred thousand and fourteen dogs thronging about her and finding one thousand and one means of harassing her. Whichever way she turned, the newcomers followed the scent, dogged her heels and flooded whatever spot her dress touched. The only course left her was to go home. As she fled through the streets, every one stopped to watch the dogs leaping high as her neck, turning her elegant toilette into a very toilet, as she ran on, helpless and steaming. It was impossible to give them the slip, the trail was too pungent. So they followed her to her residence.

While she hid in her room and her chambermaids burst into laughter behind politely raised aprons, all the dogs within a radius of a half-league came rushing up and showered so hard against the gate as to form a stream in which ducks might very well have swum. To-day this same current, now called the creek of Bièvre, flows through the grounds of the Abbey of St. Victor and past the Gobelin dye-works. Materials steeped in its waters turn a rare scarlet thanks to some special virtue of these pissdogs, as our learned Master Doribus recently pointed out in a brilliant sermon. God help us, a mill could have ground corn there, though not so much as the famous Bazacle in Toulouse on the Garonne.

Michel de Montaigne
(1533–1592)

"I have no more made my book than my book has made me," Michel de Montaigne wrote, " 'tis a book consubstantial with the author, of a peculiar design, a member of my life, and whose business is not designed for others, as that of all other books is." The book is his Essays, *and perhaps no other work has ever coincided so precisely with the personality of its author, who was an extraordinarily complex, attractive, and in some ways baffling man.*

Montaigne was born in 1533, the son of Pierre Eyquem, a wealthy merchant and mayor of Bordeaux. (Montaigne later discarded the name Eyquem and took instead the name of the family estate, the château de Montaigne in Périgord, in southwestern France.) Montaigne's father was deeply impressed with Renaissance ideas, and he attempted to give his son an experimental education that would fit him for the spirit of the new age. He sent his son to be nursed by a peasant woman in a village on his estate, so that the young Montaigne would develop a love and respect for common people. A Latin tutor came from Germany to oversee his first attempts at speech, to keep him from hearing French until he had mastered Latin, and thus to make Latin his native tongue.

When he was six, Montaigne was sent to school at the famous Collège de Guienne in Bordeaux, where he studied under a number of learned men destined to become key figures in Renaissance thought. After he had completed his course at Bordeaux, he went on to the study of law, probably at Toulouse, home of one of the famous law schools of France. When he was twenty-one, he became a member of a court and, three years later, a member of the Parlement of Bordeaux, where he was one of sixty magistrates whose duty it was to enforce the king's law. In his function as magistrate, Montaigne was an observer of, and sometimes a participant in, the religious conflicts between Catholics and Protestant Huguenots and in the brutal suppression of Huguenot "heretics." Here he seems to have developed the strong distaste for cruelty and brutal punishments that appears frequently in the Essays. The other notable influence upon Montaigne during these years was an intense friendship with another young member of the Parlement, Étienne de la Boétie, which lasted six years and ended only with the early death of La Boétie. La Boétie was a Humanist and a fine scholar who translated Xenophon and Plutarch and wrote poetry in both Latin and French.

In 1570, Montaigne resigned from the Parlement of Bordeaux and retired to his estate, "to the bosom of the learned Virgins" (the Muses), as he put it. For the rest of his life, his chief employment was the writing of his Essays, though there were many interruptions and temporary returns to active life: a year and a half of traveling in 1580–81, two terms as Mayor of Bordeaux (during which the Plague killed almost a third of the population of that city), and a period of exile from his château during the height of the Plague and the Wars of Religion. The first two volumes of his Essays were published in 1580; in 1586–88, he thoroughly revised and expanded the earlier volumes and wrote a third one. Even after the publication of the edition of 1588, he continued to revise and expand the Essays through marginal annotations during the last four years of his life. He died of a severe inflammation of the throat on September 13, 1592.

Montaigne's Essays represent a new genre in Western literature. The nineteenth-century English critic Edmund Gosse wrote, "It is not often that we can date with any approach to accuracy the arrival of a new class of literature into the world. But it was in the month of March 1571 that the essay was invented." This exaggeration neglects the long process by which Montaigne developed his characteristic form, but it does suggest the originality of his achievement. Montaigne began his work as a modest set of quotations from his readings, annotated with his own comments; a reminder of these origins remains in the many Latin quotations which punctuate the Essays in their final form. As he continued to write, however, his own comments began to outweigh the quotations and develop their own loose, rambling, almost free-associational structure. Frequently, the title of an essay serves only as the jumping-off place for a series of meditations that have little or no connection with the presumed subject. The style is easy and informal, though it can rise when appropriate to great eloquence; Montaigne's literary voice is distinctively witty, self-deprecating, and charming. Often long passages consist merely of a series of amusing and ingenious anecdotes, illustrations, and quotations spiraling around the subject. The nineteenth-century French critic Sainte-Beuve described Montaigne's style as "a continual epigram or a metaphor always renewing itself."

Montaigne's ideas have been the subject of almost continuous controversy since the Essays *were first published. Some readers, noting that he regards human reason as powerless and the world as essentially unknowable, have concluded that his work implies indifference and resignation to ignorance. Others have found the essential spirit of modern science in his skeptical, inquiring spirit and his unwillingness to take anything merely on authority. His religious views are also variously interpreted. Few of his contemporaries found anything unorthodox in the* Essays, *but the Church later found their skeptical spirit questionable and in 1676 placed them on the* Index. *Some close students of Montaigne have found him profoundly Christian, while Ralph Waldo Emerson called his essay on Montaigne "The Skeptic," and Sainte-Beuve believed that he worked deliberately to undermine the teachings of Christianity. Equally controversial, across the centuries, has been the meaning of Montaigne's preoccupation with himself. In the seventeenth century, the French scientist and philosopher Pascal spoke of Montaigne's work as "the foolish project of painting himself." Others have seen this self-preoccupation as inspired both by the classical injunction to "Know Thyself" and the Renaissance emphasis upon the importance of the individual mind, while modern readers have found in Montaigne a vivid anticipation of twentieth-century literature's intense interest in the inner world of the individual self.*

The disagreements regarding Montaigne's work probably arise from attempts to impose a unity and consistency upon them that they do not have. Critics now usually divide his thought into three stages of development. In the first stage, he was deeply influenced by the philosophy of Seneca and by the personal model of Cato of Utica. During this period he held "Stoic" ideas of indifference to death, suffering, and misfortune. A second, "Skeptical" stage is marked by his writing of the long and important Apology for Raymond Sebond *(too long to reprint here). Sebond, a Spanish professor of medicine at Toulouse, had written a Latin work called* Liber Creaturarum, *or* Natural Theology, *which Montaigne had translated into French for his father. Sebond's aim was to prove that the major tenets of Christianity could be arrived at by natural reason and reference to the natural world. In the course of writing his essay on Sebond, Montaigne came close to defending the precisely opposite view: the inability of the human mind to know anything with certainty. This skeptical view had such a hold upon Montaigne that in about 1576 he had a medal struck which depicted an evenly balanced scale above the personal motto, "Que Scay-je?" or "What do I know?" The third and last stage is often called the "Epicurean" stage; Montaigne's emphasis now shifts to the achievement of happiness through the exercise of the human faculties, physical as well as intellectual.*

This tripartite scheme seems accurate as far as it goes, but even it may imply more consistency and order in Montaigne's work than actually exists. The real core of Montaigne's work is not a consistent set of ideas, but the continual presence of the man himself. He is constantly shifting and changing but is always vividly present at center stage. It is through Montaigne's constant attention to the details of his own life that he captures not only the quality of his own personality but also the rich variety and delight of life itself. The twentieth-century novelist and critic Virginia Woolf summed up this vitality in her essay on Montaigne: "It is life that emerges more and more clearly as these essays reach not their end, but their suspension in full career. It is life that becomes more and more absorbing as death draws near, one's self, one's soul, every part of existence: that one wears silk stockings summer and winter; puts water in one's wine; has one's hair cut after dinner; must have glass to drink from; has never worn spectacles; has a loud voice; carries a switch in one's hands; bites one's tongue; fidgets with one's feet; is apt to scratch one's ears; likes meat to be high;

rubs one's teeth with a napkin (thank God, they are good!); must have curtains to one's bed; and, what is rather curious, began by liking radishes, then disliked them, and now likes them again. No fact is too little to let it slip through one's fingers."

Montaigne's spirit, as well as some of his recurring ideas and his characteristic style, are well illustrated in the three essays reprinted here. Montaigne's love of simplicity and "naturalness" is expressed vividly in the quaint but pointed essay "Of Cannibals." Montaigne, like most of his European contemporaries, was fascinated by reports of the New World; he had seen natives of Brazil at the court celebrations in Rouen in 1560 (celebrating the coming of age of Charles IX) and, as he tells us, had some Brazilian artifacts in his home. He delights in the curious details of cannibal life but, characteristically, lets his mind spiral around the implications of a comparison between the lives of these "noble savages" and his own life. "We may then call these people barbarous, in respect to the rules of reason," he writes, "but not in respect to ourselves, who in all sorts of barbarity exceed them." (This essay has an extrinsic interest in that Shakespeare adapted a passage from it, in John Florio's Elizabethan translation, and incorporated it into The Tempest.)

In the essay "Of Repentance," Montaigne comes close to what his contemporaries would have called heresy as he examines from a skeptical and ironic point of view an important religious conception. The Church enjoins penitence and contrition, a hatred of one's old life and a turning to a new life in Christ, but Montaigne builds his essay around an explanation of the blunt statement "I very rarely repent." A person may regret an action, he says, or give up "impetuous, prompt, and sudden" sins, but as for changing one's fundamental nature, being "reborn," that, Montaigne says, "is very hard for me to imagine or form." Montaigne's critics have taken this view as an attempt to justify his own self-indulgence and self-satisfaction, but Montaigne's conclusions are quite different. By denying the possibility of a sudden transformation of one's nature through divine intervention, Montaigne puts the responsibility for virtue completely upon the everyday struggles of the individual, alone with his own conscience. "The virtue of the soul," he writes, "does not consist in flying high, but in walking orderly," and his ideal is not the grandeur of an Alexander but the modesty of a Socrates, who wanted not to conquer the world but to "carry on human life conformably with its natural condition."

This emphasis upon the supremacy of individual experience over supernaturalism and general laws is developed more fully and directly in the long essay "Of Experience," which is the final essay and in many ways the climax of the three-volume series. After an opening section on the diversity and variety of life and the impossibility of imposing general laws upon it, illustrating the point by the inadequacy of the legal system (a portion of this section is omitted here), Montaigne minutely describes his own experience in living. In this earthy and amusing account, the theme gradually emerges of the importance of the body and of the concrete experiences of everyday life. The commonly endorsed morality glorifies the mind at the expense of the body, but to follow this morality is to run the risk, Montaigne says, of escaping from being human at all; in trying to be an angel, one risks becoming a beast. "The fairest lives, in my opinion, are those which regularly accommodate themselves to the common and human model; without miracle, without extravagance." This eloquent celebration of the physical world, of individual experience, and of the joy of everyday life makes Montaigne one of the most memorable spokesmen for the Renaissance spirit.

FURTHER READING (*prepared by W. J. R.*): Donald M. Frame's *Montaigne, A Biography,* 1965, a long but readable portrait by an eminent Montaigne scholar, follows the writer's life closely but does not consider his writing at length. Marcel Tetel's *Montaigne*, 1974, is a general introduction; another good one is Peter Burke's *Montaigne*, 1981, a medium-length study in the Past Masters series. Reflections on Montaigne by two creative writers provide a good introduction to the *Essays*: Ralph Waldo Emerson's "Montaigne, or The Skeptic, " in *Representative Men*, 1850, is interesting on Montaigne's skepticism; Virginia Woolf's "Montaigne," in *The Common Reader*, 1925, considers autobiography and self-knowledge. Phillip P. Hallie's *The Scar of Montaigne: An Essay in Personal Philosophy*, 1966, provides a good introductory essay on Montaigne's historical background. Hallie also examines doubt in French Renaissance thought in connection with the evolution of Montaigne's personal philosophy. Margaret M. McGowan's *Montaigne's Deceits: The Art of Persuasion in the "Essais,"* 1974, examines Montaigne's art of dissimulating in order to persuade his readers indirectly. McGowan examines his concern with surviving in his age and his interest in the difficulties of communicating. Several types of imagery and their contribution to Montaigne's persuasiveness are studied in Carol Clark's *The Web of Metaphor*, 1978. Montaigne's language is discussed in depth in Richard L. Regosin's *The Matter of My Book: Montaigne's "Essais" as the Book of the Self*, 1977. Regosin studies closely the phenomenon of objectified man as both the subject and object of discourse, considering Montaigne's own awareness of this situation and the way it shaped his style.

ESSAYS

Translated by Charles Cotton

OF CANNIBALS

When King Pyrrhus invaded Italy, having viewed and considered the order of the army the Romans sent out to meet him: "I know not," said he, "what kind of barbarians," (for so the Greeks called all other nations) "these may be; but the disposition of this army, that I see, has nothing of barbarism in it."[1] As much said the Greeks of that which Flaminius brought into their country;[2] and Philip, beholding from an eminence the order and distribution of the Roman camp formed in his kingdom by Publius Sulpicius Galba, spake to the same effect.[3] By which it appears how cautious men ought to be of taking things upon trust from vulgar opinion, and that we are to judge by the eye of reason, and not from common report.

I long had a man in my house that lived ten or twelve years in the New World, discovered in these latter days, and in that part of it where Villegaignon landed, which he called Antarctic France.[4] This discovery of so vast a country seems to be of very great consideration. I cannot be sure, that hereafter there may not be another, so many wiser men than we having been deceived in this. I am afraid our eyes are bigger than our bellies,

---

[1] Pyrrhus (318–272 B.C.) was King of Epirus. This story is told in Plutarch's *Life of Pyrrhus*.

[2] T. Quintius Flaminius (230–144 B.C.) was a Roman general. See Plutarch's *Life of Flaminius* for this story.

[3] The reference is to Philip V, King of Macedon (221–179 B.C.). This story is told by the Roman historian Livy.

[4] The French explorer Villegaignon explored Brazil (Antarctic France) in 1557.

and that we have more curiosity than capacity; for we grasp at all, but catch nothing but wind.

Plato brings in Solon, telling a story that he had heard from the priests of Sais in Egypt, that of old, and before the Deluge, there was a great island called Atlantis, situate directly at the mouth of the Straits of Gibraltar, which contained more countries than both Africa and Asia put together; and that the kings of that country, who not only possessed that isle, but extended their dominion so far into the continent that they had a country of Africa as far as Egypt, and extending in Europe to Tuscany, attempted to encroach even upon Asia, and to subjugate all the nations that border upon the Mediterranean Sea, as far as the Black Sea; and to that effect overran all Spain, the Gauls, and Italy, so far as to penetrate into Greece, where the Athenians stopped them: but that sometime after, both the Athenians, and they and their island, were swallowed by the Flood.[5]

It is very likely that this extreme irruption and inundation of water made wonderful changes and alterations in the habitations of the earth, as 'tis said that the sea then divided Sicily from Italy—

> "Haec loca, vi quondam, et vasta convulsa ruina,
> Dissiluisse ferunt, quum protenus utraque tellus
> Una foret."[6]

—Cyprus from Syria, the isle of Negropont from the continent of Boeotia, and elsewhere united lands that were separate before, by filling up the channel between them with sand and mud:

> "Sterilisque diu palus, aptaque remis,
> Vicinas urbes alit, et grave sentit aratrum."[7]

But there is no great appearance that this isle was this New World so lately discovered: for that almost touched upon Spain, and it were an incredible effect of an inundation, to have tumbled back so prodigious a mass, above twelve hundred leagues: besides that our modern navigators have already almost discovered it to be no island, but *terra firma*,[8] and continent with the East Indies on the one side, and with the lands under the two poles on the other side; or, if it be separate from them, it is by so narrow a strait and channel, that it none the more deserves the name of an island for that.

It should seem, that in this great body, there are two sorts of motions, the one natural, and the other febric,[9] as there are in ours. When I consider the impression that our river of Dordoigne has made in my time, on the right bank of its descent, and that in twenty years it has gained so much, and undermined the foundations of so many houses, I perceive it to be an extraordinary agitation: for had it always followed this course, or were hereafter to do it, the aspect of the world would be totally changed. But

---

[5] The story of Atlantis appears in Plato's *Timaeus*.

[6] "These lands, they say, once with violence and vast desolation convulsed and burst asunder, which until then were one" (Virgil, *Aeneid*).

[7] "That which was once a sterile marsh and bore vessels on its bosom now feeds neighboring cities and admits the plow" (Horace).

[8] Dry land.   [9] Feverish.

rivers alter their course, sometimes beating against the one side, and sometimes the other, and sometimes quietly keeping the channel. I do not speak of sudden inundations, the causes of which everybody understands. In Medoc,[10] by the seashore, the Sieur d'Arsac, my brother, sees an estate he had there, buried under the sands which the sea vomits before it: where the tops of some houses are yet to be seen, and where his rents and domains are converted into pitiful barren pasturage. The inhabitants of this place affirm, that of late years the sea has driven so vehemently upon them, that they have lost above four leagues of land. These sands are her harbingers: and we now see great heaps of moving sand, that march half a league before her, and occupy the land.

The other testimony from antiquity, to which some would apply this discovery of the New World, is in Aristotle; at least, if that little book of unheard-of miracles be his.[11] He there tells us, that certain Carthaginians, having crossed the Atlantic Sea without the Straits of Gibraltar, and sailed a very long time, discovered at last a great and fruitful island, all covered over with wood, and watered with several broad and deep rivers; far remote from all *terra-firma*, and that they, and others after them, allured by the goodness and fertility of the soil, went thither with their wives and children, and began to plant a colony. But the senate of Carthage perceiving their people by little and little to diminish, issued out an express prohibition, that none, upon pain of death, should transport themselves thither; and also drove out these new inhabitants; fearing, 'tis said, lest in process of time they should so multiply as to supplant themselves and ruin their state. But this relation of Aristotle no more agrees with our new-found lands than the other.

This man that I had was a plain ignorant fellow,[12] and therefore the more likely to tell truth: for your better bred sort of men are much more curious in their observation, 'tis true, and discover a great deal more, but then they gloss upon it, and to give the greater weight to what they deliver and allure your belief, they cannot forbear a little to alter the story; they never represent things to you simply as they are, but rather as they appeared to them, or as they would have them appear to you, and to gain the reputation of men of judgment, and the better to induce your faith, are willing to help out the business with something more than is really true, of their own invention. Now, in this case, we should either have a man of irreproachable veracity, or so simple that he has not wherewithal to contrive, and to give a color of truth to false relations, and who can have no ends in forging an untruth. Such a one was mine; and besides, he has at divers times brought to me several seamen and merchants who at the same time went the same voyage. I shall therefore content myself with his information, without inquiring what the cosmographers say to the business. We should have topographers to trace out to us the particular places where they have been; but for having had this advantage over us, to have seen the Holy Land, they would have the privilege, forsooth, to tell us stories of all

[10] Home of Montaigne's brother, Medoc is a district in southwestern France, northwest of Bordeaux.

[11] The book referred to is the apocryphal *Of Unheard-Of Wonders,* which contains an account of Atlantis.

[12] That is, the traveler referred to at the beginning of the essay.

the other parts of the world besides. I would have every one write what he knows, and as much as he knows, but no more; and that not in this only, but in all other subjects; for such a person may have some particular knowledge and experience of the nature of such a river, or such a fountain, who, as to other things, knows no more than what everybody does, and yet to keep a clutter with this little pittance of his, will undertake to write the whole body of physics: a vice from which great inconveniences derive their original.

Now, to return to my subject, I find that there is nothing barbarous and savage in this nation, by anything that I can gather, excepting, that every one gives the title of barbarism to everything that is not in use in his own country. As, indeed, we have no other level of truth and reason, than the example and idea of the opinions and customs of the place wherein we live: there is always the perfect religion, there the perfect government, there the most exact and accomplished usage of all things. They are savages at the same rate that we say fruit are wild, which nature produces of herself and by her own ordinary progress; whereas in truth, we ought rather to call those wild, whose natures we have changed by our artifice, and diverted from the common order. In those, the genuine, most useful and natural virtues and properties are vigorous and sprightly, which we have helped to degenerate in these, by accommodating them to the pleasure of our own corrupted palate. And yet for all this our taste confesses a flavor and delicacy, excellent even to emulation of the best of ours, in several fruits wherein those countries abound without art or culture. Neither is it reasonable that art should gain the pre-eminence of our great and powerful mother nature. We have so surcharged her with the additional ornaments and graces we have added to the beauty and riches of her own works by our inventions, that we have almost smothered her; yet in other places, where she shines in her own purity and proper luster, she marvelously baffles and disgraces all our vain and frivolous attempts.

> "Et veniunt hederae sponte sua melius;
> Surgit et in solis formosior arbutus antris;
> Et volucres nulla dulcius arte canunt."[13]

Our utmost endeavors cannot arrive at so much as to imitate the nest of the least of birds, its contexture, beauty, and convenience: not so much as the web of a poor spider.

All things, says Plato, are produced either by nature, by fortune, or by art; the greatest and most beautiful by the one or the other of the former, the least and the most imperfect by the last.[14]

These nations then seem to me to be so far barbarous, as having received but very little form and fashion from art and human invention, and consequently to be not much remote from their original simplicity. The laws of nature, however, govern them still, not as yet much vitiated with any mixture of ours: but 'tis in such purity, that I am sometimes troubled

---

[13] "The ivy grows best spontaneously, the arbutus best in shady caves, and the wild notes of birds are sweeter than art can teach" (Propertius).

[14] Montaigne is paraphrasing a passage in Plato's *Laws*.

we were not sooner acquainted with these people, and that they were not
discovered in those better times, when there were men much more able to
judge of them than we are. I am sorry that Lycurgus and Plato had no
knowledge of them:[15] for to my apprehension, what we now see in those
nations, does not only surpass all the pictures with which the poets have
adorned the golden age, and all their inventions in feigning a happy state
of man, but, moreover, the fancy and even the wish and desire of philosophy itself; so native and so pure a simplicity, as we by experience see to be
in them, could never enter into their imagination, nor could they ever
believe that human society could have been maintained with so little artifice
and human patchwork. I should tell Plato, that it is a nation wherein there
is no manner of traffic, no knowledge of letters, no science of numbers, no
name of magistrate or political superiority; no use of service, riches or
poverty, no contracts, no successions, no dividends, no properties, no employments, but those of leisure, no respect of kindred, but common, no
clothing, no agriculture, no metal, no use of corn or wine; the very words
that signify lying, treachery, dissimulation, avarice, envy, detraction, pardon, never heard of. How much would he find his imaginary republic short
of his perfection?[16] *"Viri a diis recentes."*[17]

"Hos natura modos primum dedit."[18]

As to the rest, they live in a country very pleasant and temperate, so
that, as my witnesses inform me, 'tis rare to hear of a sick person, and they
moreover assure me, that they never saw any of the natives, either para-
lytic, blear-eyed, toothless, or crooked with age. The situation of their
country is along the seashore, enclosed on the other side toward the land,
with great and high mountains, having about a hundred leagues in breadth
between. They have great store of fish and flesh, that have no resemblance
to those of ours: which they eat without any other cookery, than plain
boiling, roasting and broiling. The first that rode a horse thither, though in
several other voyages he had contracted an acquaintance and familiarity
with them, put them into so terrible a fright, with his centaur[19] appearance,
that they killed him with their arrows before they could come to discover
who he was. Their buildings are very long, and of capacity to hold two or
three hundred people, made of the barks of tall trees, reared with one end
upon the ground, and leaning to and supporting one another, at the top,
like some of our barns, of which the coverings hang down to the very
ground, and serves for the side walls. They have wood so hard, that they
cut with it, and make their swords of it, and their grills of it to broil their
meat. Their beds are of cotton, hung swinging from the roof, like our
seaman's hammocks, every man his own, for the wives lie apart from their

---

[15] Lycurgus was a Spartan lawgiver. Like Plato, he wrote of ideal societies, and, Montaigne
suggests, both would have profited from knowing the culture of the New World cannibals.
[16] The two sentences preceding are the famous passage adapted by Shakespeare in *The
Tempest,* II.i.147.
[17] "Men fresh from the gods" (Seneca).
[18] "These were the manners first taught by nature" (Virgil).
[19] A creature half horse and half man.

husbands. They rise with the sun, and so soon as they are up, eat for all day, for they have no more meals but that: they do not then drink, as Suidas[20] reports of some other people of the East that never drank at their meals; but drink very often all day after, and sometimes to a rousing pitch. Their drink is made of a certain root, and is of the color of our claret, and they never drink it but lukewarm. It will not keep above two or three days; it has a somewhat sharp, brisk taste, is nothing heady, but very comfortable to the stomach; laxative to strangers, but a very pleasant beverage to such as are accustomed to it. They make use, instead of bread, of a certain white compound, like coriander comfits;[21] I have tasted of it; the taste is sweet and a little flat. The whole day is spent in dancing. Their young men go a-hunting after wild beasts with bows and arrows; one part of their women are employed in preparing their drink the while, which is their chief employment. One of their old men, in the morning before they fall to eating, preaches to the whole family, walking from the one end of the house to the other, and several times repeating the same sentence, till he has finished the round, for their houses are at least a hundred yards long. Valor toward their enemies and love toward their wives, are the two heads of his discourse, never failing in the close, to put them in mind, that 'tis their wives who provide them their drink warm and well seasoned. The fashion of their beds, ropes, swords, and of the wooden bracelets they tie about their wrists, when they go to fight, and of the great canes, bored hollow at one end, by the sound of which they keep the cadence of their dances, are to be seen in several places, and among others, at my house. They shave all over, and much more neatly than we, without other razor than one of wood or stone. They believe in the immortality of the soul, and that those who have merited well of the gods, are lodged in that part of heaven where the sun rises, and the accursed in the west.

They have I know not what kind of priests and prophets, who very rarely present themselves to the people, having their abode in the mountains. At their arrival, there is a great feast, and solemn assembly of many villages: each house, as I have described, makes a village, and they are about a French league distant from one another. This prophet declaims to them in public, exhorting them to virtue and their duty: but all their ethics are comprised in these two articles, resolution in war, and affection to their wives. He also prophesies to them events to come, and the issues they are to expect from their enterprises, and prompts them to or diverts them from war; but let him look to't; for if he fail in his divination, and anything happen otherwise than he has foretold, he is cut into a thousand pieces, if he be caught, and condemned for a false prophet: for that reason, if any of them has been mistaken, he is no more heard of.

Divination is a gift of God, and therefore to abuse it, ought to be a punishable imposture. Among the Scythians, where their diviners failed in the promised effect, they were laid, bound hand and foot, upon carts loaded with furze and bavins, and drawn by oxen, on which they were burned to death.[22] Such as only meddle with things subject to the conduct

---

[20] A tenth-century Greek lexicographer.   [21] Cakes flavored with the herb coriander.
[22] The Scythians were the inhabitants of a region in southeastern Europe and Asia, legendary for their barbarity. "Furze and bavins" are dry heather and straw. This story appears in the work of the Greek historian Herodotus.

of human capacity, are excusable in doing the best they can: but those other fellows that come to delude us with assurances of an extraordinary faculty, beyond our understanding, ought they not to be punished, when they do not make good the effect of their promise, and for the temerity of their imposture?

They have continual war with the nations that live further within the mainland, beyond their mountains, to which they go naked, and without other arms than their bows and wooden swords, fashioned at one end like the heads of our javelins. The obstinacy of their battles is wonderful, and they never end without great effusion of blood: for as to running away, they know not what it is. Every one for a trophy brings home the head of an enemy he has killed, which he fixes over the door of his house. After having a long time treated their prisoners very well, and given them all the regales they can think of, he to whom the prisoner belongs, invites a great assembly of his friends. They being come, he ties a rope to one of the arms of the prisoner, of which, at a distance, out of his reach, he holds the one end himself, and gives to the friend he loves best the other arm to hold after the same manner; which being done, they two, in the presence of all the assembly, despatch him with their swords. After that they roast him, eat him among them, and send some chops to their absent friends. They do not do this, as some think, for nourishment, as the Scythians anciently did, but as a representation of an extreme revenge; as will appear by this: that having observed the Portuguese, who were in league with their enemies, to inflict another sort of death upon any of them they took prisoners, which was to set them up to the girdle in the earth, to shoot at the remaining part till it was stuck full of arrows, and then to hang them, they thought those people of the other world (as being men who had sown the knowledge of a great many vices among their neighbors, and who were much greater masters in all sorts of mischief than they) did not exercise this sort of revenge without a meaning, and that it must needs be more painful than theirs, they began to leave their old way, and to follow this. I am not sorry that we should here take notice of the barbarous horror of so cruel an action, but that, seeing so clearly into their faults, we should be so blind to our own. I conceive there is more barbarity in eating a man alive, than when he is dead; in tearing a body limb from limb by racks and torments, that is yet in perfect sense; in roasting it by degrees;[23] in causing it to be bitten and worried by dogs and swine (as we have not only read, but lately seen, not among inveterate and mortal enemies, but among neighbors and fellow-citizens, and, which is worse, under color of piety and religion), than to roast and eat him after he is dead.

Chrysippus and Zeno,[24] the two heads of the Stoic sect, were of opinion that there was no hurt in making use of our dead carcasses, in what way soever for our necessity, and in feeding upon them too; as our own ancestors, who being besieged by Caesar in the city of Alexia, resolved to sustain the famine of the siege with the bodies of their old men, women, and other persons who were incapable of bearing arms.[25]

---

[23] These were accepted modes of execution in Montaigne's day.
[24] Chrysippus (291–208 B.C.) and Zeno (d. 264 B.C.) were, as noted, Stoic philosophers.
[25] This story of cannibalism appears in Caesar's *Gallic Wars*.

"Vascones, ut fama est, alimentis talibus usi
Produxere animas."[26]

And the physicians make no bones of employing it to all sorts of use, either to apply it outwardly; or to give it inwardly for the health of the patient. But there never was any opinion so irregular, as to excuse treachery, disloyalty, tyranny, and cruelty, which are our familiar vices. We may then call these people barbarous, in respect to the rules of reason: but not in respect to ourselves, who in all sorts of barbarity exceed them. Their wars are throughout noble and generous, and carry as much excuse and fair pretense, as that human malady is capable of; having with them no other foundation than the sole jealousy of valor. Their disputes are not for the conquest of new lands, for these they already possess are so fruitful by nature, as to supply them without labor or concern, with all things necessary, in such abundance that they have no need to enlarge their borders. And they are moreover, happy in this, that they only covet so much as their natural necessities require: all beyond that, is superfluous to them: men of the same age call one another generally brothers, those who are younger, children; and the old men are fathers to all. These leave to their heirs in common the full possession of goods, without any manner of division, or other title than what nature bestows upon her creatures, in bringing them into the world. If their neighbors pass over the mountains to assault them, and obtain a victory, all the victors gain by it is glory only, and the advantage of having proved themselves the better in valor and virtue: for they never meddle with the goods of the conquered, but presently return into their own country, where they have no want of anything necessary, nor of this greatest of all goods, to know happily how to enjoy their condition and to be content. And those in turn do the same; they demand of their prisoners no other ransom, than acknowledgment that they are overcome: but there is not one found in an age, who will not rather choose to die than make such a confession, or either by word or look, recede from the entire grandeur of an invincible courage. There is not a man among them who had not rather be killed and eaten, than so much as to open his mouth to entreat he may not. They use them with all liberality and freedom, to the end their lives may be so much the dearer to them; but frequently entertain them with menaces of their approaching death, of the torments they are to suffer, of the preparations making in order to it, of the mangling their limbs, and of the feast that is to be made, where their carcass is to be the only dish. All which they do, to no other end, but only to extort some gentle or submissive word from them, or to frighten them so as to make them run away, to obtain this advantage that they were terrified, and that their constancy was shaken; and indeed, if rightly taken, it is in this point only that a true victory consists.

"Victoria nulla est,
Quam quae confessos animo quoque subjugat hostes."[27]

[26] "It is said that the Gascons with such meat appeased their hunger" (Juvenal).
[27] "No victory is complete which the conquered do not admit to be so" (Claudius).

The Hungarians, a very warlike people, never pretend further than to reduce the enemy to their discretion; for having forced this confession from them, they let them go without injury or ransom, excepting, at the most, to make them engage their word never to bear arms against them again. We have sufficient advantages over our enemies that are borrowed and not truly our own; it is the quality of a porter, and no effect of virtue, to have stronger arms and legs; it is a dead and corporeal quality to set in array; 'tis a turn of fortune to make our enemy stumble, or to dazzle him with the light of the sun; 'tis a trick of science and art, and that may happen in a mean base fellow, to be a good fencer. The estimate and value of a man consist in the heart and in the will: there his true honor lies. Valor is stability, not of legs and arms, but of the courage and the soul; it does not lie in the goodness of our horse or our arms: but in our own. He that falls obstinate in his courage—"*Si succiderit, de genu pugnat*"[28]—he who, for any danger of imminent death, abates nothing of his assurance; who, dying, yet darts at his enemy a fierce and disdainful look, is overcome not by us, but by fortune; he is killed, not conquered; the most valiant are sometimes the most unfortunate. There are defeats more triumphant than victories. Never could those four sister victories, the fairest the sun ever beheld, of Salamis, Plataea, Mycale, and Sicily, venture to oppose all their united glories, to the single glory of the discomfiture of King Leonidas and his men, at the pass of Thermopylae.[29] Whoever ran with a more glorious desire and greater ambition, to the winning, than Captain Iscolas to the certain loss of a battle?[30] Who could have found out a more subtle invention to secure his safety, than he did to assure his destruction? He was set to defend a certain pass of Peloponnesus against the Arcadians, which, considering the nature of the place and the inequality of forces, finding it utterly impossible for him to do, and seeing that all who were presented to the enemy, must certainly be left upon the place; and on the other side, reputing it unworthy of his own virtue and magnanimity and of the Lacedaemonian name to fail in any part of his duty, he chose a mean between these two extremes after this manner; the youngest and most active of his men, he preserved for the service and defense of their country, and sent them back; and with the rest, whose loss would be of less consideration, he resolved to make good the pass, and with the death of them, to make the enemy buy their entry as dear as possibly he could; as it fell out, for being presently environed on all sides by the Arcadians, after having made a great slaughter of the enemy, he and his were all cut in pieces. Is there any trophy dedicated to the conquerors, which was not much more due to these who were overcome? The part that true conquering is to play, lies in the encounter, not in the coming off; and the honor of valor consists in fighting, not in subduing.

But to return to my story: these prisoners are so far from discovering the least weakness, for all the terrors that can be represented to them that, on the contrary, during the two or three months they are kept, they always

[28]"If his legs fail him, he fights on his knees" (Seneca).

[29]Salamis, Plataea, Mycale, and Sicily were the sites of notable victories of the Greeks over the Persians and Carthaginians in the fifth century B.C. At Thermopylae, a narrow mountain pass in eastern Greece, a small band of Spartans held off the Persian army in 480 B.C.

[30]This story is told by the Greek historian Diodorus Siculus (first century B.C.).

appear with a cheerful countenance; importune their masters to make haste to bring them to the test, defy, rail at them, and reproach them with cowardice, and the number of battles they have lost against those of their country. I have a song made by one of these prisoners, wherein he bids them "come all, and dine upon him, and welcome, for they shall withal eat their own fathers and grandfathers, whose flesh has served to feed and nourish him. These muscles," says he, "this flesh and these veins, are your own: poor silly souls as you are, you little think that the substance of your ancestors' limbs is here yet; notice what you eat, and you will find in it the taste of your own flesh:" in which song there is to be observed an invention that nothing relishes of the barbarian. Those that paint these people dying after this manner, represent the prisoner spitting in the faces of his executioners and making wry mouths at them. And 'tis most certain, that to the very last gasp, they never cease to brave and defy them both in word and gesture. In plain truth, these men are very savage in comparison of us; of necessity, they must either be absolutely so or else we are savages; for there is a vast difference between their manners and ours.

The men there have several wives, and so much the greater number, by how much they have the greater reputation for valor. And it is one very remarkable feature in their marriages, that the same jealousy our wives have to hinder and divert us from the friendship and familiarity of other women, those employ to promote their husbands' desires, and to procure them many spouses; for being above all things solicitous of their husbands' honor, 'tis their chiefest care to seek out, and to bring in the most companions they can, forasmuch as it is a testimony of the husband's virtue. Most of our ladies will cry out, that 'tis monstrous; whereas in truth, it is not so; but a truly matrimonial virtue, and of the highest form. In the Bible, Sarah, with Leah and Rachel, the two wives of Jacob, gave the most beautiful of their handmaids to their husbands; Livia preferred the passions of Augustus to her own interest; and the wife of King Deiotarus, Stratonice, did not only give up a fair young maid that served her to her husband's embraces, but moreover carefully brought up the children he had by her, and assisted them in the succession to their father's crown.[31]

And that it may not be supposed, that all this is done by a simple and servile obligation to their common practice, or by any authoritative impression of their ancient custom, without judgment or reasoning and from having a soul so stupid, that it cannot contrive what else to do, I must here give you some touches of their sufficiency in point of understanding. Besides what I repeated to you before, which was one of their songs of war, I have another, a love-song, that begins thus: "Stay, adder, stay, that by thy pattern my sister may draw the fashion and work of a rich ribbon, that I may present to my beloved, by which means thy beauty and the excellent order of thy scales shall forever be preferred before all other serpents." Wherein the first couplet, "Stay, adder," etc., makes the burden of the song. Now I have conversed enough with poetry to judge thus much: that not only, there is nothing of barbarous in this invention, but, moreover,

---

[31] The story of Sarah and her maid Hagar appears in Genesis, chapter 16, that of Leah and Rachel in Genesis, chapter 30. The story of Livia is in Suetonius' *Life of Augustus* and that of Stratonice in Plutarch's *Bravery of Women*.

that it is perfectly Anacreontic.[32] To which may be added, that their language is soft, of a pleasing accent, and something bordering upon the Greek terminations.

Three of these people, not foreseeing how dear their knowledge of the corruptions of this part of the world will one day cost their happiness and repose, and that the effect of this commerce will be their ruin, as I presuppose it is in a very fair way (miserable men to suffer themselves to be deluded with desire of novelty and to have left the serenity of their own heaven, to come so far to gaze at ours!) were at Rouen at the time that the late King Charles IX was there.[33] The king himself talked to them a good while, and they were made to see our fashions, our pomp, and the form of a great city. After which, some one asked their opinion, and would know of them, what of all the things they had seen, they found most to be admired? To which they made answer, three things, of which I have forgotten the third, and am troubled at it, but two I yet remember. They said, that in the first place they thought it very strange, that so many tall men wearing beards, strong, and well armed, who were about the king ('tis like they meant the Swiss of his guard) should submit to obey a child, and that they did not rather choose out one among themselves to command. Secondly (they have a way of speaking in their language, to call men the half of one another), that they had observed, that there were among us men full and crammed with all manner of commodities, while, in the meantime, their halves were begging at their doors, lean, and half-starved with hunger and poverty; and they thought it strange that these necessitous halves were able to suffer so great an inequality and injustice, and that they did not take the others by the throats, or set fire to their houses.

I talked to one of them a great while together, but I had so ill an interpreter, and one who was so perplexed by his own ignorance to apprehend my meaning, that I could get nothing out of him of any moment. Asking him, what advantage he reaped from the superiority he had among his own people (for he was a captain, and our mariners called him king), he told me: to march at the head of them to war. Demanding of him further, how many men he had to follow him? he showed me a space of ground, to signify as many as could march in such a compass, which might be four or five thousand men; and putting the question to him, whether or no his authority expired with the war? he told me this remained: that when he went to visit the villages of his dependence, they plained[34] him paths through the thick of their woods, by which he might pass at his ease. All this does not sound very ill, and the last was not at all amiss, for they wear no breeches.

OF REPENTANCE

Others form man; I only report him: and represent a particular one, ill fashioned enough, and whom, if I had to model him anew, I should certainly make something else than what he is: but that's past recalling. Now,

---

[32] Like the poetry of Anacreon (c. 563–c. 478 B.C.), a Greek poet known for his love poems.
[33] King Charles IX of France died in 1574.   [34] Cleared.

though the features of my picture alter and change, 'tis not, however, unlike: the world eternally turns round; all things therein are incessantly moving, the earth, the rocks of Caucasus, and the pyramids of Egypt, both by the public motion and their own. Even constancy itself is no other but a slower and more languishing motion. I cannot fix my object; 'tis always tottering and reeling by a natural giddiness: I take it as it is at the instant I consider it; I do not paint its being, I paint its passage; not a passing from one age to another, or, as the people say, from seven to seven years, but from day to day, from minute to minute. I must accommodate my history to the hour: I may presently change, not only by fortune, but also by intention. 'Tis a counterpart of various and changeable accidents, and of irresolute imaginations, and, as it falls out, sometimes contrary: whether it be that I am then another self, or that I take subjects by other circumstances and considerations: so it is, that I may peradventure contradict myself, but, as Demades said, I never contradict the truth.[1] Could my soul once take footing, I would not essay but resolve: but it is always learning and making trial.

I propose a life ordinary and without luster: 'tis all one; all moral philosophy may as well be applied to a common and private life, as to one of richer composition: every man carries the entire form of human condition. Authors communicate themselves to the people by some especial and extrinsic mark; I, the first of any, by my universal being; as Michel de Montaigne, not as a grammarian, a poet, or a lawyer. If the world find fault that I speak too much of myself, I find fault that they do not so much as think of themselves. But is it reason, that being so particular in my way of living, I should pretend to recommend myself to the public knowledge? And is it also reason that I should produce to the world, where art and handling have so much credit and authority, crude and simple effects of nature, and of a weak nature to boot? Is it not to build a wall without stone or brick, or some such thing, to write books without learning and without art? The fancies of music are carried on by art; mine by chance. I have this, at least, according to discipline, that never any man treated of a subject he better understood and knew, than I what I have undertaken, and that in this I am the most understanding man alive: secondly, that never any man penetrated farther into his matter, nor better and more distinctly sifted the parts and sequences of it, nor ever more exactly and fully arrived at the end he proposed to himself. To perfect it, I need bring nothing but fidelity to the work; and that is there, and the most pure and sincere that is anywhere to be found. I speak truth, not so much as I would, but as much as I dare; and I dare a little the more, as I grow older; for, methinks, custom allows to age more liberty of prating, and more indiscretion of talking of a man's self. That cannot fall out here, which I often see elsewhere, that the work and the artificer contradict one another: "Can a man of such sober conversation have written so foolish a book?" Or "Do so learned writings proceed from a man of so weak conversation?" He who talks at a very ordinary rate, and writes rare matter, 'tis to say that his capacity is borrowed and not his own. A learned man is not learned in all things: but a sufficient man is

[1] Demades (d. 318 B.C.) was an Athenian orator. A version of this remark appears in Plutarch's *Life of Demosthenes*.

sufficient throughout, even to ignorance itself; here my book and I go hand in hand together. Elsewhere men may commend or censure the work, without reference to the workman; here they cannot: who touches the one, touches the other. He who shall judge of it without knowing him, will more wrong himself than me; he who does know him, gives me all the satisfaction I desire. I shall be happy beyond my desert, if I can obtain only thus much from the public approbation, as to make men of understanding perceive that I was capable of profiting by knowledge, had I had it; and that I deserved to have been assisted by a better memory.

Be pleased here to excuse what I often repeat, that I very rarely repent, and that my conscience is satisfied with itself, not as the conscience of an angel, or that of a horse, but as the conscience of a man, always adding this clause, not one of ceremony, but a true and real submission, that I speak inquiring and doubting, purely and simply referring myself to the common and accepted beliefs for the resolution. I do not teach, I only relate.

There is no vice that is absolutely a vice which does not offend, and that a sound judgment does not accuse; for there is in it so manifest a deformity and inconvenience, that, peradventure, they are in the right who say that it is chiefly begotten by stupidity and ignorance: so hard is it to imagine that a man can know without abhorring it. Malice sucks up the greatest part of its own venom, and poisons itself. Vice leaves repentance in the soul, like an ulcer in the flesh, which is always scratching and lacerating itself; for reason effaces all other grief and sorrows, but it begets that of repentance, which is so much the more grievous, by reason it springs within, as the cold and heat of fevers are more sharp than those that only strike upon the outward skin. I hold for vices (but every one according to its proportion), not only those which reason and nature condemn, but those also which the opinion of men, though false and erroneous, have made such, if authorized by law and custom.

There is likewise no virtue which does not rejoice a well-descended nature; there is a kind of, I know not what, congratulation in well doing that gives us an inward satisfaction, and a generous boldness that accompanies a good conscience: a soul daringly vicious may, peradventure, arm itself with security, but it cannot supply itself with this complacency and satisfaction. 'Tis no little satisfaction to feel a man's self preserved from the contagion of so depraved an age, and to say to himself: "Whoever could penetrate into my soul would not there find me guilty either of the affliction or ruin of any one, or of revenge or envy, or any offense against the public laws, or of innovation or disturbance, or failure of my word; and though the license of the time permits and teaches every one so to do, yet have I not plundered any Frenchman's goods, or taken his money, and have lived upon what is my own, in war as well as in peace; neither have I set any man to work without paying him his hire." These testimonies of a good conscience please, and this natural rejoicing is very beneficial to us, and the only reward that we can never fail of.

To ground the recompense of virtuous actions upon the approbation of others is too uncertain and unsafe a foundation, especially in so corrupt and ignorant an age as this, wherein the good opinion of the vulgar is injurious: upon whom do you rely to show you what is recommendable? God defend me from being an honest man, according to the descriptions of

honor I daily see every one make of himself. *"Quæ fuerant vitia, mores sunt."*[2]
Some of my friends have at times schooled and scolded me with great
sincerity and plainness, either of their own voluntary motion, or by me
entreated to it as to an office, which to a well-composed soul surpasses not
only in utility, but in kindness all other offices of friendship: I have always
received them with the most open arms, both of courtesy and acknowledgment; but, to say the truth, I have often found so much false measure, both
in their reproaches and praises, that I had not done much amiss, rather to
have done ill, than to have done well according to their notions. We, who
live private lives, not exposed to any other view than our own, ought chiefly
to have settled a pattern within ourselves by which to try our actions; and
according to that, sometimes to encourage and sometimes to correct ourselves. I have my laws and my judicature to judge of myself and apply
myself more to these than to any other rules: I do, indeed, restrain my
actions according to others; but extend them not by any other rule than my
own. You yourself only know if you are cowardly and cruel, loyal and
devout: others see you not, and only guess at you by uncertain conjectures,
and do not so much see your nature as your art; rely not therefore upon
their opinions, but stick to your own: *"Tuo tibi judicio est utendum . . . Virtutis
et vitiorum grave ipsius conscientiæ pondus est: qua sublata, jacent omnia."*[3]

But the saying that repentance immediately follows the sin seems not to
have respect to sin in its high estate, which is lodged in us as in its own
proper habitation. One may disown and retract the vices that surprise us,
and to which we are hurried by passions; but those which by a long habit
are rooted in a strong and vigorous will are not subject to contradiction.
Repentance is no other but a recanting of the will and an opposition to our
fancies, which lead us which way they please. It makes this person disown
his former virtue and continency:

> *"Quæ mens est hodie, cur eadem non puero fuit?*
> *Vel cur his animis incolumes non redeunt genæ?"*[4]

'Tis an exact life that maintains itself in due order in private. Every one
may juggle his part, and represent an honest man upon the stage: but
within, and in his own bosom, where all may do as they list, where all is
concealed, to be regular—there's the point. The next degree is to be so in
his house, and in his ordinary actions, for which we are accountable to
none, and where there is no study nor artifice. And therefore Bias, setting
forth the excellent state of a private family, says: "of which the master is the
same within, by his own virtue and temper, that he is abroad, for fear of the
laws and report of men."[5] And it was a worthy saying of Julius Drusus, to
the masons who offered him, for three thousand crowns, to put his house
in such a posture that his neighbors should no longer have the same

---

[2]"What before were vices are now right manners" (Seneca).

[3]"You might employ your own judgment upon yourself. Great is the weight of your own
conscience in the discovery of your own virtues and vices. If that is taken away, all is lost"
(Cicero).

[4]"Why was I not of the same mind when I was a boy that I am now? Or why do not the
ruddy cheeks of my youth return to help me now?" (Horace).

[5]Bias of Priene (c. 570 B.C.) was one of the "Seven Sages."

inspection into it as before; "I will give you," said he, "six thousand to make it so that everybody may see into every room."[6] 'Tis honorably recorded of Agesilaus, that he used in his journeys always to take up his lodgings in temples, to the end that the people and the gods themselves might pry into his most private actions.[7] Such a one has been a miracle to the world, in whom neither his wife nor servant has ever seen anything so much as remarkable; few men have been admired by their own domestics; no one was ever a prophet, not merely in his own house, but in his own country, says the experience of histories: 'tis the same in things of naught, and in this low example the image of a greater is to be seen. In my country of Gascony, they look upon it as a drollery to see me in print; the further off I am read from my own home, the better I am esteemed. I am fain to purchase printers in Guienne; elsewhere they purchase me. Upon this it is that they lay their foundation who conceal themselves present and living, to obtain a name when they are absent and dead. I had rather have a great deal less in hand, and do not expose myself to the world upon any other account than my present share; when I leave it I quit the rest. See this functionary whom the people escort in state, with wonder and applause, to his very door; he puts off the pageant with his robe, and falls so much the lower by how much he was higher exalted: in himself within, all is tumult and degraded. And though all should be regular there, it will require a vivid and well-chosen judgment to perceive it in these low and private actions; to which may be added, that order is a dull, somber virtue. To enter a breach, conduct an embassy, govern a people, are actions of renown: to reprehend, laugh, sell, pay, love, hate, and gently and justly converse with a man's own family, and with himself; not to relax, not to give a man's self the lie is more rare and hard, and less remarkable. By which means, retired lives, whatever is said to the contrary, undergo duties of as great or greater difficulty than the others do; and private men, says Aristotle, serve virtue more painfully and highly, than those in authority do:[8] we prepare ourselves for eminent occasions, more out of glory than conscience. The shortest way to arrive at glory, would be to do that for conscience which we do for glory: and the virtue of Alexander appears to me of much less vigor in his great theater, than that of Socrates in his mean and obscure employment.[9] I can easily conceive Socrates in the place of Alexander, but Alexander in that of Socrates, I cannot. Who shall ask the one what he can do, he will answer, "Subdue the world:" and who shall put the same question to the other, he will say, "Carry on human life conformably with its natural condition:" a much more general, weighty, and legitimate science than the other.

The virtue of the soul does not consist in flying high, but in walking orderly; its grandeur does not exercise itself in grandeur, but in mediocrity. As they who judge and try us within, make no great account of the luster of our public actions, and see they are only streaks and rays of clear water springing from a slimy and muddy bottom: so, likewise, they who

---

[6]"Julius Drusus" is an error for Marcus Livius, a second-century B.C. Roman tribune. Montaigne is citing Plutarch, *On Managing Affairs of State.*

[7]Agesilaus (c. 440–360 B.C.) was king of Sparta.   [8]*Nicomachean Ethics* X.7.

[9]Alexander the Great (356–323 B.C.) was king of Macedonia; he conquered the Greek city-states and the Persian Empire.

judge of us by this gallant outward appearance, in like manner conclude of our internal constitution; and cannot couple common faculties, and like their own, with the other faculties that astonish them, and are so far out of their sight. Therefore it is, that we give such savage forms to demons: and who does not give Tamerlane great eyebrows, wide nostrils, a dreadful visage, and a prodigious stature, according to the imagination he has conceived by the report of his name?[10] Had any one formerly brought me to Erasmus,[11] I should hardly have believed but that all was adage and apothegm he spoke to his man or his hostess. We much more aptly imagine an artisan upon his close-stool, or upon his wife, than a great president venerable by his port and sufficiency: we fancy that they, from their high tribunals, will not abase themselves so much as to live. As vicious souls are often incited by some foreign impulse to do well, so are virtuous souls to do ill; they are therefore to be judged by their settled state, when they are at home, whenever that may be; and, at all events, when they are nearer repose, and in their native station.

Natural inclinations are much assisted and fortified by education: but they seldom alter and overcome their institution: a thousand natures of my time have escaped toward virtue or vice, through a quite contrary discipline;

> "Sic ubi desuetæ silvis in carcere clausæ
> Mansuevere feræ, et vultus posuere minaces,
> Atque hominem didicere pati, si torrida parvus
> Venit in ora cruor, redeunt rabiesque furorque,
> Admonitæque tument gustato sanguine fauces;
> Fervet, et a trepido vix abstinet ira magistro;"[12]

these original qualities are not to be rooted out; they may be covered and concealed. The Latin tongue is as it were natural to me; I understand it better than French; but I have not been used to speak it, nor hardly to write it these forty years. Yet, upon extreme and sudden emotions which I have fallen into twice or thrice in my life, and once, seeing my father in perfect health fall upon me in a swoon, I have always uttered my first outcries and ejaculations in Latin; nature starting up, and forcibly expressing itself, in spite of so long a discontinuation; and this example is said of many others.

They who in my time have attempted to correct the manners of the world by new opinions, reform seeming vices, but the essential vices they leave as they were, if indeed, they do not augment them; and augmentation is, therein, to be feared; we defer all other well doing upon the account of these external reformations, of less cost and greater show, and thereby

---

[10] Tamerlane, or Tamburlaine (1336?–1405), was the Mongol conqueror of most of southern and western Asia.

[11] Erasmus (1466?–1536) was the famous Dutch Humanist, scholar, and satirist.

[12] "So savage beasts, when shut up in cages and grown unaccustomed to the woods, become tame and lay aside their fierce looks and submit to the rule of man; if again they taste blood, their rage and fury return, their jaws thirst for blood, and they scarcely forbear to assail their trembling masters" (Lucan).

expiate cheaply, for the other natural consubstantial and intestine vices.[13] Look a little into our experience: there is no man, if he listen to himself, who does not in himself discover a particular and governing form of his own, that jostles his education, and wrestles with the tempest of passions that are contrary to it. For my part, I seldom find myself agitated with surprises; I always find myself in my place, as heavy and unwieldy bodies do; if I am not at home, I am always near at hand; my dissipations do not transport me very far, there is nothing strange nor extreme in the case; and yet I have sound and vigorous turns.

The true condemnation, and which touches the common practice of men, is, that their very retirement itself is full of filth and corruption; the idea of their reformation composed; their repentance sick and faulty, very nearly as much as their sin. Some, either from having been linked to vice by a natural propension, or long practice, cannot see its deformity. Others (of which constitution I am) do indeed feel the weight of vice, but they counterbalance it with pleasure, or some other occasion; and suffer, and lend themselves to it, for a certain price, but viciously and basely. Yet there might, haply, be imagined so vast a disproportion of measure, where with justice the pleasure might excuse the sin, as we say of utility; not only if accidental, and out of sin, as in thefts, but the very exercise of sin, as in the enjoyment of women, where the temptation is violent, and 'tis said, sometimes not to be overcome.

Being the other day at Armaignac, on the estate of a kinsman of mine, I there saw a country fellow who was by every one nicknamed the thief. He thus related the story of his life; that being born a beggar, and finding that he should not be able, so as to be clear of indigence, to get his living by the sweat of his brow, he resolved to turn thief, and by means of his strength of body, had exercised this trade all the time of his youth in great security; for he ever made his harvest and vintage in other men's grounds, but a great way off, and in so great quantities, that it was not to be imagined one man could have carried away so much in one night upon his shoulders; and, moreover, was careful equally to divide and distribute the mischief he did, that the loss was of less importance to every particular man. He is now grown old, and rich for a man of his condition, thanks to his trade, which he openly confesses to every one. And to make his peace with God, he says, that he is daily ready by good offices to make satisfaction to the successors of those he has robbed, and if he do not finish (for to do it all at once he is not able) he will then leave it in charge to his heirs to perform the rest, proportionably to the wrong he himself only knows he has done to each. By this description, true or false, this man looks upon theft as a dishonest action, and hates it, but less than poverty, and simply repents; but to the extent he has thus recompensed, he repents not. This is not that habit which incorporates us into vice, and conforms even our understanding itself to it; nor is it that impetuous whirlwind that by gusts troubles and blinds our souls and for the time precipitates us, judgment and all, into the power of vice.

I customarily do what I do thoroughly and make but one step on't; I

---

[13] "Consubstantial" means "of the same substance"; "intestine" means "internal." "Natural consubstantial and intestine vices" are those which are basic and deep-seated.

have rarely any movement that hides itself and steals away from my reason, and that does not proceed in the matter by the consent of all my faculties, without division or intestine sedition; my judgment is to have all the blame or all the praise; and the blame it once has, it has always; for almost from my infancy it has ever been one; the same inclination, the same turn, the same force; and as to universal opinions, I fixed myself from my childhood in the place where I resolved to stick. There are some sins that are impetuous, prompt, and sudden; let us set them aside; but in these other sins so often repeated, deliberated, and contrived, whether sins of complexion or sins of profession and vocation, I cannot conceive that they should have so long been settled in the same resolution, unless the reason and conscience of him who has them, be constant to have them; and the repentance he boasts to be inspired with on a sudden, is very hard for me to imagine or form. I follow not the opinion of the Pythagorean sect, "that men take up a new soul when they repair to the images of the gods to receive their oracles," unless he mean that it must needs be extrinsic, new, and lent for the time; our own showing so little sign of purification and cleanness, fit for such an office.[14]

They act quite contrary to the stoical precepts, who do indeed, command us to correct the imperfections and vices we know ourselves guilty of, but forbid us therefore to disturb the repose of our souls; these make us believe that they have great grief and remorse within; but of amendment, correction, or interruption, they make nothing appear.[15] It cannot be a cure if the malady be not wholly discharged; if repentance were laid upon the scale of the balance, it would weigh down sin. I find no quality so easy to counterfeit as devotion, if men do not conform their manners and life to the profession; its essence is abstruse and occult; the appearances easy and ostentatious.

For my own part, I may desire in general to be other than I am; I may condemn and dislike my whole form, and beg of Almighty God for an entire reformation, and that He will please to pardon my natural infirmity: but I ought not to call this repentance, methinks, no more, than the being dissatisfied that I am not an angel or Cato.[16] My actions are regular, and conformable with what I am, and to my condition; I can do no better; and repentance does not properly touch things that are not in our power; sorrow does. I imagine an infinite number of natures more elevated and regular than mine; and yet I do not for all that improve my faculties, no more than my arm or will grow more strong and vigorous for conceiving those of another to be so. If to conceive and wish a nobler way of acting than that we have, should produce a repentance of our own, we must then repent us of our most innocent actions, forasmuch as we may well suppose that in a more excellent nature they would have been carried on with greater dignity and perfection; and we would that ours were so. When I reflect upon

[14] Pythagoras, the Greek philosopher, mathematician, and religious reformer (c. 582– c. 500 B.C.), taught the transmigration of souls.

[15] Stoicism was a Greek school of philosophy founded about 315 B.C. It taught, among other things, self-control and self-reformation, subduing passion and indulgence in order to attain inner freedom.

[16] Marcus Porcius Cato (95–46 B.C.)—Cato the Younger—was a Roman statesman known for his Stoical convictions and his incorruptible honesty.

the deportments of my youth, with that of my old age, I find that I have commonly behaved myself with equal order in both, according to what I understand: this is all that my resistance can do. I do not flatter myself; in the same circumstances I should do the same things. It is not a patch, but rather an universal tincture, with which I am stained. I know no repentance, superficial, half-way and ceremonious; it must sting me all over before I can call it so, and must prick my bowels as deeply and universally as God sees into me.

As to business, many excellent opportunities have escaped me for want of good management; and yet my deliberations were sound enough, according to the occurrences presented to me: 'tis their way to choose always the easiest and safest course. I find that, in my former resolves, I have proceeded with discretion, according to my own rule, and according to the state of the subject proposed, and should do the same a thousand years hence in like occasions; I do not consider what it is now, but what it was then, when I deliberated on it: the force of all counsel consists in the time; occasions and things eternally shift and change. I have in my life committed some important errors, not for want of good understanding, but for want of good luck. There are secret, and not to be foreseen, parts in matters we have in hand, especially in the nature of men; mute conditions, that make no show, unknown sometimes even to the possessors themselves, that spring and start up by incidental occasions; if my prudence could not penetrate into nor foresee them, I blame it not: 'tis commissioned no further than its own limits; if the event be too hard for me, and take the side I have refused, there is no remedy; I do not blame myself, I accuse my fortune, and not my work; this cannot be called repentance.

Phocion,[17] having given the Athenians an advice that was not followed, and the affair nevertheless succeeding contrary to his opinion, some one said to him; "Well, Phocion, art thou content that matters go so well?" "I am very well content," replied he, "that this has happened so well, but I do not repent that I counseled the other." When any of my friends address themselves to me for advice, I give it candidly and clearly, without sticking, as almost all other men do, at the hazard of the thing's falling out contrary to my opinion, and that I may be reproached for my counsel; I am very indifferent as to that, for the fault will be theirs for having consulted me, and I could not refuse them that office.

I, for my own part, can rarely blame any one but myself for my oversights and misfortunes, for indeed I seldom solicit the advice of another, if not by honor of ceremony, or excepting where I stand in need of information, special science, or as to matter of fact. But in things wherein I stand in need of nothing but judgment, other men's reasons may serve to fortify my own, but have little power to dissuade me; I hear them all with civility and patience: but to my recollection, I never made use of any but my own. With me, they are but flies and atoms, that confound and distract my will; I lay no great stress upon my opinions; but I lay as little upon those of others, and fortune rewards me accordingly: if I receive but little advice, I also give but little. I am seldom consulted, and still more seldom believed, and know

---

[17] Phocion (402–317 B.C.) was an Athenian statesman and general. This story appears in Plutarch.

no concern, either public or private, that has been mended or bettered by my advice. Even they whom fortune had in some sort tied to my direction, have more willingly suffered themselves to be governed by any other counsels than mine. And as a man who am as jealous of my repose as of my authority, I am better pleased that it should be so; in leaving me there, they humor what I profess, which is to settle and wholly contain myself within myself. I take a pleasure in being uninterested in other men's affairs, and disengaged from being their warranty, and responsible for what they do.

In all affairs that are past, be it how it will, I have very little regret; for this imagination puts me out of my pain, that they were so to fall out; they are in the great revolution of the world, and in the chain of stoical causes: your fancy cannot, by wish and imagination, move one tittle, but that the great current of things will not reverse both the past and the future.

As to the rest, I abominate that incidental repentance which old age brings along with it. He, who said of old, that he was obliged to his age for having weaned him from pleasure,[18] was of another opinion than I am; I can never think myself beholden to impotency, for any good it can do to me; *"Nec tam aversa unquam videbitur ab opere suo providentia, ut debilitas inter optima inventa sit."*[19] Our appetites are rare in old age; a profound satiety seizes us after the act; in this I see nothing of conscience; chagrin and weakness imprint in us a drowsy and rheumatic virtue. We must not suffer ourselves to be so wholly carried away by natural alterations, as to suffer our judgments to be imposed upon by them. Youth and pleasure have not formerly so far prevailed with me, that I did not well enough discern the face of vice in pleasure; neither does the distaste that years have brought me, so far prevail with me now, that I cannot discern pleasure in vice. Now that I am no more in my flourishing age, I judge as well of these things as if I were. I, who narrowly and strictly examine it, find my reason the very same it was in my most licentious age, except, perhaps, that 'tis weaker and more decayed by being grown older; and I find that the pleasure it refuses me upon the account of my bodily health, it would no more refuse now, in consideration of the health of my soul, than at any time heretofore. I do not repute it the more valiant for not being able to combat; my temptations are so broken and mortified, that they are not worth its opposition; holding but out my hands, I repel them. Should one present the old concupiscence before it, I fear it would have less power to resist it than heretofore; I do not discern that in itself it judges anything otherwise now, than it formerly did, nor that it has acquired any new light: wherefore, if there be convalescence, 'tis an enchanted one. Miserable kind of remedy, to owe one's health to one's disease! 'Tis not that our misfortune should perform this office, but the good fortune of our judgment. I am not to be made to do anything by persecutions and afflictions, but to curse them: that is for people who cannot be roused but by a whip. My reason is much more free in prosperity, and much more distracted, and put to't to digest pains than pleasures: I see best in a clear sky; health admonishes me more cheerfully, and to better purpose, than sickness. I did all that in me lay to reform and regulate

---

[18] This remark was attributed to Sophocles by Cicero.
[19] "Nor can Providence ever be seen so averse to her own work that debility should be ranked among the best things" (Quintilian).

myself from pleasures, at a time when I had health and vigor to enjoy them; I should be ashamed and envious, that the misery and misfortune of my old age should have credit over my good, healthful, sprightly, and vigorous years; and that men should estimate me, not by what I have been, but by what I have ceased to be.

In my opinion, 'tis the happy living, and not (as Antisthenes said) the happy dying, in which human felicity consists. I have not made it my business to make a monstrous addition of a philosopher's tail to the head and body of a libertine; nor would I have this wretched remainder give the lie to the pleasant, sound, and long part of my life: I would present myself uniformly throughout. Were I to live my life over again, I should live it just as I have lived it; I neither complain of the past, nor do I fear the future; and if I am not much deceived, I am the same within that I am without. 'Tis one main obligation I have to my fortune, that the succession of my bodily estate has been carried on according to the natural seasons; I have seen the grass, the blossom, and the fruit; and now see the withering; happily, however, because naturally. I bear the infirmities I have the better, because they came not till I had reason to expect them, and because also they make me with greater pleasure remember that long felicity of my past life. My wisdom may have been just the same in both ages; but it was more active, and of better grace while young and sprightly, than now it is when broken, peevish and uneasy. I repudiate, then, these casual and painful reformations. God must touch our hearts; our consciences must amend of themselves, by the aid of our reason, and not by the decay of our appetites; pleasure is, in itself, neither pale nor discolored, to be discerned by dim and decayed eyes.

We ought to love temperance for itself, and because God has commanded that and chastity; but that which we are reduced to by catarrhs, and for which I am indebted to the stone,[20] is neither chastity nor temperance; a man cannot boast that he despises and resists pleasure, if he cannot see it, if he knows not what it is, and cannot discern its graces, its force, and most alluring beauties; I know both the one and the other, and may therefore the better say it. But, methinks, our souls, in old age, are subject to more troublesome maladies and imperfections than in youth; I said the same when young and when I was reproached with the want of a beard; and I say so now that my gray hairs give me some authority. We call the difficulty of our humors and the disrelish of present things wisdom; but, in truth, we do not so much forsake vices as we change them, and, in my opinion, for worse. Besides a foolish and feeble pride, an impertinent prating, froward and insociable humors, superstition, and a ridiculous desire of riches when we have lost the use of them, I find there more envy, injustice and malice. Age imprints more wrinkles in the mind than it does on the face; and souls are never, or very rarely seen, that in growing old do not smell sour and musty. Man moves all together, both toward his perfection and decay. In observing the wisdom of Socrates, and many circumstances of his condemnation, I should dare to believe, that he in some sort himself purposely, by collusion, contributed to it, seeing that, at the age of

---

[20] The *stone* is the chronic kidney stones from which Montaigne suffered. (See "Of Experience.")

seventy years, he might fear to suffer the lofty motions of his mind to be cramped, and his wonted luster obscured. What strange metamorphoses do I see age every day make in many of my acquaintance! 'Tis a potent malady, and that naturally and imperceptibly steals into us; a vast provision of study and great precaution are required to evade the imperfections it loads us with, or at least, to weaken their progress. I find that, notwithstanding all my entrenchments, it gets foot by foot upon me; I make the best resistance I can, but I do not know to what at last it will reduce me. But fall out what will. I am content the world may know, when I am fallen, from what I fell.

from OF EXPERIENCE

There is no desire more natural than that of knowledge. We try all ways that can lead us to it; where reason is wanting, we therein employ experience.

> "Per varios usus artem experientia fecit,
> Exemplo monstrante viam,"[1]

which is a means much more weak and cheap; but truth is no great thing, that we ought not to disdain any mediation that will guide us to it. Reason has so many forms, that we know not to which to take; experience has no fewer; the consequence we would draw from the comparison of events is unsure, by reason they are always unlike. There is no quality so universal in this image of things, as diversity and variety. Both the Greeks and the Latins, and we, for the most express example of similitude, employ that of eggs: and yet there have been men, particularly one at Delphos, who could distinguish marks of difference among eggs so well, that he never mistook one for another; and, having many hens, could tell which had laid it.[2] Dissimilitude intrudes itself of itself in our works; no art can arrive at perfect similitude: neither Perrozet,[3] nor any other cardmaker, can so carefully polish and blanch the backs of his cards, that some gamesters will not distinguish them by seeing them only shuffled by another. Resemblance does not so much make one, as difference makes another. Nature has obliged herself to make nothing other, that was not unlike. . . .

I had rather understand myself well in myself, than in Cicero.[4] Of the experience I have of myself, I find enough to make me wise, if I were but a good scholar: whoever will call to mind the excess of his past anger, and to what a degree that fever transported him, will see the deformity of this passion better than in Aristotle, and conceive a more just hatred against it; whoever will remember the ills he has undergone, those that have threatened him, and the light occasions that have removed him from one state to another, will by that prepare himself for future changes, and the knowl-

---

[1] "By various proofs, experience has made art, example showing the way" (Manilus).
[2] Cicero tells of this man in his *Academica*.   [3] A famous card shark.
[4] M. Tullius Cicero (106–43 B.C.) was a Roman orator, politician, and Stoic philosopher.

edge of his condition. The life of Caesar has no greater example for us than our own: though popular and of command, 'tis still a life subject to all human accidents. Let us but listen to it; we apply to ourselves all whereof we have principal need; whoever shall call to memory how many and many times he has been mistaken in his own judgment, is he not a great fool if he does not ever after suspect it? When I find myself convinced, by the reason of another, of a false opinion, I do not so much learn what he has said to me that is new, and the particular ignorance—that would be no great acquisition—as, in general, I learn my own debility and the treachery of my understanding, whence I extract the reformation of the whole mass. In all my other errors, I do the same, and find from this rule great utility to life; I regard not the species and individual, as a stone that I have stumbled at; I learn to suspect my steps throughout, and am careful to place them right. To learn that a man has said or done a foolish thing is nothing; a man must learn that he is nothing but a fool, a much more ample and important instruction. The false steps that my memory has so often made, even then when it was most secure and confident of itself, are not idly thrown away; it may now swear to me and assure me as much as it will, I shake my ears, and dare not trust it; the first opposition that is made to its testimony, puts me into suspense, and I dare not rely upon it in anything of moment, nor warrant it in another person's concerns: and were it not that what I do for want of memory, others do more often for want of good faith, I should always, in matter of fact, rather choose to take the truth from another's mouth, than from my own. If every one would pry into the effects and circumstances of the passions that sway him, as I have done into those which I am most subject to, he would see them coming, and would a little break their impetuosity and career; they do not always seize us on a sudden; there is threatening and degrees:

> "Fluctus uti primo cœpit cum albescere vento,
> Paulatim sese tollit mare, et altius undas
> Erigit, inde imo consurgit ad æthera fundo."[5]

. . . In fine, all this hodge-podge which I scribble here, is nothing but a register of the essays of my own life, which, for the internal soundness, is exemplary enough, to take instruction against the grain; but as to bodily health, no man can furnish out more profitable experience than I, who present it pure, and no way corrupted and changed by art or opinion. Experience is properly upon its own dunghill in the subject of physic, where reason wholly gives it place: Tiberius said that whoever had lived twenty years ought to be responsible to himself for all things that were hurtful or wholesome to him, and know how to order himself without physic;[6] and he might have learned it of Socrates, who, advising his disciples to be solicitous of their health as a chief study, added that it was hard if a man of sense, having a care to his exercise and diet, did not better know than any physician what was good or ill for him. And physic itself professes

---

[5] "As at the first breath of the winds, the sea begins to foam, and swells, thence higher swells, and higher raises the waves, until at length they seem to rise to the sky" (Virgil, *Aeneid*).

[6] Montaigne seems to be drawing here upon Suetonius' life of the Roman emperor Tiberius (42 B.C–37 A.D.).

always to have experience for the test of its operations; so Plato had reason to say that, to be a right physician, it would be necessary that he who would become such, should first himself have passed through all the diseases he pretends to cure, and through all the accidents and circumstances whereof he is to judge. 'Tis but reason they should get the pox, if they will know how to cure it; for my part, I should put myself into such hands; the others but guide us, like him who paints seas and rocks and ports sitting at table, and there makes the model of a ship sailing in all security; but put him to the work itself, he knows not at which end to begin. They make such a description of our maladies, as a town-crier does of a lost horse or dog—such a color, such a height, such an ear—but bring it to him, and he knows it not, for all that. If physic should one day give me some good and visible relief, then, truly, I will cry out in good earnest:

"Tandem efficaci do manus scientiæ."[7]

The arts that promise to keep our bodies and souls in health promise a great deal; but, withal, there are none that less keep their promise. And, in our time, those who make profession of these arts among us, less manifest the effects than any other sort of men; one may say of them, at the most, that they sell medicinal drugs; but that they are physicians, a man cannot say. I have lived long enough to be able to give an account of the custom that has carried me so far; for him who has a mind to try it, as his taster, I have made the experiment. Here are some of the articles, as my memory shall supply me with them; I have no custom that has not varied according to circumstances; but I only record those that I have been best acquainted with, and that hitherto have had the greatest possession of me.

My form of life is the same in sickness as in health; the same bed, the same hours, the same meat, and even the same drink, serve me in both conditions alike; I add nothing to them but the moderation of more or less, according to my strength and appetite. My health is, to maintain my wonted state without disturbance. I see that sickness puts me off it on one side, and if I will be ruled by the physicians, they will put me off on the other; so that by fortune and by art I am out of my way. I believe nothing more certainly than this, that I cannot be hurt by the use of things to which I have been so long accustomed. 'Tis for custom to give a form to a man's life, such as it pleases him; she is all in all in that: 'tis the beverage of Circe,[8] that varies our nature as she best pleases. How many nations, and but three steps from us, think the fear of the night-dew, that so manifestly is hurtful to us, a ridiculous fancy; and our own watermen and peasants laugh at it. You make a German sick if you lay him upon a mattress, as you do an Italian if you lay him on a featherbed; and a Frenchman, if without curtains or fire. A Spanish stomach cannot hold out to eat as we can; nor ours to drink like the Swiss. A German made me very merry at Augsburg, by finding fault with our hearths, by the same arguments which we commonly make use of in decrying their stoves: for, to say the truth, the smothered heat, and then the smell of that heated matter of which the fire is com-

----

[7] "Show me an efficacious science, and I will take it by the hand" (Horace).
[8] The enchantress who, in Homer's *Odyssey*, Book X, changed Odysseus' men into swine.

posed, very much offend such as are not used to them; not me; and, indeed, the heat being always equal, constant and universal, without flame, without smoke, and without the wind that comes down our chimney, they may many ways sustain comparison with ours. Why do we not imitate the Roman architecture? for they say that anciently fires were not made in the houses, but on the outside, and at the foot of them, whence the heat was conveyed to the whole fabric by pipes contrived in the wall, which were drawn twining about the rooms that were to be warmed: which I have seen plainly described somewhere in Seneca. This German hearing me commend the conveniences and beauties of this city, which truly deserves it, began to compassionate me that I had to leave it; and the first inconvenience he alleged to me was, the heaviness of head that the chimneys elsewhere would bring upon me. He had heard some one make this complaint, and fixed it upon us, being by custom deprived of the means of perceiving it at home. All heat that comes from the fire weakens and dulls me; and yet Evenus[9] said, that fire was the best condiment of life: I rather choose any other way of making myself warm.

We are afraid to drink our wines, when toward the bottom of the cask; in Portugal those fumes are reputed delicious, and it is the beverage of princes. In short, every nation has many customs and usages that are not only unknown to other nations, but savage and miraculous in their sight. What should we do with those people who admit of no evidence that is not in print, who believe not men if they are not in a book, nor truth, if it be not of competent age? we dignify our fopperies, when we commit them to the press: 'tis of a great deal more weight to say, "I have read such a thing," than if you only say, "I have heard such a thing." But I, who no more disbelieve a man's mouth than his pen, and who know that men write as indiscreetly as they speak, and who look upon this age as one that is past, as soon quote a friend as Aulus Gellius or Macrobius;[10] and what I have seen, as what they have written. And, as 'tis held of virtue, that it is not greater for having continued longer, so do I hold of the truth, that for being older it is none the wiser. I often say that it is mere folly that makes us run after foreign and scholastic examples; their fertility is the same now that it was in the time of Homer and Plato. But is it not that we seek more honor from the quotation, than from the truth of the matter in hand? As if it were more to the purpose, to borrow our proofs from the shops of Vascosan or Plantin,[11] than from what is to be seen in our own village; or else, indeed, that we have not the wit to cull out and make useful what we see before us, and to judge of it clearly enough to draw it into example; for if we say that we want authority to give faith to our testimony, we speak from the purpose; forasmuch as, in my opinion, of the most ordinary, common, and known things, could we but find out their light, the greatest miracles of nature might be formed, and the most wonderful example, especially upon the subject of human actions.

[9] Evenus (c. 50 B.C.–c. 50 A.D.) was a Greek epigrammist.

[10] Aulus Gellius (second century A.D.) was a Latin grammarian. Macrobius (fl. c. 400 A.D.) was a Latin writer and philosopher, source of many quotations, since his seven-volume *Saturnalia* contained many quotations from earlier writers.

[11] Michel de Vascosan (d. 1576) was a French printer. Christopher Plantin (1514–1589) was a prominent printer of Antwerp.

Now, upon this subject, setting aside the examples I have gathered from books, and what Aristotle says of Andron the Argian, that he traveled over the arid sands of Lybia without drinking: a gentleman, who has very well behaved himself in several employments, said, in a place where I was, that he had ridden from Madrid to Lisbon, in the heat of summer, without any drink at all. He is very healthful and vigorous for his age, and has nothing extraordinary in the use of his life, but this, to live sometimes two or three months, nay, a whole year, as he has told me, without drinking. He is sometimes thirsty, but he lets it pass over, and he holds that it is an appetite which easily goes off of itself; and he drinks more out of caprice than either for need or pleasure.

Here is another example: 'tis not long ago that I found one of the learnedest men in France, and a man of considerable fortune, studying in a corner of a hall that they had separated for him with tapestry, and about him a rabble of his servants making all sorts of noise and confusion. He told me, and Seneca[12] almost says the same of himself, he made an advantage of this uproar; that, beaten with this rattle, he so much the more collected and retired himself into himself for contemplation, and that this tempest of voices repercussed his thoughts within himself; when a student at Padua, he had his study so long situated amid the rattle of coaches and the tumult of the square, that he not only formed himself to the contempt, but even to the use of noise, for the service of his studies. Socrates answered Alcibiades, who was astonished how he could endure the perpetual scolding of his wife, "Why," said he, "as those do who are accustomed to the ordinary noise of wheels drawing water." I am quite otherwise; I have a tender head and easily discomposed; when 'tis bent upon anything, the least buzzing of a fly tears it into pieces.

Seneca in his youth having, by the example of Sextius, put on a positive resolution of eating nothing that had had life,[13] and for a whole year dispensed with animal food, and, as he said, with pleasure: only left off, that he might not be suspected of taking up this rule from some new religion by which it was prescribed: he adopted, in like manner, from the precepts of Attalus a custom not to lie upon any sort of bedding that gave way under his weight,[14] and, even to his old age, made use of such as would not yield to any pressure. What the usage of his time made him account roughness, that of ours makes us look upon as effeminacy.

Do but observe the difference between the way of living of my laborers and my own; the Scythians[15] and Indians have nothing more remote both from my capacity and my manners. I have picked up boys from begging, to serve me: who soon after have quitted both my kitchen and livery, only that they might return to their former course of life; and I found one afterward, picking mussels out of the sewer for his dinner, whom I could neither by entreaties nor threats reclaim from the sweetness he found in indigence. Beggars have their magnificences and delights, as well as the

[12] Roman statesman, dramatist, and Stoic philosopher (c. 3 B.C.–65 A.D.).

[13] Seneca describes his vegetarianism in his *Epistles*.

[14] Attalus was a Stoic philosopher of the first century A.D.

[15] A nomadic and warlike people who lived in an area on the north shore of the Black Sea. They traded with the ancient Greeks, who regarded their name as synonymous with barbarism.

rich, and, 'tis said, their dignities and polities. These are effects of custom;
she can mold us, not only into what form she pleases (the sages say we
ought to apply ourselves to the best, which she will soon make easy to us),
but also to change and variation, which is the most noble and most useful
instruction of all she teaches us. The best of my bodily conditions is that I
am flexible and not very obstinate: I have inclinations more my own and
ordinary, and more agreeable than others; but I am diverted from them
with very little ado, and easily slip into a contrary course. A young man
ought to cross his own rules, to awaken his vigor and to keep it from growing faint and rusty; and there is no course of life so weak and sottish, as that
which is carried on by rule and discipline;

> "Ad primum lapidem vectari quum placet, hora
> Sumitur ex libro; si prurit frictus ocelli
> Angulus, inspecta genesi, collyria quærit;" [16]

he shall often throw himself even into excesses, if he will take my advice;
otherwise the least debauch will destroy him, and render him troublesome
and disagreeable in company. The worst quality in a well-bred man is over-
fastidiousness, and an obligation to a certain particular way; and it is particular, if not pliable and supple. It is a kind of reproach, not to be able, or not
to dare, to do what we see those about us do; let such as these stop at home.
It is in every man unbecoming, but in a soldier vicious and intolerable;
who, as Philopoemen said, ought to accustom himself to every variety and
inequality of life.[17]

Though I have been brought up, as much as was possible, to liberty and
independence, yet so it is that, growing old, and having by indifference
more settled upon certain forms (my age is now past instruction, and has
henceforward nothing to do but to keep itself up as well as it can), custom
has already, ere I was aware, so imprinted its character in me, in certain
things, that I look upon it as a kind of excess to leave them off; and, without
a force upon myself, cannot sleep in the day-time, nor eat between meals,
nor breakfast, nor go to bed, without a great interval between eating and
sleeping, as of three hours after supper; nor get children but before I
sleep, nor standing upon my feet; nor endure my own sweat; nor quench
my thirst either with pure water or pure wine; nor keep my head long bare,
nor cut my hair after dinner; and I should be as uneasy without my gloves
as without my shirt, or without washing when I rise from table or out of my
bed; and I could not lie without a canopy and curtains, as if they were
essential things. I could dine without a tablecoth, but without a clean napkin, after the German fashion, very incommodiously; I foul them more
than the Germans or Italians do, and make but little use either of spoon or
fork. I am sorry they did not keep up the fashion, begun after the example
of kings, to change our napkins at every service, as they do our plates. We
are told of that laborious soldier Marius, that growing old, he became nice
in his drink, and never drank but out of a particular cup of his own:[18] I, in

---

[16] "If he would be carried but a mile, he consults his almanac for the proper hour; if he but
rub the corner of his eye, he chooses the salve by his horoscope" (Juvenal).

[17] Philopoemen (252–183 B.C.) was a Greek general.

[18] Plutarch tells this story of the Roman general Marius.

like manner, have suffered myself to fancy a certain form of glasses, and not willingly to drink in common glasses, nor more than from a strange common hand: all metal offends me in comparison of a clear and transparent matter: let my eyes taste too, according to their capacity. I owe several other such niceties to custom. Nature has also, on the other side, helped me to some of hers; as not to be able to endure more than two full meals in one day, without overcharging my stomach, nor a total abstinence from one of those meals without filling myself with wind, drying up my mouth, and dulling my appetite; the finding great inconvenience from overmuch evening air; for of late years in night marches, which often happen to be all night long, after five or six hours my stomach begins to be queasy, with a violent pain in my head, so that I always vomit before the day can break. When the others go to breakfast, I go to sleep; and when I rise, I am as brisk and gay as before. I had always been told that the night dew never rises but in the beginning of the night; but for some years past, long and familiar intercourse with a lord, possessed with the opinion that the night dew is more sharp and dangerous about the declining of the sun, an hour or two before it sets, which he carefully avoids, and despises that of the night, he almost impressed upon me, not so much his reasoning as his experiences. What, shall mere doubt and inquiry strike our imagination, so as to change us? Such as absolutely and on a sudden give way to these propensions, draw total destruction upon themselves. I am sorry for several gentlemen who, through the folly of their physicians have in their youth and health wholly shut themselves up; it were better to endure a cough, than, by disuse, forever to lose the commerce of common life in things of so great utility. Malignant science to interdict us the most pleasant hours of the day! Let us keep our possession to the last; for the most part, a man hardens himself by being obstinate and corrects his constitution, as Caesar did the falling-sickness,[19] by dint of contempt. A man should addict himself to the best rules, but not enslave himself to them, except to such, if there be any such, where obligation and servitude are of profit.

Both kings and philosophers go to stool, and ladies too; public lives are bound to ceremony; mine, that is obscure and private, enjoys all natural dispensation; soldier and Gascon[20] are also qualities a little subject to indiscretion; wherefore I shall say of this act of relieving nature, that it is desirable to refer it to certain prescribed and nocturnal hours, and compel one's self to this by custom, as I have done; but not to subject one's self, as I have done in my declining years, to a particular convenience of place and seat for that purpose, and make it troublesome by long sitting: and yet, in the fouler offices, is it not in some measure excusable to require more care and cleanliness? *"Natura homo mundum et elegans animal est."*[21] Of all the actions of nature, I am the most impatient of being interrupted in that. I have seen many soldiers troubled with the unruliness of their bellies; whereas mine and I never fail of our punctual assignation, which is at leaping out of bed, if some indispensable business or sickness does not molest us.

I think then, as I said before, that sick men cannot better place them-

---

[19] Julius Caesar suffered from epilepsy (the "falling-sickness").
[20] Inhabitant of Gascony, in southwest France, thus a rustic with rather rough manners.
[21] "Man is by nature a clean and delicate creature" (Seneca).

selves anywhere in more safety, than in sitting still in that course of life wherein they have been bred and trained up; change, be it what it will, distempers and puts one out. Do you believe that chestnuts can hurt a Perigourdin or a Lucchese,[22] or milk and cheese the mountain people? We enjoin them not only a new, but a contrary, method of life; a change that the healthful cannot endure. Prescribe water to a Breton of three score and ten; shut a seaman up in a stove; forbid a Basque footman to walk: you will deprive them of motion, and in the end of air and light.[23]

> "An vivere tanti est?
> Cogimur a suetis animum suspendere rebus,
> Atque, ut vivamus, vivere desinimus. . . .
> Hos superesse reor, quibus et spirabilis aer
> Et lux, qua regimur, redditur ipsa gravis."[24]

If they do no other good, they do this at least, that they prepare patients betimes for death, by little and little undermining and cutting off the use of life.

Both well and sick, I have ever willingly suffered myself to obey the appetites that pressed upon me. I give great authority to my propensions and desires; I do not love to cure one disease by another; I hate remedies that are more troublesome than the disease itself. To be subject to the stone and subject to abstain from eating oysters, are two evils instead of one: the disease torments us on the one side, and the remedy on the other. Since we are ever in danger of mistaking, let us rather run the hazard of a mistake, after we have had the pleasure. The world proceeds quite the other way, and thinks nothing profitable that is not painful; it has great suspicion of facility. My appetite, in various things, has of its own accord happily enough accommodated itself to the health of my stomach. Relish and pungency in sauces were pleasant to me when young but my stomach disliking them since, my taste incontinently followed. Wine is hurtful to sick people, and 'tis the first thing that my mouth then finds distasteful, and with an invincible dislike. Whatever I take against my liking, does me harm; and nothing hurts me, that I eat with appetite and delight. I never received harm by any action that was very pleasant to me; and accordingly have made all medicinal conclusions largely give way to my pleasure; and I have, when I was young,

> "Quem circumcursans huc atque huc sæpe Cupido
> Fulgebat crocina splendidus in tunica,"[25]

[22] Natives of Périgord, a region in southwestern France, and of Lucca, a city in Tuscany, respectively.

[23] A Breton is a native of Brittany, in northwestern France. A Basque is a native of the western Pyrenees region in France and Spain.

[24] "Is life worth so much? They make us deprive ourselves of things to which we are accustomed; and, that we may live, we must cease to live. . . . I cannot conceive that they still live, to whom light and air, by which they live, are forbidden" (Pseudo-Gallus).

[25] "'When Cupid fluttering round me here and there shone in his rich purple mantle" (Catullus).

given myself the rein as licentiously and inconsiderately to the desire that was predominant in me, *"Et militavi non sine gloria,"*[26] as any other whomsoever; yet more in continuation and holding out, than in sally:

> "Sex me vix memini sustinuisse vices."[27]

'Tis certainly a misfortune and a miracle at once, to confess at what a tender age I first came under the subjection of love: it was indeed, by chance; for it was long before the years of choice or knowledge; I do not remember myself so far back; and my fortune may well be coupled with that of Quartilla,[28] who could not remember when she was a maid:

> "Inde tragus, celeresque pili, mirandaque matri
> Barba meæ."[29]

Physicians modify their rules according to the violent longings that happen to sick persons, ordinarily with good success; this great desire cannot be imagined so strange and vicious, but that nature must have a hand in it. And then how easy a thing is it to satisfy the fancy? In my opinion, this part wholly carries it, at least, above all the rest. The most grievous and ordinary evils are those that fancy loads us with; this Spanish saying mightily pleases in several senses; *"Defienda me Dios de my."*[30] I am sorry when I am sick, that I have not some longing that might give me the pleasure of satisfying it; all the rules of physic would hardly be able to divert me from it. I do the same when I am well; I can see very little more to be hoped or wished for. 'Twere pity a man should be so weak and languishing, as not to have even wishing left to him.

The art of physic is not so fixed, that we need be without authority for whatever we do; it changes according to climates and moons; according to Fernel and to Scaliger.[31] If your physician does not think it good for you to sleep, to drink wine, or to eat such and such meats, never trouble yourself; I will find you another that shall not be of his opinion; the diversity of medical arguments and opinions embraces all sorts of forms. I saw a miserable sick person panting and burning for thirst, that he might be cured, who was afterward laughed at for his pains by another physician, who condemned that advice as prejudicial to him: had he not tormented himself to good purpose? There lately died of the stone, a man of that profession, who had made use of extreme abstinence to contend with his disease: his fellow-physicians say that, on the contrary, this abstinence had dried him up, and baked the gravel in his kidneys.

I have observed, that both in wounds and sicknesses, speaking discomposes and hurts me, as much as any irregularity I can commit. My

---

[26]"And fought not ingloriously" (Horace).
[27]"I can scarcely remember six bouts in one night" (Ovid).
[28]Quartilla appears in Petronius' *Satyricon* (first century A.D.).
[29]"My precocious beard astonished my mother" (Martial).
[30]"God defend me from myself."
[31]Jean Fernel (1497–1558) was a famous French physician. Julius Caesar Scaliger (1484–1558) wrote commentaries on classic medical texts. Both were physicians to Henry II.

voice pains and tires me, for 'tis loud and forced; so that when I have gone to whisper some great persons about affairs of consequence, they have often desired me to moderate my voice.

This story deserves a place here. Someone in a certain Greek school speaking loud as I do, the master of the ceremonies sent to him to speak softly: "Tell him, then, he must send me," replied the other, "the tone he would have me speak in." To which the other replied, "That he should take the tone from the ears of him to whom he spake." It was well said, if to be understood: "Speak according to the affair you are speaking about to your auditor," for if it mean, "'tis sufficient that he hear you; or, govern yourself by him," I do not find it to be reason. The tone and motion of my voice carries with it a great deal of the expression and signification of my meaning, and 'tis I who am to govern it, to make myself understood: there is a voice to instruct, a voice to flatter, and a voice to reprehend. I will not only that my voice reach him, but, peradventure, that it strike and pierce him. When I rattle my footman with sharp and bitter language, it would be very pretty for him to say, "Pray, master, speak lower, I hear you very well." *"Est quædam vox ad auditum accommodata, non magnitudine, sed proprietate."* [32] Speaking is half his who speaks, and half his who hears; the latter ought to prepare himself to receive it, according to its bias; as with tennis players, he who receives the ball, shifts and prepares, according as he sees him move who strikes the stroke, and according to the stroke itself.

Experience has, moreover, taught me this, that we ruin ourselves by impatience. Evils have their life and limits, their diseases and their recovery.

The constitution of maladies is formed by the pattern of the constitution of animals; they have their fortune and their days limited from their birth; he who attempts imperiously to cut them short by force in the middle of their course, lengthens and multiplies them, and incenses instead of appeasing them. I am of Crantor's opinion, that "we are neither obstinately and willfully to oppose evils, nor truckle under them for want of courage; but that we are naturally to give way to them, according to their condition and our own." [33] We ought to grant free passage to diseases; I find they stay less with me, who let them alone; and I have lost some, reputed the most tenacious and obstinate, by their own decay, without help and without art, and contrary to its rules. Let us a little permit Nature to take her own way; she better understands her own affairs than we. "But such an one died;" and so shall you: if not of that disease, of another. And how many have not escaped dying, who have had three physicians always at their tails? Example is a vague and universal mirror, and of various reflections. If it be a delicious medicine, take it: 'tis always so much present good. I will never stick at the name nor the color, if it be pleasant and grateful to the palate: pleasure is one of the chiefest kinds of profit. I have suffered colds, gouty defluxions, relaxations, palpitations of the heart, meagrims, and other accidents, to grow old and die in time a natural death; [34] I have so lost them when I was half fit to keep them: they are sooner prevailed upon by cour-

---

[32] "There is a certain voice accommodated to the hearing, not by its loudness, but by its propriety" (Quintilian).

[33] Crantor was a Greek philosopher who lived about 300 B.C.

[34] *Defluxions* are discharges; *meagrims* are migraine headaches.

tesy than huffing. We must patiently suffer the laws of our condition; we are born to grow old, to grow weak, and to be sick, in despite of all medicine. 'Tis the first lesson the Mexicans teach their children; so soon as ever they are born they thus salute them: "Thou art come into the world, child, to endure: endure, suffer and say nothing." 'Tis injustice to lament that which has befallen any one, which may befall every one: *"Indignare, si quid in te inique proprie constitutum est."*[35]

See an old man who begs of God that he will maintain his health vigorous and entire; that is to say, that he restore him to youth:

> *"Stulte, quid hæc frustra votis puerilibus optas?"*[36]

is it not folly? his condition is not capable of it. The gout, the stone, and indigestion are symptoms of long years; as heat, rains, and winds are of long journeys. Plato does not believe that Aesculapius troubled himself to provide, by regimen to prolong life in a weak and wasted body, useless to his country and to his profession, or to beget healthful and robust children;[37] and does not think this care suitable to the divine justice and prudence, which is to direct all things to utility. My good friend, your business is done; nobody can restore you; they can, at the most, but patch you up, and prop you a little, and by that means prolong your misery an hour or two:

> "Non secus instantem cupiens fulcire ruinam,
>   Diversis contra nititur obiicibus;
> Donec certa dies, omni campage soluta,
>   Ipsum cum rebus subruat auxilium."[38]

We must learn to suffer what we cannot evade; our life, like the harmony of the world, is composed of contrary things—of diverse tones, sweet and harsh, sharp and flat, sprightly and solemn: the musician who should only effect some of these, what would he be able to do? he must know how to make use of them all, and to mix them; and so we should mingle the goods and evils which are consubstantial with our life; our being cannot subsist without this mixture, and the one part is no less necessary to it than the other. To attempt to kick against natural necessity, is to represent the folly of Ctesiphon who undertook to kick with his mule.[39]

I consult little about the alterations I feel; for these doctors take advantage; when they have you at their mercy, they cudgel your ears with their prognostics; and having once surprised me, weakened with sickness, injuriously handled me with their dogmas and magisterial fopperies—one while menacing me with great pains, and another with approaching death—by which threats I was indeed moved and shaken, but not subdued

---

[35] "Then be angry, when there is anything unjustly decreed against thee alone" (Seneca).
[36] "Why, you blockhead, pray such childish prayers in vain?" (Ovid).
[37] Aesculapius was the Greek god of healing.
[38] "Like one who, desiring to stay in impending ruin, places various props against it until, in a short time, the house, the props, and all, giving way, fall together" (Pseudo-Gallus).
[39] This story appears in Plutarch's *Of Anger*.

nor jostled from my place; and though my judgment was neither altered nor distracted, yet it was at least disturbed; 'tis always agitation and combat.

Now, I use my imagination as gently as I can, and would discharge it, if I could, of all trouble and contest; a man must assist, flatter, and deceive it, if he can; my mind is fit for that office; it needs no appearances throughout; could it persuade as it preaches, it would successfully relieve me. Will you have an example? It tells me: "that 'tis for my good to have the stone; that the structure of my age must naturally suffer some decay, and it is now time it should begin to disjoin and to confess a breach; 'tis a common necessity, and there is nothing in it either miraculous or new; I therein pay what is due to old age, and I cannot expect a better bargain; that society ought to comfort me, being fallen into the most common infirmity of my age; I see everywhere men tormented with the same disease, and am honored by the fellowship, forasmuch as men of the best quality are most frequently afflicted with it; 'tis a noble and dignified disease; that of such as are struck with it, few have it to a less degree of pain; that these are put to the trouble of a strict diet and the daily taking of nauseous potions, whereas I owe my better state purely to my good fortune; for some ordinary broths of eringo or burst-wort[40] that I have twice or thrice taken to oblige the ladies who, with greater kindness than my pain was sharp, would needs present me half of theirs, seemed to me equally easy to take and fruitless in operation, the others have to pay a thousand vows to Aesculapius, and as many crowns to their physicians, for the voiding a little gravel, which I often do by the aid of nature; even the decorum of my countenance is not disturbed in company; and I can hold my water ten hours, and as long as any man that is in perfect health. The fear of this disease," says mind, "formerly affrighted thee, when it was unknown to thee; the cries and despairing groans of those who make it worse by their impatience, begot a horror in thee. 'Tis an infirmity that punishes the members by which thou hast most offended. Thou art a conscientious fellow:"

Que venit indigne pœna, dolenda venit."[41]

"consider this chastisement; 'tis very easy in comparison of others, and inflicted with a paternal tenderness; do but observe how late it comes; it only seizes on and incommodes that part of thy life, which is, one way and another, sterile and lost; having, as it were by composition, given time for the license and pleasures of thy youth. The fear and the compassion that the people have of this disease serve thee for matter of glory; a quality, whereof if thou hast thy judgment purified, and that thy reason has somewhat cured it, thy friends, notwithstanding, discern some tincture in thy complexion. 'Tis a pleasure to hear it said of one's self: what strength of mind, what patience! Thou art seen to sweat with pain, to turn pale and red, to tremble, to vomit blood, to suffer strange contractions and convulsions, at times to let great tears drop from thine eyes, to urine thick, black, and dreadful water, or to have it suppressed by some sharp and craggy stone, that cruelly pricks and tears the neck of the bladder, while all the

---

[40] Both medicinal herbs.
[41] "We are entitled to complain of a punishment that we have not deserved" (Ovid).

while thou entertainest the company with an ordinary countenance; drolling by fits with thy people; making one in a continuous discourse, now and then making excuse for thy pain, and representing thy suffering less than it is. Dost thou call to mind the men of past time, who so greedily sought diseases to keep their virtue in breath and exercise? Put the case that nature sets thee on and impels thee to this glorious school, into which thou wouldst never have entered of thy own free will. If thou tellest me that it is a dangerous and mortal disease, what others are not so? for 'tis a physical cheat to except any that they say do not go direct to death; what matters if they go thither by accident, or if they easily slide and slip into the path that leads us to it? But thou dost not die because thou art sick; thou diest because thou art living; death kills thee without the help of sickness; and sickness has deferred death in some, who have lived longer by reason that they thought themselves always dying; to which may be added, that as in wounds, so in diseases, some are medicinal and wholesome. The stone is often no less long-lived than you; we see men with whom it has continued from their infancy even to their extreme old age; and if they had not broken company, it would have been with them longer still; you more often kill it than it kills you. And though it should present to you the image of approaching death, were it not a good office to a man of such an age, to put him in mind of his end? And, which is worse, thou hast no longer anything that should make thee desire to be cured. Whether or no, common necessity will soon call thee away. Do but consider how skillfully and gently she puts thee out of concern with life, and weans thee from the world; not forcing thee with a tyrannical subjection, like so many other infirmities which thou seest old men afflicted withal, that hold them in continual torment, and keep them in perpetual and unintermitted weakness and pains, but by warnings and instructions at intervals, intermixing long pauses of repose, as it were to give thee opportunity to meditate and ruminate upon thy lesson, at thy own ease and leisure. To give thee means to judge aright, and to assume the resolution of a man of courage, it presents to thee the state of thy entire condition, both in good and evil; and one while a very cheerful and another an insupportable life, in one and the same day. If thou embracest not death, at least thou shakest hands with it once a month; whence thou hast more cause to hope that it will one day surprise thee without menace; and that being so often conducted to the water side, but still thinking thyself to be upon the accustomed terms, thou and thy confidence will at one time or another be unexpectedly wafted over. A man cannot reasonably complain of diseases that fairly divide the time with health."

I am obliged to fortune for having so often assaulted me with the same sort of weapons; she forms and fashions me by use, hardens and habituates me, so that I can know within a little for how much I shall be quit. For want of natural memory, I make one of paper; and as any new symptom happens in my disease, I set it down, whence it falls out that, having now almost passed through all sorts of examples, if anything astounding threatens me, turning over these little loose notes, as the Sibyl's leaves,[42] I never fail of

[42] The most famous of several sibyls, or prophetesses, in classical mythology was the Cumaean Sibyl, who possessed the Sibylline Books, prophecies about Rome's destiny.

finding matter of consolation from some favorable prognostic in my past experience. Custom also makes me hope better for the time to come; for, the conduct of this clearing out having so long continued, 'tis to be believed that nature will not alter her course, and that no other worse accident will happen than what I already feel. And besides, the condition of this disease is not unsuitable to my prompt and sudden complexion; when it assaults me gently, I am afraid, for 'tis then for a great while; but it has, naturally, brisk and vigorous excesses; it claws me to purpose for a day or two. My kidneys held out an age without alteration; and I have now almost lived another, since they changed their state; evils have their periods, as well as goods; peradventure, the infirmity draws toward an end. Age weakens the heat of my stomach, and its digestion being less perfect sends this crude matter to my kidneys; why, at a certain revolution, may not the heat of my kidneys be also abated, so that they can no more petrify my phlegm, and nature find out some other way of purgation. Years have evidently helped me to drain certain rheums; and why not these excrements which furnish matter for gravel? But is there anything delightful in comparison of this sudden change, when from an excessive pain, I come, by the voiding of a stone, to recover, as by a flash of lightning, the beautiful light of health, so free and full, as it happens in our sudden and sharpest colics? Is there anything in the pain suffered, that one can counterpoise to the pleasure of so sudden an amendment? Oh, how much does health seem the more pleasant to me, after a sickness so near and so contiguous, that I can distinguish them in the presence of one another, in their greatest show; when they appear in emulation, as if to make head against and dispute it with one another! As the Stoics say that vices are profitably introduced to give value to and to set off virtue, we can, with better reason and less temerity of conjecture, say that nature has given us pain for the honor and service of pleasure and indolence. When Socrates, after his fetters were knocked off, felt the pleasure of that itching which the weight of them had caused in his legs, he rejoiced to consider the strict alliance between pain and pleasure; how they are linked together by a necessary connection, so that by turns they follow and mutually beget one another; and cried out to the good fellow Aesop, that he ought out of this consideration, to have taken matter for a fine fable.

The worst that I see in other diseases is, that they are not so grievous in their effect, as they are in their issue: a man is a whole year in recovering, and all the while full of weakness and fear. There is so much hazard, and so many steps to arrive at safety, that there is no end on't: before they have unmuffled you of a kerchief, and then of a cap, before they allow you to walk abroad and take the air, to drink wine, to lie with your wife, or eat melons, 'tis odds you relapse into some new distemper. The stone has this privilege, that it carries itself clean off: whereas the other maladies always leave behind them some impression and alteration that render the body subject to a new disease, and lend a hand to one another. Those are excusable that content themselves with possessing us, without extending farther, and introducing their followers; but courteous and kind are those whose passage brings us any profitable issue. Since I have been troubled with the stone, I find myself freed from all other accidents, much more, methinks, than I was before, and have never had any fever since; I argue that the extreme and frequent vomitings that I am subject to, purge me: and, on the other hand, my distastes for this and that, and the strange fasts I am forced to keep, digest my peccant humors,[43] and nature, with those stones, voids whatever there is in me superfluous and hurtful. Let them never tell me that it is a medicine too dear bought: for what avail so many stinking draughts, so many caustics, incisions, sweats, setons, diets, and so many other methods of cure,[44] which often, by reason we are not able to undergo their violence and importunity, bring us to our graves? So that when I have the stone, I look upon it as physic; when free from it, as an absolute deliverance.

And here is another particular benefit of my disease; which is, that it always plays its game by itself, and lets me play mine, if I have only courage to do it; for, in its greatest fury, I have endured it ten hours together on horseback. Do but endure only; you need no other regimen: play, run, dine, do this and t'other, if you can; your debauch will do you more good than harm; say as much to one that has the pox, the gout, or hernia. The other diseases have more universal obligations; rack our actions after another kind of manner, disturb our whole order, and to their consideration engage the whole state of life: this only pinches the skin; it leaves the understanding and the will wholly at our own disposal, and the tongue, the hands, and the feet; it rather awakens than stupefies you. The soul is struck with the ardor of a fever, overwhelmed with an epilepsy, and displaced by a sharp megrim, and, in short, astounded by all the diseases that hurt the whole mass, and the most noble parts; this never meddles with the soul; if anything goes amiss with her, 'tis her own fault, she betrays, dismounts, and abandons herself. There are none but fools who suffer themselves to be persuaded, that this hard and massive body which is baked in our kidneys is to be dissolved by drinks; wherefore, when it is once stirred, there is nothing to be done but to give it passage; and, for that matter, it will itself make one.

I moreover observe this particular convenience in it, that it is a disease wherein we have little to guess at: we are dispensed from the trouble into which other diseases throw us by the uncertainty of their causes, conditions, and progress; a trouble that is infinitely painful: we have no need of consultations and doctoral interpretations; the senses well enough inform us both what it is and where it is.

By such like arguments, weak and strong, as Cicero with the disease of his old age, I try to rock asleep and amuse my imagination, and to dress its wounds. If I find them worse to-morrow, I will provide new stratagems. That this is true: I am come to that pass of late, that the least motion forces pure blood out of my kidneys: what of that? I move about, nevertheless, as before, and ride after my hounds with a juvenile and insolent ardor; and hold that I have very good satisfaction for an accident of that importance, when it costs me no more but a dull heaviness and uneasiness in that part; 'tis some great stone that wastes and consumes the substance of my kidneys

---

[43] Montaigne here refers to the theory of "humors," bodily fluids which were thought to determine one's health and temperament. A "peccant humor" is a morbid or unwholesome fluid.

[44] A *caustic* is a cautery or heat treatment; a *seton* is anything inserted under the skin to keep open a passage.

and my life, which I by little and little evacuate, not without some natural pleasure, as an excrement henceforward superfluous and troublesome. Now if I feel anything stirring, do not fancy that I trouble myself to consult my pulse or my urine, thereby to put myself upon some annoying prevention; I shall soon enough feel the pain, without making it more and longer, by the disease of fear. He who fears he shall suffer, already suffers what he fears. To which may be added, that the doubts and ignorance of those who take upon them to expound the designs of nature and her internal progressions, and the many false prognostics of their art, ought to give us to understand that her ways are inscrutable and utterly unknown; there is great uncertainty, variety, and obscurity in what she either promises or threatens. Old age excepted, which is an indubitable sign of the approach of death, in all other accidents I see few signs of the future, whereon we may ground our divination. I only judge of myself by actual sensation, not by reasoning: to what end, since I am resolved to bring nothing to it but expectation and patience? Will you know how much I get by this? observe those who do otherwise, and who rely upon so many diverse persuasions and counsels; how often the imagination presses upon them, without any bodily pain. I have many times amused myself, being well and in safety, and quite free from these dangerous attacks, in communicating them to the physicians as then beginning to discover themselves in me; I underwent the decree of their dreadful conclusions, being, all the while quite at my ease, and so much the more obliged to the favor of God, and better satisfied of the vanity of this art.

There is nothing that ought so much to be recommended to youth as activity and vigilance: our life is nothing but movement. I bestir myself with great difficulty, and am slow in everything, whether in rising, going to bed, or eating: seven of the clock in the morning is early for me; and where I rule, I never dine before eleven, nor sup till after six. I formerly attributed the cause of the fevers and other diseases I fell into, to the heaviness that long sleeping had brought upon me; and have ever repented going to sleep again in the morning. Plato is more angry at excess of sleeping, than at excess of drinking.[45] I love to lie hard and alone, even without my wife, as kings do; and well covered with clothes. They never warm my bed, but since I have grown old, they give me at need warm cloths to lay at my feet and stomach. They found fault with the great Scipio, that he was a great sleeper;[46] not, in my opinion, for any other reason, than that men were displeased, that he alone should have nothing in him to be found fault with. If I am anything fastidious in my way of living, 'tis rather in my lying than anything else; but, generally, I give way and accommodate myself, as well as any one, to necessity. Sleeping has taken up a great part of my life, and I yet continue, at the age I now am, to sleep eight or nine hours together. I wean myself to my advantage, from this propension to sloth, and am evidently the better for so doing. I find the change a little hard indeed, but in three days 'tis over; and I see but few who live with less sleep, when need requires, and who more constantly exercise themselves, or to

---

[45] Plato makes this point in the *Laws*.
[46] Scipio Africanus Minor (c. 185–129 B.C.) was a Roman general and consul. His reputation for sleeping perhaps stems from the fact that he is the dreamer in Cicero's *Dream of Scipio*.

whom long journeys are less troublesome. My body is capable of a firm, but not of a violent or sudden agitation. I evade of late violent exercises, and such as make me sweat, wherein my limbs grow weary before they are hot. I can stand a whole day together, and am never weary of walking: but from my youth, I have ever preferred to ride upon paved roads; on foot, I get up to the breech in dirt; and little fellows as I am are subject in the streets to be elbowed and jostled, for want of presence; I have ever loved to repose myself, whether sitting or lying, with my heels as high or higher than my seat.

There is no profession more pleasant than the military, a profession both noble in its execution (for valor is the stoutest, proudest, and most generous of all virtues), and noble in its cause: there is no utility either more universal or more just, than the protection of the peace and grandeur of one's country. The company of so many noble, young, and active men delights you: the ordinary sight of so many tragic spectacles; the freedom of the conversation, without art; a masculine and unceremonious way of living, please you; the variety of a thousand several actions; the encouraging harmony of martial music, that ravishes and inflames both your ears and souls; the honor of this occupation, nay, even its hardships and difficulties, which Plato holds so light that, in his Republic, he makes women and children share in them, are delightful to you. You put yourselves voluntarily upon particular exploits and hazards, according as you judge of their luster and importance; and, a volunteer, find even life itself excusably employed,

> "Pulchrumque mori succurrit in armis."[47]

To fear common dangers that concern so great a multitude of men; not to dare to do what so many sorts of souls, what a whole people dare, is for a heart that is poor and mean beyond all measure: company encourages even children. If others excel you in knowledge, in gracefulness, in strength, or fortune, you have third causes to blame for that; but to give place to them in stability of mind, you can blame no one for that but yourself. Death is more abject, more languishing and troublesome in bed than in battle; fevers and catarrhs as painful and mortal as a musket-shot. Whoever has fortified himself valiantly to bear the accidents of common life, need not raise his courage to be a soldier. *"Vivere, mi Lucili, militare est."*[48]

I do not remember that I ever had the itch; and yet scratching is one of nature's sweetest gratifications, and nearest at hand; but the smart follows too near. I use it most in my ears, which are often apt to itch.

I came into the world with all my senses entire, even to perfection. My stomach is commodiously good, as also is my head and my breath; and, for the most part, uphold themselves so in the height of fevers. I have passed the age to which some nations, not without reason, have prescribed so just a term of life, that they would not suffer men to exceed it; and yet I have some intermissions, though short and inconstant, so clean and sound as to be little inferior to the health and pleasantness of my youth. I do not speak

---

[47] "It is fine to die sword in hand" (Virgil, *Aeneid*).
[48] "To live, my Lucilius, is to make war" (Seneca).

of vigor and sprightliness; 'tis not reason they should follow me beyond their limits:

> "Non hoc amplius est liminis, aut aquæ,
> Cœlestis, patiens latus."[49]

My face and eyes presently discover my condition; all my alterations begin there, and appear somewhat worse than they really are; my friends often pity me, before I feel the cause in myself. My looking-glass does not frighten me: for even in my youth it has befallen me more than once to have a scurvy complexion and of ill prognostic, without any great consequence, so that the physicians, not finding any cause within answerable to that outward alteration, attributed it to the mind and to some secret passion that tormented me within; but they were deceived. If my body would govern itself as well, according to my rule, as my mind does, we should move a little more at our ease. My mind was then not only free from trouble, but, moreover, full of joy and satisfaction, as it commonly is, half by its complexion, half by its design:

> "Nec vitiant artus ægræ contagia mentis."[50]

I am of the opinion that this temperature of my soul has often raised my body from its lapses; this is often depressed; if the other be not brisk and gay, 'tis at least tranquil and at rest. I had a quartan ague[51] four or five months, that made me look miserably ill; my mind was always, if not calm, yet pleasant. If the pain be without me, the weakness and languor do not much afflict me; I see various corporal faintings, that beget a horror in me but to name, which yet I should less fear than a thousand passions and agitations of the mind that I see about me. I make up my mind no more to run; 'tis enough that I can crawl along; nor do I more complain of the natural decadence that I feel in myself:

> "Quis tumidum guttur miratur in Alpibus?"[52]

than I regret that my duration shall not be as long and entire as that of an oak.

I have no reason to complain of my imagination; I have had few thoughts in my life that have so much as broken my sleep, except those of desire, which have awakened without afflicting me. I dream but seldom, and then of chimeras[53] and fantastic things, commonly produced from pleasant thoughts, and rather ridiculous than sad; and I believe it to be true that dreams are faithful interpreters of our inclinations; but there is art required to sort and understand them:

[49] "I am no longer able to stand waiting at a door in the rain" (Horace).
[50] "The troubles of the body never affected my mind" (Ovid).
[51] A chronic fever which recurs every fourth day.
[52] "No man is surprised to see a goiter in the Alps" (Juvenal).
[53] Any horrible or unreal creatures of the imagination.

> "Res, quæ in vita usurpant homines, cogitant, curant, vident,
> Quæque agunt vigilantes, agitantque, ea si cui in somno accidunt,
> Minus mirandum est."[54]

Plato moreover says, that 'tis the office of prudence to draw instructions of divination of future things from dreams; I don't know about this, but there are wonderful instances of it that Socrates, Xenophon,[55] and Aristotle, men of irreproachable authority, relate. Historians say that the Atlantes never dream;[56] who also never eat any animal food, which I add, forasmuch as it is, peradventure, the reason why they never dream, for Pythagoras ordered a certain preparation of diet to beget appropriate dreams.[57] Mine are very gentle, without any agitation of body or expression of voice. I have seen several of my time wonderfully disturbed by them. Theon, the philosopher, walked in his sleep, and so did Pericles' servant, and that upon the tiles and top of the house.[58]

I hardly ever choose my dish at table, but take the next at hand, and unwillingly change it for another. A confusion of meats and a clutter of dishes displease me as much as any other confusion; I am easily satisfied with few dishes; and am an enemy to the opinion of Favorinus that in a feast they should snatch from you the meat you like, and set a plate of another sort before you;[59] and that 'tis a pitiful supper, if you do not sate your guests with the rumps of various fowls, the beccafico only deserving to be all eaten.[60] I usually eat salt meats, and yet I love bread that has no salt in it; and my baker never sends up other to my table, contrary to the custom of the country. In my infancy, what they had most to correct in me was the refusal of things that children commonly best love, as sugar, sweetmeats, and march-panes.[61] My tutor contended with this aversion to delicate things, as a kind of over-nicety; and indeed 'tis nothing else but a difficulty of taste, in anything it applies itself to. Whoever cures a child of an obstinate liking for brown bread, bacon, or garlic, cures him also of pampering his palate. There are some who affect temperance and plainness, by wishing for beef and ham among pheasant and partridge; 'tis all very fine; this is delicacy upon delicacies; 'tis the taste of effeminacy that disrelishes ordinary and accustomed things; "*Per quæ luxuria divitiarum tædio ludit.*"[62] Not to make good cheer with what another is enjoying, and to be curious in what a man eats, is the essence of the vice:

> "Si modica coenare times olus omne patella."[63]

---

[54] "It is no wonder that what men practice, think, care for, see and do when waking should also run in their heads and disturb them when they are asleep" (Attius, quoted by Cicero).

[55] Greek historian (430–357 B.C.).

[56] Atlantes are inhabitants of Atlantis. That they did not eat meat or dream is reported by Herodotus.

[57] Pythagoras' instructions for stimulating dreams are reported in Cicero, *Of Divination.*

[58] Theon was a Greek Stoic philosopher. Pericles was a fifth-century B.C. Athenian statesman. The story of his servant's sleepwalking is told by Diogenes Laertius.

[59] Favorinus was a Greek rhetorician (c. 125 A.D.). He actually attacked the sort of haste Montaigne says he favored.

[60] A beccafico is a small bird eaten as a delicacy, especially in Italy.

[61] Marzipan, an almond candy.

[62] "The caprices of luxury which would escape the tediousness of riches" (Seneca).

[63] "If you cannot be content with herbs in a small dish for supper" (Horace).

There is, indeed, this difference, that, 'tis better to oblige one's appetite to things that are most easy to be had, but 'tis always vice to oblige one's self: I formerly said a kinsman of mine was over-nice, who, by being in our galleys, had unlearned the use of beds and to undress when he went to sleep.

If I had any sons I should willingly wish them my fortune: the good father that God gave me, who has nothing of me but the acknowledgment of his goodness, but truly 'tis a very hearty one, sent me from my cradle to be brought up in a poor village of his, and there continued me all the while I was at nurse, and still longer, bringing me up to the meanest and the most common way of living: *"Magna pars libertatis est bene moratus venter."*[64] Never take upon yourselves, and much less give up to your wives, the care of their nourishment; leave this to fortune, under popular and natural laws; leave it to custom to train them up to frugality and hardship, that they may rather descend from rigors than mount up to them. This humor of his yet aimed at another end to make me familiar with the people and the condition of men who most need our assistance; considering that I should rather regard them who extend their arms to me, than those who turn their backs upon me; and for this reason it was, that he provided me godfathers of the meanest fortune, to oblige and attach me to them.

Nor has his design succeeded altogether ill: for, whether upon the account of the more honor in such a condescension, or out of a natural compassion that has a very great power over me, I have an inclination toward the meaner sort of people. The faction which I should condemn in our civil wars, I should more sharply condemn, flourishing and successful; it would half reconcile me to it, should I see it miserable and overwhelmed. How much do I admire the generous humor of Chelonis, daughter and wife to kings of Sparta! while her husband, Cleombrotus, in the commotion of her city, had the advantage over Leonidas, her father, she, like a good daughter, stuck close to her father in all his misery and exile, in opposition to the conqueror.[65] But so soon as the chance of war turned, she changed her will with the change of fortune, and bravely turned to her husband's side, whom she accompanied throughout where his ruin carried him; admitting, as it appears to me, no other choice than to cleave to the side that stood most in need of her, and where she could best manifest her compassion. I am naturally more apt to follow the example of Flaminius, who rather gave his assistance to those who had most need of him than to those who had power to do him good, than I do to that of Pyrrhus, who was of an humor to truckle under the great, and to domineer over the poor.[66]

Long sittings at meat both trouble me and do me harm; for, be it for want of moderation, or that I was so accustomed when a child, I eat all the while I sit. Therefore it is that at my own house, though the meals there are the shortest, I usually sit down a little while after the rest, after the manner of Augustus:[67] but I do not imitate him in rising also before the rest of the company; on the contrary, I love to sit still a long time after, and to hear them talk, provided I am none of the talkers; for I tire and hurt myself with

[64]"A well governed stomach is a great part of liberty" (Seneca).
[65]The story of Chelonis is told by Plutarch in his *Lives of Agis and Cleomenes.*
[66]Montaigne is still drawing upon Plutarch here, his *Life of Flaminius* and *Life of Pyrrhus.*
[67]Suetonius, *Life of Augustus.*

speaking upon a full stomach, as much as I find it pleasant and very whole-some to argue and to strain my voice before dinner.

The ancient Greeks and Romans had more reason than we in sitting apart for eating, which is a principal action of life, if they were not prevented by other extraordinary business, many hours and the greatest part of the night; eating and drinking more deliberately than we do, who perform all our actions post-haste; and in extending this natural pleasure to more leisure and better use, intermixing with their meals pleasant and profitable conversation.

They whose concern it is to have a care of me, may very easily hinder me from eating anything they think will do me harm; for in such matters I never covet nor miss anything I do not see; but withal, if it once comes in my sight, 'tis in vain to persuade me to forbear; so that when I design to fast, I must be kept apart from the supper-table, and must have only so much given me, as is required for a prescribed collation; for if I sit down to table, I forget my resolution. When I order my cook to alter the manner of dressing any dish, all my family know what it means, that my stomach is out of order, and that I shall not touch it.

I love to have all meats, that will endure it, very little boiled or roasted, and prefer them very high, and even, as to several, quite gone.[68] Nothing but hardness generally offends me (of any other quality I am as patient and indifferent as any man I have known); so that, contrary to the common humor, even in fish it often happens that I find them both too fresh and too firm: not for want of teeth, which I ever had good, even to excellence, and which age does but now begin to threaten: I have always been used every morning to rub them with a napkin, and before and after dinner. God is favorable to those whom he makes to die by degrees; 'tis the only benefit of old age; the last death will be so much the less painful; it will kill but a quarter of a man or but half a one at most. I have one tooth lately fallen out without drawing and without pain: it was the natural term of its duration; and that part of my being and several others, are already dead, others half dead, of those that were most active, and in highest esteem during my vigorous years; 'tis so I melt and steal away from myself. What a folly it would be in my understanding, to apprehend the height of this fall, already so much advanced, as if it were from the very top! I hope I shall not. I, in truth, receive a principal consolation in meditating my death, that it will be just and natural, and that henceforward I cannot herein either require or hope from destiny any other but unlawful favor. Men make themselves believe that we formerly had, as greater stature, so, longer lives, but they deceive themselves; and Solon, who was of those elder times, limits the duration of life to threescore and ten years.[69] I, who have so much and so universally adored that ἄριστον μέτρον of ancient times;[70] and who have concluded the most moderate measures to be the most perfect, shall I pretend to an immeasurable and prodigious old age? Whatever happens contrary to the course of nature, may be troublesome; but what comes according to her, should always be pleasant: *"Omnia, quæ secundum naturam fiunt,*

[68] Meat which is *high* or *gone* is aged or partially spoiled.
[69] Solon (638–550 B.C.) was an Athenian lawgiver. This comment is given by Herodotus.
[70] "The mean is the best," the classical doctrine of moderation or the "golden mean."

sunt habenda in bonis."[71] And so Plato likewise says, that the death which is occasioned by wounds and diseases is violent; but that which comes upon us, old age conducting us to it, is of all others the most easy, and in some sort delicious. *"Vitam adolescentibus vis aufert, senibus maturitas."*[72] Death mixes and confounds itself throughout with life; decay anticipates its hour, and shoulders itself even into the course of our advance. I have portraits of myself taken at five and twenty, and five and thirty years of age; I compare them with that lately drawn; how variously is it no longer me; how much more is my present image unlike the former, than unlike that I shall go out of the world with? It is too much to abuse nature, to make her trot so far that she must be forced to leave us, and abandon our conduct, our eyes, teeth, legs, and all the rest, to the mercy of a foreign and begged assistance, and to resign us into the hands of art, being weary of following us herself.

I am not very fond either of salads or fruits, except melons. My father hated all sorts of sauces; I love them all. Eating too much hurts me; but, as to the quality of what I eat, I do not yet certainly know that any sort of meat disagrees with my stomach; neither have I observed that either full moon or decrease, spring or autumn, have any influence upon me. We have in us notions that are inconstant and for which no reason can be given: for example, I found radishes first grateful to my stomach, since that nauseous, and now again grateful. In several other things, I find my stomach and appetite vary after the same manner; I have changed again and again from white wine to claret, from claret to white.

I am a great lover of fish, and consequently make my fasts feasts, and feasts fasts: and I believe what some people say, that it is more easy of digestion than flesh. As I make a conscience of eating flesh upon the fish-days, so does my taste make a conscience of mixing fish and flesh; the difference between them seems to me too remote.[73]

From my youth, I have sometimes kept out of the way at meals; either to sharpen my appetite against the next morning (for, as Epicurus fasted and made lean meals to accustom his pleasure to make shift without abundance,[74] I, on the contrary, do it to prepare my pleasure to make better and more cheerful use of abundance); or else I fasted to preserve my vigor for the service of some action of body or mind; for both the one and the other of these is cruelly dulled in me by repletion; and, above all things, I hate that foolish coupling of so healthful and sprightly a goddess with that little belching god, bloated with the fumes of his liquor;[75]—or to cure my sick stomach, or for want of fit company; for I say, as the same Epicurus did, that one is not so much to regard what he eats, as with whom; and I commend Chilo, that he would not engage himself to be at Periander's feast till he first was informed who were to be the other guests;[76] no dish is so

[71] "All things that are done according to nature are to be accounted good" (Cicero).

[72] "Young men are taken away by force, old men by maturity" (Cicero). The comment by Plato is from the *Timaeus.*

[73] Fish-days are Fridays, when Catholics abstained from meat. Montaigne is saying that it goes against his conscience to mix meat and fish, just as it does to eat meat on Fridays.

[74] Epicurus (340–272 B.C.) defined philosophy as the art of making life happy; he praised physical pleasure. This story is told by Seneca in his *Epistles.*

[75] That is, Montaigne does not approve of mixing sex (Venus) and liquor (Bacchus).

[76] Chilo (c. 556 B.C.) was one of the "Seven Sages." This story is told by Plutarch in his *Banquet of the Seven Sages.*

acceptable to me, nor no sauce so appetizing, as that which is extracted from society. I think it more wholesome to eat more leisurely and less, and to eat oftener; but I would have appetite and hunger attended to; I should take no pleasure to be fed with three or four pitiful and stinted repasts a day, after a medicinal manner; who will assure me, that, if I have a good appetite in the morning, I shall have the same at supper? But, we old fellows especially, let us take the first opportune time of eating, and leave to almanac makers hopes and prognostics. The utmost fruit of my health is pleasure; let us take hold of the present and known. I avoid the invariable in these laws of fasting; he who would have one form serve him, let him avoid the continuing it; we harden ourselves in it, our strength is there stupefied and laid asleep; six months after, you shall find your stomach so inured to it, that all you have got is the loss of your liberty of doing otherwise but to your prejudice.

I never keep my legs and thighs warmer in winter than in summer; one simple pair of silk stockings is all. I have suffered myself, for the relief of my colds, to keep my head warmer; and my belly on the account of my colic; my diseases in a few days habituated themselves thereto, and disdained my ordinary provisions; we soon get from a coif[77] to a kerchief over it, from a simple cap to a quilted hat; the trimmings of the doublet must not merely serve for ornament; there must be added a hare's skin or a vulture's skin, and a cap under the hat; follow this gradation, and you will go a very fine way to work. I will do nothing of the sort, and would willingly leave off what I have begun. If you fall into any new inconvenience, all this is labor lost, you are accustomed to it; seek out some other. Thus do they destroy themselves, who submit to be pestered with these enforced and superstitious rules; they must add something more, and something more after that; there is no end on't.

For what concerns our affairs and pleasures, it is much more commodious, as the ancients did, to lose one's dinner, and defer making good cheer till the hour of retirement and repose, without breaking up a day; and so was I formerly used to do. As to health, I since by experience find, on the contrary, that it is better to dine, and that the digestion is better while awake. I am not very used to be thirsty, either well or sick; my mouth is, indeed, apt to be dry, but without thirst; and commonly I never drink but with thirst that is created by eating, and far on in the meal; I drink pretty well for a man of my pitch; in summer, and at a relishing meal, I do not only exceed the limits of Augustus, who drank but thrice, precisely;[78] but not to offend Democritus' rule, who forbade that men should stop at four times as an unlucky number,[79] I proceed at need to the fifth glass, about three half-pints; for the little glasses are my favorites, and I like to drink them off, which other people avoid as an unbecoming thing. I mix my wine sometimes with half, sometimes with the third part water; and when I am at home, by an ancient custom that my father's physician prescribed both to him and himself, they mix that which is designed for me in the buttery, two or three hours before 'tis brought in. 'Tis said, that Cranaus, king of Ath-

---

[77] A simple skullcap.   [78] This is reported in Suetonius, *Life of Augustus*.

[79] Democritus (c. 460–c. 370 B.C.) was a Greek materialist philosopher. His peculiar drinking rule is reported by Erasmus in his *Adages*.

ens, was the inventor of this custom of dashing wine with water;[80] whether useful or no, I have heard disputed. I think it more decent and wholesome for children to drink no wine till after sixteen or eighteen years of age. The most usual and common method of living is the most becoming; all particularity, in my opinion, is to be avoided; and I should as much hate a German who mixed water with his wine, as I should a Frenchman who drank it pure. Public usage gives the law in these things.

I fear a fog, and fly from smoke as from the plague; the first repairs I fell upon in my own house, were the chimneys and houses of office, the common and insupportable defects of all old buildings; and among the difficulties of war, I reckon the choking dust they make us ride in a whole day together. I have a free and easy respiration; and my colds for the most part go off without offense to the lungs, and without a cough.

The heat of summer is more an enemy to me than the cold of winter; for, besides the incommodity of heat, less remediable than cold, and besides the force of the sunbeams that strike upon the head, all glittering light offends my eyes, so that I could not now sit at dinner over against a flaming fire.

To dull the whiteness of paper, in those times when I was more wont to read, I laid a piece of glass upon my book, and found my eyes much relieved by it. I am to this hour ignorant of the use of spectacles; and I can see as far as ever I did, or any other. 'Tis true, that in the evening I begin to find a little disturbance and weakness in my sight if I read; an exercise I have always found troublesome, especially by night. Here is one step back and a very manifest one; I shall retire another; from the second to the third, and so to the fourth, so gently, that I shall be stark blind before I shall be sensible of the age and decay of my sight; so artificially do the Fatal Sisters untwist our lives.[81] And so I doubt whether my hearing begins to grow thick; and you will see I shall have half lost it, when I shall still lay the fault on the voices of those who speak to me. A man must screw up his soul to a high pitch, to make it sensible how it ebbs away.

My walking is quick and firm; and I know not which of the two, my mind or my body, I have most to do to keep in the same state. That preacher is very much my friend who can oblige my attention a whole sermon through; in places of ceremony, where every one's countenance is so starched, where I have seen the ladies keep even their eyes so fixed, I could never order it so, that some part or other of me did not lash out; so that though I was seated, I was never settled. As the philosopher Chrysippus' maid said of her master, that he was only drunk in his legs, for it was his custom to be always kicking them about in what place soever he sat; and she said it, when the wine having made all his companions drunk, he found no alteration in himself at all;[82] it may have been said of me from my infancy that I had either folly or quicksilver in my feet, so much stirring and unsettledness there is in them, wherever they are placed.

[80] Montaigne's source for this bit of trivia is unknown. Athenaeus says that one Amphictyon was the first to water his wine.

[81] The Fatal Sisters are the three Fates in Greek mythology, who spun, measured, and cut off the thread of life.

[82] Diogenes Laertius tells this story of the third-century B.C. Stoic philosopher.

'Tis indecent, besides the hurt it does to one's health, and even to the pleasure of eating, to eat so greedily as I do; I often bite my tongue, and sometimes my fingers, in my haste. Diogenes meeting a boy eating after that manner, gave his tutor a box on the ear.[83] There were men at Rome that taught people to chew, as well as to walk, with a good grace. I lose thereby the leisure of speaking, which gives great relish to the dinner-table, provided the discourse be suitable, that is, pleasant and short.

There is jealousy and envy among our pleasures; they cross and hinder one another; Alcibiades, a man who well understood how to make good cheer, banished even music from the table, that it might not disturb the entertainment of discourse, for the reason, as Plato tells us, "that it is the custom of ordinary people to call fiddlers and singing men to feasts, for want of good discourse and pleasant talk, with which men of understanding know how to entertain one another." Varro requires all this in entertainments: "Persons of graceful presence and agreeable conversation, who are neither silent nor babblers; neatness and delicacy, both of meat and place; and fair weather."[84] The art of dining well is no slight art, the pleasure not a slight pleasure; neither the greatest captains nor the greatest philosophers have disdained the use or science of eating well. My imagination has delivered three repasts to the custody of my memory, which fortune rendered sovereignly sweet to me, upon several occasions in my more flourishing age; my present state excludes me; for every one, according to the good temper of body and mind wherein he then finds himself, furnishes for his own share a particular grace and savor. I, who but crawl upon the earth, hate this inhuman wisdom, that will have us despise and hate all culture of the body; I look upon it as an equal injustice to loathe natural pleasures as to be too much in love with them. Xerxes was a coxcombical blockhead who, environed with all human delights, proposed a reward to him who could find out others;[85] but he is not much less so who cuts off any of those pleasures that nature has provided for him. A man should neither pursue nor avoid them, but receive them. I receive them, I confess, a little too warmly and kindly, and easily suffer myself to follow my natural propensions. We have no need to exaggerate their inanity; they themselves will make us sufficiently sensible of it, thanks to our sick wet-blanket mind, that puts us out of taste with them as with itself; it treats both itself and all it receives, one while better, and another worse, according to its insatiable, vagabond, and versatile essence:

"Sincerum est nisi vas, quodcunque infundis, acescit."[86]

I, who boast that I so curiously and particularly embrace the conveniences of life, find them, when I most nearly consider them, very little more than wind. But what? We are all wind throughout; and, moreover, the wind

---

[83] Diogenes (412–323 B.C.) was a Cynic philosopher. This story is told by Plutarch in *That Virtue Can Be Taught.*

[84] Aulus Gellius reports this remark of Varro, a first-century B.C. Roman scholar.

[85] Xerxes (519–464 B.C.) was King of Persia. Cicero tells the story of his search for new pleasures.

[86] "Unless the vessel be clean, it will sour whatever you put into it" (Horace).

itself, more discreet than we, loves to bluster and shift from corner to corner; and contents itself with its proper offices, without desiring stability and solidity—qualities that nothing belong to it.

The pure pleasures, as well as the pure displeasures, of the imagination, say some, are the greatest, as was expressed by the balance of Critolaus.[87] 'Tis no wonder; it makes them to its own liking, and cuts them out of the whole cloth; of this I every day see notable examples, and, peradventure, to be desired. But I, who am of a mixed and heavy condition, cannot snap so soon at this one simple object, but that I negligently suffer myself to be carried away with the present pleasures of the general human law, intellectually sensible, and sensibly intellectual. The Cyrenaic philosophers will have it that as corporal pains, so corporal pleasures are more powerful, both as double and as more just.[88] There are some, as Aristotle says, who out of a savage kind of stupidity dislike them;[89] and I know others who out of ambition do the same. Why do they not, moreover, forswear breathing? why do they not live of their own? why not refuse light, because it shines gratis, and costs them neither pains nor invention? Let Mars, Pallas, or Mercury afford them their light by which to see, instead of Venus, Ceres, and Bacchus.[90] Will they not seek the quadrature of the circle, even when on their wives?[91] I hate that we should be enjoined to have our minds in the clouds, when our bodies are at table; I would not have the mind nailed there, nor wallow there; I would have it take place there and sit, but not lie down. Aristippus maintained nothing but the body, as if he had no soul; Zeno stickled only for the soul, as if he had no body; both of them faultily.[92] Pythagoras, they say, followed a philosophy that was all contemplation; Socrates one that was all conduct and action; Plato found a mean between the two; but they only say this for the sake of talking. The true point is found in Socrates; and Plato is much more Socratic than Pythagoric, and it becomes him better. When I dance, I dance; when I sleep, I sleep. Nay, when I walk alone in a beautiful orchard, if my thoughts are some part of the time taken up with foreign occurrences, I some part of the time call them back again to my walk, to the orchard, to the sweetness of the solitude, and to myself.

Nature has with a motherly tenderness observed this, that the actions she has enjoined us for our necessity should be also pleasant to us; and she invites us to them, not only by reason, but also by appetite, and 'tis injustice to infringe her laws. When I see both Caesar and Alexander in the thickest of their greatest business, so fully enjoy human and corporal pleasures, I do not hold that they slackened their souls, but wound them up higher, by vigor of courage, subjecting these violent employments and laborious thoughts to the ordinary usage of life; wise, had they believed the last was

---

[87] A second-century B.C. peripatetic philosopher. His views of the imagination are reported by Cicero.

[88] The Cyrenaic philosophers were the followers of Aristippus of Cyrene (435?–356? B.C.), who taught that pleasure is the only rational aim in life.

[89] Montaigne is referring to Aristotle's *Ethics,* II.vii.3 and III.xi.7.

[90] Montaigne is opposing the "ethereal" gods of war, wisdom, and eloquence to the "earthy" gods of love, fertility, and wine.

[91] "Squaring the circle" was a famous intellectual problem of the Middle Ages.

[92] For Aristippus, see footnote 88. Zeno of Citium (d. 264 B.C.) was a famous Stoic philosopher.

their ordinary, the first their extraordinary vocation. We are great fools. "He has passed over his life in idleness," say we: "I have done nothing to-day." What? have you not lived? that is not only the fundamental, but the most illustrious of all your occupations. "Had I been put to the management of great affairs, I should have made it seen what I could do." Have you known how to meditate and manage your life, you have performed the greatest work of all. For a man to show and set out himself, nature has no need of fortune; she equally manifests herself in all stages, and behind a curtain as well as without one. Have you known how to regulate your conduct, you have done a great deal more than he who has composed books. Have you known how to take repose, you have done more than he who has taken cities and empires.

The great and glorious masterpiece of man is to know how to live to purpose; all other things, to reign, to lay up treasure, to build, are, at most, but little appendices and props. I delight to see a general of an army, at the foot of a breach he is presently to assault, give himself up entire and free at dinner, to talk and be merry with his friends; to see Brutus, when heaven and earth were conspired against him and the Roman liberty, stealing some hours of the night from his rounds to read and abridge Polybius, in all security.[93] 'Tis for little souls, that truckle under the weight of affairs, not from them to know how clearly to disengage themselves, not to know how to lay them aside and take them up again:

> "O fortes, pejoraque passi
> Mecum sæpe viri! nunc vino pellite curas:
> Cras ingens interabimus æquor."[94]

Whether it be in jest or earnest, that the theological and Sorbonical wine, and their feasts, are tuned into a proverb,[95] I find it reasonable they should dine so much more commodiously and pleasantly, as they have profitably and seriously employed the morning in the exercise of their schools. The conscience of having well spent the other hours, is the just and savory sauce of the dinner-table. The sages lived after that manner; and that inimitable emulation to virtue, which astonishes us both in the one and the other Cato,[96] that humor of theirs, so severe as even to be importunate, gently submits itself and yields to the laws of the human condition, of Venus and Bacchus; according to the precepts of their sect, that require the perfect sage to be as expert and intelligent in the use of natural pleasures as in all other duties of life: *"Cui cor sapiat, ei et sapiat palatus."*[97]

Relaxation and facility, methinks, wonderfully honor and best become a strong and generous soul. Epaminondas did not think that to take part, and that heartily, in songs and sport and dances with the young men of his

---

[93] This story of the Roman statesman M. Junius Brutus is told by Plutarch, *Life of Brutus*. Polybius (203?–c. 120 B.C.) was a Greek historian.

[94] "Brave spirits, who have often suffered sorrow with me, drink cares away; tomorrow we will set sail on the great sea" (Horace).

[95] Sorbonical wine is that served at the Sorbonne, or University of Paris (founded 1253).

[96] The two Catos were Cato the Elder (234–149 B.C.) and his great-grandson Cato the Younger (95–46 B.C.), both Roman statesmen known for their virtue.

[97] "He that has a learned soul has a learned palate too" (Cicero).

city, were things that in any way derogated from the honor of his glorious victories and the perfect purity of manners that was in him.[98] And among so many admirable actions of Scipio, the grandfather, a person worthy to be reputed of a heavenly extraction, there is nothing that gives him a greater grace than to see him carelessly and childishly trifling at gathering and selecting shells, and playing at quoits upon the seashore with Laelius; and, if it was foul weather, amusing and pleasing himself in representing by writing in comedies the meanest and most popular actions of men; or having his head full of that wonderful enterprise of Hannibal and Africa, visiting the schools in Sicily, and attending philosophical lectures, improving himself, to the blind envy of his enemies at Rome.[99] Nor is there anything more remarkable in Socrates than that, old as he was, he found time to make himself taught dancing and playing upon instruments, and thought it time well spent; but this same man was seen in an ecstasy, standing upon his feet a whole day and a night together, in the presence of all the Grecian army, surprised and ravished with some profound thought. He was the first who, among so many valiant men of the army, ran to the relief of Alcibiades, oppressed with the enemy; shielded him with his own body, and disengaged him from the crowd, by absolute force of arms. It was he who, in the Delian battle, raised and saved Xenophon when fallen from his horse; and who, among all the people of Athens, enraged as he was at so unworthy a spectacle, first presented himself to rescue Theramenes, whom the thirty tyrants were hauling to execution by their satellites, and desisted not from his bold enterprise but at the remonstrance of Theramenes himself, though he was only followed by two more in all. He was seen, when courted by a beauty with whom he was in love, to maintain at need a severe abstinence. He was seen ever to go to the wars, and walk upon ice, with bare feet; to wear the same robe winter and summer; to surpass all his companions in patience of bearing hardships, and to eat no more at a feast than at his own private dinner. He was seen, for seven and twenty years together, to endure hunger, poverty, the indocility of his children, and the claws of his wife, with the same countenance; and, in the end, calumny, tyranny, imprisonment, fetters, and poison. But was this man obliged to drink full bumpers by any rule of civility? he was also the man of the whole army, with whom the advantage in drinking remained. And he never refused to play at cob-nut,[1] nor to ride the hobbyhorse with children, and it became him well; for all actions, says philosophy, equally become and equally honor a wise man. We have enough wherewithal to do it, and we ought never to be weary of presenting the image of this great man in all the patterns and forms of perfections. There are very few examples of life, full and pure; and we wrong our teaching every day, to propose to ourselves those that are weak and imperfect,

---

[98] Epaminondas (418–362 B.C.) was a Theban general. His character is described in Cornelius Nepos, *Life of Epaminondas*.

[99] Although Montaigne refers to "Scipio the grandfather," some of the details suggest that he is confusing Scipio Africanus Major (234?–183 B.C.), conqueror of Hannibal, and Scipio Africanus Minor (c. 185–129 B.C.), Roman general and patron of the arts. Montaigne seems to have believed that the younger Scipio wrote Terence's comedies for him. Montaigne draws upon a number of sources for his comments on the Scipios, as he does also in the following characterization of Socrates.

[1] *Cob-nut*, as suggested, is a children's game.

scarce good for any one service, and rather pull us back; corrupters rather than correctors of manners. The people deceive themselves; a man goes much more easily indeed by the ends, where the extremity serves for a bound, a stop, and guide, than by the middle way, large and open; and according to art, more than according to nature: but withal much less nobly and commendably.

Grandeur of soul consists not so much in mounting and in pressing forward, as in knowing how to govern and circumscribe itself; it takes everything for great, that is enough, and demonstrates itself better in moderate than in eminent things. There is nothing so fine and legitimate as well and duly to play the man; nor science so arduous as well and naturally to know how to live this life; and of all the infirmities we have, 'tis the most savage to despise our being.

Whoever has a mind to send his soul abroad, when the body is ill at ease, to preserve it from the contagion, let him, by all means, do it if he can: but, otherwise, let him on the contrary favor and assist it, and not refuse to participate of its natural pleasures with a conjugal complacency, bringing to it, if it be the wiser, moderation, lest by indiscretion they should get confounded with pleasure. Intemperance is the pest of pleasure; and temperance is not its scourge, but rather its seasoning. Eudoxus, who therein established the sovereign good, and his companions, who set so high a value upon it, tasted it in its most charming sweetness, by the means of temperance, which in them was singular and exemplary.[2]

I enjoin my soul to look upon pain and pleasure with an eye equally regular, *"Eodem enim vitio est effusio animi in lætitia, quo in dolore contractio,"*[3] and equally firm; but the one gaily and the other severely, and, so far as it is able, to be as careful to extinguish the one, as to extend the other. The judging rightly of good brings along with it the judging soundly of evil; pain has something of the inevitable in its tender beginnings, and pleasure something of the evitable in its excessive end. Plato couples them together, and wills that it should be equally the office of fortitude to fight against pain, and against the immoderate and charming blandishments of pleasure; they are two fountains, from which whoever draws, when and as much as he needs, whether city, man, or beast, is very fortunate. The first is to be taken medicinally and upon necessity, and more scantily; the other for thirst, but not to drunkenness. Pain, pleasure, love, and hatred are the first things that a child is sensible of; if, when reason comes, they apply it to themselves, that is virtue.

I have a special nomenclature of my own; I "pass away time," when it is ill and uneasy, but when 'tis good I do not pass it away; "I taste it over again and stick to it;" one must run over the ill, and settle upon the good. This ordinary phrase of pastime, and passing away the time, represents the usage of those wise sort of people who think they cannot do better with their lives than to let them run out and slide away, pass them over, and balk them, and, as much as they can, ignore them, and shun them as a thing of troublesome and contemptible quality; but I know it to be another kind of thing, and find it both valuable and commodious, even in its latest decay,

---

[2] Eudoxus (409–356 B.C) was a Greek astronomer.
[3] "For it is by the same vice that we dilate ourselves in mirth and contract ourselves in sorrow" (Cicero).

wherein I now enjoy it; and nature has delivered it into our hands in such and so favorable circumstances, that we have only ourselves to blame if it be troublesome to us, or slide unprofitably away: *"Stulti vita ingrata est, trepida est, tota in futurum fertur."*[4] Nevertheless, I compose myself to lose mine without regret; but withal as a thing that is perishable by its condition, not that it troubles or annoys me. Nor does it properly well become any not to be displeased when they die, excepting such as are pleased to live. There is good husbandry in enjoying it; I enjoy it double to what others do; for the measure of its fruition depends upon the more or less of our application to it. Now especially that I perceive mine to be so short in time, I will extend it in weight; I will stop the promptitude of its flight by the promptitude of my grasp; and by the vigor of using it compensate the speed of its running away; by how much the possession of living is more short, I must make it so much deeper and more full.

Others feel the pleasure of content and prosperity; I feel it too, as well as they, but not as it slides and passes by; one should study, taste, and ruminate upon it, to render condign thanks to Him who grants it to us. They enjoy the other pleasures as they do that of sleep, without knowing it. To the end that even sleep itself should not so stupidly escape from me, I have formerly caused myself to be disturbed in my sleep, so that I might the better and more sensibly relish and taste it. I ponder with myself of content; I do not skim over, but sound it; and I bend my reason, now grown perverse and peevish, to entertain it. Do I find myself in any calm composedness? is there any pleasure that tickles me? I do not suffer it to dally with my senses only, I associate my soul to it too; not there to engage itself, but therein to take delight; not there to lose itself, but to be present there; and I employ it, on its part, to view itself in this prosperous state, to weigh and appreciate its happiness, and to amplify it. It reckons how much it stands indebted to Almighty God that its conscience and the intestine passions are in repose; that it has the body in its natural disposition, orderly and competently enjoying the soft and soothing functions, by which He of His grace is pleased to compensate the sufferings wherewith His justice at His good pleasure chastises us. It reflects how great a benefit it is to be so protected, that, which way soever it turns its eye, the heavens are calm around it. No desire, no fear or doubt, troubles the air; no difficulty, past, present, or to come, that its imagination may not pass over without offense. This consideration takes great luster from the comparison of different conditions; and therefore it is that I present to my thought, in a thousand aspects, those whom fortune or their own error torments and carries away; and those, who more like to me, so negligently and incuriously receive their good fortune. Those are men who pass away their time, indeed; they pass over the present, and that which they possess, to give themselves up to hope, and for vain shadows and images which fancy puts into their heads:

> "Morte obita quales fama est volitare figuras,
> Aut quæ sopitos deludunt somnia sensus:"[5]

---

[4] "The life of a fool is uneasy, timorous, and wholly bent upon the future" (Seneca).
[5] "Such as those forms which after death are said to flutter about; or those dreams which delude the sense in sleep" (Virgil, *Aeneid*).

which hasten and prolong their flight, according as they are pursued. The fruit and end of their pursuit is to pursue; as Alexander said, that the end of his labor was to labor:

"Nil actum credens, cum quid superesset agendum;"[6]

For my part then, I love life, and cultivate it, such as it has pleased God to bestow it upon us. I do not desire it should be without the necessity of eating and drinking; and I should think myself inexcusable to wish it had been twice as long: *"Sapiens divitiarum naturalium quæsitor accerimus:"*[7] nor that we should support ourselves by putting only a little of that drug into our mouths, by which Epimenides took away his appetite, and kept himself alive;[8] nor that we should stupidly beget children with our fingers or heels, but, rather, with reverence be it spoken, that we might voluptuously beget them with our fingers and heels; nor that the body should be without desire, and without titillation. These are ungrateful and wicked complaints. I accept kindly, and with gratitude, what nature has done for me; am well pleased with it, and proud of it. A man does wrong to the great omnipotent Giver of all things, to refuse, annul, or disfigure his gift; all goodness Himself, He has made everything good: *"Omnia quæ secundum naturam sunt, æstimatione digna sunt."*[9]

Of philosophical opinions, I preferably embrace those that are most solid, that is to say the most human, and most our own: my discourse is, suitable to my manners, low and humble; philosophy plays the child, to my thinking, when it puts itself upon its Ergos,[10] to preach to us that 'tis a barbarous alliance to marry the divine with the earthly, the reasonable with the unreasonable, the severe with the indulgent, the honest with the dishonest; that pleasure is a brutish quality, unworthy to be tasted by a wise man; that the sole pleasure he extracts from the enjoyment of a fair young wife, is a pleasure of his conscience to perform an action according to order, as to put on his boots for a profitable journey. Oh, that its followers had no more right, nor nerves, nor juice, in getting their wives' maidenhoods, than in its lessons.

That is not what Socrates says, who is its master and ours: he values, as he ought, bodily pleasure; but he prefers that of the mind, as having more force, constancy, facility, variety, and dignity. This, according to him, goes by no means alone—he is not so fantastic—but only it goes first; temperance, with him, is the moderatrix, not the adversary of pleasure. Nature is a gentle guide, but not more sweet and gentle, than prudent and just: *"Intrandum est in rerum naturam, et penitus, quid ea postulet, pervidendum."*[11] I hunt after her foot throughout; we have confounded it with artificial traces; and that academic and peripatetic good, which is, "to live according

---

[6]"Thinking nothing done, if anything is left to do" (Lucan).

[7]"A wise man eagerly desires natural riches" (Seneca).

[8]Epimenides was a seventh-century B.C. sage of Crete. The story of his taking his appetite away with a drug is told by Diogenes Laertius.

[9]"All things that are according to nature are worthy of esteem" (Cicero).

[10]*Ergos* are "therefores." When philosophy "puts itself upon its Ergos," it is emphasizing logic at the expense of common sense.

[11]"A man must search into the nature of things and examine what she requires" (Cicero).

to it," becomes, by this means, hard to limit and explain; and that of the
Stoics, cousin-german to it, which is "to consent to nature." Is it not an
error to esteem any actions less worthy, because they are necessary? And
yet they will not beat it out of my head, that it is not a very convenient
marriage of pleasure with necessity, with which, says an ancient, the gods
always conspire. To what end do we dismember by divorce a building
united by so close and brotherly a correspondence? Let us, on the contrary,
confirm it by mutual offices; let the mind rouse and quicken the heaviness
of the body, and the body stay and fix the levity of the soul. *"Qui, velut
summum bonum, laudat animæ naturam, et, tanquam malum, naturam carnis
accusat, profecto et animam carnaliter appetit, et carnem carnaliter fugit; quoniam
id vanitate sentit humana, non veritate divina."*[12] In this present that God has
made us, there is nothing unworthy our care; we stand accountable, even to
a hair; and 'tis no slight commission to man, to conduct man according to
his condition; 'tis express, plain, and the principal injunction of all, and the
Creator has seriously and strictly enjoined it. Authority has alone power to
work upon common understandings, and is of more weight in a foreign
language; therefore let us again charge with it in this place: *"Stultitiæ
proprium quis non dixerit, ignave et contumaciter facere, quæ facienda sunt; et alio
corpus impellere, alio animum; distrahique inter diversissimos motus?"*[13] To make
this apparent, ask any one, some day, to tell you what whimsies and imaginations he put into his pate, upon the account of which he diverted his
thoughts from a good meal, and regrets the time he spends in eating: you
will find there is nothing so insipid in all the dishes at your table, as this wise
meditation of his (for the most part we had better sleep than wake to the
purpose we wake); and that his discourses and notions are not worth the
worst mess there. Though they were the ecstasies of Archimedes himself,
what then?[14] I do not here speak of, nor mix with the rabble of us ordinary
men, and the vanity of the thoughts and desires that divert us, those venerable souls, elevated by the ardor of devotion and religion, to a constant and
conscientious meditation of divine things, who, by the energy of vivid and
vehement hope, prepossessing the use of the eternal nourishment, the final
aim and last step of Christian desires, the sole, constant, and incorruptible
pleasure, disdain to apply themselves to our necessitous, fluid and ambiguous conveniences, and easily resign to the body the care and use of sensual
and temporal pasture: 'tis a privileged study. Between ourselves, I have
ever observed supercelestial opinions and subterranean manners to be of
singular accord.

Aesop, that great man, saw his master make water as he walked: "What,
then," said he, "must we dung as we run?" Let us manage our time as well
as we can, there will yet remain a great deal that will be idle and ill em-

---

[12]"He who commends the nature of the soul as the supreme good and condemns the
nature of the flesh as evil certainly both carnally desires the soul and carnally flies the flesh,
because he is so possessed through human vanity and not by divine truth" (St. Augustine).

[13]"Who will not say that it is the property of folly slothfully and contumaciously to perform
what is to be done, and to bend the body one way and the mind another, and to be distracted
between wholly different motions?" (Seneca).

[14]Archimedes (287–212 B.C.) was a mathematician of Syracuse. It is said that when he
discovered an important principle of physics, he jumped out of his bath and ran naked down
the street shouting "Eureka!"

ployed. The mind has not other hours enough wherein to do its business, without disassociating itself from the body, in that little space it must have for its necessity. They would put themselves out of themselves, and escape from being men; 'tis folly; instead of transforming themselves into angels, they transform themselves into beasts; instead of elevating, they lay themselves lower. These transcendental humors affright me, like high and inaccessible cliffs and precipices; and nothing is hard for me to digest in the life of Socrates but his ecstacies and communication with demons; nothing so human in Plato as that for which they say he was called divine; and of our sciences, those seem to be the most terrestrial and low that are highest mounted; and I find nothing so humble and mortal in the life of Alexander, as his fancies about his immortalization: Philotas pleasantly quipped him in his answer: he congratulated him by letter concerning the oracle of Jupiter Hammon, which had placed him among the gods: "Upon thy account, I am glad of it, but the men are to be pitied who are to live with a man, and to obey him, who exceeds and is not contented with the measure of a man."[15] *"Diis te minorem quod geris, imperas."*[16] The pretty inscription wherewith the Athenians honored the entry of Pompey into their city, is conformable to my sense: "By so much thou art a god, as thou confessest thee a man."[17] 'Tis an absolute and, as it were, a divine perfection, for a man to know how loyally to enjoy his being. We seek other conditions, by reason we do not understand the use of our own; and go out of ourselves, because we know not how there to reside. 'Tis to much purpose to go upon stilts, for, when upon stilts, we must yet walk with our legs; and when seated upon the most elevated throne in the world, we are but seated upon our breech. The fairest lives, in my opinion, are those which regularly accommodate themselves to the common and human model; without miracle, without extravagance. Old age stands a little in need of a more gentle treatment. Let us recommend it to God, the protector of health and wisdom, but withal, let it be gay and sociable.

> "Frui paratis et valido mihi
> Latoë, dones, et, precor, integra
> Cum mente; nec turpem senectam
> Degere, nec Cithara carentem."[18]

---

[15] This story about Alexander the Great is told by Quintus Curtius.
[16] "Because thou carriest thyself lower than the gods, thou rulest" (Horace).
[17] This story appears in Plutarch's *Life of Pompey*.
[18] "Grant it to me, Apollo, that I may enjoy what I have in good health; let me be sound in body and mind; let me live in honor when old, nor let music be wanting" (Horace).

Miguel de Cervantes Saavedra
(1547–1616)

Don Quixote *is one of the greatest works of art in Western literature, but in a sense it is surprising that it should have been a work of art at all. It began its life as a humble parody of contemporary popular literature, written by an elderly failed playwright in a more or less desperate attempt to make money, possibly even as he lay in prison for shortages in his accounts as a petty government official. Cervantes may have conceived of the total work in all its complexity and grandeur from the very beginning, but it seems more likely that even he was surprised at the way the work developed, from an unpretentious extended joke to an almost mythic narrative. Growing from roots deep in the popular culture of his time, it reached the loftiest heights of man's questionings of human nature.*

Miguel de Cervantes Saavedra was born in 1547, the fourth of seven children of an impoverished physician. During Miguel's childhood the family moved from one village to another to flee from creditors. By 1564, when he was sixteen, the family had settled in Seville, where Miguel was enrolled in a Jesuit school; he seems later to have studied for a time at the University of Salamanca. Any hopes he may have had for an academic career, however, were blasted when he got involved, at the age of twenty-one, in a duel within the precincts of the royal palace in Madrid. The royal court sentenced him to lose his right hand and be exiled for ten years; Cervantes fled to Italy to escape the execution of the sentence.

He was not to return to Spain for twelve years, and those years were filled with hardships and adventures more spectacular than any in the romances he was to parody in Don Quixote. *After a brief period of service in Rome in the retinue of the cardinal-elect Giulio Acquaviva, he enlisted in the Spanish forces of the Holy League opposing Turkish control of the Mediterranean. His first engagement was the famous Battle of Lepanto. Cervantes was on board a ship called the* Marquesa *when the battle began, sick with a fever and confined to his bunk. Despite his condition, he immediately asked to be placed in the most dangerous position and fought gallantly throughout the battle. In the action, he received two shots in the chest and his left hand was shattered; he was never to recover full use of it. Cervantes received an increase in pay for his bravery and a letter of commendation from his commander, Don John of Austria, brother of King Philip II. After his convalescence, he spent four more years in the army, campaigning in Sardinia, Naples, and South Italy.*

Finally, in 1575, Cervantes set sail for Spain again in the company of his brother Rodrigo, who had joined the colors at the same time as Cervantes. Off the coast of southern France, the ship was attacked by pirates and captured, and everyone on board was carried off to Algiers to be sold as slaves. Cervantes remained in slavery for five years, conducting himself with the utmost gallantry. Four times he attempted to organize a general rising among the 24,000 Christian slaves in Algiers. All these attempts failed, and each time Cervantes took full responsibility, in spite of the potential penalty of death by torture. The Dey of Algiers, Hassan Pacha, each time pardoned him, however, since he privately admired Cervantes' courage. Rodrigo was ransomed comparatively early by his family back in Spain, but Cervantes' ransom price was much higher because of the letter of commendation to the Spanish king his captors found in his possession. He was not ransomed until 1580, half of the money coming from his hard-pressed family and the other half from sympathetic Spanish residents of Algiers.

Cervantes was thirty-three when he finally returned to Spain. He was crippled and without a job; his family was deeply in debt. Don John was by now dead, and since his memory was hated by the king, Cervantes could not use his commendation to get preferment. He spent the next twenty-five years trying desperately to earn a meager living. He wrote a number of plays, none notably successful. During his theatrical days he fell in love with an actress, Ana Franca de Rojas. They had a child, Isabel, whom Cervantes was left to rear when Ana deserted him. In 1584, at the age of thirty-seven, he married a nineteen-year-old girl, Catalina de Palacios y Salazar Vozmediano; he then had to support a household consisting of his wife, Isabel, his mother, his two sisters, and his widowed mother-in-law. He finally succeeded in getting a government post as a traveling agent charged with requisitioning supplies for the Invincible Armada, the massive fleet that Philip was preparing to launch against England in 1588. As a "commissary," he not only had to face angry mobs of villagers who resented the army's appropriation of their goods, but had to deal also with a government bureaucracy that at one point was two years behind with his salary. Cervantes was twice imprisoned for shortages in his accounts, owing to a combination of his superiors' own chaotic records, an untimely bank failure, and doubtless his own inadequacies as a bookkeeper. There is a tradition, based on an ambiguous passage in the Prologue to Book I of Don Quixote (the story was "just what might be begotten in a prison, where every discomfort is lodged and every dismal noise has its dwelling"), that he began his great novel in the prison at Seville in 1597.

However this may be, soon after his release Cervantes was hard at work on Don Quixote, *which was first published in 1605, the year in which his contemporary Shakespeare produced* King Lear. *Cervantes' book was an immediate bestseller; it went through a number of printings the first year and was very promptly translated into French, Italian, and other European languages. Its success brought Cervantes little except the satisfaction of fame; he received no royalties beyond the small initial sum paid him by the publisher.*

From the time the first part was published, Cervantes had planned a continuation, but it did not appear for ten years. In 1614, he had written fifty-nine chapters of the sequel when he learned that a pirated continuation had been published by one Alonso Fernandez de Avellaneda. Furious, he rushed through the ending of Part II, incorporating in the part he had already finished an attack upon the "false Quixote." Part II was also successful, but again it did little to relieve the author's chronic poverty. Aged and ill, he spent the last two years of his life finishing Persiles and Sigismunda, *an episodic romance he had begun in 1609. (It was published posthumously.) In the dedication to this work, written on his deathbed to his patron the Conde de Lemos, he wrote the famous lines, adapted from an old ballad, "With one foot in the stirrup, and in the anguish of death, My Lord, I write to thee." He died on April 23, 1616; ten days later in England, Shakespeare died, also on April 23 (since the English calendar was still unreformed).*

Don Quixote *is a long novel, one of the longest ever written, but it is not a word too long. An abridgment can only suggest the cumulative effect of the book's movement from primitive burlesque to the mysteriously moving climax. At the heart of the novel are the mad knight himself, his commonsensical squire Sancho, and their gradually unfolding relationship. Quixote and Sancho are inseparable, bound together like spirit and flesh as are their fictional descendants Sherlock Holmes and Dr. Watson, Stephen Dedalus and Leopold Bloom in Joyce's* Ulysses, *and Didi and Gogo in Beckett's* Waiting for Godot. *The division is not absolute: Quixote has his earthy side, and it is Sancho who clings to a dream of being governor of an island. It is not Sancho, finally, who represents the claims of unimaginative reality, but the barber and the curate, guardians of flesh and spirit in the everyday world in their respective roles as bleeder and spiritual advisor. Similarly, it is not Don Quixote himself who represents dreams kicked loose from all contact with the earth, but the romances with which he has addled himself. Quixote and Sancho are not allegorical figures but real human beings, each torn between dream and reality. The novel traces their profound, moving, and richly comic negotiation with each other. This negotiation consists of the gradual "Sanchification" of Quixote and the "Quixotification" of Sancho; the Knight moves from a world of pure delusion to a vision of real life ennobled by idealism, while Sancho begins to see the substantial world through the eyes of his master, as touched by the dream. By the end of the novel, all hope of his island gone, Sancho still longs for the quest: "Up with you this instant, out of your bed! . . . Who knows but we may find Lady Dulcinea behind a hedge, disenchanted and as fresh as a daisy!"*

As, for his protagonists, Cervantes draws upon the most fundamental of human relationships, so for his plot he turns to the most basic of narratives, the journey. The key to all the great quest stories is the goal of the quest. Odysseus, on his journey home, is in quest of Ithaca and Penelope, the world of ordinary life after the heroic but distorted world of military action. Dante, in his dream journey through the afterlife, seeks to leave the Dark Wood of worldly confusion and find the security of God's holy order. Quixote's quest remains in the Dark Wood on this earth; the dusty and sterile landscape of La Mancha, the emblem of a modern world from which it seems all glory has fled. His quest, literally for chivalric adventure, is more fundamentally for the spark of imagination that redeems ordinary life. And ultimately he finds this spark, not in absurd romances but within himself.

FURTHER READING *(prepared by W. J. R.):* Melveena McKendrick's biography *Cervantes,* 1980, is a good introduction for the general reader. Manuel Duran's *Cervantes,* 1974, a somewhat more succinct biography, contains a good introductory chapter on Spanish culture in Cervantes' time and includes a long discussion of *Don Quixote.* An excellent evaluation of Cervantes as a critical theorist can be found in E. C. Riley's *Cervantes' Theory of the Novel,* 1962, which places Cervantes' ideas in the literary context of his time and discusses such topics as structural unity, verisimilitude, and the function of history. Diverse critical approaches are represented in *Cervantes: A Collection of Critical Essays,* ed. Lowry Nelson, Jr., 1969. This volume includes Erich Auerbach's "The Enchanted Dulcinea" and Thomas Mann's "Voyage with Don Quixote." Ruth El Saffar's *Distance and Control in "Don Quixote,"* 1975, explores a wide variety of narrative techniques employed by Cervantes, concentrating on the dynamics of role-switching by the characters. John C. Weiger's *The Individuated Self,* 1979, distinguishes "individuation" from individualism in an examination of personal freedom in *Don Quixote* and is interesting on the emergence of self-knowledge in the novel. John J. Allen's *Don Quixote: Hero or Fool?: A Study in Narrative Techniques,* 1969, discusses stylistic devices, levels of fiction, and the relationship between author, reader, and character. The subject of chivalry is the starting point for a provocative study in Howard Mancing's *The Chivalric World of Don Quijote: Style, Structure, and Narrative Technique,* 1982.

DON QUIXOTE

Translated by Walter Starkie

from PART I

CHAPTER I

Which tells of the quality and manner of life of the famous gentleman Don Quixote of La Mancha

At a village of La Mancha, whose name I do not wish to remember,[1] there lived a little while ago one of those gentlemen who are wont to keep a lance in the rack, an old buckler, a lean horse, and a swift greyhound. His stew had more beef than mutton in it and most nights he ate a hodgepodge, pickled and cold. Lentil soup on Fridays, "tripe and trouble" on Saturdays,[2] and an occasional pigeon as an extra delicacy on Sundays consumed three quarters of his income. The remainder was spent on a jerkin of fine puce, velvet breeches, and slippers of the same stuff for holidays, and a suit of good, honest homespun for weekdays. His family consisted of a housekeeper about forty, a niece not yet twenty, and a lad who served him both in the field and at home and could saddle the horse or use the pruning knife. Our gentleman was about fifty years of age, of a sturdy constitution, but wizened and gaunt-featured, an early riser and a devotee of the chase. They say that his surname was Quixada or Quesada (for on this point the authors who have written on this subject differ), but we may reasonably conjecture that his name was Quixana. This, however, has very little to do with our story; enough that in its telling we swerve not a jot from the truth. You must know that the above-mentioned gentleman in his leisure moments (which was most of the year) gave himself up with so much delight and gusto to reading books of chivalry that he almost entirely neglected the exercise of the chase and even the management of his domestic affairs. Indeed his craze for this kind of literature became so extravagant that he sold many acres of arable land to purchase books of knight-errantry, and he carried off to his house as many as he could possibly find. Above all, he preferred those written by the famous Feliciano de Silva[3] because of the clarity of his writing and his intricate style, which made him value those books more than pearls, especially when he read of those courtships and letters of challenge that knights sent to ladies, often containing expressions such as: "The reason for your unreasonable treatment of my reason so enfeebles my reason that I have reason to complain of your beauty." And again: "The high heavens, which with your divinity divinely fortify you

---

[1] Cervantes was purposely vague in describing Don Quixote's birthplace. An old Spanish ballad begins "At a village in La Mancha." (Notes are adapted and expanded from those of the translator.)

[2] Spaniards ate meagerly on Saturdays, in commemoration of a victory over the Moors in 1212.

[3] A sixteenth-century writer of romances, famous for *Don Florisel de Niquea* (1532), from which the following quotation is taken.

with stars, make you the deserver of the desert that is deserved by your greatness." These and similar rhapsodies bewildered the poor gentleman's understanding, for he racked his brain day and night to unbowel their meaning, which not even Aristotle himself could have done if he had been raised from the dead for that very purpose. He was not quite convinced of the number of wounds that Don Belianís gave and received in battle, for he considered that however skillful the surgeons that cured him may have been, the worthy knight's face and body must have been bedizened with scars and scabs. Nevertheless he praised the author for concluding his book with the promise of endless adventure, and many times he felt inclined to take up his pen and finish it off himself, as it is there promised. He doubt-less would have done so, and successfully too, had he not been diverted by other plans and purposes of greater moment. He often debated with the curate of the village—a man of learning, a graduate of Sigüenza—on the relative merits of Palmerin of England and Amadis of Gaul. But Master Nicholas, the village barber, affirmed that no one could be compared with the Knight of the Sun and that if, indeed, any could be matched with him, it was Don Galaor, the brother of Amadis of Gaul, for he had a nature adapted to every whim of fortune; he was not so namby-pamby and whim-pering a knight as his brother, and as for valor, he was in every respect equal.

In short, he so immersed himself in those romances that he spent whole days and nights over his books; and thus with little sleeping and much reading, his brains dried up to such a degree that he lost the use of his reason. His imagination became filled with a host of fancies he had read in his books—enchantments, quarrels, battles, challenges, wounds, courtships, loves, tortures, and many other absurdities. So true did all this phantas-magoria from books appear to him that in his mind he accounted no history in the world more authentic. He would say that the Cid Ruiz Díaz was a very gallant knight, but not to be compared with the Knight of the Burning Sword, who with a single thwart blow cleft asunder a brace of hulking, blustering giants. He was better pleased with Bernardo del Carpio, because at Roncesvalles he had slain Roland the Enchanted by availing himself of the stratagem Hercules had employed on Antaeus, the son of the Earth, whom he squeezed to death in his arms. He praised the giant Morgante, for he alone was courteous and well bred among that monstrous brood puffed up with arrogance and insolence. Above all, he admired Rinaldo of Montalbán,[4] especially when he saw him sallying out of his castle to plunder everyone who came his way, and when beyond the seas he made off with the idol of Mohammed which, as history says, was of solid gold. But he would have parted with his housekeeper and his niece into the bargain for the pleasure of rib roasting the traitor Galalón.[5]

At last, having lost his wits completely, he stumbled upon the oddest fancy that ever entered a madman's brain. He believed that it was neces-

---

[4] One of Charlemagne's knights and the hero of Boiardo's romance *Orlando Innamorato (Roland in Love)*. Palmerin of England, Amadis of Gaul, The Knight of the Sun, The Cid Ruiz Diaz, The Knight of the Burning Sword, Bernardo del Carpio, and Morgante are all charac-ters in actual romances.

[5] Galalón, or Ganelon of Mayence, was another of Charlemagne's knights who betrayed him at Rouncevalles. See *The Song of Roland*.

sary, both for his own honor and for service of the state, that he should become a knight-errant, roaming through the world with his horse and armor in quest of adventures and practicing all that had been performed by the knights-errant of whom he had read. He would follow their life, redressing all manner of wrongs and exposing himself to continual dangers, and at last, after concluding his enterprises, he would win everlasting honor and renown. The poor gentleman fancied himself already crowned emperor of Trebizond for the valor of his arm. And thus excited by these agreeable delusions, he hastened to put his plans into operation.

The first thing he did was to refurbish some rusty armor that had belonged to his great grandfather and had lain moldering in a corner. He cleaned it and repaired it as best he could, but he found one great defect: instead of a complete helmet there was just the simple morion.[6] This want he ingeniously remedied by making a kind of visor out of pasteboard, and when it was fitted to the morion, it looked like an entire helmet. It is true that in order to test its strength and see if it was swordproof, he drew his sword and gave it two strokes, the first of which instantly destroyed the result of a week's labor. It troubled him to see with what ease he had broken the helmet in pieces, so to protect it from such an accident, he remade it and fenced the inside with a few bars of iron in such a manner that he felt assured of its strength, and without caring to make a second trial, he held it to be a most excellent helmet. Then he went to see his steed, and although it had more cracks in its hoof than there are quarters in a Spanish real[7] and more faults than Gonella's jade, which was all skin and bone,[8] he thought that neither the Bucephalus of Alexander nor the Cid's Babieca could be compared with it.[9] He spent four days deliberating over what name he would give the horse, for (as he said to himself) it was not right that the horse of so famous a knight should remain without a name. So he endeavored to find one that would express what the animal had been before he had been the mount of a knight-errant, and what he now was. It was indeed reasonable that when the master changed his state, the horse should change his name too and assume one pompous and high-sounding, as suited the new order he was about to profess. So after having devised, erased, and blotted out many other names, he finally decided to call the horse Rozinante—a name, in his opinion, lofty, sonorous, and significant, for it explained that he had been only an ordinary hack before he had been raised to his present status of first of all the hacks in the world.[10]

Now that he had given his horse a name so much to his satisfaction, he resolved to choose one for himself, and after seriously considering the matter for eight whole days, he finally determined to call himself Don Quixote. For that reason the authors who have related this most true story have deduced that his name must undoubtedly have been Quixada and not Quesada, as others would have it. Then, remembering that the valiant

[6] Headpiece of a helmet, without the visor.

[7] A *real* was a silver coin. There were eight *cuartos*, or "cracks," in a *real*.

[8] Pedro Gonella was the clown of the Duke of Ferrara in the fifteenth century; his horse, all skin and bones, was the theme of many of his jokes.

[9] Bucephalus was Alexander the Great's horse, Babieca that of Ruy Diaz, hero of the twelfth-century Spanish epic *The Cid*.

[10] *Rozin,* or *rocin,* means an ordinary horse; *ante,* before.

Amadis had not been content to call himself simply Amadis, but added thereto the name of his kingdom and native country to render it more illustrious, calling himself Amadis of Gaul, so he, like a good knight, also added the name of his province and called himself Don Quixote of La Mancha. In this way he openly proclaimed his lineage and country, and at the same time he honored it by taking its name.

Now that his armor was scoured, his morion made into a helmet, his horse and himself newly named, he felt that nothing was wanting but a lady of whom to be enamored, for a knight-errant who was loveless was a tree without leaves and fruit, a body without soul. "If," said he, "for my sins or through my good fortune I encounter some giant—a usual occurrence to knights-errant—and bowling him over at the first onset or cleaving him in twain, I finally vanquish and force him to surrender, would not it be better to have some lady to whom I may send him as a trophy? Then, when he comes into her presence, he may kneel before her and humbly say: 'Madam, I am the giant Caraculiambro, Lord of the Island of Malindrania, whom the never-adequately-praised Don Quixote of La Mancha has overcome in single combat. He has commanded me to present myself before you so that your highness may dispose of me as you wish.'" How glad was our knight when he had made these discourses to himself, but chiefly when he had found one whom he might call his lady! It happened that in a neighboring village there lived a good-looking country lass with whom he had been in love, although it is understood that she never knew or was aware of it. She was called Aldonza Lorenzo, and it was to her that he thought fit to entrust the sovereignty of his heart. He sought a name for her that would not vary too much from her own and yet would approach that of a princess or a lady of quality. At last he resolved to call her Dulcinea of El Toboso (she was a native of that town), a name in his opinion musical, uncommon, and expressive, like the others he had devised.

CHAPTER II

Which deals with our imaginative hero's first sally from his home

Once these preparations were made he was anxious to put his designs into operation without delay, for he was spurred on by the conviction that the world needed his immediate presence; so many were the grievances he intended to rectify, the wrongs he resolved to set right, the harms he meant to redress, the abuses he would reform, and the debts he would discharge. And so, without acquainting a living soul with his intentions, and wholly unobserved, one morning before daybreak (it was one of the hottest in the month of July), he armed himself cap-a-pie, mounted Rozinante, placed his ill-constructed helmet on his head, braced on his buckler, grasped his lance, and through the door of his back yard sallied forth into the open country, mightily pleased to note the ease with which he had begun his worthy enterprise. But scarcely had he issued forth when he was suddenly struck by so terrible a thought that he almost gave up his whole undertaking, for he just then remembered that he had not yet been dubbed a knight, and therefore, in accordance with the laws of chivalry, he neither

could nor ought to enter the lists against any knight. Morover, even if he
had been dubbed, he should, as a novice, have worn white armor without
any device on his shield until he had won it by force of arms. These
thoughts made him stagger in his purpose; but as his madness prevailed
over every reason, he determined to have himself knighted by the first
person he should meet, like many others of whom he had read in the books
that distracted him. As to white armor, he intended at the first opportunity
to scour his own so that it would be whiter than ermine. In this way he
calmed himself and continued his journey, letting his horse choose the way,
believing that in this consisted the true spirit of adventure.

As our brand-new adventurer proceeded, he kept conversing with himself in this manner: "Who doubts but that in future ages, when the true
story of my famous deeds is brought to light, the wise man who writes it will
describe my first sally in the morning as follows: 'Scarcely had the rubicund
Apollo spread over the face of the vast and spacious earth the golden
tresses of his beautiful hair, and scarcely had the little painted birds with
their tuneful tongues saluted in sweet and melodious harmony the coming
of rosy Aurora, who, leaving the soft couch of her jealous husband, revealed herself to mortals through the gates and balconies of the Manchegan
horizon, when the famous knight Don Quixote of La Mancha, quitting his
downy bed of ease, mounted his renowned steed, Rozinante, and began to
ride over the ancient and memorable plain of Montiel.' "[11] (And indeed he
was doing so.) Continuing his discourse, he added: "O happy era, O happy
age, wherein my famous deeds shall be revealed to the world, deeds worthy
to be engraved in bronze, sculptured in marble, and painted in pictures for
future record! O thou wise enchanter, whosoever thou mayest be, whose
duty it will be to chronicle this strange history, do not, I beseech thee,
forget my good horse, Rozinante, the everlasting companion of my wanderings." Then, as if really enamored, he cried: "O Dulcinea, my princess!
Sovereign of this captive heart! Grievous wrong hast thou done me by
dismissing me and by cruelly forbidding me by decree to appear in thy
beauteous presence. I pray thee, sweet lady, to remember this poor, enslaved heart, which for love of thee suffers so many pangs."

To such words he added a sequence of other foolish notions all in the
manner of those that his books had taught him, imitating their language as
nearly as he could. And all the while he rode slowly on while the sun rose
with such intense heat that it would have been enough to dissolve his
brains, if he had had any left. He traveled almost the whole of that day
without meeting any adventure worthy of note, wherefore he was much
troubled, for he was eager to encounter someone upon whom he could try
the strength of his doughty arm. Some authors say his first adventure was
that of the Pass of Lápice; others hold it was that of the windmills; but
according to my investigations and according to what is written in the annals of La Mancha, he traveled all that day, and at dusk both he and his
horse were tired and nearly dead with hunger. He looked around him on
every side to see whether he could discover any castle or shepherd's hut
where he might rest and find nourishment. He then saw, not far from the
road, an inn, which was as welcome to him as a star leading him not to the

---

[11] Memorable because it was the scene of a famous battle in 1369.

portals but to the very palace itself of his redemption. So he hastened on and reached it before dark.

Now there chanced to be standing at the door two young wenches who belonged to the category of women of the town, as they say. They were on their way to Seville in the company of certain carriers who halted for the night in that inn. As all our adventurer saw, thought, or imagined seemed to happen in accordance with what he had read in his books of chivalry, no sooner did he see the inn than it assumed in his eyes the semblance of a castle with four turrets, the pinnacles of which were of glittering silver, including drawbridge, deep moat, and all the appurtenances with which such castles are depicted. And so he drew near to the inn (which he thought was a castle), and at a short distance from it, he halted Rozinante, expecting that some dwarf would mount the battlements to announce by trumpet blast the arrival of a knight-errant at the castle. But when he saw that they tarried, and as Rozinante was pawing the ground impatiently in eagerness to reach the stable, he approached the inn door and there saw the two young doxies, who appeared to him to be two beautiful damsels or graceful ladies enjoying the fresh air at the castle gate. It happened also at this very moment that a swineherd, as he gathered his hogs (I ask no pardon,[12] for so they are called) from the stubblefield, blew a horn that assembled them, and instantly Don Quixote imagined it was what he expected, namely, that some dwarf was giving notice of his arrival. Therefore, with extraordinary satisfaction he went up to the inn and the ladies. But when they saw a man armed in that manner draw near with lance and buckler, they started to take to their heels, full of fear. Don Quixote, perceiving their alarm, raised his pasteboard visor, and displaying his withered and dusty countenance, accosted them gently and gravely: "I beseech your ladyships, do not flee, nor fear the least offense. The order of chivalry that I profess does not permit me to do injury to anyone, and least of all to such noble maidens as your presences denote you to be."

The wenches kept gazing earnestly, endeavoring to catch a glimpse of his face, which its ill-fashioned visor concealed; but when they heard themselves called maidens, a thing so out of the way of their profession, they could not restrain their laughter, which was so boisterous that Don Quixote exclaimed in anger: "Remember that modesty is becoming in beautiful ladies, whereas laughter without cause denotes much folly. However," added he, "I do not say this to offend you or to incur your displeasure, for my one desire is to do you honor and service." The strange language of the knight was not understood by the ladies, and this, added to his uncouth appearance, increased their laughter and his annoyance, and he would have proceeded further but for the timely appearance of the innkeeper, a man who by reason of his extreme corpulence was of very peaceable disposition. As soon as he saw that uncomely figure all armed, in accouterments so ill-sorted as were the bridle, lance, buckler, and corselet, he felt inclined to join the damsels in their mirth. But out of fear of such a medley of warlike gear, he resolved to be civil, and so he said: "Sir knight, if you are seeking a lodging, you will find all in abundance here, with the exception of a bed,

[12] Spanish peasants still beg one's pardon when mentioning pigs, a custom picked up from the neighboring Moslems, who abhor pork.

for there are none in this inn." Don Quixote, observing the humility of the governor of the fortress (for such the landlord and the inn appeared to him), answered: "Anything, sir castellan, suffices me:

> My ornaments are arms,
> My pastime is in war."

The host thought he called him a castellan because he took him to be one of the Simple-Simon Castilians,[13] whereas he was an Andalusian, one of those from the Sanlúcar shore, no less a thief than Cacus[14] and not less mischievous than a truant scholar or court page. And so he made the following reply: "If so, your worship's beds must be hard rocks and your sleep an everlasting watching;[15] wherefore you may boldly dismount and I can assure you that you can hardly miss being kept awake all year long in this house, much less one single night." Saying this, he went and held Don Quixote's stirrup, who forthwith dismounted, though with much difficulty, for he had not broken his fast all that day. He then told the host to take great care of his horse, saying that he was one of the finest pieces of horse-flesh that ever ate bread. The innkeeper looked him over but thought him not so good by half as his master had said. After stabling him, he returned to receive his guest's orders and found the damsels (who had now become reconciled to him) disarming him, but though they were able to take off the back- and breast-plates, they did not know how to undo his gorget[16] or remove his counterfeit helmet, which he had tied on with green ribbons in such a way that they could not be untied. It was necessary to cut them because the knots were so intricate, but he would not allow this to be done, and so remained all that night with his helmet on, and was the strangest and pleasantest sight imaginable.

And while he was being disarmed by those lights-o'-love whom he imagined to be ladies of quality of that castle, he said to them with great charm:

> "There never was on earth a knight
> So waited on by ladies fair
> As once was he, Don Quixote hight,
> When first he left his village dear:
> Damsels to serve him ran with speed
> And princesses to dress his steed.[17]

"Rozinante, ladies, is the name of my horse, and Don Quixote of La Mancha my own. I never intended to discover myself until deeds performed in your service should have proclaimed me, but the need of adapting to my present purpose the old ballad of Sir Lancelot has made my right name known to you prematurely. But the day will come when your ladyships shall command and I obey, and the valor of my arm make plain my desire to serve you."

---

[13] *Castellano* means both "castellan" (a governor of a castle) and "Castilian" (a native of Castile).

[14] Cacus, in Roman mythology, stole some of Hercules' cattle.

[15] The innkeeper quotes the same ballad Quixote quotes above.   [16] Throatpiece.

[17] Quixote is quoting, and altering, a ballad about Sir Lancelot, as he acknowledges below.

The girls, unaccustomed to such flourishes of rhetoric, made no reply but asked whether he would eat anything. "Fain would I break my fast," answered Don Quixote, "for I think that a little food would be of great service to me." That day happened to be a Friday and there was nothing in the inn but some pieces of fish, called in Castile pollack, in Andalusia codfish, in some parts ling, and in others troutlets, or Poor Jack. They asked him if he would eat some troutlets, for they had no other fish to offer him. "Provided there are many little trout," answered Don Quixote, "they will supply the place of one salmon trout, for it is the same to me whether I receive eight single reals or one piece of eight. Moreover, those troutlets may turn out to be like unto veal, which is better than beef, and kid, which is superior to goat. Be that as it may, let it come in quickly, for the toil and weight of arms cannot be sustained without the good government of the guts." As the air was cool, they placed the table at the door of the inn, and the landlord brought a portion of ill-soaked and worse-cooked codfish and a piece of bread as black and moldy as the knight's arms. It was a laughable sight to see him eat, for as he had his helmet and his visor up, he could not feed himself, and so one of the ladies performed that service for him. But it would have been impossible for him to drink had not the innkeeper bored a cane, and placing one end in his mouth, poured in the wine at the other end. All this he endured patiently rather than cut the ribbons of his helmet.

While he was at his meal, a hog-gelder happened to sound his reed flageolet four or five times as he came near the inn. This was a still more convincing proof to Don Quixote that he was in a famous castle where they were entertaining him with music, that the codfish was salmon trout, the bread of the purest white, the whores ladies, and the innkeeper the governor of the fortress. All this made him applaud his own resolution and his enterprising sally. There was only one thing that vexed him: he regretted that he was not dubbed a knight, for he thought that he could not lawfully undertake any adventure until he had received the order of knighthood.

CHAPTER III

Which relates the pleasant method by which Don Quixote had himself dubbed knight

As he was tormented by that thought, he made short work of his meager, pothouse supper. Then he called for his host, shut himself up with him in the stable, and fell upon his knees, saying: "I will never rise from this place, valorous knight, until your courtesy grants me the boon I seek, one that will redound to your glory and to the advantage of the human race." The innkeeper, seeing his guest at his feet and hearing such words, stared at him in bewilderment, without knowing what to do or say. He tried to make him get up, but in vain, for the latter would not consent to do so until the boon he demanded was granted. "I expected no less from your magnificence," answered Don Quixote, "and so I say unto you that the boon I have demanded and that you, out of your liberality, have granted unto me is that tomorrow morning you will dub me knight. This night I shall watch over my arms in the chapel of your castle,[18] and tomorrow, as I have said, you will fulfill my earnest desires so that I may sally forth through the four parts of the world in quest of adventures on behalf of the distressed, as is the duty of knighthood and knights-errant who, like myself, are devoted to such achievements."

The host, who was, as we said before, a bit of a wag and already had some doubts about his guest's sanity, now found all his suspicions confirmed, but he resolved to humor him so that he might have sport that night. He told the knight that his wishes were very reasonable, for such pursuits were natural to knights so illustrious as he seemed and his gallant bearing showed him to be. He added that he himself in the days of his youth had devoted himself to the same honorable profession and had wandered over various parts of the world in search of adventures; and, moreover, he had not failed to visit the curing grounds of Málaga, the Isles of Riarán, the Precinct of Seville, the Quicksilver Square of Segovia, the Olive field of Valencia, the Circle of Granada, the Strand of Sanlúcar, the Colt Fountain of Córdoba, the Taverns of Toledo, and divers other haunts where he had proved the nimbleness of his feet and the lightness of his fingers, committing wrongs in plenty, accosting many widows, deflowering sundry maidens, tricking some minors, and finally making himself known and famous to all the tribunals and courts over the length and breadth of Spain.[19] At last he had retired to this castle, where he lived on his own and on other men's revenues, entertaining therein knights-errant of every quality, solely for the great affection he bore them, and that they might share their goods with him in return for his benevolence. He further told him that in his castle there was no chapel where he could watch over his arms, for he had knocked it down to build it anew. However, in case of necessity, he might watch over the arms wherever he pleased, and therefore, he might watch that night in the castle courtyard. Then, the following morning, with God's help, the required ceremonies would be carried out in such a way that he would be dubbed a knight so effectively that nowhere in the world could one more perfect be found. He asked if Don Quixote had brought any money. "Not a farthing," answered the knight, "for I have never read in the stories of knights-errant that they ever carried money with them."

"You are mistaken," answered the landlord, "for although the stories are silent on this matter, seeing that the authors did not think it necessary to specify such obvious requirements as money and clean shirts, yet there is no reason to believe that the knights had none. On the contrary, it was an established fact that all knights-errant (whose deeds fill many a volume) carried their purses well lined against accidents, and moreover, they carried, in addition to shirts, a small chest of ointments to heal their wounds, for in the plains and deserts where they fought and were wounded, there was no one to cure them unless they were lucky enough to have some wise enchanter for friend who straightaway would send through the air in a

---

[18] In chivalric romances, the "vigil" (watching over one's arms overnight) was an important part of the ceremony of knighthood.

[19] The places the innkeeper names were all associated with robbers and thieves.

cloud some damsel or dwarf with a vial of water possessed of such power that upon tasting a single drop of it, they would instantly find their wounds as perfectly cured as if they had never received any. But when the knights had no such friend, they always insisted that their squires should be provided with money and such necessities as lint and ointments; and when they had no squires (which was very seldom), they themselves carried those things on the crupper of their horse in saddlebags so small that they were scarcely visible, for except in such a case, the custom of carrying saddlebags was not allowed among knights-errant. I must, therefore, advise you," he continued, "nay, I might even command you, seeing that you are shortly to become my godson in chivalry, never from this day forward to travel without money or without the aforesaid necessities, and you will see how serviceable you will find them when least you expect it."

Don Quixote promised to follow his injunctions carefully, and an order was given for him to watch over his armor in a large yard adjoining the inn. When the knight had collected all his arms together, he laid them on a stone trough that was close by the side of a wall. Then embracing his buckler and grasping his lance, he began with stately air to pace up and down in front of the trough, and as he began his parade, night began to close in.

The landlord, meanwhile, told all who were in the inn of the madness of his guest, the arms vigil, and the knighthood dubbing that was to come. They were astonished at such a strange kind of madness and flocked to observe him from a distance. They saw that sometimes he paced to and fro and at other times he leaned on his lance and gazed fixedly at his arms for a considerable time. It was now night, but the moon shone so clearly that she might have almost vied with the luminary that lent her splendor, and thus every action of our new knight could be seen by the spectators.

Just at this moment one of the carriers in the inn took it into his head to water his team of mules, to do which would necessitate removing Don Quixote's arms from the trough. But the knight, as he saw him approach, cried out in a loud voice: "O thou, whosoever thou art, rash knight that dost prepare to lay hands upon the arms of the most valiant knight-errant who ever girded sword, take heed and touch them not if thou wouldst not leave thy life in guerdon[20] for thy temerity." The carrier paid no heed to this warning (it would have been better for him if he had), but seizing hold of the armor by the straps, he threw it a good way from him. No sooner did Don Quixote perceive this than, raising his eyes to heaven and fixing his thoughts (as it seemed) upon his lady, Dulcinea, he said: "Assist me, O lady, in this first affront that is offered to thy vassal's heart. Let not thy favor and protection fail me in this first encounter." Uttering these and similar words, he let slip his buckler, and raising the lance in both hands, he gave the carrier such a hefty blow on the pate that he felled him to the ground in so grievous a plight that if he had followed it with a second, there would have been no need of a surgeon to cure him. This done, he put back his arms and began to pace to and fro as peacefully as before.

Soon after, another carrier, not knowing what had happened (for the first still lay unconscious), came out with the same intention of watering his mules and began to take away the arms that were encumbering the trough,

---

[20]Recompense.

when Don Quixote, not saying a word or imploring assistance from a soul, once more dropped his buckler, lifted up his lance, and without breaking it to pieces, opened the second muleteer's head in four places. All the people in the inn rushed out when they heard the noise, and the landlord among them. As soon as Don Quixote saw them, he braced on his buckler and laid his hands upon his sword, saying: "O lady of beauty, strength and vigor of my enfeebled heart! Now is the time for thee to turn the eyes of thy greatness upon this thy captive knight, who stands awaiting so great an adventure." These words, it seemed to him, filled him with such courage that if all the muleteers in the world had attacked him he would not have retreated one step. The wounded men's companions, seeing them in such an evil plight, began from afar to rain a shower of stones upon Don Quixote, who defended himself as best he could with his buckler, but he did not dare to leave the trough for fear of leaving his arms unprotected. The landlord shouted at them to let him alone, for he had told them the man was mad, and as such, he would be acquitted even if he killed every one of them. Don Quixote shouted still louder, called them caitiffs and traitors, and the lord of the castle a cowardly, baseborn knight for allowing knights-errant to be treated in such a manner. "I would make thee understand," cried he, "what a traitorous scoundrel thou art had I but been dubbed a knight. But as for you, ye vile and base rabble, I care not a fig for you; fire on, advance, draw near, and hurt me as much as you dare. Soon ye shall receive the reward for your folly and presumption." Such was the undaunted boldness with which he uttered these words that his attackers were struck with terror. And so, partly through fear and partly through the persuasive words of the landlord, they ceased to fling stones at him, and he allowed them to carry off their wounded, after which he returned to the guard of his arms with as much calm gravity as before.

The landlord did not relish the mad pranks of his guest, so he determined to make an end of them and give him his accursed order of chivalry before any further misfortune occurred. And so, going up to him, he excused himself for the insolent way those low fellows had treated him, without his knowledge or consent, adding that they had been well chastised for their rashness. He repeated what he had said before: that there was no chapel in that castle, nor was one necessary for what remained to be done; that the chief point of the knighting ceremony consisted in the accolade and the tap on the shoulders, according to the ceremonial of the order,[21] and that might be administered in the middle of a field; that he had performed the duty of watching over his armor, for he had watched more than four hours, whereas only two were required. All this Don Quixote believed and said that he was then ready to obey him, but yet begged him to conclude with all the brevity possible, for if he should be attacked again when he was armed a knight, he was determined not to leave one person alive in the castle, except those whom, out of respect for the governor of the fortress and at his request, he would spare. The governor, being warned and alarmed at possible consequences, brought out forthwith a book in which he kept his account of the straw and barley supplied to the carriers, and

---

[21] The "accolade" (a ceremonial embrace) and a ceremonial tap on the shoulders with a sword were part of the ceremony conferring knighthood.

with a stump of candle, which a boy held lighted in his hands, and accompanied by the two above-mentioned damsels, he went over to Don Quixote and ordered him to kneel. He then read in his manual as if he had been repeating some pious oration. In the midst of the prayer he raised his hand and gave him a good blow on the neck, and after that gave a royal thwack on the shoulders, all the time mumbling between his teeth as if praying. After this he commanded one of the ladies to gird on his sword, which she did with much discretion and aplomb, plenty of which was needed to prevent them all from bursting with laughter at every stage of the ceremonies; but the prowess they had beheld in the new knight made them restrain their laughter. As she girded on his sword, the good lady said: "God make you fortunate, knight, and give you success in your contests." Don Quixote demanded then how she was called that he might henceforward know to whom he was beholden for the favor received, for he was resolved to give her a share of the honor that his valor should merit. And she answered with great humility that she was called La Tolosa and was a cobbler's daughter from Toledo, who lived near Sancho Bienaya Square, and that she would always serve him and consider him her lord wherever she happened to be. Don Quixote replied, requesting her for his sake to call herself henceforth Lady Tolosa, which she promised to do. Then the other lady buckled on his spur and he addressed her in very nearly the same terms as the lady of the sword. He asked her name, and she said she was called La Molinera and was daughter of an honest miller of Antequera. He begged her to take a title and call herself Lady Molinera, at the same time making new offers of service.

Don Quixote could not rest until he found himself mounted on horseback and sallying forth in quest of adventures, and after saddling Rozinante, he mounted, but not before he had embraced his host and said so many extravagant words in thanking him for having dubbed him knight that it is impossible to tell them. The landlord, that he might speed the parting guest, answered him in no less rhetorical flourishes but in briefer words, and without asking him to pay for his lodging, he let him go with a godspeed.

CHAPTER IV

What happened to our knight when he sallied from the inn

It was about daybreak when Don Quixote sallied forth from the inn, so happy, so lively, and so excited at finding himself knighted that his very horse girths were ready to burst for joy. But calling to mind the advice of his host concerning the necessary accouterments for his travels, especially the money and the clean shirts, he resolved to return home to provide himself with them and with a squire. He had in view a certain laboring man of the neighborhood who was poor and had children but was otherwise very well fitted for the office of squire to a knight. With this thought in mind he turned Rozinante toward his village, and the horse, knowing full well the way to his stable, began to trot so briskly that his hoofs seemed hardly to strike the ground. The knight had not traveled far when he thought he heard the faint cries of someone in distress from a thicket on his right hand. No sooner had he heard them than he said: "I render thanks to heaven for such a favor. Already I have an opportunity of performing the duty of my profession and of reaping the harvest of my good ambition. Those cries must surely come from some distressed man or woman who needs my protection." Then turning his reins, he guided Rozinante toward the place from which he thought the cries came. A short distance within the wood he saw a mare tied to an oak and to another a youth of about fifteen years of age naked from the waist up. It was he who was crying out, and not without reason, for a lusty countryman was flogging him with a leather strap, and every blow he accompanied with a word of warning and advice, saying, "Keep your mouth shut and your eyes skinned." The boy answered: "I'll never do it again, master. By God's passion, I won't do it again and I promise in future to be more careful of your flock."

When Don Quixote saw what was happening, he said in an angry voice: "Discourteous knight, it is a caitiff's deed to attack one who cannot defend himself. Get up on your horse and take your lance" (for the farmer, too, had a lance leaning against the oak tree to which the mare was tied) "I will show you that you have been acting a coward's part." The countryman, at the sight of the strange apparition in armor brandishing a lance over him, gave himself up for lost and so replied submissively: "Sir knight, this youth I am chastising is a servant of mine, whom I employ to look after a flock of sheep in the neighborhood, but he is so careless that every day he loses one, and when I punish him for his negligence or rascality, he says I do it because I am a skinflint and will not pay him his wages. Upon my life and soul, he lies."

"Have you the impudence to lie in my presence, vile serf?" said Don Quixote. "By the sun that shines on us I will pierce you through and through with this lance of mine. Pay him instantly and none of your denials. If not, by almighty God who rules us all, I will annihilate you this very moment. Untie him at once."

The countryman lowered his head and without a word untied his servant. Don Quixote then asked the boy how much his master owed him. He replied nine months' wages at seven reals a month. Don Quixote, having calculated the sum, found that it came to sixty-three reals and told the farmer to pay up the money unless he wished to die. The farmer, who was shaking with fear, then answered that on the word of one in a tight corner and also upon his oath (yet he had sworn nothing), he did not owe so much, for they must deduct three pairs of shoes that he had given the boy and a real for two bloodlettings that he had when he was sick.

"That is all very well," answered Don Quixote, "but let the shoes and the bloodletting stand for the blows that you have given him for no fault of his own; if he wore out the leather of the shoes you gave him, you wore out his skin, and if the barber drew blood from him when he was sick,[22] you drew blood from him when he was in good health; so in this matter he owes you nothing."

---

[22] Barbers also functioned as surgeons.

"The trouble is, sir knight," said the countryman, "that I have no money on me. If Andrés comes home with me, I'll pay him ready money down."

"I go home with him?" said the boy. "Not on your life, sir! I would not think of doing such a thing; the moment he gets me alone he'll flay me like a Saint Bartholomew."[23]

"He will not do so," answered Don Quixote. "I have only to command and he will respect me and do my behest. So I shall let him go free and guarantee payment to you, provided he swears by the order of knighthood that he has received."

"Take heed, sir, of what you are saying," said the boy. "My master is no knight; he has not received any order of knighthood. He is Juan Haldudo the wealthy, a native of Quintanar."

"That matters little," answered Don Quixote; "there may be Haldudos who are knights, especially as every man is the son of his own works."

"That's true," said Andrés, "but what kind of works is my master the son of? Isn't he denying me the wages of my sweat and toil?"

"I'm not denying them, brother Andrés," answered the countryman. "Do, please, come with me and I swear by all the orders of knighthood there are in the world to pay you, as I said before, every real down and even perfumed into the bargain."

"I'll spare you the perfume," said Don Quixote. "Give them to him in good, honest reals and I shall be satisfied; but see to it that you carry out your oath. If not, I swear by the same oath to return and chastise you, and I am sure to find you, even if you hide away from me more successfully than a lizard. And if you want to know who it is who gives you this command, learn that I am the valiant Don Quixote of La Mancha, the undoer of wrongs and injuries. So, God be with you, and do not forget what you have promised and sworn, on pain of the penalty I have stated." With these words he spurred Rozinante and in a moment he was far away.

The countryman gazed after him, and when he saw that he had gone through the wood and was out of sight, he turned to his servant, Andrés, saying: "Come here, my boy; I want to pay you what I owe you in accordance with the commands of that undoer of wrongs."

"So you will, I swear," said Andrés; "and you had better obey the orders of that good knight—may he live a thousand years. He is such a courageous man and such a fair judge that by Saint Roch, if you don't pay me, he'll be back and he'll do what he threatened."

"And I'll swear I will too," answered the countryman, "and to show you my goodwill, I'll double the debt so that I can double the pay." Catching the boy by the arm, he tied him again to the oak and gave him such a drubbing that he left him for dead. "Now, master Andrés," said he, "call out to that undoer of wrongs and you'll find that he won't undo this one. Indeed I don't think I'm finished with you yet, for I've a mind to flay you alive as you feared a moment ago." At last he untied him and gave him leave to go off and fetch his judge to carry out the threatened sentence. As for Andrés, he went off sorely fretful, swearing that he would seek out the valiant Don

---

[23] Saint Bartholomew, one of the twelve apostles and martyrs, was said to have been flayed to death.

Quixote of La Mancha and tell him all that happened, and he would make his tormentor pay sevenfold. However, he departed in tears, while his master stayed behind laughing.

Such was the manner in which the valiant Don Quixote undid that wrong.

Meanwhile the knight was quite pleased with himself, for he believed that he had begun his feats of arms in a most successful and dignified manner, and he went on riding toward his village, saying to himself in a low voice: "Well mayest thou call thyself the happiest of all women on earth, O Dulcinea of El Toboso, peerless among beauties, for it was thy fortune to have subject to thy will so valiant and celebrated a knight as is and shall be Don Quixote of La Mancha, who, as all the world knows, received only yesterday the order of knighthood and today has undone the greatest wrong that ever ignorance designed or cruelty committed. Today from the hand of that pitiless foe he seized the lash with which he so unjustly scourged that tender child."

Just then he came to a road that branched into four directions, and forthwith he was reminded of the crossroads where knights-errant would halt to consider which road they should follow. To imitate their example, he paused for a moment's meditation, and then he slackened the reins, leaving Rozinante to choose the way. The horse followed his original intention, which was to make straight in the direction of his stable.

When Don Quixote had ridden about two miles, he saw a big company of people who, as it appeared later, were traders of Toledo on their way to buy silk in Murcia. There were six of them and they carried sunshades. They were accompanied by four servants on horseback and three muleteers on foot. No sooner had Don Quixote perceived them than he fancied a new adventure was at hand. So, imitating as closely as possible the exploits he had read about in his books, he resolved now to perform one that was admirably molded to the present circumstances. So, with a lofty bearing he fixed himself firmly in his stirrups, grasped his lance, covered himself with his buckler, and stood in the middle of the road waiting for those knights-errant to approach (for such he supposed them to be). As soon as they came within earshot, Don Quixote, raising his voice, cried out in an arrogant tone: "Let all the world stand still if all the world does not confess that there is not in all the world a fairer damsel than the Empress of La Mancha, the peerless Dulcinea of El Toboso."

At the sound of those words the traders pulled up and gazed in amazement at the grotesque being who uttered them. Both the tone and the appearance of the horseman gave clear proof of his insanity, but they wished to consider in more leisurely fashion the meaning of this confession that he insisted upon. So one of them, who was a trifle waggish in humor and had plenty of wit, addressed him as follows: "Sir knight, we do not know this lady you speak of. Show her to us, and if she is as beautiful as you say, we shall willingly and universally acknowledge the truth of your claim."

"If I were to show her to you," answered Don Quixote, "what merit would there be in acknowledging a truth so manifest to all? The important point is that you should believe, confess, affirm, swear, and defend it without setting eyes on her. If you do not, I challenge you to try battle with me, ye presumptuous and overweening band. Come on now, one by one as the traditions of chivalry declare, or else all together according to the foul custom of your breed. Here I stand waiting for you, trusting in the justice of my cause."

"Sir knight," answered the trader, "I beseech you in the name of all the princes here present not to force us to burden our consciences by confessing something we have never seen or heard, especially when it is so prejudicial to the empresses and queens of Alcarria and Extremadura.[24] Please show us some picture of that lady, even if it is no bigger than a grain of wheat, for a thread will enable us to judge the whole skein and we shall be satisfied and you yourself happy and content. I believe that we already are so much on your side that even if your lady's picture shows that one eye squints and the other drips vermilion and sulphur, yet in spite of all, to gratify you, we shall say all that you please in her favor."

"Drip indeed, you infamous scoundrels!" cried Don Quixote in a towering rage. "Nothing of the kind drips from her eyes, but only ambergris and civet in cotton wool. She is not squint-eyed nor hunchbacked, but straighter than a Guadarrama spindle. But you shall pay the penalty for the great blasphemy you have uttered against so peerless a beauty as my lady." With those words he attacked the man who had spoken to him, so fiercely with couched lance that if good fortune had not caused Rozinante to stumble and fall midway, the merchant would have paid dearly for his rashness. Rozinante fell and his master rolled a good distance over the ground. Although he tried to rise, he could not, for he was so impeded by the lance, the buckler, the spurs, the helmet, and the weight of the ancient armor. However, as he was struggling to arise, he kept on crying: "Flee not, cowardly rabble! Wait, slavish herd! It is not my fault, but the fault of my horse, that I am stretched here."

One of the muleteers of the company, who indeed was not very good-natured, when he heard the poor fallen knight say such arrogant words, could not resist the temptation to give him the answer on his ribs. So he went up to him, took the lance, broke it into pieces, and with one of them he so belabored our poor Don Quixote that in spite of his armor he thrashed him like a measure of wheat. His masters shouted to him not to beat him so much and to leave off; but the fellow was angry and would not stop the game until he had spent what remained of his rage. Then, running to get the rest of the pieces of the lance, he splintered them all on the wretched knight, who, in the midst of all this tempest of blows that rained on him, did not for a moment close his mouth, but bellowed out threats to heaven and earth and those villainous cutthroats (for so they appeared to him). At last the muleteer became wearied and the traders pursued their journey, carrying with them plenty of matter for conversation at the expense of the poor drubbed knight. And when he was alone, he tried to see if he could get up, but if he could not do so when he was hale and hearty, how could he do it when he was bruised and battered? And yet he counted himself lucky, for he thought that his misfortune was peculiar to knights-errant and he attributed the whole accident to the fault of his horse. But so bruised was his whole body that it was impossible for him to get up.

[24] Both backward, primitive regions.

CHAPTER V

In which is continued the account of our knight's mishap

Seeing that he couldn't stir, he resolved to have recourse to his usual remedy, which was to think of some incident from one of his books. His madness made him remember that of the Marquess of Mantua and Baldwin, whom Carloto left wounded on the mountainside[25]—a story familiar to children, not unknown to youths, celebrated and even believed by old men, yet for all that, no more authentic than the miracles of Mohammed. Now this story, so he thought, exactly fitted his present circumstances, so with great display of affliction he began to roll about on the ground and to repeat in a faint voice the words that the wounded knight in the wood was supposed to have said:

> "Where art thou, lady of my heart,
> That for my woe thou dost not grieve?
> Alas, thou do know'st not my distress,
> Or thou art false and pitiless."

In this manner he repeated the ballad until he came to those verses that say: "O noble Marquess of Mantua, my uncle and liege lord." By chance there happened to pass by at that very moment a peasant of his own village, a neighbor, who was returning from bringing a load of wheat to the mill. And he, seeing a man lying stretched out on the ground, came over and asked him who he was and what was the cause of his sorrowful lamentation. Don Quixote, firmly believing that the man was the Marquess of Mantua, his uncle, would not answer but continued reciting his ballad, which told of his misfortunes and of the loves of the Emperor's son with his wife, just as the book relates it. The peasant was amazed to hear those extravagant words. Then taking off his visor, which had been broken to pieces in the drubbing, he wiped the dust off his face. No sooner had he done so than he recognized him and said: "Master Quixana" (for that must have been how people called him when he had his wits and had not been transformed from a staid gentleman into a knight-errant) "who left you in such a state?" But he kept on reciting his ballad and made no answer to what he was asked. The good man then, as best as he could, took off his breast- and back-plate to see if he was wounded, but he saw no blood or scar upon him. He managed to lift him up from the ground and with the greatest difficulty hoisted him on to his ass, thinking that beast an easier mount. Then he gathered together all his arms, not omitting even the splinters of the lance, tied them into a bundle, and laid them upon Rozinante's back. Then taking the horse by the bridle and the ass by the halter, he set off toward his village, meditating all the while on the foolish words that Don Quixote kept saying. And Don Quixote on his part was no less pensive, for he was so beaten and bruised that he could hardly hold himself onto the ass, and from time to time he uttered such melancholy sighs that seemed to pierce

[25] Carloto, son of Charlemagne, was the hero of a well-known ballad, which Quixote quotes below.

the skies that the peasant felt again moved to ask him what was the cause of his sorrow. But it must have been the Devil himself who supplied him with stories so similiar to his circumstances, for at that instant, forgetting Baldwin, he remembered the Moor Abindarráez whom the governor of Antequera, Rodrigo de Narváez, took prisoner to his castle.[26] So when the peasant asked him again how he was, he answered word for word as the captive Abindarráez answered Rodrigo de Narváez, just as he had read in Montemayor's *Diana*, where the story is told. And he applied it so artfully to his own case that the peasant wished he were in Hell rather than to have to listen to such a hodgepodge of foolishness. This convinced him that his neighbor was mad, so he made haste to reach the village and thereby escape being further plagued by Don Quixote's long discourse. The latter ended by saying: "I would have you know, Master Rodrigo de Narváez, that the beauteous Jarifa I have mentioned is now the fair Dulcinea of El Toboso, for whom I have done, still do, and shall do the most famous deeds of chivalry that ever have been, are, or ever shall be seen in the world." To this the peasant answered: "Take heed, sir, that I am neither Don Rodrigo de Narváez nor the Marquess of Mantua, but Pedro Alonso, your neighbor, and you are neither Baldwin nor Abindarráez, but the honorable gentleman Master Quixana."

"I know who I am," answered Don Quixote, "and I know that I can be not only those I have mentioned but also the Twelve Peers of France and even the Nine Worthies, for my exploits will surpass all they have ever jointly or separately achieved."[27]

With this and sundry topics of conversation they reached the village at sunset, but the peasant waited until it was dark so that no one would see the belabored knight so sorrily mounted. When he thought the time had come, he entered the village and went to Don Quixote's house, which he found in an uproar. The curate and the village barber, great friends of Don Quixote, happened to be there and the housekeeper was addressing them in a loud voice: "What do you think, Master Licentiate Pedro Pérez" (that was the curate's name) "of my master's misfortune? For the past six days neither he, nor his horse, nor his buckler, nor his lance, nor his armor has appeared. Woe is me! I'm now beginning to understand, and I'm as sure of it as I am of death that those accursed books of chivalry that he continually reads have turned his brain topsy-turvy. Now that I think of it I remember hearing him say to himself many a time that he wished to become a knight-errant and go through the world in search of adventures. The Devil and Barabbas[28] take such books, for they have ruined the finest mind in all La Mancha!" The niece said the same and a little more: "You must know, Master Nicholas" (this was the name of the barber) "that it was a frequent occurrence for my uncle to read these soulless books of misadventures for

---

[26] There were a number of romance tales about the love of the captive Moor Abindarráez for the beautiful Jarifa. One version of the story is in Jorge de Montemayor's romance *Diana* (1561), which Quixote mentions.

[27] The Twelve Peers were Charlemagne's chief knights, all equal in rank. The Nine Worthies, in medieval lore, were nine famous men, three Jewish, three pagan, and three Christian, subjects of a number of tales and chronicles.

[28] The robber whom Pilate pardoned instead of Christ; see, for example, Matthew 27: 15–26.

days and nights on end. At the end of that time he would cast the book from his hands, clutch his sword, and begin to slash the walls. Then, when he was grown very weary, he would say that he had killed four giants as big as towers and that the sweat that dripped off him after his great exertions, he would say, was blood from the wounds he had received in battle. Then he would drink a great jugful of water and become calm and peaceable, saying that the water was a most precious liquor that his friend the great enchanter Esquife had given him. I, however, blame myself for all, for not having warned you of my uncle's extravagant behavior. You might have cured him before things reached such a state, and you would have burned all those excommunicated books (he has many, mind you), for they all deserve to be burned as heretics."

"I agree with that," said the curate, "and I hold that tomorrow must not pass without a public inquiry being made into them. They should be condemned to the fire to prevent them from tempting those who read them to do what my poor master must have done."

All this Don Quixote and the peasant heard. The latter finally understood the infirmity of his neighbor and began to shout: "Open your doors, all of you, to Sir Baldwin and the Marquess of Mantua, who is grievously wounded, and to the Moor Abindarráez, who is led captive by the valiant Rodrigo de Narváez, governor of Antequera."

Hearing these cries, they all rushed out and straightaway recognized their friend. They ran to embrace him, but he had not yet dismounted from the ass, for he was not able to do so. He said: "Stand back, all of you. I have been sorely wounded through the fault of my horse; carry me to my bed and, if possible, call the wise Urganda to examine and cure my wounds."

"A thousand curses," said the housekeeper then. "My heart told me clearly on which foot my master limped. Come on upstairs, sir; we'll know how to look after you here without that Urganda woman. Curses, aye, a hundred curses on those books of chivalry that have driven you to this!"

They carried him to his bed and searched his body for wounds, but could find none. He said he was all bruised after a great fall he had with his horse, Rozinante, when he was fighting ten giants, the fiercest and most overweening in the world.

"Aha!" said the curate. "So there are giants too in the dance. By the sign of the Cross I swear I'll burn the lot of them before tomorrow night."

They questioned Don Quixote a thousand times, but he would give no answer. He only asked them to give him food and allow him to sleep, for rest was what he needed most. . . .

[In a chapter omitted here, the curate and the barber examine the contents of Don Quixote's library and burn all the books on knight-errantry. They examine the title pages and comment critically on the absurd contents.]

CHAPTER VII

Of the second sally of our good knight Don Quixote of La Mancha

. . . . That same night the housekeeper burned all the books she could find in the courtyard and in the house, and some that perished in the flames deserved to be preserved forever in the archives, but fate and the laziness of the inquisitor did not allow it, and thus in their case the saying was fulfilled that the saint sometimes pays for the sinner. One of the remedies that the curate and the barber then prescribed for their friend's infirmity was to wall up the room where the books had been stored so that when he rose he should not find them, for once the cause had been removed, the effect might cease. And they agreed to tell him that an enchanter had whisked books, room, and all away. The plan was carried out with great speed.

Two days later Don Quixote got up, and the first thing he did was to go and see his books, and as he could not find the room in which he had left them, he went up and down and all over the house looking for it. He came to the place where the door used to be and felt the wall with his hands, staring around him on all sides without saying a word. At last he asked the housekeeper where was the study in which he kept his books. The housekeeper, who knew exactly what she had to answer, said: "What manner of study is your worship looking for? There are no studies or books in this house now, for the Devil in person took all away."

"It was not the Devil," said the niece, "but an enchanter who arrived on a cloud one night after you went away from here. He got down off the serpent on which he was riding and went into the room. I don't know what he did in there, but soon after he went flying out through the roof, leaving the house full of smoke. When we looked to see what he had done, we could see no books or room, but we remember very well, myself and the housekeeper, that when the wicked old man was about to depart, he said in a loud voice that owing to the secret enmity he bore against the owner of those books and of the room, he had done damage that would soon be clear. He also said that he was called Muñatón the wizard."

"Frestón was the name he wished to say," answered Don Quixote.

"I don't know," said the housekeeper, "whether he was called Frestón or Fritón; I only know that his name ended in *-tón*."

"That is true," said Don Quixote. "He is a wise enchanter, a great enemy of mine, and looks upon me with a malicious eye, for he knows by his skill and wisdom that in the course of time I shall fight in single combat with a knight whom he favors, and I shall win, in spite of all his machinations; so, he tries to do me all the hurt he can. But I affirm that he will never prevail over what has been ordained by Heaven."

"Who has any doubts on that score?" said the niece. "But, dear uncle, what have you to do with such quarrels? Is it not better to stay peacefully at home instead of roaming the world in search of better bread than is made of wheat, not to mention that many who go for wool come home shorn?"

"My dear niece," answered Don Quixote, "how far you are off the mark! Before they ever shear me, I'll have plucked and lopped off the beards of all who think they can touch the tip of a single hair of mine."

The two would not make any further reply, for they saw that his anger was rising. As a matter of fact, he remained a fortnight peacefully at home without showing any signs of wanting to repeat his former vagaries. During those days he held many pleasant arguments with his two old friends the curate and the barber. He would maintain that what the world needed most of all was plenty of knights-errant and that he himself would revive knight-errantry. The curate sometimes contradicted him; at other times he would give in to him, for had he not adopted this procedure, he could never have dealt with him.

During this interval Don Quixote made overtures to a certain laboring man, a neighbor of his and an honest fellow (if such a term can be applied to one who is poor), but with very little wit in his pate. In effect, he said so much to him and made so many promises that the poor wight resolved to set out with him and serve him as squire. Among other things Don Quixote told him that he should be most willing to go with him because some time or another he might meet with an adventure that would earn for him, in the twinkling of an eye, some island, and he would find himself governor of it. With those and other promises, Sancho Panza (for that was the fellow's name) left his wife and children and engaged himself as squire to his neighbor. Don Quixote then set about raising money, and by selling one thing, pawning another, and throwing away the lot for a mere song, he gathered a respectable sum. He furnished himself likewise with a buckler borrowed from a friend, repaired his broken helmet as best he could, and informed his squire, Sancho, of the day and hour when he intended to sally forth so that the latter might supply himself with all that was needed. He charged him particularly to carry saddlebags. Sancho said he would do so and added that he was thinking of bringing an ass with him, for he had a good one and he was not used to travel on foot. At the mention of the ass Don Quixote hesitated a little, racking his brains to remember any case of a knight-errant who was attended by a squire mounted on ass-back, but he could not remember any such case. Nevertheless, he resolved to let him take his ass, for he intended to present him with a more dignified mount when he got the opportunity, by unhorsing the first discourteous knight he came across. He also provided himself with shirts and other necessities, thus following the advice the innkeeper had given him.

After all these preparations had been made, Don Quixote, without saying farewell to his housekeeper and niece, Panza to his wife and children, set out one night from the village without being seen. They traveled so far that night that at daybreak they were sure that no one would find them, even if they were pursued.

Sancho Panza rode along on his ass like a patriarch, with his saddlebags and wineskin, full of a huge longing to see himself governor of the island his master had promised to him. Don Quixote happened to take the same road as on his first journey, that is, across the Plain of Montiel, which he now traveled with less discomfort than the last time, for as it was early in the morning, the rays of the sun did not beat down directly upon them, but slantwise, and so did not trouble them. Presently Sancho Panza said to his master: "Mind, your worship, sir knight-errant, you don't let slip from your memory the island you've promised me; I'll be able to rule it well, no matter how big it is."

To which Don Quixote replied: "I would have you know, my friend Sancho, that knights-errant of long ago were accustomed to make their squires governors of the islands or kingdoms they won, and I have resolved not to neglect so praiseworthy a custom. Nay, I wish to surpass them in it, for they sometimes, perhaps even on the majority of occasions, waited till their squires were grown old, and then when they were cloyed with service after enduring bad days and worse nights, they conferred upon them some title, such as count or at least marquess, of some valley of more or less account. But if you live and I live, I may, before six days have passed, even conquer a kingdom with a string of dependencies, which would fall in exactly with my plan of crowning you king of one of them. Do not, however, think this strange, for knights-errant of my kind meet with such extraordinary and unexpected chances that I might easily give you still more than I am promising."

"And so," answered Sancho Panza, "by that token, if I became king by one of those miracles you mention, at least my chuck[29] Juana Gutiérrez would become queen and my children princes."

"Who doubts it?" answered Don Quixote.

"I doubt it," replied Sancho Panza, "for I truly believe that even if God were to rain kingdoms down upon earth, none would sit well on the head of Mari Gutiérrez.[30] Believe me, sir, she's not worth two farthings as queen; countess would suit her better, and even then, God help her."

"Leave all in God's hands, Sancho," answered Don Quixote. "He will do what is best for her, but do not humble yourself so far as to be satisfied with anything less than the title of lord-lieutenant."

"I'll not indeed, sir," replied Sancho, "for a famous master like yourself will know what is fit for me and what I can carry."

CHAPTER VIII

Of the valiant Don Quixote's success in the terrifying and never-before-imagined adventure of the windmills, with other events worthy of happy remembrance

Just then they came in sight of thirty or forty windmills that rise from that plain, and no sooner did Don Quixote see them than he said to his squire: "Fortune is guiding our affairs better than we ourselves could have wished. Do you see over yonder, friend Sancho, thirty or forty hulking giants? I intend to do battle with them and slay them. With their spoils we shall begin to be rich, for this is a righteous war and the removal of so foul a brood from off the face of the earth is a service God will bless."

"What giants?" asked Sancho Panza.

"Those you see over there," replied his master, "with their long arms; some of them have them well-nigh two leagues in length."

"Take care, sir," cried Sancho. "Those over there are not giants but windmills, and those things that seem to be arms are their sails, which when they are whirled around by the wind turn the millstone."

"It is clear," replied Don Quixote, "that you are not experienced in adventures. Those are giants, and if you are afraid, turn aside and pray whilst I enter into fierce and unequal battle with them."

Uttering these words, he clapped spurs to Rozinante, his steed, without heeding the cries of his squire, Sancho, who warned him that he was not going to attack giants but windmills. But so convinced was he that they were

[29] A term of endearment. Juana is Sancho's wife.
[30] Gutiérrez is Juana's (or Mari's) maiden name; elsewhere she is called Juana Panza.

giants that he neither heard his squire's shouts nor did he notice what they were, though he was very near them. Instead, he rushed on, shouting in a loud voice: "Fly not, cowards and vile caitiffs; one knight alone attacks you!" At that moment a slight breeze arose and the great sails began to move. When Don Quixote saw this, he shouted again: "Although you flourish more arms than the giant Briareus, you shall pay for it!"[31]

Saying this and commending himself most devoutly to his lady, Dulcinea, whom he begged to help him in this peril, he covered himself with his buckler, couched his lance, charged at Rozinante's full gallop, and rammed the first mill in his way. He ran his lance into the sail, but the wind twisted it with such violence that it shivered the lance in pieces and dragged both rider and horse after it, rolling them over and over on the ground, sorely damaged.

Sancho Panza rushed up to his assistance as fast as his ass could gallop, and when he reached the knight, he found that he was unable to move, such was the blow that Rozinante had given him in the fall.

"God help us!" cried Sancho. "Did I not tell you, sir, to mind what you were doing, for those were only windmills? Nobody could have mistaken them unless he had windmills in his brain."

"Hold your peace, good Sancho," replied Don Quixote. "The affairs of war are, above all others, subject to continual change. Moreover, I am convinced, and that is the truth, that the magician Frestón, the one who robbed me of my study and books, has changed those giants into windmills to deprive me of the glory of victory; such is the enmity he bears against me. But in the end his evil arts will be of little avail against my doughty sword."

"God settle it in His own way," cried Sancho as he helped his master to rise and remount Rozinante, who was well-nigh disjointed by his fall.

They conversed about the recent adventure as they followed the road toward the Pass of Lápice, for there, Don Quixote said, they could not fail to find many and various adventures, seeing that it was a much frequented spot. Nevertheless he was very downcast at the loss of his lance, and in mentioning it to his squire, he said: "I remember having read of a Spanish knight called Diego Pérez de Vargas, who, when he broke his sword in a battle, tore off a huge branch from an oak and with it did such deeds of prowess that day and pounded so many Moors that he earned the surname of Machuca,[32] and so he and his descendants were called from that day onwards Vargas y Machuca. I mention this because I intend to tear from the first oak tree we meet such a branch, with which I am resolved to perform such deeds that you will consider yourself fortunate to witness, exploits that men will scarcely credit."

"God's will be done," said Sancho. "I'll believe all your worship says; but straighten yourself a bit in the saddle, for you seem to be leaning over on one side, which must be from the bruises you received in your fall."

"That is true," replied Don Quixote, "and if I do not complain, it is because knights-errant must never complain of any wound, even though their guts are protruding from them."

---

[31] Briareus was a hundred-armed, fifty-headed giant in Greek mythology. He helped Zeus to overthrow the Titans.

[32] The verb *machucar* means "to pound." The story of Diego Pérez de Vargas, a sort of Spanish Hercules, is told in another old ballad.

"If that be so, I've no more to say," answered Sancho, "but God knows I'd be glad to hear you complain when anything hurts you. As for myself, I'll never fail to complain at the smallest twinge, unless this business of not complaining applies also to squires."

Don Quixote could not help laughing at the simplicity of his squire and told him that he might complain whenever he pleased and to his heart's content, for he had never read anything to the contrary in the order of chivalry. Sancho then bade his master consider that it was now time to eat, but the latter told him to eat whenever he fancied. As for himself, he had no appetite at the moment. Sancho no sooner had obtained leave than he settled himself as comfortably as he could upon his ass, and taking out of his saddlebags some of the contents, he jogged behind his master, munching deliberately; and every now and then he would take a stiff pull at the wineskin with such gusto that the ruddiest tapster in Málaga would have envied him. While he rode on, swilling away in that manner, he did not remember any promise his master might have made to him, and so far from thinking it a labor, he thought it a life of ease to go roaming in quest of adventures, no matter how perilous they might be.

They spent that night under some trees, and from one of them Don Quixote tore a withered branch that might, at a pinch, serve him as a lance, and he fixed to it the iron head of the one he had broken. All that night he did not sleep, for he kept thinking of his lady, Dulcinea. In this way he imitated what he had read in his books, where knights spent many sleepless nights in forests and wastes, reveling in memories of their fair ladies. Not so Sancho Panza, whose belly was full of something more substantial than chicory water. He made one long sleep of it, and if his master had not roused him, not even the rays of the sun beating on his face nor the joyful warbling of the hosts of birds would have awakened him. When he got up he tested the wineskin once more and found it somewhat flabbier than the night before. This saddened him, for he thought that they were not in the way to remedy that loss as soon as would satisfy him. Don Quixote would not break his fast, for as we have said before, he was resolved to nurture himself on savory remembrances. . . .

[In the following chapters, Don Quixote attacks two monks and some muleteers who he thinks are necromancers carrying off a princess; he encounters a beautiful maiden, Marcella, who is as independent and idealistic as Quixote himself; he is beaten by herdsmen who object to Rozinante's amorous attentions to their mares; and he becomes embroiled in a dispute in an inn when he mistakenly thinks a servant girl is a beautiful princess who has fallen in love with him. This incident ends with Sancho being tossed in a blanket.]

CHAPTER XVIII

In which an account is given of the conversation that took place between Sancho Panza and his master, Don Quixote, with other adventures worth recording

. . . . Suddenly Don Quixote saw a large, dense cloud of dust rolling toward them. Turning to Sancho, he said: "This is the day, Sancho, on which shall be clearly seen the good that fate has in store for us; this is the day, I say, on which I shall show the might of my arm and on which I intend to do deeds that shall be written in the books of fame for succeeding ages. Do you see that dust cloud, Sancho? Know then that it is churned up by a mighty army composed of sundry and innumerable people who are marching this way."

"If so, there must be two armies," said Sancho, "for here on this side there is as great a cloud of dust."

Don Quixote turned around to look at it, and seeing it was so, he rejoiced, for he fancied that there were indeed two armies coming to fight each other in the midst of that spacious plain. For his imagination at all hours of the day and night was full of battles, enchantments, adventures, follies, loves, and challenges as are related in the books of chivalry, and all his words, thoughts, and actions were turned to such things. As for the clouds of dust he had seen, they were raised by two large flocks of ewes and rams that were being driven along the same road from opposite directions, which, because of the dust, could not be seen until they came near.

So earnest was Don Quixote in calling them armies that Sancho came to believe it and asked: "Well, what are we to do?"

"What?" said Don Quixote. "Why, favor and help the distressed and needy. You must know, Sancho, that the army marching toward us in front is led by the mighty emperor Alifanfarón, lord of the great island of Trapobana;[33] the other, which is marching at our back, is the army of his foe, the king of the Garamantans, Pentapolín of the Naked Arm, for he always goes into battle with his right arm bare."

"Why do these two gentlemen hate each other so much?" asked Sancho.

"They are enemies," replied Don Quixote, "because Alifanfarón is a furious pagan and is in love with the daughter of Pentapolín, a beautiful, graceful lady and a Christian. Her father refuses to give her to the pagan king unless he abandon first the false religion of Mohammed and turn Christian."

"By my beard," said Sancho, "Pentapolín does right, and I'll help as best I can."

"Then you will do your duty," said Don Quixote, "for it is not necessary to be dubbed a knight to engage in battles such as these."

"I understand," replied Sancho, "but where shall we tie this ass that we may be sure of finding him after the scuffle is over? I think it was never customary to go into battle mounted on such a beast."

"That is true," said Don Quixote. "What you must do is to leave the ass to his own devices. Let him take his chance whether he get lost or not, for after winning this battle we shall have so many horses that even Rozinante runs the risk of being exchanged for another. Now listen to me carefully while I give you an account of the principal knights in the two approaching armies. Let us withdraw to that hillock over there to get a better view of the two armies."

They did so, and standing on the top of the hill, they could have discerned the two flocks that Don Quixote had converted into armies had their eyes not been blinded by the clouds of dust. But seeing in his imagination what did not exist, he began to say in a loud voice: "The knight you see

[33] Most of the high-sounding names in this passage are imaginary. Trapobana, or Taprobana, is the ancient name given the island of Ceylon.

yonder with the yellow armor, who bears on his shield a crowned lion couchant at a damsel's feet, is the valiant Laurcalco, lord of the Silver Bridge. The other with armor flowered with gold, who bears on his shield three crowns argent on an azure field, is the fearsome Micocolembo, grand duke of Quirotia. The other, with gigantic limbs, who marches on his right, is the undaunted Brandabarbarán of Boliche, lord of the Three Arabias. He is wearing a serpent's skin and bears a gate as a shield, which, fame says, was one of those belonging to the temple that Samson pulled down when by his death he took revenge on his enemies.[34] Now turn your eyes to this other side, and there you will see, in front of this other army, the victorious and never vanquished Timonel of Carcajona, prince of New Biscay, who comes clad in armor quartered azure, vert, argent, and or. He bears on his shield a cat or on a field gules with a scroll inscribed *Miau*, which is the beginning of his mistress' name—according to report—the peerless Miaulina, daughter of Alfeñiquén, duke of Algarbe. The other, who weighs down and oppresses the back of that powerful and spirited charger, with armor as white as snow and a white shield without a device, is a novice knight of the French nation called Pierre Papin, lord of the baronies of Utrique. The other pricking with iron heel the flanks of that nimble zebra and carrying for arms the azure cups is the doughty duke of Nerbia, Espartafilardo of the Wood, who bears on his shield the device of an asparagus plant, with a motto in Castilian which says: *My fortune trails.*"

So he went on, naming many imaginary knights in each squadron as his fancy dictated and giving extemporaneously to each his armor, colors, devices, and mottoes, for he was completely carried away by his strangely deluded imagination. He continued without a pause: "That squadron in the front is composed of men of various nations: Here are they who drink of the sweet waters of the famous Xanthus; mountaineers who tread the Massilian fields; those who sift the pure and fine gold of Arabia; dwellers on the celebrated cool shores of clear Thermodon; those who drain in various ways the golden Pactolus; the Numidians, unreliable in their promises; Persians, famous for their bows and arrows; Parthians; Medes, who fight as they flee; Arabs, with their movable houses; Scythians as cruel as they are fair; Ethiopians with pierced lips; and countless other nations, whose faces I recognize and behold, although their names I do not recollect. In that other squadron come drinkers of the crystal waters of the olive-bearing Betis; men who burnish and polish their faces with the liquor of the ever-rich and golden Tagus; men who enjoy the health-giving waters of the divine Genil; dwellers in the Tartessian plain with their abundant pastures; men who enjoy the Elysian fields of Jérez; men of La Mancha rich and crowned with golden corn; men clad in iron, survivors of the ancient Gothic race; bathers in the Pisuerga, famous for its mild current; men who graze their flock on the broad pastures of the winding Guadiana, famous for its hidden current;[35] men who shiver with the cold of the wooded Pyrenees and among the white snows of the lofty Apennines; as many as all Europe contains and encloses."

[34] See Judges 16.
[35] The Guadiana river runs underground through part of La Mancha.

By God! How many provinces did he name! How many nations did he enumerate, giving to each, with wonderful speed, its peculiar attributes, so absorbed and wrapped up was he in all that he had read in his lying books! Sancho Panza hung on his words without uttering one. Now and then he turned his head to see whether he could perceive the knights and giants his master named. Seeing none, he said at last: "Master, I'll commend to the Devil any man, giant, or knight of all those you mentioned who is actually here. At least I do not see them. Perhaps all may be enchantment like last night's specters."

"Why do you say that?" said Don Quixote. "Do you not hear the neighing of the horses, the blaring of the trumpets, and the rattle of the drums?"

"I hear nothing," answered Sancho, "but the bleating of sheep and lambs." And so it was, for now the two flocks were close at hand.

"The fear you are in," said Don Quixote, "allows you neither to see nor to hear correctly, for one of the effects of fear is to disturb the senses and make things seem different from what they are. If you are so afraid, stand to one side and leave me alone, for I alone am sufficient to give the victory to the side that I shall assist." With these words he clapped spurs to Rozinante, and with lance couched, rode down the hillside like a thunderbolt.

Sancho shouted at him: "Come back, master, come back! I swear to God that those you are going to charge are only sheep and lambs. Come back! Woe to the father who begat me! What madness is this? Look! There is neither giant, nor knight, nor cats, nor arms, nor shield quartered or entire, nor azures true or bedeviled. Sinner that I am, what are you doing?"

Don Quixote, however, did not turn back, but charged on, shouting as he went: "Ho! You knights who fight under the banners of the valiant emperor Pentapolín of the Naked Arm! Follow me, all of you, and you will see how easily I will take vengeance for him on his enemy, Alifanfarón of Trapobana."

With these words he dashed into the midst of the flock of sheep and began to spear them with as much courage and fury as if he were fighting his mortal enemies. The shepherds and herdsmen who came with the flock shouted to him to stop, but seeing that words were of no avail, they unloosed their slings and began to salute his ears with stones as big as one's fist. Don Quixote took no notice of their stones but galloped to and fro, crying out: "Where are you, proud Alifanfarón? Where are you? Come to me, for I am but one knight and wish to try my strength with you, man to man, and take away your life for the wrong you do to the valiant Pentapolín." At that instant a smooth pebble hit him in the side and buried two ribs in his entrails. Finding himself in such a bad way, he thought for certain that he was killed or sorely wounded, and remembering his balsam, he took out his cruse[36] and raised it to his mouth to drink. But before he could swallow what he wanted, another pebble struck him full on the hand, broke the cruse to pieces, carried away with it three or four teeth and grinders out of his mouth, and badly crushed two fingers of his hand. And such was the force of those two blows that the poor knight fell off his horse

---

[36] An earthen pot. "Balsam" is any soothing medicine.

onto the ground. The shepherds ran up to him, and believing that they had killed him, they collected their flocks in great haste, carried away their dead sheep, which were more than seven, and departed without further inquiry.

All this time Sancho stood on the hillock watching his master's mad escapade and tearing his beard and cursing the unlucky hour and moment when he first met him. But seeing him lying on the ground and the shepherds out of sight, he came down the hill, went up to his master, and found him in a very bad way, although not quite unconscious. So he said to him: "Did I not tell you, sir, to come back, for those you went to attack were not armies, but flocks of sheep?"

"That rascal of an enchanter, my enemy, can counterfeit and make men vanish. Know, Sancho, that it is a very easy matter for such men to make us see what they please, and this malignant persecutor of mine, envious of the glory that I was to reap in this battle, has changed the squadrons of enemy into flocks of sheep. Now, for my sake, Sancho, do one thing to undeceive yourself and see the truth of what I am telling you. Get up on your ass and follow them softly, and you will see that when they have gone a little distance away, they will return to their original shapes, and ceasing to be sheep, will become grown-up, mature men as when I described them to you at first. But do not go now, for I need your assistance. Come and see how many of my teeth are missing, for I do not think I have a single one left in my mouth."

Sancho went so close that he almost thrust his eyes into his mouth, and it was precisely at the fatal moment when the balsam that had been fretting in Don Quixote's stomach came up to the surface; and with the same violence that a bullet is fired out of a gun, all that he had in his stomach discharged itself upon the beard of the compassionate squire.

"Holy Mary!" cried Sancho. "What has happened to me? The poor sinner must be at death's door, for he's puking blood at the mouth." But reflecting a little, he was soon convinced by the color, smell, and taste that it was not blood, but the balsam that he had seen him drink; and so great was the loathing he felt that his own stomach turned, and he emptied its full cargo upon his master, and both were in a precious pickle. Sancho rushed to his ass to take something out of his saddlebags to clean himself and his master, and when he did not find them, he was on the verge of losing his mind. He cursed himself again and vowed in his heart to leave his master and return to his home, although he would lose his wages for service and his hopes of becoming governor of the promised island.

Don Quixote had now risen, and keeping his left hand to his mouth lest the rest of his teeth fall out, with the other he took hold of Rozinante's bridle (who had not stirred from his master's side, such was his well-bred loyalty) and went over to his squire, who stood leaning against his ass with his cheek upon his hand, looking like the picture of a man lost in thought.

The knight, seeing him in that mood and so full of melancholy, said to him: "Learn, Sancho, that one man is not more than another unless he achieves more than another. All those storms that fall upon us are signs that soon the weather will be fair and that things will go smoothly, for it is not possible for evil or good to last forever. Hence we may infer that as our misfortunes have lasted so long, good fortunes must be near. So, you must not vex yourself about my mischances, for you have no share in them."

"How not?" replied Sancho. "I suppose him they tossed in a blanket yesterday was not my father's son? And the saddlebags that are missing today with all my chattels is someone else's misfortune?"

"What, are the saddlebags missing, Sancho?" asked Don Quixote.

"Yes, they are missing," answered Sancho.

"In that case, we have nothing to eat today," said Don Quixote.

"Very true," said Sancho, "if these fields are barren of the herbs that your worship says he knows all about and with which unfortunate knights-errant like yourself generally supply their wants."

"Nevertheless," answered Don Quixote, "at the present moment I would rather have a quarter-loaf of bread or a cottage loaf and a couple of heads of salted pilchards than all the herbs that Dioscorides describes, though his book be illustrated by Doctor Laguna.[37] But, good Sancho, get up on your ass and follow me, for God, who provides for all, will not desert us, especially being engaged, as we are, in His service. He does not abandon the gnats of the air, nor the worms of the earth, nor the tadpoles of the water, and He is so merciful that He maketh His sun shine on the good and the evil and He causeth the rain to fall upon the just and the unjust."

"Your worship," said Sancho, "were fitter to be a preacher than a knight-errant."

"Knights-errant, Sancho," said Don Quixote, "knew, and ought to know, somewhat of all things, for there have been knights-errant in past ages who were as ready to make a sermon or a speech on the king's highway as though they had taken their degrees at the University of Paris; whence it may be inferred that the lance never blunted the pen, nor the pen the lance."

"Well, may it turn out as you say," answered Sancho. "But let us be gone and endeavor to get a lodging tonight; and I pray to God we may find a place where there are no blankets, blanketeers, specters, or enchanted Moors; and if there are, may the Devil keep the lot of them."

"Ask that of God, my son," said Don Quixote, "and lead me where you please, for on this occasion I will leave the choice of lodging to you. But give me your hand and feel with your finger how many teeth and grinders I have lost on this right side of my upper jaw, for there I feel the pain."

Sancho put in his finger, and feeling about, asked: "How many grinders did your worship have before on this side?"

"Four," answered Don Quixote, "besides the wisdom tooth, all of them whole and sound."

"Mind well, master, what you say," answered Sancho.

"I say four, if not five," said Don Quixote, "for in all my life I have never had a tooth or grinder pulled from my mouth, nor has any fallen out or been destroyed by decay."

"Well then, on this lower side," said Sancho, "you have only two grinders and a half, but on the upper, not even half a one, for it is as smooth as the palm of my hand."

"Woe is me," cried Don Quixote, hearing these sad tidings from his squire. "I would rather they lopped off an arm, provided it were not my

[37] Andrés de Laguna, a famous sixteenth-century physician, translated the work of Dioscorides, a first-century A.D. Greek physician and pharmacologist.

sword arm; for you must know, Sancho, that a mouth without grinders is like a mill without grindstone, and a tooth is far more to be prized than a diamond. But all this must be suffered by those who profess the stern order of chivalry. Mount, friend, and lead the way, for I will follow you at what pace you please. . . ."

[In the succeeding sections, Don Quixote attacks a funeral party, mistakes a cloth mill for a supernatural danger, and deprives a barber of his basin, which he takes to be the "golden helmet of Mambrino," referred to in Ariosto's Orlando Furioso.]

CHAPTER XXII

Of the liberty Don Quixote gave to a number of unfortunates who were being borne, much against their will, where they had no wish to go

Cide Hamete Benengeli, the Arabian and Manchegan author,[38] relates in this most grave, high-sounding, precise, pleasant, and imaginative history that after the conversation between the famous Don Quixote of La Mancha and Sancho Panza, his squire, which is reported at the end of the twenty-first chapter, Don Quixote raised his eyes and saw coming, along the road he was taking, about a dozen men on foot strung together like beads on a great iron chain. The chain was fastened around their necks and they were handcuffed. With them were two men on horseback, and two others followed on foot. The horsemen had firelocks, and those on foot pikes and swords.

As soon as Sancho Panza saw them he said: "Here's a chain of galley slaves, men forced by the king, going to serve in the galleys."

"How! Men forced?" answered Don Quixote. "Is it possible that the king forces anybody?"

"I don't say that," answered Sancho, "but they are people condemned for their offenses to serve the king in the galleys."

"Then it is a fact," replied Don Quixote, "however you put it, that these men are being taken to their destination by force and not by their own free will."

"That is so," said Sancho.

"Then," said his master, "here is the opportunity for me to carry out my duty: to redress grievances and give help to the poor and the afflicted."

"I beg you, sir," said Sancho, "to consider that justice, which is the king himself, does no violence to these men, but only punishes those who have committed crime."

By this time the chain gang came up, and Don Quixote in very courteous words asked those in charge to be good enough to inform him why they conducted people away in that manner. One of the guardians on horseback replied that they were slaves condemned by His Majesty to the galleys and

---

[38] Cide Hamete Benengeli is the imaginary author Cervantes has earlier introduced as the writer of an old manuscript, in Arabic, containing the history of Don Quixote. This device allows the narrator to step in and out of the story, commenting on the presentation as well as on the content of the narrative.

that there was no more to be said, nor ought Don Quixote to desire any further information.

"Nevertheless," answered Don Quixote, "I would like to hear from each one of them individually the cause of his disgrace." To this the guardian on horseback answered: "Though we have here the register of the crimes of all these unlucky fellows, this is no time to produce and read them. Draw near, sir, and ask it from themselves. No doubt they'll tell you their tales, for men of their sort take delight in boasting of their rascalities."

With this leave, which Don Quixote would have taken for himself if they had not given it, he went up to the gang and asked the first man for what crimes he found himself in such straits. The man answered that it was for being in love.

"For that and no more?" cried Don Quixote. "If men are sent to the galleys for being in love, I should have been pulling an oar there long ago."

"My love was not of the kind your worship imagines," replied the galley slave. "Mine was that I loved too much a basket of fine linen, which I embraced so lovingly that if the law had not taken it from me by violence, I should not of my own free will have forsaken it even to this present day. I was caught in the act, so there was no need for torture. The case was a short one. They gave my shoulders a hundred lashes and in addition three years' hard labor in the *gurapas,* and that's an end of it."

"What are *gurapas?*" said Don Quixote.

"*Gurapas* are galleys," answered the convict, who was a young man of about twenty-four, born, as he said, at Piedrahita.

Don Quixote put the same question to the second, who returned no answer, for he seemed too downcast and melancholy to speak. But the first one spoke for him and said: "Sir, this gentleman goes for being a canary bird—I mean a musician or singer."

"Is it possible," said Don Quixote, "that musicians and singers are sent to galleys?"

"I should say so, sir," replied the galley slave. "There's nothing worse than to sing under torture."

"Well," said Don Quixote, "I, on the contrary, have heard it said: 'Who sings in grief, procures relief.'"

"Down here it's the exact opposite," said the slave, "for he who sings once, weeps the rest of his life."

"I do not understand it," said Don Quixote. One of the guards then said to him: "You know, sir, among these unsanctified folk 'to sing under torture' means to confess on the rack. They put this poor sinner to the torture, and he confessed his crime of being a rustler, which means that he was a cattle thief; and because he confessed, he was condemned to the galleys for six years, with the addition of two hundred lashes that he carries on his shoulders. He's always sad and pensive, for the other thieves bully, abuse, and despise him because he confessed and hadn't the courage to say a couple of *nos.* For as they say, 'A *nay* has as many letters as a *yea,*' and it is good luck for a criminal when there are no witnesses and proofs and his fate depends on his own tongue. In my opinion there's much truth in that."

"I think so also," said Don Quixote, and he passed on to where the third slave stood, and put to him the same question as to the others. The man replied quickly and coolly, saying: "I'm off to their ladyship the galleys because I wanted ten ducats."

"I will give you twenty with all my heart to free you from that misfortune," said Don Quixote.

"That," replied the slave, "would be like one who has money in the middle of the sea and yet is perishing of hunger because he has nowhere to buy what he needs. I say this because, if I'd had the twenty ducats your worship offers me at the right time, I would have greased the lawyer's palm with them and so sharpened my advocate's wit that I would now be strolling about in the marketplace at Toledo instead of being trailed along here like a greyhound. But God is great; patience is enough."

Don Quixote passed on to the fourth, who was a man of venerable appearance, with a white beard reaching below his chest. No sooner was he asked the reason for his being there than he began to weep and would not answer a word; but the fifth convict lent him a tongue and said: "This honest gentleman is off for four years to the galleys after having appeared in the usual procession dressed in full pomp and mounted."[39]

"That means, I suppose," said Sancho, "carried to shame in view of the whole people."

"You have said it," answered the galley slave, "and the offense for which they gave him this punishment was for having been an ear broker, and a body broker too. What I mean to say is that this gentleman goes for pimping and for fancying himself as a bit of a wizard."

"If it had been merely for pimping," said Don Quixote, "he certainly did not deserve to go rowing in the galleys, but rather to command them and be their captain. For the profession of pimp is no ordinary office, but one requiring wisdom and most necessary in any well-governed state. None but wellborn persons should practice it. In fact, it should have its overseers and inspectors, as there are of other offices, limited to a certain appointed number, like exchange brokers.[40] If this were done, many evils would be prevented, which now take place because this profession is practiced only by foolish and ignorant persons such as silly women, page boys, and mountebanks of few years' standing and less experience, who, in moments of difficulty, when the utmost skill is needed, allow the tidbit to freeze between their fingers and their mouth and scarcely know which is their right hand. I should like to go on and give reasons why it is right to make special choice of those who have to fill such an important office in the state, but this is not the place to do it. Some day I will tell my views to those who may provide a remedy; at present I only wish to say that the sorrow I felt at seeing your gray hairs and venerable countenance in so much distress for pimping has entirely vanished when I learn that you are a wizard; though I know well that there are no sorceries in the world that can affect and force the will, as some simple people imagine. Our will is free and no herb nor charm can compel it. What such gullible wenches and lying rascals do is to mix some

---

[39] Those condemned for witchcraft or wizardry were dealt with by the Holy Office. They were mounted on mules with face to the tail and led in procession through the streets accompanied by a noisy crowd. They wore a *coroza* or paper miter, carried a lighted candle, and were flogged through the streets.

[40] Don Quixote's ironic praise of pimps echoes a stock joke in sixteenth-century Spanish literature.

potion or poison that drives men crazy, claiming that it has the power to rouse love; whereas I maintain that it is impossible to force a man's will."

"That is true, sir," said the worthy old man; "and indeed I was not guilty of witchcraft; as for being a pimp, I couldn't deny it, but I never thought there was any harm in it, for all my intention was that the whole world should enjoy themselves and live together in peace and quiet without quarrels or troubles. But my good intentions could not save me from going to a place from which I have no hope of return, laden as I am with years and so worried with a bladder trouble that does not give me a moment's rest." He now began to weep as before, and Sancho felt so sorry for him that he drew from his purse a four-real piece and gave it to him as alms.

Don Quixote passed on and asked another what his offense was. He answered with much more pleasantness than the former: "I am here because I played a little too much of a game with two cousins of mine and with two other sisters who were not mine. In short, I carried the game so far with them all that the result of it was the increasing of my kindred so intricately that no devil could make it out. It was all proved against me; I hadn't a friend, and I hadn't a groat; my neck was in the utmost danger; they gave me six years in the galleys; I concurred: it's fair punishment for my guilt; I'm young; if only my life lasts, all will turn out for the best. If you, sir, have anything about you to relieve us poor devils, God will repay you in Heaven and we will have care on earth to ask God in our daily prayers to give you as long and prosperous a life and health as your kind presence deserves."

This convict was dressed in a student's habit, and one of the guards told Don Quixote that he was a great talker and a fine Latin scholar.

Behind all these came a man about thirty years of age, of very comely looks, except that he had a slight squint. He was differently tied from the rest, for he wore a chain to his leg so long that it wound around his whole body. He had, besides, around his neck two iron rings, one of which was fastened to the chain, and the other, called a keep friend or friend's foot, had two irons that came down from it to his waist, at the ends of which were fixed two manacles. These held his hands locked with a great padlock so that he could neither put his hands to his mouth nor bend down his head to his hands.

Don Quixote asked why this man was loaded with more fetters than the rest. The guard answered that it was because he had committed more crimes than all the rest put together and that he was such a desperate rascal that, though they carried him fettered in that way, they were not sure of him but feared that he might give them the slip.

"What crimes did he commit," said Don Quixote, "that have deserved no greater penalty than being sent to the galleys?"

"He is going for ten years," said the guard, "which is the same as civil death. I need only tell you that this man is the famous Ginés de Pasamonte, alias Ginesillo de Parapilla."

"Master commissary," said the galley slave, "don't go so fast and don't let us start defining names and surnames. Ginés is my name, not Ginesillo, and Pasamonte is my family name, not Parapilla as you say. Let every man first look to himself and he'll do a good deal."

"Keep a civil tongue, mister out-and-out robber," answered the commissary. "Otherwise we'll shut you up, whether you like it or not."

"I know," answered the galley slave, "that man goes as God pleases; but one day someone will know whether my name is Ginesillo de Parapilla or not."

"Don't they call you that, you lying trickster?"

"They do," answered Ginés, "but I'll make them stop calling me by that name or I'll shear them where I don't care to mention in company. And now, sir, if you have something to give us, hand it out and good-bye, for you tire us with your inquiries about other men's lives. If you want to know mine, I am Ginés de Pasamonte, whose life has been written by these very fingers of mine."

"He speaks the truth," said the commissary. "He himself has written his own history—as good a one as you could wish, and he pawned the book in jail for two hundred reals."

"Aye, and I intend to redeem it," said Ginés, "even if it stood at two hundred ducats."

"Is it good?" said Don Quixote.

"It is so good," answered Ginés, "that it means trouble for *Lazarillo de Tormes*[41] and for all that has been written or ever shall be written in that style. I assure you it deals with truths and truths so attractive and entertaining that no fiction could compare with them."

"What is the title of the book?" asked Don Quixote.

"*The Life of Ginés de Pasamonte*," answered Ginés himself.

"Is it finished yet?" asked Don Quixote.

"How can it be finished," anwered Ginés "when my life isn't finished yet? What is written tells everything from my birth down to this last time I was packed off to the galleys."

"Then you have been there before?" said Don Quixote.

"To serve God and the king," answered Ginés; "on the last occasion I was there for four years, and I know already the taste of hard tack and the lash. I'm not too sorry to return there, for I'll have an opportunity to finish my book. I've still many things to say, and in the galleys of Spain there's more than enough leisure, though I don't need much for what I have to write because I know it by heart."

"You seem to be a clever fellow," said Don Quixote.

"Aye. And an unlucky one," replied Ginés, "for bad luck always pursues genius."

"It pursues knaves," interrupted the commissary.

"I've already told you, sir commissary," answered Pasamonte, "not to go so fast. The lords of the land didn't give you that rod to mistreat us but to guide us and take us where His Majesty has ordered. If not, by Heaven— But enough! Perhaps one day the dirty work that was done in the inn may come out in the wash; in the meantime mum's the word, and let every man live well and speak better. Now let us move on, for we've had too much of this diversion."

The commissary raised his rod to strike Pasamonte in answer to his threats, but Don Quixote intervened, asking him not to ill-treat the convict since it was only fair that one who had his hands so tied should be some-

---

[41] An anonymous "rogue novel" published in 1554.

what free with his tongue. Then, turning toward the gang, he said: "I have gathered from all you have said, dearest brethren, that although they punish you for your faults, yet the pains you suffer do not please you, and that you go to them with ill will and against your inclination. I realize, moreover, that perhaps it was the lack of courage of one fellow on the rack, the want of money of another, the want of friends of a third, and finally the biased sentence of the judge that have been the cause of your not receiving the justice to which you were entitled. Now all this prompts and even compels me to perform on your behalf the task for which I was sent into the world, and for which I became a knight-errant, and to which end I vowed to succor the needy and help those who are oppressed by the powerful. But as it is prudent not to do by evil means what can be done by fair, I wish to entreat these gentlemen, your guardians and the commissary, to be kind enough to loose you and let you go in peace, for there will be plenty of men to serve the king on worthier occasions; it seems to me a harsh thing to make slaves of those whom God and nature made free. What is more, gentlemen of the guard," added Don Quixote, "these unfortunate creatures have done nothing against you yourselves. Let each man be answerable for his own sins; there is a God in Heaven who does not fail to punish the wicked nor to reward the good. It is not right that honest men should be executioners of others when they have nothing to do with the case. I ask this boon of you in a peaceable and quiet manner, and if you grant it, I shall give you my thanks. If, on the other hand, you will not grant it willingly, then shall this lance and sword of mine, wielded by my invincible arm, force you to do my bidding."

"This is a pleasant jest," answered the commissary. "You have ended your ranting with a fine joke. Do you want us to hand over to you those the king has imprisoned, as if we had the authority to let them go or you to order us to do it? Go your way, good sir, and a pleasant journey. Settle the basin straight on your pate, and don't go looking for a cat with three legs."[42]

"You are a cat, a rat, and a knave," answered Don Quixote. Without another word he ran at him so fiercely that, not giving him time to defend himself, he struck him to the ground badly wounded by his lance. It was lucky for the knight that this was the one who carried the firelock. The guards were astounded at this unexpected event. But they recovered themselves, and the horsemen drew their swords, the footmen clutched their pikes, and all of them threw themselves upon Don Quixote, who quietly waited for their attack. No doubt he would have been in great danger if the slaves, seeing a chance of liberty, had not broken the chain by which they were tied together. The confusion was such that the guards, first trying to prevent the galley slaves from getting loose, then defending themselves against Don Quixote, who attacked them, did nothing to any purpose. Sancho, for his part, helped to release Ginés de Pasamonte, who was the first that leaped free and unfettered upon the plain. The latter then set upon the fallen commissary and relieved him of his sword and firelock, with which, aiming first at one and then at another, although he never fired it,

---

[42] A proverbial expression that means "Don't go looking for the impossible."

he cleared the plain of guards, for they all fled no less from Pasamonte's firelock than from the showers of stones that the liberated slaves flung at them.

Sancho was much worried by all that had happened, for he had a shrewd suspicion that the guards who had fled would report the matter to the Holy Brotherhood,[43] who would raise the alarm and sally out in pursuit of the criminals, and he said so to his master, begging him to leave that place at once and hide themselves in the neighboring sierra.

"That is all very well," answered Don Quixote, "but I know what we should do now." Then he called all the galley slaves, who were now running hither and thither in a riotous mood and had stripped the commissary to the skin, and when they had gathered around him in a circle, he addressed them as follows: "It is the duty of well-bred people to be grateful for benefits received, and ingratitude is one of the most hateful sins in the eyes of God. I say this, sirs, because you know what favor you have received from me, and the only return I wish and demand is that you all go from here, laden with the chains from which I have just freed your necks, to the city of El Toboso. There you are to present yourselves before Lady Dulcinea of El Toboso and tell her that her Knight of the Rueful Figure sent you there to commend his service to her. You are to tell her, point by point, the details of this famous adventure, and when you have done this, you may then go whichever way you please and good luck be with you."

Ginés de Pasamonte answered for all the rest, saying: "That which you demand, sir, is impossible to perform, because we must not travel the roads together, but go alone and separate so that we may not be found by the men of the Holy Brotherhood, who will be sure to come out to search for us. What you can do, and ought to do, is to change this service and duty to the Lady Dulcinea of El Toboso into a certain number of Ave Marias and credos that we shall say for your worship's intention. And this we may do by night or by day, resting or on the run, at peace or at work; but if you think that we are now going to return to the fleshpots of Egypt—to our chains, I mean—and start off on the road to El Toboso, you might as well imagine that it's already nighttime, whereas it is not yet ten o'clock in the morning. To expect this from us is like expecting pears off an elm tree."

"I vow then," said Don Quixote in a rage, "sir whoreson, Don Ginesillo de Parapilla, or whatever you call yourself, that you will go alone, with your tail between your legs and the whole length of chain on your back."

Pasamonte, who was a truculent fellow (he now understood that Don Quixote was not very sane, seeing the foolish thing he had done by setting them free), would not stand being abused in this manner; so he winked at his companions, and they from a distance began to rain a shower of stones on Don Quixote, whose buckler gave him scant cover; and poor Rozinante paid no more attention to the spur than if his flanks were made of bronze. Sancho took cover behind his ass and thus sheltered himself against the squall of stones that burst about them. Don Quixote was less able to shield himself against the countless stones that hit him with such force that at last they stretched him on the ground. Scarcely had he fallen when the student Ginés jumped upon him, and taking the basin from his head, gave him

---

[43] A tribunal organized to punish highway robbers.

three or four blows with it on the shoulders and then struck it repeatedly on the ground, almost breaking it into pieces. They then stripped him of a tunic he wore over his armor, and they would have seized his hose too had they not been hindered by his greaves.[44] They took Sancho's cloak, leaving him in his underclothes, and after dividing among themselves the rest of the spoils, each went his own way, with more thought of escaping the Holy Brotherhood than of dragging their chains to Lady Dulcinea of El Toboso.

All that remained were the ass, Rozinante, Sancho, and Don Quixote. The ass pensively hanging his head, shaking his ears every now and then as if he thought the storm of stones was not yet over; Rozinante prostrate lying beside his master on the ground; Sancho in his underclothes, trembling at the thought of the Holy Brotherhood; and Don Quixote, in the dumps at finding himself so ill-treated by those for whom he had done so much.

[Don Quixote decides to do penance in the wilderness of the Sierra Morena as other knights-errant do who have been absent too long from their mistresses. He sends Sancho to deliver a letter to Dulcinea. Quixote then meets a young man, Cardenio (whom Quixote calls the "Knight of the Wood"), who has lost his love to a false friend, Ferdinand. Meanwhile Sancho meets the curate and the barber, and they persuade him to join in a stratagem to get Don Quixote to return to his village. They and Cardenio meet Dorothea, a woman deceived and abandoned by Cardenio's betrayer Ferdinand; she agrees to help them deceive the knight by playing the role of a princess, "Micomicona." They return to Quixote, and charmed by "Micomicona," he agrees to help her regain her "kingdom." The party stops at an inn on the way back to the village—the same inn where Sancho was tossed in a blanket. Here the curate reads them a manuscript called A Tale of Ill-Advised Curiosity, *in which a husband comes to grief through testing his wife's fidelity. The story raises some of the same questions of reality and illusion explored in the novel itself. At the inn, Cardenio is reunited with his Lucinda, and Ferdinand claims Dorothea as his true wife. A returned captive of the Turks arrives at the inn and tells the party of his experiences and his escape (experiences reminiscent of Cervantes' own). Other guests arrive, including a judge with a beautiful young daughter who is pursued by a lovesick boy posing as a muleteer. After the ugly servant woman Maritornes plays a cruel trick on Quixote, the curate and the barber place him in a barred oxcart to take him back to his village. On the journey, Sancho manages to free his master from the cart. Quixote meets a goatherd and offers to rescue his lover from a nunnery; the goatherd, however, becomes angry and beats Quixote.]*

CHAPTER LII

Of the quarrel that Don Quixote had with the goatherd, with the rare adventure of the disciplinants, which he successfully achieved with the sweat of his brow

. . . . It so happened that year that the clouds had denied the earth their moisture; so, throughout the valleys of that region, processions, public prayers, and penances were ordered to beseech Heaven to open the flood gates of its mercy and send them rain. It was for this purpose, therefore, that the people of a neighboring village were coming in procession to a holy shrine that stood on a hill at the edge of the valley. Don Quixote, as soon as he saw the strange attire of the disciplinants, did not pause to recall the

[44] Armor for the lower legs.

many occasions on which he had seen a similar sight before but immediately imagined that it was some kind of adventure that was reserved for him alone as knight-errant. He was all the more confirmed in his opinion by mistaking an image that they carried all swathed in mourning for some noble lady whom those ruffians and unmannerly churls were carrying away against her will. No sooner did this thought flash through his mind than he rushed over to Rozinante, who was grazing nearby, and taking off the bridle and buckler that hung from the pommel of the saddle, he bridled him in an instant. Then, asking Sancho for his sword, he mounted Rozinante, and bracing his buckler, he cried in a loud voice to all those present: "Now, valiant company, ye shall see how necessary it is that there be in the world knights who profess the order of knight-errantry; now, I say, shall ye see, in the restoration of that captive lady to liberty, whether knights-errant ought to be valued!"

Saying this, he clapped his heels to Rozinante (for spurs he had none), and at a half gallop (for nowhere in all this truthful history can one read that Rozinante ever went at full speed) he advanced to encounter the disciplinants, though the curate and the barber tried to stop him. But all their efforts were in vain, nor could he be stopped by the screams of Sancho, who shouted: "Master, where are you going? What devils in your heart are driving you on to attack our Catholic faith? Mind, sir! Bad 'cess to it! That is a procession of disciplinants and the lady they're carrying on the bier is the most blessed image of the Immaculate Virgin. Take heed, sir, what you're doing; this time I can assure you that it's not what you think."

Sancho wasted his breath, for his master was so set upon encountering the sheeted ones and upon freeing the lady in black that he heard not a word, and even if he had, he would not have turned back though the king himself had commanded him. When he reached the procession, he stopped Rozinante, who already wanted to rest a little, and in a hoarse, angry voice he cried out: "You there, who cover up your faces probably because you are evil, halt and pay heed to my words!"

The first to halt were those who were carrying the image. Then, one of the four priests who chanted the litanies, noticing the strange appearance of Don Quixote, the leanness of Rozinante, and other ludicrous details, answered him, saying: "Brother, if you have anything to say, say it quickly, for these brethren are scourging their flesh, and we cannot, nor is it right that we should, stop to listen to anything that may not be said in two words."

"I will say it in one," replied Don Quixote. "You must instantly free that beauteous lady whose tears and sad appearance show clearly that you are bearing her away against her will and that you have done her some grievous wrong. But I, who came into the world to redress such injuries, will not allow you to move one single step forward till you have restored to her the liberty she desires and deserves."

From these words all who heard them concluded that Don Quixote must be some madman, and they began to laugh heartily. But their laughter only served to add gunpowder to the knight's fury, for without another word he drew his sword and attacked the litter. One of those who carried it, leaving the burden to his comrades, stepped forward to encounter Don Quixote, brandishing a forked pole on which they propped the litter while resting, and with it he parried the heavy stroke that the knight aimed at him. The force of the stroke snapped the pole in two, but with the remaining stump that was left in his hand he dealt the knight such a thwack on the shoulder of his sword-arm that his buckler was unable to shield him against the rustic onslaught, and down came poor Don Quixote to the ground in a bad way. Sancho, who came panting after him, seeing him fall, called out to his assailant not to strike him again, for he was a poor enchanted knight who had done nobody any harm all his life. The peasant stopped, not, however, on account of Sancho's appeal, but because he saw that Don Quixote stirred neither hand nor foot. And, believing that he had killed him, he hastily tucked up his habit to his girdle and set off, racing like a deer across the country.

By that time everyone in Don Quixote's company had reached where he lay, but when the men in the procession saw them running in their direction and with them troopers of the Holy Brotherhood with their crossbows, they feared some trouble. So, they clustered in a circle about the image: the penitents lifted their hoods and grasped their lashes; the priests brandished their tapers, and all waited for the attack with the firm resolve to defend themselves, and if they could, to take the offensive against their aggressors. But Fortune arranged matters better than they expected, for Sancho did nothing but cast himself upon the body of his master, making over him the most sorrowful and drollest lament in the world, for he truly believed that Don Quixote was dead. Our curate was recognized by one of the priests in the procession, and this calmed the apprehension of both sides. Our curate in a few words told the second curate of Don Quixote's condition; then, he and the whole crowd of disciplinants went to see whether or not the poor knight was dead, and heard Sancho Panza proclaim with tears in his eyes: "O flower of chivalry, one single blow of a cudgel has finished the course of your well-spent years! O glory of your race, honor and credit to all La Mancha, and even to the whole world, which, now that you are gone, will be overrun with evildoers, who will no longer fear punishment for their iniquities! O liberal above all the Alexanders, since for a mere eight months' service you have given me the best island that the sea surrounds! O humble to the haughty and arrogant to the humble! Resister of perils, sufferer of affronts, lover without cause, imitator of the good, scourge of the wicked, enemy of the base! In a word, knight-errant, which is the highest thing anyone could say!"

At the cries and groans of Sancho, Don Quixote revived, and the first words he said were: "He who lives absent from thee, sweet Dulcinea, endures far greater sufferings than these. Help me, friend Sancho, to lift myself into the enchanted cart, for I am no longer in a condition to press the saddle of Rozinante; this shoulder of mine is broken to pieces."

"That I'll do with all my heart, dear master," replied Sancho, "and let us go back to our village in the company of these gentlemen, and there we will make schemes for another sally that may be more profitable to us."

"You speak well, Sancho," answered the knight. "It is prudent for us to wait until the evil influence of the stars that now reigns passes away."

The canon, the curate, and the barber approved this resolution, and after they had enjoyed Sancho Panza's fooleries to the full, they placed Don Quixote on the cart as before. The procession resumed its former order and went on its way. The goatherd took his leave of them all, and as the troopers refused to go any further, the curate paid them what he owed them. The canon then begged the curate to let him know what might happen to Don Quixote (whether he recovered from his madness or remained in it), and with this he took his leave. Thus they all parted and went their several ways.

The party now consisted only of the curate, the barber, Don Quixote, Sancho, and good Rozinante, who bore all the ups and downs as patiently as his master. The wagoner yoked his oxen, and having laid Don Quixote on a bundle of hay, plodded his way at his usual calm, deliberate pace, following the directions of the curate; and at the end of six days they reached Don Quixote's village. They made their entrance at noon, and as it happened to be Sunday, all the people were in the marketplace when the wagon passed through. Everyone rushed to see who was in it, and when they recognized their townsman, they were amazed. A boy ran off at full speed to give the news to his housekeeper and his niece that their master and uncle was coming home lean and yellow, stretched out on a bundle of hay in an oxcart. It was a pathetic thing to hear the cries of the two ladies, the blows they gave themselves, the execrations they uttered afresh against the books of chivalry, all of which were repeated when they saw Don Quixote enter the door of his house.

As soon as she received news of Don Quixote's arrival, Sancho Panza's wife ran there, and as soon as she saw Sancho, her first inquiry was whether the ass had come home in good condition. Sancho replied that he was in better health than his master.

"Thanks be to God," said she, "for this great favor. Now tell me, husband, what good have you got from your squireship? What petticoat have you brought for me? What dainty shoes for your children?"

"I've brought you nothing of the kind, dear wife," said Sancho, "But I've other things of more consequence."

"I'm glad to hear so," answered the wife. "Show me those things of more consequence. I'm dying to see them to gladden my heart, for I've been mournful and down in the mouth all those ages you've been away."

"I'll show them to you at home, wife," said Sancho. "For the present, hold your soul in patience. Please God we may sally out another time in search of adventures and you'll soon see me count or governor of an island, and not one of those around here, but the finest that can be found."

"May the Lord be pleased to grant it, husband, for we're in sore need of it. Tell me now; what's all this about islands? I don't catch your meaning."

"Honey is not for an ass's mouth," answered Sancho. "You'll see in good time, wife, aye, and you'll be all agape at hearing yourself called ladyship by all your vassals."

"What are you prating about ladyships, islands, and vassals?" cried Juana Panza, for that was the name of Sancho's wife, not because they were relatives, but because in La Mancha it is customary for wives to take their husbands' last name.

"Don't fret yourself, Juana, and be in such a hurry to know everything at once; it's enough for you to know that I'm telling the truth, so mum's the word; but I can tell you one thing by the way, namely, that there's nothing in this world so pleasant as for an honest man to be squire to a knight-errant on the prowl for adventures. It's true that most of those we encountered were not as comfortable as a body would wish, for out of a hundred adventures, ninety-nine usually turned out cross and crooked. I know by experience, for from some I came off blanketed and from others bruised and battered, but when all's said and done, it's a fine thing to be gadding about spying for chances, crossing mountains, exploring woods, climbing rocks, visiting castles, lodging in inns at our own sweet will, with devil a maravedi to pay."

While this conversation was passing between Sancho Panza and Juana Panza, his wife, Don Quixote's housekeeper and niece received the knight, undressed him, and put him into his old bed. He looked at them with squinting eyes, for he could not make out where he was. The curate told the niece to take very good care of her uncle and to be very watchful lest he should make another sally, telling her the trouble it had cost to get him home. The two women began their lamentations once more, again execrating the books of chivalry and imploring Heaven to plunge the authors of so many lies and absurdities into the bottomless abyss. In fact, they were at their wits' end, for they were afraid they might lose their master and uncle the moment he felt a little better. And events turned out as they feared.

But though the author of this history has eagerly and diligently inquired after Don Quixote's exploits on his third sally, he has not been able to discover any account of them, at least from any authentic documents. Only tradition has preserved in the memory of La Mancha that the third time Don Quixote left his home he went to Saragossa, where he took part in some famous jousts in that city, and that he had adventures there worthy of his valor and of his sound intelligence. Nor would our author have been able to discover any details of his death, nor would he even have heard of it, if Fortune had not thrown in his path an aged physician who had in his possession a leaden box that he said he had discovered among the ruined foundations of an ancient hermitage that was being rebuilt. In this box he had found certain parchments written in the Gothic script, but in Castilian verse, which contained many of his exploits and emphasized the beauty of Dulcinea of El Toboso, the shape of Rozinante, the fidelity of Sancho Panza, and the burial of Don Quixote himself, with various epitaphs and eulogies on his life and character. Such as could be deciphered and interpreted the trustworthy author of this original and matchless history has set down here, and he asks no recompense from his readers for the immense pains it has cost him to ransack all the archives of La Mancha to drag it into light. All he asks is that they should give it as much credit as sensible men are wont to give to the books of chivalry, which are held in such high esteem in the world. With this he will reckon himself well paid and satisfied, and he will be encouraged to go in search of other histories, perhaps less truthful than this one, but at least as inventive and entertaining. . . .

from PART II

CHAPTER I

What passed between the curate, the barber, and Don Quixote regarding the knight's infirmity

Cide Hamete Benengeli in the second part of this history concerning Don Quixote's third sally relates that the curate and the barber remained nearly a month without seeing him, in order not to revive past events and bring them back to his memory. But this did not prevent them from visiting his niece and his housekeeper, whom they charged to be careful to treat him well and give him to eat such food as was comforting and good for heart and brain, for they had every reason to believe that all his misfortunes proceeded from that quarter. The two women declared that they were doing so and that they would continue to lavish care and affection on their master, for they had noticed that he gave signs at times of being in his right mind. This news gave the curate and the barber great satisfaction, for it seemed to prove that they had done right in bringing him back enchanted in the ox wagon, as has been related in the last chapter of the first part of this great and accurate history. So, they resolved to visit him and test his recovery, though they thought that was scarcely possible, and they agreed not to touch in any way on knight-errantry, so as not to run the risk of ripping open wounds that were still so tender.

They paid him a visit at last and found him sitting up in his bed, dressed in a green-baize jacket and a red Toledo cap and so lean and shriveled that he looked as if he had been turned into a mummy. He welcomed them cordially and to their questions about his health he replied intelligently in very well-chosen words. In the course of conversation they discoursed on so-called affairs of state and systems of government, correcting this abuse and condemning that, reforming one practice and abolishing another, each one of the three setting himself up as a new lawgiver, a modern Lycurgus, or a brand-new Solon.[1] And to such a degree did they remodel the state that they might as well have cast it into a furnace and forged a new one. And Don Quixote spoke with such good sense on all the subjects they treated that the two examiners believed, without shadow of doubt, that he was quite recovered and in full possession of his wits. The niece and the housekeeper were present at the conversation and could not find adequate words to thank God when they saw that their master was so clear in his mind. The curate, however, changed his original plan, which was not to touch on the subject of chivalry, and resolved to test Don Quixote's recovery thoroughly to see whether it was genuine or not; so, changing from one subject to another, he came at last to talk of some news that had come from the capital. Among other things he said that they had it for certain that the Turk was descending with a powerful fleet, but no one knew what his designs were or where the mighty storm would burst. And owing to this

---

[1] The legendary Lycurgus (seventh century B.C.) reformed the Spartan constitution; Solon reformed the Athenian government in 594 B.C.

fear, which almost every year rouses men to arms, all Christendom was on the alert, and His Majesty had made provision for the defense of the coast of Naples, Sicily, and island of Malta.

"His Majesty has acted like a most prudent warrior," replied Don Quixote, "in fortifying his realms in time, so that the enemy may not find him unprepared; but if he would take my advice, I would counsel him to take one precaution of which His Majesty is not aware at the present moment."

No sooner did the curate hear this than he said to himself: "God protect you, my poor Don Quixote, for it looks to me as if you are tumbling from the pinnacle of your madness into the deep abyss of your simple-mindedness."

But the barber, who already had the same suspicions as the curate, asked Don Quixote what kind of measures he thought they should adopt, for perhaps they might be added to the long list of unpractical projects usually offered to princes.

"Mine, Mr. Scrapebeard," said Don Quixote, "are not unpractical but highly practical."

"No harm meant," replied the barber, "but experience has shown that all or most of the projects presented to His Majesty are either impossible, absurd, or damaging to the king and the country."

"But mine," rejoined Don Quixote, "is neither impossible nor ridiculous, but the easiest, the justest, the readiest, and the simplest that could enter the mind of any thinking man."

"Your worship is slow in telling us about it, Don Quixote," said the curate.

"I do not wish to tell it now," said Don Quixote, "and have it reach by tomorrow morning the ears of the lords of the Council, and for someone else to get the thanks and the reward for my pains."

"As for me," said the barber, "I give my word here and before God that I'll not repeat what you say to king, or rook, or earthly man,[2] an oath I learned from the ballad of the priest, who in the prologue warns the king against the thief who had robbed him of a hundred doubloons and his ambling mule."

"I do not know the story," said Don Quixote, "but I know that the oath is a good one, because I believe that the barber is an honest man."

"Even if he were not," said the curate, "I will go bail for him and vouch that he'll speak as much as a dumb man, under pain of any penalty imposed by the court."

"And who will go bail for your reverence?" said Don Quixote.

"My profession," replied the curate, "which is to keep secrets."

"Bless my heart!" exclaimed Don Quixote. "What else has His Majesty to do but to order by public crier all the knights-errant who are wandering about Spain to assemble at the capital on a certain day, and even if no more than half a dozen came, might there not be one among them who alone would be strong enough to annihilate the whole army of the Turk? Let your worships give me your attention and follow me. Is it, mark you, an unheard-of exploit for a single knight-errant to cut to bits an army of two hundred thousand men as if all together had but one throat or were made

---

[2] A metaphor from chess; kings and rooks are chess pieces.

of almond paste? Now tell me, how many histories are there full of such marvels? If there were living today—to my misfortune, though I shall not say to anyone else's—the famous Don Belianís or any one of those of the innumerable offspring of Amadis of Gaul![3] If any of them were living today and were to face the Turk, I would not be in the latter's shoes. But God will take care of his people and will provide someone who, if not as resolute as the knights-errant of old, will at least not be behind them in spirit. God understands me, and I say no more."

"Alas!" cried the niece, at this point. "Strike me dead if my master doesn't want to turn knight-errant again."

To which Don Quixote replied: "A knight-errant I shall die, and let the Turk make his descent or ascent whenever he will and with whatever power he can. I say once more that God understands, and I say no more."

At this the barber chimed in: "Allow me, your worships, to tell you a short tale about something that took place at Seville, for as it fits this situation like a glove, I'm dying to tell it."

Don Quixote and the curate gave him leave, and the others pricked up their ears; so, the barber began as follows: "In the madhouse at Seville was a certain man whose relations had put him there because he had lost his wits. He had graduated in common law at Osuna, but even if it had been at Salamanca, many think he would have been just as mad. This graduate, at the end of some years of confinement, convinced himself that he was sane and in his right mind, and in this frame of mind he wrote to the archbishop, imploring him earnestly and in convincing terms to order his release from the misery in which he lived, for his relatives kept him there in order to enjoy his share of the estate, and in spite of the clearest evidence, they wished to have him stay mad till his death. The archbishop, impressed by his many sensible and well-reasoned letters, ordered one of his chaplains to ascertain from the governor of the madhouse whether what the licentiate wrote was true. He asked him to speak to the madman, and if he seemed to be in his senses, to set him at liberty. The chaplain did so, and the governor informed him that the man was still mad, and that though he often talked like a person of great intelligence, in the end he would break out into wild tirades as crazy and exaggerated as his previous talk had been sensible, as he would find out by speaking to him. The chaplain wished to do so, and when he visited the madman, he talked with him for an hour and more, and in all that time he never said a queer or crazy word but spoke so sensibly that the chaplain was obliged to believe him sane. Among other things that the madman said was that the governor had an edge against him because he did not want to lose the bribes his relations paid him for declaring that he was still mad, though with lucid intervals. The greatest obstacle he had to deal with in his misfortunes, he said, was his great wealth, for in order to enjoy it his enemies misjudged him and cast doubts upon the mercy that Our Lord had done him by turning him from a beast into a man. In short, he spoke so convincingly as to throw suspicion on the governor and to make his relatives appear covetous and inhuman and himself so sane that the chaplain resolved to take him away with him, so that

---

[3] Heroes of Fernández' *Don Belianio of Greece* (1547) and the anonymous Spanish romance *Amadis of Gaul* (thirteenth or fourteenth century).

the archbishop might see him and verify the truth for himself. In all good faith, then, the worthy chaplain begged the governor to give orders for the licentiate to be given back the clothes in which he had arrived. But the governor once more bade him mind what he was doing, for the licentiate undoubtedly was still mad. However, the governor's warning could not prevail upon the chaplain to leave the madman behind; so, seeing that the archbishop had given the order, the governor obeyed, and the madman was given back his clothes, which were new and decent. When he found himself stripped of his lunatic's dress and clothed in the garb of sanity, he begged the chaplain out of charity to allow him to bid farewell to his mad companions. The chaplain told him he would like to accompany him and see the inmates who were lodged there. So they went upstairs, accompanied by some other people who were present, and the madman went up to a cage in which was a raging maniac who happened to be calm and quiet at the time, and said to him: 'My brother, see if you have any commands for me. I am going home, for God in His infinite mercy and goodness has been pleased to restore me to my senses, though I don't deserve it. Now I am sane and in my right mind, for to God's power nothing is impossible. Put great hope and trust in Him; since He has restored me to my former state, He will restore you too, if you have faith in Him. I will send you some dainties to eat, and be sure you eat them, for I must tell you that I am convinced, as one who has gone through it, that all our madness proceeds from our having our bellies empty and our brains full of wind. Take heart! Have courage! For despondency in our misfortunes weakens our health and hastens death.'

"Another madman in another cage opposite the raging lunatic's overheard all that the graduate said, and rising from an old mat on which he was lying stark naked, he asked in a loud voice who this man was who was going away cured and sane. The graduate replied: 'It is I, brother, who am going. I have no need to stay here any longer, for which I give infinite thanks to Heaven, which has done me this great favor.'

"'Mind what you say, graduate, and don't let the Devil deceive you,' answered the madman. 'Rest your feet and stay snugly and quietly at home, and you'll spare yourself the return journey.'

"'I know that I am well,' rejoined the graduate, 'and shall not have to go the rounds again.'

"'You well?' cried the madman. 'Good! We shall see. God be with you, but I vow to Jupiter, whose majesty I represent on earth, that for the sin that Seville is committing today in releasing you from this house and treating you as a sane man, I shall inflict such punishment on her as shall be remembered for centuries and centuries to come, amen. Do you not know, you mean little graduate, that I have the power to do so? For let me tell you, I am Jupiter the thunderer and hold in my hands the flaming thunderbolts with which I can and do threaten to destroy the world. But with one punishment alone I mean to chastise this ignorant city. For three whole years I will not rain on it and on all the surrounding districts, and the time is to be reckoned from the instant I utter this threat. You free, you sane, you in your right senses? And I mad and sick and in chains? I would as soon think of raining as hang myself.'

"The madman's loud burst of oratory attracted the attention of the bystanders, but our graduate, turning to our chaplain and seizing him by the hands, cried: 'Don't be concerned, my dear sir; take no notice of what this lunatic says, for if he is Jupiter and will not rain, I am Neptune, the father and god of the waters, and I will rain as often as I please and whenever it is necessary.'

"To which the chaplain replied: 'All the same, Lord Neptune, it would not be right to annoy Lord Jupiter. Your worship may remain at home, and we will come back for you another day when we have more time.'

"The governor and the bystanders burst out laughing, and the chaplain was half ashamed at their jeering. The graduate was stripped and clapped in his cage, and that is the end of my story."

"So that, Master Barber, is the story," said Don Quixote, "that suited our situation so well that you had to tell it? O Master Scrapebeard! How blind is he who cannot see through a sieve! Is it possible that your worship does not know that comparisons between wit and wit, valor and valor, beauty and beauty, birth and birth, are always hateful and cause resentment? I, Master Barber, am not Neptune, the god of the waters, and I am not setting myself up as a wise man when I am not. I only strive to convince the world of its errors in not reviving that most fortunate age in which the order of chivalry flourished. But our depraved age does not deserve to enjoy so great a blessing as did those in which knights-errant undertook and burdened their shoulders with the defense of kingdoms, the protection of damsels, the relief of children and orphans, the chastisement of the proud, and the rewarding of the humble. Most of our knights nowadays prefer to nestle in the damasks, brocades, and other rich silks they wear than in armored coats of mail. There are now no knights who sleep in the fields, exposed to the rigor of the heavens in full armor from head to foot. There is no one now who snatches a nap, as they say, resting on his lance and with his feet on the stirrups as knights-errant did of old. There is no one now to sally forth from this wood and enter that mountain, and from there to go to a wasted and deserted shore of the sea, most often stormy and tempestuous and to find there on the beach a little boat without oars, sail, mast, or tackle, and with undaunted heart to fling himself in and entrust himself to the implacable waves of the deep sea, which at one moment toss him up to the sky, and at another engulf him in the abyss. Then, exposing his chest to the irresistible tempest, he finds himself, when he least expects it, more than nine thousand miles from the place where he embarked; and leaping on to a remote and unknown shore, he undergoes experiences worthy to be inscribed not on parchment, but on brass. Today sloth triumphs over industry, idleness over labor, vice over virtue, arrogance over bravery, and theory over the practice of arms, which only lived and flourished in the Golden Age and among knights-errant. If I am not right, tell me, who was more virtuous and valiant than the renowned Amadis of Gaul? Who was wiser than Palmerin of England? Who more pleasant and dexterous than Tirante the White? Who more gallant than Lisuarte of Greece? Who a greater slasher or more slashed than Don Belianís? Who more undaunted than Perión of Gaul, or more eager to face peril than Felixmarte of Hyrcania? Or more sincere than Esplandian? Who more impetuous than Cirongilio of Thrace? Who more fearless than Rodamante? Who more prudent than King Sobrino? Who bolder than

Rinaldo? Who more invincible than Orlando? And who more high-spirited and courteous than Ruggiero, from whom are descended today the dukes of Ferrara, according to Turpin's cosmography?[4] All these knights and many more I could mention, Master Priest, were knights-errant, the light and glory of chivalry. These, and such as these, I should wish to take part in my project, and if they did, His Majesty would find himself well served at great saving of expense, and the Turk would be left tearing his beard. Therefore I wish to remain at home, since the chaplain is not taking me out, and if Jupiter, as the barber has said, will not rain, here am I who will rain whenever I please. This I say so that Master Basin may see that I understand him."

"Really, Don Quixote," said the barber, "that wasn't why I told you the tale. I meant well by it, so help me God, and your worship shouldn't take offense."

"I know best whether I took offense or not," replied Don Quixote.

The curate then remarked: "Although I've hardly said a word up to now, I should like to relieve myself of a scruple that is gnawing and scraping at my conscience upon hearing Don Quixote's last remarks."

"The curate has license for other more solemn matters," answered Don Quixote, "so he can declare his scruple, for it is unpleasant to go about with scruples on one's conscience."

"Well, with your leave," replied the curate, "I shall reveal my scruple. It is that I am unable to convince myself in any way, Don Quixote, that all this crew of knights-errant your worship has mentioned have really and truly been people of flesh and blood living in this world. On the contrary, I think that it is all fiction, fable, and lies, dreams told by men awake, or rather half asleep."

"That is another mistake," replied Don Quixote, "into which many have fallen who do not believe that such knights have ever existed. Often with different people and at different times I have tried to expose this almost universal error to the light of truth. On some occasions I have not succeeded in my purpose; on others I have, supporting my argument with evidence so infallible that I might say I have seen Amadis of Gaul with my own eyes. He was a man tall of stature and fair of face, with a well-trimmed black beard, and his looks were half mild and half severe. He was short of speech, slow to anger, and quickly appeased. Now in the same manner in which I have portrayed Amadis, I could, I believe, paint and describe all the knights-errant who wander in the histories, for I have absolute faith that they were exactly as the histories tell us, and my knowledge of their deeds and their characters makes it possible for me by sound philosophy to make out their features, their complexions, and their statures."

"How big then, my dear Don Quixote," inquired the barber, "would the giant Morgante have been in your worship's opinion?"

"As to the existence of giants," replied Don Quixote, "there are various opinions. But Holy Scripture, which cannot depart from the truth by so much as an inch, proves that they existed by telling us the story of that great Philistine, Goliath, who was seven cubits and a half tall, which is a

---

[4] The heroes mentioned are all characters in Spanish romances or in romances by Ariosto and Boiardo. *Turpin's cosmography* is a fictitious work.

prodigious height.[5] There have been also found in the island of Sicily shinbones and shoulder blades of a size that shows that their owners were giants and as tall as great towers; geometry proves this beyond a doubt. Nevertheless, I am unable to say with certainty what was the size of Morgante, although I imagine he could not have been so very tall, and I am inclined to this opinion by discovering in the history where special emphasis is laid upon his deeds that he often slept under a roof, and since he found houses to contain him, it is clear that his size was not excessive."

"That is true," said the curate, who, delighted to hear him talk such nonsense, then asked him what he felt about the features of Rinaldo of Montalbán and of Orlando and the other Peers of France, for they all were knights-errant.

"Of Rinaldo," replied Don Quixote, "I make bold to say that he was broad in face, red-complexioned, with rolling and rather prominent eyes, very thin-skinned and choleric, friendly to robbers and to vagabonds. About Roland, or Rotolando, or Orlando—for histories give him all these names—I am positively convinced that he was of middle stature, broad-shouldered, rather bowlegged, dark-complexioned, and red-bearded, with a hairy body and a threatening appearance, abrupt in speech, but very polite and well bred."

"If Orlando was no more of a gentleman than your worship has made out," said the curate, "it was no wonder that the lady Angélica the Fair rejected him for the gaiety, the dash, and the charm of the downy-cheeked Moorling to whom she gave herself. She showed good sense in falling in love with Medoro's gentleness rather than with the roughness of Orlando."[6]

"That Angélica, sir priest," answered Don Quixote, "was a giddy, wanton damsel, and a trifle flighty, and she left the world as full of her indiscretions as of her famous beauty. She scorned a thousand lords—a thousand valiant and a thousand wise lords—and contented herself with a smooth-faced little chit of a page with no other fortune than the reputation he gained by his loyalty to his friend. The great singer of her beauty, the celebrated Ariosto, did not dare, or perhaps did not care, to relate what happened to this lady after her base surrender—for no doubt her conduct was not too chaste—and left her with these lines:

'And how she won the scepter of Cathay,
Another bard will sing to a mellower lay.'

"This, no doubt, was a kind of prophecy, for poets are also called *vates*, which means diviners. This truth can be plainly seen, for since then a famous Andalusian poet has wept and sung about her tears, and another celebrated and unique Castilian poet has sung her beauty."[7]

[5] The story of Goliath is told in I Samuel 17, where his height is given as six and a half cubits, about nine feet nine inches. The giant Morgante appears in a sixteenth-century romance by Pulci.

[6] Quixote and the curate are referring to the Italian comic romance *Orlando Furioso (Roland Driven Mad)*, 1532, by Ludovico Ariosto. Quixote misquotes a couplet from this work below.

[7] The Andalusian poet is Luis Barahona de Soto, and the Castilian is Lope de Vega, both of whom wrote poems about the romance heroine Angélica.

"Tell me, Don Quixote," interposed the barber, "has there been no poet who has made some satire on this lady Angélica, among all those who have praised her?"

"I truly believe," replied Don Quixote, "that if Sacripante or Orlando had been poets, they would have given the damsel a trouncing, for it is right and natural for poets who have been scorned or not accepted by their ladies, either fictitious or modeled on those they have chosen as mistresses of their thoughts, to revenge themselves in satires and lampoons, a vengeance assuredly unworthy of generous hearts. But up to now there has come to my notice no defamatory verse against the lady Angélica, who turned the whole world topsy-turvy."

"A miracle," exclaimed the curate.

But at this point they heard the housekeeper and the niece, who had withdrawn from their conversation, making an outcry in the yard, and they all ran out to see what the noise was about.

CHAPTER II

Which deals with the notable quarrel between Sancho Panza and Don Quixote's niece and housekeeper, with other amusing incidents

The story tells that the noise Don Quixote, the curate, and the barber heard were the niece and the housekeeper screaming indignantly at Sancho Panza, who was struggling to get in and see Don Quixote, while they were holding the door against him.

"What does that feckless gadabout want in this house? Off with you to your own haunts, brother, for it's you and none other who deludes my master and leads him gallivanting over hill and dale."

To which Sancho replied: "Housekeeper of Satan! I'm the one who is deluded and led gallivanting over hill and dale, and not your master; it is he who led me on a jaunt all over the world, and you are wide off the mark. It was he who tricked me away from home, with his colloguing, promising me an island, and I'm still waiting for it."

"May those foul islands choke you," replied the niece, "damn you, Sancho. And what are those isles of yours? Are they something to eat, you glutton and gormandizer?"

"They are not anything to eat," answered Sancho, "but to govern and rule, and better than any four cities and richer than four judgeships at court."

"You shan't come in here, all the same," said the housekeeper, "you bag of mischief, you sack of villainies! Go and govern your house, till your plot, and rid your empty pate of isles and islands."

The curate and the barber were greatly amused to hear this conversation of the three, but Don Quixote was afraid Sancho would blurt out a whole heap of mischievous nonsense and touch upon points that might not be wholly to his credit. So, he called to him and bade the two women to hold their tongues and let him enter. Sancho went in, and the curate and the barber took their leave of the knight. They despaired of his cure, for they saw how fixed he was in his crazy notions and how deeply absorbed by his accursed nonsensical knight-errantry. And so the curate said to the barber: "You will see, my friend; when we least expect it, our knight will be off bush-ranging."

"I've no doubt of that," replied the barber, "but I'm less surprised at the knight's madness than at the squire's foolishness in believing the story of the isle, for I'm sure that all the disappointments imaginable will not drive it out of his head."

"May God help them," said the curate, "and let us keep our eyes open and see what comes of this crazy alliance of knight and squire. Both of them seem to be cast in the same mold, and the master's eccentricities would not be worth a farthing without the squire's foolishness."

"That's true," said the barber, "and I should be very glad to know what the two of them are talking about this moment."

"I dare wager," replied the curate, "that the niece or the housekeeper will tell us by and by, for they are not the kind to refrain from listening."

In the meantime Don Quixote had shut himself in his room with Sancho, and when they were alone, he said: "I am deeply grieved, Sancho, that you have said and still say that it was I took you from your cottage, when you know that I myself did not stay at home. We set out together, together we lived, together we wandered. One and the same fortune, one and the same destiny has fallen upon us both; if they tossed you in a blanket once, they have beaten me a hundred times, and this is the one advantage I have over you."

"That is quite right," answered Sancho, "for as your worship says, disasters belong rather to knights-errant than to their squires."

"You are mistaken, Sancho," said Don Quixote. "Remember the saying: *quando caput dolet*, etc."[8]

"I understand no language but my own," replied Sancho.

"I mean," said Don Quixote, "that when the head aches, all the limbs feel pain; and so, as I am your lord and master, I am your head, and you are a part of me because you are my servant; and for that reason the evil that touches me, or shall touch me, should hurt you, and yours should hurt me."

"So it should be," said Sancho, "but when they tossed me, the limb, in the blanket, my head was outside the wall, watching me fly through the air and not feeling any pain. But since the limbs have to suffer the head's pain, the head should also be made to suffer for the limbs."

"Do you mean to suggest, Sancho," replied Don Quixote, "that I felt no pain when they were tossing you? If that is what you say, you are wrong. You should not even think such a thing, for I felt more pain then in my spirit than you did in your body. But let us put that aside for the present, for there will be a time when we can consider the matter and come to a proper conclusion. Now tell me, Sancho, my friend, what do they say about me in the village? What opinion of me have the common people and the gentry and the knights? What do they say of my valor, of my deeds, and of my courtesy? How do they speak of the enterprise I have undertaken to revive and restore to the world the forgotten order of chivalry? In short,

---

[8] *Quando caput dolet, caetera membra dolent* is the complete proverb. Quixote translates it below: "When the head aches, all the limbs feel pain."

Sancho, I want you to tell me all that has come to your ears. You must answer me without exaggerating praise or mitigating blame. For it is the duty of loyal vassals to speak the truth to their lords without exaggerating it through flattery or lessening it through vain deference. And I would have you know, Sancho, that if the naked truth reached the ears of princes without the trappings of flattery, these times would be different, and other ages would more fitly be reputed iron than ours, which I reckon to be of gold. Take this warning, Sancho, and discreetly and faithfully give me the true answer to the questions I have asked you."

"I'll do so with all my heart, sir," replied Sancho, "on condition that your worship does not get angry at what I say, for you want me to tell you the naked truth and not to dress it in any clothes, except those I found it in."

"On no account shall I be angry," answered Don Quixote. "You can speak freely, Sancho, without beating about the bush."

"Then the first thing I'll say is that the common people take your worship for a mighty great madman, and they think I'm no less of a simpleton. The gentry say that you're not content with being a country gentleman and that you have turned yourself into a don and thrust yourself into knighthood with no more than a few miserable vinestocks and two acres of land, with a tatter behind and another in front to bless your name. The knights say they don't relish seeing the petty gentry setting themselves up against them, especially those squireens who black their shoes and darn their black stockings with green silk."

"That," said Don Quixote, "has nothing to do with me, for I am always well dressed and never patched. Ragged I may be, but ragged more from the wear and tear of my armor than from time."

"As to your worship's valor, courtesy, and exploits," continued Sancho, "there are different opinions. Some say, 'mad but droll'; others, 'valiant but unfortunate'; others, 'courteous but saucy'; and so they go sticking their noses into this and that until they don't leave a whole bone either in your body or in mine."

"Observe, Sancho," said Don Quixote, "that whenever virtue is found in an eminent degree, it is persecuted. Few or none of the famous heroes of old have escaped being slandered by malicious tongues. Julius Caesar, a most highspirited, most prudent, and most valiant captain, was branded as ambitious and not too clean either in his garments or in his morals. Alexander, whose exploits achieved for him the name of Great, was said to have been somewhat of a drunkard. And Hercules, the hero of the many labors, according to gossips was lascivious and effeminate. Don Galaor, the brother of Amadis of Gaul, is rumored to have been over-lecherous and his brother to have been a sniveler. So, Sancho, seeing that there is so much slander against good men, what they say about me may pass if it is no more than what you have told me."

"Ah, but there's the rub, body of my father!" replied Sancho.

"Is there anything more then?" asked Don Quixote.

"Faith an' we still have to skin the tail,' said Sancho. "Why, up to now it has been tarts and fancy bread, but if your worship wants to know all about the calumnies they fling at you, I'll bring you here presently one who will tell you the lot of them without missing an atom, for last night Bartolomé

Carrasco's son arrived from studying at Salamanca, where he was made a bachelor. And when I went up to welcome him, he told me that the history of your worship is already told in a book by the name of *The Ingenious Gentleman Don Quixote of La Mancha*. And he says that they also mention me in it by my own very name of Sancho Panza, and Lady Dulcinea of El Toboso, too, and many a thing that happened to us in private, which made me cross myself in amazement to think how the history writer could have got wind of what he wrote."

"You may be sure, Sancho," said Don Quixote, "that the author of our history is some wise enchanter, for nothing can be hidden from them."

"But if the author of this history was a wise enchanter," replied Sancho, "how comes it about that according to the bachelor Sansón Carrasco—for that's the man's name—the author of our history is called Cide Hamete Berengena?"

"That is a Moor's name," rejoined Don Quixote.

"So it may be," answered Sancho, "for I have heard that Moors for the most part are very fond of eggplants."[9]

"You must be mistaken, Sancho," said Don Quixote, "in the name of this Cide, which in Arabic means lord."

"Very likely," replied Sancho, "but if you would like to have me bring the bachelor here, I'll go for him like a shot."

"You will do me a great favor, my friend," said Don Quixote, "What you have told me makes me anxious, and I shall not eat a mouthful that will do me good until I am informed of everything."

"Then I'll go to fetch him," answered Sancho.

So, leaving his master, he went off to find the bachelor, with whom he returned in a short while. And between these three a most entertaining conversation took place.

CHAPTER III

Of the ridiculous conversation that passed between Don Quixote, Sancho Panza, and the bachelor Sansón Carrasco

Don Quixote remained very pensive, waiting for the bachelor Sansón Carrasco, from whom he expected to hear how he had been put into a book, as Sancho had told him. He could not convince himself that such a history could exist, for the blood of the enemies he had slain was hardly dry on the blade of his sword, yet they were already saying that his high deeds of chivalry were in print. Nevertheless, he imagined that some sage, either friend or enemy, by his magic art had given them to the press; if a friend, to magnify and exalt them above the most renowned feats of any knight-errant; if an enemy, to annihilate them and place them below the meanest ever written of some base squire, although, he said to himself, the deeds of squires were never written of. If, however, it were true that such history was in existence, seeing that it was about a knight-errant, it must of necessity be grandiloquent, lofty, distinguished, and true. This thought consoled

---

[9] The "Arabic manuscript" is supposed to have been found at Toledo, where the inhabitants were jokingly called *berengeneros* (the eggplanters).

him somewhat, but he was worried to think that its author was a Moor, as the name Cide suggested, for he could expect no truth from the Moors, since they are all impostors, forgers, and schemers. He also dreaded that his love affairs might be treated indelicately, which might lead to the disparagement and prejudice of Lady Dulcinea of El Toboso's good name. For he was anxious that it should be made quite clear that he had always been faithful to her and had always shown her respect, turning a blind eye to all queens, empresses, and damsels of every degree for her sake. And so, Sancho, when he returned with Carrasco, found him rapt and absorbed in these and countless other fancies, but the knight received the new guest with courtesy.

The bachelor, though his name was Sansón, was no giant in stature, but was a very great wag. He was of sallow complexion, very sharp witted, about twenty-four years of age, with a round face, a flat nose, and a large mouth—all signs of a mischievous disposition and of one who is fond of joking and making fun, as he showed straightaway, for no sooner did he see Don Quixote than he dropped to his knees before him, saying: "Let your mightiness give me your hands to kiss, Sir Don Quixote of La Mancha. By the habit of St. Peter[10] that I wear—though I've taken no more than the first four orders—your worship is one of the most famous knights-errant there has ever been or ever shall be in all the rotundity of the earth. Blessings on Cide Hamete Benengeli, who has written the history of your doughty deeds, and double blessings on the connoisseur who took the trouble to have it translated from Arabic into our Castilian vulgar tongue for the universal entertainment of mankind."

Don Quixote made him rise and said: "So it is true that there is a history of me and that it was a Moor and a wise man who wrote it."

"So true is it," said Sansón, "that I believe there are today in print more than twelve thousand volumes of the said history. For proof you have only to ask Portugal, Barcelona, and Valencia, where they have been printed, and it is rumored that it is being printed at Antwerp, and I am convinced that there is not a country or language in the world in which it will not be translated."[11]

"One of the things," said Don Quixote in reply, "which shall give the greatest pleasure to a virtuous and eminent man is to see himself in his lifetime printed and in the press, and with a good name on people's tongues, a good name, I repeat, for were it the contrary, no death could be so bad."

"If it is a question of a good reputation and a good name," said the bachelor, "your worship singly carries off the palm from all knights-errant, for the Moor in his language and the Christian in his have taken great pains to portray for us, quite realistically, your worship's gallantry, your great courage in facing perils, your patience in adversity and in sufferings, whether because of misfortunes or because of wounds, and the chastity and continence in the platonic loves of your worship and my lady, Doña Dulcinea of El Toboso."

---

[10] The ecclesiastical dress worn by university students.
[11] Ten editions had already been published of the first part of *Don Quixote* by 1612–13, when Cervantes is thought to have written this chapter.

"Never," butted in Sancho at this point, "have I heard Lady Dulcinea called doña, but plain Lady Dulcinea of El Toboso. So, history has gone astray."

"That's not an important objection," replied Carrasco.

"No, surely," replied Don Quixote, "but tell me, Master Bachelor, which of my deeds are most highly praised in this history?"

"About that point," answered the bachelor, "opinions vary as tastes vary. Some favor the adventure of the windmills, which seemed to your worship to be Briareuses and giants; others, the adventure of the fulling mills.[12] One is all for the description of the two armies, which afterward turned out to be two flocks of sheep; another praises the one of the corpse they were carrying to Segovia for burial. This one declares that the best of all is the freeing of the galley slaves, that one says that none equals that of the Benedictine giants and the combat with the valiant Biscayan."

"Tell me, Master Bachelor," cried Sancho, "does the adventure with the Yanguesans come in, when our good Rozinante had the notion of looking for mushrooms at the bottom of the sea?"[13]

"The sage left nothing in the inkhorn," answered Sansón. "He tells everything and touches on every point, even the capers that the worthy Sancho cut on the blanket."

"I cut no capers on the blanket," answered Sancho, "but in the air I did, and more than I would have liked."

"In my opinion," said Don Quixote, "there is no human history in the world which has not its ups and downs, especially those that deal with knight-errantry. They can never be full of lucky incidents alone."

"For all that," replied the bachelor, "some who have read your history say that they would have been glad if the author had omitted some of the countless drubbings that were given Don Quixote in his various encounters."

"Ah! There's where the truth of the story comes in," rejoined Sancho.

"Yet, they might in all fairness have kept quiet about them," said Don Quixote, "for there is no point in writing about actions that do not change or affect the truth of the story, if they tend to diminish the stature of the hero. Aeneas, I am sure, was not as pious as Virgil made him out to be, nor Ulysses as prudent as he is described in Homer."[14]

"That is true," replied Sansón, "but it is one thing to write as a poet, and another as a historian. The poet can tell or sing of things, not as they were, but as they ought to have been; the historian must relate them not as they should have been, but as they were, without adding to or subtracting from the truth."

"Well, if this Moor is out for truth," said Sancho, "then my beatings will be found there as well as my master's, for they never took measure of his worship's shoulders without measuring my whole body. But there's no wonder in that, for that same master of mine says that the limbs must take their fair share of the head's pain."

[12] Cloth mills. (The episode is omitted in this selection.)

[13] The adventures of the funeral party, the Benedictine "giants," the valiant Biscayan, and the Yanguesans are all omitted here.

[14] The references are to Virgil's *Aeneid* and Homer's *Odyssey*. *Ulysses* is Odysseus.

"You're a cunning rogue, Sancho," answered Don Quixote, "I swear your memory never fails you when you want to remember something."

"Even if I wanted to forget the cudgelings I got," said Sancho, "devil a bit would the bruises let me, for they're still as plain as paint on my ribs."

"Be quiet, Sancho," said Don Quixote, "and don't interrupt the bachelor, who, I hope, will now tell me what they say of me in this history he has referred to."

"And of me," said Sancho, "for I'm told that I am one of the principal presonages in it."

"*Personage,* not *presonages,* Sancho, my friend," said Sansón.

"So, here we have another word corrector!" rejoined Sancho. "If it goes on like this, we'll never come to the end of it in this life."

"May I be blowed, Sancho," replied the bachelor, "if you're not the second person in the history! Why, there are some who prefer to hear you talk than the best parts in the whole book, though, to be sure, there are others who say you were much too credulous in taking as Gospel truth that island Don Quixote has promised you."

"The sun is still shining on the thatch,"[15] said Don Quixote, "and in the meantime, as Sancho is growing older and riper in experience, wit, and years, he will become fitter and more able for the post of governor than he is at present."

"By God, sir," said Sancho, "any island I can't govern at my age, I'll never govern, even if I live to be as old as Methuselah.[16] The worst of it is that this isle of yours keeps itself hidden away the Lord knows where, and not that I haven't brains enough to govern it."

"Commend it to God, Sancho," said Don Quixote, "and all will be well, perhaps better than you think, for not a leaf stirs on a tree without God's will."

"That is true," said Sansón, "for if God is willing, Sancho will not lack a thousand isles, much less one."

"I have seen governors about here," said Sancho, "who, in my opinion, don't come up to the sole of my shoe. Yet, for all that they're called lordship and served on silver."

"Those are not governors of isles," answered Sansón, "but of other governments that are easier handled. Governors of isles must at least be grammarians."

"I'll deal with the *gram,*" said Sancho, "but as to the *marians,* I'll let them be, for I don't understand them. But leaving this matter of a governorship in God's hands—may He put me where I can serve Him best—let me say, Master Bachelor, that I'm mighty glad the author of this history has spoken of me in such a way that the things told of me don't give offense, for as I'm a good squire, if he'd said any derogatory things about me, not becoming the old Christian I am, our quarrel would reach the ears of the deaf."

"That would be to work miracles," said Sansón.

"Miracles or no miracles," said Sancho, "let everyone mind how he speaks or writes about persons, and not jot down helter-skelter the first thing that comes into his noddle."

---

[15] A proverbial expression, meaning "the day is not over yet" or "there is still time."
[16] 969 years, according to Genesis 5:25.

"One of the blemishes they find in this history," said the bachelor, "is that the author has inserted in it a novel called 'The Tale of Ill-Advised Curiosity'—not that it is bad or badly told, but that it is out of place and has nothing to do with the history of his worship, Don Quixote."[17]

"I'll bet," rejoined Sancho, "that the son of a dog has made a pretty kettle of fish of everything."

"Now I am sure," said Don Quixote, "that the author of my story is no sage but some ignorant prater who set himself blindly and aimlessly to write it down and let it turn out anyhow, like Orbaneja, the painter of Ubeda, who, when they asked him what he was painting, used to answer: 'Whatever it turns out.' Sometimes he would paint a cock in such a way and so little like one that it was necessary to write beside it in Gothic characters: 'This is a cock.' And so it must be with my history, which will need a commentary to be understood."

"No," replied Sansón, "for it's so plain that there is nothing in it to cause any difficulty. Children finger it, young people read it, grown men know it by heart, and old men praise it. It is so thumbed and read and so familiar to all kinds of people that no sooner do they catch sight of a lean hack than they cry out: 'There goes Rozinante.' Those who are most given to reading it are pages, for there's no lord's antechamber in which you will not find a *Don Quixote*. When one lays it down, another picks it up; some grab at it, others beg for it. This story, in fact, is the most delightful and least harmful entertainment ever seen to this day, for nowhere in it can one detect even the shadow of an indelicate expression or an uncatholic thought."

"To write in any other way," said Don Quixote, "would be to write not truths but lies, and historians who resort to lying ought to be burned like coiners of false money. But I do not know what induced the author to make use of novels and irrelevant tales when he had so much to write of in mine. No doubt he felt bound by the proverb: 'With straw or with hay, what odds we say!' For really if he had confined himself to my thoughts, my sighs, my tears, my righteous desires, and my enterprises, he could have compiled a volume greater than all the works of El Tostado, or at least as big.[18] So, my conclusion is, Master Bachelor, that one needs good judgment and ripe understanding to write histories or books of any sort whatsoever. To be witty and write humorously requires great genius. The most cunning part in a comedy is the clown's, for a man who wants to be taken for a simpleton must never be one. History is like a sacred text, for it has to be truthful, and where the truth is, there is God. But in spite of this, there are some who write books and toss them off into the world as though they were pancakes."

"There is no book so bad," said the bachelor, "that there is not something good in it."[19]

"No doubt of that," replied Don Quixote, "but it often happens that authors who have deservedly reaped and won great fame by their books

---

[17] This episode is omitted in this selection. Here and below, Cervantes is citing actual criticisms of Part I.

[18] Alonso de Madrigal, bishop of Ávila, who wrote under the pen name "El Tostado," was so prolific a writer of devotional works that there was a proverb, "He writes more than El Tostado."

[19] Carrasco is quoting the Roman naturalist Pliny the Elder.

have lost it all, or at least lessened it, when they have given them to the press."

"The reason of that is," answered Sansón, "that printed books are viewed at leisure, and so their faults are easily noticed, and the greater the fame of their authors, the more closely they are examined. Celebrated men of genius, great poets, and famous historians are always, or as a rule, envied by those who make it their pleasure and special pastime to judge the writings of others, without having published anything of their own."

"That is no wonder," said Don Quixote, "for there are many theologians who are no good in the pulpit, but excellent at recognizing the faults or excesses of those who preach."

"All that is so, Don Quixote," said Carrasco, "but I would be happy if those censors would be more merciful and less scrupulous and if they refrained from pitilessly stressing the specks on the bright sun of the work they are crabbing. For if *aliquando bonus dormitat Homerus*,[20] let them reflect how long he stayed awake to give us the light of his work with the least possible shadow. And it is possible that what seem to be faults to them are moles, which at times heighten the beauty of the face that has them. And so, I say that he who prints a book runs a very great risk, for it is absolutely impossible to write one that will satisfy and please every reader."

"The one that treats of me," said Don Quixote, "must have pleased but few."

"Rather the opposite, for as there are an infinite number of fools in the world, an infinite number of people have enjoyed that history. But there are some who have found fault and assailed the author's memory for forgetting who it was who robbed Sancho of his ass, for it is not then stated and it is only from the context that we infer that it was stolen. Yet, a little later on we find Sancho riding on this same ass, and we are never told how he turned up again. They also say that he forgot to put down what Sancho did with the hundred crowns he found in the leather bag in the Sierra Morena, for they were never mentioned again. Many people want to know what he did with them and how did he spend them, for it is one of the major omissions in the work."

"I'm not prepared now, Master Sansón," replied Sancho, "to go into details or accounts, for I feel faint in the stomach and if I don't cure it with a few swigs of the old stuff, it will put me on St. Lucy's thorn.[21] I have a drop at home, and my old woman is waiting for me. When I've had my dinner, I'll come back and answer all your worship's questions, and all the world's whether it's about my losing the ass or spending the hundred crowns."

Then, without waiting for an answer or saying another word, he went home.

Don Quixote begged and prayed the bachelor to stay and take potluck with him. He accepted the invitation and stayed for the meal, and a pair of pigeons were added to the usual fare. Knight-errantry was discussed at table, and Carrasco was careful to humor the knight. When the meal was over, they took their siesta until Sancho returned. . . .

---

[20] "Worthy Homer sometimes nods." (Horace, *Art of Poetry,* line 359.)
[21] Make me weak with hunger (proverbial).

[In the following chapters, Sancho supplies Sansón Carrasco with certain details of his and Quixote's adventures and reassures his wife Teresa that his quest with Quixote will result in his being governor of an island. Quixote's niece Antonia tries to dissuade him from further adventures, but he resolves to embark on a "third sally." He and Sancho ride out, bound first for Toboso, to see Dulcinea. There Sancho tricks Quixote by telling him that Dulcinea has been changed by enchantment into a country wench; he introduces him to three such wenches. Quixote, discouraged, rides on with Sancho; they encounter a band of strolling players. The actors have just performed a morality play called The Parliament of Death *and are costumed as Death, an angel, and a knight. The Fool of the company frightens Rozinante and Sancho's ass Dapple, who throw their riders, but Quixote yields to Sancho's advice not to do battle with these false Kings, Princes, and Emperors.]*

CHAPTER XII

Of the strange adventure that befell the gallant Don Quixote with the brave Knight of the Mirrors

Don Quixote and his squire spent the night following their encounter with Death beneath some tall and shady trees, and the former, at Sancho's persuasion, partook of the food from the store carried by Dapple. While they were at supper, Sancho said to his master: "Sir, what a fool I should have been if I had chosen for my reward the spoils of the first adventure accomplished by your worship, instead of the foals of the three mares![22] Well, well, a sparrow in the hand is better than a vulture on the wing."

"Nevertheless, Sancho," replied Don Quixote, "if you had let me attack as I wished, the Empress' gold crown and Cupid's painted wings would have fallen to you as spoils, for I would have seized them by force and put them into your hands."

"The scepters and crowns of stage emperors," answered Sancho Panza, "are never made of real gold, but only of brass or tinfoil."

"That is true," said Don Quixote, "the ornaments of the drama should not be real, but only make-believe and fiction like the drama itself. Indeed, Sancho, I want you to turn a kindly eye upon the play and in consequence upon those who represent and compose it, for they are all productive of much good to the state, placing before us at every step a mirror in which we may see vividly portrayed the action of human life. Nothing, in fact, more truly portrays us as we are and as we would be than the play and the players. Now tell me, have you never seen a play acted in which kings, emperors, pontiffs, knights, ladies, and divers other characters are introduced? One plays the bully, another the rogue; this one the merchant, that the soldier; one the wise fool, another the foolish lover. When the play is over and they have divested themselves of the dresses they wore in it, the actors are all again upon the same level."

"Yes, I've seen it," answered Sancho.

"Well, then," said Don Quixote, "the same happens in the comedy and life of this world, where some play emperors, others popes, and in short, all the parts that can be brought into a play; but when it is over, that is to say,

---

[22] The reward Quixote has promised Sancho for news of Dulcinea.

when life ends, death strips them all of the robes that distinguished one from the other, and all are equal in the grave."

"A brave comparison!" said Sancho. "Though not so new, for I've heard it many a time, as well as that one about the game of chess: so long as the game lasts, each piece has its special office, and when the game is finished, they are all mixed, shuffled, and jumbled together and stored away in the bag, which is much like ending life in the grave."

"Each day, Sancho," said Don Quixote, "you are becoming less doltish and more wise."

"Yes, master, for some of your wisdom must stick to me," said Sancho, "just as land that is of itself barren and dry will eventually, by dint of dunging and tilling, come to yield a goodly crop. What I mean to say is that your worship's talk has been the dung that has fallen upon the barren soil of my poor wit and that the time during which I have served you and enjoyed your company has been the tillage. With the help of this I hope to yield fruit that are like blessings and such that will not slide away from the paths of good breeding that you have made in my shallow understanding."

Don Quixote laughed at Sancho's affected style of speech and perceived that what he said about his improvement was true, for from time to time he spoke in a way that astonished him; though on most occasions when Sancho tried to talk in argument and in a lofty style, his speech would end by toppling down from the peak of his simplicity into the abyss of his ignorance. And where he showed his culture and his memory best was in his use of proverbs, no matter whether they came pat to the subject or not, as must have been seen already and noted in the course of this history.

In such a conversation they spent a great part of the night, but Sancho felt a wish to let down the hatches of his eyes, as he used to say when he wanted to sleep. So, having unharnessed Dapple, he left him free to crop the abundant pasture. He did not take the saddle off Rozinante, as his master's express orders were that as long as they were in the field or not sleeping under a roof, Rozinante was not to be unsaddled; it was, by the way, an ancient custom, established and observed by knights-errant, to take off the bridle and hang it on the saddlebow; but to remove the saddle from the horse—never on your life! Sancho observed this rule and gave him the same liberty he had given Dapple, whose friendship for Rozinante was so unequaled and so close that a tradition handed down from father to son says that the author of this true history wrote some chapters on the subject that, in order to preserve the propriety and decorum due to so heroic a history, he did not include. At times, however, he forgets this resolve and describes how, as soon as the two beasts were together, they would scratch one another, and how, when they were tired or satisfied, Rozinante would lay his neck across Dapple's more than half a yard beyond, and the pair would stand in that position, gazing thoughtfully at the ground, for three days, or at least, as long as they were left alone and hunger did not compel them to look for food.

It is said that the author left on record a comparison between their friendship and that of Nisus and Euryalus, and of Pylades and Orestes, and if this is true, it can be understood how steadfast must the friendship of these two animals have been to the wonder of the world and to the shame

of humankind, who fail so lamentably to preserve friendship for one another.[23] Because of this it has been said:

> Friend to friend no more draws near,
> And the jouster's cane has become a spear.[24]

And that other song that goes:

> Says friend to friend: "Here's mud in your eye!"

But let no one imagine that the author went off the tracks when he
compared the friendship of these animals to that of men, for men have
received many lessons from dumb beasts and learned many things of value,
as for example: from storks the enema, from dogs vomiting and gratitude,
from cranes watchfulness, from ants thrift, from elephants chastity, and
loyalty from the horse.

At last, Sancho fell asleep at the foot of a cork tree, and Don Quixote
dozed under a robust oak. But a short time had elapsed when a noise he
heard behind awoke the latter, and standing up, he gazed in the direction
the noise came from, and spied two men on horseback, one of whom,
letting himself slip from the saddle, said to the other: "Dismount, friend,
and take the bridles off the horses, for this spot seems to me both rich in
grass for them and in silence and solitude for my love-sick thoughts."

Saying this, he stretched himself upon the ground, and as he flung
himself down, the armor he wore clattered—a manifest proof by which
Don Quixote knew him to be a knight-errant—and going over to Sancho,
who was fast asleep, he pulled him by the arm, and after rousing him with
no small difficulty, he said to him in a low voice: "Brother Sancho, we have
an adventure."

"God send us a good one," said Sancho, "and where, master, may Mistress Adventure be?"

"Where, Sancho?" answered Don Quixote. "Turn your eyes and there
you will see stretched a knight-errant, who, I believe, is not too happy, for I
saw him fling himself off his horse and throw himself on the ground with
signs of dejection, and as he fell, his armor clattered."

"But how does your worship make out that this is an adventure?" said
Sancho.

"I do not insist," answered Don Quixote, "that this is a full adventure,
but it is the beginning of one, for this is the way adventures begin. But
listen, for he seems to be tuning a viol or lute, and by the way he is spitting
and clearing his throat, he must be preparing to sing something."

"Faith and so he is," answered Sancho. "He must be a lovesick knight."

"There is no knight-errant who is not," said Don Quixote. "Let us listen
to him, for if he sings, by that thread we shall gain a clue to his thoughts,
for the tongue speaks out of the abundance of the heart."

---

[23] Nisus and Euryalus were two friends who accompanied Aeneas to Italy, in Virgil's
Aeneid. Pylades, son of the king of Phocis, accompanied Orestes back to Argos to avenge his
father Agamemnon's death; see Aeschylus' *The Libation Bearers,* in the *Oresteia.*

[24] A line from a popular ballad.

Sancho was about to reply to his master, but the voice of the Knight of the Wood, which was neither very bad nor very good, prevented him, and the two, listening attentively, heard the following sonnet:[25]

O cruel one, bestow on me
Some token of your sovereign sway,
Which I may follow earnestly,
And never from its precepts stray.
If you would have me fade away
In silence, then account me dead,
But if you'd hear my ancient lay,
Then Love himself my cause shall plead.
My soul to contraries inured
Is made of wax and adamant,
And well prepared for Cupid's law.
Whether soft or hard my heart is yours,
To grave it leave to you I'll grant,
And to your will I'll bow with awe.

With a sigh that seemed to spring from the depths of his heart, the Knight of the Wood ended his song, and after a short pause he exclaimed in a sad and sorrowful voice: "O most beautiful and ungrateful woman in all the world! Is it possible, most serene Casildea of Vandalia, for thee to allow thy captive knight to be consumed and to perish in perpetual wandering and in harsh and unkind labors? Is it not enough that I have compelled all the knights of Navarra, of León, of Tartessus, Castile, and all the knights of La Mancha as well, to acknowledge thee to be the most beautiful lady in the world?"

"Not so," cried Don Quixote at this, "for I am of La Mancha, and I have acknowledged no such thing, nor could I, nor ought I, acknowledge anything so prejudicial to the beauty of my mistress. This knight, as you can see, Sancho, is raving. But let us listen; perhaps he will give himself away still more."

"That he will surely," answered Sancho, "for he seems the kind who'll go on mourning and groaning for a month on end."

This was not so, however, for the Knight of the Wood, overhearing voices nearby, proceeded no further with his lamentations, but sprang to his feet and called out in a loud but courteous voice: "Who goes there? Who are you? Are you by any chance one of the band of the happy or of the afflicted?"

"Of the afflicted," answered Don Quixote.

"Then come to me," replied the Knight of the Wood, "and you will come to the very fountainhead of sorrow and affliction."

Don Quixote, when he heard such gentle and courteous words, went over to him, and Sancho likewise. The melancholy knight then took Don Quixote by the arm and said: "Sit down here, sir knight. Now that I know that I have found you in this place, where solitude and the night dews, the

---

[25] Cervantes is parodying conventional love poetry of his time.

natural couch and proper dwelling of knights-errant, keep you company, I need no further proof that you belong to their number."

To which Don Quixote answered: "I am a knight, and of the order you mention; and although sorrows, misfortunes, and disasters keep their abode in my soul, they have not scored away my compassion for the misfortunes of others. From what you were singing a moment ago I gathered that yours are amorous woes—I mean, of the love you have for that ungrateful beauty whom you named in your lament."

While this conversation was proceeding, they were seated side by side upon the hard sward, in peace and good company, not in the manner of men who at break of day would have to break one another's heads.

"Are you, sir knight, perchance, in love?" inquired the Knight of the Wood.

"To my woe, I am," answered Don Quixote, "though the sorrows arising from well-placed affections should be accounted blessings rather than calamities."

"That is true," replied he of the Wood, "provided disdain does not unbalance our reason and understanding, for if exaggerated, it resembles vengeance."

"I was never disdained by my lady," said Don Quixote.

"No, surely not," said Sancho, who stood close by, "my lady is as meek as a yearling ewe and softer than butter."

"Is this your squire?" asked he of the Wood.

"Yes, he is," said Don Quixote.

"This is the first time I have ever seen a squire," said he of the Wood, "who dared to speak while his master was speaking. Anyhow, there is mine over there, who is as tall as his father, and it cannot be proved that he has ever opened his lips when I was speaking."

"By my faith," said Sancho, "I have spoken and am fit to speak before one as great, and even—But let it be, it'll be worse to stir it about."

The squire of the Wood then took Sancho by the arm, saying: "Let us two go where we can talk squirelike together, and leave these gentlemen, our masters, to butt at each other, telling the story of their loves. I wager the day will find them at it without having settled anything."

"With all my heart," said Sancho, "and I'll tell your worship who I am so that you may judge whether I deserve to be counted among the number of most talkative squires."

The two squires then withdrew to one side, and a dialogue passed between them as droll as that of their masters was serious.

CHAPTER XIII

In which the adventure of the Knight of the Wood is continued, with the wise, novel, and agreeable conversation between the two squires

The knights and squires were separated, the latter telling the stories of their lives, the former of their loves; but the history tells first of the conversation between the servants, and then follows with that between their masters. And so, it relates that he of the Wood, when they had drawn a little aside, said to Sancho: "It's a wearisome life we lead, sir, those of us who are squires to knights-errant. We certainly eat our bread in the sweat of our brows, which is one of the curses God laid on our first parents."[26]

"It may be said, too," added Sancho, "that we eat it in the chill of our bodies, for who suffers the heat and the cold worse than the wretched squires of knight-errantry? It wouldn't be so bad if we had something to eat, for sorrows are lighter when there's bread to eat, but there are times when we go a day or two without breaking our fast, unless it be on the wind that blows."

"All that can be put up with," said he of the Wood, "when we have hopes of a reward, for unless he serves an especially unlucky knight-errant, a squire is sure after a little time to find himself at least rewarded with a handsome government of some island or a tidy countship."

"I have told my master already," said Sancho, "that I'll be content with the government of some island, and he's so noble and generous that he has promised it to me many a time."

"As for me," said he of the Wood, "I'll be content with a canonry[27] for my services, and my master has already assigned me one."

"Your master," said Sancho, "must then be a knight in the ecclesiastical line and can grant such favors to his good squire, but mine is only a layman, though I do remember some wise, but in my opinion, intriguing folks who tried to persuade him to have himself made archbishop. He, however, would be nothing but an emperor, and I was trembling all the time lest he should become bitten with the fancy of going into the Church, for I didn't consider myself suitable to hold offices in it. In fact, I may as well tell you that, though I look like a man, I'm just a beast as far as the Church is concerned."

"Ah! That's where you are wrong," said he of the Wood. "Those insular governorships are not all plain sailing. Some are twisted, some poor, some dreary, and in short, the loftiest and best regulated brings with it a heavy load of worry and trouble, which the unlucky wight to whose lot it has fallen bears upon his shoulders. Far better would it be for us who profess this plague-stricken service to return to our homes and there spend our days in more pleasant occupations, such as hunting and fishing, for where in the world would you find a squire so poor as not to have a hack, a couple of greyhounds, and a fishing rod with which to while away the time in his own village?"

"I'm not short of any of these things," said Sancho. "It's true I've no hack, but I've an ass that is worth twice as much as my master's horse. God send me a bad Easter, and may it be the next one, if I would swap him, even if I got four bushels of barley to boot. You'll laugh at the value I'm putting on my Dapple, for dapple is the color of my ass. As for greyhounds, I'm in no want, for there are plenty of them in my home town, and surely the finest sport of all is where it's at other people's expense."

"Truly and earnestly, sir squire," said he of the Wood, "I've made up my mind to give up the drunken frolics of these knights of ours and go back to

---

[26] See Genesis 3:1.   [27] A minor ecclesiastical appointment.

my village and bring up my children, for I've three like three oriental pearls."

"I've two," said Sancho, "fit to be presented to the Pope in person, especially a girl whom I'm rearing to be a countess, please God, though against her mother's wishes."

"And how old is this lady who is being brought up to be a countess?" inquired he of the Wood.

"Fifteen years, more or less," replied Sancho, "but she's as tall as a lance and as fresh as an April morning and as strong as a porter."

"Those qualities," said he of the Wood, "make her fit to be not only a countess but a nymph of the greenwood. Ah, the frisky whore! What spunk the jade must have!"

To this Sancho replied somewhat sulkily: "She's no whore, nor was her mother, nor will either of them be, please God, so long as I'm alive. And do keep a civiller tongue on you. Considering that you've been reared among knights-errant, who are the last word in courtesy, I don't think your language is becoming."

"Oh, how little you understand the language of compliments, sir squire," answered he of the Wood. "Do you mean to tell me that you don't know that when a horseman lands a good lance thrust at a bull in the square, or when anyone does anything very well, the people are accustomed to say: 'How well the whoreson rogue has done it!' and what seems to be insulting in the phrase is high praise? Come, sir, let you disown the sons or daughters whose actions don't earn their parents such compliments."

"Yes, I do disown them," answered Sancho, "and in the same way you may heap the whole of whoredom straightaway on me, my wife, and my children, for all they do and say is over and above deserving of like praise. And that I may see them again, I pray God deliver me from mortal sin, which is the same as delivering me from this dangerous squire business into which I've fallen for the second time, baited and bribed by a purse with a hundred ducats in it that I found one day in the heart of the Sierra Morena.[28] And I tell you the Devil is always putting before my eyes, here, there, and everywhere, a bag full of doubloons, which I'm forever turning over with my hand and hugging it and carrying it home with me to make investments and settle rents and live like a prince. So long as I think of this, I don't care a fig for all the toils I endure with this fool of a master of mine, whom I know to be more of a madman than a knight."

"Hence the common saying that 'covetousness bursts the bag,'" said he of the Wood; "but if you mean to talk of such men, let me tell you that there is no greater in the world than my master, for he is one of those of whom it is said: 'Care for his neighbor kills the ass,' for he makes a madman of himself in order that another knight may recover the wits he has lost,[29] and he goes about looking for what, were he to find it, may, for all I know, hit him in the snout."

"Is he by any chance in love?" asked Sancho.

[28] Sancho is referring to an incident in Part I, omitted here.
[29] In the incident in the Sierra Morena, Don Quixote has tried to imitate such romance heroes as Ariosto's Orlando by going mad with love.

"He is," said he of the Wood, "with a certain Casildea of Vandalia, the rawest[30] and most hard-boiled lady in the world, but it is not on the score of rawness that he limps, for he has other greater plans rumbling in his belly; you'll hear him speak of them before long."

"No matter how smooth the road, there's sure to be some rut or hollow in it," said Sancho. "In other houses they cook beans, but in mine it is by the potful;[31] madness has always more followers and hangers-on than wisdom; but if the common saying is true, that 'to have a friend in grief gives some relief,' I may draw consolation from you, for your master is as crazy as mine."

"Crazy but valiant," answered he of the Wood, "and more roguish than crazy or valiant."

"Mine is not like that," replied Sancho. "I mean, he has nothing of the rogue in him. On the contrary, he has a soul as simple as a pitcher; he could do no harm to anyone, but good to all, nor has he any malice in him; why, a child would convince him it is night at noonday, and it is on account of this simplicity that I love him as I love the cockles of my heart, and I can't invent a way of leaving him, no matter what piece of foolishness he does."

"Nevertheless, brother and sir," said he of the Wood, "if the blind lead the blind, both are in danger of falling into the ditch. It is better for us to retire quickly and get back to our dens, for those who seek adventures don't always find good ones."

Sancho kept spitting from time to time, and as the charitable Squire of the Wood noticed that his spittle was gluey and somewhat dry, he said: "It seems to me that all this talk of ours has made our tongues stick to our palates, but I have a loosener, hanging from the saddlebow of my horse, which is quite good." And getting up, he came back a moment later with a large skin of wine and a pasty half a yard long, which is no exaggeration, for it was composed of a domestic rabbit so big that Sancho, as he held it, took it to be a goat, not to say a kid, and gazing at it, he said: "Is this what you carry along with you, sir?"

"What were you thinking then?" said the other. "Am I perchance some homespun, water-drinking squire? I carry better food supplies on my horse's crupper than a general does when he is on the march."

Sancho fell to, without any need of pressing. In the dark he gobbled lumps as large as knots on a tether, observing as he ate: "You are indeed a trusty and a loyal squire, round and sound, grand and gorgeous, as is proved by this feast, which, if it has not come here by magic, seems like it at least; and not like me, poor devil, who am only carrying in my saddlebags a scrap of cheese so hard that you could brain a giant with it, and to keep it company, a few dozen carob pods and as many filberts and walnuts. Thanks to the poverty of my master and the idea he has and the rule he follows that knights-errant must not feed on anything except dried fruits and the herbs of the field."

"By my faith," replied he of the Wood, "my stomach is not made for thistles or wild pears from the woods. Let our masters keep to their opin-

---

[30] The Spanish puns here on *crudo*, which means both "raw" and "cruel."

[31] Sancho means his bad luck comes in quantity. This paragraph is a good example of Sancho's "proverbial" style; he quotes four proverbs.

ions and laws of chivalry, and eat what is prescribed. As for me, I carry my meat baskets and this wineskin slung from my saddlebow, whether they like it or not, and I'm so devoted to her, aye, and so arrantly fond of her, that hardly a minute passes without my giving her a thousand kisses and hugs."

Saying this, he put the skin into Sancho's hands, who, raising it up, pressed it to his mouth and remained gazing at the stars for a quarter of an hour. When he had finished his drink, he let his head fall on one side, and heaving a deep sigh, he exclaimed: "Whoreson rogue, what a tip-top liquor it is!"

"There you are," said he of the Wood when he heard Sancho's exclamation. "See how you have praised my wine by calling it 'whoreson.'"

"Well," said Sancho, "I confess that I'm aware it's no dishonor to call somebody whoreson when we mean to praise him. Now tell me, sir, by the life you love best, is this Ciudad Real wine?"

"O peerless wine taster!" said he of the Wood, "From there and from nowhere else has it come, and it is a few years old, too."

"Trust me in that," said Sancho. "I knew I'd make a successful guess as to where it came from. Would you believe me, sir, when I tell you that I've such a great natural instinct in testing wines that no sooner do I smell one of them than I tell its country, its kind, its flavor and age, the changes it will undergo, and every detail concerning the wine. But you needn't wonder, for I've had in my family, on my father's side, the two finest wine tasters La Mancha has known for many a long year, and to prove what I'm saying, I'll tell you what happened to them. They were both given wine from a cask to try, and they were asked their opinion about its condition, quality, goodness or badness. One of them tested it with the tip of his tongue, the other did no more than hold it to his nose. The first said that the wine tasted of iron; the second that it had a flavor of cordovan leather. The owner declared that the cask was clean, and that the wine had no blending that could have imparted a taste of iron or leather. Notwithstanding this, the two famous wine tasters stuck to their point. Time went by, the wine was sold, and when the cask was cleaned, a small key was found in it hanging to a cordovan thong. Consider now whether one who comes of such a stock is able to give an opinion in such matters."

"Since that is so," said he of the Wood, "let us give up going in search of adventures; and since we have loaves, don't let us go looking for tarts, but return to our cots, for there God will find us if it be His will."

"I'll serve my master till he gets to Saragossa," said Sancho, "then maybe we'll come to an understanding."

Finally, the two worthy squires talked so much and drank so much that they had need of sleep to tie up their tongues and allay their thirst, for to quench it was impossible. And so the pair of them, clinging to the now nearly empty wineskin and with half-chewed morsels in their mouths, fell fast asleep; and there we will leave them for the present to relate what took place between the Knight of the Wood and him of the Rueful Figure.

CHAPTER XIV

In which the adventure of the Knight of the Wood is continued

Among the many speeches that passed between Don Quixote and the Knight of the Wood, our history tells us that the latter said to Don Quixote: "In a word, sir knight, I wish you to know that my destiny, or rather my choice, led me to become enamored of a certain lady, the peerless Casildea of Vandalia. I call her peerless, because she has no peer in bodily stature, rank, or beauty. This Lady Casildea repaid my honorable desires by forcing me, as his stepmother did Hercules,[32] to engage in many perilous exploits, promising me at the end of each that, with the end of the next, I should obtain the object of all my hopes. But my labors have gone increasing link by link until they are past counting, nor do I know which is to be the one that will finally announce the accomplishment of my honorable wishes. On one occasion she ordered me to go and challenge that famous giantess of Seville known as the Giralda,[33] who is as valiant and strong as if made of brass, and though never stirring from one spot, is the most changeable and volatile woman in the world. I came, I saw, I conquered, and I made her keep still and on one point, for none but north winds blew for more than a week. On another occasion she made me go and weigh the mighty Bulls of Guisando,[34] an enterprise that should have been recommended to porters rather than to knights. Another time she commanded me to fling myself into the pit of Cabra,[35] an unheard-of peril, and bring her back a detailed account of what is hidden in its abyss. I stopped the motion of the Giralda; I weighed the Bulls of Guisando; I descended into the pit and drew to the light of day the secrets of its abyss; yet my hopes are as dead as dead can be, and her orders and disdains as much alive as ever. And now her last command is for me to go through all provinces of Spain and compel all the knights-errant wandering about to confess that she is the most beautiful woman alive today and that I am the most valiant and the most enamored knight on earth. In accordance with her demand I have already traveled over the greater part of Spain and have vanquished many knights who have had the presumption to gainsay me. But my greatest pride and boast is that I have conquered in single combat that so famous knight Don Quixote of La Mancha, and made him confess that my Casildea is more beautiful than his Dulcinea. By this victory alone I consider that I have conquered all the knights in the world, for the said Don Quixote has vanquished them all, and since I have vanquished him, his glory, his fame, and his honor are forthwith transferred to my person, and his innumerable exploits are now set down to my account and have become mine."

Don Quixote was astounded to hear such words from the Knight of the Wood, and he was a thousand times on the point of telling him he lied and

[32] Hercules' "stepmother" was Hera, since he was the son of Zeus by the mortal Alcmena. Hera imposed the labors of Hercules.

[33] The Giralda is actually a fourteen-foot brass statue of Faith on the top of the great tower of the Cathedral of Seville.

[34] The Bulls of Guisando are four rough granite figures of animals in the district of Ávila.

[35] The pit of Cabra in the district of Córdoba is traditionally supposed to be the shaft of an ancient mine.

had the *you lie!* on the tip of his tongue, but he restrained himself as best he could in order to make him confess the lie out of his own mouth. So, he said to him calmly: "I say nothing about your worship, sir knight, having vanquished most of the knights of Spain, and even of the world, but I doubt that you have conquered Don Quixote of La Mancha. Perhaps it may have been some other knight who resembled him, though, indeed, there are few like him."

"How! Not vanquished him?" said he of the Wood. "By Heaven above us, I fought Don Quixote and vanquished him and overcame him. He is a man of tall stature, gaunt features, lanky shriveled limbs; his hair is turning gray, his nose is aquiline and a little hooked, and his moustaches are long, black, and drooping. He goes into battle under the name of the Knight of the Rueful Figure, and he has for squire a peasant called Sancho Panza. He presses the back and curbs the reins of a famous horse called Rozinante, and finally, he has for mistress of his will a certain Dulcinea of El Toboso, once upon a time known as Aldonza Lorenzo, just as mine, whose name is Casildea and who comes from Andalusia, I call Casildea of Vandalia. If all these tokens do not suffice to vindicate the truth of my words, here is my sword, which will compel incredulity itself to give credence to it."

"Softly, sir knight," said Don Quixote, "and listen to what I am about to say. You must know that this Don Quixote you speak about is the greatest friend I have in the world; in fact, I may say that I regard him as I would my very self, and by the precise tokens you have given of him I am sure that he must be the same whom you vanquished. On the other hand, I see with my eyes and feel with my hands that it is impossible for him to be the same, unless, perhaps, that particular enemy of his, who is an enchanter, may have taken his shape in order to allow himself to be vanquished so as to cheat him of the fame that his noble exploits as a knight have won him throughout the world. To confirm this I must tell you that only two days ago these said enchanters, his enemies, changed the shape and person of the fair Dulcinea of El Toboso into a vulgar and mean village lass,[36] and in the same manner they must have transformed Don Quixote. If all this does not suffice to convince you of the truth of my words, here stands Don Quixote himself: he will maintain it by arms, on foot or on horseback or in any way you wish."

With these words he stood up and grabbed his sword, waiting for the decision of the Knight of the Wood, who in a voice equally calm replied: "A good prayer needs no sureties. He who managed to vanquish you once when transformed, Señor Don Quixote, may well hope to conquer you in your person. But since it is not right for knights to perform their deeds in the dark like highwaymen and bullies, let us wait till daylight, that the sun may look down on our achievements. And it must be a condition of our battle that the vanquished shall remain entirely at the mercy of the conqueror, provided that what is imposed shall be becoming a knight."

"I am more than satisfied with these conditions," answered Don Quixote.

And so saying, they went to seek their squires, whom they found snoring in the same posture as when sleep first waylaid them. They roused

---

[36] An episode omitted here, in which Sancho plays a thoughtless trick on Quixote.

them and ordered them to prepare the steeds, for at sunrise the two knights would engage in bloody single combat. When Sancho heard the news, he was thunderstruck, fearing for the safety of his master, because of the tales that he had heard the Squire of the Wood tell of his knight's powers. Without saying a word, however, the two squires went off in search of their beasts, for the three horses and the dapple had smelled each other and were by this time all together.

On the way, he of the Wood said to Sancho: "You must know, brother, that fighting men from Andalusia are accustomed, when they are seconds in any combat, not to stand idle with their hands folded while their champions are engaged. I'm saying this to remind you that while our masters are fighting, we, too, must have a fight and knock one another to splinters."

"That custom, sir squire," replied Sancho, "may be current among the bullies and fighting men you mention, but never in any circumstances among the squires of knights-errant. At least I have never heard my master speak of such a custom, and he knows all the rules of knight-errantry by heart. But even if it is an express rule that squires should fight while their masters are fighting, I don't intend to follow it, but to pay the penalty that might be imposed on peacefully minded squires like myself, for I'm sure it will not be more than a couple of pounds of wax.[37] I would prefer to pay that, for I know it will cost me less than the plasters I'll need to heal my head, which I already reckon to be smashed in two pieces. Furthermore, I cannot fight, for I've no sword and never in my life carried one."

"I know a good remedy for that," said he of the Wood. "I've here two linen bags of the same size; you take one and I'll take the other, and we'll have a bout of bag-blows on equal terms."

"If that's the way it goes," answered Sancho, "I'm game, for such a fight will beat the dust off us rather than hurt us."

"That mustn't happen," replied the other, "for we'll put in the bags, to keep the wind from blowing them away, half a dozen fine smooth stones, all of the same weight. In this way we'll be able to pound one another without doing much damage."

"Body of my father," said Sancho, "what a nice kind of sable skins and pads of cotton wool he's putting into the bags to save breaking our heads and mashing our bones to powder! But even if they were filled with pads of raw silk, I tell you, my dear sir, there's to be no fighting for me. Let our masters fight and take their medicine, but let us eat, drink, and be merry, for Time is anxious enough to snatch away our lives from us without our going out in search of appetizers to finish them off before they reach their season and drop off the tree for very ripeness."

"Still," said he of the Wood, "we must fight, if only for half an hour."

"Not on your life," replied Sancho; "I'm not going to be so churlish or ungrateful as to pick any quarrel, no matter how trifling, with one whom I have eaten and drunk with; besides, who the devil could manage to fight in cold blood, without anger or annoyance?"

"I'll provide a remedy for that," said he of the Wood. "Before we start

---

[37] Fines payable in wax were imposed for trifling offenses; the wax was used to make church candles.

fighting I'll walk nicely and gently up to your worship and give you three or four buffets that will land you at my feet. By this means I'll rouse your choler though it be sleeping sounder than a dormouse."

"I've a trick against yours that's just as good," replied Sancho. "I'll take up a stout cudgel, and before your worship gets near enough to raise my choler, I'll send yours to sleep with such sound whacks that it will not awake unless it be in the next world, where all know that I am not the kind of man to let my face be messed about by anyone. Let each man watch out for his own arrow, though, mind you, the better way would be for everyone to let his choler sleep in peace, for no one knows the heart of his neighbor, and many a man comes for wool and goes back shorn; and God always blessed the peacemakers and cursed the peace-breakers; for if a baited cat who's shut in turns into a lion, God knows what I, who am a man, shall turn into. So, from now on I warn you, Mister Squire, that I'll put down to your account all the harm and damage that may come of our quarrel."

"I agree," said he of the Wood; "God will send the dawn and all will be as right as rain."

And now a thousand kinds of little painted birds began to warble in the trees, and with their blithe and jocund notes they seemed to welcome and salute the fresh Aurora, who already was showing her beautiful countenance through the gates and balconies of the East, shaking from her tresses countless liquid pearls. The plants, bathing in that fragrant moisture, seemed likewise to shed a spray of tiny white gems, the willow trees distilled sweet manna, the fountains laughed, the brooks murmured, and the meadows clad themselves in all their glory at her coming. But hardly had the light of the day allowed things to be seen and distinguished, when the first object that Sancho Panza caught sight of was the Squire of the Wood's nose, which was so big that it almost overshadowed his whole body. It is said, indeed, that it was of huge size, hooked in the middle, all covered with warts, and of a mulberry color like an eggplant, and that it hung down two fingers' length below his mouth. The size, the color, the warts, and the hook of the aforesaid nose made its owner's face so hideous that Sancho, as he gazed at it, began to shudder hand and foot like a child in a fit of epilepsy, and he resolved in his heart to let himself be given two hundred buffets rather than to allow his choler to provoke him into attacking that monster.

Don Quixote looked at his adversary and found that he already had his helmet on, with the visor down, so that he could not see his face, but he noticed that he was a muscular man, though not very tall in stature. Over his armor he wore a surcoat or cassock of a cloth that seemed to be of the finest gold, all bedizened with many little moons of glittering mirrors, which gave him a most gallant and showy appearance. Above his helmet fluttered a great cluster of green, yellow, and white plumes, and his lance, which was leaning against a tree, was very long and thick and had a steel point more than a palm in length.

Don Quixote noticed everything, and from what he saw he inferred that the said knight must be very powerful; but for all that he did not fear as Sancho did, but with noble courage he addressed the Knight of the Mirrors, saying: "If your great longing to fight, sir knight, has not exhausted your courtesy, I would beg you earnestly to raise your visor a little that I may see if the gallantry of your countenance corresponds with that of your accouterment."

"Whether you are vanquished or victor in this enterprise, sir knight," answered he of the Mirrors, "you will have more than enough time and opportunity to see me. If I do not now satisfy your request, it is because, in my opinion, I should wrong the beauteous Casildea of Vandalia by wasting time in raising my visor before forcing you to confess what you know I demand."

"Well," said Don Quixote, "while we are mounting our steeds you can surely tell me if I am the Don Quixote whom you said you vanquished."

"To that we answer," said he of the Mirrors, "that you are as like the knight whom I vanquished as one egg is like another, but as you say that enchanters persecute you, I dare not say whether you are the aforesaid or not."

"That is enough," said Don Quixote, "to convince me of your deception; however, to relieve you of your misapprehensions, let our horses be brought, and in less time than you would take in raising your visor, if God, my lady, and my arm prevail, I shall see your face, and you shall see that I am not the vanquished Don Quixote you consider me to be."

Therefore, cutting short further words, they mounted their horses, and Don Quixote turned Rozinante's reins in order to take up the requisite ground for charging back upon his rival, while he of the Mirrors did the same; but Don Quixote had hardly gone twenty paces when he heard himself called by the Knight of the Mirrors, who said, when each had returned halfway: "Remember, sir knight, that the condition of our battle is that the vanquished, as I said before, shall be at the disposal of the victor."

"I know it already," answered Don Quixote, "but there is a proviso that what is commanded and imposed upon the vanquished must not transgress the bounds of chivalry."

"That is understood," replied he of the Mirrors.

Just at this moment the amazing nose of the squire presented itself to Don Quixote's view, and he was no less astonished to see it than Sancho had been, so much so that he took him for some monster or else for a human being of some new species that is rarely seen on the face of the earth. Sancho, seeing his master go off to take his ground, did not want to remain alone with the nosy individual, for he was afraid that one flick of that nose on his own would end the battle as far as he was concerned and leave him stretched on the ground either because of the blow or because of fright; so, he ran after his master, holding on to one of Rozinante's stirrups, and when he thought it was time to turn about, he said: "I beg your worship, master, before you turn to charge, to help me climb up on that cork tree, from where I may witness your gallant encounter with this knight at better ease and comfort than from the ground."

"I am rather of the opinion, Sancho," said Don Quixote, "that you would even mount a scaffold to see the bulls without danger."

"To tell you the truth," replied Sancho, "the fearsome nose of that squire has me all in a dither and full of terror, so that I dare not stay near him."

"It is, indeed, such a one," said Don Quixote, "that were I not what I am, it would strike fear in me, too. So, come, I will help you to climb up where you will."

While Don Quixote stopped to let Sancho climb into the cork tree, he of the Mirrors took as much ground as he considered necessary, and thinking that Don Quixote had done likewise, without waiting for any sound of trumpet or other signal to direct them, he wheeled his horse, which was no swifter or better-looking than Rozinante, and at his top speed, which was no more than an easy trot, advanced to meet his foe, but noticing that he was busy hoisting Sancho up into the tree, he drew reins and halted midway, for which his steed was profoundly grateful, for it was unable to move. Don Quixote, imagining that his rival was careering down on top of him, drove his spurs vigorously into the lean flanks of Rozinante and made him dash along in such a way that, as the history relates, this was the one occasion when he was seen to make an attempt to gallop, for on all others he did no more than plain easy trotting; and with this unheard-of fury he charged at him of the Mirrors, who was digging the spurs into his horse up to the buttons, without being able to make him stir an inch from the spot where he had halted in his career. At this critical moment did Don Quixote bear down upon his adversary, who was in difficulties with his horse and embarrassed with his lance, for he could neither manage it nor was there time to put it into the rest. Don Quixote, however, paid scant heed to such embarrassments, but in perfect safety and without taking any risk crashed into him of the Mirrors with such force that in spite of himself, he threw him to the ground over the horse's rump and so great was the fall that he lay apparently dead, not stirring hand or foot. No sooner did Sancho see him fall than he slid down the cork tree and ran at top speed to where his master was, who, after dismounting from Rozinante, stood over the Knight of the Mirrors. Unlacing his helmet to see if he was dead and to give him air if haply he were alive, he saw — Who can say what he saw without arousing the wonder, astonishment, and awe of all who hear it? He saw, the history says, the very face, the very figure, the very aspect, the very physiognomy, the very effigy, the very image of the bachelor Sansón Carrasco. As soon as he saw him, he cried out in a loud voice: "Come, Sancho, and behold what you have to see but not to believe; make haste, my son, and learn what wizards and enchanters are able to accomplish."

Sancho came up, and when he saw the face of the bachelor Carrasco, he began to cross himself a thousand times and bless himself as many more. All this time the prostrate knight showed no signs of life, and Sancho said to Don Quixote: "In my opinion, master, you should stick your sword into the mouth of this one who looks like the bachelor Carrasco, and perhaps in him you will kill one of your enemies, the enchanters."

"That is good advice," said Don Quixote, "for the fewer enemies, the better."

Then, drawing his sword, he was about to put into operation Sancho's advice, when the Squire of the Mirrors came up, now minus the nose that had made him so hideous, and cried out in a loud voice: "Mind what you are doing, Señor Don Quixote, for that man lying at your feet is your friend the bachelor Sansón Carrasco, and I am his squire."

"And what about the nose?" said Sancho, seeing him without his former hideous appendage.

"I have it here in my pocket," said the latter, and sticking his hand into his right pocket, he drew out a clownish nose of varnished pasteboard of the kind we have already described.

Sancho, then, after peering at him more and more closely, exclaimed in a loud voice of amazement: "Holy Mary, protect us! Isn't it Tomé Cecial, my neighbor and comrade?"

"Who else would I be?" replied the unnosed squire. "Tomé Cecial I am, comrade and friend, Sancho Panza, and I'll tell you presently of the means, the vagaries, the schemings, that brought me here; but in the meantime, beg and beseech your master not to touch, maltreat, wound, or kill the Knight of the Mirrors, whom he has lying at his feet, for without doubt he is the bold and ill-advised bachelor Sansón Carrasco, our compatriot."

At this moment he of the Mirrors came to his senses, and Don Quixote no sooner saw it than he held the naked point of his sword to his face, saying: "You are a dead man, knight, unless you confess that the peerless Dulcinea of El Toboso surpasses your Casildea of Vandalia in beauty; besides, you have to promise that if you survive this combat and fall, you will go to the city of El Toboso and present yourself before her on my behalf, letting her do with you what she pleases. And if she leaves you to your own devices, you must return and look for me (the trail of my deeds will guide you in my direction) and tell me all that has taken place between her and you. These are conditions that do not depart from the terms of knight-errantry."

"I confess," said the fallen knight, "that the torn and dirty shoe of Lady Dulcinea of El Toboso is better than the ill-combed though clean beard of Calsildea, and I promise to go and return from her presence to yours and give you a complete and detailed account of what you ask me."

"You have also to confess and believe," added Don Quixote, "that the knight you vanquished was not, nor could be, Don Quixote of La Mancha, but somebody else who resembles him, just as I confess and believe that you, though you appear to be the bachelor Sansón Carrasco, are not he, but another like him, and that my enemies have conjured you up before me in his shape that I may restrain and moderate my impetuous wrath and make humane use of my glorious victory."

"I confess, judge, and consider everything to be as you confess, judge, and consider it," answered the crippled knight. "Let me rise, I pray you, if the shock of my fall will allow it, for I am indeed in a very bad way."

Don Quixote helped him to rise, with his squire Tomé Cecial, off whom Sancho never for an instant took his eyes and whom he questioned incessantly, proving thereby to his own satisfaction that the latter was truly the Tomé Cecial he said he was. But Sancho was so impressed by what his master had said about the enchanters having changed the figure of the Knight of the Mirrors into that of the bachelor Sansón Carrasco that he was unable to believe the truth of what he saw with his own eyes. In the end, both master and man remained under their delusion; and so he of the Mirrors and his squire, feeling down in the dumps and out of tune with the world, took their departure from Don Quixote and Sancho, intending to look for some place where the knight's ribs might be plastered and strapped.

Don Quixote and Sancho continued to make their way toward Saragossa, and the history leaves them at this point in order to give an account of who were the Knight of the Mirrors and his nosy squire.

CHAPTER XV

In which is told who the Knight of the Mirrors and his squire were

Don Quixote rode onward in great spirits. He was extremely pleased, elated, and vainglorious at having won a victory over such a valiant knight as he imagined him of the Mirrors to be, and from his knightly word he expected to learn whether his lady still continued to be enchanted, for the said vanquished knight was bound, on pain of ceasing to be one, to return and give him a report of what took place between himself and her. But if Don Quixote was thinking of one thing, he of the Mirrors was certainly thinking of another. In fact, the latter had no other thought at the moment than to find some place where he might get poulticed, as we have said before.

The history then says that when the bachelor Sansón Carrasco counseled Don Quixote to resume his relinquished knight-errantry, he did so in consequence of a conference he had previously held with the curate and the barber upon the measures to be taken to induce Don Quixote to stay at home in peace and quiet, without exciting himself over his accursed adventures. At that conclave it was decided by the unanimous vote of all, and at the special instance of Carrasco, that Don Quixote should be allowed to set out, as it was impossible to restrain him, that Sansón should sally forth as a knight-errant, join battle with him, for which a pretext could readily be found, and vanquish him—an easy matter they thought—and that it should be agreed and regulated that the one conquered should remain at the mercy of his conqueror. And once Don Quixote was vanquished, the knight-bachelor would order him to go back to his village and home and not leave it for two years or until some other command was imposed upon him, all of which conditions Don Quixote would carry out without fail rather than break the laws of chivalry. During the period of his seclusion, he might possibly forget his foolish notions, or else an opportunity might be found of discovering a sure remedy for his madness.

Carrasco undertook the task, and Tomé Cecial, Sancho's comrade and neighbor, a merry, scatterbrained fellow, offered his services as squire. Sansón armed himself as has been described, and Tomé Cecial, to avoid being recognized by his comrade when they met, fitted on over his natural nose the false one already mentioned. And so they followed the same road as Don Quixote and very nearly reached him in time to be present at the adventure of the cart of Death, and at last they met in the wood, where everything that the wise reader has read took place. And if it had not been for the extraordinary fancies of Don Quixote, who took it into his head that the bachelor was not the bachelor, Master Bachelor would be forever incapacitated from taking his degree as licentiate, because he did not find nests where he expected to find birds. Tomé Cecial, seeing how badly their plans had turned out and what a wretched end their expedition had come to, said to the bachelor: "For sure, Master Sansón Carrasco, we've met with our deserts. It's easy to plan and start an enterprise, but most times it's hard to get out of it safe and sound. Don Quixote is mad, and we are sane, but he comes off safe and in high spirits, while you, master, are left drubbed and downcast. Tell us, now, who is the greater madman, he who is so because he can't help it, or he who is so of his own free will?"

To which Sansón replied: "The difference between these two madmen is that he who is so perforce will be one forever, but he who is so of his own accord can leave off being one whenever he likes."

"That being so," said Tomé Cecial, "I was mad of my own accord when I agreed to become your squire, and of my own accord, I wish to leave off being one and go back home."

"You may please yourself," replied Sansón, "but to imagine that I am going home before I have given Don Quixote a beating is an absurdity, and it is not my wish to make him recover his wits that will drive me to hunt him now, but a lust for revenge, for the aching of my ribs will not let me form a more charitable resolve."

The two conversed in such a manner until they reached a town where by good fortune they found a bone-setter who cured the hapless Sansón. Then, Tomé Cecial went home, leaving the bachelor behind nursing his revenge. Our history will return to him at the proper time, but now it must frolic along with Don Quixote.

CHAPTER XVI

Of what happened when Don Quixote met a wise gentleman of La Mancha

Don Quixote continued his journey full of the joy, satisfaction, and high spirits we have described, fancying himself, owing to his late victory, the most valiant knight-errant in the world. All the adventures that might happen to him from that day on he reckoned as already successfully accomplished; he despised enchanters and enchantments; he gave no thought to the innumerable beatings he had received in the course of his knight-errantry, nor to the stoning that had knocked out half his teeth, nor to the ingratitude of the galley slaves, nor to the bold insolence of the Yanguesans who had belabored him with their staves. Finally he said to himself that if he could only discover a method of disenchanting his Lady Dulcinea, he would not envy the highest good fortune that the most fortunate knight-errant of past ages ever achieved or could achieve.

He was riding along entirely absorbed in these fancies when Sancho said to him: "Isn't it strange, master, that I've still before my eyes that monstrous and hugeous nose of my comrade Tomé Cecial?"

"Can it be, Sancho, that you really believe that the Knight of the Mirrors was the bachelor Sansón Carrasco, and his squire, Tomé Cecial, your comrade?"

"I don't know what I'm to say to that," answered Sancho. "I only know that the details he gave me about my house, my wife, and my children, no one but himself could have given me; and as for his face, once he had removed the nose, it was the very face of Tomé Cecial, for I've often seen him in my village—there was but a wall between my house and his—and the tone of his voice was just the same."

"Let us be reasonable, Sancho," replied Don Quixote. "Now tell me, how it can be argued that the bachelor Sansón Carrasco would come as a knight-errant, armed with arms offensive and defensive, to do battle with me? Have I, perchance, ever been his enemy? Have I ever given him cause to have a grudge against me? Am I his rival, or does he make profession of arms that he should envy the fame I have earned in them?"

"But what shall we say, master," replied Sancho, "about that knight, whoever he was, being the very image of the bachelor Carrasco, and his squire the dead spit of my comrade Tomé Cecial? And if that is enchantment, as your worship says, was there no other form in the world for them to take the likeness of?"

"It is all," said Don Quixote, "an artifice and trick of the malignant magicians who persecute me and who, guessing that I was to be victorious in the conflict, settled that the vanquished knight should display the face of my friend the bachelor in order that my affection for him might intervene to halt my sharp blade and restrain my mighty arm and moderate the righteous indignation of my heart, so that he who sought to rob me of my life by trickery should save his own. And in proof, you know already, Sancho, through experience, which cannot lie or deceive, how easy it is for enchanters to change some countenances into others, making the beautiful ugly and the ugly beautiful, for not two days ago you saw with your own eyes the beauty and elegance of the peerless Dulcinea in all its perfection and natural grace, while I saw her in the ugly and mean form of a coarse country wench, with cataracts in her eyes and a stinking breath from her mouth. Seeing that the perverse enchanter caused such a wicked transformation, it is no wonder that he effected that of Sansón Carrasco and of your comrade in order to snatch away my victory. Nevertheless, I console myself, because when all is said and done, I have been victorious over my enemy, no matter what shape he took."

"God knows the truth of it all," answered Sancho. Knowing as he did that the transformation of Dulcinea had been a device and trick of his own, he was not at all pleased by his master's wild fancies; but he did not like to reply, for fear of saying anything that would reveal his trickery.

While they were conversing, they were overtaken by a man who was riding on the same road behind them, mounted on a very handsome gray mare and dressed in an overcoat of fine green cloth slashed with tawny velvet and a hunting cap of the same to match. His mare's trappings were rustic and for riding with short stirrups, and were also of purple and green. He wore a Moorish scimitar hanging from a broad baldric[38] of green and gold, and his leggings were of the same make. His spurs were not gilt but covered with green lacquer and so glossy and burnished that, because they matched the rest of his apparel, they looked better than if they had been made of pure gold. When the stranger overtook them, he greeted them courteously and would have pressed on ahead, had not Don Quixote

[38] Shoulder strap.

accosted him, saying: "Gallant sir, if your worship is taking the same road as ourselves and if haste is not your object, I should be grateful if we could ride together."

"Indeed," replied the man on the mare, "I should not have passed on ahead of you if I had not been afraid that your horse would be disturbed by my mare's company."

"You may, sir," answered Sancho, "in all safety rein in your mare, for our horse is the most modest and well behaved in the world. He has never misconducted himself on such an occasion as this, and the only time he didn't behave, my master and I paid for it seven times over. Your worship, I repeat, may pull up, if you wish; why, if they served your mare to him between two courses, our horse wouldn't even look her in the face, I assure you."

The traveler drew rein and gazed with amazement at the figure and face of Don Quixote, who was riding without his helmet, which Sancho carried like a wallet on the pommel of Dapple's saddle. And the more the man in green stared at Don Quixote, the more did Don Quixote stare at the man in green, who seemed to him a man of substance. He appeared to be about fifty years of age; his gray hairs were few, his face aquiline, his expression between cheerful and grave—in short, his dress and general appearance stamped him as a man of fine endowments. What the man in green thought of Don Quixote was that he had never seen a man of that kind or physiognomy; he was amazed at his long scrawny neck, his tall body, his gaunt sallow face, his armor, his gestures and his carriage, a figure and image not seen in those parts for many a year.

Don Quixote observed how attentively the traveler was staring at him and assumed that his astonishment was due to his curiosity. So, being courteous and eager to oblige everybody, he anticipated the latter's questions and said to him: "I should not wonder if your worship were surprised at my appearance, which is both strange and out of the ordinary. But you will cease to do so when I tell you, as I do now, that I am a knight

'Of those, as people say, who ride
In quest of valiant enterprise.'

I have left my native country; I have pledged my estate; I have forsaken my comfort and delivered myself into the arms of Fortune to lead where she will. I have sought to revive the now extinct order of knight-errantry, and for many a day, stumbling here, falling there, flung down in one place and rising up in another, I have been accomplishing a great part of my design, succoring widows, protecting maidens, and relieving wives, orphans, and young children, the proper and natural office of knights-errant; and so, by my many valiant and Christian deeds I have been found worthy to appear in print in almost all, or at least most, of the nations of the earth. Thirty thousand volumes of my history have been printed, and it is on the way to be printed thirty thousand times more, if Heaven does not prevent it. In fact, to sum up all in a few words, or in one word, I must tell you that I am Don Quixote of La Mancha, otherwise called the Knight of the Rueful Figure. And though to praise oneself is degrading, I am compelled at times to sound my own, though naturally only when there is no one present to sound them. So, gentle sir, neither this horse, nor this lance, nor this shield, nor this squire, nor all these arms together, nor the sallowness of my face, nor my lanky limbs, should henceforth astonish you, now that I have informed you who I am and what profession I follow."

After saying this Don Quixote remained silent, and the man in green delayed so long in answering that he seemed unable to find words, but after a while he said: "You rightly guessed my thoughts, sir knight, when you noted my amazement, but you have not managed to dispel the wonder the sight of you causes in me. Though you say that it should be removed once I know who you are, it has not done so. On the contrary, now that I know, I am all the more perplexed and astounded. What! Is it possible that there are knights-errant in the world today and that histories are printed about real knight-errantries? I cannot persuade myself that there is anyone on earth today who favors widows, protects maidens, honors wives, and succors orphans, and I would not have believed it had I not seen it in your worship with my own eyes. Blessed be Heaven for that history of your noble and authentic chivalries, which your worship says is in print, for it will cast into oblivion the innumerable books of counterfeit knights-errant with which the world is filled, that do such harm to good morals and such damage and discredit to genuine history."

"There is much to be said," answered Don Quixote, "on this point of whether the stories of knights-errant are fictions or not."

"But is there anyone who doubts their falsity?" asked the man in green.

"I doubt it," replied Don Quixote, "but there let the matter rest. If our journey lasts, I hope, with God's help, to convince your worship that you have done wrong in going along with the stream of those who declare that they are not true."

From this last remark of Don Quixote the traveler began to suspect that he must be some crazy fellow, but he waited for further evidence to confirm his suspicions. But before they could broach any other subject, Don Quixote begged him to say who he was, since he had told him already something about his way of life.

To which the man in green replied: "I, Knight of the Rueful Figure, am a gentleman and native of a village where, please God, we shall go to dine today. I am more than moderately rich, and my name is Don Diego de Miranda. I spend my life with my wife, my children, and my friends. My pursuits are hunting and fishing, but I keep neither hawk nor hounds, but only a quiet pointer and a saucy ferret or two. I have about six dozen books, some in Spanish and some in Latin, some historical and some devotional, but books of chivalry have never even crossed my threshold. I read profane books more than devotional, provided they give me honest entertainment, delight me by their language, and startle and keep me in suspense by their plots, though there are very few of this kind in Spain. Sometimes I dine with my neighbors and friends, and very often they are my guests. My table is clean, well appointed, and never stinted. I take no pleasure in scandal and allow none in my presence; I do not pry into my neighbors' lives, nor do I spy on other men's actions. I hear Mass every day; I share my goods with the poor, without boasting of my good works, lest hypocrisy and vainglory worm themselves into my heart, for they are foes that subtly waylay even the wariest. I try to make peace between those I know to be at loggerheads. I am devoted to Our Lady and always put my trust in the infinite mercy of Our Lord."

Sancho listened most attentively to the account of the gentleman's life and occupation, and he said to himself that it was a good and holy life and that the man who led it must be able to work miracles. So, flinging himself off Dapple and hastily seizing the gentleman's right stirrup, devoutly and almost in tears he kissed his feet again and again.

At this the gentleman exclaimed: "What are you doing, brother? Why these kisses?"

"Let me kiss you," answered Sancho, "for I do believe your worship's the first saint I've seen riding with short stirrups in all the days of my life."

"I am no saint," replied the gentleman, "but a great sinner. But you, brother, must be good; your simplicity proves it."

Sancho regained his saddle, after having succeeded in extracting a laugh out of his melancholy master and causing fresh amazement in Don Diego. Don Quixote then asked the gentleman how many children he had and said that the ancient philosophers, who were devoid of the true knowledge of God, held that the highest good lay in the gifts bestowed by Nature and Fortune, and in the number of friends and good children.

"I, Don Quixote," rejoined the gentleman, "have one son, and if he did not exist, perhaps I might count myself more fortunate than I do at present, not because he is wicked, but because he is not as good as I would wish. He is eighteen years old; he has been for six years in Salamanca studying Latin and Greek, and when I wished him to proceed to the study of other sciences, I found him so steeped in the one of Poetry—if it can be called a science—that there was no way of getting him to take cheerfully to Law, which I would like him to study, or to the queen of all the sciences, Theology. I wish him to be a credit to his family, for we live in an age when our princes highly reward virtuous and deserving learning, for learning without virtue is like pearls on a dunghill. All his day he spends in discussing whether Homer expressed himself well or ill in such and such verse of the *Iliad*; whether Martial was indecent or not in some epigram; whether such and such verses of Virgil are to be understood in this way or in that. In short, all his conversation concerns the books of those poets, and those of Horace, Persius, Juvenal, and Tibullus, for he has no high opinion of modern writers in Spanish. Yet, in spite of his dislike for poetry in the vernacular, his thoughts are now absorbed in making a gloss on four verses they have sent him from Salamanca, which, I believe, refer to some literary competition."

To all this Don Quixote replied: "Children, sir, are part of their parents' bowels, and so we must love them, whether they are good or bad, as we love the souls that give us life. It is the duty of their parents to guide them from infancy along the paths of virtue, good breeding, and Christian behavior, so that, grown up, they may be the staff of their parents' old age and the glory of their posterity. But when it comes to forcing them to study this or that science, I consider it unwise, although there may be no harm in persuading them; and seeing that they are in no need of studying to earn their daily bread, as the student is lucky enough to be endowed by Heaven with parents who spare him that, my advice is that they should be permitted to pursue the branch of learning to which they are most inclined. And although that of Poetry is less useful than it is pleasurable, it is certainly not one of those that dishonor their votary. Poetry, my dear sir, I would compare to a tender, young, and ravishingly beautiful maiden, whom many other maidens, namely, all the other sciences, strive to enrich, to polish, and to adorn. And she has to exact service from all, and all of them can only become exalted through her. But this maiden refuses to be manhandled, or dragged through the streets, or exposed to the public at the market corners or in the antechambers of palaces, for she is fashioned of an alchemy of such power that anyone who knows how to treat her will transmute her into purest gold of inestimable price. He who possesses her must keep her within bounds, not letting her descend to base lampoons or impious sonnets; she must not be displayed for sale, unless in heroic poems, in mournful tragedies, or in merry and artificial comedies. She must not suffer herself to be handled by buffoons, nor by the vulgar mob, who are incapable of recognizing or valuing the treasures she enshrines. Do not imagine, sir, that by vulgar I mean only the common and humble people, for everyone who is ignorant, be he a prince or a lord, can and should be included in the category of the vulgar; so anyone with the qualifications I have mentioned who takes up and treats Poetry will become famous and his name will be held in esteem among all the civilized nations of the world. As to what you say, sir, of your son not appreciating the poetry in our Spanish tongue, I am convinced that he is wrong there, and the reason in this: the great Homer did not write in Latin because he was a Greek, nor Virgil in Greek because he was a Latin. In short, all the ancient poets wrote in the tongues they sucked with their mother's milk, and they did not go out in quest of strange ones to express the greatness of their conceptions; and this being so, it is only reasonable that the fashion should extend to all nations, and the German poet should not be undervalued because he writes in his language, nor the Castilian, nor even the Biscayan, who writes in his. But your son, sir, as I believe, does not dislike the poetry in the vulgar tongue, but only the poets who are merely vernacular and know no other tongues or other sciences to adorn, jog, and stimulate their natural inspiration. And yet, even in this we may be mistaken, for according to true belief, the poet is born—that is to say, the natural poet sallies forth from his mother's womb a poet, and with that impulse that Heaven has given him, without further study or art, he composes things that prove the truth of the saying: *est Deus in nobis,*[39] etc. Let me also say that the natural poet who makes use of art will improve himself and be much greater than the poet who relies only on his knowledge of the art. The reason is clear, for art is not better than nature, but merely perfects her. So, nature combined with art and art with nature will produce a most perfect poet. To conclude my speech, noble sir, your worship should allow your son to go where his star calls him, for if he is as good a student as he should be and if he has successfully mounted the first step of learning, which is that of the languages, he will ascend of his own accord to the summit of humane letters, which so well become a gentleman of leisure, and adorn, honor, and exalt him as miters do bishops or robes learned doctors of law. But your worship should chide your son if he

---

[39] The complete quotation is "There is a god in us; he stirs and lo! we feel his fire." (Ovid, *Festivals,* VI.5.)

writes lampoons to the prejudice of the characters of others, and punish him and tear them up; but if he writes satires after the manner of Horace, reproving vice in general terms and as elegantly as the Roman did, praise him, for a poet may lawfully castigate envy and upbraid the envious in his verses and flagellate other vices, too, provided he does not single out any particular person, though there are poets who run the risk of banishment to the Isles of Pontus for the sake of uttering one malicious jibe.[40] If the poet, however, is chaste in his morals, he will be chaste also in his verses. The pen is the tongue of the soul, and the thoughts begotten there will burgeon in whatever he writes. And when kings and princes behold the miraculous science of Poetry in subjects who are wise, virtuous, and grave, they honor, esteem, and reward them, and even crown them with the leaves of the tree that lightning never strikes, as a warning that no one should attack men whose temples are honored and adorned by such crowns."[41]

The man in green was lost in amazement at Don Quixote's reasoning, so much so that he began to alter the opinion he had formed of the knight's craziness. But in the middle of the conversation, which was not much to his taste, Sancho had strayed from the road to beg a little milk from some shepherds who were milking their ewes close by; and just as the gentleman was about to renew the conversation, highly delighted with Don Quixote's wisdom and good sense, the latter, lifting his head, saw a cart decorated with the king's colors coming along the road by which they were traveling. Imagining that this must be some new adventure, he shouted to Sancho to come and bring him his helmet. Sancho, hearing himself called, left the shepherds, and spurring on Dapple, hastened toward his master, to whom befell a stupendous and fearful adventure.

CHAPTER XVII

In which is set forth the highest point that Don Quixote's unheard-of courage ever reached, with the happily terminated adventure of the lions

Our history relates that when Don Quixote called Sancho to bring him his helmet, the latter was buying some curds from the shepherds, and being flustered by his master's pressing call, he did not know what to do with them nor how to carry them. So, in order not to lose them, as he had already paid for them, he thought it best to pour them into his master's helmet, and using this clever shift, he turned back to see what his master needed. Don Quixote cried out to him: "Give me that helmet, my friend, for either I know precious little of adventures, or what I see yonder is one that should, and does, require me to arm myself."

The man in green heard this and gazed around in all directions without seeing anything but a cart coming toward them with two or three small flags, which made him think that it was carrying the king's treasure, and so he told Don Quixote. But the knight did not believe it, for he always firmly

---

[40] Ovid was banished thus by the Emperor Augustus, presumably for writing *The Art of Love*.

[41] This refers to the laurel tree.

imagined that everything that befell him must be adventures and still more adventures. So, he replied: "Forewarned is forearmed. Nothing is lost by taking precautions, for I know by experience that I have enemies visible and invisible, and I never know when or where, nor in what moment, nor in what shape they may attack me."

And turning to Sancho, he asked him for his helmet, and as the squire had no time to take out the curds, he had to give it to him as it was. Don Quixote took it, and without noticing what was in it, he clapped it on his head hastily, and as the curds were pressed and squeezed, the whey began to pour down over Don Quixote's face and beard, which gave him such a start that he exclaimed to Sancho: "What's this, Sancho? I think my head is softening, or my brains are melting, or else I am sweating from head to foot. But if I am sweating, it is certainly not from fear, though I am truly sure the adventure I have to face is a terrible one. Give me something to wipe myself with, for this copious sweat is blinding my eyes."

Sancho held his tongue and handed him a cloth, thanking God that his master had not found out the truth.

Don Quixote wiped himself and took off the helmet to see what it was that made his head feel cool, and seeing the white mess inside the helmet, he put it up to his nose, and sniffing he said: "By my Lady Dulcinea of El Toboso, these are curds you have put here, you treacherous, impudent, ill-favored squire!"

To which with calm composure Sancho replied: "If they are curds, master, give them to me, and I'll eat them; but let the Devil eat them, for it must be he who put them there! How could you ever imagine that I would have the impudence to soil your worship's helmet? Indeed, you must already know the culprit! In faith, master, from the understanding which God has given me, I am convinced that I, too, must have enchanters who persecute me as a creature and limb of your worship, and they must have put that nasty mess there in order to rouse your patience to anger and make you drub my ribs as you are wont to do. But this time they have missed their mark, for I put my trust in my master's good sense; he must have considered that I have no curds or milk, or anything of the kind, and if I had, it is in my belly I would put them and not in the helmet."

"That may be," replied Don Quixote.

The gentleman had observed all with amazement, especially when Don Quixote, after wiping clean his head, face, beard, and helmet, put it on again, stood up in his stirrups, and feeling for his sword and grasping his lance, cried: "Now, come what may, I stand ready to face Satan himself in battle."

At this moment the cart with the flags approached. In it was nobody but the carter, who rode one of the mules, and a man who was seated in front. Don Quixote stood in front of it and said: "Whither are you going, brothers? What cart is this? What have you got in it? What flags are those?"

To this the carter replied: "The cart is mine, but in it is a fine pair of caged lions that the general is sending from Oran as a present to His Majesty, and the flags are of the king, our master, which signify that what is inside the cart is his property."

"Are the lions big?" asked Don Quixote.

"So big," said the man at the door of the cart, "that none bigger, or even as big, have ever crossed from Africa into Spain. I am the keeper and I've carried many, but never a pair like these. They are male and female; the male is in the front cage, and the female in the one behind. They are now very hungry, for they've eaten nothing today; so it would be best for your worship to stand aside, for we must make haste to reach the place where we may give them their feed."

To this Don Quixote answered, smiling slightly: "Lion cubs to me? To me lion cubs? At such a time, too? Then, by God, those gentlemen who send them here will soon see whether I am the man to be frightened by lions. Dismount, my good man, and since you are the keeper, open the cages and drive out these beasts. In the midst of this open field I will let them know who Don Quixote of La Mancha is, in spite of the enchanters who have sent them to me."

"Goodness gracious!" muttered the gentleman in green at this. "Our good knight is giving me proof of his nature. The curds, no doubt, have softened his skull and mellowed his brains."

At this point Sancho came up to him and exclaimed: "Sir, for God's sake, try and stop my master fighting with these lions; if he fights them, they'll tear us all to pieces."

"Is your master so crazy," the gentleman replied, "that you actually fear and believe he will really fight those furious beasts?"

"He's not crazy," replied Sancho, "but foolhardy."

"I'll make him stop," said the gentleman. And going up to Don Quixote, who was pressing the keeper to open the cages, he said: "Sir knight, knights-errant should engage in enterprises that hold out some prospect of success, but not in those that are entirely devoid of it, for valor that verges on temerity has more of madness about it than bravery. Moreover, these lions have not come against you, nor do they dream of doing so. They are going to be presented to His Majesty, and it is not right to detain them or hinder their journey."

"Get you gone, my dear sir," answered Don Quixote, "and look to your tame partridge and your spry ferret, and let every man look to his own duty; this is mine, and I know whether these gentlemen, the lions, are coming against me or not." Then turning to the keeper, he said sharply: "I swear, sir rascal, that if you don't open the cage at once, I'll stitch you to the cart with this lance."

The carter saw the armed phantom's grim determination and said to him: "Please, sir, for charity's sake, let me unhitch the mules and place myself in safety along with them before the lions are unleashed, for if they kill my beasts, I'm ruined for life, seeing that all I possess is this cart and the mules."

"O man of little faith!" replied Don Quixote. "Get down and unyoke, and do what you will; soon you will see that your toils were in vain and that you might have spared yourself the trouble."

The carter got down and in haste unyoked, and the keeper called out in a loud voice: "Bear witness, all who are here, how against my will and under compulsion I open the cages and let loose the lions. And I protest to this gentleman that all the harm and mischief these beasts shall do will be put to his account, together with my wages and dues as well. You, sir, take cover before I open; as for myself, I am sure they will do me no harm."

Once more the gentleman in green entreated the knight not to commit such an act of madness, for to engage in such freakish folly was to tempt Providence, but Don Quixote answered that he knew what he was up to. The gentleman warned him once more to mind what he was doing, for he was surely mistaken.

"Well, sir," replied Don Quixote, "if your worship does not wish to witness what you believe is about to be a tragedy, clap spurs to your gray mare and retire to safety."

Hearing this, Sancho besought his master with tears in his eyes to give up such an enterprise, compared with which the adventure of the windmills and the fearsome one of the fulling mills and, in fact, all the deeds his master had attempted in the whole course of his life were nothing but cakes and fancy bread. "Look sir," said he, "here there is no enchantment nor anything of the kind, for through the chinks and bars of the cage I have seen the claw of a live lion, and I'm sure that a lion with such a claw must be bigger than a mountain."

"Fear, at any rate," answered Don Quixote, "will make it seem bigger to you than half the earth. Retire, Sancho, and leave me. If I die here, you know our old compact. You will go straight to Dulcinea; I say no more."

Other words he added to those declarations that took away all hope that he would give up his insane purpose. The man in green would have resisted him, but not being so well armed, he thought it would be imprudent to fight with a madman, for he now was convinced that the knight was stark, staring mad. Don Quixote then went on pressing the keeper and repeating his threats, which gave the gentleman a chance to spur his mare, Sancho to prod Dapple, and the carter his mules—all trying to get away from the cart as far as possible before the lions erupted from their cages. Sancho wept for his master's death, for this time he truly believed he would perish at the claws of the lions, He cursed his luck and the unlucky hour when he took it into his head to return to his service. Nevertheless, in spite of all his tears and groans, he took good care to flog up Dapple so as to drive him farther away from the cart. Then, when the keeper saw that those who had fled were far enough away, he again entreated and warned Don Quixote as he had done before, but the knight replied that he heard him but would listen to no more warnings or entreaties and bade him make haste. While the keeper was opening the first cage, Don Quixote was considering whether it would be better to do battle on foot or on horseback, and in the end he decided to fight on foot, for he was afraid Rozinante would take fright at the lions. He, therefore, sprang off his horse, flung his lance aside, and braced his buckler on his arm. Then, unsheathing his sword with marvelous valor and undaunted heart, he advanced at a leisurely pace and posted himself in front of the cart, commending his soul to God and then to his lady, Dulcinea.

We now must observe that when the author of our true history came to this point, he exclaimed: "O brave and incomparably courageous Don Quixote of La Mancha! Mirror wherein all the valiant may behold themselves! You second Don Manuel of León,[42] who was the honor and glory of Spanish knights! With what words shall I describe this most fearful exploit,

---

[42] A famous knight of the time of Ferdinand and Isabella.

or how make it credible to future ages? What praises can be unfitting and unmeet for you, though hyperbole be piled on hyperbole? You on foot, you alone, you bold and undaunted with only a simple sword and no trenchant Toledo blades of the little dog make,[43] with a shield of not very bright and shining steel, you stand watchful and ready for the two fiercest lions ever bred in African forests! Let your deeds themselves, valiant Manchegan, extol you; here I leave them in all their glamor, for I lack words to glorify them."

Here the author broke off his apostrophe and proceeded to take up the thread of his history, saying:

The keeper, seeing that Don Quixote had taken up his position and that it was impossible to avoid letting loose the male lion without falling under the rage of the wrathful and undaunted knight, opened wide the doors of the first cage, containing, as we have said, the male lion. The beast was now seen to be of extraordinary size and of grim and awful aspect. The first thing he did was to turn around in the cage in which he lay and to extend his claws and stretch himself out to his full length. Then, he opened his mouth and yawned very leisurely, and with about two palms' lengths of tongue, which he put out, he licked the dust from his eyes and washed his face. When this was done, he put his head out of the cage and gazed all around with eyes like blazing coals, a sight that would have struck terror in temerity itself. Don Quixote alone stood looking at him intently, longing for him to leap out of the cart and come to close grips with him, when he hoped to hack him to pieces. Up to such a point did his unheard-of madness raise him. The noble lion, however, more courteous than arrogant, took scant notice of such childish bravado, and after looking around about him, as we have said, he turned his back and showed Don Quixote his hind parts, after which coolly and calmly he flung himself down in the cage. Seeing this, Don Quixote ordered the keeper to prod him and tease him to make him come out.

"I will not do so," replied the keeper, "for if I excite him, the first he will tear to pieces will be myself. Be content, sir, with what you have done, which leaves no more to be said on the score of courage, and don't try to tempt Fortune a second time. The lion has the door open; he's free to come out or not; since he hasn't come out up to now, he won't come out all day. Your worship's sturdy heart has been already shown to the world; no gallant champion, to my way of thinking, is bound to do more than to challenge his enemy and wait for him in the field. If his rival doesn't come, to him sticks the disgrace, and the man who waits his ground carries off the crown of victory."

"That is true," replied Don Quixote; "so, shut the door, my friend, and give me a sworn statement of what you have seen me do here, in the best form you can; to wit, that you did open for the lion, that I waited for him, that he did not come out, that still I waited for him, that still he did not come out, and that he lay down again. I am not bound to do more. Away with enchantments and God protect right, truth, and true chivalry! Shut the door, friend, while I signal to the fugitive and absent to return that they may learn of this exploit from your lips."

---

[43] A little dog was the trademark of Julián del Rey, a famous armorer of Toledo.

The keeper did so, and Don Quixote, sticking on the point of his lance the cloth with which he had wiped the shower of curds off his face, began to signal to those who were still continuing to flee, though looking around at every step, urged on by the gentleman in green. Sancho, happening to notice the signal of the white cloth, exclaimed: "May I be blowed if my master has not conquered the wild beasts, for he's calling us!"

They all stopped, and seeing that it was Don Quixote who was making the signals, losing some of their fear, they approached little by little until they clearly heard the voice of Don Quixote calling to them. At length they reached the cart, and as they came up, Don Quixote said to the carter: "Yoke your mules once more, my friend, and continue your journey, and you, Sancho, give him two gold crowns for himself and for the keeper as a compensation for the delay they have had through me."

"I'll give them with a heart and a half," said Sancho; "but what has happened to the lions? Are they alive or dead?"

Then the keeper gave a detailed account of the encounter, praising to the skies the power and valor of Don Quixote, at whose sight the cowed lion dared not to come out of his cage, though he had held the door open a good while, and that it was only because he had told the knight that it was tempting Providence to excite the lion and force him to come out, as he wanted him to do, that the knight had, against his will, allowed him to close the door.

"What do you think of this, Sancho?" said Don Quixote. "Are any enchantments able to prevail against true valor? The enchanters may be able to rob me of good luck, but of courage they cannot."

Sancho gave them the gold crowns, the carter yoked up, the keeper kissed Don Quixote's hands for the guerdon received and promised him to give an account of the brave exploit to the king himself as soon as he saw him at court.

"Then," said Don Quixote, "if His Majesty should happen to ask who performed it, you must say that it was the Knight of the Lions, for it is my wish that from this day on there may be changed, altered, and transformed the name that till now I have borne of the Knight of the Rueful Figure. In this I follow the ancient custom of knights-errant, who changed their names when they pleased or when it suited them."

The cart went on its way and Don Quixote, Sancho, and the gentleman in the green coat continued theirs.

All this while Don Diego de Miranda had not opened his mouth, so carefully was he watching and noting every word and action of Don Quixote, who appeared to him to be at once a sane man turned mad and a madman who had glimmers of sanity. The first part of this history had not yet come to his notice, for if he had read it, he would have ceased to wonder at the knight's deeds, since he would have ascertained the nature of his madness. But as he did not know it, he sometimes took him for sane, sometimes for mad. For what Don Quixote said was consistent, elegant, and well expressed, but what he did was eccentric, rash, and absurd. "What could be madder," he reflected, "than to put on a helmet full of curds and believe that enchanters had melted one's brains? And what could be rasher and more absurd than to insist on fighting with lions?"

Don Quixote interrupted his soliloquy by saying: "No doubt, Don Diego de Miranda, your worship regards me as both foolish and mad. And it would be no wonder if you did, for my actions can have no other interpretation. Nevertheless, I wish your worship to note that I am not so mad or foolish as I must have appeared to you. It is a fine sight to see a gallant knight under the eyes of his king give effective lance thrusts at a brave bull in the midst of a great square; it is a fine sight to see a knight, all armed in burnished armor, pace the lists in merry jousts before the ladies; and it is a fine sight to see all those knights who in military exercises or the like entertain, cheer, and if one may say so, honor the courts of their princes. But finer than all these is to see a knight-errant roaming through deserts and solitudes, by crossroads and forests and mountains, in quest of perilous adventures, in order to bring them to a happy and fortunate conclusion only for the sake of glory and lasting renown. It is a finer sight, I say, to see a knight-errant succoring a widow in some lonely waste than a courtier knight dallying with a maiden in the cities. All knights have their particular offices; let the courtier serve the ladies, lend pomp and circumstance to the royal court by his gay liveries, support poor knights at his beautiful table, arrange jousts, maintain tourneys, and show himself generous, liberal and lavish, and a good Christian above everything, for in this way he will fulfill his precise obligations. But let the knight-errant explore the corners of the world, penetrate the most intricate labyrinths, encounter at every step the impossible, brave the scorching rays of the sun in midsummer on high and unpeopled deserts, and in winter the grim inclemency of the winds and frosts; let no lions daunt him, nor hobgoblins scare him, nor dragons terrify him, for to seek them, attack them, and conquer them all are his principal duties. And as the lot has fallen on me to be of the number of knights-errant, I cannot then fail to attempt everything that seems to me to fall within the bounds of my duty. So, it was strictly my right to attack these lions whom I attacked just now, although I knew it to be rash temerity, for I know well what valor is, namely, a virtue that is situated between the two vicious extremes, which are cowardice and rashness. But it is far better for the brave man to mount to the height of rashness than to sink into the depths of cowardice, for just as it is easier for the generous than for the miser to be prodigal, so it is easier for the daring than for the cowardly to become truly valiant. And in the matter of encountering adventures, let your worship, Don Diego, believe me that it is better to lose the game by a card too much than by one too little, for 'this knight is rash and foolhardy' sounds better in the hearer's ears than 'such a knight is timid and cowardly.'"

"Let me admit, Don Quixote," replied Don Diego, "that all that your worship has said and done is adjusted by the balance of reason itself, and I believe that if the laws and ordinances of knight-errantry had been lost, they would be found in your worship's heart, as in their right repository and archive. . . .

[Quixote and Sancho remain four days at the home of the "Knight of the Green Coat," Don Diego de Miranda; Quixote converses with Don Lorenzo, his host's son. Riding on, they attend a village wedding. The bride, Quiteria, is marrying the wealthy Comacho rather than her real

lover, the impoverished Basilio. At the wedding, Basilio appears, stabs himself, and as a dying wish, asks to be married to Quiteria, who can then marry Comacho within a few minutes as a widow. She consents, but after the ceremony Basilio jumps up, unhurt, and claims the bride. A riot almost breaks out, but Quixote defends the newlyweds. He spends three days with them and lectures Basilio on marriage.]

CHAPTER XXII

In which is given an account of the great adventure of the cave of Montesinos, in the heart of La Mancha, which our gallant Don Quixote brought to a happy conclusion

. . . . "Remember, O wise Basilio," added Don Quixote, "that a certain sage, I know not who, held that there was not more than one good woman in all the world, and he advised everyone to think and believe that this one good woman was his own wife, and so he would live happy. I myself am not married, nor, so far, has it even come into my mind to be so; nevertheless, I would dare to give advice to anyone who might ask it, as to the mode in which he should seek a wife to marry. The first thing I would advise him is to pay more attention to reputation than to fortune, for the good woman does not win a good name solely by being good, but by appearing so, for looseness and public frivolity do greater injury to a woman's honor than secret misdeeds. If you bring a good woman to your house, it will be an easy matter to keep her good, and even improve her in that goodness. But if you bring home a bad one, you will find it a hard task to mend her ways, for it is not easy to pass from one extreme to another. I do not say it is impossible, but I consider it difficult."

Sancho, who had been listening to all this, said to himself: "Whenever I say a word that has a bit of marrow and substance about it, this master of mine straightaway says that I ought to take a pulpit in my hand and roam the world preaching fine sermons; but I say of him that when he starts stringing sentences and giving counsels, not only might he take a pulpit in his hand, but two on each finger, and go into the marketplaces with the cry, 'Who'll buy my wares?' on his lips. Devil take him for a knight-errant, what a number of things he knows! I used to think to myself that the only things he knew had to do with chivalry, but there's not a thing he doesn't peck at nor dip his spoon into."

Sancho kept mumbling to himself so loud that his master overheard him and asked: "What are you muttering about, Sancho?"

"I'm not saying or murmuring anything," said Sancho, "only saying to myself that I wish I had heard what your worship has just said before I got married. Perhaps I'd say now: 'The ox that's loose licks himself well!'"

"Is Teresa[44] so bad then, Sancho?" said Don Quixote.

"She's not too bad," replied Sancho, "but she's not very good; at least, she's not as good as I would like her to be."

"You do wrong, Sancho," said Don Quixote, "to speak ill of your wife, for she is the mother of your children."

---

[44] In Part I, Sancho's wife's name is given as Juana (or Mari) Gutiérrez; in Part II, Cervantes calls her Teresa Cascajo, apparently by mistake.

"We don't owe each other a thing," answered Sancho, "for she speaks ill of me when she's got the whim, especially when she's jealous; then Satan himself couldn't stomach her."

They remained three days with the newlyweds by whom they were treated and served as royalty. Don Quixote asked the nimble licentiate to get them a guide to conduct them to the cave of Montesinos, of which so many wonderful things were related in those parts, for he had a great wish to explore it and to see with his own eyes if the wonders reported were true. The licentiate replied that he would get him a cousin of his own, a famous scholar, one much given to reading books of chivalry, who would be very glad to guide him to the mouth of the cave and would show him the lagoons of Ruidera, which were also famous all over La Mancha, and even all over Spain. He also said that Don Quixote would enjoy his kinsman's company, who was well versed in writing books and in dedicating them to princes.

The cousin arrived later on, with a she-ass in foal, whose packsaddle was covered with a many-colored rug or sackcloth. Sancho saddled Rozinante, harnessed Dapple, and stocked his saddlebags, to which we should add those of the cousin, which likewise were well supplied. And so, commending themselves to God and taking leave of all, they set out on the road leading to the famous cave of Montesinos.[45]

On the way Don Quixote asked the cousin of what kind were his pursuits, his profession, and studies. To which he replied that his profession was that of a humanist, and his pursuits and studies were to write books for publication, all of great profit and no less entertainment to the state; that one of them was entitled *The Book of Liveries,* in which he described seven hundred and three devices, with their colors, mottoes, and ciphers, from which the gentlemen at court could select and use whichever they pleased on the occasion of festivals and revels, without having to beg them from anybody or rack their brains, as they say, to invent them to suit their wishes and purposes.

"For," he said, "I give appropriate devices to the jealous, the scorned, the forgotten, and the absent, which fit them like a glove. I have another book as well, which I mean to call *Metamorphoses,* or *The Spanish Ovid,* a new and most original work in which, while parodying Ovid, I describe the Giralda of Seville, the Angel of the Magdalen, the Gutter of Vecinguerra at Córdoba, and the Bulls of Guisando, the Sierra Morena, the fountains of Leganitos and Lavapiés in Madrid, not forgetting that of the Piojo, that of the Golden Gutter, and that of the Priora; and all these with such allegories, metaphors, and transformations that they will entertain, astonish, and instruct at the same time.[46] I also have another book that I call the

[45] There is an actual cave of Montesinos in La Mancha. It is very deep and is said to end in the feudal castle of Rochefrías.

[46] The Giralda of Seville and the Angel of the Magdalen were statues on the tops of churches in Seville and Salamanca. The Gutter of Vecinguerra was a sewer in Córdoba. The Bulls of Guisando (referred to, like the Giralda of Seville, earlier) were rough stone statues in Ávila, reportedly marking the site of one of Caesar's victories. The Sierra Morena is a range of mountains. The other wonders are fountains in Madrid. The cousin wants to imitate the Roman poet Ovid (43 B.C.–A.D. 18), whose *Metamorphoses* are a collection of mythological stories of transformations.

Supplement to Polydore Virgil,[47] which deals with the invention of things. It is a work of deep learning and research, because I clarify and verify in most elegant style the subjects of great importance that Polydore omitted. He forgot to tell us who was the first man who ever had catarrh and who was the first to use ointments to cure himself of the French pox.[48] All this I explain with the utmost precision on the testimony of twenty-five authorities. So your worship may judge whether I have not worked well, and whether this book will not be indispensable to the whole world."

Sancho, who had been listening carefully to the cousin's narrative, said to him: "Tell me, sir, and best of luck with the printing of your books, but can you inform me—of course you can, as you know everything—who was the first man who scratched his head? I'm of the opinion that it must have been our father Adam."

"Yes, it must have been," answered the cousin, "for there is no doubt Adam had a head and hair; and that being so, and as he was the first man in the world, he must sometimes have scratched himself."

"So I believe," answered Sancho; "tell me now, who was the first tumbler in the world?"

"Frankly, brother," replied the cousin, "I am not able to solve that at present, until I have gone further in my studies. I shall look into the matter when I get back to my books, and I'll answer you when we meet again, for this must not be the last time."

"Look here, sir," answered Sancho, "don't go to any trouble about it, for I've hit upon the answer to my question. The first tumbler in the world, let me tell you, was Lucifer, for when they threw or pitched him out of Heaven, he went tumbling into the pit of hell."

"You are right, my friend," said the cousin.

"That question and answer," said Don Quixote, "are not yours, Sancho. You have heard them from someone else."

"Whist, sir," answered Sancho, "for if I start questioning and answering, I shan't be done till tomorrow morning. Yes, for if it's just a matter of asking idiotic questions and giving silly replies, I needn't go begging help from the neighbors."

"You have said more than you know, Sancho," said Don Quixote, "for there are some people who tire themselves out learning and proving things that, once learned and proved, don't matter a straw as far as the mind or memory is concerned."

That day was spent in such pleasant discussions, and at night they put up in a little village that the cousin told Don Quixote was no more than six miles from the cave of Montesinos. He added that if he was determined to enter it, he would need to provide himself with ropes so that he might be tied up and lowered into its depths.

Don Quixote said that even if it reached to the abyss, he was determined to see where it ended. So, they bought about a hundred fathoms of rope, and next day at two o'clock in the afternoon they arrived at the cave. Its mouth is wide and spacious, but full of thorns and wild fig bushes and

---

[47] Polydore Virgil (c. 1470–1550) was an Italian historian who wrote a book named *On the Invention of Things.* The cousin's projects parody those of the Renaissance Humanists.
[48] A reference to the use of mercury ointments to cure syphilis.

brambles and briars, so thick and intertwined that they completely close it up.

When they caught sight of it, the cousin, Sancho, and Don Quixote dismounted, and the first two straightaway tied up the latter very firmly with the ropes, and while they were binding him and winding them around him, Sancho said: "Mind what you're doing, master; don't bury yourself alive, or put yourself where you'll be like a flask lowered down into a well to cool. Surely it's no affair of yours to be exploring this place, which must be worse than an underground dungeon."

"Tie me up and hold your peace," replied Don Quixote. "Such an enterprise as this has been reserved for me."

The guide then said: "I pray you, Señor Don Quixote, to note and examine with a hundred eyes all that is inside the cave. Perhaps there may be things that I may include in one of my books."

"The drum is in hands that will know well how to beat it," said Sancho.

When Don Quixote's binding was complete, which went over his doublet but not over his armor, he said: "It was remiss of us not to have provided ourselves of a little bell to be tied on the rope close to me. By the sound you would know that I was still descending and was alive. However, since that is impossible, let God's hand guide me."

Saying this, he fell upon his knees, and in a low voice he offered up a prayer to Heaven, beseeching God to help him and give him success in his new perilous adventure. Then, in a loud voice he cried: "O mistress of my actions and movements, most illustrious and peerless Dulcinea of El Toboso, if it is possible for the prayers and the supplications of thy venturesome lover to reach thy ears, by thy incomparable beauty I beseech thee to listen to them, for they do but beg thee not to refuse me thy favor and protection at this moment when I need them so urgently. I am about to plunge, to engulf, and to sink myself in the abyss that yawns at my feet, only to make the world recognize that if thou dost favor me, there is no impossible feat that I may not accomplish."

With those words he approached the cavern, and finding that it was not possible to let himself down or make an entrance unless by force of arm or by cutting a passage, he drew his sword and began to cut away the brambles at the mouth of the cave. At the noise he made, a great number of crows and jackdaws fluttered out so thickly and with such a rush that they knocked Don Quixote down, and if he had been as superstitious as he was a good Catholic, he would have taken it for an evil omen and would have refused to bury himself in such a place. At last, he rose to his feet, and seeing that no more crows came out, or night birds such as bats, which had flown out at the same time as the crows, he let the cousin and Sancho give him rope, and he began to lower himself into the depths of the dreaded cave. As he entered it, Sancho gave him his blessing and made a thousand signs of the Cross over him, saying: "May God and the Rock of France and the Trinity of Gaeta[49] guide you, O flower, cream, and skimming of knights-errant! There you go, you bully of the world, heart of steel, and of

---

[49] The Rock of France is a statue of the Virgin discovered in the fifteenth century, on the road between Salamanca and Cuidad Rodrigo. The chapel of the Holy Trinity of Gaeta was north of Naples.

arm of bronze. Once more, may God guide you and bring you back safe and sound to the light of this world of ours you are leaving to bury yourself in darkness."

The cousin likewise offered up similar prayers and supplications.

Don Quixote, as he descended, called out for more and more rope, and they gave it to him little by little. When his shouts, which sounded from the cave as through a funnel, could not be heard, they had already uncoiled the hundred fathoms of rope. They were of the opinion that they should pull up Don Quixote, for they had no more rope to give him. They waited, however, for about half an hour and then began to gather in the rope with great ease and without any weight, a sign that made them believe that Don Quixote had remained inside. Sancho, when he realized this, wept bitterly and pulled away in great haste in order to learn the worst. But when they came to about eighty fathoms, they felt a weight, which cheered them up considerably. At last, at ten fathoms they saw Don Quixote clearly, and Sancho shouted to him, saying: "Welcome back, master, we fancied you were staying down there to found a family."

Don Quixote answered not a word, and when they had pulled him all the way up, they saw that his eyes were shut and that he appeared to be fast asleep.

They laid him on the ground and untied him, but still he did not awake. Then, they turned him over this way and that, and so shook him and rolled him about that at last he came to himself and stretched himself as if he had just awakened from a deep sleep. Looking around him from one side to another like one who had great fear on him, he cried: "God forgive you, friends; you have snatched me from the most delightful vision that any human being has ever beheld. Now indeed I know that all the pleasant things of this life pass away like a shadow and a dream, or wither like the flowers of the field.[50] O hapless Montesinos! O sorely wounded Durandarte! O unlucky Belerma! O tearful Guadiana, and ye luckless daughters of Ruidera, who show by your waters the tears your eyes did shed!"[51]

The cousin and Sancho listened with great attention to the words of Don Quixote, who uttered them as though they were torn from his very bowels. They besought him to explain what he meant and to tell them what he had seen in the hell below.

"Hell do you call it?" said Don Quixote. "Do not call it thus, for it does not deserve such a name, as you will see presently."

He then begged them to give him something to eat, for he was very hungry. They spread the cousin's saddlecloth on the grass, visited their saddlebags, and seated together in good brotherly fellowship, they lunched and supped at the same time.

Then, when the saddlecloth was removed, Don Quixote said: "Let no one stir. Now, my sons, give me all your attention."

[50] The idea and the language are biblical. See, for example, Psalm 102:11: "My days are like an evening shadow; I wither away like grass." For the idea that "life is a dream," see Calderón's play of that title.
[51] These are all characters in chivalric romances.

CHAPTER XXIII

Of the wonderful things that the consummate Don Quixote said he had seen in the deep cave of Montesinos, whose impossibility and immensity have caused this adventure to be considered apocryphal

It was then about four o'clock in the afternoon when the sun veiled itself behind clouds and shone with subdued light, so that Don Quixote was enabled to relate without heat and discomfort what he had seen in the cave of Montesinos to his two illustrious auditors. He began as follows: "About twelve or fourteen fathoms down in the depth of this dungeon, on the right hand, there is a recess big enough to contain a large cart with its mules. A tiny ray of light enters through some chinks or crevices that are open to the earth's surface. This recess I saw when I was weary and downcast at finding myself dangling in the air by the rope and traveling down through that dark region below without any clear idea of where I was going; so, I determined to enter it and rest for a moment. I shouted to you not to let out more rope until I should ask for it, but you must not have heard me. I then gathered in the rope you were letting down, and after making a coil of it, I sat down upon it, meditating all the while on what I ought to do in order to lower myself to the bottom of the cavern, seeing that I had no one to hold me up. While I was thus perplexed, suddenly and without warning a deep sleep fell upon me, and without knowing the why or the wherefore, I awoke and found myself in the midst of the most delightful meadow that Nature could create or the most vivid imagination visualize. I opened my eyes, I rubbed them, and I found that I was not asleep but wide awake. Nevertheless, I felt my head and my heart to make sure that I myself was there and not some vain specter, but the touch, the feeling, the discourse I held with myself, proved to me that I was the same then as I am here at this moment. Then I saw before me a sumptuous royal palace or castle, with walls that seemed to be made of clear, transparent crystal, and through two great doors that opened I saw a venerable old man come toward me, clad in a long cloak of purple-colored serge that trailed on the ground. He wore over his shoulders and breast a scholar's green-satin hood, and his head was covered with a black Milanese cap, and his snow-white beard fell below his waist. He carried no arms at all, only a rosary of beads that were bigger than fair-sized walnuts—indeed, each tenth bead was like a moderate-sized ostrich egg. His bearing, his gait, his gravity, and his imposing presence, each thing by itself and all of them together, held me spellbound with admiration. He came up to me, and the first thing he did was to embrace me closely. Then he said: 'For many an age, valiant knight Don Quixote of La Mancha, we who inhabit these enchanted solitudes have waited to see you, that you may announce to the world what lies buried in the deep cavern that you have entered, called the cave of Montesinos, an exploit reserved for your invincible heart and spirit. Come with me, illustrious sir, for I wish to show you the wonders that this transparent palace contains, whereof I am the governor and perpetual chief warden, for I am Montesinos himself, after whom the cave is named.'

"No sooner had he said that he was Montesinos than I asked him if the story told in the world above was true, that he had cut the heart of his great friend Durandarte out of his breast with a little dagger and carried it to Lady Belerma, in accordance with Durandarte's instructions at the point of death.[52] He replied that the story was correct in all particulars save in the matter of the dagger, for it was not a dagger, nor little, but a burnished poniard sharper than an awl."

"That same poniard," said Sancho, "must be one of those made by Ramón de Hoces, the Sevillian."[53]

"I do not know," said Don Quixote, "but it could not have been made by that poniard maker, for Ramón de Hoces lived yesterday, whereas the affair of Roncesvalles, where this misfortune took place, was many years ago. But this matter is not of importance; it does not disturb or alter the truth of the story."

"You are right," said the cousin. "Pray proceed, Señor Don Quixote, for I am listening to you with the greatest pleasure in the world."

"And I am no less pleased to tell the story," said Don Quixote. "Well, to continue, the venerable Montesinos led me into the palace of crystal, where in a lower hall, all made of alabaster and extremely cool, there stood an elaborately carved marble tomb, on top of which I saw a knight stretched out full length, not of bronze or marble, but of actual flesh and bone. He had his right hand (which to my eyes appeared somewhat hairy and sinewy, a sign that its owner was of great muscular strength) placed over his heart, but before I could question Montesinos, he, seeing me gaze in amazement at the tomb, said: 'This is my friend Durandarte, flower and mirror of the true lovers and valiant knights of his time. He is kept enchanted here, as I am myself and many other men and women, by that Gallic enchanter Merlin,[54] who, they say, was the Devil's son; but, in my opinion, he is no Devil's son, for he knows, as the saying goes, a deal more than the Devil. How or why he enchanted us, no one knows, but time will reveal the reason at no distant date. What amazes me is that I know as surely as that it is now day that Durandarte ended his life in my arms and that after his death I extracted his heart with my own hands; indeed, it must have weighed a couple of pounds, for according to scientists, he who has a large heart is endowed with greater valor than he who has a small one. Now since the knight did really die, how comes it that he moans and complains from time to time as if he were alive?'

"As he said these words that wretched Durandarte cried aloud:

> " 'O my cousin Montesinos!
> Heed, I pray, my last request:
> When thou seest me lying dead
> And my soul from my corpse has fled,
> With thy poniard or thy dagger
> Pluck the heart from out my breast,
> And hie thee with it to Belerma.' "[55]

---

[52] This story is told in the chivalric "Ballads of Montesinos." Through this whole section, the story of the heart is told with an absurd literalness.

[53] Unidentified. Presumably a contemporary knife-maker.

[54] The wizard in the Arthurian legends. He was Welsh, not "Gallic," though he was claimed by the Bretons.

[55] Cervantes is quoting, and combining, two actual ballads.

"On hearing these words the venerable Montesinos sank upon his knees before the hapless knight, and with tears in his eyes, he exclaimed: 'Long since, Sir Durandarte, my dearest cousin, have I done what you bade me on the rueful day when I lost you. I took out your heart as best I could, without leaving the slightest piece of it in your breast; I wiped it with a lace handkerchief; I went off with it by the road to France, after having first laid you in the bosom of the earth with tears so plentiful that they sufficed to wash and cleanse my hands of the blood that stained them when I groped in your bowels. Then, O cousin of my soul, as further proof, at the first place I reached after leaving Roncesvalles, I sprinkled a few pinches of salt on your heart that it might not smell badly and that I might bring it, if not fresh, at least pickled, into the presence of Lady Belerma, whom, along with you and me, and Guadiana, your squire, and the duenna Ruidera and her seven daughters and two nieces, and other friends, Merlin the Wizard keeps here enchanted these many years. And though five hundred years have passed, not one of us has died. Ruidera and her daughters and nieces alone are missing, for Merlin, pitying them for the tears they had shed, changed them into so many lagoons, which now in the world of the living and in the province of La Mancha the people call the lagoons of Ruidera.[56] The seven daughters belong to the kings of Spain and the two nieces to the knights of a very holy order, called the Order of St. John.[57] Guadiana, your squire, who also was bewailing your fate, was changed into a river of his own name, but when he reached the surface of the earth and saw the sun of another Heaven, so great was his sorrow at finding that he was leaving you that he plunged into the bowels of the earth.[58] Nevertheless, as he cannot avoid following his natural course, from time to time he comes forth and shows himself to the sun and the world. The lagoons I have mentioned supply him with their waters, and with their help and the help of many others he enters Portugal in all his pomp and glory. But wherever he goes he shows his sadness and melancholy and takes no pride in breeding choice and tasty fish, but only coarse and tasteless kinds, very different from those of the golden Tagus.[59] All this, my cousin, I have told you many times before, but since you make me no answer, I am afraid you do not believe me, or do not hear me, which greatly distresses me, as God knows. Now I have news to give you, which, while it may not alleviate your sorrows, will by no means increase them. Learn that you have here before you (open your eyes and you will see him) that great knight about whom the magician Merlin has prophesied so many things; that Don Quixote of La Mancha, I say, who once again and to better purpose than in the past has revived in the present the already forgotten order of knight-errantry. By his aid and favor we may be disenchanted, for great deeds are reserved for great men.'

" 'And if this does not take place,' replied the hapless Durandarte in a swooning voice; 'if this may not be, then, O cousin, I say: patience and

[56] The "lagoons of Ruidera" were a series of lakes in the vicinity of the ancient Moslem castle of Ruidera.

[57] Two of the lakes (the "nieces") were in the domain of the Order of St. John.

[58] The fact that the Guadiana river in La Mancha flows underground for some distance has already been mentioned in Part I.

[59] A river in central Spain.

shuffle the cards.'[60] And turning over on his side, he relapsed into his former silence without speaking another word.

"And now a great outcry and lamentations arose, accompanied by deep groans and pitiful sobbings. I turned around and saw through the walls of crystal in another hall a procession of two lines of fair damsels all clad in mourning, with white turbans of Turkish fashion on their heads. Behind, in the rear of the procession, walked a lady, for so her dignity proclaimed her to be, also clothed in black, with a white veil so long and ample that it kissed the ground. Her turban was twice as large as the largest of any of the others; she had eyebrows that met, and her nose was rather flat; her mouth was large, but her lips were red; her teeth, which at times she showed, were few and not well set, though as white as peeled almonds. She carried in her hands a fine handkerchief, and in it, as well as I could make out, a mummified heart, for it was all dried up and pickled. Montesinos said that all those in the procession were servants of Durandarte and Belerma, who were enchanted there with their master and mistress, and that the last one, she who bore the heart wrapped up in the handkerchief, was the Lady Belerma, who with her damsels, four days a week, walked in that procession and sang, or rather wept, her sorrowful dirges over the body and wretched heart of his cousin. He added that if she appeared to me somewhat ugly, or at least, not as beautiful as fame reported, it was because of the bad nights and the worse days she spent in that enchantment, as I could see by the great dark circles around her eyes and her sickly complexion. 'And,' said he, 'her sallowness and the rings around her eyes do not come from the periodical ailment common to women, for it is many months, and even years, since it has appeared at her gates, but from the grief her own heart suffers for that object that she continually holds in her hands; it brings back to her memory the misfortune of her luckless lover. If it were not for this, scarcely would the great Dulcinea of El Toboso, so renowned in all these parts, and even in all the world, equal her in beauty, charm, and wit.'

"'Go slow, Don Montesinos,' said I. 'Tell your story rightly, for you are aware that all comparisons are odious, and there is no reason to compare one person with another. The peerless Dulcinea of El Toboso is what she is, and Doña Belerma is what she is and has been, and there let the matter rest.'

"To which he answered: 'Forgive me, Don Quixote, for I confess that I was wrong in saying that Lady Dulcinea could scarcely equal Lady Belerma, for it was enough for me to learn, I know not by what indications, that you are her knight, to make me bite my tongue rather than compare her to anything but Heaven itself.' After this satisfaction that the great Montesinos gave me, my heart recovered from the shock it had received at hearing my lady compared to Belerma."

"And yet I'm amazed," cried Sancho, "that your worship did not jump upon the old fellow and kick every bone in his body and tear out his beard, without leaving a hair in it."

"No, Sancho, my friend," said Don Quixote, "it would not have been right for me to do so, for we are all bound to show respect to the aged, even

[60] A proverb among card players.

though they be not knights, but especially to those who are and who become enchanted. I am certain that I owed him nothing in the matter of the many questions and answers that passed between us."

At this point the cousin remarked: "I cannot understand, Don Quixote, how in so short a space of time as you were down below you were able to see so many things and to say and answer so much."

"How long is it since I went down?" asked Don Quixote.

"A little more than an hour," replied Sancho.

"That cannot be," answered Don Quixote, "for night came when I was down there, and then morning, and again a night and a morning three times, so that, by my reckoning, I have been three days in these remote regions hidden from the upper world."

"My master must be right," said Sancho, "for since everything that has happened to him is by enchantment, perhaps what seems an hour to us would seem three days and nights down there."

"That must be so," said Don Quixote.

"Did you, dear sir, eat anything all that time?" asked the cousin.

"I have not broken my fast," answered Don Quixote, "nor did I feel hunger, even in my imagination."

"Do the enchanted eat?" inquired the cousin.

"They do not eat," answered Don Quixote, "nor do they void excrement, but it is thought that their nails, hair, and beard grow."

"And do the enchanted ones sleep, master?" asked Sancho.

"Certainly not," replied Don Quixote, "at any rate, during the three days I spent with them no one closed an eye; neither did I."

"This is a point," said Sancho, "where the proverb comes pat: 'Tell me the company you keep and I'll tell you what you are.' You, master, kept company with enchanted fellows who were fasting and watching. What wonder, then, that you neither ate nor slept while you were with them? But forgive me, master, if I tell you that of all you've said up to the present, God seize me—I was just going to say the devil—if I believe a single word."

"What!" cried the cousin. "Could Don Quixote tell a lie? Why, even if he wished to do so, this was no time for him to invent such a load of lies."

"I don't believe my master tells lies," answered Sancho.

"If not, what do you believe?" asked Don Quixote.

"I believe," said Sancho, "that this fellow Merlin, or these enchanters who bewitched the whole crew your worship says you saw and talked to down below, has piled your imagination with all that hodgepodge you have been telling and with everything else that you still have to tell."

"That might be, Sancho," replied Don Quixote, "but as a matter of fact, it is not so, for all that I have told you I saw with my own eyes and touched with my own hands. Now, what will you say when I tell you that among the countless marvelous things Montesinos showed me, he pointed out three peasant girls who were capering and frisking like she-goats over those delightful fields, and no sooner had I caught sight of them than I recognized one as the peerless Dulcinea of El Toboso and the other two as the same country wenches that were with her and to whom we spoke on the road from El Toboso? I asked Montesinos if he knew them. He answered that he did not, but that he thought they must be some enchanted ladies of quality, for it was but a few days since they had made their appearance in those meadows. He added that I should not be surprised at that, because many ladies of past and present times were enchanted there in various strange shapes, and among them he recognized Queen Guinevere and her duenna, Quintañona, who poured out the wine for Lancelot 'When from Brittany he came.' "[61]

As soon as Sancho Panza heard his master say this, he thought he would lose his wits, or else die with laughter, for since he knew the truth about the pretended enchanting of Dulcinea and had been himself the enchanter and the concocter of all the evidence, he made up his mind, beyond all shadow of a doubt, that his master was out of his wits and mad as a March hare. So, he said to him: "It was a bitter day, dear master, when you went below to the other world, and it was an unlucky moment when you met Señor Montesinos, who has so transmogrified you for us. Up here, master, you were in your full senses, just as God has given you, uttering your maxims and giving counsels at every turn, and not as you are now, blabbing the greatest balderdash that ever was known."

"I know you, Sancho," replied Don Quixote, "so, I pay no heed to your words."

"No more do I to yours," said Sancho, "even though you beat me or kill me for those I've spoken or mean to speak if you don't correct and mend your own. But tell me, now that we're at peace, what made you recognize the lady our mistress? If you did speak to her, what did you say, and what did she say in reply?"

"I recognized her," said Don Quixote, "because she wore the same clothes as when you showed her to me. I spoke to her, but she did not answer a word, but only turned her back on me and fled, and she ran at such a pace that an arrow would not have overtaken her. I wanted to follow her and would have done so if Montesinos had not advised me not to weary myself in doing so, for it would be vain, especially as the hour was approaching when it would be necessary for me to leave the cave. He told me, moreover, that in time he would tell me how he, Belerma, Durandarte, and all who were there were to be disenchanted. What pained me most of all was that while Montesinos was speaking to me, one of the two attendants of the hapless Dulcinea came up to me without my having seen her coming, and with tears in her eyes, she said to me in a low agitated voice: 'My Lady Dulcinea of El Toboso kisses your worship's hand and beseeches you to let her know how you are; because she is in great need, she also entreats your worship as earnestly as she can to be so good as to lend her, upon this new dimity petticoat I have here, half a dozen reals, or as many as you have, which she promises to repay in a very short time.' Such a message amazed me; so, turning to Montesinos, I said: 'Is it possible, Señor Montesinos, that persons of quality who are enchanted can suffer need?' He replied: 'Believe me, Don Quixote of La Mancha, what is called want is the fashion all over the world; it extends throughout, touches everyone, and doesn't even spare the enchanted. And since Lady Dulcinea of El Toboso sends to borrow the six reals, and the security is apparently good, there is nothing to do but to give them to her, for she must no doubt be in sore straits.'

---

[61] From the ballad on Lancelot that Don Quixote quoted in the first adventure in the inn in Part I.

" 'I will not take a pledge for her,' I replied, 'nor can I yet give her what she asks, for all I have is four reals,' which I gave her (they were those that you, Sancho, gave me the other day to hand as alms to the poor I met on the road), and I said: 'Tell your mistress, my dear friend, that I am distressed to hear of her troubles and that I wish I were a Fúcar[62] to relieve them; I would have her know that I cannot be, and ought not to be, in good health, seeing that I lack her pleasant company and witty conversation. So, I beseech her as earnestly as I can to allow herself to be seen and greeted by this her captive and foot-weary cavalier. You must tell her also that when she least expects it, she will hear that I have made a vow, like the one that the Marquess of Mantua made to avenge his nephew Baldwin when he found him dying on the mountainside, which was not to eat bread off a tablecloth, with some other trifles he added, until he had avenged him.[63] And I will do the same: not to rest, and to wander over the seven regions of the earth more diligently than the Infante Don Pedro of Portugal,[64] until I have freed her from her enchantment.'

" 'All that and more, your worship should do for my lady,' said the damsel in answer, and taking the four reals, instead of making me a curtsy she cut a caper that lifted her two yards up into the air."

"Holy God!" shouted Sancho at this point. "Is it possible that such things can happen in the world and that enchanters and enchantments can have the power to change the good sense of my master into such crazy folly? O master, master, for God's sake, mind yourself, consider your honor and give no credit to this empty balderdash that has destroyed your senses."

"You talk this way, Sancho, because you love me," said Don Quixote, "and because you are inexperienced in the affairs of the world. Everything that presents points of difficulty appears to you impossible. But after time has passed I shall tell you about some of the things I saw below that will make you believe what I have related, for its truth admits no reply or question."

CHAPTER XXIV

In which a thousand trifles are recounted, as nonsensical as they are necessary to the true understanding of this great history

The translator of this great history from the original written by its first author, Cide Hamete Benengeli, says that when he came to the adventure of the cave of Montesinos, he found written in the margin, in the hand of Hamete, these words: "I am unable to understand or to persuade myself that all that is written in the previous chapter literally happened to the valiant Don Quixote. The reason is that all the adventures until now have been feasible and probable, but this one of the cave I can find no way of accepting it as true, seeing that it exceeds all reasonable bounds. Nevertheless, I cannot possibly believe that Don Quixote, who was the most truthful

---

[62] "Fúcar" is the Spanish form of "Fugger," the name of a famous family of Bavarian bankers and financiers in the Middle Ages.

[63] The story of Carloto and Baldwin has already been told in Part I.

[64] A celebrated traveler. His account of his travels in the East was published in 1554.

gentleman and the noblest knight of the times, could tell a lie; why, he could not lie, even if they riddled him with arrows. On the other hand, when I consider the minute and detailed manner in which he has spoken, I find it still more impossible to believe that he could have fashioned such a tissue of absurdities in so short time.

"So, if this adventure seems apocryphal, it is not I who am to blame, for I write it down without vouching its truth or falsity. You, cautious reader, as you are wise, must judge for yourself, for I cannot, and should not, do more. One thing, however, is certain, that finally he retracted it on his deathbed and confessed that he had invented it, since he believed that it fitted in well with the adventures he had read of in his histories." . . .

[In a long section which follows, Don Quixote and Sancho, among other adventures, are entertained in the home of a duke and duchess who have read the First Part of their history and who play an elaborate series of practical jokes on them. The duke pretends to make Sancho the governor of an island, where he surprises everyone by the wisdom of his decisions. Meanwhile at the castle, Quixote is the victim of a series of jests, but he maintains his dignity; both he and Sancho grow in stature as the duke and duchess appear progressively more foolish. Leaving the palace, Quixote and Sancho encounter a group setting up a pastoral Arcadia, who treat them kindly. They then meet a Robin Hood-like highwayman, Roque Guinart, who befriends them. They go to Barcelona, where they are the guests of Don Antonio Moreno, who plays tricks on Quixote even more cruel than those in the castle of the duke and duchess.]

CHAPTER LXIV

Of the adventure that gave Don Quixote more sorrow than any that had ever befallen him

. . . . One morning when Don Quixote was riding out for an airing on the strand, armed cap-a-pie—for, as he often said, "my ornaments are arms, my rest the battle fray," and he was never a moment without them— he spied a knight riding toward him, armed like himself from head to foot, with a shining moon painted on his shield, who, when he came within hearing, called out to him: "Illustrious knight and never-enough-renowned Don Quixote of La Mancha, I am the Knight of the White Moon, whose unheard-of exploits perchance may have reached your ears. I come to enter into combat with you and to compel you by sword to own and confess that my mistress, whoever she may be, is incomparably more beautiful than your Dulcinea of El Toboso. If you will fairly confess this truth, you will spare your own life and me the trouble of taking it. If you are resolved to fight and if victory be mine, my terms require that you relinquish arms and the quest of adventures and retire to your home for the space of one year, where you shall live quietly and peaceably, without laying hand to your sword, for thus you will improve your temporal and spiritual welfare. But should you vanquish me, my head shall be at your mercy, my arms and my steed shall be yours, and the fame of my deeds shall be added to yours. Consider what is best for you and give me your answer without delay, for this day must decide the issue of this affair."

Don Quixote was surprised, not to say dumbfounded, as much by the arrogance of the Knight of the White Moon's challenge, as at the subject of it; so, with solemn gravity and composure he replied: "Knight of the White Moon, whose exploits have not yet come to my ears, I will make you swear that you have never set eyes upon the illustrious Dulcinea, for if you had done so, I am confident that you would never have made this claim, since the sight of her perfections must have convinced you that there never was, or ever can be, beauty comparable to hers. And so, without calling you a liar, I declare that you are mistaken and accept your challenge upon the spot, this very day. Furthermore, I accept all your conditions, with the exception of the transfer of your exploits, for they are unknown to me; I must remain contented with my own, such as they are. Choose, then, your ground and I shall do the same, and may St. Peter bless him whom God favors."

Meanwhile the viceroy, who had been informed of the arrival of the Knight of the White Moon and of the conversation that he was holding with Don Quixote, hastened to the scene of action accompanied by Don Antonio and others, firmly convinced that this must be some new jest invented by Don Antonio Moreno or by some other gentleman of the city. They arrived just as Don Quixote was wheeling Rozinante about to take his ground, and perceiving that they were on the point of attacking one another, the viceroy intervened and asked what was the reason for such a sudden encounter. The Knight of the White Moon replied that it was a question of preeminence in beauty, and then he briefly told what he had said to Don Quixote concerning the conditions of the duel. The viceroy then went up to Don Antonio and asked him in a whisper if he knew who the Knight of the White Moon was, or whether it was some trick they wished to play upon Don Quixote. Don Antonio answered that he did not know who he was, or whether the challenge was in earnest or not. The viceroy was troubled by that answer and wondered whether he ought or ought not to let the battle continue. At length, by dint of persuading himself that it was some jest, he withdrew, saying: "Gentlemen, if there be no other remedy than confession or death, and if Don Quixote is stubborn in his resolve, and you, Knight of the White Moon, are obstinate likewise, then in God's name go to it."

The Knight of the White Moon in courteous and well-chosen words thanked the viceroy for what he had done, and Don Quixote did likewise. And after recommending himself to Heaven and to his Dulcinea, he retired to take a longer compass of the ground, for he saw his opponent do the same; then, without any flourish of trumpets or any other martial instrument to give the signal for the outset, they both turned their horses around at the same instant. But he of the White Moon, who was mounted on the fleeter steed, met Don Quixote two-thirds down the course and hurtled into him with such a fierce onslaught that, without touching him with his lance, which he seemed purposely to hold aloof, he brought both horse and rider to the ground. He then sprang upon him and said as he clapped his lance to his opponent's visor: "Knight, you are vanquished and a dead man if you don't confess in accordance with the conditions of our challenge."

Don Quixote, who was bruised and stunned, without lifting his visor and as though speaking from the tomb, said in a faint low voice: "Dulcinea of El Toboso is the most beautiful woman in the world, and I am the most unfortunate knight on earth, and it isn't just that my weakness should discredit this truth. Go on, knight, press on with your lance and take away my life, since you have robbed me of my honor."

"That I shall certainly never do," said he of the White Moon. "Long may the fame of Lady Dulcinea of El Toboso's beauty live and flourish! All I demand is that the great Don Quixote should retire to his village for one year, or for a period to be fixed by me, in accordance with the agreement drawn up before this battle."

The viceroy, Don Antonio, and many others witnessed all that passed, and they heard Don Quixote promise that he would fulfill all the terms of their engagement like a genuine and punctilious knight, provided nothing was required to the prejudice of Lady Dulcinea. When this declaration was made, he of the White Moon turned about his horse, and after bowing to the viceroy, he rode at a half gallop into the city.

The viceroy commanded Don Antonio to go after him and to ascertain by all possible means who he was. Then, they raised Don Quixote from the ground, and uncovering his face, they found him pale and bathed in sweat. Rozinante was in such a plight that he was unable to stir for some time. As for Sancho, he was so sorrowful and cast down that he knew not what to say or do; he fancied that all had taken place in dreams and that the whole business was the result of enchantment. He saw his master overthrown and bound to lay aside his arms for a whole year. He imagined that his master's glory had been finally eclipsed and his own hopes from the latter's recent promises vanished like smoke in the wind. He was afraid that Rozinante might be crippled forever and his master's bones be permanently knocked out of joint, though it would be no small blessing if his madness were knocked out of him. In the end they carried the knight into the city on a hand-chair that the viceroy had sent for. The viceroy himself returned, eager to ascertain who was this Knight of the White Moon who had left Don Quixote in such a piteous state.

CHAPTER LXV

Which reveals who the Knight of the White Moon was, with the liberation of Don Gregorio and other incidents

Don Antonio Moreno rode after the Knight of the White Moon, and a great number of boys also followed, pestering him until he took refuge in an inn inside the city. Don Antonio entered there, too, as he was eager to make his acquaintance. A squire came forward to receive him and take off his armor, and he shut himself up in a lower room, where he was followed by Don Antonio, who was on tenterhooks to know who he was. Then, when the Knight of the White Moon found that the gentleman would not leave him, he said: "I know very well, sir, what you have come here for: to find out who I am. As it happens, there is no reason for me to conceal myself; so, while my servant is taking off my armor, I shall tell you the whole truth of my story, without omitting a single detail. You must know sir, that I am called the bachelor Sansón Carrasco; I come from the same town as Don Quixote of La Mancha, whose madness and folly have been the cause of deep sorrow to his friends and neighbors. I myself felt particular sympathy for his sad case, and as I believed his recovery to depend upon his remaining quietly at home, I earnestly endeavored to accomplish that end. And so, about three months ago I sallied forth myself as a knight-errant, calling myself the Knight of the Mirrors and intending to fight and vanquish him without doing him any harm and to impose as the condition of our combat that the vanquished should be at the mercy of the conqueror. Feeling certain of my success, I expected to send him home for twelve months, hoping that during that time he might be restored to health. But Fortune willed otherwise, for it was he who vanquished me; he unhorsed me, and my scheme was of no avail. He continued his journey, and I returned home vanquished, ashamed, and injured by my fall. Nevertheless, I did not abandon my scheme, as you have seen this day, and as he is so punctilious and so particular in observing the laws of knight-errantry, he is sure to perform his promise. This, sir, is my whole story, and I beseech you not to reveal me to Don Quixote, in order that my good intentions may produce their fruit and that the worthy gentleman may recover his sense, for when he is freed from the follies of chivalry, he is a man of excellent understanding."

"O sir!" replied Don Antonio. "May God forgive you for the wrong you have done in robbing the world of the most diverting madman who was ever seen. Is it not plain, sir, that his cure can never benefit mankind half as much as the pleasure he affords by his eccentricities? But I feel sure, sir, that all your art will not cure such deep-rooted madness; were it not uncharitable, I would express the hope that he may never recover, for by his cure we would lose not only the knight's good company, but also the drollery of his squire, Sancho Panza, which is enough to transform melancholy itself into mirth. All the same, I shall hold my peace and not breathe a word to him, to see whether I am right in suspecting that all Mister Carrasco's efforts will have no effect."

The bachelor answered that the business in any case was far advanced and that he was confident there would be a favorable result. And so, after Don Antonio had offered to follow the latter's instructions, the bachelor took his leave that same day. He had his armor tied on a mule; he mounted the charger on which he had done battle and left the city for home, meeting no adventure on the way worthy of mention in this true history.

Don Antonio told the viceroy everything that Carrasco had said. The viceroy was not too pleased by it, for Don Quixote's retirement would mean a loss to all those who were entertained by the tales of his mad adventures.

For six days Don Quixote was confined to his bed, dejected, melancholy, thoughtful, out of humor, and full of bleak reflections on his luckless overthrow. Sancho strove hard to comfort him, saying: "Raise your head, master, cheer up and thank your stars that you've come off without even a broken rib. Remember, sir, that 'They that give must take'; and that 'Where there are hooks there aren't always flitches.' Come now, sir, a fig for the doctor! You've no need of him. Let us be off for home, and give up this gallivanting up and down in search of adventures in lands and places, God knows where. And when you come to think of it, I'm the one who's the greater loser by this, though it's your worship who is in a worse pickle. Though with my government I gave up all desire of being a governor again, I've never lost the hankering to be a count. But I may as well say good-bye to all that if your worship gives up trying to be a king and resigns your profession of chivalry! So all my hopes end in smoke."

"Be quiet, Sancho. Do you not see that my seclusion and retirement need only last a year? After that I shall return to my honored calling, and I am bound to win a kingdom, and some countship or other for you."

"God grant you may," said Sancho, "and let sin be deaf, for I've always heard that good hopes are better than poor holdings. . . ."

[On the journey home, Quixote considers becoming a pastoral shepherd; he and Sancho meet several people from their past adventures, including the duke and duchess, who play one last trick on them. Sancho continues the self-flagellation the duke claimed was necessary to free Dulcinea from her enchantment, though he whips trees instead of himself whenever possible. Without realizing it, they arrive at their village.]

CHAPTER LXXIII

Of the omens that Don Quixote met at the entrance to his village, with other incidents that embellish and accredit this great history

As they entered the village, Cide Hamete informs us, Don Quixote noticed two boys pummeling one another on the threshing floor, and heard one say to the other: "Don't fash[65] yourself, Periquillo, for you'll never see her in all the days of your life."

Don Quixote, overhearing this, said to Sancho: "Did you catch what the boy said, 'You'll never see her in all the days of your life?'"

"Well," rejoined Sancho, "what does it matter what the boy said?"

"What?" retorted his master. "Don't you realize that such words, when applied to my affairs, clearly portend that I shall never see my Dulcinea?"

Sancho was about to answer again, but was hindered from so doing by a great hue and cry of hounds and huntsmen in full pursuit of a hare, which was so hard pressed that she came and squatted for shelter just between Dapple's feet. Immediately Sancho laid hold of her and presented her to Don Quixote, but the knight kept muttering to himself: "*Malum signum! Malum signum!*[66] A hare runs away, hounds pursue her, and Dulcinea does not appear."

"You are a strange man, sir," said Sancho. "Let us suppose that poor bunny here is Mistress Dulcinea, the greyhounds that followed her are the wicked enchanters who transmogrified her into a country lass; she races away, I catch her and hand her safe and sound to your worship, and you hold her in your arms and pet her: what harm is there in this, and what bad omen is this?"

By this time the two boys who had been fighting came up to see the hare, and when Sancho inquired why they had been fighting, he was answered by the boy who had uttered the ominous words, that he had snatched from his playmate a cage full of crickets, which he would not give back to him again. Sancho pulled a threepenny piece out of his pocket and gave it to the boy for his cage; and giving it to Don Quixote, he said: "There

[65] Worry.   [66] "A bad sign."

you are, sir; all the tokens of bad luck have been brought to nothing, and though I am a blockhead, I'm convinced all these things have no more to do with our affairs than the clouds of yesteryear. And if I remember right, I've heard the curate of our village say that no decent self-respecting Christian should give ear to such foolishness; and I've heard you yourself, master, say not many days ago that all those Christians who troubled their heads with fortune-telling rubbish were no better than nincompoops. So, without more ado let us make straight for our homes."

By now the huntsmen had come up and asked for their hare, which Don Quixote delivered up to them. They passed on, and just as they were entering the town, they perceived the curate and the bachelor Sansón Carrasco at their devotions in a small field. We must add that Sancho had thrown over Dapple and the bundle of arms, as a cover, the buckram robe painted with flames of fire that they had put on him in the duke's castle on the night when Altisidora rose from the dead.[67] He had also fitted the miter on Dapple's head, and this ornament transformed him as strangely as ever an ass was transformed in all the world. The curate and the bachelor recognized them at once and hastened toward them with open arms. Don Quixote dismounted and embraced them affectionately. Meanwhile the boys, who are as sharp-eyed as lynxes and miss no detail, sighted the ass's miter and rushed up to look at it, saying: "Have a look, boys! Here is Sancho's ass gaudier than Mingo, and Don Quixote's hack leaner than ever."[68]

Surrounded by the boys of the town and attended by the curate and the bachelor, they moved toward the house of Don Quixote, where they found the housekeeper and his niece, who had heard of their arrival, waiting for them on the doorstep. News had also reached Teresa, the wife of Sancho Panza, and she came running half-naked and with her hair all tousled, leading by the hand her daughter, Sanchica. But when she found that her husband was not quite dressed up to her notions of what a governor should wear, she said: "What's all this, husband? You look as if you'd plodded all the way on shanks' mare! You look more misgoverned than governor, I'm thinking."

"Whisht, Teresa!" said Sancho. "Many a time there's a hook but devil a flitch on it.[69] First of all, let us go home, and then I'll tell you wonders. I've money, and after all, that is what counts, and I made it by my own labors without harming a soul."

"Bring home the money, my dear," said Teresa, "no matter how or where you've earned it; after all there's nothing new in that."

Sanchica then hugged her father and asked what he had brought her, for she longed for his return as the flowers do for the dew in May. So, she caught hold of her father's waistband with one hand and pulled Dapple after her by the halter with the other, and her mother took Sancho by the arm on the other side, and away they all went to his cottage, leaving Don Quixote in his own house under the care of his niece and housekeeper with the curate and the bachelor to keep him company.

---

[67] The story of this practical joke in the duke's castle is omitted here.

[68] A reference to a popular fifteenth-century poem named *Mingo Revulgo,* in which Mingo is dressed in a blue smock and red doublet.

[69] A proverb: "Sometimes there's a hook, but no bacon on it."

Don Quixote drew the last two aside, and without observing time or season, he gave them a short account of his defeat and the obligation he lay under of remaining in his village for a year, which, like a true knight-errant, he was determined to observe most faithfully. He added that he intended to become a shepherd and spend that year in the solitude of the fields and woods, giving rein to his amorous thoughts and practising the virtues of the pastoral life. Furthermore, he begged them, if more important duties were not a hindrance, to become his companions, and he assured them that he would furnish them with sufficient sheep and cattle to enable them to belong to such a profession. He let them know that the principal part of the business was already done, for he had planned names that would fit them exactly. The curate asked him what they were, and Don Quixote replied that he was to call himself the shepherd Quixotiz, the bachelor the shepherd Carrascón, the curate the shepherd Curiambro, and Sancho Panza the shepherd Panzino. They were all astonished at Don Quixote's new strain of madness, but considering that this might be a means of preventing him from wandering from home and hoping at the same time that within the year he might be cured of his mad knight-errantry, they applauded his pastoral folly as a wise idea and offered to become his companions in carrying it out.

"Better still," said Sansón Carrasco, "as all the world is now aware that I am a very celebrated poet, I shall compose pastoral or courtly verses at every turn, or such as may best assist our cause, so that we may entertain ourselves in the lonely wastes where we may have to wander. But what is most important, gentlemen, is for each one of us to choose the name of the shepherdess he intends to celebrate in his verses, and not to have a single tree, no matter how tough its bark, on which her name is not inscribed and cut on it, as is the custom of love-sick shepherds."

"That is quite right," answered Don Quixote, "though for myself I have no need to seek for the name of any imaginary shepherdess, for I have the peerless Dulcinea of El Toboso, glory of these banks, ornament of these meadows, the prop of beauty, the cream of grace, and in short, the cynosure of all praise, however exaggerated it may be."

"That is true," said the curate, "but we must look around for indulgent shepherdesses who are easy to manage, and we may have to trim their angles if they don't square with us."

"And if they should fail," added Sansón Carrasco, "we'll give them the names in print that are known to all the world: Phyllidas, Amaryllises, Dianas, Fleridas, Galateas, and Belisardas;[70] since they're for sale in the markets, we can easily buy them and keep them for our own. If my lady—my shepherdess, I should say—by chance be called Ana, I'll celebrate her under the name of Anarda; if Francisca, I'll call her Francenia; and if Lucía, Lucinda: that is all it will come to. And if Sancho Panza is to enter our confraternity, he can celebrate his wife, Teresa Panza, under the name Teresaina."

Don Quixote smiled at the application of the name and the curate extolled his chaste and honorable resolution, repeating his offer to bear him company for as long as he could spare from compulsory duties. With this

---

[70] Common names in pastoral poetry.

they took leave of him, advising him to take care of his health and to adopt a healthy diet.

As luck would have it, the housekeeper and the niece heard the conversation between the three on the subject of the pastoral life, and no sooner had the priest and the bachelor gone than they both burst into Don Quixote's room, and the niece cried: "Mercy on us, uncle! What does this mean? We thought that you had come to stay at home and live here like a quiet, honest gentleman, and here you are longing to wander off into fresh labyrinths, becoming a 'gentle shepherd, come and go.' In truth, uncle, the straw is too old to make pipes of."

"Heaven help us, sir!" added the housekeeper. "How will your worship be able to stand the summer's heat, the winter's frost, and the howling of the wolves in the open country? Pray, sir, you mustn't think of it; it's a business for strong men who are born and bred to it from the days when they were babes in arms. And if it comes to worst, better to be a knight-errant than a shepherd. Mark my words, master, and heed my counsel; I'm not full of food and drink, but fasting, and I'm no chicken, but fifty years of age, and I say to you: Stay at home, look after your property, go to confession often, do good to the poor, and let me take the blame if you go wrong."

"My dear girls, do cease your prating," Don Quixote answered. "I know best what I have to do; only help me to my bed, for I do not feel very well. Remember that whether I be a knight-errant or an errant shepherd, you will always find me ready to provide for you, and you may rely on my good faith."

And his affectionate daughters—for so the niece and the housekeeper undoubtedly were—undressed him, put him to bed, where they brought him something to eat, and made him as comfortable as possible.

CHAPTER LXXIV

Of how Don Quixote fell ill, of the will he made, and of his death

As all human things, especially the lives of men, are not eternal, and even their beginnings are but steps to their end, and as Don Quixote was under no special dispensation of Heaven, he was snatched away by death when he least expected it. Whether his sickness was caused by his melancholic reflections on his defeat, or whether it was so preordained by Providence, he was stricken down by a violent fever that confined him to his bed for six days. All that time his good friends, the priest, the bachelor, and the barber, often visited him, and his trusty squire, Sancho Panza, never left his bedside. They were convinced that his sickness was due to his sorrow at having been defeated and his disappointment in the matter of Dulcinea's disenchantment; and so, they tried in every way to cheer him up. The bachelor begged him to pluck up his spirits and get up from his bed so that they might begin their pastoral life, adding that he had already written an eclogue that would put Sannazaro's[71] nose out of joint, and that he had bought

---

[71]Jacapo Sannazaro (1456–1533) was famous for his pastoral novel *Arcadia*.

with his own money from a shepherd of Quintanar two pedigreed dogs to watch the flock, one called Barcino and the other Butrón. But this had no effect, for Don Quixote continued to mope as before. A physician was sent for, who, after feeling his pulse, took a rather gloomy view of the case and told him that he should provide for his soul's health, for that of his body was in dangerous condition. Don Quixote received the news calmly and serenely, but his niece, his housekeeper, and his squire began to weep as bitterly as if he had been laid out already. The physician was of the opinion that melancholy and mortification had brought him to death's door. Don Quixote then asked them to leave him for a little while, as he wished to sleep. They retired, and he slept at a stretch, as they say, for more than six hours, and the housekeeper and the niece were afraid that he might not waken from it. At length he did awaken and cried out in a loud voice: "Blessed be the Almighty for this great benefit He has granted me! Infinite are His mercies, and undiminished even by the sins of men."

The niece, who was listening very attentively to these words of her uncle, found more sense in them than there was in his usual talk, at least since he had fallen ill, and she questioned him: "What do you mean, uncle? Has anything strange taken place? What mercies and what sins of men are you talking about?"

"Mercies," answered Don Quixote, "that God has just this moment granted to me in spite of all my sins. My judgment is now clear and unfettered, and that dark cloud of ignorance has disappeared, which the continual reading of those detestable books of knight-errantry had cast over my understanding. Now I see their folly and fraud, and my sole regret is that the discovery comes too late to allow me to amend my ways by reading others that would enlighten my soul. I find, dear niece, that my end approaches, but I would have it remembered that though in my life I was reputed a madman, yet in my death this opinion was not confirmed. Therefore, my dear child, call my good friends, the priest, the bachelor Sansón Carrasco, and Master Nicholas, the barber, for I wish to make my confession and my will."

There was no need for the niece to go to the trouble, for presently all three arrived at the house, and Don Quixote no sooner saw them than he said: "My dear friends, welcome the happy news! I am no longer Don Quixote of La Mancha, but Alonso Quixano, the man whom the world formerly called the Good, owing to his virtuous life. I am now the sworn enemy of Amadis of Gaul and his innumerable brood; I now abhor all profane stories of knight-errantry, for I know only too well, through Heaven's mercy and through my own personal experience, the great danger of reading them."

When his three friends heard him talk thus, they concluded that he was stricken with some new madness. Sansón then said to him: "What does all this mean, Don Quixote? Now that we have just received news that Lady Dulcinea is disenchanted, and now that we are just about to become shepherds and spend our days singing and living like princes, you talk about turning yourself into a hermit. No more foolish tales, I beg you, and come back to your senses."

"Those foolish tales," replied Don Quixote, "that up to now have been my bane may with Heaven's help turn to my advantage at my death. Dear friends, I feel that I am rapidly sinking; therefore, let us put aside all jesting. I want a priest to hear my confession, and a notary to draw up my will. At such a moment a man must not deceive his soul; therefore, I beg you to send for the notary while the priest hears my confession."

Don Quixote's words amazed his hearers, but though they were at first skeptical about the return of his sanity, they were forced to take him at his word. One of the symptoms that made them fear he was near the point of death was the suddenness with which he had recovered his intellect, for after what he had already said, he conversed with such good sense and displayed such true Christian resignation that they believed his wits had been restored at last. The curate, therefore, told the company to leave the room, and he confessed Don Quixote. In the meantime the bachelor hastened to fetch the notary, and presently he returned with him and with Sancho Panza. The latter (who had already heard from the bachelor the news of his master's plight), finding the niece and the housekeeper in tears, began to make wry faces and finally burst out crying. After the priest had heard the sick man's confession, he came out saying: "There is no doubt that Alonso Quixano is at the point of death, and there is also no doubt that he is in his entire right mind; so, we should go in and enable him to make his will."

These sad tidings burst open the floodgates of the housekeeper's, the niece's, and the good squire's swollen eyes; their tears flowed fast and furious, and a thousand sighs rose from their breasts, for, indeed, as it has been noted, the sick gentleman, whether as Alonso Quixano the Good or as Don Quixote of La Mancha, had always been so good-natured and so agreeable that he was beloved not only by his family, but by all who knew him.

The notary, with the rest of the company, then went into the sick man's chamber, and Don Quixote stated the preamble to the will, commending his soul to Heaven and including the customary Christian declarations. When he came to the legacies he said:

"Item, I give and bequeath to Sancho Panza, whom in my madness I made my squire, whatever money he has of mine in his possession; and whereas there are accounts and reckonings to be settled between us for what he has received and disbursed, my will and pleasure is that he should not be required to furnish any account of such sums, and whatever may remain due to me, which must be but little, be enjoyed by him as my free gift, and may he prosper with it. And as when I was mad, he was through my means made governor of an island, I would now, in my right senses, give him the government of a kingdom, were it in my power, for his honesty and his faithfulness deserve it.

"And now, my friend," said he, turning to Sancho, "forgive me for making you appear as mad as I was myself, and for drawing you into my errors and persuading you that there have been and still are knights-errant in the world."

"Woe is me!" cried Sancho all in tears. "Don't die on me; but take my advice and live on for many a year; the maddest trick a man can play in his life is to yield up the ghost without more ado, and without being knocked on the head or stabbed through the belly to mope away and die of the doldrums. Shame on you, master; don't let the grass grow under your feet. Up with you this instant, out of your bed, and let us put on our shepherd's clothing and off with us to the fields as we had resolved a while back. Who knows but we may find Lady Dulcinea behind a hedge, disenchanted and as fresh as a daisy. If it's your defeat that is tearing your heart, lay the blame on me and say that it was my fault in not tightening Rozinante's girths enough, and that was why you were unhorsed. You must remember, too, sir, from your books on knight-errantry how common it was for knights to jostle one another out of the saddle, and he who's lying low today may be crowning his victory tomorrow."

"Just so," said Sansón; "there is good sense in what honest Sancho says."

"Go softly, I pray you, gentlemen," replied Don Quixote; "one should never look for birds of this year in the nests of yesteryear. I was mad, but I am now in my senses; I was once Don Quixote of La Mancha, but I am now, as I said before, Alonso Quixano the Good, and I hope that my repentance and my sincere words may restore me to the same esteem as you had for me before. So now proceed, Mr. Notary.

"Item, I declare and appoint Antonia Quixano, my niece, here present, sole heiress of all my estate, both real and personal, after all my just debts and legacies have been paid and deducted out of my goods and chattels; and the first charges on the estate shall be salaries due to my housekeeper, together with twenty ducats over and above her salary wages, which I leave and bequeath her to buy a gown.

"Item, I appoint the curate and the bachelor Sansón Carrasco, here present, to be the executors of this my last will and testament.

"Item, it is my will that if my niece Antonia Quixano should wish to marry, it will be with none but a person who, upon strict investigation, shall be found never to have read a book of knight-errantry in his life; but if it should be ascertained that he is acquainted with such books and she still insists on marrying him, she is then to lose all rights to my bequest, which my executors may then distribute in charity as they think fit.

"Item, I entreat the said executors that if at any time they happen to meet with the author of a certain book entitled *The Second Part of the Exploits of Don Quixote of La Mancha*, they will in my name most heartily beg his pardon for my having been unwittingly the cause of his writing such an amount of folly and triviality as he has done. Indeed, as I depart from this life my conscience troubles me that ever I was the cause of his publishing such a book."

After finishing the will, he swooned away and stretched his body to its full length in the bed. The company were alarmed and ran to his assistance; but these fainting attacks were repeated with great frequency during the three days that he lived after he had made his will. The household was in grief and confusion; and yet, after all, the niece continued to eat her meals, the housekeeper drowned her sorrows in wine, and Sancho Panza puffed himself up with satisfaction, for the thought of a legacy possesses a magic power to remove, or at least to soothe, the pangs that the heir should otherwise feel for the death of his friend.

At length Don Quixote's last day came, after he had received all the sacraments and expressed his abhorrence of books of knight-errantry. The notary, who was present, said that he had never read of any knight who ever died in his bed so peacefully and like a good Christian as Don Quixote. And so, amid the tears and lamentations of his friends, who knelt by his bedside, he gave up the ghost, that is to say, he died. And when the priest saw that he had passed away, he bade the notary give him a certificate stating that Alonso Quixano the Good, commonly known as Don Quixote of La Mancha, had died a natural death. This he desired lest any other author, except Cide Hamete Benengeli, take the opportunity of raising him from the dead and presume to write endless histories of his pretended adventures.

Such was the death of that imaginative gentleman Don Quixote of La Mancha, whose native place Cide Hamete did not wish to ascertain, with the intention that all the towns and villages in La Mancha should vie with one another for the honor of having given him birth, as the seven cities of Greece did for Homer. We shall omit the lamentations of Sancho and those of the niece and the housekeeper, as well as the epitaphs that were composed for his tomb, and we shall only quote the following, which the bachelor Sansón Carrasco inscribed on it:

> Here lies the noble fearless knight,
> Whose valor rose to such a height;
> When Death at last did strike him down,
> His was the victory and renown.
> He reck'd the world of little prize,
> And was a bugbear in men's eyes;
> But had the fortune in his age
> To live a fool and die a sage.[72]

And said the most prudent Cide Hamete to his pen: "Here you shall rest, hanging from this rack by this copper wire, my quill. Whether you are well cut or badly pointed here you shall live long ages, unless presumptuous and unworthy historians take you down to profane you. But before they touch you, warn them in as strong terms as you are able:

> Beware, beware, all petty knaves,
> I may be touched by none:
> This enterprise, my worthy king,
> Is kept for me alone.[73]

For me alone Don Quixote was born, and I for him. He knew how to act, and I knew how to write. We two alone are as one, despite that fictitious and Tordesillescan scribe who has dared, and may dare again with his coarse and ill-trimmed ostrich quill, to write the exploits of my valorous knight.[74] This is no burden for his shoulders, no subject for his frost-bound muse; and should you by chance get to know him, do warn him to let Don Quixote's weary and moldering bones rest in the grave, and not seek, against all canons of death, to carry him off to Old Castile, compelling him to leave the tomb where he really and truly lies stretched out full

---

[72] Samuel Putnam points out that these lines are "a doggerel imitation of the epitaphs composed by village poets."

[73] A quotation from an old ballad.

[74] Another attack on the "false Quixote," whose author was reputedly from Tordesillas.

length, powerless to make a third expedition[75] and new sally. Surely his
two, which have met with approval and have delighted all the people who
knew about them, both here and abroad, are enough to make a mockery of
all the innumerable sallies undertaken by all the countless knights-errant.
Thus you will comply with your Christian profession by offering good advice to one who wishes you ill, and I shall be proud to be the first author
who ever enjoyed witnessing the full effect of his writing. For my sole aim
has been to arouse men's scorn for the false and absurd stories of knight-
errantry, whose prestige has been shaken by this tale of my true Don Quixote, and which will, without any doubt, soon crumble in ruin. Vale."[76]

[75] This should be "fourth expedition." Don Quixote had three expeditions, one alone and
two with Sancho.
[76] Farewell.

William Shakespeare
(1564–1616)

*Shakespeare's plays and poems, taken together, have a quality of impersonality, or
suprapersonality, transcending the limitations and biases that one normally finds in
a single author. If we try to understand Shakespeare through his works, he is everything and everyone. Each of his plays is its own place, with a distinctive mood,
method, and thematic emphasis; collectively, they define a mind and a sensibility that
seem nearly as inclusive as the world itself. It is appropriate, then, if also tantalizing,
that we know so little about the inner workings of the mind of Shakespeare as an
individual and artist. Nineteenth-century critical tradition tended to find autobiographical revelations in the plays and some of the poems (especially the Sonnets),
and modern psychoanalytic criticism finds in them revelations of Shakespeare's unconscious mind, but all the hard facts we have about him are impersonal or external:
records of law and vital statistics, annals of the Elizabethan and Jacobean stage, and
references to him by contemporary authors and playgoers.*

*Shakespeare was born in the town of Stratford, in the geographical heart of
England, in April, 1564. His father was a tradesman and prominent member of the
town government, his mother a descendant of a very old family. Although he did not
go to a university, he got a good education at the Stratford grammar school, especially in the Latin classics. (Ovid seems to have been one of his favorite authors.) In
1582 he married Anne Hathaway, by whom he had two daughters and a son who
died in boyhood. How and where Shakespeare spent his early twenties is obscure; by
1590 or so, however, he was active in the London theater. During the next decade he
became highly popular as a playwright and poet (among his nondramatic works are
Venus and Adonis, The Rape of Lucrece, and the famous Sonnets), apparently making a good living and also acquiring influential friends. In 1596, almost
certainly through Shakespeare's efforts, his family was granted a coat of arms. By*

1612 or so, when he stopped writing, he had composed more than three dozen plays. He died on April 23, 1616—very nearly on the same day Cervantes died.

Shakespeare wrote his plays for performance; he had little or no interest in having them printed and published. A reading audience for plays did exist, however, and many of Shakespeare's were in fact published during his lifetime—some in good versions, others in very poor ones. In 1623, seven years after Shakespeare died, the "First Folio," a comprehensive collection of almost all his plays, was issued under the supervision of two members of Shakespeare's old company. The Folio contains, among other tributes, a famous one by the eminent contemporary poet and playwright Ben Jonson. Not a man to bestow praise lightly, Jonson rated Shakespeare above all his contemporary dramatists. His true peers, according to Jonson, were Aeschylus, Sophocles, and Euripides; in comedy, Jonson asserted, Shakespeare was peerless. This tribute has proved to be an accurate prophecy of Shakespeare's reputation in later ages.

*Beginning with the First Folio, it has been customary to divide Shakespeare's plays into three categories: tragedies, comedies, and histories. But these labels are inadequate; Shakespeare's plays are typically blends of different tones and genres. Certain of the histories (*Richard the Second, *for example) can accurately be called tragedies. The comedies are of several different kinds; the early* Comedy of Errors *and* Taming of the Shrew *are mainly farcical;* A Midsummer Night's Dream *combines farce with lyrical fantasy; the "romantic" comedies of Shakespeare's middle period (including* As You Like It *and* Twelfth Night*) are warmly exuberant works that place fairly realistic characters in never-never-land settings; the "dark" comedies like* Measure for Measure *include some disturbing, uncomic elements; the late* Winter's Tale *and* Tempest *treat serious themes but with a disregard for realism that has earned for them the name romances. Some of the tragedies mingle comic episodes with their prevalent high seriousness (as in* Romeo *and* Juliet *and* Macbeth*), and several are based on history, especially that of ancient Rome (*Julius Caesar, Antony and Cleopatra, Coriolanus*).*

To enumerate briefly the qualities that make Shakespeare great is impossible, since the individual plays and poems are so different from one another. Every age from Shakespeare's time to the present has found something different in him to admire. All ages, however, have recognized his supreme skill in inventing sharply etched characters; it frequently happens that long after one has forgotten the exact story of a play one remembers its people with absolute vividness. It is true, paradoxically, that many of Shakespeare's characters represent universal types; Romeo's name has become a synonym for the fervent young lover, and the adjective Falstaffian *has entered the common vocabulary of English as an epithet for robust, expansive heartiness. But none of Shakespeare's characters is merely a type. Scores of them are fully realized persons, absolutely individualized new creations even when they are adapted from earlier sources. (Few of Shakespeare's stories were wholly invented by him.) More than anything else, it is his power to create such characters that has prompted extravagant praise of Shakespeare's "godlike" genius. Some critics, in fact, have speculated about the characters, even those Shakespeare wholly invented, almost as though they had a real existence outside of the plays. Such excesses, odd as they may seem, are understandable, for the characters do seem to speak and act as of their own volition, with the combination of inevitability and unpredictability that one finds in living human beings.*

The power to create characters and tell compelling stories underlies one tradi-

tional view of Shakespeare: that his plays are children of "nature" rather than of "art." That view of him no longer has much currency. Both in their total conception and in their craftsmanship, most Shakespearean plays are both powerful and skillfully controlled. He is expert in managing plot-lines and is particularly fond of double-plotting. King Lear *is an excellent example. The Gloucester plot is in intricate parallel and contrast with the story of the king's education in suffering, with the result that the theme has a breadth and universality it might not otherwise have.*

Perhaps the ultimate reason for Shakespeare's power is simply his mastery of language as an expressive and poetic medium. The many pages given to Shakespeare in dictionaries of quotations attest the beauty and memorability of his words. But such excerpting, which removes Shakespeare's lines from their dramatic context, also does him a disservice, suggesting as it does that he was a gnomic philosopher at large. The well known lines from Hamlet *"To thine own self be true, / And it must follow, as the night the day, / Thou canst not then be false to any man" have been quoted countless times without an awareness that in the play they illustrate a pompous old man's self-importance. The true measure of Shakespeare's language is its effectiveness in the play where it occurs; much of Shakespeare's artistry lies in his skill in giving different characters different poetic imaginations and voices. Moreover, the quality of a play's language—plain or ornate, ceremonial or colloquial, quiet or declamatory, direct or fraught with images and figures of speech—is intimately wedded to the governing themes and distinctive atmospheres. Whether the plays generated their linguistic texture or the other way around is a difficult question. Whatever the answer, it remains true that language—prose or verse—is the principal shaping force of Shakespearean drama.*

No one play can represent adequately Shakespeare's many facets, but for many people, especially in the twentieth century, King Lear *is his most powerful, disturbing, and sublime work. Its setting is a virtually prehistoric darkness (despite the medieval tone of the scene in which Edgar challenges Edmund)—an apt background for the play's ferocity, its pain, and its questionings of providence. The play is so disturbing that for a long time after it was created it was performed with a rewritten ending in which Cordelia survives to marry Edgar. In our own time, the play has come into its own, perhaps because it explores so unflinchingly the existential question of man's difficult search for meaning in a moral and natural world where agony and injustice seem to reign. The play's moral vision is very complex and has stirred controversy, especially over Shakespeare's implied answer to the problem of evil—if, indeed, he does suggest an answer. In theme and atmosphere—for example, the inscrutable mystery with which the cosmos seems to be governed—*Lear *invites comparison with ancient Greek tragedy. (The play refers continually to "the gods" rather than "God.") The parallel with Sophocles is especially compelling. In its theme of poetic justice, its story of filial and sibling relationships, its atmosphere of suffering, its tentative gropings toward positive affirmation, its imagery (of blindness, for example),* King Lear *has striking affinities with the Oedipus plays and with* Antigone.

NOTE ON SHAKESPEARE'S STAGE

The public theaters of Shakespeare's day were modeled architecturally on inn-yards, where, a generation or so earlier, plays had commonly been presented by itinerant troupes of actors. The theaters were large three-story structures, round, square, or

A reconstruction of the Fortune Theater by Walter H. Godfrey. (From Shake-speare's Theatre *by Ashley H. Thorndike.)*

multi-sided in shape, surrounding an open-air arena. *Three sides of the theater consisted of galleries, facing inward toward the arena. From the fourth side, a large platform stage, about five feet high, perhaps forty feet deep and twenty-five feet wide, projected into the arena; around it stood those spectators ("groundlings") who paid the lowest price of admission. At the back of this stage were two doors and a curtained alcove used for "discovery" scenes. There was some sort of acting space on the second level, as well, perhaps another curtained alcove and perhaps a projecting balcony, supported by posts rising from the main stage. There may have been a third level as well, occasionally used by actors but intended primarily for musicians. To avoid harassment by the Puritanically-minded London government, the theaters were built outside the city limits, especially on the south bank of the Thames. A theater could accommodate about two thousand people, drawn from every social level from the laboring class through the titled aristocracy.*

As in ancient Greek drama, spectacle was important on Shakespeare's stage. Costumes were elaborate, and the style of acting was emphatic and declamatory. All the actors were male; the female roles were played by boys. There was little or no scenery, and action flowed continuously without scene or act divisions. Because the plays were performed in the afternoon, under the sky, settings like the storm in King Lear *or night scenes had to be evoked by the play's language; the imagination of the audience thus played a crucial part, as in modern radio drama.*

Shakespeare's theater was literally what a modern director and critic has called "the empty space," to be filled by the playwright's, the actors', and the audience's imaginations. The Greek skene *building and* orchestra *were well suited for plays that took place "before the palace" and dramatized the public lives of scapegoat-*

kings. The neutral, fluid space of the Elizabethan stage was ideally suited to drama calling for the free movement of the imagination. The line between illusion and reality, nebulous in any kind of theater, was especially so in Shakespeare's, and his plays are full of scenes that question what is "real," as in King Lear, *Act IV, scene vi, in which the blind Gloucester thinks he is on the top of a cliff. Edgar knows he is "really" in a flat field, while we see that the field is as imaginary as the cliff and that he is really on a wooden stage.*

FURTHER READING *(prepared by W. J. R.):* S. Schoenbaum's *William Shakespeare: A Compact Documentary Life,* 1977, a revision of an earlier biography, discusses the major stages of Shakespeare's life and the contemporary theatrical world. For a handsome biography, full of color photographs, see Anthony Burgess's *Shakespeare,* 1970. Two fine introductions to Shakespearean criticism are *The New Century Shakespeare Handbook,* ed. Sandra Clark, 1974, and Stanley Wells' *Shakespeare: The Writer and His Work,* 1978. Clark's work contains a brief biographical sketch, notes on productions of Shakespeare's work in his own time, and numerous photographs of modern productions. Wells discusses Shakespeare's England and his theater and provides an overview of Shakespearean criticism. On Shakespeare's great tragedies, A. C. Bradley's *Shakespearean Tragedy,* 1904, is still valuable and readable. This work, which greatly influenced interpretations of the tragedies, studies *Hamlet, Othello, King Lear,* and *Macbeth.* On the history plays, see E. M. W. Tillyard's *Shakespeare's History Plays,* 1944, which discusses each of the histories individually. F. P. Wilson's *Shakespearian and Other Studies,* ed. Helen Gardner, 1969, considers the history plays, the comedies, Shakespeare's diction, and other topics. An overview of criticism is provided in *Shakespeare and His Critics,* ed. F. E. Halliday, 1947, revised 1957, which contains commentary on all the first folio plays and the minor poems. Two fine works on staging and related topics are Cécile de Banke's *Shakespearean Stage Production, Then and Now,* 1953, and S. Schoenbaum's *Shakespeare: The Globe and the World,* 1979. Banke's work is a detailed study of staging, acting, costuming, and other aspects of production relevant for the modern amateur producer of Shakespeare. Schoenbaum's work is filled with color photographs, drawings, and diagrams; modern productions of Shakespeare, including film adaptations, are also treated.

KING LEAR

Footnotes by Oscar James Campbell

DRAMATIS PERSONAE

LEAR, *king of Britain.*
KING OF FRANCE.
DUKE OF BURGUNDY.
DUKE OF CORNWALL.
DUKE OF ALBANY.
EARL OF KENT.
EARL OF GLOUCESTER.
EDGAR, *son to Gloucester.*
EDMUND, *bastard son to Gloucester.*
CURAN, *a courtier.*
OLD MAN, *tenant to Gloucester.*
DOCTOR.
FOOL.

OSWALD, *steward to Goneril.*
A CAPTAIN *employed by Edmund.*
GENTLEMAN *attendant on Cordelia.*
A HERALD.
SERVANTS *to Cornwall.*
GONERIL,
REGAN,   *daughters to Lear.*
CORDELIA,
KNIGHTS *of Lear's train,* CAPTAINS,
    MESSENGERS, SOLDIERS, *and*
    ATTENDANTS.

SCENE: *Britain.*

ACT I

SCENE I
KING LEAR'S *palace*

[*Enter* KENT, GLOUCESTER, *and* EDMUND.]
KENT. I thought the king had more affected[1] the Duke of Albany[2]
  than Cornwall.
GLOU. It did always seem so to us: but now, in the division of the
  kingdom, it appears not which of the dukes he values most; for
  equalities are so weighed,[3] that curiosity in neither can make
  choice of either's moiety.[4]
KENT. Is not this your son, my lord?
GLOU. His breeding, sir, hath been at my charge:[5] I have so often
  blushed to acknowledge him, that now I am brazed[6] to it.
KENT. I cannot conceive[7] you.   10
GLOU. Sir, this young fellow's mother could: whereupon she grew
  round-wombed, and had, indeed, sir, a son for her cradle ere she
  had a husband for her bed. Do you smell a fault?
KENT. I cannot wish the fault undone, the issue of it being so proper.[8]
GLOU. But I have, sir, a son by order of law,[9] some year[10] elder than

---

[1] Favored.   [2] An old name for Scotland.
[3] **equalities . . . weighed,** shares are so (evenly) balanced.
[4] **curiosity . . . moiety,** careful examination cannot decide which portion (moiety) is to be
preferred.
[5] Expense.   [6] Hardened.   [7] Understand.   [8] Handsome.   [9] **by . . . law,** legally.
[10] About a year.

this, who yet is no dearer in my account: though this knave came something[11] saucily into the world before he was sent for, yet was his mother fair; there was good sport at his making, and the whoreson[12] must be acknowledged. Do you know this noble gentleman, Edmund?   20

EDM. No, my lord.

GLOU. My lord of Kent: remember him hereafter as my honourable friend.

EDM. My services to your lordship.

KENT. I must love you, and sue to know you better.

EDM. Sir, I shall study deserving.[13]

GLOU. He hath been out[14] nine years, and away he shall again. The king is coming.

> [*Sennet.*[15] *Enter* KING LEAR, CORN-
> WALL, ALBANY, GONERIL, REGAN,
> CORDELIA, *and* ATTENDANTS.]

LEAR. Attend the lords of France and Burgundy, Gloucester.

GLOU. I shall, my liege.   30

> [*Exeunt* GLOUCESTER *and* ED-
> MUND.]

LEAR. Meantime we shall express our darker[16] purpose.
　　　Give me the map there. Know that we have divided
　　　In three our kingdom: and 'tis our fast intent[17]
　　　To shake all cares and business from our age;
　　　Conferring them on younger strengths, while we
　　　Unburthen'd crawl toward death. Our son of Cornwall,
　　　And you, our no less loving son of Albany,
　　　We have this hour a constant[18] will to publish[19]
　　　Our daughters' several dowers, that future strife
　　　May be prevented[20] now. The princes, France[21] and Bur-
　　　　　gundy,[22]   40
　　　Great rivals in our youngest daughter's love,
　　　Long in our court have made their amorous sojourn,
　　　And here are to be answer'd. Tell me, my daughters,—
　　　Since now we will divest us, both of rule,
　　　Interest of[23] territory, cares of state,—
　　　Which of you shall we say doth love us most?
　　　That we our largest bounty may extend
　　　Where nature doth with merit challenge.[24] Goneril,
　　　Our eldest-born, speak first.

GON. Sir, I love you more than words can wield the matter;[25]   50

---

[11] Somewhat.　　[12] Lit., son of a whore, hence bastard.　　[13] To deserve your favor.
[14] Out of England, abroad.　　[15] A series of notes sounded on a trumpet.
[16] More secret.　　[17] Firm purpose.　　[18] Firm.　　[19] Make known.　　[20] Forestalled.
[21] King of France.　　[22] Duke of Burgundy.　　[23] Claim to.
[24] **Where . . . challenge,** where your merit and my natural affection lay equal claim (to my generosity).
[25] **wield the matter,** serve to express the fact.

Dearer than eye-sight, space,[26] and liberty;[27]
Beyond what can be valued, rich or rare;
No less than life, with grace,[28] health, beauty, honour;
As much as child e'er loved, or father found;[29]
A love that makes breath poor, and speech unable;
Beyond all manner of so much[30] I love you.

COR. [*Aside*] What shall Cordelia do? Love, and be silent.

LEAR. Of all these bounds, even from this line to this,
With shadowy forests and with champains rich'd,[31]
With plenteous rivers and wide-skirted meads,　　　　　　60
We make thee lady: to thine and Albany's issue
Be this perpetual. What says our second daughter,
Our dearest Regan, wife to Cornwall? Speak.

REG. Sir, I am made
Of the self-same metal that my sister is,
And prize me at her worth.[32] In my true heart
I find she names my very deed of love;[33]
Only she comes too short: that[34] I profess
Myself an enemy to all other joys,
Which the most precious square of sense possesses;[35]　　　70
And find I am alone felicitate[36]
In your dear highness' love.[37]

COR.　　　　　　　　　　　　　[*Aside*] Then poor Cordelia!
And yet not so; since, I am sure, my love's
More richer than my tongue.[38]

LEAR. To thee and thine hereditary ever
Remain this ample third of our fair kingdom;
No less in space, validity,[39] and pleasure,
Than that conferr'd on Goneril. Now, our joy,
Although the last, not least; to whose young love
The vines of France and milk[40] of Burgundy　　　　　　80
Strive to be interess'd;[41] what can you say to draw
A third more opulent than your sisters? Speak.

COR. Nothing, my lord.

LEAR. Nothing!

COR. Nothing.

LEAR. Nothing will come of nothing: speak again.

COR. Unhappy that I am, I cannot heave
My heart into my mouth. I love your majesty
According to my bond;[42] nor more nor less.

LEAR. How, how, Cordelia! mend your speech a little,　　90
Lest it may mar your fortunes.

---

[26] Freedom from imprisonment.　　[27] Liberty of action.　　[28] Favor.
[29] **found,** i.e., in a child's love.　　[30] **all . . . much,** every sort of similar comparison.
[31] Enriched with fertile fields.
[32] **And . . . worth,** and estimate my value to be the same as hers.
[33] **very . . . love,** my love as it actually is.　　[34] In that.
[35] **Which . . . possesses,** which the most delicate test of feeling takes for joys.
[36] Made happy.　　[37] Love of your dear highness.
[38] **More . . . tongue,** i.e., greater than I can express in words.　　[39] Value.　　[40] Pastures.
[41] **to be interess'd,** to have a right in.　　[42] Obligation (as a daughter).

COR.   Good my lord,
    You have begot me, bred me, loved me: I
    Return those duties back as are right fit,[43]
    Obey you, love you, and most honour you.
    Why have my sisters husbands, if they say
    They love you all?[44] Haply, when I shall wed,
    That lord whose hand must take my plight[45] shall carry
    Half my love with him, half my care and duty:
    Sure, I shall never marry like my sisters,
    To love my father all.   100
LEAR. But goes thy heart with this?
COR.   Ay, good my lord.
LEAR. So young, and so untender?
COR. So young, my lord, and true.
LEAR. Let it be so; thy truth, then, be thy dower.
    For, by the sacred radiance of the sun,
    The mysteries[46] of Hecate,[47] and the night;
    By all the operation[48] of the orbs[49]
    From whom we do exist, and cease to be;
    Here I disclaim all my paternal care,
    Propinquity and property[50] of blood,   110
    And as a stranger to my heart and me
    Hold thee, from this, for ever. The barbarous Scythian,[51]
    Or he that makes his generation messes[52]
    To gorge his appetite, shall to my bosom
    Be as well neighbour'd, pitied, and relieved,
    As thou my sometime daughter.
KENT.   Good my liege,—
LEAR. Peace, Kent!
    Come not between the dragon[53] and his wrath.[54]
    I loved her most, and thought to set my rest[55]
    On her kind nursery.[56] Hence, and avoid[57] my sight!   120
    So be my grave my peace, as here I give
    Her father's heart from her! Call France; who stirs?
    Call Burgundy. Cornwall and Albany,
    With my two daughters' dowers digest[58] this third:
    Let pride, which she calls plainness,[59] marry her.
    I do invest you jointly with my power,
    Pre-eminence, and all the large effects[60]
    That troop with[61] majesty. Ourself, by monthly course,
    With reservation of an hundred knights,

---

[43] **as . . . fit,** which are most fitting (for a daughter).
[44] **They . . . all,** i.e., give you all their love.   [45] Pledge.   [46] Secret religious rites.
[47] Goddess of the lower world, of witchcraft and of magic.   [48] Influence.
[49] Stars.   [50] Identity.
[51] Inhabitant of Southern Russia, since classical times regarded as complete barbarians.
[52] **makes . . . messes,** makes food of his children.   [53] i.e., his crest.
[54] Object of his wrath.   [55] **set my rest,** rely entirely.   [56] Nursing.   [57] Leave.
[58] Assimilate, combine.   [59] Frankness.   [60] Lavish manifestations.
[61] March in company with.

By you to be sustain'd, shall our abode 130
Make with you by due turns. Only we still retain
The name, and all the additions[62] to a king;
The sway, revenue, execution of the rest,[63]
Belovèd sons, be yours: which to confirm,
This coronet part betwixt you.
                       [Giving the crown.]

KENT.   Royal Lear,
Whom I have ever honour'd as my king,
Loved as my father, as my master follow'd,
As my great patron thought on in my prayers,—

LEAR. The bow is bent and drawn, make from the shaft.[64]

KENT. Let it fall[65] rather, though the fork[66] invade 140
The region of my heart: be Kent unmannerly,
When Lear is mad. What wilt thou do, old man?
Think'st thou that duty shall have dread to speak,
When power to flattery bows? To plainness honour's bound,
When majesty stoops to folly. Reverse thy doom;[67]
And, in thy best consideration, check
This hideous rashness: answer my life my judgement,[68]
Thy youngest daughter does not love thee least;
Nor are those empty-hearted whose low sound
Reverbs[69] no hollowness.

LEAR.   Kent, on thy life, no more. 150

KENT. My life I never held but as a pawn
To wage[70] against thy enemies; nor fear to lose it,
Thy safety being the motive.

LEAR.   Out of my sight!

KENT. See better, Lear; and let me still remain
The true blank[71] of thine eye.

LEAR. Now, by Apollo,—

KENT.   Now, by Apollo, king,
Thou swear'st thy gods in vain.

LEAR.   O, vassal! miscreant![72]
                   [Laying his hand on his sword.]

ALB.   ⎫
CORN. ⎬ Dear sir, forbear.

KENT. Do;
Kill thy physician, and the fee bestow 160
Upon thy foul disease. Revoke thy doom;
Or, whilst I can vent clamour from my throat,
I'll tell thee thou dost evil.

LEAR.   Hear me, recreant![73]
On thine allegiance, hear me!

---

[62] Titles.   [63] The rest of my royal prerogatives.
[64] **make . . . shaft,** avoid the arrow (of my anger).   [65] Fly.   [66] Arrowhead.
[67] Judgment (pronounced against Cordelia).
[68] **answer . . . judgement,** I'll stake my life on the correctness of my opinion.
[69] Reverberates with.   [70] Stake.   [71] White center of a target.   [72] Vile wretch.
[73] Breaker of your oath (of allegiance to me).

Since thou hast sought to make us break our vow,
Which we durst never yet, and with strain'd[74] pride
To come between our sentence and our power,
Which nor our nature nor our place can bear,
Our potency[75] made good,[76] take thy reward.
Five days we do allot thee, for provision[77]   170
To shield thee from diseases[78] of the world;
And on the sixth to turn thy hated back
Upon our kingdom: if, on the tenth day following,
Thy banish'd trunk be found in our dominions,
The moment is thy death. Away! by Jupiter,
This shall not be revoked.

KENT. Fare thee well, king: sith[79] thus thou wilt appear,
Freedom lives hence, and banishment is here.
[*To* CORDELIA] The gods to their dear shelter take thee, maid,
That justly think'st, and hast most rightly said!   180
[*To* REGAN *and* GONERIL] And your large speeches may your
      deeds approve,[80]
That good effects may spring from words of love.
Thus Kent, O princes, bids you all adieu;
He'll shape his old course[81] in a country new.
                                  [*Exit.*]

                                  [*Flourish. Re-enter* GLOUCESTER,
                                  with FRANCE, BURGUNDY, *and*
                                  ATTENDANTS.]

GLOU. Here's France and Burgundy, my noble lord.
LEAR. My lord of Burgundy,
We first address towards you, who with this king
Hath rivall'd for our daughter: what, in the least,
Will you require in present dower with her,
Or cease your quest of love?

BUR.   Most royal majesty,   190
I crave no more than what your highness offer'd,
Nor will you tender less.

LEAR.   Right noble Burgundy,
When she was dear to us, we did hold her so;
But now her price is fall'n. Sir, there she stands:
If aught within that little seeming substance,[82]
Or all of it, with our displeasure pieced,
And nothing more, may fitly like[83] your grace,
She's there, and she is yours.

BUR.   I know no answer.
LEAR. Will you, with those infirmities[84] she owes,[85]
Unfriended, new-adopted to our hate,   200

---

[74] Excessive.   [75] Authority.   [76] Effective.   [77] To provide means.
[78] Distresses, pains.   [79] Since.   [80] Justify.   [81] Conduct.
[82] **that . . . substance,** that little person who only seems to be genuine.   [83] Please.
[84] Defects.   [85] Owns.

Dower'd with our curse, and stranger'd with our oath,
Take her, or leave her?

BUR.   Pardon me, royal sir;
Election makes not up on such conditions.[86]

LEAR. Then leave her, sir; for, by the power that made me,
I tell you all her wealth. [*To* FRANCE] For[87] you, great king,
I would not from your love make such a stray,
To match you where I hate; therefore beseech you
To avert your liking[88] a more worthier way
Than on a wretch whom nature is ashamed
Almost to acknowledge hers.

FRANCE.   This is most strange,   210
That she, that even but now was your best object,[89]
The argument[90] of your praise, balm of your age,
Most best, most dearest, should in this trice[91] of time
Commit a thing so monstrous, to[92] dismantle
So many folds of favour. Sure, her offence
Must be of such unnatural degree,
That monsters[93] it, or your fore-vouch'd affection
Fall'n into taint:[94] which to believe of her,
Must be a faith that reason without miracle
Could never plant in me.

COR.   I yet beseech your majesty,—   220
If for[95] I want that glib and oily art,
To speak and purpose not;[96] since what I well intend,
I'll do 't before I speak,—that you make known
It is no vicious blot,[97] murder, or foulness,[98]
No unchaste action, or dishonour'd step,
That hath deprived me of your grace and favour;
But even for want of that for which[99] I am richer,
A still-soliciting[1] eye, and such a tongue
As I am glad I have not, though not to have it
Hath lost me in your liking.[2]

LEAR.   Better thou   230
Hadst not been born than not to have pleased me better.

FRANCE. Is it but this,—a tardiness in nature[3]
Which often leaves the history unspoke
That it intends to do? My lord of Burgundy,
What say you to the lady? Love's not love
When it is mingled with regards that stand
Aloof from the entire point.[4] Will you have her?
She is herself a dowry.

---

[86] **Election . . . conditions,** i.e., choice of wife is not made under such conditions.
[87] As for.   [88] **avert your liking,** turn your affection.
[89] **your best object,** the main object of your love.   [90] Topic.   [91] Instant.   [92] As to.
[93] Makes monstrous.   [94] Decay.   [95] Because.
[96] **purpose not,** not to mean what one says.   [97] Stain made by a vice.
[98] Lack of chastity.   [99] For lack of which.   [1] Ever-begging.
[2] **lost . . . liking,** made me lose your affection.   [3] **tardiness in nature,** natural reticence.
[4] **regards . . . point,** considerations that have nothing to do with the essence of the matter.

Bur.   Royal Lear,
    Give but that portion which yourself proposed,
    And here I take Cordelia by the hand,   240
    Duchess of Burgundy.
Lear. Nothing: I have sworn; I am firm.
Bur. I am sorry, then, you have so lost a father
    That you must lose a husband.
Cor.   Peace be with Burgundy!
    Since that respects[5] of fortune are his love,
    I shall not be his wife.
France. Fairest Cordelia, that art most rich, being poor;
    Most choice, forsaken; and most loved, despised!
    Thee and thy virtues here I seize upon:
    Be it lawful I take up what's cast away.   250
    Gods, gods! 'tis strange that from their cold'st neglect
    My love should kindle to inflamed[6] respect.
    Thy dowerless daughter, king, thrown to my chance,
    Is queen of us, of ours, and our fair France:
    Not all the dukes of waterish[7] Burgundy
    Can buy this unprized[8] precious maid of me.
    Bid them farewell, Cordelia, though unkind:
    Thou losest here, a better where to find.
Lear. Thou hast her, France: let her be thine; for we
    Have no such daughter, nor shall ever see   260
    That face of hers again. Therefore be gone
    Without our grace,[9] our love, our benison.[10]
    Come, noble Burgundy.

                              [*Flourish. Exeunt all but* France,
                              Goneril, Regan, *and* Cordelia.]

France. Bid farewell to your sisters.
Cor. The jewels of our father, with wash'd eyes
    Cordelia leaves you: I know you what you are;
    And like a sister am most loath to call
    Your faults as they are named.[11] Use well our father:
    To your professèd[12] bosoms I commit him:
    But yet, alas, stood I within his grace,   270
    I would prefer[13] him to a better place.
    So, farewell to you both.
Reg. Prescribe not us our duties.
Gon.   Let your study
    Be to content your lord, who hath received you
    At fortune's alms. You have obedience scanted,[14]
    And well are worth the want that you have wanted.[15]

---

[5] Considerations.   [6] Heightened.   [7] Marshy.   [8] Unappreciated.   [9] Favor.
[10] Blessing.   [11] **as . . . named,** by their proper names.
[12] Full of professions (of love).   [13] Recommend.
[14] **At . . . alms,** i.e., when Fortune was giving alms, i.e., petty gifts; **scanted,** grudged.
[15] **And . . . wanted,** and well deserved that lack of affection (from your husband) in which
you have been lacking.

Cor. Time shall unfold what plaited[16] cunning hides:
　　Who cover faults, at last shame them derides.
　　Well may you prosper!
France.　　　　　　　　　　Come, my fair Cordelia.
　　　　　　　　　　[Exeunt France *and* Cordelia.]
Gon. Sister, it is not a little I have to say of what most nearly　　280
　　appertains to us both. I think our father will hence to-night.
Reg. That's most certain, and with you; next month with us.
Gon. You see how full of changes his age is; the observation we have
　　made of it hath not been little: he always loved our sister most; and
　　with what poor judgement he hath now cast her off appears too
　　grossly.[17]
Reg. 'Tis the infirmity of his age: yet he hath ever but slenderly
　　known himself.
Gon. The best and soundest of his time[18] hath been but rash;[19] then
　　must we look to receive from his age, not alone the imperfections　　290
　　of long-engraffed condition,[20] but therewithal[21] the unruly way-
　　wardness that infirm and choleric years bring with them.
Reg. Such unconstant starts[22] are we like[23] to have from him as this
　　of Kent's banishment.
Gon. There is further compliment[24] of leave-taking between France
　　and him. Pray you, let's hit[25] together: if our father carry author-
　　ity with such dispositions as he bears, this last surrender of his will
　　but offend[26] us.
Reg. We shall further think on't.
Gon. We must do something, and i' the heat.[27]　　　　　*[Exeunt.]*　　300

SCENE II
The Earl of Gloucester's *castle*

[Enter Edmund, *with a letter.]*
Edm. Thou, nature, art my goddess; to thy law
　　My services are bound. Wherefore should I
　　Stand in the plague of custom,[1] and permit
　　The curiosity of nations[2] to deprive me,[3]
　　For that I am some twelve or fourteen moonshines
　　Lag of[4] a brother? Why bastard? wherefore base?
　　When my dimensions are as well compact,[5]
　　My mind as generous,[6] and my shape as true,[7]

---

[16] Folded.　　[17] Obviously.　　[18] **The . . . time,** the best and soundest time of his life.
[19] Headlong, hasty.
[20] **long-engraffed condition,** temperament that has long been deeply embedded in his nature.
[21] With it.　　[22] **unconstant starts,** freakish sudden impulses.　　[23] Likely.
[24] Ceremony.　　[25] Agree.　　[26] Injure.　　[27] **i' the heat,** i.e., while the iron is hot.
[1] **Stand . . . custom,** occupy a position in which I suffer from disabilities dictated by mere custom.
[2] **curiosity of nations,** nice distinction of universal law.
[3] **deprive me,** i.e., of my just inheritance.　　[4] Behind.
[5] **dimensions . . . compact,** structure of my body is as well built.　　[6] Noble.
[7] Regular.

As honest[8] madam's issue? Why brand they us
With base? with baseness? bastardy? base, base?   10
Who, in the lusty stealth of nature, take
More composition[9] and fierce quality
Than doth, within a dull, stale, tired bed,
Go to the creating a whole tribe of fops,
Got 'tween asleep and wake? Well, then,
Legitimate Edgar, I must have your land:
Our father's love is to the bastard Edmund
As to the legitimate: fine word,—legitimate!
Well, my legitimate, if this letter speed,[10]
And my invention[11] thrive, Edmund the base   20
Shall top the legitimate. I grow; I prosper:
Now, gods, stand up for bastards!

[Enter GLOUCESTER.]

GLOU. Kent banish'd thus! and France in choler parted![12]
    And the king gone to-night! subscribed his power![13]
    Confined to exhibition![14] All this done
    Upon the gad![15] Edmund, how now! what news?
EDM. So please your lordship, none.
[Putting up the letter.]
GLOU. Why so earnestly seek you to put up that letter?
EDM. I know no news, my lord.
GLOU. What paper were you reading?   30
EDM. Nothing, my lord.
GLOU. No? What needed, then, that terrible dispatch of it[16] into your
    pocket? the quality[17] of nothing hath not such need to hide itself.
    Let's see: come, if it be nothing, I shall not need spectacles.
EDM. I beseech you, sir, pardon me:[18] it is a letter from my brother,
    that I have not all o'er-read; and for so much as I have perused, I
    find it not fit for your o'er-looking.
GLOU. Give me the letter, sir.
EDM. I shall offend, either to detain[19] or give it. The contents, as in
    part I understand them, are to blame.[20]   40
GLOU. Let's see, let's see.
EDM. I hope, for my brother's justification, he wrote this but as an
    essay[21] or taste of my virtue.
GLOU. [*Reads*] "This policy and reverence[22] of age makes the world
    bitter to the best of our times;[23] keeps our fortunes from us till our
    oldness cannot relish them. I begin to find an idle and fond bond-
    age[24] in the oppression of aged tyranny; who sways, not as it hath

---

[8] Chaste.   [9] A stronger constitution.   [10] Succeed.   [11] Scheme.   [12] Departed.
[13] **subscribed his power,** his power signed away.   [14] An allowance.
[15] Spur (of the moment).   [16] **terrible . . . it,** frantic haste to put it.   [17] Nature.
[18] Excuse my not sharing it with you.   [19] Withhold.   [20] Blameworthy.   [21] Trial.
[22] **policy and reverence,** established convention of revering the old.
[23] **best of our times,** best part of our life.
[24] **idle . . . bondage,** a useless and foolish servitude.

power, but as it is suffered.[25] Come to me, that of this I may speak
more. If our father would sleep till I waked him, you should enjoy
half his revenue for ever, and live the beloved of your brother,   50
                                                                    "EDGAR."

Hum—conspiracy!—"Sleep till I waked him,—you should enjoy
half his revenue,"—My son Edgar! Had he a hand to write this? a
heart and brain to breed it in?—When came this to you? who
brought it?

EDM. It was not brought me, my lord; there's the cunning of it; I
found it thrown in at the casement of my closet.[26]

GLOU. You know the character[27] to be your brother's?

EDM. If the matter[28] were good, my lord, I durst swear it were his;
but, in respect of[29] that, I would fain think it were not.   60

GLOU. It is his.

EDM. It is his hand, my lord; but I hope his heart is not in the contents.

GLOU. Hath he never heretofore sounded you in this business?

EDM. Never, my lord: but I have heard him oft maintain it to be fit,
that, sons at perfect age,[30] and fathers declining,[31] the father
should be as ward to the son, and the son manage his revenue.

GLOU. O villain, villain! His very opinion in the letter! Abhorred villain! Unnatural, detested, brutish villain! worse than brutish! Go,
sirrah, seek him; I'll apprehend him: abominable villain! Where   70
is he?

EDM. I do not well know, my lord. If it shall please you to suspend
your indignation against my brother till you can derive from him
better testimony of his intent, you shall run a certain course;
where,[32] if you violently proceed against him, mistaking his purpose, it would make a great gap in your own honour, and shake in
pieces the heart of his obedience. I dare pawn down my life for
him, that he hath wrote this to feel my affection[33] to your honour,
and to no further pretence of danger.[34]

GLOU. Think you so?   80

EDM. If your honour judge it meet, I will place you where you shall
hear us confer of this, and by an auricular assurance have your
satisfaction; and that without any further delay than this very evening.

GLOU. He cannot be such a monster—

EDM. Nor is not, sure.

GLOU. To his father, that so tenderly and entirely loves him. Heaven
and earth! Edmund, seek him out; wind me into him,[35] I pray
you: frame the business after your own wisdom. I would unstate
myself,[36] to be in a due resolution.[37]   90

---

[25] **who . . . suffered,** which prevails not by virtue of its power, but as a result of our submission.
[26] Private room.   [27] Handwriting.   [28] Subject matter.   [29] Regard to.
[30] Full maturity.   [31] Growing old.   [32] Whereas.
[33] **feel my affection,** test my feeling.   [34] **pretence of danger,** dangerous intention.
[35] **wind . . . him,** worm your way into his confidence for my sake.
[36] **unstate myself,** surrender the privileges of my rank.
[37] **due resolution,** proper certainty.

EDM. I will seek him, sir, presently;[38] convey[39] the business as I shall
find means, and acquaint you withal.

GLOU. These late eclipses in the sun and moon portend no good to
us: though the wisdom of nature[40] can reason it thus and thus, yet
nature finds itself scourged by the sequent effects:[41] love cools,
friendship falls off, brothers divide: in cities, mutinies;[42] in countries, discord; in palaces, treason; and the bond cracked 'twixt son
and father. This villain of mine comes under the prediction;
there's son against father: the king falls from bias[43] of nature;
there's father against child. We have seen the best of our time: 100
machinations, hollowness, treachery, and all ruinous disorders,
follow us disquietly to our graves. Find out this villain, Edmund; it
shall lose thee nothing; do it carefully. And the noble and true-
hearted Kent banished! his offence, honesty! 'Tis strange.

[Exit.]

EDM. This is the excellent foppery[44] of the world, that, when we are
sick in fortune,—often the surfeit[45] of our own behaviour,—we
make guilty of our disasters the sun, the moon, and the stars: as if
we were villains by necessity; fools by heavenly compulsion;
knaves, thieves, and treachers,[46] by spherical predominance;[47]
drunkards, liars, and adulterers, by an enforced obedience of   110
planetary influence; and all that we are evil in, by a divine
thrusting on: an admirable evasion of whoremaster man, to lay his
goatish[48] disposition to the charge of a star! My father compounded with[49] my mother under the dragon's tail; and my nativity
was under Ursa major; so that it follows, I am rough and lecherous. Tut, I should have been that I am,[50] had the maidenliest star
in the firmament twinkled on my bastardizing. Edgar—

[Enter EDGAR.]

and pat[51] he comes like the catastrophe of the old comedy: my
cue is villanous melancholy, with a sigh like Tom o' Bedlam.[52] O,
these eclipses do portend these divisions! fa, sol, la, mi.   120

EDG. How now, brother Edmund! what serious contemplation are
you in?

EDM. I am thinking, brother, of a prediction I read this other day,
what should follow these eclipses.

EDG. Do you busy yourself about that?

EDM. I promise you, the effects he writes of succeed[53] unhappily; as
of unnaturalness between the child and the parent; death,

---

[38] At once.   [39] Manage secretly.
[40] **wisdom of nature,** scientific theory.   [41] **sequent effects,** results which follow.
[42] Tumults.   [43] The curve of a bowling ball, hence "tendency."   [44] Foolishness.
[45] Overeating, indigestion.   [46] Traitors.
[47] **spherical predominance,** because of the controlling influence of some planet.
[48] Licentious.   [49] Came to terms with.   [50] **that I am,** what I am.   [51] Opportunely.
[52] Common name of lunatics of Bethlehem Hospital (Bedlam), an insane asylum, who were
sent out to beg.
[53] Follow.

dearth,[54] dissolutions of ancient amities; divisions in state, menaces and maledictions against king and nobles; needless diffi-
dences,[55] banishment of friends, dissipation of cohorts,[56] nuptial   130
breaches, and I know not what.

EDG. How long have you been a sectary astronomical?[57]

EDM. Come, come; when saw you my father last?

EDG. Why, the night gone by.

EDM. Spake you with him?

EDG. Ay, two hours together.

EDM. Parted you in good terms? Found you no displeasure in him by
word or countenance?

EDG. None at all.

EDM. Bethink yourself wherein you may have offended him: and at   140
my entreaty forbear[58] his presence till some little time hath qualified[59] the heat of his displeasure; which at this instant so rageth in
him, that with the mischief of your person[60] it would scarcely allay.

EDG. Some villain hath done me wrong.

EDM. That's my fear. I pray you, have a continent[61] forbearance till
the speed of his rage goes slower; and, as I say, retire with me to
my lodging, from whence I will fitly[62] bring you to hear my lord
speak: pray ye, go; there's my key: if you do stir abroad, go armed.

EDG. Armed, brother!

EDM. Brother, I advise you to the best; go armed: I am no honest   150
man if there be any good meaning towards you: I have told you
what I have seen and heard; but faintly, nothing like the image
and horror[63] of it: pray you, away.

EDG. Shall I hear from you anon?[64]

EDM. I do serve you in this business.

[*Exit* EDGAR.]

A credulous father! and a brother noble,
Whose nature is so far from doing harms,
That he suspects none; on whose foolish honesty
My practices[65] ride easy! I see the business.
Let me, if not by birth, have lands by wit: 160
All with me's meet that I can fashion fit.[66]   [*Exit.*]

SCENE III
The DUKE OF ALBANY'S *palace*

[*Enter* GONERIL, *and* OSWALD, *her steward.*]

GON. Did my father strike my gentleman for chiding of his fool?

OSW. Yes, madam.

---

[54] Famine.   [55] Suspicions.

[56] **dissipation of cohorts,** breaking up of military organizations.

[57] **sectary astronomical,** believer in astrology.   [58] Avoid.   [59] Lessened.

[60] **mischief . . . person,** harm to your body.   [61] Restrained.   [62] Opportunely.

[63] **image and horror,** the horrible truth.   [64] Shortly.   [65] Plots.

[66] **fashion fit,** make fitting by fraudulent management.

GON. By day and night he wrongs me; every hour
    He flashes into one gross crime or other,
    That sets us all at odds: I'll not endure it:
    His knights grow riotous, and himself upbraids us
    On every trifle. When he returns from hunting,
    I will not speak with him; say I am sick:
    If you come slack of former services,
    You shall do well; the fault of it I'll answer.   10
OSW. He's coming, madam; I hear him.
                                    [Horns within.]
GON. Put on what weary negligence you please,
    You and your fellows; I'ld have it come to question:[1]
    If he dislike it, let him to our sister,
    Whose mind and mine, I know, in that are one,
    Not to be over-ruled. Idle[2] old man,
    That still would manage those authorities
    That he hath given away! Now, by my life,
    Old fools are babes again; and must be used[3]
    With checks as[4] flatteries,—when they are seen abused.[5]   20
    Remember what I tell you.
OSW.   Well, madam.
GON. And let his knights have colder looks among you;
    What grows of it, no matter; advise your fellows so:[6]
    I would breed from hence occasions,[7] and I shall
    That I may speak: I'll write straight to my sister,
    To hold my very course. Prepare for dinner.   *[Exeunt.]*

SCENE IV
A hall in the same

[Enter KENT, *disguised.]*
KENT. If but as well I other accents borrow,
    That can my speech defuse,[1] my good intent
    May carry through itself to that full issue
    For which I razed my likeness.[2] Now, banish'd Kent,
    If thou canst serve[3] where thou dost stand condemn'd,
    So may it come, thy master, whom thou lovest,
    Shall find thee full of labours.

                        *[Horns   within.   Enter   *LEAR,
                      KNIGHTS, *and* ATTENDANTS.]

LEAR. Let me not stay a jot for dinner; go get it ready. *[Exit an*
    ATTENDANT.]* How now! what art thou?
KENT. A man, sir.   10
LEAR. What dost thou profess?[4] what wouldst thou with us?

[1] **to question,** i.e., to a showdown.   [2] Foolish.   [3] Managed.   [4] Rebukes as well as.
[5] Deceived.   [6] **advise . . . so,** tell your servants to act the same way.
[7] Opportunities.   [1] Disguise.   [2] **razed my likeness,** erased any likeness to myself.
[3] Act as a servant.   [4] **What . . . profess?** What is your profession?

KENT. I do profess to be no less than I seem; to serve him truly that
will put me in trust; to love him that is honest; to converse[5] with
him that is wise, and says little; to fear judgement; to fight when I
cannot choose;[6] and to eat no fish.[7]

LEAR. What art thou?

KENT. A very honest-hearted fellow, and as poor as the king.

LEAR. If thou be as poor for a subject as he is for a king, thou art poor
enough. What wouldst thou?

KENT. Service.   20

LEAR. Who wouldst thou serve?

KENT. You.

LEAR. Dost thou know me, fellow?

KENT. No, sir; but you have that in your countenance[8] which I would
fain call master.

LEAR. What's that?

KENT. Authority.

LEAR. What services canst thou do?

KENT. I can keep honest counsel,[9] ride, run, mar a curious[10] tale in
telling it, and deliver a plain message bluntly: that which ordinary   30
men are fit for, I am qualified in; and the best of me is diligence.

LEAR. How old art thou?

KENT. Not so young, sir, to love a woman for singing, nor so old to
dote on her for any thing: I have years on my back forty eight.

LEAR. Follow me; thou shalt serve me: if I like thee no worse after
dinner, I will not part from thee yet. Dinner, ho, dinner! Where's
my knave?[11] my fool? Go you, and call my fool hither.

[Exit an ATTENDANT.]

[Enter OSWALD.]

You, you, sirrah, where's my daughter?

OSW. So please you,—   *[Exit.]*

LEAR. What says the fellow there? Call the clotpoll[12] back. [*Exit a*   40
KNIGHT.] Where's my fool, ho? I think the world's asleep.

[Re-enter KNIGHT.]

How now! where's that mongrel?

KNIGHT. He says, my lord, your daughter is not well.

LEAR. Why came not the slave back to me when I called him?

KNIGHT. Sir, he answered me in the roundest[13] manner, he would
not.

LEAR. He would not!

KNIGHT. My lord, I know not what the matter is; but, to my judgement, your highness is not entertained[14] with that ceremonious
affection[15] as you were wont; there's a great abatement of kind-   50

---

[5] Associate.   [6] i.e., help it.
[7] **eat no fish,** i.e., a Protestant and not disloyal like the fish-eating Catholics.
[8] Bearing.   [9] Keep an honorable secret.   [10] Elaborate.   [11] Boy.   [12] Blockhead.
[13] Plainest.   [14] Treated.   [15] The affection which shows itself in formal respect.

ness appears as well in the general dependants[16] as in the duke himself also and your daughter.

LEAR. Ha! sayest thou so?

KNIGHT. I beseech you, pardon me, my lord, if I be mistaken; for my duty cannot be silent when I think your highness wronged.

LEAR. Thou but rememberest[17] me of mine own conception:[18] I have perceived a most faint[19] neglect of late; which I have rather blamed as mine own jealous curiosity[20] than as a very pretence[21] and purpose of unkindness: I will look further into 't. But where's my fool? I have not seen him this two days.   60

KNIGHT. Since my young lady's going into France, sir, the fool hath much pined away.

LEAR. No more of that; I have noted it well. Go you, and tell my daughter I would speak with her. [*Exit* KNIGHT.] Go you, call hither my fool.   [*Exit an* ATTENDANT.]

[*Re-enter* OSWALD.]

O, you sir, you, come you hither, sir: who am I, sir?

OSW. My lady's father.

LEAR. "My lady's father!" My lord's knave: you whoreson dog! you slave! you cur!

OSW. I am none of these, my lord; I beseech your pardon.   70

LEAR. Do you bandy[22] looks with me, you rascal?   [*Striking him.*]

OSW. I'll not be struck, my lord.

KENT. Nor tripped neither, you base football player.
                                                        [*Tripping up his heels.*]

LEAR. I thank thee, fellow; thou servest me, and I'll love thee.

KENT. Come, sir, arise, away! I'll teach you differences:[23] away, away! If you will measure your lubber's[24] length again, tarry: but away! go to; have you wisdom? so.
                                                        [*Pushes* OSWALD *out.*]

LEAR. Now, my friendly knave, I thank thee: there's earnest of[25] thy service.

                                                        [*Giving* KENT *money.*]

                                                        [*Enter* FOOL.]

FOOL. Let me hire him too: here's my coxcomb.   80
                                                        [*Offering* KENT *his cap.*]

LEAR. How now, my pretty knave! how dost thou?

FOOL. Sirrah, you were best[26] take my coxcomb.[27]

KENT. Why, fool?

FOOL. Why, for taking one's part that's out of favour: nay, an[28] thou canst not smile as the wind sits, thou'lt catch cold shortly: there,

---

[16] The house-servants.   [17] Remind.   [18] Idea.   [19] Half-hearted.
[20] **jealous curiosity,** overscrupulous watchfulness (for slights).
[21] **very pretence,** deliberate intention.   [22] Strike a ball back and forth (as in tennis).
[23] Proper distinctions in rank.   [24] Awkward lout's.   [25] Advance payment for.
[26] Had better.
[27] The hood crested with red like a cock's comb, worn by the professional fool.   [28] If.

take my coxcomb: why, this fellow has banished two on 's[29] daughters, and did the third a blessing against his will; if thou follow
him, thou must needs wear my coxcomb. How now, nuncle![30]
Would I had two coxcombs and two daughters!

LEAR. Why, my boy?

FOOL. If I gave them all my living, I'ld keep my coxcombs myself.
There's mine; beg another of thy daughters.

LEAR. Take heed, sirrah; the whip.

FOOL. Truth's a dog must to kennel; he must be whipped out, when
Lady the brach[31] may stand by the fire and stink.

LEAR. A pestilent gall[32] to me!

FOOL. Sirrah, I'll teach thee a speech.

LEAR. Do.

FOOL. Mark it, nuncle:
> Have more than thou showest,
> Speak less than thou knowest,
> Lend less than thou owest,[33]
> Ride more than thou goest,[34]
> Learn more than thou trowest,[35]
> Set[36] less than thou throwest;[37]
> Leave thy drink and thy whore,
> And keep in-a-door,[38]
> And thou shalt have more
> Than two tens to a score.

KENT. This is nothing, fool.

FOOL. Then 'tis like the breath of an unfee'd lawyer; you gave me
nothing for 't. Can you make no use of nothing, nuncle?

LEAR. Why, no, boy; nothing can be made out of nothing.

FOOL. [*To* KENT] Prithee, tell him, so much the rent of his land comes
to: he will not believe a fool.

LEAR. A bitter fool!

FOOL. Dost thou know the difference, my boy, between a bitter fool
and a sweet fool?

LEAR. No, lad; teach me.

FOOL. That lord[39] that counsell'd thee
> To give away thy land,
> Come place him here by me,
> Do thou for him stand:[40]
> The sweet and bitter fool
> Will presently[41] appear;
> The one in motley here,
> The other found out there.

90

100

110

120

---

[29] Of his.   [30] Contraction for "mine uncle."   [31] Bitch, personifying flattery.
[32] **pestilent gall,** annoying irritation.   [33] Ownest.   [34] Walkest.   [35] Knowest.
[36] Stake.   [37] Have a chance to throw, i.e., don't bet your all.
[38] Indoors, i.e., at home.
[39] Perhaps a reference to the Lord Skalligi in the old *King Lear* who suggests the love test.
Nobody in this play gives Lear this stupid advice.
[40] Impersonate him.   [41] Immediately.

LEAR. Dost thou call me fool, boy?

FOOL. All thy other titles thou hast given away; that thou wast born
with.   130

KENT. This is not altogether fool, my lord.

FOOL. No, faith, lords and great men will not let me; if I had a
monopoly[42] out,[43] they would have part on't:[44] and ladies too,
they will not let me have all fool to myself; they'll be snatching.
Give me an egg, nuncle, and I'll give thee two crowns.

LEAR. What two crowns shall they be?

FOOL. Why, after I have cut the egg i' the middle, and eat up the
meat, the two crowns of the egg. When thou clovest thy crown i'
the middle, and gavest away both parts, thou borest thy ass on thy
back o'er the dirt: thou hadst little wit in thy bald crown, when   140
thou gavest thy golden one away. If I speak like myself[45] in this,
let him be whipped that first finds it so.

    [*Singing*] Fools had ne'er less wit in a year;
        For wise men are grown foppish,[46]
    They know not how their wits to wear,
        Their manners are so apish.

LEAR. When were you wont to be so full of songs, sirrah?

FOOL. I have used it,[47] nuncle, ever since thou madest thy daughters
thy mother: for when thou gavest them the rod, and put'st down
thine own breeches,   150

    [*Singing*] Then they for sudden joy did weep,
        And I for sorrow sung,
    That such a king should play bo-peep,[48]
        And go the fools among.

Prithee, nuncle, keep a schoolmaster that can teach thy fool to lie:
I would fain learn to lie.

LEAR. An you lie, sirrah, we'll have you whipped.

FOOL. I marvel what kin thou and thy daughters are: they'll have me
whipped for speaking true, thou'lt have me whipped for lying;
and sometimes I am whipped for holding my peace. I had rather   160
be any kind o' thing than a fool: and yet I would not be thee,
nuncle; thou hast pared thy wit o' both sides, and left nothing i' the
middle: here comes one o' the parings.

[Enter GONERIL.*]*

LEAR. How now, daughter! what makes that frontlet[49] on? Methinks
you are too much of late i' the frown.

FOOL. Thou wast a pretty fellow when thou hadst no need to care for
her frowning; now thou art an O[50] without a figure; I am better

---

    [42] A royal patent granting a monopoly on something.   [43] Granted me.
    [44] **they . . . on't,** the lords who helped him get the monopoly would demand a share in it.
    [45] **like myself,** i.e., outspokenly.
    [46] **Fools . . . foppish,** there is nothing left for fools to do, now that wise men have become
fools (**foppish,** foolish).
    [47] **I . . . it,** it has been my custom.
    [48] **play bo-peep,** be so childish as to play "Hide and Go Seek."
    [49] Band worn on the forehead, here = frown.   [50] Cipher.

than thou art now; I am a fool, thou art nothing. [*To* GON.] Yes,
forsooth, I will hold my tongue; so your face bids me, though you
say nothing. Mum, mum, 170

> He that keeps nor crust nor crum,
> Weary of all, shall want some.

[*Pointing to* LEAR] That's a shealed peas-cod.[51]

GON. Not only, sir, this your all-licensed fool,
But other of your insolent retinue
Do hourly carp[52] and quarrel; breaking forth
In rank and not-to-be-endurèd riots. Sir,
I had thought, by making this well known unto you,
To have found a safe redress; but now grow fearful,
By what yourself too late have spoke and done, 180
That you protect this course, and put it on[53]
By your allowance;[54] which if you should, the fault
Would not 'scape censure, nor the redresses[55] sleep,
Which, in the tender of a wholesome weal,[56]
Might in their working do you that offence,
Which else were shame, that then necessity
Will call discreet proceeding.[57]

FOOL. For, you know, nuncle,
The hedge-sparrow fed the cuckoo[58] so long,
That it had it head bit off by it[59] young. 190
So, out went the candle, and we were left darkling.[60]

LEAR. Are you our daughter?

GON. Come, sir,
I would you would make use of that good wisdom,
Whereof I know you are fraught;[61] and put away
These dispositions, that of late transform you
From what you rightly are.

FOOL. May not an ass know when the cart draws the horse? Whoop,
Jug! I love thee.[62]

LEAR. Doth any here know me? This is not Lear: 200
Doth Lear walk thus? speak thus? Where are his eyes?
Either his notion[63] weakens, his discernings
Are lethargied[64]—Ha! waking?[65] 'tis not so.
Who is it that can tell me who I am?

FOOL. Lear's shadow.

LEAR. I would learn that; for, by the marks of sovereignty, knowledge, and reason, I should be false persuaded I had daughters.

FOOL. Which[66] they will make an obedient father.

---

[51] Shelled pea pod. [52] Find fault. [53] Encourage it. [54] With your approval.
[55] Acts of redress.
[56] **in the tender . . . weal,** in our care to make the commonwealth sound.
[57] **which . . . proceeding,** which would be shameful but which the demands (of the situation) would force one to call prudent action (discreet procedure).
[58] The cuckoo lays its eggs in other birds' nests. [59] **it . . . it,** its . . . its.
[60] In the dark. [61] Stored.
[62] **Whoop, Jug! . . . thee,** the tag of some song. The fool takes refuge in nonsense whenever he suspects that one of his sallies has been too impertinent.
[63] Understanding. [64] Paralyzed. [65] Am I awake? [66] Whom.

LEAR. Your name, fair gentlewoman?
GON. This admiration,[67] sir, is much o' the savour   210
     Of other your new pranks. I do beseech you
     To understand my purposes aright:
     As you are old and reverend, you should be wise.
     Here do you keep a hundred knights and squires;
     Men so disorder'd, so debosh'd[68] and bold,
     That this our court, infected with their manners,
     Shows like a riotous inn: epicurism[69] and lust
     Make it more like a tavern or a brothel
     Than a graced[70] palace. The shame itself doth speak
     For instant remedy: be then desired   220
     By her, that else will take the thing she begs,
     A little to disquantity[71] your train;
     And the remainder, that shall still depend,[72]
     To be such men as may besort[73] your age,
     And know themselves and you.
LEAR.   Darkness and devils!
     Saddle my horses; call my train together.
     Degenerate bastard! I'll not trouble thee:
     Yet have I left a daughter.
GON. You strike my people; and your disorder'd rabble
     Make servants of their betters.   230

                         [*Enter* ALBANY.]

LEAR. Woe, that too late repents,— [*To* ALB.] O, sir, are you come?
     Is it your will? Speak, sir. Prepare my horses.
     Ingratitude, thou marble-hearted fiend,
     More hideous when thou show'st thee in a child
     Than the sea-monster![74]
ALB.   Pray, sir, be patient.[75]
LEAR. [*To* GON.] Detested kite! thou liest:
     My train are men of choice and rarest parts,[76]
     That all particulars of duty know,
     And in the most exact regard support
     The worships of their name.[77] O most small fault,   240
     How ugly didst thou in Cordelia show!
     That, like an engine, wrench'd my frame of nature[78]
     From the fix'd place; drew from my heart all love,
     And added to the gall. O Lear, Lear, Lear!
     Beat at this gate, that let thy folly in,

---

[67] Pretended astonishment.   [68] Debauched.   [69] Unrestrained indulgence.
[70] Honored.   [71] Reduce the numbers of.   [72] Remain as your dependents.
[73] Befit.
[74] (1) Perhaps the hippopotamus, which had a reputation for ingratitude, or (2) any sea
monster of classical mythology.
[75] Exercise self-control.   [76] Accomplishments.
[77] **And . . . name,** And in the smallest details uphold the honorable names they bear.
[78] **like . . . nature,** like a powerful piece of mechanism, dislodged the whole structure of my
nature.

[Striking his head.]
    And thy dear judgement out! Go, go, my people.

ALB. My lord, I am guiltless, as I am ignorant
    Of what hath moved you.

LEAR.   It may be so, my lord.
    Hear, nature, hear; dear goddess, hear!
    Suspend thy purpose, if thou didst intend   250
    To make this creature fruitful!
    Into her womb convey sterility!
    Dry up in her the organs of increase;[79]
    And from her derogate[80] body never spring
    A babe to honour her! If she must teem,[81]
    Create her[82] child of spleen;[83] that it may live,
    And be a thwart[84] disnatured[85] torment to her!
    Let it stamp wrinkles in her brow of youth;
    With cadent[86] tears fret[87] channels in her cheeks;
    Turn all her mother's pains and benefits   260
    To laughter and contempt; that she may feel
    How sharper than a serpent's tooth it is
    To have a thankless child! Away, away!

[Exit.]

ALB. Now, gods that we adore, whereof comes this?

GON. Never afflict yourself to know the cause;
    But let his disposition[88] have that scope
    That dotage gives it.

[Re-enter LEAR.]

LEAR. What, fifty of my followers at a clap!
    Within a fortnight!

ALB.   What's the matter, sir?

LEAR. I'll tell thee: *[To* GON.*]* Life and death! I am ashamed   270
    That thou hast power to shame my manhood thus;
    That these hot tears, which break from me perforce,
    Should make thee worth them. Blasts and fogs[89] upon thee!
    The untented[90] woundings of a father's curse
    Pierce every sense about thee! Old fond[91] eyes,
    Beweep this cause again, I'll pluck ye out,
    And cast you, with the waters that you lose,
    To temper[92] clay. Yea, is it come to this?
    Let it be so: yet have I left a daughter,
    Who, I am sure, is kind and comfortable:[93]   280
    When she shall hear this of thee, with her nails
    She'll flay thy wolvish visage. Thou shalt find
    That I'll resume the shape which thou dost think
    I have cast off for ever: thou shalt, I warrant thee.

---

[79] Child-bearing.   [80] Deteriorated, blighted.   [81] Be fruitful.   [82] For her.
[83] Malice.   [84] Perverse.   [85] Unnatural.   [86] Falling.   [87] Wear.   [88] Mood.
[89] Fogs and mists were supposed to be laden with the seeds of pestilence.
[90] Too deep to be cleansed with a tent (a piece of lint).   [91] Foolish.   [92] Soften.
[93] Bringing comfort.

                  [*Exeunt* LEAR, KENT, *and* ATTEND-
                  ANTS.]

GON. Do you mark that, my lord?
ALB. I cannot be so partial, Goneril,
    To the great love I bear you,—
GON. Pray you, content.[94] What, Oswald, ho!
    [*To the* FOOL] You, sir, more knave than fool, after your
        master.
FOOL. Nuncle Lear, nuncle Lear, tarry and take the fool with thee.   290
    A fox, when one has caught her,
    And such a daughter,
    Should sure to the slaughter,
    If my cap would buy a halter:
    So the fool follows after.   [*Exit.*]
GON. This man hath had good counsel:—a hundred knights!
    'Tis politic[95] and safe to let him keep
    At point[96] a hundred knights: yes, that, on every dream,
    Each buzz,[97] each fancy, each complaint, dislike,
    He may enguard his dotage with their powers,   300
    And hold our lives in mercy.[98] Oswald, I say!
ALB. Well, you may fear too far.
GON.   Safer than trust too far:
    Let me still[99] take away the harms I fear,
    Not fear still to be taken:[1] I know his heart.
    What he hath utter'd I have writ my sister:
    If she sustain him and his hundred knights,
    When I have show'd the unfitness,—

                [*Re-enter* OSWALD.]

                How now, Oswald!
    What, have you writ that letter to my sister?
OSW. Yes, madam.
GON. Take you some company, and away to horse: 310
    Inform her full of my particular fear;
    And thereto add such reasons of your own
    As may compact it more.[2] Get you gone;
    And hasten your return. [*Exit* OSWALD.] No, no, my lord,
    This milky gentleness and course[3] of yours
    Though I condemn not, yet, under pardon,
    You are much more attask'd[4] for want of wisdom
    Than praised for harmful mildness.
ALB. How far your eyes may pierce I cannot tell:
    Striving to better, oft we mar what's well.   320

---

[94] Be satisfied.   [95] Prudent.   [96] Completely equipped.   [97] Rumor.
[98] At his mercy.   [99] Always.
  [1] **Let . . . taken,** let me always remove what I fear will harm me, rather than always live in fear of being attacked by some harm.
  [2] **compact it more,** give it more substance, i.e., make the argument more convincing.
  [3] **milky . . . course,** mild gentleness of this course.   [4] To be blamed.

GON. Nay, then—

ALB. Well, well; the event.[5] [*Exeunt.*]

SCENE V
Court before the same

[*Enter* LEAR, KENT, *and* FOOL.]

LEAR. Go you before to Gloucester with these letters. Acquaint my daughter no further with any thing you know than comes from her demand out of the letter. If your diligence be not speedy, I shall be there afore you.

KENT. I will not sleep, my lord, till I have delivered your letter. [*Exit.*]

FOOL. If a man's brains were in 's heels, were't not in danger of kibes?[1]

LEAR. Ay, boy.

FOOL. Then, I prithee, be merry; thy wit shall ne'er go slip-shod.[2]

LEAR. Ha, ha, ha!

FOOL. Shalt see thy other daughter will use thee kindly;[3] for though she's as like this as a crab's[4] like an apple, yet I can tell what I can tell.

LEAR. Why, what canst thou tell, my boy?

FOOL. She will taste as like this as a crab does to a crab. Thou canst tell why one's nose stands i' the middle on 's face?

LEAR. No.

FOOL. Why, to keep one's eyes of either side's nose; that what a man cannot smell out, he may spy into.

LEAR. I did her wrong—

FOOL. Canst tell how an oyster makes his shell?

LEAR. No.

FOOL. Nor I neither; but I can tell why a snail has a house.

LEAR. Why?

FOOL. Why, to put his head in; not to give it away to his daughters, and leave his horns without a case.

LEAR. I will forget my nature. So kind a father! Be my horses ready?

FOOL. Thy asses are gone about 'em. The reason why the seven stars[5] are no more than seven is a pretty reason.

LEAR. Because they are not eight?

FOOL. Yes, indeed: thou wouldst make a good fool.

LEAR. To take 't again perforce![6] Monster ingratitude!

FOOL. If thou wert my fool, nuncle, I'ld have thee beaten for being old before thy time.

LEAR. How's that?

FOOL. Thou shouldst not have been old till thou hadst been wise.

10

20

30

---

[5] **the event**, i.e., let's see what will be the outcome. [1] Chilblains.
[2] In slippers (and so in danger of chilblains).
[3] (1) according to her nature, (2) with kindness. [4] Crab-apple's. [5] Pleiades.
[6] **To . . . perforce**, I will recover my kingdom by force.

LEAR. O, let me not be mad, not mad, sweet heaven!
  Keep me in temper:[7] I would not be mad!

[*Enter* GENTLEMAN.]

  How now! are the horses ready?
GENT. Ready, my lord.   40
LEAR. Come, boy.
FOOL. She that's a maid now, and laughs at my departure,
  Shall not be a maid long, unless things be cut shorter.   [*Exeunt.*]

ACT II

SCENE I
The EARL OF GLOUCESTER'S *castle*

[*Enter* EDMUND, *and* CURAN *meets him.*]
EDM. Save thee, Curan.
CUR. And you, sir. I have been with your father, and given him notice
  that the Duke of Cornwall and Regan his duchess will be here with
  him this night.
EDM. How comes that?
CUR. Nay, I know not. You have heard of the news abroad; I mean
  the whispered ones, for they are yet but ear-kissing arguments?[1]
EDM. Not I: pray you, what are they?
CUR. Have you heard of no likely wars toward, 'twixt the Dukes of
  Cornwall and Albany?   10
EDM. Not a word.
CUR. You may do, then, in time. Fare you well, sir.   [*Exit.*]
EDM. The duke be here to-night? The better![2] best!
  This weaves itself perforce into my business.
  My father hath set guard to take my brother;
  And I have one thing, of a queasy question,[3]
  Which I must act: briefness and fortune, work!
  Brother, a word; descend:[4] brother I say!

[*Enter* EDGAR.]

  My father watches: O sir, fly this place;
  Intelligence is given where you are hid;   20
  You have now the good advantage of the night:
  Have you not spoken 'gainst the Duke of Cornwall?
  He's coming hither; now, i' the night, i' the haste,
  And Regan with him: have you nothing said
  Upon his party 'gainst the Duke of Albany?
  Advise yourself.
EDG.   I am sure on 't, not a word.

[7] Natural emotional equilibrium, i.e., sane.
[1] **ear-kissing arguments,** whispered remarks.   [2] So much the better!
[3] **of . . . question,** of a ticklish nature.
[4] Edgar is in the balcony which represents Edmund's room.

EDM. I hear my father coming: pardon me;
    In cunning[5] I must draw my sword upon you:
    Draw; seem to defend yourself; now quit you[6] well.
    Yield: come before my father. Light, ho, here!   30
    Fly, brother. Torches, torches! So, farewell.
                  [*Exit* EDGAR.]
    Some blood drawn on me would beget opinion[7] [*Wounds his arm.*]
    Of my more fierce endeavour: I have seen drunkards[8]
    Do more than this in sport. Father, father!
    Stop, stop! No help?

                  [*Enter* GLOUCESTER, *and* SER-
                  VANTS *with torches.*]

GLOU. Now, Edmund, where's the villain?
EDM. Here stood he in the dark, his sharp sword out,
    Mumbling of wicked charms, conjuring the moon
    To stand auspicious mistress,—
GLOU.   But where is he?
EDM. Look, sir, I bleed.
GLOU.   Where is the villain, Edmund?   40
EDM. Fled this way, sir. When by no means he could—
GLOU. Pursue him, ho! Go after. [*Exeunt some* SERVANTS.] By no
    means what?
EDM. Persuade me to the murder of your lordship;
    But that[9] I told him, the revenging gods
    'Gainst parricides did all their thunders bend;[10]
    Spoke, with how manifold and strong a bond
    The child was bound to the father; sir, in fine,
    Seeing how loathly opposite[11] I stood
    To his unnatural purpose, in fell motion,[12]
    With his preparèd[13] sword, he charges home
    My unprovided[14] body, lanced mine arm: 50
    But when he saw my best alarum'd spirits,[15]
    Bold in the quarrel's right, roused to the encounter,
    Or whether gasted[16] by the noise I made,
    Full suddenly he fled.
GLOU.   Let him fly far:
    Not in this land shall he remain uncaught;
    And found—dispatch.[17] The noble duke my master,
    My worthy arch and patron,[18] comes to-night:
    By his authority I will proclaim it,
    That he which finds him shall deserve our thanks,   60

---

[5] As a pretense.   [6] Acquit yourself.   [7] Give the impression.
[8] An Elizabethan gallant, when a little drunk, sometimes cut his arm to mix his blood with wine, to be drunk to his mistress's health.
[9] When.   [10] Aim.   [11] Loathingly opposed.   [12] Fierce thrust.   [13] Drawn.
[14] Undefended.   [15] **my . . . spirits,** my best energies aroused (as by a call to arms).
[16] Terrified.   [17] Finish him off.   [18] **arch and patron,** chief patron.

   Bringing the murderous coward to the stake;
   He that conceals him, death.
EDM. When I dissuaded him from his intent,
   And found him pight[19] to do it, with curst[20] speech
   I threaten'd to discover him:[21] he replied,
   "Thou unpossessing bastard! dost thou think,
   If I would stand against thee, would the reposal
   Of any trust, virtue, or worth in thee
   Make thy words faith'd?[22] No: what I should deny,—
   As this I would; ay, though thou didst produce   70
   My very character,[23]—I'ld turn it all
   To thy suggestion, plot, and damnèd practice:[24]
   And thou must make a dullard of the world,
   If they not thought the profits of my death
   Were very pregnant and potential[25] spurs
   To make thee seek it."
GLOU.   Strong and fasten'd[26] villain!
   Would he deny his letter? I never got[27] him.
          [*Tucket*[28] *within.*]
   Hark, the duke's trumpets! I know not why he comes.
   All ports[29] I'll bar;[30] the villain shall not 'scape;
   The duke must grant me that: besides, his picture   80
   I will send far and near, that all the kingdom
   May have due note of him; and of my land,
   Loyal and natural boy, I'll work the means
   To make thee capable.[31]

         [*Enter* CORNWALL, REGAN, *and*
         ATTENDANTS.]

CORN. How now, my noble friend! since I came hither,
   Which I can call but now, I have heard strange news.
REG. If it be true, all vengeance comes too short
   Which can pursue the offender. How dost, my lord?
GLOU. O, madam! my old heart is crack'd, is crack'd!
REG. What, did my father's godson seek your life?   90
   He whom my father named? your Edgar?
GLOU. O, lady, lady, shame would have it hid!
REG. Was he not companion with the riotous knights
   That tend upon my father?
GLOU. I know not, madam: 'tis too bad, too bad.
EDM. Yes, madam, he was of that consort.[32]
REG. No marvel, then, though[33] he were ill affected:[34]
   'Tis they have put him on[35] the old man's death,
   To have the expense[36] and waste of his revenues.
   I have this present evening from my sister   100

---

[19] Determined. [20] Angry. [21] Reveal his plan. [22] Believed. [23] Handwriting.
[24] Plotting. [25] **pregnant and potential,** cogent and powerful. [26] Confirmed.
[27] Begot. [28] A flourish on the trumpet, a fanfare. [29] Sea-ports. [30] Guard.
[31] i.e., of inheriting, i.e., he promises to legitimize him. [32] Company. [33] If.
[34] **ill affected,** evilly disposed. [35] **put him on,** incited him to. [36] Expenditure.

Been well inform'd of them; and with such cautions,
That if they come to sojourn at my house,
I'll not be there.

CORN.   Nor I, assure thee,[37] Regan.
Edmund, I hear that you have shown your father
A child-like office.[38]

EDM.   'Twas my duty, sir.

GLOU. He did bewray[39] his practice;[40] and received
This hurt you see, striving to apprehend him.

CORN. Is he pursued?

GLOU.   Ay, my good lord.

CORN. If he be taken, he shall never more
Be fear'd of doing harm: make your own purpose,[41]   110
How in my strength you please.[42] For you, Edmund,
Whose virtue and obedience doth this instant
So much commend itself, you shall be ours:
Natures of such deep trust we shall much need;
You we first seize on.

EDM.   I shall serve you, sir,
Truly, however else.

GLOU.   For him I thank your grace.

CORN. You know not why we came to visit you,—

REG. Thus out of season, threading[43] dark-eyed night:
Occasions, noble Gloucester, of some poise,[44]
Wherein we must have use of your advice: 120
Our father he hath writ, so hath our sister,
Of difference,[45] which[46] I least thought it fit
To answer from[47] our home; the several messengers
From hence attend dispatch.[48] Our good old friend,
Lay comforts to your bosom; and bestow
Your needful counsel to our business,
Which craves the instant use.[49]

GLOU.   I serve you, madam:
Your graces are right welcome.   [*Exeunt.*]

SCENE II
Before GLOUCESTER'S *castle*

[*Enter* KENT *and* OSWALD, *severally.*]

OSW. Good dawning to thee, friend: art of this house?

KENT. Ay.

OSW. Where may we set our horses?

KENT. I' the mire.

OSW. Prithee, if thou lovest me, tell me.

KENT. I love thee not.

---

[37] Be assured.   [38] **child-like office,** filial service.   [39] Disclose.   [40] Plot.   [41] Plans.
[42] **How . . . please,** using my authority however you please.   [43] Passing through.
[44] Weight.   [45] Quarrels.   [46] i.e., letters.   [47] Away from.
[48] **attend dispatch,** wait to be sent.   [49] **the instant use,** to be carried out instantly.

Osw. Why, then, I care not for thee.

Kent. If I had thee in Lipsbury pinfold,[1] I would make thee care
for me.

Osw. Why dost thou use me thus? I know thee not.   10

Kent. Fellow, I know thee.

Osw. What dost thou know me for?

Kent. A knave; a rascal; an eater of broken meats; a base, proud,
shallow, beggarly, three-suited,[2] hundred-pound, filthy, worsted-
stocking knave; a lily-livered,[3] action-taking knave,[4] a whoreson,
glass-gazing,[5] super-serviceable,[6] finical[7] rogue; one-trunk-inher-
iting[8] slave; one that wouldst be a bawd, in way of good service,
and art nothing but the composition[9] of a knave, beggar, coward,
pandar, and the son and heir of a mongrel bitch: one whom I will
beat into clamorous whining, if thou deniest the least syllable of   20
thy addition.[10]

Osw. Why, what a monstrous fellow art thou, thus to rail on one that
is neither known of thee nor knows thee!

Kent. What a brazen-faced varlet art thou, to deny thou knowest me!
Is it two days ago since I tripped up thy heels, and beat thee before
the king? Draw, you rogue: for, though it be night, yet the moon
shines; I'll make a sop o' the moonshine of you:[11] draw, you
whoreson cullionly barber-monger,[12] draw. [*Drawing his sword.*]

Osw. Away! I have nothing to do with thee.

Kent. Draw, you rascal: you come with letters against the king; and   30
take Vanity the puppet's part[13] against the royalty of her father:
draw, you rogue, or I'll so carbonado[14] your shanks: draw, you
rascal; come your ways.[15]

Osw. Help, ho! murder! help!

Kent. Strike, you slave; stand, rogue, stand; you neat[16] slave, strike.
[*Beating him.*]

Osw. Help, ho! murder! murder!

[*Enter* Edmund, *with his rapier
drawn,* Cornwall, Regan, Gloucester, *and* Servants.]

Edm. How now! What's the matter?

Kent. With you, goodman boy, an you please: come, I'll flesh[17] ye:
come on, young master.

---

[1] **Lipsbury pinfold,** pinfold is a pound for stray animals. Regarding Lipsbury pinfold, says
Nares: "The enclosure adjacent to my teeth, in my jaws," so, in my clutches.

[2] Alludes to the three suits a year regularly allowed to a man-servant.

[3] A white liver was devoid of blood, i.e., of courage.

[4] A man who settles his quarrels by going to the law.   [5] Vain.

[6] One who serves in ways other than honorable, e.g., as a bawd.   [7] Fussy.

[8] **one . . . inheriting,** whose possessions would fill only one trunk.   [9] Mixture.

[10] Descriptive titles.

[11] **make . . . of you,** steep you in moonshine, i.e., steep you in your own blood even if we
fight by the uncertain light of the moon.

[12] **cullionly . . . monger,** rascally haunter of barber shops (where he was beautified).

[13] **Vanity . . . part,** Lady Vanity was a character in the morality-like puppet plays.

[14] Slash.   [15] Come on then.   [16] Foppish.

[17] Feed with flesh for the first time, i.e., initiate you.

GLOU. Weapons! arms! What's the matter here?   40
CORN. Keep peace, upon your lives;
    He dies that strikes again. What is the matter?[18]
REG. The messengers from our sister and the king.
CORN. What is your difference?[19] speak.
OSW. I am scarce in breath, my lord.
KENT. No marvel, you have so bestirred your valour. You cowardly
    rascal, nature disclaims[20] in thee: a tailor made thee.[21]
CORN. Thou art a strange fellow: a tailor make a man?
KENT. Ay, a tailor, sir: a stone-cutter or a painter could not have
    made him so ill, though he had been but two hours at the trade.   50
CORN. Speak yet, how grew your quarrel?
OSW. This ancient ruffian, sir, whose life I have spared at suit of his
    gray beard,—
KENT. Thou whoreson zed![22] thou unnecessary[23] letter! My lord, if
    you will give me leave, I will tread this unbolted[24] villain into mor-
    tar, and daub the walls of a jakes[25] with him. Spare my gray beard,
    you wagtail?[26]
CORN. Peace, sirrah!
    You beastly knave, know you no reverence?
KENT. Yes, sir; but anger hath a privilege.   60
CORN. Why art thou angry?
KENT. That such a slave as this should wear a sword,
    Who wears no honesty.[27] Such smiling rogues as these,
    Like rats, oft bite the holy cords[28] a-twain
    Which are too intrinse[29] t' unloose; smooth[30] every passion
    That in the natures of their lords rebel;
    Bring oil to fire, snow to their colder moods;
    Renege,[31] affirm, and turn their halcyon beaks[32]
    With every gale and vary[33] of their masters,
    Knowing nought, like dogs, but following.   70
    A plague upon your epileptic[34] visage!
    Smile you my speeches, as I were a fool?[35]
    Goose, if I had you upon Sarum plain,[36]
    I'ld drive ye cackling home to Camelot.[37]
CORN. What, art thou mad, old fellow?
GLOU. How fell you out? say that.
KENT. No contraries hold more antipathy
    Than I and such a knave.
CORN. Why dost thou call him knave? What's his offence?

---

[18]Cause of the quarrel.   [19]Dispute.   [20]Disowns.
[21]**a . . . thee,** i.e., you are nothing but clothes.   [22]i.e., the letter "z."
[23]**unnecessary,** because "s" can express its sound.   [24]Unsifted, coarse.   [25]Privy.
[26]A ridiculously active bird.   [27]Sense of honor.
[28]**holy cords,** sacred family bonds.   [29]Intricately tied.
[30]Flatter (into uncontrolled expression).   [31]Deny.
[32]**halcyon beaks,** it was believed that if a halcyon (kingfisher) were hung by the neck, he would turn his beak into the wind.
[33]**gale and vary,** varying gale.   [34]Distorted by a (frightened) smile.
[35]Professional jester.   [36]**Sarum plain,** Salisbury plain where geese were bred.
[37]The site of King Arthur's Court.

KENT. His countenance likes me not.[38]   80
CORN. No more, perchance, does mine, nor his, nor hers.
KENT. Sir, 'tis my occupation to be plain:[39]
    I have seen better faces in my time
    Than stands on any shoulder that I see
    Before me at this instant.
CORN.   This is some fellow,
    Who, having been praised for bluntness, doth affect
    A saucy roughness, and constrains the garb[40]
    Quite from[41] his nature: he cannot flatter, he,
    An honest mind and plain, he must speak truth!
    An they will take it, so;[42] if not, he's plain.[43]   90
    These kind of knaves I know, which in this plainness
    Harbour more craft and more corrupter ends
    Than twenty silly ducking observants[44]
    That stretch their duties nicely.[45]
KENT. Sir, in good sooth, in sincere verity,[46]
    Under the allowance of your great aspect,[47]
    Whose influence, like the wreath of radiant fire
    On flickering Phoebus' front,[48]—
CORN.   What mean'st by this?
KENT. To go out of my dialect, which you discommend so much. I
    know, sir, I am no flatterer: he that beguiled you in a plain accent   100
    was a plain knave; which for my part I will not be, though I should
    win your displeasure to entreat me to 't.
CORN. What was the offence you gave him?
OSW. I never gave him any:
    It pleased the king his master very late
    To strike at me, upon his misconstruction;[49]
    When he, conjunct,[50] and flattering his displeasure,
    Tripp'd me behind; being down, insulted, rail'd,
    And put upon him such a deal of man,[51]
    That worthied him,[52] got praises of the king   110
    For him attempting who was self-subdued;[53]
    And, in the fleshment[54] of this dread exploit,
    Drew on me here again.
KENT.   None of these rogues and cowards
    But Ajax is their fool.[55]
CORN.   Fetch forth the stocks!

[38] **His . . . not,** I do not like his face.   [39] Plain-spoken.
[40] **constrains the garb,** forces himself to assume a bearing.
[41] **Quite from,** completely foreign to.   [42] Well and good.   [43] Frank.
[44] **ducking observants,** obsequious (continually bowing) courtiers.   [45] Punctiliously.
[46] Kent parodies the speech of "ducking observants."   [47] An astrological term.
[48] Forehead.   [49] Misapprehending [me].   [50] Joined with him (Lear).
[51] **deal of man,** lot of manhood, i.e., he swaggered.   [52] As made him appear worthy.
[53] **For . . . self-subdued,** for assailing one who makes no self-defense.
[54] Ferocious excitement.
[55] **Ajax . . . fool,** the cowardly swashbuckler Ajax is vastly inferior to them (in braggart
talk).

You stubborn ancient knave, you reverend braggart,
We'll teach you—

KENT.   Sir, I am too old to learn:
Call not your stocks for me: I serve the king;
On whose employment I was sent to you:
You shall do small respect, show too bold malice
Against the grace and person of my master,   120
Stocking his messenger.

CORN. Fetch forth the stocks! As I have life and honour,
There shall he sit till noon.

REG. Till noon! till night, my lord; and all night too.

KENT. Why, madam, if I were your father's dog,
You should not [56] use me so.

REG.   Sir, being his knave, I will.

CORN. This is a fellow of the self-same colour[57]
Our sister speaks of. Come, bring away[58] the stocks!
            [*Stocks brought out.*]

GLOU. Let me beseech your grace not to do so:
His fault is much, and the good king his master   130
Will check[59] him for 't: your purposed low correction
Is such as basest and contemned'st wretches
For pilferings and most common trespasses
Are punish'd with: the king must take it ill,
That he, so slightly valued in his messenger,
Should have him thus restrain'd.

CORN.   I'll answer[60] that.

REG. My sister may receive it much more worse,
To have her gentleman abused, assaulted,
For following her affairs. Put in his legs.
            [KENT *is put in the stocks.*]
Come, my good lord, away.   140
            [*Exeunt all but* GLOUCESTER *and*
            KENT.]

GLOU. I am sorry for thee, friend; 'tis the duke's pleasure,
Whose disposition, all the world well knows,
Will not be rubb'd[61] nor stopp'd: I'll entreat for thee.

KENT. Pray, do not, sir: I have watched[62] and travell'd hard;
Some time I shall sleep out, the rest I'll whistle.
A good man's[63] fortune may grow out at heels:
Give you[64] good morrow!

GLOU. The duke's to blame in this; 'twill be ill taken.   [*Exit.*]

KENT. Good king, that must approve the common saw,[65]
Thou out of heaven's benediction comest   150
To the warm sun!

---

[56] Surely would not.   [57] Sort.   [58] Along.   [59] Reprove.   [60] Be responsible for.
[61] Obstructed; a "rub" in bowling was anything that deflected the course of the ball.
[62] Stayed awake.   [63] Even a good man's.   [64] God give you.
[65] Proverb, i.e., "To run out of God's blessing [of shade] into the sun" is "to go from bad to worse."

Approach, thou beacon to this under globe,
That by thy comfortable[66] beams I may
Peruse this letter! Nothing almost sees miracles
But misery: I know 'tis from Cordelia,
Who hath most fortunately been inform'd
Of my obscurèd course;[67] [*Reads*] "And shall find time
From this enormous state,[68] seeking to give
Losses their remedies." All weary and o'erwatch'd,[69]
Take vantage,[70] heavy eyes, not to behold   160
This shameful lodging.
Fortune, good night: smile once more; turn thy wheel![71]

                                                                    [*Sleeps.*]

SCENE III
A wood

[*Enter* EDGAR.]
EDG. I heard myself proclaim'd;
        And by the happy[1] hollow of a tree
        Escaped the hunt. No port is free; no place,
        That guard, and most unusual vigilance,
        Does not attend my taking.[2] Whiles I may 'scape,
        I will preserve myself: and am bethought[3]
        To take the basest and most poorest shape
        That ever penury, in contempt of man,
        Brought near to beast: my face I'll grime with filth;
        Blanket my loins; elf[4] all my hair in knots;   10
        And with presented nakedness out-face[5]
        The winds and persecutions of the sky.
        The country gives me proof and precedent
        Of Bedlam beggars,[6] who, with roaring voices,
        Strike in their numb'd and mortified[7] bare arms
        Pins, wooden pricks,[8] nails, sprigs of rosemary;
        And with this horrible object,[9] from low[10] farms,
        Poor pelting[11] villages, sheep-cotes, and mills,
        Sometime with lunatic bans,[12] sometime with prayers,
        Enforce their charity. Poor Turlygod![13] poor Tom!   20
        That's something yet:[14] Edgar I nothing am.   [*Exit.*]

---

[66] Comforting.   [67] **obscured course,** career in disguise.
[68] The present abnormal political situation.   [69] Exhausted from lack of sleep.
[70] Advantage (of feeling sleepy).   [71] i.e., Fortune's wheel.   [1] Helpful.
[2] **attend my taking,** want to arrest me.   [3] It occurs to me.
[4] Tangle; tangled hair was thought to be the work of mischievous elves.   [5] Defy.
[6] Inhabitants of Bedlam (Bethelem Hospital), an insane asylum, were sent out on the roads
to beg.
[7] Insensible.   [8] Skewers.   [9] Spectacle.   [10] Humble.   [11] Paltry.   [12] Curses.
[13] A name beggars applied to themselves; its meaning is unknown.
[14] **That's . . . yet,** i.e., in that character I have a future.

SCENE IV
Before GLOUCESTER'S *castle*—KENT *in the stocks*

[*Enter* LEAR, FOOL, *and* GENTLEMAN.]

LEAR. 'Tis strange that they should so depart from home,
And not send back my messenger.

GENT.   As I learn'd,
The night before there was no purpose in them
Of this remove.[1]

KENT.   Hail to thee, noble master!

LEAR. Ha!
Makest thou this shame thy pastime?

KENT.   No, my lord.

FOOL. Ha, ha! he wears cruel[2] garters. Horses are tied by the heads,
dogs and bears by the neck, monkeys by the loins,[3] and men by the
legs: when a man's over-lusty at legs, then he wears wooden
nether-stocks.[4]

LEAR. What's he that hath so much thy place[5] mistook
To set thee here?

KENT.   It is both he and she;
Your son and daughter.

LEAR. No.

KENT. Yes.

LEAR. No, I say.

KENT. I say, yea.

LEAR. No, no, they would not.

KENT. Yes, they have.

LEAR. By Jupiter, I swear, no.

KENT. By Juno, I swear, ay.

LEAR.   They durst not do 't;
They could not, would not do 't; 'tis worse than murder,
To do upon respect[6] such violent outrage:
Resolve me,[7] with all modest[8] haste, which way
Thou mightst deserve, or they impose, this usage,
Coming from us.

KENT.   My lord, when at their home
I did commend your highness' letters to them,
Ere I was risen from the place that show'd
My duty kneeling, came there a reeking post,[9]
Stew'd in his haste, half breathless, panting forth
From Goneril his mistress salutations;
Deliver'd letters, spite of intermission,[10]
Which presently[11] they read: on[12] whose contents,

10

20

30

---

[1] Change of residence.   [2] Pun on crewel = worsted.
[3] **monkeys . . . loins,** the chain of pet-monkeys was so affixed.   [4] Stockings.
[5] Position (as my messenger).
[6] **upon respect,** contrary to the respect due me as their father and their King.
[7] Explain to me.   [8] Moderate.   [9] Messenger stinking from sweat.
[10] In spite of interrupting me.   [11] Immediately.   [12] As a result of.

They summon'd up their meiny,[13] straight took horse;
Commanded me to follow, and attend
The leisure of their answer; gave me cold looks:
And meeting here the other messenger,
Whose welcome, I perceived, had poison'd mine,—
Being the very fellow that of late
Display'd so saucily[14] against your highness,—   40
Having more man[15] than wit about me, drew:
He raised the house with loud and coward cries.
Your son and daughter found this trespass worth
The shame which here it suffers.

FOOL. Winter's not gone yet, if the wild-geese fly that way.
Fathers that wear rags
      Do make their children blind;
But fathers that bear bags[16]
      Shall see their children kind.
Fortune, that arrant whore,   50
Ne'er turns the key[17] to the poor.
But, for all this, thou shalt have as many dolours[18] for thy daugh-
ters as thou canst tell[19] in a year.

LEAR. O, how this mother[20] swells up toward my heart!
Hysterica passio, down, thou climbing sorrow,
Thy element's[21] below! Where is this daughter?

KENT. With the earl, sir, here within.

LEAR.   Follow me not,
Stay here.   [*Exit.*]

GENT. Made you no more offence but what you speak of?

KENT. None.   60
How chance the king comes with so small a train?

FOOL. An thou hadst been set i' the stocks for that question, thou
hadst well deserved it.[22]

KENT. Why, fool?

FOOL. We'll set thee to school to an ant, to teach thee there's no la-
bouring i' the winter. All that follow their noses are led by their
eyes but blind men; and there's not a nose among twenty but can
smell him that's stinking. Let go thy hold when a great wheel runs
down a hill, lest it break thy neck with following it; but the great
one that goes up the hill, let him draw thee after. When a wise man   70
gives thee better counsel give me mine again: I would have none
but knaves follow it, since a fool gives it.[23]
That sir[24] which serves and seeks for gain,
      And follows but for form,

---

[13] Household servants.   [14] **Display'd so saucily,** behaved so impudently.
[15] Manhood.   [16] **bear bags,** i.e., are rich.   [17] **turns the key,** i.e., opens the door.
[18] Grief, with a pun on "dollars."   [19] Count.
[20] Hysteria, supposed to be caused by wind rising from the stomach to cloud the brain
and cause dizziness.
[21] Proper sphere is.   [22] **deserved it,** i.e., for asking a silly question.
[23] The fool in stringing together these wise sayings describing Lear's situation is showing
Kent how much wiser the Fool is than he.
[24] Great man.

Will pack[25] when it begins to rain,
   And leave thee in the storm.
But I will tarry; the fool will stay,
   And let the wise man fly:
The knave turns fool that runs away;
   The fool no knave,[26] perdy.[27]

KENT. Where learned you this, fool?

FOOL. Not i' the stocks, fool.

                  [*Re-enter* LEAR, *with* GLOUCESTER.]

LEAR. Deny[28] to speak with me? They are sick? they are weary?
They have travell'd all the night? Mere fetches;[29]
The images[30] of revolt[31] and flying off.
Fetch me a better answer.

GLOU.   My dear lord,
You know the fiery quality of the duke;
How unremoveable and fix'd he is
In his own course.

LEAR. Vengeance! plague! death! confusion!
Fiery? what quality? Why, Gloucester, Gloucester,
I'ld speak with the Duke of Cornwall and his wife.

GLOU. Well, my good lord, I have inform'd them so.

LEAR. Inform'd them! Dost thou understand me, man?

GLOU. Ay, my good lord.

LEAR. The king would speak with Cornwall; the dear father
Would with his daughter speak, commands her service:
Are they inform'd of this? My breath and blood!
Fiery? the fiery duke? Tell the hot duke that—
No, but not yet: may be he is not well:
Infirmity doth still neglect all office[32]
Whereto our health is bound; we are not ourselves
When nature, being oppress'd, commands the mind
To suffer with the body: I'll forbear;
And am fall'n out with my more headier[33] will,
To take[34] the indisposed and sickly fit
For the sound man. Death on my state![35] wherefore
                  [*Looking on* KENT.]
Should he sit here? This act persuades me
That this remotion[36] of the duke and her
Is practice[37] only. Give me my servant forth.
Go tell the duke and 's wife I'ld speak with them,
Now, presently:[38] bid them come forth and hear me,
Or at their chamber-door I'll beat the drum
Till it cry sleep to death.[39]

[25] Run away.

[26] **The . . . no knave,** the fool that runs away from his master is a knave, but the fool who, like him, remains faithful is no knave.

[27] "Par dieu," literally: "by God," but is a mild oath about = "forsooth."   [28] Refuse.

[29] Pretexts.   [30] Exact likenesses, i.e., clearest signs.   [31] Gross departure from duty.

[32] Duty.   [33] Impulsive.   [34] For taking.   [35] Royal power.   [36] Removal.

[37] Trickery.   [38] At once.   [39] **cry . . . death,** murder sleep.

GLOU. I would have all well betwixt you.
                              [*Exit.*]
LEAR. O me, my heart, my rising heart! but, down!
FOOL. Cry to it, nuncle, as the cockney[40] did to the eels when she put
     'em i' the paste alive; she knapped[41] 'em o' the coxcombs[42] with a
     stick, and cried "Down, wantons, down." 'Twas her brother that, in
     pure kindness to his horse, buttered his hay.   120

                              [*Enter* CORNWALL, REGAN, GLOU-
                              CESTER, *and* SERVANTS.]

LEAR. Good morrow to you both.
CORN.   Hail to your grace![43]
                              [KENT *is set at liberty.*]
REG. I am glad to see your highness.
LEAR. Regan, I think you are; I know what reason
     I have to think so: if thou shouldst not be glad,
     I would divorce me from thy mother's tomb,
     Sepulchring[44] an adultress. [*To* KENT] O, are you free?
     Some other time for that. Belovèd Regan,
     Thy sister's naught:[45] O Regan, she hath tied
     Sharp-tooth'd unkindness, like a vulture, here:
                              [*Points to his heart.*]
     I can scarce speak to thee; thou'lt not believe   130
     With how depraved a quality[46]—O Regan!
REG. I pray you, sir, take patience:[47] I have hope
     You less know how to value her desert
     Than she to scant her duty.
LEAR.   Say, how is that?
REG. I cannot think my sister in the least
     Would fail her obligation: if, sir, perchance
     She have restrain'd the riots of your followers,
     'Tis on such ground, and to such wholesome end,
     As clears her from all blame.
LEAR. My curses on her!
REG.   O, sir, you are old;   140
     Nature in you stands on the very verge
     Of her confine:[48] you should be ruled and led
     By some discretion, that discerns your state[49]
     Better than you yourself. Therefore, I pray you,
     That to our sister you do make return;
     Say you have wrong'd her, sir.
LEAR.   Ask her forgiveness?
     Do you but mark how this becomes the house:[50]
     "Dear daughter, I confess that I am old;
                              [*Kneeling.*]

---

[40] Cook, perhaps a London cook who knows nothing about eels.   [41] Rapped.
[42] Jocular for heads.   [43] i.e., Majesty.   [44] i.e., as containing.   [45] Wicked.
[46] Character.   [47] **take patience,** be calm.   [48] Assigned boundary.
[49] i.e., mental state.   [50] **becomes the house,** is a fitting family relationship.

Age is unnecessary:[51] on my knees I beg
That you'll vouchsafe me raiment, bed, and food."   150
REG. Good sir, no more; these are unsightly tricks:
Return you to my sister.
LEAR.   [*Rising*] Never, Regan:
She hath abated me of half my train;[52]
Look'd black upon me; struck me with her tongue,
Most serpent-like, upon the very heart:
All the stored vengeances of heaven fall
On her ingrateful top! Strike her young bones,[53]
You taking[54] airs, with lameness!
CORN.   Fie, sir, fie!
LEAR. You nimble lightnings, dart your blinding flames
Into her scornful eyes! Infect her beauty,   160
You fen-suck'd fogs, drawn by the powerful sun,
To fall[55] and blast her pride!
REG. O the blest gods! so will you wish on me,
When the rash mood is on.
LEAR. No, Regan, thou shalt never have my curse:
Thy tender-hefted[56] nature shall not give
Thee o'er to harshness: her eyes are fierce; but thine
Do comfort and not burn. 'Tis not in thee
To grudge my pleasures, to cut off my train,
To bandy hasty words, to scant my sizes,[57]   170
And in conclusion to oppose the bolt
Against my coming in: thou better know'st
The offices[58] of nature, bond of childhood,[59]
Effects of courtesy,[60] dues of gratitude;
Thy half o' the kingdom hast thou not forgot,
Wherein I thee endow'd.
REG.   Good sir, to the purpose.[61]
LEAR. Who put my man i' the stocks?
                         [*Tucket within.*]
CORN.   What trumpet's that?
REG. I know 't, my sister's: this approves her letter,
That she would soon be here.

                    [*Enter* OSWALD.]

                         Is your lady come?
LEAR. This is a slave, whose easy-borrow'd[62] pride   180
Dwells in the fickle grace of her he follows.
Out, varlet,[63] from my sight!
CORN.   What means your grace?
LEAR. Who stock'd my servant? Regan, I have good hope

[51] **Age is unnecessary,** old people are of no use.
[52] **abated . . . train,** reduced my retinue by half.   [53] i.e., Goneril's youthful figure.
[54] Infecting.   [55] Fall upon.   [56] Swayed by tender feelings.   [57] Allowances.
[58] Duties.   [59] **bond of childhood,** the duties of a child to its parents.
[60] **effects of courtesy,** courteous action.   [61] Talk sense.   [62] Easily assumed.
[63] Scoundrel.

Thou didst not know on 't. Who comes here? O heavens,

[*Enter* GONERIL.]

If you do love old men, if your sweet sway
Allow[64] obedience, if yourselves are old,
Make it your cause; send down, and take my part!
[*To* GON.] Art not ashamed to look upon this beard?
O Regan, wilt thou take her by the hand?

GON. Why not by the hand, sir? How have I offended?   190
All's not offence that indiscretion finds
And dotage terms so.

LEAR.   O sides, you are too tough;
Will you yet hold? How came my man i' the stocks?

CORN. I set him there, sir: but his own disorders
Deserved much less advancement.[65]

LEAR.   You! did you?

REG. I pray you, father, being weak, seem so.
If, till the expiration of your month,
You will return and sojourn with my sister,
Dismissing half your train, come then to me:
I am now from home, and out of that provision   200
Which shall be needful for your entertainment.[66]

LEAR. Return to her, and fifty men dismiss'd?
No, rather I abjure all roofs, and choose
To wage[67] against the enmity o' the air;
To be a comrade with the wolf and owl,—
Necessity's sharp pinch! Return with her?
Why, the hot-blooded France, that dowerless took
Our youngest born, I could as well be brought
To knee[68] his throne, and, squire-like,[69] pension beg
To keep base life afoot. Return with her?   210
Persuade me rather to be slave and sumpter[70]
To this detested groom.[71]   [*Pointing at* OSWALD.]

GON.   At your choice, sir.

LEAR. I prithee, daughter, do not make me mad:
I will not trouble thee, my child; farewell:
We'll no more meet, no more see one another:
But yet thou art my flesh, my blood, my daughter;
Or rather a disease that's in my flesh,
Which I must needs call mine: thou art a boil,
A plague-sore, an embossèd[72] carbuncle,
In my corrupted blood. But I'll not chide thee;   220
Let shame come when it will, I do not call it:
I do not bid the thunder-bearer shoot,
Nor tell tales of thee to high-judging Jove:
Mend when thou canst; be better at thy leisure:

---

[64] Approve.   [65] Honor.   [66] Maintenance.   [67] Wage war with.   [68] Kneel before.
[69] As if I were a servant.   [70] Packhorse, drudge.   [71] Menial.   [72] Swollen.

    I can be patient; I can stay with Regan,
    I and my hundred knights.
REG.   Not altogether so:
    I look'd not for you yet, nor am provided
    For your fit welcome. Give ear, sir, to my sister;
    For those that mingle reason with your passion[73]
    Must be content to think you old, and so—   230
    But she knows what she does.
LEAR.   Is this well spoken?
REG. I dare avouch[74] it, sir: what, fifty followers?
    Is it not well? What should you need of more?
    Yea, or so many, sith that both charge[75] and danger
    Speak 'gainst so great a number? How, in one house,
    Should many people, under two commands,
    Hold amity? 'Tis hard; almost impossible.
GON. Why might not you, my lord, receive attendance
    From those that she calls servants or from mine?
REG. Why not, my lord? If then they chanced to slack[76] you,   240
    We could control them. If you will come to me,—
    For now I spy a danger,—I entreat you
    To bring but five and twenty: to no more
    Will I give place or notice.[77]
LEAR. I gave you all—
REG.   And in good time you gave it.
LEAR. Made you my guardians, my depositaries;[78]
    But kept a reservation to be follow'd
    With such a number. What, must I come to you
    With five and twenty, Regan? said you so?
REG. And speak 't again, my lord; no more with me.   250
LEAR. Those wicked creatures yet do look well-favour'd,[79]
    When others are more wicked; not being the worst
    Stands in some rank of praise. [*To* GON.] I'll go with thee:
    Thy fifty yet doth double five-and-twenty,
    And thou art twice her love.
GON.   Hear me, my lord:
    What need you five and twenty, ten, or five,
    To follow in a house where twice so many
    Have a command to tend you?
REG.   What need one?
LEAR. O, reason[80] not the need: our basest beggars
    Are in the poorest thing superfluous:[81]   260
    Allow not nature more than nature needs,
    Man's life is cheap as beast's: thou art a lady;
    If only to go warm were gorgeous,

[73] **mingle . . . passion,** consider your violence in the light of reason.
[74] Affirm.   [75] Expense.   [76] Neglect.   [77] Recognition.   [78] Trustees.
[79] Handsome.   [80] Discuss.
[81] **Are . . . superfluous,** have in their most meagre possessions more than the barest necessities.

Why, nature needs not what thou gorgeous wear'st,
Which scarcely keeps thee warm. But, for true need,—
You heavens, give me that patience,[82] patience I need!
You see me here, you gods, a poor old man,
As full of grief as age; wretched in both!
If it be you that stir these daughters' hearts
Against their father, fool me not so much   270
To bear it tamely;[83] touch me with noble anger,
And let not women's weapons, water-drops,
Stain my man's cheeks! No, you unnatural hags,
I will have such revenges on you both,
That all the world shall—I will do such things,—
What they are, yet I know not; but they shall be
The terrors of the earth.[84] You think I'll weep;
No, I'll not weep:
I have full cause of weeping; but this heart
Shall break into a hundred thousand flaws,[85]   280
Or ere I'll weep. O fool, I shall go mad!
                              [*Exeunt* LEAR, GLOUCESTER,
                              KENT, *and* FOOL. *Storm and*
                              tempest.]

CORN. Let us withdraw; 'twill be a storm.
REG. This house is little: the old man and his people
        Cannot be well bestow'd.[86]
GON. 'Tis his own blame;[87] hath put himself from rest,
        And must needs taste[88] his folly.
REG. For his particular,[89] I'll receive him gladly,
        But not one follower.
GON.   So am I purposed.
        Where is my lord of Gloucester?
CORN. Follow'd the old man forth: he is return'd.   290

                    [*Re-enter* GLOUCESTER.]

GLOU. The king is in high rage.
CORN.   Whither is he going?
GLOU. He calls to horse; but will I know not whither.
CORN. 'Tis best to give him way; he leads himself.
GON. My lord, entreat him by no means to stay.
GLOU. Alack, the night comes on, and the bleak winds
        Do sorely ruffle;[90] for many miles about
        There's scarce a bush.
REG.   O, sir, to wilful men,
        The injuries that they themselves procure
        Must be their schoolmasters. Shut up your doors:
        He is attended with a desperate train;   300
        And what they may incense[91] him to, being apt[92]

---

[82] Endurance.
[83] **fool . . . tamely,** do not make me so much of a weakling as to endure it tamely.
[84] **The . . . earth,** deeds to terrify the whole world.   [85] Fragments.   [86] Lodged.
[87] Fault.   [88] i.e., digest.   [89] As for him alone.   [90] Bluster.   [91] Incite.   [92] Ready.

To have his ear abused,[93] wisdom bids fear.
CORN. Shut up your doors, my lord; 'tis a wild night:
My Regan counsels well: come out o' the storm.   [*Exeunt.*]

ACT III

SCENE I
A heath

[*Storm still. Enter* KENT *and a* GENTLEMAN, *meeting.*]
KENT. Who's there, besides foul weather?
GENT. One minded like the weather, most unquietly.
KENT. I know you. Where's the king?
GENT. Contending with the fretful element;
Bids the wind blow the earth into the sea,
Or swell the curlèd waters 'bove the main,[1]
That things[2] might change or cease; tears his white hair,
Which the impetuous blasts, with eyeless[3] rage,
Catch in their fury, and make nothing of;[4]
Strives in his little world of man[5] to outscorn   10
The to-and-fro-conflicting wind and rain.
This night, wherein the cub-drawn[6] bear would couch,[7]
The lion and the belly-pinchèd wolf
Keep their fur dry, unbonneted[8] he runs,
And bids what will take all.[9]
KENT.   But who is with him?
GENT. None but the fool; who labours to out-jest
His heart-struck injuries.
KENT.   Sir, I do know you;
And dare, upon the warrant of my note,[10]
Commend a dear thing[11] to you. There is division,
Although as yet the face of it be cover'd   20
With mutual cunning, 'twixt Albany and Cornwall;
Who have—as who have not, that their great stars
Throned and set high?—servants, who seem no less,[12]
Which are to France the spies and speculations[13]
Intelligent of our state;[14] what hath been seen,
Either in snuffs[15] and packings[16] of the dukes,
Or the hard rein which both of them have borne

---

[93] Deceived.   [1] Mainland.   [2] World.   [3] **eyeless,** hence undirected, indiscriminate.
[4] **make nothing of,** show no respect for.
[5] **little . . . man,** man was regarded as a universe (macrocosm) in miniature (microcosm).
[6] Sucked dry by her cubs.   [7] Lie protected from the storm.   [8] Without a hat.
[9] **take all,** the cry of a gambler when he stakes his last penny; so a gesture of desperation.
[10] Knowledge (of the situation).
[11] **Commend . . . thing,** entrust a momentous matter.
[12] **no less,** not more nor less than servants.   [13] Observers.
[14] **Intelligent . . . state,** giving information about our political situation.
[15] Resentments.   [16] Plots.

Against the old kind king; or something deeper,
Whereof perchance these are but furnishings;[17]
But, true it is, from France there comes a power[18]   30
Into this scatter'd[19] kingdom; who already,
Wise in our negligence, have secret feet[20]
In some of our best ports, and are at point[21]
To show their open banner. Now to you:
If on my credit[22] you dare build so far
To[23] make your speed to Dover, you shall find
Some that will thank you, making just[24] report
Of how unnatural and bemadding sorrow
The king hath cause to plain.[25]
I am a gentleman of blood and breeding;   40
And, from some knowledge and assurance, offer
This office[26] to you.
GENT. I will talk further with you.
KENT.   No, do not.
    For confirmation that I am much more
    Than my out-wall,[27] open this purse, and take
    What it contains. If you shall see Cordelia,—
    As fear not but you shall,—show her this ring;
    And she will tell you who your fellow[28] is
    That yet you do not know. Fie on this storm!
    I will go seek the king.   50
GENT. Give me your hand: have you no more to say?
KENT. Few words, but, to effect,[29] more than all yet;
    That, when we have found the king,—in which your pain
    That way,[30] I'll this,—he that first lights on him
    Holla the other.   [*Exeunt severally.*]

SCENE II
Another part of the heath—storm still

[*Enter* LEAR *and* FOOL.]
LEAR. Blow, winds, and crack your cheeks! rage! blow!
    You cataracts and hurricanoes,[1] spout
    Till you have drench'd our steeples, drown'd the cocks![2]
    You sulphurous and thought-executing[3] fires,
    Vaunt-couriers[4] to oak-cleaving thunderbolts,
    Singe my white head! And thou, all-shaking thunder,
    Smite flat the thick rotundity o' the world!

---

[17] Deceptive shows.   [18] Armed force.   [19] Divided.   [20] Infantry.
[21] **at point,** all ready.   [22] **my credit,** your trust in me.   [23] As to.
[24] **making just,** if you make accurate.   [25] Complain.   [26] Duty.
[27] Exterior, i.e., the garb of a serving man.   [28] Companion.
[29] **to effect,** in their importance.   [1] Water-spouts.
[30] **your . . . way,** i.e., your efforts to find him lie in that direction.
[2] Weathercocks.   [3] Having the speed of thought.   [4] Forerunners.

Crack nature's moulds,[5] all germens[6] spill[7] at once,
That make ingrateful man!

FOOL. O nuncle, court holy-water[8] in a dry house is better than this   10
rain-water out o' door. Good nuncle, in, and ask thy daughters'
blessing: here's a night pities neither wise man nor fool.

LEAR. Rumble thy bellyful! Spit, fire! spout, rain!
Nor rain, wind, thunder, fire, are my daughters:
I tax[9] not you, you elements, with unkindness;
I never gave you kingdom, call'd you children,
You owe me no subscription:[10] then let fall
Your horrible pleasure; here I stand, your slave,
A poor, infirm, weak, and despised old man:
But yet I call you servile ministers,[11]   20
That have with two pernicious daughters join'd
Your high engender'd[12] battles[13] 'gainst a head
So old and white as this. O! O! 'tis foul!

FOOL. He that has a house to put 's head in has a good head-piece.
The cod-piece[14] that will house
Before the head has any,
The head and he shall louse;[15]
So beggars marry many.
The man that makes his toe
What he his heart should make[16]   30
Shall of a corn cry woe,
And turn his sleep to wake.
For there was never yet fair woman but she made mouths in a
glass.[17]

LEAR. No, I will be the pattern of all patience;
I will say nothing.

[*Enter* KENT.]

KENT. Who's there?

FOOL. Marry, here's grace[18] and a cod-piece; that's a wise man and a
fool.

KENT. Alas, sir, are you here? things that love night   40
Love not such nights as these; the wrathful skies
Gallow[19] the very wanderers of the dark,
And make them keep their caves: since I was man,
Such sheets of fire, such bursts of horrid thunder,
Such groans of roaring wind and rain, I never
Remember to have heard: man's nature cannot carry[20]
The affliction[21] nor the fear.

---

[5] i.e., molds in which nature fashions men.   [6] Seeds.   [7] Destroy.
[8] **court holy-water,** i.e., flattery.   [9] Reproach.   [10] Obedience.   [11] Agents.
[12] Engendered on high.   [13] Battalions.
[14] An appendage worn on the front of men's trousers.
[15] **The cod-piece . . . louse,** the man who begets children before he has a house will live a lousy existence.
[16] **The . . . make,** the man who puts his heart where his toe should be.
[17] **made . . . glass,** grimaced before a looking-glass.   [18] An honorable gentleman.
[19] Terrify.   [20] Bear.   [21] The bodily pain.

LEAR.   Let the great gods,
That keep this dreadful pother[22] o'er our heads,
Find out their enemies now. Tremble, thou wretch,
That hast within thee undivulgèd crimes,   50
Unwhipp'd of justice: hide thee, thou bloody hand;
Thou perjured, and thou simular man of[23] virtue
That art incestuous: caitiff,[24] to pieces shake,
That under covert and convenient seeming[25]
Hast practised on[26] man's life: close pent-up guilts,
Rive your concealing continents,[27] and cry
These dreadful summoners[28] grace.[29] I am a man
More sinn'd against than sinning.

KENT.   Alack, bare-headed!
Gracious my lord, hard by here is a hovel;
Some friendship will it lend[30] you 'gainst the tempest: 60
Repose you there; while I to this hard[31] house—
More harder than the stones whereof 'tis raised;
Which even but now, demanding after[32] you,
Denied[33] me to come in—return, and force
Their scanted courtesy.

LEAR.   My wits begin to turn.
Come on, my boy: how dost, my boy? art cold?
I am cold myself. Where is this straw, my fellow?
The art[34] of our necessities is strange,
That can make vile things precious. Come, your hovel.
Poor fool and knave, I have one part in my heart   70
That's sorry yet for thee.

FOOL. [*Singing*] He that has and a little tiny wit,—
      With hey, ho, the wind and the rain,—
Must make content with his fortunes fit,
      For the rain it raineth every day.

LEAR. True, my good boy. Come, bring us to this hovel.
                                        [*Exeunt* LEAR *and* KENT.]

FOOL. This is a brave[35] night to cool a courtezan.
I'll speak a prophecy ere I go:
When priests are more in word than matter;[36]
When brewers mar their malt with water;   80
When nobles are their tailors' tutors;
No heretics burn'd, but wenches' suitors;
When every case in law is right;
No squire in debt, nor no poor knight;
When slanders do not live in tongues;
Nor cutpurses come not to throngs;
When usurers tell[37] their gold i' the field;
And bawds and whores do churches build;

---

[22] Uproar.   [23] **simular man of,** pretender to.   [24] Despicable creature.
[25] Hypocrisy.   [26] Plotted against.   [27] **Rive . . . continents,** rip open your coverings.
[28] Police of an ecclesiastical court.   [29] **cry . . . grace,** beg for mercy.   [30] Afford.
[31] Cruel.   [32] Asking for.   [33] Forbade.   [34] A reference to alchemy.   [35] Fine.
[36] **more . . . matter,** better in their talk than in deeds.   [37] Count.

Then shall the realm of Albion[38]
Come to great confusion:[39]
Then comes the time, who lives to see 't,
That going[40] shall be used with feet.
This prophecy Merlin[41] shall make; for I live before his time.
[Exit.]

90

SCENE III
GLOUCESTER's *castle*

[Enter GLOUCESTER *and* EDMUND.*]*
GLOU. Alack, alack, Edmund, I like not this unnatural dealing. When
I desired their leave that I might pity him, they took from me the
use of mine own house; charged me, on pain of their perpetual
displeasure, neither to speak of him, entreat for him, nor any way
sustain[1] him.
EDM. Most savage and unnatural!
GLOU. Go to; say you nothing. There's a division betwixt the dukes;
and a worse matter than that: I have received a letter this night; 'tis
dangerous to be spoken; I have locked the letter in my closet:
these injuries the king now bears will be revenged home;[2] there's
part of a power[3] already footed:[4] we must incline to the king.[5] I
will seek him, and privily[6] relieve him: go you and maintain talk
with the duke, that my charity be not of him perceived: if he ask
for me, I am ill, and gone to bed. Though I die for it, as no less is
threatened me, the king my old master must be relieved. There is
some strange thing toward,[7] Edmund; pray you, be careful. *[Exit.]*
EDM. This courtesy, forbid thee,[8] shall the duke
Instantly know; and of that letter too:
This seems a fair deserving,[9] and must draw me
That which my father loses; no less than all:
The younger rises when the old doth fall. *[Exit.]*

10

20

SCENE IV
The heath—before a hovel

[Enter LEAR, KENT, *and* FOOL.*]*
KENT. Here is the place, my lord; good my lord, enter:
The tyranny of the open night's[1] too rough
For nature to endure. *[Storm still.]*
LEAR. Let me alone.
KENT. Good my lord, enter here.

---

[38] Britain. [39] Ruin. [40] Walking.
[41] Magician and prophet of King Arthur's Court. [1] Relieve. [2] Fully. [3] Army.
[4] Landed. [5] **incline to the King,** take the King's part. [6] Secretly.
[7] In preparation. [8] Forbidden to thee.
[9] **This . . . deserving,** this will seem a meritorious action.
[1] **open night,** night in the open.

LEAR.   Wilt break my heart?
KENT. I had rather break mine own. Good my lord, enter.
LEAR. Thou think'st 'tis much that this contentious storm
    Invades us to the skin: so 'tis to thee;
    But where the greater malady is fix'd,
    The lesser is scarce felt. Thou 'ldst shun a bear;
    But if thy flight lay toward the raging sea,   10
    Thou 'ldst meet the bear i' the mouth.[2] When the mind's free,[3]
    The body's delicate:[4] the tempest in my mind
    Doth from my senses take all feeling else
    Save what beats there. Filial ingratitude!
    Is it not as[5] this mouth should tear this hand
    For lifting food to 't? But I will punish home:
    No, I will weep no more. In such a night
    To shut me out! Pour on; I will endure.
    In such a night as this! O Regan, Goneril!
    Your old kind father, whose frank[6] heart gave all,—   20
    O, that way madness lies; let me shun that;
    No more of that.
KENT.   Good my lord, enter here.
LEAR. Prithee, go in thyself; seek thine own ease:
    This tempest will not give me leave to ponder
    On things would hurt me more. But I'll go in.
    [*To the* FOOL] In, boy; go first. You houseless poverty,—
    Nay, get thee in. I'll pray, and then I'll sleep.
               [FOOL *goes in.*]
    Poor naked wretches, wheresoe'er you are,
    That bide[7] the pelting of this pitiless storm,
    How shall your houseless heads and unfed sides,   30
    Your loop'd and window'd[8] raggedness, defend you
    From seasons such as these? O, I have ta'en
    Too little care of this! Take physic, pomp;
    Expose thyself to feel what wretches feel,
    That thou mayst shake the superflux[9] to them,
    And show the heavens more just.
EDG. [*Within*] Fathom[10] and half, fathom and half! Poor Tom!
              [*The* FOOL *runs out from the hovel.*]
FOOL. Come not in here, nuncle, here's a spirit. Help me, help me!
KENT. Give me thy hand. Who's there?
FOOL. A spirit, a spirit: he says his name's poor Tom.   40
KENT. What art thou that dost grumble there i' the straw? Come
    forth.

              [*Enter* EDGAR *disguised as a mad-
              man.*]

---

[2]**i' the mouth,** face to face.   [3]i.e., from trouble.   [4]Sensitive.   [5]As if.
[6]Generous.   [7]Endure.
[8]**loop'd and window'd,** the two words are synonymous, meaning "full of holes."
[9]Superfluity (i.e., what pomp does not need).
[10]**Fathom, etc.,** Tom pretends to be a sailor, taking soundings in a storm at sea.

Edg. Away! the foul fiend follows me!
  Through the sharp hawthorn blows the cold wind.
  Hum! go to thy cold bed, and warm thee.
Lear. Hast thou given all to thy two daughters?
  And art thou come to this?
Edg. Who gives any thing to poor Tom? whom the foul fiend hath
  led through fire and through flame, through ford and whirlpool,
  o'er bog and quagmire; that hath laid knives under his pillow,[11]   50
  and halters in his pew;[12] set ratsbane by his porridge; made him
  proud of heart, to ride on a bay trotting-horse over four-inched
  bridges, to course[13] his own shadow for a traitor. Bless thy five
  wits! Tom's a-cold,—O, do de, do de, do de. Bless thee from
  whirlwinds, star-blasting, and taking![14] Do poor Tom some charity, whom the foul fiend vexes: there could I have him[15] now,—
  and there,—and there again, and there.

                    [*Storm still.*]

Lear. What, have his daughters brought him to this pass?
  Couldst thou save nothing? Didst thou give them all?
Fool. Nay, he reserved a blanket, else we had been all shamed.   60
Lear. Now, all the plagues that in the pendulous[16] air
  Hang faded o'er men's faults light on thy daughters!
Kent. He hath no daughters, sir.
Lear. Death, traitor! nothing could have subdued[17] nature[18]
  To such a lowness but his unkind daughters.
  Is it the fashion, that discarded fathers
  Should have thus little mercy on their flesh?[19]
  Judicious punishment! 'twas this flesh begot
  Those pelican daughters.[20]
Edg. Pillicock[21] sat on Pillicock-hill: 70
  Halloo, halloo, loo, loo!
Fool. This cold night will turn us all to fools and madmen.
Edg. Take heed o' the foul fiend: obey thy parents; keep thy word
  justly; swear not; commit[22] not with man's sworn spouse; set not
  thy sweet heart on proud array. Tom's a-cold.
Lear. What hast thou been?
Edg. A serving-man, proud in heart and mind; that curled my hair;
  wore gloves in my cap;[23] served the lust of my mistress' heart, and
  did the act of darkness with her; swore as many oaths as I spake
  words, and broke them in the sweet face of heaven: one that slept   80
  in the contriving of lust, and waked to do it: wine loved I deeply,
  dice dearly; and in woman out-paramoured[24] the Turk:[25] false

[11] **knives . . . pillow,** i.e., tempted him to commit suicide.
[12] A gallery of a house, not a church pew.   [13] Chase.   [14] Infection.
[15] **there . . . him,** i.e., he snatches at vermin.   [16] Overhanging.   [17] Reduced.
[18] i.e., man's nature.
[19] **mercy . . . flesh,** Edgar has stuck thorns or skewers into his flesh.
[20] **pelican daughters,** it was believed that young pelicans fed on their mother's blood.
[21] Suggested by *pelican;* it meant darling.   [22] i.e., commit adultery.
[23] **gloves . . . cap,** a gallant often wore his lady's glove in his hat.
[24] Had more mistresses than.   [25] The Sultan.

of heart, light of ear,[26] bloody of hand; hog in sloth, fox in stealth, wolf in greediness, dog in madness, lion in prey. Let not the creaking of shoes nor the rustling of silks betray thy poor heart to woman: keep thy foot out of brothels, thy hand out of plackets,[27] thy pen from lenders' books, and defy the foul fiend.
Still through the hawthorn blows the cold wind:
Says suum, mun, ha, no, nonny.
Dolphin[28] my boy, my boy, sessa![29] let him trot by.   90

[Storm still.]

LEAR. Why, thou wert better in thy grave than to answer[30] with thy uncovered body this extremity of the skies.[31] Is man no more than this? Consider him well. Thou owest the worm no silk, the beast no hide, the sheep no wool, the cat[32] no perfume. Ha! here's three on's are sophisticated! Thou art the thing itself: unaccommodated man[33] is no more but such a poor, bare, forked animal as thou art. Off, off, you lendings![34] come, unbutton here.

[Tearing off his clothes.]

FOOL. Prithee, nuncle, be contented; 'tis a naughty[35] night to swim in. Now a little fire in a wild field were like an old lecher's heart; a small spark, all the rest on 's body cold. Look, here comes a walk-   100
ing fire.

[Enter GLOUCESTER, with a torch.]

EDG. This is the foul fiend Flibbertigibbet: he begins at curfew, and walks till the first cock; he gives the web and the pin,[36] squints the eye, and makes the hare-lip; mildews the white[37] wheat, and hurts the poor creature of earth.
Saint Withold[38] footed[39] thrice the 'old;[40]
He met the night-mare,[41] and her nine-fold;[42]
        Bid her alight,
        And her troth plight,[43]
And, aroint[44] thee, witch, aroint thee!   110

KENT. How fares your grace?[45]
LEAR. What's he?
KENT. Who's there? What is 't you seek?
GLOU. What are you there? Your names?
EDG. Poor Tom; that eats the swimming frog, the toad, the tadpole, the wall-newt and the water;[46] that in the fury of his heart, when the foul fiend rages, eats cow-dung for sallets;[47] swallows the old

---

[26] **light of ear,** foolishly credulous of evil gossip.   [27] Slits in petticoats.
[28] **Dolphin, my boy,** reference to a ballad ridiculing the French Dauphin.
[29] Hurry, go it.   [30] Oppose.   [31] **extremity . . . skies,** violence of the storm.
[32] Civet cat.
[33] **unaccommodated man,** man unprovided with clothes and other furnishings of civilization.
[34] Lent by art to the natural man.   [35] Very wicked.
[36] **web and the pin,** old term for "cataract."   [37] i.e., ripening.   [38] i.e., St. Vitalis.
[39] Walked across.   [40] Wold, an upland plain.   [41] A demon.   [42] Nine offspring.
[43] Pledge her faith (to do no harm).   [44] Begone.   [45] Majesty.
[46] **wall . . . water,** the wall-lizard and the water-lizard.   [47] Salads.

rat and the ditch-dog; drinks the green mantle[48] of the standing[49]
pool; who is whipped from tithing to tithing,[50] and stock-punished,[51]
and imprisoned; who hath had three suits to his back, six shirts to   120
his body, horse to ride, and weapon to wear;
       But mice and rats, and such small deer,[52]
       Have been Tom's food for seven long year.
Beware my follower.[53] Peace, Smulkin; peace, thou fiend!
GLOU. What, hath your grace no better company?
EDG. The prince of darkness is a gentleman:
       Modo he's call'd, and Mahu.
GLOU. Our flesh and blood is grown so vile, my lord,
       That it doth hate what gets[54] it.
EDG. Poor Tom's a-cold.   130
GLOU. Go in with me: my duty cannot suffer[55]
       To obey in all your daughters' hard commands:
       Though their injunction be to bar my doors,
       And let this tyrannous night take hold upon you,
       Yet have I ventured to come seek you out,
       And bring you where both fire and food is ready.
LEAR. First let me talk with this philosopher.[56]
       What is the cause of thunder?
KENT. Good my lord, take his offer; go into the house.
LEAR. I'll talk a word with this same learned Theban.[57]   140
       What is your study?[58]
EDG. How to prevent[59] the fiend, and to kill vermin.
LEAR. Let me ask you one word in private.
KENT. Importune him once more to go, my lord;
       His wits begin to unsettle.
GLOU. Canst thou blame him?   [*Storm still.*]
       His daughters seek his death; ah, that good Kent!
       He said it would be thus, poor banish'd man!
       Thou say'st the king grows mad; I'll tell thee, friend,
       I am almost mad myself: I had a son,   150
       Now outlaw'd from my blood; he sought my life,
       But lately, very late: I loved him, friend:
       No father his son dearer: truth to tell thee,
       The grief hath crazed my wits. What a night's this!
       I do beseech your grace,—
LEAR.   O, cry you mercy,[60] sir.
       Noble philosopher, your company.
EDG. Tom's a-cold.
GLOU. In, fellow, there, into the hovel: keep thee warm.
LEAR. Come, let's in all.
KENT.   This way, my lord.
LEAR.   With him;
       I will keep still[61] with my philosopher.   160

---

[48] Scum.   [49] Stagnant.   [50] **tithing to tithing,** parish to parish.
[51] Put in the stocks.   [52] Animal.   [53] Attendant fiend.   [54] Begets.   [55] Permit me.
[56] Scientist.   [57] i.e., Greek philosopher.   [58] Specialty.
[59] Forestall.   [60] **cry you mercy,** beg your pardon (for not paying attention).   [61] Always.

KENT. Good my lord, soothe[62] him; let him take the fellow.
GLOU. Take him you on.
KENT. Sirrah, come on; go along with us.
LEAR. Come, good Athenian.
GLOU. No words, no words: hush.
EDG. Child[63] Rowland[64] to the dark tower came,
  His word was still,—Fie, foh, and fum,
   I smell the blood of a British man.   *[Exeunt.]*

SCENE V
GLOUCESTER'S *castle*

[Enter CORNWALL *and* EDMUND.*]*
CORN. I will have my revenge ere I depart his house.
EDM. How, my lord, I may be censured,[1] that nature thus gives way to
 loyalty, something fears me[2] to think of.
CORN. I now perceive, it was not altogether your brother's evil dispo-
 sition made him seek his death; but a provoking merit,[3] set a-work
 by a reproveable badness in himself.[4]
EDM. How malicious is my fortune, that I must repent to be just![5]
 This is the letter he spoke of, which approves[6] him an intelligent
 party[7] to the advantages of France.[8] O heavens! that this treason
 were not, or not I the detector!   10
CORN. Go with me to the duchess.
EDM. If the matter of this paper be certain, you have mighty business
 in hand.
CORN. True or false, it hath made thee earl of Gloucester. Seek out
 where thy father is, that he may be ready for our apprehension.[9]
EDM. *[Aside]* If I find him comforting[10] the king, it will stuff his suspicion more fully.—I will persevere in my course of loyalty, though
 the conflict be sore between that and my blood.[11]
CORN. I will lay trust upon thee; and thou shalt find a dearer father
 in my love.   *[Exeunt.]* 20

SCENE VI
A chamber in a farmhouse adjoining the castle

[Enter GLOUCESTER, LEAR, KENT, FOOL, *and* EDGAR.*]*
GLOU. Here is better than the open air; take it thankfully. I will piece
 out the comfort with what addition I can: I will not be long from
 you.

---

 [62] Humor. [63] A candidate for knighthood.
 [64] Charlemagne's nephew and legendary hero. The line is probably a snatch from a lost
ballad.
 [1] Judged. [2] **something fears me,** I am somewhat frightened.
 [3] **provoking merit,** i.e., the fact that your father deserved to die also incited him.
 [4] i.e., Gloucester. [5] Righteous. [6] Proves. [7] **intelligent party,** a spy.
 [8] King of France. [9] Arrest. [10] Giving aid and comfort. [11] Natural instincts.

KENT. All the power of his wits have given way to his impatience: the
gods reward your kindness!   [*Exit* GLOUCESTER.]

EDG. Fraieretto[1] calls me; and tells me Nero is an angler in the lake of
darkness. Pray, innocent,[2] and beware the foul fiend.

FOOL. Prithee, nuncle, tell me whether a madman be a gentleman or
a yeoman?[3]

LEAR. A king, a king!   10

FOOL. No, he's a yeoman that has a gentleman to his son; for he's a
mad yeoman that sees his son a gentleman before him.[4]

LEAR. To have a thousand with red burning spits
    Come hissing in upon 'em,—

EDG. The foul fiend bites my back.

FOOL. He's mad that trusts in the tameness of a wolf, a horse's health,
a boy's love, or a whore's oath.

LEAR. It shall be done; I will arraign them straight.
    [*To* EDGAR] Come, sit thou here, most learned justicer;[5]
    [*To the* FOOL] Thou, sapient sir, sit here. Now, you she foxes!   20

EDG. Look, where he stands and glares!
    Wantest thou eyes at trial,[6] madam?
        Come o'er the bourn,[7] Bessy, to me,—[8]

FOOL. Her boat hath a leak,
    And she must not speak
    Why she dares not come over to thee.

EDG. Thou foul fiend haunts poor Tom in the voice of a nightingale.
Hopdance[9] cries in Tom's belly for two white[10] herring. Croak
not,[11] black angel; I have no food for thee.

KENT. How do you, sir? Stand you not so amazed:[12]   30
    Will you lie down and rest upon the cushions?

LEAR. I'll see their trial first. Bring in the evidence.[13]
    [*To* EDGAR] Thou robed man of justice, take thy place;
    [*To the* FOOL] And thou, his yoke-fellow of equity,
    Bench[14] by his side: [*To* KENT] you are o' the commission,[15]
    Sit you too.

EDG. Let us deal justly.
    Sleepest or wakest thou, jolly shepherd?
        Thy sheep be in the corn;[16]
    And for one blast[17] of thy minikin[18] mouth,   40
    Thy sheep shall take no harm.
    Purr! the cat is gray.

LEAR. Arraign her first; 'tis Goneril. I here take my oath before this
honourable assembly, she kicked the poor king her father.

FOOL. Come hither, mistress. Is your name Goneril?

---

[1] The name of a fiend.   [2] Simpleton.
[3] A small landed proprietor, in rank lower than a gentleman.
[4] **before him,** before he is one.   [5] Judge.
[6] **Wantest . . . trial?** Don't you see you have a spectator at your trial, i.e., the fiend?
[7] Brook.   [8] **Come . . . me,** first line of an old ballad.   [9] A fiend.   [10] Fresh.
[11] **Croak not,** addressed to his rumbling belly.   [12] In a daze.   [13] Witnesses.
[14] Sit on the judge's bench.   [15] A commissioned Justice of the Peace.
[16] Wheat field.   [17] The time it takes to blow one blast.   [18] Pretty little.

LEAR. She cannot deny it.

FOOL. Cry you mercy, I took you for a joint-stool.[19]

LEAR. And here's another, whose warp'd[20] looks proclaim
    What store[21] her heart is made on. Stop her there!
    Arms, arms, sword, fire! Corruption in the place![22]   50
    False justicer, why hast thou let her 'scape?

EDG. Bless thy five wits!

KENT. O pity! Sir, where is the patience now,
    That you so oft have boasted to retain?

EDG. [*Aside*] My tears begin to take his part so much,
    They'll mar my counterfeiting.

LEAR. The little dogs and all,
    Tray, Blanch, and Sweet-heart, see, they bark at me.

EDG. Tom will throw his head at them.
    Avaunt, you curs!   60
        Be thy mouth or black or white,
        Tooth that poisons if it bite;
        Mastiff, greyhound, mongrel grim,
        Hound or spaniel, brach or lym,[23]
        Or bobtail tike[24] or trundle-tail,[25]
        Tom will make them weep and wail:
        For, with throwing thus my head,
        Dogs leap the hatch,[26] and all are fled.
    Do de, de, de. Sessa![27] Come, march to wakes and fairs and mar-
    ket-towns. Poor Tom, thy horn is dry.[28]   70

LEAR. Then let them anatomize[29] Regan; see what breeds about her
    heart. Is there any cause in nature that makes these hard hearts?
    [*To* EDGAR] You, sir, I entertain[30] for one of my hundred; only I
    do not like the fashion of your garments: you will say they are
    Persian[31] attire; but let them be changed.

KENT. Now, good my lord, lie here and rest awhile.

LEAR. Make no noise, make no noise; draw the curtains:[32] so, so, so.
    We'll go to supper i' the morning. So, so, so.[33]

FOOL. And I'll go to bed at noon.

                [*Re-enter* GLOUCESTER.]

GLOU. Come hither, friend: where is the king my master?   80

KENT. Here, sir; but trouble him not, his wits are gone.

GLOU. Good friend, I prithee, take him in thy arms;
    I have o'erheard a plot of death upon[34] him:
    There is a litter ready; lay him in 't,
    And drive towards Dover, friend, where thou shalt meet
    Both welcome and protection. Take up thy master:

---

[19] Stool made by a joiner.   [20] Distorted.   [21] Stuff.
[22] **Corruption . . . place,** bribery in the court.   [23] **brach or lym,** bitch or bloodhound.
[24] Cur.   [25] Drooping-tail.   [26] Lower half of a divided [Dutch] door.
[27] about = "Let's go!"   [28] **horn is dry,** a beggar's appeal for drink; horn was a bottle.
[29] Dissect.   [30] Engage.   [31] Gorgeous.   [32] i.e., imaginary bed curtains.
[33] **So . . . so,** an indication that Lear goes through the motions of drawing curtains.
[34] Against.

If thou shouldst dally[35] half an hour, his life,
With thine, and all that offer to defend him,
Stand in assurèd loss:[36] take up, take up;
And follow me, that will to some provision[37]   90
Give thee quick conduct.

KENT.   Oppressèd nature sleeps;
This rest might yet have balm'd thy broken sinews,[38]
Which, if convenience will not allow,
Stand in hard cure.[39] [*To the* FOOL] Come, help to bear thy
    master;
Thou must not stay behind.

GLOU.   Come, come, away.
                    [*Exeunt all but* EDGAR.]

EDG. When we our betters see bearing our woes,
We scarcely think our miseries our foes.
Who alone suffers suffers most i' the mind,
Leaving free[40] things and happy shows[41] behind:
But then the mind much sufferance[42] doth o'erskip,[43]   100
When grief hath mates, and bearing[44] fellowship.
How light and portable[45] my pain seems now,
When that which makes me bend makes the king bow,
He childed as I father'd![46] Tom, away!
Mark the high noises;[47] and thyself bewray,[48]
When false opinion, whose wrong thought defiles thee,
In thy just proof,[49] repeals[50] and reconciles thee.
What[51] will hap more to-night, safe 'scape the king!
Lurk, lurk.[52]   [*Exit.*]

SCENE VII
GLOUCESTER's castle

[*Enter* CORNWALL, REGAN, GONERIL, EDMUND, *and* SERVANTS.]

CORN. Post speedily to my lord your husband; show him this letter:
    the army of France is landed. Seek out the villain Gloucester.
                    [*Exeunt some of the* SERVANTS.]

REG. Hang him instantly.

GON. Pluck out his eyes.

CORN. Leave him to my displeasure. Edmund, keep you our sister
    company: the revenges we are bound to take upon your traitorous
    father are not fit for your beholding. Advise the duke, where you

---

[35] Delay.   [36] **Stand . . . loss,** are sure to be lost.   [37] i.e., for safety.
[38] **balm'd . . . sinews,** healed your racked nerves.
[39] **Stand . . . cure,** are hard to cure.
[40] Carefree.   [41] **happy shows,** appearances of happiness.   [42] Suffering.
[43] Escape.   [44] i.e., of sorrow.   [45] Endurable.
[46] **childed . . . father'd,** having children like my father (in cruelty).
[47] **high noises,** sounds of discord among the high and mighty.
[48] You reveal yourself, i.e., put off your disguise.
[49] **In . . . proof,** on proof that you are guiltless.   [50] Restores (i.e., to favor).
[51] Whatever.   [52] Hide.

are going, to a most festinate preparation:[1] we are bound to the
like.[2] Our posts[3] shall be swift and intelligent[4] betwixt us. Farewell,
dear sister: farewell, my lord of Gloucester.[5]   10

[*Enter* OSWALD.]

How now! where's the king?
Osw. My lord of Gloucester[6] hath convey'd him hence:
    Some five or six and thirty of his knights,
    Hot questrists[7] after him, met him at gate;
    Who, with some other of the lords dependants,
    Are gone with him towards Dover; where they boast
    To have well-armèd friends.
CORN.   Get horses for your mistress.
GON. Farewell, sweet lord, and sister.
CORN. Edmund, farewell.

                [*Exeunt* GONERIL, EDMUND, *and*
                OSWALD.]
            Go seek the traitor Gloucester,
Pinion[8] him like a thief, bring him before us.   20

                [*Exeunt other* SERVANTS.]
Though well we may not pass[9] upon his life
Without the form of justice, yet our power
Shall do a courtesy[10] to our wrath, which men
May blame, but not control. Who's there? the traitor?

                [*Enter* GLOUCESTER, *brought in by
                two or three.*]

REG. Ingrateful fox! 'tis he.
CORN. Bind fast his corky[11] arms.
GLOU. What mean your graces? Good my friends, consider
    You are my guests: do me no foul play, friends.
CORN. Bind him, I say.

                [SERVANTS *bind him.*]
REG.   Hard, hard. O filthy traitor!
GLOU. Unmerciful lady as you are, I'm none.   30
CORN. To this chair bind him. Villain, thou shalt find—

                [REGAN *plucks his beard.*]
GLOU. By the kind gods, 'tis most ignobly done
    To pluck me by the beard.
REG. So white, and such a traitor!
GLOU.   Naughty[12] lady,
    These hairs, which thou dost ravish from my chin,
    Will quicken,[13] and accuse thee: I am your host:

---

[1] **to . . . preparation,** to make a most hasty preparation (for war).
[2] **bound to the like,** getting ready for the like preparation.
[3] Messengers.   [4] Carry information.
[5] i.e., Edmund, who has been given the title as a reward for his treachery.
[6] The old Earl.   [7] Searchers.   [8] i.e., bind his elbows together.   [9] Pass judgment.
[10] Act in accordance with.   [11] Withered.   [12] Wicked.   [13] Come to life.

With robbers' hands my hospitable favours[14]
You should not ruffle[15] thus. What will you do?
CORN. Come, sir, what letters had you late from France?
REG. Be simple[16] answerer, for we know the truth.   40
CORN. And what confederacy have you with the traitors
    Late footed[17] in the kingdom?
REG. To whose hands have you sent the lunatic king?
    Speak.
GLOU.   I have a letter guessingly set down,
    Which came from one that's of a neutral heart,
    And not from one opposed.
CORN.   Cunning.
REG.   And false.
CORN. Where hast thou sent the king?
GLOU. To Dover.
REG. Wherefore to Dover? Wast thou not charged at peril[18]—
CORN. Wherefore to Dover? Let him first answer that.   50
GLOU. I am tied to the stake, and I must stand the course.[19]
REG. Wherefore to Dover, sir?
GLOU. Because I would not see thy cruel nails
    Pluck out his poor old eyes; nor thy fierce sister
    In his anointed[20] flesh stick boarish fangs.
    The sea, with such a storm as his bare head
    In hell-black night endured, would have buoy'd up,[21]
    And quench'd the stelled fires:[22]
    Yet, poor old heart, he holp[23] the heavens to rain.
    If wolves had at thy gate howl'd[24] that stern time,   60
    Thou shouldst have said "Good porter, turn the key,"
    All cruels else subscribed:[25] but I shall see
    The wingèd vengeance overtake such children.
CORN. See 't shalt thou never. Fellows, hold the chair.
    Upon these eyes of thine I'll set my foot.
GLOU. He that will think to live till he be old,
    Give me some help! O cruel! O you gods!
REG. One side will mock another;[26] the other too.
CORN. If you see vengeance,—
FIRST SERV.   Hold your hand, my lord:
    I have served you ever since I was a child;   70
    But better service have I never done you
    Than now to bid you hold.
REG.   Hold now, you dog!

---

[14] **hospitable favours,** the features of your host.   [15] Treat with violence.
[16] Straightforward.   [17] Landed.   [18] Under peril (of death).
[19] Attack (of the dogs in bear-baiting).
[20] i.e., with the consecrated oil at his coronation.   [21] Heaved aloft.
[22] **stelled fires,** the fires of the stars.   [23] Helped.   [24] i.e., for shelter.
[25] **All ... subscribed,** all other cruel creatures except you gave way (to their need for shelter).
[26] **One ... another,** i.e., one good eye will mock the other blind one.

FIRST SERV. If you did wear a beard upon your chin,
    I'd shake it on this quarrel.[27] What do you mean?
CORN. My villain![28]   [*They draw and fight.*]
FIRST SERV. Nay, then, come on, and take the chance of anger.
REG. Give me thy sword. A peasant stand up thus!
                                    [*Takes a sword, and runs at him
                                    behind.*]
FIRST SERV. O, I am slain! My lord, you have one eye left
    To see some mischief[29] on him. O!
                                    [*Dies.*]
CORN. Lest it see more, prevent[30] it. Out, vile jelly!   80
    Where is thy lustre now?
GLOU. All dark and comfortless. Where's my son Edmund?
    Edmund, enkindle all the sparks of nature,
    To quit[31] this horrid act.
REG.   Out, treacherous villain!
    Thou call'st on him that hates thee: it was he
    That made the overture[32] of thy treasons to us;
    Who is too good to pity thee.
GLOU. O my follies! then Edgar was abused.[33]
    Kind gods, forgive me that,[34] and prosper him!
REG. Go thrust him out at gates, and let him smell   90
    His way to Dover. [*Exit one with* GLOUCESTER.] How is 't, my
    lord? how look you?
CORN. I have received a hurt: follow me, lady.
    Turn out that eyeless villain; throw this slave
    Upon the dunghill. Regan, I bleed apace:[35]
    Untimely[36] comes this hurt: give me your arm.
                                    [*Exit* CORNWALL, *led by* REGAN.]
SEC. SERV. I'll never care what wickedness I do,
    If this man come to good.
THIRD SERV.   If she live long,
    And in the end meet the old course of death,
    Women will all turn monsters.[37]
SEC. SERV. Let's follow the old earl, and get the Bedlam[38]   100
    To lead him where he would: his roguish madness
    Allows itself to any thing.[39]
THIRD SERV. Go thou: I'll fetch some flax and whites of eggs
    To apply to his bleeding face. Now, heaven help him!
                                    [*Exeunt severally.*]

---

[27] This cause (over which I quarrel with you).   [28] Bondman, serf.   [29] Harm.
[30] Forestall.   [31] Repay, revenge.   [32] Disclosure.   [33] Deceived (by Edmund).
[34] i.e., my treatment of Edgar.   [35] Fast.   [36] Inopportunely.
[37] **Women . . . monsters,** because they will know there is no divine justice.
[38] Lunatic, i.e., Edgar.
[39] **Allows . . . thing,** permits him to do anything with impunity.

ACT IV

SCENE I
The heath

[*Enter* EDGAR.]

EDG. Yet better thus, and known to be contemn'd,[1]
    Than still contemn'd and flatter'd. To be worst,
    The lowest and most dejected thing of fortune,
    Stands still in esperance,[2] lives not in fear:
    The lamentable change is from the best;
    The worst returns to laughter.[3] Welcome, then,
    Thou unsubstantial air that I embrace!
    The wretch that thou hast blown unto the worst
    Owes nothing to thy blasts. But who comes here?

                    [*Enter* GLOUCESTER, *led by an*
                    OLD MAN.]

    My father, poorly led?[4] World, world, O world!   10
    But that thy strange mutations[5] make us hate thee,
    Life would not yield to age.

OLD MAN. O, my good lord, I have been your tenant, and your fa-
    ther's tenant, these fourscore years.

GLOU. Away, get thee away; good friend, be gone:
    Thy comforts can do me no good at all;
    Thee they may hurt.

OLD MAN. Alack, sir, you cannot see your way.

GLOU. I have no way,[6] and therefore want no eyes;
    I stumbled when I saw: full oft 'tis seen,   20
    Our means secure us,[7] and our mere defects
    Prove our commodities.[8] O dear son Edgar,
    The food[9] of thy abusèd[10] father's wrath!
    Might I but live to see thee in my touch,
    I'd say I had eyes again!

OLD MAN.   How now! Who's there?

EDG. [*Aside*] O gods! Who is 't can say "I am at the worst"?
    I am worse then e'er I was.

OLD MAN.   'Tis poor mad Tom.

EDG. [*Aside*] And worse I may be yet: the worst is not
    So long as we can say "This is the worst."

OLD MAN. Fellow, where goest?

GLOU.   Is it a beggar-man?   30

OLD MAN. Madman and beggar too.

---

[1] Despised.   [2] Hope.
[3] **returns to laughter,** changes to happiness.
[4] **poorly led,** led by one poor old man, instead of his former attendants.
[5] Changes (of fortune).   [6] **I . . . way,** no course in life is left me.
[7] **Our . . . secure us,** prosperity makes us careless and overconfident.
[8] **our mere . . . commodities,** our very deprivations prove to be benefits.
[9] i.e., object.   [10] Deceived.

GLOU. He has some reason, else he could not beg.
      I' the last night's storm I such a fellow saw;
      Which made me think a man a worm: my son
      Came then into my mind; and yet my mind
      Was then scarce friends with him: I have heard more since.
      As flies to wanton[11] boys, are we to the gods,
      They kill us for their sport.

EDG.   [*Aside*] How should this be?
      Bad is the trade that must play fool to sorrow,
      Angering[12] itself and others.—Bless thee, master!   40

GLOU. Is that the naked fellow?

OLD MAN.   Ay, my lord.

GLOU. Then, prithee, get thee gone: if, for my sake,
      Thou wilt o'ertake us, hence a mile or twain,
      I' the way toward Dover, do it for ancient love;
      And bring some covering for this naked soul,
      Who I'll entreat to lead me.

OLD MAN.   Alack, sir, he is mad.

GLOU. 'Tis the times' plague,[13] when madmen lead the blind.
      Do as I bid thee, or rather do thy pleasure;[14]
      Above the rest,[15] be gone.

OLD MAN. I'll bring him the best 'parel that I have,   50
      Come on 't what will.   [*Exit.*]

GLOU. Sirrah, naked fellow,—

EDG. Poor Tom's a-cold. [*Aside*] I cannot daub it[16] further.

GLOU. Come hither, fellow.

EDG. [*Aside*] And yet I must.—Bless thy sweet eyes, they bleed.

GLOU. Knowst thou the way to Dover?

EDG. Both stile and gate, horse-way and foot-path. Poor Tom hath
    been scared out of his good wits: bless thee, good man's son, from
    the foul fiend! five fiends have been in poor Tom at once; of lust,
    as Obidicut; Hobbididance, prince of dumbness; Mahu, of steal-   60
    ing; Modo, of murder; Flibbertigibbet, of mopping and mowing,[17]
    who since[18] possesses chambermaids and waiting-women. So, bless
    thee, master!

GLOU. Here, take this purse, thou whom the heavens' plagues
      Have humbled to all strokes:[19] that I am wretched
      Makes thee the happier: heavens, deal so still![20]
      Let the superfluous and lust-dieted man,[21]
      That slaves your ordinance,[22] that will not see
      Because he doth not feel, feel your power quickly;
      So distribution[23] should undo[24] excess,   70
      And each man have enough. Dost thou know Dover?

---

[11] Playful.   [12] Distressing.   [13] **times' plague,** world's calamity.
[14] **thy pleasure,** what you wish.   [15] **above the rest,** above all.   [16] **daub it,** dissemble.
[17] **mopping and mowing,** grimacing and making faces.   [18] i.e., since a long time ago.
[19] **Have . . . strokes,** have humbled you so that you accept every sort of adversity.
[20] **deal so still,** i.e., continue to treat men overconfident in their prosperity as you have me.
[21] **superfluous . . . man,** the man who has all that he needs, all that he lusts after.
[22] **slaves your ordinance,** that makes heaven's will subservient to his own.
[23] Distributive justice.   [24] Correct.

EDG. Ay, master.

GLOU. There is a cliff, whose high and bending head
　　　Looks fearfully[25] in the confinèd[26] deep.[27]
　　　Bring me but to the very brim of it,
　　　And I'll repair the misery thou dost bear
　　　With something rich about me: from that place
　　　I shall no leading need.

EDG. 　　　　　　　　　　　Give me thy arm:
　　　Poor Tom shall lead thee. 　　　　　　　*[Exeunt.]*

SCENE II
Before the DUKE OF ALBANY's *palace*

[Enter GONERIL *and* EDMUND.*]*

GON. Welcome, my lord: I marvel our mild husband
　　　Not met us on the way.

　　　　　　　　　　　　[Enter OSWALD.*]*

　　　　　　　　　　　Now, where's your master?

OSW. Madam, within; but never man so changed.
　　　I told him of the army that was landed;
　　　He smiled at it: I told him you were coming;
　　　His answer was "The worse:" of Gloucester's treachery,
　　　And of the loyal service of his son,
　　　When I inform'd him, then he call'd me sot,[1]
　　　And told me I had turn'd the wrong side out:[2]
　　　What most he should dislike seems pleasant to him;　　　10
　　　What like, offensive.

GON. *[To* EDM.*]* 　　　　　Then shall you go no further.
　　　It is the cowish[3] terror of his spirit,
　　　That dares not undertake:[4] he'll not feel wrongs
　　　Which tie him to an answer. Our wishes on the way[5]
　　　May prove effects.[6] Back, Edmund, to my brother;
　　　Hasten his musters and conduct his powers:[7]
　　　I must change[8] arms[9] at home, and give the distaff
　　　Into my husband's hands. This trusty servant
　　　Shall pass between us: ere long you are like to hear,
　　　If you dare venture in your own behalf,　　　20
　　　A mistress's command. Wear this; spare speech;
　　　　　　　　　　　[Giving a favor.]
　　　Decline your head: this kiss, if it durst speak,
　　　Would stretch thy spirits up into the air:
　　　Conceive,[10] and fare thee well.

---

[25] In a way to arouse terror in anyone who looks over it down to the sea.
[26] Shut in. 　[27] **confined deep,** i.e., the Straits of Dover.
[1] Fool. 　[2] **turn'd . . . out,** completely misinterpreted the situation. 　[3] Cowardly.
[4] Take the initiative. 　[5] **on the way,** expressed on our way here.
[6] **prove effects,** come to pass. 　[7] Forces. 　[8] Exchange.
[9] Emblems of our professions. 　[10] Understand.

EDM. Yours in the ranks of death.

GON.   My most dear Gloucester!

[*Exit* EDMUND.]

O, the difference of man and man!
To thee a woman's services are due:
My fool[11] usurps[12] my body.

OSW.   Madam, here comes my lord.

[*Exit.*]

[*Enter* ALBANY.]

GON. I have been worth the whistle.[13]

ALB.   O Goneril!

You are not worth the dust which the rude wind   30
Blows in your face. I fear your disposition:[14]
That nature, which contemns its origin,
Cannot be border'd certain in itself;[15]
She that herself will sliver and disbranch[16]
From her material sap,[17] perforce must wither
And come to deadly use.[18]

GON. No more; the text is foolish.

ALB. Wisdom and goodness to the vile seem vile:
Filths savour but themselves.[19] What have you done?
Tigers, not daughters, what have you perform'd?   40
A father, and a gracious[20] agèd man,
Whose reverence even the head-lugg'd[21] bear would lick,
Most barbarous, most degenerate! have you madded.[22]
Could my good brother suffer you to do it?
A man, a prince, by him so benefited!
If that the heavens do not their visible[23] spirits
Send quickly down to tame these vile offences,
It will come,[24]
Humanity must perforce prey on itself,
Like monsters of the deep.

GON.   Milk-liver'd[25] man!   50

That bear'st a cheek for blows, a head for wrongs:
Who hast not in thy brows an eye discerning[26]
Thine honour[27] from thy suffering; that not know'st
Fools[28] do those villains pity who are punish'd
Ere they have done their mischief. Where's thy drum?
France[29] spreads his banners in our noiseless[30] land,

---

[11] i.e., fool of a husband.   [12] Possesses without right.   [13] **the whistle,** whistling for.
[14] Temperament.   [15] **Cannot . . . itself,** can have no sure restraints in its own nature.
[16] **sliver and disbranch,** both mean "break off."
[17] **material sap,** its nourishing substance (i.e., the sap of the tree).
[18] **deadly use,** i.e., to destruction.
[19] **Filths . . . themselves,** everything tastes filthy to the filthy.   [20] Kindly.
[21] Pulled along by the head, showing he is surly.   [22] Driven insane.
[23] In visible form.   [24] **It will come,** this will be the result.
[25] White-livered, cowardly.   [26] Able to distinguish.
[27] **Thine honour,** things you can endure with honor.   [28] i.e., only fools.
[29] The King of France.   [30] Quiet, i.e., unprepared for warlike resistance.

       With plumèd helm thy state[31] begins to threat;
       Whiles thou, a moral[32] fool, sit'st still, and criest
       "Alack, why does he so?"
ALB.   See thyself, devil!
       Proper[33] deformity seems not in the fiend   60
       So horrid as in woman.
GON.   O vain[34] fool!
ALB. Thou changèd[35] and self-cover'd[36] thing, for shame,
       Be-monster[37] not thy feature. Were 't my fitness[38]
       To let these hands obey my blood,[39]
       They art apt[40] enough to dislocate and tear
       Thy flesh and bones: howe'er[41] thou art a fiend,
       A woman's shape doth shield thee.
GON. Marry, your manhood now[42]—

                 [Enter a MESSENGER.*]*

ALB. What news?
MESS. O, my good lord, the Duke of Cornwall's dead;   70
       Slain by his servant, going to put out
       The other eye of Gloucester.
ALB.   Gloucester's eyes!
MESS. A servant that he bred, thrill'd with remorse,[43]
       Opposed against the act, bending[44] his sword
       To[45] his great master; who, thereat enraged,
       Flew on him, and amongst them fell'd[46] him dead;
       But not without that harmful stroke, which since
       Hath pluck'd him after.[47]
ALB.   This shows you are above,
       You justicers, that these our nether crimes
       So speedily can venge! But, O poor Gloucester!   80
       Lost he his other eye?
MESS.   Both, both, my lord.
       This letter, madam, craves a speedy answer;
       'Tis from your sister.
GON. *[Aside]* One way I like this well;
       But being widow, and my Gloucester with her,
       May all the building in my fancy pluck
       Upon my hateful[48] life: another way,
       The news is not so tart.[49]—I'll read, and answer.
                    [Exit.]

---

[31] Realm.   [32] Moralizing.   [33] Suitable to a fiend.   [34] Silly, futile.
[35] Transformed.   [36] i.e., covering your real fiend's nature with a woman's form.
   [37] **Be-monster . . . feature,** don't allow your whole appearance to be changed to that of a monster.
   [38] **were't my fitness,** if it were proper for me.   [39] Passion.   [40] Ready.
   [41] However much.   [42] **your . . . now,** what a fine specimen of manhood you are now!
   [43] Pity.   [44] Directing.   [45] Against.   [46] They felled.
   [47] **pluck'd him after,** i.e., pulled Cornwall down after him.
   [48] **May . . . hateful,** may pull down all my castles in the air (her plan to marry Edmund) and make my life a hated ruin.
   [49] Painful.

ALB. Where was his son when they did take his eyes?
MESS. Come with my lady hither.
ALB.   He is not here.   90
MESS. No, my good lord; I met him back[50] again.
ALB. Knows he the wickedness?
MESS. Ay, my good lord; 'twas he inform'd against him;
    And quit the house on purpose, that their punishment
    Might have the freer course.
ALB.   Gloucester, I live
    To thank thee for the love thou show'dst the king,
    And to revenge thine eyes. Come hither, friend:
    Tell me what more thou know'st.   [*Exeunt.*]

SCENE III
The French camp near Dover

[*Enter* KENT *and a* GENTLEMAN.]
KENT. Why the King of France is so suddenly gone back know you
    the reason?
GENT. Something he left imperfect in the state, which since his com-
    ing forth is thought of; which imports[1] to the kingdom so much
    fear and danger that his personal return was most required and
    necessary.
KENT. Who hath he left behind him general?
GENT. The Marshal of France, Monsieur La Far.
KENT. Did your letters pierce the queen to any demonstration of
    grief?   10
GENT. Ay, sir; she took them, read them in my presence;
    And now and then an ample tear trill'd[2] down
    Her delicate cheek; it seem'd she was a queen
    Over her passion;[3] who, most rebel-like,
    Sought to be king o'er her.
KENT.   O, then it moved her.
GENT. Not to a rage:[4] patience and sorrow strove
    Who should express her goodliest.[5] You have seen
    Sunshine and rain at once: her smiles and tears
    Were like a better way:[6] those happy smilets,[7]
    That play'd on her ripe lip, seem'd not to know   20
    What guests were in her eyes; which[8] parted thence,
    As pearls from diamonds dropp'd. In brief,
    Sorrow would be a rarity most beloved,
    If all could so become it.[9]
KENT.   Made she no verbal question?[10]
GENT. 'Faith, once or twice she heaved the name of "father"

---

[50]On his way back.   [1]Portends.   [2]Trickled.
[3]Emotion, i.e., grief.   [4]Outburst (of grief).
[5]**express her goodliest,** give her the most beautiful expression.
[6]**like . . . way,** like mingled sunshine and rain, only more beautiful.   [7]Little smiles.
[8]i.e., the tears.   [9]**all . . . become it,** it were so becoming to all (as to her).
[10]**Made . . . question?** Did she say nothing? (**question,** speech).

    Pantingly forth, as if it press'd her heart;
    Cried "Sisters! sisters! Shame of ladies! sisters!
    Kent! father! sisters! What, i' the storm? i' the night?
    Let pity not be believed!"[11] There she shook
    The holy water from her heavenly eyes,   30
    And clamour moisten'd:[12] then away she started
    To deal with grief alone.
KENT.   It is the stars,
    The stars above us, govern our conditions;[13]
    Else one self[14] mate and mate could not beget
    Such different issues. You spoke not with her since?
GENT. No.
KENT. Was this before the king return'd?
GENT.   No, since.
KENT. Well, sir, the poor distressèd Lear's i' the town;
    Who sometime,[15] in his better tune,[16] remembers
    What we are come about, and by no means   40
    Will yield[17] to see his daughter.
GENT.   Why, good sir?
KENT. A sovereign[18] shame so elbows[19] him: his own unkindness,
    That stripp'd her from his benediction,[20] turn'd her
    To foreign casualties,[21] gave her dear rights
    To his dog-hearted daughters, these things sting
    His mind so venomously, that burning shame
    Detains him from Cordelia.
GENT.   Alack, poor gentleman!
KENT. Of Albany's and Cornwall's powers[22] you heard not?
GENT. 'Tis so, they are afoot.
KENT. Well, sir, I'll bring you to our master Lear,   50
    And leave you to attend him: some dear[23] cause
    Will in concealment wrap me up awhile;
    When I am known aright, you shall not grieve
    Lending me[24] this acquaintance. I pray you, go
    Along with me.   [*Exeunt.*]

SCENE IV
The same—a tent

[*Enter, with drum and colours,* CORDELIA, DOCTOR, *and* SOLDIERS.]
COR. Alack, 'tis he: why, he was met even now
    As mad as the vex'd sea; singing aloud;
    Crown'd with rank fumiter and furrow-weeds,[1]

---

[11] Believed in.   [12] **clamour moisten'd,** moistened her cries of grief (by weeping).
[13] Temperaments.   [14] **one self,** one and the same.   [15] Sometimes.
[16] **better tune,** more lucid intervals.   [17] Assent.   [18] Overmastering.
[19] Stands at his elbow.   [20] Parting blessing.
[21] **foreign casualties,** hazards in a foreign land.   [22] Troops.
[23] Important.   [24] **Lending me,** for having granted me.
[1] **rank . . . furrow-weeds,** luxuriant fumitory (earth-smoke) and weeds growing in furrows
of a plowed field.

With bur-docks, hemlock, nettles, cuckoo-flowers,[2]
Darnel, and all the idle[3] weeds that grow
In our sustaining corn.[4] A century[5] send forth;
Search every acre in the high-grown field,
And bring him to our eye. [*Exit an* OFFICER.] What can man's
    wisdom[6]
In the restoring his bereavèd sense?
He that helps him take all my outward worth.[7]   10
DOCT. There is means, madam:
    Our foster-nurse of nature[8] is repose,
    The which he lacks; that to provoke[9] in him,
    Are many simples operative,[10] whose power
    Will close the eye of anguish.
COR.   All blest secrets,[11]
    All you unpublish'd virtues[12] of the earth,
    Spring with my tears! be aidant and remediate[13]
    In the good man's distress! Seek, seek for him;
    Lest his ungovern'd rage[14] dissolve the life
    That wants the means[15] to lead it.

                           [*Enter a* MESSENGER.]

MESS.   News, madam;   20
    The British powers are marching hitherward.
COR. 'Tis known before; our preparation stands
    In expectation of[16] them. O dear father,
    It is thy business that I go about;
    Therefore great France
    My mourning and important[17] tears hath pitied.
    No blown[18] ambition doth our arms incite,
    But love, dear love, and our aged father's right:
    Soon may I hear and see him!   [*Exeunt.*]

SCENE V
GLOUCESTER'S *castle*

[*Enter* REGAN *and* OSWALD.]
REG. But are my brother's powers set forth?
OSW.   Ay, madam.
REG. Himself in person there?
OSW.   Madam, with much ado:[1]
    Your sister is the better soldier.

---

[2] Flowers blooming when the cuckoo is abroad, i.e., in April and May—perhaps cowslips.
[3] Useless.   [4] **sustaining corn,** wheat that gives sustenance.
[5] Detail of a hundred men.   [6] **What . . . wisdom,** what can science do.   [7] Property.
[8] **Our foster . . . of,** the nurse that fosters our nature.   [9] Induce.
[10] **simples operative,** effective medicinal herbs.   [11] Private remedies.
[12] **unpublish'd virtues,** secret efficacious medicinal plants.
[13] **be . . . remediate,** be helpful and remedial.   [14] Delirium.
[15] **the means,** i.e., his reason.   [16] **In . . . of,** ready to meet.   [17] Importunate.
[18] Swollen.   [1] **with much ado,** as a result of much effort.

REG. Lord Edmund spake not with your lord at home?
Osw. No, madam.
REG. What might import[2] my sister's letter to him?
Osw. I know not, lady.
REG. 'Faith, he is posted[3] hence on serious matter.[4]
    It was great ignorance,[5] Gloucester's eyes being out,
    To let him live: where he arrives he moves   10
    All hearts against us: Edmund, I think, is gone,
    In pity of his misery, to dispatch
    His nighted life; moreover, to descry
    The strength o' the enemy.
Osw. I must needs after him, madam, with my letter.
REG. Our troops set forth to-morrow: stay with us;
    The ways are dangerous.
Osw.   I may not, madam:
    My lady charged my duty in this business.
REG. Why should she write to Edmund? Might not you
    Transport her purposes by word? Belike,[6]   20
    Something—I know not what: I'll love thee much,
    Let me unseal the letter.
Osw.   Madam, I had rather—
REG. I know your lady does not love her husband;
    I am sure of that: and at her late being here
    She gave strange oeillades[7] and most speaking looks
    To noble Edmund. I know you are of her bosom.[8]
Osw. I, madam?
REG. I speak in understanding; you are, I know 't:
    Therefore I do advise you, take this note:
    My lord is dead; Edmund and I have talk'd;[9]   30
    And more convenient[10] is he for my hand
    Than for your lady's: you may gather more.[11]
    If you do find him, pray you, give him this;
    And when your mistress hears thus much[12] from you,
    I pray, desire her call her wisdom to her.
    So, fare you well.
    If you do chance to hear of that blind traitor,
    Preferment[13] falls on him that cuts him off.
Osw. Would I could meet him, madam! I should show
    What party I do follow.
REG.   Fare thee well.   *[Exeunt.]*   40

---

[2] Mean. [3] **is posted,** has ridden fast. [4] Business. [5] Stupidity. [6] Probably.
[7] Amorous glances. [8] **of her bosom,** in her confidence.
[9] **have talk'd,** have come to an understanding (about marrying). [10] Suitable.
[11] **gather more,** i.e., make further inferences.
[12] **thus much,** as much as I have told you. [13] Advancement.

SCENE VI
Fields near Dover

[*Enter* GLOUCESTER, *and* EDGAR *dressed like a peasant.*]
GLOU. When shall we come to the top of that same hill?
EDG. You do climb up it now: look, how we labour.
GLOU. Methinks the ground is even.
EDG.   Horrible steep.
    Hark, do you hear the sea?
GLOU.   No, truly.
EDG. Why, then, your other senses grow imperfect
    By your eyes' anguish.
GLOU.   So may it be, indeed:
    Methinks thy voice is alter'd; and thou speak'st
    In better phrase and matter than thou didst.
EDG. You're much deceived: in nothing am I changed
    But in my garments.
GLOU.   Methinks you're better spoken.[1]   10
EDG. Come on, sir; here's the place: stand still. How fearful
    And dizzy 'tis, to cast one's eyes so low!
    The crows and choughs[2] that wing the midway air
    Show scarce so gross[3] as beetles: half way down
    Hangs one that gathers samphire,[4] dreadful trade!
    Methinks he seems no bigger than his head:
    The fishermen, that walk upon the beach,
    Appear like mice; and yond tall anchoring bark,
    Diminish'd to her cock;[5] her cock, a buoy
    Almost too small for sight: the murmuring surge,   20
    That on the unnumber'd[6] idle[7] pebbles chafes,
    Cannot be heard so high. I'll look no more;
    Lest my brain turn, and the deficient sight[8]
    Topple[9] down headlong.
GLOU.   Set me where you stand.
EDG. Give me your hand: you are now within a foot
    Of the extreme verge: for all beneath the moon
    Would I not leap upright.[10]
GLOU.   Let go my hand.
    Here, friend, 's another purse; in it a jewel
    Well worth a poor man's taking: fairies[11] and gods
    Prosper it with thee! Go thou farther off;   30
    Bid me farewell, and let me hear thee going.
EDG. Now fare you well, good sir.
GLOU.   With all my heart.

---

[1] i.e., you speak with more propriety.
[2] Crow-like birds, something like grackles.   [3] Large.
[4] An aromatic herb, gathered from the face of cliffs by men lowered by a rope.
[5] Cock-boat, tender.   [6] Innumerable.   [7] Useless, barren.
[8] **the . . . sight,** my sight failing.   [9] Cause me to topple.   [10] i.e., even straight up.
[11] fairies, because they were supposed to make it increase miraculously.

EDG. Why I do trifle thus with his despair
    Is done to cure it.
GLOU. [*Kneeling*]   O you mighty gods!
    This world I do renounce, and in your sights,
    Shake patiently my great affliction off:
    If I could bear it longer, and not fall
    To quarrel with[12] your great opposeless[13] wills,
    My snuff[14] and loathèd part of nature should
    Burn itself out. If Edgar live, O, bless him!   40
    Now, fellow, fare thee well.   [*He falls forward.*]
EDG.   Gone, sir; farewell.
    And yet I know not how conceit[15] may rob
    The treasury of life,[16] when life itself
    Yields to the theft:[17] had he been where he thought,
    By this, had thought been past. Alive or dead?
    Ho, you sir! friend! Hear you, sir! speak!
    Thus might he pass[18] indeed: yet he revives.
    What are you, sir?
GLOU.   Away, and let me die.
EDG. Hadst thou been aught but gossamer,[19] feathers, air,
    So many fathom down precipitating,   50
    Thou 'dst shiver'd like an egg: but thou dost breathe;
    Hast heavy substance; bleed'st not; speak'st; art sound.
    Ten masts at each[20] make not the altitude
    Which thou hast perpendicularly fell:
    Thy life's a miracle. Speak yet again.
GLOU. But have I fall'n, or no?
EDG. From the dread summit of this chalky bourn.[21]
    Look up a-height;[22] the shrill-gorged[23] lark so far
    Cannot be seen or heard: do but look up.
GLOU. Alack, I have no eyes.   60
    Is wretchedness deprived that benefit,
    To end itself by death? 'Twas yet some comfort,
    When misery could beguile[24] the tyrant's rage,
    And frustrate his proud will.
EDG.   Give me your arm:
    Up: so. How is 't? Feel you your legs? You stand.
GLOU. Too well, too well.
EDG.   This is above all strangeness.
    Upon the crown o' the cliff, what thing was that
    Which parted from you?
GLOU.   A poor unfortunate beggar.
EDG. As I stood here below, methought his eyes
    Were two full moons; he had a thousand noses,   70
    Horns whelk'd[25] and waved like the enridgèd sea:

[12] Rebel against.   [13] Irresistible.   [14] Burnt and smoking wick.   [15] Imagination.
[16] Life's treasury.   [17] **Yields . . . theft,** i.e., death's theft of the treasury of life.
[18] Die.   [19] Floating cobweb.   [20] **at each,** end to end.   [21] Boundary.   [22] On high.
[23] Shrill-throated.   [24] Cheat.   [25] Twisted.

It was some fiend; therefore, thou happy father,
Think that the clearest[26] gods, who make them honours
Of men's impossibilities,[27] have preserved thee.

GLOU. I do remember now: henceforth I'll bear
    Affliction till it do cry out itself
    "Enough, enough," and die. That thing you speak of,
    I took it for a man; often 'twould say
    "The fiend, the fiend:" he led me to that place.

EDG. Bear free[28] and patient thoughts. But who comes here?   80

> [*Enter* LEAR, *fantastically dressed
> with wild flowers.*]

The safer[29] sense will ne'er accommodate[30]
His master thus.

LEAR. No, they cannot touch[31] me for coining;[32]
    I am the king himself.

EDG. O thou side-piercing sight!

LEAR. Nature's above art in that respect. There's your press-money.[33]
    That fellow handles his bow like a crow-keeper:[34] draw me a cloth-
    ier's yard.[35] Look, look, a mouse! Peace, peace; this piece of toasted
    cheese will do 't. There's my gauntlet; I'll prove[36] it on a giant.
    Bring up the brown bills.[37] O, well flown, bird![38] i' the clout,[39] i'   90
    the clout: hewgh![40] Give the word.[41]

EDG. Sweet marjoram.

LEAR. Pass.

GLOU. I know that voice.

LEAR. Ha! Goneril, with a white beard! They flattered me like a dog;
    and told me I had white hairs in my beard ere the black ones were
    there. To say "ay" and "no" to every thing that I said!—"Ay" and
    "no" too was no good divinity. When the rain came to wet me once,
    and the wind to make me chatter; when the thunder would not
    peace[42] at my bidding; there I found 'em, there I smelt 'em out.   100
    Go to, they are not men o' their words: they told me I was every
    thing; 'tis a lie, I am not ague-proof.

GLOU. The trick[43] of that voice I do well remember:
    Is 't not the king?

LEAR.   Ay, every inch a king:
    When I do stare, see how the subject quakes.
    I pardon that man's life. What was thy cause?
    Adultery?
    Thou shalt not die: die for adultery! No:
    The wren goes to 't, and the small gilded fly

---

[26] Most glorious.   [27] **men's impossibilities,** things impossible to men.
[28] i.e., from grief.   [29] Saner.   [30] Equip.   [31] Arrest.
[32] Making counterfeit money.   [33] Money to a recruit pressed into military service.
[34] A boy stationed to scare away crows.
[35] **clothier's yard,** arrow a cloth-yard in length.   [36] Defend it by combat.
[37] Halberds, painted brown to prevent rust.   [38] i.e., arrow.   [39] Bulls-eye.
[40] Imitation of the whizzing of the arrow.   [41] Password.   [42] Hold its peace.
[43] Peculiarity.

Does lecher in my sight.   110
Let copulation thrive; for Gloucester's bastard son
Was kinder to his father than my daughters
Got 'tween the lawful sheets.
To 't, luxury,[44] pell-mell! for I lack soldiers.
Behold yond simpering dame,
Whose face between her forks presages snow;[45]
That minces virtue,[46] and does shake the head
To hear of pleasure's name;
The fitchew,[47] nor the soilèd[48] horse, goes to 't
With a more riotous appetite.   120
Down from the waist they are Centaurs,[49]
Though women all above:
But[50] to the girdle do the gods inherit,[51]
Beneath is all the fiends';
There's hell, there's darkness, there's the sulphurous pit,
Burning, scalding, stench, consumption; fie, fie, fie! pah, pah!
Give me an ounce of civet,[52] good apothecary, to sweeten my
imagination: there's money for thee.
GLOU. O, let me kiss that hand!
LEAR. Let me wipe it first; it smells of mortality.   130
GLOU. O ruin'd piece[53] of nature! This great world
　　Shall so wear out to nought.[54] Dost thou know me?
LEAR. I remember thine eyes well enough. Dost thou squiny[55] at me?
　　No, do thy worst, blind Cupid;[56] I'll not love. Read thou this chal-
　　lenge; mark but the penning of it.
GLOU. Were all the letters suns, I could not see one.
EDG. I would not take[57] this from report; it is,
　　And my heart breaks at it.
LEAR. Read.
GLOU. What, with the case[58] of eyes?   140
LEAR. O, ho, are you there with me?[59] No eyes in your head, nor no
　　money in your purse? Your eyes are in a heavy case,[60] your purse
　　in a light: yet you see how this world goes.
GLOU. I see it feelingly.
LEAR. What, art mad? A man may see how this world goes with no
　　eyes. Look with thine ears: see how yond justice rails upon yond
　　simple[61] thief. Hark, in thine ear: change places; and, handy-
　　dandy,[62] which is the justice, which is the thief? Thou hast seen a
　　farmer's dog bark at a beggar?
GLOU. Ay, sir.   150

---

[44] Lust.　　[45] i.e., chastity.
[46] **minces virtue,** makes a show of virtue by her mincing (affected) bearing.
[47] Skunk, a supposedly oversexed animal.　　[48] Fed full with spring grass.
[49] Lustful fabulous monsters, half man, half horse.　　[50] Only.　　[51] Rule.
[52] Perfume.　　[53] Masterpiece.
[54] **Shall . . . nought,** shall likewise come to nothing.　　[55] Squint.
[56] **blind Cupid,** the sign usually hung over a brothel.　　[57] Accept, believe.
[58] Sockets.　　[59] **are . . . me?** i.e., Is that what you are telling me?
[60] **heavy case,** bad condition, with a pun on case-socket.　　[61] Mere.
[62] **handy-dandy,** "Which hand will you have?" (a formula in a well-known child's game).

LEAR. And the creature run from the cur? There thou mightst be-
        hold the great image[63] of authority: a dog's obeyed in office.
        Thou rascal beadle, hold thy bloody hand!
        Why dost thou lash that whore? Strip thine own back;
        Thou hotly lust'st to use her in that kind[64]
        For which thou whipp'st her. The usurer hangs the cozener.[65]
        Through tatter'd clothes small vices do appear;
        Robes and furr'd gowns hide all. Plate sin with gold,[66]
        And the strong lance of justice hurtless breaks;
        Arm it in rags, a pigmy's straw does pierce it.   160
        None does offend, none I say, none; I'll able[67] 'em:
        Take that[68] of me, my friend, who have the power
        To seal the accuser's lips. Get thee glass eyes;[69]
        And, like a scurvy politician,[70] seem
        To see the things thou dost not. Now, now, now, now:
        Pull off my boots: harder, harder: so.
EDG. O, matter and impertinency[71] mix'd!
        Reason in madness!
LEAR. If thou wilt weep my fortunes, take my eyes.
        I know thee well enough; thy name is Gloucester: 170
        Thou must be patient; we came crying hither:
        Thou know'st, the first time that we smell the air,
        We wawl and cry. I will preach to thee: mark.
GLOU. Alack, alack the day!
LEAR. When we are born, we cry that we are come
        To this great stage of fools: this's a good block;[72]
        It were a delicate stratagem, to shoe
        A troop of horse with felt: I'll put 't in proof;[73]
        And when I have stol'n upon these sons-in-law,
        Then, kill, kill, kill, kill, kill, kill!   180

                              [*Enter a* GENTLEMAN, *with* ATTEN-
                                        DANTS.]

GENT. O, here he is: lay hand upon him. Sir,
        Your most dear daughter—
LEAR. No rescue? What, a prisoner? I am even
        The natural fool of fortune.[74] Use me well;
        You shall have ransom. Let me have surgeons;
        I am cut to the brains.
GENT.   You shall have any thing.
LEAR. No seconds? all myself?
        Why, this would make a man a man of salt,[75]

---

[63] Figure.   [64] Way.   [65] Cheater, sharper.
[66] **Plate . . . with gold,** clothe sin in golden armor-plates.   [67] Authorize.
[68] i.e., an imaginary pardon.   [69] Spectacles.   [70] **scurvy politician,** vile trickster.
[71] **matter and impertinency,** sense and incoherence.   [72] Hat.
[73] **put 't in proof,** make a trial of it.
[74] **The . . . fortune,** man reduced by fortune to the condition of a fool.
[75] Of salt tears.

To use his eyes for garden water-pots,
Ay, and laying autumn's dust.
GENT.   Good sir,—   190
LEAR. I will die bravely,[76] like a bridegroom. What!
I will be jovial: come, come; I am a king,
My masters, know you that.
GENT. You are a royal one, and we obey you.
LEAR. Then there's life in 't. Nay, if you get it, you shall get it with
running. Sa, sa, sa, sa.[77]   [*Exit running;* ATTENDANTS *follow.*]
GENT. A sight most pitiful in the meanest wretch,
Past speaking of in a king! Thou hast one daughter,
Who redeems nature from the general[78] curse
Which twain have brought her to.   200
EDG. Hail, gentle[79] sir.
GENT.   Sir, speed you: what's your will?
EDG. Do you hear aught, sir, of a battle toward?[80]
GENT. Most sure and vulgar:[81] every one hears that,
Which[82] can distinguish sound.
EDG.   But, by your favour,
How near's the other army?
GENT. Near and on speedy foot; the main descry[83]
Stands on the hourly thought.[84]
EDG.   I thank you, sir: that's all.
GENT. Though that the queen on special cause is here,
Her army is moved on.
EDG.   I thank you, sir.
                                              [*Exit* GENTLEMAN.]
GLOU. You ever-gentle gods, take my breath from me;   210
Let not my worser spirit[85] tempt me again
To die before you please!
EDG.   Well pray you, father.
GLOU. Now, good sir, what are you?
EDG. A most poor man, made tame to fortune's blows;
Who, by the art of known and feeling[86] sorrows,
Am pregnant to[87] good pity. Give me your hand,
I'll lead you to some biding.[88]
GLOU.   Hearty thanks:
The bounty[89] and the benison[90] of heaven
To boot,[91] and boot![92]

[*Enter* OSWALD.]

OSW.   A proclaim'd prize! Most happy!

---

[76] In fine clothes.   [77] **Sa . . . sa,** a hunter's cry to urge on the dogs.   [78] Universal.
[79] Noble.   [80] At hand.   [81] i.e., known to everyone.   [82] Who.
[83] **the main descry,** the view of the main body of troops.
[84] **Stands . . . thought,** is expected any time.   [85] Worse side of my nature.
[86] Heartfelt.   [87] **pregnant to,** able to conceive.   [88] Abiding place.   [89] Favor.
[90] Blessing.   [91] **To boot,** besides.   [92] **and boot,** and may it be your reward.

That eyeless head of thine was first framed flesh 220
To raise my fortunes. Thou old unhappy traitor,
Briefly thyself remember:[93] the sword is out
That must destroy thee.

GLOU. Now let thy friendly hand
Put strength enough to 't.

[EDGAR *interposes.*]

OSW. Wherefore, bold peasant,
Darest thou support a publish'd[94] traitor? Hence;
Lest that the infection of his fortune take
Like hold on thee. Let go his arm.

EDG. Chill[95] not let go, zir, without vurther 'casion.

OSW. Let go, slave, or thou diest!

EDG. Good gentleman, go your gait, and let poor volk pass. An 230
chud[96] ha' bin zwaggered out of my life, 'twould not ha' bin zo
long as 'tis by a vortnight. Nay, come not near th' old man;
keep out, che vor ye,[97] or ise[98] try whether your costard[99] or
my ballow[1] be the harder: chill be plain with you.

OSW. Out, dunghill!

EDG. Chill pick your teeth, zir: come; no matter vor your foins.[2]

[*They fight, and* EDGAR *knocks
him down.*]

OSW. Slave, thou hast slain me: villain, take my purse:
If ever thou wilt thrive, bury my body;
And give the letters which thou find'st about me
To Edmund earl of Gloucester; seek him out 240
Upon the British party:[3] O, untimely death!

[*Dies.*]

EDG. I know thee well: a serviceable villain;
As duteous[4] to the vices of thy mistress
As badness would desire.

GLOU. What, is he dead?

EDG. Sit you down, father; rest you.
Let's see these pockets: the letters that he speaks of
May be my friends. He's dead; I am only sorry
He had no other death's-man.[5] Let us see:
Leave,[6] gentle wax; and, manners, blame us not:
To know our enemies' minds, we'ld rip their hearts; 250
Their papers, is more lawful.

[*Reads*] "Let our reciprocal vows be remembered. You have many
opportunities to cut him off: if your will want not, time and place
will be fruitfully[7] offered. There is nothing done, if he return the
conqueror: then am I the prisoner, and his bed my gaol; from the
loathed warmth whereof deliver me, and supply the place for your
labour.

---

[93] **thyself remember,** repent your past sins.   [94] Publicly proclaimed.
[95] I will. The following passage is in stage rustic dialect.   [96] If I could.
[97] **che vor ye,** I warn you.   [98] I will.   [99] Apple, slang for head.   [1] Cudgel.
[2] Sword thrusts.   [3] **British party,** side of the British.   [4] Compliant.
[5] Executioner.   [6] Allow me.   [7] Amply.

"Your—wife, so I would say—
    Affectionate servant,[8]
        GONERIL."   260
O undistinguish'd space[9] of woman's will![10]
A plot upon her virtuous husband's life;
And the exchange my brother! Here, in the sands,
Thee I'll rake up,[11] the post[12] unsanctified
Of murderous lechers: and in the mature time[13]
With this ungracious[14] paper strike the sight
Of the death-practised duke:[15] for him 'tis well
That of thy death and business I can tell.

GLOU. The king is mad: how stiff is my vile sense,[16]
That I stand up, and have ingenious feeling[17]   270
Of my huge sorrows! Better I were distract:[18]
So should my thoughts be sever'd from my griefs,
And woes by wrong imaginations lose
The knowledge of themselves.

EDG.   Give me your hand:
                    [*Drum afar off.*]
Far off, methinks, I hear the beaten drum:
Come, father, I'll bestow you with a friend.   [*Exeunt.*]

SCENE VII

A tent in the French camp—LEAR *on a bed asleep, soft*
music playing; GENTLEMAN, *and others attending*

[*Enter* CORDELIA, KENT, *and* DOCTOR.]

COR. O thou good Kent, how shall I live and work,
To match thy goodness? My life will be too short,
And every measure[1] fail me.

KENT. To be acknowledged, madam, is o'erpaid.
All my reports go with the modest truth;[2]
Nor more nor clipp'd,[3] but so.

COR.   Be better suited:[4]
These weeds[5] are memories[6] of those worser hours:
I prithee, put them off.

KENT.   Pardon me, dear madam;
Yet to be known shortens my made intent:[7]
My boon I make it,[8] that you know me not   10
Till time and I think meet.

---

[8]**servant,** lover.   [9]**undistinguish'd space,** limitless range.   [10]Lust.
[11]Bury hastily.   [12]Messenger.   [13]**in . . . time,** when the time is ripe.
[14]Wicked.   [15]**death . . . duke,** duke whose death is plotted.
[16]**stiff . . . sense,** strong is my sanity.   [17]**ingenious feeling,** keen consciousness.
[18]Insane.   [1]i.e., measuring out (of benefits).
[2]**modest truth,** moderate statement of the facts.   [3]Abridged.   [4]Clothed.
[5]Garments.   [6]Reminders.
[7]**shortens . . . intent,** makes me fall short of my prearranged plan.
[8]**My . . . it,** I ask it as a favor to me.

COR. Then be 't so, my good lord. [*To the* DOCTOR] How does the king?
DOCT. Madam, sleeps still.
COR. O you kind gods,
    Cure this great breach in his abusèd nature!
    The untuned and jarring senses, O, wind up[9]
    Of this child-changèd[10] father!
DOCT.   So please your Majesty
    That we may wake the king: he hath slept long.
COR. Be govern'd by your knowledge, and proceed
    I' the sway of your own will. Is he array'd?   20
GENT. Ay, madam; in the heaviness of his sleep
    We put fresh garments on him.
DOCT. Be by, good madam, when we do awake him;
    I doubt not of his temperance.[11]
COR.   Very well.
DOCT. Please you, draw near. Louder the music there!
COR. O my dear father! Restoration hang
    Thy medicine on my lips; and let this kiss
    Repair those violent harms that my two sisters
    Have in thy reverence made![12]
KENT.   Kind and dear princess!
COR. Had you not been their father, these white flakes   30
    Had challenged pity of them. Was this a face
    To be opposed against the warring winds?
    To stand against the deep dread-bolted[13] thunder?
    In the most terrible and nimble stroke
    Of quick, cross[14] lightning? to watch—poor perdu![15]—
    With this thin helm?[16] Mine enemy's dog,
    Though he had bit me, should have stood that night
    Against my fire; and wast thou fain,[17] poor father,
    To hovel thee with swine, and rogues[18] forlorn,
    In short and musty straw? Alack, alack!   40
    'Tis wonder that thy life and wits at once
    Had not concluded all.[19] He wakes; speak to him.
DOCT. Madam, do you; 'tis fittest.
COR. How does my royal lord? How fares your majesty?
LEAR. You do me wrong to take me out o' the grave:
    Thou art a soul in bliss; but I am bound
    Upon a wheel of fire, that[20] mine own tears
    Do scald like molten lead.
COR.   Sir, do you know me?
LEAR. You are a spirit, I know: when did you die?
COR. Still, still, far wide![21]   50
DOCT. He's scarce awake: let him alone awhile.

---

[9] i.e., tighten the strings (as of a musical instrument) of his untuned senses.
[10] Whose nature has become childish.   [11] Self-control, i.e., sanity.
[12] **in thy . . . made,** done to you to whom they owe reverence.
[13] With its dreadful bolts.   [14] Zigzag.
[15] A soldier on an isolated post of great danger.   [16] i.e., hair.   [17] Glad.
[18] Tramps.   [19] Altogether come to an end.   [20] So that.   [21] i.e., of the mark.

LEAR. Where have I been? Where am I? Fair daylight?
I am mightily abused.[22] I should e'en die with pity,
To see another thus. I know not what to say.
I will not swear these are my hands: let's see;
I feel this pin prick. Would I were assured
Of my condition![23]

COR.   O, look upon me, sir,
And hold your hands in benediction o'er me:
No, sir, you must not kneel.

LEAR.   Pray, do not mock me:
I am a very foolish fond[24] old man,   60
Fourscore and upward, not an hour more nor less;
And, to deal plainly,
I fear I am not in my perfect mind.
Methinks I should know you, and know this man;
Yet I am doubtful: for I am mainly[25] ignorant
What place this is; and all the skill[26] I have
Remembers not these garments; nor I know not
Where I did lodge last night. Do not laugh at me;
For, as I am a man, I think this lady
To be my child Cordelia.

COR.   And so I am, I am.   70

LEAR. Be your tears wet? yes, 'faith. I pray, weep not:
If you have poison for me, I will drink it.
I know you do not love me; for your sisters
Have, as I do remember, done me wrong:
You have some cause, they have not.

COR.   No cause, no cause.

LEAR. Am I in France?

KENT.   In your own kingdom, sir.

LEAR. Do not abuse[27] me.

DOCT. Be comforted, good madam: the great rage,[28]
You see, is kill'd in him: and yet it is danger
To make him even o'er the time[29] he has lost.   80
Desire him to go in; trouble him no more
Till further settling.[30]

COR. Will 't please your highness walk?[31]

LEAR.   You must bear with me:
Pray you now, forget and forgive: I am old and foolish.

                        [*Exeunt all but* KENT *and* GEN-
                            TLEMAN.]

GENT. Holds it true, sir, that the Duke of Cornwall was so slain?

KENT. Most certain, sir.

GENT. Who is conductor of his people?

KENT. As 'tis said, the bastard son of Gloucester.

---

[22] Deluded.   [23] Situation.   [24] Doting.   [25] Completely.   [26] Intelligence.
[27] Deceive.   [28] Delirium.
[29] **even o'er the time,** fill the interval by recalling what happened.
[30] **Till . . . settling,** until he becomes calmer.   [31] i.e., come with me.

GENT. They say Edgar, his banished son, is with the Earl of Kent in
    Germany.   90
KENT. Report is changeable. 'Tis time to look about; the powers[32] of
    the kingdom approach apace.
GENT. The arbitrement[33] is like to be bloody.
    Fare you well, sir.   [*Exit.*]
KENT. My point and period[34] will be throughly wrought,[35]
    Or well or ill, as this day's battle's fought.   [*Exit.*]

ACT V

SCENE I

The British camp, near Dover

[*Enter, with drum and colours,* EDMUND, REGAN, GENTLEMEN, *and* SOLDIERS.]
EDM. Know of the duke if his last purpose hold,
    Or whether since he is advised[1] by aught
    To change the course: he's full of alteration
    And self-reproving: bring his constant pleasure.[2]
                    [*To a* GENTLEMAN, *who goes out.*]
REG. Our sister's man is certainly miscarried.[3]
EDM. 'Tis to be doubted, madam.
REG.   Now, sweet lord,
    You know the goodness I intend upon you:
    Tell me—but truly—but then speak the truth,
    Do you not love my sister?
EDM.   In honour'd love.
REG. But have you never found my brother's way   10
    To the forfended[4] place?
EDM.   That thought abuses[5] you.
REG. I am doubtful[6] that you have been conjunct[7]
    And bosom'd[8] with her, as far as we call hers.[9]
EDM. No, by mine honour, madam.
REG. I never shall endure her: dear my lord,
    Be not familiar with her.
EDM.   Fear me not:[10]
    She and the duke her husband!

             [*Enter, with drum and colours,* AL-
             BANY, GONERIL, *and* SOLDIERS.]

GON. [*Aside*] I had rather lose the battle than that sister
    Should loosen him and me.
ALB. Our very loving sister, well be-met.[11]   20

---

[32] Armed forces.   [33] Forcing of the decision.
[34] **My point and period,** the final attainment of my ends.   [35] Worked out.
[1] Induced.   [2] **constant pleasure,** settled decision.   [3] Come to grief.   [4] Forbidden.
[5] Dishonors.   [6] **am doubtful,** suspect.   [7] Joined.   [8] Intimate.
[9] **as . . . hers,** i.e., in all that she has.   [10] **Fear me not,** don't worry about me.
[11] Met.

Sir, this I hear; the king is come to his daughter,
With others whom the rigour of our state[12]
Forced to cry out.[13] Where I could not be honest,[14]
I never yet was valiant: for[15] this business,
It toucheth us, as France[16] invades our land,
Not bolds[17] the king, with others, whom, I fear,
Most just and heavy causes[18] make oppose.[19]

EDM. Sir, you speak nobly.

REG.   Why is this reason'd?[20]

GON. Combine together 'gainst the enemy;
For these domestic and particular[21] broils   30
Are not the question here.

ALB.   Let's then determine
With the ancient of war[22] on our proceedings.

EDM. I shall attend you presently at your tent.

REG. Sister, you'll go with us?

GON. No.

REG. 'Tis most convenient;[23] pray you, go with us.

GON. [*Aside*] O, ho, I know the riddle.[24]—I will go.

> [*As they are going out, enter* EDGAR
> *disguised.*]

EDG. If e'er your grace had speech with man so poor,
Hear me one word.

ALB.   I'll overtake you. Speak.

> [*Exeunt all but* ALBANY *and* EDGAR.]

EDG. Before you fight the battle, ope this letter.   40
If you have victory, let the trumpet sound
For him that brought it: wretched though I seem,
I can produce a champion that will prove
What is avouchèd there. If you miscarry,[25]
Your business of the world hath so an end,
And machination[26] ceases. Fortune love you!

ALB. Stay till I have read the letter.

EDG.   I was forbid it.
When time shall serve, let but the herald cry,
And I'll appear again.

ALB. Why, fare thee well: I will o'erlook[27] thy paper. [*Exit* EDGAR.]   50

> [*Re-enter* EDMUND.]

EDM. The enemy's in view; draw up your powers.
Here is the guess of their true strength and forces

---

[12] Administration.   [13] Protest.   [14] Honorable.   [15] As for.
[16] The King of France.   [17] Emboldens.   [18] **heavy causes,** weighty reasons.
[19] **make oppose,** force to oppose us.
[20] **Why . . . reason'd,** Why do you search for reasons [for an action]?
[21] Family and personal.   [22] **ancient of war,** veteran soldiers.   [23] Fitting.
[24] Hidden reason (i.e., you want to be alone with Edmund).   [25] i.e., are killed.
[26] Intrigue (against you).   [27] Glance at.

By diligent discovery;[28] but your haste[29]
Is now urged on you.

ALB.   We will greet the time.[30]   [*Exit.*]

EDM. To both these sisters have I sworn my love;
Each jealous[31] of the other, as the stung
Are of the adder. Which of them shall I take?
Both? one? or neither? Neither can be enjoy'd,
If both remain alive: to take the widow
Exasperates, makes mad her sister Goneril;   60
And hardly shall I carry out my side,[32]
Her husband being alive. Now then we'll use
His countenance[33] for the battle; which being done,
Let her who would be rid of him devise
His speedy taking off. As for the mercy
Which he intends to Lear and to Cordelia,
The battle done, and they within our power,
Shall never see his pardon; for my state
Stands on me to defend, not to debate.[34]   [*Exit.*]

SCENE II
A field between the two camps

[*Alarum*[1] *within. Enter, with drum and colours,* LEAR, CORDELIA, *and* SOL-
DIERS, *over the stage; and exeunt.*]

                                        [*Enter* EDGAR *and* GLOUCESTER.]

EDG. Here, father, take the shadow of this tree
For your good host; pray that the right may thrive:
If ever I return to you again,
I'll bring you comfort.

GLOU.   Grace[2] go with you, sir!
                                        [*Exit* EDGAR.]

                                        [*Alarum and retreat within. Re-
                                        enter* EDGAR.]

EDG. Away, old man; give me thy hand; away!
King Lear hath lost, he and his daughter ta'en:
Give me thy hand; come on.

GLOU. No farther, sir; a man may rot even here.

EDG. What, in ill thoughts again? Men must endure
Their going hence, even as their coming hither: 10
Ripeness[3] is all: come on.

GLOU.   And that's true too.   [*Exeunt.*]

---

[28] Scouting.   [29] **your haste,** prompt action on your part.
[30] **greet the time,** meet the situation.   [31] Suspiciously afraid.   [32] Plans.
[33] Authority.   [34] **my state . . . debate,** my situation requires defense by arms, not
debate (as to the justification of my actions).
   [1] A call to arms.   [2] The protection of the gods.   [3] Readiness (for death).

SCENE III
The British camp near Dover

[*Enter, in conquest, with drum and colours,* EDMUND; LEAR *and* CORDELIA,
prisoners; CAPTAIN, SOLDIERS, &c.]

EDM. Some officers take them away: good guard,
    Until their greater pleasures[1] first be known
    That are to censure[2] them.
COR.   We are not the first
    Who, with best meaning, have incurr'd the worst.
    For thee, oppressèd king, am I cast down;
    Myself could else out-frown false fortune's frown.
    Shall we not see these daughters and these sisters?
LEAR. No, no, no, no! Come, let's away to prison:
    We two alone will sing like birds i' the cage:
    When thou dost ask me blessing, I'll kneel down,   10
    And ask of thee forgiveness: so we'll live,
    And pray, and sing, and tell old tales, and laugh
    At gilded butterflies,[3] and hear poor rogues[4]
    Talk of court news; and we'll talk with them too,
    Who loses and who wins; who's in, who's out;
    And take upon 's the mystery of things,[5]
    As if we were God's spies: and we'll wear out,[6]
    In a wall'd prison, packs[7] and sects of great ones,
    That ebb and flow by the moon.
EDM.   Take them away.
LEAR. Upon such sacrifices, my Cordelia,   20
    The gods themselves throw incense. Have I caught thee?
    He that parts us shall bring a brand from heaven,
    And fire us hence like foxes.[8] Wipe thine eyes;
    The good-years[9] shall devour them, flesh and fell,[10]
    Ere they shall make us weep: we'll see 'em starve first.
    Come.   [*Exeunt* LEAR *and* CORDELIA,
                        guarded.]
EDM.   Come hither, captain; hark.
    Take thou this note[11] [*giving a paper*]; go follow them to prison:
    One step I have advanced thee; if thou dost
    As this instructs thee, thou dost make thy way
    To noble fortunes: know thou this, that men   30
    Are as the time is:[12] to be tender-minded
    Does not become a sword: thy great employment

---

[1] **their greater pleasures,** the wishes of those of higher rank.
[2] Pass judgment upon.   [3] i.e., dandified courtiers.   [4] Wretches.
[5] **take . . . things,** assume that we can explain the mysteries of human life.
[6] i.e., forget.   [7] Parties.
[8] **fire . . . foxes,** foxes can be driven from their holes by smoke and fire.
[9] Evils, perhaps "pestilence."   [10] Skin.
[11] i.e., an order for the execution of Lear and Cordelia.
[12] **as . . . is,** as the situation demands.

    Will not bear question;[13] either say thou'lt do 't,
    Or thrive by other means.[14]

CAPT.   I'll do' t, my lord.

EDM. About it; and write happy[15] when thou hast done.
    Mark, I say, instantly; and carry it[16] so
    As I have set it down.

CAPT. I cannot draw a cart, nor eat dried oats;
    If it be man's work, I'll do it.   [*Exit.*]

                              [*Flourish. Enter* ALBANY, GON-
                              ERIL, REGAN, *another* CAPTAIN,
                              and SOLDIERS.]

ALB. Sir, you have shown to-day your valiant strain.[17]   40
    And fortune led you well: you have the captives
    That were the opposites of[18] this day's strife:
    We do require them of you, so to use them
    As we shall find their merits and our safety
    May equally determine.

EDM.   Sir, I thought it fit
    To send the old and miserable king
    To some retention and appointed guard;[19]
    Whose age has charms in it, whose title more,
    To pluck the common bosom[20] on his side,
    And turn our impress'd lances[21] in our eyes   50
    Which[22] do command them. With him I sent the queen;
    My reason all the same; and they are ready
    To-morrow, or at further space, to appear
    Where you shall hold your session. At this time
    We sweat and bleed: the friend hath lost his friend;
    And the best quarrels,[23] in the heat, are cursed
    By those that feel their sharpness:
    The question of Cordelia and her father
    Requires a fitter place.[24]

ALB.   Sir, by your patience,[25]
    I hold you but a subject of this war,   60
    Not as a brother.

REG.   That's as we list to grace him.[26]
    Methinks our pleasure[27] might have been demanded,
    Ere you had spoke so far. He led our powers;
    Bore the commission of my place and person;[28]

---

[13] Permit discussion.   [14] **other means,** i.e., than my favor.
[15] **write happy,** write yourself down as fortunate.   [16] Carry it out.
[17] Stock.   [18] **the opposites of,** our opponents in.
[19] **some retention . . . guard,** to the custody of some guards appointed for the purpose.
[20] **pluck . . . bosom,** enlist the sympathies of the common soldiers.
[21] **impress'd lances,** drafted troops.   [22] Who.   [23] Causes.
[24] i.e., than the battlefield.   [25] i.e., if you will pardon my plain talk.
[26] **That's . . . him,** that depends on how far I wish to honor him.
[27] Wishes in the matter.
[28] **Bore . . . person,** exercised the authority of my rank and person.

The which immediacy[29] may well stand up,
And call itself your brother.

GON.   Not so hot:
In his own grace[30] he doth exalt himself,
More than in your addition.[31]

REG.   In my rights,
By me invested, he compeers[32] the best.

GON. That were the most,[33] if he should husband you.   70

REG. Jesters do oft prove prophets.

GON.   Holla, holla!
That eye that told you so look'd but a-squint.[34]

REG. Lady, I am not well; else I should answer
From a full-flowing stomach.[35] General,
Take thou my soldiers, prisoners, patrimony;
Dispose of them, of me; the walls are thine:[36]
Witness the world, that I create thee here
My lord and master.

GON.   Mean you to enjoy him?

ALB. The let-alone lies not in your good will.[37]

EDM. Nor in thine, lord.

ALB.   Half-blooded[38] fellow, yes.   80

REG. [*To* EDMUND] Let the drum strike, and prove[39] my title thine.

ALB. Stay yet; hear reason. Edmund, I arrest thee
On capital treason; and, in thine attaint,[40]
This gilded serpent [*pointing to* GONERIL.]. For your claim,[41]
     fair sister,
I bar it in the interest of my wife;
'Tis she is sub-contracted[42] to this lord,
And I, her husband, contradict your bans.
If you will marry, make your loves to me,
My lady is bespoke.

GON.   An interlude![43]

ALB. Thou art arm'd, Gloucester: let the trumpet sound: 90
If none appear to prove upon thy head
Thy heinous, manifest, and many treasons,
There is my pledge [*throwing down a glove*]; I'll prove it on thy
     heart,
Ere I taste bread, thou art in nothing[44] less
Than I have here proclaim'd thee.

---

[29]**The which immediacy,** and this fact of immediate representation [of me].
[30]His personal deserts.   [31]**your addition,** the title you gave him.   [32]Equals.
[33]**the most,** most fully realized.
[34]**That eye . . . asquint,** a reference to the proverb, "Love being jealous, makes a good eye look asquint."
[35]Anger.   [36]**the walls are thine,** i.e., you have taken my outer defenses by storm.
[37]**let-alone . . . will,** the prohibition does not depend on what you wish.   [38]Bastard.
[39]i.e., by combat.   [40]**in . . . attaint,** i.e., as a sharer in your corruption.
[41]i.e., to Edmund.
[42]i.e., has made a contract depending on the abrogation of a previous one.
[43]Comedy (a reference to Albany's elaborate irony).   [44]No respect.

REG.   Sick, O, sick!

GON. [*Aside*] If not, I'll ne'er trust medicine.

EDM. There's my exchange [*throwing down a glove*]: what[45] in the world
       he is
    That names me traitor, villain-like he lies:
    Call by thy trumpet: he that dares approach,
    On him, on you, who not? I will maintain   100
    My truth and honour firmly.

ALB. A herald, ho!

EDM.   A herald, ho, a herald!

ALB. Trust to thy single virtue;[46] for thy soldiers,
    All levied in my name, have in my name
    Took their discharge.

REG.   My sickness grows upon me.

ALB. She is not well; convey her to my tent.   [*Exit* REGAN, *led.*]

[*Enter a* HERALD.]

    Come hither, herald,—Let the trumpet sound,—
    And read out this.

CAPT. Sound, trumpet![47] [*A trumpet sounds.*]

HER. [*Reads*] "If any man of quality or degree[48] within the lists of the   110
    army will maintain upon Edmund, supposed Earl of Gloucester,
    that he is a manifold traitor, let him appear by the third sound of
    the trumpet: he is bold in his defence."

EDM. Sound!   [*First trumpet.*]

HER. Again!   [*Second trumpet.*]

HER. Again!   [*Third trumpet.*]

                                        [*Trumpet answers within.*]

[*Enter* EDGAR, *at the third sound,*
armed, with a trumpet before him.]

ALB. Ask him his purposes, why he appears
    Upon this call o' the trumpet.

HER.   What are you?
    Your name, your quality? and why you answer
    This present summons?

EDG.   Know, my name is lost;   120
    By treason's tooth bare-gnawn and canker-bit:[49]
    Yet am I noble as the adversary
    I come to cope.[50]

ALB.   Which is that adversary?

EDG. What's he that speaks for Edmund Earl of Gloucester?

EDM. Himself: what say'st thou to him?

EDG.   Draw thy sword,
    That, if my speech offend a noble heart,
    Thy arm[51] may do thee justice: here is mine.
    Behold, it is the privilege of mine honours,[52]

---

[45] Whoever and whatever.   [46] Valor.   [47] Trumpeter.
[48] **quality or degree,** rank or high social position.   [49] Eaten away by a canker-worm.
[50] Cope with.   [51] Weapon.   [52] **mine honours,** my rank, i.e., as knight.

My oath,[53] and my profession: I protest,
Maugre[54] thy strength, youth, place, and eminence,   130
Despite thy victor sword and fire-new[55] fortune,
Thy valour and thy heart,[56] thou art a traitor;
False to thy gods, thy brother, and thy father;
Conspirant[57] 'gainst this high-illustrious prince;
And, from the extremest upward[58] of thy head
To the descent[59] and dust below thy foot,
A most toad-spotted[60] traitor. Say thou "No,"
This sword, this arm, and my best spirits, are bent
To prove upon thy heart, whereto I speak,
Thou liest.   140
EDM. In wisdom[61] I should ask thy name;
But, since thy outside looks so fair and warlike,
And that thy tongue some say of breeding[62] breathes,
What safe and nicely[63] I might well delay
By rule of knighthood, I disdain and spurn:
Back do I toss these treasons[64] to thy head;
With the hell-hated[65] lie o'erwhelm thy heart;
Which, for[66] they yet glance by and scarcely bruise,
This sword of mine shall give them instant way,
Where they shall rest for ever. Trumpets, speak!   150

              [Alarums. They fight. EDMUND falls.]

ALB. Save him, save him!
GON.   This is mere practice,[67] Gloucester:
By the law of arms thou wast not bound to answer[68]
An unknown opposite;[69] thou art not vanquish'd,
But cozen'd[70] and beguiled.
ALB.   Shut your mouth, dame,
Or with this paper[71] shall I stop it. Hold, sir;
Thou worse than any name, read thine own evil:
No tearing, lady; I perceive you know it.

              [Gives the letter to EDMUND.]

GON. Say, if I do, the laws are mine, not thine:[72]
Who can arraign me for 't?
ALB.   Most monstrous! oh!
Know'st thou this paper?
GON.   Ask me not what I know.   *[Exit.]*   160
ALB. Go after her: she's desperate; govern[73] her.

---

[53] i.e., which I swore when dubbed knight, i.e., to protect the honor of knighthood from such evils as treason.
[54] In spite of.   [55] Brand-new.   [56] Courage.   [57] Conspirator.   [58] Top.
[59] Lowest part [of you].   [60] Marked with poisonous spots.
[61] **In wisdom,** i.e., a knight was not obliged to accept the challenge of an unknown opponent.
[62] **say of breeding,** accent of a gentleman.
[63] **safe and nicely,** safely and punctiliously.   [64] Accusations of treason.
[65] Hateful as hell.   [66] Because.   [67] **mere practice,** out-and-out foul play.
[68] Accept the challenge of.   [69] Opponent.   [70] Cheated.
[71] i.e., her love letter which Edgar has found on Oswald's body.
[72] **the laws . . . thine,** I, as ruler, make the laws, not you.   [73] Restrain.

EDM. What you have charged me with, that have I done;
And more, much more; the time will bring it out:
'Tis past, and so am I. But what art thou
That hast this fortune[74] on me? If thou'rt noble,
I do forgive thee.

EDG.   Let's exchange charity.
I am no less in blood than thou art, Edmund;
If more, the more thou hast wrong'd me.
My name is Edgar, and thy father's son.
The gods are just, and of our pleasant vices   170
Make instruments to plague us:
The dark and vicious place where thee he got[75]
Cost him his eyes.

EDM.   Thou hast spoken right, 'tis true;
The wheel[76] is come full circle; I am here.

ALB. Methought thy very gait[77] did prophesy
A royal nobleness: I must embrace thee:
Let sorrow split my heart, if ever I
Did hate thee or thy father!

EDG.   Worthy[78] prince, I know't.

ALB. Where have you hid yourself?
How have you known the miseries of your father?   180

EDG. By nursing them, my lord. List a brief tale;
And when 'tis told, O, that my heart would burst!
The bloody proclamation to escape,[79]
That follow'd me so near,—O, our lives' sweetness!
That we the pain of death would hourly die
Rather than die at once![80]—taught me to shift
Into a madman's rags; to assume a semblance
That very dogs disdain'd: and in this habit
Met I my father with his bleeding rings,
Their precious stones new lost; became his guide,   190
Led him, begg'd for him, saved him from despair;
Never,—O fault![81]—reveal'd myself unto him,
Until some half-hour past, when I was arm'd:
Not sure, though hoping, of this good success,
I ask'd his blessing, and from first to last
Told him my pilgrimage: but his flaw'd[82] heart,
Alack, too weak the conflict to support!
'Twixt two extremes of passion, joy and grief,
Burst smilingly.

EDM.   This speech of yours hath moved me,
And shall perchance do good: but speak you on;   200
You look as you had something more to say.

---

[74]Success.   [75]Begot.   [76]i.e., of Fortune.   [77]Bearing.   [78]Honorable.
[79]**The . . . escape,** in order to escape from the proclamation for my arrest.
[80]**That . . . once,** that we prefer to suffer the pain of death hour by hour than to die at once.
[81]Mistake.   [82]Cracked.

ALB. If there be more, more woeful, hold it in;
    For I am almost ready to dissolve,[83]
    Hearing of this.
EDG.   This would have seem'd a period[84]
    To such as love not sorrow; but another,
    To amplify too much, would make much more,
    And top extremity.[85]
    Whilst I was big in clamour[86] came there in a man,
    Who, having seen me in my worst estate,[87]
    Shunn'd my abhorr'd society; but then, finding
    Who 'twas that so endured, with his strong arms
    He fasten'd on my neck, and bellow'd out
    As he'ld burst heaven; threw him on my father;
    Told the most piteous tale of Lear and him
    That ever ear received: which in recounting
    His grief grew puissant,[88] and the strings of life[89]
    Began to crack: twice then the trumpets sounded,
    And there I left him tranced.[90]
ALB.   But who was this?
EDG. Kent, sir, the banish'd Kent; who in disguise
    Follow'd his enemy king, and did him service
    Improper for[91] a slave.

                    [*Enter a* GENTLEMAN, *with a*
                    bloody knife.]

GENT. Help, help, O, help!
EDG.   What kind of help?
ALB.   Speak, man.
EDG. What means that bloody knife?
GENT.   'Tis hot, it smokes;
    It came even from the heart of—O, she's dead!
ALB. Who dead? speak, man.
GENT. Your lady, sir, your lady: and her sister
    By her is poisoned; she hath confess'd it.
EDM. I was contracted to them both: all three
    Now marry in an instant.
EDG.   Here comes Kent.
ALB. Produce their bodies, be they alive or dead:
    This judgement of the heavens, that makes us tremble,
    Touches us not with pity.   [*Exit* GENTLEMAN.]

                [*Enter* KENT.]

            O, is this he?
    The time will not allow the compliment[92]
    Which very manners urges.

---

[83] i.e., in tears.   [84] End (of sorrow).   [85] **top extremity,** exceed the extreme limit.
[86] **big in clamour,** loud in lament.   [87] Condition.   [88] Overpowering.
[89] **strings of life,** heart-strings.   [90] In a swoon.   [91] Even for.   [92] Ceremony.

210

220

230

KENT.   I am come
    To bid my king and master aye[93] good night:
    Is he not here?
ALB.   Great thing of[94] us forgot!
    Speak, Edmund, where's the king? and where's Cordelia?
    See'st thou this object, Kent?

                       [*The bodies of* GONERIL *and* RE-
                       GAN *are brought in.*]

KENT. Alack, why thus?
EDM.   Yet Edmund was beloved:
    The one the other poison'd for my sake,   240
    And after slew herself.
ALB. Even so. Cover their faces.
EDM. I pant for life: some good I mean to do,
    Despite of mine own nature. Quickly send,
    Be brief in it, to the castle; for my writ
    Is on the life of Lear on Cordelia:
    Nay, send in time.
ALB.   Run, run, O, run!
EDG. To who, my lord? Who hath the office? send
    Thy token of reprieve.
EDM. Well thought on: take my sword,   250
    Give it the captain.
ALB.   Haste thee, for thy life.   [*Exit* EDGAR.]
EDM. He hath commission from thy wife and me
    To hang Cordelia in the prison, and
    To lay the blame upon her own despair,
    That she fordid[95] herself.
ALB. The gods defend her! Bear him hence awhile.

                       [EDMUND *is borne off.*]

                       [*Re-enter* LEAR, *with* CORDELIA
                       dead in his arms; EDGAR, CAP-
                       TAIN, *and others following.*]

LEAR. Howl, howl, howl, howl! O, you are men of stones:
    Had I your tongues and eyes, I'ld use them so
    That heaven's vault should crack. She's gone for ever!
    I know when one is dead, and when one lives;   260
    She's dead as earth. Lend me a looking-glass;
    If that her breath will mist or stain the stone,[96]
    Why, then she lives.
KENT.   Is this the promised end?[97]
EDG. Or image[98] of that horror?
ALB.   Fall, and cease![99]

---

[93] Forever.   [94] By.   [95] Destroyed.   [96] Crystal mirror.
[97] i.e., of the world, the Last Judgment.   [98] Exact likeness.
[99] **Fall, and cease,** i.e., let Doomsday come and all things cease to be.

LEAR. This feather stirs; she lives! if it be so,
　　　It is a chance which does redeem[1] all sorrows
　　　That ever I have felt.
KENT. [*Kneeling*] O my good master!
LEAR. Prithee, away.
EDG.　　　　　　　'Tis noble Kent, your friend.
LEAR. A plague upon you, murderers, traitors all!
　　　I might have saved her; now she's gone for ever!　　　　270
　　　Cordelia, Cordelia! stay a little. Ha!
　　　What is 't thou say'st? Her voice was ever soft,
　　　Gentle, and low, an excellent thing in woman.
　　　I kill'd the slave that was a-hanging thee.
CAPT. 'Tis true, my lords, he did.
LEAR.　　　　　　　　　　Did I not, fellow?
　　　I have seen the day, with my good biting falchion[2]
　　　I would have made them skip: I am old now,
　　　And these same crosses[3] spoil me. Who are you?
　　　Mine eyes are not o' the best: I'll tell you straight.[4]
KENT. If fortune brag of two she loved and hated,　　　　280
　　　One of them we behold.[5]
LEAR. This is a dull sight. Are you not Kent?
KENT.　　　　　　　　　　　　The same,
　　　Your servant Kent. Where is your servant Caius?
LEAR. He's a good fellow, I can tell you that;
　　　He'll strike, and quickly too: he's dead and rotten.
KENT. No, my good lord; I am the very man,—
LEAR. I'll see that[6] straight.
KENT. That, from your first of difference and decay,[7]
　　　Have follow'd your sad steps.
LEAR.　　　　　　　　　　You are welcome hither.
KENT. Nor no man else:[8] all's cheerless, dark, and deadly.　　　290
　　　Your eldest daughters have fordone[9] themselves,
　　　And desperately[10] are dead.
LEAR.　　　　　　　　　Ay, so I think.
ALB. He knows not what he says: and vain it is
　　　That we present us to him.
EDG.　　　　　　　　Very bootless.

　　　　　　　　　　[*Enter a* CAPTAIN.]

CAP. Edmund is dead, my lord.
ALB.　　　　　　　　That's but a trifle here.
　　　You lords and noble friends, know our intent.
　　　What comfort to this great decay[11] may come

---

[1] Repay.　　[2] A curved, broad-bladed sword.　　[3] Troubles.　　[4] Straightway.
[5] **One . . . behold,** certainly no more than two men in all human history have experienced such violent ups and downs of Fortune as Lear.
[6] **see that,** see to that.
[7] **from . . . decay,** from the beginning of the decline and decay of your fortunes.
[8] **Nor . . . else,** not I nor any one else.　　[9] Killed.　　[10] In despair.
[11] **great decay,** great man fallen into decay.

    Shall be applied: for us, we will resign
    During the life of this old majesty,
    To him our absolute power:[12] [*To* EDGAR *and* KENT] you, to
      your rights;   300
    With boot,[13] and such addition as your honours
    Have more than merited. All friends shall taste
    The wages of their virtue, and all foes
    The cup of their deservings. O, see, see!
LEAR. And my poor fool[14] is hang'd! No, no, no life!
    Why should a dog, a horse, a rat, have life,
    And thou no breath at all? Thou'lt come no more,
    Never, never, never, never, never!
    Pray you, undo this button: thank you, sir.
    Do you see this? Look on her, look, her lips,   310
    Look there, look there!   [*Dies.*]
EDG.   He faints! My lord, my lord!
KENT. Break, heart; I prithee, break!
EDG.   Look up, my lord.
KENT. Vex not his ghost:[15] O, let him pass! he hates him much
    That would upon the rack of this tough world
    Stretch him out longer.
EDG.   He is gone, indeed.
KENT. The wonder is, he hath endured so long:
    He but usurp'd his life.[16]
ALB. Bear them from hence. Our present business
    Is general woe. [*To* KENT *and* EDGAR] Friends of my soul, you
      twain
    Rule in this realm, and the gored state sustain.   320
KENT. I have a journey, sir, shortly to go;
    My master calls me,[17] I must not say no.
ALB. The weight of this sad time we must obey;
    Speak what we feel, not what we ought to say.
    The oldest[18] hath borne most: we that are young
    Shall never see so much, nor live so long.[19]
            [*Exeunt, with a dead march.*]

---

[12] **our absolute power,** the sovereign power I now exercise.
[13] Something given in the bargain.
[14] i.e., Cordelia; "fool" was used as a term of endearment. [15] Departing spirit.
[16] **usurp'd his life,** i.e., lived longer than the usual term of life.
[17] i.e., to follow him through Death. [18] i.e., Lear and Gloucester.
 [19] **Shall . . . long,** i.e., even if we shall live as long as Lear has, we should never experience
so much misery.

John Donne
(1572–1631)

The first thing the reader of John Donne's poems is likely to be struck by is their tone of voice. We read "For God's sake hold your tongue, and let me love," and we are suddenly hearing an extraordinary voice: vital, energetic, flashing mercurially from the abrupt and colloquial to the gnarled and difficult, thirsty to drink all experience and all learning, from the earthiest to the most sublime, tirelessly histrionic, whipping dramatic masks on and off with dazzling speed, simultaneously attentive to the brain, the soul, and the genitals. It is, in short, a Renaissance voice. If Hamlet had been a poet, we feel that he would not have written the piece of doggerel to the "beautified Ophelia" that Polonius quotes; he is more likely to have written John Donne's poems.

Donne was born in 1572, during an intensely anti-Catholic age in England, into a devoutly Roman Catholic family in London. His father was a prosperous dealer in iron and hardware; his mother was the daughter of John Heywood, the Elizabethan satirist and playwright. Many details of Donne's early life are missing, but it appears that he spent his youth to the age of twenty-five in a variety of pursuits, all directed toward finding some way to make a place for himself as a Catholic in a fervently Protestant world. He enrolled at Oxford when he was twelve and remained there until he was almost sixteen. (Catholic parents often sent their children to the university at a very early age in order to avoid their having to take the Oath of Supremacy, required of university students at the age of sixteen, acknowledging Queen Elizabeth as "Supreme Governor" of the church. In any case, Donne would not have been allowed, as a Catholic, to take a degree at either Oxford or Cambridge.) Upon leaving Oxford, he seems to have traveled for as much as four years in Italy and Spain. When he was nineteen, he returned to London and became a law student at the Inns of Court. If contemporary reports are to be trusted, he made the most of the life of a London law student; he was said to be "not dissolute, but very neat [witty and fashionable], a great visitor of ladies, a great frequenter of plays, a great writer of conceited verses." He seems to have combined his life as a fashionable man about town, however, with that of a serious student, not only of the law but also of theology. He surveyed, as he later wrote, "the body of divinity, as it was then controverted betwixt the Reformed and the Roman Church"; the result was that he ceased to be a practicing Catholic, although he did not become an Anglican until some years later. Leaving the Inns of Court in 1596, Donne got a taste of war, sailing under Sir Walter Raleigh to attack the Spanish shipping in Cadiz harbor and under the Earl of Essex to engage Spanish treasure ships off the Azores. Upon his return, since he was no longer a Catholic, he was able to obtain a position as secretary to Sir Thomas Egerton, Keeper of the Great Seal. The way to success seemed open; in 1601, Donne served as Member of Parliament for one of several constituencies controlled by Egerton.

These great expectations ended abruptly, however, when Donne, after three years in Egerton's service, secretly married Ann More, the seventeen-year-old niece of Egerton's wife. Egerton himself had no particular objection to the marriage, but Ann's father, Sir George More, was infuriated: he forced Egerton to dismiss Donne immediately; he had Donne, along with two friends who had abetted him, committed to prison; and he appealed the marriage to the Court of High Commission. Donne, in his letter to Ann telling her of his dismissal, concluded: "John Donne, Ann Donne, undone."

Donne was released from prison after two months and his marriage was ratified by the Archbishop of Canterbury, but his career was in ruins. For the next dozen years, between the ages of twenty-nine and forty-one, he was hard put to earn a living for his growing family. (He and Ann had twelve children, seven of whom survived childhood.) Much of his time during these years was spent in seeking preferment at Court, trying to get the secretaryship or ambassadorship for which his service with Egerton was to have prepared him, and in assisting Thomas Morton, one of King James's chaplains, in the preparation of Protestant propaganda intended to convert Catholics "by weight of reason" rather than by law.

Finally, in 1615, at the age of forty-three, Donne yielded to pressure from Morton and from King James and took Anglican Holy Orders. Almost immediately he was appointed Reader in Divinity at Lincoln's Inn, where he preached to a fashionable and intelligent congregation of lawyers and courtiers. Donne's wit, eloquence, and histrionic flair served him well in the pulpit, and he soon became famous for his sermons. He became Dean of St. Paul's in 1621, and during the remaining ten years of his life he continued to preach his eloquent and dramatic sermons, one hundred and sixty of which survive. Obsessed with death, he preached his own funeral sermon a few weeks before he died and had his portrait painted in his shroud. He wrote "Hymn to God, My God, in My Sickness" on his deathbed. Death came in 1631.

Donne's witty and highly wrought poems have often tested the poetic sensibilities of succeeding ages. In his own time, his works were prized by followers who found in them an alternative to the content and language of Elizabethan lyricism, which had grown somewhat mechanical and facile with age. But the "Metaphysical" style went out of fashion about thirty years after Donne's death, and neither the eighteenth nor the nineteenth century had much use for him. Though intellectual, he lacked the clarity and universality the Neoclassicists sought; though passionate, he lacked the un-ironic directness that pleased Romantic tastes. In the early twentieth century he was rediscovered by readers dissatisfied with the exhausted poetic rhetoric of the late nineteenth century, as his original readers had been with the fag end of sixteenth-century poetry. In Donne these moderns found the toughness of mind, the passionate intensity, and the openness to a wide range of experience that they sought in their new poetry. The result has been the elevation of Donne to a major place among English poets, a position he continued to hold long after the struggle for a modern poetry was won.

Donne is an intensely dramatic poet—most of his poems present a particular speaker addressing a particular listener in a specific place—and what he dramatizes is himself. His is a voice that can move dazzlingly from a harsh, colloquial line to a singingly beautiful one, or from a moment of cynical, shallow wit to one of intense and simple feeling. When his poems are read dramatically, their wit often seems a defense against despair; death is never far from Donne's mind, even in his lightest moods. There is always the bone beneath the "subtle wreath of hair," and even to make love is to "die." Donne's distinctive voice, even after the witty paradoxes and the intellectual fireworks have ceased to startle, is likely to continue to ring in the reader's ear.

FURTHER READING (*prepared by W. J. R.*): R. C. Bald's *John Donne: A Life*, ed. Wesley Milgate, 1970, is a good introduction to both Donne and his poetry. John Carey's *John Donne: Life, Mind, and Art*, 1981, is also a good interpretation of the man and poet. An older biography, Edmund Gosse's *The Life and Letters of John Donne*, 1899, rpt. 1959, is still useful. Arnold Stein's *John Donne's Lyrics: The Elo-*

quence of Action, 1962, is a good comprehensive critical study of the poetry. James Winny's *A Preface to Donne*, 1970, contains excellent introductory material on Donne's religious, intellectual, and literary backgrounds. Several poems are also studied individually, including "The Sun Rising" and "Batter my Heart." *Donne, Songs and Sonnets: A Casebook*, ed. Julian Lovelock, 1973, provides a biographical introduction, a sampling of early criticism of Donne's poetry, and selections from twentieth-century criticism by C. S. Lewis, Arnold Stein, and others. For an overview of the decline and rise of Donne's reputation, see Murray Roston's *The Soul of Wit*, 1974, which also discusses the divine poems, considering at length the paradox of Donne as rake and religious writer. J. B. Leishman's *The Monarch of Wit*, 1951, 6th ed. 1962, begins with a general discussion of Donne's place in seventeenth-century poetry and then treats the epigrams and satires, songs and sonnets, and the divine poems in detail in separate sections. The tercentenary year of Donne's death—1931—was celebrated with *A Garland for John Donne*, ed. Theodore Spencer, 1931, rpt. 1958. Eight essays on fairly general topics are collected in this volume, the lead essay being T. S. Eliot's "Donne in Our Time." More recent critical perspectives are represented in *Essential Articles for the Study of John Donne's Poetry*, ed. John R. Roberts, 1975, which discusses Donne's reputation, his prosody, his love poetry, and other topics.

THE GOOD-MORROW

I wonder by my troth, what thou and I
Did, till we lov'd? were we not wean'd till then?
But suck'd on country pleasures,[1] childishly?
Or snorted we in the seven sleepers' den?[2]
'Twas so; but this,[3] all pleasures fancies be.   5
If ever any beauty I did see,
Which I desir'd, and got, 'twas but a dream of thee.

And now good-morrow to our waking souls,
Which watch not one another out of fear;
For love all love of other sights controls,   10
And makes one little room[4] an everywhere.
Let sea-discoverers to new worlds have gone,
Let maps to other, worlds on worlds have shown,
Let us possess one world, each hath one, and is one.[5]

My face in thine eye, thine in mine appears,   15
And true plain hearts do in the faces rest;
Where can we find two better hemispheres[6]
Without sharp North, without declining West?
What ever dies, was not mixt equally;[7]

---

[1] Rural pleasures, but also a sexual pun.
[2] The seven sleepers were seven Christian youths of Ephesus who were said to have taken refuge in a cave during the persecution of the Emperor Decius and slept for two centuries.
[3] Compared to this love.   [4] Their bedroom.
[5] That is, each has the world of the other, and each is a world to the other.
[6] Donne may have been thinking of "cordiform" maps which depicted each hemisphere as a heart.
[7] An axiom in alchemy. *Equally* here means "uniformly."

If our two loves be one, or thou and I   20
Love so alike that none do slacken, none can die.

SONG

Go, and catch a falling star,
  Get with child a mandrake root,[1]
Tell me, where all past years are,
  Or who cleft the Devil's foot,[2]
Teach me to hear Mermaids singing,   5
  Or to keep off envy's stinging,
       And find
       What wind
Serves to advance an honest mind.

If thou be'st born to strange sights,   10
  Things invisible to see,
Ride ten thousand days and nights,
  Till age snow white hairs on thee,
Thou, when thou return'st, wilt tell me
All strange wonders that befell thee,   15
       And swear
       No where
Lives a woman true, and fair.

If thou find'st one, let me know,
  Such a Pilgrimage were sweet;   20
Yet do not, I would not go,
  Though at next door we might meet,
Though she were true, when you met her,
And last, till you write your letter,
       Yet she   5
       Will be
False, ere I come, to two, or three.

THE CANONIZATION

For God's sake hold your tongue, and let me love;
  Or chide my palsy, or my gout,
My five grey hairs, or ruin'd fortune flout;
  With wealth your state, your mind with arts improve,
    Take you a course,[1] get you a place,[2]   5

[1] The forked root of the mandrake looks like the lower half of a human body.
[2] The devil is said to be recognizable by his cloven hoof.
[1] That is, a course of action leading to worldly success.   [2] A job.

Observe his Honour, or his Grace,[3]
Or the King's real, or his stamped face[4]
Contemplate; what you will, approve,[5]
So you will let me love.

Alas, alas, who's injur'd by my love?   10
What merchant's ships have my sighs drown'd?
Who says my tears have overflow'd his ground?
When did my colds a forward spring remove?
When did the heats which my veins fill
Add one more to the plaguy bill?[6]   15
Soldiers find wars, and lawyers find out still
Litigious men, which quarrels move,[7]
Though she and I do love.

Call us what you will, we are made such by love;
Call her one, me another fly,[8]   20
We're tapers too, and at our own cost die,[9]
And we in us find the Eagle and the Dove.[10]
The Phoenix riddle[11] hath more wit
By us; we two being one, are it.
So to one neutral thing both sexes fit,   25
We die and rise the same,[12] and prove
Mysterious by this love.

We can die by it, if not live by love,
And if unfit for tombs and hearse[13]
Our legend be, it will be fit for verse;   30
And if no piece of Chronicle we prove,[14]
We'll build in sonnets pretty rooms;[15]
As well a well-wrought urn becomes
The greatest ashes, as half-acre tombs,
And by these hymns, all shall approve   35
Us canonized for Love:

[3] 1) A judge or a nobleman, 2) the qualities of honor and grace.
[4] Stamped on a coin.   [5] Try out, test.
[6] The list of deaths from the plague.   [7] Who start quarrels.
[8] The taper-fly, which was attracted to flame and burned itself in it, was said to be hermaphroditic and resurrectable.
[9] Sexual intercourse was thought to shorten life. Therefore lovers are like candles, which get shorter as they burn. *Die* is a slang term for having sexual intercourse.
[10] Symbols, in medieval literature, of righteousness and mercy.
[11] The Phoenix bird, which was resurrected from its own ashes, was also said to be hermaphroditic.
[12] In sexual intercourse, we become sexless (*neutral*), because one sex cancels out the other. But after intercourse, we mysteriously are two different sexes again. *Die* and *rise* also have sexual meanings.
[13] Funereal poems were pinned to hearses.
[14] If we are not recorded in history, or if we do not beget children as described in I Chronicles 1–9.
[15] Mausoleum rooms and stanzas (in Italian).

And thus invoke us; You whom reverend love
    Made one another's hermitage;
You, to whom love was peace, that now is rage;
    Who did the whole world's soul contract, and drove   40
        Into the glasses of your eyes[16]
        (So made such mirrors, and such spies,
That they did all to you epitomize,)
    Countries, Towns, Courts: beg from above
    A pattern of your love![17]   45

THE FUNERAL

Whoever comes to shroud me, do not harm
    Nor question much
That subtle wreath of hair, which crowns my arm;[1]
The mystery, the sign you must not touch,
    For 'tis my outward Soul,   5
Viceroy to that, which then to heaven being gone,
    Will leave this to control,
And keep these limbs, her Provinces, from dissolution.

For if the sinewy thread my brain lets fall
    Through every part,[2]   10
Can tie those parts, and make me one of all;
These hairs which upward grew, and strength and art
    Have from a better brain,
Can better do 't;[3] except[4] she meant that I
    By this should know my pain,   15
As prisoners then are manacled, when they're condemn'd to die.

Whate'er she meant by it, bury it with me,
    For since I am
Love's martyr, it might breed idolatry,
If into others' hands these Reliques came;   20
    As 'twas humility
To afford to it all that a Soul can do,[5]
    So, 'tis some bravery,
That since you would save none of me, I bury some of you.

---

[16] That is, drove the whole world into each other's eyes by gazing at each other.
[17] Ask the god of love for a pattern of your love.
[1] Such bracelets found on corpses are described by several medieval writers, including Giraldus Cambrensis.
[2] The nervous system which makes him one being.
[3] That is, tie the parts of the body together.   [4] Unless.
[5] It was submission to give to it all that a soul can do.

THE SUN RISING

Busy old fool, unruly Sun,
    Why dost thou thus,
Through windows, and through curtains call on us?
Must to thy motions lovers' seasons run?
    Saucy, pedantic wretch, go chide   5
    Late school-boys, and sour prentices,
  Go tell Court-huntsmen, that the King will ride,
  Call country ants to harvest offices;[1]
Love, all alike, no season knows, nor clime,
Nor hours, days, months, which are the rags of time.   10

    Thy beams so reverend, and strong
    Why shouldst thou think?
I could eclipse and cloud them with a wink,
But that I would not lose her sight so long:
    If her eyes have not blinded thine,
    Look, and to-morrow late, tell me,   15
  Whether both th' Indias of spice and mine[2]
  Be where thou left'st them, or lie here with me.
Ask for those Kings whom thou saw'st yesterday,
And thou shalt hear, All here in one bed lay.   20

    She's all States, and all Princes, I,
    Nothing else is.
Princes do but play us; compar'd to this,
All honour's mimic; all wealth alchemy.[3]
    Thou, sun, art half as happy as we,   25
    In that the world's contracted thus;[4]
  Thine age asks ease, and since thy duties be
  To warm the world, that's done in warming us.
Shine here to us, and thou art everywhere;
This bed thy centre is, these walls, thy sphere.[5]   30

SONG

Sweetest love, I do not go,
    For weariness of thee,
Nor in hope the world can show
    A fitter Love for me;

---

[1] Duties.   [2] The East Indies (spices) and the West Indies (gold mines).
[3] Counterfeit.   [4] Contracted into the space of the bed.
[5] The sun's orbit in the Ptolemaic system.

But since that I
Must die at last, 'tis best,
To use my self in jest
    Thus by feign'd deaths to die.[1]

Yesternight the Sun went hence,
    And yet is here to-day;
He hath no desire nor sense,
    Nor half so short a way:
      Then fear not me,
But believe that I shall make
Speedier journeys, since I take
    More wings and spurs than he.

O how feeble is man's power,
    That if good fortune fall,
Cannot add another hour,
    Nor a lost hour recall!
      But come bad chance,
And we join to it our strength,
And we teach it art and length,[2]
    Itself o'er us to advance.

When thou sigh'st, thou sigh'st not wind,
    But sigh'st my soul away,
When thou weep'st, unkindly kind,[3]
    My life's blood doth decay.
      It cannot be
That thou lov'st me, as thou say'st,
If in thine my life thou waste,
    Thou art the best of me.

Let not thy divining heart
    Forethink me any ill,
Destiny may take thy part,
    And may thy fears fulfil;
      But think that we
Are but turn'd aside to sleep;
They who one another keep
    Alive, ne'er parted be.

THE ECSTASY[1]

Where, like a pillow on a bed,
    A pregnant bank swell'd up, to rest

---

[1] It is best to get used to death by dying feigned deaths in jest.   [2] Longer life.
[3] Kind to weep, unkind because her weeping grieves the speaker.
[1] Mental transport or rapture from the contemplation of divine things.

The violet's reclining head,
    Sat we two, one another's best.[2]
Our hands were firmly cemented
    With a fast balm, which thence did spring,[3]   5
Our eye-beams twisted, and did thread
    Our eyes, upon one double string;
So t' intergraft[4] our hands, as yet
    Was all the means to make us one,   10
And pictures in our eyes to get
    Was all our propagation.
As 'twixt two equal Armies, Fate
    Suspends uncertain victory,
Our souls, (which to advance their state,   15
    Were gone out,) hung 'twixt her, and me.
And whilst our souls negotiate there,
    We like sepulchral statues lay;
All day, the same our postures were,
    And we said nothing, all the day.   20
If any, so by love refin'd,
    That he soul's language understood,
And by good love were grown all mind,
    Within convenient distance stood,
He (though he knew not which soul spake,   25
    Because both meant, both spake the same)
Might thence a new concoction[5] take,
    And part far purer than he came.
This Ecstasy doth unperplex
    (We said) and tell us what we love,   30
We see by this, it was not sex,
    We see, we saw not what did move:
But as all several souls contain
    Mixture of things, they know not what,
Love these mix'd souls doth mix again,   35
    And makes both one, each this and that.
A single violet transplant,
    The strength, the colour, and the size,
(All which before was poor, and scant,)
    Redoubles still, and multiplies.   40
When love, with one another so
    Interinanimates[6] two souls,
That abler soul, which thence doth flow,
    Defects of loneliness controls.
We then, who are this new soul, know,   45

[2] Each other's best pillow.
[3] The balm (perspiration) sprang from the hands themselves.
[4] Unite by mutual grafting, as in horticulture.
[5] In alchemy, a process of purification by heat.
[6] *Interinanimates* means both "mutually breathes life into" and "mutually removes the consciousness of." The two souls breathe life into each other, and the *abler soul* which results is unconscious of division.

Of what we are compos'd, and made,
For, th' Atomies of which we grow,
   Are souls, whom no change can invade.
But O alas, so long, so far
   Our bodies why do we forbear?   50
They are ours, though they are not we, We are
   The intelligences, they the spheres.[7]
We owe them thanks, because they thus,
   Did us, to us, at first convey,
Yielded their forces, sense, to us,   55
   Nor are dross to us, but allay.[8]
On man heaven's influence works not so,
   But that it first imprints the air,[9]
So soul into the soul may flow,
   Though it to body first repair.   60
As our blood labours to beget
   Spirits,[10] as like souls as it can,
Because such fingers need[11] to knit
   That subtle knot, which makes us man:
So must pure lovers' souls descend   65
   T' affections, and to faculties,[12]
Which sense may reach and apprehend,
   Else a great Prince[13] in prison lies.
To our bodies turn we then, that so
   Weak men on love reveal'd may look;   70
Love's mysteries in souls do grow,
   But yet the body is his book,
And if some lover, such as we,
   Have heard this dialogue of one,[14]
Let him still mark us, he shall see   75
   Small change, when we're to bodies gone.

THE FLEA

Mark but this flea, and mark in this,
How little that which thou deny'st me is;
   It suck'd me first, and now sucks thee,

---

[7] We (the souls) are the directors, our bodies are the provinces.

[8] *Dross* is worthless waste from smelting. An *allay* is an alloy, made by blending two metals when they are molten.

[9] The influence of the heavenly bodies can work on man only through the air in which they revolve.

[10] In Renaissance medicine, *spirits* were vapors in the blood which mediated between body and soul.

[11] Are needed.   [12] To passions and to powers of action.

[13] The "abler soul" referred to in line 43.

[14] One person has spoken the poem, but it comes from two.

And in this flea, our two bloods mingled be;[1]
Thou know'st that this cannot be said 5
A sin, nor shame, nor loss of maidenhead,
    Yet this enjoys before it woo,
    And pamper'd swells with one blood made of two,
    And this, alas, is more than we would do.

Oh stay, three lives in one flea spare, 10
Where we almost, yea more than married are.
This flea is you and I, and this
Our marriage bed, and marriage temple is;
Though parents grudge, and you, we're met,
And cloistered in these living walls of jet. 15
    Though use make you apt to kill me,
    Let not to that, self murder added be,
    And sacrilege,[2] three sins in killing three.

Cruel and sudden, hast thou since
Purpled thy nail, in blood of innocence?
Wherein could this flea guilty be, 20
Except in that drop which it suck'd from thee?
Yet thou triumph'st, and say'st that thou
Find'st not thyself, nor me the weaker now;
    'Tis true, then learn how false, fears be;
    Just so much honour, when thou yield'st to me, 25
    Will waste, as this flea's death took life from thee.

A VALEDICTION: FORBIDDING MOURNING[1]

As virtuous men pass mildly away,
    And whisper to their souls, to go,
Whilst some of their sad friends do say,
    The breath goes now, and some say, no:

So let us melt, and make no noise, 5
    No tear-floods, nor sigh-tempests move,
'Twere profanation of our joys
    To tell the laity our love.

Moving of th' earth brings harms and fears,
    Men reckon what it did and meant, 10

---

[1] The three united in the flea—the flea himself, the lover, and the mistress—thus echo the Trinity, an idea that recurs throughout the poem.
[2] Sacrilege because the flea is a "marriage temple."
[1] Donne wrote this poem to his wife when he went to the Continent with Sir Robert Drury in 1611.

But trepidation of the spheres,[2]
   Though greater far, is innocent.

Dull sublunary[3] lovers' love
   (Whose soul is sense[4]) cannot admit
Absence, because it doth remove   15
   Those things which elemented[5] it.

But we by a love, so much refin'd,
   That ourselves know not what it is,
Inter-assurèd of the mind,
   Care less eyes, lips, and hands to miss.   20

Our two souls therefore, which are one,
   Though I must go, endure not yet[6]
A breach, but an expansion,
   Like gold to aery thinness beat.

If they be two, they are two so   25
   As stiff twin compasses[7] are two,
Thy soul the fixed foot, makes no show
   To move, but doth, if th' other do.

And though it in the centre sit,
   Yet when the other far doth roam,   30
It leans, and hearkens after it,
   And grows erect, as that comes home.

Such wilt thou be to me, who must
   Like th' other foot, obliquely[8] run;
Thy firmness makes my circle just,   35
   And makes me end, where I begun.

LOVE'S DIET

To what a cumbersome unwieldiness
And burdenous corpulence my love had grown,
   But that I did, to make it less,
   And keep it in proportion,
Give it a diet, made it feed upon   5
That which love worst endures, *discretion*.

---

[2]*Trepidation* was the term used for the trembling of the outermost sphere (the *primum mobile*) in the Ptolemaic universe; this gave movement to the other spheres. The word also means "fear" of heavenly disturbances.

[3]Beneath the moon; earthly.   [4]Dependent upon sensual gratification.

[5]Created or composed.

[6]Nevertheless do not allow.   [7]That is, the two legs of a compass.

[8]Not in a straight line. The lover travels in a circle, and then, when the compass is closed, returns to his starting place.

Above one sigh a day I allow'd him not,
Of which my fortune, and my faults had part;
   And if sometimes by stealth he got
    A she sigh from my mistress' heart,
And thought to feast on that, I let him see
'Twas neither very sound, nor meant to me.[1]   10

If he wrung from me a tear, I brined[2] it so
With scorn or shame, that him it nourish'd not;
   If he suck'd hers, I let him know
    'Twas not a tear, which he had got,   15
His drink was counterfeit, as was his meat;
For, eyes which roll towards all, weep not, but sweat.

Whatever he would dictate, I writ that,
But burnt my letters; when she writ to me,   20
   And that that favour made him fat,
    I said, if any title be
Convey'd by this, Ah, what doth it avail,
To be the fortieth name in an entail?[3]

Thus I reclaim'd my buzzard[4] love, to fly   25
At what, and when, and how, and where I choose;
   Now negligent of sport I lie,
    And now as other falconers use,
I spring[5] a mistress, swear, write, sigh and weep:
And the game kill'd, or lost, go talk, and sleep.   30

ELEGY XIX
TO HIS MISTRESS GOING TO BED

Come, Madam, come, all rest my powers defy,
Until I labour, I in labour lie.[1]
The foe oft-times having the foe in sight,
Is tired with standing though he never fight.[2]
Off with that girdle, like heaven's Zone glistering,   5
But a far fairer world encompassing.
Unpin that spangled breastplate which you wear,
That th' eyes of busy fools may be stopt there.

---

[1] This is a difficult line. It probably means either, "The *she sigh* was neither a true ("very")
sound, nor meant *for* me," or "The *she sigh* was to me neither a true sound nor sincerely
intended."
  [2] Salted.
  [3] An *entail* is a paper documenting a line of descent of ownership or inheritance. The lover
doubts that he will win the mistress, since he is so far down on the list.
  [4] That is, rapacious but slow.   [5] Rouse from hiding, as in hunting with falcons.
  [1] Until I get to work at sexual intercourse, I lie in agony waiting.
  [2] Note sexual double meanings.

Unlace yourself, for that harmonious chime
Tells me from you, that now it is bed time.   10
Off with that happy busk,[3] which I envy,
That still can be, and still can stand so nigh.
Your gown going off, such beauteous state reveals,
As when from flowry meads th' hill's shadow steals.
Off with that wiry Coronet and show   15
The hairy Diadem which on you doth grow:
Now off with those shoes, and then safely tread
In this love's hallow'd temple, this soft bed.
In such white robes, heaven's Angels used to be
Receiv'd by men; thou Angel bring'st with thee   20
A heaven like Mahomet's Paradise;[4] and though
Ill spirits walk in white, we easily know,
By this these Angels from an evil sprite,
Those set our hairs, but these our flesh upright.
    Licence my roving hands, and let them go,   25
Before, behind, between, above, below.
O my America! my new-found-land,
My kingdom, safeliest when with one man mann'd,
My Mine of precious stones, My Empery,
How blest am I in this discovering thee!   30
To enter in these bonds, is to be free;
Then where my hand is set, my seal[5] shall be.
    Full nakedness! All joys are due to thee,
As souls unbodied, bodies uncloth'd must be,
To taste whole joys. Gems which you women use   35
Are like Atlanta's balls,[6] cast in men's views,
That when a fool's eye lighteth on a Gem,
His earthly soul may covet theirs, not them.
Like pictures, or like books' gay coverings made
For lay-men, are all women thus array'd;   40
Themselves are mystic books, which only we
(Whom their imputed grace will dignify)
Must see reveal'd. Then since that I may know,[7]
As liberally,[8] as to a Midwife, show
Thyself: cast all, yea, this white linen hence,   45
There is no penance due to innocence.
    To teach thee, I am naked first; why then
What needst thou have more covering than a man.

---

[3] Corset.   [4] The paradise of Islam was supposed to be full of fleshly pleasure.
[5] Both "impression" and "sign of ownership."
[6] Atalanta (usually so spelled) lost a race to Hippomenes because she paused three times to
pick up three golden apples which Venus had given him and which he threw in her path.
[7] Both "have knowledge" and "have intercourse."   [8] Both "freely" and "lewdly."

HOLY SONNETS

X

Death be not proud, though some have called thee
Mighty and dreadful, for, thou art not so,
For, those, whom thou think'st, thou dost overthrow,
Die not, poor death, nor yet canst thou kill me.
From rest and sleep, which but thy pictures be,　　　　　5
Much pleasure, then from thee, much more must flow,
And soonest our best men with thee do go,
Rest of their bones, and soul's delivery.
Thou art slave to Fate, Chance, kings, and desperate men,
And dost with poison, war, and sickness dwell,　　　　10
And poppy, or charms can make us sleep as well,
And better than thy stroke; why swell'st thou then?
One short sleep past, we wake eternally,
And death shall be no more; death, thou shalt die.

XIV

Batter my heart, three-person'd God; for, you
As yet but knock, breathe, shine, and seek to mend;
That I may rise, and stand, o'erthrow me, and bend
Your force, to break, blow, burn and make me new.
I, like an usurp'd town, to another due,　　　　　　5
Labour to admit you, but Oh, to no end,
Reason your viceroy in me, me should defend,
But is captiv'd, and proves weak or untrue.
Yet dearly I love you, and would be loved fain,
But am betroth'd unto your enemy:　　　　　　　10
Divorce me, untie, or break that knot again,
Take me to you, imprison me, for I
Except you enthral me, never shall be free,
Nor ever chaste, except you ravish me.

A HYMN TO GOD THE FATHER

I

Wilt Thou forgive that sin where I begun,[1]
　　Which is my sin, though it were done before?[2]
Wilt Thou forgive that sin, through which I run,

---

[1] Original sin.　　[2] Note the pun on Donne's name, here and below.

And do run still: thou still I do deplore?
 When Thou hast done, Thou hast not done,   5
  For I have more.

II

Wilt Thou forgive that sin by which I have won
 Others to sin? and, made my sin their door?
Wilt Thou forgive that sin which I did shun
 A year, or two: but wallowed in, a score?   10
 When Thou hast done, Thou hast not done,
  For I have more.

III

I have a sin of fear, that when I have spun
 My last thread, I shall perish on the shore;[3]
Swear by Thyself, that at my death Thy son   15
 Shall shine as He shines now, and heretofore;
 And, having done that, Thou hast done,
  I fear no more.

[3] As opposed to going to heaven.

Don Pedro Calderón de la Barca
(1600–1681)

Don Pedro Calderón de la Barca was the greatest dramatic writer of the so-called Siglo de Oro, *"The Golden Century," of Spanish art and culture. The era produced the novelist and playwright Miguel de Cervantes (author of* Don Quixote*); the painters El Greco, Ribera, Zurbarán, and Valázquez; and Calderón's fellow playwrights Lope de Vega (author of over fifteen hundred plays), Tirso de Molina (author of over four hundred), and a host of others. This period of flowering in art and especially in the theater is comparable to the contemporary golden age of art and drama in England.*

Calderón was born into a noble Madrid family in 1600. He was educated at a Jesuit school in Madrid, at the University of Alcalá, and at the University of Salamanca, where he received a degree in canonical law in 1619. Instead of going into the church, however, he served in the army in Italy and Flanders, eventually returning to Madrid and the court of Philip IV. Handsome, urbane, and witty, he quickly became a leading figure there. His first plays were performed in 1623, and during the next few years he wrote voluminously for the theater. He became court theater director when the famous playwright Lope de Vega died in 1635; by 1637, when the first two volumes of Calderón's collected plays were published, he had written sixty-six. (The total was eventually to exceed two hundred.) In 1650, Calderón left the court, gave up writing for public performance, and took holy orders, saddened by the deaths, within a short time, of his two brothers and his mistress, by whom he had had a son. He served for a time as a chaplain in Toledo, then returned to Madrid as private chaplain to Philip IV. During this last period of his life, he wrote seventy autos sacramentales *for performance at the Corpus Christi festivals in Madrid. These short religious plays, Spanish versions of medieval liturgical drama, were allegorical works performed on street wagons for popular audiences during the annual festivals. Calderón died in 1681.*

Sixteenth- and seventeenth-century Spanish theaters were, like English ones, basically courtyards with an open space in the middle surrounded by balconies and rooms from which spectators watched the action. There was a large, bare stage at one end of the courtyard, with an inner stage that could be closed off by a curtain, and a balcony that served as an upper stage. The physical similarities of the stages for which Calderón and Shakespeare wrote account for the similarities in their dramatic technique: both writers made use of scenes moving freely from one setting to another, a large cast of characters, and a double plot, in which two stories are woven together with continuous implicit comparisons and contrasts.

But there are also many differences between the Spanish and English theaters, differences that may at first pose problems for the non-Spanish reader. One is the language: Calderón and his contemporaries delighted in long, elaborate speeches relished for their own sake and in defiance of conversational realism. Such rhetorical artificiality, called conceptismo *in Spain, was a common feature of Baroque style all over Europe. It appeared as* préciosité *in France, as* marinismo *in Italy, and as "Euphuism" in England, where Shakespeare parodied it amusingly in* Love's Labors Lost. *Segismund's first speech is one of many examples in* Life Is a Dream, *and Calderón himself, like Shakespeare, parodies the style at one point, in Clarion's first speech in the third scene of Act III. Such lengthy speeches are balanced by equally artificial passages of balanced, one-line exchanges. Even single sentences are sometimes divided between two characters, as in Stella's and Astolfo's greeting to the king in the last scene of Act I.*

There are also a number of other special features of classical Spanish drama, features which Life Is a Dream *illustrates at the same time that it raises them to the highest level of art. Character tends to be conventionalized and subordinated to action.* Life Is a Dream *is built around a small group of stock characters: a romantic hero, a pair of lovers, an old man, a king, and a fool. Spanish playwrights were much more inclined than even the English writers were to ignore the neoclassical "unities" of time, place, and action. Lope de Vega, in both theory and practice, strongly defended the mixing of tragedy and comedy and the ignoring of the unities; his practice, he argued, was truer to the variety of nature than were rule-bound plays.* Life Is a Dream *well illustrates the extravagance and improbability of the action of many Spanish plays, although it makes that action a resonant symbol of human life. And finally, Spanish drama is much more deeply religious than English drama. Even in secular plays man's life is regarded as a religious pilgrimage, and a recurring concept is expressed by the word* desengaño, *which means literally "disillusionment" but which might better be translated "illumination." The Spanish protagonist wanders through a world of confusing surfaces and deceptions until at a climactic moment the scales fall from his eyes and he suddenly sees himself in the context of eternity and spiritual reality. Segismund, who achieves this vision after he is returned to his prison, describes it in the great last speech of Act II, the most famous speech in Spanish drama.*

One of the most striking features of Life Is a Dream *is its combination of the most primitive folk materials with the loftiest philosophy. For his plot, Calderón draws upon two ancient folk tales, both Oriental in origin. In the story of Barlaam and Josephat, a pagan king hears that his newborn son Josephat will become a Christian. He therefore isolates the son in a mountain prison, but the holy hermit Barlaam finds Josephat and converts him to Christianity. The other story is from the* Arabian Nights: *someone is drugged, given one day of royal power, and later told it was all a dream. (Boccaccio, in the* Decameron, *and Shakespeare, in* The Taming of the Shrew, *both employ variants of this story.)*

In Calderón's hands, these fairy-tale materials are transformed into a profound study of human life. The play can be read as deeply Christian: Segismund is Everyman, confined in the cave of worldly illusion and spiritual darkness. His chains are his own earthly instincts, and his task is to free himself from these chains and attain salvation. King Basil, in this context, becomes a God-figure as he tests his erring son and sets him upon the road to self-mastery. But from another point of view, Basil is far from blameless, and the play becomes a study in the human conflict between fate and self-determination. The king reminds us not only of Josephat's father but also of the father of Oedipus, who also tried to avert a threatening prophecy by condemning his own son. Basil boasts that the stars have been his "chiefest study" all his life; ironically, by focusing his attention too closely upon the unworldly, he does a great injustice to his own son and throws his kingdom into disarray, until the son who was supposedly to be the destroyer of the kingdom becomes its savior. Modern, psychology-conscious readers are likely to see in King Basil not so much God as the castrating father of childhood fantasy. (Biographers have pointed out how many of Calderón's plays deal with tyrannical, unjust fathers and the violence that erupts from father-son conflict. The roots of this theme may lie in Calderón's own relationship with his harsh and autocratic father.) The progress of Segismund, involuntary killer of his mother and victim of his father, is toward self-mastery and reconciliation, from the infantile rage of his first appearance at court to the maturity of the lofty-minded hero of the last act.

These themes, and many others, are all implicit in the play's title metaphor of life as dream. The starting point for this metaphor may be the Christian view of life as merely a passing dream from which we awake into eternity. But Calderón's use of the metaphor transcends the narrowly doctrinal, especially in the way the metaphor is embedded in the basic structure of the play. Segismund, suddenly transported from his cave and set down in the splendor of the court, is deceived by an illusion. (Or perhaps the court is the reality, and his cave-life the illusion, arranged and stage-managed by a playwright-father.) But we, watching the play, are watching an illusion of an illusion, a dream of a dream. The English-language reader, faced with such complexities, is likely to be reminded of Shakespeare's comparable use of the metaphors of life as theater and life as dream in Hamlet *and* A Midsummer Night's Dream, *plays among which* Life Is a Dream *takes its place as a masterpiece of dramatic art.*

FURTHER READING *(prepared by W. J. R.):* Background information on the Spanish Golden Age can be found in Everett W. Hesse's *Calderón de la Barca,* 1967, a good introduction to Calderón's drama that classifies it by seven types and discusses each of them. James E. Maraniss's *On Calderón,* 1978, contains a general discussion of Calderón's drama and chapters on seven plays, including *Life Is a Dream.* Further information on the historical period is available in Margaret Wilson's *Spanish Drama of The Golden Age,* 1969, along with sections on Lope de Vega, Tirso de Molina, and

Calderón. Michael D. McGaha's *Approaches to the Theater of Calderón,* 1982, is a comprehensive collection of essays on Calderón's theater, major plays (including *Life Is a Dream*), and influence. Diverse critical approaches are represented in *Critical Essays on the Theatre of Calderón,* ed. Bruce W. Wardropper, 1965; a section on *Life Is a Dream* includes essays on structure, the role of Rosaura, and other topics. John V. Bryan's *Calderón de la Barca: Imagery, Rhetoric and Drama,* 1977, covers dramatic language, imagery, the conceit, and other topics. John V. Bryan's "Rosaura Liberated, or A Woman's Rebellion," in *University of British Columbia Hispanic Studies,* ed. Harold Livermore, 1974, discusses the importance of the subplot in *Life Is a Dream,* analyzing thoroughly the question of Rosaura's honor. Robert Ter Horst's "From Comedy to Tragedy: Calderón and the New Tragedy," *Modern Language Notes,* 92 (1977), 181–201, is about the development of a new kind of tragedy from the comedy of Spain's Golden Age; the transition is examined as it is reflected in several Calderón plays.

LIFE IS A DREAM

Translated by Roy Campbell

DRAMATIS PERSONAE

BASIL, *King of Poland*
SEGISMUND, *Prince*
ASTOLFO, *Duke of Muscovy*
CLOTALDO, *old man*
CLARION, *a comical servant*

ROSAURA, *a lady*
STELLA, *a princess*
Soldiers, guards, musicians,
   servants, retinues, women

The scene is laid in the court of Poland, a nearby fortress, and the open country.

ACT I

On one side a craggy mountain: on the other a rude tower whose base serves as a prison for SEGISMUND. *The door facing the spectators is open. The action begins at nightfall.*

[ROSAURA, *dressed as a man, appears on the rocks climbing down to the plain: behind her comes* CLARION.]
ROSAURA. You headlong hippogriff[1] who match the gale
  In rushing to and fro, you lightning-flicker
  Who give no light, you scaleless fish, you bird
  Who have no coloured plumes, you animal
  Who have no natural instinct, tell me whither
  You lead me stumbling through this labyrinth
  Of naked crags! Stay here upon this peak

---

[1] A legendary creature, half horse and half griffin. A griffin was itself a hybrid, with an eagle's head and wings and a lion's body.

And be a Phaëthon[2] to the brute-creation!
For I, pathless save only for the track
The laws of destiny dictate for me   10
Shall, blind and desperate, descend this height
Whose furrowed brows are frowning at the sun.
How rudely, Poland, you receive a stranger
(Hardly arrived, but to be treated hardly)
And write her entry down in blood with thorns.
My plight attests this well, but after all,
Where did the wretchèd ever pity find?

CLARION. Say *two* so wretchèd. Don't you leave me out
When you complain! If we two sallied out
From our own country, questing high adventure,   20
And after so much madness and misfortune
Are still two here, and were two when we fell
Down those rough crags—shall I not be offended
To share the trouble yet forego the credit?

ROSAURA. I did not give you shares in my complaint
So as not to rob you of the right to sorrow
Upon your own account. There's such relief
In venting grief that a philosopher
Once said that sorrows should not be bemoaned
But sought for pleasure.

CLARION.   Philosopher?   30
I call him a long-bearded, drunken sot
And would they'd cudgelled him a thousand blows
To give him something worth his while lamenting!
But, madam, what should we do, by ourselves,
On foot and lost at this late hour of day,
Here on this desert mountain far away—
The sun departing after fresh horizons?

ROSAURA. Clarion, how can I answer, being both
The partner of your plight and your dilemma?

CLARION. Would anyone believe such strange events?   40

ROSAURA. If there my sight is not deceived by fancy,
In the last timid light that yet remains
I seem to see a building.

CLARION.   Either my hopes
Are lying or I see the signs myself.

ROSAURA. Between the towering crags, there stands so small
A royal palace that the lynx-eyed sun
Could scarce perceive it at midday, so rude
In architecture that it seems but one
Rock more down-toppled from the sun-kissed crags
That form the jaggèd crest.

CLARION.   Let's go closer,   50

---

[2] Phaëthon, in Greek mythology, drove the chariot of his father the Sun too near the earth, which he almost set on fire.

For we have stared enough: it would be better
To let the inmates make us welcome.
ROSAURA.   See:
    The door, or, rather, that funereal gap,
    Is yawning wide—whence night itself seems born,
    Flowing out from its black, rugged centre.
                              [*A sound of chains is heard.*]
CLARION. Heavens! What's that I hear?
ROSAURA.   I have become
    A block immovable of ice and fire.
CLARION. Was that a little chain? Why, I'll be hanged
    If that is not the clanking ghost of some
    Past galley-slave—my terror proves it is!   60
SEGISMUND. Oh, miserable me! Unhappy me!
ROSAURA. How sad a cry that is! I fear new trials
    And torments.
CLARION.   It's a fearful sound.
ROSAURA.   Oh, come,
    My Clarion, let us fly from suffering!
CLARION. I'm in such sorry trim, I've not the spirit
    Even to run away.
ROSAURA.   And if you had,
    You'd not have seen that door, not known of it.
    When one's in doubt, the common saying goes
    One walks between two lights.
CLARION.   I'm the reverse.
    It's not that way with me.
ROSAURA.   What then disturbs you?   70
CLARION. I walk in doubt between two darknesses.
ROSAURA. Is not that feeble exhalation there
    A light? That pallid star whose fainting tremors,
    Pulsing a doubtful warmth of glimmering rays,
    Make even darker with its spectral glow
    That gloomy habitation? Yes! because
    By its reflection (though so far away)
    I recognise a prison, grim and sombre,
    The sepulchre of some poor living carcase.
    And, more to wonder at, a man lies there   80
    Clothed in the hides of savage beasts, with limbs
    Loaded with fetters, and a single lamp
    For company. So, since we cannot flee,
    Let us stay here and listen to his plaint
    And what his sorrows are.
SEGISMUND.   Unhappy me!
    Oh, miserable me! You heavens above,
    I try to think what crime I've done against you
    By being born. Although to have been born,
    I know, is an offence, and with just cause
    I bear the rigours of your punishment: 90

Since to be born is man's worst crime. But yet
I long to know (to clarify my doubts)
What greater crime, apart from being born,
Can thus have earned my greater chastisement.
Aren't others born like me? And yet they seem
To boast a freedom that I've never known.
The bird is born, and in the hues of beauty
Clothed with its plumes, yet scarce has it become
A feathered posy—or a flower with wings—
When through ethereal halls it cuts its way,   100
Refusing the kind shelter of its nest.
And I, who have more soul than any bird,
Must have less liberty?
The beast is born, and with its hide bright-painted,
In lovely tints, has scarce become a spangled
And starry constellation (thanks to the skilful
Brush of the Painter) than its earthly needs
Teach it the cruelty to prowl and kill,
The monster of its labyrinth of flowers.
Yet I, with better instincts than a beast,   110
Must have less liberty?
The fish is born, the birth of spawn and slime,
That does not even live by breathing air.
No sooner does it feel itself a skiff
Of silver scales upon the wave than swiftly
It roves about in all directions taking
The measure of immensity as far
As its cold blood's capacity allows.
Yet I, with greater freedom of the will,
Must have less liberty?   120
The brook is born, and like a snake unwinds
Among the flowers. No sooner, silver serpent,
Does it break through the blooms than it regales
And thanks them with its music for their kindness,
Which opens to its course the majesty
Of the wide plain. Yet I, with far more life,
Must have less liberty?
This fills me with such passion, I become
Like the volcano, Etna, and could tear
Pieces of my own heart out of my breast!   130
What law, justice, or reason can decree
That man alone should never know the joys
And be alone excepted from the rights
God grants a fish, a bird, a beast, a brook?

ROSAURA. His words have filled me full of fear and pity.
SEGISMUND. Who is it overheard my speech? Clotaldo?
CLARION. Say "yes!"
ROSAURA.   It's only a poor wretch, alas,
    Who in these cold ravines has overheard
    Your sorrows.

SEGISMUND.   Then I'll kill you
                                              [*Seizes her.*]
    So as to leave no witness of my frailty.   140
    I'll tear you into bits with these strong arms!
CLARION. I'm deaf. I wasn't able to hear that.
ROSAURA. If you were human born, it is enough
    That I should kneel to you for you to spare me.
SEGISMUND. Your voice has softened me, your presence halted me,
    And now, confusingly, I feel respect
    For you. Who are you? Though here I have learned
    So little of the world, since this grim tower
    Has been my cradle and my sepulchre;
    And though since I was born (if you can say   150
    I really have been born) I've only seen
    This rustic desert where in misery
    I dwell alone, a living skeleton,
    An animated corpse; and though till now,
    I never spoke, save to one man who hears
    My griefs and through whose converse I have heard
    News of the earth and of the sky; and though,
    To astound you more, and make you call me
    A human monster, I dwell here, and am
    A man of the wild animals, a beast   160
    Among the race of men; and though in such
    Misfortune, I have studied human laws,
    Instructed by the birds, and learned to measure
    The circles of the gentle stars, you only
    Have curbed my furious rage, amazed my vision,
    And filled with wonderment my sense of hearing.
    Each time I look at you, I feel new wonder!
    The more I see of you, the more I long
    To go on seeing more of you. I think
    My eyes are dropsical, to go on drinking   170
    What it is death for them to drink, because
    They go on drinking that which I am dying
    To see and that which, seen, will deal me death.
    Yet let me gaze on you and die, since I
    Am so bewitched I can no longer think
    What not seeing you would do to me—the sight
    Itself being fatal! that would be more hard
    Than dying, madness, rage, and fiercest grief:
    It would be life—worst fate of all because
    The gift of life to such a wretchèd man   180
    Would be the gift of death to happiness!
ROSAURA. Astonished as I look, amazed to hear,
    I know not what to say nor what to ask.
    All I can say is that heaven guided me
    Here to be comforted, if it is comfort
    To see another sadder than oneself.
    They say a sage philosopher of old,

Being so poor and miserable that he
Lived on the few plain herbs he could collect,
One day exclaimed: "Could any man be poorer   190
Or sadder than myself?"—when, turning round,
He saw the very answer to his words.
For there another sage philosopher
Was picking up the scraps he'd thrown away.
I lived cursing my fortune in this world
And asked within me: "Is there any other
Suffers so hard a fate?" Now out of pity
You've given me the answer. For within me
I find upon reflection that my griefs
Would be as joys to you and you'd receive them   200
To give you pleasure. So if they perchance
In any measure may afford relief,
Listen attentively to my misfortune
And take what is left over for yourself.
I am. . .

CLOTALDO. [*Within.*] Guards of the tower! You sluggards
    Or cowards, you have let two people pass
    Into the prison bounds. . .

ROSAURA.   Here's more confusion!

SEGISMUND. That is Clotaldo, keeper of my prison.
    Are my misfortunes still not at an end?

CLOTALDO. Come. Be alert, and either seize or slay them   210
    Before they can resist!

VOICES. [*Within.*]   Treason! Betrayal!

CLARION. Guards of the tower who let us pass unhindered,
    Since there's a choice, to seize us would be simpler.

                            [*Enter* CLOTALDO *with soldiers. He
                            holds a pistol and they all wear
                            masks.*]

CLOTALDO. [*Aside to the soldiers.*]
    Cover your faces, all! It's a precaution
    Imperative that nobody should know us
    While we are here.

CLARION.   What's this? A masquerade?

CLOTALDO. O you, who ignorantly passed the bounds
    And limits of this region, banned to all—
    Against the king's decree which has forbidden
    That any should find out the prodigy   220
    Hidden in these ravines—yield up your weapons
    Or else this pistol, like a snake of metal,
    Will spit the piercing venom of two shots
    With scandalous assault upon the air.

SEGISMUND. Tyrannic master, ere you harm these people
    Let my life be the spoil of these sad bonds
    In which (I swear it by Almighty God)
    I'll sooner rend myself with hands and teeth

Amid these rocks than see them harmed and mourn
Their suffering.
CLOTALDO.   Since you know, Segismund,   230
That your misfortunes are so huge that, even
Before your birth, you died by heaven's decree,
And since you know these walls and binding chains
Are but the brakes and curbs to your proud frenzies,
What use is it to bluster?

                              [*To the guards.*]
                    Shut the door
Of this close prison! Hide him in its depths!
SEGISMUND. Ah, heavens, how justly you denied me freedom!
For like a Titan[3] I would rise against you,
Pile jasper mountains high on stone foundations
And climb to burst the windows of the sun!   240
CLOTALDO. Perhaps you suffer so much pain today
Just to forestall that feat.
ROSAURA.   Now that I see
How angry pride offends you, I'd be foolish
Not to plead humbly at your feet for life.
Be moved by me to pity. It would be
Notoriously harsh that neither pride
Nor humbleness found favour in your eyes!
CLARION. And if neither Humility nor Pride
Impress you (characters of note who act
And motivate a thousand mystery plays[4])   250
Let me, here, who am neither proud nor humble,
But merely something halfway in between,
Plead to you both for shelter and for aid.
CLOTALDO. Ho, there!
SOLDIER.   Sir?
CLOTALDO.   Take their weapons. Bind their eyes
So that they cannot see the way they're led.
ROSAURA. This is my sword. To nobody but you
I yield it, since you're, after all, the chief.
I cannot yield to one of meaner rank.
CLARION. My sword is such that I will freely give it
To the most mean and wretched.

                              [*To one soldier.*]
                    Take it, you!   260
ROSAURA. And if I have to die, I'll leave it to you
In witness of your mercy. It's a pledge
Of great worth and may justly be esteemed
For someone's sake who wore it long ago.

---

[3] In Greek mythology, one of a family of giants who overthrew their parents Uranus and Gaea and were themselves overthrown by the Olympian gods.
[4] Clarion is comically referring to the medieval mystery plays (or, more strictly, morality plays) in which the characters are personifications of abstractions. See the Introduction to *Everyman.*

CLOTALDO. [*Apart.*] Each moment seems to bring me new misfortune!
ROSAURA. Because of that, I ask you to preserve
    This sword with care. Since if inconstant Fate
    Consents to the remission of my sentence,
    It has to win me honour. Though I know not
    The secret that it carries, I do know   270
    It has got one—unless I trick myself—
    And prize it just as the sole legacy
    My father left me.
CLOTALDO.   Who then was your father?
ROSAURA. I never knew.
CLOTALDO.   And why have you come here?
ROSAURA. I came to Poland to avenge a wrong.
CLOTALDO. [*Apart.*]
    Sacred heavens!

> [*On taking the sword he becomes
> very perturbed.*]

        What's this? Still worse and worse.
I am perplexed and troubled with more fears.
                [*Aloud.*]
    Tell me: who gave that sword to you?
ROSAURA.   A woman.
CLOTALDO. Her name?
ROSAURA.   A secret I am forced to keep.
CLOTALDO. What makes you think this sword contains a secret?   280
ROSAURA. That she who gave it to me said: "Depart
    To Poland. There with subtlety and art
    Display it so that all the leading people
    And noblemen can see you wearing it,
    And I know well that there's a lord among them
    Who will both shelter you and grant you favour."
    But, lest he should be dead, she did not name him.
CLOTALDO. [*Aside.*] Protect me, heavens! What is this I hear?
    I cannot say if real or imagined
    But here's the sword I gave fair Violante   290
    In token that, whoever in the future
    Should come from her to me wearing this sword,
    Would find in me a tender father's love.
    Alas, what can I do in such a pass,
    When he who brings the sword to win my favour
    Brings it to find his own red death instead
    Arriving at my feet condemned already?
    What strange perplexity! How hard a fate!
    What an inconstant fortune to be plagued with!
    This is my son not only by all signs   300
    But also by the promptings of my heart,
    Since, seeing him, my heart seems to cry out
    To him, and beat its wings, and, though unable
    To break the locks, behaves as one shut in,
    Who, hearing noises in the street outside,

Cranes from the window-ledge. Just so, not knowing
What's really happening, but hearing sounds,
My heart runs to my eyes which are its windows
And out of them flows into bitter tears.
Protect me, heaven! What am I to do?   310
To take him to the king is certain death.
To hide him is to break my sacred oath
And the strong law of homage. From one side
Love of one's own, and from the other loyalty—
Call me to yield. Loyalty to my king
(Why do I doubt?) comes before life and honour.
Then live my loyalty, and let him die!
When I remember, furthermore, he came
To avenge an injury—a man insulted
And unavenged is in disgrace. My son   320
Therefore he is not, nor of noble blood.
But if some danger has mischanced, from which
No one escapes, since honour is so fragile
That any act can smash it, and it takes
A stain from any breath of air, what more
Could any nobleman have done than he,
Who, at the cost of so much risk and danger,
Comes to avenge his honour? Since he's so brave
He is my son, and my blood's in his veins.
And so betwixt the one doubt and the other,   330
The most important mean between extremes
Is to go to the king and tell the truth—
That he's my son, to kill, if so he wishes.
Perhaps my loyalty thus will move his mercy
And if I thus can merit a live son
I'll help him to avenge his injury.
But if the king prove constant in his rigour
And deal him death, he'll die in ignorance
That I'm his father.

                                       [*Aloud to* ROSAURA *and* CLARION.]
            Come then, strangers, come!
And do not fear that you have no companions   340
In your misfortunes, since, in equal doubt,
Tossed between life and death, I cannot guess
Which is the greater evil or the less.

          A hall at the royal palace, in court

[*Enter* ASTOLFO *and soldiers at one side: from the other side* PRINCESS
STELLA *and ladies. Military music and salvos.*]
ASTOLFO. To greet your excellent bright beams
    As brilliant as a comet's rays,
    The drums and brasses mix their praise

With those of fountains, birds, and streams.
With sounds alike, in like amaze,
Your heavenly face each voice salutes,
Which puts them in such lively fettle,   350
The trumpets sound like birds of metal,
The songbirds play like feathered flutes.
And thus they greet you, fair señora—
The salvos, as their queen, the brasses,
As to Minerva when she passes,
The songbirds to the bright Aurora,
And all the flowers and leaves and grasses
As doing homage unto Flora,[5]
Because you come to cheat the day
Which now the night has covered o'er—   360
Aurora in your spruce array,
Flora in peace, Pallas in war,
But in my heart the queen of May.
STELLA. If human voice could match with acts
     You would have been unwise to say
     Hyperboles that a few facts
     May well refute some other day
     Confounding all this martial fuss
     With which I struggle daringly,
     Since flatteries you proffer thus   370
     Do not accord with what I see.
     Take heed that it's an evil thing
     And worthy of a brute accursed,
     Loud praises with your mouth to sing
     When in your heart you wish the worst.
ASTOLFO. Stella, you have been badly misinformed
     If you doubt my good faith. Here let me beg you
     To listen to my plea and hear me out.
     The third Eugtorgius died, the King of Poland.
     Basil, his heir, had two fair sisters who   380
     Bore you, my cousin, and myself. I would not
     Tire you with all that happened here. You know
     Clorilene was your mother who enjoys,
     Under a better reign, her starry throne.
     She was the elder. Lovely Recisunda
     (Whom may God cherish for a thousand years!)
     The younger one, my mother and your aunt,
     Was wed in Muscovy. Now to return:
     Basil has yielded to the feebleness
     Of age, loves learnèd study more than women,   390
     Has lost his wife, is childless, will not marry.
     And so it comes that you and I both claim
     The heirdom of the realm. You claim that you

─────────

[5] Minerva (equivalent of the Greek Pallas Athena), Aurora, and Flora are the Roman goddesses of, respectively, wisdom, the dawn, and gardens.

Were daughter to the elder daughter. I
Say that my being born a man, although
Son of the younger daughter, gives me title
To be preferred. We've told the king, our uncle,
Of both of our intentions. And he answered
That he would judge between our rival claims,
For which the time and place appointed was   400
Today and here. For that same reason I
Have left my native Muscovy. With that
Intent I come—not seeking to wage war
But so that you might thus wage war on me!
May Love, wise god, make true what people say
(Your "people" is a wise astrologer)
By settling this through your being chosen queen—
Queen and my consort, sovereign of my will;
My uncle crowning you, for greater honour;
Your courage conquering, as it deserves;   410
My love applauding you, its emperor!
STELLA. To such chivalrous gallantry, my breast
    Cannot hold out. The imperial monarchy
    I wish were mine only to make it yours—
    Although my love is not quite satisfied
    That you are to be trusted since your speech
    Is somewhat contradicted by that portrait
    You carry in the locket round your neck.
ASTOLFO. I'll give you satisfaction as to that.
[Drums.]
    But these loud instruments will not permit it   420
    That sound the arrival of the king and council.
[Enter KING BASIL with his
following.]

STELLA. Wise Thales. . .
ASTOLFO.   Learned Euclid[6]. . .
STELLA. Among the signs. . .
ASTOLFO.   Among the stars. . .
STELLA. Where you preside in power. . .
ASTOLFO.   Where you reside. . .
STELLA. And plot their paths. . .
ASTOLFO.   And trace their fiery trails. . .
STELLA. Describing. . .
ASTOLFO.   . . .Measuring and judging them. . .
STELLA. Please read my stars that I, in humble bonds. . .
ASTOLFO. Please read them, so that I in soft embraces. . .
STELLA. May twine as ivy to this tree!
ASTOLFO.   May find
    Myself upon my knees before these feet!   430
BASIL. Come and embrace me, niece and nephew. Trust me,
    Since you're both loyal to my loving precepts,

---

[6] Thales and Euclid were celebrated classical astronomers and mathematicians.

And come here so affectionately both—
In nothing shall I leave you cause to cavil,
And both of you as equals will be treated.
The gravity of what I have to tell
Oppresses me, and all I ask of you
Is silence: the event itself will claim
Your wonderment. So be attentive now,
Belovèd niece and nephew, illustrious courtiers,   440
Relatives, friends, and subjects! You all know
That for my learning I have merited
The surname of The Learnèd, since the brush
Of great Timanthes, and Lisippus' marbles[7]—
Stemming oblivion (consequence of time)—
Proclaimed me to mankind Basil the Great.
You know the science that I most affect
And most esteem is subtle mathematics
(By which I forestall time, cheat fame itself)
Whose office is to show things gradually.   450
For when I look my tables up and see,
Present before me, all the news and actions
Of centuries to come, I gain on Time—
Since Time recounts whatever I have said
After I say it. Those snowflaking haloes,
Those canopies of crystal spread on high,
Lit by the sun, cut by the circling moon,
Those diamond orbs, those globes of radiant crystal
Which the bright stars adorn, on which the signs
Parade in blazing excellence, have been   460
My chiefest study all through my long years.
They are the volumes on whose adamantine
Pages, bound up in sapphire, heaven writes,
In lines of burnished gold and vivid letters,
All that is due to happen, whether adverse
Or else benign. I read them in a flash,
So quickly that my spirit tracks their movements—
Whatever road they take, whatever goal
They aim at. Would to heaven that before
My genius had been the commentary   470
Writ in their margins, or the index to
Their pages, that my life had been the rubble,
The ruin, and destruction of their wrath,
And that my tragedy in them had ended,
Because, to the unlucky, even their merit
Is like a hostile knife, and he whom knowledge
Injures is but a murderer to himself.
And this I say myself, though my misfortunes

---

[7] Timanthes (c. 400 B.C.) was a celebrated Greek painter, Lysippus (356–323 B.C.) a celebrated Greek sculptor. Basil does not mean that he was literally painted or sculpted by these
men; he is using their names generically for all painters and sculptors.

Say it far better, which, to marvel at,
I beg once more for silence from you all.   480
With my late wife, the queen, I had a son,
Unhappy son, to greet whose birth the heavens
Wore themselves out in prodigies and portents.
Ere the sun's light brought him live burial
Out of the womb (for birth resembles death)
His mother many times, in the delirium
And fancies of her sleep, saw a fierce monster
Bursting her entrails in a human form,
Born spattered with her lifeblood, dealing death,
The human viper of this century!   490
The day came for his birth, and every presage
Was then fulfilled, for tardily or never
Do the more cruel ones prove false. At birth
His horoscope was such that the bright sun,
Stained in its blood, entered ferociously
Into a duel with the moon above.
The whole earth seemed a rampart for the strife
Of heaven's two lights, who—though not hand-to-hand—
Fought light-to-light to gain the mastery!
The worst eclipse the sun has ever suffered   500
Since Christ's own death horrified earth and sky.
The whole earth overflowed with conflagrations
So that it seemed the final paroxysm
Of existence. The skies grew dark. Buildings shook.
The clouds rained stones. The rivers ran with blood.
In this delirious frenzy of the sun,
Thus, Segismund was born into the world,
Giving a foretaste of his character
By killing his own mother, seeming to speak thus
By his ferocity: "I am a man,   510
Because I have begun now to repay
All kindnesses with evil." To my studies
I went forthwith, and saw in all I studied
That Segismund would be the most outrageous
Of all men, the most cruel of all princes,
And impious of all monarchs, by whose acts
The kingdom would be torn up and divided
So as to be a school of treachery
And an academy of vices. He,
Risen in fury, amidst crimes and horrors,   520
Was born to trample me (with shame I say it)
And make of my grey hairs his very carpet.
Who is there but believes an evil Fate?
And more if he discovers it himself,
For self-love lends its credit to our studies.
So I, believing in the Fates, and in
The havoc that their prophecies predestined,
Determined to cage up this newborn tiger

To see if on the stars we sages have
Some power. I gave out that the prince had died   530
Stillborn, and, well-forewarned, I built a tower
Amidst the cliffs and boulders of yon mountains
Over whose tops the light scarce finds its way,
So stubbornly their obelisks and crags
Defend the entry to them. The strict laws
And edicts that I published then (declaring
That nobody might enter the forbidden
Part of the range) were passed on that account.
There Segismund lives to this day, a captive,
Poor and in misery, where, save Clotaldo,   540
His guardian, none have seen or talked to him.
The latter has instructed him in all
Branches of knowledge and in the Catholic faith,
Alone the witness of his misery.
There are three things to be considered now:
Firstly, Poland, that I love you greatly,
So much that I would free you from the oppression
And servitude of such a tyrant king.
He would not be a kindly ruler who
Would put his realm and homeland in such danger.   550
The second fact that I must bear in mind
Is this: that to deny my flesh and blood
The rights which law, both human and divine,
Concedes, would not accord with Christian charity,
For no law says that, to prevent another
Being a tyrant, I may be one myself,
And if my son's a tyrant, to prevent him
From doing outrage, I myself should do it.
Now here's the third and last point I would speak of,
Namely, how great an error it has been   560
To give too much belief to things predicted,
Because, even if his inclination should
Dictate some headlong, rash precipitancies,
They may perhaps not conquer him entirely,
For the most accursèd destiny, the most
Violent inclination, the most impious
Planet—all can but influence, not force,
The free will which man holds direct from God.
And so, between one motive and another
Vacillating discursively, I hit   570
On a solution that will stun you all.
I shall tomorrow, but without his knowing
He is my son—your king—place Segismund
(For that's the name with which he was baptised)
Here on my throne, beneath my canopy,
Yes, in my very place, that he may govern you
And take command. And you must all be here
To swear him fealty as his loyal subjects.

Three things may follow from this test, and these
I'll set against the three which I proposed.   580
The first is that should the prince prove prudent,
Stable, and benign—thus giving the lie
To all that prophecy reports of him—
Then you'll enjoy in him your rightful ruler
Who was so long a courtier of the mountains
And neighbour to the beasts. Here is the second:
If he prove proud, rash, cruel, and outrageous,
And with a loosened rein gallop unheeding
Across the plains of vice, I shall have done
My duty, and fulfilled my obligation   590
Of mercy. If I then re-imprison him,
That's incontestably a kingly deed—
Not cruelty but merited chastisement.
The third thing's this: that if the prince should be
As I've described him, then—by the love I feel
For you, my vassals—I shall give you worthier
Rulers to wear the sceptre and the crown;
Because your king and queen will be my nephew
And niece, each with an equal right to rule,
Each gaining the inheritance he merits,   600
And joined in faith of holy matrimony.
This I command you as a king, I ask you
As a kind father, as a sage I pray you,
As an experienced old man I tell you,
And (if it's true, as Spanish Seneca[8]
Says, that the king is slave unto his nation)
This, as a humble slave, I beg of you.
ASTOLFO. If it behoves me to reply (being
The person most involved in this affair)
Then, in the name of all, let Segismund   610
Appear! It is enough that he's your son!
ALL. Give us our prince: we want him for our king!
BASIL. Subjects, I thank you for your kindly favour.
Accompany these, my two Atlases,[9]
Back to their rooms. Tomorrow you shall see him.
ALL. Long live the great King Basil! Long live Basil!

> [*Exeunt all, accompanying* STELLA
> *and* ASTOLFO. *The* KING *remains.*]
> [*Enter* CLOTALDO *with* ROSAURA
> *and* CLARION.]

CLOTALDO. May I have leave to speak, sire?
BASIL.   Oh, Clotaldo!
You're very welcome.
CLOTALDO.   Thus to kneel before you

---

[8] Seneca was a Roman philosopher who was born in Spain about 4 B.C.
[9] In Greek mythology, Atlas was a Titan who bore the earth on his shoulders. Basil is flatteringly suggesting that Stella and Astolfo divide the world between them.

Is always welcome, sire—yet not today
When sad and evil Fate destroys the joy   620
Your presence normally concedes.
BASIL.   What's wrong?
CLOTALDO. A great misfortune, sire, has come upon me
Just when I should have met it with rejoicing.
BASIL. Continue.
CLOTALDO.   Sire, this beautiful young man
Who inadvertently and daringly
Came to the tower, wherein he saw the prince,
Is my . . .
BASIL.   Do not afflict yourself, Clotaldo.
Had it not been just now, I should have minded,
I must confess. But I've revealed the secret,
And now it does not matter if he knows it.   630
Attend me afterwards. I've many things
To tell you. You in turn have many things
To do for me. You'll be my minister,
I warn you, in the most momentous action
The world has ever seen. These prisoners, lest you
Should think I blame your oversight, I'll pardon.
                              [*Exit.*]
CLOTALDO. Long may you live, great sire! A thousand years!
                              [*Aside.*]
Heaven improves our fates. I shall not tell him
Now that he is my son, since it's not needed
Till he's avenged.   640
                              [*Aloud.*]
Strangers, you may go free.
ROSAURA. Humbly I kiss your feet.
CLARION.   Whilst I'll just *miss* them—
Old friends will hardly quibble at one letter.
ROSAURA. You've granted me my life, sir. I remain
Your servant and eternally your debtor.
CLOTALDO. No! It was not your life I gave you. No!
Since any wellborn man who, unavenged,
Nurses an insult does not live at all.
And seeing you have told me that you came
For that sole reason, it was not life I spared—   650
Life in disgrace is not a life at all.
                              [*Aside.*]
I see this spurs him.
ROSAURA.   Freely I confess it—
Although you spared my life, it was no life.
But I will wipe my honour's stain so spotless
That after I have vanquished all my dangers
Life well may seem a shining gift from you.
CLOTALDO. Take here your burnished steel: 'twill be enough,
Bathed in your enemies' red blood, to right you.

For steel that once was mine (I mean of course
Just for the time I've had it in my keeping)   660
Should know how to avenge you.
ROSAURA. Now, in your name I gird it on once more
And on it I will swear to take revenge
Although my foe were even mightier.
CLOTALDO. Is he so powerful?
ROSAURA.   So much so that . . .
Although I have no doubt in your discretion . . .
I say no more because I'd not estrange
Your clemency.
CLOTALDO. You would have won me had you told me, since
That would prevent me helping him.   670
                          [*Aside.*]
If only I could discover who he is!
ROSAURA. So that you'll not think that I value lightly
Such confidence, know that my adversary
Is no less than Astolfo, Duke of Muscovy.
CLOTALDO. [*Aside.*] (I hardly can withstand the grief it gives me
For it is worse than aught I could imagine!
Let us inquire of him some further facts.)
                          [*Aloud.*]
If you were born a Muscovite, your ruler
Could never have affronted you. Go back
Home to your country. Leave this headstrong valour.   680
It will destroy you.
ROSAURA.   Though he's been my prince,
I know that he has done me an affront.
CLOTALDO. Even though he slapped your face, that's no affront.
                        [*Aside.*]
O heavens!
ROSAURA.   My insult was far deeper!
CLOTALDO.   Tell it:
Since nothing I imagine could be deeper.
ROSAURA. Yes. I will tell it, yet, I know not why,
With such respect I look upon your face,
I venerate you with such true affection,
With such high estimation do I weigh you,
That I scarce dare to tell you—these men's clothes   690
Are an enigma, not what they appear.
So now you know. Judge if it's no affront
That here Astolfo comes to wed with Stella
Although betrothed to me. I've said enough.
             [*Exeunt* ROSAURA *and* CLARION.]
CLOTALDO. Here! Listen! Wait! What mazed confusion!
It is a labyrinth wherein the reason
Can find no clue. My family honour's injured.
The enemy's all powerful. I'm a vassal
And she's a woman. Heavens! Show a path

Although I don't believe there is a way!   700
There's nought but evil bodings in the sky.
The whole world is a prodigy, say I.

ACT II

A Hall in the Royal Palace

[*Enter* BASIL *and* CLOTALDO.]
CLOTALDO. All has been done according to your orders.
BASIL. Tell me, Clotaldo, how it went?
CLOTALDO.   Why, thus:
    I took to Segismund a calming drug
    Wherein are mixed herbs of especial virtue,
    Tyrannous in their overpowering strength,
    Which seize and steal and alienate man's gift
    Of reasoning, thus making a live corpse
    Of him. His violence evaporated
    With all his faculties and senses too.
    There is no need to prove it's possible   10
    Because experience teaches us that medicine
    Is full of natural secrets, that there is no
    Animal, plant, or stone that has not got
    Appointed properties. If human malice
    Explores a thousand poisons which deal death,
    Who then can doubt, that being so, that other
    Poisons, less violent, cause only sleep?
    But (leaving that doubt aside, as proven false
    By every evidence) hear then the sequel:
    I went down into Segismund's close prison   20
    Bearing the drink wherein, with opium,
    Henbane and poppies had been mixed. With him
    I talked a little while of the humanities,
    In which dumb Nature has instructed him,
    The mountains and the heavens and the stars,
    In whose divine academies he learned
    Rhetoric from the birds and the wild creatures.
    To lift his spirit to the enterprise
    Which you require of him, I chose for subject
    The swiftness of a stalwart eagle, who,   30
    Deriding the base region of the wind,
    Rises into the sphere reserved for fire,
    A feathered lightning, an untethered comet.
    Then I extolled such lofty flight and said:
    "After all, he's the king of birds, and so
    Takes precedence, by right, over the rest."
    No more was needful for, in taking up
    Majesty for his subject, he discoursed

With pride and high ambition, as his blood
Naturally moves, incites, and spurs him on   40
To grand and lofty things, and so he said
That in the restless kingdom of the birds
There should be those who swear obedience, too!
"In this, my miseries console me greatly,
Because if I'm a vassal here, it's only
By force, and not by choice. Of my own will
I would not yield in rank to any man."
Seeing that he grew furious—since this touched
The theme of his own griefs—I gave the potion
And scarcely had it passed from cup to breast   50
Before he yielded all his strength to slumber.
A chill sweat ran through all his limbs and veins.
Had I not known that this was mere feigned death
I would have thought him dead. Then came the men
To whom you've trusted this experiment,
Who placed him in a coach and brought him here
To your own rooms, where all things were prepared
In royalty and grandeur as befitting
His person. In your own bed they have laid him
Where, when the torpor wanes, they'll do him service   60
As if he were Your Majesty himself.
All has been done as you have ordered it,
And if I have obeyed you well, my lord,
I'd beg a favour (pardon me this freedom)—
To know what your intention is in thus
Transporting Segismund here to the palace.

BASIL. Your curiosity is just, Clotaldo,
And yours alone I'll satisfy. The star
Which governs Segismund, my son, in life,
Threatens a thousand tragedies and woes.   70
And now I wish to see whether the stars
(Which never lie—and having shown to us
So many cruel signs seem yet more certain)
May yet be brought to moderate their sentence,
Whether by prudence charmed or valour won,
For man does have the power to rule his stars.
I would examine this, bringing him here
Where he may know he is my son, and make
Trial of his talent. If magnanimously
He conquers and controls himself, he'll reign,   80
But if he proves a tyrant and is cruel,
Back to his chains he'll go. Now, you will ask,
Why did we bring him sleeping in this manner
For the experiment? I'll satisfy you,
Down to the smallest detail, with my answer.
If he knows that he is my son today,
And if tomorrow he should find himself

Once more reduced to prison, to misery,
He would despair entirely, knowing truly
Who, and whose son, he is. What consolation   90
Could he derive, then, from his lot? So I
Contrive to leave an exit for such grief,
By making him believe it was a dream.
By these means we may learn two things at once:
First, his character—for he will really be
Awake in all he thinks and all his actions;
Second, his consolation—which would be
(If he should wake in prison on the morrow,
Although he saw himself obeyed today)
That he might understand he had been dreaming,   100
And he will not be wrong, for in this world,
Clotaldo, all who live are only dreaming.

CLOTALDO. I've proofs enough to doubt of your success,
   But now it is too late to remedy it.
   From what I can make out, I think he's wakened
   And that he's coming this way, by the sound.

BASIL. I shall withdraw. You, as his tutor, go
   And guide him through his new bewilderments
   By answering his queries with the truth.

CLOTALDO. You give me leave to tell the truth of it?   110

BASIL. Yes, because knowing all things, he may find
   Known perils are the easiest to conquer.
                                               [*Exit* BASIL.]
                                               [*Enter* CLARION.]

CLARION. It cost me four whacks to get here so quickly.
   I caught them from a red-haired halberdier
   Sprouting a ginger beard over his livery,
   And I've come to see what's going on.
   No windows give a better view than those
   A man brings with him in his head, not asking
   For tickets of admission or paid seats,
   Since at all functions, festivals, or feasts   120
   He looks out with the same nice self-composure.

CLOTALDO. [*Aside.*] Here's Clarion who's the servant of that person—
   That trader in woes, importer from Poland
   Of my disgrace.
                            [*Aloud.*]
                  Come, Clarion, what news?

CLARION. Item the first: encouraged by the fact
   Your clemency's disposed to venge her insult,
   Rosaura has resumed her proper clothing.

CLOTALDO. That's right: it's less indecorous and bold.

CLARION. Item: she's changed her name, and given out
   That she's your niece. And now they've made so much   130
   Of her that she's been raised to maid of honour
   To the unique and only princess, Stella.

CLOTALDO. That's right: her honour stands to my account.

CLARION. Indeed she merely bides the time till you
    Will settle all accounts about her honour.
CLOTALDO. Biding the time is wise, for in the end
    It's Time that's going to settle all accounts!
CLARION. Item: that she's attended like a queen,
    Because they take her for your niece. Item:
    That I, who trudged along with her, am dying   140
    Of hunger. Nobody remembers me,
    Nor yet remembers that I'm like my name
    And (should I sound my Clarion) could tell
    All to the king and Stella and Astolfo.
    For I am both a Clarion and a servant—
    Two things which ill-accord with secrecy.
    If silence should, by chance, let slip my hand,
    Then there's a chorus which would fit me well:
    "Dawn-breaking Clarion plays no better tune!"
CLOTALDO. You've reason for complaint. I'll satisfy it   150
    If you'll but serve me . . .
CLARION.   Hush, here's Segismund!
                      [Enter musicians, singing, and ser-
                      vants arraying SEGISMUND, *who*
                      seems amazed.]
SEGISMUND. Heavens above! What's this that I am seeing?
    I wonder at it all, with naught of fear!
    But with a mighty doubt, I disbelieve it!
    I?—in a sumptuous palace? I—encircled
    With rich brocades and silks? I—overwhelmed
    With servants in such brilliant liveries?
    I—to awake in such a gorgeous bed?
    I—in the middle of so many footmen
    Who clothe me in rich garments? I'm awake: 160
    It would be false to take this for a dream.
    Am I not Segismund? Heavens! disabuse me
    If I'm mistaken. Say, what could have happened
    In my imagination while I slept—
    That I should find myself in such a place?
    But why should I worry, whatever it was?
    I'll let myself be served and entertained—
    Befall what may.
FIRST SERVANT. *[Aside to* SECOND SERVANT *and* CLARION.] He's very
    melancholy!
SECOND SERVANT. Who would not be, considering all that's happened
    To him?
CLARION. I would not be!
SECOND SERVANT.   You, speak to him.   170
FIRST SERVANT. Shall they begin to sing again?
SEGISMUND.   Why, no,
    I would not have them sing.
SECOND SERVANT.   You're so distraught,
    I wish you entertained.

SEGISMUND.   My griefs are such
   That no mere voices can amuse me now—
   Only the martial music pleased my mind.
CLOTALDO. Your Highness, mighty prince, give me your hand
   To kiss. I'm glad to be the first to offer
   Obedience at your feet.
SEGISMUND. [*Aside.*] This is Clotaldo.
   How is it he, that tyrannised my thralldom,
   Should now be treating me with such respect?   180
                    [*Aloud.*]
   Tell me what's happening all round me here.
CLOTALDO. With the perplexities of your new state,
   Your reason will encounter many doubts,
   But I shall try to free you from them all
   (If that may be) because you now must know
   You are hereditary Prince of Poland.
   If you have been withdrawn from public sight
   Under restraint, it was in strict obedience
   To Fate's inclemency, which will permit
   A thousand woes to fall upon this empire   190
   The moment that you wear the sovereign's crown.
   But trusting that you'll prudently defeat
   Your own malignant stars (since they can be
   Controlled by magnanimity) you've been
   Brought to this palace from the tower you knew
   Even while your soul was yielded up to sleep.
   My lord the king, your father, will be coming
   To see you, and from him you'll learn the rest.
SEGISMUND. Then, vile, infamous traitor, what have I
   To know more than this fact of who I am,   200
   To show my pride and power from this day onward?
   How have you played your country such a treason
   As to deny me, against law and right,
   The rank which is my own?
CLOTALDO.   Unhappy me!
SEGISMUND. You were a traitor to the law, a flattering liar
   To your own king, and cruel to myself.
   And so the king, the law, and I condemn you,
   After such fierce misfortunes as I've borne,
   To die here by my hands.
SECOND SERVANT.   My lord!
SEGISMUND.   Let none
   Get in the way. It is in vain. By God!   210
   If you intrude, I'll throw you through the window,
SECOND SERVANT. Clotaldo, fly!
CLOTALDO.   Alas, poor Segismund!
   That you should show such pride, all unaware
   That you are dreaming this.
                  [*Exit.*]
SECOND SERVANT.   Take care! Take care!

SEGISMUND. Get out!

SECOND SERVANT.   He was obeying the king's orders.

SEGISMUND. In an injustice, no one should obey
    The king, and I'm his prince.

SECOND SERVANT.   He had no right
    To look into the rights and wrongs of it.

SEGISMUND. You must be mad to answer back at me.

CLARION. The prince is right. It's you who're in the wrong!   220

SECOND SERVANT. Who gave you right to speak?

CLARION.   I simply took it.

SEGISMUND. And who are you?

CLARION.   I am the go-between,
    And in this art I think I am a master—
    Since I'm the greatest jackanapes alive.

SEGISMUND. [*To* CLARION.]
    In all this new world, you're the only one
    Of the whole crowd who pleases me.

CLARION.   Why, my lord,
    I am the best pleaser of Segismunds
    That ever was: ask anybody here!

                        [*Enter* ASTOLFO.]

ASTOLFO. Blessèd the day, a thousand times, my prince,
    On which you landed here on Polish soil   230
    To fill with so much splendour and delight
    Our wide horizons, like the break of day!
    For you arise as does the rising sun
    Out of the rugged mountains, far away.
    Shine forth then! And although so tardily
    You bind the glittering laurels on your brows,
    The longer may they last you still unwithered.

SEGISMUND. God save you.

ASTOLFO.   That you do not know me, sir,
    Is some excuse for greeting me without
    The honour due to me. I am Astolfo   240
    The Duke of Muscovy. You are my cousin.
    We are of equal rank.

SEGISMUND.   Then if I say,
    "God save you," do I not display good feeling?
    But since you take such note of who you are,
    The next time that I see you, I shall say
    "God save you *not*," if you would like that better.

SECOND SERVANT. [*To* ASTOLFO.]
    Your Highness, make allowance for his breeding
    Amongst the mountains. So he deals with all.

                    [*To* SEGISMUND.]
    Astolfo does take precedence, Your Highness—

SEGISMUND. I have no patience with the way he came   250
    To make his solemn speech, then put his hat on!

SECOND SERVANT. He's a grandee!

SEGISMUND.   I'm grander than grandees!

SECOND SERVANT. For all that, there should be respect between you,
    More than among the rest.
SEGISMUND.   And who told you
    To mix in my affairs?

                          [Enter STELLA.]

STELLA. Many times welcome to Your Royal Highness,
    Now come to grace the dais that receives him
    With gratitude and love. Long may you live
    August and eminent, despite all snares,
    And count your life by centuries, not years!   260
SEGISMUND. *[Aside to CLARION.]*
    Now tell me, who's this sovereign deity
    At whose divinest feet Heaven lays down
    The fleece of its aurora in the east?
CLARION. Sir, it's your cousin Stella.
SEGISMUND.   She were better
    Named "sun" than "star"!

                    [To STELLA.]
              Though your speech was fair,
    Just to have seen you and been conquered by you
    Suffices for a welcome in itself.
    To find myself so blessed beyond my merit
    What can I do but thank you, lovely Stella,
    For you could add more brilliance and delight   270
    To the most blazing star? When you get up
    What work is left the sun to do? O give me
    Your hand to kiss, from out whose cup of snow
    The solar horses drink the fires of day!
STELLA. Be a more gentle courtier.
ASTOLFO.   I am lost.
SECOND SERVANT. I know Astolfo's hurt. I must divert him.

                    [To SEGISMUND.]
    Sir, you should know that thus to woo so boldly
    Is most improper. And, besides, Astolfo . . .
SEGISMUND. Did I not tell you not to meddle with me?
SECOND SERVANT. I only say what's just.
SEGISMUND.   All this annoys me.   280
    Nothing seems just to me but what I want.
SECOND SERVANT. Why, sir, I heard you say that no obedience
    Or service should be lent to what's unjust.
SEGISMUND. You also heard me say that I would throw
    Anyone who annoys me from that balcony.
SECOND SERVANT. With men like me you cannot do such things.
SEGISMUND. No? Well, by God, I'll have to prove it then!

                  [He takes him in his arms and
                  rushes out, followed by many, to re-
                  turn soon after.]

ASTOLFO. What on earth have I seen? Can it be true?
STELLA. Go, all, and stop him!

SEGISMUND. [*Returning.*]　　　　　From the balcony
　　He's fallen in the sea. How strange it seems!　　　　　　　290
ASTOLFO. Measure your acts of violence, my lord:
　　From crags to palaces, the distance is
　　As great as that between man and the beasts.
SEGISMUND. Well, since you are for speaking out so boldly,
　　Perhaps one day you'll find that on your shoulders
　　You have no head to place your hat upon.
　　　　　　　　　　　　　[*Exit* ASTOLFO.]
　　　　　　　　　　　　　[*Enter* BASIL.]
BASIL. What's happened here?
SEGISMUND.　　　　　　　　　Nothing at all. A man
　　Wearied me, so I threw him in the sea.
CLARION. [*To* SEGISMUND.] Be warned. That is the king.
BASIL.　　　　　　　　　　　　　On the first day,
　　So soon, your coming here has cost a life?　　　　　　　300
SEGISMUND. He said I couldn't: so I won the bet.
BASIL. It grieves me, Prince, that, when I hoped to see you
　　Forewarned, and overriding Fate, in triumph
　　Over your stars, the first thing I should see
　　Should be such rigour—that your first deed here
　　Should be a grievous homicide. Alas!
　　With what love, now, can I offer my arms,
　　Knowing your own have learned to kill already?
　　Who sees a dirk, red from a mortal wound,
　　But does not fear it? Who can see the place　　　　　　310
　　Soaking in blood, where late a man was murdered,
　　But even the strongest must respond to nature?
　　So in your arms seeing the instrument
　　Of death, and looking on a blood-soaked place,
　　I must withdraw myself from your embrace,
　　And though I thought in loving bonds to bind
　　Your neck, yet fear withholds me from your arms.
SEGISMUND. Without your loving arms I can sustain
　　Myself as usual. That such a loving father
　　Could treat me with such cruelty, could thrust me　　　320
　　From his side ungratefully, could rear me
　　As a wild beast, could hold me for a monster,
　　And pray that I were dead, that such a father
　　Withholds his arms from winding round my neck,
　　Seems unimportant, seeing that he deprives
　　Me of my very being as a man.
BASIL. Would to heaven I had never granted it,
　　For then I never would have heard your voice,
　　Nor seen your outrages.
SEGISMUND.　　　　　　　Had you denied
　　Me being, then I would not have complained,　　　　　330
　　But that you took it from me when you gave it—
　　That is my quarrel with you. Though to give

Is the most singular and noble action,
It is the basest action if one gives
Only to take away.
BASIL.   How well you thank me
    For being raised from pauper to a prince!
SEGISMUND. In this what is there I should thank you for?
    You tyrant of my will! If you are old
    And feeble, and you die, what can you give me
    More than what is my own by right of birth?   340
    You are my father and my king, therefore
    This grandeur comes to me by natural law.
    Therefore, despite my present state, I'm not
    Indebted to you, rather can I claim
    Account of all those years in which you robbed me
    Of life and being, liberty, and honour.
    You ought to thank me that I press no claim
    Since you're my debtor, even to bankruptcy.
BASIL. Barbarous and outrageous brute! The heavens
    Have now fulfilled their prophecy: I call   350
    Them to bear witness to your pride. Although
    You know now, disillusioned, who you are,
    And see yourself where you take precedence,
    Take heed of this I say: be kind and humble
    Since it may be that you are only dreaming,
    Although it seems to you you're wide-awake.
                            [*Exit* BASIL.]
SEGISMUND. Can I perhaps be dreaming, though I seem
    So wide-awake? No: I am not asleep,
    Since I can touch, and realise what I
    Have been before, and what I am today.   360
    And if you even now relented, Father,
    There'd be no cure since I know who I am
    And you cannot, for all your sighs and groans,
    Cheat me of my hereditary crown.
    And if I was submissive in my chains
    Before, then I was ignorant of what I am,
    Which I now know (and likewise know that I
    Am partly man but partly beast as well).
                      [*Enter* ROSAURA *in woman's*
                                clothing.]
ROSAURA. [*Aside.*] I came in Stella's train. I am afraid
    Of meeting with Astolfo, since Clotaldo   370
    Says he must not know who I am, not see me,
    Because (he says) it touches on my honour.
    And well I trust Clotaldo since I owe him
    The safety of my life and honour both.
CLARION. What pleases you, and what do you admire
    Most, of the things you've seen here in the world?
SEGISMUND. Why, nothing that I could not have foreseen—
    Except the loveliness of women! Once,

I read among the books I had out there
That who owes God most grateful contemplation   380
Is Man: who is himself a tiny world.
But I think who owes God more grateful study
Is Woman—since she is a tiny heaven,
Having as much more beauty than a man
As heaven than earth. And even more, I say,
If she's the one that I am looking at.

ROSAURA. [*Aside.*] That is the prince. I'll go.

SEGISMUND.   Stop! Woman! Wait!
Don't join the sunset with the breaking day
By fading out so fast. If east and west
Should clash like that, the day would surely suffer   390
A syncope.[10] But what is this I see?

ROSAURA. What I am looking at I doubt, and yet
Believe.

SEGISMUND. [*Aside.*] This beauty I have seen before.

ROSAURA. [*Aside.*] This pomp and grandeur I have seen before
Cooped in a narrow dungeon.

SEGISMUND. [*Aside.*]   I have found
My life at last.

                          [*Aloud.*]
             Woman (for that sole word
Outsoars all wooing flattery of speech
From one that is a man), woman, who are you?
If even long before I ever saw you
You owed me adoration as your prince,   400
How much the more should you be conquered by me
Now I recall I've seen you once before!
Who are you, beauteous woman?

ROSAURA. [*Aside.*]   I'll pretend.
                          [*Aloud.*]
In Stella's train, I am a luckless lady.

SEGISMUND. Say no such thing. You are the sun from which
The minor star that's Stella draws its life,
Since she receives the splendour of your rays.
I've seen how in the kingdom of sweet odours,
Commander of the squadrons of the flowers,
The rose's deity presides, and is   410
Their empress by divine right of her beauty.
Among the precious stones which can be listed
In the academy of mines, I've seen
The diamond much preferred above the rest,
And crowned their emperor, for shining brightest.
In the revolving empire of the stars
The morning star takes pride among the others.
In their perfected spheres, when the sun calls

---

[10] A suspension of life or activity.

The planets to his council, he presides
And is the very oracle of day.   420
Then if among stars, gems, planets, and flowers
The fairest are exalted, why do you
Wait on a lesser beauty than yourself
Who are, in greater excellence and beauty,
The sun, the morning star, the diamond, and the rose!

[Enter CLOTALDO, *who remains
by the stage-curtain.]*

CLOTALDO. [*Aside.*]
   I wish to curb him, since I brought him up.
   But, what is this?
ROSAURA.   I reverence your favour,
   And yet reply, rhetorical, with silence,
   For when one's mind is clumsy and untaught,
   He answers best who does not speak at all.   430
SEGISMUND. Stay! Do not go! How can you wish to go
   And leave me darkened by my doubts?
ROSAURA.   Your Highness,
   I beg your leave to go.
SEGISMUND.   To go so rudely
   Is not to beg my leave but just to take it.
ROSAURA. But if you will not grant it, I must take it.
SEGISMUND. That were to change my courtesy to rudeness.
   Resistance is like venom to my patience.
ROSAURA. But even if this deadly, raging venom
   Should overcome your patience, yet you dare not
   And could not treat me with dishonour, sir.   440
SEGISMUND. Why, just to see then if I can, and dare to—
   You'll make me lose the fear I bear your beauty,
   Since the impossible is always tempting
   To me. Why, only now I threw a man
   Over this balcony who said I couldn't:
   And so to find out if I can or not
   I'll throw your honour through the window too.
CLOTALDO. [*Aside.*]
   He seems determined in this course. Oh, heavens!
   What's to be done that for a second time
   My honour's threatened by a mad desire?   450
ROSAURA. Then with good reason it was prophesied
   Your tyranny would wreak this kingdom
   Outrageous scandals, treasons, crimes, and deaths.
   But what can such a creature do as you
   Who are not even a man, save in the name—
   Inhuman, barbarous, cruel, and unbending
   As the wild beasts amongst whom you were nursed?
SEGISMUND. That you should not insult me in this way
   I spoke to you most courteously, and thought
   I'd thereby get my way; but if you curse me thus   460
   Even when I am speaking gently, why,

By the living God, I'll really give you cause.
Ho there! Clear out, the lot of you, at once!
Leave her to me! Close all the doors upon us.
Let no one enter!

> [*Exeunt* CLARION *and other attend-
> ants.*]

ROSAURA.   I am lost . . . I warn you . . .
SEGISMUND. I am a tyrant and you plead in vain.
CLOTALDO. [*Aside.*]
  Oh, what a monstrous thing! I must restrain him
  Even if I die for it.

> [*Aloud.*]

            Sir! Wait! Look here!
SEGISMUND. A second time you have provoked my anger,
  You feeble, mad old man! Do you prize lightly   470
  My wrath and rigour that you've gone so far?
CLOTALDO. Brought by the accents of her voice, I came
  To tell you you must be more peaceful
  If still you hope to reign, and warn you that
  You should not be so cruel, though you rule—
  Since this, perhaps, is nothing but a dream.
SEGISMUND. When you refer to disillusionment
  You rouse me near to madness. Now you'll see,
  Here as I kill you, if it's truth or dreaming!

> [*As he tries to pull out his dagger,*
> CLOTALDO *restrains him and
> throws himself on his knees before
> him.*]

CLOTALDO. It's thus I'd save my life: and hope to do so—   480
SEGISMUND. Take your presumptuous hand from off this steel.
CLOTALDO. Till people come to hold your rage and fury
  I shall not let you go.
ROSAURA.   O heavens!
SEGISMUND.   Loose it,

> [*They struggle.*]

  I say, or else—you interfering fool—
  I'll crush you to your death in my strong arms!
ROSAURA. Come quickly! Here's Clotaldo being killed!

> [*Exit.*]

> [ASTOLFO *appears as* CLOTALDO
> *falls on the floor, and the former
> stands between* SEGISMUND *and*
> CLOTALDO.]

ASTOLFO. Why, what is this, most valiant prince? What? Staining
  Your doughty steel in such old, frozen blood?
  For shame! For shame! Sheathe your illustrious weapon!
SEGISMUND. When it is stained in his infamous blood!   490
ASTOLFO. At my feet here he has found sanctuary
  And there he's safe, for it will serve him well.
SEGISMUND. Then serve me well by dying, for like this

I will avenge myself for your behaviour
In trying to annoy me first of all.
ASTOLFO. To draw in self-defence offends no king,
Though in his palace.

> [ASTOLFO *draws his sword and they*
> *fight.*]

CLOTALDO. [*To* ASTOLFO.] Do not anger him!

> [*Enter* BASIL, STELLA, *and attend-*
> *ants.*]

BASIL. Hold! Hold! What's this? Fighting with naked swords?
STELLA. [*Aside.*] It is Astolfo! How my heart misgives me!
BASIL. Why, what has happened here?
ASTOLFO.   Nothing, my Lord,   500
Since you've arrived.

> [*Both sheathe their swords.*]

SEGISMUND.   Much, though you *have* arrived.
I tried to kill the old man.
BASIL.   Had you no
Respect for those white hairs?
CLOTALDO.   Sire, since they're only
Mine, as you well can see, it does not matter!
SEGISMUND. It is in vain you'd have me hold white hairs
In such respect, since one day you may find
Your own white locks prostrated at my feet
For still I have not taken vengeance on you
For the foul way in which you had me reared.

> [*Exit.*]

BASIL. Before that happens you will sleep once more   510
Where you were reared, and where what's happened may
Seem just a dream (being mere earthly glory).

> [*All save* ASTOLFO *and* STELLA
> *leave.*]

ASTOLFO. How seldom does prediction fail, when evil!
How oft, foretelling good! Exact in harm,
Doubtful in benefit! Oh, what a great
Astrologer would be one who foretold
Nothing but harms, since there's no doubt at all
That they are always due! In Segismund
And me the case is illustrated clearly.
In him, crimes, cruelties, deaths, and disasters   520
Were well predicted, since they all came true.
But in my own case, to predict for me
(As I foresaw beholding rays which cast
The sun into the shade and outface heaven)
Triumphs and trophies, happiness and praise,
Was false—and yet was true: it's only just
That when predictions start with promised favours
They should end in disdain.
STELLA.   I do not doubt

Your protestations are most heartfelt; only
They're not for me, but for another lady   530
Whose portrait you were wearing round your neck
Slung in a locket when you first arrived.
Since it is so, she only can deserve
These wooing flatteries. Let her repay you
For in affairs of love, flatteries and vows
Made for another are mere forged credentials.

> [ROSAURA *enters but waits by the curtain.*]

ROSAURA. [*Aside.*] Thanks be to God, my troubles are near ended!
    To judge from what I see, I've naught to fear.
ASTOLFO. I will expel that portrait from my breast
    To make room for the image of your beauty   540
    And keep it there. For there where Stella is
    Can be no room for shade, and where the sun is
    No place for any star. I'll fetch the portrait.

> [*Aside.*]

Forgive me, beautiful Rosaura, that,
When absent, men and women seldom keep
More faith than this.

> [*Exit.*]
> [ROSAURA *comes forward.*]

ROSAURA. [*Aside.*] I could not hear a word, I was afraid
    That they would see me.
STELLA.   Oh, Astrea!
ROSAURA.   My lady!
STELLA. I am delighted that you came. Because
    To you alone would I confide a secret.   550
ROSAURA. Thereby you greatly honour me, your servant.
STELLA. Astrea, in the brief time I have known you
    I've given you the latchkey of my will.
    For that, and being who you are, I'll tell you
    A secret which I've very often hidden
    Even from myself.
ROSAURA.   I am your slave.
STELLA.   Then, briefly:
    Astolfo, who's my cousin (the word cousin
    Suffices, since some things are plainly said
    Even by thinking them), is to wed me
    If Fortune thus can wipe so many cares   560
    Away with one great joy. But I am troubled
    In that, the day he first came here, he carried
    A portrait of a lady round his neck.
    I spoke to him about it courteously.
    He was most amiable, he loves me well,
    And now he's gone for it. I am embarrassed
    That he should give it me himself. Wait here,
    And tell him to deliver it to you.

Do not say more. Since you're discreet and fair:
You'll surely know just what love is.

[Exit.]

ROSAURA.   Great heavens!   570
How I wish that I did not! For who could be
So prudent or so skilful as would know
What to advise herself in such a case?
Lives there a person on this earth today
Who's more beset by the inclement stars,
Who has more cares besieging him, or fights
So many dire calamities at once?
What can I do in such bewilderment
Wherein it seems impossible to find
Relief or comfort? Since my first misfortune   580
No other thing has chanced or happened to me
But was a new misfortune. In succession
Inheritors and heirs of their own selves
(Just like the Phoenix, his own son and father[11])
Misfortunes reproduce themselves, are born,
And live by dying. In their sepulchre
The ashes they consume are hot forever.
A sage once said misfortunes must be cowards
Because they never dare to walk alone
But come in crowds. I say they are most valiant   590
Because they always charge so bravely on
And never turn their backs. Who charges with them
May dare all things because there is no fear
That they'll ever desert him; and I say it
Because in all my life I never once
Knew them to leave me, nor will they grow tired
Of me till, wounded and shot through and through
By Fate, I fall into the arms of death.
Alas, what can I do in this dilemma?
If I reveal myself, then old Clotaldo,   600
To whom I owe my life, may take offence,
Because he told me to await the cure
And mending of my honour in concealment.
If I don't tell Astolfo who I am
And he detects me, how can I dissimulate?
Since even if I say I am not I,
The voice, the language, and the eyes will falter,
Because the soul will tell them that they lie.
What shall I do? It is in vain to study
What I should do, when I know very well   610
That, whatsoever way I choose to act,
When the time comes I'll do as sorrow bids,
For no one has control over his sorrows.

---

[11] In Egyptian legend, the Phoenix was a bird that lived for five or six centuries and then consumed itself in fire and rose from its own ashes, thus becoming its own son and father.

Then since my soul dares not decide its actions
Let sorrow fill my cup and let my grief
Reach its extremity and, out of doubts
And vain appearances, once and for all
Come out into the light—and Heaven shield me!

[Enter ASTOLFO.]

ASTOLFO. Here, lady, is the portrait . . . but . . . great God!
ROSAURA. Why does Your Highness halt, and stare astonished?   620
ASTOLFO. Rosaura! Why, to see you here!
ROSAURA.   Rosaura?
    Sir, you mistake me for some other lady.
    I am Astrea, and my humble station
    Deserves no perturbation such as yours.
ASTOLFO. Enough of this pretence, Rosaura, since
    The soul can never lie. Though as Astrea
    I see you now, I love you as Rosaura.
ROSAURA. Not having understood Your Highness' meaning
    I can make no reply except to say
    That Stella (who might be the star of Venus)   630
    Told me to wait here and to tell you from her
    To give to me the portrait you were fetching
    (Which seems a very logical request)
    And I myself will take it to my lady.
    Thus Stella bids: even the slightest things
    Which do me harm are governed by some star.
ASTOLFO. Even if you could make a greater effort
    How poorly you dissimulate, Rosaura!
    Tell your poor eyes they do not harmonise
    With your own voice, because they needs must jangle   640
    When the whole instrument is out of time.
    You cannot match the falsehood of your words
    With the sincerity of what you're feeling.
ROSAURA. All I can say is—that I want the portrait.
ASTOLFO. As you require a fiction, with a fiction
    I shall reply. Go and tell Stella this:
    That I esteem her so, it seems unworthy
    Only to send the counterfeit to her
    And that I'm sending her the original.
    And you, take the original along with you,   650
    Taking yourself to her.
ROSAURA.   When a man starts
    Forth on a definite task, resolved and valiant,
    Though he be offered a far greater prize
    Than what he seeks, yet he returns with failure
    If he returns without his task performed.
    I came to get that portrait. Though I bear
    The original with me, of greater value,
    I would return in failure and contempt
    Without the copy. Give it me, Your Highness,
    Since I cannot return without it.

ASTOLFO.   But
   If I don't give it you, how can you do so?
ROSAURA. Like this, ungrateful man! I'll take it from you.
                      [She tries to wrest it from him.]

ASTOLFO. It is in vain.
ROSAURA.   By God, it shall not come
   Into another woman's hands!
ASTOLFO.   You're terrifying!
ROSAURA. And you're perfidious!
ASTOLFO.   Enough, my dear
   Rosaura!
ROSAURA. I, your dear? You lie, you villain!
                [They are both clutching the portrait.]
                [Enter STELLA.]
STELLA. Astrea and Astolfo, what does this mean?
ASTOLFO. *[Aside.]* Here's Stella.
ROSAURA. *[Aside.]*   Love, grant me the strength to win
   My portrait.
             [To STELLA.]
     If you want to know, my lady,
   What this is all about, I will explain.   670
ASTOLFO. *[To ROSAURA, aside.]* What do you mean?
ROSAURA.   You told me to await
   Astolfo here and ask him for a portrait
   On your behalf. I waited here alone
   And as one thought suggests another thought,
   Thinking of portraits, I recalled my own
   Was here inside my sleeve. When one's alone,
   One is diverted by a foolish trifle
   And so I took it out to look at it.
   It slipped and fell, just as Astolfo here,
   Bringing the portrait of the other lady,   680
   Came to deliver it to you as promised.
   He picked my portrait up, and so unwilling
   Is he to give away the one you asked for,
   Instead of doing so, he seized upon
   The other portrait which is mine alone
   And will not give it back though I entreated
   And begged him to return it. I was angry
   And tried to snatch it back. That's it he's holding,
   And you can see yourself if it's not mine.
STELLA. Let go the portrait.
               [She snatches it from him.]
ASTOLFO.   Madam!
STELLA.   The draughtsman   690
   Was not unkind to truth.
ROSAURA.   Is it not mine?
STELLA. Why, who could doubt it?
ROSAURA.   Ask him for the other.

STELLA. Here, take your own, Astrea. You may leave us.
ROSAURA. [*Aside.*] Now I have got my portrait, come what will.
                              [*Exit.*]
STELLA. Now give me up the portrait that I asked for
  Although I'll see and speak to you no more.
  I do not wish to leave it in your power
  Having been once so foolish as to beg it.
ASTOLFO. [*Aside.*] Now how can I get out of this foul trap?
                              [*To* STELLA.]
  Beautiful Stella, though I would obey you,   700
  And serve you in all ways, I cannot give you
  The portrait, since. . .
STELLA.   You are a crude, coarse villain
  And ruffian of a wooer. For the portrait—
  I do not want it now, since, if I had it,
  It would remind me I had asked you for it.
                              [*Exit.*]
ASTOLFO. Listen! Look! Wait! Let me explain!
                              [*Aside.*]
                                        Oh, damn
  Rosaura! How the devil did she get
  To Poland for my ruin and her own?

The prison of SEGISMUND *in the tower*

[SEGISMUND *lying on the ground loaded with fetters and clothed in skins as
before.* CLOTALDO, *two attendants, and* CLARION.]
CLOTALDO. Here you must leave him—since his reckless pride
  Ends here today where it began.
ATTENDANT.   His chain   710
  I'll rivet as it used to be before.
CLARION. O Prince, you'd better not awake too soon
  To find how lost you are, how changed your fate,
  And that your fancied glory of an hour
  Was but a shade of life, a flame of death!
CLOTALDO. For one who knows so well to wield his tongue
  It's fit a worthy place should be provided
  With lots of room and lots of time to argue.
  This is the fellow that you have to seize
                              [*To the attendants.*]
  And that's the room in which you are to lock him.   720
                              [*Points to the nearest cell.*]
CLARION. Why me?
CLOTALDO.   Because a Clarion who knows
  Too many secrets must be kept in gaol—
  A place where even clarions are silent.
CLARION. Have I, by chance, wanted to kill my father

Or thrown an Icarus[12] from a balcony?
Am I asleep or dreaming? To what end
Do you imprison me?
CLOTALDO.   You're Clarion.
CLARION. Well, say I swear to be a cornet now,
    A silent one, a wretched instrument. . . ?

> [*They hustle him off.* CLOTALDO
> *remains.*]
> [*Enter* BASIL, *wearing a mask.*]

BASIL. Clotaldo.
CLOTALDO.   Sire . . . and is it thus alone   730
    Your Majesty has come?
BASIL.   Vain curiosity
    To see what happens here to Segismund.
CLOTALDO. See where he lies, reduced to misery!
BASIL. Unhappy prince! Born at a fatal moment!
    Come waken him, now he has lost his strength
    With all the opium he's drunk.
CLOTALDO.   He's stirring
    And talking to himself.
BASIL.   What is he dreaming?
    Let's listen now.
SEGISMUND.   He who chastises tyrants
    Is a most pious prince . . . Now let Clotaldo
    Die by my hand . . . my father kiss my feet. . .   740
CLOTALDO. He threatens me with death!
BASIL.   And me with insult
    And cruelty.
CLOTALDO.   He'd take my life away.
BASIL. And he'd humiliate me at his feet.
SEGISMUND. [*Still in a dream.*]
    Throughout the expanse of this world's theatre
    I'll show my peerless valour, let my vengeance
    Be wreaked, and the Prince Segismund be seen
    To triumph—over his father . . . but, alas!
                                    [*Awakening.*]
    Where am I?
BASIL. [*To* CLOTALDO.] Since he must not see me here,
    I'll listen further off. You know your cue.
                                    [*Retires to one side.*]
SEGISMUND. Can this be I? Am I the same who, chained   750
    And long imprisoned, rose to such a state?
    Are you not still my sepulchre and grave,
    You dismal tower? God! What things I have dreamed!
CLOTALDO. [*Aside.*] Now I must go to him to disenchant him.
                                    [*Aloud.*]
    Awake already?

---

[12] In Greek mythology, Icarus was the son of Daedalus. In escaping from imprisonment on wings made of wax, he flew too near the sun, melted the wax, and perished in the sea.

SEGISMUND.   Yes: it was high time.
CLOTALDO. What? Do you have to spend all day asleep?
    Since I was following the eagle's flight
    With tardy discourse, have you still lain here
    Without awaking?
SEGISMUND.   No. Nor even now
    Am I awake. It seems I've always slept,   760
    Since, if I've dreamed what I've just seen and heard
    Palpably and for certain, then I am dreaming
    What I see now—nor is it strange I'm tired,
    Since what I, sleeping, see, tells me that I
    Was dreaming when I thought I was awake.
CLOTALDO. Tell me your dream.
SEGISMUND.   That's if it *was* a dream!
    No, I'll not tell you what I dreamed; but what
    I lived and saw, Clotaldo, I *will* tell you.
    I woke up in a bed that might have been
    The cradle of the flowers, woven by Spring.   770
    A thousand nobles, bowing, called me Prince,
    Attiring me in jewels, pomp, and splendour.
    My equanimity you turned to rapture
    Telling me that I was the Prince of Poland.
CLOTALDO. I must have got a fine reward!
SEGISMUND.   Not so:
    For as a traitor, twice, with rage and fury,
    I tried to kill you.
CLOTALDO.   Such cruelty to me?
SEGISMUND. I was the lord of all, on all I took revenge,
    Except I loved one woman . . . I believe
    That *that* was true, though all the rest has faded.   780
                      [*Exit* BASIL.]
CLOTALDO. [*Aside.*] I see the king was moved, to hear him speak.
                        [*Aloud.*]
    Talking of eagles made you dream of empires,
    But even in your dreams it's good to honour
    Those who have cared for you and brought you up.
    For Segismund, even in dreams, I warn you
    Nothing is lost by trying to do good.
                        [*Exit.*]
SEGISMUND. That's true, and therefore let us subjugate
    The bestial side, this fury and ambition,
    Against the time when we may dream once more,
    As certainly we shall, for this strange world   790
    Is such that but to live here is to dream.
    And now experience shows me that each man
    Dreams what he is until he is awakened.
    The king dreams he's a king and in this fiction
    Lives, rules, administers with royal pomp.
    Yet all the borrowed praises that he earns
    Are written in the wind, and he is changed

(How sad a fate!) by death to dust and ashes.
What man is there alive who'd seek to reign
Since he must wake into the dream that's death.   800
The rich man dreams his wealth which is his care
And woe. The poor man dreams his sufferings.
He dreams who thrives and prospers in this life.
He dreams who toils and strives. He dreams who injures,
Offends, and insults. So that in this world
Everyone dreams the thing he is, though no one
Can understand it. I dream I am here,
Chained in these fetters. Yet I dreamed just now
I was in a more flattering, lofty station.
What is this life? A frenzy, an illusion,   810
A shadow, a delirium, a fiction.
The greatest good's but little, and this life
Is but a dream, and dreams are only dreams.

ACT III

The tower

[*Enter* CLARION.]

CLARION. I'm held in an enchanted tower, because
    Of all I know. What would they do to me
    For all I don't know, since—for all I know—
    They're killing me by starving me to death.
    O that a man so hungry as myself
    Should live to die of hunger while alive!
    I am so sorry for myself that others
    May well say "I can well believe it," since
    This silence ill accords with my name "Clarion,"
    And I just can't shut up. My fellows here?   10
    Spiders and rats—fine feathered songsters those!
    My head's still ringing with a dream of fifes
    And trumpets and a lot of noisy humbug
    And long processions as of penitents
    With crosses, winding up and down, while some
    Faint at the sight of blood besmirching others.
    But now to tell the truth, I am in prison.
    For knowing secrets, I am kept shut in,
    Strictly observed as if I were a Sunday,
    And feeling sadder than a Tuesday, where   20
    I neither eat nor drink. They say a secret
    Is sacred and should be as strictly kept
    As any saint's day on the calendar.
    Saint Secret's Day for me's a working day
    Because I'm never idle then. The penance
    I suffer here is merited, I say:
    Because being a lackey, I was silent,

Which, in a servant, is a sacrilege.

[*A noise of drums and trumpets.*]

FIRST SOLDIER. [*Within.*]
 Here is the tower in which he is imprisoned.
 Smash in the door and enter, everybody!   30
CLARION. Great God! They've come to seek me. That is certain
 Because they say I'm here. What can they want?

[*Enter several soldiers.*]

FIRST SOLDIER. Go in.
SECOND SOLDIER. He's here!
CLARION.   No, he's not here!
ALL THE SOLDIERS.   Our lord!
CLARION. What, are they drunk?
FIRST SOLDIER.   You are our rightful prince.
 We do not want and never shall allow
 A stranger to supplant our trueborn prince.
 Give us your feet to kiss!
ALL THE SOLDIERS.   Long live the prince!
CLARION. Bless me, if it's not real! In this strange kingdom
 It seems the custom, everyday, to take
 Some fellow and to make him prince and then   40
 Shut him back in this tower. That *must* be it!
 So I must play my role.
ALL THE SOLDIERS.   Give us your feet.
CLARION. I can't. They're necessary. After all
 What sort of use would be a footless prince?
SECOND SOLDIER. All of us told your father, as one man,
 We want no prince of Muscovy but you!
CLARION. You weren't respectful to my father? Shame!
FIRST SOLDIER. It was our loyalty that made us tell him.
CLARION. If it was loyalty, you have my pardon.
SECOND SOLDIER. Restore your empire. Long live Segismund! 50
CLARION. [*Aside.*] That is the name they seem to give to all
 These counterfeited princes.

[*Enter* SEGISMUND.]

SEGISMUND.   Who called Segismund?
CLARION. [*Aside.*] I seem to be a hollow sort of prince.
FIRST SOLDIER. Which of you's Segismund?
SEGISMUND.   I am.
SECOND SOLDIER. [*To* CLARION.]   Then, why,
 Rash fool, did you impersonate the prince
 Segismund?
CLARION. What? I, Segismund? Yourselves
 Be-Segismunded me without request.
 All yours was both the rashness and the folly.
FIRST SOLDIER. Prince Segismund, whom we acclaim our lord,
 Your father, great King Basil, in his fear   60
 That heaven would fulfil a prophecy
 That one day he would kneel before your feet
 Wishes now to deprive you of the throne

And give it to the Duke of Muscovy.
For this he called a council, but the people
Discovered his design and knowing, now,
They have a native king, will have no stranger.
So scorning the fierce threats of destiny,
We've come to seek you in your very prison,
That aided by the arms of the whole people,   70
We may restore you to the crown and sceptre,
Taking them from the tyrant's grasp. Come, then:
Assembling here, in this wide desert region,
Hosts of plebeians, bandits, and freebooters,
Acclaim you king. Your liberty awaits you!
Hark to its voice!

                                                    [Shouts within.]
                          Long life to Segismund!
SEGISMUND. Once more, you heavens will that I should dream
       Of grandeur, once again, 'twixt doubts and shades,
       Behold the majesty of pomp and power
       Vanish into the wind, once more you wish   80
       That I should taste the disillusion and
       The risk by which all human power is humbled,
       Of which all human power should live aware.
       It must not be. I'll not be once again
       Put through my paces by my fortune's stars.
       And since I know this life is all a dream,
       Depart, vain shades, who feign, to my dead senses,
       That you have voice and body, having neither!
       I want no more feigned majesty, fantastic
       Display, nor void illusions, that one gust   90
       Can scatter like the almond tree in flower,
       Whose rosy buds, without advice or warning,
       Dawn in the air too soon and then, as one,
       Are all extinguished, fade, and fall, and wither
       In the first gust of wind that comes along!
       I know you well. I know you well by now.
       I know that all that happens in yourselves
       Happens as in a sleeping man. For me
       There are no more delusions and deceptions
       Since I well know this life is all a dream.   100
SECOND SOLDIER. If you think we are cheating, just sweep
       Your gaze along these towering peaks, and see
       The hosts that wait to welcome and obey you.
SEGISMUND. Already once before I've seen such crowds
       Distinctly, quite as vividly as these:
       And yet it was a dream.
SECOND SOLDIER.   No great event
       Can come without forerunners to announce it
       And this is the real meaning of your dream.
SEGISMUND. Yes, you say well. It was the fore-announcement
       And just in case it was correct, my soul,   110

(Since life's so short) let's dream the dream anew!
But it must be attentively aware
That we'll awake from pleasure in the end.
Forewarned of that, the shock's not so abrupt,
The disillusion's less. Evils anticipated
Lose half their sting. And armed with this precaution—
That power, even when we're sure of it, is borrowed
And must be given back to its true owner—
We can risk anything and dare the worst.
Subjects, I thank you for your loyalty.   120
In me you have a leader who will free you,
Bravely and skilfully, from foreign rule.
Sound now to arms, you'll soon behold my valour.
Against my father I must march and bring
Truth from the stars. Yes: he must kneel to me.

[Aside.]

But yet, since I may wake before he kneels,
Perhaps I'd better not proclaim what may not happen.
ALL. Long live Segismund!

[Enter CLOTALDO.]

CLOTALDO.   Gracious heavens! What is
This riot here?
SEGISMUND.   Clotaldo!
CLOTALDO.   Sir!

[Aside.]

He'll prove

His cruelty on me.
CLARION.   I bet he throws him   130
Over the mountain.
CLOTALDO.   At your royal feet
I kneel, knowing my penalty is death.
SEGISMUND. Rise, rise, my foster father, from the ground,
For you must be the compass and the guide
In which I trust. You brought me up, and I
Know what I owe your loyalty. Embrace me!
CLOTALDO. What's that you say?
SEGISMUND.   I know I'm in a dream,
But I would like to act well, since good actions,
Even in a dream, are not entirely lost.
CLOTALDO. Since doing good is now to be your glory,   140
You will not be offended that I too
Should do what's right. You march against your father!
I cannot give you help against my king.
Here at your feet, my lord, I plead for death.
SEGISMUND. [*Aloud.*] Villain!

[Aside.]

But let us suffer this annoyance.

Though my rage would slay him, yet he's loyal.
A man does not deserve to die for that.
How many angry passions does this leash

Restrain in me, this curb of knowing well
That I must wake and find myself alone!   150
SECOND SOLDIER. All this fine talk, Clotaldo, is a cruel
    Spurn of the public welfare. We are loyal
    Who wish our own prince to reign over us.
CLOTALDO. Such loyalty, after the king were dead,
    Would honour you. But while the king is living
    He is our absolute, unquestioned lord.
    There's no excuse for subjects who oppose
    His sovereignty in arms.
FIRST SOLDIER.   We'll soon see well
    Enough, Clotaldo, what this loyalty
    Is worth.
CLOTALDO. You would be better if you had some.   160
    It is the greatest prize.
SEGISMUND.   Peace, peace, I pray you.
CLOTALDO. My lord!
SEGISMUND.   Clotaldo, if your feelings
    Are truly thus, go you, and serve the king;
    That's prudence, loyalty, and common sense.
    But do not argue here with anyone
    Whether it's right or wrong, for every man
    Has his own honour.
CLOTALDO.   Humbly I take my leave.
                          [Exit.]
SEGISMUND. Now sound the drums and march in rank and order
    Straight to the palace.
ALL.   Long live Segismund!
SEGISMUND. Fortune, we go to reign! Do not awake me   170
    If I am dreaming! Do not let me fall
    Asleep if it is true! To act with virtue
    Is what matters, since if this proves true,
    That truth's sufficient reason in itself;
    If not, we win us friends against the time
    When we at last awake.

A room in the royal palace

[*Enter* BASIL *and* ASTOLFO.]
BASIL. Whose prudence can rein in a bolting horse?
    Who can restrain a river's pride, in spate?
    Whose valour can withstand a crag dislodged
    And hurtling downwards from a mountain peak?   180
    All these are easier by far than to hold back
    A crowd's proud fury, once it has been roused.
    It has two voices, both proclaiming war,
    And you can hear them echoing through the mountains,

Some shouting "Segismund," others "Astolfo."
The scene I set for swearing of allegiance
Lends but an added horror to this strife:
It has become the back cloth to a stage
Where Fortune plays out tragedies in blood.

ASTOLFO. My lord, forget the happiness and wealth   190
You promised me from your most blessèd hand.
If Poland, which I hope to rule, refuses
Obedience to my right, grudging me honour,
It is because I've got to earn it first.
Give me a horse, that I with angry pride
May match the thunder in my voice and ride
To strike, like lightning, terror far and wide.

                                    [*Exit* ASTOLFO.]

BASIL. No remedy for what's infallible!
What is foreseen is perilous indeed!
If something has to be, there's no way out;   200
In trying to evade it, you but court it.
This law is pitiless and horrible.
Thinking one can evade the risk, one meets it:
My own precautions have been my undoing,
And I myself have quite destroyed my kingdom.

                                    [*Enter* STELLA.]

STELLA. If you, my lord, in person do not try
To curb the vast commotion that has started
In all the streets between the rival factions,
' You'll see your kingdom, swamped in waves of crimson,
Swimming in its own blood, with nothing left   210
But havoc, dire calamity, and woe.
So frightful is the damage to your empire
That, seen, it strikes amazement; heard, despair.
The sun's obscured, the very winds are hindered.
Each stone is a memorial to the dead.
Each flower springs from a grave while every building
Appears a mausoleum, and each soldier
A premature and walking skeleton.

                                    [*Enter* CLOTALDO.]

CLOTALDO. Praise be to God, I reach your feet alive!
BASIL. Clotaldo! What's the news of Segismund?   220
CLOTALDO. The crowd, a headstrong monster blind with rage,
Entered his dungeon tower and set him free.
He, now exalted for the second time,
Conducts himself with valour, boasting how
He will bring down the truth out of the stars.
BASIL. Give me a horse, that I myself, in person,
May vanquish such a base, ungrateful son!
For I, in the defence of my own crown,
Shall do by steel what science failed to do.

                                    [*Exit.*]

STELLA. I'll be Bellona[13] to your Sun, and try　　　　　　　230
　　To write my name next yours in history.
　　I'll ride as though I flew on outstretched wings
　　That I may vie with Pallas.[14]

　　　　　　　　　　　　　　　　　[*Exit.*]
　　　　　　　　　　　　　　　[*Enter* ROSAURA, *holding back*
　　　　　　　　　　　　　　　CLOTALDO.]

ROSAURA. I know that all is war, Clotaldo, yet
　　Although your valour calls you to the front,
　　First hear me out. You know quite well that I
　　Arrived in Poland poor and miserable,
　　Where, shielded by your valour, I found mercy.
　　You told me to conceal myself, and stay
　　Here in the palace, hiding from Astolfo.　　　　　240
　　He saw me in the end, and so insulted
　　My honour that (although he saw me clearly)
　　He nightly speaks with Stella in the garden.
　　I have the key to it and I will show you
　　How you can enter there and end my cares.
　　Thus bold, resolved, and strong, you can recover
　　My honour, since you're ready to avenge me
　　By killing him.
CLOTALDO.　　　　It's true that I intended,
　　Since first I saw you (having heard your tale)
　　With my own life to rectify your wrongs.　　　　250
　　The first step that I took was bid you dress
　　According to your sex, for fear Astolfo
　　Might see you as you were, and deem you wanton.
　　I was devising how we could recover
　　Your honour (so much did it weigh on me)
　　Even though we had to kill him. (A wild plan—
　　Though since he's not my king, I would not flinch
　　From killing him.) But then, when suddenly
　　Segismund tried to kill me, it was he
　　Who saved my life with his surpassing valour.　　260
　　Consider: how can I requite Astolfo
　　With death for giving me my life so bravely,
　　And when my soul is full of gratitude?
　　So torn between the two of you I stand—
　　Rosaura, whose life I saved, and Astolfo,
　　Who saved my life. What's to be done? Which side
　　To take, and whom to help, I cannot judge.
　　What I owe you in that I gave you life
　　I owe to him in that he gave me life.
　　And so there is no course that I can take　　　　270
　　To satisfy my love. I am a person
　　Who has to act, yet suffer either way.
ROSAURA. I should not have to tell so brave a man

---

[13] Roman goddess of war.　　　[14] Athena, protector of wise warriors.

That if it is nobility to give,
It's baseness to receive. That being so
You owe no gratitude to him, admitting
That it was he who gave you life, and you
Who gave me life, since he forced you to take
A meaner role, and through me you assumed
A generous role. So you should side with me: 280
My cause is so far worthier than his own
As giving is than taking.

CLOTALDO.   Though nobility
Is with the giver, it is gratitude
That dwells with the receiver. As a giver
I have the name of being generous:
Then grant me that of being grateful too
And let me earn the title and be grateful,
As I am liberal, giving or receiving.

ROSAURA. You granted me my life, at the same time
Telling me it was worthless, since dishonoured,   290
And therefore was no life. Therefore from you
I have received no life at all. And since
You should be liberal first and grateful after
(Since so you said yourself) I now entreat you
Give me the life, the life you never gave me!
As giving magnifies the most, give first
And then be grateful after, if you will!

CLOTALDO. Won by your argument, I will be liberal.
Rosaura, I shall give you my estate
And you shall seek a convent, there to live.   300
This measure is a happy thought, for, see,
Fleeing a crime, you find a sanctuary.
For when the empire's threatened with disasters
And is divided thus, I, born a noble,
Am not the man who would augment its woes.
So with this remedy which I have chosen
I remain loyal to the kingdom, generous
To you, and also grateful to Astolfo.
And thus I choose the course that suits you best.
Were I your father, what could I do more?   310

ROSAURA. Were you my father, then I would accept
The insult. Since you are not, I refuse.

CLOTALDO. What do you hope to do then?

ROSAURA.   Kill the duke!

CLOTALDO. A girl who never even knew her father
Armed with such courage?

ROSAURA.   Yes.

CLOTALDO.   What spurs you on?

ROSAURA. My good name.

CLOTALDO.   In Astolfo you will find. . .

ROSAURA. My honour rides on him and strikes him down!

CLOTALDO. Your king, too, Stella's husband!

ROSAURA.   Never, never
   Shall that be, by almighty God, I swear!
CLOTALDO. Why, this is madness!
ROSAURA.   Yes it is!
CLOTALDO.   Restrain it.   320
ROSAURA. That I cannot.
CLOTALDO.   Then you are lost forever!
ROSAURA. I know it!
CLOTALDO.   Life and honour both together!
ROSAURA. I well believe it!
CLOTALDO.   What do you intend?
ROSAURA. My death.
CLOTALDO.   This is despair and desperation.
ROSAURA. It's honour.
CLOTALDO.   It is nonsense.
ROSAURA.   It is valour.
CLOTALDO. It's frenzy.
ROSAURA.   Yes, it's anger! Yes, it's fury!
CLOTALDO. In short you cannot moderate your passion?
ROSAURA. No.
CLOTALDO.   Who is there to help you?
ROSAURA.   I, myself.
CLOTALDO. There is no cure?
ROSAURA.   There is no cure!
CLOTALDO.   Think well
   If there's not some way out. . .
ROSAURA.   Some other way   330
   To do away with me. . .
                             [Exit.]
CLOTALDO.   If you are lost,
   My daughter, let us both be lost together!

In the country

[*Enter* SEGISMUND *clothed in skins. Soldiers marching.* CLARION. *Drums beating.*]
SEGISMUND. If Rome, today, could see me here, renewing
   Her olden triumphs, she might laugh to see
   A wild beast in command of mighty armies,
   A wild beast, to whose fiery aspirations
   The firmament were all too slight a conquest!
   But stoop your flight, my spirit. Do not thus
   Be puffed to pride by these uncertain plaudits
   Which, when I wake, will turn to bitterness   340
   In that I won them only to be lost.
   The less I value them, the less I'll miss them.
                     [A trumpet sounds.]
CLARION. Upon a rapid courser (pray excuse me,

Since if it comes to mind I must describe it)
In which it seems an atlas was designed
Since if its body is earth, its soul is fire
Within its breast, its foam appears the sea,
The wind its breath, and chaos its condition,
Since in its soul, its foam, its breath and flesh,
It seems a monster of fire, earth, sea, and wind,   350
Upon the horse, all of a patchwork colour,
Dappled, and rushing forward at the will
Of one who plies the spur, so that it flies
Rather than runs—see how a woman rides
Boldly into your presence.[15]

SEGISMUND.   Her light blinds me.
CLARION. Good God! Why, here's Rosaura!
SEGISMUND.   It is heaven
That has restored her to my sight once more.

> [*Enter* ROSAURA *with sword and*
> *dagger in riding costume.*]

ROSAURA. Generous Segismund, whose majesty
Heroically rises in the lustre
Of his great deeds out of his night of shadows,   360
And as the greatest planet, in the arms
Of his aurora, lustrously returns
To plants and roses, over hills and seas,
When, crowned with gold, he looks abroad, dispersing
Radiance, flashing his rays, bathing the summits,
And broidering the fringes of the foam,
So may you dawn upon the world, bright sun
Of Poland, that a poor unhappy woman
May fall before your feet and beg protection
Both as a woman and unfortunate—   370
Two things that must oblige you, sire, as one
Who prize yourself as valiant, each of them
More than suffices for your chivalry.
Three times you have beheld me now, three times
Been ignorant of who I am, because
Three times you saw me in a different clothing.
The first time you mistook me for a man,
Within that rigorous prison, where your hardships
Made mine seem pleasure. Next time, as a woman,
You saw me, when your pomp and majesty   380
Were as a dream, a phantasm, a shade.
The third time is today when, as a monster
Of both the sexes, in a woman's costume
I bear a soldier's arms. But to dispose you
The better to compassion, hear my story.
My mother was a noble in the court

[15]Clarion's speech is a parody of exaggerated style—including Calderón's. [Translator's note.]

Of Moscow, who, since most unfortunate,
Must have been beautiful. Then came a traitor
And cast his eyes on her (I do not name him,
Not knowing who he is). Yet I deduce   390
That he was valiant too from my own valour,
Since he gave form to me—and I could wish
I had been born in pagan times, that I might
Persuade myself he was some god of those
Who rain in showers of gold, turn into swans
Or bulls, for Danaës, Ledas, or Europas.[16]
That's strange: I thought I was just rambling on
By telling old perfidious myths, yet find
I've told you how my mother was cajoled.
Oh, she was beautiful as no one else   400
Has been, but was unfortunate like all.
He swore to wed her (that's an old excuse)
And this trick reached so nearly to her heart
That thought must weep, recalling it today.
The tyrant left her only with his sword
As Aeneas left Troy.[17] I sheathed its blade here
Upon my thigh, and I will bare it too
Before the ending of this history.
Out of this union, this poor link which neither
Could bind the marriage nor handcuff the crime,   410
Myself was born, her image and her portrait,
Not in her beauty, but in her misfortune,
For mine's the same. That's all I need to say.
The most that I can tell you of myself
Is that the man who robbed me of the spoils
And trophies of my honour is Astolfo.
Alas! to name him my heart rages so
(As hearts will do when men name enemies).
Astolfo was my faithless and ungrateful
Lord, who (quite forgetful of our happiness,   420
Since of a past love even the memory fades)
Came here to claim the throne and marry Stella
For she's the star who rises as I set.
It's hard to credit that a star should sunder
Lovers the stars had made conformable!
So hurt was I, so villainously cheated,
That I became mad, brokenhearted, sick,
Half wild with grief, and like to die, with all
Hell's own confusion ciphered on my mind
Like Babel's incoherence.[18] Mutely I told   430

[16]Zeus, the chief of the Greek Olympian gods, seduced Danaë, Leda, and Europa in the
forms of a shower of gold, a swan, and a bull, respectively.

[17]Calderón is apparently alluding to Aeneas's abandoning of Dido. But this took place in
Carthage, not in Troy.

[18]At the Tower of Babel, in Genesis 11:1-9, God confused human languages in order to
punish man's presumption in attempting to build a tower to Heaven.

My griefs (since woes and griefs declare themselves
Better than can the mouth, by their effects),
When, with my mother (we were by ourselves),
She broke the prison of my pent-up sorrows
And from my breast they all rushed forth in troops.
I felt no shyness, for in knowing surely
That one to whom one's errors are recounted
Has also been an ally in her own,
One finds relief and rest, since bad example
Can sometimes serve for a good purpose too.   440
She heard my plaint with pity, and she tried
To palliate my sorrows with her own.
How easily do judges pardon error
When they've offended too! An example,
A warning, in herself, she did not trust
To idleness, or the slow cure of time,
Nor try to find a remedy for her honour
In my misfortunes, but, with better counsel,
She bade me follow him to Poland here
And with prodigious gallantry persuade him   450
To pay the debt to honour that he owes me.
So that it would be easier to travel,
She bade me don male clothing, and took down
This ancient sword which I am wearing now.
Now it is time that I unsheathe the blade
As I was bid, for, trusting in its sign,
She said: "Depart to Poland, show this sword
That all the nobles may behold it well,
And it may be that one of them will take
Pity on you, and counsel you, and shield you."   460
I came to Poland and, you will remember,
Entered your cave. You looked at me in wonder.
Clotaldo passionately took my part
To plead for mercy to the king, who spared me,
Then, when he heard my story, bade me change
Into my own clothes and attend on Stella,
There to disturb Astolfo's love and stop
Their marriage. Again you saw me in woman's dress
And were confused by the discrepancy.
But let's pass to what's new: Clotaldo, now   470
Persuaded that Astolfo must, with Stella,
Come to the throne, dissuades me from my purpose,
Against the interests of my name and honour.
But seeing you, O valiant Segismund,
Are claiming your revenge, now that the heavens
Have burst the prison of your rustic tower,
(Wherein you were the tiger of your sorrows,
The rock of sufferings and direful pains)
And sent you forth against your sire and country,
I come to aid you, mingling Dian's silks   480

With the hard steel of Pallas.[19] Now, strong Captain,
It well behoves us both to stop this marriage—
Me, lest my promised husband should be wed,
You, lest, when their estates are joined, they weigh
More powerfully against your victory.
I come, as a mere woman, to persuade you
To right my shame; but, as a man, I come
To help you battle for your crown. As woman,
To melt your heart, here at your feet I fall;
But, as a man, I come to serve you bravely   490
Both with my person and my steel, and thus,
If you today should woo me as a woman,
Then I should have to kill you as a man would
In honourable service of my honour;
Since I must be three things today at once—
Passionate, to persuade you: womanly,
To ply you with my woes: manly, to gain
Honour in battle.

SEGISMUND.   Heavens! If it is true I'm dreaming,
Suspend my memory, for in a dream
So many things could not occur. Great heavens!   500
If I could only come free of them all!
Or never think of any! Who ever felt
Such grievous doubts? If I but dreamed that triumph
In which I found myself, how can this woman
Refer me to such sure and certain facts?
Then all of it was true and not a dream.
But if it be the truth, why does my past life
Call it a dream? This breeds the same confusion.
Are dreams and glories so alike, that fictions
Are held for truths, realities for lies?   510
Is there so little difference in them both
That one should question whether what one sees
And tastes is true or false? What? Is the copy
So near to the original that doubt
Exists between them? Then if that is so,
And grandeur, power, majesty, and pomp,
Must all evaporate like shades at morning,
Let's profit by it, this time, to enjoy
That which we only can enjoy in dreams.
Rosaura's in my power: my soul adores her beauty.   520
Let's take the chance. Let love break every law
On which she has relied in coming here
And kneeling, trustful, prostrate at my feet.
This is a dream. If so, dream pleasures now
Since they must turn to sorrows in the end!
But with my own opinions, I begin

---

[19]Diana was the Roman goddess of virginity and the hunt, while Pallas is the Greek
Athena, goddess of wisdom and war.

Once again to convince myself. Let's think.
If it is but vainglory and a dream,
Who for mere human vainglory would lose
True glory? What past blessing is not merely   530
A dream? Who has known heroic glories,
That deep within himself, as he recalls them,
Has never doubted that they might be dreams?
But if this all should end in disenchantment,
Seeing that pleasure is a lovely flame
That's soon converted into dust and ashes
By any wind that blows, then let us seek
That which endures in thrifty, lasting fame
In which no pleasures sleep, nor grandeurs dream.
Rosaura's without honour. In a prince   540
It's worthier to restore it than to steal it.
I shall restore it, by the living God,
Before I win my throne! Let's shun the danger
And fly from the temptation which is strong!
Then sound to arms!

                [*To a soldier.*]

Today I must give battle before darkness
Buries the rays of gold in green-black waves!
ROSAURA. My lord! Alas, you stand apart, and offer
  No word of pity for my plight. How is it
  You neither hear nor see me nor even yet   550
  Have turned your face on me?
SEGISMUND.   Rosaura, for your honour's sake
  I must be cruel to you, to be kind.
My voice must not reply to you because
My honour must reply to you. I am silent
Because my deeds must speak to you alone.
I do not look at you since, in such straits,
Having to see your honour is requited,
I must not see your beauty.

                [*Exit with soldiers.*]

ROSAURA. What strange enigma's this? After such trouble
  Still to be treated with more doubtful riddles!   560

                [*Enter* CLARION.]

CLARION. Madam, may you be visited just now?
ROSAURA. Why, Clarion, where have you been all this time?
CLARION. Shut in the tower, consulting cards
  About my death: "to be or not to be."
  And it was a near thing.
ROSAURA.   Why?
CLARION.   Because I know
  The secret who you are: in fact, Clotaldo. . .

                [*Drums.*]

  But hush! What noise is that?
ROSAURA.   What can it be?
CLARION. From the beleaguered palace a whole squadron

Is charging forth to harry and defeat
That of fierce Segismund.

ROSAURA.   Why, what a coward   570
 Am I, not to be at his side, the terror
 And scandal of the world, while such fierce strife
 Presses all round in lawless anarchy.

           [*Exit.*]

VOICES OF SOME. Long live our king!
VOICES OF OTHERS.   Long live our liberty!
CLARION. Long live both king and liberty, Yes, live!
 And welcome to them both! I do not worry.
 In all this pother, I behave like Nero
 Who never grieved at what was going on.[20]
 If I had anything to grieve about
 It would be me, myself. Well hidden here,   580
 Now, I can watch the sport that's going on.
 This place is safe and hidden between crags,
 And since death cannot find me here, two figs for death!

      [*He hides. Drums and the clash of
      arms are heard.*]
      [*Enter* BASIL, CLOTALDO, *and*
      ASTOLFO, *fleeing.*]

BASIL. Was ever king so hapless as myself
 Or father more ill used?
CLOTALDO.   Your beaten army
 Rush down, in all directions, in disorder.
ASTOLFO. The traitors win!
BASIL.   In battles such as these
 Those on the winning side are ever "loyal,"
 And traitors the defeated. Come, Clotaldo,
 Let's flee from the inhuman cruelty   590
 Of my fierce son!

      [*Shots are fired within.* CLARION
      falls wounded.*]

CLARION.   Heavens, save me!
ASTOLFO.   Who is this
 Unhappy soldier bleeding at our feet?
CLARION. I am a most unlucky man who, wishing
 To guard myself from death, have sought it out
 By fleeing from it. Shunning it, I found it,
 Because, to death, no hiding-place is secret.
 So you can argue that whoever shuns it
 Most carefully runs into it the quickest.
 Turn, then, once more into the thick of battle:
 There is more safety there amidst the fire   600
 And clash of arms than here on this secluded
 Mountain, because no hidden path is safe

---

[20] The Roman emperor Nero proverbially ignored the burning of Rome; he fiddled as it
burned.

From the inclemency of Fate; and so,
Although you flee from death, yet you may find it
Quicker than you expect, if God so wills.

                              [*He falls dead.*]

BASIL. "If God so wills" . . . With what strange eloquence
This corpse persuades our ignorance and error
To better knowledge, speaking from the mouth
Of its fell wound, where the red liquid flowing
Seems like a bloody tongue which teaches us   610
That the activities of man are vain
When they are pitted against higher powers.
For I, who wished to liberate my country
From murder and sedition, gave it up
To the same ills from which I would have saved it.

CLOTALDO. Though Fate, my lord, knows every path, and finds
Him whom it seeks even in the midst of crags
And thickets, it is not a Christian judgment
To say there is no refuge from its fury.
A prudent man can conquer Fate itself.   620
Though you are not exempted from misfortune,
Take action to escape it while you can!

ASTOLFO. Clotaldo speaks as one mature in prudence,
And I as one in valour's youthful prime.
Among the thickets of this mount is hidden
A horse, the very birth of the swift wind.
Flee on him, and I'll guard you in the rear.

BASIL. If it is God's will I should die, or if
Death waits here for my coming, I will seek
Him out today, and meet him face to face.   630

                    [*Enter* SEGISMUND, STELLA,
                      ROSAURA, *soldiers, and their train.*]

A SOLDIER. Amongst the thickets of this mountain
The king is hiding.

SEGISMUND.   Seek him out at once!
Leave no foot of the summit unexplored
But search from stem to stem and branch to branch!

CLOTALDO. Fly, sir!

BASIL.   What for?

ASTOLFO.   What do you mean to do?

BASIL. Astolfo, stand aside!

CLOTALDO.   What is your wish?

BASIL. To take a cure I've needed for some time.

                              [*To* SEGISMUND.]

If you have come to seek me, here I am.

                              [*Kneeling.*]

Your father, prince, kneels humbly at your feet.
The white snow of my hair is now your carpet.   640
Tread on my neck and trample on my crown!
Lay low and drag my dignity in dust!
Take vengeance on my honour! Make a slave

Of me and, after all I've done to thwart them,
Let Fate fulfil its edict and claim homage
And Heaven fulfil its oracles at last!

SEGISMUND. Illustrious court of Poland, who have been
The witnesses of such unwonted wonders,
Attend to me, and hear your prince speak out.
What Heaven decrees and God writes with his finger   650
(Whose prints and ciphers are the azure leaves
Adorned with golden lettering of the stars)
Never deceives nor lies. They only lie
Who seek to penetrate the mystery
And, having reached it, use it to ill purpose.
My father, who is here to evade the fury
Of my proud nature, made me a wild beast:
So, when I, by my birth of gallant stock,
My generous blood, and inbred grace and valour,
Might well have proved both gentle and forbearing,   660
The very mode of life to which he forced me,
The sort of bringing up I had to bear
Sufficed to make me savage in my passions.
What a strange method of restraining them!
If one were to tell any man: "One day
You will be killed by an inhuman monster,"
Would it be the best method he could choose
To wake that monster when it was asleep?
Of if they told him: "That sword which you're wearing
Will be your death," what sort of cure were it   670
To draw it forth and aim it at his breast?
Or if they told him: "Deep blue gulfs of water
Will one day be your sepulchre and grave
Beneath a silver monument of foam,"
He would be mad to hurl himself in headlong
When the sea highest heaved its showy mountains
And crystalline sierras plumed with spray.
The same has happened to the king as to him
Who wakes a beast which threatens death, to him
Who draws a naked sword because he fears it,   680
To him who dives into the stormy breakers.
Though my ferocious nature (hear me now)
Was like a sleeping beast, my inborn rage
A sheathèd sword, my wrath a quiet ripple,
Fate should not be coerced by man's injustice—
This rouses more resentment. So it is
That he who seeks to tame his fortune must
Resort to moderation and to measure.
He who foresees an evil cannot conquer it
Thus in advance, for though humility   690
Can overcome it, this it can do only
When the occasion's there, for there's no way

To dodge one's fate and thus evade the issue.
Let this strange spectacle serve as example—
This prodigy, this horror, and this wonder,
Because it is no less than one, to see,
After such measures and precautions taken
To thwart it, that a father thus should kneel
At his son's feet, a kingdom thus be shattered.
This was the sentence of the heavens above,　　　　　　　　700
Which he could not evade, much though he tried.
Can I, younger in age, less brave, and less
In science than the king, conquer that fate?
　　　　　　　　　　　　　　　[*To the* KING.]
Sire, rise, give me your hand, now that the heavens
Have shown you that you erred as to the method
To vanquish them. Humbly I kneel before you
And offer you my neck to tread upon.
BASIL. Son, such a great and noble act restores you
　　Straight to my heart. Oh, true and worthy prince!
　　You have won both the laurel and the palm.　　　　　710
　　Crown yourself with your deeds! For you *have* conquered!
ALL. Long live Segismund! Long live Segismund!
SEGISMUND. Since I have other victories to win,
　　The greatest of them all awaits me now:
　　To conquer my own self. Astolfo, give
　　Your hand here to Rosaura, for you know
　　It is a debt of honour and must be paid.
ASTOLFO. Although, it's true, I owe some obligations—
　　She does not know her name or who she is,
　　It would be base to wed a woman who . . .　　　　　720
CLOTALDO. Hold! Wait! Rosaura's of as noble stock
　　As yours, Astolfo. In the open field
　　I'll prove it with my sword. She is my daughter
　　And that should be enough.
ASTOLFO.　　　　　　　　　What do you say?
CLOTALDO. Until I saw her married, righted, honoured,
　　I did not wish for it to be discovered.
　　It's a long story but she is my daughter.
ASTOLFO. That being so, I'm glad to keep my word.
SEGISMUND. And now, so that the princess Stella here
　　Will not remain disconsolate to lose　　　　　　730
　　A prince of so much valour, here I offer
　　My hand to her, no less in birth and rank.
　　Give me your hand.
STELLA.　　　　　　　I gain by meriting
　　So great a happiness.
SEGISMUND.　　　　　And now, Clotaldo,
　　So long so loyal to my father, come
　　To my arms. Ask me anything you wish.
FIRST SOLDIER. If thus you treat a man who never served you,

What about me who led the revolution
And brought you from your dungeon in the tower?
What will you give me?
SEGISMUND.   That same tower and dungeon   740
From which you never shall emerge till death.
No traitor is of use after his treason.
BASIL. All wonder at your wisdom!
ASTOLFO.   What a change
Of character!
ROSAURA.   How wise and prudent!
SEGISMUND.   Why
Do you wonder? Why do you marvel, since
It was a dream that taught me and I still
Fear to wake up once more in my close dungeon?
Though that may never happen, it's enough
To dream it might, for thus I came to learn
That all our human happiness must pass   750
Away like any dream, and I would here
Enjoy it fully ere it glide away,
Asking (for noble hearts are prone to pardon)
Pardon for faults in the actors or the play.

John Milton
(*1608–1674*)

*John Milton was one of the world's greatest and most influential poets, the author of
the definitive English epic, the last towering figure of the European Renaissance, and
a prominent partisan, on the Puritan and Republican side, in the momentous English Civil War, fought in the seventeenth century over issues of church and civil
government. The issues of his day in certain ways mark the beginning of the modern
political era.*

*Milton was born in London in 1608; his father, disinherited for converting from
Roman Catholicism to Protestantism, was a successful businessman (and a gifted
musician) who found it proper, the family having risen in the world, to give his son
John the best of humanist educations, through private tutors and at St. Paul's
School. The precocious evidence John gave of intellectual and poetic ability made the
church, rather than a more worldly profession, seem his natural calling, and, although Milton later in his life chose not to be ordained, he remained grateful that his
education had not been narrow and merely pragmatic. In 1625 he entered Cambridge University; there, after problems with his first tutor, he achieved distinction,
though he chafed at what he considered the university's intellectual conservatism. At
Cambridge he earned the nickname "The Lady" because of his delicate good looks, his
religious seriousness, and the ascetic tendencies that (as his later life would reveal)
coexisted with a passionate and even sensuous side of his character. In 1629 he wrote*

his first great poem in English (he composed in Latin and Italian also), the Ode on
the Morning of Christ's Nativity, *which anticipates* Paradise Lost *by its references to the overcoming of the heathen gods at the coming of Christ. After taking his
B.A. in 1629 and his M.A. in 1632, he retired to his father's estate, where he studied
intensively, preparing himself, as he felt, for some great enterprise in literature or
public life. Before the age of thirty, when this period of retirement ended, Milton had
also written* L'Allegro *and* Il Penseroso *(twin poems praising, respectively, the
cheerful and contemplative characters), the brief masque* Arcades, *the longer
masque* Comus *(a platonic celebration of the triumph of virtue and chastity over evil
and sensuality), and* Lycidas, *a pastoral elegy that some critics consider the greatest
lyric poem in English. Written to commemorate the premature death of an acquaintance,* Lycidas *dramatizes Milton's concern over the mystery and injustice of death,
the possible unfulfillment of his own hopes in life, and the assurance of spiritual
victory through submission to divine Providence—all this in the context of an almost
unbelievably rich pattern of classical allusion and creative imitation.*

*In 1638 Milton left England to spend fifteen months on the Continent, mainly in
Florence, Rome, and Naples. During this "grand tour," he met a number of eminent
men of learning and culture, including Hugo Grotius, the Dutch expositor of international law, and Galileo, who at the time was in trouble with the Church because of
his speculations in astronomy. Milton was for the most part gratified by his reception,
which gave him increased confidence in his powers. It is both characteristic and
prophetic that, as Milton later put it, he "openly defended . . . the reformed religion
in the very metropolis of popery" despite plots said to have been hatched against him
by the Jesuits. He aborted a trip to Sicily and Greece when he learned of the outbreak
of civil disturbances in England, and some months later he was back there. Around
the time of his return, King Charles I was forced to convene a hostile Parliament;
over the next two decades, during which many battles were fought between the
Royalists/Episcopalians and their Republican/Puritan antagonists, the Presbyterian
party first rose to power, being succeeded later by an even more radical party of
Independents; Charles I was beheaded in 1649; a republic (the "Commonwealth")
was declared; Oliver Cromwell was named Lord Protector (dictator, virtually) between 1653 and his death in 1658; his ineffectual son Richard succeeded him but
abdicated; and finally, to Milton's dismay, the monarchy was restored in 1660 in the
person of the heretofore exiled Charles II.*

*After returning from his Italian tour, Milton pondered an ambitious literary
work, particularly a drama on an English or scriptural subject, and it is possible that
he did begin a play on his favorite topic, the fall of man, which he later chose for his
epic. But his sense of commitment to the cause of religious and civil freedom as he
understood it made him put aside his ambitious literary plans for the greater part of
two decades, during which he composed many treatises and pamphlets directed
against his personal and political enemies and those of the revolutionary government.
His first efforts dealt with the evils of the episcopal system (rule by bishops) in the
Church of England, an issue that Milton conceived to be part of the larger issue of
general human freedom. An ill-considered marriage, which for a time was broken
off, prompted a series of tracts boldly arguing for the legality of divorce on grounds of
incompatibility, a position that in its alleged libertinism alienated not only the Royalists but the Presbyterians as well. In 1644, in opposition to a Parliamentary censor-
ship law, he wrote* Areopagitica, *a classic rationale for freedom of the press and
individual responsibility that, curiously, uses arguments against an artificially sheltered, untested virtue that seem at least to be similar to those Satan and Eve use in*

Book IX of Paradise Lost *to justify eating the fruit of the Tree of Knowledge of Good and Evil. He also wrote on education, history, and theology. In 1649, the year Charles was beheaded, he wrote* The Tenure of Kings and Magistrates, *a tract that earned him the favor of the regicide regime by arguing that a king's tenure and very life were subject to the will of the people. Milton was made Latin Secretary in the government, a post that involved foreign correspondence and official defenses of the regime against its opponents at home and abroad. But his eyesight, which for some time had been failing, deteriorated until total blindness came in 1652, after which time he was gradually relieved of official duties and was able (especially after 1654) to turn his energies again to literature. Milton was sustained in part by his belief that loss of literal vision was compensated by a strengthened inner light and vision—a hope that was later expressed movingly in the hymn to light that opens Book III of* Paradise Lost. *In the latter 1650s he began his epic* Paradise Lost, *which he completed by 1665; it was published in 1667, in a ten-book version that he later altered to twelve. Meanwhile, the restoration of the Royalists brought Milton's life into peril, though for reasons not entirely clear he was released, after being arrested, with just a fine. Thereafter, despite reduced financial circumstances and some friction with his relatives, he lived a fairly regular and outwardly uneventful life, composing verse (the inspiration for which is said to have come mainly in the winter during the hours before dawn), singing and playing music, walking in his garden, meditating and being read to, receiving admiring visitors. In 1671 were published the "short epic"* Paradise Regained *(a sequel to* Paradise Lost *that centers on Christ's resistance to Satan's temptations in the wilderness as narrated, for example, in the fourth chapter of Matthew's gospel) and the drama* Samson Agonistes. *The latter, based on the story of Samson in Judges 13–16, has irresistible autobiographical relevance as the story of a blinded hero, living his last days in captivity, who undergoes a spiritual renewal and finally triumphs over his wicked captors.* Samson Agonistes *has been praised as the nearest English equivalent of ancient Greek drama and as a work on the same level of greatness as* Paradise Lost. *Thus Milton's stature as a poet is attested in all three traditional poetic modes: lyric (his sonnets must be mentioned along with works already named), epic, and drama. After a final pamphlet in 1673 warning against resurgent "popery" under Charles II, Milton died, in 1674, of gout.*

In Paradise Lost *Milton aimed at grandeur, comprehensiveness, and universal relevance. This is most clearly true in the choice of subject itself, for to Christians no theme could be more awesome than that of the fall of man, which "Brought death into the world, and all our woe" (I.3) and the counterpoised Redemption that is outlined theologically in Book III and historically in Book XII. It was a theme, Milton tells us, that he was "long choosing and beginning late" (IX.26). The question to what extent the poem transcends the interests of Christian theology has been much debated. Milton's approach can be cited on both sides: on one hand, he is careful to integrate into his poem the whole fabric of pagan antiquity, thus achieving something like mythic universality; on the other hand, he takes pains to distinguish the distorted versions of truth expressed by the pagans from the literal and naked truth of biblical revelation on which his epic is based. The pagan gods, for example, are the true devils in disguise. Aiming at universality, Milton subordinates in* Paradise Lost *the notes of political and religious partisanship he sounds in his tracts. His political opposition to the restored monarchy appears chiefly by innuendo, and although there is in the poem some peculiarly Miltonic theology (his apparently unorthodox view of the Trinity, for example), and some direct sectarian invective like his attack on Catholic monasticism*

(III.474–97), his treatment of the Son's redeeming self-sacrifice is essentially in the mainstream of Christian tradition.

Whatever limitations Milton's theology, idiosyncratic or more broadly Christian, may imply for the persuasiveness of his answers, it is hardly questionable that he defines compellingly the ultimate issues explored in all theodicies (attempts to "justify God's ways")—questions of cosmic justice, the origin of physical suffering and of moral evil, and the relationship of these to human free will. Indeed, the motif of liberty is at the heart of Paradise Lost and is perhaps the most vital link between the values of the poem and those Milton cherished in his personal and public life. Moreover, his treatment of liberty is complex. His belief that man stands or falls essentially on his own, without either the compulsion or the effective help of earthly authority, is part both of radical Protestantism and of modern libertarianism. Yet it is also true that the Son's obedient submission to the Father is for Milton the prototype of all true liberty. Paradise Lost thus raises some questions about the relationship between absolute human autonomy and acquiescence in the cosmic order that assert themselves in any age, under any system.

Milton's claim to have raised the subject matter of epic to a new level of grandeur and truth is itself part of the epic tradition. In this claim he is following the precedent of Virgil, who (to apply a phrase of Milton's) also tried to be "doctrinal and exemplary to a nation" by implicitly substituting for Homeric objectivity and concern with war a set of values that, while still communal, are more inward, ethical, philosophical. Like Virgil, Milton tells a story whose historical, and not merely mythical, dimension is important to him. The matter is of the greatest possible public import. Yet Milton, while insisting on the literal existence of hell, heaven, and the earthly paradise, gives them also an extended spiritual dimension. Hell is a state of mind, one that Satan creates for himself and carries with him everywhere he goes. Paradise is lost by Adam and Eve, but Book XII assures them that, through faith in and imitation of the redeeming Son of God, they can achieve "A Paradise within thee, happier far" (XII.587) than the one they forfeited. In a passage where he both acknowledges and repudiates his epic ancestry, Milton substitutes for "Wars, hitherto the only argument / Heroic deemed" the "better fortitude / Of patience and heroic martyrdom" (IX.28–32). It is enormously significant that in Paradise Regained he balances against the "disobedience" (Paradise Lost, I.1) of the fallen Adam not the climax of Jesus' public life in the Passion and Resurrection but the most private incident in his career, the obedience to his Father manifested in the Temptation in the Wilderness.

Much of the power of Paradise Lost comes from qualities that might seem alien to the opinionated Milton: a kind of evenhandedness or at least intellectual and imaginative empathy that he extends to ideas and characters opposed to what he is championing. Easily the best example is Satan, one of the supreme triumphs of literary characterization. Shelley and other interpreters in the Romantic tradition went so far as to consider him the real hero of the poem. That was surely not Milton's intent, yet it remains true that Satan is given dramatic autonomy. He is treated with grandeur, in, for example, Books I and II, and sometimes with touches of pathos as in the soliloquy that opens Book IV. (Ironically, as it has seemed to some readers, the Milton who in life defended rebellion against monarchy identifies the insubordinate Satan in the epic poem as the origin of evil.) Belial, whom Milton calls "lewd," "gross," and one who could "make the worse appear / The better reason" (I.490–491; II.113–114), is endowed with breathtaking imagination and made to utter a noble encomium on the human mind, "this intellectual being, / Those thoughts that wander through eternity" (II.147–148). And, as mentioned earlier, Satan and Eve *sound somewhat like* Areopagitica. *Such anomalies can suggest a failure by Milton to control the tone of the poem or else, as William Blake's* Marriage of Heaven and Hell *charges, a lapse in self-knowledge by Milton. Against which it might be argued that in true epics heroes and heroism have worthy, however evil, adversaries. If the temptations and errors of Satan and mankind had no plausibility and seductive power, their fall would seem not tragic but fatuous.*

Paradise Lost *is a consummate work of art, in architecture and surface. The sublime hymn to light in Book III, for example, serves structurally to emphasize the emergence of Satan, and the poem, from the sulphurous horror of hell and darkness to the ambrosial brightness of heaven. These same transitional lines also mark the elaborate parallelism between the council-scenes of Books II and III, including the antithetical offers by Satan and the Son of God respectively to destroy man and to save him, and the elaborate parody of the divine Trinity in the infernal trinity of Satan, Sin, and Death. Closer-grained effects are equally skillful and deliberate; the "No light, but rather darkness visible" of hell (I.63) contrasts with the Deity, "Dark with excessive bright" (III.380). Figures of speech are powerful; the modulation of the metaphysical praise of light into Milton's mourning for his personal blindness is capped by a sublime metaphor in which the outward-radiating natural sun that fertilizes the world and dispels darkness becomes the emblem of a fertilizing spiritual sun that shines toward a center:*

> *So much the rather thou celestial Light*
> *Shine inward, and the mind through all her powers*
> *Irradiate, there plant eyes, all mist from thence*
> *Purge and disperse, that I may see and tell*
> *Of things invisible to mortal sight. (III.51–55)*

The grand style in Paradise Lost, *the style generally called "Miltonic," is the high ceremonial one that Milton recognized as appropriate to epic. Vowel sounds are often sonorous ("To bellow through the vast and boundless deep"—I.177). Half-repetitions (the "Miltonic turn") have an effect that can be both epigrammatic and swelling ("to have found their Chief / Not in despair, to have found themselves not lost / In loss itself"—I.524–26). Exotic, evocative proper names are heaped on one another (I.579–87). Long-extended similes are used as in Homer and Virgil (I.302–13, 768–92), often with even greater psychological suggestiveness. Sentences are prolonged through whole "verse paragraphs," the sense drawn out inexorably from one line to the next—sustaining elevation of tone or creating suspense or introducing bold imaginative surprises that one is not allowed to linger over as climaxes.*

In fact, however, the poem has many voices. The speeches in the infernal council in Book II are not just magniloquent; they are specifically modeled on parliamentary oratory. Moreover, even this section is varied within itself, the headlong Moloch sounding not at all like the subtle, intellectually speculative Belial. Satan's soliloquy in Book IV is in itself a mixture of tones, from subdued remorse to anguish to desperate recklessness. Adam and Eve can address each other like royal consorts in their unfallen state but with colloquial acrimony at the end of Book IX after their fall. Milton abandoned the dramatic genre for the epic, but he retained the variety of speech one finds in the best dramas.

Although Shakespeare may have been rated as highly, Milton's influence on English literature in the 150 years following his death in 1674 was much greater, indeed incalculable. To imitate Shakespeare, who created in his plays and poems a score of different worlds, is nearly equivalent to imitating the whole variety of human experience. But Milton's work, despite its wide variety of genre and tone, has a kind of finished architectural coherence that, blending with the events of his life and his forcefully expressed ideas, has the effect of a single massive literary and personal presence. He dominated the eighteenth-century imagination as Newton dominated its science, partly because of his grandeur of manner, partly because of the fascination of his theological argument, partly because he synthesized while he transformed a vast body of ancient and Renaissance culture. The English Romantic poets, especially Blake, Wordsworth, Shelley, and Keats, all took Milton, in one way or another, as a touchstone for their most considered statements about human values and the place of humanity in the cosmic order.

FURTHER READING *(prepared by W. J. R.):* William Riley Parker's *Milton: A Biography,* 2 vols., 1968, is the definitive modern biography; as an introduction, Douglas Bush's *John Milton: A Sketch of His Life and Writings,* 1964, is recommended. Arnold Stein's *Answerable Style: Essays on "Paradise Lost,"* 1953, is an excellent study of the poem. C. S. Lewis's *A Preface to "Paradise Lost,"* 1942, rev. 1960, discusses the poem's ideas and style in a lively, rigorous fashion, in the contexts of classical and Christian tradition. An excellent introduction is David M. Miller's *John Milton: Poetry,* 1978, which includes a biographical introduction and discussions of *Paradise Lost, Paradise Regained,* and *Samson Agonistes,* in a manner suitable for general readers. Northrop Frye's *The Return of Eden,* 1965, contains excellent essays, including Frye's celebrated analysis of foreground and background action in *Paradise Lost.* Douglas Bush's *"Paradise Lost" in Our Time,* 1945, discusses the negative reaction to Milton's epic in the twentieth century, Milton's religion and ethics, methods of characterization, and other topics. Helen Gardner's *A Reading of "Paradise Lost,"* 1965, contains a helpful discussion of the modern meaning of *Paradise Lost;* an appendix contains Gardner's earlier (1948) and important essay on Satan and his appeal as a heroic figure. Joan Webber's *Milton and His Epic Tradition,* 1979, surveys early epics beginning with Homer and relates this tradition to *Paradise Lost* and *Paradise Regained. New Essays on "Paradise Lost,"* ed. Thomas Kranidas, 1971, contains good essays on the theme of Book III, innocence and experience in *Paradise Lost,* the Fall, and other topics. Don Cameron Allen's *The Harmonious Vision,* 1954, deals with nearly all of Milton's poetry in an attempt to define the overall unity of Milton's thought.

PARADISE LOST

Selected Notes by James Holly Hanford

THE VERSE: The measure is English heroic verse without rime, as that of Homer in Greek, and of Virgil in Latin; rime being no necessary adjunct or true ornament of poem or good verse, in longer works especially, but the invention of a barbarous age, to set off wretched matter and lame metre; graced indeed since by the use of some famous modern poets, carried away by custom, but much to their own vexation, hindrance, and constraint to express many things otherwise, and for the most part worse than else they would have expressed them. Not without cause, therefore, some both Italian and Spanish poets of prime note have rejected rime both in longer and shorter works, as have also, long since, our best English tragedies, as a thing of itself, to all judicious ears, trivial and of no true musical delight; which consists only in apt numbers, fit quantity of syllables, and the sense variously drawn out from one verse into another, not in the jingling sound of like endings, a fault avoided by the learned ancients both in poetry and all good oratory. This neglect then of rime so little is to be taken for a defect, though it may seem so perhaps to vulgar readers, that it rather is to be esteemed an example set, the first in English, of ancient liberty recovered to heroic poem from the troublesome and modern bondage of riming.

BOOK I

THE ARGUMENT

This first book proposes first in brief the whole subject, Man's disobedience, and the loss thereupon of Paradise wherein he was placed: then touches the prime cause of his fall, the Serpent, or rather Satan in the Serpent; who revolting from God, and drawing to his side many legions of angels, was by the command of God driven out of Heaven with all his crew into the great Deep. Which action passed over, the poem hastes into the midst of things, presenting Satan with his angels now fallen into Hell, described here, not in the center (for Heaven and Earth may be supposed as yet not made, certainly not yet accursed) but in a place of utter darkness, fitliest called Chaos. Here Satan with his angels lying on the burning lake, thunderstruck and astonished, after a certain space recovers, as from confusion, calls up him who next in order and dignity lay by him; they confer of their miserable fall. Satan awakens all his legions, who lay till then in the same manner confounded; they rise: their numbers, array of battle, their chief leaders named, according to the idols known afterwards in Canaan and the countries adjoining. To these Satan directs his speech, comforts them with hope yet of regaining Heaven, but tells them lastly of a new world and new kind of creature to be created, according to an ancient prophecy or report in Heaven; for that angels were long before this visible creation, was the opinion of many ancient Fathers. To find out the truth of this prophecy, and what to determine thereon, he refers to a full council. What his associates thence attempt. Pandemonium the palace of Satan rises, suddenly built out of the Deep; the infernal peers there sit in council.

Of Man's first disobedience, and the fruit*
Of that forbidden tree, whose mortal taste
Brought death into the world, and all our woe,
With loss of Eden, till one greater Man
Restore us, and regain the blissful seat,
Sing Heavenly Muse, that on the secret top

---

*All footnotes are by Hanford unless otherwise stated. Some notes are abridged. The Arguments are by Milton.

1 ff. Milton follows the conventional epic procedure in his opening. For the various elements or steps in this procedure, cf. *Iliad* i. 1 ff., *Aeneid* i. 1 ff.

2. mortal, deadly.

6. Heavenly Muse. The Christian poets adopted the classical muse of Astronomy, whose name (Urania, the Heavenly) qualified her for the new office, as the patroness of their divine inspiration. Milton identifies her with the Holy Spirit of Scripture and so turns his invocation into a prayer.

Of Oreb, or of Sinai, didst inspire
That shepherd, who first taught the chosen seed,
In the beginning how the Heavens and Earth
Rose out of Chaos; or if Sion hill
Delight thee more, and Siloa's brook that flowed
Fast by the oracle of God, I thence
Invoke thy aid to my adventurous song,
That with no middle flight intends to soar
Above the Aonian mount, while it pursues
Things unattempted yet in prose or rhyme.
And chiefly thou O Spirit, that dost prefer
Before all temples the upright heart and pure,
Instruct me, for thou knowest; thou from the first
Wast present, and with mighty wings outspread
Dove-like sat'st brooding on the vast Abyss
And madest it pregnant: what in me is dark
Illumine, what is low raise and support;
That to the height of this great argument
I may assert Eternal Providence,
And justify the ways of God to men.
    Say first, for Heaven hides nothing from thy view,
Nor the deep tract of Hell, say first what cause
Moved our grand parents in that happy state,
Favored of Heaven so highly, to fall off
From their Creator, and transgress his will
For one restraint, lords of the world besides?
Who first seduced them to that foul revolt?
The infernal Serpent; he it was, whose guile,
Stirred up with envy and revenge, deceived
The Mother of Mankind; what time his pride
Had cast him out from Heaven, with all his host
Of rebel angels, by whose aid aspiring
To set himself in glory above his peers,
He trusted to have equalled the Most High,
If he opposed; and with ambitious aim

---

7. of Oreb or of Sinai. Cf. Exod. 19:20 and Deut. 4:10. Milton carefully follows Scripture even in its apparent contradiction.

8. That shepherd, Moses.

10. Sion hill, Mount Zion, one of the hills on which the city of Jerusalem is built.

11. Siloa's brook, "the waters of Shiloah that go softly" (Isa. 8:6).

12. Fast by the oracle of God, i.e., close to the Temple of Jerusalem.

15. Above the Aonian mount. Milton means that his theme is loftier than any that the Pagan poets could sing. The **Aonian mount** is Helicon, sacred to the muses.

21. Gen. 1:1, 2. The Hebrew word translated in the Authorized Version "moved" can also be rendered "brooded." The Holy Spirit takes the form of a dove in Luke 3:22.

24. argument, subject.   **25. assert,** maintain the cause of.

26. justify, make apparent the justice of. The real issue in Milton's mind is whether an intelligent and righteous will rules man's destiny, or a blind or capricious or malicious one. The justification hinges on (1) the affirmation of man's freedom and responsibility, and (2) the scheme of salvation through Christ which is set forth in the poem as a whole.

29. our grand parents, i.e., our original ancestors, Adam and Eve.

32. for, because of.

Against the throne and monarchy of God,
Raised impious war in Heaven and battle proud
With vain attempt. Him the Almighty Power
Hurled headlong flaming from the ethereal sky
With hideous ruin and combustion down
To bottomless perdition, there to dwell
In adamantine chains and penal fire,
Who durst defy the Omnipotent to arms.
   Nine times the space that measures day and night   50
To mortal men, he with his horrid crew
Lay vanquished, rolling in the fiery gulf
Confounded though immortal. But his doom
Reserved him to more wrath; for now the thought
Both of lost happiness and lasting pain
Torments him; round he throws his baleful eyes,
That witnessed huge affliction and dismay
Mixed with obdurate pride and steadfast hate.
At once as far as angel's ken he views
The dismal situation waste and wild: 60
A dungeon horrible, on all sides round
As one great furnace flamed, yet from those flames
No light, but rather darkness visible
Served only to discover sights of woe,
Regions of sorrow, doleful shades, where peace
And rest can never dwell, hope never comes
That comes to all; but torture without end
Still urges, and a fiery deluge, fed
With ever-burning sulphur unconsumed:
Such place Eternal Justice had prepared   70
For those rebellious, here their prison ordained
In utter darkness, and their portion set
As far removed from God and light of Heaven
As from the center thrice to the utmost pole.
Oh how unlike the place from whence they fell!
There the companions of his fall, o'erwhelmed
With floods and whirlwinds of tempestuous fire,
He soon discerns, and weltering by his side
One next himself in power, and next in crime,
Long after known in Palestine, and named   80

---

53. Confounded, defeated and ruined.   **57. witnessed,** bore witness to, expressed.
59. angel's ken, an angel's range of vision.
63. darkness visible, darkness not quite absolute. The words perhaps express also the idea
of the darkness having a positive quality.
64. discover, reveal.
66. Cf. Dante, *Inferno,* iii: "All hope abandon, ye who enter here."
68. urges, afflicts.
72. utter, outer—as in Scripture. But there is also a suggestion of the modern sense.
74. from the center thrice to the utmost pole. The center is the center of the earth; the
utmost pole is the pole of the outermost sphere of the visible heavens. The distance from hell
to the empyrean (the supreme heaven) is ordinarily felt by Milton to be much greater than this
exact calculation makes it.

Beëlzebub. To whom the Arch-Enemy,
And thence in Heaven called Satan, with bold words
Breaking the horrid silence thus began.
    "If thou beest he; but Oh how fallen! how changed
From him, who in the happy realms of light
Clothed with transcendent brightness didst outshine
Myriads, though bright: if he whom mutual league,
United thoughts and counsels, equal hope
And hazard in the glorious enterprise,
Joined with me once, now misery hath joined   90
In equal ruin: into what pit thou seest
From what height fallen, so much the stronger proved
He with his thunder, and till then who knew
The force of those dire arms? Yet not for those,
Nor what the potent victor in his rage
Can else inflict, do I repent or change,
Though changed in outward luster, that fixed mind
And high disdain, from sense of injured merit,
That with the Mightiest raised me to contend,
And to the fierce contention brought along   100
Innumerable force of spirits armed
That durst dislike his reign, and, me preferring,
His utmost power with adverse power opposed
In dubious battle on the plains of Heaven,
And shook his throne. What though the field be lost?
All is not lost; the unconquerable will,
And study of revenge, immortal hate,
And courage never to submit or yield:
And what is else not to be overcome?
That glory never shall his wrath or might   110
Extort from me. To bow and sue for grace
With suppliant knee, and deify his power
Who from the terror of this arm so late
Doubted his empire, that were low indeed,
That were an ignominy and shame beneath
This downfall; since by fate the strength of gods
And this empyreal substance cannot fail,
Since through experience of this great event,
In arms not worse, in foresight much advanced,
We may with more successful hope resolve   120
To wage by force or guile eternal war,
Irreconcilable to our grand foe,
Who now triumphs, and in the excess of joy

81. Beëlzebub. Cf. Matt. 12:24. **Arch-Enemy.** Satan in Hebrew means "adversary."
84 ff. If thou beest he, etc. The sentence is not completed. The entire speech is made disjointed to indicate Satan's emotional stress.
110. That glory, i.e., the glory of subduing Satan's will.   **114. Doubted,** feared for.
116 ff. since by fate, etc. Satan denies that he was created by and is therefore subordinate to God. His egotism makes him a polytheist or more specifically a Manichee.
120. successful hope, hope of success.

Sole reigning holds the tyranny of Heaven."
    So spake the apostate Angel, though in pain,
Vaunting aloud, but racked with deep despair;
And him thus answered soon his bold compeer.
    "O Prince, O Chief of many thronèd Powers,
That led the embattled Seraphim to war
Under thy conduct, and in dreadful deeds   130
Fearless, endangered Heaven's perpetual King,
And put to proof his high supremacy,
Whether upheld by strength, or chance, or fate;
Too well I see and rue the dire event,
That with sad overthrow and foul defeat
Hath lost us Heaven, and all this mighty host
In horrible destruction laid thus low,
As far as gods and heavenly essences
Can perish: for the mind and spirit remains
Invincible, and vigor soon returns,   140
Though all our glory extinct, and happy state
Here swallowed up in endless misery.
But what if he our conqueror (whom I now
Of force believe almighty, since no less
Than such could have o'erpowered such force as ours)
Have left us this our spirit and strength entire,
Strongly to suffer and support our pains,
That we may so suffice his vengeful ire,
Or do him mightier service as his thralls
By right of war, whate'er his business be,   150
Here in the heart of Hell to work in fire,
Or do his errands in the gloomy deep;
What can it then avail, though yet we feel
Strength undiminished, or eternal being
To undergo eternal punishment?"
    Whereto with speedy words the Arch-Fiend replied.
"Fallen Cherub, to be weak is miserable,
Doing or suffering: but of this be sure,
To do aught good never will be our task,
But ever to do ill our sole delight,   160
As being the contrary to his high will
Whom we resist. If then his providence
Out of our evil seek to bring forth good,
Our labor must be to pervert that end,
And out of good still to find means of evil;
Which oft-times may succeed, so as perhaps
Shall grieve him, if I fail not, and disturb
His inmost counsels from their destined aim.

128–29. thronèd Powers, Seraphim. The angelic orders in Dante and the Catholic theologians are, from lowest to highest, as follows: Angels, Archangels, Principalities, Powers, Virtues, Dominions, Thrones, Cherubim, Seraphim. Milton uses many of these names interchangeably.
    148. suffice, satisfy.   **167. if I fail not,** unless I mistake.

But see the angry victor hath recalled
His ministers of vengeance and pursuit
Back to the gates of Heaven; the sulphurous hail
Shot after us in storm, o'erblown hath laid
The fiery surge, that from the precipice
Of Heaven received us falling, and the thunder,
Winged with red lightning and impetuous rage,
Perhaps hath spent his shafts, and ceases now
To bellow through the vast and boundless deep.
Let us not slip the occasion, whether scorn,
Or satiate fury yield it from our foe.
Seest thou yon dreary plain, forlorn and wild,
The seat of desolation, void of light,
Save what the glimmering of these livid flames
Casts pale and dreadful? Thither let us tend
From off the tossing of these fiery waves,
There rest, if any rest can harbor there,
And re-assembling our afflicted powers,
Consult how we may henceforth most offend
Our enemy, our own loss how repair,
How overcome this dire calamity,
What reinforcement we may gain from hope;
If not, what resolution from despair."
    Thus Satan talking to his nearest mate
With head uplift above the wave, and eyes
That sparkling blazed; his other parts besides,
Prone on the flood, extended long and large,
Lay floating many a rood, in bulk as huge
As whom the fables name of monstrous size,
Titanian or Earth-born, that warred on Jove,
Briareos or Typhon, whom the den
By ancient Tarsus held, or that sea-beast
Leviathan, which God of all his works
Created hugest that swim the ocean stream:
Him haply slumbering on the Norway foam,
The pilot of some small night-foundered skiff,
Deeming some island, oft, as seamen tell,
With fixèd anchor in his scaly rind,
Moors by his side under the lee, while night
Invests the sea, and wishèd morn delays:

170

180

190

200

178. Let us not slip, Let us not let slip.   **186. afflicted powers,** routed forces.
197. as whom, as those whom.
198. Titanian, or Earth-born. The Titans and Giants in classical mythology were sons of Heaven (Uranus) and Earth (Ge).
199. Briareos or Typhon. The former was a Titan, the latter a Giant.
201. Leviathan. Cf. Psalms 104:26, and Job 41. The monster was often associated with the whale or the crocodile. Milton does not specifically identify it with either, although he suggests characteristics of both.
203 ff. This is an old traveller's story, the most familiar version being in the *Arabian Nights*.
night-foundered, i.e., lost in the darkness as completely as a sunken ship is lost in the ocean.
208. invests, covers as with a garment.

So stretched out huge in length the Arch-Fiend lay
Chained on the burning lake; nor ever thence   210
Had risen or heaved his head, but that the will
And high permission of all-ruling Heaven
Left him at large to his own dark designs,
That with reiterated crimes he might
Heap on himself damnation, while he sought
Evil to others, and enraged might see
How all his malice served but to bring forth
Infinite goodness, grace and mercy shown
On Man by him seduced, but on himself
Treble confusion, wrath and vengeance poured.   220
    Forthwith upright he rears from off the pool
His mighty stature; on each hand the flames
Driven backward slope their pointing spires, and rolled
In billows, leave in the midst a horrid vale.
Then with expanded wings he steers his flight
Aloft, incumbent on the dusky air
That felt unusual weight, till on dry land
He lights, if it were land that ever burned
With solid, as the lake with liquid fire,
And such appeared in hue; as when the force   230
Of subterranean wind transports a hill
Torn from Pelorus, or the shattered side
Of thundering Ætna, whose combustible
And fuellèd entrails thence conceiving fire,
Sublimed with mineral fury, aid the winds,
And leave a singèd bottom all involved
With stench and smoke: such resting found the sole
Of unblest feet. Him followed his next mate,
Both glorying to have scaped the Stygian flood
As gods, and by their own recovered strength,   240
Not by the sufferance of supernal power.
    "Is this the region, this the soil, the clime,"
Said then the lost Archangel, "this the seat
That we must change for Heaven, this mournful gloom
For that celestial light? Be it so, since he
Who now is sovran can dispose and bid
What shall be right. Farthest from him is best,
Whom reason hath equalled, force hath made supreme
Above his equals. Farewell happy fields
Where joy for ever dwells: Hail horrors, hail   250
Infernal world, and thou profoundest Hell
Receive thy new possessor: one who brings
A mind not to be changed by place or time.

---

226. incumbent, leaning on.   **232. Pelorus,** Cape Faro in Sicily, near Mt. Aetna.
235. sublimed, sublimated, converted to gaseous form, but also with the original sense of
lifted up; **the winds,** i.e., the winds or gases within the earth which were supposed to be the
cause of earthquakes.
236. involved, wrapped in.   **244. change for,** take in exchange for.
246. sovran, sovereign, supreme in power.

The mind is its own place, and in itself
Can make a Heaven of Hell, a Hell of Heaven.
What matter where, if I be still the same,
And what I should be, all but less than he
Whom thunder hath made greater? Here at least
We shall be free; the Almighty hath not built
Here for his envy, will not drive us hence: 260
Here we may reign secure, and in my choice
To reign is worth ambition, though in Hell:
Better to reign in Hell than serve in Heaven.
But wherefore let we then our faithful friends,
The associates and co-partners of our loss,
Lie thus astonished on the oblivious pool,
And call them not to share with us their part
In this unhappy mansion; or once more
With rallied arms to try what may be yet
Regained in Heaven, or what more lost in Hell?"   270
    So Satan spake, and him Beëlzebub
Thus answered. "Leader of those armies bright,
Which but the Omnipotent none could have foiled,
If once they hear that voice, their liveliest pledge
Of hope in fears and dangers, heard so oft
In worst extremes, and on the perilous edge
Of battle when it raged, in all assaults
Their surest signal, they will soon resume
New courage and revive, though now they lie
Grovelling and prostrate on yon lake of fire,   280
As we erewhile, astounded and amazed;
No wonder, fallen such a pernicious height!"
    He scarce had ceased when the superior Fiend
Was moving toward the shore; his ponderous shield,
Ethereal temper, massy, large, and round,
Behind him cast; the broad circumference
Hung on his shoulders like the moon, whose orb
Through optic glass the Tuscan artist views
At evening from the top of Fesolë,
Or in Valdarno, to descry new lands,   290

254–55. The supremacy of the mind is one of Milton's favorite ideas. The corollary of this utterance of Satan's is to be found in IV, 20–23.

257–58. all but less than, etc. Usually interpreted as "all but equal to" or "less only than," but other or additional meanings are possible. "What I should be" is, in Satan's mind, God's equal. He would rather be anything but inferior and, since the mind is its own place, he *can* be equal in everything but power. The confusion of grammar is no greater than the confusion of frustrated human emotion.

266. oblivious, causing forgetfulness. Milton is thinking of the classical Lethe.

276. edge. Latin *acies*, edge, means also battle line.

288. the Tuscan artist, Galileo, whom Milton had visited during his stay in Italy.

289. Fesolë, Fiesole, a small town located on a hill just outside Florence.

290. Valdarno, the valley of the Arno, in which Florence is located. Galileo's last residence was at Arcetri, west of the main part of the city. He was blind or almost so when Milton visited him and lamented that he could no longer look at the universe which his discoveries had made more wonderful.

Rivers or mountains in her spotty globe.
His spear, to equal which the tallest pine
Hewn on Norwegian hills, to be the mast
Of some great ammiral, were but a wand,
He walked with, to support uneasy steps
Over the burning marle, not like those steps
On Heaven's azure; and the torrid clime
Smote on him sore besides, vaulted with fire.
Nathless he so endured, till on the beach
Of that inflamëd sea, he stood and called   300
His legions, angel forms, who lay entranced,
Thick as autumnal leaves that strew the brooks
In Vallombrosa, where the Etrurian shades
High over-arched embower; or scattered sedge
Afloat, when with fierce winds Orion armed
Hath vexed the Red-Sea coast, whose waves o'erthrew
Busiris and his Memphian chivalry
While with perfidious hatred they pursued
The sojourners of Goshen, who beheld
From the safe shore their floating carcasses   310
And broken chariot wheels; so thick bestrewn
Abject and lost lay these, covering the flood,
Under amazement of their hideous change.
He called so loud, that all the hollow deep
Of Hell resounded. "Princes, Potentates,
Warriors, the flower of Heaven, once yours, now lost,
If such astonishment as this can seize
Eternal spirits; or have ye chosen this place
After the toil of battle to repose
Your wearied virtue, for the ease you find   320
To slumber here, as in the vales of Heaven?
Or in this abject posture have ye sworn
To adore the conqueror, who now beholds
Cherub and Seraph rolling in the flood
With scattered arms and ensigns, till anon
His swift pursuers from Heaven gates discern
The advantage, and descending tread us down
Thus drooping, or with linkëd thunderbolts

294. ammiral, admiral, flagship.   **296. marle,** soil.   **299. Nathless,** nevertheless.
302 ff. Note the series of brilliant Homeric similes used to emphasize the numbers of the
fallen angels. They are compared (1) when lying on the lake, to fallen leaves and floating
sea-weed; (2) when flying, to a cloud of locusts; (3) when alighted, to a huge invading army.
303. Vallombrosa, a district about eighteen miles from Florence, containing a famous
monastery which Milton is said to have visited. The name is Italian for "shady valley."
305. Orion, a constellation proverbially associated with storms.
307 ff. Cf. Exod. 14. **Busiris** was an ancient Egyptian king, whom Milton for some reason
identifies with the Pharaoh whose hosts were drowned in the Red Sea. **Memphian** is here
equivalent to Egyptian, Memphis being the ancient capital of Egypt. **The sojourners of Goshen** are of course the Israelites.
312. Abject, cast down (Latin *abjectus*).   **320. virtue,** valor, strength (Latin *virtus*).
328. linkëd thunderbolts. The thunderbolts are compared to linked cannon balls.

Transfix us to the bottom of this gulf.
Awake, arise, or be for ever fallen!"   330
    They heard and were abashed, and up they sprung
Upon the wing, as when men wont to watch
On duty, sleeping found by whom they dread,
Rouse and bestir themselves ere well awake.
Nor did they not perceive the evil plight
In which they were, or the fierce pains not feel;
Yet to their general's voice they soon obeyed
Innumerable. As when the potent rod
Of Amram's son in Egypt's evil day
Waved round the coast, up called a pitchy cloud   340
Of locusts, warping on the eastern wind,
That o'er the realm of impious Pharaoh hung
Like night, and darkened all the land of Nile:
So numberless were those bad angels seen
Hovering on wing under the cope of Hell
'Twixt upper, nether, and surrounding fires;
Till, as a signal given, the uplifted spear
Of their great Sultan waving to direct
Their course, in even balance down they light
On the firm brimstone, and fill all the plain;   350
A multitude, like which the populous North
Poured never from her frozen loins, to pass
Rhene or the Danaw, when her barbarous sons
Came like a deluge on the South, and spread
Beneath Gibraltar to the Libyan sands.
Forthwith from every squadron and each band
The heads and leaders thither haste where stood
Their great commander; godlike shapes and forms
Excelling human, Princely Dignities,
And Powers that erst in Heaven sat on thrones;   360
Though of their names in heavenly records now
Be no memorial, blotted out and rased
By their rebellion from the Books of Life.
Nor had they yet among the sons of Eve
Got them new names, till wandering o'er the Earth,

335. Nor did they not, i.e., they did.
338 ff. As when the potent rod, etc. Cf. Exod. 10:12–15. Moses was Amram's son.
340. pitchy, dark as pitch.
341. warping, working slowly forward with a bending or swerving motion. The term is primarily nautical.
345. cope, vault or canopy.
351. A multitude, etc. Milton concentrates in a simile the history of the barbarian invasions of the Roman Empire. Successive inroads were made by the Goths, the Vandals, and the Huns.
353. Rhene, the Rhine (from Latin *Rhenus*). **Danaw,** the Danube (from German *Donau*).
355. Beneath Gibraltar, i.e., south of Gibraltar. The Vandals crossed from Spain into North Africa.
364 ff. Nor had they yet, etc. The idea that the fallen angels become the pagan divinities goes back to early Patristic sources. The identification furnishes Milton with abundant biblical and mythological data regarding the inhabitants of hell.

Through God's high sufferance for the trial of Man,
By falsities and lies the greatest part
Of mankind they corrupted to forsake
God their Creator, and the invisible
Glory of him that made them to transform   370
Oft to the image of a brute, adorned
With gay religions full of pomp and gold,
And devils to adore for deities:
Then were they known to men by various names,
And various idols through the heathen world.
   Say, Muse, their names then known, who first, who last,
Roused from the slumber on that fiery couch,
At their great Emperor's call, as next in worth
Came singly where he stood on the bare strand,
While the promiscuous crowd stood yet aloof.   380
   The chief were those who from the pit of Hell
Roaming to seek their prey on Earth, durst fix
Their seats long after next the seat of God,
Their altars by his altar, gods adored
Among the nations round, and durst abide
Jehovah thundering out of Sion, throned
Between the Cherubim; yea, often placed
Within his sanctuary itself their shrines,
Abominations; and with cursèd things
His holy rites and solemn feasts profaned,   390
And with their darkness durst affront his light.
First Moloch, horrid king besmeared with blood
Of human sacrifice, and parents' tears,
Though for the noise of drums and timbrels loud
Their children's cries unheard, that passed through fire
To his grim idol. Him the Ammonite
Worshipped in Rabba and her watery plain,
In Argob and in Basan, to the stream
Of utmost Arnon. Nor content with such
Audacious neighborhood, the wisest heart   400
Of Solomon he led by fraud to build
His temple right against the temple of God
On that opprobrious hill, and made his grove
The pleasant valley of Hinnom, Tophet thence

386–87. throned Between the Cherubim. Cf. Ps. 80:1. The reference is to the golden figures placed over the Ark of the Covenant.

392 ff. First Moloch, etc. The list of the principal demons is parallel to Homer's catalogue of the ships (*Iliad* ii. 484 ff.) and Virgil's of the Trojan warriors (*Aeneid* vii. 641 ff.). A new appeal to the Muse is made by both ancient authors at this point.

392. Moloch. Cf. II Kings 23:10, etc.

398–99. Argob, Basan, Arnon, all on the east side of the Jordan. These, like many of the other names in the passage, are used more for their suggestive sound than for their precise signification.

403. that opprobrious hill, the Mount of Olives, called after Solomon's offense "the mount of corruption." Cf. II Kings 23:13.

404. Hinnom, a ravine southwest of Jerusalem. **Tophet,** cf. II Kings 23:10; Jer. 7:31.

And black Gehenna called, the type of Hell.
Next Chemos, the óbscene dread of Moab's sons,
From Aroar to Nebo, and the wild
Of southmost Abarim; in Hesebon
And Horonaim, Seon's realm, beyond
The flowery dale of Sibma clad with vines, 410
And Elealè to the Asphaltic pool.
Peor his other name, when he enticed
Israel in Sittim on their march from Nile
To do him wanton rites, which cost them woe.
Yet thence his lustful orgies he enlarged
Even to that hill of scandal, by the grove
Of Moloch homicide, lust hard by hate;
Till good Josiah drove them thence to Hell.
With these came they, who from the bordering flood
Of old Euphrates to the brook that parts 420
Egypt from Syrian ground, had general names
Of Baalim and Ashtaroth, those male,
These feminine. For spirits when they please
Can either sex assume, or both; so soft
And uncompounded is their essence pure,
Not tied or manacled with joint or limb,
Nor founded on the brittle strength of bones,
Like cumbrous flesh; but in what shape they choose,
Dilated or condensed, bright or obscure,
Can execute their airy purposes, 430
And works of love or enmity fulfil.
For those the race of Israel oft forsook
Their living Strength, and unfrequented left
His righteous altar, bowing lowly down
To bestial gods; for which their heads as low
Bowed down in battle, sunk before the spear
Of despicable foes. With these in troop
Came Astoreth, whom the Phoenicians called
Astarte, Queen of Heaven, with crescent horns;
To whose bright image nightly by the moon 440
Sidonian virgins paid their vows and songs;
In Sion also not unsung, where stood

406. Chemos, the god of the Moabites, practically identical with Moloch.
407 ff. Aroar, etc., i.e. from the southern boundary of the Moabites to Mt. Nebo (Pisgah) on the north.
411. Asphaltic pool, the Dead Sea, so called from the asphalt or bitumen which it contains.
413–14. Cf. Num. 25:1–5. **418.** Cf. II Kings 23.
422. Baalim and Ashtaroth. The Phoenician and Canaanitish people worshiped Baal and Astoreth (Astarte) under various manifestations, collectively designated by the plurals ending in *-im* (masculine) and *-oth* (feminine).
425. uncompounded, simple, not mixed. Milton's idea is that the angelic substance belongs to the realm of the abstract and general rather than of the concrete and particular. This Platonic notion underlies his whole representation of heaven.
439. Astarte, a moon goddess, also symbolized by the planet Venus. She was the counterpart of the Greek Aphrodite.

Her temple on the offensive mountain, built
By that uxorious king, whose heart though large,
Beguiled by fair idolatresses, fell
To idols foul. Thammuz came next behind,
Whose annual wound in Lebanon allured
The Syrian damsels to lament his fate
In amorous ditties all a summer's day,
While smooth Adonis from his native rock   450
Ran purple to the sea, supposed with blood
Of Thammuz yearly wounded: the love-tale
Infected Sion's daughters with like heat,
Whose wanton passions in the sacred porch
Ezekiel saw, when by the vision led
His eye surveyed the dark idolatries
Of alienated Judah. Next came one
Who mourned in earnest, when the captive ark
Maimed his brute image, head and hands lopt off
In his own temple, on the grunsel edge,   460
Where he fell flat, and shamed his worshippers:
Dagon his name, sea monster, upward man
And downward fish; yet had his temple high
Reared in Azotus, dreaded through the coast
Of Palestine, in Gath and Ascalon,
And Accaron and Gaza's frontier bounds.
Him followed Rimmon, whose delightful seat
Was fair Damascus, on the fertile banks
Of Abbana and Pharphar, lucid streams.
He also against the house of God was bold;   470
A leper once he lost and gained a king,
Ahaz his sottish conqueror, whom he drew
God's altar to disparage and displace
For one of Syrian mode, whereon to burn
His odious offerings, and adore the gods
Whom he had vanquished. After these appeared
A crew who under names of old renown,
Osiris, Isis, Orus, and their train,

444. That uxorious king, Solomon. Cf. I Kings 11:1–5.
446. Thammuz, identical with the Greek Adonis, was god of the solar year and symbol of fertility. Mourning for his death in the autumn and rejoicing at his revival in the spring were important Pagan ceremonials in Babylonia and Phoenicia, and later in Egypt and Greece.
450. Adonis. The reference here is not to the god himself but to a small river rising in the Lebanon mountains. Its discoloration by red sediment occasioned the belief to which Milton alludes.
456. dark, secret.
457 ff. Cf. I Sam. 5:1–5. Dagon was the national god of the Philistines.
460. grunsel, ground-sill, threshold.
464 ff. Azotus, Gath, Ascalon, Accaron, Gaza, the five chief cities of the Philistines.
467. Rimmon, a Syrian deity.   **471. a leper,** Naaman. Cf. II Kings 5.
472. Ahaz, a king of Judah. Cf. II Kings 16.
478. Osiris, the chief male deity of the Egyptians, was worshiped under the form of a sacred bull. **Isis,** the sister and wife of Osiris, was represented with the head or horns of a cow. **Orus,** or Horus, son of Osiris and Isis, was generally represented with the head of a hawk.

With monstrous shapes and sorceries abused
Fanatic Egypt and her priests, to seek   480
Their wandering gods disguised in brutish forms
Rather than human. Nor did Israel scape
The infection, when their borrowed gold composed
The calf in Oreb; and the rebel king
Doubled that sin in Bethel and in Dan,
Likening his Maker to the grazèd ox,
Jehovah, who in one night when he passed
From Egypt marching, equalled with one stroke
Both her first-born and all her bleating gods.
Belial came last, than whom a spirit more lewd   490
Fell not from Heaven, or more gross to love
Vice for itself. To him no temple stood
Or altar smoked; yet who more oft than he
In temples and at altars, when the priest
Turns atheist, as did Eli's sons, who filled
With lust and violence the house of God.
In courts and palaces he also reigns
And in luxurious cities, where the noise
Of riot ascends above their loftiest towers,
And injury and outrage; and when night   500
Darkens the streets, then wander forth the sons
Of Belial, flown with insolence and wine.
Witness the streets of Sodom, and that night
In Gibeah, when the hospitable door
Exposed a matron, to avoid worse rape.
    These were the prime in order and in might;
The rest were long to tell, though far renowned,
The Ionian gods, of Javan's issue held
Gods, yet confessed later than Heaven and Earth,
Their boasted parents; Titan, Heaven's first-born,   510
With his enormous brood, and birthright seized
By younger Saturn; he from mightier Jove,
His own and Rhea's son, like measure found;
So Jove usurping reigned. These, first in Crete

---

479. abused, deceived.
482 ff. Cf. Exod. 32. The borrowed gold was that taken from the Egyptians (Exod. 12:35).
484. the rebel king, Jeroboam. Cf. I Kings 12:28, 29.   **487 ff.** Cf. Exod. 12:29.
490 ff. Belial was not originally a proper name, but an abstract noun meaning "wickedness." In the New Testament it is sometimes used as synonymous with Satan: e.g., in II Cor. 6:15. Milton makes Belial the embodiment of effeminacy and lust, far more depraved than Satan.
493–505. These famous lines suggest conditions under Charles II but could apply more generally. The biblical term "sons of Belial" was common in the mouth of Puritans.
495. Eli's sons. Cf. I Sam. 2:12 ff.
502. flown, flushed (literally), and swollen (metaphorically).
505. Cf. Gen. 19:4–8; Judg. 19:22–24.
508. Ionian, Greek (the word being used generically). **Javan's issue,** the offspring of Javan, son of Japheth (cf. Gen. 10:2); i.e., the Greeks.
509. confessed later, i.e., admitted to be of later origin. The Greeks themselves made Heaven and Earth the ancestors of their deities.
510. Titan, here specifically Oceanus, eldest of the Titans.

And Ida known, thence on the snowy top
Of cold Olympus ruled the middle air,
Their highest Heaven; or on the Delphian cliff,
Or in Dodona, and through all the bounds
Of Doric land; or who with Saturn old
Fled over Adria to the Hesperian fields,   520
And o'er the Celtic roamed the utmost isles.

All these and more came flocking; but with looks
Downcast and damp, yet such wherein appeared
Obscure some glimpse of joy, to have found their Chief
Not in despair, to have found themselves not lost
In loss itself; which on his countenance cast
Like doubtful hue. But he, his wonted pride
Soon recollecting, with high words that bore
Semblance of worth, not substance, gently raised
Their fainting courage, and dispelled their fears.   530
Then straight commands that, at the warlike sound
Of trumpets loud and clarions, be upreared
His mighty standard; that proud honor claimed
Azazel as his right, a Cherub tall;
Who forthwith from the glittering staff unfurled
The imperial ensign, which full high advanced
Shone like a meteor streaming to the wind,
With gems and golden luster rich emblazed,
Seraphic arms and trophies; all the while
Sonorous metal blowing martial sounds;   540
At which the universal host up sent
A shout that tore Hell's concave, and beyond
Frighted the reign of Chaos and old Night.
All in a moment through the gloom were seen
Ten thousand banners rise into the air
With orient colors waving; with them rose
A forest huge of spears; and thronging helms
Appeared, and serried shields in thick array
Of depth immeasurable. Anon they move

---

515. Ida, the reputed birthplace of Jove.
516. middle air. The older phyics divided the air into three regions.
517. Delphian cliff. Mount Parnassus above Delphi, seat of the famous oracle of Apollo.
520. Adria, the Adriatic Sea. **Hesperian fields,** Italy.
521. Celtic. The noun "fields" is understood from the preceding line. **the utmost isles,** Britain.
531 ff. Then straight commands, etc. Milton represents the host of Satan as an army disciplined according to the military science of the ancients. **Phalanx** (l. 550 ff.) is the Greek term for battalion. The **Dorian mood** is one of three modes or scales of ancient Greek music; it is represented by Plato (*Republic* iii. 399) as fittest to inspire valor. **Flutes** (of which the **recorder** is a variety) are mentioned by Thucydides as the instruments to the sound of which the Spartans marched to battle. **Soft** seems like an inappropriate adjective, but Milton's idea is that the highest courage is not a furor of the blood but a temperate resolution of the soul inspired by thoughtfulness. The music also helps to reconcile the fallen angels to their lot. A whole philosophy of art in its relation to action is implied in these lines.
536. advanced, uplifted.   **543. reign,** kingdom.
546. orient, bright, lustrous.   **548. serried,** locked together.

In perfect phalanx to the Dorian mood 550
Of flutes and soft recorders; such as raised
To height of noblest temper heroes old
Arming to battle, and instead of rage
Deliberate valor breathed, firm and unmoved
With dread of death to flight or foul retreat;
Nor wanting power to mitigate and swage
With solemn touches troubled thoughts, and chase
Anguish and doubt and fear and sorrow and pain
From mortal or immortal minds. Thus they,
Breathing united force with fixëd thought, 560
Moved on in silence to soft pipes that charmed
Their painful steps o'er the burnt soil; and now
Advanced in view they stand, a horrid front
Of dreadful length and dazzling arms, in guise
Of warriors old, with ordered spear and shield,
Awaiting what command their mighty Chief
Had to impose. He through the armëd files
Darts his experienced eye, and soon traverse
The whole battalion views, their order due,
Their visages and stature as of gods; 570
Their number last he sums. And now his heart
Distends with pride, and hardening in his strength
Glories; for never since created Man,
Met such embodied force, as named with these
Could merit more than that small infantry
Warred on by cranes: though all the giant brood
Of Phlegra with the heroic race were joined
That fought at Thebes and Ilium, on each side
Mixed with auxiliar gods; and what resounds
In fable or romance of Uther's son 580
Begirt with British and Armoric knights;
And all who since, baptized or infidel,
Jousted in Aspramont, or Montalban,

563. horrid, bristling.

567 ff. Satan glances first along the files from front to rear, then along the ranks from right to left.

573. since created man, i.e., since man's creation.

575. that small infantry, the Pigmies, whose unsuccessful struggle with the cranes is mentioned by Homer (*Iliad* iii. 3–6). Milton says that compared to Satan's host all the famous hosts of legend joined together would be as insignificant as a Pigmy army. **Infantry** may be a pun.

577. Phlegra, the scene of the battle between the giants and the gods.

579. on each . . . gods. In the *Iliad* and elsewhere, the gods are represented as joining with the Greeks and Trojans in battle.

580. Uther's son, King Arthur.

581. British and Armoric knights. Some of Arthur's knights came from the island of Britain, some from the peninsula of Armorica, modern Brittany.

583 ff. The references here are to places celebrated in the wars of the Christians and Saracens as narrated in the Italian romances, notably in Ariosto's *Orlando Furioso*. **Aspramont** and **Montalban** were in France, **Trebisond** in Asia Minor. Charlemagne was not killed at Fontarabbia as these lines seem to imply. But the rear-guard of his army was cut to pieces in the pass of Roncesvalles (about forty miles from Fontarabbia), and among those slain was Roland (Orlando), the most famous of his twelve "peers."

Damasco, or Marocco, or Trebisond,
Or whom Biserta sent from Afric shore
When Charlemain with all his peerage fell
By Fontarabbia. Thus far these beyond
Compare of mortal prowess, yet observed
Their dread commander. He above the rest
In shape and gesture proudly eminent   590
Stood like a tower; his form had yet not lost
All her original brightness, nor appeared
Less than Archangel ruined, and the excess
Of glory obscured: as when the sun new-risen
Looks through the horizontal misty air
Shorn of his beams, or from behind the moon
In dim eclipse disastrous twilight sheds
On half the nations, and with fear of change
Perplexes monarchs. Darkened so, yet shone
Above them all the Archangel; but his face   600
Deep scars of thunder had intrenched, and care
Sat on his faded cheek, but under brows
Of dauntless courage, and considerate pride
Waiting revenge. Cruel his eye, but cast
Signs of remorse and passion to behold
The fellows of his crime, the followers rather
(Far other once beheld in bliss), condemned
For ever now to have their lot in pain,
Millions of spirits for his fault amerced
Of Heaven, and from eternal splendors flung   610
For his revolt, yet faithful how they stood,
Their glory withered: as when Heaven's fire
Hath scathed the forest oaks or mountain pines,
With singèd top their stately growth though bare
Stands on the blasted heath. He now prepared
To speak; whereat their doubled ranks they bend
From wing to wing, and half enclose him round
With all his peers: attention held them mute.
Thrice he assayed, and thrice in spite of scorn,
Tears such as angels weep, burst forth; at last   620
Words interwove with sighs found out their way.
  "O myriads of immortal spirits, O Powers
Matchless, but with the Almighty, and that strife
Was not inglorious, though the event was dire,
As this place testifies, and this dire change
Hateful to utter. But what power of mind
Foreseeing or presaging, from the depth

594–99. **as when the sun ... monarchs.** According to John Toland, these lines were
objected to by the censor as suggesting a prophecy of the downfall of Charles II.
  603. **considerate,** well-considered, thoughtful.
  605. **remorse and passion,** pity and intense sorrow.
  609. **amerced of,** deprived of as if by a fine.   624. **event,** outcome.

Of knowledge past or present, could have feared
How such united force of gods, how such
As stood like these, could ever know repulse?   630
For who can yet believe, though after loss,
That all these puissant legions, whose exile
Hath emptied Heaven, shall fail to re-ascend
Self-raised, and re-possess their native seat.
For me, be witness all the host of Heaven,
If counsels different, or danger shunned
By me, have lost our hopes. But he who reigns
Monarch in Heaven, till then as one secure
Sat on his throne, upheld by old repute,
Consent or custom, and his regal state   640
Put forth at full, but still his strength concealed,
Which tempted our attempt, and wrought our fall.
Henceforth his might we know, and know our own,
So as not either to provoke, or dread
New war provoked; our better part remains
To work in close design, by fraud or guile
What force effected not; that he no less
At length from us may find, who overcomes
By force, hath overcome but half his foe.
Space may produce new worlds; whereof so rife   650
There went a fame in Heaven that he ere long
Intended to create, and therein plant
A generation, whom his choice regard
Should favor equal to the sons of Heaven.
Thither, if but to pry, shall be perhaps
Our first eruption, thither or elsewhere;
For this infernal pit shall never hold
Celestial spirits in bondage, nor the Abyss
Long under darkness cover. But these thoughts
Full counsel must mature. Peace is despaired,   660
For who can think submission! War then, war
Open or understood, must be resolved."
   He spake; and to confirm his words, out flew
Millions of flaming swords, drawn from the thighs
Of mighty Cherubim; the sudden blaze
Far round illumined Hell. Highly they raged
Against the Highest, and fierce with graspèd arms
Clashed on their sounding shields the din of war,
Hurling defiance toward the vault of Heaven.
   There stood a hill not far, whose grisly top   670
Belched fire and rolling smoke; the rest entire
Shone with a glossy scurf, undoubted sign

---

   646 ff. In turning from **force** to **close design,** Satan shows his familiarity with the two well-recognized Machiavellian methods of gaining power.
   651. fame, rumor.   **660. despaired,** i.e., despaired of.

That in his womb was hid metallic ore,
The work of sulphur. Thither winged with speed
A numerous brigad hastened: as when bands
Of pioneers with spade and pickaxe armed
Forerun the royal camp, to trench a field,
Or cast a rampart. Mammon led them on,
Mammon, the least erected spirit that fell
From Heaven, for even in Heaven his looks and thoughts   680
Were always downward bent, admiring more
The riches of Heaven's pavement, trodden gold,
Than aught divine or holy else enjoyed
In vision beatific. By him first
Men also, and by his suggestion taught,
Ransacked the center, and with impious hands
Rifled the bowels of their mother Earth
For treasures better hid. Soon had his crew
Opened into the hill a spacious wound
And digged out ribs of gold. Let none admire   690
That riches grow in Hell; that soil may best
Deserve the precious bane. And here let those
Who boast in mortal things, and wondering tell
Of Babel, and the works of Memphian kings,
Learn how their greatest monuments of fame,
And strength, and art, are easily outdone
By spirits reprobate, and in an hour
What in an age they with incessant toil
And hands innumerable scarce perform.
Nigh on the plain, in many cells prepared,   700
That underneath had veins of liquid fire
Sluiced from the lake, a second multitude
With wondrous art founded the massy ore,
Severing each kind, and scummed the bullion dross.
A third as soon had formed within the ground
A various mould, and from the boiling cells
By strange conveyance filled each hollow nook,
As in an organ from one blast of wind
To many a row of pipes the sound-board breathes.
Anon out of the earth a fabric huge   710
Rose like an exhalation, with the sound

674. **The work of sulphur.** Sulphur and quicksilver were held by the alchemists to be the
"parents" of the metals.

676. **pioneers,** engineers.

678. **Mammon.** The word was originally a common noun, meaning "riches." Cf. Matt.
6:24; Luke 16:9–13.

679. **erected,** high-souled, noble.

684. **vision beatific.** *Visio beatifica* was the phrase regularly used by medieval theologians to
describe the experience of "seeing" God.

690. **admire,** wonder.

694. **Babel.** Cf. Gen. 11:1–9. **the works of Memphian kings,** i.e., the Pyramids of the
Pharaohs. **Memphian** is equivalent to Egyptian, as in 307 above.

703. **founded,** fused, melted.

Of dulcet symphonies and voices sweet,
Built like a temple, where pilasters round
Were set, and Doric pillars overlaid
With golden architrave; nor did there want
Cornice or frieze with bossy sculptures graven;
The roof was fretted gold. Not Babylon,
Nor great Alcairo such magnificence
Equalled in all their glories, to enshrine
Belus or Serapis their gods, or seat   720
Their kings, when Egypt with Assyria strove
In wealth and luxury. The ascending pile
Stood fixed her stately height, and straight the doors
Opening their brazen folds discover wide
Within, her ample spaces, o'er the smooth
And level pavement; from the archëd roof
Pendent by subtle magic many a row
Of starry lamps and blazing cressets fed
With naphtha and asphaltus yielded light
As from a sky. The hasty multitude   730
Admiring entered, and the work some praise,
And some the architect: his hand was known
In Heaven by many a towered structure high,
Where sceptred angels held their residence,
And sat as princes, whom the supreme King
Exalted to such power, and gave to rule,
Each in his Hierarchy, the Orders bright.
Nor was his name unheard or unadored
In ancient Greece; and in Ausonian land
Men called him Mulciber; and how he fell   740
From Heaven, they fabled, thrown by angry Jove
Sheer o'er the crystal battlements: from morn
To noon he fell, from noon to dewy eve,
A summer's day; and with the setting sun
Dropped from the zenith like a falling star,
On Lemnos the Ægæan isle. Thus they relate,
Erring; for he with this rebellious rout
Fell long before; nor aught availed him now

713 ff. Built like . . . gold. Note Milton's careful use of architectural terms to suggest the style of an ancient Greek temple. It has been plausibly suggested that he had also in mind Saint Peter's Church in Rome. **Pilasters** are square columns supporting the master beam or **architrave,** on which are placed the **frieze** and **cornice.** By **bossy sculptures** are meant figures or ornaments projected in relief. The roof of **fretted gold** is one adorned with inwrought patterns.
718. Alcairo, the ancient city of Memphis, near the site of modern Cairo.
720. Belus, the god Bel or Baal, whose great temple at Babylon is mentioned by Herodotus (*History* i. 181–83). **Serapis,** an Egyptian deity practically identified with Osiris. The most famous of his temples was at Alexandria, but there was also one at Memphis.
732 ff. the architect. Milton is alluding to the Greek god Hephaestus (the Roman Vulcan or Mulciber), who built the palaces on Olympus.
737. Milton accepts the medieval idea of the angelic hierarchies without going into detail about it.
739. Ausonian land, Italy.

To have built in Heaven high towers; nor did he scape
By all his engines, but was headlong sent   750
With his industrious crew to build in Hell.
    Meanwhile the wingèd heralds by command
Of sovran power, with awful ceremony
And trumpet's sound, throughout the host proclaim
A solemn council forthwith to be held
At Pandemonium, the high capitol
Of Satan and his peers; their summons called
From every band and squarèd regiment
By place or choice the worthiest; they anon
With hundreds and with thousands trooping came   760
Attended. All access was thronged, the gates
And porches wide, but chief the spacious hall
(Though like a covered field, where champions bold
Wont ride in armed, and at the Soldan's chair
Defied the best of Paynim chivalry
To mortal combat or career with lance)
Thick swarmed, both on the ground and in the air,
Brushed with the hiss of rustling wings. As bees
In spring time, when the sun with Taurus rides,
Pour forth their populous youth about the hive   770
In clusters; they among fresh dews and flowers
Fly to and fro, or on the smoothèd plank,
The suburb of their straw-built citadel,
New rubbed with balm, expatiate and confer
Their state affairs. So thick the airy crowd
Swarmed and were straitened; till the signal given,
Behold a wonder! they but now who seemed
In bigness to surpass Earth's giant sons,
Now less than smallest dwarfs, in narrow room
Throng numberless, like that Pygmean race   780
Beyond the Indian mount, or fairy elves,
Whose midnight revels, by a forest side
Or fountain, some belated peasant sees,
Or dreams he sees, while overhead the Moon
Sits arbitress, and nearer to the Earth
Wheels her pale course; they on their mirth and dance
Intent, with jocund music charm his ear;

750. **engines,** devices, inventions.   753. **awful,** awe-inspiring.
    756. **Pandemonium,** the abode of all the demons. The name, which is a Miltonic coinage, may have been suggested by *Pantheon,* the abode of all the gods.
    757 ff. **their summons,** etc. The council is in reality a sort of military Parliament.
    763–66. The allusion is to the single combats between Pagans and Crusaders described in the Italian romances of chivalry. **Soldan** is a variant of Sultan.
    769. **when the Sun with Taurus rides,** i.e., when the sun is in the zodiacal sign of the Bull (between April 19 and May 20).
    774. **expatiate and confer,** walk abroad and discuss.   776. **straitened,** crowded.
    780 ff. See note on 575 above. The **Indian mount** is probably Imaus in the Himalayas.
    781 ff. Milton is here drawing on the traditions of English fairy poetry.
    785. **arbitress,** spectator.

At once with joy and fear his heart rebounds.
Thus incorporeal spirits to smallest forms
Reduced their shapes immense, and were at large, 790
Though without number still, amidst the hall
Of that infernal court. But far within,
And in their own dimensions like themselves,
The great Seraphic Lords and Cherubim
In close recess and secret conclave sat,
A thousand demi-gods on golden seats,
Frequent and full. After short silence then
And summons read, the great consult began.

BOOK II

THE ARGUMENT

The consultation begun, Satan debates whether another battle is to be hazarded for the recovery of Heaven: some advise it, others dissuade. A third proposal is preferred, mentioned before by Satan, to search the truth of that prophecy or tradition in Heaven concerning another world, and another kind of creature, equal, or not much inferior, to themselves, about this time to be created. Their doubt who shall be sent on this difficult search; Satan, their chief, undertakes alone the voyage; is honoured and applauded. The council thus ended, the rest betake them several ways and to several employments, as their inclinations lead them, to entertain the time till Satan return. He passes on his journey to Hell gates, finds them shut, and who sat there to guard them; by whom at length they are opened, and discover to him the great gulf between Hell and Heaven; with what difficulty he passes through, directed by Chaos, the Power of that place, to the sight of this new world which he sought.

High on a throne of royal state, which far
Outshone the wealth of Ormus and of Ind,
Or where the gorgeous East with richest hand
Showers on her kings barbaric pearl and gold,
Satan exalted sat, by merit raised
To that bad eminence; and from despair
Thus high uplifted beyond hope, aspires
Beyond thus high, insatiate to pursue
Vain war with Heaven, and by success untaught,
His proud imaginations thus displayed. 10
    "Powers and Dominions, Deities of Heaven,
For since no deep within her gulf can hold
Immortal vigor, though oppressed and fallen,

---

790. were at large, had ample room.   **793. like themselves,** i.e., in their own shapes.
795. recess, retirement.   **797. frequent,** crowded.
    2. Ormus, a city on the Persian Gulf, famous as a market for precious stones. It is often mentioned by Renaissance travelers. **Ind,** India.
    4. barbaric pearl and gold. The sprinkling of powdered pearls and gold dust on a monarch at his coronation was an Oriental custom.
    9. success, i.e., ill-success, the outcome of his former attempt.

I give not Heaven for lost. From this descent
Celestial Virtues rising, will appear
More glorious and more dread than from no fall,
And trust themselves to fear no second fate.
Me though just right, and the fixed laws of Heaven
Did first create your leader, next, free choice,
With what besides, in counsel or in fight,   20
Hath been achieved of merit, yet this loss
Thus far at least recovered, hath much more
Established in a safe unenvied throne
Yielded with full consent. The happier state
In Heaven, which follows dignity, might draw
Envy from each inferior; but who here
Will envy whom the highest place exposes
Foremost to stand against the Thunderer's aim
Your bulwark, and condemns to greatest share
Of endless pain? Where there is then no good   30
For which to strive, no strife can grow up there
From faction; for none sure will claim in Hell
Precedence, none whose portion is so small
Of present pain, that with ambitious mind
Will covet more. With this advantage then
To union, and firm faith, and firm accord,
More than can be in Heaven, we now return
To claim our just inheritance of old,
Surer to prosper than prosperity
Could have assured us; and by what best way,   40
Whether of open war or covert guile,
We now debate; who can advise, may speak."
        He ceased, and next him Moloch, sceptred king,
Stood up, the strongest and the fiercest spirit
That fought in Heaven; now fiercer by despair.
His trust was with the Eternal to be deemed
Equal in strength, and rather than be less
Cared not to be at all; with that care lost
Went all his fear: of God, or Hell, or worse
He recked not, and these words thereafter spake.   50
        "My sentence is for open war. Of wiles,
More unexpert, I boast not; them let those
Contrive who need, or when they need, not now.
For while they sit contriving, shall the rest,
Millions that stand in arms, and longing wait

---

17. trust themselves, etc., i.e., their experience has given them such confidence that they
will not fear to fall again.
        24 ff. Satan, like Belial (112 ff.), knows how to "make the worse appear the better reason."
        50. thereafter spake, spoke accordingly.
        51. sentence, judgment, opinion (Latin *sententia*). Moloch is the type of blunt warrior who
knows no other method of winning an object than to fight for it. Milton must have known such
among the leaders of the Commonwealth.

The signal to ascend, sit lingering here
Heaven's fugitives, and for their dwelling-place
Accept this dark opprobrious den of shame,
The prison of his tyranny who reigns
By our delay? No, let us rather choose, 60
Armed with Hell flames and fury, all at once
O'er Heaven's high towers to force resistless way,
Turning our tortures into horrid arms
Against the Torturer; when to meet the noise
Of his almighty engine he shall hear
Infernal thunder, and for lightning see
Black fire and horror shot with equal rage
Among his angels, and his throne itself
Mixed with Tartarean sulphur and strange fire,
His own invented torments. But perhaps 70
The way seems difficult and steep to scale
With upright wing against a higher foe.
Let such bethink them, if the sleepy drench
Of that forgetful lake benumb not still,
That in our proper motion we ascend
Up to our native seat; descent and fall
To us is adverse. Who but felt of late
When the fierce foe hung on our broken rear
Insulting, and pursued us through the deep,
With what compulsion and laborious flight 80
We sunk thus low? The ascent is easy then;
The event is feared; should we again provoke
Our stronger, some worse way his wrath may find
To our destruction; if there be in Hell
Fear to be worse destroyed; what can be worse
Than to dwell here, driven out from bliss, condemned
In this abhorrëd deep to utter woe;
Where pain of unextinguishable fire
Must exercise us without hope of end
The vassals of his anger, when the scourge 90
Inexorably, and the torturing hour
Calls us to penance? More destroyed than thus
We should be quite abolished and expire.
What fear we then? what doubt we to incense

63. **tortures,** i.e., the flames which torture.
65. **engine,** instrument—referring to the thunderbolt.
69. **Tartarean,** infernal (from Tartarus, a classical name for hell).
73. **such,** i.e., those who reason thus. **sleepy drench,** sleep-producing drink. The word **drench** suggests contempt.
74. **forgetful,** causing forgetfulness. Cf. I, 266 and note.
75–77. The natural (**proper**) motion of Spirits, as of fire, is upward. For them to fall is therefore unnatural (**adverse**).
79. **Insulting.** The original Latin meaning (*insultans,* leaping upon) is implied.
82. **event,** outcome (as in I, 624). 89. **exercise,** torment.
94. **what doubt we,** i.e., why do we hesitate.

His utmost ire? which to the height enraged,
Will either quite consume us, and reduce
To nothing this essential, happier far
Than miserable to have eternal being;
Or if our substance be indeed divine,
And cannot cease to be, we are at worst   100
On this side nothing; and by proof we feel
Our power sufficient to disturb his Heaven,
And with perpetual inroads to alarm,
Though inaccessible, his fatal throne;
Which if not victory is yet revenge."
He ended frowning, and his look denounced
Desperate revenge, and battle dangerous
To less than gods. On the other side up rose
Belial, in act more graceful and humane;
A fairer person lost not Heaven; he seemed   110
For dignity composed and high exploit;
But all was false and hollow; though his tongue
Dropped manna, and could make the worse appear
The better reason, to perplex and dash
Maturest counsels: for his thoughts were low;
To vice industrious, but to nobler deeds
Timorous and slothful: yet he pleased the ear,
And with persuasive accent thus began.
   "I should be much for open war, O Peers,
As not behind in hate, if what was urged   120
Main reason to persuade immediate war,
Did not dissuade me most, and seem to cast
Ominous conjecture on the whole success:
When he who most excels in fact of arms,
In what he counsels and in what excels
Mistrustful, grounds his courage on despair
And utter dissolution, as the scope
Of all his aim, after some dire revenge.
First, what revenge? The towers of Heaven are filled
With armèd watch, that render all access   130
Impregnable; oft on the bordering deep
Encamp their legions, or with óbscure wing
Scout far and wide into the realm of Night,
Scorning surprise. Or could we break our way
By force, and at our heels all Hell should rise
With blackest insurrection, to confound

   97. essential, essence, spiritual being.
   104. fatal, upheld by fate. Admitting that the throne is so upheld, Moloch is forced to grant
its inaccessibility.
   106. denounced, proclaimed.   **109. act,** bearing.
   113. manna. Cf. Exod. 16:31: "the taste of it was like wafers made with honey."
   119 ff. Cf. with the abrupt beginning of Moloch's speech the insinuating oratory of Belial.
Like a skilled debater, he turns his opponent's own argument against him.
   124. fact of arms, feat of arms (Latin *factum*, deed).
   136. blackest insurrection. Cf. 65–70. Belial answers Moloch point by point.

Heaven's purest light, yet our great enemy
All incorruptible would on his throne
Sit unpolluted, and the ethereal mould
Incapable of stain would soon expel   140
Her mischief, and purge off the baser fire,
Victorious. Thus repulsed, our final hope
Is flat despair; we must exasperate
The almighty victor to spend all his rage,
And that must end us, that must be our cure,
To be no more; sad cure; for who would lose,
Though full of pain, this intellectual being,
Those thoughts that wander through eternity,
To perish rather, swallowed up and lost
In the wide womb of uncreated Night,   150
Devoid of sense and motion? And who knows,
Let this be good, whether our angry foe
Can give it, or will ever? How he can
Is doubtful; that he never will is sure.
Will he, so wise, let loose at once his ire,
Belike through impotence, or unaware,
To give his enemies their wish, and end
Them in his anger, whom his anger saves
To punish endless? 'Wherefore cease we then?'
Say they who counsel war; 'we are decreed,   160
Reserved, and destined to eternal woe;
Whatever doing, what can we suffer more,
What can we suffer worse?' Is this then worst,
Thus sitting, thus consulting, thus in arms?
What when we fled amain, pursued and struck
With Heaven's afflicting thunder, and besought
The Deep to shelter us? this Hell then seemed
A refuge from those wounds. Or when we lay
Chained on the burning lake? that sure was worse.
What if the breath that kindled those grim fires   170
Awaked should blow them into sevenfold rage
And plunge us in the flames? or from above
Should intermitted vengeance arm again
His red right hand to plague us? What if all
Her stores were opened, and this firmament
Of Hell should spout her cataracts of fire,
Impendent horrors, threatening hideous fall
One day upon our heads; while we perhaps
Designing or exhorting glorious war,

---

139. mould, substance.
141. Her mischief, i.e., the damage or pollution caused by hell-fire.
152. Let this be good, i.e., granting that this (annihilation) is desirable.
156. Belike, no doubt. As frequently in Shakespeare, the word implies irony. **impotence,** lack of self-control.
165. What when, i.e., how was it when. **amain,** with all haste, precipitately.
177. impendent, overhanging.

Caught in a fiery tempest shall be hurled   180
Each on his rock transfixed, the sport and prey
Of racking whirlwinds, or for ever sunk
Under yon boiling ocean, wrapped in chains;
There to converse with everlasting groans,
Unrespited, unpitied, unreprieved,
Ages of hopeless end; this would be worse.
War therefore, open or concealed, alike
My voice dissuades; for what can force or guile
With him, or who deceive his mind, whose eye
Views all things at one view? He from Heaven's height   190
All these our motions vain, sees and derides;
Not more almighty to resist our might
Than wise to frustrate all our plots and wiles.
Shall we then live thus vile, the race of Heaven
Thus trampled, thus expelled to suffer here
Chains and these torments? Better these than worse,
By my advice; since fate inevitable
Subdues us, and omnipotent decree,
The victor's will. To suffer, as to do,
Our strength is equal, nor the law unjust   200
That so ordains: this was at first resolved,
If we were wise, against so great a foe
Contending, and so doubtful what might fall.
I laugh when those who at the spear are bold
And venturous, if that fail them, shrink and fear
What yet they know must follow, to endure
Exile, or ignominy, or bonds, or pain,
The sentence of their conqueror: this is now
Our doom; which if we can sustain and bear,
Our súpreme foe in time may much remit   210
His anger, and perhaps, thus far removed,
Not mind us not offending, satisfied
With what is punished; whence these raging fires
Will slacken, if his breath stir not their flames.
Our purer essence then will overcome
Their noxious vapor, or inured not feel,
Or changed at length, and to the place conformed
In temper and in nature, will receive
Familiar the fierce heat, and void of pain;
This horror will grow mild, this darkness light,   220
Besides what hope the never-ending flight
Of future days may bring, what chance, what change

182. **racking,** twisting, torturing.
185. Note how the repetition of the prefix intensifies the effect of utter hopelessness.
186. **of hopeless end,** without hope of end.   191. **motions,** proposals, plots.
213. **With what is punished,** i.e., with the punishment already inflicted.
219. **Familiar the fierce heat,** etc., i.e., the fierce heat, by becoming familiar, will be no longer painful. The considerations which move Belial are in complete accordance with his character and philosophy.

Worth waiting, since our present lot appears
For happy though but ill, for ill not worst,
If we procure not to ourselves more woe."
  Thus Belial with words clothed in reason's garb,
Counselled ignoble ease, and peaceful sloth,
Not peace; and after him thus Mammon spake.
  "Either to disenthrone the King of Heaven
We war, if war be best, or to regain   230
Our own right lost. Him to unthrone we then
May hope, when everlasting Fate shall yield
To fickle Chance, and Chaos judge the strife:
The former, vain to hope, argues as vain
The latter; for what place can be for us
Within Heaven's bound, unless Heaven's Lord supreme
We overpower? Suppose he should relent
And publish grace to all, on promise made
Of new subjection; with what eyes could we
Stand in his presence humble, and receive   240
Strict laws imposed, to celebrate his throne
With warbled hymns, and to his Godhead sing
Forced halleluiahs; while he lordly sits
Our envied Sovran, and his altar breathes
Ambrosial odors and ambrosial flowers,
Our servile offerings. This must be our task
In Heaven, this our delight; how wearisome
Eternity so spent in worship paid
To whom we hate. Let us not then pursue,
By force impossible, by leave obtained   250
Unacceptable, though in Heaven, our state
Of splendid vassalage, but rather seek
Our own good from ourselves, and from our own
Live to ourselves, though in this vast recess,
Free, and to none accountable, preferring
Hard liberty before the easy yoke
Of servile pomp. Our greatness will appear
Then most conspicuous, when great things of small,
Useful of hurtful, prosperous of adverse
We can create, and in what place soe'er   260
Thrive under evil, and work ease out of pain
Through labor and endurance. This deep world
Of darkness do we dread? How oft amidst
Thick clouds and dark doth Heaven's all-ruling Sire
Choose to reside, his glory unobscured,
And with the majesty of darkness round
Covers his throne; from whence deep thunders roar,
Mustering their rage, and Heaven resembles Hell!

---

  224. For happy, etc., i.e., viewed as a happy situation the present one is bad, but it is not so
bad as it might be.
  234. argues, proves.   **249. pursue,** seek to regain.

As he our darkness, cannot we his light
Imitate when we please? This desert soil   270
Wants not her hidden luster, gems and gold;
Nor want we skill or art, from whence to raise
Magnificence; and what can Heaven show more?
Our torments also may in length of time
Become our elements, these piercing fires
As soft as now severe, our temper changed
Into their temper; which must needs remove
The sensible of pain. All things invite
To peaceful counsels, and the settled state
Of order, how in safety best we may   280
Compose our present evils, with regard
Of what we are and where, dismissing quite
All thoughts of war: ye have what I advise."
   He scarce had finished, when such murmur filled
The assembly, as when hollow rocks retain
The sound of blustering winds, which all night long
Had roused the sea, now with hoarse cadence lull
Seafaring men o'erwatched, whose bark by chance
Or pinnace anchors in a craggy bay
After the tempest: such applause was heard   290
As Mammon ended, and his sentence pleased,
Advising peace; for such another field
They dreaded worse than Hell: so much the fear
Of thunder and the sword of Michaël
Wrought still within them; and no less desire
To found this nether empire, which might rise
By policy and long process of time,
In emulation opposite to Heaven.
Which when Beëlzebub perceived, than whom,
Satan except, none higher sat, with grave   300
Aspéct he rose, and in his rising seemed
A pillar of state; deep on his front engraven
Deliberation sat and public care;
And princely counsel in his face yet shone,
Majestic though in ruin: sage he stood,
With Atlantean shoulders fit to bear

   271. Wants not, is not without.
   278. sensible, sense. The use of an adjective for a noun is a Latinism which Milton frequently adopts.
   281. Compose, adjust.
   290 ff. such applause, etc. Mammon's proposal is an improvement on Belial's in that it supplies an activity consistent with the abandonment of a futile renewal of the attempt on Heaven. But the desire for revenge expressed by Moloch and felt by all the demons remains to be satisfied.
   299. Beëlzebub. Cf. I, 79–81 and note. In the Old Testament the name is applied to the sun-god of the Philistines.
   302. front, forehead.
   306. Atlantean shoulders, shoulders like those of Atlas, who in Greek mythology supported the heavens.

The weight of mightiest monarchies; his look
Drew audience and attention still as night
Or summer's noontide air, while thus he spake.
    "Thrones and imperial Powers, Offspring of Heaven,   310
Ethereal Virtues; or these titles now
Must we renounce, and changing style, be called
Princes of Hell? for so the popular vote
Inclines, here to continue, and build up here
A growing empire; doubtless; while we dream,
And know not that the King of Heaven hath doomed
This place our dungeon, not our safe retreat
Beyond his potent arm, to live exempt
From Heaven's high jurisdiction, in new league
Banded against his throne, but to remain   320
In strictest bondage, though thus far removed,
Under the inevitable curb, reserved
His captive multitude. For he, be sure,
In height or depth, still first and last will reign
Sole king, and of his kingdom lose no part
By our revolt, but over Hell extend
His empire, and with iron scepter rule
Us here, as with his golden those in Heaven.
What sit we then projecting peace and war?
War hath determined us, and foiled with loss   330
Irreparable; terms of peace yet none
Vouchsafed or sought; for what peace will be given
To us enslaved, but custody severe,
And stripes, and arbitrary punishment
Inflicted? and what peace can we return,
But to our power hostility and hate,
Untamed reluctance, and revenge though slow,
Yet ever plotting how the conqueror least
May reap his conquest, and may least rejoice
In doing what we must in suffering feel?   340
Nor will occasion want, nor shall we need
With dangerous expedition to invade
Heaven, whose high walls fear no assault or siege
Or ambush from the Deep. What if we find
Some easier enterprise? There is a place
(If ancient and prophetic fame in Heaven
Err not), another world, the happy seat
Of some new race called Man, about this time
To be created like to us, though less
In power and excellence, but favored more   350
Of him who rules above; so was his will

313. **the popular vote,** i.e., the state of opinion indicated by the applause given Mammon.
315. **doubtless.** The word is used sarcastically.
330. **determined us,** ended us or perhaps determined our future.
336. **to our power,** up to the limits of our power.
337. **Untamed reluctance,** untamable resistance.   346. **fame,** rumor.

Pronounced among the gods, and by an oath,
That shook Heaven's whole circumference, confirmed.
Thither let us bend all our thoughts, to learn
What creatures there inhabit, of what mould
Or substance, how endued, and what their power,
And where their weakness, how attempted best,
By force or subtlety. Though Heaven be shut,
And Heaven's high Arbitrator sit secure
In his own strength, this place may lie exposed,   360
The utmost border of his kingdom, left
To their defence who hold it; here perhaps
Some advantageous act may be achieved
By sudden onset, either with Hell fire
To waste his whole creation, or possess
All as our own, and drive as we were driven,
The puny habitants; or if not drive,
Seduce them to our party, that their God
May prove their foe, and with repenting hand
Abolish his own works. This would surpass   370
Common revenge, and interrupt his joy
In our confusion, and our joy upraise
In his disturbance; when his darling sons
Hurled headlong to partake with us, shall curse
Their frail original, and faded bliss,
Faded so soon. Advise if this be worth
Attempting, or to sit in darkness here
Hatching vain empires." Thus Beëlzebub
Pleaded his devilish counsel, first devised
By Satan, and in part proposed; for whence,   380
But from the author of all ill, could spring
So deep a malice, to confound the race
Of Mankind in one root, and Earth with Hell
To mingle and involve, done all to spite
The great Creator? But their spite still serves
His glory to augment. The bold design
Pleased highly those infernal States, and joy
Sparkled in all their eyes; with full assent
They vote: whereat his speech he thus renews.
    "Well have ye judged, well ended long debate,   390
Synod of gods, and like to what ye are,

354. Thither let us, etc. Beëlzebub's proposal does not exclude Mammon's, which had
itself appropriated Belial's; but it goes beyond both in supplying a rational project of revenge.
The whole movement of the discussion has been constructively forward toward the formation
of a policy satisfactory to all, and Beëlzebub, who is Satan's mouthpiece, has been simply
waiting the opportune moment to introduce Satan's own scheme. His intelligence is far more
comprehensive than that of the preceding speakers. It is easy to believe that Milton had been
present at deliberations of the Council of State, and that he had noted with care the play of
mind in them.
    356. endued, equipped.   **375. original,** originator, i.e., Adam.
    380. in part proposed, i.e., in his earlier speech, I, 645 ff.
    382. confound, destroy completely.   **387. States,** princes or representatives.

Great things resolved; which from the lowest deep
Will once more lift us up, in spite of Fate,
Nearer our ancient seat; perhaps in view
Of those bright confines, whence with neighboring arms
And opportune excursion we may chance
Re-enter Heaven; or else in some mild zone
Dwell not unvisited of Heaven's fair light
Secure, and at the brightening orient beam
Purge off this gloom; the soft delicious air,   400
To heal the scar of these corrosive fires
Shall breathe her balm. But first whom shall we send
In search of this new world? whom shall we find
Sufficient? who shall tempt with wandering feet
The dark unbottomed infinite Abyss
And through the palpable obscure find out
His uncouth way, or spread his aîry flight
Upborne with indefatigable wings
Over the vast abrupt, ere he arrive
The happy isle; what strength, what art can then   410
Suffice, or what evasion bear him safe
Through the strict senteries and stations thick
Of angels watching round? Here he had need
All circumspection, and we now no less
Choice in our suffrage; for on whom we send,
The weight of all and our last hope relies."
   This said, he sat; and expectation held
His look suspense, awaiting who appeared
To second, or oppose, or undertake
The perilous attempt; but all sat mute,   420
Pondering the danger with deep thoughts; and each
In other's countenance read his own dismay
Astonished; none among the choice and prime
Of those Heaven-warring champions could be found
So hardy as to proffer or accept
Alone the dreadful voyage; till at last
Satan, whom now transcendent glory raised
Above his fellows, with monarchal pride
Conscious of highest worth, unmoved thus spake.
   "O Progeny of Heaven, empyreal Thrones,   430
With reason hath deep silence and demur
Seized us, though undismayed. Long is the way
And hard, that out of Hell leads up to light;
Our prison strong, this huge convex of fire,
Outrageous to devour, immures us round

---

404. tempt, attempt, try.   **406. palpable obscure,** tangible darkness.
407. uncouth, unknown, strange.
409. the vast abrupt, the region of Chaos, which is a gulf or breach (Lat. *abruptum*), an emptiness.
412. stations, outposts, guards.   **415. choice in our suffrage,** care in our selection.
418. suspense, suspended.   **431. demur,** hesitation.

Ninefold, and gates of burning adamant
Barred over us prohibit all egress.
These passed, if any pass, the void profound
Of unessential Night receives him next
Wide gaping, and with utter loss of being   440
Threatens him, plunged in that abortive gulf.
If thence he scape into whatever world,
Or unknown region, what remains him less
Than unknown dangers and as hard escape.
But I should ill become this throne, O Peers,
And this imperial sovranty, adorned
With splendor, armed with power, if aught proposed
And judged of public moment, in the shape
Of difficulty or danger, could deter
Me from attempting. Wherefore do I assume   450
These royalties, and not refuse to reign,
Refusing to accept as great a share
Of hazard as of honor, due alike
To him who reigns, and so much to him due
Of hazard more, as he above the rest
High honored sits? Go therefore mighty Powers,
Terror of Heaven, though fallen; intend at home,
While here shall be our home, what best may ease
The present misery, and render Hell
More tolerable; if there be cure or charm   460
To respite or deceive, or slack the pain
Of this ill mansion; intermit no watch
Against a wakeful foe, while I abroad
Through all the coasts of dark destruction seek
Deliverance for us all: this enterprise
None shall partake with me." Thus saying rose
The Monarch, and prevented all reply;
Prudent, lest from his resolution raised
Others among the chief might offer now
(Certain to be refused) what erst they feared;   470
And so refused might in opinion stand
His rivals, winning cheap the high repute
Which he through hazard huge must earn. But they
Dreaded not more the adventure than his voice
Forbidding; and at once with him they rose;
Their rising all at once was as the sound

439. unessential, having no real being. Night and Chaos are thought of by Milton as merely negative, not really created.
441. abortive, prematurely brought forth and therefore unformed.
445 ff. But I should ill, etc. Satan's offer is parallel to that of Christ in III, 217 ff.
450. Me. Note the emphasis given by the meter.
457. intend, plan, consider.   **461. deceive,** beguile.
467. prevented, anticipated (a good example of the transition from the older, literal meaning of the word to the modern).
468. from his resolution raised, encouraged by his bravery.

Of thunder heard remote. Towards him they bend
With awful reverence prone; and as a god
Extol him equal to the Highest in Heaven.
Nor failed they to express how much they praised,   480
That for the general safety he despised
His own: for neither do the spirits damned
Lose all their virtue; lest bad men should boast
Their specious deeds on Earth, which glory excites,
Or close ambition varnished o'er with zeal.
    Thus they their doubtful consultations dark
Ended rejoicing in their matchless chief:
As when from mountain tops the dusky clouds
Ascending, while the North wind sleeps, o'erspread
Heaven's cheerful face, the louring element   490
Scowls o'er the darkened landscape snow or shower;
If chance the radiant sun with farewell sweet
Extend his evening beam, the fields revive,
The birds their notes renew, and bleating herds
Attest their joy, that hill and valley rings.
O shame to men! Devil with devil damned
Firm concord holds, men only disagree
Of creatures rational, though under hope
Of heavenly grace; and God proclaiming peace,
Yet live in hatred, enmity, and strife   500
Among themselves, and levy cruel wars,
Wasting the Earth, each other to destroy:
As if (which might induce us to accord)
Man had not hellish foes enow besides,
That day and night for his destruction wait!
    The Stygian council thus dissolved; and forth
In order came the grand infernal Peers;
Midst came their mighty Paramount, and seemed
Alone the antagonist of Heaven, nor less
Than Hell's dread Emperor, with pomp supreme,   510
And god-like imitated state; him round
A globe of fiery Seraphim enclosed
With bright emblazonry, and horrent arms.
Then of their session ended they bid cry
With trumpet's regal sound the great result.

477–79. This deification of Satan is a precedent for the idolatries of men.
   483. **virtue,** merit—but not moral goodness, for that, Milton would hold, is inconsistent with disobedience to God.
   484. **specious deeds,** deeds which, though having all the appearance of being public-spirited and self-sacrificing, are really the fruit of personal ambition masquerading as zeal for the common good. Under Milton's theory the demons can furnish a precedent for all that is great and magnanimous in men except the one essential of a righteous will. He never forgets that Satan and the rest are angels fallen.
   490. **element,** sky.   492. **If chance,** if it chances that.
   509. **Alone the antagonist,** i.e., worthy in himself to be the antagonist.
   512. **globe,** circle, as in the Roman military sense of *globus*.   513. **horrent,** bristling.

Toward the four winds four speedy Cherubim
Put to their mouths the sounding alchemy
By herald's voice explained; the hollow Abyss
Heard far and wide, and all the host of Hell
With deafening shout, returned them loud acclaim.   520
   Thence more at ease their minds and somewhat raised
By false presumptuous hope, the rangèd powers
Disband, and wandering, each his several way
Pursues, as inclination or sad choice
Leads him perplexed, where he may likeliest find
Truce to his restless thoughts, and entertain
The irksome hours, till his great chief return.
Part on the plain, or in the air sublime,
Upon the wing, or in swift race contend,
As at the Olympian games or Pythian fields;   530
Part curb their fiery steeds, or shun the goal
With rapid wheels, or fronted brigads form:
As when to warn proud cities war appears
Waged in the troubled sky, and armies rush
To battle in the clouds; before each van
Prick forth the airy knights, and couch their spears,
Till thickest legions close; with feats of arms
From either end of Heaven the welkin burns.
Others with vast Typhœan rage more fell
Rend up both rocks and hills, and ride the air   540
In whirlwind; Hell scarce holds the wild uproar:
As when Alcides from Œchalia crowned
With conquest, felt the envenomed robe, and tore
Through pain up by the roots Thessalian pines,
And Lichas from the top of Œta threw
Into the Euboic sea. Others more mild,
Retreated in a silent valley, sing
With notes angelical to many a harp
Their own heroic deeds and hapless fall
By doom of battle; and complain that Fate   550
Free Virtue should enthrall to Force or Chance.

    517. sounding alchemy, i.e., trumpets made of so-called "alchemy gold."
    523 ff. and wandering, etc. Milton makes the recreations of the demons parallel to those of men, and equally expressive of their various temperaments. The milder spirits are the poets and philosophers.
    528. sublime, aloft.
    530. The **Olympian games,** held every four years at Olympia in honor of Zeus, and the **Pythian,** held at Delphi in honor of Apollo (slayer of the Python), were the two great athletic festivals of ancient Greece.
    531. Part curb, etc. This is poetic diction for "engage in horse or chariot racing."
    532. fronted brigads form, i.e., to carry on a kind of mock combat or tourney.
    542. Alcides is another name for Hercules. Poisoned by a robe received from his wife, he in his agony hurled into the sea his companion, Lichas, who had brought the robe to him. Afterwards he ascended Mt. Œta in Thessaly, where he burned himself to death. Cf. Sophocles, *Trachiniae,* which opens with the news of Hercules' conquest of King Eurytus of Œchalia.
    551. Free Virtue, i.e., the individualistic expansion of the soul.

Their song was partial, but the harmony
(What could it less when spirits immortal sing?)
Suspended Hell, and took with ravishment
The thronging audience. In discourse more sweet
(For eloquence the soul, song charms the sense)
Others apart sat on a hill retired
In thoughts more elevate, and reasoned high
Of providence, foreknowledge, will, and fate,
Fixed fate, free will, foreknowledge absolute,   560
And found no end, in wandering mazes lost.
Of good and evil much they argued then,
Of happiness and final misery,
Passion and apathy, and glory and shame,
Vain wisdom all, and false philosophy;
Yet with a pleasing sorcery could charm
Pain for a while or anguish, and excite
Fallacious hope, or arm the obdurèd breast
With stubborn patience as with triple steel.
Another part, in squadrons and gross bands,   570
On bold adventure to discover wide
That dismal world, if any clime perhaps
Might yield them easier habitation, bend
Four ways their flying march, along the banks
Of four infernal rivers that disgorge
Into the burning lake their baleful streams;
Abhorrèd Styx, the flood of deadly hate;
Sad Acheron of sorrow, black and deep;
Cocytus, named of lamentation loud
Heard on the rueful stream; fierce Phlegethon,   580
Whose waves of torrent fire inflame with rage.
Far off from these a slow and silent stream,
Lethe, the river of oblivion, rolls
Her watery labyrinth, whereof who drinks
Forthwith his former state and being forgets,
Forgets both joy and grief, pleasure and pain.
Beyond this flood a frozen continent
Lies dark and wild, beat with perpetual storms
Of whirlwind and dire hail, which on firm land
Thaws not, but gathers heap, and ruin seems   590
Of ancient pile; all else deep snow and ice,

552. **partial,** imperfect, because they have lost their hold on the divine source of poetic truth. There is a reflection here of Milton's verdict on ancient pagan literature.

557 ff. **Others apart sat,** etc. Loss of true faith compels the invention of philosophy. The Stoic is most popular, as affording the best remedy in misfortune by its doctrine of **apathy** or insensibility to suffering.

568. **obdurèd,** hardened.   570. **gross,** compact.

577 ff. Milton, like Dante, provides for the four rivers of the classical Hades in his Christian hell. Lethe ("forgetfulness") is usually thought of as separate from the others, and Milton so represents it.

A gulf profound as that Serbonian bog
Betwixt Damiata and Mount Casius old,
Where armies whole have sunk; the parching air
Burns frore, and cold performs the effect of fire.
Thither by harpy-footed Furies haled,
At certain revolutions all the damned
Are brought; and feel by turns the bitter change
Of fierce extremes, extremes by change more fierce,
From beds of raging fire to starve in ice   600
Their soft ethereal warmth, and there to pine
Immovable, infixed, and frozen round,
Periods of time; thence hurried back to fire.
They ferry over this Lethean sound
Both to and fro, their sorrow to augment,
And wish and struggle, as they pass, to reach
The tempting stream, with one small drop to lose
In sweet forgetfulness all pain and woe,
All in one moment, and so near the brink;
But Fate withstands, and to oppose the attempt   610
Medusa with Gorgonian terror guards
The ford, and of itself the water flies
All taste of living wight, as once it fled
The lip of Tantalus. Thus roving on
In cónfused march forlorn, the adventurous bands,
With shuddering horror pale, and eyes aghast,
Viewed first their lamentable lot, and found
No rest. Through many a dark and dreary vale
They passed, and many a region dolorous,
O'er many a frozen, many a fiery Alp,   620
Rocks, caves, lakes, fens, bogs, dens, and shades of death,
A universe of death, which God by curse
Created evil, for evil only good,
Where all life dies, death lives, and Nature breeds,
Perverse, all monstrous, all prodigious things,
Abominable, inutterable, and worse
Than fables yet have feigned, or fear conceived,

592–93. The **Serbonian bog** is Lake Serbonis in Lower Egypt. **Damiata** (mentioned by Ariosto, Tasso, and Dante) is a city at the mouth of the Nile.
595. frore, frozen. Milton is fond of such contradictions as **burns frore.**
600. to starve in ice. The meaning is clearer than the grammar. They are moved from beds of fire to have their warmth perish (starve) in ice.
610 ff. Milton introduces into hell the monsters of classical mythology, apparently regarding them as native inhabitants at the time of the fallen angels' arrival.
611. Medusa, one of the three Gorgons, whose horrible countenances, crowned with snakes for hair, turned all beholders to stone.
614. Tantalus, a mythical king of Lydia, whose punishment in the lower world was to stand in a pool of water which receded whenever he tried to drink.
621. Note that the line is made up entirely of monosyllables. The effect is one of monotonous desolation.
625. prodigious, unnatural.

Gorgons and Hydras, and Chimæras dire.
   Meanwhile the Adversary of God and Man,
Satan with thoughts inflamed of highest design,   630
Puts on swift wings, and toward the gates of Hell
Explores his solitary flight; sometimes
He scours the right-hand coast, sometimes the left;
Now shaves with level wing the deep, then soars
Up to the fiery concave towering high.
As when far off at sea a fleet descried
Hangs in the clouds, by equinoctial winds
Close sailing from Bengala, or the isles
Of Ternate and Tidore, whence merchants bring
Their spicy drugs: they on the trading flood   640
Through the wide Ethiopian to the Cape,
Ply stemming nightly toward the pole. So seemed
Far off the flying Fiend. At last appear
Hell bounds high reaching to the horrid roof,
And thrice threefold the gates; three folds were brass,
Three iron, three of adamantine rock,
Impenetrable, impaled with circling fire,
Yet unconsumed. Before the gates there sat
On either side a formidable shape;
The one seemed woman to the waist, and fair,   650
But ended foul in many a scaly fold
Voluminous and vast, a serpent armed
With mortal sting. About her middle round
A cry of Hell-hounds never ceasing barked
With wide Cerberean mouths full loud, and rung
A hideous peal; yet, when they list, would creep,
If aught disturbed their noise, into her womb,
And kennel there, yet there still barked and howled
Within unseen. Far less abhorred than these
Vexed Scylla bathing in the sea that parts   660
Calabria from the hoarse Trinacrian shore;
Nor uglier follow the night-hag, when, called
In secret, riding through the air she comes,

---

628. The **Hydra** was a nine-headed serpent; the **Chimæra** a firebreathing monster, part lion, part goat, and part dragon. Cf. *Aeneid* vi.

637. equinoctial winds, the trade winds which blow from the east at the time of the equinoxes.

638. Close, i.e., in close formation or perhaps close-hauled. **Bengala,** Bengal.

639. Ternate and Tidore, two of the so-called "spice islands" or Moluccas.

641. the wide Ethiopian to the Cape, the Indian Ocean to the Cape of Good Hope.

642. stemming, pressing forward.   **647. impaled,** surrounded.

660. The rock Scylla is located in the Straits of Messina, between southern Italy **(Calabria)** and Sicily **(the Trinacrian shore)**. According to classical myth, Scylla was originally a beautiful nymph, who flung herself into the sea after being hideously transformed by the magic herbs of Circe.

662–66. There is much genuine witch superstition in this passage. The **night-hag** is Hecate, goddess of the underworld and of witchcraft.

Lured with the smell of infant blood, to dance
With Lapland witches, while the laboring moon
Eclipses at their charms. The other shape,
If shape it might be called that shape had none
Distinguishable in member, joint, or limb;
Or substance might be called that shadow seemed,
For each seemed either; black it stood as Night,   670
Fierce as ten Furies, terrible as Hell,
And shook a dreadful dart; what seemed his head
The likeness of a kingly crown had on.
Satan was now at hand, and from his seat
The monster moving onward came as fast,
With horrid strides; Hell trembled as he strode.
The undaunted Fiend what this might be admired,
Admired, not feared; God and his Son except,
Created thing nought valued he nor shunned;
And with disdainful look thus first began.   680
     "Whence and what art thou, execrable Shape,
That darest, though grim and terrible, advance
Thy miscreated front athwart my way
To yonder gates? Through them I mean to pass,
That be assured, without leave asked of thee.
Retire, or taste thy folly, and learn by proof,
Hell-born, not to contend with spirits of Heaven."
     To whom the goblin, full of wrath, replied:
"Art thou that traitor angel, art thou he,
Who first broke peace in Heaven and faith, till then   690
Unbroken, and in proud rebellious arms
Drew after him the third part of Heaven's sons
Conjured against the Highest, for which both thou
And they, outcast from God, are here condemned
To waste eternal days in woe and pain?
And reckon'st thou thyself with spirits of Heaven,
Hell-doomed, and breath'st defiance here and scorn
Where I reign king, and to enrage thee more,
Thy king and lord? Back to thy punishment,
False fugitive, and to thy speed add wings,   700
Lest with a whip of scorpions I pursue
Thy lingering, or with one stroke of this dart
Strange horror seize thee, and pangs unfelt before."
     So spake the grisly terror, and in shape,

---

     665. laboring moon. The epithet is based on the Latin use of *laborare* to mean "suffer eclipse."
     670. each seemed either, i.e., substance and shadow were indistinguishable.
     677. admired, wondered.
     678–79. not feared . . . shunned. Milton means that Satan feared *no* created thing, but only God and his Son.
     688. goblin, demon, fiend.   **693. conjured,** sworn together, banded by oath.
     697. Hell-doomed. Death uses the term in direct retort to Satan's "Hell-born" (687).

So speaking and so threatening, grew tenfold
More dreadful and deform. On the other side,
Incensed with indignation, Satan stood
Unterrified, and like a comet burned,
That fires the length of Ophiuchus huge
In the arctic sky, and from his horrid hair   710
Shakes pestilence and war. Each at the head
Levelled his deadly aim; their fatal hands
No second stroke intend; and such a frown
Each cast at the other, as when two black clouds
With Heaven's artillery fraught, come rattling on
Over the Caspian, then stand front to front
Hovering a space, till winds the signal blow
To join their dark encounter in mid air:
So frowned the mighty combatants, that Hell
Grew darker at their frown, so matched they stood;   720
For never but once more was either like
To meet so great a foe. And now great deeds
Had been achieved, whereof all Hell had rung,
Had not the snaky sorceress that sat
Fast by Hell gate and kept the fatal key,
Risen, and with hideous outcry rushed between.
    "O father, what intends thy hand," she cried,
"Against thy only son? What fury O son,
Possesses thee to bend that mortal dart
Against thy father's head? and know'st for whom;   730
For him who sits above and laughs the while
At thee ordained his drudge, to execute
Whate'er his wrath, which he calls justice, bids,
His wrath which one day will destroy ye both!"
    She spake, and at her words the hellish pest
Forbore; then these to her Satan returned:
    "So strange thy outcry, and thy words so strange
Thou interposest, that my sudden hand
Prevented spares to tell thee yet by deeds
What it intends; till first I know of thee,   740
What thing thou art, thus double-formed, and why
In this infernal vale first met thou call'st
Me father, and that phantasm call'st my son.
I know thee not, nor ever saw till now
Sight more detestable than him and thee."
    To whom thus the portress of Hell gate replied:
"Hast thou forgot me then, and do I seem
Now in thine eye so foul? once deemed so fair

---

709. Ophiuchus, "the Serpent-bearer." Milton erroneously locates this constellation in northern heavens because Satan is said in Scripture to come from the "parts of the North."

716. The Caspian Sea is frequently mentioned in Renaissance literature as a region of storms.

722. so great a foe, i.e., Christ.   **736. these,** i.e., these words.

In Heaven, when at the assembly, and in sight
Of all the Seraphim with thee combined   750
In bold conspiracy against Heaven's King,
All on a sudden miserable pain
Surprised thee; dim thine eyes, and dizzy swum
In darkness, while thy head flames thick and fast
Threw forth, till on the left side opening wide,
Likest to thee in shape and countenance bright,
Then shining heavenly fair, a goddess armed
Out of thy head I sprung. Amazement seized
All the host of Heaven; back they recoiled afraid
At first, and called me *Sin*, and for a sign   760
Portentous held me; but familiar grown,
I pleased, and with attractive graces won
The most averse, thee chiefly, who full oft
Thyself in me thy perfect image viewing
Becam'st enamored; and such joy thou took'st
With me in secret, that my womb conceived
A growing burden. Meanwhile war arose,
And fields were fought in Heaven; wherein remained
(For what could else) to our almighty foe
Clear victory, to our part loss and rout   770
Through all the Empyrean; down they fell
Driven headlong from the pitch of Heaven, down
Into this Deep, and in the general fall
I also; at which time this powerful key
Into my hand was given, with charge to keep
These gates for ever shut, which none can pass
Without my opening. Pensive here I sat
Alone, but long I sat not, till my womb,
Pregnant by thee, and now excessive grown,
Prodigious motion felt and rueful throes.   780
At last this odious offspring whom thou seest
Thine own begotten, breaking violent way
Tore through my entrails, that with fear and pain
Distorted, all my nether shape thus grew
Transformed; but he my inbred enemy
Forth issued, brandishing his fatal dart
Made to destroy. I fled, and cried out *Death;*
Hell trembled at the hideous name, and sighed
From all her caves, and back resounded *Death.*
I fled; but he pursued (though more, it seems,   790
Inflamed with lust than rage) and swifter far,
Me overtook, his mother, all dismayed,
And in embraces forcible and foul

749 ff. The birth of Sin from the head of Satan is like that of Minerva from the head of
Jove. The rebellious angels, though at first startled, found her alluring. Now in hell she
appears in her true ugliness.

772. pitch, height.

Engendering with me, of that rape begot
These yelling monsters that with ceaseless cry
Surround me, as thou saw'st, hourly conceived
And hourly born, with sorrow infinite
To me; for when they list, into the womb
That bred them they return, and howl and gnaw
My bowels, their repast; then bursting forth   800
Afresh, with conscious terrors vex me round,
That rest or intermission none I find.
Before mine eyes in opposition sits
Grim Death my son and foe, who sets them on,
And me his parent would full soon devour
For want of other prey, but that he knows
His end with mine involved; and knows that I
Should prove a bitter morsel, and his bane,
Whenever that shall be; so Fate pronounced.
But thou O father, I forewarn thee, shun   810
His deadly arrow; neither vainly hope
To be invulnerable in those bright arms,
Though tempered heavenly; for that mortal dint,
Save he who reigns above, none can resist."
   She finished; and the subtle Fiend his lore
Soon learned, now milder, and thus answered smooth.
   "Dear daughter, since thou claim'st me for thy sire,
And my fair son here show'st me, the dear pledge
Of dalliance had with thee in Heaven, and joys
Then sweet, now sad to mention, through dire change   820
Befallen us unforeseen, unthought of, know
I come no enemy, but to set free
From out this dark and dismal house of pain,
Both him and thee, and all the heavenly host
Of spirits that in our just pretences armed,
Fell with us from on high. From them I go
This uncouth errand sole, and one for all
Myself expose, with lonely steps to tread
The unfounded deep, and through the void immense
To search with wandering quest a place foretold   830
Should be, and, by concurring signs, ere now
Created vast and round, a place of bliss
In the purlieus of Heaven, and therein placed
A race of upstart creatures, to supply
Perhaps our vacant room, though more removed,

---

809. so Fate pronounced. Like Satan, Sin recognizes Fate as the supreme power. Cf.I, 116.
813. tempered heavenly, hardened by heavenly process. **dint,** blow.
815. lore, lesson. Satan now proceeds to show himself as "the father of lies."
825. pretences, claims.
827. This uncouth errand sole, alone on this uncertain errand.
829. unfounded, without foundation, bottomless.   **833. purlieus,** outskirts.
835–37. Satan attributes fear and meanness to God in the creation of man at a safe distance (**more removed**) from Heaven.

Lest Heaven surcharged with potent multitude
Might hap to move new broils. Be this or aught
Than this more secret now designed, I haste
To know; and this once known, shall soon return,
And bring ye to the place where thou and Death   840
Shall dwell at ease, and up and down unseen
Wing silently the buxom air, embalmed
With odors; there ye shall be fed and filled
Immeasurably, all things shall be your prey."
    He ceased, for both seemed highly pleased, and Death
Grinned horrible a ghastly smile, to hear
His famine should be filled, and blessed his maw
Destined to that good hour. No less rejoiced
His mother bad, and thus bespake her sire.
    "The key of this infernal pit, by due   850
And by command of Heaven's all-powerful King
I keep, by him forbidden to unlock
These adamantine gates; against all force
Death ready stands to interpose his dart,
Fearless to be o'ermatched by living might.
But what owe I to his commands above
Who hates me, and hath hither thrust me down
Into this gloom of Tartarus profound,
To sit in hateful office here confined,
Inhabitant of Heaven and heavenly-born,   860
Here in perpetual agony and pain,
With terrors and with clamors compassed round
Of mine own brood, that on my bowels feed?
Thou art my father, thou my author, thou
My being gavest me; whom should I obey
But thee, whom follow? Thou wilt bring me soon
To that new world of light and bliss, among
The gods who live at ease, where I shall reign
At thy right hand voluptuous, as beseems
Thy daughter and thy darling, without end."   870
    Thus saying, from her side the fatal key,
Sad instrument of all our woe, she took;
And towards the gate rolling her bestial train,
Forthwith the huge portcullis high up drew,
Which but herself not all the Stygian powers
Could once have moved; then in the key-hole turns
The intricate wards, and every bolt and bar
Of massy iron or solid rock with ease
Unfastens. On a sudden open fly
With impetuous recoil and jarring sound   880
The infernal doors, and on their hinges grate
Harsh thunder, that the lowest bottom shook

---

842. buxom, yielding, buoyant.
865. whom should I obey. Sin disobeys God, as it is her nature to do.

Of Erebus. She opened, but to shut
Excelled her power; the gates wide open stood,
That with extended wings a bannered host
Under spread ensigns marching might pass through
With horse and chariots ranked in loose array;
So wide they stood, and like a furnace mouth
Cast forth redounding smoke and ruddy flame.
Before their eyes in sudden view appear   890
The secrets of the hoary deep, a dark
Illimitable ocean without bound,
Without dimension; where length, breadth, and height,
And time, and place, are lost; where eldest Night
And Chaos, ancestors of Nature, hold
Eternal anarchy, amidst the noise
Of endless wars, and by confusion stand.
For Hot, Cold, Moist, and Dry, four champions fierce,
Strive here for mastery, and to battle bring
Their embryon atoms; they around the flag   900
Of each his faction, in their several clans,
Light-armed or heavy, sharp, smooth, swift, or slow,
Swarm populous, unnumbered as the sands
Of Barca or Cyrene's torrid soil,
Levied to side with warring winds, and poise
Their lighter wings. To whom these most adhere,
He rules a moment; Chaos umpire sits,
And by decision more embroils the fray
By which he reigns; next him high arbiter
Chance governs all. Into this wild Abyss,   910
The womb of Nature and perhaps her grave,
Of neither sea, nor shore, nor air, nor fire,
But all these in their pregnant causes mixed
Confusedly, and which thus must ever fight,
Unless the Almighty Maker them ordain

---

883. Erebus, one of the classical names for hell. In its strictest sense, it denoted the region between Hades and the upper world.

889. redounding, overflowing, surging.

890 ff. Cf. Ovid's description of Chaos, *Metamorphoses* i.

895. Nature, the created universe.

898. Hot, Cold, Moist, and Dry, i.e., the attributes of the four elements (fire, earth, water, air), out of which, in the older Physics, all substances were composed.

900. embryon atoms. The atoms were the germinal units of matter in the Epicurean system as expounded by Lucretius, who calls them *semina rerum* and represents them as having different shapes.

903 ff. as the sands . . . wings. The figure implies that the sands are raised (**levied**) by the winds to serve as ballast (**poise their lighter wings**). **Levied** has its military connotation (i.e., the sands are levied like troops of soldiers) as well as its literal meaning. **Lighter** has the force of "too light" (a Latinism).

904. Barca, Cyrene, cities in northern Africa.

906. To whom these most adhere, i.e., the attribute (**Hot, Cold,** etc.) which attracts the most atoms.

913. pregnant causes, potential elements. The differentiation of the elements is not yet accomplished.

His dark materials to create more worlds,
Into this wild Abyss the wary Fiend
Stood on the brink of Hell and looked a while,
Pondering his voyage; for no narrow frith
He had to cross. Nor was his ear less pealed   920
With noises loud and ruinous (to compare
Great things with small) than when Bellona storms,
With all her battering engines bent to raze
Some capital city; or less than if this frame
Of Heaven were falling, and these elements
In mutiny had from her axle torn
The steadfast Earth. At last his sail-broad vans
He spreads for flight, and in the surging smoke
Uplifted spurns the ground; thence many a league
As in a cloudy chair ascending rides   930
Audacious, but that seat soon failing, meets
A vast vacuity: all unawares
Fluttering his pennons vain plumb down he drops
Ten thousand fathom deep, and to this hour
Down had been falling, had not by ill chance
The strong rebuff of some tumultuous cloud
Instinct with fire and niter hurried him
As many miles aloft; that fury stayed,
Quenched in a boggy Syrtis, neither sea,
Nor good dry land, nigh foundered on he fares,   940
Treading the crude consistence, half on foot,
Half flying; behoves him now both oar and sail.
As when a gryphon through the wilderness
With wingèd course o'er hill or moory dale,
Pursues the Arimaspian, who by stealth
Had from his wakeful custody purloined
The guarded gold: so eagerly the Fiend
O'er bog or steep, through strait, rough, dense, or rare,
With head, hands, wings, or feet pursues his way,
And swims or sinks, or wades, or creeps, or flies.   950
At length a universal hubbub wild
Of stunning sounds and voices all confused
Borne through the hollow dark assaults his ear
With loudest vehemence; thither he plies,
Undaunted to meet there whatever power

---

919. frith, firth, channel.   **920. pealed,** deafened.
922. Bellona, Roman goddess of war.   **927. vans,** vanes, wings.
933. pennons, pinions, wings.   **937. instinct,** imbued, charged.
939. Syrtis, quicksand. The Syrtes were two gulfs on the north coast of Africa, much dreaded for their quicksands.
941. crude consistence, unrefined mixture.
943. gryphon, griffin, a mythical monster with the head and wings of an eagle and the body of a lion. According to Pliny (*Natural History* vii. 2) and others, the griffins had in their possession vast gold mines which the Arimaspians, the one-eyed inhabitants of Scythia, were continually trying to obtain.
948. dense or rare, matter condensed or rarefied. Cf. the phrase "through thick and thin."

Or spirit of the nethermost Abyss
Might in that noise reside, of whom to ask
Which way the nearest coast of darkness lies
Bordering on light; when straight behold the throne
Of Chaos, and his dark pavilion spread   960
Wide on the wasteful Deep; with him enthroned
Sat sable-vested Night, eldest of things,
The consort of his reign; and by them stood
Orcus and Ades, and the dreaded name
Of Demogorgon; Rumor next and Chance,
And Tumult and Confusion all embroiled,
And Discord with a thousand various mouths.
    To whom Satan turning boldly, thus. "Ye Powers
And Spirits of this nethermost Abyss,
Chaos and ancient Night, I come no spy,   970
With purpose to explore or to disturb
The secrets of your realm, but by constraint
Wandering this darksome desert, as my way
Lies through your spacious empire up to light,
Alone and without guide, half lost, I seek
What readiest path leads where your gloomy bounds
Confine with Heaven; or if some other place
From your dominion won, the Ethereal King
Possesses lately, thither to arrive
I travel this profound. Direct my course;   980
Directed no mean recompense it brings
To your behoof, if I that region lost,
All usurpation thence expelled, reduce
To her original darkness and your sway
(Which is my present journey) and once more
Erect the standard there of ancient Night;
Yours be the advantage all, mine the revenge."
    Thus Satan; and him thus the Anarch old
With faltering speech and visage incomposed
Answered. "I know thee, stranger, who thou art,   990
That mighty leading angel, who of late
Made head against Heaven's King, though overthrown.
I saw and heard, for such a numerous host
Fled not in silence through the frighted deep
With ruin upon ruin, rout on rout,
Confusion worse confounded; and Heaven gates

---

964. Orcus and Ades, Latin and Greek names for Pluto, god of the underworld.
964–65. dreaded name of Demogorgon, i.e., Demogorgon, whose name is dreaded (a Latinism). Perhaps the name is a corruption of *demiourgos*, which was used by Neoplatonic writers to designate a creative agency inferior to God.
977. confine with, border on.
981 ff. Satan diplomatically gives the impression that his journey was undertaken in the special interest of Chaos.
989. incomposed, discomposed. Chaos is a symbol of spiritual as well as of material disorder. His features exhibit his tumultuous passions.

Poured out by millions her victorious bands
Pursuing. I upon my frontiers here
Keep residence; if all I can will serve
That little which is left so to defend,   1000
Encroached on still through our intestine broils
Weakening the scepter of old Night: first Hell
Your dungeon stretching far and wide beneath;
Now lately Heaven and Earth, another world
Hung o'er my realm, linked in a golden chain
To that side Heaven from whence your legions fell.
If that way be your walk, you have not far;
So much the nearer danger; go and speed;
Havoc and spoil and ruin are my gain."
    He ceased; and Satan stayed not to reply,   1010
But glad that now his sea should find a shore,
With fresh alacrity and force renewed
Springs upward like a pyramid of fire
Into the wild expanse, and through the shock
Of fighting elements, on all sides round
Environed, wins his way; harder beset
And more endangered, than when Argo passed
Through Bosporus betwixt the justling rocks;
Or when Ulysses on the larboard shunned
Charybdis, and by the other whirlpool steered.   1020
So he with difficulty and labor hard
Moved on, with difficulty and labor he;
But he once passed, soon after when Man fell,
Strange alteration! Sin and Death amain
Following his track, such was the will of Heaven,
Paved after him a broad and beaten way
Over the dark Abyss, whose boiling gulf
Tamely endured a bridge of wondrous length
From Hell continued reaching the utmost orb
Of this frail world; by which the spirits perverse   1030
With easy intercourse pass to and fro
To tempt or punish mortals, except whom
God and good angels guard by special grace.
    But now at last the sacred influence
Of light appears, and from the walls of Heaven
Shoots far into the bosom of dim Night
A glimmering dawn; here Nature first begins

    1001. still, constantly.
    1004. Heaven here means the sky of the newly created world; in 1006 it means the Empyrean.
    1016 ff. The reference is to the expedition of Jason in search of the Golden Fleece. The **justling rocks** are the Symplegades (from the Greek verb meaning "to strike together"), so called because they dashed against each other at intervals, crushing the vessels that attempted to sail between them. For the adventure of Ulysses with Charybdis and Scylla (**the other Whirlpool**), cf. *Odyssey* xii.
    1024. amain, with haste.
    1029. the utmost orb, i.e., the outermost of the nine spheres surrounding the earth.

Her farthest verge, and Chaos to retire
As from her outmost works a broken foe,
With tumult less and with less hostile din,   1040
That Satan with less toil, and now with ease
Wafts on the calmer wave by dubious light
And like a weather-beaten vessel holds
Gladly the port, though shrouds and tackle torn;
Or in the emptier waste, resembling air,
Weighs his spread wings, at leisure to behold
Far off the empyreal Heaven, extended wide
In circuit, undetermined square or round,
With opal towers and battlements adorned
Of living sapphire, once his native seat;   1050
And fast by hanging in a golden chain,
This pendent world, in bigness as a star
Of smallest magnitude close by the moon.
Thither full fraught with mischievous revenge,
Accurst, and in a cursèd hour, he hies.

BOOK III

THE ARGUMENT

God, sitting on his throne, sees Satan flying towards this World, then newly created; shows him to the Son, who sat at his right hand; foretells the success of Satan in perverting mankind; clears his own justice and wisdom from all imputation, having created Man free and able enough to have withstood his tempter; yet declares his purpose of grace towards him, in regard he fell not of his own malice, as did Satan, but by him seduced. The Son of God renders praises to his Father for the manifestation of his gracious purpose towards Man; but God again declares that grace cannot be extended towards Man without the satisfaction of Divine Justice: Man hath offended the majesty of God by aspiring to Godhead, and therefore, with all his progeny, devoted to death, must die, unless some one can be found sufficient to answer for his offence, and undergo his punishment. The Son of God freely offers himself a ransom for Man: the Father accepts him, ordains his incarnation, pronounces his exaltation above all names in Heaven and Earth; commands all the angels to adore him: they obey, and hymning to their harps in full choir, celebrate the Father and the Son. Meanwhile Satan alights upon the bare convex of this World's outermost orb; where wandering he first finds a place since called the Limbo of Vanity; what persons and things fly up thither; thence comes to the gate of Heaven, described ascending by stairs, and the waters above the firmament that flow about it. His passage thence to the orb of the sun: he finds there Uriel, the regent of that orb, but first changes himself into the shape of a meaner angel, and pretending a zealous desire to behold the new creation, and Man whom God had placed here, inquires of him the place of his habitation, and is directed; alights first on Mount Niphates.

1039. her, Nature's.   **1043. holds,** i.e., holds his course toward.
1050. living, vivid.
1052. This pendent world, i.e., the entire visible universe with its encircling spheres.

Hail holy Light, offspring of Heaven first-born,
Or of the Eternal coeternal beam
May I express thee unblamed? since God is light,
And never but in unapproachèd light,
Dwelt from eternity, dwelt then in thee,
Bright effluence of bright essence increate.
Or hear'st thou rather pure ethereal stream,
Whose fountain who shall tell? Before the sun,
Before the Heavens thou wert, and at the voice
Of God, as with a mantle didst invest   10
The rising world of waters dark and deep,
Won from the void and formless infinite.
Thee I revisit now with bolder wing,
Escaped the Stygian pool, though long detained
In that obscure sojourn, while in my flight
Through utter and through middle darkness borne
With other notes than to the Orphean lyre
I sung of Chaos and eternal Night,
Taught by the heavenly Muse to venture down
The dark descent, and up to re-ascend,   20
Though hard and rare: thee I revisit safe,
And feel thy sovran vital lamp; but thou
Revisit'st not these eyes, that roll in vain
To find thy piercing ray, and find no dawn;
So thick a drop serene hath quenched their orbs,
Or dim suffusion veiled. Yet not the more
Cease I to wander where the Muses haunt
Clear spring, or shady grove, or sunny hill,
Smit with the love of sacred song; but chief
Thee Sion, and the flowery brooks beneath   30
That wash thy hallowed feet, and warbling flow,
Nightly I visit; nor sometimes forget
Those other two equalled with me in fate,
So were I equalled with them in renown,
Blind Thamyris and blind Mæonides,
And Tiresias and Phineus prophets old:
Then feed on thoughts, that voluntary move
Harmonious numbers; as the wakeful bird

2–3. May I, without blame, call thee coeternal with God?

6. Light is God's essence and as such is uncreated; but it is also what flows from him (effluence) and was the first created thing.

7–8. Or hear'st. Milton now says that the relation of the effluence to the essence is a mystery.

16. utter, outer, i.e., Hell.

17. Orphean lyre. There was an Orphic hymn to night. Milton means that his poem is of higher inspiration, being based on Scripture.

25. drop serene, a translation of the medical term *gutta serena*, used of blindness in which the eye is not clouded. The "clear drop" is a humor which blocks the optic nerve.

26. dim suffusion, cataract.

29. sacred song, poetry, which is divine as coming from the muses.

30. To visit the brooks by Sion is to read Scripture.   **35. Mæonides,** Homer.

Sings darkling, and in shadiest covert hid
Tunes her nocturnal note. Thus with the year   40
Seasons return; but not to me returns
Day, or the sweet approach of even or morn,
Or sight of vernal bloom, or summer's rose,
Or flocks, or herds, or human face divine;
But cloud instead, and ever-during dark
Surrounds me, from the cheerful ways of men
Cut off, and for the book of knowledge fair
Presented with a universal blank
Of Nature's works to me expunged and razed,
And wisdom at one entrance quite shut out.   50
So much the rather thou celestial Light
Shine inward, and the mind through all her powers
Irradiate, there plant eyes, all mist from thence
Purge and disperse, that I may see and tell
Of things invisible to mortal sight.
   Now had the Almighty Father from above,
From the pure Empyrean where he sits
High throned above all height, bent down his eye,
His own works and their works at once to view.
About him all the sanctities of Heaven   60
Stood thick as stars, and from his sight received
Beatitude past utterance; on his right
The radiant image of his glory sat,
His only Son; on Earth he first beheld
Our two first parents, yet the only two
Of mankind, in the happy garden placed,
Reaping immortal fruits of joy and love,
Uninterrupted joy, unrivalled love
In blissful solitude. He then surveyed
Hell and the gulf between, and Satan there   70
Coasting the wall of Heaven on this side Night
In the dun air sublime, and ready now
To stoop with wearied wings and willing feet
On the bare outside of this World, that seemed
Firm land imbosomed without firmament,
Uncertain which, in ocean or in air.
Him God beholding from his prospect high,
Wherein past, present, future he beholds,

72. sublime, elevated.

74–76. Satan is ready to light on the *primum mobile,* the outer shell of the created universe, not on the earth itself. The substance of this shell is indeterminate. The "firmament" is the visible sky, which separates the waters above from the waters beneath the earth. The shell is "without," i.e., outside of this firmament, or perhaps rather not composed of it, as the other spheres must be. The "waters above" are described in III, 518. They constitute the crystalline sphere, inside the *primum mobile,* but also make a sea on top of it. Milton is not only adjusting the biblical account of creation to the Ptolemaic idea of the spheres but making the conception philosophic as well. The *primum mobile* is a link between God and his universe.

76. uncertain which, it being uncertain whether the shell hung in water or in air. Milton suggests that the business about the firmament and the waters is obscure, as indeed it is.

Thus to his only Son foreseeing spake.
     "Only begotten Son, seest thou what rage   80
Transports our Adversary, whom no bounds
Prescribed, no bars of Hell, nor all the chains
Heaped on him there, nor yet the main Abyss
Wide interrupt can hold; so bent he seems
On desperate revenge, that shall redound
Upon his own rebellious head. And now
Through all restraint broke loose he wings his way
Not far off Heaven, in the precincts of light,
Directly towards the new-created World,
And Man there placed, with purpose to assay   90
If him by force he can destroy, or worse,
By some false guile pervert; and shall pervert;
For Man will hearken to his glozing lies,
And easily transgress the sole command,
Sole pledge of his obedience; so will fall
He and his faithless progeny. Whose fault?
Whose but his own? Ingrate, he had of me
All he could have; I made him just and right,
Sufficient to have stood, though free to fall.
Such I created all the Ethereal Powers   100
And spirits, both them who stood and them who failed;
Freely they stood who stood, and fell who fell.
Not free, what proof could they have given sincere
Of true allegiance, constant faith, or love,
Where only what they needs must do, appeared,
Not what they would? what praise could they receive?
What pleasure I from such obedience paid,
When will and reason (reason also is choice)
Useless and vain, of freedom both despoiled,
Made passive both, had served necessity,   110
Not me. They therefore as to right belonged,
So were created, nor can justly accuse
Their Maker, or their making, or their fate,
As if predestination overruled
Their will, disposed by absolute decree
Or high foreknowledge; they themselves decreed
Their own revolt, not I. If I foreknew,
Foreknowledge had no influence on their fault,
Which had no less proved certain unforeknown.
So without least impulse or shadow of fate,   120
Or aught by me immutably foreseen,
They trespass, authors to themselves in all,
Both what they judge and what they choose; for so
I formed them free, and free they must remain,

---

114 ff. Predestination, in Milton's theology, was a conditional decree of God, not an absolute one, as in strict Calvinism. Milton is not the first or the last thinker to maintain the paradox that God foresees but not immutably.

Till they enthrall themselves: I else must change
Their nature, and revoke the high decree
Unchangeable, eternal, which ordained
Their freedom; they themselves ordained their fall.
The first sort by their own suggestion fell,
Self-tempted, self-depraved; Man falls, deceived   130
By the other first; Man therefore shall find grace,
The other none. In mercy and justice both,
Through Heaven and Earth, so shall my glory excel,
But mercy first and last shall brightest shine."
    Thus while God spake, ambrosial fragrance filled
All Heaven, and in the blessed spirits elect
Sense of new joy ineffable diffused.
Beyond compare the Son of God was seen
Most glorious; in him all his Father shone
Substantially expressed; and in his face   140
Divine compassion visibly appeared,
Love without end, and without measure grace,
Which uttering thus he to his Father spake.
    "O Father, gracious was that word which closed
Thy sovran sentence, that Man should find grace;
For which both Heaven and Earth shall high extol
Thy praises with the innumerable sound
Of hymns and sacred songs, wherewith thy throne
Encompassed shall resound thee ever blest.
For should Man finally be lost, should Man   150
Thy creature late so loved, thy youngest son
Fall circumvented thus by fraud, though joined
With his own folly? that be from thee far,
That far be from thee, Father, who art judge
Of all things made, and judgest only right.
Or shall the Adversary thus obtain
His end, and frustrate thine, shall he fulfil
His malice, and thy goodness bring to nought,
Or proud return though to his heavier doom,
Yet with revenge accomplished, and to Hell   160
Draw after him the whole race of mankind,
By him corrupted? or wilt thou thyself
Abolish thy creation, and unmake,
For him, what for thy glory thou hast made?
So should thy goodness and thy greatness both
Be questioned and blasphemed without defence."
    To whom the great Creator thus replied.
"O Son, in whom my soul hath chief delight,
Son of my bosom, Son who art alone
My word, my wisdom, and effectual might,   170
All hast thou spoken as my thoughts are, all
As my eternal purpose hath decreed:
Man shall not quite be lost, but saved who will,
Yet not of will in him, but grace in me

Freely vouchsafed; once more I will renew
His lapsëd powers, though forfeit and enthralled
By sin to foul exorbitant desires;
Upheld by me, yet once more he shall stand
On even ground against his mortal foe,
By me upheld, that he may know how frail   180
His fallen condition is, and to me owe
All his deliverance, and to none but me.
Some I have chosen of peculiar grace
Elect above the rest; so is my will.
The rest shall hear me call, and oft be warned
Their sinful state, and to appease betimes
The incensëd Deity, while offered grace
Invites; for I will clear their senses dark,
What may suffice, and soften stony hearts
To pray, repent, and bring obedience due.   190
To prayer, repentance, and obedience due,
Though but endeavored with sincere intent,
Mine ear shall not be slow, mine eye not shut.
And I will place within them as a guide
My umpire Conscience, whom if they will hear,
Light after light well used they shall attain,
And to the end persisting, safe arrive.
This my long sufferance and my day of grace
They who neglect and scorn shall never taste;
But hard be hardened, blind be blinded more,   200
That they may stumble on, and deeper fall;
And none but such from mercy I exclude.
But yet all is not done; Man disobeying,
Disloyal breaks his fealty, and sins
Against the high supremacy of Heaven,
Affecting Godhead, and so losing all,
To expiate his treason hath nought left,
But to destruction sacred and devote,
He with his whole posterity must die;
Die he or justice must; unless for him   210
Some other able, and as willing, pay
The rigid satisfaction, death for death.
Say Heavenly Powers, where shall we find such love?
Which of ye will be mortal to redeem

175–76. Man's free will, like Satan's, has lapsed with his disobedience. Because his sin came from an outside suggestion his power to choose good is renewed by an act of Grace, as Satan's is not.

184. Elect. In Calvinistic thought the elect include all who are to be saved, in contrast to the "reprobate," who are predestined before their birth to be damned; with Milton, on the other hand, the elect are only a special group of saints to whom goodness and salvation come easily. The rest of mankind are prone to sin but capable of repentance.

203 ff. God's immutable decree cannot be evaded. If justice is to be satisfied there must be death for sin. The solution is the sacrifice of Christ, who, like Adam, is the representative of mankind.

Man's mortal crime, and just the unjust to save?
Dwells in all Heaven charity so dear?"
 He asked, but all the heavenly choir stood mute,
And silence was in Heaven; on Man's behalf
Patron or intercessor none appeared,
Much less that durst upon his own head draw   220
The deadly forfeiture, and ransom set.
And now without redemption all mankind
Must have been lost, adjudged to Death and Hell
By doom severe, had not the Son of God,
In whom the fulness dwells of love divine,
His dearest mediation thus renewed.
 "Father, thy word is passed, Man shall find grace;
And shall grace not find means, that finds her way,
The speediest of thy wingèd messengers,
To visit all thy creatures, and to all   230
Comes unprevented, unimplored, unsought?
Happy for Man, so coming; he her aid
Can never seek, once dead in sins and lost;
Atonement for himself or offering meet,
Indebted and undone, hath none to bring.
Behold me then, me for him, life for life
I offer; on me let thine anger fall;
Account me Man; I for his sake will leave
Thy bosom, and this glory next to thee
Freely put off, and for him lastly die   240
Well pleased; on me let Death wreak all his rage;
Under his gloomy power I shall not long
Lie vanquished; thou hast given me to possess
Life in myself for ever; by thee I live;
Though now to Death I yield, and am his due
All that of me can die, yet that debt paid,
Thou wilt not leave me in the loathsome grave
His prey, nor suffer my unspotted soul
For ever with corruption there to dwell;
But I shall rise victorious, and subdue   250
My vanquisher, spoiled of his vaunted spoil;
Death his death's wound shall then receive, and stoop
Inglorious, of his mortal sting disarmed.
I through the ample air in triumph high
Shall lead Hell captive maugre Hell, and show
The powers of darkness bound. Thou at the sight
Pleased, out of Heaven shalt look down and smile,
While by thee raised I ruin all my foes,
Death last, and with his carcass glut the grave:
Then with the multitude of my redeemed,   260
Shall enter Heaven long absent, and return,

---

236 ff. Christ's highly dramatic offer, with its reception, is in studied contrast to Satan's in Book II, 430 ff.

Father, to see thy face, wherein no cloud
Of anger shall remain, but peace assured
And reconcilement; wrath shall be no more
Thenceforth, but in thy presence joy entire."
   His words here ended, but his meek aspéct
Silent yet spake, and breathed immortal love
To mortal men, above which only shone
Filial obedience. As a sacrifice
Glad to be offered, he attends the will   270
Of his great Father. Admiration seized
All Heaven, what this might mean, and whither tend
Wondering; but soon the Almighty thus replied.
   "O thou in Heaven and Earth the only peace
Found out for mankind under wrath, O thou
My sole complacence! well thou know'st how dear
To me are all my works, nor Man the least
Though last created, that for him I spare
Thee from my bosom and right hand, to save,
By losing thee a while, the whole race lost!   280
Thou therefore whom thou only canst redeem,
Their nature also to thy nature join;
And be thyself Man among men on Earth,
Made flesh, when time shall be, of virgin seed,
By wondrous birth; be thou in Adam's room
The head of all mankind, though Adam's son.
As in him perish all men, so in thee
As from a second root shall be restored,
As many as are restored; without thee, none.
His crime makes guilty all his sons; thy merit   290
Imputed shall absolve them who renounce
Their own both righteous and unrighteous deeds,
And live in thee transplanted, and from thee
Receive new life. So Man, as is most just,
Shall satisfy for Man, be judged and die,
And dying rise, and rising with him raise
His brethren, ransomed with his own dear life.
So heavenly love shall outdo hellish hate,
Giving to death, and dying to redeem,
So dearly to redeem what hellish hate   300
So easily destroyed, and still destroys
In those who, when they may, accept not grace.
Nor shalt thou by descending to assume
Man's nature, lessen or degrade thine own.
Because thou hast, though throned in highest bliss
Equal to God, and equally enjoying
God-like fruition, quitted all to save
A world from utter loss, and hast been found
By merit more than birthright Son of God,
Found worthiest to be so by being good,   310
Far more than great or high; because in thee

Love hath abounded more than glory abounds;
Therefore thy humiliation shall exalt
With thee thy manhood also to this throne;
Here shalt thou sit incarnate, here shalt reign
Both God and Man, Son both of God and Man,
Anointed universal King. All power
I give thee; reign for ever, and assume
Thy merits; under thee as Head supreme
Thrones, Princedoms, Powers, Dominions, I reduce.   320
All knees to thee shall bow, of them that bide
In Heaven, or Earth, or under Earth in Hell;
When thou attended gloriously from Heaven
Shalt in the sky appear, and from thee send
The summoning Archangels to proclaim
Thy dread tribunal, forthwith from all winds
The living, and forthwith the cited dead
Of all past ages to the general doom
Shall hasten, such a peal shall rouse their sleep.
Then all thy saints assembled, thou shalt judge   330
Bad men and angels; they arraigned shall sink
Beneath thy sentence; Hell, her numbers full,
Thenceforth shall be for ever shut. Meanwhile
The World shall burn, and from her ashes spring
New Heaven and Earth, wherein the just shall dwell,
And after all their tribulations long
See golden days, fruitful of golden deeds,
With Joy and Love triumphing, and fair Truth.
Then thou thy regal scepter shalt lay by,
For regal scepter then no more shall need;   340
God shall be all in all. But all ye gods,
Adore him, who to compass all this dies,
Adore the Son, and honor him as me."
   No sooner had the Almighty ceased, but all
The multitude of angels with a shout
Loud as from numbers without number, sweet
As from blest voices, uttering joy, Heaven rung
With jubilee, and loud hosannas filled
The eternal regions. Lowly reverent
Towards either throne they bow, and to the ground   350
With solemn adoration down they cast
Their crowns inwove with amarant and gold,
Immortal amarant, a flower which once
In Paradise, fast by the Tree of Life
Began to bloom, but soon for Man's offence
To Heaven removed where first it grew, there grows
And flowers aloft shading the Fount of Life,
And where the River of Bliss through midst of Heaven
Rolls o'er Elysian flowers her amber stream;
With these that never fade the spirits elect   360
Bind their resplendent locks inwreathed with beams;

Now in loose garlands thick thrown off, the bright
Pavement, that like a sea of jasper shone,
Impurpled with celestial roses smiled.
Then crowned again their golden harps they took,
Harps ever tuned, that glittering by their side
Like quivers hung, and with preamble sweet
Of charming symphony they introduce
Their sacred song, and waken raptures high;
No voice exempt, no voice but well could join   370
Melodious part, such concord is in Heaven.
    Thee Father first they sung Omnipotent,
Immutable, Immortal, Infinite,
Eternal King; thee Author of all being,
Fountain of light, thyself invisible
Amidst the glorious brightness where thou sitt'st
Throned inaccessible, but when thou shadest
The full blaze of thy beams, and through a cloud
Drawn round about thee like a radiant shrine,
Dark with excessive bright thy skirts appear,   380
Yet dazzle Heaven, that brightest Seraphim
Approach not, but with both wings veil their eyes.
Thee next they sang, of all creation first,
Begotten Son, Divine Similitude,
In whose conspicuous countenance, without cloud
Made visible, the Almighty Father shines,
Whom else no creature can behold; on thee
Impressed the effulgence of his glory abides,
Transfused on thee his ample Spirit rests.
He Heaven of Heavens and all the powers therein   390
By thee created, and by thee threw down
The aspiring Dominations. Thou that day
Thy Father's dreadful thunder didst not spare,
Nor stop thy flaming chariot wheels, that shook
Heaven's everlasting frame, while o'er the necks
Thou drovest of warring angels disarrayed.
Back from pursuit, thy powers with loud acclaim
Thee only extolled, Son of thy Father's might,
To execute fierce vengeance on his foes,
Not so on Man; him through their malice fallen,   400
Father of mercy and grace, thou didst not doom
So strictly, but much more to pity incline.
No sooner did thy dear and only Son
Perceive thee purposed not to doom frail Man
So strictly, but much more to pity inclined,
He to appease thy wrath, and end the strife
Of mercy and justice in thy face discerned,
Regardless of the bliss wherein he sat
Second to thee, offered himself to die
For Man's offence. O unexampled love,   410
Love nowhere to be found less than divine,

Hail, Son of God, Savior of men, thy name
Shall be the copious matter of my song
Henceforth, and never shall my harp thy praise
Forget, nor from thy Father's praise disjoin.
   Thus they in Heaven, above the starry sphere,
Their happy hours in joy and hymning spent.
Meanwhile, upon the firm opacous globe
Of this round World, whose first convex divides
The luminous inferior orbs, enclosed   420
From Chaos and the inroad of Darkness old,
Satan alighted walks. A globe far off
It seemed, now seems a boundless continent
Dark, waste, and wild, under the frown of Night
Starless exposed, and ever-threatening storms
Of Chaos blustering round, inclement sky;
Save on that side which from the wall of Heaven,
Though distant far some small reflexion gains
Of glimmering air less vexed with tempest loud.
Here walked the Fiend at large in spacious field.   430
As when a vulture on Imaus bred,
Whose snowy ridge the roving Tartar bounds,
Dislodging from a region scarce of prey
To gorge the flesh of lambs or yeanling kids
On hills where flocks are fed, flies toward the springs
Of Ganges or Hydaspes, Indian streams;
But in his way lights on the barren plains
Of Sericana, where Chineses drive
With sails and wind their cany wagons light:
So on this windy sea of land, the Fiend   440
Walked up and down alone bent on his prey,
Alone, for other creature in this place,
Living or lifeless to be found was none,
None yet, but store hereafter from the Earth
Up hither like aerial vapors flew
Of all things transitory and vain, when sin
With vanity had filled the works of men.
Both all things vain, and all who in vain things
Built their fond hopes of glory or lasting fame,
Or happiness in this or the other life;   450
All who have their reward on earth, the fruits
Of painful superstition and blind zeal,
Nought seeking but the praise of men, here find
Fit retribution, empty as their deeds;
All the unaccomplished works of Nature's hand,
Abortive, monstrous, or unkindly mixed,
Dissolved on Earth, fleet hither, and in vain,

   431. As when a vulture. The vulture flies southwest from a mountain range in central Asia, across the western plains of China (called Sericana in old maps), to the fertile plains of Northern India.
   436. Hydaspes, classical name for the Jehlam River.

Till final dissolution, wander here,
Not in the neighboring moon, as some have dreamed;
Those argent fields more likely habitants,   460
Translated saints, or middle spirits hold
Betwixt the angelical and human kind.
Hither of ill-joined sons and daughters born,
First from the ancient world those giants came
With many a vain exploit, though then renowned;
The builders next of Babel on the plain
Of Sennaar, and still with vain design
New Babels, had they wherewithal, would build;
Others came single: he who to be deemed
A god, leaped fondly into Ætna flames,   470
Empedocles; and he who to enjoy
Plato's Elysium, leaped into the sea,
Cleombrotus, and many more too long,
Embryos and idiots, eremites and friars
White, black, and grey, with all their trumpery.
Here pilgrims roam, that strayed so far to seek
In Golgotha him dead who lives in Heaven;
And they who to be sure of Paradise,
Dying put on the weeds of Dominic,
Or in Franciscan think to pass disguised;   480
They pass the planets seven, and pass the fixed,
And that crystalline sphere whose balance weighs
The trepidation talked, and that first moved;
And now Saint Peter at Heaven's wicket seems
To wait them with his keys, and now at foot
Of Heaven's ascent they lift their feet, when lo!
A violent cross wind from either coast
Blows them transverse, ten thousand leagues awry
Into the devious air; then might ye see
Cowls, hoods and habits with their wearers tossed   490
And fluttered into rags; then reliques, beads,
Indulgences, dispenses, pardons, bulls,
The sport of winds. All these upwhirled aloft
Fly o'er the backside of the World far off

471. Empedocles leaped into the crater of Mount Etna to make his name live forever.
472. Plato's Elysium, the after-world as described in the *Phaedo.*
479–80. Milton's fanatical hatred of the Roman church blinds him to the beauty of everything in its tradition. He has read Dante's great tribute to the Dominican and Franciscan orders, yet he thinks of them only as the refuge for hypocrites who make haste to take the robe on their deathbed to make sure of Heaven. Readers have been justly offended by this passage on artistic as well as religious grounds. But Milton believed that the greatest danger to true faith, as inculcated in the poem, lay in reliance on man-made traditions and outward forms. The material is not inappropriate, therefore, in this book, where the central doctrines of Christianity are set forth.
481. the fixed, the sphere of the fixed stars.
482–83. The balance of the crystalline sphere determined the much talked of swaying or libration, which in the Ptolemaic system belonged to the celestial system, in the Copernican, of course, to the earth. **First moved,** the *primum mobile,* which imparted motion to the other spheres.

Into a limbo large and broad, since called
The Paradise of Fools; to few unknown
Long after, now unpeopled and untrod.
    All this dark globe the Fiend found as he passed,
And long he wandered, till at last a gleam
Of dawning light turned thitherward in haste   500
His travelled steps; far distant he descries
Ascending by degrees magnificent
Up to the wall of Heaven a structure high,
At top whereof, but far more rich appeared
The work as of a kingly palace gate
With frontispiece of diamond and gold
Embellished; thick with sparkling orient gems
The portal shone, inimitable on Earth
By model, or by shading pencil drawn.
The stairs were such as whereon Jacob saw   510
Angels ascending and descending, bands
Of guardians bright, when he from Esau fled
To Padan-Aram in the field of Luz,
Dreaming by night under the open sky,
And waking cried, "This is the gate of Heaven."
Each stair mysteriously was meant, nor stood
There always, but drawn up to Heaven sometimes
Viewless, and underneath a bright sea flowed
Of jasper, or of liquid pearl, whereon
Who after came from Earth, sailing arrived,   520
Wafted by angels, or flew o'er the lake
Rapt in a chariot drawn by fiery steeds.
The stairs were then let down, whether to dare
The Fiend by easy ascent, or aggravate
His sad exclusion from the doors of bliss.
Direct against which opened from beneath,
Just o'er the blissful seat of Paradise,
A passage down to the Earth, a passage wide,
Wider by far than that of after-times
Over Mount Sion, and, though that were large,   530
Over the Promised Land to God so dear,
By which, to visit oft those happy tribes,
On high behests his angels to and fro
Passed frequent, and his eye with choice regard
From Paneas, the fount of Jordan's flood,
To Beërsaba, where the Holy Land
Borders on Egypt and the Arabian shore;
So wide the opening seemed, where bounds were set
To darkness, such as bound the ocean wave.
    Satan from hence, now on the lower stair   540

---

510. For Jacob's vision see Gen. 28:10–19.
535. Paneas, Dan on the north boundary of the Holy Land. God surveyed all Palestine
through the opening "from Dan to Beersheba."

That scaled by steps of gold to Heaven gate
Looks down with wonder at the sudden view
Of all this World at once. As when a scout
Through dark and desert ways with peril gone
All night, at last by break of cheerful dawn
Obtains the brow of some high-climbing hill,
Which to his eye discovers unaware
The goodly prospect of some foreign land
First seen, or some renowned metropolis
With glistering spires and pinnacles adorned,   550
Which now the rising sun gilds with his beams.
Such wonder seized, though after Heaven seen,
The spirit malign, but much more envy seized
At sight of all this World beheld so fair.
Round he surveys, and well might, where he stood,
So high above the circling canopy
Of Night's extended shade; from eastern point
Of Libra to the fleecy star that bears
Andromeda far off Atlantic seas
Beyond the horizon; then from pole to pole   560
He views in breadth, and without longer pause
Down right into the World's first region throws
His flight precipitant, and winds with ease
Through the pure marble air his oblique way
Amongst innumerable stars, that shone
Stars distant, but nigh hand seemed other worlds,
Or other worlds they seemed, or happy isles,
Like those Hesperian Gardens famed of old,
Fortunate fields, and groves, and flowery vales,
Thrice happy isles, but who dwelt happy there   570
He stayed not to inquire. Above them all
The golden sun in splendor likest Heaven
Allured his eye. Thither his course he bends,
Through the calm firmament; but up or down,
By center, or eccentric, hard to tell,
Or longitude, where the great luminary
Aloof the vulgar constellations thick,
That from his lordly eye keep distance due,
Dispenses light from far; they as they move
Their starry dance in numbers that compute   580
Days, months, and years, towards his all-cheering lamp
Turn swift their various motions, or are turned
By his magnetic beam, that gently warms
The Universe, and to each inward part

  558. the fleecy star, the sign of Aries, the Ram, opposite Libra and just below the constellation of Andromeda.
  562. first region. The air was divided into upper, middle, and lower regions.
  564. marble, lucent and shining, like some marble.
  574. up or down, etc. Satan's course was devious and obscure, its ambiguity being perhaps
heightened by the uncertainty whether one should call the earth or the sun the center.

With gentle penetration, though unseen,
Shoots invisible virtue even to the deep:
So wondrously was set his station bright.
　　There lands the Fiend, a spot like which perhaps
Astronomer in the sun's lucent orb
Through his glazed optic tube yet never saw. 590
The place he found beyond expression bright,
Compared with aught on Earth, metal or stone;
Not all parts like, but all alike informed
With radiant light, as glowing iron with fire.
If metal, part seemed gold, part silver clear;
If stone, carbuncle most or chrysolite,
Ruby or topaz, to the twelve that shone
In Aaron's breast-plate, and a stone besides,
Imagined rather oft than elsewhere seen,
That stone, or like to that, which here below 600
Philosophers in vain so long have sought;
In vain, though by their powerful art they bind
Volatile Hermes, and call up unbound
In various shapes old Proteus from the sea,
Drained through a limbec to his native form.
What wonder then if fields and regions here
Breathe forth elixir pure, and rivers run
Potable gold, when with one virtuous touch
The arch-chemic sun, so far from us remote,
Produces, with terrestrial humor mixed, 610
Here in the dark so many precious things
Of color glorious and effect so rare?
Here matter new to gaze the Devil met
Undazzled; far and wide his eye commands,
For sight no obstacle found here, nor shade,
But all sunshine, as when his beams at noon
Culminate from the equator, as they now
Shot upward still direct, whence no way round
Shadow from body opaque can fall, and the air,
Nowhere so clear, sharpened his visual ray 620
To objects distant far, whereby he soon
Saw within ken a glorious angel stand,
The same whom John saw also in the sun.
His back was turned, but not his brightness hid;
Of beaming sunny rays, a golden tiar
Circled his head, nor less his locks behind
Illustrious on his shoulders fledge with wings
Lay waving round; on some great charge employed
He seemed, or fixed in cogitation deep.

588–90. Galileo had discovered the sun spots with his telescope.
591 ff. Milton revels in the picturesque terms of Alchemy.
608–9. One touch of the sun's power, mixed with the moisture of earth, produces flowers, jewels, etc.
623. Rev. 19:17.

Glad was the spirit impure, as now in hope   630
To find who might direct his wandering flight
To Paradise the happy seat of Man,
His journey's end and our beginning woe.
But first he casts to change his proper shape,
Which else might work him danger or delay.
And now a stripling Cherub he appears,
Not of the prime, yet such as in his face
Youth smiled celestial, and to every limb
Suitable grace diffused, so well he feigned;
Under a coronet his flowing hair   640
In curls on either cheek played, wings he wore
Of many a colored plume sprinkled with gold,
His habit fit for speed succinct, and held
Before his decent steps a silver wand.
He drew not nigh unheard; the angel bright,
Ere he drew nigh, his radiant visage turned,
Admonished by his ear, and straight was known
The Archangel Uriel, one of the seven
Who in God's presence, nearest to his throne
Stand ready at command, and are his eyes   650
That run through all the Heavens, or down to the Earth
Bear his swift errands over moist and dry,
O'er sea and land. Him Satan thus accosts:
    "Uriel, for thou of those seven spirits that stand
In sight of God's high throne, gloriously bright,
The first art wont his great authentic will
Interpreter through highest Heaven to bring,
Where all his sons thy embassy attend;
And here art likeliest by supreme decree
Like honor to obtain, and as his eye   660
To visit oft this new creation round;
Unspeakable desire to see and know
All these his wondrous works, but chiefly Man,
His chief delight and favor, him for whom
All these his works so wondrous he ordained,
Hath brought me from the choirs of Cherubim
Alone thus wandering. Brightest Seraph tell
In which of all these shining orbs hath Man
His fixèd seat, or fixèd seat hath none,
But all these shining orbs his choice to dwell;   670
That I may find him, and with secret gaze,
Or open admiration him behold
On whom the great Creator hath bestowed
Worlds, and on whom hath all these graces poured;
That both in him and all things, as is meet,
The Universal Maker we may praise;
Who justly hath driven out his rebel foes

---

637. not of the prime, not yet in the prime of life.

To deepest Hell, and to repair that loss
Created this new happy race of men
To serve him better: wise are all his ways." 680
    So spake the false dissembler unperceived;
For neither man nor angel can discern
Hypocrisy, the only evil that walks
Invisible, except to God alone,
By his permissive will, through Heaven and Earth;
And oft though Wisdom wake, Suspicion sleeps
At Wisdom's gate, and to Simplicity
Resigns her charge, while Goodness thinks no ill
Where no ill seems: which now for once beguiled
Uriel, though regent of the sun, and held 690
The sharpest-sighted spirit of all in Heaven;
Who to the fraudulent impostor foul,
In his uprightness answer thus returned.
    "Fair Angel, thy desire which tends to know
The works of God, thereby to glorify
The great Work-master, leads to no excess
That reaches blame, but rather merits praise
The more it seems excess, that led thee hither
From thy empyreal mansion thus alone,
To witness with thine eyes what some perhaps 700
Contented with report hear only in Heaven:
For wonderful indeed are all his works,
Pleasant to know, and worthiest to be all
Had in remembrance always with delight;
But what created mind can comprehend
Their number, or the wisdom infinite
That brought them forth, but hid their causes deep?
I saw when at his word the formless mass,
This World's material mould, came to a heap,
Confusion heard his voice, and wild uproar 710
Stood ruled, stood vast infinitude confined;
Till at his second bidding Darkness fled,
Light shone, and order from disorder sprung.
Swift to their several quarters hasted then
The cumbrous elements, earth, flood, air, fire,
And this ethereal quintessence of Heaven
Flew upward, spirited with various forms,
That rolled orbicular, and turned to stars
Numberless, as thou seest, and how they move;
Each had his place appointed, each his course; 720
The rest in circuit walls this Universe.
Look downward on that globe whose hither side

708 ff. This account of creation owes much to Plato's *Timaeus*, which is the basic philosophical authority for the theory of one primordial matter out of which God formed the universe, instead of by fiat out of nothing.
    715 ff. The four elements form the earth. A fifth essence rises above them and becomes the stars and the surrounding wall of the universe.

With light from hence, though but reflected, shines;
That place is Earth the seat of Man, that light
His day, which else as the other hemisphere,
Night would invade, but there the neighbouring moon
(So call that opposite fair star) her aid
Timely interposes, and her monthly round
Still ending, still renewing, through mid Heaven,
With borrowed light her countenance triform   730
Hence fills and empties to enlighten the Earth,
And in her pale dominion checks the night.
That spot to which I point is Paradise,
Adam's abode, those lofty shades his bower.
Thy way thou canst not miss, me mine requires."
    Thus said, he turned, and Satan bowing low,
As to superior spirits is wont in Heaven,
Where honor due and reverence none neglects,
Took leave, and toward the coast of Earth beneath,
Down from the ecliptic, sped with hoped success,   740
Throws his steep flight in many an airy wheel,
Nor stayed, till on Niphates' top he lights.

BOOK IV

THE ARGUMENT

*Satan, now in prospect of Eden, and nigh the place where he must now attempt
the bold enterprise which he undertook alone against God and Man, falls into
many doubts with himself, and many passions, fear, envy, and despair; but at
length confirms himself in evil, journeys on to Paradise, whose outward prospect
and situation is described, overleaps the bounds, sits in the shape of a cormorant
on the Tree of Life, as highest in the Garden, to look about him. The Garden
described; Satan's first sight of Adam and Eve; his wonder at their excellent form
and happy state, but with resolution to work their fall; overhears their discourse;
thence gathers that the Tree of Knowledge was forbidden them to eat of under
penalty of death, and thereon intends to found his temptation by seducing them to
transgress; then leaves them a while, to know further of their state by some other
means. Meanwhile Uriel, descending on a sunbeam, warns Gabriel, who had in
charge the gate of Paradise, that some evil spirit had escaped the Deep, and
passed at noon by his sphere, in the shape of a good angel, down to Paradise;
discovered after by his furious gestures in the mount. Gabriel promises to find him
ere morning. Night coming on, Adam and Eve discourse of going to their rest:
their bower described; their evening worship. Gabriel, drawing forth his bands of
night-watch to walk the round of Paradise, appoints two strong angels to Adam's
bower, lest the evil spirit should be there doing some harm to Adam or Eve
sleeping; there they find him at the ear of Eve, tempting her in a dream, and
bring him, though unwilling, to Gabriel; by whom questioned, he scornfully*

---

    730. triform, Latin *triformis*, referring to the goddess's threefold incarnation as Luna in the
sky, Diana on earth, and Hecate in the underworld.
    742. Niphates, a mountain in the Taurus range in Armenia.

answers, prepares resistance, but hindered by a sign from Heaven, flies out of Paradise.

O for that warning voice, which he who saw
The Apocalypse heard cry in Heaven aloud,
Then when the Dragon, put to second rout,
Came furious down to be revenged on men,
"Woe to the inhabitants on Earth!" that now,
While time was, our first parents had been warned
The coming of their secret foe, and scaped,
Haply so scaped, his mortal snare; for now
Satan, now first inflamed with rage, came down,
The tempter ere the accuser of mankind,   10
To wreak on innocent frail Man his loss
Of that first battle, and his flight to Hell.
Yet not rejoicing in his speed, though bold,
Far off and fearless, nor with cause to boast,
Begins his dire attempt, which nigh the birth
Now rolling, boils in his tumultuous breast,
And like a devilish engine back recoils
Upon himself; horror and doubt distract
His troubled thoughts, and from the bottom stir
The Hell within him, for within him Hell   20
He brings, and round about him, nor from Hell
One step no more than from himself can fly
By change of place. Now conscience wakes despair
That slumbered, wakes the bitter memory
Of what he was, what is, and what must be
Worse; of worse deeds worse sufferings must ensue.
Sometimes towards Eden which now in his view
Lay pleasant, his grievèd look he fixes sad,
Sometimes towards Heaven and the full-blazing sun,
Which now sat high in his meridian tower.   30
Then much revolving, thus in sighs began.
  "O thou that with surpassing glory crowned,
Look'st from thy sole dominion like the god
Of this new world; at whose sight all the stars
Hide their diminished heads; to thee I call,
But with no friendly voice, and add thy name
O Sun, to tell thee how I hate thy beams
That bring to my remembrance from what state
I fell, how glorious once above thy sphere;
Till pride and worse ambition threw me down   40

1 ff. This opening passage is based on the vision of St. John recorded in Rev. 12.
  10. The tempter ere the accuser. In St. John's vision, Satan, routed from heaven for the second time, comes down to earth as "the accuser of our brethren" (Rev. 12:10). But, as Milton points out, he first came to earth in the role of tempter. The word "devil" is a corruption of the Greek *diabolos*, meaning literally "slanderer" or "accuser."
  11. wreak, avenge.   **27.** The literal meaning of **Eden** is "delight."
  31. much revolving, pondering many things.

Warring in Heaven against Heaven's matchless King.
Ah wherefore! He deserved no such return
From me, whom he created what I was
In that bright eminence, and with his good
Upbraided none; nor was his service hard.
What could be less than to afford him praise,
The easiest recompense, and pay him thanks,
How due! Yet all his good proved ill in me,
And wrought but malice; lifted up so high
I 'sdeined subjection, and thought one step higher   50
Would set me highest, and in a moment quit
The debt immense of endless gratitude,
So burdensome still paying, still to owe;
Forgetful what from him I still received,
And understood not that a grateful mind
By owing owes not, but still pays, at once
Indebted and discharged; what burden then?
Oh had his powerful destiny ordained
Me some inferior angel, I had stood
Then happy; no unbounded hope had raised   60
Ambition. Yet why not? some other Power
As great might have aspired, and me though mean
Drawn to his part; but other Powers as great
Fell not, but stand unshaken, from within
Or from without, to all temptations armed.
Hadst thou the same free will and power to stand?
Thou hadst. Whom hast thou then or what to accuse,
But Heaven's free love dealt equally to all?
Be then his love accurst, since love or hate,
To me alike it deals eternal woe.   70
Nay cursed be thou; since against his thy will
Chose freely what it now so justly rues.
Me miserable! which way shall I fly
Infinite wrath and infinite despair?
Which way I fly is Hell; myself am Hell;
And in the lowest deep a lower deep
Still threatening to devour me opens wide,
To which the Hell I suffer seems a Heaven.
O then at last relent: is there no place
Left for repentance, none for pardon left?   80
None left but by submission; and that word
Disdain forbids me, and my dread of shame
Among the spirits beneath, whom I seduced
With other promises and other vaunts
Than to submit, boasting I could subdue

---

41. Cf. I, 116, 117 and note. The uncompromising egotism of Satan's public utterances now gives way to a secret admission of God's supremacy.

50. 'sdeined, disdained.   **51. quit,** requite, pay.

52–57. Satan means that gratitude is in itself payment, whereas payment alone does not release from a debt of gratitude.

The Omnipotent. Ay me, they little know
How dearly I abide that boast so vain,
Under what torments inwardly I groan;
While they adore me on the throne of Hell,
With diadem and scepter high advanced   90
The lower still I fall, only supreme
In misery; such joy ambition finds.
But say I could repent, and could obtain
By act of grace my former state; how soon
Would height recall high thoughts, how soon unsay
What feigned submission swore: ease would recant
Vows made in pain, as violent and void.
For never can true reconcilement grow
Where wounds of deadly hate have pierced so deep;
Which would but lead me to a worse relapse   100
And heavier fall: so should I purchase dear
Short intermission bought with double smart.
This knows my Punisher; therefore as far
From granting he, as I from begging peace.
All hope excluded thus, behold instead
Of us, outcast, exiled, his new delight,
Mankind created, and for him this World.
So farewell hope, and with hope farewell fear,
Farewell remorse! All good to me is lost;
Evil be thou my good; by thee at least   110
Divided empire with Heaven's King I hold
By thee, and more than half perhaps will reign;
As Man ere long, and this new World shall know."
    Thus while he spake, each passion dimmed his face
Thrice changed with pale, ire, envy, and despair,
Which marred his borrowed visage, and betrayed
Him counterfeit, if any eye beheld.
For heavenly minds from such distempers foul
Are ever clear. Whereof he soon aware,
Each perturbation smoothed with outward calm,   120
Artificer of fraud; and was the first
That practised falsehood under saintly show,
Deep malice to conceal, couched with revenge.
Yet not enough had practised to deceive
Uriel once warned; whose eye pursued him down
The way he went, and on the Assyrian mount
Saw him disfigured, more than could befall
Spirit of happy sort. His gestures fierce
He marked and mad demeanor, then alone,
As he supposed, all unobserved, unseen.   130
    So on he fares, and to the border comes

87. **abide,** suffer for.   90. **advanced,** elevated. **Me** (89) is the word modified.
    115. **Thrice changed with pale,** i.e., each of the passions (**ire, envy, and despair**) dims the natural luster of his countenance. **Pale** is of course used as a noun.
    123. **couched with,** lying hidden with.   126. **the Assyrian mount,** Niphates.

Of Eden, where delicious Paradise,
Now nearer, crowns with her enclosure green,
As with a rural mound the champaign head
Of a steep wilderness, whose hairy sides
With thicket overgrown, grotesque and wild,
Access denied; and overhead up grew
Insuperable height of loftiest shade,
Cedar, and pine, and fir, and branching palm,
A sylvan scene, and as the ranks ascend   140
Shade above shade, a woody theater
Of stateliest view. Yet higher than their tops
The verdurous wall of Paradise up sprung;
Which to our general sire gave prospect large
Into his nether empire neighboring round.
And higher than that wall a circling row
Of goodliest trees loaden with fairest fruit,
Blossoms and fruits at once of golden hue
Appeared, with gay enamelled colors mixed;
On which the sun more glad impressed his beams   150
Than in fair evening cloud, or humid bow,
When God hath showered the earth; so lovely seemed
That landscape. And of pure now purer air
Meets his approach, and to the heart inspires
Vernal delight and joy, able to drive
All sadness but despair; now gentle gales
Fanning their odoriferous wings dispense
Native perfumes, and whisper whence they stole
Those balmy spoils. As when to them who sail
Beyond the Cape of Hope, and now are past   160
Mozambic, off at sea north-east winds blow
Sabæan odors from the spicy shore
Of Araby the Blest, with such delay
Well pleased they slack their course, and many a league
Cheered with the grateful smell old Ocean smiles.
So entertained those odorous sweets the Fiend
Who came their bane, though with them better pleased
Than Asmodëus with the fishy fume,
That drove him, though enamored, from the spouse
Of Tobit's son, and with a vengeance sent   170
From Media post to Egypt, there fast bound.

---

132 ff. Eden is apparently thought of as embracing the greater part of the Tigris and
Euphrates region. Paradise is a garden in the east of Eden.
    134. champaign head, level summit.
    145. nether empire, i.e., the outlying territories of Eden.
    149. enamelled, bright and variegated.
    167 ff. The allusion is to an episode related in the apocryphal Book of Tobit, 8. Tobit's son
is married to a maiden of Media, who is beloved by the evil spirit Asmodeus; to get rid of this
spirit he is instructed by the angel Raphael to burn the heart and liver of a fish. The odor
drives Asmodeus into Egypt, where the angel binds him.

Now to the ascent of that steep savage hill
Satan had journeyed on, pensive and slow;
But further way found none, so thick entwined,
As one continued brake, the undergrowth
Of shrubs and tangling bushes had perplexed
All path of man or beast that passed that way.
One gate there only was, and that looked east
On the other side; which when the Arch-Felon saw,
Due entrance he disdained, and in contempt,   180
At one slight bound high overleaped all bound
Of hill or highest wall, and sheer within
Lights on his feet. As when a prowling wolf,
Whom hunger drives to seek new haunt for prey,
Watching where shepherds pen their flocks at eve
In hurdled cotes amid the field secure,
Leaps o'er the fence with ease into the fold;
Or as a thief bent to unhoard the cash
Of some rich burgher, whose substantial doors,
Cross-barred and bolted fast, fear no assault,   190
In at the window climbs, or o'er the tiles:
So clomb this first grand thief into God's fold;
So since into his Church lewd hirelings climb.
Thence up he flew, and on the Tree of Life,
The middle tree and highest there that grew,
Sat like a cormorant; yet not true life
Thereby regained, but sat devising death
To them who lived; nor on the virtue thought
Of that life-giving plant, but only used
For prospect, what well used had been the pledge   200
Of immortality. So little knows
Any, but God alone, to value right
The good before him, but perverts best things
To worst abuse, or to their meanest use.
Beneath him with new wonder now he views
To all delight of human sense exposed
In narrow room Nature's whole wealth, yea more,
A Heaven on Earth, for blissful Paradise
Of God the garden was, by him in the east
Of Eden planted; Eden stretched her line   210
From Auran eastward to the royal towers
Of great Seleucia, built by Grecian kings,
Or where the sons of Eden long before
Dwelt in Telassar. In this pleasant soil

---

172. **savage,** woody.   176. **perplexed,** made difficult.
181. **bound . . . bound.** Note the play on words.   194. **Tree of Life.** Cf. Gen. 2:9.
196. **like a cormorant,** i.e., in the shape of a ravenous bird of prey.
211. **Auran,** a district of Syria, about fifty miles south of Damascus.
212. **Seleucia,** a city on the Tigris, about twenty miles southeast of modern Bagdad.
214. **Telassar,** an ancient site in Mesopotamia.

His far more pleasant garden God ordained;
Out of the fertile ground he caused to grow
All trees of noblest kind for sight, smell, taste;
And all amid them stood the Tree of Life,
High-eminent, blooming ambrosial fruit
Of vegetable gold; and next to life   220
Our death the Tree of Knowledge grew fast by,
Knowledge of good bought dear by knowing ill.
Southward through Eden went a river large,
Nor changed his course, but through the shaggy hill
Passed underneath ingulfed, for God had thrown
That mountain as his garden mould, high raised
Upon the rapid current, which through veins
Of porous earth with kindly thirst up drawn,
Rose a fresh fountain, and with many a rill
Watered the garden; thence united fell   230
Down the steep glade, and met the nether flood,
Which from his darksome passage now appears,
And now divided into four main streams,
Runs diverse, wandering many a famous realm
And country whereof here needs no account;
But rather to tell how, if art could tell,
How from that sapphire fount the crispèd brooks,
Rolling on orient pearl and sands of gold,
With mazy error under pendent shades
Ran nectar, visiting each plant, and fed   240
Flowers worthy of Paradise, which not nice art
In beds and curious knots, but Nature boon
Poured forth profuse on hill and dale and plain,
Both where the morning sun first warmly smote
The open field, and where the unpierced shade
Imbrowned the noon-tide bowers. Thus was this place,
A happy rural seat of various view;
Groves whose rich trees wept odorous gums and balm,
Others whose fruit burnished with golden rind
Hung amiable, Hesperian fables true,   250
If true, here only, and of delicious taste.
Betwixt them lawns, or level downs, and flocks
Grazing the tender herb, were interposed,

219. blooming, bearing.
223 ff. Southward . . . no account. Cf. Gen. 2:10. In IX, 71–73 Milton identifies this river with the Tigris.
233. four main streams. Cf. Gen. 2:10–14.   **238. orient,** lustrous.
239. error, wandering (the literal meaning of Latin *error*).
241–42. The natural profusion of Paradise is contrasted with the artificial arrangement of an Italian garden. **nice,** fastidious. **boon,** bounteous. This passage played a part in supporting later preference for the so-called English garden and for the love of natural scenery generally.
247. various view, varied aspect.
250–51. Milton means that here, if anywhere, was to be found such fruit as classical myth attributed to the Garden of the Hesperides. **amiable,** lovely.

Or palmy hillock, or the flowery lap
Of some irriguous valley spread her store,
Flowers of all hue, and without thorn the rose.
Another side, umbrageous grots and caves
Of cool recess, o'er which the mantling vine
Lays forth her purple grape, and gently creeps
Luxuriant; meanwhile murmuring waters fall   260
Down the slope hills, dispersed, or in a lake,
That to the fringèd bank with myrtle crowned
Her crystal mirror holds, unite their streams.
The birds their choir apply; airs, vernal airs,
Breathing the smell of field and grove, attune
The trembling leaves, while universal Pan,
Knit with the Graces and the Hours in dance,
Led on the eternal Spring. Not that fair field
Of Enna, where Proserpine gathering flowers
Herself a fairer flower by gloomy Dis   270
Was gathered, which cost Ceres all that pain
To seek her through the world; nor that sweet grove
Of Daphne by Orontes, and the inspired
Castalian spring, might with this Paradise
Of Eden strive; nor that Nyseian isle,
Girt with the river Triton, where old Cham
Whom Gentiles Ammon call and Lybian Jove,
Hid Amalthea and her florid son
Young Bacchus from his stepdame Rhea's eye;
Nor where Abassin kings their issue guard,   280
Mount Amara, though this by some supposed
True Paradise, under the Ethiop line
By Nilus' head, enclosed with shining rock,
A whole day's journey high, but wide remote
From this Assyrian garden, where the Fiend
Saw undelighted all delight, all kind
Of living creatures new to sight and strange.

255. irriguous, well-watered.

266 ff. Classical writers often made "the dance of the Hours" symbolic of the orderly succession of the seasons.

269 ff. Enna, etc. Proserpine (Greek Persephone), the daughter of Ceres, goddess of agriculture (Greek Demeter), was abducted by Dis, god of the underworld, from her garden in Enna (in Sicily). After a long search, Ceres found her daughter in the underworld and arranged that she should spend part of her time there and part on the earth. The myth obviously describes the alternation of the seasons. (Editors' note.)

273. Daphne, a town situated on the river **Orontes,** about five miles from Antioch. It contained a grove and fountain sacred to Apollo, the fountain being named after the more famous **Castalian spring** at Delphi.

275. that Nyseian isle, the island of Nysa, situated in the midst of the river **Triton** in northern Africa. The identification of Jupiter Ammon with Noah's son Ham (**Cham**) is an interesting Miltonic touch.

281. Mount Amara, a high hill on the Abyssinian plateau, the place of seclusion where, according to tradition, the Abyssinian princes were sent to be educated.

282. Ethiop line, the equator.

Two of far nobler shape erect and tall,
God-like erect, with native honor clad
In naked majesty seemed lords of all,   290
And worthy seemed, for in their looks divine
The image of their glorious Maker shone,
Truth, wisdom, sanctitude severe and pure,
Severe but in true filial freedom placed;
Whence true authority in men; though both
Not equal, as their sex not equal seemed;
For contemplation he and valor formed,
For softness she and sweet attractive grace;
He for God only, she for God in him.
His fair large front and eye sublime declared   300
Absolute rule; and hyacinthine locks
Round from his parted forelock manly hung
Clustering, but not beneath his shoulders broad:
She as a veil down to the slender waist
Her unadornëd golden tresses wore
Dishevelled, but in wanton ringlets waved
As the vine curls her tendrils, which implied
Subjection, but required with gentle sway,
And by her yielded, by him best received,
Yielded with coy submission, modest pride,   310
And sweet reluctant amorous delay.
Nor those mysterious parts were then concealed;
Then was not guilty shame; dishonest shame
Of Nature's works, honor dishonorable,
Sin-bred, how have ye troubled all mankind
With shows instead, mere shows of seeming pure,
And banished from man's life his happiest life,
Simplicity and spotless innocence.
So passed they naked on, nor shunned the sight
Of God or angel, for they thought no ill;   320
So hand in hand they passed, the loveliest pair
That ever since in love's embraces met:
Adam the goodliest man of men since born
His sons, the fairest of her daughters Eve.
Under a tuft of shade that on a green
Stood whispering soft, by a fresh fountain side
They sat them down; and after no more toil
Of their sweet gardening labor than sufficed

289. **God-like erect.** Milton makes man's upright stature a symbol of his superiority to the brutes and of his instinctive aspiration.

295 ff. Throughout the poem Milton carefully distinguishes between the relative endowments and obligations of man and woman. The sexes are not equal, he insists, and authority quite properly belongs to the male. But the position which he accords woman, when considered in the light of theological tradition, is exceedingly high.

300. **front,** brow.   301. **hyacinthine,** i.e., dark in color.

306. **wanton,** loose, unbound.   313. **dishonest,** unchaste.

323. **the goodliest man of men since born,** etc. The idiom is obviously illogical, but it has ample precedent in Elizabethan English as well as in Greek and Latin.

To recommend cool Zephyr, and made ease
More easy, wholesome thirst and appetite   330
More grateful, to their supper-fruits they fell,
Nectarine fruits which the compliant boughs
Yielded them, sidelong as they sat recline
On the soft downy bank damasked with flowers.
The savory pulp they chew, and in the rind
Still as they thirsted scoop the brimming stream;
Nor gentle purpose, nor endearing smiles
Wanted, nor youthful dalliance, as beseems
Fair couple linked in happy nuptial league,
Alone as they. About them frisking played   340
All beasts of the earth, since wild, and of all chase
In wood or wilderness, forest or den;
Sporting the lion ramped, and in his paw
Dandled the kid; bears, tigers, ounces, pards,
Gambolled before them; the unwieldy elephant
To make them mirth used all his might, and wreathed
His lithe proboscis; close the serpent sly
Insinuating, wove with Gordian twine
His braided train, and of his fatal guile
Gave proof unheeded; others on the grass   350
Couched, and now filled with pasture gazing sat,
Or bedward ruminating; for the sun
Declined was hasting now with prone career
To the Ocean Isles, and in the ascending scale
Of Heaven the stars that usher evening rose:
When Satan still in gaze, as first he stood,
Scarce thus at length failed speech recovered sad.
   "Oh Hell! what do mine eyes with grief behold!
Into our room of bliss thus high advanced
Creatures of other mould, earth-born perhaps,   360
Not spirits, yet to heavenly spirits bright
Little inferior; whom my thoughts pursue
With wonder, and could love, so lively shines
In them divine resemblance, and such grace
The hand that formed them on their shape hath poured.
Ah gentle pair, ye little think how nigh
Your change approaches, when all these delights
Will vanish and deliver ye to woe,
More woe, the more your taste is now of joy;
Happy, but for so happy ill secured   370
Long to continue, and this high seat your Heaven

---

333. recline, i.e., reclining.   **334. damasked,** ornamented with a variegated pattern.
337. purpose, conversation.   **343. ramped,** reared on his hind legs.
   348. Gordian twine, intricate tangle. The reference is to the famous Gordian knot, which no one could untie but which Alexander the Great finally cut with his sword.
   352. ruminating, chewing the cud.
   354. the Ocean Isles, i.e., the extreme west. Milton may here have in mind the Azores, as in 592; but the figure is used by classical writers without definite geographical reference.

Ill fenced for Heaven to keep out such a foe
As now is entered; yet no purposed foe
To you whom I could pity thus forlorn
Though I unpitied. League with you I seek,
And mutual amity so strait, so close,
That I with you must dwell, or you with me
Henceforth; my dwelling haply may not please
Like this fair Paradise, your sense, yet such
Accept your Maker's work; he gave it me,   380
Which I as freely give; Hell shall unfold,
To entertain you two, her widest gates,
And send forth all her kings; there will be room,
Not like these narrow limits, to receive
Your numerous offspring; if no better place,
Thank him who puts me loath to this revenge
On you who wrong me not, for him who wronged.
And should I at your harmless innocence
Melt, as I do, yet public reason just,
Honor and empire with revenge enlarged,   390
By conquering this new World, compels me now
To do what else though damned I should abhor."
   So spake the Fiend, and with necessity,
The tyrant's plea, excused his devilish deeds.
Then from his lofty stand on that high tree
Down he alights among the sportful herd
Of those four-footed kinds, himself now one,
Now other, as their shape served best his end
Nearer to view his prey, and unespied
To mark what of their state he more might learn   400
By word or action marked. About them round
A lion now he stalks with fiery glare;
Then as a tiger, who by chance hath spied
In some purlieu two gentle fawns at play,
Straight couches close, then rising changes oft
His couchant watch, as one who chose his ground
Whence rushing he might surest seize them both
Griped in each paw; when Adam first of men
To first of women Eve thus moving speech,
Turned him all ear to hear new utterance flow.   410
   "Sole partner and sole part of all these joys,
Dearer thyself than all, needs must the Power
That made us, and for us this ample World,
Be infinitely good, and of his good
As liberal and free as infinite,
That raised us from the dust and placed us here

389. By excusing his crime on the ground of political expediency, Satan once more demonstrates his proficiency in Machiavellian statecraft. Cf. I. 645–47, and note. That he can feel human pity is a survival of the divine endowment which he has perverted.
   411. Note the double play on words: **partner . . . part; sole . . . sole.** The first *sole* is used in the ordinary sense of "only," the second in the sense of "unrivaled," or "chief."

In all this happiness, who at his hand
Have nothing merited, nor can perform
Aught whereof he hath need, he who requires
From us no other service than to keep   420
This one, this easy charge, of all the trees
In Paradise that bear delicious fruit
So various, not to taste that only Tree
Of Knowledge, planted by the Tree of Life,
So near grows death to life, whate'er death is,
Some dreadful thing no doubt; for well thou know'st
God hath pronounced it death to taste that Tree;
The only sign of our obedience left
Among so many signs of power and rule
Conferred upon us, and dominion given   430
Over all other creatures that possess
Earth, air, and sea. Then let us not think hard
One easy prohibition, who enjoy
Free leave so large to all things else, and choice
Unlimited of manifold delights;
But let us ever praise him, and extol
His bounty, following our delightful task
To prune these growing plants, and tend these flowers,
Which were it toilsome, yet with thee were sweet."
    To whom thus Eve replied. "O thou for whom   440
And from whom I was formed flesh of thy flesh,
And without whom am to no end, my guide
And head, what thou hast said is just and right.
For we to him indeed all praises owe,
And daily thanks, I chiefly who enjoy
So far the happier lot, enjoying thee
Pre-eminent by so much odds, while thou
Like consort to thyself canst nowhere find.
That day I oft remember, when from sleep
I first awaked, and found myself reposed   450
Under a shade on flowers, much wondering where
And what I was, whence thither brought, and how.
Not distant far from thence a murmuring sound
Of waters issued from a cave and spread
Into a liquid plain, then stood unmoved
Pure as the expanse of Heaven; I thither went
With unexperienced thought, and laid me down
On the green bank, to look into the clear
Smooth lake, that to me seemed another sky.
As I bent down to look, just opposite   460
A shape within the watery gleam appeared
Bending to look on me: I started back,
It started back, but pleased I soon returned,
Pleased it returned as soon with answering looks
Of sympathy and love; there I had fixed
Mine eyes till now, and pined with vain desire,

Had not a voice thus warned me. 'What thou seest,
What there thou seest, fair creature, is thyself,
With thee it came and goes; but follow me,
And I will bring thee where no shadow stays   470
Thy coming, and thy soft embraces, he
Whose image thou art, him thou shalt enjoy
Inseparably thine; to him shalt bear
Multitudes like thyself, and thence be called
Mother of human race.' What could I do
But follow straight, invisibly thus led?
Till I espied thee, fair indeed and tall,
Under a platane; yet methought less fair,
Less winning soft, less amiably mild,
Than that smooth watery image; back I turned,   480
Thou following cried'st aloud, 'Return fair Eve,
Whom fliest thou? whom thou fliest, of him thou art,
His flesh, his bone; to give thee being I lent
Out of my side to thee, nearest my heart,
Substantial life, to have thee by my side
Henceforth an individual solace dear.
Part of my soul I seek thee, and thee claim
My other half.' With that thy gentle hand
Seized mine, I yielded, and from that time see
How beauty is excelled by manly grace   490
And wisdom, which alone is truly fair."
   So spake our general mother, and with eyes
Of conjugal attraction unreproved,
And meek surrender, half embracing leaned
On our first father; half her swelling breast
Naked met his under the flowing gold
Of her loose tresses hid. He in delight
Both of her beauty and submissive charms
Smiled with superior love, as Jupiter
On Juno smiles, when he impregns the clouds   500
That shed May flowers; and pressed her matron lip
With kisses pure. Aside the Devil turned
For envy, yet with jealous leer malign
Eyed them askance, and to himself thus plained.
   "Sight hateful, sight tormenting! thus these two
Imparadised in one another's arms,
The happier Eden, shall enjoy their fill
Of bliss on bliss, while I to Hell am thrust,
Where neither joy nor love, but fierce desire,
Among our other torments not the least,   510

470. stays, awaits.   **479. less amiably mild,** i.e., less fitted to inspire love.
486. individual, inseparable.   **493. unreproved,** unreprovable.
500. impregns, impregnates. Hera typifies the lower air or haze which surrounds the
earth, Zeus the upper air (aether). The mingling of the two produces the spring with its
flowers.
504. plained, complained, murmured.

Still unfulfilled with pain of longing pines;
Yet let me not forget what I have gained
From their own mouths. All is not theirs, it seems;
One fatal tree there stands, of Knowledge called,
Forbidden them to taste. Knowledge forbidden?
Suspicious, reasonless. Why should their Lord
Envy them that? can it be sin to know,
Can it be death? and do they only stand
By ignorance, is that their happy state,
The proof of their obedience and their faith?   520
O fair foundation laid whereon to build
Their ruin! Hence I will excite their minds
With more desire to know, and to reject
Envious commands, invented with design
To keep them low whom knowledge might exalt
Equal with gods. Aspiring to be such,
They taste and die; what likelier can ensue?
But first with narrow search I must walk round
This garden, and no corner leave unspied;
A chance but chance may lead where I may meet   530
Some wandering spirit of Heaven, by fountain side,
Or in thick shade retired, from him to draw
What further would be learned. Live while ye may,
Yet happy pair; enjoy, till I return,
Short pleasures, for long woes are to succeed."
   So saying, his proud step he scornful turned,
But with sly circumspection, and began
Through wood, through waste, o'er hill, o'er dale, his roam.
Meanwhile in utmost longitude, where Heaven
With Earth and Ocean meets, the setting sun   540
Slowly descended, and with right aspect
Against the eastern gate of Paradise
Levelled his evening rays. It was a rock
Of alabaster, piled up to the clouds,
Conspicuous far, winding with one ascent
Accessible from Earth, one entrance high;
The rest was craggy cliff, that overhung
Still as it rose, impossible to climb.
Betwixt these rocky pillars Gabriel sat,
Chief of the angelic guards, awaiting night;   550
About him exercised heroic games
The unarmed youth of Heaven, but nigh at hand
Celestial armory, shields, helms, and spears,

---

521 ff. Satan's own experience has taught him the allurement of godlike power, and the outcome of any attempt to gain it. He therefore has little difficulty in determining the most effective temptation. Cf. IX, 705 ff.
   530. A chance but, there is a chance that.
   539. in utmost longitude, in the extreme west.
   541. with right aspect, i.e., directly opposite. The setting sun, now on a level with the rock which forms the eastern gate of Paradise, throws its beams horizontally against the inner side.

Hung high, with diamond flaming and with gold.
Thither came Uriel, gliding through the even
On a sun beam, swift as a shooting star
In autumn thwarts the night, when vapors fired
Impress the air, and shows the mariner
From what point of his compass to beware
Impetuous winds. He thus began in haste.   560
  "Gabriel, to thee thy course by lot hath given
Charge and strict watch that to this happy place
No evil thing approach or enter in;
This day at height of noon came to my sphere
A spirit, zealous, as he seemed, to know
More of the Almighty's works, and chiefly Man
God's latest image. I described his way
Bent all on speed, and marked his airy gait;
But in the mount that lies from Eden north,
Where he first lighted, soon discerned his looks   570
Alien from Heaven, with passions foul obscured.
Mine eye pursued him still, but under shade
Lost sight of him; one of the banished crew
I fear, hath ventured from the Deep, to raise
New troubles; him thy care must be to find."
  To whom the wingèd warrior thus returned.
"Uriel, no wonder if thy perfect sight,
Amid the sun's bright circle where thou sitt'st,
See far and wide. In at this gate none pass
The vigilance here placed, but such as come   580
Well known from Heaven; and since meridian hour
No creature thence. If spirit of other sort,
So minded, have o'erleaped these earthy bounds
On purpose, hard thou know'st it to exclude
Spiritual substance with corporeal bar.
But if within the circuit of these walks
In whatsoever shape he lurk, of whom
Thou tell'st, by morrow dawning I shall know."
  So promised he, and Uriel to his charge
Returned on that bright beam, whose point now raised   590
Bore him slope downward to the sun now fallen
Beneath the Azores; whether the prime orb,

555. **Uriel.** The name means literally "Light of God." Cf. III, 645 ff.
557. **thwarts,** crosses.
561. The Scriptural references to Gabriel (Dan. 8, 9; Luke 1) depict him as a peaceful messenger of God. Milton makes him a great warrior, second only to Michael.
567. **God's latest image.** Christ is of course the first, and after him are the angels.
568. **his airy gait,** i.e., the course which he took through the air.
580. **vigilance,** guard. The abstract is used for the concrete.
590. **that bright beam, whose point now raised.** The sunbeam, which was horizontal when Uriel arrived at the gate of Paradise (555, 556), is now inclined upward.
592 **ff.** Milton shows his knowledge of both the Ptolemaic and the Copernican systems of astronomy, without committing himself as to which is right.
592. **the prime orb,** the sun.

Incredible how swift, had thither rolled
Diurnal, or this less volubil Earth
By shorter flight to the east, had left him there
Arraying with reflected purple and gold
The clouds that on his western throne attend.
  Now came still Evening on, and Twilight gray
Had in her sober livery all things clad;
Silence accompanied, for beast and bird,   600
They to their grassy couch, these to their nests
Were slunk, all but the wakeful nightingale;
She all night long her amorous descant sung;
Silence was pleased. Now glowed the firmament
With living sapphires; Hesperus that led
The starry host, rode brightest, till the Moon
Rising in clouded majesty, at length
Apparent queen unveiled her peerless light,
And o'er the dark her silver mantle threw.
When Adam thus to Eve. "Fair consort, the hour   610
Of night, and all things now retired to rest
Mind us of like repose, since God hath set
Labor and rest, as day and night to men
Successive, and the timely dew of sleep
Now falling with soft slumberous weight inclines
Our eye-lids; other creatures all day long
Rove idle, unemployed, and less need rest;
Man hath his daily work of body or mind
Appointed, which declares his dignity,
And the regard of Heaven on all his ways;   620
While other animals unactive range,
And of their doings God takes no account.
To-morrow ere fresh morning streak the east
With first approach of light, we must be risen,
And at our pleasant labor, to reform
Yon flowery arbors, yonder alleys green,
Our walks at noon, with branches overgrown,
That mock our scant manuring, and require
More hands than ours to lop their wanton growth.
Those blossoms also, and those dropping gums,   630
That lie bestrown unsightly and unsmooth,
Ask riddance, if we mean to tread with ease;
Meanwhile, as Nature wills, night bids us rest."
  To whom thus Eve with perfect beauty adorned.
"My author and disposer, what thou bidd'st
Unargued I obey; so God ordains.
God is thy law, thou mine; to know no more
Is woman's happiest knowledge and her praise.

---

594. volubil, swiftly rolling.   **603. descant,** a song, or rather a soprano part.
605. Hesperus, the evening star.   **608. Apparent,** manifest.
628. manuring, cultivating.

With thee conversing I forget all time,
All seasons and their change, all please alike.   640
Sweet is the breath of Morn, her rising sweet,
With charm of earliest birds; pleasant the Sun
When first on this delightful land he spreads
His orient beams, on herb, tree, fruit, and flower,
Glistering with dew; fragrant the fertile Earth
After soft showers; and sweet the coming on
Of grateful Evening mild, then silent Night
With this her solemn bird and this fair Moon,
And these the gems of Heaven, her starry train:
But neither breath of Morn when she ascends   650
With charm of earliest birds, nor rising Sun
On this delightful land, nor herb, fruit, flower,
Glistering with dew, nor fragrance after showers,
Nor grateful Evening mild, nor silent Night,
With this her solemn bird, nor walk by moon,
Or glittering star-light, without thee is sweet.
But wherefore all night long shine these? for whom
This glorious sight, when sleep hath shut all eyes?"
    To whom our general ancestor replied.
"Daughter of God and Man, accomplished Eve,   660
Those have their course to finish, round the Earth
By morrow evening, and from land to land
In order, though to nations yet unborn,
Ministering light prepared, they set and rise;
Lest total Darkness should by night regain
Her old possession, and extinguish life
In nature and all things; which these soft fires
Not only enlighten, but with kindly heat
Of various influence foment and warm,
Temper or nourish, or in part shed down   670
Their stellar virtue on all kinds that grow
On Earth, made hereby apter to receive
Perfection from the sun's more potent ray.
These then, though unbeheld in deep of night,
Shine not in vain, nor think, though men were none,
That Heaven would want spectators, God want praise;
Millions of spiritual creatures walk the Earth
Unseen, both when we wake, and when we sleep.
All these with ceaseless praise his works behold

640. all seasons, i.e., all times of the day. Spring is the only season of the year that Eve has yet experienced.

642. charm, song.

650 ff. Note how the imagery of the preceding nine lines is repeated with subtle variations in phrasing. Milton frequently makes effective use of repetition, but nowhere else does he work it into so elaborate a pattern. He is adorning or sophisticating a Homeric device, as he does in his use of similes, and in his structural adaptation of the epic throwback.

665. total Darkness, i.e., the darkness of Chaos. Cf. II, 984.

667 ff. The doctrine of stellar influence, which formed the basis of astrology, was still widely current in the seventeenth century. Milton seems to take its validity for granted.

Both day and night. How often from the steep 680
Of echoing hill or thicket have we heard
Celestial voices to the midnight air,
Sole, or responsive each to other's note,
Singing their great Creator; oft in bands
While they keep watch, or nightly rounding walk,
With heavenly touch of instrumental sounds
In full harmonic number joined, their songs
Divide the night, and lift our thoughts to Heaven."
    Thus talking, hand in hand alone they passed
On to their blissful bower; it was a place 690
Chosen by the sovran Planter, when he framed
All things to Man's delightful use; the roof
Of thickest covert was inwoven shade,
Laurel and myrtle, and what higher grew
Of firm and fragrant leaf; on either side
Acanthus, and each odorous bushy shrub
Fenced up the verdant wall; each beauteous flower,
Iris all hues, roses, and jessamine
Reared high their flourished heads between, and wrought
Mosaic; underfoot the violet, 700
Crocus, and hyacinth with rich inlay
Broidered the ground, more colored than with stone
Of costliest emblem. Other creature here,
Beast, bird, insect, or worm durst enter none;
Such was their awe of Man. In shadier bower
More sacred and sequestered, though but feigned,
Pan or Sylvanus never slept, nor Nymph
Nor Faunus haunted. Here in close recess
With flowers, garlands, and sweet-smelling herbs
Espousèd Eve decked first her nuptial bed, 710
And heavenly choirs the hymenæan sung,
What day the genial angel to our sire
Brought her in naked beauty more adorned,
More lovely than Pandora, whom the gods
Endowed with all their gifts, and O too like
In sad event, when to the unwiser son
Of Japhet brought by Hermes, she ensnared
Mankind with her fair looks, to be avenged

688. Divide the night, i.e., into watches.
703. emblem, embossed or inlaid ornamentation.
707. Pan, Sylvanus, and **Faunus** were classical deities of the fields and woods. The quali-fying **though but feigned** phrase, used with reference to their haunts, implies a judgment on much of the subject matter of pagan poetry. Milton frequently asserts the superior truth of his own materials. Cf. 250, 251, and note.
712. genial, nuptial, instrumental to marriage.
714 ff. The allusion is to a myth related by Hesiod. To be avenged on Prometheus, who had stolen fire from heaven for the use of mortals, Jove sent to earth **Pandora** ("the all-gifted"), on whom each of the gods had bestowed some fatal charm. Hermes conducted her to Epimetheus, the **unwiser son of Japhet,** who married her, despite the warning of his brother. Thereupon all the ills which she had brought from heaven were released to afflict humanity.

On him who had stole Jove's authentic fire.
   Thus at their shady lodge arrived, both stood,   720
Both turned, and under open sky adored
The God that made both sky, air, Earth, and Heaven,
Which they beheld, the moon's resplendent globe
And starry pole: "Thou also mad'st the night,
Maker Omnipotent, and thou the day,
Which we in our appointed work employed
Have finished happy in our mutual help
And mutual love, the crown of all our bliss
Ordained by thee, and this delicious place
For us too large, where thy abundance wants   730
Partakers, and uncropped falls to the ground.
But thou hast promised from us two a race
To fill the Earth, who shall with us extol
Thy goodness infinite, both when we wake,
And when we seek, as now, thy gift of sleep."
   This said unanimous, and other rites
Observing none, but adoration pure
Which God likes best, into their inmost bower
Handed they went; and eased the putting off
These troublesome disguises which we wear,   740
Straight side by side were laid, nor turned, I ween,
Adam from his fair spouse, nor Eve the rites
Mysterious of connubial love refused;
Whatever hypocrites austerely talk
Of purity and place and innocence,
Defaming as impure what God declares
Pure, and commands to some, leaves free to all.
Our Maker bids increase; who bids abstain
But our destroyer, foe to God and Man?
Hail wedded Love, mysterious law, true source   750
Of human offspring, sole propriety
In Paradise of all things common else.
By thee adulterous lust was driven from men
Among the bestial herds to range; by thee,
Founded in reason, loyal, just, and pure,
Relations dear, and all the charities
Of father, son, and brother first were known.
Far be it, that I should write thee sin or blame,
Or think thee unbefitting holiest place,
Perpetual fountain of domestic sweets,   760
Whose bed is undefiled and chaste pronounced,
Present or past, as saints and patriarchs used.

   719. authentic, original.   **739. Handed,** hand in hand.
   744 ff. Whatever hypocrites, etc. Throughout this passage, Milton is quite obviously taking issue with the advocates of monasticism and celibacy.
   751. sole propriety, sole property. Their love for each other is the one thing in Paradise which Adam and Eve have as their exclusive possession.
   756. charities, affections.

Here Love his golden shafts employs, here lights
His constant lamp, and waves his purple wings,
Reigns here and revels; not in the bought smile
Of harlots, loveless, joyless, unendeared,
Casual fruition; nor in court-amours,
Mixed dance, or wanton mask, or midnight ball,
Or serenate, which the starved lover sings
To his proud fair, best quitted with disdain.   770
These lulled by nightingales, embracing slept,
And on their naked limbs the flowery roof
Showered roses, which the morn repaired. Sleep on
Blest pair; and O yet happiest if ye seek
No happier state, and know to know no more.
    Now had night measured with her shadowy cone
Half way up hill this vast sublunar vault,
And from their ivory port the Cherubim
Forth issuing at the accustomed hour stood armed
To their night-watches in warlike parade,   780
When Gabriel to his next in power thus spake.
    "Uzziel, half these draw off, and coast the south
With strictest watch; these other wheel the north;
Our circuit meets full west." As flame they part,
Half wheeling to the shield, half to the spear.
From these, two strong and subtle spirits he called
That near him stood, and gave them thus in charge.
    "Ithuriel and Zephon, with winged speed
Search through this garden; leave unsearched no nook;
But chiefly where those two fair creatures lodge,   790
Now laid perhaps asleep secure of harm.
This evening from the sun's decline arrived
Who tells of some infernal spirit seen
Hitherward bent (who could have thought?) escaped
The bars of Hell, on errand bad no doubt:
Such where ye find, seize fast, and hither bring."
    So saying, on he led his radiant files,
Dazzling the moon; these to the bower direct

767. **nor in court-amours,** etc. Milton may be thinking specifically of the court of Charles II; but he is also thinking of the general chivalric tradition, the artificial conventions of which he believes to be irreconcilable with the ideal domestic relationship.

769. **serenate,** serenade. **starved,** i.e., suffering from cold.

775. **know to know no more,** i.e., are wise enough not to seek further knowledge.

776 ff. Night is the shadow of the earth cast by the sun. Since the sun is the larger body, the shadow, if viewed in its totality, would be a cone; and if the point of the cone had moved halfway from the horizon to the zenith (**half way up hill**), one-fourth of the night would be past. In other words, assuming the days and nights to be of equal length, the time would be nine o'clock.

778. **port,** gate. The Cherubim are appropriately assigned to sentinel duty because of their superior power of vision.

785. **Half wheeling to the shield, half to the spear,** i.e., half turning to the left, half to the right. The terms "shield side" and "spear side" were used by both the Greeks and the Romans.

786. **subtle,** i.e., quick to observe.   791. **secure of,** without fear of.

793. **Who,** i.e., one who.   798. **these,** i.e., Ithuriel and Zephon.

In search of whom they sought. Him there they found
Squat like a toad, close at the ear of Eve;   800
Assaying by his devilish art to reach
The organs of her fancy, and with them forge
Illusions as he list, phantasms and dreams;
Or if, inspiring venom, he might taint
The animal spirits that from pure blood arise
Like gentle breaths from rivers pure, thence raise
At least distempered, discontented thoughts,
Vain hopes, vain aims, inordinate desires
Blown up with high conceits engendering pride.
Him thus intent Ithuriel with his spear   810
Touched lightly; for no falsehood can endure
Touch of celestial temper, but returns
Of force to its own likeness. Up he starts
Discovered and surprised. As when a spark
Lights on a heap of nitrous powder, laid
Fit for the tun some magazine to store
Against a rumored war, the smutty grain
With sudden blaze diffused, inflames the air:
So started up in his own shape the Fiend.
Back stept those two fair angels half amazed   820
So sudden to behold the grisly king;
Yet thus, unmoved with fear, accost him soon.
    "Which of those rebel spirits adjudged to Hell
Com'st thou, escaped thy prison; and transformed,
Why sat'st thou like an enemy in wait
Here watching at the head of these that sleep?"
    "Know ye not then," said Satan, filled with scorn,
"Know ye not me? Ye knew me once no mate
For you, there sitting where ye durst not soar;
Not to know me argues yourselves unknown,   830
The lowest of your throng; or if ye know,
Why ask ye, and superfluous begin
Your message, like to end as much in vain?"
    To whom thus Zephon, answering scorn with scorn.
"Think not, revolted spirit, thy shape the same,
Or undiminished brightness, to be known
As when thou stood'st in Heaven upright and pure;
That glory then, when thou no more wast good,
Departed from thee, and thou resemblest now
Thy sin and place of doom obscure and foul.   840
But come, for thou, be sure, shalt give account
To him who sent us, whose charge is to keep
This place inviolable, and these from harm."
    So spake the Cherub, and his grave rebuke

---

813. **Of force,** of necessity, perforce.
829. **there sitting where ye durst not soar,** i.e., in the higher places of heaven. Ithuriel and Zephon had belonged to a lower order of angels than Satan.
830. **argues,** proves.   843. **these,** i.e., Adam and Eve.

Severe in youthful beauty, added grace
Invincible. Abashed the Devil stood,
And felt how awful goodness is, and saw
Virtue in her shape how lovely; saw, and pined
His loss; but chiefly to find here observed
His luster visibly impaired; yet seemed   850
Undaunted. "If I must contend," said he,
"Best with the best, the sender not the sent;
Or all at once; more glory will be won,
Or less be lost." "Thy fear," said Zephon bold,
"Will save us trial what the least can do
Single against thee wicked, and thence weak."
   The Fiend replied not, overcome with rage;
But like a proud steed reined, went haughty on,
Champing his iron curb. To strive or fly
He held it vain; awe from above had quelled   860
His heart, not else dismayed. Now drew they nigh
The western point, where those half-rounding guards
Just met, and closing stood in squadron joined
Awaiting next command. To whom their chief
Gabriel from the front thus called aloud.
   "O friends, I hear the tread of nimble feet
Hasting this way, and now by glimpse discern
Ithuriel and Zephon through the shade,
And with them comes a third, of regal port,
But faded splendor wan; who by his gait   870
And fierce demeanor seems the Prince of Hell,
Not likely to part hence without contest;
Stand firm, for in his look defiance lours."
   He scarce had ended, when those two approached
And brief related whom they brought, where found,
How busied, in what form and posture couched.
To whom with stern regard thus Gabriel spake.
"Why hast thou, Satan, broke the bounds prescribed
To thy transgressions, and disturbed the charge
Of others, who approve not to transgress   880
By thy example, but have power and right
To question thy bold entrance on this place;
Employed it seems to violate sleep, and those
Whose dwelling God hath planted here in bliss?"
   To whom thus Satan, with contemptuous brow.
"Gabriel, thou hadst in Heaven the esteem of wise,
And such I held thee; but this question asked
Puts me in doubt. Lives there who loves his pain?
Who would not, finding way, break loose from Hell,
Though thither doomed? Thou wouldst thyself, no doubt,   890

   861 ff. Note the military exactness of Milton's description. The maneuver ordered by
Gabriel (782–84) has been executed, and the full angelic guard is now drawn up along the
western extremity of Paradise.
   869. port, bearing.   **886. the esteem of wise,** the repute of being wise.

And boldly venture to whatever place
Farthest from pain, where thou mightst hope to change
Torment with ease, and soonest recompense
Dole with delight, which in this place I sought;
To thee no reason; who know'st only good,
But evil hast not tried. And wilt object
His will who bound us? let him surer bar
His iron gates, if he intends our stay
In that dark durance. Thus much what was asked.
The rest is true, they found me where they say;   900
But that implies not violence or harm."
    Thus he in scorn. The warlike angel moved,
Disdainfully half smiling thus replied.
"O loss of one in Heaven to judge of wise,
Since Satan fell, whom folly overthrew,
And now returns him from his prison scaped,
Gravely in doubt whether to hold them wise
Or not, who ask what boldness brought him hither
Unlicensed from his bounds in Hell prescribed;
So wise he judges it to fly from pain   910
However, and to scape his punishment.
So judge thou still, presumptuous, till the wrath,
Which thou incurr'st by flying, meet thy flight
Sevenfold, and scourge that wisdom back to Hell,
Which taught thee yet no better, that no pain
Can equal anger infinite provoked.
But wherefore thou alone? wherefore with thee
Came not all Hell broke loose? is pain to them
Less pain, less to be fled or thou than they
Less hardy to endure? Courageous chief,   920
The first in flight from pain, hadst thou alleged
To thy deserted host this cause of flight,
Thou surely hadst not come sole fugitive."
    To which the Fiend thus answered frowning stern.
"Not that I less endure, or shrink from pain,
Insulting angel, well thou know'st I stood
Thy fiercest, when in battle to thy aid
The blasting vollied thunder made all speed
And seconded thy else not dreaded spear.
But still thy words at random, as before,   930
Argue thy inexperience what behooves
From hard assays and ill successes past
A faithful leader, not to hazard all

---

904. O loss of one in Heaven to judge of wise, i.e., What a loss Heaven has sustained in the loss of one so well qualified to judge of wisdom.

911. However, in whatever manner.

921. The first in flight, etc. Satan has taken great pride in the courage demanded by his journey of exploration (cf. II, 430–66; 826–31). Gabriel's insistence that it was entered upon through cowardice is therefore peculiarly fitted to exasperate him.

926–27. I stood Thy fiercest, i.e., I withstood thy fiercest attack.

Through ways of danger by himself untried.
I therefore, I alone first undertook
To wing the desolate Abyss, and spy
This new-created World, whereof in Hell
Fame is not silent, here in hope to find
Better abode, and my afflicted powers
To settle here on Earth, or in mid air;   940
Though for possession put to try once more
What thou and thy gay legions dare against;
Whose easier business were to serve their Lord
High up in Heaven, with songs to hymn his throne,
And practised distances to cringe, not fight."
   To whom the warrior angel soon replied.
"To say and straight unsay, pretending first
Wise to fly pain, professing next the spy,
Argues no leader but a liar traced,
Satan, and couldst thou 'faithful' add? O name,   950
O sacred name of faithfulness profaned!
Faithful to whom? to thy rebellious crew?
Army of fiends, fit body to fit head;
Was this your discipline and faith engaged,
Your military obedience, to dissolve
Allegiance to the acknowledged Power Supreme?
And thou sly hypocrite, who now wouldst seem
Patron of liberty, who more than thou
Once fawned, and cringed, and servilely adored
Heaven's awful Monarch? wherefore but in hope   960
To dispossess him, and thyself to reign?
But mark what I areed thee now: Avaunt;
Fly thither whence thou fledst. If from this hour
Within these hallowed limits thou appear,
Back to the infernal pit I drag thee chained,
And seal thee so, as henceforth not to scorn
The facile gates of Hell too slightly barred."
   So threatened he, but Satan to no threats
Gave heed, but waxing more in rage replied.
   "Then when I am thy captive talk of chains,   970
Proud limitary Cherub, but ere then
Far heavier load thyself expect to feel
From my prevailing arm, though Heaven's King
Ride on thy wings, and thou with thy compeers,
Used to the yoke, drawest his triumphant wheels

938. **Fame,** report.
942. **gay,** bright, shining. Having lost his own brilliance, Satan disparages the quality in
those who have retained it.
945. **practised distances to cringe,** i.e., to make the obeisances prescribed by court eti-
quette.
962. **areed,** advise.
971. **limitary,** i.e., set to guard the frontiers (Latin *limites*). Satan uses the word in sarcastic
allusion to the "hallowed limits" spoken of by Gabriel (964).

In progress through the road of Heaven star-paved."
    While thus he spake, the angelic squadron bright
Turned fiery red, sharpening in mooned horns
Their phalanx, and began to hem him round
With ported spears, as thick as when a field   980
Of Ceres ripe for harvest waving bends
Her bearded grove of ears, which way the wind
Sways them; the careful ploughman doubting stands
Lest on the threshing-floor his hopeful sheaves
Prove chaff. On the other side Satan alarmed
Collecting all his might dilated stood,
Like Teneriff or Atlas unremoved:
His stature reached the sky, and on his crest
Sat Horror plumed; nor wanted in his grasp
What seemed both spear and shield. Now dreadful deeds   990
Might have ensued, nor only Paradise
In this commotion, but the starry cope
Of Heaven perhaps, or all the elements
At least had gone to wrack, disturbed and torn
With violence of this conflict, had not soon
The Eternal to prevent such horrid fray
Hung forth in Heaven his golden scales, yet seen
Betwixt Astræa and the Scorpion sign,
Wherein all things created first he weighed,
The pendulous round Earth with balanced air   1000
In counterpoise, now ponders all events,
Battles and realms: in these he put two weights
The sequel each of parting and of fight;
The latter quick up flew, and kicked the beam;
Which Gabriel spying, thus bespake the Fiend.
    "Satan, I know thy strength, and thou know'st mine,
Neither our own, but given; what folly then
To boast what arms can do, since thine no more

---

978. in mooned horns, in the form of a crescent.
    980. with ported spears, i.e., with spears held slantwise against the body, points to the left,
preparatory to leveling them for the charge. The command "Port arms" is still used in the
modern manual.
    980–81. a field of Ceres, i.e., a field of grain (Ceres being the ancient goddess of agricul-
ture).
    985. alarmed, aroused, put on guard.
    987. Teneriff, a high peak on one of the Canary Islands. **Atlas,** a range of mountains in
northern Africa. According to classical myth, the heavens rested on its summit. **unremoved,**
unremovable.
    993. all the elements, i.e., the fabric of the terrestrial universe, as distinct from "the starry
cope."
    997 ff. The passage is based on the famous figure of the golden scales in *Iliad* viii. Milton,
however, makes two significant additions: he identifies the scales with the zodiacal constellation Libra, which is located between Virgo (**Astræa**) and the Scorpion; and he further identifies them with the scales mentioned in Isa. 40:12, as being used by God to weigh the elements
of the universe.
    1001. ponders, weighs (the literal meaning of Latin *ponderare*).
    1003. the sequel, i.e., the consequence to Satan.

Than Heaven permits, nor mine, though doubled now
To trample thee as mire: for proof look up, 1010
And read thy lot in yon celestial sign
Where thou art weighed, and shown how light, how weak,
If thou resist." The Fiend looked up, and knew
His mounted scale aloft: nor more; but fled
Murmuring; and with him fled the shades of Night.

BOOK V: THE ARGUMENT

Morning approached, Eve relates to Adam her troublesome dream; he likes it not, yet comforts her; they come forth to their day labors; their morning hymn at the door of their bower. God, to render Man inexcusable, sends Raphael to admonish him of his obedience, of his free estate, of his enemy near at hand—who he is, and why his enemy, and whatever else may avail Adam to know. Raphael comes down to Paradise; his appearance described; his coming discerned by Adam afar off, sitting at the door of his bower; he goes out to meet him, brings him to his lodge, entertains him with the choicest fruits of Paradise got together by Eve; their discourse at table. Raphael performs his message, minds Adam of his state and of his enemy; relates, at Adam's request, who that enemy is, and how he came to be so, beginning from his first revolt in Heaven, and the occasion thereof; how he drew his legions after him to the parts of the North, and there incited them to rebel with him, persuading all but only Abdiel, a Seraph, who in argument dissuades and opposes him, then forsakes him.

BOOK VI: THE ARGUMENT

Raphael continues to relate how Michael and Gabriel were sent forth to battle against Satan and his angels. The first fight described; Satan and his Powers retire under night. He calls a council; invents devilish engines, which, in the second day's fight, put Michael and his angels to some disorder; but they at length, pulling up mountains, overwhelmed both the force and machines of Satan. Yet, the tumult not so ending, God, on the third day, sends Messiah his Son, for whom he had reserved the glory of that victory. He, in the power of his Father, coming to the place, and causing all his legions to stand still on either side, with his chariot and thunder driving into the midst of his enemies, pursues them, unable to resist, towards the wall of Heaven; which opening, they leap down with horror and confusion into the place of punishment prepared for them in the deep. Messiah returns with triumph to his Father.

BOOK VII: THE ARGUMENT

Raphael, at the request of Adam, relates how and wherefore this World was first created: that God, after the expelling of Satan and his angels out of Heaven, declared his pleasure to create another World, and other creatures to dwell therein; sends his Son with glory, and attendance of angels, to perform the work of creation in six days: the angels celebrate with hymns the performance thereof, and his reascension into Heaven.

1014. nor more, i.e., made no further show of resistance.

BOOK VIII: THE ARGUMENT

Adam inquires concerning celestial motions; is doubtfully answered, and exhorted to search rather things more worthy of knowledge. Adam assents, and still desirous to detain Raphael, relates to him what he remembered since his own creation: his placing in Paradise, his talk with God concerning solitude and fit society, his first meeting and nuptials with Eve. His discourse with the angel thereupon; who, after admonitions repeated, departs.

BOOK IX

THE ARGUMENT

Satan, having compassed the Earth, with meditated guile returns as a mist by night into Paradise; enters into the serpent sleeping. Adam and Eve in the morning go forth to their labors, which Eve proposes to divide in several places, each laboring apart: Adam consents not, alleging the danger, lest that enemy, of whom they were forewarned, should attempt her found alone. Eve, loth to be thought not circumspect or firm enough, urges her going apart, the rather desirous to make trial of her strength; Adam at last yields. The Serpent finds her alone: his subtle approach, first gazing, then speaking, with much flattery extolling Eve above all other creatures. Eve, wondering to hear the Serpent speak, asks how he attained to human speech and such understanding, not till now; the Serpent answers, that by tasting of a certain tree in the garden he attained both to speech and reason, till then void of both. Eve requires him to bring her to that tree, and finds it to be the Tree of Knowledge forbidden. The Serpent, now grown bolder, with many wiles and arguments induces her at length to eat; she, pleased with the taste, deliberates a while whether to impart thereof to Adam or not; at last brings him of the fruit; relates what persuaded her to eat thereof. Adam, at first amazed, but perceiving her lost, resolves through vehemence of love to perish with her, and, extenuating the trespass, eats also of the fruit. The effects thereof in them both; they seek to cover their nakedness; then fall to variance and accusation of one another.

No more of talk where God or angel guest
With Man, as with his friend, familiar used
To sit indulgent, and with him partake
Rural repast, permitting him the while
Venial discourse unblamed. I now must change
Those notes to tragic; foul distrust and breach
Disloyal on the part of man, revolt
And disobedience; on the part of Heaven
Now alienated, distance and distaste,

1 ff. The long conversation between Raphael and Adam, forming the substance of Books V–VIII, has introduced the antecedent action and illuminated more fully the existing situation. Now before entering upon the climax of his narrative, Milton pauses for a brief meditative interlude. The personal allusions in the opening lines of this book are of exceptional interest.

6–12. Cf. I, 3. The theme announced at the beginning of the poem is repeated in expanded form.

Anger and just rebuke, and judgment given,　　　　　　　　　　　　　　10
That brought into this World a world of woe,
Sin and her shadow Death, and Misery
Death's harbinger. Sad task, yet argument
Not less but more heroic than the wrath
Of stern Achilles on his foe pursued
Thrice fugitive about Troy wall; or rage
Of Turnus for Lavinia disespoused;
Or Neptune's ire or Juno's, that so long
Perplexed the Greek and Cytherea's son;
If answerable style I can obtain　　　　　　　　　　　　　　　　　　　20
Of my celestial patroness, who deigns
Her nightly visitation unimplored,
And dictates to me slumbering, or inspires
Easy my unpremeditated verse;
Since first this subject for heroic song
Pleased me long choosing and beginning late;
Not sedulous by nature to indite
Wars, hitherto the only argument
Heroic deemed, chief mastery to dissect
With long and tedious havoc fabled knights　　　　　　　　　　　　　30
In battles feigned; the better fortitude
Of patience and heroic martyrdom
Unsung; or to describe races and games,
Or tilting furniture, imblazoned shields,
Impresses quaint, caparisons and steeds,
Bases and tinsel trappings, gorgeous knights
At joust and tournament; then marshalled feast
Served up in hall with sewers and seneshals,
The skill of artifice or office mean,
Not that which justly gives heroic name　　　　　　　　　　　　　　40
To person or to poem. Me of these
Nor skilled nor studious, higher argument
Remains, sufficient of itself to raise

---

13 ff. Having restated his theme, Milton here asserts its superiority to the themes of the three great classical epics: (1) the *Iliad*, which deals with **the wrath of stern Achilles;** (2) the *Odyssey*, which relates the outcome of **Neptune's ire** against the Greek Odysseus; (3) the *Aeneid*, the first part of which is motivated by the hostility of **Juno** toward Aeneas (**Cytherea's son**), and the second part by the anger of **Turnus** at the loss of **Lavinia.**

20. answerable style, i.e., a style commensurate with the dignity of the theme.

21–23. Cf. III, 29–40. The implication is that with Milton composition was a spontaneous process, based on a passive reception of impressions and ideas.

25 ff. From the Cambridge MS. it is evident that the subject of *Paradise Lost* (together with various other subjects drawn from biblical and British history) was in Milton's mind by 1640 or soon after. The actual composition of the epic could not have been begun much before 1658.

33. races and games. Milton is thinking of the detailed accounts in *Iliad* xxiii, and *Aeneid* v. His own references to such games (II, 528–38; IV, 551, 552) are brief.

34. tilting furniture, etc., i.e., the trappings of chivalry.

35. impresses, devices on shields.

36. bases, kilt-like garments worn by knights on horseback.

41–43. Me . . . remains. To me, who am, etc., there remains.

That name, unless an age too late, or cold
Climate, or years damp my intended wing
Depressed, and much they may, if all be mine,
Not hers who brings it nightly to my ear.
   The sun was sunk, and after him the star
Of Hesperus, whose office is to bring
Twilight upon the Earth, short arbiter   50
'Twixt day and night, and now from end to end
Night's hemisphere had veiled the horizon round;
When Satan who late fled before the threats
Of Gabriel out of Eden, now improved
In meditated fraud and malice, bent
On Man's destruction, maugre what might hap
Of heavier on himself, fearless returned.
By night he fled, and at midnight returned
From compassing the Earth, cautious of day,
Since Uriel, regent of the sun, descried   60
His entrance, and forewarned the Cherubim
That kept their watch; thence full of anguish driven,
The space of seven continued nights he rode
With darkness, thrice the equinoctial line
He circled, four times crossed the car of Night
From pole to pole, traversing each colure;
On the eighth returned, and on the coast averse
From entrance or cherubic watch, by stealth
Found unsuspected way. There was a place,
Now not, though sin, not time, first wrought the change,   70
Where Tigris at the foot of Paradise
Into a gulf shot under ground, till part
Rose up a fountain by the Tree of Life;
In with the river sunk, and with it rose
Satan involved in rising mist, then sought
Where to lie hid; sea he had searched and land
From Eden over Pontus, and the pool
Mæotis, up beyond the river Ob;
Downward as far antarctic; and in length

44–45. an age too late, i.e., too late a period in the world's history. The notion of universal retrogression was fairly common in the seventeenth century. Though Milton had argued against the theory, he here shows that he is not unaffected by fear that it may be true. **or cold Climate.** The idea that a northern climate is unfavorable to works of the mind goes back to Aristotle.

56. maugre, in spite of.

66. traversing each colure. The colures are two great circles intersecting at the poles, one passing through the equinoxes, the other (at right angles to it) through the solstices. Satan follows each of these lines from south to north and back, keeping always within the earth's shadow.

69 ff. Cf. IV, 223–30. Satan makes his entrance from the north side. Satan's wanderings, first described astronomically, are here described geographically. Northward he had gone over the Black Sea (**Pontus**) and the Sea of Azof (**the pool Mæotis**), beyond the Siberian river **Ob** to the pole; thence southward to the Antarctic. Westward he had gone along the Syrian river **Orontes,** over the Mediterranean and Atlantic to the Isthmus of Panama (**Darien**), and from there across the Pacific to India (the land of **Ganges and Indus**).

West from Orontes to the ocean barred   80
At Darien, thence to the land where flows
Ganges and Indus. Thus the orb he roamed
With narrow search, and with inspection deep
Considered every creature, which of all
Most opportune might serve his wiles, and found
The serpent subtlest beast of all the field.
Him after long debate, irresolute
Of thoughts revolved, his final sentence chose
Fit vessel, fittest imp of fraud, in whom
To enter, and his dark suggestions hide   90
From sharpest sight; for in the wily snake,
Whatever sleights none would suspicious mark,
As from his wit and native subtlety
Proceeding, which in other beasts observed,
Doubt might beget of diabolic power
Active within beyond the sense of brute.
Thus he resolved, but first from inward grief
His bursting passion into plaints thus poured.
"O Earth, how like to Heaven, if not preferred
More justly, seat worthier of Gods, as built   100
With second thoughts, reforming what was old!
For what God after better worse would build?
Terrestrial Heaven, danced round by other Heavens
That shine, yet bear their bright officious lamps,
Light above light, for thee alone, as seems,
In thee concentring all their precious beams
Of sacred influence. As God in Heaven
Is center, yet extends to all, so thou
Centring receivest from all those orbs; in thee,
Not in themselves, all their known virtue appears   110
Productive in herb, plant, and nobler birth
Of creatures animate with gradual life
Of growth, sense, reason, all summed up in Man.
With what delight could I have walked thee round,
If I could joy in aught, sweet interchange
Of hill and valley, rivers, woods, and plains,
Now land, now sea, and shores with forest crowned,
Rocks, dens, and caves; but I in none of these
Find place or refuge; and the more I see
Pleasures about me, so much more I feel   120
Torment within me, as from the hateful siege
Of contraries; all good to me becomes
Bane, and in Heaven much worse would be my state.
But neither here seek I, no nor in Heaven

82. orb, the world.   **88. sentence,** decision.   **89. imp,** offspring.

99 ff. "O Earth," etc. Cf. Satan's soliloquy on first gaining sight of Eden, IV, 32 ff. As then, he is torn by passion, but now there is less of remorse, more of bitterness and despair.

103. danced round by other Heavens. Milton frequently compares the motion of the heavenly bodies to a dance.

To dwell, unless by mastering Heaven's Supreme;
Nor hope to be myself less miserable
By what I seek, but others to make such
As I, though thereby worse to me redound:
For only in destroying I find ease
To my relentless thoughts; and him destroyed,   130
Or won to what may work his utter loss,
For whom all this was made, all this will soon
Follow, as to him linked in weal or woe;
In woe then, that destruction wide may range.
To me shall be the glory sole among
The infernal Powers, in one day to have marred
What he Almighty styled, six nights and days
Continued making, and who knows how long
Before had been contriving, though perhaps
Not longer than since I in one night freed   140
From servitude inglorious well nigh half
The angelic name, and thinner left the throng
Of his adorers. He to be avenged,
And to repair his numbers thus impaired,
Whether such virtue spent of old now failed
More angels to create, if they at least
Are his created, or to spite us more,
Determined to advance into our room
A creature formed of earth, and him endow,
Exalted from so base original,   150
With heavenly spoils, our spoils. What he decreed
He effected; Man he made, and for him built
Magnificent this World, and Earth his seat,
Him lord pronounced, and, O indignity!
Subjected to his service angel wings,
And flaming ministers to watch and tend
Their earthy charge. Of these the vigilance
I dread, and to elude, thus wrapped in mist
Of midnight vapor glide obscure, and pry
In every bush and brake, where hap may find   160
The serpent sleeping, in whose mazy folds
To hide me, and the dark intent I bring.
O foul descent! that I who erst contended
With Gods to sit the highest, am now constrained
Into a beast, and, mixed with bestial slime,
This essence to incarnate and imbrute,
That to the height of deity aspired;
But what will not ambition and revenge
Descend to? Who aspires must down as low
As high he soared, obnoxious first or last   170

---

142. name, race, stock.

163 ff. Cf. IV, 835–40. Satan's imbruting himself within the serpent is the final step in his progressive degeneration. His own words explain the symbolism.

170. obnoxious, liable, subject.

To basest things. Revenge, at first though sweet,
Bitter ere long back on itself recoils;
Let it; I reck not, so it light well aimed,
Since higher I fall short, on him who next
Provokes my envy, this new favorite
Of Heaven, this man of clay, son of despite,
Whom us the more to spite his Maker raised
From dust: spite then with spite is best repaid."
   So saying, through each thicket dank or dry,
Like a black mist low creeping, he held on   180
His midnight search, where soonest he might find
The serpent. Him fast sleeping soon he found
In labyrinth of many a round self-rolled,
His head the midst, well stored with subtle wiles;
Not yet in horrid shade or dismal den,
Nor nocent yet, but on the grassy herb
Fearless unfeared he slept. In at his mouth
The Devil entered, and his brutal sense,
In heart or head, possessing soon inspired
With act intelligential, but his sleep   190
Disturbed not, waiting close the approach of morn.
   Now whenas sacred light began to dawn
In Eden on the humid flowers, that breathed
Their morning incense, when all things that breathe,
From the Earth's great altar send up silent praise
To the Creator, and his nostrils fill
With grateful smell, forth came the human pair
And joined their vocal worship to the choir
Of creatures wanting voice; that done, partake
The season, prime for sweetest scents and airs;   200
Then commune how that day they best may ply
Their growing work; for much their work outgrew
The hands' dispatch of two gardening so wide.
And Eve first to her husband thus began.
   "Adam, well may we labor still to dress
This garden, still to tend plant, herb, and flower,
Our pleasant task enjoined, but till more hands
Aid us, the work under our labor grows,
Luxurious by restraint; what we by day
Lop overgrown, or prune, or prop, or bind,   210
One night or two with wanton growth derides
Tending to wild. Thou therefore now advise
Or hear what to my mind first thoughts present:
Let us divide our labors, thou where choice
Leads thee, or where most needs, whether to wind
The woodbine round this arbor, or direct
The clasping ivy where to climb, while I

199–200. partake the season, i.e., share the beauties of the morning. As in IV, 640, **season** refers to the time of day.

In yonder spring of roses intermixed
With myrtle, find what to redress till noon.
For while so near each other thus all day   220
Our task we choose, what wonder if so near
Looks intervene and smiles, or object new
Casual discourse draw on, which intermits
Our day's work, brought to little, though begun
Early, and the hour of supper comes unearned."
    To whom mild answer Adam thus returned.
"Sole Eve, associate sole, to me beyond
Compare above all living creatures dear,
Well hast thou motioned, well thy thoughts employed
How we might best fulfil the work which here   230
God hath assigned us, nor of me shalt pass
Unpraised; for nothing lovelier can be found
In woman, than to study household good,
And good works in her husband to promote.
Yet not so strictly hath our Lord imposed
Labor, as to debar us when we need
Refreshment, whether food, or talk between,
Food of the mind, or this sweet intercourse
Of looks and smiles, for smiles from reason flow,
To brute denied, and are of love the food,   240
Love not the lowest end of human life.
For not to irksome toil, but to delight
He made us, and delight to reason joined.
These paths and bowers doubt not but our joint hands
Will keep from wilderness with ease, as wide
As we need walk, till younger hands ere long
Assist us. But if much converse perhaps
Thee satiate, to short absence I could yield;
For solitude sometimes is best society,
And short retirement urges sweet return.   250
But other doubt possesses me, lest harm
Befall thee severed from me; for thou know'st
What hath been warned us, what malicious foe
Envying our happiness, and of his own
Despairing, seeks to work us woe and shame
By sly assault; and somewhere nigh at hand
Watches, no doubt, with greedy hope to find
His wish and best advantage, us asunder,
Hopeless to circumvent us joined, where each
To other speedy aid might lend at need;   260
Whether his first design be to withdraw
Our feälty from God, or to disturb
Conjugal love, than which perhaps no bliss
Enjoyed by us excites his envy more;

---

    218. spring, clump, thicket.   **229. motioned,** proposed.
    245. wilderness, wildness (i.e., too luxuriant growth of vegetation).

Or this, or worse, leave not the faithful side
That gave thee being, still shades thee and protects.
The wife, where danger or dishonor lurks,
Safest and seemliest by her husband stays,
Who guards her, or with her the worst endures."
    To whom the virgin majesty of Eve,   270
As one who loves, and some unkindness meets,
With sweet austere composure thus replied.
    "Offspring of Heaven and Earth, and all Earth's lord,
That such an enemy we have, who seeks
Our ruin, both by thee informed I learn,
And from the parting angel overheard
As in a shady nook I stood behind,
Just then returned at shut of evening flowers.
But that thou shouldst my firmness therefore doubt
To God or thee, because we have a foe   280
May tempt it, I expected not to hear.
His violence thou fear'st not, being such,
As we, not capable of death or pain,
Can either not receive, or can repel.
His fraud is then thy fear, which plain infers
Thy equal fear that my firm faith and love
Can by his fraud be shaken or seduced;
Thoughts, which how found they harbor in thy breast,
Adam, misthought of her to thee so dear?"
    To whom with healing words Adam replied.   290
"Daughter of God and Man, immortal Eve,
For such thou art, from sin and blame entire;
Not diffident of thee do I dissuade
Thy absence from my sight, but to avoid
The attempt itself, intended by our foe.
For he who tempts, though in vain, at least asperses
The tempted with dishonor foul, supposed
Not incorruptible of faith, not proof
Against temptation. Thou thyself with scorn
And anger wouldst resent the offered wrong,   300
Though ineffectual found. Misdeem not then,
If such affront I labor to avert
From thee alone, which on us both at once
The enemy, though bold, will hardly dare,
Or daring, first on me the assault shall light.
Nor thou his malice and false guile contemn;
Subtle he needs must be, who could seduce
Angels, nor think superfluous others' aid.
I from the influence of thy looks receive
Access in every virtue, in thy sight   310

265. **Or this, or worse,** i.e., whether his design (261) be this or worse.
276. **from the parting angel,** i.e., from Raphael as he was parting from Adam.
292. **entire,** untouched.   310. **access,** growth, increase.

More wise, more watchful, stronger, if need were
Of outward strength; while shame, thou looking on,
Shame to be overcome or overreached,
Would utmost vigor raise, and raised unite.
Why shouldst not thou like sense within thee feel
When I am present, and thy trial choose
With me, best witness of thy virtue tried."
So spake domestic Adam in his care
And matrimonial love; but Eve, who thought
Less attributed to her faith sincere,   320
Thus her reply with accent sweet renewed.
    "If this be our condition, thus to dwell
In narrow circuit straitened by a foe,
Subtle or violent, we not endued
Single with like defence, wherever met,
How are we happy, still in fear of harm?
But harm precedes not sin: only our foe
Tempting affronts us with his foul esteem
Of our integrity; his foul esteem
Sticks no dishonor on our front, but turns   330
Foul on himself; then wherefore shunned or feared
By us? who rather double honor gain
From his surmise proved false, find peace within,
Favor from Heaven, our witness, from the event.
And what is faith, love, virtue, unassayed
Alone, without exterior help sustained?
Let us not then suspect our happy state
Left so imperfect by the Maker wise,
As not secure to single or combined.
Frail is our happiness, if this be so,   340
And Eden were no Eden thus exposed."
    To whom thus Adam fervently replied.
"O Woman, best are all things as the will
Of God ordained them; his creating hand
Nothing imperfect or deficient left
Of all that he created, much less Man,
Or aught that might his happy state secure,
Secure from outward force: within himself
The danger lies, yet lies within his power;
Against his will he can receive no harm.   350

318. **domestic,** devoted to home life and its duties.   **320. less,** too little.
328. **affronts.** The literal meaning "strikes on the forehead" is implied (Latin *ad + frons*).
Note how the image is expanded in the two lines following.
335. **And what is faith, love, virtue,** etc., i.e., what value have these qualities unless they
have been tested and found able to stand by their own merits. Milton here puts in the mouth
of Eve an argument which he himself used in *Areopagitica.* Cf. the famous passage: "I cannot
praise a fugitive and cloistered virtue," etc.
339. **to single or combined,** i.e., to us singly or together.
341. **no Eden,** no place of delight. Cf. note on IV, 27, 28.
348 ff. **within himself . . . no harm.** The principle of human responsibility is fundamental
to Milton's whole philosophy.

But God left free the will, for what obeys
Reason is free, and Reason he made right,
But bid her well be ware, and still erect,
Lest by some fair appearing good surprised
She dictate false, and misinform the will
To do what God expressly hath forbid.
Not then mistrust, but tender love enjoins,
That I should mind thee oft, and mind thou me.
Firm we subsist, yet possible to swerve,
Since Reason not impossibly may meet   360
Some specious object by the foe suborned,
And fall into deception unaware,
Not keeping strictest watch, as she was warned.
Seek not temptation then, which to avoid
Were better, and most likely if from me
Thou sever not; trial will come unsought.
Wouldst thou approve thy constancy, approve
First thy obedience; the other who can know,
Not seeing thee attempted, who attest?
But if thou think trial unsought may find   370
Us both securer than thus warned thou seem'st,
Go; for thy stay, not free, absents thee more;
Go in thy native innocence, rely
On what thou hast of virtue, summon all,
For God towards thee hath done his part, do thine."
    So spake the patriarch of mankind, but Eve
Persisted; yet submiss, though last, replied.
    "With thy permission then, and thus forewarned,
Chiefly by what thy own last reasoning words
Touched only, that our trial, when least sought,   380
May find us both perhaps far less prepared,
The willinger I go, nor much expect
A foe so proud will first the weaker seek;
So bent, the more shall shame him his repulse."
    Thus saying, from her husband's hand her hand
Soft she withdrew, and like a wood-nymph light,
Oread or Dryad, or of Delia's train,
Betook her to the groves, but Delia's self
In gait surpassed and goddess-like deport,
Though not as she with bow and quiver armed,   390
But with such gardening tools as art yet rude,
Guiltless of fire had formed, or angels brought.
To Pales, or Pomona, thus adorned,

---

353. **still erect,** ever alert.   367. **approve,** give proof of, confirm.
371. **securer,** i.e., "less prepared" (381).
387. **Oread or Dryad,** a nymph of the mountains or of the trees. **Delia,** the goddess Diana, born on the island of Delos.
392. **Guiltless of fire.** The uses of fire are not discovered until after the fall.
393 ff. **Pales** was a Roman goddess of flocks, **Pomona** of fruits, **Ceres** of agriculture; **Vertumnus** was god of the changing seasons.

Likest she seemed, Pomona when she fled
Vertumnus, or to Ceres in her prime,
Yet virgin of Proserpina from Jove.
Her long with ardent look his eye pursued
Delighted, but desiring more her stay.
Oft he to her his charge of quick return
Repeated, she to him as oft engaged   400
To be returned by noon amid the bower,
And all things in best order to invite
Noontide repast, or afternoon's repose.
O much deceived, much failing, hapless Eve,
Of thy presumed return! event perverse!
Thou never from that hour in Paradise
Found'st either sweet repast or sound repose;
Such ambush, hid among sweet flowers and shades,
Waited with hellish rancor imminent
To intercept thy way, or send thee back   410
Despoiled of innocence, of faith, of bliss.
    For now, and since first break of dawn the Fiend,
Mere serpent in appearance, forth was come,
And on his quest, where likeliest he might find
The only two of mankind, but in them
The whole included race, his purposed prey.
In bower and field he sought, where any tuft
Of grove or garden-plot more pleasant lay,
Their tendance or plantation for delight,
By fountain or by shady rivulet.   420
He sought them both, but wished his hap might find
Eve separate; he wished, but not with hope
Of what so seldom chanced; when to his wish,
Beyond his hope, Eve separate he spies,
Veiled in a cloud of fragrance, where she stood,
Half spied, so thick the roses bushing round
About her glowed, oft stooping to support
Each flower of slender stalk, whose head though gay
Carnation, purple, azure, or specked with gold,
Hung drooping unsustained; them she upstays   430
Gently with myrtle band, mindless the while
Herself, though fairest unsupported flower,
From her best prop so far, and storm so nigh.
Nearer he drew, and many a walk traversed
Of stateliest covert, cedar, pine, or palm,
Then voluble and bold, now hid, now seen
Among thick-woven arborets and flowers
Imbordered on each bank, the hand of Eve:

396. yet virgin of, not yet the mother of.
402. And all things in best order, i.e., to have all things in best order.
432. Herself . . . flower. The metaphor is repeated from IV, 270.
436. voluble, rolling (Latin *volubilis*).   **437. arborets,** small trees, shrubs.
438. hand, handiwork.

Spot more delicious than those gardens feigned
Or of revived Adonis, or renowned 440
Alcinous, host of old Laertes' son,
Or that, not mystic, where the sapient king
Held dalliance with his fair Egyptian spouse.
Much he the place admired, the person more.
As one who long in populous city pent,
Where houses thick and sewers annoy the air,
Forth issuing on a summer's morn to breathe
Among the pleasant villages and farms
Adjoined, from each thing met conceives delight,
The smell of grain, or tedded grass, or kine, 450
Or dairy, each rural sight, each rural sound;
If chance with nymph-like step fair virgin pass,
What pleasing seemed, for her now pleases more,
She most, and in her look sums all delight.
Such pleasure took the Serpent to behold
This flowery plat, the sweet recess of Eve
Thus early, thus alone; her heavenly form
Angelic, but more soft and feminine,
Her graceful innocence, her every air
Of gesture or least action overawed 460
His malice, and with rapine sweet bereaved
His fierceness of the fierce intent it brought.
That space the Evil One abstracted stood
From his own evil, and for the time remained
Stupidly good, of enmity disarmed,
Of guile, of hate, of envy, of revenge;
But the hot hell that always in him burns,
Though in mid Heaven, soon ended his delight,
And tortures him now more, the more he sees
Of pleasure not for him ordained; then soon 470
Fierce hate he recollects, and all his thoughts
Of mischief, gratulating, thus excites.
   "Thoughts, whither have ye led me, with what sweet
Compulsion thus transported to forget
What hither brought us, hate, not love, nor hope
Of Paradise for Hell, hope here to taste
Of pleasure, but all pleasure to destroy,
Save what is in destroying; other joy

439 ff. The gardens of Alcinous, the Phaeacian ruler who entertained Odysseus (**old Laertes' son**), are described in *Odyssey* vii. The garden of Solomon (**the sapient king**) is mentioned in Scripture; hence, from Milton's point of view, it is not **feigned** or **mystic** (i.e., mythical) like the others. Cf. Song of Sol. 7:2, and I Kings 3:1.
   440, 442. Or . . . or, either . . . or.
   445 ff. The attitude toward nature revealed in this simile anticipates Wordsworth's. Note especially the idea that natural objects, lovely in themselves, are enhanced in meaning by their human associations. Milton's treatment is ordinarily more impersonal.
   446. annoy, pollute, render noisome.
   450. tedded grass, grass just mown and spread out for drying.
   465. stupidly good, i.e., stupefied into goodness.

To me is lost. Then let me not let pass
Occasion which now smiles, behold alone   480
The woman, opportune to all attempts,
Her husband, for I view far round, not nigh,
Whose higher intellectual more I shun,
And strength, of courage haughty, and of limb
Heroic built, though of terrestrial mould,
Foe not informidable, exempt from wound,
I not; so much hath Hell debased, and pain
Enfeebled me, to what I was in Heaven.
She fair, divinely fair, fit love for Gods,
Not terrible, though terror be in love   490
And beauty, not approached by stronger hate,
Hate stronger, under shew of love well feigned,
The way which to her ruin now I tend."
    So spake the Enemy of mankind, enclosed
In serpent, inmate bad, and toward Eve
Addressed his way, not with indented wave,
Prone on the ground as since, but on his rear,
Circular base of rising folds, that towered
Fold above fold a surging maze; his head
Crested aloft, and carbuncle his eyes;   500
With burnished neck of verdant gold, erect
Amidst his circling spires, that on the grass
Floated redundant. Pleasing was his shape,
And lovely, never since of serpent kind
Lovelier; not those that in Illyria changed
Hermione and Cadmus, or the god
In Epidaurus; nor to which transformed
Ammonian Jove, or Capitoline was seen,
He with Olympias, this with her who bore
Scipio the height of Rome. With tract oblique   510
At first, as one who sought access, but feared
To interrupt, sidelong he works his way.
As when a ship by skilful steersman wrought
Nigh river's mouth or foreland, where the wind
Veers oft, as oft so steers, and shifts her sail;
So varied he, and of his tortuous train

    485. of terrestrial mould, of earthly substance.
    500. carbuncle, i.e., deep red, suggesting passion.
    502. spires, coils.   505. changed, took the place of.
    506. Hermione and her husband Cadmus, king of Thebes, were changed into serpents at
their own request, in order to escape the miseries of human life. The god of medicine,
Aesculapius, took the form of a serpent when going from Epidaurus to Rome for the purpose
of staying a pestilence.
    507. nor to which transformed, etc., i.e., nor those serpents into which Jove was seen
transformed. According to a myth told by Plutarch, Jupiter Ammon (Ammonian Jove) was
the father of Alexander the Great, having been observed in the shape of a serpent with
Olympias, Alexander's mother. A similar myth portrayed Jupiter Capitolinus as the father of
Scipio Africanus.

Curled many a wanton wreath in sight of Eve,
To lure her eye; she busied heard the sound
Of rustling leaves, but minded not, as used
To such disport before her through the field,   520
From every beast, more duteous at her call,
Than at Circean call the herd disguised.
He bolder now, uncalled before her stood,
But as in gaze admiring. Oft he bowed
His turret crest, and sleek enamelled neck,
Fawning, and licked the ground whereon she trod.
His gentle dumb expression turned at length
The eye of Eve to mark his play; he glad
Of her attention gained, with serpent tongue
Organic, or impulse of vocal air,   530
His fraudulent temptation thus began:
     "Wonder not, sovran mistress, if perhaps
Thou canst, who art sole wonder, much less arm
Thy looks, the heaven of mildness, with disdain,
Displeased that I approach thee thus, and gaze
Insatiate, I thus single, nor have feared
Thy awful brow, more awful thus retired.
Fairest resemblance of thy Maker fair,
Thee all things living gaze on, all things thine
By gift, and thy celestial beauty adore,   540
With ravishment beheld, there best beheld
Where universally admired; but here
In this enclosure wild, these beasts among,
Beholders rude, and shallow to discern
Half what in thee is fair, one man except,
Who sees thee? (and what is one?) who shouldst be seen
A Goddess among Gods, adored and served
By angels numberless, thy daily train."
     So glozed the Tempter, and his proem tuned;
Into the heart of Eve his words made way,   550
Though at the voice much marvelling; at length
Not unamazed she thus in answer spake.
     "What may this mean? Language of man pronounced
By tongue of brute, and human sense expressed?
The first at least of these I thought denied
To beasts, whom God on their creation-day
Created mute to all articulate sound;
The latter I demur, for in their looks

---

517. wanton, playful.
522. Circean call. The allusion is to the well-known myth of Circe, an enchantress who changed men into beasts and kept them in complete subjection to her will.
529. with serpent tongue, etc. Satan either uses the serpent's vocal organs directly or causes his words seemingly to come from them.
544. shallow, i.e., too shallow.   **549. glozed,** smoothed over his real motive with flattery.
558. demur, remain in doubt about.

Much reason, and in their actions, oft appears.
Thee, Serpent, subtlest beast of all the field   560
I knew, but not with human voice endued;
Redouble then this miracle, and say,
How cam'st thou speakable of mute, and how
To me so friendly grown above the rest
Of brutal kind, that daily are in sight?
Say, for such wonder claims attention due."
    To whom the guileful Tempter thus replied.
"Empress of this fair World, resplendent Eve,
Easy to me it is to tell thee all
What thou command'st, and right thou shouldst be obeyed.   570
I was at first as other beasts that graze
The trodden herb, of abject thoughts and low,
As was my food, nor aught but food discerned
Or sex, and apprehended nothing high:
Till on a day roving the field, I chanced
A goodly tree far distant to behold
Loaden with fruit of fairest colors mixed,
Ruddy and gold. I nearer drew to gaze;
When from the boughs a savory odor blown,
Grateful to appetite, more pleased my sense   580
Than smell of sweetest fennel or the teats
Of ewe or goat dropping with milk at even,
Unsucked of lamb or kid, that tend their play.
To satisfy the sharp desire I had
Of tasting those fair apples, I resolved
Not to defer; hunger and thirst at once,
Powerful persuaders, quickened at the scent
Of that alluring fruit, urged me so keen.
About the mossy trunk I wound me soon,
For high from ground the branches would require   590
Thy utmost reach or Adam's: round the tree
All other beasts that saw, with like desire
Longing and envying stood, but could not reach.
Amid the tree now got, where plenty hung
Tempting so nigh, to pluck and eat my fill
I spared not, for such pleasure till that hour
At feed or fountain never had I found.
Sated at length, ere long I might perceive
Strange alteration in me, to degree
Of reason in my inward powers, and speech   600
Wanted not long, though to this shape retained.
Thenceforth to speculations high or deep
I turned my thoughts, and with capacious mind
Considered all things visible in Heaven,

563. How cam'st thou speakable of mute, i.e., how did you, being mute, become capable of speech.

581. According to popular belief, serpents were especially fond of fennel and were in the habit of sucking milk from sheep and goats.

Or Earth, or middle, all things fair and good;
But all that fair and good in thy divine
Semblance, and in thy beauty's heavenly ray
United I beheld; no fair to thine
Equivalent or second, which compelled
Me thus, though importune perhaps, to come   610
And gaze, and worship thee of right declared
Sovran of creatures, universal Dame."
   So talked the spirited sly Snake; and Eve
Yet more amazed unwary thus replied.
   "Serpent, thy overpraising leaves in doubt
The virtue of that fruit, in thee first proved.
But say, where grows the tree, from hence how far?
For many are the trees of God that grow
In Paradise, and various, yet unknown
To us; in such abundance lies our choice,   620
As leaves a greater store of fruit untouched,
Still hanging incorruptible, till men
Grow up to their provision, and more hands
Help to disburden Nature of her birth."
   To whom the wily Adder, blithe and glad.
"Empress, the way is ready, and not long;
Beyond a row of myrtles, on a flat,
Fast by a fountain, one small thicket past
Of blowing myrrh and balm; if thou accept
My conduct, I can bring thee thither soon."   630
   "Lead then," said Eve. He leading swiftly rolled
In tangles, and made intricate seem straight,
To mischief swift. Hope elevates, and joy
Brightens his crest, as when a wandering fire,
Compact of unctuous vapor, which the night
Condenses, and the cold environs round,
Kindled through agitation to a flame,
Which oft, they say, some evil spirit attends,
Hovering and blazing with delusive light,
Misleads the amazed night-wanderer from his way   640
To bogs and mires, and oft through pond or pool,
There swallowed up and lost, from succor far.
So glistered the dire Snake, and into fraud
Led Eve our credulous mother, to the tree
Of prohibition, root of all our woe;
Which when she saw, thus to her guide she spake.
   "Serpent, we might have spared our coming hither,

---

605. middle, i.e., the air.   **612. universal Dame,** mistress of the universe.
613. spirited, i.e., inspired by Satan.   **622. incorruptible,** incapable of decay.
624. birth, i.e., the products to which she has given birth.   **629. blowing,** blossoming.
634 ff. This description of the ignis fatuus combines a semiscientific explanation with a popular superstition. Whether Milton actually believed the phenomenon the work of an evil spirit he does not say.
643. fraud, offense, harm.

Fruitless to me, though fruit be here to excess,
The credit of whose virtue rest with thee,
Wondrous indeed, if cause of such effects.   650
But of this tree we may not taste nor touch;
God so commanded, and left that command
Sole daughter of his voice; the rest, we live
Law to ourselves, our reason is our law."
   To whom the Tempter guilefully replied.
"Indeed? Hath God then said that of the fruit
Of all these garden trees ye shall not eat,
Yet lords declared of all in Earth or air?"
   To whom thus Eve yet sinless. "Of the fruit
Of each tree in the garden we may eat,   660
But of the fruit of this fair tree amidst
The garden, God hath said, 'Ye shall not eat
Thereof, nor shall ye touch it, lest ye die.'"
   She scarce had said, though brief, when now more bold
The Tempter, but with show of zeal and love
To Man, and indignation at his wrong,
New part puts on, and as to passion moved,
Fluctuates disturbed, yet comely and in act
Raised, as of some great matter to begin.
As when of old some orator renowned   670
In Athens or free Rome, where eloquence
Flourished, since mute, to some great cause addressed,
Stood in himself collected, while each part,
Motion, each act won audience ere the tongue,
Sometimes in height began, as no delay
Of preface brooking through his zeal of right.
So standing, moving, or to height upgrown,
The Tempter all impassioned thus began.
   "O sacred, wise, and wisdom-giving Plant,
Mother of science, now I feel thy power   680
Within me clear, not only to discern
Things in their causes, but to trace the ways
Of highest agents, deemed however wise.
Queen of this Universe, do not believe
Those rigid threats of death; ye shall not die:
How should ye? by the fruit? it gives you life
To knowledge; by the threatener? look on me,
Me who have touched and tasted, yet both live,

---

653. the rest, as for the rest.

661–63. Milton here follows very closely the phraseology of Gen. 3:1–3.

668. fluctuates. The word is used literally. Milton means that the serpent moves his body to and fro, in order to give visible expression to his assumed emotion.

679 ff. "O sacred, wise . . ." The serpent's speech is a masterpiece of persuasion, uniting intense emotional fervor with closely packed and seemingly irrefutable arguments. Milton does not wish to make Eve too easy a victim.

680. science, knowledge (Latin *scientia*).   **687. To,** in addition to.

And life more perfect have attained than fate
Meant me, by venturing higher than my lot. 690
Shall that be shut to Man, which to the beast
Is open? or will God incense his ire
For such a petty trespass, and not praise
Rather your dauntless virtue, whom the pain
Of death denounced, whatever thing death be,
Deterred not from achieving what might lead
To happier life, knowledge of good and evil;
Of good, how just? of evil, if what is evil
Be real, why not known, since easier shunned?
God therefore cannot hurt ye, and be just; 700
Not just, not God; not feared then, nor obeyed:
Your fear itself of death removes the fear.
Why then was this forbid? Why but to awe,
Why but to keep ye low and ignorant,
His worshippers; he knows that in the day
Ye eat thereof, your eyes that seem so clear,
Yet are but dim, shall perfectly be then
Opened and cleared, and ye shall be as Gods,
Knowing both good and evil as they know.
That ye should be as Gods, since I as Man, 710
Internal Man, is but proportion meet,
I of brute human, ye of human Gods.
So ye shall die perhaps, by putting off
Human, to put on Gods, death to be wished,
Though threatened, which no worse than this can bring.
And what are Gods, that Man may not become
As they, participating godlike food?
The Gods are first, and that advantage use
On our belief, that all from them proceeds;
I question it, for this fair Earth I see, 720
Warmed by the sun, producing every kind,
Them nothing. If they all things, who enclosed
Knowledge of good and evil in this tree,
That whoso eats thereof, forthwith attains
Wisdom without their leave? and wherein lies
The offence, that Man should thus attain to know?
What can your knowledge hurt him, or this tree
Impart against his will, if all be his?
Or is it envy, and can envy dwell
In heavenly breasts? These, these and many more 730
Causes import your need of this fair fruit.
Goddess humane, reach then, and freely taste!"
   He ended, and his words replete with guile
Into her heart too easy entrance won.
Fixed on the fruit she gazed, which to behold

---

732. humane, gracious, gentle in demeanor.

Might tempt alone, and in her ears the sound
Yet rung of his persuasive words, impregned
With reason, to her seeming, and with truth;
Meanwhile the hour of noon drew on, and waked
An eager appetite, raised by the smell   740
So savory of that fruit, which with desire,
Inclinable now grown to touch or taste,
Solicited her longing eye; yet first
Pausing a while, thus to herself she mused.
   "Great are thy virtues, doubtless, best of fruits,
Though kept from Man, and worthy to be admired,
Whose taste, too long forborne, at first assay
Gave elocution to the mute, and taught
The tongue not made for speech to speak thy praise.
Thy praise he also who forbids thy use   750
Conceals not from us, naming thee the Tree
Of Knowledge, knowledge both of good and evil;
Forbids us then to taste, but his forbidding
Commends thee more, while it infers the good
By thee communicated, and our want;
For good unknown sure is not had, or had
And yet unknown, is as not had at all.
In plain then, what forbids he but to know,
Forbids us good, forbids us to be wise?
Such prohibitions bind not. But if Death   760
Bind us with after-bands, what profits then
Our inward freedom? In the day we eat
Of this fair fruit, our doom is, we shall die.
How dies the Serpent? He hath eaten and lives,
And knows, and speaks, and reasons, and discerns,
Irrational till then. For us alone
Was death invented? or to us denied
This intellectual food, for beasts reserved?
For beasts it seems; yet that one beast which first
Hath tasted, envies not, but brings with joy   770
That good befallen him, author unsuspect,
Friendly to man, far from deceit or guile.
What fear I then, rather what know to fear
Under this ignorance of good and evil,
Of God or death, of law or penalty?
Here grows the cure of all, this fruit divine,
Fair to the eye, inviting to the taste,
Of virtue to make wise; what hinders then

   737. impregned, impregnated.
   739–43. Physical appetite is an important factor in Eve's decision, but she does not admit it
to herself.
   758. In plain, frankly (i.e., in plain terms).
   771. author unsuspect, informant not to be suspected.
   778. Of virtue, i.e., having the power.

To reach, and feed at once both body and mind?"
  So saying, her rash hand in evil hour   780
Forth reaching to the fruit, she plucked, she eat.
Earth felt the wound, and Nature from her seat
Sighing through all her works gave signs of woe,
That all was lost. Back to the thicket slunk
The guilty Serpent, and well might, for Eve
Intent now only on her taste, nought else
Regarded; such delight till then, as seemed,
In fruit she never tasted, whether true
Or fancied so, through expectation high
Of knowledge, nor was Godhead from her thought.   790
Greedily she ingorged without restraint,
And knew not eating death. Satiate at length,
And heightened as with wine, jocund and boon,
Thus to herself she pleasingly began.
  "O sovran, virtuous, precious of all trees
In Paradise, of operation blest
To sapience, hitherto obscured, infamed,
And thy fair fruit let hang, as to no end
Created; but henceforth my early care,
Not without song, each morning, and due praise,   800
Shall tend thee, and the fertile burden ease
Of thy full branches offered free to all;
Till dieted by thee I grow mature
In knowledge, as the Gods who all things know;
Though others envy what they cannot give;
For had the gift been theirs, it had not here
Thus grown. Experience, next to thee I owe,
Best guide; not following thee, I had remained
In ignorance, thou open'st Wisdom's way,
And givest access, though secret she retire.   810
And I perhaps am secret; Heaven is high,
High and remote to see from thence distinct
Each thing on Earth; and other care perhaps
May have diverted from continual watch
Our great Forbidder, safe with all his spies

781. eat. Milton regularly uses this form of the preterite. Since the pronunciation corresponds to the spelling, lines 781 and 782 form a rhymed couplet, giving effective emphasis to a crucial point in the action.
    791. Greedily she ingorged without restraint. In terms of human ethics as opposed to theology, Milton interprets the sin of Adam and Eve as a sin of excess, a violation of temperance. Eve's initial greed is therefore a symbol of all the other forms of excess in which she and Adam afterwards indulge.
    792. knew not eating, i.e., knew not that she was eating.   **793. boon,** gay.
    795. virtuous, precious of all trees, i.e., most virtuous, most precious, etc. The idiom is classical.
    796–97. of operation blest To sapience, i.e., so blest as to have the power of conferring wisdom.
    797. infamed, not known.   **815. safe,** not likely to do harm.

About him. But to Adam in what sort
Shall I appear? Shall I to him make known
As yet my change, and give him to partake
Full happiness with me, or rather not,
But keep the odds of knowledge in my power   820
Without copartner? so to add what wants
In female sex, the more to draw his love,
And render me more equal, and perhaps,
A thing not undesirable, sometime
Superior; for inferior who is free?
This may be well. But what if God have seen
And death ensue? then I shall be no more,
And Adam wedded to another Eve,
Shall live with her enjoying, I extinct;
A death to think. Confirmed then I resolve   830
Adam shall share with me in bliss or woe.
So dear I love him, that with him all deaths
I could endure, without him live no life."
     So saying, from the tree her step she turned,
But first low reverence done, as to the power
That dwelt within, whose presence had infused
Into the plant sciential sap, derived
From nectar, drink of Gods. Adam the while
Waiting desirous her return, had wove
Of choicest flowers a garland to adorn   840
Her tresses, and her rural labors crown,
As reapers oft are wont their harvest queen.
Great joy he promised to his thoughts, and new
Solace in her return, so long delayed;
Yet oft his heart, divine of something ill,
Misgave him; he the faltering measure felt;
And forth to meet her went, the way she took
That morn when first they parted. By the Tree
Of Knowledge he must pass; there he her met,
Scarce from the tree returning; in her hand   850
A bough of fairest fruit that downy smiled,
New gathered, and ambrosial smell diffused.
To him she hasted; in her face excuse
Came prologue, and apology to prompt,

817 ff. Shall I to him, etc. The first fruits of Eve's sin are selfishness and jealousy—the negation of her original qualities.

835–36. Eve's perverted conception of God quickly manifests itself in idolatry.

837. sciential, capable of bestowing knowledge.

838–44. Adam the while . . . delayed. The situation closely parallels that in *Iliad* xxii, where Andromache is described making preparations for Hector's return, not knowing that he is already slain.

845. divine of, foreboding.

846. faltering measure, i.e., the uneven beating of his heart.

853–54. in her face . . . prompt. Milton means that the appearance of Eve's face served as a fitting introduction to her verbal apology. The stage imagery is perhaps intended to suggest her insincerity; she approaches Adam in an assumed character.

Which with bland words at will she thus addressed.
   "Hast thou not wondered, Adam, at my stay?
Thee I have missed, and thought it long, deprived
Thy presence, agony of love till now
Not felt, nor shall be twice, for never more
Mean I to try what rash untried I sought,   860
The pain of absence from thy sight. But strange
Hath been the cause, and wonderful to hear:
This tree is not as we are told, a tree
Of danger tasted, nor to evil unknown
Opening the way, but of divine effect
To open eyes, and make them Gods who taste;
And hath been tasted such. The Serpent wise,
Or not restrained as we, or not obeying,
Hath eaten of the fruit, and is become
Not dead as we are threatened, but thenceforth   870
Endued with human voice and human sense,
Reasoning to admiration, and with me
Persuasively hath so prevailed, that I
Have also tasted, and have also found
The effects to correspond, opener mine eyes,
Dim erst, dilated spirits, ampler heart,
And growing up to Godhead; which for thee
Chiefly I sought, without thee can despise.
For bliss, as thou hast part, to me is bliss;
Tedious, unshared with thee, and odious soon.   880
Thou therefore also taste, that equal lot
May join us, equal joy, as equal love;
Lest thou not tasting, different degree
Disjoin us, and I then too late renounce
Deity for thee, when fate will not permit."
   Thus Eve with countenance blithe her story told;
But in her cheek distemper flushing glowed.
On the other side, Adam, soon as he heard
The fatal trespass done by Eve, amazed,
Astonied stood and blank, while horror chill   890
Ran through his veins, and all his joints relaxed;
From his slack hand the garland wreathed for Eve
Down dropped, and all the faded roses shed.
Speechless he stood and pale, till thus at length
First to himself he inward silence broke.
   "O fairest of creation, last and best
Of all God's works, creature in whom excelled
Whatever can to sight or thought be formed,
Holy, divine, good, amiable, or sweet!
How art thou lost, how on a sudden lost,   900

---

   872. to admiration, in a way to be admired.
   877–78. which for . . . chiefly I sought. Eve ends her plea with an open falsehood.
Cf. 816–25.

Defaced, deflowered, and now to death devote!
Rather how hast thou yielded to transgress
The strict forbiddance, how to violate
The sacred fruit forbidden! Some cursèd fraud
Of enemy hath beguiled thee, yet unknown,
And me with thee hath ruined, for with thee
Certain my resolution is to die;
How can I live without thee, how forgo
Thy sweet converse and love so dearly joined,
To live again in these wild woods forlorn?   910
Should God create another Eve, and I
Another rib afford, yet loss of thee
Would never from my heart; no, no! I feel
The link of nature draw me: flesh of flesh,
Bone of my bone thou art, and from thy state
Mine never shall be parted, bliss or woe."
   So having said, as one from sad dismay
Recomforted, and after thoughts disturbed
Submitting to what seemed remediless,
Thus in calm mood his words to Eve he turned.   920
   "Bold deed thou hast presumed, adventurous Eve,
And peril great provoked, who thus hast dared,
Had it been only coveting to eye
That sacred fruit, sacred to abstinence,
Much more to taste it under ban to touch.
But past who can recall, or done undo?
Not God Omnipotent, nor Fate. Yet so
Perhaps thou shalt not die; perhaps the fact
Is not so heinous now, foretasted fruit,
Profaned first by the Serpent, by him first   930
Made common and unhallowed ere our taste,
Nor yet on him found deadly; he yet lives,
Lives, as thou saidst, and gains to live as Man
Higher degree of life, inducement strong
To us, as likely tasting to attain
Proportional ascent, which cannot be
But to be Gods, or angels, demi-gods.
Nor can I think that God, Creator wise,
Though threatening, will in earnest so destroy
Us his prime creatures, dignified so high,   940
Set over all his works, which in our fall,
For us created, needs with us must fail,
Dependent made; so God shall uncreate,
Be frustrate, do, undo, and labor lose,
Not well conceived of God, who though his power
Creation could repeat, yet would be loth

---

   901. devote, doomed, accursed.   **914 ff. flesh of flesh,** etc. Cf. Gen. 2:23.
   928. fact, deed (Latin *factum*).
   932. he yet lives, etc. Having determined his course on nonrational grounds, Adam proceeds to rationalize just as Eve had done.

Us to abolish, lest the Adversary
Triumph and say: 'Fickle their state whom God
Most favors, who can please him long? Me first
He ruined, now mankind; whom will he next?' 950
Matter of scorn not to be given the Foe;
However, I with thee have fixed my lot,
Certain to undergo like doom: if death
Consort with thee, death is to me as life;
So forcible within my heart I feel
The bond of nature draw me to my own,
My own in thee, for what thou art is mine;
Our state cannot be severed; we are one,
One flesh; to lose thee were to lose myself."
   So Adam, and thus Eve to him replied. 960
"O glorious trial of exceeding love,
Illustrious evidence, example high!
Engaging me to emulate, but short
Of thy perfection, how shall I attain,
Adam, from whose dear side I boast me sprung,
And gladly of our union hear thee speak,
One heart, one soul in both; whereof good proof
This day affords, declaring thee resolved,
Rather than death or aught than death more dread
Shall separate us, linked in love so dear, 970
To undergo with me one guilt, one crime,
If any be, of tasting this fair fruit,
Whose virtue (for of good still good proceeds,
Direct, or by occasion) hath presented
This happy trial of thy love, which else
So eminently never had been known.
Were it I thought death menaced would ensue
This my attempt, I would sustain alone
The worst, and not persuade thee, rather die
Deserted, than oblige thee with a fact 980
Pernicious to thy peace, chiefly assured
Remarkably so late of thy so true,
So faithful love unequalled; but I feel
Far otherwise the event, not death, but life
Augmented, opened eyes, new hopes, new joys,
Taste so divine, that what of sweet before
Hath touched my sense, flat seems to this and harsh.
On my experience, Adam, freely taste,
And fear of death deliver to the winds."
   So saying, she embraced him, and for joy 990
Tenderly wept, much won that he his love
Had so ennobled, as of choice to incur

---

   953. certain, resolved.
   977–83. Were it I thought . . . unequalled. Cf. 826–33. **oblige,** render liable to punishment.

Divine displeasure for her sake, or death.
In recompense (for such compliance bad
Such recompense best merits) from the bough
She gave him of that fair enticing fruit
With liberal hand; he scrupled not to eat
Against his better knowledge, not deceived,
But fondly overcome with female charm.
Earth trembled from her entrails, as again   1000
In pangs, and Nature gave a second groan;
Sky loured, and muttering thunder, some sad drops
Wept at completing of the mortal sin
Original; while Adam took no thought,
Eating his fill, nor Eve to iterate
Her former trespass feared, the more to soothe
Him with her loved society, that now
As with new wine intoxicated both
They swim in mirth, and fancy that they feel
Divinity within them breeding wings   1010
Wherewith to scorn the Earth. But that false fruit
Far other operation first displayed,
Carnal desire inflaming: he on Eve
Began to cast lascivious eyes, she him
As wantonly repaid; in lust they burn,
Till Adam thus 'gan Eve to dalliance move.
    "Eve, now I see thou art exact of taste,
And elegant, of sapience no small part,
Since to each meaning savor we apply,
And palate call judicious; I the praise   1020
Yield thee, so well this day thou hast purveyed.
Much pleasure we have lost, while we abstained
From this delightful fruit, nor known till now
True relish, tasting; if such pleasure be
In things to us forbidden, it might be wished
For this one tree had been forbidden ten.
But come; so well refreshed, now let us play,
As meet is, after such delicious fare;
For never did thy beauty since the day
I saw thee first and wedded thee, adorned   1030
With all perfections, so inflame my sense
With ardor to enjoy thee, fairer now
Than ever, bounty of this virtuous tree."

1000 ff. Earth trembled, etc. The idea that the fall was marked by convulsions of the earth and other signs of nature's grief is a literary and theological tradition. While it has no direct scriptural authority, it may have been suggested by the analogous portents accompanying the crucifixion of Christ (Matt. 27:51).

1003–4. the mortal sin Original. This is Milton's only use in the poem of the theological term "original sin."

1019. The word **savor** is derived from Latin *sapere*, which means both "to taste" and "to be wise." Milton represents Adam as playing on this double meaning in explaining why Eve's *taste* can properly be called **judicious.**

So said he, and forbore not glance or toy
Of amorous intent, well understood
Of Eve, whose eye darted contagious fire.
Her hand he seized, and to a shady bank,
Thick overhead with verdant roof embowered,
He led her nothing loth; flowers were the couch,
Pansies, and violets, and asphodel,   1040
And hyacinth, Earth's freshest softest lap.
There they their fill of love and love's disport
Took largely, of their mutual guilt the seal,
The solace of their sin, till dewy sleep
Oppressed them, wearied with their amorous play.
   Soon as the force of that fallacious fruit,
That with exhilarating vapor bland
About their spirits had played, and inmost powers
Made err, was now exhaled, and grosser sleep,
Bred of unkindly fumes, with conscious dreams   1050
Encumbered, now had left them, up they rose
As from unrest, and each the other viewing,
Soon found their eyes how opened, and their minds
How darkened; innocence, that as a veil
Had shadowed them from knowing ill, was gone,
Just confidence, and native righteousness,
And honor from about them, naked left
To guilty Shame. He covered, but his robe
Uncovered more. So rose the Danite strong,
Herculean Samson, from the harlot-lap   1060
Of Philistean Delilah, and waked
Shorn of his strength, they destitute and bare
Of all their virtue. Silent, and in face
Confounded, long they sat, as strucken mute,
Till Adam, though not less than Eve abashed,
At length gave utterance to these words constrained.
   "O Eve, in evil hour thou didst give ear
To that false worm, of whomsoever taught
To counterfeit Man's voice, true in our fall,
False in our promised rising; since our eyes   1070
Opened we find indeed, and find we know
Both good and evil, good lost and evil got,
Bad fruit of knowledge, if this be to know,
Which leaves us naked thus, of honor void,
Of innocence, of faith, of purity,
Our wonted ornaments now soiled and stained,
And in our faces evident the signs
Of foul concupiscence; whence evil store,

1034. **toy,** caress.   1050. **unkindly,** contrary to nature.
1058. **He covered,** etc. i.e., shame covered them with his robe, but in so doing revealed to them their nakedness.
1059. **So rose the Danite strong,** etc. Cf. Judg. 16:4–20.   1068. **worm.** serpent.

Even shame, the last of evils; of the first
Be sure then. How shall I behold the face   1080
Henceforth of God or angel, erst with joy
And rapture so oft beheld? those heavenly shapes
Will dazzle now this earthly, with their blaze
Insufferably bright. Oh might I here
In solitude live savage, in some glade
Obscured, where highest woods impenetrable
To star or sunlight, spread their umbrage broad
And brown as evening! Cover me ye pines,
Ye cedars, with innumerable boughs
Hide me, where I may never see them more.   1090
But let us now, as in bad plight, devise
What best may for the present serve to hide
The parts of each from other that seem most
To shame obnoxious, and unseemliest seen,
Some tree whose broad smooth leaves together sewed,
And girded on our loins, may cover round
Those middle parts, that this new comer, Shame,
There sit not, and reproach us as unclean."
    So counselled he, and both together went
Into the thickest wood; there soon they chose   1100
The fig-tree, not that kind for fruit renowned,
But such as at this day to Indians known
In Malabar or Decan spreads her arms
Branching so broad and long, that in the ground
The bended twigs take root, and daughters grow
About the mother tree, a pillared shade
High overarched, and echoing walks between;
There oft the Indian herdsman shunning heat
Shelters in cool, and tends his pasturing herds
At loop-holes cut through thickest shade. Those leaves   1110
They gathered, broad as Amazonian targe,
And with what skill they had, together sewed,
To gird their waist, vain covering if to hide
Their guilt and dreaded shame; Oh how unlike
To that first naked glory. Such of late
Columbus found the American so girt
With feathered cincture, naked else and wild
Among the trees on isles and woody shores.
Thus fenced, and as they thought, their shame in part
Covered, but not at rest or ease of mind,   1120
They sat them down to weep, nor only tears
Rained at their eyes, but high winds worse within
Began to rise, high passions, anger, hate,

1079. the last of evils, i.e., the greatest (Latin *extremus*). **the first,** i.e., the lesser.
1094. obnoxious. Cf. note on 170.
1103. Malabar refers to the western coast of Hindustan, especially the southern part.
Decan, or **Deccan,** is a name applied to the entire peninsula.
1111. Amazonian targe, shield of the Amazons.

Mistrust, suspicion, discord, and shook sore
Their inward state of mind, calm region once
And full of peace, now tossed and turbulent;
For Understanding ruled not, and the Will
Heard not her lore, both in subjection now
To sensual Appetite, who from beneath
Usurping over sovran Reason claimed   1130
Superior sway. From thus distempered breast,
Adam, estranged in look and altered style,
Speech intermitted thus to Eve renewed.
    "Would thou hadst hearkened to my words, and stayed
With me, as I besought thee, when that strange
Desire of wandering this unhappy morn,
I know not whence possessed thee; we had then
Remained still happy, not as now, despoiled
Of all our good, shamed, naked, miserable.
Let none henceforth seek needless cause to approve   1140
The faith they owe; when earnestly they seek
Such proof, conclude, they then begin to fail."
    To whom soon moved with touch of blame thus Eve.
"What words have passed thy lips, Adam severe!
Imputest thou that to my default, or will
Of wandering, as thou call'st it, which who knows
But might as ill have happened thou being by,
Or to thyself perhaps? Hadst thou been there,
Or here the attempt, thou couldst not have discerned
Fraud in the Serpent, speaking as he spake;   1150
No ground of enmity between us known,
Why he should mean me ill, or seek to harm.
Was I to have never parted from thy side?
As good have grown there still a lifeless rib.
Being as I am, why didst not thou the head
Command me absolutely not to go,
Going into such danger as thou saidst?
Too facile then, thou didst not much gainsay,
Nay didst permit, approve, and fair dismiss.
Hadst thou been firm and fixed in thy dissent,   1160
Neither had I transgressed, nor thou with me."
    To whom then first incensed Adam replied.
"Is this the love, is this the recompense

1127 ff. For Understanding . . . sway. The tripartite division of the soul, which underlies
this passage, is Platonic. Cf. 351–56.
    1141. owe, possess.
    1163 ff. Adam's statement is a fascinating mixture of right and wrong judgment, self-
knowledge, and self-deception. In Milton's theory he is the superior being, but his reasoning is
flawed by passion: "Understanding ruled not." Lines 1166–67 are certainly not a fair representation of the facts, being inconsistent with what he said in lines 908–10, above: "How can I
live without thee?" On the other hand, he has come to the point of partly recognizing his own
weakness: "And perhaps I also erred." How detached Milton himself is in all this it is really
very difficult to say.

Of mine to thee, ingrateful Eve, expressed
Immutable when thou wert lost, not I,
Who might have lived and joyed immortal bliss,
Yet willingly chose rather death with thee?
And am I now upbraided, as the cause
Of thy transgressing? not enough severe,
It seems, in thy restraint. What could I more?   1170
I warned thee, I admonished thee, foretold
The danger, and the lurking enemy
That lay in wait; beyond this had been force,
And force upon free will hath here no place.
But confidence then bore thee on, secure
Either to meet no danger or to find
Matter of glorious trial; and perhaps
I also erred in overmuch admiring
What seemed in thee so perfect, that I thought
No evil durst attempt thee, but I rue   1180
That error now, which is become my crime,
And thou the accuser. Thus it shall befall
Him who to worth in women overtrusting
Lets her will rule; restraint she will not brook,
And left to herself, if evil thence ensue,
She first his weak indulgence will accuse."
Thus they in mutual accusation spent
The fruitless hours, but neither self-condemning,
And of their vain contest appeared no end.

BOOK X: THE ARGUMENT

*Man's transgression known, the guardian angels forsake Paradise, and return
up to Heaven to approve their vigilance, and are approved; God declaring that
the entrance of Satan could not be by them prevented. He sends his Son to judge
the transgressors; who descends, and gives sentence accordingly; then in pity
clothes them both, and reascends. Sin and Death, sitting till then at the gates of
Hell, by wondrous sympathy feeling the success of Satan in this new world, and
the sin by Man there committed, resolve to sit no longer confined in Hell, but to
follow Satan, their sire, up to the place of Man. To make the way easier from Hell
to this world to and fro, they pave a broad highway or bridge over Chaos, according to the track that Satan first made; then, preparing for Earth, they meet him,
proud of his success, returning to Hell; their mutual gratulation. Satan arrives
at Pandemonium; in full assembly relates, with boasting, his success against
Man; instead of applause is entertained with a general hiss by all his audience,
transformed, with himself also, suddenly into serpents, according to his doom
given in Paradise; then, deluded with a show of the Forbidden Tree springing up
before them, they greedily reaching to take of the fruit chew dust and bitter ashes.
The proceedings of Sin and Death; God foretells the final victory of his Son over
them, and the renewing of all things; but for the present commands his angels to
make several alterations in the heavens and elements. Adam, more and more
perceiving his fallen condition, heavily bewails, rejects the condolement of Eve;*

1164. expressed, demonstrated.

*she persists, and at length appeases him: then, to evade the curse likely to fall on
their offspring, proposes to Adam violent ways, which he approves not, but,
conceiving better hope, puts her in mind of the late promise made them, that her
seed should be revenged on the Serpent, and exhorts her with him to seek peace of
the offended Deity by repentance and supplication.*

BOOK XI: THE ARGUMENT

*The Son of God presents to his Father the prayers of our first parents now
repenting, and intercedes for them. God accepts them, but declares that they must
no longer abide in Paradise; sends Michael with a band of Cherubim to
dispossess them, but first to reveal to Adam future things; Michael's coming
down. Adam shows to Eve certain ominous signs; he discerns Michael's approach; goes out to meet him; the Angel denounces their departure. Eve's lamentation. Adam pleads, but submits; the Angel leads him up to a high hill; sets
before him in vision what shall happen till the Flood.*

from BOOK XII

THE ARGUMENT

*The Angel Michael continues from the Flood to relate what shall succeed; then,
in the mention of Abraham, comes by degrees to explain, who that Seed of the
Woman shall be which was promised Adam and Eve in the Fall; his incarnation,
death, resurrection, and ascension; the state of the Church till his second coming.
Adam greatly satisfied and recomforted by these relations and promises descends
the hill with Michael; wakens Eve, who all this while had slept, but with gentle
dreams composed to quietness of mind and submission. Michael in either hand
leads them out of Paradise, the fiery sword waving behind them, and the Cherubim taking their stations to guard the place.*

Here Adam interposed. "O sent from Heaven,   270
Enlightener of my darkness, gracious things
Thou hast revealed, those chiefly which concern
Just Abraham and his seed. Now first I find
Mine eyes true opening, and my heart much eased,
Erewhile perplexed with thoughts what would become
Of me and all mankind; but now I see
His day, in whom all nations shall be blest,
Favor unmerited by me, who sought
Forbidden knowledge by forbidden means.
This yet I apprehend not, why to those   280
Among whom God will deign to dwell on Earth
So many and so various laws are given;
So many laws argue so many sins
Among them; how can God with such reside?"
    To whom thus Michael. "Doubt not but that sin
Will reign among them, as of thee begot;

And therefore was law given them to evince
Their natural pravity, by stirring up
Sin against law to fight; that when they see
Law can discover sin, but not remove,
Save by those shadowy expiations weak,
The blood of bulls and goats, they may conclude
Some blood more precious must be paid for Man,
Just for unjust, that in such righteousness
To them by faith imputed, they may find
Justification towards God, and peace
Of conscience, which the law by ceremonies
Cannot appease, nor man the moral part
Perform, and not performing cannot live.
So law appears imperfect, and but given
With purpose to resign them in full time
Up to a better covenant, disciplined
From shadowy types to truth, from flesh to spirit,
From imposition of strict laws, to free
Acceptance of large grace, from servile fear
To filial, works of law to works of faith.
And therefore shall not Moses, though of God
Highly beloved, being but the minister
Of law, his people into Canaan lead;
But Joshua whom the Gentiles Jesus call,
His name and office bearing, who shall quell
The adversary Serpent, and bring back
Through the world's wilderness long-wandered Man
Safe to eternal Paradise of rest.
Meanwhile they in their earthly Canaan placed
Long time shall dwell and prosper, but when sins
National interrupt their public peace,
Provoking God to raise them enemies,
From whom as oft he saves them penitent
By judges first, then under kings; of whom
The second, both for piety renowned
And puissant deeds, a promise shall receive
Irrevocable, that his regal throne
For ever shall endure; the like shall sing
All prophecy: that of the royal stock
Of David (so I name this king) shall rise
A Son, the Woman's Seed to thee foretold,
Foretold to Abraham, as in whom shall trust

290

300

310

320

---

287. evince, to demonstrate. In Milton's theology the Mosaic law was given "for the hardness of men's hearts." It was abrogated by the new testament of love in Christ, the "better covenant" of line 302.

303. shadowy types. Christian interpretation found allegorical illustrations of the truth everywhere in Old Testament history. Thus the burnt offerings are a symbol of the true sacrifice of a contrite heart; Moses is a mediator and foreshadows the office of the Redeemer; Joshua, leading his people into the promised land, is again Christ making possible salvation for the elect.

All nations, and to kings foretold, of kings
The last, for of his reign shall be no end.   330
But first a long succession must ensue,
And his next son for wealth and wisdom famed,
The clouded ark of God till then in tents
Wandering, shall in a glorious temple enshrine.
Such follow him, as shall be registered
Part good, part bad, of bad the longer scroll,
Whose foul idolatries and other faults
Heaped to the popular sum, will so incense
God, as to leave them, and expose their land,
Their city, his temple, and his holy ark   340
With all his sacred things, a scorn and prey
To that proud city, whose high walls thou saw'st
Left in confusion, Babylon thence called.
There in captivity he lets them dwell
The space of seventy years, then brings them back,
Remembering mercy, and his covenant sworn
To David, stablished as the days of Heaven.
Returned from Babylon by leave of kings
Their lords, whom God disposed, the house of God
They first re-edify, and for a while   350
In mean estate live moderate, till grown
In wealth and multitude, factious they grow;
But first among the priests dissension springs,
Men who attend the altar, and should most
Endeavor peace; their strife pollution brings
Upon the temple itself; at last they seize
The scepter and regard not David's sons,
Then lose it to a stranger, that the true
Anointed King Messiah might be born
Barred of his right; yet at his birth a star   360
Unseen before in Heaven proclaims him come,
And guides the eastern sages, who inquire
His place, to offer incense, myrrh, and gold;
His place of birth a solemn angel tells
To simple shepherds, keeping watch by night;
They gladly thither haste, and by a choir
Of squadroned angels hear his carol sung.
A Virgin is his mother, but his Sire
The Power of the Most High; he shall ascend
The throne hereditary, and bound his reign   370
With Earth's wide bounds, his glory with the Heavens."
　　He ceased, discerning Adam with such joy
Surcharged, as had like grief been dewed in tears,
Without the vent of words, which these he breathed.
　　"O prophet of glad tidings, finisher

---

332. his next son. Solomon. See I Kings 6–7 and II Chron. 3–4.
373. had, would have.

Of utmost hope! now clear I understand
What oft my steadiest thoughts have searched in vain,
Why our great Expectation should be called
The Seed of Woman: Virgin Mother, hail,
High in the love of Heaven, yet from my loins   380
Thou shalt proceed, and from thy womb the Son
Of God Most High; so God with Man unites.
Needs must the Serpent now his capital bruise
Expect with mortal pain: say where and when
Their fight, what stroke shall bruise the Victor's heel."
     To whom thus Michael. "Dream not of their fight
As of a duel, or the local wounds
Of head or heel: not therefore joins the Son
Manhood to Godhead, with more strength to foil
Thy enemy; nor so is overcome   390
Satan, whose fall from Heaven, a deadlier bruise,
Disabled not to give thee thy death's wound;
Which he, who comes thy Savior, shall recure,
Not by destroying Satan, but his works
In thee and in thy seed. Nor can this be,
But by fulfilling that which thou didst want,
Obedience to the law of God, imposed
On penalty of death, and suffering death,
The penalty to thy transgression due,
And due to theirs which out of thine will grow: 400
So only can high justice rest appaid.
The law of God exact he shall fulfil
Both by obedience and by love, though love
Alone fulfil the law; thy punishment
He shall endure by coming in the flesh
To a reproachful life and cursèd death,
Proclaiming life to all who shall believe
In his redemption, and that his obedience
Imputed becomes theirs by faith, his merits
To save them, not their own, though legal works.   410
For this he shall live hated, be blasphemed,
Seized on by force, judged, and to death condemned
A shameful and accursed, nailed to the cross
By his own nation, slain for bringing life;
But to the cross he nails thy enemies,
The law that is against thee, and the sins
Of all mankind, with him there crucified,
Never to hurt them more who rightly trust
In this his satisfaction; so he dies,
But soon revives, Death over him no power   420
Shall long usurp; ere the third dawning light
Return, the stars of morn shall see him rise

---

383. capital, of the head, but with the idea also of "chief."

Out of his grave, fresh as the dawning light,
Thy ransom paid, which Man from Death redeems,
His death for Man, as many as offered life
Neglect not, and the benefit embrace
By faith not void of works. This godlike act
Annuls thy doom, the death thou shouldst have died,
In sin for ever lost from life; this act
Shall bruise the head of Satan, crush his strength   430
Defeating Sin and Death, his two main arms,
And fix far deeper in his head their stings
Than temporal death shall bruise the Victor's heel,
Or theirs whom he redeems, a death like sleep,
A gentle wafting to immortal life.
Nor after resurrection shall he stay
Longer on Earth than certain times to appear
To his disciples, men who in his life
Still followed him; to them shall leave in charge
To teach all nations what of him they learned   440
And his salvation, them who shall believe
Baptizing in the profluent stream, the sign
Of washing them from guilt of sin to life
Pure, and in mind prepared, if so befall,
For death, like that which the Redeemer died.
All nations they shall teach; for from that day
Not only to the sons of Abraham's loins
Salvation shall be preached, but to the sons
Of Abraham's faith wherever through the world;
So in his seed all nations shall be blest.   450
Then to the Heaven of Heavens he shall ascend
With victory, triumphing through the air
Over his foes and thine; there shall surprise
The Serpent, Prince of air, and drag in chains
Through all his realm, and there confounded leave;
Then enter into glory, and resume
His seat at God's right hand, exalted high
Above all names in Heaven; and thence shall come,
When this world's dissolution shall be ripe,
With glory and power to judge both quick and dead,   460
To judge the unfaithful dead, but to reward
His faithful, and receive them into bliss,
Whether in Heaven or Earth, for then the Earth
Shall all be Paradise, far happier place
Than this of Eden, and far happier days."
  So spake the Archangel Michael, then paused,
As at the world's great period; and our Sire
Replete with joy and wonder thus replied.
  "O goodness infinite, goodness immense!
That all this good of evil shall produce,   470
And evil turn to good; more wonderful

Than that which by creation first brought forth
Light out of darkness! full of doubt I stand,
Whether I should repent me now of sin
By me done and occasioned, or rejoice
Much more, that much more good thereof shall spring,
To God more glory, more good will to men
From God, and over wrath grace shall abound.
But say, if our Deliverer up to Heaven
Must reascend, what will betide the few   480
His faithful, left among the unfaithful herd,
The enemies of truth; who then shall guide
His people, who defend? will they not deal
Worse with his followers than with him they dealt?"
    "Be sure they will," said the Angel; "but from Heaven
He to his own a Comforter will send,
The promise of the Father, who shall dwell
His Spirit within them, and the law of faith
Working through love, upon their hearts shall write,
To guide them in all truth, and also arm   490
With spiritual armor, able to resist
Satan's assaults, and quench his fiery darts,
What man can do against them, not afraid,
Though to the death, against such cruelties
With inward consolations recompensed,
And oft supported so as shall amaze
Their proudest persecutors. For the Spirit
Poured first on his Apostles, whom he sends
To evangelize the nations, then on all
Baptized, shall them with wondrous gifts endue   500
To speak all tongues, and do all miracles,
As did their Lord before them. Thus they win
Great numbers of each nation to receive
With joy the tidings brought from Heaven: at length
Their ministry performed, and race well run,
Their doctrine and their story written left,
They die; but in their room, as they forewarn,
Wolves shall succeed for teachers, grievous wolves,
Who all the sacred mysteries of Heaven
To their own vile advantages shall turn   510
Of lucre and ambition, and the truth
With superstitions and traditions taint,

473 ff. The paradox which makes the Fall of Man at once the greatest of human calamities
and the occasion of man's highest experience of good is a commonplace of Christian thinking.
    508 ff. Wolves shall succeed for teachers. In this review of the perversion of the Church
Milton touches on every essential point in the attack of Protestant against Catholic, of Puritan
against Anglican. The clergy have substituted "man-made tradition" for the "plain truth of
Scripture"; they have sought rank and title instead of imitating the simplicity of the early
church; they have invoked secular power for the suppression of dissent; they have taught that
authority and not inner conviction should rule the individual in matters of belief, and that
salvation may be obtained by ritualistic observance rather than by repentance. Milton had
been saying these things more or less all his life.

Left only in those written records pure,
Though not but by the Spirit understood.
Then shall they seek to avail themselves of names,
Places and titles, and with these to join
Secular power, though feigning still to act
By spiritual, to themselves appropriating
The Spirit of God, promised alike and given
To all believers; and from that pretence,   520
Spiritual laws by carnal power shall force
On every conscience; laws which none shall find
Left them enrolled, or what the Spirit within
Shall on the heart engrave. What will they then
But force the Spirit of Grace itself, and bind
His consort Liberty; what but unbuild
His living temples, built by faith to stand,
Their own faith, not another's: for on earth
Who against faith and conscience can be heard
Infallible? yet many will presume: 530
Whence heavy persecution shall arise
On all who in the worship persevere
Of Spirit and Truth; the rest, far greater part,
Will deem in outward rites and specious forms
Religion satisfied; Truth shall retire
Bestuck with slanderous darts, and works of faith
Rarely be found. So shall the world go on,
To good malignant, to bad men benign,
Under her own weight groaning till the day
Appear of respiration to the just,   540
And vengeance to the wicked, at return
Of Him so lately promised to thy aid,
The Woman's Seed, obscurely then foretold,
Now amplier known thy Savior and thy Lord,
Last in the clouds from Heaven to be revealed
In glory of the Father, to dissolve
Satan with his perverted world, then raise
From the conflagrant mass, purged and refined,
New Heavens, new Earth, ages of endless date
Founded in righteousness and peace and love,   550
To bring forth fruits joy and eternal bliss."
   He ended; and thus Adam last replied.
"How soon hath thy prediction, Seer blest,
Measured this transient world, the race of time,
Till time stand fixed: beyond is all abyss,
Eternity, whose end no eye can reach.
Greatly instructed I shall hence depart,
Greatly in peace of thought, and have my fill
Of knowledge, what this vessel can contain;
Beyond which was my folly to aspire.   560
Henceforth I learn, that to obey is best,
And love with fear the only God, to walk

As in his presence, ever to observe
His providence, and on him sole depend,
Merciful over all his works, with good
Still overcoming evil, and by small
Accomplishing great things, by things deemed weak
Subverting worldly strong, and worldly wise
By simply meek; that suffering for truth's sake
Is fortitude to highest victory,   570
And to the faithful death the gate of life;
Taught this by his example whom I now
Acknowledge my Redeemer ever blest."
    To whom thus also the Angel last replied.
"This having learned, thou hast attained the sum
Of wisdom; hope no higher, though all the stars
Thou knew'st by name, and all the ethereal powers,
All secrets of the deep, all Nature's works,
Or works of God in heaven, air, earth, or sea,
And all the riches of this world enjoy'dst,   580
And all the rule, one empire; only add
Deeds to thy knowledge answerable, add faith,
Add virtue, patience, temperance, add love,
By name to come called charity, the soul
Of all the rest: then wilt thou not be loth
To leave this Paradise, but shalt possess
A Paradise within thee, happier far.
Let us descend now therefore from this top
Of speculation; for the hour precise
Exacts our parting hence; and see the guards,   590
By me encamped on yonder hill, expect
Their motion, at whose front a flaming sword,
In signal of remove, waves fiercely round;
We may no longer stay: go, waken Eve;
Her also I with gentle dreams have calmed
Portending good, and all her spirits composed
To meek submission: thou at season fit
Let her with thee partake what thou hast heard,
Chiefly what may concern her faith to know,
The great deliverance by her seed to come   600
(For by the Woman's Seed) on all mankind.
That ye may live, which will be many days,
Both in one faith unanimous though sad,
With cause for evils past, yet much more cheered
With meditation on the happy end."
    He ended, and they both descend the hill;
Descended, Adam to the bower where Eve
Lay sleeping ran before, but found her waked;
And thus with words not sad she him received.
    "Whence thou return'st, and whither went'st, I know;   610

591–92. expect their motion, await the moment of moving.

For God is also in sleep, and dreams advise,
Which he hath sent propitious, some great good
Presaging, since with sorrow and heart's distress
Wearied I fell asleep. But now lead on;
In me is no delay; with thee to go,
Is to stay here; without thee here to stay,
Is to go hence unwilling; thou to me
Art all things under Heaven, all places thou,
Who for my wilful crime art banished hence.
This further consolation yet secure   620
I carry hence; though all by me is lost,
Such favor I unworthy am vouchsafed,
By me the Promised Seed shall all restore."
  So spake our mother Eve, and Adam heard
Well pleased, but answered not; for now too nigh
The Archangel stood, and from the other hill
To their fixed station, all in bright array
The Cherubim descended; on the ground
Gliding meteorous, as evening mist
Risen from a river o'er the marish glides,   630
And gathers ground fast at the laborer's heel
Homeward returning. High in front advanced,
The brandished sword of God before them blazed
Fierce as a comet; which with torrid heat,
And vapor as the Libyan air adust,
Began to parch that temperate clime; whereat
In either hand the hastening angel caught
Our lingering parents, and to the eastern gate
Led them direct, and down the cliff as fast
To the subjected plain; then disappeared.   640
They looking back, all the eastern side beheld
Of Paradise, so late their happy seat,
Waved over by that flaming brand, the gate
With dreadful faces thronged and fiery arms.
Some natural tears they dropped, but wiped them soon;
The world was all before them, where to choose
Their place of rest, and Providence their guide.
They hand in hand with wandering steps and slow,
Through Eden took their solitary way.

614 ff. Eve's words suggest those of Ruth, "Whither thou goest I will go," but also Andromache's to Hector in the *Iliad*.

Chronology

Political and Social Events	Intellectual and Cultural Events

B.C.

13th *c.* Hebrew Exodus from Egypt into Canaan

1193–1184 Trojan War

ca. 1100 Dorians migrate into Peloponnesus

953 Dedication of Temple at Jerusalem

          10th *c.* Oral traditions of Jews attain first written form (the J strand); oral epics in circulation among the Greeks

931 Jews split into the Northern Kingdom of Israel and the Southern Kingdom of Judah

826 Founding of Carthage

776 First Olympic games in Greece

753 Traditional date of founding of Rome by Romulus and Remus

750–500 Era of Greek colonization

          6th *c.* Rise of free statuary and Doric and Ionic temple architecture

597 Babylonian captivity of the Jews

6th *c.* Ascendancy of the Persian empire

          586 The piper Sakadas wins the pipe contest at the Greek Pythian games with a piece representing Apollo's fight with a dragon

538 The Persians under Cyrus capture Babylon and free the Jews

          585 Thales makes the first prediction of a solar eclipse

          534 Thespis' dramatic performances in Athens

509 Traditional date of the founding of the Roman Republic

490 Athenians defeat Persians at the Battle of Marathon

480 The Greek fleet defeats the Persians at the Battle of Salamis

461–429 The Periclean Age in Athens

          432 The Parthenon completed

431–404 Peloponnesian War and the fall of Athens

          429 The Acropolis completed

          399 The death of Socrates

336–323 Conquests of Alexander

          334 Foundation of the Library at Alexandria

264–146 Punic Wars

146 Roman conquest of Greece

          ca. 150 Frieze from the Altar of Zeus at Pergamon

Old Testament (10th–2nd c.)

Homer (8th c.)

Sappho (7th–6th c.)

Aeschylus (ca. 525–456)

Sophocles (496–406)

Euripides (ca. 480–406)

Aristophanes (ca. 450–ca. 386)

Plato (ca. 427–ca. 348)

Aristotle (384–322)

Political and Social Events	*Intellectual and Cultural Events*
60 First Triumvirate (Pompey, Julius Caesar, Crassus)	
58–50 Caesar's Gallic Wars	
44 Assassination of Caesar	
43 Second Triumvirate (Antony, Octavian, Lepidus)	
27–A.D. 14 Augustus Caesar Emperor of Rome	
ca. 4 Birth of Christ	
A.D.	
ca. 29 Crucifixion of Christ	
64 Burning of Rome and first Christian persecutions	
70 Titus, son of Emperor Vespasian, suppresses a Jewish revolt, destroys the Temple at Jerusalem, and massacres and exiles Jews (the *Diaspora,* or Scattering)	70 Colosseum begun at Rome
	81 Arch of Titus completed at Rome
84 Roman conquest of Britain	
	118–126 Construction of the Pantheon at Rome
132 Jews rebel again, recapture Jerusalem, and set up a state of Israel	
135 Jewish revolt crushed; the Final Diaspora	
250 Decius, Emperor of Rome, makes emperor-worship compulsory and orders persecution of Christians	211–217 Construction of Roman Baths of Caracalla
286 Emperor Diocletian divides the Empire into Eastern and Western Empires	
323–337 Constantine Emperor in the East. He moves the capital to Constantinople and allows Christianity in the Empire	
351 Emperor Julian attempts to reintroduce paganism in place of Christianity	
395 Emperor Theodosius makes Christianity the official religion of Rome	

Catullus (*ca.* 84–*ca.* 54)

Virgil (70–19)

Ovid (43 B.C.–A.D. 17)

New Testament (1st and 2nd *c.*)

Political and Social Events	Intellectual and Cultural Events
401 Pope Innocent I claims universal jurisdiction over the Roman Church	413 St. Augustine, *The City of God* *ca.* 450 Establishment of the seven liberal arts as regular course of study
476 The end of the Roman Empire	

✻ THE MIDDLE AGES

	527–565 Construction of the Hagia Sophia, Constantinople
622–624 Beginning of Mohammedan Era and Holy War	622 Hegira of Mohammed
711 Conquest of Spain by Arabs	
	ca. 750 Arabic science brought to Europe
768–814 Charlemagne Ruler of Franks and Holy Roman Emperor	
9th *c.* Feudal system develops among the Franks and spreads across Europe	9th *c.* Music cultivated in monasteries; development of "sequences" (elaborated passages) in liturgical music
856–875 Vikings overrun England	
	ca. 925 The *Quem Quaeritis* trope, earliest surviving example of the staged sections of the Mass which were to form the basis of medieval drama
	ca. 1025 Guido of Arezzo's earliest writings on the theory of music
1066 Norman conquest of England	*ca.* 1080 The Bayeux Tapestry
	1086 The Domesday Book compiled in England
	1094 Construction begins on St. Mark's Cathedral, Venice
1095–1291 Period of the Crusades	1145 Chartres Cathedral begun
	ca. 1150 Troubadours flourish in Provence; rise of universities in Europe; flourishing of Scholasticism
	1163 Cornerstone laid for Notre Dame in Paris

- *Song of Roland* (ca. 1100)

Icelandic saga
(12th–14th c.)

- *Aucassin and Nicolette* (12th c.)

Political and Social Events	*Intellectual and Cultural Events*
	1167 Oxford University founded
	1170 Beginning of the University of Paris
	ca. 1200 Trouvères flourish in northern France, Minnesingers in Germany
	1209 Cambridge University founded
	1213–1380 Construction of the Alhambra
1233 Inquisition established in Spain	
	ca. 1240 The motet becomes the most important form of polyphonic composition
	ca. 1250 Period of the *ars antiqua* polyphonic style in music
	1270 St. Thomas Aquinas, *Summa Theologica*
1271 Beginning of Marco Polo's travels	
	1300–1370 Period of *ars nova* in France, the "new art" of musical composition
1309–1378 The "Babylonian Captivity": papal see removed to Avignon, France	1305 Giotto, the Arena chapel frescoes
	1308 Duccio begins painting the Siena panels
	1327 Petrarch meets Laura
1337–1453 The Hundred Years' War between France and England	
1348 Outbreak of Black Death in Europe	
	1360 Guillaume Machaut, Mass of Notre Dame
	1376 Wycliffe's translation of the Bible
1431 Joan of Arc burned as a witch	1426 Jan and Hubert Van Eyck begin the Ghent Altarpiece
	1436 Guillaume Dufay, *Nuper rosarum flores*
	ca. 1450 Ascendancy of humanism in Italy
1453 Fall of Constantinople to Ottoman Turks ends the Byzantine Empire and marks the end of the Middle Ages	

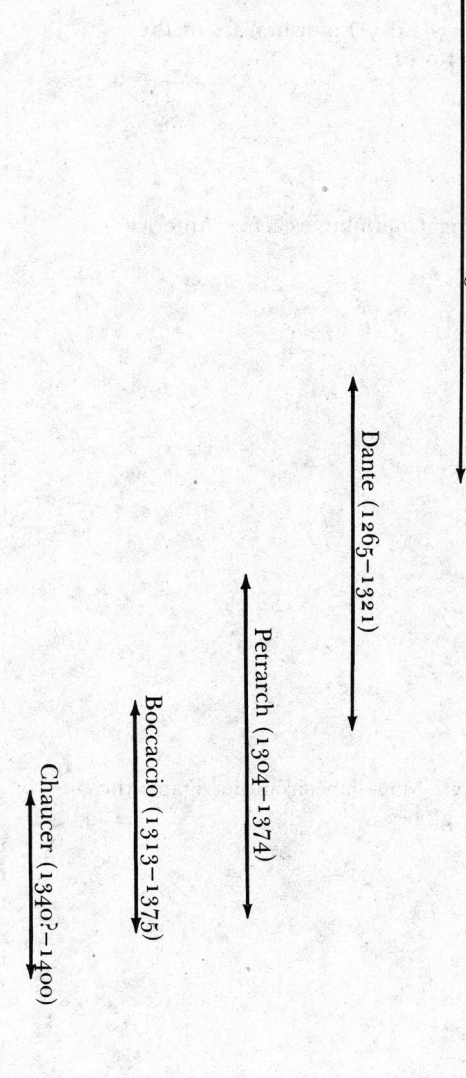

(Icelandic saga)

Dante (1265–1321)

Petrarch (1304–1374)

Boccaccio (1313–1375)

Chaucer (1340?–1400)

❧ THE RENAISSANCE

Political and Social Events	Intellectual and Cultural Events
	1454 Printing by movable type perfected by Gutenberg
1455–1485 English Wars of the Roses	
	1478 Lorenzo de' Medici patronizes arts in Florence; Sandro Botticelli, *La Primavera*
	1487 Giovanni Bellini, San Giobbe Altarpiece
1492 Columbus reaches America	
	1495 Hieronymus Bosch, *Temptation of St. Anthony;* Leonardo da Vinci, *The Last Supper*
	1501 Publication of Josquin des Prez's first book of masses
	1503 Leonardo da Vinci, the *Mona Lisa*
	1504 Michelangelo Buonarotti, *David*
	1506 St. Peter's begun in Rome
	1508 Michelangelo begins Sistine Chapel ceiling
	1511 Desiderius Erasmus' *Praise of Folly*
	1516 Raphael, the *Sistine Madonna;* Lodovico Ariosto, *Orlando Furioso*
	1517 Martin Luther nails his ninety-five theses to a church door in Wittenberg to begin the German Reformation
1522 Magellan circumnavigates the globe	
	1525 Titian, *Deposition*
	1533 First Italian madrigals
	1540 Society of Jesus (the Jesuits) founded
	1547 Benvenuto Cellini, *Perseus*
	1554 Giovanni Palestrina, first book of Masses
	1555 Pieter Breughel the Elder, *The Wedding Dance*
1572 Saint Bartholomew's Day massacre: French Protestants massacred	
	1575–1625 The school of "English virginalist" composers, including William Byrd, Thomas Morley, and Orlando Gibbons
1588 England defeats the invading Spanish Armada	

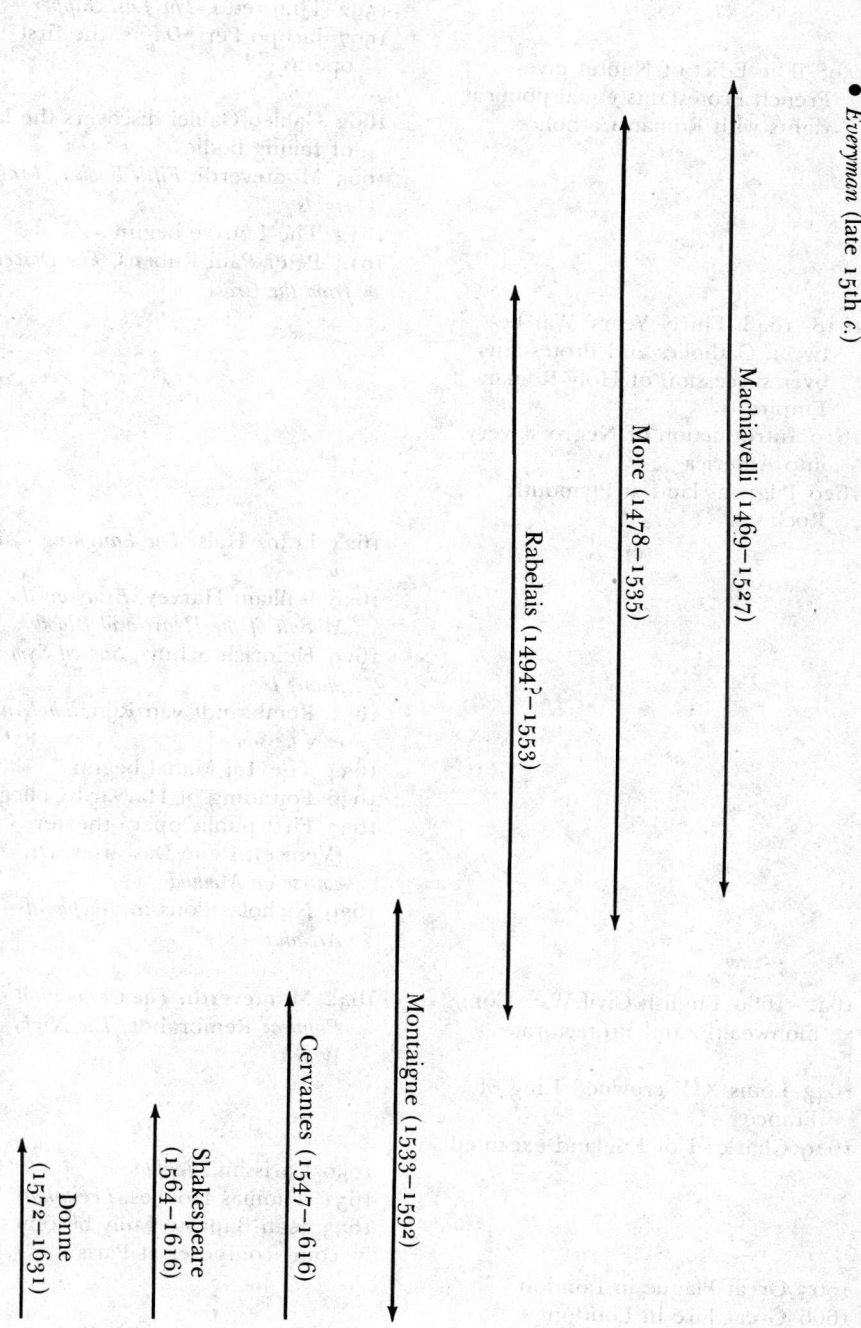

● *Everyman* (late 15th c.)

Machiavelli (1469–1527)

More (1478–1535)

Rabelais (1494?–1553)

Montaigne (1533–1592)

Cervantes (1547–1616)

Shakespeare (1564–1616)

Donne (1572–1631)

Political and Social Events	Intellectual and Cultural Events
	1592 Tintoretto, *The Last Supper*
	1597 Jacopo Peri, *Dafne* (the first opera)
1598 The Edict of Nantes gives French Protestants equal political rights with Roman Catholics	
	1602 Galileo Galilei discovers the law of falling bodies
	1605 Monteverdi, *Fifth Book of Madrigals*
	1612 The Louvre begun
	1614 Peter Paul Rubens, *The Descent from the Cross*
1618–1648 Thirty Years' War between Catholics and Protestants over succession of Holy Roman Empire	
1619 Introduction of Negro slavery into America	
1620 Pilgrims land at Plymouth Rock	
	1624 Franz Hals, *The Laughing Cavalier*
	1628 William Harvey, *Essay on the Motion of the Heart and Blood*
	1629 Heinrich Schütz, *Sacred Symphony I*
	1631 Rembrandt van Rijn, *The Anatomy Lesson*
	1634 The Taj Mahal begun
	1636 Founding of Harvard College
	1637 First public opera theater (Venice); René Descartes, *Discourse on Method*
	1639 Nicholas Poussin, *Shepherds in Arcadia*
1642–1660 English Civil War, Commonwealth, and Protectorate	1642 Monteverdi, *The Coronation of Poppea;* Rembrandt, *The Night Watch*
1643 Louis XIV crowned King of France	
1649 Charles I of England executed	
	1650 Carissimi, *Jephta*
	1651 Thomas Hobbes, *Leviathan*
	1653 Jean-Baptiste Lully becomes court composer at Paris
1665 Great Plague in London	
1666 Great Fire in London	

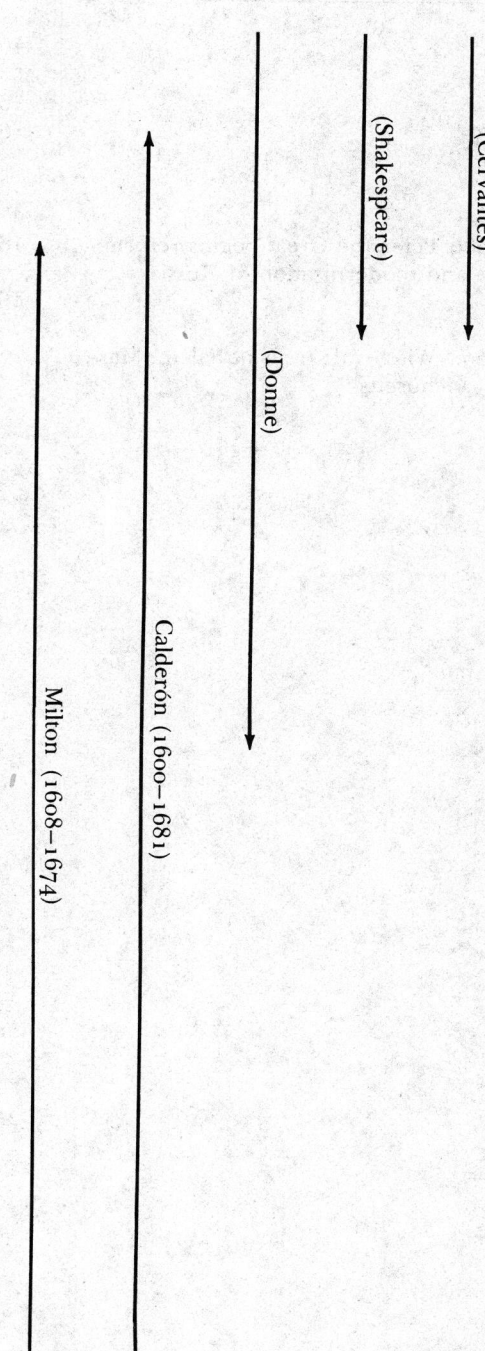

Political and Social Events	Intellectual and Cultural Events
	1667 Giovanni Lorenzo Bernini, colonnade of St. Peter's
	1670 Blaise Pascal, *Pensées*
	1675 Sir Christopher Wren begins St. Paul's Cathedral
	1687 Isaac Newton, *Principia Mathematica*
1689 Peter the Great begins reform and modernization of Russia	1689 Henry Purcell, *Dido and Aeneas*
1692 Witchcraft trials at Salem, Massachusetts	1690 John Locke, *An Essay Concerning Human Understanding*

Index

※※※※※※※

Note: First lines of short poems and titles of books of the Bible are in roman type. Titles of other long works are in italics. Titles of short works are in italics in the general alphabetical listing but in roman type when listed as sub-entries under their authors' names.

The Aeneid, from, 924
AESCHYLUS, 464
  The Oresteia, 467
    Agamemnon, 468
    The Eumenides, 555
    The Libation Bearers, 520
Agamemnon, 468
Alcestis, 709
All you that hear in scattered rhymes the sound, 1588
The Ancient World, Introduction, 1
Antigone, 642
The Apology, 854
ARISTOPHANES, 753
  Lysistrata, 755
ARISTOTLE, 873
  Nicomachean Ethics, from, 892
  Poetics, from, 876
As virtuous men pass mildly away, 2101
Aucassin and Nicolette, 1207, 1209
Authun and the Bear, 1203

Batter my heart, three-person'd God; for, you, 2105
Bible. *See* The Old Testament; The New Testament
Bless the Lord, O my soul, 126
BOCCACCIO, GIOVANNI, 1595
  The Decameron, from, 1597
    The First Day, 1597
    Third Day, Tenth Tale, 1608
    Fourth Day, Second Tale, 1613
    Fifth Day, Eighth Tale, 1619
    Fifth Day, Ninth Tale, 1623
    Fifth Day, Tenth Tale, 1626
    Tenth Day, Tenth Tale, 1633
    Conclusion, 1641
Busy old fool, unruly Sun, 2097
By the rivers of Babylon, there we sat down, 129

CALDERÓN DE LA BARCA, PEDRO, 2106
  Life Is a Dream, 2109
Of Cannibals, 1830
The Canonization, 2094
The Canterbury Tales, from, 1474
CATULLUS, 909
  Come, Lesbia, let us live and love (5), 913
  Dear brother, I have come these many miles (101), 919
  Dress now in sorrow (3), 912
  Egnatius has white teeth (39), 914
  Furius, Aurelius, bound to Catullus (11), 916
  He is changed to a god (51), 912
  If man can find rich consolation (76), 915
  I hate and love (85), 913
  My life, my love, you say our love will last forever (109), 914
  Poor damned Catullus (8), 915
  Twilight and star we hope to see arise (62), 917
  Who shall receive my new-born book (1), 911
CERVANTES SAAVEDRA, MIGUEL DE, 1884
  Don Quixote, from, 1887
    Part I, from, 1887
    Part II, from, 1928
CHAUCER, GEOFFREY, 1471
  The Canterbury Tales, from, 1474
    The Knight's Interruption of the Monk's Tale, 1531
    The Nun's Priest's Tale, 1532
    The Pardoner's Tale, Prologue to, 1517
    The Pardoner's Tale, 1520
    Prologue, 1474
    The Wife of Bath's Tale, Prologue to, 1492

CHAUCER (Continued)
  The Wife of Bath's Tale, 1510
Come, Lesbia, let us live and love, 913
Come, Madam, come, all rest my
    powers defy, 2103
Conclusion (The Decameron), 1641

DANTE ALIGHIERI, 1234
  The Divine Comedy, 1240
    Inferno, 1240
    Paradise, from, 1428
    Purgatory, from, 1379
Dear brother, I have come these many
    miles, through strange lands to
    this Eastern Continent, 919
Death be not proud, though some
    have called thee, 2105
The Decameron, from, 1597
*Discourses on the First Decade of Titus
    Livius,* from, 1672
The Divine Comedy, 1240
DONNE, JOHN, 2091
  The Canonization, 2094
  The Ecstasy, 2098
  Elegy XIX: To His Mistress Going
    to Bed, 2103
  The Flea, 2100
  The Funeral, 2096
  The Good-Morrow, 2093
  Holy Sonnets, from, 2105
    Batter my heart (XIV), 2105
    Death be not proud (X), 2105
  A Hymn to God the Father, 2105
  Love's Diet, 2102
  Song: Go, and catch a falling star,
    2094
  Song: Sweetest love, I do not go,
    2097
  The Sun Rising, 2097
  A Valediction: Forbidding
    Mourning, 2101
Don Quixote, from, 1887
Dress now in sorrow, O all, 912

The Ecstasy, 2098
Egnatius has white teeth and
    therefore always pleasant,
    always smiling, 914
Elegy XIX: To His Mistress Going to Bed,
    2103
Ethics, Nicomachean, from, 892
The Eumenides, 555
EURIPIDES, 673
  Alcestis, 709
  Medea, 675

Everyman, 1545, 1548
The Exodus Saga, 53
Of Experience, from, 1851
The eyes I spoke of once in words
    that burn, 1594

Fierce heart and bitter, and most cruel
    will, 1593
Fifth Day, Eighth Tale (The Decameron),
    1619
Fifth Day, Ninth Tale (The Decameron),
    1623
Fifth Day, Tenth Tale (The Decameron),
    1626
The First Day (The Decameron), 1597
The Flea, 2100
For God's sake hold your tongue, and
    let me love, 2094
*Fourth Day, Second Tale (The
    Decameron),* 1613
From thought to thought, from
    mountainside to mountain,
    1591
The Funeral, 2096
Furius, Aurelius, bound to Catullus,
    916

Gargantua and Pantagruel, from, 1748
Genesis, from, 20
Go, and catch a falling star, 2094
The Good-Morrow, 2093
The Gospel According to Saint Luke,
    from, 1091
The Gospel According to Saint
    Matthew, 1045

He is changed to a god he who looks
    on her, 912
He is more than a hero, 460
He that dwelleth in the secret place of
    the Most High, 125
Holy Sonnets, from, 2105
HOMER, 133
  The Odyssey, 136
Hrafnkel the Priest of Frey, 1184
A Hymn to God the Father, 2105

ICELANDIC SAGA, 1182
  Authun and the Bear, 1203
  Hrafnkel the Priest of Frey, 1184
I find no peace, and have no arms for
    war, 1593
If man can find rich consolation,
    remembering his good deeds
    and all he has done, 915

I hate and love, 913
I have had not one word from her,
     462
I have often asked you, 463
I keep lamenting over days gone by,
     1594
Inferno, 1240
It was that very day on which the sun,
     1589
It was you, Atthis, who said, 462
I wonder by my troth, what thou and
     I, 2093

Job, from, 95
Jonah, 130

King Lear, 2003
*The Knight's Interruption of the Monk's
     Tale*, 1531

Lament for a maidenhead, 458
The Libation Bearers, 520
Life Is a Dream, 2109
The Lord is my shepherd, 125
Love's Diet, 2102
Luke, The Gospel According to Saint,
     from, 1091
Lysistrata, 755

MACHIAVELLI, NICCOLÒ, 1644
     *Discourses on the First Decade of Titus
          Livius*, from, 1672
     The Prince, from, 1647
Mark but this flea, and mark in this,
     2100
Matthew, The Gospel According to
     Saint, 1045
Medea, 675
Metamorphoses (Ovid), from, 1006
The Middle Ages, Introduction, 1097
MILTON, JOHN, 2164
     Paradise Lost, from, 2169
MONTAIGNE, MICHEL DE, 1826
     Of Cannibals, 1830
     Of Experience, from, 1851
     Of Repentance, 1840
MORE, THOMAS, 1674
     Utopia, 1679
          Book I, 1679
          Book II, 1701
My life, my love, you say our love will
     last forever, 914

THE NEW TESTAMENT, 1041
     The Gospel According to Saint
          Luke, from, 1091

THE NEW TESTAMENT (Continued)
     The Gospel According to Saint
          Matthew, 1045
Nicomachean Ethics, from, 892
The Nun's Priest's Tale, 1532

The Odyssey, 136
Oedipus the King, 593
THE OLD TESTAMENT, 16
     The Exodus Saga, 53
     Genesis, from, 20
     Job, from, 95
     Jonah, 130
     Psalms, from, 124
          Bless the Lord, O my soul (Psalm
               103), 126
          By the rivers of Babylon, there
               we sat down (Psalm 137), 129
          He that dwelleth in the secret
               place of the Most High (Psalm
               91), 125
          The Lord is my shepherd (Psalm
               23), 125
          O Lord our Lord, how excellent
               is thy name in all the earth!
               (Psalm 8), 124
          O Lord, thou hast searched me,
               and known me (Psalm 139), 129
          Out of the depths have I cried
               unto thee, O Lord (Psalm 130),
               128
          When Israel went out of Egypt
               (Psalm 114), 127
O Lord our Lord, how excellent is thy
     name in all the earth!, 124
O Lord, thou hast searched me, and
     known me, 129
The Oresteia, 467
Out of the depths have I cried unto
     thee, O Lord, 128
OVID, 1004
     Metamorphoses, from, 1006

The Parable of the Cave (from *The
     Republic*), 850
Paradise (Dante), from, 1428
Paradise Lost, from, 2169
The Pardoner's Tale, 1520
The Pardoner's Tale, Prologue to, 1517
PETRARCH, FRANCIS, 1585
     Rhymes, from, 1588
          All you that hear in scattered
               rhymes (I), 1588
          The eyes I spoke of once in words
               that burn (CCXCII), 1594

PETRARCH (Continued)
Fierce heart and bitter, and most cruel will (CCLXV), 1593
From thought to thought, from mountainside to mountain (CXXIX), 1591
I find no peace, and have no arms for war (CXXXIV), 1593
I keep lamenting over days gone by (CCCLXV), 1594
It was that very day on which the sun (III), 1589
Upon the breeze she spread her golden hair (XC), 1589
Waters fresh and sweet and clear (CXXVI), 1590

PLATO, 807
The Apology, 854
The Republic, from: The Parable of the Cave, 850
Symposium (The Banquet), 810
Poetics (Aristotle), from, 876
Poor damned Catullus, here's no time for nonsense, 915
Prayer to my lady of Paphos, 459
The Prince, from, 1647
Prologue (The Canterbury Tales), 1474
Psalms, from, 124
Purgatory, from, 1379

RABELAIS, FRANÇOIS, 1745
Gargantua and Pantagruel, from, 1748
The First Book, from, 1749
The Second Book, from, 1788
The Renaissance, Introduction, 1569
Of Repentance, 1840
The Republic, from: *The Parable of the Cave*, 850
Rhymes (Petrarch), from, 1588
Roland, The Song of, from, 1106, 1110

SAPPHO, 455
He is more than a hero, 460
I have had not one word from her, 462
I have often asked you, 463
It was you, Atthis, who said, 462
Lament for a maidenhead, 458
Prayer to my lady of Paphos, 459
To an army wife, in Sardis, 461
We drink your health, 457
Yes, Atthis, you may be sure, 460

SAPPHO (Continued)
You know the place, 458
SHAKESPEARE, WILLIAM, 1998
King Lear, 2003
Song: Go, and catch a falling star, 2094
The Song of Roland, from, 1106, 1110
Song: Sweetest love, I do not go, 2097
SOPHOCLES, 591
Antigone, 642
Oedipus the King, 593
The Sun Rising, 2097
Sweetest love, I do not go, 2097
Symposium (The Banquet), 810

Tenth Day, Tenth Tale (The Decameron), 1633
Third Day, Tenth Tale (The Decameron), 1608
To an army wife, in Sardis, 461
To what a cumbersome unwieldiness, 2102
Twilight and star we hope to see arise, pouring bright rain from Mount Olympus down, 917

Upon the breeze she spread her golden hair, 1589
Utopia, 1679

A Valediction: Forbidding Mourning, 2101
VIRGIL, 920
The Aeneid, from, 924

Waters fresh and sweet and clear, 1590
We drink your health, 457
When Israel went out of Egypt, 127
Where, like a pillow on a bed, 2098
Whoever comes to shroud me, do not harm, 2096
Who shall receive my new-born book, 911
The Wife of Bath's Tale, 1510
The Wife of Bath's Tale, Prologue to, 1492
Wilt Thou forgive that sin where I begun, 2105

Yes, Atthis, you may be sure, 460
You know the place: then, 458